S0-FCZ-696

S. Pub. 108–18

2003–2004

OFFICIAL

Congressional Directory

108th CONGRESS

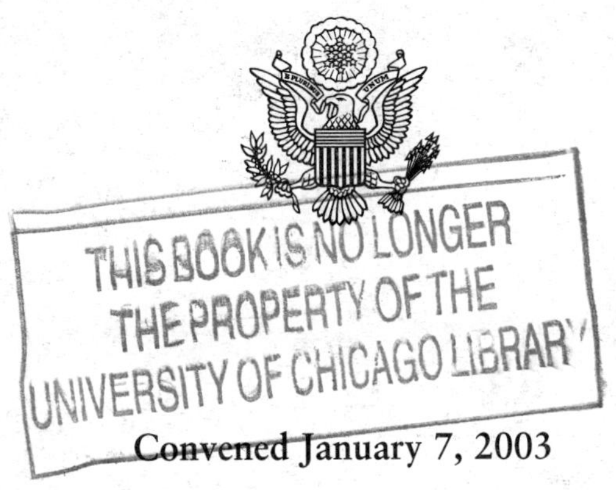

Convened January 7, 2003

Joint Committee on Printing
United States Congress

United States Government Printing Office
Washington, DC

Printed on recycled paper

NOTES

Closing date for compilation of the Congressional Directory was July 11, 2003.

[Republicans in roman, Democrats in *italic*, Independents in SMALL CAPS.]

The following changes have occurred in the membership of the 108th Congress since the election of November 5, 2002:

Name	Resigned or [Died]	Successor	Elected or [Appointed]	Sworn in
REPRESENTATIVES				
Ed Case, 2d HI	....	....	Jan. 4, 2003 [1] ...	Jan. 7, 2003
Larry Combest, 19th TX	May 31, 2003 ...	Randy Neugebauer	June 3, 2003	June 5, 2003

[1] The special election held on January 4, 2003, was to fill this seat for the 108th Congress. The separate special election held on November 30, 2002 (see table below), was to fill this seat for the remainder of the 107th Congress only.

The following changes occurred in the membership of the 107th Congress after the election of November 3, 2000:

Name	Resigned, [Died], or (Expelled)	Successor	Elected or [Appointed]	Sworn in
SENATORS				
Mel Carnahan, MO [1]	[Oct. 16, 2000]	*Jean Carnahan*	[Dec. 4, 2000]	Jan. 3, 2001
James M. Jeffords, VT [2]	....	....	....	
Paul D. Wellstone, MN	[Oct. 25, 2002]	DEAN M. BARKLEY ...	[Nov. 4, 2002]	Nov. 12, 2002
James M. Talent, MO [3]	....	....	Nov. 5, 2002	Jan. 7, 2003
Phil Gramm, TX	Nov. 30, 2002 ...	John Cornyn	[Dec. 1, 2002]	Jan. 7, 2003
Frank H. Murkowski, AK [4]	Dec. 1, 2002	Lisa Murkowski	[Dec. 20, 2002]	Jan. 7, 2003
REPRESENTATIVES				
Julian C. Dixon, 32d CA [5]	[Dec. 8, 2000]	*Diane E. Watson*	June 5, 2001	June 7, 2001
Bud Shuster, 9th PA	Feb. 5, 2001	Bill Shuster	May 15, 2001 ..	May 17, 2001
Norman Sisisky, 4th VA	[Mar. 29, 2001]	J. Randy Forbes	June 19, 2001 ..	June 26, 2001
John Joseph Moakley, 9th MA.	[May 28, 2001]	*Stephen F. Lynch*	Oct. 16, 2001 ...	Oct. 23, 2001
Asa Hutchinson, 3d AR [6] ...	Aug. 6, 2001	John Boozman	Nov. 20, 2001 ..	Nov. 29, 2001
Floyd Spence, 2d SC	[Aug. 16, 2001]	Joe Wilson	Dec. 18, 2001 ..	Dec. 19, 2001
Joe Scarborough, 1st FL	Sept. 6, 2001	Jeff Miller	Oct. 16, 2001 ...	Oct. 23, 2001
Steve Largent, 1st OK	Feb. 15, 2002	John Sullivan	Jan. 8, 2002	Feb. 27, 2002
James A. Traficant, Jr., 17th OH [7]	(July 24, 2002)	....	....	
VIRGIL S. GOODE, JR., 5th VA [8]	....	....	....	
Tony P. Hall, 3d OH [9]	Sept. 9, 2002	....	....	
Patsy Mink, 2d HI	[Sept. 28, 2002]	*Ed Case*	Nov. 30, 2002 [10]	

[1] Died during the campaign, but was elected in the general election, after which the seat was declared vacant.

[2] Changed party affiliation from Republican to Independent on June 6, 2001.

[3] Senator Talent officially replaced Senator Carnahan after the certification of election results, which was not completed until after the Senate had adjourned sine die on November 20, 2002.

[4] Resigned on December 1, 2002, the day before being sworn in as Governor of Alaska.

[5] Died as a member-elect of the 107th Congress.

[6] Resigned to become Administrator of the Drug Enforcement Administration.

[7] Expelled from the House of Representatives pursuant to H. Res. 495. The seat remained vacant for the remainder of the 107th Congress.

[8] Changed party affiliation from Independent to Republican on August 1, 2002.

[9] Resigned to become U.S. Ambassador to the U.N. Food and Agriculture Agencies. The seat remained vacant for the remainder of the 107th Congress.

[10] The special election held on this date was to fill this seat for the remainder of the 107th Congress only, which had already adjourned sine die. Representative-elect Case was not sworn in during the 107th Congress.

FOREWORD

The Congressional Directory is one of the oldest working handbooks within the United States government. While there were unofficial directories for Congress in one form or another beginning with the 1st Congress in 1789, the Congressional Directory published in 1847 for the 30th Congress is considered by scholars and historians to be the first official edition because it was the first to be ordered and paid for by Congress. With the addition of biographical sketches of legislators in 1867, the Congressional Directory attained its modern format.

The Congressional Directory is published by the United States Senate in partnership with the Government Printing Office, at the direction of the Joint Committee on Printing under the authority of Title 44, Section 721 of the U.S. Code.

JOINT COMMITTEE ON PRINTING

Robert W. Ney, Representative from Ohio, *Chairman.*

Saxby Chambliss, Senator from Georgia, *Vice Chairman.*

House

John T. Doolittle, of California.
John Linder, of Georgia.
John B. Larson, of Connecticut.
Robert A. Brady, of Pennsylvania.

Senate

Thad Cochran, of Mississippi.
Gordon Smith, of Oregon.
Daniel K. Inouye, of Hawaii.
Mark Dayton, of Minnesota.

The 2003–2004 Congressional Directory was compiled by the Government Printing Office, under the direction of the Joint Committee on Printing by:

Project Manager.—Michael M. Sardone.

Deputy Project Manager.—Charles H. Potter II.

Editors: Nicole Timmons; Joann Sharp; Shirley Craven.

Typographers: Don Davis; Kathie Connor.

Special Assistance.—Peter Byrd, Capitol Guide Service.

State District Maps.—Election Data Services, Inc.

Representatives' Zip Codes.—House Office of Mailing Services / U.S. Postal Service.

For sale by the Superintendent of Documents, U.S. Government Printing Office

Internet: bookstore.gpo.gov Phone: toll free (866) 512–1800; DC area (202) 512–1800

Fax: (202) 512–2250 Mail: Stop SSOP, Washington, DC 20402–0001

Paper Cover ISBN–0–16–051420–7

Casebound ISBN–0–16–051421–5

CONTENTS

Name Index on page 1103

108th Congress*

THE VICE PRESIDENT

RICHARD B. CHENEY, Republican, of Wyoming, born on January 30, 1941, in Lincoln, NE; education: B.A., and M.A., degrees from the University of Wyoming; public service: served on the Cost of Living Council and Office of Economic Opportunity in the Nixon Administration; served as Assistant to the President and White House Chief of Staff for President Gerald R. Ford; elected to the U.S. House of Representatives in 1978, and reelected 5 times, through 1988; in the House he served as Chairman of the House Republican Conference and House Minority Whip; in 1989 he was nominated to be Secretary of Defense by President George H.W. Bush, and was confirmed by the U.S. Senate; he served from 1989 to 1993; on July 3, 1991, President Bush awarded Secretary Cheney the Presidential Medal of Freedom; after leaving the Department of Defense, he joined the Halliburton Company serving as Chairman of the Board and Chief Executive Officer; religion: Methodist; family: married to Lynne Cheney, 1964; two daughters; elected Vice President of the United States on November 7, 2000; took the oath of office on January 20, 2001.

The Ceremonial Office of the Vice President is S–212 in the Capitol. The Vice President has offices in the Dirksen Senate Office Building, the Eisenhower Executive Office Building (EEOB) and the White House (West Wing).

Chief of Staff.—Lewis Libby, EEOB, Room 276, 456–9000.
Deputy Chief of Staff.—Dean McGrath, EEOB, Room 276, 456–9000.
Counsel to the Vice President.—David Addington, EEOB, Room 268, 456–9089.
Counselor to the Vice President.—Catherine Martin, EEOB, Room 272, 456–9042.
Principal Deputy Assistant to the Vice President for National Security Affairs.—Eric Edelman, EEOB, Room 298, 456–9501.
Assistant to the Vice President for Legislative Affairs.—Candi Wolff, EEOB, Room 285, 456–6774.
Staff Assistant (Senate).—Sara Nokes, U.S. Capitol, Room S–212, 224–2424.
Assistant to the Vice President for Domestic Policy.—Cesar Conda, EEOB, Room 288, 456–2728.
Executive Assistant to the Vice President.—Debra Heiden, West Wing, 456–7549.
Deputy Assistant to the Vice President and Director of Operations.—Claire O'Donnell, EEOB, Room 269, 456–6770.
Assistant to the Vice President and Chief of Staff to Mrs. Cheney.—Lea Berman, EEOB, Room 200, 456–7458.
Deputy Assistant to the Vice President and Director of Scheduling.—Elizabeth Kleppe, EEOB, Room 279, 456–6773.
Director of Correspondence.—Cecelia Boyer, EEOB, Room 265, 456–9002.

---

*Biographies are based on information furnished or authorized by the respective Senators and Representatives.

ALABAMA

(Population 2000, 4,447,100)

SENATORS

RICHARD C. SHELBY, Republican, of Tuscaloosa, AL; born in Birmingham, AL, May 6, 1934; attended the public schools; A.B., University of Alabama, 1957; LL.B., University of Alabama School of Law, 1963; attorney; admitted to the Alabama bar in 1961 and commenced practice in Tuscaloosa; member, Alabama State Senate, 1970–78; law clerk, Supreme Court of Alabama, 1961–62; city prosecutor, Tuscaloosa, 1963–71; U.S. Commissioner, Northern District of Alabama, 1966–70; special assistant Attorney General, State of Alabama, 1968–70; chairman, legislative council of the Alabama Legislature, 1977–78; former president, Tuscaloosa County Mental Health Association; member of Alabama Code Revision Committee, 1971–75; member: Phi Alpha Delta legal fraternity, Tuscaloosa County; Alabama and American bar associations; First Presbyterian Church of Tuscaloosa; Exchange Club; American Judicature Society; Alabama Law Institute; married the former Annette Nevin in 1960; two children: Richard C., Jr. and Claude Nevin; committees: Appropriations; chairman, Banking, Housing, and Urban Affairs; Governmental Affairs; Special Committee on Aging; elected to the 96th Congress on November 7, 1978; reelected to the three succeeding Congresses; elected to the U.S. Senate on November 4, 1986; reelected to each succeeding Senate term.

Office Listings

http://shelby.senate.gov

110 Hart Senate Office Building, Washington, DC 20510 .... (202) 224–5744
Administrative Assistant.—Phil Rivers. FAX: 224–3416
Personal Secretary / Appointments.—Anne Caldwell.
Press Secretary.—Andrea Andrews.
P.O. Box 2570, Tuscaloosa, AL 35403 .... (205) 759–5047
Federal Building, Room 321, 1800 5th Avenue North, Birmingham, AL 35203 .... (205) 731–1384
308 U.S. Court House, 113 St. Joseph Street, Mobile, AL 36602 .... (251) 694–4164
One Church Street, Room C–561, Montgomery, AL 36104 .... (334) 223–7303
Huntsville International Airport, 1000 Glenn Hearn Boulevard, Box 20127, Huntsville, AL 35824 .... (256) 772–0460

* * *

JEFFERSON BEAUREGARD SESSIONS III, Republican, of Mobile, AL; born in Hybart, AL, on December 24, 1946; education: graduated Wilcox County High School, Camden, AL; B.A., Huntingdon College, Montgomery, AL, 1969; J.D., University of Alabama, Tuscaloosa, 1973; U.S. Army Reserves, captain, 1973–86; employment: attorney; admitted to the Alabama bar in 1973 and commenced practice for Guin, Bouldin and Porch in Russellville, 1973–75; Assistant U.S. Attorney, South District of Alabama, 1975–77; attorney for Stockman & Bedsole, 1977–81; U.S. Attorney, South District of Alabama, 1981–93; attorney for Stockman, Bedsole and Sessions, 1993–94; Attorney General, State of Alabama, 1994–96; member: Huntingdon College Board of Trustees; Samford University, Board of Overseers; delegate, General Conference, United Methodist Church; Montgomery Lions Club; Mobile United Methodist Inner City Mission; American Bar Association; Ashland Place United Methodist Church; married: the former Mary Blackshear, 1969; children: Ruth, Mary Abigail and Samuel; committees: Armed Services; Budget; Health, Education, Labor, and Pensions; Joint Economic Committee; Judiciary; elected to the U.S. Senate on November 5, 1996; reelected to each succeeding Senate term.

Office Listings

http://sessions.senate.gov

335 Russell Senate Office Building, Washington, DC 20510 .... (202) 224–4124
Chief of Staff.—Armand DeKeyser. FAX: 224–3149
Scheduler.—Stormie Janzen.
Executive Assistant.—Peggi Jeffreys.
Press Secretary.—Mike Brumas.
341 Vance Federal Bldg., 1800 Fifth Avenue North, Birmingham, AL 35203 .... (205) 731–1500
Field Representative.—Shannon McClure.
Colonial Bank Cntr., Suite 187, 41 W. I–65 Service Rd. N., Mobile, AL 36608 .... (251) 414–3083
Field Representative.—Phillip May.
200 Clinton Avenue, NW, Suite 802, Huntsville, AL 35801 .... (256) 533–0979
Field Representative.—Lisa Ramsey.
7550 Halcyon Summit Drive, Suite 150, Montgomery, AL 36117 .... (334) 244–7017
State Director.—Chuck Spurlock.

REPRESENTATIVES

FIRST DISTRICT

JO BONNER, Republican, of Mobile, AL; born on November 19, 1959; education: B.A., in Journalism, University of Alabama, 1982; organizations: Rotary Club; Mobile Area Chamber of Commerce; University of Alabama Alumni Association; Leadership Mobile; Junior League of Mobile; International Committee for the Mobile Tricentennial; professional: congressional aide to Representative Sonny Callahan, serving as Press Secretary, 1985–1989; and Chief of Staff, 1989–2002; family: married to Janee; children: Jennifer Lee and Josiah Robins, III; elected to the 108th Congress on November 5, 2002.

Office Listings

www.house.gov/bonner

315 Cannon House Office Building, Washington, DC 20515 .... (202) 225–4931
Chief of Staff.—Alan Spencer. FAX: 225–0562
Legislative Director.—Nancy Tippins.
Scheduler.—Marcy Pack.
1141 Montlimar Drive, Suite 3010, Mobile, AL 36609 .... (251) 690–2811
(800) 288–8721

Counties: BALDWIN, CLARKE (part), ESCAMBIA, MOBILE, MONROE, WASHINGTON. Population (2000), 635,300.

ZIP Codes: 36420, 36425–27, 36432, 36436, 36439, 36441, 36444–46, 36451, 36456–58, 36460–62, 36470–71, 36475, 36480–83, 36502–05, 36507, 36509, 36511–13, 36515, 36518, 36521–30, 36532–33, 36535–36, 36538–39, 36541–45, 36547–51, 36553, 36555–56, 36558–62, 36564, 36567–69, 36571–72, 36575–85, 36587, 36590, 36601–13, 36615–19, 36621–22, 36628, 36633, 36640, 36652, 36660, 36663, 36670–71, 36685, 36688–89, 36691, 36693, 36695, 36720–23, 36726, 36728, 36741, 36751, 36762, 36768–69, 36784

* * *

SECOND DISTRICT

TERRY EVERETT, Republican, of Enterprise, AL; born February 15, 1937, in Dothan, AL; attended Enterprise State Junior College; journalist; newspaper publisher; professional: Premium Home Builders; Everett Land Development Company; Union Springs Newspapers, Inc.; owner and operator, Hickory Ridge Farms; Alabama Press Association; chairman of the board, Union Springs Newspapers, Inc.; married to Barbara Pitts Everett; committees: Agriculture; Armed Services; Intelligence; Veterans' Affairs; elected on November 3, 1992 to the 103rd Congress; reelected to each succeeding Congress.

Office Listings

http://www.house.gov/everett

2312 Rayburn House Office Building, Washington, DC 20515 .... (202) 225–2901
Administrative Assistant.—Wade Heck. FAX: 225–8913
Legislative Director.—Lindsay Davis.
Press Secretary.—Mike Lewis.
Scheduler.—Kathleen Tonore.
3500 Eastern Boulevard, No. 250, Montgomery, AL 36116 .... (334) 277–9113
256 Honeysuckle Road, Suite #15, Dothan, AL 36305 .... (334) 794–9680
101 North Main Street, Opp, AL 36467 .... (334) 493–9253

Counties: AUTAUGA, BARBOUR, BULLOCK, BUTLER, COFFEE, CONECUH, COVINGTON, CRENSHAW, DALE, ELMORE, GENEVA, HENRY, HOUSTON, LOWNDES, MONTGOMERY (part), PIKE. Population (2000), 635,300.

ZIP Codes: 35010, 36003, 36005–06, 36008–10, 36015–17, 36020, 36022, 36024–43, 36046–49, 36051–54, 36061–62, 36064–69, 36071–72, 36078–82, 36089, 36091–93, 36101–18, 36120–21, 36123–25, 36130, 36132, 36135, 36140–42, 36177, 36191, 36301–05, 36310–14, 36316–23, 36330–31, 36340, 36343–46, 36349–53, 36360–62, 36370–71, 36373–76, 36401, 36420, 36426, 36429, 36432, 36442, 36449, 36453–56, 36467, 36471, 36473–77, 36483, 36502, 36524, 36703, 36749, 36752, 36758, 36761, 36775, 36785

* * *

THIRD DISTRICT

MIKE ROGERS, Republican, of Saks, AL; born on July 16, 1958, in Hammond, IN; education: B.A., Jacksonville State University, 1981; M.P.A., Jacksonville State University, 1984; J.D., Birmingham School of Law, 1991; profession: Attorney; awards: Anniston Star Citizen of the Year, 1998; public service: Calhoun County Commissioner, 1987–1991; Alabama House of Representatives, 1994–2002; family: married to Beth; children: Emily, Evan, and Elliot; elected to the 108th Congress on November 5, 2002.

Office Listings

http://www/house.gov/mike-rogers

514 Cannon House Office Building, Washington, DC 20515 .... (202) 225–3261
Chief of Staff.—Rob Jesmer. FAX: 226–8485
Press Secretary.—Marshall Macomber.
Office Manager.—Debby McBride.
1129 Noble Street, 104 Federal Building, Anniston, AL 36201 .... (256) 236–5655
2216 Executive Park Drive, Opelika, AL 36801 .... (334) 745–6221
7550 Halcyon Summit Drive, Montgomery, AL 36117 .... (334) 277–4210

Counties: CALHOUN, CHAMBERS, CHEROKEE, CLAY, CLEBURNE, COOSA (part), LEE, MACON, MONTGOMERY (part), RANDOLPH, RUSSELL, TALLADEGA, TALLAPOOSA. Population (2000), 635,300.

ZIP Codes: 35010–11, 35014, 35032, 35034–35, 35040, 35042, 35044–45, 35072, 35082, 35085, 35089, 35094, 35096, 35115, 35120, 35136, 35146, 35149–51, 35160–61, 35171, 35188, 35204, 35208, 35210, 35213–14, 35901, 35905, 35959–61, 35967, 35973, 35983–84, 36006, 36020, 36022, 36023–27, 36029–31, 36036, 36039, 36043, 36045–47, 36051, 36054, 36057, 36064–65, 36069, 36075, 36078, 36080, 36083, 36087–89, 36091–92, 36104–08, 36116–17, 36119, 36130–31, 36201–07, 36250–51, 36253–58, 36260–69, 36271–80, 36749–50, 36801–04, 36830–32, 36849–56, 36858–63, 36865–71, 36874–75, 36877, 36879

* * *

FOURTH DISTRICT

ROBERT B. ADERHOLT, Republican, of Haleyville, AL; born in Haleyville, AL, on July 22, 1965; education: graduate, Birmingham Southern University; J.D., Cumberland School of Law, Samford University; employment: attorney; assistant legal advisor to Governor Fob James, 1995–96; Haleyville municipal judge, 1992–96; George Bush delegate, Republican National Convention, 1992; Republican nominee for the 17th District, Alabama House of Representatives, 1990; married: the former Caroline McDonald; children: Mary Elliott; committees: Appropriations; elected to the 105th Congress; reelected to each succeeding Congress.

Office Listings

1433 Longworth House Office Building, Washington, DC 20515 .... (202) 225–4876
Chief of Staff.—Mark Busching. FAX: 225–5587
Legislative Director.—Mark Dawson.
Communications Director.—Wade Newton.
Scheduler / Office Manager.—Tiffany Noel.
247 Carl Elliott Building, 1710 Alabama Avenue, Room 247, Jasper, AL 35501 .... (205) 221–2310
District Director.—Bill Harris.
205 Fourth Avenue, NE., Suite 104, Cullman, AL 35055 .... (256) 734–6043
Director of Constituent Services.—Jennifer Butler.
107 Federal Building, 600 Broad Street, Gadsden, AL 35901 .... (256) 546–0201
Field Representative.—Jason Harper.

Counties: BLOUNT, CULLMAN, DEKALB, ETOWAH, FAYETTE, FRANKLIN, LAMAR, MARION, MARSHALL, MORGAN (part), PICKENS (part), ST. CLAIR (part), WALKER, WINSTON. Population (2000), 635,300.

ZIP Codes: 35006, 35013, 35016, 35019, 35031, 35033, 35038, 35049, 35053, 35055–58, 35062–63, 35070, 35077, 35079, 35083, 35087, 35097–98, 35121, 35126, 35130–31, 35133, 35146, 35148, 35172, 35175, 35179–80, 35205–07, 35212–13, 35215, 35441, 35447, 35461, 35466, 35481, 35501–04, 35540–46, 35548–55, 35559–60, 35563–65, 35570–82, 35584–87, 35592–94, 35601, 35603, 35619, 35621–22, 35640, 35651, 35653–54, 35670, 35672–73, 35747, 35754–55, 35760, 35765, 35769, 35771, 35775–76, 35901–07, 35950–54, 35956–57, 35959–64, 35966–68, 35971–76, 35978–81, 35983–84, 35986–90, 36064, 36117, 36271–72, 36275

* * *

FIFTH DISTRICT

ROBERT E. (BUD) CRAMER, JR., Democrat, of Huntsville, AL; born in Huntsville, August 22, 1947; graduated, Huntsville High School, 1965; B.A., University of Alabama, Tuscaloosa, 1969, ROTC; J.D., University of Alabama School of Law, Tuscaloosa, 1972; U.S. Army, 1972; captain, U.S. Army Reserves, 1976–78; attorney; instructor, University of Alabama School of Law, Tuscaloosa; director of clinical studies program, 1972–73; assistant district attorney, Madison County, AL, 1973–75; private law practice, Huntsville, AL, 1975–80; district attorney,

Madison County, 1981–90; member: Alabama District Attorneys Association; National District Attorneys Association; founder, National Children's Advocacy Center, Huntsville; National Center for Missing and Exploited Children Advisory Council; American Bar Association, 1975–present; State of Alabama Bar Association, 1972–present; American Bar Association's National Legal Resource Center for Child Advocacy and Protection; awards and honors: received certificate of appreciation, presented by President Ronald Reagan, for outstanding dedication and commitment in promoting safety and well-being of children from the President's Child Safety Partnership, 1987; 1986 recipient of the Vincent De Francis Award, presented by the American Humane Association; selected as National Public Citizen of the Year, 1984; Alabama District Attorneys Investigators Association, ''District Attorney of the Year, 1986''; Methodist; widower; one daughter: Hollan C. Gaines; committees: Appropriations; House Permanent Select Committee on Intelligence; elected to the 102nd Congress, November 6, 1990; reelected to each succeeding Congress.

Office Listings

http://www.house.gov/cramer

2368 Rayburn House Office Building, Washington, DC 20515 .... (202) 225–4801
  Administrative Assistant.—Carter Wells.
  Executive Assistant.—Val Watson.
  Legislative Director.—Jenny Bottegal.
626 Clinton Avenue, West, Huntsville, AL 35801 .... (256) 551–0190
  District Coordinator.—Howell Lee.
Morgan County Courthouse, Box 668, Decatur, AL 35602 .... (256) 355–9400
1011 George Wallace Boulevard, Tuscumbia, AL 35674 .... (256) 381–3450

Counties: COLBERT, JACKSON, LAUDERDALE, LAWRENCE, LIMESTONE, MADISON, MORGAN (part). Population (2000), 635,300.

ZIP Codes: 35016, 35205–06, 35209–10, 35212, 35215, 35540, 35582, 35601–03, 35609–20, 35630–34, 35640, 35643, 35645–54, 35660–62, 35671–74, 35677, 35699, 35739–42, 35744–46, 35748–52, 35755–69, 35771–74, 35776, 35801–16, 35824, 35893–96, 35898–99, 35958, 35966, 35978–79, 36104

* * *

SIXTH DISTRICT

SPENCER BACHUS, Republican, of Vestavia Hills, AL; born in Birmingham, AL, December 28, 1947; education: B.A., Auburn University, 1969; J.D., University of Alabama, 1972; employment: law firm, Bachus, Dempsey, Carson, and Steed, senior partner; member: Hunter Street Baptist Church; Alabama State Representative and Senator; school board; Republican Party Chair; children: Warren, Stuart, Elliott, Candace, and Lisa; committees: Financial Services; Judiciary; Transportation and Infrastructure; elected to the 103rd Congress, November 3, 1992; reelected to each succeeding Congress.

Office Listings

http://www.house.gov/bachus

442 Cannon House Office Building, Washington, DC 20515 .... (202) 225–4921
  Chief of Staff.—Larry Lavender.
  Press Secretary.—Evan Keefer.
  Legislative Director.—Shayne Gill.
1900 International Park Drive, Suite 107, Birmingham, AL 35243 .... (205) 969–2296
Northport Civic Center, P.O. Box 569, 3500 McFarland Boulevard, Northport, AL 35476 .... (205) 333–9894
703 Second Avenue, North, P.O. Box 502, Clanton, AL 35046 .... (205) 280–0704

Counties: BIBB, CHILTON, COOSA (part), JEFFERSON (part), SHELBY, ST. CLAIR (part), TUSCALOOSA (part). CITIES AND TOWNSHIPS: Adamsville, Alabaster, Argo, Brookside, Brookwood, Calera, Cardiff, Clanton, Columbiana, County Line, Fultondale, Gardendale, Graysville, Harpersville, Helena, Homewood, Hoover, Hueytown, Irondale, Jemison, Kimberly, Leeds, Maytown, Montevallo, Morris, Mountain Brook, Mulga, North Johns, Northport, Pelham, Pell City, Pleasant Grove, Ragland, Sumiton, Sylvan Springs, Thorsby, Trafford, Trussville, Vestavia Hills, Vincent, Warrior, West Jefferson, Wilsonville, Wilton, and portions of Bessemer, Birmingham, Tarrant, Tuscaloosa, and West Blocton. Population (2000), 635,300.

ZIP Codes: 35004–07, 35015, 35022–23, 35035, 35040, 35043, 35046, 35048, 35051–52, 35054, 35060, 35062–63, 35068, 35071, 35073–74, 35078–80, 35085, 35091, 35094, 35096, 35111–12, 35114–20, 35123–28, 35130–31, 35133, 35135, 35137, 35139, 35142–44, 35146–48, 35151, 35171–73, 35175–76, 35178, 35180–88, 35201–03, 35205–07, 35209–10, 35212–17, 35219, 35222–26, 35230, 35233, 35235–37, 35240, 35242–46, 35249, 35253–55, 35259–61, 35266, 35277–83, 35285, 35287–99, 35402–03, 35406–07, 35444, 35446, 35452, 35456–58, 35466, 35468, 35473, 35475–76, 35480, 35482, 35490, 35546, 35579, 35953, 35987, 36006, 36051, 36064, 36091, 36750, 36758, 36790, 36792–93

SEVENTH DISTRICT

ARTUR DAVIS, Democrat, of Birmingham, AL; born in Montgomery, AL, on October 9, 1967; education: Harvard University, graduated *magna cum laude;* Harvard Law School, graduated *cum laude;* profession: Attorney; public service: interned with U.S. Senator Howell Heflin (D–AL); interned with the Southern Poverty Law Center; clerked for Federal Judge Myron Thompson; served as an Assistant U.S. Attorney for four years; community service: volunteer work for the Birmingham Public School System; served as a legal and political commentator for Birmingham's Fox 6 News; religion: Baptist; elected to the 108th Congress on November 5, 2002.

Office Listings

http://www.house.gov/arturdavis

208 Cannon House Office Building, Washington, DC 20515 .... (202) 225–2665
Chief of Staff.—Dana Gresham. FAX: 226–9567
Deputy Chief of Staff / Communications Director.—Corey Ealons.
Legislative Director.—Amy Chevalier Efantis.
1728 3rd Avenue North, Birmingham, AL 35203 .... (205) 254–1960
908 Alabama Avenue, Federal Building, Suite 112, Selma, AL 36701 .... (334) 877–4414
102 East Washington Street, Suite F, Demopolis, AL 36732 .... (334) 287–0860
205 North Washington Street, UWA Station 40, Suites 236–237, Livingston, AL 35470 .... (205) 652–5834
1118 Greensboro Avenue, Suite 336, Tuscaloosa, AL 35401 .... (205) 752–5380

Counties: CHOCTAW, CLARKE (part), DALLAS, GREENE, HALE, JEFFERSON (part), MARENGO, PERRY, PICKENS (part), SUMTER, TUSCALOOSA (part), WILCOX. Population (2000), 635,300.

ZIP Codes: 35005–06, 35020–23, 35034, 35036, 35041–42, 35061, 35064, 35068, 35071, 35073–74, 35079, 35111, 35117, 35126–27, 35173, 35175, 35184, 35188, 35203–15, 35217–18, 35221–22, 35224, 35228–29, 35233–35, 35238, 35243, 35401, 35404–06, 35440–44, 35446–49, 35452–53, 35456, 35459–60, 35462–64, 35466, 35469–71, 35473–78, 35480–81, 35485–87, 35490–91, 35546, 35601, 35603, 35640, 35754, 36030, 36032, 36040, 36064, 36105, 36435–36, 36451, 36482, 36524, 36540, 36545, 36558, 36701–03, 36720, 36722–23, 36726–28, 36732, 36736, 36738, 36740–42, 36744–45, 36748–54, 36756, 36758–59, 36761–69, 36773, 36775–76, 36782–86, 36790, 36792–93, 36901, 36904, 36906–08, 36910, 36912–13, 36915–16, 36919, 36921–22, 36925

ALASKA

(Population 2000, 626,932)

SENATORS

TED STEVENS, Republican, of Girdwood, AK; born in Indianapolis, IN, on November 18, 1923; education: graduated, UCLA, 1947; Harvard Law School, 1950; military service: served as a first lieutenant (pilot), 1943–46; 14th Air Force in China, 1944–45; employment: practiced law in Washington, DC, and Fairbanks, AK, 1950–53; U.S. Attorney, Fairbanks, AK, 1953–56; legislative counsel, U.S. Department of the Interior, 1956–57; assistant to the Secretary of the Interior (Fred Seaton), 1958–59; appointed solicitor of the Department of the Interior by President Eisenhower, 1960; opened law office, Anchorage, AK, 1961; Alaska House of Representatives, 1964–68; has served in U.S. Senate since December 24, 1968; assistant Republican leader, 1977–85; committees: chairman, Appropriations; Commerce, Science, and Transportation; Governmental Affairs; Rules and Administration; Joint Committee on the Library; Special Committee on Aging; married Catherine Chandler of Anchorage, AK; one daughter; five children with first wife, Ann Cherrington (deceased, 1978); member: American, Federal, California, Alaska, and District of Columbia bar associations; member: Rotary, American Legion, Veterans of Foreign Wars, Igloo No. 4 Pioneers of Alaska; Senate President Pro Tempore.

Office Listings

http://stevens.senate.gov

522 Hart Senate Office Building, Washington, DC 20510 .... (202) 224–3004
Chief of Staff.—David Russell.
Legislative Director.—George Lowe.
Administrative Director.—John Hozey.
Scheduling Director.—DeLynn Henry.
Press Secretary.—Melanie Alvord.
222 West Seventh Avenue, No. 2, Anchorage, AK 99513 .... (907) 271–5915
Federal Building, Room 206, Box 4, 101 12th Avenue, Fairbanks, AK 99701 .... (907) 456–0261
Federal Building, Room 971, Box 20149, Juneau, AK 99802 .... (907) 586–7400
130 Trading Bay Road, Suite 350, Kenai, AK 99611 .... (907) 283–5808
540 Water Street, Suite 101, Ketchikan, AK 99901 .... (907) 225–6880

* * *

LISA MURKOWSKI, Republican, of Anchorage, AK; born on May 22, 1957, in Ketchikan, AK; education: Willamette University, 1975–77; Georgetown University, 1978–80, B.A., Economics; Willamette College of Law, 1982–85, J.D.; occupation: Attorney; professional: private law practice; Alaska and Anchorage Bar Associations: First Bank Board of Directors; organizations: Catholic Social Services; YWCA; Alaskans for Drug-Free Youth; Alaska Federation of Republican Women; Arctic Power; public service: Anchorage Equal Rights Commission; Anchorage District Court Attorney, 1987–89; Task Force on the Homeless, 1990–91; Alaska State Representative, 1998–2002; family: married to Verne Martell; children: Nicholas and Matthew; appointed to the U.S. Senate on December 20, 2002.

Office Listings

http://murkowski.senate.gov

322 Hart Senate Office Building, Washington, DC 20510 .... (202) 224–6665
Chief of Staff.—Justin Stiefel. FAX: 224–5301
Legislative Director.—Jon DeVore.
Scheduler.—Kristen Daimler.
510 L Street, #550, Anchorage, AK 99501 .... (907) 271–3735
101 12th Avenue, Room 216, Fairbanks, AK 99701 .... (907) 456–0233
709 W. 9th, Room 971, Juneau, AK 99802 .... (907) 586–7400

REPRESENTATIVE

AT LARGE

DON YOUNG, Republican, of Fort Yukon, AK; born in Meridian, CA, on June 9, 1933; education: A.A., Yuba Junior College; B.A., Chico State College, Chico, CA; Honorary Doctorate of Laws, University of Alaska, Fairbanks; State House of Representatives, 1966–70; U.S.

Army, 41st Tank Battalion, 1955–57; elected member of the State Senate, 1970–73; served on the Fort Yukon City Council for six years, serving four years as mayor; educator for nine years; river boat captain; member: National Education Association, Elks, Lions, Jaycees; married: Lula Fredson of Fort Yukon; children: Joni and Dawn; committees: chairman, Transportation and Infrastructure; Resources; Select Committee on Homeland Security; elected to the 93rd Congress in a special election, March 6, 1973, to fill the vacancy created by the death of Congressman Nick Begich; reelected to each succeeding Congress.

Office Listings

http://www.house.gov/donyoung

2111 Rayburn House Office Building, Washington, DC 20515 .... (202) 225–5765
Administrative Assistant.—Michael Anderson. FAX: 225–0425
Press Secretary.—Grant Thompson.
Executive Assistant / Office Manager.—Sara Parsons.
222 West Seventh Avenue, No. 3, Anchorage, AK 99513 .... (907) 271–5978
101 12th Avenue, Box 10, Fairbanks, AK 99701 .... (907) 456–0210
971 Federal Building, Box 21247, Juneau, AK 99802 .... (907) 586–7400
540 Water Street, Ketchikan, AK 99901 .... (907) 225–6880
130 Trading Bay Road, Suite 350, Kenai, AK 99611 .... (907) 283–5808
851 East Westpoint Drive, #307, Wasilla, AK 99654 .... (907) 376–7665

Population (2000), 626,932.

ZIP Codes: 99501–24, 99540, 99546–59, 99561, 99563–69, 99571–81, 99583–91, 99599, 99602–15, 99619–22, 99624–41, 99643–45, 99647–72, 99674–95, 99697, 99701–12, 99714, 99716, 99720–27, 99729–30, 99732–34, 99736–86, 99788–89, 99791, 99801–03, 99811, 99820–21, 99824–27, 99829–30, 99832–33, 99835–36, 99840–41, 99850, 99901, 99903, 99918–19, 99921–23, 99925–29, 99950

ARIZONA

(Population 2000, 5,140,683)

SENATORS

JOHN McCAIN, Republican, of Phoenix, AZ; born in the Panama Canal Zone, August 29, 1936; graduated Episcopal High School, Alexandria, VA, 1954; graduated, U.S. Naval Academy, Annapolis, MD, 1958; National War College, Washington, DC, 1973; retired captain (pilot), U.S. Navy, 1958–81; military awards: Silver Star, Bronze Star, Legion of Merit, Purple Heart, and Distinguished Flying Cross; chair, International Republican Institute; married to the former Cindy Hensley; seven children: Doug, Andy, Sidney, Meghan, Jack, Jim, and Bridget; committees: Armed Services; chairman, Commerce, Science and Transportation; Indian Affairs; elected to the 98th Congress in November, 1982; reelected to the 99th Congress in November, 1984; elected to the U.S. Senate in November, 1986; reelected to each succeeding Senate term.

Office Listings

http://mccain.senate.gov

241 Russell Senate Office Building, Washington, DC 20510 .... (202) 224–2235
Administrative Assistant.—Mark Salter. TDD: 224–7132
Legislative Director.—Christine Dodd.
Communications Director.—Marshall Wittmann.
Scheduler.—Ellen Cahill.
Office Manager.—Heidi Karpen.
2400 East Arizona Biltmore Circle, Suite 1150, Phoenix, AZ 85016 .... (602) 952–2410
TDD: 952–0170
4450 South Rural Road, Suite B–130, Tempe, AZ 85282 .... (480) 897–6289
450 West Paseo Redondo, Suite 200, Tucson, AZ 85701 .... (602) 670–6334

* * *

JON KYL, Republican, of Phoenix, AZ; born in Oakland, NE on April 25, 1942; education: graduated Bloomfield High School, Bloomfield, IA, 1960; B.A., University of Arizona, Tucson, 1964 (Phi Beta Kappa, Phi Kappa Phi); LL.B., University of Arizona, 1966; employment: editor-in-chief, *Arizona Law Review*; attorney, admitted to the Arizona State bar, 1966; former partner in Phoenix law firm of Jennings, Strouss and Salmon, 1966–86; chairman, Phoenix Chamber of Commerce (1984–85); married: the former Caryll Louise Collins; children: Kristine and Jon; committees: Energy and Natural Resources; Finance; Judiciary; chairman, Republican Policy Committee; elected to the 100th Congress on November 4, 1986; reelected to each succeeding Congress; elected to the U.S. Senate in November, 1994; reelected to each succeeding Senate term.

Office Listings

http://kyl.senate.gov

730 Hart Senate Office Building, Washington, DC 20515 .... (202) 224–4521
Chief of Staff.—Tim Glazewski.
Senior Policy Advisor.—Jeff Kuhnreich.
Legislative Director.—Elizabeth Maier.
Office Director.—Sherry Reichel.
Scheduler.—Jill Cernock.
Press Secretary.—Andrew Wilder.
Suite 120, 2200 East Camelback Road, Phoenix, AZ 85016 .... (602) 840–1891
Suite 220, 7315 North Oracle, Tucson, AZ 85704 .... (520) 575–8633

REPRESENTATIVES

FIRST DISTRICT

RICK RENZI, Republican, of Flagstaff, AZ; born on June 11, 1958, in Sierra Vista, AZ; education: B.S., Northern Arizona University, 1980; J.D., Catholic University, 2002; profession: businessman; founded Renzi and Co., an insurance company designed to help non-profit organizations; while working on his law degree, he served as a legal extern for members of Arizona's congressional delegation; researched legal issues on religious freedoms, Federal land policies, and private property rights; family: married to Roberta; twelve children; elected to the 108th Congress on November 5, 2002.

Office Listings

http://www.house.gov/renzi

418 Cannon House Office Building, Washington, DC 20515 .... (202) 225–2315
Chief of Staff.—Jimmy Jayne. FAX: 226–9739
Legislative Director.—Joanne Keene.
Scheduler.—Anna Hackett.
2707 S. White Mountain Road, Suite E, Show Low, AZ 85901 .... (928) 537–2800

Counties: APACHE, COCONINO, GILA, GRAHAM, GREENLEE, NAVAJO (part), PINAL (part), YAVAPAI. CITIES AND TOWNSHIPS: Flagstaff, Prescott, Payson, Show Low, and Casa Grande. Population (2000), 641,329.

ZIP Codes: 85218, 85221–23, 85228, 85230–32, 85235, 85237, 85241, 85245, 85247, 85272–73, 85291–92, 85324, 85332, 85362, 85501–02, 85530–36, 85539–48, 85550–54, 85618, 85623, 85631, 85653, 85901–02, 85911–12, 85920, 85922–42, 86001–04, 86011, 86015–18, 86020, 86022–25, 86028–29, 86031–33, 86035–36, 86038, 86040, 86044–47, 86052–54, 86301–05, 86312–14, 86320–27, 86329–43, 86351, 86503, 86505, 86514–15, 86520, 86535, 86538, 86540, 86544–45, 86547, 86549, 86556

* * *

SECOND DISTRICT

TRENT FRANKS, Republican, of Phoenix, AZ; born on June 19, 1957, in Uravan, CO; education: attended Ottawa University; graduate of the Center for Constitutional Studies; professional: small business owner; oil field and drilling engineer; Executive Director, Arizona Family Research Institute; conservative writer, and former radio commentator, with Family Life Radio and NBC affiliate KTKP 1280 AM; public service: Arizona House of Representatives, 1985–87; appointed in 1987 to head the Arizona Governor's Office for Children; religion: Baptist; member, North Phoenix Baptist Church; family: married to Josephine; elected to the 108th Congress on November 5, 2002.

Office Listings

http://www.house.gov/franks

1237 Longworth House Office Building, Washington, DC 20515 .... (202) 225–4576
Chief of Staff.—John Graves. FAX: 225–6328
Legislative Director.—Doyle Scott.
Press Secretary.—Elaine Dalbo.
7121 W. Bell Road, Suite 200, Glendale, AZ 85308 .... (623) 776–7911

Counties: COCONINO (part), LAPAZ (part), MARICOPA (part), MOHAVE, NAVAJO (part), YAVAPAI (part). Population (2000), 641,329.

ZIP Codes: 85029, 85037, 85051, 85098, 85301–10, 85312, 85318, 85320, 85326, 85335, 85338, 85340, 85342, 85345, 85351, 85355, 85358, 85360–61, 85363, 85372–76, 85378–83, 85385, 85387, 85390, 86021, 86030, 86034, 86039, 86042–43, 86401–06, 86411–13, 86426–27, 86429–46

* * *

THIRD DISTRICT

JOHN B. SHADEGG, Republican, of Phoenix, AZ; born in Phoenix on October 22, 1949; graduated Camelback High School; B.A., University of Arizona, Tucson, 1972; J.D., University of Arizona, 1975; Air National Guard, 1969–75; admitted to the Arizona bar, 1976; law offices of John Shadegg; special counsel, Arizona House Republican Caucus, 1991–92; special assistant attorney general, 1983–90; advisor, U.S. Sentencing Commission; founding director/executive committee member, Goldwater Institute for Public Policy; member/former president, Crime Victim Foundation; chairman, Arizona Juvenile Justice Advisory Council; advisory board, Salvation Army; vestry, Christ Church of the Ascension Episcopal, 1989–91; member, Law Society, ASU College of Law; chairman, Arizona Republican Caucus, 1985–87; chairman, Proposition 108—Two-Thirds Tax Limitation Initiative, 1992; member, Fiscal Accountability and Reform Efforts (FARE) Committee, 1991–92; counsel, Arizonans for Wildlife Conservation (no on Proposition 200), 1992; Victims Bill of Rights Task Force, 1989–90; member, Growing Smarter Committee, (yes on Proposition 303), 1998; married to Shirley Shadegg; two children: Courtney and Stephen; committees: Energy and Commerce; Financial Services; assistant whip, Republican Policy Committee; Republican Steering Committee; Republican Study Committee; Select Committee on Homeland Security; subcommittees: Capital Markets, Insurance, and Government Sponsored Enterprises; vice chairman, Commerce, Trade, and Consumer Protection; Domestic Monetary Policy, Technology and Economic Growth; chairman, Emergency Preparedness and Response;

Energy and Air Quality; Health; Infrastructure and Border Security; Intelligence and Counterterrorism; Oversight and Investigation; elected to the 104th Congress; reelected to each succeeding Congress.

Office Listings

http://johnshadegg.house.gov

306 Cannon House Office Building, Washington, DC 20515 .... (202) 225–3361
Chief of Staff.—Elise Finley. FAX: 225–3462
Legislative Director.—Lance Wenger.
Scheduler.—Kristin Nelthorpe.
Press Secretary.—John Pappas.
301 East Bethany Home Road, Suite C–178, Phoenix, AZ 85012 .... (602) 263–5300
District Chief of Staff.—Sean Noble.

Counties: MARICOPA (part). CITIES AND TOWNSHIPS: Carefree, Cave Creek, Paradise Valley, and Phoenix (part). Population (2000), 641,329.

ZIP Codes: 85012–24, 85027–29, 85032, 85046, 85050–51, 85053–54, 85060, 85071, 85075, 85078–80, 85082, 85098–99, 85250–51, 85253–54, 85262, 85308, 85310, 85327, 85331, 85377

* * *

FOURTH DISTRICT

ED PASTOR, Democrat, of Phoenix, AZ; born in Claypool, AZ, on June 28, 1943; education: attended public schools in Miami, AZ; graduate of Arizona State University; B.A., chemistry, 1966; J.D., Arizona University, 1974; member, Governor Raul Castro's staff; taught chemistry, North High School; former deputy director of Guadalupe Organization, Inc.; elected supervisor, board of supervisors, Maricopa County; served board of directors for the National Association of Counties; vice chairman, Employment Steering Committee; president, Arizona County Supervisors Association; member, executive committee of the Arizona Association of Counties; resigned, May, 1991; elected by special election on September 24, 1991, to fill the vacancy caused by the resignation of Morris K. Udall; reelected in November, 1992, to the 103rd Congress; appointed to Democratic Steering and Policy Committee; member: Appropriations Committee, Subcommittee on Energy and Water Development; Subcommittee on Rural Development, Agriculture and Related Agencies; reelected to the 104th Congress in November, 1994; member: Committee on Agriculture; Subcommittee on General Commodities; Subcommittee on Risk Management and Specialty Crops; House Committee on Oversight; Joint Committee on the Library of Congress; chairman, Hispanic Caucus; reelected to the 105th Congress in November, 1996; appointed a Deputy Minority Whip; member, Appropriations Committee; Subcommittee on Energy and Water Development; Subcommittee on Transportation; Committee on Standards of Official Conduct; reelected to the 106th Congress in November, 1998; appointed a Chief Deputy Minority Whip; member, Appropriations Committee; Subcommittee on Energy and Water Development; Subcommittee on Transportation; Subcommittee on Legislative; reelected to the 107th Congress in November, 2000; appointed Chief Deputy Minority Whip; committees: Appropriations; Standards of Official Conduct; subcommittees: Energy and Water Development; Transportation; reelected to the 108th Congress in November 2002; appointed a Chief Deputy Minority Whip; member, Appropriations Committee; Subcommittee on District of Columbia; Subcommittee on Energy and Water Development; Subcommittee on Transportation, Treasury and Independent Agencies; married: Verma Pastor; two daughters: Yvonne and Laura; board of directors, Neighborhood Housing Services of America; National Association of Latino Elected Officials; served as director at large, ASU Alumni Association; founding board member, ASU Los Diablos Alumni Association; served on board of directors of the National Council of La Raza; Arizona Joint Partnership Training Council; National Conference of Christians and Jews; Friendly House; Chicanos Por La Causa; Phoenix Economic Growth Corporation; Sun Angel Foundation; vice president, Valley of the Sun United Way; advisory member, Boys Club of Metropolitan Phoenix.

Office Listings

http://www.house.gov/pastor

2465 Rayburn House Office Building, Washington, DC 20515 .... (202) 225–4065
Executive Assistant.—Laura Campos.
411 N. Central Avenue, Suite 150, Phoenix, AZ 85004 .... (602) 256–0551
District Director.—Ron Piceno.

Counties: MARICOPA (part). Population (2000), 641,329.

ZIP Codes: 85001–09, 85012–19, 85025–26, 85030–31, 85033–36, 85038, 85040–44, 85051, 85061–64, 85066–69, 85072–74, 85076, 85082, 85099, 85283, 85301, 85303, 85309, 85311, 85339, 86045, 86329, 86337

FIFTH DISTRICT

J.D. HAYWORTH, Republican, of Scottsdale, AZ; born in High Point, NC, on July 12, 1958; graduated, High Point Central High School, 1976; B.A., speech communications and political science, *cum laude*, North Carolina State University, Raleigh, 1980; broadcaster; public relations consultant; insurance agent; member: Rotary Club of Phoenix (Paul Harris Fellow); Boy Scouts of America (Eagle Scout); married Mary Denise Yancey Hayworth, 1989; three children: Nicole, Hannah, and John Micah; committees: Resources; Ways and Means; elected to the 104th Congress; reelected to each succeeding Congress.

Office Listings

http://www.house.gov/hayworth

2434 Rayburn House Office Building, Washington, DC 20515 .... (202) 225–2190
Administrative Assistant.—Joe Eule. FAX: 225–3263
Legislative Director.—Katharine Mottley.
Executive Assistant.—Tricia Evans.
Legislative Assistants: Suzanne Geroux, Ryan Serote, Todd Sommers.
14300 North Northside Boulevard, Suite 101, Scottsdale, AZ 85260 .... (480) 926–4151

Counties: MARICOPA (part). CITIES AND TOWNSHIPS: Chandler (part), Fountain Hills, Mesa (part), Phoenix (part), Rio Verde, Scottsdale, Tempe. Ahwatukee, the Salt River Pima Indian Reservation, and the Fort McDowell Yavapai Apache Indian Reservation. Population (2000), 641,329.

ZIP Codes: 85008, 85018, 85044–45, 85048, 85070, 85076, 85201–03, 85210, 85213, 85215, 85224–26, 85250–64, 85267–69, 85271, 85274, 85280–85, 85287, 85331

* * *

SIXTH DISTRICT

JEFF FLAKE, Republican, of Mesa, AZ; born in Snowflake, AZ, on December 31, 1962; education: Brigham Young University; B.A., International Relations; M.A., Political Science; religion: Mormon; served a mission in South Africa and Zimbabwe; occupation: businessman; employment: Shipley, Smoak & Henry (public affairs firm); Executive Director, Foundation for Democracy; Executive Director, Goldwater Institute; married: Cheryl; children: Ryan, Alexis, Austin, Tanner, and Dallin; elected to the 107th Congress on November 7, 2000; reelected to each succeeding Congress.

Office Listings

http://www.house.gov/flake

424 Cannon House Office Building, Washington, DC 20515 .... (202) 225–2635
Chief of Staff.—Steve Voeller. FAX: 226–4386
Office Manager.—Jana Kigin.
Press Secretary.—Matthew Specht.
1640 South Stapley, #215, Mesa, AZ 85204 .... (480) 833–0092

Counties: MARICOPA (part), PINAL (part). CITIES AND TOWNSHIPS: Apache Junction, Chandler, Gilbert, Mesa, and Queen Creek. Population (2000), 641,329.

ZIP Codes: 85201, 85203–08, 85210–20, 85224–25, 85227, 85233–34, 85236, 85242, 85244, 85246, 85248–49, 85254, 85275, 85277–78, 85290, 85296–97, 85299

* * *

SEVENTH DISTRICT

RAÚL M. GRIJALVA, Democrat, of Tulsa, AZ; born on February 19, 1948; education: Sunnyside High School, Tucson, AZ; B.A., University of Arizona; professional: former Assistant Dean for Hispanic Student Affairs, University of Arizona; former Director of the El Pueblo Neighborhood Center; public service: Tucson Unified School District Governing Board, 1974–1986; Pima County Board of Supervisors, 1989–2002; family: married to Ramona; three daughters; elected to the 108th Congress on November 5, 2002.

Office Listings

http://www.house.gov/grijalva

1440 Longworth House Office Building, Washington, DC 20515 .... (202) 225–2435
Chief of Staff.—Ana Ma. FAX: 225–1541
Legislative Director.—Glenn Miller.
Press Liaison / Scheduler.—Ruben Reyes.
810 East 22nd Street, Suite 102, Tucson, AZ 85713 .... (520) 622–6788

Counties: LA PAZ (part), MARICOPA (part), PIMA (part), PINAL (part), SANTA CRUZ (part), YUMA. Population (2000), 641,329.

ZIP Codes: 85033, 85035, 85037, 85043, 85221–22, 85226, 85228, 85232, 85239, 85242, 85248–49, 85273, 85321–23, 85325–26, 85328–29, 85333–34, 85336–37, 85339–41, 85343–44, 85346–50, 85352–54, 85356–57, 85359, 85364–67, 85369, 85371, 85601, 85621, 85628, 85631, 85633–34, 85639–40, 85648, 85653, 85662, 85701–03, 85705–06, 85711, 85713–14, 85716–17, 85719, 85721–26, 85733–36, 85743, 85745–46, 85754

* * *

EIGHTH DISTRICT

JIM KOLBE, Republican, of Tucson, AZ; born in Evanston, IL, June 28, 1942; education: graduated, U.S. Capitol Page School, Washington, DC, 1960; B.A., political science, Northwestern University, Evanston, IL, 1965; M.B.A., Stanford University, CA, 1967; study abroad program, International School of America, 1962–63; served in Vietnam, U.S. Navy, lieutenant, 1967–69; lieutenant commander, U.S. Naval Reserves (inactive); employment: vice president, Wood Canyon Corporation, Sonoita, AZ; consultant, real estate development and political affairs; Arizona State Senator, 1977–82; special assistant to Governor Ogilvie of Illinois, 1972–73; board of directors, Tucson Community Food Bank; committees: Appropriations; elected to the 99th Congress on November 6, 1984; reelected to each succeeding Congress.

Office Listings

http://www.house.gov/kolbe

2266 Rayburn House Office Building, Washington, DC 20515 .... (202) 225–2542
Chief of Staff.—Fran McNaught.
Office Manager/Scheduler.—Patrick Baugh.
Suite 112, 1661 North Swan, Tucson, AZ 85712 .... (520) 881–3588
District Director.—Patricia Klein.
Suite B–160, 77 Calle Portal, Sierra Vista, AZ 85635 .... (520) 459–3115

Counties: COCHISE, PIMA (part), PINAL (part), SANTA CRUZ. Population (2000), 641,329.

ZIP Codes: 85602–03, 85605–11, 85613–17, 85619–20, 85622, 85624–27, 85629–30, 85632, 85635–38, 85641, 85643–46, 85650, 85652–55, 85670, 85704–16, 85718–19, 85728, 85730–32, 85736–45, 85747–52

ARKANSAS

(Population 2000, 2,673,400)

SENATORS

BLANCHE L. LINCOLN, Democrat, of Helena, AR; born in Helena, AR, on September 30, 1960; graduate of Helena Central High School; daughter of the late Jordan Bennett Lambert, Jr., and Martha Kelly Lambert; B.S., in biology, at Randolph Macon Woman's College, Lynchburg, VA, 1982; also attended the University of Arkansas, Fayetteville; member, Chi Omega sorority; American Red Cross volunteer; married to Dr. Stephen R. Lincoln; mother of twin boys, Bennett and Reece; committees: Agriculture, Nutrition, and Forestry; Finance; Special Committee on Aging; Select Committee on Ethics; subcommittees: ranking member, Forestry, Conservation and Rural Revitalization; elected to the U.S. House of Representatives for the 103rd and 104th Congresses; elected to the U.S. Senate on November 3, 1998.

Office Listings

http://lincoln.senate.gov

355 Dirksen Senate Office Building, Washington, DC 20510 .... (202) 224–4843
Chief of Staff.—Steve Patterson. FAX: 228–1371
Legislative Director.—Kelly Rucker Bingel.
Press Secretary.—Drew Goesl.
Scheduler.—Katie Davies.
912 West Fourth Street, Little Rock, AR 72201 .... (501) 375–2993
6700 McKennon Boulevard, Suite 122, Fort Smith, AR 72903 .... (479) 782–9215
Federal Building, Suite 315, 615 South Main, Jonesboro, AR 72401 .... (870) 910–6896
Drew County Courthouse, 210 South Main Street, Monticello, AR 71655 .... (870) 367–6925
Miller County Courthouse, 400 Laurel Street, #101, Texarkana, AR 71854 .... (870) 774–3106

* * *

MARK PRYOR, Democrat, of Little Rock, AR; born on January 10, 1963, in Fayetteville, AR; education: B.A., University of Arkansas, 1985; J.D., University of Arkansas, 1988; profession: Attorney; employment: Wright, Lindsey & Jennings (law firm); public service: elected, Arkansas House of Representatives, 1990; elected, Arkansas Attorney General, 1998; family: married to Jill; children: Adams and Porter; his father, David Pryor, was a former Governor and U.S. Senator from Arkansas; elected to the U.S. Senate on November 5, 2002.

Office Listings

http://pryor.senate.gov

217 Russell Senate Office Building, Washington, DC 20510 .... (202) 224–2353
Chief of Staff.—Bob Russell. FAX: 228–0908
Legislative Director.—Walter Pryor.
Communications Director.—Rodell Mollineau.
Administrative Director.—Shannon Lane.
Federal Building, Room 2527, 700 West Capitol Street, Little Rock, AR 72201 ..... (501) 324–6336

REPRESENTATIVES

FIRST DISTRICT

MARION BERRY, Democrat, of Gillett, AR; born in Bayou Meto Community, August 27, 1942; graduated, DeWitt High School; B.S., pharmacy, University of Arkansas, 1965; partner and general manager, family farm; appointed Special Assistant to the President for Agricultural Trade and Food Assistance, 1993; member, Domestic Policy Council, The White House, 1993–96; member, Arkansas Soil and Water Conservation Commission, 1986–94, serving as chairman in 1992; Gillett City Councilman, 1976–80; married the former Carolyn Lowe in 1962; two children: Ann Coggin and Mitchell; co-chairman, Democratic Blue Dog Coalition's Health Care Task Force; co-chair, House Affordable Medicines Task Force; Congressional Methamphetamine Caucus; Congressional Missing and Exploited Children's Caucus; Congressional Rural Caucus; Congressional Silk Road Caucus; co-chair, Congressional Soybean Caucus; Congressional Steel Caucus; House Renewable Energy and Energy Efficiency Caucus; New Democrat Coalition; Rural Health Care Coalition; Brain Injury Caucus; Rural Working Group; committees: Appropriations; subcommittees: Energy and Water Development; Homeland Security; elected to the 105th Congress; reelected to each succeeding Congress.

Office Listings

http://www.house.gov/berry

1113 Longworth House Office Building, Washington, DC 20515 .... (202) 225–4076
Chief of Staff.—Thad Huguley. FAX: 225–5602
Press Secretary.—Josh Earnest.
Legislative Director.—Chad Causey.
108 East Huntington Avenue, Jonesboro, AR 72401 .... (870) 972–4600
116 North First Street, Suite C–1, Cabot, AR 72023 .... (501) 843–3043

Counties: ARKANSAS, BAXTER, CLAY, CLEBURNE, CRAIGHEAD, CRITTENDEN, CROSS, FULTON, GREENE, INDEPENDENCE, IZARD, JACKSON, LAWRENCE, LEE, LONOKE, MISSISSIPPI, MONROE, PHILLIPS, POINSETT, PRAIRIE, RANDOLPH, ST. FRANCIS, SEARCY, SHARP, STONE, WOODRUFF. Population (2000), 668,360.

ZIP Codes: 72003, 72005–07, 72014, 72017, 72020–21, 72023–24, 72026, 72029, 72031, 72036–38, 72040–44, 72046, 72048, 72051, 72055, 72059–60, 72064, 72067, 72069, 72072–76, 72083, 72086, 72101–02, 72108, 72112, 72121, 72123, 72130–31, 72134, 72137, 72139–40, 72142–43, 72153, 72160, 72165–66, 72169–70, 72175–76, 72179, 72189, 72301, 72303, 72310–13, 72315–16, 72319–22, 72324–33, 72335–36, 72338–42, 72346–48, 72350–55, 72358–60, 72364–70, 72372–74, 72376–77, 72383–84, 72386–87, 72389–92, 72394–96, 72401–04, 72410–17, 72419, 72421–22, 72424–45, 72447, 72449–51, 72453–62, 72464–67, 72469–76, 72478–79, 72482, 72501, 72503, 72512–13, 72515, 72517, 72519–34, 72536–40, 72542–46, 72550, 72553–56, 72560–62, 72564–69, 72571–73, 72575–79, 72581, 72583–85, 72587, 72610, 72613, 72617, 72623, 72626, 72629, 72631, 72633, 72635–36, 72639, 72642, 72645, 72650–51, 72653–54, 72658, 72663, 72669, 72675, 72679–80, 72685–86

* * *

SECOND DISTRICT

VIC SNYDER, Democrat, of Little Rock, AR; born in Medford, OR, September 27, 1947; graduated from Medford High School, 1965; corporal, U.S. Marine Corps, 1967–69, including one year in Vietnam with Headquarters Company, First Marine Division; B.A., chemistry, 1975, Willamette University, Salem, OR; M.D., 1979, University of Oregon Health Sciences Center, Portland; family practice residency, 1979–82, University of Arkansas for Medical Sciences; family practice physician in central Arkansas, 1982–present; medical missions to Cambodian refugee camps in Thailand, El Salvadoran refugee camps in Honduras, a West African mission hospital in Sierra Leone, and an Ethiopian refugee camp in Sudan; J.D., 1988, University of Arkansas at Little Rock School of Law; Arkansas State Senator, 1991–96; committees: Armed Services; Veterans Affairs; elected to the 105th Congress; reelected to each succeeding Congress.

Office Listings

http://www.house.gov/snyder

1330 Longworth House Office Building, Washington, DC 20515 .... (202) 225–2506
Staff Director.—Ed Fry. FAX: 225–5903
Press Secretary/District Scheduler.—Jennifer Oglesby.
Legislative Director.—Mike Casey.
3118 Federal Building, 700 West Capitol Avenue, Little Rock, AR 72201 .... (501) 324–5941
District Director.—Amanda Nixon White.

Counties: CONWAY, FAULKNER, PERRY, PULASKI, SALINE, VAN BUREN, WHITE, YELL. Population (2000), 668,176.

ZIP Codes: 71772, 71909, 72001–02, 72010–13, 72015–18, 72020, 72022–23, 72025, 72027–28, 72030–35, 72039, 72045–47, 72052–53, 72057–61, 72063, 72065–68, 72070, 72076, 72078–82, 72085, 72087–89, 72099, 72102–04, 72106–08, 72110–11, 72113–22, 72124–27, 72131, 72135–37, 72139, 72141–43, 72145, 72149, 72153, 72156–57, 72164, 72167, 72173, 72178, 72180–81, 72183, 72190, 72199, 72201–07, 72209–12, 72214–17, 72219, 72221–23, 72225, 72227, 72231, 72260, 72295, 72419, 72568, 72629, 72645, 72679, 72823–24, 72827–29, 72833–34, 72838, 72841–42, 72853, 72857, 72860, 72943

* * *

THIRD DISTRICT

JOHN BOOZMAN, Republican, of Rogers, AR; born on December 10, 1950, in Shreveport, LA; education: Northside High School, Fort Smith, AR; University of Arkansas, completing his pre-optometry requirements; graduated, Southern College of Optometry, 1977; profession: optometrist; entered private practice as a co-founder of the Boozman-Hof Eye Clinic; community service: volunteer optometrist at the Arkansas School for the Blind, and at area clinics; public service: Rogers School Board, serving two terms; member: state and local cattlemen's associations; Benton County Fair Board; Fellowship of Christian Athletes; Arkansas Athletes Outreach Board; religion: Baptist; family: married the former Cathy Marley; three daughters; elected to the 107th Congress, by special election, on November 20, 2001; reelected to each succeeding Congress.

Office Listings

http://www.house.gov/boozman

1708 Longworth House Office Building, Washington, DC 20515 .... (202) 225–4301
Deputy Chief of Staff.—Matthew Sagely. FAX: 225–5713
Press Secretary.—Patrick Creamer.
Scheduler.—Elizabeth Yeager.
30 South 6th Street, Room 240, Fort Smith, AR 72901 .... (479) 782–7787
402 N. Walnut Street, Suite 210, Harrison, AR 72601 .... (870) 741–6900
207 West Center Street, Fayetteville, AR 72701 .... (479) 442–5258
Chief of Staff.—Steve Gray.

Counties: BENTON, BOONE, CARROLL, CRAWFORD, FRANKLIN, JOHNSON, MADISON, MARION, NEWTON, POPE, SEBASTIAN, WASHINGTON. Population (2000), 668,479.

ZIP Codes: 71937, 71944–45, 71953, 71972–73, 72063, 72080, 72601–02, 72611, 72613, 72615–16, 72619, 72624, 72628, 72630–34, 72638–41, 72644–45, 72648, 72653, 72655, 72660–63, 72666, 72668, 72670, 72672, 72675, 72677, 72679, 72682–83, 72685–87, 72701–04, 72711–12, 72714–19, 72721–22, 72727–30, 72732–42, 72744–45, 72747, 72749, 72751–53, 72756–58, 72760–62, 72764–66, 72768–70, 72773–74, 72776, 72801–02, 72811–12, 72820–21, 72823, 72830, 72832, 72837–43, 72845–47, 72852, 72854, 72856–58, 72860, 72901–06, 72908, 72913–14, 72916–19, 72921, 72923, 72927–28, 72930, 72932–38, 72940–41, 72944–49, 72951–52, 72955–57, 72959

* * *

FOURTH DISTRICT

MIKE ROSS, Democrat, of Prescott, AR; born on August 2, 1961, in Texarkana, AR; education: Hope High School; B.A., University of Arkansas at Little Rock, 1987; employment: small businessman; owner of Ross Pharmacy, Inc., in Prescott, AR; public service: Chief of Staff to Arkansas Lt. Governor Winston Bryant, 1985–89; three term State Senator, 1991–2000; organizations: Executive Director, Arkansas Youth Suicide Prevention Commission, 1985–89; First United Methodist Church in Prescott, AR; awards: National Association of Social Workers Public Citizen of the Year, 1999; Arkansas State Police Association Distinguished Service Award; Arkansas Kids Count Coalition Achievement Award; married: Holly; children: Alex and Sydney Beth; elected to the 107th Congress on November 7, 2000; reelected to each succeeding Congress.

Office Listings

http://www.house.gov/ross

314 Cannon House Office Building, Washington, DC 20515 .... (202) 225–3772
Chief of Staff.—Erik Greathouse. FAX: 225–1314
Legislative Director.—Monique Frazier.
Communications Director.—Marie DesOrmeaux.
District Director.—Chris Masingill.
221 West Main Street, Prescott, AR 71857 .... (870) 887–6787
2300 West 29th, Suite 1A, Pine Bluff, AR 71603 .... (870) 536–3376
112 Buena Vista, Hot Springs, AR 71913 .... (501) 520–5892
Union County Courthouse, Suite 406, 101 North Washington Street, El Dorado, AR 71730 .... (870) 881–0681

Counties: ASHLEY, BRADLEY, CALHOUN, CHICOT, CLARK, CLEVELAND, COLUMBIA, DALLAS, DESHA, DREW, GARLAND, GRANT, HEMPSTEAD, HOT SPRING, HOWARD, JEFFERSON, LAFAYETTE, LINCOLN, LITTLE RIVER, LOGAN, MILLER, MONTGOMERY, NEVADA, OUACHITA, PIKE, POLK, SCOTT, SEVIER, UNION. Population (2000), 668,385.

ZIP Codes: 71601–03, 71611–13, 71630–31, 71635, 71638–40, 71642–44, 71646–47, 71651–63, 71665–67, 71670–71, 71674–78, 71701, 71711, 71720–22, 71724–26, 71728, 71730–31, 71740, 71742–45, 71747–54, 71758–59, 71762–66, 71768, 71770, 71772, 71801–02, 71820, 71822–23, 71825–28, 71831–42, 71844–47, 71851–55, 71857–62, 71864–66, 71901–03, 71909–10, 71913–14, 71920–23, 71929, 71932–33, 71935, 71937, 71940–45, 71949–50, 71952–53, 71956–62, 71964–65, 71968–73, 71998–99, 72004, 72015, 72046, 72055, 72057, 72065, 72072–73, 72079, 72084, 72087, 72104–05, 72128–29, 72132–33, 72150, 72152, 72160, 72167–68, 72175, 72182, 72379, 72826–27, 72833–35, 72838, 72841–42, 72851, 72855, 72863, 72865, 72924, 72926–28, 72933, 72943–44, 72949–51, 72958

CALIFORNIA

(Population 2000, 33,871,648)

SENATORS

DIANNE FEINSTEIN, Democrat, of San Francisco, CA; born June 22, 1933 in San Francisco; education: B.A., Stanford University, 1955; elected to San Francisco Board of Supervisors, 1970–78; president of Board of Supervisors: 1970–71, 1974–75, 1978; mayor of San Francisco, 1978–88; candidate for governor of California, 1990. Recipient: Distinguished Woman Award, *San Francisco Examiner;* Achievement Award, Business and Professional Women's Club, 1970; Golden Gate University, California, LL.D. (hon.), 1979; SCOPUS Award for Outstanding Public Service, American Friends of the Hebrew University of Jerusalem; University of Santa Clara, D.P.S. (hon.); University of Manila, D.P.A. (hon.), 1981; Antioch University, LL.D. (hon.), 1983; Los Angeles Anti-Defamation League of B'nai B'rith's Distinguished Service Award, 1984; French Legion d'Honneur from President Mitterand, 1984; Mills College, LL.D. (hon.), 1985; U.S. Army's Commander's Award for Public Service, 1986; Brotherhood/Sisterhood Award, National Conference of Christians and Jews, 1986; Paulist Fathers Award, 1987; Episcopal Church Award for Service, 1987; U.S. Navy Distinguished Civilian Award, 1987; Silver Spur Award for Outstanding Public Service, San Francisco Planning and Urban Renewal Association, 1987; All Pro Management Team Award for No. 1 Mayor, *City and State* Magazine, 1987; Community Service Award Honoree for Public Service, 1987; American Jewish Congress, 1987; President's Award, St. Ignatius High School, San Francisco, 1988; Coro Investment in Leadership Award, 1988; President's Medal, University of California at San Francisco, 1988; University of San Francisco, D.H.L. (hon.), 1988. Member: Coro Foundation, Fellowship, 1955–56; California Women's Board of Terms and Parole, 1960–66, executive committee; U.S. Conference of Mayors, 1983–88; Mayor's Commission on Crime, San Francisco; Bank of California, director, 1988–89; San Francisco Education Fund's Permanent Fund, 1988–89; Japan Society of Northern California, 1988–89; Inter-American Dialogue, 1988-present; Trilateral Commission, 1988; Biderberg Foreign Policy Conference, Baden, Germany, 1991; married: Dr. Bertram Feinstein (dec.); married on January 20, 1980, to Richard C. Blum; children: one child; three stepchildren; religion: Jewish; committees: Appropriations; Energy and Natural Resources; Judiciary; Rules and Administration; Select Committee on Intelligence; elected to the U.S. Senate, by special election, on November 3, 1992, to fill the vacancy caused by the resignation of Senator Pete Wilson; reelected to each succeeding Senate term.

Office Listings

http://feinstein.senate.gov

331 Hart Senate Office Building, Washington, DC 20510 .... (202) 224–3841
Chief of Staff.—Mark Kadesh.
Legislative Director.—Michael Schiffer.
Director of Communications.—Howard Gantman.
750 B Street, Suite 1030, San Diego, CA 92101 .... (619) 231–9712
Federal Office Building, Suite 2446, 1130 O Street, Fresno, CA 93721 .... (559) 485–7430
One Post Street, Suite 2450, San Francisco, CA 94104 .... (415) 393–0707
11111 San Monica Boulevard, Suite 915, Los Angles, CA 90025 .... (310) 914–7300

* * *

BARBARA BOXER, Democrat, of Greenbrae, CA; born in Brooklyn, NY, November 11, 1940; education: B.A., economics, Brooklyn College, 1962; employment: stockbroker and economic researcher with securities firms on Wall Street, 1962–65; journalist and associate editor, *Pacific Sun* newspaper, 1972–74; congressional aide, Fifth Congressional District, California, 1974–76; elected Marin County Board of Supervisors, 1976–82; first woman president, Marin County Board of Supervisors; married: Stewart Boxer, 1962; children: Doug and Nicole; elected November 2, 1982 to 98th Congress; reelected to the 99th–102nd Congresses; committees: Commerce, Science, and Transportation; Environment and Public Works; Foreign Relations; subcommittees: Aviation; Communications; Competition, Foreign Commerce, and Infrastructure; International Operations and Terrorism; Near Eastern and South Asian Affairs; Superfund and Waste Management; Surface Transportation and Merchant Marine; Transportation and Infrastructure; Western Hemisphere, Peace Corps, and Narcotics Affairs; elected to the U.S. Senate on November 3, 1992; reelected to each succeeding Senate term.

Office Listings

http://boxer.senate.gov

112 Hart Senate Office Building, Washington, DC 20510 .... (202) 224–3553
Administrative Assistant.—Karen Olick.
Legislative Director.—Matthew Baumgart.
Communications Director.—David Sandretti.
1700 Montgomery Street, Suite 240, San Francisco, CA 94111 .... (415) 403–0100
Chief of Staff.—Sam Chapman.
312 North Spring Street, Suite 1748, Los Angeles, CA 90012 .... (213) 894–5000
501 I Street, Suite 7–600, Sacramento, CA 95814 .... (916) 448–2787
201North E Street, Suite 210, San Bernadino, CA 92401 .... (909) 888–8525
600 B Street, Suite 2240, San Diego, CA 92101 .... (619) 239–3884
1130 O Street, Suite 2450, Fresno, CA 93721 .... (209) 497–5109

REPRESENTATIVES

FIRST DISTRICT

MIKE THOMPSON, Democrat, of Napa Valley, CA; born on January 24, 1951, in St. Helena, CA; graduated, St. Helena High School, St. Helena, CA; U.S. Army, 1969–72; Purple Heart; B.A., Chico State University, 1982; M.A., Chico State University, 1996; teacher at San Francisco State University, and Chico State University; elected to the California State Senate, 2nd District, 1990–98; chairman of the Budget Committee; married to Janet; two children: Christopher and Jon; committees: Agriculture; Budget; Transportation and Infrastructure; elected to the 106th Congress; reelected to each succeeding Congress.

Office Listings

http://www.house.gov/mthompson http://www.house.gov/writerep

119 Cannon House Office Building, Washington, DC 20515 .... (202) 225–3311
Legislative Director.—Mandy Kenney. FAX: 225–4335
1040 Main Street, Suite 101, Napa, CA 94559 .... (707) 226–9898
Chief of Staff/Press Secretary.—Ed Matovcik.
317 Third Street, Suite 1, Eureka, CA 95501 .... (707) 269–9595
Post Office Box 2208, Fort Bragg, CA 95437 .... (707) 962–0933
712 Main Street, Suite 1, Woodland, CA 95695 .... (530) 662–5272

Counties: DEL NORTE COUNTY. CITIES AND TOWNSHIPS: Crescent City, Fortdeck, Gasquet, Klamath, Prison, Smith River. HUMBOLDT COUNTY. CITIES AND TOWNSHIPS: Alderpoint, Areata, Bayside, Blocksburg, Blue Lake, Burcka, Carlotta, Eureka, Ferndale, Fortuna, Garberville, Hoopa, Hydsevilie, Kneeland, Korbel, Loleta, McKinlayville, Myers Flat, Orick, Petrolia, Redcrest, Redway, Rio Del, Scotia, Trinidad, Whitehorn, Willow Çreek. LAKE COUNTY. CITIES AND TOWNSHIPS: Clearlake, Clearlake Oaks, Clearlake Park, Cobb, Glenhaven, Kelseyville, Lakeport, Lower Lake, Lucerne, Middletown, Nice, Upper Lake. MENDOCINO COUNTY. CITIES AND TOWNSHIPS: Albion, Boonville, Calpella, Compiche, Covelo, Elk, Finley, Fort Bragg, Gualala, Hopland, Laytonville, Little River, Manchester, Mendocino, Philo, Piercy, Point Arena, Potter Valley, Redwood Valley, Talmage, Ukiah, Willits, Yorkville. NAPA COUNTY. CITIES AND TOWNSHIPS: American Canyon, Angwin, Aetna Springs, Calistoga, Deer Park, Oakville, Pope Valley, Rutherford, St. Helena. SONOMA COUNTY (part). CITIES AND TOWNSHIPS: Alexander Valley, Cloverdale, Geyserville, Healdsburg, Mark West, Santa Rosa (part), Sonoma, Windsor. YOLO COUNTY (part). CITIES AND TOWNSHIPS: Davis, West Sacramento, Winters, and Woodland. Population (2000), 639,087.

ZIP Codes: 94503, 94508, 94515, 94558–59, 94562, 94567, 94573–74, 94576, 94581, 94589–90, 94599, 95403–04, 95409–10, 95415–18, 95420, 95422–29, 95432–33, 95435, 95437, 95441–43, 95445, 95448–49, 95451–54, 95456–61, 95463–64, 95466, 95468–70, 95476, 95481–82, 95485, 95487–88, 95490, 95492–94, 95501–03, 95511, 95514, 95518–19, 95521, 95524–26, 95528, 95531–32, 95534, 95536–38, 95540, 95542–43, 95545–51, 95553–56, 95558–60, 95562, 95564–65, 95567, 95569–71, 95573, 95585, 95587, 95589, 95605, 95612, 95615–16, 95618, 95691, 95694–95, 95776, 95798–99, 95899

* * *

SECOND DISTRICT

WALLY HERGER, Republican, of Marysville, CA; born in Sutter County, CA, May 20, 1945; education: graduated East Nicolaus High School; attended California State University, Sacramento, CA; cattle rancher; small businessman; East Nicolaus High School Board of Trustees, 1977–80; California State Assemblyman, 1980–86; member: National Federation of Independent Business; Sutter County Taxpayers Association; Yuba-Sutter Farm Bureau; California Cattlemen's Association; California Chamber of Commerce; Big Brothers/Big Sisters Board of Directors; South Yuba Rotary Club; married: to the former Pamela Sargent; children: eight; committees: Ways and Means; subcommittees: chairman, Human Resources; Trade; elected to the 100th Congress, November 4, 1986; reelected to each succeeding Congress.

Office Listings

2268 Rayburn House Office Building, Washington, DC 20515 .... (202) 225–3076
Administrative Assistant.—John P. Magill.
Legislative Director.—Steve Thompson.
Press Secretary.—Daniel MacLean.
Executive Assistant/Scheduler.—Cherstyn Monson.
Suite 104, 55 Independence Circle, Chico, CA 95973 .... (530) 893–8363
District Director.—Fran Peace.
410 Hemsted Drive, Suite 115, Redding, CA 96002 .... (530) 223–5898

Counties: BUTTE (part), COLUSA, GLENN, SHASTA, SISKIYOU, SUTTER, TEHAMA, TRINITY, YOLO (part), YUBA. Population (2000), 639,087.

ZIP Codes: 95526–27, 95552, 95563, 95568, 95595, 95606–07, 95627, 95637, 95645, 95653, 95659, 95668, 95674, 95676, 95679, 95692, 95697–98, 95837, 95901, 95903, 95912–14, 95917–20, 95922, 95925–29, 95932, 95935–39, 95941–43, 95947–48, 95950–51, 95953–55, 95957–58, 95960–63, 95967, 95969–74, 95976–79, 95981–82, 95987–88, 95991–93, 96001–03, 96007–08, 96010–11, 96013–14, 96016–17, 96019, 96021–25, 96027–29, 96031–35, 96037–41, 96044, 96046–52, 96055–59, 96061–65, 96067, 96069–71, 96073–76, 96078–80, 96084–97, 96099, 96101, 96103–04, 96114, 96118, 96122, 96124, 96134, 96137, 96161

* * *

THIRD DISTRICT

DOUG OSE, Republican, of Sacramento, CA; born in Sacramento, CA, on June 27, 1955; education: Rio Americano High School; B.S., Business Administration, University of California at Berkeley; religion: Lutheran; organizations: former member, Citrus Heights Incorporation Project Board of Directors; former member, California State Automobile Association Board of Directors; former member, Citrus Heights Chamber of Commerce; former member, Sacramento Housing and Redevelopment Commission; member, Sacramento Rotary Club; married: Lynnda Ose, 1989; children: Erika and Emily; committees: Agriculture; Financial Services; Government Reform; subcommittees: vice chairman, Capital Markets, Insurance, and Government Sponsored Enterprises; Criminal Justice, Drug Policy and Human Resources; Department Operations, Oversight, Nutrition and Forestry; Domestic and International Monetary Policy, Trade and Technology; chairman, Energy Policy, Natural Resources and Regulatory Affairs; Housing and Community Opportunity; vice chairman, Livestock and Horticulture; Technology, Information Policy, Intergovernmental Relations and the Census; elected to the 106th Congress; reelected to each succeeding Congress.

Office Listings

http://www.house.gov/ose

236 Cannon House Office Building, Washington, DC 20515 .... (202) 225–5716
Chief of Staff.—Dan Skopec. FAX: 226–1298
Legislative Director.—James Kaplan.
Press Secretary.—Yier Shi.
4400 Auburn Boulevard, Suite 110, Sacramento, CA 95841 .... (916) 489–3684
District Director.—Dan Sharp.

Counties: ALPINE, AMADOR, CALAVERAS, SACRAMENTO (part), SOLANO (part). CITIES AND TOWNSHIPS: Amador, Arden-Arcade, Carmichael, Citrus Heights, Elk Grove, Fair Oaks, Folsom, Foothill Farms, Galt, Gold River, Ione, Jackson, Laguna, Laguna West, LaRiviera, North Highland, Rancho Cordova, Rancho Murieta, Rio Linda, Rio Vista, Roseville, Sacramento, Vineyard, and Wilton. Population (2000), 639,088.

ZIP Codes: 94571, 94585, 95221–26, 95228–30, 95232–33, 95236, 95245–52, 95254–55, 95257, 95601, 95608, 95610–11, 95615, 95620–21, 95624, 95626, 95628–30, 95632, 95638–40, 95642, 95646, 95652, 95654–55, 95660, 95662, 95665–66, 95668–71, 95673, 95675, 95683, 95685, 95688–90, 95693–94, 95699, 95742, 95758–59, 95763, 95821, 95825–30, 95832, 95835–37, 95841–43, 95864, 96021–22, 96029, 96035, 96055, 96061, 96080, 96120

* * *

FOURTH DISTRICT

JOHN T. DOOLITTLE, Republican, of Rocklin, CA; born in Glendale, CA, October 30, 1950; education: graduated Cupertino High School, Cupertino, CA, 1968; University of California at Santa Cruz, 1972; University of the Pacific, McGeorge School of Law, 1978; employment: lawyer; member: California bar; elected to the California State Senate, 1980; reelected 1984 and 1988; served as chairman of the Senate Republican Caucus, May 1987–April 1990; married: the former Julia Harlow, 1979; children: John, Jr. and Courtney Doolittle; elected to the 102nd Congress, November 6, 1990; reelected to each succeeding Congress.

Office Listings

http://www.house.gov/doolittle

2410 Rayburn House Office Building, Washington, DC 20515 .... (202) 225–2511
Chief of Staff.—David Lopez.
Executive Assistant.—Alisha Perkins. FAX: 225–5444
Legislative Director.—Greg Orlando.
4230 Douglas Boulevard, Suite 200, Granite Bay, CA 95746 .... (916) 786–5560
District Director / Deputy Chief of Staff.—Richard Robinson.

Counties: BUTTE (part), EL DORADO, LASSEN, MODOC, NEVADA, PLACER, PLUMAS, SACRAMENTO (part), SIERRA. Population (2000), 639,088.

ZIP Codes: 95602–04, 95609, 95613–14, 95617, 95619, 95623, 95626, 95628–31, 95633–36, 95648, 95650–51, 95656, 95658, 95661–64, 95667–68, 95672, 95677–78, 95681–82, 95684, 95701, 95703, 95709, 95712–15, 95717, 95720–22, 95724, 95726, 95728, 95735–36, 95741, 95746–47, 95762, 95765, 95816, 95910, 95915–16, 95922–24, 95930, 95934, 95940–41, 95944–47, 95949, 95956, 95959–60, 95965–66, 95968, 95971, 95975, 95977, 95980, 95983–84, 95986, 96006, 96009, 96015, 96020, 96054, 96056, 96068, 96101, 96103–30, 96132–33, 96135–37, 96140–43, 96145–46, 96148, 96150–52, 96154–56, 96158, 96160–62

* * *

FIFTH DISTRICT

ROBERT T. MATSUI, Democrat, of Sacramento, CA, born in Sacramento, September 17, 1941; education: graduated, C.K. McClatchy High School, 1959; A.B., University of California, Berkeley, 1963; J.D., Hastings College of Law, University of California, 1966; employment: admitted to the California bar in 1967 and commenced practice in Sacramento; Sacramento City Council, District 8, 1971–75; reelected, 1975–78; chairman, budget-finance committee, 1976–78; vice mayor, 1977; chairman, law and legislative committee, 1978; chairman, U.S. Congressman John E. Moss reelection campaign committee; member, California Democratic Central Committee, 1973–78; president, Active 20–30 Club, 1972; vice president, Sacramento Safety Council; board member, United Crusade and Sacramento Rotary Club; officer and director, Sacramento Metropolitan Chamber of Commerce; Jaycee Young Man of the Year, 1973; married: the former Doris K. Okada, 1966; children: Brian Robert; member, Ways and Means Committee; elected to the 96th Congress, November 7, 1978; reelected to each succeeding Congress.

Office Listings

http://www.house.gov/matsui

2310 Rayburn House Office Building, Washington, DC 20515 .... (202) 225–7163
Chief of Staff.—Chuck Brimmer. FAX: 225–0566
Executive Assistant.—Shirley Queja.
501 I Street, 12–600, Sacramento, CA 95814 .... (916) 498–5600
District Director.—Anne Sanger.

Counties: SACRAMENTO COUNTY (part). CITIES: Sacramento (part). Population (2000), 639,088.

ZIP Codes: 94204–09, 94211, 94229–30, 94232, 94234–37, 94239–40, 94244, 94246–49, 94252, 94254, 94256–59, 94261–63, 94267–69, 94271, 94273–74, 94277–80, 94282, 94284–91, 94293–99, 95660, 95670, 95758, 95812–20, 95822–29, 95831–35, 95838, 95840–43, 95851–53, 95860, 95864–67, 95887, 95894

* * *

SIXTH DISTRICT

LYNN C. WOOLSEY, Democrat, of Petaluma, CA; born in Seattle, WA, on November 3, 1937; graduated from Lincoln High School, Seattle; B.S., University of San Francisco, 1981; president and founder, Woolsey Personnel Service, 1980–92; human resources manager, Harris Digital Telephone Systems, 1969–80; elected member, Petaluma City Council, 1984–92; vice mayor, 1989 and 1992; member: Sonoma County National Women's Political Caucus, chair; Sonoma County Commission on the Status of Women, chair; Business and Professional Women; National Organization for Women; Sierra Club; Sonoma County Hazardous Materials Management Commission, chair; Association of Bay Area Governments, Regional Hazardous Materials Representative; CAL Energy Commission, advisory committee; Education Task Force of the California Delegation Bipartisan Caucus, co-chair; the Renewable Energy Caucus; the Congressional Human Rights Caucus; the Missing and Exploited Children's Caucus (founding member); the Congressional Task Force on Health and Tobacco; the Internet Caucus; the Congressional Task Force on International HIV/AIDS; the Congressional Friends of Animals; and the Livable Communities Task Force; chair of the Children's Task Force; co-chair of the Democratic Caucus Task Force on Welfare Reform; vice chair of the Progressive Caucus; member of the House Democratic leadership as an Assistant Whip; ranking member of the Education Reform subcommittee of the House Education and Workforce committee, and a senior Democrat on the Energy subcommittee of the House Science committee; four children: Joseph Critchett, Michael Woolsey, Ed Critchett, and Amy Critchett; two grandchildren; elected on November 3, 1992 to the 103rd Congress; reelected to each succeeding Congress.

Office Listings

http://www.house.gov/woolsey

2263 Rayburn House Office Building, Washington, DC 20515 .... (202) 225–5161
Chief of Staff.—Nora Matus.
Press Secretary.—Susannah Cernojevich.
1101 College Avenue, Suite 200, Santa Rosa, CA 95404 .... (707) 542–7182
District Director.—Wendy Friefeld.
1050 Northgate Drive, Suite 140, San Rafael, CA 94903 .... (415) 507–9554

Counties: MARIN, SONOMA (part). CITIES AND TOWNSHIPS: Santa Rosa, Sebastapol, Cotati, Petaluma, and Sonoma to Golden Gate Bridge. Population (2000), 639,087.

ZIP Codes: 94901, 94903–04, 94912–15, 94920, 94922–31, 94933, 94937–42, 94945–57, 94960, 94963–66, 94970–79, 94998–99, 95401–07, 95409, 95412, 95419, 95421, 95430–31, 95436, 95439, 95441–42, 95444, 95446, 95448, 95450, 95452, 95462, 95465, 95471–73, 95476, 95480, 95486, 95492, 95497

* * *

SEVENTH DISTRICT

GEORGE MILLER, Democrat, of Martinez, CA; born in Richmond, CA, May 17, 1945; education: attended Martinez public schools; Diablo Valley College; graduated, 1968, San Francisco State College; J.D., 1972, University of California at Davis School of Law; member: California State bar; Davis Law School Alumni Association; served five years as legislative aide to Senate majority leader, California State Legislature; past chairman and member of Contra Costa County Democratic Central Committee; past president of Martinez Democratic Club; married: the former Cynthia Caccavo; children: George and Stephen; committees: ranking member, Education and the Workforce; member, Resources; elected to the 94th Congress, November 5, 1974; reelected to each succeeding Congress.

Office Listings

http://www.house.gov/georgemiller george.miller@mail.house.gov

2205 Rayburn House Office Building, Washington, DC 20515 .... (202) 225–2095
Chief of Staff/Press Secretary.—Daniel Weiss.
Personal Secretary.—Sylvia Arthur.
1333 Willow Pass Road, Suite 203, Concord, CA 94520 .... (925) 602–1880
District Director.—David A. Tucker.
Room 281, 3220 Blume Drive, Richmond, CA 94806 .... (510) 262–6500
Field Representative.—Latressa Alford.
1410 Georgia Street, Vallejo, CA 94590 .... (707) 645–1888
Field Representative.—Kathy Hoffman.

Counties: CONTRA COSTA (part), SOLANO (part). CITIES AND TOWNSHIPS: Benicia, Clayton, Concord (part), Crockett, El Sobrante, Green Valley (part), Hercules, Martinez, Pinole, Pittsburg, Port Costa, Richmond, Rodeo, San Pablo, Sulsun Valley (part), Vacaville, and Vallejo. Population (2000), 639,088.

ZIP Codes: 94503, 94510, 94517, 94519–25, 94527, 94529, 94533–34, 94547, 94553, 94564–65, 94569, 94572, 94585, 94589–92, 94801–08, 94820, 94875, 95687–88, 95696

* * *

EIGHTH DISTRICT

NANCY PELOSI, Democrat, of San Francisco, CA; born in Baltimore, MD, March 26, 1940; daughter of the late Representative Thomas D'Alesandro, Jr., of MD; education: graduated, Institute of Notre Dame High School, 1958; B.A., Trinity College, Washington, DC (major, political science; minor, history), 1962; northern chair, California Democratic Party, 1977–81; state chair, California Democratic Party, 1981–83; chair, 1984 Democratic National Convention Host Committee; finance chair, Democratic Senatorial Campaign Committee, 1985–86; member:

Democratic National Committee; California Democratic Party Executive Committee; San Francisco Library Commission; Board of Trustees, LSB Leakey Foundation; married: Paul F. Pelosi, 1963; children: Nancy Corinne, Christine, Jacqueline, Paul, Jr., and Alexandra; elected by special election, June 2, 1987, to the 100th Congress to fill the vacancy caused by the death of Sala Burton; reelected to each succeeding Congress; elected Minority Leader for the 108th Congress.

Office Listings

http://www.house.gov/pelosi sf.nancy@mail.house.gov

2371 Rayburn House Office Building, Washington, DC 20515 .... (202) 225–4965
Chief of Staff.—Terri McCullough. FAX: 225–8259
Office Manager.—Paula Short.
Room 14370, 450 Golden Gate Avenue, San Francisco, CA 94102 .... (415) 556–4862
District Director.—Catherine Dodd.

Counties: SAN FRANCISCO COUNTY (part). CITIES: San Francisco (part). Population (2000), 639,088.

ZIP Codes: 94101–12, 94114–15, 94117–26, 94128–47, 94150–52, 94155–56, 94158–66, 94168, 94170, 94172, 94175, 94177, 94188, 94199

* * *

NINTH DISTRICT

BARBARA LEE, Democrat, of Oakland, CA; born in El Paso, TX, on July 16, 1946; education: graduated, San Fernando High School; B.A., Mills College, 1973; MSW, University of California, Berkeley, 1975; congressional aide and public servant; senior advisor and chief of staff to Congressman Ronald V. Dellums in Washington, DC, and Oakland, CA, 1975–87; California State Assembly, 1990–96; California State Senate, 1996–98; Assembly committees: Housing and Land Use; Appropriations; Business and Professions; Industrial Relations; Judiciary; Revenue and Taxation; board member, California State Coastal Conservancy, District Export Council, and California Defense Conversion Council; committees: Financial Services; International Relations; elected to the 105th Congress on April 7, 1998, by special election, to fill the remaining term of retiring Representative Ronald V. Dellums; reelected to each succeeding Congress.

Office Listings

http://www.house.gov/lee

1724 Longworth House Office Building, Washington, DC 20515 .... (202) 225–2661
Legislative Director / Administrative Assistant.—Julie Little. FAX: 225–9817
Office Manager / Executive Assistant.—Myat (Phyllis) Khaing.
Press Secretary.—Stuart Chapman.
1301 Clay Street, Suite 1000–N, Oakland, CA 94612 .... (510) 763–0370
Chief of Staff.—Sandré Swanson.

Counties: ALAMEDA COUNTY. CITIES: Alameda, Albany, Berkeley, Emeryville, Kensington, Piedmont. OAKLAND COUNTY (part). Population (2000), 639,088.

ZIP Codes: 94541–42, 94546, 94552, 94577–80, 94588, 94601–13, 94615, 94617–26, 94643, 94649, 94659–62, 94666, 94701–10, 94712, 94720

* * *

TENTH DISTRICT

ELLEN O. TAUSCHER, Democrat, of Alamo, CA; born in East Newark, NJ, November 15, 1951; graduated, Harrison High School, Harrison, NJ, 1969; B.S., early childhood education, Seton Hall University, NJ; founder and CEO, The Registry Companies, first national child care provider pre-employment screening service, 1992–present; one of the first women to hold a seat on the New York Stock Exchange (1977–79); Wall Street trader and investment banker, 1979–88; author of *The Child Care Source Book*; created the Tauscher Foundation, which has provided $150,000 to California and Texas elementary schools for purchase of computer equipment; member: NARAL, CARAL, Planned Parenthood, Seton Hall University Board of Regents; endorsed by Emily's List; co-chair, Dianne Feinstein's 1992, and 1994, U.S. Senatorial campaigns; married William Y. Tauscher in 1989; one child: Katherine; committees: Armed Services; Transportation and Infrastructure; elected to the 105th Congress; reelected to each succeeding Congress.

Office Listings

http://www.house.gov/tauscher

1034 Longworth House Office Building, Washington, DC 20515 .... (202) 225–1880
Chief of Staff.—Peter Muller. FAX: 225–5914
Legislative Director.—John Fisher.
1801 North California Boulevard, Suite 103, Walnut Creek, CA 94596 .... (925) 932–8899
District Director.—Lisa Tucker.
2000 Cadenasso Drive, Suite A, Fairfield, CA 94533 .... (707) 428–7792
420 West Third Street, Antioch, CA 94509 .... (925) 757–7187

Counties: CONTRA COSTA (part), ALAMEDA (part), SACRAMENTO (part), SOLANO (part). CITIES AND TOWNSHIPS: Alamo, Antioch, Blackhawk, Bethel Island, Brentwood, Byron, Clayton, Concord (part), Danville, Diablo, Dublin, Fairfield (part), Lafayette, Livermore, Moraga, Oakley, Orinda, Pleasant Hill, and Walnut Creek. Population (2000), 639,088.

ZIP Codes: 94507, 94509–12, 94516, 94518, 94520–21, 94523, 94530–31, 94533–35, 94548–51, 94556, 94561, 94563, 94570–71, 94575, 94585, 94588, 94595–98, 94706–08, 94803, 95377, 95391, 95620, 95625, 95641, 95680, 95690

* * *

ELEVENTH DISTRICT

RICHARD W. POMBO, Republican, of Tracy, CA; born in Tracy, CA, on January 8, 1961; attended California State University at Pomona; rancher; Tracy, CA, City Councilman, 1990–91; cofounder, San Joaquin County Citizens Land Alliance; member, Tracy Rotary Club; married to Annette Pombo since 1983; children: Richard Jr., Rena, and Rachel; committees: Agriculture; chairman, Resources; subcommittees: Department Operations, Oversight, Nutrition, and Forestry; Livestock and Horticulture; elected on November 3, 1992, to the 103rd Congress; reelected to each succeeding Congress.

Office Listings

http://www.house.gov/pombo

2411 Rayburn House Office Building, Washington, DC 20515 .... (202) 225–1947
Chief of Staff.—Steven J. Ding. FAX: 226–0861
Communications Director.—Doug Heye.
Legislative Director.—Jessica Carter.
Scheduler.—Catherine Kennett.
2495 West March Lane, Suite 104, Stockton, CA 95207 .... (209) 951–3091
District Director.—Nicole Goehring.

Counties: ALAMEDA (part), CONTRA COSTA (part), SAN JOAQUIN (part), SANTA CLARA (part). CITIES AND TOWNSHIPS: Blackhawk, Brentwood, Byron, Clements, Danville, Diablo, Discovery Bay, Dublin, Escalon, Farmington, Linden, Lockeford, Lodi, Manteca, Morada, Morgan Hill, Pleasanton, Ripon, San Ramon, Stockton, Sunol, Tracy, and Woodbridge. Population (2000), 639,088.

ZIP Codes: 94506–07, 94509, 94513–14, 94526, 94528, 94539, 94550, 94566, 94568, 94583, 94586, 94588, 95020, 95023, 95037–38, 95046, 95127, 95132, 95135, 95138, 95140, 95204, 95207, 95209–12, 95215, 95219–20, 95227, 95230, 95234, 95236–37, 95240–42, 95253, 95258, 95267, 95297, 95304, 95320, 95336–37, 95361, 95366, 95376–77, 95391, 95686

* * *

TWELFTH DISTRICT

TOM LANTOS, Democrat, of San Mateo, CA; born in Budapest, February 1, 1928; during World War II active in anti-Nazi underground; came to the United States in 1947 on academic scholarship; B.A., University of Washington, 1949; M.A., University of Washington, 1950; Ph.D., University of California, 1953, Phi Beta Kappa; professor of economics; consultant, TV news analyst and commentator; member, Millbrae Board of Education, 1950–66; administrative assistant, economic and foreign policy adviser, U.S. Senate; married: Annette Tillemann; two married daughters: Annette Tillemann-Dick and Katrina Lantos-Swett; 17 grandchildren; committees: ranking member, International Relations; Government Reform; co-chairman of the permanent U.S. Congressional Delegation to the European Parliament of the European Union; co-chairman, Congressional Human Rights Caucus; member, U.S. Holocaust Memorial Council; elected to the 97th Congress on November 4, 1980; reelected to each succeeding Congress.

Office Listings

http://www.house.gov/lantos

2413 Rayburn House Office Building, Washington, DC 20515 .... (202) 225–3531
Administrative Assistant.—Robert R. King.
Office Manager.—Rudolf Rohonyi.
Suite 410, 400 South El Camino Real, San Mateo, CA 94402 .... (650) 342–0300
District Representative.—Evelyn Szelenyi.

Counties: SAN MATEO COUNTY (part). CITIES: Brisbane, Burlingame, Colma, Daly City, Foster City, Hillsborough, Millbrae, Montara, Moss Beach, Pacifica, Redwood Shores, San Bruno, San Mateo, South San Francisco. SAN FRANCISCO COUNTY (part). CITIES: San Francisco (part). Population (2000), 639,088.

ZIP Codes: 94005, 94010–11, 94013–17, 94021, 94030, 94037–38, 94044, 94061–63, 94065–66, 94070, 94080, 94083, 94099, 94112, 94116–17, 94122, 94127–28, 94131–32, 94143, 94401–09, 94497

* * *

THIRTEENTH DISTRICT

FORTNEY PETE STARK, Democrat, of Fremont, CA; born in Milwaukee, WI, on November 11, 1931; graduated from Wauwatosa, WI, High School, 1949; Massachusetts Institute of Technology, B.S., 1953; University of California, Berkeley, M.B.A., 1960; East Bay Skills Center, Oakland, G.E.D. (honorary), 1972; served in U.S. Air Force, 1955–57, first lieutenant; banker, founder, and president, Security National Bank, Walnut Creek, CA, 1963–72; trustee, California Democratic Council; chairman, board of trustees, Starr King School of Ministry, Berkeley; trustee, Graduate Theological Union, Berkeley; sponsor, Northern California American Civil Liberties Union; board member: Housing Development Corporation and Council for Civic Unity; director, Common Cause, 1971–72; children: Jeffrey Peter, Beatrice Stark Winslow, Thekla Stark Wainwright, Sarah Stark Ramirez, Fortney Stark III, Hannah and Andrew; married: Deborah Roderick; committee: Ways and Means (senior member); elected to the 93rd Congress, November 7, 1972; reelected to each succeeding Congress.

Office Listings

239 Cannon House Office Building, Washington, DC 20515 .... (202) 225–5065
Administrative Assistant.—Debbie Curtis. FAX: 226–3805
Personal Assistant.—Deborah Chusmir.
39300 Civic Center Drive, Fremont, CA 94538 .... (510) 494–1388
District Administrator.—Jo Cazenave.

Counties: ALAMEDA COUNTY (part). CITIES AND TOWNSHIPS: Alameda, Castro Valley (part), Fremont, Hayward, Milpitas, Newark, Oakland (part), San Leandro, San Lorenzo, Sunnyvale (part), Sunol, and Union City. Population (2000), 639,088.

ZIP Codes: 94501–02, 94536–46, 94552, 94555, 94557, 94560, 94566, 94577–80, 94586–88, 94603, 94605, 94621, 94622

* * *

FOURTEENTH DISTRICT

ANNA G. ESHOO, Democrat, of Atherton, CA; born on December 13, 1942; attended, Canada College; San Mateo supervisor, 1983–92; served on the House Committees on Science, Space, and Technology, and Merchant Marine and Fisheries; Democratic Regional Whip since 1993; selected to co-chair the House Medical Technology Caucus, 1994; committees: Energy and Commerce; House Permanent Select Committee on Intelligence; subcommittees: Telecommunications and the Internet; Health; elected on November 3, 1992, to the 103rd Congress; reelected to each succeeding Congress.

Office Listings

http://www-eshoo.house.gov

205 Cannon House Office Building, Washington, DC 20515 .... (202) 225–8104
Chief of Staff.—Eric Olson. FAX: 225–8890
Press Secretary.—Dawn Bergantino.
Executive Assistant.—Megan O'Reilly.
Legislative Director.—Anne Wilson.
698 Emerson Street, Palo Alto, CA 94301 .... (650) 323–2984
Chief of Staff.—Karen Chapman.

Counties: SAN MATEO (part), SANTA CLARA (part), SANTA CRUZ (part). CITIES AND TOWNSHIPS: Amesti, Aptos, Atherton, Belmont, Ben Lomond, Bonny Doon, Boulder Creek, Brookdale, Corralitos, Davenport, East Palo Alto, Felton, Half Moon Bay, Interlaken, La Honda, Los Altos, Los Altos Hills, Menlo Park, Monte Sereno, Mountain View, Palo Alto, Portola Valley, Redwood City, San Carlos, Scotts Valley, Stanford, Sunnyvale, and Woodside. Population (2000), 639,088.

ZIP Codes: 94002, 94018–28, 94035, 94039–43, 94060–64, 94074, 94085–89, 94301–06, 94309, 95003, 95005–08, 95014, 95017–18, 95030, 95033, 95041, 95051, 95060, 95065–67, 95070–71, 95073, 95076, 95130

* * *

FIFTEENTH DISTRICT

MICHAEL M. HONDA, Democrat, of San Jose, CA; born on June 27, 1941, in Walnut Creek, CA; education: San Jose State University, received degrees in Biological Sciences and Spanish, and a Masters Degree in Education; awards: California Federation of Teachers Legislator of the Year; Outreach Paratransit Services Humanitarian Award; AEA Legislator of the Year; Service Employees International Union Home Care Champion Award; Asian Law Alliance Community Impact Award; AFL–CIO Distinguished Friend of Labor Award; public service: Peace Corps; San Jose Planning Commission; San Jose Unified School Board; Santa Clara County Board of Supervisors; California State Assemblyman; married: Jeanne; children: Mark and Michelle; elected to the 107th Congress on November 7, 2000; reelected to each succeeding Congress.

Office Listings

http://www.house.gov/honda

1713 Longworth House Office Building, Washington, DC 20515 .... (202) 225–2631
Legislative Director.—Chris Mitchell. FAX: 225–2699
Senior Counsel.—Bob Sakaniwa.
Communications Director.—Ruben Pulido.
1999 South Bascom Avenue, Suite 815, Campbell, CA 95008 .... (408) 558–8085
Constituents Services Assistant.—Cathy Ming-Hyde.

Counties: SANTA CLARA COUNTY (part). CITIES AND TOWNSHIPS: Campbell, Cambrian Park, Cupertino, Fruitdale, Gilroy, Lexington Hill, Los Gatos, Milpitas, San Jose (part), and Santa Clara (part). Population (2000), 639,088.

ZIP Codes: 94024, 94087, 95002, 95008–09, 95011, 95014–15, 95020–21, 95026, 95030–33, 95035–37, 95044, 95050–56, 95070, 95101, 95112, 95117–18, 95120, 95123–34, 95150, 95153–55, 95157, 95160–61, 95170

* * *

SIXTEENTH DISTRICT

ZOE LOFGREN, Democrat, of San Jose, CA; born in San Mateo, CA, December 21, 1947; graduated Gunn High School, 1966; B.A., Stanford University, Stanford, CA, 1970; J.D., Santa Clara Law School, Santa Clara, CA, 1975; admitted to the California bar, 1975; District of Columbia bar, 1981; Supreme Court, 1986; member: board of trustees, San Jose Evergreen Community College District, 1979–81; board of supervisors, Santa Clara County, CA, 1981–94; married: John Marshall Collins, 1978; children: Sheila and John; committees: Judiciary; Science; Select Committee on Homeland Security; subcommittees: Courts, the Internet, and Intellectual Property; Environment, Technology and Standards; Immigration, Border Security, and Claims; Research; elected to the 104th Congress; reelected to each succeeding Congress.

Office Listings

http://www.house.gov/lofgren

102 Cannon House Office Building, Washington, DC 20515 .... (202) 225–3072
Chief of Staff.—David Thomas. FAX: 225–3336
Communications Director.—Steve Adamske.
Executive Assistant / Scheduler.—Lauren Gillespie.
635 North First Street, Suite B, San Jose, CA 95112 .... (408) 271–8700
Chief of Staff.—Sandra Soto.

Counties: SANTA CLARA COUNTY (part). CITIES AND TOWNSHIPS: San Jose (part), San Martin, and unincorporated portions of southern Santa Clara County. Population (2000), 639,088.

ZIP Codes: 95008, 95013, 95020, 95035, 95037, 95042, 95046, 95103, 95106, 95108–13, 95115–16, 95118–28, 95131–36, 95138–40, 95148, 95151–52, 95156, 95158–59, 95164, 95172–73, 95190–94, 95196

SEVENTEENTH DISTRICT

SAM FARR, Democrat, of Carmel, CA; born on July 4, 1941; attended Carmel, CA, public schools; B.S., biology, Willamette University, Salem, OR; studied at the Monterey Institute of International Studies; served in the Peace Corps for two years in Colombia, South America; worked as a consultant and employee of the California Assembly; elected to the California Assembly, 1980–93; member: Committees on Education, Insurance, and Natural Resources; married to Shary Baldwin; one daughter: Jessica; elected on June 8, 1993, by special election, to fill the vacancy caused by the resignation of Representative Leon Panetta; reelected to each succeeding Congress.

Office Listings

http://www.house.gov/farr

1221 Longworth House Office Building, Washington, DC 20515 .... (202) 225–2861
Administrative Assistant.—Rochelle Dornatt.
Legislative Director.—Debbie Merrill.
Press Secretary.—Sarah Rosen.
701 Ocean Avenue, Santa Cruz, CA 95060 .... (831) 429–1976
100 West Alisal, Salinas, CA 93901 .... (831) 424–2229

Counties: MONTEREY, SAN BENITO, SANTA CRUZ (southern half). Population (2000), 639,088.

ZIP Codes: 93426, 93450–51, 93901–02, 93905–08, 93912, 93915, 93920–28, 93930, 93932–33, 93940, 93942–44, 93950, 93953–55, 93960, 93962, 95001, 95003–04, 95010, 95012, 95019, 95023–24, 95039, 95043, 95045, 95060–65, 95073, 95075–77

* * *

EIGHTEENTH DISTRICT

DENNIS A. CARDOZA, Democrat, of Atwater, CA; born on March 31, 1959, in Merced, CA; education: B.A., University of Maryland, 1982; profession: businessman; public service: Atwater City Council, 1984–1987; California State Assembly, 1996–2002; awards: California State Sheriff's Association Legislator of the Year; Small Business Roundtable Legislator of the Year; Small Business Association Legislator of the Year; and University of California Legislator of the Year, for his work on behalf of U.C. Merced; religion: Catholic; family: married to Kathleen McLoughlin; children: Joey, Brittany, and Elaina; elected to the 108th Congress on November 5, 2002.

Office Listings

http://www.house.gov/cardoza

503 Cannon House Office Building, Washington, DC 20515 .... (202) 225–6131
Administrative Assistant.—Jennifer Walsh. FAX: 225–0819
Senior Policy Advisor.—Robin Adam.
Legislative Director.—Gary Palmquist.
415 West 18th Street, Merced, CA 95340 .... (209) 383–4455
Chief of Staff.—Mark Garrett.

Counties: FRESNO (part), MADERA (part), MERCED, SAN JOAQUIN (part), STANISLAUS (part). CITIES AND TOWNSHIPS: Atwater, Ceres, Dos Palos, Gustine, Lathrop, Livingston, Los Banos, Modesto (part), Newman, Patterson, and Stockton (part). Population (2000), 639,088.

ZIP Codes: 93606, 93610, 93620, 93622, 93630, 93635, 93637, 93661, 93665, 93706, 93722, 95201–08, 95210, 95213, 95215, 95231, 95269, 95296, 95301, 95303–04, 95307, 95312–13, 95315, 95317, 95319, 95322, 95324, 95326, 95330, 95333–34, 95336–37, 95340–41, 95344, 95348, 95350–54, 95357–58, 95360, 95363, 95365, 95369, 95374, 95380, 95385, 95387–88, 95397

* * *

NINETEENTH DISTRICT

GEORGE RADANOVICH, Republican, of Mariposa, CA; born June 20, 1955; graduated, Mariposa County High School; B.A., California State Polytechnic University, 1978; assistant manager, Yosemite Bank, 1980–83; opened Mariposa County's first winery, 1986; charter member and president of the Mariposa Wine Grape Growers Association; founder, Mariposa Creek Parkway, 1985; treasurer, Mariposa Historical Society, 1982–83; member: Wine Institute; California Farm Bureau; California Association of Wine Grape Growers; Chambers of Commerce; California Ag Leadership, class XXI; chairman: Mariposa County Board of Supervisors;

Mariposa County Planning Commission; executive director of the California State Mining and Mineral Museum Association; committees: Energy and Commerce; Resources; subcommittees: Commerce, Trade, and Consumer Protection; Energy and Air Quality; Environment and Hazardous Materials; National Parks, Recreation and Public Lands; Water and Power; former chairman, Western Caucus, 106th Congress; founding member of the Wine Caucus; elected to the 104th Congress; reelected to each succeeding Congress.

Office Listings

http://www.radanovich.house.gov

438 Cannon House Office Building, Washington, DC 20515 .... (202) 225–4540
Chief of Staff.—John McCamman. FAX: 225–3402
Scheduler.—Jill Wyman.
2350 West Shaw, Suite 137, Fresno, CA 93711 .... (559) 449–2490
District Director.—Debbie Hurley.
121 Main, Suite D, Turlock, CA 95380 .... (209) 656–8660

Counties: FRESNO (part), MADERA (part), MARIPOSA (part), STANISLAUS (part), TUOLUMNE. CITIES AND TOWNSHIPS: Ahwahnee, Auberry (part), Bass Lake, Big Oak Flat, Cathey's Valley, Ceres (part), Chinese Camp, Chowchilla (part), Coarsegold, Columbia, Coleville (part), Coulterville, Crows Landing (part), Dardanelle, Denair, El Portal, Farmington (part), Firebaugh (part), Fish Camp, Fresno (part), Groveland, Hickman, Hornitos, Hughson, Kerman (part), Keyes, La Grange, Long Barn, Madera, Mariposa, Mendota (part), Midpines, Mi Wuk Village, Moccasin, Modesto (part), North Fork, Oakdale (part), Oakhurst, O'Neals, Pinecrest, Raymond, Riverbank, Salida, San Joaquin (part), Snelling (part), Sonora, Soulsbyville, Standard, Strawberry, Tranquillity (part), Tuolumne, Turlock (part), Twain Harte, Vernalis (part), Waterford, Wishon, and Yosemite National Park. Population (2000), 639,088.

ZIP Codes: 93601–02, 93604, 93610–11, 93614, 93622–23, 93626, 93630, 93637–40, 93643–45, 93650, 93653, 93660, 93668–69, 93704–06, 93710–11, 93720, 93722, 93726, 93728–29, 93741, 93755, 93765, 93780, 93784, 93790–94, 95230, 95305–07, 95309–11, 95313–14, 95316, 95318, 95321, 95323, 95325–29, 95335, 95338, 95345–47, 95350–51, 95355–57, 95360–61, 95364, 95367–68, 95370, 95372–73, 95375, 95379–80, 95382–83, 95386, 95389

* * *

TWENTIETH DISTRICT

CALVIN M. DOOLEY, Democrat, of Fresno, CA; born in Hanford, CA, January 11, 1954; M.S., management, Sloan Fellow, Stanford University, 1986–87; B.S., agricultural economics, University of California at Davis; administrative assistant to State Senator Rose Ann Vuich; past vice president, Tulare County Farm Bureau; married: the former Linda Phillips; children: Brooke and Emily; committees: Agriculture; Resources; subcommittees: Conservation, Credit, Rural Development and Research; Department Operations, Oversight, Nutrition, and Forestry; General Farm Commodities and Risk Management; Water and Power; co-founder and executive council member, New Democratic Coalition; co-chair, Western Water Caucus; co-chair, Congressional Biotechnology Caucus; Education and Industry Liaison, Oil and Gas Forum; co-chair, Democratic Caucus Health Care Task Force; member, Rural Health Care Coalition; past co-chair, Western Water Caucus; elected to the 102nd Congress on November 6, 1990; reelected to each succeeding Congress.

Office Listings

http://www.house.gov/dooley

1201 Longworth House Office Building, Washington, DC 20515 .... (202) 225–3341
Chief of Staff.—Lisa Quigley.
Legislative Director.—Lori Denham.
1060 Fulton Mall, Suite 1015, Fresno, CA 93721 .... (559) 441–7496
(800) 464–4294

Counties: FRESNO (part), KERN (part), KINGS. Population (2000), 639,088.

ZIP Codes: 93202–04, 93206, 93210, 93212, 93215–16, 93220, 93230, 93232, 93234, 93239, 93241–42, 93245–46, 93249–50, 93263, 93266, 93280, 93282, 93301, 93305, 93307, 93383, 93387, 93518, 93607–09, 93616, 93620, 93622, 93624–25, 93627, 93631, 93640, 93648, 93652, 93656–57, 93660, 93662, 93668, 93701–09, 93712, 93714–18, 93721–22, 93724–25, 93727–28, 93744–45, 93750, 93760–62, 93764, 93771–79, 93786, 93844, 93888

* * *

TWENTY-FIRST DISTRICT

DEVIN NUNES, Republican, of Pixley, CA; born on October 1, 1973, in Tulare County, CA; education: A.A., College of the Sequoias; B.S., Agricultural Business, and a Masters Degree in Agriculture, from California Polytechnic State University, San Luis Obispo; graduate,

California Agriculture Leadership Fellowship Program; profession: farmer and businessman; elected, College of the Sequoias Board of Trustees, 1996; reelected, 2000; appointed by President George W. Bush to serve as California State Director of the U.S. Department of Agriculture Rural Development Office, 2001; religion: Catholic; elected to the 108th Congress on November 5, 2002.

Office Listings

http://www.nunes.house.gov

1017 Longworth House Office Building, Washington, DC 20515 .... (202) 225–2523
Chief of Staff.—Johnny Amaral. FAX: 225–3404
Legislative Director.—Damon Nelson.
Executive Assistant.—Jennifer Buckley.
113 North Church Street, Suite 208, Visalia, CA 93291 .... (559) 733–3861
264 Clovis Avenue, Suite 206, Clovis, CA 93612 .... (559) 323–5235

Counties: TULARE COUNTY, FRESNO COUNTY (part). Population (2000), 639,088.

ZIP Codes: 93201, 93207–08, 93212, 93215, 93218–19, 93221, 93223, 93227, 93235, 93237, 93242, 93244, 93247, 93256–58, 93260–62, 93265, 93267, 93270–72, 93274–75, 93277–79, 93286, 93290–92, 93602–03, 93605, 93609, 93611–13, 93615–16, 93618, 93621, 93625–26, 93628, 93631, 93633–34, 93641–42, 93646–49, 93651, 93654, 93656–57, 93662, 93664, 93666–67, 93670, 93673, 93675, 93703, 93710, 93720, 93726–27, 93740, 93747

* * *

TWENTY-SECOND DISTRICT

WILLIAM M. THOMAS, Republican, of Bakersfield, CA; born in Wallace, ID, on December 6, 1941; graduated, Garden Grove High School, 1959; A.A., Santa Ana Community College, 1961; B.A., San Francisco State University, 1963; M.A., San Francisco State University, 1965; professor, Bakersfield Community College, 1965–74; served in California State Assembly, 1974–78; member: Agriculture; Revenue and Taxation; and Rules committees; selected by the American Council of Young Political Leaders as a delegate to the Soviet Union, 1977; chairman, Ways and Means Committee; chairman, Joint Committee on Taxation; married to the former Sharon Lynn Hamilton, 1968; two children: Christopher and Amelia; elected to the 96th Congress on November 7, 1978; reelected to each succeeding Congress.

Office Listings

http://www.house.gov/billthomas

2208 Rayburn House Office Building, Washington, DC 20515 .... (202) 225–2915
Administrative Assistant.—Mary Sue Englund.
Scheduler.—Renee Edelen.
4100 Empire Drive, Suite 150, Bakersfield, CA 93309 .... (661) 327–3611
6500 Palma Avenue, Suite 210, Atascadero, CA 93422 .... (805) 461–1034

Counties: KERN COUNTY (part). CITIES AND TOWNSHIPS: Arvin, Bakersfield, Bodfish, Boron, Caliente, California City, Cantil, China Lake, Edison, Edwards, Fellows, Frazier Park, Glennville, Havilah, Inyokern, Keene, Kernville, Lake Isabella, Lebec, Maricopa, McKittrick, Mojave, Monolith, North Edwards, Onyx, Randsberg, Ridgecrest, Rosamond, Taft, Tehachapi, Tupman, Weldon, Willow Springs, Wofford Heights, Woody. SAN LUIS OBISPO COUNTY (part). CITIES AND TOWNSHIPS: Arroyo Grande, Paso Robles, San Miguel, Atascadero, Shandon, Templeton, San Luis Obispo, Nipomo (part), Grover Beach (part). LOS ANGELES COUNTY (part). Population (2000) 639,088.

ZIP Codes: 91390, 92832, 92834, 93203, 93205–06, 93215, 93222, 93224–26, 93238, 93240–41, 93243, 93249–52, 93255, 93263, 93268, 93276, 93283, 93285, 93287, 93301–09, 93311–14, 93380, 93384–86, 93388–90, 93401–02, 93405, 93407, 93409–10, 93420, 93422–23, 93426, 93428, 93430, 93432, 93442, 93444, 93446–47, 93451, 93453–54, 93461, 93465, 93501–02, 93504–05, 93516, 93518–19, 93522–24, 93527–28, 93531–32, 93534–36, 93539, 93554–56, 93558, 93560–61, 93581, 93584, 93596

* * *

TWENTY-THIRD DISTRICT

LOIS CAPPS, Democrat, of Santa Barbara, CA; born in Ladysmith, WI, January 10, 1938; education: graduated Flathead County High School, Kalispell, MT, 1955; B.S. in Nursing, Pacific Lutheran University, 1959; M.A. in Religion, Yale University, 1964; M.A. in Education, University of California at Santa Barbara, 1990; employment: head nurse, Yale New Haven Hospital; staff nurse, Visiting Nurses Association, Hamden, CT; elementary district nurse, Santa Barbara School District; director, Teenage Pregnancy and Parenting Project, Santa Barbara County; director, Santa Barbara School District Parent and Child Education Center; instructor of early childhood education, Santa Barbara City College; board member: American Red Cross, American Heart Association, Family Service Agency, Santa Barbara Women's Political Committee; married: Walter Capps, 1960; children: Lisa, Todd, and Laura; committees: Budget; Energy and Commerce; elected by special election on March 10, 1998, to the 105th Congress, to fill the vacancy caused by the death of her husband Rep. Walter Capps; reelected to each succeeding Congress.

Office Listings

http://www.house.gov/capps

1707 Longworth House Office Building, Washington, DC 20515 .... (202) 225–3601
Chief of Staff.—Jeremy Rabinovitz. FAX: 225–5632
Legislative Director.—Randolph Harrison.
Press Secretary.—Brigid O'Brien.
Executive Assistant.—Erin Shaughnessy.
1411 Marsh Street, Suite 205, San Luis Obispo, CA 93401 .... (805) 546–8348
District Representatives: Betsy Umhofer, Greg Haas.
1216 State Street, Suite 403, Santa Barbara, CA 93101 .... (805) 730–1710
District Director.—Sharon Siegel.
141 South A Street, Suite 204, Oxnard, CA 93030 .... (805) 385–3440
District Representative.—Chris Henson.

Counties: SAN LUIS OBISPO COUNTY (part). CITIES AND TOWNSHIPS: Baywood-Los Osos, Cambria, Cayucos, Grover Beach, Morro Bay, Nipomo, Oceano, Pismo Beach, San Luis Obispo. SANTA BARBARA COUNTY (part). CITIES AND TOWNSHIPS: Carpinteria, Goleta, Guadalupe, Isla Vista, Mission Canyon, Montecito, Santa Barbara, Santa Maria, Summerland, Toro Canyon. VENTURA COUNTY (part). CITIES AND TOWNSHIPS: Channel Island, El Rio, Oxnard, Port Hueneme, and San Buenaventura (part). Population (2000), 639,088.

ZIP Codes: 92832, 93001, 93003, 93013–14, 93030–36, 93041, 93043–44, 93067, 93101–03, 93105–11, 93116–18, 93120–21, 93130, 93140, 93150, 93160, 93190, 93199, 93401–03, 93405–06, 93408, 93412, 93420–21, 93424, 93428, 93430, 93433–35, 93442–45, 93448–49, 93452, 93454–56, 93458, 93483

* * *

TWENTY-FOURTH DISTRICT

ELTON GALLEGLY, Republican, of Simi Valley, CA; born in Huntington Park, CA, on March 7, 1944; education: graduated Huntington Park High School, 1962; attended Los Angeles State College; businessman; member, Simi Valley City Council, 1979; mayor, city of Simi Valley, 1980–86; committees: International Relations; Resources; Judiciary; Permanent Select Committee on Intelligence; subcommittees: Immigration, Border Security and Claims; Europe; Intelligence Policy and National Security; chairman, International Terrorism, Nonproliferation and Human Rights; Courts, the Internet and Intellectual Property; National Parks, Recreation and Public Lands; Technical and Tactical Intelligence; Terrorism and Homeland Security; Congressional Aerospace Caucus; Congressional Autism Caucus; Congressional Automotive Caucus; Congressional Fire Services Caucus; chairman, Task Force on Urban Search and Rescue; Congressional Caucus to Fight and Control Methamphetamine; Congressional Friends of Animals; Congressional Human Rights Caucus; Congressional Task Force on Alzheimer's Disease; Congressional Task Force on Tobacco and Health; Congressional Wine Caucus; Diabetes Caucus; Fairness Caucus; House Renewable Energy and Energy Efficiency Caucus; Older Americans Caucus; Congressional Taiwan Caucus; Western Caucus; former vice-chairman and chairman, Ventura County Association of Governments; former member, board of directors, Moorpark College Foundation; delegate to 1988 Republican National Convention; married the former Janice L. Shrader, 1974; four children: Shawn G., Shawn P., Kevin, and Shannon; elected to the 100th Congress on November 4, 1986; reelected to each succeeding Congress.

Office Listings

2427 Rayburn House Office Building, Washington, DC 20515 .... (202) 225–5811
Chief of Staff.—Richard Mereu.
Administrative Assistant.—Patrick Murphy.
Press Secretary.—Tom Pfeifer.
Office Manager.—Rose Adams.
2829 Townsgate Road, Suite 315, Thousand Oaks, CA 91361 .... (805) 497–2224
District Chief of Staff.—Brian Miller. (800) 423–0023

Counties: VENTURA COUNTY (part). CITIES AND TOWNSHIPS: Bell Canyon, Camarillo, Fillmore, Moorpark, Newbury Park, Oak Park, Oak View, Ojai, Piru, Santa Paula, Simi Valley, Somis, Thousand Oaks, Ventura, Westlake Village. SANTA BARBARA COUNTY (part). CITIES AND TOWNSHIPS: Buellton, Lompoc, Los Alamos, Los Olivos, Orcutt, Santa Barbara, Santa Ynez, and Solvang. Population (2000), 639,088.

ZIP Codes: 91301, 91304, 91307, 91311, 91319–20, 91358–62, 91377, 91406, 91413, 93001, 93003–07, 93009–13, 93015–16, 93020–24, 93030, 93033, 93036, 93040–42, 93060–66, 93094, 93099, 93105, 93111, 93117, 93225, 93252, 93254, 93427, 93429, 93436–38, 93440–41, 93454–55, 93457–58, 93460, 93463–64

TWENTY-FIFTH DISTRICT

HOWARD P. (BUCK) McKEON, Republican, of Santa Clarita, CA; born in Los Angeles, CA, on September 9, 1938; education: graduated, Verdugo Hills High School, Tujunga, CA; B.S., Brigham Young University; owner, Howard and Phil's Western Wear; mayor and city councilman, Santa Clarita, 1987–92; member: board of directors, Canyon Country Chamber of Commerce; California Republican State Central Committee; advisory council, Boy Scouts of America; president and trustee, William S. Hart School District, 1979–87; chairman and director, Henry Mayo Newhall Memorial Hospital, 1983–87; chairman and founding director, Valencia National Bank, 1987–92; honorary chairman, Red Cross Community Support Campaign, 1992; honorary chairman, Leukemia Society Celebrity Program, 1990 and 1994; president, Republican Freshman Class of the 103rd Congress; married: to the former Patricia Kunz, 1962; children: Tamara, Howard D., John Matthew, Kimberly, David Owen, and Tricia; elected on November 3, 1992, to the 103rd Congress; reelected to each succeeding Congress.

Office Listings

http://www.house.gov/mckeon

2351 Rayburn House Office Building, Washington, DC 20515 .... (202) 225–1956
Chief of Staff.—Bob Cochran. FAX: 226–0683
Executive Assistant / Appointments.—Samantha Roe.
District Director.—Scott Wilk.
23929 West Valencia Boulevard, Suite 410, Santa Clarita, CA 91355 .... (661) 254–2111
1008 West Avenue, M–14, Suite E1, Palmdale, CA 93551 .... (661) 274–9688

Counties: INYO, LOS ANGELES (part), MONO, SAN BERNARDINO (part). CITIES AND TOWNSHIPS: Acton, Adelanto, Baker, Barstow, Benton, Big Pine, Bishop, Bridgeport, Castaic, Canyon Country, Coleville, Death Valley, Edwards, Ft. Irwin, Helendale, Hesperia (part), Hinkley, Independence, Inyokern (part), June Lake, Keeler, La Crescenta (part), Lancaster, Littlerock, Little Lake, Little Vinning, Llano, Lone Pine, Mammoth Lakes, Newberry Springs (part), Newhall, Nipton (part), Olancha, Oro Grande (part), Palmdale, Pearblossom, Phelan, Pinon Hills, Ridgecrest (part), Santa Clarita, Shoshone, Stevenson Ranch, Sunland, Sylmar (part), Tecopa, Topaz, Trona, Tujunga, Valencia, Valyerno (part), Victorville, and Yermo. Population (2000), 639,087.

ZIP Codes: 91042, 91214, 91310, 91321–22, 91350–51, 91354–55, 91380–81, 91383–87, 91390, 92301, 92309–12, 92328, 92342, 92345, 92347, 92364–65, 92368, 92371–72, 92384, 92389, 92392–94, 92398, 92832, 93510, 93512–17, 93524, 93526–27, 93529–30, 93534–35, 93541–46, 93549–53, 93560, 93562, 93586, 93590–92, 93599, 96107, 96133

* * *

TWENTY-SIXTH DISTRICT

DAVID DREIER, Republican, of San Dimas, CA; born in Kansas City, MO, on July 5, 1952; Claremont McKenna College, B.A. (*cum laude*), political science, 1975; Claremont Graduate School, M.A., American Government, 1976; Winston S. Churchill Fellow; Phi Sigma Alpha; director, corporate relations, Claremont McKenna College, 1975–78; member: board of governors, James Madison Society; Republican State Central Committee of California; Los Angeles Town Hall; named Outstanding Young Man of America and Outstanding Young Californian, 1976 and 1978; director, marketing and government affairs, Industrial Hydrocarbons, 1979–80; vice president, Dreier Development, 1985–present; author of congressional reform package incorporated into the House Rules; committees: chairman, Rules; elected to the 97th Congress on November 4, 1980; reelected to each succeeding Congress.

Office Listings

http://www.house.gov/dreier

237 Cannon House Office Building, Washington, DC 20515 .... (202) 225–2305
Chief of Staff.—Bradley W. Smith. FAX: 225–7018
Administrative Assistant.—Janice McKinney.
Legislative Director.—Todd Gillenwater.
2220 East Route 66, Suite 225, Glendora, CA 91740 .... (626) 852–2626

Counties: LOS ANGELES (part). CITIES: Altadena, Arcadia, Bradbury, Claremont, Covina, El Monte, Glendora, La Canada Flintridge, La Crescenta, La Verne, Monrovia, Montrose, Pasadena, San Antonio Heights, San Dimas, San Gabriel, San Marino, Sierra Madre, Walnut. SAN BERNARDINO (part). CITIES: Montclair, Rancho Cucamonga, Upland, and Wrightwood. Population (2000), 639,088.

ZIP Codes: 91001, 91006–07, 91010–12, 91016–17, 91020–21, 91023–25, 91066, 91077, 91104, 91107–08, 91118, 91131, 91185, 91187, 91191, 91214, 91390, 91410, 91701, 91711, 91730, 91737, 91739–41, 91750, 91759, 91763, 91773, 91775, 91784, 91786, 91789, 92329, 92336, 92345, 92358, 92371–72, 92397, 92407

TWENTY-SEVENTH DISTRICT

BRAD SHERMAN, Democrat, of Sherman Oaks, CA; born in Los Angeles, October 24, 1954; education: B.A., *summa cum laude,* UCLA, 1974; J.D., *magna cum laude,* Harvard Law School, 1979; employment: admitted to the California bar in 1979 and began practice in Los Angeles; attorney, CPA, certified tax law specialist; elected to the California State Board of Equalization, 1990, serving as chairman, 1991–95; committees: Financial Services; International Relations; Science; subcommittees: ranking member, International Terrorism, Nonproliferation and Human Rights; elected to the 105th Congress; reelected to each succeeding Congress.

Office Listings

1030 Longworth House Office Building, Washington, DC 20515 .... (202) 225–5911
Chief of Staff.—Ron Carleton. FAX: 225–5879
Legislative Director.—Ryan Donovan.
Communications Director.—Matthew Farrauto.
Legislative Correspondent.—Laura Marsh.
5000 Van Nuys Boulevard, Suite 420, Sherman Oaks, CA 91403 .... (818) 501–9200
District Director.—Mike Gatto.

Counties: LOS ANGELES COUNTY (part). Population (2000), 639,088.

ZIP Codes: 91040–41, 91043, 91303–06, 91309, 91311–12, 91316, 91324–30, 91335, 91337, 91342–46, 91352, 91356–57, 91364, 91367, 91371, 91394–96, 91401, 91403, 91405–06, 91409, 91411, 91416, 91423, 91426, 91436, 91470, 91482, 91495–96, 91504–07, 91510, 91601, 91605–06

* * *

TWENTY-EIGHTH DISTRICT

HOWARD L. BERMAN, Democrat, of Mission Hills, CA (representing the San Fernando Valley and parts of Los Angeles); born April 15, 1941 in Los Angeles; education: B.A., international relations, UCLA, 1962; LL.B., UCLA School of Law, 1965; California Assembly Fellowship Program, 1965–70; Vista volunteer, 1966–67; admitted to the California bar, 1966; practiced law until election to California Assembly in 1972; named assembly majority leader in first term; served as chair of the Assembly Democratic Caucus and policy research management committee; member: regional board of the Anti-Defamation League; past president, California Federation of Young Democrats; married: Janis; children: Brinley and Lindsey; committees: International Relations; Judiciary; subcommittees: ranking member, Courts, the Internet, and Intellectual Property; elected to the 98th Congress on November 2, 1982; reelected to each succeeding Congress.

Office Listings

http://www.house.gov/berman

2221 Rayburn House Office Building, Washington, DC 20515 .... (202) 225–4695
Chief of Staff.—Gene Smith.
Legislative Director.—Doug Campbell.
Executive Assistant/Appointments.—Nancy Milburn.
14546 Hamlin Street, Suite 202, Van Nuys, CA 91411 .... (818) 994–7200
Administrative Assistant.—Bob Blumenfield.

Counties: LOS ANGELES COUNTY (part). Portions of the city of Los Angeles, including all or part of the communities of Arleta, Encino, North Hollywood, North Hills, Pacoima, Panorama City, San Fernando, Sherman Oaks, Studio City, Valley Village, and Van Nuys. Population (2000), 639,087.

ZIP Codes: 90028, 90046, 90049, 90068, 91316, 91331, 91333–34, 91340–43, 91345, 91352–53, 91356, 91388, 91392–93, 91401–08, 91411–12, 91423, 91436, 91497, 91499, 91505, 91601–12, 91614–18

* * *

TWENTY-NINTH DISTRICT

ADAM B. SCHIFF, Democrat, of Burbank, CA; born on June 20, 1960, in Framingham, MA; education: B.A., Stanford University, 1982; J.D., Harvard University, 1985; employment: Attorney; U.S. Attorney's Office, served as a criminal prosecutor; chosen by the Dept. of Justice to assist the Czechoslovakian government in reforming their criminal justice system; public service: elected to the California State Senate, 1996; involved in numerous community service activities; awards: Dept. of Justice Special Achievement Award; Council of State Governments Toll Fellowship; California League of High Schools Legislator of the Year; family: married to the former Eve Sanderson; children: Alexa; elected to the 107th Congress on November 7, 2000; reelected to each succeeding Congress.

Office Listings

http://www.house.gov/schiff

326 Cannon House Office Building, Washington, DC 20515 .... (202) 225–4176
Chief of Staff.—Gail Ravnitzky. FAX: 225–5828
Communications Director.—Elizabeth Alexander.
Executive Assistant.—Caron Spector.
35 South Raymond Avenue, Suite 205, Pasadena, CA 91105 .... (626) 304–2727
District Director.—Ann Peifer.

Counties: LOS ANGELES COUNTY (part). CITIES: Alhambra, Altadena, Burbank, Glendale, Griffith Park, Monterey Park, Pasadena, San Gabriel, South Pasadena, and Temple City. Population (2000), 639,088.

ZIP Codes: 90004–06, 90010, 90020, 90026–27, 90029, 90035–36, 90038–39, 90046, 90048, 90064, 90068, 91001, 91003, 91007, 91011, 91030–31, 91046, 91101–10, 91114–17, 91121, 91123–26, 91129, 91175, 91182, 91184, 91186, 91188–89, 91201–10, 91214, 91221–22, 91224–26, 91501–06, 91508, 91521–23, 91775–76, 91780, 91801, 91803–04

* * *

THIRTIETH DISTRICT

HENRY A. WAXMAN, Democrat, of Los Angeles, CA; born in Los Angeles, CA, on September 12, 1939; education: B.A., political science, UCLA, 1961; J.D., School of Law; admitted to the California State bar, 1965; served three terms as California State Assemblyman; former chairman, California Assembly Health Committee; Select Committee on Medical Malpractice; and Committee on Elections and Reapportionment; president, California Federation of Young Democrats, 1965–67; member: Guardians of the Jewish Home for the Aged; American Jewish Congress; Sierra Club; committees: Energy and Commerce; ranking member, Government Reform; married: the former Janet Kessler, 1971; children: Carol Lynn and Michael David; elected to the 94th Congress on November 5, 1974; reelected to each succeeding Congress.

Office Listings

http://www.house.gov/waxman

2204 Rayburn House Office Building, Washington, DC 20515 .... (202) 225–3976
Chief of Staff.—Philip M. Schiliro. FAX: 225–4099
Administrative Assistant.—Patricia Delgado.
Personal Secretary / Office Manager.—Amanda Molson.
8436 West Third Street, Suite 600, Los Angeles, CA 90048 .... (323) 651–1040
District Director.—Lisa Pinto.

Counties: LOS ANGELES COUNTY (part). CITIES AND TOWNSHIPS: Agoura Hills, Bel-Air, Beverly Hills, Brentwood, Calabasas, Canoga Park, Century City, Chatsworth, Hidden Hills, Malibu, Northridge, Pacific Palisades, Pico-Robertson, Santa Monica, Tarzana, Topanga, West Hills, West Hollywood, Westlake Village, West Los Angeles, Westwood, and Woodland Hills. Population (2000), 639,088.

ZIP Codes: 90024–25, 90027–29, 90032, 90034–36, 90038–39, 90046, 90048–49, 90057, 90063–64, 90067–69, 90072–73, 90075–77, 90095, 90209–13, 90263–65, 90272, 90290–91, 90401–11, 91301–04, 91307–08, 91311, 91313, 91324, 91356, 91361–65, 91367, 91372, 91376, 91399

* * *

THIRTY-FIRST DISTRICT

XAVIER BECERRA, Democrat, of Los Angeles, CA; born in Sacramento, CA, on January 26, 1958; graduated, McClatchy High School, Sacramento, 1976; B.A., Stanford University, 1980; J.D., Stanford Law School, 1984; admitted to California bar, 1985; attended Universidad de Salamanca, 1978–79; staff attorney, ''Reggie Fellow,'' Legal Assistance Corporation of Central Massachusetts, 1984–85; administrative assistant for State Senator Art Torres, California State Legislature, 1986; Deputy Attorney General, Office of the Attorney General, State of California, 1987–90; Assemblyman, California State Legislature, 1990–92; member: Mexican American State Legislators Policy Institute; Mexican American Bar Association; chairperson: Hispanic Employee Advisory Committee to the State Attorney General, 1989;

honorary member: Association of California State Attorneys and Administrative Law Judges; former member: steering committee, Greater Eastside Voter Registration Project; Construction and General Laborers Union, Local 185 (Sacramento); married to Dr. Carolina Reyes; elected on November 3, 1992, to the 103rd Congress; reelected to each succeeding Congress.

Office Listings

http://www.house.gov/becerra

1119 Longworth House Office Building, Washington, DC 20515 .... (202) 225–6235
Chief of Staff.—Krista Atteberry. FAX: 225–2202
1910 Sunset Boulevard, Suite 560, Los Angeles, CA 90026 .... (213) 483–1425
District Director.—Laura Arciniega.

Counties: LOS ANGELES COUNTY (part). CITIES: Los Angeles (part). Population (2000), 639,088.

ZIP Codes: 90004–07, 90011–12, 90015, 90018, 90020–22, 90026, 90028–29, 90031–32, 90037–39, 90041–42, 90048, 90057–58, 90065, 90072

* * *

THIRTY-SECOND DISTRICT

HILDA L. SOLIS, Democrat, of El Monte, CA; born in Los Angeles, CA, on October 20, 1957; education: B.A., California Polytechnic University, Pomona; M.S., University of Southern California; employment: White House Office of Hispanic Affairs during the Carter Administration; management analyst, U.S. Office of Management and Budget; Rio Hondo Community College Board of Trustees; Los Angeles County Insurance Commission; public service: California State Assembly, 1992–94; California State Senate, 1994–2000; first Latina to serve in the State Senate; recognized and honored by numerous community and civic organizations; elected to the 107th Congress on November 7, 2000; reelected to each succeeding Congress.

Office Listings

http://www.house.gov/solis

1725 Longworth House Office Building, Washington, DC 20515 .... (202) 225–5464
Chief of Staff.—Laura Rodriguez. FAX: 225–5467
District Director.—Yvette Martinez.
4401 Santa Anita Avenue, Suite 211, El Monte, CA 91731 .... (626) 448–1271
4716 Cesar Chavez Avenue, Building A, East Los Angeles, CA 90022 .... (323) 307–9904

Counties: LOS ANGELES COUNTY (part). CITIES: Azusa, Baldwin Park, Covina, Duarte, El Monte, South El Monte, Irwindale, Monterey Park, Rosemead, San Gabriel, South San Gabriel, and portions of East Los Angeles, Citrus CDP, Glendora, Industry City, Los Angeles, Temple City, Vincent CDP, and West Covina. Population (2000), 639,087.

ZIP Codes: 90022, 90032, 90034–36, 90044–45, 90047–48, 90063–64, 90066–67, 90089, 91009–10, 91016, 91702, 91706, 91722–24, 91731–33, 91740, 91754–55, 91770, 91790–93

* * *

THIRTY-THIRD DISTRICT

DIANE E. WATSON, Democrat, of Los Angeles, CA; education: Bachelor of Arts Degree in Education from the University of California, Los Angeles; Master of Science Degree in School Psychology from California State University, Los Angeles; attended the John F. Kennedy School of Government at Harvard University and earned a Ph.D. in Educational Administration from the Claremont Graduate University; professional: served as an elementary school teacher, acting principal, assistant superintendent of child welfare and attendance, and school psychologist; served on the faculty at both California State University, Los Angeles, and Long Beach; Health Occupations Specialist, California Department of Education; awards: named Legislator of the Year by numerous California universities, associations, and organizations; public service: Los Angeles Unified School District Board Member; served in the California State Senate for 20 years; served as U.S. Ambassador to Micronesia, 1999–2001; elected to the 107th Congress, by special election, on June 5, 2001; reelected to each succeeding Congress.

Office Listings

125 Cannon House Office Building, Washington, DC 20515 .... (202) 225–7084
Chief of Staff.—Rodney Emery. FAX: 225–2422
Legislative Director/Press Secretary.—Bert Hammond.
4322 Wilshire Boulevard, Suite 302, Los Angeles, CA 90010 .... (323) 965–1422

Counties: LOS ANGELES COUNTY (part). CITIES: Culver City, Los Angeles City (part), communities of Ladera Heights and View Park-Windsor Hills. Population (2000), 639,088.

ZIP Codes: 90004–08, 90010–11, 90016, 90018–20, 90022, 90026–29, 90033–39, 90043–45, 90047–48, 90053, 90056–58, 90062–64, 90066, 90068, 90070, 90078, 90083, 90093, 90099, 90103, 90230–33, 90291–92, 90302

* * *

THIRTY-FOURTH DISTRICT

LUCILLE ROYBAL-ALLARD, Democrat, of Los Angeles, CA; born on June 12, 1941, in Los Angeles, CA; B.A., California State University, Los Angeles, 1965; served in the California State Assembly, 1987–92; the first woman to serve as the chair of the California Democratic Congressional Delegation in the 105th Congress; elected on November 3, 1992 to the 103rd Congress, the first Mexican-American woman elected to Congress; in the 106th Congress, she became the first Latina in history to be appointed to the House Appropriations Committee; committees: Appropriations; Standards of Official Conduct; subcommittees: Homeland Security; Labor, Health and Human Services, and Education; first woman to chair the Congressional Hispanic Caucus for the 106th Congress; married to Edward T. Allard III; two children: Lisa Marie and Ricardo; two stepchildren: Angela and Guy Mark; reelected to each succeeding Congress.

Office Listings

http://www.house.gov/roybal-allard

2330 Rayburn House Office Building, Washington, DC 20515 .... (202) 225–1766
Chief of Staff.—Ellen Riddleberger. FAX: 226–0350
Associate Staff for Appropriations.—Don DeArmon.
Executive Assistant.—Lisa Pablo.
255 East Temple Street, Suite 1860, Los Angeles, CA 90012–3334 .... (213) 628–9230
District Director.—Ana Figueroa-Davis.

Counties: LOS ANGELES COUNTY (part). CITIES: Bell, Belflower, Bell Gardens, Boyle Heights, Chinatown (part), Commerce, Cudahy, Downey, Downtown Los Angeles, East Los Angeles (part), Florence (part), Huntington Park, Little Tokyo, Maywood, Pico Union (part), South Park, Vernon, and Westlake. Population (2000), 639,088.

ZIP Codes: 90001–03, 90011–15, 90017, 90021–23, 90025–26, 90030, 90033, 90040, 90051, 90054–55, 90057–58, 90060, 90063, 90071, 90074, 90079, 90081, 90084, 90086–88, 90091, 90096, 90101–02, 90201–02, 90239–42, 90255, 90270, 90280, 90703, 90706–07, 90712–13, 90723

* * *

THIRTY-FIFTH DISTRICT

MAXINE WATERS, Democrat, of Los Angeles, CA; born in St. Louis, MO, August 15, 1938; B.A., California State University; honorary degrees: Harris-Stowe State College, St. Louis, MO, and Central State University, Wilberforce, OH, Spelman College, Atlanta, GA, North Carolina A&T State University, Howard University, Central State University, Bishop College, Morgan State University; elected to California State Assembly, 1976; reelected every two years thereafter; member: Assembly Democratic Caucus, Board of TransAfrica Foundation, National Women's Political Caucus; chairperson, Ways and Means Subcommittee on State Administration; chair, Joint Committee on Public Pension Fund Investments; married to Sidney Williams, former U.S. Ambassador to the Commonwealth of the Bahamas; two children: Karen and Edward; founding member, National Commission for Economic Conversion and Disarmament; member of the board, Center for National Policy; Clara Elizabeth Jackson Carter Foundation (Spelman College); Minority AIDS Project; Chief Deputy Minority Whip; committees: chair, Democratic Caucus Special Committee on Election Reform; Financial Services, Judiciary; elected to the 102nd Congress on November 6, 1990; reelected to each succeeding Congress.

Office Listings

2344 Rayburn House Office Building, Washington, DC 20515 .... (202) 225–2201
Chief of Staff.—[Vacant].
Press Secretary.—[Vacant].
Executive Assistant / Office Manager.—Betty Edwards.
Executive Assistant / Scheduler.—Joyce Freeland.
10124 South Broadway, Los Angeles, CA 90003 .... (323) 757–8900
District Director.—Mike Murase.

Counties: LOS ANGELES COUNTY (part). CITIES: Gardena, Hawthorne, Inglewood, Lawndale, Los Angeles (part), Playa Del Ray, and Torrance. Population (2000), 639,088.

ZIP Codes: 90001–03, 90007, 90009, 90037, 90044–45, 90047, 90052, 90056, 90059, 90061, 90066, 90082, 90094, 90189, 90247–51, 90260–61, 90293, 90301–13, 90397–98, 90504, 90506

* * *

THIRTY-SIXTH DISTRICT

JANE HARMAN, Democrat, of Venice, CA; born on June 28, 1945, in New York, NY; education: University High School, Los Angeles, CA, 1962; B.A., Smith College, Northampton, MA, 1966; J.D., Harvard University Law School, Cambridge, MA, 1969; profession: Attorney; admitted to the District of Columbia Bar, 1969; counsel for Jones, Day, Reavis and Pogue (law firm); Director and General Counsel for Harman International Industries; Special Counsel, Department of Defense, 1979; Regents' Professor at UCLA, 1999; organizations: L.A. County High Technology Committee; South Bay Alliance for Choice; Center for National Policy; International Human Rights Law Group; member of the Visiting Committee of the John F. Kennedy School of Government, Harvard University; National Commission on Terrorism; family: married to Sidney Harman, 1980; children: Brian Lakes Frank, Hilary Lakes Frank, Daniel Geier Harman, and Justine Leigh Harman; elected to the 103rd, 104th, and 105th Congresses; candidate for Governor of California, 1998; committees: ranking member, Permanent Select Committee on Intelligence; Select Committee on Homeland Security; elected to the 107th Congress on November 7, 2000; reelected to each succeeding Congress.

Office Listings

http://www.house.gov/harman

2400 Rayburn House Office Building, Washington, DC 20515 .... (202) 225–8220
Chief of Staff.—John Hess. FAX: 226–7290
Legislative Director.—David Flanders.
Scheduler.—Vanessa Moore.
2321 East Rosecrans Boulevard, Suite 3270, El Segundo, CA 90245 .... (310) 643–3636
544 North Avalon Boulevard, Suite 307, Wilmington, CA 90744 .... (310) 549–8282

Counties: LOS ANGELES COUNTY (part). CITIES: El Segundo, Harbor City, Hermosa Beach, Lawndale, Lennox, Los Angeles (part), Manhattan Beach, Marina Del Rey, Playa Del Rey, Redondo Beach, San Pedro, Torrance, Venice, Westchester, West Carson (part), and Wilmington. Population (2000), 639,087.

ZIP Codes: 90009, 90025, 90034, 90039, 90045, 90064, 90066, 90080, 90245, 90248, 90254, 90266–67, 90277–78, 90291–92, 90294–96, 90304, 90404–05, 90501–10, 90710, 90717, 90731–34, 90744, 90748

* * *

THIRTY-SEVENTH DISTRICT

JUANITA MILLENDER-MCDONALD, Democrat, of Carson, CA; born in Birmingham, AL, on September 7, 1938; education: graduated from University of Redlands, CA; graduate work at California State University–Long Beach and University of Southern California; employment: teacher, director of gender equity programs; coordinator of Career Education, Los Angeles Unified School District; member, California State Assembly, 1992–96, serving as California's representative, Education Commission of the States (executive committee), and vice chair, Commerce Committee, National Conference of State Legislatures; first woman chair, Assembly Revenue and Taxation Committee, 1995–96; first woman chair, Assembly Insurance Committee, 1994; first woman vice chair, Assembly Governmental Organization Committee, 1993; mayor pro tempore, Carson City Council, 1991–92; member, Carson City Council, 1990; life member, NAACP; member, Alpha Kappa Alpha Sorority; board of directors, Southern California SCLC; board of trustees, Second Baptist Church; serves on the National Commission on Teaching and America's Future; married since 1955 to James McDonald, Jr.; children: Valerie, Angela, Sherryll, and Keith; committees: House Administration; Small Business; Transportation and Infrastructure; elected to the 105th Congress; reelected to each succeeding Congress.

Office Listings

http://www.house.gov/millender-mcdonald

1514 Longworth House Office Building, Washington, DC 20515 .... (202) 225–7924
Chief of Staff.—Shirley Cooks. FAX: 225–7926
Legislative Director.—Damon Dozier.
Scheduler/Legislative Correspondent.—Dany Khy.
Press Secretary.—Cinnamon Burnim.
970 West 190th Street, East Tower, Suite 900, Torrance, CA 90502 .... (310) 538–1190

Counties: LOS ANGELES COUNTY (part). CITIES: Carson, Compton, and Long Beach (part). Population (2000), 639,088.

ZIP Codes: 90002–03, 90044, 90059, 90061, 90220–24, 90247, 90501–02, 90713, 90723, 90745–47, 90749, 90755, 90801–10, 90813–15, 90822, 90842, 90844–48, 90888, 90899

* * *

THIRTY-EIGHTH DISTRICT

GRACE F. NAPOLITANO, Democrat, of Los Angeles, CA; born in Brownsville, TX, on December 4, 1936; maiden name: Flores; education: Brownsville High School, Brownsville, TX; Cerritos College; Southmost College; profession: Transportation Coordinator, Ford Motor Company; elected to Norwalk, CA, City Council, 1986; became mayor of Norwalk, CA, 1989; elected to the California Assembly, 58th District, 1992–98; married: Frank Napolitano; children: Yolanda Dyer, Fred Musquiz, Edward Musquiz, Michael Musquiz, and Cynthia Dowling; organizations: Norwalk Lions Club; Veterans of Foreign Wars (auxiliary); American Legion (auxiliary); Soroptimist International; past director, Cerritos College Foundation; director, Community Family Guidance Center; League of United Latin American Citizens; director, Los Angeles County Sanitation District; director, Los Angeles County Vector Control (Southeast District); director, Southeast Los Angeles Private Industry Council; director, Los Angeles County Sheriff's Authority; National Women's Political Caucus; past national board secretary, United States-Mexico Sister Cities Association; committees: International Relations; Resources; Small Business; subcommittees: Energy and Mineral Resources; International Terrorism, Nonproliferation and Human Rights; Water and Power; Western Hemisphere; elected to the 106th Congress; reelected to each succeeding Congress.

Office Listings

http://www.house.gov/napolitano

1609 Longworth House Office Building, Washington, DC 20515 .... (202) 225–5256
Chief of Staff.—Charles Fuentes. FAX: 225–0027
Legislative Director.—Kate Krause.
Legislative Assistants: Daniel Chao, Kelly Alderson.
Executive Assistant/Office Manager.—Michelle Rickman.
11627 East Telegraph Road, Suite 100, Santa Fe Springs, CA 90670 .... (562) 801–2134
District Director.—Raymond Cordova.

Counties: LOS ANGELES COUNTY (part). Population (2000), 639,088.

ZIP Codes: 90601, 90605–06, 90640, 90650–52, 90659–62, 90665, 90670, 90703, 90731, 90806, 91715–16, 91744–47, 91766–70, 91789–90, 91792, 91795

* * *

THIRTY-NINTH DISTRICT

LINDA T. SÁNCHEZ, Democrat, of Lakewood, CA; born on January 28, 1969, in Orange, CA; education: B.A., University of California, Berkeley; J.D., U.C.L.A. Law School; passed bar exam in 1995; profession: Attorney; she has practiced in the areas of appellate, civil rights, and employment law; recent employment: International Brotherhood of Electrical Workers Local 441; National Electrical Contractors Association; and Orange County Central Labor Council Executive Secretary, AFL–CIO; organizations: National Women's Political Caucus; Women in Leadership; religion: Catholic; family: married to Mark Valentine; elected to the 108th Congress on November 5, 2002.

Office Listings

http://www.house.gov/lindasanchez

1007 Longworth House Office Building, Washington, DC 20515 .... (202) 225–6676
Chief of Staff.—Janice Morris. FAX: 226–1012
Legislative Director.—Karen Minatelli.
4007 Paramount Boulevard, Suite 106, Lakewood, CA 90712 .... (562) 429–8499

Counties: LOS ANGELES COUNTY (part). Population (2000), 639,088.

ZIP Codes: 90001–02, 90059, 90255, 90262, 90280, 90601–06, 90608–10, 90637–39, 90670, 90701–03, 90706, 90711–16, 90723, 90805, 90807–08

FORTIETH DISTRICT

EDWARD R. ROYCE, Republican, of Fullerton, CA; born on October 12, 1951 in Los Angeles, CA; education: B.A., California State University, Fullerton, 1977; employment: small business owner; controller; corporate tax manager; California State Senate, 1982–92; member: Fullerton Chamber of Commerce; board member, Literacy Volunteers of America; California Interscholastic Athletic Foundation board of advisers; married: Marie Therese Porter, 1985; elected on November 3, 1992 to the 103rd Congress; reelected to each succeeding Congress.

Office Listings

http://www.house.gov/royce

2202 Rayburn House Office Building, Washington, DC 20515 .... (202) 225–4111
Chief of Staff.—Joan Bates Korich. FAX: 226–0335
Legislative Director.—Amy Porter.
Press Secretary.—Julianne Lignelli.
305 North Harbor Boulevard, Suite 300, Fullerton, CA 92832 .... (714) 992–8081
District Director.—Jennifer Cowen.

Counties: ORANGE COUNTY. The north and west part including the cities of Anaheim (part), Buena Park, Cypress, Fullerton, La Palma, Los Alamitos, Orange (part), Placentia, Stanton, Villa Park, Westminster, and Yorba Linda. Population (2000), 639,088.

ZIP Codes: 90620–24, 90630, 90638, 90680, 90720–21, 91759, 92804, 92806, 92831–33, 92835, 92845, 92861, 92865–71

* * *

FORTY-FIRST DISTRICT

JERRY LEWIS, Republican, of Redlands, CA; born in Seattle, WA, October 21, 1934; education: graduated, San Bernardino High School, 1952; B.A., UCLA, 1956; graduate intern in public affairs, Coro Foundation; life underwriter; former member, San Bernardino School Board; served in California State Assembly, 1968–78; insurance executive, 1959–78; married to Arlene Willis; seven children; elected to the 96th Congress, November 7, 1978; reelected to each succeeding Congress.

Office Listings

http://www.house.gov/jerrylewis

2112 Rayburn House Office Building, Washington, DC 20515 .... (202) 225–5861
Administrative Assistant.—Arlene Willis. FAX: 225–6498
Associate Staff / Appropriations Committee.—Carl Kime.
Deputy Chief of Staff / Communications Director.—Jim Specht.
1150 Brookside Avenue, No. J5, Redlands, CA 92373 .... (909) 862–6030
District Representative.—Corrine Spears.

Counties: RIVERSIDE (part), SAN BERNARDINO (part). CITIES AND TOWNSHIPS: Adelanto, Amboy, Angelus Oaks, Apple Valley, Argus, Arrowbear Lake, Banning, Beaumont, Big Bear City, Big Bear Lake, Blue Jay, Bryn Mawr, Big River, Cabazon, Cadiz, Calimesa, Cedar Glen, Cedar Pines Park, Cherry Valley, Cima, Colton (part), Crestline, Crest Park, Daggett, Desert Hot Springs, Earp, East Highlands, Essex, Fawnskin, Forest Falls, Grand Terrace, Green Valley Lake, Havasu Lake, Hesperia, Highland, Joshua Tree, Kelso, Lake Arrowhead, Landers, Loma Linda, Lucerne Valley, Ludlow, Mentone, Morongo Valley, Mountain Pass, Needles, Newberry Springs, Nipton, Oro Grande, Parker Dam, Redlands, Rim Forest, Running Springs, San Bernardino (part), San Jacinto, Sky Forest, Spring Valley Lake, Sugarloaf, Twentynine Palms, Twin Peaks, Valle Vista, Vidal, Yucaipa, and Yucca Valley. Population (2000), 639,088.

ZIP Codes: 92220, 92223, 92230, 92240–42, 92252, 92256, 92258, 92267–68, 92277–78, 92280, 92282, 92284–86, 92304–05, 92307–08, 92311, 92313–15, 92317–18, 92320–27, 92332–33, 92338–42, 92345–46, 92350, 92352, 92354, 92356–57, 92359, 92363–66, 92368–69, 92371, 92373–75, 92378, 92382, 92385–86, 92391–92, 92399, 92404–05, 92407–08, 92410, 92424, 92427, 92544, 92555, 92557, 92581–83

* * *

FORTY-SECOND DISTRICT

GARY G. MILLER, Republican, of Diamond Bar, CA; born in Huntsville, AR, October 16, 1948; married: Cathy Miller; four children: Brian, Elizabeth, Loren, and Matthew; education: Loma Vista Elementary School, Whittier, CA; California High School, Whittier, CA; Lowell High School, LaHabra, CA; Mount San Antonio College, Walnut, CA; military service: private, U.S. Army, 1967; profession: developer; owner, G. Miller Development Company; public service: Diamond Bar, CA, City Council, 1989–95; Mayor, 1992; California State Assembly, 1995–98; committees: Financial Services; Transportation and Infrastructure; elected to the 106th Congress; reelected to each succeeding Congress.

Office Listings

http://www.house.gov/garymiller

1037 Longworth House Office Building, Washington, DC 20515 .... (202) 225–3201
Chief of Staff.—John Rothrock. FAX: 226–6962
Legislative Director.—Lesli McCollum.
Executive Director.—Kevin McKee.
1800 East Lambert Road, Suite 150, Brea, CA 92821 .... (714) 257–1142
District Director.—Steven Thornton.

Counties: LOS ANGELES (part), ORANGE (part), and SAN BERNARDINO (part). CITIES AND TOWNSHIPS: Anaheim (part), Brea (part), Chino, Chino Hills, Diamond Bar, La Habra, La Habra Heights (part), Las Flores (part), Mission Viejo, Placentia (part), Rancho Santa Margarita, Rowland Heights (part), Yorba Linda (part) and Whittier (part). Population (2000), 639,088.

ZIP Codes: 90601–05, 90607, 90631–33, 91708–10, 91729, 91743, 91748, 91758, 91765, 92676, 92679, 92688, 92691–92, 92807–08, 92821–23, 92833, 92885–87

* * *

FORTY-THIRD DISTRICT

JOE BACA, Democrat, of San Bernardino County, CA; born in Belen, NM, on January 23, 1947; education: graduated from California State University, Los Angeles, with a bachelor's degree in Sociology; professional: GTE Corp. (community relations); Interstate World Travel (owner); military service: Army; public service: elected to the California State Assembly, 1992, and served as Assistant Speaker Pro Tempore, and the Speaker's Federal Government Liaison, 1997–1998; elected to the California State Senate, 1998; awards: American Legion California Legislator of the Year; VFW Outstanding Legislator; League of Women Voters Citizen of Distinction; San Bernardino Kiwanis Club Kiwanian of the Year; Boy Scouts of America Distinguished Citizen; married: Barbara (four children); elected to the 106th Congress on November 16, 1999, by special election; reelected to each succeeding Congress.

Office Listings

328 Cannon House Office Building, Washington, DC 20515 .... (202) 225–6161
Chief of Staff.—Linda Macias. FAX: 225–8671
Executive Assistant.—Deanna Gomez.
Press Secretary.—Paul Todd.
201 North E Street, Suite 102, San Bernardino, CA 92401 .... (909) 885–2222
District Director.—Michael Townsend.

Counties: SAN BERNARDINO COUNTY (part). CITIES: Colton, Fontana, Ontario, Redlands (part), Rialto, and San Bernardino. Population (2000), 639,087.

ZIP Codes: 91758, 91761–62, 91764, 92316, 92324, 92334–37, 92346, 92376–77, 92401–08, 92410–13, 92415, 92418, 92423

* * *

FORTY-FOURTH DISTRICT

KEN CALVERT, Republican, of Corona, CA; born June 8, 1953 in Corona; education: Chaffey College (CA), A.A., 1973; San Diego State University, B.A. in economics, 1975; employment: congressional aide to Rep. Victor V. Veysey, CA; general manager, Jolly Fox Restaurant, Corona, 1975–79; Marcus W. Meairs Co., Corona, 1979–81; president and general manager, Ken Calvert Real Properties, 1981–92; County Youth Chairman, Rep. Veysey's District, 1970, then 43rd District, 1972; Corona/Norco Youth Chairman for Nixon, 1968 and 1972; Reagan-Bush campaign worker, 1980; co-chair, Wilson for Senate Campaign, 1982; Riverside Republican Party, chairman, 1984–88; co-chairman, George Deukmejian election, 1978, 1982 and 1986; co-chairman, George Bush election, 1988; co-chairman, Pete Wilson Senate elections, 1982 and 1988; co-chairman, Pete Wilson for Governor election, 1990; member: Riverside County Republican Winners Circle, charter member; Corona/Norco Republican Assembly, former vice president; Lincoln Club of Riverside County, chairman and charter member,

1986–90; Corona Rotary Club, president, 1991; Corona Elks; Navy League of Corona/Norco; Corona Chamber of Commerce, past president, 1990; Norco Chamber of Commerce; County of Riverside Asset Leasing, past chairman; Corona/Norco Board of Realtors; Monday Morning Group; Corona Group, past chairman; Economic Development Partnership, executive board; Corona Community Hospital Corporate 200 Club; Silver Eagles (March AFB Support Group), charter member; Corona Airport Advisory Commission; Generic Drug Equity Caucus, co-chair; Caucus to Fight and Control Methamphetamine, co-chair; Manufactured Housing Caucus, co-chair; Defense Study Group; Hellenic Caucus; Fire Caucus; National Guard & Reserve Caucus; Human Rights Caucus; Baltic Caucus; Travel and Tourism Caucus; Coalition for Autism Research and Education; Diabetes Caucus; Missing and Exploited Children's Caucus; Zero Capital Gains Tax Caucus; Medical Technology Caucus; Law Enforcement Caucus; Correctional Officers Caucus; Western Caucus; Sportsman's Caucus; Native American Caucus; Coastal Caucus; committees: Armed Services; Resources; Science; subcommittees: chairman, Water and Power; elected on November 3, 1992 to the 103rd Congress, reelected to each succeeding Congress.

Office Listings

http://www.house.gov/calvert

2201 Rayburn House Office Building, Washington, DC 20515 .... (202) 225–1986
Chief of Staff.—Dave Ramey. FAX: 225–2004
Legislative Director.—Maria Bowie.
Press Secretary.—Rebecca Rudman.
District Manager.—Linda Fisher.
3400 Central Avenue, Suite 200, Riverside, CA 92506 .... (909) 784–4300
100 Avenida Presidio, Suite A, San Clemente, CA 92672 .... (949) 496–2343

Counties: ORANGE COUNTY (part). CITIES AND TOWNSHIPS: Coto d' Casa, Ledera Ranch, Margarita, Rancho Santa, San Clemente, San Juan Capistrano. RIVERSIDE COUNTY (part). CITIES AND TOWNSHIPS: Corona, March AFB, Mira Loma, Norco, Perris (part), and Riverside. Population (2000), 639,088.

ZIP Codes: 92501–09, 92513–18, 92521–22, 92532, 92557, 92570, 92596, 92672–75, 92679, 92694, 92860, 92879–83

* * *

FORTY-FIFTH DISTRICT

MARY BONO, Republican, of Palm Springs, CA; born in Cleveland, OH, October 24, 1961; daughter of Clay Whitaker, retired physician and surgeon, and Karen, retired chemist; Bachelor of Fine Arts in Art History, University of Southern California, 1984; Woman of the Year, 1993, San Gorgonio Chapter of the Girl Scouts of America for her assistance to victims of a tragic Girl Scout bus crash in Palm Springs; board member: Palm Springs International Film Festival; first lady of Palm Springs and active in a wide range of community charities and service organizations; leadership role in support of the D.A.R.E. program, Olive Crest Home for Abused Children, Tiempos de Los Ninos; certified personal fitness instructor in martial arts (Karate, Tae Kwan Do); accomplished gymnast with Gymnastics Olympica; appointed chair, Congressional Salton Sea Task Force; married Sonny Bono, 1986; two children: Chesare Elan and Chianna Maria; committees: Energy and Commerce; subcommittees: Commerce, Trade and Consumer Protection; Energy and Air Quality; Environment and Hazardous Materials; Health; Telecommunications and the Internet; elected by special election on April 7, 1998 to the 105th Congress, to fill the vacancy caused by the death of her husband Rep. Sonny Bono; reelected to each succeeding Congress.

Office Listings

http://www.house.gov/bono

404 Cannon House Office Building, Washington, DC 20515 .... (202) 225–5330
Chief of Staff.—Frank Cullen. FAX: 225–2961
Legislative Director.—Linda Valter.
Communications Director.—Cindy Hartley.
Scheduler/Executive Assistant.—Andrea Miller.
707 East Tahquitz Canyon Way, Suite 9, Palm Springs, CA 92262 .... (760) 320–1076
District Director.—Lou Penrose.
1600 E. Florida Avenue, Suite 301, Hemet, CA 92544 .... (909) 658–2312
District Representative.—Karen Brown.

Counties: RIVERSIDE COUNTY (part). CITIES AND TOWNSHIPS: Bermuda Dunes, Blythe, Cathedral City, Coachella, East Blythe, East Hemet, Hemet, Homeland, Idyllwild-Pine, Indian Wells, Indio, Lakeview, La Quinta, Mecca, Moreno Valley, Murrieta, Nuevo, Palm Desert, Palm Springs, Rancho Mirage, Thousand Palms, and Winchester. Population (2000), 639,088.

ZIP Codes: 92201, 92203, 92210–11, 92220, 92225–26, 92234–36, 92239–41, 92253–55, 92260–64, 92270, 92274, 92276, 92282, 92536, 92539, 92543–46, 92548–49, 92551–57, 92561–64, 92567, 92571, 92584–86, 92590–92, 92595–96

FORTY-SIXTH DISTRICT

DANA ROHRABACHER, Republican, of Huntington Beach, CA; born in Coronado, CA, on June 21, 1947; graduated Palos Verdes High School, CA, 1965; attended Los Angeles Harbor College, Wilmington, CA, 1965–67; B.A., Long Beach State College, CA, 1969; M.A., University of Southern California, Los Angeles, 1975; writer/journalist; speechwriter and special assistant to the President, The White House, Washington, D.C., 1981–88; assistant press secretary, Reagan/Bush Committee, 1980; reporter, City News Service/Radio News West, and editorial writer, *Orange County Register*, 1972–80; elected on November 8, 1988, to the 101st Congress; reelected to each succeeding Congress.

Office Listings

http://www.house.gov/rohrabacher

2338 Rayburn House Office Building, Washington, DC 20515 .... (202) 225–2415
Chief of Staff/Legislative Director.—Richard T. (Rick) Dykema. FAX: 225–0145
Communications Director.—Aaron Lewis.
101 Main Street, Suite 380, Huntington Beach, CA 92648 .... (714) 960–6483
District Director.—Kathleen M. Hollingsworth.

Counties: ORANGE COUNTY (part). Communities of Fountain Valley, Huntington Beach, Costa Mesa, Westminster (part), Seal Beach, Santa Ana (part), Midway City, Garden Grove (part), Newport Beach (part), Sunset Beach, Surfside. LOS ANGELES COUNTY (part). Communities of Avalon, Long Beach (part), Palos Verdes, Palos Verdes Estates, Rancho Palos Verdes, Rolling Hills, Rolling Hills Estates, and San Pedro (part). Population (2000), 639,088.

ZIP Codes: 90274–75, 90704, 90731–32, 90740, 90742–44, 90802–04, 90808, 90813–15, 90822, 90831–35, 90840, 90853, 92626–28, 92646–49, 92655, 92683, 92702, 92708, 92711–12, 92725, 92735, 92799, 92841, 92843–44

* * *

FORTY-SEVENTH DISTRICT

LORETTA SANCHEZ, Democrat, of Anaheim, CA; born in Lynwood, CA, on January 7, 1960; education: graduate of Chapman University; M.B.A., American University; specializes in assisting public agencies with finance matters; member, Blue Dog Coalition; Law Enforcement Caucus; Congressional Women's, and Hispanic Caucuses; married: Steven Brixey; committees: Armed Services; Select Committee on Homeland Security; elected to the 105th Congress; reelected to each succeeding Congress.

Office Listings

http://www.house.gov/sanchez

1230 Longworth House Office Building, Washington, DC 20515 .... (202) 225–2965
Chief of Staff.—Lee Godown. FAX: 225–5859
Office Director.—Peter Ludgin.
Legislative Assistants: Dan Barba, Kristen Cummings, Ann Norris.
Office Manager/Scheduler.—Shane Skinner.
12397 Lewis Street, Suite 101, Garden Grove, CA 92840 .... (714) 621–0102
District Director.—Raul Luna.

Counties: ORANGE COUNTY (part). CITIES: Anaheim (west and north-south of the Anaheim Stadium-Disneyland corridor), Fullerton, Garden Grove, Orange, and Santa Ana. Population (2000), 639,087.

ZIP Codes: 90680, 92609, 92616, 92619, 92623, 92650, 92652, 92654, 92658, 92679, 92697–98, 92701–04, 92706–07, 92735, 92781, 92801–02, 92804–05, 92812, 92815–17, 92825, 92832–33, 92840–41, 92843–44, 92850, 92868

* * *

FORTY-EIGHTH DISTRICT

CHRISTOPHER COX, Republican, of Newport Beach, CA; born in St. Paul, Ramsey County, MN, October 16, 1952; graduated, St. Thomas Academy, St. Paul, 1970; B.A., University of Southern California, Los Angeles, 1973; J.D., Harvard Law School, Cambridge, MA, 1977; M.B.A., Harvard Business School, Boston, MA, 1977; attorney; admitted to the California bar in 1978 and commenced practice in Los Angeles; law clerk, U.S. Court of Appeals, San Francisco, CA, and Honolulu, HI, 1977–78; associate, Latham and Watkins, Newport Beach, CA, 1978–84; cofounder, Context Corporation, St. Paul, MN, 1984–86; partner, Latham and Watkins, Newport Beach, CA, 1984–86; senior associate counsel to the President, The White House, 1986–88; member: Republican Associates, California Republican Assembly, and Rotary

Club of Orange County; committees: Energy and Commerce; chairman, Select Committee on Homeland Security; married: Rebecca Gernhardt Cox; children: Charles, Kathryn and Kevin; elected November 8, 1988, to the 101st Congress; reelected to each succeeding Congress.

Office Listings

http://cox.house.gov christoper.cox@mail.house.gov

2402 Rayburn House Office Building, Washington, DC 20515 .... (202) 225–5611
Chief of Staff.—Peter Uhlmann. FAX: 225–9177
Scheduler.—Kassie Stewart.
Office Manager.—Marilyn Cosenza.
Senior Legislative Assistant.—Muhammad Hutasuhut.
One Newport Place, Suite 420, Newport Beach, CA 92660 .... (949) 756–2244
District Representative.—James M. Fournier.

Counties: ORANGE COUNTY (part). CITIES: Aliso Viejo (part), Anaheim (part), Corona del Mar, Dana Point, Foothill Ranch, Irvine, Laguna Beach, Laguna Hills, Laguna Woods, Lake Forest, Mission Viejo, Newport Beach, Orange, Santa Ana (part), and Tustin. Population (2000), 639,089.

ZIP Codes: 92602–04, 92606–07, 92610, 92612, 92614, 92618, 92620, 92624–25, 92629–30, 92651, 92653, 92656–57, 92660–63, 92674–75, 92677–79, 92690, 92693, 92705, 92780, 92782

* * *

FORTY-NINTH DISTRICT

DARRELL E. ISSA, Republican, of Vista, CA; born in Cleveland, OH, on November 1, 1953; education: Siena Heights College; military service: U.S. Army; attended college on an ROTC scholarship; profession: Businessman; founder and CEO of Directed Electronics, Inc.; immediate past Chairman, Consumer Electronics Association; Board of Directors, Electronics Industry Association; awards: Inc. Magazine's Entrepreneur of the Year; public service: Co-Chairman of the campaign to pass the California Civil Rights Initiative (Proposition 209); Chairman of the Volunteer Committee for the 1996 Republican National Convention; Chairman of the San Diego County Lincoln Club; candidate for the U.S. Senate in 1998; married: Kathy; children: William; elected to the 107th Congress on November 7, 2000; reelected to each succeeding Congress.

Office Listings

http://www.house.gov/issa

211 Cannon House Office Building, Washington, DC 20515 .... (202) 225–3906
Chief of Staff.—Dale Neugebauer. FAX: 225–3303
Legislative Director.—Paige Anderson.
Press Secretary.—Frederick Hill.
Scheduler.—Suzy Augustyn.
1800 Thibodo Road, #310, Vista, CA 92083 .... (760) 599–5000

Counties: RIVERSIDE (part), SAN DIEGO (part). Population (2000), 639,087

ZIP Codes: 92003, 92025–28, 92036, 92049, 92051–52, 92054–61, 92065–66, 92068–70, 92081–86, 92088, 92128, 92530, 92532, 92548, 92562–63, 92567, 92570–72, 92584–87, 92589–93, 92595–96, 92599

* * *

FIFTIETH DISTRICT

RANDY (DUKE) CUNNINGHAM, Republican, of Del Mar, CA; born in Los Angeles, CA, December 8, 1941; graduated, Shelbina High School, Shelbina, MO; University of Missouri, B.S. in education, 1964, and M.S. in education, 1965; M.B.A., National University, San Diego, CA; dean, School of Aviation and Flight Training, and businessman; coached swim teams at Hinsdale and at the University of Missouri, training 36 All Americans, two Olympic gold and silver medalists; member: Naval Aviation Hall of Fame, 1986–present; Golden Eagles, 1985–present; Miramar Aviation Hall of Fame, 1974–present; American Fighter Aces Association, 1972–present; author of ''Fox Two,'' on his experiences as a naval aviator, and produced ''Top Gun—The Story Behind the Story'' video about his career as a fighter pilot instructor at Miramar NAS; joined the Navy at the age of 25 and became one of the most highly decorated fighter pilots in the Vietnam War; retired in 1987 with the rank of commander; married the former Nancy Jones; three children: Randall Todd, April, and Carrie; committees: Appropriations; Permanent Select Committee on Intelligence; subcommittees: Defense; Labor, HHS and Education; District of Columbia; elected to the 102nd Congress on November 6, 1990; reelected to each succeeding Congress.

Office Listings

http://www.house.gov/cunningham

2350 Rayburn House Office Building, Washington, DC 20515 .... (202) 225–5452
Chief of Staff.—Dave Heil. FAX: 225–2558
Legislative Director.—Nancy Lifset.
Executive Assistant.—Susan B. Woodworth.
Press Secretary.—Harmony Allen.
613 West Valley Parkway, Suite 320, Escondido, CA 92025 .... (760) 737–8438
District Director.—Nathan Fletcher.

Counties: San Diego County (part). Population (2000), 639,087.

ZIP Codes: 92007–09, 92013–14, 92018, 92023–27, 92029–30, 92033, 92037, 92046, 92067, 92069, 92075, 92078–79, 92081–84, 92091, 92096, 92109–11, 92117, 92121–22, 92126–30, 92145, 92172, 92177, 92191, 92196, 92198

* * *

FIFTY-FIRST DISTRICT

BOB FILNER, Democrat, of San Diego, CA; born on September 4, 1942, in Pittsburgh, PA; B.A., Cornell University, Ithaca, NY, 1963; M.A., University of Delaware, 1969; Ph.D., Cornell University, 1973; professor, San Diego State University, 1970–92; San Diego Board of Education, 1979–83 (president, 1982); San Diego City Council, 1987–92 (deputy mayor, 1990); member: Sierra Club, NAACP, Navy League, Gray Panthers, Economic Conversion Council, Common Cause, ACLU, ADL, NWPC, MAPA; married in 1985 to Jane Merrill Filner; children: Erin and Adam; elected on November 3, 1992 to the 103rd Congress; reelected to each succeeding Congress.

Office Listings

http://www.house.gov/filner

2428 Rayburn House Office Building, Washington, DC 20515 .... (202) 225–8045
Chief of Staff.—Tony Buckles. FAX: 225–9073
Executive Assistant.—Kim Messineo.
Legislative Director.—Ian Pfeiffer.
Senior Legislative Assistant.—Sharon Schultze.
333 F Street, Suite A, Chula Vista, CA 91910 .... (619) 422–5963
1101 Airport Road, Suite D, Imperial, CA 92251 .... (760) 355–8800

Counties: San Diego County (part), Imperial County. Cities: Brawley, Calexico, Calipatria, Chula Vista, El Centro, Holtville, Imperial, National City, San Diego (part), San Ysidro, and Westmorland. Population (2000), 639,087.

ZIP Codes: 91902, 91905–06, 91908–15, 91917, 91921, 91934, 91945, 91947, 91950, 91963, 91977, 91980, 92102, 92105, 92113–15, 92136, 92139, 92143, 92149, 92153–54, 92173, 92179, 92222, 92227, 92231–33, 92243–44, 92249–51, 92257, 92259, 92266, 92273–75, 92281, 92283

* * *

FIFTY-SECOND DISTRICT

DUNCAN HUNTER, Republican, of Alpine, CA; born in Riverside, CA, May 31, 1948; education: graduated, Rubidoux High School, 1966; J.D., Western State University, 1976; first lieutenant, U.S. Army Airborne, 1969–71; profession: trial lawyer; admitted to the California bar, 1976; commenced practice in San Diego; member: Baptist Church, Navy League; married: the former Lynne Layh, 1973; committees: chairman, Armed Services; Select Committee on Homeland Security; children: Duncan Duane and Robert Samuel; elected to the 97th Congress, November 4, 1980; reelected to each succeeding Congress.

Office Listings

http://www.house.gov/hunter

2265 Rayburn House Office Building, Washington, DC 20515 .... (202) 225–5672
Administrative Assistant.—Victoria Middleton. FAX: 225–0235
Office Manager/Appointment Secretary.—Melinda Patterson.
Press Secretary.—Michael Harrison.
366 South Pierce Street, El Cajon, CA 92020 .... (619) 579–3001

Counties: SAN DIEGO COUNTY (part). CITIES AND TOWNSHIPS: Alpine, Barona I.R., Borrego Springs, Boulder Park, Boulevard, Campo, Descanso, Dulzura, El Cajon, Guatay, Indian Res., Jacumba, Jamul, Lakeside, La Mesa, Lemon Grove, Mount Laguna, Pine Valley, Potrero, Poway, Ramona, San Diego, Santee, Spring Valley, Tecate, and Palo Verde. Population (2000), 639,087.

ZIP Codes: 91901, 91903, 91905–06, 91916–17, 91931, 91935, 91941–45, 91948, 91962, 91976–79, 92004, 92019–22, 92025, 92036, 92040, 92064–66, 92071–72, 92074, 92090, 92108, 92111, 92115, 92117, 92119–20, 92123–24, 92126, 92128–29, 92131, 92142, 92150, 92158–60, 92190, 92193–94, 92197, 92199

* * *

FIFTY-THIRD DISTRICT

SUSAN A. DAVIS, Democrat, of San Diego, CA; born on April 13, 1944, in Cambridge, MA; education: B.S., University of California at Berkeley; M.A., University of North Carolina; public service: served three terms in the California State Assembly; served nine years on the San Diego City School Board; former President of the League of Women Voters of San Diego; awards: California School Boards Association Legislator of the Year; League of Middle Schools Legislator of the Year; family: married to Steve; children: Jeffrey and Benjamin; grandson: Henry; elected to the 107th Congress on November 7, 2000; reelected to each succeeding Congress.

Office Listings

http://www.house.gov/susandavis

1224 Longworth House Office Building, Washington DC 20515 .... (202) 225–2040
Chief of Staff.—Lisa Sherman. FAX: 225–2948
Press Secretary.—Aaron Hunter.
Scheduler.—Cynthia Patton.
4305 University Avenue, Suite 515, San Diego, CA 92105 .... (619) 280–5353
District Director.—Todd Gloria.

Counties: SAN DIEGO COUNTY (part). Population (2000), 639,087.

ZIP Codes: 91932–33, 91945–46, 91977, 92037–39, 92092–93, 92101–18, 92120–23, 92132–38, 92140, 92147, 92152, 92155, 92161, 92163–71, 92175–76, 92178, 92182, 92184, 92186–87, 92192, 92195

COLORADO

(Population 2000, 4,301,261)

SENATORS

BEN NIGHTHORSE CAMPBELL, Republican, of Ignacio, CO; born in Auburn, CA, on April 13, 1933; attended Placer High School, Auburn, CA, 1951; quit high school to join Air Force (where he got his GED); attended graduation exercises and received a diploma in 1991; B.A., San Jose State, 1957; attended Meiji University in Toyko, Japan, as special research student, 1960–64; served in U.S. Air Force in Korea, airman second class, 1951–53; jewelry designer who has won more than 200 first-place and best-of-show awards; rancher who raised, trained, and showed horses; All-American in judo, captain of the U.S. Olympic Judo Team in 1964, gold medal in the Pan-American Games of 1963; elected to Colorado State Legislature in 1982, serving 1983–86 on the Agriculture and Natural Affairs and Business and Labor committees; appointed advisor to the Colorado Commission on International Trade and Colorado Commission on the Arts and Humanities; voted by colleagues one of ''Ten Best Legislators'' in the Denver Post-News Center 4 survey, 1984; ''1984 Outstanding Legislator'' award from Colorado Bankers Association; inducted into the Council of 44 Chiefs, Northern Cheyenne Indian Tribe; member of Durango Chamber of Commerce, American Quarter Horse Association, American Paint Horse Association, American Brangus Association, American Indian Education Association, Colorado Pilots Association, Aircraft Owners and Pilot Association; senior technical advisor, U.S. Judo Association; married: Linda Price, July 23, 1966; children: Colin and Shanan; elected to the 100th Congress, November 4, 1986; reelected to the 101st and 102nd Congresses; elected to the U.S. Senate on November 3, 1992; reelected on November 3, 1998; 108th Congress Deputy Majority Whip; committees: chairman, Indian Affairs; Appropriations; Energy and Natural Resources; Veterans' Affairs; subcommittees: chairman, Treasury and General Government; chairman, Commission on Security and Cooperation in Europe (Helsinki Commission).

Office Listings

http://campbell.senate.gov

380 Russell Senate Office Building, Washington, DC 20510 .... (202) 224–5852
Chief of Staff.—Ginnie Kontnik.
Deputy Chief of Staff.—Kristan Mack.
Press Secretary.—Camden Hubbard.
6950 East Belleview, Suite 200, Greenwood Village, CO 80111 .... (303) 843–4100
Aspinall Federal Building, 400 Rood Avenue, #213, Grand Junction, CO 81501 .... (970) 241–6631
503 North Main Street, Suite 648, Pueblo, CO 81003 .... (719) 542–6987
3500 John F. Kennedy Parkway, Room 209, Ft. Collins, CO 80525 .... (970) 206–1788
212 North Wahsatch Avenue, Suite 203, Colorado Springs, CO 80903 .... (719) 636–9092
679 East 2nd Avenue, Suite B, Durango, CO 81301 .... (970) 385–9877

* * *

WAYNE ALLARD, Republican, of Loveland, CO; born in Fort Collins, CO, December 2, 1943; graduated, Fort Collins High School, 1963; preveterinary studies, Colorado State University, 1964; Doctor of Veterinary Medicine, Colorado State University, 1968; received veterinarian license in Colorado; Chief Health Officer, Loveland, CO, 1970–78; Larimer County Board of Health, 1978–82; Colorado State Senate, 1982–90; chair, Health and Human Services Committee and majority caucus; member: American Veterinary Medical Association, National Federation of Independent Business, Chamber of Commerce, Loveland Rotary, American Animal Hospital Association, American Board of Veterinary Practitioners, Companion Animal; married: the former Joan Elizabeth Malcolm; children: Christi and Cheryl; committees: Armed Services; Banking, Housing, and Urban Affairs; Budget; Environment and Public Works; subcommittees: chairman, Housing and Transportation; chairman, Strategic Forces; Emerging Threats and Capabilities; Financial Institutions; Fisheries, Wildlife and Water; Readiness and Management Support; Securities and Investment; Superfund and Waste Management. Deputy Majority Whip. In February 2001, appointed by Senate Majority Leader Trent Lott to serve on the High Tech Task Force and the National Security Working Group; chairman, Senate Renewable Energy and Energy Efficiency Caucus, and the Veterinary Caucus; elected to the 102nd Congress, November 6, 1990; reelected to each succeeding Congress; elected to the U.S. Senate on November 6, 1996; reelected to each succeeding Senate term.

Office Listings

http://allard.senate.gov

525 Dirksen Senate Office Building, Washington, DC 20510 .... (202) 224–5941
Chief of Staff.—Sean Conway. FAX: 224–6471
Scheduler.—Erin Von Tersch.
Press Secretary.—Dick Wadhams.
7340 East Caley, Suite 215, Englewood, CO 80111 .... (303) 220–7414
5401 Stone Creek Circle, Suite 203, Loveland, CO 80538 .... (970) 461–3530
111 S. Tejon Street, Suite 300, Colorado Springs, CO 80903 .... (719) 634–6071
411 Thatcher Building, Fifth and Main Streets, Pueblo, CO 81003 .... (719) 545–9751
215 Federal Building, 400 Rood Avenue, Grand Junction, CO 81501 .... (970) 245–9553

REPRESENTATIVES

FIRST DISTRICT

DIANA DEGETTE, Democrat, of Denver, CO; born on July 29, 1957, in Tachikowa, Japan; B.A., political science, *magna cum laude*, The Colorado College, 1979; J.D., New York University School of Law, 1982 (Root Tilden Scholar); attorney with McDermott, Hansen, and Reilly; Colorado Deputy State Public Defender, Appellate Division, 1982–84; Colorado House of Representatives, 1992–96; board of directors, Planned Parenthood, Rocky Mountain Chapter; member and formerly on board of governors, Colorado Bar Association; member, Colorado Women's Bar Association; past memberships: board of trustees, The Colorado College; Denver Women's Commission; board of directors, Colorado Trial Lawyers Association; former editor, *Trial Talk* magazine; listed in 1994–96 edition of *Who's Who in America*; elected to the 105th Congress; reelected to each succeeding Congress.

Office Listings

1530 Longworth House Office Building, Washington, DC 20515 .... (202) 225–4431
Chief of Staff.—Lisa B. Cohen. FAX: 225–5657
Appointment Secretary.—Michael Carey.
Press Secretary.—Josh Freed.
600 Grant Street, Suite 202, Denver, CO 80203 .... (303) 844–4988
District Administrator.—Greg Diamond.

Counties: ADAMS (part), ARAPAHOE (part), DENVER, JEFFERSON (part). Population (2000), 614,465.

ZIP Codes: 80110–11, 80113, 80121, 80123, 80127, 80150–51, 80155, 80201–12, 80214–24, 80226–32, 80235–39, 80243–44, 80246–52, 80255–57, 80259, 80261–62, 80264–66, 80270–71, 80273–75, 80279, 80281, 80285, 80290–95, 80299

* * *

SECOND DISTRICT

MARK UDALL, Democrat, of Boulder, CO; born on July 18, 1950, in Tucson, AR; son of Morris ''Mo'' Udall, U.S. Representative, 1961–91, and candidate for President of the United States, 1976; education: B.A., Williams College, 1972; employment: course director, educator, and executive director, Outward Bound, 1985–95; Colorado State House of Representatives, District 13, 1997–98; married: Maggie Fox; two children; committees: Agriculture; Resources; Science; elected to the 106th Congress; reelected to each succeeding Congress.

Office Listings

http://www.house.gov/markudall

115 Cannon House Office Building, Washington, DC 20515 .... (202) 225–2161
Chief of Staff.—Alan Salazar. FAX: 226–7840
Legislative Director.—Stan Sloss.
Press Secretary.—Lawrence Pecheco.
Appointment Secretary.—Lisa Carpenter.
8601 Turnpike Drive, Suite 206, Westminster, CO 80031 .... (303) 650–7820
P.O. Box 325, Minturn, CO 81645 .... (970) 827–4154

Counties: ADAMS (part), BOULDER (part), BROOMFIELD, CLEAR CREEK, EAGLE, GILPIN, GRAND, JEFFERSON (part), SUMMIT, WELD (part). Population (2000), 614,465.

ZIP Codes: 80003, 80005, 80007, 80020–21, 80025–28, 80030–31, 80035–36, 80038, 80212, 80221, 80229, 80233–34, 80241, 80260, 80263, 80301–10, 80314, 80321–23, 80328–29, 80403, 80422–24, 80426–28, 80435–36, 80438–39,

80442–44, 80446–47, 80451–52, 80455, 80459, 80463, 80466, 80468, 80471, 80474, 80476–78, 80481–82, 80497–98, 80503–04, 80510, 80514, 80516, 80520, 80530, 80540, 80544, 80602, 80614, 80640, 81620–21, 81623, 81631–32, 81637, 81645, 81649, 81655, 81657–58

* * *

THIRD DISTRICT

SCOTT McINNIS, Republican, of Glenwood Springs, CO; born and raised in Glenwood Springs; graduated from Glenwood Springs High School; attended Mesa College in Grand Junction; received B.A. in business administration from Fort Lewis College in Durango; earned law degree from St. Mary's University in San Antonio; worked as police officer in Glenwood Springs, 1976; director of the Valley View Hospital; director of personnel at Holy Cross Electric Association; served in the Colorado legislature; chaired the Committee on Agriculture, Livestock, and Natural Resources; served on the Judiciary, Local Government and Appropriations Committee for 10 years; House majority leader, 1990–92; the only elected official ever to receive the Florence Sabin Award for contributions to rural health care and received several awards from the United Veterans Commission of Colorado; member, Colorado Tourism Board; Colorado Ski Country's Legislator of the Year and Legislative Achievement of the Decade; received the Lee Atwater Leadership Award for outstanding contributions and extraordinary achievements in public service; received the National Federation of Independent Business and Guardian of Small Business Award; married: the former Lori Smith; children: Daxon, Tessa, and Andrea; committees: Resources; Ways and Means; subcommittees: chairman, Forests and Forest Health; Human Resources; Oversight; member, NATO Parliamentary Assembly; elected November 3, 1992 to the 103rd Congress; reelected to each succeeding Congress.

Office Listings

320 Cannon House Office Building, Washington, DC 20515 .... (202) 225–4761
Chief of Staff.—Michael Hesse. FAX: 226–0622
Legislative Director.—Christopher Hatcher.
Press Secretary.—Blair Jones.
225 North 5th Street, Suite 702, Grand Junction, CO 81501 .... (970) 245–7107
134 West B Street, Pueblo, CO 81003 .... (719) 543–8200
160 Rock Point Drive, Suite A, Durango, CO 81301 .... (970) 259–2754
Hotel Colorado, 526 Pine Street, Suite 111, Glenwood Springs, CO 81601 .... (970) 928–0637

Counties: Alamosa, Archuleta, Conejos, Costilla, Custer, Delta, Dolores, Garfield, Gunnison, Hinsdale, Huerfano, Jackson, La Plata, Las Animas, Mesa, Mineral, Moffat, Montezuma, Montrose, Otero (part), Ouray, Park, Pitkin, Pueblo, Rio Blanco, Rio Grande, Routt, Saguache, San Juan, San Miguel. Population (2000), 614,467.

ZIP Codes: 80423–24, 80428, 80430, 80434–35, 80443, 80446–47, 80456, 80459, 80463, 80467, 80469, 80473, 80479–80, 80483, 80487–88, 80498, 81001–12, 81019–20, 81022–25, 81027, 81029, 81033, 81039–41, 81043–44, 81046, 81049–50, 81054–55, 81058–59, 81062, 81064, 81067, 81069, 81077, 81081–82, 81089, 81091, 81101–02, 81120–38, 81140–41, 81143–44, 81146–49, 81151–55, 81157, 81201, 81210–12, 81215, 81220–26, 81228, 81230–33, 81235–37, 81239–41, 81243, 81248, 81251–53, 81301–03, 81320–21, 81323–32, 81334–35, 81401–02, 81410–11, 81413–16, 81418–20, 81422–35, 81501–06, 81520–27, 81601–02, 81610–12, 81615, 81621, 81623–26, 81630, 81633, 81635–36, 81638–43, 81646–48, 81650, 81652–56

* * *

FOURTH DISTRICT

MARILYN N. MUSGRAVE, Republican, of Fort Morgan, CO; born on January 27, 1949; raised in Weld County, CO; education: graduated, Eaton High School, and Colorado State University; professional: school teacher; businesswoman (agricultural business); public service: Fort Morgan School Board; State House of Representatives, and State Senate; elected State Senate Republican Caucus Chairman; religion: First Assembly of God Church; family: married to Steve Musgrave; four children; elected to the 108th Congress on November 5, 2002.

Office Listings

http://www.house.gov/musgrave

1208 Longworth House Office Building, Washington, DC 20515 .... (202) 225–4676
Chief of Staff.—Guy Short. FAX: 225–5870
Senior Legislative Analyst / Scheduler.—Krista Brinkley.
Legislative Aide.—John Headley.
Office Manager / Executive Assistant.—Michele Rager.
5401 Stone Creek Circle, #204, Loveland, CO 80538 .... (970) 663–3536
705 South Division Avenue, Sterling, CO 80751 .... (970) 522–1788

Counties: BACA, BOULDER (part), CHEYENNE, CROWLEY, KENT, KIOWA, KIT CARSON, LARIMER, LINCOLN, LOGAN, MORGAN, PHILLIPS, PROWERS, OTERO (part), SEDGEWICK, WASHINGTON, WELD (part), YUMA. Population (2000), 614,466.

ZIP Codes: 80501–04, 80510–13, 80515, 80517, 80521–28, 80530, 80532–43, 80545–47, 80549–51, 80553, 80603, 80610–12, 80615, 80620–24, 80631–34, 80638–39, 80642–46, 80648–54, 80701, 80705, 80720–23, 80726–29, 80731–37, 80740–47, 80749–51, 80754–55, 80757–59, 80801–02, 80804–05, 80807, 80810, 80812, 80815, 80818, 80821–26, 80828, 80830, 80832–34, 80836, 80861–62, 81021, 81024, 81027, 81029–30, 81033–34, 81036, 81038, 81041, 81043–47, 81049–50, 81052, 81054, 81057, 81059, 81062–64, 81071, 81073, 81076, 81084, 81087, 81090, 81092

* * *

FIFTH DISTRICT

JOEL HEFLEY, Republican, of Colorado Springs, CO; born in Ardmore, OK, on April 18, 1935; education: graduated, Classen High School, Oklahoma City, OK, 1953; B.A., Oklahoma Baptist University, Shawnee, 1957; M.A., Oklahoma State University, Stillwater, 1962; Gates Fellow, Harvard University, Cambridge, MA, 1984; management consultant; executive director, Community Planning and Research Council, 1966–86; Colorado State House of Representatives, 1977–78; Colorado State Senate, 1979–86; assistant minority whip, 1989–94; committees: Armed Services; chairman, Standards of Official Conduct; married: the former Lynn Christian, 1961; children: Janna, Lori, and Juli; elected to the 100th Congress on November 4, 1986; reelected to each succeeding Congress.

Office Listings

2372 Rayburn House Office Building, Washington, DC 20515 .... (202) 225–4422
Scheduler.—Rebecca Anfinson. FAX: 225–1942
104 South Cascade Avenue, Suite 105, Colorado Springs, CO 80903 .... (719) 520–0055
Chief of Staff.—Connie Solomon.

Counties: CHAFFEE, EL PASO, FREMONT, LAKE, PARK (part), TELLER. Population (2000), 614,467.

ZIP Codes: 80104, 80106, 80132–33, 80135, 80420, 80432, 80438, 80440, 80443, 80448–49, 80456, 80461, 80475, 80808–09, 80813–14, 80816–17, 80819–20, 80827, 80829–33, 80835, 80840–41, 80860, 80863–64, 80866, 80901, 80903–22, 80925–26, 80928–37, 80940–47, 80949–50, 80960, 80962, 80970, 80977, 80995, 80997, 81008, 81154, 81201, 81211–12, 81221, 81223, 81226–28, 81233, 81236, 81240–42, 81244, 81251, 81253

* * *

SIXTH DISTRICT

THOMAS G. TANCREDO, Republican, of Littleton, CO; born on December 20, 1945, in North Denver, CO; graduated, Holy Family High School, 1964; B.A., University of North Colorado, 1968; elected to the Colorado State Legislature in 1976, and served until 1982; appointed, Secretary of Education's Regional Representative, served from 1982 to 1992, during the Reagan and Bush administrations; in 1993, accepted presidency of the Independence Institute, a public policy research organization in Golden, CO; Christian; married to Jackie; two children: Ray and Randy; committees: Budget; International Relations; Resources; elected to the 106th Congress; reelected to each succeeding Congress.

Office Listings

http://www.house.gov/tancredo tom.tancredo@mail.house.gov

1130 Longworth House Office Building, Washington, DC 20515 .... (202) 225–7882
Chief of Staff.—Jacque Ponder. FAX: 226–4623
Legislative Director.—Mac Zimmerman.
Scheduler.—Rachel Hayes.
6099 S. Quebec Street, #200, Centennial, CO 80111 .... (720) 283–9772
1800 West Littleton Boulevard, Littleton, CO 80120 .... (720) 283–7575

Counties: ARAPAHOE (part), DOUGLAS, ELBERT, JEFFERSON (part), PARK (part). Population (2000), 614,466.

ZIP Codes: 80013–16, 80018, 80046, 80101–09, 80111–12, 80116–18, 80120–31, 80134–38, 80160–63, 80165–66, 80225, 80231, 80235–36, 80247, 80401, 80403, 80421, 80425, 80433, 80437, 80439, 80453–54, 80457, 80465, 80470, 80808, 80828, 80830–33, 80835

SEVENTH DISTRICT

BOB BEAUPREZ, Republican, of Arvada, CO; born on September 22, 1948 in Lafayette, CO; education: graduated, University of Colorado, 1970, with a B.S. degree in Education; professional: dairy farmer; Chairman and CEO, Heritage Bank; community service: Colorado Republican Party; serving as a Precinct Committeeman, Chairman of a Congressional District, County Chairman, and State Chairman (1999–2002); family: married to Claudia; four children; elected to the 108th Congress on November 5, 2002.

Office Listings

http://www.house.gov/beauprez

511 Cannon House Office Building, Washington, DC 20515 .... (202) 225–2645
Chief of Staff.—Sean Murphy. FAX: 225–5278
Legislative Director.—Dale Jones.
Scheduler.—Valery Pech.
4251 Kipling Street, Suite 370, Wheat Ridge, CO 80033 .... (303) 940–5821

Counties: ADAMS (part), ARAPAHOE (part), JEFFERSON (part). CITIES AND TOWNSHIPS: Arvada (part), Aurora, Bennett, Brighton, Commerce City, Edgewater, Golden, Lakewood (part), and Wheat Ridge. Population (2000), 614,465.

ZIP Codes: 80001–07, 80010–14, 80017–19, 80021–22, 80030, 80033–34, 80040–42, 80044–45, 80047, 80102–03, 80105, 80123, 80127, 80136–37, 80212, 80214–16, 80221, 80226–35, 80241, 80247, 80401–03, 80419, 80465, 80601–03, 80640, 80642–43, 80654

CONNECTICUT

(Population 2000, 3,405,565)

SENATORS

CHRISTOPHER J. DODD, Democrat, of East Haddam, CT; born in Willimantic, CT, on May 27, 1944, son of Thomas J. and Grace Murphy Dodd; graduated, Georgetown Preparatory School, 1962; B.A., English Literature, Providence College, 1966; J.D., University of Louisville School of Law, 1972; admitted to Connecticut bar, 1973; served in U.S. Army Reserves, 1969–75; Peace Corps volunteer, Dominican Republic, 1966–68; married to Jackie Clegg; one child, Grace; founded the Senate Children's Caucus; House committees: served on the Rules Committee, Judiciary Committee, and Science and Technology Committee; appointed to the Select Committee on the Outer Continental Shelf and the Select Committee on Assassinations; committees: Foreign Relations; Banking, Housing and Urban Affairs; Health, Education, Labor, and Pensions; ranking member, Rules and Administration; appointed to the Commission on Security and Cooperation in Europe; elected to the 94th Congress, November 5, 1974; reelected to the 95th and 96th Congresses; elected to the U.S. Senate, November 4, 1980; reelected to each succeeding Senate term.

Office Listings

http://dodd.senate.gov

448 Russell Senate Office Building, Washington, DC 20510 .... (202) 224–2823
Chief of Staff.—Sheryl Cohen.
Legislative Director.—Shawn Maher.
Putnam Park, 100 Great Meadow Road, Wethersfield, CT 06109 .... (860) 258–6940
State Director.—Ed Mann.

* * *

JOSEPH I. LIEBERMAN, Democrat, of New Haven, CT; born in Stamford, CT, on February 24, 1942; education: attended Stamford public schools; B.A., Yale University, 1964; law degree, Yale Law School, 1967; Connecticut State Senate, 1970–80; majority leader, 1974–80; honorary degrees: Yeshiva University, University of Hartford; Connecticut's 21st attorney general, 1983; reelected in 1986; author of ''The Power-Broker'' (Houghton Mifflin Company, 1966), a biography of late Democratic Party chairman John M. Bailey; ''The Scorpion and the Tarantula'' (Houghton Mifflin Company, 1970), a study of early efforts to control nuclear proliferation; ''The Legacy'' (Spoonwood Press, 1981), a history of Connecticut politics from 1930–80; ''Child Support in America'' (Yale University Press, 1986); ''In Praise of Public Life'' (Simon and Schuster, 2000); and ''An Amazing Adventure'' (Simon and Schuster, 2003); married: Hadassah Lieberman; children: Matthew, Rebecca, Ethan, and Hana; committees: ranking member, Governmental Affairs; Armed Services; Environment and Public Works; Small Business and Entrepreneurship; member, Democratic Leadership Council; Democratic candidate for Vice President, 2000; elected on November 8, 1988, to the U.S. Senate; releected to each succeeding Senate term.

Office Listings

http://lieberman.senate.gov

706 Hart Senate Office Building, Washington, DC 20510 .... (202) 224–4041
Administrative Assistant.—Clarine Nardi Riddle. FAX: 224–9750
Executive Assistant.—Melissa Winter.
Legislative Director.—William B. Bonvillian.
One Constitution Plaza, 7th Floor, Hartford, CT 06103 .... (860) 549–8463
State Directors: Laura Cahill, Joan Jacobs.

REPRESENTATIVES

FIRST DISTRICT

JOHN B. LARSON, Democrat, of East Hartford, CT; born in Hartford, CT, on July 22, 1948; married: Leslie Larson; children: Carolyn, Laura, and Raymond; education: Mayberry Elementary School, East Hartford, CT; East Hartford High School; B.A., Central Connecticut State University; Senior Fellow, Yale University, Bush Center for Child Development and Social Policy; employment: high school teacher, 1972–77; insurance broker, 1978–98; president, Larson and Lyork; public service: Connecticut State Senate, 12 years, President Pro Tempore, 8 years;

committees: Armed Services; ranking member, House Administration; Science; subcommittees: Readiness; Space and Aeronautics; Tactical Air and Land Forces; elected to the 106th Congress; reelected to each succeeding Congress.

Office Listings

http://www.house.gov/larson

1005 Longworth House Office Building, Washington, DC 20515 .... (202) 225–2265
Legislative Director.—Jonathan Renfrew. FAX: 225–1031
Press Secretary.—Michael Timothy Kirk.
Scheduler.—Evelene Corrigan.
221 Main Street, Hartford, CT 06106–1864 .... (860) 278–8888
Chief of Staff.—Elliot Ginsberg.

Counties: HARTFORD (part), LITCHFIELD (part), MIDDLESEX (part). Population (2000), 681,113.

ZIP Codes: 06002, 06006, 06010–11, 06016, 06021, 06023, 06025–28, 06033, 06035, 06037, 06040–41, 06045, 06057, 06060–61, 06063–65, 06067, 06073–74, 06088, 06090–91, 06094–96, 06098, 06101–12, 06114–15, 06117–20, 06123, 06126–29, 06131–34, 06137–38, 06140–47, 06150–56, 06160–61, 06176, 06180, 06183, 06199, 06416, 06422, 06444, 06457, 06467, 06479–80, 06489, 06759, 06790

* * *

SECOND DISTRICT

ROB SIMMONS, Republican, of Stonington, CT; born on January 11, 1943, in New York, NY; education: B.A., Haverford College, 1965; Harvard University, 1979; military service: U.S. Army, 1965–69; U.S. Army Reserve; employment: CIA, 1969–79; staff of Senator John H. Chafee (R–RI), 1979–81; staff director of the Senate Select Committee on Intelligence, 1981–85; public service: Connecticut State Representative, 1991–2000; organizations: Stonington Police Commission, 1987–88; Stonington Community Center, 1986–88; Stonington Republican Town Committee, 1986–present; American Legion Post 58; religion: Episcopal; married: Heidi Paffard; children: Jane and Robert; elected to the 107th Congress on November 7, 2000; reelected to each succeeding Congress.

Office Listings

http://www.house.gov/simmons

215 Cannon House Office Building, Washington, DC 20515 .... (202) 225–2076
Chief of Staff / Legislative Director.—Todd Mitchell. FAX: 225–4977
Press Secretary.—Nathan Raab.
37 Pearl Street, Enfield, CT 06082 .... (860) 741–4053
2 Courthouse Square, Norwich, CT 06360 .... (860) 886–0139

Counties: HARTFORD (part), MIDDLESEX (part), NEW LONDON, TOLLAND, WINDHAM. Population (2000), 681,113.

ZIP Codes: 06029, 06033, 06040, 06043, 06066, 06071–73, 06075–78, 06080, 06082–84, 06093, 06226, 06230–35, 06237–39, 06241–51, 06254–56, 06258–60, 06262–69, 06277–82, 06320, 06330–40, 06349–51, 06353–55, 06357, 06359–60, 06365, 06370–80, 06382–85, 06387–89, 06409, 06412–15, 06417, 06419–20, 06422–24, 06426, 06438–39, 06441–43, 06447, 06456–57, 06459, 06469, 06474–75, 06498

* * *

THIRD DISTRICT

ROSA L. DELAURO, Democrat, of New Haven, CT; born in New Haven, March 2, 1943; education: graduated, Laurelton Hall High School; attended London School of Economics, Queen Mary College, London, 1962–63; B.A., *cum laude*, history and political science, Marymount College, NY, 1964; M.A., international politics, Columbia University, NY, 1966; employment: executive assistant to Mayor Frank Logue, city of New Haven, 1976–77; executive assistant/development administrator, city of New Haven, 1977–78; chief of staff, Senator Christopher Dodd, 1980–87; executive director, Countdown '87, 1987–88; executive director, Emily's List, 1989–90; married: Stanley Greenberg; children: Anna, Kathryn, and Jonathan; elected to the 102nd Congress on November 6, 1990; reelected to each succeeding Congress.

Office Listings

2262 Rayburn House Office Building, Washington, DC 20515 .... (202) 225–3661
Chief of Staff.—Richard Woodruff.
Legislative Director.—Rebecca Salay.
Executive Assistant.—Nancy Mulry.
59 Elm Street, New Haven, CT 06510 .... (203) 562–3718
District Director.—Jennifer Cosenza.

Counties: FAIRFIELD (part), MIDDLESEX (part), NEW HAVEN (part). CITIES AND TOWNSHIPS: Ansonia, Beacon Falls, Bethany, Branford, Derby, Durham (part), East Haven, Guilford, Hamden, Middlefield, Middletown (part), Milford, Naugatuck, New Haven, North Branford, North Haven, Orange, Prospect, Seymour, Shelton (part), Stratford, Wallingford, Waterbury (part), West Haven, and Woodbridge. Population (2000), 681,113.

ZIP Codes: 06401, 06403, 06405, 06410, 06418, 06422, 06437, 06450, 06455, 06457, 06460, 06471–73, 06477, 06481, 06483–84, 06492–94, 06501–21, 06524–25, 06530–38, 06540, 06607, 06614–15, 06706, 06708, 06712, 06762, 06770

* * *

FOURTH DISTRICT

CHRISTOPHER SHAYS, Republican, of Bridgeport, CT; born in Stamford on October 18, 1945; education: graduated, Darien High School, Darien, CT, 1964; B.A., Principia College, Elsah, IL, 1968; M.B.A., New York University Graduate School of Business, 1974; M.P.A., New York University Graduate School of Public Administration, 1978; member, Peace Corps, Fiji Islands, 1968–70; employment: business consultant; college instructor, realtor; executive aide, Trumbull First Selectman, 1971–72; Connecticut House of Representatives, 1974–87; married: Betsi Shays, 1968; children: Jeramy; elected by special election, August 18, 1987, to the 100th Congress to fill the vacancy caused by the death of Stewart B. McKinney; reelected to each succeeding Congress.

Office Listings

http://www.house.gov/shays rep.shays@mail.house.gov

1126 Longworth House Office Building, Washington, DC 20515 .... (202) 225–5541
Chief of Staff.—Betsy Wright Hawkings. FAX: 225–9629
Legislative Director.—Len Wolfson.
Executive Assistant.—Diana White.
888 Washington Boulevard, Stamford, CT 06901–2927 .... (203) 357–8277
10 Middle Street, Bridgeport, CT 06604–4223 .... (203) 579–5870
District Director.—Paul Pimentel.

Counties: FAIRFIELD (part), NEW HAVEN (part). CITIES AND TOWNSHIPS: Bridgeport, Darien, Easton, Fairfield, Greenwich, Monroe, New Canaan, Norwalk, Oxford, Redding, Ridgefield, Shelton, Stamford, Trumbull Weston, Westport, and Wilton. Population (2000), 681,113.

ZIP Codes: 06468, 06478, 06483–84, 06491, 06601–02, 06604–08, 06610–12, 06673, 06699, 06807, 06820, 06824–25, 06828–31, 06836, 06838, 06840, 06850–58, 06860, 06870, 06875–81, 06883, 06888–90, 06896–97, 06901–07, 06910–14, 06920–22, 06925–28

* * *

FIFTH DISTRICT

NANCY L. JOHNSON, Republican, of New Britain, CT; born in Chicago, IL, January 5, 1935, daughter of Gertrude Smith (deceased), and Noble W. Lee (deceased); education: attended University of Chicago Laboratory School, 1951; University of Chicago, 1953; B.A., Radcliffe College, *cum laude,* Cambridge, MA, 1957; attended University of London (English Speaking Union Scholarship), 1958; Connecticut State Senate, 1977–82; member, board of directors, United Way of New Britain; president, Sheldon Community Guidance Clinic; Unitarian Universalists Society of New Britain; founding president, Friends of New Britain Public Library; member: board of directors, New Britain Bank and Trust; New Britain Museum of American Art; adjunct professor (political science), Central Connecticut State College; married: Dr. Theodore Herbert Johnson, 1958; children: Lindsey, Althea, and Caroline; elected on November 2, 1982, to the 98th Congress; reelected to each succeeding Congress.

Office Listings

2113 Rayburn House Office Building, Washington, DC 20515 .... (202) 225–4476
Chief of Staff.—Dave Karvelas. FAX: 225–4488
Press Secretary.—Brian Schuebert.
Scheduler.—Megan Shelley.
1 Grove Street, New Britain, CT 06053 .... (860) 223–8412
District Director.—Ken Hiscoe.
20 East Main Street, Suite 222, Waterbury, CT 06702 .... (203) 573–1418
198 Main Street, Suite 1, Danbury, CT 06810 .... (203) 790–6856
22 West Main Street, Meriden, CT 06451 .... (203) 630–1903

Counties: FAIRFIELD (part), HARTFORD (part), LITCHFIELD, NEW HAVEN (part). CITIES: Danbury, Meriden, New Britain, Torrington (part), and Waterbury (part). Population (2000), 681,113.

ZIP Codes: 06001, 06013, 06018–20, 06022, 06024, 06030–32, 06034, 06039, 06050–53, 06058–59, 06062, 06068–70, 06079, 06081, 06085, 06087, 06089, 06092, 06107, 06404, 06408, 06410–11, 06440, 06450–51, 06454, 06470, 06482, 06487–88, 06701–06, 06708, 06710, 06716, 06720–26, 06749–59, 06762–63, 06776–79, 06781–87, 06790–91, 06793–96, 06798, 06801, 06804, 06810–14, 06816–17

DELAWARE

(Population 2000, 783,600)

SENATORS

JOSEPH R. BIDEN, JR., Democrat, of Wilmington, DE; born in Scranton, PA, on November 20, 1942; educated at St. Helena's School, Wilmington, DE; Archmere Academy, Claymont, DE; A.B., history and political science, University of Delaware; J.D., Syracuse University College of Law; married: Jill Tracy Biden; children: Joseph R. Biden III, Robert Hunter Biden, and Ashley Blazer Biden; admitted to the bar, December 1968, Wilmington, DE; engaged in private practice until 1972; served on New Castle County Council, 1970–72; committees: ranking member, Foreign Relations; Judiciary; elected to the U.S. Senate on November 7, 1972; reelected to each succeeding Senate term.

Office Listings

http://biden.senate.gov senator@biden.senate.gov

221 Russell Senate Office Building, Washington, DC 20510 .... (202) 224–5042
Chief of Staff.—Danny O'Brien. FAX: 224–0139
Legislative Director.—Jane Woodfin. TDD: 224–4048
Communications Director.—Norm Kurz.
1105 North Market Street, Suite 2000, Wilmington, DE 19801–1233 .... (302) 573–6345
24 NW Front Street, Windsor Building, Suite 101, Milford, DE 19963 .... (302) 424–8090

* * *

TOM CARPER, Democrat, of Wilmington, DE; born on January 23, 1947, in Beckley, WV; education: B.A., Ohio State University, 1968; M.B.A., University of Delaware, 1975; military service: U.S. Navy, served during Vietnam War; public service: Delaware State Treasurer, 1977–1983; U.S. House of Representatives, 1983–1993; Governor of Delaware, 1993–2001; organizations: National Governors' Association; American Legacy Foundation; Jobs for America's Graduates; religion: Presbyterian; family: married to the former Martha Ann Stacy; children: Ben and Christopher; elected to the U.S. Senate on November 7, 2000.

Office Listings

http://carper.senate.gov

513 Hart Senate Office Building, Washington, DC 20510 .... (202) 224–2441
Chief of Staff.—Jonathon Jones. FAX: 228–2190
Legislative Director.—Shiela Murphy.
Office Manager.—Judy Rainey.
Deputy Press Secretary.—Jennifer Connell.
2215 Federal Building, 300 South New Street, Dover, DE 19904 .... (302) 674–3308
State Director.—Brian Bushweller.
3021 Federal Building, 844 King Street, Wilmington, DE 19801 .... (302) 573–6291

REPRESENTATIVE

AT LARGE

MICHAEL N. CASTLE, Republican, of Wilmington, DE; born on July 2, 1939 in Wilmington; graduate of Tower Hill School, 1957; B.S., economics, Hamilton College, Clinton, NY, 1961; J.D., Georgetown University Law School, 1964; attorney; admitted to the District of Columbia and Delaware bars, 1964; commenced practice in Wilmington; Delaware House of Representatives, 1966–67; Delaware Senate, 1968–76; Lieutenant Governor of Delaware, 1981–85; Governor, 1985–92; awarded honorary degrees: Wesley College, 1986; Widener College, 1986; Delaware State University, 1986; Hamilton College, 1991; Jefferson Medical College, Philadelphia, PA, 1992; active in the National Governors Association, serving three years as chairman of the Human Resources Committee; co-vice chairman for NGA's Task Force on Health Care with President Clinton; past president of the Council of State Governments; past chairman of the Southern Governors Association; chaired the Republican Governors Association, 1988; American Diabetes Association's C. Everett Koop Award for Health Promotion and Awareness, 1992; member: Delaware Bar Association, American Bar Association; former member: National Governors Association, Republican Governors Association, National Assessment Governing Board, Council of State Governors, Southern Governors Association; honorary board of directors, Delaware Greenways; committees: Financial Services; Education and the Workforce; subcommittees: chairman, Education Reform; Financial Institutions and Consumer Credit; Capital Markets, Insurance and Government Sponsored Enterprises; Domestic and International Monetary Policy, Trade, and Technology; 21st Century Competitiveness; task forces: co-chairman, Congressional Task Force to the National Campaign to Reduce Teen Pregnancy; House Social Security Task Force; House Tobacco Task Force; married: Jane DiSabatino, 1992; elected to the 103rd Congress on November 3, 1992; reelected to each succeeding Congress.

Office Listings

http://www.house.gov/castle

1233 Longworth House Office Building, Washington, DC 20515 .... (202) 225–4165
Chief of Staff.—Paul Leonard. FAX: 225–2291
Press Secretary.—Jonathan Dean.
201 North Walnut Street, Suite 107, Wilmington, DE 19801 .... (302) 428–1902
Office Director.—Jeff Dayton. FAX: 428–1905
J. Allen Frear Federal Building, 300 South New Street, Dover, DE 19904 .... (302) 736–1666

Counties: KENT, NEW CASTLE, SUSSEX. CITIES AND TOWNSHIPS: Brookside, Camden, Claymont, Delaware City, Dover, Edgemoor, Elsmere, Georgetown, Harrington, Highland, Acres, Kent Acres, Laurel, Lewes, Middletown, Milford, Millsboro, New Castle, Newark, Pike Creek, Rising Sun-Lebanon, Rodney Village, Seaford, Smyrna, Stanton, Talleyville, Wilmington, Wilmington Minor, and Woodside East. Population (2000), 783,600.

ZIP Codes: 19701–03, 19706–18, 19720–21, 19725–26, 19730–36, 19801–10, 19850, 19880, 19884–87, 19890–99, 19901–06, 19930–31, 19933–34, 19936, 19938–41, 19943–47, 19950–56, 19958, 19960–64, 19966–71, 19973, 19975, 19977, 19979–80

FLORIDA

(Population 2000, 15,982,378)

SENATORS

BOB GRAHAM, Democrat, of Miami Lakes, FL; born in Coral Gables, FL, November 9, 1936; education: graduated, Miami High School, 1955; B.S., University of Florida, Gainesville, 1959; LL.B., Harvard Law School, Cambridge, MA, 1962; employment: lawyer; admitted to the Florida bar, 1962; builder and cattleman; elected to the Florida State House of Representatives, 1966; Florida State Senate, 1970–78; Governor of Florida, 1978–86; married: the former Adele Khoury in 1959; children: Gwendolyn Patricia, Glynn Adele, Arva Suzanne, and Kendall Elizabeth; committees: Energy and Natural Resources; Environment and Public Works; Finance; Veterans' Affairs; elected to the U.S. Senate on November 4, 1986; reelected to each succeeding Senate term.

Office Listings

http://graham.senate.gov

524 Hart Senate Office Building, Washington, DC 20510 .... (202) 224–3041
Administrative Assistant.—Henry Menn.
Legislative Director.—Bryant Hall.
2252 Killearn Center Boulevard, 3rd Floor, Tallahassee, FL 32309–3573 .... (850) 907–1100
State Director.—Mary Chiles.
625 East Twiggs Street, Suite 500, Tampa, FL 33602 .... (813) 228–2476
150 Southeast 2nd Avenue, Suite 1025, Miami, FL 33131 .... (305) 536–7293

* * *

BILL NELSON, Democrat, of Tallahassee, FL, born on September 29, 1942, in Miami, FL; education: Melbourne High School, 1960; B.A., Yale University, 1965; J.D. University of Virginia School of Law, 1968; professional: attorney; admitted to the Florida Bar, 1968; captain, U.S. Army Reserve, 1965–1971; active duty, 1968–1970; public service: Florida State House of Representatives, 1973–1979; U.S. House of Representatives, 1979–1991; Florida Treasurer, Insurance Commissioner, and State Fire Marshal, 1995–2001; Astronaut: payload specialist on the space shuttle *Columbia*, January, 1986; family: married to the former Grace Cavert; children: Bill Jr. and Nan Ellen; elected to the U.S. Senate on November 7, 2000.

Office Listings

http://billnelson.senate.gov

716 Hart Senate Office Building, Washington, DC 20510 .... (202) 224–5274
Chief of Staff.—Sheila Nix. FAX: 228–2183
Deputy Chief of Staff, Communications.—Dan McLaughlin.
Deputy Chief of Staff, Administration.—Brenda Strickland.
Legislative Director.—Dan Shapiro.
U.S. Courthouse Annex, 111 North Adams Street, Tallahassee, FL 32301 .... (850) 942–6415
State Director.—Pete Mitchell.
801 North Florida Avenue, 4th Floor, Tampa, FL 33602 .... (813) 225–7040
2925 Salzedo Street, Coral Gables, FL 33134 .... (305) 536–5999
3416 University Drive, Ft. Lauderdale, FL 33328 .... (954) 693–4851
500 Australian Avenue, Suite 125, West Palm Beach, FL 33401 .... (561) 514–0189
225 East Robinson Street, Suite 410, Orlando, FL 32801 .... (407) 872–7161
1301 Riverplace Boulevard, Suite 2281, Jacksonville, FL 32207 .... (904) 346–4500

REPRESENTATIVES

FIRST DISTRICT

JEFF MILLER, Republican, of Chumuckla, FL; born on June 27, 1959, in St. Petersburg, FL; education: B.S., University of Florida, 1984; employment: real estate broker; public service: Executive Assistant to the Commissioner of Agriculture, 1984–88; Environmental Land Management Study Commission, 1992; Santa Rosa County Planning Board Vice Chairman, 1996–98; elected to the Florida House of Representatives in 1998; reelected in 2000; served as House Majority Whip: organizations: Kiwanis Club of Milton; Florida Historical Society; Santa Rosa County United Way; Milton Pregnancy Resource Center Advisory Board; Gulf Coast Council of Boy Scouts; Florida FFA Foundation; religion: Methodist; family: married to Vicki Griswold; children: Scott and Clint; elected to the 107th Congress, by special election, on October 16, 2001; reelected to each succeeding Congress.

Office Listings

331 Cannon House Office Building, Washington, DC 20515 .... (202) 225–4136
Chief of Staff.—Dan McFaul.
Legislative Director.—Marcus Dunn.
Scheduler.—Jamie Lawley.
Legislative Counsels: Helen Walker, Steve Holton, Chris Kuzmuk.
4300 Bayou Boulevard, Suite 17–C, Pensacola, FL 32503 .... (850) 479–1183
District Director.—Kris Tande.
348 SW Miracle Strip Parkway, Unit 21, Ft. Walton Beach, FL 32548 .... (850) 664–1266
Okaloosa County Director.—Lois Hoyt.

Counties: ESCAMBIA, HOLMES, OKALOOSA (part), SANTA ROSA, WALTON (part), WASHINGTON. CITIES AND TOWNSHIPS: Bonifay, Carryville, Crestview, DeFuniak Springs, Destin, Fountain, Freeport, Ft. Walton Beach, Gulf Breeze, Jay, Laurel Hill, Lynn Haven, Milton, Noma, Pace, Panama City, Paxton, Pensacola, Sunnyside, Westville, and Youngstown. Population (2000), 639,295.

ZIP Codes: 32420–22, 32425, 32427–28, 32431, 32433–35, 32437–40, 32446, 32452, 32455, 32457, 32462–64, 32466, 32501–09, 32511–14, 32516, 32520–24, 32526, 32530–31, 32533–42, 32544, 32547–49, 32559–72, 32577–79, 32580, 32583, 32588, 32591, 32598

* * *

SECOND DISTRICT

ALLEN BOYD, Democrat, of Monticello, FL; born in Valdosta, GA, June 6, 1945; graduated, Jefferson County High School, Monticello, 1963; B.S., Florida State University, 1969; partner and general manager, F.A. Boyd and Sons, Inc., family farm corporation; first lieutenant, U.S. Army 101st Airborne Division, Vietnam, 1969–71, receiving the CIB and other decorations; Florida House of Representatives, 1989–96; elected majority whip; chaired Governmental Operations Committee (1992–94) and House Democratic Conservative Caucus (Blue Dogs); member: Peanut Producers Association; Farm Bureau; Cattlemen's Association; local historical association; Chamber of Commerce; and Kiwanis; board member, National Cotton Council; member, First United Methodist Church; married: the former Stephannie Ann Roush, 1970; children: Fred Allen Boyd III (d), Suzanne, John, and David; elected to the 105th Congress; reelected to each succeeding Congress.

Office Listings

http:/www.house.gov/boyd

107 Cannon House Office Building, Washington, DC 20515 .... (202) 225–5235
Administrative Assistant.—Libby Greer. FAX: 225–5615
Legislative Director.—Jason Quaranto.
Legislative Assistant/Systems Manager.—Craig Stevens.
Legislative Assistants: Danny Collins, Charla Penn.
Executive Assistant/Scheduler.—Robin Lee.
301 South Monroe Street, No. 108, Tallahassee, FL 32301 .... (850) 561–3979
District Director.—Jerry Smithwick.
30 W. Government Street, Panama City, FL 32401 .... (850) 785–0812
District Representative.—Bobby Pickles.

Counties: BAY, CALHOUN, DIXIE, FRANKLIN, GADSDEN, GULF, JACKSON, JEFFERSON (part), LAFEYETTE, LEON (part), LIBERTY, SUWANNE, TAYLOR, WALKULLA, WALTON (part). Population (2000), 639,295.

ZIP Codes: 32008, 32013, 32024, 32038, 32055, 32060, 32062, 32064, 32066, 32071, 32094, 32096, 32126, 32140, 32170, 32175, 32267, 32301–18, 32320–24, 32326–34, 32336, 32343–44, 32346–48, 32351–53, 32355–62, 32395, 32399, 32401–13, 32417, 32420–21, 32423–24, 32426, 32428, 32430–32, 32437–38, 32440, 32442–49, 32454, 32456–57, 32459–61, 32465–66, 32541, 32550, 32578, 32628, 32648, 32680, 32692

* * *

THIRD DISTRICT

CORRINE BROWN, Democrat, of Jacksonville, FL; born in Jacksonville on November 11, 1946; B.S., Florida A&M University, 1969; master's degree, Florida A&M University, 1971; education specialist degree, University of Florida; honorary doctor of law, Edward Waters College; faculty member: Florida Community College in Jacksonville; University of Florida; and Edward Waters College; served in the Florida House of Representatives for 10 years; first woman elected chairperson of the Duval County Legislative Delegation; served as a consultant to the Governor's Committee on Aging; committees: Transportation and Infrastructure;

Veterans' Affairs; member: Congressional Black Caucus; Women's Caucus; and Progressive Caucus; one child: Shantrel; elected on November 3, 1992, to the 103rd Congress; reelected to each succeeding Congress.

Office Listings

http://www.house.gov/corrinebrown

2444 Rayburn House Office Building, Washington, DC 20515 .... (202) 225–0123
Chief of Staff.—E. Ronnie Simmons. FAX: 225–2256
Executive Assistant/Scheduler.—Darla E. Smallwood.
Legislative Director.—Nick Martinelli.
Senior Legislative Assistant.—Kim Bright.
101 East Union Street, Suite 202, Jacksonville, FL 32202 .... (904) 354–1652
219 Lime Avenue, Orlando, FL 32802 .... (407) 872–0656

Counties: ALACHUA (part), CLAY (part), DUVAL (part), LAKE (part), MARION (part), ORANGE (part), PUTNAM (part), SEMINOLE (part), VOLUSIA (part). Population (2000), 639,295.

ZIP Codes: 32003, 32007, 32043, 32066, 32073, 32102, 32105, 32112–13, 32130–31, 32134, 32138, 32140, 32147–49, 32160, 32177, 32179–80, 32182, 32185, 32190, 32201–11, 32215–16, 32218–19, 32231–32, 32234, 32236, 32238–39, 32244, 32247, 32254, 32277, 32601–04, 32627, 32631, 32640–41, 32653–54, 32662, 32666–67, 32681, 32702–03, 32712–13, 32720–24, 32736, 32751, 32757, 32763, 32767–68, 32771–73, 32776, 32789, 32798, 32801, 32804–05, 32808–11, 32818–19, 32835, 32839, 32855, 32858, 32861, 32868, 33142, 33160–61, 33179, 34488, 34761

* * *

FOURTH DISTRICT

ANDER CRENSHAW, Republican, of Jacksonville, FL; born on September 1, 1944, in Jacksonville, FL; education: B.A., University of Georgia, 1966; J.D., University of Florida, 1969; profession: investment banker; religion: Episcopal; public service: former member of the Florida House of Representatives and the Florida State Senate; served as President of the Florida State Senate; family: married to Kitty; children: Sarah and Alex; elected to the 107th Congress on November 7, 2000; reelected to each succeeding Congress.

Office Listings

http://www.house.gov/crenshaw

127 Cannon House Office Building, Washington, DC 20515 .... (202) 225–2501
Chief of Staff.—John Ariale. FAX: 225–2504
Legislative Director.—Erica Striebel.
Communications Director.—Ken Lundberg.
1061 Riverside Avenue, Suite 100, Jacksonville, FL 32204 .... (904) 598–0481
District Director.—Jacqueline Smith.
212 North Marion Avenue, Suite 209, Lake City, FL 32055 .... (386) 365–3316

Counties: BAKER, COLUMBIA, DUVAL (part), HAMILTON, JEFFERSON (part), LEON (part), MADISON, NASSAU, UNION. CITIES AND TOWNSHIPS: Greenville, Hilliard, Jacksonville (part), Jacksonville Beach, Jasper, Jennings, Lake Butler, Lake City, Lee, Macclenny, Madison, Monticello, Nassau Village-Ratliff, Palm Valley, Tallahassee (part), White Springs, and Yulee. Population (2000), 639,295.

ZIP Codes: 32009, 32011, 32024–26, 32034–35, 32038, 32040–41, 32046, 32052–56, 32058–59, 32061, 32063, 32072, 32083, 32087, 32094, 32096–97, 32204–05, 32207, 32210–12, 32214, 32216–18, 32223–29, 32233–35, 32237, 32240–41, 32244–46, 32250, 32255–58, 32266, 32277, 32301, 32311, 32317, 32331, 32336–37, 32340–41, 32344–45, 32350, 32643, 32697, 33142

* * *

FIFTH DISTRICT

GINNY BROWN-WAITE, Republican, of Brooksville, FL; born on October 5, 1943, in Albany, NY; education: B.S., State University of New York, 1976; Russell Sage College, 1984; Labor Studies Program Certification, Cornell University; professional: served as a Legislative Director in the New York State Senate for almost 18 years; public service: Hernando County, FL, Commissioner; Florida State Senate, 1992–2002; served as Senate Majority Whip, and President Pro Tempore; recipient of numerous awards for community service; family: married to Harvey; three daughters; elected to the 108th Congress on November 5, 2002.

Office Listings

http://www.house.gov/brown-waite

1516 Longworth House Office Building, Washington, DC 20515 .... (202) 225–1002
Chief of Staff.—Brian Walsh. FAX: 226–6559
Scheduler.—Pete Meachum.
Legislative Director.—Serena Underwood.
Press Secretary.—Caryn McLeod.
20 North Main Street, Room 200, Brooksville, FL 34601 .... (352) 799–8354
38008 Meridian Avenue, Suite A, Dade City, FL 33525 .... (352) 567–6707

Counties: CITRUS, HERNANDO, LAKE (part), LEVY (part), MARION (part), PASCO (part), POLK (part), SUMTER. CITIES AND TOWNSHIPS: Brooksville, Dade City, and Clermont. Population (2000), 639,295.

ZIP Codes: 32159, 32162, 32621, 32625–26, 32635, 32639, 32644, 32658, 32668, 32683, 32696, 32778, 32825, 33513–14, 33521, 33523–26, 33537–38, 33540–44, 33548–49, 33556, 33558–59, 33574, 33576, 33585, 33593, 33597, 33809–10, 33849, 33868, 34218, 34220, 34423, 34428–34, 34436, 34442, 34445–53, 34460–61, 34464–65, 34481–82, 34484, 34487, 34498, 34601–11, 34613–14, 34636, 34639, 34653–55, 34661, 34667, 34669, 34711–13, 34731, 34736–37, 34748, 34753, 34755, 34762, 34785, 34787–89, 34797

* * *

SIXTH DISTRICT

CLIFF STEARNS, Republican, of Ocala, FL; born in Washington, DC, April 16, 1941; graduated, Woodrow Wilson High, Washington, DC, 1959; B.S., electrical engineering, George Washington University, Washington, DC, 1963; Air Force ROTC Distinguished Military Graduate; graduate work, University of California, Los Angeles, 1965; served, U.S. Air Force (captain), 1963–67; businessman; past president: Silver Springs Kiwanis; member: Marion County/Ocala Energy Task Force, Tourist Development Council, Ocala Board of Realtors, American Hotel/Motel Association in Florida, American Hotel/Motel Association of the United States, Grace Presbyterian Church; board of directors, Boys Club of Ocala; trustee: Munroe Regional Hospital; married to the former Joan Moore; three children: Douglas, Bundy, and Scott; elected November 8, 1988, to the 101st Congress; reelected to each succeeding Congress.

Office Listings

http://www.house.gov/stearns

2370 Rayburn House Office Building, Washington, DC 20515 .... (202) 225–5744
Administrative Assistant.—Jack Seum. FAX: 225–3973
Legislative Director.—Alan Hill.
Executive Assistant.—Joan Smutko.
115 Southeast 25th Avenue, Ocala, FL 34471 .... (352) 351–8777
District Manager.—Judy Moore.
5700 S.W. 34th Street, #425, Gainesville, FL 32608 .... (352) 337–0003
1726 Kinglsey Avenue S.E., Suite 8, Orange Park, FL 32073 .... (904) 269–3203

Counties: ALACHUA (part), BRADFORD, CLAY (part), DUVAL (part), GILCHREST, LAKE (part), LEVY (part), MARION (part). CITIES AND TOWNSHIPS: Ocala (part), Gainesville (part), Leesburg, Orange Park, Middleburg, and Jacksonville (part). Population (2000), 639,295.

ZIP Codes: 32003, 32006, 32008, 32030, 32042–44, 32050, 32054, 32058, 32065, 32067–68, 32073, 32079, 32083, 32091, 32099, 32111, 32113, 32133, 32140, 32158–59, 32162, 32179, 32183, 32195, 32205, 32210, 32215, 32219–22, 32234, 32244, 32254, 32276, 32601, 32603, 32605–12, 32614–16, 32618–19, 32621–22, 32631, 32633–34, 32643, 32653, 32655–56, 32658, 32663–64, 32666–69, 32681, 32686, 32693–94, 32696, 33142, 33160–61, 34420–21, 34432, 34436, 34470–76, 34478, 34480–83, 34491–92, 34731, 34748–49

* * *

SEVENTH DISTRICT

JOHN L. MICA, Republican, of Winter Park, FL; born in Binghamton, NY, on January 27, 1943; education: graduated, Miami-Edison High School, Miami, FL; B.A., University of Florida, 1967; employment: president, MK Development; managing general partner, Cellular Communications; former government affairs consultant, Mica, Dudinsky and Associates; executive director, Local Government Study Commissions, Palm Beach County, 1970–72; executive director, Orange County Local Government Study Commission, 1972–74; Florida State House of Representatives, 1976–80; administrative assistant, U.S. Senator Paula Hawkins, 1980–85; Florida State Good Government Award, 1973; one of five Florida Jaycees Outstanding Young Men of America, 1978; member: Kiwanis, U.S. Capitol Preservation Commission, Tiger Bay Club, co-chairman, Speaker's Task Force for a Drug Free America, Florida Blue Key; brother of former Congressman Daniel A. Mica; married: the former Patricia Szymanek, 1972; children: D'Anne Leigh and John Clark; elected on November 3, 1992 to the 103rd Congress; reelected to each succeeding Congress.

Office Listings

http://www.house.gov/mica

2445 Rayburn House Office Building, Washington, DC 20515 .... (202) 225–4035
Chief of Staff.—Russell L. Roberts. FAX: 226–0821
Executive Assistant / Scheduler.—Mary Klappa.
Legislative Director.—Gary Burns.
668 N. Orlando Avenue, Suite 218, Maitland, FL 32751 .... (407) 657–8080
840 Deltona Boulevard, Deltona, FL 32725 .... (386) 860–1499
770 W. Granada Boulevard, Ormond Beach, FL 32174 .... (386) 676–7750
3000 N. Ponce de Leon Boulevard, St. Augustine, FL .... (904) 810–5048
613 St. Johns Avenue, Palatka, FL 32177 .... (386) 328–1622
1 Florida Park Drive, Palm Coast, FL 32127 .... (386) 246–6042

Counties: ORANGE COUNTY (part). CITIES AND TOWNSHIPS: Maitland (part), Winter Park (part). SEMINOLE COUNTY. CITIES AND TOWNSHIPS: Altamonte Springs (part), Casselberry (part), Heathrow, Lake Mary, Longwood, Sanford (part), Winter Springs (part). VOLUSIA COUNTY (part). CITIES AND TOWNSHIPS: Daytona Beach (part), Debary (part), Deland (part), Deltona (part), Holly Hill, Lake Helen, Orange City, Ormond Beach, Pierson (part). FLAGLER COUNTY. CITIES AND TOWNSHIPS: Beverly Beach, Bunnell, Flagler Beach, Marineland, Palm Coast. ST. JOHNS COUNTY. CITIES AND TOWNSHIPS: Hastings, Ponte Vedra Beach, St. Augustine, St. Augustine Beach. PUTNAM COUNTY (part). CITIES AND TOWNSHIPS: Crescent City, Palatka (part), Pomona Park, and Welaka. Population, (2000), 639,295.

ZIP Codes: 32004, 32033, 32080, 32082, 32084–86, 32092, 32095, 32110, 32112, 32114–22, 32125, 32130–31, 32135–37, 32139, 32142, 32145, 32151, 32157, 32164, 32173–78, 32180–81, 32187, 32189, 32193, 32198, 32259–60, 32701, 32706–08, 32713–15, 32718, 32720, 32724–25, 32728, 32730, 32738, 32744, 32746–47, 32750–53, 32763–64, 32771, 32773–74, 32779, 32789, 32791–92, 32795, 32799

* * *

EIGHTH DISTRICT

RIC KELLER, Republican, of Orlando, FL; born on September 5, 1964, in Johnson City, TN; education: Boone High School, 1982; B.S., East Tennessee State University, 1986; J.D., Vanderbilt University, 1992; occupation: Attorney; partner in the law firm of Rumberger, Kirk & Caldwell; community service: Chairman of the Board of Directors of the Orlando/Orange County COMPACT Program; co-author of two amendments to Florida's Constitution (the Everglades Polluter Pays amendment, and the Everglades Trust Fund amendment); religion: United Methodist; divorced; children: Nick and Christy; elected to the 107th Congress on November 7, 2000; reelected to each succeeding Congress.

Office Listings

http://www.house.gov/keller

419 Cannon House Office Building, Washington, DC 20515 .... (202) 225–2176
Chief of Staff.—Jason Miller. FAX: 225–0999
Legislative Director.—Jaclyn Norris.
Scheduler.—Mandy Leigh Runnels.
605 East Robinson Street, Suite 650, Orlando, FL 32801 .... (407) 872–1962
District Director.—Mike Miller.

Counties: ORANGE (part), OSCEOLA (part), MARION (part), LAKE (part). CITIES AND TOWNSHIPS: Astatula, Azalea, Bay Hill, Bay Lake, Belle Isle, Belleview, Celebration, Conway, Doctor Phillips (part), Edgewood, Eustis, Fairview Shores (part), Howey in the Hills (part), Holden Heights (part), Leesburg (part), Meadow Wood (part), Mid Florida Lakes, Montverde, Oakland, Ocala Part, Ocoee, Orlando (part), Silver Springs Shores (part), Sky Lakes, Tavares, Umatilla (part), Union Park (part), Williamsburg, Windermere, Winter Garden, and Winter Park (part). Population (2000), 639,295.

ZIP Codes: 32113, 32179, 32192, 32617, 32702–03, 32710, 32726–27, 32735–36, 32756–57, 32777–78, 32784, 32789, 32792, 32801–07, 32809–12, 32814, 32817–19, 32821–22, 32824–25, 32827, 32829–30, 32835–37, 32839, 32853–54, 32856–57, 32859–60, 32862, 32867, 32869, 32872, 32877, 32885–87, 32890–91, 32893, 32896–98, 33030, 33032–33, 33161, 33186, 34470–72, 34475, 34479–80, 34488–89, 34705, 34711, 34729, 34734, 34740, 34746–47, 34756, 34760–61, 34777–78, 34786–88

* * *

NINTH DISTRICT

MICHAEL BILIRAKIS, Republican, of Palm Harbor, FL; born July 16, 1930, in Tarpon Springs, FL; raised in western Pennsylvania; B.S. in engineering, University of Pittsburgh, 1955–59; accounting, George Washington University, Washington, DC, 1959–60; J.D., University of Florida, Gainesville, 1961–63; U.S. Air Force, 1951–55; attorney and small businessman, petroleum engineer, aerospace contract administrator, geophysical engineer (offshore oil exploration), steelworker, and judge of various courts for eight years; honors in college include Phi Alpha Delta Annual Award for Outstanding Law Graduate and president of the student body of School of Engineering and Mines; honors after college, civil activities, and organizations include Citizen of the Year Award for Greater Tarpon Springs, 1972–73; founder and charter president of Tarpon Springs Volunteer Ambulance Service; past president and four-year director of Greater Tarpon Springs Chamber of Commerce; past president, Rotary Club of Tarpon Springs; board of governors, Pinellas Suncoast Chamber of Commerce; board of development, Anclote Manor Psychiatric Hospital, AHEPA; elected commander, Post 173 American Legion, Holiday, FL (1977–79, two terms); 33rd degree Mason and Shriner; member: West Pasco Bar Association, American Judicature Society, Florida and American bar associations, University of Florida Law Center Association, Gator Booster, American Legion, and Veterans of Foreign Wars; holds college level doctorate teaching certificate; member: Juvenile Diabetes Association, Elks, Eastern Star and White Shrine of Jerusalem, Royaler of Jesters of Egypt Temple Shrine District, Air Force Association; former member: Clearwater Bar Association, National Contract Management Association, American Society of Mining, Metallurgical and Petroleum Engineers, and Creative Education Foundation; married the former Evelyn Miaoulis, 1959; two children: Manuel and Gus; elected to the 98th Congress, November 2, 1982; reelected to each succeeding Congress.

Office Listings

http://www.house.gov/bilirakis

2269 Rayburn House Office Building, Washington, DC 20515 .... (202) 225–5755
Administrative Assistant.—Rebecca Hyder. FAX: 225–4085
Legislative Director.—Sarah Owen.
Communications Director/Legislative Assistant.—Christy Stefadouros.
Deputy Administrative Assistant/Scheduler.—Douglas Menorca.
35111 US Highway 19 North, Suite 301, Palm Harbor, FL 34684 .... (727) 773–2871
Director of District Operations.—Sonja Stefanadis.
10330 North Dale Mabry, Suite 205, Tampa, FL 33618 .... (813) 960–8173

Counties: HILLSBOROUGH (part), PASCO (part), PINELLAS (part). CITIES AND TOWNSHIPS: Bearss, Bloomingdale, Brandon (part), Carrollwood Village, Citrus Park (part), Clearwater, Countryside, Crystal Springs, Dale Mabry, Eastlake Woodlands, Elfers, Fishhawk, Holiday, Hudson, Hunters Green, Lutz, New Port Richey, Odessa, Oldsmar, Palm Harbor, Plant City, Safety Harbor, Seffner, Seven Springs, Tarpon Springs, Temple Terrace (part), Thonotosassa, Trinity, Valrico, and Veterans Village. Population (2000), 639,296.

ZIP Codes: 33030, 33032–33, 33175, 33186, 33511, 33527, 33530, 33539–40, 33542, 33547–49, 33556, 33558–59, 33563, 33565–67, 33569, 33583–84, 33587, 33592, 33594–95, 33598, 33612–13, 33617–18, 33624–26, 33637, 33647, 33688, 33755–59, 33761, 33763–66, 33769, 33810, 34652–56, 34667–69, 34673–74, 34677, 34679–80, 34683–85, 34688–91, 34695

* * *

TENTH DISTRICT

C.W. BILL YOUNG, Republican, of Largo, FL; born in Harmarville, PA, December 16, 1930; elected Florida's only Republican State Senator in 1960; reelected 1964, 1966, 1967 (special election), and 1968, serving as minority leader from 1963 to 1970; national committeeman, Florida Young Republicans, 1957–59; state chairman, Florida Young Republicans, 1959–61; member, Florida Constitution Revision Commission, 1965–67; he and his wife, Beverly, have three sons; committees: chairman, Appropriations; Select Committee on Homeland Security; Republican Executive Committee on Committees; elected to the 92nd Congress, November 3, 1970; reelected to each succeeding Congress.

Office Listings

2407 Rayburn House Office Building, Washington, DC 20515 .... (202) 225–5961
Chief of Staff.—Harry Glenn. FAX: 225–9764
Scheduler.—Jane Porter.
Legislative Director.—Brad Stine.
360 Central Avenue, Suite 1480, St. Petersburg, FL 33701 .... (727) 893–3191
Administrative Assistant.—George N. Cretekos.
801 West Bay Drive, Suite 606, Largo, FL 33770 .... (727) 581–0980

Counties: PINELLAS COUNTY (part). Population (2000), 639,295.

ZIP Codes: 33701–16, 33729, 33731–32, 33734, 33736–38, 33740–44, 33755–56, 33760–65, 33767, 33770–82, 33784–86, 34660, 34681–84, 34697–98

ELEVENTH DISTRICT

JIM DAVIS, Democrat, of Tampa, FL; born October 11, 1957, in Tampa; B.A., Washington and Lee University, 1979; J.D., University of Florida Law School, 1982; admitted to the Florida bar in 1982 and began practice with Carlton Fields law firm in Tampa; partner, Bush, Ross, Gardner, Warren and Rudy law firm, 1988–96; member, Florida House of Representatives, 1988–96, serving as majority leader from 1994 to 1996; member of the Tampa, Brandon and Riverview chambers of commerce and Old Seminole Heights Preservation Committee; married to Peggy Bessent Davis since 1986; two sons, Peter and William; elected to the 105th Congress, and selected Democratic freshman class president; reelected to each succeeding Congress.

Office Listings

http://www.house.gov/jimdavis

409 Cannon House Office Building, Washington, DC 20515 .... (202) 225–3376
Chief of Staff.—Karl Koch. FAX: 225–5652
Deputy Chief of Staff/Legislative Director.—Tricia Barrentine.
Scheduler/Executive Assistant.—Joan R. Hall.
Press Secretary.—Diane Pratt-Heavner.
3315 Henderson Boulevard, No. 100, Tampa, FL 33609 .... (813) 354–9217
District Director.—John Kynes.

Counties: HILLSBOROUGH COUNTY (part). CITIES: Apollo Beach (part), Bloomingdale (part), Brandon (part), Carrollwood, Del Rio, East Lake-Orient Park, Egypt Lake, Gibsonton, Lake Magdalene (part), Mango (part), Palm River-Clair Mel, Riverview, Tampa, Temple Terrace, and Town 'N' Country. Population (2000), 639,295.

ZIP Codes: 33030, 33033–34, 33142, 33160–61, 33189, 33534, 33549, 33569–70, 33572, 33586, 33601–26, 33629–31, 33633–35, 33637, 33650, 33655, 33660–64, 33672–75, 33677, 33679–82, 33684–87, 33690, 33697, 33701, 33705, 33707, 33710–13, 33730, 33733, 33747, 34205, 34208, 34221–22

* * *

TWELFTH DISTRICT

ADAM H. PUTNAM, Republican, of Bartow, FL; born on July 31, 1974, in Bartow, FL; education: Bartow High School; University of Florida, B.S., Food and Resource Economics; employment: farmer; rancher; awards: Outstanding Male Graduate of the University of Florida; Who's Who in American Politics; organizations: Florida 4–H Foundation; Sheriff's Youth Villa Board of Associates; Chamber of Commerce; Polk County Farm Bureau; married: Melissa; public service: Florida House of Representatives, 1996–2000; elected to the 107th Congress on November 7, 2000; reelected to each succeeding Congress.

Office Listings

http://www.house.gov/putnam

506 Cannon House Office Building, Washington, DC 20515 .... (202) 225–1252
Chief of Staff.—John Hambel. FAX: 226–0585
Executive Assistant.—Chanel Dedes.
Legislative Director.—Karen Williams.
Director of Communications.—Shawn Dhar.
650 East Davidson Street, Bartow, FL 33830 .... (863) 534–3530
District Director.—Matthew Joyner.

Counties: HILLSBOROUGH (part), OSCEOLA (part), POLK (part). CITIES AND TOWNSHIPS: Apollo Beach, Auburndale, Babson Park, Bartow, Brandon (part), Davenport, Dundee, Eagle Lake, Fort Meade, Frostproof, Gibsonton, Haines City, Highland City, Hillcrest Heights, Indian Lake Estates, Lakeland (part), Lake Alfred, Lake Hamilton, Lake Wales, Mulberry, Plant City (part), Poinciana (part), Polk City (part), Riverview (part), Ruskin (part), Seffner, Sun City Center, Tampa (part), Temple Terrace (part), Thonotosassa, Wimauma, and Winter Haven. Population (2000), 639,296.

ZIP Codes: 33030, 33033, 33170, 33183, 33186, 33503, 33508–11, 33527, 33534, 33547, 33550, 33563–64, 33566–73, 33575, 33584, 33592, 33594, 33598, 33610, 33617, 33619, 33637, 33689, 33801–07, 33809–11, 33813, 33815, 33820, 33823, 33825, 33827, 33830–31, 33834–41, 33843–47, 33850–51, 33853–56, 33859–60, 33863, 33867–68, 33877, 33880–85, 33888, 33896–98, 34758–59

* * *

THIRTEENTH DISTRICT

KATHERINE HARRIS, Republican, of Sarasota, FL; born on April 5, 1957, in Key West, FL; education: bachelor's degree, Agnes Scott College, in history; master's degree, Harvard University, in international trade and negotiations; professional: IBM marketing executive, and vice president of a commercial real estate firm; public service: Florida State Senate, 1994–1998; Florida Secretary of State, 1999–2002; awards: Florida Arts Advocacy Award; Florida Economic Development Council Legislator of the Year; Milton N. Fisher Award for International Trade Advocacy; Florida United Business Association Outstanding Legislator Award; Sarasota Humanitarian of the Year Award; family: married to Anders Ebbeson; one child, Louise; elected to the 108th Congress on November 5, 2002.

Office Listings

http://www.house.gov/harris

116 Cannon House Office Building, Washington, DC 20515 .... (202) 225–5015
Chief of Staff.—Dan Berger. FAX: 226–0828
Legislative Director.—Melissa Figge.
Scheduler.—Bonnie Kidd.
1991 Main Street, Suite 181, Sarasota, FL 34236 .... (941) 951–6643
District Director.—Hartley O'Brien.
1112 Manatee Avenue West, Suite 902, Bradenton, FL 34205 .... (941) 747–9081

Counties: CHARLOTTE (part), DESOTO, HARDEE, MANATEE (part), SARASOTA. Population (2000), 639,295.

ZIP Codes: 33138, 33160–61, 33598, 33834, 33865, 33873, 33890, 33946–47, 34201–12, 34215–19, 34221–24, 34228–43, 34250–51, 34260, 34264–70, 34272, 34274–78, 34280–82, 34284–89, 34292–93, 34295

* * *

FOURTEENTH DISTRICT

PORTER J. GOSS, Republican, of Sanibel, FL; born in Waterbury, CT, November 26, 1938; B.A., Yale University, New Haven, CT, 1960; served, U.S. Army, second lieutenant, 1960–62; clandestine services officer, CIA, 1962–72; newspaper publisher, small business owner; councilman/mayor, city of Sanibel, 1974–82; chairman, Lee County Commission, 1985–86; commissioner, Lee County, District 1, 1983–88; director, National Audubon Society; chairman, State Advisory Committee on Coastal Management; vice chairman, West Coast Inland Navigational District; past chairman, Metropolitan Planning Organization; port commissioner, Southwest Florida Regional Airport; member: Southwest Florida Mental Health District Board, Canterbury School, Lee County Mental Health Center, Sanibel-Captiva Conservation Foundation, Westminster Presbyterian Church; married to the former Mariel Robinson; four children: Leslie, Chauncey, Mason, and Gerrit; elected November 8, 1988, to the 101st Congress; reelected to each succeeding Congress.

Office Listings

http://www.house.gov/goss

108 Cannon House Office Building, Washington, DC 20515 .... (202) 225–2536
Chief of Staff.—Sheryl Wooley. FAX: 225–6820
Legislative Director.—Joey Hefferon.
Office Manager/Scheduler.—Maggie Knutson.
Press Secretary.—Julie Almacy.
Suite 303, Barnett Center, 2000 Main Street, Fort Myers, FL 33901 .... (239) 332–4677
Suite 212, Building F, 3301 Tamiami Trail East, Naples, FL 34112 .... (239) 774–8060

Counties: CHARLOTTE (part), COLLIER (part), LEE. Population (2000), 639,295.

ZIP Codes: 33030, 33033, 33160, 33186, 33189, 33901–22, 33924, 33927–28, 33931–32, 33936, 33945–46, 33948, 33953–57, 33965, 33970–72, 33981, 33990–91, 33993–94, 34101–10, 34112–14, 34116, 34119, 34133–36, 34140, 34142, 34145–46, 34224

* * *

FIFTEENTH DISTRICT

DAVE WELDON, Republican, of Palm Bay, FL; born in Long Island, NY, August 31, 1953; graduated Farmingdale High School, Farmingdale, NY, 1971; B.S., biochemistry, State University of New York, Stony Brook, 1978; M.D., State University of New York, Buffalo, 1981; U.S. Army Major, 1981–87; physician, internal medicine; member: American College of Physicians, Florida Medical Association, Brevard County Medical Society, Retired Officers Association, Good Samaritan Club, Brevard Veterans Council, Vietnam Veterans of Brevard, American Legion; founder, Space Coast Family Forum; married: Nancy Weldon, 1979; children: Katherine and David; committees: Appropriations; subcommittees: Labor, Health and Human Services, Education and Related Agencies; VA, HUD, and Independent Agencies; District of Columbia; elected to the 104th Congress; reelected to each succeeding Congress.

Office Listings

http://www.house.gov/weldon

2347 Rayburn House Office Building, Washington, DC 20515 .... (202) 225–3671
Chief of Staff.—Dana Gartzke. FAX: 225–3516
Deputy Chief of Staff.—Stuart Burns.
Office Manager/Personal Secretary.—Barbara Reynolds.
Legislative Director.—Paul Webster.
Senior Legislative Assistant.—Brendan Curry.
Building C, 2725 Judge Fran Jamieson Way, Melbourne, FL 32940 .... (321) 632–1776
District Director.—J.B. Kump.
2000 16th Avenue, Indian River County Courthouse, Room 157, Vero Beach, FL 32960 .... (772) 778–3534

Counties: BREVARD (part), INDIAN RIVER, OSCEOLA (part), POLK (part). Population (2000), 639,295.

ZIP Codes: 32815, 32899, 32901–12, 32919–20, 32922–26, 32931–32, 32934–37, 32940–41, 32948–53, 32955–58, 32960–71, 32976, 32978, 33837, 33848, 33858, 33868, 33896–98, 34739, 34741–47, 34758–59, 34769–73, 34972

* * *

SIXTEENTH DISTRICT

MARK FOLEY, Republican, of West Palm Beach, FL; born in Newton, MA, on September 8, 1954; graduated Lake Worth High School, Lake Worth, FL; attended Palm Beach Community College, Lake Worth; president, Foley Smith and Associates, Inc., real estate company; Florida House of Representatives, 1990–92; Florida Senate (Agriculture Committee chairman), 1992–94; Lake Worth city commissioner, 1977; Lake Worth vice mayor, 1983–84; committees: Ways and Means; deputy whip; chairman, Entertainment Task Force; elected to the 104th Congress; reelected to each succeeding Congress.

Office Listings

http://www.house.gov/foley

104 Cannon House Office Building, Washington, DC 20515 .... (202) 225–5792
Chief of Staff.—Kirk Fordham. FAX: 225–3132
Press Secretary.—Christopher Paulitz.
Legislative Director.—Elizabeth Nicolson.
4440 PGA Boulevard, Suite 406, Palm Beach Gardens, FL 33410 .... (561) 627–6192
District Manager.—Don Kislewski.
County Annex Building, 250 Northwest Country Club Drive, Port St. Lucie, FL 34986 .... (772) 878–3181
District Manager.—Ann Decker.
18500 Murdock Circle, Suite 536, Port Charlotte, FL 33948 .... (941) 627–9100

Counties: CHARLOTTE (part), GLADES, HENDRY (part), HIGHLANDS, MARTIN (part), OKEECHOBEE, PALM BEACH (part), ST. LUCIE (part). Population (2000), 639,295.

ZIP Codes: 33138, 33160–61, 33170, 33186, 33410–12, 33414, 33418, 33421, 33440, 33455, 33458, 33467, 33469–71, 33475, 33477–78, 33825–26, 33852, 33857, 33862, 33870–72, 33875–76, 33917, 33920, 33930, 33935, 33938, 33944, 33948–55, 33960, 33972, 33975, 33980, 33982–83, 34142, 34945–47, 34949–53, 34956–58, 34972–74, 34981–88, 34990–92, 34994–97

* * *

SEVENTEENTH DISTRICT

KENDRICK B. MEEK, Democrat, of Miami, FL; born on September 6, 1966; education: B.S., Florida A&M University, 1989; organizations: NAACP; 100 Black Men of America, Inc.; Greater Miami Service Corps; Omega Psi Phi Fraternity; awards: Mothers Against Drunk Driving Outstanding Service Award; Ebony Magazine's 50 Leaders of Tomorrow; Adams-Powell Civil Rights Award; public service: Florida House of Representatives, 1994–1998; Florida State Senate, 1998–2002; family: married to Leslie Dixon; children: Lauren and Kendrick B., Jr.; son of former Florida U.S. Representative Carrie P. Meek; elected to the 108th Congress on November 5, 2002.

Office Listings

http://www.house.gov/kenmeek

1039 Longworth House Office Building, Washington, DC 20515 .... (202) 225–4506
Chief of Staff.—John Schelble. FAX: 226–0777
Senior Advisor.—Misty Brown.
Legislative Director.—Tasha Cole.
Scheduler.—Lisa Kohnke.
111 N.W. 183rd Street, Suite 315, Miami, FL 33169 .... (305) 690–5905
District Office Director.—Anthony Williams.

Counties: DADE (part), BROWARD (part). Population (2000), 639,296.

ZIP Codes: 33008–09, 33013, 33020–25, 33054–56, 33081, 33083, 33090, 33092, 33101, 33110, 33127, 33136–38, 33142, 33147, 33150–51, 33156, 33160–62, 33164, 33167–69, 33179–81, 33197, 33238, 33242, 33247, 33256, 33261

* * *

EIGHTEENTH DISTRICT

ILEANA ROS-LEHTINEN, Republican, of Miami, FL; born July 15, 1952 in Havana, Cuba; B.A., English, Florida International University; M.S., educational leadership, Florida International University; doctoral candidate in education, University of Miami; certified Florida school teacher; founder and former owner, Eastern Academy; elected to Florida House of Representatives, 1982; elected to Florida State Senate, 1986; former president, Bilingual Private School Association; regular contributor to leading Spanish-language newspaper; during House tenure, married then-State Representative Dexter Lehtinen; children: Amanda Michelle and Patricia Marie; member: International Relations and Government Reform committees; elected on August 29, 1989 to the 101st Congress; reelected to each succeeding Congress.

Office Listings

2160 Rayburn House Office Building, Washington, DC 20515 .... (202) 225–3931
Chief of Staff.—Arthur Estopinan. FAX: 225–5620
Deputy Administrative Assistant.—Christine del Portillo.
Legislative Director.—Fred Ratliff.
Press Secretary.—Alex Cruz.
Suite 100, 9210 Sunset Drive, Miami, FL 33173 .... (305) 275–1800

Counties: DADE (part), MONROE (part). CITIES AND TOWNSHIPS: Coral Gables, Florida City, Homestead, Key Biscayne, Miami, Miami Beach, South Miami, and West Miami. Population (2000), 639,295.

ZIP Codes: 33001, 33030, 33032–34, 33036–37, 33039–45, 33050–52, 33070, 33109, 33111–12, 33114, 33119, 33121, 33124–36, 33139–46, 33149, 33154–59, 33165, 33170, 33174, 33176, 33186, 33189–90, 33195, 33197, 33199, 33231, 33233–34, 33239, 33243, 33245, 33255, 33257, 33265, 33296, 33299

* * *

NINETEENTH DISTRICT

ROBERT WEXLER, Democrat, of Boca Raton, FL; born on January 2, 1961 in Queens, NY; graduate of Hollywood Hills High School; University of Florida, 1982; George Washington University Law School, 1985; admitted to the Florida bar in 1985; attorney; Florida State Senator, 1990–96; member: Palm Beach Planning and Zoning Commission, 1989–90, Palm Beach County Democratic Executive Committee, 1989–92, Palm Beach County Affordable Housing Committee, 1990–91, Florida Bar Association, South Palm Beach County Jewish Federation, Palm Beach County Anti-Defamation League; married to the former Laurie Cohen; three children; committees: International Relations; Judiciary; subcommittees: Asia and the Pacific; Courts, the Internet, and Intellectual Property; ranking member, Europe; elected to the 105th Congress; reelected to each succeeding Congress.

Office Listings

213 Cannon House Office Building, Washington, DC 20515 .... (202) 225–3001
Chief of Staff.—Eric Johnson. FAX: 225–5974
Press Secretary.—Lale Mamaux.
2500 North Military Trail, Suite 100, Boca Raton, FL 33431 .... (561) 988–6302
District Director.—Wendy Lipsich.
5790 Margate Boulevard, Margate, FL 33063 .... (954) 972–6454

Counties: BROWARD (part), PALM BEACH (part). CITIES AND TOWNSHIPS: Boca Raton, Boynton Beach, Coconut Creek, Coral Springs, Deerfield Beach, Delray Beach, Lauderhill, Lake Worth, Margate, North Lauderdale, Parkland, Pompano Beach, Sunrise and Tamarac. Population (2000) 639,295.

ZIP Codes: 33063–66, 33068–69, 33071, 33073, 33075–77, 33093, 33140, 33155, 33309, 33321, 33401, 33406, 33409, 33411, 33413–15, 33417, 33422, 33426, 33428, 33431, 33433–34, 33436–37, 33441–42, 33445–46, 33448, 33454, 33461–63, 33466–67, 33474, 33481–82, 33484, 33486–88, 33496–99

* * *

TWENTIETH DISTRICT

PETER DEUTSCH, Democrat, of Ft. Lauderdale, FL; born in New York, NY, on April 1, 1957; education: graduated, Horace Mann School, New York City, 1975; B.A., Swarthmore College, 1979; J.D., Yale Law School, New Haven, CT, 1982; employment: attorney; admitted to Florida bar, 1983; elected to the Florida State House, 1982; member, Jewish Foundation Board of Directors; married: the former Lori Ann Coffino, 1989; children: Johnathan Michael and Danielle Brooke; committees: Energy and Commerce; subcommittees: Commerce, Trade and Consumer Protection; Environment and Hazardous Materials; Telecommunications and the Internet; ranking member, Oversight and Investigations; elected on November 3, 1992 to the 103rd Congress; reelected to each succeeding Congress.

Office Listings

http://www.house.gov/deutsch

2303 Rayburn House Office Building, Washington, DC 20515 .... (202) 225–7931
Chief of Staff.—Marcus Jadotte. FAX: 225–8456
Legislative Director.—Elizabeth Assey.
Scheduler/Office Manager.—Evonne Marche.
District Director.—Jennifer Irving.
10100 Pines Boulevard, Pembroke Pines, FL 33026 .... (954) 437–3936
19200 West Country Club Drive, Third Floor, Aventura, FL 33180 .... (305) 936–5724

Counties: BROWARD COUNTY (part). CITIES: Dania Beach (part), Davie (part), Lazy Lake, Plantation (part), Wilton Manors, Weston. DADE COUNTY (part). CITIES: Bay Harbor Island (part), North Bay Village, and Sunny Isles. Population (2000), 639,295.

ZIP Codes: 33004, 33009, 33019–21, 33024, 33026, 33030, 33033, 33084, 33137, 33139–41, 33147, 33154, 33156, 33160–61, 33170, 33180–81, 33301, 33304–05, 33309, 33311–15, 33317–19, 33321–32, 33334, 33336, 33338, 33345, 33351, 33355, 33394

* * *

TWENTY-FIRST DISTRICT

LINCOLN DIAZ-BALART, Republican, of Miami, FL; born in Havana, Cuba on August 13, 1954; graduated, American School of Madrid, Spain, 1972; B.A., New College of the University of South Florida, Sarasota, 1976; J.D., Case Western Reserve University Law School, 1979; attorney; admitted to the Florida bar, 1979; partner, Fowler, White, Burnett, Hurley, Banick and Strickroot, P.A., Miami; Florida State House, 1986–89; Florida State Senate, 1989–92; founding member, Miami-Westchester Lions Club; member, Organization for Retarded Citizens; married the former Cristina Fernandez, 1976; two children: Lincoln Gabriel and Daniel; committees: Foreign Affairs; Rules; House Republican Policy Committee; Select Committee on Homeland Security; subcommittees: vice-chair, Legislative and Budget Process; Majority Assistant Whip; Congressional Human Rights Caucus; elected on November 3, 1992 to the 103rd Congress; re-elected to each succeeding Congress.

Office Listings

http://www.house.gov/diaz-balart

2244 Rayburn House Office Building, Washington, DC 20515 .... (202) 225–4211
Chief of Staff/Administrative Assistant.—Stephen D. Vermillion III.
Legislative Director.—Stephen Cote.
Deputy Press Secretary.—Angelica Alfonso.
8525 NW 53 Terrace, Suite 102, Miami, FL 33166 .... (305) 470–8555
District Director.—Ana M. Carbonell.

Counties: DADE COUNTY (part). CITIES AND TOWNSHIPS: Central Kendall (part), Doral, Fontainebleau (part), Hialeah, Miami Lakes, Miami Springs, Miramar, Pembroke Pines, Richmond Heights (part), Sweetwater, Virginia Gardens, and Westchester (part). Population (2000), 639,295.

ZIP Codes: 33002, 33010–17, 33027–29, 33054–55, 33082, 33102, 33107, 33116, 33122, 33126, 33143, 33148, 33152, 33155–58, 33165–66, 33172–74, 33176, 33178, 33186, 33188, 33266, 33283

* * *

TWENTY-SECOND DISTRICT

E. CLAY SHAW, JR., Republican, of Fort Lauderdale, FL; born in Miami, FL, April 19, 1939; education: graduated, Miami Edison Senior High School, 1957; B.S., Stetson University, Deland, FL, 1961; M.B.A., University of Alabama, 1963; J.D., Stetson University College of Law, 1966; employment: former certified public accountant; lawyer; admitted to the Florida State bar in 1966 and commenced practice in Fort Lauderdale; admitted to practice before the federal court in the Southern District of Florida and the U.S. Supreme Court; assistant city attorney, Fort Lauderdale, 1968; chief city prosecutor, 1968–69; assistant municipal judge, 1969–71; city commissioner, 1971–72; vice mayor, 1973–75; mayor, 1975–80; member: executive committee, U.S. Conference of Mayors; executive committee, Republican National Committee; president, National Conference of Republican Mayors; U.S. special ambassador, Papua, New Guinea (President Ford); director, Fort Lauderdale Chamber of Commerce; vice chairman, Sun Belt Mayor's Task Force; Broward County Charter Commission; national vice chairman, Mayors for Reagan, 1980; member, St. Anthony's Church; married: the former Emilie Costar, 1960; children: Mimi Shaw Carter, Jennifer Shaw Wilder, E. Clay Shaw III, and John Charles Shaw; elected to the 97th Congress, November 4, 1980; reelected to each succeeding Congress.

Office Listings

http://www.house.gov/shaw

2408 Rayburn House Office Building, Washington, DC 20515 .... (202) 225–3026
Chief of Staff.—Eric Eikenberg. FAX: 225–8398
Press Secretary.—Wendy Rosen.
1512 East Broward Boulevard, Fort Lauderdale, FL 33301 .... (954) 522–1800
District Director.—Joel Gustafson.
222 Lakeview Avenue, Suite 225, West Palm Beach, FL 33401 .... (561) 832–3007

Counties: BROWARD (part), PALM BEACH (part). CITIES: Aventura, Bal Harbour, Bay Harbor Islands, Biscayne Park, Boca Raton, Boynton Beach, Bring Breezes, Cloud Lake, Dania, Deerfield Beach, Delray Beach, Fort Lauderdale, Glen Ridge, Golden Beach, Gulf Stream, Hallandale, Highland Beach, Hillsboro Beach, Hollywood, Hypoluxo, Indian Creek, Juno Beach, Lake Park, Lake Worth, Lantana, Lauderdale by the Sea, Lazy Lake, Lighthouse Point, Manalapan, North Bay Village, North Palm Beach, Oakland Park, Ocean Ridge, Palm Beach, Palm Beach Gardens, Palm Beach Shores, Pembroke Park, Pompano Beach, Rivera Beach, Sea Ranch Lakes, South Palm Beach, Surfside, West Palm Beach, and Wilton Manors. Population (2000), 639,295.

ZIP Codes: 33004, 33009, 33015, 33033, 33060–62, 33064–65, 33067, 33071–74, 33076, 33097, 33128, 33153, 33155–56, 33161, 33163, 33165, 33179, 33186, 33189, 33280, 33301, 33303–09, 33312, 33314–17, 33324, 33328, 33334–35, 33339, 33346, 33348, 33401, 33403–08, 33410–12, 33415, 33418–20, 33424, 33426–27, 33429, 33431–36, 33441–45, 33458, 33460–64, 33468, 33477–78, 33480, 33483, 33486–87

* * *

TWENTY-THIRD DISTRICT

ALCEE L. HASTINGS, Democrat, of Miramar, FL; born in Altamonte Springs, FL, on September 5, 1936; graduated, Crooms Academy, Sanford, FL, 1954; B.A., Fisk University, Nashville, TN, 1958; Howard University, Washington, DC; J.D., Florida A&M University, Tallahassee, 1963; attorney; admitted to the Florida bar, 1963; circuit judge, U.S. District Court for the Southern District of Florida; member: African Methodist Episcopal Church, NAACP, Miami-Dade Chamber of Commerce, Family Christian Association, ACLU, Southern Poverty Law Center, National Organization for Women, Planned Parenthood, Women and Children First, Inc., Sierra Club, Cousteau Society, Broward County Democratic Executive Committee, Dade County Democratic Executive Committee, Lauderhill Democratic Club, Hollywood Hills Democratic Club, Pembroke Pines Democratic Club, Urban League, National Bar Association, Florida Chapter of the National Bar Association, T.J. Reddick Bar Association, National Conference of Black Lawyers, Simon Wiesenthal Center, The Furtivist Society; Progressive Black Police Officers Club, International Black Firefighters Association; three children: Alcee Lamar II, Chelsea, and Leigh; elected on November 3, 1992, to the 103rd Congress; reelected to each succeeding Congress.

Office Listings

http://www.house.gov/alceehastings

2235 Rayburn House Office Building, Washington, DC 20515 .... (202) 225–1313
Chief of Staff.—Arthur W. Kennedy.
Administrative Assistant / Legislative Director.—Fred Turner.
2701 West Oakland Park Boulevard, Suite 200, Ft. Lauderdale, FL 33311 .... (954) 733–2800
5725 Corporate Way, Suite 208, West Palm Beach, FL 33407 .... (561) 684–0565

Counties: BROWARD (part), HENDRY (part), MARTIN (part), PALM BEACH (part), ST. LUCIE (part). Population (2000), 639,295.

ZIP Codes: 33025, 33027–28, 33033, 33060, 33064, 33066, 33068–69, 33142, 33155–56, 33158, 33160–61, 33179, 33269, 33301–02, 33304–05, 33309–13, 33315, 33317, 33319–22, 33330–32, 33334, 33340, 33349, 33351, 33359, 33401–09, 33411, 33413–17, 33425, 33430, 33435, 33437–41, 33444–45, 33447, 33459–62, 33465, 33467, 33470, 33476, 33483, 33493, 34945–48, 34950–51, 34954, 34956, 34972, 34974, 34979, 34981, 34986–87

* * *

TWENTY-FOURTH DISTRICT

TOM FEENEY, Republican, of Oviedo, FL; born on May 21, 1958, in Abington, PA; education: B.A., Pennsylvania State University, 1980; J.D., University of Pittsburgh, 1983; professional: Attorney; business interests: Real Estate; religion: Presbyterian; organizations: Cornerstone, Inc., Distribution Center Board of Directors; City of Light Business Leadership Council; Mosley's High-Tech Tutoring Board of Directors; East Orange, Southwest Volusia, Sanford, and Oviedo Chambers of Commerce; James Madison Institute Board of Directors; OIA Kidsway, Inc., Board of Directors; Orange and Seminole County Republican Executive Committees; The Empowerment Network; American Legislative Exchange Council National Education Task Force; public service: Florida House of Representatives, 1990–1994, and 1996–2002; Republican nominee for Lieutenant Governor, 1994; Florida Speaker of the House of Representatives, 2000–2002; family: married to Ellen Stewart; children: Tommy and Sean; elected to the 108th Congress on November 5, 2002.

Office Listings

http://www.house.gov/feeney

323 Cannon House Office Building, Washington, DC 20515 .... (202) 225–2706
Chief of Staff.—Jason Roe. FAX: 226–2269
Legislative Director.—Brandon Steinmann.
Executive Assistant.—Sherry Dudley.
12424 Research Parkway, Suite 135, Orlando, FL 32826 .... (407) 208–1106
1000 City Center Circle, Second Floor, Port Orange, FL 32129 .... (386) 756–9798
400 South Street, Suite 413, Titusville, FL 32780 .... (321) 264–6113

Counties: BREVARD (part), ORANGE (part), SEMINOLE (part), VOLUSIA (part). Population (2000), 639,295.

ZIP Codes: 32114, 32118–19, 32123–24, 32127–29, 32132, 32141, 32168–70, 32701, 32703–04, 32707–09, 32712, 32714, 32716, 32719, 32732–33, 32738–39, 32751, 32754, 32757, 32759, 32762, 32764–66, 32775, 32779–83, 32789–90, 32792–94, 32796, 32798, 32810, 32816–17, 32820, 32824–29, 32831–33, 32878, 32922, 32926–27, 32953–54, 32959, 33313, 33319, 33337, 33388

* * *

TWENTY-FIFTH DISTRICT

MARIO DIAZ-BALART, Republican, of Miami, FL; born on September 25, 1961, in Fort Lauderdale, FL; education: University of South Florida; professional: President, Gordon Diaz-Balart and Partners (public relations and marketing business); religion: Catholic; public service: Administrative Assistant to the Mayor of Miami, 1985–1988; Florida House of Representatives, 1988–1992, and 2000–2002; Florida State Senate, 1992–2000; committees: Budget; Transportation and Infrastructure; elected to the 108th Congress on November 5, 2002.

Office Listings

http://www.house.gov/mariodiaz-balart

313 Cannon House Office Building, Washington, DC 20515 .... (202) 225–2778
Chief of Staff.—Omar Franco. FAX: 226–0346
Legislative Director.—Charles Cooper.
12851 SW 42nd Street, Suite 131, Miami, FL 33175 .... (305) 225–6866
District Director.—Miguel Otero.
4715 Golden Gate Parkway, Suite 1, Naples, FL 34116 .... (239) 348–1620
District Representative.—Stephen Hart.

Counties: COLLIER (part), DADE (part). Population (2000), 639,295.

ZIP Codes: 33015–16, 33018, 33030–35, 33157, 33166, 33170, 33175–78, 33182–87, 33189–90, 33193–94, 33196, 34113–14, 34116–17, 34120, 34137–39, 34141–43

GEORGIA

(Population 2000, 8,186,453)

SENATORS

ZELL MILLER, Democrat, of Young Harris, GA; born on February 24, 1932, in Young Harris, GA; education: graduated from Young Harris College, 1951; received a bachelor's degree, 1957, and a master's degree, 1958, in History from the University of Georgia; military service: U.S. Marine Corps, 1953–56; public service: elected Mayor of Young Harris, GA, 1959; elected to the Georgia State Senate, 1960; Director, Georgia Board of Probation, 1965–66; Deputy Director, Georgia Dept. of Corrections, 1967–68; Executive Secretary to the Governor of Georgia, 1968–71; Executive Director of the Georgia Democratic Party, 1971–73; member, Georgia State Board of Pardons and Paroles, 1973–75; Lieutenant Governor of Georgia; 1975–91; Governor of Georgia, 1991–99; professional: teacher at the University of Georgia, Emory University, and Young Harris College, 1999–2000; married: Shirley Carver Miller; children: Murphy and Matthew; appointed to the U.S. Senate on July 24, 2000; elected to the U.S. Senate on November 7, 2000.

Office Listings

http://miller.senate.gov

257 Dirksen Senate Office Building, Washington, DC 20510 .... (202) 224–3643
Chief of Staff.—Alex Albert. FAX: 228–2090
Legislative Director.—Mary Ann Chaffee.
Office Manager.—Patty Parmer.
State Director.—Toni Brown.
1175 Peachtree Street NE., 100 Colony Square, Suite 300, Atlanta, GA 30361 .... (404) 347–2202

* * *

SAXBY CHAMBLISS, Republican, of Moultrie, GA; born in Warrenton, NC, November 10, 1943; graduated, C.E. Byrd High School, Shreveport, LA, 1962; B.A., University of Georgia, 1966; J.D., University of Tennessee College of Law, 1968; served on the state bar of Georgia's Disciplinary Review Panel, 1969; member: Moultrie-Colquitt County Economic Development Authority; Colquitt County Economic Development Corporation; married the former Julianne Frohbert, 1966; two children: Lia Chambliss Baker, and C. Saxby (Bo), Jr.; elected to the 104th Congress; reelected to each succeeding Congress; elected to the U.S. Senate on November 5, 2002.

Office Listings

saxby_chambliss@chambliss.senate.gov

416 Russell Senate Office Building, Washington, DC 20510 .... (202) 224–3521
Chief of Staff.—Krister Holladay. FAX: 224–0103
Office Manager.—Donna Davis.
Executive Assistant.—Teresa Ervin.
100 Galleria, Suite 1340, Atlanta, GA 30339 .... (770) 763–9090
State Director.—Greg Wright.
950 Plantation Centre, Macon, GA 31210 .... (478) 476–0788
Field Representative.—Bill Stembridge.
419–A South Main Street, Moultrie, GA 31768 .... (229) 985–2112
Field Representative.—Debbie Cannon.

REPRESENTATIVES

FIRST DISTRICT

JACK KINGSTON, Republican, of Savannah, GA; born on April, 24, 1955 in Bryan, TX; education: Michigan State University, 1973–74; University of Georgia, 1974–78; insurance salesman; vice president, Palmer and Cay/Carswell; Georgia State Legislature, 1984–92; member: Savannah Health Mission, Isle of Hope Community Association, Christ Church; married: Elizabeth Morris Kingston, 1979; children: Betsy, John, Ann, and Jim; committee: Appropriations; subcommittees: chairman, Legislative Appropriations; Agriculture, Rural Development, FDA and Related Agencies; Military Construction; vice chairman, Republican Conference for the 108th Congress; elected on November 3, 1992 to the 103rd Congress; reelected to each succeeding Congress.

Office Listings

http://www.house.gov/kingston

2242 Rayburn House Office Building, Washington, DC 20515 .... (202) 225–5831
Chief of Staff.—Bill Johnson. FAX: 226–2269
Legislative Director.—Laura Quattlebaum.
Legislative Assistant.—Emily Howard.
Communications Director.—Robyn Ridgley.
One Diamond Causeway, Suite 7, Savannah, GA 31405 .... (912) 352–0101
P.O. Box 40, Baxley, GA 31515 .... (912) 367–7403
Brunswick Federal Building, 805 Gloucester Street, Room 304, Brunswick, GA 31520 .... (912) 265–9010
P.O. Box 9348, Warner Robins, GA 31095 .... (478) 923–8987

Counties: Appling, Atkinson, Bacon, Ben Hill, Berrier, Brantley, Bryan (part), Camden, Charlton, Chatham (part), Clinch, Coffee, Colquitt (part), Cook, Echols, Glynn, Houston (part), Irwin, Jeff Davis, Lanier, Liberty, Long, Lowndes (part), McIntosh, Pierce, Pulaski (part), Ware, Wayne, Wilcox (part). Population (2000), 629,761.

ZIP Codes: 30426–27, 31001, 31005, 31008, 31015, 31028, 31030, 31036, 31047, 31069, 31071–72, 31079, 31088, 31091–93, 31098, 31301, 31304–05, 31309–10, 31313–16, 31319–20, 31323, 31327–28, 31331, 31333, 31406, 31409–11, 31416, 31419, 31422, 31501–03, 31510, 31512–13, 31515–16, 31518–25, 31527, 31532–35, 31537, 31539, 31542–43, 31545–48, 31550–58, 31560–69, 31598–99, 31602, 31604–05, 31620, 31622–24, 31627, 31630–32, 31634–37, 31639, 31641–42, 31645, 31647–50, 31699, 31722, 31733, 31749–50, 31760, 31768–69, 31773–74, 31778, 31783, 31788, 31790, 31794, 31798

* * *

SECOND DISTRICT

SANFORD D. BISHOP, Jr., Democrat, of Albany, GA; born on February 4, 1947, in Mobile, AL; education: attended Mobile County public schools; B.A., Morehouse College, 1968; J.D., Emory University, 1971; employment: attorney; admitted to the Georgia and Alabama bars; Georgia House of Representatives, 1977–91; Georgia Senate, 1991–93; former member: Executive Board, Boy Scouts of America; YMCA; Sigma Pi Phi Fraternity; Kappa Alpha Psi Fraternity; 32nd Degree Mason, Shriner; member: Mt. Zion Baptist Church, Albany, GA; committee: Appropriations; elected to the 103rd Congress; reelected to each succeeding Congress.

Office Listings

http://www.house.gov/bishop

2429 Rayburn House Office Building, Washington, DC 20515 .... (202) 225–3631
Chief of Staff.—Nadine Chatman. FAX: 225–2203
Legislative Director.—Roger Manno.
Legislative Assistants: Ben Bell, Femeia Adamson.
Communications Director.—Selby McCach.
Administrative Assistant / Scheduler.—Diana Rodriguez.
Albany Towers, 235 W. Roosevelt Avenue, Suite 114, Albany, GA 31701 .... (229) 439–8067
District Director.—Kenneth Cutts.
101 S. Main Street, Dawson, GA 31742 .... (229) 995–3991
Field Representative.—Elaine Gillespie.
401 North Patterson Street, Room 255, Federal Building, Valdosta, GA 31601 .... (229) 247–9705
Field Representative.—Michael Bryant.
18 Ninth Street, Suite 201, Columbus, GA 31901 .... (706) 320–9477
Field Representatives: Marvin Cohen, Elaine Gillespie.

Counties: Baker, Brooks, Calhoun, Chattahoochee, Clay, Colquitt (part), Crisp, Decatur, Dougherty, Early, Grady, Lee, Lowndes (part), Miller, Mitchell, Muscogee (part), Quitman, Randolph, Seminole, Stewart, Sumter, Terrell, Thomas, Tift, Turner, Webster, Worth. Population (2000), 629,735.

ZIP Codes: 30150, 30290, 31010, 31015, 31039, 31068–69, 31072, 31092, 31201, 31204, 31211, 31217, 31328, 31601–03, 31605–06, 31625–26, 31629, 31636–38, 31641, 31643, 31698, 31701–12, 31714, 31716, 31719–22, 31727, 31730, 31733, 31735, 31738–39, 31743–44, 31747, 31749, 31753, 31756–58, 31763–65, 31768, 31771–72, 31775–76, 31778–84, 31787–96, 31799, 31803, 31805, 31814–15, 31821, 31824–25, 31832, 31901–07, 31914, 31995, 31997–99, 39813, 39815, 39817–19, 39823–29, 39832, 39834, 39836–37, 39840–42, 39845–46, 39851–52, 39854, 39859, 39861–62, 39866–67, 39870, 39877, 39885–86, 39897

* * *

THIRD DISTRICT

JIM MARSHALL, Democrat, of Macon, GA; born on March 31, 1948; education: graduated from high school in Mobile, AL, in 1966; received a National Merit Scholarship to attend Princeton University, and graduated in 1972; military service: U.S. Army; infantry combat in

Vietnam; served as an Airborne-Ranger reconnaissance platoon sergeant; decorated for heroism; received Purple Heart and two Bronze Stars; professional: graduated from Boston University Law School, 1977; joined the Mercer University Law School faculty in 1979; public service: participates in numerous community service activities; elected Mayor of Macon, GA, in 1995; family: married to Camille; children: Mary and Robert; elected to the 108th Congress on November 5, 2002.

Office Listings

http://jimmarshall.house.gov

502 Cannon House Office Building, Washington, DC 20515 .... (202) 225–6531
Chief of Staff.—John Kirincich. FAX: 225–3013
Legislative Director.—Bradley Edgell.
Communications Director.—Doug Moore.
682 Cherry Street, Suite 300, Macon, GA 31201 .... (478) 464–0255

Counties: BALDWIN, BIBB (part), BLECKLEY, CANDLER, CRAWFORD, DODGE, DOOLY, EMANUEL, EVANS, HANCOCK, HOUSTON (part), JOHNSON, JONES (part), LAURENS, MACON, MARION, MONROE, MONTGOMERY, PEACH, PULASKI (part), SCHLEY, TATTNALL, TAYLOR, TELFAIR, TOOMBS, TREUTLEN, TWIGGS, WASHINGTON, WHEELER, WILCOX (part), WILKINSON. Population (2000), 629,748.

ZIP Codes: 30204, 30233, 30401, 30410–14, 30417, 30420–21, 30423, 30425, 30427–29, 30436, 30438–39, 30441, 30445, 30447–48, 30450–54, 30457, 30464, 30470–71, 30473–75, 30477, 30499, 30678, 30820, 31001–03, 31006–09, 31011–23, 31025, 31027–42, 31044–46, 31049–52, 31054–55, 31057–63, 31065–72, 31075–78, 31081–84, 31086–99, 31201–13, 31216–17, 31220, 31294–97, 31328, 31544, 31549, 31601–02, 31632, 31711, 31735, 31801, 31803, 31806, 31812, 31824

* * *

FOURTH DISTRICT

DENISE L. MAJETTE, Democrat, of Decatur, GA; born in Brooklyn, NY, on May 18, 1955; education: graduated, Yale University, with a degree in History, 1976; J.D., Duke University School of Law, 1979; professional: Attorney; Legal Aid Society; adjunct professor of law, Wake Forest University; law clerk, DeKalb County Superior Court Judge R. Keegan Federal; law assistant, Georgia Court of Appeals Judge Robert Benham; special assistant, Georgia Attorney General's office; partner, law firm of Jenkins, Nelson & Welch; Administrative Law Judge, Georgia State Board of Worker's Compensation; Judge, State Court of DeKalb County, 1993–2002; organizations: Georgia State Bar Association; American Bar Association; DeKalb Bar Association; Georgia Association of Black Women Attorneys; awards: Georgia State University Black Law Students' Association Judge's Community Recognition Award; religion; member, Antioch AME Church in Stone Mountain, GA; family: married to Rogers J. Mitchell, Jr.; two children; elected to the 108th Congress on November 5, 2002.

Office Listings

http://www.house.gov/majette

1517 Longworth House Office Building, Washington, DC 20515 .... (202) 225–1605
Chief of Staff.—Michael Williams. FAX: 226–0691
Legislative Director.—Michaeleen Crowell.
Communications Director.—Jeannie Layson.
2050 Lawrenceville Highway, Suite D–46, Decatur, GA 30033 .... (404) 633–0927
District Director.—Steven Haynes

Counties: DEKALB (part), GWINNETT (part). CITIES: Avondale Estates, Chamblee, Clarkston, Decatur, Doraville, Dunwoody, Lithonia, and Stone Mountain. Population (2000), 629,690.

ZIP Codes: 30002–03, 30012, 30021, 30030–38, 30058, 30071–72, 30074, 30079, 30083–88, 30091–92, 30094, 30306–07, 30316, 30319, 30322, 30324, 30329, 30338, 30340–41, 30345–47, 30350, 30356, 30359–60, 30362, 30366, 30376, 31107, 31119, 31141, 31145, 39901

* * *

FIFTH DISTRICT

JOHN LEWIS, Democrat, of Atlanta, GA; born in Pike County, AL on February 21, 1940; graduated Pike County Training School, Brundidge, AL, 1957; B.A., American Baptist Theological Seminary, Nashville, TN, 1961; B.A., Fisk University, Nashville, TN, 1963; civil rights leader; Atlanta City Council, 1982–86; member: Martin Luther King Center for Social Change,

African American Institute, Robert F. Kennedy Memorial; married the former Lillian Miles in 1968; one child, John Miles Lewis; committees: Budget; Ways and Means; subcommittees: Health; appointed senior chief deputy Democratic whip for the 108th Congress; elected to the 100th Congress on November 4, 1986; reelected to each succeeding Congress.

Office Listings

http://www.house.gov/johnlewis

343 Cannon House Office Building, Washington, DC 20515 .... (202) 225–3801
Chief of Staff.—Michael Collins. FAX: 225–0351
Suite 1920, 100 Peachtree Street NW, Atlanta, GA 30303 .... (404) 659–0116
Director of Constituent Services.—Love Williams.

Counties: CLAYTON (part), COBB (part), DEKALB (part), FULTON (part). Population (2000), 629,727.

ZIP Codes: 30067, 30075–76, 30080, 30082, 30126, 30213, 30272, 30296, 30301–21, 30324–34, 30336–37, 30339, 30342–44, 30346, 30348–50, 30354–55, 30357–58, 30361, 30364, 30368–71, 30374–75, 30377–79, 30384, 30392, 30394, 30904, 30909, 31032, 31106, 31126, 31131–32, 31156, 31192–93, 31328

* * *

SIXTH DISTRICT

JOHNNY ISAKSON, Republican, of Marietta, GA; born on December 28, 1944, in Fulton County, GA; married: Dianne Isakson; three children: John, Kevin, and Julie; religion: Methodist; education: University of Georgia; profession: real estate executive; president, Northside Realty; public service: Georgia State House of Representatives, 1976–1990; Georgia State Senate, 1992–1996; appointed Chairman of the Georgia Board of Education, 1996; awards: Republican National Committee ''Best Legislator in America,'' 1989; organizations: chairman of the board, Georgian Club; trustee, Kennesaw State University; board of directors, Metro Atlanta and Georgia Chambers of Commerce; past president, Cobb Chamber of Commerce; executive committee, National Association of Realtors; president, Realty Alliance; advisory board, Federal National Mortgage Association; committees: Education and the Workforce; Transportation and Infrastruture; elected to the 106th Congress on February 23, 1999, by special election; reelected to each succeeding Congress.

Office Listings

http://www.house.gov/isakson

132 Cannon House Office Building, Washington, DC 20515 .... (202) 225–4501
Chief of Staff.—Heath Garrett. FAX: 225–4656
Legislative Director.—Glee Smith.
Press Secretary.—Tricia Chastain.
Scheduler.—Tempe Landrum.
6000 Lake Forrest Drive, Suite 110, Atlanta, GA 30328 .... (404) 252–5239

Counties: CHEROKEE (part), COBB (part), FULTON (part). CITIES AND TOWNSHIPS: Dunwoody, Marietta, Roswell, Sandy Springs, and Smyrna (part). Population (2000), 629,725.

ZIP Codes: 30004–07, 30009–10, 30022–24, 30041, 30060, 30062, 30064–68, 30075–77, 30092, 30096–97, 30101–02, 30106, 30115, 30127, 30141, 30144, 30152, 30156, 30160, 30168, 30188–89, 30327–28, 30339, 30342, 30350, 31032, 31146, 31150, 31156, 31602, 31632

* * *

SEVENTH DISTRICT

JOHN LINDER, Republican, of Duluth, GA; born on September 9, 1942, in Deer River, MN; graduate, Deer River High School, 1957; B.S., 1963, and D.D.S., 1967, University of Minnesota; captain, U.S. Air Force, 1967–69; former dentist; president, Linder Financial Corporation; Georgia State Representative, 1975–80, 1983–90; member: Georgia GOP, Rotary Club, American Legion; married: Lynne Peterson Linder, 1963; children: Matt and Kristine; elected on November 3, 1992, to the 103rd Congress; reelected to each succeeding Congress.

Office Listings

http://www.house.gov/linder

1727 Longworth House Office Building, Washington, DC 20515 .... (202) 225–4272
Chief of Staff.—Rob Woodall. FAX: 225–4696
Legislative Director.—Don Green.
Scheduler.—Joy Burch.
Press Secretary.—Scott Haggard.
90 North Street, Suite 360, Canton, GA 30114 .... (770) 479–1888
2805 Peachtree Industrial Boulevard, Suite 213, Duluth, GA 30097 .... (770) 232–3005

Counties: BARTOW (part), CHEROKEE (part), FORSYTH (part), GWINNETT (part), PAULDING (part). Population (2000), 629,725.

ZIP Codes: 30004–05, 30012, 30017, 30019, 30024, 30039–47, 30049, 30052, 30071, 30078, 30087, 30092, 30095–97, 30101–03, 30107, 30114–15, 30120–21, 30123, 30127, 30132, 30134, 30137, 30141–43, 30145–46, 30153, 30157, 30168–69, 30178–80, 30183–84, 30188–89, 30515, 30518–19, 31139

* * *

EIGHTH DISTRICT

MAC COLLINS, Republican, of Hampton, GA; born in Jackson, October 15, 1944; education: graduated, Jackson High School, 1962; employment: owner, Collins Trucking Company, Inc.; Georgia State Senate, 1989–92; chairman, Butts County Commission, 1977–80; chairman, Butts County Republican Party, 1981–82; director, Georgia Forestry Association; 32nd degree Mason; member: American Legislative Exchange Council and National Conference of State Legislatures; married: the former Julie Watkins, 1964; children: Crystal, Mike, Andy, and April; committees: Ways and Means; Permanent Select Committee on Intelligence; deputy majority whip; elected on November 3, 1992 to the 103rd Congress; reelected to each succeeding Congress.

Office Listings

http://www.house.gov/maccollins

1131 Longworth House Office Building, Washington, DC 20515 .... (202) 225–5901
Chief of Staff.—Bo Bryant. FAX: 225–2515
Legislative Director.—Michael Joyce.
Executive Assistant.—Patricia Koch.
Press Secretary.—Dan Kidder.
1125 Meredith Park Drive, McDonough, GA 30253 .... (678) 583–6500
Eastern Regional District Director.—Fred Chitwood.
5820 Veterans Parkway, #305, Columbus, GA 31904 .... (706) 327–7228
Western Regional District Director.—Chuck Hunsaker.
20 Baker Road, Suite #9, Newnan, GA 30265 .... (770) 683–4622

Counties: BIBB COUNTY (part). CITIES AND TOWNSHIPS: Macon, Payne. BUTTS COUNTY (part). CITIES AND TOWNSHIPS: Flovilla, Jackson, Jenkinsburg. CARROLL COUNTY (part). CITIES AND TOWNSHIPS: Bowdon, Carrollton, Mount Zion, Roopville, Temple, Villa Rica, Whitesburg. COWETA COUNTY (part). CITIES AND TOWNSHIPS: Grantville, Haralson, Lone Oak (also Meriwether), Luthersville, Moreland, Newnan, Palmetto, Senoia, Sharpsburg, Turin. DOUGLAS COUNTY (part). CITIES AND TOWNSHIPS: Austell, Douglasville, Lithia Springs, Winston. FAYETTE COUNTY. CITIES AND TOWNSHIPS: Brooks, Fayetteville, Peachtree City, Tyrone, Woolsey. HARRIS COUNTY (part). CITIES AND TOWNSHIPS: Cataula, Ellerslie, Fortson, Hamilton, Midland, Pine Mountain, Pine Mountain Valley, Shiloh, Waverly Hall, West Point. HENRY COUNTY (part). CITIES AND TOWNSHIPS: Hampton, Locust Grove, McDonough, Stockbridge. JASPER COUNTY (part). CITIES AND TOWNSHIPS: Monticello, Shady Dale. JONES COUNTY (part). CITIES AND TOWNSHIPS: Gray, Haddcock. LAMAR COUNTY. CITIES AND TOWNSHIPS: Aldora, Barnesville, Milner. MUSCOGEE COUNTY (part). CITIES AND TOWNSHIPS: Bibb City, Columbus. NEWTON COUNTY (part). CITIES AND TOWNSHIPS: Covington, Mansfield, Newborn, Oxford, Porterdale. PIKE COUNTY. CITIES AND TOWNSHIPS: Concord, Meansville, Molena, Williamson, Zebulon. ROCKDALE COUNTY (part). CITIES AND TOWNSHIPS: Conyers. SPALDING COUNTY (part). CITIES AND TOWNSHIPS: Griffin, Orchard Hill, Sunny Side. TROUP COUNTY (part). CITIES AND TOWNSHIPS: Hogansville, LaGrange. UPSON COUNTY (part). CITIES AND TOWNSHIPS: Thomaston, and Yatesville. Population (2000), 629,700.

ZIP Codes: 30013–14, 30016, 30055–56, 30094, 30108, 30110, 30116–17, 30122, 30133–35, 30154, 30170, 30179–80, 30185, 30187, 30204–06, 30213–17, 30220, 30223–24, 30228–30, 30233–34, 30236, 30238, 30240–41, 30248, 30252–53, 30256–59, 30263–66, 30268–69, 30271, 30273, 30275–77, 30281, 30284–86, 30289–90, 30292, 30295, 30904, 31002, 31004, 31016, 31024, 31029, 31032, 31038, 31046, 31064, 31066, 31085, 31097, 31204, 31210–11, 31220–21, 31602, 31632, 31801, 31804, 31807–08, 31811, 31820, 31822–23, 31826, 31829–31, 31833, 31904, 31907–09, 31993

* * *

NINTH DISTRICT

CHARLIE NORWOOD, Republican, of Evans, GA; born in Valdosta, GA, July 27, 1941; graduated, Baylor Military High School, Chattanooga, TN, 1959; B.S., Georgia Southern University, Statesboro, 1964; D.D.S., Georgetown University Dental School, Washington, DC,

1967; served as captain, U.S. Army, 1967–69, including tour of duty in Vietnam with the 173rd Airborne Brigade; awarded the Combat Medic Badge and two Bronze Stars; dentistry practice, Augusta, GA, 1969; elected president of the Georgia Dental Association, 1983; member, Trinity-on-the-Hill United Methodist Church, Augusta, GA; started several small businesses over the years, including Northwood Tree Nursery in Evans, GA, and Park Avenue Fabrics in Augusta, GA; married: Gloria Norwood, 1962; children: Charles and Carlton; two grandchildren; committees: Education and the Workforce; Energy and Commerce; subcommittees: chairman, Workforce Protections; vice chairman, Health; Energy and Air Quality; Select Education; elected on November 8, 1994, to the 104th Congress; reelected to each succeeding Congress.

Office Listings

2452 Rayburn House Office Building, Washington, DC 20515 .... (202) 225–4101
Chief of Staff.—John Walker.
Legislative Director.—Lem Smith.
Deputy Chief of Staff.—Rodney Whitlock.
Legislative Assistant.—Jennie Derge.
Communications Director.—Duke Hipp.
1056 Claussen Road, Suite 226, Augusta, GA 30907 .... (706) 733–7066
District Director.—Michael Shaffer.
315 West Savannah Street, Toccoa, GA 30577 .... (706) 886–2776
District Director.—Dessie Martin.

Counties: BANKS, BARROW, COLUMBIA, ELBERT, FRANKLIN, GREENE, HABERSHAM, HART, JACKSON, LINCOLN, LUMPKIN, MADISON, MCDUFFIE, MORGAN, NEWTON (part), OCONEE, OGLETHORPE (part), PUTNAM, RABUN, RICHMOND (part), STEPHENS, TOWNS, UNION, WALTON (part), WHITE, WILKES. Population (2000), 629,762.

ZIP Codes: 30011, 30014, 30016, 30018, 30025, 30052, 30054–56, 30510–12, 30514, 30516–17, 30520–23, 30525, 30528–31, 30533, 30535, 30537–38, 30544–49, 30552–53, 30557–58, 30562–63, 30565, 30567–68, 30571–73, 30575–77, 30580–82, 30596–99, 30607, 30619–25, 30627–30, 30633–35, 30638–39, 30641–43, 30645–48, 30650, 30655–56, 30660, 30662–63, 30665–69, 30671, 30673, 30677–78, 30680, 30683, 30802, 30806, 30808–09, 30813–14, 30817–18, 30824, 30904–05, 30907, 30909, 30917, 31024, 31026, 31033, 31038, 31061, 31064, 31907

* * *

TENTH DISTRICT

NATHAN DEAL, Republican, of Clermont, GA; born in Millen, GA, on August 25, 1942; education: graduated, Washington County High School, Sandersville, 1960; B.A., Mercer University, Macon, GA, 1964; J.D., Mercer University, Walter F. George School of Law, Macon, GA, 1966; admitted to the Georgia bar, 1966; captain, U.S. Army, 1966–68; Georgia State Senate, 1981–92; president pro tempore, 1991–92; married: the former Emilie Sandra Dunagan, 1966; children: Jason, Mary Emily, Carrie, and Katie; elected on November 3, 1992, to the 103rd Congress; reelected to each succeeding Congress.

Office Listings

http://www.house.gov/deal

2437 Rayburn House Office Building, Washington, DC 20515 .... (202) 225–5211
Chief of Staff.—Chris Riley.
Press Secretaries: Chris Riley, Todd Smith.
108 W. Lafayette Square, Suite 102, Lafayette, GA 30728 .... (706) 638–7042
P.O. Box 1015, Gainesville, GA 30503 .... (770) 535–2592
Suite 108, 415 East Walnut Avenue, Dalton, GA 30721 .... (706) 226–5320

Counties: CATOOSA, DADE, DAWSON, FANNIN, FORSYTH (part), GILMER, GORDON, GWINNETT (part), HALL, MURRAY, PICKENS, ROCKDALE (part), WALKER, WALTON (part), and WHITFIELD. CITIES AND TOWNSHIPS: Auburn, Blue Ridge, Braselton, Buford, Calhoun, Chatsworth, Chickamauga, Clermont, Cohutta, Conyers, Cumming, Dacula, Dalton, Dawsonville, East Ellijay, Ellijay, Eton, Fairmount, Flowery Branch, Fort Oglethorpe, Gainesville, Gillsville, Grayson, Jasper, LaFayette, Lawrenceville, Loganville, Lookout Mountain, Lula, McCaysville, Morgantown, Nelson, Oakwood, Plainville, Ranger, Rest Haven, Resaca, Ringgold, Rossville, Snellville, Talking Rock, Trenton, Tunnel Hill, and Varnell. Population (2000), 629,702.

ZIP Codes: 30011–13, 30017, 30019, 30028, 30039–41, 30045, 30052, 30078, 30103, 30107, 30139, 30143, 30148, 30151, 30171, 30175, 30177, 30501–04, 30506–07, 30510, 30512–13, 30517–19, 30522, 30527, 30534, 30539–43, 30548, 30554–55, 30559–60, 30564, 30566, 30572, 30575, 30701, 30703, 30705, 30707–08, 30710–11, 30719–22, 30724–26, 30728, 30731–36, 30738–42, 30746–47, 30750–53, 30755–57, 30811, 31002

ELEVENTH DISTRICT

PHIL GINGREY, Republican, of Marietta, GA; born on July 10, 1942, in Augusta, GA; education: B.S., Georgia Tech, 1965; M.D., Medical College of Georgia, 1969; profession: Physician; set up a pro-life OB-GYN practice; organizations: Cobb County Medical Society; Medical Association of Georgia; American Medical Association; Georgia OB-GYN Society; public service: Marietta School Board, 1993–1997; Georgia State Senate, 1999–2002; family: married to Billie Ayers; children: Billy, Gannon, Phyllis, and Laura; elected to the 108th Congress on November 5, 2002.

Office Listings

http://www.house.gov/gingrey

1118 Longworth House Office Building, Washington, DC 20515 .... (202) 225–2931
Chief of Staff.—Mitch Hunter. FAX: 225–2944
Legislative Director.—Rob Herriott.
Executive Assistant / Office Manager.—Catherine Gabrysh.
219 Roswell Street, Marietta, GA 30060 .... (770) 429–1776
600 East 1st Street, Rome, GA 30161 .... (706) 290–1776

Counties: BARTOW (part), CARROLL (part), CHATTOOGA, COBB (part), COWETA (part), DOUGLAS (part), FLOYD, HARALSON, HARRIS (part), HEARD, MERIWETHER, MUSCOGEE (part), PAULDING (part), POLK, TALBOT, TROUP (part), UPSON (part). Population (2000) 629,730.

ZIP Codes: 30008, 30060–64, 30066–67, 30069, 30080–82, 30090, 30103–06, 30108–13, 30116–22, 30124–27, 30129, 30134–35, 30137–40, 30145, 30147, 30149–50, 30153, 30161–65, 30168, 30170–73, 30176, 30178–80, 30182–84, 30217–20, 30222, 30230, 30240–41, 30251, 30259, 30261, 30263, 30276, 30286, 30293, 30548, 30701, 30730–31, 30733, 30747, 30753, 31016, 31058, 31072, 31079, 31097, 31801, 31810, 31812, 31816, 31822, 31826–27, 31830–31, 31833, 31836, 31904, 31906–07, 31917

* * *

TWELFTH DISTRICT

MAX BURNS, Republican, of Sylvania, GA; born on November 8, 1948, in Millen, GA; education: Bachelor of Industrial Engineering, Georgia Tech, 1973; Masters in Business Information Systems, Georgia State University, 1977; Ph.D. in Business Administration, Georgia State University, 1987; Senior Fulbright Scholar; military service: U.S. Army Reserves, First Lieutenant; occupations: Professor of Information Systems, Georgia Southern University; beef and timber farmer; public service: Screven County Commission, 1993–1998; religion: Baptist; family: married to Lora; children: Andrew and Nathan; elected to the 108th Congress on November 5, 2002.

Office Listings

http://burns.house.gov

512 Cannon House Office Building, Washington, DC 20515 .... (202) 225–2823
Chief of Staff.—Chris Ingram. FAX: 225–3377
Legislative Director.—Christy Seyfert.
Scheduler / Deputy Press Secretary.—Jaillene Erickson.
2743 Perimeter Parkway, Suite 200, Building 130, Augusta, GA 30909 .... (706) 854–4595
District Director.—Nancy Bobbitt.
115 North Main Street, Statesboro, GA 30458 .... (912) 764–4589
6605 Abercorn Street, Suite 102, Savannah, GA 31405 .... (912) 352–1736

Counties: BRYAN (part), BULLOCH, BURKE, CHATHAM (part), CLARKE, EFFINGHAM, GLASCOCK, JEFFERSON, JENKINS, OGLETHORPE (part), RICHMOND (part), SCREVEN, TALIAFERRO, WARREN. CITIES AND TOWNSHIPS: Augusta, Athens, Savannah, and Statesboro. Population (2000) 629,735.

ZIP Codes: 30413, 30415, 30417, 30424–26, 30434, 30439, 30441–42, 30446, 30449–50, 30452, 30455–56, 30458–61, 30467, 30471, 30477, 30601–09, 30612, 30619, 30631, 30660, 30664, 30667, 30669, 30678, 30683, 30803, 30805, 30807–08, 30810, 30812–13, 30815–16, 30818–24, 30828, 30830, 30833, 30901, 30903–04, 30906–07, 30909, 30911–14, 30916, 30919, 30999, 31045, 31206, 31302–03, 31307–08, 31312, 31314, 31318, 31321–22, 31324, 31326, 31329, 31401–08, 31412, 31414–15, 31418–22

* * *

THIRTEENTH DISTRICT

DAVID SCOTT, Democrat, of Atlanta, GA; born on June 27, 1945, in Aynor, SC; education: Florida A&M University, graduated with honors, 1967; University of Pennsylvania Wharton School of Finance, MBA degree, graduated with honors, 1969; profession: businessman; owner and CEO, Dayn-Mark Advertising; public service: Georgia House of Representatives, 1974–1982; Georgia State Senate, 1982–2002; family: married to Alfredia Aaron, 1969; children: Dayna and Marcye; elected to the 108th Congress on November 5, 2002.

Office Listings

http://davidscott.house.gov

417 Cannon House Office Building, Washington, DC 20515 .... (202) 225–2939
Chief of Staff.—Rob Griner. FAX: 225–4628
Executive Assistant / Office Manager.—Angie Borja.
Legislative Director.—Donni Turner.

173 North Main Street, Jonesboro, GA 30236 .... (770) 210–5073
District Director.—Shelia Edwards.

Counties: BUTTS (part), CLAYTON (part), DEKALB (part), FAYETTE (part), FULTON (part), GWINNETT (part), HENRY (part), NEWTON (part), ROCKDALE (part), SPAULDING (part), WALTON (part). Population (2000) 629,732.

ZIP Codes: 30012–16, 30025–26, 30029, 30034, 30038–39, 30044–45, 30047–48, 30054, 30058, 30070–71, 30084, 30087, 30093–94, 30096–99, 30212–16, 30223–24, 30228, 30233–34, 30236–38, 30248, 30250, 30252–53, 30260, 30268, 30273–74, 30281, 30287–88, 30291, 30294, 30296–98, 30315–16, 30331, 30337, 30340, 30349, 30353–54, 30368, 30380, 30385–90, 30396, 30398–99, 30655–56

HAWAII

(Population 2000, 1,211,537)

SENATORS

DANIEL K. INOUYE, Democrat, of Honolulu, HI; born in Honolulu, September 7, 1924; A.B., government and economics, University of Hawaii, 1950; J.D., George Washington University Law School, 1952; majority leader, Territorial House of Representatives, 1954–58; Territorial Senate, 1958–59; enlisted as private, 442nd Infantry Regimental Combat Team, 1943; battlefield commission, second lieutenant, 1944; served in France and Italy; retired captain, U.S. Army; Methodist; married the former Margaret Shinobu Awamura of Honolulu; one son, Daniel Ken Inouye, Jr.; committees: Appropriations; Commerce, Science and Transportation; vice chairman, Indian Affairs; Joint Committee on Printing; Rules and Administration; elected on July 28, 1959, to the 86th Congress; reelected to the 87th Congress; elected to the U.S. Senate on November 6, 1962; reelected to each succeeding Senate term.

Office Listings

http://inouye.senate.gov

722 Hart Senate Office Building, Washington, DC 20510 .... (202) 224–3934
Administrative Assistant.—Patrick H. DeLeon. TDD: 224–1233
Office Manager.—Beverly MacDonald.
Personal Secretary.—Sally Watanabe.
Legislative Director.—Margaret Cummisky.
Suite 7–212, 300 Ala Moana Boulevard, Honolulu, HI 96850 .... (808) 541–2542
Hilo Auxiliary Office, 101 Aupuni Street, No. 205, Hilo, HI 96720 .... (808) 935–0844

* * *

DANIEL K. AKAKA, Democrat, of Honolulu, HI; born in Honolulu, September 11, 1924; graduated, Kamehameha High School, 1942; University of Hawaii, 1948–66, bachelor of education, professional certificate, master of education; served in the U.S. Army, 1945–47; teacher, 1953–60; vice principal, 1960; principal, 1963–71; program specialist, 1968–71; director, 1971–74; director and special assistant in human resources, 1975–76; member, Kawaiahao Church; board of directors, Hanahauoli School; Act 4 Educational Advisory Commission; Library Advisory Council; Na Hookama O Pauahi Scholarship Committee, Kamehameha Schools; commissioner, Manpower and Full Employment Commission; Minister of Music, Kawaiahao Church; married to the former Mary Mildred Chong; five children: Millannie, Daniel, Jr., Gerard, Alan, and Nicholas; elected to the 95th Congress in November, 1976; reelected to each succeeding Congress; appointed to the U.S. Senate in April, 1990, to fill the vacancy caused by the death of Senator Spark Matsunaga; elected to complete the unexpired term in November, 1990; reelected to each succeeding Senate term.

Office Listings

http://akaka.senate.gov

141 Hart Senate Office Building, Washington, DC 20510 .... (202) 224–6361
Administrative Assistant.—James Sakai. FAX: 224–2126
Legislative Director.—Melissa U. Hampe.
Office Manager/Personal Secretary.—Patricia L. Hill.
Prince Kuhio Federal Building, 300 Ala Moana Boulevard, Room 3–106, P.O. Box 50144, Honolulu, HI 96850 .... (808) 522–8970
State Director.—Michael T. Kitamura.
101 Aupuni Street, Suite 213, Hilo, HI 96720 .... (808) 935–1114

REPRESENTATIVES

FIRST DISTRICT

NEIL ABERCROMBIE, Democrat, of Honolulu, HI; born in Buffalo, NY, June 26, 1938; graduated from Williamsville High School, Williamsville, NY; B.A., Union College, 1959; Ph.D., University of Hawaii, 1974; candidate for election to the U.S. Senate, 1970; Hawaii House of Representatives, 1974–78; Hawaii State Senate, 1978–86; elected to the U.S. House of Representatives on September 20, 1986, to fill the vacancy caused by the resignation of Cecil Heftel; Honolulu City Council, 1988–90; married: to Nancie Caraway; elected to the 102nd Congress, November 6, 1990; reelected to each succeeding Congress.

Office Listings

http://www.house.gov/abercrombie

1502 Longworth House Office Building, Washington, DC 20515 .... (202) 225–2726
Chief of Staff.—Cathy Mangino.
Legislative Director.—Tom Wanley.
Communications Director.—Mike Slackman.
Room 4–104, 300 Ala Moana Boulevard, Honolulu, HI 96850 .... (808) 541–2570
Deputy Chief of Staff.—Amy Asselbaye.

Counties: HONOLULU COUNTY (part). CITIES AND TOWNSHIPS: Aiea Pearl City, Ewa Beach, Honolulu, Mililani, and Waipahu (part). Population (2000), 606,718.

ZIP Codes: 96701, 96706, 96782, 96789, 96797, 96801–28, 96830, 96835–44, 96846–50, 96853, 96858–61

* * *

SECOND DISTRICT

ED CASE, Democrat, of Honolulu, HI; born on September 27, 1952, in Hilo, HI; education: Hawai'i Preparatory Academy, 1970; B.A., Williams College, 1975; J.D., University of California/Hastings College of Law, 1981; profession: attorney; employment: Law Clerk, Hawai'i Supreme Court Chief Justice William Richardson, 1981–1982; Carlsmith Ball (law firm), 1983–2002; partner, 1989–2002; managing partner 1992–1994; public service: Legislative Assistant, U.S. Representative/Senator Spark Matsunaga, 1975–1978; Manoa Neighborhood Board, 1985–1989; Hawai'i State House of Representatives, 1994–2002; Majority Leader, 1999–2000; Candidate, Governor of Hawai'i, 2002; family: married to the former Audrey Nakamura; children: David, Megan, James, and David; elected to the 107th Congress, by special election, on November 30, 2002; reelected to the 108th Congress, by special election, on January 4, 2003.

Office Listings

http://www.house.gov/case ed.case@mail.house.gov

128 Cannon House Office Building, Washington, DC 20515 .... (202) 225–4906
Chief of Staff.—Esther Kia'aina. FAX: 225–4987
Deputy Chief of Staff.—Pamela Hayashi Okimoto.
Legislative Director.—Anne Stewart.
Room 5104, Prince Kuhio Federal Building, PO Box 50124, Honolulu, HI 96850 .. (808) 541–1986
State Director.—Jimmy Nakatani.

Counties: HAWAI'I COUNTY. CITIES: Hawi, Hilo, Honoka'a, Kailua-Kona, Na'alehu, Kealakekua, Pahoa, Ocean View, Volcano, Waimea, Waikoloa. MAUI COUNTY. CITIES: Hana, Kahului, Kaunakakai, Lahaina, Lana'i City, Makawao, Wailuku. KALAWAO COUNTY. CITY: Kalaupapa. HONOLULU COUNTY (part). CITIES: Hale'iwa, Honolulu (part), Kailua, Kane'ohe, Kapolei, La'ie, Makakilo, Nanakuli, Wahiawa, Waialua, Wai'anae, Waimanalo. KAUA'I COUNTY. CITIES: Hanalei, Hanapepe, Kalaheo, Kapa'a, Kekaha, Kilauea, Koloa, Lihue, Waimea. NORTHWESTERN HAWAIIAN ISLANDS. ISLANDS OF: Becker, French Frigate Shoals, Gardener Pinnacles, Hermes and Kure Atolls, Laysan, Lisianski, Maro Reef, Nihoa, and Pearl. Population (2000), 604,819.

ZIP Codes: 96703–05, 96707–10, 96712–22, 96725–34, 96737–57, 96759–74, 96776–81, 96783–86, 96788–93, 96795–97, 96854, 96857, 96862–63

IDAHO

(Population 2000, 1,293,953)

SENATORS

LARRY E. CRAIG, Republican, of Payette, ID; born July 20, 1945, in Council, ID; attended Midvale public schools; graduated, University of Idaho; student body president, University of Idaho, 1968–69; USANG 1970–72; graduate work in economics and the politics of developing nations, George Washington University, 1970; Idaho State president and national vice president, Future Farmers of America, 1966–67; Idaho State Senate (three terms); chairman, Senate Commerce and Labor Committee; member: National Foundation for Defense Analysis; Idaho State Republican Executive Committee, 1976–78; president, Young Republican League of Idaho, 1976–77; chairman, Republican Central Committee, Washington County, 1971–72; board of directors, National Rifle Association; policy chairman, Republican Study Committee, 1990; farmer-rancher, Midvale area, for 10 years; married to the former Suzanne Thompson; three children: Mike, Shae, and Jay; Senate co-chairman, Congressional Coalition on Adoption; co-founder and co-chair, Senate Private Property Rights Caucus; co-chairman, Congressional Leaders United for a Balanced Budget (CLUBB); committees: Appropriations; Energy and Natural Resources; Veterans' Affairs; Judiciary; chairman, Special Committee on Aging; elected to the 97th Congress on November 4, 1980; reelected to each succeeding Congress; elected to the U.S. Senate on November 6, 1990; reelected to each succeeding Senate term.

Office Listings

http://craig.senate.gov

520 Hart Senate Office Building, Washington, DC 20510 .... (202) 224–2752
Chief of Staff.—Michael O. Ware. FAX: 228–1067
Executive Assistant/Scheduler.—Jodi Lindley.
Legislative Director/Counsel.—Brooke M. Roberts.
Press Secretary.—Will Hart.
304 North Eighth Street, Room 149, Boise, ID 83702 .... (208) 342–7985
610 Hubbard, Suite 121, Coeur d'Alene, ID 83814 .... (208) 667–6130
846 Main Street, Lewiston, ID 83501 .... (208) 743–0792
801 E. Sherman Street, Room 193, Pocatello, ID 83201 .... (208) 236–6817
560 Filer Avenue, Suite A, Twin Falls, ID 83301 .... (208) 734–6780
490 Memorial Drive, Suite 101, Idaho Falls, ID 83402 .... (208) 523–5541

* * *

MICHAEL D. CRAPO, Republican, of Idaho Falls, ID; born in Idaho Falls on May 20, 1951; graduated, Idaho Falls High School, 1969; B.A., Brigham Young University, Provo, UT, 1973; J.D., Harvard University Law School, Cambridge, MA, 1977; attorney; admitted to the California bar, 1977; admitted to the Idaho bar, 1979; law clerk, Hon. James M. Carter, Judge of the U.S. Court of Appeals for the Ninth Circuit, San Diego, CA, 1977–78; associate attorney, Gibson, Dunn, and Crutcher, San Diego, 1978–79; attorney, Holden, Kidwell, Hahn and Crapo, 1979–92; partner, 1983–92; Idaho State Senate, 1984–92, assistant majority leader, 1987–89, president pro tempore, 1989–92; member: American Bar Association, Boy Scouts of America, Idaho Falls Rotary Club, 1984–88; married: the former Susan Diane Hasleton, 1974; children: Michelle, Brian, Stephanie, Lara, and Paul; committees: Agriculture, Nutrition, and Forestry; Banking, Housing, and Urban Affairs; Budget; Environment and Public Works; Small Business and Entrepreneurship; subcommittees: chairman, Fisheries, Wildlife, and Water; Forestry, Conservation, and Rural Revitalization; Western Water Caucus; co-chairman, Nuclear Cleanup Caucus; Deputy Republican Whip; elected on November 3, 1992, to the 103rd Congress; reelected to each succeeding Congress; elected to the U.S. Senate on November 3, 1998.

Office Listings

http://crapo.senate.gov

239 Dirksen Senate Office Building, Washington, DC 20510 .... (202) 224–6142
Chief of Staff (Boise).—John Hoehne.
Administrative Assistant.—Peter Fischer.
Communications Director.—Susan Wheeler.
Legislative Director.—Ken Flanz.
304 North Eighth Street, Room 338, Boise, ID 83702 .... (208) 334–1776
1000 Northwest Boulevard, Suite 300, Coeur d'Alene, ID .... (208) 664–5490
111 Main Street, Suite 140, Lewiston, ID 83501 .... (208) 743–1492
801 E. Sherman, Suite 178, Pocatello, ID 83201 .... (208) 236–6775

524 E. Cleveland, Suite 220, Caldwell, ID 73605 .... (208) 455–0360
490 Memorial Drive, Suite 102, Idaho Falls, ID 83404 .... (208) 522–9779
202 Falls Avenue, Suite 2, Twin Falls, ID 83301 .... (208) 734–2515

REPRESENTATIVES

FIRST DISTRICT

C.L. (BUTCH) OTTER, Republican, of Star, ID; born on May 3, 1942, in Caldwell, ID; education: College of Idaho, B.A., Political Science; Mindanao State University in the Philippines, Honorary Doctorate; employment: businessman; J.R. Simplot Co.; Kyn Ten Oil Drilling Co.; organizations: Idaho International Trade Council; Elks Club; Ducks Unlimited; National Rifle Association; Idaho Agricultural Leadership Council; public service: Idaho Army National Guard, 1968–73; Idaho House of Representatives, 1972–76; Lt. Governor of Idaho, 1987–2000; elected to the 107th Congress; reelected to each succeeding Congress.

Office Listings

http://www.house.gov/otter

1711 Longworth House Office Building, Washington, DC 20515 .... (202) 225–6611
Chief of Staff.—Jeff Malmen. FAX: 225–3029
Communications Director.—Mark Warbis.
Legislative Director.—Jani Revier.
802 W. Bannock Street, Suite 101, Boise, ID 83702 .... (208) 336–9831
District Director.—Tana Cory.
610 W. Hubbard, Suite 206, Coeur d'Alene, ID 83814 .... (208) 667–0127
111 Main Street, Suite 170, Lewiston, ID 83501 .... (208) 298–0030

Counties: ADA (part), ADAMS, BENEWAH, BOISE, BONNER, BOUNDARY, CANYON, CLEARWATER, GEM, IDAHO, KOOTENAI, LATAH, LEWIS, NEZ PERCE, OWYHEE, PAYETTE, SHOSHONE, VALLEY, WASHINGTON. Population (2000), 648,774.

ZIP Codes: 83501, 83520, 83522–26, 83530–31, 83533, 83535–37, 83539–49, 83552–55, 83602, 83604–07, 83610–12, 83615–17, 83619, 83622, 83624, 83626–32, 83634–39, 83641–45, 83647, 83650–57, 83660–61, 83666, 83669–72, 83676–77, 83680, 83686–87, 83702, 83704–06, 83708–09, 83711, 83713–14, 83716, 83719, 83799, 83801–06, 83808–16, 83821–27, 83830, 83832–37, 83839–58, 83860–61, 83864–74, 83876–77

* * *

SECOND DISTRICT

MICHAEL K. SIMPSON, Republican, of Blackfoot, ID; born in Burley, ID, on September 8, 1950; education: graduated, Blackfoot High School, 1968; Utah State University, 1972; Washington University School of Dental Medicine, 1977; employment: dentist, private practice; Blackfoot, ID, City Council, 1981–85; Idaho State Legislature, 1985–98; Idaho Speaker of the House 1992–98; married: Kathy Simpson; committees: Appropriations; elected to the 106th Congress; reelected to each succeeding Congress.

Office Listings

http://www.house.gov/simpson mike.simpson@mail.house.gov

1339 Longworth House Office Building, Washington, DC 20515 .... (202) 225–5531
Chief of Staff.—Lindsay Slater. FAX: 225–8216
Scheduler.—Vicki Kinney.
Legislative Director.—John Revier.
Press Secretary.—Lucinda Willits.
802 West Bannock, Suite 600, Boise, ID 83702 .... (208) 334–1953
628 Blue Lakes Boulevard North, Twin Falls, ID 83301 .... (208) 734–7219
490 Memorial Drive, Suite 103, Idaho Falls, ID 83402 .... (208) 523–6701
801 E. Sherman, Suite 194, Pocatello, ID 83201 .... (208) 478–4160

Counties: ADA (part), BANNOCK, BEAR LAKE, BINGHAM, BLAINE, BONNEVILLE, BUTTE, CAMAS, CARIBOU, CASSIA, CLARK, CUSTER, ELMORE, FRANKLIN, FREMONT, GOODING, JEFFERSON, JEROME, LEMHI, LINCOLN, MADISON, MINIDOKA, ONEIDA, POWER, TETON, TWIN FALLS. Population (2000), 645,179.

ZIP Codes: 83201–06, 83209–15, 83217–18, 83220–21, 83223, 83226–30, 83232–39, 83241, 83243–46, 83250–56, 83261–63, 83271–72, 83274, 83276–78, 83281, 83283, 83285–87, 83301–03, 83311–14, 83316, 83318, 83320–25, 83327–28, 83330, 83332–38, 83340–44, 83346–50, 83352–55, 83401–06, 83415, 83420–25, 83427–29, 83431, 83433–36, 83438, 83440–46, 83448–52, 83454–55, 83460, 83462–69, 83601–02, 83604, 83623–24, 83627, 83633–34, 83647–48, 83701–09, 83712, 83714–17, 83720–33, 83735, 83744, 83756

ILLINOIS

(Population, 2000 12,419,293)

SENATORS

RICHARD J. DURBIN, Democrat, of Springfield, IL; born in East St. Louis, IL, on November 21, 1944; son of William and Ann Durbin; graduated, Assumption High School, East St. Louis; B.S., foreign service and economics, Georgetown University, Washington, DC, 1966; J.D., Georgetown University Law Center, 1969; attorney, admitted to the Illinois bar in 1969 and began practice in Springfield; legal counsel to Lieutenant Governor Paul Simon, 1969–72; legal counsel to Illinois Senate Judiciary Committee, 1972–82; parliamentarian, Illinois Senate, 1969–82; president, New Members Democratic Caucus, 98th Congress; associate professor of medical humanities, Southern Illinois University School of Medicine, Springfield; married the former Loretta Schaefer, 1967; three children: Christine, Paul, and Jennifer; committees: Governmental Affairs; Judiciary; Appropriations; Rules and Administration; Intelligence; Assistant Democratic Floor Leader; elected to the 98th Congress, November 2, 1982; reelected to each succeeding Congress; elected to the U.S. Senate on November 5, 1996; reelected to each succeeding Senate term.

Office Listings

http://durbin.senate.gov

332 Dirksen Senate Office Building, Washington, DC 20510 .... (202) 224–2152
Chief of Staff.—Ed Greelegs. FAX: 228–0400
Legislative Director.—Tom Faletti. TTY: 224–8180
Executive Assistant.—Kathy Anderson.
Press Secretary.—Joe Shoemaker.
230 South Dearborn, Kluczynski Building 38th Floor, Chicago, IL 60604 .... (312) 353–4952
Chief of Staff.—Mike Daly.
525 South Eighth Street, Springfield, IL 62703 .... (217) 492–4062
Director.—Bill Houlihan.
701 N. Court Street, Marion, IL 62959 .... (618) 998–8812

* * *

PETER G. FITZGERALD, Republican, of Inverness, IL; born in Elgin, IL, on October 20, 1960; graduated from Portsmouth Abbey, 1978; B.A., Dartmouth College, 1982; J.D., University of Michigan School of Law, 1986; corporate attorney; State Senator in Illinois General Assembly, 1992–98; married: Nina; one child: Jake; committees: Agriculture, Nutrition, and Forestry; Commerce, Science, and Transportation; Governmental Affairs; Special Committee on Aging; Small Business and Entrepreneurship; elected to the U.S. Senate on November 3, 1998.

Office Listings

http://fitzgerald.senate.gov

555 Dirksen Senate Office Building, Washington, DC 20510 .... (202) 224–2854
Chief of Staff.—Gregory J. Gross. FAX: 228–1372
Legislative Director.—Joseph Watson.
Press Secretary.—Brian Stoller.
Office Manager.—Sherri R. Hupart.
230 South Dearborn Street, #3900, Chicago, IL 60604 .... (312) 886–3506
State Director.—Margaret A. Hickey.
520 South Eighth Street, Springfield, IL 62703 .... (217) 492–5089
Central Illinois Director.—David E. Curtin.
Ginger Creek Village, #7B, Glen Carbon, IL 62034 .... (618) 692–0364
Southern Illinois Director.—Christine M. Sullivan.
115 West First Street, #100, Dixon, IL 61021 .... (815) 288–3140
Northern Illinois Director.—Jason T. Anderson.

REPRESENTATIVES

FIRST DISTRICT

BOBBY L. RUSH, Democrat, of Chicago, IL; born on November 23, 1946 in Georgia; served in U.S. Army, 1963–68; B.A., with honors, Roosevelt University, Chicago; M.A., University of Illinois, Chicago; Democratic Ward Committeeman, second ward, Chicago, 1984, 1988; Democratic State Central Committeeman, First Congressional District, 1990; deputy chairman, Illinois Democratic Party, 1990; Department of Commerce and Community Affairs Illinois Enterprise Zone Award; Operation PUSH Outstanding Young Man Award; Henry Booth House Outstanding Community Service Award; South End Jaycees Outstanding Business and Professional Achievement Award; Chicago Black United Communities Distinguished Political Leadership Award; cofounder, Illinois Black Panther Party; married to Carolyn Rush; five children; elected on November 3, 1992, to the 103rd Congress; reelected to each succeeding Congress.

Office Listings

http://www.house.gov/rush

2416 Rayburn House Office Building, Washington, DC 20515 .... (202) 225–4372
Legislative Director.—Yardly Pollas-Kimble. FAX: 226–0333
Executive Assistant/Scheduler.—Lenette Myers.
Press Secretary.—Robyn Wheeler.
700–706 East 79th Street, Chicago, IL 60619 .... (773) 224–6500
District Office Director.—Sheila Jackson.

Counties: COOK COUNTY (part). CITIES AND TOWNSHIPS: Alsip (part), Blue Island, Chicago (part), Evergreen Park, Merrionette Park, and Oak Lawn. Population (2000), 653,647.

ZIP Codes: 60406, 60426, 60445, 60450, 60452–53, 60456, 60462–64, 60467, 60469, 60472, 60477–78, 60482, 60544, 60609, 60615–17, 60619–21, 60628–29, 60632, 60636–37, 60643, 60649, 60652–53, 60655, 60803, 60805, 60827

* * *

SECOND DISTRICT

JESSE L. JACKSON, JR., Democrat, of Chicago, IL; born in Greenville, SC, March 11, 1965; education: B.S., business management, *magna cum laude,* North Carolina A&T State University, 1987; M.A., Chicago Theological Seminary, 1989; J.D., University of Illinois College of Law, 1993; member, Congressional Black Caucus, Congressional Progressive Caucus; elected Secretary of the Democratic National Committee's Black Caucus; national field director, National Rainbow Coalition, 1993–95; member, Rainbow/Push Action Network; married: the former Sandra Lee Stevens; committees: Appropriations; elected to the 104th Congress (special election); reelected to each succeeding Congress.

Office Listings

http://www.house.gov/jackson

2419 Rayburn House Office Building, Washington, DC 20515 .... (202) 225–0773
Chief of Staff.—Kenneth Edmonds. FAX: 225–0899
Legislative Director.—George Seymore.
Legislative Assistant.—Charles Dujon.
Executive Assistant/Scheduler.—DeBorah Posey.
17926 South Halsted, Homewood, IL 60430 .... (708) 798–6000
District Director.—Rick Bryant.
2120 East 71st Street, Chicago, IL 60649 .... (773) 241–6500

Counties: COOK (part), WILL (part). CITIES AND TOWNSHIPS: Blue Island, Burnham, Calumet City, Calumet Park, Chicago (part), Chicago Heights, Country Club Hills Crestwood, Dixmoor, Dolton, East Hazel Crest, Flossmoor, Ford Heights, Glenwood, Harvey, Hazel Crest, Homewood, Lansing, Lynwood, Markham, Matteson, Midlothian, Monee (part), Oak Forest, Olympia Fields, Park Forest, Phoenix, Posen, Richton Park, Riverdale, Robbins, Sauk Village, South Chicago Heights, South Holland, Steger (part), Tinley Park, Thornton, and University Park (part). Population (2000), 653,647.

ZIP Codes: 60406, 60409, 60411–12, 60417, 60419, 60422–23, 60425–26, 60429–30, 60438, 60443, 60445, 60449, 60452, 60461, 60466, 60471, 60473, 60475–78, 60615, 60617, 60620, 60628, 60633, 60636–37, 60643, 60649, 60827

* * *

THIRD DISTRICT

WILLIAM O. LIPINSKI, Democrat, of Chicago, IL; born in Chicago on December 22, 1937; education: graduated, St. Patrick High School, Chicago, 1956; attended Loras College, Dubuque, IA, 1956–57; employment: served in U.S. Army Reserves, 1961–67; alderman, Chicago City Council, 1975–83; chairman, City Council Education Committee; delegate, Democratic National Convention, 1976, 1984, 1988, 1992, and 1996; past president, Kiwanis Club; member: Polish National Alliance, Chicago Historical Society; 23rd Ward Democratic Committeeman, 1974–present; married: the former Rose Marie Lapinski, 1962; children: Laura and Dan; award: Man of the Year, Area 4, Chicago Park District, January 1983; committee: Transportation and

Infrastructure; subcommittees: Aviation; ranking member, Highways, Transit, and Pipelines; Railroads; elected on November 2, 1982, to the 98th Congress; reelected to each succeeding Congress.

Office Listings

2188 Rayburn House Office Building, Washington, DC 20515 .... (202) 225–5701
Chief of Staff.—Michael McLaughlin. FAX: 225–1012
Legislative Director / Senior Policy Advisor.—Jason Tai.
Executive Assistant.—Jennifer Murer.
Legislative Assistants: Ashley Musselman, Ryan Quinn, Ted Bush.
5832 South Archer Avenue, Chicago, IL 60638 .... (312) 886–0481
District Director.—Jerry Hurckes.
5239 W. 95th Street, Oak Lawn, IL 60453 .... (708) 952–0860
Staff Assistant.—Lenore Goodfriend.
19 W. Hillgrove, LaGrange, IL 60525 .... (708) 352–0524

Counties: COOK COUNTY (part). CITIES AND TOWNSHIPS: Alsip, Argo, Bedford Park, Berwyn, Bridgeview, Burr Ridge, Chicago, Chicago Ridge, Cicero, Countryside, Hickory Hills, Hinsdale, Hometown, Hodgkins, Indian Head Park, Justice Burbank, LaGrange, Lyons, McCook, North Riverside, Oak Lawn, Oak Park, Palos Hills, Palos Park, Proviso, Riverside, Stickney, Summit Brookfield, Western Springs, Willow Springs, and Worth. Population (2000), 653,647

ZIP Codes: 60126, 60130, 60154, 60162, 60402, 60415, 60426, 60430, 60453–59, 60463–65, 60477, 60480, 60482, 60499, 60501, 60513, 60521, 60525–27, 60534, 60546, 60558, 60570, 60608–09, 60616, 60620, 60623, 60629, 60632, 60636, 60638, 60643, 60652, 60655, 60803–05

* * *

FOURTH DISTRICT

LUIS V. GUTIERREZ, Democrat, of Chicago, IL; born on December 10, 1953, in Chicago; B.A., Northeastern Illinois University, 1974; Chicago Alderman; social worker, State of Illinois; teacher; married: 1977 to Soraida Arocho Gutierrez; children: Omaira and Jessica; elected on November 3, 1992, to the 103rd Congress; reelected to each succeeding Congress.

Office Listings

2367 Rayburn House Office Building, Washington, DC 20515 .... (202) 225–8203
Chief of Staff.—Jennice Fuentes. FAX: 225–7810
Deputy Chief of Staff.—Enrique Fernandez.
Professional Staff Member / Legislative Assistant.—Annie Toro.
Press Secretary.—Scott Frotman.
3455 West North Avenue, Chicago, IL 60647 .... (773) 384–1655
1310 West 18th Street, Chicago, IL 60608 .... (312) 666–3882

Counties: COOK COUNTY (part). CITIES: Berkeley (part), Brookfield (part), Chicago (part), Ciero (part), Elmwood Park (part), Forest Park (part), Hillside (part), Maywood (part), Melrose Park (part), Northlake (part), Oak Park (part), Stickney (part), Stone Park (part), and Westchester (part). Population (2000), 653,647.

ZIP Codes: 60130, 60141, 60153–55, 60160, 60162–65, 60304–05, 60402, 60443, 60446, 60473, 60513, 60526, 60542, 60546, 60608–09, 60612, 60614, 60616, 60618, 60622–23, 60625, 60629, 60632, 60639, 60641, 60644, 60647, 60651, 60707, 60804

* * *

FIFTH DISTRICT

RAHM EMANUEL, Democrat, of Chicago, IL; born on November 29, 1959, in Chicago, IL; education: B.A., Liberal Arts, Sarah Lawrence College, 1981; M.A., Speech and Communication, Northwestern University, 1985; professional: Illinois Public Action (consumer rights organization); managing director, Dresdner Kleinwort Wasserstein (global investment bank); Democratic Party activities: worked on Paul Simon's successful U.S. Senate campaign, 1984; national campaign director, Democratic Congressional Campaign Committee, 1988; senior advisor and chief fundraiser for Richard M. Daley's successful Mayoral campaign, 1989; public service: Assistant to the President under President Bill Clinton, 1993–2000; family: married to Amy; children: Zachariah, Ilana, and Leah; elected to the 108th Congress on November 8, 2002.

Office Listings

http://www.house.gov/emanuel

1319 Longworth House Office Building, Washington, DC 20515 .... (202) 225–4061
Chief of Staff.—Elizabeth Sears Smith. FAX: 225–5603
Communications Director.—Cecelia Prewett.
Executive Assistant / Scheduler.—Preeti Chaudhari.
Legislative Director.—Pete Spiro.
3742 West Irving Park Road, Chicago, IL 60618 .... (773) 267–5926

Counties: COOK COUNTY (part). Population (2000), 653,647.

ZIP Codes: 60018, 60106, 60131, 60153, 60160–61, 60164–65, 60171, 60176, 60504, 60525, 60613–14, 60618, 60625, 60630–31, 60634, 60639–41, 60646, 60656–57, 60659–60, 60677, 60706–07, 60712, 60714

* * *

SIXTH DISTRICT

HENRY J. HYDE, Republican, of Wood Dale, IL; born in Chicago, April 18, 1924; graduated St. George High School, Evanston, IL, 1942; B.S.S., Georgetown University, 1947; J.D., Loyola University School of Law, Chicago, 1949; ensign, U.S. Navy, 1944–46; commander, U.S. Naval Reserves (retired); admitted to the Illinois bar, January 9, 1950; State Representative in Illinois General Assembly, 1967–74; majority leader, Illinois House of Representatives, 1971–72; married the late Jeanne Simpson, 1947; four children: Henry Jr., Robert, Anthony, Laura; elected to the 94th Congress, November 5, 1974; reelected to each succeeding Congress.

Office Listings

http://www.house.gov/hyde

2110 Rayburn House Office Building, Washington, DC 20515 .... (202) 225–4561
Administrative Assistant.—Judy Wolverton.
Suite 200, 50 East Oak Street, Addison, IL 60101 .... (630) 832–5950
Executive Assistants: Patrick Durante, Alice Horstman.

Counties: COOK (part), DUPAGE (part). CITIES AND TOWNSHIPS: Addison, Arlington Heights (part), Bensenville, Bloomingdale, Carol Stream, Des Plaines (part), Elk Grove, Elk Grove Village, Elmhurst, Glen Ellyn, Glendale Heights, Hanover Park Streamwood (part), Itasca, Leyden Proviso, Lombard, Maine, Milton, Oak Brook (part), Oak Brook Terrace, Roselle, Villa Park, Wayne (part), Westchester, Westmont (part), Wheaton, Winfield, and York. Population (2000), 615,419.

ZIP Codes: 60005, 60007–09, 60016–18, 60056, 60067, 60101, 60103, 60105–08, 60116–17, 60120, 60125–26, 60128, 60131–33, 60137–39, 60143, 60148, 60157, 60172–73, 60176, 60181, 60185, 60187–95, 60197, 60199, 60399, 60515, 60523, 60532, 60559, 60563, 60666, 60688, 60701

* * *

SEVENTH DISTRICT

DANNY K. DAVIS, Democrat, of Chicago, IL; born in Parkdale, AR, on September 6, 1941; B.A., Arkansas A.M. & N. College, 1961; M.A., Chicago State University; Ph.D., Union Institute, Cincinnati, OH; educator and health planner-administrator; board of directors, National Housing Partnership; Cook County Board of Commissioners, 1990–96; former alderman of the Chicago City Council's 29th ward, receiving the Independent Voters of Illinois ''Best Alderman Award'' for 1980–81, 1981–82, and 1989–90; co-chair, Clinton-Gore-Braun '92; founder and past president, Westside Association for Community Action; past president, National Association of Community Health Centers; 1987 recipient of the Leon M. Despres Award; married to Vera G. Davis; two sons: Jonathan and Stacey; committees: Education and the Workforce; Government Reform; Small Business; elected to the 105th Congress; reelected to each succeeding Congress.

Office Listings

http://www.house.gov/dannydavis

1222 Longworth House Office Building, Washington, DC 20515 .... (202) 225–5006
Chief of Staff.—Richard Boykin. FAX: 225–5641
Legislative Director.—Caleb Gilchrist.
Director of Issues and Communications.—Ira Cohen.
3333 West Arthington Street, Suite 130, Chicago, IL 60624 .... (773) 533–7520
1030 South 17th Avenue, Maywood, IL 60153 .... (708) 345–6857

Counties: COOK COUNTY (part). CITIES AND TOWNSHIPS: Bellwood, Berkley (part), Broadview, Chicago (part), Forest Park (part), Hillside (part), Maywood (part), Oak Park, River Forest, and Westchester (part). Population (2000), 653,647.

ZIP Codes: 60104, 60130, 60141, 60153–55, 60160, 60162–63, 60301–05, 60546, 60601–12, 60614–16, 60621–24, 60636–37, 60639, 60644, 60651, 60653–54, 60661, 60663–65, 60667–75, 60678–81, 60683–88, 60690–91, 60693–97, 60707, 60804

* * *

EIGHTH DISTRICT

PHILIP M. CRANE, Republican, of Wauconda, IL; born in Chicago, November 3, 1930; educated at DePauw University, Hillsdale College, University of Michigan, and University of Vienna, and received M.A. and Ph.D. degrees from Indiana University; honorary doctor of laws, Grove City College, Grove City, PA, 1973; honorary doctor of political science, Francisco Marroquin University, Guatemala, 1979; U.S. Army, active duty, 1954–56; two years, advertising manager, Hopkins Syndicate, Inc.; taught at Indiana University for three years before moving to Bradley University, Peoria, IL, in 1963, where he taught United States and Latin American history until 1967; director of schools, Westminster Academy, Northbrook, IL, 1967–68; in 1962, employed by the Republican Party as a public relations expert; in 1964, served as director of research for the Illinois Goldwater Organization; at the request of Richard Nixon, served as one of his advisors and researchers on political and national issues, 1964–68; in 1976 served as chairman of Illinois Citizens for Reagan Committee; trustee of Hillsdale College; chairman, American Conservative Union, 1977–79; director of the Intercollegiate Studies Institute; serves with more than 60 U.S. Senators and Representatives on the National Advisory Board of Young Americans for Freedom; chairman of Republican Study Committee, 1983; appointed by President Reagan to the Commission on the Bicentennial of the United States Constitution; married Arlene Catherine Johnson of Chicago; eight children: Catherine Anne, Susanna Marie, Jennifer Elizabeth, Rebekah Caroline, George Washington V, Rachel Ellen, Sarah Emma, and Carrie Esther; committee: Ways and Means; subcommittees: chairman, Trade; Health; elected to the 91st Congress by special election, November 25, 1969, to fill the vacancy caused by the resignation of Donald Rumsfeld; reelected to each succeeding Congress.

Office Listings

http://www.house.gov/crane

233 Cannon House Office Building, Washington, DC 20515 .... (202) 225–3711
Chief of Staff.—James Hayes.
Deputy Chief of Staff.—Michele Taulton.
Legislative Director.—Shalla Ross.
Press Secretary.—Sara Perkins.
1100 W. Northwest Highway, Palatine, IL 60067 .... (847) 358–9160
District Representative.—Dennis O'Sullivan.
300 North Milwaukee Avenue, Suite C, Lake Villa, IL 60046 .... (847) 265–9000

Counties: COOK COUNTY. CITIES: Barrington (part), Hoffman Estates (part) Palatine (part), Schaumburg (part). LAKE COUNTY (part). CITIES: Antioch, Barrington (part), Beach Park (part), Fox Lake, Grayslake (part), Gurnee (part), Hawthorne Woods, Ingleside, Kildeer, Lake Villa, Lake Zurich, Lindenhurst, Long Grove (part), Mundelein, Park City (part), Round Lake, Volo, Wadsworth, Wauconda, Winthrop Harbor, Zion (part). MCHENRY COUNTY (part). CITIES: Bull Valley, Greenwood, Hebron, Holiday Hills, Island Lake (part), Johnsburg, Lakemoor, Lilymoor, McHenry (part), Prairie Grove (part), Richmond, Ringwood, Spring Grove, Wonder Lake, Woodstock (part). Population (2000), 653,647.

ZIP Codes: 60002, 60004–05, 60007–08, 60010–14, 60020 21, 60030–31, 60033–34, 60038, 60041–42, 60046–51, 60055, 60060, 60067, 60071–75, 60081, 60083–85, 60087, 60094–99, 60103, 60107, 60118, 60120, 60133, 60159, 60168, 60172–73, 60179, 60192–96

* * *

NINTH DISTRICT

JANICE D. SCHAKOWSKY, Democrat, of Evanston, IL; born in Chicago, IL, on May 26, 1944; B.A., University of Illinois, 1965; consumer advocate; program director, Illinois Public Action; executive director, Illinois State Council of Senior Citizens, 1985–90; State Representative, 18th District, Illinois General Assembly, 1991–99; served on Labor and Commerce, Human Service Appropriations, Health Care, and Electric Deregulation Committees; religion: Jewish; married: Robert Creamer; three children: Ian, Mary, and Lauren; committees: Energy and Commerce; elected to the 106th Congress; reelected to each succeeding Congress.

Office Listings

http://www.house.gov/schakowsky

515 Cannon House Office Building, Washington, DC 20515 .... (202) 225–2111
Chief of Staff.—Cathy Hurwit. FAX: 226–6890
Press Secretary.—Nadeam Elshami.
Appointments Secretary.—Kim Muzeroll.
5533 Broadway, Chicago, IL 60640 .... (773) 506–7100
District Director.—Leslie Combs.

Counties: COOK COUNTY (part). CITIES: Chicago (part), Evanston, Glenview, Golf, Lincolnwood, Morton Grove, Niles, and Skokie. Population (2000), 653,647.

ZIP Codes: 60016, 60018–19, 60025, 60029, 60053, 60056, 60068, 60076–77, 60091, 60176, 60201–04, 60208, 60611, 60613, 60626, 60630–31, 60640, 60645–46, 60656–57, 60659–60, 60706, 60712, 60714

* * *

TENTH DISTRICT

MARK STEVEN KIRK, Republican, of Highland Park, IL; born on September 15, 1959, in Champaign, IL; education: New Trier East High School, Winnetka, IL, 1977; B.A., Cornell University, 1981; J.D., Georgetown University, 1992; profession: Attorney; military service: Lt. Commander, U.S. Navy Reserve; employment: Administrative Assistant to Rep. John Porter (R–IL), 1984–90; World Bank, served as an International Finance Corp. officer; Dept. of State, served as Special Assistant to the Assistant Secretary for Inter-American Affairs; Baker & McKenzie (law firm); House Committee on International Relations, served as Counsel; married: Kimberly Vertolli; elected to the 107th Congress on November 7, 2000; reelected to each succeeding Congress.

Office Listings

http://www.house.gov/kirk

1531 Longworth House Office Building, Washington, DC 20515 .... (202) 225–4835
Chief of Staff.—Doug O'Brien.
Legislative Director.—Jeannette Windon.
102 Wilmot Road, Suite 200, Deerfield, IL 60015 .... (847) 940–0202
Press Secretary.—Matt Towson.

Counties: COOK (part), LAKE (part). Population (2000), 653,647.

ZIP Codes: 60004–06, 60008, 60010, 60015–16, 60022, 60025–26, 60030–31, 60035, 60037, 60040, 60043–45, 60047–48, 60056, 60060–62, 60064–65, 60067, 60069–70, 60074, 60078–79, 60082–83, 60085–93, 60173, 60195, 60201

* * *

ELEVENTH DISTRICT

JERRY WELLER, Republican, of Morris, IL; born in Streator, IL, July 7, 1957; graduated, Dwight High School, 1975; B.A., agriculture, University of Illinois, 1979; aide to Congressman Tom Corcoran, 1980–81; aide to John R. Block (U.S. Secretary of Agriculture), 1981–85; former State Representative, 1988–94; National Republican Legislative Association Legislator of the Year; listed in the 1990 *Almanac of Illinois Politics*; committees: International Relations; Ways and Means; subcommittees: Asia and the Pacific; Oversight; Western Hemisphere; Select Revenue Measures; assistant majority whip; House Republican Steering Committee; elected to the 104th Congress; reelected to each succeeding Congress.

Office Listings

http://www.house.gov/weller

1210 Longworth House Office Building, Washington, DC 20515 .... (202) 225–3635
Chief of Staff.—Jeanette Forcash. FAX: 225–3521
Executive Assistant.—Danielle Hernandez.
Legislative Director.—Alan Tennille.
Deputy Chief of Staff/Press Secretary.—Ben Fallon.
2701 Black Road, Suite 201, Joliet, IL 60435 .... (815) 740–2028
District Manager.—Reed Wilson.

Counties: BUREAU (part), GRUNDY, KANKAKEE, LA SALLE, LIVINGSTON (part), MCLEAN (part), WILL (part), and WOODFORD (part). Population (2000), 653,658.

ZIP Codes: 60401, 60407–11, 60416–17, 60420–21, 60423–24, 60430–37, 60442, 60444–45, 60447–51, 60466, 60468, 60470, 60474–75, 60477, 60479, 60481, 60504, 60518, 60531, 60541, 60544, 60548–49, 60551–52, 60557, 60625, 60640, 60646, 60660, 60901–02, 60910, 60912–15, 60917, 60919, 60922, 60935, 60940–41, 60944, 60950, 60954, 60961, 60964, 61238, 61240–41, 61254, 61262, 61273, 61301, 61312, 61314–17, 61320–23, 61325–26, 61328–30, 61332, 61334, 61337–38, 61341–42, 61344–45, 61348–50, 61354, 61356, 61358–62, 61364, 61368, 61370–74, 61376–77, 61379, 61701–02, 61704, 61725, 61732, 61736, 61744–45, 61748, 61752, 61754, 61760–61, 61772, 61774, 61790

* * *

TWELFTH DISTRICT

JERRY F. COSTELLO, Democrat, of Belleville, IL; born in East St. Louis, IL, on September 25, 1949; education: graduated, Assumption High, East St. Louis, 1968; A.A., Belleville Area College, IL, 1970; B.A., Maryville College of the Sacred Heart, St. Louis, MO, 1973; employment: law enforcement official, 1970–80; elected chairman of the county board, St. Clair County, 1980–88; member: East-West Gateway Coordinating Council, Metro Counties of Illinois, Southwestern Illinois Leadership Council, Southwestern Illinois Small Business Finance Alliance, Light Rail Transit Committee; chairman, St. Clair Heart Fund drive, and United Way drive, 1985; co-chairman of the St. Clair County March of Dimes, 1988; married: the former Georgia Jean Cockrum, 1968; children: Jerry II, Gina Keen, and John; committees: Transportation and Infrastructure; Science; elected by special election to the 100th Congress on August 9, 1988, to fill the vacancy caused by the death of Charles Melvin Price; reelected to each succeeding Congress.

Office Listings

http://www.house.gov/costello

2454 Rayburn House Office Building, Washington, DC 20515	(202) 225–5661
Administrative Assistant.—David Gillies.	FAX: 225–0285
1363 Niedringhaus Avenue, Granite City, IL 62040	(618) 451–7065
8787 State Street, Suite 210, East Saint Louis, IL 62203	(618) 397–8833
155 Lincoln Place Court, Belleville, IL 62221	(618) 233–8026
201 East Nolen Street, West Frankfort, IL 62896	(618) 937–6402
250 West Cherry Street, Carbondale, IL 62901	(618) 529–3791
1330 Swanwick Street, Chester, IL 62233	(618) 826–3043

Counties: ALEXANDER, FRANKLIN, JACKSON, MADISON (part), MONROE, PERRY, PULASKI, RANDOLPH, ST. CLAIR, UNION, WILLIAMSON (part). Population (2000), 653,647.

ZIP Codes: 62002, 62010, 62018, 62024–25, 62035, 62040, 62048, 62059–60, 62071, 62084, 62087, 62090, 62095, 62201–08, 62217, 62220–26, 62232–34, 62236–44, 62246, 62248, 62254–61, 62263–65, 62268–69, 62272, 62274, 62277–80, 62282, 62284–86, 62288–89, 62292–95, 62297–98, 62812, 62819, 62822, 62831–32, 62836, 62840, 62846, 62859–60, 62865, 62883–84, 62888, 62890, 62896–97, 62901–03, 62905–07, 62912, 62914–18, 62920, 62922–24, 62926–27, 62932–33, 62939–42, 62948–52, 62956–59, 62961–64, 62966, 62969–71, 62973–76, 62983, 62987–88, 62990, 62992–94, 62996–99

* * *

THIRTEENTH DISTRICT

JUDY BIGGERT, Republican, of Hinsdale, IL; born in Chicago, IL, on August 15, 1937; education: graduated from New Trier High School, 1955; B.A., Stanford University, 1959; J.D., Northwestern University School of Law; employment: attorney, 1975–present; Illinois House of Representatives (81st District), 1993–98; Assembly committees: Judiciary; Human Services; Appropriations; Labor and Commerce; and Conflict of Interest; Assistant House Republican Leader, 1995–99; has served on numerous local civic and community organizations and groups; committees: Education and Workforce; Financial Services; Science; Standards of Official Conduct; subcommittees: Capital Markets, Insurance and Government Sponsored Enterprises; vice-chair, Domestic and International Monetary Policy, Trade, and Technology; Education Reform; chair, Energy; Environment, Technology, and Standards; Financial Institutions and Consumer Credit; vice-chair, Workforce Protections; married: Rody P. Biggert; children: Courtney, Alison, Rody, and Adrienne; Episcopalian; elected to the 106th Congress; reelected to each succeeding Congress.

Office Listings

1213 Longworth House Office Building, Washington, DC 20515	(202) 225–3515
Chief of Staff/Press Secretary.—Kathy Lydon.	FAX: 225–9420
Legislative Director.—Paul Doucette.	
Scheduler.—Jeff Hennie.	
115 West 55th Street, Suite 100, Clarendon Hills, IL 60514	(630) 655–2052

Counties: COOK (part), DUPAGE (part), WILL (part). Population (2000), 653,647.

ZIP Codes: 60181, 60431–32, 60435, 60439–41, 60446, 60448, 60451, 60462–65, 60467, 60477, 60482, 60490–91, 60504–05, 60507, 60514–17, 60519, 60521–23, 60525, 60527, 60532, 60540, 60543–44, 60555, 60559, 60561, 60563–68, 60572, 60597–99

* * *

FOURTEENTH DISTRICT

J. DENNIS HASTERT, Republican, of Yorkville, IL; born in Aurora, IL, on January 2, 1942; graduated, Oswego High School, 1960; B.A., Wheaton College, IL, 1964; M.S., Northern Illinois University, DeKalb, 1967; teacher/coach, Yorkville High School; partner, family restaurant business; member, Illinois General Assembly House of Representatives, 1980–86; Republican spokesman for the Appropriations II Committee; chairman, Joint Committee on Public Utility Regulation; member, Legislative Audit Commission; named one of Illinois' 20 top legislators in 1985 by *Chicago Sun-Times*; member, Yorkville Lions Club; board of directors, Aurora Family Support Center; married the former Jean Kahl in 1973; two children: Joshua and Ethan; elected to the 100th Congress on November 4, 1986; reelected to each succeeding Congress; elected Speaker of the House for the 106th Congress; reelected Speaker for the 107th and 108th Congresses.

Office Listings

http://www.house.gov/hastert

235 Cannon House Office Building, Washington, DC 20515 .... (202) 225–2976
Chief of Staff.—Scott Palmer. FAX: 225–0697
Scheduler.—Helen Morrell.
Legislative Director.—Anthony Reed.
27 North River Street, Batavia, IL 60510 .... (630) 406–1114
Office Manager.—Lisa Post.
119 West First Street, Dixon, IL 61021 .... (815) 288–0680

Counties: BUREAU (part), DEKALB (part), DUPAGE (part), HENRY (part), KANE, KENDALL, LEE, WHITESIDE (part). CITIES AND TOWNSHIPS: Amboy, Ashton, Aurora, Barrington Hills (part), Bartlett (part), Batavia, Big Rock, Bristol, Burlington, Carol Stream (part), Carpentersville, Clare, Compton, Cornell, Cortland, DeKalb, Dixon, Dundee, East and West, Earlville, Elburn, Elgin, Esmond, Forreston, Franklin Grove, Geneva, Genoa, Gilberts, Hampshire, Harmon, Hinckley, Kaneville, Kingston, Kirkland, Lee, Leland, Malta, Maple Park, Mendota, Millbrook, Millington, Minooka (part), Montgomery, Mooseheart, Nelson, Newark, North Aurora, Oswego, Paw Paw, Plano, Plato Center, St. Charles, Sandwich, Shabbona, Sleepy Hollow, Somonauk, South Elgin, Steward, Sublette, Sugar Grove, Sycamore, Virgil, Warrenville (part), Wasco, Waterman, Wayne, West Brooklyn, West Chicago, Wheaton (part), Winfield, and Yorkville. Population (2000), 653,647.

ZIP Codes: 60010, 60102–03, 60109–10, 60112, 60115, 60118–23, 60134, 60136, 60140, 60142, 60144, 60147, 60150–52, 60170, 60174–75, 60177–78, 60183–87, 60190, 60431, 60447, 60450, 60504–06, 60510–12, 60518, 60520, 60530–31, 60536–39, 60541–45, 60548, 60550, 60552–56, 60560, 60563, 60568, 60640, 60660, 61006, 61021, 61031, 61042, 61057–58, 61068, 61071, 61081, 61234–35, 61238, 61240–41, 61243, 61250, 61254, 61258, 61270, 61273–74, 61277, 61283, 61310, 61318, 61324, 61330–31, 61342, 61344, 61346, 61349, 61353, 61367, 61376, 61378, 61434, 61443

* * *

FIFTEENTH DISTRICT

TIMOTHY V. JOHNSON, Republican, of Sidney, IL; born on July 23, 1946, in Champaign, IL; education: B.A., University of Illinois, Phi Beta Kappa; J.D., University of Illinois College of Law, graduated with high honors; occupation: Attorney; public service: Urbana, IL, City Council, 1971–75; Illinois House of Representatives, 1976–2000; Deputy Majority Leader; Champaign County, IL, Republican Party Chairman, 1990–96; elected to the 107th Congress on November 7, 2000; reelected to each succeeding Congress.

Office Listings

http://www.house.gov/timjohnson

1229 Longworth House Office Building, Washington, DC 20515 .... (202) 225–2371
Chief of Staff.—Jerome T. Clarke. FAX: 226–0791
Legislative Director.—Erik Woehrmann.
Legislative Correspondent.—Stephen Borg.
2004 Fox Drive, Champaign, IL 61820 .... (217) 403–4690

Counties: CHAMPAIGN, CLARK, COLES, CRAWFORD, CUMBERLAND, DEWITT, DOUGLAS, EDGAR, EDWARDS (part), FORD, GALLATIN (part), IROQUOIS, LAWRENCE (part), LIVINGSTON (part), MACON (part), MCLEAN (part), MOULTRIE, PIATT, SALINE (part), VERMILION, WABASH (part), WHITE (part). CITIES AND TOWNSHIPS: Bloomington-Normal (part), Champaign-Urbana, Charleston-Mattoon, Danville, Decatur (part), Mount Carmel (part), and Pontiac. Population (2000), 653,647.

ZIP Codes: 60420, 60423, 60437, 60449, 60460, 60518, 60531, 60551–52, 60901–02, 60911–14, 60917–22, 60924, 60926–34, 60936, 60938–42, 60945–46, 60948–49, 60951–53, 60955–57, 60959–64, 60966–70, 60973–74, 61252, 61270, 61311,

61313, 61319, 61321, 61333, 61364, 61401, 61434, 61448–49, 61530, 61701–02, 61704, 61709–10, 61720, 61722, 61724, 61726–28, 61730–31, 61735, 61737, 61739–41, 61743, 61748–50, 61752–53, 61758, 61761, 61764, 61769–70, 61772–73, 61775–78, 61791, 61799, 61801–03, 61810–18, 61820–22, 61824–26, 61830–34, 61839–59, 61862–66, 61870–78, 61880, 61882–84, 61910–14, 61917, 61919–20, 61924–25, 61928–33, 61936–38, 61940–44, 61949, 61951, 61953, 61955–56, 62401, 62410, 62413, 62420–21, 62423, 62427–28, 62432–33, 62435–36, 62439–42, 62445, 62447, 62449, 62451, 62454, 62460, 62462, 62466–69, 62474, 62477–78, 62481, 62521–22, 62526, 62532, 62544, 62549–50, 62701–03, 62821, 62827, 62844, 62863, 62867, 62869, 62871, 62930, 62934, 62946, 62984

* * *

SIXTEENTH DISTRICT

DONALD A. MANZULLO, Republican, of Egan, IL; born on March 24, 1944, in Rockford, IL; education: B.A., American University, Washington, DC, 1987; J.D., Marquette University Law School, Milwaukee, WI, 1970; president, Ogle County Bar Association, 1971, 1973; advisor, Oregon Ambulance Corporation; founder, Oregon Youth, Inc.; admitted to Illinois bar, 1970; member: State of Illinois and City of Oregon chambers of commerce, Friends of Severson Dells, Natural Land Institute, Ogle County Historic Society, Northern Illinois Alliance for the Arts, Aircraft Owners and Pilots Association, Ogle County Pilots Association, Kiwanis International, Illinois Farm Bureau, Ogle County Farm Bureau, National Federation of Independent Business, Citizens Against Government Waste; married: Freda Teslik Manzullo, 1982; children: Niel, Noel, and Katherine; elected on November 3, 1992, to the 103rd Congress; reelected to each succeeding Congress.

Office Listings

2228 Rayburn House Office Building, Washington, DC 20515 .... (202) 225–5676
Chief of Staff.—Adam Magary.
415 South Mulford Road, Rockford, IL 61108 .... (815) 394–1231
Director of Communications.—Rich Carter.
181 Virginia Avenue, Crystal Lake, IL 60014 .... (815) 356–9800
Caseworker.—Nada Geddes.

Counties: BOONE, CARROLL, DEKALB (part), JO DAVIESS, MCHENRY (part), OGLE, STEPHENSON, WHITESIDE (part), WINNEBAGO. Population (2000), 653,647.

ZIP Codes: 60001, 60010, 60012–14, 60021, 60033–34, 60039, 60042, 60050–51, 60098, 60102, 60111, 60113, 60115, 60129, 60135, 60140, 60142, 60145–46, 60150, 60152, 60156, 60178, 60180, 60530, 61001, 61006–08, 61010–16, 61018–21, 61024–25, 61027–28, 61030–32, 61036, 61038–39, 61041, 61043–44, 61046–54, 61059–65, 61067–68, 61070–75, 61077–81, 61084–85, 61087–89, 61091, 61101–12, 61114–15, 61125–26, 61130–32, 61230, 61250–52, 61261, 61266, 61270, 61285

* * *

SEVENTEENTH DISTRICT

LANE EVANS, Democrat, of Rock Island, IL; born in Rock Island on August 4, 1951; graduated, Alleman High School, Rock Island, 1969; B.A., Augustana College, Rock Island, 1974; J.D., Georgetown University Law Center, Washington, DC, 1978; admitted to Illinois bar in 1978 and commenced practice in Rock Island; served in U.S. Marine Corps, 1969–71; attorney for the Western Illinois Legal Foundation, 1978–79; national staff, Kennedy for President campaign, 1980; entered private practice as a partner in Community Legal Clinic, 1982; legal representative for ACLU, APRI, and LULAC, 1979; awards: Vietnam Veterans of America ''National Legislator of the Year'' (1985), President's Award for Outstanding Achievement, 1990; elected on November 2, 1982, to the 98th Congress; reelected to each succeeding Congress.

Office Listings

2211 Rayburn House Office Building, Washington, DC 20515 .... (202) 225–5905
Administrative Assistant.—Dennis King. FAX: 225–5396
Office Manager.—Eda Robinson.
Press Secretary.—Steve Vetzner.
1535 47th Avenue, Room 5, Moline, IL 61265 .... (309) 793–5760
District Representative.—Phil Hare.
261 North Broad, Suite 5, Galesburg, IL 61401 .... (309) 342–4411

Counties: ADAMS (part), CALHOUN, CHRISTIAN (part), FAYETTE (part), FULTON, GREENE (part), HANCOCK, HENDERSON, HENRY (part), JERSEY (part), KNOX (part), MACON (part), MACOUPIN, MADISON (part), MCDONOUGH, MERCER, MONTGOMERY (part), PIKE (part), ROCK ISLAND, SANGAMON (part), SHELBY (part), WARREN, WHITESIDE (part). Population (2000), 653,647.

ZIP Codes: 61037, 61071, 61081, 61201, 61204, 61230–33, 61236–37, 61239–42, 61244, 61251, 61256–57, 61259–65, 61272, 61275–76, 61278–79, 61281–82, 61284, 61299, 61318, 61342, 61364, 61401–02, 61410–20, 61422–23, 61425,

61427, 61430–43, 61447–48, 61450, 61452–55, 61458–60, 61462, 61465–78, 61480, 61482, 61484, 61486, 61488–90, 61501, 61519–20, 61524, 61531, 61533, 61542–44, 61553, 61560, 61563, 61569, 61572, 61611, 61701, 61761, 62001–02, 62006, 62009, 62011–14, 62017, 62019, 62021, 62023, 62027, 62031–33, 62036–37, 62044–45, 62047, 62049–53, 62056, 62058, 62063, 62065, 62069–70, 62074–75, 62077–79, 62082, 62085–86, 62088–89, 62091–94, 62097–98, 62262, 62301, 62305–06, 62311, 62313, 62316, 62320–21, 62326, 62329–30, 62334, 62336, 62338, 62341, 62343, 62345, 62348, 62351, 62354–56, 62358, 62360–61, 62366–67, 62370, 62373–74, 62376, 62379–80, 62431, 62513–15, 62520–23, 62525–26, 62537, 62539, 62544, 62549–51, 62557, 62560–61, 62572, 62615, 62624, 62626, 62629–30, 62640, 62644, 62649, 62661, 62667, 62670, 62672, 62674, 62683, 62685, 62690, 62692, 62701–05, 62707–08, 62713, 62781, 62794, 62796

* * *

EIGHTEENTH DISTRICT

RAY LAHOOD, Republican, of Peoria, IL; born December 6, 1945, in Peoria; education: graduate of Spalding High School; Canton Junior College, Canton, IL; B.S., education and sociology, Bradley University, Peoria, IL, 1971; previous memberships: Academy of Our Lady/ Spalding Board of Education (president), Notre Dame High School Board (president), Peoria Area Retarded Citizens Board of Directors, Bradley University National Alumni Board (president) and Peoria Area Chamber of Commerce Board; junior high school teacher, director of Rock Island County Youth Services Bureau, chief planner for Bi-State Metropolitan Planning Commission, administrative assistant to Congressman Tom Railsback and chief of staff for Congressman Bob Michel; member, Illinois House of Representatives, 1982; Peoria Economic Development Council Board of Directors, Heartland Water Resources Council, Children's Hospital of Illinois Advisory Board, Peoria Rotary Club, Junior League Community Advisory Committee, United Way Pillars Society and Holy Family Church; married: Kathy Dunk LaHood, 1967; children: Darin, Amy, Sam, and Sara; committees: Appropriations; House Permanent Select Committee on Intelligence; elected on November 8, 1994, to the 104th Congress; reelected to each succeeding Congress.

Office Listings

http://www.house.gov/lahood

1424 Longworth House Office Building, Washington, DC 20515 .... (202) 225–6201
Chief of Staff.—Diane Liesman. FAX: 225–9249
Deputy Chief of Staff.—Joan Mitchell.
100 Monroe Street NE, Room 100, Peoria, IL 61602 .... (309) 671–7027
District Chief of Staff.—Brad McMillan.
209 West State Street, Jacksonville, IL 62650 .... (217) 245–1431
Office Manager.—Barb Baker.
3050 Montvale Drive, Suite D, Springfield, IL 62704 .... (217) 793–0808
Office Manager.—Donna Rapps Miller.

Counties: ADAMS (part), BROWN, BUREAU (part), CASS, KNOX (part), LOGAN, MACON (part), MARSHALL, MASON, MCLEAN, MENARD, MORGAN, PEORIA, PIKE (part), PUTNAM, SANGAMON (part), SCHUYLER, SCOTT, STARK, TAZEWELL, WOODFORD (part). Population (2000), 653,647.

ZIP Codes: 61314, 61320–21, 61326–27, 61330, 61334–36, 61340, 61345, 61349, 61362–63, 61369–70, 61375, 61377, 61401, 61410, 61414, 61421, 61424, 61426, 61428, 61434, 61436, 61440, 61443, 61448–49, 61451–52, 61455, 61458, 61467, 61472, 61479, 61483–85, 61488–89, 61491, 61501, 61516–17, 61523, 61525–26, 61528–37, 61539–42, 61545–48, 61550, 61552, 61554–55, 61558–62, 61564–65, 61567–72, 61601–07, 61610–12, 61614–16, 61625, 61628–30, 61632–41, 61643–44, 61650–56, 61704, 61721, 61723, 61729, 61733–34, 61738, 61742, 61747, 61749, 61751, 61755–56, 61759–61, 61771, 61774, 61778, 61830, 62305, 62311–12, 62314, 62319–20, 62323–25, 62338–40, 62344, 62346–47, 62349, 62352–53, 62357, 62359–60, 62362–63, 62365, 62367, 62375, 62378, 62501, 62512, 62515, 62518–22, 62524, 62526, 62535, 62539, 62541, 62543, 62548, 62551, 62554, 62561, 62573, 62601, 62610–13, 62615, 62617–18, 62621–22, 62624–25, 62627–29, 62631, 62633–35, 62638–39, 62642–44, 62650–51, 62655–56, 62660–68, 62670–71, 62673, 62675, 62677, 62681–82, 62684, 62688, 62690–95, 62701–07, 62713, 62715, 62719, 62721–22, 62726, 62736, 62739, 62746, 62756–57, 62761, 62765, 62767, 62769, 62776–77, 62781, 62786, 62791, 62796

* * *

NINETEENTH DISTRICT

JOHN SHIMKUS, Republican, of Collinsville, IL; born on February 21, 1958, in Collinsville; graduated from Collinsville High School; B.S., West Point Military Academy, West Point, NY, 1980; teaching certificate, Christ College, Irvine, CA, 1990; MBA, Southern Illinois University, Edwardsville, 1997; U.S. Army Reserves, 1980–85; government and history teacher, Collinsville High School; Collinsville township trustee, 1989; Madison county treasurer, 1990–96; married the former Karen Muth, 1987; children: David, Daniel, and Joshua; elected to the 105th Congress; reelected to each succeeding Congress.

Office Listings

http://www.house.gov/shimkus

513 Cannon House Office Building, Washington, DC 20515 .... (202) 225–5271
Chief of Staff.—Craig Roberts. FAX: 225–5880
Legislative Director.—Ray Fitzgerald.
3130 Chatham Road, Suite C, Springfield, IL 62704 .... (217) 492–5090
District Director.—Deb Detmeys.
508 West Main, Collinsville, IL 62234 .... (618) 344–3065
221 East Broadway, Suite 102, Centralia, IL 62801 .... (618) 532–9676
120 South Fair, Olney, IL 62450 .... (618) 392–7737
110 East Locust Street, Room 12, Harrisburg, IL 62946 .... (618) 252–8271

Counties: BOND, CHRISTIAN (part), CLAY, CLINTON, EDWARDS (part), EFFINGHAM, FAYETTE (part), GALLATIN (part), GREENE (part), HAMILTON, HARDIN, JASPER, JEFFERSON, JERSEY (part), JOHNSON, LAWRENCE (part), MADISON (part), MARION, MASSAC, MONTGOMERY (part), POPE, RICHLAND, SALINE (part), SANGAMON (part), SHELBY (part), WABASH (part), WASHINGTON, WAYNE, WHITE (part), WILLIAMSON (part). Population (2000), 653,647.

ZIP Codes: 61957, 62001–02, 62010, 62012, 62015–17, 62019, 62021–22, 62024–26, 62028, 62030, 62034–35, 62040, 62044, 62046, 62049, 62051–52, 62054, 62056, 62061–62, 62067, 62074–76, 62080–81, 62083, 62086, 62088, 62094, 62097, 62214–16, 62218–19, 62230–31, 62234, 62237, 62245–47, 62249–50, 62252–55, 62257–58, 62262–63, 62265–66, 62268–69, 62271, 62273, 62275, 62281, 62284, 62293–94, 62338, 62401, 62410–11, 62413–14, 62417–28, 62431–36, 62438–52, 62454, 62458–69, 62471, 62473–81, 62510, 62513, 62515, 62517, 62520–22, 62526, 62530–31, 62533–34, 62536, 62538–40, 62545–48, 62550, 62553, 62555–58, 62560, 62563, 62565, 62567–68, 62570–72, 62615, 62629, 62689–90, 62703–04, 62707, 62716, 62723, 62762–64, 62766, 62791, 62801, 62803, 62805–12, 62814–25, 62827–31, 62833–44, 62846, 62848–72, 62874–87, 62889–99, 62908–10, 62912, 62917, 62919, 62921–23, 62926, 62928, 62930–31, 62934–35, 62938–39, 62941, 62943, 62946–47, 62953–56, 62959–60, 62965, 62967, 62972, 62977, 62979, 62982–85, 62987, 62991, 62995

INDIANA

(Population 2000, 6,080,485)

SENATORS

RICHARD G. LUGAR, Republican, of Indianapolis, IN; born in Indianapolis, April 4, 1932; education: graduated, Shortridge High School, 1950; B.A., Denison University, Granville, OH; Rhodes Scholar, B.A., M.A., Pembroke College, Oxford, England, 1956; served in the U.S. Navy, 1957–60; businessman; treasurer, Lugar Stock Farms, Inc., a livestock and grain operation; vice president and treasurer, 1960–67, Thomas L. Green and Co., manufacturers of food production machinery; member, Indianapolis Board of School Commissioners, 1964–67; mayor of Indianapolis, 1968–75; member, advisory board, U.S. Conference of Mayors, 1969–75; National League of Cities, advisory council, 1972–75, president, 1971; Advisory Commission on Intergovernmental Relations, 1969–75, vice chairman, 1971–75; board of trustees, Denison University and the University at Indianapolis; advisory board, Indiana University-Purdue University at Indianapolis; visiting professor of political science, director of public affairs, Indiana Central University; 31 honorary doctorates; recipient of Fiorello LaGuardia Award, 1975; GOP National Convention Keynote Speaker, 1972; SFRC chairman, 1985–86; NRSC chairman, 1983–84; member, St. Luke's Methodist Church; married the former Charlene Smeltzer, 1956; four children; committees: Agriculture, Nutrition and Forestry; chairman, Foreign Relations; elected to the U.S. Senate on November 2, 1976; reelected to each succeeding Senate term.

Office Listings

http://lugar.senate.gov

306 Hart Senate Office Building, Washington, DC 20510 .... (202) 224–4814
  Administrative Assistant.—Martin W. Morris.
  Legislative Director.—Chris Geeslin.
  Press Secretary.—Andy Fisher.
  Scheduler.—Amy Oberhelman.
10 West Market Street, Room 1180, Indianapolis, IN 46204 .... (317) 226–5555
Federal Building, Room 122, 101 NW Martin Luther King Boulevard, Evansville, IN 47708 .... (812) 465–6313
Federal Building, Room 3158, 1300 South Harrison Street, Fort Wayne, IN 46802 (260) 422–1505
175 West Lincolnway, Suite G–1, Valparaiso, IN 46383 .... (219) 548–8035
Federal Center, Room 103, 1201 East 10th Street, Jeffersonville, IN 47132 .... (812) 288–3377

* * *

EVAN BAYH, Democrat, of Indianapolis, IN, born in Terre Haute, IN, December 26, 1955; education: graduated St. Albans School, Washington, DC, 1974; received a B.A. with honors in business economics from Indiana University, 1978; J.D. from University of Virginia Law School, 1982; admitted to the District of Columbia and Indiana bars, 1984; law clerk for the Southern District of Indiana court, 1982–83; attorney with Hogan and Hartson, Washington, 1983–84; attorney for Bayh, Tabbert and Capehart, Washington, 1985; attorney for Bingham Summers, Welsh and Spilman, Indianapolis, 1986; elected as Secretary of State of Indiana, 1986–89; elected Governor of Indiana, 1988; reelected 1992; chairman of the Democratic Governors' Association, 1994; chairman of the National Education Goals Panel, 1995; chairman of the Education Commission of the States, 1995; Above and Beyond Award from Indiana Black Expo, 1995; Breaking the Glass Ceiling Award Women Executives in State Government, 1996; keynote speaker at the National Democratic Convention, 1996; member of the executive committee on the National Governors' Association, 1996; Red Poling Chair, business economics at Indiana University, 1997; twin sons, Birch Evans IV, and Nicholas Harrison; married: Susan Breshears, April 13, 1985; committees: Banking, Housing and Urban Affairs; Energy and Natural Resources; Special Committee on Aging; Select Committee on Intelligence; Small Business and Entrepreneurship; Armed Services; chairman, Democratic Leadership Council; elected to the U.S. Senate on November 3, 1998.

Office Listings

http://bayh.senate.gov

463 Russell Senate Office Building, Washington, DC 20510 .... (202) 224–5623
  Chief of Staff.—Tom Sugar. FAX: 228–1377
  Executive Assistant.—Clare Glynn.
  Legislative Director.—Charlie Salem.
  Scheduler.—Sarah Rozensky.
130 South Main Street, Suite 110, South Bend, IN 44601 .... (574) 236–8302
1650 Market Tower, 10 W. Market Street, Indianapolis, IN 46204 .... (317) 554–0750

10 Martin Luther King, Jr. Boulevard, Evansville, IN 47708 .... (812) 465–6500
1300 South Harrison Street, Ft. Wayne, IN 46802 .... (219) 426–3151
1201 East 10th Street, Suite 106, Jeffersonville, IN 47130 .... (812) 218–2317
Hammond Courthouse, Suite 3200, 5400 Federal Plaza, Hammond, IL 46320 .... (219) 852–2763

REPRESENTATIVES

FIRST DISTRICT

PETER J. VISCLOSKY, Democrat, of Merrillville, IN; born in Gary, IN, on August 13, 1949; graduated, Andrean High School, Merrillville, 1967; B.S., accounting, Indiana University Northwest, Gary, 1970; J.D., University of Notre Dame Law School, Notre Dame, IN, 1973; LL.M., international and comparative law, Georgetown University Law Center, Washington, DC, 1982; profession: attorney; admitted to the Indiana State bar, 1974, the District of Columbia Bar, 1978, and the U.S. Supreme Court Bar, 1980; associate staff, U.S. House of Representatives, Committee on Appropriations, 1977–80, Committee on the Budget, 1980–82; practicing attorney, Merrillville law firm, 1983–84; two children: John Daniel and Timothy Patrick; committees: Appropriations; subcommittees: Defense; ranking member, Energy and Water Development; elected to the 99th Congress on November 6, 1984; reelected to each succeeding Congress.

Office Listings

http://www.house.gov/visclosky

2313 Rayburn House Office Building, Washington, DC 20515 .... (202) 225–2461
Administrative Assistant.—Richard Kaelin. FAX: 225–2493
Appropriations Director.—Peder Maarbjerg.
Executive Assistant/Scheduler.—Katherine Bensen-Piscopo.
Press Assistant.—Cliston Brown.
701 East 83rd Avenue, #9, Merrillville, IN 46410 .... (219) 795–1844
District Director.—Mark Savinski. (888) 423–7383

Counties: BENTON, JASPER, LAKE, NEWTON, PORTER (part). Population (2000), 675,767.

ZIP Codes: 46301–04, 46307–08, 46310–12, 46319–25, 46327, 46341–42, 46345, 46347–49, 46355–56, 46360, 46366, 46368, 46372–73, 46375–77, 46379–85, 46390, 46392–94, 46401–11, 47917, 47921–22, 47942–44, 47948, 47951, 47963–64, 47970–71, 47977–78, 47984, 47986, 47995

* * *

SECOND DISTRICT

CHRIS CHOCOLA, Republican, of Bristol, IN; born on February 24, 1962, in Jackson, MI; education: graduated, *summa cum laude,* from Hillsdale College, 1984, with a double major in Business Administration and Political Economy; J.D., *magna cum laude,* Thomas Cooley Law School, 1988; profession: businessman; Chief Executive Officer, CTB International Corp.; community organizations: Rotary International; Oaklawn Psychiatric Center; South Bend Center for the Homeless; family: married to Sarah; children: Caroline and Colin; elected to the 108th Congress on November 5, 2002.

Office Listings

http://www.house.gov/chocola

510 Cannon House Office Building, Washington, DC 20515 .... (202) 225–3915
Chief of Staff.—Brooks Kochvar. FAX: 225–6798
Legislative Director.—Rob Vernon.
Scheduler.—Michele Madasz.
Press Secretary.—Alison Harden.
100 East Wayne Street, Suite 330, South Bend, IN 46601 .... (574) 251–0596
444 Mall Road, Logansport, IN 46947 .... (574) 753–4700

Counties: CARROLL, CASS, ELKHART (part), FULTON, LAPORTE, MARSHALL, PORTER (part), PULASKI, ST. JOSEPH, STARKE, WHITE (part). CITIES: Elkhart, Kokomo, LaPorte, Logansport, Monticello, Mishawaka, Plymouth, Rochester, South Bend, and Westville. Population (2000), 675,767.

ZIP Codes: 46041, 46051, 46056, 46065, 46143, 46301, 46304, 46340–42, 46345–46, 46348, 46350, 46352, 46360–61, 46365–66, 46371, 46374, 46382–83, 46390–91, 46501, 46504, 46506, 46511, 46513–17, 46524, 46526, 46528, 46530–32, 46534, 46536–37, 46539, 46544–46, 46550, 46552, 46554, 46556, 46561, 46563, 46570, 46572, 46574, 46595, 46601, 46604, 46613–17, 46619–20, 46624, 46626, 46628–29, 46634–35, 46637, 46660, 46680, 46699, 46901–02, 46910, 46912–13, 46915–17, 46920, 46922–23, 46926, 46929, 46931–32, 46939, 46942, 46945, 46947, 46950–51,

46960–61, 46967–68, 46970, 46975, 46977–79, 46982, 46985, 46988, 46994, 46996, 46998, 47920, 47923, 47925–26, 47946, 47950, 47957, 47959, 47960, 47997

* * *

THIRD DISTRICT

MARK E. SOUDER, Republican, of Fort Wayne, IN; born in Grabill, IN, July 18, 1950; graduated from Leo High School, 1968; B.S., Indiana University, Fort Wayne, 1972; M.B.A., University of Notre Dame Graduate School of Business, 1974; partner, Historic Souder's of Grabill; majority owner of Souder's General Store; vice president, Our Country Home, fixture manufacturing business; attends Emmanuel Community Church; served as economic development liaison for then-Representative Dan Coats (IN–4th District); appointed Republican staff director of the House Select Committee on Children, Youth and Families, 1984; legislative director and deputy chief of staff for former Senator Coats; member: Grabill Chamber of Commerce, former head of Congressional Action Committee of Ft. Wayne Chamber of Commerce; married the former Diane Zimmer, 1974; three children: Brooke, Nathan, and Zachary; committees: Government Reform; Resources; Select Committee on Homeland Security; elected to the 104th Congress; reelected to each succeeding Congress.

Office Listings

http://www.house.gov/souder

1227 Longworth House Office Building, Washington, DC 20515 .... (202) 225–4436
Chief of Staff.—Angela Flood. FAX: 225–3479
Scheduler.—Dawn Gerson.
1300 South Harrison, Room 3105, Fort Wayne, IN 46802 .... (260) 424–3041
District Director.—Mark Wickersham.
102 West Lincoln Avenue, 1st Source Building, Suite 250, Goshen, IN 46526 .... (574) 533–5802
700 Park Avenue, The Boathouse, Suite D, Winona Lake, IN 46590 .... (574) 269–1940

Counties: ALLEN (part), DEKALB, ELKHART (part), KOSCIUSKO, LAGRANGE, NOBLE, STEUBEN, WHITLEY. Population (2000), 675,617.

ZIP Codes: 46502, 46504, 46506–08, 46510, 46516, 46524, 46526–28, 46538–40, 46542–43, 46550, 46553, 46555, 46562, 46565–67, 46571, 46573, 46580–82, 46590, 46701, 46703–06, 46710, 46721, 46723, 46725, 46730, 46732, 46737–38, 46741–43, 46746–48, 46750, 46755, 46760–61, 46763–65, 46767, 46771, 46773–74, 46776–77, 46779, 46783–89, 46793–99, 46801–09, 46814–16, 46818–19, 46825, 46835, 46845, 46850–69, 46885, 46895–99, 46910, 46962, 46975, 46982

* * *

FOURTH DISTRICT

STEVE BUYER, Republican, of Monticello, IN; born in Rensselaer, IN, November 26, 1958; education: graduated from North White High School in 1976; B.S., business administration, The Citadel, 1980; J.D., Valparaiso University School of Law, 1984; admitted to the Virginia and Indiana bars; profession: U.S. Army Judge Advocate General Corps, 1984–87, assigned Deputy to the Attorney General of Indiana, 1987–88; family law practice, 1988–92; U.S. Army Reserves, 1980–present; major; legal counsel for the 22nd Theatre Army in Operations Desert Shield and Desert Storm; married: to the former Joni Lynn Geyer; children: Colleen and Ryan; committees: Energy and Commerce; Veterans' Affairs; subcommittees: Energy and Air Quality, Environment and Hazardous Materials; chairman, Oversight and Investigations; Health; co-chairman, National Guard and Reserve Components Caucus; Assistant Whip; elected to the 103rd Congress, November 3, 1992; reelected to each succeeding Congress.

Office Listings

http://www.house.gov/buyer

2230 Rayburn House Office Building, Washington, DC 20515 .... (202) 225–5037
Administrative Assistant.—Mike Copher.
Scheduler/Office Manager.—Danelle Bowsher.
Legislative Director.—Myrna Dugan.
Press Secretary.—Laura Zuckerman.
148 North Perry Road, Plainfield, IN 46168 .... (317) 838–0404
District Director.—Brandt Hershman.
100 S. Main Street, Monticello, IN 47960 .... (574) 583–9819

Counties: BOONE, CLINTON, FOUNTAIN (part), HENDRICKS, JOHNSON (part), LAWRENCE (part), MARION (part), MONROE (part), MONTGOMERY, MORGAN, TIPPECANOE, WHITE (part). Population (2000), 675,617.

ZIP Codes: 46035, 46039, 46041, 46049–50, 46052, 46057–58, 46060, 46065, 46067, 46069, 46071, 46075, 46077, 46102–03, 46106, 46111–13, 46118, 46120–23, 46125, 46131, 46142–43, 46147, 46149, 46151, 46157–58, 46160, 46165–68, 46172, 46175, 46180–81, 46183–84, 46214, 46221, 46224, 46231, 46234, 46241, 46254, 46268, 46278, 46920, 46923, 46979, 47108, 47260, 47264, 47403–04, 47420–21, 47429–30, 47433, 47436–37, 47446, 47451, 47456, 47460, 47462–64, 47467, 47470, 47901–07, 47909, 47916, 47918, 47920, 47923–24, 47929–30, 47932–41, 47944, 47949, 47952, 47954–55, 47958–60, 47962, 47965, 47967–68, 47970–71, 47978, 47980–81, 47983, 47987–90, 47992, 47994–96

* * *

FIFTH DISTRICT

DAN BURTON, Republican, of Indianapolis, IN; born in Indianapolis, June 21, 1938; graduated, Shortridge High School, 1956; Indiana University, 1956–57, Cincinnati Bible Seminary, 1958–60; served in the U.S. Army, 1957–58; U.S. Army Reserves, 1958–64; businessman, insurance and real estate firm owner since 1968; served, Indiana House of Representatives, 1967–68 and 1977–80; Indiana State Senate, 1969–70 and 1981–82; president: Volunteers of America, Indiana Christian Benevolent Association, Committee for Constitutional Government, and Family Support Center; member, Jaycees; 33rd degree Mason, Scottish rite division; married the former Barbara Jean Logan, 1959; three children: Kelly, Danielle Lee, and Danny Lee II; elected on November 2, 1982, to the 98th Congress; reelected to each succeeding Congress.

Office Listings

http://www.house.gov/burton

2185 Rayburn House Office Building, Washington, DC 20515 .... (202) 225–2276
Administrative Assistant.—Mark Walker. FAX: 225–0016
Executive Assistant.—Claudia Keller.
Office Manager.—Diane Menorca.
Press Secretary.—John Cardarelli.
8900 Keystone at the Crossing, Suite 1050, Indianapolis, IN 46240 .... (317) 848–0201
District Director.—Michael Delph.

Counties: Grant, Hamilton, Hancock, Howard (part), Huntington, Johnson (part), Marion (part), Miami, Shelby, Tipton, Wabash. Population (2000), 675,794.

ZIP Codes: 46030–34, 46036, 46038, 46040, 46045, 46047, 46049, 46055, 46060–61, 46064, 46068–70, 46072, 46074, 46076–77, 46082, 46110, 46115, 46117, 46124, 46126, 46129–31, 46140, 46143, 46148, 46150, 46154, 46161–63, 46176, 46182, 46184, 46186, 46217, 46220, 46226–27, 46229, 46236–37, 46239–40, 46250, 46256, 46259–60, 46280, 46290, 46307, 46347, 46355, 46379–80, 46702, 46713–14, 46725, 46750, 46766, 46770, 46783, 46787, 46792, 46901–04, 46910–11, 46914, 46919, 46921, 46926, 46928–30, 46932–33, 46936–38, 46940–41, 46943, 46946, 46951–53, 46957–59, 46962, 46965, 46970–71, 46974–75, 46979–80, 46982, 46984, 46986–87, 46989–92, 46995, 47234, 47246, 47272, 47342, 47384

* * *

SIXTH DISTRICT

MIKE PENCE, Republican, of Columbus, IN; born on June 7, 1959, in Columbus, IN; education: Hanover College, 1981; J.D., Indiana University School of Law, 1986; former Republican nominee for the U.S. House of Representatives in the 2nd District in 1988 and 1990; President, Indiana Policy Review Foundation, 1991–93; radio broadcaster: the Mike Pence Show, syndicated statewide in Indiana; married: Karen; children: Michael, Charlotte, and Audrey; elected to the 107th Congress on November 7, 2000; reelected to each succeeding Congress.

Office Listings

http://mikepence.house.gov

1605 Longworth House Office Building, Washington, DC 20515 .... (202) 225–3021
Chief of Staff.—Bill Smith. FAX: 225–3382
Legislative Director.—Trip Radtke.
Press Secretary.—Matt Lloyd.
Paramount Centre, 1134 Meridian, Anderson, IN 46016 .... (765) 640–2919
District Director.—Lani Czarniecki.

Counties: Allen (part), Adams, Bartholomew (part), Blackford, Dearborn (part), Decatur, Delaware, Fayette, Franklin, Henry, Jay, Johnson (part), Madison, Randolph, Rush, Shelby (part), Union, Wayne, Wells. Population (2000), 675,669.

ZIP Codes: 46001, 46011–18, 46036, 46040, 46044, 46048, 46051, 46056, 46063–64, 46070, 46104, 46110, 46115, 46124, 46126–27, 46131, 46133, 46140, 46142, 46144, 46146, 46148, 46150–51, 46155–56, 46160–62, 46164, 46173, 46176,

46181–82, 46186, 46711, 46714, 46731, 46733, 46740, 46745, 46750, 46759, 46766, 46769–70, 46772–73, 46777–78, 46780–83, 46791–92, 46797–98, 46809, 46816, 46819, 46928, 46952–53, 46989, 46991, 47003, 47006, 47010, 47012, 47016, 47022, 47024–25, 47030, 47035–37, 47060, 47201, 47203, 47225–26, 47234, 47240, 47244, 47246, 47261, 47263, 47265, 47272, 47280, 47283, 47302–08, 47320, 47322, 47324–27, 47330–31, 47334–42, 47344–46, 47348, 47351–62, 47366–71, 47373–75, 47380–88, 47390, 47392–94, 47396, 47448

* * *

SEVENTH DISTRICT

JULIA CARSON, Democrat, of Indianapolis, IN; born in Louisville, KY, July 8, 1938; education: graduated, Crispus Attucks High School, Indianapolis, IN, 1955; attended: Martin University, Indianapolis, IN; Indiana University-Purdue University at Indianapolis; employment: manager and businesswoman; Indiana House of Representatives, 1972–76; Indiana State Senate, 1976–90; as Indianapolis center township trustee, 1990–96, she targeted fraud and waste to eliminate the city's $20-million debt; twice named Woman of the Year by the *Indianapolis Star*; children: two; committees: Financial Services; Transportation and Infrastructure; subcommittees: Financial Institutions and Consumer Credit; Housing and Community Opportunity; Highways, Transit, and Pipelines; Railroads; elected on November 5, 1996, to the 105th Congress; reelected to each succeeding Congress.

Office Listings

http://www.juliacarson.house.gov

1535 Longworth House Office Building, Washington, DC 20515 .... (202) 225–4011
Deputy Chief of Staff.—Deron Roberson. FAX: 225–5633
Legislative Director.—Marti Thomas.
Legislative Assistants: Lee Footer, Michael Wallace, Kerry Horgan.
Executive Assistant.—Aarti Nayak.
300 East Fall Creek Parkway, Suite 201, Indianapolis, IN 46205 .... (317) 283–6516
Chief of Staff.—S. Sargent (Sarge) Visher.

Counties: MARION COUNTY. City of Indianapolis (part), township of Center, parts of the townships of Decatur, Lawrence, Perry, Pike, Warren, Washington, and Wayne, included are the cities of Beech Grove and Lawrence (part). Population (2000), 675,456.

ZIP Codes: 46107, 46160, 46201–09, 46211, 46214, 46216–22, 46224–31, 46234–35, 46237, 46239–42, 46244, 46247, 46249, 46251, 46253–55, 46260, 46266, 46268, 46274–75, 46277–78, 46282–83, 46285, 46291, 46295–96, 46298

* * *

EIGHTH DISTRICT

JOHN N. HOSTETTLER, Republican, of Blairsville, IN; born in Evansville, IN, on June 19, 1961; education: graduated from North Posey High School, Poseyville, IN, 1979; B.S.M.E., Rose-Hulman Polytechnic University, 1983; employment: performance engineer, Southern Indiana Gas and Electric; religion: Baptist; married: the former Elizabeth Hamman, 1983; children: Matthew, Amanda, Jaclyn and Jared; committees: Judiciary; Armed Services; subcommittees: The Constitution; chairman, Immigration, Border Security, and Claims; Projection Forces; Readiness; elected to the 104th Congress; reelected to each succeeding Congress.

Office Listings

http://www.house.gov/hostettler

1214 Longworth House Office Building, Washington, DC 20515 .... (202) 225–4636
Chief of Staff.—Carl Little. FAX: 225–3284
Press Secretary.—Michael Jahr.
Federal Building, Room 124, 101 NW Martin Luther King, Jr. Boulevard, Evansville, IN 47708 .... (812) 465–6484
Toll Free (Indiana only) .... (800) 321–9830
328 North Second Street, Suite 304, Vincennes, IN 47591 .... (812) 882–0632
District Director.—Eric Holcomb.

Counties: CLAY, DAVIESS, FOUNTAIN (part), GIBSON, GREENE, KNOX, MARTIN, OWEN, PARKE, PIKE, POSEY, PUTNAM, SULLIVAN, VANDERBURGH, VERMILLION, VIGO, WARREN, WARRICK. Population (2000), 675,564.

ZIP Codes: 46105, 46120–21, 46128, 46135, 46165–66, 46170–72, 46175, 47403–04, 47424, 47427, 47429, 47431–33, 47438–39, 47441, 47443, 47445–46, 47449, 47453, 47455–57, 47459–60, 47462, 47465, 47469–71, 47501, 47512, 47516, 47519, 47522–24, 47527–29, 47535, 47537, 47541–42, 47553, 47557–58, 47561–62, 47564, 47567–68, 47573, 47578, 47581, 47584–85, 47590–91, 47596–98, 47601, 47610–14, 47616, 47618–20, 47629–31, 47633, 47637–40,

47647–49, 47654, 47660, 47665–66, 47670, 47683, 47701–06, 47708, 47710–16, 47719–22, 47724–25, 47727–28, 47730–37, 47739–41, 47744, 47747, 47750, 47801–05, 47807–09, 47811–12, 47830–34, 47836–38, 47840–42, 47845–66, 47868–72, 47874–76, 47878–82, 47884–85, 47917–18, 47921, 47928, 47932, 47952, 47966, 47969–70, 47974–75, 47982, 47987, 47989, 47991–93

* * *

NINTH DISTRICT

BARON P. HILL, Democrat, of Seymour, IN; born in Seymour, IN, on June 23, 1953; education: graduated, Seymour High School, 1971; B.A., Furman University, 1975; elected to the Indiana House of Representatives, 1982–90; served on the House Rules Committee, and was Assistant Whip for the Democratic Caucus; financial analyst with Merrill Lynch; married: the former Betty Schepman; children: Jennifer, Cara, and Elizabeth; committees: Agriculture; Armed Services; Joint Economic Committee; elected to the 106th Congress; reelected to each succeeding Congress.

Office Listings

1024 Longworth House Office Building, Washington, DC 20515 .... (202) 225–5315
Chief of Staff.—Ryan Guthrie. FAX: 226–6866
Executive Assistant.—Anne Ruach.
Communications Director.—Scott Downes.
Legislative Director.—Joel Elliott.
590 Missouri Avenue, Suite 203, Jeffersonville, IN 47130 .... (812) 288–3999
District Director.—Luke Clippinger.

Counties: BARTHOLOMEW (part), BROWN, CLARK, CRAWFORD, DEARBORN (part), DUBOIS, FLOYD, HARRISON, JACKSON, JEFFERSON, MONROE (part), OHIO, ORANGE, PERRY, RIPLEY, SCOTT, SPENCER, SWITZERLAND, WASHINGTON. Population (2000), 675,599.

ZIP Codes: 46151, 46160, 46164, 46181, 47001, 47006, 47011, 47017–23, 47025, 47031–34, 47037–43, 47102, 47104, 47106–08, 47110–12, 47114–20, 47122–26, 47129–47, 47150–51, 47160–67, 47170, 47172, 47174, 47177, 47199, 47201–03, 47220, 47223–24, 47227–32, 47235–36, 47240, 47243–45, 47247, 47249–50, 47260, 47264–65, 47270, 47273–74, 47281–83, 47401–08, 47426, 47432, 47434–36, 47448, 47452, 47454, 47458, 47462, 47468–69, 47513–15, 47520–21, 47523, 47525, 47527, 47531–32, 47536–37, 47541–42, 47545–47, 47549–52, 47556, 47564, 47574–77, 47579–81, 47586, 47588, 47590, 47601, 47611, 47615, 47617, 47634–35, 47637

IOWA

(Population 2000, 2,926,324)

SENATORS

CHARLES E. GRASSLEY, Republican, of Cedar Falls, IA; born in New Hartford, IA, September 17, 1933; graduated, New Hartford Community High School, 1951; B.A., University of Northern Iowa, 1955; M.A., University of Northern Iowa, 1956; doctoral studies, University of Iowa, 1957–58; farmer; member, Iowa State Legislature, 1959–74; Farm Bureau, State and County Historical Society, Masons, Baptist Church, and International Association of Machinists, 1962–71; married: the former Barbara Ann Speicher, 1954; children: Lee, Wendy, Robin Lynn, Michele Marie, and Jay Charles; committees: Agriculture; Budget; chairman, Finance; Judiciary; Joint Committee on Taxation; co-chairman, International Narcotics Control Caucus; elected to the 94th Congress, November 5, 1974; reelected to the 95th and 96th Congresses; elected to the U.S. Senate, November 4, 1980; reelected to each succeeding Senate term.

Office Listings

http://grassley.senate.gov

135 Hart Senate Office Building, Washington, DC 20510 .... (202) 224–3744
Chief of Staff.—Ken Cunningham. FAX: 224–6020
Director of Communications.—Jill Kozeny.
Legislative Director.—Kolan Davis.
721 Federal Building, 210 Walnut Street, Des Moines, IA 50309 .... (515) 284–4890
State Administrator.—Henry C. Wulff.
206 Federal Building, 101 First Street SE, Cedar Rapids, IA 52401 .... (319) 363–6832
103 Federal Courthouse Building, 320 Sixth Street, Sioux City, IA 51101 .... (712) 233–1860
210 Waterloo Building, 531 Commercial Street, Waterloo, IA 50701 .... (319) 232–6657
131 West 3rd Street, Suite 180, Davenport, IA 52801 .... (319) 322–4331
307 Federal Building, 8 South Sixth Street, Council Bluffs, IA 51501 .... (712) 322–7103

* * *

TOM HARKIN, Democrat, of Cumming, IA; born in Cumming, IA, on November 19, 1939; education: graduated from Dowling Catholic High School, Des Moines, IA; B.S., Iowa State University, Ames, 1962; LL.B., Catholic University of America, Washington, DC, 1972; U.S. Navy, 1962–67; military service: LCDR, U.S. Naval Reserves; admitted to the bar, 1972, Des Moines, IA; married: the former Ruth Raduenz, 1968; children: Amy and Jenny; committees: Agriculture, Nutrition, and Forestry; Appropriations; Health, Education, Labor, and Pensions; Small Business and Entrepreneurship; elected to the 94th Congress on November 5, 1974; reelected to four succeeding Congresses; elected to the U.S. Senate on November 6, 1984; reelected to each succeeding Senate term.

Office Listings

http://harkin.senate.gov

731 Hart Senate Office Building, Washington, DC 20510 .... (202) 224–3254
Chief of Staff.—Peter Reinecke. TDD: 224–4633
Legislative Director.—Brian Ahlberg.
Press Secretary.—Allison Dobson.
Federal Building, Room 733, 210 Walnut Street, Des Moines, IA 50309 .... (515) 284–4574
150 First Avenue NE, Suite 370, Cedar Rapids, IA 52401 .... (319) 365–4504
1606 Brady Street, Suite 323, Davenport, IA 52801 .... (563) 322–1338
Federal Building, Room 110, 320 Sixth Street, Sioux City, IA 51101 .... (712) 252–1550
Federal Building, Room 315, 350 West Sixth Street, Dubuque, IA 52001 .... (563) 582–2130

REPRESENTATIVES

FIRST DISTRICT

JIM NUSSLE, Republican, of Manchester, IA; born in Des Moines, IA, June 27, 1960; graduated, Carl Sandburg High School, 1978; attended Ronshoved Hojskole, Denmark, 1978–79; Luther College, Decorah, IA, 1983; Drake University Law School, Des Moines, IA, 1985; admitted to the bar, January 1986; Delaware County Attorney, 1986–90; family: married to Karen; children: Sarah and Mark; committees: chairman, Budget; Ways and Means; subcommittee: Trade; elected to the 102nd Congress; reelected to each succeeding Congress.

Office Listings

http://www.house.gov/nussle

303 Cannon House Office Building, Washington, DC 20515 .... (202) 225–2911
Chief of Staff.—Rich Meade. FAX: 225–9129
3641 Kimball Avenue, Waterloo, IA 50702 .... (319) 235–1109
2255 John F. Kennedy Road, Dubuque, IA 52002 .... (563) 557–7740
209 West 4th Street, Davenport, IA 52801 .... (563) 326–1841
712 West Main Street, Manchester, IA 52057 .... (563) 927–5141
District Administrator.—Cheryl Madlom.

Counties: BLACK HAWK, BREMER, BUCHANAN, BUTLER, CLAYTON, CLINTON, DELAWARE, DUBUQUE, FAYETTE, JACKSON, JONES, SCOTT. Population (2000), 585,302.

ZIP Codes: 50601–02, 50604–08, 50611, 50613–14, 50619, 50622–23, 50625–26, 50629, 50631, 50634, 50636, 50641, 50643–44, 50647–51, 50654–55, 50660, 50662, 50664–68, 50670–71, 50674, 50676–77, 50681–82, 50701–04, 50706–07, 50799, 52001–04, 52030–33, 52035–50, 52052–54, 52056–57, 52060, 52064–66, 52068–79, 52099, 52135, 52141–42, 52147, 52156–59, 52164, 52166, 52169, 52171, 52175, 52205, 52207, 52210, 52212, 52223, 52226, 52237, 52252, 52254, 52305, 52309–10, 52312, 52320–21, 52323, 52326, 52329–30, 52362, 52701, 52722, 52726–33, 52736, 52742, 52745–48, 52750–51, 52753, 52756–58, 52765, 52767–68, 52771, 52773–74, 52777, 52801–09

* * *

SECOND DISTRICT

JAMES A. LEACH, Republican, of Davenport, IA; born in Davenport on October 15, 1942; graduated, Davenport High School, 1960; B.A., Princeton University, 1964; M.A., School of Advanced International Studies, Johns Hopkins University, 1966; further graduate studies at the London School of Economics, 1966–68; staff member of U.S. Congressman Donald Rumsfeld, 1965–66; foreign service officer assigned to the Department of State, 1968–69; administrative assistant to the director of the Office of Economic Opportunity, 1969–70; foreign service officer assigned to the Arms Control and Disarmament Agency, 1970–73; member: U.S. delegation to the Geneva Disarmament Conference, 1971–72; U.S. delegation to the United Nations General Assembly, 1972; U.S. delegation to the United Nations Conference on Natural Resources, 1975; U.S. Advisory Commission on International Educational and Cultural Affairs, 1975–76; Federal Home Loan Bank Board of Des Moines, 1975–76; president, Flamegas Companies, Inc., family business, 1973–76; organizations: Bettendorf Chamber of Commerce; National Federation of Independent Business; Davenport Elks; Moose; and Rotary; religion: Episcopal Church; family: married to the former Elisabeth Foxley; two children: Gallagher and Jenny; committees: Financial Services; International Relations; elected to the 95th Congress on November 2, 1976; reelected to each succeeding Congress.

Office Listings

http://www.house.gov/leach

2186 Rayburn House Office Building, Washington, DC 20515 .... (202) 225–6576
Administrative Assistant.—Bill Tate. FAX: 226–1278
Legislative Director.—Mary Andrus.
Office Manager.—Sarah Morgan.
214 Jefferson Street, Burlington, IA 52601 .... (319) 754–1106
129 12th Street, SE., Cedar Rapids, IA 52403 .... (319) 363–4773
125 South Dubuque Street, Iowa City, IA 52240 .... (319) 351–0789
105 East 3rd Street, Room 201, Ottumwa, IA 52501 .... (641) 684–4024

Counties: APPANOOSE, CEDAR, DAVIS, DES MOINES, HENRY, JEFFERSON, JOHNSON, LEE, LINN, LOUISA, MUSCATINE, VAN BUREN, WAPELLO, WASHINGTON, WAYNE. Population (2000), 585,241.

ZIP Codes: 50008, 50052, 50060, 50123, 50147, 50165, 50238, 52201–02, 52213–14, 52216, 52218–19, 52227–28, 52233, 52235, 52240–48, 52253, 52255, 52302, 52305–06, 52314, 52317, 52319–20, 52322–24, 52327–28, 52333, 52336–38, 52340–41, 52344, 52350, 52352–53, 52356, 52358–59, 52401–11, 52497–99, 52501, 52530–31, 52533, 52535–38, 52540, 52542, 52544, 52548–49, 52551, 52553–57, 52560, 52565–67, 52570–74, 52580–81, 52583–84, 52588, 52590, 52593–94, 52601, 52619–21, 52623–27, 52630–32, 52635, 52637–42, 52644–56, 52658–60, 52720–21, 52731, 52737–39, 52747, 52749, 52752, 52754–55, 52759–61, 52766, 52769, 52772, 52776, 52778

* * *

THIRD DISTRICT

LEONARD L. BOSWELL, Democrat, of Davis City, IA; born in Harrison County, MO, on January 10, 1934; education: graduated from Lamoni High School, 1952; B.A., Graceland College, Lamoni, IA, 1969; military service: lieutenant colonel, U.S. Army, 1956–76; awards: two

Distinguished Flying Crosses, two Bronze Stars, Soldier's Medal; Iowa State Senate, 1984–96; Iowa State Senate President, 1992–96; lay minister, RLDS Church; member: American Legion, Disabled American Veterans of Foreign Wars, Iowa Farm Bureau, Iowa Cattlemen's Association, Graceland College Board of Trustees; Farmer's Co-op Grain and Seed Board of Directors, 1979–93 (president for 13 years); married Darlene (Dody) Votava Boswell, 1955; three children: Cindy, Diana and Joe; committees: Agriculture; Transportation and Infrastructure; Permanent Select Committee on Intelligence; subcommittees: Aviation; General Farm Commodities and Risk Management; Livestock and Horticulture; Human Intelligence, Analysis and Counterintelligence; Railroads; Terrorism and Homeland Security; The Coalition (Blue Dogs); co-chair and member emeritus, Mississippi River Caucus; co-chair, Methamphetamine Caucus; elected to the 105th Congress; reelected to each succeeding Congress.

Office Listings

http://www.house.gov/boswell

1427 Longworth House Office Building, Washington, DC 20515 .... (202) 225–3806
Administrative Assistant.—E.H. (Ned) Michalek. FAX: 225–5608
Legislative Director / Communications Director.—Eric Witte.
Executive Assistant.—Sandy Carter.
Senior Legislative Assistant.—Jason Briggs.
300 East Locust Street, Suite 320, Des Moines, IA 50309 .... (515) 282–1909
District Director.—Jay Byers.

Counties: BENTON, GRUNDY, IOWA, JASPER, KEOKUK, LUCAS, MAHASKA, MARION, MONROE, POLK, POWESHIEK, TAMA. Population (2000), 585,305.

ZIP Codes: 50007, 50009, 50015, 50021, 50027–28, 50032, 50035, 50044, 50047, 50049, 50054, 50057, 50061–62, 50068, 50073, 50104, 50109, 50111–12, 50116, 50119, 50127, 50131, 50135–39, 50143, 50148, 50150–51, 50153, 50156–58, 50163, 50168–71, 50173, 50206–08, 50214, 50219, 50222, 50225–26, 50228, 50232, 50237–38, 50240, 50242–43, 50251–52, 50255–58, 50265–66, 50268, 50272, 50301–23, 50325, 50327–36, 50338–40, 50347, 50350, 50359–64, 50367–69, 50380–81, 50391–96, 50398, 50601, 50604, 50609, 50612–13, 50621, 50624, 50627, 50632, 50635, 50638, 50642–43, 50651–52, 50657, 50660, 50665, 50669, 50672–73, 50675, 50680, 50936, 50940, 50947, 50950, 50980–81, 52203–04, 52206, 52208–09, 52211, 52213, 52215, 52217, 52220–22, 52224–25, 52228–29, 52231–32, 52236, 52248–49, 52251, 52257, 52301, 52307–08, 52313, 52315–16, 52318, 52322, 52324–25, 52332, 52334–35, 52339, 52342, 52345–49, 52351, 52354–55, 52361, 52404, 52531, 52534, 52543, 52550, 52552, 52561–63, 52568–69, 52576–77, 52585–86, 52591, 52595

* * *

FOURTH DISTRICT

TOM LATHAM, Republican, of Alexander, IA; born July 14, 1948, in Hampton, IA; education: attended Alexander Community School; graduated Cal (Latimer) Community College, 1966; attended Wartburg College, 1966–67; Iowa State University, 1976–70; agriculture business major; employment: marketing representative, independent insurance agent, bank teller and bookkeeper; member and past president, Nazareth Lutheran Church; past chairman, Franklin County Extension Council; secretary, Republican Party of Iowa; 5th District representative, Republican State Central Committee; co-chairman, Franklin County Republican Central Committee; Iowa delegation whip; member: 1992 Republican National Convention, Iowa Farm Bureau Federation, Iowa Soybean Association, American Seed Trade Association, Iowa Corn Growers Association, Iowa Seed Association, Agribusiness Association of Iowa, I.S.U. Extension Citizens Advisory Council; married: Mary Katherine (Kathy) Latham, 1975; children: Justin, Jennifer, and Jill; elected to the 104th Congress; reelected to each succeeding Congress.

Office Listings

http://www.house.gov/latham

440 Cannon House Office Building, Washington, DC 20515 .... (202) 225–5476
Chief of Staff.—Michael R. Gruber. FAX: 225–3301
Press Secretary.—James D. Carstensen.
Legislative Director.—Kevin Berents.
Scheduler.—Kathryn Kurlander.
213 North Duff Avenue, Suite 1, Ames, IA 50010 .... (515) 232–2885
District Director.—Clarke Scanlon.
812 Highway 18 East, P.O. Box 532, Clear Lake, IA 50428 .... (641) 357–5225
Regional Representative.—Lois Clark.
1426 Central Avenue, Suite A, Fort Dodge, IA 50501 .... (515) 573–2738
Staff Assistant.—Jim Oberhelman.

Counties: ALLAMAKEE, BOONE, CALHOUN, CERRO GORDO, CHICKASAW, DALLAS, EMMET, FLOYD, FRANKLIN, GREENE, HAMILTON, HANCOCK, HARDIN, HOWARD, HUMBOLDT, KOSSUTH, MADISON, MARSHALL, MITCHELL, PALO ALTO, POCAHONTAS, STORY, WARREN, WEBSTER, WINNEBAGO, WINNESHIEK, WORTH, WRIGHT. Population (2000), 585,305.

ZIP Codes: 50001, 50003, 50005–06, 50010–14, 50028, 50031, 50033–34, 50036–41, 50046–47, 50050–51, 50055–56, 50058–59, 50061, 50063–64, 50066, 50069–72, 50075, 50078, 50101–02, 50105–07, 50109, 50118, 50120, 50122, 50124–26, 50129–30, 50132, 50134, 50139, 50141–42, 50145–46, 50148–49, 50151–52, 50154–56, 50158, 50160–62, 50166–67, 50201, 50206, 50210–13, 50217–18, 50220, 50222–23, 50225, 50227, 50229–31, 50233–36, 50239–41, 50244, 50246–49, 50252, 50257–59, 50261, 50263, 50266, 50269, 50271, 50273, 50276, 50278, 50320, 50323, 50325, 50401–02, 50420–21, 50423–24, 50426–28, 50430–36, 50438–41, 50444, 50446–61, 50464–73, 50475–84, 50501, 50510–11, 50514–33, 50536, 50538–46, 50548, 50551–52, 50554, 50556–63, 50566, 50568–71, 50573–75, 50577–79, 50581–83, 50586, 50590–91, 50593–95, 50597–99, 50601, 50603, 50605, 50609, 50616, 50619–21, 50625, 50627–28, 50630, 50632–33, 50635–36, 50645, 50653, 50658–59, 50661, 50672, 50674, 50680, 51334, 51342, 51344, 51358, 51364–65, 51433, 51443, 51449, 51453, 51462, 51510, 52101, 52132–34, 52136, 52140, 52144, 52146, 52149, 52151, 52154–56, 52159–63, 52165, 52168, 52170–72

* * *

FIFTH DISTRICT

STEVE KING, Republican, of Odebolt, IA; born on May 28, 1949, in Storm Lake, IA; education: graduated, Denison Community High School; attended Northwest Missouri State University; profession: agri-businessman; owner and operator of King Construction Company; public service: Iowa State Senate, 1996–2002; religion: Catholic; family: married to Marilyn; children: David, Michael, and Jeff; elected to the 108th Congress on November 5, 2002.

Office Listings

http://www.house.gov/steveking

1432 Longworth House Office Building, Washington, DC 20515	(202) 225–4426
Chief of Staff.—Chuck Laudner.	FAX: 225–3193
Deputy Chief of Staff.—Brenna Findley.	
Legislative Director.—Paula Steiner.	
607 Lake Avenue, Storm Lake, IA 50588	(712) 732–4197
526 Nebraska Street, Sioux City, IA 51101	(712) 224–4692
40 Pearl Street, Council Bluffs, IA 51503	(712) 325–1404

Counties: Adair, Adams, Audubon, Buena Vista, Carroll, Cass, Cherokee, Clarke, Clay, Crawford, Decatur, Dickinson, Fremont, Guthrie, Harrison, Ida, Lyon, Mills, Monona, Montgomery, O'Brien, Osceola, Page, Plymouth, Pottawattamie, Ringgold, Sac, Shelby, Sioux, Taylor, Union, Woodbury. Population (2000), 584,967.

ZIP Codes: 50002, 50020, 50022, 50025–26, 50029, 50042, 50048, 50058, 50065, 50067, 50070, 50074, 50076, 50103, 50108, 50110, 50115, 50117, 50119, 50123, 50128, 50133, 50140, 50144, 50146, 50149, 50151, 50155, 50164, 50174, 50210, 50213, 50216, 50222, 50233, 50250, 50254, 50257, 50262, 50264, 50273–77, 50510, 50535, 50565, 50567–68, 50576, 50583, 50585, 50588, 50592, 50801, 50830–31, 50833, 50835–37, 50839–43, 50845–49, 50851, 50853–54, 50857–64, 51001–12, 51014–16, 51018–20, 51022–31, 51033–41, 51044–56, 51058–63, 51101–06, 51108–09, 51111, 51201, 51230–32, 51234–35, 51237–50, 51301, 51331, 51333, 51338, 51340–41, 51343, 51345–47, 51350–51, 51354–55, 51357, 51360, 51363–64, 51366, 51401, 51430–33, 51436, 51439–52, 51454–55, 51458–61, 51463, 51465–67, 51501–03, 51510, 51520–21, 51523, 51525–37, 51540–46, 51548–49, 51551–66, 51570–73, 51575–79, 51591, 51593, 51601–03, 51630–32, 51636–40, 51645–54, 51656

KANSAS

(Population 2000, 2,688,418)

SENATORS

SAM BROWNBACK, Republican, of Topeka, KS; born in Garrett, KS, on September 12, 1956; graduated from Prairie View High School, 1974; B.S., with honors, Kansas State University, Manhattan, KS, 1978; J.D., University of Kansas, Lawrence, 1982; Kansas Bar; attorney, broadcaster, teacher; U.S. House of Representatives, 1994–96; State Secretary of Agriculture, 1986–93; White House Fellow, Office of the U.S. Trade Representative, 1990–91; member: Topeka Fellowship Council, Kansas Bar Association, Kansas State University and Kansas University alumni associations; married: the former Mary Stauffer, 1982; children: Abby, Andy, Liz, Mark and Jenna; committees: Commerce, Science, and Transportation; Foreign Relations; Joint Economic Committee; elected to the U.S. Senate in November, 1996, to fill the remainder of the vacancy caused by the resignation of Senator Bob Dole; reelected to each succeeding Senate term.

Office Listings

http://brownback.senate.gov

303 Hart Senate Office Building, Washington, DC 20510 .... (202) 224–6521
Chief of Staff.—David Kensinger. FAX: 228–1265
Scheduler.—Tina Hervey.
Communications Director.—Eric Hotmire.
612 South Kansas, Topeka, KS 66603 .... (785) 233–2503
Kansas Scheduler.—Denise Coatney.
1001–C North Broadway, Pittsburg, KS 66762 .... (316) 231–6040
Grant Director.—Anne Emerson.
225 North Market, Suite 120, Wichita, KS 67202 .... (620) 264–8066
State Director.—Chuck Alderson.
11111 West 95th, Suite 245, Overland Park, KS 66214 .... (913) 492–6378
Casework Director.—Shawn Cowing.
811 N. Main, Suite A, Garden City, KS 67846 .... (620) 275–1124
Regional Director.—Dennis Mesa.

* * *

PAT ROBERTS, Republican, of Dodge City, KS; born in Topeka, KS, April 20, 1936; graduated, Holton High School, Holton, KS, 1954; B.S., journalism, Kansas State University, Manhattan, KS, 1958; captain, U.S. Marine Corps, 1958–62; editor and reporter, Arizona newspapers, 1962–67; aide to Senator Frank Carlson, 1967–68; aide to Representative Keith Sebelius, 1969–80; U.S. House of Representatives, 1980–96; founding member: bipartisan Caucus on Unfunded Mandates, House Rural Health Care Coalition; shepherded the 1996 Freedom to Farm Act through the House and Senate; awards: honorary American Farmer, Future Farmers of America; 1993 Wheat Man of the Year, Kansas Association of Wheat Growers; Golden Carrot Award, Public Voice; Golden Bulldog Award, Watchdogs of the Treasury; numerous Guardian of Small Business awards, National Federation of Independent Business; 1995 Dwight D. Eisenhower Medal, Eisenhower Exchange Fellowship; 2001 U.S. Marine Corps Semper Fidelis Award; married: the former Franki Fann, 1969; children: David, Ashleigh, and Anne-Wesley; committees: Agriculture, Nutrition, and Forestry; Armed Services; Select Committee on Ethics; chairman, Select Committee on Intelligence; elected to the U.S. Senate in November, 1996; reelected to each succeeding Senate term.

Office Listings

http://roberts.senate.gov

109 Hart Senate Office Building, Washington, DC 20510 .... (202) 224–4774
Chief of Staff.—Jackie Cottrell. FAX: 224–3514
Legislative Director.—Keith Yehle.
Scheduler.—Maggie Ward.
100 Military Plaza, P.O. Box 550, Dodge City, KS 67801 .... (620) 227–2244
District Director.—Debbie Pugh.
155 North Market Street, Suite 120, Wichita, KS 67202 .... (316) 263–0416
District Director.—Karin Wisdom.
Frank Carlson Federal Building, 444 SE Quincy, Room 392, Topeka, KS 66683 .... (785) 295–2745
District Director.—Gilda Lintz.
11900 College Boulevard, Overland Park, KS 66210 .... (913) 451–9343
District Director.—Ramona Corbin.

REPRESENTATIVES

FIRST DISTRICT

JERRY MORAN, Republican, of Hays, KS; born in Great Bend, KS, May 29, 1954; B.S., economics, 1976, and J.D., 1981, University of Kansas; M.B.A. candidate, Fort Hays State University; partner, Jeter and Moran, Attorneys at Law, Hays, KS; former bank officer and university instructor; represented 37th District in Kansas Senate, 1989–97, serving as vice president in 1993–95 and majority leader in 1995–97; Special Assistant Attorney General, State of Kansas, 1982–85; Deputy Attorney, Rooks County, 1987–95; governor, board of governors, University of Kansas School of Law, 1990 (vice president, 1993–94; president, 1994–95); member: board of directors, Kansas Chamber of Commerce and Industry, 1996–97; Hays Chamber of Commerce; Northwest Kansas and Ellis County bar associations; Phi Alpha Delta legal fraternity; Rotary Club; Lions International; board of trustees, Fort Hays State University Endowment Association; founding co-chair, Congressional Rural Caucus; co-chair, Rural Health Care Coalition; commissioner, Dwight D. Eisenhower Memorial Commission; married: Robba Moran; children: Kelsey and Alex; committees: Agriculture; Transportation and Infrastructure; Veterans' Affairs; subcommittees: chairman, General Farm Commodities and Risk Management; vice-chairman, Health; elected to the 105th Congress; reelected to each succeeding Congress.

Office Listings

http://www.house.gov/moranks01

1519 Longworth House Office Building, Washington, DC 20515 .... (202) 225–2715
Chief of Staff.—Jon Hixson. FAX: 225–5124
Legislative Director.—Kim Rullman.
Press Secretary.—Travis Murphy.
Office Manager—Lindsay McPhail.
1200 Main Street, Suite 402, P.O. Box 249, Hays KS 67601–0249 .... (785) 628–6401
District Representatives: Eric Depperschmidt, Lisa Dethloff.
1 North Main, Suite 525, Hutchinson, KS 67504–1128 .... (620) 665–6138
District Director.—Kirk Johnson.

Counties: BARBER, BARTON, CHASE, CHEYENNE, CLARK, CLAY, CLOUD, COMANCHE, DECATUR, DICKINSON, EDWARDS, ELLIS, ELLSWORTH, FINNEY, FORD, GEARY (part), GOVE, GRAHAM, GRANT, GRAY, GREELEY, GREENWOOD (part), HAMILTON, HASKELL, HODGEMAN, JEWELL, KEARNY, KIOWA, LANE, LINCOLN, LOGAN, LYON, MCPHERSON, MARION (part), MARSHALL, MEADE, MITCHELL, MORRIS, MORTON, NEMAHA (part), NESS, NORTON, OSBORNE, OTTAWA, PAWNEE, PHILLIPS, PRATT, RAWLINS, RENO, REPUBLIC, RICE, ROOKS, RUSH, RUSSELL, SALINE, SCOTT, SEWARD, SHERIDAN, SHERMAN, SMITH, STAFFORD, STANTON, STEVENS, THOMAS, TREGO, WABAUNSEE, WALLACE, WASHINGTON, WICHITA. Population (2000), 672,105.

ZIP Codes: 66401, 66403–04, 66406–08, 66411–13, 66423, 66427, 66431, 66438, 66441, 66501–02, 66507–08, 66514, 66518, 66523, 66526, 66534, 66536, 66538, 66541, 66544, 66547–48, 66610, 66614–15, 66801, 66830, 66833–35, 66838, 66840, 66843, 66845–46, 66849–51, 66853–54, 66858–62, 66864–66, 66868–70, 66872–73, 66901, 66930, 66932–33, 66935–46, 66948–49, 66951–53, 66955–56, 66958–64, 66966–68, 66970, 67009, 67020–21, 67028–29, 67035, 67053–54, 67057, 67059, 67061–63, 67065–66, 67068, 67070, 67073, 67104, 67107–09, 67112, 67114, 67124, 67127, 67134, 67138, 67143, 67151, 67155, 67335, 67401–02, 67410, 67416–18, 67420, 67422–23, 67425, 67427–28, 67430–32, 67436–39, 67441–52, 67454–60, 67464, 67466–68, 67470, 67473–76, 67478, 67480–85, 67487, 67490–92, 67501–02, 67504–05, 67510–16, 67518–26, 67529–30, 67543–48, 67550, 67552–54, 67556–57, 67559–61, 67563–68, 67570, 67572–76, 67578–79, 67581, 67583–85, 67601, 67621–23, 67625–29, 67631–32, 67634–35, 67637–40, 67642–51, 67653–61, 67663–65, 67667, 67669, 67671–75, 67701, 67730–41, 67743–45, 67748–49, 67751–53, 67756–58, 67761–62, 67764, 67801, 67831, 67834–42, 67844, 67846, 67849–51, 67853–55, 67857, 67859–65, 67867, 67869–71, 67876–80, 67882, 67901, 67905, 67950–54

* * *

SECOND DISTRICT

JIM RYUN, Republican, of Topeka, KS; born on April 29, 1947, in Wichita, KS; graduated, Wichita East High School, 1965; B.S., photojournalism, University of Kansas; product development consultant, president of Jim Ryun Sports, Inc., professional photographer, and author of two books; represented the U.S. in three consecutive Olympics (1964, 1968, 1972): silver medal in the 1500-meter race, 1968, and World Record Holder in the 880-yard, one-mile, and 1500-meter races; awards: Sports Illustrated Sportsman of the Year, 1966; AAU Sullivan Award; Jaycees of America Top Ten Young Men of the United States, 1968; married: Anne Snider Ryun, 1969; children: Heather, Ned, Drew, and Catharine; elected to the 105th Congress; reelected to each succeeding Congress.

Office Listings

http://www.house.gov/ryun

2433 Rayburn House Office Building, Washington, DC 20515 .... (202) 225–6601
Chief of Staff.—Mark Kelly. FAX: 225–7986
Press Secretary.—Chad Hayward.
Legislative Director.—Jim Richardson.

800 SW Jackson Street, Suite 100, Topeka, KS 66612 .... (785) 232–4500
District Director.—Michelle Butler.
The Stilwell Hotel, 701 North Broadway, Pittsburg, KS 66762 .... (620) 232–6100
Regional Representative.—Jim Allen.

Counties: ALLEN, ANDERSON, ATCHISON, BOURBON, BROWN, CHEROKEE, COFFEY, CRAWFORD, DONIPHAN, DOUGLAS (part), FRANKLIN, GEARY, JACKSON, JEFFERSON, LABETE, LEAVENWORTH, LINN, MIAMI, NEMAHA (part), NEOSHO, OSAGE, POTTAWATOMIE, RILEY, SHAWNEE, WILSON, WOODSON. Population (2000), 672,102.

ZIP Codes: 66002, 66006–08, 66010, 66012–17, 66020–21, 66023–27, 66032–33, 66035–36, 66039–50, 66052–54, 66056, 66058, 66060, 66064, 66066–67, 66070–73, 66075–80, 66083, 66086–88, 66090–91, 66093–95, 66097, 66109, 66112, 66401–04, 66407, 66409, 66413–20, 66422, 66424–29, 66431–32, 66434, 66436, 66439–40, 66442, 66449, 66451, 66502–03, 66505–06, 66509–10, 66512, 66515–17, 66520–24, 66527–28, 66531–40, 66542–44, 66546–50, 66552, 66554, 66601, 66603–12, 66614–22, 66624–26, 66628–29, 66636–37, 66642, 66647, 66652–53, 66667, 66675, 66683, 66692, 66699, 66701, 66710–14, 66716–17, 66720, 66724–25, 66728, 66732–36, 66738–43, 66746, 66748–49, 66751, 66753–63, 66767, 66769–73, 66775–83, 66834, 66839, 66849, 66852, 66854, 66856–57, 66864, 66868, 66870–71, 66933, 67047, 67330, 67332, 67335–37, 67341–42, 67351, 67354, 67356–57

* * *

THIRD DISTRICT

DENNIS MOORE, Democrat, of Lenexa, KS; born on November 8, 1945, in Anthony, KS; education: Jefferson Elementary School, and Charles Curtis Intermediate School, Wichita, KS; B.A., University of Kansas, 1967; J.D., Washburn University of Law, 1970; profession: attorney; admitted to Kansas Bar, 1970, first practiced in Topeka, KS; Assistant Attorney General of Kansas, 1971–73; Johnson County District Attorney, 1977–89; Johnson County Community College Board of Trustees, 1993–99; member, American Legion; married: Stephene Moore; seven children: Todd, Scott, Andrew, Felicia Barge, Valerie Rock, Nathan Hansen, and Adam Hansen; military: U.S. Army, 2nd Lieutenant, 1970; U.S. Army Reserves, Captain, 1970–73; committees: Budget; Financial Services; Science; subcommittees: Capital Markets, Insurance and Government Sponsored Enterprises; Financial Institutions and Consumer Credit; Oversight and Investigations; Research; Space and Aeronautics; elected to the 106th Congress; reelected to each succeeding Congress.

Office Listings

http://www.house.gov/moore

431 Cannon House Office Building, Washington, DC 20515 .... (202) 225–2865
Chief of Staff.—Howard Bauleke. FAX: 225–2807
Scheduler.—Andrew Funk.
Communications Director.—Christie Appelhanz.
8417 Santa Fe Drive, Room 101, Overland Park, KS 66212 .... (913) 383–2013
District Director.—Kaye Cleaver.
500 State Avenue, Room 176, Kansas City, KS 66101 .... (913) 621–0832
647 Massachusetts Street, #212, Lawrence, KS 66044 .... (785) 842–9313
Constituent Services Director.—Becky Fast.

Counties: DOUGLAS (part), JOHNSON, WYANDOTTE. Population (2000), 672,124.

ZIP Codes: 66006–07, 66012–13, 66018–19, 66026, 66030–31, 66035–36, 66044–47, 66049–51, 66053, 66061–64, 66071, 66077, 66083, 66085, 66092, 66101–06, 66109–13, 66115, 66117–19, 66160, 66201–27, 66250–51, 66276, 66282–83, 66285–86

* * *

FOURTH DISTRICT

TODD TIAHRT, Republican, of Goddard, KS; born in Vermillion, SD, June 15, 1951; attended South Dakota School of Mines and Technology; B.A., Evangel College, Springfield, MO, 1975; M.B.A., Southwest Missouri State, 1989; proposal manager, The Boeing Company; married the former Vicki Holland, 1976; three children: Jessica, John, and Luke; member, Appropriations Committee; elected to the 104th Congress; reelected to each succeeding Congress.

Office Listings

http://www.house.gov/tiahrt

2441 Rayburn House Office Building, Washington, DC 20515 .... (202) 225–6216
Administrative Assistant.—Jeff Kahrs. FAX: 225–3489
Legislative Director.—Amy Claire Brusch.
Scheduler.—Melissa James.
Communications Director.—Chuck Knapp.
155 North Market Street, Suite 400, Wichita, KS 67202 .... (316) 262–8992
District Director.—Robert Noland.

Counties: BUTLER, CHAUTAUQUA, COWLEY, ELK, GRENWOOD (part), HARPER, HARVEY, KINGMAN, MONTGOMERY, SEDGWICK, SUMNER. Population (2000), 672,101.

ZIP Codes: 66840, 66842, 66853, 66863, 66866, 66870, 67001–05, 67008–10, 67012–13, 67016–20, 67022–26, 67030–31, 67035–39, 67041–42, 67045, 67047, 67049–52, 67055–56, 67058, 67060–62, 67067–68, 67070, 67072, 67074, 67101, 67103, 67105–08, 67110–12, 67114, 67117–20, 67122–23, 67131–33, 67135, 67137–38, 67140, 67142, 67144, 67146–47, 67149–52, 67154, 67156, 67159, 67201–21, 67226, 67230, 67235, 67260, 67275–78, 67301, 67333–35, 67337, 67340, 67344–47, 67349, 67351–53, 67355, 67360–61, 67363–64, 67522, 67543

KENTUCKY

(Population 2000, 4,041,769)

SENATORS

MITCH McCONNELL, Republican, of Louisville, KY; born in Colbert County, AL, on February 20, 1942; education: graduated Manual High School, Louisville, 1960, president of the student body; B.A. with honors, University of Louisville, 1964, president of the student council, president of the student body of the College of Arts and Sciences; J.D., University of Kentucky Law School, 1967, president of student bar association, outstanding oral advocate; employment: attorney, admitted to the Kentucky bar, 1967; chief legislative assistant to U.S. Senator Marlow Cook, 1968–70; Deputy Assistant U.S. Attorney General, 1974–75; Judge/Executive of Jefferson County, KY, 1978–84; chairman, National Republican Senatorial Committee, 1997–2000; chairman, Joint Congressional Committee on Inaugural Ceremonies, 1999–2001; Senate Majority Whip, 2002–present; married to Elaine Chao on February 6, 1993; children: Elly, Claire, and Porter; committees: Agriculture, Nutrition, and Forestry; Appropriations; Rules and Administration; subcommittees: chairman, Foreign Operations; elected to the U.S. Senate on November 6, 1984; reelected to each succeeding Senate term.

Office Listings

http://mcconnell.senate.gov

361A Russell Senate Office Building, Washington, DC 20510 .... (202) 224–2541
Chief of Staff.—William H. Piper. FAX: 224–2499
Scheduler.—Peggy Morgan.
Press Secretary.—Robert Steurer.
601 West Broadway, Suite 630, Louisville, KY 40202 .... (502) 582–6304
State Director.—Larry Cox.
1885 Dixie Highway, Suite 345, Fort Wright, KY 41011 .... (606) 578–0188
300 South Main Street, Suite 310, London, KY 40740 .... (606) 864–2026
Professional Arts Building, Suite 100, 2320 Broadway, Paducah, KY 42001 .... (502) 442–4554
771 Corporate Drive, Suite 530, Lexington, KY 40507 .... (606) 224–8286
Federal Building, Room 102, 241 Main Street, Bowling Green, KY 42101 .... (502) 781–1673

* * *

JIM BUNNING, Republican, of Southgate, KY; born in Southgate, October 23, 1931; education: graduated, St. Xavier High School, Cincinnati, OH, 1949; B.S., Xavier University, Cincinnati, OH, 1953; employment: professional baseball player, Hall of Fame; investment broker and agent; president, Jim Bunning Agency, Inc.; member of Kentucky State Senate (minority floor leader), 1979–83; member: Ft. Thomas City Council, 1977–79; appointed member, Ohio, Kentucky, and Indiana Regional Council of Governments, Cincinnati, OH; National Committeeman, Republican National Committee, 1983–92; appointed member, President's National Advisory Board on International Education Programs, 1984–88; member: board of directors of Kentucky Special Olympics, Ft. Thomas (KY) Lions Club, Brighton Street Center Community Action Group; married: the former Mary Catherine Theis, 1952; children: Barbara, Jim, Joan, Cathy, Bill, Bridgett, Mark, David and Amy; elected to the 100th Congress, November 4, 1986; reelected to each succeeding Congress; elected to the U.S. Senate in November, 1998; committees: Banking, Housing, and Urban Affairs; Budget; Energy and Natural Resources; Finance; Veterans' Affairs.

Office Listings

http://bunning.senate.gov

316 Hart Senate Office Building, Washington, DC 20515 .... (202) 224–4343
Personnel Assistant/Scheduler.—Amy Douglas. FAX: 228–1373
Chief of Staff.—Jon Deuser.
Legislative Director.—David Young.
Press Secretary.—Michael Reynard.
1717 Dixie Highway, Suite 220, Fort Wright, KY 41011 .... (859) 341–2602
State Director.—Debbie McKinney.
The Federal Building, 423 Frederica Street, Room 305, Owensboro, KY 42301 ..... (270) 689–9085
717 Corporate Drive, Lexington, KY 40503 .... (606) 219–2239
1100 South Main Street, Suite 12, Hopkinsville, KY 42240 .... (270) 885–1212

REPRESENTATIVES

FIRST DISTRICT

ED WHITFIELD, Republican, of Hopkinsville, KY; born in Hopkinsville, May 25, 1943; education: graduated, Madisonville High School, Madisonville, KY; B.S., University of Kentucky, Lexington, 1965; J.D., University of Kentucky, 1969; attended American University's Wesley Theological Seminary, Washington, DC; military service: first lieutenant, U.S. Army Reserves, 1967–73; employment: attorney, private practice, 1970–79; vice president, CSX Corporation, 1979–90; admitted to bar: Kentucky, 1970, and Florida, 1993; employment: began practice in 1970 in Hopkinsville, KY; member, Kentucky House, 1973, one term; married: Constance Harriman Whitfield; children: Kate; elected to the 104th Congress; reelected to each succeeding Congress.

Office Listings

301 Cannon House Office Building, Washington, DC 20515 .... (202) 225–3115
Chief of Staff.—Karen Long. FAX: 225–3547
Scheduler/Office Manager.—Melissa Joiner.
Legislative Director.—Jason Van Pelt.
1403 South Main Street, Hopkinsville, KY 42240 .... (270) 885–8079
District Director.—Michael Pape.
P.O. Box 717, Monroe County Courthouse, Tompkinsville, KY 42167 .... (270) 487–9509
Field Representative.—Sandy Simpson.
222 First Street, Suite 206A, Henderson, KY 42420 .... (270) 826–4180
Field Representative.—Ed West.
100 Fountain Avenue, Room 104, Paducah, KY 42001 .... (270) 442–6901
Field Representative.—David Mast.

Counties: ADAIR, ALLEN, BALLARD, BUTLER, CALDWELL, CALLOWAY, CARLISLE, CASEY, CHRISTIAN, CLINTON, CRITTENDEN, CUMBERLAND, FULTON, GRAVES, HENDERSON, HICKMAN, HOPKINS, LINCOLN (part), LIVINGSTON, LOGAN, LYON, MARSHALL, MCCRACKEN, MCLEAN, METCALF, MONROE, MUHLENBERG, OHIO (part), RUSSELL, SIMPSON, TODD, TRIGG, UNION, WEBSTER. Population (2000), 673,629.

ZIP Codes: 40009, 40328, 40437, 40442, 40448, 40464, 40484, 40489, 42001–03, 42020–25, 42027–29, 42031–33, 42035–41, 42044–45, 42047–51, 42053–56, 42058, 42060–61, 42063–64, 42066, 42069–71, 42076, 42078–79, 42081–88, 42101, 42104, 42120, 42122–24, 42129, 42133–35, 42140–41, 42150–51, 42153–54, 42164, 42166–67, 42170, 42201–04, 42206, 42209–211, 42214–17, 42219–21, 42223, 42232, 42234, 42236, 42240–41, 42251–52, 42254, 42256, 42261–62, 42265–67, 42273–74, 42276, 42280, 42283, 42286–88, 42301, 42320–28, 42330, 42332–34, 42337, 42339, 42344–45, 42347, 42349–50, 42352, 42354, 42356, 42367–69, 42371–72, 42374–76, 42402–04, 42406, 42408–11, 42413, 42419–20, 42431, 42436–37, 42440–42, 42444–45, 42450–53, 42455–64, 42516, 42528, 42539, 42541, 42544, 42565–67, 42602–03, 42629, 42642, 42711, 42715, 42717, 42720–21, 42728, 42731, 42733, 42735, 42740–43, 42746, 42749, 42753, 42759, 42786

* * *

SECOND DISTRICT

RON LEWIS, Republican, of Cecilia, KY; born in South Shore, KY, September 14, 1946; graduated, McKell High School, 1964; B.A., University of Kentucky, 1969; M.A., higher education, Morehead State University, 1981; U.S. Navy Officer Candidate School, 1972; laborer, Morehead State, Armco Steel Corporation; Kentucky Highway Department, Eastern State Hospital; sales for Ashland Oil; teacher, Watterson College, 1980; minister, White Mills Baptist Church; member, Elizabethtown Chamber of Commerce; past president, Hardin and Larue County jail ministry; member, Serverus Valley Ministerial Association; honored for his voting record by League of Private Property Rights, Council for Citizens Against Government Waste, National Federation of Independent Business; married: the former Kayi Gambill, 1966; children: Ronald Brent and Allison Faye; committees: Government Reform; Ways and Means; subcommittees: Human Resources; National Security, Emerging Threats, and International Relations; Select Revenue Measures; Social Security; elected to the 104th Congress; reelected to each succeeding Congress.

Office Listings

http://www.house.gov/ronlewis

2418 Rayburn House Office Building, Washington, DC 20515 .... (202) 225–3501
Chief of Staff.—Helen Devlin.
Legislative Director.—Eric Bergren.
Press Secretary.—Kathy Reding.
Scheduler.—Kelley Ayers.
1690 Ring Road, Suite 260, Elizabethtown, KY 42701 .... (270) 765–4360
District Administrator.—Keith Rogers.
Warren Co. Justice Ctr, 1001 Center St., Suite 300, Bowling Green, KY 42101 ..... (270) 842–9896
1100 Walnut Street, Suite P15 B, Owensboro, KY 42301 .... (270) 688–8858

Counties: Barren, Breckinridge, Bullitt, Daviess, Edmonson, Grayson, Green, Hancock, Hardin, Hart, Jefferson (part), Larue, Marion, Meade, Nelson, Ohio (part), Shelby, Spencer, Taylor, Warren, Washington. Population (2000), 673,244.

ZIP Codes: 40003–04, 40008–09, 40012–13, 40018–20, 40022–23, 40033, 40037, 40040, 40046–49, 40051–52, 40057, 40060–63, 40065–69, 40071, 40076, 40078, 40104, 40107–11, 40115, 40117–19, 40121, 40129, 40140, 40142–46, 40150, 40152–53, 40155, 40157, 40159–62, 40164–65, 40170–71, 40175–78, 40219, 40229, 40245, 40272, 40291, 40299, 40328, 40330, 40342, 40448, 40468, 40601, 42101–04, 42122–23, 42127–31, 42133, 42141–42, 42152, 42156–57, 42159–60, 42163, 42166, 42170–71, 42201, 42206–07, 42210, 42251, 42257, 42259, 42270, 42274–75, 42283, 42285, 42301–04, 42320, 42327, 42333–34, 42338, 42343, 42347–49, 42351–52, 42355–56, 42361, 42364, 42366, 42368, 42370, 42375–78, 42701–02, 42712–13, 42716, 42718–19, 42721–22, 42724, 42726, 42728–29, 42732–33, 42740, 42743, 42746, 42748–49, 42754–55, 42757–58, 42762, 42764–65, 42776, 42782–84, 42788

* * *

THIRD DISTRICT

ANNE M. NORTHUP, Republican, of Louisville, KY; born on January 22, 1948, in Louisville; education: graduated from Sacred Heart Academy, Louisville, 1966; graduated from St. Mary's College, Notre Dame, IN, 1970; Kentucky State Legislature, 1987–96; legislative appointments: Co-Chair congressional Coalition on Adoption; Founder and co-chair of the House Reading Caucus; 1998 Chairwoman of Speaker's Task Force on Education; 1998 Speaker's Drug Free Task Force; member: House Committee on Appropriations, Health Care on the Horizon Caucus; Public Pension Reform Caucus; Housing Opportunity Caucus; Education Caucus; Caucus on Disabilities; Diabetes Caucus; House Cancer Awareness Working Group; awards: 2000 Legislator of the Year for the Association of the Equipment Distributors; 2000 Chamber of Commerce Spirit of Enterprise Award; 2000 Watchdog of the Treasury Bulldog Award; 2000 Citizens for a Sound Economy Jefferson Award; 1999 Southern Economic Development Council Honor Roll of Legislative Achievement in Economic Development; the NFIB Guardian of Small Business Award; 2000 Citizen of the Year Award; Optimist Club of Louisville 2000 Literacy Leadership Award; 2000 Small Business Advocate; Hero of the Taxpayer 2000; 2000 Housing Hero Award; 2000 Community Healthcare Champion Award; Friend of the Farm Bureau 2000; member, Holy Spirit Catholic Church; Greater Louisville, Inc.; Rotary Club of Louisville; Leadership Louisville; Metropolitan Republican Women's Club; National Order of Women Legislators; Ladies Auxiliary to the VFW; married: Robert Wood Northup, 1969; children: David, Katie, Joshua, Kevin, Erin, Mark; elected to the 105th Congress; reelected to each succeeding Congress.

Office Listings

http://www.house.gov/northup

1004 Longworth House Office Building, Washington, DC 20515 .... (202) 225–5401
Chief of Staff.—Terry Carmack. FAX: 225–5776
Legislative Director.—Clinton Blair.
Press Secretary.—Jenn Mascott.
Scheduler.—Amanda Haynes.
600 Martin Luther King, Jr. Place, Suite 216, Louisville, KY 40202 .... (502) 582–5129
District Director.—Sherri Craig.

Counties: Jefferson County. Population (2000), 674,032.

ZIP Codes: 40018, 40023, 40025, 40027, 40041, 40059, 40109, 40118, 40201–25, 40228–29, 40231–33, 40241–43, 40245, 40250–53, 40255–59, 40261, 40266, 40268–70, 40272, 40280–83, 40285, 40287, 40289–99

* * *

FOURTH DISTRICT

KEN LUCAS, Democrat, of Boone County, KY; born in Kenton County, KY, August 22, 1933; education: B.S., in Commerce, University of Kentucky, 1955; M.B.A., Xavier University, 1970; military service: pilot, U.S. Air Force, 1955–57; Major, Air National Guard, 1957–67; profession: financial planner, Sagemark Consulting of Lincoln Financial (formerly CIGNA); former president and executive committee chairman, Boone State Bank; director, Fifth Third Bank; director, The Drees Company; president, Florence Christian Services, Inc.; regent emeritus, Northern Kentucky University; elder, Florence Christian Church; member, St. Luke Hospital Foundation Board; former chairman, Northern Kentucky Chamber of Commerce; former board member, Kentucky State Chamber of Commerce; former NKY chairman, Fine Arts Fund of Greater Cincinnati; public service: Florence, KY, City Council, 1967–74; Boone County, KY, Commissioner, 1974–82; Boone County, KY, Judge-Executive, 1992–98; married: Mary K. Lucas, 1961; children: Lance, Shannon, Kendall, Trent, and Tiffany; committees: Agriculture; Budget; elected to the 106th Congress; reelected to each succeeding Congress.

Office Listings

http://www.house.gov/kenlucas

1205 Longworth House Office Building, Washington, DC 20515 .... (202) 225–3465
Chief of Staff.—Cheryl Brownell. FAX: 225–0003
Scheduler / Staff Assistant.—Kathryn Ray.
Legislative Director.—Colleen Monahan Smith.
Senior Legislative Assistant / Press Secretary.—Joe Clabes.
277 Buttermilk Pike, Fort Mitchell, KY 41017 .... (859) 426–0080
District Director.—Angie Cain.
1405 Greenup Avenue, Suite 236, Ashland, KY 41101 .... (606) 324–9898
Assistant Constituent Services Director.—Marilyn Mason.

Counties: BATH (part), BOONE, BOYD, BRACKEN, CAMPBELL, CARROLL, CARTER, ELLIOTT, FLEMING, GALLATIN, GRANT, GREENUP, HARRISON, HENRY, KENTON, LEWIS, MASON, NICHOLAS, OLDHAM, OWEN, PENDLETON, ROBERTSON, SCOTT (part), TRIMBLE. Population (2000), 673,588.

ZIP Codes: 40006–07, 40010–11, 40014, 40019, 40026, 40031–32, 40036, 40045, 40050, 40055–59, 40066, 40068, 40070, 40075, 40077, 40241, 40245, 40311, 40324, 40329, 40334, 40346, 40350–51, 40353, 40355, 40358–61, 40363, 40366, 40370–71, 40374, 40379, 40601, 41001–08, 41010–12, 41014–19, 41022, 41030–31, 41033–35, 41037, 41039–46, 41048–49, 41051–56, 41059, 41061–65, 41071–76, 41080–81, 41083, 41085–86, 41091–98, 41101–02, 41105, 41114, 41121, 41128–29, 41132, 41135, 41137, 41139, 41141–44, 41146, 41149, 41156, 41159, 41164, 41166, 41168–69, 41171, 41173–75, 41179–81, 41183, 41189, 41472, 42254, 45275, 45277, 45298, 45944, 45999

* * *

FIFTH DISTRICT

HAROLD ROGERS, Republican, of Somerset, KY; born in Barrier, KY, December 31, 1937; graduated, Wayne County High School, 1955; attended Western Kentucky University, 1956–57; A.B., University of Kentucky, 1962; LL.B., University of Kentucky Law School, 1964; lawyer, admitted to the Kentucky State bar, 1964; commenced practice in Somerset; member, North Carolina and Kentucky National Guard, 1957–64; associate, Smith and Blackburn, 1964–67; private practice, 1967–69; Commonwealth Attorney, Pulaski and Rockcastle Counties, KY, 1969–80; delegate, Republican National Convention, 1972, 1976, 1980, 1984, and 1988; Republican nominee for Lieutenant Governor, KY, 1979; past president, Kentucky Commonwealth Attorneys Association; member and past president, Somerset-Pulaski County Chamber of Commerce and Pulaski County Industrial Foundation; founder, Southern Kentucky Economic Development Council, 1986; member, Chowder and Marching Society, 1981–present; member, Energy and Commerce Committee, 1981–82; member, House Appropriations Committee, 1983–present; Select Committee on Homeland Security; married the former Shirley McDowell, 1957; three children: Anthony, Allison, and John Marshall; elected to the 97th Congress, November 4, 1980; reelected to each succeeding Congress.

Office Listings

http://www.house.gov/rogers

2406 Rayburn House Office Building, Washington, DC 20515 .... (202) 225–4601
Administrative Assistant.—Will Smith. FAX: 225–0940
Office Manager.—Julia Casey.
Communications Director.—Leslie Cupp.
551 Clifty Street, Somerset, KY 42501 .... (606) 679–8346
District Administrator.—Robert L. Mitchell.
601 Main Street, Hazard, KY 41701 .... (606) 439–0794
119 College Street, Suite 2, Room 212, Pikeville, KY 41501 .... (606) 432–4388

Counties: BATH (part), BELL, BREATHITT, CLAY, FLOYD, HARLAN, JACKSON, JOHNSON, KNOTT, KNOX, LAUREL, LAWRENCE, LEE, LESLIE, LETCHER, MAGOFFIN, MARTIN, MCCREARY, MENIFEE, MORGAN, OWSLEY, PERRY, PIKE, PULASKI, ROCKCASTLE, ROWAN, WAYNE, WHITLEY, WOLFE. Population (2000), 673,670.

ZIP Codes: 40313, 40316–17, 40319, 40322, 40329, 40336–37, 40346, 40351, 40358, 40360, 40371, 40387, 40402–03, 40409, 40419, 40421, 40434, 40445, 40447, 40456, 40460, 40467, 40481, 40486, 40488, 40492, 40701–02, 40724, 40729–30, 40734, 40737, 40740–45, 40751, 40754–55, 40759, 40763, 40769, 40771, 40801, 40803, 40806–08, 40810, 40813, 40815–16, 40818–20, 40823–24, 40826–31, 40840, 40843–45, 40847, 40849, 40854–56, 40858, 40862–63, 40865, 40868, 40870, 40873–74, 40902–03, 40906, 40913–15, 40921, 40923, 40927, 40930, 40932, 40935, 40939–41, 40943–44, 40946, 40949, 40951, 40953, 40955, 40958, 40962, 40964–65, 40972, 40977, 40979, 40981–83, 40988, 40995, 40997, 40999, 41124, 41129, 41132, 41159–60, 41164, 41168, 41180, 41201, 41203–04, 41214, 41216, 41219, 41222, 41224, 41226, 41230–32, 41234, 41238, 41240, 41250, 41254–57, 41260, 41262–65, 41267–68, 41271, 41274, 41301, 41307, 41310–11, 41313–14, 41317, 41332–33, 41338–39, 41342, 41344, 41347–48, 41351–52, 41360, 41362, 41364–68, 41385–86, 41390, 41397, 41408, 41410, 41413, 41419, 41421–22, 41425–26, 41433, 41451, 41459, 41464–65, 41472, 41477, 41501–03, 41512–14, 41517, 41519–20, 41522, 41524, 41526–28, 41531, 41534–35, 41537–40, 41542–44, 41546–49, 41553–55, 41557–64, 41566–68, 41571–72, 41601–07, 41612, 41615–16, 41619, 41621–22, 41630–32, 41635–36, 41640, 41642–43, 41645, 41647, 41649–51, 41653, 41655, 41659–60, 41663, 41666–67, 41669, 41701–02, 41712–14, 41719, 41721–23, 41725, 41727, 41729, 41731, 41735–36, 41739–40, 41743, 41745–47, 41749, 41751,

41754, 41759–60, 41762–64, 41766, 41772–78, 41804, 41810, 41812, 41815, 41817, 41819, 41821–22, 41824–26, 41828, 41831–40, 41843–45, 41847–49, 41855, 41858–59, 41861–62, 42501–03, 42518–19, 42533, 42544, 42553, 42558, 42564, 42567, 42603, 42631, 42633–35, 42638, 42642, 42647, 42649, 42653

* * *

SIXTH DISTRICT

ERNIE FLETCHER, Republican, of Lexington, KY; born in Mount Sterling, KY, on November 12, 1952; graduated, LaFayette High School, 1970; B.S., University of Kentucky, 1974; USAF, 1974–79; University of Kentucky College of Medicine, 1984; physician; family medical practice; CEO, St. Joseph Medical Foundation; elected to Kentucky House of Representatives, 1994–96; married to Glenna Foster, 1971; two children: Rachel and Benjamin; committees: Energy and Commerce; elected to the 106th Congress; reelected to each succeeding Congress.

Office Listings

http://www.house.gov/fletcher

1117 Longworth House Office Building, Washington, DC 20515 .... (202) 225–4706
Chief of Staff.—Pamela Mattox. FAX: 225–2122
Legislative Director.—Phillip Brown.
Deputy Chief of Staff / Scheduler.—Caroline Atkins.
860 Corporate Drive, Suite 105, Lexington, KY 40503 .... (859) 219–1366
District Office Manager.—Lorrie Parker.

Counties: ANDERSON, BOURBON, BOYLE, CLARK, ESTILL, FAYETTE, FRANKLIN, GARRARD, JESSAMINE, LINCOLN (part), MADISON, MERCER, MONTGOMERY, POWELL, SCOTT (part), WOODFORD. Population (2000), 673,626.

ZIP Codes: 40003, 40046, 40076, 40078, 40310–12, 40320, 40324, 40328, 40330, 40334, 40336–37, 40339–40, 40342, 40346–48, 40353, 40355–57, 40361–62, 40370, 40372, 40374, 40376, 40379–80, 40383–86, 40390–92, 40403–05, 40409–10, 40419, 40422–23, 40437, 40440, 40444–47, 40452, 40461, 40464, 40468, 40472–73, 40475–76, 40484, 40489, 40495, 40502–17, 40522–24, 40526, 40533, 40536, 40544, 40546, 40550, 40555, 40574–83, 40588, 40591, 40598, 40601–04, 40618–22, 41031, 41901–06, 42567

LOUISIANA

(Population 2000, 4,468,976)

SENATORS

JOHN BREAUX, Democrat, of Crowley, LA; born in Crowley, LA, on March 1, 1944; education: graduated, St. Michael's High School, Crowley, LA, 1961; B.A., political science, University of Southwestern Louisiana, Lafayette, 1964; J.D., Louisiana State University, Baton Rouge, 1967; employment: law partner, Brown, McKernan, Ingram, and Breaux, 1967–68; legislative assistant to Congressman Edwin W. Edwards, 1968–69; district assistant to Congressman Edwards, 1969–72; member: Louisiana Bar Association and Acadia Parish Bar Association; board of directors, International Rice Festival Association; member: Crowley Jaycees; Crowley Chamber of Commerce; Pi Lambda Beta, prelaw fraternity; Phi Alpha Delta, law fraternity; Lambda Chi Alpha, social fraternity; Student Bar Association, L.S.U.; U.S.L. tennis team; Moot Court finalist, L.S.U., 1966; winner, American Legion Award; married: the former Lois Gail Daigle in 1964; children: John I. Jr., William Lloyd, Elizabeth Andre, and Julia Agnes; two granddaughters: Anna Kate and Campbell McKay Sheperdson; elected to the 92nd Congress by special election, 7th District of Louisiana, September 30, 1972; reelected to the seven succeeding Congresses; chairman, Subcommittee on the Conservation of Wildlife and Fisheries and the Environment, 1979–86; elected to U.S. Senate on November 4, 1986; chairman, Democratic Senatorial Campaign Committee, 1989–90; member and chairman, Democratic Leadership Council (1991–93); elected Democratic chief deputy whip, 104th Congress; committees: Commerce, Science, and Transportation; Finance; Rules and Administration; Special Committee on Aging; subcommittees: Social Security and Family Policy; Health Care; Taxation and IRS Oversight; Science, Technology, and Space; Aviation; Communications; Oceans and Fisheries; Surface Transportation and Merchant Marine; in January 1998, he was selected by the White House and House and Senate leaders to chair the National Bipartisan Commission on the Future of Medicare. Also in 1998, he co-chaired the National Commission on Retirement Policy, which produced legislation to help reform Social Security; reelected to a 2nd term on November 3, 1992; reelected to each succeeding Senate term.

Office Listings

http://breaux.senate.gov

503 Hart Senate Office Building, Washington, DC 20510 .... (202) 224–4623
Chief of Staff.—Fred Hatfield.
Legislative Director.—Sarah Walter.
Executive Assistant.—Diana Bostic.
Communications Director.—Bette Phelan.
Federal Courthouse Building, 800 Lafayette Street, Suite 1300, Lafayette, LA 70501 .... (337) 262–6871
2237 South Acadian Thruway, Suite 802, Baton Rouge, LA 70808 .... (225) 248–0104
1900 N. 18th Street, Suite 805, Monroe, LA 71201 .... (318) 325–3320
Hale Boggs Federal Building, Suite 1005, 501 Magazine Street, New Orleans, LA 70130 .... (504) 589–2531

* * *

MARY L. LANDRIEU, Democrat, of New Orleans, LA; born in Alexandria, VA, on November 23, 1955; education: B.A., Louisiana State University, 1977; real estate broker, specializing in townhouse development; represented New Orleans House District 90 in Louisiana Legislature, 1979–87; State Treasurer, 1987–95; vice chair, Louisiana Council on Child Abuse; member, Business and Professional Women; majority council member, Emily's List; past national president, Women's Legislative Network; past vice president, Women Executives in State Government; delegate to every Democratic National Convention since 1980; married: E. Frank Snellings; children: Connor, and Mary Shannon; committees: Appropriations; Energy and Natural Resources; Small Business and Entrepreneurship; Congressional Coalition on Adoption; elected to the U.S. Senate on November 5, 1996; reelected to each succeeding Senate term.

Office Listings

http://landrieu.senate.gov

724 Hart Senate Office Building, Washington, DC 20510 .... (202) 224–5824
Chief of Staff.—Norma Jane Sabiston. FAX: 224–9735
Scheduler.—Dorothy Makris.
Executive Assistant.—Jill Wren.
Legislative Director.—Jason Matthews.
Hale Boggs Federal Building, Room 1010, 501 Magazine Street, New Orleans, LA 70130 .... (504) 589–2427

U.S. Courthouse, 300 Fannin Street, Room 2240, Shreveport, LA 71101–3086 .... (318) 676–3085
U.S. Federal Court House, 707 Florida Street, Room 326, Baton Rouge, LA 70801 .. (225) 389–0395
Hibernia Tower, One Lakeshore Drive, Suite 1260, Lake Charles, LA 70629 .... (337) 436–6650

REPRESENTATIVES

FIRST DISTRICT

DAVID VITTER, Republican, of Metairie, LA; born on May 3, 1961; married: Wendy Baldwin Vitter; four children: Sophie, Lise, Airey, and Jack; education: Harvard University; Oxford University Rhodes Scholar; Tulane University School of Law; profession: lawyer (business attorney); adjunct law professor, Tulane and Loyola Universities; religion: Catholic; public service: elected to the Louisiana House of Representatives in 1991, reelected in 1995; awards: Alliance for Good Government ''Legislator of the Year''; Victims and Citizens Against Crime ''Outstanding Legislator'' and ''Lifetime Achievement Award''; elected to the 106th Congress on May 29, 1999, by special election; reelected to each succeeding Congress.

Office Listings

http://www.house.gov/vitter

414 Cannon House Office Building, Washington, DC 20515 .... (202) 225–3015
Chief of Staff / Legislative Director.—Kyle Ruckert. FAX: 225–0739
Communications Director.—Tonya Newman.
Scheduler / Office Manager.—Amanda Mayer.
300 East Thomas Street, Hammond, LA 70401 .... (985) 542–9616
2800 Veterans Boulevard, Suite 201, Metairie, LA 70002 .... (504) 589–2753

Parishes: JEFFERSON (part), ORLEANS (part), ST. CHARLES (part), ST. TAMMANY, TANGIPAHOA, WASHINGTON. Population (2000), 638,355.

ZIP Codes: 70001–06, 70009–11, 70033, 70047, 70053, 70055–56, 70058, 70060, 70062, 70064–65, 70072, 70087, 70094, 70115, 70118–19, 70121–24, 70160, 70181, 70183–84, 70401–04, 70420, 70422, 70426–27, 70429, 70431, 70433–38, 70442–48, 70450–52, 70454–67, 70469–71

* * *

SECOND DISTRICT

WILLIAM J. JEFFERSON, Democrat, of New Orleans, LA; born in Lake Providence, LA, on March 14, 1947; graduated, G.W. Griffin High School, Lake Providence, LA, 1965; B.A., Political Science and English, Southern University and A&M College, Baton Rouge, LA, 1969; J.D., Harvard Law School, Cambridge, MA, 1972; LL.M., Georgetown University, 1996; admitted to the bar, New Orleans, LA, 1972; attorney, Jefferson, Bryan, Jupiter, Lewis and Blanson, New Orleans, LA; first lieutenant, U.S. Army, J.A.G. Corps, 1975; member, board of trustees, Greater St. Stephen's Baptist Church; Urban League of Greater New Orleans; Southern University Foundation Board; Louisiana State Senate, March, 1980 to January, 1991; family: married the former Andrea Green in 1970; five children: Jamila, Jalila, Jelani, Nailah, and Akilah; elected to the 102nd Congress; reelected to each succeeding Congress.

Office Listings

240 Cannon House Office Building, Washington, DC 20515 .... (202) 225–6636
Administrative Assistant.—Lionel Collins.
Executive Assistant.—Roberta Hopkins.
Communications Director.—Devona Dolliole.
1012 Hale Boggs Federal Building, 501 Magazine Street, New Orleans, LA 70130 .. (504) 589–2274
District Office Manager.—Stephanie Butler.

Parishes: JEFFERSON (part), ORLEANS (part). Population (2000), 638,562.

ZIP Codes: 70001, 70003, 70053–54, 70056, 70058, 70062–63, 70065, 70067, 70072–73, 70094, 70096, 70112–19, 70121–31, 70139–43, 70145–46, 70148–54, 70156–67, 70170, 70172, 70174–79, 70182, 70185–87, 70189–90, 70195

* * *

THIRD DISTRICT

W.J. (BILLY) TAUZIN, Republican, of Thibodaux, LA; born in Chackbay, LA, June 14, 1943; graduated, Thibodaux High School, 1961; B.A., History, Prelaw, Nicholls State University, 1964; honor student, Hall of Fame graduate, student body president, 1962–64; J.D.,

Louisiana State University, 1967, while serving four years in Louisiana State Senate, legislative aide; lawyer; admitted to the Louisiana bar in 1968; commenced practice in Houma, LA.; law partner, Marcel, Marcel, Fanguy and Tauzin, 1968–72; private practice, 1972; partner, Sonnier and Tauzin, 1976; married Cecile Bergeron Tauzin; five children by previous marriage: Kristie René, W.J. (Billy) III, John Ashton, Thomas Nicholas, and Michael James; served in Louisana State Legislature, 1971–80; committees: chairman, Energy and Commerce; senior member, Resources; Select Committee on Homeland Security; elected to the 96th Congress, May 22, 1980, in a special election to fill the vacancy caused by the resignation of David C. Treen; reelected to each succeeding Congress.

Office Listings

http://www.house.gov/tauzin

2183 Rayburn House Office Building, Washington, DC 20515 .... (202) 225–4031
Chief of Staff.—Mimi Simoneaux.
Federal Building, Suite 107, Houma, LA 70360 .... (985) 876–3033
District Representative.—Jeri Theriot.
210 East Main Street, New Iberia, LA 70560 .... (337) 367–8231
District Representative.—Jan Viator.
Ascension Parish Courthouse East, 828 South Irma Boulevard, Gonzales, LA 70737 .... (225) 621–8490
District Representative.—Ina Smiley.
8201 West Judge Perez Drive, Chalmette, LA 70043 .... (504) 271–1707
District Coordinator.—Sandy Kain.

Parishes: ASCENSION (part), ASSUMPTION, IBERIA, JEFFERSON (part), LAFOURCHE, PLAQUEMINES, ST. BERNARD, ST. CHARLES (part), ST. JAMES, ST. JOHN THE BAPTIST, ST. MARTIN, ST. MARY, TERREBONNE. Population (2000), 638,322.

ZIP Codes: 70030–32, 70036–41, 70043–44, 70047, 70049–52, 70056–58, 70067–72, 70075–76, 70078–87, 70090–92, 70301–02, 70310, 70339–46, 70353–54, 70356–61, 70363–64, 70371–75, 70377, 70380–81, 70390–95, 70397, 70512–14, 70517–19, 70521–23, 70528, 70538, 70540, 70544, 70552, 70560, 70562–63, 70569, 70582, 70592, 70723, 70725, 70734, 70737, 70743, 70763, 70778, 70792

* * *

FOURTH DISTRICT

JIM MCCRERY, Republican, of Shreveport, LA; born in Shreveport, September 18, 1949; graduated Leesville High, Los Angeles, 1967; B.A., Louisiana Tech University, Ruston, 1971; J.D., Louisiana State University, Baton Rouge, 1975; attorney; admitted to the Louisiana bar in 1975 and commenced practice in Leesville, LA; Jackson, Smith, and Ford (Leesville), 1975–78; assistant city attorney, Shreveport, 1979–80; district manager, U.S. Representative Buddy Roemer, 1981–82; legislative director, U.S. Representative Buddy Roemer, 1982–84; board of directors, Louisiana Association of Business and Industry, 1986–87; chairman, Regulatory Affairs Committee, Louisiana Forestry Association, 1987; regional manager for Government Affairs, Georgia-Pacific Corporation, 1984–88; committee: Ways and Means; subcommittee: chairman, Select Revenue Measures; elected by special election to the 100th Congress, April 16, 1988, to fill the vacancy caused by the resignation of Charles E. (Buddy) Roemer; reelected to each succeeding Congress.

Office Listings

http://www.house.gov/mccrery

2104 Rayburn House Office Building, Washington, DC 20515 .... (202) 225–2777
Chief of Staff.—Bob Brooks. FAX: 225–8039
6425 Youree Drive, Suite 350, Shreveport, LA 71105 .... (318) 798–2254
District Manager.—Linda Wright.
Southgate Plaza Shopping Center, 1606 South Fifth Street, Leesville, LA 71446 .... (337) 238–0778

Parishes: ALLEN (part), BEAUREGARD, BIENVILLE, BOSSIER, CADDO, CLAIBORNE, DESOTO, GRANT, NATCHITOCHES, RED RIVER, SABINE, VERNON, WEBSTER. Population (2000), 638,466.

ZIP Codes: 70633–34, 70637–39, 70644, 70648, 70651–57, 70659–60, 70662, 71001–04, 71006–09, 71016, 71018–19, 71021, 71023–25, 71027–34, 71036–40, 71043–52, 71055, 71058, 71060–61, 71063–73, 71075, 71078–80, 71082, 71101–13, 71115, 71118–20, 71129–30, 71133–38, 71148–49, 71151–54, 71156, 71161–66, 71171–72, 71222, 71235, 71251, 71256, 71268, 71275, 71360, 71403–04, 71406–07, 71411, 71414, 71416–17, 71419, 71423, 71426–29, 71432, 71434, 71438–39, 71443, 71446–47, 71449–50, 71452, 71454–63, 71467–69, 71474–75, 71486, 71496–97

FIFTH DISTRICT

RODNEY ALEXANDER, Democrat, of Quitman, LA; born on December 5, 1946, in Bienville, LA; education: attended Louisiana Tech University; profession: businessman, with a background in the insurance and construction industries; organizations: member, Louisiana Farm Bureau and the National Rifle Association; public service: Jackson Parish Police Jury, 1970–1985; served as President during the last seven years of his tenure; Louisiana House of Representatives, 1987–2002; religion: Baptist; family: married to Nancy; three children; elected to the 108th Congress on December 7, 2002.

Office Listings

http://www.house.gov/alexander

316 Cannon House Office Building, Washington, DC 20515 .... (202) 225–8490
Chief of Staff.—Wooten Johnson. FAX: 225–5639
Press Secretary.—Ellis Brachman.
Policy Director.—Peter Conroy.
1900 Stubbs Avenue, Suite B, Monroe, LA 71201 .... (318) 322–3500
1412 Centre Court, Suite 402, Alexandria, LA 71301 .... (318) 445–0818

Parishes: ALLEN (part), AVOYELLES, CALDWELL, CATAHOULA, CONCORDIA, EVANGELINE (part), EAST CARROLL, FRANKLIN, IBERVILLE (part), JACKSON, LASALLE, LINCOLN, MADISON, MOREHOUSE, OUACHITA, POINT COUPEE (part), RAPIDES, RICHLAND, TENSAS, UNION, WEST CARROLL, WIN. Population (2000), 638,517.

ZIP Codes: 70532, 70554, 70576, 70585–86, 70655–57, 70759–60, 70764–65, 70772, 70781, 70783, 71001, 71031, 71201–03, 71207–13, 71218–23, 71225–27, 71229–30, 71232–35, 71237–38, 71240–43, 71245, 71247, 71249–51, 71253–54, 71256, 71259–61, 71263–64, 71266, 71268–70, 71272–73, 71275–77, 71279–82, 71284, 71286, 71291–92, 71294–95, 71301–03, 71306–07, 71309, 71315–16, 71320, 71322–31, 71333–34, 71336, 71339–43, 71346, 71348, 71350–51, 71354–57, 71360–63, 71365–69, 71371, 71373, 71375, 71377–78, 71401, 71404–05, 71407, 71409–10, 71415, 71417–18, 71422–25, 71427, 71430–33, 71435, 71438, 71440–41, 71447–48, 71454–55, 71457, 71463, 71465–67, 71471–73, 71477, 71479–80, 71483, 71485

* * *

SIXTH DISTRICT

RICHARD H. BAKER, Republican, of Baton Rouge, LA; born in New Orleans, LA, on May 22, 1948; education: graduated, University High School; Louisiana State University, Baton Rouge; employment: real estate broker; Louisiana House of Representatives, 1972–86; chairman, Committee on Transportation, Highways, and Public Works, 1980–86; member: Southern Legislative Conference, ALEC, Central Area Homebuilders, East Baton Rouge Airport Commission, Baton Rouge Lodge No. 372 Central Region Planning Commission; married: the former Kay Carpenter in 1969; children: Brandon and Julie; committees: Financial Services; Transportation and Infrastructure; Veteran's Affairs; subcommittees: Aviation; chairman, Capital Markets, Insurance and Government Sponsored Enterprises; Financial Institutions and Consumer Credit; Health; Highways and Transit and Pipelines; Housing and Community Opportunities; Water Resources and Environment; elected to the 100th Congress on November 4, 1986; reelected to each succeeding Congress.

Office Listings

341 Cannon House Office Building, Washington, DC 20515 .... (202) 225–3901
Administrative Assistant.—Paul Sawyer. FAX: 225–7313
Office Manager/Executive Assistant.—Lynn Kirk.
5555 Hilton Avenue, Suite 100, Baton Rouge, LA 70808 .... (225) 929–7711
Chief of Staff.—Christina Kyle Casteel.

Parishes: ASCENSION (part), EAST BATON ROUGE, EAST FELICIANA, IBERVILLE (part), LIVINGSTON, POINTE COUPEE (part), ST. HELENA, WEST BATON ROUGE (part), WEST FELICIANA. CITIES: Addis, Albany, Angola, Baker, Batchelor, Baton Rouge, Bayou Goula, Blanks, Brittany, Brusly, Bueche, Carville, Clinton, Denham Springs, Duplessis, Erwinville, Ethel, Fordoche, French Settlement, Geismar, Glynn, Gonzales, Greenburg, Greenwell Springs, Grosse Tete, Hardwood, Holden, Innis, Jackson, Jarreau, Labarre, Lakeland, Lettsworth, Livingston, Livonia, Lottie, Maringouin, Maurepas, Morganza, New Roads, Norwood, Oscar, Pine Grove, Plaquemine, Port Allen, Prairieville, Pride, Rosedale, Rougon, Slaughter, Sorrento, Springfield, St. Amant, St. Francisville, St. Gabriel, Sunshine, Torbert, Tunica, Ventress, Wakefield, Walker, Watson, Weyanoke, White Castle, Wilson, and Zachary. Population (2000), 638,324.

ZIP Codes: 70403, 70422, 70436, 70441, 70443–44, 70449, 70453, 70462, 70466, 70586, 70704, 70706–07, 70710–12, 70714–15, 70718–19, 70721–22, 70726–30, 70732–34, 70736–40, 70744, 70747–49, 70752–57, 70759–62, 70764, 70767, 70769–70, 70772–78, 70780, 70782–89, 70791, 70801–23, 70826, 70831, 70833, 70835–37, 70874, 70879, 70883–84, 70892–96, 70898

SEVENTH DISTRICT

CHRISTOPHER JOHN, Democrat, of Crowley, LA; born in Crowley, January 5, 1960; education: graduated, Notre Dame High School, Acadia Parish, 1978; B.A., business administration, Louisiana State University, 1982; vice president in charge of office operations, John N. John Truckline, Inc.; aide to father, Louisiana State Representative John N. John, Jr., 1974–82; elected chairman of Acadiana Delegation while serving in Louisiana House of Representatives, 1988–96; charter member, Crowley Chamber of Commerce; member: Crowley Kiwanis Club, Acadia Chapter of Ducks Unlimited, Knights of Columbus; past vice president, Acadiana Sportsmen's League; former Crowley City Councilman; married: Payton Smith; elected to the 105th Congress; reelected to each succeeding Congress.

Office Listings

http://www.house.gov/john

403 Cannon House Office Building, Washington, DC 20515 .... (202) 225–2031
Chief of Staff.—Gordon Taylor. FAX: 225–5724
800 Lafayette Street, Suite 1400, Lafayette, LA 70501 .... (337) 235–6322
Executive Assistant.—Stephen Stefanski.
1011 Lakeshore Drive, Suite 306, Lake Charles, LA 70601 .... (337) 433–1747
Executive Assistant.—Lynn Jones.

Parishes: ACADIA, CALCASIEU, CAMERON, EVANGELINE, JEFFERSON DAVIS, LAFAYETTE, ST. LANDRY, VERMILION. Population (2000), 638,430.

ZIP Codes: 70501–12, 70515–18, 70520, 70524–29, 70531–35, 70537, 70541–43, 70546, 70548–51, 70554–56, 70558–59, 70570–71, 70575, 70577–78, 70580–81, 70583–84, 70586, 70589, 70591–92, 70596, 70598, 70601–02, 70605–07, 70609, 70611–12, 70615–16, 70630–33, 70640, 70643, 70645–48, 70650, 70655, 70658, 70661, 70663–65, 70668–69, 70750, 71322, 71345, 71353, 71356, 71358, 71362

MAINE

(Population, 2000 1,274,923)

SENATORS

OLYMPIA J. SNOWE, Republican, of Auburn, ME; born in Augusta, ME, February 21, 1947; education: graduated from Edward Little High School, Auburn, ME, 1965; B.A., University of Maine, Orono, 1969; member, Holy Trinity Greek Orthodox Church of Lewiston-Auburn; active member of civic and community organizations; elected to the Maine House of Representatives, 1973, to the seat vacated by the death of her first husband, the late Peter Snowe; reelected for a full two-year term in 1974; elected to the Maine Senate, 1976; chaired the Joint Standing Committee on Health and Institutional Services; elected to the 96th Congress on November 7, 1978—the youngest Republican woman, and first Greek-American woman elected; reelected to the 97th through 103rd Congresses; past member: House Budget Committee; House Foreign Affairs Committee; leading member of the former House Select Committee on Aging, ranking Republican on its Subcommittee on Human Services; Senate committees: Commerce, Science and Transportation; Finance; chair, Small Business and Entrepreneurship; Select Committee on Intelligence; subcommittees: Health Care; International Trade; Taxation and IRS Oversight; Aviation; Communications; chair, Oceans, Fisheries and Coast Guard; Surface Transportation and Merchant Marine; past member: Budget; Armed Services; Foreign Relations; married to former Maine Governor John R. McKernan, Jr.; elected to the U.S. Senate on November 8, 1994; reelected to each succeeding Senate term.

Office Listings

http://snowe.senate.gov

154 Russell Senate Office Building, Washington, DC 20510 .... (202) 224–5344
Chief of Staff.—Jane A. Calderwood.
Executive Assistant.—Kelly Becker.
Communications Director.—W. Davis Lackey, Jr.
Legislative Director.—Carolyn L. Holmes.
2 Great Falls Plaza, Suite 7B, Auburn, ME 04210 .... (207) 786–2451
Regional Representative.—Diane Jackson.
40 Western Avenue, Suite 408C, Augusta, ME 04330 .... (207) 622–8292
Regional Representative.—John S. Cummings, Jr.
One Cumberland Place, Suite 306, Bangor, ME 04401 .... (207) 945–0432
Regional Representative.—Gail Kelly.
231 Main Street, P.O. Box 215, Biddeford, ME 04005 .... (207) 282–4144
Regional Representative.—Peter Morin.
3 Canal Plaza, Suite 601, P.O. Box 188, Portland, ME 04112 .... (207) 874–0883
State Director.—Charles E. Summers, Jr.
169 Academy Street, Suite 3, Presque Isle, ME 04769 .... (207) 764–5124
Regional Representative.—Ken White.

* * *

SUSAN COLLINS, Republican, of Bangor, ME; born on December 7, 1952, in Caribou, ME; graduated, Caribou High School, 1971; B.A., *magna cum laude,* Phi Beta Kappa, St. Lawrence University, Canton, NY; Outstanding Alumni Award, St. Lawrence University, 1992; staff director, Senate Subcommittee on the Oversight of Government Management, 1981–87; for 12 years, principal advisor on business issues to former Senator William S. Cohen; Commissioner of Professional and Financial Regulation for Maine Governor John R. McKernan, Jr., 1987; New England administrator, Small Business Administration, 1992–93; appointed Deputy Treasurer of Massachusetts, 1993; executive director, Husson College Center for Family Business, 1994–96; committees: Armed Services; chairman, Governmental Affairs; Joint Economic; Special Committee on Aging; elected to the U.S. Senate on November 5, 1996; reelected to each succeeding Senate term.

Office Listings

http://collins.senate.gov

172 Russell Senate Office Building, Washington, DC 20510 .... (202) 224–2523
Chief of Staff.—Steven Abbott. FAX: 224–2693
Press Secretary.—Felicia Knight.
Legislative Director.—Jennifer Hemingway.
P.O. Box 655, 202 Harlow Street, Room 204, Bangor, ME 04401 .... (207) 945–0417
State Representative.—Judy Cuddy.
168 Capitol Street, Augusta, ME 04330 .... (207) 622–8414
State Representative.—William Card.

160 Main Street, Biddeford, ME 04005 .... (207) 283–1101
State Representative.—William Vail.
11 Lisbon Street, Lewiston, ME 04240 .... (207) 784–6969
State Director.—Randy Bumps.
25 Sweden Street, Suite A, Caribou, ME 04736 .... (207) 493–5873
State Representative.—Philip Bosse.
One City Center, Suite 100, Portland, ME 04101 .... (207) 780–3575

REPRESENTATIVES

FIRST DISTRICT

THOMAS H. ALLEN, Democrat, of Portland, ME; born in Portland, April 16, 1945; education: graduated, Deering High School, Portland; Bowdoin College, Phi Beta Kappa; Oxford University, Rhodes scholar; Harvard University, J.D.; Bowdin College Board of Trustees; board of directors of Shalom House and the United Way of Greater Portland; president, Portland Stage Company; Executive and Legislative Policy committees; Maine Municipal Association; chair, Governor's Task Force on Foster Care; Portland City Council and Mayor; married: Diana Allen; children: Gwen and Kate; committees: Energy and Commerce; elected to the 105th Congress; reelected to each succeeding Congress.

Office Listings

http://www.tomallen.house.gov

1717 Longworth House Office Building, Washington, DC 20515 .... (202) 225–6116
Chief of Staff.—Jacqueline Potter. FAX: 225–5590
Executive Assistant.—Jolene Chonko.
Legislative Director.—Todd Stein.
Legislative Assistants: James Bradley, Rachel Gallant, Susan Lexer, Anne Nadzo, Matt Nelson, Kate Turner.
234 Oxford Street, Portland, ME 04101 .... (207) 774–5019
Office Manager / Scheduler.—Stephanie Betzold.

Counties: CUMBERLAND, KENNEBEC (part), KNOX, LINCOLN, SAGADAHOC, YORK. Population (2000), 637,461.

ZIP Codes: 03901–11, 04001–11, 04013–15, 04017, 04019–21, 04024, 04027–30, 04032–34, 04038–40, 04042–43, 04046–50, 04053–57, 04061–64, 04066, 04069–79, 04082–87, 04090–98, 04101–10, 04112, 04116, 04122–24, 04259–60, 04265, 04284, 04287, 04330, 04332–33, 04336, 04338, 04341–55, 04357–60, 04363–64, 04530, 04535–39, 04541, 04543–44, 04547–48, 04551, 04553–56, 04558, 04562–65, 04567–68, 04570–76, 04578–79, 04841, 04843, 04846–56, 04858–65, 04901, 04910, 04917–18, 04922, 04926–27, 04935, 04937, 04941, 04949, 04952, 04962–63, 04973, 04987–89, 04992

* * *

SECOND DISTRICT

MICHAEL H. MICHAUD, Democrat, of East Millinocket, ME; born on January 18, 1955; education: graduate, Harvard University John F. Kennedy School of Government Program for Senior Executives in State and Local Government; previous occupation: mill worker; community service: actively involved in a variety of local, regional, and statewide civic and economic development organizations; public service: Maine House of Representatives, 1980–1994; Maine State Senate, 1994–2002; religion: Catholic; elected to the 108th Congress on November 5, 2002.

Office Listings

http://www.house.gov/michaud

437 Cannon House Office Building, Washington, DC 20515 .... (202) 225–6306
Chief of Staff.—Peter Chandler. FAX: 225–2943
Legislative Director.—Matt Robison.
Scheduler.—Diane Smith.
202 Harlow Street, Room 235, Bangor, ME 04401 .... (207) 942–6935
179 Lisbon Street, Ground Floor, Lewiston, ME 04240 .... (207) 782–3704
445 Main Street, Presque Isle, ME 04769 .... (207) 764–1036

Counties: ANDROSCOGGIN, AROOSTOOK, FRANKLIN, HANCOCK, KENNEBEC (part), OXFORD, PENOBSCOT, PISCATAQUIS, SOMERSET, WALDO, WASHINGTON. Population (2000), 637,461.

ZIP Codes: 04010, 04016, 04022, 04037, 04041, 04051, 04068, 04088, 04210–12, 04216–17, 04219–28, 04230–31, 04234, 04236–41, 04243, 04250, 04252–58, 04261–63, 04266–68, 04270–71, 04274–76, 04278, 04280–83, 04285–86, 04288–92, 04294, 04354, 04401–02, 04406, 04408, 04410–24, 04426–31, 04434–35, 04438, 04441–44, 04448–51, 04453–57, 04459–64, 04467–69, 04471–76, 04478–79, 04481, 04485, 04487–93, 04495–97, 04549, 04605–07, 04609, 04611–17, 04619, 04622–31, 04634–35, 04637, 04640, 04642–46, 04648–50, 04652–58, 04660, 04662, 04664, 04666–69, 04671–77, 04679–81, 04683–86, 04691, 04693–94, 04730, 04732–47, 04750–51, 04756–66, 04768–70, 04772–77, 04779–81, 04783, 04785–88, 04848–51, 04857, 04903, 04911–12, 04915, 04920–25, 04928–30, 04932–33, 04936–45, 04947, 04949–58, 04961, 04964–67, 04969–76, 04978–79, 04981–88, 04992

MARYLAND

(Population 2000, 5,296,486)

SENATORS

PAUL S. SARBANES, Democrat, of Baltimore, MD; born in Salisbury, MD, February 3, 1933, son of Spyros and Matina Sarbanes; graduated, Wicomico Senior High School, 1950; A.B., Princeton University, 1954, *magna cum laude* and Phi Beta Kappa; Rhodes scholar, Balliol College, Oxford, England, 1954–57, first-class B.A. honours in School of Philosophy, Politics and Economics; LL.B., *cum laude,* Harvard Law School, 1960; admitted to practice by Maryland Court of Appeals, 1960; law clerk to Judge Morris A. Soper, U.S. Court of Appeals for the Fourth Circuit, 1960–61; associate in Baltimore law firms Piper and Marbury, 1961–62, and Venable, Baetjer and Howard, 1965–70; administrative assistant to Walter W. Heller, chairman of the Council of Economic Advisers, 1962–63; executive director, Charter Revision Commission of Baltimore City, 1963–64; elected to the Maryland House of Delegates in November 1966, serving from 1967–71; member, Greek Orthodox Cathedral of the Annunciation, Baltimore, MD; married: Christine Dunbar of Brighton, England; three children and five grandchildren; committees: ranking member, Banking, Housing, and Urban Affairs; Budget; Foreign Relations; Joint Economic; elected to 92nd Congress on November 3, 1970; reelected to 93rd and 94th Congresses; elected to the U.S. Senate on November 2, 1976; reelected to each succeeding Senate term.

Office Listings

http://sarbanes.senate.gov

309 Hart Senate Office Building, Washington, DC 20510 .... (202) 224–4524
Chief of Staff.—Julie Kehrli. FAX: 224–1651
Legislative Director.—Kristi Kennedy. TDD: 224–3452
Appointment Secretary.—Elise Gillette.
Press Secretary.—Jesse Jacobs.
100 South Charles Street, Tower I, Suite 1710, Baltimore, MD 21201 .... (410) 962–4436
1110 Bonifant Street, Suite 450, Silver Spring, MD 20910 .... (301) 589–0797
113 Baltimore Street, Suite 201, Cumberland, MD 21502 .... (301) 724–0695
110 W. Church Street, Suite D, Salisbury, MD 21801 .... (410) 860–2131
15499 Potomac River Drive, Box 409, Cobb Island, MD 20625 .... (301) 259–2404

* * *

BARBARA A. MIKULSKI, Democrat, of Baltimore, MD; born in Baltimore on July 20, 1936; education: B.A., Mount St. Agnes College, 1958; M.S.W., University of Maryland School of Social Work, 1965; former social worker for Catholic Charities and city of Baltimore; served as an adjunct professor, Department of Sociology, Loyola College; elected to the Baltimore City Council, 1971; Democratic nominee for the U.S. Senate in 1974, winning 43 percent of vote; elected to the U.S. House of Representatives in November, 1976; first woman appointed to the Energy and Commerce Committee; also served on the Merchant Marine and Fisheries Committee; became the first woman representing the Democratic Party to be elected to a Senate seat not previously held by her husband, and the first Democratic woman ever to serve in both houses of Congress; committees: Appropriations; Health, Education, Labor, and Pensions; Select Committee on Intelligence; subcommittees: ranking member, Aging; Commerce, Justice, State and the Judiciary; Foreign Operations; Homeland Security; Interior; Transportation, Treasury, and General Government; ranking member, VA, HUD, and Independent Agencies; Secretary, Democratic Conference; first woman to be elected to a leadership post; elected to the U.S. Senate in November, 1986, with 61 percent of the vote; reelected in November, 1992, with 71 percent of the vote; reelected in November, 1998, with 71 percent of the vote.

Office Listings

http://mikulski.senate.gov

709 Hart Senate Office Building, Washington, DC 20510 .... (202) 224–4654
Chief of Staff.—Jennifer Luray.
Deputy Chief of Staff/Legislative Director.—Julia Frifield.
Communications Director.—Liz Lubow.
1629 Thames Street, Suite 400, Baltimore, MD 2123 .... (410) 962–4510
State Director.—Mike Morrill.
60 West Street, Suite 202, Annapolis, MD 21401 .... (410) 263–1805
6404 Ivy Lane, Suite 406, Greenbelt, MD 20770 .... (301) 345–5517
94 West Washington Street, Hagerstown, MD 21740 .... (301) 797–2826
1201 Pemberton Drive, Suite 1E, Building B, Salisbury, MD 21801 .... (410) 546–7711

REPRESENTATIVES

FIRST DISTRICT

WAYNE T. GILCHREST, Republican, of Kennedyville, MD; born on April 15, 1946, in Rahway, NJ; education: graduated from Rahway High School, 1964; attended Wesley College, Dover, DE; B.A. in History, Delaware State College, Dover, 1973; graduate studies, Loyola University, Baltimore, MD, 1984–present; military service: served in the U.S. Marine Corps, 1964–68; awarded the Purple Heart, Bronze Star, Navy Commendation Medal, Navy Unit Citation, and others; employment: government and history teacher, Kent County High School, 1973–present; member: Kent County Teachers Association, American Legion, Veterans of Foreign Wars, Order of the Purple Heart; religion: Kennedyville Methodist Church; married: the former Barbara Rawley; children: Kevin, Joel, and Katie; elected to the 102nd Congress; reelected to each succeeding Congress.

Office Listings

2245 Rayburn House Office Building, Washington, DC 20515 .... (202) 225–5311
Chief of Staff.—Tony Caligiuri. FAX: 225–0254
Office Manager / Scheduler.—Kathy Hicks.
Legislative Director.—Jeri Finke.
Press Secretary / District Director.—Cathy Bassett.
315 High Street, Suite 105, Chestertown, MD 21620 .... (410) 778–9407
District Office Manager.—Karen Willis.
One Plaza East, Salisbury, MD 21801 .... (410) 749–3184
District Office Manager.—Monica Bell.
45 North Main Street, Bel Air, MD 21014 .... (410) 838–2517
District Office Manager.—Shirley Stoyer.

Counties: ANNE ARUNDEL (part), BALTIMORE (part), CAROLINE, CECIL, DORCHESTER, HARFORD (part), KENT, QUEEN ANNE'S, SOMERSET, TALBOT, WICOMICO, WORCESTER. Population (2000), 662,062.

ZIP Codes: 21001, 21009, 21012–15, 21018, 21023, 21028, 21030–32, 21034, 21047, 21050–51, 21054, 21057, 21078, 21082, 21084–85, 21087, 21092–93, 21108, 21111, 21113, 21122, 21128, 21131, 21136, 21144, 21146, 21156, 21162, 21206, 21225–26, 21234, 21236, 21240, 21286, 21401–05, 21411–12, 21601, 21606–07, 21609–10, 21612–13, 21617, 21619–20, 21622–29, 21631–32, 21634–36, 21638–41, 21643–45, 21647–73, 21675–79, 21681–85, 21687, 21690, 21801–04, 21810–11, 21813–14, 21817, 21821–22, 21824, 21826, 21829–30, 21835–38, 21840–43, 21849–53, 21856–57, 21861–67, 21869, 21871–72, 21874–75, 21890, 21901–04, 21911–22, 21930

* * *

SECOND DISTRICT

C.A. DUTCH RUPPERSBERGER, Democrat, of Cockeysville, MD; born on January 30, 1946, in Baltimore, MD; education: Baltimore City College; University of Maryland, College Park; J.D., University of Baltimore Law School, 1970; profession: Attorney; partner, Ruppersberger, Clark, and Mister (law firm); public service: Baltimore County Assistant State's Attorney; Baltimore County Council; Baltimore County Executive, 1994–2002; family: married to the former Kay Murphy; children: Corey and Jill; elected to the 108th Congress on November 5, 2002.

Office Listings

http://dutch.house.gov

1630 Longworth House Office Building, Washington, DC 20515 .... (202) 225–3061
Chief of Staff.—Jim Cauley. FAX: 225–3094
Press Secretary.—Rick Binetti.
Scheduler.—Brenda Connolly.
The Atrium, 375 West Padonia Road, Suite 200, Timonium, MD 21093 .... (410) 628–2701
District Office Manager.—Tara Oursler.

Counties: ANNE ARUNDEL (part), BALTIMORE CITY (part), BALTIMORE COUNTY (part), HARFORD (part). Population (2000), 662,060.

ZIP Codes: 20755, 21001, 21005, 21009–10, 21017, 21022, 21027, 21030–31, 21034, 21040, 21047, 21050–52, 21056–57, 21060–62, 21065, 21071, 21076–78, 21085, 21087, 21090, 21093–94, 21104, 21111, 21113, 21117, 21122–23, 21130, 21133, 21136, 21144, 21162–63, 21204, 21206, 21208, 21212–14, 21219–22, 21224–27, 21230, 21234, 21236–37, 21239, 21244, 21252, 21284–86

THIRD DISTRICT

BENJAMIN L. CARDIN, Democrat, of Baltimore, MD; born in Baltimore, October 5, 1943; education: attended Baltimore public schools; graduated Baltimore City College, 1961; B.A., University of Pittsburgh, PA, 1964, *cum laude*; J.D., University of Maryland, Baltimore, 1967, (first in class); employment: attorney; admitted to Maryland bar November 1967 and began practice in Baltimore; member of the Maryland House of Delegates, 1967–86; Speaker of House of Delegates, 1979–86; chairman, Ways and Means Committee, 1974–79; vice chairman, Ways and Means Committee, 1971–73; member, Presidential Advisory Committee on Federalism; chairman, State Federal Assembly, National Council of State Legislators, 1980–81; member, National Council of State Legislators, executive committee; member, Council of State Governments, executive committee, 1979–86; co-chairman, Legislative Policy Committee, Maryland General Assembly, 1979–86; trustee, Baltimore Museum of Art; member, Baltimore Jewish Community Relations Council; trustee, Baltimore Council on Foreign Affairs; member, Associated Jewish Charities Welfare Fund; member, board of visitors of the University of Maryland School of Law; trustee, Goucher College; former chairman, Maryland Legal Services Corporation; MACO Legislator of the Year Award, 1984; ranking member, Commission on Security and Cooperation in Europe; married: the former Myrna Edelman, 1964; committees: Ways and Means; Select Committee on Homeland Security; subcommitttees: ranking member, Human Resources; Social Security; elected to the 100th Congress, November 4, 1986; reelected to each succeeding Congress.

Office Listings

http://www.cardin.house.gov

2207 Rayburn House Office Building, Washington, DC 20515 .... (202) 225–4016
Chief of Staff.—Christopher Lynch. FAX: 225–9219
Office Manager.—Amy Daiger.
600 Wyndhurst Avenue, Suite 230, Baltimore, MD 21210 .... (410) 433–8886
District Director.—Bailey Fine.
Press Secretary.—Susan Sullam.

Counties: ANNE ARUNDEL (part), BALTIMORE (part), HOWARD (part), BALTIMORE CITY (part). TOWNS: Arbutus (part), Crofton, Ellicott City (part), Elkridge, Glen Burnie (part), Halethrope, Lansdowne, Linthicum (part), Maryland City, Odenton (part), Owings Mills, Parkville (part), Pikesville, Reisterstown, Russett City (part), Severn (part), and Towson (part). Population (2000), 662,062.

ZIP Codes: 20701, 20723–24, 20755, 20759, 20794, 21022, 21029, 21032, 21035, 21037, 21043–46, 21054–55, 21060–61, 21071, 21075–77, 21090, 21093, 21098, 21108, 21113–14, 21117, 21122, 21136, 21139, 21144, 21146, 21150, 21153, 21201–02, 21204–06, 21208–15, 21218, 21222–25, 21227–31, 21234, 21236–37, 21239, 21281–82, 21285–86, 21401–05, 21411–12

* * *

FOURTH DISTRICT

ALBERT RUSSELL WYNN, Democrat, of Largo, MD; born in Philadelphia, PA, on September 10, 1951; graduated DuVal High School, Lanham, 1969; B.S., University of Pittsburgh, PA, 1973; attended Howard University Graduate School of Political Science, 1974; J.D., Georgetown University Law School, Washington, DC, 1977; attorney; admitted to the Maryland bar, 1979; Maryland House of Delegates, 1983–86; Maryland State Senate, 1987–92; executive director, Prince George's County Consumer Protection Commission, 1979–82; member: Kappa Alpha Psi Fraternity; J. Franklyn Bourne Bar Association; board of directors, Consumer Credit Counseling Service; Prince George's County Economic Development Corporation; Ploughman and Fisherman; committees: Energy and Commerce; elected on November 3, 1992, to the 103rd Congress; reelected to each succeeding Congress.

Office Listings

http://www.wynn.house.gov

434 Cannon House Office Building, Washington, DC 20515 .... (202) 225–8699
Chief of Staff.—Curt Clifton. FAX: 225–8714
Legislative Director.—Ken Nealy.
Press Secretary.—Amaya Smith.
9200 Basil Court, Suite 221, Largo, MD 20774 .... (301) 773–4094
18200 Georgia Avenue, Suite E, Olney, MD 20832 .... (301) 929–3462

Counties: MONTGOMERY (part), PRINCE GEORGE'S (part). CITIES AND TOWNSHIPS: Bladensburg, Brentwood, Brookeville, Capitol Heights, Cheverly, Colmar Manor, Cottage City, District Heights, Edmonston, Fairmount Heights, Glenarden, Landover Hills, Largo, Laytonsville, Morningside, Mount Rainier, New Carrollton, North Brentwood, Olney, Riverdale, Rockville, Seat Pleasant, University Park, and Upper Marlboro. Population (2000), 662,062.

ZIP Codes: 20703, 20706–07, 20710, 20720–21, 20731, 20735, 20737, 20743–48, 20750, 20752–53, 20757, 20762, 20769, 20772, 20774–75, 20777, 20781–85, 20788, 20790–92, 20797, 20799, 20830, 20832–33, 20841, 20853, 20855, 20860–62, 20866, 20868, 20871–72, 20874, 20876–77, 20879, 20882, 20886, 20901, 20903–06, 20910–12, 21771, 21797

* * *

FIFTH DISTRICT

STENY H. HOYER, Democrat, of Mechanicsville, MD; born in New York, NY, June 14, 1939; education: graduated Suitland High School; B.S., University of Maryland, 1963; J.D., Georgetown University Law Center, 1966; Honorary Doctor of Public Service, University of Maryland, 1988; admitted to the Maryland Bar Association, 1966; employment: practicing attorney, 1966–90; Maryland State Senate, 1967–79; vice chairman, Prince George's County, MD, Senate delegation, 1967–69; chairman, Prince George's County, MD, Senate delegation, 1969–75; president, Maryland State Senate, 1975–79; member, State Board for Higher Education, 1978–81; married: Judith Pickett, deceased, February 6, 1997; children: Susan, Stefany, and Anne; committees: Appropriations; subcommittees: Labor, Health and Human Services, Education, and Related Agencies; Democratic Steering Committee; Democratic Whip; elected to the 97th Congress on May 19, 1981, by special election; reelected to each succeeding Congress.

Office Listings

http://www.hoyer.house.gov

1705 Longworth House Office Building, Washington, DC 20515 .... (202) 225–4131
Chief of Staff.—Cory Alexander.
Legislative Director.—Geoff Plague.
U.S. Federal Courthouse, Suite 310, 6500 Cherrywood Lane, Greenbelt, MD 20770 .... (301) 474–0119
401 Post Office Road, Suite 202, Waldorf, MD 20602 .... (301) 843–1577

Counties: ANNE ARUNDEL (part), CALVERT, CHARLES, PRINCE GEORGE'S (part), ST. MARY'S. Population (2000), 662,060.

ZIP Codes: 20601–04, 20606–13, 20615–30, 20632, 20634–37, 20639–40, 20643, 20645–46, 20650, 20653, 20656–62, 20664, 20667, 20670, 20674–78, 20680, 20682, 20684–90, 20692–93, 20695, 20697, 20704–09, 20711, 20714–21, 20725–26, 20732–33, 20735–38, 20740–42, 20744, 20748–49, 20751, 20754, 20758, 20764–65, 20768–74, 20776, 20778–79, 20781–84, 20904, 21035, 21037, 21054, 21106, 21113, 21140

* * *

SIXTH DISTRICT

ROSCOE G. BARTLETT, Republican, of Frederick, MD; born June 3, 1926, in Moreland, KY; B.A., Columbia Union College, 1947; M.A., 1948, and Ph.D., University of Maryland, 1952; still an active farmer, prior to his election to Congress, he had retired after owning and operating a small business for ten years; awarded 20 patents for inventions during his scientific career as a professor and research engineer; held positions at Loma Linda University, the Navy's School of Aviation Medicine, John Hopkins Applied Physics Laboratory, and at IBM; married to Ellen; 10 children; committees: Armed Services; Science; vice chairman, Small Business; subcommittees: Energy; Space and Aeronautics; chairman, Projection Forces; Regulatory Reform and Oversight; Terrorism, Unconventional Threats and Capabilities; elected to the 103rd Congress; reelected to each succeeding Congress.

Office Listings

http://www.bartlett.house.gov

2412 Rayburn House Office Building, Washington, DC 20515 .... (202) 225–2721
Chief of Staff.—Gregg Cox. FAX: 512–1859
Legislative Director.—John Biddison.
Office Manager / Scheduler.—Barb Calligan.
11377 Robinwood Drive, Hagerstown, MD 21742 .... (301) 797–6043
7360 Guilford Drive, Suite 101, Frederick, MD 21704 .... (301) 694–3030
15 Main Street, Suite 110, Westminster, MD 21157 .... (410) 857–1115
1 Frederick Street, Cumberland, MD 21502 .... (301) 724–3105

Counties: ALLEGANY, CARROLL, FREDERICK, GARRETT, BALTIMORE (part), HARFORD (part), WASHINGTON. CITIES AND TOWNSHIPS: Baltimore, Boonsboro, Cumberland, Emmitsburg, Frederick, Frostburg, Funkstown, Hagerstown, Hancock, Middletown, Mount Airy, Oakland, Reisterstown, Sharpsburg, Smithburg, Thurmont, Timonium, Walkersville, Westminster, Williamsport, Woodsboro. Also includes Antietam National Battlefield and Camp David. Population (2000), 662,060.

ZIP Codes: 20842, 20871–72, 20876, 20882, 21014, 21020, 21029–30, 21034, 21036, 21041–43, 21047–48, 21050, 21053, 21074–75, 21084, 21088, 21102, 21104–05, 21111, 21120, 21131–32, 21136, 21152, 21154–55, 21157–58,

21160–61, 21163, 21501–05, 21520–24, 21528–32, 21536, 21538–43, 21545, 21550, 21555–57, 21560–62, 21701–05, 21709–11, 21713–23, 21727, 21733–34, 21740–42, 21746–50, 21754–59, 21762, 21766–67, 21769–71, 21773–84, 21787–88, 21790–91, 21793, 21795, 21797–98

* * *

SEVENTH DISTRICT

ELIJAH E. CUMMINGS, Democrat, of Baltimore, MD; born in Baltimore, MD, on January 18, 1951; education: graduated, Baltimore City College High School, 1969; B.S., political science, Phi Beta Kappa, Howard University, Washington, DC, 1973; J.D., University of Maryland Law School, 1976; employment: attorney; admitted to the Maryland bar in 1976; delegate, Maryland State Legislature, 1982–96; chairman, Maryland Legislative Black Caucus, 1984; speaker pro tempore, Maryland General Assembly, 1995–96; vice chairman, Constitutional and Administrative Law Committee; vice chairman, Economic Matters Committee; president, sophomore class, student government treasurer and student government president at Howard University; member: Governor's Commission on Black Males; New Psalmist Baptist Church, Baltimore, MD; active in civic affairs, and recipient of numerous community awards; one child: Jennifer; committees: Government Reform; Transportation and Infrastructure; subcommittees: ranking member, Criminal Justice, Drug Policy and Human Resources; Wellness and Human Rights; Highways, Transit and Pipelines; Railroads; chair, Congressional Black Caucus; co-chair of the House AIDS Working Group; Task Force on Health Care Reform; elected to the 104th Congress by special election in April, 1996; reelected to each succeeding Congress.

Office Listings

http://www.house.gov/cummings

1632 Longworth House Office Building, Washington, DC 20515 .... (202) 225–4741
Chief of Staff.—Vernon Simms. FAX: 225–3178
Legislative Assistants: Gwen Clinton, Asi Ofosu.
1010 Park Avenue, Suite 105, Baltimore, MD 21201 .... (410) 685–9199
754 Frederick Road, Catonsville, MD 21228 .... (410) 719–8777

Counties: BALTIMORE (part), HOWARD (part), BALTIMORE CITY (part). Population (2000), 662,060.

ZIP Codes: 20701, 20723, 20759, 20763, 20777, 20794, 20833, 21029, 21036, 21042–45, 21075, 21104, 21117, 21133, 21163, 21201–03, 21205–18, 21223–24, 21227–31, 21233, 21235, 21239, 21241, 21244, 21250–51, 21263–65, 21268, 21270, 21273–75, 21278–80, 21283, 21287–90, 21297–98, 21723, 21737–38, 21765, 21771, 21784, 21794, 21797

* * *

EIGHTH DISTRICT

CHRIS VAN HOLLEN, Democrat, of Kensington, MD; born on January 10, 1959; education: B.A., Swarthmore College, 1982; Masters in Public Policy, Harvard University, 1985; J.D., Georgetown University, 1990; professional: Attorney; legislative assistant to former Maryland U.S. Senator Charles McC. Mathias, Jr.; staff member, U.S. Senate Committee on Foreign Relations; senior legislative advisor to former Maryland Governor William Donald Schaefer; public service: elected, Maryland House of Delegates, 1990; elected, Maryland State Senate, 1994; family: married to Katherine; children: Anna, Nicholas, and Alexander; elected to the 108th Congress on November 5, 2002.

Office Listings

http://www.senate.gov/vanhollen

1419 Longworth House Office Building, Washington, DC 20515 .... (202) 225–5341
Chief of Staff / Legislative Director.—Kay Casstevens. FAX: 225–0375
Legislative Director.—Phil Alperson.
Press Secretary.—Marilyn Campbell.
51 Monroe Street, Suite 507, Rockville, MD 20850 .... (301) 424–3501
District Director.—Joan Kleinman.

Counties: MONTGOMERY (part), PRINCE GEORGES (part). Population (2000), 662,060.

ZIP Codes: 20712, 20722, 20782–83, 20787, 20810–18, 20824–25, 20827, 20837–39, 20841–42, 20847–55, 20857, 20859, 20871, 20874–80, 20883–86, 20889, 20891–92, 20894–99, 20901–08, 20910, 20912–16, 20918, 20997

MASSACHUSETTS

(Population 2000, 6,349,097)

SENATORS

EDWARD M. KENNEDY, Democrat, of Barnstable, MA; born in Boston, MA, February 22, 1932, son of Joseph P. and Rose F. Kennedy; graduated, Milton Academy, 1950; A.B., Harvard College, 1956; International Law School, The Hague, the Netherlands, 1958; LL.B., University of Virginia Law School, 1959; enlisted in the U.S. Army as a private and served in France and Germany, 1951–53; married to Victoria Reggie Kennedy; children: Kara, Edward M., Jr., Patrick J., Curran, and Caroline; committees: ranking member, Health, Education, Labor and Pensions; Judiciary; Armed Services; Joint Economic Committee; elected to the U.S. Senate on November 6, 1962, to fill the unexpired term of his brother John F. Kennedy; reelected November 3, 1964; reelected to each succeeding Senate term.

Office Listings

http://kennedy.senate.gov

315 Russell Senate Office Building, Washington, DC 20510 .... (202) 224–4543
Chief of Staff.—Mary Beth Cahill. FAX: 224–2417
Legislative Director.—Carey Parker. TDD: 224–1819
2400 John F. Kennedy Federal Building, Boston, MA 02203 .... (617) 565–3170
State Administrative Director.—Barbara Souliotis. TDD: 565–4045

* * *

JOHN F. KERRY, Democrat, of Boston, MA; born in Denver, CO, December 11, 1943; graduated, St. Paul's School, Concord, NH, 1962; B.A., Yale University, New Haven, CT, 1966; J.D., Boston College Law School, Boston, MA, 1976; served, U.S. Navy, discharged with rank of lieutenant; decorations: Silver Star, Bronze Star with Combat ''V'', three Purple Hearts, various theatre campaign decorations; attorney, admitted to Massachusetts bar, 1976; appointed first assistant district attorney, Middlesex County, 1977; elected lieutenant governor, Massachusetts, 1982; married to Teresa Heinz; appointed to Democratic Leadership for 104th and 105th Congresses; committees: Commerce, Science, and Transportation; Finance; Foreign Relations; Small Business and Entrepreneurship; elected to the U.S. Senate on November 6, 1984; reelected to each succeeding Senate term.

Office Listings

http://kerry.senate.gov

304 Russell Senate Office Building, Washington, DC 20510 .... (202) 224–2742
Administrative Assistant.—David McKean. FAX: 224–8525
Legislative Director.—George Abar.
Personal Secretary.—Patricia Ferrone.
One Bowdoin Square, 10th Floor, Boston, MA 02114 .... (617) 565–8519
Suite 311, 222 Milliken Place, Fall River, MA 02722 .... (508) 677–0522
One Financial Plaza, Springfield, MA 01103 .... (413) 747–3942

REPRESENTATIVES

FIRST DISTRICT

JOHN W. OLVER, Democrat, of Amherst, MA; born on September 3, 1936, in Honesdale, PA; education: B.S., Rensselaer Polytechnic Institute, 1955; M.A., Tufts University, 1956; taught for two years at Franklin Technical Institute, Boston, MA; Ph.D., Massachusetts Institute of Technology, 1961; chemistry professor, University of Massachusetts-Amherst; Massachusetts House, 1968–72; Massachusetts Senate, 1972–91; became first Democrat since the Spanish-American War to represent the First Congressional District, 1991; elected by special election on June 4, 1991, to fill the vacancy caused by the death of Silvio Conte; married: Rose Olver; children: Martha; committees: Appropriations; subcommittees: Interior; ranking member, Transportation and Treasury; elected on June 4, 1991, by special election, to the 102nd Congress; reelected to each succeeding Congress.

Office Listings

http://www.house.gov/olver

1027 Longworth House Office Building, Washington, DC 20515 .... (202) 225–5335
Chief of Staff.—Hunter Ridgway.
Press Secretary / Scheduler.—Nicole Letourneau.
Legislative Director.—Bob Letteney.
463 Main Street, Fitchburg, MA 01420 .... (978) 342–8722
Office Manager.—Peggy Kane.
57 Suffolk Street, Suite 310, Holyoke, MA 01040 .... (413) 532–7010
District Director.—Jon Niedzielski.
78 Center Street, Pittsfield, MA 01201 .... (413) 442–0946
Office Manager.—Cindy Clark.

Counties: BERKSHIRE, FRANKLIN, HAMPDEN (part), HAMPSHIRE (part), MIDDLESEX (part), WORCESTER (part). Population (2000), 634,479.

ZIP Codes: 01002–05, 01007–08, 01011–12, 01026–27, 01029, 01031–34, 01037–41, 01050, 01054, 01059, 01066, 01068–75, 01077, 01080–82, 01084–86, 01088–90, 01093–94, 01096–98, 01102, 01107, 01201–03, 01220, 01222–27, 01229–30, 01235–38, 01240, 01242–45, 01247, 01252–60, 01262–64, 01266–67, 01270, 01301–02, 01330–31, 01337–44, 01346–47, 01349–51, 01355, 01360, 01364, 01366–68, 01370, 01373, 01375–76, 01378–80, 01420, 01430–31, 01436, 01438, 01440–41, 01452–53, 01462–63, 01468–69, 01473–75, 01477, 01531, 01564, 01585

* * *

SECOND DISTRICT

RICHARD E. NEAL, Democrat, of Springfield, MA; born in Springfield, February 14, 1949; graduated, Springfield Technical High School, 1968; B.A., American International College, Springfield, 1972; M.A., University of Hartford Barney School of Business and Public Administration, CT, 1976; instructor and lecturer; assistant to mayor of Springfield, 1973–78; Springfield City Council, 1978–84; mayor, city of Springfield, 1984–88; member: Massachusetts Mayors Association; Adult Education Council; American International College Alumni Association; Boys Club Alumni Association; Emily Bill Athletic Association; Cancer Crusade; John Boyle O'Reilly Club; United States Conference of Mayors; Valley Press Club; Solid Waste Advisory Committee for the State of Massachusetts; Committee on Leadership and Government; Mass Jobs Council; trustee: Springfield Libraries and Museums Association, Springfield Red Cross, Springfield YMCA; married to Maureen; four children: Rory Christopher, Brendan Conway, Maura Katherine, and Sean Richard; elected on November 8, 1988, to the 101st Congress; reelected to each succeeding Congress.

Office Listings

http://www.house.gov/neal

2133 Rayburn House Office Building, Washington, DC 20515 .... (202) 225–5601
Administrative Assistant.—Ann Jablon. FAX: 225–8112
Executive Assistant.—Sarah Bontempo.
Press Secretary.—Bill Tranghese.
Federal Building, Room 309, 1550 Main Street, Springfield, MA 01103 .... (413) 785–0325
District Manager.—James Leydon.
4 Congress Street, Milford, MA 01757 .... (508) 634–8198
Office Manager.—Virginia Purcell.

Counties: HAMPDEN (part), HAMPSHIRE (part), NORFOLK (part), WORCESTER (part). Population (2000), 634,444.

ZIP Codes: 01001, 01009–10, 01013–14, 01020–22, 01027–28, 01030, 01035–36, 01053, 01056–57, 01060–63, 01069, 01075, 01079–81, 01083, 01092, 01095, 01101–09, 01111, 01115–16, 01118–19, 01128–29, 01133, 01138–39, 01144, 01151–52, 01199, 01504, 01506–09, 01515–16, 01518–19, 01521, 01524–27, 01529, 01534–38, 01540, 01542, 01550, 01560, 01562, 01566, 01568–71, 01585–86, 01588, 01590, 01607, 01611, 01747, 01756–57

* * *

THIRD DISTRICT

JAMES P. MCGOVERN, Democrat, of Worcester, MA; born in Worcester, November 20, 1959; education: B.A., M.P.A., American University; legislative director and senior aide to Congressman Joe Moakley (D–South Boston); led the 1989 investigation into the murders of six Jesuit priests and two lay women in El Salvador; managed George McGovern's (D–SD) 1984 presidential campaign in Massachusetts and delivered his nomination speech at the Democratic

National Convention; board of directors, Jesuit International Volunteers; former volunteer, Mt. Carmel House, an emergency shelter for battered and abused women; married: Lisa Murray McGovern; committees: Rules; subcommittees: Technology and the House; elected to the 105th Congress; reelected to each succeeding Congress.

Office Listings

http://www.house.gov/mcgovern

430 Cannon House Office Building, Washington, DC 20515 .... (202) 225–6101
Chief of Staff.—Ed Augustus. FAX: 225–5759
Legislative Director.—Cindy Buhl.
Press Secretary.—Michael Mershon.
34 Mechanic Street, Worcester, MA 01608 .... (508) 831–7356
District Director.—Gladys Rodriguez-Parker.
1 Park Street, Attleboro, MA 02703 .... (508) 431–8025
District Representative.—Shirley Coelho.
218 South Main Street, Room 204, Fall River, MA 02721 .... (508) 677–0140
District Representative.—Patrick Norton.
255 Main Street, Room 104, Marlborough, MA 01752 .... (508) 460–9292
District Representative.—Matthew Pacheco.

Counties: BRISTOL (part), MIDDLESEX (part), NORFOLK (part), WORCESTER (part). CITIES AND TOWNSHIPS: Ashland, Attleborough, Auburn, Boylston, Clinton, Fall River (part), Franklin, Holden, Holliston, Hopkinton, Marlborough, Medway, North Attleborough, Northborough, Paxton, Plainville, Princeton, Rehoboth, Rutland, Seekonk, Shrewsbury, Somerset, Southborough, Swansea, West Boylston, Westborough, Worcester, and Wrentham. Population (2000), 634,585.

ZIP Codes: 01501, 01505, 01510, 01517, 01520, 01522, 01527, 01532, 01541, 01543, 01545–46, 01580–83, 01601–15, 01653–55, 01721, 01745–46, 01748–49, 01752, 01772, 01784, 02038, 02053, 02070, 02093, 02703, 02720–21, 02723–26, 02760–63, 02769, 02771, 02777

* * *

FOURTH DISTRICT

BARNEY FRANK, Democrat, of Newton, MA; born in Bayonne, NJ, March 31, 1940; graduated, Bayonne High School, 1957; B.A., Harvard College, 1962; graduate student in political science, Harvard University, 1962–67; teaching fellow in government, Harvard College, 1963–66; J.D., Harvard University, 1977; admitted to the Massachusetts bar, 1979; executive assistant to Mayor Kevin White of Boston, 1968–71; administrative assistant to U.S. Congressman Michael F. Harrington, 1971–72; member, Massachusetts Legislature, 1973–80; partner: Sergio Pombo; elected to the 97th Congress, November 4, 1980; reelected to each succeeding Congress.

Office Listings

http://www.house.gov/frank

2252 Rayburn House Office Building, Washington, DC 20515 .... (202) 225–5931
Chief of Staff.—Peter Kovar. FAX: 225–0182
Deputy Chief of Staff / Scheduler.—Maria Giesta.
Administrative Assistant.—Peter Kovar.
29 Crafts Street, Newton, MA 02458 .... (617) 332–3920
District Director.—Dorothy Reichard.
558 Pleasant Street, Room 309, New Bedford, MA 02740 .... (508) 999–6462
Office Manager.—Elsie Souza.
29 Broadway, The Jones Building, Taunton, MA 02780 .... (508) 822–4796
Office Manager.—Garth Patterson.

Counties: BRISTOL (part), MIDDLESEX (part), NORFOLK (part), PLYMOUTH (part). CITIES AND TOWNSHIPS: Acushnet, Berkley, Brookline, Dartmouth, Dighton, Dover, Fairhaven, Fall River (part), Foxboro, Freetown, Halifax, Lakeville, Mansfield, Marion, Mattapoisett, Middleborough, Millis, New Bedford, Newton, Norfolk, Norton, Raynham, Rochester, Sharon, Sherborn, Taunton, Wareham, Wellesley, and Westport. Population (2000), 634,624.

ZIP Codes: 02021, 02030, 02032, 02035, 02048, 02053–54, 02056, 02067, 02130, 02135, 02215, 02330, 02333, 02338, 02344, 02346–47, 02349, 02360, 02367, 02445–47, 02456–62, 02464–68, 02472, 02476, 02481–82, 02492–93, 02495, 02532, 02538, 02558, 02571, 02576, 02702, 02712, 02714–15, 02717–23, 02738–48, 02764, 02766–70, 02779–80, 02783, 02790–91

* * *

FIFTH DISTRICT

MARTIN T. MEEHAN, Democrat, of Lowell, MA; born in Lowell, December 30, 1956; graduated from Lowell High School, 1974; B.A., University of Lowell, 1978; M.P.A., Suffolk University, Boston, MA, 1981; J.D., Suffolk University Law School, 1986; attorney; admitted to the Massachusetts bar, 1986; First Assistant District Attorney for Middlesex County; Deputy Secretary of State; married Ellen Murphy, July 1996; committees: Armed Services; Judiciary; elected on November 3, 1992, to the 103rd Congress; reelected to each succeeding Congress.

Office Listings

http://www.house.gov/meehan

2229 Rayburn House Office Building, Washington, DC 20515 .... (202) 225–3411
Chief of Staff.—William J. McCann. FAX: 226–0771
Press Secretary.—Stacy Kerr.
11 Kearney Square, Lowell, MA 01852 .... (978) 459–0101
305 Essex Street, 4th Floor, Lawrence, MA 01840 .... (978) 681–6200
Haverhill City Hall, 2nd Floor, Room 201A, 4 Summer Street, Haverhill, MA 01830 .... (978) 521–1845

Counties: ESSEX (part), MIDDLESEX (part), WORCESTER (part). CITIES AND TOWNSHIPS: Acton, Andover, Ayer, Berlin, Bolton, Boxborough, Carlisle, Chelmsford, Concord, Dillerjca, Drocut, Dunstable, Groton, Harvard, Haverhill, Hudson, Lawrence, Lancaster, Littleton, Lowell, Maynard, Methuen, Shirley, Stow, Sudbury, Tewksbury, Tyngsborough, Wayland, and Westford. Population (2000), 635,326.

ZIP Codes: 01432, 01450–51, 01453, 01460, 01464, 01467, 01470–72, 01503, 01523, 01561, 01718–20, 01740–42, 01749, 01754, 01775–76, 01778, 01810, 01812, 01821–22, 01824, 01826–27, 01830, 01832, 01835, 01840–44, 01850–54, 01862–63, 01865–66, 01876, 01879, 01886, 01899, 02493, 05501, 05544

* * *

SIXTH DISTRICT

JOHN F. TIERNEY, Democrat, of Salem, MA; born on September 18, 1951, in Salem; graduated, Salem High School; B.A., political science, Salem State College, 1973; J.D., Suffolk University, 1976; attorney, admitted to the Massachusetts bar in 1976; sole practitioner, 1976–80; partner, Tierney, Kalis and Lucas, 1981–96; member: Salem Chamber of Commerce, 1976–96 (president, 1995); trustee, Salem State College, 1992–97; married Patrice M. Tierney, 1997; committees: Education and the Workforce; Government Reform; subcommittees: Employer-Employee Relations; ranking member, Energy Policy, Natural Resources and Regulatory Affairs; National Security, Emerging Threats and International Relations; 21st Century Competitiveness; elected to the 105th Congress; reelected to each succeeding Congress.

Office Listings

http://www.house.gov/tierney

120 Cannon House Office Building, Washington, DC 20515 .... (202) 225–8020
Chief of Staff.—Christine Pelosi. FAX: 225–5915
Legislative Director.—Perry Lange.
Executive Assistant.—Abby Wolfson.
17 Peabody Square, Peabody, MA 01960 .... (978) 531–1669
District Director.—Gary Barrett.
Room 410, Lynn City Hall, Lynn, MA 01902 .... (781) 595–7375

Counties: ESSEX, MIDDLESEX. CITIES AND TOWNSHIPS: Amesbury, Bedford, Beverly, Boxford, Burlington, Danvers, Essex, Georgetown, Gloucester, Groveland, Hamilton, Ipswich, Lynn, Lynnfield, Manchester by the Sea, Marblehead, Merrimac, Middletown, Nahant, Newbury, Newburyport, North Andover, North Reading, Peabody, Reading (part), Rockport, Rowley, Salem, Salisbury, Saugus, Swampscott, Topsfield, Wenham, West Newbury, Wakefield, and Wilmington. Population (2000), 636,554.

ZIP Codes: 01730–31, 01801, 01803, 01805, 01810, 01821, 01833–34, 01845, 01860, 01864, 01867, 01880, 01885, 01887, 01889, 01901–08, 01910, 01913, 01915, 01921–23, 01929–31, 01936–38, 01940, 01944–45, 01949–52, 01960–61, 01965–66, 01969–71, 01982–85

* * *

SEVENTH DISTRICT

EDWARD J. MARKEY, Democrat, of Malden, MA; born in Malden, July 11, 1946; graduated, Malden Catholic High School, 1964; B.A., Boston College, 1968; J.D., Boston College Law School, 1972; lawyer; served in the U.S. Army Reserves, 1968–73; member, Massachusetts House of Representatives, 1973–76; elected to the 94th Congress, November 2, 1976, to fill the vacancy caused by the death of Representative Torbert H. Macdonald; at the same time elected to the 95th Congress; reelected to each succeeding Congress.

Office Listings

http://www.house.gov/markey

2108 Rayburn House Office Building, Washington, DC 20515 .... (202) 225–2836
Chief of Staff.—David Moulton.
Executive Assistant.—Nancy Morrissey.
Legislative Director.—Jeff Duncan.
5 High Street, Suite 101, Medford, MA 02155 .... (781) 396–2900
188 Concord Street, Suite 102, Framingham, MA 01701 .... (508) 875–2900

Counties: MIDDLESEX (part), SUFFOLK (part). CITIES AND TOWNSHIPS: Arlington (part), Belmont, Everett, Framingham (part), Lexington (part), Lincoln, Malden, Medford, Melrose, Natick, Revere, Stoneham, Waltham (part), Watertown, Wayland (part), Weston, Winchester, Winthrop, and Woburn. Population (2000), 634,287.

ZIP Codes: 01701–05, 01731, 01760, 01773, 01776, 01778, 01801, 01803, 01806–08, 01813, 01815, 01888, 01890, 02138, 02144, 02148–49, 02151–53, 02155–56, 02176, 02180, 02420–21, 02451–55, 02461, 02466, 02471–72, 02474–76, 02478–79, 02493

* * *

EIGHTH DISTRICT

MICHAEL E. CAPUANO, Democrat, of Somerville, MA; born in Somerville, MA, on January 1, 1952; graduated, Somerville High School, 1969; B.A., Dartmouth College, 1973; J.D., Boston College Law School, 1977; admitted to the Massachusetts Bar, 1977; Alderman in Somerville, MA, 1977–79; Alderman-at-Large, 1985–89; elected Mayor for five terms, 1990 to January, 1999, when he resigned to be sworn in as a U.S. Representative; committees: Financial Services; Transportation and Infrastructure; subcommittees: Aviation; Capital Markets, Insurance and Government-Sponsored Enterprises; Highways, Transit and Pipelines; Housing and Community Opportunity; Democratic Regional Whip; married Barbara Teebagy of Somerville, MA, in 1974; two children: Michael and Joseph; elected to the 106th Congress; reelected to each succeeding Congress.

Office Listings

http://www.house.gov/capuano

1232 Longworth House Office Building, Washington, DC 20515 .... (202) 225–5111
Chief of Staff.—Robert Primus. FAX: 225–9322
Office Manager / Scheduler.—Mary Doherty.
Senior Legislative Assistants: Jon Skarin, Christopher Huckleberry.
Legislative Assistant.—Christine Locke.
110 First Street, Cambridge, MA 02141 .... (617) 621–6208
District Director.—Michael J. Gorman.

Counties: MIDDLESEX (part), SUFFOLK (part). CITIES AND TOWNSHIPS: Boston (part), Cambridge, Chelsea, and Somerville. Population (2000), 634,835.

ZIP Codes: 02108–11, 02113–22, 02124–26, 02128–31, 02133–36, 02138–45, 02150–51, 02155, 02163, 02199, 02215–17, 02228, 02238–39, 02295, 02297, 02446, 02458, 02467, 02472, 02478

* * *

NINTH DISTRICT

STEPHEN F. LYNCH, Democrat, of South Boston, MA; born on March 31, 1955, in South Boston; education: South Boston High School, 1973; B.S., Wentworth Institute of Technology; J.D., Boston College Law School; Master in Public Administration, JFK School of Government, Harvard University; professional: Attorney; former President of Ironworkers Local #7; organizations: South Boston Boys and Girls Club; Boston Children's Museum; Colonel Daniel Marr Boys and Girls Club; Chinatown Trust Fund; South Boston Harbor Academy Charter School; Friends for Children; public service: elected to the Massachusetts House of Representatives in 1994, and the State Senate in 1996; family: married to Margaret; one child: Victoria; committees: Financial Services; Government Reform; elected to the 107th Congress, by special election, on October 16, 2001; reelected to each succeeding Congress.

Office Listings

319 Cannon House Office Building, Washington, DC 20515 .... (202) 225–8273
Chief of Staff.—Kevin Ryan. FAX: 225–3984
Legislative Director.—Caroline Powers.
Legislative Counsel.—Kerry McGinn.
Executive Assistant.—Greta Hebert.

Moakley Federal Courthouse, 1 Courthouse Way, Suite 3110, Boston, MA 02210 (617) 428–2000
District Director.—Stacey Walker.
166 Main Street, Brockton, MA 02401 .... (508) 586–5555

Counties: BRISTOL (part), NORFOLK (part), PLYMOUTH (part), SUFFOLK (part). Population (2000), 634,062.

ZIP Codes: 02021, 02026–27, 02032, 02052, 02062, 02071–72, 02081, 02090, 02101–10, 02112, 02114, 02116, 02122, 02124–27, 02130–32, 02136–37, 02151, 02169–71, 02184–87, 02196, 02201–12, 02222, 02241, 02266, 02283–84, 02293, 02297, 02301–05, 02322, 02324–25, 02333–34, 02337, 02341, 02343, 02350, 02356–57, 02368, 02375, 02379, 02382, 02467, 02481, 02492, 02494

* * *

TENTH DISTRICT

WILLIAM D. DELAHUNT, Democrat, of Quincy, MA; born in Boston, MA, on July 18, 1941; B.A., political science, Middlebury College, VT; M.A., J.D., Boston College Law School, 1967; U.S. Coast Guard Reserves, 1963–71; admitted to the Massachusetts Bar in 1967 and began practice in Boston; assistant majority leader, Massachusetts House of Representatives, 1973–75; Norfolk County District Attorney, 1975–96; president, Massachusetts District Attorneys Association, 1985; member, Council of Young American Political Leaders fact-finding mission to Poland, 1979; named citizen of the Year by South Shore Coalition for Human Rights, 1983; delegate, Human Rights Project fact-finding mission to Cuba, 1988; member, Anti-Defamation League of B'nai B'rith fact-finding mission to Israel, 1990; chairman, Development Committee, South Shore Association for Retarded Citizens; Democratic State Committeeman, Norfolk District; advisory board member, Jane Doe Safety Fund; honoree of the Boston Area Rape Crisis Center for contribution to preventing sexual assault, 1993; New England Region honoree, Anti-Defamation League, 1994; Massachusetts Bar Association Public Service Award, 1994; member, Board of Directors, RYKA Rose Foundation; committees: Judiciary; International Relations; co-chair, Coast Guard Caucus; Older Americans Caucus; Democratic Task Force on Crime; Law Enforcement Caucus; Congressional Human Rights Caucus; Democratic Steering Committee; two daughters: Kirsten and Kara; elected to the 105th Congress; reelected to each succeeding Congress.

Office Listings

1317 Longworth House Office Building, Washington, DC 20515 .... (202) 225–3111
Chief of Staff.—Steve Schwadron. FAX: 225–5658
146 Main Street, Hyannis, MA 02601 .... (508) 771–0666
Regional Representative.—Mark Forest.
1250 Hancock Street, Suite 802N, Quincy, MA 02169 .... (617) 770–3700
Regional Representative.—Corinne Young.

Counties: BARNSTABLE, DUKES, NANTUCKET, NORFOLK (part), PLYMOUTH (part). Population (2000), 635,901.

ZIP Codes: 02018, 02020, 02025, 02035, 02040–41, 02043–45, 02047, 02050–51, 02055, 02059–61, 02065–66, 02169–71, 02184, 02186, 02188–91, 02269, 02327, 02330–32, 02339–41, 02345, 02351, 02355, 02358–62, 02364, 02366–67, 02370, 02381, 02532, 02534–37, 02539–43, 02552–54, 02556–57, 02559, 02561–65, 02568, 02573–75, 02584, 02601, 02630–35, 02637–39, 02641–53, 02655, 02657, 02659–64, 02666–73, 02675, 02713

MICHIGAN

(Population 2000, 9,938,444)

SENATORS

CARL M. LEVIN, Democrat, of Detroit, MI; born in Detroit, MI, on June 28, 1934; graduated, Central High School, Detroit, 1952; Swarthmore College, Swarthmore, PA, 1956; Harvard Law School, Boston, MA, 1959; lawyer; Grossman, Hyman and Grossman, Detroit, 1959–64; assistant attorney general and general counsel for Michigan Civil Rights Commission, 1964–67; chief appellate defender for city of Detroit, 1968–69; counsel, Schlussel, Lifton, Simon, Rands and Kaufman, 1971–73; counsel, Jaffe, Snider, Raitt, Garratt and Heuer, 1978–79; admitted to the Michigan bar in 1959; member, City Council of Detroit, 1969–77; president, City Council of Detroit, 1974–77; member: Congregation T'Chiyah; American, Michigan and Detroit bar associations; former instructor at Wayne State University and the University of Detroit; married the former Barbara Halpern, 1961; three daughters: Kate, Laura, and Erica; elected to the U.S. Senate on November 7, 1978; reelected to each succeeding Senate term.

Office Listings

http://levin.senate.gov

269 Russell Senate Office Building, Washington, DC 20510 .... (202) 224–6221
Administrative Assistant.—David Lyles.
Legislative Director.—Rich Arenberg.
Executive Secretary.—Susan Cameron.
Press Secretary.—Tara Andringa.
McNamara Building, Room 1860, 477 Michigan Avenue, Detroit, MI 48226 .... (313) 226–6020
Federal Building, Room 720, 110 Michigan Street, NW, Grand Rapids, MI 49503.. (616) 456–2531
1810 Michigan National Tower, 124 West Allegan Street, Lansing, MI 48933 .... (517) 377–1508
524 Ludington Street, Suite LL103, Escanaba, MI 49829 .... (906) 789–0052
615 North Washington, Suite 402, Saginaw, MI 48607 .... (989) 754–2494
30500 VanDyke, Suite 206, Warren, MI 48093 .... (810) 573–9145
207 Grandview Parkway, Suite 104, Traverse City, MI 49684 .... (616) 947–9569

* * *

DEBBIE STABENOW, Democrat, of Lansing, MI; born on April 29, 1950, in Gladwin, MI; education: Clare High School; B.A., Michigan State University, 1972; M.S.W., Michigan State University, 1975; public service: Ingham County, MI, Commissioner, 1975–1978, chairperson for two years; Michigan State House of Representatives, 1979–1990; Michigan State Senate, 1991–1994; religion: Methodist; married to Thomas Athans; two children: Todd and Michelle; elected to the U.S. House of Representatives in 1996 and 1998; elected to the U.S. Senate on November 7, 2000.

Office Listings

http://stabenow.senate.gov

702 Hart Senate Office Building, Washington, DC 20510 .... (202) 224–4822
Chief of Staff / Legislative Director.—Sander Lurie. FAX: 228–0325
Communications Director.—David Lemmon.
Executive Assistant / Scheduler.—Sally Cluthe.
280 East Saginaw Street, East Lansing, MI 48823 .... (517) 203–1760
Marquette Building, 243 West Congress, Suite 550, Detroit, MI 48226 .... (313) 961–4330
3230 Broadmoor Street, Suite B, Grand Rapids, MI 49512 .... (616) 975–0052
2503 South Linden Road, Flint, MI 48532 .... (810) 720–4172

REPRESENTATIVES

FIRST DISTRICT

BART STUPAK, Democrat, of Menominee, MI; born in Milwaukee, WI, on February 29, 1952; graduated, Gladstone High School, Gladstone, MI, 1970; B.S., Saginaw Valley State College, 1977; J.D., Thomas Cooley Law School, 1981; attorney; admitted to the Michigan bar, 1981; Michigan State House of Representatives, 1989–90; member: Elks Club; State Employees Retirement Association; Sons of the American Legion; Wildlife Unlimited; National Rifle Association; Knights of Columbus; national committeeman, Boy Scouts of America; married to the former Laurie Ann Olsen; two children: Ken and Bart, Jr. (deceased); elected on November 3, 1992, to the 103rd Congress; reelected to each succeeding Congress.

Office Listings

http://www.house.gov/stupak

2352 Rayburn House Office Building, Washington, DC 20515	(202) 225–4735
Chief of Staff.—Scott Schloegel.	FAX: 225–4744
Legislative Director.—Lynne Jensen.	
Press Secretary.—Leslie Thomsen.	
District Administrator.—Tom Baldini.	
512 East Houghton Avenue, West Branch, MI 48661	(989) 345–2258
902 Ludington Street, Escanaba, MI 49829	(906) 786–4504
1229 West Washington, Marquette, MI 49855	(906) 228–3700
111 East Chisholm, Alpena, MI 49707	(989) 356–0690
2 South 6th Street, Suite 3, Crystal Falls, MI 49920	(906) 875–3751
616 Sheldon Avenue, Room 213, Houghton, MI 49931	(906) 482–1371
200 Division Street, Petoskey, MI 49770	(231) 348–0657

Counties: ALCONA, ALGER, ALPENA, ANTRIM, ARENAC, BARAGA, BAY (part), CHARLEVOIX, CHEBOYGAN, CHIPPEWA, CRAWFORD, DELTA, DICKINSON, EMMET, GOGEBIC, HOUGHTON, IRON, KEWEENAW, LUCE, MACKINAC, MARQUETTE, MENOMINEE, MONTMORENCY, OGEMAW, ONTONAGON, OSCODA, OTSEGO, PRESQUE ISLE, SCHOOLCRAFT. Population (2000), 662,563.

ZIP Codes: 48610–13, 48618–19, 48621, 48623–24, 48628, 48631, 48634–36, 48642, 48647, 48650, 48652–54, 48658–59, 48661, 48703, 48705–06, 48721, 48728, 48730, 48737–40, 48742–43, 48745, 48748–50, 48756, 48761–66, 48770, 49611–12, 49615, 49622, 49627, 49629, 49648, 49659, 49676, 49701, 49705–07, 49709–13, 49715–30, 49733–40, 49743–49, 49751–53, 49755–57, 49759–62, 49764–66, 49768–70, 49774–77, 49779–85, 49788, 49790–93, 49795–97, 49799, 49801–02, 49805–08, 49812, 49814–22, 49825–27, 49829, 49831, 49833–41, 49845, 49847–49, 49852–55, 49858, 49861–64, 49866, 49868, 49870–74, 49876–81, 49883–87, 49891–96, 49901–03, 49905, 49908, 49910–13, 49915–22, 49925, 49927, 49929–31, 49934–35, 49938, 49945–48, 49950, 49952–53, 49955, 49958–65, 49967–71

* * *

SECOND DISTRICT

PETER HOEKSTRA, Republican, of Holland, MI; born in Groningen, the Netherlands, on October 30, 1953; education: graduated, Holland Christian High School; B.A., Hope College, Holland, 1975; M.B.A., University of Michigan, 1977; employment: vice president for product management, Herman Miller, Inc.; married: the former Diane Johnson; children: Erin, Allison, and Bryan; elected on November 3, 1992, to the 103rd Congress; reelected to each succeeding Congress.

Office Listings

http://www.house.gov/hoekstra

2234 Rayburn House Office Building, Washington, DC 20515	(202) 225–4401
Chief of Staff.—John Vanfossen.	FAX: 226–0779
Legislative Director.—Justin Wormmeester.	
Scheduler / Executive Assistant.—Kathleen Whitfield.	
District Director of Policy.—Jon DeWitte.	
184 South River, Holland, MI 49423	(616) 395–0030
900 Third Street, Suite 203, Muskegon, MI 49440	(231) 722–8386
210½ North Mitchell Street, Cadillac, MI 49601	(231) 775–0050

Counties: ALLEGAN (part), BENZIE, KENT (part), LAKE, MANISTEE, MASON, MUSKEGON, NEWAYGO, OCEANA, OTTAWA, WEXFORD. Population (2000), 662,563.

ZIP Codes: 49010, 49078, 49080, 49303–04, 49307, 49309, 49312, 49314–15, 49318–19, 49321, 49323, 49327–30, 49333, 49336–38, 49343, 49345–46, 49348–49, 49401–06, 49408–13, 49415, 49417–31, 49434–37, 49440 46, 49448 49, 49451 61, 49463–64, 49544, 49601, 49613–14, 49616–20, 49623, 49625–26, 49628, 49630, 49633–35, 49638, 49640, 49642–45, 49649–50, 49655–56, 49660, 49663, 49668, 49675, 49677, 49683, 49688–89

* * *

THIRD DISTRICT

VERNON J. EHLERS, Republican, of Grand Rapids, MI; born on February 6, 1934, in Pipestone, MN; educated at home by his parents; attended Calvin College; undergraduate degree in physics and Ph.D. in nuclear physics, University of California at Berkeley; taught and did research at Berkeley for 6 years; returned to Calvin College; taught physics and became chairman, Physics Department; served on various boards and commissions; member, Michigan House and Senate; first research physicist in Congress; while on Science Committee in 1997–98, was selected to rewrite the nation's science policy; introduced National Science Education Acts aimed at reforming K–12 science, mathematics, engineering, and technology education; as member of House Administration Committee, guided the program to revamp the House computer system, connect it to the Internet, and allow all citizens to access House documents; member and former elder, Eastern Avenue Christian Reformed Church, Grand Rapids, MI; family: married to the former Johanna Meulink; four adult children: Heidi, Brian, Marla, and Todd; three grandchildren; committees: vice chairman, Joint Committee on the Library of Congress; Education and the Workforce; House Administration; Science; Transportation and Infrastructure; subcommittees: chairman, Environment, Technology, and Standards; elected to the 103rd Congress, by special election, on December 7, 1993; reelected to each succeeding Congress.

Office Listings

http://www.house.gov/ehlers

1714 Longworth House Office Building, Washington, DC 20515 .... (202) 225–3831
Chief of Staff.—Bill McBride.
Deputy Chief of Staff / Legislative Director.—Cameron Wilson.
Executive Assistant / Scheduler.—Loraine Kehl.
Press Secretary.—Jon Brandt.
110 Michigan Street, NW, Suite 166, Grand Rapids, MI 49503 .... (616) 451–8383
Community Services Director.—Jeanne Englehart.

Counties: BARRY, IONIA, KENT (part). CITIES: Belding, Cedar Springs, East Grand Rapids, Grand Rapids, Grandville, Hastings, Ionia, Kentwood, Lowell, Portland, Rockford, Walker, and Wyoming. Population (2000), 662,563.

ZIP Codes: 48809, 48815, 48834, 48837–38, 48845–46, 48849, 48851, 48860–61, 48865, 48870–71, 48873, 48875, 48881, 48887, 48890, 48897, 49017, 49021, 49035, 49046, 49050, 49058, 49060, 49073, 49080, 49083, 49301–02, 49306, 49315–17, 49319, 49321, 49325–26, 49331, 49333, 49341, 49343–45, 49347–48, 49351, 49355–57, 49418, 49468, 49501–10, 49512, 49514–16, 49518, 49523, 49525, 49530, 49544, 49546, 49548, 49550, 49555, 49560, 49588, 49599

* * *

FOURTH DISTRICT

DAVE CAMP, Republican, of Midland, MI; born in Midland, July 9, 1953; graduated, H.H. Dow High School, Midland, 1971; B.A., Albion College, Albion, MI, 1975, *magna cum laude*; J.D., University of San Diego, 1978; attorney, member of State Bar of Michigan, State Bar of California, District of Columbia bar, U.S. Supreme Court; U.S. District Court, Eastern District of Michigan and Southern District of California; Midland County Bar Association; law practice, Midland, 1979–91; Special Assistant Attorney General, 1980–84; administrative assistant to Congressman Bill Schuette, Michigan's 10th Congressional District, 1985–87; State Representative, Michigan's 102nd district, 1989–91; committees: Ways and Means; Select Committee on Homeland Security; subcommittees: Health; Trade; Human Resources; chairman, Corrections Day Advisory Group; assistant majority whip; National Republican Congressional Committee; Executive Committee; Rural Health Care Coalition; 1998 Adoption Hall of Fame Inductee; American Farm Bureau Federation 1998 Golden Plow award recipient; married: attorney Nancy Keil of Midland, 1994; three children; elected to Congress on November 6, 1990; reelected to each succeeding Congress.

Office Listings

http://www.house.gov/camp

137 Cannon House Office Building, Washington, DC 20515 .... (202) 225–3561
Chief of Staff.—Jim Brandell. FAX: 225–9679
Communications Director.—Deanne Brady.
Legislative Director.—Deirdre Onizuk.
Scheduler.—Tim Cummings.
135 Ashman Street, Midland, MI, 48640 .... (989) 631–2552
121 East Front Street, Suite 202, Traverse City, MI 49684 .... (231) 929–4711

Counties: CLARE COUNTY. CITIES: Clare, Farwell, Harrison, Lake, Lake George. CLINTON COUNTY. CITY: Carland. GRAND TRAVERSE COUNTY. CITIES: Acme, Fife Lake, Grawn, Interlochen, Kingsley, Mayfield, Old Mission, Traverse City, Williamsburg. GRATIOT COUNTY. CITIES: Alma, Ashley, Bannister, Breckenridge, Elm Hall, Elwell, Ithaca, Middleton, North Star, Perrinton, Pompeii, Riverdale, Sumner, St. Louis, Wheeler. ISABELLA COUNTY. CITIES: Blanchard, Millbrook, Mt. Pleasant, Rosebush, Shepherd, Weidman, Winn. KALKASKA COUNTY. CITIES: Kalkaska, Rapid City, South Boardman. LEELANAU COUNTY. CITIES: Cedar, Empire, Glen Arbor, Lake Leelanau, Leland, Maple City, Northport, Omena, Suttons Bay. MECOSTA COUNTY. CITIES: Barryton, Big Rapids, Canadian Lakes, Chippewa Lakes, Mecosta, Morley, Paris, Remus, Stanwood. MIDLAND COUNTY. CITIES: Coleman, Edenville, Hope, Laporte, Midland, North Bradley, Poseyville, Sanford. MISSAUKEE COUNTY. CITIES: Falmouth, Lake City, McBain, Merritt, Moorestown. MONTCALM COUNTY. CITIES: Alger, Butternut, Carson City, Cedar Lake, Coral, Crystal, Edmore, Entrican, Fenwick, Gowen, Greenville, Howard City, Lakeview, Langston, Maple Hill, McBride, Pierson, Sand Lake, Sheridan, Sidney, Six Lakes, Stanton, Trufant, Vestaburg, Vickeryville. OSCEOLA COUNTY. CITIES: Evart, Hersey, LeRoy, Marion, Reed City, Sears, Tustin. ROSCOMMON COUNTY. CITIES: Higgins Lake, Houghton Lake, Houghton Lake Heights, Prudenville, Roscommon, St. Helen. SAGINAW COUNTY (part). CITIES: Birch Run, Brant, Bridgeport, Burt, Carrolton, Chesaning, Fosters, Freeland, Fremont, Hemlock, Merrill, Oakley, Richland, Saginaw, Shields, Spalding, St. Charles, University Center. SHIAWASSEE COUNTY (part). CITIES: Bancroft, Caledonia, Chapin, Corunna, Henderson, Laingsburg, Morrice, New Haven, New Lothrup, Owosso, Perry, Shaftsburg, Venice, and Vernon. Population (2000), 662,563.

ZIP Codes: 48415, 48417, 48429, 48433, 48436, 48449, 48457, 48460, 48476, 48601–04, 48608–09, 48614–18, 48620, 48622–30, 48632–33, 48637, 48640–42, 48649, 48651–53, 48655–57, 48662, 48667, 48670, 48674, 48686, 48706, 48722, 48724, 48801–02, 48804, 48806–07, 48809, 48811–12, 48817–18, 48829–32, 48834, 48837–38, 48841, 48845, 48847, 48850, 48852–53, 48856, 48858–59, 48862, 48866–67, 48874–75, 48877–80, 48883–86, 48888–89, 48891, 48893, 48896, 49305, 49307, 49310, 49320, 49322–23, 49326, 49328–29, 49332, 49336–40, 49342–43, 49346–47, 49601, 49610, 49612, 49620–21, 49630–33, 49636–37, 49639–40, 49643, 49646, 49649, 49651, 49653–55, 49657, 49659, 49663–67, 49670, 49673–74, 49676–77, 49679–80, 49682–86, 49688, 49690, 49696, 49738

* * *

FIFTH DISTRICT

DALE E. KILDEE, Democrat, of Flint, MI; born in Flint, September 16, 1929; graduated, St. Mary High School, 1947; B.A., Sacred Heart Seminary, Detroit, 1952; M.A., University of Michigan, Ann Arbor, 1961; graduate studies in history and political science, University of Peshawar, Pakistan, under Rotary Foundation Fellowship; teacher, University of Detroit High School, 1954–56; Flint Central High School, 1956–64; served as State Representative, 1965–74; State Senator, 1975–77; member: Optimists, Urban League, Knights of Columbus, Phi Delta Kappa national honorary fraternity, American Federation of Teachers; life member, National Association for the Advancement of Colored People; married to the former Gayle Heyn, 1965; three children: David, Laura, and Paul; elected to the 95th Congress, November 2, 1976; reelected to each succeeding Congress.

Office Listings

2107 Rayburn House Office Building, Washington, DC 20515 .... (202) 225–3611
Administrative Assistant.—Christopher J. Mansour. FAX: 225–6393
Legislative Director.—Callig Coffman.
Personal Secretary.—Greta Moore.
432 North Saginaw, Suite 410, Flint, MI 48502 .... (810) 239–1437
District Director, all Districts.—Tiffany Anderson-Flynn. (800) 662–2685
515 North Washington Avenue, Suite 401, Saginaw, MI 48607 .... (989) 755–8904
916 Washington Avenue, Suite 205, Bay City, MI 48708 .... (989) 891–0990

Counties: BAY (part), GENESEE, SAGINAW (part), TUSCOLA. Population (2000), 662,563.

ZIP Codes: 48411, 48415, 48417–18, 48420–21, 48423, 48426, 48429–30, 48433, 48435–39, 48449, 48451, 48453, 48457–58, 48460, 48462–64, 48473, 48501–07, 48509, 48519, 48529, 48531–32, 48550–57, 48601–07, 48623, 48631, 48663, 48701, 48706–08, 48710, 48722–23, 48726–27, 48729, 48732–36, 48741, 48744, 48746–47, 48757–60, 48767–69, 48787

* * *

SIXTH DISTRICT

FRED UPTON, Republican, of St. Joseph, MI; born in St. Joseph, on April 23, 1953; graduated, Shattuck School, Fairbault, MN, 1971; B.A., journalism, University of Michigan, Ann Arbor, 1975; field manager, Dave Stockman Campaign, 1976; staff member, Congressman Dave Stockman, 1976–80; legislative assistant, Office of Management and Budget, 1981–83; deputy director of Legislative Affairs, 1983–84; director of Legislative Affairs, 1984–85; member: First Congregational Church, Emil Verbin Society; married to the former Amey Rulon-Miller; elected to the 100th Congress on November 4, 1986; reelected to each succeeding Congress.

Office Listings

2161 Rayburn House Office Building, Washington, DC 20515 .... (202) 225–3761
Administrative Assistant.—Joan Hillebrands. FAX: 225–4986
Executive Assistant.—Rachel Williams.
800 Centre, Suite 106, 800 Ship Street, St. Joseph, MI 49085 .... (269) 982–1986
157 South Kalamazoo Mall, Suite 180, Kalamazoo, MI 49006 .... (269) 385–0039

Counties: ALLEGAN (part), BERRIEN, CALHOUN (part), CASS, KALAMAZOO, ST. JOSEPH, VAN BUREN. CITIES AND TOWNSHIPS: Allegan, Augusta, Bangor, Baroda, Benton Harbor, Berrien Springs, Berrien Center, Bloomingdale, Breedsville, Bridgman, Buchanan, Burr Oak, Cassopolis, Centreville, Climax, Coloma, Colon, Comstock, Constantine, Covert, Decatur, Delton, Dowagiac, Eau Claire, Edwardsburg, Fulton, Galesburg, Galien, Gobles, Grand Junction, Hagar Shores, Harbert, Hartford, Hickory Corners, Jones, Kalamazoo, Kendall, Lacota, Lakeside, Lawrence, Lawton, Leonidas, Marcellus, Mattawan, Mendon, Nazareth, New Troy, New Buffalo, Niles, Nottawa, Oshtemo, Otsego, Paw Paw, Plainwell, Portage, Pullman, Richland, Riverside, Sawyer, Schoolcraft, Scotts, Sodus, South Haven, St. Joseph, Stevensville, Sturgis, Three Oaks, Three Rivers, Union Pier, Union, Vandalia, Vicksburg, Watervliet, and White Pigeon. Population (2000), 662,563.

ZIP Codes: 48867, 49001–15, 49017, 49019, 49022–24, 49026–27, 49030–32, 49034, 49038–43, 49045, 49047–48, 49051–53, 49055–57, 49060–67, 49070–72, 49074–75, 49077–81, 49083–85, 49087–88, 49090–91, 49093, 49095,

49097–99, 49101–04, 49106–07, 49111–13, 49115–17, 49119–21, 49125–30, 49311, 49315–16, 49323, 49328, 49333, 49335, 49344, 49348, 49408, 49416, 49450

* * *

SEVENTH DISTRICT

NICK SMITH, Republican, of Addison, MI; born in Addison, on November 5, 1934; attended Addison Community Schools; B.A., Michigan State University, East Lansing, MI, 1957; M.S., University of Delaware, 1959; served as captain, military intelligence, U.S. Air Force, 1959–61; elected to Addison Township as trustee, supervisor, and county board member; member: Addison Community Hospital Board; State chairman, Agriculture Stabilization and Conservation Service; director, Michigan Farm Bureau; National Director of Energy for the U.S. Department of Agriculture; Michigan House of Representatives, 1978–82; Michigan State Senate, 1982–92; member: National Delegation on U.S.-Soviet Cooperation and Trade; awards: Kellogg Foundation Fellow, Outstanding Young Men of America; married the former Bonnalyn Atwood, 1960; four children: Julianna Smith Bellinger, Bradley LeGrand, Elizabeth Smith Burnette, and Stacia Kathleen; committees: Agriculture; International Relations; Science; elected on November 3, 1992, to the 103rd Congress; reelected to each succeeding Congress.

Office Listings

http://www.house.gov/nicksmith

2305 Rayburn House Office Building, Washington, DC 20515 .... (202) 225–6276
Administrative Assistant.—Kurt Schmautz.
Executive Assistant.—Mary Christ.
110 First Street, Suite A, Jackson, MI 49201 .... (517) 783–4486
Chief of Staff.—Keith Brown.
249 W. Michigan, Battle Creek, MI 49015 .... (616) 965–9066

Counties: BRANCH, CALHOUN (part), EATON, HILLSDALE, JACKSON, LENAWEE, WASHTENAW (part). Population (2000), 662,563.

ZIP Codes: 48103, 48105, 48115, 48118, 48130, 48158, 48160, 48167, 48170, 48175–76, 48178, 48189, 48601, 48813, 48821, 48827, 48837, 48849, 48861, 48876, 48890, 48906, 48908, 48911, 48917, 49011, 49014–18, 49020–21, 49028–30, 49033, 49036, 49040, 49051–52, 49058, 49068–69, 49073, 49076, 49082, 49089, 49092, 49094, 49096, 49201–04, 49220–21, 49224, 49227–30, 49232–42, 49245–59, 49261–69, 49271–72, 49274–77, 49279, 49281–89

* * *

EIGHTH DISTRICT

MIKE ROGERS, Republican, of Brighton, MI; born on June 2, 1963, in Livingston County, MI; education: B.S., Adrian College, also attended the University of Michigan as an Army ROTC member; military service: U.S. Army; 1st Lieutenant, served in a rapid deployment unit as a Company Commander; employment: FBI Special Agent, assigned to public corruption and organized crime units; businessman; co-founder of E.B.I. Builders, Inc.; organizations: American Heart Association; Women's Resource Center; Brighton Rotary Club; Society of Former Special Agents of the FBI; religion: Methodist; married: Diane; children: Erin and Jonathan; elected to the 107th Congress on November 7, 2000; reelected to each succeeding Congress.

Office Listings

http://www.house.gov/mikerogers

133 Cannon House Office Building, Washington, DC 20515 .... (202) 225–4872
Chief of Staff.—Matt Strawn. FAX: 225–5820
Legislative Director.—Heather Keiser.
Press Secretary.—Sylvia Warner.
1327 East Michigan Avenue, Lansing, MI 48912 .... (517) 702–8000

Counties: CLINTON, INGHAM, LIVINGSTON, OAKLAND (part), SHIAWASSE (part). Population (2000), 662,563.

ZIP Codes: 48114, 48116, 48137, 48139, 48143, 48169, 48178, 48189, 48329, 48346–48, 48350, 48353, 48356–57, 48359–62, 48366–67, 48370–71, 48380, 48386, 48414, 48418, 48428–30, 48436, 48438–39, 48442, 48451, 48455, 48462, 48504, 48507, 48805, 48807–08, 48816–17, 48819–27, 48831, 48833, 48835–37, 48840, 48842–45, 48848, 48854–55, 48857, 48863–64, 48866–67, 48872–73, 48875, 48879, 48882, 48892, 48894–95, 48901, 48906, 48909–13, 48915–19, 48921–22, 48924, 48929–30, 48933, 48937, 48950–51, 48956, 48980, 49078, 49080, 49251, 49264, 49285

NINTH DISTRICT

JOE KNOLLENBERG, Republican, of Bloomfield Hills, MI; born in Mattoon, IL, on November 28, 1933; graduated Eastern Illinois University, B.S.; operated family insurance agency; Troy Chamber of Commerce, past vice chairman; Birmingham Cable TV Community Advisory Board, past member; St. Bede's Parish Council, past president and board member; Evergreen School PTA, past president; Bloomfield Glens Homeowners Association, past president; Cranbrook Homeowners Association, past president; Southfield Ad Hoc Park and Recreational Development Committee, past coordinator; Southfield Mayor's Wage and Salary Committee, past member; married to the former Sandra Moco; two sons, Martin and Stephen; elected to the Freshman Class Leadership, liaison to the National Republican Congressional Committee; committees: Appropriations; subcommittees: chairman, Military Construction; Foreign Operations, Export Financing, and Related Programs; Veterans Affairs, HUD, and Independent Agencies; elected on November 3, 1992, to the 103rd Congress; reelected to each succeeding Congress.

Office Listings

http://www.house.gov/knollenberg

2349 Rayburn House Office Building, Washington, DC 20515 .... (202) 225–5802
Chief of Staff.—Jeff Onizuk. FAX: 226–2356
Legislative Director.—Craig Albright.
Press Secretary.—Christopher Close.
30833 Northwestern Highway, Suite 100, Farmington Hills, MI 48334 .... (248) 851–1366

Counties: OAKLAND (part). CITIES AND TOWNSHIPS: Auburn Hills, Berkley, Beverly Hills, Bingham Farms, Birmingham, Birmingham Farms, Bloomfield Hills, Bloomfield, Clawson, Farmington, Farmington Hills, Franklin, Keego Harbo, Lake Angelus, Oakland, Orchard Lake Village, Orion (part), Pontiac, Rochester, Rochester Hills, Royal Oak (part), Sylvan Lake, Troy, Waterford, and West Bloomfield. Population (2000), 662,563.

ZIP Codes: 48007, 48009, 48012, 48017, 48025, 48067–68, 48072–73, 48083–85, 48098–99, 48167, 48301–04, 48306–09, 48320–36, 48340–43, 48346, 48359–60, 48362–63, 48367, 48370, 48382, 48387, 48390, 48398

* * *

TENTH DISTRICT

CANDICE S. MILLER, Republican, of Harrison Township, MI; born on May 7, 1954, in St. Clair Shores, MI; education: attended Macomb Community College and Northwood University; public service: Harrison Township Board of Trustees, 1979; Harrison Township Supervisor, 1980–1992; Macomb County Treasurer, 1992–1994; Michigan Secretary of State, 1994–2002; previous employment: worked in a family-owned marina business before she became involved in public service; religion: Presbyterian; family: married to Macomb County Circuit Court Judge Donald Miller; children: Wendy; elected to the 108th Congress on November 5, 2002.

Office Listings

http://www.house.gov/candicemiller

508 Cannon House Office Building, Washington, DC 20515 .... (202) 225–2106
Chief of Staff.—Jamie Roe. FAX: 226–1169
Legislative Director.—Sean Moran.
Legislative Assistant.—Kimberly R. Bird.
48653 Van Dyke Avenue, Shelby Township, MI 48317 .... (586) 997–5010

Counties: HURON, LAPEER, MACOMB (part), SAINT CLAIR, SANILAC. Population (2000), 662,562.

ZIP Codes: 48001–06, 48014, 48022–23, 48027–28, 48032, 48039–42, 48044–45, 48047–51, 48054, 48059–65, 48074, 48079, 48094–97, 48306, 48310–18, 48371, 48401, 48410, 48412–13, 48416, 48419, 48421–23, 48426–28, 48432, 48434–35, 48438, 48440–41, 48444–46, 48450, 48453–56, 48461–72, 48475, 48720, 48725–27, 48729, 48731, 48735, 48741, 48744, 48754–55, 48759–60, 48767

* * *

ELEVENTH DISTRICT

THADDEUS G. MCCOTTER, Republican, of Livonia, MI; born on August 22, 1965, in Detroit, MI; education: B.A., University of Detroit, 1987; J.D., University of Detroit Law School, 1990; profession: Attorney; public service: elected to the Schoolcraft Community College Trustees, 1989; elected to the Wayne County Commission, 1992; elected to the Michigan State Senate, 1998; awards: Michigan Jaycees Outstanding Michigander, 2001; Police

Officers Association of Michigan Legislator of the Year, 2002; religion: Catholic; family: married to Rita; children: George, Timothy, and Emilia; elected to the 108th Congress on November 5, 2002.

Office Listings

http://www.house.gov/mccotter

415 Cannon House Office Building, Washington, DC 20515 .... (202) 225–8171
Chief of Staff.—Kurt Berryman. FAX: 225–2667
Legislative Director.—David Woodruff.
17197 N. Laurel Park Drive, Suite 161, Livonia, MI 48152 .... (734) 632–0314

Counties: WAYNE COUNTY. CITIES: Livonia, Canton Township, Plymouth City, Plymouth Township, Northville City, Northville Township, Belleville, Van Buren Township, Wayne, Westland, Garden City, Redford Township, Dearborn Heights (part). OAKLAND COUNTY. CITIES: Novi, South Lyon, Lyon Township, Milford, Wixom, Walled Lake, Commerce Township, White Lake, Highland, and Waterford (part). Population (2000), 662,563.

ZIP Codes: 48111–12, 48127, 48135–36, 48141, 48150–54, 48165, 48167, 48170, 48174, 48178, 48184–88, 48239–40, 48327, 48329, 48346, 48356–57, 48374–77, 48380–83, 48386–87, 48390–91, 48393

* * *

TWELFTH DISTRICT

SANDER M. LEVIN, Democrat, of Royal Oak, MI; born in Detroit, MI, on September 6, 1931; education: graduated, Central High School, Detroit, 1949; B.A., University of Chicago, 1952; M.A., Columbia University, New York, NY, 1954; LL.B., Harvard University, Cambridge, MA, 1957; employment: attorney, admitted to the Michigan bar in 1958 and commenced practice in Detroit, MI; member: Oakland Board of Supervisors, 1961–64; Michigan Senate, 1965–70; Democratic floor leader in State Senate; served on the Advisory Committee on the Education of Handicapped Children in the Department of Health, Education, and Welfare, 1965–68; chairman, Michigan Democratic Party, 1968–69; Democratic candidate for governor, 1970 and 1974; fellow, Kennedy School of Government, Institute of Politics, Harvard University, 1975; assistant administrator, Agency for International Development, 1977–81; married: the former Victoria Schlafer, 1957; children: Jennifer, Andrew, Madeleine, and Matthew; elected on November 2, 1982, to the 98th Congress; reelected to each succeeding Congress.

Office Listings

http://www.house.gov/levin

2300 Rayburn Office House Building, Washington, DC 20515 .... (202) 225–4961
Administrative Assistant.—Hilarie Chambers.
Scheduler.—Karen Kampa.
27085 Gratiot Avenue, Roseville, MI 48066 .... (586) 498–7122
District Administrator.—Diana McBroom.
25900 Greenfield Road, Room 212, Oak Park, MI 48237 .... (248) 968–2025

Counties: MACOMB (part), OAKLAND (part). CITIES: Center Line, Clinton Township, East Pointe, Ferndale, Fraser, Hazel Park, Huntington Woods, Lake Township, Lathrup Village, Madison Heights, Mt. Clemens, Oak Park, Pleasant Ridge, Roseville, Royal Oak (part), Royal Oak Township, Southfield, St. Clair Shores, Sterling Heights (part), and Warren. Population (2000), 662,563.

ZIP Codes: 48015, 48021, 48025–26, 48030, 48034–38, 48043, 48046, 48066–67, 48069–71, 48075–76, 48080–82, 48086, 48088–93, 48220, 48236–37, 48310, 48312, 48397

* * *

THIRTEENTH DISTRICT

CAROLYN C. KILPATRICK, Democrat, of Detroit, MI; born in Detroit, on June 25, 1945; attended Ferris State University; graduate, Western Michigan University, 1972; M.S., Education Administration, University of Michigan, 1977; teacher; served in Michigan House of Representatives, 1979–96; member, Detroit Substance Abuse Advisory Council; former chair, Michigan Legislative Black Caucus; participated in first-of-its-kind African Trade Mission; delegate, U.N. International Women's Conference; led Michigan Department of Agriculture delegation to the International Agriculture Show, Nairobi, Kenya; awards: Anthony Wayne Award for leadership, Wayne State University; Burton-Abercrombie Award, 15th Democratic Congressional District;

Distinguished Legislator Award, University of Michigan; named Woman of the Year by Gentlemen of Wall Street, Inc.; listed in *Who's Who in Black America* and *Who's Who in American Politics*; two children: Kwame and Ayanna; committee: Appropriations; elected to the 105th Congress; reelected to each succeeding Congress.

Office Listings

http://www.house.gov/kilpatrick

1610 Longworth House Office Building, Washington, DC 20515 .... (202) 225–2261
Chief of Staff.—Kimberly Rudolph. FAX: 225–5730
Executive Assistant.—Gerri Houston.
Legislative Director.—Gene Fisher.
Press Secretary.—Denise Toliver.
1274 Library Street, Suite 1B, Detroit, MI 48226 .... (313) 965–9004

Counties: WAYNE COUNTY (part). Population (2000), 628,363.

ZIP Codes: 48146, 48178, 48192, 48195, 48201–18, 48220, 48222, 48224–26, 48229–34, 48236, 48238, 48242–44, 48255, 48260, 48264–69, 48272, 48275, 48277–79

* * *

FOURTEENTH DISTRICT

JOHN CONYERS, JR., Democrat, of Detroit, MI; born on May 16, 1929, in Detroit; son of John and Lucille Conyers; graduated from Wayne State University (B.A., 1957); graduated from Wayne State Law School (LL.B., June 1958); served as officer in the U.S. Army Corps of Engineers, one year in Korea; awarded combat and merit citations; married to Monica Esters-Conyers; engaged in many civil rights and labor activities; legislative assistant to Congressman John D. Dingell, December 1958 to May 1961; appointed Referee for the Workmen's Compensation Department, State of Michigan, by Governor John B. Swainson in October 1961; former vice chairman of Americans for Democratic Action; vice chairman of the National Advisory Council of the ACLU; member: Kappa Alpha Psi; Wolverine Bar; NAACP; Tuskegee Airmen, Inc.; ranking member, Judiciary Committee; organizations: Congressional Black Caucus; Congressional Urban Caucus; Progressive Caucus; elected to the 89th Congress on November 3, 1964; reelected to each succeeding Congress.

Office Listings

http://www.house.gov/conyers john.conyers@mail.house.gov

2426 Rayburn House Office Building, Washington, DC 20515 .... (202) 225–5126
Legislative Director.—Cynthia Martin. FAX: 225–0072
Federal Courthouse, Suite 669, 231 West Lafayette, Detroit, MI 48226 .... (313) 961–5670
Chief of Staff.—Ray Plowden.

Counties: WAYNE COUNTY (part). CITIES AND TOWNSHIPS: Allen Park, Detroit, Dearborn (part), Gibraltar, Grosse Ile, Hamtramack, Highland Park, Melvindale, Riverview, Southgate, and Trenton. Population (2000), 662,563.

ZIP Codes: 48101–02, 48120–22, 48124, 48126–27, 48138, 48173, 48180, 48183, 48192, 48195, 48203–04, 48206, 48210–12, 48219, 48221, 48223, 48227–28, 48235, 48238–40

* * *

FIFTEENTH DISTRICT

JOHN D. DINGELL, Democrat, of Dearborn, MI; born in Colorado Springs, CO, July 8, 1926; B.S., Georgetown University, 1949; J.D., Georgetown University Law School, 1952; World War II veteran; assistant Wayne County prosecutor, 1953–55; married to the former Deborah Insley; member: Migratory Bird Conservation Commission; committees: ranking member, Energy and Commerce Committee; elected to the 84th Congress in a special election to fill the vacant seat of his late father, the Honorable John D. Dingell, December 13, 1955; reelected to the 85th and each succeeding Congress.

Office Listings

http://www.house.gov/dingell

2328 Rayburn House Office Building, Washington, DC 20515 .... (202) 225–4071
Chief of Staff.—Rick Kessler.
Communications Director.—Mike Hacker.

19855 West Outer Drive, Suite 103–E, Dearborn, MI 48124 .... (313) 278–2936
District Coordinator.—Terry Spryszak.
23 East Front Street, Suite 103, Monroe, MI 48161 .... (734) 243–1849

Counties: WAYNE COUNTY (part). CITIES AND TOWNSHIPS: Brownstown Township, Dearborn (part), Dearborn Heights (part), Flat Rock, Gibraltar, Rockwood, Romulus, Taylor, Woodhaven. MONROE COUNTY. CITIES AND TOWNSHIPS: Azalia, Carleton, Dundee, Erie, Ida, Lambertville, LaSalle, Luna Pier, Maybee, Milan (part), Monroe, Newport, Ottawa Lake, Petersburg, Samaria, S. Rockwood, Temperance. WASHTENAW COUNTY (part). CITIES AND TOWNSHIPS: Ann Arbor, Pittsfield Township, York Township, Superior Township, Ypsilanti, and Ypsilanti Township. Population (2000), 662,563.

ZIP Codes: 48103–11, 48113, 48117, 48123–28, 48131, 48133–34, 48140–41, 48144–45, 48157, 48159–62, 48164, 48166, 48170, 48173–74, 48176–77, 48179–80, 48182–84, 48186, 48190–92, 48197–98, 48228, 48239, 49228–29, 49238, 49267, 49270, 49276

MINNESOTA

(Population 2000, 4,919,479)

SENATORS

MARK DAYTON, Democrat, of Minneapolis, MN; born on January 26, 1947, in Minneapolis; education: B.A., Yale University, 1969; occupations: worked as a teacher in the New York, NY, public school system, 1969–1971; also worked as a counselor and administrator for a Boston, MA, social services agency, 1971–1975; religion: Presbyterian; public service: legislative assistant to Senator Walter Mondale, 1975–1976; assistant to Minnesota Governor Rudy Perpich, 1977–1978; Minnesota Commissioner of Energy and Economic Development, 1983–1986; Minnesota State Auditor, 1991–1995; elected to the U.S. Senate on November 7, 2000.

Office Listings

http://dayton.senate.gov

346 Russell Senate Office Building, Washington, DC 20510 .... (202) 224–3244
Chief of Staff.—Sarah Dahlin. FAX: 228–2186
Office Manager.—Matthew McGowan.
Legislative Director.—Lani Kawamura.
Scheduler.—Karin Rogge.
Federal Building, Suite 298, Fort Snelling, MN 55111 .... (612) 727–5220
Deputy Chief of Staff.—Marc Kimball.
401 DeMers Avenue, East Grand Forks, MN 56721 .... (218) 773–1110
P.O. Box 608, Renville, MN 56284 .... (320) 905–3007
222 Main Street, Suite 200, P.O. Box 937, Biwabik, MN 55708 .... (218) 865–4480

* * *

NORM COLEMAN, Republican, of St. Paul, MN; born on August 17, 1949, in Brooklyn, NY; education: B.A., Hofstra University; J.D., University of Iowa; profession: Attorney; public service: served for 17 years in the Minnesota Attorney General's office, holding the positions of Chief Prosecutor and Solicitor General of Minnesota; Mayor of St. Paul, MN, 1993–2001; Republican candidate for Governor of Minnesota, 1998; family: married to Laurie; children: Jacob and Sarah; elected to the U.S. Senate on November 5, 2002.

Office Listings

http://coleman.senate.gov

320 Hart Senate Office Building, Washington, DC 20510 .... (202) 224–5641
Chief of Staff.—Tom Mason. FAX: 224–1152
Legislative Director.—Jeff Harrison.
2550 University Avenue West, Suite 100N, St. Paul, MN 55114 .... (651) 645–0323

REPRESENTATIVES

FIRST DISTRICT

GIL GUTKNECHT, Republican, of Rochester, MN; born in Cedar Falls, IA, on March 20, 1951; education: graduated, Cedar Falls High School; B.A., University of Northern Iowa; employment: real estate broker and auctioneer; served as State Representative, 1982–94, floor leader, House Republican Caucus; married: Mary Catherine Gutknecht, 1972; children: Margie, Paul, and Emily; elected to the 104th Congress; reelected to each succeeding Congress.

Office Listings

http://www.house.gov/gutknecht

425 Cannon House Office Building, Washington, DC 20515 .... (202) 225–2472
Chief of Staff.—Stephanie Brand.
Legislative Director.—Rhett Butler.
Executive Assistant.—Sarah Derrick.
Legislative Assistants: James Beabout, Verna Regier, Brandon Lerch.
1530 Greenview Drive, SW., Suite 108, Rochester, MN 55902 .... (507) 252–9841

Counties: BLUE EARTH COUNTY. CITIES: Amboy, Eagle Lake, Garden City, Good Thunder, Lake Crystal, Madison Lake, Mankato, Mapleton, Pemberton, St. Clair, Vernon Center. BROWN COUNTY. CITIES: Comfrey, Hanska, New Ulm, Sleepy Eye, Springfield. COTTONWOOD COUNTY. CITIES: Mountain Lake, Storedon, Westbrook. DODGE COUNTY. CITIES: Claremont, Dodge Center, Hayfield, Kasson, Mantorville, West Concord, Windom. FARIBAULT COUNTY. CITIES: Blue Earth, Bricelyn, Delavan, Easton, Elmore, Frost, Huntley, Kiester, Minnesota Lake, Walters, Wells, Winnebago. FILLMORE COUNTY. CITIES: Canton, Chatfield, Fountain, Harmony, Lanesboro, Mabel, Ostrander, Peterson, Preston, Rushford, Spring Valley, Whalan, Wykoff. FREEBORN COUNTY. CITIES: Albert Lea, Alden, Clarks Grove, Conger, Emmons, Freeborn, Geneva, Glenville, Hartland, Hayward, Hollandale, London, Manchester, Myrtle, Oakland, Twin Lakes. HOUSTON COUNTY. CITIES: Brownsville, Caledonia, Eitzen, Hokah, Houston, La Crescent, Spring Grove. JACKSON COUNTY. CITIES: Heron, Jackson, Lake Field. MARTIN COUNTY. CITY: Fairmont. MOWER COUNTY. CITIES: Adams, Austin, Brownsdale, Dexter, Elkton, Grand Meadow, Lansing, LeRoy, Lyle, Rose Creek, Sargeant, Taopi, Waltham. MURRAY COUNTY. CITIES: Fulda, Slayton. NICOLLET COUNTY. CITIES: North Mankato, St. Peter. NOBLES COUNTY. CITIES: Adrian, Worthington. OLMSTED COUNTY. CITIES: Byron, Dover, Eyota, Oronoco, Rochester, Stewartville, Viola. PIPESTONE COUNTY. CITIES: Edgerton, Jasper, Pipestone Ruthton. ROCK COUNTY. CITY: Lurverne. STEELE COUNTY. CITIES: Blooming Prairie, Ellendale, Hope, Medford, Meriden, Owatonna. WABASHA COUNTY. CITIES: Elgin, Hammond, Kellogg, Lake City, Mazeppa, Milleville, Plainview, Reads Landing, Theilman, Wabasha. WASECA COUNTY. CITIES: Janesville, New Richland, Otisco, Waldorf, Waseca. WATONWAN COUNTY. CITIES: Madelia, St. James. WINONA COUNTY. CITIES: Altura, Dakota, Goodview, Homer, Lewiston, Minnesota City, Rollingstone, St. Charles, Stockton, Utica, and Winona. Population (2000), 614,935.

ZIP Codes: 55021, 55027, 55041, 55049, 55052, 55060, 55901–06, 55909–10, 55912, 55917–27, 55929, 55931–36, 55939–47, 55949–57, 55959–65, 55967–77, 55979, 55981–83, 55985, 55987–88, 55990–92, 56001–03, 56006–07, 56009–11, 56013–14, 56016, 56019–21, 56023–29, 56031, 56033–34, 56036–37, 56039, 56041–43, 56045–48, 56050–51, 56054–55, 56058, 56060, 56062–63, 56065, 56068, 56072–74, 56078, 56080–83, 56085, 56087–91, 56093, 56096–98, 56101, 56110–11, 56114–23, 56125, 56127–29, 56131, 56134, 56136–41, 56143–47, 56149–53, 56155–56, 56158–62, 56164–68, 56170–74, 56176–77, 56180–81, 56183, 56185–87, 56266

* * *

SECOND DISTRICT

JOHN KLINE, Republican, of Lakeville, MN; born on September 6, 1947, in Allentown, PA; education: B.A., Rice University, 1969; M.P.A., Shippensburg University, 1988; military service: U.S. Marine Corps, 1969–1994; retired at the rank of Colonel; organizations: Boy Scouts of America; Marine Corps League; Veterans of Foreign Wars; Marine Corps Association; American Legion; Retired Officers Association; past president, Marine Corps Coordinating Council of Minnesota; religion: Methodist; family: married to Vicky; children: Kathy and Dan; elected to the 108th Congress on November 5, 2002.

Office Listings

http://www.house.gov/kline

1429 Longworth House Office Building, Washington, DC 20515 .... (202) 225–2271
Chief of Staff.—Steven Sutton. FAX: 225–2595
Legislative Director.—Jim McGuire.
Executive Assistant.—Brooke Dorobiala.
Press Secretary.—Angelyn Wollen.
101 West Burnsville Parkway, Suite 201, Burnsville, MN 55337 .... (952) 808–1213

Counties: CARVER COUNTY. CITIES: Chanhassen, Chaska, Waconia, Victoria. DAKOTA COUNTY (part). CITIES: Apple Valley, Burnsville, Eagan, Farmington, Hastings, Inver Grove Heights. GOODHUE COUNTY. CITIES: Cannon Falls, Pine Island, Red Wing, Zumbrota. LE SUEUR COUNTY. CITIES: Le Sueur, Le Center, Montgomery. RICE COUNTY. CITIES: Faribault, Northfield. SCOTT COUNTY. CITIES: Shakopee, Savage, Prior Lake, New Prague, Jordan, Belle Plaine. WASHINGTON COUNTY (part). CITIES: Woodbury (part), and Cottage Grove. Population (2000), 614,934.

ZIP Codes: 55001, 55009–10, 55016, 55018–20, 55021, 55024, 55026–27, 55031, 55033, 55041, 55044, 55046, 55049, 55052–54, 55057, 55065–66, 55068, 55076–77, 55085, 55087–89, 55103, 55118, 55121–25, 55129, 55306, 55313, 55315, 55317–18, 55322, 55328, 55330–31, 55336–37, 55339, 55350, 55352, 55360, 55367–68, 55371–75, 55378–79, 55382–83, 55386–88, 55393–94, 55397, 55399, 55550–54, 55556–60, 55562, 55564–68, 55573, 55575, 55580–91, 55594, 55946, 55951, 55953, 55956, 55963, 55983, 55985, 55992, 56011, 56014, 56017, 56022–26, 56028, 56030–32, 56035, 56037, 56039, 56042, 56044, 56046–47, 56050, 56052, 56056–58, 56063, 56065, 56068–69, 56071, 56096

* * *

THIRD DISTRICT

JIM RAMSTAD, Republican, of Minnetonka, MN; born in Jamestown, ND, May 6, 1946; education: University of Minnesota, B.A., Phi Beta Kappa, 1968; George Washington University, J.D. with honors, 1973; military service: first lieutenant, U.S. Army Reserves, 1968–74; elected to the Minnesota Senate, 1980; reelected 1982, 1986; assistant minority leader; attorney; adjunct professor; Representative of the Year by the National Association of Police Organizations, 1997, 2000; Legislator of the Year by the National Association of Alcoholism and Drug

Addiction Counselors, 1998; Legislator of the Year by the National Mental Health Association, 1999; Fulbright Distinguished Public Service Award; committee: Ways and Means; elected to the 102nd Congress, November 6, 1990; reelected to each succeeding Congress.

Office Listings

103 Cannon House Office Building, Washington, DC 20515 .... (202) 225–2871
Administrative Assistant.—Dean Peterson.
Legislative Director.—Karin Hope.
Executive Assistant / Scheduler.—Valerie Nelson.
1809 Plymouth Road South, Suite 300, Minnetonka, MN 55305 .... (952) 738–8200
District Director.—Lance Olson.

Counties: ANOKA (part), HENNEPIN (part). CITIES AND TOWNSHIPS: Bloomington, Brooklyn Center, Brooklyn Park, Champlin, Coon Rapids, Corcoran, Dayton, Deephaven, Eden Prarie, Edina, Excelsior, Greenwood, Hassan, Hopkins, Independence, Long Lake, Loretto, Maple Grove, Maple Plain, Medicine Lake, Medina, Minnetonka Beach, Minnetonka, Minnetrista, Mound, Orono, Osseo, Plymouth, Rogers, Saint Bonifacius, Shorewood, Spring Park, Tonka Bay, Wayzata, and Woodland. Population (2000), 614,935.

ZIP Codes: 55304–05, 55311, 55316, 55323, 55327, 55331, 55340–41, 55343–48, 55356–57, 55359, 55361, 55364, 55369, 55373–75, 55378, 55384, 55387–88, 55391–92, 55410, 55416, 55420, 55422–26, 55428–31, 55433, 55435–39, 55441–48, 55569–72, 55574, 55576–79, 55592–93, 55595–99

* * *

FOURTH DISTRICT

BETTY McCOLLUM, Democrat, of North St. Paul, MN; born on July 12, 1954, in Minneapolis, MN; education: A.A., Inver Hills Community College; B.S., College of St. Catherine; employment: teacher and sales manager; single; children: Sean and Katie; public service: North St. Paul City Council, 1986–1992; Minnesota House of Representatives, 1992–2000; organizations: Girl Scouts of America; VFW Ladies' Auxiliary; and American Legion Ladies' Auxiliary; elected Midwest Regional Whip 2002; committees: Education and the Workforce; International Relations; Resources; appointments: Democratic Steering and Policy Committee; National Council on the Arts; Regional Whip; elected to the 107th Congress on November 7, 2000; reelected to each succeeding Congress.

Office Listings

http://www.house.gov/mccollum

1029 Longworth House Office Building, Washington, DC 20515 .... (202) 225–6631
Chief of Staff.—Bill Harper. FAX: 225–1968
Communications Director.—Stacy Stordahl.
Office Director.—Shelly Schafer.
165 Western Avenue North, Suite 17, St. Paul, MN 55102 .... (651) 224–9191
Communications / District Director.—Joshua Straka.

Counties: DAKOTA (part), RAMSEY, WASHINGTON (part). Population (2000), 614,935.

ZIP Codes: 55016, 55042, 55055, 55071, 55075–77, 55090, 55101–10, 55112–20, 55125–29, 55133, 55144, 55146, 55150, 55155, 55161, 55164–66, 55168–70, 55172, 55175, 55177, 55182, 55187–88, 55190–91, 55199, 55421, 55432, 55449

* * *

FIFTH DISTRICT

MARTIN OLAV SABO, Democrat-Farmer-Labor, of Minneapolis, MN; born in Crosby, ND, February 28, 1938; education: graduated Alkabo High School, ND, 1955; B.A., Augsburg College, Minneapolis, MN, 1959; graduate studies, University of Minnesota, 1960; served in the Minnesota House of Representatives, 1961–78; served as House Democrat-Farmer-Labor minority leader, 1969–73; Speaker of the House, 1973–78; presidential appointee to the National Advisory Commission on Intergovernmental Relations; president, National Conference of State Legislatures; president, National Legislative Conference; chairman, Intergovernmental Relations Committee of the National Conference of State Legislatures; Nuclear Test Ban Leadership Award, 1992; Arms Control Leadership Award, 1988; Endowment for Leadership in Community and Public Service, established in his name, 1994; Distinguished Service Award from the Committee on Education Funding, 1994; inducted into the Scandinavian American Hall of

Fame, October 12, 1994; honorary lifetime member, Hospital and Nursing Home Employees Union, Local No. 113, SEIU AFL–CIO; Minneapolis Jaycees Man of the Year Award, 1973–74; Augsburg College Distinguished Alumnus Citation; Lloyd M. Short Merit Award of the Minnesota Chapter of the American Society for Public Administration; chair, House Budget committee, 1993–1994; committees: Appropriations; Democratic Policy Committee; subcommittees: Commerce, Justice, State and Judiciary; Defense; ranking member, Homeland Security; married: the former Sylvia Lee, 1963; children: Karin and Julie; 5 grandchildren; elected to the 96th Congress, November 7, 1978; reelected to each succeeding Congress.

Office Listings

http://www.house.gov/sabo

2336 Rayburn House Office Building, Washington, DC 20515 .... (202) 225–4755
Chief of Staff.—Michael Erlandson.
Press Secretary.—Travis Talvitie.
Office Manager.—Bonnie Gottwald.
286 Commerce at the Crossings, 250 Second Avenue South, Minneapolis, MN 55401 .... (612) 664–8000

Counties: ANOKA (part), HENNEPIN (part), RAMSEY (part). CITIES: Columbia Heights, Crystal, Ft. Snelling, Fridley, Golden Valley, Hilltop, Hopkins (part), Minneapolis, New Hope, Richfield, Robbinsdale, St. Anthony, St. Louis Park, and Spring Lake Park, Population (2000), 614,935.

ZIP Codes: 55111–12, 55305, 55343, 55401–30, 55432–33, 55440–41, 55450, 55454–55, 55458–60, 55470, 55472, 55474, 55479–80, 55483–88

* * *

SIXTH DISTRICT

MARK R. KENNEDY, Republican, of Watertown, MN; born on April 11, 1957, in Benson, MN; education: B.A., St. John's University; M.B.A., University of Michigan; profession: businessman; employment: certified public accountant, Arthur Andersen; executive positions with Department 56, Shopko Stores, and Pillsbury; organizations: Minnesota Rough Riders Issues Forum; Center of the American Experiment; Lions Club; married: Debbie; children: Charles, Emily, Sarah, and Peter; committees: Financial Services; Transportation and Infrastructure; elected to the 107th Congress on November 7, 2000; reelected to each succeeding Congress.

Office Listings

http://markkennedy.house.gov

1415 Longworth House Office Building, Washington, DC 20515 .... (202) 225–2331
Chief of Staff.—Pat Shortridge. FAX: 225–6475
Executive Assistant.—Elisa Thiede.
Legislative Director.—Edward Skala.
District Director.—Mark Matuska.
1111 Highway 25 North, Suite 204, Buffalo, MN 55313 .... (763) 684–1600
22 Wilson Avenue, NE., Suite 104, P.O. Box 6010, St. Cloud, MN 56302 .... (320) 259–0992
14660 Fitzgerald Avenue, North, Suite 100, Hugo, MN 55038 .... (651) 653–5933

Counties: ANOKA (part), BENTON, SHERBURNE, STEARNS (part), WASHINGTON (part), WRIGHT. CITIES: Andover, Anoka, Blaine, Elk River, Forest Lake, Lino Lakes, St. Cloud, Stillwater, Ramsey, and Woodbury. Population (2000), 614,935.

ZIP Codes: 55001, 55003, 55005–06, 55011, 55014, 55025, 55031, 55038, 55042–43, 55047, 55070, 55073, 55079, 55082–83, 55092, 55110, 55112, 55115, 55125, 55128–29, 55301–04, 55308–09, 55313, 55319–21, 55328–30, 55341, 55349, 55353, 55358–59, 55362–63, 55365, 55371, 55373–74, 55376, 55380–82, 55388–90, 55395, 55398, 55412–13, 55417–18, 55429–30, 55432, 55434, 55448–49, 56301, 56303–04, 56307, 56310, 56314, 56320, 56329–31, 56340, 56352, 56357, 56362, 56367–68, 56373–75, 56377, 56379, 56387–88, 56393, 56395–99

* * *

SEVENTH DISTRICT

COLLIN C. PETERSON, Democrat, of Detroit Lakes, MN; born in Fargo, ND, June 29, 1944; graduated from Glyndon (MN) High School, 1962; B.A., Moorhead State University, 1966: (business administration and accounting); U.S. Army National Guard, 1963–69; CPA, owner and partner; Minnesota State Senator, 1976–86; member: AOPA, Safari Club, Ducks

Unlimited, American Legion, Sea Plane Pilots Association, Pheasants Forever, Benevolent Protective Order of Elks, Cormorant Lakes Sportsmen Club; three children: Sean, Jason, and Elliott; elected to the 102nd Congress, November 6, 1990; reelected to each succeeding Congress.

Office Listings

http://collinpeterson.house.gov

2159 Rayburn House Office Building, Washington, DC 20515 .... (202) 225–2165
Assistants: Liz Bolstad, Mark Brownell, Robin Goracke, Chris Iacaruso, Cherie Slayton, Katherine Telleen.
Lake Avenue Plaza Building, Suite 107, 714 Lake Avenue, Detroit Lakes, MN 56501 .... (218) 847–5056
Minnesota Wheat Growers Building, 2603 Wheat Drive, Red Lake, MN 56750 ..... (218) 253–4356
320 Southwest Fourth Street, Centre Point Mall, Willmar, MN 56201 .... (320) 235–1061

Counties: BECKER, BELTRAMI (part), BIG STONE, CHIPPEWA, CLAY, CLEARWATER, DOUGLAS, GRANT, KANDIYOHI, KITTSON, LAC QUI PARLE, LAKE OF THE WOODS, LINCOLN, LYON, MAHNOMEN, MARSHALL, MCLEOD, MEEKER, NORMAN, OTTER TAIL, PENNINGTON, POLK, POPE, RED LAKE, REDWOOD, RENVILLE, ROSEAU, SIBLEY, STEARNS (part), STEVENS, SWIFT, TODD, TRAVERSE, WILKIN, YELLOW MEDICINE. Population (2000) 614,935.

ZIP Codes: 55307, 55310, 55312, 55314, 55321, 55324–25, 55329, 55332–36, 55338–39, 55342, 55350, 55353–55, 55366, 55368, 55370, 55381–82, 55385, 55389, 55395–96, 55409, 55970, 56011, 56044, 56054, 56058, 56083, 56085, 56087, 56113, 56115, 56129, 56132, 56136, 56142, 56149, 56152, 56157, 56164, 56166, 56169–70, 56175, 56178, 56180, 56201, 56207–12, 56214–16, 56218–32, 56235–37, 56239–41, 56243–45, 56248–49, 56251–53, 56255–58, 56260, 56262–67, 56270–71, 56273–74, 56276–85, 56287–89, 56291–97, 56301–04, 56307–12, 56314–16, 56318–21, 56323–24, 56326–27, 56329, 56331–32, 56334, 56336, 56339–40, 56343, 56345, 56347, 56349, 56352, 56354–55, 56360–62, 56368, 56372–74, 56377–79, 56381–82, 56385, 56387, 56393, 56395–99, 56433–34, 56436–38, 56440, 56443, 56446, 56453, 56458, 56461, 56464, 56466–67, 56470, 56475, 56477–79, 56481–82, 56501–02, 56510–11, 56514–25, 56527–29, 56531, 56533–38, 56540–54, 56556–57, 56560–63, 56565–81, 56583–94, 56601, 56619, 56621, 56623, 56633–34, 56644, 56646–47, 56650–52, 56661, 56663, 56666–67, 56670–71, 56673, 56676, 56678, 56682–87, 56701, 56710–11, 56713–16, 56720–29, 56731–38, 56740–42, 56744, 56748, 56750–51, 56754–63

* * *

EIGHTH DISTRICT

JAMES L. OBERSTAR, Democrat, of Chisholm, MN; born in Chisholm, September 10, 1934; graduated, Chisholm High School, 1952; B.A., *summa cum laude*, French and political science, College of St. Thomas, St. Paul, MN, 1956; M.A., European area studies, College of Europe, Bruges, Belgium, 1957; Laval University, Canada; Georgetown University, former teacher of English, French, and Creole; served as administrative assistant to the late Congressman John A. Blatnik, 1963–74; administrator of the House Public Works Committee, 1971–74; co-chair, Congressional Travel and Tourism Caucus; Democratic Study Group; Great Lakes Task Force; National Water Alliance; Northeast Midwest Congressional Coalition; Steel Caucus; Conference of Great Lakes Congressmen (chairman); married: Jean Kurth, 1993; children: Thomas Edward, Katherine Noelle, Anne-Therese, Monica Rose, Charlie, and Lindy; committee: Transportation and Infrastructure, ranking Democrat; elected to the 94th Congress, November 5, 1974; reelected to each succeeding Congress.

Office Listings

http://www.house.gov/oberstar

2365 Rayburn House Office Building, Washington, DC 20515 .... (202) 225–6211
Administrative Assistant.—William Richard.
Office Manager.—Marianne Buckley.
Legislative Director.—Chip Gardiner.
Communications Director.—Mary Kerr.
231 Federal Building, Duluth, MN 55802 .... (218) 727–7474
District Manager.—Jackie Morris.
Chisholm City Hall, 316 West Lake Street, Chisholm, MN 55719 .... (218) 254–5761
District Representative.—Peter Makowski.
Brainerd City Hall, 501 Laurel Street, Brainerd, MN 56401 .... (218) 828–4400
District Representative.—Ken Hasskamp.
38625 14th Avenue, Suite 300B, North Branch, MN 55056 .... (651) 277–1234
District Representative.—Deven Nelson.

Counties: AITKIN, BELTRAMI (part), CARLTON, CASS, CHISAGO, COOK, CROW WING, HUBBARD, ISANTI, ITASCA, KANABEC, KOOCHICHING, LAKE, MILLE LACS, MORRISON, PINE, ST. LOUIS, WADENA. CITIES: Brainerd, Chisholm, Cloquet, Duluth, Grand Rapids, Hibbing, International Falls, and Little Falls. Population (2000), 614,935.

ZIP Codes: 55002, 55005–08, 55012–13, 55017, 55025, 55029–30, 55032, 55036–37, 55040, 55045, 55051, 55056, 55063, 55067, 55069–70, 55072–74, 55078–80, 55084, 55092, 55330–31, 55362, 55371, 55377, 55398, 55408, 55601–07, 55609, 55612–16, 55701–13, 55716–26, 55730–36, 55738, 55741–42, 55744–46, 55748–53, 55756–58, 55760,

55763–69, 55771–72, 55775, 55777, 55779–87, 55790–93, 55795–98, 55801–08, 55810–12, 55814–16, 56028, 56058, 56304, 56307, 56309–11, 56313–15, 56317–19, 56323, 56325–33, 56335–36, 56338–45, 56347, 56350, 56353–61, 56363–64, 56367–69, 56371, 56373, 56376–77, 56381–82, 56384, 56386, 56389, 56401, 56425, 56430–31, 56433–35, 56437, 56441–44, 56446–50, 56452–53, 56455–56, 56458–59, 56461, 56464–70, 56472–75, 56477, 56479, 56481–82, 56484, 56601, 56623, 56626–31, 56633, 56636–37, 56639, 56641, 56647, 56649, 56653–55, 56657–63, 56668–69, 56672, 56678–81, 56683, 56688

MISSISSIPPI

(Population 2000, 2,844,658)

SENATORS

THAD COCHRAN, Republican, of Jackson, MS; born in Pontotoc, MS, December 7, 1937; education: B.A., University of Mississippi, 1959; J.D., University of Mississippi Law School, 1965; received a Rotary Foundation Fellowship and studied international law and jurisprudence at Trinity College, University of Dublin, Ireland, 1963–64; military service: served in U.S. Navy, 1959–61; employment: admitted to Mississippi bar in 1965; board of directors, Jackson Rotary Club, 1970–71; Outstanding Young Man of the Year Award, Junior Chamber of Commerce in Mississippi, 1971; president, young lawyers section of Mississippi State bar, 1972–73; married: the former Rose Clayton of New Albany, MS, 1964; two children and a grandson; elected to the 93rd Congress, November 7, 1972; reelected to 94th and 95th Congresses; elected to the U.S. Senate, November 7, 1978, for the six-year term beginning January 3, 1979; subsequently appointed by the governor, December 27, 1978, to fill the vacancy caused by the resignation of Senator James O. Eastland; reelected to each subsequent Senate term; chairman of the Senate Republican Conference, 1990–96; committees: Appropriations; chairman, Agriculture, Nutrition, and Forestry; Rules and Administration; Joint Committee on the Library of Congress; Joint Committee on Printing; co-chairman, National Security Working Group.

Office Listings

http://cochran.senate.gov

113 Dirksen Senate Office Building, Washington, DC 20510 .... (202) 224–5054
Chief of Staff.—Mark E. Keenum.
Legislative Director.—Clayton Heil.
Office Manager.—Fred Pagan.
Scheduler.—Doris Wagley.
188 East Capitol Street, Suite 614, Jackson, MS 39201 .... (601) 965–4459
P.O. Box 1434, Oxford, MS 38655 .... (601) 236–1018
14094 Customs Boulevard, Suite 201, Gulfport, MS 39503 .... (228) 867–9710

* * *

TRENT LOTT, Republican, of Pascagoula, MS; born on October 9, 1941, in Grenada, MS; son of Chester P. and Iona (Watson) Lott; University of Mississippi, B.P.A., 1963, J.D., 1967; served as field representative for the University of Mississippi, 1963–65; acting Law Alumni Secretary of the Ole Miss Alumni Association, 1966–67; practiced law in Pascagoula in 1967 with Bryan and Gordon law firm; administrative assistant to Congressman William M. Colmer, 1968–72; member: Sigma Nu social fraternity, Phi Alpha Delta legal fraternity, Jackson County Bar Association, American Bar Association, the Masons, First Baptist Church of Pascagoula; married Patricia E. Thompson of Pascagoula, 1964; two children: Chester T., Jr. and Tyler Elizabeth; elected to the 93rd Congress, November 7, 1972; reelected to each succeeding Congress; member, Judiciary Committee, Merchant Marine and Fisheries, 93rd Congress; Committee on Rules and Post Office and Civil Service Committee, 94th and 95th Congresses; chairman, House Republican Research Committee, 96th Congress; House Republican Whip, Committee on Rules, 97th–100th Congresses; member, Committee on Small Business, 101st Congress; member, Committee on Budget, 102nd Congress; chairman, Republican Committee on Committees, 102nd Congress; member, Committee on Energy and Natural Resources, Joint Committee on the Reorganization of Congress, Secretary of Republican Conference, 103rd Congress; member, Committee on Ethics, 101st and 102nd Congresses; member, Committee on Armed Services, Committee on Commerce, Science and Transportation, 101st–103rd Congresses; elected to the U.S. Senate on November 8, 1988; reelected in 1994 and 2000; Senate Republican Whip, 1995–1996; Senate Republican Leader, 1996–2003; committees: Commerce, Science, and Transportation (chairman of Aviation Subcommittee); Finance; chairman, Rules and Administration; Select Committee on Intelligence; Joint Committee on the Library of Congress.

Office Listings

http://lott.senate.gov

487 Russell Senate Office Building, Washington, DC 20510 .... (202) 224–6253
Chief of Staff.—William Gottshall. FAX: 224–2262
Scheduler.—Hardy Lott.
Press Secretary.—Lee Youngblood.
Legislative Director.—Jim Sartucci.

245 East Capitol Street, Suite 226, Jackson, MS 39201 .... (601) 965–4644
3100 South Pascagoula Street, Pascagoula, MS 39567 .... (228) 762–5400
1 Government Plaza, Suite 428, Gulfport, MS 39502 .... (228) 863–1988
911 Jackson Avenue, Suite 127, Oxford, MS 38655 .... (662) 234–3774
200 East Washington Street, Suite 145, Greenwood, MS 38930 .... (662) 453–5681

REPRESENTATIVES

FIRST DISTRICT

ROGER F. WICKER, Republican, of Tupelo, MS; born in Pontotoc, MS, July 5, 1951; education: graduated, Pontotoc High School; University of Mississippi: B.A., 1973, J.D., 1975; president, Associated Student Body, 1972–73; Mississippi Law Journal, 1973–75; Air Force ROTC; U.S. Air Force, 1976–80; lieutenant colonel, U.S. Air Force Reserve, 1980–present; U.S. House of Representatives Rules Committee staff for Representative Trent Lott, 1980–82; private law practice, 1982–94; Lee County Public Defender, 1984–87; Tupelo City Judge pro tempore, 1986–87; Mississippi State Senate, 1988–94, chairman: Elections Committee (1992), Public Health and Welfare Committee (1993); member: Lions Club; University of Mississippi Hall of Fame; Sigma Nu Fraternity; Omicron Delta Kappa; Phi Delta Phi; religion: deacon, adult choir, of the First Baptist Church, Tupelo, MS; married: Gayle Long Wicker; children: Margaret, Caroline and McDaniel; committees: Appropriations; Budget; deputy majority whip; Republican Policy Committee; elected to the 104th Congress, November 8, 1994; president, Republican freshman class, 1995; reelected to each succeeding Congress.

Office Listings

http://www.house.gov/wicker

2455 Rayburn House Office Building, Washington, DC 20515 .... (202) 225–4306
Chief of Staff.—John Keast.
500 West Main Street, Suite 210, P.O. Box 1482, Tupelo, MS 38802 .... (662) 844–5437
Administrative Assistant / Press Secretary.—Kyle Steward.
8700 Northwest Drive, Suite 102, P.O. Box 70, Southaven, MS 38671 .... (662) 342–3942
1360 Sunset Drive, Suite 2, Grenada, MS 38901 .... (662) 294–1321
523 Main Street, Columbus, MS 39701 .... (662) 327–0748

Counties: ALCORN, BENTON, CALHOUN, CHICKASAW, CHOCTAW, CLAY, DESOTO, GRENADA, ITTAWAMBA, LAFAYETTE, LEE, LOWNDES, MARSHALL, MONROE, PANOLA, PONTOTOC, PRENTISS, TATE, TIPPAH, TISHOMINGO, UNION, WEBSTER (part), WINSTON (part), YALOBUSHA. Population (2000), 711,160.

ZIP Codes: 38601–03, 38606, 38610–11, 38618–21, 38625, 38627, 38629, 38632–35, 38637–38, 38641–42, 38647, 38649–52, 38654–55, 38658–59, 38661, 38663, 38665–66, 38668, 38670–74, 38677, 38679–80, 38683, 38685–86, 38801–04, 38820–21, 38824–29, 38833–35, 38838–39, 38841, 38843–44, 38846–52, 38854–60, 38862–66, 38868–71, 38873–80, 38901–02, 38913–16, 38920, 38922, 38925–27, 38929, 38940, 38948–49, 38951, 38953, 38955, 38960–61, 38965, 39108, 39339, 39701–05, 39710, 39730, 39735–37, 39740–41, 39743–46, 39750–56, 39759, 39766–67, 39769, 39771–73, 39776

* * *

SECOND DISTRICT

BENNIE G. THOMPSON, Democrat, of Bolton, MS; born in Bolton, MS, on January 28, 1948; graduated, Hinds County Agriculture High School; B.A., Tougaloo College, 1968; M.S., Jackson State University, 1972; teacher; Bolton Board of Aldermen, 1969–73; mayor of Bolton, 1973–79; Hinds County Board of Supervisors, 1980–93; married to the former London Johnson, Ph.D.; one daughter: BendaLonne; committees: Agriculture; Select Committee on Homeland Security; subcommittees: ranking member, Emergency Preparedness and Response; member: Congressional Black Caucus; Sunbelt Caucus; Rural Caucus; Progressive Caucus; Housing Assistance Council; NAACP 100 Black Men of Jackson, MS; Southern Regional Council; Kappa Alpha Psi Fraternity; elected to the 103rd Congress in a special election; reelected to each succeeding Congress.

Office Listings

http://www.house.gov/thompson thompsonms2nd@mail.house.gov

2432 Rayburn House Office Building, Washington, DC 20515 .... (202) 225–5876
Administrative Assistant.—Marsha G. McCraven. FAX: 225–5898
Communications Director.—Lanier Avant.
Office Manager.—Minnie Langham.

107 West Madison Street, P.O. Box 610, Bolton, MS 39041–0610 .... (601) 866–9003
District Director.—Charlie Horhn.
263 East Main Street, Marks, MS 38646 .... (662) 326–9003
Mound Bayou City Hall, Room 134, 106 West Green Street, Mound Bayou, MS 38762 .... (662) 741–9003
509 Highway 82 West, Greenwood, MS 38930 .... (662) 455–9003
910 Courthouse Lane, Greenville, MS 38701 .... (662) 335–9003

Counties: Attala Bolivar, Carroll, Claiborne, Coahoma, Copiah, Hinds (part), Holmes, Humphreys, Issaquena, Jefferson, Leake (part), Leflore, Madison (part), Montgomery, Quitman, Sharkey, Sunflower, Tallahatchie, Tunica, Warren, Washington, Yazoo. Population (2000), 711,164.

ZIP Codes: 38606, 38609, 38614, 38617, 38621–23, 38626, 38628, 38630–31, 38639, 38643–46, 38664–65, 38669–70, 38676, 38701–04, 38720–23, 38725–26, 38730–33, 38736–40, 38744–46, 38748–49, 38751, 38753–54, 38756, 38758–62, 38764–65, 38767–69, 38771–74, 38776, 38778, 38780–82, 38901, 38912, 38917, 38920–21, 38923–25, 38927–28, 38930, 38935, 38940–41, 38943–48, 38950, 38952–54, 38957–59, 38961–64, 38966–67, 39038–41, 39045–46, 39051, 39054, 39056, 39058–61, 39063, 39066–67, 39069, 39071–72, 39077–79, 39083, 39086, 39088, 39090, 39095–97, 39107–08, 39110, 39113, 39115, 39120, 39144, 39146, 39150, 39154, 39156–57, 39159–60, 39162–63, 39166, 39169–71, 39173–77, 39179–83, 39191–92, 39194, 39201–07, 39209–10, 39212–13, 39215–17, 39225, 39235, 39269, 39271–72, 39282–84, 39286, 39289, 39296, 39653, 39661, 39668, 39745, 39747, 39767

* * *

THIRD DISTRICT

CHARLES W. (CHIP) PICKERING, Jr., Republican, of Laurel, MS; born on August 10, 1963; B.A., Business Administration, University of Mississippi, 1986; M.B.A., Baylor University; farmer; legislative aide to Senate Majority Leader Trent Lott, 1992–96; Bush administration appointee, U.S. Department of Agriculture, 1989–91; Southern Baptist missionary to Budapest, Hungary, 1986–87; married to the former Leisha Jane Prather; children: Will, Ross, Jackson, Asher, and Harper; committees: Agriculture; Energy and Commerce; assistant whip at large; subcommittees: Energy and Air Quality; General Farm Commodities and Risk Management; Health; Livestock and Horticulture; Telecommunications and the Internet; Congressional Wireless Caucus; elected to the 105th Congress; reelected to each succeeding Congress.

Office Listings

http://www.house.gov/pickering

229 Cannon House Office Building, Washington, DC 20515 .... (202) 225–5031
Chief of Staff.—Susan Butler. FAX: 225–5797
Press Secretary.—Brian Perry.
Legislative Director.—John Rounsaville.
Scheduler.—Marcy Scoggins.
110–D Airport Road, Pearl, MS 39208 .... (601) 932–2410
District Director.—Stanley Shows.
823 22nd Avenue, Meridian, MS 39301 .... (601) 693–6681
Staff Assistants: Lynne Compton, Carol Mabry.
1 Research Boulevard, Suite 201, Starkville, MS 39759 .... (662) 324–0007
District Representative.—Henry Moseley.
230 South Whitworth Street, Brookhaven, MS 39601 .... (601) 823–3400
Staff Assistant.—Mary Martha Dixon.
308 Franklin Street, Natchez, MS 39120 .... (601) 442–2515

Counties: Adans, Amite, Covington, Franklin, Hinds (part), Jasper (part), Jeff Davis, Jones (part), Kemper, Lauderdale, Lawrence, Leake (part), Lincoln, Madison (part), Marion (part), Neshoba, Newton, Noxubee, Oktibbeha, Pike, Rankin, Scott, Simpson, Smith, Walthall, Webster (part), Wilkinson, Winston. Population (2000), 711,164.

ZIP Codes: 39041–44, 39046–47, 39051, 39057, 39062, 39069, 39071, 39073–74, 39078, 39080, 39082–83, 39087, 39090, 39092, 39094, 39098, 39108–12, 39114, 39116–17, 39119–22, 39130, 39140, 39145, 39148–49, 39151–53, 39157–58, 39161, 39165, 39167–68, 39189–91, 39193, 39202, 39206, 39208–09, 39211, 39213, 39216, 39218, 39232, 39236, 39288, 39298, 39301–05, 39307, 39309, 39320, 39323, 39325–28, 39332, 39335–39, 39341–42, 39345–46, 39350, 39352, 39354, 39358–59, 39361, 39364–65, 39402, 39421–22, 39427–29, 39439, 39443, 39460, 39474, 39478–80, 39482–83, 39601–03, 39629–33, 39635, 39638, 39641, 39643, 39645, 39647–49, 39652–54, 39656–57, 39661–69, 39701, 39735, 39739, 39743, 39750, 39755, 39759–60, 39762, 39769

* * *

FOURTH DISTRICT

GENE TAYLOR, Democrat, of Bay St. Louis, MS; born in New Orleans, LA, on September 17, 1953; graduated from De LaSalle High School, New Orleans, LA, 1971; B.A., Tulane University, New Orleans, LA, 1974; graduate studies in business and economics,

University of Southern Mississippi, August 1978–April 1980; U.S. Coast Guard Reserves, 1971–84, first class petty officer, search and rescue boat skipper; sales representative, Stone Container Corporation, 1977–89; city councilman, Bay St. Louis, 1981–83; State Senator, 1983–89; member: American Legion; Rotary; Boys and Girls Club of the Gulf Coast; committees: Armed Services; Transportation and Infrastructure; married the former Margaret Gordon, 1978; three children: Sarah, Emily, Gary; elected to the 101st Congress, by special election, on October 17, 1989, to fill the vacancy caused by the death of Larkin Smith; reelected to each succeeding Congress.

Office Listings

http://www.house.gov/genetaylor

2311 Rayburn House Office Building, Washington, DC 20515 .... (202) 225–5772
Chief of Staff.—Wayne Weidie. FAX: 225–7074
Legislative Director.—Stephen Peranich.
Executive Assistant.—Courtney Littig.
2424 Fourteenth Street, Gulfport, MS 39501 .... (228) 864–7670
District Manager.—Beau Gex.
215 Federal Building, 701 Main Street, Hattiesburg, MS 39401 .... (601) 582–3246
1314 Government Street, Ocean Springs, MS 39564 .... (228) 872–7950
527 Central Avenue, Laurel, MS 39440 .... (601) 425–3905

Counties: CLARKE, FORREST, GEORGE, GREENE, HANCOCK, HARRISON, JACKSON, JASPER (part), JONES, LAMAR, MARION (part), PEARL RIVER, PERRY, STONE, WAYNE. CITIES AND TOWNSHIPS: Biloxi, Gulfport, Hattiesburg, Laurel, and Pascagoula. Population (2000), 711,170.

ZIP Codes: 39301, 39307, 39322, 39324, 39330, 39332, 39347–48, 39355–56, 39360, 39362–63, 39366–67, 39401–04, 39406, 39422–23, 39425–26, 39429, 39436–37, 39439–43, 39451–52, 39455–57, 39459, 39461–66, 39470, 39475–78, 39480–82, 39501–03, 39505–07, 39520–22, 39525, 39529–35, 39540, 39552–53, 39555–56, 39558, 39560–69, 39571–74, 39576–77, 39581, 39595

MISSOURI

(Population 2000, 5,595,211)

SENATORS

CHRISTOPHER S. (KIT) BOND, Republican, of Mexico, MO; born on March 6, 1939, in St. Louis, MO; B.A., *cum laude*, Woodrow Wilson School of Public and International Affairs of Princeton University, 1960; J.D., valedictorian, University of Virginia, 1963; held a clerkship with the U.S. Court of Appeals for the Fifth Circuit, 1964; practiced law in Washington, DC, and returned to Missouri, 1967; assistant attorney general of Missouri, 1969; state auditor, 1970; Governor of Missouri, 1973–77, 1981–85; children: Samuel Reid Bond; committees: Small Business and Entrepreneurship; Appropriations; Environment and Public Works; Health, Education, Labor and Pensions; Intelligence; elected to the U.S. Senate on November 4, 1986; reelected to each succeeding Senate term.

Office Listings

http://bond.senate.gov

274 Russell Senate Office Building, Washington, DC 20510 .... (202) 224–5721
Chief of Staff.—Julie Dammann. FAX: 224–8149
Legislative Director.—Brian Klippenstein.
Legal Counsel.—Jack Bartling.
Scheduling Secretary.—Amy Gibson.
911 Main Street, Suite 2224, Kansas City, MO 64105 .... (816) 417–7141
7700 Bonhomme, Suite 615, Clayton, MO 63105 .... (314) 725–4484
1700 S. Campbell, Suite E, Springfield, MO 65807 .... (417) 864–8258
Federal Building, Room 140, 339 Broadway, Cape Girardeau, MO 63701 .... (573) 334–7044
308 East High, Suite 202, Jefferson City, MO 65101 .... (314) 634–2488

* * *

JAMES M. TALENT, Republican, of Chesterfield, MO; born on October 18, 1956, in St. Louis, MO; graduated from Kirkwood High School, 1973; B.A., Washington University, St. Louis, 1978; J.D., University of Chicago Law School, 1981; Attorney; admitted to the Missouri bar, 1981; clerk for Judge Richard Posner, U.S. Court of Appeals, 7th Circuit; associate of Moller, Talent, Kuelthau, and Welch; counsel of Lashly and Baer; Missouri State House of Representatives, 1985–92, elected minority leader, 1989–92; member: West County Chamber of Commerce; Chesterfield Chamber of Commerce; Twin Oaks Presbyterian Church; married the former Brenda Lyons, 1984; three children: Michael, Kate, and Chrissy; elected on November 3, 1992, to the 103rd Congress; not a candidate for reelection to the House in 2000; elected to the U.S. Senate on November 5, 2002.

Office Listings

http://talent.senate.gov

493 Russell Senate Office Building, Washington, DC 20510 .... (202) 224–6154
Chief of Staff.—Mark N. Strand. FAX: 228–1518
Legislative Director.—Brett Thompson.
Legislative Counsel.—Faith Cristol.
Communications Director.—Rich Chrismer.
122 East High Street, Second Floor, Jefferson City, MO 65101 .... (573) 636–1070
State Director.—Donna Spickert.
Thomas F. Eagleton Federal Courthouse, 111 South Tenth Street, Suite 23.350, St. Louis, MO 63102 .... (314) 436–3416
H&H Building, 400 Broadway, Suite 520, Cape Girardeau, MO 63701 .... (573) 651–0964
300 John Q. Hammonds Parkway, Suite 111, Springfield, MO 65806 .... (417) 831–2735
Federal Office Building, 400 East 9th Street, Suite 40 Plaza Level, Kansas City, MO 64106 .... (816) 421–1639

REPRESENTATIVES

FIRST DISTRICT

WM. LACY CLAY, Democrat, of St. Louis, MO; born on July 27, 1956, in St. Louis, MO; education: Springbrook High School, Silver Spring, MD, 1974; B.S., University of Maryland, 1983, with a degree in government and politics, and a certificate in paralegal studies; public service: Missouri House of Representatives, 1983–91; Missouri State Senate, 1991–2000; non-profit organizations: St. Louis Gateway Classic Sports Foundation; Mary Ryder Homes; William L. Clay Scholarship and Research Fund; married: Ivie Lewellen Clay; children: Carol, and William III; elected to the 107th Congress on November 7, 2000; reelected to each succeeding Congress.

Office Listings

http://www.house.gov/clay

131 Cannon House Office Building, Washington, DC 20515 .... (202) 225–2406
Chief of Staff.—Harriett Pritchett Grigsby. FAX: 225–1725
Legislative Director.—Michele Bogdanovich.
Press Secretary.—Ishmael-Lateef Ahmed.
625 North Euclid Avenue, Suite 200, St. Louis, MO 63108 .... (314) 367–1970
8525 Page Boulevard, St. Louis, MO 63114 .... (314) 890–0349

Counties: ST. LOUIS (part). Population (2000), 621,690.

ZIP Codes: 63031–34, 63042–44, 63074, 63101–08, 63110, 63112–15, 63117, 63119–22, 63124, 63130–38, 63141, 63145–47, 63150, 63155–56, 63160, 63164, 63166–67, 63169, 63171, 63177–80, 63182, 63188, 63190, 63195–99

* * *

SECOND DISTRICT

W. TODD AKIN, Republican, of St. Louis, MO; born on July 5, 1947, in New York, NY; education: B.S., WPI, 1971; military service: Officer, U.S. Army Engineers; professional: engineer and businessman; employment: IBM; Laclede Steel; taught International Marketing, undergraduate level; public service: appointed to the Bicentennial Commission of the U.S. Constitution, 1987; Missouri House of Representatives, 1988–2000; organizations: Boy Scouts of America; Missouri Right to Life; Mission Gate Prison Ministry; family: married to Lulli; children: Wynn, Perry, Micah, Ezra, Hanna and Abigail; elected to the 107th Congress on November 7, 2000; reelected to each succeeding Congress.

Office Listings

http://www.house.gov/akin

117 Cannon House Office Building, Washington, DC 20515 .... (202) 225–2561
Chief of Staff.—Rob Schwarzwalder. FAX: 225–2563
Scheduler.—Amanda Carman.
301 Sovereign Court, Suite 201, St. Louis, MO 63011 .... (314) 590–0029
District Director.—Patrick Werner.

Counties: LINCOLN, ST. CHARLES (part), ST. LOUIS (part). Population (2000), 621,690.

ZIP Codes: 63001, 63005–06, 63011, 63017, 63021–22, 63024–26, 63038, 63040, 63043, 63049, 63069, 63088, 63099, 63110, 63114, 63117, 63119, 63122–29, 63131, 63134, 63141, 63144–46, 63301–04, 63333–34, 63338, 63343–44, 63346–49, 63359, 63362, 63366–67, 63369–70, 63373, 63376–77, 63379, 63381, 63383, 63385–87, 63389–90

* * *

THIRD DISTRICT

RICHARD A. GEPHARDT, Democrat, of St. Louis, MO; born in St. Louis, MO, on January 31, 1941; graduated, Southwest High School, 1958; education: B.S., Northwestern University, 1962; J.D., University of Michigan Law School, 1965; admitted to the Missouri bar in 1965; commenced practice in St. Louis; attorney, partner, Thompson and Mitchell law firm, 1965–77; served in Missouri Air National Guard, 1965–71; chairman, Young Lawyer's Section, the Bar Association of Metropolitan St. Louis, 1971–73; Democratic Committeeman, 1968–71; alderman of 14th ward, city of St. Louis, 1971–77; member: Third Baptist Church (St. Louis), Kiwanis, Boy Scouts of America, Children's United Research Effort, Missouri Bar Association, and the Bar Association of Metropolitan St. Louis; married: the former Jane Ann Byrnes, 1966; children: Matthew, Christine, and Katherine; member, Democratic Caucus; past chairman, Democratic Leadership Council; former House Democratic Leader; elected to the 95th Congress on November 2, 1976; reelected to each succeeding Congress.

Office Listings

http://dickgephardt.house.gov

1236 Longworth House Office Building, Washington, DC 20515 .... (202) 225–2671
Administrative Assistant.—Kevin Gunn.
Legislative Director.—Sean Kennedy.
11140 South Towne Square, Room 201, St. Louis, MO 63123 .... (314) 894–3400
Administrative Assistant.—Mary Renick.

Counties: JEFFERSON, SAINTE GENEVIEVE, ST. LOUIS (part). CITIES: St. Louis (part). Population (2000), 621,690.

ZIP Codes: 63010, 63012, 63015–16, 63019–20, 63023, 63025–26, 63028, 63030, 63036, 63041, 63047–53, 63057, 63060, 63065–66, 63069–72, 63087, 63102, 63104–05, 63109–11, 63116–19, 63122–30, 63132, 63139, 63143–44, 63151, 63157–58, 63163, 63627–28, 63640, 63645, 63661, 63670, 63673

* * *

FOURTH DISTRICT

IKE SKELTON, Democrat, of Lexington, MO; born in Lexington, MO, on December 20, 1931; graduated, Lexington High School, 1949; attended Wentworth Military Academy, Lexington; graduated, University of Missouri: A.B., 1953, LL.B., 1956; attended University of Edinburgh (Scotland), 1953; lawyer; admitted to the Missouri bar in 1956 and commenced practice in Lexington; elected, State Senate, 1970; reelected, 1974; prosecuting attorney, Lafayette County, 1957–60; special assistant attorney general, 1961–63; member: Phi Beta Kappa honor society, Missouri Bar Association, Lions, Elks, Masons, Boy Scouts, First Christian Church; married the former Susan B. Anding, 1961; three children: Ike, James, and Page; elected to the 95th Congress on November 2, 1976; reelected to each succeeding Congress.

Office Listings

http://www.house.gov/skelton

2206 Rayburn House Office Building, Washington, DC 20515 .... (202) 225–2876
Chief of Staff.—Robert Hagedorn.
Administrative Assistant.—Whitney Frost.
Legislative Director.—Dana O'Brien.
Press Secretary.—Lara Battles.
514–B North West 7 Highway, Blue Springs, MO 64014 .... (816) 228–4242
Chief of Staff.—Robert Hagedorn.
908 Thompson Boulevard, Sedalia, MO 65301 .... (660) 826–2675
1401 Southwest Boulevard, Jefferson City, MO 65109 .... (573) 635–3499
219 North Adams, Lebanon, MO 65536 .... (417) 532–7964

Counties: BARTON, BATES, BENTON, CAMDEN (part), CASS (part), CEDAR, COLE, DADE, DALLAS, HENRY, HICKORY, JACKSON (part), JOHNSON, LACLEDE, LAFAYETTE, MONITEAU, MORGAN, PETTIS, POLK (part), PULASKI, RAY, SALINE, ST. CLAIR, VERNON, WEBSTER. Population (2000), 621,690.

ZIP Codes: 64001, 64011, 64013–14, 64016–17, 64019–22, 64024, 64029, 64034–37, 64040, 64058, 64061–62, 64067, 64071, 64074–77, 64080, 64082, 64084–86, 64088, 64090, 64093, 64096–97, 64624, 64637, 64668, 64670–71, 64701, 64720, 64722–26, 64728, 64730, 64733, 64735, 64738–48, 64750, 64752, 64755–56, 64759, 64761–63, 64765, 64767, 64769–72, 64776, 64778–81, 64783–84, 64788, 64790, 64832, 64855, 65011, 65018, 65020, 65023, 65025–26, 65032, 65034, 65037–38, 65040, 65042, 65046, 65049–50, 65052–53, 65055, 65065, 65072, 65074, 65076, 65078–79, 65081, 65084, 65101–11, 65287, 65301–02, 65305, 65320–21, 65323–27, 65329–30, 65332–40, 65344–45, 65347–51, 65354–55, 65360, 65452, 65457, 65459, 65461, 65463, 65470, 65473, 65534, 65536, 65543, 65550, 65552, 65556–67, 65572, 65583–84, 65590–91, 65601, 65603–04, 65607, 65632, 65634–36, 65640, 65644, 65646, 65648–50, 65652, 65661–62, 65668, 65674, 65682, 65685, 65706, 65713, 65722, 65724, 65727, 65732, 65735, 65742, 65746, 65752, 65757, 65764, 65767, 65774, 65779, 65783, 65785–87

* * *

FIFTH DISTRICT

KAREN McCARTHY, Democrat, of Kansas City, MO; born in Haverhill, MA, March 18, 1947; education: graduated, Shawnee Mission East High School, Shawnee Mission, KS, 1965; University of Kansas, Lawrence, 1969; B.S. (English) and M.A. (English), University of Missouri, Kansas City, 1976; M.B.A., University of Kansas, 1986; educator; Stern Brothers and Company Investment Bankers; Midwest Research Institute; Marion Merrell Dow; Missouri State Representative; president, National Conference of State Legislatures; president, Leadership America Alumni Board; Harvard Fellow, Institute of Politics, Kennedy School of Government; Japan Fellow, U.S.-Japan Leadership Program; National Democratic Institute for International

Affairs instructor; American Council of Young Political Leaders; member, University of Kansas School of Business Board of Advisors; member: Missouri House of Representatives, 1977–95; chair, Ways and Means Committee, 1983–95; elected to the 104th Congress; reelected to each succeeding Congress.

Office Listings

1436 Longworth House Office Building, Washington, DC 20515 .... (202) 225–4535
Chief of Staff.—[Vacant]. FAX: 225–4403
Administrative Assistant / Communications Director.—Matt Nerzig.
Legislative Director.—Susan Hunter.
400 East 9th Street, Suite 9350, Kansas City, MO 64106 .... (816) 842–4545
301 West Lexington, Room 217, Independence, MO 64050 .... (816) 833–4545
District Aide.—Nicki Cardwell.

Counties: CASS COUNTY (part), JACKSON COUNTY (part). CITIES AND TOWNSHIPS: Grandview, Greenwood, Independence, Kansas City, Lee's Summit, Raytown, and Sugar Creek. Population (2000), 621,691.

ZIP Codes: 64012, 64014–15, 64029–30, 64034, 64050–58, 64061, 64063–65, 64070, 64075, 64078, 64080–83, 64086, 64101–02, 64105–06, 64108–14, 64120–21, 64123–34, 64136–39, 64141, 64145–49, 64170–71, 64179–80, 64184–85, 64187–88, 64191–94, 64196–99, 64701, 64734, 64944, 64999

* * *

SIXTH DISTRICT

SAM GRAVES, Republican, of Tarkio, MO; born on November 7, 1963, in Fairfax, MO; education: B.S., University of Missouri-Columbia, 1986; profession: farmer; organizations: Missouri Farm Bureau; Northwest Missouri State University Agriculture Advisory Committee; University Extension Council; Rotary Club; awards: Associated Industries Voice of Missouri Business Award; Tom Henderson Award; Tarkio Community Betterment Award; Missouri Physical Therapy Association Award; public service: elected to the Missouri House of Representatives, 1992; and the Missouri State Senate, 1994; religion: Baptist; family: married to Lesley; children: Megan, Emily, and Sam III; committees: Agriculture; Small Business; Transportation and Infrastructure; elected to the 107th Congress on November 7, 2000; reelected to each succeeding Congress.

Office Listings

http://www.house.gov/graves

1513 Longworth House Office Building, Washington, DC 20515 .... (202) 225–7041
Chief of Staff.—Jeff Roe. FAX: 225–8221
Press Secretary.—Jacob DiPietre.
201 S. Eighth Street, Room 330, St. Joseph, MO 64501 .... (816) 233–9818
113 Blue Jay Drive, Suite 100, Liberty, MO 64068 .... (816) 792–3976

Counties: ANDREW, ATCHISON, BUCHANAN, CALDWELL, CARROLL, CHARITON, CLAY, CLINTON, COOPER, DAVIESS, DEKALB, GENTRY, GRUNDY, HARRISON, HOLT, HOWARD, LINN, LIVINGSTON, MERCER, NODAWAY, PLATTE, PUTNAM, SCHUYLER, SULLIVAN, WORTH. Population (2000), 621,690.

ZIP Codes: 63535–36, 63541, 63544–46, 63548, 63551, 63556–61, 63565–67, 64014–15, 64017–18, 64024, 64028–29, 64035–36, 64048, 64056–58, 64060, 64064, 64066, 64068–69, 64072–73, 64075, 64077, 64079, 64084–85, 64088–89, 64092, 64098, 64116–19, 64144, 64150–58, 64161, 64163–68, 64190, 64195, 64401–02, 64420–24, 64426–34, 64436–49, 64451, 64453–59, 64461, 64463, 64465–71, 64473–77, 64479–94, 64496–99, 64501–08, 64601, 64620, 64622–25, 64628, 64630–33, 64635–61, 64664, 64667–68, 64670–74, 64676, 64679, 64681–83, 64686, 64688–89, 64763, 65018, 65025, 65046, 65068, 65081, 65230, 65233, 65236–37, 65243–44, 65246, 65248, 65250, 65254, 65256–57, 65261, 65274, 65276, 65279, 65281, 65286–87, 65301, 65322, 65347–48, 65350, 65354

* * *

SEVENTH DISTRICT

ROY BLUNT, Republican, of Strafford, MO; born in Niangua, MO, January 10, 1950; Majority Whip; committees: Energy and Commerce; Republican Leadership Steering Committee; House Delegate to National Historical Publications and Records Commission; House Delegate to North Atlantic Assembly; member, Family Caucus and the Travel-Tourism Caucus; before election to Congress, president of Southwest Baptist University; author; two-term Missouri Secretary of State; Greene County, Missouri Clerk and chief election officer; past chair: Missouri Housing Development Commission, Governor's Council on Literacy; past co-chairman, Missouri Opportunity 2000 Commission; past member, Project Democracy Commission for Voter Participation in the United States; board member, American Council of Young Political Leaders; served as first chairman of the Missouri Prison Fellowship; named one of the Ten

Outstanding Young Americans, 1986; children: Matt, Secretary of State of Missouri and Naval reserve officer; Amy, a lawyer in the Kansas City area; and Andy, an attorney in Jefferson City; elected to the 105th Congress; reelected to each succeeding Congress.

Office Listings

http://www.majoritywhip.gov http://blunt.house.gov

H–329, U.S. Capitol Building (Office of the Majority Whip), Washington, DC 20515 .... (202) 225–0197
Chief of Staff.—Gregg Hartley.
Communications Director.—Burson Taylor.
Director of Scheduling.—Richard Eddings.
217 Cannon House Office Building, Washington, DC 20515 .... (202) 225–6536
Chief of Staff.—Amy Field. FAX: 225–5604
2740–B East Sunshine, Springfield, MO 65804 .... (417) 889–1800
District Director.—Sharon Nahon.
Northpark Mall, 101 Range Line Road, Box 20, Joplin, MO 64801 .... (417) 781–1041

Counties: Barry, Christian, Greene, Jasper, Lawrence, McDonald, Newton, Polk (part), Stone, Taney (part). Population (2000), 621,690.

ZIP Codes: 64748, 64755–56, 64766, 64769, 64801–04, 64830–36, 64840–44, 64847–50, 64853–59, 64861–70, 64873–74, 65603–05, 65608–20, 65622–27, 65629–31, 65633, 65635, 65637–38, 65640–41, 65645–50, 65652–58, 65661, 65663–64, 65666, 65669, 65672–76, 65680–82, 65686, 65702, 65705, 65707–08, 65710, 65712, 65714–15, 65720–21, 65723, 65725–30, 65733–34, 65737–42, 65744–45, 65747, 65752–57, 65759–62, 65765–73, 65781, 65784–85, 65801–10, 65814, 65817, 65890, 65898–99

* * *

EIGHTH DISTRICT

JO ANN EMERSON, Republican, of Cape Girardeau, MO; born in Washington, DC, September 16, 1950; B.A., political science, Ohio Wesleyan University, Delaware, OH, 1972; Senior Vice President of Public Affairs, American Insurance Association; director, State Relations and Grassroots Programs, National Restaurant Association; deputy communications director, National Republican Congressional Committee; member: PEO Women's Service Group, Cape Girardeau, MO; Copper Dome Society, Southeast Missouri State University; advisory committee, Children's Inn, National Institutes of Health; advisory board, Arneson Institute for Practical Politics and Public Affairs, Ohio Weslyan University; married: Ron Gladney, 2000; children: Victoria and Katharine; six stepchildren: Elizabeth, Abigail, Victoria, Stephanie, Alison, Jessica, and Sam; committees: Appropriations; subcommittees: Agriculture, Rural Development, and Related Agencies; Energy and Water Development; Homeland Security; elected on November 5, 1996, by special election, to the 104th Congress: reelected to each succeeding Congress.

Office Listings

http://www.house.gov/emerson

2440 Rayburn House Office Building, Washington, DC 20515 .... (202) 225–4404
Deputy Chief of Staff.—Jordan Bernstein. FAX: 226–0326
Legislative Director.—Grant Erdel.
Communications Director.—Michelle Dimarob.
Executive Assistant / Scheduler.—Atalie Ebersole.
339 Broadway, Cape Girardeau, MO 63701 .... (573) 335–0101
Chief of Staff.—Lloyd Smith.
612 Pine Street, Rolla, MO 65401 .... (573) 364–2455
22 East Columbia, Farmington, MO 63640 .... (573) 756–9755

Counties: Bollinger, Butler, Cape Girardeau, Carter, Crawford, Dent, Douglas, Dunklin, Howell, Iron, Madison, Mississippi, New Madrid, Oregon, Ozark, Pemiscot, Perry, Phelps, Reynolds, Ripley, St. Francois, Scott, Shannon, Stoddard, Taney (part), Texas, Washington, Wayne, Wright. Population (2000), 621,690.

ZIP Codes: 63028, 63030, 63036, 63071, 63080, 63087, 63601, 63620–26, 63628–33, 63636–38, 63640, 63648, 63650–51, 63653–56, 63660, 63662–66, 63674–75, 63701–03, 63730, 63732, 63735–40, 63742–48, 63750–52, 63755, 63758, 63760, 63763–64, 63766–67, 63769–72, 63774–76, 63779–85, 63787, 63801, 63820–30, 63833–34, 63837, 63839–41, 63845–53, 63855, 63857, 63860, 63862–63, 63866–70, 63873–82, 63901–02, 63931–45, 63950–57, 63960–67, 65401–02, 65409, 65436, 65438–41, 65444, 65446, 65449, 65453, 65456, 65459, 65461–62, 65464, 65466, 65468, 65479, 65483–84, 65501, 65529, 65532, 65541–42, 65546, 65548, 65550, 65552, 65555, 65557, 65564–66, 65570–71, 65586, 65588–89, 65606, 65608–09, 65614, 65616, 65618, 65620, 65626–27, 65629, 65637–38, 65652–53, 65655, 65660, 65662, 65666–67, 65676, 65679–80, 65688–90, 65692, 65701–02, 65704, 65711, 65713, 65715, 65717, 65720, 65729, 65731, 65733, 65740–41, 65744, 65746, 65753, 65755, 65759–62, 65766, 65768, 65773, 65775, 65777–78, 65784, 65788–91, 65793

NINTH DISTRICT

KENNY C. HULSHOF, Republican, of Columbia, MO; born on May 22, 1958, in Sikeston, MO; graduated from Thomas W. Kelly High School, Benton, MO; agriculture economics degree, University of Missouri School of Agriculture, 1980; J.D., University of Mississippi Law School, 1983; attorney, admitted to Missouri and Mississippi bars in 1983; Assistant Public Defender, 32nd judicial circuit, 1983–86; Assistant Prosecuting Attorney, Cape Girardeau, MO, 1986–89; Assistant Attorney General, State of Missouri, 1989–96; member: Newman Center Catholic Church, Boone County Farm Bureau, Farm House Foundation, Ducks Unlimited; committee: Ways and Means; married Renee Howell Hulshof, 1994; elected to the 105th Congress; reelected to each succeeding Congress.

Office Listings

http://www.house.gov/hulshof

412 Cannon House Office Building, Washington, DC 20515 .... (202) 225–2956
Chief of Staff.—Manning Feraci. FAX: 225–5712
Administrative Assistant.—Matt Miller.
Executive Assistant / Scheduler.—Lena Johnson.
33 Broadway, Suite 280, Columbia, MO 65203 .... (573) 449–5111
201 N. 3rd Street, Hannibal, MO 63401 .... (573) 221–1200
516 Jefferson Street, Washington, MO 63090 .... (636) 239–4001

Counties: ADAIR, AUDRAIN, BOONE, CALLAWAY, CAMDEN (part), CLARK, CRAWFORD, FRANKLIN, GASCONADE, KNOX, LEWIS, MACON, MARIES, MARION, MILLER, MONROE, MONTGOMERY, OSAGE, PIKE, RALLS, RANDOLPH, ST. CHARLES (part), SCOTLAND, SHELBY, WARREN. Population (2000), 621,690.

ZIP Codes: 63005, 63013–15, 63037, 63039, 63041, 63055–56, 63060, 63068–69, 63072–73, 63077, 63079–80, 63084, 63089–91, 63303–04, 63330, 63332–34, 63336, 63339, 63341–42, 63344–45, 63348–53, 63357, 63359, 63361, 63363, 63365–67, 63376, 63378, 63381–85, 63388, 63390, 63401, 63430–43, 63445–48, 63450–54, 63456–69, 63471–74, 63501, 63530–34, 63536–40, 63543–44, 63546–47, 63549, 63552, 63555, 63557–59, 63563, 64631, 64658, 64856, 65001, 65010, 65013–14, 65016–17, 65024, 65026, 65031–32, 65035–36, 65039–41, 65043, 65047–49, 65051, 65054, 65058–59, 65061–67, 65069, 65072, 65074–77, 65080, 65082–83, 65085, 65101, 65201–03, 65205, 65211–12, 65215–18, 65230–32, 65239–40, 65243–44, 65247, 65251, 65255–60, 65262–65, 65270, 65275, 65278–85, 65299, 65337, 65441, 65443, 65446, 65449, 65452–53, 65456, 65459, 65486, 65535, 65559–60, 65565, 65580, 65582, 65586, 65591

MONTANA

(Population 2000, 902,195)

SENATORS

MAX BAUCUS, Democrat, of Helena, MT; born in Helena, December 11, 1941; graduated, Helena High School, 1959; B.A. in economics, Stanford University, 1964; LL.B., Stanford University Law School, 1967; attorney, Civil Aeronautics Board, 1967–71; attorney, George and Baucus law firm, Missoula, MT; married to the former Wanda Minge; one child, Zeno; member, Montana and District of Columbia bar associations; served in Montana House of Representatives, 1973–74; committees: ranking member, Finance; Agriculture, Nutrition, and Forestry; Joint Committee on Taxation; Environment and Public Works; elected to the 94th Congress, November 5, 1974; reelected to the 95th Congress; elected to the U.S. Senate, November 7, 1978, for the six-year term beginning January 3, 1979; subsequently appointed on December 15, 1978, to fill the vacancy caused by the resignation of Senator Paul Hatfield; reelected to each succeeding Senate term.

Office Listings

http://baucus.senate.gov

511 Hart Senate Office Building, Washington, DC 20510 .... (202) 224–2651
  Chief of Staff.—Jeff Forbes.
  Legislative Director.—Zak Andersen.
  Press Secretary.—Michael Seigel.
  DC Scheduler.—Julie Wirkkala.
207 North Broadway, Billings, MT 59101 .... (406) 657–6790
P.O. Box 1689, Bozeman, MT 59771 .... (406) 586–6104
Silver Bow Center, 125 West Granite, Butte, MT 59701 .... (406) 782–8700
118 Fifth Street South, Great Falls, MT 59401 .... (406) 761–1574
23 South Last Chance Gulch, Helena, MT 59601 .... (406) 449–5480
  Communications Director.—Bill Lombardi.
220 First Avenue East, Kalispell, MT 59901 .... (406) 756–1150
211 North Higgins, Room 102, Missoula, MT 59802 .... (406) 329–3123
  State Chief of Staff.—Jim Foley. (800) 332–6106

* * *

CONRAD BURNS, Republican, of Billings, MT; born in Gallatin, MO, on January 25, 1935; graduated, Gallatin High School, 1952; attended University of Missouri, Columbia, 1953–54; served, U.S. Marine Corps, corporal, 1955–57; farm broadcaster and auctioneer; county commissioner, Yellowstone County, 1986; member: Rotary, American Legion, National Association of Farm Broadcasters, American Association of Farm Broadcasters, Atonement Lutheran Church; married to the former Phyllis Kuhlmann; two children: Keely and Garrett; committees: Appropriations, Budget; Commerce, Science, and Transportation; Energy and Natural Resources; Small Business and Entrepreneurship; elected to the U.S. Senate on November 8, 1988; reelected to each succeeding Senate term.

Office Listings

http://burns.senate.gov

187 Dirksen Senate Office Building, Washington, DC 20510 .... (202) 224–2644
  Chief of Staff / General Counsel.—Will Brooke.
  Legislative Director.—Ric Molen.
  Executive Assistant / Scheduler.—Angela Schulze.
  Administrative Director.—Margo Rushing.
208 North Montana Avenue, Suite 202–A, Helena, MT 59601 .... (406) 449–5401
222 North 32nd Street, Suite 400, Billings, MT 59101 .... (406) 252–0550
321 First Avenue North, Great Falls, MT 59401 .... (406) 452–9585
200 East Broadway, Missoula Federal Building, Missoula, MT 59807 .... (406) 329–3528
324 West Towne, Glendive, MT 59330 .... (406) 365–2391
211 Haggerty Lane, Bozeman, MT 59715 .... (406) 586–4450
125 West Granite, Suite 211, Butte, MT 59701 .... (406) 723–3277
1845 Highway 93 South, Suite 210, Kalispell, MT 59901 .... (406) 257–3360

REPRESENTATIVE

AT LARGE

DENNIS R. REHBERG, Republican, of Billings, MT; born on October 5, 1955, in Billings, MT; education: B.A., Washington State University, 1977; employment: rancher; manages the Rehberg Ranch; public service: interned in the Montana State Senate, 1977–79; legislative assistant to Rep. Ron Marlenee (R–MT), 1979–82; elected to the Montana House of Representatives, 1984; appointed Lt. Governor of Montana in 1991; elected Lt. Governor in 1992; Chairman, Drought Advisory Committee; Worker's Compensation Task Force; and the Montana Rural Development Council; Republican nominee for the U.S. Senate, 1996; married: Janice; children: A.J., Katie, and Elsie; elected to the 107th Congress on November 7, 2000; reelected to each succeeding Congress.

Office Listings

http://www.house.gov/rehberg

516 Cannon House Office Building, Washington, DC 20515 .... (202) 225–3211
Chief of Staff.—Erik Iverson. FAX: 225–5687
Communications Director.—Brad Keena.
1201 Grand Avenue, Suite 1, Billings, MT 59102 .... (406) 256–1019
District Director.—Randy Vogel.

Counties: BEAVERHEAD, BIG HORN, BLAINE, BROADWATER, CARBON, CARTER, CASCADE, CHOUTEAU, CUSTER, DANIELS, DAWSON, DEER LODGE, FALLON, FERGUS, FLATHEAD, GALLATIN, GARFIELD, GLACIER, GOLDEN VALLEY, GRANITE, HILL, JEFFERSON, JUDITH BASIN, LAKE, LEWIS AND CLARK, LIBERTY, LINCOLN, MADISON, MCCONE, MEAGHER, MINERAL, MISSOULA, MUSSELLSHELL PARK, PETROLEUM, PHILLIPS, PONDERA, POWDER RIVER, POWELL, PRAIRIE, RAVALLI, RICHLAND, ROOSEVELT, ROSEBUD, SANDERS, SHERIDAN, SILVER BOW, STILLWATER, SWEET GRASS, TETON, TOOLE, TREASURE, VALLEY, WHEATLAND, WIBAUX, YELLOWSTONE. Population (2000), 902,195.

ZIP Codes: 59001–04, 59006–08, 59010–16, 59018–20, 59022, 59024–39, 59041, 59043–44, 59046–47, 59050, 59052–55, 59057–59, 59061–72, 59074–79, 59081–89, 59101–08, 59201, 59211–15, 59217–19, 59221–23, 59225–26, 59230–31, 59240–44, 59247–48, 59250, 59252–63, 59270, 59273–76, 59301, 59311–19, 59322–24, 59326–27, 59330, 59332–33, 59336–39, 59341, 59343–45, 59347, 59349, 59351, 59353–54, 59401–06, 59410–12, 59414, 59416–22, 59424–25, 59427, 59430, 59432–36, 59440–48, 59450–54, 59456–57, 59460–69, 59471–72, 59474, 59477, 59479–80, 59482–87, 59489, 59501, 59520–32, 59535, 59537–38, 59540, 59542, 59544–47, 59601–02, 59604, 59620, 59623–24, 59626, 59631–36, 59638–45, 59647–48, 59701–03, 59710–11, 59713–22, 59724–25, 59727–33, 59735–36, 59739–41, 59743, 59745–52, 59754–56, 59758–62, 59771–73, 59801–04, 59806–08, 59812, 59820–21, 59823–35, 59837, 59840–48, 59851, 59853–56, 59858–60, 59863–68, 59870–75, 59901, 59903–04, 59910–23, 59925–37

NEBRASKA

(Population 2000, 1,711,263)

SENATORS

CHUCK HAGEL, Republican, of Omaha, NE; born in North Platte, NE, on October 4, 1946; education: graduated, St. Bonaventure High School, Columbus, NE, 1964; Brown Institute for Radio and Television, Minneapolis, MN; University of Nebraska, Omaha; military service: served with U.S. Army in Vietnam, 1968, receiving two Purple Hearts, other decorations; profession: president, McCarthy and Company, Omaha, NE; president and CEO, Private Sector Council (PSC), Washington, DC; deputy director and CEO, Economic Summit of Industrialized Nations (G–7 Summit), 1990; president and CEO, World USO; cofounder, director, and executive vice president, VANGUARD Cellular Systems, Inc.; cofounder and chairman of VANGUARD subsidiary, Communications Corporation International, Ltd.; president, Collins, Hagel and Clarke, Inc.; former deputy administrator, Veterans' Administration; former administrative assistant to Congressman John Y. McCollister (R–NE); former newscaster and talk show host, Omaha radio stations KBON and KLNG; member: American Legion; Veterans of Foreign Wars; Disabled American Veterans; Military Order of the Purple Heart; Business-Government Relations Council, Washington, DC; Council for Excellence in Government; University of Nebraska Chancellors Club; board of directors, Omaha Chamber of Commerce; board of trustees: Bellevue University, Hastings College, Heartland Chapter of the American Red Cross; chairman: Building Campaign, Great Plains Chapter of Paralyzed Veterans of America; 10th Anniversary Vietnam Veterans' Memorial; board of directors and national advisory committee, Friends of the Vietnam Veterans' Memorial; board of directors, Arlington National Cemetery Historical Society; chairman of the board, No Greater Love, Inc.; awards: first-ever World USO Leadership Award; International Men of Achievement; Outstanding Young Men of America; Distinguished Alumni Award, University of Nebraska, Omaha, 1988; Freedom Foundation (Omaha Chapter) 1993 Recognition Award; married: the former Lilibet Ziller, 1985; children: Allyn and Ziller; committees: Banking, Housing and Urban Affairs; Foreign Relations; Select Committee on Intelligence; subcommittees: chair, International Trade and Finance; chair, International Economic Policy, Export and Trade Promotion; elected to the U.S. Senate on November 5, 1996; reelected to each succeeding Senate term.

Office Listings

http://hagel.senate.gov

248 Russell Senate Office Building, Washington, DC 20510 .... (202) 224–4224
Legislative Director.—Daniel Archer. FAX: 224–5213
Office Manager.—Marilouis Hudgins.
Communications Director.—Michael Buttry.
11301 Davenport Street, Suite 2, Omaha, NE 68154 .... (402) 758–8981
State Director.—Tom Janssen.
294 Federal Building, 100 Centennial Mall North, Lincoln, NE 68508 .... (402) 476–1400
Constituent Services Director.—Dorothy Anderson.
4009 Sixth Avenue, Suite 9, Kearney, NE 68845 .... (308) 236–7602
Constituent Services Representative.—Julie Brooker.
115 Railway Street, C102, Scottsbluff, NE 69361 .... (308) 632–6032
State Agriculture Director.—Mary B. Crawford.

* * *

BEN NELSON, Democrat, of Omaha, NE; born on May 17, 1941, in McCook, NE; education: University of Nebraska at Lincoln; received a bachelor's degree in 1963, a master's degree in 1965, and a law degree in 1970; profession: Attorney; employment: Director, Nebraska Department of Insurance; President and CEO of the Central National Insurance Group; Executive Vice President and Chief of Staff of the National Association of Insurance Commissioners; Kennedy, Holland, DeLacy, and Svoboda (law firm); awards: Thomas Jefferson Freedom Award; George W. Norris Award; National Eagle Scout Association Distinguished Eagle Award; family: married to Diane; four children; Governor of Nebraska, 1991–1999; elected to the U.S. Senate on November 7, 2000.

Office Listings

http://bennelson.senate.gov

720 Hart Senate Office Building, Washington, DC 20510 .... (202) 224–6551
Chief of Staff.—Tim Becker. FAX: 228–0012
Communications Director.—David DiMartino.
Federal Building, Room 287, Centennial Mall North, Lincoln, NE 68508 .... (402) 441–4600
7602 Pacific Street, Suite 205, Omaha, NE 68154 .... (402) 391–3411

REPRESENTATIVES

FIRST DISTRICT

DOUG BEREUTER, Republican, of Lincoln, NE; born in York, NE, on October 6, 1939, son of Rupert and Evelyn Bereuter; graduated, Utica High School, Utica, NE, 1957; B.A., University of Nebraska, Lincoln, 1961; Sigma Alpha Epsilon; M.C.P., Harvard University, 1966; M.P.A., Harvard University, 1973; counterintelligence officer, First Infantry Division, U.S. Army, 1963–65; urban development consultant in states surrounding Nebraska; associate professor at University of Nebraska and Kansas State University; visiting lecturer, Harvard University; State Senator, Nebraska Unicameral Legislature, 1974–78; vice chairman, Appropriations Committee and Committee on Administrative Rules and Regulations, 1977–78; chaired the Urban Development Committee of the National Conference of State Legislatures, 1977–78; member, Select Committee on Post-Secondary Education Coordination, 1977–78; Legislative Conservationist of the Year Award by the Nebraska and National Wildlife Federation in 1980; division director, Nebraska Department of Economic Development, 1967–68; director, State Office of Planning and Programming, 1968–70; appointee, Federal-State Relations Coordinator for Nebraska State Government, 1967–70; member: State Crime Commission 1969–71; Phi Beta Kappa; Sigma Xi; member, President's Council, Nebraska Wesleyan University; married: Louise Meyer Bereuter, 1962; children: Eric and Kirk; member: State Department Commission on Security and Economic Assistance, 1983–84, National Commission on Agricultural Trade and Export Policy 1985–86; congressional delegate to the United Nations, 1987; committees: Financial Services; International Relations; Transportation and Infrastructure; vice chairman, Select Committee on Intelligence; chairman, House Delegation to the NATO Parliamentary Assembly; elected to the 96th Congress; reelected to each succeeding Congress.

Office Listings

http://www.house.gov/bereuter

2184 Rayburn House Office Building, Washington, DC 20515 .... (202) 225–4806
Chief of Staff.—Susan Olson.
Office Manager.—Robin Evans.
Scheduler.—Sue Hager.
301 South 13th Street, Suite 100, P.O. Box 82887, Lincoln, NE 68508 .... (402) 438–1598
District Office Manager.—Roger Massey.
629 North Broad Street, P.O. Box 377, Fremont, NE 68025 .... (402) 727–0888
Office Manager.—Jon Peterson.

Counties: BURT, BUTLER, CASS, CEDAR (part), COLFAX, CUMING, DAKOTA, DIXON, DODGE, GAGE, JOHNSON, LANCASTER, MADISON, NEMAHA, OTOE, PAWNEE, RICHARDSON, SARPY (part), SAUNDERS, SEWARD, STANTON, THURSTON, WASHINGTON, WAYNE. Population (2000), 570,421.

ZIP Codes: 68001–04, 68007–09, 68014–20, 68023, 68025–26, 68028–31, 68033–34, 68036–42, 68044–48, 68050, 68055, 68057–59, 68061–68, 68070–73, 68112, 68122–23, 68133, 68136, 68138, 68142, 68144, 68152, 68301, 68304–05, 68307, 68309–10, 68313–14, 68316–21, 68323–24, 68328–33, 68336–37, 68339, 68341–49, 68351, 68355, 68357–60, 68364, 68366–68, 68371–72, 68376, 68378, 68380–82, 68401–05, 68407, 68409–10, 68413–15, 68417–24, 68428, 68430–31, 68433–34, 68437–39, 68441–43, 68445–48, 68450, 68452–58, 68460–67, 68501–10, 68512, 68514, 68516, 68520–24, 68526, 68528–29, 68532, 68542, 68583, 68588, 68601, 68621, 68624, 68626, 68629, 68631–33, 68635, 68641–44, 68648–49, 68658–59, 68661–62, 68666–67, 68669, 68701–02, 68710, 68715–17, 68723–24, 68727–28, 68731–33, 68739–41, 68743, 68745, 68747–49, 68751–52, 68757–58, 68767–68, 68770–71, 68776, 68779, 68781, 68784–85, 68787–88, 68790–92

* * *

SECOND DISTRICT

LEE TERRY, Republican, of Omaha, NE; born in Omaha, NE, on January 29, 1962; education: B.A., University of Nebraska, 1984; J.D., Creighton Law School, 1987; attorney; elected to the Omaha, NE, City Council, 1990–98; served as vice president and president, and on the audit, legislative, and cable television committees; religion: Methodist; married: Robyn; children: Nolan, Ryan, and Jack; committees: Energy and Commerce; elected to the 106th Congress; reelected to each succeeding Congress.

Office Listings

http://www.house.gov/terry

1524 Longworth House Office Building, Washington, DC 20515 .... (202) 225–4155
Chief of Staff.—Eric Hultman. FAX: 226–5452
Legislative Director.—Jamie Karl.
Appointment Secretary.—Shelly Blake.
Press Secretary.—Jeffrey Connor.
11640 Arbor Street, Suite 100, Omaha, NE 68144 .... (402) 397–9944
District Director.—Molly Koozer-Lloyd.

Counties: DOUGLAS, SARPY (part). CITIES: Bellevue, Bennington, Boys Town, Elkhorn, Gretna, La Vista, Omaha, Offutt AFB, Papillion, Plattsmouth, Ralston, Springfield, Valley, and Waterloo. Population (2000), 570,421.

ZIP Codes: 68005, 68007, 68010, 68016, 68022, 68028, 68046, 68056, 68064, 68069, 68101–14, 68116–20, 68122–24, 68127–28, 68130–39, 68142, 68144–45, 68147, 68152, 68154–55, 68157, 68164, 68172, 68175–76, 68178–83, 68197–98

* * *

THIRD DISTRICT

TOM OSBORNE, Republican, of Lemoyne, NE; born on February 23, 1937, in Hastings, NE; education: B.A., History, Hastings College; M.A., Educational Psychology, University of Nebraska; Ph.D., Educational Psychology, University of Nebraska; employment: Educator; Head Football Coach at the University of Nebraska, 1973–1998; won three National Championships, 1994, 1995, and 1997; author of several books; married: Nancy; three children; community service: developed and underwrote the Team Mates Mentoring Program for at-risk students; elected to the 107th Congress on November 7, 2000; reelected to each succeeding Congress.

Office Listings

http://www.house.gov/osborne

507 Cannon House Office Building, Washington, DC 20515 .... (202) 225–6435
Deputy Chief of Staff.—Christina Muedeking.
Legislative Director.—Erin Duncan.
Press Secretary.—Jennifer Hayes.
819 Diers Avenue, Suite 3, Grand Island, NE 68803 .... (308) 381–5555
Chief of Staff.—Bruce Rieker.
21 E. 20th Street, Scottsbluff, NE 69361 .... (308) 632–3333
Rural Initiatives Director.—Scot Blehm.

Counties: ADAMS, ANTELOPE, ARTHUR, BANNER, BLAINE, BOONE, BOX BUTTE, BOYD, BROWN, BUFFALO, CEDAR (part), CHASE, CHERRY, CHEYENNE, CLAY, CUSTER, DAWES, DAWSON, DEUEL, DUNDY, FILLMORE, FRANKLIN, FRONTIER, FURNAS, GARDEN, GARFIELD, GOSPER, GRANT, GREELEY, HALL, HAMILTON, HARLAN, HAYES, HITCHCOCK, HOLT, HOOKER, HOWARD, JEFFERSON, KEARNEY, KEITH, KEYA PAHA, KIMBALL, KNOX, LINCOLN, LOGAN, LOUP, MCPHERSON, MERRICK, MORRILL, NANCE, NUCKOLLS, PERKINS, PHELPS, PIERCE, PLATTE, POLK, RED WILLOW, ROCK, SALINE, SCOTTS BLUFF, SHERIDAN, SHERMAN, SIOUX, THAYER, THOMAS, VALLEY, WEBSTER, WHEELER, YORK. Population (2000), 570,421.

ZIP Codes: 68303, 68310, 68313, 68315–16, 68319, 68322, 68325–27, 68333, 68335, 68338–43, 68350–52, 68354, 68359, 68361–62, 68365, 68367, 68370–71, 68375, 68377, 68401, 68405–06, 68416, 68423–24, 68429, 68436, 68440, 68444–45, 68452–53, 68460, 68464–65, 68467, 68601–02, 68620–23, 68627–28, 68631, 68634, 68636–38, 68640, 68642–44, 68647, 68651–55, 68658, 68660, 68662–66, 68701, 68711, 68713–14, 68717–20, 68722–27, 68729–30, 68734–36, 68738–39, 68742, 68746–48, 68752–53, 68755–56, 68758–61, 68763–67, 68769, 68771, 68773–74, 68777–78, 68780–81, 68783, 68786, 68789, 68792, 68801–03, 68810, 68812–18, 68820–28, 68831–38, 68840–50, 68852–56, 68858–66, 68869–76, 68878–79, 68881–83, 68901–02, 68920, 68922–30, 68932–50, 68952, 68954–61, 68964, 68966–67, 68969–82, 69001, 69020–30, 69032–34, 69036–46, 69101, 69103, 69120–23, 69125, 69127–35, 69138, 69140–57, 69160–63, 69165–71, 69190, 69201, 69210–12, 69214, 69216–21, 69301, 69331, 69333–37, 69339–41, 69343, 69345–48, 69350–58, 69360–61, 69363, 69365–67

NEVADA

(Population 2000, 1,998,257)

SENATORS

HARRY REID, Democrat, of Searchlight NV; born in Searchlight on December 2, 1939; graduated, Basic High School, Henderson, NV, 1957; associate degree in science, Southern Utah State College, 1959; B.S., Utah State University, Phi Kappa Phi, 1961; J.D., George Washington School of Law, Washington, DC, 1964; admitted to the Nevada State bar in 1963, a year before graduating from law school; while attending law school, worked as a U.S. Capitol police officer; city attorney, Henderson, 1964–66; member and chairman, South Nevada Memorial Hospital Board of Trustees, 1967–69; elected: Nevada State Assembly, 1969–70; Lieutenant Governor, State of Nevada, 1970–74; served, executive committee, National Conference of Lieutenant Governors; chairman, Nevada Gaming Commission, 1977–81; member: Nevada State, Clark County and American bar associations; married the former Landra Gould in 1959; five children: Lana, Rory, Leif, Josh, and Key; committees: Appropriations; Environment and Public Works; vice chairman, Select Committee on Ethics; Special Committee on Aging; Indian Affairs; Assistant Democratic Leader; elected to the 98th Congress on November 2, 1982, and reelected to the 99th Congress; elected to the U.S. Senate on November 4, 1986; reelected to each succeeding Senate term.

Office Listings

http://reid.senate.gov

528 Hart Senate Office Building, Washington, DC 20510 .... (202) 224–3542
Chief of Staff.—Susan McCue. FAX: 224–7327
Deputy Chief of Staff.—David McCullum.
Executive Assistant.—Janice Shelton.
Legislative Director.—Kai Anderson.
600 East Williams Street, Room 302, Carson City, NV 89701 .... (775) 882–7343
333 Las Vegas Boulevard South, Suite 8016, Las Vegas, NV 89101 .... (702) 388–5020
400 S. Virginia Street, No. 902, Reno, NV 89501 .... (775) 686–5750

* * *

JOHN ENSIGN, Republican, of Las Vegas, NV; born in Roseville, CA, on March 25, 1958; education: E.W. Clark High School, Las Vegas, NV, 1976; B.S., University of Nevada at Las Vegas, 1976–79; Oregon State University, 1981; Colorado State University, 1985; profession: veterinarian; organizations: Las Vegas Southwest Rotary; Las Vegas Chamber of Commerce; Sigma Chi (fraternal organization); Meadows Christian Fellowship; married: Darlene Ensign, 1987; children: Trevor, Siena, and Michael; committees: Armed Services; Budget; Commerce, Science, and Transportation; Health, Education, Labor, and Pensions; Small Business and Entrepreneurship; Veterans' Affairs; elected to the U.S. House of Representatives in 1994; reelected in 1996; elected to the U.S. Senate on November 7, 2000.

Office Listings

http://ensign.senate.gov

364 Russell Senate Office Building, Washington, DC 20510 .... (202) 224–6244
Chief of Staff.—Scott Bensing. FAX: 228–2193
Scheduler.—Valerie Largent.
Legislative Director.—Pam Thiessen.
Communications Director.—Jack Finn.
333 Las Vegas Boulevard South, Suite 8203, Las Vegas, NV 89101 .... (702) 388–6605
State Director.—Sonja Joya.
600 East William Street, Suite 304, Carson City, NV 89701 .... (775) 885–9111
Rural Coordinator.—Kevin Kirkeby.
400 S. Virginia Street, Suite 738, Reno, NV 89501 .... (775) 686–5770
Northern Nevada Director.—Verita Black Prothro.

REPRESENTATIVES

FIRST DISTRICT

SHELLEY BERKLEY, Democrat, of Las Vegas, NV; born in New York, NY, January 20, 1951; education: graduate of Clark County, NV, public school system; B.A., University of Nevada at Las Vegas, 1972; J.D., University of San Diego School of Law, 1976; employment:

attorney; Nevada State Assembly, 1982–84; former deputy director of the Nevada State Commerce Department; hotel executive; vice-chair, Nevada University and Community College System Board of Regents, 1990–98; has served on numerous civic, business, and professional organizations; married: Larry Lehrner; children: Max and Sam; committees: International Relations; Veterans Affairs; Transportation and Infrastructure; elected to the 106h Congress; reelected to each succeeding Congress.

Office Listings

http://www.house.gov/berkley

439 Cannon House Office Building, Washington, DC 20515 .... (202) 225–5965
Chief of Staff.—Richard Urey. FAX: 225–3119
Legislative Director.—Mark Guiton.
Communications Director.—Michael O'Donovan.
Scheduler.—Joanne Jensen.
2340 Paseo Del Prado, Suite D–106, Las Vegas, NV 89102 .... (702) 220–9823
District Director.—Tod Story.

Counties: CLARK COUNTY (part). CITIES: Las Vegas (part), and North Las Vegas (part). Population (2000), 666,088.

ZIP Codes: 89030–33, 89036, 89084, 89086, 89101–04, 89106–10, 89114–17, 89119, 89121–22, 89125–35, 89137, 89142–46, 89149–56, 89160, 89170, 89177, 89185, 89193

* * *

SECOND DISTRICT

JIM GIBBONS, Republican, of Reno, NV; born in Sparks, NV, December 16, 1944; education: B.S., geology, and M.S., mining geology, University of Nevada at Reno; J.D., Southwestern University; admitted to the Nevada bar in 1982 and began practice in Reno; military service: colonel, U.S. Air Force, 1967–71; vice commander of the Nevada Air Guard since 1975; employment: pilot, Delta Airlines; mining geologist; mining and water rights attorney; Nevada State Assemblyman, 1989–93; member: advisory board, Committee to Aid Abused Women; Nevada Landman's Association; American Association of Petroleum Landsmen; Nevada Bar Association; National Conference Board; University of Nevada Alumni Association; Reno Board of Realtors; board of directors, Nevada Council on Economic Education; Nevada Development Authority; married: Theresa D. Snelling in 1986; children: Christopher, Jennifer, and Jimmy; committees: Armed Services; Intelligence; vice chairman, Resources; Select Committee on Homeland Security; elected to the 105th Congress; reelected to each succeeding Congress.

Office Listings

100 Cannon House Office Building, Washington, DC 20515 .... (202) 225–6155
Chief of Staff.—Robert Uithoven. FAX: 225–5679
Press Secretary.—Amy Spanbauer.
Legislative Director.—Margaret McElroy.
Legislative Assistants: Sandra Keil, Cory Kennedy, Ken Madura, Dan Waters.
400 South Virginia Street, Suite 502, Reno, NV 89501 .... (775) 686–5760
District Director.—Betty Jo Gerber.
600 Las Vegas Blvd., Suite 680, Las Vegas, NV 89101 .... (702) 255–1651
Constituent Representative.—Judy Rice.
491 Fourth Street, Elko, NV 89801 .... (775) 777–7920
Constituent Representative.—Betty Jo Gerber.

Counties: CARSON CITY, CHURCHILL, CLARK (part), DOUGLAS, ELKO, ESMERALDA, EUREKA, HUMBOLDT, LANDER, LINCOLN, LYON, MINERAL, NYE, PERSHING, STOREY, WASHOE, WHITE PINE. Population (2000), 666,087.

ZIP Codes: 89001, 89003, 89008, 89010, 89013, 89017, 89019–24, 89026–27, 89030–31, 89041–43, 89045, 89047–49, 89052, 89060–61, 89115, 89124, 89137, 89139, 89141, 89156, 89191, 89301, 89310–11, 89314–19, 89402–15, 89418–36, 89438–40, 89442, 89444–52, 89460, 89496, 89501–07, 89509–13, 89515, 89520–21, 89523, 89533, 89557, 89570, 89701–06, 89711–14, 89721, 89801–03, 89815, 89820–26, 89828, 89830–32, 89834–35, 89883

* * *

THIRD DISTRICT

JON C. PORTER, Republican, of Boulder City, NV; born on May 16, 1955, in Fort Dodge, IA; education: attended Briar Cliff College in Sioux City, IA; profession: insurance business; worked with the Farmers Insurance Group; public service: former Mayor (1987–1991), and City Councilman (1983–1993), in Boulder City; elected to the Nevada State Senate, 1994; awards:

Nevada League of Cities' Elected Official of the Year; Clark County School District's Crystal Apple Award; religion: Catholic; family: married to Laurie; children: J. Chris and Nicole; elected to the 108th Congress on November 5, 2002.

Office Listings

http://www.house.gov/porter

218 Cannon House Office Building, Washington, DC 20515 .... (202) 225–3252
Chief of Staff.—Windsor Freemyer. FAX: 225–2185
Legislative Director.—Mike McEleney.
Office Manager.—Polly Walker.
Press Secretary.—Traci Scott.
2501 North Green Valley Parkway, Suite 112D, Henderson, NV 89014 .... (702) 387–4941
District Director.—Kay Finfrock.

Counties: CLARK COUNTY (part). Population (2000), 666,082.

ZIP Codes: 89004–05, 89007, 89009, 89011–12, 89014–16, 89018, 89025, 89028–30, 89039–40, 89046, 89052–53, 89070, 89074, 89077, 89101–4, 89108–11, 89113, 89117–24, 89128–29, 89134–36, 89138–39, 89141–42, 89146–49, 89156, 89159, 89162–63, 89170, 89173, 89177, 89180, 89185, 89191, 89193, 89195, 89199

NEW HAMPSHIRE

(Population 2000, 1,235,786)

SENATORS

JUDD GREGG, Republican, of Rye, NH; born in Nashua, NH, on February 14, 1947; graduated Phillips Exeter Academy, 1965; A.B., Columbia University, New York City, 1969; J.D., 1972, and LL.M., 1975, Boston University; attorney, admitted to the New Hampshire bar, 1972; commenced practice in Nashua, NH; practiced law, 1975–80; member, Governor's Executive Council, 1978–80; married to the former Kathleen MacLellan, 1973; three children: Molly, Sarah, and Joshua; committees: Appropriations; Budget; chairman, Health, Education, Labor, and Pensions; elected to the 97th Congress, November 4, 1980, and reelected to the 98th–100th Congresses; elected Governor of New Hampshire, 1988–92; elected to the U.S. Senate on November 3, 1992; reelected to each succeeding Senate term.

Office Listings

http://gregg.senate.gov

393 Russell Senate Office Building, Washington, DC 20510 .... (202) 224–3324
Chief of Staff.—Joel Maiola.
Administrative Assistant.—Vasiliki Christopoulos.
Legislative Director.—Kevin Koonce.
Communications Director.—Erin Rath.
125 North Main Street, Concord, NH 03301 .... (603) 225–7115
41 Hooksett Road, Unit #2, Manchester, NH 03104 .... (603) 622–7979
16 Pease Boulevard, Portsmouth, NH 03801 .... (603) 431–2171
60 Pleasant Street, Berlin, NH 03570 .... (603) 752–2604

* * *

JOHN E. SUNUNU, Republican, of Bedford, NH; born on September 10, 1964, in Boston, MA; graduated, Salem High School, Salem, NH, 1982; B.S., mechanical engineering, Massachusetts Institute of Technology, 1986; M.S., mechanical engineering, Massachusetts Institute of Technology, 1987; M.B.A., Harvard University Business School, Boston, MA, 1991; Chief Financial Officer and Director of Operations, Teletrol Systems, Inc.; married to Catherine Halloran Sununu, 1988; three children: John Hayes, Grace, and Charlotte; elected to the 105th Congress; reelected to each succeeding Congress; elected to the U.S. Senate on November 5, 2002.

Office Listings

http://sununu.senate.gov

111 Russell Senate Office Building, Washington, DC 20510 .... (202) 224–2841
Chief of Staff.—Paul Collins. FAX: 228–4131
Legislative Director.—Gregg Willhauck.
Communications Director.—Barbara Riley.
One New Hampshire Avenue, Suite 120, Portsmouth, NH 03801 .... (603) 430–9560
1589 Elm Street, Suite 3, Manchester, NH 03101 .... (603) 647–7500

REPRESENTATIVES

FIRST DISTRICT

JEB BRADLEY, Republican, of Wolfeboro, NH; born on October 20, 1952; education: Governor Dummer Academy (prep school), Byfield, MA; Tufts University, Medford, MA; profession: businessman; owner of a health food store and a paint contracting business; also developed commercial and residential real estate; public service: served on the local planning board and budget committee; New Hampshire State Representative, 1990–2002; family: married to Barbara; children: Jan, Ramona, Urs, and Sebastian; elected to the 108th Congress on November 5, 2002.

Office Listings

http://www.house.gov/bradley

1218 Longworth House Office Building, Washington, DC 20515 .... (202) 225–5456
Chief of Staff.—Debra Vanderbeek. FAX: 225–5822
Legislative Director.—Michael Liles.
Press Secretary.—T.J. Crawford.

1095 Elm Street, Manchester, NH 03101 .... (603) 641–9536
104 Washington Street, Dover, NH 03820 .... (603) 743–4813

Counties: BELKNAP (part), CARROLL, HILLSBOROUGH (part), ROCKINGHAM, STAFFORD. CITIES: Bedford, Conway, Derry, Dover, Exeter, Goffstown, Laconia, Londonderry, Manchester, Merrimack, Portsmouth, and Rochester. Population (2000), 617,575.

ZIP Codes: 03032, 03034, 03036–38, 03040–42, 03044–45, 03053–54, 03077, 03101–06, 03108–11, 03218, 03220, 03225–27, 03237, 03246–47, 03249, 03253–54, 03256, 03259, 03261, 03263, 03269, 03290–91, 03298–99, 03307, 03801–05, 03809–10, 03812–22, 03824–27, 03830, 03832–33, 03835–60, 03862, 03864–75, 03878, 03882–87, 03890, 03894, 03896–97

* * *

SECOND DISTRICT

CHARLES F. BASS, Republican, of Peterborough, NH; born on January 8, 1952, in Boston, MA; graduated, Holderness School, Plymouth, NH, 1970; B.A., Dartmouth College, NH, 1974; vice president, High Standard Inc., Dublin, NH; chairman, Columbia Architectural Products, Beltsville, MD; New Hampshire State Representative, 1982–88; vice chairman, Judiciary Committee; New Hampshire State Senate 1988–92; chairman, Public Affairs and Ethics committees; co-chairman, Economic Development Committee; member: Monadnock Rotary Club (president, 1992–93); Amoskeag Veterans; Altermont Lodge, FA&M; trusteeships: New Hampshire Higher Education Assistance Foundation, Monadnock Conservancy, New Hampshire Humanities Council; committees: Energy and Commerce; married Lisa Levesque Bass, 1989; two children: Lucy and Jonathan; elected to the 104th Congress; reelected to each succeeding Congress.

Office Listings

http://www.house.gov/bass cbass@mail.house.gov

2421 Rayburn House Office Building, Washington, DC 20515 .... (202) 225–5206
Chief of Staff.—Darwin Cusack.
Legislative Director.—Tad Furtado.
Press Secretary.—Sally Tibbetts.
142 North Main Street, Concord, NH 03301 .... (603) 226–0249
170 Main Street, Nashua, NH 03062 .... (603) 889–8772
76 Main Street, Suite 2C, Littleton, NH 03561 .... (603) 444–1271
1 West Street, Suite 208, Keene, NH 03431 .... (603) 358–4094

Counties: BELKNAP (part), CHESHIRE, COOS, GRAFTON, HILLSBOROUGH (part), MERRIMACK (part), ROCKINGHAM (part), SULLIVAN. Population (2000), 618,211.

ZIP Codes: 03031, 03033, 03037, 03043, 03045–49, 03051–52, 03055, 03057, 03060–64, 03070–71, 03073, 03076, 03079, 03082, 03084, 03086–87, 03215–17, 03220–24, 03226, 03229–31, 03233–35, 03238, 03240–45, 03251–52, 03255, 03257–58, 03260–64, 03266, 03268–69, 03272–76, 03278–82, 03284, 03287, 03289, 03293, 03301–05, 03307, 03431, 03435, 03440–52, 03455–58, 03461–62, 03464–70, 03561, 03570, 03574–76, 03579–85, 03587–90, 03592–93, 03595, 03597–98, 03601–05, 03607–09, 03740–41, 03743, 03745–46, 03748–56, 03765–66, 03768–71, 03773–74, 03777, 03779–82, 03784–85, 03811

NEW JERSEY

(Population 2000 8,414,350)

SENATORS

JON S. CORZINE, Democrat, of Hoboken, NJ; born on January 1, 1947, in Willey's Station, IL; education: B.A., University of Illinois, 1969 (Phi Beta Kappa); M.B.A., University of Chicago, 1973; military service: U.S. Marine Corps Reserve, 1969–1975; family: three children; occupation: businessman; Chairman and CEO of Goldman Sachs (investment bank); organizations: co-chairman, YMCA Second Century Campaign; director, Family Services of Summit; chairman, New Jersey Performing Arts Center Council of Trustees; Progressive Policy Institute; awards: Time Magazine's Top 50 Technology Executives, 1997; chair, President's Commission to Study Capital Budgeting, 1997–1999; elected to the U.S. Senate on November 7, 2000.

Office Listings

http://corzine.senate.gov

502 Hart Senate Office Building, Washington, DC 20510 .... (202) 224–4744
Chief of Staff.—Tom Shea. FAX: 228–2197
Press Secretary.—David Wald.
Office Manager.—Margaret Van Tassell.
1 Gateway Center, 11th Floor, Newark, NJ 07102 .... (973) 645–3030
208 Whitehorse Pike, Suite 18, Barrington, NJ 08007–1322 .... (856) 757–5353

* * *

FRANK LAUTENBERG, Democrat, of Cliffside Park, NJ; born in Paterson, NJ, on January 23, 1924; education: Nutley High School, Nutley, NJ, 1941; B.S., Economics, Columbia University School of Business, New York, NY, 1949; U.S. Army Signal Corps, 1942–46; data processing firm founder, and CEO, 1952–82; commissioner, Port Authority of New York and New Jersey, 1978–82; commissioner, New Jersey Economic Development Authority; member: U.S. Holocaust Memorial Council; Advisory Council of the Graduate School of Business, Columbia University; four children: Ellen, Nan, Lisa and Joshua; elected to the U.S. Senate on November 2, 1982; appointed by the Governor on December 27, 1982, to complete the unexpired term of Senator Nicholas F. Brady; reelected in 1988 and 1994; not a candidate for reelection in 2000; replaced Senator Robert Torricelli as the Democratic candidate for the U.S. Senate in October 2002; elected to the U.S. Senate on November 5, 2002.

Office Listings

http://lautenberg.senate.gov

324 Hart Senate Office Building, Washington, DC 20510 .... (202) 224–3224
Chief of Staff.—Tim Yehl. FAX: 228–4054
Chief Counsel.—Dan Katz.
Legislative Director.—Gray Maxwell.
Communications Director.—Alex Formuzis.
1 Gateway Center, Suite 102, Newark, NJ 07102 .... (973) 639–8700

REPRESENTATIVES

FIRST DISTRICT

ROBERT E. ANDREWS, Democrat, of Haddon Heights, NJ; born in Camden, NJ, on August 4, 1957; education: graduated, Triton High School, Runnemede, NJ, 1975; B.S., political science, Bucknell University, *summa cum laude*, Phi Beta Kappa, Lewisburg, PA, 1979; J.D., *magna cum laude*, Cornell Law School, Cornell Law Review, Ithaca, NY, 1982; Camden County Freeholder, 1986–90; Camden County Freeholder Director, 1988–90; married: Camille Spinello; children: Jacquelyn and Josi; committees: Education and the Workforce; Select Committee on Homeland Security; elected by special election on November 6, 1990, to the 101st Congress, to fill the vacancy caused by the resignation of James Florio; elected at the same time to the 102nd Congress; reelected to each succeeding Congress.

Office Listings

http://www.house.gov/andrews

2439 Rayburn House Office Building, Washington, DC 20515 .... (202) 225–6501
Chief of Staff.—Matt Walker. FAX: 225–6583
506A White Horse Pike, Haddon Heights, NJ 08035 .... (856) 546–5100
District Director.—Amanda Caruso.

Counties: BURLINGTON COUNTY. CITIES AND TOWNSHIPS: Maple Shade, Palmyra, Riverton. CAMDEN COUNTY. CITIES AND TOWNSHIPS: Audubon, Audubon Park, Barrington, Bellmawr, Berlin, Berlin Township, Brooklawn, Camden, Chesilhurst, Clementon, Collingswood, Gibbsboro, Gloucester City, Gloucester Township, Haddon Heights, Haddon Township (part), Hi-Nella, Laurel Springs, Lawnside, Lindenwold, Magnolia, Mt. Ephraim, Oaklyn, Pennsauken, Pine Hill, Pine Valley, Runnemede, Somerdale, Stratford, Tavistock, Voorhees, Winslow, Woodlynne. GLOUCESTER COUNTY. CITIES AND TOWNSHIPS: Deptford, E. Greenwich, Greenwich, Logan Township, Mantua (part), Monroe, National Park, Paulsboro, Washington Township, and Wenonah. Population (2000), 647,258.

ZIP Codes: 08002–04, 08007, 08009, 08012, 08014, 08018, 08020–21, 08026–33, 08035, 08037, 08043, 08045, 08049, 08051–52, 08056, 08059, 08061–63, 08065–66, 08071, 08076–80, 08081, 08083–86, 08089–91, 08093–97, 08099, 08101–10

* * *

SECOND DISTRICT

FRANK A. LOBIONDO, Republican; born in Bridgeton, NJ, on May 12, 1946; education: graduated, St. Joseph's University, Philadelphia, PA, 1968; employment: operations manager, LoBiondo Brothers Motor Express, 1968–94; Cumberland County Freeholder, 1985–87; New Jersey General Assembly, 1988–94; currently serves as Member of Congress (1995–present); committees: Transportation and Infrastructure; subcommittees: Aviation; chairman, Coast Guard and Maritime Transportation; awards and honors: honorary Coast Guard Chief Petty Officer; Board of Directors, Young Mens Christian Association; Honorary Rotarian; Taxpayer Hero award; Watchdog of the Treasury award; ''Super Friend of Seniors'' award; two-time winner of the ''Friend of the National Parks'' award; March of Dimes FDR award for community service; 2001 President's award, Literacy Volunteers of America, NJ, Inc.; elected to the 104th Congress; reelected to each succeeding Congress.

Office Listings

http://www.house.gov/lobiondo

225 Cannon House Office Building, Washington, DC 20515 .... (202) 225–6572
Chief of Staff.—Mary Annie Harper. FAX: 225–3318
Executive Assistant.—Theresa Spinola.
5914 Main Street, Mays Landing, NJ 08330 .... (609) 625–5008
District Director.—Joan Dermanoski.

Counties: BURLINGTON (part). CITIES AND TOWNSHIPS: Shamong, Washington, Waterford. CAMDEN COUNTY (part). ATLANTIC COUNTY. CITIES AND TOWNSHIPS: Absecon, Atlantic City, Brigantine, Buena, Cardiff, Collings Lake, Cologne, Corbin City, Dorothy, Egg Harbor, Estell Manor, Galloway, Hammonton, Landisville, Leeds Point, Linwood, Longport, Margate, Mays Landing, Milmay, Minotola, Mizpah, Newtonville, Northfield, Oceanville, Pleasantville, Pomona, Port Republic, Richland, Somers Point, Ventnor. CAPE MAY COUNTY. CITIES AND TOWNSHIPS: Avalon, Bargaintown, Beesley's, Belleplain, Burleigh, Cape May, Cape May C.H., Cape May Point, Cold Springs, Del Haven, Dennisville, Dias Creek, Eldora, Erma, Fishing Creek, Goshen, Green Creek, Greenfield, Marmora, Ocean City, Ocean View, Rio Grande, Sea Isle, South Dennis, South Seaville, Stone Harbor, Strathmere, Tuckahoe, Villas, Whitesboro, Wildwood, Woodbine. CUMBERLAND COUNTY. CITIES AND TOWNSHIPS: Bridgeton, Cedarville, Centerton, Deerfield, Delmont, Dividing Creek, Dorchester, Elwood, Fairton, Fortescue, Greenwich, Heislerville, Hopewell, Leesburg, Mauricetown, Millville, Newport, Port Elizabeth, Port Norris, Rosenhayn, Shiloh, Vineland. GLOUCESTER COUNTY (part). CITIES AND TOWNSHIPS: Clayton, Ewan, Franklinville, Glassboro, Harrisonville, Malaga, Mantua, Mickleton, Mullica Hill, Newfield, Pitman, Richwood, Sewell, Swedesboro, Williamstown, Woodbury. SALEM COUNTY. CITIES AND TOWNSHIPS: Alloway, Carney's Point, Daretown, Deepwater, Elmer, Elsinboro, Hancocks Bridge, Monroeville, Norma, Pedricktown, Penns Grove, Pennsville, Quinton, Salem, and Woodstown. Population (2000), 647,258.

ZIP Codes: 08001, 08004, 08009, 08019–20, 08023, 08025, 08028, 08037–39, 08051, 08056, 08061–62, 08067, 08069–72, 08074, 08079–80, 08085, 08088–89, 08094, 08098, 08201–05, 08210, 08212–15, 08217–21, 08223, 08225–26, 08230–32, 08234, 08240–48, 08250–52, 08260, 08270, 08302, 08310–24, 08326–30, 08332, 08340–50, 08352–53, 08360–62, 08401–04, 08406

* * *

THIRD DISTRICT

JIM SAXTON, Republican, of Mt. Holly, NJ; born in Nicholson, PA, January 22, 1943; education: graduated, Lackawanna Trail High School, Factoryville, PA, 1961; B.A., Education, East Stroudsburg State College, PA, 1965; graduate courses in elementary education, Temple University, Philadelphia, PA, 1968; profession: public school teacher, 1965–68; realtor, owner of Jim Saxton Realty Company, 1968–85; New Jersey General Assembly, 1976–82; State Senate, 1982–84; chairman, State Republican Platform Committee, 1983; former member: Chamber of Commerce, Association of the U.S. Air Force, Leadership Foundation of New Jersey, Boy Scouts of America, Rotary International; former chairman: American Cancer Committee; children: Jennifer and Martin; elected to the 98th Congress, by special election, on November 6, 1984; reelected to each succeeding Congress.

Office Listings

339 Cannon House Office Building, Washington, DC 20515 .... (202) 225–4765
Chief of Staff.—Mark A. O'Connell. FAX: 225–0778
Executive Assistant.—Sarah White.
100 High Street, Mount Holly, NJ 08060 .... (609) 261–5800
District Representative / Business Manager.—Sandra Condit.
1 Maine Avenue, Cherry Hill, NJ 08002 .... (856) 428–0520
247 Main Street, Toms River, NJ 08753 .... (732) 914–2020

Counties: BURLINGTON (part), CAMDEN (part), OCEAN (part). Population (2000), 647,257.

ZIP Codes: 08002–06, 08008–11, 08015–16, 08019, 08034, 08036, 08043, 08046, 08048, 08050, 08053–55, 08057, 08060, 08064–65, 08068, 08073, 08075, 08077, 08087–88, 08092, 08109, 08215, 08224, 08352, 08501, 08511, 08562, 08618, 08640–41, 08690, 08721–23, 08731–32, 08734–35, 08739–41, 08751–59

* * *

FOURTH DISTRICT

CHRISTOPHER H. SMITH, Republican, of Robbinsville, NJ; born in Rahway, NJ, on March 4, 1953; B.A., Trenton State College, 1975; attended Worcester College, England, 1974; businessman; executive director, New Jersey Right to Life Committee, Inc., 1976–78; married to the former Marie Hahn, 1976; children: Melissa Elyse, Christopher, and Michael; religion: Catholic; committees: chairman, Veterans' Affairs; vice-chairman, International Relations; co-chairman, Commission on Security and Cooperation in Europe; co-chairman, Congressional Pro-Life Caucus; elected to the 97th Congress, November 4, 1980; reelected to each succeeding Congress.

Office Listings

http://www.house.gov/chrissmith

2373 Rayburn House Office Building, Washington, DC 20515 .... (202) 225–3765
Chief of Staff.—Mary Noonan. FAX: 225–7768
Press Secretary.—Nick Manetto.
Office Manager.—Kristie Rodgers.
1540 Kuser Road, Suite A9, Hamilton, NJ 08619 .... (609) 585–7878
Regional Director.—Joyce Golden.
108 Lacey Road, Whiting, NJ 08759 .... (732) 350–2300
Regional Director.—Loretta Charbonneau.

Counties: BURLINGTON COUNTY. MUNICIPALITIES: Bordentown City, Bordentown Township, Burlington City, Burlington Township, Chesterfield, Fieldsboro, Florence, Mansfield, Springfield. MERCER COUNTY. MUNICIPALITIES: East Windsor, Hamilton, Highstown, Trenton (part), Washington Township. MONMOUTH COUNTY. MUNICIPALITIES: Allentown, Brielle, Colts Neck, Farmingdale, Freehold (part), Freehold Borough, Howell, Manasquan, Millstone Township, Roosevelt, Sea Girt, Spring Lake Heights, Upper Freehold, Wall. OCEAN COUNTY. MUNICIPALITIES: Bay Head, Brick, Jackson, Lakehurst, Lakewood, Manchester, Mantoloking, Plumstead, Pt. Pleasant, and Pt. Pleasant Beach. Population (2000), 647,258.

ZIP Codes: 07710, 07715, 07719, 07722, 07726–28, 07731, 07753, 07762, 08010, 08016, 08022, 08041–42, 08060, 08068, 08075, 08501, 08505, 08510, 08512, 08514–15, 08518, 08520, 08526–27, 08533, 08535, 08554–55, 08561, 08601–07, 08609–11, 08619–20, 08625, 08629, 08638, 08645–48, 08650, 08666, 08690–91, 08695, 08701, 08720, 08723–24, 08730, 08733, 08736, 08738, 08742, 08750, 08753, 08757, 08759

* * *

FIFTH DISTRICT

SCOTT GARRETT, Republican, of Wantage Township, NJ; born on July 7, 1959, in Englewood, NJ; education: High Point Regional High School, 1977; B.A., Montclair State University, 1981; J.D., Rutgers University Law School, 1984; profession: Attorney; counsel attorney with law firm of Sellar Richardson; organizations: Big Brothers, Big Sisters; Sussex County Chamber of Commerce; Sussex County Board of Agriculture; public service: New Jersey State Assemblyman, 1990–2002; family: married to Mary Ellen; children: Jennifer and Brittany; elected to the 108th Congress on November 5, 2002.

Office Listings

http://www.house.gov/garrett

1641 Longworth House Office Building, Washington, DC 20515 .... (202) 225–4465
Chief of Staff.—Evan Kozlow. FAX: 225–9048
Legislative Director.—Jackie Moran.
Press Secretary.—Steve O'Halloran.
210 Route 4 East, Suite 206, Paramus, NJ 07652 .... (201) 712–0330
93 Main Street, Newton, NJ 07860 .... (973) 300–2000

Counties: BERGEN (part), PASSAIC (part), SUSSEX, WARREN. Population (2000), 647,257.

ZIP Codes: 07401, 07403, 07416–23, 07428, 07430, 07432, 07435–36, 07438–39, 07446, 07450–52, 07456, 07458, 07460–63, 07465, 07480–81, 07495, 07498, 07620–21, 07624, 07626–28, 07630, 07640–42, 07645–49, 07652–53, 07656, 07661–62, 07670, 07675–77, 07820–23, 07825–27, 07829, 07831–33, 07838–40, 07844, 07846, 07848, 07851, 07855, 07860, 07863, 07865, 07871, 07875, 07877, 07879–82, 07890, 08802, 08804, 08808, 08865–86

* * *

SIXTH DISTRICT

FRANK PALLONE, JR., Democrat, of Long Branch, NJ; born in Long Branch, October 30, 1951; B.A., Middlebury College, Middlebury, VT, 1973; M.A., Fletcher School of Law and Diplomacy, 1974; J.D., Rutgers University School of Law, 1978; member of the bar: Florida, New York, Pennsylvania, and New Jersey; attorney, Marine Advisory Service; assistant professor, Cook College, Rutgers University Sea Grant Extension Program; counsel, Monmouth County, NJ, Protective Services for the Elderly; instructor, Monmouth College; Long Branch City Council, 1982–88; New Jersey State Senate, 1983–88; married the former Sarah Hospodor, 1992; elected to the 100th Congress, by special election, on November 8, 1988, to fill the vacancy caused by the death of James J. Howard; reelected to each succeeding Congress.

Office Listings

420 Cannon House Office Building, Washington, DC 20515 .... (202) 225–4671
Chief of Staff.—Jeff Carroll. FAX: 225–9665
Legislative Director.—Kathy Kulkarni.
Press Secretary.—Andrew Souvall.
District Director.—Paul Dement.
504 Broadway, Long Branch, NJ 07740 .... (732) 571–1140
67/69 Church Street, Kilmer Square, New Brunswick, NJ .... (732) 249–8892
Suite 104, I.E.I. Airport Plaza, Highway 36, Hazlet, NJ .... (732) 264–9104

Counties: MONMOUTH COUNTY. CITIES AND TOWNSHIPS: Aberdeen, Allenhurst, Asbury Park, Atlantic Highlands, Avon-by-the-Sea, Belmar, Bradley Beach, Deal, Hazlet, Highlands, Interlaken, Keansburg, Keyport, Loch Arbour, Long Branch, Manalapan (part), Marlboro (part), Matawan, Middletown (part), Monmouth Beach, Neptune City, Neptune Twp., Ocean, Red Bank, Sea Birght, South Belmar, Union Beach, West Long Branch. MIDDLESEX COUNTY. CITIES AND TOWNSHIPS: Dunellen, Edison (part), Highland Park, Metuchen, Middlesex, New Brunswick, Old Bridge (part), Piscataway, Sayerville, South Amboy. SOMERSET COUNTY. CITIES: Franklin. UNION COUNTY. CITIES: Plainfield. Population (2000), 647,257.

ZIP Codes: 07060–63, 07080, 07701–02, 07704, 07709–12, 07715–21, 07723–24, 07726, 07730, 07732, 07734–35, 07737, 07740, 07746–48, 07750–56, 07758, 07760, 07764, 08812, 08816–18, 08820, 08830–31, 08837, 08840, 08846, 08854–55, 08857, 08859, 08871–73, 08877–79, 08899, 08901, 08903–04, 08906, 08922, 08933, 08988–89

* * *

SEVENTH DISTRICT

MIKE FERGUSON, Republican, of Warren, NJ; born on July 2, 1970, in Ridgewood, NJ; education: Delbarton School, Morristown, NJ; B.A., University of Notre Dame; M.P.P., Georgetown University; profession: educator and small businessman; Executive Director, Better Schools Foundation; Executive Director, Catholic Campaign of America; Director, Save Our Schoolchildren; President, Strategic Education Initiatives, Inc.; organizations: National Federation of Independent Business; Knights of Columbus; Epilepsy Foundation of New Jersey; Sierra Club; Friendly Sons of St. Patrick; National Italian American Association; religion: Roman Catholic; family: married to Maureen; three children; elected to the 107th Congress on November 7, 2000; reelected to each succeeding Congress.

Office Listings

http://www.house.gov/ferguson

214 Cannon House Office Building, Washington, DC 20515 .... (202) 225–5361
Chief of Staff.—Chris Jones. FAX: 225–9460
Legislative Director.—Alex DelPizzo.
Scheduler.—Meredith Atkinson.
Press Secretary.—Bailey Wood.
792 Chimney Rock Road, Suite E, Martinsville, NJ 08836 .... (908) 757–7835
District Director.—Marcus Rayner.

Counties: MIDDLESEX COUNTY. MUNICIPALITIES: Edison (part), South Plainfield, Woodbridge (part). UNION COUNTY. MUNICIPALITIES: Berkeley Heights, Clark, Cranford, Fanwood, Garwood, Kenilworth, Linden, Mountainside, New Providence, Roselle Park, Scotch Plains, Springfield, Summit, Union, Westfield, Winfield. HUNTERDON COUNTY. MUNICIPALITIES: Alexandria, Bethlehem, Bloomsbury, Califon, Clinton Township, Clinton, Flemington, Glen Gardner, Hampton, High Bridge, Holland, Lebanon, Lebanon Township, Milford, Oldwick, Raritan, Readington, Tewksbury, Union. SOMERSET COUNTY. MUNICIPALITIES: Bedminster, Bernardsville, Bound Brook, Branchburg, Bridgewater, Far Hills, Green Brook, Hillsborough, Manville, Montgomery Township, Millstone, North Plainfield, Peapack-Gladstone, Rocky Hill, South Bound Brook, Warren, and Watchung. Population (2000), 647,257.

ZIP Codes: 07001, 07008, 07016, 07023, 07027, 07033, 07036, 07040, 07059–60, 07062–64, 07066–67, 07069, 07076, 07080–81, 07083, 07090–92, 07095, 07204, 07830, 07901–02, 07921–22, 07924, 07931, 07934, 07974, 07977–79, 08502, 08504, 08540, 08551, 08553, 08558, 08801–02, 08804–05, 08807, 08809, 08812, 08820–22, 08825–27, 08829–30, 08832–37, 08840, 08844, 08848, 08853, 08858, 08863, 08867, 08870, 08876, 08880, 08885, 08887–89

* * *

EIGHTH DISTRICT

BILL PASCRELL, JR., Democrat, of Paterson, NJ; born in Paterson, January 27, 1937; B.A., journalism, and M.A., philosophy, Fordham University; veteran, U.S. Army and Army Reserves; educator; New Jersey General Assembly, 1988–96: elected Minority Leader Pro Tempore; mayor of Paterson, 1990–96; named Mayor of the Year by bipartisan NJ Conference of Mayors, 1996; started Paterson's first Economic Development Corporation; married to the former Elsie Marie Botto; three children: William III, Glenn, and David; committees: Transportation and Infrastructure; Select Committee on Homeland Security; subcommittees: Aviation; Emergency Preparedness and Response; Highways, Transit and Pipelines; Infrastructure and Border Security; Water Resources and the Environment; elected to the 105th Congress; reelected to each succeeding Congress.

Office Listings

http://www.house.gov/pascrell

1722 Longworth House Office Building, Washington, DC 20515 .... (202) 225–5751
Office Manager.—Selvin J. White, Jr. FAX: 225-5782
Legislative Director.—Ben Rich.
200 Federal Plaza, Suite 500, Paterson, NJ 07505 .... (201) 523–5152
Chief of Staff.—Ed Farmer.

Counties: ESSEX COUNTY. CITIES: Belleville, Bloomfield, Cedar Grove. Glen Ridge, Livingston, Maplewood, Montclair, Nutley, South Orange, Verona, West Orange. PASSAIC COUNTY. CITIES: Clifton, Haledon, Little Falls, North Haledon, Passaic, Paterson, Pompton Lakes, Prospect Park, Totowa, Wayne, and West Paterson. Population (2000), 647,258

ZIP Codes: 07003–04, 07009, 07011–15, 07028, 07039, 07042–44, 07052, 07055, 07079, 07107, 07109–10, 07424, 07442, 07470, 07474, 07477, 07501–14, 07522, 07524, 07533, 07538, 07543–44

* * *

NINTH DISTRICT

STEVEN R. ROTHMAN, Democrat, of Fair Lawn, NJ; born in Englewood, NJ, October 14, 1952; graduate, Tenafly High School, 1970; B.A., Syracuse University, Syracuse, NY, 1974; LL.B., Washington University School of Law, St. Louis, MO, 1977; attorney; as two-term mayor of Englewood, NJ, spearheaded business growth and installed a fiscally conservative management team, transforming Englewood's bond rating from one of the worst to the best in Bergen County; Judge, Bergen County Surrogate Court, 1993–96; founding member, New Democratic Coalition; authored the Secure Our Schools Act; two children; committees: Appropriations; subcommittees: Foreign Operations, Export Financing and Related Programs; Transportation, Treasury and Independent Agencies; elected to the 105th Congress; reelected to each succeeding Congress.

Office Listings

http://www.house.gov/rothman

1607 Longworth House Office Building, Washington, DC 20515 .... (202) 225–5061
Chief of Staff.—Chuck Young. FAX: 225–5851
Executive Assistant / Scheduler.—Mary Flanagan.
Communications Director.—Jeff Lieberson.
Legislative Director.—Rob Zucker.
25 Main Street, Court Plaza, Hackensack, NJ 07601–7089 .... (201) 646–0808
District Director.—Brendan Gill.
130 Central Avenue, Jersey City, NJ 07306–2118 .... (201) 798–1366
Office Director.—Al Zampella.

Counties: BERGEN COUNTY. CITIES AND TOWNS: Bogota, Carlstadt, Cliffside Park, East Rutherford, Edgewater, Elmwood Park, Englewood, Englewood Cliffs, Fair Lawn, Fairview, Fort Lee, Garfield, Hackensack, Hasbrouck Heights, Leonia, Little Ferry, Lodi, Lyndhurst, Maywood, Moonachie, New Milford (part), North Arlington, Palisades Park, Ridgefield, Ridgefield Park, Rutherford, Saddle Brook, South Hackensack, Teaneck, Teterboro, Wallington, Wood Ridge. HUDSON COUNTY. CITIES AND TOWNS: Kearny (ward 1: districts 1, 2, and 6; ward 3; and ward 4: districts 5–7), Secaucus, North Bergen, Jersey City. PASSAIC COUNTY (part). BOROUGH: Hawthorne. Population (2000), 647,258.

ZIP Codes: 07010, 07020, 07022, 07024, 07026, 07031–32, 07042, 07047, 07057, 07070–75, 07094, 07096–97, 07099, 07306–08, 07407, 07410, 07601–08, 07631–32, 07643–44, 07646, 07650, 07657, 07660, 07663, 07666, 07670

* * *

TENTH DISTRICT

DONALD M. PAYNE, Democrat, of Newark, NJ; born in Newark, July 16, 1934; graduated, Barringer High School, Newark, 1952; B.A., Seton Hall University, South Orange, NJ, 1957; businessman; elected to the Essex County Board of Chosen Freeholders, 1972–78; elected to the Newark Municipal Council, 1982–88; president, YMCA of the USA, 1970–73; member: NAACP, Council on Foreign Relations, Bethlehem Baptist Church; former chairman, Congressional Black Caucus; serves on the advisory council of the U.S. Committee for UNICEF; Advisory Commission on Intergovernmental Relations; board of directors: Congressional Black Caucus Foundation, National Endowment for Democracy; committees: Education and the Workforce; International Relations; Democratic Steering Committee; subcommittees: ranking member, Africa; Employer-Employee Relations; 21st Century Competitiveness; Western Hemisphere; Workforce Protections; widower; three children; elected on November 8, 1988, to the 101st Congress; reelected to each succeeding Congress.

Office Listings

2209 Rayburn House Office Building, Washington, DC 20515 .... (202) 225–3436
Chief of Staff.—Maxine James. FAX: 225–4160
Legislative Director / Press Secretary.—Kerry McKenney.
50 Walnut Street, Room 1016, Newark, NJ 07102 .... (973) 645–3213
District Representative.—Robert Cottingham, Jr.
333 North Broad Street, Elizabeth, NJ 07202 .... (908) 629–0222

Counties: ESSEX COUNTY. CITIES AND TOWNSHIPS: East Orange, Irvington, Maplewood Millburn, Montclair (part), Newark (part), Orange, South Orange, West Orange. HUDSON COUNTY. CITIES AND TOWNSHIPS: Bayonne (part), Jersey City (part). UNION COUNTY. CITIES AND TOWNSHIPS: Elizabeth (part), Hillside, Linden, Rahway, Roselle, and Union (part). Population (2000), 647,258.

ZIP Codes: 07002, 07017–19, 07028, 07036, 07040–42, 07044, 07050–52, 07065, 07078–79, 07083, 07088, 07101–03, 07105–08, 07111–12, 07114–75, 07184, 07188–89, 07191–95, 07197–99, 07201–03, 07205–08, 07304–05

* * *

ELEVENTH DISTRICT

RODNEY P. FRELINGHUYSEN, Republican, of Morristown, NJ; born in New York, NY, April 29, 1946; graduated Hobart College, NY, 1969; attended graduate school in Connecticut; named Legislator of the Year by the Veterans of Foreign Wars, the New Jersey Association of Mental Health Agencies, and the New Jersey Association of Retarded Citizens; honored by numerous organizations; served in the New Jersey General Assembly, 1983–94; chairman, Assembly Appropriations Committee, 1988–89 and 1992–94; member: Morris County Board of Chosen Freeholders, 1974–83 (director, 1980); served on: Welfare and Mental Health boards; Human Services and Private Industry councils; served, U.S. Army, 93rd Engineer Battalion; honorably discharged, 1971; member: American Legion, and Veterans of Foreign Wars; Morris

County state and federal aid coordinator and administrative assistant, 1972; married: Virginia Frelinghuysen; children: Louisine and Sarah; committees: Appropriations; subcommittees: District of Columbia; Energy and Water Development; Defense; elected to the 104th Congress in November, 1994; reelected to each succeeding Congress.

Office Listings

http://www.house.gov/frelinghuysen

2442 Rayburn House Office Building, Washington, DC 20515 .... (202) 225–5034
Chief of Staff.—Nancy Fox.
Press Secretary.—Mark Broadhurst.
Legislative Director.—Steve Wilson.
Scheduler.—Carolyn Kappen.
30 Schuyler Place, 2nd Floor, Morristown, NJ 07960 .... (973) 984–0711

Counties: ESSEX COUNTY. CITIES AND TOWNSHIPS: Caldwell, Essex Fells, Fairfield Township, Livingston, Millburn (part), North Caldwell, Roseland, West Caldwell. MORRIS COUNTY. CITIES AND TOWNSHIPS: Bernardsville, municipalities of Boonton Town, Boonton Township, Brookside, Budd Lake, Butler, Califon, Cedar Knolls, Chatham Borough, Chatham Township, Chester Borough, Chester Township, Convent Station, Denville, Dover Town, East Hanover, Flanders, Florham Park, Gillette, Green Pond, Green Village, Hanover, Harding, Hibernia, Ironia, Jefferson, Kenvill, Kinnelon, Lake Hiawatha, Lake Hopatcong, Landing, Ledgewood, Lincoln Park, Long Valley, Madison, Mendham Borough, Mendham Township, Millington, Mine Hill, Montville, Morris Plains, Morris Township, Morristown, Mount Arlington, Mountain Lakes, Mount Olive, Mount Tabor, Netcong, Newfoundland, New Vernon, Oak Ridge, Parsippany-Troy Hills, Passaic Township, Pequannock, Picatinny, Pine Brook, Randolph, Riverdale, Rockaway Borough, Rockaway Township, Roxbury, Schooley's Mountain, Stanhope, Stirling, Succasunna, Towaco, Victory Gardens, Washington Township, Wharton, and Whippany. PASSAIC COUNTY. CITIES: Bloomingdale. SOMERSET COUNTY. CITIES AND TOWNSHIPS: Bernards Township, Bridgewater (part), Raritan Borough, and Somerville. SUSSEX COUNTY. CITIES AND TOWNSHIPS: Byram, Hopatcong, Sparta, and Stanhope. Population (2000), 647,258.

ZIP Codes: 07004–07, 07021, 07034–35, 07039, 07041, 07045–46, 07054, 07058, 07068, 07078, 07082, 07405, 07438, 07440, 07444, 07457, 07801–03, 07806, 07821, 07828, 07830, 07834, 07836–37, 07840, 07842–43, 07845, 07847, 07849–50, 07852–53, 07856–57, 07866, 07869–71, 07874, 07876, 07878, 07885, 07920, 07926–28, 07930, 07932–36, 07938–40, 07945–46, 07950, 07960–63, 07970, 07976, 07980–81, 07983, 07999, 08807, 08869, 08876, 08896

* * *

TWELFTH DISTRICT

RUSH D. HOLT, Democrat, of Hopewell Township, NJ; born in Weston, WV, on October 15, 1948; son of the youngest person ever to be elected to the U.S. Senate; B.A., Carleton College, 1970; M.S. and Ph.D., physics, New York University, 1981; physicist; New York City Environmental Protection Administration, 1972–74; teaching fellow, New York University, 1974–80; Congressional Science Fellow, U.S. House of Representatives, Office of Representative Bob Edgar, 1982–83; professor, Swarthmore College, 1980–88; acting chief, Nuclear & Scientific Division, Office of Strategic Forces, U.S. Department of State, 1987–89; assistant director, Princeton Plasma Physics Laboratory, Princeton, NJ, 1989–97; Protestant; married to Margaret Lancefield; three children: Michael, Dejan, and Rachel; committees: Education and the Workforce; Intelligence; elected to the 106th Congress; reelected to each succeeding Congress.

Office Listings

http://holt.house.gov

1019 Longworth House Office Building, Washington, DC 20515 .... (202) 225–5801
Chief of Staff.—Jim Papa. FAX: 225–6025
Legislative Director.—Bill Goold.
Press Secretary.—Jim Kapsis.
Executive Assistant.—Margie Ellis.
50 Washington Road, West Windsor, NJ 08550 .... (609) 750–9365

Counties: HUNTERDON COUNTY. CITIES AND TOWNSHIPS: Delaware, East Amwell, Franklin, Frenchtown, Kingwood, Lambertville, Stockton, West Amwell. MERCER COUNTY. CITIES AND TOWNSHIPS: Ewing, Hopewell Borough, Hopewell Township, Lawrence, Pennington, Princeton Borough, Princeton Township, West Windsor. MIDDLESEX COUNTY. CITIES AND TOWNSHIPS: Cranbury, East Brunswick, Helmetta, Jamesburg, Monroe, North Brunswick, Old Bridge, Plainsboro Township, South River, Spotswood, South Brunswick. MONMOUTH COUNTY. CITIES AND TOWNSHIPS: Eatontown, Englishtown, Fair Haven, Freehold Township, Holmdel, Little Silver, Manalapan, Marlboro, Middletown, Oceanport, Rumson, Shrewsbury Borough, Shrewsbury Township, Tinton Falls. SOMERSET COUNTY. CITIES AND TOWNSHIPS: Franklin Township. Population (2000), 647,258.

ZIP Codes: 07701–04, 07712, 07724, 07726, 07728, 07733, 07738–39, 07746, 07748, 07751, 07753, 07757, 07760, 07763, 07765, 07777, 07799, 08512, 08525, 08528, 08530, 08534, 08536, 08540–44, 08550–51, 08556–57, 08559–60, 08570, 08608–09, 08611, 08618–19, 08628, 08638, 08648, 08690, 08801, 08803, 08809–10, 08816, 08822–25, 08828, 08831, 08844, 08850, 08852, 08857, 08859, 08867–68, 08873, 08875, 08882, 08884, 08890, 08901–02, 08905, 08922

THIRTEENTH DISTRICT

ROBERT MENENDEZ, Democrat, of Hoboken, NJ; born in New York City, NY, on January 1, 1954; education: graduated, Union Hill High School, 1972; B.A., St. Peter's College, Jersey City, NJ, 1976; J.D., Rutgers Law School, Newark, NJ, 1979; employment: attorney; admitted to the New Jersey bar, 1980; elected to the Union City Board of Education, 1974–78; mayor of Union City, 1986–92; New Jersey Assembly, 1987–91; New Jersey State Senate, 1991–92; chairman, New Jersey Hispanic Leadership Program; Vice Chair, Democratic Caucus, 1998–2002; member, New Jersey Hispanic Elected Officials Organization; New Jersey Mayors Coalition; president and co-founder, Alliance Civic Association; elected Chairman, Democratic Caucus, 2002; children: Alicia and Robert; elected on November 3, 1992, to the 103rd Congress; reelected to each succeeding Congress.

Office Listings

http://www.house.gov/menendez

2238 Rayburn House Office Building, Washington, DC 20515 .... (202) 225–7919
Office Manager / Scheduler.—Judi Wolford. FAX: 226–0792
Legislative Director.—Chris Schloesser.
911 Bergen Avenue, Jersey City, NJ 07306 .... (201) 222–2828
654 Avenue C, Bayonne, NJ 07002 .... (201) 823–2900
263 Hobart Street, Perth Amboy, NJ 08861 .... (732) 324–6212
3109 Bergenline Avenue, Union City, NJ 07087 .... (201) 558–0800

Counties: ESSEX (part), HUDSON (part), MIDDLESEX (part), UNION (part). CITIES AND TOWNSHIPS: Bayonne (part), Carteret, East Newark, Elizabeth (part), Guttenberg, Harrison Township, Hoboken, Jersey City (part), Kearny (part), Linden (part), Newark, North Bergen (part), Port Reading, Perth Amboy, Sewaren, Union City, Weehawken, West New York, and Woodbridge (part). Population (2000), 647,258.

ZIP Codes: 07002–03, 07008, 07029–30, 07036, 07047, 07064, 07077, 07086–87, 07093, 07095, 07102–05, 07107, 07114, 07201–02, 07206, 07302–11, 08861–62

NEW MEXICO

(Population 2000, 1,819,046)

SENATORS

PETE V. DOMENICI, Republican, of Albuquerque, NM; born in Albuquerque, May 7, 1932; education: graduate of St. Mary's High School, 1954; University of New Mexico, B.S., 1966; Denver University, LL.D., 1958; employment: admitted to New Mexico bar, 1958; elected to Albuquerque City Commission, 1966; chairman (ex officio mayor), 1967; married: Nancy Burk, 1958; children: Lisa, Peter, Nella, Clare, David, Nanette, Helen, and Paula; committees: Appropriations; Budget; chairman, Energy and Natural Resources; Indian Affairs; elected to the U.S. Senate on November 7, 1972; reelected to each succeeding Senate term.

Office Listings

http://domenici.senate.gov

328 Hart Senate Office Building, Washington, DC 20510 .... (202) 224–6621
Chief of Staff.—Steve Bell.
Administrative / Systems Director.—Lynden Armstrong.
Legislative Director.—Edward Hild.
Press Secretary.—Chris Gallegos.
201 3rd Street NW, Suite 700, Albuquerque, NM 87102 .... (505) 346–6791
Federal Building, Loretto Town Centre, 505 South Main, Suite 118, Las Cruces, NM 88005 .... (505) 526–5475
Room 302, 120 South Federal Place, Santa Fe, NM 87501 .... (505) 988–6511
Federal Building, 140 Roswell, NM 88201 .... (505) 623–6170

* * *

JEFF BINGAMAN, Democrat, of Santa Fe, NM; born in El Paso, TX, on October 3, 1943; raised in Silver City, NM; graduate of Western High (now Silver High), 1961; B.A., government, Harvard University, 1965; J.D., Stanford Law School, 1968; served in the U.S. Army Reserves, 1968–74; served as Assistant New Mexico Attorney General, 1969, as counsel to the State constitutional convention; private practice, 1970–78; served as New Mexico Attorney General, 1979–82; member: Methodist Church; married to the former Anne Kovacovich; one son: John; committees: ranking member, Energy and Natural Resources; Finance; Health, Education, Labor, and Pensions; Joint Economic Committee; elected to the U.S. Senate on November 2, 1982; reelected to each succeeding Senate term.

Office Listings

http://bingaman.senate.gov

703 Hart Senate Office Building, Washington, DC 20510 .... (202) 224–5521
Administrative Assistant.—Bernie Toon. TDD: 224–1792
Legislative Director.—Trudy Vincent.
Communications Secretary.—Jude McCartin.
Personal Assistant.—Virginia White.
Loretto Town Centre, Suite 148, 505 South Main, Las Cruces, NM 88001 .... (505) 523–6561
625 Silver Avenue SW, Suite 130, Albuquerque, NM 87102 .... (505) 346–6601
105 West Third Street, Suite 409, Roswell, NM 88201 .... (505) 622–7113
119 East Marcy, Suite 101, Santa Fe, NM 87501 .... (505) 988–6647
118 Bridge Street, Suite 3, Las Vegas, NM 87701 .... (505) 454–8824

REPRESENTATIVES

FIRST DISTRICT

HEATHER WILSON, Republican, of Albuquerque, NM; born on December 30, 1960, in Keene, NH; George S. Emerson Elementary School, Fitzwilliam, NH; Keene High School, NH; B.S., United States Air Force Academy; Rhodes Scholar, Oxford University, England; Masters and Doctoral degrees in Philosophy (international relations); United States Air Force, Captain, 1978–89; President, Keystone International, Inc., 1991–95; New Mexico Sec. Of Children, Youth, and Families; 1995–98; married: Jay R. Hone, 1991; children: Scott, Joshua, and Caitlin Hone; committees: Armed Services; Energy and Commerce; subcommittees: Energy and Air

Quality; Environment and Hazardous Materials; Health; Strategic Forces; Readiness; Telecommunications and the Internet; elected to the 105th Congress on June 23, 1998, by special election; reelected to each succeeding Congress.

Office Listings

http://www.house.gov/wilson

318 Cannon House Office Building, Washington, DC 20515 .... (202) 225–6316
Chief of Staff.—Bryce Dustman. FAX: 225–4975
Legislative Director.—Clint Williamson.
Executive Assistant.—Barbara Cohen.
20 First Plaza, NW., Suite 603, Albuquerque, NM 87102 .... (505) 346–6781
Scheduler.—Katherine Carraro.

Counties: BERNALILLO (part), SANDOVAL (part), SANTA FE (part), TORRANCE, VALENCIA (part). CITIES AND TOWNSHIPS: Albuquerque, Belen (part), Estancia, Los Lunas (part), Moriarty, Mountainair, and Rio Rancho (part). Population (2000), 606,391.

ZIP Codes: 87001–02, 87004, 87008–09, 87015–16, 87031–32, 87035–36, 87042–43, 87047–48, 87059–61, 87063, 87068, 87070, 87101–25, 87131, 87151, 87153–54, 87158, 87176, 87181, 87184–85, 87187, 87190–99, 88301, 88321

* * *

SECOND DISTRICT

STEVAN PEARCE, Republican, of Hobbs, NM; born on August 24, 1947, in Lamesa, TX; education: B.B.A., New Mexico State University; M.B.A., Eastern New Mexico University; profession: businessman; owner and operator of Lea Fishing Tools, Inc., an oilfield services company; military service: U.S. Air Force pilot, 1970–76; attained the rank of Captain; awarded the Distinguished Flying Cross; public service: New Mexico House of Representatives, 1996–2000; religion: Baptist; family: married to Cynthia; children: Lori; elected to the 108th Congress on November 5, 2002.

Office Listings

http://www.house.gov/pearce

1408 Longworth House Office Building, Washington, DC 20515 .... (202) 225–2365
Chief of Staff.—Jim Richards. FAX: 225–9599
Press Secretary.—Gail Gitcho.
Scheduler.—Peggy Mallow.
1717 West 2nd Street, Suite 100, Roswell, NM 88201 .... (505) 622–0055
400 North Telshor, Suite E, Las Cruces, NM 88011 .... (505) 522–2219
1923 North Dal Paso, Hobbs, NM 88240 .... (505) 392–8325
District Representative.—Bob Carter.
111 School of Mines Road, Socorro, NM 87801 .... (505) 838–7516

Counties: BERNALILLO (part), CATRON, CHAVES, CIBOLA, DEBACA, DONA ANA, EDDY, GRANT, GUADALUPE, HIDALGO, LEA, LINCOLN, LUNA, MCKINLEY (part), OTERO, SIERRA, SOCORRO, VALENCIA (part). Population (2000), 606,406.

ZIP Codes: 87002, 87005–07, 87011, 87014, 87020–23, 87026, 87028, 87031, 87034, 87038, 87040, 87045, 87049, 87051, 87062, 87068, 87105, 87121, 87315, 87321, 87327, 87357, 87711, 87724, 87801, 87820–21, 87823–25, 87827–32, 87901, 87930–31, 87933, 87935–37, 87939–43, 88001–09, 88011–12, 88020–21, 88023–34, 88036, 88038–49, 88051–56, 88058, 88061–63, 88065, 88072, 88081, 88114, 88116, 88119, 88134, 88136, 88201–03, 88210–11, 88220–21, 88230–32, 88240–42, 88244, 88250, 88252–56, 88260, 88262–65, 88267–68, 88301, 88310–12, 88314, 88316–18, 88323–25, 88330, 88336–55, 88417, 88431, 88435

* * *

THIRD DISTRICT

TOM UDALL, Democrat, of Santa Fe, NM; born in Tucson, AZ, on May 18, 1948; son of U.S. Representative (1955–61), and Secretary of the Interior (1961–1969), Stewart Udall; education: McLean, VA, High School; B.A., Prescott College, 1970; Cambridge (England) University, 1975; J.D., University of New Mexico, 1977; employment: law clerk for Chief Justice Oliver Seth of the Tenth Circuit Court of Appeals, Santa Fe, NM; assistant U.S. Attorney, 1977–81; private attorney, 1981; chief counsel, New Mexico Health and Environment Department, 1983–84; New Mexico Attorney General, 1990–98; married: Jill Z. Cooper; one child; committees: Resources; Small Business; Veterans Affairs; elected to the 106th Congress; reelected to each succeeding Congress.

Office Listings

http://www.house.gov/tomudall

502 Cannon House Office Building, Washington, DC 20515 .... (202) 225–6190
Chief of Staff.—Tom Nagle. FAX: 226–1331
Legislative Director.—Mike Collins.
Press Secretary.—Glen Loveland.
Appointment Secretary.—Donda Morgan.
811 St. Michaels Drive, Suite 104, Santa Fe, NM 87505 .... (505) 984–8950
District Director.—Michele Jacquez-Ortiz.
321 N. Connelly Street, P.O. Box 868, Clovis, NM 88102–0868 .... (505) 763–7616
800 Municipal Drive, Farmington, NM 87401 .... (505) 324–1005
Constituent Services Representative.—Pete Valencia.
110 W. Aztec, Gallup, NM 87301 .... (505) 863–0582
Outreach and Community Service Representative.—Rose Custer.
1700 N. Grand Avenue, P.O. Box 160, Las Vegas, NM 87701 .... (505) 454–4080
Field Representative / Veterans Liaison.—Thomas Garcia.
3900 Southern Boulevard, SE, Room 105–A, Rio Rancho, NM 87124 .... (505) 994–0499
Field Representative.—Sarah Cobb.

Counties: BERNALILLO (part), COLFAX, CURRY, HARDING, LOS ALAMOS, MCKINLEY (part), MORA, QUAY, RIO ARRIBA, ROOSEVELT, SANDOVAL (part), SAN JUAN, SAN MIGUEL, SANTA FE (part), TAOS, UNION. Population (2000), 606,249.

ZIP Codes: 87001, 87004, 87010, 87012–13, 87015, 87017–18, 87024–25, 87027, 87029, 87037, 87041, 87044–48, 87052–53, 87056, 87064, 87072, 87083, 87114, 87120, 87123–24, 87144, 87174, 87301–02, 87305, 87310–13, 87316–17, 87319–23, 87325–26, 87328, 87347, 87364–65, 87375, 87401–02, 87410, 87412–13, 87415–21, 87455, 87461, 87499, 87501–25, 87527–33, 87535, 87537–40, 87543–45, 87548–49, 87551–54, 87556–58, 87560, 87562, 87564–67, 87569, 87571, 87573–83, 87592, 87594, 87701, 87710, 87712–15, 87718, 87722–23, 87728–36, 87740, 87742–43, 87745–47, 87749–50, 87752–53, 88101–03, 88112–13, 88115–16, 88118, 88120–26, 88130, 88132–35, 88401, 88410–11, 88414–16, 88418–19, 88421–22, 88424, 88426–27, 88430, 88433–34, 88436–37, 88439

NEW YORK

(Population 2000, 18,976,457)

SENATORS

CHARLES E. SCHUMER, Democrat, of Brooklyn and Queens, NY; born in Brooklyn on November 23, 1950; education: graduated valedictorian, Madison High School; Harvard University, *magna cum laude*, 1971; J.D. with honors, Harvard Law School, 1974; employment: admitted to the New York State bar in 1975; elected to the New York State Assembly, 1974; served on Judiciary, Health, Education, and Cities committees; chairman, subcommittee on City Management and Governance, 1977; chairman, Committee on Oversight and Investigation, 1979; reelected to each succeeding legislative session until December 1980; married: Iris Weinshall, 1980; children: Jessica Emily and Alison Emma; committees: Banking, Housing, and Urban Affairs; Energy and Natural Resources; Judiciary; Rules and Administration; subcommittees: ranking member, Administrative Oversight and the Courts; Antitrust, Business Rights, and Competition; ranking member, Economic Policy; Housing and Transportation; Immigration; Securities and Investment; elected to the 97th Congress on November 4, 1980; reelected to each succeeding Congress; elected to the U.S. Senate on November 3, 1998.

Office Listings

http://schumer.senate.gov

313 Hart Senate Office Building, Washington, DC 20510 .... (202) 224–6542
Chief of Staff.—Mike Lynch. FAX: 228–3027
Communications Director.—Phil Singer.
Executive Assistant.—Joe Harris.
757 Third Avenue, Suite 1702, New York, NY 10017 .... (212) 486–4430
Leo O'Brien Building, Room 420, Albany, NY 12207 .... (518) 431–4070
111 West Huron, Room 620, Buffalo, NY 14202 .... (716) 846–4111
100 State Street, Room 3040, Rochester, NY 14614 .... (716) 263–5866
100 South Clinton, Room 841, Syracuse, NY 13261–7318 .... (315) 423–5471
Federal Office Building, 15 Henry Street, #B6, Binghamton, NY 13901 .... (607) 772–6792
Two Greenway Plaza, 145 Pine Lawn Road and 300 N, Melville, NY 11747 .... (631) 753–0978
P.O. Box A, Red Hook, NY 12571 .... (914) 285–9741

* * *

HILLARY RODHAM CLINTON, Democrat, of Chappaqua, NY; born on October 26, 1947, in Chicago, IL; education: B.A., Wellesley College, 1969; J.D., Yale University, 1973; profession: Attorney; employment: Children's Defense Fund; U.S. House of Representatives' Judiciary Committee; University of Arkansas at Fayetteville; and private legal practice; family: married to former Arkansas Governor and President William Jefferson Clinton, 1975; one daughter: Chelsea, 1980; First Lady of Arkansas, 1979–1981, and 1983–1993; First Lady of the United States, 1993–2001; author: *It Takes a Village and Other Lessons Children Teach Us; Dear Socks, Dear Buddy: Kids' Letters to the First Pets; An Invitation to the White House*; religion: Methodist; recipient of numerous awards; elected to the U.S. Senate on November 7, 2000.

Office Listings

http://clinton.senate.gov

476 Russell Senate Office Building, Washington, DC 20510 .... (202) 224–4451
Chief of Staff.—Tamera Luzzatto. FAX: 228–0282
Press Secretary.—Philippe Reines.
Communications Director.—Karen Dunn.
Scheduler.—Lona Valmoro.
Federal Office Building, 1 Clinton Square, Room 821, Albany, NY 12207 .... (518) 431–0120
Guaranty Building, 28 Church Street, Suite 208, Buffalo, NY 14202 .... (716) 854–9725
Federal Office Building, 100 State Street, Room 3280, Rochester, NY 14614 .... (585) 263–6250
Federal Office Building, 100 South Clinton Street, P.O. Box 7378, Syracuse, NY 13261 .... (315) 448–0470
P.O. Box 273, Lowville, NY 13367 .... (315) 376–6118
P.O. Box 617, Hartsdale, NY 10530 .... (914) 725–9294
Three Greenway Plaza, 155 Pinclawn Road, Suite 250 North, Melville, NY 11747 .... (631) 249–2825

REPRESENTATIVES

FIRST DISTRICT

TIMOTHY H. BISHOP, Democrat, of Southampton, NY; born on June 1, 1950, in Southampton; education: Southampton High School, 1968; A.B., in History, from Holy Cross College; M.P.A., Long Island University, 1981; profession: educator; Provost of Southampton College, 1986–2002; community service: Southampton Rotary Club Scholarship Committee; Southampton Town Board of Ethics; Eastern Long Island Coastal Conservation Alliance; Bridgehampton Childcare and Recreation Center; religion: Catholic; family: married to Kathryn; children: Molly and Meghan; elected to the 108th Congress on November 5, 2002.

Office Listings

http:/www.house.gov/timbishop

1133 Longworth House Office Building, Washington, DC 20515 .... (202) 225–3826
Chief of Staff.—Doug Dodson. FAX: 225–3143
Legislative Director.—Aprill Springfield.
Communications Director / Legislative Assistant.—Jon Schneider.
3680 Route 112, Suite C, Coram, NY 11727 .... (631) 696–6500

Counties: SUFFOLK COUNTY (part). CITIES: Brookhaven, Smithtown (part), Southampton, and Montauk. Population (2000), 654,360.

ZIP Codes: 00501, 00544, 11713, 11715, 11719–20, 11727, 11733, 11738, 11741–42, 11745, 11754–55, 11763–64, 11766–68, 11772, 11776–80, 11784, 11786–90, 11792, 11794, 11901, 11930–35, 11937, 11939–42, 11944, 11946–65, 11967–73, 11975–78, 11980

* * *

SECOND DISTRICT

STEVE ISRAEL, Democrat, of Huntington, NY; born on May 30, 1958, in Brooklyn, NY; education: B.A., George Washington University, 1982; profession: public relations and marketing executive; public service: Legislative Assistant for Rep. Richard Ottinger (D–NY), 1980–83; Suffolk County Executive for Intergovernmental Relations, 1988–91; elected to the Huntington Town Board, 1993; reelected two times; organizations: Institute on the Holocaust; Touro Law Center; Nature Conservancy; Audubon Society; awards: Child Care Council of Suffolk Leadership Award; Anti-Defamation League and Sons of Italy Purple Aster Award; elected to the 107th Congress on November 7, 2000; reelected to each succeeding Congress.

Office Listings

http://www.house.gov/israel

429 Cannon House Office Building, Washington, DC 20515 .... (202) 225–3335
Chief of Staff.—Mark Siegel. FAX: 225–4669
Deputy Chief of Staff.—Jonathan Vogel.
Legislative Director.—Francis Creighton.
150 Motor Parkway, Suite 108, Hauppauge, NY 11788 .... (631) 951–2210
District Director.—Holli Dunayer. (516) 505–1448

Counties: NASSAU COUNTY (part), SUFFOLK COUNTY (part). CITIES: Asharoken, Bay Shore (part), Bayport, Bohemia, Brentwood, Brightwaters (part), Centerport, Central Islip, Cold Springs Harbor, Commack, Copiague (part), Deer Park, Dix Hills, East Farmingdale, East Northport, Eaton's Neck, Elwood, Fort Salonga (part), Great River, Greenlawn, Halesite, Hauppauge, Holbrook, Huntington, Huntington Station, Islandia, Islip (part), Islip Terrace, Jericho (part), King's Park (part), Lindenhurst (part), Lloyd Harbor, Melville, North Amityville, Northport, Oakdale, Ocean Beach, Old Bethpage (part), Plainview, Ronkonkoma, Sayville, Smithtown (part), South Huntington, Syosset (part), West Babylon, West Hills, West Islip (part), West Sayville, Wheatley Heights, Woodbury and Wyandanch. Population (2000), 654,360.

ZIP Codes: 11701, 11703–06, 11714–18, 11721–22, 11724–26, 11729–31, 11735, 11737, 11739–43, 11746–47, 11749–54, 11757, 11760, 11767–70, 11772, 11775, 11779, 11782, 11787–88, 11791, 11796–98, 11801, 11803–04

* * *

THIRD DISTRICT

PETER T. KING, Republican, of Seaford, NY; born on April 5, 1944 in Manhattan, NY; education: B.A., St. Francis College, NY, 1965; J.D., University of Notre Dame Law School, IN, 1968; military service: served, U.S. Army Reserve National Guard, specialist 5, 1968–73;

admitted to New York bar, 1968; employment: attorney; Deputy Nassau County Attorney, 1972–74, executive assistant to the Nassau County Executive, 1974–76; general counsel, Nassau Off-Track Betting Corporation, 1977; Hempstead Town Councilman, 1978–81; Nassau County Comptroller, 1981–92; member: Ancient Order of Hiberians, Long Island Committee for Soviet Jewry, Sons of Italy, Knights of Columbus, 69th Infantry Veterans Corps, American Legion; married: Rosemary Wiedl King, 1967; children: Sean and Erin; elected on November 3, 1992 to the 103rd Congress; reelected to each succeeding Congress.

Office Listings

http://www.house.gov/king

436 Cannon House Office Building, Washington, DC 20515 .... (202) 225–7896
Chief of Staff.—Robert O'Connor. FAX: 226–2279
Legislative Director / Press Secretary.—Kevin Fogarty.
Special Assistant.—Nicole Longo.
1003 Park Boulevard, Massapequa Park, NY 11762 .... (516) 541–4225
District Director.—Anne Rosenfeld.
Suffolk County .... (631) 541–4225

Counties: NASSAU (part), SUFFOLK (part). CITIES AND TOWNSHIPS: Amityville (part), Babylon (part), Baldwin (part), Bayshore (part), Bayville, Bellmore (part), Bethpage, Brightwaters (part), Brookville, Cedar Beach, Centre Island, Copiague (part), Cove Neck, East Islip (part), East Norwich, Farmingdale (part), Freeport (part), Gilgo Beach, Glen Cove, Glen Head, Glenwood Landing, Greenvale (part), Harbor Isle, Hicksville, Island Park, Islip (part), Jericho, Lattingtown, Laurel Hollow, Levittown, Lido Beach, Lindenhurst (part), Locust Grove (part), Locust Valley, Long Beach, Massapequa, Massapequa Park, Matinecock, Merrick (part), Mill Neck, Muttontown, North Babylon (part), North Bellmore (part), North Lindenhurst (part), Oak Beach, Oceanside (part), Old Bethpage, Old Brookville, Old Westbury, Oyster Bay, Oyster Bay Cove, Plainview (part), Point Lookout, Sea Cliff (part), Seaford, Syosset (part), Wantagh, West Babylon (part), West Bayshore (part), Westbury (part), West Islip, and Woodbury (part). Population (2000), 654,361.

ZIP Codes: 11510, 11520, 11542, 11545, 11547–48, 11558, 11560–61, 11566, 11568–69, 11572, 11576, 11579, 11590, 11599, 11701–04, 11706, 11709–10, 11714, 11718, 11724, 11726, 11730, 11732, 11735–37, 11751, 11753, 11756–58, 11762, 11765, 11771, 11773–74, 11783, 11791, 11793, 11795, 11797, 11801–04, 11815, 11819, 11854–55

* * *

FOURTH DISTRICT

CAROLYN McCARTHY, Democrat, of Mineola, NY; born in Brooklyn, NY, January 5, 1944; education: graduated, Mineola High School, 1962; graduated, nursing school, 1964; employment: licensed practical nurse in ICU Section, Glen Cove Hospital; married: Dennis McCarthy, 1967; widowed on December 7, 1993, when her husband was killed and her only son, Kevin, severely wounded in the Long Island Railroad Massacre; turned personal nightmare into a crusade against violence—speaking out with other families of the Long Island tragedy, not just to the victims of the shooting but to crime victims across the country; honorary member of the board, Americans Against Gun Violence; member: board of directors for ''Guns for Goods''; board of directors, New Yorkers Against Gun Violence; board of directors, New York City ''Stop the Violence'' campaign; committees: Education and the Workforce; Financial Services; subcommittees: Capital Markets, Insurance and Government Sponsored Enterprises; Employer-Employee Relations; Financial Institutions and Consumer Credit; 21st Century Competitiveness; elected to the 105th Congress; reelected to each succeeding Congress.

Office Listings

http://www.house.gov/carolynmccarthy

106 Cannon House Office Building, Washington, DC 20515 .... (202) 225–5516
Chief of Staff.—Jim Hart. FAX: 225–5758
District Director.—Mary Ellen Mendelsohn.
Executive Assistant.—Christopher Hoven.
Communications Director.—Mark Sokolove.
200 Garden City Plaza, Suite 320, Garden City, NY 11530 .... (516) 739–3008

Counties: NASSAU (part). CITIES AND TOWNSHIPS: Atlantic Beach, Baldwin (part), Bellerose (part), Carle Place, Cedarhurst, East Meadow, East Rockaway, East Williston, Elmont, Floral Park (part), Franklin Square, Freeport (part), Garden City, Garden City Park (part), Hempstead, Hewlett, Inwood, Lakeview, Lawrence, Lynbrook, Malverne, Merrick (part), Mineola, New Cassel, New Hyde Park, North Bellmore, North New Hyde Park, Oceanside (part), Rockville Centre, Roosevelt, Salisbury, Stewart Manor, South Floral Park, South Valley Stream, Uniondale, Valley Stream, West Hempstead, Westbury, Williston Park (part), Woodmere, and Woodsburgh. Population (2000) 654,360.

ZIP Codes: 11001–03, 11010, 11040, 11042, 11096, 11501, 11509–10, 11514, 11516, 11518, 11520, 11530–31, 11535–36, 11549–57, 11559, 11561, 11563–66, 11568, 11570–72, 11575, 11577, 11580–83, 11588, 11590, 11592–99, 11710, 11793

FIFTH DISTRICT

GARY L. ACKERMAN, Democrat, of Queens, NY; born in Brooklyn, NY, November 19, 1942; education: graduate, Queens College, Flushing, NY; attended St. John's University, Jamaica, NY; public school teacher; newspaper editor; businessman; New York State Senate, 1979–83; married: the former Rita Tewel; children: Lauren, Corey, and Ari; elected by special election on March 1, 1983, to the 98th Congress, to fill the vacancy caused by the death of Representative Benjamin Rosenthal; reelected to each succeeding Congress.

Office Listings

http://www.house.gov/ackerman

2243 Rayburn House Office Building, Washington, DC 20515 .... (202) 225–2601
Administrative Assistant.—Jedd Moskowitz.
218–14 Northern Boulevard, Bayside, NY 11361 .... (718) 423–2154
District Office Administrator.—Moya Berry.

Counties: NASSAU (part), QUEENS (part). CITIES AND TOWNSHIPS: Auburndale, Bay Terrace, Bayside, Bell Park Gardens, Bell Park Manor, Centre Island, Clearview, Corona, Deepdale, Douglaston, Douglaston Manor, East Elmhurst, East Hills, Flushing, Fresh Meadows, Glen Oaks, Great Neck, Great Neck Estates, Great Neck Gardens, Great Neck Plaza, Greenvale, Herricks, Hillcrest, Hollis Court Gardens, Hollis Hills, Jackson Heights, Jamaica Estates, Kensington, Kew Gardens Hills, Kings Point, Lake Success, Lefrak City, Linden Hill, Little Neck, Malba, Manor Haven, North Shore Towers, Oakland Gardens, Pomonok, Port Washington, Port Washington North, Queensboro Hill, Roslyn, Roslyn Estates, Roslyn Harbor, Roslyn Heights, Russell Gardens, Saddle Rock, Saddle Rock Estates, Sands Point, Searington, Thomaston, University Gardens, West Neck, and Windsor Park. Population (2000), 654,361.

ZIP Codes: 11004–05, 11020–24, 11030, 11040, 11042, 11050–55, 11351–52, 11354–58, 11360–66, 11368–69, 11372–73, 11375, 11379, 11423, 11426–27, 11432, 11507, 11542, 11548, 11560, 11568, 11576–77, 11596

* * *

SIXTH DISTRICT

GREGORY W. MEEKS, Democrat, of Far Rockaway, NY; born in Harlem, NY, on September 25, 1953; married: Simone-Marie Meeks, 1997; children: Aja, Ebony, and Nia-Ayana; education: P.S. 183; Robert F. Wagner Junior High School; Julia Richman High School, New York, NY; bachelor degree, Adelphi University, 1971–75; J.D., Howard University School of Law, 1975–78; employment: lawyer, admitted to bar, 1979; Queens District Attorney's Office, 1978–83, serving as Assistant District Attorney; Judge, New York State Workers' Compensation Board; public service: New York State Assemblyman, 1992–97; organizations: Alpha Phi Alpha Fraternity; Congressional Black Caucus; Council of Black-Elected Democrats; National Bar Association; Task Force on Financial Services; committees: Financial Services; International Relations; subcommittees: Africa; Capital Markets, Insurance, and Government Sponsored Enterprises; Asia and the Pacific; Financial Institutions and Consumer Credit; active member of the Congressional Black Caucus; elected to the 105th Congress on February 3, 1998; reelected to each succeeding Congress.

Office Listings

http://www.house.gov/meeks

1710 Longworth House Office Building, Washington, DC 20515 .... (202) 225–3461
Chief of Staff.—Jameel Aalim-Johnson. FAX: 226–4169
Legislative Director.—Melvenia Gueye.
Office Manager / Scheduler.—Pat Fisher.
196–06 Linden Boulevard, St. Albans, NY 11412 .... (718) 949–5600
District Director.—Patrick Jenkins.
1931 Mott Avenue, Room 305, Far Rockaway, NY 11691 .... (718) 327–9791
Community Liaison.—Edward Williams.
106–11 Liberty Avenue, 2nd Floor, Richmond Hill, NY 11419 .... (718) 738–4200
Community Liaison.—Erline Nelson.

Counties: QUEENS COUNTY (part). CITIES AND TOWNSHIPS: Arverne, Cambria Heights, Edgemere, Far Rockaway, Floral Park, Glen Oaks, Hammels, Hollis, Howard Beach, Jamaica, Jamaica Estates, Kew Gardens, Laurelton, New Hyde Park, Ozone Park, Queens Village, Richmond Hill, Rosedale, St. Albans, South Jamaica, South Ozone Park, Springfield Gardens, and Woodhaven. Population (2000), 654,361.

ZIP Codes: 11001, 11004, 11040, 11405, 11411–20, 11422–23, 11425–36, 11439, 11451, 11484, 11690–93

SEVENTH DISTRICT

JOSEPH CROWLEY, Democrat, of Elmhurst, Queens, NY; born in New York, NY, on March 16, 1962; graduated: Power Memorial High School, 1981; B.A., Queens College, 1985; elected to the New York State Assembly, 1986–98; Assembly Committees: Racing and Wagering; Banking, Consumer Affairs, and Protection; Election Law; Labor and Housing; religion: Roman Catholic; married to Kasey Nilson; committees: Financial Services; International Relations; elected to the 106th Congress; reelected to each succeeding Congress.

Office Listings

http://house.gov/crowley

312 Cannon House Office Building, Washington, DC 20510 .... (202) 225–3965
Chief of Staff.—Christopher McCannell. FAX: 225–1909
Office Manager.—John Olmsted.
Legislative Director.—Kevin Casey.
3425 East Tremont Avenue, Suite 1–3, Bronx, NY 10465 .... (718) 931–1400
82–11 37th Avenue, Suite 705, Jackson Heights, NY 10372 .... (718) 779–1400
177 Dreiser Loop, Room 3, Bronx, NY 10475 .... (718) 320–2314

Counties: BRONX (part), QUEENS (part). Population (2000), 654,360.

ZIP Codes: 10458, 10460–62, 10464–67, 10469, 10472–75, 10805, 11103–04, 11354, 11356, 11368–73, 11377–78, 11380

* * *

EIGHTH DISTRICT

JERROLD NADLER, Democrat, of New York, NY; born in Brooklyn, NY, on June 13, 1947; education: graduated from Stuyvesant High School, 1965; B.A., Columbia University, 1970; J.D., Fordham University, 1978; New York State Assembly, 1977–92; member: American Jewish Congress; ACLU; National Abortion Rights Action League; AIPAC; National Organization for Women; Assistant Whip; committees: Judiciary; Transportation and Infrastructure; married: 1976; one child; elected to the 102nd Congress on November 3, 1992, to fill the vacancy caused by the death of Representative Ted Weiss; at the same time elected to the 103rd Congress; reelected to each succeeding Congress.

Office Listings

http://www.house.gov/nadler

2334 Rayburn House Office Building, Washington, DC 20515 .... (202) 225–5635
Legislative Director.—John Doty. FAX: 225–6923
Administrative Assistant.—Brett Heimov.
201 Varick Street, Suite 669, New York, NY 10014 .... (212) 367–7350
Chief of Staff.—Amy Rutkin.
445 Neptune Avenue, Brooklyn, NY 11224 .... (718) 373–3198
Brooklyn Director.—Robert Gottheim.

Counties: KINGS (part), NEW YORK (part). Population (2000), 654,360.

ZIP Codes: 10001–08, 10010–14, 10016, 10018–20, 10023–24, 10036, 10038, 10041, 10043, 10047–48, 10069, 10072, 10080–82, 10087, 10095, 10101–02, 10108–09, 10113–14, 10116–19, 10121, 10123–24, 10129, 10132–33, 10149, 10199, 10203, 10211–13, 10242, 10249, 10256, 10259–61, 10265, 10268–82, 10285–86, 10292, 10467, 11204, 11214–15, 11218–20, 11223–24, 11230–32, 11235

* * *

NINTH DISTRICT

ANTHONY D. WEINER, Democrat, of Brooklyn, NY; born in Brooklyn, NY, on September 4, 1964; education: graduated, Brooklyn Tech High School; B.A., State University of New York at Plattsburgh, 1985; employment: served in the New York City Council, 1992–98; selected to serve as Freshman Whip, 106th Congress; committees: Judiciary; Science; Transportation and Infrastructure; subcommittees: Aviation; Commercial and Administrative Law; Courts, the Internet, and Intellectual Property; Highways, Transit and Pipelines; Space and Aeronautics; elected to the 106th Congress; reelected to each succeeding Congress.

Office Listings

http://www.house.gov/weiner

501 Cannon House Office Building, Washington, DC 20515 .... (202) 225–6616
Chief of Staff.—Veronica Sullivan. FAX: 226–7253
Executive Assistant.—Amy Kletnick.
Special Assistant.—Debi Roder.
Senior Policy Advisor.—Lamar Robertson.
80–02 Kew Gardens Road, Suite 5000, Kew Gardens, NY 11415 .... (718) 520–9001
90–16 Rockaway Beach Boulevard, Rockaway, NY 11693 .... (718) 318–9255
1800 Sheepshead Bay Road, Brooklyn, NY 11235 .... (718) 743–0441
District Director.—Veronica Sullivan.

Counties: KINGS COUNTY (part). CITIES AND TOWNSHIPS: Bergen Beach, Brighton Beach, Canasie, Flatbush, Flatlands, Gerritsen Beach, Georgetowne, Kensington, Manhattan Beach, Marine Park, Midwood, Mill Basin, Park Slope, Parkville, Sheepshead Bay, Windsor Terrace. QUEENS COUNTY (part). CITIES AND TOWNSHIPS: Belle Harbor, Breezy Point, Briarwood, Broad Channel, Corona, Elmhurst, Far Rockaway, Forest Hills, Glendale, Hamilton Beach, Howard Beach, Kew Gardens, Lindenwood, Middle Village, Neponsit, Ozone Park, Rego Park, Richmond Hill, Ridgewood, Rockway Point, Roxbury, West Lawrence, and Woodhaven. Population (2000), 654,360.

ZIP Codes: 11204, 11208, 11210, 11218, 11223, 11229–30, 11234–36, 11358, 11361, 11364–67, 11373–75, 11378–79, 11381, 11385, 11414–18, 11421, 11424, 11427, 11432, 11435, 11693–95, 11697

* * *

TENTH DISTRICT

EDOLPHUS TOWNS, Democrat, of Brooklyn, NY; born in Chadbourn, NC, on July 21, 1934; graduated, West Side High School, Chadbourn, 1952; B.S., North Carolina A&T State University, Greensboro, 1956; master's degree in social work, Adelphi University, Garden City, NY, 1973; U.S. Army, 1956–58; teacher, Medgar Evers College, Brooklyn, NY, and for the New York City public school system; deputy hospital administrator, 1965–71; deputy president, Borough of Brooklyn, 1976–82; member: Kiwanis, Boy Scouts Advisory Council, Salvation Army, Phi Beta Sigma Fraternity; married the former Gwendolyn Forbes in 1960; two children: Darryl and Deidra; committees: Energy and Commerce; Government Reform; subcommittees: Commerce, Trade and Consumer Protection; ranking member, Government Efficiency and Financial Management; Health; Telecommunications and the Internet; elected on November 2, 1982, to the 98th Congress; reelected to each succeeding Congress.

Office Listings

http://www.house.gov/towns

2232 Rayburn House Office Building, Washington, DC 20515 .... (202) 225–5936
Chief of Staff.—Brenda Pillors. FAX: 225–1018
Legal Counsel.—Cherri Branson.
Office Manager / Scheduler.—Gerri Taylor.
1110 Pennsylvania Avenue, Store #5, Brooklyn, NY 11207 .... (718) 272–1175
26 Court Street, Suite 1510, Brookyln, NY 11241 .... (718) 855–8018
District Director.—Karen Johnson.
1670 Fulton Street, Brooklyn, NY 11213 .... (718) 774–5682

Counties: KINGS COUNTY (part). Population (2000), 654,361.

ZIP Codes: 11201–03, 11205–08, 11210–13, 11216–17, 11221, 11230, 11233–34, 11236, 11238–39, 11245, 11247–48, 11251, 11256

* * *

ELEVENTH DISTRICT

MAJOR R. OWENS, Democrat, of Brooklyn, NY; born in Memphis, TN, June 28, 1936; education: attended Hamilton High School, Memphis, TN; B.A., with high honors Morehouse College, 1956; M.S., Atlanta University, 1957; chairman, Brooklyn Congress of Racial Equality; vice president, Metropolitan Council of Housing, 1964; community coordinator, Brooklyn Public Library, 1965; executive director, Brownsville Community Council, 1966; commissioner, New York City Community Development Agency, 1968–73; director, community media library program at Columbia University, 1974; New York State Senate, 1974–82; chairman, Senate Democratic Operations Committee; Brooklyn borough president declared September 10, 1971, ''Major R. Owens Day''; served on International Commission on Ways of Implementing Social

Policy to Ensure Maximum Public Participation and Social Justice for Minorities at The Hague, the Netherlands, 1972; published author and lecturer on library science; featured speaker, White House Conference on Libraries, 1979; recognized authority in community development; married: Maria A. Owens of New York City; the children of their blended family are Christopher, Geoffrey, Millard, Carlos, and Cecelia; appointed chairman of the House Subcommittee on Select Education and Civil Rights, 1987; chairman of the Congressional Black Caucus Budget Task Force; appointed chairman of the Congressional Black Caucus Education Braintrust from the 98th Congress to the present; committees: Education and the Workforce; Government Reform; elected to the 98th Congress, November 2, 1982; reelected to each succeeding Congress.

Office Listings

2309 Rayburn House Office Building, Washington, DC 20515 .... (202) 225–6231
Chief of Staff / Administrative Assistant.—Jacqueline Ellis. FAX: 226–0112
Legislative Director.—Larry Walker.
Legislative Assistant.—Norman A. Meyer.
Executive Assistant.—Debbie Aledo-Simpson.
289 Utica Avenue, Brooklyn, NY 11213 .... (718) 773–3100
1414 Cortelyou Road, Brooklyn, NY 11226 .... (718) 940–3213

Counties: KINGS COUNTY (part). Population (2000), 654,361.

ZIP Codes: 11201, 11203, 11210, 11212–13, 11215–18, 11225–26, 11230–31, 11233–34, 11236, 11238, 11241–42

* * *

TWELFTH DISTRICT

NYDIA M. VELÁZQUEZ, Democrat, of New York, NY; born in Yabucoa, Puerto Rico, March 28, 1953; education: University of Puerto Rico, B.A. in political science, 1974; New York University, M.A. in political science, 1976; employment: faculty member, University of Puerto Rico, 1976–81; adjunct professor, Hunter College of the City University of New York, 1981–83; special assistant to Congressman Ed Towns, 1983; member, City Council of New York, 1984–86; national director of Migration Division Office, Department of Labor and Human Resources of Puerto Rico, 1986–89; director, Department of Puerto Rican Community Affairs in the United States, 1989–92; elected on November 3, 1992, to the 103rd Congress; reelected to each succeeding Congress.

Office Listings

http://www.house.gov/velazquez

2241 Rayburn House Office Building, Washington, DC 20515 .... (202) 225–2361
Chief of Staff.—Michael Day. FAX: 226–0327
Communications Director.—Wendy Belzer.
268 Broadway, 2nd Floor, Brooklyn, NY 11211 .... (718) 599–3658
16 Court Street, Suite 1006, Brooklyn, NY 11241 .... (718) 222–5819
173 Avenue B, New York, NY 10009 .... (212) 673–3997

Counties: KINGS (part), NEW YORK (part), QUEENS (part). Population (2000), 654,360.

ZIP Codes: 10002, 10009, 10012–13, 10038, 11101, 11104, 11201, 11205–08, 11211, 11215, 11218–23, 11231–32, 11237, 11377–79, 11385–86, 11416, 11421

* * *

THIRTEENTH DISTRICT

VITO FOSSELLA, Republican, of Staten Island, NY; born on March 9, 1965; education: Public School 39, South Beach; Intermediate School 2, Midland Beach; Monsignor Farrell High School; B.S., University of Pennsylvania Wharton School; Fordham University School of Law; employment: lawyer, admitted to New York bar, 1994; New York City Council, 1994–97; married: Mary Pat Fossella, 1990; children: Dylan and Griffin; organizations: Ancient Order of Hibernians; South Shore Rotary; Staten Island Bucks; committees: Energy and Commerce; Financial Services; elected to the 105th Congress, by special election, on November 4, 1997; reelected to each succeeding Congress.

Office Listings

http://www.house.gov/fossella

1239 Longworth House Office Building, Washington, DC 20515 .... (202) 225–3371
Chief of Staff.—Tom Quaadman. FAX: 226–1272
Office Manager.—Vicki J. Hook.
Legislative Director.—Brendon Weiss.
4434 Amboy Road, Second Floor, Staten Island, NY 10312 .... (718) 356–8400
District Director.—Sherry Diamond
9818 4th Avenue, Brooklyn, NY 11209 .... (718) 630–5277
Office Manager.—Eileen Long.

Counties: KINGS (part), RICHMOND. Population (2000), 654,361.

ZIP Codes: 10301–10, 10312–14, 11204, 11209, 11214, 11219–20, 11223, 11228, 11252

* * *

FOURTEENTH DISTRICT

CAROLYN B. MALONEY, Democrat, of New York City, NY; born on February 19, 1948 in Greensboro, NC; B.A., Greensboro College, Greensboro, NC, 1968; various positions, New York City Board of Education, 1970–77; legislative aide, New York State Assembly, senior program analyst, 1977–79; executive director of advisory council, 1979–82; director of special projects, New York State Senate Office of the Minority Leader; New York City council member, 1982–93; chairperson, New York City Council Committee on Contracts; member: Council Committee on Aging, National Organization of Women, Common Cause, Sierra Club, Americans for Democratic Action, New York City Council Committee on Housing and Buildings, Citizens Union, Grand Central Business Improvement District, Harlem Urban Development Corporation (1982–91), Commission on Early Childhood Development Programs, Council of Senior Citizen Centers of New York City, 1982–87; married Clifton H. W. Maloney, 1976; two children: Virginia Marshall Maloney and Christina Paul Maloney; elected on November 3, 1992, to the 103rd Congress; reelected to each succeeding Congress.

Office Listings

http://www.house.gov/maloney

2331 Rayburn House Office Building, Washington, DC 20515 .... (202) 225–7944
Administrative Assistant.—Ben Chevat. FAX: 225–4709
Legislative Director.—Robin Bachman.
1651 Third Avenue, Suite 311, New York, NY 10128 .... (212) 860–0606
28–11 Astoria Boulevard, Long Island City, NY 11102 .... (718) 932–1804

Counties: NEW YORK (part), QUEENS (part). CITIES AND TOWNSHIPS: Astoria, Manhattan (part), Queens (part), Long Island City, Roosevelt Island, Sunnyside (part), and Woodside (part). Population (2000), 654,361.

ZIP Codes: 10001–03, 10009–10, 10012, 10016–24, 10026, 10028–29, 10036, 10044, 10055, 10103–07, 10110–12, 10119–20, 10122, 10126, 10128, 10130–31, 10138, 10150–60, 10162–79, 10185, 11101–06, 11120, 11369–70, 11375, 11377

* * *

FIFTEENTH DISTRICT

CHARLES B. RANGEL, Democrat-Liberal, of New York, NY; born in Harlem, NY, on June 11, 1930; attended DeWitt Clinton High School; served in U.S. Army, 1948–52; awarded the Purple Heart, Bronze Star for Valor, U.S. and Korean presidential citations, and three battle stars while serving in combat with the Second Infantry Division in Korea; honorably discharged with rank of staff sergeant; after military duty, completed high school, 1953; graduated from New York University School of Commerce, student under the G.I. bill; 1957 dean's list; graduated from St. John's University School of Law, dean's list student under a full three-year scholarship, 1960; lawyer; admitted to practice in the courts of the State of New York, U.S. Federal Court, Southern District of New York, and U.S. Customs Court; appointed assistant U.S. attorney, Southern District of New York, 1961; legal counsel, New York City Housing and Redevelopment Board, Neighborhood Conservation Bureau; general counsel, National Advisory Commission on Selective Service, 1966; served two terms in the New York State Assembly, 1966–70; active in 369th Veterans Association; Community Education Program; and Martin Luther King, Jr., Democratic Club; married Alma Carter; two children: Steven and Alicia; elected to the 92nd Congress, November 3, 1970; reelected to each succeeding Congress.

Office Listings

http://www.house.gov/rangel

2354 Rayburn House Office Building, Washington, DC 20515 .... (202) 225–4365
Administrative Assistant.—George A. Dalley. FAX: 225–0816
163 West 125th Street, New York, NY 10027 .... (212) 663–3900
District Administrator.—Vivian E. Jones.

Counties: BRONX (part), NEW YORK (part), QUEENS (part). Population (2000), 654,361.

ZIP Codes: 10023–27, 10029–35, 10037, 10039–40, 10115–16, 10169, 10463, 11105

* * *

SIXTEENTH DISTRICT

JOSÉ E. SERRANO, Democrat, of Bronx, NY; born in Mayagüez, PR, October 24, 1943; education: Dodge Vocational High School, Bronx, NY; attended Lehman College, City University of New York, NY; served with the U.S. Army Medical Corps, 1964–66; employed by the Manufacturers Hanover Bank, 1961–69; Community School District 7, 1969–74; New York State Assemblyman, 1974–90; chairman, Consumer Affairs Committee, 1979–83; chairman, Education Committee, 1983–90; married in 1979 to the former Mary Staucet; five children: Lisa Trapenese, Jose Marco, Benjamin, Jonathan Brucker, and Justine Brucker; committees: Appropriations; subcommittees: ranking member, Commerce, Justice, State, Judiciary; Homeland Security; elected to the 101st Congress, by special election, March 28, 1990, to fill the vacancy caused by the resignation of Robert Garcia; reelected to each succeeding Congress.

Office Listings

http://www.house.gov/serrano

2227 Rayburn House Office Building, Washington, DC 20515 .... (202) 225–4361
Chief of Staff.—Ellyn Toscano.
Executive Assistant.—Pichy Marty.
Legislative Director.—Lucy Hand.
Scheduler.—Josefina Bello.
890 Grand Concourse, Bronx, NY 10451–2828 .... (718) 538–5400
District Director.—Cheryl Simmons-Oliver.

Counties: BRONX COUNTY (part). CITIES AND TOWNSHIPS: Bronx. Population (2000), 654,360.

ZIP Codes: 10451–60, 10463, 10468, 10472–74

* * *

SEVENTEENTH DISTRICT

ELIOT L. ENGEL, Democrat, of Bronx, NY; born in Bronx, NY, on February 18, 1947; education: B.A., Hunter-Lehman College, 1969; M.A., City University of New York, 1973; New York Law School, 1987; married: Patricia Ennis Engel, 1980; children: Julia, Jonathan, and Philip; teacher and counselor in the New York City public school system, 1969–77; elected to the New York legislature, 1977–88; chaired the Assembly Committee on Alcoholism and Substance Abuse and subcommittee on Mitchell-Lama Housing (twelve years prior to his election to Congress); committees: Energy and Commerce; Inernational Relations; subcommittees: Telecommunications and the Internet; Health; Middle East and Central Asia; Europe; member: Congressional Human Rights Caucus; Democratic Study Group on Health; Long Island Sound Caucus; co-chairman, Albanian Issues Caucus; board member, Congressional Ad Hoc Committee on Irish Affairs; elected on November 8, 1988, to the 101st Congress; reelected to each succeeding Congress.

Office Listings

http://www.house.gov/engel

2264 Rayburn House Office Building, Washington, DC 20515 .... (202) 225–2464
Administrative Assistant / Legal Counsel.—Jason Steinbaum.
Office Manager.—Michelle Shwimer.
3655 Johnson Avenue, Bronx, NY 10463 .... (718) 796–9700
Chief of Staff.—William Weitz.
6 Gramatan Avenue, Mt. Vernon, NY 10550 .... (914) 699–4100
261 West Nyack Road, West Nyack, NY 10994 .... (845) 358–7800

Counties: BRONX (part), WESTCHESTER (part). CITIES AND TOWNSHIPS: Parts of Bronx, Yonkers, Mount Vernon, New Rochelle and Pelham. Population (2000), 654,360.

ZIP Codes: 10458, 10463, 10466–71, 10475, 10522, 10533, 10550–53, 10557–58, 10591, 10701, 10704–06, 10708, 10901, 10913, 10920, 10931, 10952, 10954, 10956, 10960, 10962, 10964–65, 10968, 10970, 10974, 10976–77, 10983, 10989, 10994

* * *

EIGHTEENTH DISTRICT

NITA M. LOWEY, Democrat, of Harrison, NY; born in New York, NY, July 5, 1937; education: graduated, Bronx High School of Science, 1955; B.S., Mount Holyoke College, 1959; assistant to Secretary of State for Economic Development and Neighborhood Preservation, and deputy director, Division of Economic Opportunity, 1975–85; Assistant Secretary of State, 1985–87; member: boards of directors, Close-Up Foundation; Effective Parenting Information for Children; Windward School, Downstate (New York Region); Westchester Jewish Conference; Westchester Opportunity Program; National Committee of the Police Corps; Women's Network of the YWCA; Legal Awareness for Women; National Women's Political Caucus of Westchester; American Jewish Committee of Westchester; married: Stephen Lowey, 1961; children: Dana, Jacqueline, and Douglas; elected on November 8, 1988, to the 101st Congress; reelected to each succeeding Congress.

Office Listings

http://www.house.gov/lowey

2329 Rayburn House Office Building, Washington, DC 20515 .... (202) 225–6506
Chief of Staff.—Clare Coleman. FAX: 225–0546
Executive Assistant.—Randy Stokes.
Suite 310, 222 Mamaroneck Avenue, White Plains, NY 10605 .... (914) 428–1707
District Administrator.—Patricia Keegan.

Counties: ROCKLAND (part), WESTCHESTER (part). CITIES AND TOWNSHIPS: Ardsley, Ardsley on the Hundson, Briarcliff Manor; Bronxville, Chappaqua, Congers, Crestwood, Dobbs Ferry, Eastchester, Elmsford, Harrison, Hartsdale, Hasting-on-Hudson, Haverstraw, Hawthorne, Irvington, Larchmont, Mamaroneck, Maryknoll, Millwood, Mt. Kisco, New City, New Rochelle, North Castle, Ossining, Pelham, Pleasantville, Port Chester, Purchase, Rye, Rye Brook, Scarsdale, Sleepy Hollow, Tarrytown, Thornwood, Tuckahoe, Valhalla, Valley Cottage (part), West Harrison, West Haverstraw, White Plains, and Yonkers. Population (2000), 654,360.

ZIP Codes: 10502, 10504, 10506, 10510, 10514, 10522–23, 10528, 10530, 10532–33, 10538, 10543, 10546, 10549, 10562, 10570, 10573, 10577, 10580, 10583, 10591, 10594–95, 10601–07, 10610, 10650, 10701–10, 10801–05, 10920, 10923, 10927, 10956, 10989, 10993–94

* * *

NINETEENTH DISTRICT

SUE W. KELLY, Republican, of Katonah, NY; born in Lima, OH, September 26, 1936; graduated, Lima Central High School; B.A., Denison University, Granville, OH, 1958; M.A., Sarah Lawrence College, Bronxville, NY, 1985; educator; small business owner; patient advocate; rape crisis counselor; community leader; member: League of Women Voters; American Association of University Women; PTA; Bedford Recreation Committee; Bedford Presbyterian Church; married Edward W. Kelly, 1960; four children: Eric, Sean, Charity, and Tim; committees: Transportation and Infrastructure; Small Business; and Financial Services; elected to the 104th Congress; reelected to each succeeding Congress.

Office Listings

http://www.house.gov/suekelly

1127 Longworth House Office Building, Washington, DC 20515 .... (202) 225–5441
Chief of Staff.—Mike Giuliani.
Legislative Director.—Nick Curran.
Press Secretary.—Robert Ostrander.
21 Old Main Street, Room 107, Fishkill, NY 12524 .... (845) 897–5200
District Director.—Jerry Nappi.
255 Main Street, 3rd Floor, Goshen, NY 10924 .... (845) 291–4100

Counties: DUTCHESS COUNTY (part). CITIES AND TOWNSHIPS: Beacon, Castle Point, Chelsea, Dover Plains, Fishkill, Glenham, Holmes, Hopewell Junction, Hughsonville, Pawling, Poughkeepsie, Stormville, Wappingers Falls, Wingdale. ORANGE COUNTY (part). CITIES AND TOWNSHIPS: Amith, Arden, Bear Mountain, Bellvale, Blooming Grove, Burnside, Campbell

Hall, Central Valley, Chester, Cornwall, Cornwall-on-Hudson, Craigville, Cuddebackville, Durlandville, Eagle Valley, Edenville, Finchville, Finnegan's Corner, Firthcliffe, Florida, Fort Montgomery, Gardnerville, Goddefroy, Goshen, Greenwood Lake, Guymard, Harriman, Highland Falls, Highland Mills, Huguenot, Johnson, Kiryas Joel, Little Britain, Little York, Maybrook, Monroe, Montgomery, Mountainville, New Hampton, New Milford, New Vernon, New Windsor, Newburgh, Otisville, Oxford Depot, Phillipsburg, Pine Island, Port Jervis, Ridgebury, Rock Tavern, Salisbury Mills, Slate Hill, Sloatsburg, Southfields, Sparrowbush, Sterling Forest, Stony Ford, Suffern, Sugarloaf, Tuxedo, Tuxedo Park, Unionville, Vails Gate, Wallkill, Warwick, Washingtonville, West Point, Westbrookville, Westtown, Wickham Village. PUTNAM COUNTY. CITIES AND TOWNSHIPS: Baldwin Place, Brewster, Carmel, Cold Spring, Kent, Lake Peekskill, Mahopac, Mahopac Falls, Patterson, Putnam Valley. ROCKLAND COUNTY. CITIES AND TOWNSHIPS: Garnerville, Haverstraw, Pomona, Stony Point, Thiells, Tomkins Cove. WESTCHESTER COUNTY. CITIES AND TOWNSHIPS: Amawalk, Baldwin Place, Bedford, Bedford Hills, Buchanan, Cortlandt Manor, Crompound, Cross River, Croton Falls, Croton-on-Hudson, Golden's Bridge, Jefferson Valley, Katonah, Lincolndale, Mohegan Lake, Montrose, Mt. Kisco, North Salem, Peekskill, Pound Ridge, Purdys, Shenorock, Shrub Oak, Somers, South Salem, Verplanck, Waccabuc, and Yorktown Heights. Population (2000), 654,361.

ZIP Codes: 10501, 10504–07, 10509, 10511–12, 10516–21, 10524, 10526–27, 10530, 10535–37, 10540–42, 10545, 10547–49, 10551, 10558, 10560, 10562, 10566–67, 10571–72, 10576, 10578–79, 10587–90, 10596–98, 10602, 10911, 10916–18, 10921–26, 10928, 10930, 10940–41, 10943, 10950, 10953, 10958, 10963, 10969–70, 10973, 10975, 10979–80, 10984, 10986–87, 10990, 10992, 10996–98, 11518, 11542, 11568, 11572, 11701–02, 11704, 11706–09, 11721, 11724, 11730–31, 11740, 11757, 11768, 11797, 12508, 12510–12, 12518, 12520, 12522, 12524, 12527, 12531, 12533, 12537–38, 12540, 12543, 12549, 12552–53, 12555, 12563–64, 12570, 12575, 12577–78, 12582, 12584, 12590, 12592, 12594, 12601–04, 12729, 12746, 12771, 12780, 12785

* * *

TWENTIETH DISTRICT

JOHN E. SWEENEY, Republican, of Clifton Park, NY; born in Troy, NY, on August 9, 1955; B.A., Russell Sage College, Troy, NY, 1981; J.D., Western New England School of Law, 1990; attorney, New York; New York State Commissioner of Labor, 1995–97; Deputy Secretary to the Governor, 1997–98; children: Kelly, John, and Mary; committees: Appropriations; Select Committee on Homeland Security; subcommittees: Transportation, Treasury, and Independent Agencies; Commerce, Justice, State, and the Judiciary; Homeland Security; Infrastructure and Border Security; Intelligence and Counterterrorism; elected to the 106th Congress; reelected to each succeeding Congress.

Office Listings

http://www.house.gov/sweeney

416 Cannon House Office Building, Washington, DC 20515 .... (202) 225–5614
Chief of Staff.—Martin Torrey. FAX: 225–6234
Press Secretary.—Kevin Madden.
939 Route 146, Suite 430, Clifton Park, NY 12065 .... (518) 371–8839
Senator Charles D. Cook Office Building, 111 Main Street, Delhi, NY 13753 .... (607) 746–9700
560 Warren Street, Room 302, Hudson, NY 12534 .... (518) 828–0181
21 Bay Street, Glens Falls, NY 12801 .... (518) 792–3031

Counties: COLUMBIA, DELAWARE (part), DUTCHESS (part), ESSEX (part), GREENE, RENSSELAER (part), SARATOGA (part), OTSEGO (part), WARREN, and WASHINGTON. Population (2000), 654,360.

ZIP Codes: 12010, 12015, 12017–20, 12022, 12024–25, 12027–29, 12033, 12037, 12040, 12042, 12046, 12050–52, 12057–60, 12062, 12065, 12074–76, 12083, 12086–87, 12089–90, 12093–94, 12106, 12115, 12118, 12123–25, 12130, 12132–34, 12136, 12138, 12140, 12143, 12148, 12151, 12153–56, 12165, 12167–70, 12172–74, 12176, 12180, 12182, 12184–85, 12192, 12195–96, 12198, 12405–07, 12413–14, 12418, 12421–24, 12427, 12430–31, 12434, 12438–39, 12442, 12444, 12450–51, 12454–55, 12459–60, 12463, 12468–70, 12473–74, 12480, 12482, 12485, 12492, 12496, 12501–03, 12507, 12513–14, 12516–17, 12521–23, 12526, 12529, 12533–34, 12538, 12540, 12545–46, 12565, 12567, 12569–72, 12578, 12580–81, 12583, 12585, 12590, 12592, 12594, 12601, 12603, 12776, 12801, 12803–04, 12808–11, 12814–17, 12819–24, 12827–28, 12831–39, 12841, 12843–46, 12848–50, 12853–56, 12859–63, 12865–66, 12870–74, 12878, 12883–87, 12942–43, 12946, 12977, 12983, 13326, 13450, 13488, 13731, 13739–40, 13750, 13752–53, 13755, 13757, 13775, 13782, 13786, 13788, 13804, 13806–07, 13820, 13838, 13842, 13846, 13849, 13856, 13860

* * *

TWENTY-FIRST DISTRICT

MICHAEL R. MCNULTY, Democrat, of Green Island, NY; born in Troy, Rensselaer County, NY, September 16, 1947; education: graduated St. Joseph's Institute, Barrytown, NY, 1965; attended Loyola University, Rome Center, Rome, Italy, 1967–68; B.A., Holy Cross College, Worcester, MA, 1969; attended Hill School of Insurance, New York City, 1970; insurance broker; town supervisor, Green Island, NY, 1969–77; Mayor, village of Green Island, 1977–83; New York State Assembly, 1983–88; member: Albany County Democratic Executive Committee; Green Island Democratic Committee; New York State Democratic Committee; board of directors, Capital Region Technology Development Council; delegate, Democratic National Convention, 1972; married: the former Nancy Ann Lazzaro, 1971; children: Michele, Angela, Nancy, and Maria; elected on November 8, 1988, to the 101st Congress; reelected to each succeeding Congress.

Office Listings

http://www.house.gov/mcnulty

2210 Rayburn House Office Building, Washington, DC 20515 .... (202) 225–5076
Chief of Staff.—David Torian. FAX: 225–5077
Press Secretary.—Michael Wojnar.
Legislative Director.—Jim Glenn.
Leo W. O'Brien Federal Building, Albany, NY 12207 .... (518) 465–0700
U.S. Office, Schenectady, NY 12305 .... (518) 374–4547
33 Second Street, Troy, NY 12180 .... (518) 271–0822
2490 Riverfront Center, Amsterdam, NY 12010 .... (518) 843–3400
233 West Main Street, Room 10, Johnstown, NY 12095 .... (518) 762–3568

Counties: ALBANY, FULTON (part), MONTGOMERY, RENSSELAER (part), SARATOGA (part), SCHOHARIE, and SCHENECTADY. Population (2000), 654,361.

ZIP Codes: 12007–10, 12016, 12019, 12027, 12031, 12033, 12035–36, 12041, 12043, 12045–47, 12053–54, 12056, 12061, 12063–64, 12066–73, 12077–78, 12082–87, 12092–93, 12095, 12107, 12110, 12116, 12120–23, 12128, 12131, 12137, 12141, 12143–44, 12147, 12149–50, 12157–61, 12166–67, 12175, 12177, 12179–83, 12186–89, 12193–94, 12197–98, 12201–12, 12214, 12220, 12222–40, 12242–50, 12252, 12255–57, 12260–61, 12288, 12301–09, 12325, 12345, 12434, 12469, 13317, 13320, 13339, 13410, 13428, 13452, 13459

* * *

TWENTY-SECOND DISTRICT

MAURICE D. HINCHEY, Democrat, of Hurley, NY; born in New York, NY, on October 27, 1938; graduated, Saugerties High School, 1956; B.S., State College, New Paltz, NY, 1968; M.A., State College, New Paltz, 1969; seaman first class, U.S. Navy, 1956–59; teacher; public administrator; elected to the New York State Assembly, 1975–92; member: New York Council of State Governments; National Conference of State Legislatures; three children: Maurice Scott, Josef, and Michelle Rebecca; elected on November 3, 1992 to the 103rd Congress; reelected to each succeeding Congress.

Office Listings

http://www.house.gov/hinchey

2431 Rayburn House Office Building, Washington, DC 20515 .... (202) 225–6335
Chief of Staff.—Wendy Darwell.
Legislative Director.—Dianne Miller.
Press Secretary.—Kevin O'Connell.
291 Wall Street, Kingston, NY 12401 .... (846) 331–4466
100A Federal Building, Binghamton, NY 13901 .... (607) 773–2768
123 S. Cayuga Street, Suite 201, Ithaca, NY 14850 .... (607) 273–1388

Counties: BROOME COUNTY (part); CITIES AND TOWNS OF: Binghamton, Conklin, Kirkwood, Sanford, Union (includes villages of Endicott and Johnson City), Vestal, and Windsor. DELAWARE COUNTY (part); TOWNS OF: Deposit, Hancock, and Tompkins. DUTCHESS COUNTY (part). CITIES: Poughkeepsie. ORANGE COUNTY (part); CITIES AND TOWNS OF: Crawford, Middletown, Montgomery (includes village of Walden), Newburgh, and Wallkill (part). SULLIVAN COUNTY; CITIES AND TOWNS OF: Bethel, Callicoon, Cochecton, Delaware, Fallsburg, Forestburgh, Fremont, Highland, Liberty, Lumberland, Mamakating, Neversink, Rockland, Thompson, and Tusten. TIOGA COUNTY (part). CITIES AND TOWNS: Barton, Nichols, Owego (part), and Spencer. TOMPKINS COUNTY (part). CITIES AND TOWNS: Danby, and Ithaca. ULSTER COUNTY. CITIES AND TOWNS: Denning, Esopus, Gardiner, Hardenburgh, Hurley, Kingston, Lloyd, Marbletown, Marlborough, New Paltz, Olive, Plattekill, Rochester, Rosendale, Saugerties, Shandaken, Shawangunk, Ulster, Wawarsing (includes village of Ellenville), and Woodstock. Population (2000), 654,361.

ZIP Codes: 10915, 10919, 10932, 10940–41, 10985, 12401–02, 12404, 12406, 12409–12, 12416, 12419–20, 12428–29, 12432–33, 12435–36, 12440–41, 12443, 12446, 12448–49, 12451–53, 12455–58, 12461, 12464–66, 12469, 12471–72, 12475, 12477, 12480–81, 12483–84, 12486–87, 12489–91, 12493–95, 12498, 12504, 12506, 12515, 12525, 12528, 12530, 12541–44, 12547–51, 12561, 12566, 12568, 12574–75, 12583, 12586, 12588–89, 12601, 12603, 12701, 12719–27, 12729, 12732–34, 12736–38, 12740–43, 12745, 12747–52, 12754, 12758–60, 12762–70, 12775–84, 12786–92, 12814, 12853, 12857–58, 12879, 12883, 12928, 12983, 13068, 13501, 13730, 13732, 13734, 13737, 13743, 13748–49, 13754, 13756, 13760, 13774, 13783, 13790, 13795, 13811–13, 13820, 13826, 13850, 13856, 13864–65, 13901–05, 14817, 14850–51, 14853, 14859, 14867, 14883, 14889, 14892

* * *

TWENTY-THIRD DISTRICT

JOHN M. MCHUGH, Republican, of Pierrepoint Manor, NY; born in Watertown, NY, on September 29, 1948; education: graduated from Watertown High School, 1966; B.A., Utica College of Syracuse University; M.A., Nelson A. Rockefeller Graduate School of Public Affairs; assistant to the city manager, Watertown; liaison with local governments for New York State

Senator H. Douglas Barclay; New York State Senate, 1984–92; committees: Government Reform; Armed Services; International Relations; subcommitees: chairman, Total Force; chairman, Special Panel on Postal Reform and Oversight; Readiness; Criminal Justice, Drug Policy and Human Resources; Energy Policy, Natural Resources and Regulatory Affairs; Middle East and Central Asia; co-chairman, Army Caucus; elected on November 3, 1992, to the 103rd Congress; reelected to each succeeding Congress.

Office Listings

http://www.house.gov/mchugh

2333 Rayburn House Office Building, Washington, DC 20515 .... (202) 225–4611
Chief of Staff.—Robert Taub.
Administrative Secretary.—Donna M. Bell.
205 South Peterboro Street, Canastota, NY 13032 .... (315) 697–2063
28 North School Street, P.O. Box 800, Mayfield, NY 12117 .... (518) 661–6486
104 Federal Building, Plattsburgh, NY 12901 .... (518) 563–1406
120 Washington Street, Suite 200, Watertown, NY 13601 .... (315) 782–3150

Counties: CLINTON, ESSEX (part), FRANKLIN, FULTON (part), HAMILTON, JEFFERSON, LEWIS, MADISON, ONEIDA (part), OSWEGO, ST. LAWRENCE. Population (2000), 654,361.

ZIP Codes: 12010, 12023, 12025, 12032, 12036, 12070, 12078, 12086, 12095, 12108, 12117, 12134, 12139, 12164, 12167, 12190, 12812, 12842, 12847, 12851–52, 12857, 12864, 12883, 12901, 12903, 12910–24, 12926–30, 12932–37, 12939, 12941, 12944–46, 12949–50, 12952–53, 12955–62, 12964–67, 12969–70, 12972–76, 12978–81, 12983, 12985–87, 12989, 12992–93, 12996–98, 13028, 13030, 13032–33, 13035–37, 13042–44, 13052, 13061, 13064, 13069, 13072, 13074, 13076, 13082–83, 13093, 13103–04, 13107, 13111, 13114–15, 13121–23, 13126, 13131–32, 13134–36, 13142, 13144–45, 13156, 13158, 13163, 13167, 13301–04, 13308–10, 13313–16, 13318–19, 13321–23, 13325–29, 13332–35, 13337–43, 13345–46, 13348, 13350, 13352, 13354–55, 13357, 13360–65, 13367–68, 13401–03, 13406–11, 13413, 13415, 13417–18, 13421, 13424–25, 13428, 13431, 13433, 13435–41, 13449–50, 13452, 13455–57, 13460–61, 13465, 13468–69, 13471, 13473, 13475, 13477–80, 13482–86, 13488–95, 13501–05, 13599, 13601–03, 13605–08, 13611–28, 13630–43, 13645–52, 13654–62, 13664–85, 13687–88, 13690–97, 13699

* * *

TWENTY-FOURTH DISTRICT

SHERWOOD BOEHLERT, Republican, of New Hartford, NY; born in Utica, NY, on September 28, 1936; education: graduated from Whitesboro Central High School; Utica College, B.A., 1961; military service: served in the U.S. Army, 1956–58; employment: 1961–64, manager of Public Relations, Wyandotte Chemicals Corporation; 1964–72, chief of staff for Congressman Alexander Pirnie; 1973–79, chief of staff for Congressman Donald J. Mitchell; elected 1979, Oneida County Executive; member: board of directors, Utica College Foundation; St. John the Evangelist Church, New Hartford; numerous awards including honorary doctoral degrees from Syracuse University, Colgate University and Cazenovia College; married: the former Marianne Willey; four children; committees: chairman, Science; Transportation and Infrastructure; House Permanent Select Committee on Intelligence; elected on November 2, 1982 to the 98th Congress; reelected to each succeeding Congress.

Office Listings

http://www.house.gov/boehlert

2246 Rayburn House Office Building, Washington, DC 20515 .... (202) 225–3665
Chief of Staff.—Dean D'Amore.
Executive Assistant.—John Konkus.
Alexander Pirnie Federal Office Building, Room 200, 10 Broad Street, Utica, NY 13501 .... (315) 793–8146
District Director.—Jeanne Donalty.

Counties: BROOME (part), CAYUGA (part), CHENANGO, CORTLAND, HERKIMER (part), ONEIDA (part), ONTARIO (part), OTSEGO (part), SENECA, TIOGA (part), TOMPKINS (part). Population (2000), 654,361.

ZIP Codes: 13021–22, 13024, 13026, 13032–34, 13040, 13042, 13045, 13052–54, 13056, 13062, 13065, 13068, 13071–74, 13077, 13080–81, 13083, 13087, 13092, 13101–02, 13117–18, 13124, 13136, 13139–41, 13147–48, 13152, 13155, 13157–60, 13162, 13165–66, 13302–05, 13308–09, 13312, 13315, 13317–20, 13322–29, 13331–33, 13335, 13337–40, 13342–43, 13345, 13348, 13350, 13353–54, 13357, 13360–61, 13363, 13365, 13367–68, 13403–04, 13406–07, 13411, 13413, 13415–17, 13420–21, 13424–26, 13431, 13433, 13436–42, 13452, 13454, 13456, 13460–61, 13464, 13468–73, 13475–78, 13480, 13485–86, 13489–93, 13495, 13501–02, 13601, 13603, 13605–08, 13611–26, 13628, 13630, 13632–43, 13645–52, 13654–56, 13658–62, 13664–69, 13672–85, 13687, 13690–97, 13699, 13730, 13733–34, 13736, 13738, 13743–47, 13752–54, 13758, 13760, 13776–78, 13780, 13784, 13787, 13790, 13794, 13796–97, 13801–03, 13807–11, 13813–15, 13820, 13825–27, 13830, 13832–33, 13835, 13838, 13840–41, 13843–45, 13848–49, 13856, 13859, 13861–64, 14433, 14443, 14456, 14468–69, 14489, 14504, 14521, 14532, 14541, 14548, 14571, 14588, 14817, 14841, 14847, 14850–52, 14854, 14860, 14867, 14881–83, 14886

TWENTY-FIFTH DISTRICT

JAMES T. WALSH, Republican, of Syracuse, NY; born in Syracuse, June 19, 1947, son of U.S. Representative William F. Walsh; education: B.A., St. Bonaventure University, Olean, NY, 1970; employment: marketing executive; president, Syracuse Common Council; member: Syracuse Board of Estimates; board of trustees of Erie Canal Museum; advisory council of the Catholic Schools Drug-Free Schools and Communities Consortium; Valley Men's Club; South Side Businessmen's Club; Nine Mile Republican Club; Onondaga Anglers Association; Oneida Lake Association; Otisco Lake Association; married: the former Diane Elizabeth Ryan, 1974; children: James (Jed), Benjamin, and Maureen; elected on November 8, 1988, to the 101st Congress; reelected to each succeeding Congress.

Office Listings

http://www.house.gov/walsh

2369 Rayburn House Office Building, Washington, DC 20515 .... (202) 225–3701
Chief of Staff.—Art Jutton. FAX: 225–4042
Scheduler.—Jodi Major.
Legislative Assistant.—Martha Carmen.
P.O. Box 7306, Syracuse, NY 13261 .... (315) 423–5657
District Representative.—Virginia Carmody.
1180 Canandaigua Road, Palmyra, NY 14522 .... (315) 597–6138

Counties: CAYUGA (part), MONROE (part), ONONDAGA, and WAYNE. CITIES AND TOWNSHIPS: Arcadia, Butler, Camillus, Cato, Cicero, Clay, Conquest (part), DeWitt, Elbridge, Fabius, Galen, Geddes, Huron, Ira, Irondequoit (part), LaFayette, Lyons, Lysander, Macedon, Manlius, Marcellus, Marion, Onondaga, Ontario, Otisco, Palmyra, Penfield (part), Pompey, Rose, Salina, Savannah, Skaneateles, Sodus, Spafford, Sterling, Syracuse, Tully, Van Buren, Victory, Walworth, Webster, Williamson, and Wolcott. Population (2000), 654,361.

ZIP Codes: 13020–21, 13027, 13029–31, 13033, 13035, 13037, 13039–41, 13051–53, 13057, 13060, 13063–64, 13066, 13068–69, 13077–78, 13080, 13082, 13084, 13088, 13090, 13104, 13108, 13110–13, 13116–17, 13119–20, 13122, 13126, 13135, 13137–38, 13140–41, 13143, 13146, 13148, 13152–54, 13156, 13159, 13164–66, 13201–12, 13214–15, 13217–21, 13224–25, 13235, 13244, 13250–52, 13261, 13290, 14413, 14432–33, 14449–50, 14489, 14502, 14505, 14513, 14516, 14519–20, 14522, 14526, 14537–38, 14542, 14551, 14555, 14563–64, 14568, 14580, 14589–90, 14609, 14617, 14621–22, 14625

* * *

TWENTY-SIXTH DISTRICT

THOMAS M. REYNOLDS, Republican, of Springville, NY; born in Springville, NY, on September 3, 1950; attended Kent State University; Erie County legislator, 1982–88; New York State Assembly, 1988–98; former director, Better Business Bureau; Cooperative Extension and Central Referral Service; member: House Administration and Rules Committees; he and his wife, Donna, are the parents of four children; elected to the 106th Congress; reelected to each succeeding Congress.

Office Listings

http://www.house.gov/reynolds

332 Cannon House Office Building, Washington, DC 20515 .... (202) 225–5265
Chief of Staff.—Michael Brady. FAX: 225–5910
Executive Assistant.—Karen Kaumeier.
Legislative Director.—John Willis.
500 Essjay Road, Suite 260, Williamsville, NY 14221 .... (716) 634–2324
1577 Ridge Road West, Rochester, NY 14615 .... (585) 663–5570

Counties: ERIE (part), GENESEE, LIVINGSTON, MONROE (part), NIAGARA (part), ORLEANS (part), WYOMING. Population (2000), 654,361.

ZIP Codes: 14001, 14004–05, 14008–09, 14011–13, 14020–21, 14024, 14026, 14030–32, 14036, 14038–39, 14043, 14051, 14054, 14056, 14058–59, 14066–68, 14082–83, 14086, 14094–95, 14098, 14103, 14105, 14113, 14120, 14125, 14130–32, 14139, 14143, 14145, 14167, 14215, 14221, 14224–26, 14228, 14231, 14260, 14304, 14410–11, 14414, 14416, 14420, 14422–23, 14427–30, 14435, 14437, 14452, 14454, 14462, 14464, 14466, 14468, 14470–72, 14476–77, 14479–82, 14485–88, 14510–12, 14514–15, 14517, 14525, 14530, 14533, 14536, 14539, 14545–46, 14549–50, 14556–60, 14569, 14571–72, 14591–92, 14606, 14612, 14615–16, 14624, 14626, 14822, 14836, 14846

* * *

TWENTY-SEVENTH DISTRICT

JACK QUINN, Republican, of Hamburg, NY; born on April 13, 1951, in Buffalo, NY; education: B.A., Siena College, Loudonville, NY, 1973; M.A., State University of New York, Buffalo, 1978; teacher; councilman, Hamburg, 1982–84; town supervisor, Hamburg, 1985–92;

founder, DARE, 1984; married: the former Mary Beth McAndrews, 1974; children: Jack III, and Kara Elizabeth; elected on November 3, 1992, to the 103rd Congress; reelected to each succeeding Congress.

Office Listings

http://www.house.gov/quinn

2448 Rayburn House Office Building, Washington, DC 20515 .... (202) 225–3306
Legislative Director.—Beth Thompson. FAX: 226–0347
Senior Legislative Assistant.—Steve Stallmer.
Communication Director.—Mike Tetuan.
Legislative Correspondent.—C.W. Estoff.
Brisbane Building, 403 Main Street, Suite 240, Buffalo, NY 14203–2199 .... (716) 845–5257
Chief of Staff.—Mary Lou Palmer.

Counties: CHAUTAUQUA, ERIE (part). CITIES AND TOWNSHIPS: Boston, Brant, Buffalo (part), Cheektowaga, Colden, Concord, Collins, East Aurora, Eden, Elma, Evans, Hamburg, Holland, Lackawanna, North Boston, North Collins, Orchard Park, Sardinia, and Seneca. Population (2000), 654,361.

ZIP Codes: 14004, 14006, 14010, 14025–27, 14030, 14033–35, 14037, 14040, 14043, 14047–48, 14052, 14055, 14057, 14059, 14061–63, 14069–70, 14075, 14080–81, 14085–86, 14091, 14102, 14110–12, 14127, 14134–36, 14138–41, 14145, 14166, 14169–70, 14201–03, 14206–16, 14218–22, 14224–27, 14233, 14240–41, 14264–65, 14267, 14269, 14272, 14276, 14280, 14504, 14701–04, 14710, 14712, 14716, 14718, 14720, 14722–24, 14726, 14728, 14732–33, 14736, 14738, 14740, 14742, 14747, 14750, 14752, 14756–58, 14767, 14769, 14775, 14781–82, 14784–85, 14787

* * *

TWENTY-EIGHTH DISTRICT

LOUISE MCINTOSH SLAUGHTER, Democrat, of Fairport, NY; born in Harlan County, KY, August 14, 1929; graduated from University of Kentucky with a B.S. in bacteriology; master's degree in public health; elected to Monroe County legislature, two terms, 1976–79; elected to New York State Assembly, two terms, 1982–86; Distinguished Public Health Legislation Award, American Public Health Association, 1998; married to Robert Slaughter; three daughters; four grandchildren; minority whip at large; committees: Rules; Select Committee on Homeland Security; elected to the 100th Congress on November 4, 1986; reelected to each succeeding Congress.

Office Listings

http://www.house.gov/slaughter

2469 Rayburn House Office Building, Washington, DC 20515 .... (202) 225–3615
Chief of Staff.—Cynthia Pellegrini.
Legislative Director.—Sally Schaeffer.
Communications Director.—Megan Thompson.
3120 Federal Building, 100 State Street, Rochester, NY 14614 .... (716) 232–4850
465 Main Street, Suite 105, Buffalo, NY 14203 .... (716) 853–5813
1910 Pine Avenue, Niagara Falls, NY 14301 .... (716) 282–1274

Counties: Erie (part), Monroe (part), Niagara (part), Orleans (part). CITIES AND TOWNSHIPS: Appleton, Barker, Brighton, Buffalo, Burt, East Rochester, Fairport, Grand Island, Greece, Hamlin, Hilton, Irondequoit, Kendall, Kent, Lewiston, Lyndonville, Model City, Morton, Newfane, Niagara Falls, Olcott, Penfield, Perinton, Ransomville, Rochester, Sanborn, Stella Niagara, Tonawanda, Waterport, Wilson and Youngstown. Population (2000), 654,361.

ZIP Codes: 14008, 14012, 14028, 14067, 14072, 14092, 14094, 14098, 14107–09, 14126, 14131–32, 14144, 14150–51, 14172, 14174, 14202–03, 14205–12, 14214–15, 14217, 14222–23, 14225–26, 14263, 14270, 14273, 14301–05, 14411, 14420, 14445, 14450, 14464, 14468, 14470, 14476–77, 14508, 14526, 14534, 14571, 14602–25, 14627, 14638–39, 14642–47, 14649–53, 14660, 14664, 14673

* * *

TWENTY-NINTH DISTRICT

AMO HOUGHTON, Republican, of Corning, NY; born in Corning on August 7, 1926; grandson of former Congressman Alanson B. Houghton of New York; graduated, St. Paul's School, Concord, NH; B.A., Harvard University, Cambridge, MA, 1950; M.A., Harvard Business School, 1952; honorary doctoral degrees: Alfred University, NY, 1963; Albion College, MI, 1964; Centre College, Danville, KY, 1966; Clarkson College of Technology, Potsdam, NY, 1968; Elmira College, NY, 1982; Hartwick College, Oneonta, NY, 1983; Houghton College, NY, 1983; St. Bonaventure University, NY, 1987; Hobart and William Smith College, 1991; honorary degrees: SUNY, Fredonia, NY, 2000; served in the U.S. Marine Corps, 1945–46; executive officer, Corning Glass Works, Corning, NY, 1951–86; member: Grace Commission;

Business Council of New York State; Business Advisory Commission for Governor of New York; Labor-Industry Coalition for International Trade; Corning Chamber of Commerce; Corning Rotary Club; Corning Elk's Club; trustee, Brookings Institution; committees: International Relations; Ways and Means; subcommittees: Africa; Trade; chairman, Oversight; married to Priscilla Dewey Houghton; elected to the 100th Congress on November 4, 1986; reelected to each succeeding Congress.

Office Listings

http://houghton.house.gov

1111 Longworth House Office Building, Washington, DC 20515 .... (202) 225–3161
Staff Director.—William (Mac) McKenney. FAX: 225–5574
Office Manager.—Bonnie Matles.
Legislative Director.—Robert Van Wicklin.
32 Denison Parkway West, Corning, NY 14830 .... (607) 937–3333
20 Pleasant Street, Canandaigua, NY 14424 .... (585) 394–0220

Counties: ALLEGANY, CATTARAUGUS, CHEMUNG, MONROE (part), ONTARIO (part), SCHUYLER, STEUBEN, YATES. Population (2000), 654,361.

ZIP Codes: 14009, 14024, 14029–30, 14041–42, 14060, 14065, 14070, 14081, 14101, 14129, 14133, 14138, 14141, 14168, 14171, 14173, 14414–15, 14418, 14423–25, 14428, 14432, 14437, 14441, 14445, 14450, 14453, 14456, 14461, 14463, 14466–67, 14469, 14471–72, 14475, 14478, 14482, 14485, 14487, 14489, 14502, 14504, 14506–07, 14512–14, 14518, 14522, 14526–27, 14529, 14532, 14534, 14536, 14543–44, 14546–48, 14559–61, 14564, 14572, 14585–86, 14606, 14610, 14618, 14620, 14623–25, 14706–09, 14711, 14714–15, 14717, 14719, 14721, 14726–27, 14729–31, 14735, 14737–39, 14741, 14743–45, 14747–48, 14751, 14753–55, 14760, 14766, 14770, 14772, 14774, 14777–79, 14783, 14786, 14788, 14801–10, 14812–16, 14818–27, 14830–31, 14836–46, 14855–59, 14861, 14863–65, 14867, 14869–74, 14876–80, 14884–87, 14889, 14891–95, 14897–98, 14901–05, 14925

NORTH CAROLINA

(Population 2000, 8,049,313)

SENATORS

JOHN EDWARDS, Democrat, of Raleigh, NC; born in Seneca, SC, on June 10, 1953; education: graduated from North Moore High School, Robbins, NC, 1971; B.S., North Carolina State University, 1974; J.D., University of North Carolina at Chapel Hill, 1977; employment: attorney; religion: Methodist; married: Elizabeth; children: Kate, Emma Claire and Jack; committees: Health, Education, Labor and Pensions; Judiciary; Small Business and Entrepreneurship; Select Committee on Intelligence; elected to the U.S. Senate on November 3, 1998.

Office Listings

http://edwards.senate.gov

225 Dirksen Senate Office Building, Washington, DC 20510 .... (202) 224–3154
Chief of Staff.—Miles Lackey. FAX: 228–1374
Scheduler.—Alexis Bar.
Press Secretary.—Michael Briggs.
Legislative Director.—Robert Gordon.
301 Century Post Office Building, 300 Fayetteville St. Mall, Raleigh, NC 27601 .... (919) 856–4245
State Director.—Brad Thompson.
Federal Courthouse, Suite 219, 401 West Trade Street, Charlotte, NC 28202 .... (704) 344–6154
125 South Elm Street, Suite 401, Greensboro, NC 27401 .... (336) 333–5311
Federal Office Building, Suite 200, 151 Patton Avenue, Asheville, NC 28801 .... (828) 285–0760
401 West First Street, Suite 1–C, Greenville, NC 27835 .... (252) 931–1111

* * *

ELIZABETH H. DOLE, Republican, of North Carolina; born on July 29, 1936, in Salisbury, NC; education: B.A., Duke University, 1958; M.A., Harvard University, 1960; J.D., Harvard University, 1965; Phi Beta Kappa; public service: Deputy Assistant to President Nixon for Consumer Affairs, 1971–73; member, Federal Trade Commission, 1973–79; Assistant to President Reagan for Public Liaison, 1981–83; Secretary of Transportation, 1983–87, under President Reagan; Secretary of Labor, 1989–91, under President George H.W. Bush; President, American Red Cross, 1991–99; awards: National Safety Council's Distinguished Service Award; National Commission Against Drunk Driving Humanitarian Award; Women Executives in State Government Lifetime Achievement Award; North Carolina Award; National Religious Broadcasters' Board of Directors Award; League of Women Voters Leadership Award; organizations: Duke University Board of Trustees, 1974–85; Harvard University Board of Overseers, 1990–96; married to former Senator Bob Dole (R–KS); elected to the U.S. Senate on November 5, 2002.

Office Listings

htttp://dole.senate.gov

120 Russell Senate Office Building, Washington, DC 20510 .... (202) 224–6342
Chief of Staff.—Frank Hill. FAX: 224–1100
Legislative Counsel / Policy Director.—Scott Quesenberry.
Communications Director.—Mary Brown Brewer.
310 New Bern Avenue, Suite 122, Raleigh NC 27601 .... (919) 856–4630
225 North Main Street, Suite 404, Salisbury, NC 28144 .... (704) 633–5011

REPRESENTATIVES

FIRST DISTRICT

FRANK W. BALLANCE, Jr., Democrat, of Warrenton, NC; born on February 15, 1942, in Windsor, NC; education: B.A., North Carolina Central University, 1963; law degree, North Carolina Central University, 1965; profession: Attorney; military service: North Carolina National Guard, 1968–1971; public service: North Carolina House of Representatives, 1982–1986; North Carolina State Senate, 1988–2002; religion: Baptist; family: married to Bernadine Smallwood Ballance, 1969; children: Garey, Angela, and Valerie; elected to the 108th Congress on November 5, 2002.

Office Listings

http://www.house.gov/ballance

413 Cannon House Office Building, Washington, DC 20515 .... (202) 225–3101
Chief of Staff.—Corliss James.
Senior Legislative Assistant.—Dana Hopings.
Executive Assistant.—Darnise Pearson.
415 East Boulevard, Suite 100, Williamston, NC 27892 .... (252) 789–4939
Warren Corners Shopping Center, Unit 7, P.O. Box 280, Norlina, NC 27563 .... (252) 456–3091

Counties: BEAUFORT (part), BERTIE, CHOWAN, CRAVEN (part), EDGECOMBE, GATES, GRANVILLE VANCE (part), GREENE, HALIFAX, HARTFORD, JONES (part), MARTIN, NORTHAMPTON, PASQUOTANK, PERQUIMANS, PITT (part), WARREN, WASHINGTON, WAYNE (part), WILSON (part). Population (2000), 619,178.

ZIP Codes: 27507, 27530–31, 27533–34, 27536–37, 27551, 27553, 27556, 27563, 27565, 27570, 27584, 27586, 27589, 27594, 27801, 27803–06, 27809, 27811–14, 27817–23, 27825, 27827–29, 27831–35, 27837, 27839–47, 27849–50, 27852–55, 27857–58, 27860–64, 27866–67, 27869–74, 27876–77, 27879, 27881, 27883–84, 27886–95, 27897, 27906–07, 27909–10, 27919, 27922, 27924, 27926, 27928, 27930, 27932, 27935, 27937–38, 27942, 27944, 27946, 27957, 27962, 27967, 27969–70, 27979–80, 27983, 27985–86, 28216, 28226, 28502–04, 28513, 28523, 28526, 28530, 28538, 28551, 28554–55, 28560–63, 28573, 28580, 28585–86, 28590

* * *

SECOND DISTRICT

BOB ETHERIDGE, Democrat, of Lillington, NC; born in Sampson County, NC, August 7, 1941; B.S., business administration, 1965, Campbell University, NC; graduate studies in economics, North Carolina State University, 1967; U.S. Army, 1965–67; businessman, bank director, licensed realtor; North Carolina General Assembly, 1978–88; North Carolina Superintendent of Public Instruction, 1988–96; Harnett County commissioner, 1972–76, serving as chairman of the board in 1974–76; past member: National Council of Chief State School Officers; Governor's Executive Cabinet; advisory board, Mathematics / Science Education Network; Board of the North Carolina Council on Economic Education; board of trustees, North Carolina Symphony; board of trustees, University of North Carolina Center for Public Television; Harnett County Mental Health Board; North Carolina Law and Order Commission; member and past president, Occoneechee Boy Scout Council; received Lillington Jaycees Distinguished Service Award and Lillington Community Service Award; elder, Presbyterian Church; married the former Faye Cameron in 1965; three children: Brian, Catherine, and David; committees: Agriculture; Select Committee on Homeland Security; elected to the 105th Congress; reelected to each succeeding Congress.

Office Listings

http://www.house.gov/etheridge

1533 Longworth House Office Building, Washington, DC 20515 .... (202) 225–4531
Chief of Staff.—Julie Dwyer. FAX: 225–5662
Legislative Director.—Pat Devlin.
Press Secretary.—Sara Yawn.
Executive Assistant.—Anedra M. Woods.
225 Hillsborough Street, Suite 490, Raleigh, NC 27603 .... (919) 829–9122
609 First Street, Lillington, NC 27564 .... (910) 814–0335

Counties: CHATHAM, CUMBERLAND, FRANKLIN, HARNETT, JOHNSTON, LEE, NASH, SAMPSON (part), VANCE, WAKE (part), WILSON (part). Population (2000), 619,178.

ZIP Codes: 27207–08, 27213, 27237, 27252, 27256, 27298, 27312, 27325, 27330–32, 27344, 27349, 27355, 27405, 27501, 27504–06, 27508, 27520–21, 27524–26, 27529, 27536–37, 27540, 27542–44, 27546, 27549, 27552, 27555, 27557, 27559, 27562, 27564, 27568–70, 27576–77, 27589, 27591–93, 27596–97, 27601–03, 27605–07, 27610, 27614, 27625, 27698, 27801–04, 27807, 27809, 27816, 27822, 27829, 27850, 27856, 27863, 27878, 27880, 27882, 27891, 27893–94, 27896, 28301, 28303, 28307–08, 28310–11, 28314, 28323, 28326, 28328, 28334–35, 28339, 28341, 28355–56, 28365–66, 28368, 28382, 28385, 28390, 28393, 28441, 28444, 28447, 28453, 28458, 28466, 28478

* * *

THIRD DISTRICT

WALTER B. JONES, Republican, of Farmville, NC; born in Farmville, February 10, 1943; education: graduated Hargrave Military Academy, Chatham, VA, 1961; B.A., Atlantic Christian College, Wilson, NC, 1966; served in North Carolina National Guard; self-employed, sales; member: North Carolina House of Representatives, 1983–92; married: Joe Anne Whitehurst

Jones; one child, Ashley Elizabeth Jones Scarborough; committees: Armed Services; Financial Services; Resources; elected to the 104th Congress; reelected to each succeeding Congress.

Office Listings

422 Cannon House Office Building, Washington, DC 20515 .... (202) 225–3415
Chief of Staff.—Glen Downs. FAX: 225–3286
Office Manager.—Emily Chapman.
Press Secretary.—Lanier Swann.
1105 C Corporate Drive, Greenville, NC 27858 .... (252) 931–1003
District Office Manager.—Millicent A. Lilley.

Counties: BEAUFORT (part), CAMDEN, CARTERET, CRAVEN (part), CURRITUCK, DARE, DUPLIN (part), HYDE, JONES (part), LENOIR (part), MARTIN (part), ONSLOW (part), PAMLICO, PASQUOTANK (part), PENDER (part), PITT (part), SAMPSON, TYRRELL and WAYNE (part). CITIES: Atlantic Beach, Ayden (part), Beaufort, Belhaven, Burgaw, Clinton, Elizabeth City (part), Emerald Isle, Fremont, Goldsboro, Greenville (part), Havelock, Jacksonville (part), Kill Devil Hills, Kinston (part), Kitty Hawk, Morehead City, Mount Olive, Nags Head, New Bern (part), Newport, River Bend, Trent Woods, Wallace (part), Washington (part) and Winterville. Population (2000), 619,178.

ZIP Codes: 27530–32, 27534, 27542, 27557, 27569, 27803–04, 27807–10, 27814, 27817, 27822, 27824, 27826, 27828–30, 27834, 27836–37, 27851–52, 27856, 27858, 27860, 27863, 27865, 27868, 27871, 27875, 27879, 27880, 27882–83, 27885, 27888–89, 27892–93, 27896, 27909, 27915–17, 27920–21, 27923, 27925, 27927–29, 27936, 27939, 27941, 27943, 27947–50, 27953–54, 27956, 27958–60, 27962, 27964–66, 27968, 27972–74, 27976, 27978, 27981–82, 28333, 28341, 28445, 28454, 28460, 28501, 28504, 28508–13, 28515–16, 28518–22, 28524–29, 28531–33, 28537, 28539–47, 28551–53, 28555–57, 28560, 28562, 28564, 28570–72, 28574–75, 28577–87, 28589–90, 28594

* * *

FOURTH DISTRICT

DAVID E. PRICE, Democrat, of Chapel Hill, NC; born in Erwin, TN, August 17, 1940; education: B.A., Morehead Scholar, University of North Carolina; Bachelor of Divinity, 1964, and Ph.D., political science, 1969, Yale University; professor of political science and public policy, Duke University; author of four books on Congress and the American political system; served North Carolina's Fourth District in the U.S. House of Representatives, 1987–94; in the 102nd Congress, wrote and pushed to passage the Scientific and Advanced Technology Bill and sponsored the Home Ownership Assistance Act; past chairman and executive director, North Carolina Democratic Party; Hubert Humphrey Public Service Award, American Political Science Association, 1990; member, North Carolina's Transit 2001 Commission; past chairman of the board and Sunday School teacher, Binkley Memorial Baptist Church; married: Lisa Price; children: Karen and Michael; committees: Appropriations; subcommittees: Homeland Security; Legislative; VA-HUD; elected to the 100th–103rd Congresses; elected to the 105th Congress; reelected to each succeeding Congress.

Office Listings

http://www.house.gov/price

2162 Rayburn House Office Building, Washington, DC 20515 .... (202) 225–1784
Chief of Staff.—Jean-Louise Beard. FAX: 225–2014
Legislative Director: Darek Newby.
Special Assistant.—Catherine Liao.
Systems Manager.—Jenny Chang.
5400 Trinity Place, Suite 205, Raleigh, NC 27607 .... (919) 859–5999
District Director.—Rose Auman.
88 Vilcom Circle, Suite 140, Chapel Hill, NC 27514 .... (919) 967–7924
411 W. Chapel Hill Street, Durham, NC 27701 .... (919) 688–3004

Counties: CHATHAM (part), DURHAM, ORANGE, WAKE (part). Population (2000), 619,178.

ZIP Codes: 27228, 27231, 27243, 27278, 27302, 27312, 27330, 27501–03, 27510–17, 27519, 27523, 27526, 27529, 27539–41, 27560, 27562, 27572, 27583, 27592, 27599, 27603, 27606–07, 27610, 27612–15, 27617, 27623–24, 27656, 27675–76, 27690, 27695, 27699, 27701–05, 27707–13, 27715, 27717, 27722

* * *

FIFTH DISTRICT

RICHARD BURR, Republican, of Winston-Salem, NC; born in Charlottesville, VA on November 30, 1955; education: graduated Reynolds High School, Winston-Salem, NC, 1974; B.A., Communications, Wake Forest University, Winston-Salem, NC, 1978; sales manager, Carswell Distributing; member: Reynolds Rotary Club; committees: vice chairman, Energy and Commerce; Select Committee on Intelligence; married: Brooke Fauth Burr, 1984; children: two; elected to the 104th Congress; reelected to each succeeding Congress.

Office Listings

http://www.house.gov/burr richard.burrnc05@mail.house.gov

1526 Longworth House Office Building, Washington, DC 20515 .... (202) 225–2071
Chief of Staff.—John Versaggi. FAX: 225–2995
Policy Director.—Chris Joyner.
Special Projects / Communications Director.—Kimrey Rhinehardt
Legislative Assistants: Jenny Hansen, Brian Vanderbloemen, Sam White.
2000 West First Street, Piedmont Plaza Two, Room 508, Winston-Salem, NC 27104 .... (336) 631–5125
District Staff Director.—Dean Myers.

Counties: ALEXANDER COUNTY. CITIES: Bethlehem, Hiddenite, Stony Point, Taylorsville. ALLEGANY COUNTY. CITIES: Ennice, Glade Valley, Laurel Springs, Sparta. ASHE COUNTY. CITIES: Crumpler, Glendale Springs, Grassy Creek, Jefferson, Lansing, Scottville, Todd, Warrensville, West Jefferson. DAVIE COUNTY. CITIES: Advance, Cooleemee, Mocksville. FORSYTH COUNTY (part). CITIES: Bethania, Clemmons, Kernersville, King, Lewisville, Pfafftown, Rural Hall, Tobaccoville, Walkertown, Winston-Salem. IREDELL COUNTY (part). CITIES: Harmony, Love Valley, Mooresville, Olin, Statesville, Turnersburg, Troutman. ROCKINGHAM COUNTY (part). CITIES: Madison, Stokesdale. STOKES COUNTY. CITIES: Danbury, Germanton, Lawsonville, King, Pine Hall, Pinnacle, Sandy Ridge, and Walnut Cove. SURRY COUNTY. CITIES: Ararat, Dobson, Elkin, Flat Rock, Mount Airy, Pilot Mountain, Siloam, Toast, Westfield, White Plains. WATAUGA COUNTY. CITIES: Beech Mountain, Blowing Rock, Boone, Deep Gap, Seven Devils, Sugar Grove, Triplett, Vilas, Zionville. WILKES COUNTY. CITIES: Boomer, Cricket, Hays, Fairplains, Ferguson, Millers Creek, Moravian Falls, Mulberry, N. Wilkesboro, Oiln, Pleasant Hill, Roaring River, Ronda, Thurmond, Traphill, Wilkesboro. YADKIN COUNTY. CITIES: Arlington, Booneville, East Bend, Hamptonville, Jonesville, Turnersburg, and Yadkinville. Population (2000), 619,178.

ZIP Codes: 27006–07, 27009–14, 27016–25, 27028, 27030, 27040–43, 27045–47, 27049–53, 27055, 27094, 27098–99, 27101–09, 27111, 27113–17, 27120, 27127, 27130, 27150–51, 27155–57, 27199, 27201–02, 27235, 27244, 27265, 27284–85, 27305, 27314–15, 27320, 27326, 27343, 27357–58, 27360, 27379, 27565, 27582, 27893, 28115, 28125, 28166, 28601, 28604–08, 28615, 28617–18, 28621–27, 28629–31, 28634–36, 28640, 28642–45, 28649, 28651, 28654, 28656, 28659–60, 28663, 28665, 28668–70, 28672, 28675–79, 28681, 28683–85, 28688–89, 28691–94, 28697–99

* * *

SIXTH DISTRICT

HOWARD COBLE, Republican, of Greensboro, NC; born in Greensboro, March 18, 1931; attended Appalachian State University, Boone, NC, 1949–50; A.B., history, Guilford College, Greensboro, NC, 1958; J.D., University of North Carolina School of Law, Chapel Hill, 1962; enlisted in U.S. Coast Guard as a seaman recruit, 1952; active duty, 1952–56 and 1977–78; reserve duty, 1960–82; presently holds rank of captain; last reserve duty assignment, commanding officer, U.S. Coast Guard Reserve Unit, Wilmington, NC; attorney; admitted to North Carolina bar, 1966; field claim representative and superintendent, auto insurance, 1961–67; elected to North Carolina House of Represenives, 1969; assistant U.S. attorney, Middle District of North Carolina, 1969–73; commissioner (secretary), North Carolina Department of Revenue, 1973–77; North Carolina House of Representatives, 1979–83; practiced law with law firm of Turner, Enochs and Sparrow, Greensboro, NC, 1979–84; member: Alamance Presbyterian Church, American Legion, Veterans of Foreign Wars of the United States, Lions Club, Greensboro Bar Association, North Carolina Bar Association, North Carolina State Bar; North Carolina State co-chairman, American Legislative Exchange Council, 1983–84; elected to the 99th Congress on November 6, 1984; reelected to each succeeding Congress.

Office Listings

http://www.house.gov/coble howard.coble@mail.house.gov

2468 Rayburn House Office Building, Washington, DC 20515 .... (202) 225–3065
Chief of Staff / Press Secretary.—Missy Branson. FAX: 225–8611
Executive Assistant.—Mary Elizabeth Tillman.
2102 North Elm Street, Suite B, Greensboro, NC 27408–5100 .... (336) 333–5005
Office Manager.—Chris Beaman.
155 Northpoint Avenue, Suite 200B, High Point, NC 27262–7723 .... (336) 886–5106
District Representative.—Nancy Mazza.
241 Sunset Avenue, Suite 101, Asheboro, NC 27203–5658 .... (336) 626–3060
District Representative.—Rebecca Redding.
272D Old Concord Road, Suite 2404, Salisbury, NC 28146–8388 .... (704) 645–8082
District Representative.—Terri Welch.
124 West Elm Stret, P.O. Box 812, Graham, NC 27253–0812 .... (336) 229–0159
District Representative.—Janine Osborne.

Counties: ALAMANCE (part), DAVIDSON (part), GUILFORD (part), MOORE, RANDOLPH, ROWAN (part). Population (2000), 620,590.

ZIP Codes: 27201–05, 27208–09, 27214–17, 27220, 27230, 27233, 27235, 27239, 27242, 27244, 27248–49, 27252–53, 27258–65, 27281–84, 27288–89, 27292, 27295, 27298–99, 27301–02, 27310, 27312–13, 27316–17, 27325, 27330, 27340–42, 27344, 27349–50, 27355–61, 27370–71, 27373–74, 27376–77, 27401–10, 27415–17, 27419–20, 27425, 27427, 27429, 27435, 27438, 27455, 27495, 27498–99, 27607, 27612–13, 27640, 27803–04, 28023, 28041, 28071–72, 28081, 28083, 28088, 28125, 28127, 28137–38, 28144, 28146–47, 28315, 28326–27, 28347, 28350, 28370, 28373–74, 28387–88, 28394

* * *

SEVENTH DISTRICT

MIKE MCINTYRE, Democrat, of Lumberton, NC; born in Robeson County, August 6, 1956; education: B.A., Phi Beta Kappa Morehead Scholar, 1978, and J.D., 1981, University of North Carolina; upon graduation, received the Algernon Sydney Sullivan Award for ''unselfish interest in the welfare of his fellow man''; profession: attorney; past president, Lumberton Economic Advancement for Dowtown; formerly on board of directors of Lumberton Rotary Club, Chamber of Commerce and a local group home for the mentally handicapped; active in the Boy Scouts of America, and Lumberton PTA; married: the former Dee Strickland; two children; elected to the 105th Congress; reelected to each succeeding Congress.

Office Listings

http://www.house.gov/mcintyre

228 Cannon House Office Building, Washington, DC 20515 .... (202) 225–2731
Chief of Staff / Press Secretary.—Dean Mitchell. FAX: 225–5773
Deputy Chief of Staff.—Audrey Lesesne.
Chief of Constituent Services.—Vivian Lipford.
Legislative Director.—Jeff Hogg.
Federal Building, 301 Green Street, Room 218, Fayetteville, NC 28401 .... (910) 323–0260
District Director.—Martha McLean.
201 North Front Street, Suite 440, Wilmington, NC 28401 .... (910) 815–4959
Constituent Services Assistant.—Pam Campbell-Dereef.
701 Elm Street, Lumberton, NC 28358 .... (910) 671–6223
District Executive Assistant.—Marie Thompson.

Counties: BLADEN, BRUNSWICK, COLUMBUS, CUMBERLAND (part), DUPLIN (part), NEW HANOVER, PENDER, ROBESON, SAMPSON (part). Population (2000), 619,178.

ZIP Codes: 28301–06, 28309, 28311–12, 28318–20, 28325, 28328, 28331–32, 28334, 28337, 28340–42, 28344, 28348–49, 28356–60, 28362, 28364–66, 28369, 28371–72, 28375, 28377–78, 28383–86, 28390–93, 28395, 28398–99, 28401–12, 28420–25, 28428–36, 28438–39, 28441–59, 28461–70, 28472, 28478–80, 28513, 28518, 28521, 28572, 28574

* * *

EIGHTH DISTRICT

ROBIN HAYES, Republican, of Concord, NC; born in Concord, NC, on August 14, 1945; education: B.A., history, Duke University, 1967; employment: owner and operator, Mt. Pleasant Hosiery Mill; member, North Carolina House of Representatives, 1992–96; married: Barbara Weiland, 1968; children: Winslow and Bob; appointed to the Armed Services Committee Panel on Morale, Welfare, and Recreation for the 106th Congress; appointed to Special Oversight Panel on Terrorism for the 107th Congress; committees: Agriculture; Armed Services; Transportation and Infrastructure; chairman, Congressional Sportsmen's Caucus; chairman, Special Operations Forces Caucus; Assistant Majority Whip; elected to the 106th Congress; reelected to each succeeding Congress.

Office Listings

http://www.hayes.house.gov

130 Cannon House Office Building, Washington, DC 20515 .... (202) 225–3715
Administrative Assistant.—Andrew Duke. FAX: 225–4036
Legislative Director.—Jennifer Thompson.
Scheduler.—Annie Stull.
137 Union Street South, Concord, NC 28025 .... (704) 786–1612
District Director.—Richard Hudson.
230 East Franklin Street, Rockingham, NC 28379 .... (910) 997–2070

Counties: ANSON, CABARRUS (part), CUMBERLAND (part), HOKE, MECKLENBURG (part), MONTGOMERY, RICHMOND, SCOTLAND (part), STANLY, UNION (part). Population (2000), 619,178.

ZIP Codes: 27209, 27215, 27229, 27247, 27253, 27281, 27284, 27306, 27312, 27320, 27341, 27356, 27358, 27371, 27405, 27534, 27803–04, 27893, 28001–02, 28007, 28009, 28025–27, 28036, 28071, 28075, 28081–83, 28091, 28097,

28102–04, 28107–12, 28119, 28124, 28127–29, 28133, 28135, 28137–38, 28159, 28163, 28167, 28170, 28174, 28204–05, 28209–13, 28215, 28217–18, 28220, 28223, 28227, 28229, 28262, 28270, 28278, 28301, 28303–06, 28308, 28311, 28314–15, 28325, 28329–30, 28338, 28343, 28345, 28347, 28349, 28351–53, 28357, 28361, 28363–64, 28367, 28371, 28376–77, 28379–80, 28382, 28386, 28396

* * *

NINTH DISTRICT

SUE WILKINS MYRICK, Republican, of Charlotte, NC; born in Tiffin, OH, August 1, 1941; education: graduated Port Clinton High School, Port Clinton, OH; attended Heidelberg College; employment: former president and CEO, Myrick Advertising and Myrick Enterprises; mayor of Charlotte, NC, 1987–91; Charlotte City Council, 1983–85; active with the National League of Cities and the U.S. Conference of Mayors; served on former President Bush's Affordable Housing Commission; member: Charlotte Chamber of Commerce; Muscular Dystrophy Association; March of Dimes; Elks Auxiliary; PTA; Cub Scout den mother; United Methodist Church; founder, Charitable Outreach Society; married Ed Myrick, 1977; five children; elected to the 104th Congress; reelected to each succeeding Congress; committee: Rules.

Office Listings

http://www.myrick.house.gov

230 Cannon House Office Building, Washington, DC 20515 .... (202) 225–1976
Administrative Assistant.—Ashley Hoy. FAX: 225–3389
Executive Assistant.—Hollie Arnold.
6525 Morrison Boulevard, Suite 402, Charlotte, NC 28211 .... (704) 362–1060
318 South Street, Gastonia, NC 28052 .... (704) 861–1976

Counties: GASTON (part), MECKLENBURG (part), UNION. Population (2000), 619,178.

ZIP Codes: 28006, 28012, 28016–17, 28031–34, 28036, 28042, 28052–56, 28070, 28077–80, 28086, 28092–93, 28098, 28101, 28103–07, 28110, 28112, 28114, 28120, 28126, 28130, 28134, 28136, 28150–52, 28164, 28169, 28173–74, 28201, 28203–04, 28206–11, 28213–17, 28222, 28226–27, 28241, 28247, 28250, 28253, 28261–62, 28269–71, 28273–74, 28277–78, 28287

* * *

TENTH DISTRICT

CASS BALLENGER, Republican, of Hickory, NC; born in Hickory, December 6, 1926; education: graduated, Episcopal High School, Alexandria, VA, 1944; attended University of North Carolina, Chapel Hill, 1944–45; B.A., Amherst College, Amherst, MA, 1948; military service: served in U.S. Naval Air Corps, aviation cadet, 1944–45; employment: founder and president, Plastic Packaging, Inc.; North Carolina House of Representatives, 1974–76; North Carolina Senate, 1976–86; member: Catawba County Board of Commissioners, 1966–74 (chairman, 1970–74); Advisory Budget Commission, White House Advisory Committee, Community Ridge Day Care Center, Hickory Rotary Club, Hickory United Fund, Lenoir-Rhyne College Board of Development, Salvation Army Board of Directors, Florence Crittenton Home Board of Directors, Greater Hickory Chamber of Commerce (director); sustaining member, North Carolina School of the Arts; patron: North Carolina Symphony, North Carolina Arts Society; married: the former Donna Davis, 1952; children: Lucinda Ballenger-Brinkley, Melissa Ballenger Jordan, and Dorothy Davis Ballenger Weaver; grandchildren: Matthew Jordan, William Eriksen Jordan, Lucy; deputy whip, 104th Congress; committees: Education and the Workforce; International Relations: elected to the 99th Congress, November 4, 1986, to complete the unexpired term of James Broyhill; reelected to each succeeding Congress.

Office Listings

http://www.house.gov/ballenger

2182 Rayburn House Office Building, Washington, DC 20515 .... (202) 225–2576
Chief of Staff.—Dan Gurley. FAX: 225–0316
Legislative Director.—Roberta Hood.
Executive Assistant.—Jessica Swinehart.
P.O. Box 1830, Hickory, NC 28603 .... (704) 327–6100
District Director.—Tommy Luckadoo.

Counties: AVERY, BURKE, CALDWELL, CATAWBA, CLEVELAND, GASTON (part), IREDELL (part), LINCOLN, MITCHELL, and RUTHERFORD (part). CITIES AND TOWNSHIPS: Hickory, Lenoir, Morganton, Shelby, and Mooresville. Population (2000), 619,178.

ZIP Codes: 28006, 28010, 28016–21, 28024, 28033, 28036–38, 28040, 28042–43, 28052, 28073–74, 28076, 28080, 28086, 28089–90, 28092, 28114–15, 28117, 28139, 28150, 28152, 28164, 28166–69, 28601–07, 28609–13, 28616, 28619, 28621–22, 28624–25, 28628–30, 28633, 28635–38, 28641, 28645–47, 28650, 28652–55, 28657–58, 28661–62, 28664, 28666–67, 28671, 28673, 28676–78, 28680–82, 28687, 28690, 28699, 28705, 28720, 28740, 28746, 28752, 28761, 28765, 28777

* * *

ELEVENTH DISTRICT

CHARLES H. TAYLOR, Republican, of Brevard, NC; born in Brevard on January 23, 1941; graduated from Brevard High School; B.A., Wake Forest University, 1963; J.D., Wake Forest University, 1966; tree farmer; member: North Carolina Board of Transportation, North Carolina Energy Policy Council; vice chairman, Western North Carolina Environmental Council; chairman, North Carolina Parks and Recreation Council; member, North Carolina State House, 1967–73; minority leader, 1969–73; North Carolina State Senator and minority leader, 1973–75; married to the former Elizabeth Owen; three children: Owen, Bryan, and Charles Robert; member, Board of Visitors to the Military Academy; committees: Appropriations; subcommittees: Commerce, State, Justice and the Judiciary; chairman, Interior; elected to the 102nd Congress on November 6, 1990; reelected to each succeeding Congress.

Office Listings

231 Cannon House Office Building, Washington, DC 20515 .... (202) 225–6401
Chief of Staff.—Roger France.
Scheduler.—Steve Green.
22 South Pack Square, Suite 330, Asheville, NC 28801 .... (828) 251–1988
111 West Second Street, Suite 100, Rutherfordton, NC 28139 .... (828) 286–8750
211 Seventh Avenue West, Hendersonville, NC 28791 .... (828) 697–8539
Cherokee County Courthouse, Murphy, NC 28906 .... (828) 837–3249
515 South Haywood Street, Suite 118, Waynesville, NC 28787 .... (828) 456–7559

Counties: BUNCOMBE, CHEROKEE, CLAY, GRAHAM, HAYWOOD, HENDERSON, JACKSON, MCDOWELL, MACON, MADISON, POLK, RUTHERFORD (part), SWAIN, TRANSYLVANIA, YANCEY. Population (2000), 619,177.

ZIP Codes: 28043, 28114, 28139, 28160, 28701–02, 28704, 28707–45, 28747–58, 28760–63, 28766, 28768, 28770–79, 28781–93, 28801–06, 28810, 28813–16, 28901–06, 28909

* * *

TWELFTH DISTRICT

MELVIN L. WATT, Democrat, of Charlotte, NC; born in Charlotte on August 26, 1945; education: graduated, York Road High School, Charlotte, 1963; B.S., business adminisration, University of North Carolina, Chapel Hill, 1967; J.D., Yale University Law School, New Haven, CT, 1970; employment: attorney; admitted to the District of Columbia bar, 1970, admitted to the North Carolina bar, 1971; began practice with Chambers, Stein, Ferguson and Becton, 1971–92; North Carolina State Senate, 1985–86; life member: NAACP; member: Mount Olive Presbyterian Church; Mecklenburg County Bar Association, past president; Johnston C. Smith University Board of Visitors; Central Piedmont Community College Foundation; North Carolina Association of Black Lawyers; North Carolina Association of Trial Lawyers; Legal Aid of Southern Piedmont; NationsBank Community Development Corporation; Charlotte Chamber of Commerce; Sports Action Council; Auditorium-Coliseum-Civic Center Authority; United Way; Mint Museum; Inroads, Inc.; Family Housing Services; Public Education Forum; Dilworth Community Development Association; Cities in Schools; West Charlotte Business Incubator; Housing Authority Scholarship Board; Morehead Scholarship Selection Committee, Forsyth Region; married: the former Eulada Paysour, 1968; children: Brian and Jason; elected on November 3, 1992, to the 103rd Congress; reelected to each succeeding Congress.

Office Listings

http://www.house.gov/watt

2236 Rayburn House Office Building, Washington, DC 20515 .... (202) 225–1510
Chief of Staff.—Joyce Brayboy. FAX: 225–1512
1230 West Morehead Street, Suite 306, Charlotte, NC 28208 .... (704) 344–9950
301 South Greene Street, Suite 210, Greensboro, NC 27401 .... (336) 275–9950
District Director.—Pam Stubbs.

Counties: CABARRUS COUNTY (part). DAVIDSON COUNTY (part). CITIES AND TOWNSHIPS: Lexington, and Thomasville. FORSYTH COUNTY (part). CITIES AND TOWNSHIPS: Winston-Salem (part). GUILFORD COUNTY (part). CITIES AND TOWNSHIPS: High Point (part), Greensboro (part). MECKLENBURG COUNTY. CITIES AND TOWNSHIPS: Charlotte (part). ROWAN COUNTY. CITIES: Salisbury. Population (2000), 619,178.

ZIP Codes: 27010, 27012–13, 27019, 27040, 27045, 27051, 27054, 27101, 27103–07, 27110, 27127, 27214, 27260, 27262–63, 27265, 27282, 27284, 27292–95, 27299, 27310, 27320, 27351, 27360, 27401, 27403, 27405–11, 27534, 27803–04, 27893, 28023, 28027, 28035–36, 28039, 28078, 28081, 28115, 28123, 28125, 28134, 28144–47, 28159, 28202–17, 28219, 28221, 28224, 28226–28, 28230–37, 28240, 28242–43, 28254–56, 28258, 28260, 28262, 28265–66, 28269–70, 28272–73, 28275, 28278, 28280–82, 28284–85, 28289–90, 28296–97

* * *

THIRTEENTH DISTRICT

BRAD MILLER, Democrat, of Raleigh, NC; born on May 19, 1953, in Fayetteville, NC; education: B.A., Political Science, University of North Carolina, 1975; Master's Degree, Political Science, London School of Economics, 1978; J.D., Columbia University Law School, 1979; profession: Attorney; law clerk to Circuit Court of Appeals Judge J. Dickson Phillips, Jr., 1979–80; has practiced law in Raleigh since 1980, and has been in private practice since 1991; public service: North Carolina House of Representatives, 1992–94; North Carolina State Senate, 1996–2002; religion: Episcopal; family: married to Esther Hall; elected to the 108th Congress on November 5, 2002.

Office Listings

http://www.house.gov/bradmiller

1505 Longworth House Office Building, Washington, DC 20515 .... (202) 225–3032
Chief of Staff.—Mark Harkins. FAX: 225–0181
Legislative Director.—Thomas Koonce.
Press Secretary.—Joe Bonfiglio.
Scheduler.—Eleanor Blaine.
100 East Six Forks Road, Suite 309, Raleigh, NC 27609 .... (919) 781–9101
400 West Market Street, Suite 104, Greensboro, NC 27401 .... (336) 574–2909

Counties: ALAMANCE (part), CASWELL, GRANVILLE (part), GUILFORD (part), PERSON, ROCKINGHAM (part), WAKE (part). Population (2000), 619,178.

ZIP Codes: 27025, 27027, 27046, 27048, 27212, 27214–17, 27231, 27244, 27249, 27253, 27258, 27288–89, 27291, 27301–02, 27305, 27311–12, 27314–15, 27320, 27323, 27326, 27343, 27375, 27379, 27401, 27403, 27405–10, 27412, 27455, 27507, 27509, 27511, 27522, 27525–26, 27541, 27544–45, 27565, 27571–74, 27581–83, 27587–88, 27591, 27596–97, 27601, 27603–17, 27619–20, 27622, 27625, 27627–29, 27634–36, 27640, 27650, 27658, 27661, 27668, 27690, 27698

NORTH DAKOTA

(Population 2000, 642,200)

SENATORS

KENT CONRAD, Democrat, of Bismarck, ND; born in Bismarck on March 12, 1948; graduated from Wheelus High School, Tripoli, Libya, 1966; attended the University of Missouri, Columbia, 1967; B.A., Stanford University, CA, 1971; M.B.A., George Washington University, Washington, DC, 1975; assistant to the Tax Commissioner, Bismarck, 1974–80; director, Management Planning and Personnel, North Dakota Tax Department, March–December 1980; Tax Commissioner, State of North Dakota, 1981–86; married Lucy Calautti, February 1987; one child by former marriage: Jessamyn Abigail; elected to the U.S. Senate on November 4, 1986; committees: Agriculture, Nutrition and Forestry; ranking member, Budget; Finance; Indian Affairs; was not a candidate for a second term to Senate seat he had won in 1986; subsequently elected by special election on December 4, 1992, to fill the vacancy caused by the death of Senator Quentin Burdick, whose term would have expired on January 3, 1995; took the oath of office on December 14, 1992, and continued his Senate service without interruption; reelected to each succeeding Senate term.

Office Listings

http://conrad.senate.gov

530 Hart Senate Office Building, Washington, DC 20510 .... (202) 224–2043
Chief of Staff.—Bob Van Heuvelen. FAX: 224–7776
Legislative Director.—Tom Mahr.
220 East Rosser Avenue, Room 228, Bismarck, ND 58501 .... (701) 258–4648
State Director.—Lynn Clancy.
657 Second Avenue North, Room 306, Fargo, ND 58102 .... (701) 232–8030
TDD: 232–2139
102 North Fourth Street, Suite 104, Grand Forks, ND 58203 .... (701) 775–9601
100 First Street, SW, Room 105, Minot, ND 58701 .... (701) 852–0703

* * *

BYRON L. DORGAN, Democrat, of Bismarck, ND; born in Dickinson, ND, on May 14, 1942; education: graduated, Regent High School, 1961; B.S., University of North Dakota, 1965; M.B.A., University of Denver, 1966; employment: North Dakota State Tax Commissioner, 1969–80, the only elected state tax commissioner in the nation; received 80 percent of the vote in 1976 tax commissioner reelection bid; chairman, Multi-State Tax Commission, 1972–74; executive committee member, National Association of Tax Administrators, 1972–75; selected by the *Washington Monthly* as one of the outstanding state officials in the United States, 1975; chosen by one of North Dakota's leading newspapers as the individual with the greatest influence on State government, 1977; elected to Congress, 1980; elected president of Democratic freshman class during first term; reelected, 1982, with 72 percent of the vote; reelected to Congress in 1984 with 78.5 percent of the vote, setting three election records in North Dakota—largest vote ever received by a statewide candidate, largest vote by a U.S. House candidate, and largest majority by a U.S. House candidate; his 242,000 votes in 1984 were the most received anywhere in the nation by an opposed House candidate; reelected to each succeeding Congress; served on three congressional committees during first term in Congress: Agriculture, Small Business, and Veterans' Affairs; named to the Ways and Means Committee, January 1983; called the real successor to Bill Langer and the State's most exciting office holder in generations, by the 1983 *Book of America*; 1990 *New York Times* editorial said, ''Mr. Dorgan sets an example for political statesmanship''; named to Select Committee on Hunger in 1985; chairman, International Task Force on Select Committee on Hunger; elected to the U.S. Senate on November 3, 1992; first sworn in on December 15, 1992, to fill the remainder of the term in North Dakota's open Senate seat, then sworn in January 5, 1993, for six-year term; reelected to each succeeding Senate term; committees: Appropriations; Commerce, Science and Transportation; Energy and Natural Resources; Indian Affairs; chairman, Democratic Policy Committee, 106th, 107th, and 108th Congresses; assistant Democratic Leader for Policy, 106th and 107th Congresses; assistant Democratic Floor Leader, 104th and 105th Congresses; assistant Democratic Floor Leader, ex officio, 106th and 107th Congresses; married: Kim Dorgan; children: Scott, Shelly (deceased), Brendon, and Haley.

Office Listings

http://dorgan.senate.gov

713 Hart Senate Office Building, Washington, DC 20510 .... (202) 224–2551
Chief of Staff.—Jim Messina. FAX: 224–1193
Communications Director.—Barry E. Piatt.
Office Manager.—Dana McCallum.
State Director.—Bob Valeu.
220 East Rosser Avenue, Room 312, Bismarck, ND 58502 .... (701) 250–4618
112 Roberts Street, Fargo, ND 58102 .... (701) 239–5389
102 North Fourth Street, Room 108, Grand Forks, ND 58201 .... (701) 746–8972
100 First Street SW, Suite 105, Minot, ND 58701 .... (701) 852–0703

REPRESENTATIVE

AT LARGE

EARL POMEROY, Democrat-NPL, of Valley City, ND; born on September 2, 1952 in Valley City; education: B.A. and J.D., University of North Dakota, Grand Forks, 1974, 1979; graduate research in legal history at the University of Durham, England, 1975–76; employment: attorney; admitted to North Dakota bar, 1979; North Dakota House of Representatives, 1980–84; Insurance Commissioner of North Dakota, 1985–92; president, National Association of Insurance Commissioners, 1990; children: Kathryn and Scott; committees: Agriculture; Ways and Means; elected to the 103rd Congress on November 3, 1992; reelected to each succeeding Congress.

Office Listings

http://www.house.gov/pomeroy

1110 Longworth House Office Building, Washington, DC 20515 .... (202) 225–2611
Chief of Staff.—Bob Siggins. FAX: 226–0893
Legislative Director.—Aleta Botts.
Press Secretary.—Julianne Fisher.
Federal Building, 220 East Rosser Avenue, Room 328, Bismarck, ND 58501 .... (701) 224–0355
Federal Building, 657 Second Avenue, Room 266, North, Fargo, ND 58102 .... (701) 235–9760
State Director.—Gail Skaley.

Population (2000), 642,200.

ZIP Codes: 58001–02, 58004–09, 58011–13, 58015–18, 58021, 58027, 58029, 58030–33, 58035–36, 58038, 58040–43, 58045–49, 58051–54, 58056–65, 58067–69, 58071–72, 58074–79, 58081, 58102–09, 58121–22, 58124–26, 58201–06, 58208, 58210, 58212, 58214, 58216, 58218–20, 58222–25, 58227–31, 58233, 58235–41, 58243–44, 58249–51, 58254–62, 58265–67, 58269–78, 58281–82, 58301, 58310–11, 58313, 58316–19, 58321, 58323–25, 58327, 58329–32, 58335, 58338–39, 58341, 58343–46, 58348, 58351–53, 58355–57, 58359, 58361–63, 58365–70, 58372, 58374, 58377, 58379–82, 58384–86, 58401–02, 58405, 58413, 58415–16, 58418, 58420–26, 58428–31, 58433, 58436, 58438–45, 58448, 58451–52, 58454–56, 58458, 58460–61, 58463–64, 58466–67, 58472, 58474–84, 58486–88, 58490, 58492, 58494–97, 58501–07, 58520–21, 58523–24, 58528–33, 58535, 58538, 58540–42, 58544–45, 58549, 58552, 58554, 58558–66, 58568–73, 58575–77, 58579–81, 58601–02, 58620–23, 58625–27, 58630–32, 58634, 58636, 58638–47, 58649–56, 58701–05, 58707, 58710–13, 58716, 58718, 58721–23, 58725, 58727, 58730–31, 58733–37, 58740–41, 58744, 58746–48, 58750, 58752, 58755–63, 58765, 58768–73, 58775–76, 58778–79, 58781–85, 58787–90, 58792–95, 58801–02, 58830–31, 58833, 58835, 58838, 58843–45, 58847, 58849, 58852–54, 58856

OHIO

(Population 2000, 11,353,140)

SENATORS

MIKE DEWINE, Republican, of Columbus, OH; born in Springfield, OH, January 5, 1947; Yellow Springs High School; B.S., Miami University, Oxford, OH, 1969; graudated, J.D., Ohio Northern University, 1972; attorney, admitted to the Ohio State bar, 1972; Greene County assistant and prosecuting attorney, 1976–80; Ohio State Senator, 1980–82; U.S. Representative, 1983–91; Lieutenant Governor of Ohio, 1991–95; married the former Frances Struewing, 1967; eight children: Patrick, Jill, Becky, John, Brian, Alice, Mark, and Anna; committees: Appropriations; Health, Education, Labor, and Pensions; Judiciary; Select Committee on Intelligence; elected to the U.S. Senate on November 8, 1994; reelected to each succeeding Senate term.

Office Listings

http://dewine.senate.gov

140 Russell Senate Office Building, Washington, DC 20510 .... (202) 224–2315
Chief of Staff.—Laurel Dawson. FAX: 224–6519
Communications Director.—Mike Dawson.
Legislative Director.—Paul Palagyi.
Press Secretary.—Amanda Flaig.
312 Walnut Street, Room 2030, Cincinnati, OH 45202 .... (513) 763–8260
Regional Director.—Shannon Jones.
600 Superior Avenue East, Room 2450, Cleveland, OH 44114 .... (216) 522–7272
Regional Director.—Michelle Gillcrest.
37 West Broad Street, Room 300, Columbus, OH 43215 .... (614) 469–5186
Regional Director.—Scott Corbitt.
121 Putnam Street, Suite 102, Marietta, OH 45750 .... (614) 373–2317
District Representative.—Karen Sloan.
420 Madison Avenue, Room 1225, Toledo, OH 43604 .... (419) 259–7535
District Representative.—Scott Noyes.
100 West Main Street, 2nd Floor, Xenia, OH 45385 .... (937) 376–3080
State Director.—Barbara Schenck.

* * *

GEORGE V. VOINOVICH, Republican, of Cleveland, OH; born in Cleveland, on July 15, 1936; B.A., Ohio University, 1958; J.D., College of Law, Ohio State University, 1961; Honorary Doctorate of Law, Ohio University, 1981; Honorary Doctorate of Public Administration, Findlay University, 1993; public service: Assistant Attorney General, Ohio, 1963; member, Ohio House of Representatives, 1967–71; Cuyahoga County Auditor, 1971–76; Cuyahoga County Commissioner, 1977–78; Lieutenant Governor, Ohio, 1979; Mayor, Cleveland, OH, 1979–86; 65th Governor of Ohio, 1990–98; President, National League of Cities, 1985; chairman, National Governor's Association, 1997–98; Catholic; married: Janet Voinovich; three children: George, Betsy, and Peter; committees: Governmental Affairs; Environment and Public Works; Foreign Relations; Select Committee on Ethics; elected to the U.S. Senate on November 3, 1998.

Office Listings

http://voinovich.senate.gov

317 Hart Senate Office Building, Washington, DC 20510 .... (202) 224–3353
Chief of Staff.—Ted Hollingsworth. FAX: 228–1382
Legislative Director.—Aric Newhouse.
Press Secretary.—Scott Milburn.
Office Manager.—Monica Heil.
1240 East Ninth Street, Suite 2955, Cleveland, OH 44199 .... (216) 522–7095
Regional Representative.—Nicholas Gattozzi.
37 West Broad Street, Suite 310, Columbus, OH 43215 .... (614) 469–6774
State Director.—Beth Hansen.
37 East 7th Street, Room 2615, Cincinnati, OH 45202 .... (513) 684–3265
District Representative.—Tony Condia.
420 Madison Avenue, Room 1210, Toledo, OH 43604 .... (419) 259–3895
District Representative.—Dennis Fligor.
37 West Broad Street, Suite 320, Columbus, OH 43215 .... (614) 409–6774
Constituent Services Director.—Jeannine Keating.

REPRESENTATIVES

FIRST DISTRICT

STEVE CHABOT, Republican, of Cincinnati, OH; born in Cincinnati, OH, January 22, 1953; attended LaSalle High School, Cincinnati; B.A., College of William and Mary, Williamsburg, VA, 1975; J.D., Salmon P. Chase College of Law, 1978; former school teacher; private practice lawyer, 1978–94; Hamilton County commissioner, 1990–94; member, Cincinnati City Council, 1985–90; chairman, County Council's Urban Development and Law and Public Safety committees; married: Donna Chabot, 1973; children: Randy and Erica; committees: Judiciary; International Relations; Small Business; subcommittees: chairman, The Constitution; Middle East and Central Asia; Asia and the Pacific; Crime, Terrorism, and Homeland Security; Commercial and Administrative Law; Tax, Finance, and Exports; elected to the 104th Congress; reelected to each succeeding Congress.

Office Listings

129 Cannon House Office Building, Washington, DC 20515 .... (202) 225–2216
Chief of Staff.—Gary Lindgren. FAX: 225–3012
Legislative Director.—Kevin Fitzpatrick.
Office Manager.—Amy Spolrich.
Carew Tower, 441 Vine Street, Room 3003, Cincinnati, OH 45202 .... (513) 684–2723
District Director.—Mike Cantwell.

Counties: BUTLER (part), HAMILTON (part). Population (2000), 630,730.

ZIP Codes: 45001–02, 45013–14, 45030, 45033, 45040–41, 45051–54, 45056, 45070, 45201–21, 45223–25, 45229, 45231–34, 45236–41, 45246–48, 45250–53, 45258, 45262–64, 45267–71, 45273–74, 45277, 45280, 45296, 45298–99

* * *

SECOND DISTRICT

ROB PORTMAN, Republican, of Cincinnati, OH; born in Cincinnati, December 19, 1955; education: graduated Cincinnati Country Day School; B.A., Dartmouth College, 1979; J.D., University of Michigan Law School, 1984; admitted to the Ohio and Washington, DC bars, 1984; employment: attorney, private practice, (six years); associate counsel to former President Bush, 1989; deputy assistant to the president and director, White House Office of Legislative Affairs, 1989–91; married: Jane Dudley Portman, 1986; three children; committees: Budget; Ways and Means; co-chair, National Commission on Restructuring the Internal Revenue Service; Chairman of the House Republican Leadership, and Liaison to the White House; elected by special election on May 4, 1993, to fill the vacancy caused by the resignation of William Gradison; reelected to the each succeeding Congress.

Office Listings

http://www.house.gov/portman

238 Cannon House Office Building, Washington, DC 20515 .... (202) 225–3164
Chief of Staff.—Rob Lehman.
Legislative Director.—Barbara Pate.
Communications Director.—Jim Morrell.
8044 Montgomery Road, Suite 540, Cincinnati, OH 45236 .... (513) 791–0381
District Manager.—Nan Cahall.

Counties: ADAMS, BROWN, CLERMONT, HAMILTON (part), PIKE, SCIOTO (part), WARREN (part). Population (2000), 630,730.

ZIP Codes: 45034, 45036, 45039–40, 45054, 45065, 45068, 45101–03, 45105–07, 45111–13, 45115, 45118–22, 45130–31, 45133, 45140, 45142, 45144–45, 45147–48, 45150, 45152–54, 45156–58, 45160, 45162, 45167–68, 45171, 45174, 45176, 45202, 45206–09, 45212–13, 45222, 45226–27, 45230, 45235–37, 45241–46, 45249, 45254–55, 45601, 45612–13, 45616, 45618, 45624, 45630, 45642, 45646, 45648, 45650, 45652, 45657, 45660–63, 45671, 45679, 45683–84, 45687, 45690, 45693, 45697

* * *

THIRD DISTRICT

MICHAEL R. TURNER, Republican, of Dayton, OH; born on January 11, 1960; education: B.A., Ohio Northern University, 1982; J.D., Case Western Reserve University Law School, 1985; M.B.A., University of Dayton, 1992; profession: Attorney; president, JMD Development (real estate company); corporate counsel, MTC International (holding company); organizations: Ohio Bar Association; California Bar Association; public service: Mayor of Dayton, 1994–2002; family: married to Lori; children: Jessica and Carolyn; elected to the 108th Congress on November 5, 2002.

Office Listings

http://www.house.gov/miketurner

1740 Longworth House Office Building, Washington, DC 20515 .... (202) 225–6465
Chief of Staff.—Stacy Palmer-Barton. FAX: 225–6754
Legislative Director.—Melissa Decker.
120 West Third Street, Suite 305, Dayton, OH 45402 .... (937) 225–2843

Counties: CLINTON, HIGHLAND, MONTGOMERY (part), WARREN (part). Population (2000), 630,730.

ZIP Codes: 45005, 45032, 45036, 45040, 45042, 45044, 45054, 45066, 45068, 45107, 45110, 45113–14, 45118, 45123, 45132–33, 45135, 45138, 45140, 45142, 45146, 45148, 45155, 45159, 45164, 45166, 45169, 45177, 45206, 45240–41, 45309, 45315, 45322, 45325, 45327, 45335, 45338, 45342–45, 45354, 45371, 45377, 45381, 45401–10, 45412–20, 45422, 45426–29, 45431–32, 45437, 45439–41, 45448–49, 45454, 45458–59, 45463, 45469–70, 45475, 45479, 45481–82, 45490, 45612, 45660, 45679, 45697

* * *

FOURTH DISTRICT

MICHAEL G. OXLEY, Republican, of Findlay, OH; born in Findlay, February 11, 1944, son of George Garver and Marilyn Maxine; education: graduated, Findlay Senior High School, 1962; B.A., government, Miami University, Oxford, OH, 1966; J.D., Ohio State University College of Law, Columbus, 1969; admitted to Ohio bar, 1969; employment: FBI special agent, Washington, DC, Boston, and New York City, 1969–72; attorney, Oxley, Malone, Fitzgerald, Hollister, 1972–81; elected to Ohio House of Representatives, 1972, from 82nd District, which includes all or parts of four northwestern Ohio counties; reelected, 1974, 1976, 1978, and 1980; member: financial institutions committee and State government committee; ranking minority member, judiciary and criminal justice committee; member: Trinity Lutheran Church, Findlay, OH; American, Ohio, and Findlay Bar Associations; Sigma Chi Fraternity; Omicron Delta Kappa Men's Honorary Fraternity; Society of Former Special Agents of the FBI; Rotary International; Ohio Association of Township Trustees and Clerks; Ohio Farm Bureau; Findlay Area Chamber of Commerce; married: the former Patricia Pluguez of Philadelphia, 1971; children: Chadd; committees: chairman, Financial Services; elected to the 97th Congress, June 25, 1981, in a special election to fill the vacancy caused by the death of Tennyson Guyer; reelected to each succeeding Congress.

Office Listings

http://oxley.house.gov

2308 Rayburn House Office Building, Washington, DC 20515 .... (202) 225–2676
Administrative Assistant.—Jim Conzelman.
Legislative Director / Press Secretary.—Timothy M. Johnson.
Office Manager / Personal Secretary.—Debi Deimling.
3121 West Elm Plaza, Lima, OH 45805–2516 .... (419) 999–6455
100 East Main Cross Street, Findlay, OH 45840–3311 .... (419) 423–3210
24 West Third Street, Room 314, Mansfield, OH 44902–1299 .... (419) 522–5757

Counties: ALLEN, AUGLAIZE, CHAMPAIGN, HANCOCK, HARDIN, LOGAN, MARION, MORROW, RICHLAND, SHELBY, WYANDOT (part). Population (2000), 630,730.

ZIP Codes: 43003, 43009, 43011, 43019, 43044–45, 43047, 43050, 43060, 43067, 43070, 43072, 43074, 43078, 43083–84, 43301–02, 43306, 43310–11, 43314–26, 43330–38, 43340–51, 43356–60, 43516, 44802, 44804–05, 44813, 44817, 44822, 44827, 44830, 44833, 44837, 44843, 44849, 44862, 44864–65, 44875, 44878, 44901–07, 44999, 45013, 45302, 45306, 45312, 45317, 45326, 45333–34, 45336, 45340, 45344, 45353, 45356, 45360, 45363, 45365, 45380, 45388–89, 45404, 45414, 45420, 45424, 45431–32, 45502, 45801–02, 45804–10, 45812, 45814, 45816–17, 45819–20, 45822, 45830, 45833, 45835–36, 45839–41, 45843–45, 45850, 45854, 45856, 45858–59, 45862, 45865, 45867–72, 45877, 45881, 45884–85, 45887–90, 45894–97

* * *

FIFTH DISTRICT

PAUL E. GILLMOR, Republican, of Old Fort, OH; born in Tiffin, OH, February 1, 1939; education: graduated, Old Fort High School, Old Fort, OH, 1957; B.A., Ohio Wesleyan University, Delaware, 1961; J.D., University of Michigan Law School, Ann Arbor, 1964; military service: served in the U.S. Air Force, captain, 1965–66; employment: attorney; admitted to the Ohio bar, 1965; commenced practice in Tiffin, OH; Ohio State Senate, 1967–88; minority leader and president, Ohio State Senate; married the former Karen Lako, 1983; five children: Linda, Julie, Paul Michael, Adam, and Connor; committees: Energy and Commerce; Financial Services; subcommittees: chairman, Environment and Hazardous Materials; elected to the 101st Congress on November 8, 1988; reelected to each succeeding Congress.

Office Listings

http://gillmor.house.gov

1203 Longworth House Office Building, Washington, DC 20515 .... (202) 225–6405
Administrative Assistant.—Mark Wellman.
Executive Assistant / Scheduler.—Kelley Kurtz.
120 Jefferson Street, Second Floor, Port Clinton, OH 43452 .... (419) 734–1999
613 West Third Street, Defiance, OH 43512 .... (419) 782–1996
130 Shady Lane Drive, Norwalk, OH 44857 .... (419) 668–0206

Counties: ASHLAND (part), CRAWFORD, DEFIANCE, FULTON, HENRY, HURON, LUCAS (part), MERCER (part), PAULDING, PUTNAM, SANDUSKY, SENECA, VAN WERT, WILLIAMS, WOOD, WYANDOT (part). Population (2000), 630,730.

ZIP Codes: 43302, 43314, 43316, 43323, 43337, 43351, 43402–03, 43406–07, 43410, 43413–14, 43416, 43420, 43430–31, 43435, 43437, 43441–43, 43447, 43449–51, 43457, 43460, 43462–67, 43469, 43501–02, 43504–06, 4351012, 43515–27, 43529–36, 43540–43, 43545, 43547–58, 43565–67, 43569–71, 43605, 43619, 43654, 44035, 44235, 44287, 44802, 44805, 44807, 44809, 44811, 44815, 44817–18, 44820, 44825–28, 44830, 44833, 44836–37, 44841, 44844–51, 44853–57, 44859–61, 44865–67, 44874–75, 44878, 44880–83, 44887–90, 45813, 45815, 45817, 45821–22, 45827–28, 45830–33, 45837–38, 45844, 45846, 45848–49, 45851, 45853, 45855–56, 45858, 45861–64, 45868, 45872–77, 45879–80, 45882, 45886–87, 45889, 45891, 45893–94, 45898–99

* * *

SIXTH DISTRICT

TED STRICKLAND, Democrat, of Lucasville, OH: born in Lucasville, August 4, 1941; education: B.A., history, Asbury College, 1963; M. Div., Asbury College, 1967; M.A., 1967; M.A., Ph.D. (1980), counseling psychology, University of Kentucky; employment: psychologist and educator; director of a Methodist children's home; professor at Shawnee State University; and consulting psychologist at Southern Ohio Correctional Facility; married: Francis Smith Strickland; committees: Energy and Commerce; Veterans' Affairs; elected to the 103rd and 105th Congresses; reelected to each succeeding Congress.

Office Listings

336 Cannon House Office Building, Washington, DC 20515 .... (202) 225–5705
Chief of Staff.—John Haseley. FAX: 225–5907
Legislative Director.—Michelle Dallafior.
Press Secretary.—Chad Tanner.
Scheduler.—Stephanie Foster.
11692 Gallia Pike, Wheelersburg, OH 45694 .... (740) 574–2676
Toll Free Number. (888) 706–1833
254 Front Street, Marietta, OH 45750 .... (740) 376–0868
District Director.—Jess Goode.
374 Boardman-Poland Road, Boardman, OH 44512 .... (330) 965–4220
35 South Fifth Street, Martins Ferry, OH 43935 .... (740) 633–2275

Counties: ATHENS (part), BELMONT, COLUMBIANA, GALLIA, JEFFERSON, LAWRENCE, MAHONING (part), MEIGS, MONROE, NOBLE, SCIOTO (part), WASHINGTON. Population (2000), 630,730.

ZIP Codes: 43711, 43713, 4371619, 43724, 43728, 43732, 43747, 43752, 43754, 43757, 43759, 43772–73, 43778–80, 43786–89, 43793, 43901–03, 43905–10, 43912–17, 43920, 43925–26, 43930–35, 43937–48, 43950–53, 43961–64, 43967–68, 43970–71, 43973, 43977, 43983, 43985, 44401, 44406, 44408, 44412–13, 44415–16, 44422–23, 44427, 44429, 44431–32, 44441–45, 44449, 44451–52, 44454–55, 44460, 44481, 44490, 44492–93, 44502, 44507, 44511–15, 44601, 44609, 44619, 44625, 44634, 44657, 44665, 44672, 45014, 45040, 45054, 45065, 45067–68, 45107, 45110, 45113–14, 45123, 45132–33, 45135, 45138, 45140, 45142, 45146, 45148, 45155, 45159, 45162, 45164, 45166, 45172, 45177, 45419, 45614, 45619–20, 45623, 45629, 45631, 45636, 45638, 45643, 45645, 45648, 45653, 45656, 45658–59, 45662, 45669, 45674–75, 45677–78, 45680, 45682, 45685–86, 45688, 45694, 45696, 45699, 45701, 45710–15, 45720–21, 45723–24, 45727, 45729, 45732, 45734–35, 45739, 45741–46, 45750, 45760–61, 45764, 45766–73, 45775–80, 45783–84, 45786–89

* * *

SEVENTH DISTRICT

DAVID L. HOBSON, Republican, of Springfield, OH; born in Cincinnati, OH, October 17, 1936; education: graduated from Withrow High School, Cincinnati, 1954; B.A., Ohio Wesleyan University, Delaware, OH, 1958; J.D., Ohio State College of Law, Columbus, 1963; admitted to the Kentucky bar, 1965; airman, Ohio Air National Guard, 1958–63; businessman; member: VFW Post No. 1031, Springfield Rotary, Shrine Club No. 5121, Moose No. 536, Elks No. 51; member: board of Ohio Wesleyan University; appointed to Ohio State Senate, 1982; Ohio State Senator, 1982–90; majority whip, 1986–88; president pro tempore, 1988–90; committees: Appropriations; married: the former Carolyn Alexander, 1958; children: Susan Marie, Lynn Martha, Douglas Lee; elected to the 102nd Congress on November 6, 1990; reelected to each succeeding Congress.

Office Listings

http://www.house.gov/hobson

2346 Rayburn House Office Building, Washington, DC 20515 .... (202) 225–4324
Chief of Staff.—Wayne Struble.
Legislative Director.—Kenny Kraft.
Washington Scheduler.—Ginny Gano.
5 West North Street, Suite 200, P.O. Box 269, Springfield, OH 45501–0269 .... (937) 325–0474
212 South Broad Street, Room 55, Lancaster, OH 43130–4389 .... (740) 654–5149

Counties: CLARK, FAIRFIELD, FAYETTE, FRANKLIN (part), GREENE, PERRY, PICKAWAY, ROSS (part). Population (2000), 630,730.

ZIP Codes: 43009–10, 43044, 43046, 43062, 43068, 43076, 43078, 43102–03, 43105–07, 43109–10, 43112–13, 43115–17, 43125, 43128, 43130, 43135–38, 43140, 43142–43, 43145–48, 43150, 43153–57, 43160, 43163–64, 43199, 43207, 43213, 43217, 43227, 43232, 43314, 43730–31, 43739, 43748, 43758, 43760–61, 43764, 43766, 43777, 43782–83, 45123, 45135, 45169, 45301, 45305, 45307, 45314, 45316, 45319, 45323–24, 45335, 45341, 45344, 45349, 45368–70, 45372, 45384–85, 45387, 45424, 45430–35, 45440, 45458–59, 45501–06, 45601, 45628, 45644, 45671, 45732

* * *

EIGHTH DISTRICT

JOHN A. BOEHNER, Republican, of West Chester, OH; born in Reading, OH, on November 17, 1949; education: graduated, Moeller High School, Cincinnati, OH, 1968; B.S., Xavier University, 1977; president, Nucite Sales, Inc.; Ohio House of Representatives, 1984–90; ranking Republican member, Commerce and Labor Committee; Energy and Environment Committee; Judiciary and Criminal Justice; elected, Union Township Trustees, 1981; elected, president, Union Township Board of Trustees, 1984; member: St. John Catholic Church; Ohio Farm Bureau; Lakota Hills Homeowners Association; Knights of Columbus, Pope John XXIII; Union Chamber of Commerce; American Heart Association Board; Butler County Mental Health Association; YMCA Capital Campaign; Union Elementary School PTA; Middletown Chamber of Commerce; American Legion Post 218 of Middletown Butler County Trustees and Clerks Association; married the former Deborah Gunlack, 1973; two children: Lindsay, Tricia; committees: chairman, Education and the Workforce; vice chairman, Agriculture; elected to the 102nd Congress; reelected to each succeeding Congress.

Office Listings

http://johnboehner.house.gov

1011 Longworth House Office Building, Washington, DC 20515 .... (202) 225–6205
Chief of Staff.—Mike Sommers. FAX: 225–0704
Press Secretary.—Steve Forde.
8200 Beckett Park Drive, Suite 202, Hamilton, OH 45011 .... (513) 870–0300
12 South Plum Street, Troy, Ohio 45373 .... (937) 339–1524

Counties: BUTLER (part), DARKE, MERCER (part), MIAMI, MONTGOMERY (part), PREBLE. Population (2000), 630,730.

ZIP Codes: 45003–05, 45011–15, 45018, 45025–26, 45036, 45042–44, 45050, 45055–56, 45061–64, 45067, 45069, 45071, 45073, 45099, 45241, 45246, 45303–04, 45308–12, 45317–18, 45320–22, 45325–28, 45330–32, 45337–39, 45344, 45346–48, 45350–52, 45356, 45358–59, 45361–62, 45365, 45371, 45373–74, 45378, 45380–83, 45388, 45390, 45402–04, 45406, 45414, 45424, 45431–32, 45822, 45826, 45828, 45845–46, 45860, 45865–66, 45869, 45883, 45885

* * *

NINTH DISTRICT

MARCY KAPTUR, Democrat, of Toledo, OH; born in Toledo on June 17, 1946; Roman Catholic; graduated, St. Ursula Academy, Toledo, 1964; B.A., University of Wisconsin, Madison, 1968; Master of Urban Planning, University of Michigan, Ann Arbor, 1974; attended University of Manchester, England, 1974; urban planner; assistant director for urban affairs, domestic policy staff, White House, 1977–79; member: American Planning Association and American

Institute of Certified Planners board of directors; National Center for Urban Ethnic Affairs advisory committee; University of Michigan Urban Planning Alumni Association; NAACP Urban League; Polish Museum; Polish American Historical Association; Lucas County Democratic Party Executive Committee; Democratic Women's Campaign Association; Little Flower Parish Church; member: Appropriations Committee; co-chair: Congressional Competitiveness Caucus; House Auto Parts Task Force; Northeast-Midwest Congressional Coalition; Ukrainian Caucus; elected on November 2, 1982, to the 98th Congress; reelected to each succeeding Congress.

Office Listings

http://www.house.gov/kaptur

2366 Rayburn House Office Building, Washington, DC 20515 .... (202) 225–4146
Chief of Staff.—Roger Szemraj.
Administrative Assistant.—Steve Katich.
Legislative Director.—Steve Fought.
Office Manager / Scheduler.—Norma Olsen.
One Maritime Plaza, Suite 600, Toledo, OH 43604 .... (419) 259–7500

Counties: ERIE COUNTY. CITIES AND TOWNSHIPS: Bellevue, Berlin Heights, Berlinville, Birmingham, Bloomingville, Bronson, Castalia, Chatham, Clarksfield, Collins, East Townsend, Fitchville, Hartland, Huron, Kimball, Litchfield, Milan, Mitiwanga, Monroeville, New London, Norwalk, Nova, Olena, Ridgefield, River Corners, Ruggles, Ruggles Beach, Sandusky, Shinrock, Spencer, Steuben, Sullivan, Wakeman, West Clarksfield. LORAIN COUNTY. CITIES AND TOWNSHIPS: Amherst, Beaver Park, Belden, Beulah Beach, Brownhelm, Columbia Station, Elyria, Grafton, Henrietta, Kipton, Lagrange, Linwood Park, Lorain, North Eaton, Oberlin, Ridgeville, Rochester, South Amherst, Vermilion, Wellington. LUCAS COUNTY (part). CITIES AND TOWNSHIPS: Berkey, Curtice, Gypsum, Harbor View, Holland, Maumee, Monclova, Northwood, Oregon, Swanton, Sylvania, Toledo, Waterville, Whitehouse, Woodville. OTTAWA COUNTY. CITIES AND TOWNSHIPS: Bay Shore, Bono, Catawba Island, Clay Center, Danbury, Eagle Beach, Elliston, Elmore, Gem Beach, Genoa, Graytown, Hessville, Isle St. George, Kelleys Island, Lacarne, Lakeside, Lindsey, Marblehead, Martin, Oak Harbor, Port Clinton, Portage, Put-in-Bay, Rocky Ridge, Springbrook, Vickery, Washington, Wayne, Whites Landing, and Williston. Population (2000), 630,730.

ZIP Codes: 43408, 43412, 43416, 43430, 43432–34, 43436, 43438–40, 43442, 43445–47, 43449, 43452, 43456, 43458, 43464, 43468–69, 43504, 43528, 43537, 43542, 43558, 43560, 43566, 43571, 43601–18, 43620, 43623–24, 43635, 43652, 43656–57, 43659–61, 43666–67, 43681–82, 43697, 43699, 44001, 44028, 44035, 44044, 44049–50, 44053, 44074, 44089–90, 44253, 44256, 44275, 44280, 44811, 44814, 44816, 44824, 44826, 44839, 44846–47, 44851, 44857, 44859, 44870–71, 44880, 44889

* * *

TENTH DISTRICT

DENNIS J. KUCINICH, Democrat, of Cleveland, OH; born in Cleveland, October 8, 1946; B.A., M.A., speech and communications, Case Western Reserve University, 1973; editor, professor; Ohio Senate, 1994–96; named outstanding Ohio Senator by National Association of Social Workers for his work on health and social welfare issues; Mayor of Cleveland, 1977–79; Clerk of the Municipal Court, 1975–77; Cleveland City Councilman, 1969–75; one child, Jackie; committees: Education and the Workforce; Government Reform; subcommittees: ranking member, National Security, Emerging Threats and International Relations; Education Reform; Energy Policy, Natural Resources, and Regulatory Affairs; Workforce Protections; elected to the 105th Congress; reelected to each succeeding Congress.

Office Listings

http://www.house.gov/kucinich

1730 Longworth House Office Building, Washington, DC 20515 .... (202) 225–5871
Administrative Director.—Doug Gordon. FAX: 225–5745
14400 Detroit Avenue, Lakewood, OH 44107 .... (216) 228–8850

Counties: CUYAHOGA COUNTY (part). CITIES AND TOWNSHIPS: Bay Village, Berea, Brooklyn, Brooklyn Heights, Cleveland, Cuyahaga Heights, Fairview Park, Lakewood, Newberg Heights, North Olmsted, Olmsted Falls, Olmsted Township, Parma, Rocky River, Seven Hills, Strongsville, and Westlake. Population (2000), 630,730.

ZIP Codes: 44017, 44070, 44102, 44105, 44107, 44109, 44111, 44113, 44115–16, 44125–27, 44129–31, 44134–42, 44144–46, 44149, 44181

* * *

ELEVENTH DISTRICT

STEPHANIE TUBBS JONES, Democrat, of Cleveland, OH; born in Cleveland, OH, on September 10, 1949; B.A., Case Western Reserve University, 1971; J.D., Case Western Reserve University, 1974; Prosecutor, Cuyahoga County, OH; Judge of Common Pleas and Municipal Courts; Baptist; married to Mervyn; one child; committees: Ways and Means; Standards of Official Conduct; elected to the 106th Congress; reelected to each succeeding Congress.

Office Listings

http://www.house.gov/tubbsjones

1009 Longworth House Office Building, Washington, DC 20515 .... (202) 225–7032
Chief of Staff.—Patrice Willoughby. FAX: 225–1339
Scheduler.—Nikia Graster.
3645 Warrensville Center Road, Suite 204, Shaker Heights, OH 44122 .... (216) 522–4900

Counties: CUYAHOGA COUNTY (part). CITIES: Beachwood (part), Bedford Heights, Brooklyn (part), Cleveland (part), Cleveland Heights, East Cleveland, Euclid, Garfield Heights (part), Linndale, Maple Heights (part), Oakwood (part), Orange, Richmond Heights (part), Shaker Heights, South Euclid, University Heights, Warrensville Heights, and Woodmere. Population (2000), 630,730.

ZIP Codes: 44022, 44101–06, 44108–10, 44112–15, 44117–25, 44127–28, 44132, 44137, 44143, 44146, 44178, 44185, 44188–95, 44197–99

* * *

TWELFTH DISTRICT

PATRICK J. TIBERI, Republican, of Columbus, OH; born on October 21, 1962, in Columbus, OH; education: B.A., Ohio State University, 1985; employment: real estate agent; assistant to Representative John Kasich (R–OH); public service: Ohio House of Representatives, 1992–2000; served as Majority Leader; organizations: American Red Cross Columbus Chapter Advisory Board; Westerville Chamber of Commerce; Columbus Board of Realtors; Military Veterans and Community Service Commission; Sons of Italy; awards: Fraternal Order of Police Outstanding Legislator; Watchdog of the Treasury Award; American Red Cross Volunteer Service Award; married: Denice; elected to the 107th Congress on November 7, 2000; reelected to each succeeding Congress.

Office Listings

http://www.house.gov/tiberi

113 Cannon House Office Building, Washington, DC 20515 .... (202) 225–5355
Chief of Staff.—Chris Zeigler. FAX: 226–4523
Legislative Director.—Adam Francis.
Communications Director.—Bruce Cuthbertson.
2700 East Dublin-Granville Road, Suite 525, Columbus, OH 43231 .... (614) 523–2555
District Director.—Sally Testa.

Counties: DELAWARE, FRANKLIN (part), LICKING (part). Population (2000), 630,730.

ZIP Codes: 43001–04, 43011, 43013, 43015–18, 43021, 43023, 43025–27, 43031–33, 43035, 43040, 43046, 43054–56, 43061–62, 43064–66, 43068, 43071, 43073–74, 43080–82, 43085–86, 43105, 43147, 43201, 43203, 43205–07, 43209, 43211, 43213–15, 43218–19, 43224, 43226–27, 43229–32, 43235–36, 43240, 43334, 43342, 43344, 43356

* * *

THIRTEENTH DISTRICT

SHERROD BROWN, Democrat, of Lorain, OH; born on November 9, 1952 in Mansfield, OH; education: B.A., Yale University, 1974; M.A., education, Ohio State University, 1979; M.A., Public Administration, Ohio State University, 1981; Ohio House of Representatives, 1975–83; Ohio Secretary of State, 1983–91; Eagle Scout, Boy Scouts of America; children: Emily and Elizabeth; elected to the 103rd Congress; reelected to each succeeding Congress.

Office Listings

http://www.house.gov/sherrodbrown

2332 Rayburn House Office Building, Washington, DC 20515 .... (202) 225–3401
Chief of Staff.—Donna Pignatelli. FAX: 225–2266
Press Secretary.—Ted Miller.
205 W. 20th Street, M–230, Elyria, OH 44052 .... (440) 934–5100
1655 W. Market Street, Akron, OH 44313 .... (330) 865–8450

Counties: CUYAHOGA (part), LORAIN (part), MEDINA (part), SUMMIT (part). CITIES AND TOWNSHIPS: Akron, Lorain, Elyria, N. Ridgeville, Brunswick, Strongsville, and N. Royalton. Population (2000), 630,730.

ZIP Codes: 44001, 44011–12, 44028, 44035–36, 44039, 44044, 44052–55, 44133, 44136, 44141, 44147, 44149, 44203, 44210, 44212, 44216, 44221–24, 44230, 44233, 44253, 44256, 44264, 44280–81, 44286, 44301–04, 44306–14, 44317, 44319–22, 44325–26, 44328, 44333–34, 44372, 44393, 44398–99, 44614, 44645, 44685, 44720

FOURTEENTH DISTRICT

STEVEN C. LATOURETTE, Republican, of Madison Village, OH; born on July 22, 1954; education: graduated, Cleveland Heights High School, 1972; B.A., University of Michigan, 1976; J.D., Cleveland State University, 1979; employment: assistant public defender, Lake County, OH, Public Defender's Office, 1980–83; associated with Painesville firm of Cannon, Stern, Aveni and Krivok, 1983–86; Baker, Hackenberg and Collins, 1986–88; prosecuting attorney, Lake County, OH, 1988–94; served on the Lake County Budget Commission; executive board of the Lake County Narcotics Agency; chairman, County Task Force on Domestic Violence; trustee, Cleveland Policy Historical Society; director, Regional Forensic Laboratory; member: Lake County Association of Police Chiefs, Ohio Prosecuting Attorneys Association, and National District Attorneys Association; appointed to serve as a fellow of the American College of Prosecuting Attorneys; married: Susan; children: Sarah, Sam, Clare, and Amy; committees: Financial Services; Government Reform; Standards of Official Conduct; Transportation and Infrastructure; subcommittees: chairman, Economic Development, Public Buildings and Emergency Management; Financial Institutions and Consumer Credit; Government Efficiency and Financial Management; Highways, Transit and Pipelines; National Security, Emerging Threats and International Relations; Oversight and Investigations; Water Resources and the Environment; elected to the 104th Congress; reelected to each succeeding Congress.

Office Listings

http://www.house.gov/latourette

2453 Rayburn House Office Building, Washington, DC 20515 .... (202) 225–5731
Chief of Staff.—Matt Wallen. FAX: 225–3307
Communications Director.—Deborah Setliff.
Executive Assistant / Scheduler.—Kathy Kato.
1 Victoria Place, Room 320, Painesville, OH 44077 .... (440) 352–3939

Counties: ASHTABULA, CUYAHOGA (part), GEAUGA, LAKE, PORTAGE (part), SUMMIT (part), TRUMBULL (part). Population (2000), 630,730.

ZIP Codes: 44003–05, 44010, 44021–24, 44026, 44030, 44032–33, 44040–41, 44045–48, 44056–57, 44060–62, 44064–65, 44067–68, 44072–73, 44076–77, 44080–82, 44084–88, 44092–97, 44099, 44124, 44139, 44141, 44143, 44202, 44221, 44223–24, 44231, 44234, 44236–37, 44240, 44255, 44262, 44264, 44278, 44404, 44410, 44417–18, 44428, 44439, 44450, 44470, 44491

* * *

FIFTEENTH DISTRICT

DEBORAH PRYCE, Republican, of Columbus, OH; born on July 29, 1951 in Warren, OH; education: B.A., *cum laude,* Ohio State University, Columbus, 1973; J.D., Capital University Law School, Columbus, OH, 1976; attorney; admitted to the Ohio bar in 1976; administrative law judge, Ohio Department of Insurance, 1976–78; first assistant city prosecutor, senior assistant city attorney, and assistant city attorney, Columbus City Attorney's Office, 1978–85; judge, Franklin County Municipal Court, presiding judge for two terms; Ohio Supreme Court Victims of Crime Award, 1986–92; YWCA Woman of the Year Award, 1995; member, Ohio Supreme Court Committee on Dispute Resolution; chairperson, Municipal Court Subcommittee; 2001 Ohio Women's Hall of Fame Inductee; Board member, National Fund for the U.S. Botanic Garden; Board member, John F. Kennedy Center for the Performing Arts; American Council of Young Political Leaders, delegate to Australia, 1986; session member, former deacon and stewardship chair, Indianola Presbyterian Church; children: Caroline (deceased), and Mia; 103rd Congress freshman class policy director; 104th Congress transition team; elected Republican Conference Secretary for the 105th Congress; elected Republican Conference Vice Chairman, 107th Congress; elected Republican Conference Chair, 108th Congress; Chair, House Rules Committee Subcommittee on Legislative and Budget Process; on leave with seniority, Financial Services Committee; Deputy Whip, NRCC Executive Committee; elected to the 103rd Congress; reelected to each succeeding Congress.

Office Listings

http://www.house.gov/pryce

221 Cannon House Office Building, Washington, DC 20515 .... (202) 225–2015
Chief of Staff.—Lori Salley.
Legislative Director.—Shiloh Reiher.
Executive Assistant.—Sara Rogers.
500 S. Front Street, Room1130,Columbus, OH 43215 .... (614) 469–5614
District Director.—Marcee McCreary.

Counties: FRANKLIN (part), MADISON, UNION. Population (2000), 630,730.

ZIP Codes: 43007, 43015–17, 43026, 43029, 43036, 43040–41, 43044–45, 43060–61, 43064–67, 43077, 43084–85, 43110, 43119, 43123, 43125–26, 43137, 43140, 43143, 43146, 43151, 43153, 43162, 43196, 43198, 43201–04, 43206–07, 43210–12, 43214–16, 43220–24, 43228–29, 43231–32, 43234–35, 43251, 43260, 43265–66, 43268, 43270–72, 43279, 43287, 43291, 43299, 43302, 43319, 43340, 43342, 43344, 43358, 45368–69

* * *

SIXTEENTH DISTRICT

RALPH REGULA, Republican, of Navarre, OH; born in Beach City, OH, December 3, 1924; education: B.A., Mount Union College, Alliance, OH, 1948; LL.B., William McKinley School of Law, Canton, OH, 1952; military service: U.S. Navy, 1944–46; employment: attorney at law; admitted to Ohio bar and began practice in Navarre, OH, 1952; Ohio House of Representatives, 1965–66, and Ohio Senate, 1967–72; member: Ohio State Board of Education, 1960–64; Saint Timothy Episcopal Church, Massillon, OH; board of trustees, Mount Union College; honorary member, board of advisors, Walsh College; Kiwanis; Grange; trustee, Stark County Historical Society; married: Mary Ann Rogusky, 1950; children: Martha, David, and Richard; committee: Appropriations; elected to the 93rd Congress, November 7, 1972; reelected to each succeeding Congress.

Office Listings

http://www.house.gov/regula

2306 Rayburn House Office Building, Washington, DC 20515 .... (202) 225–3876
Executive Assistant.—Sylvia Snyder. FAX: 225–3059
Appropriations.—Lori Rowley.
Legal Counsel.—Karen Buttaro.
Chief of Staff / Press Secretary.—Connie Veillette.
4150 Belden Village Street NW, Suite 408, Canton, OH 44718 .... (330) 489–4414
District Staff Director.—Robert Mullen.

Counties: ASHLAND (part), MEDINA (part), STARK, WAYNE. Population (2000), 630,730.

ZIP Codes: 44090, 44201, 44203, 44214–17, 44230, 44233, 44235, 44251, 44253–54, 44256, 44258, 44260, 44270, 44273–76, 44280–82, 44287, 44321, 44333, 44601, 44606, 44608, 44611–14, 44618, 44624, 44626–27, 44630, 44632, 44634, 44636, 44638, 44640–41, 44643, 44645–48, 44650, 44652, 44657, 44659, 44662, 44666–67, 44669–70, 44676–77, 44680, 44685, 44688–89, 44691, 44701–12, 44714, 44718, 44720–21, 44730, 44735, 44750, 44760, 44767, 44799, 44805, 44822, 44838, 44840, 44842–43, 44864, 44866, 44878, 44880, 44903

* * *

SEVENTEENTH DISTRICT

TIM RYAN, Democrat, of Niles, OH; born on July 16, 1973; education: B.S., Bowling Green University, 1995; J.D., Franklin Pierce Law Center, 2000; awarded a National Italian American Foundation Scholarship; profession: Attorney; internship, Trumbull County Prosecutor's Office; also worked as a congressional legislative aide in Washington, DC; organizations: former president, Trumbull County Young Democrats; former chairman, Earning by Learning Program in Warren, OH; public service: Ohio State Senate, 2000–2002; religion: Catholic; elected to the 108th Congress on November 5, 2002.

Office Listings

http://timryan.house.gov

222 Cannon House Office Building, Washington, DC 20515 .... (202) 225–5261
Chief of Staff.—Mary Anne Walsh. FAX: 225–3719
Scheduler.—Erin Stone.
Constituent and Communications Liaison.—Jennifer Hoelzer.
197 West Market Street, Warren, OH 44481 .... (330) 373–0074
241 Federal Plaza West, Youngstown, OH 44503 .... (330) 740–0193

Counties: MAHONING (part), PORTAGE (part), SUMMIT (part), TRUMBULL (part). Population (2000), 630,730.

ZIP Codes: 44201, 44211, 44221, 44223–24, 44231–32, 44236, 44240–43, 44250, 44255, 44260, 44265–66, 44272, 44278, 44285, 44288, 44302–06, 44308, 44310–13, 44315–16, 44319, 44402–06, 44410–12, 44417–18, 44420, 44424–25, 44429–30, 44436–38, 44440, 44444, 44446, 44449–50, 44453, 44470–71, 44473, 44481–86, 44488, 44491, 44501–07, 44509–12, 44514–15, 44555, 44599, 44632, 44685, 44720

EIGHTEENTH DISTRICT

ROBERT W. NEY, Republican, of St. Clairsville, OH; born in Wheeling, WV, July 5, 1954; education: graduated, St. John's High School, Bellaire, OH; B.S., Ohio State University, Columbus, OH; Ohio House of Representatives, 1981–82, and Ohio Senate, 1984–94; Ohio Senate Chairman, Finance Committee; member: Elks, Lions, Kiwanis, and NRA; married: Elizabeth Ney; children: Robert William II, and Kayla Marie; committees: chairman, House Administration; Financial Services; Transportation and Infrastructure; chairman, Joint Committee on Printing; subcommittee chairman, Housing and Community Opportunity; Deputy Majority Whip; elected to the 104th Congress; relected to each succeeding Congress.

Office Listings

http://www.house.gov/ney bobney@mail.house.gov

2438 Rayburn House Office Building, Washington, DC 20515 .... (202) 225–6265
Chief of Staff.—Will Heaton. FAX: 225–3394
Legislative Director.—Greg Mesack.
Scheduler.—Sarah Habansky.
Legislative Assistants: J.P. Dutton, Chris Otillio.
146 A West Main Street, St. Clairsville, OH 43950 .... (740) 699–2704
Toll-free, Ohio only. (866) 464–4618
District Director.—John Poe.
126 East Second Street, Suite D, Chillicothe, OH 45601 .... (740) 779–1634
200 Broadway, Jackson, OH 45640 .... (740) 288–1430
152 Second Street, NE., Hilton-Fairfield Building #200, New Philadelphia, OH 44663 .... (330) 364–6380
District Representative.—Lesley Applegarth.
Masonic Temple Building, 38 North Fourth Street, Room 502, Zanesville, OH 43701 .... (614) 452–7023
District Representative.—Joe Rose.

Counties: ATHENS (part), BELMONT (PART), CARROLL, COSHOCTON, GUERNSEY, HARRISON, HOCKING, HOLMES, JACKSON, KNOX, LICKING (part), MONROE, MORGAN, MUSKINGUM, ROSS (part), TUSCARAWAS, VINTON. Population (2000), 630,730.

ZIP Codes: 43005–06, 43008, 43011, 43014, 43019, 43022–23, 43025, 43028, 43030, 43037, 43048, 43050, 43055–56, 43058, 43071, 43076, 43080, 43093, 43098, 43101–02, 43107, 43111, 43127, 43130, 43135, 43138, 43144, 43149, 43152, 43155, 43158, 43160, 43701–02, 43718, 43720–25, 43727–28, 43730–36, 43738–40, 43746, 43749–50, 43755–56, 43758, 43760, 43762, 43766–68, 43771–73, 43777–78, 43780, 43787, 43791, 43802–05, 43811–12, 43821–22, 43824, 43828, 43830, 43832, 43836–37, 43840, 43842–45, 43901, 43903, 43906–08, 43910, 43927–28, 43933, 43945, 43950, 43972–74, 43976–77, 43981, 43983–84, 43986, 43988, 44427, 44607–08, 44610–12, 44615, 44617, 44620–22, 44624–29, 44631, 44633, 44637–39, 44643–44, 44651, 44653–54, 44656–57, 44660–61, 44663, 44671, 44675–76, 44678–83, 44687–90, 44693, 44695, 44697, 44699, 44730, 44813, 44822, 44842, 45123, 45601, 45612–13, 45617, 45621–22, 45628, 45633–34, 45640, 45644, 45647, 45651, 45653–54, 45656, 45672–73, 45681–82, 45685, 45690, 45692, 45695, 45698, 45701, 45710–11, 45715–16, 45719, 45732, 45740–41, 45761, 45764, 45766, 45780, 45782, 45786

OKLAHOMA

(Population 2000, 3,450,654)

SENATORS

DON NICKLES, Republican, of Ponca City, OK; born in Ponca City, on December 6, 1948; graduated, Ponca City High School, 1967; B.S., Business Administration, Oklahoma State University, 1971; served in National Guard, 1970–76; Vice President and General Manager, Nickles Machine Corporation; served in Oklahoma State Senate, 1979–80; cofounder and member, Oklahoma Coalition for Peace Through Strength; served on the boards of: Ponca City United Way, St. Mary's Catholic Church Parish Council, Chamber of Commerce, Kay County Council for Retarded Children; chairman of the National Republican Senatorial Committee, 1988–90; chairman, Republican Policy Committee, 1991–95; Assistant Republican Leader, 1996–2002; chairman, Committee on the Budget since 2003; member: Rotary Club; Fellowship of Christian Athletes; married to the former Linda Lou Morrison; four children: Don, Jenny, Kim, and Robyn; other committees: Energy and Natural Resources; Finance; Rules and Administration; elected to the U.S. Senate on November 4, 1980; reelected to each succeeding Senate term.

Office Listings

http://nickles.senate.gov

133 Hart Senate Office Building, Washington, DC 20510 .... (202) 224–5754
Administrative Assistant.—Bret Bernhardt. FAX: 224–6008
Legislative / Communications Director.—Brook Simmons.
Office Manager.—Pamela Fleming.
100 North Broadway, Suite 1820, Oklahoma City, OK 73102 .... (405) 231–4941
711 D Avenue, SW., Suite 202, Lawton, OK 73501 .... (580) 357–9878
3310 Mid-Continent Tower, 409 South Boston, Tulsa, OK 74103 .... (918) 581–7651
1914 Lake Road, Ponca City, OK 74604 .... (580) 767–0116

* * *

JAMES M. INHOFE, Republican, of Tulsa, OK; born in Des Moines, IA, on November 17, 1934; education: graduated Central High School, Tulsa, OK, 1953; B.A., University of Tulsa, OK, 1959; military service: served in the U.S. Army, private first class, 1957–58; employment: businessman; active pilot; president, Quaker Life Insurance Company; Oklahoma House of Representatives, 1967–69; Oklahoma State Senate, 1969–77; Mayor of Tulsa, OK, 1978–84; religion: member, First Presbyterian Church of Tulsa; married: the former Kay Kirkpatrick; children: Jim, Perry, Molly, and Katy; eleven grandchildren; committees: Armed Services; chairman, Environment and Public Works; Indian Affairs; elected to the 100th Congress on November 4, 1986; reelected to each succeeding Congress; elected to the U.S. Senate on November 8, 1994, finishing the unexpired term of Senator David Boren; reelected to each succeeding Senate term.

Office Listings

http://inhofe.senate.gov

453 Russell Senate Office Building, Washington, DC 20510 .... (202) 224–4721
Press Secretary.—Gary Hoitsma.
Chief of Staff.—Glenn Powell.
Legislative Director.—Chad Bradley.
Scheduler.—Wendi Price.
Suite 530, 1924 South Utica, Tulsa, OK 74104 .... (918) 748–5111
1900 N.W. Expressway, Suite 1210, Oklahoma City, OK 73118 .... (405) 608–4381
Suite 104, 302 North Independence, Enid, OK 73701 .... (405) 234–5104
Suite 106, 215 East Choctaw, McAlester, OK 74501 .... (918) 426–0933

REPRESENTATIVES

FIRST DISTRICT

JOHN SULLIVAN, Republican, of Tulsa, OK; born on January 1, 1965, in Tulsa; education: B.B.A., Northeastern State University, 1992; professional: fuel sales, Love's Country Stores; public service: Oklahoma House of Representatives, 1995-2002; organizations: vice president, Tulsa County Republican Men's Club; member, Tulsa County Young Republicans; member, St. John's Medical Center Community Liaison Board; family: married to Judith; children: Thomas, Meredith, and Sydney; elected to the 107th Congress, by special election, on January 8, 2002; reelected to each succeeding Congress.

Office Listings

http://sullivan.house.gov

114 Cannon House Office Building, Washington, DC 20510 .... (202) 225–2211
Chief of Staff.—Elizabeth Bartheld. FAX: 225–9187
Scheduler.—Arden Herrington.
2424 East 21st Street, Suite 510, Tulsa, OK 74114 .... (918) 749–0014
Chief of Staff.—Richard Hedgecock.

Counties: CREEK (part), ROGERS (part), TULSA, WAGONER, WASHINGTON. Population (2000), 690,131.

ZIP Codes: 74003–06, 74008, 74011–14, 74021–22, 74029, 74033, 74037, 74039, 74041, 74043, 74047–48, 74050–51, 74053, 74055, 74061, 74063, 74066, 74070, 74073, 74080, 74082–83, 74101–08, 74110, 74112, 74114–17, 74119–21, 74126–30, 74132–37, 74141, 74145–50, 74152–53, 74155–59, 74169–72, 74182–84, 74186–87, 74189, 74192–94, 74337, 74352, 74403, 74429, 74434, 74436, 74446, 74454, 74458, 74467, 74477

* * *

SECOND DISTRICT

BRAD CARSON, Democrat, of Claremore, OK; born on March 11, 1967, in Winslow, AZ; education: B.A., Baylor University; M.A., Oxford University (Rhodes Scholar); J.D., University of Oklahoma; recognized as Outstanding Law School Graduate; profession: Attorney; Special Assistant to the Secretary of Defense for Special Projects; organizations: Legal Services of Eastern Oklahoma; Cherokee Bar Association; Oklahoma Bar Association; awards: 1996 Exceptional Contribution to Legal Services Award; religion: Baptist; family: married to Julie; elected to the 107th Congress on November 7, 2000; reelected to each succeeding Congress.

Office Listings

http://carson.house.gov

317 Cannon House Office Building, Washington, DC 20515 .... (202) 225–2701
Chief of Staff.—Chebon Marshall. FAX: 225–3038
Deputy Chief of Staff.—Cathie McCarley.
Press Secretary.—Brad Luna.
215 State Street, Suite 815, Muskogee, OK 74401 .... (918) 687–2533

Counties: ADAIR, ATOKA, BRYAN, CHEROKEE, CHOCTAW, COAL, CRAIG, DELAWARE, HASKELL, HUGHES, JOHNSTON, LATIMER, LEFLORE, MAYES, MCCURTAIN, MCINTOSH, MUSKOGEE, NOWATA, OKFUSKEE, OKMULGEE, OTTAWA, PITTSBURG, PUSHMATAHA, ROGERS, SEQUOYAH. Population (2000), 690,130.

ZIP Codes: 73432, 73447, 73449–50, 73455, 73460–61, 74006, 74010, 74015–19, 74021, 74027, 74031, 74036, 74042, 74047–48, 74053, 74055, 74072, 74079–80, 74083, 74301, 74330–33, 74335, 74337–40, 74342–47, 74349–50, 74352, 74354–55, 74358–70, 74401–03, 74421–23, 74425–32, 74434–38, 74440–42, 74444–45, 74447, 74450–52, 74455–57, 74459–65, 74468–72, 74501–02, 74521–23, 74525, 74528–31, 74533–36, 74538, 74540, 74543, 74545–47, 74549, 74552–63, 74565, 74567, 74569–72, 74574, 74576–78, 74701–02, 74720–24, 74726–31, 74733–38, 74740–41, 74743, 74745, 74747–48, 74750, 74752–56, 74759–61, 74764, 74766, 74827, 74829, 74833, 74836, 74839, 74845, 74848, 74850, 74856, 74859–60, 74871, 74878, 74880, 74883, 74901–02, 74930–32, 74935–37, 74939–49, 74951, 74953–57, 74959–60, 74962–66

* * *

THIRD DISTRICT

FRANK D. LUCAS, Republican, of Cheyenne, OK; born in Cheyenne, January 6, 1960; attended Oklahoma State University, Stillwater, 1982; rancher and farmer; served in Oklahoma State House of Representatives, 1989–94; secretary, Oklahoma House Republican Caucus, 1991–94; member: Oklahoma Farm Bureau, Oklahoma Cattlemen's Association, and Oklahoma Shorthorn Association; married to Lynda Bradshaw Lucas; three children: Jessica, Ashlea, and Grant; elected to the 103rd Congress, by special election, in May 1994; reelected to each succeeding Congress.

Office Listings

http://www.house.gov/lucas

2342 Rayburn House Office Building, Washington, DC 20515 .... (202) 225–5565
Administrative Assistant / Legislative Director.—Nicole Scott. FAX: 225–8698
Press Secretary.—Jim Luetkemeyer.
Scheduler / Office Manager.—Jessica Reinsch.
Legislative Assistants: Richard Blackwood, Amber Coulter, Marna Harris.
10952 Northwest Expressway, Suite B, Yukon, OK 73099 .... (405) 373–1958
Chief of Staff.—Stacey Glasscock.

720 South Husband, Suite 7, Stillwater, OK 74075 .... (405) 624–6407
Field Representative.—Julie Arntz.
2728 Williams Avenue, Suite F, Woodward, OK 73801 .... (580) 256–5752
Field Representative.—Bryce Marlatt.

Counties: ALFALFA, BEAVER, BECKHAM, BLAINE, CADDO, CANADIAN (part), CIMARRON, CREEK (part), CUSTER, DEWEY, ELLIS, GARFIELD, GRANT, GREER, HARMON, HARPER, JACKSON, KINGFISHER, KAY, KIOWA, LINCOLN, LOGAN, MAJOR, NOBLE, OSAGE, PAWNEE, PAYNE, ROGER MILLS, TEXAS, WASHITA, WOODS, AND WOODWARD. CITIES: Altus, Clinton, El Reno, Elk City, Enid, Guthrie, Guymon, Oklahoma City (part), Perry, Ponce City, Sapulpa (part), Stillwater, Tulsa (part), Weatherford, Woodward and Yukon. Population (2000), 690,131.

ZIP Codes: 73001, 73003, 73005–07, 73009, 73014–17, 73021–22, 73024, 73027–29, 73033–34, 73036, 73038, 73040–45, 73047–48, 73050, 73053–54, 73056, 73058–59, 73061–64, 73073, 73077–79, 73085, 73090, 73092, 73094, 73096–97, 73099, 73127, 73437, 73501, 73521–23, 73526, 73532, 73537, 73539, 73544, 73547, 73549–50, 73554, 73556, 73559–60, 73564, 73566, 73571, 73601, 73620, 73622, 73624–28, 73632, 73638–39, 73641–42, 73644–48, 73650–51, 73654–55, 73658–64, 73666–69, 73673, 73701–03, 73705–06, 73716–20, 73722, 73724, 73726–31, 73733–39, 73741–44, 73746–47, 73749–50, 73753–64, 73766, 73768, 73770–73, 73801–02, 73832, 73834–35, 73838, 73840–44, 73847–48, 73851–53, 73855, 73857–60, 73901, 73931–33, 73937–39, 73942, 73944–47, 73949–51, 74001–03, 74010, 74020, 74022–23, 74026, 74028, 74030, 74032, 74034–35, 74038–39, 74044–47, 74051–52, 74054, 74056, 74058–60, 74062–63, 74066–68, 74070–71, 74073–79, 74081, 74084–85, 74106, 74126–27, 74131–32, 74601–02, 74604, 74630–33, 74636–37, 74640–41, 74643–44, 74646–47, 74650–53, 74824, 74832, 74834, 74851, 74855, 74859, 74864, 74869, 74875, 74881

* * *

FOURTH DISTRICT

TOM COLE, Republican, of Moore, OK; born on April 28, 1949, in Shreveport, LA; education: B.A., Grinnell College, 1971; M.A. Yale University, 1974; Ph.D., University of Oklahoma, 1984; Watson Fellow, 1971–72; and a Fulbright Fellow, 1977–78; professional: former college professor of history and politics; President, Cole Hargrave Snodgrass & Associates (political consulting firm); public service: Oklahoma State Senate, 1988–91; Oklahoma Secretary of State, 1995–99; has served as Chairman, and Executive Director, of the Oklahoma Republican Party; Executive Director, National Republican Congressional Committee; and Chief of Staff of the Republican National Committee; family: married to Ellen; one child: Mason; religion: United Methodist; elected to the 108th Congress on November 5, 2002.

Office Listings

http://www.house.gov/cole

501 Cannon House Office Building, Washington, DC 20515 .... (202) 225–6165
Chief of Staff.—Leslie Sowell. FAX: 225–3512
Legislative Director / Legal Counsel.—Rob Johnson.
Senior Legislative Director.—Chris Carron.
Press Secretary.—Julie Bley.
2420 Springer Drive, Suite 120, Norman, OK 73069 .... (405) 329–6500
711 SW., D Avenue, Suite 201, Lawton, OK 73501 .... (580) 357–2131

Counties: CANADIAN (part), CARTER, CLEVELAND, COMANCHE, COTTON, GARVIN, GRADY, JEFFERSON, LOVE, MARSHALL, MCCLAIN, MURRAY, OKLAHOMA (part), PONTOTOC, STEPHENS, TILLMAN. Population (2000), 690,131.

ZIP Codes: 73002, 73004, 73006, 73010–11, 73017–20, 73023, 73026, 73030–32, 73036, 73051–52, 73055, 73057, 73059, 73064–65, 73067–72, 73074–75, 73079–80, 73082, 73086, 73089, 73092–93, 73095, 73098–99, 73110, 73115, 73127–30, 73135, 73139–40, 73145, 73149–50, 73153, 73159–60, 73165, 73169–70, 73173, 73179, 73189, 73401–03, 73425, 73430, 73433–44, 73446, 73448, 73453, 73456, 73458–59, 73463, 73476, 73481, 73487–88, 73491, 73501–03, 73505–07, 73520, 73527–31, 73533–34, 73536, 73538, 73540–43, 73546, 73548, 73551–53, 73555, 73557, 73559, 73561–62, 73564–70, 73572–73, 74820–21, 74825, 74831, 74842–44, 74851, 74857, 74865, 74871–72

* * *

FIFTH DISTRICT

ERNEST J. ISTOOK, JR., Republican, of Oklahoma City, OK; born in Fort Worth, TX, on February 11, 1950; education: graduated, Castleberry High School, Ft. Worth, 1967; B.A., Baylor University, 1971; J.D., Oklahoma City University, 1976; emploment: attorney; admitted to the Oklahoma bar, 1977; reporter, WKY, KOMA, 1972–77; city councilman, Warr Acres, 1982–86; library board chairman, Oklahoma City, 1985–86; director, Warr Acres Chamber of Commerce, 1986–92; Oklahoma State House of Representatives, 1986–92; married: the former Judy Bills, 1973; children: Butch, Chad, Amy, Diana, and Emily; committees: Appropriations; Select Committee on Homeland Security; elected on November 3, 1992, to the 103rd Congress; reelected to each succeeding Congress.

Office Listings

http://www.house.gov/istook

2404 Rayburn House Office Building, Washington, DC 20515 .... (202) 225–2132
Chief of Staff.—John Albaugh. FAX: 226–1463
Legislative Director.—Kevin Johnson.
Administrative Assistant.—Carrie Hobbs.
Scheduler.—Kim Rubin.
5400 North Grand Boulevard, Suite 505, Oklahoma City, OK 73112 .... (405) 942–3636
102 South 5th, Ponca City, OK 74601 .... (580) 762–6778
117 West 5th Street, Suite 403, Bartlesville, OK 74003 .... (918) 336–5546

Counties: OKLAHOMA (part), POTTAWATOMIE, and SEMINOLE. CITIES: Arcadia, Bethany, Bethel Acres, Choctaw, Cromwell, Del City, Earlsboro, Edmond, Forrest Park, Harrah, Johnson, Jones, Konawa, Lake Aluma, Lima, Luther, Macomb, Maud, Midwest City (part), Nichols Hills, Nicoma Park, Oklahoma City, Pink, Sasakwa, Seminole, Shawnee, Smith Village, Spencer, St. Louis, Tecumesh, The Village, Tribbey, Valley Brook, Wanette, Warr Acres, Wewoka, and Woodlawn Park. Population (2000), 690,131.

ZIP Codes: 73003, 73007–08, 73013, 73020, 73034, 73045, 73049, 73054, 73066, 73078, 73083–84, 73101–32, 73134–37, 73139, 73141–44, 73146–49, 73151–52, 73154–57, 73159, 73162, 73164, 73169, 73172–73, 73178–79, 73184–85, 73190, 73194–96, 73198, 74801–02, 74804, 74818, 74826, 74830, 74837, 74840, 74849, 74851–52, 74854, 74857, 74859, 74866–68, 74873, 74878, 74884

OREGON

(Population 2000, 3,421,399)

SENATORS

RON WYDEN, Democrat, of Portland, OR; born in Wichita, KS, on May 3, 1949; education: graduated from Palo Alto High School, 1967; B.A. in political science, with distinction, Stanford University, 1971; J.D., University of Oregon Law School, 1974; employment: attorney; member, American Bar Association; former director, Oregon Legal Services for the Elderly; former public member, Oregon State Board of Examiners of Nursing Home Administrators; cofounder and codirector, Oregon Gray Panthers, 1974–80; children: Adam David and Lilly Anne; elected to the 97th Congress, November 4, 1980; reelected to each succeeding Congress; committees: Budget; Commerce, Science and Transportation; Energy and Natural Resources; Environment and Public Works; Special Committee on Aging; Select Committee on Intelligence; elected to the U.S. Senate on January 30, 1996, to fill the unexpired term of Senator Bob Packwood; reelected to each succeeding Senate term.

Office Listings

http://wyden.senate.gov

516 Hart Senate Office Building, Washington, DC 20510 .... (202) 224–5244
Chief of Staff.—Josh Kardon.
Legislative Director.—Carole Grunberg.
Communications Director.—Lisa Wade Raasch.
Scheduler.—Bruce Ehrle.
700 NE Multnomah Street, Suite 450, Portland, OR 97232 .... (503) 326–7525
151 West Seventh Avenue, Suite 435, Eugene, OR 97401 .... (541) 431–0229
The Federal Courthouse, 310 West Sixth Street, Room 118, Medford, OR 97501 ... (541) 858–5122
The Jamison Building, 131 NW Hawthorne Avenue, Suite 107, Bend, OR 97701 .. (541) 330–9142
SAC Annex Building, 105 Fir Street, Suite 201, LaGrande, OR 97850 .... (541) 962–7691
777 13th Street, SE, Suite 110, Salem, OR 97310 .... (503) 589–4555

* * *

GORDON HAROLD SMITH, Republican, of Pendleton, OR; born May 25, 1952, in Pendleton, B.A., 1976, Brigham Young University; LL.B, 1979, Southwestern University; served as law clerk to Justice H. Vernon Payne of the New Mexico Supreme Court and practiced law in Arizona; elected to State of Oregon Senate, 1993; elected Oregon Senate President, 1994; president/owner of Smith Frozen Foods, Inc., since 1981; committees: Special Committee on Aging; Commerce, Science, and Transportation; Energy and Natural Resources; Finance; Indian Affairs; Rules and Administration; married: Sharon Lankford Smith, 1975; three children: Brittany, Garrett, and Morgan; elected to the U.S. Senate on November 5, 1996; reelected to each succeeding Senate term.

Office Listings

http://gsmith.senate.gov

404 Russell Senate Office Building, Washington, DC 20510 .... (202) 224–3753
Chief of Staff.—John Easton.
Legislative Director.—Penny Schiller.
Director of Administration.—Sue Keenom.
Communications Director.—Chris Matthews.
121 S.W. Salmon, Suite 1250, Portland, OR 97204 .... (503) 326–3386
Jager Building, 116 S. Main Street, Suite 3, Pendleton, OR 97801 .... (541) 278–1129
Federal Building, 211 E. 7th Avenue, Room 202, Eugene, OR 97401 .... (541) 465–6750
Security Plaza, 1175 E. Main Street, Suite 2D, Medford, OR 97504 .... (541) 608–9102
Jamison Building, 131 NW Hawthorne Avenue, Suite 107, Bend, OR 97701 .... (541) 318–1298

REPRESENTATIVES

FIRST DISTRICT

DAVID WU, Democrat, of Portland, OR; born in Taiwan on April 8, 1955; moved to the United States, with his family, in October, 1961; married: Michelle; two children: Matthew, Sarah; education: B.S., Stanford University, 1977; attended, Harvard University Medical School; law degree, Yale University, 1982; profession: lawyer; co-founder of Cohen & Wu (law firm), 1988; first Chinese American member of the U.S. House of Representatives; chairman,

Congressional Asian Pacific American Caucus; member, New Democrat Coalition; committees: Education and the Workforce; Science; subcommittees: 21st Century Competiveness; Employer-Employee Relations; Space and Aeronautics; Energy; elected to the 106th Congress; reelected to each succeeding Congress.

Office Listings

http://www.house.gov/wu

1023 Longworth House Office Building, Washington, DC 20515 .... (202) 225–0855
Chief of Staff.—Julie Tippens. FAX: 225–9497
Executive Assistant.—Ajah Maloney.
Press Secretary.—Cameron Johnson.
620 SW Main Street, Suite 606, Portland, OR 97205 .... (503) 326–2901

Counties: CLATSOP, COLUMBIA, MULTNOMAH (part), WASHINGTON, YAMHILL. Population (2000), 684,277.

ZIP Codes: 97005–08, 97016, 97018, 97035, 97048, 97051, 97053–54, 97056, 97062, 97064, 97070, 97075–78, 97101–03, 97106, 97109–11, 97113–17, 97119, 97121, 97123–25, 97127–28, 97132–33, 97138, 97140, 97144–46, 97148, 97201, 97204–05, 97207–10, 97219, 97221, 97223–25, 97228–29, 97231, 97239–40, 97251, 97253–55, 97258, 97272, 97280–81, 97291, 97296, 97298, 97378, 97396, 97498

* * *

SECOND DISTRICT

GREG WALDEN, Republican, of Hood River, OR; born on January 10, 1957, in The Dalles, OR; married: Mylene Walden; one child: Anthony David Walden; education: graduated from the University of Oregon, 1981; B.S. in Journalism; owner, Columbia Gorge Broadcasters, Inc.; member, and Assistant Majority Leader, Oregon State Senate, 1995–97; member, Oregon State House of Representatives, 1989–95, and Majority Leader, 1991–93; National Republican Legislators Association Legislator of the Year, 1993; Oregon Jaycees Outstanding Young Oregonian, 1991; member, Associated Oregon Industries; Oregon Health Sciences Foundation; Hood River Rotary Club; Hood River Elk's Club; National Federation of Independent Business; Hood River Chamber of Commerce; Hood River Memorial Hospital; Columbia Bancorp; committees: Energy and Commerce; Resources; subcommittees: vice chairman, Oversight and Investigations; Energy and Air Quality; Telecommunications and the Internet; Water and Power; elected to the 106th Congress; reelected to each succeeding Congress.

Office Listings

http://www.walden.house.gov

1404 Longworth House Office Building, Washington, DC 20515 .... (202) 225–6730
Chief of Staff.—Brian MacDonald. FAX: 225–5774
Legislative Director.—Brian Hard.
Executive Assistant.—Joel Willard.
843 East Main, Suite 400, Medford, OR 97504 .... (541) 776–4646
District Director.—John Snider. (800) 533–3303

Counties: BAKER, CROOK, DESCHUTES, GILLIAM, GRANT, HARNEY, HOOD RIVER, JACKSON, JEFFERSON, JOSEPHINE (part), KLAMATH, LAKE, MALHEUR, MORROW, SHERMAN, UMATILLA, UNION, WALLOWA, WASCO, WHEELER. Population (2000), 684,280.

ZIP Codes: 97001, 97014, 97021, 97029, 97031, 97033, 97037, 97039–41, 97044, 97050, 97057–58, 97063, 97065, 97116, 97425, 97501–04, 97520, 97522, 97524–28, 97530, 97533, 97535–37, 97539–41, 97544, 97601–04, 97620 27, 97630, 97632–41, 97701–02, 97707–12, 97720–22, 97730–39, 97741, 97750–54, 97756, 97758–61, 97801, 97810, 97812–14, 97817–20, 97823–28, 97830, 97833–46, 97848, 97850, 97856–57, 97859, 97861–62, 97864–65, 97867–70, 97873–77, 97880, 97882–86, 97901–11, 97913–14, 97917–18, 97920

* * *

THIRD DISTRICT

EARL BLUMENAUER, Democrat, of Portland, OR; born on August 16, 1948 in Portland; graduated from Centennial High School; Lewis and Clark College; J.D., Northwestern School of Law; assistant to the president, Portland State University; served in Oregon State Legislature 1973–78; chaired Revenue and School Finance Committee; Multnomah County Commissioner, 1978–85; Portland City Commissioner 1986–96; served on Governor's Commission on Higher

Education; National League of Cities Transportation Committee; National Civic League Board of Directors; Oregon Environmental Council; Oregon Public Broadcasting; two children: Jon and Anne; elected to the U.S. House of Representatives on May 21, 1996, to fill the vacancy created by Representative Ron Wyden's election to the U.S. Senate; reelected to each succeeding Congress.

Office Listings

http://www.house.gov/blumenauer

2446 Rayburn House Office Building, Washington, DC 20515 .... (202) 225–4811
Administrative Assistant.—Mariia Zimmerman. FAX: 225–8941
Communications Director.—Kathie Eastman.
Legislative Director.—James Koski.
729 Northeast Oregon Street, Suite 115, Portland, OR 97232 .... (503) 231–2300
District Director.—Julia Pomeroy.

Counties: MULTNOMAH (part), CLAKAMUS (part). Population (2000), 684,279.

ZIP Codes: 97004, 97009, 97011, 97014–15, 97017, 97019, 97022–24, 97028, 97030, 97035, 97045, 97049, 97055, 97060, 97067, 97080, 97124, 97133, 97202–03, 97206, 97210–18, 97220, 97222, 97227, 97229–33, 97236, 97238, 97242, 97256, 97266–67, 97269, 97282–83, 97286, 97290, 97292–94, 97299

* * *

FOURTH DISTRICT

PETER A. DEFAZIO, Democrat, of Springfield, OR; born in Needham, MA, May 27, 1947; B.A., Tufts University, 1969; M.S., University of Oregon, 1977; aide to Representative Jim Weaver, 1977–82; Lane County commissioner, 1983–86; committees: Transportation and Infrastructure; Select Committee on Homeland Security; elected to the 100th Congress, November 4, 1986; reelected to each succeeding Congress.

Office Listings

http://www.house.gov/defazio

2134 Rayburn House Office Building, Washington, DC 20515 .... (202) 225–6416
Administrative Assistant.—Penny Dodge.
Legislative Director.—Tom Vinson.
151 West Seventh Avenue, Suite 400, Eugene, OR 97401 .... (541) 465–6732
District Director.—Karmen Fore. (800) 944–9603
125 Central Avenue, Room 350, Coos Bay, OR 97420 .... (541) 269–2609
612 SE Jackson Street, Room 9, Roseburg, OR 97470 .... (541) 440–3523

Counties: BENTON (part), COOS, CURRY, DOUGLAS, JOSEPHINE (part), LANE, LINN. CITIES: Eugene, Roseburg, and Coos Bay. Population (2000), 684,280.

ZIP Codes: 97321–22, 97324, 97326–27, 97329–30, 97333, 97335–36, 97345–46, 97348, 97350, 97352, 97355, 97358, 97360–61, 97370, 97374, 97377, 97383, 97386, 97389, 97401–17, 97419–20, 97423–24, 97426–32, 97434–44, 97446–59, 97461–67, 97469–70, 97472–73, 97476–82, 97484, 97486–99, 97523, 97526–27, 97530–34, 97537–38, 97543–44

* * *

FIFTH DISTRICT

DARLENE HOOLEY, Democrat, of West Linn, OR; born on April 4, 1939; B.S., Education, Oregon State University; employment: teacher and girls' sports coach; past member: Oregon House of Representatives, West Linn City Council, Clackamas County Board of Commissioners; children: Chad and Erin; committees: Budget; Financial Services; Veterans' Affairs; subcommittees: ranking member, Oversight and Investigations; Capital Markets, Insurance and Government Sponsored Enterprises; Domestic and International Monetary Policy, Trade and Technology; Financial Institutions and Consumer Credit; Health; elected to the 105th Congress; reelected to each succeeding Congress.

Office Listings

http://www.house.gov/hooley

2430 Rayburn House Office Building, Washington, DC 20515 .... (202) 225–5711
Chief of Staff / Press.—Joan Mooney. FAX: 225–5699
Executive Assistant / Scheduler.—Anne Marie Feeney.
Legislative Director.—Mark Dedrick.

315 Mission Street, Suite 101, Salem, OR 97302 .... (503) 588–9100
District Director.—Willie Smith.
21570 Williamette Drive West, Linn, OR 97068 .... (503) 557–1324

Counties: BENTON (part); CLACKAMAS (part); LINCOLN; MARION; MULTNOMAH (part); POLK; TILLAMOOK. CITIES: Corvallis, Portland, Salem, and Tillamook. Population (2000), 684,333.

ZIP Codes: 97002, 97004, 97010, 97013, 97015, 97017, 97020, 97023, 97026–27, 97032, 97034–36, 97038, 97042, 97045, 97062, 97068, 97070–71, 97101, 97107–08, 97112, 97118, 97122, 97130–31, 97134–37, 97140–41, 97143, 97147, 97149, 97201, 97219, 97222, 97239, 97267–68, 97301–14, 97321, 97324–25, 97330–31, 97333, 97338–39, 97341–44, 97346–47, 97350–52, 97357–62, 97364–73, 97375–76, 97380–81, 97383–85, 97388, 97390–92, 97394, 97396, 97498

PENNSYLVANIA

(Population 2000, 12,281,054)

SENATORS

ARLEN SPECTER, Republican, of Philadelphia, PA; born in Wichita, KS, February 12, 1930; education: graduated, Russell High School, Russell, KS, 1947; University of Pennsylvania, 1951, B.A., international relations, Phi Beta Kappa; Yale Law School, LL.B., 1956; board of editors, *Law Journal*; military service: served in U.S. Air Force, 1951–53, attaining rank of first lieutenant; employment: member, law firm of Dechert, Price and Rhoads before and after serving two terms as district attorney of Philadelphia, 1966–74; married: former Joan Levy, who was elected to the city council of Philadelphia in 1979; children: Shanin and Stephen; served as assistant counsel to the Warren Commission, 1964; served on Pennsylvania's State Planning Board, The White House Conference on Youth, The National Commission on Criminal Justice, and the Peace Corps National Advisory Council; committees: Appropriations; Judiciary; Government Affairs; chairman, Veterans' Affairs; elected to the U.S. Senate on November 4, 1980; reelected to each succeeding Senate term.

Office Listings

http://specter.senate.gov arlen_specter@specter.senate.gov

711 Hart Senate Office Building, Washington, DC 20510 .... (202) 224–9020
Chief of Staff.—Carey A. Lackman. FAX: 228–3430
Legislative Director.—[Vacant].
Office Manager.—Alegra Hassan.
Communications Director.—William Reynolds.
600 Arch Street, Suite 9400, Philadelphia, PA 19106 .... (215) 597–7200
Federal Building, Liberty Avenue and Grant Street, Suite 2031, Pittsburgh, PA 15222 .... (412) 644–3400
Federal Building, Room 107, Sixth and State Streets, Erie, PA 16501 .... (814) 453–3010
Federal Building, Room 1104, 228 Walnut Street, Harrisburg, PA 17101 .... (717) 782–3951
Federal Building, Suite 3814, 504 West Hamilton Street, Allentown, PA 18101 .... (610) 434–1444
310 Spruce Street, No. 201, Scranton, PA 18503 .... (570) 346–2006
7 North Wilkes Barre Boulevard, Stegmaier Building, Room 377M, Wilkes Barre, PA 18702 .... (570) 826–6265

* * *

RICHARD JOHN SANTORUM, Republican, of Penn Hills, PA; born in Winchester, VA, May 10, 1958; graduated Carmel High School, 1976; B.A., Pennsylvania State University, 1980; M.B.A., University of Pittsburgh, 1981; J.D., Dickinson School of Law, 1986; admitted to the Pennsylvania bar; administrative assistant to State Senator J. Doyle Corman (R–Centre), 1981–86: director of the Senate Local Government Committee, 1981–84; director of the Senate Transportation Committee, 1984–86; associate attorney, Kirkpatrick and Lockhart, Pittsburgh, PA, 1986–90; married Karen Garver Santorum, 1990; six children: Elizabeth Anne, Richard John, Jr., Daniel James, Sarah Maria, Peter Kenneth, Patrick Francis; committees: Finance; Banking, Housing, and Urban Affairs; Rules and Administration; Special Committee on Aging; subcommittee chairman, Social Security and Family Policy; chairman, Senate Republican Conference; elected to the 102nd Congress; reelected to each succeeding Congress; elected to the U.S. Senate on November 8, 1994; reelected to each succeeding Senate term.

Office Listings

http://santorum.senate.gov

511 Dirksen Senate Office Building, Washington, DC 20510 .... (202) 224–6324
Chief of Staff.—Michael Hershey. FAX: 228–0604
Executive Assistant.—Ramona Ely.
Legislative Director.—Wayne Palmer.
Office Manager.—Jeff Stoltzfoos.
1705 West 26th Street, Erie, PA 16508 .... (814) 454–7114
555 Walnut Street, Harrisburg, PA 17101 .... (717) 231–7540
Federal Building, Suite 3802, 504 West Hamilton Street, Allentown, PA 18101 .... (610) 770–0142
Regency Square, Suite 202, Route 220 North, Altoona, PA 16001 .... (814) 946–7023
Widener Building, One South Penn Square, Suite 960, Philadelphia, PA 19107 .... (215) 864–6900
Landmarks Building, One Station Square, Suite 250, Pittsburgh, PA 15219 .... (412) 562–0533
527 Linden Street, Scranton, PA 18503 .... (717) 344–8799

REPRESENTATIVES

FIRST DISTRICT

ROBERT A. BRADY, Democrat, of Philadelphia, PA; born in Philadelphia, PA, April 7, 1945; graduated from St. Thomas More High School; carpenter; union official; assistant Sergeant-At-Arms, Philadelphia City Council, 1975–83; Deputy Mayor for Labor, W. Wilson Goode Administration; consultant to Pennsylvania State Senate; Pennsylvania Turnpike Commissioner; board of director's, Philadelphia Redevelopment Authority; Democratic Party Executive; ward leader; chairman, Philadelphia Democratic Party; member of Pennsylvania Democratic State Committee, and Democratic National Committee; Catholic; married: Debra Brady; two children: Robert and Kimberly; committees: Armed Services; House Administration; elected to the 105th Congress on May 21, 1998, to fill the unexpired term of Representative Tom Foglietta; reelected to each succeeding Congress.

Office Listings

http://www.house.gov/robertbrady

206 Cannon House Office Building, Washington, DC 20515 .... (202) 225–4731
Chief of Staff.—Stan White. FAX: 225–0088
Legislative Director.—J. Mark Trumbore.
Appointments Secretary.—Nicole Barcliff.
Press Secretary.—Karen Warrington.
1907 South Broad Street, Philadelphia, PA 19148 .... (215) 389–4627
The Colony Building, 511–13 Welsh Street, 1st Floor, Chester, PA 19103 .... (610) 874–7094

Counties: PHILADELPHIA (part). CITIES AND TOWNSHIPS: Chester City, Chester Township, Eddystone Borough, Colwyn Borough, Ridley Township (part), Tinicum Township (part), Darby Township (part), and Yeadon Borough. Population (2000), 630,730.

ZIP Codes: 19012–16, 19018, 19022–23, 19029, 19032, 19036, 19050, 19078–79, 19086, 19092–93, 19101, 19105–09, 19111–13, 19120, 19122–26, 19130–34, 19137–51, 19153–54, 19160–62, 19170–73, 19175, 19177–78, 19181–82, 19185, 19187–88

* * *

SECOND DISTRICT

CHAKA FATTAH, Democrat, of Philadelphia, PA; born in Philadelphia; attended Overbrook High School, Community College of Philadelphia, University of Pennsylvania's Wharton School; M.A., University of Pennsylvania's Fels School of State and Local Government, 1986; Harvard University's John F. Kennedy School of Government; recognized for outstanding leadership in *Time* magazine, and in *Ebony* magazine as one of 50 Future Leaders; recipient, Pennsylvania Public Interest Coalition's State Legislator of the Year Award; Pennsylvania State Senate, 1988–94; State House of Representatives, 1982–88; created the Jobs Project; in Pennsylvania House of Representatives, sponsored 1987 Employment Opportunities Act; supported Ben Franklin Technology Center, a conduit for securing government contracts for African-American and women-owned businesses; founded Graduate Opportunities Conference; chairman of the executive committee of the Pennsylvania Higher Education Assistance Agency; convened and led a task force, Child Development Initiative; supported measures to reform the Philadelphia Housing Authority; formed the Drug-Free Program; founded the American Cities Foundation; trustee, Lincoln University and Community College of Philadelphia; member, Mt. Carmel Baptist Church; married to the former Renée Chenault; three children; committees: Appropriations; subcommittees: ranking member, District of Columbia; Veterans Affairs, HUD, and Independent Agencies; elected to the 104th Congress; reelected to each succeeding Congress.

Office Listings

http://www.house.gov/fattah

2301 Rayburn House Office Building, Washington, DC 20515 .... (202) 225–4001
Chief of Staff.—Michelle Anderson Lee.
Legislative Director.—Debra Anderson.
Communications Director/Policy Advisor.—Rebecca Kirszner.
4104 Walnut Street, Philadelphia, PA 19104 .... (215) 387–6404
6632 Germantown Avenue, Philadelphia, PA 19119 .... (215) 848–9386

Counties: MONTGOMERY (part), PHILADELPHIA (part). Population (2000), 630,730.

ZIP Codes: 19012, 19027, 19038, 19053, 19095, 19102–04, 19107, 19110–11, 19118–21, 19123–24, 19126–32, 19138–41, 19143–46, 19150–51, 19161–62, 19170, 19173, 19178, 19184, 19187, 19191–94, 19196–97

THIRD DISTRICT

PHIL ENGLISH, Republican, of Erie, PA; born in Erie, June 20, 1956; B.A., University of Pennsylvania, political science; chief of staff, State Senator Melissa Hart; executive director, State Senate Finance Committee; married Christiane Weschler-English, 1992; committees: Joint Economic Committee; Ways and Means; elected to the 104th Congress; reelected to each succeeding Congress.

Office Listings

http://www.house.gov/english

1410 Longworth House Office Building, Washington, DC 20515 .... (202) 225–5406
Chief of Staff.—Bob Holste. FAX: 225–3103
Office Manager.—Nancy Billet.
Press Secretary.—Idil Oyman.
Legislative Director.—David Stewart.
Modern Toal Square, 310 French Street, Suite 107, Erie, PA 16507 .... (814) 456–2038
312 Chestnut Street, Suite 114, Meadville, PA 16335 .... (814) 724–8414
City Annex Building, 900 North Hermitage Road, Suite 6, Hermitage, PA 16148 .. (724) 342–6132
101 East Dramond Street, Suite 213, Butler PA 16001 .... (724) 285–7005

Counties: ARMSTRONG (part), BUTLER (part), CRAWFORD (part), ERIE, MERCER (part), VENANGO (part), WARREN (part). Population (2000), 630,730.

ZIP Codes: 16001–03, 16016–18, 16020, 16022–23, 16025, 16027–30, 16033–35, 16037–41, 16045–46, 16048–53, 16055–57, 16059, 16061, 16110–11, 16113–14, 16124–25, 16127, 16130–31, 16133–34, 16137, 16142–43, 16145–46, 16148, 16150–51, 16153–54, 16156, 16159, 16201, 16210, 16218, 16222–24, 16226, 16229, 16232, 16242, 16244–45, 16249–50, 16253, 16259, 16261–63, 16311–12, 16314, 16316–17, 16319, 16323, 16327, 16329, 16335, 16340, 16342, 16345, 16350–51, 16354, 16360, 16362, 16365–69, 16371–74, 16388, 16401–07, 16410–13, 16415, 16417, 16420–24, 16426–28, 16430, 16432–36, 16438, 16440–44, 16475, 16501–12, 16514–15, 16522, 16530–34, 16538, 16541, 16544, 16546, 16550, 16553–54, 16563, 16565

* * *

FOURTH DISTRICT

MELISSA A. HART, Republican, of Bradford Woods, PA; born on April 4, 1962, in Pittsburgh, PA; education: B.A., Washington and Jefferson College; J.D., University of Pittsburgh; profession: Attorney; employment: Doepken, Keevican & Weiss (law firm); public service: elected to the Pennsylvania State Senate, 1990; reelected in 1994, and 1998; served as chairman of the State Senate Finance Committee; House committees: Financial Services; Judiciary; and Science; elected to the 107th Congress on November 7, 2000; reelected to each succeeding Congress.

Office Listings

http://www.house.gov/hart

1508 Longworth House Office Building, Washington, DC 20515 .... (202) 225–2565
Administrative Assistant.—William Ries. FAX: 226–2274
Legislative Director.—Christian Marchant.
Press Secretary.—Brendan Benner.
501 Lawrence Avenue, Ellwood City, PA 16117 .... (724) 752–0490
District Director.—Patrick Geho.
4655 Route 8, Suite 124G, Coventry Square Shopping Center, Allison Park, PA 15101 .... (412) 492–0161
District Director.—Patrick Geho.

Counties: ALLEGHENY (part), BEAVER, BUTLER (part), LAWRENCE, MERCER (part), WESTMORELAND (part). Population (2000), 630,730.

ZIP Codes: 15001, 15003, 15005–07, 15009–10, 15014–15, 15024, 15026–27, 15030, 15032, 15042–44, 15046, 15049–52, 15056, 15059, 15061, 15065–66, 15068–69, 15074, 15076–77, 15081, 15084–86, 15090–91, 15095–96, 15101, 15108, 15116, 15127, 15139, 15143–44, 15146, 15202, 15209, 15212, 15214–15, 15223, 15229, 15235, 15237–39, 15601, 15626, 15632, 15650, 15668, 16002, 16024–25, 16033, 16037, 16040, 16046, 16051–52, 16055–57, 16059, 16061, 16063, 16066, 16101–03, 16105, 16107–08, 16112, 16115–17, 16120–21, 16123, 16127, 16132, 16136, 16140–43, 16148, 16155–57, 16159–61, 16172, 16229

FIFTH DISTRICT

JOHN E. PETERSON, Republican, of Pleasantville, PA; born in Titusville, PA, on December 25, 1938; education: attended Pennsylvania State University; military service: served in U.S. Army, 1958–64; employment: past owner of supermarket; served in Pennsylvania House of Representatives, 1977–84, and in Pennsylvania Senate, 1985–96; Pleasantville Borough Councilman, 1968–77; past president: Pleasantville Lions Club, Titusville Chamber of Commerce, Pleasantville PTA, and Pleasantville Borough Council; formerly served on: board of directors of Titusville Hospital; and University of Pittsburgh's Titusville and Bradford campuses; advisory board of Pennsylvania State University School of Forest Resources; and advisory committee of the University of Pittsburgh Graduate School of Public Health; married: Saundra J. Watson in 1966; children: Richard; committees: Appropriations; Resources; elected to the 105th Congress; reelected to each succeeding Congress.

Office Listings

123 Cannon House Office Building, Washington, DC 20515 .... (202) 225–5121
Chief of Staff.—Jordan Clark. FAX: 225–5796
Legislative Director.—Jeff Vorberger.
Senior Legislative Assistant.—Brian Sowa.
Press Secretary.—Paul Feenstra.
127 West Spring Street, Suite C, Titusville, PA 16354 .... (814) 827–3985
1524 West College Avenue, State College, PA 16801 .... (814) 238–1776

Counties: CAMERON, CENTRE, CLARION, CLEARFIELD (part), CLINTON, CRAWFORD (part), ELK, FOREST, JEFFERSON, LYCOMING (part), MCKEAN, MIFFLIN (part), POTTER, TIOGA, VENANGO (part), WARREN (part). Population (2000), 630,730.

ZIP Codes: 15711, 15715, 15730, 15733, 15744, 15753, 15757, 15764, 15767, 15770, 15772, 15776, 15778, 15780–81, 15784, 15801, 15821, 15823–25, 15827–29, 15831–32, 15834, 15840–41, 15845–49, 15851, 15853, 15856–57, 15860–61, 15863–66, 15868, 15870, 16028, 16036, 16049, 16054, 16058, 16153, 16213–14, 16217, 16220–22, 16224–26, 16230, 16232–35, 16239–40, 16242, 16248, 16254–58, 16260, 16301, 16311, 16313–14, 16317, 16319, 16321–23, 16326–29, 16331–34, 16340–47, 16351–54, 16361–62, 16364–65, 16370–71, 16373–75, 16404, 16416, 16434, 16620, 16627, 16645, 16651, 16661, 16663, 16666–77, 16681, 16686, 16701, 16720, 16724–35, 16738, 16740, 16743–46, 16748–50, 16801–05, 16820–23, 16825–30, 16832–41, 16843–45, 16847–56, 16858–61, 16863–66, 16868, 16870–79, 16881–82, 16901, 16911–12, 16914–15, 16917–18, 16920–23, 16927–30, 16932–33, 16935–40, 16942–43, 16946–48, 16950, 17004, 17009, 17029, 17044, 17051, 17063, 17084, 17099, 17701–02, 17720–21, 17723–24, 17726–27, 17729, 17738–40, 17744–45, 17747–48, 17750–52, 17754, 17759–60, 17764–65, 17767, 17769, 17773, 17776–79, 17810, 17841

* * *

SIXTH DISTRICT

JIM GERLACH, Republican, of Upper Uwchlan Township, PA; born on February 25, 1955, in Ellwood City, PA; education: B.A., Dickinson College, 1977; J.D., Dickinson School of Law, 1980; profession: Attorney; former special counsel to the regional law firm of Fox, Rothschild, O'Brien & Frankel; community service: Brandywine Hospital and Trauma Center, board of directors; MECA (Mission for Educating Children with Autism), board of directors; Dickinson College Board of Trustees; Chester County Agricultural Development Council; West Brandywine Township Zoning Hearing Board; public service: Pennsylvania House of Representatives, 1991–1994; Pennsylvania State Senate, 1995–2002; children: Katie, Jimmy, and Robby; elected to the 108th Congress on November 5, 2002.

Office Listings

http://www.house.gov/gerlach

1541 Longworth House Office Building, Washington, DC 20515 .... (202) 225–4315
Chief of Staff.—Linda Pedigo. FAX: 225–8440
Legislative Director.—Pete Kirkham.
Press Secretary.—Kelli Phiel.
1230 Pottstown Pike, Suite 4, Glenmoore, PA 19343 .... (610) 458–8010
501 North Park Road, Wyomissing, PA 19610 .... (610) 376–7630
580 Main Street, Suite #4, Trappe, PA 19426 .... (610) 409–2780

Counties: BERKS (part), CHESTER (part), MONTGOMERY (part). Population (2000), 630,730.

ZIP Codes: 17527, 17555, 17569, 18011, 18031, 18041, 18056, 18062, 18070, 18092, 19003–04, 19010, 19025, 19031, 19034–35, 19041, 19066, 19072, 19085, 19087, 19096, 19131, 19151, 19301, 19310, 19312, 19316, 19320, 19333, 19335, 19341, 19343–45, 19353–55, 19358, 19365–67, 19369, 19371–72, 19376, 19380, 19382, 19401, 19403–04, 19409, 19421, 19423, 19425–26, 19428, 19430, 19432, 19438, 19442, 19444, 19446, 19457, 19460, 19462, 19464–65, 19468, 19470, 19473–75, 19480–85, 19490, 19493–96, 19503–05, 19508, 19511–12, 19518–20, 19522–23, 19525, 19530, 19535, 19538–40, 19542–43, 19545, 19547–48, 19562, 19565, 19601–02, 19604–12

SEVENTH DISTRICT

CURT WELDON, Republican, of Thornbury, PA; born in Marcus Hook, PA, on July 22, 1947; education: B.A., West Chester State College, PA, 1969; graduate work, Cabrini College, Wayne, PA; Temple and St. Joseph's Universities, Philadelphia, PA; business executive; administrator and teacher; mayor of Marcus Hook Borough, 1977–82; member, Delaware County Council, 1981–86; chairman, Delaware Valley Regional Planning Commission; member: Lower Delco Lions Club, United Way of Southeastern Pennsylvania, American Red Cross in Media, Marcus Hook Fire Company, Viscose Fire Company, Sacred Heart Medical Center, Neumann College, Delaware County Industrial Development Authority, Delaware County Community Action Agency, Delaware County Hero Scholarship Fund, Boy Scout Troop No. 418, Darby-Colwyn-William Penn School District Education Association; awards: 1984 Man of the Year from Delaware County Irish-American Association; 1984 Man of the Year from the Chester Business and Professional Association; married: the former Mary Gallagher in 1972; children: Karen, Kristen, Kimberly, Curt, and Andrew; elected to the 100th Congress on November 4, 1986; reelected to each succeeding Congress.

Office Listings

http://www.house.gov/curtweldon curtpa07@mail.house.gov

2466 Rayburn House Office Building, Washington, DC 20515 .... (202) 225–2011
Administrative Assistant.—Michael Conallen. FAX: 225–8137
Scheduler.—Amy Leedecke.
1554 Garrett Road, Upper Darby, PA 19082 .... (610) 259–0700
District Representative.—Kelly Colvin.

Counties: CHESTER (part), DELAWARE (part), MONTGOMERY (part). Population (2000), 630,730.

ZIP Codes: 19003, 19008, 19010, 19013–15, 19017–18, 19022–23, 19026, 19028–29, 19032–33, 19036–37, 19039, 19041, 19043, 19050, 19052, 19061, 19063–65, 19070, 19073–74, 19076, 19078–83, 19085–89, 19091, 19094, 19096, 19098, 19153, 19301, 19312, 19317, 19319, 19331, 19333, 19339–40, 19342, 19355, 19373, 19380, 19382, 19397–99, 19403, 19405–08, 19415, 19420, 19426, 19428–29, 19453, 19456, 19460, 19462, 19468, 19484–85

* * *

EIGHTH DISTRICT

JAMES C. GREENWOOD, Republican, of Erwinna, PA; born on May 4, 1951, in Philadelphia, PA; graduated: Council Rock High School; B.A., Dickinson College, Carlisle, PA, 1973; legislative assistant, Pennsylvania State Representative John S. Renninger, 1972–76; head house parent, The Woods Schools, 1974–76; campaign coordinator, Renninger for Congress Committee, 1976; caseworker, Bucks County Children and Youth Social Service Agency, 1977–80; Pennsylvania State Representative, 1980–86; Pennsylvania State Senator, 1986–93; chairman: Joint State Government Commission Task Force on Services to Children and Youth, Pennsylvania Legislative Children's Caucus; member: Joint State Government Commission Task Force on Commonwealth Efficiency Study; vice chairman, Assembly on the Legislature of the National Conference of State Legislatures; board of directors: Pennsylvania Trauma Systems Foundation, Pennsylvania Energy Development Authority, Pennsylvania Higher Education Assistance Agency; member: Governor's Commission for Children and Families, Children's Trust Fund Board, Joint Legislative Air and Water Pollution Control and Conservation Committee; Committee on the Environment of the Eastern Regional Conference of the Council of State Governments, Permanency Planning Task Force; board of directors: Bucks County Council on Alcoholism, Parents Anonymous, Today Inc., The Woods Schools; committees: Energy and Commerce; Education and the Workforce; subcommittees: chairman, Oversight and Investigations; Health; Environment and Hazardous Materials; Education Reform; Select Education; married: the former Christina Paugh; children: Robert, Laura, Kathryn; elected on November 3, 1992, to the 103rd Congress; reelected to each succeeding Congress.

Office Listings

http://www.house.gov/greenwood

2436 Rayburn House Office Building, Washington, DC 20515 .... (202) 225–4276
Administrative Assistant.—Jordan P. Krauss. FAX: 225–9511
Scheduler.—Karen Cologne.
Legislative Director.—Judy Borger.
69 East Oakland Avenue, Doylestown, PA 18901 .... (215) 348–7511
One Oxford Valley, Suite 800, Langhorne, PA 19047 .... (215) 752–7711
District Director.—Sean Slack.

Counties: BUCKS, MONTGOMERY (part), PHILADELPHIA (part). Population (2000), 630,730.

ZIP Codes: 18036, 18039, 18041–42, 18054–55, 18073, 18077, 18081, 18901, 18910–17, 18920–23, 18925–35, 18938, 18940, 18942–44, 18946–47, 18949–51, 18953–56, 18960, 18962–64, 18966, 18968–70, 18972, 18974, 18976–77, 18980–81, 18991, 19001–02, 19006–08, 19020–21, 19025, 19030, 19034, 19038, 19040, 19044, 19047–49, 19053–59, 19067, 19075, 19090, 19114, 19116, 19154–55, 19440, 19454

* * *

NINTH DISTRICT

BILL SHUSTER, Republican, of Hollidaysburg, PA; born on January 10, 1961, in McKeesport, PA; education: Everett High School, Bedford County, PA; B.A., Dickinson College; M.B.A., American University; profession: businessman; employment: Goodyear Tire & Rubber Corp.; Bandag, Inc.; Shuster Chrysler (President and General Manager); organizations: Member, Zion Lutheran Church; National Federation of Independent Business; National Rifle Association; Y.M.C.A.; Precious Life, Inc.; Rotary Club; Director, Pennsylvania Automotive Association; Board of Trustees, Homewood Home Retirement Community; Sigma Chi Fraternity; family: married to Rebecca; two children: Ali and Garrett; elected to the 107th Congress, by special election, on May 15, 2001; reelected to each succeeding Congress.

Office Listings

http://www.house.gov/shuster

1108 Longworth House Office Building, Washington, DC 20515 .... (202) 225–2431
  Chief of Staff.—Alex Mistri. FAX: 225–2486
  Legislative Director.—Michael Joyce.
  Scheduler.—Elizabeth Carter.
310 Penn Street, Hollidaysburg, PA 16648 .... (814) 696–6318
179 East Queen Street, Chambersburg, PA 17201 .... (717) 264–8308
645 Philadelphia Street, Suite 304, Indiana, PA 15701 .... (724) 463–0516
118 West Main Street, Suite 302, Somerset, PA 15501 .... (814) 443–3918

Counties: Bedford, Blair, Cambria (part), Clearfield (part), Cumberland (part), Fayette (part), Franklin, Fulton, Huntingdon, Indiana (part), Juniata, Mifflin, Perry (part), Somerset (part). Population (2000), 630,730.

ZIP Codes: 15411, 15416, 15421, 15424–25, 15431, 15436–37, 15440, 15445, 15451, 15459, 15462, 15464–65, 15469–70, 15478–79, 15501, 15510, 15521–22, 15530, 15532–42, 15545, 15549–54, 15557–60, 15562–65, 15681, 15701, 15712–14, 15716–17, 15720–25, 15727–29, 15731–32, 15734, 15738–39, 15741–42, 15746–48, 15750, 15752–54, 15756–59, 15763, 15765, 15767, 15771–72, 15774–75, 15777, 15783, 15840, 15920, 15924, 15926, 15929, 15931, 15936, 15940, 15944, 15946, 15949, 15954, 15961, 15963, 16211, 16222, 16246, 16256, 16601–03, 16611, 16613, 16616–17, 16619, 16621–25, 16627, 16629–31, 16633–41, 16644, 16646–48, 16650–52, 16654–57, 16659–62, 16664–65, 16667–75, 16678–80, 16682–86, 16689, 16691–95, 16823, 16833, 16844, 16861, 16865, 16871, 16877, 17002, 17004, 17006, 17013–14, 17021, 17024, 17035, 17037, 17040, 17044–45, 17047, 17049, 17051–54, 17056, 17058–60, 17062, 17065–66, 17068, 17071, 17074–76, 17081–82, 17086, 17090, 17094, 17201, 17210–15, 17217, 17219–25, 17228–29, 17231–33, 17235–41, 17243–44, 17246–47, 17249–57, 17260–68, 17270–72, 17307, 17324

* * *

TENTH DISTRICT

DON SHERWOOD, Republican, of Tunkhannock, PA; born on March 5, 1941, in Nicholson, PA; education: Nicholson Elementary School; Lackawanna Trail High School; Wyoming Seminary Preparatory School; Dartmouth College, degree in Economics; military: U.S. Army, 1963–65, active duty service as a 1st Lieutenant; profession: small businessman; owner and chief executive officer of Sherwood Chevrolet and Horiacher-Sherwood Forestry Equipment; business organizations: vice president, Northeastern Pennsylvania Chevrolet Dealers Association; director, Pennsylvania Chevrolet Dealers Area Marketing Group; Pennsylvania Hardware Lumber Manufacturing Association; Pennsylvania Farmers Association; married: Carol Evans, 1972; three children: Jesse, Dana, and Maria; public service: Tunkhannock Area School Board, 1975–98; committees: Appropriations; elected to the 106th Congress; reelected to each succeeding Congress.

Office Listings

http://www.house.gov/sherwood

1223 Longworth House Office Building, Washington, DC 20515 .... (202) 225–3731
  Chief of Staff.—John Enright. FAX: 225–9594
  Press Secretary.—Jake O'Donnell.
  Scheduler.—Matt Allen.
1146 Northern Boulevard, Clarks Summit, PA 18411 .... (570) 585–8190
  District Director.—Jerry Morgan.
330 Pine Street, Suite 202, Williamsport, PA 17701 .... (570) 327–9359

Counties: Bradford, Lackawanna (part), Luzerne (part), Lycoming (part), Montour, Northumberland, Pike, Snyder, Sullivan, Susquehanna, Union, Wayne, Wyoming. Population (2000), 630,730.

ZIP Codes: 16910, 16914, 16925–26, 16930, 16932, 16936, 16945, 16947, 17017, 17045, 17063, 17086, 17701, 17703, 17705, 17724, 17728, 17730, 17731, 17735, 17737, 17742, 17749, 17756, 17758, 17762–63, 17765, 17768, 17771–72, 17774, 17777, 17801, 17810, 17812–15, 17820–24, 17827, 17829–37, 17840–42, 17844–45, 17847, 17850–51, 17853, 17855–57, 17860–62, 17864–68, 17870, 17872, 17876–77, 17880–87, 17889, 18301, 18324–26, 18328, 18336–37, 18340, 18371, 18403, 18405, 18407, 18410–11, 18413–17, 18419–21, 18424–28, 18430–31, 18433–41, 18443–49, 18451–65, 18469–73, 18512, 18612, 18614–16, 18618–19, 18622–23, 18625–30, 18632, 18636, 18640–41, 18653–54, 18656–57, 18704, 18708, 18801, 18810, 18812–18, 18820–34, 18837, 18840, 18842–48, 18850–51, 18853–54

* * *

ELEVENTH DISTRICT

PAUL E. KANJORSKI, Democrat, of Nanticoke, PA; born in Nanticoke, April 2, 1937; U.S. Capitol Page School, Washington, DC, 1954; attended, Wyoming Seminary, Kingston, PA, Temple University, Philadelphia, PA, Dickinson School of Law, Carlisle, PA; served in U.S. Army, private, 1960–61; attorney, admitted to Pennsylvania State bar, 1966; began practice in Wilkes Barre, PA, November 7, 1966; committees: Financial Services; Government Reform; ranking member, Capital Markets, Insurance, and Government-Sponsored Enterprises; married to the former Nancy Marie Hickerson; one daughter, Nancy; elected to the 99th Congress on November 6, 1984; reelected to each succeeding Congress.

Office Listings

http://www.house.gov/kanjorski

2353 Rayburn House Office Building, Washington, DC 20515 .... (202) 225–6511
Chief of Staff.—Karen Feather.
Legislative Director.—Todd Harper.
Executive Assistant.—Donna Giobbi.
Press Secretary.—Ben Turner.
The Stegmaier Building, 7 North Wilkes Barre Boulevard, Suite 400–M, Wilkes Barre, PA 18702–5283 .... (570) 825–2200

Counties: CARBON, COLUMBIA, LACKAWANNA (part), LUZERNE (part), MONROE. Population (2000), 630,730.

ZIP Codes: 17814–15, 17820–21, 17824, 17839, 17846, 17858–59, 17878, 17888, 17920, 17985, 18012, 18030, 18058, 18071, 18201–02, 18210–12, 18216, 18219, 18221–25, 18229–30, 18232, 18234–35, 18237, 18239–41, 18244, 18246–47, 18249–51, 18254–56, 18301, 18320–23, 18325–27, 18330–35, 18341–42, 18344, 18346–50, 18352–57, 18360, 18370, 18372, 18424, 18434, 18445, 18447, 18466, 18501–05, 18507–10, 18512, 18514–15, 18517–19, 18522, 18540, 18577, 18601–03, 18610–12, 18617, 18621–22, 18624, 18631, 18634–35, 18640–44, 18651, 18655, 18660–61, 18690, 18701–11, 18761–67, 18769, 18773–74

* * *

TWELFTH DISTRICT

JOHN P. MURTHA, Democrat, of Johnstown, PA; graduated, Ramsey High School, Mount Pleasant, PA; Kiskiminetas Spring School; B.A. in economics, University of Pittsburgh; graduate study at Indiana University of Pennsylvania; married Joyce Bell; three children: Donna Sue and twin sons, John and Patrick; served in Marine Corps as an enlisted Marine commissioned as an officer; discharged as a first lieutenant; maintained active reserve officer status; volunteered for one year of active duty in Vietnam as a major; served with 1st Marines, a Marine infantry regiment, 1966–67, south of Danang; awarded Bronze Star Medal with combat ''V'', two Purple Heart medals, Vietnamese Cross of Gallantry, and service medals; retired colonel, U.S. Marine Corps Reserves; elected to Pennsylvania House of Representatives in 1969, served continuously until elected to U.S. House of Representatives; recipient of Pennsylvania Distinguished Service Medal and Pennsylvania Meritorious Service Medal (the commonwealth's two highest honors); created the John P. Murtha Award for student assistance at the University of Pittsburgh at Johnstown; received Honorary Doctor of Humanities, Mount Aloysius Junior College; committee: Appropriations; elected to the 93rd Congress, February 5, 1974; reelected to each succeeding Congress.

Office Listings

http://www.house.gov/murtha

2423 Rayburn House Office Building, Washington, DC 20515 .... (202) 225–2065
Executive Assistant.—William N. Allen.
Administrator.—Winifred Frederick.
Scheduling Coordinator.—Jane Phipps.
P.O. Box 780, Johnstown, PA 15907 .... (814) 535–2642
District Administrative Assistant.—John Hugya.

Counties: ALLEGHENY COUNTY (part). CITIES AND TOWNSHIPS: Brackenridge, East Deer, and Tarentum; ARMSTRONG COUNTY (part). CITIES AND TOWNSHIPS: Apollo, Bethel, Burrell, Cadogan, Elderton, Ford City, Ford Cliff, Freeport, Gilpin, Kiskiminetas, Kittanning, Leechburg, Manor, Manorville, North Apollo, North Buffalo, Parks, Plumcreek, South Bend, and South Buffalo; CAMBRIA COUNTY (part). CITIES AND TOWNSHIPS: Adams, Barr, Blacklick, Brownstown, Cambria, Carrolltown, Cassandra, Conemaugh, Cresson, Croyle, Daisytown, Dale, East Carroll, East Conemaugh, East Taylor, Ebensburg, Ehrenfeld, Ferndale, Franklin, Geistown, Jackson, Johnstown, Lilly, Lorain, Lower Yoder, Middle Taylor, Munster, Nanty Glo, Portage, Richland, Sankertown, Scalp Level, South Fork, Southmonth, Stonycreek, Summerhill, Upper Yoder, Vintondale, Washington, Westmont, West Carroll, West Taylor, Wilmore. FAYETTE COUNTY (part). CITIES AND TOWNSHIPS: Belle Vernon, Brownsville, Bullskin, Connellsville, Dawson, Dunbar, Everson, Fayette City, Franklin, Georges, German, Jefferson, Lower Tyrone, Luzerne, Masontown, Menallen, Newell, Nicholson, North Union, Perry, Perryopolis, Point Marion, Redstone, Saltlick, South Union, Springhill, Upper Tyrone, Uniontown, Vanderbilt, Washington. GREENE COUNTY, INDIANA COUNTY (part). CITIES AND TOWNSHIPS: Cherryhill, Clymer, Indiana, Pine, White. SOMERSET COUNTY (part). CITIES AND TOWNSHIPS: Benson, Boswell, Conemaugh, Hooversville, Jefferson, Jenner, Jennerstown, Lincoln, Middlecreek, Paint, Quemahoning, Seven Springs, Stoystown, Windber. WASHINGTON COUNTY (part). CITIES AND TOWNSHIPS: Allenport, Beallsville, Bentleyville, California, Canonsburg, Canton, Carroll, Centerville, Charleroi, Chartier, Coal Center, Cokeburg, Deemston, Donora, Dunlevy, East Bethlehem, East Washington, Elco, Ellsworth, Fallowfield, Finleyville, Houston, Long Branch, Marianna, Monongahela, New Eagle, North Bethlehem, North Charleroi, North Strabane, Roscoe, Somerset, South Strabane, Speers, Stockdale, Twilight, Union, Washington, West Bethlehem, West Brownsville, West Pike Run. WESTMORELAND COUNTY (part). CITIES AND TOWNSHIPS: Allegheny, Arnold, Avonmore, Bell, Bessemer, Bolivar, Bovard, Bridgeport, Crabtree, Derry, Dorothy, Duncan, East Herminie, East Huntingdon, East Vandergrift, Fairfield, Hannastown, Heccla, Hempfield, Hugus, Hyde Park, Jacobs Creek, Latrobe, Laurel Run, Lloydsville, Lowber, Lower Burrell, Loyalhanna, Luxor, Mammoth, Mechlings, Mineral, Monessen, Mount Pleasant, New Alexandria, New Florence, New Kensington, North Belle Vernon, North Washington, Oklahoma, Paulton, Port Royal, Rillton, Rostraver, Salem, Scottdale, Seward, Sewickley, Smithton, South Huntingdon, Spring Garden, St. Clair, Sutersville, United, Unity, Upper Burrell, Vandergrift, Washington, Wayne, Westmoreland, West Herminie, West Leechburg, West Newton, Wyano, and Yukon. Population (2000), 630,730.

ZIP Codes: 15012, 15022, 15030, 15033, 15038, 15062–63, 15067–68, 15072, 15083, 15087, 15089, 15301, 15310, 15313–17, 15320, 15322, 15324–25, 15327, 15329–34, 15336–38, 15341–42, 15344–49, 15351–54, 15357–60, 15362–64, 15366, 15368, 15370, 15377, 15380, 15401, 15410–13, 15415, 15417, 15419–20, 15422–25, 15427–36, 15438, 15442–44, 15446–47, 15449–51, 15454–56, 15458, 15460–61, 15463, 15466–68, 15472–77, 15479–80, 15482–86, 15488–90, 15492, 15501–02, 15520, 15531, 15541, 15544, 15547–48, 15551, 15555, 15557, 15561, 15563, 15601, 15610, 15613, 15618, 15620–22, 15624–25, 15627, 15629, 15631, 15633, 15635, 15637, 15641–42, 15644, 15646, 15650, 15655–56, 15660–62, 15664, 15666, 15670–71, 15673–74, 15677–78, 15680–90, 15701, 15705, 15710, 15714, 15717, 15722, 15728, 15732, 15736–37, 15745, 15748, 15760–62, 15765, 15773–74, 15779, 15901–02, 15904–07, 15909, 15921–23, 15925, 15927–28, 15930–31, 15934–38, 15940, 15942–46, 15948, 15951–63, 16023, 16055, 16201, 16212, 16215, 16226, 16228–29, 16236, 16238, 16240, 16249, 16262, 16630, 16641, 16668–69

* * *

THIRTEENTH DISTRICT

JOSEPH M. HOEFFEL, Democrat, of Montgomery County, PA; born on September 3, 1950, in Philadelphia, PA; education: graduated from William Penn Charter School, Boston University, and Temple Unviersity School of Law; served as a State Representative, for the Abington area, 1976–84; served as a County Commissioner for Montgomery County, PA, 1992–98; married: Francesca Montori, 1977; children: Mary and Jake; committees: International Relations; Transportation and Infrastructure; subcommittees: Europe; Highways, Transit and Pipelines; Middle East and Central Asia; Water Resources and Environment; elected to the 106th Congress; reelected to each succeeding Congress.

Office Listings

426 Cannon House Office Building, Washington, DC 20515 .... (202) 225–6111
Chief of Staff.—Joshua D. Shapiro. FAX: 226–0611
Press Secretary.—Frank X. Custer.
Executive Assistant / Scheduler.—Carmela R. Gipprich.
7219 Frankford Avenue, Philadelphia, PA 19135 .... (215) 335–3355
District Director.—Jack Dempsey.
20 East Butler Avenue, Ambler, PA 19002 .... (215) 540–8444
District Director.—Joan Nagel.

County: MONTGOMERY COUNTY; CITIES AND TOWNSHIPS: Abington Wards (part), Hatfield, Horsham, Lower Frederick, Lower Gwynedd, Lower Moreland, Lower Salford, Malborough (part), Montgomery, New Hanover, Plymouth (part), Springfield, Towamencin, Upper Dublin (part), Upper Frederick, Upper Gwynedd, Upper Moreland (part), Upper Salford, Whitemarsh (part), Whitpain. Boroughs of Ambler, Bryn Athyn, Green Lane, Hatboro, Hatfield, Jenkintown, Lansdale, North Wales, Rockledge, Schwenksville. PHILADELPHIA COUNTY; CITY OF: Philadelphia (part). Population (2000), 630,730.

ZIP Codes: 18054, 18074, 18914–15, 18932, 18936, 18957–58, 18964, 18969, 18979, 19001–02, 19006, 19009, 19019, 19025, 19027, 19038, 19040, 19044, 19046, 19075, 19090, 19096, 19111, 19114–16, 19118, 19120, 19124, 19128, 19134–37, 19149, 19152, 19154–55, 19244, 19255, 19422, 19424, 19428, 19435–38, 19440–41, 19443–44, 19446, 19450–51, 19454–55, 19462, 19464, 19473, 19477–78, 19486–87, 19489, 19492, 19504, 19512, 19525

* * *

FOURTEENTH DISTRICT

MICHAEL F. DOYLE, Democrat, of Swissvale, PA; born in Swissvale, PA, August 5, 1953; graduated, Swissvale Area High School, 1971; B.S., Pennsylvania State University, 1975; co-owner, Eastgate Insurance Agency, Inc., 1983; elected and served as finance and recreation chairman, Swissvale, Borough Council, 1977–81; member: Leadership Pittsburgh Alumni Association, Lions Club, Ancient Order of the Hibernians, Italian Sons and Daughters of America, and Penn State Alumni Association; member: Democratic Caucus, Democratic Study Group, Pennsylvania Democratic Delegation, Congressional Steel Caucus, Travel and Tourism CMO, Ad Hoc Committee on Irish Affairs, and National Italian-American Foundation; married Susan Beth Doyle, 1975; four children: Michael, David, Kevin, and Alexandra; committees: Energy and Commerce; Standards of Official Conduct; founder and co-chair, Coalition for Autism Research and Education; elected November 8, 1994, to the 104th Congress; reelected to each succeeding Congress.

Office Listings

http://www.house.gov/doyle rep.doyle@mail.house.gov

401 Cannon House Office Building, Washington, DC 20515 .... (202) 225–2135
Administrative Assistant.—David Lucas.
Legislative Director.—Sharon Grant.
Office Manager / Scheduler.—Ellen Young.
225 Ross Street, Pittsburgh, PA 15219 .... (412) 261–5091
11 Duff Road, Penn Hills, PA 15235 .... (412) 241–6055
District Director.—Paul D'Alesandro.
627 Lysle Boulevard, McKeesport, PA 15132 .... (412) 664–4049

County: ALLEGHENY COUNTY (part); CITIES AND TOWNSHIPS OF: Avalon, Baldwin Borough, Baldwin Township, Blawnox, Braddock, Braddock Hills, Chalfant, Clairton, Coraopolis, Dravosburg, Duquesne, E. McKeesport, E. Pittsburgh, Edgewood, Elizabeth Borough, Elizabeth Township, Etna, Forest Hills, Glassport, Ingram, Kennedy, Liberty, Lincoln, McKees Rocks, McKeesport, Millvale, Monroeville, Mt. Oliver, Munhall, Neville, North Braddock, North Versailles, O'Hara Township, Penn Hills, Pitcairn, Pittsburgh, Port Vue, Rankin, Reserve, Robinson, Stowe, Swissvale, Sharpsburg, Turtle Creek, Verona, Versailles, Wall, West Homestead, West Mifflin, Whitaker, Wilkins, Wilkinsburg, and Wilmerding. Population (2000), 630,730.

ZIP Codes: 15025, 15034–35, 15037, 15044–45, 15063, 15104, 15106, 15108, 15110, 15112, 15116, 15120, 15122, 15132–37, 15140, 15145–48, 15201–19, 15221–27, 15230, 15232–36, 15238–40, 15242, 15244, 15250–51, 15253, 15255, 15257–62, 15264–65, 15267–68, 15272, 15274, 15278–79, 15281–83, 15285–86, 15290, 15295

* * *

FIFTEENTH DISTRICT

PATRICK J. TOOMEY, Republican, of Allentown, PA; born on November 17, 1961, in Providence, RI; education: B.A., Harvard University, 1984; professional: investment banker; international financial consultant; restaurateur; elected to Allentown, PA, Government Study Commission, 1994; religion: Catholic; married: Kris Toomey; one child; committees: Budget; Financial Services; Small Business; elected to the 106th Congress; reelected to each succeeding Congress.

Office Listings

http://www.house.gov/toomey

224 Cannon House Office Building, Washington, DC 20515 .... (202) 225–6411
Chief of Staff.—Mark Dion. FAX: 226–0778
Scheduler.—Kate Galm.
Press Secretary.—Aimee Steel.
2020 Hamilton Street, Allentown, PA 18104–1392 .... (610) 439–8861

Counties: LEHIGH COUNTY. CITIES OF: Kempton, Kutztown, Limeport, Neffs. MONTGOMERY COUNTY. CITIES OF: Abington, Barto, Earlington, Franconia, Harleysville, Perkiomenville, Pottstown, Sassamansville, Sellersville, Souderton, Sumneytown, Telford, Tylersport. NORTHAMPTON COUNTY. CITIES OF: Ackermanville, Catasauqua, and Flicksville. Population (2000), 630,730.

ZIP Codes: 18001–03, 18010–11, 18013–18, 18020, 18025, 18031–32, 18034–38, 18040–46, 18049–55, 18059–60, 18062–70, 18072–74, 18076–80, 18083–88, 18091–92, 18098–99, 18101–06, 18109, 18175, 18195, 18343, 18351, 18918, 18924, 18951, 18964, 18969, 18971, 19438, 19464, 19472, 19504–05, 19512, 19525, 19529–30, 19539

* * *

SIXTEENTH DISTRICT

JOSEPH R. PITTS, Republican, of Kennett Square, PA; born in Lexington, KY, October 10, 1939; education: B.A., philosophy and religion, Asbury College, KY; military service: served in U.S. Air Force, 1963–69, rising from second lieutenant to captain; employment: nursery business owner and operator; math and science teacher, Great Valley High School, Malvern, PA, 1969–72; teacher, Mortonsville Elementary School, Versailles, KY; member: Pennsylvania

House of Representatives, 1972–96, serving as chairman of Appropriations Committee, 1989–96, and of Labor Relations Committee, 1981–88; married: the former Virginia M. Pratt in 1961; children: Karen, Carol, and Daniel; elected to the 105th Congress; reelected to each succeeding Congress.

Office Listings

http://www.house.gov/pitts

204 Cannon House Office Building, Washington, DC 20515 .... (202) 225–2411
Chief of Staff.—Gabe Neville.
Legislative Director.—Ken Miller.
Press Secretary.—Derek Karchner.
P.O. Box 837, Unionville, PA 19375 .... (610) 444–4581

Counties: LANCASTER, BERK (part). CITIES AND TOWNSHIPS: Reading, Bern, Lower Heidelberg, South Heidelberg, Spring. BOROUGH OF: Wernersville. CHESTER COUNTY (part). CITIES AND TOWNSHIPS: Birmingham, East Bradford, East Fallowfield, East Marlborough, East Nottingham, Elk, Franklin, Highland, Kennett, London Britain, London Grove, Londonderry, Lower Oxford, New Garden, New London, Newlin, Penn, Pennsbury, Upper Oxford, West Fallowfield, West Marlborough, West Nottingham. BOROUGHS OF: Avondale, Kennett Square, Oxford, Parkesburg, West Chester, and West Grove. Population (2000), 630,730.

ZIP Codes: 17501–09, 17512, 17516–22, 17527–29, 17532–38, 17540, 17543, 17545, 17547, 17549–52, 17554–55, 17557, 17560, 17562–70, 17572–73, 17575–76, 17578–85, 17601–08, 19106, 19310–11, 19317–20, 19330, 19342, 19346–48, 19350–52, 19357, 19360, 19362–63, 19365, 19374–75, 19380–83, 19390, 19395, 19464, 19501, 19540, 19543, 19565, 19601–02, 19604–05, 19608–11

* * *

SEVENTEENTH DISTRICT

TIM HOLDEN, Democrat, of St. Clair, PA; born in Pottsville, PA, on March 5, 1957; education: attended St. Clair High School, St. Clair; Fork Union Military Academy; University of Richmond, Richmond, VA; B.A., Bloomsburg State College, 1980; sheriff of Schuylkill County, PA, 1985–93; licensed insurance broker and real estate agent, John J. Holden Insurance Agency and Holden Realty Company, St. Clair; member: Pennsylvania Sheriffs Association; Fraternal Order of Police; St. Clair Fish and Game Association; Benevolent and Protective Order of the Elks Lodge 1533; Congressional Hellenic Caucus; co-chair, Correctional Officers Caucus; Firefighter's Caucus; Mining Caucus; co-chair, Law Enforcement Caucus; co-chair, Northeast Agriculture Caucus; Sportsmens Causus; Steel Caucus; Blue Dog Coalition; Rural Caucus; Rural Health Care Caucus; Alzheimer's Caucus; Congressional Beef Caucus; Pork Industry Congressional Caucus; Commuter Caucus; Diabetes Caucus; Water Infrastructure Caucus; Friends of Ireland; Ad-Hoc Committee for Irish Affairs; Autism Caucus; Congressional Cement Caucus; Wine Caucus; elected to the 103rd Congress; reelected to each succeeding Congress.

Office Listings

2417 Rayburn House Office Building, Washington, DC 20515 .... (202) 225–5546
Chief of Staff.—Trish Reilly-Hudock. FAX: 226–0996
Legislative Director.—Ari Strauss.
Projects Director.—Bill Hanley.
Scheduler.—Theresa Weber.
101 North Centre Street, Suite 303, Pottsville, PA 17901 .... (570) 622–4212
The Corbit Building, 147 North 5th Street, Reading, PA 19601 .... (610) 371–9931

Counties: BERKS (part), DAUPHIN, LEBANON, PERRY (part), SCHUYLKILL. Population (2000), 630,730.

ZIP Codes: 17003, 17005, 17010, 17016–18, 17020, 17022–24, 17026, 17028, 17030, 17032–34, 17036, 17038–39, 17041–42, 17045–46, 17048, 17053, 17057, 17061–62, 17064, 17067–69, 17073–74, 17077–78, 17080, 17083, 17085, 17087–88, 17097–98, 17101–13, 17120–30, 17140, 17177, 17502, 17830, 17836, 17901, 17921–23, 17925, 17929–36, 17938, 17941–46, 17948–49, 17951–54, 17957, 17959–61, 17963–68, 17970, 17972, 17974, 17976, 17978–83, 17985, 18211, 18214, 18218, 18220, 18231, 18237, 18240–42, 18245, 18248, 18250, 18252, 18255, 19506–07, 19510, 19512, 19516, 19518, 19522, 19526, 19529–30, 19533–34, 19536, 19541, 19544, 19547, 19549–51, 19554–55, 19559–60, 19564–65, 19567, 19601, 19604–06

* * *

EIGHTEENTH DISTRICT

TIM MURPHY, Republican, of Upper St. Clair, PA; born on September 12, 1952, in Cleveland, OH; education: B.S., Wheeling Jesuit University, 1974; M.A., Cleveland State University, 1976; Ph.D., University of Pittsburgh, 1979; profession: Psychologist; holds two adjunct faculty positions at the University of Pittsburgh; Associate Professor in the Department of Public Health, and in the Department of Pediatrics; public service: Pennsylvania State Senate, 1996–2002; religion: Catholic; family: married to Nan Missig; children: Bevin; elected to the 108th Congress on November 5, 2002.

Office Listings

http://murphy.house.gov

226 Cannon House Office Building, Washington, DC 20515 .... (202) 225–2301
Chief of Staff.—Patrick Sheehan
Legislative Director.—J.P. Delmore.
Office Manager / Scheduler.—Rebecca Smith.
504 Washington Road, Pittsburgh, PA 15228 .... (412) 344–5583

Counties: ALLEGHENY (part), WASHINGTON (part), WESTMORELAND (part). CITIES AND TOWNSHIPS: Pittsburgh (part), Greensburg, and Jeannette. Population (2000), 630,730.

ZIP Codes: 15001, 15004, 15017–22, 15025–26, 15028, 15031, 15033, 15036–37, 15044, 15046–47, 15053–55, 15057, 15060, 15063–64, 15071, 15075, 15078, 15082–83, 15085, 15088–89, 15102, 15106, 15108, 15126, 15129, 15131, 15136, 15142, 15146, 15205, 15209, 15212, 15215–16, 15220–21, 15226–28, 15231, 15234–36, 15238, 15241, 15243, 15270, 15277, 15301, 15311–12, 15314, 15317, 15321, 15323, 15329–30, 15332, 15339–40, 15342, 15345, 15350, 15361, 15363, 15365, 15367, 15376–79, 15448, 15501, 15601, 15605–06, 15611–12, 15615–17, 15619, 15622–23, 15626, 15628, 15632, 15634, 15636–40, 15642, 15644, 15647, 15650, 15655, 15658, 15663, 15665, 15668, 15672, 15675–76, 15679, 15683, 15687–88, 15691–93, 15695–97

* * *

NINETEENTH DISTRICT

TODD RUSSELL PLATTS, Republican, of York County, PA; born on March 5, 1962, in York County, PA; education: York Suburban High School, 1980; Shippensburg University of Pennsylvania; 1984, B.S. in Public Administration; Pepperdine University School of Law, 1991, Juris Doctorate; employment: Attorney; married: Leslie; children: T.J. and Kelsey; organizations: York County Transportation Coalition; Statewide Children's Health Insurance Program Advisory Council; York Metropolitan Planning Organization; public service: Pennsylvania House of Representatives, 1992–2000; elected to the 107th Congress on November 7, 2000; reelected to each succeeding Congress.

Office Listings

http://www.house.gov/platts

1032 Longworth House Office Building, Washington, DC 20515 .... (202) 225–5836
Press Secretary.—Suzanne Graney. FAX: 226–1000
2209 East Market Street, York, PA 17402 .... (717) 600–1919
Chief of Staff.—Bryan Tate.
22 Chambersburg Street, Gettysburg, PA 17325 .... (717) 338–1919
59 West Louther Street, Carlisle, PA 17013 .... (717) 249–0190

Counties: ADAMS COUNTY. CITIES OF: Abbottstown, Arendtsville, Aspers, Bendersville, Biglerville, East Berlin, Fairfield, Gardners, Gettysburg, Littlestown, McKnightstown, McSherrystown, New Oxford, Orrtanna. CUMBERLAND COUNTY. CITIES OF: Boiling Springs, Carlisle, Camp Hill, East Pennsboro, Enola, Grantham, Lemoyne, Mechanicsburg, Mt. Holly Springs, Newburg, New Cumberland, Newville, Shippensburg, Shiremanstown, Summerdale, Walnut Bottom, West Fairview, Wormleysburg; townships of Hampden (part), Lower Allen, Middlesex, Monroe, Shippensburg, Silver Spring, South Newton, Southampton, Upper Allen, the boroughs of Camp Hill, Carlisle, Lemoyne, Mt. Holly Springs, New Cumberland, Shippensburg (part), Shiremanstown, Wormleysburg. YORK COUNTY. CITIES AND TOWNSHIPS: Airville, Brodbecks, Brogue, Dallastown, Delta, Dillsburg, Dover, Emigsville, East Prospect, Etters, Felton, Fawn Grove, Glen Rock, Hanover, Hellam, Jacobus, Lewisberry, Loganville, Manchester, Mount Wolf, New Freedom, New Park, Red Lion, Spring Grove, Shrewsbury, Stewartstown, Seven Valleys, Thomasville, Wellsville, Windsor, Wrightsville, York, York Haven, York New Salem, Yoe, and York Springs. Population (2000), 647,065.

ZIP Codes: 17001, 17007–08, 17011–13, 17019, 17025, 17027, 17043, 17050, 17053, 17055, 17065, 17070, 17072, 17089–90, 17093, 17222, 17257, 17301–04, 17306–07, 17309–27, 17329, 17331–33, 17337, 17339–40, 17342–45, 17347, 17349–50, 17352–56, 17358, 17360–66, 17368, 17370–72, 17401–07, 17415

RHODE ISLAND

(Population 2000, 1,048,319)

SENATORS

JACK REED, Democrat, of Cranston, RI; born in Providence, RI, November 12, 1949; graduated, La Salle Academy, Providence, RI, 1967; B.S., U.S. Military Academy, West Point, NY, 1971; M.P.P., Kennedy School of Government, Harvard University, 1973; J.D., Harvard Law School, 1982; served in the U.S. Army, 1967–79; associate professor, Department of Social Sciences, U.S. Military Academy, West Point, NY, 1978–79; 2nd BN (Abn) 504th Infantry, 82nd Airborne Division, Fort Bragg, NC; platoon leader, company commander, battalion staff officer, 1973–77; military awards: Army commendation medal with Oak Leaf Cluster, ranger, senior parachutist, jumpmaster, expert infantryman's badge; lawyer; admitted to the Washington, DC bar, 1983; elected to the Rhode Island State Senate, 1985–90; committees: Armed Services; Banking, Housing, and Urban Affairs; Health, Education, Labor, and Pensions; Joint Economic Committee; elected to the 102nd Congress on November 6, 1990; served three terms in the U.S. House of Representatives; elected to the U.S. Senate, November 5, 1996; reelected to each succeeding Senate term.

Office Listings

http://reed.senate.gov

320 Hart Senate Office Building, Washington, DC 20510 .... (202) 224–4642
Administrative Assistant.—J.B. Poersch.
Office Manager.—Mary Perko.
Legislative Director.—Neil Campbell.
Press Secretary.—Greg McCarthy.
201 Hillside Road, Suite 200, Cranston, RI 02920 .... (401) 943–3100
Chief of Staff.—Raymond Simone.
U.S. District Courthouse, One Exchange Terrace, Suite 408, Providence, RI 02903 (401) 528–5200

* * *

LINCOLN D. CHAFEE, Republican, of Warwick, RI; born in Warwick, RI; March 26, 1953; education: Brown University, B.A. degree in Classics, 1975; after graduation he attended horseshoeing school in Bozeman, MT; professional: blacksmith; Cranston Print Works; Rhode Island Forging Steel; and General Dynamics' Electric Boat; public service: elected to the Rhode Island Constitutional Convention, 1985; Warwick, RI, City Council, 1986; and Warwick, RI, Mayor, 1992; in 1998 he was elected by his peers as President of the Rhode Island League of Cities and Towns; married to the former Stephanie Danforth; three children: Louisa, Caleb, and Thea; appointed to the U.S. Senate on November 2, 1999; elected to the U.S. Senate on November 7, 2000.

Office Listings

http://chafee.senate.gov

141A Russell Senate Office Building, Washington, DC 20510 .... (202) 224–2921
Chief of Staff.—David A. Griswold. FAX: 228–2853
Appointments Secretary.—Kathy Wilmoth.
Press Secretary.—Jeff Neal.
320 Thames Street, Newport, RI 02840 .... (401) 845–0700
170 Westminster Street, Providence, RI 02903 .... (401) 453–5294

REPRESENTATIVES

FIRST DISTRICT

PATRICK J. KENNEDY, Democrat, of Providence, RI; born on July 14, 1967, in Brighton, MA; graduated, Phillips Academy, Andover, MA; B.A., Providence College, Providence, RI, 1991; Rhode Island State Legislature, 1988–94; member: Rhode Island Special Olympics (board of directors), Rhode Island March of Dimes, Rhode Island Lung Association, Rhode Island Mental Health Association, Rhode Island Chapter of National Committee for the Prevention of Child Abuse; elected to the 104th Congress; reelected to each succeeding Congress.

Office Listings

http://www.house.gov/patrickkennedy

407 Cannon House Office Building, Washington, DC 20515 .... (202) 225–4911
Chief of Staff.—Sean Richardson. FAX: 225–3290
Legislative Director.—Kimber Colton.
Executive Assistant.—Terri Alford.
Press Secretary.—Ernesto Anguilla.
249 Roosevelt Avenue, Suite 200, Pawtucket, RI 02860 .... (401) 729–5600
District Director.—George Zainyeh.

Counties: BRISTOL, NEWPORT, PROVIDENCE (part). CITIES AND TOWNSHIPS: Barrington, Bristol, Burrillville, Central Falls, Cumberland, East Providence, Jamestown, Lincoln, Little Compton, Middleton, Newport, North Providence, North Smithfield, Providence, Pawtucket, Portsmouth, Smithfield, Tiverton, Warren, and Woonsocket. Population (2000), 524,157.

ZIP Codes: 02801, 02802, 02806, 02809, 02824, 02826, 02828, 02830, 02835, 02837, 02838, 02839, 02840, 02841, 02842, 02858, 02859, 02860, 02861, 02862, 02863, 02864, 02865, 02871, 02872, 02876, 02878, 02885, 02895, 02896, 02903, 02904, 02906, 02908, 02909, 02911, 02912, 02914, 02915, 02916, 02917, 02918, 02940

* * *

SECOND DISTRICT

JAMES R. LANGEVIN, Democrat, of Warwick, RI; born on April 22, 1964, in Providence, RI; education: Rhode Island College, B.A., Political Science / Public Administration, 1990; Harvard University, Masters of Public Administration, 1994; community service: American Red Cross; March of Dimes; Lions Club of Warwick; PARI Independent Living Center; Knights of Columbus; public service: Secretary, 1986 Rhode Island Constitutional Convention; Rhode Island State Representative, 1989–95; Rhode Island Secretary of State, 1995–2000; elected to the 107th Congress; reelected to each succeeding Congress.

Office Listings

http://www.house.gov/langevin

109 Cannon House Office Building, Washington, DC 20515 .... (202) 225–2735
Chief of Staff.—Kristin Nicholson. FAX: 225–5976
Office Manager.—Stu Rose.
The Summit South, 300 Centerville Road, Suite 200, Warwick, RI 02886 .... (401) 732–9400
District Director.—Ken Wild.

Counties: KENT, PROVIDENCE (part), WASHINGTON. CITIES AND TOWNSHIPS: Charleston, Coventry, Cranston, Exeter, Foster, Glocester, Greenwich (East and West), Hopkinton, Johnston, Kingstown (North and South), Narragansett, New Shoreham, Providence (part), Richmond, Warwick, West Warwick, Westerly, and Sctuate. Population (2000), 538,032.

ZIP Codes: 02804, 02807–08, 02812–18, 02822–23, 02825, 02827–29, 02831–33, 02836, 02852, 02857, 02873–75, 02877, 02879–83, 02886–89, 02891–94, 02898, 02901–05, 02907–11, 02917, 02919–21

SOUTH CAROLINA

(Population 2000, 4,012,012)

SENATORS

ERNEST F. HOLLINGS, Democrat, of Charleston, SC; born in Charleston, January 1, 1922; son of Wilhelmine Meyer and Adolph G. Hollings; graduated, The Citadel, B.A., 1942; University of South Carolina, LL.B., 1947; LL.D. The Citadel, June 1959; lawyer; member of Charleston County, South Carolina, and American bar associations; admitted to practice before South Carolina Supreme Court, U.S. District Court, U.S. Circuit Court of Appeals, U.S. Tax Court, U.S. Customs Court, and U.S. Supreme Court; member, St. John's Lutheran Church; member, Court of Adjudication, Lutheran Church in America; Armed Forces, 1942–45, served overseas from Africa to Austria, 33 months; 353rd Antiaircraft Artillery; 3rd, 36th, and 45th Divisions, captain; member, highest honor society at The Citadel—The Round Table; president of the alumni (the Association of Citadel Men), 1954; at the University of South Carolina Law School—member, Honor Society, Wig and Robe, *South Carolina Law Review,* and president of Law Federation; honorary doctor of letters degree, Benedict College, Columbia, SC, 1971; Charleston Junior Chamber of Commerce Distinguished Service Award as Young Man of the Year, 1953; U.S. Junior Chamber of Commerce, one of ten Outstanding Young Men of the United States, 1954; South Carolina Veteran of the Year, 1957; member, Hibernian Society, Arion Society, Sertoma Club; Charleston Rifle Club; Mason, LeCandeur No. 36, AFM; Shriner, Omar Temple; BPOE Lodge No. 242; American Legion, Post No. 10; Charleston Chamber of Commerce; Veterans of Foreign Wars; Captain John L. Weeks Post No. 3142; elected to South Carolina General Assembly from Charleston County, 1948, 1950, and 1952; chairman, Charleston County legislative delegation; speaker pro tempore, South Carolina House of Representatives; elected twice by unanimous vote, 1951, 1953; elected lieutenant governor, November 2, 1954; elected governor, November 4, 1958; served as Governor, 1959–63; appointed to Hoover Commission May 15, 1955; appointed by President Eisenhower to Advisory Commission on Intergovernmental Relations, December 1959; reappointed by President Kennedy, February 1962; chairman, Regional Advisory Council on Nuclear Energy; instituted technical training program in South Carolina, Nuclear Space Commission, and Commission on Higher Education; married to the former Rita Louise Liddy of Charleston, SC; four children: Michael Milhous, Helen Hayne, Patricia Salley, and Ernest Frederick Hollings III; author of "The Case Against Hunger—A Demand for a National Policy," 1970; committees: ranking member, Commerce, Science, and Transportation Committee; other committee assignments: Appropriations; Budget; elected to the U.S. Senate, November 8, 1966, to complete the unexpired term of the late Senator Olin D. Johnston; reelected to each succeeding Senate term.

Office Listings

http://hollings.senate.gov

125 Russell Senate Office Building, Washington, DC 20510 .... (202) 224–6121
Chief of Staff.—Joab Lesesne.
Executive Assistant.—Betty Pittleman.
State Assistant.—Trip King III.
Appointments Secretary.—Robin McCain.
Room 1551, 1835 Assembly Street, Columbia, SC 29201 .... (803) 765–5731
Custom House, Suite 112, 200 East Bay Street, Charleston, SC 29401 .... (843) 727–4525
126 Federal Building, Greenville, SC 29603 .... (864) 233–5366

* * *

LINDSEY GRAHAM, Republican, of Seneca, SC; born in Seneca, July 9, 1955; education: graduated, Daniel High School, Central, SC; B.A., University of South Carolina, 1977; awarded J.D., 1981; military service: joined the U.S. Air Force, 1982; served in the Base Legal Office and as Area Defense Counsel; assigned to Rhein Main Air Force Base, Germany, 1984; circuit trial counsel, U.S. Air Forces; Meritorious Service Medal for Active Duty Tour in Europe; Base Staff Judge Advocate in McEntire Air National Guard Base, SC, 1989–1994; presently, Lt. Col. in Air Force Reserves; employment: established private law practice, 1988; former member, South Carolina House of Representatives; Home Health Care Legislator of the Year, 1992; Assistant County Attorney for Oconee County, 1988–92; City Attorney for Central, SC, 1990–94; member: Seneca Sertoma; Walhalla Rotary; Anderson Chamber of Commerce; American Legion Post 120; Retired Officers Association; served as fundraising chairman, Oconee County Chapter of the American Cancer Society; board member, Rosa Clark Free Medical Clinic in

Seneca, SC; appointed to the Judicial Arbitration Commission by the Chief Justice of the Supreme Court; religion: attends Corinth Baptist Church; elected to the 104th Congress on November 8, 1994; reelected to each succeeding Congress; elected to the U.S. Senate on November 5, 2002.

Office Listings

http://lgraham.senate.gov

290 Russell Senate Office Building, Washington, DC 20510 .... (202) 224–5972
Chief of Staff.—Richard Perry. FAX: 224–1189
Legislative Director.—Aleix Jarvis.
Scheduler.—Ellen Bradley.
101 East Washington Street, Suite 220, Greenville, SC 29601 .... (864) 250–1417
530 Johnnie Dodds Boulevard, Suite 203, Mt. Pleasant, SC 29464 .... (843) 849–3887

* * *

REPRESENTATIVES

FIRST DISTRICT

HENRY E. BROWN, JR., Republican, of Hanahan, SC; born on December 20, 1935, in Lee County, SC; education: Berkeley High School; Baptist College; and The Citadel; occupation: Businessman; Piggly Wiggly Carolina Co., Inc.; helped develop the Lowcountry Investment Corp.; awards: National Republican Legislator of the Year; South Carolina Taxpayers Watchdog Award; South Carolina Association of Realtors Legislator of the Year; honorary degree, Doctor of Business Administration, The Citadel; family: married to Billye; three children; public service: Hanahan City Council, 1981–85; South Carolina House of Representatives, 1985–2000; elected to the 107th Congress on November 7, 2000; reelected to each succeeding Congress.

Office Listings

http://www.house.gov/henrybrown

1124 Longworth House Office Building, Washington, DC 20515 .... (202) 225–3176
Chief of Staff.—Stovall Witte.
Legislative Director.—Joe Glebocki.
Press Secretary.—Denver Merrill.
5900 Core Avenue, Charleston, SC 29406 .... (843) 747–4175
District Director.—Kathy Crawford.

Counties: BERKELEY (part), CHARLESTON (part), DORCHESTER (part), GEORGETOWN (part), HORRY. Population (2000), 668,668.

ZIP Codes: 29401–07, 29410, 29412–14, 29416–20, 29422–25, 29429, 29436, 29439–40, 29442, 29445, 29449, 29451, 29455–58, 29461, 29464–66, 29469–70, 29472, 29474–75, 29482–85, 29487, 29511, 29526–28, 29544–45, 29566, 29568–69, 29572, 29575–79, 29581–82, 29585, 29587–88, 29597–98

* * *

SECOND DISTRICT

JOE WILSON, Republican, of Springdale, SC; born on July 31, 1947, in Charleston, SC; education: graduated, Washington & Lee University, Lexington, VA; University of South Carolina School of Law; professional: attorney; Kirkland, Wilson, Moore, Taylor & Thomas (law firm); served on the staff of Senator Strom Thurmond and Congressman Floyd Spence; former Deputy General Counsel for the U.S. Department of Energy; former Judge of the town of Springdale, SC; military service: U.S. Army Reserves, 1972-1975; currently a Colonel in the South Carolina Army National Guard as a Staff Judge Advocate for the 218th Mechanized Infantry Brigade; organizations: Cayce-West Columbia Rotary Club; Sheriff's Department Law Enforcement Advisory Council; Reserve Officers Association; Lexington County Historical Society; Columbia Home Builders Association; County Community and Resource Development Committee; American Heart Association; Mid-Carolina Mental Health Association; Cayce-West Columbia Jaycees; Kidney Foundation; South Carolina Lung Association; Alston-Wilkes Society; Cayce-West Metro Chamber of Commerce; Columbia World Affairs Council; Fellowship of Christian Athletes, Sinclair Lodge 154; Jamil Temple; Woodmen of the World; Sons of Confederate Veterans; Military Order of the World Wars; Lexington, Greater Irmo, Chapin, Columbia, West Metro, and Batesburg-Leesville Chambers of Commerce; West Metro and Dutch Fork Women's Republican Clubs; and Executive Council of the Indian Waters Council, Boy Scouts of America; awards: U.S. Chamber of Commerce Spirit of Enterprise Award, 2001; Americans for Tax Reform Friend of the Taxpayer Award, 2001; public service: South Carolina State Senate, 1984-2001; family: married to Roxanne Dusenbury McCrory; four sons; elected to the 107th Congress, by special election, on December 18, 2001; reelected to each succeeding Congress.

Office Listings

http://joewilson.house.gov

212 Cannon House Office Building, Washington, DC 20515	(202) 225–2452
Chief of Staff.—Eric Dell.	FAX: 225–2455
Press Secretary.—Wesley Denton.	
Legislative Director.—Laurin Groover.	
903 Port Republic Street, P.O. Box 1538, Beaufort, SC 29901	(843) 521–2530
1700 Sunset Boulevard (U.S. 378), Suite 1, West Columbia, SC 29169	(803) 939–0041

Counties: AIKEN (part), ALLENDALE, BARNWELL, BEAUFORT, CALHOUN (part), HAMPTON, JASPER, LEXINGTON, ORANGEBURG (part), RICHLAND (part). CITIES AND TOWNSHIPS: Aiken (part), Allendale, Ballentine, Barnwell, Batesburg, Beaufort, Blackville, Bluffton, Blythewood, Brunson, Cayce, Chapin, Columbia (part), Coosawhatchie, Cope, Cordova, Crocketville, Daufuskie Island, Early Branch, Elko, Estill, Fairfax, Furman, Garnett, Gaston, Gifford, Gilbert, Hampton, Hardeeville, Hilda, Hilton Head Island, Irmo, Islandston, Kline, Leesville, Lexington, Livingston, Luray, Martin, Miley, Montmorenci, Neeses, North, Norway, Orangeburg, Pelion, Pineland, Port Royal, Ridgeland, Ruffin, Scotia, Springfield, St. Helena Island, St. Matthews (part), State Park, Swansea, Sycamore, Tillman, Ulmer, Varnville, West Columbia, White Rock, Williams, Williston, Windsor, and Yemassee. Population (2000), 668,668.

ZIP Codes: 29002, 29006, 29016, 29033, 29036, 29045, 29053–54, 29063, 29070–73, 29075, 29078, 29107, 29112–13, 29115–16, 29118, 29123, 29128, 29130, 29135, 29137, 29142, 29146–47, 29160, 29164, 29169–72, 29177, 29180, 29203–07, 29209–10, 29212, 29219, 29221, 29223–24, 29226–27, 29229, 29260, 29290, 29292, 29405, 29412–13, 29436, 29470, 29472, 29801, 29803, 29805, 29810, 29812–13, 29817, 29826–27, 29836, 29839, 29843, 29846, 29849, 29853, 29901–07, 29909–11, 29913–16, 29918, 29920–28, 29932–36, 29938–41, 29943–45

* * *

THIRD DISTRICT

J. GRESHAM BARRETT, Republican, of Westminster, SC; born on February 14, 1961, in Oconee, SC; education: B.S., Business Administration, The Citadel, 1983; military service: U.S. Army, 1983–1987; profession: small businessman; owner and operator of Barrett's Furniture; organizations: Westminster Rotary Club; Oconee County Boy Scouts; Westminster Chamber of Commerce; Oconee County Red Cross; religion: Baptist; attends Westminster Baptist Church; public service: South Carolina House of Representatives, 1987–2002; family: married to Natalie; children: Madison, Jeb, and Ross; elected to the 108th Congress on November 5, 2002.

Office Listings

http://www.house.gov/barrett

1523 Longworth House Office Building, Washington, DC 20515	(202) 225–5301
Chief of Staff.—William (Lance) Williams.	FAX: 225–3216
Legislative Director.—Sandra Campbell.	
315 South McDuffie Street, Anderson, SC 29622	(864) 224–7401
115 Enterprise Court, Suite B, Greenwood, SC 29649	(864) 223–8251
233 Pendleton Street, NW., Aiken, SC 29801	(803) 649–5571

Counties: ABBEVILLE, AIKEN (part), ANDERSON, EDGEFIELD, GREENWOOD, LAURENS (part), MCCORMICK, OCONEE, PICKENS, SALUDA. Population (2000), 668,669.

ZIP Codes: 29006, 29037, 29070, 29105, 29127–29, 29138, 29166, 29178, 29325, 29332, 29334–35, 29351, 29355, 29360, 29370, 29384, 29388, 29406, 29611, 29620–28, 29630–33, 29635, 29638–49, 29653–59, 29661, 29664–67, 29669–73, 29675 79, 29682, 29684 86, 29689, 29691 93, 29695 97, 29801 05, 29808 09, 29816, 29819, 29821 22, 29824, 29828–29, 29831–32, 29834–35, 29838, 29840–42, 29844–45, 29847–48, 29850–51, 29853, 29856, 29860–61

* * *

FOURTH DISTRICT

JIM DEMINT, Republican, of Greenville, SC; born in Greenville, SC, on September 2, 1951; education: graduated, West Hampton High School, Greenville, SC, 1969; B.S., University of Tennessee, 1973; MBA, Clemson University, 1981; certified management consultant and certified quality trainer; advertising and marketing businessman; started his own company, DeMint Marketing; active in Greenville, SC, business and educational organizations; married: Debbie; children; Mitchell Road Presbyterian Church; committees: Education and the Workforce; Small Business; Transportation and Infrastructure; elected to the 106th Congress; reelected to each succeeding Congress.

Office Listings

http://www.demint.house.gov

432 Cannon House Office Building, Washington, DC 20515 .... (202) 225–6030
Chief of Staff.—Matt Hoskins. FAX: 226–1177
Office Manager/Scheduler.—Ellen Weaver.
Legislative Director.—Chuck Royal.
Federal Building, 145 North Church Street, BTC #56, Suite 302, Spartanburg, SC 29306 .... (864) 582–6422
Federal Building, 300 East Washington Street, Suite 101, Greenville, SC 29601 .... (864) 232–1141

Counties: GREENVILLE, LAURENS (part), SPARTANBURG, UNION. Population (2000), 668,669.

ZIP Codes: 29031, 29178, 29301–07, 29316, 29318–24, 29329–31, 29333–36, 29338, 29346, 29348–49, 29353, 29356, 29364–65, 29368–69, 29372–79, 29385–86, 29388, 29390–91, 29395, 29564, 29601–17, 29627, 29635–36, 29644–45, 29650–52, 29654, 29661–62, 29669, 29673, 29680–81, 29683, 29687–88, 29690, 29698

* * *

FIFTH DISTRICT

JOHN M. SPRATT, JR., Democrat, of York, SC; born in Charlotte, NC, November 1, 1942; education: graduated, York High School, 1960; A.B., Davidson College, 1964; president of student body and Phi Beta Kappa, Davidson College; M.A., economics, Oxford University, Corpus Christi College (Marshall Scholar), 1966; LL.B., Yale Law School, 1969; admitted to the South Carolina Bar in 1969; military service: active duty, U.S. Army, 1969–71, discharged as captain; served as member of Operations Analysis Group, Office of the Assistant Secretary of Defense (Comptroller), received Meritorious Service Medal; employment: private practice of law 1971–82, Spratt, McKeown and Spratt in York, SC; York County attorney, 1973–82; president, Bank of Fort Mill, 1973–82; president, Spratt Insurance Agency, Inc.; president, York Chamber of Commerce; chairman, Winthrop College Board of Visitors; chairman, Divine Saviour Hospital Board; board of visitors, Davidson and Coker Colleges; president, Western York County United Fund; board of directors, Piedmont Legal Services; House of Delegates, South Carolina bar; elder, First Presbyterian Church, York; committees: Armed Services; ranking member, Budget; married: Jane Stacy Spratt, 1968; children: Susan, Sarah, and Catherine; elected to the 98th Congress, November 2, 1982; reelected to each succeeding Congress.

Office Listings

http://www.house.gov/spratt

1401 Longworth House Office Building, Washington, DC 20515 .... (202) 225–5501
Chief of Staff.—Ellen Buchanan. FAX: 225–0464
Press Secretary.—Chuck Fant.
P.O. Box 350, Rock Hill, SC 29731 .... (803) 327–1114
District Administrator.—Robert Hopkins.
39 East Calhoun Street, Sumter, SC 29150 .... (803) 773–3362
88 Public Square, Darlington, SC 29532–0025 .... (843) 393–3998

Counties: CHEROKEE, CHESTER, CHESTERFIELD, DARLINGTON, DILLON, FAIRFIELD, FLORENCE (part), KERSHAW, LANCASTER, LEE (part), MARLBORO, NEWBERRY, SUMTER (part), YORK. Population (2000), 668,668.

ZIP Codes: 29009–10, 29014–16, 29020, 29031–32, 29036–37, 29040, 29045, 29055, 29058, 29065, 29067, 29069, 29074–75, 29078–79, 29101–02, 29104, 29106, 29108, 29122, 29126–28, 29130, 29132, 29145, 29150–54, 29161, 29163, 29175–76, 29178, 29180, 29203, 29218, 29307, 29323, 29330, 29332, 29340–42, 29355, 29372, 29501, 29506, 29512, 29516, 29520, 29525, 29532, 29536, 29540, 29543, 29547, 29550–51, 29563, 29565, 29567, 29570, 29573–74, 29581, 29584, 29592–94, 29596, 29654, 29702–04, 29706, 29708–10, 29712, 29714–18, 29720–22, 29724, 29726–32, 29734, 29741–45

* * *

SIXTH DISTRICT

JAMES E. CLYBURN, Democrat, of Columbia, SC; born in Sumter, SC, on July 21, 1940; education: graduated, Mather Academy, Camden, SC, 1957; B.S., South Carolina State University, Orangeburg, 1962; attended University of South Carolina Law School, Columbia, 1972–74; South Carolina State Human Affairs Commissioner; Assistant to the Governor for Human Resource Development; executive director, South Carolina Commission for Farm Workers, Inc.; director, Neighborhood Youth Corps and New Careers; counselor, South Carolina Employment Security Commission; member: NAACP, lifetime member; Southern Regional Council; Omega

Psi Phi Fraternity, Inc.; Arabian Temple, No. 139; Nemiah Lodge No. 51 F&AM; married: the former Emily England; children: Mignon, Jennifer and Angela; elected Vice Chairman, Democratic Caucus, 2002; elected on November 3, 1992, to the 103rd Congress; reelected to each succeeding Congress.

Office Listings

http://www.house.gov/clyburn

2135 Rayburn House Office Building, Washington, DC 20515 .... (202) 225–3315
Administrative Assistant.—Yelberton Watkins. FAX: 225–2313
Legislative Director.—Danny Cromer.
Legislative Assistant.—Barvetta Singletary.
Policy Advisor.—Jaime Harrison.
1703 Gervais Street, Columbia, SC 29201 .... (803) 799–1100
District Director.—Robert Nance.
181 East Evans Street, Suite 314, Post Office Box 6286, Florence, SC 29502 .... (803) 662–1212
Joseph Floyd Manor, Suite 7, 2106 Mt. Pleasant Street, Charleston, SC 29405 .... (843) 965–5578

Counties: BAMBERG COUNTY. CITIES AND TOWNSHIPS: Bamberg, Denmark, Erhardt, Olar. BERKELEY COUNTY (part). CITIES AND TOWNSHIPS: Bethera, Cross, Daniel Island, Huger, Jamestown, Pineville, Russellville, Saint Stephen, Wando. CALHOUN COUNTY (part). CITY OF: Cameron (part), Creston, Fort Motte, St. Matthews. CHARLESTON COUNTY (part). CITIES AND TOWNSHIPS: Adams Run, Charleston (part), Edisto Island, Hollywood, Johns Island (part), Ravenel (part), Wadmalaw Island (part). CLARENDON COUNTY. CITIES AND TOWNSHIPS: Alcolu, Davis Station, Gable, Manning, New Zion, Rimini, Summerton, Turbeville. COLLETON COUNTY. CITIES AND TOWNSHIPS: Ashton, Cottageville, Green Pond, Hendersonville, Islandton, Jacksonboro, Lodge (part), Ritter, Round O, Smoaks, Walterboro (part), Williams. DORCHESTER COUNTY (part). CITIES AND TOWNSHIPS: Dorchester, Harleyville, Reevesville, Ridgeville, Rosinville, Saint George. FLORENCE COUNTY (part). CITIES AND TOWNSHIPS: Coward, Effingham, Florence (part), Johnsonville, Lake City, Olanta, Pamplico, Quinby (part), Scranton, Timmonsville. GEORGETOWN COUNTY (part). CITIES AND TOWNSHIPS: Andrews, Outland, Sampit. MARION COUNTY. CITIES AND TOWNSHIPS: Centenary, Gresham, Marion, Mullins, Nichols, Rains, Sellers. LEE COUNTY (part). CITIES AND TOWNSHIPS: Elliott, Lynchburg. ORANGEBURG COUNTY (part). CITIES AND TOWNSHIPS: Bowman, Branchville (part), Cardova, Cope (part), Elloree, Eutawville, Holly Hill, Norway, Orangeburg (part), Rowesville, Santee, Vance. RICHLAND COUNTY (part). CITIES AND TOWNSHIPS: Blythewood, Columbia (part), Eastover, Gadsden, Hopkins (part). SUMTER COUNTY (part). CITIES AND TOWNSHIPS: Mayesville, Oswego, Pinewood, Sumter (part). WILLIAMSBURG COUNTY. CITIES AND TOWNSHIPS: Cades, Greeleyville, Hemingway, Kingstree, Lane, Nesmith, Salters, and Trio. Population (2000), 668,670.

ZIP Codes: 29001, 29003, 29006, 29010, 29018, 29030, 29038–42, 29044–48, 29051–52, 29056, 29059, 29061–62, 29078, 29080–82, 29102, 29104, 29107, 29111, 29113–15, 29117–18, 29125, 29128, 29130, 29133, 29135, 29142–43, 29146, 29148, 29150, 29153–54, 29161–63, 29168, 29201–05, 29208–09, 29211, 29214–17, 29220, 29223, 29225, 29228, 29230, 29240, 29250, 29403, 29405–06, 29409, 29415, 29418, 29426, 29430–38, 29440, 29446–50, 29452–53, 29461, 29466, 29468, 29470–72, 29474–77, 29479, 29481, 29488, 29492–93, 29501–06, 29510, 29518–19, 29530, 29541, 29546, 29554–56, 29560, 29565, 29571, 29574, 29580–81, 29583, 29589–92, 29817, 29843, 29929, 29931, 29945

SOUTH DAKOTA

(Population 2000, 754,844)

SENATORS

TOM DASCHLE, Democrat, of Aberdeen, SD; born in Aberdeen on December 9, 1947; attended private and public schools; B.A., South Dakota State University, 1969; served in U.S. Air Force Strategic Air Command, first lieutenant, 1969–72; representative for financial investment firm; legislative assistant to former South Dakota Senator James Abourezk; member, American Legion, Catholic Church, South Dakota Jaycees; awards: only the third South Dakotan in 43 years to receive the Ten Outstanding Young Men from the U.S. Jaycees (1981), National Commander's Award by the Disabled American Veterans (1980), Person of the Year by the National Association of Concerned Veterans, Eminent Service Award by East River (South Dakota) Electric Power Cooperative, Friend of Education by the South Dakota Education Association; VFW Congressional Award, Veterans of Foreign Wars, 1997; founder, American Grown Foundation (1987); board member, Rural Voice; married the former Linda Hall in 1984; three children: Kelly, Nathan, and Lindsay; elected to the 96th Congress, November 7, 1978; and reelected to the three succeeding Congresses; elected Rocky Mountain region whip (1979); served as whip-at-large (1982–86), elected to the House Steering and Policy Committee (1983); elected to the U.S. Senate on November 4, 1986; reelected to each succeeding Senate term; elected Senate Democratic Leader in December, 1994, for the 104th Congress; reelected leader for the 105th, 106th, 107th, and 108th Congresses.

Office Listings

http://daschle.senate.gov

509 Hart Senate Office Building, Washington, DC 20510 .... (202) 224–2321
Administrative Assistant.—Laura Petrou.
Administrative Director.—Kelly Fado.
Press Secretary.—Don Pfeiffer.
Deputy Press Secretary.—Jake Maas.
320 N. Main Avenue, Suite B, Sioux Falls, SD 57101 .... (605) 334–9596
State Director.—Steve Erpenbach.
320 S. First Street, Suite 101, Aberdeen, SD 57402 .... (605) 225–8823
1313 West Main Street, Rapid City, SD 57709 .... (605) 348–7551

* * *

TIM JOHNSON, Democrat, of Vermillion, SD, born in Canton, SD, December 28, 1946; education: B.A., University of South Dakota, 1969; Phi Beta Kappa; M.A., political science, University of South Dakota, 1970; post-graduate study in political science, Michigan State University, 1970–71; J.D., University of South Dakota, 1975; married: Barbara Brooks, 1969; children: Brooks, Brendan and Kelsey Marie; Lutheran; budget advisor to the Michigan State Senate Appropriations Committee, 1971–72; admitted to the South Dakota bar in 1975 and began private law practice in Vermillion; served as Clay County Deputy State's Attorney, 1985; elected to the South Dakota House of Representatives, 1978; reelected, 1980; elected to the South Dakota State Senate, 1982; reelected, 1984; served on the Joint Appropriations Committee and the Senate Judiciary Committee; named Outstanding Citizen of Vermillion (1983); received South Dakota Education Association's ''Friend of Education'' Award (1983); Billy Sutton Award for Legislative Achievement (1984); elected to the U.S. House of Representatives, 1986; reelected to each succeeding Congress; delegate, Democratic National Convention, 1988–92; member: President's Export Council, 1999; committees: Appropriations; Banking, Housing and Urban Affairs; Budget; Energy and Natural Resources; Indian Affairs; elected to the U.S. Senate on November 5, 1996; reelected to each succeeding Senate term.

Office Listings

http://johnson.senate.gov

324 Hart Senate Office Building, Washington, DC 20510 .... (202) 224–5842
Chief of Staff.—Drey Samuelson.
Administrative Assistant.—Bob Martin.
Legislative Director.—Susan Hansen.
Communications Director.—Julianne Fisher.
715 S. Minnesota Avenue, Sioux Falls, SD 57104 .... (605) 332–8896
State Director.—Sharon Boysen.

REPRESENTATIVE

AT LARGE

WILLIAM J. JANKLOW, Republican, of Brandon, SD; born on September 13, 1939, in Chicago, IL; education: B.S., Business Administration, University of South Dakota, 1964; law degree, University of South Dakota, 1966; military service: U.S. Marine Corps, 1956–1959; profession: Attorney; religion: Lutheran; public service: South Dakota Attorney General, 1974–1978; South Dakota Governor, 1979–1987, and 1994–2002; family: married to Mary Dean; children: Pamela, Shonna, and Russell; elected to the 108th Congress on November 5, 2002.

Office Listings

http://www.house.gov/janklow

1504 Longworth House Office Building, Washington, DC 20515 .... (202) 225–2801
Chief of Staff.—Chris Braendlin. FAX: 225–5823
Scheduler.—Janie Beeman.
Systems Administrator.—Tammy Sumner.
2600 South Minnesota Avenue, Suite 100, Sioux Falls, SD 57105 .... (605) 367–8371
District Director.—Dave Volk.
2525 West Main Street, Suite 210, Rapid City, SD 57702 .... (605) 394–5280
10 Sixth Avenue, SW, Aberdeen, SD 57401 .... (605) 626–3440

Population (2000), 754,844.

ZIP Codes: 57001–07, 57010, 57012–18, 57020–22, 57024–59, 57061–73, 57075–79, 57101, 57103–10, 57117–18, 57186, 57188–89, 57192–98, 57201, 57212–14, 57216–21, 57223–27, 57231–39, 57241–43, 57245–49, 57251–53, 57255–66, 57268–74, 57276, 57278–79, 57301, 57311–15, 57317, 57319, 57321–26, 57328–32, 57334–35, 57337, 57339–42, 57344–46, 57348–50, 57353–56, 57358–59, 57361–71, 57373–76, 57379–86, 57399, 57401–02, 57420–22, 57424, 57426–30, 57432–42, 57445–46, 57448–52, 57454–57, 57460–61, 57465–77, 57479, 57481, 57501, 57520–23, 57528–29, 57531–34, 57536–38, 57540–44, 57547–48, 57551–53, 57555, 57559–60, 57562–64, 57566–72, 57574, 57576–77, 57579–80, 57584–85, 57601, 57620–23, 57625–26, 57630–34, 57636, 57638–42, 57644–46, 57648–52, 57656–61, 57701–03, 57706, 57709, 57714, 57716–20, 57722, 57724–25, 57730, 57732, 57735, 57737–38, 57741, 57744–45, 57747–48, 57750–52, 57754–56, 57758–64, 57766–67, 57769–70, 57772–73, 57775–77, 57779–80, 57782–83, 57785, 57787–88, 57790–94, 57799

TENNESSEE

(Population 2000, 5,689,283)

SENATORS

WILLIAM H. FRIST, Republican, of Nashville, TN; born on February 22, 1952 in Nashville; education: graduated, Montgomery Bell Academy, Nashville, 1970; A.B., Princeton University, Woodrow Wilson School of Public and International Affairs, 1974; M.D., Harvard Medical School, 1978, with honors; residency in general surgery (1978–84) and thoracic surgery (1983–84), Massachusetts General Hospital; cardiovascular and transplant fellowship, Stanford University Medical Center, 1985–86; heart and lung transplant surgeon; founding director, Vanderbilt Transplant Center; teaching faculty, Vanderbilt University Medical Center, 1986–93; staff surgeon, Nashville Veterans' Administration Hospital; board certified in both general surgery and cardiothoracic surgery; Medical Center Ethics Committee, 1991–93; chairman, Tennessee Medicaid Task Force, 1992–93; recipient: Distinguished Service Award, Tennessee Medical Association; president, Middle Tennessee Heart Association; member: Smithsonian Institution's Board of Regents, Princeton University Board of Trustees, American College of Surgeons, Society of Thoracic Surgeons, Southern Thoracic Surgical Association, American College of Chest Physicians; American Medical Association, Tennessee Medical Association, American Society of Transplant Surgeons, Association of Academic Surgery, International Society for Heart and Lung Transplantation, Tennessee Transplant Society, Alpha Omega Alpha, Rotary Club, United Way de Tocqueville Society; board member: YMCA Foundation of Metropolitan Nashville, Sergeant York Historical Association; commercial pilot; author of 100 scientific articles, chapters and abstracts (subjects: fibroblast growth factor, thoracic surgery, artificial heart, transplantation, immunosuppression); author of *Transplant* (Atlantic Monthly Press, 1989); co-editor, *Grand Rounds in Transplantation* (Chapman and Hall, 1995); married Karyn McLaughlin Frist, 1981; three children: Harrison, Jonathan, and Bryan; committees: Health, Education, Labor, and Pensions; Finance; Rules and Administration; Senate Majority Leader; elected to the U.S. Senate on November 8, 1994; reelected to each succeeding Senate term.

Office Listings

http://frist.senate.gov

461 Dirksen Senate Office Building, Washington, DC 20510 .... (202) 224–3344
Chief of Staff.—Howard Liebengood.
Legislative Director.—Andrea Becker.
Communications Director.—Nick Smith.
Executive Assistant / Scheduler.—Ramona Lessen.
28 White Bridge Road, Suite 211, Nashville, TN 37205 .... (615) 352–9411
State Director.—Bart VerHulst.
5100 Poplar Avenue, Suite 514, Memphis, TN 38137 .... (901) 683–1910
James Building, 735 Broad Street, Suite 701, Chattanooga, TN 37402 .... (423) 894–2203
200 East Main Street, Suite 111, Jackson, TN 38301 .... (731) 425–9655
10368 Wallace Alley Street, Suite 7, Kingsport, TN 37663 .... (423) 323–1252
Twelve Oaks Executive Park, Building One, Suite 170, 5401 Kingston Pike, Knoxville, TN 37919 .... (865) 602–7977

* * *

LAMAR ALEXANDER, Republican, of Nashville, TN; born on July 3, 1940, in Maryville, TN; education: Vanderbilt University, graduating Phi Beta Kappa, with honors in Latin American history; New York University Law School; served as Law Review editor; professional: clerk to Judge John Minor Wisdom, U.S. Court of Appeals in New Orleans; legislative assistant to Senator Howard Baker (R–TN), 1967; executive assistant to Bryce Harlow, counselor to President Nixon, 1969; President, University of Tennessee, 1988–1991; Co-Director, Empower America, 1994–1995; Chairman, Co-nect, an education and school improvement company; public service: Republican nominee for Governor of Tennessee, 1974; elected Governor of Tennessee in 1978, and reelected in 1982, serving from 1979–1987; U.S. Secretary of Education, 1991–1993; community service: chairman, Salvation Army Red Shield Family Initiative; and the Museum of Appalachia in Norris, TN; received Tennessee Conservation League Conservationist of the Year Award; family: married to Honey Alexander; four children; committees: Energy and Natural Resources; Foreign Relations; Health, Education, Labor, and Pensions; Joint Economic Committee; elected to the U.S. Senate on November 5, 2002.

Office Listings

http://alexander.senate.gov

302 Hart Senate Office Building, Washington, DC 20510 .... (202) 224–4944
Chief of Staff.—Tom Ingram. FAX: 228–3398
Legislative Director.—Richard Hertling.
Administrative Assistant.—Trina Tyrer.
Executive Assistant / Scheduler.—Bonnie Sansonetti.
3322 West End Avenue, Suite 120, Nashville, TN 37203 .... (615) 736–5129
Howard H. Baker, Jr. U.S. Courthouse; 800 Market Street, Suite 112, Knoxville, TN 37902 .... (865) 545–4253
Federal Building, 167 North Main Street, Suite 1068, Memphis, TN 38103 .... (901) 544–4224
Federal Building, 109 South Highland Street, Suite B–9, Jackson, TN 38301 .... (731) 423–9344
Joel E. Solomon Federal Building, 900 Georgia Avenue, Suite 260, Chattanooga, TN 37402 .... (423) 752–5337
Tri-Cities Regional Airport, Terminal Building, Suite 101, Blountville, TN 37663 (423) 245–3353

REPRESENTATIVES

FIRST DISTRICT

WILLIAM L. JENKINS, Republican, of Rogersville, TN; born on November 29, 1936 in Detroit, MI; education: graduated from Rogersville High School, 1954; B.B.A from Tennessee Tech, Cookville, 1957; military service: served in the U.S. Army Military Police, second lieutenant, 1959–60; J.D., University of Tennessee College of Law, Knoxville, TN, 1961; admitted to the Tennessee bar, 1962; employment: attorney; farmer; Commissioner of Conservation; Circuit Judge; energy advisor to Governor Lamar Alexander; TVA board member; State Representative to Tennessee General Assembly, 1962–70; Speaker of the House, 1968–70; delegate to the Republican National Convention, 1988; member: American Legion, Masonic Lodge, Tennessee Bar Association, Tennessee Farm Bureau; married: Mary Kathryn Jenkins, 1959; children: Rebecca, Georgeanne Price, William, Jr., Douglas; elected to the 105th Congress; reelected to each succeeding Congress.

Office Listings

1207 Longworth House Office Building, Washington, DC 20515 .... (202) 225–6356
Chief of Staff.—Brenda J. Otterson. FAX: 225–5714
Executive Assistant.—Dennis LeNard.
Legislative Director.—Richard Vaughn.
320 West Center Street, Kingsport, TN 57660 .... (423) 247–8161

Counties: CARTER, COCKE, GREENE, HAMBLEN, HANCOCK, HAWKINS, JEFFERSON, JOHNSON, SEVIER, SULLIVAN, UNICOI, WASHINGTON. Population (2000), 632,143.

ZIP Codes: 37601–02, 37604–05, 37614–18, 37620–21, 37625, 37640–45, 37650, 37656–60, 37662–65, 37680–84, 37686–88, 37690–92, 37694, 37699, 37711, 37713, 37722, 37725, 37727, 37731, 37738, 37743–45, 37752–53, 37760, 37764–65, 37778, 37809–11, 37813–16, 37818, 37821–22, 37843, 37857, 37860, 37862–65, 37868–69, 37873, 37876–77, 37879, 37881, 37890–91

* * *

SECOND DISTRICT

JOHN J. DUNCAN, JR., Republican, of Knoxville, TN; born in Lebanon, TN, July 21, 1947; education: University of Tennessee, B.S. degree in journalism, 1969; National Law Center, George Washington University, J.D. degree, 1973; served in both the Army National Guard and the U.S. Army Reserves, retiring with the rank of captain; private law practice in Knoxville, 1973–81; appointed State Trial Judge by Governor Lamar Alexander in 1981 and elected to a full eight-year term in 1982 without opposition, receiving the highest number of votes of any candidate on the ballot that year; member: American Legion 40 and 8, Elks, Sertoma Club, Masons, Scottish Rite and Shrine; present or past board member: Red Cross, Girl's Club, YWCA, Sunshine Center for the Mentally Retarded, Beck Black Heritage Center, Knoxville Union Rescue Mission, Senior Citizens Home Aid Service; religion: active elder at Eastminster Presbyterian Church; married: the former Lynn Hawkins; children: Tara, Whitney, John J. III, and Zane; committees: Government Reform; Transportation and Infrastructure; Resources; elected to both the 100th Congress (special election) and the 101st Congress in separate elections held on November 8, 1988; reelected to each succeeding Congress.

Office Listings

http://www.house.gov/duncan

2400 Rayburn House Office Building, Washington, DC 20515 .... (202) 225–5435
Chief of Staff.—Bob Griffitts. FAX: 225–6440
Deputy Chief of Staff.—Don Walker.
Legislative Director.—Bert Robinson.
Press Secretary.—Rob Haralson.
6 East Madison Avenue, Athens, TN 37303 .... (423) 745–4671
800 Market Street, Suite 100, Knoxville, TN 37902 .... (423) 523–3772
District Director.—Bob Griffitts.
262 East Broadway, Maryville, TN 37804 .... (423) 984–5464

Counties: BLOUNT, KNOX (part), LOUDON, MCMINN, MONROE. CITIES AND TOWNSHIPS: Alcoa, Athens, Englewood, Etowah, Farragut, Halls (Knox Co.), Knoxville, Lenoir City, Loudon, Madisonville, Maryville, Powell, Seymour (part), and Sweetwater. Population (2000), 632,144.

ZIP Codes: 37303, 37309, 37311–12, 37314, 37322–23, 37325, 37329, 37331, 37353–54, 37369–71, 37385, 37701, 37709, 37721, 37725, 37737, 37742, 37754, 37764, 37771–72, 37774, 37777, 37779, 37801–04, 37806–07, 37820, 37826, 37830, 37846, 37849, 37853, 37865, 37871, 37874, 37876, 37878, 37880, 37882, 37885–86, 37901–02, 37909, 37912, 37914–24, 37927–33, 37938–40, 37950, 37990, 37995–98

* * *

THIRD DISTRICT

ZACH WAMP, Republican, of Chattanooga, TN; born on October 28, 1957 in Fort Benning, GA; graduated, McCallie School, Chattanooga, 1976; attended University of North Carolina at Chapel Hill and University of Tennessee; member, Red Bank Baptist Church; commercial and industrial real estate broker; named Chattanooga Business Leader of the Year; chairman, Hamilton County Republican Party; regional director, Tennessee Republican Party; received Tennessee Jaycees' Outstanding Young Tennessean Award in 1996, U.S. Chamber of Commerce Spirit of Enterprise Award, Citizens Against Government Waste ''A'' Rating, National Taxpayers Union Friend of the Taxpayers Award; recognized by the Citizens Taxpayers Association of Hamilton County, the National Federation of Independent Business and the Concord Coalition for casting tough votes to reduce spending; married Kimberly Watts Wamp, 1985; two children: Weston and Coty; committees: Appropriations; subcommittees: Energy and Water; Homeland Security; Interior; elected to the 104th Congress; reelected to each succeeding Congress.

Office Listings

http://www.house.gov/wamp

2447 Rayburn House Office Building, Washington, DC 20515 .... (202) 225–3271
Chief of Staff.—Helen Hardin. FAX: 225–3494
Legislative Director.—Rob Hobart.
Press Secretary.—Susan Haigler.
Scheduler.—Randy Forrester.
900 Georgia Avenue, Suite 126, Chattanooga, TN 37402 .... (423) 756–2342
District Director.—Sarah Bryan.
Federal Building, Suite 100, 200 Administration Road, Oak Ridge, TN 37830 .... (865) 576–1976
District Director.—Linda Ponce.

Counties: ANDERSON, BRADLEY, CLAIBORNE, GRAINGER, HAMILTON, JEFFERSON (part), MEIGS, POLK, RHEA, ROANE (part), UNION. Population (2000), 632,143.

ZIP Codes: 37302, 37304, 37307–12, 37315–17, 37320–23, 37325–26, 37332–33, 37336–38, 37341, 37343, 37350–51, 37353, 37361–64, 37369, 37373, 37375, 37377, 37379, 37381, 37384, 37391, 37397, 37401–12, 37414–16, 37419, 37421–22, 37424, 37450, 37705, 37707–10, 37715–17, 37719, 37721, 37724–26, 37730, 37752, 37754, 37760, 37763–64, 37769, 37771, 37774, 37779, 37806–07, 37811, 37820–21, 37824–26, 37828, 37830–31, 37840, 37846, 37848–49, 37851, 37861, 37866, 37869–71, 37874, 37876–77, 37879–81, 37888, 37890, 37931, 37938

* * *

FOURTH DISTRICT

LINCOLN DAVIS, Democrat, of Pall Mall, TN; born on September 13, 1943; education: Alvin C. York Agricultural Institute, 1962; B.S., Agronomy, Tennessee Technological University, 1966; profession: farmer and general contractor; civic organizations: Tennessee State Jaycees; Pickett County Chamber of Commerce; Upper Cumberland Developmental District; Boy Scouts; public service: Mayor of Byrdstown, TN, 1978–1982; Tennessee State Representative, 1980–1984; Tennessee State Senator, 1996–2002; religion: Baptist; family: married to Lynda; children: Larissa, Lynn, and Libby; elected to the 108th Congress on November 5, 2002.

Office Listings

http://www.house.gov/lincolndavis

504 Cannon House Office Building, Washington, DC 20515 .... (202) 225–6831
Chief of Staff.—Beecher Frasier. FAX: 226–5172
Legislative Director.—Cicely Simpson.
Press Secretary.—Tom Hayden.
1064 North Gateway Avenue, Rockwood, TN 37854 .... (865) 354–3323
629 North Main Street, Jamestown, TN 38556 .... (931) 879–2361
1804 Carmack Boulevard, Suite A, Columbia, TN 38401 .... (931) 490–8699

Counties: Bledsoe, Campbell, Coffee, Cumberland, Fentress, Franklin, Giles, Grundy, Hickman (part), Lawrence, Lewis, Lincoln, Marion, Maury, Moore, Morgan, Pickett, Roane (part), Scott, Sequatchie, Van Buren, Warren, White, Williamson (part). Population (2000), 632,143.

ZIP Codes: 37018, 37025–26, 37033, 37037, 37047, 37062, 37064, 37078, 37091, 37096, 37098, 37110–11, 37129–33, 37137, 37144, 37160, 37166, 37171, 37174, 37179, 37183, 37190, 37301, 37305–06, 37313, 37318, 37324, 37327–28, 37330, 37334–35, 37337, 37339–40, 37342, 37345, 37347–49, 37352, 37355–57, 37359–60, 37365–67, 37374–83, 37387–89, 37394, 37396–98, 37419, 37714–15, 37719, 37721, 37723, 37726, 37729, 37732–33, 37748, 37755–57, 37762–63, 37766, 37769–71, 37773, 37778, 37819, 37829, 37840–41, 37845, 37847, 37852, 37854, 37867, 37869–70, 37872, 37880, 37887, 37892, 38370, 38401–02, 38449, 38451, 38453–57, 38459–64, 38468–69, 38472–78, 38481–83, 38486–88, 38504, 38506, 38549–50, 38553, 38555–59, 38565, 38571–72, 38574, 38577–79, 38581, 38583, 38585, 38587, 38589

* * *

FIFTH DISTRICT

JIM COOPER, Democrat, of Nashville, TN; born on June 19, 1954; education: University of North Carolina at Chapel Hill, B.A., History & Economics, 1975; Rhodes Scholar, Oxford University, 1977; J.D., Harvard Law School, 1980; admitted to Tennessee bar, 1980; employment: Attorney; Waller, Lansden, Dortch, and Davis (law firm), 1980–1982; Managing Director, Equitable Securities, 1995–1999; Adjunct Professor, Vanderbilt University Owen School of Management, 1995–2002; partner, Brentwood Capital Advisors LLC, 1999–2002; public service: elected to the U.S. House of Representatives, 1982; reelected 5 times; served, 1983–1995; unsuccessful candidate for U.S. Senate, 1994; family: married to Martha Hays; children: Mary, Jamie, and Hayes; elected to the 108th Congress on November 5, 2002.

Office Listings

http://www.cooper.house.gov

1536 Longworth House Office Building, Washington, DC 20515 .... (202) 225–4311
Chief of Staff.—Greg Hinote. FAX: 226–1035
Legislative Director.—Thomas Fields.
706 Church Street, Suite 101, Nashville, TN 37203 .... (615) 736–5295

Counties: Cheatham (part), Davidson, Wilson (part). Population (2000), 632,143.

ZIP Codes: 37011, 37013, 37015, 37027, 37032, 37034–35, 37064, 37070–72, 37076, 37080, 37082, 37086–88, 37090, 37115–16, 37121–22, 37135, 37138, 37143, 37146, 37189, 37201–22, 37224, 37227–30, 37232, 37234–36, 37238–50

* * *

SIXTH DISTRICT

BART GORDON, Democrat, of Murfreesboro, TN; born January 24, 1949, Murfreesboro; graduated, Central High School, Murfreesboro, 1967; B.S. *cum laude*, Middle Tennessee State University, Murfreesboro, 1971; J.D., University of Tennessee College of Law, Knoxville, 1973; admitted to the Tennessee State bar, 1974; opened private law practice in Murfreesboro, 1974; elected to the Tennessee Democratic Party's executive committee, 1974; appointed executive director of the Tennessee Democratic Party, 1979; elected the first full-time chairman of the Tennessee Democratic Party, 1981; resigned chairmanship, 1983, to successfully seek congressional seat; member, St. Mark's Methodist Church, Murfreesboro; past chairman: Rutherford County United Givers Fund and Rutherford County Cancer Crusade; board member: Rutherford County Chamber of Commerce, MTSU Foundation; married, Leslie Peyton Gordon; children: Peyton Margaret; committees: Energy and Commerce; Science; elected to the 99th Congress on November 6, 1984; reelected to each succeeding Congress.

Office Listings

http://www.house.gov/gordon

2304 Rayburn House Office Building, Washington, DC 20515 .... (202) 225–4231
Chief of Staff.—Chuck Atkins. FAX: 225–6887
Executive Assistant / Scheduler.—Julie Eubank.
P.O. Box 1986, 106 South Maple Street, Murfreesboro, TN 37133 .... (615) 896–1986
District Chief of Staff.—Kent Syler.
P.O. Box 1140, 15 South Jefferson, Cookeville, TN 38501 .... (931) 528–5907
101 Fifth Avenue West, Suite D, Springfield, TN 37172 .... (615) 382–9712

Counties: BEDFORD, CANNON, CLAY, DEKALB, JACKSON, MACON, MARSHALL, OVERTON, PUTNAM, ROBERTSON, RUTHERFORD, SMITH, SUMNER, TROUSDALE, WILSON (part). CITIES AND TOWNSHIPS: Cookeville, Gallatin, Hendersonville, Lafayette, Lebanon, Lewisburg, Livingston, Murfreesboro, Shelbyville, and Springfield. Population (2000), 632,143.

ZIP Codes: 37010, 37012, 37014, 37016, 37018–20, 37022, 37026, 37030–32, 37034, 37037, 37046–49, 37057, 37059–60, 37063, 37066, 37072–75, 37077, 37080, 37083, 37085–87, 37090–91, 37095, 37110, 37118–19, 37122, 37127–28, 37135–36, 37141, 37144–46, 37148–53, 37160–62, 37166–67, 37172, 37174, 37180, 37183–84, 37186, 37188, 37190, 37357, 37360, 37388, 38451, 38472, 38501–03, 38505–06, 38541–45, 38547–48, 38551–52, 38554, 38560, 38562–64, 38567–70, 38573–75, 38580–83, 38588–89

* * *

SEVENTH DISTRICT

MARSHA BLACKBURN, Republican, of Franklin, TN; born in Laurel, MS, on June 6, 1952; education: Mississippi State University, Bachelor of Science, 1973; occupation; retail marketing; public service: American Council of Young Political Leaders; Executive Director, Tennessee Film, Entertainment, and Music Commission; Chairman, Governor's Prayer Breakfast; Tennessee State Senate, 1998–2002; Minority Whip; community service: Rotary Club; Chamber of Commerce; Arthritis Foundation; Nashville Symphony Guild Board; Tennessee Biotechnology Association; March of Dimes; American Lung Association; awards: Chi Omega Alumnae Greek Woman of the Year, 1999; Middle Tennessee 100 Most Powerful People, 1999–2002; family: married to Chuck; children: Mary Morgan Ketchel and Chad; elected to the 108th Congress on November 5, 2002.

Office Listings

http://www.house.gov/blackburn

509 Cannon House Office Building, Washington, DC 20515 .... (202) 225–2811
Chief of Staff.—Steve Brophy. FAX: 225–3004
Legislative Director.—Michael Platt.
Executive Assistant.—Ryan Loskarn.
7975 Stage Hill Boulevard, Suite 1, Memphis, TN 38133 .... (901) 382–5811
City Hall Mall, 201 3rd Avenue S., Suite 117, Franklin, TN 37064 .... (615) 591–5161

Counties: CHEATHAM (part), CHESTER, DAVIDSON (part), DECATUR, FAYETTE, HARDEMAN, HARDIN, HENDERSON, HICKMAN (part), MCNAIRY, MONTGOMERY (part), PERRY, SHELBY (part), WAYNE, WILLIAMSON (part). Population (2000), 632,139.

ZIP Codes: 37010, 37014–15, 37024–25, 37027, 37032–33, 37035–36, 37040–43, 37046, 37052, 37055, 37060, 37062, 37064–65, 37067–69, 37079, 37082, 37096–98, 37101, 37135, 37137, 37140, 37155, 37174, 37179, 37187, 37191, 37211, 37215, 37220–21, 38002, 38004, 38008, 38010–11, 38014, 38016–18, 38027–29, 38036, 38039, 38042, 38044–46, 38048–49, 38052–53, 38057, 38060–61, 38066–69, 38075–76, 38088, 38128, 38133–34, 38138–39, 38141, 38163, 38183–84, 38310–11, 38313, 38315, 38321, 38326–29, 38332, 38334, 38339–41, 38345, 38347, 38351–52, 38356–57, 38359, 38361, 38363, 38365–68, 38370–72, 38374–76, 38379–81, 38388, 38390, 38392–93, 38425, 38450, 38452, 38463, 38471, 38475, 38485–86

* * *

EIGHTH DISTRICT

JOHN S. TANNER, Democrat, of Union City, TN; born at Dyersburg Army Air Base in Halls, TN, on September 22, 1944; attended elementary and high school in Union City; B.S., University of Tennessee at Knoxville, 1966; J.D., University of Tennessee at Knoxville, 1968; served, U.S. Navy, lieutenant, 1968–72; Tennessee Army National Guard, colonel, 1974–2000; attorney; admitted to the Tennessee bar in 1968 and commenced practice in Union City; member, Elam, Glasgow, Tanner and Acree law firm until 1988; businessman; elected to Tennessee House of Representatives, 1976–88; chairman, House Committee on Commerce, 1987–88; member: Obion County Chamber of Commerce; Obion County Cancer Society; Union City Rotary Club, Paul Harris Fellow; Obion County Bar Association; American Legion; Masons; First

Christian Church (Disciples of Christ) of Union City; married: the former Betty Ann Portis; children: Elizabeth Tanner Atkins and John Portis; two grandchildren; committees: Ways and Means; member: Blue Dog Coalition; Congressional Sportsmen's Caucus; elected to the 101st Congress on November 8, 1988; reelected to each succeeding Congress.

Office Listings

http://www.house.gov/tanner

1226 Longworth House Office Building, Washington, DC 20515 .... (202) 225–4714
Administrative Assistant.—Vickie Walling. FAX: 225–1765
Legislative Director.—Douglas Thompson.
Press Secretary.—Randy Ford.
Personal Secretary.—Kathy Becker.
203 West Church Street, Union City, TN 38261 .... (731) 885–7070
District Director.—Joe Hill.
Federal Building, Room B–7, Jackson, TN 38301 .... (731) 423–4848
8120 Highway 51 North, Suite 3, Millington, TN 38053 .... (901) 873–5690

Counties: BENTON, CARROLL, CROCKETT, DICKSON, DYER, GIBSON, HAYWOOD, HENRY, HOUSTON, HUMPHREYS, LAKE, LAUDERDALE, MADISON, MONTGOMERY (part), OBION, SHELBY (part), STEWART, TIPTON, WEAKLEY. Population (2000), 632,142.

ZIP Codes: 37015, 37023, 37025, 37028–29, 37036, 37040, 37043–44, 37050–52, 37055–56, 37058, 37061–62, 37078–79, 37097, 37101, 37134, 37142, 37165, 37171, 37175, 37178, 37181, 37185, 37187, 38001, 38004, 38006–07, 38011–12, 38015, 38019, 38021, 38023–25, 38030, 38034, 38037, 38040–41, 38047, 38049–50, 38053–55, 38058–59, 38063, 38069–71, 38075, 38077, 38079–80, 38083, 38127–29, 38135, 38201, 38220–26, 38229–33, 38235–38, 38240–42, 38251, 38253–61, 38271, 38281, 38301–03, 38305, 38308, 38313–14, 38316–18, 38320–21, 38324, 38330–31, 38333, 38336–38, 38341–44, 38346, 38348, 38355–56, 38358, 38362, 38366, 38369, 38378, 38380, 38382, 38387, 38389–92

* * *

NINTH DISTRICT

HAROLD E. FORD, JR., Democrat, of Memphis, TN; born in Memphis, May 11, 1970; son of the Honorable Harold E. Ford (D, TN–09, 1974–96) and Dorothy Bowles Ford; B.A. in American History, University of Pennsylvania, 1992; cofounded monthly newspaper, ''The Vision'' while at the University of Pennsylvania; J.D., University of Michigan School of Law, 1996; special assistant, Department of Commerce Economic Development Administration; Special Assistant, Justice/Civil Rights Cluster, President Clinton's 1992 transition team; aide to U.S. Senator James Sasser, Senate Budget Committee; coordinator of 1992 and 1994 reelection campaigns of U.S. Representative Harold E. Ford; member: Mt. Moriah-East Baptist Church; committees: Budget; Financial Services; subcommittees: Capital Markets, Insurance, and Government Sponsored Enterprises; Financial Institutions and Consumer Credit; elected to the 105th Congress; reelected to each succeeding Congress.

Office Listings

http://www.house.gov/ford

325 Cannon House Office Building, Washington, DC 20515 .... (202) 225–3265
Chief of Staff.—Mark Schuermann. FAX: 225–5663
Legislative Director.—Scott Keefer.
Executive Assistant.—Amy Mollenkamp.
Communications Director.—Anthony Coley.
Federal Office Building, Suite 369, 167 North Main Street, Memphis, TN 38103 ... (901) 544–4131

County: SHELBY COUNTY (part). CITY OF: Memphis. Population (2000), 632,143.

ZIP Codes: 37501, 38016–18, 38101, 38103–09, 38111–20, 38122, 38124–28, 38130–37, 38139, 38141–42, 38145–48, 38151–52, 38157, 38159, 38161, 38165–68, 38173–75, 38177, 38181–82, 38186–88, 38190, 38193–95, 38197

TEXAS

(Population 2000, 20,851,820)

SENATORS

KAY BAILEY HUTCHISON, Republican, of Dallas, TX; raised in La Marque, TX; education: graduate of The University of Texas at Austin, and University of Texas School of Law; Texas House of Representatives, 1972–76; appointed vice chair of the National Transportation Safety Board, 1976; senior vice president and general counsel, RepublicBank Corporation, and later co-founded Fidelity National Bank of Dallas; owned McCraw Candies, Inc.; political and legal correspondent for KPRC–TV, Houston; religion: Episcopalian, married: Ray Hutchison; member: development boards of SMU and Texas A&M schools of business; trustee of The University of Texas Law School Foundation; elected Texas State Treasurer, 1990; committees: Appropriations; Commerce, Science and Transportation; Rules and Administration; Veterans' Affairs; elected to the U.S. Senate, by special election, on June 5, 1993, to fill the vacancy caused by the resignation of Senator Lloyd Bentsen; reelected to each succeeding Senate term.

Office Listings

http://hutchison.senate.gov

284 Russell Senate Office Building, Washington, DC 20510 .... (202) 224–5922
Chief of Staff.—Ruth Cymber. FAX: 224–0776
Legislative Director.—Joseph Mondello.
State Director.—Lindsey Parham.
961 Federal Building, 300 East 8th Street, Austin, TX 78701 .... (512) 916–5834
10440 North Central Expressway, Suite 1160, LB 606, Dallas, Texas 75231 .... (214) 361–3500
1919 Smith Street, Suite 800, Houston, TX 77024 .... (713) 653–3456
222 E. Van Buren, Suite 404, Harlingen, TX 77002 .... (956) 423–2253
500 Chestnut Street, Suite 1570, Abilene, Texas 79602 .... (325) 676–2839
145 Duncan Drive, Suite 120, San Antonio, Texas 78230 .... (210) 340–2885

* * *

JOHN CORNYN, Republican, of San Antonio, TX; born on February 2, 1952, in Houston, TX; education: graduated, Trinity University, and St. Mary's School of Law, San Antonio, TX; Masters of Law, University of Virginia, Charlottesville, VA; profession: Attorney; public service: Bexar County District Court Judge; Presiding Judge, Fourth Administrative Judicial Region; Texas Supreme Court, 1990–1997; Texas Attorney General, 1999–2002; community service: Salvation Army Adult Rehabilitation Council; World Affairs Council of San Antonio; Lutheran General Hospital Board; awards: Outstanding Texas Leader Award, 2000; James Madison Award, 2001; elected to the U.S. Senate on November 5, 2002; appointed to the U.S. Senate on December 2, 2002.

Office Listings

http://cornyn.senate.gov

517 Hart Senate Office Building, Washington, DC 20510 .... (202) 224–2934
Chief of Staff.—Pete Olson. FAX: 228–2856
Legislative Director.—Beth Jayari.
Communications Director.—Don Stewart.
24 Greenway Plaza, Suite 1705, Houston, TX 77046 .... (713) 572–3337
5005 LBJ Freeway, Suite 1150, Farmers Branch, TX 75244 .... (214) 767–3000
100 East Ferguson Street, Suite 1004, Tyler, TX 75702 .... (903) 593–0902
221 West 6th Street, Suite 1530, Austin, TX 78701 .... (512) 469–6034
812 Federal Building, 1205 Texas Avenue, Lubbock, TX 79401 .... (806) 472–7533
222 East Van Buren, Suite 404, Harlingen, TX 78550 .... (956) 423–6118

REPRESENTATIVES

FIRST DISTRICT

MAX SANDLIN, Democrat, of Marshall, TX; born on September 29, 1952 in Texarkana, AR; education: graduated, Atlanta High School, TX; B.A., Baylor University, Waco, TX, 1975; J.D., Baylor University School of Law, 1978; admitted to the bar, Marshall, TX, 1978; board certified in family law; employment: county judge, Harrison County, 1986–89; county court of law judge, Harrison County, 1989–96; partner, Sandlin & Buckner, 1982–96; vice president, Howell and Sandlin, Inc., 1989–96; president, East Texas Fuels, Inc., 1992–96; coach, Marshall Youth Baseball, Softball and Basketball Association; member: Texas Ranger Association Foundation; Marshall Chamber of Commerce; East Texas Housing and Finance Corporation (board of directors and treasurer); Oil, Gas and Mineral Law section of the State Bar of Texas; awards: National Mock Trial Championship Team; Outstanding Young Alumni, Baylor University; Texas Department of Human Services award for services to abused children; children: Hillary, Max III, Emily, Christian; elected to the 105th Congress; reelected to each succeeding Congress.

Office Listings

http://www.house.gov/sandlin

324 Cannon House Office Building, Washington, DC 20515 .... (202) 225–3035
- Chief of Staff.—Paul F. Rogers.
- Press Secretary.—Danielle Allen.
- Legislative Director.—Andy Lewin.
- Office Manager / Scheduler.—Karen Brooke.

1300 East Pinecrest Drive, Suite 700, Marshall, TX 75670 .... (903) 938–8386
P.O. Box 248, New Boston, TX 75570 .... (903) 628–5594
P.O. Box 538, Sulphur Springs, TX 75482–0538 .... (903) 885–8682
202 East Pilar Street, Room 304, Nacogdoches, TX 75961 .... (936) 559–0063

Counties: BOWIE, CAMP, CASS, DELTA, FRANKLIN, HARRISON, HOPKINS, HUNT (part), LAMAR, MARION, MORRIS, NACOGDOCHES (part), PANOLA, RED RIVER, RUSK, SHELBY, TITUS, UPSHUR, WOOD. Population (2000), 651,619.

ZIP Codes: 75135, 75160–61, 75169, 75189, 75401–04, 75410–12, 75415–17, 75420–23, 75425–26, 75428–29, 75431–37, 75440–42, 75444, 75446, 75448–53, 75455–58, 75460–62, 75468–74, 75477–78, 75480–83, 75486–87, 75493–94, 75496–97, 75501, 75503–05, 75507, 75550–51, 75554–56, 75558–74, 75599, 75601–06, 75630–31, 75633, 75636–45, 75647, 75650–54, 75656–59, 75661–62, 75666–72, 75680–89, 75691–92, 75694, 75755, 75760, 75765, 75773, 75783–84, 75788–89, 75861, 75935, 75943, 75946, 75954, 75958, 75961, 75963–65, 75973–75

* * *

SECOND DISTRICT

JIM TURNER, Democrat, of Crockett, TX; born on February 6, 1946; education: B.A., M.A., business administration, and LL.B., University of Texas; military service: captain, U.S. Army; represented Fifth District in Texas Senate; Texas House of Representatives, 1981–84; Special Counsel for Legislative Affairs and Executive Assistant to the Governor, 1984–85; chairman, Texas Commission on Children and Youth, 1993; member, Select Committee on Public Education and Texas Punishment Standards Commission, 1993; sponsored legislation to establish, and served as member of the State Ethics Commission; former mayor of Crockett; past president, Crockett Chamber of Commerce; deacon and Sunday School teacher, First Baptist Church; named Legislator of the Year by the Texas Association for the Education of Young Children and Outstanding State Senator by the Texas Youth Commission; married: Ginny Turner; children: John and Susan; committees: Armed Services; ranking member, Select Committee on Homeland Security; subcommittees: Tactical Air and Land Forces; Terrorism, Unconventional Threats and Capabilities; House Blue Dogs; elected to the 105th Congress; reelected to each succeeding Congress.

Office Listings

http://www.house.gov/turner

330 Cannon House Office Building, Washington, DC 20515 .... (202) 225–2401
- Chief of Staff.—Elizabeth Hurley Burks. FAX: 225–5955
- Legislative Director / General Counsel.—Trent Ashby.
- Executive Assistant.—Rachel Redington.
- Press Secretary.—Jennie McCue.

701 North First Street, Room 201, Lufkin, TX 75901–3008 .... (936) 637–1770
- District Caseworkers: Norma Butler, Jerry Huffman.

420 West Green Avenue, Orange, TX 77630 .... (409) 883–4990
- Field Representative.—Ann Gray.

1202 Sam Houston Avenue, Suite 5, Huntsville, TX 77340 .... (936) 291–3097

Counties: ANGELINA, CHEROKEE, GRIMES, HARDIN, HOUSTON, JASPER, LIBERTY, MONTGOMERY (part), NACOGDOCHES (part), NEWTON, ORANGE, POLK, SABINE, SAN AUGUSTINE, SAN JACINTO, TRINITY, TYLER, WALKER. Population (2000), 651,619.

ZIP Codes: 75757, 75759, 75764, 75766, 75772, 75780, 75784–85, 75789, 75834–35, 75839, 75844–45, 75847, 75849, 75851–52, 75856, 75858, 75862, 75865, 75901–04, 75915, 75925–26, 75928–34, 75936–39, 75941–42, 75944, 75947–49, 75951, 75956, 75959–61, 75965–66, 75968–69, 75972, 75976–80, 77301–03, 77306, 77320, 77326–28, 77331–32, 77334–35, 77340–42, 77350–51, 77354, 77356–60, 77363–64, 77367–69, 77371–72, 77374, 77376, 77378, 77399, 77519, 77533, 77535, 77538, 77561, 77564, 77574–75, 77582, 77585, 77611–12, 77614–17, 77624–26, 77630–32, 77639, 77656–57, 77659, 77660, 77662–64, 77670, 77830–31, 77861, 77868, 77872, 77875–76

THIRD DISTRICT

SAM JOHNSON, Republican, of Dallas, TX; born San Antonio, TX, October 11, 1930; education: B.S., business administration, Southern Methodist University, Dallas, TX, 1951; M.A., international affairs, George Washington University, Washington, DC, 1974; military service: served in Air Force, 29 years: Korea and Vietnam (POW in Vietnam, six years, ten months); director, Air Force Fighter Weapons School; flew with Air Force Thunderbirds Precision Flying Demonstration Team; graduate of Armed Services Staff College and National War College; military awards: two Silver Stars, two Legions of Merit, Distinguished Flying Cross, one Bronze Star with Valor, two Purple Hearts, four Air Medals, and three Outstanding Unit awards; ended career with rank of colonel and Air Division commander; retired, 1979; employment: opened homebuilding company, 1979; served seven years in Texas House of Representatives; Smithsonian Board of Regents; U.S. / Russian Joint Commission on POW / MIA; member: Executive Board of Dedman College, Southern Methodist University; Associated Texans Against Crime; Texas State Society; married the former Shirley L. Melton, 1950; three children, Dr. James Robert Johnson, Shirley Virginia (Gini) Mulligan, Beverly Briney; elected to Texas State House of Representatives, 1984; elected to the 102nd Congress by special election on May 18, 1991, to fill the vacancy caused by the resignation of Steve Bartlett; reelected to each succeeding Congress.

Office Listings

http://www.house.gov/samjohnson

1211 Longworth House Office Building, Washington, DC 20515 .... (202) 225–4201
Chief of Staff.—Cody Lusk.
Legislative Director.—Rebekah Hamilton.
Communications Director.—McCall Cameron.
Executive Assistant.—Elizabeth Bowden.
2929 North Central Expressway, Suite 240, Richardson, TX 75074 .... (972) 470–0892

Counties: COLLIN (part), DALLAS, (part). CITIES AND TOWNSHIPS: Allen, Frisno, Garland, McKinney, Plano, Princeton, Richardson, Rowlett, Sachse, and Wylie. Population (2000), 651,620.

ZIP Codes: 75002, 75007, 75009, 75013, 75023–26, 75030, 75034–35, 75040–42, 75044–48, 75069–71, 75074–75, 75078, 75080–82, 75085–86, 75088–89, 75093–94, 75098, 75245, 75248, 75252, 75287, 75355, 75367, 75370, 75378, 75382, 75407, 75409, 75424, 75442, 75454

* * *

FOURTH DISTRICT

RALPH M. HALL, Democrat, of Rockwall, TX; born in Fate, TX, May 3, 1923; graduated, Rockwall High School, 1941; attended Texas Christian University, University of Texas, and received LL.B., Southern Methodist University, 1951; lieutenant (senior grade), U.S. Navy, carrier pilot, 1942–45; lawyer; admitted to the Texas bar in 1951 and commenced practice in Rockwall; former president and chief executive officer, Texas Aluminum Corporation; past general counsel, Texas Extrusion Company, Inc.; past organizer, chairman, board of directors, now chairman of board, Lakeside National Bank of Rockwall (now Lakeside Bancshares, Inc.); past chairman, board of directors, Lakeside News, Inc.; past vice chairman, board of directors, Bank of Crowley; president, North and East Trading Company; vice president, Crowley Holding Co.; county judge, Rockwall County, 1950–62; member, Texas State Senate, 1962–72; member: First Methodist Church; American Legion Post 117; VFW Post 6796, Rockwall Rotary Club, and Rotary Clubs International; committees: Energy and Commerce, ranking member, Science; married the former Mary Ellen Murphy, 1944; three sons: Hampton, Brett and Blakeley; elected to the 97th Congress, November 4, 1980; reelected to each succeeding Congress.

Office Listings

http://www.house.gov/ralphhall

2405 Rayburn House Office Building, Washington, DC 20515 .... (202) 225–6673
Chief of Staff.—Janet Perry Poppleton. FAX: 225–3332
Legislative Director.—Grace Warren.
104 North San Jacinto Street, Rockwall, TX 75087–2508 .... (972) 771–9118
District Assistant.—Tom Hughes.
101 East Pecan Street, Suite 114, Sherman, TX 75090–5989 .... (903) 892–1112
District Assistant.—Judy Rowton.
211 West Ferguson Street, Suite 211, Tyler, TX 75072–7222 .... (903) 597–3729
District Assistant.—Martha Glover.

Counties: COLLIN COUNTY (part). CITIES AND TOWNSHIPS: Anna, Blue Ridge, Caddo Mills, Celina, Copeville, Farmersville, Josephine, Lavon, McKinney, Melissa, Nevada, Prosper, Weston, Westminster. COOKE COUNTY. CITIES AND TOWNSHIPS: Decatur, Era, Forestburg, Gainesville, Greenwood, Lake Kiowa, Lindsay, Muenster, Myra, Rosston, Sanger, Slidell, Valley View. FANNIN COUNTY. CITIES AND TOWNSHIPS: Bailey, Bells, Bonham, Dodd City, Ector, Gober, Honeygrove, Ivanhoe, Ladonia, Leonard, Randolph, Ravenna, Savoy, Telephone, Trenton, Windom. GRAYSON COUNTY. CITIES AND TOWNSHIPS: Collinsville, Denison, Gordonville, Gunter, Howe, Pilot Point, Pottsboro, Sadler, Sherman, Southmayd, Tioga, Tom Bean, Whitesboro, Whitewright, Van Alstyne. GREGG COUNTY. CITIES AND TOWNSHIPS: Easton, Gladewater, Judson, Kilgore, Lair Hill, Longview, White Oak. HUNT COUNTY (part). CITIES AND TOWNSHIPS: Greenville, Quinlan. KAUFMAN COUNTY (part). CITIES AND TOWNSHIPS: Crandall, Elmo, Forney, Gun Barrel City, Kaufman, Kemp, Mabank, Rosser, Scurry, Seagoville, Terrell. RAINS COUNTY. CITIES AND TOWNSHIPS: Alba, Emory, Golden, Lone Oak, Point. ROCKWALL COUNTY. CITIES AND TOWNSHIPS: Fate, Heath, Rowlett, Rockwall, Royse City. SMITH COUNTY. CITIES AND TOWNSHIPS: Arp, Bullard, Flint, Lindale, Mineola, New London, New Summerfield, Overton, Troup, Tyler, Whitehouse, Winona. VAN ZANDT COUNTY. CITIES AND TOWNSHIPS: Athens, Ben Wheeler, Canton, Edgewood, Fruitvale, Grand Saline, Murchison, Van, and Wills Point. Population (2000), 651,620.

ZIP Codes: 75009, 75013, 75020–21, 75032, 75058, 75069, 75076, 75087–92, 75097–98, 75103, 75114, 75117–18, 75121, 75124, 75126–27, 75132, 75140, 75142–43, 75147, 75156, 75158–61, 75164, 75166, 75169, 75173, 75189, 75409–10, 75413–14, 75418, 75420, 75423–24, 75438–40, 75442–43, 75446–47, 75449, 75452–54, 75459, 75472, 75474–76, 75479, 75485, 75488–92, 75495–97, 75601–08, 75615, 75645, 75647, 75660, 75662–63, 75666, 75684, 75693, 75701–09, 75711–13, 75750, 75752, 75754, 75756–58, 75762, 75771, 75773, 75778–92, 75798–99, 76209, 76233–34, 76238–41, 76245, 76250, 76252–53, 76263–66, 76268, 76271–73

* * *

FIFTH DISTRICT

JEB HENSARLING, Republican, of Dallas, TX; born on May 29, 1957, in Stephenville, TX; education: B.A., economics, Texas A&M University, 1979; J.D., University of Texas School of Law, 1982; profession: businessman; vice president, Maverick Capital, 1993–1996; owner, San Jacinto Ventures, 1996–2002; vice president, Green Mountain Energy Co., 1999–2001; community service: American Cancer Society for the Dallas Metro Area; Children's Education Fund; Habitat for Humanity; religion: Christian; family: married to Melissa; children: Claire; elected to the 108th Congress on November 5, 2002.

Office Listings

http://www.house.gov/hensarling

423 Cannon House Office Building, Washington, DC 20515 .... (202) 225–3484
Chief of Staff.—Brian Thomas. FAX: 226–4888
Legislative Director.—Dee Buchanan.
Press Secretary.—Mike Walz.
10675 East Northwest Highway, Suite 1685, Dallas, TX 75238 .... (214) 349–9996
100 East Corsicana Street, Suite 208, Athens, TX 77571 .... (903) 675–8288

Counties: ANDERSON, DALLAS (part), FALLS, HENDERSON, KAUFMAN (part), LEON, LIMESTONE, FREESTONE, MADISON, MCLENNAN (part), ROBERTSON. Population (2000), 651,620.

ZIP Codes: 75041, 75043, 75049, 75088–89, 75098, 75114, 75124–26, 75134, 75141–43, 75146–50, 75156–59, 75163, 75172, 75180–82, 75185, 75187, 75214, 75217–18, 75227–28, 75231, 75238, 75243, 75253, 75336, 75357, 75359, 75630, 75710, 75751–52, 75756, 75758, 75763, 75770, 75773, 75778–79, 75782, 75801–03, 75831–33, 75838–40, 75844, 75846, 75848, 75850, 75852–53, 75855, 75859–61, 75880, 75882, 75884, 75886, 76034, 76036, 76095, 76111, 76163, 76446, 76450, 76519, 76524, 76570, 76578–79, 76624, 76629–30, 76632, 76635, 76642, 76648, 76653, 76655–56, 76661, 76664, 76667, 76673, 76678, 76680, 76682, 76685–87, 76693, 76703, 77807, 77837, 77850, 77855–56, 77859, 77864–65, 77867, 77870–72, 77882

* * *

SIXTH DISTRICT

JOE BARTON, Republican, of Ennis, TX; born in Waco, TX, September 15, 1949; graduated Waco High School, 1968; B.S., industrial engineering, Texas A&M University, College Station, 1972; M.S., industrial administration, Purdue University, West Lafayette, IN, 1973; plant manager, assistant to the vice president, Ennis Business Forms, Inc., 1973–81; awarded White House Fellowship, 1981–82; served as aide to James B. Edwards, Secretary, Department of Energy; member, Natural Gas Decontrol Task Force in the Office of Planning, Policy and Analysis; worked with the Department of Energy task force in support of the President's Private Sector Survey on Cost Control; natural gas decontrol and project cost control consultant, Atlantic Richfield Company; cofounder, Houston County Volunteer Ambulance Service, 1976; vice president, Houston County Industrial Development Authority, 1980; chairman, Crockett Parks and Recreation Board, 1979–80; vice president, Houston County Chamber of Commerce, 1977–80; member, Dallas Energy Forum; three children: Brad, Alison and Kristin; Methodist; elected to the 99th Congress on November 6, 1984; reelected to each succeeding Congress.

Office Listings

http://www.joebarton.house.gov

2109 Rayburn House Office Building, Washington, DC 20515 .... (202) 225–2002
Administrative Assistant.—Heather Couri. FAX: 225–3052
Deputy Chief of Staff / Communications Director.—Samantha Jordan.
Legislative Director.—Ryan Long.
Scheduler.—Andrea Rodriguez.
Suite 201, 303 West Knox, Ennis, TX 75119–3942 .... (817) 543–1000
6001 West I–20, Suite 200, Arlington, TX 76107 .... (817) 543–1000

Counties: ELLIS, HILL, JOHNSON, NAVARRO, TARRANT (part). CITIES AND TOWNSHIPS: Arlington, Alvarado, Bardwell, Burleson (part), Cleburne, Corsicana, Crowley (part), Dawson, Ennis (part), Everman, Ferris, Fort Worth (part), Frost, Grand Prairie (part), Godley, Grandview, Hillsboro, Hubbard, Itasca, Italy, Joshua, Keene, Keens, Mansfield, Maypearl, Midlothian, Milford, Oak Leaf, Palmer, Pecan Hill (part), Red Oak (part), Rice, Richland, Rio Vista, Venus, Waxahachie, and Whitney. Population (2000), 651,620.

ZIP Codes: 75052, 75101–02, 75104–05, 75109–10, 75119–20, 75125, 75144, 75146, 75151–55, 75165, 75167–68, 75859, 76001–03, 76009–10, 76012–18, 76020, 76028, 76031, 76033, 76035–36, 76041, 76044, 76049–50, 76052, 76055, 76058–61, 76063–65, 76070, 76084, 76092–94, 76096–99, 76108, 76112, 76120, 76123, 76126, 76131–34, 76140, 76155, 76162, 76179, 76182, 76244, 76262, 76621–23, 76626–28, 76631, 76635–36, 76639, 76641, 76645, 76648, 76650–51, 76660, 76666, 76670, 76673, 76675–76, 76679, 76681, 76691–93

* * *

SEVENTH DISTRICT

JOHN ABNEY CULBERSON, Republican, of Harris County, TX; born on August 24, 1956, in Houston, TX; education: B.A., Southern Methodist University; J.D., South Texas College of Law; occupation: Attorney; family: married to Belinda Burney, 1989; children: Caroline; awards: Citizens for a Sound Economy Friend of the Taxpayer Award; Texas Eagle Forum Freedom and Family Award; Houston Jaycees Outstanding Young Houstonian Award; public service: Texas House of Representatives, 1987–2000; elected to the 107th Congress on November 7, 2000; reelected to each succeeding Congress.

Office Listings

http://www.house.gov/culberson

1728 Longworth House Office Building, Washington, DC 20515 .... (202) 225–2571
Chief of Staff.—Bill Crow. FAX: 225–4381
Legislative Director.—Tont Essalih.
Office Manager.—Jamie Harper.
10000 Memorial Drive, Suite 620, Houston, TX 77024–3490 .... (713) 682–8828
District Director.—Jan Crow.

County: HARRIS COUNTY (part). Population (2000), 651,620.

ZIP Codes: 77019, 77024, 77027, 77031, 77036, 77040–43, 77046, 77055–57, 77063, 77072, 77074, 77077, 77079–80, 77082–84, 77094–95, 77098–99, 77215, 77218, 77224, 77227, 77237, 77242–44, 77254, 77256–57, 77263, 77269, 77272, 77279–82, 77284, 77411, 77413, 77433, 77449–50, 77477

* * *

EIGHTH DISTRICT

KEVIN BRADY, Republican, of The Woodlands, TX; born in Vermillion, SD, April 11, 1955; education: B.S., business, University of South Dakota; employment: served in Texas House of Representatives, 1991–96, the first Republican to capture the 15th District seat since the 1800s; awards: Achievement Award, Texas Conservative Coalition; Outstanding Young Texan (one of five), Texas Jaycees; Ten Best Legislators for Families and Children, State Bar of Texas; Legislative Standout, Dallas Morning News; Scholars Achievement Award for Excellence in Public Service, North Harris Montgomery Community College District; Victims Rights Equalizer Award, Texans for Equal Justice Center; Support for Family Issues Award, Texas Extension Homemakers Association; chair, Council of Chambers of Greater Houston; president, East Texas Chamber Executive Association; president, South Montgomery County Woodlands Chamber of Commerce, 1985-present; director, Texas Chamber of Commerce Executives; Rotarian; religion: attends Saints Simon and Jude Catholic Church; married: Cathy Brady; elected to the 105th Congress; reelected to each succeeding Congress.

Office Listings

http://www.house.gov/brady

428 Cannon House Office Building, Washington, DC 20515 .... (202) 225–4901
Chief of Staff.—Doug Centilli.
Press Secretary.—Sarah Tunstall.
Legislative Director.—David Malech.
200 River Pointe Drive, Suite 304, Conroe, TX 77304 .... (936) 441–5700
616 FM 1960 West, Suite 220, Houston, TX 77090 .... (281) 895–8892
District Director.—Heather Montgomery.

COUNTIES: HARRIS, (part), MONTGOMERY (part). CITIES AND TOWNSHIPS: Conroe (part), Houston (part), Humble (part), Kingwood, Oak Ridge North, Panorama Village, Pinehurst, Shenandoah, Spring, The Woodlands, and Tomball. Population (2000), 651,619.

ZIP Codes: 77040, 77064–66, 77068–70, 77073, 77086, 77090, 77273, 77290, 77301–06, 77316, 77318, 77325, 77328, 77333, 77336, 77338–39, 77345–47, 77353–58, 77362, 77365, 77373, 77375, 77377–89, 77391, 77393, 77396, 77429, 77433, 77447, 77532, 77873

* * *

NINTH DISTRICT

NICK LAMPSON, Democrat, of Beaumont, TX; born in Beaumont, February 14, 1945; education: graduated, South Park High School, Beaumont, TX, 1964; B.S., biology, Lamar University, Beaumont, 1968; M.Ed., Lamar University, 1971; teacher; elected Jefferson County Tax Assessor-Collector; member: Young Men's Business League; Clean Air and Water; Sierra International; Knights of Columbus; married: the former Susan Floyd; children: Hillary, Stephanie; committees: Science; Transportation and Infrastructure; elected to the 105th Congress; reelected to each succeeding Congress.

Office Listings

http://www.house.gov/lampson

405 Cannon House Office Building, Washington, DC 20515 .... (202) 225–6565
Chief of Staff.—Tom Combs. FAX: 225–5547
Legislative Director.—David Lofye.
Executive Assistant.—Jennifer Milek.
Suite 322, 300 Willow Street, Beaumont, TX 77701 .... (409) 838–0061
Suite 216, 601 Rosenberg, Galveston, TX 77550 .... (409) 762–5877

Counties: CHAMBERS, GALVESTON, HARRIS (part), JEFFERSON. CITIES OF: Baytown, Beaumont, Galveston, Port Arthur, and Texas City. Population (2000), 651,619.

ZIP Codes: 77044, 77049, 77058, 77062, 77089, 77258, 77346, 77362, 77364, 77369, 77396, 77435, 77510–11, 77514, 77517–18, 77520–22, 77532, 77535, 77539, 77546, 77549–55, 77560, 77562–63, 77565, 77568, 77573–75, 77580–82, 77590–92, 77597–98, 77613, 77617, 77619, 77622–23, 77625–27, 77629, 77631, 77640–43, 77650–51, 77655, 77659–61, 77663–65, 77701–08, 77710, 77713, 77720, 77725–26

* * *

TENTH DISTRICT

LLOYD DOGGETT, Democrat, of Austin, TX; born October 6, 1946 in Austin; education: graduated, Austin High School; B.B.A., University of Texas, Austin, 1967; J.D., University of Texas, 1970; president, University of Texas Student Body; associate editor, *Texas Law Review*; Outstanding Young Lawyer, Austin Association of Young Lawyers; president, Texas Consumer Association; religion: member, First United Methodist Church; admitted to the Texas State bar, 1971; Texas State Senate, 1973–85, elected at age 26; Senate author of 124 state laws and Senate sponsor of 63 House bills enacted into law; elected president pro tempore of Texas Senate; served as acting governor; named Outstanding Young Texan by Texas Jaycees; Arthur B. DeWitty Award for outstanding achievement in human rights, Austin NAACP; honored for work by Austin Rape Crisis Center, Planned Parenthood of Austin; Austin Chapter, American Institute of Architects; Austin Council on Alcoholism; Disabled American Veterans; justice on Texas Supreme Court, 1989–94; chairman, Supreme Court Task Force on Judicial Ethics, 1992–94; Outstanding Judge (Mexican-American Bar of Texas), 1993; adjunct professor, University of Texas School of Law, 1989–94; James Madison Award, Texas Freedom of Information Foundation, 1990; First Amendment Award, National Society of Professional Journalists, 1990; committees: Ways and Means; subcommittees: Health; Select Revenue Measures; member: cofounder, House Information Technology Roundtable; Democratic Caucus Task Force on Education; Congressional Task Force on Tobacco and Health; Democratic Caucus Task Force on Child Care; married: Libby Belk Doggett, 1969; children: Lisa and Cathy; elected to the 104th Congress; reelected to each succeeding Congress.

Office Listings

http://www.house.gov/doggett

201 Cannon House Office Building, Washington, DC 20515 .... (202) 225–4865
Chief of Staff.—Michael J. Mucchetti.
Systems Administrator.—Gina Maraboto.
Press Secretary.—Julie Davis.
Staff Assistant.—Kevin Clune.
300 East 8th Street, Suite 763, Austin, TX 78701 .... (512) 916–5921
District Director.—Kristi Willis.

County: TRAVIS COUNTY (part). Population (2000), 651,619.

ZIP Codes: 73301, 73344, 78610, 78612, 78615, 78617, 78621, 78634, 78641, 78651–53, 78659–60, 78664, 78691, 78701–05, 78708–16, 78718–25, 78727–29, 78731, 78739, 78741, 78744–45, 78747–48, 78751–68, 78772–74, 78778–81, 78783, 78785–86, 78788–789, 78799

* * *

ELEVENTH DISTRICT

CHET EDWARDS, Democrat, of Waco, TX; born in Corpus Christi, TX, November 24, 1951; education: graduated Memorial High School, Houston, TX, 1970; B.A., Texas A&M University, College Station, 1974; M.B.A., Harvard Business School, Boston, MA, 1981; served as legislative assistant to Texas Congressman Olin ''Tiger'' Teague, 1974–77; marketing representative, Trammell Crow Company, 1981–85; president, Edwards Communications, Inc.; member, Texas State Senate, 1983–90; married: to the former Lea Ann Wood; children: John Thomas and Garrison Alexander; elected to the 102nd Congress, November 6, 1990; reelected to each succeeding Congress.

Office Listings

http:/www.house.gov/edwards

2459 Rayburn House Office Building, Washington, DC 20515 .... (202) 225–6105
Administrative Assistant.—Chris Chwastyk. FAX: 225–0350
Press Secretary.—David Helfert.
600 Austin Avenue, Suite 29, Waco, TX 76710 .... (254) 752–9600
Deputy District Director.—Myrtle Johnson.
116 South East Street, Belton, TX 76513 .... (254) 933–2904
District Director.—Sam Murphey.
624 South Austin Avenue, Suite 210, Georgetown, TX 78626 .... (512) 864–3186

Counties: BELL, BOSQUE, CORYELL, HAMILTON, LAMPASAS, MCLENNAN, MILAM, MILLS, SAN SABA, WILLIAMSON (part). CITIES OF: Georgetown, Killeen, Temple, and Waco. Population (2000), 651,620.

ZIP Codes: 76436, 76501–05, 76508, 76511, 76513, 76518–20, 76522–28, 76531, 76533–34, 76537–44, 76547–50, 76554, 76556–59, 76561, 76564–67, 76569–71, 76577–79, 76596–99, 76621–22, 76624, 76629–30, 76633–34, 76637–38, 76640, 76643–44, 76649, 76652, 76654–55, 76657, 76664–65, 76671, 76682, 76684, 76689–91, 76701–02, 76704–08, 76710–12, 76714–16, 76797–99, 76801, 76824, 76832, 76842, 76844, 76853, 76864, 76869–72, 76877–80, 76890, 77857, 78577, 78610, 78626–28, 78634, 78642, 78673

* * *

TWELFTH DISTRICT

KAY GRANGER, Republican, of Fort Worth, TX; born in Greenville, TX, January 18, 1943; education: B.S., *magna cum laude*, 1965, and Honorary Doctorate of Humane Letters, 1992, Texas Wesleyan University; owner, Kay Granger Insurance Agency, Inc.; former public school teacher; elected Mayor of Fort Worth, 1991, serving three terms; during her tenure, Fort Worth received All-America City Award from the National Civic League; former Fort Worth Councilwoman; past chair, Fort Worth Zoning Commission; past board member: Dallas-Fort Worth International Airport; North Texas Commission; Fort Worth Convention and Visitors Bureau; U.S. Conference of Mayors Advisory Board; Business and Professional Women's Woman of the Year, 1989; three grown children: J.D., Brandon and Chelsea; first woman Republican to represent Texas in the U.S. House; committees: Appropriations; Select Committee on Homeland Security; Deputy Republican Whip; elected to the 105th Congress; reelected to each succeeding Congress.

Office Listings

http://www.house.gov/granger

435 Cannon House Office Builiding, Washington, DC 20515 .... (202) 225–5071
Chief of Staff.—Barrett Karr. FAX: 225–5683
Legislative Director.—Nora Bomar.
Scheduler.—Trish Horowitz.
1701 River Run Road, Suite 407, Fort Worth, TX 76107 .... (817) 338–0909
District Director.—Barbara Ragland. (817) 335–5852

Counties: PARKER (part), TARRANT (part). Population (2000), 651,619.

ZIP Codes: 76008, 76020–23, 76028, 76031, 76033, 76035–36, 76039–40, 76044, 76049–50, 76052–54, 76058, 76063, 76066–67, 76071, 76082, 76084–88, 76092, 76101–02, 76104, 76106–18, 76120–21, 76124, 76126–27, 76129–33, 76135–37, 76147–48, 76161, 76164, 76177, 76179–81, 76185, 76191–93, 76195–99, 76248, 76262, 76439, 76462, 76485–87, 76490

* * *

THIRTEENTH DISTRICT

MAC THORNBERRY, Republican, of Clarendon, TX; born in Clarendon, TX, July 15, 1958; education: valedictorian graduate of Clarendon High School; B.A., Texas Tech University; University of Texas, law degree; employment: rancher, attorney; admitted to the Texas bar, 1983; member: Texas and Southwestern Cattle Raisers; co-chair of the Congressional Oil and Gas Forum; Rural Health Care Coalition, and co-founder/co-chair of Defense Study Group; married: Sarah Adams, 1986; children: Will and Mary Kemp; committees: Armed Services; Budget; Select Committee on Homeland Security; subcommittees: chairman, Cybersecurity, Science, and Research and Development; Emergency Preparedness and Response; Intelligence and Counterterrorism; Terrorism, Unconventional Threats and Capabilities; Strategic Forces; elected to the 104th Congress; reelected to each succeeding Congress.

Office Listings

http://www.house.gov/thornberry

2457 Rayburn House Office Building, Washington, DC 20515 .... (202) 225–3706
Administrative Assistant.—Lou Zickar. FAX: 225–3486
Office Manager.—Tim Kennedy.
905 South Filmore, Suite 520, Amarillo, TX 79101 .... (806) 371–8844
Chief of Staff.—Sylvia Nugent.
4245 Kemp, Suite 315, Wichita Falls, TX 76308 .... (940) 692–1700
District Office Manager.—Brent Oden.

Counties: ARCHER, ARMSTRONG, BAYLOR, BRISCOE, CARSON, CASTRO, CHILDRESS, CLAY, COLLINGSWORTH, COTTLE, CROSBY, DALLAM, DEAF SMITH, DICKENS, DONLEY, FLOYD, FOARD, GARZA (part), GRAY, HALE, HANSFORD, HARDEMAN, HARTLEY, HEMPHILL, HUTCHINSON, KING, KNOX, LAMB (part), LIPSCOMB, MONTAGUE, MOORE, MOTLEY, OCHILTREE, OLDHAM, POTTER, RANDALL, ROBERTS, SHERMAN, SWISHER, WHEELER, WICHITA, WILBARGER. Population (2000), 651,619.

ZIP Codes: 76228, 76230, 76234, 76239, 76249, 76251–52, 76255, 76261, 76265, 76270, 76301–02, 76305–11, 76351–52, 76354, 76357, 76360, 76363–67, 76369–71, 76373–74, 76377, 76379–80, 76384–85, 76389, 79001–03, 79005, 79007–08, 79010–15, 79018–19, 79021–22, 79024, 79027, 79029, 79031–36, 79039–46, 79052, 79054, 79056–59, 79061–66, 79068, 79070, 79072–73, 79077–88, 79092, 79094–98, 79101–11, 79114, 79116–21, 79124, 79159, 79165–66, 79168, 79170, 79172, 79174–75, 79178, 79180–81, 79184–87, 79201, 79220–21, 79223, 79225–27, 79229–31, 79233–37, 79239, 79241, 79243–45, 79248, 79250–52, 79255–59, 79261, 79311–13, 79322, 79330, 79343, 79347, 79357, 79364, 79369–70, 79383, 79505, 79529

* * *

FOURTEENTH DISTRICT

RON PAUL, Republican, of Surfside Beach, TX; born in Pittsburgh, PA, August 20, 1935; education: B.A., Gettysburg College, 1957; M.D., Duke College of Medicine, North Carolina, 1961; captain, U.S. Air Force, 1963–68; employment: obstetrician and gynecologist; represented Texas' 22nd District in the U.S. House of Representatives, 1976–1977, and 1979–85; married: the former Carol Wells in 1957; children: Ronnie, Lori, Pyeatt, Rand, Robert and Joy LeBlanc; committees: Financial Services; International Relations; elected to the 105th Congress; reelected to each succeeding Congress.

Office Listings

http://www.house.gov/paul

203 Cannon House Office Building, Washington, DC 20515 .... (202) 225–2831
Chief of Staff.—Tom Lizardo.
Legislative Director.—Norman Singleton.
Press Secretary.—Jeff Deist.
312 South Main, Suite 228, Victoria, TX 77901 .... (512) 576–1231
200 W. 2nd Street, Suite 210, Freeport, TX 77541 .... (409) 230–0000

Counties: ARANSAS, BASTROP (part), BRAZORIA (part), CALDWELL, CALHOUN, COLORADO, DEWITT, FAYETTE, GONZALES, GUADALUPE, HAYS (part), JACKSON, KARNES, LAVACA, MATAGORDA, REFUGIO, VICTORIA, WHARTON, WILSON. Population (2000), 651,619.

ZIP Codes: 77404, 77412, 77414–15, 77419–20, 77422, 77426, 77428, 77430–32, 77434–37, 77440, 77442–44, 77446, 77448, 77453–58, 77460, 77463, 77465, 77467–68, 77470, 77474–75, 77480, 77482–83, 77486, 77488, 77515, 77531, 77541–42, 77566, 77901–05, 77950–51, 77954, 77957, 77961–62, 77964, 77968–71, 77973–79, 77982–84, 77986–88, 77990–91, 77994–95, 78064, 78101, 78108, 78111–19, 78121–24, 78130, 78140–41, 78143–44, 78147, 78151, 78154–56, 78159–61, 78164, 78223, 78335–36, 78340, 78358, 78377, 78381–82, 78390, 78393, 78602, 78604, 78606, 78610, 78612, 78614, 78616–17, 78622, 78629, 78632, 78635–36, 78638, 78640, 78644, 78648, 78655–56, 78658, 78661–63, 78666–67, 78670–71, 78673–74, 78677, 78932–35, 78938, 78940–43, 78945–46, 78948–54, 78956–57, 78959–63

* * *

FIFTEENTH DISTRICT

RUBÉN HINOJOSA, Democrat, of Mercedes, TX; born in Mercedes, August 20, 1940; B.B.A., 1962, and M.B.A., 1980, University of Texas; president and chief financial officer, H&H Foods, Inc.; board of directors, National Livestock and Meat Board and Texas Beef Industry Council, 1989–93; past president and past chairman of the board of directors, Southwestern Meat Packers Association; chairman and member of board of trustees, South Texas Community College, 1993–96; past public member, Texas State Bar Board of Directors; former adjunct professor, Pan American University School of Business; elected member, Texas State Board of Education, 1975–84; past director, Rio Grande Valley Chamber of Commerce; Knapp Memorial Hospital Board of Trustees; and Our Lady of Mercy Church Board of Catholic Advisors; past member, board of trustees, Mercedes Independent School District; former U.S. Jaycee Ambassador to Colombia and Ecuador; married to Martha L. Hinojosa; five children: Ruben, Jr., Laura, Iliana, Kaitlin, and Karen; elected to the 105th Congress; reelected to each succeeding Congress.

Office Listings

http://www.house.gov/hinojosa

2463 Rayburn House Office Building, Washington, DC 20515 .... (202) 225–2531
Chief of Staff.—Roy Dye. FAX: 225–5688
Legislative Director.—Connie Humphrey.
Senior Advisor.—Greg Davis.
Press Secretary.—Israel Rocha.
311 North 15th Street, McAllen, TX 78501 .... (956) 682–5545
District Director.—Salomon Torres.
107 South St. Mary's Street, Beeville, TX 78102 .... (361) 358–8400
District Director.—Judy McAda.

Counties: BEE, BROOKS, GOLIAD, HIDALGO (part), KLEGERG (part), LIVE OAK, NUECES (part), SAN PATRICIO. CITIES AND TOWNSHIPS: Agua Dulce, Alamo, Beeville, Bishop, Donna, Driscoll, Edcouch, Edinburg, Elroy, Elsa, Goliad, Gregory, Kingsville, LaVilla, Mathis, McAllen, Mercedes, Mission, Odem, Pharr, Portland, Robstown, San Juan, Sinton, Taft, Three Rivers, and Weslaco. Population: (2000) 651,619.

ZIP Codes: 77905, 77954, 77960, 77963, 77967, 77974, 77989, 77993–94, 78022, 78060, 78071, 78075, 78102, 78104, 78107, 78119, 78125, 78142, 78145–46, 78151, 78162, 78330, 78332, 78335–36, 78343, 78350, 78352–53, 78355, 78359, 78362–64, 78368, 78370, 78372, 78374, 78380, 78383, 78387, 78389–91, 78501–05, 78516, 78537–41, 78543, 78549, 78557–58, 78561–63, 78565, 78569–70, 78572–74, 78577, 78579–80, 78589, 78595–96, 78599

* * *

SIXTEENTH DISTRICT

SILVESTRE REYES, Democrat, of El Paso, TX; born in Canutillo, TX, on November 10, 1944; graduated, Canutillo High School, 1964; associate degree, El Paso Community College, 1976; attended University of Texas, Austin, 1964–65, and El Paso, 1965–66; served in U.S. Army, 1966–68, Vietnam combat veteran; U.S. Border Patrol, chief patrol agent, 26½ years, retired December 1, 1995; member: Canutillo School Board, 1968–69, 21st Century Democrats, El Paso County Democrats, and Unite El Paso; married the former Carolina Gaytan, 1968; three children: Monica, Rebecca and Silvestre Reyes, Jr.; elected on November 5, 1996, to the 105th Congress; reelected to each succeeding Congress.

Office Listings

http://www.house.gov/reyes

1527 Longworth House Office Building, Washington, DC 20515 .... (202) 225–4831
Chief of Staff.—Perry Finney Brody. FAX: 225–2016
Press Secretary.—Ashley Atwell.
Scheduler / Office Manager.—Liza Lynch.
Suite 400, 310 North Mesa, El Paso, TX 79901 .... (915) 534–4400
Deputy Chief of Staff.—Sal Payan.

Counties: EL PASO (part). CITIES AND TOWNSHIPS: Anthony, Canutillo, Clint, El Paso, Fabens, Horizon City, San Elizario, Socorro, Tornillo, Vinton, and Westway. Population (2000), 651,619.

ZIP Codes: 79821, 79835–36, 79838–39, 79849, 79901–08, 79910, 79912–18, 79920, 79922–27, 79929–32, 79934–38, 79940–55, 79958, 79960–61, 79968, 79976, 79978, 79980, 79995–99, 88510–21, 88523–36, 88538–50, 88553–63, 88565–90, 88595

* * *

SEVENTEENTH DISTRICT

CHARLES W. STENHOLM, Democrat, of Abilene, TX; born in Stamford, TX, October 26, 1938; education: graduated, Stamford High School, 1957; graduated, Tarleton State Junior College, 1959; B.S., Texas Tech University, 1961; M.S., Texas Tech University, 1962; honorary doctor of laws, McMurry University; honorary doctor of laws, Abilene Christian University; honorary doctor of laws, Hardin-Simmons University; farmer; past president, Rolling Plains Cotton Growers and Texas Electric Cooperatives; former member, Texas State ASC Committee; former State Democratic executive committeeman, 30th senatorial district; member: Stamford Exchange Club; and Lions Club; past president: Stamford Chamber of Commerce; United Way; and Little League; member: Bethel Lutheran Church; married: the former Cynthia (Cindy) Ann Watson; children: Chris, Cary and Courtney Ann; elected to the 96th Congress, November 7, 1978; reelected to each succeeding Congress.

Office Listings

http://www.house.gov/stenholm

1211 Longworth House Office Building, Washington, DC 20515 .... (202) 225–6605
Administrative Assistant / Press Assistant.—Rebecca Tice. FAX: 225–2234
Legislative Director.—Ed Lorenzen.
P.O. Box 1237, Stamford, TX 79553 .... (915) 773–3623
1500 Industrial Boulevard, Suite 101, Abilene, TX 79602 .... (915) 673–7221
2121 Knickerbocker Road, San Angelo, Texas 76904 .... (915) 942–8881

Counties: BORDEN, BROWN, CALLAHAN, COKE, COLEMAN, COMANCHE, CONCHO, DAWSON, EASTLAND, ERATH, FISHER, GARZA (part), GLASSCOCK, HASKELL, HOOD, IRION, JACK, JONES, KENT, MCCULLOCH, MITCHELL, NOLAN, PALO PINTO, RUNNELS, SCHLEICHER, SCURRY, SHACKELFORD, SOMERVELL, STEPHENS, STERLING, STONEWALL, TAYLOR, THROCKMORTON, TOM GREEN, WISE, YOUNG. Population (2000), 651,619.

ZIP Codes: 76020, 76023, 76033, 76035, 76043, 76048–49, 76052, 76066–68, 76070–71, 76073, 76077–78, 76082, 76087, 76225, 76230, 76234, 76246–47, 76249, 76259, 76267, 76270, 76363, 76365, 76371–72, 76374, 76388–89, 76401–02, 76424, 76426–27, 76429–33, 76435–37, 76442–46, 76448–50, 76452–55, 76457–72, 76474–76, 76481, 76483–84, 76486–87, 76490–91, 76531, 76649, 76690, 76801–04, 76821, 76823, 76825, 76827–28, 76834, 76836–37, 76841–42, 76845, 76852, 76855, 76857–58, 76861–62, 76865–66, 76871–73, 76875, 76878, 76882, 76884, 76886–88, 76890, 76901–06, 76908–09, 76930, 76933–37, 76939–41, 76945, 76949, 76951, 76953, 76955, 76957–58, 77047, 79331, 79345, 79351, 79356, 79370, 79377, 79501–04, 79506, 79508, 79510–12, 79516–21, 79525–30, 79532–41, 79543–50, 79553, 79556, 79560–63, 79565–67, 79601–08, 79697–99, 79706, 79713, 79720, 79738–39, 79782

* * *

EIGHTEENTH DISTRICT

SHEILA JACKSON LEE, Democrat, of Houston, TX; born in Queens, NY, on January 12, 1950; graduated, Jamaica High School; B.A., Yale University, New Haven, CT, 1972; J.D., University of Virginia Law School, 1975; practicing attorney for 12 years; AKA Sorority; Houston Area Urban League; American Bar Association; staff counsel, U.S. House Select Committee on Assassinations, 1977–78; admitted to the Texas bar, 1975; city council (at large), Houston, 1990–94; Houston Municipal Judge, 1987–90; married Dr. Elwyn Cornelius Lee, 1973; two children: Erica Shelwyn and Jason Cornelius Bennett; elected to the 104th Congress; reelected to each succeeding Congress.

Office Listings

http://www.jacksonlee.house.gov

2435 Rayburn Cannon House Office Building, Washington, DC 20515 .... (202) 225–3816
Administrative Assistant.—Sophia King.
Legislative Director.—Lisa Kinard.
Communications Director.—Nkenge Harman.
Scheduler.—Gail Mathapo.
1919 Smith Street, Suite 1180, Mickey Leland Building, Houston, TX 77002 .... (713) 655–0050
District Director.—Cynthia Buggage.
420 West 19th Street, Houston, TX 77008 .... (713) 861–4070

Counties: HARRIS COUNTY (part). CITY OF: Houston. Population (2000), 651,620.

ZIP Codes: 77001–10, 77013, 77016, 77018–24, 77026, 77028–30, 77033, 77035, 77038, 77040–41, 77045, 77047–48, 77051–52, 77054–55, 77064, 77066–67, 77076, 77078, 77080, 77086–88, 77091–93, 77097–98, 77201–06, 77208, 77210, 77212, 77216, 77219, 77221, 77226, 77230, 77233, 77238, 77240–41, 77251–53, 77255, 77265–66, 77277, 77288, 77291–93, 77297–99

* * *

NINETEENTH DISTRICT

RANDY NEUGEBAUER, Republican, of Lubbock, TX; born on December 24, 1949, in St. Louis, MO; education: Texas Tech University, 1972; professional: small businessman (home building industry); organizations: West Texas Home Builders Association; Land Use and Developers Council; Texas Association of Builders; National Association of Home Builders; Campus Crusade for Christ; public service: Lubbock City Council, 1992–1998; served as Mayor Pro Tempore, 1994–1996; leader of coalition to create the Ports-to-Plains Trade Corridor; awards: Lubbock Chamber of Commerce Distinguished Service Award; Reese Air Force Base Friend of Reese Award; religion: Baptist; family: married to Dana; two children; elected to the 108th Congress, by special election, on June 3, 2003.

Office Listings

1026 Longworth House Office Building, Washington, DC 20515 .... (202) 225–4005
Chief of Staff.—Anthony Hulen. FAX: 225–9615
Communications Director.—Thais Conway.
Federal Building, 1205 Texas Avenue, Room 810, Lubbock, TX 79401 .... (806) 763–1611
District Director.—Jimmy Clark.

Counties: ANDREWS, BAILEY, COCHRAN, CRANE, ECTOR, GAINES, HOCKLEY, HOWARD, LAMP (part), LOVING, LUBBOCK, LYNN, MARTIN, MIDLAND, PARMER, TERRY, WARD, WINKLER, YOAKUM. Population (2000), 651,619.

ZIP Codes: 79009, 79031, 79035, 79053, 79064, 79311–14, 79316, 79320, 79323–26, 79329, 79331, 79336, 79338–39, 79342–47, 79350–51, 79353, 79355–56, 79358–60, 79363–64, 79366–67, 79371–73, 79376–82, 79401–04, 79406–16, 79423–24, 79430, 79452–53, 79457, 79464, 79490–91, 79493, 79499, 79511, 79701–08, 79710–14, 79719–21, 79731, 79733, 79741–42, 79745, 79748–49, 79754–56, 79758–66, 79768–69, 79776–77, 79779, 79782–83, 79788–89

* * *

TWENTIETH DISTRICT

CHARLES A. GONZALEZ, Democrat, of San Antonio, TX; born in San Antonio, TX, on May 5, 1945; son of former Representative Henry Gonzalez, who served the 20th district from 1961–99; education: Thomas A. Edison High School, 1965; B.A., University of Texas at Austin, 1969; J.D., St. Mary's School of Law, 1972; elementary school teacher; private attorney, 1972–82; Municipal Court Judge; County Court at Law Judge, 1983–87; District Judge, 1989–97; committees: Financial Services; Small Business; Select Committee on Homeland Security; Democratic Regional Whip; chair, Congressional Hispanic Caucus Civil Rights Task Force; elected to the 106th Congress; reelected to each succeeding Congress.

Office Listings

327 Cannon House Office Building, Washington, DC 20515 .... (202) 225–3236
Chief of Staff.—Kevin Kimble. FAX: 225–1915
Executive Assistant.—Rose Ann Maldonado.
Legislative Assistant.—Tony Zaffirini.
Press Secretary.—Adrian Saenz.
Federal Building, B–124, 727 East Durango Boulevard, San Antonio, TX 78206 ... (210) 472–6195

Counties: BEXAR COUNTY (part). CITIES OF: Alamo Heights (part), Atascosa (part), Balcones Heights, Castle Hills (part), Lackland AFB, Leon Valley (part), Macdona Somerset (part), San Antonio (part), Terrell Hills (part), and Von Ormy (part). Population (2000), 651,619.

ZIP Codes: 78002, 78009, 78039, 78052, 78054, 78069, 78073, 78201–05, 78207–13, 78215–18, 78224–30, 78233–34, 78236–38, 78240–43, 78245, 78250–52, 78254, 78264, 78268, 78279–80, 78284–85, 78288–89, 78291–99

* * *

TWENTY-FIRST DISTRICT

LAMAR S. SMITH, Republican, of San Antonio, TX; born in San Antonio on November 19, 1947; education: graduated from Texas Military Institute, San Antonio, 1965; B.A., Yale University, New Haven, CT, 1969; management intern, Small Business Administration, Washington, DC, 1969–70; business and financial writer, *The Christian Science Monitor*, Boston, MA, 1970–72; J.D., Southern Methodist University School of Law, Dallas, TX, 1975; admitted to the State bar of Texas, 1975, and commenced practice in San Antonio with the firm of Maebius and Duncan, Inc.; elected chairman of the Republican Party of Bexar County, TX, 1978 and 1980; elected District 57–F State Representative, 1981; elected Precinct 3 Commissioner of Bexar County, 1982 and 1984; partner, Lamar Seeligson Ranch, Jim Wells County, TX; married: Beth Schaefer; children: Nell Seeligson and Tobin Wells; committees: Judiciary; Science; Select Committee on Homeland Security; subcommittees: chairman, Courts, the Internet, and Intellectual Property; elected to the 100th Congress on November 4, 1986; reelected to each succeeding Congress.

Office Listings

http://lamarsmith.house.gov

2231 Rayburn House Office Building, Washington, DC 20515 .... (202) 225–4236
Chief of Staff / Assistant to the Chairman.—John Lampmann. FAX: 225–8628
Administrative Assistant / Scheduler.—Jennifer Brown.
Guaranty Federal Building, Suite 640, 1100 North East Loop 410, San Antonio, TX 78209 .... (210) 821–5024
District Director.—O'Lene Stone.
1006 Junction Highway, Kerrville, TX 78028 .... (830) 895–1414

Counties: BANDERA, BEXAR (part), BLANCO, BURNET, COMAL, GILLESPIE, HAYS (part), KENDALL, KERR, KIMBLE, LLANO, MASON, MENARD, TRAVIS (part). Population (2000), 651,619.

ZIP Codes: 76820, 76825, 76831–32, 76841–42, 76848–49, 76854, 76856, 76859, 76869, 76874, 76883, 76885, 78003–04, 78006, 78010, 78013, 78015, 78023–25, 78027–29, 78055, 78058, 78063, 78070, 78074, 78130–33, 78135, 78148, 78150, 78154, 78163, 78209, 78213, 78216–18, 78230–33, 78239, 78247, 78258–61, 78265–66, 78270, 78280, 78287, 78605–11, 78613, 78618–20, 78623–24, 78626–27, 78630–31, 78635–36, 78638–39, 78641–43, 78645–46, 78648, 78652, 78654, 78657, 78663, 78666, 78669, 78671–72, 78674–76, 78680, 78682–83, 78726, 78730, 78732–39, 78746, 78749–50, 78755, 78759, 78780, 78861, 78883, 78885

* * *

TWENTY-SECOND DISTRICT

TOM DELAY, Republican, of Sugar Land, TX; born in Laredo, TX, April 8, 1947; graduated Calallan High School, Corpus Christi, 1965; attended Baylor University, Waco, TX, 1967; B.S., University of Houston, TX, 1970; businessman; Texas House of Representatives, 1979–84; member: Oyster Creek Rotary; Fort Bend 100 Club; Chamber of Commerce; board member, Youth Opportunities Unlimited; married to the former Christine Furrh; one child: Danielle; elected by colleagues to the No. 3 leadership post as Majority Whip for the 104th through the 107th Congresses; elected as Majority Leader for the 108th Congress; elected to the 99th Congress on November 6, 1984; reelected to each succeeding Congress.

Office Listings

http://tomdelay.house.gov

242 Cannon House Office Building, Washington, DC 20515 .... (202) 225–5951
Chief of Staff.—Tim Berry. FAX: 225–5241
Administrative Assistant.—Carl Thorsen.
Director of Communications.—Stuart James.
Legislative Director.—David James.
Legislative Assistant.—Christopher Lynch.
Legislative Correspondent.—Hope Henry.
Director of Finance / Special Events.—Amy Lorenzini.
Policy Director.—Juliane Sullivan.
Staff Assistant.—Keagan Resler.
Suite 118, 10701 Corporate Drive, Stafford, TX 77477 .... (281) 240–3700

Counties: BRAZORIA COUNTY. CITIES AND TOWNSHIPS: Alvin, Angleton, Danbury, Lake Jackson, Liverpool, Manvel, Pearland, Rosharon. FORT BEND COUNTY. CITIES AND TOWNSHIPS: Beasley, Fresno, Fulshear, Guy, Houston, Katy, Kindleton, Meadows Place, Missouri City, Needville, Orchard, Richmond, Rosenberg, Simonton, Stafford, Sugar Land, Thompson. HARRIS COUNTY. CITIES AND TOWNSHIPS: Deer Park, Friendswood, Houston (part), LaPorte, Pasadena (part), Seabrook / Taylor Lake and Village / El Lago (part). Population (2000), 651,619.

ZIP Codes: 77031, 77034, 77053, 77058–59, 77062, 77075, 77083, 77085, 77089, 77099, 77236, 77259, 77274, 77289, 77406, 77412, 77415, 77417, 77419–20, 77423, 77430, 77435–36, 77441, 77444, 77450–51, 77459, 77461, 77464, 77469, 77471, 77476–79, 77481, 77485–87, 77489, 77493–94, 77496–97, 77503–05, 77507, 77511–12, 77515–16, 77531, 77534, 77536, 77541, 77545–46, 77566, 77571, 77577–78, 77581, 77583–84, 77586, 77588, 77598

* * *

TWENTY-THIRD DISTRICT

HENRY BONILLA, Republican, of San Antonio, TX; born in San Antonio on January 2, 1954; graduated from South San Antonio High School, 1972; B.J., University of Texas, Austin, 1976; Executive Producer for Public Affairs, KENS–TV, San Antonio; Executive News Producer, KENS–TV, San Antonio; co-chair of Congressional Border Caucus; vice-chair of U.S. / Mexico Congressional Caucus; founding member of Congressional Hispanic Conference; co-chair of Community Health Center Causus; awards: American Cancer Society Public Policy Leadership Award; American Diabetes Association Public Policy Leadership Award; 60 Plus Associations, Hero of the American Tax Payer Award; Champion of Small Business; National Job Corps Award, Policymaker of the Year; National Retail Federation Retail Champion of the Year; National Association of Manufacturers, Free Trade Alliance Award; National Federation of Independent Business Guardian of Small Business; U.S. Chamber of Commerce Spirit of Enterprise Award; U.S. Hispanic Chamber of Commerce President's Award; U.T. Health Science Center at San Antonio Star Award; married: former Deborah JoAnn Knapp, 1981; children: Alicia Knapp and Austin Elliot; committees: Appropriations; subcommittees: chairman, Agriculture, Rural Development, Food and Drug Administration and Related Agencies; Defense; Foreign Operations, Export Financing and Related Programs; elected to the 103rd Congress; reelected to each succeeding Congress.

Office Listings

http://www.house.gov/bonilla

2458 Rayburn House Office Building, Washington, DC 20515 .... (202) 225–4511
Chief of Staff.—Marcus Lubin. FAX: 225–2237
Press Secretary.—Taryn Fritz.
11120 Wurzbach, Suite 300, San Antonio, TX 78230 .... (210) 697–9055
District Director.—Phil Ricks.
1300 Matamoros Street, Suite 113B, Laredo, TX 78040 .... (956) 726–4682
111 East Broadway, Suite 101, Del Rio, TX 78840 .... (830) 774–6547
107 W. Avenue E., #14, Alpine, TX 79830 .... (432) 837–1313

Counties: BEXAR COUNTY. CITIES AND TOWNSHIPS: Boerne, Cross Mountain, Dominion, Fair Oaks Ranch, Grey Forest, Helotes, Hill Country Village, Hollywood Park, Leon Springs, Leon Valley, San Antonio, Scenic Oaks, Shavano Park, Timberwood Park. BREWSTER COUNTY. CITIES AND TOWNSHIPS: Alpine, Big Bend National Park, Castolon, Chisos Basin, Lajitas, Marathon, Rio Grande Village, Study Butte, Terlingua. CROCKETT COUNTY. CITY OF: Ozona. CULBERSON COUNTY. CITIES AND TOWNSHIPS: Kent, Lobo, Nickle Creek, Pine Springs, and Van Horn. DIMMIT COUNTY. CITIES AND TOWNSHIPS: Asherton, Big Wells, Brundage, Carrizo Springs, Catarina, Valley Wells, and Winter Haven. EDWARDS COUNTY. CITIES AND TOWNSHIPS: Barksdale, Carta Valley, Rocksprings. EL PASO COUNTY. CITIES AND TOWNSHIPS: Clint, El Paso, Fabens, Fort Bliss, Homestead Meadows, Horizon City, San Azario, Socorro, Sparks, Tornillo. HUDSPETH COUNTY. CITIES AND TOWNSHIPS: Acala, Allamore, Cornudas, Dell City, Esperanza, Finlay, Fort Hancock, Hot Wells, Hueca, McNary, Salt Flat, Sierra Blanca. JEFF DAVIS COUNTY. CITIES AND TOWNSHIPS: Fort Davis, Valentine. KINNEY COUNTY. CITIES AND TOWNSHIPS: Brackettville, Fort Clark Springs, Spofford. MAVERICK COUNTY. CITIES AND TOWNSHIPS: Eagle Pass, El India, Normandy, Quemado. MEDINA COUNTY. CITIES AND TOWNSHIPS: Castroville, Devine, D'Hanis,

Dunlay, Honda, Lacoste, Mico, Natalia, Riomedina, Lytle, and Yancey. PECOS COUNTY. CITIES AND TOWNSHIPS: Bakersfield, Buena Vista, Coyanosa, Fort Stockton, Girvin, Imperial, Iraan, Sheffield. PRESIDIO COUNTY. CITIES AND TOWNSHIPS: Adobes, Candelaria, Casa Pierda, Fort Leaton State Park, Marfa, Presidio, Redford, Ruidosa, Shafter. REAGAN COUNTY. CITIES AND TOWNSHIPS: Best, Big Lake, Santa Rita. REAL COUNTY. CITIES AND TOWNSHIPS: Leakey, Camp Wood. REEVES COUNTY. CITIES AND TOWNSHIPS: Arno, Balmorhea, Orla, Pecos, Saragosa, Toyah, Toyahvale, Verhalen. SUTTON COUNTY. CITY OF: Sonora. TERRELL COUNTY. CITIES AND TOWNSHIPS: Dryden, Sanderson. UPTON COUNTY. CITIES AND TOWNSHIPS: McCamey, Midkiff, Rankin. UVALDE COUNTY. CITIES AND TOWNSHIPS: Blewett, Cline, Concan, Dabney, Knippa, Montell, Reagan Wells, Sabinal, Utopia. VAL VERDE COUNTY. CITIES AND TOWNSHIPS: Comstock, Del Rio, Juno, Langtry, Laughlin AFB, Loma Alta, Pandale, Pumpville. WEBB COUNTY. CITIES AND TOWNSHIPS: Aguilares, Bruni, Callaghan, Chupadero Springs, El Cenizo, Laredo, Miranda City, Oilton, Webb. ZAVALA COUNTY. CITIES AND TOWNSHIPS: Batesville, Crystal City, and La Pryor. Population (2000) 651,619.

ZIP Codes: 76930, 76932, 76943, 76950, 78006, 78009, 78015–16, 78023–24, 78039–46, 78049, 78052, 78056–57, 78059, 78066, 78216, 78230–33, 78240, 78245–51, 78253–58, 78260, 78269, 78278, 78344, 78369, 78371, 78801–02, 78827–30, 78832–34, 78836–43, 78847, 78850–53, 78860–61, 78870–73, 78877, 78879–81, 78884, 78886, 79706, 79718, 79730, 79734–35, 79739–40, 79743–44, 79752, 79755, 79770, 79772, 79778, 79780–81, 79785–86, 79830–32, 79834, 79836–37, 79839, 79842–43, 79845–49, 79851–55, 79927–28, 79938

* * *

TWENTY-FOURTH DISTRICT

MARTIN FROST, Democrat, of Arlington, TX; born in Glendale, CA, January 1, 1942; education: graduated R.L. Paschal High School, Fort Worth, TX, 1960; B.A. and B.J., University of Missouri, Columbia, MO, 1964; J.D., Georgetown Law Center, Washington, DC, 1970; served in U.S. Army Reserves, 1966–72; lawyer; law clerk for Federal Judge Sarah T. Hughes; legal commentator for channel 13; vice president and board member, Dallas Democratic Forum, 1976–77; admitted to the Texas bar in 1970 and commenced practice in Dallas; active leader in civic, community, and political affairs; board member, Oak Cliff Chamber of Commerce; American Cancer Society; and Oak Cliff Conservation League; member: Oak Cliff Lions Club; American Jewish Committee; Congregation Beth El in Fort Worth; Dallas and Texas bar associations; staff writer for the *Congressional Quarterly Weekly,* 1965–67; married: Kathryn George Frost, Major General, U.S. Army; children: Alanna, Mariel and Camille; ranking member, Rules Committee; elected to the 96th Congress, November 7, 1978; reelected to each succeeding Congress.

Office Listings

http://www.house.gov/frost

2256 Rayburn House Office Building, Washington, DC 20515 .... (202) 225–3605
Administrative Assistant.—Susan McAvoy. FAX: 225–4951
Executive Assistant.—Vera Lou Durigon.
Legislative Director.—Fernando Gomez.
3020 South East Loop 820, Fort Worth, TX 76140 .... (817) 293–9231
District Director.—Cinda Crawford.
506 Bank of America, 400 South Zang Boulevard, Dallas, TX 75208 .... (214) 948–3401
101 East Rundle Mills, Suite 108, Arlington, TX 76011 .... (817) 303–1530

Counties: DALLAS (part), TARRANT (part). CITIES AND TOWNSHIPS: Fort Worth, Dallas, Arlington, Duncanville, Grand Prairie, and Cedar Hill. Population (2000), 651,619.

ZIP Codes: 75050–54, 75104, 75106, 75116, 75137–38, 75203, 75208, 75211, 75224, 75233, 75236, 75249, 75368, 75398, 76001–02, 76004–07, 76010–13, 76015, 76017–19, 76040–41, 76053, 76065, 76102–05, 76110–12, 76115, 76117–20, 76124, 76134, 76140

* * *

TWENTY-FIFTH DISTRICT

CHRIS BELL, Democrat, of Houston, TX; born on November 23, 1959; education: University of Texas at Austin, 1982, journalism degree; South Texas College of Law, law degree, 1992; professional: Attorney, with Beirne, Maynard & Parsons, LLP; journalist; television and radio reporter; awards: Texas Associated Press Best Radio Reporter Award; Omicron Delta Kappa Leader of the Year Award; Friends of the Homeless Award; community service: Big Brothers Big Sisters of the Gulf Coast Region; American Diabetes Association; Houston Area Parkinson Society; Palmer Memorial Episcopal Church Way Station; religion: Episcopal; public service: Houston City Council, 1997–2001; family: married to Alison Ayres Bell; children: Atlee and Connally; elected to the 108th Congress on November 5, 2002.

Office Listings

http://www.house.gov/bell

216 Cannon House Office Building, Washington, DC 20515 .... (202) 225–7508
Chief of Staff.—John M. Gonzalez. FAX: 225–2947
Communications Director.—Eric Burns.
Legislative Director.—Justin Hamilton.
Scheduler.—David Burns.
7707 Fannin Street, Suite 203, Houston, TX 77054 .... (713) 383–8600
District Director.—Larry Payne.
6307 Fairmont Parkway, Pasadena, TX 77505 .... (281) 473–4334

Counties: HARRIS (part), FORT BEND (part). Population (2000), 651,619.

ZIP Codes: 77004–05, 77015, 77017, 77019, 77025, 77027, 77030–31, 77034–36, 77045–49, 77051, 77053–54, 77056–57, 77059, 77061, 77071–72, 77074–75, 77081, 77085, 77087, 77089, 77096, 77098–99, 77213, 77225, 77231, 77234–35, 77245, 77271, 77275, 77401–02, 77477, 77489, 77501–08, 77514, 77520–21, 77530, 77532, 77536, 77545, 77562–63, 77571–72, 77583, 77598

* * *

TWENTY-SIXTH DISTRICT

MICHAEL C. BURGESS, Republican, of Denton County, TX; born on December 23, 1950; education: North Texas State University, Bachelor and Masters degrees in Physiology; received his M.D. from the University of Texas Medical School in Houston; and received a Masters degree in Medical Management from the University of Texas in Dallas; completed medical residency programs at Parkland Hospital in Dallas; professional: founder of Private Practice Specialty Group for Obstetrics and Gynecology; former Chief of Staff and Chief of Obstetrics for Lewisville Medical Center; organizations: past president, Denton County Medical Society; Denton County delegate to the Texas Medical Association; alternate delegate to the American Medical Association; family: married to Laura; three children; elected to the 108th Congress on November 5, 2002.

Office Listings

http://www.house.gov/burgess

1721 Longworth House Office Building, Washington, DC 20515 .... (202) 225–7772
Chief of Staff.—Barry Brown. FAX: 225–2919
Legislative Director.—Randi Reid.
Press Secretary.—Lori McMahon.
1660 South Stemmons Freeway, Suite 230, Lewisville, TX 75067 .... (972) 434–9700

Counties: COLLIN (part), DENTON, TARRANT (part), WISE (part). Population (2000) 651,619.

ZIP Codes: 75007, 75009–11, 75019, 75022, 75027–29, 75034–35, 75056–57, 75060–61, 75065, 75067–71, 75077–78, 75093, 75261, 75287, 75381, 76006, 76011–12, 76021–22, 76034, 76039–40, 76051–54, 76092, 76095, 76112, 76120, 76137, 76155, 76177, 76180, 76201–10, 76226–27, 76234, 76247–49, 76258–59, 76262, 76266, 76272, 76299

* * *

TWENTY-SEVENTH DISTRICT

SOLOMON P. ORTIZ, Democrat, of Corpus Christi, TX; born in Robstown, TX, June 3, 1937; attended Robstown High School; attended Del Mar College, Corpus Christi; officers certificate, Institute of Applied Science, Chicago, IL, 1962; officers certificate, National Sheriffs Training Institute, Los Angeles, CA, 1977; served in U.S. Army, Sp4c. 1960–62; insurance agent; Nueces County constable, 1965–68; Nueces County commissioner, 1969–76; Nueces County sheriff, 1977–82; member: Congressional Hispanic Caucus (chairman, 102nd Congress); Congressional Hispanic Caucus Institute (chairman of the board, 102nd Congress); Army Caucus; Depot Caucus; Sheriffs' Association of Texas; National Sheriffs' Association; Corpus Christi Rotary Club; American Red Cross; United Way; honors: *Who's Who Among Hispanic Americans;* Man of the Year, International Order of Foresters (1981); Conservation Legislator of the Year for the Sportsman Clubs of Texas (1986); Boss of the Year by the American Businesswomen Association (1980); National Government Hispanic Business Advocate, U.S. Hispanic Chamber of Commerce (1992); Leadership Award, Latin American Management Association (1991); National Security Leadership Award, American Security Council (1992); Tree of Life Award, Jewish National Fund (1987); Quality of Life Award (USO) 2001; children: Yvette and Solomon, Jr.; elected on November 2, 1982, to the 98th Congress; reelected to each succeeding Congress.

Office Listings

2470 Rayburn House Office Building, Washington, DC 20515 .... (202) 225–7742
Chief of Staff.—Florencio H. Rendon. FAX: 226–1134
Executive Assistant / Scheduling.—Rhiannon Burruss.
Legislative Director.—David Garcia.
Press Secretary.—Cathy Travis.
3649 Leopard, Suite 510, Corpus Christi, TX 78408 .... (361) 883–5868
3505 Boca Chica Boulevard, Suite 200, Brownsville, TX 78521 .... (956) 541–1242

Counties: CAMERON, KENEDY (part), KLEBERG (part), NUECES (part), WILLACY. Population (2000), 651,619.

ZIP Codes: 78336, 78338–39, 78343, 78347, 78351, 78363, 78373, 78379–80, 78385, 78401–19, 78426–27, 78460, 78463, 78465–78, 78480, 78520–23, 78526, 78535, 78550–53, 78559, 78566–69, 78575, 78578, 78580, 78583, 78586, 78590, 78592–94, 78597–98

* * *

TWENTY-EIGHTH DISTRICT

CIRO D. RODRIGUEZ, Democrat, of San Antonio, TX; born in Piedras Negras, Mexico; attended San Antonio College; B.A. in Political Science, St. Mary's University; M.A., Our Lady of the Lake University; Harlendale Independent School District School Board; served in the Texas State House of Representatives, 1987–97; taught undergraduate and graduate courses at Worden School of Social Work; caseworker, Texas Department of Mental Health and Mental Retardation; faculty associate, Our Lady of the Lake University; consultant, Intercultural Development Research Association; chair, Congressional Hispanic Caucus; Missing and Exploited Children Caucus; National Guard and Reserve Components Caucus; Impact Aid Coalition Education Caucus; Border Caucus; Census Caucus; Congressional Youth Leadership Council; married to Carolina Pena; one daughter: Xochil Daria; committees: Armed Services; Resources; Veterans Affairs; elected to the 105th Congress in a special election; reelected to each succeeding Congress.

Office Listings

http://rodriguez.house.gov

1507 Longworth House Office Bulding, Washington, DC 20515–4328 .... (202) 225–1640
Chief of Staff.—Jeff Mendelsohn. FAX: 225–1641
Legislative Director.—Julie Merberg.
Scheduler / Staff Assistant.—Belinda Garza.
Press Secretary.—Sean Foertsch.
1313 South East Military Drive, Suite 115, San Antonio, TX 78214–2851 .... (210) 924–7383
District Director.—Norma Reyes.
400 East Gravis Street, 2nd Floor, San Diego, Texas 78384 .... (512) 279–3907
301 Lincoln Avenue, Roma, TX 78584 .... (956) 847–1111

Counties: ATASCOSA, BEXAR (part), DUVAL, FRIO, HILDAGO (part), JIM HOGG, JIM WELLS, LA SALLE, MCMULLEN, STARR, ZAPATA. Population (2000), 651,620.

ZIP Codes: 78001–02, 78005, 78007–08, 78011–12, 78014, 78017, 78019, 78021, 78026, 78050, 78052, 78057, 78061–62, 78064–65, 78067, 78069, 78072–73, 78076, 78101, 78108–09, 78112–13, 78123–24, 78132, 78152, 78154–55, 78202–05, 78209–11, 78214–15, 78218–25, 78233, 78235, 78239, 78244, 78247, 78263–64, 78283, 78332–33, 78341–42, 78344, 78349, 78355, 78357, 78360–61, 78363, 78372, 78375–76, 78380, 78383–84, 78536, 78545, 78547–48, 78557, 78560, 78563–64, 78572, 78574, 78576, 78582, 78584–85, 78588, 78591, 78595

* * *

TWENTY-NINTH DISTRICT

GENE GREEN, Democrat, of Houston, TX; born on October 17, 1947, in Houston, TX; education: B.A., University of Houston, 1971; admitted, Texas bar, 1977; employment: business manager; attorney; Texas State Representative, 1973–85; Texas State Senator, 1985–92; member: Houston Bar Association; Texas Bar Association; American Bar Association; Communications Workers of America; Aldine Optimist Club; Gulf Coast Conservation Association; Texas Historical Society; Lindale Lions Club; Democratic Deputy Whip; committees: Energy and Commerce; Standards of Official Conduct; subcommittees: Commerce, Trade, and Consumer Protection; Environment and Hazardous Materials; Health; Telecommunications and the Internet; member: Congressional Steel Caucus; Urban Caucus; Sportsmen's Caucus; co-chair, Congressional Urban Healthcare Caucus; married: January 23, 1970, to Helen Albers; children: Angela and Christopher; elected on November 3, 1992, to the 103rd Congress; reelected to each succeeding Congress.

Office Listings

http://www.house.gov/green

2335 Rayburn House Office Building, Washington, DC 20515 .... (202) 225–1688
Chief of Staff / Administrative Assistant.—Marc Gonzales. FAX: 225–9903
Legislative Director.—Sharon Scribner.
Press Secretary.—Celinda Gonzalez.
Legislative Assistants: Lantie Ferguson, Andrew Wallace.
256 North Sam Houston Parkway East, Suite 29, Houston, TX 77060 .... (281) 999–5879
District Director.—Rhonda Jackson.
11811 I–10 East, Suite 430, Houston, TX 77029 .... (713) 330–0761

Counties: HARRIS COUNTY (part). CITIES AND TOWNSHIPS: Houston, Humble (part), Pasadena (part), Channelview, Galena Park, Jacinto City, La Porte (part), and South Houston. Population (2000), 651,620.

ZIP Codes: 77003, 77009, 77011–17, 77020, 77022–23, 77028–29, 77032, 77034, 77037–39, 77044, 77049–50, 77060, 77066–69, 77073, 77076, 77078, 77087–88, 77090–91, 77093, 77207, 77217, 77220, 77222–23, 77228–29, 77248–49, 77261–62, 77267–68, 77270, 77287, 77315, 77338, 77396, 77501–04, 77506, 77520, 77530, 77536, 77547, 77587

* * *

THIRTIETH DISTRICT

EDDIE BERNICE JOHNSON, Democrat, of Dallas, TX; born on December, 3, 1935 in Waco, TX; education: nursing diploma, St. Mary's at Notre Dame, 1955; B.S., nursing, Texas Christian, 1967; M.P.A, Southern Methodist, 1976; proprietor, Eddie Bernice Johnson and Associates consulting and airport concession management; Texas House of Representatives, 1972–77; Carter administration appointee, 1977–81; Texas State Senate, 1986–92; member, St. John Baptist Church, Dallas; member, American Nurses Association; member, Links, Inc., Dallas Chapter; member, Dallas Black Chamber of Commerce; life member, NAACP; member, Charter 100 of Dallas; member, Girlfriends, Inc.; honorary member, Delta Kappa Gama Society International Women Educators Organization, Epsilon Chapter; life member, YWCA; executive committee member, United Way of Metropolitan Dallas; member, Women's Council of Dallas; member and past president, National Council of Negro Women; member, Democratic Women of Dallas County; member, Dallas Urban League; member, Dallas County Democratic Progressive Voters League; member, past national vice president and past national secretary, National Order of Women Legislators; member, National Black Nurses Association; member, Goals for Dallas; Emma V. Kelly Achievement Award, Grant Temple Daughters of IBPOE of W, 1973; first woman to chair a major House committee in the Texas Legislature; Libertarian of the Year, ACLU, 1978; Women Helping Women Award, Soroptimist International of Dallas and Southwest Region, 1979; Outstanding Citizenship Award, National Conference of Christians and Jews, 1985; NAACP Juanita Craft Award in Politics, NAACP, Dallas Chapter, 1989; Legislative Action Award, Texas Association of Community Action Agencies, 1989; ''She Knows Where She is Going,'' Girls Inc., 1990; Distinguished Public Service Award, Prairie View A&M University, 1990; Eartha M.M. White Award, outstanding achievement as a businesswoman, National Business League, 1990; Outstanding Service Award, KKDA Radio, 1991; National Association of Negro Business and Professional Women and Clubs Achievement in Government, 1991; Outstanding Service Award, Sigma Pi Phi Fraternity, 1991; Certificate of Commendation, City of Dallas, 1991; Outstanding Service Award, the Child Care Group, 1991; Legislator of the Year Award, Dallas Alliance for the Mentally Ill, 1991; Mental Health Association of Greater Dallas Prism Award, 1991; member, Alpha Kappa Alpha Sorority, Inc., Dallas Chapter; 1993 Meritorious Award, the National Black Nurses Foundation, Inc.; 1993 Award for Achievement in Equal Employment Opportunity, U.S. Department of Energy; NAACP–Arlington Branch, Special Service Award, 1993; South Dallas Business & Professional Women's Club, Inc., President's Award, 1993; 1994 Leadership Commendation, Campaign To Keep America Warm; Texas Senate Black Caucus Mickey Leland Award, 1994, U.S. Department of Energy Hall of Fame Black History Month, 1995; U.S. Department of Energy Leadership Award, 1999; Zeta Phi Beta Sorority Governmental Affairs Award, 1999; NABTP Mickey Leland Award for Excellence in Diversity, 2000; National Association of School Nurses, Inc., Legislative Award, 2000; The State of Texas Honorary Texan issued by the Governor of Texas, 2000; Links, Inc., Co-Founders Award, 2000; 100 Black Men of America, Inc., Woman of the Year, 2001; National Black Caucus of State Legislators Image Award, 2001; National Conference of Black Mayors, Inc. President's Award, 2001; 2002 Alpha Kappa Alpha Trailblazer; Thurgood Marshall Scholarship Community Leader 2002; Phi Beta Sigma Fraternity Woman of the Year 2002; CBCF Outstanding Leadership 2002; chair, (107th Congress), Congressional Black Caucus; Congressional Womens' Caucus; congressional caucuses: Asian-Pacific; Airpower; Army; Arts; Biomedical Research; Women's Issues; Children's Working Group; Fire Services; Oil & Gas Educational Forum; Study Group on Japan; co-chair, Task Force on International HIV / AIDS; Urban; Medical Technology; Livable Communities Task Force; Congressional Human Rights Caucus; Congressional Korean Caucus; Congressional Singapore Caucus; Tex-21 Transportation Caucus; children: Dawrence Kirk; elected on November 3, 1992, to the 103rd Congress; reelected to each succeeding Congress.

Office Listings

http://www.house.gov/ebjohnson

1511 Longworth House Office Building, Washington, DC 20515 .... (202) 225–8885
Chief of Staff.—Beverly Fields.
Legislative Director.—Murat Gokcigdem.
Scheduler / Executive Assistant (DC).—Elisabeth Howie.
Legislative Assistants: Josiah Daniel, Cathleen Harrington, Edlecia Sherrod.
2501 Cedar Springs Road, Suite 550, Dallas, TX 75201 .... (214) 922–8885
District Director.—Roscoe Smith.
1634 B West Irving Boulevard, Irving, TX 75061 .... (972) 253–8885
Special Assistant.—Mardi Chev.

Counties: DALLAS (part). CITIES AND TOWNSHIPS: Cedar Hill, Dallas, De Soto, Duncanville, Farmer's Branch, Glenn Heights, Grand Prairie, Grapeville, Hutchins, Irving, Lancaster, Mesquite and Ovilla. Population (2000), 651,620.

ZIP Codes: 75014–17, 75019, 75037–39, 75050, 75060–63, 75104, 75115–16, 75123, 75134, 75137, 75141, 75146, 75149–50, 75154, 75172, 75201–04, 75207–10, 75212, 75215–17, 75219–24, 75226–28, 75232–33, 75235–37, 75241–42, 75245–47, 75250, 75258, 75260, 75262–67, 75270, 75277, 75283–87, 75301, 75303, 75310, 75312–13, 75315, 75320, 75323, 75326, 75339, 75342, 75353, 75356, 75363–64, 75371, 75373, 75376, 75380, 75386–97

* * *

THIRTY-FIRST DISTRICT

JOHN R. CARTER, Republican, of Round Rock, TX; born on November 6, 1941, in Houston, TX; education: Texas Tech University, 1964; University of Texas Law School, 1969; profession: Attorney; private law practice; public service: appointed and elected a Texas District Court Judge, 1981–2001; awards: recipient and namesake of the Williamson County ''John R. Carter Lifetime Achievement Award''; family: married to Erika Carter; children: Gilianne, John, Theodore, and Erika Danielle; elected to 108th Congress on November 5, 2002.

Office Listings

http://www.house.gov/carter

408 Cannon House Office Building, Washington, DC 20515 .... (202) 225–3864
Administrative Assistant.—Travis Lucas. FAX: 225–5886
Scheduler.—Julie Leake.
Legislative Director.—Ryan Henry.
One Financial Centre, 1717 North IH 35, Round Rock, TX 78664 .... (512) 246–1600
111 University Drive, East, Suite 216, College Station, TX 77840 .... (979) 846–6068

Counties: AUSTIN, BASTROP (part), BRAZOS (part), BURLESON (part), HARRIS (part), LEE, WALLER, WASHINGTON, WILLIAMSON (part). Population (2000), 651,209.

ZIP Codes: 76511, 76530, 76556, 76567, 76574, 76577–78, 77041, 77065, 77070, 77084, 77095, 77355, 77363, 77410, 77418, 77423, 77426, 77429, 77433, 77445, 77447, 77449–50, 77466, 77473–74, 77484–85, 77492–94, 77801–03, 77805–08, 77833–36, 77838, 77840–45, 77852–53, 77862–63, 77866, 77868, 77878–81, 78363, 78602, 78612–13, 78615, 78621, 78626, 78628, 78634, 78641–42, 78650, 78659, 78664, 78681, 78717, 78728–29, 78759, 78931, 78933, 78940, 78942, 78944–48, 78950, 78954, 78957

* * *

THIRTY-SECOND DISTRICT

PETE SESSIONS, Republican, of Dallas, TX; born on March 22, 1955; graduate, Southwestern University, 1978; worked for Southwestern Bell, and Bell Communications Research (formerly Bell Labs), 1978–94, rising to the position of district manager; past vice president for public policy, National Center for Policy Analysis, 1994–95; board member, East Dallas YMCA; past chairman, East Dallas Chamber of Commerce; past district chairman, White Rock Council of the Boy Scouts of America; member, East Dallas Rotary Club; married to Juanita Sessions; two children, Bill and Alex; committees: Rules; Select Committee on Homeland Security; chairman, Results Caucus; elected on November 5, 1996, to the 105th Congress; reelected to each succeeding Congress.

Office Listings

http://www.house.gov/sessions

1318 Longworth House Office Building, Washington, DC 20515 .... (202) 225–2231
Chief of Staff.—Guy Harrison. FAX: 225–5878
Communications Director.—Gina Carty.
Legislative Director.—Josh Saltzman.
Park Central VII, 12750 Merit Drive, Suite 1434, Dallas, TX 75251 .... (972) 392–0505

County: DALLAS (part). CITIES AND TOWNSHIPS: Addison, Carrollton (part), Coppell, Dallas (part), Farmer's Branch, Garland (part), Highland Park, Irving (part), Richardson (part), and University Park. Population (2000), 651,619.

ZIP Codes: 75001, 75006–07, 75011, 75019, 75039, 75041–42, 75062–63, 75080–83, 75099, 75204–06, 75209, 75214, 75219–20, 75223, 75225–26, 75229–31, 75234–35, 75238, 75240, 75243–44, 75246, 75248, 75251–52, 75254, 75275, 75287, 75354, 75360, 75372, 75374, 75378–81, 75389, 75391, 76051

UTAH

(Population 2000, 2,233,169)

SENATORS

ORRIN G. HATCH, Republican, of Salt Lake City, UT; born in Pittsburgh, PA, on March 22, 1934; education: B.S., Brigham Young University, Provo, UT, 1959; LL.B., University of Pittsburgh, 1962; practiced law in Salt Lake City, UT, and Pittsburgh, PA; senior partner, Hatch and Plumb law firm, Salt Lake City; worked his way through high school, college, and law school at the metal lathing building trade; member, AFL–CIO; holds ''AV'' rating in Martindale-Hubbell Law Directory; member, Salt Lake County Bar Association, Utah Bar Association, American Bar Association, Pennsylvania Bar Association, Allegheny County Bar Association, numerous other professional and fraternal organizations; member, Church of Jesus Christ of Latter-Day Saints; honorary doctorate, University of Maryland; honorary doctor of laws: Pepperdine University and Southern Utah State University; honorary national ski patroller; Help Eliminate Litter and Pollution (HELP) Association; author of numerous national publications; married: Elaine Hansen of Newton, UT; children: Brent, Marcia, Scott, Kimberly, Alysa and Jess; committees: Aging; Finance; Indian Affairs; chairman, Judiciary; Select Committee on Intelligence; Joint Committee on Taxation; elected to the U.S. Senate on November 2, 1976; reelected to each succeeding Senate term.

Office Listings

http://hatch.senate.gov

104 Hart Senate Office Building, Washington, DC 20510 .... (202) 224–5251
Chief of Staff.—Patricia Knight.
Communications Director.—Adam Elggren.
Federal Building, Suite 8402, Salt Lake City, UT 84138 .... (801) 524–4380
State Director.—Melanie Bowen.
Federal Building, 324 25th Street, Suite 1006, Ogden, UT 84401 .... (801) 625–5672
51 South University Avenue, Suite 320, Provo, UT 84606 .... (801) 375–7881
197 East Tabernacle, Room 2, St. George, UT 84770 .... (435) 634–1795
2390 West Highway 56, P.O. Box 99, Cedar City, UT 84720 .... (435) 586–8435

* * *

ROBERT F. BENNETT, Republican, of Salt Lake City, UT; born September 18, 1933 in Salt Lake City; education: B.S., University of Utah, 1957; chief executive officer of Franklin Quest, Salt Lake City; chief congressional liaison; U.S. Department of Transportation chairman of Utah Education Strategic Planning Commission; awards: ''Entrepreneur of the Year,'' *Inc.* magazine, 1989, Light of Learning Award, 1989; High-Tech Legislator of the Year; author, *Gaining Control*; married: Joyce McKay; children: James, Julie, Robert, Wendy, Heather, and Heidi; committees: Appropriations; Banking, Housing, and Urban Affairs; Governmental Affairs; Joint Economic Committee; Small Business and Entrepreneurship; member, Church of Jesus Christ of Latter-Day Saints; honorary doctorates: Westminster College; Salt Lake Community College; elected to the U.S. Senate on November 3, 1992; reelected to each succeeding Senate term.

Office Listings

http://bennett.senate.gov

431 Dirksen Senate Office Building, Washington, DC 20510 .... (202) 224–5444
Chief of Staff.—Chip Yost.
Legislative Director.—Corine Bradshaw.
Office Manager.—Sandy Knickman.
Communications Director.—Mary Jane Collipriest.
Wallace F. Bennett Federal Building, Suite 4225, Salt Lake City, UT 84138 .... (801) 524–5933
State Director.—Tim Sheehan.
Federal Building, 324 25th Street, Suite 1410, Ogden, UT 84401 .... (801) 625–5675
51 South University Avenue, Provo, UT 84601–4424 .... (801) 379–2525
Federal Building, 196 E. Tabernacle Street, St. George, UT 84770–3474 .... (435) 628–5514
2390 West Highway 56, Suite 4B, Cedar City, UT 84720 .... (435) 865–1335

REPRESENTATIVES

FIRST DISTRICT

ROB BISHOP, Republican, of Brigham City, UT; born on July 13, 1951, in Kaysville, UT; education: B.A., Political Science, University of Utah, 1974; graduated *magna cum laude;* profession: high-school teacher; public service: Utah House of Representatives, 1979–1994; served as Speaker of the House his last two years; elected, chairman of the Utah Republican Party, 1997, and served for two terms; religion: Church of Jesus Christ of Latter-day Saints; family: married to Jeralynn Hansen; children: Shule, Jarom, Zenock, Maren and Jashon; elected to the 108th Congress on November 5, 2002.

Office Listings

http://www.house.gov/robbishop

124 Cannon House Office Building, Washington, DC 20515 .... (202) 225–0453
Chief of Staff.—Scott Parker. FAX: 225–5857
Legislative Assistants: Justin Harding, Miriam Harmer.
Scheduler / Office Manager.—Jennifer Griffith.
1017 Federal Building, 324 25th Street, Ogden, UT 84401 .... (801) 625–0107

Counties: BOX ELDER, CACHE, DAVIS, JUAB (part), MORGAN, RICH, SALT LAKE (part), SUMMIT, TOOELE, WEBER. Population (2000), 744,389.

ZIP Codes: 84010–11, 84014–18, 84022, 84024–25, 84028–29, 84033–34, 84036–38, 84040–41, 84044, 84050, 84054–56, 84060–61, 84064, 84067–69, 84071, 84074–75, 84080, 84083, 84086–87, 84089, 84098, 84101–06, 84110–11, 84114–16, 84119–20, 84122, 84125–28, 84130–31, 84133–34, 84136, 84138–39, 84141, 84144–45, 84147, 84150–51, 84180, 84189–90, 84199, 84201, 84244, 84301–02, 84304–41, 84401–05, 84407–09, 84412, 84414–15, 84628

* * *

SECOND DISTRICT

JIM MATHESON, Democrat, of Salt Lake City, UT; born on March 21, 1960, in Salt Lake City, UT; education: B.A., Harvard University; M.B.A., University of California at Los Angeles (UCLA); profession: energy consultant; employment: Bonneville Pacific; Energy Strategies, Inc.; The Matheson Group; organizations: Environmental Policy Institute; Salt Lake Public Utilities Board; Scott M. Matheson Leadership Forum; religion: Mormon; married: Amy; children: Will; elected to the 107th Congress on November 7, 2000; reelected to each succeeding Congress.

Office Listings

http://www.house.gov/matheson

410 Cannon House Office Building, Washington, DC 20515 .... (202) 225–3011
Chief of Staff.—Stacey Alexander. FAX: 225–5638
Executive Assistant.—Wendy Ware.
240 E. Morris Avenue, #235, Salt Lake City, UT 84115 .... (801) 486–1236
District Director.—Alene Bentley.
321 North Mall Drive, #E101B, St. George, UT 84790 .... (435) 627–0880

Counties: CARBON, DAGGETT, DUCHENSNE, EMERY, GARFIELD, GRAND, IRON, KANE, PIUTE, SALT LAKE (part), SAN JUAN, UNITAH, UTAH (part), WASATCH, WASHINGTON, WAYNE. Population (2000), 744,390.

ZIP Codes: 84001–04, 84007–08, 84020–21, 84023, 84026–27, 84031–32, 84035, 84039, 84043, 84046–47, 84049, 84051–53, 84062–63, 84066, 84070, 84072–73, 84076, 84078–79, 84082, 84085, 84090–94, 84102–03, 84105–09, 84112–13, 84115–17, 84119, 84121, 84123–24, 84132, 84143, 84148, 84152, 84157–58, 84165, 84171, 84501, 84510–13, 84515–16, 84518, 84520–23, 84525–26, 84528–37, 84539, 84540, 84542, 84604, 84710, 84712, 84714–23, 84725–26, 84729, 84732–38, 84740–43, 84745–47, 84749–50, 84753, 84755–65, 84767, 84770–76, 84779–84, 84790–91

* * *

THIRD DISTRICT

CHRIS CANNON, Republican, of Mapleton, UT; born in Salt Lake City, UT, October 20, 1950; education: B.S., University Studies, Brigham Young University, 1974; graduate work at Harvard School of Business, 1974–75; J.D., Brigham Young University, 1977–80; employment: admitted to the Utah bar in 1980 and began practice in Provo, UT; attorney, Robinson, Seiler and Glazier; former associate solicitor and deputy associate solicitor, Department of the Interior;

cofounder, Geneva Steel, Provo; founder, Cannon Industries, Salt Lake City; president and, subsequently, chairman, of Cannon Industries, Salt Lake City; member, Utah Republican Party Elephant Club and Finance Committee; Utah Chairman, Lamar Alexander for President; Utah Finance Chairman, Bush-Quayle '92; married: the former Claudia Ann Fox in 1978; religion: Church of Jesus Christ of Latter-day Saints; children: Rachel, Jane, Laura, Emily, Elizabeth, Jonathan, Matthew, Katherine; elected to the 105th Congress; reelected to each succeeding Congress.

Office Listings

http://chriscannon.house.gov cannon.ut03@mail.house.gov

118 Cannon House Office Building, Washington, DC 20515 .... (202) 225–7751
Chief of Staff.—Joe Hunter. FAX: 225–5629
Executive Assistant.—Chris MacKay.
Legislative Director.—Todd Thorpe.
Legislative Assistants: Rob Morgan, Cody Stewart.
51 South University Avenue, Suite 319, Provo, UT 84606 .... (801) 379–2500

Counties: BEAVER, JUAB (part), MILLARD, SALT LAKE (part), SANPETE, SEVIER, UTAH (part). Population (2000), 744,390.

ZIP Codes: 84003, 84006, 84013, 84042–44, 84047, 84057–59, 84062, 84065, 84070, 84084, 84088, 84095, 84097, 84107, 84118–20, 84123, 84128, 84170, 84184, 84199, 84601–06, 84620–24, 84626–27, 84629–40, 84642–57, 84660, 84662–65, 84667, 84701, 84711, 84713, 84724, 84728, 84730–31, 84739, 84744, 84751–52, 84754, 84766

VERMONT

(Population 2000, 608,827)

SENATORS

PATRICK J. LEAHY, Democrat, of Burlington, VT; born in Montpelier, VT, March 31, 1940, son of Howard and Alba Leahy; graduate of St. Michael's High School, Montpelier, 1957; B.A., St. Michael's College, 1961; J.D., Georgetown University, 1964; lawyer, admitted to the Vermont bar, 1964; admitted to the District of Columbia bar, 1979; admitted to practice before the U.S. Supreme Court, 1968; the Second Circuit Court of Appeals in New York, 1966, the Federal District Court of Vermont, 1965, and the Vermont Supreme Court, 1964; State's Attorney, Chittenden County, 1966–74; vice president, National District Attorneys Association, 1971–74; married: the former Marcelle Pomerleau, 1962; children: Kevin, Alicia and Mark; committees: Agriculture, Nutrition and Forestry; Appropriations; ranking member, Judiciary; subcommittees: Administrative Oversight and the Courts; Antitrust, Competition Policy and Consumer Rights; Commerce, Justice, State and the Judiciary; Defense; ranking member, Foreign Operations; Forestry, Conservation and Rural Revitalization; Homeland Security; Immigration, Border Security and Citizenship; Interior and Related Agencies; VA, HUD and Independent Agencies; ranking member, Research, Nutrition and General Legislation; first Democrat and youngest person in Vermont to be elected to the U.S. Senate; elected to the Senate on November 5, 1974; reelected to each succeeding Senate term.

Office Listings

http://leahy.senate.gov

433 Russell Senate Office Building, Washington, DC 20510 .... (202) 224–4242
Chief of Staff.—Luke Albee.
Deputy Chief of Staff.—Clara Kircher.
Legislative Director.—John P. Dowd.
Press Secretary.—David Carle.
Federal Building, Room 338, Montpelier, VT 05602 .... (802) 229–0569
Office Director.—Robert G. Paquin.
199 Main Street, Courthouse Plaza, Burlington, VT 05401 .... (802) 863–2525
State Director.—Chuck Ross.

* * *

JAMES M. JEFFORDS, Independent, of Shrewsbury, VT; born in Rutland, VT, on May 11, 1934; attended public schools in Rutland; received B.S.I.A. degree from Yale, New Haven, CT, 1956; graduate work, Harvard, Cambridge, MA, 1962, LL.B.; served in the U.S. Navy as lieutenant (jg.); captain, U.S. Naval Reserves (retired June 1990); admitted to the Vermont bar, 1962, and began practice in Rutland; State Senator, 1967–68; Attorney General, State of Vermont, 1969–73; committees: ranking member, Environment and Public Works; Health, Education, Labor, and Pensions; Finance; Veterans' Affairs; Special Committee on Aging; Northeast-Midwest Coalition; married to Elizabeth Daley; two children: Leonard and Laura; elected to the 94th Congress, November 5, 1974; reelected to each succeeding Congress; elected to the U.S. Senate on November 8, 1988; reelected to each succeeding Senate term.

Office Listings

http://jeffords.senate.gov

413 Dirksen Senate Office Building, Washington, DC 20510 .... (202) 224–5141
Chief of Staff.—Susan Boardman Russ.
Legislative Director.—Sherry Kaiman.
Office Manager.—Jim Eismeier.
Scheduler / Personal Assistant.—Trecia McEvoy.
58 State Street, Montpelier, VT 05602 .... (802) 223–5273
Lindholm Building, 2 South Main Street, Rutland, VT 05701 .... (802) 773–3875
30 Main Street, Suite 350, Burlington, VT 05401 .... (802) 658–6001

REPRESENTATIVE

AT LARGE

BERNARD SANDERS, Independent, of Burlington, VT; born in Brooklyn, NY, on September 8, 1941; education: graduated from Madison High School, Brooklyn; B.S., Political Science, University of Chicago, 1964; employment: carpenter, writer, college professor; Mayor of Burlington, VT, 1981–89; married: the former Jane O'Meara, 1988; children: Levi, Heather, Carina and David; elected to the 102nd Congress on November 6, 1990; reelected to each succeeding Congress.

Office Listings

http://bernie.house.gov

2233 Rayburn House Office Building, Washington, DC 20515 .... (202) 225–4115
Chief of Staff.—Jeff Weaver. FAX: 225–6790
Executive Assistant.—Roxanne Scott.
Legislative Director.—Warren Gunnels.
Communications Director.—Joel Barkin.
1 Church Street, Second Floor, Burlington, VT 05401 .... (802) 862–0697

Population (2000), 608,827.

ZIP Codes: 05001, 05009, 05030–43, 05045–56, 05058–62, 05065, 05067–77, 05079, 05081, 05083–86, 05088–89, 05091, 05101, 05141–43, 05146, 05148–56, 05158–59, 05161, 05201, 05250–55, 05257, 05260–62, 05301–04, 05340–46, 05350–63, 05401–07, 05439–66, 05468–74, 05476–79, 05481–83, 05485–92, 05494–95, 05601–04, 05609, 05620, 05633, 05640–41, 05647–58, 05660–67, 05669–82, 05701–02, 05730–48, 05750–51, 05753, 05757–70, 05772–78, 05819–30, 05832–33, 05836–43, 05845–51, 05853, 05855, 05857–63, 05866–68, 05871–75, 05901–07

VIRGINIA

(Population 2000, 7,078,515)

SENATORS

JOHN W. WARNER, Republican, of Alexandria, VA; born February 18, 1927; grandson of John W. and Mary Tinsley Warner of Amherst County, VA, son of the late Dr. John W. Warner and Martha Budd Warner; left high school in 1944 to serve in the U.S. Navy, released from active duty, third class electronics technician, July 1946; graduated Washington and Lee University (engineering), 1949; entered University of Virginia Law School, 1949; U.S. Marine Corps, second tour of active military duty as a first lieutenant, September, 1950 to May, 1952, with service in Korea, October, 1951 to May, 1952 as a ground communications officer with Marine Air Group 33, 1st Marine Air Wing; received LL.B. from University of Virginia, 1953; former owner and operator of Atoka, a cattle and crops farm, 1961–94; law clerk to E. Barrett Prettyman, late chief judge for the U.S. Court of Appeals for D.C. Circuit, 1953–54; private law practice, 1954–56; assistant U.S. attorney, 1956–60; private law practice, 1960–69; trustee, Protestant Episcopal Cathedral, Mount St. Albans, 1967–72; member, board of trustees, Washington and Lee University, 1968–79; presidential appointments: Under Secretary, U.S. Navy, February 1969–April 1972; Secretary, U.S. Navy, May 1972–April 1974; Department of Defense delegate to Law of Sea Conferences, 1969–72, head of U.S. delegation for Incidents at Sea Conference, treaty signed in Moscow, May 1972; administrator, American Revolution Bicentennial Administration, April 1974–October 1976; committees: chairman, Armed Services; Environment and Public Works; Health, Education, Labor, and Pensions; Select Committee on Intelligence; National Security Working Group; Commission on Roles and Capabilities of U.S. Intelligence; U.S. Delegate to the 12th special session of the U.N. General Assembly devoted to disarmament, 1982; appointed in 1985 as a Senate observer to the Geneva arms control talks with the Soviet Union; elected to the U.S. Senate on November 7, 1978, and took the oath of office in Richmond, VA, on January 2, 1979; reelected to each succeeding Senate term.

Office Listings

http//warner.senate.gov

225 Russell Senate Office Building, Washington, DC 20510 .... (202) 224–2023
Chief of Staff.—Susan Magill.
Executive Assistant / Scheduler.—Anna Reilly.
Communications Director.—John Ullyot.
Office Manager.—Scott Stangeland.
235 Federal Building, 180 West Main Street, Abingdon, VA 24210 .... (276) 628–8158
600 East Main Street, Richmond, VA 23219 .... (804) 771–2579
4900 World Trade Center, Norfolk, VA 23510 .... (757) 441–3079
1003 First Union Bank Building, 213 South Jefferson Street, Roanoke, VA 24011.. (540) 857–2676

* * *

GEORGE ALLEN, Republican, of Chesterfield County, VA; born on March 8, 1952, in Whittier, CA; education: B.A., University of Virginia, 1974; Juris Doctorate, University of Virginia, 1977; profession: attorney; businessman: Commonwealth Biotechnologies, Inc.; Xybernaut Corp.; organizations: Virginia Council on Economic Education; Virginia-Israel Advisory Board; Richmond Historic Riverfront Foundation; Atlantic Rural Exposition Board; Boy Scouts of America, Stonewall Jackson Council; public service: Virginia House of Delegates, 1983–1991; U.S. House of Representatives, 1991–1993; Governor of Virginia, 1994–1998; family: married to Susan; children: Forrest, Brooke, and Tyler; elected to the U.S. Senate on November 7, 2000.

Office Listings

http://allen.senate.gov

204 Russell Senate Office Building, Washington, DC 20510 .... (202) 224–4024
Chief of Staff.—Michael Thomas. FAX: 224–5432
Deputy Chief of Staff.—Teresa DeRoco.
Legislative Director.—Paul Unger.
Scheduler.—Carlos Munoz.
507 E. Franklin Street, Richmond, VA 23219 .... (804) 771–2221
3140 Chaparral Drive, Building C, Suite 101, Roanoke, VA 24018 .... (540) 772–4236
2214 Rock Hill Road, Suite 100, Herndon, VA 20170 .... (703) 435–0039

REPRESENTATIVES

FIRST DISTRICT

JO ANN DAVIS, Republican, of Yorktown, VA; born on June 29, 1950, in Rowan County, NC; education: Kecoughtan High School, Hampton, VA; Hampton Roads Business College; profession: Real Estate Broker; established Davis Management Co., 1988; and Jo Ann Davis Realty, 1990; organizations: Peninsula Chamber of Commerce; Better Business Bureau; National Association of Realtors; Mothers Against Drunk Driving; York County Business Association; family: married to Chuck Davis; children: Charlie and Chris; public service: Virginia House of Delegates, 1997–2000; elected to the 107th Congress on November 7, 2000; reelected to each succeeding Congress.

Office Listings

http://www.house.gov/joanndavis

1123 Longworth House Office Building, Washington, DC 20515 .... (202) 225–4261
Chief of Staff.—Chris Connelly.
Legislative Director / Deputy Chief of Staff.—Tim Baroody.
Scheduler / Office Manager.—Abby Moon.
4904–B George Washington Memorial Highway, Yorktown, VA 23692 .... (757) 874–6687
District Director.—Angela Welch.
4500 Plank Road, Suite 105–A, Fredericksburg, VA 22407 .... (540) 548–1086
623 Tappahannock Blvd., P.O. Box 3106, Tappahannock, VA 22560 .... (804) 443–0668

Counties: CAROLINE (part), ESSEX, FAUQUIER (part), GLOUCESTER, JAMES CITY, KING AND QUEEN, KING GEORGE, KING WILLIAM, LANCASTER, MATHEWS, MIDDLESEX, NORTHUMBERLAND, PRINCE WILLIAM (part), RICHMOND, SPOTSYLVANIA (part), STAFFORD, WESTMORELAND, YORK. CITIES AND TOWNSHIPS: Bowling Green, Chancellorsville, Cobbs Creek, Colonial Beach, Dumfries, Falmouth, Fredericksburg, Hampton (part), Kilmarnock, Lightfoot, Montross, Newport News (part), Poquoson, Quantico, Saluda, Seaford, Tappahannock, Toano, Triangle, Warsaw, West Point, White Stone, Williamsburg, and Yorktown. Population (2000), 643,514.

ZIP Codes: 20106, 20112, 20115, 20119, 20128, 20138–39, 20181, 20186–87, 22026, 22134–35, 22172, 22191, 22193, 22401–08, 22412, 22427, 22430, 22432, 22435–38, 22442–43, 22446, 22448, 22451, 22454, 22456, 22460, 22463, 22469, 22471–73, 22476, 22480–82, 22485, 22488, 22501, 22503–04, 22507–09, 22511, 22513–14, 22517, 22520, 22523–24, 22526, 22528–30, 22535, 22538–39, 22544–48, 22552–56, 22558, 22560, 22570, 22572, 22576–81, 22639, 22712, 22720, 22728, 22734, 22739, 22742, 23001, 23003, 23009, 23011, 23017–18, 23021, 23023–25, 23031–32, 23035, 23043, 23045, 23050, 23056, 23061–62, 23064, 23066, 23068–72, 23076, 23079, 23081, 23085–86, 23089–92, 23106–10, 23115, 23117, 23119, 23125–28, 23130–31, 23138, 23148–49, 2315356, 23161, 23163, 23168–69, 23175–78, 23180–81, 23183–88, 23190–91, 23354, 23601–03, 23605–06, 23608–09, 23612, 23662–63, 23665–67, 23669–70, 23681, 23690–94, 23696

* * *

SECOND DISTRICT

EDWARD L. SCHROCK, Republican, of Virginia Beach, VA; born in Middletown, OH, on April 6, 1941; education: B.A., Alderson-Broaddus College; M.A., American University; military service: U.S. Navy, 1964–88, retired with the rank of Captain; employment: investment broker; organizations: Friends of the Virginia Beach Public Library; Cape Henry Collegiate School Parent / Faculty Association; Library of Virginia Foundation Board; Lee's Friends (cancer victim support organization); Governor's Commission on Information Technology; married: Judith; children: Randy; religion: Baptist; public service: Virginia State Senate, 1995–2000; elected to the 107th Congress on November 7, 2000; reelected to each succeeding Congress.

Office Listings

http://schrock.house.gov

322 Cannon House Office Building, Washington, DC 20515 .... (202) 225–4215
Chief of Staff.—Rob Catron. FAX: 225–4218
Press Secretary.—Tom Gordy.
4772 Euclid Road, Suite E, Virginia Beach, VA 23462 .... (757) 497–6859
District Director.—Jim Deangio.
23386 Front Street, Accomac, VA 23301 .... (757) 787–7836

Counties: ACCOMACK, NORTHAMPTON. CITIES: Hampton (part), Norfolk (part), and Virginia Beach. Population (2000), 643,510.

ZIP Codes: 23301–03, 23306–08, 23310, 23313, 23316, 23336–37, 23341, 23345, 23347, 23350, 23354, 23356–59, 23389, 23395, 23398–99, 23401, 23404–05, 23407–10, 23412–23, 23426–27, 23429, 23440–43, 23450–67, 23471, 23479–80, 23482–83, 23486, 23488, 23502–03, 23505–08, 23511–13, 23515, 23518–19, 23521, 23529, 23541, 23551, 23605, 23651, 23661, 23663–66, 23669

THIRD DISTRICT

ROBERT C. SCOTT, Democrat, of Newport News, VA; born in Washington, DC, on April 30, 1947; education: graduated from Groton High School; B.A., Harvard University; J.D., Boston College Law School; served in the Massachusetts National Guard; employment: attorney; admitted to the Virginia bar; Virginia House of Representatives, 1978–83; Virginia State Senate, 1983–92; member: Sigma Pi Phi Fraternity; Peninsula Chamber of Commerce; NAACP; Alpha Phi Alpha Fraternity; March of Dimes Board of Directors; Peninsula Legal Aid Center Board of Directors; elected on November 3, 1992 to the 103rd Congress; reelected to each succeeding Congress.

Office Listings

wttp://www.house.gov/scott

2464 Rayburn House Office Building, Washington, DC 20515 .... (202) 225–8351
Chief of Staff.—Joni L. Ivey.
Special Assistant.—Randi Estes.
Legislative Director.—Lee Perselay.
Legislative Assistants: Diane Beedle, LaQuita Honeysucker.
2600 Washington Avenue, Suite 1010, Newport News, VA 23607 .... (757) 380–1000
501 North Second Street, Suite 401, Richmond, VA 23219–1321 .... (804) 644–4845

Counties: CHARLES CITY, HENRICO (part), NEW KENT, SURRY. CITIES: Hampton (part), Norfolk (part), Portsmouth and Richmond (part). Population (2000), 643,476.

ZIP Codes: 23011, 23030, 23059–60, 23075, 23089, 23111, 23124, 23140–41, 23147, 23150, 23181, 23185, 23218–25, 23227–28, 23230–32, 23234, 23240–41, 23249–50, 23260–61, 23269–70, 23272, 23274–76, 23278–79, 23282, 23284–86, 23290–93, 23295, 23298, 23501–02, 23504–05, 23507–10, 23513–14, 23517–18, 23520, 23523, 23530, 23601–09, 23628, 23630–31, 23653, 23661, 23663–64, 23666–70, 23701–05, 23707–09, 23839, 23842, 23846, 23860, 23875, 23881, 23883, 23888, 23898–99

* * *

FOURTH DISTRICT

J. RANDY FORBES, Republican, of Chesapeake, VA; born on February 17, 1952, in Chesapeake, VA; education: B.A., Randolph-Macon College; J.D., University of Virginia School of Law; occupation: Attorney; religion: Baptist; public service: Virginia House of Delegates, 1990–1997; Virginia State Senate, 1997–2001; Republican House Floor Leader, 1994–1997; Republican Senate Floor Leader, 1998–2001; Chairman of the Republican Party of Virginia, 1996–2000; family: married to Shirley; four children: Neil, Jamie, Jordan, and Justin; elected to the 107th Congress, by special election, on June 19, 2001; reelected to each succeeding Congress.

Office Listings

307 Cannon House Office Building, Washington, DC 20515 .... (202) 225–6365
Chief of Staff.—Dee Gilmore. FAX: 226–1170
Communications Director.—Christine Shott.
Legislative Director.—Andy Halataei.
636 Cedar Road, Suite 200, Chesapeake, VA 23322 .... (757) 382–0080
District Representative.—Ryan K. Mottley.
2903 Boulevard, Suite B, Colonial Heights, VA 23834 .... (804) 526–4969
District Representative.—Jason Gray.
425 H. South Main Street, Emporia, VA 23847 .... (434) 634–5575
District Field Representative.—Rick Franklin.

Counties: AMELIA, BRUNSWICK (part), CHESTERFIELD (part), DINWIDDIE, GREENSVILLE, ISLE OF WIGHT (part), NOTTOWAY, POWHATAN, PRINCE GEORGE (part), SOUTHAMPTON, SUSSEX. Population (2000), 643,477.

ZIP Codes: 23002, 23083, 23101, 23105, 23112–14, 23120, 23139, 23234, 23236–37, 23304, 23314–15, 23320–28, 23397, 23424, 23430–39, 23487, 23501, 23801, 23803–06, 23821, 23824, 23827–34, 23836–38, 23840–42, 23844–45, 23847, 23850–51, 23856–57, 23860, 23866–67, 23872–76, 23878–79, 23882, 23884–85, 23887–91, 23894, 23897–98, 23920, 23922, 23930, 23938, 23950, 23955

* * *

FIFTH DISTRICT

VIRGIL H. GOODE, JR., Republican, of Rocky Mount, VA; born in Richmond, VA, October 17, 1946; education: B.A., University of Richmond, 1969; J.D., University of Virginia Law School, 1973; served in Virginia Army National Guard; admitted to the Virginia bar in 1973;

attorney; member, Virginia State Senate, 1973–97; former member: Ruritan Chamber of Commerce; Jaycees; married: Lucy Dodson Goode, 1991; children: Catherine; elected to the 105th Congress; reelected to each succeeding Congress.

Office Listings

http://www.house.gov/goode

1520 Longworth House Office Building, Washington, DC 20515 .... (202) 225–4711
Chief of Staff.—Tom Hance. FAX: 225–5681
Legislative Assistant / Office Manager.—Ward Anderson.
Scheduler.—Judy E. Mattox.
Virgil Goode Building, 70 East Court Street, Suite 215, Rocky Mount, VA 24151.. (540) 484–1254

Counties: ALBEMARLE COUNTY. CITIES AND TOWNSHIPS: Charlotteville, Batesville, Covesville, Esmont, Greenwood, Hatton, Ivy, Keene, Keswick, North Garden, Scottsville. APPOMATTOX COUNTY. CITIES AND TOWNSHIPS: Appomattox, Evergreen, Pamplin, Spout Spring. BEDFORD COUNTY. CITIES AND TOWNSHIPS: Bedford, Big Island, Goodview, Coleman Falls, Forest, Goode, Huddleston, Lowry, Thaxton. BRUNSWICK COUNTY. BUCKINGHAM COUNTY. CITIES AND TOWNSHIPS: Andersonville, Arvonia, Buckingham, Dillwyn, Buckingham, New Canton. CAMPBELL COUNTY. CITIES AND TOWNSHIPS: Altavista, Brookneal, Concord, Evington, Gladys, Long Island, Lynch Station, Naruna, Rustburg. CHARLOTTE COUNTY. CITIES AND TOWNSHIPS: Barnesville, Charlotte Court House, Cullen, Drakes Branch, Keysville, Phenix, Randolph, Red House, Red Oak, Saxe, Wylliesburg. CUMBERLAND COUNTY. CITIES AND TOWNSHIPS: Carterville, Cumberland. DANVILLE COUNTY. CITY: Danville. FLUVANNA COUNTY. CITIES AND TOWNSHIPS: Bremo Bluff, Bybee, Carysbrook, Columbia, Fort Union, Kents Store, Palmyra, Troy. FRANKLIN COUNTY. CITIES AND TOWNSHIPS: Boones Mill, Callaway, Ferrum, Glade Hill, Henry, Redwood, Penhook, Rocky Mount, Union Hall, Waidsboro, Wirtz. GREENE COUNTY. HALIFAX COUNTY. CITIES AND TOWNSHIPS: Alton, Clover, Cluster Springs, Crystal Hall, Denniston, Halifax, Ingram, Lennig, Mayo, Nathalie, Republican Grove, Scottsburg, Turbeville, Vernon Hill, Virgilina. HENRY COUNTY. CITIES AND TOWNSHIPS: Axton, Bassett, Collinsville, Fieldale, Ridgeway, Spencer, Stanleytown. LUNENBURG COUNTY. CITIES AND TOWNSHIPS: Tamworth, Dundas, Fort Mitchell, Kenbridge, Lunenburg, Rehoboth, Victoria. MARTINSVILLE COUNTY. CITY: Martinsville. MECKLENBURG COUNTY. CITIES AND TOWNSHIPS: Baskerville, Blackridge, Boydton, Bracey, Chase City, Clarksville, Forksville, LaCross, Palmer Springs, Skipwith, South Hill, Union Level Buffalo Junction, Nelson. NELSON COUNTY. CITIES AND TOWNSHIPS: Afton, Arrington, Faber, Lovingston, Massies Mill, Nellysford, Montebello, Gladstone, Norwood, Piney River, Roseland, Schuyler, Shipman, Tye River, Tyro, Wingina. PITTSYLVANIA COUNTY. CITIES AND TOWNSHIPS: Blairs, Callands, Cascade, Chatham, Pittsville, Sandy Level, Dry Fork, Gretna, Hurt, Java, Keeling, Ringgold, Sutherlin. PRINCE EDWARD COUNTY. CITIES AND TOWNSHIPS: Green Bay, Farmville, Darlington, Heights, Green Bay, Hampden-Sydney, Meherrin, Prospect, Rice, and South Boston. Population (2000), 643,497.

ZIP Codes: 22901–11, 22920, 22922–24, 22931–32, 22935–38, 22940, 22942–43, 22945–47, 22949, 22952, 22954, 22958–59, 22963–65, 22967–69, 22971, 22973–74, 22976, 22987, 23004, 23022, 23027, 23038, 23040, 23055, 23084, 23093, 23123, 23139, 23821, 23824, 23843, 23845, 23856–57, 23868, 23887, 23889, 23893, 23901, 23909, 23915, 23917, 23919–24, 23927, 23934, 23936–39, 23941–44, 23947, 23950, 23952, 23954, 23958–60, 23962–64, 23966–68, 23970, 23974, 23976, 24012, 24053–55, 24059, 24064–65, 24067, 24069, 24076, 24078–79, 24082, 24088–89, 24091–92, 24095, 24101–02, 24104, 24112–15, 24120–22, 24133, 24137, 24139, 24146, 24148, 24151, 24153, 24161, 24168, 24171, 24174, 24176–77, 24179, 24184–85, 24312, 24464, 24483, 24501–02, 24504, 24517, 24520, 24522–23, 24527–31, 24534–35, 24538–41, 24543–44, 24549–51, 24553–54, 24556–58, 24562–63, 24565–66, 24569–71, 24574, 24576–77, 24580–81, 24585–86, 24588–90, 24592–94, 24597–99

* * *

SIXTH DISTRICT

BOB GOODLATTE, Republican, of Roanoke, VA; born on September 22, 1952 in Holyoke, MA; education: B.A., Bates College, Lewiston, ME, 1974; J.D., Washington and Lee University, 1977; Massachusetts bar, 1977, Virginia bar, 1978; employment: began practice in Roanoke, VA, 1979; district director for Congressman M. Caldwell Butler, 1977–79; attorney, sole practitioner, 1979–81; partner, 1981–92; chairman, sixth district, VA, Republican Committee, 1983–88; member, Civitan Club of Roanoke (president, 1989–90); former member, Building Better Boards Advisory Council; member, Parent Teachers Association, Fishburn Park Elementary School; deputy majority whip; member, House Republican Policy Committee; committees: chairman, Agriculture; Select Committee on Homeland Security; Judiciary; subcommittees: Courts, the Internet, and Intellectual Property; Crime, Terrorism and Homeland Security; Infrastructure and Border Security; Cybersecurity, Science, and Research and Development; married: Maryellen Flaherty, 1974; children: Jennifer and Robert; elected on November 3, 1992, to the 103rd Congress; reelected to each succeeding Congress.

Office Listings

http://www.house.gov/goodlatte

2240 Rayburn House Office Building, Washington, DC 20515 .... (202) 225–5431
Chief of Staff.—Shelley Husband. FAX: 225–9681
Legislative Counsel.—Branden Ritchie.
Communications Director.—Elyse Bauer.
10 Franklin Road, SE, 540 Crestar Plaza, Roanoke, VA 24011 .... (540) 857–2672
District Director.—Pete Larkin.
919 Main Street, Suite 300, Lynchburg, VA 24504 .... (804) 845–8306
7 Court Square, Staunton, VA 24401 .... (540) 885–3861
2 South Main Street, First Floor, Suite A, Harrisonburg, VA 22801 .... (540) 432–2391

Counties: ALLEGHANY (part), AMHERST, AUGUSTA, BATH, BEDFORD (part), BOTETOURT, HIGHLAND, ROANOKE (part), ROCKBRIDGE, ROCKINGHAM (part), SHENANDOAH. CITIES: Buena Vista, Covington (part), Harrisonburg, Lexington, Lynchburg, Roanoke, Salem, Staunton, and Waynesboro. Population (2000), 643,504.

ZIP Codes: 22626, 22641, 22644–45, 22652, 22654, 22657, 22660, 22664, 22801–03, 22807, 22810–12, 22815, 22820–21, 22824, 22827, 22830–34, 22840–48, 22850, 22853, 22920, 22922, 22939, 22952, 22967, 22980, 24001–20, 24022–38, 24040, 24042–44, 24048, 24053, 24059, 24064–66, 24070, 24077, 24079, 24083, 24085, 24087, 24090, 24101, 24121–22, 24130, 24153, 24156, 24174–75, 24178–79, 24401–02, 24411–13, 24415–16, 24421–22, 24426, 24430–33, 24435, 24437–42, 24445, 24450, 24458–60, 24463, 24465, 24467–69, 24471–73, 24476–77, 24479, 24482–87, 24501–06, 24512–15, 24521, 24523, 24526, 24533, 24536, 24550–51, 24553, 24555–56, 24572, 24574, 24578–79, 24595

* * *

SEVENTH DISTRICT

ERIC CANTOR, Republican, of Henrico County, VA; born on June 6, 1963, in Henrico County, VA; education: George Washington University, Bachelor's Degree, 1985; College of William and Mary, Law Degree, 1988; Columbia University, Masters Degree, 1989; occupation: Attorney; organizations: Western Henrico Rotary; Henrico County Republican Committee; President, Virginia-Israel Foundation; Virginia Holocaust Museum Board of Trustees; Elk Hill Farm Board of Trustees; family: married to Diana; three children; elected to the Virginia House of Delegates, 1991; elected to the 107th Congress on November 7, 2000; reelected to each succeeding Congress.

Office Listings

http://www.house.gov/cantor

329 Cannon House Office Building, Washington, DC 20515 .... (202) 225–2815
Chief of Staff.—Boyd Marcus. FAX: 225–0011
Legislative Director.—Bill Dolbow.
Press Secretary.—Rob Collins.
5040 Sadler Place, Suite 110, Glen Allen, VA 23060 .... (804) 771–2809
763 Madison Road, Suite 207, Culpeper, VA 22701 .... (540) 825–8960

Counties: CAROLINE (part), CHESTERFIELD (part), CULPEPER, GOOCHLAND, HANOVER, HENRICO (part), LOUISIA, MADISON, ORANGE, PAGE, RAPPAHANNOCK, SPOTSYLVANIA (part). CITIES: Richmond (part). Population (2000), 643,499.

ZIP Codes: 20106, 20119, 20186, 22407, 22433, 22508, 22534, 22542, 22546, 22553, 22565, 22567, 22580, 22610, 22623, 22627, 22630, 22640, 22650, 22701, 22709, 22711, 22713–16, 22718–19, 22721–27, 22729–38, 22740–41, 22743, 22746–49, 22827, 22835, 22849, 22851, 22903, 22923, 22942, 22947–48, 22957, 22960, 22972, 22974, 22989, 23005, 23015, 23024, 23038–39, 23047, 23058–60, 23063, 23065, 23067, 23069, 23084, 23093, 23102–03, 23111–14, 23116–17, 23120, 23124, 23129, 23146, 23153, 23160, 23162, 23170, 23173, 23192, 23221–30, 23233–36, 23242, 23255, 23273, 23280, 23288–89, 23294–95

* * *

EIGHTH DISTRICT

JAMES P. MORAN, Democrat, of Alexandria, VA; born on May 16, 1945, in Buffalo, NY; College of Holy Cross, B.A.; Bernard Baruch Graduate School of Finance—City University of New York; University of Pittsburgh Graduate School of Public and International Affairs, M.P.A.; served on City Council of Alexandria, 1979–82; Vice Mayor of Alexandria from 1982–84, Mayor from 1985–90; founding member of the New Democrat Coalition, a group of more than 75 centrist House Democrats committed to fiscal responsibility, improvements to education, and maintaining America's economic competitiveness; co-chair of the Congressional Prevention Coalition; named as one of two ''High Technology Legislators of the Year'' by the Information Technology Industry Council; in 2000 named to the ''Legislative Hall of Fame'' by the American Electronics Association for his work on technology issues; five children: James, Michael, Patrick, Mary, and Dorothy; committees: Appropriations; Budget; subcommittees: Defense; Interior; ranking member, Legislative; elected to the 102nd Congress on November 6, 1990; reelected to each succeeding Congress.

Office Listings

http://www.house.gov/moran

2239 Rayburn House Office Building, Washington, DC 20515 .... (202) 225–4376
Chief of Staff / Administrative Assistant.—Melissa Koloszar. FAX: 225–0017
Legislative Director.—Tim Aiken.
5115 Franconia Road, Suite B, Alexandria, VA 22310 .... (703) 971–4700
District Director.—Susie Warner.

Counties: ARLINGTON, FAIRFAX (part). CITIES: Alexandria, and Falls Church. Population (2000), 643,503.

ZIP Codes: 20170–71, 20190–91, 20194–96, 20206, 20231, 20301, 20310, 20330, 20350, 20406, 20453, 22003, 22027, 22031, 22037, 22040–44, 22046–47, 22060, 22079, 22101–03, 22107–09, 22122, 22124, 22150–51, 22159, 22180–82, 22201–07, 22209–17, 22219, 22222, 22225–27, 22229–30, 22234, 22240–45, 22301–07, 22310–15, 22320–21, 22331–34, 22336

* * *

NINTH DISTRICT

RICK BOUCHER, Democrat, of Abingdon, VA; born in Washington County, VA, on August 1, 1946; education: graduated from Abingdon High School in 1964; B.A. degree from Roanoke College in 1968; J.D. degree from the University of Virginia School of Law in 1971; employment: associate, Milbank, Tweed, Hadley and McCloy, New York, NY; partner, Boucher and Boucher, Abingdon, VA; elected to the Virginia State Senate in 1975 and reelected in 1979; former chairman of the Oil and Gas Subcommittee of the Virginia Coal and Energy Commission; former member: Virginia State Crime Commission; Virginia Commission on Interstate Cooperation; Law and Justice Committee of the National Conference of State Legislatures; member: board of directors of the First Virginia Bank, Damascus; Abingdon United Methodist Church; Kappa Alpha order; Phi Alpha Delta legal fraternity; American Bar Association; Virginia Bar Association; Association of the Bar of the City of New York; recipient of the Abingdon Jaycees Outstanding Young Businessman Award, 1975; committees: Energy and Commerce; Judiciary; assistant whip; elected to the 98th Congress on November 2, 1982; reelected to each succeeding Congress.

Office Listings

http://www.house.gov/boucher ninthnet@mail.house.gov

2187 Rayburn House Office Building, Washington, DC 20515 .... (202) 225–3861
Chief of Staff.—Becky Coleman. FAX: 225–0442
Deputy Chief of Staff/Comunications Director.—Sharon Ringley.
188 East Main Street, Abingdon, VA 24210 .... (540) 628–1145
District Administrator.—Linda Di Yorio.
1 Cloverleaf Square, Suite C–1, Big Stone Gap, VA 24219 .... (540) 523–5450
112 North Washington Avenue, P.O. Box 1268, Pulaski, VA 24301 .... (540) 980–4310

Counties: ALLEGHANY (part), BLAND, BUCHANAN, CARROLL, CRAIG, DICKENSON, FLOYD, GILES, GRAYSON, HENRY (part), LEE, MONTGOMERY, PATRICK, PULASKI, ROANOKE (part), RUSSELL, SCOTT, SMYTH, TAZEWELL, WASHINGTON, WISE, WYTHE. CITIES: Bristol, Covington (part) Galax, Norton, and Radford. Population (2000), 643,514.

ZIP Codes: 24018–19, 24053, 24055, 24058–64, 24068, 24070, 24072–73, 24076, 24079, 24082, 24084, 24086–87, 24089, 24091, 24093–94, 24104–05, 24111–12, 24120–22, 24124, 24126–29, 24131–34, 24136, 24138, 24141–43, 24147–50, 24153, 24162, 24165, 24167, 24171, 24175, 24177, 24185, 24201–03, 24209–12, 24215–21, 24224–26, 24228, 24230, 24236–37, 24239, 24243–46, 24248, 24250–51, 24256, 24258, 24260, 24263, 24265–66, 24269–73, 24277, 24279–83, 24290, 24292–93, 24301, 24311–19, 24322–28, 24330, 24333, 24340, 24343, 24347–48, 24350–52, 24354, 24360–61, 24363, 24366, 24368, 24370, 24374–75, 24377–78, 24380–82, 24422, 24426, 24448, 24457, 24474, 24502, 24526, 24550–51, 24556, 24601–09, 24612–14, 24618–20, 24622, 24624, 24627–28, 24630–31, 24634–35, 24637, 24639–41, 24646–47, 24649, 24651, 24656–58

* * *

TENTH DISTRICT

FRANK R. WOLF, Republican, of Vienna, VA; born in Philadelphia, PA, January 30, 1939; B.A., Pennsylvania State University, 1961; LL.B., Georgetown University Law School, 1965; served in the U.S. Army Signal Corps (Reserves); lawyer, admitted to the Virginia State bar; legislative assistant for former U.S. Congressman Edward G. Biester, Jr., 1968–71; assistant to Secretary of the Interior Rogers C.B. Morton, 1971–74; Deputy Assistant Secretary for Congressional and Legislative Affairs, Department of the Interior, 1974–75; member, Vienna Presbyterian Church; married to the former Carolyn Stover; five children: Frank, Jr., Virginia, Anne, Brenda, and Rebecca; elected to the 97th Congress, November 4, 1980; reelected to each succeeding Congress.

Office Listings

http://www.house.gov/wolf

241 Cannon House Office Building, Washington, DC 20515 .... (202) 225–5136
Chief of Staff/Press Secretary.—Dan Scandling. FAX: 225–0437
Legislative Director.—Janet Shaffron.
13873 Park Center Road, Suite 130, Herndon, VA 20171 .... (703) 709–5800
Director of Constituent Services.—Judy McCary.
110 North Cameron Street, Winchester, VA 22601 .... (540) 667–0900

Counties: CLARKE, FAIRFAX (part), FAUQUIER (part), FREDERICK, LOUDOUN, PRINCE WILLIAM (part), WARREN. CITIES: Manassas, Manassas Park, and Winchester. Population (2000), 643,512.

ZIP Codes: 20101–05, 20107–13, 20115–18, 20120–22, 20129–32, 20134–35, 20137, 20140–44, 20146–49, 20151–53, 20158–60, 20163–67, 20170–72, 20175–78, 20180, 20184–90, 20194, 20197–98, 22026, 22033, 22043–44, 22046, 22066–67, 22101, 22106, 22184–85, 22193, 22207, 22556, 22601–04, 22610–11, 22620, 22622, 22624–25, 22630, 22637, 22639, 22642–43, 22645–46, 22649, 22654–57, 22663

* * *

ELEVENTH DISTRICT

TOM DAVIS, Republican, of Falls Church, VA; born in Minot, ND, January 5, 1949; graduated, U.S. Capitol Page School; graduated, Amherst College with honors in political science; law degree, University of Virginia; attended officer candidate school; served in the U.S. Army Reserves; member: Fairfax County Board of Supervisors, 1980–94, Chairman, 1992–94; vice president and general counsel of PRC, Inc., McLean, VA; past president, Washington Metropolitan Council of Governments; founding member and past president, Bailey's Crossroads Rotary Club; married the former Peggy Rantz, 1973; three children: Carlton, Pamela, and Shelley; committees: chairman, Government Reform; elected to the 104th Congress; reelected to each succeeding Congress.

Office Listings

http://www.house.gov/tomdavis

2348 Rayburn House Office Building, Washington, DC 20515 .... (202) 225–1492
Chief of Staff.—David Thomas. FAX: 225–3071
Legislative Director.—Bill Womack.
Executive Assistant.—Gabriele Forsyth.
4415 Annandale Road, Annandale, VA 22003 .... (703) 916–9610
District Director.—Dave Foreman.
Telecommuting District Office .... (703) 437–1726
Constituent Service Director.—Ann Rust.
Dominion Center, 13554 Minnieville Road, Woodbridge, VA 22192 .... (703) 590–4599
Constituent Service Director.—Brian Gordon.

Counties: FAIRFAX (part), PRINCE WILLIAM (part). CITIES: Alexandria (part), Annandale, Burke, Centreville (part), Clifton, Fairfax (part), Fairfax Station, Herndon (part), Lorton, Manassas (part), Oakton, Occoquan, Springfield (part), Vienna (part), and Woodbridge. Population (2000), 643,509.

ZIP Codes: 20069–70, 20109–10, 20112, 20119–22, 20124, 20136–37, 20155–56, 20168–69, 20171, 20181–82, 22003, 22009, 22015, 22027, 22030–33, 22035, 22038–39, 22044, 22060, 22079, 22081–82, 22102, 22116, 22118–21, 22124–25, 22150–53, 22156, 22158–61, 22180–83, 22185, 22191–95, 22199, 22308–09, 22312

WASHINGTON

(Population 2000, 5,894,121)

SENATORS

PATTY MURRAY, Democrat, of Seattle, WA; born on October 11, 1950 in Seattle; education: B.A., Washington State University, 1972; teacher; lobbyist; Shoreline Community College; parent education instructor for Crystal Springs, 1984–87; citizen lobbyist for environmental and educational issues, 1983–88; school board member, 1985–89; elected Board of Directors, Shoreline School District, 1985–89; Washington State Senate, 1988–92; Democratic Whip, 1990–92; State Senate committees: Education; Ways and Means; Commerce and Labor; Domestic Timber Processing Select Committee; Open Government Select Committee; School Transportation Safety Task Force chairperson; Washington State Legislator of the Year, 1990; married: Rob Murray; children: Randy and Sara; committees: Appropriations; Budget; Health, Education, Labor and Pensions; Veterans' Affairs; elected to the U.S. Senate on November 3, 1992; reelected to each succeeding Senate term.

Office Listings

http://murray.senate.gov

173 Russell Senate Office Building, Washington, DC 20510 .... (202) 224–2621
Chief of Staff.—Rick Desimone. FAX: 224–0238
Legislative Director.—Ben McMakin. TDD: 224–4430
2988 Jackson Federal Building, 915 Second Avenue, Seattle, WA 98174 .... (206) 553–5545
State Director.—John Engber.
The Marshall House, 1323 Officer's Row, Vancouver, WA 98661 .... (360) 696–7797
District Director.—Mindi Linquist.
601 West Main Avenue, Suite 1213, Spokane, WA 99201 .... (509) 624–9515
District Director.—Judy Olson.
2930 Wetmore Avenue, Suite 903, Everett, WA 98201 .... (425) 259–6515
District Director.—Rachelle Hein.
402 E. Yakima Avenue, Suite 390, Yakima, WA 98901 .... (509) 453–7462
District Director.—Mary McBride.

* * *

MARIA CANTWELL, Democrat, of Edmonds, WA; born on October 13, 1958, in Indianapolis, IN; education: B.A., Miami University, Miami, OH, 1980; professional: businesswoman; RealNetworks, Inc.; organizations: South Snohomish County Chamber of Commerce; Alderwood Rotary; Mountlake Terrace Friends of the Library; public service: Washington State House of Representatives, 1987–1992; U.S. House of Representatives, 1992–1994; committees: Commerce, Science and Transportation; Energy and Natural Resources; Indian Affairs; Small Business and Entrepreneurship; religion: Roman Catholic; elected to the U.S. Senate on November 7, 2000.

Office Listings

http://cantwell.senate.gov

717 Hart Senate Office Building, Washington, DC 20510 .... (202) 224–3441
Chief of Staff.—Caroline R. Fredrickson. FAX: 228–0514
Legislative Director.—Dan Sakura.
Office Manager.—Carolyn Mosley.
Communications Director.—Jed Lewinson.
915 Second Avenue, Seattle, WA 98174 .... (206) 220–6400
State Director and Deputy Chief of Staff.—Kurt Beckett. (888) 648–7328
697 U.S. Courthouse, Spokane, WA 99201 .... (509) 353–2507
The Marshall House, 1313 Officer's Row, Vancouver, WA 98661 .... (360) 696–7838
825 Jadwin Avenue, G–58–A, Richland, WA 99352 .... (509) 946–8106
930 Wetmore Avenue, Suite 9B, Everett, WA 98201 .... (888) 648–7328

REPRESENTATIVES

FIRST DISTRICT

JAY INSLEE, Democrat, of Bainbridge Island, WA; born on February 9, 1951, in Seattle, WA; education: graduated, Ingraham High School, 1969; B.A., University of Washington, 1973; J.D., Willamette School of Law, 1976; employment: attorney, 1976–92; Washington State

House of Representatives, 1988–92, 14th Legislative District; served on Appropriations; Housing; Judiciary; and Financial Institutions and Insurance Committees; represented the 4th District in the U.S. House of Representatives, 1993–95; attorney, 1995–96; Regional Director, U.S. Department of Health and Human Services, 1997–98; married: Trudi; three children: Jack, Connor, and Joe; committees: Financial Services; Resources; subcommittees: Capital Markets, Insurance and Government Sponsored Enterprises; ranking member, Forests and Forest Health; Oversight and Investigations; Water and Power; elected to the U.S. House of Representatives, from the 1st District, for the 106th Congress; reelected to each succeeding Congress.

Office Listings

http://www.house.gov/inslee

308 Cannon House Office Building, Washington, DC 20515 .... (202) 225–6311
Chief of Staff.—Joby Shimomura. (800) 422–5521
Legislative Director.—Brian Bonlender.
Scheduler.—Sharmila Kotelawala.
Communications Director.—Sara O'Connell.
21905 64th Avenue West, Suite 101, Mountlake Terrace, WA 98043 .... (425) 640–0233
17701 Fjord Drive NE, Suite A–112, Liberty Bay Marina, Poulsbo, WA 98370 ..... (360) 598–2342
District Director.—Kennie Endelman.

Counties: KING (part), KITSAP (part), SNOHOMISH (part). CITIES AND TOWNSHIPS: Bainbridge Island, Bothell, Bremerton, Brier, Duvall, Edmonds, Everett, Hansville, Indianola, Kenmore, Keyport, Kingston, Kirkland, Lake Forest (part), Lynnwood, Mill Creek, Monroe, Mountlake Terrace, Mukilteo, Port Gamble, Poulsbo, Redmond, Rollingbay, Seabeck, Seattle, Shoreline, Silverdale, Snohomish, Suquamish, and Woodinville. Population (2000), 654,904.

ZIP Codes: 98011–12, 98019–20, 98021, 98026, 98028, 98033–34, 98036–37, 98041, 98043, 98046, 98052, 98061, 98072–74, 98077, 98082–83, 98110, 98133, 98155, 98160, 98177, 98204, 98208, 98272, 98275, 98290, 98296, 98311–12, 98315, 98340, 98342, 98345–46, 98364, 98370, 98380, 98383, 98392–93

* * *

SECOND DISTRICT

RICK LARSEN, Democrat, of Lake Stevens, WA; born on June 15, 1965, in Arlington, WA; education: B.A., Pacific Lutheran University; M.P.A., University of Minnesota; employment: economic development official at the Port of Everett; worked as a Director of Public Affairs for a health provider association; public service: Snohomish County Council; religion: Methodist; married: Tiia Karlen; children: Robert and Per; elected to the 107th Congress on November 7, 2000; reelected to each succeeding Congress.

Office Listings

http:/www.house.gov/larsen

1529 Longworth House Office Building, Washington, DC 20515 .... (202) 225–2605
Deputy Chief of Staff / Legislative Director.—Jennifer Pharaoh. FAX: 225–4420
Press Secretary.—Charla Neuman.
2930 Wetmore Avenue, Suite 9E, Everett, WA 98201 .... (425) 252–3188
Chief of Staff.—Jeff Bjornstad.
104 West Magnolia, Room 303, Bellingham, WA 98225 .... (360) 733–4500

Counties: ISLAND, KING (part), SAN JUAN, SKAGIT, SNOHOMISH (part), WHATCOM. CITIES AND TOWNSHIPS: Bellingham, Everett, and Mount Vernon. Population (2000), 654,903.

ZIP Codes: 98201, 98203–08, 98213, 98220–33, 98235–41, 98243–45, 98247–53, 98255–64, 98266–67, 98270–84, 98286–88, 98290–97

* * *

THIRD DISTRICT

BRIAN BAIRD, Democrat, of Vancouver, WA; born March 7, 1956 in Chauma, NM; B.S., University of Utah, 1977; M.S., University of Wyoming, 1980; Ph.D., University of Wyoming, 1984; profession: licensed clincial psychologist; has practiced in Washington State and Oregon; Professor and former Chairman of the Department of Psychology at Pacific Lutheran University; has worked in a variety of medical environments prior to election to the U.S. Congress; elected President of the Democratic Freshman Class for the 106th Congress; Democratic Regional Whip; committees: Budget; Science; Transportation and Infrastructure; elected to the 106th Congress; reelected to each succeeding Congress.

Office Listings

http://www.house.gov/baird

1721 Longworth House Office Building, Washington, DC 20515 .... (202) 225–3536
Chief of Staff.—Joe Shoemaker. FAX: 225–3478
Legislative Director.—Ryan Hedgepeth.
Press Secretary.—Anne Linskey.
1220 Main Street, Suite 360, Vancouver, WA 98660 .... (360) 695–6292
District Director.—Jeanne Bennett.
120 Union Avenue, Suite 105, Olympia, WA 98501 .... (360) 352–9768

Counties: CLARK COUNTY. CITIES AND TOWNSHIPS: Amboy, Ariel, Battle Ground, Brush Prairie, Camas, Heisson, La Center, Ridgefield, Vancouver, Washougal, Woodland, Yacolt. COWLITZ COUNTY. CITIES AND TOWNSHIPS: Carrolls, Castle Rock, Cougar, Kalama, Kelso, Longview, Ryderwood, Silverlake, Toutle. LEWIS COUNTY. CITIES AND TOWNSHIPS: Adna, Centralia, Chehalis, Cinebar, Curtis, Doty, Ethel, Galvin, Glenoma, Mineral, Morton, Mossyrock, Napavine, Onalaska, Packwood, Pe Ell, Randle, Salkum, Silver Creek, Toledo, Vader, Winlock. PACIFIC COUNTY. CITIES AND TOWNSHIPS: Bay Center, Chinook, Ilwaco, Lebam, Long Beach, Menlo, Nahcotta, Naselle, Ocean Park, Oysterville, Raymond, Seaview, South Bend, Tokeland. PIERCE COUNTY. CITIES AND TOWNSHIPS: Elbe. SKAMANIA COUNTY (part). CITIES AND TOWNSHIPS: Carson, North Bonneville, Stevenson, Underwood. THURSTON COUNTY (part). CITIES AND TOWNSHIPS: Buroda, Littlerock, Olympia, Tenino, and Rochester. WAHKIAKUM COUNTY. CITIES AND TOWNSHIPS: Cathlamet, Grays River, Rosburg, and Skamokawa. Population (2000), 654,898.

ZIP Codes: 98304, 98328, 98330, 98336, 98355–56, 98361, 98377, 98501–09, 98511–13, 98522, 98527, 98531–33, 98537–39, 98541–42, 98544, 98547, 98554, 98556–57, 98559, 98561, 98564–65, 98568, 98570, 98572, 98576–77, 98579, 98581–83, 98585–86, 98589–91, 98593, 98595–97, 98601–04, 98606–07, 98609–12, 98614, 98616, 98621–22, 98624–26, 98628–29, 98631–32, 98635, 98637–45, 98647–51, 98660–66, 98668, 98671–72, 98674–75, 98682–87

* * *

FOURTH DISTRICT

DOC HASTINGS, Republican, of Pasco, WA; born in Spokane, WA, on February 7, 1941; education: graduated, Pasco High School, 1959; attended Columbia Basin College and Central Washington State University, Ellensburg, WA; military service: U.S. Army Reserves, 1963–69; employment: president, Columbia Basin Paper and Supply; board of directors, Yakima Federal Savings and Loan; member: Washington State House of Representatives, 1979–87; Republican Caucus chairman, assistant majority leader, and National Platform Committee, 1984; president: Pasco Chamber of Commerce; Pasco Downtown Development Association; Pasco Jaycees (chamber president); committees: Budget; Rules; Standards of Official Conduct; subcommittees: Legislative and Budget Process; chairman, Franklin County Republican Central Committee, 1974–78; delegate, Republican National Convention, 1976–84; married: Claire Hastings, 1967; children: Kirsten, Petrina and Colin; elected to the 104th Congress; reelected to each succeeding Congress.

Office Listings

http://www.house.gov/hastings

1323 Longworth House Office Building, Washington, DC 20515 .... (202) 225–5816
Administrative Assistant.—Ed Cassidy. FAX: 225–3251
Scheduler / Office Manager.—Ilene Clauson.
Press Secretary.—Jessica Baker.
2715 St. Andrews Loop, Suite D, Pasco, WA 99302 .... (509) 543–9396
302 East Chestnut, Yakima, WA 98901 .... (509) 452–3243

Counties: ADAMS COUNTY (part). CITIES: Othello. BENTON COUNTY. CITIES AND TOWNSHIPS: Benton City, Kennewick, Paterson, Plymouth, Prosser, Richland, West Richland. CHELAN COUNTY. CITIES AND TOWNSHIPS: Ardenvoir, Cashmere, Chelan, Chelan Falls, Dryden, Entiat, Leavenworth, Malaga, Manson, Monitor, Peshastin, Stehekin, Wenatchee. DOUGLAS COUNTY. CITIES AND TOWNSHIPS: Bridgeport, Leahy, Mansfield, Orondo, Palisades, Rock Island, Waterville, Wenatchee. FRANKLIN COUNTY. CITIES AND TOWNSHIPS: Connell, Eltopia, Kahlotus, Mesa, Pasco, Windust. GRANT COUNTY. CITIES AND TOWNSHIPS: Beverly, Coulee City, Electric City, Ephrata, George, Grand Coulee, Hartline, Marlin, Mattawa, Moses Lake, Quincy, Royal City, Soap Lake, Stratford, Warden, Wilson Creek. KITTITAS COUNTY. CITIES AND TOWNSHIPS: Cle Elum, Easton, Ellensburg, Hyak, Kittitas, Ronald, Roslyn, South Cle Elum, Thorp, Vantage. KLICKITAT COUNTY. CITIES AND TOWNSHIPS: Alderdale, Appleton, Bickleton, Bingen, Centerville, Dallesport, Glenwood, Goldendale, Husum, Klickitat, Lyle, Roosevelt, Trout Lake, White Salmon, Wishram. SKAMANIA COUNTY (part), YAKIMA COUNTY. CITIES AND TOWNSHIPS: Brownstown, Buena, Cowiche, Grandview, Granger, Harrah, Mabton, Moxee, Naches, Outlook, Parker, Selah, Sunnyside, Tieton, Toppenish, Wapato, White Swan, Yakima, and Zillah. Population (2000), 654,901.

ZIP Codes: 98602, 98605, 98610, 98613, 98617, 98619–20, 98623, 98628, 98635, 98648, 98650–51, 98670, 98672–73, 98801–02, 98807, 98811–13, 98815–17, 98819, 98821–24, 98826, 98828–32, 98834, 98836–37, 98843, 98845, 98847–48, 98850–53, 98857–58, 98860, 98901–04, 98907–09, 98920–23, 98925–26, 98930, 98932–44, 98946–48, 98950–53, 99103, 99115–16, 99123–24, 99133, 99135, 99155, 99301–02, 99320–22, 99326, 99330, 99335–38, 99343–46, 99349–50, 99352–53, 99356–57

FIFTH DISTRICT

GEORGE R. NETHERCUTT, JR., Republican, of Spokane, WA; born in Spokane, on October 7, 1944; education: graduated from North Central High School; B.A., Washington State University, 1967; J.D., Gonzaga University School of Law, 1971; served as law clerk to Federal Judge Ralph Plummer, U.S. District Court, Anchorage, AK; served as staff counsel and chief of staff to U.S. Senator Ted Stevens (R–Alaska), 1972–77; private law practice; served as town attorney for eastern Washington communities of Reardan, Creston and Almira; cofounder, Vanessa Behan Crisis Nursery; past president, INLAND Northwest Chapter Juvenile Diabetes Foundation; past chairman, Spokane County Republican Party; member: Spokane Central Lions; Sigma Nu Fraternity; Spokane Masonic Lodge No. 34; Scottish rite; El Katif Shrine; Masonic Temple Foundation Trustees; Spokane School Levy Advisory Foundation; committees: Appropriations; Science; married: the former Mary Beth Socha of Summerville, SC; children: Meredith and Elliott; elected to the 104th Congress on November 8, 1994; reelected to each succeeding Congress.

Office Listings

http://www.house.gov/nethercutt

2443 Rayburn House Office Building, Washington, DC 20515 .... (202) 225–2005
Chief of Staff.—Amy Flachbart.
Legislative Director.—Paul Kavinoky.
Press Secretary.—April Gentry.
Scheduler/Office Manager.—Julie Blackorby.
920 West Riverside, Suite 594, Spokane, WA 99201 .... (509) 353–2374
29 South Palouse, Walla Walla, WA 99362 .... (509) 529–9358
555 South Main Street, Colville, WA 99114 .... (509) 684–3481

Counties: ADAMS (part), ASOTIN, COLUMBIA, FERRY, GARFIELD, LINCOLN, PEND OREILLE, OKANAGAN, SPOKANE, STEVENS, WALLA WALLA, WHITMAN. Population (2000), 654,901.

ZIP Codes: 98812, 98814, 98819, 98827, 98829, 98832–34, 98840–41, 98844, 98846, 98849, 98855–57, 98859, 98862, 99001, 99003–06, 99008–09, 99011–14, 99016–23, 99025–27, 99029–34, 99036–37, 99039–40, 99101–05, 99107, 99109–11, 99113–14, 99116–19, 99121–22, 99125–26, 99128–31, 99133–41, 99143–44, 99146–61, 99163–67, 99169–71, 99173–74, 99176, 99179–81, 99185, 99201–20, 99223–24, 99228, 99251–52, 99256, 99258, 99260, 99302, 99323–24, 99326, 99328–29, 99333, 99335, 99341, 99344, 99347–48, 99356, 99359–63, 99371, 99401–03

* * *

SIXTH DISTRICT

NORMAN D. DICKS, Democrat, of Bremerton, WA; born in Bremerton, December 16, 1940; education: graduated, West Bremerton High School, 1959; B.A., political science, University of Washington, 1963; J.D., University of Washington School of Law, 1968; admitted to Washington bar, 1968; joined the staff of Senator Warren G. Magnuson in 1968 as legislative assistant and appropriations assistant, named administrative assistant in 1973, and held that post until he resigned to campaign for Congress in February 1976; in Congress he received a first-term appointment to the House Appropriations Committee, where he currently still serves; appointed to the Select Committee on Homeland Security, 2003; subcommittees: Intelligence and Counterterrorism; Infrastructure and Border Security; Defense; ranking member, Interior and Related Agencies; Military Construction; member: Democratic Caucus; Washington, DC, and Washington State Bars; serves on the Board of Visitors of the U.S. Air Force Academy, and is a member of the Puget Sound Naval Bases Association, and the Navy League of the United States; married: the former Suzanne Callison, 1967; children: David and Ryan; elected to the 95th Congress; reelected to each succeeding Congress.

Office Listings

2467 Rayburn House Office Building, Washington, DC 20515 .... (202) 225–5916
Legislative Director.—Pete Modaff.
Press Secretary.—George Behan.
1717 Pacific Avenue, Suite 2244, Tacoma, WA 98402 .... (253) 593–6536
District Director.—Bryan McConaughy.
500 Pacific Avenue, Suite 301, Bremerton, WA 98310 .... (360) 479–4011
Deputy District Director.—Cheri Williams.
322 E. 5th Street, Port Angeles, WA 98362 .... (360) 452–3370
District Representative.—Mary Schuneman.

Counties: CLALLAM COUNTY. CITIES AND TOWNSHIPS: Forks, Port Angeles, La Push, Sequim, Sekiu, Neah Bay. GRAYS HARBOR COUNTY. CITIES AND TOWNSHIPS: Aberdeen, Hoquiam, Montesano, Ocean City, Ocean Shores, Moclips, Westport. JEFFERSON COUNTY. CITIES AND TOWNSHIPS: Port Townsend, Quilcene. KITSAP COUNTY (part). CITIES AND TOWNSHIPS: Bremerton (part), Port Orchard, Gorst. MASON COUNTY. CITIES AND TOWNSHIPS: Shelton, Belfair, Allyn, Union. PIERCE COUNTY (part). CITIES AND TOWNSHIPS: Tacoma (part), Gig Harbor, Lakebay, and Lakewood. Population (2000), 654,902.

ZIP Codes: 98305, 98310–12, 98314, 98320, 98322, 98324–26, 98329, 98331–33, 98335, 98337, 98339, 98343, 98349–51, 98353, 98357–59, 98362–63, 98365–68, 98373, 98376, 98378, 98380–82, 98384, 98386, 98394–95, 98401–09, 98411–13, 98415–16, 98418, 98442, 98444–45, 98464–67, 98471, 98477, 98481, 98492, 98497–99, 98502, 98520, 98524, 98526, 98528, 98535–37, 98541, 98546–48, 98550, 98552, 98555, 98557, 98560, 98562–63, 98566, 98568–69, 98571, 98575, 98584, 98587–88, 98592, 98595

* * *

SEVENTH DISTRICT

JIM McDERMOTT, Democrat, of Seattle, WA; born in Chicago, IL, on December 28, 1936; education: B.S., Wheaton College, Wheaton, IL, 1958; M.D., University of Illinois Medical School, Chicago, 1963; residency in adult psychiatry, University of Illinois Hospitals, 1964–66; residency in child psychiatry, University of Washington Hospitals, Seattle, 1966–68; served, U.S. Navy Medical Corps, lieutenant commander, 1968–70; psychiatrist; Washington State House of Representatives, 1971–72; Washington State Senate, 1975–87; Democratic nominee for governor, 1980; regional medical officer, Sub-Saharan Africa, U.S. Foreign Service, 1987–88; practicing psychiatrist and assistant clinical professor of psychiatry, University of Washington, Seattle, 1970–83; member: Washington State Medical Association; King County Medical Society; American Psychiatric Association; religion: St. Mark's Episcopal Church, Seattle; children: Katherine and James; committees: Ways and Means; subcommittees: Health; Human Resources; elected on November 8, 1988, to the 101st Congress; reelected to each succeeding Congress.

Office Listings

1035 Longworth House Office Building, Washington, DC 20515 .... (202) 225–3106
Administrative Assistant.—Jan Shinpoch.
Executive Assistant.—Beverly Swain.
1809 Seventh Avenue, Suite 1212, Seattle, WA 98101–1313 .... (206) 553–7170
District Administrator.—Jane Sanders.

Counties: KING COUNTY (part). CITIES AND TOWNSHIPS: Vashon, Burton, Dockton, and Seattle (part). Population (2000), 654,902.

ZIP Codes: 98013, 98055, 98070, 98101–09, 98111–19, 98121–22, 98124–27, 98129, 98131, 98133–34, 98136, 98139, 98141, 98144–46, 98151, 98154–55, 98161, 98164–66, 98168, 98171, 98174–75, 98177–78, 98181, 98184–85, 98190–91, 98194–95, 98199

* * *

EIGHTH DISTRICT

JENNIFER DUNN, Republican, of Bellevue, WA; born on July 29, 1941 in Seattle, WA; B.A., Stanford University, 1963; chairman, Washington State Republican Party, 1981–92; member, Republican National Committee: vice chairman, Western Region; U.S. delegate to the 30th United Nations Commission on the Status of Women, 1984, 1990; member, Preparatory Commission for the 1985 World Conference on the Status of Women; presidential appointee: President's Advisory Council on Voluntary Services; President's Advisory Council on Historic Preservation; Executive Committee of the Small Business Administration Advisory Council; received Shavano Summit Award for Excellence in National Leadership, Hillsdale College, 1984; member: Seattle Junior League; Board of Epiphany School; Advisory Board for KUOW–FM (National Public Radio); Metropolitan Opera National Council; Henry M. Jackson Foundation; International Women's Forum; and International Republican Institute; committees: Ways and Means; Select Committee on Homeland Security; served on House elected leadership team in 1997–98; two children: Bryant and Reagan; elected to the 103rd Congress; reelected to each succeeding Congress.

Office Listings

http://www.house.gov/dunn

1501 Longworth House Office Building, Washington, DC 20515 .... (202) 225–7761
Chief of Staff.—Doug Badger. FAX: 225–8673
Office Manager / Scheduler.—Kate Fernstrom.
Legislative Director.—Vergil Cabasco.
Communications Director.—Jen Burita.
2737 78th Avenue, SE, Suite 202, Mercer Island, WA 98040 .... (206) 275–3438
District Contact.—Travis Sines.

Counties: KING COUNTY (part). CITIES AND TOWNSHIPS: Auburn, Baring, Beaux Arts Village, Bellevue, Black Diamond, Carnation, Duvall, Enumclaw, Fall City, Issaquah, Kent, Mercer Island, Maple Valley, New Castle, North Bend, Preston, Redmond (part), Renton (part), Skykomish, Snoqualmie, Summit, Woodinville. PIERCE COUNTY. CITIES AND TOWNSHIPS: Ashford, Bonney Lake, Buckley, Carbonado, Eatonville, Elbe, Graham, Orting, Roy, South Prairie, Spanaway, and Wilkeson. Population (2000), 654,905.

ZIP Codes: 98002, 98004–10, 98014–15, 98019, 98022, 98024–25, 98027, 98029–31, 98033, 98035, 98038–40, 98042, 98045, 98050–53, 98055–56, 98058–59, 98064–65, 98068, 98074–75, 98077, 98092, 98304, 98321, 98323, 98328, 98330, 98338, 98344, 98348, 98352, 98360, 98372–75, 98385, 98387, 98390, 98396–98, 98446

* * *

NINTH DISTRICT

ADAM SMITH, Democrat, of Tacoma, WA; born on June 15, 1965, in Washington, DC; graduated from Tyee High School, 1983; graduated from Fordham University, NY, 1987; law degree, University of Washington, 1990; admitted to the Washington bar in 1991; prosecutor for the city of Seattle; Washington State Senate, 1990–96; member, Kent Drinking Driver Task Force; board member, Judson Park Retirement Home; married Sara Smith, 1993; committees: Armed Services; International Relations; elected to the 105th Congress; reelected to each succeeding Congress.

Office Listings

227 Cannon House Office Building, Washington, DC 20515 .... (202) 225–8901
Chief of Staff.—Ali Wade. FAX: 225–5893
Office Manager.—Kate Gibbons.
Communications Director.—Katharine Lister.
1717 Pacific Avenue, #2135, Tacoma, WA 98402 .... (253) 593–6600
District Director.—Linda Danforth.

Counties: KING (part), PIERCE (part), THURSTON (part). CITIES: Federal Way, Kent, Olympia (part), Puyallup, Renton, Seattle (part), and Tacoma. Population (2000), 654,902.

ZIP Codes: 98001–03, 98023, 98030–32, 98047, 98054–58, 98062–63, 98071, 98089, 98092–93, 98131–32, 98136, 98138, 98146, 98148, 98158, 98166, 98168, 98171, 98178, 98188, 98198, 98303, 98327–28, 98338, 98354, 98371–75, 98387–88, 98390, 98402, 98404, 98409, 98421–22, 98424, 98430–31, 98433, 98438–39, 98443–47, 98466–67, 98493, 98498–99, 98501, 98503, 98506, 98509, 98513, 98516, 98558, 98576, 98580, 98597

WEST VIRGINIA

(Population 2000, 1,808,344)

SENATORS

ROBERT C. BYRD, Democrat, of Sophia, WV; born November 20, 1917; Baptist; married Erma Ora James; two daughters: Mrs. Mohammad (Mona Byrd) Fatemi and Mrs. Jon (Marjorie Byrd) Moore; six grandchildren: Erik, Darius and Fredrik Fatemi, and Michael (deceased), Mona and Mary Anne Moore; and three great-grandchildren; committees: ranking member, Appropriations; Armed Services; Budget; Rules and Administration; sworn in to the U.S. Senate on January 3, 1959; reelected to each succeeding Senate term.

Office Listings

http://byrd.senate.gov

311 Hart Senate Office Building, Washington, DC 20510 .... (202) 224–3954
Chief of Staff.—Barbara Videnieks.
Administrative Assistant.—Ann Adler.
Press Secretary.—Tom Gavin.
300 Virginia Street East, Suite 2630, Charleston, WV 25301 .... (304) 342–5855
State Director.—Anne Barth.

* * *

JOHN D. ROCKEFELLER IV, Democrat, of Charleston, WV; born in New York City, NY, June 18, 1937; education: graduated, Phillips Exeter Academy, Exeter, NH, 1954; A.B., Harvard University, Cambridge, MA, 1961; honorary degrees: J.D., West Virginia University; Marshall University; Davis and Elkins College; Dickinson College; University of Alabama; University of Cincinnati; doctor of humanities, West Virginia Institute of Technology; doctor of public service, Salem College; Vista volunteer, Emmons, WV, 1964; West Virginia House of Delegates, 1966–68; elected Secretary of State of West Virginia, 1968; president, West Virginia Wesleyan College, 1973–76; Governor of West Virginia, 1976–84; married: the former Sharon Percy; children: John, Valerie, Charles and Justin; committees: Commerce, Science, and Transportation; Finance; Veterans' Affairs; Foreign Relations; Intelligence; Joint Committee on Taxation; elected to the U.S. Senate on November 6, 1984; reelected to each succeeding Senate term.

Office Listings

http://rockefeller.senate.gov

531 Hart Senate Office Building, Washington, DC 20510 .... (202) 224–6472
Chief of Staff.—Kerry Ates. FAX: 224–7665
Legislative Director.—Ellen Doneski.
Communications Director.—Wendy Morigi.
405 Capitol Street, Suite 308, Charleston, WV 25301 .... (304) 347–5372
207 Prince Street, Beckley, WV 25801 .... (304) 253–9704
118 Adams Street, Suite 301, Fairmont, WV 26554 .... (304) 367–0122
225 W. King Street, Suite 307, Martinsburg, WV 25401 .... (304) 262–9285

REPRESENTATIVES

FIRST DISTRICT

ALAN B. MOLLOHAN, Democrat, of Fairmont, WV; born in Fairmont on May 14, 1943; son of former Congressman Robert H. Mollohan and Helen Holt Mollohan; education: graduated, Greenbrier Military School, Lewisburg, WV, 1962; A.B., College of William and Mary, Williamsburg, VA, 1966; J.D., West Virginia University College of Law, Morgantown, 1970; captain, U.S. Army Reserves, 1970–83; admitted to the West Virginia bar in 1970 and commenced practice in Fairmont; admitted to the District of Columbia bar in 1975; member, First Baptist Church, Fairmont; married: the former Barbara Whiting, 1976; children: Alan, Robert, Andrew, Karl and Mary Kathryn; elected on November 2, 1982, to the 98th Congress; reelected to each succeeding Congress.

Office Listings

2302 Rayburn House Office Building, Washington, DC 20515 .... (202) 225–4172
Chief of Staff.—Colleen McCarty.
Scheduler.—Ann Marie Packo.
Legislative Director.—Gavin Clingham.
Press Secretary.—Ron Hudok.
209 Post Office Building, P.O. Box 1400, Clarksburg, WV 26302–1400 .... (304) 623–4422
Federal Building, Room 232, P.O. Box 720, Morgantown, WV 26507–0720 .... (304) 292–3019
Federal Building, Room 2040, 425 Juliana Street, Parkersburg, WV 26101–0145 ... (304) 428–0493
Federal Building, Room 316, 1125 Chapline Street, Wheeling, WV 26003–2900 .... (304) 232–5390

Counties: BARBOUR, BROOKE, DODDRIDGE, GILMER, GRANT, HANCOCK, HARRISON, MARION, MARSHALL, MINERAL, MONONGALIA, OHIO, PLEASANTS, PRESTON, RITCHIE, TAYLOR, TUCKER, TYLER, WETZEL, WOOD. CITIES AND TOWNSHIPS: Albright, Alma, Alvy, Anmoore, Arthur, Arthurdate, Auburn, Aurora, Baldwin, Barrackville, Baxter, Bayard, Beech Bottom, Belington, Belleville, Belleville, Bellview, Belmont, Bens Run, Benwood, Berea, Bethany, Big Run, Blacksville, Blandville, Booth, Brandonville, Bretz, Bridgeport, Bristol, Brownton, Bruceton Mills, Burlington, Burnt House, Burton, Cabins, Cairo, Cameron, Carolina, Cassville, Cedarville, Center Point, Central Station, Century, Chester, Clarksburg, Coburn, Colfax, Colliers, Core, Corinth, Cove, Coxs Mills, Cuzzart, Dallas, Davis, Davisville, Dawmont, Dellslow, Dorcas, Eglon, Elk Garden, Ellenboro, Elm Grove, Enterprise, Eureka, Everettville, Fairmont, Fairview, Farmington, Flemington, Flower, Follansbee, Folsom, Fort Ashby, Fort Neal, Four states, Friendly, Galloway, Gilmer, Glen Dale, Glen Easton, Glenville, Goffs, Gormania, Grafton, Grant Town, Granville, Greenwood, Gypsy, Hambleton, Harrisville, Hastings, Haywood, Hazelton, Hebron, Hendricks, Hepzibah, Highland, Hundred, Idamay, Independence, Industrial, Jacksonburg, Jere, Jordan, Junior, Keyser, Kingmont, Kingwood, Knob Fork, Lahmansville, Letter Gap, Lima, Linn, Littleton, Lockney, Lost Creek, Lumberport, MacFarlan, Mahone, Maidsville, Mannington, Masontown, Maysville, McMechen, McWhorter, Meadowbrook, Medley, Metz, Middlebourne, Mineralwells, Moatsville, Monongah, Montana Mines, Morgantown, Moundsville, Mount Clare, Mount Storm, Mountain, New Creek, New Cumberland, New England, New Manchester, New Martinsville, New Milton, Newberne, Newburg, Newell, Normantown, North Parkersburg, Nutter Fort, Osage, Owings, Paden City, Parkersburg, Parsons, Pennsboro, Pentress, Perkins, Petersburg, Petroleum, Philippi, Piedmont, Pine Grove, Porters Falls, Proctor, Pullman, Pursglove, Rachel, Reader, Red Creek, Reedsville, Reynoldsville, Riegeley, Rivesville, Rocket Center, Rockport, Rosedale, Rosemont, Rowlesburg, Saint George, Saint Marys, Salem, Sand Fork, Shinnston, Shirley, Shocks, Short Creek, Simpson, Sistersville, Smithburg, Smithfield, Smithville, Spelter, Stonewood, Stouts Mill, Stumptown, Tanner, Terra Alta, Thomas, Thornton, Toll Gate, Troy, Triadelphia, Tunnelton, Valley Grove, Vienna, Volga, Wadestown, Walker, Wallace, Wana, Warwood, Washington, Watson, Waverly Weirton, Wellsburg, Wendel, West Liberty, West Milford, West Union, Westover, Wheeling Wick, Wilbur, Wiley Ford, Wileyville, Williamstown, Wilson, Wilsonburg, Windsor Heights, Wolf Summit, Worthington, and Wyatt. Population (2000), 602,543.

ZIP Codes: 25258, 25267, 26003, 26030–41, 26047, 26050, 26055–56, 26058–60, 26062, 26070, 26074–75, 26101–06, 26120–21, 26133–34, 26142–43, 26146–50, 26155, 26159, 26161–62, 26164, 26167, 26169–70, 26175, 26178, 26180–81, 26184, 26186–87, 26201, 26238, 26250, 26254, 26260, 26263, 26269, 26271, 26275–76, 26283, 26287, 26289, 26292, 26301–02, 26306, 26320–21, 26323, 26325, 26327, 26330, 26332, 26334–35, 26337, 26339, 26342, 26346–49, 26351, 26354, 26361–62, 26366, 26369, 26374, 26377–78, 26384–86, 26404–05, 26408, 26410–12, 26415–16, 26419, 26421–22, 26424–26, 26430–31, 26434–38, 26440, 26443–44, 26448, 26451, 26456, 26463, 26501–02, 26504–08, 26519–21, 26524–25, 26527, 26529, 26531, 26534, 26537, 26541–44, 26546–47, 26554–55, 26559–63, 26566, 26568, 26570–72, 26574–76, 26578, 26581–82, 26585–88, 26590–91, 26611, 26623, 26636, 26638, 26705, 26710, 26716–17, 26719–20, 26726, 26731, 26734, 26739, 26743, 26750, 26753, 26764, 26767, 26833, 26847, 26852, 26855

* * *

SECOND DISTRICT

SHELLEY MOORE CAPITO, Republican, of Charleston, WV; born on November 26, 1953, in Glen Dale, WV; education: B.S., Duke University; M.Ed., University of Virginia; profession: career counselor; employment: West Virginia State College; West Virginia Board of Regents; organizations: Community Council of Kanawha Valley; YWCA; West Virginia Interagency Council for Early Intervention; Habitat for Humanity; public service: elected to the West Virginia House of Delegates, 1996; reelected in 1998; awards: Coalition for a Tobacco-Free West Virginia Legislator of the Year; co-chair, Women's Caucus; religion: Presbyterian; family: married to Charles L. Capito, Jr.; three children; elected to the 107th Congress on November 7, 2000; reelected to each succeeding Congress.

Office Listings
http://www.house.gov/capito

1431 Longworth House Office Building, Washington, DC 20515 .... (202) 225–2711
Chief of Staff.—Mark Johnson.
Office Manager.—Alison Bibbee.
Legislative Director.—Robert Steptoe.
4815 MacCorkle Avenue, Southeast, Charleston, WV 25304 .... (304) 925–5964
300 Foxcroft Avenue, Suite 102, Martinsburg, WV 25401 .... (304) 264–8810

Counties: BERKELEY, BRAXTON, CALHOUN, CLAY, HAMPSHIRE, HARDY, JACKSON, JEFFERSON, KANAWHA, LEWIS, MASON, MORGAN, PENDLETON, PUTNAM, RANDOLPH, ROANE, UPSHUR, WIRT. Population (2000), 602,245.

ZIP Codes: 25002–03, 25005, 25011, 25015, 25019, 25025–26, 25030, 25033, 25035, 25039, 25043, 25045–46, 25054, 25059, 25061, 25063–64, 25067, 25070–71, 25075, 25079, 25081–83, 25085–86, 25088, 25102–03, 25106–07, 25109–13, 25123–26, 25132–34, 25136, 25139, 25141, 25143, 25147, 25150, 25156, 25159–60, 25162, 25164, 25168, 25177,

25187, 25201–02, 25211, 25213–14, 25231, 25234–35, 25239, 25241, 25243–45, 25247–48, 25251–53, 25259–62, 25264–68, 25270–71, 25275–76, 25279, 25281, 25285–87, 25301–06, 25309, 25311–15, 25317, 25320–39, 25350, 25356–58, 25360–62, 25364–65, 25375, 25392, 25396, 25401–02, 25410–11, 25413–14, 25419–23, 25425, 25427–32, 25434, 25437–38, 25440–44, 25446, 25502–03, 25510, 25515, 25520, 25523, 25526, 25541, 25550, 25560, 25569, 26133, 26136–38, 26141, 26143, 26147, 26151–52, 26160–61, 26164, 26173, 26180, 26201–02, 26205, 26210, 26215, 26218, 26224, 26228–30, 26234, 26236–38, 26241, 26253–54, 26257, 26259, 26261, 26263, 26267–68, 26270, 26273, 26276, 26278, 26280, 26282–83, 26285, 26293–94, 26296, 26321, 26335, 26338, 26342–43, 26351, 26372, 26376, 26378, 26384–85, 26412, 26430, 26443, 26447, 26452, 26546, 26590, 26601, 26610–11, 26615, 26617, 26619, 26621, 26623–24, 26627, 26629, 26631, 26636, 26638–39, 26641, 26651, 26656, 26660, 26662, 26667, 26671, 26675–76, 26678–79, 26681, 26684, 26690–91, 26704–05, 26707, 26710–11, 26714, 26717, 26722, 26731, 26739, 26743, 26750, 26755, 26757, 26761, 26763–64, 26801–02, 26804, 26807–08, 26810, 26812, 26814–15, 26817–18, 26823–24, 26836, 26838, 26845, 26847, 26851–52, 26865–66, 26884, 26886

* * *

THIRD DISTRICT

NICK J. RAHALL II, Democrat, of Beckley, WV; born in Beckley, May 20, 1949; graduated, Woodrow Wilson High School, Beckley, 1967; A.B., Duke University, Durham, NC, 1971; graduate work, George Washington University, Washington, DC; colonel in U.S. Air Force Civil Air Patrol; president of the West Virginia Society of Washington, DC; business executive; sales representative, WWNR radio station; president, Mountaineer Tour and Travel Agency, 1974; president, West Virginia Broadcasting; named: Coal Man of the Year, *Coal Industry News,* 1979; ''Young Democrat of the Year'', Young Democrats, 1980; 1984 West Virginia American Legion Distinguished Service Award recipient; delegate, Democratic national conventions, 1972, 1976, 1980, 1984; member: Rotary; Elks; Moose; Eagles; NAACP; National Rifle Association; AF & AM; RAM; Mount Hope Commandery; Shrine Club; Benie Kedeem Temple in Charleston; Beckley Presbyterian Church; chairman and founder, Congressional Coal Group; Democratic Leadership Council; Congressional Arts Caucus; Congressional Black Caucus; Congressional Fitness Caucus; International Workers' Rights Caucus; ITS Caucus; Qatar Caucus; Congressional Rural Caucus; Congressional Steel Caucus; Congressional Textile Caucus; Congressional Travel and Tourism Caucus; Congressional Truck Caucus; Wine Caucus; Automobile Task Force; Democratic Congressional Campaign Committee; Democratic Study Group; Energy and Environment Study Conference; three children: Rebecca Ashley, Nick Joe III, and Suzanne Nicole; committees: ranking member, Resources; Transportation and Infrastructure; elected to the 95th Congress on November 2, 1976; reelected to each succeeding Congress.

Office Listings

nrahall@mail.house.gov http://www.house.gov/rahall

2307 Rayburn House Office Building, Washington, DC 20515 .... (202) 225–3452
Administrative Assistant.—Kent Keyser. FAX: 225–9061
Chief Counsel.—Jim Zoia.
Legislative Assistants: Christine Gleichert, Thomas Lynch.
Press Secretary.—Kent Keyser.
815 Fifth Avenue, Huntington, WV 25701 .... (304) 522–6425
106 Main Street, Beckley, WV 25801 .... (304) 252–5000
220 Dingess Street, Logan, WV 25601 .... (304) 752–4934
1005 Federal Building, Bluefield, WV 24701 .... (304) 325–6222

Counties: BOONE, CABELL, FAYETTE, GREENBRIER, LINCOLN, LOGAN, MCDOWELL, MERCER, MINGO, MONROE, NICHOLAS, POCAHONTAS, RALEIGH, SUMMERS, WAYNE, WEBSTER, WYOMING. Population (2000), 603,556.

ZIP Codes: 24701, 24712, 24714–16, 24719, 24724, 24726, 24729, 24731–33, 24736–40, 24747, 24751, 24801, 24808, 24811, 24813, 24815–18, 24820–31, 24834, 24836, 24839, 24842–57, 24859–62, 24866–74, 24878–82, 24884, 24887–88, 24892, 24894–99, 24901–02, 24910, 24915–18, 24920, 24924–25, 24927, 24931, 24934–36, 24938, 24941, 24943–46, 24950–51, 24954, 24957, 24961–63, 24966, 24970, 24974, 24976–77, 24981, 24983–86, 24991, 24993, 25002–04, 25007–10, 25021–22, 25024, 25028, 25031, 25036, 25040, 25043–44, 25047–49, 25051, 25053, 25057, 25059–60, 25062, 25076, 25081, 25083, 25085, 25090, 25093, 25108, 25114–15, 25118–19, 25121, 25130, 25136, 25139–40, 25142, 25148–49, 25152, 25154, 25161, 25165, 25169, 25173–74, 25180–81, 25183, 25185–86, 25193, 25202–06, 25208–09, 25213, 25501, 25504–08, 25510–12, 25514, 25517, 25520–21, 25523–24, 25526, 25529–30, 25534–35, 25537, 25540–41, 25544–45, 25547, 25555, 25557, 25559, 25562, 25564–65, 25567, 25570–73, 25601, 25606–08, 25611–12, 25614, 25617, 25621, 25624–25, 25628, 25630, 25632, 25634–39, 25644, 25646–47, 25649–54, 25661, 25665–67, 25669–72, 25674, 25676, 25678, 25682, 25685–88, 25690–92, 25694, 25696, 25699, 25701–29, 25755, 25770–79, 25801–02, 25810–13, 25816–18, 25820, 25823, 25825–27, 25831–33, 25836–37, 25839–41, 25843–49, 25851, 25853–57, 25859–60, 25862, 25864–66, 25868, 25870–71, 25873, 25875–76, 25878–80, 25882, 25901–02, 25904, 25906–09, 25911, 25913–22, 25927–28, 25931–32, 25934, 25936, 25938, 25942–43, 25951, 25958, 25961–62, 25965–67, 25969, 25971–72, 25976–79, 25981, 25984–86, 25989, 26202–03, 26205–06, 26208–09, 26217, 26222, 26230, 26234, 26261, 26264, 26266, 26288, 26291, 26294, 26298, 26610, 26617, 26639, 26651, 26656, 26660, 26662, 26674, 26676, 26678–81, 26684, 26690–91

WISCONSIN

(Population 2000, 5,363,675)

SENATORS

HERB KOHL, Democrat, of Milwaukee, WI; born in Milwaukee on February 7, 1935; graduated, Washington High School, Milwaukee, 1952; B.A., University of Wisconsin, Madison, 1956; M.B.A., Harvard Graduate School of Business Administration, Cambridge, MA, 1958; LL.D., Cardinal Stritch College, Milwaukee, WI, 1986 (honorary); served, U.S. Army Reserves, 1958–64; businessman; president, Herbert Kohl Investments; owner, Milwaukee Bucks NBA basketball team; past chairman, Milwaukee's United Way Campaign; State Chairman, Democratic Party of Wisconsin, 1975–77; honors and awards: Pen and Mike Club Wisconsin Sports Personality of the Year, 1985; Wisconsin Broadcasters Association Joe Killeen Memorial Sportsman of the Year, 1985; Greater Milwaukee Convention and Visitors Bureau Lamplighter Award, 1986; Wisconsin Parkinson's Association Humanitarian of the Year, 1986; Kiwanis Milwaukee Award, 1987; committees: Appropriations; Judiciary; Special Committee on Aging; elected to the U.S. Senate on November 8, 1988; reelected to each succeeding Senate term.

Office Listings

http://kohl.senate.gov senator_kohl@kohl.senate.gov

330 Hart Senate Office Building, Washington, DC 20510 .... (202) 224–5653
Chief of Staff.—Paul Bock.
Legislative Director.—Kate Sparks.
Communications Director.—Lynn Becker.
Executive Assistant.—Arlene Branca.
310 W. Wisconsin Avenue, Suite 950, Milwaukee, WI 53203 .... (414) 297–4451
14 West Muffin Street, Suite 207, Madison, WI 53703 .... (608) 264–5338
402 Graham Avenue, Suite 206, Eau Claire, WI 54701 .... (715) 832–8424
4321 West College Avenue, Suite 235, Appleton, WI 54914 .... (920) 738–1640
425 State Street, Suite 202, LaCrosse, WI 54601 .... (608) 796–0045

* * *

RUSSELL FEINGOLD, Democrat, of Middleton, WI; born on March 2, 1953, in Janesville, WI; graduated from Craig High School, Janesville, WI, 1971; B.A., University of Wisconsin-Madison, 1975; Rhodes Scholar, Oxford University, 1977; J.D., Harvard Law School, 1979; practicing attorney with Foley and Lardner, and with LaFollette and Sinykin, both in Madison, WI, 1979–85; Wisconsin State Senate, January 1983 to January 1993; married to Mary Feingold; four children: daughters Jessica and Ellen, and stepsons Sam Speerschneider and Ted Speerschneider; committees: Budget; Foreign Relations; Judiciary; Special Committee on Aging; elected to the U.S. Senate on November 3, 1992; reelected to each succeeding Senate term.

Office Listings

http://feingold.senate.gov

506 Hart Senate Office Building, Washington, DC 20510 .... (202) 224–5323
Administrative Assistant.—Mary Irvine.
Legislative Director.—Bill Dauster.
Press Secretary.—Ari Geller.
517 East Wisconsin Avenue, Milwaukee, WI 53202 .... (414) 276–7282
1600 Aspen Commons, Room 100, Middleton, WI 53562 .... (608) 828–1200
State Coordinator.—Janet Piraino.
401 Fifth Street, Room 410, Wausau, WI 54401 .... (715) 848–5660
425 State Street, Room 225, LaCrosse, WI 54603 .... (608) 782–5585
1640 Main Street, Green Bay, WI 54302 .... (920) 465–7508

REPRESENTATIVES

FIRST DISTRICT

PAUL RYAN, Republican, of Janesville, WI; born in Janesville, WI, on January 29, 1970; education: Joseph A. Craig High School; economic and political science degrees, Miami University in Ohio; employment: marketing consultant, Ryan Inc., Central (construction firm); aide to former U.S. Senator Bob Kasten (R–WI); advisor to former Vice Presidential candidate Jack

Kemp, and U.S. Drug Czar Bill Bennett; also served as a legislative director in the U.S. Senate; organizations: Janesville Bowmen, Inc.; Ducks Unlimited; committees: Ways and Means; Joint Economic; elected to the 106th Congress; reelected to each succeeding Congress.

Office Listings

http://www.house.gov/ryan

1217 Longworth House Office Building, Washington, DC 20515 .... (202) 225–3031
Administrative Assistant.—Joyce Meyer. FAX: 225–3393
Legislative Director.—Leah Uhlmann.
Scheduler.—Nichole Robison.
20 South Main Street, Suite 10, Janesville, WI 53545 .... (608) 752–4050
5712 7th Avenue, Kenosha, WI 53140 .... (262) 654–1901
304 6th Street, Racine, WI 53403 .... (262) 637–0510

Counties: KENOSHA, MILWAUKEE (part), RACINE, ROCK (part), WALWORTH (part), WAUKESHA (part). Population (2000), 670,458.

ZIP Codes: 53101–05, 53108–09, 53114–15, 53119–21, 53125–26, 53128–30, 53132, 53138–44, 53146–54, 53156–59, 53167–68, 53170–72, 53176–77, 53179, 53181–82, 53184–85, 53189–92, 53194–95, 53207, 53219–21, 53228, 53401–08, 53501, 53505, 53511, 53525, 53534, 53538, 53545–48, 53563, 53585

* * *

SECOND DISTRICT

TAMMY BALDWIN, Democrat, of Madison, WI; born on February 11, 1962, in Madison, WI; education: graduated from Madison West High School, 1980; A.B., mathematics and government, Smith College, 1984; J.D., University of Wisconsin Law School, 1989; employment: attorney, 1989–92; elected to the Dane County Board of Supervisors, 1986–94; elected to the State Assembly from the 78th district, 1993–99; committees: Budget; Judiciary; elected to the 106th Congress; reelected to each succeeding Congress.

Office Listings

http://tammybaldwin.house.gov

1022 Longworth House Office Building, Washington, DC 20515 .... (202) 225–2906
Chief of Staff.—Bill Murat. FAX: 225–6942
Legislative Director.—Kris Pratt.
Appointment Secretary.—Maureen Hekmat.
Press Secretary.—Jonathan Beeton.
10 East Doty Street, Suite 405, Madison, WI 53703 .... (608) 258–9800
District Director.—Mark Webster.
400 East Grand Avenue, Suite 402, Beloit, WI 53511 .... (608) 362–2800

Counties: COLUMBIA, DANE, GREEN, JEFFERSON (part), ROCK (part), SAUK (part), WALWORTH (part). Population (2000), 670,457.

ZIP Codes: 53038, 53094, 53098, 53190, 53501–02, 53504, 53508, 53511–12, 53515–17, 53520–23, 53527–29, 53531–32, 53534, 53536–38, 53542, 53544–46, 53548–51, 53555, 53558–63, 53566, 53570–72, 53574–76, 53578, 53581–83, 53589–91, 53593–94, 53596–98, 53701–08, 53711, 53713–19, 53725–26, 53744, 53777–79, 53782–94, 53901, 53911, 53913, 53916, 53923, 53925–26, 53928, 53932–33, 53935, 53951, 53954–57, 53959–60, 53965, 53968–69

* * *

THIRD DISTRICT

RON KIND, Democrat, of La Crosse, WI; born in La Crosse, March 16, 1963; education: B.A., Harvard University, 1985; M.A., London School of Economics, 1986; J.D., University of Minnesota Law School, 1990; admitted to the Wisconsin bar, 1990; state prosecutor, La Crosse County District Attorney's Office; board of directors, La Crosse Boys and Girls Club; Coulee Council on Alcohol and Drug Abuse; Wisconsin Harvard Club; Wisconsin Bar Association; La Crosse County Bar Association; married: Tawni Zappa in 1994; one son, Jonathan; committees: Budget; Education and the Workforce; Resources; elected to the 105th Congress; reelected to each succeeding Congress.

Office Listings

1406 Longworth House Office Building, Washington, DC 20515 .... (202) 225–5506
Chief of Staff / Legislative Director.—Cindy Brown. FAX: 225–5739
Press Secretary.—Scot Ross.
Executive Assistant.—Erik Olson.
Senior Policy Advisor.—Darin Schroeder.
205 5th Avenue South, Suite 227, La Crosse, WI 54601 .... (608) 782–2558
District Director.—Loren Kannenberg.
131 S. Barstow Street, Suite 301, Eau Claire, WI 54701 .... (715) 831–9214
Staff Assistant / Case Worker.—Mark Aumann.

Counties: BUFFALO, CLARK (part), CRAWFORD, DUNN, EAU CLAIRE, GRANT, IOWA, JACKSON, JUNEAU, LA CROSSE, LAFAYETTE, MONROE, PEPIN, PIERCE, RICHLAND, SAUK (part), ST. CROIX, TREMPEALEAU, VERNON. Population (2000), 670,462.

ZIP Codes: 53503–04, 53506–07, 53510, 53516–18, 53522, 53526, 53530, 53533, 53535, 53540–41, 53543–44, 53553–54, 53556, 53560, 53565, 53569, 53573, 53577–78, 53580–84, 53586–88, 53595, 53599, 53801–13, 53816–18, 53820–21, 53824–27, 53913, 53924, 53929, 53937, 53940–44, 53948, 53950–51, 53958–59, 53961–62, 53965, 53968, 54001–05, 54007, 54009–11, 54013–17, 54020–28, 54082, 54420, 54436–37, 54446, 54449, 54456–57, 54460, 54466, 54479, 54488, 54493, 54601–03, 54610–12, 54614–16, 54618–32, 54634–46, 54648–62, 54664–67, 54669–70, 54701–03, 54720–30, 54733–43, 54746–47, 54749–51, 54754–65, 54767–73

* * *

FOURTH DISTRICT

GERALD D. KLECZKA, Democrat, of Milwaukee, WI; born in Milwaukee, November 26, 1943; education: graduated Don Bosco High School, Milwaukee, 1961; attended University of Wisconsin, Milwaukee; served in the Wisconsin Air National Guard, 1963–69; served in Wisconsin Assembly, 1969–74; Wisconsin Senate, 1975–84; member: LaFarge Lifelong Learning Institute; Thomas More Foundation; Polish National Alliance-Milwaukee Society; Polish American Congress; South Side Democratic Party Unit; State and Milwaukee County Democratic Party; married: the former Bonnie L. Scott, 1978; elected to the 98th Congress, by special election, April 3, 1984; reelected to each succeeding Congress.

Office Listings

http://www.house.gov/kleczka

2217 Rayburn House Office Building, Washington, DC 20515 .... (202) 225–4572
Administrative Assistant.—Win Boerckel.
Press Secretary.—[Vacant].
5032 West Forest Home Avenue, Milwaukee, WI 53219 .... (414) 297–1140
Chief of Staff.—Kathryn Hein.
4900 West Burleigh Street, Milwaukee, WI 53210 .... (414) 297–1331

Counties: MILWAUKEE (part). CITIES AND TOWNSHIPS: Milwaukee (part), Cudahy, South Milwaukee, St. Francis, West Allis (part), and West Milwaukee. Population (2000), 670,458.

ZIP Codes: 53110, 53154, 53172, 53201–28, 53233–35, 53237, 53268, 53270, 53277–78, 53280–81, 53284–85, 53288, 53290, 53293, 53295

* * *

FIFTH DISTRICT

F. JAMES SENSENBRENNER, JR., Republican, of Menomonee Falls, WI; born in Chicago, IL, June 14, 1943; education: graduated from Milwaukee Country Day School, 1961; A.B., Stanford University, 1965; J.D., University of Wisconsin Law School, 1968; admitted to the Wisconsin bar, 1968; commenced practice in Cedarburg, WI; admitted to practice before the U.S. Supreme Court in 1972; attorney; elected to the Wisconsin Assembly in 1968, reelected in 1970, 1972, and 1974; elected to Wisconsin Senate in a special election in 1975, and reelected in 1976, serving as assistant minority leader; staff member of former U.S. Congressman J. Arthur Younger of California in 1965; member: Waukesha County Republican Party; Wisconsin Bar Association; Riveredge Nature Center; Friends of Museums; and American Philatelic Society; married: the former Cheryl Warren, 1977; children: Frank James III, and Robert Alan; committees: chairman, Judiciary; elected to the 96th Congress, November 7, 1978; reelected to each succeeding Congress.

Office Listings

http://www.house.gov/sensenbrenner sensenbrenner@mail.house.gov

2449 Rayburn House Office Building, Washington, DC 20515 .... (202) 225–5101
Chief of Staff.—Tom Schreibel.
Deputy Chief of Staff.—Rich Zipperer.
Scheduler/Office Manager.—Jill C. Wade.
Press Secretary.—Raj Bharwani.
Room 154, 120 Bishops Way, Brookfield, WI 53005 .... (262) 784–1111
Chief of Staff.—Tom Schreibel.

Counties: JEFFERSON (part), MILWAUKEE (part), OZAUKEE, WASHINGTON, WAUKESHA (part). Population (2000), 670,458.

ZIP Codes: 53002, 53004–05, 53007–08, 53012–13, 53017–18, 53021–22, 53024, 53027, 53029, 53033, 53037–38, 53040, 53045–46, 53051–52, 53056, 53058, 53060, 53064, 53066, 53069, 53072, 53074, 53076, 53080, 53085–86, 53089–90, 53092, 53095, 53097–98, 53118, 53122, 53127, 53137, 53146, 53151, 53156, 53178, 53183, 53186–90, 53208–14, 53217, 53219, 53222–23, 53225–28, 53263, 53538, 53549

* * *

SIXTH DISTRICT

THOMAS E. PETRI, Republican, of Fond du Lac, WI; born in Marinette, WI, on May 28, 1940; education: graduated, Lowell P. Goodrich High School, 1958; B.A., Harvard University, Cambridge, MA, 1962; J.D., Harvard Law School, 1965; admitted to the Wisconsin state and Fond du Lac county bar associations, 1965; commenced practice in Fond du Lac in 1970; lawyer; law clerk to Federal Judge James Doyle, 1965; Peace Corps volunteer, 1966–67; White House aide, 1969; elected to the Wisconsin State Senate in 1972; reelected in 1976, and served until April, 1979; married; one daughter; elected to the 96th Congress, by special election, on April 3, 1979, to fill the vacancy caused by the death of William A. Steiger; reelected to each succeeding Congress.

Office Listings

http://www.house.gov/petri

2462 Rayburn House Office Building, Washington, DC 20515 .... (202) 225–2476
Administrative Assistant/Legislative Director.—Debra Gebhardt.
Communications Director.—Niel Wright.
Office Manager.—Linda Towse.
490 West Rolling Meadows Drive, Suite B, Fond du Lac, WI 54937 .... (920) 922–1180
District Director.—Sue Kerkman-Jung.
115 Washington Avenue, Oshkosh, WI 54901 .... (920) 231–6333

Counties: ADAMS, CALUMET (part), DODGE, FOND DU LAC, GREEN LAKE, JEFFERSON (part), MANITOWOC, MARQUETTE, OUTAGAMIE (part), SHEBOYGAN, WAUSHARA, WINNEBAGO. Population (2000), 670,459.

ZIP Codes: 53001, 53003, 53006, 53010–11, 53013–16, 53019–21, 53023, 53026–27, 53031–32, 53034–36, 53039, 53042, 53044, 53047–50, 53057, 53059, 53061–63, 53065–66, 53070, 53073, 53075, 53078–79, 53081–83, 53085, 53088, 53091, 53093–94, 53098–99, 53137, 53205, 53207, 53215, 53221, 53557, 53579, 53594, 53901, 53910, 53916–17, 53919–20, 53922–23, 53925–27, 53930–34, 53936, 53939, 53946–47, 53949–50, 53952–54, 53956, 53963–65, 53968, 54110, 54115, 54123, 54126, 54129–30, 54136, 54140, 54160, 54169, 54207–08, 54214–16, 54220–21, 54227–28, 54230, 54232, 54240–41, 54245, 54247, 54413, 54457, 54486, 54494, 54499, 54613, 54619, 54638, 54648, 54660, 54755, 54901–04, 54906, 54909, 54911, 54913–15, 54921–23, 54927, 54930, 54932–37, 54941, 54943–44, 54947, 54950, 54952, 54956–57, 54960, 54963–68, 54970–71, 54974, 54976, 54979–86

* * *

SEVENTH DISTRICT

DAVID R. OBEY, Democrat, of Wausau, WI; born in Okmulgee, OK, on October 3, 1938; education: graduated Wausau High School, 1956; M.A. in political science, University of Wisconsin, 1960 (graduate work in Russian government and foreign policy); elected to the Wisconsin Legislature from Marathon County's 2nd District at the age of 24; reelected three times; assistant Democratic floor leader; married: Joan Lepinski of Wausau, WI, 1962; children: Craig David and Douglas David; ranking member, House Committee on Appropriations; ranking member, Subcommittee on Labor, Health and Human Services, and Education; ex officio member of all subcommittees; former chairman, Joint Economic Committee; elected to the 91st Congress, by special election, on April 1, 1969, to fill the vacancy created by the resignation of Melvin R. Laird; reelected to each succeeding Congress.

Office Listings

http://www.house.gov/obey

2314 Rayburn House Office Building, Washington, DC 20515 .... (202) 225–3365
Staff Director.—William H. Stone.
Scheduler.—Carly M. Burns.
Press Secretary.—Thomas Powell-Bullock.
401 5th Street, Suite 406A, Wausau, WI 54403 .... (715) 842–5606
District Representative.—Doug Hill.
1401 Tower Avenue, Suite 307, Superior, WI 54880 .... (715) 398–4426

Counties: ASHLAND, BARRON, BAYFIELD, BURNETT, CHIPPEWA, CLARK (part), DOUGLAS, IRON, LANGLADE (part), LINCOLN, MARATHON, ONEIDA (part), POLK, PORTAGE, PRICE, RUSK, SAWYER, TAYLOR, WASHBURN, WOOD. Population (2000), 670,462.

ZIP Codes: 54001, 54004–07, 54009, 54017, 54020, 54024, 54026, 54401–12, 54414–15, 54417–18, 54420–29, 54432–35, 54437, 54439–43, 54447–49, 54451–52, 54454–55, 54457–60, 54462–63, 54466–67, 54469–76, 54479–81, 54484–85, 54487–90, 54492, 54494–95, 54498–99, 54501, 54513–15, 54517, 54524–27, 54529–32, 54534, 54536–38, 54545–47, 54550, 54552, 54555–56, 54559, 54563–65, 54703, 54724, 54726–33, 54739, 54745, 54748, 54757, 54762–63, 54766, 54768, 54771, 54774, 54801, 54805–06, 54810, 54812–14, 54816–22, 54824, 54826–30, 54832, 54834–50, 54853–59, 54861–62, 54864–65, 54867–68, 54870–76, 54880, 54888–91, 54893, 54895–96, 54909, 54921, 54945, 54966, 54977, 54981

* * *

EIGHTH DISTRICT

MARK GREEN, Republican, of Green Bay, WI; born in Boston, MA, on June 1, 1960; B.A., University of Wisconsin-Eau Claire; J.D., University of Wisconsin Law School-Madison, 1987; attorney; elected to Wisconsin State Assembly, 4th District, 1992–98; he and his wife Sue have three children: Rachel, Anna, and Alex; committees: Financial Services; International Relations; Judiciary; Republican Policy Committee; Assistant Majority Whip; elected to the 106th Congress; reelected to each succeeding Congress.

Office Listings

http://ww.house.gov/markgreen mark.green@mail.house.gov

1314 Longworth House Office Building, Washington, DC 20515 .... (202) 225–5665
Chief of Staff.—Mark Graul. FAX: 225–5729
Communications Director.—Chris Tuttle.
Executive Assistant.—Nicole Vernon.
700 East Walnut Street, Green Bay, WI 54301 .... (920) 437–1954
District Director.—Chad Weininger.
609–A W. College Avenue, Appleton, WI 54911 .... (920) 380–0061
District Caseworker.—Kathy McCarthy.

Counties: BROWN, CALUMET (part), DOOR, FLORENCE, FOREST, KEWAUNEE, LANGLADE (part), MARINETTE, MENOMINEE, OCONTO, ONEIDA (part), OUTAGAMIE (part), SHAWANO, VILAS, WAUPACA. Population (2000), 670,461.

ZIP Codes: 54101–04, 54106–07, 54110–15, 54119–21, 54124–28, 54130–31, 54135, 54137–41, 54143, 54149–57, 54159, 54161–62, 54165–66, 54169–71, 54173–75, 54177, 54180, 54182, 54201–02, 54204–05, 54208–13, 54216–17, 54226–27, 54229–30, 54234–35, 54241, 54246, 54301–08, 54311, 54313, 54324, 54344, 54408–09, 54414, 54416, 54418, 54424, 54427–28, 54430, 54435, 54450, 54452, 54462–65, 54485–87, 54491, 54499, 54501, 54511–12, 54519–21, 54529, 54531, 54538–43, 54545, 54548, 54554, 54557–58, 54560–62, 54564, 54566, 54568, 54911–15, 54919, 54922, 54926, 54928–29, 54931, 54933, 54940, 54942, 54944–50, 54952, 54956, 54961–62, 54965, 54969, 54975, 54977–78, 54981, 54983, 54990

WYOMING

(Population 2000, 493,782)

SENATORS

CRAIG THOMAS, Republican, of Casper, WY; born February 17, 1933 in Cody, WY; education: graduated from Cody High School; B.S., University of Wyoming, 1955; military service: served in the U.S. Marine Corps, captain, 1955–59; small businessman; vice president, Wyoming Farm Bureau, 1959–66; American Farm Bureau, 1966–75; general manager, Wyoming Rural Electric Association, 1975–89; member: Wyoming House of Representatives, 1984–89; committees: Energy and Natural Resources; Environment and Public Works; Finance; Indian Affairs; Select Committee on Ethics; married: Susan Thomas; children: Peter, Paul, Lexi and Patrick; elected to the U.S. House of Representatives, by special election, on April 25, 1989, to fill the vacancy caused by the resignation of Dick Cheney; reelected to each succeeding Congress; elected to the U.S. Senate in November, 1994; reelected to each succeeding Senate term.

Office Listings

http://thomas.senate.gov

307 Dirksen Senate Office Building, Washington, DC 20510 .... (202) 224–6441
    Chief of Staff.—Chris Jahn. FAX: 224–1724
    Legislative Director.—Shawn Whitman.
    Press Secretary.—Carrie Sloan.
    Administrative Director.—David Brewster.
2201 Federal Building, Casper, WY 82601 .... (307) 261–6413
    State Director.—Bobbi Brown.
2120 Capitol Avenue, Suite 2013, Cheyenne, WY 82001 .... (307) 772–2451
    Field Representative.—Mary Paxson.
2632 Foothills Boulevard, Suite 101, Rock Springs, WY 82901 .... (307) 362–5012
    Field Representative.—Pati Smith.
325 West Main, Suite F, Riverton, WY 82501 .... (307) 856–6642
    Field Representative.—Pam Buline.
2 North Main Street, Suite 206, Sheridan, WY 82801 .... (307) 672–6456
    Field Representative.—Matt Jones.

* * *

MICHAEL B. ENZI, Republican, of Gillette, WY; born in Bremerton, WA, February 1, 1944; B.S., accounting, George Washington University, 1966; M.B.A., Denver University, 1968; served in Wyoming National Guard, 1967–73; accounting manager and computer programmer, Dunbar Well Service, 1985–97; director, Black Hills Corporation, a New York Stock Exchange company, 1992–96; member, founding board of directors, First Wyoming Bank of Gillette, 1978–88; owner, with wife, of NZ Shoes; served in Wyoming House of Representatives, 1987–91, and in Wyoming State Senate, 1991–96; Mayor of Gillette, 1975–82; commissioner, Western Interstate Commission for Higher Education, 1995–96; served on the Education Commission of the States, 1989–93; president, Wyoming Association of Municipalities, 1980–82; president, Wyoming Jaycees, 1973–74; member: Lions Club; elder, Presbyterian Church; Eagle Scout; married Diana Buckley in 1969; three children: Amy, Brad, and Emily; committees: Budget; Health, Education, Labor and Pensions; Banking, Housing, and Urban Affairs; Foreign Relations; Small Business and Entrepreneurship; Special Committee on Aging; elected to the U.S. Senate in November, 1996; reelected to each succeeding Senate term.

Office Listings

http://enzi.senate.gov senator@enzi.senate.gov

290 Russell Senate Office Building, Washington, DC 20510 .... (202) 224–3424
    Chief of Staff.—George (Flip) McConnaughey.
    Legislative Director.—Katherine Brunett-McGuire.
    Press Secretary.—Coy Knobel.
    Office Manager.—Christen Petersen.
Federal Building, Suite 2007, Cheyenne, WY 82001 .... (307) 772–2477
400 S. Kendrick, Suite 303, Gillette, WY 82716 .... (307) 682–6268
Federal Center, Suite 3201, 100 East B Street, Casper, WY 82601 .... (307) 261–6572
1285 Sheridan Avenue, Suite 210, Cody, WY 82414 .... (307) 527–9444
P.O. Box 12470, Jackson, WY 83002 .... (307) 739–9507

REPRESENTATIVE

AT LARGE

BARBARA CUBIN, Republican, of Casper, WY; graduated, Natrona County High School; B.S., Creighton University, 1969; manager; substitute teacher; social worker; chemist; founding member of the Casper Suicide Prevention League; Casper Service League; president, Southridge Elementary School Parent/Teacher Organization; Mercer House, president and executive member; Casper Self Help Center, board member; Seton House, board member; Central Wyoming Rescue Mission, volunteer cook and server; Wyoming State Choir; Casper Civic Chorale; Cub Scout leader; Sunday School teacher at Saint Stephen's Episcopal Church; past memberships: executive committee of the Energy Council; chairman, Center for Legislators Energy and Environment Research (CLEER); National Council of State Legislatures; vice chairman, Energy Committee; 1994 Edison Electric Institutes' Wyoming Legislator of the Year and Toll Fellowship from the Council of State Governments, 1990; Wyoming House of Representatives committees, 1987–92: Minerals, Business and Economic Development; Revenue; Transportation; chair, Joint Interim Economic Development Subcommittee; Wyoming Senate committees, 1993–94: Travel, Recreation, Wildlife, and Cultural Resources; Revenue; Republican activities: chair, Wyoming Senate Conference, 1992–94; precinct committeewoman, 1988–94; legislative liaison and member, Natrona County Republican Women; 1992 Wyoming State Convention Parliamentarian; delegate, Wyoming State Convention, 1990, 1992, and 1994; State Legislative Candidate Recruitment Committee for the Wyoming Republican Party in 1988, 1990, and 1992; married: Frederick W. (Fritz) Cubin; children: William (Bill) and Frederick III (Eric); committees: Energy and Commerce; Resources; subcommittees: chair, Energy and Mineral Resources; National Parks, Recreation, and Public Lands; Commerce, Trade, and Consumer Protection; Telecommunications and the Internet; Health; Deputy Majority Whip; elected to the 104th Congress; reelected to each succeeding Congress.

Office Listings

http://www.house.gov/cubin

1114 Longworth House Office Building, Washington, DC 20515 .... (202) 225–2311
Chief of Staff.—Tom Wiblemo. FAX: 225–3057
Legislative Director.—Dennis Ellis.
Senior Legislative Assistant.—Jonni McCrann.
Press Secretary.—Joe Milczewski.
100 East B Street, Suite 4003, Casper, WY 82601 .... (307) 261–6595
State Director.—Kyra Hageman.
2120 Capitol Avenue, Suite 2015, Cheyenne, WY 82001 .... (307) 772–2595
District Representative.—Katie Legerski.
2515 Foothill Boulevard, Suite 204, Rock Springs, WY 82901 .... (307) 362–4095
District Representative.—Bonnie Cannon.

Population (2000), 493,782.

ZIP Codes: 82001, 82003, 82005–10, 82050–55, 82058–61, 82063, 82070–73, 82081–84, 82190, 82201, 82210, 82212–15, 82217–19, 82221–25, 82227, 82229, 82240, 82242–44, 82301, 82310, 82321–25, 82327, 82329, 82331–32, 82334–36, 82401, 82410–12, 82414, 82420–23, 82426, 82428, 82430–35, 82440–43, 82450, 82501, 82510, 82512–16, 82520, 82523–24, 82601–02, 82604–05, 82609, 82615, 82620, 82630, 82633, 82635–40, 82642–44, 82646, 82648–49, 82701, 82710–12, 82714–18, 82720–21, 82723, 82725, 82727, 82729–32, 82801, 82831–40, 82842, 82844–45, 82901–02, 82922–23, 82925, 82929–39, 82941–45, 83001–02, 83011–14, 83025, 83101, 83110–16, 83118–24, 83126–28

AMERICAN SAMOA

(Population 2000, 57,291)

DELEGATE

ENI F.H. FALEOMAVAEGA, Democrat, of Vailoatai, AS; graduate of Kahuku High School, Hawaii, 1962; B.A., Brigham Young University, 1966; J.D., University of Houston Law School, 1972; LL.M., University of California, Berkeley, 1973; enlisted in U.S. Army, 1966–69, Vietnam veteran; captain, USAR, Judge Advocate General Corps, 1982–92; adminstrative assistant to American Samoa's Delegate to Washington, 1973–75; staff counsel, Committee on Interior and Insular Affairs, 1975–81; deputy attorney general, American Samoa, 1981–84; elected Lieutenant Governor, American Samoa, 1984–89; Congressional Human Rights Caucus; Congressional Travel and Tourism Caucus; Democratic Study Group; Congressional Arts Caucus; Congressional Hispanic Caucus; admitted to U.S. Supreme Court and American Samoa bars; National Conference of Lieutenant Governors; National Association of Secretaries of State; Veterans of Foreign Wars; Navy League of the United States; National American Indian Prayer Breakfast Group; Pago Pago Lions Club; committees: International Relations; Resources; Small Business; married to Hinanui Bambridge Cave of Tahiti; five children; elected as the American Samoan Delegate to the 101st Congress on November 8, 1988; reelected to each succeeding Congress.

Office Listings

http://www.house.gov/faleomavaega

2422 Rayburn House Office Building, Washington, DC 20515 .... (202) 225–8577
Deputy Chief of Staff.—Lisa Williams. FAX: 225–8757
Office Manager.—Vili Lei.
Legislative Director.—Leilani Judy.
P.O. Drawer X, Pago Pago, AS 96799 .... (684) 633–1372

ZIP Codes: 96799

* * *

DISTRICT OF COLUMBIA

(Population 2000, 572,059)

DELEGATE

ELEANOR HOLMES NORTON, Democrat, of Washington, DC; born in Washington, DC, on June 13, 1937; education: graduated from Dunbar High School, 1955; B.A., Antioch College, 1960; M.A., Yale Graduate School, 1963; J.D., Yale Law School, 1964; honorary degrees: Tougalvo University, 1992; University of Southern Connecticut, 1992; Fisk University, 1991; University of Hartford, 1990; Ohio Wesleyan University, 1990; Wake Forest University, 1990; Colgate University, 1989; Drury College, 1989; Florida International University, 1989; St. Lawrence University, 1989; University of Wisconsin, 1989; Rutgers University, 1988; St. Joseph's College, 1988; University of Lowell, 1988; Sojourner-Douglas College, 1987; Salem State College, 1987; Haverford College, 1986; Lesley College, 1986; New Haven University, 1986; University of San Diego, 1986; Bowdoin College, 1985; Antioch College, 1985; Tufts University, 1984; University of Massachusetts, 1983; Smith College, 1983; Medical College of Pennsylvania, 1983; Spelman College, 1982; Syracuse University, 1981; Yeshiva University, 1981; Lawrence University, 1981; Emanuel College, 1981; Wayne State University, 1980; Gallaudet College, 1980; Denison University, 1980; New York University, 1978; Howard University, 1978; Brown University, 1978; Wilberforce University, 1978; Georgetown University, 1977; City College of New York, 1975; Marymount College, 1974; Princeton University, 1973; Bard College, 1971; Cedar Crest College, 1969; chair, Equal Employment Opportunity Commission, 1977–81; professor of law, Georgetown University, 1982–90; chair, New York Commission on Human Rights, 1970–76; executive assistant to the mayor of New York City (concurrent appointment); law clerk, Judge A. Leon Higginbotham, Federal District Court, 3rd Circuit; attorney, admitted to practice by examination in the District of Columbia and Pennsylvania and in the U.S. Supreme Court; One Hundred Most Important Women (*Ladies Home Journal*, 1988); One Hundred Most Powerful Women in Washington (The *Washingtonian* magazine, September 1989); Ralph E. Shikes Bicentennial Fellow, Harvard Law School, 1987; Visiting Phi Beta Kappa Scholar, 1985; Visiting Fellow, Harvard University, John F. Kennedy School of Government, spring 1984; Distinguished Public Service Award, Center for National Policy, 1985; Chancellor's Distinguished Lecturer, University of California Law School (Boalt Hall) at Berkeley, 1981; Yale Law School Association Citation of Merit Medal to the Outstanding Alumnus of the Law School, 1980; Harper Fellow, Yale Law School, 1976, (for ''a person . . . who has made a distinguished contribution to the public life of the nation . . .''); Rockefeller Foundation, trustee, 1982–90; Community Foundation of Greater Washington, board; Yale Corporation, 1982–88; Council on Foreign Relations; Overseas Development Council; U.S. Committee to Monitor the Helsinki accords; Carter Center, Atlanta, Georgia; boards of Martin Luther King, Jr. Center for Social Change and Environmental Law Institute; Workplace Health Fund; committees: Government Reform; Transportation and Infrastructure; Select Committee on Homeland Security; subcommittees: Aviation; Civil Service and Agency Organization; Criminal Justice, Drug Policy and Human Resources; ranking member, Economic Development, Public Buildings and Emergency Management; Emergency Preparedness and Response; Intelligence and Counterterrorism; divorced; two children: John and Katherine; elected to the 102nd Congress on November 6, 1990; reelected to each succeeding Congress.

Office Listings

http://www.house.gov/norton

2136 Rayburn House Office Building, Washington, DC 20515 .... (202) 225–8050
Chief of Staff.—Julia Hudson. FAX: 225–3002
Legislative Director.—Rosalind Parker.
Executive Assistant.—Vernard Portis.
Communications Director.—Doxie McCoy.

ZIP Codes: 20001–13, 20015–20, 20024, 20026–27, 20029–30, 20032–33, 20035–45, 20047, 20049–53, 20055–71, 20073–77, 20080, 20088, 20090–91, 20099, 20201–04, 20206–08, 20210–13, 20215–24, 20226–33, 20235, 20237, 20239–42, 20244–45, 20250, 20254, 20260, 20268, 20270, 20277, 20289, 20301, 20303, 20306–07, 20310, 20314–15, 20317–19, 20330, 20340, 20350, 20370, 20372–76, 20380, 20388–95, 20398, 20401–16, 20418–29, 20431, 20433–37, 20439–42, 20444, 20447, 20451, 20453, 20456, 20460, 20463, 20469, 20472, 20500, 20503–10, 20515, 20520–27, 20530–36, 20538–44, 20546–49, 20551–55, 20557, 20559–60, 20565–66, 20570–73, 20575–77, 20579–81, 20585–86, 20590–91, 20593–94, 20597, 20599

* * *

GUAM

(Population 2000, 154,805)

DELEGATE

MADELEINE Z. BORDALLO, Democrat, born on May 31, 1933, in Graceville, MN; education: Associate Degree in Music, St. Katherine's College, St. Paul, MN, 1953; First Lady of Guam 1975–1978, and 1983–1986; Guam Senator, five terms, 1981–1982, and 1987–1994; two term Lt. Governor of Guam 1995–2002; National Committee Chairwoman for the National Democratic Party 1964–present; family: husband Ricardo J. Bordallo (deceased); daughter Deborah, and granddaughter Nicole; committees: Armed Services; Resources; Small Business; elected to the 108th Congress on November 5, 2002.

Office Listings

http://www.house.gov/bordallo madeline.bordallo@mail.house.gov

2427 Cannon House Office Building, Washington, DC 20515 .... (202) 225–1188
Chief of Staff.—John Whitt. FAX: 226–0341
Press Secretary.—Jean Hudson.
Scheduler.—Rosanne Meno.
120 Father Duenas Avenue, Suite 107, Hagatna, GU 96910 .... (671) 477–4272

ZIP Codes: 96910, 96912–13, 96915–17, 96919, 96921, 96923, 96926, 96928–29, 96931–32

* * *

PUERTO RICO

(Population 2000, 3,808,610)

RESIDENT COMMISSIONER

ANÍBAL ACEVEDO-VILÁ, Popular Democratic Party, of Puerto Rico; born on February 13, 1962, in Hato Rey, PR; education: Political Science degree, University of Puerto Rico, Rio Piedras Campus, 1982; law degree, University of Puerto Rico, 1985; profession: Attorney;

served as Legislative Advisor for Puerto Rico Gov. Rafael Hernández Colón, 1989–1992; public service: elected President of the Popular Democratic Party; elected to two terms in the Puerto Rico House of Representatives; elected to Congress on November 7, 2000.

Office Listings

http://www.house.gov/acevedo-vila

126 Cannon House Office Building, Washington, DC 20515 .... (202) 225–2615
Chief of Staff.—Carlos G. Dalmau. FAX: 225–2154
Senior Legislative Director.—Paul Weiss.
Press Secretary.—Juanita Colombani.
Legislative Assistant.—Ileana Fas.
Distict Office, P.O. Box 9023958, San Juan, PR 00902 .... (787) 723–6333
District Director.—Lorna Rodriguez.

ZIP Codes: 00601–06, 00610–14, 00616–17, 00622–25, 00627, 00631, 00636–38, 00641, 00646–48, 00650, 00652–62, 00664, 00667, 00669–70, 00674, 00676–78, 00680–83, 00685, 00687–88, 00690, 00692–94, 00698, 00701, 00703–05, 00707, 00714–21, 00723, 00725–42, 00744–45, 00751, 00754, 00757, 00765–69, 00771–73, 00775, 00777–78, 00780, 00782–86, 00791–92, 00794–95, 00901–36, 00938, 00940, 00949–63, 00965–66, 00968–71, 00975–79, 00981–88

* * *

VIRGIN ISLANDS

(Population 2000, 108,612)

DELEGATE

DONNA M. CHRISTENSEN, Democrat, of St. Croix, VI; B.S., St. Mary's College, Notre Dame, IN, 1966; M.D., George Washington University School of Medicine, 1970; physician, family medicine; Acting Commissioner of Health, 1994–95; medical director, St. Croix Hospital, 1987–88; founding member and vice president, Virgin Islands Medical Institute; trustee, National Medical Association; past secretary and two-time past president, Virgin Islands Medical Society; founding member and trustee, Caribbean Youth Organization; member: Democratic National Committee; Virgin Islands Democratic Territorial Committee (past vice chair); Substance Abuse Coalition; St. Dunstan's Episcopal School Board of Directors; Caribbean Studies Association; Women's Coalition of St. Croix; St. Croix Environmental Association; past chair, Christian Education Committee; Friedensthal Moravian Church; past member: Virgin Islands Board of Education; Democratic Platform Committee; cohost, Straight Up TV interview program, 1993; married: Chris Christensen; children: two daughters: Rabiah Layla and Karida Yasmeen; member: Congressional Black Caucus; Congressional Women's Caucus; committees: Small Business; Resources; Select Committee on Homeland Security; elected to the 105th Congress; reelected to each succeeding Congress.

Office Listings

1510 Longworth House Office Building, Washington, DC 20515 .... (202) 225–1790
Chief of Staff.—Monique Clendinen Watson. FAX: 225–5517
Legislative Director.—Brian Modeste.
Office Manager.—Steven Steele.
Executive Assistant / Scheduler.—Shelley Thomas.
Nisky Center, 2nd Floor, Suite 207, St. Thomas, VI 00802 .... (340) 774–4408
Office Assistant.—Joyce Jackson.
Sunny Isle Shopping Center, Space No. 25, P.O. Box 5980, St. Croix, VI 00823 .. (340) 778–5900
District Manager.—Claire Roker.

ZIP Codes: 00801–05, 00820–24, 00830–31, 00840–41, 00850–51

STATE DELEGATIONS

Number before names designates Congressional district. Republicans in roman; Democrats in *italic*; Independents in SMALL CAPS; Resident Commissioner and Delegates in **boldface**.

ALABAMA

SENATORS
Richard C. Shelby
Jeff Sessions

REPRESENTATIVES
[Republicans 5, Democrats 2]

1. Jo Bonner
2. Terry Everett
3. Mike Rogers
4. Robert B. Aderholt
5. *Robert E. (Bud) Cramer*
6. Spencer Bachus
7. *Artur Davis*

ALASKA

SENATORS
Ted Stevens
Lisa Murkowski

REPRESENTATIVE
[Republican 1]
At Large - Don Young

ARIZONA

SENATORS
John McCain
Jon Kyl

REPRESENTATIVES
[Republicans 6, Democrats 2]

1. Rick Renzi
2. Trent Franks
3. John B. Shadegg
4. *Ed Pastor*
5. J.D. Hayworth
6. Jeff Flake
7. *Raúl M. Grijalva*
8. Jim Kolbe

ARKANSAS

SENATORS
Blanche L. Lincoln
Mark Pryor

REPRESENTATIVES
[Republicans 1, Democrats 3]

1. *Marion Berry*
2. *Vic Snyder*
3. John Boozman
4. *Mike Ross*

CALIFORNIA

SENATORS
Dianne Feinstein
Barbara Boxer

REPRESENTATIVES
[Republicans 20, Democrats 33]

1. *Mike Thompson*
2. Wally Herger
3. Doug Ose
4. John T. Doolittle
5. *Robert T. Matsui*
6. *Lynn Woolsey*
7. *George Miller*
8. *Nancy Pelosi*
9. *Barbara Lee*
10. *Ellen O. Tauscher*

11. Richard W. Pombo
12. *Tom Lantos*
13. *Fortney Pete Stark*
14. *Anna G. Eshoo*
15. *Michael M. Honda*
16. *Zoe Lofgren*
17. *Sam Farr*
18. *Dennis A. Cardoza*
19. George Radanovich
20. *Calvin M. Dooley*
21. Devin Nunes
22. William M. Thomas
23. Lois Capps
24. Elton Gallegly
25. Howard P. (Buck) McKeon
26. David Dreier
27. *Brad Sherman*
28. *Howard L. Berman*
29. *Adam B. Schiff*
30. *Henry A. Waxman*
31. *Xavier Becerra*
32. *Hilda L. Solis*
33. *Diane E. Watson*
34. *Lucille Roybal-Allard*
35. *Maxine Waters*
36. *Jane Harman*
37. *Juanita Millender-McDonald*
38. *Grace F. Napolitano*
39. *Linda T. Sánchez*
40. Edward R. Royce
41. Jerry Lewis
42. Gary G. Miller
43. *Joe Baca*
44. Ken Calvert
45. Mary Bono
46. Dana Rohrabacher
47. *Loretta Sanchez*
48. Christopher Cox
49. Darrell E. Issa
50. Randy (Duke) Cunningham
51. *Bob Filner*
52. Duncan Hunter
53. *Susan A. Davis*

COLORADO

SENATORS
Ben Nighthorse Campbell
Wayne Allard

REPRESENTATIVES
[Republicans 5, Democrats 2]

1. *Diana DeGette*
2. *Mark Udall*
3. Scott McInnis
4. Marilyn N. Musgrave
5. Joel Hefley
6. Thomas G. Tancredo
7. Bob Beauprez

CONNECTICUT

SENATORS
Christopher J. Dodd
Joseph I. Lieberman

REPRESENTATIVES
[Republicans 3, Democrats 2]

1. *John B. Larson*
2. Rob Simmons
3. *Rosa L. DeLauro*
4. Christopher Shays
5. Nancy L. Johnson

DELAWARE

SENATORS
Joseph R. Biden, Jr.
Thomas Carper

REPRESENTATIVE
[Republican 1]

At Large - Michael N. Castle

FLORIDA

SENATORS
Bob Graham
Bill Nelson

REPRESENTATIVES
[Republicans 18, Democrats 7]

1. Jeff Miller
2. *Allen Boyd*
3. *Corrine Brown*
4. Ander Crenshaw
5. Ginny Brown-Waite
6. Cliff Stearns
7. John L. Mica
8. Ric Keller
9. Michael Bilirakis
10. C.W. Bill Young
11. *Jim Davis*
12. Adam H. Putnam
13. Katherine Harris
14. Porter J. Goss

15. Dave Weldon
16. Mark Foley
17. *Kendrick B. Meek*
18. Ileana Ros-Lehtinen
19. *Robert Wexler*
20. *Peter Deutsch*
21. Lincoln Diaz-Balart
22. E. Clay Shaw, Jr.
23. *Alcee L. Hastings*
24. Tom Feeney
25. Mario Diaz-Balart

GEORGIA

SENATORS
Zell Miller
Saxby Chambliss

REPRESENTATIVES
[Republicans 8, Democrats 5]

1. Jack Kingston
2. *Sanford D. Bishop, Jr.*
3. *Jim Marshall*
4. *Denise L. Majette*
5. *John Lewis*
6. Johnny Isakson
7. John Linder
8. Mac Collins
9. Charlie Norwood
10. Nathan Deal
11. Phil Gingrey
12. Max Burns
13. *David Scott*

HAWAII

SENATORS
Daniel K. Inouye
Daniel K. Akaka

REPRESENTATIVES
[Democrats 2]

1. *Neil Abercrombie*
2. *Ed Case*

IDAHO

SENATORS
Larry Craig
Michael Crapo

REPRESENTATIVES
[Republicans 2]

1. C.L. (Butch) Otter
2. Michael K. Simpson

ILLINOIS

SENATORS
Richard J. Durbin
Peter G. Fitzgerald

REPRESENTATIVES
[Republicans 10, Democrats 9]

1. *Bobby L. Rush*
2. *Jesse L. Jackson, Jr.*
3. *William O. Lipinski*
4. *Luis V. Gutierrez*
5. *Rahm Emanuel*
6. Henry J. Hyde
7. *Danny K. Davis*
8. Philip M. Crane
9. *Janice D. Schakowsky*
10. Mark Steven Kirk
11. Jerry Weller
12. *Jerry F. Costello*
13. Judy Biggert
14. J. Dennis Hastert
15. Timothy V. Johnson
16. Donald A. Manzullo
17. *Lane Evans*
18. Ray LaHood
19. John Shimkus

INDIANA

SENATORS
Richard G. Lugar
Evan Bayh

REPRESENTATIVES
[Republicans 6, Democrats 3]

1. *Peter J. Visclosky*
2. Chris Chocola
3. Mark E. Souder
4. Steve Buyer
5. Dan Burton
6. Mike Pence
7. *Julia Carson*
8. John N. Hostettler
9. *Baron P. Hill*

IOWA

SENATORS
Charles E. Grassley
Tom Harkin

REPRESENTATIVES
[Republicans 4, Democrats 1]
1. Jim Nussle
2. James A. Leach
3. *Leonard L. Boswell*
4. Tom Latham
5. Steve King

KANSAS

SENATORS
Samuel Dale Brownback
Pat Roberts

REPRESENTATIVES
[Republicans 3, Democrats 1]
1. Jerry Moran
2. Jim Ryun
3. *Dennis Moore*
4. Todd Tiahrt

KENTUCKY

SENATORS
Mitch McConnell
Jim Bunning

REPRESENTATIVES
[Republicans 5, Democrats 1]
1. Ed Whitfield
2. Ron Lewis
3. Anne M. Northup
4. *Ken Lucas*
5. Harold Rogers
6. Ernie Fletcher

LOUISIANA

SENATORS
John B. Breaux
Mary Landrieu

REPRESENTATIVES
[Republicans 4, Democrats 3]
1. David Vitter
2. *William J. Jefferson*
3. W.J. (Billy) Tauzin
4. Jim McCrery
5. *Rodney Alexander*
6. Richard H. Baker
7. *Christopher John*

MAINE

SENATORS
Olympia J. Snowe
Susan Collins

REPRESENTATIVES
[Democrats 2]
1. *Thomas H. Allen*
2. *Michael H. Michaud*

MARYLAND

SENATORS
Paul S. Sarbanes
Barbara A. Mikulski

REPRESENTATIVES
[Republicans 2, Democrats 6]
1. Wayne T. Gilchrest
2. *C.A. Dutch Ruppersberger*
3. *Benjamin L. Cardin*
4. *Albert Russell Wynn*
5. *Steny H. Hoyer*
6. Roscoe G. Bartlett
7. *Elijah E. Cummings*
8. *Chris Van Hollen*

MASSACHUSETTS

SENATORS
Edward M. Kennedy
John F. Kerry

REPRESENTATIVES
[Democrats 10]

1. *John W. Olver*
2. *Richard E. Neal*
3. *James P. McGovern*
4. *Barney Frank*
5. *Martin T. Meehan*
6. *John F. Tierney*
7. *Edward J. Markey*
8. *Michael E. Capuano*
9. *Stephen F. Lynch*
10. *William D. Delahunt*

MICHIGAN

SENATORS
Carl Levin
Debbie Stabenow

REPRESENTATIVES
[Republicans 9, Democrats 6]

1. *Bart Stupak*
2. Peter Hoekstra
3. Vernon J. Ehlers
4. Dave Camp
5. *Dale E. Kildee*
6. Fred Upton
7. Nick Smith
8. Mike Rogers
9. Joe Knollenberg
10. Candice S. Miller
11. Thaddeus G. McCotter
12. *Sander M. Levin*
13. *Carolyn C. Kilpatrick*
14. *John Conyers, Jr.*
15. *John D. Dingell*

MINNESOTA

SENATORS
Mark Dayton
Norm Coleman

REPRESENTATIVES
[Republicans 4, Democrats 4]

1. Gil Gutknecht
2. John Kline
3. Jim Ramstad
4. *Betty McCollum*
5. *Martin Olav Sabo*
6. Mark R. Kennedy
7. *Collin C. Peterson*
8. *James L. Oberstar*

MISSISSIPPI

SENATORS
Thad Cochran
Trent Lott

REPRESENTATIVES
[Republicans 2, Democrats 2]

1. Roger F. Wicker
2. *Bennie G. Thompson*
3. Charles W. (Chip) Pickering
4. *Gene Taylor*

MISSOURI

SENATORS
Christopher S. Bond
James Talent

REPRESENTATIVES
[Republicans 5, Democrats 4]

1. *Wm. Lacy Clay*
2. W. Todd Akin
3. *Richard A. Gephardt*
4. *Ike Skelton*
5. *Karen McCarthy*
6. Sam Graves
7. Roy Blunt
8. Jo Ann Emerson
9. Kenny C. Hulshof

MONTANA

SENATORS
Max Baucus
Conrad Burns

REPRESENTATIVE
[Republican 1]

At Large - Dennis R. Rehberg

NEBRASKA

SENATORS
Chuck Hagel
Ben Nelson

REPRESENTATIVES
[Republicans 3]

1. Doug Bereuter
2. Lee Terry
3. Tom Osborne

NEVADA

SENATORS
Harry Reid
John Ensign

REPRESENTATIVES
[Republicans 2, Democrats 1]

1. *Shelley Berkley*
2. Jim Gibbons
3. Jon C. Porter

NEW HAMPSHIRE

SENATORS
Judd Gregg
John Sununu

REPRESENTATIVES
[Republicans 2]

1. Jeb Bradley
2. Charles F. Bass

NEW JERSEY

SENATORS
Jon S. Corzine
Frank Lautenberg

REPRESENTATIVES
[Republicans 5, Democrats 8]

1. *Robert E. Andrews*
2. Frank LoBiondo
3. Jim Saxton
4. Christopher H. Smith
5. Scott Garrett
6. *Frank Pallone, Jr.*
7. Mike Ferguson
8. *Bill Pascrell, Jr.*
9. *Steven R. Rothman*
10. *Donald M. Payne*
11. Rodney P. Frelinghuysen
12. *Rush D. Holt*
13. *Robert Menendez*

NEW MEXICO

SENATORS
Pete V. Domenici
Jeff Bingaman

REPRESENTATIVES
[Republicans 2, Democrats 1]

1. Heather Wilson
2. Stevan Pearce
3. *Tom Udall*

NEW YORK

SENATORS
Charles E. Schumer
Hillary Rodham Clinton

REPRESENTATIVES
[Republicans 10, Democrats 19]

1. *Timothy H. Bishop*
2. *Steve Israel*
3. Peter T. King
4. *Carolyn McCarthy*
5. *Gary L. Ackerman*
6. *Gregory W. Meeks*
7. *Joseph Crowley*
8. *Jerrold Nadler*
9. *Anthony D. Weiner*
10. *Edolphus Towns*
11. *Major R. Owens*
12. *Nydia M. Velázquez*
13. Vito Fossella
14. *Carolyn B. Maloney*

15. *Charles B. Rangel*
16. *José E. Serrano*
17. *Eliot L. Engel*
18. *Nita M. Lowey*
19. Sue W. Kelly
20. John E. Sweeney
21. *Michael R. McNulty*
22. *Maurice D. Hinchey*
23. John M. McHugh
24. Sherwood Boehlert
25. James T. Walsh
26. Thomas M. Reynolds
27. Jack Quinn
28. *Louise McIntosh Slaughter*
29. Amo Houghton

NORTH CAROLINA

SENATORS
John Edwards
Elizabeth Dole

REPRESENTATIVES
[Republicans 7, Democrats 6]

1. *Frank W. Ballance, Jr.*
2. *Bob Etheridge*
3. Walter B. Jones
4. *David E. Price*
5. Richard M. Burr
6. Howard Coble
7. *Mike McIntyre*
8. Robin Hayes
9. Sue Wilkins Myrick
10. Cass Ballenger
11. Charles H. Taylor
12. *Melvin L. Watt*
12. *Brad Miller*

NORTH DAKOTA

SENATORS
Kent Conrad
Byron L. Dorgan

REPRESENTATIVE
[Democrat 1]

At Large - *Earl Pomeroy*

OHIO

SENATORS
Mike DeWine
George V. Voinovich

REPRESENTATIVES
[Republicans 12, Democrats 6]

1. Steve Chabot
2. Rob Portman
3. Michael R. Turner
4. Michael G. Oxley
5. Paul E. Gillmor
6. *Ted Strickland*
7. David L. Hobson
8. John A. Boehner
9. *Marcy Kaptur*
10. *Dennis J. Kucinich*
11. *Stephanie Tubbs Jones*
12. Patrick J. Tiberi
13. *Sherrod Brown*
14. Steven C. LaTourette
15. Deborah Pryce
16. Ralph Regula
17. *Timothy J. Ryan*
18. Robert W. Ney

OKLAHOMA

SENATORS
Don Nickles
James M. Inhofe

REPRESENTATIVES
[Republicans 4, Democrats 1]

1. John Sullivan
2. *Brad Carson*
3. Frank D. Lucas
4. Tom Cole
5. Ernest J. Istook, Jr.

OREGON

SENATORS
Ron Wyden
Gordon Smith

REPRESENTATIVES
[Republican 1, Democrats 4]

1. *David Wu*

2. Greg Walden
3. *Earl Blumenauer*
4. *Peter A. DeFazio*
5. *Darlene Hooley*

PENNSYLVANIA

SENATORS
Arlen Specter
Rick Santorum

REPRESENTATIVES
[Republicans 12, Democrats 7]

1. *Robert A. Brady*
2. *Chaka Fattah*
3. Phil English
4. Melissa A. Hart
5. John E. Peterson
6. Jim Gerlach
7. Curt Weldon
8. James C. Greenwood
9. Bill Shuster
10. Don Sherwood
11. *Paul E. Kanjorski*
12. *John P. Murtha*
13. *Joseph M. Hoeffel*
14. *Michael F. Doyle*
15. Patrick J. Toomey
16. Joseph R. Pitts
17. *Tim Holden*
18. Tim Murphy
19. Todd Russell Platts

RHODE ISLAND

SENATORS
Jack Reed
Lincoln D. Chafee

REPRESENTATIVES
[Democrats 2]

1. *Patrick J. Kennedy*
2. *James R. Langevin*

SOUTH CAROLINA

SENATORS
Ernest F. Hollings
Lindsey Graham

REPRESENTATIVES
[Republicans 4, Democrats 2]

1. Henry E. Brown, Jr.
2. Joe Wilson
3. J. Gresham Barrett
4. Jim DeMint
5. *John M. Spratt, Jr.*
6. *James E. Clyburn*

SOUTH DAKOTA

SENATORS
Thomas A. Daschle
Tim Johnson

REPRESENTATIVE
[Republican 1]

At Large - William J. Janklow

TENNESSEE

SENATORS
Bill Frist
Lamar Alexander

REPRESENTATIVES
[Republicans 4, Democrats 5]

1. William L. Jenkins
2. John J. Duncan, Jr.
3. Zach Wamp
4. *Lincoln Davis*
5. *Jim Cooper*
6. *Bart Gordon*
7. Marsha Blackburn
8. *John S. Tanner*
9. *Harold E. Ford, Jr.*

TEXAS

SENATORS
Kay Bailey Hutchison
John Cornyn

REPRESENTATIVES
[Republicans 15, Democrats 17]

1. *Max Sandlin*
2. *Jim Turner*
3. Sam Johnson
4. *Ralph M. Hall*
5. Jeb Hensarling
6. Joe Barton
7. John Abney Culberson
8. Kevin Brady
9. *Nick Lampson*
10. *Lloyd Doggett*
11. *Chet Edwards*
12. Kay Granger
13. Mac Thornberry
14. Ron Paul
15. *Rubén Hinojosa*
16. *Silvestre Reyes*
17. *Charles W. Stenholm*
18. *Sheila Jackson Lee*
19. Randy Neugebauer
20. *Charles A. Gonzalez*
21. Lamar S. Smith
22. Tom DeLay
23. Henry Bonilla
24. *Martin Frost*
25. *Chris Bell*
26. Michael C. Burgess
27. *Solomon P. Ortiz*
28. *Ciro Rodriguez*
29. *Gene Green*
30. *Eddie Bernice Johnson*
31. John R. Carter
32. Pete Sessions

UTAH

SENATORS
Orrin G. Hatch
Robert F. Bennett

REPRESENTATIVES
[Republicans 2, Democrats 1]

1. Rob Bishop
2. *Jim Matheson*
3. Christopher B. Cannon

VERMONT

SENATORS
Patrick J. Leahy
JAMES M. JEFFORDS

REPRESENTATIVE
[Independent 1]

At Large - BERNARD SANDERS

VIRGINIA

SENATORS
John W. Warner
George Allen

REPRESENTATIVES
[Republicans 8, Democrats 3]

1. Jo Ann Davis
2. Edward L. Schrock
3. *Robert C. Scott*
4. J. Randy Forbes
5. Virgil H. Goode, Jr.
6. Robert W. Goodlatte
7. Eric Cantor
8. *James P. Moran*
9. *Rick Boucher*
10. Frank R. Wolf
11. Tom Davis

WASHINGTON

SENATORS
Patty Murray
Maria Cantwell

REPRESENTATIVES
[Republicans 3, Democrats 6]

1. *Jay Inslee*
2. *Rick Larsen*
3. *Brian Baird*
4. Doc Hastings
5. George R. Nethercutt, Jr.
6. *Norman D. Dicks*
7. *Jim McDermott*
8. Jennifer Dunn
9. *Adam Smith*

WEST VIRGINIA

SENATORS
Robert C. Byrd
John D. Rockefeller IV

REPRESENTATIVES
[Republicans 1, Democrats 2]
1. *Alan B. Mollohan*
2. Shelley Moore Capito
3. *Nick J. Rahall II*

WISCONSIN

SENATORS
Herb Kohl
Russell D. Feingold

REPRESENTATIVES
[Republicans 4, Democrats 4]
1. Paul Ryan
2. *Tammy Baldwin*
3. *Ron Kind*
4. *Gerald D. Kleczka*
5. F. James Sensenbrenner, Jr.
6. Thomas E. Petri
7. *David R. Obey*
8. Mark Green

WYOMING

SENATORS
Craig Thomas
Michael B. Enzi

REPRESENTATIVE
[Republican 1]
At Large - Barbara Cubin

AMERICAN SAMOA

DELEGATE
[Democrat 1]
Eni F.H. Faleomavaega

DISTRICT OF COLUMBIA

DELEGATE
[Democrat 1]
Eleanor Holmes Norton

GUAM

DELEGATE
[Democrat 1]
Madeleine Z. Bordallo

PUERTO RICO

RESIDENT COMMISSIONER
[Popular Democratic Party 1]
Aníbal Acevedo-Vilá

VIRGIN ISLANDS

DELEGATE
[Democrat 1]
Donna M. Christensen

ALPHABETICAL LIST

SENATORS

Alphabetical list of Senators, Representatives, Delegates, and Resident Commissioner. Republicans in roman (51); Democrats in *italic* (48); Independent in SMALL CAPS (1).

Akaka, Daniel K., HI
Alexander, Lamar, TN
Allard, Wayne, CO
Allen, George, VA
Baucus, Max, MT
Bayh, Evan, IN
Bennett, Robert F., UT
Biden, Joseph R., Jr., DE
Bingaman, Jeff, NM
Bond, Christopher S., MO
Boxer, Barbara, CA
Breaux, John B., LA
Brownback, Sam, KS
Bunning, Jim, KY
Burns, Conrad R., MT
Byrd, Robert C., WV
Campbell, Ben Nighthorse, CO
Cantwell, Maria, WA
Carper, Thomas R., DE
Chafee, Lincoln D., RI
Chambliss, Saxby, GA
Clinton, Hillary Rodham, NY
Cochran, Thad, MS
Coleman, Norm, MN
Collins, Susan M., ME
Conrad, Kent, ND
Cornyn, John, TX
Corzine, Jon S., NJ
Craig, Larry E., ID
Crapo, Michael D., ID
Daschle, Thomas A., SD
Dayton, Mark, MN
DeWine, Mike, OH
Dodd, Christopher J., CT
Dole, Elizabeth H., NC
Domenici, Pete V., NM
Dorgan, Byron L., ND
Durbin, Richard J., IL
Edwards, John, NC
Ensign, John, NV
Enzi, Michael B., WY
Feingold, Russell D., WI
Feinstein, Dianne, CA
Fitzgerald, Peter G., IL
Frist, Bill, TN
Graham, Bob, FL
Graham, Lindsey O., SC
Grassley, Charles E., IA
Gregg, Judd, NH
Hagel, Chuck, NE
Harkin, Tom, IA
Hatch, Orrin G., UT
Hollings, Ernest F., SC
Hutchison, Kay Bailey, TX
Inhofe, James M., OK
Inouye, Daniel K., HI
JEFFORDS, JAMES M., VT
Johnson, Tim, SD
Kennedy, Edward M., MA
Kerry, John F., MA
Kohl, Herb, WI
Kyl, Jon, AZ
Landrieu, Mary L., LA
Lautenberg, Frank, NJ
Leahy, Patrick J., VT
Levin, Carl, MI
Lieberman, Joseph I., CT
Lincoln, Blanche L., AR
Lott, Trent, MS
Lugar, Richard G., IN
McCain, John, AZ
McConnell, Mitch, KY
Mikulski, Barbara A., MD
Miller, Zell, GA
Murkowski, Lisa, AK
Murray, Patty, WA
Nelson, Ben, NE
Nelson, Bill, FL
Nickles, Don, OK
Pryor, Mark, AR
Reed, Jack, RI
Reid, Harry, NV
Roberts, Pat, KS
Rockefeller, John D., IV, WV
Santorum, Rick, PA
Sarbanes, Paul S., MD
Schumer, Charles E., NY
Sessions, Jeff, AL
Shelby, Richard C., AL
Smith, Gordon, OR
Snowe, Olympia J., ME
Specter, Arlen, PA
Stabenow, Deborah Ann, MI
Stevens, Ted, AK
Sununu, John E., NH
Talent, James M., MO
Thomas, Craig, WY
Voinovich, George V., OH
Warner, John W., VA
Wyden, Ron, OR

REPRESENTATIVES

Republicans in roman (229); Democrats in *italic* (205); Independents in SMALL CAPS (1); Resident Commissioner and Delegates in **boldface** (5); [Vacant] (0); total 440.

Abercrombie, Neil, HI (1st)
Ackerman, Gary L., NY (5th)
Aderholt, Robert B., AL (4th)
Akin, W. Todd, MO (2nd)
Alexander, Rodney, LA (5th)
Allen, Thomas H., ME (1st)
Andrews, Robert E., NJ (1st)
Baca, Joe, CA (43rd)
Bachus, Spencer, AL (6th)
Baird, Brian, WA (3rd)
Baker, Richard H., LA (6th)
Baldwin, Tammy, WI (2nd)
Ballance, Frank W., Jr., NC (1st)
Ballenger, Cass, NC (10th)
Barrett, J. Gresham, SC (3rd)
Bartlett, Roscoe G., MD (6th)
Barton, Joe, TX (6th)
Bass, Charles F., NH (2nd)
Beauprez, Bob, CO (7th)
Becerra, Xavier, CA (31st)
Bell, Chris, TX (25th)
Bereuter, Doug, NE (1st)
Berkley, Shelley, NV (1st)
Berman, Howard L., CA (28th)
Berry, Marion, AR (1st)
Biggert, Judy, IL (13th)
Bilirakis, Michael, FL (9th)
Bishop, Rob, UT (1st)
Bishop, Sanford D., Jr., GA (2nd)
Bishop, Timothy H., NY (1st)
Blackburn, Marsha, TN (7th)
Blumenauer, Earl, OR (3rd)
Blunt, Roy, MO (7th)
Boehlert, Sherwood, NY (24th)
Boehner, John A., OH (8th)
Bonilla, Henry, TX (23rd)
Bonner, Jo, AL (1st)
Bono, Mary, CA (45th)
Boozman, John, AR (3rd)
Boswell, Leonard L., IA (3rd)
Boucher, Rick, VA (9th)
Boyd, Allen, FL (2nd)
Bradley, Jeb, NH (1st)
Brady, Kevin, TX (8th)
Brady, Robert A., PA (1st)
Brown, Corrine, FL (3rd)
Brown, Henry E., Jr., SC (1st)
Brown, Sherrod, OH (13th)
Brown-Waite, Ginny, FL (5th)
Burgess, Michael C., TX (26th)
Burns, Max, GA (12th)
Burr, Richard M., NC (5th)
Burton, Dan, IN (5th)
Buyer, Steve, IN (4th)
Calvert, Ken, CA (44th)
Camp, Dave, MI (4th)
Cannon, Christopher B., UT (3rd)
Cantor, Eric, VA (7th)
Capito, Shelley Moore, WV (2nd)
Capps, Lois, CA (23rd)
Capuano, Michael E., MA (8th)
Cardin, Benjamin L., MD (3rd)
Cardoza, Dennis A., CA (18th)
Carson, Brad, OK (2nd)
Carson, Julia M., IN (7th)
Carter, John R., TX (31st)
Case, Ed, HI (2nd)
Castle, Michael N., DE (At Large)
Chabot, Steve, OH (1st)
Chocola, Chris, IN (2nd)
Clay, Wm. Lacy, MO (1st)
Clyburn, James E., SC (6th)
Coble, Howard, NC (6th)
Cole, Tom, OK (4th)
Collins, Mac, GA (8th)
Conyers, John, Jr., MI (14th)
Cooper, Jim, TN (5th)
Costello, Jerry F., IL (12th)
Cox, Christopher, CA (48th)
Cramer, Robert E. (Bud), Jr., AL (5th)
Crane, Philip M., IL (8th)
Crenshaw, Ander, FL (4th)
Crowley, Joseph, NY (7th)
Cubin, Barbara, WY (At Large)
Culberson, John Abney, TX (7th)
Cummings, Elijah E., MD (7th)
Cunningham, Randy (Duke), CA (50th)
Davis, Artur, AL (7th)
Davis, Danny K., IL (7th)
Davis, Jim, FL (11th)
Davis, Jo Ann, VA (1st)
Davis, Lincoln, TN (4th)
Davis, Susan A., CA (53rd)
Davis, Tom, VA (11th)
Deal, Nathan, GA (10th)
DeFazio, Peter A., OR (4th)
DeGette, Diana, CO (1st)
Delahunt, William D., MA (10th)
DeLauro, Rosa L., CT (3rd)
DeLay, Tom, TX (22nd)
DeMint, Jim, SC (4th)
Deutsch, Peter, FL (20th)
Diaz-Balart, Lincoln, FL (21st)
Diaz-Balart, Mario FL (25th)
Dicks, Norman D., WA (6th)
Dingell, John D., MI (15th)

Doggett, Lloyd, TX (10th)
Dooley, Calvin M., CA (20th)
Doolittle, John T., CA (4th)
Doyle, Michael F., PA (14th)
Dreier, David, CA (26th)
Duncan, John J., Jr., TN (2nd)
Dunn, Jennifer, WA (8th)
Edwards, Chet, TX (11th)
Ehlers, Vernon J., MI (3rd)
Emanuel, Rahm, IL (5th)
Emerson, Jo Ann, MO (8th)
Engel, Eliot L., NY (17th)
English, Phil, PA (3rd)
Eshoo, Anna G., CA (14th)
Etheridge, Bob, NC (2nd)
Evans, Lane, IL (17th)
Everett, Terry, AL (2nd)
Farr, Sam, CA (17th)
Fattah, Chaka, PA (2nd)
Feeney, Tom, FL (24th)
Ferguson, Mike, NJ (7th)
Filner, Bob, CA (51st)
Flake, Jeff, AZ (6th)
Fletcher, Ernie, KY (6th)
Foley, Mark, FL (16th)
Forbes, J. Randy, VA (4th)
Ford, Harold E., Jr., TN (9th)
Fossella, Vito, NY (13th)
Frank, Barney, MA (4th)
Franks, Trent, AZ (2nd)
Frelinghuysen, Rodney P., NJ (11th)
Frost, Martin, TX (24th)
Gallegly, Elton, CA (24th)
Garrett, Scott, NJ (5th)
Gephardt, Richard A., MO (3rd)
Gerlach, Jim, PA (6th)
Gibbons, Jim, NV (2nd)
Gilchrest, Wayne T., MD (1st)
Gillmor, Paul E., OH (5th)
Gingrey, Phil, GA (11th)
Gonzalez, Charles A., TX (20th)
Goode, Virgil H., Jr., VA (5th)
Goodlatte, Robert W. (Bob), VA (6th)
Gordon, Bart, TN (6th)
Goss, Porter J., FL (14th)
Granger, Kay, TX (12th)
Graves, Samuel, MO (6th)
Green, Gene, TX (29th)
Green, Mark, WI (8th)
Greenwood, James C., PA (8th)
Grijalva, Raúl M., AZ (7th)
Gutierrez, Luis V., IL (4th)
Gutknecht, Gil, MN (1st)
Hall, Ralph M., TX (4th)
Harman, Jane, CA (36th)
Harris, Katherine, FL (13th)
Hart, Melissa A., PA (4th)
Hastert, J. Dennis, IL (14th)
Hastings, Alcee L., FL (23rd)
Hastings, Doc, WA (4th)
Hayes, Robin, NC (8th)
Hayworth, J.D., AZ (5th)
Hefley, Joel, CO (5th)
Hensarling, Jeb, TX (5th)
Herger, Wally, CA (2nd)
Hill, Baron P., IN (9th)
Hinchey, Maurice D., NY (22nd)
Hinojosa, Rubén, TX (15th)
Hobson, David L., OH (7th)
Hoeffel, Joseph M., PA (13th)
Hoekstra, Peter, MI (2nd)
Holden, Tim, PA (17th)
Holt, Rush D., NJ (12th)
Honda, Michael M., CA (15th)
Hooley, Darlene, OR (5th)
Hostettler, John N., IN (8th)
Houghton, Amo, NY (29th)
Hoyer, Steny H., MD (5th)
Hulshof, Kenny C., MO (9th)
Hunter, Duncan, CA (52nd)
Hyde, Henry J., IL (6th)
Inslee, Jay, WA (1st)
Isakson, Johnny, GA (6th)
Israel, Steve, NY (2nd)
Issa, Darrell E., CA (49th)
Istook, Ernest J., Jr., OK (5th)
Jackson, Jesse L., Jr., IL (2nd)
Jackson Lee, Sheila, TX (18th)
Janklow, William J., SD (At Large)
Jefferson, William J., LA (2nd)
Jenkins, William L., TN (1st)
John, Christopher, LA (7th)
Johnson, Eddie Bernice, TX (30th)
Johnson, Nancy L., CT (5th)
Johnson, Sam, TX (3rd)
Johnson, Timothy V., IL (15th)
Jones, Stephanie Tubbs, OH (11th)
Jones, Walter B., NC (3rd)
Kanjorski, Paul E., PA (11th)
Kaptur, Marcy, OH (9th)
Keller, Ric, FL (8th)
Kelly, Sue W., NY (19th)
Kennedy, Mark R., MN (6th)
Kennedy, Patrick J., RI (1st)
Kildee, Dale E., MI (5th)
Kilpatrick, Carolyn C., MI (13th)
Kind, Ron, WI (3rd)
King, Peter T., NY (3rd)
King, Steve, IA (5th)
Kingston, Jack, GA (1st)
Kirk, Mark Steven, IL (10th)
Kleczka, Gerald D., WI (4th)
Kline, John, MN (2nd)
Knollenberg, Joe, MI (9th)
Kolbe, Jim, AZ (8th)
Kucinich, Dennis J., OH (10th)
LaHood, Ray, IL (18th)
Lampson, Nick, TX (9th)
Langevin, James R., RI (2nd)
Lantos, Tom, CA (12th)
Larsen, Rick, WA (2nd)
Larson, John B., CT (1st)
Latham, Tom, IA (4th)
LaTourette, Steven C., OH (14th)
Leach, James A., IA (2nd)
Lee, Barbara, CA (9th)
Levin, Sander M., MI (12th)
Lewis, Jerry, CA (41st)
Lewis, John, GA (5th)
Lewis, Ron, KY (2nd)
Linder, John, GA (7th)
Lipinski, William O., IL (3rd)

LoBiondo, Frank A., NJ (2nd)
Lofgren, Zoe, CA (16th)
Lowey, Nita M., NY (18th)
Lucas, Frank D., OK (3rd)
Lucas, Ken, KY (4th)
Lynch, Stephen F., MA (9th)
Majette, Denise L., GA (4th)
Maloney, Carolyn B., NY (14th)
Manzullo, Donald A., IL (16th)
Markey, Edward J., MA (7th)
Marshall, Jim, GA (3rd)
Matheson, Jim, UT (2nd)
Matsui, Robert T., CA (5th)
McCarthy, Carolyn, NY (4th)
McCarthy, Karen, MO (5th)
McCollum, Betty, MN (4th)
McCotter, Thaddeus G., MI (11th)
McCrery, Jim, LA (4th)
McDermott, Jim, WA (7th)
McGovern, James P., MA (3rd)
McHugh, John M., NY (23rd)
McInnis, Scott, CO (3rd)
McIntyre, Mike, NC (7th)
McKeon, Howard P. (Buck), CA (25th)
McNulty, Michael R., NY (21st)
Meehan, Martin T., MA (5th)
Meek, Kendrick B., FL (17th)
Meeks, Gregory W., NY (6th)
Menendez, Robert, NJ (13th)
Mica, John L., FL (7th)
Michaud, Michael H., ME (2nd)
Millender-McDonald, Juanita, CA (37th)
Miller, Brad, NC (13th)
Miller, Candice S., MI (10th)
Miller, Gary G., CA (42nd)
Miller, George, CA (7th)
Miller, Jeff, FL (1st)
Mollohan, Alan B., WV (1st)
Moore, Dennis, KS (3rd)
Moran, James P., VA (8th)
Moran, Jerry, KS (1st)
Murphy, Tim, PA (18th)
Murtha, John P., PA (12th)
Musgrave, Marilyn N., CO (4th)
Myrick, Sue Wilkins, NC (9th)
Nadler, Jerrold, NY (8th)
Napolitano, Grace F., CA (38th)
Neal, Richard E., MA (2nd)
Nethercutt, George R., Jr., WA (5th)
Neugebauer, Randy, TX (19th)
Ney, Robert W., OH (18th)
Northup, Anne M., KY (3rd)
Norwood, Charlie, GA (9th)
Nunes, Devin, CA (21st)
Nussle, Jim, IA (1st)
Oberstar, James L., MN (8th)
Obey, David R., WI (7th)
Olver, John W., MA (1st)
Ortiz, Solomon P., TX (27th)
Osborne, Tom, NE (3rd)
Ose, Doug, CA (3rd)
Otter, C.L. (Butch), ID (1st)
Owens, Major R., NY (11th)
Oxley, Michael G., OH (4th)
Pallone, Frank, Jr., NJ (6th)
Pascrell, Bill, Jr., NJ (8th)
Pastor, Ed, AZ (4th)
Paul, Ron, TX (14th)
Payne, Donald M., NJ (10th)
Pearce, Stevan, NM (2nd)
Pelosi, Nancy, CA (8th)
Pence, Mike, IN (6th)
Peterson, Collin C., MN (7th)
Peterson, John E., PA (5th)
Petri, Thomas E., WI (6th)
Pickering, Charles W. (Chip) Jr., MS (3rd)
Pitts, Joseph R., PA (16th)
Platts, Todd Russell, PA (19th)
Pombo, Richard W., CA (11th)
Pomeroy, Earl, ND (At Large)
Porter, Jon C., NV (3rd)
Portman, Rob, OH (2nd)
Price, David E., NC (4th)
Pryce, Deborah H., OH (15th)
Putnam, Adam, FL (12th)
Quinn, Jack, NY (27th)
Radanovich, George, CA (19th)
Rahall, Nick J., II, WV (3rd)
Ramstad, Jim, MN (3rd)
Rangel, Charles B., NY (15th)
Regula, Ralph, OH (16th)
Rehberg, Dennis R., MT (At Large)
Renzi, Rick, AZ (1st)
Reyes, Silvestre, TX (16th)
Reynolds, Thomas M., NY (26th)
Rodriguez, Ciro D., TX (28th)
Rogers, Harold, KY (5th)
Rogers, Mike, AL (3rd)
Rogers, Mike, MI (8th)
Rohrabacher, Dana, CA (46th)
Ros-Lehtinen, Ileana, FL (18th)
Ross, Mike, AR (4th)
Rothman, Steven R., NJ (9th)
Roybal-Allard, Lucille, CA (34th)
Royce, Edward R., CA (40th)
Ruppersberger, C.A. Dutch, MD (2nd)
Rush, Bobby L., IL (1st)
Ryan, Paul, WI (1st)
Ryan, Timothy J., OH (17th)
Ryun, Jim, KS (2nd)
Sabo, Martin Olav, MN (5th)
Sánchez, Linda T., CA (39th)
Sanchez, Loretta, CA (47th)
SANDERS, BERNARD, VT (At Large)
Sandlin, Max, TX (1st)
Saxton, Jim, NJ (3rd)
Schakowsky, Janice D., IL (9th)
Schiff, Adam B., CA (29th)
Schrock, Edward L., VA (2nd)
Scott, David, GA (13th)
Scott, Robert C., VA (3rd)
Sensenbrenner, F. James, Jr., WI (5th)
Serrano, José E., NY (16th)
Sessions, Pete, TX (32nd)
Shadegg, John B., AZ (3rd)
Shaw, E. Clay, Jr., FL (22nd)
Shays, Christopher, CT (4th)
Sherman, Brad, CA (27th)
Sherwood, Don, PA (10th)
Shimkus, John, IL (19th)
Shuster, Bill, PA (9th)
Simmons, Rob, CT (2nd)

Simpson, Michael K., ID (2nd)
Skelton, Ike, MO (4th)
Slaughter, Louise McIntosh, NY (28th)
Smith, Adam, WA (9th)
Smith, Christopher H., NJ (4th)
Smith, Lamar S., TX (21st)
Smith, Nick, MI (7th)
Snyder, Vic, AR (2nd)
Solis, Hilda L., CA (32nd)
Souder, Mark E., IN (3rd)
Spratt, John M., Jr., SC (5th)
Stark, Fortney Pete, CA (13th)
Stearns, Cliff, FL (6th)
Stenholm, Charles W., TX (17th)
Strickland, Ted, OH (6th)
Stupak, Bart, MI (1st)
Sullivan, John, OK (1st)
Sweeney, John E., NY (20th)
Tancredo, Thomas G., CO (6th)
Tanner, John S., TN (8th)
Tauscher, Ellen O., CA (10th)
Tauzin, W.J. (Billy), LA (3rd)
Taylor, Charles H., NC (11th)
Taylor, Gene, MS (4th)
Terry, Lee, NE (2nd)
Thomas, William M., CA (22nd)
Thompson, Bennie G., MS (2nd)
Thompson, Mike, CA (1st)
Thornberry, Mac, TX (13th)
Tiahrt, Todd, KS (4th)
Tiberi, Patrick J., OH (12th)
Tierney, John F., MA (6th)
Toomey, Patrick J., PA (15th)
Towns, Edolphus, NY (10th)
Turner, Jim, TX (2nd)
Turner, Michael R., OH (3rd)
Udall, Mark, CO (2nd)
Udall, Tom, NM (3rd)
Upton, Fred, MI (6th)
Van Hollen, Chris, MD (8th)
Velázquez, Nydia M., NY (12th)
Visclosky, Peter J., IN (1st)
Vitter, David, LA (1st)
Walden, Greg, OR (2nd)
Walsh, James T., NY (25th)
Wamp, Zach, TN (3rd)
Waters, Maxine, CA (35th)
Watson, Diane E., CA (33rd)
Watt, Melvin L., NC (12th)
Waxman, Henry A., CA (30th)
Weiner, Anthony D., NY (9th)
Weldon, Curt, PA (7th)
Weldon, Dave, FL (15th)
Weller, Jerry, IL (11th)
Wexler, Robert, FL (19th)
Whitfield, Ed, KY (1st)
Wicker, Roger F., MS (1st)
Wilson, Heather, NM (1st)
Wilson, Joe, SC (2nd)
Wolf, Frank R., VA (10th)
Woolsey, Lynn C., CA (6th)
Wu, David, OR (1st)
Wynn, Albert Russell, MD (4th)
Young, C.W. Bill, FL (10th)
Young, Don, AK (At Large)

DELEGATES
Bordallo, Madeleine Z., GU
Christensen, Donna M., VI
Faleomavaega, Eni F.H., AS
Norton, Eleanor Holmes, DC

RESIDENT COMISSIONER
Acevedo-Vilá, Aníbal, PR

108th Congress
Nine-Digit Postal ZIP Codes

Senate Post Office (20510): The four-digit numbers in these tables were assigned by the Senate Committee on Rules and Administration. Mail to all Senate offices is delivered by the main Post Office in the Dirksen Senate Office Building.

Senate Committees

Committee on Agriculture, Nutrition, and Forestry	–6000
Committee on Appropriations	–6025
Committee on Armed Services	–6050
Committee on Banking, Housing, and Urban Affairs.	–6075
Committee on the Budget	–6100
Committee on Commerce, Science, and Transportation.	–6125
Committee on Energy and Natural Resources	–6150
Committee on Environment and Public Works	–6175
Committee on Finance	–6200
Committee on Foreign Relations	–6225
Committee on Governmental Affairs	–6250
Committee on Health, Education, Labor and Pensions.	–6300
Committee on Indian Affairs	–6450
Committee on the Judiciary	–6275
Committee on Rules and Administration	–6325
Committee on Small Business and Entrepreneurship.	–6350
Committee on Veterans' Affairs	–6375
Committee on Aging (Special)	–6400
Committee on Ethics (Select)	–6425
Committee on Intelligence (Select)	–6475

Joint Committee Offices, Senate Side

Joint Economic Committee	–6602
Joint Committee on the Library	–6625
Joint Committee on Printing	–6650
Joint Committee on Taxation	–6675

Senate Leadership Offices

President Pro Tempore	–7000
Chaplain	–7002
Majority Leader	–7010
Assistant Majority Leader	–7012
Secretary for the Majority	–7014
Minority Leader	–7020
Assistant Minority Leader	–7022
Secretary for the Minority	–7024
Democratic Policy Committee	–7050
Republican Conference	–7060
Secretary to the Republican Conference	–7062
Republican Policy Committee	–7064
Republican Steering Committee	–7066
Arms Control Observer Group	–7070

Senate Officers

Secretary of the Senate	–7100
Curator of Art and Antiquities	–7102
Disbursing Office	–7104
Document Room	–7106
Historian	–7108
Interparliamentary Services	–7110
Senate Library	–7112
Office of Senate Security	–7114
Office of Public Records	–7116
Office of Official Recorders of Debates	–7117
Stationery Room	–7118
Office of Printing Services	–7120
U.S. Capitol Preservation Commission	–7122
Office of Conservation and Preservation	–7124
Senate Gift Shop	–7128
Legal Counsel, Employment Management Relations.	–7130
Senate Sergeant at Arms	–7200
General Counsel	–7201
Facilities	–7204
Finance Division	–7205
Hair Care Services	–7206
Procurement	–7207
Capitol Guides	–7209
Parking	–7210
Employee Assistance Program Office	–7211
Human Resources	–7212
Health Promotion Seminars	–7213
Placement	–7214
Senate Office of Education and Training	–7215
Photographic Studio	–7261
Capitol Police	–7218
Senate Post Office	–7263
Senate Recording Studio	–7222
Congressional Special Services Office	–7228
Customer Relations	–7230
CR-Customer Support	–7231

Other Offices on the Senate Side

Senate Legal Counsel	–7250
Central Operations (CO)—Administration	–7260
CO-Photo Studio	–7261
CO-Parking/ID	–7262
CO-Post Office	–7263
CO-Printing Graphics & Direct Mail—Production.	–7264
CO-Recording	–7265
CO-Printing Graphics & Direct Mail—Reprographics.	–7266
Chief of Operations	–7270
Deputy Chief of Operations	–7271
Senate Legislative Counsel	–7275
Program Management	–7276
Systems Architecture	–7277
Office Operations (OO)—Administration	–7280
OO-IT/Telecom Support	–7281
OO-Equipment Services	–7282
OO-Communication Installation & Support	–7283
OO-Desktop/LAN Support	–7284
OO-State Office Liasion	–7285
Technical Operations (TO)—Administration	–7290
TO-Applications Development	–7291
TO-Web & Technology Assessment	–7292
TO-Network Engineering & Management	–7293
TO-Enterprise It Systems	–7294
TO-Voice & RF Systems	–7295
TO-Inter/Intranet Services	–7296
Architect of the Capitol	–8000
Superintendent of Senate Buildings	–8002
Restaurant	–8050
Office of Technology Assessment	–8025

Amtrak Ticket Office	–9010
Airlines Ticket Office (CATO)	–9014
Child Care Center	–9022
Credit Union	–9026
Periodical Press Gallery	–7234
Press Gallery	–7238
Press Photo Gallery	–7242
Radio and TV Gallery	–7246
Webster Hall	–7248
Office of Compliance	–9061
Social Security Liaison	–9064
Veterans Liaison	–9054
Western Union	–9058
Office of Senate Fair Employment Practices	–9060
Frank Delano Roosevelt Memorial Commission	–9066
Caucus on International Narcotics Control	–9070
Army Liaison	–9082
Air Force Liaison	–9083
Coast Guard Liaison	–9084
Navy Liaison	–9085
Marine Liaison	–9087

House Post Office (20515): The four-digit numbers in these tables were assigned by the Postmaster of the House of Representatives. Mail to all House offices is delivered by the main Post Office in the Longworth House Office Building.

House Committees, Leadership and Officers

U.S. House of Representatives	–0001
Cannon House Office Building	–0002
Rayburn House Office Building	–0003
Longworth House Office Building	–0004
O'Neill House Office Building	–0005
Ford House Office Building	–0006
The Capitol	–0007
Office of the Chaplain	–6655
Committee on Agriculture	–6001
Committee on Appropriations	–6015
Committee on Armed Services	–6035
Committee on the Budget	–6065
Committee on Education and the Workforce	–6100
Committee on Energy and Commerce	–6115
Committee on Financial Services	–6050
Committee on Government Reform	–6143
Committee on House Administration	–6157
Committee on International Relations	–6128
Committee on the Judiciary	–6216
Committee on Resources	–6201
Committee on Rules	–6269
Committee on Science	–6301
Committee on Small Business	–6315
Committee on Standards of Official Conduct	–6328
Committee on Transportation and Infrastructure	–6256
Committee on Veterans' Affairs	–6335
Committee on Ways and Means	–6348
Select Committee on Homeland Security	–6480
Select Committee on Intelligence	–6415

Joint Committee Offices, House Side

Joint Economic Committee	–6432
Joint Committee on the Library of Congress	–6439
Joint Committee on Printing	–6445
Joint Committee on Taxation	–6453

House Leadership Offices

Office of the Speaker	–6501
Office of the Majority Leader	–6502
Office of the Majority Whip	–6503
Office of the Deputy Majority Whip	–6504
Democratic Caucus	–6524
Democratic Congressional Campaign Committee	–6525
Democratic Personnel Committee	–6526
Democratic Steering and Policy Committee	–6527
Democratic Cloakroom	–6528
Office of the Democratic Leader	–6537
Office of the Democratic Whip	–6538
House Republican Conference	–6544
House Republican Research Committee	–6545
Legislative Digest (Republican Conference)	–6546
Republican Congressional Committee, National	–6547
Republican Policy Committee	–6549
Republican Cloakroom	–6650

House Officers

Office of the Clerk	–6601
Office of History and Preservation	–6612
Office of Employment and Counsel	–6622
House Page School	–9996
House Page Dorm	–6606
Legislative Computer Systems	–6618
Office of Legislative Operations	–6602
Legislative Resource Center	–6612
Official Reporters	–6615
Office of Publication Services	–6611
Chief Administrative Officer	–6861
First Call	–6660
Administrative Counsel	–6660
Periodical Press Gallery	–6624
Press Gallery	–6625
Radio/TV Correspondents' Gallery	–6627
HIR Call Center	–6165
HIR Information Systems Security	–6165
Outplacement Services	–9920
Office of Employee Assistance	–6619
ADA Services	–6860
Personnel and Benefits	–9980
Child Care Center	–0001
Payroll	–9920
Members' Services	–9970
Office Supply Service	–6860
House Gift Shop	–6860
Mail List/Processing	–6860
Mailing Services	–6860
Contractor Management	–6860
Photography	–6623
House Recording Studio	–6613
Furniture Support Services	–6610
House Office Service Center	–6860
Budget	–6604
Financial Counseling	–6604
Procurement Desktop Help	–9940
Office of the Sergeant at Arms	–6611

House Commissions and Offices

Congressional-Executive Commission on the People's Republic of China.	–0001
Commission on Security and Cooperation in Europe.	–6460
Commission on Congressional Mailing Standards	–6461
Office of the Law Revision Counsel	–6711
Office of Emergency Planning, Preparedness and Operations.	–6462

Office of the Legislative Counsel	–6721
Office of the Parliamentarian	–6731
General Counsel	–6532
Architect of the Capitol	–6906
Attending Physician	–6907
Congressional Budget Office	–6925

Liaison Offices

Air Force	–6854
Army	–6855
Coast Guard	–6856
Navy	–6857
Office of Personnel Management	–6858
Veterans' Administration	–6859

TERMS OF SERVICE

EXPIRATION OF THE TERMS OF SENATORS

CLASS III.—SENATORS WHOSE TERMS OF SERVICE EXPIRE IN 2005

[34 Senators in this group: Democrats, 19; Republicans, 15]

Name	Party	Residence
Bayh, Evan	D.	Indianapolis, IN.
Bennett, Robert F.	R.	Salt Lake City, UT.
Bond, Christopher S.	R.	Mexico, MO.
Boxer, Barbara	D.	Greenbrae, CA.
Breaux, John B.	D.	Crowley, LA.
Brownback, Samuel Dale [1]	R.	Topeka, KS.
Bunning, Jim	R.	Southgate, KY.
Campbell, Ben Nighthorse [2]	R.	Ignacio, CO.
Crapo, Michael D.	R.	Idaho Falls, ID.
Daschle, Thomas A.	D.	Aberdeen, SD.
Dodd, Christopher J.	D.	Norwich, CT.
Dorgan, Byron L.[3]	D.	Bismarck, ND.
Edwards, John	D.	Raleigh, NC.
Feingold, Russell D.	D.	Middleton, WI.
Fitzgerald, Peter G.	R.	Inverness, IL.
Graham, Bob	D.	Miami Lakes, FL.
Grassley, Charles E.	R.	New Hartford, IA.
Gregg, Judd	R.	Greenfield, NH.
Hollings, Ernest F.	D.	Charleston, SC.
Inouye, Daniel K.	D.	Honolulu, HI.
Leahy, Patrick J.	D.	Burlington, VT.
Lincoln, Blanche L.	D.	Hughes, AR.
McCain, John	R.	Phoenix, AZ.
Mikulski, Barbara A.	D.	Baltimore, MD.
Miller, Zell [4]	D.	Young Harris, GA.
Murkowski, Lisa [5]	R.	Anchorage, AK.
Murray, Patty	D.	Seattle, WA.
Nickles, Don	R.	Ponca City, OK.
Reid, Harry	D.	Las Vegas, NV.
Schumer, Charles E.	D.	Brooklyn, NY.
Shelby, Richard C.[6]	R.	Tuscaloosa, AL.
Specter, Arlen	R.	Philadelphia, PA.
Voinovich, George V.	R.	Cleveland, OH.
Wyden, Ron [7]	D.	Portland, OR.

[1] Senator Brownback was elected on November 5, 1996 to fill the remainder of the term of Senator Bob Dole. He took the oath of office on November 27, 1996. This seat was filled by Senator Sheila Frahm, who had been appointed, ad interim, on June 11, 1996 by the Governor.

[2] Senator Campbell changed parties March 3, 1995.

[3] Senator Dorgan was elected to a 6-year term on Nov. 3, 1992, and subsequently was appointed by the Governor Dec. 14, 1992 to fill the vacancy caused by the resignation of Senator Kent Conrad.

[4] Senator Miller was appointed on July 24, 2000, by the Governor of Georgia, to fill the vacancy caused by the death of Senator Paul Coverdell. He was then elected to finish the last 4 years of the term on November 7, 2000.

[5] Senator Lisa Murkowski was appointed on December 20, 2002 by the Governor of Alaska to fill the vacancy caused by the resignation of Senator Frank Murkowski who was elected Governor on November 5, 2002.

[6] Senator Shelby changed parties on November 5, 1994.

[7] Senator Wyden was elected on January 30, 1996, to fill the vacancy caused by the resignation of Senator Bob Packwood.

CLASS I.—SENATORS WHOSE TERMS OF SERVICE EXPIRE IN 2007

[33 Senators in this group: Democrats, 17; Republicans, 15; Independents, 1]

Name	Party	Residence
Akaka, Daniel K.[1]	D.	Honolulu, HI.
Allen, George	R.	Chesterfield County, VA.
Bingaman, Jeff	D.	Santa Fe, NM.
Burns, Conrad R.	R.	Billings, MT.
Byrd, Robert C.	D.	Sophia, WV.
Cantwell, Maria	D.	Edmonds, WA.
Carper, Thomas	D.	Wilmington, DE.
Chafee, Lincoln D.[2]	R.	Warwick, RI.
Clinton, Hillary Rodham	D.	Chappaqua, NY.
Conrad, Kent[3]	D.	Bismarck, ND.
Corzine, Jon S.	D.	Summit, NJ.
Dayton, Mark	D.	Minneapolis, MN.
DeWine, Mike	R.	Cedarville, OH.
Ensign, John	R.	Las Vegas, NV.
Feinstein, Dianne[4]	D.	San Francisco, CA.
Frist, William H.	R.	Nashville, TN.
Hatch, Orrin G.	R.	Salt Lake City, UT.
Hutchison, Kay Bailey[5]	R.	Dallas, TX.
Jeffords, James M.[6]	I.	Shrewsbury, VT.
Kennedy, Edward M.	D.	Boston, MA.
Kohl, Herb	D.	Milwaukee, WI.
Kyl, Jon	R.	Phoenix, AZ.
Lieberman, Joseph I.	D.	New Haven, CT.
Lott, Trent	R.	Pascagoula, MS.
Lugar, Richard G.	R.	Indianapolis, IN.
Nelson, Ben	D.	Omaha, NE.
Nelson, Bill	D.	Tallahassee, FL.
Santorum, Rick	R.	Pittsburgh, PA.
Sarbanes, Paul S.	D.	Baltimore, MD.
Snowe, Olympia J.	R.	Auburn, ME.
Stabenow, Debbie	D.	Lansing, MI.
Talent, James M.[7]	R.	Chesterfield, MO.
Thomas, Craig	R.	Casper, WY.

[1] Senator Akaka was appointed Apr. 28, 1990 by the Governor of Hawaii to fill the vacancy caused by the death of Senator Spark M. Matsunaga, and took the oath of office on May 16, 1990. He was elected in a special election on Nov. 6, 1990, for the remainder of the unexpired term.

[2] Senator Lincoln D. Chafee was appointed on November 2, 1999, by the Governor of Rhode Island, to fill the vacancy caused by the death of Senator John H. Chafee. He was then elected to a full term on November 7, 2000.

[3] Senator Conrad resigned his term from Class III after winning a special election on Dec. 4, 1992, to fill the vacancy caused by the death of Senator Quentin Burdick. Senator Conrad's seniority in the Senate continues without a break in service. He took the oath of office on Dec. 15, 1992.

[4] Senator Feinstein won the special election held on Nov. 3, 1992, to fill the vacancy caused by the resignation of Senator Pete Wilson. She took the oath of office on Nov. 10, 1992. This seat was filled, pending the election, by Senator John Seymour who was appointed by the Governor of California on January 7, 1991.

[5] Senator Hutchison won the special election held on June 5, 1993, to fill remainder of the term of Senator Lloyd Bentsen. She took the oath of office on June 14, 1993. She won the seat from Senator Bob Krueger, who had been appointed by the Governor of Texas on Jan. 21, 1993.

[6] Senator Jeffords changed party affiliation from Republican to Independent on June 6, 2001.

[7] Senator Talent won the general election held on November 5, 2002, against Senator Jean Carnahan.

CLASS II.—SENATORS WHOSE TERMS OF SERVICE EXPIRE IN 2009

[33 Senators in this group: Republicans, 21; Democrats, 12]

Name	Party	Residence
Alexander, Lamar	R.	Nashville, TN.
Allard, Wayne	R.	Loveland, CO.
Baucus, Max	D.	Missoula, MT.
Biden, Joseph R., Jr.	D.	Hockessin, DE.
Chambliss, Saxby	R.	Moultrie, GA.
Cochran, Thad	R.	Jackson, MS.
Coleman, Norm	R.	St. Paul, MN.
Collins, Susan	R.	Bangor, ME.
Cornyn, John	R.	San Antonio, TX.
Craig, Larry E.	R.	Boise, ID.
Dole, Elizabeth H.	R.	Salisbury, NC.
Domenici, Pete V.	R.	Albuquerque, NM.
Durbin, Richard J.	D.	Springfield, IL.
Enzi, Michael B.	R.	Gillette, WY.
Graham, Lindsey	R.	Seneca, SC.
Hagel, Chuck	R.	Omaha, NE.
Harkin, Tom	D.	Cumming, IA.
Inhofe, James M.	R.	Tulsa, OK.
Kerry, John F.	D.	Boston, MA.
Johnson, Tim	D.	Vermillion, SD.
Landrieu, Mary	D.	Baton Rouge, LA.
Lautenberg, Frank R.	D.	Cliffside Park, NJ.
Levin, Carl	D.	Detroit, MI.
McConnell, Mitch	R.	Louisville, KY.
Pryor, Mark	D.	Little Rock, AR.
Reed, Jack	D.	Cranston, RI.
Roberts, Pat	R.	Dodge City, KS.
Rockefeller, John D., IV	D.	Charleston, WV.
Sessions, Jeff	R.	Mobile, AL.
Smith, Gordon	R.	Pendleton, OR.
Stevens, Ted	R.	Anchorage, AK.
Sununu, John E.	R.	Bedford, NH.
Warner, John W.	R.	Middleburg, VA.

CONTINUOUS SERVICE OF SENATORS

[Republicans in roman (51); Democrats in *italic* (48); Independents in SMALL CAPS (1); total, 100]

Rank	Name	State	Beginning of present service
1	*Byrd, Robert C.*†	West Virginia	Jan. 3, 1959.
2	*Kennedy, Edward M.*[1]	Massachusetts	Nov. 7, 1962. ‡
3	*Inouye, Daniel K.*†	Hawaii	Jan. 3, 1963.
4	*Hollings, Ernest F.*[2]	South Carolina	Nov. 9, 1966. ‡
5	Stevens, Ted[3]	Alaska	Dec. 24, 1968.
6	*Biden, Joseph R., Jr.*	Delaware	Jan. 3, 1973.
	Domenici, Pete V.	New Mexico	
7	*Leahy, Patrick J.*	Vermont	Jan. 3, 1975.
8	Hatch, Orrin G.	Utah	Dec. 30, 1976.
	Lugar, Richard G.	Indiana	
9	*Sarbanes, Paul S.*†	Maryland	Jan. 3, 1977.
10	*Baucus, Max*†[4]	Montana	Dec. 15, 1978.
11	Cochran, Thad†[5]	Mississippi	Dec. 27, 1978.
12	Warner, John W.[6]	Virginia	Jan. 2, 1979.
13	*Levin, Carl*	Michigan	Jan. 3, 1979.
14	*Dodd, Christopher J.*†	Connecticut	Jan. 3, 1981.
	Grassley, Charles E.†	Iowa	
	Nickles, Don	Oklahoma	
	Specter, Arlen	Pennsylvania	
15	*Bingaman, Jeff*	New Mexico	Jan. 3, 1983.
16	*Kerry, John F.*[7]	Massachusetts	Jan. 2, 1985.
17	*Harkin, Tom*†	Iowa	
	McConnell, Mitch	Kentucky	
18	*Rockefeller, John D., IV*[8]	West Virginia	Jan. 15, 1985.
19	Bond, Christopher S.	Missouri	Jan. 3, 1987.
	Breaux, John B.†	Louisiana	
	Conrad, Kent	North Dakota	
	Daschle, Thomas A.†	South Dakota	
	Graham, Bob	Florida	
	McCain, John†	Arizona	
	Mikulski, Barbara A.†	Maryland	
	Reid, Harry†	Nevada	
	Shelby, Richard C.†	Alabama	
20	Burns, Conrad	Montana	Jan. 3, 1989.
	JEFFORDS, JAMES M.†[9]	Vermont	
	Kohl, Herb	Wisconsin	
	Lieberman, Joseph I.	Connecticut	
	Lott, Trent†	Mississippi	
21	*Akaka, Daniel K.*†[10]	Hawaii	Apr. 28, 1990.
22	Craig, Larry E.†	Idaho	Jan. 3, 1991.
23	*Feinstein, Dianne*[11]	California	Nov. 10, 1992.‡
24	*Dorgan, Byron*†[12]	North Dakota	Dec. 14, 1992.
25	Bennett, Robert F.	Utah	Jan. 3, 1993.
	Boxer, Barbara†	California	
	Campbell, Ben Nighthorse†[13]	Colorado	
	Feingold, Russell	Wisconsin	
	Gregg, Judd†	New Hampshire	
	Murray, Patty	Washington	
26	Hutchison, Kay Bailey[14]	Texas	June 5, 1993.
27	Inhofe, James M.†[15]	Oklahoma	Nov. 16, 1994. ‡
28	DeWine, Mike†	Ohio	Jan. 3, 1995
	Frist, Bill	Tennessee	
	Kyl, Jon†	Arizona	
	Santorum, Rick†	Pennsylvania	

CONTINUOUS SERVICE OF SENATORS—CONTINUED

[Republicans in roman (51); Democrats in *italic* (48); Independents in SMALL CAPS (1); total, 100]

Rank	Name	State	Beginning of present service
	Snowe, Olympia J.†	Maine	
	Thomas, Craig †	Wyoming	
29	*Wyden, Ron* † [16]	Oregon	Feb. 6, 1996. ‡
30	Brownback, Samuel Dale † [17]	Kansas	Nov. 6, 1996. ‡
31	Hagel, Chuck	Nebraska	Jan. 3, 1997.
	Allard, Wayne †	Colorado	
	Collins, Susan	Maine	
	Durbin, Richard J. †	Illinois	
	Enzi, Michael B.	Wyoming	
	Johnson, Tim †	South Dakota	
	Landrieu, Mary	Louisiana	
	Reed, Jack †	Rhode Island	
	Roberts, Pat †	Kansas	
	Sessions, Jeff	Alabama	
	Smith, Gordon	Oregon	
32	*Bayh, Evan*	Indiana	Jan. 3, 1999.
	Bunning, Jim †	Kentucky	
	Crapo, Michael D.†	Idaho	
	Edwards, John	North Carolina	
	Fitzgerald, Peter G.	Illinois	
	Lincoln, Blanche L. †	Arkansas	
	Schumer, Charles E. †	New York	
	Voinovich, George V.	Ohio	
33	Chafee, Lincoln D.[18]	Rhode Island	Nov. 2, 1999.
34	*Miller, Zell* [19]	Georgia	Jul. 24, 2000.
35	Allen, George †	Virginia	Jan. 3, 2001.
	Cantwell, Maria †	Washington	
	Carper, Thomas †	Delaware	
	Clinton, Hillary Rodham	New York	
	Corzine, Jon S.	New Jersey	
	Dayton, Mark	Minnesota	
	Ensign, John †	Nevada	
	Nelson, Ben	Nebraska	
	Nelson, Bill †	Florida	
	Stabenow, Debbie †	Michigan	
36	Talent, James M. † [20]	Missouri	Nov. 6, 2002. ‡
37	Cornyn, John [21]	Texas	Dec. 2, 2002.
38	Murkowski, Lisa [22]	Alaska	Dec. 20, 2002.
39	Alexander, Lamar	Tennessee	Jan. 3, 2003.
	Chambliss, Saxby †	Georgia	
	Coleman, Norm	Minnesota	
	Dole, Elizabeth H.	North Carolina	
	Graham, Lindsey †	South Carolina	
	Lautenberg, Frank R. [23]	New Jersey	
	Pryor, Mark	Arkansas	
	Sununu, John †	New Hampshire	

† Served in the House of Representatives previous to service in the Senate.

‡ Senators elected to complete unexpired terms begin their terms on the day following the election.

[1] Senator Kennedy was elected Nov. 6, 1962, to complete the unexpired term caused by the resignation of Senator John F. Kennedy.

[2] Senator Hollings was elected Nov. 8, 1966, to complete the unexpired term caused by the death of Senator Olin D. Johnston.

[3] Senator Stevens was appointed Dec. 23, 1968 by the Governor to fill the vacancy caused by the death of Senator Edward L. Bartlett.

[4] Senator Baucus was elected Nov. 7, 1978, for the 6-year term commencing Jan. 3, 1979; subsequently appointed Dec. 15, 1978, to fill the vacancy caused by the resignation of Senator Paul Hatfield.

[5] Senator Cochran was elected Nov. 6, 1978, for the 6-year term commencing Jan. 3, 1979; subsequently appointed Dec. 27, 1978, to fill the vacancy caused by the resignation of Senator James Eastland.

[6] Senator Warner was elected Nov. 6, 1978, for the 6-year term commencing Jan. 3, 1979; subsequently appointed Jan. 2, 1979, to fill the vacancy caused by the resignation of Senator William Scott.

[7] Senator Kerry was elected Nov. 6, 1984, for the 6-year term commencing Jan. 3, 1985; subsequently appointed Jan. 2, 1985, to fill the vacancy caused by the resignation of Senator Paul E. Tsongas.

[8] Senator Rockefeller was elected Nov. 6, 1984, for the 6-year term commencing Jan. 3, 1985; did not take his seat until Jan. 15, 1985.

[9] Senator Jeffords changed party affiliation from Republican to Independent on June 6, 2001.

[10] Senator Akaka was appointed Apr. 28, 1990 by the Governor to fill the vacancy caused by the death of Senator Spark M. Matsunaga. Subsequently elected on Nov. 6, 1990 to complete the unexpired term.

[11] Senator Feinstein was elected on Nov. 3, 1992 to fill the vacancy caused by the resignation of Senator Pete Wilson. She replaced appointed Senator John Seymour when she took the oath of office on Nov. 10, 1992.

[12] Senator Dorgan was elected to a 6-year term on Nov. 3, 1992 and subsequently was appointed by the Governor on Dec. 14, 1992 to complete the unexpired term of Senator Kent Conrad.

[13] Senator Campbell changed parties on March 3, 1995.

[14] Senator Hutchison won a special election on June 5, 1993 to fill the vacancy caused by the resignation of Senator Lloyd Bentsen. She won the seat from Senator Bob Krueger, who had been appointed on Jan. 21, 1993 by the Governor.

[15] Senator Inhofe was elected to fill an unexpired term until January 3, 1997.

[16] Senator Wyden was elected on January 30, 1996 to fill the vacancy caused by the resignation of Senator Bob Packwood.

[17] Senator Brownback was elected on November 5, 1996 to fill the vacancy caused by the resignation of Senator Bob Dole. He replaced appointed Senator Sheila Frahm when he took the oath of office on November 27, 1996.

[18] Senator Lincoln D. Chafee was appointed on November 2, 1999, by the Governor of Rhode Island, to fill the vacancy caused by the death of Senator John H. Chafee. He was then elected to a full term on November 7, 2000.

[19] Senator Miller was appointed on July 24, 2000, by the Governor of Georgia, to fill the vacancy caused by the death of Senator Paul Coverdell. He was then elected to finish the last 4 years of the term on November 7, 2000.

[20] Senator Talent was elected to fill an unexpired term until January 3, 2007.

[21] Senator Cornyn was appointed on December 2, 2002 to fill the vacancy caused by the resignation of Senator Phil Gramm.

[22] Senator Lisa Murkowski was appointed on December 20, 2002 to fill the vacancy caused by the resignation of Senator Frank Murkowski.

[23] Senator Lautenberg previously served in the Senate from December 27, 1982 until January 3, 2001.

CONGRESSES IN WHICH REPRESENTATIVES HAVE SERVED, WITH BEGINNING OF PRESENT SERVICE

[* Elected to fill a vacancy; Republicans in roman (229); Democrats in *italic* (205); Independents in SMALL CAPS (1); Resident Commissioner and Delegates in **boldface** (5); total, 440]

Name	State	Congresses (inclusive)	Beginning of present service
25 terms, consecutive			
Dingell, John D.	MI	*84th to 108th	Dec. 13, 1955
20 terms, consecutive			
Conyers, John, Jr.	MI	89th to 108th	Jan. 3, 1965
18 terms, consecutive			
Crane, Philip M.	IL	*91st to 108th	Nov. 25, 1969
Obey, David R.	WI	*91st to 108th	Apr. 1, 1969
17 terms, consecutive			
Rangel, Charles B.	NY	92d to 108th	Jan. 3, 1971
Young, C.W. Bill	FL	92d to 108th	Jan. 3, 1971
16 terms, consecutive			
Murtha, John P.	PA	*93d to 108th	Feb. 5, 1974
Regula, Ralph	OH	93d to 108th	Jan. 3, 1973
Stark, Fortney Pete	CA	93d to 108th	Jan. 3, 1973
Young, Don	AK	*93d to 108th	Mar. 6, 1973
15 terms, consecutive			
Hyde, Henry J.	IL	94th to 108th	Jan. 3, 1975
Markey, Edward J.	MA	*94th to 108th	Nov. 2, 1976
Miller, George	CA	94th to 108th	Jan. 3, 1975
Oberstar, James L.	MN	94th to 108th	Jan. 3, 1975
Waxman, Henry A.	CA	94th to 108th	Jan. 3, 1975
14 terms, consecutive			
Dicks, Norman D.	WA	95th to 108th	Jan. 3, 1977
Gephardt, Richard A.	MO	95th to 108th	Jan. 3, 1977
Kildee, Dale E.	MI	95th to 108th	Jan. 3, 1977
Leach, James A.	IA	95th to 108th	Jan. 3, 1977
Rahall, Nick J., II	WV	95th to 108th	Jan. 3, 1977
Skelton, Ike	MO	95th to 108th	Jan. 3, 1977
13 terms, consecutive			
Bereuter, Doug	NE	96th to 108th	Jan. 3, 1979
Frost, Martin	TX	96th to 108th	Jan. 3, 1979
Lewis, Jerry	CA	96th to 108th	Jan. 3, 1979
Matsui, Robert T.	CA	96th to 108th	Jan. 3, 1979
Petri, Thomas E.	WI	*96th to 108th	Apr. 3, 1979
Sabo, Martin Olav	MN	96th to 108th	Jan. 3, 1979
Sensenbrenner, F. James, Jr.	WI	96th to 108th	Jan. 3, 1979
Stenholm, Charles W.	TX	96th to 108th	Jan. 3, 1979
Tauzin, W.J. (Billy)	LA	*96th to 108th	May 17, 1980
Thomas, Bill	CA	96th to 108th	Jan. 3, 1979
12 terms, consecutive			
Dreier, David	CA	97th to 108th	Jan. 3, 1981
Frank, Barney	MA	97th to 108th	Jan. 3, 1981

CONGRESSES IN WHICH REPRESENTATIVES HAVE SERVED, WITH BEGINNING OF PRESENT SERVICE—CONTINUED

[* Elected to fill a vacancy; Republicans in roman (229); Democrats in *italic* (205); Independents in SMALL CAPS (1); Resident Commissioner and Delegates in **boldface** (5); total, 440]

Name	State	Congresses (inclusive)	Beginning of present service
Hall, Ralph M.	TX	97th to 108th	Jan. 3, 1981
Hoyer, Steny H.	MD	*97th to 108th	May 19, 1981
Hunter, Duncan	CA	97th to 108th	Jan. 3, 1981
Lantos, Tom	CA	97th to 108th	Jan. 3, 1981
Oxley, Michael G.	OH	*97th to 108th	June 25, 1981
Rogers, Harold	KY	97th to 108th	Jan. 3, 1981
Shaw, E. Clay, Jr.	FL	97th to 108th	Jan. 3, 1981
Smith, Christopher H.	NJ	97th to 108th	Jan. 3, 1981
Wolf, Frank R.	VA	97th to 108th	Jan. 3, 1981
11 terms, consecutive			
Ackerman, Gary L.	NY	*98th to 108th	Mar. 1, 1983
Berman, Howard L.	CA	98th to 108th	Jan. 3, 1983
Bilirakis, Michael	FL	98th to 108th	Jan. 3, 1983
Boehlert, Sherwood	NY	98th to 108th	Jan. 3, 1983
Boucher, Rick	VA	98th to 108th	Jan. 3, 1983
Burton, Dan	IN	98th to 108th	Jan. 3, 1983
Evans, Lane	IL	98th to 108th	Jan. 3, 1983
Johnson, Nancy L.	CT	98th to 108th	Jan. 3, 1983
Kaptur, Marcy	OH	98th to 108th	Jan. 3, 1983
Kleczka, Gerald D.	WI	98th to 108th	Apr. 3, 1984
Levin, Sander M.	MI	98th to 108th	Jan. 3, 1983
Lipinski, William O.	IL	98th to 108th	Jan. 3, 1983
Mollohan, Alan B.	WV	98th to 108th	Jan. 3, 1983
Ortiz, Solomon P.	TX	98th to 108th	Jan. 3, 1983
Owens, Major R.	NY	98th to 108th	Jan. 3, 1983
Saxton, Jim	NJ	*98th to 108th	Nov. 6, 1984
Spratt, John M., Jr.	SC	98th to 108th	Jan. 3, 1983
Towns, Edolphus	NY	98th to 108th	Jan. 3, 1983
10 terms, consecutive			
Ballenger, Cass	NC	*99th to 108th	Nov. 4, 1986
Barton, Joe	TX	99th to 108th	Jan. 3, 1985
Coble, Howard	NC	99th to 108th	Jan. 3, 1985
DeLay, Tom	TX	99th to 108th	Jan. 3, 1985
Gordon, Bart	TN	99th to 108th	Jan. 3, 1985
Kanjorski, Paul E.	PA	99th to 108th	Jan. 3, 1985
Kolbe, Jim	AZ	99th to 108th	Jan. 3, 1985
Visclosky, Peter J.	IN	99th to 108th	Jan. 3, 1985
9 terms, consecutive			
Baker, Richard H.	LA	100th to 108th	Jan. 3, 1987
Cardin, Benjamin L.	MD	100th to 108th	Jan. 3, 1987
Costello, Jerry F.	IL	*100th to 108th	Aug. 9, 1988
DeFazio, Peter A.	OR	100th to 108th	Jan. 3, 1987
Duncan, John J., Jr.	TN	*100th to 108th	Nov. 8, 1988
Gallegly, Elton	CA	100th to 108th	Jan. 3, 1987
Hastert, J. Dennis	IL	100th to 108th	Jan. 3, 1987
Hefley, Joel	CO	100th to 108th	Jan. 3, 1987
Herger, Wally	CA	100th to 108th	Jan. 3, 1987
Houghton, Amo	NY	100th to 108th	Jan. 3, 1987

CONGRESSES IN WHICH REPRESENTATIVES HAVE SERVED, WITH BEGINNING OF PRESENT SERVICE—CONTINUED

[* Elected to fill a vacancy; Republicans in roman (229); Democrats in *italic* (205); Independents in SMALL CAPS (1); Resident Commissioner and Delegates in **boldface** (5); total, 440]

Name	State	Congresses (inclusive)	Beginning of present service
Lewis, John	GA	100th to 108th	Jan. 3, 1987
McCrery, Jim	LA	*100th to 108th	Apr. 16, 1988
Pallone, Frank, Jr.	NJ	*100th to 108th	Nov. 8, 1988
Pelosi, Nancy	CA	*100th to 108th	June 2, 1987
Shays, Christopher	CT	*100th to 108th	Aug. 18, 1987
Slaughter, Louise McIntosh	NY	100th to 108th	Jan. 3, 1987
Smith, Lamar S.	TX	100th to 108th	Jan. 3, 1987
Upton, Frederick S.	MI	100th to 108th	Jan. 3, 1987
Weldon, Curt	PA	100th to 108th	Jan. 3, 1987
8 terms, consecutive			
Andrews, Robert E.	NJ	*101st to 108th	Nov. 6, 1990
Cox, Christopher	CA	101st to 108th	Jan. 3, 1989
Engel, Eliot L.	NY	101st to 108th	Jan. 3, 1989
Gillmor, Paul E.	OH	101st to 108th	Jan. 3, 1989
Goss, Porter J.	FL	101st to 108th	Jan. 3, 1989
Lowey, Nita M.	NY	101st to 108th	Jan. 3, 1989
McDermott, Jim	WA	101st to 108th	Jan. 3, 1989
McNulty, Michael R.	NY	101st to 108th	Jan. 3, 1989
Neal, Richard E.	MA	101st to 108th	Jan. 3, 1989
Payne, Donald M.	NJ	101st to 108th	Jan. 3, 1989
Rohrabacher, Dana	CA	101st to 108th	Jan. 3, 1989
Ros-Lehtinen, Ileana	FL	*101st to 108th	Aug. 29, 1989
Serrano, José E.	NY	*101st to 108th	Mar. 20, 1990
Stearns, Cliff	FL	101st to 108th	Jan. 3, 1989
Tanner, John S.	TN	101st to 108th	Jan. 3, 1989
Taylor, Gene	MS	*101st to 108th	Oct. 17, 1989
Walsh, James T.	NY	101st to 108th	Jan. 3, 1989
8 terms, not consecutive			
Abercrombie, Neil	HI	*99th, 102d to 108th.	Jan. 3, 1991
Paul, Ron	TX	94th, 96th to 98th, 105th to 108th.	Jan. 3, 1997
Price, David E.	NC	100th to 103d, 105th to 108th.	Jan 3. 1997
7 terms, consecutive			
Boehner, John A.	OH	102d to 108th	Jan. 3, 1991
Camp, Dave	MI	102d to 108th	Jan. 3, 1991
Cramer, Robert (Bud), Jr.	AL	102d to 108th	Jan. 3, 1991
Cunningham, Randy (Duke)	CA	102d to 108th	Jan. 3, 1991
DeLauro, Rosa L.	CT	102d to 108th	Jan. 3, 1991
Dooley, Calvin M.	CA	102d to 108th	Jan. 3, 1991
Doolittle, John T.	CA	102d to 108th	Jan. 3, 1991
Edwards, Chet	TX	102d to 108th	Jan. 3, 1991
Gilchrest, Wayne T.	MD	102d to 108th	Jan. 3, 1991
Hobson, David L.	OH	102d to 108th	Jan. 3, 1991
Jefferson, William J.	LA	102d to 108th	Jan. 3, 1991
Johnson, Sam	TX	*102d to 108th	May 18, 1991
Moran, James P.	VA	102d to 108th	Jan. 3, 1991
Nadler, Jerrold	NY	*102d to 108th	Nov. 4, 1992

CONGRESSES IN WHICH REPRESENTATIVES HAVE SERVED, WITH BEGINNING OF PRESENT SERVICE—CONTINUED

[* Elected to fill a vacancy; Republicans in roman (229); Democrats in *italic* (205); Independents in SMALL CAPS (1); Resident Commissioner and Delegates in **boldface** (5); total, 440]

Name	State	Congresses (inclusive)	Beginning of present service
Nussle, Jim	IA	102d to 108th	Jan. 3, 1991
Olver, John W.	MA	*102d to 108th	June 4, 1991
Pastor, Ed	AZ	*102d to 108th	Sep. 24, 1991
Peterson, Collin C.	MN	102d to 108th	Jan. 3, 1991
Ramstad, Jim	MN	102d to 108th	Jan. 3, 1991
SANDERS, BERNARD	VT	102d to 108th	Jan. 3, 1991
Taylor, Charles H.	NC	102d to 108th	Jan. 3, 1991
Waters, Maxine	CA	102d to 108th	Jan. 3, 1991
7 terms, not consecutive			
Cooper, Jim	TN	98th to 103d and 108th.	Jan. 3, 2003
6 terms, consecutive			
Bachus, Spencer	AL	103d to 108th	Jan. 3, 1993
Bartlett, Roscoe G.	MD	103d to 108th	Jan. 3, 1993
Becerra, Xavier	CA	103d to 108th	Jan. 3, 1993
Bishop, Sanford D., Jr.	GA	103d to 108th	Jan. 3, 1993
Bonilla, Henry	TX	103d to 108th	Jan. 3, 1993
Brown, Corrine	FL	103d to 108th	Jan. 3, 1993
Brown, Sherrod	OH	103d to 108th	Jan. 3, 1993
Buyer, Steve	IN	103d to 108th	Jan. 3, 1993
Calvert, Ken	CA	103d to 108th	Jan. 3, 1993
Castle, Michael N.	DE	103d to 108th	Jan. 3, 1993
Clyburn, James E.	SC	103d to 108th	Jan. 3, 1993
Collins, Mac	GA	103d to 108th	Jan. 3, 1993
Deal, Nathan	GA	103d to 108th	Jan. 3, 1993
Deutsch, Peter	FL	103d to 108th	Jan. 3, 1993
Diaz-Balart, Lincoln	FL	103d to 108th	Jan. 3, 1993
Dunn, Jennifer	WA	103d to 108th	Jan. 3, 1993
Ehlers, Vernon	MI	103d to 108th	Dec. 7, 1993
Eshoo, Anna G.	CA	103d to 108th	Jan. 3, 1993
Everett, Terry	AL	103d to 108th	Jan. 3, 1993
Farr, Sam	CA	*103d to 108th	June 8, 1993
Filner, Bob	CA	103d to 108th	Jan. 3, 1993
Goodlatte, Robert W. (Bob)	VA	103d to 108th	Jan. 3, 1993
Green, Gene	TX	103d to 108th	Jan. 3, 1993
Greenwood, James C.	PA	103d to 108th	Jan. 3, 1993
Gutierrez, Luis V.	IL	103d to 108th	Jan. 3, 1993
Hastings, Alcee L.	FL	103d to 108th	Jan. 3, 1993
Hinchey, Maurice D.	NY	103d to 108th	Jan. 3, 1993
Hoekstra, Peter	MI	103d to 108th	Jan. 3, 1993
Holden, Tim	PA	103d to 108th	Jan. 3, 1993
Istook, Ernest J., Jr.	OK	103d to 108th	Jan. 3, 1993
Johnson, Eddie Bernice	TX	103d to 108th	Jan. 3, 1993
King, Peter T.	NY	103d to 108th	Jan. 3, 1993
Kingston, Jack	GA	103d to 108th	Jan. 3, 1993
Knollenberg, Joseph	MI	103d to 108th	Jan. 3, 1993
Lewis, Ron	KY	*103d to 108th	May 17, 1994
Linder, John	GA	103d to 108th	Jan. 3, 1993
Lucas, Frank	OK	*103d to 108th	May 10, 1994
Maloney, Carolyn B.	NY	103d to 108th	Jan. 3, 1993

CONGRESSES IN WHICH REPRESENTATIVES HAVE SERVED, WITH BEGINNING OF PRESENT SERVICE—CONTINUED

[* Elected to fill a vacancy; Republicans in roman (229); Democrats in *italic* (205); Independents in SMALL CAPS (1); Resident Commissioner and Delegates in **boldface** (5); total, 440]

Name	State	Congresses (inclusive)	Beginning of present service
Manzullo, Donald A.	IL	103d to 108th	Jan. 3, 1993
McHugh, John M.	NY	103d to 108th	Jan. 3, 1993
McInnis, Scott	CO	103d to 108th	Jan. 3, 1993
McKeon, Howard P. (Buck)	CA	103d to 108th	Jan. 3, 1993
Meehan, Martin T.	MA	103d to 108th	Jan. 3, 1993
Menendez, Robert	NJ	103d to 108th	Jan. 3, 1993
Mica, John L.	FL	103d to 108th	Jan. 3, 1993
Pombo, Richard W.	CA	103d to 108th	Jan. 3, 1993
Pomeroy, Earl	ND	103d to 108th	Jan. 3, 1993
Portman, Rob	OH	*103d to 108th	May 4, 1993
Pryce, Deborah	OH	103d to 108th	Jan. 3, 1993
Quinn, Jack	NY	103d to 108th	Jan. 3, 1993
Roybal-Allard, Lucille	CA	103d to 108th	Jan. 3, 1993
Royce, Ed	CA	103d to 108th	Jan. 3, 1993
Rush, Bobby L.	IL	103d to 108th	Jan. 3, 1993
Scott, Robert C. (Bobby)	VA	103d to 108th	Jan. 3, 1993
Smith, Nick	MI	103d to 108th	Jan. 3, 1993
Stupak, Bart	MI	103d to 108th	Jan. 3, 1993
Thompson, Bennie G.	MS	*103d to 108th	Apr. 13, 1993
Thurman, Karen L.	FL	103d to 108th	Jan. 3, 1993
Velázquez, Nydia M.	NY	103d to 108th	Jan. 3, 1993
Watt, Melvin L.	NC	103d to 108th	Jan. 3, 1993
Woolsey, Lynn	CA	103d to 108th	Jan. 3, 1993
Wynn, Albert Russell.	MD	103d to 108th	Jan. 3, 1993
5 terms, consecutive			
Bass, Charles F.	NH	104th to 108th	Jan. 3, 1995
Blumenauer, Earl	OR	*104th to 108th	May 21, 1996
Burr, Richard M.	NC	104th to 108th	Jan. 3, 1995
Chabot, Steve	OH	104th to 108th	Jan. 3, 1995
Cubin, Barbara	WY	104th to 108th	Jan. 3, 1995
Cummings, Elijah E.	MD	*104th to 108th	Apr. 16, 1996
Davis, Tom	VA	104th to 108th	Jan. 3, 1995
Doggett, Lloyd	TX	104th to 108th	Jan. 3, 1995
Doyle, Michael F.	PA	104th to 108th	Jan. 3, 1995
Emerson, Jo Ann	MO	*104th to 108th	Nov. 5, 1996
English, Phil	PA	104th to 108th	Jan. 3, 1995
Fattah, Chaka	PA	104th to 108th	Jan. 3, 1995
Foley, Mark	FL	104th to 108th	Jan. 3, 1995
Frelinghuysen, Rodney P.	NJ	104th to 108th	Jan. 3, 1995
Gutknecht, Gil	MN	104th to 108th	Jan. 3, 1995
Hastings, Doc	WA	104th to 108th	Jan. 3, 1995
Hayworth, J.D.	AZ	104th to 108th	Jan. 3, 1995
Hostettler, John N.	IN	104th to 108th	Jan. 3, 1995
Jackson Lee, Sheila	TX	104th to 108th	Jan. 3, 1995
Jackson, Jesse, Jr.	IL	*104th to 108th	Dec. 12, 1995
Jones, Walter B.	NC	104th to 108th	Jan. 3, 1995
Kelly, Sue	NY	104th to 108th	Jan. 3, 1995
Kennedy, Patrick J.	RI	104th to 108th	Jan. 3, 1995
LaHood, Ray	IL	104th to 108th	Jan. 3, 1995
Latham, Tom	IA	104th to 108th	Jan. 3, 1995
LaTourette, Steven	OH	104th to 108th	Jan. 3, 1995

CONGRESSES IN WHICH REPRESENTATIVES HAVE SERVED, WITH BEGINNING OF PRESENT SERVICE—CONTINUED

[* Elected to fill a vacancy; Republicans in roman (229); Democrats in *italic* (205); Independents in SMALL CAPS (1); Resident Commissioner and Delegates in **boldface** (5); total, 440]

Name	State	Congresses (inclusive)	Beginning of present service
LoBiondo, Frank	NJ	104th to 108th	Jan. 3, 1995
Lofgren, Zoe	CA	104th to 108th	Jan. 3, 1995
McCarthy, Karen	MO	104th to 108th	Jan. 3, 1995
Millender-McDonald, Juanita	CA	*104th to 108th	Mar. 26, 1996
Myrick, Sue Wilkins	NC	104th to 108th	Jan. 3, 1995
Nethercutt, George	WA	104th to 108th	Jan. 3, 1995
Ney, Robert W.	OH	104th to 108th	Jan. 3, 1995
Norwood, Charlie	GA	104th to 108th	Jan. 3, 1995
Portman, Rob	OH	104th to 108th	Jan. 3, 1995
Radanovich, George	CA	104th to 108th	Jan. 3, 1995
Ryun, Jim	KS	*104th to 108th	Nov. 27, 1996
Shadegg, John	AZ	104th to 108th	Jan. 3, 1995
Souder, Mark E.	IN	104th to 108th	Jan. 3, 1995
Thornberry, Mac	TX	104th to 108th	Jan. 3, 1995
Tiahrt, Todd	KS	104th to 108th	Jan. 3, 1995
Wamp, Zachary Paul	TN	104th to 108th	Jan. 3, 1995
Weldon, Dave	FL	104th to 108th	Jan. 3, 1995
Weller, Jerry	IL	104th to 108th	Jan. 3, 1995
Whitfield, Ed	KY	104th to 108th	Jan. 3, 1995
Wicker, Roger	MS	104th to 108th	Jan. 3, 1995
5 terms, not consecutive			
Harman, Jane	CA	103d to 105th, 107th and 108th.	Jan. 3, 2001
Strickland, Ted	OH	103d, 105th to 108th.	Jan. 3, 1997
4 terms			
Aderholt, Robert	AL	105th to 108th	Jan. 3, 1997
Allen, Thomas H.	ME	105th to 108th	Jan. 3, 1997
Berry, Marion	AR	105th to 108th	Jan. 3, 1997
Blagójevich, Rod	IL	105th to 108th	Jan. 3, 1997
Blunt, Roy	MO	105th to 108th	Jan. 3, 1997
Bono, Mary	CA	*105th to 108th	Apr. 7, 1998
Boswell, Leonard L.	IA	105th to 108th	Jan. 3, 1997
Boyd, Allen	FL	105th to 108th	Jan. 3, 1997
Brady, Kevin	TX	105th to 108th	Jan. 3, 1997
Brady, Robert A.	PA	*105th to 108th	May. 19, 1998
Cannon, Christopher B.	UT	105th to 108th	Jan. 3, 1997
Capps, Lois	CA	*105th to 108th	Mar. 10, 1998
Carson, Julia M.	IN	105th to 108th	Jan. 3, 1997
Cooksey, John	LA	105th to 108th	Jan. 3, 1997
Davis, Danny K.	IL	105th to 108th	Jan. 3, 1997
Davis, Jim	FL	105th to 108th	Jan. 3, 1997
DeGette, Diana	CO	105th to 108th	Jan. 3, 1997
Delahunt, William D.	MA	105th to 108th	Jan. 3, 1997
Etheridge, Bob	NC	105th to 108th	Jan. 3, 1997
Ford, Harold E., Jr.	TN	105th to 108th	Jan. 3, 1997
Fossella, Vito	NY	*105th to 108th	Nov. 4, 1997
Gibbons, Jim	NE	105th to 108th	Jan. 3, 1997
Goode, Virgil H., Jr.	VA	105th to 108th	Jan. 3, 1997
Granger, Kay	TX	105th to 108th	Jan. 3, 1997

CONGRESSES IN WHICH REPRESENTATIVES HAVE SERVED, WITH BEGINNING OF PRESENT SERVICE—CONTINUED

[* Elected to fill a vacancy; Republicans in roman (229); Democrats in *italic* (205); Independents in SMALL CAPS (1); Resident Commissioner and Delegates in **boldface** (5); total, 440]

Name	State	Congresses (inclusive)	Beginning of present service
Hinojosa, Rubén	TX	105th to 108th	Jan. 3, 1997
Hooley, Darlene	OR	105th to 108th	Jan. 3, 1997
Hulfshof, Kenny	MO	105th to 108th	Jan. 3, 1997
Hutchinson, Asa	AR	105th to 108th	Jan. 3, 1997
Jenkins, William L. (Bill)	TN	105th to 108th	Jan. 3, 1997
John, Chris	LA	105th to 108th	Jan. 3, 1997
Kilpatrick, Carolyn C.	MI	105th to 108th	Jan. 3, 1997
Kind, Ron	WI	105th to 108th	Jan. 3, 1997
Kucinich, Dennis J.	OH	105th to 108th	Jan. 3, 1997
Lampson, Nick	TX	105th to 108th	Jan. 3, 1997
Lee, Barbara	CA	*105th to 108th	Apr. 7, 1998
McCarthy, Carolyn	NY	105th to 108th	Jan. 3, 1997
McGovern, James P.	MA	105th to 108th	Jan. 3, 1997
McIntyre, Mike	NC	105th to 108th	Jan. 3, 1997
Meeks, Gregory W.	NY	*105th to 108th	Feb. 3, 1998
Moran, Jerry	KS	105th to 108th	Jan. 3, 1997
Northup, Anne M.	KY	105th to 108th	Jan. 3, 1997
Pascrell, Bill, Jr.	NJ	105th to 108th	Jan. 3, 1997
Peterson, John E.	PA	105th to 108th	Jan. 3, 1997
Pickering, Charles W. (Chip), Jr.	MS	105th to 108th	Jan. 3, 1997
Pitts, Joseph R.	PA	105th to 108th	Jan. 3, 1997
Reyes, Silvestre	TX	105th to 108th	Jan. 3, 1997
Rodriguez, Ciro	TX	*105th to 108th	Apr. 12, 1997
Rothman, Steven R.	NJ	105th to 108th	Jan. 3, 1997
Sanchez, Loretta	CA	105th to 108th	Jan. 3, 1997
Stolin, Max	TX	105th to 108th	Jan. 3, 1997
Sessions, Pete	TX	105th to 108th	Jan. 3, 1997
Sherman, Brad	CA	105th to 108th	Jan. 3, 1997
Shimkus, John	IL	105th to 108th	Jan. 3, 1997
Smith, Adam	WA	105th to 108th	Jan. 3, 1997
Snyder, Vic	AR	105th to 108th	Jan. 3, 1997
Tauscher, Ellen O.	CA	105th to 108th	Jan. 3, 1997
Tierney, John	MA	105th to 108th	Jan. 3, 1997
Turner, Jim	TX	105th to 108th	Jan. 3, 1997
Wexler, Robert	FL	105th to 108th	Jan. 3, 1997
Wilson, Heather	NM	*105th to 108th	Jun. 23, 1998
4 terms, not consecutive			
Inslee, Jay	WA	*103d, 106th to 108th.	Jan. 3, 1999
3 terms			
Baca, Joe	CA	*106th to 108th	Nov. 17, 1999
Baird, Brian	WA	106th to 108th	Jan. 3, 1999
Baldwin, Tammy	WI	106th to 108th	Jan. 3, 1999
Berkley, Shelley	NV	106th to 108th	Jan. 3, 1999
Biggert, Judy	IL	106th to 108th	Jan. 3, 1999
Capuano, Michael E.	MA	106th to 108th	Jan. 3, 1999
Crowley, Joseph	NY	106th to 108th	Jan. 3, 1999
DeMint, Jim	SC	106th to 108th	Jan. 3, 1999
Fletcher, Ernie.	KY	106th to 108th	Jan. 3, 1999
Gonzalez, Charles A.	TX	106th to 108th	Jan. 3, 1999

CONGRESSES IN WHICH REPRESENTATIVES HAVE SERVED, WITH BEGINNING OF PRESENT SERVICE—CONTINUED

[* Elected to fill a vacancy; Republicans in roman (229); Democrats in *italic* (205); Independents in SMALL CAPS (1); Resident Commissioner and Delegates in **boldface** (5); total, 440]

Name	State	Congresses (inclusive)	Beginning of present service
Green, Mark	WI	106th to 108th	Jan. 3, 1999
Hayes, Robin	NC	106th to 108th	Jan. 3, 1999
Hill, Baron P.	IN	106th to 108th	Jan. 3, 1999
Hoeffel, Joseph M.	PA	106th to 108th	Jan. 3, 1999
Holt, Rush D.	NJ	106th to 108th	Jan. 3, 1999
Isakson, Johnny	GA	*106th to 108th	Feb. 23, 1999
Jones, Stephanie Tubbs	OH	106th to 108th	Jan. 3, 1999
Larson, John B.	CT	106th to 108th	Jan. 3, 1999
Lucas, Ken	KY	106th to 108th	Jan. 3, 1999
Miller, Gary G.	CA	106th to 108th	Jan. 3, 1999
Moore, Dennis	KS	106th to 108th	Jan. 3, 1999
Napolitano, Grace F.	CA	106th to 108th	Jan. 3, 1999
Ose, Doug	CA	106th to 108th	Jan. 3, 1999
Reynolds, Thomas M.	NY	106th to 108th	Jan. 3, 1999
Ryan, Paul	WI	106th to 108th	Jan. 3, 1999
Schakowsky, Janice D.	IL	106th to 108th	Jan. 3, 1999
Sherwood, Don	PA	106th to 108th	Jan. 3, 1999
Simpson, Michael K.	ID	106th to 108th	Jan. 3, 1999
Sweeney, John E.	NY	106th to 108th	Jan. 3, 1999
Tancredo, Thomas G.	CO	106th to 108th	Jan. 3, 1999
Terry, Lee	NE	106th to 108th	Jan. 3, 1999
Thompson, Mike	CA	106th to 108th	Jan. 3, 1999
Toomey, Patrick J.	PA	106th to 108th	Jan. 3, 1999
Udall, Mark	CO	106th to 108th	Jan. 3, 1999
Udall, Tom	NM	106th to 108th	Jan. 3, 1999
Vitter, David	LA	*106th to 108th	May 29, 1999
Walden, Greg	OR	106th to 108th	Jan. 3, 1999
Weiner, Anthony D.	NY	106th to 108th	Jan. 3, 1999
Wu, David	OR	106th to 108th	Jan. 3, 1999
2 terms			
Akin, W. Todd	MO	107th and 108th	Jan. 3, 2001
Boozman, John	AR	*107th and 108th	Nov. 20, 2001
Brown, Henry E., Jr.	SC	107th and 108th	Jan. 3, 2001
Cantor, Eric	VA	107th and 108th	Jan. 3, 2001
Capito, Shelley Moore	WV	107th and 108th	Jan. 3, 2001
Carson, Brad	OK	107th and 108th	Jan. 3, 2001
Case, Ed	HI	*107th and 108th	Nov. 30, 2002
Clay, Wm. Lacy	MO	107th and 108th	Jan. 3, 2001
Crenshaw, Ander	FL	107th and 108th	Jan. 3, 2001
Culberson, John	TX	107th and 108th	Jan. 3, 2001
Davis, Jo Ann	VA	107th and 108th	Jan. 3, 2001
Davis, Susan	CA	107th and 108th	Jan. 3, 2001
Ferguson, Mike	NJ	107th and 108th	Jan. 3, 2001
Flake, Jeff	AZ	107th and 108th	Jan. 3, 2001
Forbes, J. Randy	VA	*107th and 108th	June 19, 2001
Graves, Samuel	MO	107th and 108th	Jan. 3, 2001
Hart, Melissa A.	PA	107th and 108th	Jan. 3, 2001
Honda, Mike	CA	107th and 108th	Jan. 3, 2001
Israel, Steve	NY	107th and 108th	Jan. 3, 2001
Issa, Darrell	CA	107th and 108th	Jan. 3, 2001
Johnson, Timothy V.	IL	107th and 108th	Jan. 3, 2001

CONGRESSES IN WHICH REPRESENTATIVES HAVE SERVED, WITH BEGINNING OF PRESENT SERVICE—CONTINUED

[* Elected to fill a vacancy; Republicans in roman (229); Democrats in *italic* (205); Independents in SMALL CAPS (1); Resident Commissioner and Delegates in **boldface** (5); total, 440]

Name	State	Congresses (inclusive)	Beginning of present service
Keller, Ric	FL	107th and 108th	Jan. 3, 2001
Kennedy, Mark	MN	107th and 108th	Jan. 3, 2001
Kirk, Mark	IL	107th and 108th	Jan. 3, 2001
Langevin, James	RI	107th and 108th	Jan. 3, 2001
Larsen, Rick	WA	107th and 108th	Jan. 3, 2001
Lynch, Stephen F.	MA	*107th and 108th	Oct. 16, 2001
Matheson, Jim	UT	107th and 108th	Jan. 3, 2001
McCollum, Betty	MN	107th and 108th	Jan. 3, 2001
Miller, Jeff	FL	*107th and 108th	Oct. 16, 2001
Osborne, Tom	NE	107th and 108th	Jan. 3, 2001
Otter, C.L. (Butch)	ID	107th and 108th	Jan. 3, 2001
Pence, Mike	IN	107th and 108th	Jan. 3, 2001
Platts, Todd Russell	ID	107th and 108th	Jan. 3, 2001
Putnam, Adam	FL	107th and 108th	Jan. 3, 2001
Rehberg, Dennis	MT	107th and 108th	Jan. 3, 2001
Rogers, Mike	MI	107th and 108th	Jan. 3, 2001
Ross, Mike	AR	107th and 108th	Jan. 3, 2001
Schiff, Adam	CA	107th and 108th	Jan. 3, 2001
Schrock, Edward	VA	107th and 108th	Jan. 3, 2001
Shuster, Bill	PA	*107th and 108th	May 15, 2001
Simmons, Rob	CT	107th and 108th	Jan. 3, 2001
Solis, Hilda	CA	107th and 108th	Jan. 3, 2001
Sullivan, John	OK	*107th and 108th	Jan. 8, 2002
Tiberi, Patrick	OH	107th and 108th	Jan. 3, 2001
Watson, Diane E.	CA	*107th and 108th	June 5, 2001
Wilson, Joe	SC	*107th and 108th	Dec. 18, 2001
1 term			
Alexander, Rodney	LA	108th	Jan. 3, 2003
Ballance, Frank W., Jr.	NC	108th	Jan. 3, 2003
Barrett, Gresham	SC	108th	Jan. 3, 2003
Beauprez, Bob	CO	108th	Jan. 3, 2003
Bell, Chris	TX	108th	Jan. 3, 2003
Bishop, Rob	UT	108th	Jan. 3, 2003
Blackburn, Marsha	TN	108th	Jan. 3, 2003
Bonner, Jo	AL	108th	Jan. 3, 2003
Bradley, Jeb	NH	108th	Jan. 3, 2003
Brown-Waite, Ginny	FL	108th	Jan. 3, 2003
Burgess, Michael	TX	108th	Jan. 3, 2003
Burns, Max	GA	108th	Jan. 3, 2003
Cardoza, Dennis	CA	108th	Jan. 3, 2003
Carter, John R.	TX	108th	Jan. 3, 2003
Chocola, Chris	IN	108th	Jan. 3, 2003
Cole, Tom	OK	108th	Jan. 3, 2003
Davis, Artur	AL	108th	Jan. 3, 2003
Davis, Lincoln	TN	108th	Jan. 3, 2003
Diaz-Balart, Mario	FL	108th	Jan. 3, 2003
Emanuel, Rahm	IL	108th	Jan. 3, 2003
Feeney, Tom	FL	108th	Jan. 3, 2003
Franks, Trent	AZ	108th	Jan. 3, 2003
Garrett, Scott	NJ	108th	Jan. 3, 2003
Gerlach, Jim	PA	108th	Jan. 3, 2003

CONGRESSES IN WHICH REPRESENTATIVES HAVE SERVED, WITH BEGINNING OF PRESENT SERVICE—CONTINUED

[* Elected to fill a vacancy; Republicans in roman (229); Democrats in *italic* (205); Independents in SMALL CAPS (1); Resident Commissioner and Delegates in **boldface** (5); total, 440]

Name	State	Congresses (inclusive)	Beginning of present service
Gingrey, Phil	GA	108th	Jan. 3, 2003
Grijalva, Raúl M.	AZ	108th	Jan. 3, 2003
Harris, Katherine	FL	108th	Jan. 3, 2003
Hensarling, Jeb	TX	108th	Jan. 3, 2003
Janklow, William J.	SD	108th	Jan. 3, 2003
King, Steve	IA	108th	Jan. 3, 2003
Kline, John	MN	108th	Jan. 3, 2003
Majette, Denise	GA	108th	Jan. 3, 2003
Marshall, Jim	GA	108th	Jan. 3, 2003
McCotter, Thaddeus G.	MI	108th	Jan. 3, 2003
Meek, Kendrick B.	FL	108th	Jan. 3, 2003
Michaud, Michael H.	ME	108th	Jan. 3, 2003
Miller, Brad	NC	108th	Jan. 3, 2003
Miller, Candice S.	MI	108th	Jan. 3, 2003
Murphy, Tim	PA	108th	Jan. 3, 2003
Musgrave, Marilyn N.	CO	108th	Jan. 3, 2003
Neugebauer, Randy	TX	*108th	June 3, 2003
Nunes, Devin	CA	108th	Jan. 3, 2003
Pearce, Stevan	NM	108th	Jan. 3, 2003
Porter, Jon C.	NV	108th	Jan. 3, 2003
Renzi, Rick	AZ	108th	Jan. 3, 2003
Rogers, Mike	AL	108th	Jan. 3, 2003
Ruppersberger, C.A. Dutch	MD	108th	Jan. 3, 2003
Ryan, Timothy J.	OH	108th	Jan. 3, 2003
Sánchez, Linda	CA	108th	Jan. 3, 2003
Scott, David	GA	108th	Jan. 3, 2003
Turner, Mike	OH	108th	Jan. 3, 2003
Van Hollen, Chris	MD	108th	Jan. 3, 2003
RESIDENT COMMISSIONER			
Acevedo-Vilá, Aníbal [1]	PR	107th and 108th	Jan. 3, 2001
DELEGATES			
Christensen, Donna M.	VI	105th to 108th	Jan. 3, 1997
Faleomavaega, Eni F.H.	AS	101st to 108th	Jan. 3, 1989
Norton, Eleanor Holmes	DC	102d to 108th	Jan. 3, 1991
Bordallo, Madeleine Z.	GU	108th	Jan. 3, 2003

[1] Popular Democratic Party.

NOTE: Members elected by special election are considered to begin service on the date of the election, except for those elected after a sine die adjournment. If elected after the Congress has adjourned for the session, Members are considered to begin their service on the day after the election.

STANDING COMMITTEES OF THE SENATE

[Republicans in roman; Democrats in *italic*; Independents in SMALL CAPS]

[Room numbers beginning with SD are in the Dirksen Building, SH in the Hart Building, SR in the Russell Building, and S in The Capitol]

Agriculture, Nutrition, and Forestry

328A Russell Senate Office Building 20510–6000

phone 224–2035, fax 224–1725, TTY/TDD 224–2587

http://agriculture.senate.gov

meets first and third Wednesdays of each month

Thad Cochran, of Mississippi, *Chairman.*

Richard G. Lugar, of Indiana.
Mitch McConnell, of Kentucky.
Pat Roberts, of Kansas.
Peter Fitzgerald, of Illinois.
Saxby Chambliss, of Georgia.
Norm Coleman, of Minnesota.
Mike Crapo, of Idaho.
James M. Talent, of Missouri.
Elizabeth Dole, of North Carolina.
Charles E. Grassley, of Iowa.

Tom Harkin, of Iowa.
Patrick J. Leahy, of Vermont.
Kent Conrad, of North Dakota.
Thomas A. Daschle, of South Dakota.
Max Baucus, of Montana.
Blanche L. Lincoln, of Arkansas.
Zell Miller, of Georgia.
Debbie Stabenow, of Michigan.
E. Benjamin Nelson, of Nebraska.
Mark Dayton, of Minnesota.

SUBCOMMITTEES

[The chairman and ranking minority member are ex officio (non-voting) members of all subcommittees on which they do not serve.]

Forestry, Conservation, and Rural Revitalization

Mike Crapo, of Idaho, *Chairman.*

Richard G. Lugar, of Indiana.
Norm Coleman, of Minnesota.
James M. Talent, of Missouri.
Mitch McConnell, of Kentucky.
Pat Roberts, of Kansas.

Blanche L. Lincoln, of Arkansas.
Mark Dayton, of Minnesota.
Patrick J. Leahy, of Vermont.
Thomas A. Daschle, of South Dakota.
E. Benjamin Nelson, of Nebraska.

Marketing, Inspection, and Product Promotion

James M. Talent, of Missouri, Chairman.

Pat Roberts, of Kansas.
Peter Fitzgerald, of Illinois.
Saxby Chambliss, of Georgia.
Charles E. Grassley, of Iowa.

Max Baucus, of Montana.
E. Benjamin Nelson, of Nebraska.
Kent Conrad, of North Dakota.
Debbie Stabenow, of Michigan.

Production and Price Competitiveness

Elizabeth Dole, of North Carolina, *Chair.*

Mitch McConnell, of Kentucky.
Pat Roberts, of Kansas.
Saxby Chambliss, of Georgia.
Norm Coleman, of Minnesota.
Charles E. Grassley, of Iowa.

Kent Conrad, of North Dakota.
Thomas A. Daschle, of South Dakota.
Zell Miller, of Georgia.
Max Baucus, of Montana.
Blanche L. Lincoln, of Arkansas.

Research, Nutrition, and General Legislation

Peter Fitzgerald, of Illinois, *Chairman.*

Richard G. Lugar, of Indiana.
Mitch McConnell, of Kentucky.
Mike Crapo, of Idaho.
Elizabeth Dole, of North Carolina.

Patrick J. Leahy, of Vermont.
Debbie Stabenow, of Michigan.
Zell Miller, of Georgia.
Mark Dayton, of Minnesota.

STAFF

Committee on Agriculture, Nutrition, and Forestry (SR–328A), 224–2035, fax 224–1725.
Staff Director.—Hunt Shipman.
Chief Counsel.—David L. Johnson.
Counsel.—Lance Koshwar.
Chief Economist.—Andrew Morton.
Administrative Assistant.—Amanda Dawson.
Senior Professional Staff.—Hunter Moorehead.
Professional Staff: Judy Myers, Matt O'Mara, Molly Phillips.
Legislative Correspondents: Ellis Fisher, Beth Hamilton.
Staff Assistant.—Frank Newkirk.
Hearing Clerk.—Vershawn Perkins.
Chief Clerk.—Robert Sturm.
GPO Editor.—Natoshka Faxio-Douglas.
Minority Staff Director/Counsel.—Mark Halverson, 4–2035, fax 8–4576.
Counsels: Allison Fox, Eric Juzenas.
Legislative Staff Assistant.—John Farrell.
Professional Staff: Richard Bender, Karil Bialostosky, Amy Fredregill, Sara Hopper, Susan Keith, Jay Klug, Mary Langowski, Doug O'Brien, Lloyd Ritter.
Economist.—Stephanie Mercier.

Appropriations

S–128 The Capitol 20510–6025, phone 224–3471

http://appropriations.senate.gov

meets upon call of the chairman

Ted Stevens, of Alaska, *Chairman.*

Thad Cochran, of Mississippi.
Arlen Specter, of Pennsylvania.
Pete V. Domenici, of New Mexico.
Christopher S. Bond, of Missouri.
Mitch McConnell, of Kentucky.
Conrad Burns, of Montana.
Richard C. Shelby, of Alabama.
Judd Gregg, of New Hampshire.
Robert F. Bennett, of Utah.
Ben Nighthorse Campbell, of Colorado.
Larry Craig, of Idaho.
Kay Bailey Hutchison, of Texas.
Mike DeWine, of Ohio.
Sam Brownback, of Kansas.

Robert C. Byrd, of West Virginia.
Daniel K. Inouye, of Hawaii.
Ernest F. Hollings, of South Carolina.
Patrick J. Leahy, of Vermont.
Tom Harkin, of Iowa.
Barbara A. Mikulski, of Maryland.
Harry Reid, of Nevada.
Herb Kohl, of Wisconsin.
Patty Murray, of Washington.
Byron L. Dorgan, of North Dakota.
Dianne Feinstein, of California.
Richard J. Durbin, of Illinois.
Tim Johnson, of South Dakota.
Mary L. Landrieu, of Louisiana.

SUBCOMMITTEES

[The chairman and ranking minority member are ex officio members of all subcommittees on which they do not serve.]

Agriculture, Rural Development, and Related Agencies

Robert F. Bennett, of Utah, *Chairman.*

Thad Cochran, of Mississippi.
Arlen Specter, of Pennsylvania.
Christopher S. Bond, of Missouri.
Mitch McConnell, of Kentucky.
Conrad Burns, of Montana.
Larry Craig, of Idaho.
Sam Brownback, of Kansas.

Herb Kohl, of Wisconsin.
Tom Harkin, of Iowa.
Byron L. Dorgan, of North Dakota.
Dianne Feinstein, of California.
Richard J. Durbin, of Illinois.
Tim Johnson, of South Dakota.
Mary L. Landrieu, of Louisiana.

Commerce, Justice, State, and the Judiciary

Judd Gregg, of New Hampshire, *Chairman.*

Ted Stevens, of Alaska.
Pete V. Domenici, of New Mexico.
Mitch McConnell, of Kentucky.
Kay Bailey Hutchison, of Texas.
Ben Nighthorse Campbell, of Colorado.
Sam Brownback, of Kansas.

Ernest F. Hollings, of South Carolina.
Daniel K. Inouye, of Hawaii.
Barbara A. Mikulski, of Maryland.
Patrick J. Leahy, of Vermont.
Herb Kohl, of Wisconsin.
Patty Murray, of Washington.

Defense

Ted Stevens, of Alaska, *Chairman.*

Thad Cochran, of Mississippi.
Arlen Specter, of Pennsylvania.
Pete V. Domenici, of New Mexico.
Christopher S. Bond, of Missouri.
Mitch McConnell, of Kentucky.
Richard C. Shelby, of Alabama.
Judd Gregg, of New Hampshire.
Kay Bailey Hutchison, of Texas.
Conrad Burns, of Montana.

Daniel K. Inouye, of Hawaii.
Ernest F. Hollings, of South Carolina.
Robert C. Byrd, of West Virginia.
Patrick J. Leahy, of Vermont.
Tom Harkin, of Iowa.
Byron L. Dorgan, of North Dakota.
Harry Reid, of Nevada.
Dianne Feinstein, of California.

District of Columbia

Mike DeWine, of Ohio, *Chairman.*

Sam Brownback, of Kansas.
Kay Bailey Hutchison, of Texas.

Mary L. Landrieu, of Louisiana.
Richard J. Durbin, of Illinois.

Energy and Water Development

Pete V. Domenici, of New Mexico, *Chairman.*

Thad Cochran, of Mississippi.
Mitch McConnell, of Kentucky.
Robert F. Bennett, of Utah.
Conrad Burns, of Montana.
Larry Craig, of Idaho.
Christopher S. Bond, of Missouri.

Harry Reid, of Nevada.
Robert C. Byrd, of West Virginia.
Ernest F. Hollings, of South Carolina.
Patty Murray, of Washington.
Byron L. Dorgan, of North Dakota.
Dianne Feinstein, of California.

Foreign Operations

Mitch McConnell, of Kentucky, *Chairman.*

Arlen Specter, of Pennsylvania.
Judd Gregg, of New Hampshire.
Richard C. Shelby, of Alabama.
Robert F. Bennett, of Utah.
Ben Nighthorse Campbell, of Colorado.
Christopher S. Bond, of Missouri.
Mike DeWine, of Ohio.

Patrick J. Leahy, of Vermont.
Daniel K. Inouye, of Hawaii.
Tom Harkin, of Iowa.
Barbara A. Mikulski, of Maryland.
Richard J. Durbin, of Illinois.
Tim Johnson, of South Dakota.
Mary L. Landrieu, of Louisiana.

Homeland Security

Thad Cochran, of Mississippi, *Chairman.*

Ted Stevens, of Alaska.
Arlen Specter, of Pennsylvania.
Pete V. Domenici, of New Mexico.
Mitch McConnell, of Kentucky.
Richard C. Shelby, of Alabama.
Judd Gregg, of New Hampshire.
Ben Nighthorse Campbell, of Colorado.
Larry Craig, of Idaho.

Robert C. Byrd, of West Virginia.
Daniel K. Inouye, of Hawaii.
Ernest F. Hollings, of South Carolina.
Patrick J. Leahy, of Vermont.
Tom Harkin, of Iowa.
Barbara A. Mikulski, of Maryland.
Herb Kohl, of Wisconsin.
Patty Murray, of Washington.

Interior

Conrad Burns, of Montana, *Chairman.*

Ted Stevens, of Alaska.
Thad Cochran, of Mississippi.
Pete V. Domenici, of New Mexico.
Robert F. Bennett, of Utah.
Judd Gregg, of New Hampshire.
Ben Nighthorse Campbell, of Colorado.
Sam Brownback, of Kansas.

Byron L. Dorgan, of North Dakota.
Robert C. Byrd, of West Virginia.
Patrick J. Leahy, of Vermont.
Ernest F. Hollings, of South Carolina.
Harry Reid, of Nevada.
Dianne Feinstein, of California.
Barbara A. Mikulski, of Maryland.

Labor, Health and Human Services, and Education

Arlen Specter, of Pennsylvania, *Chairman.*

Thad Cochran, of Mississippi.
Judd Gregg, of New Hampshire.
Larry Craig, of Idaho.
Kay Bailey Hutchison, of Texas.
Ted Stevens, of Alaska.
Mike DeWine, of Ohio.
Richard C. Shelby, of Alabama.

Tom Harkin, of Iowa.
Ernest F. Hollings, of South Carolina.
Daniel K. Inouye, of Hawaii.
Harry Reid, of Nevada.
Herb Kohl, of Wisconsin.
Patty Murray, of Washington.
Mary L. Landrieu, of Louisiana.

Legislative Branch

Ben Nighthorse Campbell, of Colorado, *Chairman.*

Robert F. Bennett, of Utah.
Ted Stevens, of Alaska.

Richard J. Durbin, of Illinois.
Tim Johnson, of South Dakota.

Military Construction

Kay Bailey Hutchison, of Texas, *Chairman.*

Conrad Burns, of Montana.
Larry Craig, of Idaho.
Mike DeWine, of Ohio.
Sam Brownback, of Kansas.

Dianne Feinstein, of California.
Daniel K. Inouye, of Hawaii.
Tim Johnson, of South Dakota.
Mary L. Landrieu, of Louisiana.

Transportation / Treasury and General Government

Richard C. Shelby, of Alabama, *Chairman.*

Arlen Specter, of Pennsylvania.
Christopher S. Bond, of Missouri.
Robert F. Bennett, of Utah.
Ben Nighthorse Campbell, of Colorado.
Kay Bailey Hutchison, of Texas.
Mike DeWine, of Ohio.
Sam Brownback, of Kansas.

Patty Murray, of Washington.
Robert C. Byrd, of West Virginia.
Barbara A. Mikulski, of Maryland.
Harry Reid, of Nevada.
Herb Kohl, of Wisconsin.
Richard J. Durbin, of Illinois.
Byron L. Dorgan, of North Dakota.

VA, HUD, and Independent Agencies

Christopher S. Bond, of Missouri, *Chairman.*

Conrad Burns, of Montana.
Richard C. Shelby, of Alabama.
Larry Craig, of Idaho.
Pete V. Domenici, of New Mexico.
Mike DeWine, of Ohio.
Kay Bailey Hutchison, of Texas.

Barbara A. Mikulski, of Maryland.
Patrick J. Leahy, of Vermont.
Tom Harkin, of Iowa.
Robert C. Byrd, of West Virginia.
Tim Johnson, of South Dakota.
Harry Reid, of Nevada.

STAFF

Committee on Appropriations (S–128), 224–7363.
Staff Director.—Jim Morhard.
Deputy Staff Director.—Lisa Sutherland.
General Counsel.—Andy Givens.
Chief Clerk.—Dona Pate.
Deputy General Counsel.—Christine Drager.
Communications Director.—Tim Boulay.
Professional Staff: John J. Conway (SD–114); Mary Dietrich; Robert W. Putnam (SD–114).
Security Manager.—Justin Weddle (SD–114).
Assistant Chief Clerk.—Mazie R. Mattson (SD–119).
Staff Assistants: Wendi D. Dow, LaShawnda Smith.
Minority Staff Director.—Terry Sauvain (S–125A), 4–7292.
Deputy Staff Director.—Charles Kieffer.
Chief Clerk.—Edie Stanley (S–112).
Communications Director.—Tom Gavin.
Professional Staff: Suzanne Bentzel (S–112), Nora Martin (SD–134), Leslie Staples (S–112), William Simpson (SH–123), Chris Watkins (SH–123).
Staff Assistant.—Elnora Harvey (SH–123).
Subcommittee on Agriculture, Rural Development, and Related Agencies (SD–188), 4–5270.
Clerk.—Pat Raymond.
Professional Staff.—Fitz Elder.
Staff Assistant.—Hunter Moorhead.
Minority Clerk.—Galen Fountain (SH–123), 4–8090.
Professional Staff: Jessica Arden, William Simpson (SH–123).
Staff Assistant.—Meaghan L. McCarthy (SD–144).
Subcommittee on Commerce, Justice, State, and Judiciary (S–146A), 4–7277.
Clerk.—Kevin Linskey.
Professional Staff: Dennis Balkham, Katherine Hennessey, Jill Shapiro Long.
Staff Assistant.—Jessica Roberts.
Minority Clerk.—Lila Helms (SH–123), 4–9073.
Professional Staff: Kate Eltrich, Chad Schulken.
Subcommittee on Defense (SD–119), 4–7255.
Clerk.—Sid Ashworth.
Professional Staff: Jennifer Chartrand, Alycia Farrell, Menda Fife, Tom Hawkins, Robert J. Henke, Lesley Kalan, Mazie R. Mattson, Kraig Siracuse, Brian Wilson.
Staff Assistant.—Nicole Royal.
Minority Clerk.—Charles J. Houy (SD–117).
Professional Staff: Nicole Rutberg Di Resta (SD–115), Betsy Schmid (SD–115).
Subcommittee on District of Columbia (SD–128), 4–7643.
Clerk.—Mary Dietrich.
Minority Clerk.—Kate Eltrich (SH–123), 4–6933.
Subcommittee on Energy and Water Development (SD–127), 4–7260.
Clerk.—Clay Sell.
Professional Staff.—Tammy Perrin.
Staff Assistant.—Erin McHale.
Minority Clerk.—Drew Willison (SD–156), 4–8119.
Professional Staff.—Nancy Olkewicz.
Subcommittee on Foreign Operations (SD–142), 4–2255.
Clerk.—Paul Grove.
Staff Assistant.—Brendan Wheeler.
Minority Clerk.—Tim Rieser (SH–123), 4–8202.
Professional Staff.—Mark Lippert.
Subcommittee on Homeland Security (SD–136), 4–4319.
Clerk.—Rebecca Davies.
Professional Staff: James Hayes, Rachelle Schroeder, Les Spivey.
Staff Assistant.—Joshua Manley.
Minority Clerk.—Charles Kieffer (S–125A), 4–6870.
Professional Staff: Scott Nance (SD–196), Alexa Sewell (SD–128), Chip Walgren (SD–196).

Subcommittee on Interior and Related Agencies (SD–132), 4–7233.
Clerk.—Bruce Evans.
Professional Staff: Ginny James, Leif Fonnesbeck, Ryan Thomas.
Staff Assistant.—Larissa Sommer.
Minority Clerk.—Peter Kiefhaber (SD–160), 8–0774.
Professional Staff: Brooke Livingston.

Subcommittee on Labor, Health and Human Services, and Education (SD–184), 4–7230.
Clerk.—Bettilou Taylor.
Professional Staff: Mark Laisch, Sudip Shrikant Parikh, Candice Rogers, Jim Sourwine.
Staff Assistant.—Carole Geagley.
Minority Clerk.—Ellen Murray (SH–123), 4–7288.
Professional Staff.—Erik Fatemi, Adrienne Hallett.

Subcommittee on Legislative Branch (SD–127) 4–7238.
Clerk.—Carolyn E. Apostolou.
Staff Assistant.—Erin McHale.
Minority Clerk.—Terrence E. Sawain (S–125), 4–0335.
Professional Staff.—Drew Willison (SD–156).

Subcommittee on Military Construction (SD–140), 4–5245.
Clerk.—Dennis Ward.
Minority Clerk.—Christina Evans (SH–123), 4–8224.
Professional Staff.—B.G. Wright.

Subcommittee on Transportation/Treasury and General Government (SD–133), 4–4869.
Clerk.—Paul Doerrer.
Professional Staff.—Lula Edwards, Shannon Hines.
Staff Assistant.—Jacque Esai.
Minority Clerk.—Peter Rogoff (SD–144), 4–7281.
Professional Staff.—Diana Gourlay, Kate Hallahan.
Staff Assistant.—Meaghan L. McCarthy.

Subcommittee on VA, HUD, and Independent Agencies (SD–130), 4–8252.
Clerk.—Jon Kamarck.
Professional Staff.—Allen Cutler, Cheh Kim.
Staff Assistant.—Jennifer Storipan.
Minority Clerk.—Paul Carliner (SD–128).
Professional Staff.—Gabrielle A. Batkin, Alexa Sewell.

Editorial and Printing (SD–126): Richard L. Larson, 4–7265; Wayne W. Hosier (GPO), 4–7267; Doris Jackson (GPO), 4–7217; Heather Sturgess (GPO), 4–7266.

Clerical Assistants (SD–120): Joseph C. Chase, 4–0331; Norman L. Edwards, 4–7264.

Armed Services

228 Russell Senate Office Building 20510–6050

phone 224–3871, http://www.senate.gov/~armed_services

meets every Tuesday and Thursday

John Warner, of Virginia, *Chairman.*

John McCain, of Arizona.
James M. Inhofe, of Oklahoma.
Pat Roberts, of Kansas.
Wayne Allard, of Colorado.
Jeff Sessions, of Alabama.
Susan M. Collins, of Maine.
John Ensign, of Nevada.
James M. Talent, of Missouri.
Saxby Chambliss, of Georgia.
Lindsey O. Graham, of South Carolina.
Elizabeth Dole, of North Carolina.
John Cornyn, of Texas.

Carl Levin, of Michigan.
Edward M. Kennedy, of Massachusetts.
Robert C. Byrd, of West Virginia.
Joseph I. Lieberman, of Connecticut.
Jack Reed, of Rhode Island.
Daniel K. Akaka, of Hawaii.
Bill Nelson, of Florida.
E. Benjamin Nelson, of Nebraska.
Mark Dayton, of Minnesota.
Evan Bayh, of Indiana.
Hillary Rodham Clinton, of New York.
Mark Pryor, of Arkansas.

SUBCOMMITTEES

[The chairman and the ranking minority member are ex officio (non-voting) members of all subcommittees on which they do not serve.]

Airland

Jeff Sessions, of Alabama, *Chairman.*

John McCain, of Arizona.
James M. Inhofe, of Oklahoma.
Pat Roberts, of Kansas.
James M. Talent, of Missouri.
Saxby Chambliss, of Georgia.
Elizabeth Dole, of North Carolina.

Joseph I. Lieberman, of Connecticut.
Daniel K. Akaka, of Hawaii.
Mark Dayton, of Minnesota.
Evan Bayh, of Indiana.
Hillary Rodham Clinton, of New York.
Mark Pryor, of Arkansas.

Emerging Threats and Capabilities

Pat Roberts, of Kansas, *Chairman.*

Wayne Allard, of Colorado.
Susan M. Collins, of Maine.
John Ensign, of Nevada.
James M. Talent, of Missouri.
Saxby Chambliss, of Georgia.
Lindsey O. Graham, of South Carolina.
Elizabeth Dole, of North Carolina.
John Cornyn, of Texas.

Jack Reed, of Rhode Island.
Edward M. Kennedy, of Massachusetts.
Robert C. Byrd, of West Virginia.
Joseph I. Lieberman, of Connecticut.
Daniel K. Akaka, of Hawaii.
Bill Nelson, of Florida.
Evan Bayh, of Indiana.
Hillary Rodham Clinton, of New York.

Personnel

Saxby Chambliss, of Georgia, *Chairman.*

Susan M. Collins, of Maine.
Elizabeth Dole, of North Carolina.
John Cornyn, of Texas.

E. Benjamin Nelson, of Nebraska.
Edward M. Kennedy, of Massachusetts.
Mark Pryor, of Arkansas.

Readiness and Management Support

John Ensign, of Nevada, *Chairman.*

John McCain, of Arizona.
James M. Inhofe, of Oklahoma.
Pat Roberts, of Kansas.
Wayne Allard, of Colorado.
Jeff Sessions, of Alabama.
James M. Talent, of Missouri.
Saxby Chambliss, of Georgia.
John Cornyn, of Texas.

Daniel K. Akaka, of Hawaii.
Robert C. Byrd, of West Virginia.
Bill Nelson, of Florida.
E. Benjamin Nelson, of Nebraska.
Mark Dayton, of Minnesota.
Evan Bayh, of Indiana.
Hillary Rodham Clinton, of New York.
Mark Pryor, of Arkansas.

Seapower

James M. Talent, of Missouri, *Chairman.*

John McCain, of Arizona.
Susan M. Collins, of Maine.
Lindsey O. Graham, of South Carolina.

Edward M. Kennedy, of Massachusetts.
Joseph I. Lieberman, of Connecticut.
Jack Reed, of Rhode Island.

Strategic Forces

Wayne Allard, of Colorado, *Chairman.*

James M. Inhofe, of Oklahoma.
Jeff Sessions, of Alabama.
John Ensign, of Nevada.
Lindsey O. Graham, of South Carolina.
John Cornyn, of Texas.

Bill Nelson, of Florida.
Robert C. Byrd, of West Virginia.
Jack Reed, of Rhode Island.
E. Benjamin Nelson, of Nebraska.
Mark Dayton, of Minnesota.

STAFF

Committee on Armed Services (SR–228), 224–3871.
Staff Director.—Judith A. Ansley.
Chief Clerk.—Marie Fabrizio Dickinson.
Assistant Chief Clerk and Security Manager.—Cindy Pearson.
General Counsel.—Scott W. Stucky.
Counsels: L. David Cherington, Ann M. Mittermeyer, Richard F. Walsh.
Professional Staff Members: Charles W. Alsup, Brian R. Green, Willliam C. Greenwalt, Carolyn M. Hanna, Mary Alice A. Hayward, Ambrose R. Hock, Gregory T. Kiley, Patricia L. Lewis, Thomas L. MacKenzie, Lucian L. Niemeyer, Paula J. Philbin, Lynn F. Rusten, Joseph T. Sixeas.
Nominations Clerk.—Gabriella Eisen.
Systems Administrator.—Gary J. Howard.
Printing and Documents Clerk.—June M. Borawski.
Special Assistant.—Jennifer D. Cave.
Security Clerk.—Kenneth Barbee.
Staff Assistants: Michael N. Berger, Leah C. Brewer, Andrew W. Florell, Andrew Kent, Jennifer Key, Sara R. Mareno, Nicholas W. West.
Receptionist.—Pendred K. Wilson.
Democratic Staff Director.—Richard D. DeBobes.
Administrative Assistant to the Minority.—Christine E. Cowart.
Counsels: Madelyn R. Creedon, Gerald J. Leeling, Peter K. Levine.
Professional Staff: Daniel J. Cox, Jr., Kenneth M Crosswait, Evelyn N. Farkas, Richard W. Fieldhouse, Creighton Greene, Jeremy L. Hekhuis, Maren R. Leed, Arun A. Seraphin, Christina D. Still, Mary Louise Wagner.
Special Assistant.—Bridget M. Whalan.
Subcommittee on Airland:
Majority Professional Staff: Ambrose R. Hock, Thomas L. MacKenzie.
Minority Professional Staff: Daniel J. Cox, Jr., Creighton Greene.
Subcommittee on Emerging Threats and Capabilities:
Majority Professional Staff: Charles W. Alsup, Carolyn M. Hanna, Mary Alice A. Hayward, Paula J. Philbin, Lynn F. Rusten, Joseph T. Sixeas.
Minority Professional Staff: Madelyn R. Creedon, Evelyn N. Farkas, Richard W. Fieldhouse, Maren Leed, Peter K. Levine, Arun A. Seraphin.

Subcommittee on Personnel:
Majority Professional Staff: Patricia L. Lewis, Richard F. Walsh.
Minority Professional Staff.—Gerald J. Leeling.
Subcommittee on Readiness and Management Support:
Majority Professional Staff: William C. Greenwalt, Gregory T. Kiley, Ann M. Mittermeyer, Lucian L. Niemeyer, Joseph T. Sixeas.
Minority Professional Staff: Maren R. Leed, Peter K. Levine, Christina D. Still.
Subcommittee on Seapower:
Majority Professional Staff: Ambrose R. Hock, Thomas L. MacKenzie.
Minority Professional Staff: Daniel J. Cox, Jr., Creighton Greene.
Subcommittee on Strategic Forces:
Majority Professional Staff: Charles W. Alsup, L. David Cherington, Brian R. Green,
Minority Professional Staff: Madelyn R. Creedon, Kenneth M. Crosswait, Richard W. Fieldhouse, .
Majority Professional Staff for:
Acquisition Policy.—William C. Greenwalt.
Arms Control/Counterproliferation.—Mary Alice A. Hayward.
Army Programs.—Ambrose R. Hock.
Aviation Systems.—Thomas L. MacKenzie.
Budget Tracking.—Gregory T. Kiley.
Civilian Nominations: Scott W. Stucky, Richard F. Walsh.
Combating Terrorism/Homeland Defense.—Paula J. Philbin.
Counterdrug Programs.—Charles W. Alsup.
Defense Security Assistance.—Joseph T. Sixeas.
Energy Issues.—L. David Cherington.
Environmental Issues.—Ann M. Mittermeyer.
Export Controls: William C. Greenwalt, Mary Alice A. Hayward.
Foreign Policy: Charles W. Alsup, Lynn F. Rusten.
Information Security.—Charles W. Alsup.
Intelligence Issues.—Charles W. Alsup.
Marine Corps Ground Procurement and R&D Issues.—Ambrose R. Hock.
Military Construction/Base Closures.—Lucian L. Niemeyer.
Military Health Care.—Patricia L. Lewis.
Military Nominations.—Richard F. Walsh.
Military Strategy.—Charles W. Alsup.
Missile Defense.—Brian Green.
Personnel Issues: Patricia L. Lewis, Richard F. Walsh.
Readiness/Operations and Maintenance: William C. Greenwalt, Joseph T. Sixeas.
Readiness, Logistics and Training.—Joseph T. Sixeas.
Science and Technology.—Carolyn M. Hanna.
Shipbuilding Programs.—Thomas L. MacKenzie.
Special Operations Forces.—Charles W. Alsup.
Strategic Programs.—Brian R. Green.
Threat Reduction Programs.—Mary Alice A. Hayward.
Minority Professional Staff for:
Acquisition Policy.—Peter K. Levine.
Arms Control/Counterproliferation.—Richard W. Fieldhouse.
Army Programs.—Daniel J. Cox, Jr.
Aviation Systems.—Creighton Greene.
Budget Tracking.—Creighton Greene.
Civilian Nominations.—Peter K. Levine.
Combating Terrorism/Domestic Preparedness.—Evelyn N. Farkas.
Counterdrug Programs.—Evelyn N. Farkas.
Defense Security Assistance.—Evelyn N. Farkas.
Energy Issues: Madelyn R. Creedon, Mary Louise Wagner.
Environmental Issues.—Peter K. Levine.
Export Controls.—Evelyn N. Farkas.
Foreign Policy: Richard D. DeBobes, Evelyn N. Farkas.
Homeland Defense.—Evelyn N. Farkas.
Information Security.—Creighton Greene.
Intelligence Issues.—Kenneth M. Crosswait.
Marine Corps Ground Procurement and R&D Issues.—Daniel J. Cox, Jr.
Military Construction/Base Closures.—Christina D. Still.
Military Health Care.—Gerald J. Leeling.
Military Nominations.—Gerald J. Leeling.
Military Strategy.—Richard D. DeBobes.
Missile Defense: Kenneth M. Crosswait, Richard W. Fieldhouse.

Morale, Welfare, Recreation.—Gerald J. Leeling.
Personnel Issues.—Gerald J. Leeling.
Readiness and Training / Operations and Maintenance.—Maren R. Leed.
Readiness Logistics / Operations and Maintenance.—Maren R. Leed.
Science and Technology.—Arun A. Seraphin.
Shipbuilding Programs.—Creighton Greene.
Special Operations Forces.—Evelyn N. Farkas.
Strategic Programs.—Madelyn R. Creedon.
Threat Reduction Programs.—Madelyn R. Creedon.

Banking, Housing, and Urban Affairs

534 Dirksen Senate Office Building 20510

phone 224–7391, http://banking.senate.gov

meets last Tuesday of each month

Richard C. Shelby, of Alabama, *Chairman.*

Robert F. Bennett, of Utah.
Wayne Allard, of Colorado.
Michael B. Enzi, of Wyoming.
Chuck Hagel, of Nebraska.
Rick Santorum, of Pennsylvania.
Jim Bunning, of Kentucky.
Mike Crapo, of Idaho.
John E. Sununu, of New Hampshire.
Elizabeth Dole, of North Carolina.
Lincoln D. Chafee, of Rhode Island.

Paul S. Sarbanes, of Maryland.
Christopher J. Dodd, of Connecticut.
Tim Johnson, of South Dakota.
Jack Reed, of Rhode Island.
Charles E. Schumer, of New York.
Evan Bayh, of Indiana.
Zell Miller, of Georgia.
Thomas R. Carper, of Delaware.
Debbie Stabenow, of Michigan.
Jon S. Corzine, of New Jersey.

SUBCOMMITTEES

[The chairman and ranking minority member are ex officio members of all subcommittees.]

Economic Policy

Jim Bunning, of Kentucky, *Chairman.*

Elizabeth Dole, of North Carolina.
Richard Shelby, of Alabama.

Charles E. Schumer, of New York.
Zell Miller, of Georgia.

Financial Institutions

Robert F. Bennett, of Utah, *Chairman.*

Elizabeth Dole, of North Carolina.
Lincoln D. Chafee, of Rhode Island.
Wayne Allard, of Colorado.
Rick Santorum, of Pennsylvania.
Chuck Hagel, of Nebraska.
Jim Bunning, of Kentucky.

Tim Johnson, of South Dakota.
Zell Miller, of Georgia.
Thomas R. Carper, of Delaware.
Christopher J. Dodd, of Connecticut.
Jack Reed, of Rhode Island.
Evan Bayh, of Indiana.
Debbie Stabenow, of Michigan.

Housing and Transportation

Wayne Allard, of Colorado, *Chairman.*

Rick Santorum, of Pennsylvania.
Robert F. Bennett, of Utah.
Lincoln D. Chafee, of Rhode Island.
Michael B. Enzi, of Wyoming.
John E. Sununu, of New Hampshire.
Richard C. Shelby, of Alabama.

Jack Reed, of Rhode Island
Debbie Stabenow, of Michigan.
Jon S. Corzine, of New Jersey.
Christopher J. Dodd, of Connecticut.
Thomas R. Carper, of Delaware.
Charles E. Schumer, of New York.

International Trade and Finance

Chuck Hagel, of Nebraska, *Chairman.*

Michael B. Enzi, of Wyoming.
Mike Crapo, of Idaho.
John E. Sununu, of New Hampshire.
Elizabeth Dole, of North Carolina.
Lincoln D. Chafee, of Rhode Island.

Evan Bayh, of Indiana
Zell Miller, of Georgia.
Tim Johnson, of South Dakota.
Thomas R. Carper, of Delaware.
Jon S. Corzine, of New Jersey.

Securities and Investment

Michael B. Enzi, of Wyoming, *Chairman.*

Mike Crapo, of Idaho.
John E. Sununu, of New Hampshire.
Chuck Hagel, of Nebraska.
Jim Bunning, of Kentucky.
Robert F. Bennett, of Utah.
Wayne Allard, of Colorado.
Rick Santorum, of Pennsylvania.

Christopher J. Dodd, of Connecticut.
Tim Johnson, of South Dakota.
Jack Reed, of Rhode Island.
Charles E. Schumer, of New York.
Evan Bayh, of Indiana.
Debbie Stabenow, of Michigan.
Jon S. Corzine, of New Jersey.

STAFF

Committee on Banking, Housing, and Urban Affairs (SD–534), 224–7391.
Staff Director.—Kathy Casey.
Chief Counsel.—Doug Nappi.
Counsel.—Mark Oesterle.
Deputy Press Secretary.—Andrew Gray.
Legislative Assistant.—Sherry Little.
Special Assistant.—Jennifer Amatos.
Subcommittee Staff Directors:
Economic Policy.—Steve Patterson.
Financial Institutions.—Mike Nielsen.
Housing and Transportation.—Tewana Wilkerson.
International Trade and Finance.—Catherine Cruz Wojtasik.
Securities and Investment.—Mike Thompson.
Minority Staff Director/Chief Counsel.—Steven Harris.
Senior Counsel.—Martin Gruenberg.
Counsels: Jennifer Fogel-Bublick, Lynsey Graham, Sarah Kline, Dean Shahinian, Patience Singleton.
Professional Staff.—Jonathan Miler.
Economist.—Aaron Klein.
Legislative Assistants: Karolina Arias, Laurie Better, Erin Hansen.
Communications Director.—Jesse Jacobs.
Chief Clerk/Systems Administrator.—Joseph Kolinski.
Deputy Chief Clerk.—J.P. Green.
Editor.—George Whittle.
Editorial Assistant.—Irene Whiston.

Budget

624 Dirksen Senate Office Building 20510–6100

phone 224–0642, http://budget.senate.gov

meets first Thursday of each month

Don Nickles, of Oklahoma, *Chairman.*

Pete V. Domenici, of New Mexico.
Charles E. Grassley, of Iowa.
Judd Gregg, of New Hampshire.
Wayne Allard, of Colorado.
Conrad Burns, of Montana.
Michael Enzi, of Wyoming.
Jeff Sessions, of Alabama.
Jim Bunning, of Kentucky.
Mike Crapo, of Idaho.
John Ensign, of Nevada.
John Cornyn, of Texas.

Kent Conrad, of North Dakota.
Ernest F. Hollings, of South Carolina.
Paul S. Sarbanes, of Maryland.
Patty Murray, of Washington.
Ron Wyden, of Oregon.
Russell D. Feingold, of Wisconsin.
Tim Johnson, of South Dakota.
Robert C. Byrd, of West Virginia.
Bill Nelson, of Florida.
Debbie Stabenow, of Michigan.
Jon Corzine, of New Jersey.

(No Subcommittees)

STAFF

Committee on Budget (SD–624), 224–0642.
Majority Staff Director.—Hazen Marshall, 4–2469.
Deputy Staff and Policy Director.—Stacey Hughes, 4–4973.
Chief Counsel.—Beth Smerko Felder, 4–0531.
Special Counsel.—Bob Taylor, 4–3293.
Chief Economist.—Dan Brandt, 4–0797.
Junior Economist.—Anne Oswalt, 4–0536.
Press Secretary.—Gayle Osterberg, 4–6011.
Senior Policy Analyst for Defense and International Affairs.—Roy Phillips, 4–0529.
Senior Analyst for—
Income Security.—Amy Angelier, 4–5369.
Government Finance and Management.—Jim Hearn, 4–2370.
Transportation.—Don Kent, 4–8463.
Veteran Affairs and Social Security.—Maureen O'Neill, 4–1602.
Community and Regional Development.—David Ortega, 4–5398.
Education and General Science.—David Pappone, 4–0564.
Budget Review/Revenues.—Cheri Reidy, 4–0557.
Natural Resources/Energy/Agriculture.—Margaret Stewart, 4–0539.
Budget Review.—Jennifer Winkler, 4–7928.
Health Policy Director.—Megan Hauck, 4–2465.
Tax Policy Director.—Rachel Jones, 4–8695.
Staff and Legislative Coordinator.—Jody Hernandez, 4–4999.
Press Assistant.—Lauren Baylor, 4–0857.
Webmaster.—David Myers, 4–6815.
Staff Assistants: Cara Duckworth, 4–2574; Ron Floyd, 4–0838.
Non-designated:
Chief Clerk.—Lynne Seymour, 4–0191.
Computer Systems Administrator.—George Woodall, 4–6576.
Publications Department.—Letitia Fletcher, 4–0855.
Staff Assistants: Lee Greenwood, 4–0565; Tim Nolan, 4–0796.
Minority Staff Director.—Mary Naylor, 4–0862.
Deputy Staff Directors: Sue Nelson, 4–0560; Jim Horney, 4–0865.
General Counsel.—Lisa Konwinski, 4–2757.
Senior Analyst for—
Education and Appropriations.—Shelley Amdur, 4–9731.
Revenues.—Steve Bailey, 4–2835.
Agriculture and Trade.—Tim Galvin, 4–8463.
Budget Analyst.—Barry Strumpf, 4–0550.

Communications Director.—Stu Nagurka, 4–7436.
Deputy Communications Director.—Steve Posner, 4–7925.
Graphics Production Coordinator.—Kobye Noel, 4–3728.
Chief Economist.—Lee Price, 4–6588.
Analyst for—
Income Security and Medicaid.—Jim Esquea, 4–5811.
Budget.—Mike Jones, 4–0833.
Social Security, Transportation, and Community Development.—Sarah Kuehl, 4–0559.
General Government.—John Righter, 4–0544.
International Affairs and National Security.—Dakota Rudesill, 4–0872.
Webmaster Junior Analyst.—Rock Cheung, 4–0538.
Staff Assistants: Lawrence Hershon, 4–3023; Erin Keogh, 4–0571; Jessie LaVine, 4–0547.

Commerce, Science, and Transportation

508 Dirksen Senate Office Building 20510–6125
phone 224–5115, TTY/TDD 224–8418 www.senate.gov/~commerce

meets first and third Tuesdays of each month

John McCain, of Arizona, *Chairman.*

Ted Stevens, of Alaska.
Conrad R. Burns, of Montana.
Trent Lott, of Mississippi.
Kay Bailey Hutchison, of Texas.
Olympia J. Snowe, of Maine.
Sam Brownback, of Kansas.
Gordon Smith, of Oregon.
Peter G. Fitzgerald, of Illinois.
John Ensign, of Nevada.
George Allen, of Virginia.
John E. Sununu, of New Hampshire.
Ernest F. Hollings, of South Carolina.
Daniel K. Inouye, of Hawaii.
John D. Rockefeller IV, of West Virginia.
John F. Kerry, of Massachusetts.
John B. Breaux, of Louisiana.
Byron L. Dorgan, of North Dakota.
Ron Wyden, of Oregon.
Barbara Boxer, of California.
Bill Nelson, of Florida.
Maria Cantwell, of Washington.
Frank Lautenberg, of New Jersey.

SUBCOMMITTEES

[The chairman and ranking minority member are ex officio members of all subcommittees.]

Aviation

Trent Lott, of Mississippi, *Chairman.*

Ted Stevens, of Alaska.
Conrad R. Burns, of Montana.
Kay Bailey Hutchison, of Texas.
Olympia J. Snowe, of Maine.
Sam Brownback, of Kansas.
Gordon Smith, of Oregon.
Peter G. Fitzgerald, of Illinois.
John Ensign, of Nevada.
George Allen, of Virginia.
John E. Sununu, of New Hampshire.
Ernest F. Hollings, of South Carolina.
John D. Rockefeller IV, of West Virginia.
Daniel K. Inouye, of Hawaii.
John B. Breaux, of Louisiana.
Byron L. Dorgan, of North Dakota.
Ron Wyden, of Oregon.
Bill Nelson, of Florida.
Barbara Boxer, of California.
Maria Cantwell, of Washington.
Frank Lautenberg, of New Jersey.

Communications

Conrad R. Burns, of Montana, *Chairman.*

Ted Stevens, of Alaska.
Trent Lott, of Mississippi.
Kay Bailey Hutchison, of Texas.
Olympia J. Snowe, of Maine.
Sam Brownback, of Kansas.
Gordon Smith, of Oregon.
Peter G. Fitzgerald, of Illinois.
John Ensign, of Nevada.
George Allen, of Virginia.
John E. Sununu, of New Hampshire.
Ernest F. Hollings, of South Carolina.
Daniel K. Inouye, of Hawaii.
John D. Rockefeller IV, of West Virginia.
John F. Kerry, of Massachusetts.
John B. Breaux, of Louisiana.
Byron L. Dorgan, of North Dakota.
Ron Wyden, of Oregon.
Barbara Boxer, of California.
Bill Nelson, of Florida.
Maria Cantwell, of Washington.

Competition, Foreign Commerce, and Infrastructure

Gordon Smith, of Oregon, *Chairman.*

Conrad R. Burns, of Montana.
Sam Brownback, of Kansas.
Peter G. Fitzgerald, of Illinois.
John Ensign, of Nevada.
John E. Sununu, of New Hampshire.
Byron L. Dorgan, of North Dakota.
Barbara Boxer, of California.
Bill Nelson, of Florida.
Maria Cantwell, of Washington.
Frank Lautenberg, of New Jersey.

Consumer Affairs and Product Safety

Peter G. Fitzgerald, of Illinois, *Chairman.*

Conrad R. Burns, of Montana.
Gordon Smith, of Oregon.

Ron Wyden, of Oregon.
Byron L. Dorgan, of North Dakota.

Oceans, Fisheries, and Coast Guard

Olympia J. Snowe, of Maine, *Chairman.*

Ted Stevens, of Alaska.
Trent Lott, of Mississippi.
Kay Bailey Hutchison, of Texas.
Gordon Smith, of Oregon.
John E. Sununu, of New Hampshire.

Ernest F. Hollings, of South Carolina.
John F. Kerry, of Massachusetts.
Daniel K. Inouye, of Hawaii.
John B. Breaux, of Louisiana.
Maria Cantwell, of Washington.

Science, Technology, and Space

Sam Brownback, of Kansas, *Chairman.*

Ted Stevens, of Alaska.
Conrad R. Burns, of Montana.
Trent Lott, of Mississippi.
Kay Bailey Hutchison, of Texas.
John Ensign, of Nevada.
George Allen, of Virginia.
John E. Sununu, of New Hampshire.

John B. Breaux, of Louisiana
John D. Rockefeller IV, of West Virginia.
John F. Kerry, of Massachusetts.
Byron L. Dorgan, of North Dakota.
Ron Wyden, of Oregon.
Bill Nelson, of Florida.
Frank Lautenberg, of New Jersey.

Surface Transportation and Merchant Marine

Kay Bailey Hutchison, of Texas, *Chairman.*

Ted Stevens, of Alaska.
Conrad R. Burns, of Montana.
Trent Lott, of Mississippi.
Olympia J. Snowe, of Maine.
Sam Brownback, of Kansas.
Gordon Smith, of Oregon.
George Allen, of Virginia.

Daniel K. Inouye, of Hawaii.
John D. Rockefeller IV, of West Virginia.
John F. Kerry, of Massachusetts.
John B. Breaux, of Louisiana.
Ron Wyden, of Oregon.
Barbara Boxer, of California.
Frank Lautenberg, of New Jersey.

STAFF

Committee on Commerce, Science, and Transportation (SD–508), 224–5115.
Republican Staff Director/General Counsel.—Jeanne Bumpus.
Deputy Staff Director.—Ann Begeman.
Press Secretary.—Rebecca Hanks.
Democratic Staff Director/Chief Counsel.—Kevin D. Kayes.
General Counsel.—Gregg Elias.

Staff:
James M. Assey, Jr.
Lloyd G. Ator
Bill Bailey
Heather Bartsch
Ann Begeman
Carl Bentzel
Chris Bertram
Carli Bertrand*
Jessica Bonanno
Chris Bonanti*
Mark Bruegger
Jeanne Bumpus
Lee Carosi
Pablo Carrillo
Rob Chamberlin
Pablo Chavez
Channon Clements
Cassandra Coleman*
Helen Colosimo
John Cullen
Floyd DesChamps
Gregg Ellias
Theresa Eugene
Jeff Ferguson*
Bridget Ferriss*
Carlos Fierro
Robert Foster
Amy Fraenkel
Robert Freeman
Jack Fulmer*
Yvonne T. Gowdy
Rebecca Hanks
Debbie Hersman
Alexsis Horowitz
Sarah Jolly
E. Vanessa Jones
Kevin Kayes
Rebecca A. Kojm
Angela Kouters
Ken LaSala
Nancy Lewis*
Chan Lieu

Kristine Lynch
Susan MacDonald
Paul Martino
Nathan Mattison
Cathy McCullough
Allison McMahan
Jeremy Miller
Drew Minkiewicz
Matthew Morrissey
Kenneth Nahigian
Marvin Nixon
Debbie Paul
Mary Phillips
Virginia Pounds
Joe Raymond
Sean Russell
Ivy Shannon
Alyson Schuck
Shay Singh
Margaret Spring
David Strickland
Katie Strumpf
Gael Sullivan
Jean Toal Eisen
Joani Wales
Rachel Welch
Sam Whitehorn
David Wonnenberg
Erika Young

**Associated with the Committee.*

Energy and Natural Resources

364 Dirksen Senate Office Building 20510

phone 224–4971, fax 224–6163, http://energy.senate.gov

meets third Wednesday of each month

Pete V. Domenici, of New Mexico, *Chairman.*

Don Nickles, of Oklahoma.
Larry E. Craig, of Idaho.
Ben Nighthorse Campbell, of Colorado.
Craig Thomas, of Wyoming.
Lamar Alexander, of Tennessee.
Lisa Murkowski, of Alaska.
James M. Talent, of Missouri.
Conrad Burns, of Montana.
Gordon H. Smith, of Oregon.
Jim Bunning, of Kentucky.
Jon Kyl, of Arizona.

Jeff Bingaman, of New Mexico.
Daniel K. Akaka, of Hawaii.
Byron L. Dorgan, of North Dakota.
Bob Graham, of Florida.
Ron Wyden, of Oregon.
Tim Johnson, of South Dakota.
Mary L. Landrieu, of Louisiana.
Evan Bayh, of Indiana.
Dianne Feinstein, of California.
Charles E. Schumer, of New York.
Maria Cantwell, of Washington.

SUBCOMMITTEES

[The chairman and the ranking minority member are ex officio members of all subcommittees.]

Energy

Lamar Alexander, of Tennessee, *Chairman.*

Don Nickles, of Oklahoma.
James M. Talent, of Missouri.
Jim Bunning, of Kentucky.
Craig Thomas, of Wyoming.
Lisa Murkowski, of Alaska.
Larry E. Craig, of Idaho.
Conrad Burns, of Montana.

Bob Graham, of Florida.
Daniel K. Akaka, of Hawaii.
Tim Johnson, of South Dakota.
Mary L. Landrieu, of Louisiana.
Evan Bayh, of Indiana.
Charles E. Schumer, of New York.
Maria Cantwell, of Washington.

National Parks

Craig Thomas, of Wyoming, *Chairman.*

Don Nickles, of Oklahoma.
Ben Nighthorse Campbell, of Colorado.
Lamar Alexander, of Tennessee.
Conrad Burns, of Montana.
Gordon H. Smith, of Oregon.
Jon Kyl, of Arizona.

Daniel K. Akaka, of Hawaii.
Byron L. Dorgan, of North Dakota.
Bob Graham, of Florida.
Mary L. Landrieu, of Louisiana.
Evan Bayh, of Indiana.
Charles E. Schumer, of New York.

Public Lands and Forests

Larry E. Craig, of Idaho, *Chairman.*

Conrad Burns, of Montana.
Gordon H. Smith, of Oregon.
Jon Kyl, of Arizona.
Ben Nighthorse Campbell, of Colorado.
Lamar Alexander, of Tennessee.
Lisa Murkowski, of Alaska.
James M. Talent, of Missouri.

Ron Wyden, of Oregon.
Daniel K. Akaka, of Hawaii.
Byron L. Dorgan, of North Dakota.
Tim Johnson, of South Dakota.
Mary L. Landrieu, of Louisiana.
Evan Bayh, of Indiana.
Dianne Feinstein, of California.

Water and Power

Lisa Murkowski, of Alaska, *Chairman.*

Ben Nighthorse Campbell, of Colorado.
Gordon H. Smith, of Oregon.
Jon Kyl, of Arizona.
Larry E. Craig, of Idaho.
James M. Talent, of Missouri.
Jim Bunning, of Kentucky.
Craig Thomas, of Wyoming.

Byron L. Dorgan, of North Dakota.
Bob Graham, of Florida.
Ron Wyden, of Oregon.
Tim Johnson, of South Dakota.
Dianne Feinstein, of California.
Charles E. Schumer, of New York.
Maria Cantwell, of Washington.

STAFF

Committee on Energy and Natural Resources (SD–364), 224–4971, fax 224–6163.

Staff Director.—Alex Flint, 4–1004

Deputy Staff Director.—Carole McGuire, 4–0537.

Chief Counsel.—Jim Beirne, 4–2564.

*Counsels:*Kellie Donnelly, 4–9360; Lisa Epifani, 4–5269; Shelly Randel, 4–7933.

Deputy Chief Counsel.—Judy Pensabene, 4–1327.

Chief Clerk.—Carol Craft, 4–7153.

Communications Director.—Marnie Funk, 4–6977.

Staff Scientist.—Bryan Hannegan, 4–7932.

Executive Clerk.—Kristin Phillips, 4–5305.

Professional Staff: Frank Gladies, 4–2878; Pete Lyons, 4–5861; Scott O'Malia, 4–2039.

Senior Staff Assistant.—Jo Meuse, 4–4971.

Staff Assistants: Shane Perkins, 4–7555; Jared Stubbs, 4–7556; Justin Tillinghast, 4–2694.

BLM Fellow.—Dick Bouts, 4–7574.

Bevinetto Fellow.—Pete Lucero, 4–6293.

Press Intern.—Patience Gaydos, 4–7875.

Presidential Management Intern.—Joe Hartenstine, 4–9313.

Research Assistant.—Jennifer Owen, 4–1219.

Fellows: Thomas Lillie, 4–5161; Erik Webb, 4–4756.

Democratic Staff Director.—Robert Simon, 4–9201.

Chief Clerk.—Vicki Thorne, 4–3607.

Chief Counsel.—Sam Fowler, 4–7571.

Senior Counsels: Patty Beneke, 4–5451; David Brooks, 4–9863.

Counsels: Mike Connor, 4–5479; Deborah Estes, 4–5360; Kira Finkler, 4–8164; Scott Miller, 4–5488.

Communications Director.—Bill Wicker, 4–5243.

Professional Staff: Leon Lowery, 4–2209; Jennifer Michael, 4–7143.

Legislative Assistant.—Jonathan Black, 4–6722.

Staff Assistants: Shelley Brown, 4–5915; Amanda Goldman, 4–6836; Malini Sekhar, 4–7934.

Calendar Clerk.—Mia Bennett, 4–7147.

Financial Clerk.—Nancy Hall, 4–3606.

Systems Administrator.—Dave McAdam, 4–7163.

Printer/Editor.—Richard Smit, 4–3118.

Printer.—Jack Sprinkle, 4–7302.

Environment and Public Works

410 Dirksen Senate Office Building 20510–6175

phone 224–6176, www.senate.gov/~epw

meets first and third Thursdays of each month

James M. Inhofe, of Oklahoma, *Chairman.*

John W. Warner, of Virginia.
Christopher S. Bond, of Missouri.
George V. Voinovich, of Ohio.
Mike Crapo, of Idaho.
Lincoln Chafee, of Rhode Island.
John Cornyn, of Texas.
Lisa Murkowski, of Alaska.
Craig Thomas, of Wyoming.
Wayne Allard, of Colorado.

JAMES M. JEFFORDS, of Vermont.
Max Baucus, of Montana.
Harry Reid, of Nevada.
Bob Graham, of Florida.
Joseph I. Lieberman, of Connecticut.
Barbara Boxer, of California.
Ron Wyden, of Oregon.
Thomas R. Carper, of Delaware.
Hillary Rodham Clinton, of New York.

SUBCOMMITTEES

[The chairman and the ranking minority member are ex officio (non-voting) members of all subcommittees on which they do not serve.]

Clean Air, Wetlands, and Climate Change

George V. Voinovich, of Ohio, *Chairman.*

Christopher S. Bond, of Missouri.
Mike Crapo, of Idaho.
John Cornyn, of Texas.
Craig Thomas, of Wyoming.

Thomas R. Carper, of Delaware.
Joseph I. Lieberman, of Connecticut.
Harry Reid, of Nevada.
Hillary Rodham Clinton, of New York.

Fisheries, Wildlife, and Water

Mike Crapo, of Idaho, *Chairman.*

John W. Warner, of Virginia.
Lisa Murkowski, of Alaska.
Craig Thomas, of Wyoming.
Wayne Allard, of Colorado.

Bob Graham, of Florida.
Max Baucus, of Montana.
Ron Wyden, of Oregon.
Hillary Rodham Clinton, of New York.

Superfund and Waste Management

Lincoln Chafee, of Rhode Island, *Chairman.*

Wayne Allard, of Virginia.
John W. Warner, of Missouri.
Christopher S. Bond, of Colorado.

Barbara Boxer, of California.
Ron Wyden, of Oregon.
Thomas R. Carper, of Delaware.

Transportation and Infrastructure

Christopher S. Bond, of Missouri, *Chairman.*

John W. Warner, of Virginia.
George V. Voinovich, of Ohio.
Lincoln Chafee, of Rhode Island.
John Cornyn, of Texas.
Lisa Murkowski, of Alaska.

Harry Reid, of Montana.
Max Baucus, of Nevada.
Bob Graham, of Florida.
Joseph I. Lieberman, of Connecticut.
Barbara Boxer, of California.

STAFF

Committee on Environment and Public Works (SD–410), phone 224–6176.
Recording for Committee Agenda, 224–1179.
Majority fax (SD–410), 224–5167; (SH–415), 224–2322.
Staff Director.—Andrew Wheeler.
Deputy Staff Director for Environment.—Louis Renjel.
Deputy Staff Director for Transportation.—Ruth Van Mark.
Chief Counsel.—Aloysius Hogan.
Counsels: Ryan Jackson, John Shanahan.
Chief Clerk.—Alicia Butler.
Executive Assistant.—Debbie Leggitt.
Systems Administrator.—RaeAnn Phipps.
Communications Director.—Mike Catanzaro.
Deputy Communications Director.—Jared Young.
Senior Professional Staff: Martin Hall, Michele Nellenbach.
Professional Staff: Genevieve Erny, Angelina Giancarlo, James O'Keeffe.
Editorial Director.—Duane Nystrom.
Legislative Correspondents: Loyed Gill, Suzanne Matwyshen-Gillen.
Legislative Fellow.—Mitch Surrett.
GPO Detailee.—Brenda Samuels.
Staff Assistants: Matt Dempsey, Kristy Rose.
Research Analysts: James Qualters, Nathan Richmond.
Minority fax (SD–456), 224–1273; (SH–508), 224–0574.
Minority Staff Director.—Ken Connolly.
Deputy Staff Director.—Edward Barron.
Executive Assistant.—Carolyn Dupree.
Chief Counsel.—Alison Taylor.
Counsels: Mary Katherine Ishee, J.C. Sandberg.
Senior Policy Advisors: Jo-Ellen Darcy, Jeff Squires.
Executive Clerk/Office Manager.—Margaret Wetherald.
Professional Staff: Geoff Brown, Shannon Heyck-Williams, Doug Jordan, Chris Miller, Catharine Ransom, Bryan Richardson, Cameron Taylor.
Legislative Correspondent.—Matthew Kooperman.
Research Assistant.—Elizabeth Ryan.
Fellows: Erik Steavens, Malcolm Woolf.
Chief Clerk.—Alicia Butler.
Systems Administrator.—RaeAnn Phipps.
Editorial Director.—Duane Nystrom.

Finance

219 Dirksen Senate Office Building 20510

phone 224–4515, fax 224–0554, http://finance.senate.gov

meets second and fourth Tuesdays of each month

Charles E. Grassley, of Iowa, *Chairman.*

Orrin G. Hatch, of Utah.
Don Nickles, of Oklahoma.
Trent Lott, of Mississippi.
Olympia J. Snowe, of Maine.
Jon Kyl, of Arizona.
Craig Thomas, of Wyoming.
Rick Santorum, of Pennsylvania.
Bill Frist, of Tennessee.
Gordon Smith, of Oregon.
Jim Bunning, of Kentucky.

Max Baucus, of Montana.
John D. Rockefeller IV, of West Virginia.
Thomas A. Daschle, of South Dakota.
John B. Breaux, of Louisiana.
Kent Conrad, of North Dakota.
Bob Graham, of Florida.
JAMES M. JEFFORDS, of Vermont.
Jeff Bingaman, of New Mexico.
John F. Kerry, of Massachusetts.
Blanche L. Lincoln, of Arkansas.

SUBCOMMITTEES

[The chairman and the ranking minority member are ex officio (non-voting) members of all subcommittees on which they do not serve.]

Health Care

Jon Kyl, of Arizona, *Chairman.*

Olympia J. Snowe, of Maine.
Bill Frist, of Tennessee.
Jim Bunning, of Kentucky.
Don Nickles, of Oklahoma.
Craig Thomas, of Wyoming.
Rick Santorum, of Pennsylvania.
Gordon Smith, of Oregon.
Orrin G. Hatch, of Utah.
Trent Lott, of Mississippi.

John D. Rockefeller IV, of West Virginia.
Thomas A. Daschle, of South Dakota.
Bob Graham, of Florida.
JAMES M. JEFFORDS, of Vermont.
Jeff Bingaman, of New Mexico.
John F. Kerry, of Massachusetts.
Blanche L. Lincoln, of Arkansas.
John B. Breaux, of Louisiana.
Max Baucus, of Montana.

International Trade

Craig Thomas, of Wyoming, *Chairman.*

Orrin G. Hatch, of Utah.
Charles E. Grassley, of Iowa.
Gordon Smith, of Oregon.
Olympia J. Snowe, of Maine.
Bill Frist, of Tennessee.
Trent Lott, of Mississippi.
Jim Bunning, of Kentucky.

Max Baucus, of Montana.
John D. Rockefeller IV, of West Virginia.
Kent Conrad, of North Dakota.
Bob Graham, of Florida.
JAMES M. JEFFORDS, of Vermont.
Thomas A. Daschle, of South Dakota.
John F. Kerry, of Massachusetts.

Long-Term Growth and Debt Reduction

Gordon Smith, of Oregon, *Chairman.*

Trent Lott, of Mississippi.
Jon Kyl, of Arizona.

Bob Graham, of Florida.
Kent Conrad, of North Dakota.

Social Security and Family Policy

Rick Santorum, of Pennsylvania, *Chairman.*

Charles E. Grassley, of Iowa.
Jon Kyl, of Arizona.
Jim Bunning, of Kentucky.
Don Nickles, of Oklahoma.
Olympia J. Snowe, of Maine.
Bill Frist, of Tennessee.
John B. Breaux, of Louisiana.
Thomas A. Daschle, of South Dakota.
John F. Kerry, of Massachusetts.
John D. Rockefeller IV, of West Virginia.
Jeff Bingaman, of New Mexico.
Blanche L. Lincoln, of Arkansas.

Taxation and IRS Oversight

Don Nickles, of Oklahoma, *Chairman.*

Orrin G. Hatch, of Utah.
Trent Lott, of Mississippi.
Olympia J. Snowe, of Maine.
Craig Thomas, of Wyoming.
Rick Santorum, of Pennsylvania.
Gordon Smith, of Oregon.
Kent Conrad, of North Dakota.
Jeff Bingaman, of New Mexico.
Blanche L. Lincoln, of Arkansas.
John B. Breaux, of Louisiana.
Max Baucus, of Montana.
JAMES M. JEFFORDS, of Vermont.

STAFF

Committee on Finance (SD–219), 224–4515, fax 228–0554.
Staff Director/Chief Counsel.—Kolan Davis.
Deputy Staff Director.—Ted Totman.
Special Counsel to the Chairman/Chief Investigative Counsel.—Emilia DiSanto.
Investigative Counsel.—Dan Donovan.
Investigator.—John Drake.
Investigative Staff Assistant.—Ed Wallace.
Archivist.—Josh LeVasseur.
Chief Clerk.—Carla Martin.
Deputy Clerk.—Amber Williams.
Chief Editor.—Bob Merulla.
Chief Health Counsel.—Linda Fishman.
Tax Counsel/Senior Counsel to the Chairman.—Dean Zerbe.
Chief Tax Counsel.—Mark Prater.
Tax Counsels: Diann Howland, Ed McClellan, Christy Mistr, Elizabeth Paris.
Tax Staff Assistant.—Brad Cannon.
Trade Counsel.—Stephen Schaefer.
Trade Professional Staff Member.—Carrie Clark.
Trade Staff Assistant.—Zach Paulsen.
Hearing Clerk.—Mark Blair.
Chief International Trade.—Everett Eissenstat.
Chief Social Security Analyst.—Steve Robinson.
International Trade Counsel.—David Johanson.
Press Secretary.—Jill Gerber.
Communications Director.—Jill Kozeny.
Staff Assistants: Jewel Harper, Julia McCaul, Erin Nugent, Marko Serbinsky.
System Administrator.—Geoffery Burrell.
Health Policy Advisors: Jennifer Bell, Mark Hayes, Leah Kegler, Colin Roskey, Becky Shipp.
Health Staff Assistant.—Alicia Ziemiecki.
Minority Staff Director.—Jeff Forbes.
Senior Advisor.—John Angell.
Executive Assistant to the Minority Staff Director.—Lara Birkes.
Chief International Trade Counsel.—Tim Punke.
Trade Counsels: Shara Aranoff, John Gilliland, Brian Pomper.
Associate Trade Advisor.—Andy Harig.
Chief Tax Counsel.—Russ Sullivan.
Senior Budget Advisor.—Alan Cohen.
Chief Health Counsel.—Liz Fowler.
Health Investigative Counsel.—Andrea Cohen.
Chief Investigator.—Patrick Heck.

Investigator.—Anita Horn Rizek.
General Counsel.—Bill Dauster.
Counsel.—Matt Jones.
Press Secretary.—Laura Hayes.
Professional Staff Members of:
  Medicare: Jon Blum, Pat Bousliman.
  Social Security.—Tom Klouda.
  Welfare.—Doug Steiger.
Professional Staff Member.—Kate Kirchgraber, Dawn Levy.
Tax Research Assistant.—Liz Liebschutz.
Tax Assistant.—Jonathan Selib.

Foreign Relations

446 Dirksen Senate Office Building 20510–6225

phone 224–4651, http://foreign.senate.gov

meets each Tuesday

Richard G. Lugar, of Indiana, *Chairman.*

Chuck Hagel, of Nebraska.
Lincoln D. Chafee, of Rhode Island.
George Allen, of Virginia.
Sam Brownback, of Kansas.
Michael B. Enzi, of Wyoming.
George V. Voinovich, of Ohio.
Lamar Alexander, of Tennessee.
Norm Coleman, of Minnesota.
John E. Sununu, of New Hampshire.
Joseph R. Biden Jr., of Delaware.
Paul S. Sarbanes, of Maryland.
Christopher J. Dodd, of Connecticut.
John F. Kerry, of Massachusetts.
Russell D. Feingold, of Wisconsin.
Barbara Boxer, of California.
Bill Nelson, of Florida.
John D. Rockefeller IV, of West Virginia.
Jon S. Corzine, of New Jersey.

SUBCOMMITTEES

[The chairman and ranking minority member are ex officio (non-voting) members of all subcommittees on which they do not serve.]

African Affairs

Lamar Alexander, of Tennessee, *Chairman.*

Sam Brownback, of Kansas.
Norm Coleman, of Minnesota.
John E. Sununu, of New Hampshire.
Russell D. Feingold, of Wisconsin.
Christopher J. Dodd, of Connecticut.
Bill Nelson, of Florida.

East Asian and Pacific Affairs

Sam Brownback, of Kansas, *Chairman.*

Lamar Alexander, of Tennessee.
Chuck Hagel, of Nebraska.
George Allen, of Virginia.
George V. Voinovich, of Ohio.
John F. Kerry, of Massachusetts.
John D. Rockefeller IV, of West Virginia.
Russell D. Feingold, of Wisconsin.
Jon S. Corzine, of New Jersey.

European Affairs

George Allen, of Virginia, *Chairman.*

George V. Voinovich, of Ohio.
Chuck Hagel, of Nebraska.
John E. Sununu, of New Hampshire.
Lincoln D. Chafee, of Rhode Island.
Joseph R. Biden Jr., of Delaware.
Paul S. Sarbanes, of Maryland.
Christopher J. Dodd, of Connecticut.
John F. Kerry, of Massachusetts.

International Economic Policy, Export and Trade Promotion

Chuck Hagel, of Nebraska, *Chairman.*

Lincoln D. Chafee, of Rhode Island.
Michael B. Enzi, of Wyoming.
Lamar Alexander, of Tennessee.
Norm Coleman, of Minnesota.
Paul S. Sarbanes, of Maryland.
John D. Rockefeller IV, of West Virginia.
Jon S. Corzine, of New Jersey.
Christopher J. Dodd, of Connecticut.

International Operations and Terrorism

John E. Sununu, of New Hampshire, *Chairman.*

Michael B. Enzi, of Wyoming.
George Allen, of Virginia.
George V. Voinovich, of Ohio.
Sam Brownback, of Kansas.

Bill Nelson, of Florida.
Joseph R. Biden Jr., of Delaware.
Russell D. Feingold, of Wisconsin.
Barbara Boxer, of California.

Near Eastern and South Asian Affairs

Lincoln D. Chafee, of Rhode Island, *Chairman.*

Chuck Hagel, of Nebraska.
Sam Brownback, of Kansas.
George V. Voinovich, of Ohio.
Norm Coleman, of Minnesota.

Barbara Boxer, of California.
Jon S. Corzine, of New Jersey.
John D. Rockefeller IV, of West Virginia.
Paul S. Sarbanes, of Maryland.

Western Hemisphere, Peace Corps, and Narcotics Affairs

Norm Coleman, of Minnesota, *Chairman.*

Lincoln D. Chafee, of Rhode Island.
George Allen, of Virginia.
Michael B. Enzi, of Wyoming.
John E. Sununu, of New Hampshire.

Christopher J. Dodd, of Connecticut.
Barbara Boxer, of California.
Bill Nelson, of Florida.
Joseph R. Biden Jr., of Delaware.
John F. Kerry, of Massachusetts.

STAFF

Committee on Foreign Relations (SD–450), 224–4651.
Staff Director.—Kenneth Myers, Jr.
Deputy Staff Director.—Dan Diller.
Chief Counsel.—Paul Clayman.
Deputy Chief Counsels: Stephanie Henning, Michael Mattler.
Press Secretary.—Andy Fisher.
Senior Professional Staff: Jay Branegan, Mark Helmke, Mary Locke, Keith Luse, Kenneth Myers III, Kim Savit.
Professional Staff: Jessica Fugate, Carl Meacham, Thomas Moore, Michael Phelan.
Administrative Director.—Katherine Maloney.
Legislative Assistants: Cristina Tallarigo, Ellona Wilner.
Intern Coordinator.—C. Derickson Stowe.
Democratic Staff Director.—Antony Blinken (SD–439), 4–3953.
Chief Counsel.—Brian McKeon.
Special Assistant to the Staff Director.—Jessica Dalton.
Professional Staff: Gregory Aftandilian, Jonah Blank, Heather Flynn, Michael Haltzel, Frank Jannuzi, Jofi Joseph, Edward Levine, Erin Logan, Janice O'Connell, Nancy Stetson, Puneet Talwar.
Legislative Research Assistant.—Stacy Kessler.
Office Manager.—Joanna Woodward.
Systems Administrator.—Alan Browne.
Director for Protocol/Foreign Travel.—Sandy Mason.
Chief Clerk.—Susan Oursler.
Executive Clerk.—Angela Evans.
Executive Assistant to the Chief Clerk.—Megan McCray.
Hearing Clerk.—Bertie Bowman.
Printing Clerks: Michael Bennett, David Evans.
Staff Assistant.—Deborah M. Johnson.
Clerical Assistants: Matthew McMillan, Thomas B. Wharton.

Governmental Affairs

340 Dirksen Senate Office Building 20510

phone 224–4751, http://www.senate.gov/~gov_affairs

Hearing Room—SD–342 Dirksen Senate Office Building

meets first Thursday of each month

Susan M. Collins, of Maine, *Chairman.*

Ted Stevens, of Alaska.
George V. Voinovich, of Ohio.
Norm Coleman, of Minnesota.
Arlen Specter, of Pennsylvania.
Robert F. Bennett, of Utah.
Peter G. Fitzgerald, of Illinois.
John E. Sununu, of New Hampshire.
Richard C. Shelby, of Alabama.

Joseph I. Lieberman, of Connecticut.
Carl Levin, of Michigan.
Daniel K. Akaka, of Hawaii.
Richard J. Durbin, of Illinois.
Thomas R. Carper, of Delaware.
Mark Dayton, of Minnesota.
Frank Lautenberg, of New Jersey.
Mark Pryor, of Arkansas.

SUBCOMMITTEES

[The chairman and the ranking minority member are ex officio members of all subcommittees.]

Financial Management, the Budget, and International Security (FMBIS)

Peter G. Fitzgerald, of Illinois, *Chairman.*

Ted Stevens, of Alaska.
George V. Voinovich, of Ohio.
Arlen Specter, of Pennsylvania.
Robert F. Bennett, of Utah.
John E. Sununu, of New Hampshire.
Richard C. Shelby, of Alabama.

Daniel K. Akaka, of Hawaii.
Carl Levin, of Michigan.
Thomas R. Carper, of Delaware.
Mark Dayton, of Minnesota.
Frank Lautenberg, of New Jersey.
Mark Pryor, of Arkansas.

Oversight of Government Management, the Federal Workforce and the District of Columbia (OGM)

George V. Voinovich, of Ohio, *Chairman.*

Ted Stevens, of Alaska.
Norm Coleman, of Minnesota.
Robert F. Bennett, of Utah.
Peter G. Fitzgerald, of Illinois.
John E. Sununu, of New Hampshire.

Richard J. Durbin, of Illinois.
Daniel K. Akaka, of Hawaii.
Thomas R. Carper, of Delaware.
Frank Lautenberg, of New Jersey.
Mark Pryor, of Arkansas.

Permanent Subcommittee on Investigations (PSI)

Norm Coleman, of Minnesota, *Chairman.*

Ted Stevens, of Alaska.
George V. Voinovich, of Ohio.
Arlen Specter, of Pennsylvania.
Robert F. Bennett, of Utah.
Peter G. Fitzgerald, of Illinois.
John E. Sununu, of New Hampshire.
Richard C. Shelby, of Alabama.

Carl Levin, of Michigan.
Daniel K. Akaka, of Hawaii.
Richard J. Durbin, of Illinois.
Thomas R. Carper, of Delaware.
Mark Dayton, of Minnesota.
Frank Lautenberg, of New Jersey.
Mark Pryor, of Arkansas.

STAFF

Committee on Governmental Affairs (SD–340), 224–4751.
Staff Director/Counsel.—Michael Bopp.
Chief Investigative Counsel.—David Kass.
Senior Counsel: Jason A. Foster, Johanna Hardy, Alec D. Rogers.
Counsels: James McKay, Rob Owen.
Professional Staff: Jane Alonso, Claire Barnard, Kim Corthell, James P. Dohoney, Lynn Dondis, Ann Fisher, Priscilla Hanley, Bonnie Heald, David Hunter, Jon Kakasenko, Tim Raducha-Grace.
Executive Assistant.—Jennifer Gagnon.
Chief Clerk.—Darla Cassell.
Financial Clerk.—John Gleason.
Publications Clerk.—Pat Hogan.
Systems Administrator/Webmaster.—Ryan Davis.
Archivist/Librarian.—Tom Eisinger.
Assistant Press Secretary.—Megan Sowards.
Investigator.—Eileen Fisher.
Staff Assistants: Alexandra Charles, Courtney Cheney, Meghan Foley, John A. Woodcock.
U.S. Coast Guard Detailee.—Claudia C. Gelzer.
Minority Staff Director/Counsel.—Joyce Rechtschaffen (SH–604), 224–2627.
Office Manager/Executive Assistant to the Minority Staff Director.—Janet Burrell.
Communications Director.—Leslie Phillips.
Communications Advisor.—Joshua Greenman.
Chief Counsel.—Laurie Rubenstein.
Counsels: Beth Grossman, Holly Idelson, Kevin Landy, Cynthia Gooen Lesser, Lawrence B. Novey, Susan Propper, Kathryn J. Seddon (SD–330).
Professional Staff: Michael L. Alexander, David Barton, David M. Berick (SD–330), Patrick Hart (SD–330), Donny R. Williams, Jason M. Yanussi.
Deputy Press Secretary.—Sari Levy.
Staff Assistant.—Megan Finlayson.
Research Assistants: Jennifer Hamilton, Adam Sedgewick (SD–330), Wendy Wang.
Subcommittee on Financial Management, the Budget, and International Security (FMBIS) (SH–446), 4–4551.
Staff Director.—Michael J. Russell, 4–2254.
Chief Clerk.—Amanda Linaburg.
Minority Staff Director.—Richard J. Kessler (SH–439), 4–4551.
Deputy Staff Director.—Nanci Langley.
Professional Staff.—Garrick Groves.
Counsel.—Jennifer Tyree.
Fellow.—Joshua Handler.
Subcommittee on Oversight of Government Management, The Federal Workforce, and the District of Columbia (SH–442), 4–3682.
Staff Director.—Andrew Richardson.
Counsel.—Amanda Nichols.
Professional Staff: Michael Dovilla, John Salamone.
Legislative Aide.—Theresa Prych.
Staff Assistant.—Kevin Doran.
Subcommittee Clerk.—Cynthia Simmons.
Minority Staff Director/Chief Counsel.—Marianne Upton (SD–326), 4–5538.
Counsels: Emily J. Kirk, Bill Weber.
Professional Staff.—Susan Soyka Hardesty.
Legislative Correspondent.—Sanchi Bhandary.
Staff Assistants: John Daley, Brian McLaughlin.
Permanent Subcommittee on Investigations (SR–199), 4–3721.
General Counsel.—Joseph Kennedy.
Professional Staff: Bernadette Kilroy, Grant Lebens, Jay Thweatt.
Chief Clerk.—Mary Robertson, 4–3721.
Minority Staff Director/Chief Counsel.—Elise J. Bean, 4–9505.
Counsels: Dan M. Berkovitz, Robert L. Roach, Laura Stuber.
Professional Staff.—James J. Duckman.
Detailees: James S. Elliott, Beth Merillat-Bianchi, Kesha L. Pitt.

Health, Education, Labor, and Pensions

428 Dirksen Senate Office Building 20510–6300

phone 224–0767, http://labor.senate.gov

meets second and fourth Wednesdays of each month

Judd Gregg, of New Hampshire, *Chairman.*

Bill Frist, of Tennessee.
Michael B. Enzi, of Wyoming.
Lamar Alexander, of Tennessee.
Christopher S. Bond, of Missouri.
Mike DeWine, of Ohio.
Pat Roberts, of Kansas.
Jeff Sessions, of Alabama.
John Ensign, of Nevada.
Lindsey O. Graham, of South Carolina.
John W. Warner, of Virginia.

Edward M. Kennedy, of Massachusetts.
Christopher J. Dodd, of Connecticut.
Tom Harkin, of Iowa.
Barbara A. Mikulski, of Maryland.
JAMES M. JEFFORDS, of Vermont.
Jeff Bingaman, of New Mexico.
Patty Murray, of Washington.
Jack Reed, of Rhode Island.
John Edwards, of North Carolina.
Hillary Rodham Clinton, of New York.

SUBCOMMITTEES

[The chairman and ranking minority member are ex officio members of all subcommittees on which they do not serve.]

Aging

Christopher Bond, of Missouri, *Chairman.*

Lamar Alexander, of Tennessee.
Mike Dewine, of Ohio.
Pat Roberts, of Kansas.
John Ensign, of Nevada.
John W. Warner, of Virginia.

Barbara A. Mikulski, of Maryland.
Edward M. Kennedy, of Massachusetts.
Patty Murray, of Washington.
John Edwards, of North Carolina.
Hillary Rodham Clinton, of New York.

Children and Families

Lamar Alexander, of Tennessee, *Chairman.*

Michael B. Enzi, of Wyoming.
Christopher S. Bond, of Missouri.
Mike DeWine, of Ohio.
Pat Roberts, of Kansas.
Jeff Sessions, of Alabama.
John Ensign, of Nevada.
Lindsey O. Graham, of South Carolina.
John W. Warner, of Virginia.

Christopher J. Dodd, of Connecticut.
Tom Harkin, of Iowa.
JAMES M. JEFFORDS, of Vermont.
Jeff Bingaman, of New Mexico.
Patty Murray, of Washington.
Jack Reed, of Rhode Island.
John Edwards, of North Carolina.
Hillary Rodham Clinton, of New York.

Employment, Safety, and Training

Michael B. Enzi, of Wyoming, *Chairman.*

Lamar Alexander, of Tennessee.
Christopher S. Bond, of Missouri.
Pat Roberts, of Kansas.
Jeff Sessions, of Alabama.

Patty Murray, of Washington.
Christopher J. Dodd, of Connecticut.
Tom Harkin, of Iowa.
JAMES M. JEFFORDS, of Vermont.

Substance Abuse and Mental Health Services

Mike DeWine, of Ohio, *Chairman.*

Michael B. Enzi, of Wyoming.
Jeff Sessions, of Alabama.
John Ensign, of Alabama.

Edward M. Kennedy, of Massachusetts.
Jeff Bingaman, of New Mexico.
Jack Reed, of Rhode Island.

STAFF

Committee on Health, Education, Labor, and Pensions (SD–428), 224–5375, fax 228–5044, TDD 224–1975.

Staff Director.—Sharon R. Soderstrom (SH–835), 4–6770.

Deputy Staff Director.—Townsend L. McNitt (SH–835).

Health Policy Director.—Vincent J. Ventimiglia (SH–727).

Chief Counsel.—Stephanie J. Monroe (SH–835).

Counsel/Labor: David L. Thompson (SH–833), Anne B. White (SH–833).

Counsel/Health.—Steven E. Irizarry (SH–727).

Counsel/Education.—Tracy A. Locklin (SH–833).

Policy Director for Education.—Denzel E. McGuire (SH–833).

Health Research Assistant.—Katy French (SH–727).

Legislative Assistants/Health: Jeremy Craig Burton (SH–632A), 4–3598; Elizabeth Scanlon (SH–632A), 4–8978.

Director of Communications.—Christine Iverson (SH–725).

Office Manager.—Bonnie L. Walchak (SH–835).

Professional Staff Members: William Lucia (SH–833); Kimberly D. Monk (SH–727).

Research Assistants: Edwin Egee (SH–609); Rebecca G. Liston (SH–835); Chuenee Sampson (SH–833); Kelly Scott (SH–833).

Staff Assistants: Joshua Shields (SH–725); Christina Sink (SH–727); Richard Weiblinger (SH–727).

Chief Clerk.—Denis O'Donovan (SH–426), 4–3656.

Editor.—Uwe E. Timpke (SH–422), 4–7657.

Systems Administrator.—Frank Zhang (SH–422), 4–9570.

Legislative Clerk.—Stephen L. Chapman (SH–426), 4–5375.

Staff Assistant.—Mary M. Smith (SH–428), 4–5375.

Minority Staff Director/Chief Counsel.—Michael J. Myers (SD–646), 4–0767.

Health Staff Director.—David Nexon (SH–527), 4–7675.

Deputy Health Staff Directors: David Bowen (SH–527); Dora Hughes (SH–527).

Chief Counsel/Policy.—Jeffrey Teitz (SD–648), 4–0767.

Policy Director for Disabilities and Public Health.—Constance M. Garner (SD–644), 4–5441.

Disability Counsel.—Mary Giliberti (SH–113), 4–3254.

Labor Counsel.—Portia Wu (SH–639), 4–5441.

Counsel/Labor.—Holly B. Fetchner (SH–639), 4–5441.

Senior Counsel/Education: Michael Dannenburg (SH–622B), 4–5501; Roberto Rodriguez (SH–622B), 4–5501.

Counsel/Education.—Danica L. Petroshius (SH–642), 4–0767.

Labor Policy Advisor.—Julie P. Kashen (SH–639), 4–0767.

Education Advisor.—Jane Oates (SH–622B), 4–5501.

Education Research Assistant.—Dana J. Fiordaliso (SH–622B), 4–0767.

Professional Staff Member.—Justin W. King (SH–404A), 4–5585.

Legislative Aide.—Martin Walsh (SD–424), 4–0767.

Legislative Assistants: Mary Giliberti (SH–113), 4–3254; Jay McCarthy (SD–424), 4–0767; Chani Wiggins (SH–113), 4–3254.

Staff Assistants: Amelia P. Dungan (SH–527), 4–7675; Christopher K. Mitchell (SD–644), 4–0767; Emma Vadehra (SH–622B), 4–5501; Kathleen M. Wildman (SH–639), 4–5441.

Subcommittee on Aging (SH–132), 4–4838.

Majority Staff Director.—Kara Vlasaty.

Professional Staff.—Thomas M. Horgan.

Legislative Assistant.—Julie A. Jolly.

Staff Assistant.—Elizabeth A. Perlak.

Minority Staff Director.—Rhonda Richards (SH–113), 4–9243.

Professional Staff.—Stephanie Sterling.

Subcommittee on Children and Families (SH–632), 4–5800.

Majority Staff Director.—Marguerite Sallee.

Health Policy Advisor.—Page Curry.

Professional Staff: Kristin Bannerman, Joseph Cwiklinski.

Minority Staff Director.—Grace A. Reef (SH–404), 4–5630.

Professional Staff: Benjamin B. Berwick, James Fenton, Julius Lloyd Horwich.

Subcommittee on Employment, Safety, and Training (SH–615), 4–7229.

Majority Staff Director.—Ilyse W. Schuman.

Professional Staff Member.—Steven J. Northrup.

Legislative Aide.—Allen S. Fleming.

Minority Staff Director.—William Kamela (SH–801B), 4–4925.
Staff Assistant.—Heather Honaker.

Subcommittee on Substance Abuse and Mental Health Services (SH–527), 4–7675.
Minority Staff Director.—Karla Carpenter (SH–607).
Professional Staff Members: Abby Kral, Lindsay A. Morris.
Staff Assistant.—Angela Oswald.

Judiciary

224 Dirksen Senate Office Building 20510–6275

phone 224–5225, fax 224–9102, http://www.senate.gov/~judiciary

meets upon call of the chairman

Orrin G. Hatch, of Utah, *Chairman.*

Charles E. Grassley, of Iowa.
Arlen Specter, of Pennsylvania.
Jon Kyl, of Arizona.
Mike DeWine, of Ohio.
Jeff Sessions, of Alabama.
Lindsey Graham, of South Carolina.
Larry Craig, of Idaho.
Saxby Chambliss, of Georgia.
John Cornyn, of Texas.

Patrick Leahy, of Vermont.
Edward M. Kennedy, of Massachusetts.
Joseph R. Biden, Jr., of Delaware.
Herbert H. Kohl, of Wisconsin.
Dianne Feinstein, of California.
Russell D. Feingold, of Wisconsin.
Charles E. Schumer, of New York.
Richard Durbin, of Illinois.
John Edwards, of North Carolina.

SUBCOMMITTEES

Administrative Oversight and the Courts

Jeff Sessions, of Alabama, *Chairman.*

Charles E. Grassley, of Iowa.
Arlen Specter, of Pennsylvania.
Larry Craig, of Idaho.
John Cornyn, of Texas.

Charles E. Schumer, of New York.
Patrick Leahy, of Vermont.
Russell D. Feingold, of Wisconsin.
Richard Durbin, of Illinois.

Antitrust, Competition Policy and Consumer Rights

Mike DeWine, of Ohio, *Chairman.*

Orrin G. Hatch, of Utah.
Arlen Specter, of Pennsylvania.
Lindsey Graham, of South Carolina.
Saxby Chambliss, of Georgia.

Herbert H. Kohl, of Wisconsin.
Patrick Leahy, of Vermont.
Russell D. Feingold, of Wisconsin.
John Edwards, of North Carolina.

Constitution, Civil Rights and Property Rights

John Cornyn, of Texas, *Chairman.*

Jon Kyl, of Arizona.
Lindsey Graham, of South Carolina.
Larry Craig, of Idaho.
Saxby Chambliss, of Georgia.

Russell D. Feingold, of Wisconsin.
Edward M. Kennedy, of Massachusetts.
Charles E. Schumer, of New York.
Richard Durbin, of Illinois.

Crime, Corrections and Victims' Rights

Lindsey Graham, of South Carolina, *Chairman.*

Orrin G. Hatch, of Utah.
Charles E. Grassley, of Iowa.
Jeff Sessions, of Alabama.
Larry Craig, of Idaho.
John Cornyn, of Texas.

Joseph R. Biden, Jr., of Delaware.
Herbert H. Kohl, of Wisconsin.
Dianne Feinstein, of California.
Richard Durbin, of Illinois.
John Edwards, of North Carolina.

Immigration, Border Security and Citizenship

Saxby Chambliss, of Georgia, *Chairman.*

Charles E. Grassley, of Iowa.
Jon Kyl, of Arizona.
Mike DeWine, of Ohio.
Jeff Sessions, of Alabama.
Larry Craig, of Idaho.
John Cornyn, of Texas.

Edward M. Kennedy, of Massachusetts.
Patrick Leahy, of Vermont.
Dianne Feinstein, of California.
Charles E. Schumer, of New York.
Richard Durbin, of Illinois.
John Edwards, of North Carolina.

Terrorism, Technology and Homeland Security

Jon Kyl, of Arizona, *Chairman.*

Orrin G. Hatch, of Utah.
Arlen Specter, of Pennsylvania.
Mike DeWine, of Ohio.
Jeff Sessions, of Alabama.
Saxby Chambliss, of Georgia.

Dianne Feinstein, of California.
Edward M. Kennedy, of Massachusetts.
Joseph R. Biden, Jr., of Delaware.
Herbert H. Kohl, of Wisconsin.
John Edwards, of North Carolina.

STAFF

Committee on the Judiciary (SD–224), 224–5225, fax 224–9102.
Chief Counsel/Staff Director.—Mark Delrahim.
Assistants to the Chief Counsel: Jessica Caramanica, Beth Ann Snell.
Deputy Chief Counsel/Nominations.—Rena Comisac.
Deputy Chief Counsel.—Alex Dahl.
Senior Counsel.—Bruce Artim.
Counsels: René Augustine, David Best, Katherine Bloemendal, Bill Castle, David Codevilla, Dabney Friedrich, Ryan Higginbotham, David Jones, Harold Kim, Cherylyn LeBon, Dorothy Mitchell, Reed O'Conner, Kevin O'Scandlin, Rebecca Seidel, Patrick Shen, Mike Volkov.
Professional Staff Members: Chris Campbell, Pattie DeLoatche.
Chief Clerk.—Jane Butterfield, 224–1444.
Deputy Chief Clerk.—Roslyne Turner, 224–6928.
Hearings Clerk.—Katie Stahl, 224–9376.
Librarian.—Kurt Carroll, 224–9250.
Systems Administrator.—Brian Wikner, 224–8251.
Health Policy Fellow.—Mark Carlson.
Legal Fellows: Jon Eskelson, Tanya Green, Jay Greissing, Payam Soliemanzadeh.
Investigator.—Amy Haywood.
Legislative Staff Assistants: Ted Lehman, Jason Lundell, Martin Millette, Jennifer Wagner.
Legislative Correspondent.—Swen Prior.
Press Secretary.—Margarita Tapia.
Receptionists: Matt Bunker, Lissa Camacho, Jacob Johnson.
GPO Printers.—Preble Marimon, Heinz Mohle, Cecilia Morcombe.
Minority Staff Director/Chief Counsel.—Bruce Cohen (SD–152), 224–7703, fax 224–9516.
Legislative Staff Assistant to Chief Counsel.—Phil Toomajian.
Senior Counsels: Julie Katzman, Ed Pagano.
Legislative Staff Assistant to Ed Pagano.—Jessica Berry.
Counsels: Susan Davies, Tim Lynch, Richard Phillips.
Chief Nominations Counsel.—Lisa Graves.
Senior Nominations Counsel.—Helaine Greenfield.
Nominations Counsels: Leesa Klepper, Kristine Lucius.
Nominations Clerk.—Rachel Arfa.
Professional Staff Member.—Tara Magner.
Legislative Correspondents: Christine McKennerney, Liz Parry.
Congressional Fellow.—Linda Demaine.
Legislative Staff Assistant.—Ben Huebner.
Detailee.—Sandy Wilkinson.
Staff Assistants: Dan Fine, Ed Layfayette.

Subcommittee on Administrative Oversight and the Courts
Majority Chief Counsel.—William Smith, 224–7572.
Deputy Chief Counsel.—Ajit Pai.
Legislative Counsels: Cindy Barnes, Andrea Sander.
Minority Chief Counsel.—Jeff Berman, 224–6542.
Counsel.—Cynthia Bauerly.
Legislative Correspondent.—Lilah Pomerance.
Detailee.—James Flood.

Subcommittee on Antitrust, Competition Policy, and Consumer Rights
Majority Chief Counsel/Staff Director.—Peter Levitas, 224–9494.
Counsels: Evelyn Fortier, Steve Taylor.
Clerk.—Robin Blackwell.
Detailee.—Bill Jones.

Minority Chief Counsel.—Jeffrey Miller, 224–3406.
Counsels: Seth Bloom, Jon Schwantes.
Professional Staff Member.—Libby Reder.
Legislative Aide.—Caroline Nonna.
Detailee.—Ross Arlends.

Subcommittee on the Constitution, Civil Rights, and Property Rights
Majority Chief Counsel.—James Ho, 224–2934.
Minority Chief Counsel.—Bob Schiff, 224–5573.
Clerk.—Kirsten White.
Detailee.—Alex Busansky.

Subcommittee on Crime, Corrections, and Victims' Rights
Majority Legislative Assistant.—James Galyean, 224–5972.
Minority Chief Counsel/Staff Director.—Neil McBride, 224–0558.
Counsels: Jonathan Meyer, Tonya Robinson, Eric Rosen, Louisa Terrell.
Senior Advisor.—Marcia Lee.

Subcommittee on Immigration, Border Security, and Citizenship
Majority Staff Director.—Joe Jacqot, 224–3521.
Chief Counsel.—John Gillies.
Legislative Director.—Martha Scott Poindexter.
Legislative Correspondent.—Camilla McLean.
Minority Chief Counsel.—Jim Flug, 224–7878.
Counsels: Olati Johnson, Janice Kaguyutan, Esther Olavarria, Robert (Robin) Toone.
Legislative Aide.—Julia Sessions.

Subcommittee on Terrorism, Technology, and Homeland Security
Majority Chief Counsel.—Stephen Higgins, 224–6791.
Counsel.—Joe Matal.
Legislative Correspondent/Clerk.—Matt Letourneau.
Minority Chief Counsel/Staff Director.—David Hantman, 224–4933.
Counsels: Matthew Lamberti, Tom Oscherwitz, LaVita Strickland.
Legislative Aides: Dempsey Hughes, Jason Knapp.

Rules and Administration

305 Russell Senate Office Building 20510–6325

phone 224–6352, http://rules.senate.gov

[Legislative Reorganization Act of 1946]

meets second and fourth Wednesday of each month

Trent Lott, of Mississippi, *Chairman.*

Ted Stevens, of Alaska.
Mitch McConnell, of Kentucky.
Thad Cochran, of Mississippi.
Rick Santorum, of Pennsylvania.
Don Nickles, of Oklahoma.
Kay Bailey Hutchison, of Texas.
Bill Frist, of Tennessee.
Gordon Smith, of Oregon.
Saxby Chambliss, of Georgia.

Christopher J. Dodd, of Connecticut.
Robert C. Byrd, of West Virginia.
Daniel K. Inouye, of Hawaii.
Dianne Feinstein, of California.
Charles E. Schumer, of New York.
John B. Breaux, of Louisiana.
Thomas A. Daschle, of South Dakota.
Mark Dayton, of Minnesota.
Richard J. Durbin, of Illinois.

(No Subcommittees)

STAFF

Committee on Rules and Administration (SR–305), 224–6352.
Staff Director.—Susan Wells, 4–6352.
Deputy Staff Director/Director for IT Policy.—Liz McAlhany, 4–4951.
Chief Counsel.—Ken Jones, 4–6764.
Director for Administration and Policy.—Chris Shunk, 4–9528.
Chief Clerk.—Sue Wright, 4–2536.
Executive Assistant.—Scott Walker, 4–1208.
Professional Staff.—Sam Young, 4–7569.
Staff Assistants: Katie Friesen 4–8925, Galey Tatum, 4–4508.
Democratic Staff Director/Chief Counsel.—Kennie Gill, 4–6351.
Democratic Elections Counsel.—Veronica Gillespie, 4–5648.
Administrative Assistant to Democratic Staff Director.—Carole Blessington, 4–0278.
Staff Assistant.—Courtney Cotter, 4–2475.

Small Business and Entrepreneurship

428A Russell Senate Office Building 20510

phone 224–5175, fax 224–6619, http://www.senate.gov/~sbc

[Created pursuant to S. Res. 58, 81st Congress]

meets first Wednesday of each month

Olympia J. Snowe, of Maine, *Chairman.*

Christopher S. Bond, of Missouri.
Conrad Burns, of Montana.
Robert F. Bennett, of Utah.
Michael Enzi, of Wyoming.
Peter G. Fitzgerald, of Illinois.
Michael D. Crapo, of Idaho.
George Allen, of Virginia.
John Ensign, of Nevada.
Norm Coleman, of Minnesota.

John F. Kerry, of Massachusetts.
Carl Levin, of Michigan.
Tom Harkin, of Iowa.
Joseph I. Lieberman, of Connecticut.
Mary Landrieu, of Louisiana.
John Edwards, of North Carolina.
Maria Cantwell, of Washington.
Evan Bayh, of Indiana.
Mark Pryor, of Arkansas.

(No Subcommittees)

STAFF

Committee on Small Business and Entrepreneurship (SR–428A), 224–5175, fax 224–6619.
Majority Staff Director/Tax Counsel.—Mark E. Warren
Regulatory Affairs Counsel.—Marc D. Freedman.
Counsel.—Daniel Donovan III.
Communications Director.—Craig Orfield.
Committee Aide.—Matt Hutson.
Executive Assistant.—Samantha Hamilton.
Professional Staff Assistants: Matt Reid, Jamie Suzor.
Chief Clerk.—Lena Lawrence.
Hearing Clerk.—Lindsey Ledwin.
Minority Staff Director/Chief Counsel.—Patty Forbes.
Assistant to the Staff Director.—Rebecca Shore-Suslowitz.
Counsel.—Lisa Rosenberg.
Professional Staff: John Phillips, Kevin Wheeler.
Press Secretary.—Dayna Hanson.
Senior Legislative Assistant for Economic and Tax Policy.—Jeff Hamond.
Junior Legislative Assistant.—Marc Comer.
Legislative Correspondent.—T Coviello.
Committee Aide.—Salvatore Ciolino.
Staff Assistant.—Sarah Martin.

Veterans' Affairs

SR–412 Russell Senate Office Building 20510

phone 224–9126, http://www.senate.gov/~veterans

meets first Wednesday of each month

Arlen Specter, of Pennsylvania, *Chairman.*

Ben Nighthorse Campbell, of Colorado.
Larry E. Craig, of Idaho.
Kay Bailey Hutchison, of Texas.
Jim Bunning, of Kentucky.
John Ensign, of Nevada.
Lindsey O. Graham, of South Carolina
Lisa Murkowski, of Alaska.

Bob Graham, of Florida.
John D. Rockefeller IV, of West Virginia.
JAMES M. JEFFORDS, of Vermont.
Daniel K. Akaka, of Hawaii.
Patty Murray, of Washington.
Zell Miller, of Georgia.
E. Benjamin Nelson, of Nebraska.

(No Subcommittees)

STAFF

Committee on Veterans' Affairs (SR–412), 224–9126.
Majority Chief Counsel / Staff Director.—William F. Tuerk.
Associate Counsel.—David J. Goetz.
Executive Assistant.—Linda H. Reamy.
Professional Staff Member.—Jonathan A. Towers.
Professional Staff Assistant.—William T. Cahill.
Staff Assistant.—Katie Mucklow.
Legislative Aides: Alexa K. Grollman, Christopher P. McNamee.
Minority Staff (SH–202), 224–2074.
Staff Director / Chief Counsel.—Bryant Hall.
Deputy Staff Director for—
Benefits Programs/General Counsel.—Mary J. Schoelen.
Health Programs.—Kim E. Lipsky.
Legislative Correspondent.—Amanda Krohn.
Professional Staff Members: Tandy Barrett, Julie E. Fischer, Edward B. Pusey.
Legislative Assistant.—Alexandra Sardegna.
Non-Designated:
Chief Clerk.—Dennis G. Doherty.
Systems Administrator / Legislative Clerk.—Bernard X. Readmond.

SELECT AND SPECIAL COMMITTEES OF THE SENATE

Committee on Indian Affairs

838 Hart Senate Office Building 20510–2251

phone 224–2251, fax 224–5929, http://indian.senate.gov

[Created pursuant to S. Res. 4, 95th Congress; amended by S. Res. 71, 103d Congress]

meets first Tuesday of each month

Ben Nighthorse Campbell, of Colorado, *Chairman.*

Daniel K. Inouye, of Hawaii, *Vice Chairman.*

John McCain, of Arizona.
Pete V. Domenici, of New Mexico.
Craig Thomas, of Wyoming.
Orrin G. Hatch, of Utah.
James M. Inhofe, of Oklahoma.
Gordon Smith, of Oregon.
Lisa Murkowski, of Alaska.

Kent Conrad, of North Dakota.
Harry Reid, of Nevada.
Daniel K. Akaka, of Hawaii.
Byron L. Dorgan, of North Dakota.
Tim Johnson, of South Dakota.
Maria Cantwell, of Washington.

STAFF

Majority Staff Director/Chief Counsel.—Paul Moorehead.
Executive Assistant.—Morgan Litchfield.
Senior Counsel.—John Tahsuda.
Counsel.—Jim Hall.
Professional Staff.—Lee Frazier.
Minority Staff Director/Chief Counsel.—Patricia Zell.
Executive Assistant.—[Vacant].
Senior Counsels: Carl Christensen, Colin Kippen.
Counsels: Janet Erickson, Diana Kupchella.

Select Committee on Ethics

220 Hart Senate Office Building 20510, phone 224–2981, fax 224–7416

[Created pursuant to S. Res. 338, 88th Congress; amended by S. Res. 110, 95th Congress]

George V. Voinovich, of Ohio, *Chairman.*

Harry Reid, of Nevada, *Vice Chairman.*

Pat Roberts, of Kansas.
Craig Thomas, of Wyoming.

Daniel K. Akaka, of Hawaii.
Blanche L. Lincoln, of Arkansas.

STAFF

Staff Director / Chief Counsel.—Robert L. Walker.
Counsels: Kenyen Brown, Eric Witiw.
Chief Clerk.—Annette M. Gillis.
Professional Staff.—John Lewter.
Systems Administrator.—Danny Remington.
Staff Assistants: Greg Gomes, Courtney Kaezyk, Dawne Vernon.

Select Committee on Intelligence

211 Hart Senate Office Building 20510–6475, phone 224–1700

http://www.senate.gov/~intelligence

[Created pursuant to S. Res. 400, 94th Congress]

Pat Roberts, of Kansas, *Chairman.*

John D. Rockefeller IV, of West Virginia, *Vice Chairman.*

Orrin G. Hatch, of Utah.
Mike DeWine, of Ohio.
Christopher S. Bond, of Missouri.
Trent Lott, of Mississippi.
Olympia J. Snowe, of Maine.
Chuck Hagel, of Nebraska.
Saxby Chambliss, of Georgia.
John W. Warner, of Virginia.

Carl Levin, of Michigan.
Dianne Feinstein, of California.
Ron Wyden, of Oregon.
Richard Durbin, of Illinois.
Evan Bayh, of Indiana.
John Edwards, of North Carolina.
Barbara A. Mikulski, of Maryland.

Ex Officio

William H. Frist, of Tennessee.

Thomas A. Daschle, of South Dakota.

STAFF

Staff Director.—Bill Duhnke.
Minority Staff Director.—Chris Mellon.
Chief Clerk.—Kathleen P. McGhee.

Special Committee on Aging

G–31 Dirksen Senate Office Building 20510, phone 224–5364, fax 224–8660

http://aging.senate.gov

[Reauthorized pursuant to S. Res. 4, 95th Congress]

Larry E. Craig, of Idaho, *Chairman.*

Richard C. Shelby, of Alabama.
Susan M. Collins, of Maine.
Michael B. Enzi, of Wyoming.
Gordon Smith, of Oregon.
James M. Talent, of Missouri.
Peter G. Fitzgerald, of Illinois.
Orrin G. Hatch, of Utah.
Elizabeth Dole, of North Carolina.
Ted Stevens, of Alaska.
Rick Santorum, of Pennsylvania.

John Breaux, of Louisiana.
Harry Reid, of Nevada.
Herb Kohl, of Wisconsin.
James M. Jeffords, of Vermont.
Russell D. Feingold, of Wisconsin.
Ron Wyden, of Oregon.
Blanche L. Lincoln, of Arkansas.
Evan Bayh, of Indiana.
Thomas R. Carper, of Delaware.
Debbie Stabenow, of Michigan.

STAFF

Staff Director.—Lupe Wissel.
Executive Assistant.—Zola McMurray.
Chief Policy Advisor/Counsel.—Andrew Patzman.
Senior Policy Advisor.—Scott Nystrom.
Senior Investigators/Counsels: Ron Crump, Omar Valverde.
Senior Health Policy Advisor.—Dana Bostic Lukken.
Press Secretary.—Maria Vallejo.
Communications Director.—Jeff Schrade.
Legislative Correspondent.—Trenton Wright.
Staff Assistants: Stacy Smith, Brian Wonderlich.

Minority Staff (SH–628), 224–1467, fax 224–9926.
Staff Director.—Michelle Easton
Chief Clerk/Systems Administrator.—Patricia Hameister.
Chief Investigative Counsel.—Lauren Fuller.
Investigative Counsel.—Cecil Swamidoss.
Press Secretary.—Scott Mulhauser.
Professional Staff: Elaine Dalpiaz, Janet Forlini, Phil Thevenet.

National Republican Senatorial Committee

425 Second Street NE., 20002, phone 675–6000, fax 675–6058

George Allen, of Virginia, *Chairman.*

STAFF

Executive Director.—Jay Timmons.
Treasurer.—Stan Huckaby.
Director of:
Finance.—Nicole Sexton.
Corporate Affairs.—Ed Rahal.
Communications.—Dan Allen.
Research.—Gary Feld.
Legal Counsel.—Steve Hoersting.
Political Director.—Patrick Davis.

Linda Bond
Ted Borie
Thomas Breen
John Byrd
Keith Carter
Krista Cole
Taylor Craig
Patrick Davis
Mark Drake
Jonathan Finger
Ashleigh Foard
Megan Foran
Blair Foutch
Heidi Frederickson
Sandy Fuentes
Will Fulgeras
David Gershanik
John Gibson
Leslie Grabias
Matt Granish
Vince Haley
Daniel Kayede
Mary Kinner
Mike Kroeger
Rachel Lavender
Renee Limoge
Shahla Mansoori
Fraley Marshall
Thomas Maxwell
Mike McSherry
Court Michau
Carmen Miller
Megan Morgan
Liz Murray
Tara Nelson
Joseph Osborne
Laura Petrilino
Gretchen Purser
Doug Robinson
Brian Rogers
Frank Sadler
Tricia Sell
Beth Sherrard
Bill Spence
Stephen Taylor
Jim Tobin
Elizabeth Verrill
Tricia Waite
Hannah Walker
Eric Wang
David Welch
Erica White
Kevin Wright
Evan Yost

Republican Policy Committee

347 Russell Senate Office Building, phone 224–2946
fax 224–1235, http://rpc.senate.gov

Jon Kyl, of Arizona, *Chairman.*

STAFF

Staff Director.—Lawrence Willcox.
Deputy Staff Director.—Katie Gumerson.
Administrative Director.—Craig Cheney.
Analysts:
Defense Policy.—Margaret Hemenway.
Foreign Policy.—Rich Douglas.
Public Lands, Energy, and Environmental Policy.—John Peschke.
Judiciary Issues.—Steven Duffield.
Labor, Education, Welfare Policy.—Kyle Hicks.
Health Care Policy.—Diane Major.
Tax, Budget, and Economic Policy.—Eric Schlect.

Professional Staff:
Editor.—Judy Gorman Prinkey.
System Administrator/RVA Analyst.—Tom Pulju.
Station Manager/Special Projects.—Carolyn Laird.
Station Operators/Project Assistants: Chad Luck, Brooke Smith.

Senate Republican Conference

405 Hart Senate Office Building, phone 224–2764
http://src.senate.gov

Chairman.—Rick Santorum, of Pennsylvania.
Vice Chair.—Kay Bailey Hutchison, of Texas.
Committee Chairmen:
Policy.—Jon Kyl, of Arizona.
NRSC.—George Allen, of Virginia.

STAFF

Conference of the Majority (SH–405), 224–2764.
Staff Director.—Mark Rodgers.
Assistant to the Staff Director.—Rebecca Kessler.
Deputy Staff Director/Communications Director.—Robert Traynham.
Assistant to Deputy Staff Director/Office Consultant.—Tonya Bah.
Art Director.—Chris Angrisani.
Senior Graphic Designer.—Laura Gill.
Graphic Designer.—Katie Wise.
Director of Information Technology.—Tim Petty.
Technology Specialist.—Rebecca Cotton.
Systems Administrator.—Eric Miller.
Television Services Director.—Henry Peterson, Jr.
Photographer.—Chris Ahlberg.
Photographer/Editor.—Cyrus Pearson.
Producer.—Deirdre M. Woodbyrne.
Radio Services Director.—Dave Hodgdon.
Booker for Radio Productions.—Alex Kauffman.
Director of Coalitions.—Barbara Ledeen.
Senior Communications Advisor.—Drew Cantor.
Office Manager.—Eden Gordon.
Communications Managers: Sarah Berk, Elizabeth Keys.
Staff Assistant.—Jennifer Mahurin.
Vice Chair of the Conference Staff (SR–287), 224–1326
Staff Director.—David Davis.
Professional Staff Member.—Jeffrey Lee.

Democratic Policy Committee

419 Hart Senate Office Building, phone 224–3232

Byron Dorgan, of North Dakota, *Chairman.*

Patty Murray, of Washington, Regional Chair.
Evan Bayh, of Indiana, Regional Chair.
Jack Reed, of Rhode Island, Regional Chair.
Mary L. Landrieu, of Louisiana, Regional Chair.
Ernest F. Hollings, of South Carolina.
John D. Rockefeller IV, of West Virginia.
Thomas A. Daschle, of South Dakota.
Daniel K. Akaka, of Hawaii.
Russell D. Feingold, of Wisconsin.
Joseph I. Lieberman, of Connecticut.
Dianne Feinstein, of California.
Ron Wyden, of Oregon.
Tim Johnson, of South Dakota.
Charles E. Schumer, of New York.
Blanche L. Lincoln, of Arkansas.
Zell Miller, of Georgia.
Bill Nelson, of Florida.
Thomas R. Carper, of Delaware.
Jon S. Corzine, of New Jersey.
Mark Dayton, of Minnesota.
Harry Reid, of Nevada, ex officio.
Barbara Mikulski, of Maryland, ex officio.

STAFF

Staff Director.—Chuck Cooper.
Assistant to the Staff Director.—Emily Tyler.
Research Director.—Tim Gaffaney.
Policy Advisors: Bethany Dickerson, Evan Gottesman, Brian Hickey, Isaac Reyes, Celine Senseney, Peter Umhofer, Ted Zegers.
Publications Director.—Doug Connelly.
Publications Specialists: Alex Fisher, Katharine Moore, Chris Tishue.
Votes Analysts: Clare Amoruso, Kristin Hedger, Michael Mozden.

Steering and Coordination Committee

712 Hart Senate Office Building, phone 224–9048

Hillary Rodham Clinton, of New York, *Chair.*

John F. Kerry, of Massachusetts.
Daniel K. Inouye, of Hawaii.
Robert C. Byrd, of West Virginia.
Edward M. Kennedy, of Massachusetts.
Joseph R. Biden, Jr., of Delaware.
Patrick J. Leahy, of Vermont.
Christopher J. Dodd, of Connecticut.
Tom Harkin, of Iowa.
Max Baucus, of Montana.
Bob Graham, of Florida.
Kent Conrad, of North Dakota.
Carl Levin, of Michigan.
Herbert H. Kohl, of Wisconsin.
Barbara Boxer, of California.
John B. Breaux, of Louisiana.
Thomas A. Daschle, of South Dakota.
Jeff Bingaman, of New Mexico.
Paul Sarbanes, of Maryland.
Harry Reid, of Nevada.
Richard J. Durbin, of Illinois.
John Edwards, of North Carolina.

STAFF

Staff Director.—Jodi Sakol.
Associate Directors: Josh Ackil, Leslie Brown, Sarah Lucas, Ilia Rodriguez.

Technology and Communications Committee

619 Hart Senate Office Building, phone 224–1430

Thomas A. Daschle, of South Dakota, *Chairman.*

Ernest F. Hollings, of South Carolina.
Patty Murray, of Washington.
Jeff Bingaman, of New Mexico.
Christopher J. Dodd, of Connecticut.
Kent Conrad, of North Dakota.
Tim Johnson, of South Dakota.
John Edwards, of North Carolina.
Hillary Rodham Clinton, of New York.
Harry Reid, of Nevada, ex officio.
Barbara Mikulski, of Maryland, ex officio.
John B. Breaux, of Louisiana, ex officio.

STAFF

Staff Director.—Joseph Trahern.
Deputy Staff Director.—Sarah Feinberg.
Administrator.—Mary Helen Fuller.
Radio Producer.—Russ Kelley.
Editors: Ike Blake, Toby Hayman, Mike Million.
TV Producer.—Nathan Ackerman.
Internet Technology Advisers: Brian Barrie, Jeff Hecker.
Videographers: Clare Flood, Brian Jones, Kevin Kelleher.
Press Assistant.—Sara Gragert.

Senate Democratic Conference

709 Hart Senate Office Building, phone 224–4654, fax 224–8858

Secretary.—Barbara A. Mikulski, of Maryland.
Liaison to Leadership.—Jennifer Luray.

Democratic Senatorial Campaign Committee

430 South Capitol Street SE., 20003, phone 224–2447, fax 485–3120

Jon S. Corzine, of New Jersey, *Chairman.*

Debbie Stabenow, of Michigan, *Vice Chairman.*

Thomas A. Daschle, of South Dakota, *Democratic Leader.*

STAFF

Executive Director.—Andrew Grossman.
Communications Director.—Michael Siegel.
Political.—Paul Tewes.
Director, Research.—Benjamin Jones.
Deputy Director, Research.—Matt McKenna.
Finance Director.—Diana Rogalle.
Deputy Finance Director.—Adrienne Donato.
Director of New York Fundraising.—Amanda Steck.
Director of Corporate Affairs.—Allison Griner.
Leadership Circle/DSCC Roundtable.—Julie Walden.
Comptroller.—Darlene Setter.
General Counsel: Bob Bauer, Marc Elias.
Office Manager.—Bill Clapp.
Senior Political Advisor.—Cornell Belcher.
Assistant to the Chairman.—Megan Mulcahy.
Press Secretary.—Brad Woodhouse.
Director of:
Western Regional Finance.—Colleen Browne.
Marketing.—Meaghan Burdick.
Women's Senate Network.—Gabrielle Guevara.
National Field.—Joe Hansen.
Business Roundtable.—Eli Joseph.
Finance Communications.—Cara Morris.
Events and Facilities.—Patti Ogle.
Senate Victory Club.—Tom Perron.
Research Associate.—Brad Katz.

OFFICERS AND OFFICIALS OF THE SENATE

Capitol Telephone Directory, 224–3121

Senate room prefixes:

Capitol—S, Russell Senate Office Building—SR

Dirksen Senate Office Building—SD, Hart Senate Office Building—SH

PRESIDENT OF THE SENATE

Vice President of the United States and President of the Senate.—Richard B. Cheney.

The Ceremonial Office of the Vice President is S–212 in the Capitol. The Vice President has offices in the Dirksen Office Building, Eisenhower Executive Office Building (EEOB) and the White House (West Wing).

Chief of Staff.—Lewis Libby, EEOB, Room 276, 456–9000.
Deputy Chief of Staff.—Dean McGrath, EEOB, Room 276, 456–9000.
Counsel to the Vice President.—David Addington, EEOB, Room 268, 456–9089.
Counselor to the Vice President.—Catherine Martin, EEOB, Room 272, 456–9042.
Principal Deputy Assistant to the Vice President for National Security Affairs.—Eric Edelman, EEOB, Room 298, 456–9501.
Assistant to the Vice President for Legislative Affairs.—Candi Wolff, EEOB, Room 285, 456–6774.
Staff Assistant (Senate).—Sara Nokes, U.S. Capitol, Room S–212, 224–2424.
Assistant to the Vice President for Domestic Policy.—Cesar Conda, EEOB, Room 288, 456–2728.
Executive Assistant to the Vice President.—Debra Heiden, West Wing, 456–7549.
Deputy Assistant to the Vice President and Director of Operations.—Claire O'Donnell, EEOB, Room 269, 456–6770.
Assistant to the Vice President and Chief of Staff to Mrs. Cheney.—Lea Berman, EEOB, Room 200, 456–7458.
Deputy Assistant to the Vice President and Director of Scheduling.—Elizabeth Kleppe, EEOB, Room 279, 456–6773.
Director of Correspondence.—Cecelia Boyer, EEOB, Room 265, 456–9002.

PRESIDENT PRO TEMPORE

S–240 The Capitol, phone 224–1034

President Pro Tempore of the Senate.—Ted Stevens.

MAJORITY LEADER

S–230 The Capitol, phone 224–3135, fax 224–4639

Majority Leader.—Bill Frist.
Chief of Staff.—Lee Rawls.
Assistant to the Chief of Staff.—Parker Wood.
Chief Counsel.—Alex Vogel.
Counsel.—Manuel Miranda.
Policy Advisors.—Libby Jarvis, Rohit Kumar, Bill Wichterman.
National Security Affairs Advisor.—Steve Biegun.
Press Secretary.—Nick Smith.
Deputy Press Secretary.—Antonia Ferrier.
Deputy Communications Director.—Paul Jacobson.

Director of Budget & Appropriations.—Bill Hoagland.
Director of Special Projects.—Holly Hammond Nass.
Director of Health Policy.—Dean Rosen.
Executive Assistant.—Ramona Lessen.
Legislative Correspondents: Robert Duncan, Steve Kline, Allison Winnike.
Office Administrator.—Liana Mitchell.
Floor Advisor.—Martin Gold.
Special Assistant.—Brook Whitfield.
Transition Staff.—Eric Ueland.
Personal Assistant.—Tom Craig.
Staff Assistants: Abby Clinton, Meg Gregory.

MAJORITY WHIP

S–208 The Capitol, phone 224–2708, fax 224–3913

Majority Whip.—Mitch McConnell.
Chief of Staff.—Kyle Simmons.
Policy Director.—Michael Solon.
Legal Counsel.—John Abegg.
Floor Counsel.—Brian Lewis.
Whip Liaisons: Malloy McDaniel, Laura Pemberton.
Floor Assistant.—Amy Swonger.
Director of Administration.—Nan Mosher.
Personal Assistant.—B.J. Stieglitz.
Staff Assistants: Kelly Kotch, Theresa Williams.

DEMOCRATIC LEADER

S–221 The Capitol, phone 224–5556

Democratic Leader.—Thomas A. Daschle.
Chief of Staff.—Peter Rouse.
Deputy Chief of Staff.—Nancy Erickson.
Chief Counsel / Policy Director.—Mark Childress.
Staff Director, Leadership Committees.—Mark Patterson.
Counsel.—Michele Ballantyne.
Scheduler.—Amber Danter.
Assistant Scheduler.—Nancy Hogan.
Special Assistants: Pat Sarcone, Darcell Savage.
Administrative Director.—Kelly Fado.
Communications Director.—Ranit Schmelzer.
Deputy Communications Director.—Jay Carson.
Senior Speechwriter / Deputy Communications Director.—Molly Rowley.
Speechwriters: Jeff Nussbaum, Daniel Franklin.
Office Manager, Press Office.—Chris Bois.
Press Assistant, Press Office.—Elizabeth Lietz.

ASSISTANT DEMOCRATIC LEADER

S–321 The Capitol, phone 224–2158

Assistant Democratic Leader.—Harry Reid.
Chief of Staff.—Susan McCue.
General Counsel.—James Ryan.
Executive Assistant to Senator.—Janice Shelton.
Executive Assistant to Chief of Staff.—Lindsay Rhodes.
Floor Manager.—Gary Myrick.
Floor Assistant.—Kristy Skupa.
Scheduler.—Romayne Houle.

OFFICE OF THE SECRETARY

S–312 The Capitol, phone 224–3622

EMILY J. REYNOLDS, Secretary of the Senate; elected and sworn in as the 31sth Secretary of the Senate on January 7, 2003; born and raised in the State of Tennessee; graduate of Stephens College, Columbia, MO; Chief of Staff to U.S. Senator Bill Frist, 2001–2002; State Director for U.S. Senator Bill Frist, 1995–2000; Deputy Campaign Manager and Finance Director, Dr. Bill Frist for U.S. Senate, 1994; Active in several U.S. Senate campaigns, and Bush / Quayle, 1992; served as Deputy Director of National Coalitions, 1985–1993; Special Assistant, U.S. Senate Majority Leader, Howard H. Baker, Jr., 1980–1984; Associate Director of Admissions, Stephens College, 1978–1980.

Secretary of the Senate.—Emily J. Reynolds (S–312), 224–3622.
Administrative Assistant.—[Vacant].
Senior Office Services Administrator.—[Vacant] (SB–36), 224–1483.
Assistant Secretary of the Senate.—Mary Suit Jones (S–414C), 224–2114.
General Counsel.—Bruce Kasold, 224–3448.
Counsel.—Adam Bramwell, 224–8789.
Accounts Manager.—Zoraida Torres (S–333), 224–7099.
Special Projects Manager (LIS/XML).—Marsha Misenhimer (SD–B40i), 224–2500.
Bill Clerk.—Mary Anne Clarkson (S–123), 224–2120.
Captioning Services, Director.—Peter Jepsen (ST–54), 224–4321.
Conservation and Preservation, Bookbinder.—Carl Fritter, (S–416), 224–4550.
Curator.—Diane Skvarla (S–411), 224–2955.
Daily Digest, Editor.—Linda E. Sebold (S–410), 224–2658.
Assistant Editor.—Ken Dean, 224–2658.
Disbursing Office, Financial Clerk.—Timothy S. Wineman (SH–127), 224–3205.
Assistant Financial Clerk.—David L. Lingle, 224–3208.
Enrolling Clerk.—Thomas J. Lundregan (S–139), 224–8427.
Assistant Enrolling Clerk.—Joseph M. Monahan, 224–7108.
Executive Clerk.—Michelle Haynes (S–138), 224–4341.
Senior Assistant Executive Clerk.—Stacy Sullivan, 224–5246.
Historian.—Richard A. Baker (SH–201), 224–6900.
Associate Historian.—Donald A. Ritchie, 224–6816.
Assistant Historian.—Betty K. Koed, 224–0753.
Human Resources, Director.—Michelle Jezycki (SH–231B), 224–3625.
Information Systems, Administrator.—Dan Kulnis (ST–58), 224–0795.
Webmaster.—Cheri Allen, 224–2020.
Interparliamentary Services, Director.—Sally Walsh (SH–808), 224–3047.
Journal Clerk.—Scott Sanborn (S–135), 224–4650.
Legislative Clerk.—David J. Tinsley (S–134), 224–4350.
Assistant Legislative Clerk.—Kathleen Alvarez, 224–3630.
Librarian.—Gregory C. Harness (SR–B15), 224–3313.
Official Reporters of Debates, Chief Reporter.—Jerald D. Linell (S–410A), 224–7525.
Coordinator of the Record.—Eileen Milton, 224–1238.
Morning Business Editor.—Jack Hickman (S–123), 224–3079.
Parliamentarian.—Alan S. Frumin (S–133), 224–6128.
Senior Assistant Parliamentarian.—Elizabeth MacDonough, 224–6128.
Printing and Document Services, Director.—Karen Moore (SH–B04), 224–0205.
Assistant to the Director.—Doug Bowers, 224–7960.
Public Records, Superintendent.—Pamela B. Gavin (SH–232), 224–0762.
Assistant Superintendent.—Elizabeth Williams, 224–0329.
Campaign Finance.—Raymond Davis, 224–0761.
Ethics and Disclosure.—Jon Jensen, 224–0763.
Lobbying and Foreign Travel.—Erica Omorogieva, 224–0758.
Senate Chief Counsel for Employment.—Jean Manning (SH–103), 224–5424.
Senate Gift Shop, Director.—Ernie LePire (SDG–42), 224–7308.
Senate Page School, Principal.—Kathryn S. Weeden, 224–3926.
Senate Security, Director.—Michael P. DiSilvestro (S–407), 224–5632.
Deputy Director.—Margaret Garland, 224–5632.
Stationery, Keeper of the Stationery.—Michael J. McGhee (SD–B43), 224–6838.
Assistant Keeper of the Stationery.—Michael V. McNeal, 224–3381.
Senate Office of Education and Training, Director.—Peggy Greenberg (SH–121), 224–5969.

OFFICE OF THE CHAPLAIN

S–332 The Capitol, phone 224–2510, fax 224–9686

BARRY C. BLACK, Chaplain, U.S. Senate; born in Baltimore, MD, on November 1, 1948; education: Bachelor of Arts, Theology, Oakwood College, 1970; Master of Divinity, Andrews Theological Seminary, 1973; Master of Arts, Counseling, North Carolina Central University, 1978; Doctor of Ministry, Theology, Eastern Baptist Seminary, 1982; Master of Arts, Management, Salve Regina University, 1989; Doctor of Philosophy, Psychology, United States International University, 1996; military service: U.S. Navy, 1976–2003; rising to the rank of Rear Admiral; Chief of Navy Chaplains, 2000–2003; awards: Legion of Merit Medal; Defense Meritorious Service Medal; Meritorious Service Medals (two awards); Navy and Marine Corps Commendation Medals (two awards); 1995 NAACP Renowned Service Award; family: married to Brenda; three children: Barry II, Brendan, and Bradford.

Chaplain of the Senate.—Barry C. Black.

OFFICE OF THE SERGEANT AT ARMS

S–321 The Capitol, phone 224–2341, fax 224–7690

BILL PICKLE, Sergeant at Arms, U.S. Senate; began service on March 17, 2003; education: American University, and Metro State College in Denver; he holds a degree in Political Science; military service: served with the First Air Cavalry Division in Vietnam from 1968–1969 as an infantry sergeant, and medivac helicopter door gunnery; awards: Bronze Star; Purple Heart; Army Commendation Medal; Combat Infantryman Badge; and seven Air Medals; professional: served with the U.S. Secret Service for 26 years, attaining the positions of Deputy Assistant Director for Human Resources and Training, and as Special Agent in Charge of the Vice Presidential Protective Division; prior to coming to the Senate, he served as Deputy Inspector General for the Department of Labor, and was the Transportation Security Administration's first Federal Security Director; family: married, with two children.

Sergeant at Arms.—Bill Pickle.
Deputy Sergeant at Arms.—Keith Kennedy.
Administrative Assistant.—Rick Edwards.
Executive Assistants: Becky Daugherty, Laura Parker, Julie Urian.
Director of—
Capitol Facilities.—Skip Rouse (Capitol Basement), 224–4171.
Capitol Guide Service.—[Vacant] (Capitol Rotunda), 224–5750.
Office Support Services.—Esther Gordon (Postal Square), 224–1113.
Joint Office of Education and Training.—Peggy Greenberg (SH–121), 224–5969.
IT Support Services.—Kim Winn (Postal Square), 224–1113.
Office of Senate Security.—Chuck Kaylor (acting), (Postal Square), 224–1113.
Technology Development.—Tracy Williams (Postal Square), 224–1113.
Human Resources.—Doug Fertig (SH–143), 224–2889.
Financial Officer.—Chris Dey (Postal Square), 224–1113.
Postmaster.—Harry Green (SDB–23), 224–5353.
Manager, Hair Care Services.—Mario D'Angelo (SRB–70), 224–4560.
Supervisor, State Office Liaison.—Jeanne Tessieri (Postal Square), 224–5409.
Chief, U.S. Capitol Police.—Terrance W. Gainer (119 D Street NE), 224–9806.

OFFICE OF THE MAJORITY SECRETARY

S–337 The Capitol, phone 224–3835, fax 224–2860

Secretary for the Majority.—David Schiappa (S–337).
Assistant Secretary for the Majority.—Denise Ramonas (S–229).

S–226 Majority Cloakroom, phone 224–6191

Cloakroom Assistants: Conner Collins, Noelle Ringel, Robert White.

S–229 Republican Legislative Scheduling, phone 224–5456

Legislative Scheduler.—Tam Clement.
Floor Assistant.—Dan Dukes (S–226), phone 224–6191.
Administrative Assistant.—Marilyn J. Sayler (S–337).

OFFICE OF THE MINORITY SECRETARY

S–309 The Capitol, phone 224–3735

Secretary for the Minority.—Martin P. Paone.
Assistant Secretary for the Minority.—Lula J. Davis (S–118), 224–5551.
Administrative Assistant to the Secretary.—Nancy Iacomini.

S–225 Democratic Cloakroom, phone 224–4691

Cloakroom Assistants: Joe Lapia, Michelle Marciniak, Erik Pederson, Bret Wincup.

OFFICE OF THE LEGISLATIVE COUNSEL

668 Dirksen Senate Office Building, phone 224–6461, fax 224–0567

Legislative Counsel.—James W. Fransen.
Deputy Legislative Counsel.—William F. Jensen III.
Senior Counsels: Anthony C. Coe, Gary L. Endicott, Mark J. Mathiesen, Gregory A. Scott.
Assistant Counsels: Charles E. Armstrong, Laura M. Ayoud, William R. Baird, Darcie E. Chan, Polly W. Craighill, Susan M. Cullen, Ruth Ann Ernst, Heather L. Flory, John A. Goetcheus, Janine L. Johnson, Elizabeth Aldridge King, Mark S. Koster, James G. Scott, Timothy D. Trushel.
Staff Attorneys: Kevin M. Davis, Stephanie Easley, Amy E. Gaynor, Matthew D. McGhie, Mark M. McGunagle, Eric J. Shufflebarger, Jennifer L. Testut.
Systems Integrator.—Thomas E. Cole.
Office Manager.—Donna L. Pasqualino.
Assistant Office Manager.—Joanne T. Cole.
Staff Assistants: Kimberly Bourne, Ahmika V. Isaac, Barbara J. Lyskawa, Rebekah J. Musgrove, Diane E. Nesmeyer, Gretchen E. Walter.
Receptionist.—Patricia E. Harris.

OFFICE OF SENATE LEGAL COUNSEL

642 Hart Senate Office Building, phone 224–4435, fax 224–3391

Senate Legal Counsel.—Patricia Mack Bryan.
Deputy Senate Legal Counsel.—Morgan J. Frankel.
Assistant Senate Legal Counsels: Thomas E. Caballero, Grant R. Vinik.
Systems Administrator/Legal Assistant.—Sara Fox Jones.
Administrative Assistant.—Kathleen M. Parker.

STANDING COMMITTEES OF THE HOUSE

[Republicans in roman; Democrats in *italic*; Independents in SMALL CAPS; Resident Commissioner and Delegates in **boldface**]

[Room numbers beginning with H are in the Capitol, with CHOB in the Cannon House Office Building, with LHOB in the Longworth House Office Building, with RHOB in the Rayburn House Office Building, with H1 in O'Neill House Office Building, and with H2 in the Ford House Office Building]

Agriculture

1301 Longworth House Office Building, phone 225–2171, fax 225–0917

http://www.house.gov/agriculture

meets first Wednesday of each month

Bob Goodlatte, of Virginia, *Chairman.*

John A. Boehner, of Ohio, *Vice Chairman.*

Richard W. Pombo, of California.
Nick Smith, of Michigan.
Terry Everett, of Alabama.
Frank D. Lucas, of Oklahoma.
Jerry Moran, of Kansas.
William L. Jenkins, of Tennessee.
Gil Gutknecht, of Minnesota.
Doug Ose, of California.
Robin Hayes, of North Carolina.
Charles W. (Chip) Pickering, of Mississippi.
Timothy V. Johnson, of Illinois.
Tom Osborne, of Nebraska.
Mike Pence, of Indiana.
Dennis R. Rehberg, of Montana.
Sam Graves, of Missouri.
Adam H. Putnam, of Florida.
William J. Janklow, of South Dakota.
Max Burns, of Georgia.
Jo Bonner, of Alabama.
Mike Rogers, of Alabama.
Steven King, of Iowa.
Chris Chocola, of Indiana.
Marilyn N. Musgrave, of Colorado.
Devin Nunes, of California.
Randy Neugebauer, of Texas.

Charles W. Stenholm, of Texas.
Collin C. Peterson, of Minnesota.
Calvin M. Dooley, of California.
Tim Holden, of Pennsylvania.
Bennie G. Thompson, of Mississippi.
Mike McIntyre, of North Carolina.
Bob Etheridge, of North Carolina.
Baron P. Hill, of Indiana.
Joe Baca, of California.
Mike Ross, of Arkansas.
Aníbal Acevedo-Vilá, of Puerto Rico.
Ed Case, of Hawaii.
Rodney Alexander, of Louisiana.
Frank W. Ballance, Jr., of North Carolina.
Dennis A. Cardoza, of California.
David Scott, of Georgia.
Jim Marshall, of Georgia.
Earl Pomeroy, of North Dakota.
Leonard L. Boswell, of Iowa.
Ken Lucas, of Kentucky.
Mike Thompson, of California.
Mark Udall, of Colorado.
Rick Larsen, of Washington.
Lincoln Davis, of Tennessee.

SUBCOMMITTEES

[The chairman and ranking minority member are ex officio (voting) members of all subcommittees on which they do not serve.]

Conservation, Credit, Rural Development, and Research

Frank D. Lucas, of Oklahoma, *Chairman.*

Tom Osborne, of Nebraska, *Vice Chairman.*

Jerry Moran, of Kansas.
Sam Graves, of Missouri.
Adam H. Putnam, of Florida.
Max Burns, of Georgia.
Jo Bonner, of Alabama.
Mike Rogers, of Alabama.
Steven King, of Iowa.

Tim Holden, of Pennsylvania.
Ed Case, of Hawaii.
Frank W. Ballance, Jr., of North Carolina.
Collin C. Peterson, of Minnesota.
Calvin M. Dooley, of California.
Bob Etheridge, of North Carolina.
Aníbal Acevedo-Vilá, of Puerto Rico.
Jim Marshall, of Georgia.
Mike McIntyre, of North Carolina.

Department Operations, Oversight, Nutrition, and Forestry

Gil Gutknecht, of Minnesota, *Chairman.*

Dennis R. Rehberg, of Montana, *Vice Chairman.*

Richard W. Pombo, of California.
Nick Smith, of Michigan.
Doug Ose, of California.
Adam H. Putnam, of Florida.
William J. Janklow, of South Dakota.
Jo Bonner, of Alabama.
Steven King, of Iowa.
Devin Nunes, of California.

Calvin M. Dooley, of California.
Joe Baca, of California.
Aníbal Acevedo-Vilá, of Puerto Rico.
Dennis A. Cardoza, of California.
Tim Holden, of Pennsylvania.
Baron P. Hill, of Indiana.
Frank W. Ballance, Jr., of North Carolina.
Mike Thompson, of California.
Lincoln Davis, of Tennessee.

General Farm Commodities and Risk Management

Jerry Moran, of Kansas, *Chairman.*

Nick Smith, of Michigan, *Vice Chairman.*

John A. Boehner, of Ohio.
Terry Everett, of Alabama.
Frank D. Lucas, of Oklahoma.
William L. Jenkins, of Tennessee.
Charles W. (Chip) Pickering, of Mississippi.
Timothy V. Johnson, of Illinois.
Mike Pence, of Indiana.
Dennis R. Rehberg, of Montana.
Sam Graves, of Missouri.
Max Burns, of Georgia.
Chris Chocola, of Indiana.
Marilyn N. Musgrave, of Colorado.

Collin C. Peterson, of Minnesota.
Bennie G. Thompson, of Mississippi.
Rodney Alexander, of Louisiana.
Mike Ross, of Arkansas.
Calvin M. Dooley, of California.
Earl Pomeroy, of North Dakota.
Leonard L. Boswell, of Iowa.
Bob Etheridge, of North Carolina.
Baron P. Hill, of Indiana.
Ed Case, of Hawaii.
Dennis A. Cardoza, of California.
Jim Marshall, of Georgia.
Rick Larsen, of Washington.
Lincoln Davis, of Tennessee.

Livestock and Horticulture

Robin Hayes, of North Carolina, *Chairman.*

Doug Ose, of California, *Vice Chairman.*

Richard W. Pombo, of California.
Charles W. (Chip) Pickering, of Mississippi.
Tom Osborne, of Nebraska.
Mike Pence, of Indiana.
Adam H. Putnam, of Florida.
William J. Janklow, of South Dakota.
Mike Rogers, of Alabama.
Chris Chocola, of Indiana.
Marilyn N. Musgrave, of Colorado.

Mike Ross, of Arkansas.
Dennis A. Cardoza, of California.
David Scott, of Georgia.
Collin C. Peterson, of Minnesota.
Rodney Alexander, of Louisiana.
Ken Lucas, of Kentucky.
Leonard L. Boswell, of Iowa.
Mark Udall, of Colorado.
Rick Larsen, of Washington.
Joe Baca, of California.

Specialty Crops and Foreign Agriculture Programs

William L. Jenkins, of Tennessee, *Chairman.*

Terry Everett, of Alabama, *Vice Chairman.*

Gil Gutknecht, of Minnesota.
Robin Hayes, of North Carolina.
Dennis R. Rehberg, of Montana.
Mike Rogers, of Alabama.
Devin Nunes, of California.

Mike McIntyre, of North Carolina.
Bob Etheridge, of North Carolina.
Baron P. Hill, of Indiana.
David Scott, of Georgia.
Jim Marshall, of Georgia.
Bennie G. Thompson, of Mississippi.
Rodney Alexander, of Louisiana.

STAFF

Committee on Agriculture (1301 LHOB), 225–2171, fax 225–0917.
Chief of Staff.—Bill O'Conner.
Deputy Chief of Staff.—Brent Gattis.
Chief Clerk.—Callista Gingrich.
Administrator.—Diane Keyser.
Printing Editor.—Jim Cahill.
Director, Information Systems.—Merrick Munday.
Assistant Clerk.—Kelly Rogers.
Chief Counsel.—Kevin Kramp.
Associate Counsels: Anne Hazlette, Stephanie Myers.
Legislative Clerk.—Debbie Smith.
Communications Director.—Elyse Bauer.
Chief Economist.—Craig Jagger.
Senior Professional Staff: Dave Ebersole, Lynn Gallagher, Alan Mackey, Pete Thompson.
Professional Staff: Kathleen Elder, John Goldberg, Elizabeth Parker, Jason Vaillancourt.
Legislative Assistants: Claire Folbre, Matt Leggett, Ryan O'Neal, Matt Schertz, Tyler Wegmeyer.
Subcommittee Staff Directors:
Conservation, Credit, Rural Development and Research.—Ryan Weston.
Department Operations, Oversight, Nutrition and Forestry.—Sam Diehl.
General Farm Commodities and Risk Management.—Jon Hixson.
Livestock and Horticulture.—Pam Scott.
Specialty Crops and Foreign Agriculture Programs.—Pelham Straughn.
Minority Staff Director.—Stephen Haterius (1305 LHOB), 5–0317.
Minority Deputy Staff Director/Press.—John Haugen, 5–6872.
Counsel/Legislative Director.—Vernie Hubert, 5–0317.
Deputy Counsel.—Andy Baker (1002B LHOB), 5–3069.
Assistant Counsel.—Quinton Robinson (LHOB 1002A), 5–8903.
Economist.—Howard Conley (1041 LHOB), 5–2349.
Professional Staff: Andy Johnson (1002B LHOB), 5–6395; Anne Simmons (1002A LHOB), 5–1494; Lisa Kelley (1002A LHOB), 5–4453; John Riley (1305 LHOB), 5–7987; Russell Middleton (1002B LHOB), 5–1496.
Office Manager.—Sharon Rusnak (1305 LHOB), 5–0317.

Appropriations

H–218 The Capitol, phone 225–2771

http://www.house.gov/appropriations

meets first Wednesday of each month

C.W. Bill Young, of Florida, *Chairman.*

Ralph Regula, of Ohio.
Jerry Lewis, of California.
Harold Rogers, of Kentucky.
Frank R. Wolf, of Virginia.
Jim Kolbe, of Arizona.
James T. Walsh, of New York.
Charles H. Taylor, of North Carolina.
David L. Hobson, of Ohio.
Ernest J. Istook, Jr., of Oklahoma.
Henry Bonilla, of Texas.
Joe Knollenberg, of Michigan.
Jack Kingston, of Georgia.
Rodney P. Frelinghuysen, of New Jersey.
Roger F. Wicker, of Mississippi.
George R. Nethercutt, Jr., of Washington.
Randy (Duke) Cunningham, of California.
Todd Tiahrt, of Kansas.
Zach Wamp, of Tennessee.
Tom Latham, of Iowa.
Anne M. Northup, of Kentucky.
Robert B. Aderholt, of Alabama.
Jo Ann Emerson, of Missouri.
Kay Granger, of Texas.
Virgil H. Goode, Jr., of Virginia.
John T. Doolittle, of California.
Ray LaHood, of Illinois.
John E. Sweeney, of New York.
David Vitter, of Louisiana.
Don Sherwood, of Pennsylvania.
Dave Weldon, of Florida.
Michael K. Simpson, of Idaho.
John Abney Culberson, of Texas.
Mark Steven Kirk, of Illinois.
Ander Crenshaw, of Florida.

David R. Obey, of Wisconsin.
John P. Murtha, of Pennsylvania.
Norman D. Dicks, of Washington.
Martin Olav Sabo, of Minnesota.
Steny H. Hoyer, of Maryland.
Alan B. Mollohan, of West Virginia.
Marcy Kaptur, of Ohio.
Peter J. Visclosky, of Indiana.
Nita M. Lowey, of New York.
José E. Serrano, of New York.
Rosa L. DeLauro, of Connecticut.
James P. Moran, of Virginia.
John W. Olver, of Massachusetts.
Ed Pastor, of Arizona.
David E. Price, of North Carolina.
Chet Edwards, of Texas.
Robert E. (Bud) Cramer, Jr., of Alabama.
Patrick J. Kennedy, of Rhode Island.
James E. Clyburn, of South Carolina.
Maurice D. Hinchey, of New York.
Lucille Roybal-Allard, of California.
Sam Farr, of California.
Jesse L. Jackson, Jr., of Illinois.
Carolyn C. Kilpatrick, of Michigan.
Allen Boyd, of Florida.
Chaka Fattah, of Pennsylvania.
Steven R. Rothman, of New Jersey.
Sanford D. Bishop, Jr., of Georgia.
Marion Berry, of Arkansas.

SUBCOMMITTEES

[The chairman and ranking minority member are ex officio (voting) members of all subcommittees on which they do not serve.]

Agriculture, Rural Development, Food and Drug Administration, and Related Agencies

Henry Bonilla, of Texas, *Chairman.*

James T. Walsh, of New York.
Jack Kingston, of Georgia.
George R. Nethercutt, Jr., of Washington.
Tom Latham, of Iowa.
Jo Ann Emerson, of Missouri.
Virgil H. Goode, Jr., of Virginia.
Ray LaHood, of Illinois.

Marcy Kaptur, of Ohio.
Rosa L. DeLauro, of Connecticut.
Maurice D. Hinchey, of New York.
Sam Farr, of California.
Allen Boyd, of Florida.

Commerce, Justice, State, and the Judiciary

Frank R. Wolf, of Virginia, *Chairman.*

Harold Rogers, of Kentucky.
Jim Kolbe, of Arizona.
Charles H. Taylor, of North Carolina.
Ralph Regula, of Ohio.
David Vitter, of Louisiana.
John E. Sweeney, of New York.
Mark Steven Kirk, of Illinois.

José E. Serrano, of New York.
Alan B. Mollohan, of West Virginia.
Robert E. (Bud) Cramer, Jr., of Alabama.
Patrick J. Kennedy, of Rhode Island.
Martin Olav Sabo, of Minnesota.

Defense

Jerry Lewis, of California, *Chairman.*

C.W. Bill Young, of Florida.
David L. Hobson, of Ohio.
Henry Bonilla, of Texas.
George R. Nethercutt, Jr., of Washington.
Randy (Duke) Cunningham, of California.
Rodney P. Frelinghuysen, of New Jersey.
Todd Tiahrt, of Kansas.
Roger F. Wicker, of Mississippi.

John P. Murtha, of Pennsylvania.
Norman D. Dicks, of Washington.
Martin Olav Sabo, of Minnesota.
Peter J. Visclosky, of Indiana.
James P. Moran, of Virginia.

District of Columbia

Rodney P. Frelinghuysen, of New Jersey, *Chairman.*

Ernest J. Istook, Jr., of Oklahoma.
Randy (Duke) Cunningham, of California.
John T. Doolittle, of California.
Dave Weldon, of Florida.
John Abney Culberson, of Texas.

Chaka Fattah, of Pennsylvania.
Ed Pastor, of Arizona.
Robert E. (Bud) Cramer, Jr., of Alabama.

Energy and Water Development

David L. Hobson, of Ohio, *Chairman.*

Rodney P. Frelinghuysen, of New Jersey.
Tom Latham, of Iowa.
Zach Wamp, of Tennessee.
Jo Ann Emerson, of Missouri.
John T. Doolittle, of California.
John E. Peterson, of Pennsylvania.
Michael K. Simpson, of Idaho.

Peter J. Visclosky, of Indiana.
Chet Edwards, of Texas.
Ed Pastor, of Arizona.
James E. Clyburn, of South Carolina.
Marion Berry, of Arkansas.

Foreign Operations, Export Financing, and Related Programs

Jim Kolbe, of Arizona, *Chairman.*

Joe Knollenberg, of Michigan.
Jerry Lewis, of California.
Roger F. Wicker, of Mississippi.
Henry Bonilla, of Texas.
David Vitter, of Louisiana.
Ander Crenshaw, of Florida.
Mark Steven Kirk, of Illinois.

Nita M. Lowey, of New York.
Jesse L. Jackson, Jr., of Illinois.
Carolyn C. Kilpatrick, of Michigan.
Steven R. Rothman, of New Jersey.
Marcy Kaptur, of Ohio.

Homeland Security

Harold Rogers, of Kentucky, *Chairman.*

C.W. Bill Young, of Florida.
Frank R. Wolf, of Virginia.
Zach Wamp, of Tennessee.
Tom Latham, of Iowa.
Jo Ann Emerson, of Missouri.
Kay Granger, of Texas.
John E. Sweeney, of New York.
Don Sherwood, of Pennsylvania.
Martin Olav Sabo, of Minnesota.
David E. Price, of North Carolina.
José E. Serrano, of New York.
Lucille Roybal-Allard, of California.
Marion Berry, of Arkansas.
Alan B. Mollohan, of West Virginia.

Interior

Charles H. Taylor, of North Carolina, *Chairman.*

Ralph Regula, of Ohio.
Jim Kolbe, of Arizona.
George R. Nethercutt, Jr., of Washington.
Zach Wamp, of Tennessee.
John E. Peterson, of Pennsylvania.
Don Sherwood, of Pennsylvania.
Ander Crenshaw, of Florida.
Norman D. Dicks, of Washington.
John P. Murtha, of Pennsylvania.
James P. Moran, of Virginia.
Maurice D. Hinchey, of New York.
John W. Olver, of Massachusetts.

Labor, Health and Human Services, and Education

Ralph Regula, of Ohio, *Chairman.*

Ernest J. Istook, Jr., of Oklahoma.
Roger F. Wicker, of Mississippi.
Anne M. Northup, of Kentucky.
Randy (Duke) Cunningham, of California.
Kay Granger, of Texas.
John E. Peterson, of Pennsylvania.
Don Sherwood, of Pennsylvania.
Dave Weldon, of Florida.
Michael K. Simpson, of Idaho.
David R. Obey, of Wisconsin.
Steny H. Hoyer, of Maryland.
Nita M. Lowey, of New York.
Rosa L. DeLauro, of Connecticut.
Jesse L. Jackson, Jr., of Illinois.
Patrick J. Kennedy, of Rhode Island.
Lucille Roybal-Allard, of California.

Legislative

Jack Kingston, of Georgia, *Chairman.*

Ray LaHood, of Illinois.
Todd Tiahrt, of Kansas.
John Abney Culberson, of Texas.
Mark Steven Kirk, of Illinois.
James P. Moran, of Virginia.
David E. Price, of North Carolina.
James E. Clyburn, of South Carolina.

Military Construction

Joe Knollenberg, of Michigan, *Chairman.*

James T. Walsh, of New York.
Robert B. Aderholt, of Alabama.
Kay Granger, of Texas.
Virgil H. Goode, Jr., of Virginia.
David Vitter, of Louisiana.
Jack Kingston, of Georgia.
Ander Crenshaw, of Florida.
Chet Edwards, of Texas.
Sam Farr, of California.
Allen Boyd, of Florida.
Sanford D. Bishop, Jr., of Georgia.
Norman D. Dicks, of Washington.

Transportation, Treasury, and Independent Agencies

Ernest J. Istook, Jr., of Oklahoma, *Chairman.*

Frank R. Wolf, of Virginia.
Jerry Lewis, of California.
Harold Rogers, of Kentucky.
Todd Tiahrt, of Kansas.
Anne M. Northup, of Kentucky.
Robert B. Aderholt, of Alabama.
John E. Sweeney, of New York.
John Abney Culberson, of Texas.
John W. Olver, of Massachusetts.
Steny H. Hoyer, of Maryland.
Ed Pastor, of Arizona.
Carolyn C. Kilpatrick, of Michigan.
James E. Clyburn, of South Carolina.
Steven R. Rothman, of New Jersey.

VA, HUD, and Independent Agencies

James T. Walsh, of New York, *Chairman.*

David L. Hobson, of Ohio.
Joe Knollenberg, of Michigan.
Anne M. Northup, of Kentucky.
Virgil H. Goode, Jr., of Virginia.
Robert B. Aderholt, of Alabama.
Ray LaHood, of Illinois.
Dave Weldon, of Florida.
Michael K. Simpson, of Idaho.
Alan B. Mollohan, of West Virginia.
Marcy Kaptur, of Ohio.
David E. Price, of North Carolina.
Robert E. (Bud) Cramer, Jr., of Alabama.
Chaka Fattah, of Pennsylvania.
Sanford D. Bishop, Jr., of Georgia.

STAFF

Committee on Appropriations (H–218), 225–2771.
Clerk and Staff Director.—James W. Dyer.
Staff Assistants: Dale Oak, John Blazey, Therese McAuliffe.
Communications Director.—John Scofield.
Administrative Assistant.—Di Kane.
Administrative Aides: Sandy Farrow, John Howard, Jane Porter.
Office Assistant.—Theodore Powell.
Editor.—Larry Boarman (B–301A RHOB), 5–2851.
Administrative Aide.—Cathy Edwards.
Computer Operations (B–305 RHOB), 5–2718: Timothy J. Buck, Carrie Campbell, Vernon Hammett, Linda Muir, Jay Sivulich.
Minority Staff Director.—Scott Lilly (1016 LHOB), 5–3481.
Staff Assistants: David Reich, William H. Stone.
Administrative Aides: Robert Bonner, Melody Clark, Mandy Swann.
Surveys and Investigations Staff (H2–283 FHOB), 5–3881.
Chief.—Robert Reitwiesner.
Deputy Director.—Robert Pearre.
Investigators: Dennis K. Lutz, Douglas D. Nosik, L. Michael Welsh, Herman C. Young.
Administrative Officer.—Ann McCoy.
Secretaries: Victoria V. Decatur-Brodeur, Jane Graham, Regina L. Martinez, Johannah P. O'Keefe, Tracey E. Russell, Joyce C. Stoyer.
Subcommittee on Agriculture, Rural Development, Food and Drug Administration, and Related Agencies (2362 RHOB), 5–2638.
Staff Assistants: Martin Delgado, Maureen Hollohan, Henry Moore.
Administrative Aide.—Joanne Perdue.
Minority Staff Assistant.—Martha Foley (1016 LHOB), 5–3481.
Subcommittee on Commerce, Justice, State, and the Judiciary (H–309), 5–3351.
Staff Assistants: Leslie Albright, Christine Kojac, John Martens, Mike Ringler.
Minority Staff Assistants: Rob Nabors, David Pomerantz (1016 LHOB), 5–3481.
Subcommittee on Defense (H–149), 5–2847.
Staff Assistants: Douglas Gregory, Alicia Jones, Kevin Jones, Paul Juola, Greg Lankler, Kris Mallard, Steven Nixon, Betsy Phillips, Kevin M. Roper, John Shank, Paul Terry, Sarah Young.
Administrative Aides: Clelia Alvarado, Sherry Young.
Minority Staff Assistant.—David Morrison (1016 LHOB), 5–3481.
Subcommittee on the District of Columbia (H–147), 5–5338.
Staff Assistant.—Carol Murphy.
Minority Staff Assistant.—Rob Nabors (1016 LHOB), 5–3481.

Subcommittee on Energy and Water Development (2362 RHOB), 5–3421.
Staff Assistants: Kevin Cook, Dennis Kern, Bob Schmidt.
Administrative Aide.—Tracy LaTurner.
Minority Staff Assistant.—David Kilian (1016 LHOB), 5–3481.

Subcommittee on Foreign Operations, Export Financing, and Related Programs (H–150), 5–2041.
Staff Assistants: Charles O. Flickner, Jr., Alice Grant, Scott Gudes.
Administrative Aide.—Lorinda Maes.
Minority Staff Assistant.—Mark W. Murray (1016 LHOB), 5–3481.

Subcommittee on Homeland Security (B–307 RHOB), 5–5834.
Staff Assistants: Jeff Ashford, Stephanie Gupta, Tom McLemore, Michelle Mrdeza, Jeanne Wilson.
Administrative Aide.—Tammy Hughes.
Minority Staff Assistant.—Beverly Pheto.

Subcommittee on Interior (B–308 RHOB), 5–3081.
Staff Assistants: Loretta C. Beaumont, Joel Kaplan, Christopher Topik, Deborah A. Weatherly.
Administrative Aide.—Andria Oliver.
Minority Staff Assistant.—Mike Stevens (1016 LHOB), 5–3481.

Subcommittee on Labor, Health and Human Services, and Education (2358 RHOB), 5–3508.
Staff Assistants: Susan Firth, Craig Higgins, Nicole Kunko, Sue Quantius, Francine Salvador, Meg Thompson.
Minority Staff Assistants: Linda Pagelsen, David Reich, Cheryl Smith (1016 LHOB), 5–3481.

Subcommittee on Legislative (H–147), 5–5338.
Staff Assistants: Liz Dawson, Chuck Turner.
Minority Staff Assistant.—Tom Forhan (1016 LHOB), 5–3481.

Subcommittee on Military Construction (B–300 RHOB), 5–3047.
Staff Assistants: Valerie Baldwin, Brian Potts.
Administrative Aide.—Mary Arnold.
Minority Staff Assistant.—Tom Forhan (1016 LHOB), 5–3481.

Subcommittee on Transportation, Treasury and Independent Agencies (2358 RHOB), 5–2141.
Staff Assistants: Kurt Dodd, Richard Efford, Walter Hearne, Leigha Shaw, Cheryle Tucker.
Minority Staff Assistant.—Mike Malone (1016 LHOB), 5–3481.

Subcommittee on VA, HUD, and Independent Agencies (H–143), 5–3241.
Staff Assistants: Dena Baron, Jennifer Miller, Timothy Peterson, Jennifer Whitson.
Minority Staff Assistants: Michelle Burkett, Mike Stephens (1016 LHOB), 5–3481.

Armed Services

2120 Rayburn House Office Building, phone 225–4151, fax 225–9077

http://www.house.gov/hasc

Duncan Hunter, of California, *Chairman.*

Curt Weldon, of Pennsylvania.
Joel Hefley, of Colorado.
Jim Saxton, of New Jersey.
John M. McHugh, of New York.
Terry Everett, of Alabama.
Roscoe G. Bartlett, of Maryland.
Howard P. (Buck) McKeon, of California.
Mac Thornberry, of Texas.
John N. Hostettler, of Indiana.
Walter B. Jones, of North Carolina.
Jim Ryun, of Kansas.
Jim Gibbons, of Nevada.
Robin Hayes, of North Carolina.
Heather Wilson, of New Mexico.
Ken Calvert, of California.
Rob Simmons, of Connecticut.
Jo Ann Davis, of Virginia.
Ed Schrock, of Virginia.
W. Todd Akin, of Missouri.
J. Randy Forbes, of Virginia.
Jeff Miller, of Florida.
Joe Wilson, of South Carolina.
Frank A. LoBiondo, of New Jersey.
Tom Cole, of Oklahoma.
Jeb Bradley, of New Hampshire.
Rob Bishop, of Utah.
Michael Turner, of Ohio.
John Kline, of Minnesota.
Candice S. Miller, of Michigan.
Phil Gingrey, of Georgia.
Mike Rogers, of Alabama.
Trent Franks, of Arizona.

Ike Skelton, of Missouri.
John M. Spratt, Jr., of South Carolina.
Solomon P. Ortiz, of Texas.
Lane Evans, of Illinois.
Gene Taylor, of Mississippi.
Neil Abercrombie, of Hawaii.
Marty Meehan, of Massachusetts.
Silvestre Reyes, of Texas.
Vic Snyder, of Arkansas.
Jim Turner, of Texas.
Adam Smith, of Washington.
Loretta Sanchez, of California.
Mike McIntyre, of North Carolina.
Ciro D. Rodriguez, of Texas.
Ellen O. Tauscher, of California.
Robert A. Brady, of Pennsylvania.
Baron P. Hill, of Indiana.
John B. Larson, of Connecticut.
Susan A. Davis, of California.
James R. Langevin, of Rhode Island.
Steve Israel, of New York.
Rick Larsen, of Washington.
Jim Cooper, of Tennessee.
Jim Marshall, of Georgia.
Kendrick B. Meek, of Florida.
Madeleine Z. Bordallo, of Guam.
Rodney Alexander, of Louisiana.
Tim Ryan, of Ohio.

SUBCOMMITTEES

Projection Forces

Roscoe G. Bartlett, of Maryland, *Chairman.*

Rob Simmons, of Connecticut.
Jo Ann Davis, of Virginia.
Ed Schrock, of Virginia.
Jim Saxton, of New Jersey.
John N. Hostettler, of Indiana.
Ken Calvert, of California.
Jeb Bradley, of New Hampshire.
John Kline, of Minnesota.

Gene Taylor, of Mississippi.
Neil Abercrombie, of Hawaii.
Ellen O. Tauscher, of California.
James R. Langevin, of Rhode Island.
Steve Israel, of New York.
Jim Marshall, of Georgia.
Rodney Alexander, of Louisiana.

Readiness

Joel Hefley, of Colorado, *Chairman.*

Howard P. (Buck) McKeon, of California.
John N. Hostettler, of Indiana.
Walter B. Jones, of North Carolina.
Jim Ryun, of Kansas.
Robin Hayes, of North Carolina.
Heather Wilson, of New Mexico.
Ken Calvert, of California.
J. Randy Forbes, of Virginia.
Jeff Miller, of Florida.
Tom Cole, of Oklahoma.
Rob Bishop, of Utah.
Candice S. Miller, of Michigan.
Mike Rogers, of Alabama.
Trent Franks, of Arizona.
John M. McHugh, of New York.

Solomon P. Ortiz, of Texas.
Lane Evans, of Illinois.
Gene Taylor, of Mississippi.
Neil Abercrombie, of Hawaii.
Silvestre Reyes, of Texas.
Vic Snyder, of Arkansas.
Ciro D. Rodriguez, of Texas.
Robert A. Brady, of Pennsylvania.
Baron P. Hill, of Indiana.
John B. Larson, of Connecticut.
Susan A. Davis, of California.
Rick Larsen, of Washington.
Jim Marshall, of Georgia.
Madeleine Z. Bordallo, of Guam.

Strategic Forces

Terry Everett, of Alabama, *Chairman.*

Mac Thornberry, of Texas.
Curt Weldon, of Pennsylvania.
Heather Wilson, of New Mexico.
Rob Bishop, of Utah.
Michael Turner, of Ohio.
Mike Rogers, of Alabama.
Trent Franks, of Arizona.

Silvestre Reyes, of Texas.
John M. Spratt, Jr., of South Carolina.
Loretta Sanchez, of California.
Ellen O. Tauscher, of California.
Kendrick B. Meek, of Florida.
Tim Ryan, of Ohio.

Tactical Air and Land Forces

Curt Weldon, of Pennsylvania, *Chairman.*

Jim Gibbons, of Nevada.
W. Todd Akin, of Missouri.
Jeb Bradley, of New Hampshire.
Michael Turner, of Ohio.
Phil Gingrey, of Georgia.
Terry Everett, of Alabama.
Howard P. (Buck) McKeon, of California.
Walter B. Jones, of North Carolina.
Jim Ryun, of Kansas.
Rob Simmons, of Connecticut.
Ed Schrock, of Virginia.
J. Randy Forbes, of Virginia.
Joel Hefley, of Colorado.
Heather Wilson, of New Mexico.
Frank A. LoBiondo, of New Jersey.

Neil Abercrombie, of Hawaii.
Ike Skelton, of Missouri.
John M. Spratt, Jr., of South Carolina.
Solomon P. Ortiz, of Texas.
Lane Evans, of Illinois.
Jim Turner, of Texas.
Adam Smith, of Washington.
Mike McIntyre, of North Carolina.
Robert A. Brady, of Pennsylvania.
John B. Larson, of Connecticut.
Steve Israel, of New York.
Jim Cooper, of Tennessee.
Kendrick B. Meek, of Florida.
Rodney Alexander, of Louisiana.

Terrorism, Unconventional Threats and Capabilities

Jim Saxton, of New Jersey, *Chairman.*

Heather Wilson, of New Mexico.
Frank A. LoBiondo, of New Jersey.
John Kline, of Minnesota.
Jeff Miller, of Florida.
Roscoe G. Bartlett, of Maryland.
Mac Thornberry, of Texas.
Jim Gibbons, of Nevada.
Robin Hayes, of North Carolina.
Jo Ann Davis, of Virginia.
W. Todd Akin, of Missouri.
Joel Hefley, of Colorado.

Marty Meehan, of Massachusetts.
Jim Turner, of Texas.
Adam Smith, of Washington.
Mike McIntyre, of North Carolina.
Ciro D. Rodriguez, of Texas.
Baron P. Hill, of Indiana.
Susan A. Davis, of California.
James R. Langevin, of Rhode Island.
Rick Larsen, of Washington.
Jim Cooper, of Tennessee.

Total Force

John M. McHugh, of New York, *Chairman.*

Tom Cole, of Oklahoma.
Candice S. Miller, of Michigan.
Phil Gingrey, of Georgia.
Jim Saxton, of New Jersey.
Jim Ryun, of Kansas.
Ed Schrock, of Virginia.
Robin Hayes, of North Carolina.
Vic Snyder, of Arkansas.
Marty Meehan, of Massachusetts.
Loretta Sanchez, of California.
Ellen O. Tauscher, of California.
Jim Cooper, of Tennessee.
Madeleine Z. Bordallo, of Guam.

STAFF

Committee on Armed Services (2120 RHOB), 225–4151; fax 225–9077.
Staff Director.—Robert S. Rangel.
Executive Assistant to the Staff Director.—Laura R. Haas.
General Counsel.—Hugh N. Johnston, Jr.
Counsels: Uyen T. Dinh, Mary Ellen Fraser, Virginia H. Johnson, J. Henry Schweiter.
Professional Staff: Hugh P. Brady, Harry E. Cartland, John D. Chapla, Erin C. Conaton, Joseph V. Fengler, J.J. Gertler, Thomas E. Hawley, Lynn W. Henselman, Michael R. Higgins, James M. Lariviere, Robert W. Lautrup, Bill R. Marck, Jr., Eric J. Massa, William H. Natter, John J. Pollard III, Jean D. Reed, Douglas C. Roach, Roger M. Smith, Richard I. Stark, Jr., Kenneth A. Steadman, Eric R. Sterner, John F. Sullivan, Dudley L. Tademy, Rita D. Thompson, B. Ryan Vaart, Debra S. Wada, Nancy M. Warner, Brenda J. Wright.
Communications: Harald Stavenas, Meghan L. Wedd.
Legislative Operations: Linda M. Burnette, Alexis R. Lasselle.
Research Assistants: Justin P. Bernier, Mary E. Petrella, Jesse D. Tolleson.
Staff Assistants: Frank A. Barnes, Diane W. Bowman, Curtis B. Flood, Katherine K. Gordon, Betty B. Gray, Danleigh S. Halfast, Dave B. Heaton, Daniel T. Hilton, Preston J. Johnson, Elizabeth L. McAlpine, Lori Shaffer, Angela M. Sowa, Ernest B. Warrington, Jr.

Budget

309 Cannon House Office Building 20515–6065, phone 226–7270, fax 226–7174
http://www.house.gov/budget

meets second Wednesday of each month

Jim Nussle, of Iowa, *Chairman.*

Christopher Shays, of Connecticut (Speaker's Designee / Vice Chairman).
Gil Gutknecht, of Minnesota.
Mac Thornberry, of Texas.
Jim Ryun, of Kansas.
Patrick J. Toomey, of Pennsylvania.
Doc Hastings, of Washington.
Rob Portman, of Ohio.
Edward Schrock, of Virginia.
Henry E. Brown, Jr., of South Carolina.
Ander Crenshaw, of Florida.
Adam Putnam, of Florida.
Roger Wicker, of Mississippi.
Kenny C. Hulshof, of Missouri.
Thomas G. Tancredo, of Colorado.
David Vitter, of Louisiana.
Jo Bonner, of Alabama.
Trent Franks, of Arizona.
Scott Garrett, of New Jersey.
Gresham Barrett, of South Carolina.
Thaddeus McCotter, of Michigan.
Mario Diaz-Balart, of Florida.
Jeb Hensarling, of Texas.
Ginny Brown-Waite, of Florida.

John M. Spratt, Jr., of South Carolina.
James P. Moran, of Virginia.
Darlene Hooley, of Oregon.
Tammy Baldwin, of Wisconsin.
Dennis Moore, of Kansas.
John Lewis, of Georgia.
Richard E. Neal, of Massachusetts.
Rosa DeLauro, of Connecticut.
Chet Edwards, of Texas.
Robert C. (Bobby) Scott, of Virginia.
Harold Ford, of Tennessee.
Lois Capps, of California.
Mike Thompson, of California.
Brian Baird, of Washington.
Jim Cooper, of Tennessee.
Artur Davis, of Alabama.
Rahm Emanuel, of Illinois.
Denise Majette, of Georgia.
Ron Kind, of Wisconsin.

(No Subcommittees)

Committee on Budget (309 CHOB), 226–7270; fax 226–7174.
Chief of Staff.—Rich Meade.
Chief Council/Deputy Staff Director.—Jim Bates.
Executive Assistant.—Teri Dorn.
Administrative Officer.—Marsha Douglas.
Director of—
Budget Review.—Dan Kowalski.
Communications.—Sean Spicer.
Assistant Director of Communications.—Angela Kuck.
Press Secretary.—Kyle Downey.
Electronic Communications.—Steve Webber.
Policy.—Pat Knudsen.
Strategic Planning.—Kim Boyer.
Chief Economist.—John Kitchen.
Counsels: Paul Restuccia, Rob Borden, Charlene Smith.
Analysts: Chuck Berwick, Jim Cantwell, Bret Coulson, Lynn Kremer, Mike Lofgren, Roger Mahan, Jason McKitrick, Otto Mucklo, Ed Puccerella, Takako Tsuji, Peter Warren, Chris Wydler.
Information Systems Manager.—Dick Magee.
Systems Administrator.—Jose Guillen.
Special Assistants: Will Meade, Ryan Romito.
Minority Staff Director.—Tom Kahn, (B71 Cannon), 226–7200, fax 226–7233.
Assistant to Staff Director.—Linda Bywaters.
Office Manager.—Shelia McDowell.
Director of Policy.—Joe Minarik.
Chief Economist.—Jim Klumpner.
Counsel.—Lisa Venus.
Analysts: Sarah Abernathy, Arthur Burris, Jennifer Friedman, Mike McCord, Diana Meredith, Kimberly Overbeek, Antonio Santalucia, Andrea Weathers.
Staff Assistant.—Andrew Smullian.

Education and the Workforce

2181 Rayburn House Office Building, phone 225–4527, fax 225–9571

http://edworkforce.house.gov

meets second Wednesday of each month

John A. Boehner, of Ohio, *Chairman.*

Thomas E. Petri, of Wisconsin.
Cass Ballenger, of North Carolina.
Peter Hoekstra, of Michigan.
Howard P. (Buck) McKeon, of California.
Michael N. Castle, of Delaware.
Sam Johnson, of Texas.
James C. Greenwood, of Pennsylvania.
Charlie Norwood, of Georgia.
Fred Upton, of Michigan.
Vernon J. Ehlers, of Michigan.
Jim DeMint, of South Carolina.
Johnny Isakson, of Georgia.
Judy Biggert, of Illinois.
Todd Russell Platts, of Pennsylvania.
Patrick J. Tiberi, of Ohio.
Ric Keller, of Florida.
Tom Osborne, of Nebraska.
Joe Wilson, of South Carolina.
Thomas Cole, of Oklahoma.
Jon C. Porter, of Nevada.
John Kline, of Minnesota.
John R. Carter, of Texas.
Marilyn N. Musgrave, of Colorado.
Marsha Blackburn, of Tennessee.
Phil Gingrey, of Georgia.
Max Burns, of Georgia.

George Miller, of California.
Dale E. Kildee, of Michigan.
Major R. Owens, of New York.
Donald M. Payne, of New Jersey.
Robert E. Andrews, of New Jersey.
Lynn C. Woolsey, of California.
Rubén Hinojosa, of Texas.
Carolyn McCarthy, of New York.
John F. Tierney, of Massachusetts.
Ron Kind, of Wisconsin.
Dennis J. Kucinich, of Ohio.
David Wu, of Oregon.
Rush D. Holt, of New Jersey.
Susan Davis, of California.
Betty McCollum, of Minnesota.
Danny Davis, of Illinois.
Ed Case, of Hawaii.
Raúl M. Grijalva, of Arizona.
Denise L. Majette, of Georgia.
Chris Van Hollen, of Maryland.
Timothy J. Ryan, of Ohio.
Timothy H. Bishop, of New York.

SUBCOMMITTEES

[The chairman and ranking minority member are ex officio (non-voting) members of all subcommittees on which they do not serve.]

Education Reform

Michael N. Castle, of Delaware, *Chairman.*

Tom Osborne, of Nebraska.
James C. Greenwood, of Pennsylvania.
Fred Upton, of Michigan.
Vernon J. Ehlers, of Michigan.
Jim DeMint, of South Carolina.
Judy Biggert, of Illinois.
Todd Russell Platts, of Pennsylvania.
Ric Keller, of Florida.
Joe Wilson, of South Carolina.
Marilyn N. Musgrave, of Colorado.

Lynn C. Woolsey, of California.
Susan Davis, of California.
Danny Davis, of Illinois.
Ed Case, of Hawaii.
Raúl M. Grijalva, of Arizona.
Ron Kind, of Wisconsin.
Dennis J. Kucinich, of Ohio.
Chris Van Hollen, of Maryland.
Denise L. Majette, of Georgia.

Employer-Employee Relations

Sam Johnson, of Texas, *Chairman.*

Jim DeMint, of South Carolina.
John A. Boehner, of Ohio.
Cass Ballenger, of North Carolina.
Howard P. (Buck) McKeon, of California.
Todd Russell Platts, of Pennsylvania.
Patrick J. Tiberi, of Ohio.
Joe Wilson, of South Carolina.
Thomas Cole, of Oklahoma.
John Kline, of Minnesota.
John R. Carter, of Texas.
Marilyn N. Musgrave, of Colorado.
Marsha Blackburn, of Tennessee.

Robert E. Andrews, of New Jersey.
Donald M. Payne, of New Jersey.
Carolyn McCarthy, of New York.
Dale E. Kildee, of Michigan.
John F. Tierney, of Massachusetts.
David Wu, of Oregon.
Rush D. Holt, of New Jersey.
Betty McCollum, of Minnesota.
Ed Case, of Hawaii.
Raúl M. Grijalva, of Arizona.

Select Education

Peter Hoekstra, of Michigan, *Chairman.*

Jon C. Porter, of Nevada.
James C. Greenwood, of Pennsylvania.
Charlie Norwood, of Georgia.
Phil Gingrey, of Georgia.
Max Burns, of Georgia.

Rubén Hinojosa, of Texas.
Susan Davis, of California.
Danny Davis, of Illinois.
Timothy J. Ryan, of Ohio.

Workforce Protections

Charlie Norwood, of Georgia, *Chairman.*

Judy Biggert, of Illinois.
Cass Ballenger, of North Carolina.
Peter Hoekstra, of Michigan.
Johnny Isakson, of Georgia.
Ric Keller, of Florida.
John Kline, of Minnesota.
Marsha Blackburn, of Tennessee.

Major R. Owens, of New York.
Dennis J. Kucinich, of Ohio.
Lynn C. Woolsey, of California.
Denise L. Majette, of Georgia.
Donald M. Payne, of New Jersey.
Timothy H. Bishop, of New York.

21st Century Competitiveness

Howard P. (Buck) McKeon, of California, *Chairman.*

Johnny Isakson, of Georgia.
John A. Boehner, of Ohio.
Thomas E. Petri, of Wisconsin.
Michael N. Castle, of Delaware.
Sam Johnson, of Texas.
Fred Upton, of Michigan.
Vernon J. Ehlers, of Michigan.
Patrick J. Tiberi, of Ohio.
Ric Keller, of Florida.
Tom Osborne, of Nebraska.
Thomas Cole, of Oklahoma.
Jon C. Porter, of Nevada.
John R. Carter, of Texas.
Phil Gingrey, of Georgia.
Max Burns, of Georgia.

Dale E. Kildee, of Michigan.
John F. Tierney, of Massachusetts.
Ron Kind, of Wisconsin.
David Wu, of Oregon.
Rush D. Holt, of New Jersey.
Betty McCollum, of Minnesota.
Carolyn McCarthy, of New York.
Chris Van Hollen, of Maryland.
Timothy J. Ryan, of Ohio.
Major R. Owens, of New York.
Donald M. Payne, of New Jersey.
Robert E. Andrews, of New Jersey.
Rubén Hinojosa, of Texas.

STAFF

Committee on Education and the Workforce (2181 RHOB), 225–4527.

Staff Director.—Paula Nowakowski.

Deputy to the Staff Director.—Amy Lozupone.

General Counsel.—Jo-Marie St. Martin.

Counselor to the Chairman.—George Canty.

Director of Workforce Policy.—Ed Gilroy.

Deputy Director of Workforce Policy.—Molly Salmi (B–346A RHOB), 5–7101.

Workforce Policy Counsel.—Christine Roth (B–346A RHOB), 5–7101.

Coalitions Director for Workforce Policy.—Greg Maurer.

Director of Education and Human Resources Policy.—Sally G. Lovejoy.

Deputy Director of Education and Human Resources Policy.—Krisann Pearce (H2–230 FHOB), 5–6558.

Coalitions Director for Education Policy.—Maria Miller.

Chief Clerk/Assistant to the General Counsel.—Linda Stevens.

Committee Clerk/Intern Coordinator.—Deborah L. Samantar.

GPO Liaison.—Laura Thomas.

Financial Administrator.—Dianna J. Ruskowsky (2257A RHOB), 5–4527.

Senior Administrative Staff.—Linda Loughner (2257A RHOB), 5–4527.

Senior Budget Analyst.—Cindy Herrle (B–346A RHOB), 5–7101.

Web/Information Technology Manager.—Cindy Von Gogh (2178 RHOB), 5–4527.

Senior Systems Administrator.—Dray Thorne (2178 RHOB), 5–4527.

Systems Administrator.—Billy Benjamin (2178 RHOB), 5–4527.

Communications Director.—Dave Schnittger.

Communications Advisor.—Kevin Smith.

Communications Coordinator.—Parker Hamilton.

Press Secretary.—Alexa Marrero.

Director, Media Affairs.—Joshua Holly.

Professional Staff: David Cleary (H2–230 FHOB), 5–6558; David Connolly, Jr. (B–346A RHOB), 5–7101; Pam Davidson (H2–230 RHOB), 5–6558; Stacey Dion (B–346A RHOB), 5–7101; Kristin (Wolgemuth) Fitzgerald (B–346A RHOB), 5–7101; Kevin Frank (B–346A RHOB) 5–7101; Kate Gorton (H2–230 FHOB), 5–6558; Melanie Looney (H2–230 FHOB), 5–6558; Stephanie Milburn (B–346A RHOB), 5–7101; Jim Paretti (B–346A RHOB) 5–7101; Alison Ream (H2–230 FHOB), 5–6558; Whitney Rhoades (H2–230 FHOB), 5–6558; Stephen Settle (B–346A RHOB), 5–7101; Kathleen Smith (H2–230 FHOB) 5–6558; Rich Stombres (H2–230 FHOB), 5–6558; Loren Sweatt (B–346A RHOB), 5–7101; Robert Sweet (H2–230 FHOB), 5–6558.

Executive Assistants: Allison Dembeck; Kim Proctor.

Legislative Assistants: Julian Baer (H2–230 FHOB), 5–6558; Travis McCoy (B–346A RHOB), 5–7101; Holli Traud (H2–230 FHOB), 5–6558; Elizabeth Wheel (H2–230 FHOB), 5–6558.

Administrative Staff: Billie Irving (B–346A RHOB), 5–7101; Lisa Paschal (H2–230 FHOB), 5–6558.

Receptionist/Staff Assistant.—Shemika Jamison.

Minority Staff Director.—John Lawrence, (2101 RHOB), 5–3725.

General Counsel.—Mark Zuckerman, 5–3725.

Deputy Staff Director.—Charlie Barone, 5–3725.

Administrative Assistant. Ann Owens, 5–3725.

Administrative Staff.—Joycelyn Johnson, 5–3725.

Communications Director.—Daniel Weiss (2205 RHOB), 5–2095.

Counsel/Education and Oversight.—Cheryl Johnson (1040 LHOB), 5–3725.

Legislative Associate/Education: Ellynne Bannon (1107 LHOB), 6–2068; Denise Forte (1107 LHOB), 6–2068; Ruth Friedman (1107 LHOB), 6–2068; Ricardo Martinez (1040 LHOB), 5–3725; Alex Nock (1107 LHOB), 6–2068; Lynda Theil (1040 LHOB), 5–3725.

Senior Legislative Associate/Labor.—Peter Rutledge (1040 LHOB), 5–3725.

Staff Assistant/Education.—Joe Novotny (1107 LHOB), 6–2068.

Legislative Associate/Labor.—Maria Cuprill (112 CHOB), 6–1881.

Staff Assistant/Labor.—Dan Rawlins (112 CHOB), 6–1881.

Labor Counsel/Coordinator.—Michele Varnhagen (112 CHOB), 6–1881.

Energy and Commerce

2125 Rayburn House Office Building, phone 225–2927

http://www.house.gov/commerce

meets fourth Tuesday of each month

W.J. (Billy) Tauzin, of Louisiana, *Chairman.*

Richard Burr, of North Carolina, *Vice Chairman.*

Michael Bilirakis, of Florida.
Joe Barton, of Texas.
Fred Upton, of Michigan.
Cliff Stearns, of Florida.
Paul E. Gillmor, of Ohio.
James C. Greenwood, of Pennsylvania.
Christopher Cox, of California.
Nathan Deal, of Georgia.
Ed Whitfield, of Kentucky.
Charlie Norwood, of Georgia.
Barbara Cubin, of Wyoming.
John Shimkus, of Illinois.
Heather Wilson, of New Mexico.
John B. Shadegg, of Arizona.
Charles W. (Chip) Pickering, of Mississippi.
Vito Fossella, of New York.
Roy Blunt, of Missouri.
Steve Buyer, of Indiana.
George Radanovich, of California.
Charles F. Bass, of New Hampshire.
Joseph R. Pitts, of Pennsylvania.
Mary Bono, of California.
Greg Walden, of Oregon.
Lee Terry, of Nebraska.
Ernie Fletcher, of Kentucky.
Mike Ferguson, of New Jersey.
Mike Rogers, of Michigan.
Darrell E. Issa, of California.
C.L. (Butch) Otter, of Idaho.

John D. Dingell, of Michigan.
Henry A. Waxman, of California.
Edward J. Markey, of Massachusetts.
Ralph M. Hall, of Texas.
Rick Boucher, of Virginia.
Edolphus Towns, of New York.
Frank Pallone, Jr., of New Jersey.
Sherrod Brown, of Ohio.
Bart Gordon, of Tennessee.
Peter Deutsch, of Florida.
Bobby L. Rush, of Illinois.
Anna G. Eshoo, of California.
Bart Stupak, of Michigan.
Eliot L. Engel, of New York.
Albert Russell Wynn, of Maryland.
Gene Green, of Texas.
Karen McCarthy, of Missouri.
Ted Strickland, of Ohio.
Diana DeGette, of Colorado.
Lois Capps, of California.
Michael F. Doyle, of Pennsylvania.
Christopher John, of Louisiana.
Thomas H. Allen, of Maine.
Jim Davis, of Florida.
Janice D. Schakowsky, of Illinois.
Hilda L. Solis, of California.

SUBCOMMITTEES

[The chairman and ranking minority member are ex officio (voting) members of all subcommittees on which they do not serve.]

Commerce, Trade, and Consumer Protection

Cliff Stearns, of Florida, *Chairman.*

John B. Shadegg, of Arizona, *Vice Chairman.*

Fred Upton, of Michigan.
Ed Whitfield, of Kentucky.
Barbara Cubin, of Wyoming.
John Shimkus, of Illinois.
George Radanovich, of California.
Charles F. Bass, of New Hampshire.
Joseph R. Pitts, of Pennsylvania.
Mary Bono, of California.
Lee Terry, of Nebraska.
Ernie Fletcher, of Kentucky.
Mike Ferguson, of New Jersey.
Darrell E. Issa, of California.
C.L. (Butch) Otter, of Idaho.
W.J. (Billy) Tauzin, of Louisiana.

Janice D. Schakowsky, of Illinois.
Hilda L. Solis, of California.
Edward J. Markey, of Massachusetts.
Edolphus Towns, of New York.
Sherrod Brown, of Ohio.
Jim Davis, of Florida.
Peter Deutsch, of Florida.
Bart Stupak, of Michigan.
Gene Green, of Texas.
Karen McCarthy, of Missouri.
Ted Strickland, of Ohio.
Diana DeGette, of Colorado.
John D. Dingell, of Michigan.

Energy and Air Quality

Joe Barton, of Texas, *Chairman.*

John Shimkus, of Illinois, *Vice Chairman.*

Christopher Cox, of California.
Richard Burr, of North Carolina.
Ed Whitfield, of Kentucky.
Charlie Norwood, of Georgia.
Heather Wilson, of New Mexico.
John B. Shadegg, of Arizona.
Charles W. (Chip) Pickering, of Mississippi.
Vito Fossella, of New York.
Steve Buyer, of Indiana.
George Radanovich, of California.
Mary Bono, of California.
Greg Walden, of Oregon.
Mike Rogers, of Michigan.
Darrell E. Issa, of California.
C.L. (Butch) Otter, of Idaho.
W.J. (Billy) Tauzin, of Louisiana.

Rick Boucher, of Virginia.
Albert Russell Wynn, of Maryland.
Thomas H. Allen, of Maine.
Henry A. Waxman, of California.
Edward J. Markey, of Massachusetts.
Ralph M. Hall, of Texas.
Frank Pallone, Jr., of New Jersey.
Sherrod Brown, of Ohio.
Bobby L. Rush, of Illinois.
Karen McCarthy, of Missouri.
Ted Strickland, of Ohio.
Lois Capps, of California.
Michael F. Doyle, of Pennsylvania.
Christopher John, of Louisiana.
John D. Dingell, of Michigan.

Environment and Hazardous Materials

Paul E. Gillmor, of Ohio, *Chairman.*

Vito Fossella, of New York, *Vice Chairman.*

James C. Greenwood, of Pennsylvania.
John Shimkus, of Illinois.
Heather Wilson, of New Mexico.
Steve Buyer, of Indiana.
George Radanovich, of California.
Charles F. Bass, of New Hampshire.
Joseph R. Pitts, of Pennsylvania.
Mary Bono, of California.
Lee Terry, of Nebraska.
Ernie Fletcher, of Kentucky.
Darrell E. Issa, of California.
Mike Rogers, of Michigan.
C.L. (Butch) Otter, of Idaho.
W.J. (Billy) Tauzin, of Louisiana.

Hilda L. Solis, of California.
Thomas H. Allen, of Maine.
Frank Pallone, Jr., of New Jersey.
Michael F. Doyle, of Pennsylvania.
Jim Davis, of Florida.
Janice D. Schakowsky, of Illinois.
Peter Deutsch, of Florida.
Bobby L. Rush, of Illinois.
Bart Stupak, of Michigan.
Albert Russell Wynn, of Maryland.
Gene Green, of Texas.
Diana DeGette, of Colorado.
John D. Dingell, of Michigan.

Health

Michael Bilirakis, of Florida, *Chairman.*

Charlie Norwood, of Georgia, *Vice Chairman.*

Joe Barton, of Texas.
Fred Upton, of Michigan.
James C. Greenwood, of Pennsylvania.
Nathan Deal, of Georgia.
Richard Burr, of North Carolina.
Ed Whitfield, of Kentucky.
Barbara Cubin, of Wyoming.
Heather Wilson, of New Mexico.
John B. Shadegg, of Arizona.
Charles W. (Chip) Pickering, of Mississippi.
Steve Buyer, of Indiana.
Joseph R. Pitts, of Pennsylvania.
Ernie Fletcher, of Kentucky.
Mike Ferguson, of New Jersey.
Mike Rogers, of Michigan.
W.J. (Billy) Tauzin, of Louisiana.

Sherrod Brown, of Ohio.
Henry A. Waxman, of California.
Ralph M. Hall, of Texas.
Edolphus Towns, of New York.
Frank Pallone, Jr., of New Jersey.
Anna G. Eshoo, of California.
Bart Stupak, of Michigan.
Eliot L. Engel, of New York.
Gene Green, of Texas.
Ted Strickland, of Ohio.
Lois Capps, of California.
Bart Gordon, of Tennessee.
Diana DeGette, of Colorado.
Christopher John, of Louisiana.
John D. Dingell, of Michigan.

Oversight and Investigations

James C. Greenwood, of Pennsylvania, *Chairman.*

Greg Walden, of Oregon, *Vice Chairman.*

Michael Bilirakis, of Florida.
Cliff Stearns, of Florida.
Richard Burr, of North Carolina.
Charles F. Bass, of New Hampshire.
Mike Ferguson, of New Jersey.
Mike Rogers, of Michigan.
W.J. (Billy) Tauzin, of Louisiana.

Peter Deutsch, of Florida.
Diana DeGette, of Colorado.
Jim Davis, of Florida.
Janice D. Schakowsky, of Illinois.
Henry A. Waxman, of California.
Bobby L. Rush, of Illinois.
John D. Dingell, of Michigan.

Telecommunications and the Internet

Fred Upton, of Michigan, *Chairman.*

Cliff Stearns, of Florida, *Vice Chairman.*

Michael Bilirakis, of Florida.
Joe Barton, of Texas.
Paul E. Gillmor, of Ohio.
Christopher Cox, of California.
Nathan Deal, of Georgia.
Ed Whitfield, of Kentucky.
Barbara Cubin, of Wyoming.
John Shimkus, of Illinois.
Heather Wilson, of New Mexico.
Charles W. (Chip) Pickering, of Mississippi.
Vito Fossella, of New York.
Charles F. Bass, of New Hampshire.
Mary Bono, of California.
Greg Walden, of Oregon.
Lee Terry, of Nebraska.
W.J. (Billy) Tauzin, of Louisiana.

Edward J. Markey, of Massachusetts.
Bobby L. Rush, of Illinois.
Karen McCarthy, of Missouri.
Michael F. Doyle, of Pennsylvania.
Jim Davis, of Florida.
Rick Boucher, of Virginia.
Edolphus Towns, of New York.
Bart Gordon, of Tennessee.
Peter Deutsch, of Florida.
Anna G. Eshoo, of California.
Bart Stupak, of Michigan.
Eliot L. Engel, of New York.
Albert Russell Wynn, of Maryland.
Gene Green, of Texas.
John D. Dingell, of Michigan.

STAFF

Committee on Energy and Commerce (2125 RHOB), 225–2927; fax 225–1919.
Staff Director.—David E. Marventano.
Deputy Staff Director.—Nydia Bonnin.
Deputy Chief of Staff.—Patrick Morrisey.
General Counsel.—James Barnette.
Chief Counsel, Oversight and Investigations.—Mark Paoletta.
Communications Director.—Ken Johnson.
Deputy Communications Directors: Mary Ellen Grant, Vikki Riley, Arturo Silva, Jon Tripp.
Counsels: Jason Bentley, Linda Bloss-Baum, David Cavicke, Charles Clapton, Anthony Cooke, William Cooper, Sean Cunningham, Brent Del Monte, Tom Dilenge, Nandan Kenkeremath, Brian McCullough, Robert Meyers, Patrick Ronan, Jennifer Safavian, Ray Shepherd, Manisha Singh, Alan Slobodin, Jessica Wallace, Howard Waltzman, Kelly Zerzan.
Policy Coordinators: Ramsen Betfarhad, Andrew Black, Jerry Couri, Will Nordwind, Steven Tilton.
Professional Staff Members: Dwight Cates, Brad Conway, Rebecca Hermard, Robert Simison, Peter Spencer, Shannon Vildostegui, Ann Washington, Kathleen Weldon.
Legislative Clerks: Will Carty, Yong Choe, Eugenia Edwards, Hollyn Kidd, Peter Kielty, Jill Latham.
Special Assistant.—Jaylyn Connaughton.
Administrative and Human Resources Coordinator.—Linda Walker.
Assistant to the Administrative Coordinator.—Audrey Murdoch.
Comptroller.—Anthony Sullivan.
Systems Administrator.—John Clocker.
Printer.—Joseph Patterson.
Archivist.—Jerome Sikorski.
Project Assistant.—William O'Brien.
Staff Assistants: Michael Abraham, Seth Benhard, William Harvard, Jennifer Robertson.

Financial Services

2129 Rayburn House Office Building, phone 225–7502

http://www.house.gov/financialservices

meets first Tuesday of each month

Michael G. Oxley, of Ohio, *Chairman.*

James A. Leach, of Iowa.
Doug Bereuter, of Nebraska.
Richard H. Baker, of Louisiana.
Spencer Bachus, of Alabama.
Michael N. Castle, of Delaware.
Peter T. King, of New York.
Edward R. Royce, of California.
Frank D. Lucas, of Oklahoma.
Robert W. Ney, of Ohio.
Sue W. Kelly, of New York.
Ron Paul, of Texas.
Paul E. Gillmor, of Ohio.
Jim Ryun, of Kansas.
Steven C. LaTourette, of Ohio.
Donald A. Manzullo, of Illinois.
Walter B. Jones, of North Carolina.
Doug Ose, of California.
Judy Biggert, of Illinois.
Mark Green, of Wisconsin.
Patrick J. Toomey, of Pennsylvania.
Christopher Shays, of Connecticut.
John B. Shadegg, of Arizona.
Vito Fossella, of New York.
Gary G. Miller, of California.
Melissa A. Hart, of Pennsylvania.
Shelley Moore Capito, of West Virginia.
Patrick J. Tiberi, of Ohio.
Mark R. Kennedy, of Minnesota.
Tom Feeney, of Florida.
Jeb Hensarling, of Texas.
Scott Garrett, of New Jersey.
Tim Murphy, of Pennsylvania.
Ginny Brown-Waite, of Florida.
J. Gresham Barrett, of South Carolina.
Katherine Harris, of Florida.
Rick Renzi, of Arizona.

Barney Frank, of Massachusetts.
Paul E. Kanjorski, of Pennsylvania.
Maxine Waters, of California.
Carolyn B. Maloney, of New York.
Luis V. Gutierrez, of Illinois.
Nydia M. Velázquez, of New York.
Melvin L. Watt, of North Carolina.
Gary L. Ackerman, of New York.
Darlene Hooley, of Oregon.
Julia Carson, of Indiana.
Brad Sherman, of California.
Gregory W. Meeks, of New York.
Barbara Lee, of California.
Jay Inslee, of Washington.
Dennis Moore, of Kansas.
Charles A. Gonzalez, of Texas.
Michael E. Capuano, of Massachusetts.
Harold E. Ford, Jr., of Tennessee.
Rubén Hinojosa, of Texas.
Ken Lucas, of Kentucky.
Joseph Crowley, of New York.
Wm. Lacy Clay, of Missouri.
Steve Israel, of New York.
Mike Ross, of Arkansas.
Carolyn McCarthy, of New York.
Joe Baca, of California.
Jim Matheson, of Utah.
Stephen F. Lynch, of Massachusetts.
Brad Miller, of North Carolina.
Rahm Emanuel, of Illinois.
David Scott, of Georgia.
Artur Davis, of Alabama.

BERNARD SANDERS, of Vermont.

SUBCOMMITTEES

[The chairman and ranking minority member are ex officio (voting) members of all subcommittees on which they do not serve.]

Capital Markets, Insurance, and Government-Sponsored Enterprises

Richard H. Baker, of Louisiana, *Chairman.*

Doug Ose, of California.
Christopher Shays, of Connecticut.
Paul E. Gillmor, of Ohio.
Spencer Bachus, of Alabama.
Michael N. Castle, of Delaware.
Peter T. King, of New York.
Frank D. Lucas, of Oklahoma.
Edward R. Royce, of California.
Donald A. Manzullo, of Illinois.
Sue W. Kelly, of New York.
Robert W. Ney, of Ohio.
John B. Shadegg, of Arizona.
Jim Ryun, of Kansas.
Vito Fossella, of New York.
Judy Biggert, of Illinois.
Mark Green, of Wisconsin.
Gary G. Miller, of California.
Patrick J. Toomey, of Pennsylvania.
Shelley Moore Capito, of West Virginia.
Melissa A. Hart, of Pennsylvania.
Mark R. Kennedy, of Minnesota.
Patrick J. Tiberi, of Ohio.
Ginny Brown-Waite, of Florida.
Katherine Harris, of Florida.
Rick Renzi, of Arizona.

Paul E. Kanjorski, of Pennsylvania.
Gary L. Ackerman, of New York.
Darlene Hooley, of Oregon.
Brad Sherman, of California.
Gregory W. Meeks, of New York.
Jay Inslee, of Washington.
Dennis Moore, of Kansas.
Charles A. Gonzalez, of Texas.
Michael E. Capuano, of Massachusetts.
Harold E. Ford, Jr., of Tennessee.
Rubén Hinojosa, of Texas.
Ken Lucas, of Kentucky.
Joseph Crowley, of New York.
Steve Israel, of New York.
Mike Ross, of Arkansas.
Wm. Lacy Clay, of Missouri.
Carolyn McCarthy, of New York.
Joe Baca, of California.
Jim Matheson, of Utah.
Stephen F. Lynch, of Massachusetts.
Brad Miller, of North Carolina.
Rahm Emanuel, of Illinois.
David Scott, of Georgia.

Domestic and International Monetary Policy, Trade and Technology

Peter T. King, of New York, *Chairman.*

Judy Biggert, of Illinois.
James A. Leach, of Iowa.
Michael N. Castle, of Delaware.
Ron Paul, of Texas.
Donald A. Manzullo, of Illinois.
Doug Ose, of California.
John B. Shadegg, of Arizona.
Mark R. Kennedy, of Minnesota.
Tom Feeney, of Florida.
Jeb Hensarling, of Texas.
Tim Murphy, of Pennsylvania.
J. Gresham Barrett, of South Carolina.
Katherine Harris, of Florida.

Carolyn B. Maloney, of New York.
BERNARD SANDERS, of Vermont.
Melvin L. Watt, of North Carolina.
Maxine Waters, of California.
Barbara Lee, of California.
Paul E. Kanjorski, of Pennsylvania.
Brad Sherman, of California.
Darlene Hooley, of Oregon.
Luis V. Gutierrez, of Illinois.
Nydia M. Velázquez, of New York.
Joe Baca, of California.
Rahm Emanuel, of Illinois.

Financial Institutions and Consumer Credit

Spencer Bachus, of Alabama, *Chairman.*

Steven C. LaTourette, of Ohio.
Doug Bereuter, of Nebraska.
Richard H. Baker, of Louisiana.
Michael N. Castle, of Delaware.
Edward R. Royce, of California.
Frank D. Lucas, of Oklahoma.
Sue W. Kelly, of New York.
Paul E. Gillmor, of Ohio.
Jim Ryun, of Kansas.
Walter B. Jones, of North Carolina.
Judy Biggert, of Illinois.
Patrick J. Toomey, of Pennsylvania.
Vito Fossella, of New York.
Melissa A. Hart, of Pennsylvania.
Shelley Moore Capito, of West Virginia.
Patrick J. Tiberi, of Ohio.
Mark R. Kennedy, of Minnesota.
Tom Feeney, of Florida.
Jeb Hensarling, of Texas.
Scott Garrett, of New Jersey.
Tim Murphy, of Pennsylvania.
Ginny Brown-Waite, of Florida.
J. Gresham Barrett, of South Carolina.
Rick Renzi, of Arizona.

BERNARD SANDERS, of Vermont.
Carolyn B. Maloney, of New York.
Melvin L. Watt, of North Carolina.
Gary L. Ackerman, of New York.
Brad Sherman, of California.
Gregory W. Meeks, of New York.
Luis V. Gutierrez, of Illinois.
Dennis Moore, of Kansas.
Charles A. Gonzalez, of Texas.
Paul E. Kanjorski, of Pennsylvania.
Maxine Waters, of California.
Nydia M. Velázquez, of New York.
Darlene Hooley, of Oregon.
Julia Carson, of Indiana.
Harold E. Ford, Jr., of Tennessee.
Rubén Hinojosa, of Texas.
Ken Lucas, of Kentucky.
Joseph Crowley, of New York.
Steve Israel, of New York.
Mike Ross, of Arkansas.
Carolyn McCarthy, of New York.
Artur Davis, of Alabama.

Housing and Community Opportunity

Robert W. Ney, of Ohio, *Chair.*

Mark Green, of Wisconsin.
Doug Bereuter, of Nebraska.
Richard H. Baker, of Louisiana.
Peter T. King, of New York.
Walter B. Jones, of North Carolina.
Doug Ose, of California.
Patrick J. Toomey, of Pennsylvania.
Christopher Shays, of Connecticut.
Gary G. Miller, of California.
Melissa A. Hart, of Pennsylvania.
Patrick J. Tiberi, of Ohio.
Katherine Harris, of Florida.
Rick Renzi, of Arizona.

Maxine Waters, of California.
Nydia M. Velázquez, of New York.
Julia Carson, of Indiana.
Barbara Lee, of California.
Michael E. Capuano, of Massachusetts.
BERNARD SANDERS, of Vermont.
Melvin L. Watt, of North Carolina.
Wm. Lacy Clay, of Missouri.
Stephen F. Lynch, of Massachusetts.
Brad Miller, of North Carolina.
David Scott, of Georgia.
Artur Davis, of Alabama.

Oversight and Investigations

Sue W. Kelly, of New York, *Chair.*

Ron Paul, of Texas.
Steven C. LaTourette, of Ohio.
Mark Green, of Wisconsin.
John B. Shadegg, of Arizona.
Vito Fossella, of New York.
Jeb Hensarling, of Texas.
Scott Garrett, of New Jersey.
Tim Murphy, of Pennsylvania.
Ginny Brown-Waite, of Florida.
J. Gresham Barrett, of South Carolina.

Luis V. Gutierrez, of Illinois.
Jay Inslee, of Washington.
Dennis Moore, of Kansas.
Joseph Crowley, of New York.
Carolyn B. Maloney, of New York.
Charles A. Gonzalez, of Texas.
Rubén Hinojosa, of Texas.
Jim Matheson, of Utah.
Stephen F. Lynch, of Massachusetts.

STAFF

Committee on Financial Services (2129 RHOB), 225–7502.
Chief Counsel / Staff Director.—Robert Foster.
Deputy Staff Director / Communications Director.—Peggy Peterson.
Parliamentarian / Director of Legislative Operations.—Hugh Halpern.
Assistant Communications Director for Research.—Madeline Burns.
Assistant Communications Directors: Scott Duncan, Brookly McLaughlin.
Senior Counsels: James Clinger, Andrew Cochran, Robert Gordon, Clinton Jones, Carter McDowell, Tom Montgomery, Linda Dallas Rich.
Counsels: Justin Daly, David Eppstein, Kyle Gilster, Karen Lynch, Kevin MacMillan, Tom McCrocklin, Charles Symington, Frank Tillotson.
Senior Professional Staff: Cindy Chetti, Joe Pinder.
Professional Staff: John Butler, Paul Kangas.
Director of Coalitions.—Bob Bolster.
Administrative Assistant.—Angela Gambo.
Executive Assistant.—Dale Dorr.
Calendar, Documents and Systems Administrator.—Kim Trimble.
Executive Staff Assistants: Susan Cole, Rosemary Keech, Janice Zanardi.
Staff Assistants: Tucker Foote, Angela Palmer, Beverly Price, Matt Timothy, Earnestine Worelds.
Minority Staff Director.—Jeanne Roslanowick (B–301C RHOB), 225–4247.
Counsels: Ava Boyd, Erika Jeffers, Scott Olson, Lawranne Stewart, Ken Swab.
Communications Director.—S. Kay Gibbs.
Press Secretary.—Jennifer Gore.
Senior Policy Analyst.—Dean Sagar.
Economist.—Scott Morris.
Senior Professional Staff.—Jaime Lizarraga.
Professional Staff: Donald Auerbach, Warren Gunnels, Todd Harper, Patricia Lord, Daniel McGlinchey, Annie Toro, John Wilson, Roberta Youmans.
Staff Assistant.—Alanna Porter.

Government Reform

2154 Rayburn House Office Building, phone 225–5074, fax 225–3974, TTY 225–6852

http://www.house.gov/reform

meets second Tuesday of each month

Tom Davis, of Virginia, *Chairman.*

Dan Burton, of Indiana.
Christopher Shays, of Connecticut.
Ileana Ros-Lehtinen, of Florida.
John M. McHugh, of New York.
John L. Mica, of Florida.
Mark E. Souder, of Indiana.
Steven C. LaTourette, of Ohio.
Doug Ose, of California.
Ron Lewis, of Kentucky.
Jo Ann Davis, of Virginia.
Todd Russell Platts, of Pennsylvania.
Chris Cannon, of Utah.
Adam H. Putnam, of Florida.
Edward L. Schrock, of Virginia.
John J. Duncan, Jr., of Tennessee.
John Sullivan, of Oklahoma.
Nathan Deal, of Georgia.
Candice S. Miller, of Michigan.
Tim Murphy, of Pennsylvania.
Michael R. Turner, of Ohio.
John R. Carter, of Texas.
William J. Janklow, of South Dakota.
Marsha Blackburn, of Tennessee.

Henry A. Waxman, of California.
Tom Lantos, of California.
Major R. Owens, of New York.
Edolphus Towns, of New York.
Paul E. Kanjorski, of Pennsylvania.
Carolyn B. Maloney, of New York.
Elijah E. Cummings, of Maryland.
Dennis J. Kucinich, of Ohio.
Danny K. Davis, of Illinois.
John F. Tierney, of Massachusetts.
Wm. Lacy Clay, of Missouri.
Diane E. Watson, of California.
Stephen F. Lynch, of Massachusetts.
Chris Van Hollen, of Maryland.
Linda T. Sánchez, of California.
C.A. Dutch Ruppersberger, of Maryland.
Eleanor Holmes Norton, of the District of Columbia.
Jim Cooper, of Tennessee.
Chris Bell, of Texas.

BERNARD SANDERS, of Vermont.

SUBCOMMITTEES

[The chairman and ranking minority member are ex officio (voting) members of all subcommittees]

Civil Service and Agency Organization

Jo Ann Davis, of Virginia, *Chairwoman.*

Tim Murphy, of Pennsylvania.
John L. Mica, of Florida.
Mark E. Souder, of Indiana.
Adam H. Putnam, of Florida.
Nathan Deal, of Georgia
Marsha Blackburn, of Tennessee.

Danny K. Davis, of Illinois.
Major R. Owens, of New York.
Chris Van Hollen, of Maryland.
Eleanor Holmes Norton, of the District of Columbia.
Jim Cooper, of Tennessee.

Criminal Justice, Drug Policy, and Human Resources

Mark E. Souder, of Indiana, *Chairman.*

Nathan Deal, of Georgia.
John M. McHugh, of New York.
John L. Mica, of Florida.
Doug Ose, of California.
Jo Ann Davis, of Virginia.
Edward L. Schrock, of Virginia.
John R. Carter, of Texas.
Marsha Blackburn, of Tennessee.

Elijah E. Cummings, of Maryland.
Danny K. Davis, of Illinois.
Wm. Lacy Clay, of Missouri.
Linda T. Sánchez, of California.
C.A. Dutch Ruppersberger, of Maryland.
Eleanor Holmes Norton, of the District of Columbia.
Chris Bell, of Texas.

Energy Policy, Natural Resources, and Regulatory Affairs

Doug Ose, of California, *Chairman.*

William J. Janklow, of South Dakota.
Christopher Shays, of Connecticut.
John M. McHugh, of New York.
Chris Cannon, of Utah.
John Sullivan, of Oklahoma.
Nathan Deal, of Georgia.
Candice S. Miller, of Michigan.

John F. Tierney, of Massachusetts.
Tom Lantos, of California.
Paul E. Kanjorski, of Pennsylvania.
Dennis J. Kucinich, of Ohio.
Chris Van Hollen, of Maryland.
Jim Cooper, of Tennessee.

Government Efficiency and Financial Management

Todd Russell Platts, of California, *Chairman.*

Marsha Blackburn, of Tennessee.
Steven C. LaTourette, of Ohio.
John Sullivan, of Oklahoma.
Candice S. Miller, of Michigan.
Michael R. Turner, of Ohio.

Edolphus Towns, of New York.
Paul E. Kanjorski, of Pennsylvania.
Major R. Owens, of New York.
Carolyn B. Maloney, of New York.

Human Rights and Wellness

Dan Burton, of Indiana, *Chairman.*

Chris Cannon, of Utah.
Christopher Shays, of Connecticut.
Ileana Ros-Lehtinen, of Florida.

Diane E. Watson, of California.
BERNARD SANDERS, of Vermont.
Elijah E. Cummings, of Maryland.

National Security, Emerging Threats and International Relations

Christopher Shays, of Connecticut, *Chairman.*

Michael R. Turner, of Ohio.
Dan Burton, of Indiana.
Steven C. LaTourette, of Ohio.
Ron Lewis, of Kentucky.
Todd Russell Platts, of Pennsylvania.
Adam H. Putnam, of Florida.
Edward L. Schrock, of Virginia.
John J. Duncan, Jr., of Tennessee.
Tim Murphy, of Pennsylvania.
William J. Janklow, of South Dakota.

Dennis J. Kucinich, of Ohio.
Tom Lantos, of California.
BERNARD SANDERS, of Vermont.
Stephen F. Lynch, of Massachusetts.
Carolyn B. Maloney, of New York.
Linda T. Sánchez, of California.
C.A. Dutch Ruppersberger, of Maryland.
Chris Bell, of Texas.
John F. Tierney, of Massachusetts.

Technology, Information Policy, Intergovernmental Relations and the Census

Adam Putnam, of Florida, *Chairman.*

Candice S. Miller, of Michigan.
Doug Ose, of California.
Tim Murphy, of Pennsylvania.
Michael R. Turner, of Ohio.

Wm. Lacy Clay, of Missouri.
Diane E. Watson, of California.
Stephen F. Lynch, of Massachusetts.

STAFF

Committee on Government Reform (2157 RHOB), 225–5074.

Staff Director.—Peter Sirh.

Deputy Staff Director.—Melissa Wojciak.

Chief Counsel.—Keith Ausbrook.

Senior Legislative Policy Director/Counsel.—Ellen Brown.

Counsel/Parliamentarian.—Randall Kaplan.

Counsel: John Callender, Howie Denis, John Hunter, Jim Moore, Ann Marie Turner, David Young.

Director of Communications.—David Marin.

Deputy Director of Communications.—Scott Kopple.

Professional Staff: Mason Alinger, Drew Crockett, Edward Kidd, Jacquelin Mason, Michael May, Victoria Proctor, Grace Washbourne.

Chief Clerk.—Teresa Austin.

Deputy Chief Clerk.—Joshua Gillespie.

Financial Administrator.—Robin Butler.

Office Manager.—Allyson Blandford.

Legislative Assistants: Jason Chung, Shalley Kim, Michael Layman, Susie Schulte.

Chief Information Officer.—Corinne Zaccagnini.

Computer Systems Manager.—Leneal Scott.

Staff Assistants: Brien Beattie, Lori Gavaghan, Ryan Kelly.

Minority Staff Director.—Phil Schiliro (B–350A RHOB), 225–5051.

Chief Counsel.—Phil Barnett.

Deputy Chief Counsels: Kristin Amerling, Christopher Lu, Michael Yeager.

Counsels: Michelle Ash, Jon Bouker, Sarah Despres, Greg Dotson, Tony Haywood, Elizabeth Mundinger, Dave Rapallo, Alexandra Teitz, Paul Weinberger.

Professional Staff: Brian Cohen, David McMillan, Tania Shand, Josh Sharfstein, Mark Stephenson, Denise Wilson.

Senior Policy Advisor.—Karen Lightfoot.

Chief Clerk.—Earley Green.

Assistant Clerks: Teresa Coufal, Jean Gosa.

Research Assistants: Andrew Su, Chris Traci.

Special Assistant.—Katie Goodwin.

Staff Assistants: Christopher Davis, Therese Foote.

Information Manager.—Nancy Scola.

Subcommittee on Civil Service and Agency Organization (B–373 RHOB), 5–5147.

Staff Director.—Ronald Martinson.

Senior Counsel/Deputy Chief Counsel.—Chad Bungard.

Professional Staff.—Heea Vazirani-Fales.

Communications Director.—Robert White.

Legislative Counsel.—Vaughn Murphy.

Clerk.—Christopher Barkley.

Subcommittee on Criminal Justice, Drug Policy, and Human Resources (B–373B RHOB), 5–2577.

Staff Director.—Chris Donesa.

Counsel.—Nicholas Coleman.

Professional Staff.—Roland R. Foster.

Counsel/Professional Staff.—Elizabeth Meyer.

Clerk.—Nicole Garrett.

Subcommittee on Energy Policy, Natural Resources, and Regulatory Affairs (B–377 RHOB), 5–4407.

Staff Director.—Dan Skopec.

Deputy Staff Director.—Barbara Kahlow.

Press Secretary.—Yier Shi.

Clerk.—Melanie Tory.

Subcommittee on Government Efficiency and Financial Management (B–349C RHOB), 5–3741.

Staff Director.—Michael Hettinger.

Professional Staff: Larry Brady, Kara Galles.

Counsel.—Dan Daly.

Clerk.—Amy Laudeman.

Subcommittee on National Security, Emerging Threats, and International Relations (B–372 RHOB), 5–2548.

Staff Director/Counsel.—Lawrence J. Halloran.

Senior Policy Analyst.—R. Nicholas Palarino.

Chief Investigator.—Vincent Chase.

Professional Staff: Thomas Costa, Kristine McElroy.

Clerk.—Robert Briggs.

Subcommittee on Technology Policy, Information Policy, Intergovernmental Relations and Census (B–349A RHOB), 5–6751.

Staff Director.—Robert Dix.

Professional Staff: Scott Klein, Lori Martin, Chip Walker.

Counsel.—John Hambel.

Clerk.—Ursula Wojiechowski.

Subcommittee on Wellness and Human Rights (B–371C RHOB), 5–6427.

Staff Director.—Mark Walker.

Professional Staff: Elizabeth Clay, John Rowe.

Counsel.—Liz Birt.

Clerk.—Mindi Walker.

House Administration

1309 Longworth House Office Building, phone 225–8281, fax 225–9957

http://www.house.gov/cha

meets second Wednesday of each month

Robert W. Ney, of Ohio, *Chairman.*

Vernon J. Ehlers, of Michigan.
John L. Mica, of Florida.
John Linder, of Georgia.
John T. Doolittle, of California.
Thomas M. Reynolds, of New York.

John B. Larson, of Connecticut.
Juanita Millender-McDonald, of California.
Robert A. Brady, of Pennsylvania.

(No Subcommittees)

STAFF

Committee on House Administration (1309 LHOB), 225–8281.
Staff Director.—Paul Vinovich.
Deputy Staff Director.—Channing Nuss.
Counsels: Fred Hay, Matt Petersen.
Policy Director.—Maria Robinson
Technology Director.—John Erickson.
Coalitions Director.—Aaron Poe.
Professional Staff Members: Darren Feist, George Hadijski, Alec Hoppes, Jeff Janas, Chet Kalis, Pat Leahy.
Office Manager.—Will Le.
Communications Director.—Brian Walsh.
Systems Administrators: John Erickson, John Konya.
Executive Assistant to the Chairman.—Chris Krueger.
Executive Assistant to the Staff Director.—Jennifer Hing.
Staff Assistants: Ray Robbins, Payam Zakipour.
Minority Staff Director.—George F. Shevlin, IV, 1216 LHOB, 225–2061.
Chief Counsel.—Charles T. Howell.
Professional Staff: Kellie Cass Broussard, Connie Goode, Michael L. Harrison, Ellen A. McCarthy, Mary Elizabeth McHugh, Matt Pinkus.
Technology Director.—Sterling Spriggs.
Communications Director.—Elizabeth Ann Bellizzi.
Office Manager.—Tiffani J. Mendivil.
Assistant to the Staff Director.—Catherine Le Tran.

Franking Commission (1338, LHOB), 5–9337.
Staff Director.—Jack Dail.
Staff Assistants: Michael Frohlich, Richard Landon.
Minority Staff Director.—Ellen A. McCarthy.
Professional Staff.—Connie Goode.
Staff Assistant.—Tiffani J. Mendivil.

International Relations

2170 Rayburn House Office Building, phone 225–5021

http://www.house.gov/international_relations

meets first Tuesday of each month

Henry J. Hyde, of Illinois, *Chairman.*

James A. Leach, of Iowa.
Doug Bereuter, of Nebraska.
Christopher H. Smith, of New Jersey.
Dan Burton, of Indiana.
Elton Gallegly, of California.
Ileana Ros-Lehtinen, of Florida.
Cass Ballenger, of North Carolina.
Dana Rohrabacher, of California.
Edward R. Royce, of California.
Peter T. King, of New York.
Steve Chabot, of Ohio.
Amo Houghton, of New York.
John M. McHugh, of New York.
Thomas G. Tancredo, of Colorado.
Ron Paul, of Texas.
Nick Smith, of Michigan.
Joseph R. Pitts, of Pennsylvania.
Jeff Flake, of Arizona.
Jo Ann Davis, of Virginia.
Mark Green, of Wisconsin.
Jerry Weller, of Illinois.
Mike Pence, of Indiana.
Thaddeus G. McCotter, of Michigan.
William J. Janklow, of South Dakota.
Katherine Harris, of Florida.

Tom Lantos, of California.
Howard L. Berman, of California.
Gary L. Ackerman, of New York.
Eni F.H. Faleomavaega, of American Samoa.
Donald M. Payne, of New Jersey.
Robert Menendez, of New Jersey.
Sherrod Brown, of Ohio.
Brad Sherman, of California.
Robert Wexler, of Florida.
Eliot L. Engel, of New York.
William D. Delahunt, of Massachusetts.
Gregory W. Meeks, of New York.
Barbara Lee, of California.
Joseph Crowley, of New York.
Joseph M. Hoeffel, of Pennsylvania.
Earl Blumenauer, of Oregon.
Shelley Berkley, of Nevada.
Grace F. Napolitano, of California.
Adam B. Schiff, of California.
Diane E. Watson, of California.
Adam Smith, of Washington.
Betty McCollum, of Minnesota.
Chris Bell, of Texas.

SUBCOMMITTEES

[The chairman and ranking minority member are ex officio (non-voting) members of all subcommittees on which they do not serve.]

Africa

Edward R. Royce, of California, *Chairman.*

Amo Houghton, of New York.
Thomas G. Tancredo, of Colorado.
Jeff Flake, of Arizona.
Mark Green, of Wisconsin.

Donald M. Payne, of New Jersey.
Gregory W. Meeks, of New York.
Barbara Lee, of California.
Betty McCollum, of Minnesota.

Asia and the Pacific

James A. Leach, of Iowa, *Chairman.*

Dan Burton, of Indiana.
Doug Bereuter, of Nebraska.
Christopher H. Smith, of New Jersey.
Dana Rohrabacher, of California.
Edward R. Royce, of California.
Steve Chabot, of Ohio.
Ron Paul, of Texas.
Jeff Flake, of Arizona.
Jerry Weller, of Illinois.
Thomas G. Tancredo, of Colorado.

Eni F.H. Faleomavaega, of American Samoa.
Sherrod Brown, of Ohio.
Earl Blumenauer, of Oregon.
Diane E. Watson, of California.
Adam Smith, of Washington.
Gary L. Ackerman, of New York.
Brad Sherman, of California.
Robert Wexler, of Florida.
Gregory W. Meeks, of New York.

Europe

Doug Bereuter, of Nebraska, *Chairman.*

Dan Burton, of Indiana.
Elton Gallegly, of California.
Peter T. King, of New York.
Jo Ann Davis, of Virginia.
Thaddeus G. McCotter, of Michigan.
William J. Janklow, of South Dakota.
Robert Wexler, of Florida.
Eliot L. Engel, of New York.
William D. Delahunt, of Massachusetts.
Barbara Lee, of California.
Joseph M. Hoeffel, of Pennsylvania.
Earl Blumenauer, of Oregon.

International Terrorism, Nonproliferation, and Human Rights

Elton Gallegly, of California, *Chair.*

Christopher H. Smith, of New Jersey.
Dana Rohrabacher, of California.
Peter T. King, of New York.
Joseph R. Pitts, of Pennsylvania.
Mark Green, of Wisconsin.
Cass Ballenger, of North Carolina.
Thomas G. Tancredo, of Colorado.
Nick Smith, of Michigan.
Mike Pence, of Indiana.
Brad Sherman, of California.
Robert Menendez, of New Jersey.
Joseph Crowley, of New York.
Shelley Berkley, of Nevada.
Grace F. Napolitano, of California.
Adam B. Schiff, of California.
Diane Watson, of California.
Chris Bell, of Texas.

The Middle East and Central Asia

Ileana Ros-Lehtinen, of Florida, *Chairman.*

Steve Chabot, of Ohio.
John M. McHugh, of New York.
Nick Smith, of Michigan.
Jo Ann Davis, of Virginia.
Mike Pence, of Indiana.
Thaddeus G. McCotter, of Michigan.
William J. Janklow, of South Dakota.
Joseph R. Pitts, of Pennsylvania.
Katherine Harris, of Florida.
Gary L. Ackerman, of New York.
Howard L. Berman, of California.
Eliot L. Engel, of New York.
Joseph Crowley, of New York.
Joseph M. Hoeffel, of Pennsylvania.
Shelley Berkley, of Nevada.
Adam B. Schiff, of California.
Chris Bell, of Texas.

The Western Hemisphere

Cass Ballenger, of North Carolina, *Chairman.*

Ron Paul, of Texas.
Jerry Weller, of Illinois.
Katherine Harris, of Florida.
James A. Leach, of Iowa.
Ileana Ros-Lehtinen, of Florida.
Robert Menendez, of New Jersey.
William D. Delahunt, of Massachusetts.
Grace F. Napolitano, of California.
Eni F.H. Faleomavaega, of American Samoa.
Donald M. Payne, of New Jersey.

STAFF

Committee on International Relations (2170 RHOB), 225–5021.
Staff Director/General Counsel.—Thomas E. Mooney.
Deputy Staff Director.—John Walker Roberts.
Senior Counsel.—Bob Jones.
Investigative Counsel.— John P. Mackey.
Counsels: Frank Cotter, Kirsti Garlock.
Counsel/Parliamentarian.—Dan Freeman.
Senior Professional Staff/Counsel.—Hillel Weinberg.
Senior Professional Staff: Kristen Gilley, Francis C. Record.
Professional Staff: Blaine Aaron, Lara Alameh, Joan Condon, Dennis Halpin, Patricia Katyoka, John Lis, Doug Seay.
Communications Director.—Sam Stratman.
Security Officer.—Laura Rush.

Administrative Director/Executive Assistant to General Counsel.—Sheila Klein.
Financial Administrator.—Jim Farr.
Information Resource Manager.—Sharon Hammersla.
Legislative Correspondence Manager.—Elizabeth Singleton.
Senior Staff Associate/Travel Coordinator.—Jo Weber.
Protocol Officer.—Linda Solomon.
Printing Manager.—Shirley Alexander.
Staff Associates: Liberty Dunn, Marilyn Owen.
Special Assistants: Fran Marcucci, Joseph Painter, Amy Serck.
Assistant Systems Administrator.—Patrick Troy.
Democratic Staff Director.—Robert R. King (B–360 RHOB), 225–6735.
Deputy Staff Director.—Peter M. Yeo.
Chief Counsel.—David S. Abramowitz.
Deputy Chief Counsel.—Paul Oostburg Sanz.
Senior Policy Advisor.—Kay A. King.
Professional Staff: David Fite, David Killion, Alan Makovsky, Pearl Alice Marsh, Tanya Mazin, Robin Roizman.
Press Secretary.—Matt Gobush.
Clerk.—Carol G. Doherty.
Staff Associate.—Keith O'Neil.
Subcommittee on Africa (255 FHOB), 226–7812.
Staff Director.—Tom Sheehy.
Democratic Professional Staff.—Noelle Lusane.
Professional Staff.—Malik M. Chaka.
Staff Associate.—Greg Galvin.
Subcommittee on Asia and the Pacific (B–358 RHOB), 226–7825.
Staff Director.—Jamie McCormick.
Democratic Professional Staff.—Lisa Williams.
Professional Staff/Counsel.—Douglas Anderson.
Staff Associate.—Tiernen Miller.
Subcommittee on Europe (2401A RHOB), 226–7820.
Staff Director.—Vince Morelli.
Democratic Professional Staff.—Jonathan Katz.
Professional Staff.—Patrick Prisco.
Staff Associate.—Beverly Hallock.
Subcommittee on International Terrorism, Nonproliferation, and Human Rights (253 FHOB), 225–3345.
Staff Director.—Richard Mereu.
Democratic Professional Staff.—Don McDonald.
Professional Staff.—Renee Austell.
Staff Associate.—Joe Windrem.
Subcommittee on the Middle East and Central Asia (257 RHOB), 226–9940.
Staff Director.—Yleem Poblete.
Democratic Professional Staff.—David S. Adams.
Professional Staff.—[Vacant].
Staff Associate.—Matthew Zweig.
Subcommittee on the Western Hemisphere (259 FHOB), 226–9970.
Staff Director.—Caleb McCarry.
Democratic Professional Staff.—Pedro Pablo Permuy.
Professional Staff.—Ted Brennan.
Staff Associate.—Jean Carroll.

Judiciary

2138 Rayburn House Office Building, phone 225–3951

http://www.house.gov/judiciary

meets every Tuesday

F. James Sensenbrenner, Jr., of Wisconsin, *Chairman.*

Henry J. Hyde, of Illinois.
Howard Coble, of North Carolina.
Lamar S. Smith, of Texas.
Elton Gallegly, of California.
Bob Goodlatte, of Virginia.
Steve Chabot, of Ohio.
William L. Jenkins, of Tennessee.
Chris Cannon, of Utah.
Spencer Bachus, of Alabama.
John N. Hostettler, of Indiana.
Mark Green, of Wisconsin.
Ric Keller, of Florida.
Melissa A. Hart, of Pennsylvania.
Jeff Flake, of Arizona.
Mike Pence, of Indiana.
J. Randy Forbes, of Virginia.
Steve King, of Iowa.
John Carter, of Texas.
Tom Feeney, of Florida.
Marsha Blackburn, of Tennessee.

John Conyers, Jr., of Michigan.
Howard L. Berman, of California.
Rick Boucher, of Virginia.
Jerrold Nadler, of New York.
Robert C. Scott, of Virginia.
Melvin L. Watt, of North Carolina.
Zoe Lofgren, of California.
Sheila Jackson Lee, of Texas.
Maxine Waters, of California.
Martin T. Meehan, of Massachusetts.
William D. Delahunt, of Massachusetts.
Robert Wexler, of Florida.
Tammy Baldwin, of Wisconsin.
Anthony Weiner, of New York.
Adam B. Schiff, of California.
Linda Sánchez, of California.

SUBCOMMITTEES

[The chairman and the ranking minority member are ex officio (non-voting) members of all subcommittees on which they do not serve.]

Commercial and Administrative Law

Chris Cannon, of Utah, *Chairman.*

Howard Coble, of North Carolina.
Jeff Flake, of Arizona.
John Carter, of Texas.
Marsha Blackburn, of Tennessee.
Steve Chabot, of Ohio.
Tom Feeney, of Florida.

Melvin L. Watt, of North Carolina.
Jerrold Nadler, of New York.
Tammy Baldwin, of Wisconsin.
William D. Delahunt, of Massachusetts.
Anthony Weiner, of New York.

The Constitution

Steve Chabot, of Ohio, *Chairman.*

Steve King, of Iowa.
William L. Jenkins, of Tennessee.
Spencer Bachus, of Alabama.
John N. Hostettler, of Indiana.
Melissa A. Hart, of Pennsylvania.
Tom Feeney, of Florida.
J. Randy Forbes, of Virginia.

Jerrold Nadler, of New York.
John Conyers, Jr., of Michigan.
Robert C. Scott, of Virginia.
Melvin L. Watt, of North Carolina.
Adam B. Schiff, of California.

Courts, the Internet, and Intellectual Property

Lamar S. Smith, of Texas, *Chairman.*

Henry J. Hyde, of Illinois.
Elton Gallegly, of California.
Bob Goodlatte, of Virginia.
William L. Jenkins, of Tennessee.
Spencer Bachus, of Alabama.
Mark Green, of Wisconsin.
Ric Keller, of Florida.
Melissa A. Hart, of Pennsylvania.
Mike Pence, of Indiana.
J. Randy Forbes, of Virginia.
John Carter, of Texas.

Howard L. Berman, of California.
John Conyers, Jr., of Michigan.
Rick Boucher, of Virginia.
Zoe Lofgren, of California.
Maxine Waters, of California.
Martin T. Meehan, of Massachusetts.
William D. Delahunt, of Massachusetts.
Robert Wexler, of Florida.
Tammy Baldwin, of Wisconsin.
Anthony Weiner, of New York.

Crime, Terrorism, and Homeland Security

Howard Coble, of North Carolina, *Chairman.*

Tom Feeney, of Florida.
Bob Goodlatte, of Virginia.
Steve Chabot, of Ohio.
Mark Green, of Wisconsin.
Ric Keller, of Florida.
Mike Pence, of Indiana.
J. Randy Forbes, of Virginia.

Robert C. Scott, of Virginia.
Adam B. Schiff, of California.
Sheila Jackson Lee, of Texas.
Maxine Waters, of California.
Martin T. Meehan, of Massachusetts.

Immigration, Border Security, and Claims

John N. Hostettler, of Indiana, *Chairman.*

Jeff Flake, of Arizona.
Marsha Blackburn, of Tennessee.
Lamar S. Smith, of Texas.
Elton Gallegly, of California.
Chris Cannon, of Utah.
Steve King, of Iowa.
Melissa A. Hart, of Pennsylvania.

Sheila Jackson Lee, of Texas.
Linda Sánchez, of California.
Zoe Lofgren, of California.
Howard L. Berman, of California.
John Conyers, Jr., of Michigan.

STAFF

Committee on the Judiciary (2138 RHOB), 225–3951.
Chief of Staff/General Counsel.—Philip Kiko.
Staff Director/Deputy General Counsel.—Steve Pinkos.
Chief Legislative Counsel/Parliamentarian.—Joseph Gibson.
Counsel: Thad Bingel, Rob Tracci.
Chief Clerk/Administrator.—Tish Schwartz.
Assistant to Chief of Staff/General Counsel.—Christine Layman.
Legislative and Executive Assistant.—Chris Cylke.
Office Manager.—Michele Manon Utt.
Communications Director.—Jeff Lungren.
Press Secretary.—Terry Shawn.
Finance Clerk.—Diane Hill.
Legislative Clerk.—James David Binsted.
Computer Specialist.—Vladimir Cerga.
Calendar Clerk.—Lynn Alcock (B–29 CHOB), 5–5026.
Publications Clerk.—Joe McDonald (B–29 CHOB), 5–0408.
Receptionist.—Ann Jemison.
Printing Clerk.—Douglas Alexander.
Oversight Counsel: Art Arthur, James Daley, Patricia DeMarco, Melissa McDonald.
Senior Investigator.—Brian Zimmer.
Coalition and Projects Director.—Paul Zanowski.
Information Systems Manager.—Kerli Philippe.
Editor.—Anne M. Binsted.
Staff Assistant.—Bobby Parmiter.

Minority Chief Counsel.—Perry Apelbaum (2142 RHOB), 5–6504.
Financial and Administrative Officer.—Anita Johnson.
Senior Counsel.—Burt Wides.
General Counsel.—Ted Kalo.
Counsels: Gregory Barnes, Stacey Dansky, Alec French, Sampak Garg, Lillian German, Michone Johnson, Keenan Keller, Stephanie Moore, Nolan Rappaport, Bobby Vassar, Kirsten Wells.
Professional Staff: Danielle Brown, David G. Lachmann.
Legislative Assistants: Carolyn Donnelly, Teresa Vest.
Staff Assistants: Veronica Eligan, Susanna Gutierrez.

Subcommittee on Commercial and Administrative Law (B–353 RHOB), 5–2825.
Chief Counsel.—Raymond V. Smietanka.
Counsels: Susan Jensen, Diane Taylor.
Staff Assistant.—Christine Baldwin.
Minority Counsel.—Stephanie Moore (B–351C RHOB), 5–6906.

Subcommittee on the Constitution (H2–362 FHOB), 6–7680.
Chief Counsel.—Crystal Roberts.
Counsels: D. Michael Hurst, Paul Taylor.
Staff Assistant.—Catherine Graham.
Minority Professional Staff.—David Lachmann (B–336 RHOB), 5–2022.

Subcommittee on Courts, the Internet, and Intellectual Property (B–351A RHOB), 5–5741.
Chief Counsel.—Blaine Merritt.
Counsels: Debra Laman Rose, David Whitney.
Staff Assistant.—Eunice Goldring.
Minority Counsel.—Alec French (B–336 RHOB), 5–2329.

Subcommittee on Crime, Terrorism, and Homeland Security (207 CHOB), 5–3926.
Chief Counsel.—Jay Apperson.
Counsels: Katy Crooks, Sean McLaughlin, Beth Sokul.
Staff Assistant.—Sharon Atkinson.
Minority Counsel.—Bobby Vassar (B–336 RHOB), 5–2329.

Subcommittee on Immigration, Border Security, and Claims (B–370B RHOB), 5–5727.
Chief Counsel.—George Fishman.
Counsel.—Lora Ries.
Professional Staff.—Cynthia Blackston.
Staff Assistant.—Emily Sanders.
Minority Counsel.—Nolan Rappaport (B–336 RHOB), 5–2329.

Resources

1324 Longworth House Office Building, phone 225–2761

http://www.house.gov/resources

meets each Wednesday

Richard W. Pombo, of California, *Chairman.*

Jim Gibbons, of Nevada, *Vice Chairman.*

Don Young, of Alaska.
W.J. (Billy) Tauzin, of Louisiana.
Jim Saxton, of New Jersey.
Elton Gallegly, of California.
John J. Duncan, Jr., of Tennessee.
Wayne T. Gilchrest, of Maryland.
Ken Calvert, of California.
Scott McInnis, of Colorado.
Barbara Cubin, of Wyoming.
George P. Radanovich, of California.
Walter B. Jones, of North Carolina.
Chris Cannon, of Utah.
John E. Peterson, of Pennsylvania.
Mark E. Souder, of Indiana.
Greg Walden, of Oregon.
Thomas G. Tancredo, of Colorado.
J.D. Hayworth, of Arizona.
Tom Osborne, of Nebraska.
Jeff Flake, of Arizona.
Dennis R. Rehberg, of Montana.
Rick Renzi, of Arizona.
Tom Cole, of Oklahoma.
Stevan Pearce, of New Mexico.
Rob Bishop, of Utah.
Devin Nunes, of California.
Randy Neugebauer, of Texas.

Nick J. Rahall II, of West Virginia.
Dale E. Kildee, of Michigan.
Eni F.H. Faleomavaega, of American Samoa.
Neil Abercrombie, of Hawaii.
Solomon P. Ortiz, of Texas.
Frank Pallone, Jr., of New Jersey.
Calvin M. Dooley of California.
Donna M. Christensen, of the Virgin Islands.
Ron Kind, of Wisconsin.
Jay Inslee, of Washington.
Grace F. Napolitano, of California.
Tom Udall, of New Mexico.
Mark Udall, of Colorado.
Aníbal Acevedo-Vilá, of Puerto Rico.
Brad Carson, of Oklahoma.
Raúl M. Grijalva, of Arizona.
Dennis A. Cardoza, of California.
Madeleine Z. Bordallo, of Guam.
George Miller, of California.
Edward J. Markey, of Massachusetts.
Rubén Hinojosa, of Texas.
Ciro D. Rodriguez, of Texas.
Joe Baca, of California.
Betty McCollum, of Minnesota.

SUBCOMMITTEES

[The chairman and ranking minority member are ex officio (non-voting) members of all subcommittees on which they do not serve.]

Energy and Mineral Resources

Barbara Cubin, of Wyoming, *Chair.*

W.J. (Billy) Tauzin, of Louisiana.
Chris Cannon, of Utah.
Jim Gibbons, of Nevada.
Mark E. Souder, of Indiana.
Dennis R. Rehberg, of Montana.
Tom Cole, of Oklahoma.
Stevan Pearce, of New Mexico.
Rob Bishop, of Utah.
Devin Nunes, of California.

Ron Kind, of Wisconsin.
Eni F.H. Faleomavaega, of American Samoa.
Solomon P. Ortiz, of Texas.
Grace F. Napolitano, of California.
Tom Udall, of New Mexico.
Brad Carson, of Oklahoma.
Edward J. Markey, of Massachusetts.

Fisheries Conservation, Wildlife, and Oceans

Wayne T. Gilchrest, of Maryland, *Chairman.*

Don Young, of Alaska.
W.J. (Billy) Tauzin, of Louisiana.
Jim Saxton, of New Jersey.
Mark E. Souder, of Indiana.
Walter B. Jones, of North Carolina.
Randy Neugebauer, of Texas.

Frank Pallone, Jr., of New Jersey.
Eni F.H. Faleomavaega, of American Samoa.
Neil Abercrombie, of Hawaii.
Solomon P. Ortiz, of Texas.
Madeleine Z. Bordallo, of Guam.
Ron Kind, of Wisconsin.

Forests and Forest Health

Scott McInnis, of Colorado, *Chairman.*

John J. Duncan, Jr., of Tennessee.
Walter B. Jones, of North Carolina.
John E. Peterson, of Pennsylvania.
Thomas G. Tancredo, of Colorado.
J.D. Hayworth, of Arizona.
Jeff Flake, of Arizona.
Dennis R. Rehberg, of Montana.
Rick Renzi, of Arizona.
Stevan Pearce, of New Mexico.

Jay Inslee, of Washington.
Dale E. Kildee, of Michigan.
Tom Udall, of New Mexico.
Mark Udall, of Colorado.
Aníbal Acevedo-Vilá, of Puerto Rico.
Brad Carson, of Oklahoma.
Betty McCollum, of Minnesota.

National Parks, Recreation, and Public Lands

George P. Radanovich, of California, *Chairman.*

Elton Gallegly, of California.
John J. Duncan, Jr., of Tennessee.
Wayne T. Gilchrest, of Maryland.
Barbara Cubin, of Wyoming.
Walter B. Jones, of North Carolina.
Chris Cannon, of Utah.
John E. Peterson, of Pennsylvania.
Jim Gibbons, of Nevada.
Mark E. Souder, of Indiana.
Rob Bishop, of Utah.

Donna M. Christensen, of the Virgin Islands.
Dale E. Kildee, of Michigan.
Ron Kind, of Wisconsin.
Tom Udall, of New Mexico.
Mark Udall, of Colorado.
Aníbal Acevedo-Vilá, of Puerto Rico.
Raúl M. Grijalva, of Arizona.
Dennis A. Cardoza, of California.
Madeleine Z. Bordallo, of Guam.

Water and Power

Ken Calvert, of California, *Chairman.*

George P. Radanovich, of California.
Greg Walden, of Oregon.
Thomas G. Tancredo, of Colorado.
J.D. Hayworth, of Arizona.
Tom Osborne, of Nebraska.
Rick Renzi, of Arizona.
Stevan Pearce, of New Mexico.
Devin Nunes, of California.

Grace F. Napolitano, of California.
Calvin M. Dooley of California.
Jay Inslee, of Washington.
Raúl M. Grijalva, of Arizona.
Dennis A. Cardoza, of California.
George Miller, of California.
Ciro D. Rodriguez, of Texas.
Joe Baca, of California.

STAFF

Committee on Resources (1324 LHOB), 225–2761.
Chief of Staff.—Steve Ding.
Executive Assistant to the Chief of Staff.—Linda Livingston.
Chief Counsel.—Lisa Pittman (1320 LHOB), 5–7800.
Deputy Chief Counsel.—Vince Sampson, 5–6869.
Legislative Assistant to the Chief Counsel.—Joanna MacKay, 5–7800.
Chief Financial Officer.—Lisa Wallace (1327A LHOB), 5–8133.
Chief Clerk.—Nancy Laheeb (1328 LHOB), 5–7611.
Legislative Calendar Clerk.—Ann Vogt, 5–5282.
Communications Director.—Doug Heye (1334 LHOB), 6–9019.
Communications Coordinator.—Matthew Streit.
Press Secretary.—Brian Kennedy (1334 LHOB), 6–6915.
Systems Administrators: Ed Van Scoyoc, Matt Vaccaro (1322 LHOB), 5–1975.
Senior Policy Director.—Todd Willens (1331 LHOB), 5–2761.
Professional Staff: Tom Brierton (1413P LHOB), 5–2761; Kurt Christensen (1413P LHOB), 5–2761; Matt S. Miller (1324 LHOB).
Senior Advisor.—Dan Kish (1331 LHOB) 5–2761.
Staff Assistant.—Matt Lauver.
Editors and Printers: Kathleen Miller, Natalie Nixon (550 Ford), 6–3529.

Minority Staff Director.—James H. Zoia (1329 LHOB), 225–6065.
Chief Counsel.—Jeffrey Petrich.
Administrator.—Linda Booth.
Staff Assistants: Jennifer Gould; Tracey Parker (186 LHOB), 6–2311.
Press Secretary.—Helen Machado (269 FHOB), 6–2311.
Assistant Press Secretary.—Kristen Bossi.

Subcommittee on Energy and Mineral Resources (1626 LHOB), 225–9297; fax 225–5255.
Staff Director.—Jack Belcher.
Clerk.—Lucas Frances.
Minority Staff: Deborah van Hoffman Lazone, Ben Winburn (186 FHOB), 226–2311.

Subcommittee on Fisheries Conservation, Wildlife, and Oceans (H2–188 FHOB), 226–0200; fax 225–1542.
Staff Director.—Harry Burroughs.
Legislative Staff: Bonnie Bruce, Dave Whaley.
Clerk.—Michael Correia.
Minority Staff.—Dave Jansen, Lori Sonken, Catherine Ware (186 FHOB), 226–2311.

Subcommittee on Forests and Forest Health (1337 LHOB), 225–0691; fax 225–0521.
Staff Director.—Josh Penry.
Legislative Staff.—Amie Brown; Erica Tergeson.
Clerk.—Teresa Fierro.
Minority Staff.—Erica Rosenberg, Lori Sonken (269 FHOB), 226–2311.

Subcommittee on National Parks, Recreation, and Public Lands (1333 LHOB), 226–7736; fax 226–2301.
Staff Director.—Rob Howarth.
Clerk.—Casey Hammond.
Minority Staff.—David Watkins, Richard Healy (186 FHOB), 226–2311.

Subcommittee on Water and Power (1522 LHOB), 225–8331; fax 226–6953.
Staff Director.—Joshua Johnson.
Legislative Staff.—Kiel Weaver.
Clerk.—Daisy Minter.
Minority Staff.—J. Stevens Lanich (186 FHOB), Lori Sonken, (269 FHOB), 226–2311.

Office of Native American and Insular Affairs (140 CHOB), 226–9725; fax 225–7094.
Staff Director.—Christopher Fluhr, 5–6523.
Legislative Staff: Cynthia Ahwinona.
Minority Staff.—Tony Babauta, Marie Howard Fabrizio, Heather Hausburg, (186 FHOB), 226–2311.

Rules

H–312 The Capitol, phone 225–9191

http://www.house.gov/rules

meets every Tuesday

David Dreier, of California, *Chairman.*

Porter Goss, of Florida, *Vice Chairman.*

John Linder, of Georgia.
Deborah Pryce, of Ohio.
Lincoln Diaz-Balart, of Florida.
Doc Hastings, of Washington.
Sue Wilkins Myrick, of North Carolina.
Pete Sessions, of Texas.
Thomas M. Reynolds, of New York.

Martin Frost, of Texas.
Louise M. Slaughter, of New York.
James P. McGovern, of Massachusetts.
Alcee L. Hastings, of Florida.

SUBCOMMITTEES

Legislative and Budget Process

Deborah Pryce, of Ohio, *Chair.*

Lincoln Diaz-Balart, *Vice Chairman.*

Porter Goss, of Florida.
Doc Hastings, of Washington.
David Dreier, of California.

Louise M. Slaughter, of New York.
Martin Frost, of Texas.

Technology and the House

John Linder, of Georgia, *Chairman.*

Sue Wilkins Myrick, of North Carolina, *Vice Chairman.*

Pete Sessions, of Texas.
Thomas M. Reynolds, of New York.
David Dreier, of California.

James P. McGovern, of Massachusetts.
Alcee L. Hastings, of Florida.

STAFF

Committee on Rules (H–312 The Capitol), 225–9191.
Staff Director.– Bill Pitts.
Press Secretary.—Jo Powers.
Policy Director.—Amy Heerink.
Professional Staff: Stephanie Blanto, Adam Jarvis, Dan Mathews, George Rogers, Celeste West.
Legislative Clerk.—Eileen Harley.
Staff Assistant.—Kelly Blanchard.
Minority Staff Director.—Kristi Walseth (H–152), 5–9091.
Professional Staff: John A. Daniel, Katherine Sophie Hayford, (234 CHOB), 5–9486.
Associate Staff: Clyde Henderson, 5–3615; Keith Stern, 5–6101; Fred Turner, 5–1313.
Subcommittee on Legislative and Budget Process (421 CHOB), 225–2015.
Staff Director.—J.C. Scott.
Minority Staff Director.—Clyde Henderson (2347 RHOB), 5–3615.
Subcommittee on Technology and the House (421 CHOB), 225–4272.
Staff Director.—Don Green.
Minority Staff Director.—Keith Stern (LHOB), 5–6465.

Science

2320 Rayburn House Office Building, phone 225–6371, fax 226–0113
http://www.house.gov/science

meets second and fourth Wednesdays of each month

Sherwood Boehlert, of New York, *Chairman.*

Lamar S. Smith, of Texas.
Curt Weldon, of Pennsylvania.
Dana Rohrabacher, of California.
Joe Barton, of Texas.
Ken Calvert, of California.
Nick Smith, of Michigan.
Roscoe G. Bartlett, of Maryland.
Vernon J. Ehlers, of Michigan.
Gil Gutknecht, of Minnesota.
George R. Nethercutt, Jr., of Washington.
Frank D. Lucas, of Oklahoma.
Judy Biggert, of Illinois.
Wayne T. Gilchrest, of Maryland.
W. Todd Akin, of Missouri.
Timothy V. Johnson, of Illinois.
Melissa A. Hart, of Pennsylvania.
John Sullivan, of Oklahoma.
J. Randy Forbes, of Virginia.
Phil Gingrey, of Georgia.
Rob Bishop, of Utah.
Michael C. Burgess, of Texas.
Jo Bonner, of Alabama.
Tom Feeney, of Florida.
Randy Neugebauer, of Texas.

Ralph M. Hall, of Texas.
Bart Gordon, of Tennessee.
Jerry F. Costello, of Illinois.
Eddie Bernice Johnson, of Texas.
Lynn C. Woolsey, of California.
Nick Lampson, of Texas.
John B. Larson, of Connecticut.
Mark Udall, of Colorado.
David Wu, of Oregon.
Michael M. Honda, of California.
Chris Bell, of Texas.
Brad Miller, of North Carolina.
Lincoln Davis, of Tennessee.
Sheila Jackson Lee, of Texas.
Zoe Lofgren, of California.
Brad Sherman, of California.
Brian Baird, of Washington.
Dennis Moore, of Kansas.
Anthony D. Weiner, of New York.
Jim Matheson, of Utah.
Dennis A. Cardoza, of California.

SUBCOMMITTEES

[The chairman and ranking minority member are ex officio (voting) members of all subcommittees on which they do not serve.]

Energy

Judy Biggert, of Illinois, *Chairman.*

Curt Weldon, of Pennsylvania.
Roscoe G. Bartlett, of Maryland.
Vernon J. Ehlers, of Michigan.
George R. Nethercutt, Jr., of Washington.
W. Todd Akin, of Missouri.
Melissa A. Hart, of Pennsylvania.
Phil Gingrey, of Georgia.
Jo Bonner, of Alabama.

Nick Lampson, of Texas.
Jerry F. Costello, of Illinois.
Lynn C. Woolsey, of California.
David Wu, of Oregon.
Michael M. Honda, of California.
Brad Miller, of North Carolina.
Lincoln Davis, of Tennessee.

Environment, Technology, and Standards

Vernon J. Ehlers, of Michigan, *Chairman.*

Nick Smith, of Michigan.
Gil Gutknecht, of Minnesota.
Judy Biggert, of Illinois.
Wayne T. Gilchrest, of Maryland.
Timothy V. Johnson, of Illinois.
Michael C. Burgess, of Texas.

Mark Udall, of Colorado.
Brad Miller, of North Carolina.
Lincoln Davis, of Tennessee.
Brian Baird, of Washington.
Jim Matheson, of Utah.
Zoe Lofgren, of California.

Research

Nick Smith, of Michigan, *Chairman.*

Lamar S. Smith, of Texas.
Dana Rohrabacher, of California.
Gil Gutknecht, of Minnesota.
Frank D. Lucas, of Oklahoma.
W. Todd Akin, of Missouri.
Timothy V. Johnson, of Illinois.
Melissa A. Hart, of Pennsylvania.
John Sullivan, of Oklahoma.
Phil Gingrey, of Georgia.

Eddie Bernice Johnson, of Texas.
Michael M. Honda, of California.
Zoe Lofgren, of California.
Dennis A. Cardoza, of California.
Brad Sherman, of California.
Dennis Moore, of Kansas.
Jim Matheson, of Utah.
Sheila Jackson Lee, of Texas.

Space and Aeronautics

Dana Rohrabacher, of California, *Chairman.*

Lamar S. Smith, of Texas.
Curt Weldon, of Pennsylvania.
Joe Barton, of Texas.
Ken Calvert, of California.
Roscoe G. Bartlett, of Maryland.
George R. Nethercutt, Jr., of Washington.
Frank D. Lucas, of Oklahoma.
John Sullivan, of Oklahoma.
J. Randy Forbes, of Virginia.
Rob Bishop, of Utah.
Michael C. Burgess, of Texas.
Jo Bonner, of Alabama.
Tom Feeney, of Florida.

Bart Gordon, of Tennessee.
John B. Larson, of Connecticut.
Chris Bell, of Texas.
Nick Lampson, of Texas.
Mark Udall, of Colorado.
David Wu, of Oregon.
Eddie Bernice Johnson, of Texas.
Sheila Jackson Lee, of Texas.
Brad Sherman, of California.
Dennis Moore, of Kansas.
Anthony D. Weiner, of New York.

STAFF

Committee on Science (2320 RHOB), 225–6371, fax 226–0113.
Chief of Staff.—David Goldston, 5–8772.
Chief Counsel.—Barry Beringer, 5–8772.
Deputy Chief of Staff: Scott Giles (Research; Space and Aeronautics), 5–1199, John Mimikakis (Energy; Environment, Technology, and Standards), 5–1199, fax 5–3170.
Communications Director.—Heidi Tringe, 5–4275.
Projects Director.—Tim Clancy, 5–1199, fax 5–3170.
Associate General Counsel.—Mike Bloomquist, 5–1199.
Financial Administrator.—Dave Laughter, 5–8772.
Deputy Communications Director/Administrative Clerk.—Jeff Donald, 5–4275.
Legislative Clerk.—Vivian Tessieri.
Systems Administrator.—Larry Whittaker.
Printer.—Jude Ruckel.
Special Assistant to the Chief of Staff.—Adam Shampaine, 5–8772.
Special Assistant to the Chief Counsel.—Jason Cervenak, 5–8772.
Legislative Assistant.—Joe Pouliot, 5–1199.
Staff Assistants: Leslie Caudle, 5–1199, Colin Hubbell.
Minority Staff Director.—Bob Palmer (394 FHOB), 5–6375, fax 5–3895.
Chief Counsel.—Jim Turner.
Professional Staff.—Chris King, James Paul, Dan Pearson.
Counsel: Mike Lynch, Marsha Shasteen.
Senior Staff Assistant.—Mary Sanchez.
Staff Assistant.—Terese McDonald.
Subcommittee on Energy (390 FHOB) 5–9662, fax 6–6983.
Staff Director.—Gabe Rozsa.
Professional Staff, Chairman's Designee.—[Vacant].
Professional Staff: Eli Hopson, Tina Kaarsburg.
Staff Assistant.—Kate Sullivan.
Minority Staff Director.—Charlie Cook.

Subcommittee on Environment, Technology, and Standards (2319 RHOB), 5–8844, fax 5–4438.
Staff Director.—Eric Webster.
Professional Staff, Chairman's Designee.—[Vacant].
Professional Staff: Susannah Foster, Olwen Huxley, Marty Spitzer.
AAAS Fellow.—Amy Carroll.
NIH Detailee.—Kevin Wheeler.
Staff Assistant.—Elyse Stratton.
Minority Professional Staff: Jean Frucci, Mike Quear.
Staff Assistant.—Marty Ralston.

Subcommittee on Research (B–374 RHOB), 5–7858, fax 5–7815.
Staff Director.—Peter Rooney.
Professional Staff, Chairman's Designee.—Dan Byers.
Professional Staff: Greg Garcia, Elizabeth Grossman, Kara Haas.
NIH Detailee.—Kevin Wheeler.
Staff Assistant.—Jeremy Johnson.
Minority Professional Staff.—Jim Wilson.

Subcommittee on Space and Aeronautics (B–374 RHOB), 5–7858, fax 5–6415.
Staff Director.—Bill Adkins.
Professional Staff, Chairman's Designee.—Ruben Van Mitchell.
Professional Staff: Ed Feddeman, Ken Monroe, Chris Shank.
Staff Assistant.—Tom Hammond.
Minority Professional Staff.—Dick Obermann.

Small Business

2361 Rayburn House Office Building, phone 225–5821, fax 225–3587

http://www.house.gov/smbiz

meets second Thursday of each month

Donald A. Manzullo, of Illinois, *Chairman.*

Roscoe G. Bartlett, of Maryland.
Sue W. Kelly, of New York.
Steve Chabot, of Ohio.
Patrick J. Toomey, of Pennsylvania.
Jim DeMint, of South Carolina.
Sam Graves, of Missouri.
Edward L. Schrock, of Virginia.
W. Todd Akin, of Missouri.
Shelley Moore Capito, of West Virginia.
Bill Shuster, of Pennsylvania.
Marilyn N. Musgrave, of Colorado.
Trent Franks, of Arizona.
Jim Gerlach, of Pennsylvania.
Jeb Bradley, of New Hampshire.
Bob Beauprez, of Colorado.
Chris Chocola, of Indiana.
Steve King, of Iowa.
Thaddeus McCotter, of Michigan.

Nydia M. Velázquez, of New York.
Juanita Millender-McDonald, of California.
Tom Udall, of New Mexico.
Frank Ballance, of North Carolina.
Eni Faleomavaega, of American Samoa.
Donna M. Christensen, of Virgin Islands.
Danny K. Davis, of Illinois.
Charles A. Gonzalez, of Texas.
Grace F. Napolitano, of California.
Aníbal Acevedo-Vilá, of Puerto Rico.
Ed Case, of Hawaii.
Madeleine Bordallo, of Guam.
Denise Majette, of Georgia.
Jim Marshall, of Georgia.
Michael Michaud, of Maine.
Linda Sánchez, of California.
Brad Miller, of North Carolina.

SUBCOMMITTEES

[The chairman and ranking minority member are ex officio (non-voting) members of all subcommittees on which they do not serve.]

Regulatory Reform and Oversight

Edward L. Schrock, of Virginia, *Chairman.*

Roscoe G. Bartlett, of Maryland.
Sue W. Kelly, of New York.
Trent Franks, of Arizona.
Jeb Bradley, of New Hampshire.
Steve King, of Iowa.
Thaddeus McCotter, of Michigan.

Charles A. Gonzalez, of Texas.
Donna M. Christensen, of Virgin Islands.
Aníbal Acevedo-Vilá, of Puerto Rico.
Denise Majette, of Georgia.

Rural Enterprises, Agriculture, and Technology

Sam Graves, of Missouri, *Chairman.*

Bill Shuster, of Pennsylvania.
Sue W. Kelly, of New York.
Shelley Moore Capito, of West Virginia.
Marilyn N. Musgrave, of Colorado.
Patrick J. Toomey, of Pennsylvania.

Frank Ballance, of North Carolina.
Michael Michaud, of Maine.
Donna M. Christensen, of Virgin Islands.
Ed Case, of Hawaii.
Madeleine Bordallo, of Guam.

Tax, Finance, and Exports

Patrick J. Toomey, of Pennsylvania, *Chairman.*

Steve Chabot, of Ohio.
Marilyn N. Musgrave, of Colorado.
Jim Gerlach, of Pennsylvania.
Bob Beauprez, of Colorado.
Trent Franks, of Arizona.
Jim DeMint, of South Carolina.
Chris Chocola, of Indiana.

Juanita Millender-McDonald, of California.
Jim Marshall, of Georgia.
Frank Ballance, of North Carolina.
Danny K. Davis, of Illinois.
Aníbal Acevedo-Vilá, of Puerto Rico.
Denise Majette, of Georgia.
Michael Michaud, of Maine.

Workforce, Empowerment, and Government Programs

W. Todd Akin, of Missouri, *Chairman.*

Jim DeMint, of South Carolina.
Shelley Moore Capito, of West Virginia.
Jeb Bradley, of New Hampshire.
Chris Chocola, of Indiana.
Steve King, of Iowa.
Thaddeus McCotter, of Michigan.

Tom Udall, of New Mexico.
Danny K. Davis, of Illinois.
Charles A. Gonzalez, of Texas.
Grace F. Napolitano, of California.
Ed Case, of Hawaii.
Madeleine Bordallo, of Guam.

STAFF

Committee on Small Business (2361 RHOB), 225–5821, fax 225–3587.
Chief of Staff/Chief Counsel.—Matt Szymanski.
Policy Director.—Phil Eskeland.
Chief Clerk.—Nancy Piper.
General Counsel.—Nelson Crowther.
Counsels: Greg Dean (Finance); Barry Pineles (Regulatory).
Communications Director.—Rich Carter.
Press/Systems Manager.—Mike Arlinsky.
Legislative Director.—Patrick Wilson.
Legislative Assistant.—Laura Smith.
Finance Administrator/Special Assistant.—Christy Markva.
Professional Staff/Special Assistant—Ian Deason.
Staff Assistant.—Sean Deverey.
Oversight Counsel.—Brad Knox.
Chief Tax Counsel.—Jim Clark.
Commerce Detailee.—Mike Fullerton.
Minority Staff Director.—Michael Day (B–343C RHOB), 225–4038, fax 225–7209.
Office Manager.—Mory Garcia.
Communications Director.—Wendy Belzer.
Deputy Communications Director.—Kate Davis.
Professional Staff: LeAnn Delaney, Jordan Haas, Adam Minehardt, Tim Slattery.
Subcommittee on Regulatory Reform and Oversight (2361 RHOB), 225–5821, fax 225–3587.
Professional Staff.—Rosario Palmieri.
Subcommittee on Tax, Finance, and Exports (B–363 RHOB), 225–5821, fax 225–3587.
Professional Staff.—Joe Hartz.
Subcommittee on Workforce, Empowerment, and Government Programs (2361 RHOB), 225–5821, fax 225–3587.
Professional Staff.—Thomas Bezas.
Subcommittee on Rural Enterprises, Agriculture, and Technology (B–363 RHOB), 225–5821, fax 225–3587.
Professional Staff.—Piper Largent.

Standards of Official Conduct

HT–2 The Capitol, phone 225–7103, fax 225–7392

Joel Hefley, of Colorado, *Chairman.*

Doc Hastings, of Washington.
Judy Biggert, of Illinois.
Kenny C. Hulshof, of Missouri.
Steven C. LaTourette, of Ohio.

Alan B. Mollohan, of West Virginia.
Stephanie Tubbs Jones, of Ohio.
Gene Green, of Texas.
Lucille Roybal-Allard, of California.
Michael F. Doyle, of Pennsylvania.

(No Subcommittees)

STAFF

Chief Counsel / Staff Director.—John E. Vargo.
Counsel to the Chairman.—Virginia H. Johnson.
Assistant to the Ranking Minority Member.—Colleen McCarty.
Counsels: Carol E. Dixon, Kenneth E. Kellner, Paul M. Lewis, Bernadette C. Sargeant, John C. Sassaman, Jr., Reed D. Slack.
System Administrator.—Christine Stevens.
Staff Assistant.—Brooke Watson.
Administrative Assistant.—Joanne White.

Transportation and Infrastructure

2165 Rayburn House Office Building, phone 225–9446, fax 225–6782

http://www.house.gov/transportation

meets first Wednesday of each month

Don Young, of Alaska, *Chairman.*

Thomas E. Petri, of Wisconsin.
Sherwood Boehlert, of New York.
Howard Coble, of North Carolina.
John J. Duncan, Jr., of Tennessee.
Wayne T. Gilchrest, of Maryland.
John L. Mica, of Florida.
Peter Hoekstra, of Michigan.
Jack Quinn, of New York.
Vernon J. Ehlers, of Michigan.
Spencer Bachus, of Alabama.
Steven C. LaTourette, of Ohio.
Sue W. Kelly, of New York.
Richard H. Baker, of Louisiana.
Robert W. Ney, of Ohio.
Frank A. LoBiondo, of New Jersey.
Jerry Moran, of Kansas.
Gary G. Miller, of California.
Jim DeMint, of South Carolina.
Doug Bereuter, of Nebraska.
Johnny Isakson, of Georgia.
Robin Hayes, of North Carolina.
Rob Simmons, of Connecticut.
Shelley Moore Capito, of West Virginia.
Henry E. Brown, Jr., of South Carolina.
Timothy V. Johnson, of Illinois.
Dennis R. Rehberg, of Montana.
Todd Russell Platts, of Pennsylvania.
Sam Graves, of Missouri.
Mark R. Kennedy, of Minnesota.
Bill Shuster, of Pennsylvania.
John Boozman, of Arkansas.
John Sullivan, of Oklahoma.
Chris Chocola, of Indiana.
Bob Beauprez, of Colorado.
Michael C. Burgess, of Texas.
Max Burns, of Georgia.
Stevan Pearce, of New Mexico.
Jim Gerlach, of Pennsylvania.
Mario Diaz-Balart, of Florida.
Jon C. Porter, of Nevada.

James L. Oberstar, of Minnesota.
Nick J. Rahall II, of West Virginia.
William O. Lipinski, of Illinois.
Peter A. DeFazio, of Oregon.
Jerry F. Costello, of Illinois.
Eleanor Holmes Norton, of the District of Columbia.
Jerrold Nadler, of New York.
Robert Menendez, of New Jersey.
Corrine Brown, of Florida.
Bob Filner, of California.
Eddie Bernice Johnson, of Texas.
Gene Taylor, of Mississippi.
Juanita Millender-McDonald, of California.
Elijah E. Cummings, of Maryland.
Earl Blumenauer, of Oregon.
Ellen O. Tauscher, of California.
Bill Pascrell, Jr., of New Jersey.
Leonard L. Boswell, of Iowa.
Tim Holden, of Pennsylvania.
Nick Lampson, of Texas.
Brian Baird, of Washington.
Shelley Berkley, of Nevada.
Brad Carson, of Oklahoma.
Jim Matheson, of Utah.
Michael M. Honda, of California.
Rick Larsen, of Washington.
Michael E. Capuano, of Massachusetts.
Anthony D. Weiner, of New York.
Julia Carson, of Indiana.
Joseph M. Hoeffel, of Pennsylvania.
Mike Thompson, of California.
Timothy H. Bishop, of New York.
Michael H. Michaud, of Maine.
Lincoln Davis, of Tennessee.

SUBCOMMITTEES

[The chairman and ranking minority member are ex officio (voting) members of all subcommittees on which they do not serve.]

Aviation

John L. Mica, of Florida, *Chairman.*

Thomas E. Petri, of Wisconsin.
John J. Duncan, Jr., of Tennessee.
Jack Quinn, of New York.
Vernon J. Ehlers, of Michigan.
Spencer Bachus, of Alabama.
Sue W. Kelly, of New York.
Richard H. Baker, of Louisiana.
Frank A. LoBiondo, of New Jersey.
Jerry Moran, of Kansas.
Johnny Isakson, of Georgia.
Robin Hayes, of North Carolina.
Timothy V. Johnson, of Illinois.
Dennis R. Rehberg, of Montana.
Sam Graves, of Missouri.
Mark R. Kennedy, of Minnesota.
Bill Shuster, of Pennsylvania.
John Boozman, of Arkansas.
John Sullivan, of Oklahoma.
Chris Chocola, of Indiana.
Bob Beauprez, of Colorado.
Stevan Pearce, of New Mexico.
Jim Gerlach, of Pennsylvania.
Mario Diaz-Balart, of Florida.
Jon C. Porter, of Nevada.

Peter A. DeFazio, of Oregon.
Leonard L. Boswell, of Iowa.
William O. Lipinski, of Illinois.
Jerry F. Costello, of Illinois.
Eleanor Holmes Norton, of the District of Columbia.
Robert Menendez, of New Jersey.
Corrine Brown, of Florida.
Eddie Bernice Johnson, of Texas.
Juanita Millender-McDonald, of California.
Ellen O. Tauscher, of California.
Bill Pascrell, Jr., of New Jersey.
Tim Holden, of Pennsylvania.
Shelley Berkley, of Nevada.
Brad Carson, of Oklahoma.
Jim Matheson, of Utah.
Michael M. Honda, of California.
Rick Larsen, of Washington.
Michael E. Capuano, of Massachusetts.
Anthony D. Weiner, of New York.
Nick J. Rahall II, of West Virginia.
Bob Filner, of California.

Coast Guard and Maritime Transportation

Frank A. LoBiondo, of New Jersey, *Chairman.*

Howard Coble, of North Carolina.
Wayne T. Gilchrest, of Maryland.
Peter Hoekstra, of Michigan.
Jim DeMint, of South Carolina.
Rob Simmons, of Connecticut.
Mario Diaz-Balart, of Florida.

Bob Filner, of California.
Peter A. DeFazio, of Oregon.
Corrine Brown, of Florida.
Juanita Millender-McDonald, of California.
Nick Lampson, of Texas.
Mike Thompson, of California.

Economic Development, Public Buildings, and Emergency Management

Steven C. LaTourette, of Ohio, *Chairman.*

Shelley Moore Capito, of West Virginia.
Michael C. Burgess, of Texas.
Max Burns, of Georgia.
Jim Gerlach, of Pennsylvania.

Eleanor Holmes Norton, of the District of Columbia.
Lincoln Davis, of Tennessee.
Brad Carson, of Oklahoma.
Michael H. Michaud, of Maine.

Highways, Transit and Pipelines

Thomas E. Petri, of Wisconsin, *Chairman.*

Sherwood Boehlert, of New York.
Howard Coble, of North Carolina.
John J. Duncan, Jr., of Tennessee.
John L. Mica, of Florida.
Peter Hoekstra, of Michigan.
Jack Quinn, of New York.
Steven C. LaTourette, of Ohio.
Sue W. Kelly, of New York.
Richard H. Baker, of Louisiana.
Robert W. Ney, of Ohio.
Frank A. LoBiondo, of New Jersey.
Jerry Moran, of Kansas.
Jim DeMint, of South Carolina.
Doug Bereuter, of Nebraska.
Johnny Isakson, of Georgia.
Robin Hayes, of North Carolina.
Rob Simmons, of Connecticut.
Shelley Moore Capito, of West Virginia.
Henry E. Brown, Jr., of South Carolina.
Timothy V. Johnson, of Illinois.
Dennis R. Rehberg, of Montana.
Todd Russell Platts, of Pennsylvania.
Sam Graves, of Missouri.
Mark R. Kennedy, of Minnesota.
Bill Shuster, of Pennsylvania.
John Boozman, of Arkansas.
Bob Beauprez, of Colorado.
Michael C. Burgess, of Texas.
Max Burns, of Georgia.

William O. Lipinski, of Illinois.
Nick J. Rahall II, of West Virginia.
Jerrold Nadler, of New York.
Eddie Bernice Johnson, of Texas.
Gene Taylor, of Mississippi.
Juanita Millender-McDonald, of California.
Elijah E. Cummings, of Maryland.
Ellen O. Tauscher, of California.
Bill Pascrell, Jr., of New Jersey.
Tim Holden, of Pennsylvania.
Brian Baird, of Washington.
Shelley Berkley, of Nevada.
Brad Carson, of Oklahoma.
Jim Matheson, of Utah.
Michael M. Honda, of California.
Rick Larsen, of Washington.
Michael E. Capuano, of Massachusetts.
Earl Blumenauer, of Oregon.
Nick Lampson, of Texas.
Anthony D. Weiner, of New York.
Julia Carson, of Indiana.
Joseph M. Hoeffel, of Pennsylvania.
Mike Thompson, of California.
Timothy H. Bishop, of New York.
Michael H. Michaud, of Maine.

Railroads

Jack Quinn, of New York, *Chairman.*

Thomas E. Petri, of Wisconsin.
Sherwood Boehlert, of New York.
Howard Coble, of North Carolina.
John L. Mica, of Florida.
Spencer Bachus, of Alabama.
Jerry Moran, of Kansas.
Gary G. Miller, of California.
Jim DeMint, of South Carolina.
Rob Simmons, of Connecticut.
Shelley Moore Capito, of West Virginia.
Todd Russell Platts, of Pennsylvania.
Sam Graves, of Missouri.
Jon C. Porter, of Nevada.

Corrine Brown, of Florida.
Nick J. Rahall II, of West Virginia.
Peter A. DeFazio, of Oregon.
Jerrold Nadler, of New York.
Bob Filner, of California.
Elijah E. Cummings, of Maryland.
Earl Blumenauer, of Oregon.
Leonard L. Boswell, of Iowa.
Julia Carson, of Indiana.
Michael H. Michaud, of Maine.
William O. Lipinski, of Illinois.
Jerry F. Costello, of Illinois.

Water Resources and Environment

John J. Duncan, Jr., of Tennessee, *Chairman.*

Sherwood Boehlert, of New York.
Wayne T. Gilchrest, of Maryland.
Vernon J. Ehlers, of Michigan.
Steven C. LaTourette, of Ohio.
Sue W. Kelly, of New York.
Richard H. Baker, of Louisiana.
Robert W. Ney, of Ohio.
Gary G. Miller, of California.
Johnny Isakson, of Georgia.
Robin Hayes, of North Carolina.
Henry E. Brown, Jr., of South Carolina.
Bill Shuster, of Pennsylvania.
John Boozman, of Arkansas.
John Sullivan, of Oklahoma.
Chris Chocola, of Indiana.
Stevan Pearce, of New Mexico.
Jim Gerlach, of Pennsylvania.
Mario Diaz-Balart, of Florida.

Jerry F. Costello, of Illinois.
Robert Menendez, of New Jersey.
Gene Taylor, of Mississippi.
Nick Lampson, of Texas.
Brian Baird, of Washington.
Joseph M. Hoeffel, of Pennsylvania.
Mike Thompson, of California.
Timothy H. Bishop, of New York.
Lincoln Davis, of Tennessee.
Eleanor Holmes Norton, of the District of Columbia.
Jerrold Nadler, of New York.
Eddie Bernice Johnson, of Texas.
Earl Blumenauer, of Oregon.
Ellen O. Tauscher, of California.
Bill Pascrell, Jr., of New Jersey.

STAFF

Committee on Transportation and Infrastructure (2165 RHOB), 225–9446, fax 225–6782.
Chief of Staff.—Lloyd Jones.
Administrator.—Christine Kennedy.
Chief Counsel.—Elizabeth Megginson.
Deputy Chief Counsel/Parliamentarian.—Charles Ziegler.
Special Assistant to the Chief Counsel.—Kimberlee Saranko.
Director of Committee Facilities/Travel.—Jimmy Miller.
Special Counsel.—Raga Elim.
Executive Assistant to Chief of Staff.—Debbie Callis.
Policy Director.—Fraser Verrusio.
Financial Administrator.—Will Stevens.
Communications Director.—Steve Hansen.
Deputy Communications Director.—Justin Harclerode.
Manager, Information Systems.—Keven Sard.
Assistant Systems Administrator.—Sonia Tutiven.
Web and Graphics Editor.—Christopher Hewett.
Staff Assistants: John Bressler, Ryan Young.
Senior Counsel/Investigations.—Bob Faber (586 FHOB), 5–5504.
Investigative Counsel.—Derek Miller.
Legislative Staff Assistant.—Charles Yessaian.
Professional Staff Member, Investigations.—Joseph Graziano.
Editor.—Gilda Fuentez (B–329 RHOB), 5–9960.
Legislative Calendar Clerk.—Tracy Mosebey.
Minority Committee Staff (2163 RHOB), 225–4472, fax 226–1270.
Staff Director.—David Heymsfeld.
Chief Counsel.—Ward McCarragher.
Counsel.—Kathleen Donnelly.
Systems Administrator.—Sheila Lockwood.
Financial Administrator.—Dara Schlieker.
Director of Communications.—Jim Berard (2167–A RHOB), 5–6260.
Counsel, Investigations.—Trinita Brown (585 FHOB), 6–4697.
Subcommittee on Aviation (2251 RHOB), 6–3220, fax 5–4629.
Majority Staff Director/Senior Counsel.—David Schaffer.
Counsel.—Holly E. Woodruff Lyons.
Legislative Staff Assistant.—Steven Beaulieu.
Professional Staff: Sharon Barkeloo, Adam Tsao.
Minority Staff Director.—Stacie Soumbeniotis, 5–9161.
Counsel.—Giles Giovinazzi.
Staff Assistant.—Michael Herren.

Subcommittee on Coast Guard and Maritime Transportation (507 FHOB), 6–3552, fax 6–2524.
Majority Counsel.—Mark Zachares.
Senior Legislative Staff Assistant.—Marsha Canter.
Professional Staff.—John Rayfield.
Minority Staff Director.—John Cullather (585 FHOB), 6–3587.
Staff Assistant.—Rose Hamlin.
Subcommittee on Economic Development, Public Buildings, and Emergency Management (591 FHOB), 5–3014, fax 6–1898.
Staff Director.—Matthew Wallen.
Majority Counsel.—Dan Schulman.
Legislative Staff Assistant.—Kri Demirjian.
Minority Staff Director.—Susan Brita (585 FHOB), 5–9961.
Counsel, Emergency Management.—Trinita Brown.
Staff Assistant.—Rose Hamlin.
Subcommittee on Highways, Transit and Pipelines (B–370A RHOB), 5–6715, fax 5–4623.
Majority Staff Director.—Levon Boyagian.
Counsel.—Graham Hill.
Legislative Staff Assistants: Melissa Theriault, Amy Warder.
Professional Staff: Joyce Rose, James Tymon.
Minority Senior Staff Director.—Clyde Woodle (B–375 RHOB), 5–9989, fax 4–4627.
Staff Director for:
Highway Issues.—Kenneth House.
Hazardous Materials and Pipelines.—Frank Mulvey (2251 RHOB), 5–3274.
Staff Assistant.—Eric Schyndle.
Subcommittee on Railroads (589 FHOB), 6–0727, fax 6–3475.
Majority Staff Director/Senior Counsel.—Glenn Scammel.
Counsel.—John Brennan.
Legislative Staff Assistant.—Travis Johnson.
Minority Staff Director.—Frank Mulvey (2251 RHOB), 5–3274, fax 5–4629.
Staff Assistant.—Michael Herren.
Subcommittee on Water Resources and Environment (B–376 RHOB), 5–4360, fax 6–5435.
Majority Staff Director/Senior Counsel.—Susan Bodine.
Counsel.—Jonathan Pawlow.
Senior Legislative Staff Assistant.—Donna Campbell.
Legislative Staff Assistant.—Fess Cassels.
Professional Staff: John Anderson, Geoff Bowman.
Minority Staff Director.—Kenneth Kopocis (B–375 RHOB), 5–0060, fax 5–4627.
Counsel.—Ryan Seiger.
Chief Economist.—Art Chan.
Staff Assistant.—Pamela Keller.

Veterans' Affairs

335 Cannon House Office Building, phone 225–3527, fax 225–5486

http://www.veterans.house.gov

meets second Wednesday of each month

Chris Smith, of New Jersey, *Chairman.*

Mike Bilirakis, of Florida.
Terry Everett, of Alabama.
Steve Buyer, of Indiana.
Jack Quinn, of New York.
Cliff Stearns, of Florida.
Jerry Moran, of Kansas.
Richard Baker, of Louisiana.
Rob Simmons, of Connecticut.
Henry E. Brown, Jr., of South Carolina.
Jeff Miller, of Florida.
John Boozman, of Arkansas.
Jeb Bradley, of New Hampshire.
Bob Beauprez, of Colorado.
Ginny Brown-Waite, of Florida.
Rick Renzi, of Arizona.
Tim Murphy, of Pennsylvania.

Lane Evans, of Illinois.
Bob Filner, of California.
Luis V. Gutierrez, of Illinois.
Corrine Brown, of Florida.
Vic Snyder, of Arkansas.
Ciro D. Rodriguez, of Texas.
Michael H. Michaud, of Maine.
Darlene Hooley, of Oregon.
Silvestre Reyes, of Texas.
Ted Strickland, of Ohio.
Shelley Berkley, of Nevada.
Tom Udall, of New Mexico.
Susan Davis, of California.
Tim Ryan, of Ohio.

SUBCOMMITTEES

Benefits

Henry E. Brown, Jr., of South Carolina, *Chairman.*

Jack Quinn, of New York.
Jeff Miller, of Florida.
Jeb Bradley, of New Hampshire.
Ginny Brown-Waite, of Florida.

Michael Michaud, of Maine.
Susan Davis, of California.
Silvestre Reyes, of Texas.
Corrine Brown, of Florida.

Health

Rob Simmons, of Connecticut, *Chairman.*

Jerry Moran, of Kansas.
Richard Baker, of Louisiana.
Jeff Miller, of Florida.
John Boozman, of Arkansas.
Jeb Bradley, of New Hampshire.
Bob Beauprez, of Colorado.
Ginny Brown-Waite, of Florida.
Rick Renzi, of Arizona.
Cliff Stearns, of Florida.
Tim Murphy, of Pennsylvania.

Ciro D. Rodriguez, of Texas.
Bob Filner, of California.
Vic Snyder, of Arkansas.
Ted Strickland, of Ohio.
Shelley Berkley, of Nevada.
Tim Ryan, of Ohio.
Luis V. Gutierrez, of Illinois.
Corrine Brown, of Florida.
Darlene Hooley, of Oregon.

Oversight and Investigations

Steve Buyer, of Indiana, *Chairman.*

Mike Bilirakis, of Florida.
Terry Everett, of Alabama.
John Boozman, of Arkansas.

Darlene Hooley, of Oregon.
Lane Evans, of Illinois.
Bob Filner, of California.
Ciro D. Rodriguez, of Texas.

STAFF

Committee on Veterans' Affairs (335 CHOB), 225–3527, fax 225–5486.
Chief Counsel/Staff Director.—Patrick Ryan, 5–3527.
Deputy Chief Counsel.—Kingston Smith, 5–8604.
Deputy Staff Director.—Arthur Wu, 6–3670.
Legislative Coordinator.—Jeannie McNally, 5–9112.
Administrative/Financial Assistant/Chief Clerk.—Mary McDermott, 5–8557.
Director of Information Systems.—Steve Kirkland, 5–3698.
Communications Director.—Peter Dickinson.
Office Manager.—Bernadine Dotson.
Staff Assistants: Summer Larson, 6–0972; Tanya Skypeck.
Printing Clerk.—Jerry Tan (400 CHOB), 5–3535.
Staff Advisor.—Mary M. Noonan (2373 RHOB), 5–3765.
Senior Investigator.—Andrew Napoli (2373 RHOB), 5–3765.
Democratic Staff Director.—Michael Durishin (333 CHOB), 5–9756.
Democratic Professional Staff.—Kevin Gash (333 CHOB), 5–9756.
Subcommittee on Benefits (337 CHOB), 225–9164.
Staff Director.—Darryl Kehrer.
Professional Staff.—Paige McManus.
Staff Assistant.—Devon Seibert.
Democratic Staff Director.—Mary Ellen McCarthy (333 CHOB), 5–9756.
Democratic Counsel.—Geoffrey Collver (333 CHOB), 5–9756.
Democratic Executive Assistant.—Leah Booth (333 CHOB), 5–9756.
Subcommittee on Health (338 CHOB), 225–9154.
Staff Director.—John Bradley.
Professional Staff: Dolores Dunn, Kathleen Greve.
Research Assistant.—Stacy Zelenski.
Democratic Staff Director.—Susan Edgerton (333 CHOB), 5–9756.
Democratic Executive Assistant.—Sarah Keller-Likins (333 CHOB), 5–9756.
Subcommittee on Oversight and Investigations (337A CHOB), 225–3569.
Staff Director.—Arthur Wu.
Professional Staff.—Veronica Crowe.
Staff Assistant.—Jonathan McKay.
Democratic Staff Director.—Len Sistek (333 CHOB), 5–9756.
Democratic Professional Staff.—Ruth Mahnken (333 CHOB), 5–9756.
Democratic Administrative/Executive Assistant.—Deborah Smith (333 CHOB), 5–9756.

Ways and Means

1102 Longworth House Office Building, phone 225–3625

http://waysandmeans.house.gov

meets second Wednesday of each month

William M. Thomas, of California, *Chairman.*

Philip M. Crane, of Illinois.
E. Clay Shaw, Jr., of Florida.
Nancy L. Johnson, of Connecticut.
Amo Houghton, of New York.
Wally Herger, of California.
Jim McCrery, of Louisiana.
Dave Camp, of Michigan.
Jim Ramstad, of Minnesota.
Jim Nussle, of Iowa.
Sam Johnson, of Texas.
Jennifer Dunn, of Washington.
Mac Collins, of Georgia.
Rob Portman, of Ohio.
Phil English, of Pennsylvania.
J.D. Hayworth, of Arizona.
Jerry Weller, of Illinois.
Kenny C. Hulshof, of Missouri.
Scott McInnis, of Colorado.
Ron Lewis, of Kentucky.
Mark Foley, of Florida.
Kevin Brady, of Texas.
Paul Ryan, of Wisconsin.
Eric Cantor, of Virginia

Charles B. Rangel, of New York.
Fortney Pete Stark, of California.
Robert T. Matsui, of California.
Sander M. Levin, of Michigan.
Benjamin L. Cardin, of Maryland.
Jim McDermott, of Washington.
Gerald D. Kleczka, of Wisconsin.
John Lewis, of Georgia.
Richard E. Neal, of Massachusetts.
Michael R. McNulty, of New York.
William J. Jefferson, of Louisiana.
John S. Tanner, of Tennessee.
Xavier Becerra, of California.
Lloyd Doggett, of Texas.
Earl Pomeroy, of North Dakota.
Max Sandlin, of Texas.
Stephanie Tubbs Jones, of Ohio.

SUBCOMMITTEES

[The chairman and ranking minority member are ex officio (non-voting) members of all subcommittees.]

Health

Nancy L. Johnson, of Connecticut, *Chair.*

Jim McCrery, of Louisiana.
Philip M. Crane, of Illinois.
Sam Johnson, of Texas.
Dave Camp, of Michigan.
Jim Ramstad, of Minnesota.
Phil English, of Pennsylvania.
Jennifer Dunn, of Washington.

Fortney Pete Stark, of California.
Gerald D. Kleczka, of Wisconsin.
John Lewis, of Georgia.
Jim McDermott, of Washington.
Lloyd Doggett, of Texas.

Human Resources

Wally Herger, of California, *Chairman.*

Nancy L. Johnson, of Connecticut.
Scott McInnis, of Colorado.
Jim McCrery, of Louisiana.
Dave Camp, of Michigan.
Phil English, of Pennsylvania.
Ron Lewis, of Kentucky.
Eric Cantor, of Virginia.

Benjamin L. Cardin, of Maryland.
Fortney Pete Stark, of California.
Sander M. Levin, of Michigan.
Jim McDermott, of Washington.
Charles B. Rangel, of New York.

Oversight

Amo Houghton, of New York, *Chairman.*

Rob Portman, of Ohio.
Jerry Weller, of Illinois.
Scott McInnis, of Colorado.
Mark Foley, of Florida.
Sam Johnson, of Texas.
Paul Ryan, of Wisconsin.
Eric Cantor, of Virginia.

Earl Pomeroy, of North Dakota.
Gerald D. Kleczka, of Wisconsin.
Michael R. McNulty, of New York.
John S. Tanner, of Tennessee.
Max Sandlin, of Texas.

Select Revenue Measures

Jim McCrery, of Louisiana, *Chairman.*

J.D. Hayworth, of Arizona.
Jerry Weller, of Illinois.
Ron Lewis, of Kentucky.
Mark Foley, of Florida.
Kevin Brady, of Texas.
Paul Ryan, of Wisconsin.
Mac Collins, of Georgia.

Michael R. McNulty, of New York.
William J. Jefferson, of Louisiana.
Max Sandlin, of Texas.
Lloyd Doggett, of Texas.
Stephanie Tubbs Jones, of Ohio.

Social Security

E. Clay Shaw, Jr., of Florida, *Chairman.*

Sam Johnson, of Texas.
Mac Collins, of Georgia.
J.D. Hayworth, of Arizona.
Kenny C. Hulshof, of Missouri.
Ron Lewis, of Kentucky.
Kevin Brady, of Texas.
Paul Ryan, of Wisconsin.

Robert T. Matsui, of California.
Benjamin L. Cardin, of Maryland.
Earl Pomeroy, of North Dakota.
Xavier Becerra, of California.
Stephanie Tubbs Jones, of Ohio.

Trade

Philip M. Crane, of Illinois, *Chairman.*

E. Clay Shaw, Jr., of Florida.
Amo Houghton, of New York.
Dave Camp, of Michigan.
Jim Ramstad, of Minnesota.
Jennifer Dunn, of Washington.
Wally Herger, of California.
Phil English, of Pennsylvania.
Jim Nussle, of Iowa.

Sander M. Levin, of Michigan.
Charles B. Rangel, of New York.
Richard E. Neal, of Massachusetts.
William J. Jefferson, of Louisiana.
Xavier Becerra, of California.
John S. Tanner, of Tennessee.

STAFF

Committee on Ways and Means (1102 LHOB), 225–3625.
Chief of Staff.—Allison Giles.
Chief Counsel.—John Kelliher.
Chief Tax Counsel.—Bob Winters (1135 LHOB), 5–5522.
Tax Counsel.—Lisa Rydland.
Senior Tax and Budget Advisor.—Shahira Knight.
Senior Economist.—Alex Brill.
Professional Staff.—Greg Nickerson.
Senior Staff Assistant.—Billy Mulvihill.
Calendar Clerk.—Carren Turko.
Senior Committee Clerk.—Traci Altman.
Assistant Hearing Clerk.—William Covey.
Director of IS.—Melody Buras.
Assistant Director of IS.—Darren Gunlock.
Professional Staff.—Peter Davila.
Committee Administrator.—Julie Hasler.

Press Secretary.—Molly Millerwise.
Communications Director.—Christin Tinsworth.
Senior Staff Assistant.—Robert Vanden Heuvel.
Office Manager.—Adam Martinez.
Webmaster/Markup Clerk.—Diane Kirkland.
Senior Staff Assistant.—Jack Dusik.
Staff Assistant.—Risa Salsburg.
Documents Clerk.—Reggie Greene.
Minority Staff Director/Chief Counsel.—Janice Mays (1106 LHOB), 5–4021.
Chief Tax Counsel.—John Buckley.
Tax Counsels: Mildeen Worrell, Beth Kuntz Vance.
Chief Economist.—[Vacant].
Communications Director.—Daniel Maffei.
Deputy Communications Director.—Jennifer Whitson.
Professional Staff: Karlin McNeill, Sonja Nesbitt, Kathryn Olson.
Professional Staff Assistants: Aruna Kalyanam, Maureen Pritchard, Anthony Tait, Judy Talbert.
Systems Administrator.—Antoine Walker.
Subcommittee on Health (1136 LHOB), 5–3943.
Staff Director.—John McManus.
Professional Staff: Joelle Oishi, Madeleine Smith, Joel White, Deborah Williams.
Senior Staff Assistant.—Alisha Wallenstein.
Minority Professional Staff.—Cybele Bjorklund.
Subcommittee on Human Resources (B–317 RHOB), 5–1025.
Staff Director.—Matt Weidinger.
Professional Assistants: Christine Devere, Margo Smith.
Senior Staff Assistant.—Doug Sahmel.
Minority Professional Staff.—Nick Gwyn.
Subcommittee on Oversight (1136 LHOB), 5–7601.
Staff Director.—Kirk Walder.
Professional Staff: Payson Peabody, Kimberly Reed.
Senior Staff Assistant.—Jenny Wolff.
Subcommittee on Select Revenue Measures (1135 LHOB), 6–5911.
Staff Director.—Jeff McMillen.
Subcommittee on Social Security (B–316 RHOB), 5–9263.
Staff Director.—Kim Hildred.
Professional Staff: Rachel Forward, Sophia Wright.
Senior Staff Assistant.—Jay Solly.
Subcommittee on Trade (1104 LHOB), 5–6649.
Staff Director.—Angela Ellard.
Senior Professional Staff.—Meredith Broadbent.
Professional Staff: David Kirk Kavanaugh, Stephanie Lester.
Senior Staff Assistant.—Michael Morrow.
Minority Chief Trade Counsel.—Timothy Reif (1106 LHOB), 5–4021.
Trade Counsel.—Viji Rangaswami.

SELECT AND SPECIAL COMMITTEES OF THE HOUSE

Permanent Select Committee on Intelligence

H–405 The Capitol, phone 225–4121

[Created pursuant to H. Res. 658, 95th Congress]

Porter J. Goss, of Florida, *Chairman.*

Doug Bereuter, of Nebraska.
Sherwood Boehlert, of New York.
Jim Gibbons, of Nevada.
Ray LaHood, of Illinois.
Randy (Duke) Cunningham, of California.
Peter Hoekstra, of Michigan.
Richard M. Burr, of North Carolina.
Terry Everett, of Alabama.
Elton Gallegly, of California.
Mac Collins, of Georgia.

Jane Harman, of California.
Alcee L. Hastings, of Florida.
Silvestre Reyes, of Texas.
Leonard L. Boswell, of Iowa.
Collin C. Peterson, of Minnesota.
Robert E. (Bud) Cramer, Jr., of Alabama.
Anna G. Eshoo, of California.
Rush D. Holt, of New Jersey.
C.A. Dutch Ruppersberger, of Maryland.

SUBCOMMITTEES

[The Speaker and Minority Leader are ex officio (non-voting) members of the committee.]

Human Intelligence, Analysis and Counterintelligence

Jim Gibbons, of Nevada, *Chairman.*

Sherwood Boehlert, of New York.
Randy (Duke) Cunningham, of California.
Peter Hoekstra, of Michigan.
Richard M. Burr, of North Carolina.
Terry Everett, of Alabama.
Mac Collins, of Georgia.

Leonard L. Boswell, of Iowa.
C.A. Dutch Ruppersberger, of Maryland.
Silvestre Reyes, of Texas.
Collin C. Peterson, of Minnesota.
Robert E. (Bud) Cramer, Jr., of Alabama.

Intelligence Policy and National Security

Doug Bereuter, of Nebraska, *Chairman.*

Ray LaHood, of Illinois.
Randy (Duke) Cunningham, of California.
Peter Hoekstra, of Michigan.
Richard M. Burr, of North Carolina.
Elton Gallegly, of California.

Anna G. Eshoo, of California.
Alcee L. Hastings, of Florida.
Rush D. Holt, of New Jersey.
C.A. Dutch Ruppersberger, of Maryland.

Technical and Tactical Intelligence

Peter Hoekstra, of Michigan, *Chairman.*

Sherwood Boehlert, of New York.
Jim Gibbons, of Nevada.
Randy (Duke) Cunningham, of California.
Terry Everett, of Alabama.
Elton Gallegly, of California.
Mac Collins, of Georgia.
Robert E. (Bud) Cramer, Jr., of Alabama.
Rush D. Holt, of New Jersey.
Anna G. Eshoo, of California.
Collin C. Peterson, of Minnesota.
C.A. Dutch Ruppersberger, of Maryland.

Terrorism and Homeland Security

Ray LaHood, of Illinois, *Chairman.*

Doug Bereuter, of Nebraska.
Jim Gibbons, of Nevada.
Richard M. Burr, of North Carolina.
Terry Everett, of Alabama.
Elton Gallegly, of California.
Mac Collins, of Georgia.
Alcee L. Hastings, of Florida.
Silvestre Reyes, of Texas.
Collin C. Peterson, of Minnesota.
Leonard L. Boswell, of Iowa.
Robert E. (Bud) Cramer, Jr., of Alabama.

STAFF

Staff Director/Chief Legal Officer.—Patrick Murray.
Deputy Staff Director.—Merrell Moorhead.
General Counsel.—Chris Barton.
Chief Clerk.—Claire Young.
Special Assistant to the Staff Director.—Dee Jackson.
Director of Security.—Bill McFarland.
Systems Administrator.—Brandon Smith.
Minority Professional Staff: Bob Emmett, John Keefe, Beth Larson, Marcel Lettre, Kirk McConnell.
Counsel/Professional Staff.—Wyndee Parker.
Democratic Counsel.—Chris Healy.
Staff Assistant.—Ilene Romack.
Subcommittee on Human Intelligence, Analysis and Counterintelligence.
Staff Director.—Brant Basset.
Professional Staff.—Barbara Bennett.
Subcommittee on Intelligence Policy and National Security.
Staff Director.—Mike Ennis.
Professional Staff/Counsel.—Michele Lang.
Subcommittee on Technical and Tactical Intelligence.
Staff Director.—Mike Meermans.
Professional Staff: Riley Purdue, Kathleen Reilly, John Stopher.
Subcommittee on Terrorism and Homeland Security.
Professional Staff.—Jim Lewis.
Staff Assistant.—Kevin Schmidt.

Select Committee on Homeland Security

433 Cannon House Office Building phone 226–8417, fax 226–3399

Christopher Cox, of California, *Chairman.*

Jennifer Dunn, of Washington.
C.W. Bill Young, of Florida.
Don Young, of Alaska.
F. James Sensenbrenner, of Wisconsin.
W.J. (Billy) Tauzin, of Louisiana.
David Dreier, of California.
Duncan Hunter, of California.
Harold Rogers, of Kentucky.
Sherwood Boehlert, of New York.
Christopher Shays, of Connecticut.
Lamar Smith, of Texas.
Curt Weldon, of Pennsylvania.
Porter Goss, of Florida.
Dave Camp, of Michigan.
Lincoln Diaz-Balart, of Florida.
Robert W. Goodlatte, of Virginia.
Ernest Istook, of Oklahoma.
Peter King, of New York.
John Linder, of Georgia.
John Shadegg, of Arizona.
Mark Souder, of Indiana.
Mac Thornberry, of Texas.
Jim Gibbons, of Nevada.
Kay Granger, of Texas.
Pete Sessions, of Texas.
John Sweeney, of New York.

Jim Turner, of Texas.
Bennie G. Thompson, of Mississippi.
Loretta Sanchez, of California.
Edward J. Markey, of Massachusetts.
Norman D. Dicks, of Washington.
Barney Frank, of Massachusetts.
Jane Harman, of California.
Benjamin L. Cardin, of Maryland.
Louise Slaughter, of New York.
Peter A. DeFazio, of Oregon.
Nita M. Lowey, of New York.
Robert E. Andrews, of New Jersey.
Eleanor Holmes Norton, of the District of Columbia.
Zoe Lofgren, of California.
Karen McCarthy, of Missouri.
Sheila Jackson Lee, of Texas.
Bill Pascrell, Jr., of North Carolina.
Donna M. Christensen, of the Virgin Islands.
Bob Etheridge, of North Carolina.
Charles Gonzalez, of Texas.
Ken Lucas, of Kentucky.
James R. Langevin, of Rhode Island.
Kendrick B. Meek, of Florida.

SUBCOMMITTEES

Cybersecurity, Science, and Research and Development

Mac Thornberry, of Texas, *Chairman.*

Pete Sessions, of Texas.
Sherwood Boehlert, of New York.
Lamar Smith, of Texas.
Curt Weldon, of Pennsylvania.
Dave Camp, of Michigan.
Robert W. Goodlatte, of Virginia.
Peter King, of New York.
John Linder, of Georgia.
Mark Souder, of Indiana.
Jim Gibbons, of Nevada.
Kay Granger, of Texas.

Zoe Lofgren, of California.
Loretta Sanchez, of California.
Robert E. Andrews, of New Jersey.
Sheila Jackson Lee, of Texas.
Donna M. Christensen, of the Virgin Islands.
Bob Etheridge, of North Carolina.
Charles Gonzalez, of Texas.
Ken Lucas, of Kentucky.
James R. Langevin, of Rhode Island.
Kendrick B. Meek, of Florida.

Emergency Preparedness and Response

John Shadegg, of Arizona, *Chairman.*

Curt Weldon, of Pennsylvania.
W.J. (Billy) Tauzin, of Louisiana.
Christopher Shays, of Connecticut.
Dave Camp, of Michigan.
Lincoln Diaz-Balart, of Florida.
Peter King, of New York.
Mark Souder, of Indiana.
Mac Thornberry, of Texas.
Jim Gibbons, of Nevada.
Kay Granger, of Texas.
Pete Sessions, of Texas.

Bennie G. Thompson, of Mississippi.
Jane Harman, of California.
Benjamin L. Cardin, of Maryland.
Peter A. DeFazio, of Oregon.
Nita M. Lowey, of New York.
Eleanor Holmes Norton, of the District of Columbia.
Bill Pascrell, Jr., of North Carolina.
Donna M. Christensen, of the Virgin Islands.
Bob Etheridge, of North Carolina.
Ken Lucas, of Kentucky.

Infrastructure and Border Security

Dave Camp, of Michigan, *Chairman.*

Kay Granger, of Texas.
Jennifer Dunn, of Washington.
Don Young, of Alaska.
Duncan Hunter, of California.
Lamar Smith, of Texas.
Lincoln Diaz-Balart, of Florida.
Robert W. Goodlatte, of Virginia.
Ernest Istook, of Oklahoma.
John Shadegg, of Arizona.
Mark Souder, of Indiana.
John Sweeney, of New York.

Loretta Sanchez, of California.
Edward J. Markey, of Massachusetts.
Norman D. Dicks, of Washington.
Barney Frank, of Massachusetts.
Benjamin L. Cardin, of Maryland.
Louise Slaughter, of New York.
Peter A. DeFazio, of Oregon.
Sheila Jackson Lee, of Texas.
Bill Pascrell, Jr., of North Carolina.
Charles Gonzalez, of Texas.

Intelligence and Counterterrorism

Jim Gibbons, of Nevada, *Chairman.*

John Sweeney, of New York.
Jennifer Dunn, of Washington.
C.W. Bill Young, of Florida.
Harold Rogers, of Kentucky.
Christopher Shays, of Connecticut.
Lamar Smith, of Texas.
Porter Goss, of Florida.
Peter King, of New York.
John Linder, of Georgia.
John Shadegg, of Arizona.
Mac Thornberry, of Texas.

James R. Langevin, of Rhode Island.
Edward J. Markey, of Massachusetts.
Norman D. Dicks, of Washington.
Barney Frank, of Massachusetts.
Jane Harman, of California.
Nita M. Lowey, of New York.
Robert E. Andrews, of New Jersey.
Eleanor Holmes Norton, of the District of Columbia.
Karen McCarthy, of Missouri.
Kendrick B. Meek, of Florida.

Rules

Lincoln Diaz-Balart, of Florida, *Chairman.*

Jennifer Dunn, of Washington.
F. James Sensenbrenner, of Wisconsin.
David Dreier, of California.
Curt Weldon, of Pennsylvania.
Porter Goss, of Florida.
John Linder, of Georgia.
Pete Sessions, of Texas.

Louise Slaughter, of New York.
Bennie G. Thompson, of Mississippi.
Loretta Sanchez, of California.
Zoe Lofgren, of California.
Karen McCarthy, of Missouri.
Kendrick B. Meek, of Florida.

STAFF

Committee on Homeland Security (433 CHOB), 6–8417.
Majority Staff Director.—John C. Gannon
Deputy Staff Director/Chief Counsel.—Uttam A.S. Dhillon.
Chief Financial Officer.—Dawn M. Criste.
Senior Advisor for Intelligence Information Sharing.—Stephen W. DeVine.
Communications Directors.—Vincent Francis Sollitto, Elizabeth Tobias.

Professional Staff Members.—Stephen M. Cote, Julie Vincent Gunlock, Charles R. Korsmos, Carolyn E. Lukas.
Chief Clerk/Office Manager.—Michael S. Twinchek.
Minority Staff Director and Chief Counsel.—David H. Schanzer (1413B LHOB), 6–2616.
Senior Policy Advisor.—Scott D. Bates.
Budget Director.—Mark T. Magee.
Special Assistant to the Staff Director.—S. Camille Camacho.
Professional Staff Members/Counsels: Carla Buckner, Jessica Herrera, Lorraine Lewis, Sue Ramanathan.
Professional Staff: David Grannis, Jason R. McNamara, Allen Thompson, Traci A. Williams.

National Republican Congressional Committee

320 First Street, SE., 20003, phone 479–7000

Thomas M. Reynolds, of New York, *Chairman.*

Chairman, Executive Committee.—Sue Wilkins Myrick, of North Carolina.
Chairman of:
Candidate Recruitment.—John E. Sweeney, of New York.
Finance.—Mike Rogers, of Michigan.
Get-out-the-vote.—Howard P. (Buck) McKeon, of California.
Communications–Message.—Mike Pence, of Indiana.
Community Partnerships.—Jerry Weller, of Illinois.
Education–Training.—John B. Shadegg, of Arizona.
Incumbent Development.—Phil English, of Pennsylvania.
Incumbent Review.—Robert W. Ney, of Ohio.
Incumbent Support: Kevin Brady, of Texas, and Melissa A. Hart, of Pennsylvania.
Coalitions/Outreach.—Pete Sessions, of Texas.

EXECUTIVE COMMITTEE MEMBERS

John A. Boehner, of Ohio.
Eric Cantor, of Virginia.
Tom Cole, of Oklahoma.
Ander Crenshaw, of Florida.
John Abney Culberson, of Texas.
Mario Diaz-Balart, of Floria.
David Dreier, of California.
Jennifer Dunn, of Washington.
Jo Ann Emerson, of Missouri.
Phil English, of Pennsylvania.
Tom Feeney, of Florida.
Mike Ferguson, of New Jersey.
Sam Graves, of Missouri.
Mark Green, of Wisconsin.
Doc Hastings, of Washington.
Jeb Hensarling, of Texas.
David L. Hobson, of Ohio.
Sue W. Kelly, of New York.
Mark Steven Kirk, of Illinois.
Jim McCrery, of Louisiana.
Howard P. (Buck) McKeon, of California.
Candice S. Miller, of Michigan.
Jerry Moran, of Kansas.
Sue Wilkins Myrick, of North Carolina.
Robert W. Ney, of Ohio.
Charlie Norwood, of Georgia.
Rob Portman, of Ohio.
Adam Putnam, of Florida.
Mike Rogers, of Michigan.
Ed Royce, of California.
Pete Sessions, of Texas.
John B. Shadegg, of Arizona.
Don Sherwood, of Pennsylvania.
John E. Sweeney, of New York.
Todd Tiahrt, of Kansas.
Patrick J. Tiberi, of Ohio.
Fred Upton, of Michigan.
Greg Walden, of Oregon.
Zach Wamp, of Tennessee.
Jerry Weller, of Illinois.
Roger F. Wicker, of Mississippi.

Ex Officio Members from the Leadership
J. Dennis Hastert, of Illinois.
Tom Delay, of Texas.
Roy Blunt, of Missouri.
Deborah Pryce, of Ohio.
Chris Cox, of California.

STAFF

Executive Director.—Sally Vastola.
Deputy Executive Director.—Donna Anderson.
Political Director.—Mike McElwain.

Director of:
Communications.—Carl Forti.
Finance.—Joe Rachinsky.
Research.—Mike Shields.
Counsel.—Don McGahn.

House Policy Committee

2471 Rayburn House Office Building, phone, 225–6168

http://policy.house.gov

meets at the call of the Chair or the Speaker

Christopher Cox, of California, *Chairman.*

Republican Leadership:
Speaker.—J. Dennis Hastert, of Illinois.
Majority Leader.—Tom DeLay, of Texas.
Majority Whip.—Roy Blunt, of Missouri.
Conference Chairman.—Deborah Pryce, of Ohio.
Conference Vice Chair.—Jack Kingston, of Georgia.
Conference Secretary.—John Doolittle, of California.
NRCC Chairman.—Thomas Reynolds, of New York.
Leadership Chairman.—Rob Portman, of Ohio.
106th Class Representative.—Ernie Fletcher, of Kentucky.
107th Class Representative.—Ander Crenshaw, of Florida.

Committee Chairmen:
Rules Committee.—David Dreier, of California.
Ways and Means Committee.—Bill Thomas, of California.
Appropriations Committee.—C.W. Bill Young, of Florida.
Budget Committee.—Jim Nussle, of Iowa.
Energy and Commerce Committee.—Billy Tauzin, of Louisiana.

At Large Representatives (Appointed by the Speaker of the House):
Vito Fossella, of New York.
Bob Goodlatte, of Virginia.
Henry J. Hyde, of Illinois.
Joe Knollenberg, of Michigan.
Ron Lewis, of Kentucky.
Doug Ose, of California.
John Shadegg, of Arizona.
Nick Smith, of Michigan.
Cliff Stearns, of Florida.
Dave Weldon, of Florida.
Jerry Weller, of Illinois.

Class Representatives:
105th Congress.—Kenny C. Hulshof, of Missouri.
Sophomore Class.—Mark Green, of Wisconsin.
Freshman Class.—Todd Platts, of Pennsylvania.

STAFF

House Policy Committee (2471 RHOB), 225–6168.
Executive Director.—Paul Wilkinson.
Director, Communications.—Kate Whitman.
Chief Counsel.—William Schulz.
CPA.—Thomas Anfinson.
Clerk.—Natalya Anfilofyeva.

House Republican Conference

1010 Longworth House Office Building, phone 225–5107, fax 225–0809

Deborah Pryce, of Ohio, *Chairman.*

Jack Kingston, of Georgia, *Vice Chair.*

John Doolittle, of California, *Secretary.*

STAFF

Chief of Staff.—Kathryn Lehman.
Deputy Chief of Staff.—Lori Salley.
Assistant to the Chief of Staff.—Brooks Brunson.
Director of Policy and Coalitions.—Andrew Shore.
Deputy Director of Policy/Counsel.—J.C. Scott.
Coalitions Coordinator.—John DeStefano.
Policy Analyst.—Kelly Bulliner.
Manager of Committee Relations.—Michael Tomberlin.
Senior Policy Advisor.—Shalla Ross.
Scheduler.—Sara Rogers.
Special Assistant to the Chairman.—Chris Frech.
Special Projects Coordinator.—Amata Radewagen.
Systems Administrator.—Leith Robothman.
Conference Coordinator.—Matt Sturges.
Staff Assistants: Jim Billimoria, Larissa Pennington.
Communications Director.—Greg Crist.
Press Secretary.—Jessica Incitto.
Deputy Press Secretary.—Andrea Tantaros.
Press Assistant.—Shannon Flaherty, 226–1156.
Committee Liaison.—Joel Roberson.

House Republican Steering Committee

H–209 The Capitol, phone, 225–2204

J. Dennis Hastert, of Illinois, *Chairman.*

Tom DeLay, of Texas.
Roy Blunt, of Missouri.
Eric Cantor, of Virginia.
Deborah Pryce, of Ohio.
Christopher Cox, of California.
Jack Kingston, of Georgia.
John T. Doolittle, of California.
Thomas M. Reynolds, of New York.
Tom Davis, of Virginia.
C.W. Bill Young, of Florida.
W.J. (Billy) Tauzin, of Louisiana.
David Dreier, of California.
Bill Thomas, of California.
Ken Calvert, of California.
Adam H. Putnam, of Florida.
Doc Hastings, of Washington.
John B. Shadegg, of Arizona.
Joe Barton, of Texas.
Tom Latham, of Iowa.
Dave Camp, of Michigan.
John McHugh, of New York.
Curt Weldon, of Pennsylvania.
Ralph Regula, of Ohio.
Hal Rogers, of Kentucky.
Mac Collins, of Georgia.
Don Young, of Alaska.
John Culberson, of Texas.
John R. Carter, of Texas.

Democratic Congressional Campaign Committee

430 South Capitol Street SE., 20003, phone (202) 863–1500

Executive Committee:
Robert T. Matsui, of California, *Chair.*
Nancy Pelosi, of California, *Democratic Leader.*
Charles B. Rangel, of New York, *Executive Board Chair.*

John D. Dingell, of Michigan, *Chairman's Council.*
Nita Lowey, of New York, *Chair Emeritus.*
Patrick J. Kennedy, of Rhode Island, *Chair Emeritus.*
Martin Frost, of Texas, *Chair Emeritus.*
Rahm Emanuel, of Illinois, *Committee Vice Chair.*
Charlie Gonzalez, of Texas, *Committee Vice Chair.*
Ed Markey, of Massachusetts, *Committee Vice Chair.*
Kendrick Meek, of Florida, *Committee Vice Chair.*
Lucille Roybal-Allard, of California, *Committee Vice Chair.*
Mike Thompson, of California, *Business Council Chair.*
Janice D. Schakowsky, of Illinois, *Women LEAD Chair.*

STAFF

Executive Director.—James J. Bonham, 485–3510, fax 485–3512.
Political Director.—Peter Cari, 485–3507, fax 485–3436.
Communications Director.—Kori Bernards, 485–3440, fax 485–3535.
Director of Field and Base Vote.—Glenn Rushing, 485–3434, fax 485–3436.
National Finance Director.—Brian L. Wolff, 485–3509, fax 485–3427.
Deputy National Finance Directors: Lane M. Luskey, 485–3525; Nicole Runge, 485–3526.
Marketing and Membership Director.—Liz Fisher Jalali, 485–3421, fax 485–3511.
Chief Financial Officer.—Ann Marie Habershaw, 485–3529, fax 485–3536.
Member Services.—485–3508.

Democratic Steering and Policy Committee

H–204 The Capitol, phone 225–0100

Chairman.—Nancy Pelosi, Representative from California.
Co-Chairs:
Steering.—Rosa DeLauro, Representative from Connecticut.
Policy.—George Miller, Representative from California.

STAFF

Democratic Policy Committee (H–130), 225–0100, fax 226–0938.
Policy Advisors: Scott Boule, 225–4965; Kit Judge; Lara Levison, 225–4965; Mike Sheehy; Leanita Shelby; Melissa Shannon, 225–4965.
Research Associate.—Margie Capron.

Democratic Steering Committee 225–0100, fax 225–4188.
Senior Advisor.—George Kundanis.

Democratic Caucus

1420 Longworth House Office Building, phone 226–3210, fax 225–9253

democratic.caucus@mail.house.gov

Robert Menendez, of New Jersey, *Chairman.*

James E. Clyburn, of South Carolina, *Vice Chairman.*

STAFF

Executive Director.—Jim Datri.
Policy Director.—Karissa Willhite.
Communications Director/Senior Advisor.—Andrew Kauders.
Caucus Planning Director.—Wendy Hartmann.
Special Projects Director.—Blair Watters.
Outreach Director.—Ivan Zapien.

General Counsel.—George Henry.
Assistant to the Executive Director.—Allie Neill.
Staff Assistants: Justin Field, Amber Goodwin.
Parliamentarian.—Matt Pinkus.
Chief of Staff to the Vice Chair.—Yelberton Watkins.
Legislative Director to the Vice Chair.—Danny Cromer.
Senior Policy Advisor to the Vice Chair.—Andrea Martin.
Legislative Assistant to the Vice Chair.—Barvetta Singletary.
Special Assistant to the Vice Chair.—Jaime Harrison.

OFFICERS AND OFFICIALS OF THE HOUSE

OFFICE OF THE SPEAKER

H–232 The Capitol, phone 225–0600, fax 226–1996

http://speaker.house.gov

The Speaker.—J. Dennis Hastert.
Chief of Staff.—Scott B. Palmer.
Deputy Chief of Staff.—Michael Stokke.
Director of Administration.—Christy Surprenant.
Director of Policy.—Bill Hughes.
Assistants to the Speaker for Policy: Kevin Fromer, Kiki Kless, Bill Koetzle, Tim Kurth, Margaret Peterlin, Jim Rendon, Chris Walker, Darren Willcox.
Director of Speaker Operations.—Samuel Lancaster.
General Counsel.—Theodore J. Van Der Meid.
Scheduler.—Helen Morrell.
Systems Administrator.—Jeff Schwartz.
Executive Assistant.—Jennifer Connelly.
Office Manager.—Rachel Hodges.

SPEAKER'S PRESS OFFICE

H–326 The Capitol, phone 225–2800

Communications Director.—Pete Jeffries.
Press Secretary.—John Feehery.
Deputy Press Secretary.—Paige Ralston.
Press Assistant.—Jennie Page.
Writer.—Amy Drake.

SPEAKER'S FLOOR OFFICE

H–210 The Capitol, phone 225–2204

Senior Floor Director.—Seth Webb.
Floor Assistants: Karen Haas, Jay Pierson.

OFFICE OF THE MAJORITY LEADER

H–107 The Capitol, phone 225–4000, fax 225–5117

Majority Leader.—Tom DeLay.
Chief of Staff.—Tim Berry.
Special Assistant to the Chief of Staff.—Elizabeth Pauls.
Deputy Chief of Staff.—Dan Flynn.
Policy Director.—Juliane Sullivan.
Communications Director.—Stuart Roy.
Press Secretary.—Jonathan Grella.
Deputy Press Secretary.—Laura Blackann.
Speechwriter.—Michael Connolly.

Senior Policy Advisor.—Cassie Bevan.
Policy Analyst.—Deana Funderburk.
Senior Advisor, Director of National Security Policy.—Brett Shogren.
Policy Advisor.—Jack Victory.
Deputy Chief of Staff/Legislative Operations.—Brett Loper.
Senior Floor Assistant.—Danielle Simonetta.
Floor Assistant.—Jonathan Robilotto.
Director of Finance and Special Events.—Amy Lorenzini.
Scheduler.—Dawn Loffredo.
Office Manager.—Ellen Schlachter.
Staff Assistant.—Lilia Bruni.
Director of Information Technology.—Ed Mullen.
Deputy Director of Information Technology.—Josh Shultz.

OFFICE OF THE MAJORITY WHIP

H–329 The Capitol, phone 225–0197

Majority Whip.—Roy Blunt.
Chief of Staff.—Gregg Hartley.
Deputy Chief of Staff/Director of Member Services.—Mildred Webber.
Director of Policy Analysis & Management/Deputy Chief of Staff.—Brian Gaston.
Director of Floor Operations.—Amy Steinmann.
Deputy Director of Floor Operations.—Kirk Boyle.
Chief Floor Assistant.—Sam Langholz.
Communications Director.—Burson Taylor.
Press Secretary.—David James.
Deputy Press Secretary.—Laurent Crenshaw.
Director of Scheduling.—Richard Eddings.
Director of Coalitions.—Sam Geduldig.

OFFICE OF THE CHIEF DEPUTY MAJORITY WHIP

H–330 The Capitol, phone 225–0197

Chief Deputy Majority Whip.—Eric Cantor.
Chief of Staff.—Steve Stombres.
Special Assistant.—Matt Jesse.

OFFICE OF THE DEMOCRATIC LEADER

H–204 The Capitol, phone 225–0100

Democratic Leader.—Nancy Pelosi.
Chief of Staff.—George Crawford.
Executive Assistant/Director of Scheduling.—Cortney Bright.
Senior Advisor.—George Kundanis.
Communications Director.—Brendan Daly.
Communications Counsel.—Melissa Skolfield.
Office Manager.—Paula Short.
Deputy Scheduler/Staff Assistant.—Tom Manatos.
Assistant to the Chief of Staff.—Deborah Spriggs.
Executive/Personal Assistant.—Catlin O'Neill.
Deputy Chief of Staff.—Cecile Richards.
Executive Floor Assistant.—Jerry Hartz.
Floor Assistant.—Howard Moon.
Counsel to the Leader.—Bernie Raimo.
Director of Intergovernmental Relations.—Lorraine Miller.

OFFICE OF THE DEMOCRATIC WHIP

H–306 The Capitol, phone 225–3130, fax 226–0663

http://democraticwhip.house.gov

Democratic Whip.—Steny Hoyer.
Chief of Staff.—Cory Alexander.
Executive Assistant/Appointments.—Kathy May.
Office Manager.—Erica Rossi.
Floor Director.—Rob Cogorno.
Floor Assistant/Member Services Director.—Brian Romick.
Communications Director.—David Ransom.
Press Secretary.—Stacey Farnen.
Senior Policy Advisors: Keith Aboucher, Scott DeFife, Gina Mahony.
Director of Information Technology.—Stephen Dwyer.

CHIEF DEPUTY DEMOCRATIC WHIPS

Deputy Democratic Whips:
John Lewis.
Ed Pastor.
Joseph Crowley.
Max Sandlin.
Baron P. Hill.
Jan Schakowsky.
Ron Kind.
Maxine Waters.

OFFICE OF THE CLERK

H–154 The Capitol, phone 225–7000

JEFF TRANDAHL, native of Spearfish, South Dakota; 1983 Graduate of Spearfish High School; Bachelor of Arts in Government/Politics, English emphasis, from the University of Maryland, 1987. Professional experience includes: Office of United States Senator James Abdnor (R–SD) from 1983 to 1987; Office of Congresswoman Virginia Smith (R–NE) and the House Committee on Appropriations from 1987 to 1990; Office of Congressman Pat Roberts (R–KS) and the Committee on House Administration from 1990 to 1995; Assistant to the Clerk of the U.S. House of Representatives from 1995 to 1996; Chief Administrative Officer (acting) for the U.S. House of Representatives from 1996 to 1997; Deputy Clerk of the House of Representatives from 1997 to 1999; appointed Clerk of the House of Representatives on January 1, 1999, and elected Clerk of the House of Representatives on January 6, 1999. Involved in various social and professional organizations.

Clerk.—Jeff Trandahl.
Deputy Clerk.—Martha C. Morrison.
Assistants to the Clerk: Daniel J. Strodel, Gerasimos C. Vans.
Chief of—
Legislative Computer Systems.—Joe Carmel, (2401 RHOB), 225–1182.
Legislative Operations.—Gigi Kelaher, (HT–13), 225–7925.
Legislative Resource Center.—Deborah Turner, (B–106 CHOB), 226–5200.
Office of Publication Services.—Janice Wallace-Robinson, (B–28 CHOB), 225–1908.
Office of History and Preservation.—Kenneth Kato, (B–106 CHOB), 226–5200.
Official Reporter.—Susan Hanback, (1718 LHOB), 225–2627.
Service Groups—
Majority Chief of Pages.—Peggy Sampson, 225–7350.
Minority Chief of Pages.—Wren Ivester, 225–7330.
Congresswoman's Suite.—225–4196.
Members and Family Committee.—225–0622.
Prayer Room.—225–8070.
Office of House Employment Counsel.—Gloria Lett Ferguson, (1036 LHOB), 225–7075.

CHIEF ADMINISTRATIVE OFFICER

HB–30 The Capitol, phone 225–6969

[Authorized by House Resolution 423, 102nd Congress, enacted April 9, 1992]

JAMES M. EAGEN III, Chief Administrative Officer of the House of Representatives; native of Clarks Summit, PA; B.A. in History, Gettysburg College, Gettysburg, PA, 1979; M.A. in International Relations, American University School of International Services, Washington, D.C., 1982; Congressman Steve Gunderson (R–WI), Legislative Assistant, 1982–83; Administrative Assistant, 1983–85; Congressman William F. Goodling (R–PA), Administrative Assistant, 1985–1991; House Committee on Education and Labor, Minority Staff Director, 1991–94; House Committee on Education and the Workforce, Majority Staff Director, 1995–97; elected August 1, 1997, as Chief Administrative Officer of the House of Representatives.

Chief Administrative Officer.—James M. Eagen III.
Deputy Chief Administrative Officer for Operations.—Will Plaster, H2–217 FHOB, 225–6969.
Deputy Chief Administrative Officer for Strategy.—Philip Flewallen, H2–217 FHOB, 225–6969.
Administrative Counsel.—Bill Cable, H2–217 FHOB, 225–6969.
Executive Assistant.—Marikka Green, HB–30 The Capitol, 225–6969.
Associate Administrator for—
Finance.—Bernice Brosious, H2–331 FHOB, 225–6514.
House Information Resources.—Dan Doody, H2–631 FHOB, 225–9276.
House Support Services.—Helene Flanagan, H2–B29, 225–2033.
Human Resources.—Kathy Wyszynski, H2–B29, 225–2450.
Procurement.—Bill Dellar, H2–359A FHOB, 225–2921.

CHAPLAIN

HB–25 The Capitol, phone 225–2509, fax 225–1776

DANIEL P. COUGHLIN, Chaplain, House of Representatives; residence: St. Clement Parish, Chicago, IL; attended St. Mary of the Lake University, Mundelein, IL, and received a degree in Sacred Theology; ordained a Roman Catholic Priest on May 3, 1960; also attended Loyola University, Chicago, IL, and received a degree in Pastoral Studies; Director of the Office for Divine Worship, Archdiocese of Chicago, under John Cardinal Cody, 1969–1984; Director of the Cardinal Stritch Retreat House, Mundelein, IL, 1990–1995; Vicar for Priests under Francis Cardinal George, and Joseph Cardinal Bernardin, Archbishops of Chicago, 1995–2000; elected House Chaplain on March 23, 2000.

Chaplain of the House.—Daniel P. Coughlin.

HOUSE INFORMATION RESOURCES

Ford House Office Building, H2–631, 20515, phone 225–9276, fax 226–6017

Associate Administrator.—Dan Doody.

OFFICE OF THE ATTENDING PHYSICIAN

H–166 The Capitol, phone 225–5421

(After office hours, call Capitol Operator 224–2145)

Attending Physician.—Dr. John F. Eisold.
Chief of Staff.—Christopher R. Picaut
Administrative Assistant.—Keith Pray.

OFFICE OF INSPECTOR GENERAL

Ford House Office Building, H2–385, phone 226–1250

Inspector General.—Steven A. McNamara.
Deputy Inspector General.—Christian Hendricks.
Administrative Assistant.—Susan M. Kozubski.
Director, Performance and Financial Audits.—G. Kenneth Eichelman.
Auditors-in-Charge: Opal Marie Hughes, Gary A. Muller.
Auditors: Stephen M. Connard, Stuart W. Josephs, Julie A. Poole.
Director, Information Systems Audits.—Belinda J. Finn.
Auditors-in-Charge: Theresa M. Grafenstine, Steven L. Johnson.
Auditors: Donna K. Hughes, Stephen D. Lockhart, Keith A. Sullenberger.
Director, Computer Assisted Audit Techniques.—Michael E. Benner.
Director, Contract Audit Services.—John E. Byrd.
Assistant Director, Contract Audit Services.—Susan L. Sharp.
Auditor.—Jennie E. Fairbanks.
Director, Investigations.—Michael W. Nye.

OFFICE OF THE LAW REVISION COUNSEL

Ford House Office Building, H2–304, 20515–6711, phone 226–2411, fax 225–0010

Law Revision Counsel.—John R. Miller.
Deputy Counsel.—Jerald J. Director.
Senior Counsels: Peter G. LeFevre, Kenneth I. Paretzky, Richard B. Simpson.
Assistant Counsels: Frances E. Kraus, Derrick L. Lindsey, Edward T. Mulligan, Ralph V. Seep, Alan G. Skutt, Robert M. Sukol, Deborah Z. Yee.
Staff Assistants: Debra L. Johnson, Amanda Prather.
Printing Editors.—Terisa L. Allison, Robert E. Belcher.
Senior Systems Engineer.—Eric Loach.

OFFICE OF THE LEGISLATIVE COUNSEL

136 Cannon House Office Building, phone 225–6060

Legislative Counsel.—Pope Barrow.
Deputy Legislative Counsel.—Douglass Bellis.
Senior Counsels: Timothy Brown, Steven Cope, Robert Cover, Ira Forstater, Stanley Grimm, Edward Grossman, Jean Harmann, Yvonne Haywood, Lawrence Johnston, Edward Leong, David Mendelsohn, Sandra Strokoff, Robert Weinhagen, James Wert.
Assistant Counsels: Wade Ballou, Warren Burke, Paul C. Callen, Sherry Chriss, Henry Christrup, Lisa M. Daly, Tobias A. Dorsey, Matthew Eckstein, Susan Fleishman, Rosemary Gallagher, Pete Goodloe, James Grossman, Curt C. Haensel, Gregory M. Kostka, Pierre Poisson, Hank Savage, Mark A. Synnes, Noah L. Wofsy, Brady Young.
Office Administrator.—Renate Stehr.
Assistant Office Administrator.—Nancy Cassavechia.
Staff Assistants: Debra Birch, Victoria Cirks, Donna Clarner, Pamela Griffiths, Kelly Meryweather, Tom Meryweather, Carolyn Ryan, David Topper, Joseph Woodell.
Information Systems Analyst.—Willie Blount.
Publications Coordinator.—Craig Sterkx.

OFFICE OF THE PARLIAMENTARIAN

H–209 The Capitol, phone 225–7373

Parliamentarian.—Charles W. Johnson III.
Deputy Parliamentarians: Thomas G. Duncan, John V. Sullivan.
Assistant Parliamentarians: Muftiah M. McCartin, Thomas J. Wickham, Ethan Lauer.
Chief Clerk.—Gay S. Topper.
Assistant Clerk.—Brian C. Cooper.
Precedent Editor.—Deborah W. Khalili.
Information Technology Manager.—Bryan J. Feldblum.

OFFICE OF THE SERGEANT AT ARMS

H–124 The Capitol, phone 225–2456

WILSON (BILL) LIVINGOOD, Sergeant at Arms of the U.S. House of Representatives; born on October 1, 1936 in Philadelphia, PA; B.S., Police Administration, Michigan State University; career record: special agent, U.S. Secret Service's Dallas Field Office, 1961–69; assistant to the special agent in charge of the Presidential Protective Division, 1969; special agent in charge of the Office of Protective Forces, 1970; inspector, Office of Inspection, 1978–82; special agent in charge, Houston Field Office, 1982–86; deputy assistant director, Office of Training, 1986–89; executive assistant to the Director of Secret Service, 1989–95; elected 36th Sergeant at Arms of the U.S. House of Representatives on January 4, 1995, for the 104th Congress; reelected for each succeeding Congress.

Sergeant at Arms.—Wilson (Bill) Livingood.
Deputy Sergeant at Arms.—Kerri Hanley.
Executive Assistant.—Kathleen Joyce.
Staff Assistants: Doris Boyd, Karen Forriest, KaSandra Greenhow, Susan Lowe, Tanya McBride, Micaela Fernandez.
Directors—
Police Services/Special Events.—Don Kellaher.
Identification Services.—Melissa Franger.
Chamber Security.—Bill Sims.
Assistant Supervisor.—Richard Wilson.
House Garages and Parking Security.—Rod Myers.
Assistants to the Sergeant at Arms: Pam Ahearn, Kevin Brennan, Nina Dues, Teresa Johnson, Jim Kaelin, Jack Kelliher, Ted Daniel.
Appointments/Public Information Center: Sam Jeffries, Robin Pegues.

OFFICE OF EMERGENCY PLANNING, PREPAREDNESS, AND OPERATIONS

H2–192 Ford House Office Building, phone 226–0950

Director.—Curt Coughlin.
Deputy Director.—Lawrence Himmelsbach.
Special Assistant to the Director.—Robert Noll.
Assistant Director for—
Operations.—Michael P. Susalla.
Planning.—Eric M. Kruse.
Preparedness.—John E. Veatch.
Executive Assistant.—Linda R. Shealy.
Program Manager.—Traci L. Brasher.
Staff Assistant.—Lynsi Pfleegor.
USCP Liaison.—William B. Rosenbaum.

JOINT COMMITTEES

Joint Economic Committee

G01 Dirksen Senate Office Building 20510–6432, phone 224–5171

[Created pursuant to sec. 5(a) of Public Law 304, 79th Congress]

Robert F. Bennett, Senator from Utah, *Chairman.*

Jim Saxton, Representative from New Jersey, *Vice Chairman.*

SENATE

Sam Brownback, of Kansas.
Jeff Sessions, of Alabama.
John E. Sununu, of New Hampshire.
Lamar Alexander, of Tennessee.
Susan M. Collins, of Maine.

Jack Reed, of Rhode Island.
Edward M. Kennedy, of Massachusetts.
Paul S. Sarbanes, of Maryland.
Jeff Bingaman, of New Mexico.

HOUSE

Paul Ryan, of Wisconsin.
Jennifer Dunn, of Washington.
Phil English, of Pennsylvania.
Adam H. Putnam, of Florida.
Ron Paul, of Texas.

Fortney Pete Stark, of California.
Carolyn B. Maloney, of New York.
Melvin L. Watt, of North Carolina.
Baron P. Hill, of Indiana.

STAFF

Joint Economic Committee (SD–G01), 224–5171, fax 224–0240.
Executive Director.—Donald Marron.
Finance Director.—Colleen Healy.
Senior Policy Advisor.—Gary Blank (SD–G03), 4–7943.
Senior Policy Analyst.—Rowdy Yeates (SD–G07), 4–6593.
Senior Health Economist.—Michael O'Grady (SH–805).
Senior Economists: Ike Brannon (SH–805), 4–0378; Reed Garfield (SH–805), 4–0376; Tim Kane, 4–0367; Jeff Wrase (SD–G07), 4–2335.
Economist.—Brian Jenn, 4–0368.
Press Secretary.—Rebecca Wilder, 4–0379.
Professional Staff.—Trish Kent (SH–805), 4–2989.
Research Assistant.—Sean Davis.
Staff Assistant.—Melissa Branson, 4–7171.
Information Systems Director.—John Falls, 4–5906.
Chief Economist to Vice Chairman.—Chris Frenze (1538 LHOB), 5–3923.
Chief Macroeconomist to Vice Chairman.—Robert Keleher (368 FHOB), 6–3227.
Senior Economists to Vice Chairman: Jason Fichtner (1537 LHOB), 5–0371; Dan Miller (1537 LHOB), 5–2223; Robert O'Quinn (246 FHOB), 6–4065; Kurt Schuler (246 FHOB), 6–2485.
Analyst to Vice Chairman.—Brian Higginbotham (1537 LHOB), 5–0370.
Executive Assistant to the Chief Economist to the Vice Chairman.—Connie Foster (1537 LHOB), 6–3231.
Minority Staff Director.—Wendell Primus (SH–805), 4–0372, fax 224–5568.
Chief Economist/Deputy Director.—Chad Stone (SH–804),
Deputy Director.—Frank Sammartino (SH–804), 4–7056.4–2675.
Press Secretary.—Nan Gibson (SH–804), 4–0377.
Senior Economist/Special Assistant to Staff Director.—Daphne V. Clones-Federing (SH–804), 4–5436.

Principal Economists: Diane Rogers (SH–804), 4–7683; Matthew Salomon (SH–804), 4–0373.
Economist.—John McInerney (244 FHOB), 6–2487.
Research Assistants: Joshua Shakin (SH–804), 4–9065; Hayden Smith (246 FHOB), 5–6024.
Staff Assistant.—Rachel Klastorin (SH–804), 4–0372.

Joint Committee on the Library of Congress

S–240 The Capitol, 20515, phone 224–1034

Ted Stevens, Senator from Alaska, *Chairman.*

Vernon J. Ehlers, Representative from Michigan, *Vice Chairman.*

SENATE

Trent Lott, of Mississippi.
Thad Cochran, of Mississippi.
Christopher J. Dodd, of Connecticut.
Charles E. Schumer, of New York.

HOUSE

Robert W. Ney, of Ohio.
Jack Kingston, of Georgia.
John B. Larson, of Connecticut.
Juanita Millender-McDonald, of California.

STAFF

Staff Director.—Jennifer Mies.
Deputy Staff Director.—Bill McBride.

Joint Committee on Printing

1309 Longworth House Office Building, 20515, phone 225–8281

[Created by act of August 3, 1846 (9 Stat. 114); U.S. Code 44, Section 101]

Robert W. Ney, Representative from Ohio, *Chairman.*

Saxby Chambliss, Senator from Georgia, *Vice Chairman.*

HOUSE

John T. Doolittle, of California.
John Linder, of Georgia.
John B. Larson, of Connecticut.
Robert A. Brady, of Pennsylvania.

SENATE

Thad Cochran, of Mississippi.
Gordon Smith, of Oregon.
Daniel K. Inouye, of Hawaii.
Mark Dayton, of Minnesota.

STAFF

Staff Director.—Maria Robinson.
Deputy Staff Director.—Martha Scott Poindexter.

Joint Committee on Taxation

1015 Longworth House Office Building 20515–6453, phone 225–3621

http://www.house.gov/jct

[Created by Public Law 20, 69th Congress]

William M. Thomas, Representative from California, *Chairman.*

Clarles E. Grassley, Senator from Iowa, *Vice Chairman.*

HOUSE

Philip M. Crane, of Illinois.
E. Clay Shaw, Jr., of Florida.
Charles B. Rangel, of New York.
Fortney Pete Stark, of California.

SENATE

Orrin G. Hatch, of Utah.
Don Nickles, of Oklahoma.
Max Baucus, of Montana.
John D. Rockefeller IV, of West Virginia.

STAFF

Joint Committee on Taxation (1015 LHOB), 225–3621.
Chief of Staff.—George K. Yin.
Deputy Chiefs of Staff: Bernard A. Schmitt (594 FHOB), 6–7575; Mary M. Schmitt (1620 LHOB), 5–7377.
Associate Deputy Chiefs of Staff: Thomas F. Koerner (595 FHOB), 6–7575; Carolyn E. Smith (1620 LHOB), 5–7377.
Administrative Assistant.—Kathleen M. Dorn.
Chief Clerk.—John H. Bloyer (1620 LHOB), 5–7377.
Senior Legislation Counsels: Harold E. Hirsch (1620 LHOB), 5–7377; Laurie A. Matthews (1620 LHOB), 5–7377; Cecily W. Rock (1620 LHOB), 5–7377; Melvin C. Thomas, Jr. (1620 LHOB), 5–7377.
Legislation Counsels: Ray Beeman (SD–204), 4–5561; Roger Colinvaux (SD–204), 4–5561; Nikole Flax (1604 LHOB), 5–7377; Deirdre James (1620 LHOB), 5–7377; Trisha McDermott (SD–204), 4–5561; Joseph W. Nega (1620 LHOB), 5–7377; David Noren (1604 LHOB), 5–7377; Carol Sayegh (1620 LHOB), 5–7377; Ronald Schultz (1620 LHOB), 5–7377; Gretchen Sierra (1604 LHOB), 5–7377; Allison Wielobob (1620 LHOB), 5–7377; Barry L. Wold (SD–204), 4–5561.
Senior Economists: Thomas A. Barthold (1620 LHOB), 5–7377; Patrick A. Driessen (560A FHOB), 6–7575; Ronald A. Jeremias (593 FHOB), 6–7575; Pamela H. Moomau (593 FHOB), 6–7575; William T. Sutton (560B FHOB), 6–7575.
Economists: Mary Ann Borrelli (579A FHOB), 6–7575; John W. Diamond (579B FHOB), 6–7575; Timothy Dowd (578 FHOB), 6–7575; Christopher P. Giosa (561 FHOB), 6–7575; Robert P. Harvey (561 FHOB), 6–7575; Thomas Holtmann (578 FHOB), 6–7575; Gary Koenig (595 FHOB), 6–7575; John F. Navratil (1620 LHOB), 5–7377; Christopher Overend (574B FHOB), 6–7575; Michacl A. Udell (574A FHOB), 6–7575.
Accountants: Brian Meighan (SD–204), 4–5561; Tara Zimmerman (1604 LHOB), 5–7377.
Chief Statistical Analyst.—Melani M. Houser (966 FHOB), 6–7575.
Statistical Analyst.—Tanya Butler (596 FHOB), 6–7575.
Director of Tax Resources.—Tracy S. Nadel (1015 LHOB), 5–3621.
Tax Resources Specialist.—Melissa A. O'Brien (SD–462), 4–0494.
Senior Refund Counsel.—Norman J. Brand (3565 IRS), 622–3580.
Refund Counsels: Carl E. Bates (3565 IRS), 622–3580; Robert C. Gotwald (3565 IRS), 622–3580.
Document Production Specialist.—Christine J. Simmons (1620 LHOB), 5–7377.
Executive Assistants: B. Jean Best (596 LHOB), 6–7575; Jayne Gribbin (SD–204), 4–5561; Lucia J. Rogers (1015 LHOB), 5–3621; Patricia C. Smith (1620 LHOB), 5–7377; Sharon Watts (3565 IRS), 662–3580.

Senior Computer Specialist.—William J. Dahl (577 FHOB), 6–7575.
Computer Specialist.—Hal G. Norman (577 FHOB), 6–7575.
Data Research Analyst.—Brent Trigg (561 FHOB), 6–7575.
Senior Staff Assistant.—Debra L. McMullen (1620 LHOB), 5–2647.
Staff Assistants: Sean R. Corcoran (1620 LHOB), 5–2647; Neval E. McMullen (1620 LHOB), 5–2647; Kristine Means (1620 LHOB), 5–2647.

ASSIGNMENTS OF SENATORS TO COMMITTEES

[Republicans in roman (51); Democrats in *italic* (48); Independent in SMALL CAPS (1); total, 100]

Senator	Committees (Standing, Joint, Special, Select)
Akaka	Armed Services. Energy and Natural Resources. Governmental Affairs. Indian Affairs. Veterans' Affairs. Select Committee on Ethics.
Alexander	Energy and Natural Resources. Foreign Relations. Health, Education, Labor, and Pensions. Joint Economic Committee.
Allard	Armed Services. Banking, Housing, and Urban Affairs. Budget. Environment and Public Works.
Allen	Commerce, Science, and Transportation. Foreign Relations. Small Business and Entrepreneurship.
Baucus	Agriculture, Nutrition, and Forestry. Environment and Public Works. Finance. Joint Committee on Taxation.
Bayh	Armed Services. Banking, Housing, and Urban Affairs. Energy and Natural Resources. Small Business and Entrepreneurship. Select Committee on Intelligence. Special Committee on Aging.
Bennett	Appropriations. Banking, Housing, and Urban Affairs. Governmental Affairs. Small Business and Entrepreneurship. Joint Economic Committee, *chairman.*
Biden	Foreign Relations. Judiciary.
Bingaman	Energy and Natural Resources. Finance. Health, Education, Labor, and Pensions. Joint Economic Committee.
Bond	Appropriations. Environment and Public Works. Health, Education, Labor, and Pensions. Small Business and Entrepreneurship. Select Committee on Intelligence.
Boxer	Commerce, Science, and Transportation. Environment and Public Works. Foreign Relations.

Senator	Committees (Standing, Joint, Special, Select)
Breaux	Commerce, Science, and Transportation. Finance. Rules and Administration. Special Committee on Aging.
Brownback	Appropriations. Commerce, Science, and Transportation. Foreign Relations. Joint Economic Committee.
Bunning	Banking, Housing, and Urban Affairs. Budget. Energy and Natural Resources. Finance. Veterans' Affairs.
Burns	Appropriations. Budget. Commerce, Science, and Transportation. Energy and Natural Resources. Small Business and Entrepreneurship.
Byrd	Appropriations. Armed Services. Budget. Rules and Administration.
Campbell	Indian Affairs, *chairman.* Appropriations. Energy and Natural Resources. Veterans' Affairs.
Cantwell	Commerce, Science, and Transportation. Energy and Natural Resources. Indian Affairs. Small Business and Entrepreneurship.
Carper	Banking, Housing, and Urban Affairs. Environment and Public Works. Governmental Affairs. Special Committee on Aging.
Chafee	Banking, Housing, and Urban Affairs. Environment and Public Works. Foreign Relations.
Chambliss	Agriculture, Nutrition, and Forestry. Armed Services. Judiciary. Rules and Administration. Joint Committee on Printing. Select Committee on Intelligence.
Clinton	Armed Services. Environment and Public Works. Health, Education, Labor, and Pensions.
Cochran	Agriculture, Nutrition, and Forestry, *chairman.* Appropriations. Rules and Administration. Joint Committee on the Library of Congress. Joint Committee on Printing.
Coleman	Agriculture, Nutrition, and Forestry. Foreign Relations. Governmental Affairs. Small Business and Entrepreneurship.

Senator	Committees (Standing, Joint, Special, Select)
Collins	Governmental Affairs, *chairman.* Armed Services. Joint Economic Committee. Special Committee on Aging.
Conrad	Agriculture, Nutrition, and Forestry. Budget. Finance. Indian Affairs.
Cornyn	Armed Services. Budget. Environment and Public Works. Judiciary.
Corzine	Banking, Housing, and Urban Affairs. Budget. Foreign Relations.
Craig	Appropriations. Energy and Natural Resources. Judiciary. Veterans' Affairs. Special Committee on Aging, *chairman.*
Crapo	Agriculture, Nutrition, and Forestry. Banking, Housing, and Urban Affairs. Budget. Environment and Public Works. Small Business and Entrepreneurship.
Daschle	Agriculture, Nutrition, and Forestry. Finance. Rules and Administration.
Dayton	Agriculture, Nutrition, and Forestry. Armed Services. Governmental Affairs. Rules and Administration. Joint Committee on Printing.
DeWine	Appropriations. Health, Education, Labor, and Pensions. Judiciary. Select Committee on Intelligence.
Dodd	Banking, Housing, and Urban Affairs. Foreign Relations. Health, Education, Labor, and Pensions. Rules and Administration. Joint Committee on the Library of Congress.
Dole	Agriculture, Nutrition, and Forestry. Armed Services. Banking, Housing, and Urban Affairs. Special Committee on Aging.
Domenici	Energy and Natural Resources, *chairman.* Appropriations. Budget. Indian Affairs.
Dorgan	Appropriations. Commerce, Science, and Transportation. Energy and Natural Resources. Indian Affairs.

Senator	Committees (Standing, Joint, Special, Select)
Durbin	Appropriations. Governmental Affairs. Judiciary. Rules and Administration. Select Committee on Intelligence.
Edwards	Health, Education, Labor, and Pensions. Judiciary. Small Business and Entrepreneurship. Select Committee on Intelligence.
Ensign	Armed Services. Budget. Commerce, Science, and Transportation. Health, Education, Labor, and Pensions. Small Business and Entrepreneurship. Veterans' Affairs.
Enzi	Banking, Housing, and Urban Affairs. Budget. Foreign Relations. Health, Education, Labor, and Pensions. Small Business and Entrepreneurship. Special Committee on Aging.
Feingold	Budget. Foreign Relations. Judiciary. Special Committee on Aging.
Feinstein	Appropriations. Energy and Natural Resources. Judiciary. Rules and Administration. Select Committee on Intelligence.
Fitzgerald	Agriculture, Nutrition, and Forestry. Commerce, Science, and Transportation. Governmental Affairs. Small Business and Entrepreneurship. Special Committee on Aging.
Frist	Finance. Health, Education, Labor, and Pensions. Rules and Administration.
Graham, Bob, of Florida	Energy and Natural Resources. Environment and Public Works. Finance. Veterans' Affairs.
Graham, Lindsey, of South Carolina.	Armed Services. Health, Education, Labor, and Pensions. Judiciary. Veterans' Affairs.
Grassley	Finance, *chairman.* Agriculture, Nutrition, and Forestry. Budget. Judiciary. Joint Committee on Taxation.
Gregg	Health, Education, Labor, and Pensions, *chairman.* Appropriations. Budget.
Hagel	Banking, Housing, and Urban Affairs. Foreign Relations. Select Committee on Intelligence.

Senator	Committees (Standing, Joint, Special, Select)
Harkin	Agriculture, Nutrition, and Forestry. Appropriations. Health, Education, Labor, and Pensions. Small Business and Entrepreneurship.
Hatch	Judiciary, *chairman.* Finance. Indian Affairs. Joint Committee on Taxation. Select Committee on Aging. Select Committee on Intelligence.
Hollings	Appropriations. Budget. Commerce, Science, and Transportation.
Hutchison	Appropriations. Commerce, Science, and Transportation. Rules and Administration. Veterans' Affairs.
Inhofe	Environment and Public Works, *chairman.* Armed Services. Indian Affairs.
Inouye	Appropriations. Commerce, Science, and Transportation. Indian Affairs. Rules and Administration. Joint Committee on Printing.
JEFFORDS	Environment and Public Works. Finance. Health, Education, Labor, and Pensions. Veterans' Affairs. Special Committee on Aging.
Johnson	Appropriations. Banking, Housing, and Urban Affairs. Budget. Energy and Natural Resources. Indian Affairs.
Kennedy	Armed Services. Health, Education, Labor, and Pensions. Judiciary. Joint Economic Committee.
Kerry	Commerce, Science, and Transportation. Finance. Foreign Relations. Small Business and Entrepreneurship.
Kohl	Appropriations. Judiciary. Special Committee on Aging.
Kyl	Energy and Natural Resources. Finance. Judiciary.
Landrieu	Appropriations. Energy and Natural Resources. Small Business and Entrepreneurship.
Lautenberg	Commerce, Science, and Transportation. Governmental Affairs.

Senator	Committees (Standing, Joint, Special, Select)
Leahy	Agriculture, Nutrition, and Forestry. Appropriations. Judiciary.
Levin	Armed Services. Governmental Affairs. Small Business and Entrepreneurship. Select Committee on Intelligence.
Lieberman	Armed Services. Environment and Public Works. Governmental Affairs. Small Business and Entrepreneurship.
Lincoln	Agriculture, Nutrition, and Forestry. Finance. Select Committee on Ethics. Special Committee on Aging.
Lott	Rules and Administration, *chairman.* Commerce, Science, and Transportation. Finance. Joint Committee on the Library of Congress. Select Committee on Intelligence.
Lugar	Foreign Relations, *chairman.* Agriculture, Nutrition, and Forestry.
McCain	Commerce, Science, and Transportation, *chairman.* Armed Services. Indian Affairs.
McConnell	Agriculture, Nutrition, and Forestry. Appropriations. Rules and Administration.
Mikulski	Appropriations. Health, Education, Labor, and Pensions. Select Committee on Intelligence.
Miller	Agriculture, Nutrition, and Forestry. Banking, Housing, and Urban Affairs. Veterans' Affairs.
Murkowski	Energy and Natural Resources. Environment and Public Works. Indian Affairs. Veterans' Affairs.
Murray	Appropriations. Budget. Health, Education, Labor, and Pensions. Veterans' Affairs.
Nelson, Bill, of Florida	Armed Services. Budget. Commerce, Science, and Transportation. Foreign Relations.
Nelson, Ben, of Nebraska	Agriculture, Nutrition, and Forestry. Armed Services. Veterans' Affairs.
Nickles	Budget, *chairman.* Energy and Natural Resources. Finance. Rules and Administration. Joint Committee on Taxation.

Senator	Committees (Standing, Joint, Special, Select)
Pryor	Armed Services. Governmental Affairs. Small Business and Entrepreneurship.
Reed, of Rhode Island	Armed Services. Banking, Housing, and Urban Affairs. Health, Education, Labor, and Pensions. Joint Economic Committee.
Reid, of Nevada	Appropriations. Environment and Public Works. Indian Affairs. Select Committee on Ethics. Special Committee on Aging.
Roberts	Agriculture, Nutrition, and Forestry. Armed Services. Health, Education, Labor, and Pensions. Select Committee on Ethics. Select Committee on Intelligence, *chairman.*
Rockefeller	Commerce, Science, and Transportation. Finance. Foreign Relations. Veterans' Affairs. Joint Committee on Taxation. Select Committee on Intelligence.
Santorum	Banking, Housing, and Urban Affairs. Finance. Rules and Administration. Special Committee on Aging.
Sarbanes	Banking, Housing, and Urban Affairs. Budget. Foreign Relations. Joint Economic Committee.
Schumer	Banking, Housing, and Urban Affairs. Energy and Natural Resources. Judiciary. Rules and Administration. Joint Committee on the Library of Congress.
Sessions	Armed Services. Budget. Health, Education, Labor, and Pensions. Judiciary. Joint Economic Committee.
Shelby	Banking, Housing, and Urban Affairs, *chairman.* Appropriations. Governmental Affairs. Special Committee on Aging.
Smith	Commerce, Science, and Transportation. Energy and Natural Resources. Finance. Indian Affairs. Rules and Administration. Joint Committee on Printing. Special Committee on Aging.
Snowe	Small Business and Entrepreneurship, *chairman.* Commerce, Science, and Transportation. Finance. Select Committee on Intelligence.

Senator	Committees (Standing, Joint, Special, Select)
Specter	Veterans' Affairs, *chairman.* Appropriations. Governmental Affairs. Judiciary.
Stabenow	Agriculture, Nutrition, and Forestry. Banking, Housing, and Urban Affairs. Budget. Special Committee on Aging.
Stevens	Appropriations, *chairman.* Commerce, Science, and Transportation. Governmental Affairs. Rules and Administration. Joint Committee on the Library of Congress, *chairman.* Special Committee on Aging.
Sununu	Banking, Housing, and Urban Affairs. Commerce, Science, and Transportation. Foreign Relations. Governmental Affairs. Joint Economic Committee.
Talent	Agriculture, Nutrition, and Forestry. Armed Services. Energy and Natural Resources. Special Committee on Aging.
Thomas	Energy and Natural Resources. Environment and Public Works. Finance. Indian Affairs. Select Committee on Ethics.
Voinovich	Environment and Public Works. Foreign Relations. Governmental Affairs. Select Committee on Ethics, *chairman.*
Warner	Armed Services, *chairman.* Environment and Public Works. Health, Education, Labor, and Pensions. Select Committee on Intelligence.
Wyden	Budget. Commerce, Science, and Transportation. Energy and Natural Resources. Environment and Public Works. Select Committee on Intelligence. Special Committee on Aging.

ASSIGNMENTS OF REPRESENTATIVES TO COMMITTEES

[Republicans in roman (229); *Democrats* in *italic* (205); Independents in SMALL CAPS (1); Resident Commissioner and Delegates in **boldface** (5); [Vacant] (0); total, 440]

Representative	Committees (Standing, Joint, Special, and Select)
Abercrombie	Armed Services. Resources.
Acevedo-Vilá	Agriculture. Resources. Small Business.
Ackerman	Financial Services. International Relations.
Aderholt	Appropriations.
Akin	Armed Services. Science. Small Business.
Alexander	Agriculture. Armed Services.
Allen	Energy and Commerce.
Andrews	Education and the Workforce. Select Committee on Homeland Security.
Baca	Agriculture. Financial Services. Resources.
Bachus	Financial Services. Judiciary. Transportation and Infrastructure.
Baird	Budget. Science. Transportation and Infrastructure.
Baker	Financial Services. Transportation and Infrastructure. Veterans' Affairs.
Baldwin	Budget. Judiciary.
Ballance	Agriculture. Small Business.
Ballenger	Education and the Workforce. International Relations.
Barrett	Budget. Financial Services.
Bartlett	Armed Services. Science. Small Business.

Representative	Committees (Standing, Joint, Special, and Select)
Barton	Energy and Commerce. Science.
Bass	Energy and Commerce.
Beauprez	Small Business. Transportation and Infrastructure. Veterans' Affairs.
Becerra	Ways and Means.
Bell	Government Reform. International Relations. Science.
Bereuter	Financial Services. International Relations. Transportation and Infrastructure. Select Committee on Intelligence.
Berkley	International Relations. Transportation and Infrastructure. Veterans' Affairs.
Berman	International Relations. Judiciary.
Berry	Appropriations.
Biggert	Education and the Workforce. Financial Services. Science. Standards of Official Conduct.
Bilirakis	Energy and Commerce. Veterans' Affairs.
Bishop, Rob, of Utah	Armed Services. Resources. Science.
Bishop, Sanford D., Jr., of Georgia.	Appropriations.
Bishop, Timothy H., of New York.	Education and the Workforce. Transportation and Infrastructure.
Blackburn	Education and the Workforce. Government Reform. Judiciary.
Blumenauer	International Relations. Transportation and Infrastructure.
Blunt	Majority Whip. Energy and Commerce.
Boehlert	Science, *chairman.* Transportation and Infrastructure. Select Committee on Homeland Security. Select Committee on Intelligence.
Boehner	Education and the Workforce, *chairman.* Agriculture.
Bonilla	Appropriations.
Bonner	Agriculture. Budget. Science.

Representative	Committees (Standing, Joint, Special, and Select)
Bono	Energy and Commerce.
Boozman	Transportation and Infrastructure. Veterans' Affairs.
Bordallo	Armed Services. Resources. Small Business.
Boswell	Agriculture. Transportation and Infrastructure. Select Committee on Intelligence.
Boucher	Energy and Commerce. Judiciary.
Boyd	Appropriations.
Bradley	Armed Services. Small Business. Veterans' Affairs.
Brady, Kevin, of Texas	Ways and Means.
Brady, Robert A., of Pennsylvania.	Armed Services. House Administration. Joint Committee on Printing.
Brown, Corrine, of Florida	Transportation and Infrastructure. Veterans' Affairs.
Brown, Henry E., Jr., of South Carolina.	Budget. Transportation and Infrastructure. Veterans' Affairs.
Brown, Sherrod, of Ohio	Energy and Commerce. International Relations.
Brown-Waite	Budget. Financial Services. Veterans' Affairs.
Burgess	Science. Transportation and Infrastructure.
Burns	Agriculture. Education and the Workforce. Transportation and Infrastructure.
Burr	Energy and Commerce. Select Committee on Intelligence.
Burton	Government Reform. International Relations.
Buyer	Energy and Commerce. Veterans' Affairs.
Calvert	Armed Services. Resources. Science.
Camp	Ways and Means. Select Committee on Homeland Security.
Cannon	Government Reform. Judiciary. Resources.
Cantor	Ways and Means.

Representative	Committees (Standing, Joint, Special, and Select)
Capito	Financial Services. Small Business. Transportation and Infrastructure.
Capps	Budget. Energy and Commerce.
Capuano	Financial Services. Transportation and Infrastructure.
Cardin	Ways and Means. Select Committee on Homeland Security.
Cardoza	Agriculture. Resources. Science.
Carson, Brad, of Oklahoma	Resources. Transportation and Infrastructure.
Carson, Julia, of Indiana	Financial Services. Transportation and Infrastructure.
Carter	Education and the Workforce. Government Reform. Judiciary.
Case	Agriculture. Education and the Workforce. Small Business.
Castle	Education and the Workforce. Financial Services.
Chabot	International Relations. Judiciary. Small Business.
Chocola	Agriculture. Small Business. Transportation and Infrastructure.
Christensen	Resources. Small Business. Select Committee on Homeland Security.
Clay	Financial Services. Government Reform.
Clyburn	Appropriations.
Coble	Judiciary. Transportation and Infrastructure.
Cole	Armed Services. Education and the Workforce. Resources.
Collins	Ways and Means. Select Committee on Intelligence.
Conyers	Judiciary.
Cooper	Armed Services. Budget. Government Reform.
Costello	Science. Transportation and Infrastructure.

Representative	Committees (Standing, Joint, Special, and Select)
Cox	Select Committee on Homeland Security, *chairman.* Energy and Commerce.
Cramer	Appropriations. Select Committee on Intelligence.
Crane	Ways and Means. Joint Committee on Taxation.
Crenshaw	Appropriations. Budget.
Crowley	Financial Services. International Relations.
Cubin	Energy and Commerce. Resources.
Culberson	Appropriations.
Cummings	Government Reform. Transportation and Infrastructure.
Cunningham	Appropriations. Select Committee on Intelligence.
Davis, Artur, of Alabama	Budget. Financial Services.
Davis, Danny K., of Illinois	Education and the Workforce. Government Reform. Small Business.
Davis, Jim, of Florida	Energy and Commerce.
Davis, Jo Ann, of Virginia	Armed Services. Government Reform. International Relations.
Davis, Lincoln, of Tennessee	Agriculture. Science. Transportation and Infrastructure.
Davis, Susan A., of California	Armed Services. Education and the Workforce. Veterans' Affairs.
Davis, Tom, of Virginia	Government Reform, *chairman.*
Deal	Energy and Commerce. Government Reform.
DeFazio	Transportation and Infrastructure. Select Committee on Homeland Security.
DeGette	Energy and Commerce.
Delahunt	International Relations. Judiciary.
DeLauro	Appropriations. Budget.
DeLay	Majority Leader.
DeMint	Education and the Workforce. Small Business. Transportation and Infrastructure.
Deutsch	Energy and Commerce.

Representative	Committees (Standing, Joint, Special, and Select)
Diaz-Balart, Lincoln, of Florida.	Rules. Select Committee on Homeland Security.
Diaz-Balart, Mario, of Florida	Budget. Transportation and Infrastructure.
Dicks	Appropriations. Select Committee on Homeland Security.
Dingell	Energy and Commerce.
Doggett	Ways and Means.
Dooley	Agriculture. Resources.
Doolittle	Appropriations. House Administration. Joint Committee on Printing.
Doyle	Energy and Commerce. Standards of Official Conduct.
Dreier	Rules, *chairman.* Select Committee on Homeland Security.
Duncan	Government Reform. Resources. Transportation and Infrastructure.
Dunn	Ways and Means. Joint Economic Committee. Select Committee on Homeland Security.
Edwards	Appropriations. Budget.
Ehlers	Education and the Workforce. House Administration. Science. Transportation and Infrastructure. Joint Committee on the Library of Congress.
Emanuel	Budget. Financial Services.
Emerson	Appropriations.
Engel	Energy and Commerce. International Relations.
English	Ways and Means. Joint Economic Committee.
Eshoo	Energy and Commerce. Select Committee on Intelligence.
Etheridge	Agriculture. Select Committee on Homeland Security.
Evans	Armed Services. Veterans' Affairs.
Everett	Agriculture. Armed Services. Veterans' Affairs. Select Committee on Intelligence.
Faleomavaega	International Relations. Resources. Small Business.

Representative	Committees (Standing, Joint, Special, and Select)
Farr	Appropriations.
Fattah	Appropriations.
Feeney	Financial Services. Judiciary. Science.
Ferguson	Energy and Commerce.
Filner	Transportation and Infrastructure. Veterans' Affairs.
Flake	International Relations. Judiciary. Resources.
Fletcher	Energy and Commerce.
Foley	Ways and Means.
Forbes	Armed Services. Judiciary. Science.
Ford	Budget. Financial Services.
Fossella	Energy and Commerce. Financial Services.
Frank	Financial Services. Select Committee on Homeland Security.
Franks	Armed Services. Budget. Small Business.
Frelinghuysen	Appropriations.
Frost	Rules.
Gallegly	International Relations. Judiciary. Resources. Select Committee on Intelligence.
Garrett	Budget. Financial Services.
Gephardt	[No committee assignments at press time].
Gerlach	Small Business. Transportation and Infrastructure.
Gibbons	Armed Services. Resources. Select Committee on Homeland Security. Select Committee on Intelligence.
Gilchrest	Resources. Science. Transportation and Infrastructure.
Gillmor	Energy and Commerce. Financial Services.
Gingrey	Armed Services. Education and the Workforce. Science.

Representative	Committees (Standing, Joint, Special, and Select)
Gonzalez	Financial Services. Small Business. Select Committee on Homeland Security.
Goode	Appropriations.
Goodlatte	Agriculture, *chairman.* Judiciary. Select Committee on Homeland Security.
Gordon	Energy and Commerce. Science.
Goss	Select Committee on Intelligence, *chairman.* Rules. Select Committee on Homeland Security.
Granger	Appropriations. Select Committee on Homeland Security.
Graves	Agriculture. Small Business. Transportation and Infrastructure.
Green, Gene, of Texas	Energy and Commerce. Standards of Official Conduct.
Green, Mark, of Wisconsin	Financial Services. International Relations. Judiciary.
Greenwood	Education and the Workforce. Energy and Commerce.
Grijalva	Education and the Workforce. Resources.
Gutierrez	Financial Services. Veterans' Affairs.
Gutknecht	Agriculture. Budget. Science.
Hall	Energy and Commerce. Science.
Harman	Select Committee on Homeland Security. Select Committee on Intelligence.
Harris	Financial Services. International Relations.
Hart	Financial Services. Judiciary. Science.
Hastert	Speaker of the House. Select Committee on Intelligence.
Hastings, Alcee L., of Florida	Rules. Select Committee on Intelligence.
Hastings, Doc, of Washington	Budget. Rules. Standards of Official Conduct.
Hayes	Agriculture. Armed Services. Transportation and Infrastructure.

Representative	Committees (Standing, Joint, Special, and Select)
Hayworth	Resources. Ways and Means.
Hefley	Standards of Official Conduct, *chairman.* Armed Services.
Hensarling	Budget. Financial Services.
Herger	Ways and Means.
Hill	Agriculture. Armed Services. Joint Economic Committee.
Hinchey	Appropriations.
Hinojosa	Education and the Workforce. Financial Services.
Hobson	Appropriations.
Hoeffel	International Relations. Transportation and Infrastructure.
Hoekstra	Education and the Workforce. Transportation and Infrastructure. Select Committee on Intelligence.
Holden	Agriculture. Transportation and Infrastructure.
Holt	Education and the Workforce. Select Committee on Intelligence.
Honda	Science. Transportation and Infrastructure.
Hooley	Budget. Financial Services. Veterans' Affairs.
Hostettler	Armed Services. Judiciary.
Houghton	International Relations. Ways and Means.
Hoyer	Appropriations. Democratic Whip.
Hulshof	Budget. Standards of Official Conduct. Ways and Means.
Hunter	Armed Services, *chairman.* Select Committee on Homeland Security.
Hyde	International Relations, *chairman.* Judiciary.
Inslee	Financial Services. Resources.
Isakson	Education and the Workforce. Transportation and Infrastructure.
Israel	Armed Services. Financial Services.
Issa	Energy and Commerce.

Representative	Committees (Standing, Joint, Special, and Select)
Istook	Appropriations. Select Committee on Homeland Security.
Jackson	Appropriations.
Jackson Lee	Judiciary. Science. Select Committee on Homeland Security.
Janklow	Agriculture. Government Reform. International Relations.
Jefferson	Ways and Means.
Jenkins	Agriculture. Judiciary.
John	Energy and Commerce.
Johnson, Eddie Bernice, of Texas.	Science. Transportation and Infrastructure.
Johnson, Nancy L., of Connecticut.	Ways and Means.
Johnson, Sam, of Texas	Education and the Workforce. Ways and Means.
Johnson, Timothy V., of Illinois.	Agriculture. Science. Transportation and Infrastructure.
Jones, Stephanie Tubbs, of Ohio.	Standards of Official Conduct. Ways and Means.
Jones, Walter B., of North Carolina.	Armed Services. Financial Services. Resources.
Kanjorski	Financial Services. Government Reform.
Kaptur	Appropriations.
Keller	Education and the Workforce. Judiciary.
Kelly	Financial Services. Small Business. Transportation and Infrastructure.
Kennedy, Mark R., of Minnesota.	Financial Services. Transportation and Infrastructure.
Kennedy, Patrick J., of Rhode Island.	Appropriations.
Kildee	Education and the Workforce. Resources.
Kilpatrick	Appropriations.
Kind	Budget. Education and the Workforce. Resources.
King, Peter T., of New York	Financial Services. International Relations. Select Committee on Homeland Security.

Representative	Committees (Standing, Joint, Special, and Select)
King, Steve, of Iowa	Agriculture. Judiciary. Small Business.
Kingston	Appropriations. Joint Committee on the Library of Congress.
Kirk	Appropriations.
Kleczka	Ways and Means.
Kline	Armed Services. Education and the Workforce.
Knollenberg	Appropriations.
Kolbe	Appropriations.
Kucinich	Education and the Workforce. Government Reform.
LaHood	Appropriations. Select Committee on Intelligence.
Lampson	Science. Transportation and Infrastructure.
Langevin	Armed Services. Select Committee on Homeland Security.
Lantos	Government Reform. International Relations.
Larsen	Agriculture. Armed Services. Transportation and Infrastructure.
Larson	Armed Services. House Administration. Science. Joint Committee on the Library of Congress. Joint Committee on Printing.
Latham	Appropriations.
LaTourette	Financial Services. Government Reform. Standards of Official Conduct. Transportation and Infrastructure.
Leach	Financial Services. International Relations.
Lee	Financial Services. International Relations.
Levin	Ways and Means.
Lewis, Jerry, of California	Appropriations.
Lewis, John, of Georgia	Budget. Ways and Means.
Lewis, Ron, of Kentucky	Government Reform. Ways and Means.
Linder	House Administration. Rules. Select Committee on Homeland Security. Joint Committee on Printing.

Representative	Committees (Standing, Joint, Special, and Select)
Lipinski	Transportation and Infrastructure.
LoBiondo	Armed Services. Transportation and Infrastructure.
Lofgren	Judiciary. Science. Select Committee on Homeland Security.
Lowey	Appropriations. Select Committee on Homeland Security.
Lucas, Frank D., of Oklahoma.	Agriculture. Financial Services. Science.
Lucas, Ken, of Kentucky	Agriculture. Financial Services. Select Committee on Homeland Security.
Lynch	Financial Services. Government Reform.
Majette	Budget. Education and the Workforce. Small Business.
Maloney	Financial Services. Government Reform. Joint Economic Committee.
Manzullo	Small Business, *chairman.* Financial Services.
Markey	Energy and Commerce. Resources. Select Committee on Homeland Security.
Marshall	Agriculture. Armed Services. Small Business.
Matheson	Financial Services. Science. Transportation and Infrastructure.
Matsui	Ways and Means.
McCarthy, Carolyn, of New York.	Education and the Workforce. Financial Services.
McCarthy, Karen, of Missouri	Energy and Commerce. Select Committee on Homeland Security.
McCollum	Education and the Workforce. International Relations. Resources.
McCotter	Budget. International Relations. Small Business.
McCrery	Ways and Means.
McDermott	Ways and Means.
McGovern	Rules.
McHugh	Armed Services. Government Reform. International Relations.

Representative	Committees (Standing, Joint, Special, and Select)
McInnis	Resources. Ways and Means.
McIntyre	Agriculture. Armed Services.
McKeon	Armed Services. Education and the Workforce.
McNulty	Ways and Means.
Meehan	Armed Services. Judiciary.
Meek	Armed Services. Select Committee on Homeland Security.
Meeks	Financial Services. International Relations.
Menendez	International Relations. Transportation and Infrastructure.
Mica	Government Reform. House Administration. Transportation and Infrastructure.
Michaud	Small Business. Transportation and Infrastructure. Veterans' Affairs.
Millender-McDonald	House Administration. Small Business. Transportation and Infrastructure. Joint Committee on the Library of Congress.
Miller, Brad, of North Carolina.	Financial Services. Science. Small Business.
Miller, Candice S., of Michigan.	Armed Services. Government Reform.
Miller, Gary, of California	Financial Services. Transportation and Infrastructure.
Miller, George, of California	Education and the Workforce. Resources.
Miller, Jeff, of Florida	Armed Services. Veterans' Affairs.
Mollohan	Appropriations. Standards of Official Conduct.
Moore	Budget. Financial Services. Science.
Moran, James P., of Virginia	Appropriations. Budget.
Moran, Jerry, of Kansas	Agriculture. Transportation and Infrastructure. Veterans' Affairs.
Murphy	Financial Services. Government Reform. Veterans' Affairs.

Representative	Committees (Standing, Joint, Special, and Select)
Murtha	Appropriations.
Musgrave	Agriculture. Education and the Workforce. Small Business.
Myrick	Rules.
Nadler	Judiciary. Transportation and Infrastructure.
Napolitano	International Relations. Resources. Small Business.
Neal	Budget. Ways and Means.
Nethercutt	Appropriations. Science.
Neugebauer	Agriculture. Resources. Science.
Ney	House Administration, *chairman.* Joint Committee on Printing, *chairman.* Financial Services. Transportation and Infrastructure. Joint Committee on the Library of Congress.
Northup	Appropriations.
Norton	Government Reform. Transportation and Infrastructure. Select Committee on Homeland Security.
Norwood	Education and the Workforce. Energy and Commerce.
Nunes	Agriculture. Resources.
Nussle	Budget, *chairman.* Ways and Means.
Oberstar	Transportation and Infrastructure.
Obey	Appropriations.
Olver	Appropriations.
Ortiz	Armed Services. Resources.
Osborne	Agriculture. Education and the Workforce. Resources.
Ose	Agriculture. Financial Services. Government Reform.
Otter	Energy and Commerce.
Owens	Education and the Workforce. Government Reform.

Representative	Committees (Standing, Joint, Special, and Select)
Oxley	Financial Services, *chairman.*
Pallone	Energy and Commerce. Resources.
Pascrell	Transportation and Infrastructure. Select Committee on Homeland Security.
Pastor	Appropriations.
Paul	Financial Services. International Relations. Joint Economic Committee.
Payne	Education and the Workforce. International Relations.
Pearce	Resources. Transportation and Infrastructure.
Pelosi	Democratic Leader. Select Committee on Intelligence.
Pence	Agriculture. International Relations. Judiciary.
Peterson, Collin C., of Minnesota.	Agriculture. Select Committee on Intelligence.
Peterson, John E., of Pennsylvania.	Appropriations. Resources.
Petri	Education and the Workforce. Transportation and Infrastructure.
Pickering	Agriculture. Energy and Commerce.
Pitts	Energy and Commerce. International Relations.
Platts	Education and the Workforce. Government Reform. Transportation and Infrastructure.
Pombo	Resources, *chairman.* Agriculture.
Pomeroy	Agriculture. Ways and Means.
Porter	Education and the Workforce. Transportation and Infrastructure.
Portman	Budget. Ways and Means.
Price	Appropriations.
Pryce	Rules.
Putnam	Agriculture. Budget. Government Reform. Joint Economic Committee.
Quinn	Transportation and Infrastructure. Veterans' Affairs.

Representative	Committees (Standing, Joint, Special, and Select)
Radanovich	Energy and Commerce. Resources.
Rahall	Resources. Transportation and Infrastructure.
Ramstad	Ways and Means.
Rangel	Ways and Means. Joint Committee on Taxation.
Regula	Appropriations.
Rehberg	Agriculture. Resources. Transportation and Infrastructure.
Renzi	Financial Services. Resources. Veterans' Affairs.
Reyes	Armed Services. Veterans' Affairs. Select Committee on Intelligence.
Reynolds	House Administration. Rules.
Rodriguez	Armed Services. Resources. Veterans' Affairs.
Rogers, Harold, of Kentucky	Appropriations. Select Committee on Homeland Security.
Rogers, Mike, of Alabama	Agriculture. Armed Services.
Rogers, Mike, of Michigan	Energy and Commerce.
Rohrabacher	International Relations. Science.
Ros-Lehtinen	Government Reform. International Relations.
Ross	Agriculture. Financial Services.
Rothman	Appropriations.
Roybal-Allard	Appropriations. Standards of Official Conduct.
Royce	Financial Services. International Relations.
Ruppersberger	Armed Services. Government Reform. Select Committee on Intelligence.
Rush	Energy and Commerce.
Ryan, of Ohio	Armed Services. Education and the Workforce. Veterans' Affairs.
Ryan, of Wisconsin	Ways and Means. Joint Economic Committee.

Representative	Committees (Standing, Joint, Special, and Select)
Ryun	Armed Services. Budget. Financial Services.
Sabo	Appropriations.
Sánchez, Linda T., of California.	Government Reform. Judiciary. Small Business.
Sanchez, Loretta, of California	Armed Services. Select Committee on Homeland Security.
SANDERS	Financial Services. Government Reform.
Sandlin	Ways and Means.
Saxton	Armed Services. Resources. Joint Economic Committee.
Schakowsky	Energy and Commerce.
Schiff	International Relations. Judiciary.
Schrock	Armed Services. Budget. Government Reform. Small Business.
Scott, David, of Georgia	Agriculture. Financial Services.
Scott, Robert C., of Virginia	Budget. Judiciary.
Sensenbrenner	Judiciary, *chairman.* Select Committee on Homeland Security.
Serrano	Appropriations.
Sessions	Rules. Select Committee on Homeland Security.
Shadegg	Energy and Commerce. Financial Services. Select Committee on Homeland Security.
Shaw	Ways and Means. Joint Committee on Taxation.
Shays	Budget. Financial Services. Government Reform. Select Committee on Homeland Security.
Sherman	Financial Services. International Relations. Science.
Sherwood	Appropriations.
Shimkus	Energy and Commerce.
Shuster	Small Business. Transportation and Infrastructure.

Representative	Committees (Standing, Joint, Special, and Select)
Simmons	Armed Services. Transportation and Infrastructure. Veterans' Affairs.
Simpson	Appropriations.
Skelton	Armed Services.
Slaughter	Rules. Select Committee on Homeland Security.
Smith, Adam, of Washington	Armed Services. International Relations.
Smith, Christopher H., of New Jersey.	Veterans' Affairs, *chairman.* International Relations.
Smith, Lamar S., of Texas	Judiciary. Science. Select Committee on Homeland Security.
Smith, Nick, of Michigan	Agriculture. International Relations. Science.
Snyder	Armed Services. Veterans' Affairs.
Solis	Energy and Commerce.
Souder	Government Reform. Resources. Select Committee on Homeland Security.
Spratt	Armed Services. Budget.
Stark	Ways and Means. Joint Committee on Taxation. Joint Economic Committee.
Stearns	Energy and Commerce. Veterans' Affairs.
Stenholm	Agriculture.
Strickland	Energy and Commerce. Veterans' Affairs.
Stupak	Energy and Commerce.
Sullivan	Government Reform. Science. Transportation and Infrastructure.
Sweeney	Appropriations. Select Committee on Homeland Security.
Tancredo	Budget. International Relations. Resources.
Tanner	Ways and Means.
Tauscher	Armed Services. Transportation and Infrastructure.
Tauzin	Energy and Commerce, *chairman.* Resources. Select Committee on Homeland Security.

Representative	Committees (Standing, Joint, Special, and Select)
Taylor, Charles H., of North Carolina.	Appropriations.
Taylor, Gene, of Mississippi	Armed Services. Transportation and Infrastructure.
Terry	Energy and Commerce.
Thomas	Ways and Means, *chairman.* Joint Committee on Taxation, *chairman.*
Thompson, Bennie G., of Mississippi.	Agriculture. Select Committee on Homeland Security.
Thompson, Mike, of California	Agriculture. Budget. Transportation and Infrastructure.
Thornberry	Armed Services. Budget. Select Committee on Homeland Security.
Tiahrt	Appropriations.
Tiberi	Education and the Workforce. Financial Services.
Tierney	Education and the Workforce. Government Reform.
Toomey	Budget. Financial Services. Small Business.
Towns	Energy and Commerce. Government Reform.
Turner, Jim, of Texas	Armed Services. Select Committee on Homeland Security.
Turner, Michael R., of Ohio	Armed Services. Government Reform.
Udall, Mark, of Colorado	Agriculture. Resources. Science.
Udall, Tom, of New Mexico	Resources. Small Business. Veterans' Affairs.
Upton	Education and the Workforce. Energy and Commerce.
Van Hollen	Education and the Workforce. Government Reform.
Velázquez	Financial Services. Small Business.
Visclosky	Appropriations.
Vitter	Appropriations. Budget.
Walden	Energy and Commerce. Resources.
Walsh	Appropriations.
Wamp	Appropriations.

Representative	Committees (Standing, Joint, Special, and Select)
Waters	Financial Services. Judiciary.
Watson	Government Reform. International Relations.
Watt	Financial Services. Judiciary. Joint Economic Committee.
Waxman	Energy and Commerce. Government Reform.
Weiner	Judiciary. Science. Transportation and Infrastructure.
Weldon, Curt, of Pennsylvania	Armed Services. Science. Select Committee on Homeland Security.
Weldon, Dave, of Florida	Appropriations.
Weller	International Relations. Ways and Means.
Wexler	International Relations. Judiciary.
Whitfield	Energy and Commerce.
Wicker	Appropriations. Budget.
Wilson, Heather, of New Mexico.	Armed Services. Energy and Commerce.
Wilson, Joe, of South Carolina	Armed Services. Education and the Workforce.
Wolf	Appropriations.
Woolsey	Education and the Workforce. Science.
Wu	Education and the Workforce. Science.
Wynn	Energy and Commerce.
Young, C.W. Bill, of Florida	Appropriations, *chairman*. Select Committee on Homeland Security.
Young, Don, of Alaska	Transportation and Infrastructure, *chairman*. Resources. Select Committee on Homeland Security.

CONGRESSIONAL ADVISORY BOARDS COMMISSIONS, AND GROUPS

BOARD OF VISITORS TO THE AIR FORCE ACADEMY

[Title 10, U.S.C., Section 9355(a)]

Wayne Allard, of Colorado
Larry E. Craig, of Idaho
Ernest F. Hollings, of South Carolina

C.W. Bill Young, of Florida
Joel Hefley, of Colorado
Heather Wilson, of New Mexico
Norman D. Dicks, of Washington
Mike Thompson, of California

BOARD OF VISITORS TO THE MILITARY ACADEMY

[Title 10, U.S.C., Section 4355(a)]

Rick Santorum, of Pennsylvania
Mike DeWine, of Ohio
Jack Reed, of Rhode Island
Mary Landrieu, of Louisiana

Charles H. Taylor, of North Carolina
Sue Kelly, of New York
John M. McHugh, of New York
Maurice D. Hinchey, of New York
Ellen O. Tauscher, of California

BOARD OF VISITORS TO THE NAVAL ACADEMY

[Title 10, U.S.C., Section 6968(a)]

John McCain, of Arizona
Thad Cochran, of Mississippi
Paul Sarbanes, of Maryland
Barbara Mikulski, of Maryland

Wayne T. Gilchrest, of Maryland
Randy (Duke) Cunningham, of California
Steny Hoyer, of Maryland
John S. Tanner, of Tennessee
Mike McIntyre, of North Carolina

BOARD OF VISITORS TO THE COAST GUARD ACADEMY

[Title 14 U.S.C., Section 194(a)]

John McCain, of Arizona
Peter G. Fitzgerald, of Illinois
Ernest F. Hollings, of South Carolina
Patty Murray, of Washington

Rob Simmons, of Connecticut
Don Young, of Alaska
Howard Coble, of North Carolina
Bob Filner, of California
Frank LoBiondo, of New Jersey

BROADCASTING BOARD OF GOVERNORS

330 Independence Avenue SW., Suite 3360, 20237
phone 401–3736, fax 401–6605

[Created by Public Law 103–236]

Chairman.—Kenneth Y. Tomlinson.

GOVERNORS

Edward E. Kaufman
Robert M. Ledbetter, Jr.
Norm Pattiz
Joaquin F. Blaya
Blanquita Walsh Cullum
D. Jeffrey Hirschberg
Steven J. Simmons
Colin L. Powell
(ex officio)

STAFF

Executive Director.—Brian T. Conniff.
Deputy Executive Director.—Bruce Sherman.
Legal Counsel.—Carol Booker.
Program Review Officer.—Bruce Sherman.
Congressional Coordinator.—Susan Andross.
Communications Coordinator.—Joan Mower.
Chief Financial Officer.—Kelley Lehman Sullivan.
Executive Assistant.—Brenda Hardnett.
Research and Planning Coordinator.—Sherwood Demitz.
Program Review and Planning Officer.—Jim Morrow.
Special Projects Officer.—Oanh Tran.
Program Coordinator.—Bonnie Thompson.
Staff Assistants.—Mariam Azizkeya, Lori Dodson, Clark Pearson.

CANADA–UNITED STATES INTERPARLIAMENTARY GROUP

Senate Hart Building, Room 808, 224–3047

[Created by Public Law 86–42, 22 U.S.C., 1928a–1928d, 276d–276g]

Senate Delegation:
Chairman.—Mike Crapo, Senator from Idaho.
Vice Chairman.—[Vacant].
Director, Interparliamentary Services.—Sally Walsh.

COMMISSION ON CONGRESSIONAL MAILING STANDARDS

1309 Longworth House Office Building, phone 225–9337

[Created by Public Law 93–191]

Chairman.—Robert W. Ney, Representative from Ohio.
Robert B. Aderholt, Representative from Alabama.
John E. Sweeney, Representative from New York.
John B. Larson, Representative from Connecticut.
Bennie G. Thompson, Representative from Mississippi.
Rush D. Holt, Representative from New Jersey.

STAFF

Staff Director.—Jack Dail, 225–9337.
Staff Assistant.—Michael Frolich.

COMMISSION ON SECURITY AND COOPERATION IN EUROPE

234 Ford House Office Building, phone 225–1901, fax 226–4199

http://www.csce.gov

Christopher H. Smith, of New Jersey, *Chairman.*
Ben Nighthorse Campbell, of Colorado, *Co-Chairman.*

LEGISLATIVE BRANCH COMMISSIONERS

Senate

Sam Brownback, of Kansas.
Gordon H. Smith, of Oregon.
Kay Bailey Hutchison, of Texas.
Saxby Chambliss, of Georgia.
Christopher J. Dodd, of Connecticut.
Bob Graham, of Florida.
Russell D. Feingold, of Wisconsin.
Hillary Rodham Clinton, of New York.

House

Frank R. Wolf, of Virginia.
Joseph R. Pitts, of Pennsylvania.
Robert B. Aderholt, of Alabama.
Anne M. Northup, of Kentucky.
Benjamin L. Cardin, of Maryland.
Louise McIntosh Slaughter, of New York.
Alcee L. Hastings, of Florida.

EXECUTIVE BRANCH COMMISSIONERS

Department of State.—Lorne W. Craner.
Department of Defense.—Jack Dyer Crouch II.
Department of Commerce.—William Henry Lash III.

COMMISSION STAFF

Chief of Staff.—Dorothy Douglas Taft.
Deputy Chief of Staff.—Ronald J. McNamara.
Communications Director.—Ben Anderson.
Staff Assistants: Quena Gonzalez, Jennifer Winter.
Senior Advisor.—Elizabeth B. Pryor.
Staff Advisors: Orest Deychakiwsky, John Finerty, Chadwick R. Gore, Robert Hand, Janice Helwig, Michael Ochs.
Counsel for International Law.—Erika B. Schlager.
General Counsel.—Maureen T. Walsh.
Counsels: Marlene Kaufmann, H. Knox Thames.

CONGRESSIONAL AWARD FOUNDATION

379 Ford House Office Building 20515, phone (202) 226–0130, fax (202) 226–0131

[Created by Public Law 96–114]

Chairman.—Thomas D. Campbell, Thomas D. Campbell and Associates Inc., (609) 823–8551.
Vice Chairmen:
John M. Falk, Esq., Compressus, Inc., (202) 742–4307.
Charles F. Smithers, Jr., UBS PaineWebber, (212) 333–8900.
Secretary.—Edwin S. Jayne, AFSCME, (202) 429–1188.
Treasurer.—Kim Talley, American Airlines, (202) 496–5666.
National Director.—William E. Kelley, (202) 226–0130.

Members:

Paxton Baker, BET (202) 608–2052.
Max Baucus, Senator from Montana, (202) 224–2651.
Dolores M. Beilenson, Chevy Chase, MD, (301) 652–9125.
Dr. Clinton Bristow, Jr., Alcorn State University, (601) 877–6131.
Mary Bunning, (202) 224–4343.
Michael Carozza, Bristol-Myers Squibb Company, (202) 783–8659.
Larry E. Craig, Senator from Idaho, (202) 224–2752.
Barbara Cubin, Representative from Wyoming, (202) 225–2311.
George B. Gould, National Association of Letter Carriers, (202) 662–2833.
Janice Griffin, Griffin & Associates, (202) 785–6770.
Robert B. Harding, Esq., (703) 241–7468.
J. Steven Hart, Esq., Williams & Jensen, P.C., (202) 659–8201.
David W. Hunt, Esq., White & Case, L.L.P., (202) 626–3604.
Judy Istook, (202) 225–2132.
Timothy J. Keating, Honeywell International, (202) 662–2613.
Robert Kelley, St. Louis Labor Council, (202) 439–5001.
William E. Kelley, Congressional Award Foundation, (202) 226–0130.
General Richard L. Lawson, USAF (Ret.), (202) 822–6120.
Kevin B. Lefton, (315) 422–6275.
Reynaldo L. Martinez, Strategic Dimensions, (703) 941–4420.
John A. McCallum, The TAG Foundation, (404) 817–3333.
Linda Mitchell, Mississippi State University Extension Service, (662) 534–7776.
Sir James Murray K.C.M.G., New York, NY, (718) 852–3320.
Andrew F. Ortiz, J.D., M.P.A., Arizona Cleaning the Air, (602) 224–0524 ext. 2055.
Nancy Gibson Prowitt, Alcade & Fay, (703) 841–0626.
Altagracia Ramos, Hispanic Youth Foundation, (937) 427–3565.
Galen J. Reser, Pepsi Co., Inc., (914) 253–2862.
Felix R. Sanchez, TerraCom, Inc., (202) 965–5151.
Daniel B. Scherder, The Willard Group, (703) 893–8409.
William F. Sittmann, National Association of Chain Drug Stores, (703) 837–4161.
Debbie Snyder, EDS, (972) 605–4432.
Kimberly Talley, American Airlines, Inc., (202) 496–5666.
Rex B. Wackerle, Prudential Insurance Co., (202) 293–1141.

CONGRESSIONAL CLUB

2001 New Hampshire Avenue, NW., 20008, phone 332–1155, fax 797–0698

President.—Mary Lucas.
Vice Presidents:
(1st) Vicki Piahrt.
(2d) Eulada Watt.
(3d) Judy Istook.
(4th) Sylvia Sabo.
(5th) Lana Bethune.
(6th) Vivia Bishop.
Treasurer.—Lea Ann Edwards.
Corresponding Secretary.—Laura Bateman.
Recording Secretary.—Jinny Bartlett.

HOUSE OFFICE BUILDING COMMISSION

H–232 The Capitol, phone 225–0600

[Title 40, U.S.C. 175–176]

Chairman.—J. Dennis Hastert, Speaker of the House of Representatives.
Tom DeLay, House Majority Leader.
Nancy Pelosi, House Minority Leader.

HOUSE OF REPRESENTATIVES PAGE BOARD

H–154 The Capitol, phone 225–7000

[Established by House Resolution 611, 97th Congress]

Chairman.—John Shimkus, Representative from Illinois.

Members:

Heather Wilson, Representative from New Mexico.

Dale Kildee, Representative from Michigan.

Jeff Trandahl, Clerk of the House.

Wilson (Bill) Livingood, Sergeant at Arms of the House.

Staff Contact:

Grace Crews, Office of the Clerk, Page Program Coordinator.

JAPAN–UNITED STATES FRIENDSHIP COMMISSION

1110 Vermont Avenue NW., Suite 800, 20005, phone 418–9800, fax 418–9802

[Created by Public Law 94–118]

Chairman.—Dr. Richard J. Samuels, Massachusetts Institute of Technology.

Vice Chairman.—Dr. Amy Y. Heinrich, Columbia University.

Executive Director.—Dr. Eric J. Gangloff.

Assistant Executive Director.—Margaret P. Mihori.

Assistant Executive Director, CULCON.—Pamela L. Fields.

Secretary.—Sylvia L. Dandridge.

Members:

James A. Kelly, Assistant Secretary of State for East Asian and Pacific Affairs, U.S. Department of State.

The Honorable Dana Gioia, Chairman, National Endowment for the Arts.

Bruce Cole, Chairman, National Endowment for the Humanities.

The Honorable Thomas Petri, U.S. House of Representatives.

The Honorable John D. Rockefeller IV, U.S. Senate.

Dr. Patricia Steinhoff, University of Hawaii.

Dr. Linda Kerber, University of Iowa.

Theodore R. Life, Filmmaker.

Ira Wolf, Washington, D.C.

The Honorable James McDermott, U.S House of Representatives.

Dr. Richard E. Dyck, President, TCS Japan, KK

The Honorable Patricia De Stacy Harrison, Assistant Secretary of State for Educational and Cultural Affairs.

Doris O. Matsui, Senior Advisor, Collier, Shannon Scott PLLC

Francis Y. Sogi, Life Partner, Kellev Dive & Warren.

Frank P. Stanek, President, International Business Development, Universal Studios Recreation Group, Universal Studios.

The Honorable Sally Stroup, Assistant Secretary of Education for Post-Secondary Education.

MEXICO–UNITED STATES INTERPARLIAMENTARY GROUP

Senate Hart Building, Room 808, phone 224–3047

[Created by Public Law 82–420, 22 U.S.C. 276h–276k]

Senate Delegation:

Chairman.—Jeff Sessions, of Alabama.

Vice Chairman.—Christopher J. Dodd, of Connecticut.

House Delegation:

Chairman.—Jim Kolbe, of Arizona.

STAFF

Contact, Interparliamentary Services.—Julia Hart.

MIGRATORY BIRD CONSERVATION COMMISSION

4401 North Fairfax Drive, Room 622, Arlington, VA 22203
phone (703) 358–1716 fax (703) 358–2223

[Created by act of February 18, 1929, 16 U.S.C. 715a]

Chairman.—Gale Norton, Secretary of the Interior.
John Breaux, Senator from Louisiana.
Thad Cochran, Senator from Mississippi.
John D. Dingell, Representative from Michigan.
Curt Weldon, Representative from Pennsylvania.
Ann Veneman, Secretary of Agriculture.
[Vacant], Administrator of Environmental Protection Agency.
Secretary.—A. Eric Alvarez.

NATO PARLIAMENTARY ASSEMBLY

Headquarters: Place du Petit Sablon 3, B–1000 Brussels, Belgium

[Created by Public Law 84–689, 22 U.S.C., 1928z]

Senate Delegation:
Chairman.—Gordon Smith, Senator from Oregon.
Vice Chairman.—Joseph Biden, Senator from Delaware.

House of Representatives Delegation:
Chairman.—Douglas Bereuter, Representative from Nebraska.

STAFF

Secretary, Senate Delegation.—Julia Hart, Interparliamentary Services, SH–808, 224–3047.
Secretary, House Delegation.—Susan Olsen, Office of Rep. Douglas Bereuter, 2184 Rayburn House Office Building, 20515, 225–4806.

PERMANENT COMMITTEE FOR THE OLIVER WENDELL HOLMES DEVISE FUND

Library of Congress 20540, phone 707–5383

[Created by act of Congress approved Aug. 5, 1955 (Public Law 246, 84th Congress), to administer Oliver Wendell Holmes Devise Fund, established by same act]

Chairman ex officio.—James H. Billington.
Administrative Officer for the Devise.—James H. Hutson, 707–5383.

SENATE NATIONAL SECURITY WORKING GROUP

113 Dirksen Senate Office Building 20510, phone 224–3941

Administrative Co-Chairman.—Thad Cochran, Senator from Mississippi.
Administrative Co-Chairman.—Robert C. Byrd, Senator from West Virginia.
Co-Chairman.—Ted Stevens, Senator from Alaska.
Co-Chairman.—Jon Kyl, Senator from Arizona.
Co-Chairman.—Trent Lott, Senator from Mississippi.
Co-Chairman.—Carl Levin, Senator from Michigan.
Co-Chairman.—Joseph R. Biden, Jr., Senator from Delaware.

Members:
Bill Frist, Senator from Tennessee.
Richard G. Lugar, Senator from Indiana.
John Warner, Senator from Virginia.
Wayne Allard, Senator from Colorado.
Jeff Sessions, Senator from Alabama.
Don Nickles, Senator from Oklahoma.
Tom Daschle, Senator from South Dakota.
Edward M. Kennedy, Senator from Massachusetts.
Paul S. Sarbanes, Senator from Maryland.
John F. Kerry, Senator from Massachusetts.
Richard J. Durbin, Senator from Illinois.
Bryon L. Dorgan, Senator from North Dakota.
Bill Nelson, Senator from Florida.

STAFF

Republican Staff Director.—Stewart Holmes, 224–3941.
Democratic Staff Director.—Christina Evans, 224–3088.

SENATE OFFICE BUILDING COMMISSION

[Created by the act of April 28, 1904 (33 Stat. 481), as amended by the act of July 11, 1947 (61 Stat. 307), the act of August 1, 1953 (67 Stat. 328), and the act of August 3, 1956 (70 Stat. 966)]

[Membership Not Available At Press Time].

U.S. ASSOCIATION OF FORMER MEMBERS OF CONGRESS

233 Pennsylvania Avenue SE., Suite 200, 20002–1107
phone (202) 543–8676, fax 543–7145

The nonpartisan United States Association of Former Members of Congress was founded in 1970 as a nonprofit, educational, research and social organization. It has been chartered by the United States Congress and has approximately 600 members who represented American citizens in both the U.S. Senate and House of Representatives. The Association promotes improved public understanding of the role of Congress as a unique institution as well as the crucial importance of representative democracy as a system of government, both domestically and internationally.

President.—Larry LaRocco, of Idaho.
Vice President.—Jack Buechner, of Missouri.
Treasurer.—Jim Slattery, of Kansas.
Secretary.—John J. Rhodes III, of Arizona.
Immediate Past President.—John N. Erlenborn, of Illinois.
Honorary Co-Chairmen: Gerald R. Ford, of Michigan; Walter F. Mondale, of Minnesota.
Executive Director.—Linda A. Reed.
Counselors: Mark Andrews, of North Dakota; J. Glenn Beall, Jr., of Maryland; Donald G. Brotzman, of Colorado; Robert Kastenmeier, of Wisconsin; Matthew F. McHugh, of New York; Philip E. Ruppe, of Michigan; Carlton R. Sickles, of Maryland; James W. Symington, of Missouri.

U.S. CAPITOL HISTORICAL SOCIETY

200 Maryland Avenue NE., 20002, phone 543–8919, fax 544–8244

[Congressional Charter, October 20, 1978, Public Law 95–493, 95th Congress, 92 Stat. 1643]

Chairman of the Board.—The Honorable E. Thomas Coleman.
President.—The Honorable Ron Sarasin.
Treasurer.—L. Neale Cosby.
General Secretary.—Suzanne C. Dicks.
Vice Presidents: Brenda T. Day, The Honorable Thomas S. Foley, Erik Winborn, Jean Thompson, Robert E. Cole.

EXECUTIVE COMMITTEE

Robert E. Cole
The Honorable E. Thomas Coleman
L. Neale Cosby
Suzanne C. Dicks
Michael Dineen
The Honorable Ron Sarasin
Jean Thompson
Erik Winborn
Sharon Archer
Brenda T. Day
The Honorable Thomas S. Foley
The Honorable Louis Stokes

STAFF

Chief Historian.—Donald R. Kennon.
Associate Historian and Communications Director.—Felicia Bell.
Director of Development.—Rebecca Evans.
Manager, Member Programs.—Oki Radich.
Manager, Corporate Committee.—Marilyn Green.
Director, Retail Sales.—Diana Wailes.
Director of Finance.—Paul McGuire.
Senior Manager for Special Projects.—Steve Livengood.
Director of Outreach.—Andrew Dodge.

U.S. CAPITOL PRESERVATION COMMISSION

[Created pursuant to Public Law 100–696]

Co-Chairmen:
J. Dennis Hastert, Speaker of the House.
Ted Stevens, Senate President Pro Tempore.

House Members:
Tom DeLay, Majority Leader.
Nancy Pelosi, Minority Leader.
Robert W. Ney.
John Larson.
Chaka Fattah.
C.W. Bill Young.
John Mica.
Steven LaTourette.

Senate Members:
Bill Frist, Majority Leader.
Thomas A. Daschle, Minority Leader.
Trent Lott.
Christopher J. Dodd.
Robert Bennett.
Richard J. Durbin.
Ben Nighthorse Campbell.

Architect of the Capitol.—Alan M. Hantman.

U.S. HOUSE OF REPRESENTATIVES FINE ARTS BOARD

1309 Longworth House Office Building, phone 225–8281

[Created by Public Law 101–696]

Chairman.—Robert W. Ney, of Ohio.

Members:
Vernon J. Ehlers, of Michigan.
Jack Kingston, of Georgia.
John B. Larson, of Connecticut.
Juanita Millender-McDonald, of California.

U.S. SENATE COMMISSION ON ART

S–411 The Capitol, phone 224–2955

[Created by Public Law 100–696]

Chairman.—Bill Frist, of Tennessee.
Vice Chairman.—Thomas A. Daschle, of South Dakota.

Members:
Ted Stevens, of Alaska.
Christopher J. Dodd, of Connecticut.
Trent Lott, of Mississippi.

STAFF

Executive Secretary.—Emily J. Reynolds.
Curator.—Diane K. Skvarla.
Administrator.—Scott M. Strong.
Associate Curator.—Melinda K. Smith.
Registrar.—Deborah Wood.
Museum Specialist.—Richard L. Doerner.

OTHER CONGRESSIONAL OFFICIALS AND SERVICES

ARCHITECT OF THE CAPITOL

ARCHITECT'S OFFICE

SB–15 The Capitol, phone 228–1793, fax 228–1893, http://www.aoc.gov

Architect of the Capitol.—Alan M. Hantman.
Assistant Architect of the Capitol.—Michael G. Turnbull, 228–1221.
Administrative Assistant.—Amita Poole, 228–1701.
Director of:
Administrative Operations.—Hector Suarez, 228–1205.
Engineering.—Scott Birkhead, 226–5630.
Safety, Fire & Environmental Programs.—Susan Adams, 226–0630.
Chief Financial Officer.—Gary Glovinsky, 228–1819.
Budget Officer.—Edgar Bennett, 228–1225.
Communications Officer.—Eva Malecki, 228–1681.
General Counsel.—Charles Tyler, 225–1210.
Executive Officer, U.S. Botanic Garden.—Holly Shimizu, 225–6670.
Landscape Architect.—Matthew Evans, 224–6645.
Curator.—Barbara Wolanin, 228–1222.

U.S. CAPITOL

HT–42, Capitol Superintendent's Service Center, phone 228–8800, fax 225–7351

Superintendent.—Carlos Elias, 226–4859.
Assistant Superintendent.—Don White, 228–1875.

SENATE OFFICE BUILDINGS

G45 Dirksen Senate Office Building, phone 224–3141, fax 224–0652

Superintendent.—Lawrence Stoffel, 224–5023.
Deputy Superintendent.—Robin Morey, 224–6951.
Assistant Superintendents: Mark Sciarritta, Greg Simmons, Marvin Simpson, John St. Louis, 224–7686.

HOUSE OFFICE BUILDINGS

B–341 Rayburn House Office Building, phone 225–4141, fax 225–3003

Superintendent.—Frank Tiscione, 225–7012.
Deputy Superintendent.—Robert Gleich, 225–4142.
Assistant Superintendents: Peter Aitcheson, Sterling Thomas, Bill Wood, 225–4142.

CAPITOL TELEPHONE EXCHANGE

6110 Postal Square Building, phone 224–3121

Supervisor: Joan Sartori.

CHILD CARE CENTERS

HOUSE OF REPRESENTATIVES CHILD CARE CENTER

**147 Ford House Office Building,
Virginia Avenue and 3rd Street SW., 20515,
phone 225–9684, fax 225–6908**

Director.—Melissa Mangano.

SENATE EMPLOYEES' CHILD CARE CENTER

**United States Senate, Washington, DC 20510
phone 224–1461, fax 228–3686**

Director.—Shirley V. Letourneau.

COMBINED AIRLINES TICKET OFFICES (CATO)

**1925 North Lynn Street Suite 801, Arlington VA 22209
phone (703) 522–8664, fax (703) 522–0616**

General Manager.—Charles A. Dinardo.
Assistant General Manager.—Susan B. Willis.

**B–222 Longworth House Office Building
phone (703) 522–2286, fax (202) 226–5992**

Supervisor.—Michelle Gelzer.

**B–24 Russell Senate Office Building
phone (703) 522–2286, fax (202) 393–1981**

Supervisor.—Sonja Noll.

CONGRESSIONAL DAILY DIGEST

HOUSE SECTION

HT–13 The Capitol, phone 225–2868 (committees), 225–7497 (chamber)

Editors for—
Committee Meetings.—Maura Patricia Kelly.
Chamber Action.—Elsa B. Thompson.

SENATE SECTION

S–421 The Capitol, phone 224–2658, fax 224–1220

Editor.—Linda E. Sebold.
Assistant Editor.—Ken Dean.

CONGRESSIONAL RECORD INDEX OFFICE

U.S. Government Printing Office, Room C–738
North Capitol and H Streets NW 20401, phone 512–0275

Director.—Marcia Oleszewski (acting), 512–2010, ext. 3–1975.
Deputy Director.—Philip C. Hart (acting), 512–2010, ext. 3–1973.
Historian of Bills.—Barbre A. Brunson, 512–2010, ext. 3–1957.
Editors: Grafton J. Daniels, Tucker Greer, Philip C. Hart, Michael M. Sardone.
Indexers: Dorothy G. Bryant, Ytta B. Carr, Jason Parsons, Patricia J. Slater.

CAPITOL GUIDE SERVICE AND CONGRESSIONAL SPECIAL SERVICES OFFICE

ST–13 The Capitol 20510, Recorded Information 225–6827
Special Services 224–4048, TTY 224–4049

Director.—Tom Stevens, 224–3235.
Assistant Director (Administration).—Kevin Barry, 224–8399 (TTY).
Assistant Director (Special Services Office).—David Hauck, Crypt, 224–4048.
Assistant Director (Tours).—Sharon Nevitt, 224–4526.
Assistant Director (Training).—Tripp Jones, 224–3010.

LIAISON OFFICES

AIR FORCE

B–322 Rayburn House Office Building, phone 225–6656, fax 685–2592

Chief.—Lt. Col. Laura Shoaf.
Deputy Chief.—Lt. Col. Richard McGivern.
Action Officers: MAJ David Foglesong, MAJ Dawn Suitor.
Legislative Liaison Specialist.—Alice Geishecker.
Legislative Liaison Assistant.—S. Sgt. Lloyd Jenkins.

182 Russell Senate Office Building, phone 224–2481, fax 685–2575

Chief.—BG David Edmonds.
Liaison Officers: Lt. Col. John McCance, Lt. Col. L.C. Coffey, MAJ Ted Fordyce, SMSgt. Monica Rodriguez.
Legislative Liaison Specialist.—Beth Unklesbay.

ARMY

B–325 Rayburn House Office Building, phone 225–3853, fax 685–2674

Chief.—Col. Michael DeYoung.
Liaison Officers: LtCol. Larnell Exum, LtCol. Jim Garrison, LtCol. Michael Legg, Maj. Susan Riopel, LtCol. Malcom Shorter, LtCol. Eric Wagner.
Administrative Assistant.—SSG. Carol S. Murray.
Chief Congressional Caseworker.— Gail Warren.
Congressional Caseworker—Bob Nelson, Jr.

183 Russell Senate Office Building, phone 224–2881, fax 685–2570

Chief.—Col. John Schorsch.
Deputy Chief.—LtCol. Lon Pribble.
Liaison Officer.—Maj. Gean McGinnis.
Administrative Assistant.—SSG. Cynthia Gray.
Chief, Casework Liaison.—Margaret T. Tyler.
Casework Liaison Officer.—Trulesta Pauling.

COAST GUARD

B–320 Rayburn House Office Building, phone 225–4775, fax 426–6081

Liaison Officer.—Cdr. Karl Schultz.
Assistant Liaison Officers: Lt. Jo-Ann Feigofsky, Lt. Christian Lee.

183 Russell Senate Office Building, phone 224–2913, fax 755–1695

Liaison Officer.—Cdr. Timothy A. Cook.
Liaison Assistant.—Liz Moses.

NAVY / MARINE CORPS

B–324 Rayburn House Office Building, phone Navy 685–6079; Marine Corps 225–7124

Director.—Capt. Dale Lumme, USN.
Deputy Director.—Cdr. Lorin Selby, USN.
USN Liaison Officers: LtCdr. John Gilliland, USN (contracts); Lt. Tiffany Landis, USN; Lt. Frank Cristinzio, USN; Lt. Roy Zaletski, USN; Lt. Laura Booth, USN.
Director USMC.—LtCol. Michael Shupp, USMC.
USMC Liaison Officers: Maj. Bill McCollough, USMC; Capt. Samuel Bryce, USMC.
Office Manager/Administrative Clerk.—Sgt. Ana Morell, USMC.
House Staff NCO.—Sgt. Lorence Chance.

182 Russell Senate Office Building, phone: Navy 224–4682; Marine Corps 224–4681

Director.—Capt. Mark Ferguson, USN.
Deputy Director.—Cdr. Jim Stein, USN.
USN Liaison Officers: Lt. Matt Schnappauf, Lt. Deborah Loomis.
Assistant Liaison Officer.—YNC(SW) James Evans.
Director, USMC.—Col. Arthur White.
Deputy Director, USMC.—Maj. Mike Tiddy.
Assistant Liaison Officers: GySgt. Tom Hogdahl, USMC; SSG. Carmen Breiding, USMC.

GENERAL ACCOUNTING OFFICE

Room 7125, 441 G Street 20548, phone 512–4400

Congressional Relations Director.—Gloria L. Jarmon.
Legislative Advisers: Doris Cannon, 512–4507; Glenn Davis, 512–4301; Valeria Gist, 512–8092; Rahul Gupta 512–2662; Richard P. Roscoe, 512–3505; Jerry Skelly, 512–9918; Mary Frances Widner, 512–3804.
Associate Legislative Adviser.—Carolyn McCowan, 512–3503.

OFFICE OF PERSONNEL MANAGEMENT

B–332 Rayburn House Office Building, phone 225–4955 or 632–6296

Chief.—Charlene E. Luskey.
Senior Civil Service Representative.—Elnora E. Lewis.
Administrative Assistant.—Kirk H. Brightman.

VETERANS' AFFAIRS

B–328 Rayburn House Office Building, phone 225–2280, fax 453–5225

Director.—Patricia Covington.
Assistant Director.—Paul Downs.
Liaison Assistant.—Yvette Wilkins.
Representatives: Richard Armstrong, Pamela Mugg.

321 Hart Senate Office Building, phone 224–5351, fax 453–5218

Director.—Patricia Covington.
Assistant Director.—Paul Downs.
Liaison Assistant.—Michelle Newman.
Representatives: Erica Jones, Stuart Weiner.

PAGE SCHOOLS

SENATE

Daniel Webster Senate Page Residence 20510, fax 224–1838

Principal.—Kathryn S. Weeden, 224–3926.
English.—Frances Owens, 8–1024.
Mathematics.—Raymond Cwalina, 8–1018.
Science.—Duncan Forbes, 8–1025.
Social Studies.—Michael Bowers, 8–1012.
Administrative Assistant.—Lorraine Foreman, 4–3927.

HOUSE OF REPRESENTATIVES

LJ–A11 Library of Congress 20540–9996, phone 225–9000, fax 225–9001

Principal.—Linda G. Miranda.
Administrative Assistant.—Sue Ellen Stickley.
English.—Lona Carwile-Klein.
Guidance.—Donna D. Wilson.
Languages: Sebastian Hobson, French; Linda G. Miranda, Spanish.
Mathematics.—Barbara R. Bowen.
Science.—Tom Levatino.
Social Studies.—Ronald L. Weitzel.
Technology.—Darryl Gonzalez.

U.S. CAPITOL POLICE

119 D Street, NE., 20510–7218

Office of the Chief 224–9806, Command Center 224–0908
Communications 224–5151, Emergency 224–0911

U.S. CAPITOL POLICE BOARD

Sergeant at Arms, U.S. Senate.—Bill Pickle.
Sergeant at Arms, U.S. House of Representatives.—Wilson (Bill) Livingood.
Architect of the Capitol.—Alan M. Hantman.

OFFICE OF THE CHIEF

Chief of Police.—Terrance W. Gainer.
Administrative Assistant.—Lt. Matthew R. Verderosa.
General Counsel.—John T. Caulfield.
Deputy Counsel.—Gretchen DeMar.
Office of:
Strategic Planning/Inspections.—Sgt. Ricardo Anderson.
Internal Affairs.—Lt. Thomas L. Smith.
Public Information.—Officer Jessica Gissubel.
Chief of Staff.—Kristan Trugman.

CHIEF OF OPERATIONS

Assistant Chief.—Robert R. Howe.
Administration Assistant.—Sgt. Jane Frederick.
Command Center: Insp. Price S. Goldston, Insp. Mark Herbst, Insp. Joseph Parisi, Capt. Caroline Fields, Capt. Lawrence Loughery, Capt. Mark Sullivan, Capt. William Uber.
Special Events.—Lt. Matthew K. Perkins.

OPERATIONAL SERVICES BUREAU

Bureau Commander.—Deputy Chief James P. Rohan.
Hazardous Incident Response Division.—Robert Murphy.
Patrol/Mobile Response Division.—Capt. Robert Dicks.

PROTECTIVE SERVICES BUREAU

Bureau Commander.—Deputy Chief Steven D. Bahrns.
Investigations Division.—Capt. Yancey H. Garner.
Dignitary Protection Division.—Capt. Thomas Reynolds.

SECURITY SERVICES BUREAU

Bureau Commander.—Robert M. Greeley.
Physical Security Division.—Robert F. Ford.
Technical Countermeasures Division.—Michael Marinucci.
Construction Security Division.—Insp. Michael Jarboe.

UNIFORM SERVICES BUREAU

Bureau Commander.—Deputy Chief Christopher McGaffin.
Executive Assistant.—Sgt. Michelle M. Hafler.
Capitol Division Commander.—Inspector David F. Callaway.
House Division Commander.—Inspector Gregory Parman.
Senate Division Commander.—Inspector Vickie Frye.

CHIEF ADMINISTRATIVE OFFICER

Chief Administrative Officer.—John M. McWilliam.
Deputy Chief Administrative Officer.—Deputy Chief Marsha Krug.

Director, Office of:
Financial Management.—Mary Jean Jablonicky.
Human Resources.—Deputy Chief Marsha Krug (acting).
Information Systems.—James R. Getter.
Logistics.—J. Bruce Holmberg.
Commander, Training Services Bureau.—Deputy Chief Larry D. Thompson.

WESTERN UNION TELEGRAPH CO.

242–A Cannon House Office Building, phone 225–4553/4554, fax 225–5499

Manager.—Gladys R. Crockett.

STATISTICAL INFORMATION

VOTES CAST FOR SENATORS IN 1998, 2000, AND 2002

[Compiled from official statistics obtained by the Clerk of the House. Figures in the last column, for the 2002 election, may include totals for more candidates than the ones shown.]

State	Vote						Total vote cast in 2002
	1998		2000		2002		
	Republican	Democrat	Republican	Democrat	Republican	Democrat	
Alabama	817,973	474,568			792,561	538,878	1,353,023
Alaska	165,227	43,743			179,438	24,133	229,548
Arizona	696,577	275,224	1,108,196				
Arkansas	295,870	385,878			370,735	433,386	804,121
California	3,575,078	4,410,056	3,886,853	5,932,522			
Colorado	829,370	464,754			717,893	648,130	1,416,082
Connecticut	312,177	628,306	448,077	828,902			
Delaware			142,891	181,566	94,793	135,253	232,314
Florida	1,463,755	2,436,407	2,705,348	2,989,487			
Georgia	918,540	791,904	920,478	1,413,224	1,071,352	932,422	2,031,604
Hawaii	70,964	315,252	84,701	251,215			
Idaho	262,966	107,375			266,215	132,975	408,544
Illinois	1,709,041	1,610,496			1,325,703	2,103,766	3,486,851
Indiana	552,732	1,012,244	1,427,944	683,273			
Iowa	648,480	289,049			447,892	554,278	1,023,075
Kansas	474,639	229,718			641,075		776,850
Kentucky	569,817	563,051			731,679	399,634	1,131,313
Louisiana	314,580	630,395			596,642	638,654 [1]	1,235,296
Maine			437,689	197,183	295,041	209,858	504,899
Maryland	444,637	1,062,810	715,178	1,230,013			
Massachusetts			334,341	1,889,494		1,605,976	2,220,301
Michigan			1,994,693	2,061,952	1,185,545	1,896,614	3,129,287
Minnesota			1,047,474	1,181,553	1,116,697	1,078,627	2,254,639
Mississippi			654,941	314,090	533,269		630,495
Missouri	830,625	690,208	1,142,852	1,191,812	935,032	913,778	1,877,620
Montana			208,082	194,430	103,611	204,853	326,537
Nebraska			337,977	353,093	397,438	70,290	480,217
Nevada	208,220	208,621	330,687	238,260			
New Hampshire	213,477	88,883			227,229	207,478	447,135
New Jersey			1,420,267	1,511,237	928,439	1,138,193	2,112,604
New Mexico			225,517	363,744	314,193	168,863	483,056
New York	1,680,203	2,386,314	2,724,589	3,562,415			
North Carolina	945,943	1,029,237			1,248,664	1,047,983	2,331,181
North Dakota	75,013	134,747	111,069	176,470			
Ohio	1,922,087	1,482,054	2,665,512	1,595,066			
Oklahoma	570,682	268,898			583,579	369,789	1,018,424
Oregon	377,739	682,425			712,287	501,898	1,267,221
Pennsylvania	1,814,180	1,028,839	2,481,962	2,154,908			
Rhode Island			222,588	161,023	69,808	253,774	323,582
South Carolina	488,238	563,377			600,010	487,359	1,102,948
South Dakota	95,431	162,884			166,949	167,481	337,501
Tennessee			1,255,444	621,152	891,498	728,232	1,642,432
Texas			4,078,954	2,025,024	2,496,243	1,955,758	4,514,012
Utah	316,652	163,172	504,803	242,569			
Vermont	48,051	154,567	189,133	73,352			
Virginia			1,420,460	1,296,093	1,229,894		1,489,422
Washington	785,377	1,103,184	1,197,208	1,199,437			
West Virginia			121,635	469,215	160,902	275,281	436,183
Wisconsin	852,272	890,059	940,744	1,563,238			
Wyoming			157,622	47,087	133,710	49,570	183,280

[1] Louisiana law requires a runoff election between the top two candidates in the general election if none of the candidates receives 50 percent of the total votes cast. The runoff election was held on December 7, 2002.

VOTES CAST FOR REPRESENTATIVES, RESIDENT COMMISSIONER, AND DELEGATES IN 1998, 2000, AND 2002

[The figures, compiled from official statistics obtained by the Clerk of the House, show the votes for the Republican and Democratic nominees, except as otherwise indicated. Figures in the last column, for the 2002 election, may include totals for more candidates than the ones shown. The 2002 congressional districts reflect changes in apportionments resulting from the 2000 census.]

State and district	Vote cast in 1998		State and district	Vote cast in 2000		State and district	Vote cast in 2002		Total vote cast in 2002
	Republican	Democrat		Republican	Democrat		Republican	Democrat	
AL:			AL:			AL:			
1st	112,872	....	1st	151,188	....	1st	108,102	67,507	178,687
2d	131,428	58,136	2d	151,830	64,958	2d	129,233	55,495	187,965
3d	101,731	73,357	3d	147,317	....	3d	91,169	87,351	181,223
4th	106,297	82,065	4th	140,009	86,400	4th	139,705	....	161,101
5th	58,536	134,819	5th	186,059	....	5th	48,226	143,029	195,171
6th	154,761	60,657	6th	212,751	....	6th	178,171	....	198,346
7th	....	136,431	7th	46,134	148,243	7th	....	153,735	166,309
AK:			AK:			AK:			
At large	139,676	77,232	At large	190,862	45,372	At large	169,685	39,357	227,725
AZ:			AZ:			AZ:			
1st	98,840	54,108	1st	123,289	97,455	1st	85,967	79,730	174,687
2d	23,628	57,178	2d	32,990	84,034	2d	100,359	61,217	167,502
3d	137,618	66,979	3d	198,367	94,676	3d	104,847	47,173	155,751
4th	102,722	49,538	4th	140,396	71,803	4th	18,381	44,517	66,065
5th	103,952	91,030	5th	172,986	101,564	5th	103,870	61,559	169,812
6th	106,891	88,001	6th	186,687	108,317	6th	103,094	49,355	156,337
						7th	38,474	61,256	103,818
						8th	126,930	67,328	200,428
AR:			AR:			AR:			
1st	....	[1]	1st	79,437	120,266	1st	64,357	129,701	194,058
2d	72,737	100,334	2d	93,692	126,957	2d	....	142,752	153,626
3d	154,780	....	3d	[1]	....	3d	141,478	....	143,055
4th	92,346	68,194	4th	104,017	108,143	4th	77,904	119,633	197,537
CA:			CA:			CA:			
1st	64,692	121,713	1st	66,987	155,638	1st	60,013	118,669	185,216
2d	128,372	70,837	2d	168,172	72,075	2d	117,747	52,455	178,985
3d	100,621	86,471	3d	129,254	93,067	3d	121,732	67,136	194,918
4th	155,306	85,394	4th	197,503	97,974	4th	147,997	72,860	228,506
5th	47,307	130,715	5th	55,945	147,025	5th	34,749	92,726	131,578
6th	69,295	158,446	6th	80,169	182,116	6th	62,052	139,750	209,563
7th	38,290	125,842	7th	44,154	159,692	7th	36,584	97,849	138,376
8th	20,781	148,027	8th	25,298	181,847	8th	20,063	127,684	160,441
9th	22,431	140,722	9th	21,033	182,352	9th	25,333	135,893	166,917
10th	103,299	127,134	10th	134,863	160,429	10th	....	126,390	167,197
11th	95,496	56,345	11th	120,635	79,539	11th	104,921	69,035	173,956
12th	36,562	128,135	12th	44,162	158,404	12th	38,381	105,597	154,984
13th	38,050	101,671	13th	44,499	129,012	13th	26,852	86,495	121,723
14th	53,719	129,663	14th	59,338	161,720	14th	48,346	117,055	171,678
15th	111,876	70,059	15th	99,866	128,545	15th	41,251	87,482	133,022
16th	27,494	85,503	16th	37,213	115,118	16th	32,182	72,370	107,986
17th	52,470	103,719	17th	51,557	143,219	17th	40,334	101,632	149,296
18th	....	118,842	18th	56,465	121,003	18th	47,528	56,181	109,593
19th	131,105	....	19th	144,517	70,578	19th	106,209	47,403	157,802
20th	39,183	60,599	20th	57,563	66,235	20th	25,628	47,627	74,770
21st	115,989	....	21st	142,539	49,318	21st	87,544	32,584	124,198
22d	85,927	109,517	22d	113,094	135,538	22d	120,473	38,988	164,285
23d	96,322	64,032	23d	119,479	89,918	23d	62,604	95,752	162,222
24th	69,501	103,491	24th	70,169	155,398	24th	120,585	58,755	185,006
25th	114,013	....	25th	138,628	73,921	25th	80,775	38,674	124,336
26th	....	69,000	26th	96,500	....	26th	95,360	50,081	149,530
27th	80,702	73,875	27th	94,518	113,708	27th	48,996	79,815	128,811
28th	90,607	61,721	28th	116,557	81,804	28th	23,926	73,771	103,326
29th	40,282	131,561	29th	45,784	180,295	29th	40,616	76,036	121,541
30th	13,441	58,230	30th	11,788	83,223	30th	54,989	130,604	185,593
31st	19,786	61,173	31st	89,600	....	31st	12,674	54,569	67,243
32d	14,622	112,253	32d	19,924	137,447	32d	23,366	58,530	85,079
33d	6,364	43,310	33d	8,260	60,510	33d	16,699	97,779	118,449
34th	32,321	76,471	34th	33,445	105,980	34th	17,090	48,734	65,824
35th	....	78,732	35th	12,582	100,569	35th	18,094	72,401	93,407
36th	88,843	84,624	36th	111,199	115,651	36th	50,328	88,198	143,751
37th	12,301	70,026	37th	12,762	93,269	37th	20,154	63,445	87,012
38th	71,386	59,767	38th	87,266	85,498	38th	23,126	62,600	88,027
39th	97,366	52,815	39th	129,294	64,398	39th	38,925	52,256	95,346
40th	97,406	47,897	40th	151,069	....	40th	92,422	40,265	136,642
41st	68,310	52,264	41st	104,695	66,361	41st	91,326	40,155	135,533

VOTES CAST FOR REPRESENTATIVES, RESIDENT COMMISSIONER, AND DELEGATES IN 1998, 2000, AND 2002—CONTINUED

[The figures, compiled from official statistics obtained by the Clerk of the House, show the votes for the Republican and Democratic nominees, except as otherwise indicated. Figures in the last column, for the 2002 election, may include totals for more candidates than the ones shown. The 2002 congressional districts reflect changes in apportionments resulting from the 2000 census.]

State and district	Vote cast in 1998		State and district	Vote cast in 2000		State and district	Vote cast in 2002		Total vote cast in 2002
	Republican	Democrat		Republican	Democrat		Republican	Democrat	
42d	45,328	62,207	42d	53,239	90,585	42d	98,476	42,090	145,246
43d	83,012	56,373	43d	140,201	....	43d	20,821	45,374	68,340
44th	97,013	57,697	44th	123,738	79,302	44th	76,686	38,021	120,463
45th	94,296	60,022	45th	136,275	71,066	45th	87,101	43,692	133,533
46th	33,388	47,964	46th	40,928	70,381	46th	108,807	60,890	176,265
47th	132,711	57,938	47th	181,365	83,186	47th	24,346	42,501	70,178
48th	138,948	....	48th	160,627	74,073	48th	122,884	51,058	179,549
49th	90,516	86,400	49th	105,515	113,400	49th	94,594	....	122,497
50th	....	77,354	50th	38,526	95,191	50th	111,095	55,855	172,701
51st	126,229	71,706	51st	172,291	81,408	51st	40,430	59,541	102,787
52d	116,251	....	52d	131,345	63,537	52d	118,561	43,526	168,010
						53d	43,891	72,252	116,180
CO:			CO:			CO:			
1st	52,452	116,628	1st	56,291	141,831	1st	49,884	111,718	168,582
2d	108,385	113,946	2d	109,338	155,725	2d	75,564	123,504	205,522
3d	156,501	74,479	3d	199,204	87,921	3d	143,433	68,160	217,972
4th	131,318	89,973	4th	209,078	....	4th	115,359	87,499	209,955
5th	155,790	55,609	5th	253,330	....	5th	128,118	45,587	184,677
6th	111,374	82,662	6th	141,410	110,568	6th	158,851	71,327	237,501
						7th	81,789	81,668	172,879
CT:			CT:			CT:			
1st	69,668	97,681	1st	59,331	151,932	1st	66,968	134,698	201,688
2d	57,860	99,567	2d	114,380	111,520	2d	117,434	99,674	217,108
3d	42,090	109,726	3d	60,037	156,910	3d	54,757	121,557	185,364
4th	94,767	40,988	4th	119,155	84,472	4th	113,197	62,491	175,695
5th	76,051	78,394	5th	98,229	118,932	5th	113,626	90,616	209,454
6th	101,630	69,201	6th	143,698	75,471				
DE:			DE:			DE:			
At large	199,811	57,446	At large	211,797	96,488	At large	164,605	61,011	228,405
FL:			FL:			FL:			
1st	140,525	....	1st	(2)	....	1st	152,635	51,972	204,626
2d	....	138,440	2d	71,754	185,579	2d	75,275	152,164	227,439
3d	53,530	66,621	3d	75,228	102,143	3d	60,747	88,462	149,213
4th	(2)	....	4th	203,090	94,587	4th	171,152	....	171,661
5th	....	132,005	5th	100,244	180,338	5th	121,998	117,758	254,671
6th	(2)	....	6th	(2)	....	6th	141,570	75,046	216,616
7th	(2)	....	7th	171,018	99,531	7th	142,147	96,444	238,591
8th	104,298	54,245	8th	125,253	121,295	8th	123,497	66,099	189,596
9th	(2)	....	9th	210,318	....	9th	169,369	67,623	237,008
10th	(2)	....	10th	146,799	....	10th	(2)	....	(2)
11th	46,176	85,262	11th	149,465	....	11th	....	(2)	(2)
12th	(2)	....	12th	125,224	94,395	12th	(2)	....	(2)
13th	(2)	....	13th	175,918	99,568	13th	139,048	114,739	253,809
14th	(2)	....	14th	242,614	....	14th	(2)	....	(2)
15th	129,278	75,654	15th	176,189	117,511	15th	146,414	85,433	231,857
16th	(2)	....	16th	176,153	108,782	16th	176,171	....	223,340
17th	....	(2)	17th	....	(2)	17th	....	113,749	113,822
18th	(2)	....	18th	(2)	....	18th	103,512	42,852	149,787
19th	....	(2)	19th	67,789	171,080	19th	60,477	156,747	217,224
20th	....	(2)	20th	....	(2)	20th	....	(2)	(2)
21st	84,018	28,378	21st	(2)	....	21st	(2)	....	(2)
22d	(2)	....	22d	105,855	105,256	22d	131,930	83,265	217,115
23d	....	(2)	23d	27,630	89,179	23d	27,986	96,347	124,338
						24th	135,576	83,667	219,243
						25th	81,845	44,757	126,602
GA:			GA:			GA:			
1st	92,229	....	1st	131,684	58,776	1st	103,661	40,026	143,687
2d	59,305	77,953	2d	83,870	96,430	2d	....	102,925	102,925
3d	123,064	....	3d	150,200	86,309	3d	73,866	75,394	149,260
4th	64,146	100,622	4th	90,277	139,579	4th	35,202	118,045	153,247
5th	29,877	109,177	5th	40,606	137,333	5th	....	116,259	116,259
6th	164,966	68,366	6th	256,595	86,666	6th	163,525	41,204	204,729
7th	85,982	69,293	7th	126,312	102,272	7th	138,997	37,124	176,121
8th	87,993	53,079	8th	113,380	79,051	8th	142,505	39,422	181,927
9th	122,713	....	9th	183,171	60,360	9th	123,313	45,974	169,287
10th	88,527	60,004	10th	122,590	71,309	10th	129,242	....	129,242
11th	120,909	53,510	11th	199,652	....	11th	69,427	65,007	134,434
						12th	77,479	62,904	140,383
						13th	47,405	70,011	117,416
HI:			HI:			HI:			
1st	68,905	116,693	1st	44,989	108,517	1st	45,032	131,673	180,733
2d	50,423	144,254	2d	65,906	112,856	2d	71,661	100,671	179,251
ID:			ID:			ID:			
1st	113,231	91,653	1st	173,743	84,080	1st	120,743	80,269	206,141
2d	91,337	77,736	2d	158,912	58,265	2d	135,605	57,769	198,882

VOTES CAST FOR REPRESENTATIVES, RESIDENT COMMISSIONER, AND DELEGATES IN 1998, 2000, AND 2002—CONTINUED

[The figures, compiled from official statistics obtained by the Clerk of the House, show the votes for the Republican and Democratic nominees, except as otherwise indicated. Figures in the last column, for the 2002 election, may include totals for more candidates than the ones shown. The 2002 congressional districts reflect changes in apportionments resulting from the 2000 census.]

State and district	Vote cast in 1998		State and district	Vote cast in 2000		State and district	Vote cast in 2002		Total vote cast in 2002
	Republican	Democrat		Republican	Democrat		Republican	Democrat	
IL:			IL:			IL:			
1st	18,429	151,890	1st	23,915	172,271	1st	29,776	149,068	183,656
2d	16,075	148,985	2d	19,906	175,995	2d	32,567	151,443	184,010
3d	44,012	115,887	3d	47,005	145,498	3d	....	156,042	156,042
4th	10,529	54,244	4th	....	89,487	4th	12,778	67,339	84,513
5th	33,687	95,738	5th	....	142,161	5th	46,008	106,514	159,435
6th	111,603	49,906	6th	133,327	92,880	6th	113,174	60,698	173,872
7th	....	130,984	7th	26,872	164,155	7th	25,280	137,933	165,756
8th	104,242	47,614	8th	141,918	90,777	8th	95,275	70,626	165,926
9th	33,448	107,878	9th	45,344	147,002	9th	45,307	118,642	168,836
10th	138,429	....	10th	121,582	115,924	10th	128,611	58,300	186,911
11th	100,597	70,458	11th	132,384	102,485	11th	124,192	68,893	193,085
12th	65,409	99,605	12th	....	183,208	12th	58,440	131,580	190,020
13th	121,889	77,78	13th	193,250	98,768	13th	139,546	59,069	198,615
14th	117,304	50,844	14th	188,597	66,309	14th	135,198	47,165	182,363
15th	104,255	65,054	15th	125,943	110,679	15th	134,650	64,131	206,617
16th	143,686	....	16th	178,174	88,781	16th	133,339	55,488	188,827
17th	94,072	100,128	17th	108,853	132,494	17th	76,519	127,093	203,612
18th	158,175	....	18th	173,706	85,317	18th	192,567	....	192,567
19th	87,614	122,430	19th	85,137	155,101	19th	133,956	110,517	244,473
20th	121,103	76,475	20th	161,393	94,382				
IN:			IN:			IN:			
1st	33,503	92,634	1st	56,200	148,683	1st	41,909	90,443	135,111
2d	99,608	62,452	2d	106,023	80,885	2d	95,081	86,253	188,458
3d	61,041	84,625	3d	98,822	107,438	3d	92,566	50,509	146,606
4th	93,671	54,286	4th	131,051	74,492	4th	112,760	41,314	158,008
5th	101,567	58,504	5th	132,051	81,427	5th	129,442	45,283	179,855
6th	135,250	31,472	6th	199,207	74,881	6th	118,436	63,871	185,653
7th	109,712	44,823	7th	135,869	66,764	7th	64,379	77,478	145,840
8th	92,785	81,871	8th	116,879	100,488	8th	98,952	88,763	192,865
9th	87,787	92,973	9th	102,219	126,420	9th	87,169	96,654	188,957
10th	47,017	69,682	10th	62,233	91,689				
IA:			IA:			IA:			
1st	106,419	79,529	1st	164,972	96,283	1st	112,280	83,779	196,455
2d	104,613	83,405	2d	139,906	110,327	2d	108,130	94,767	207,171
3d	78,063	107,947	3d	83,810	156,327	3d	97,285	115,367	215,985
4th	129,942	67,550	4th	169,267	101,112	4th	115,430	90,784	210,774
5th	132,730	....	5th	159,367	67,593	5th	113,257	68,853	182,237
KS:			KS:			KS:			
1st	152,775	36,618	1st	214,328	....	1st	189,976	....	208,561
2d	108,527	69,521	2d	164,951	71,709	2d	127,477	79,160	210,977
3d	93,938	103,376	3d	144,672	154,505	3d	102,882	110,095	219,389
4th	94,785	62,737	4th	131,871	101,980	4th	115,691	70,656	190,963
KY:			KY:			KY:			
1st	95,308	77,402	1st	132,115	95,806	1st	117,600	62,617	180,217
2d	113,285	62,848	2d	160,800	74,537	2d	122,773	51,431	176,288
3d	100,690	92,865	3d	142,106	118,875	3d	118,228	110,846	229,074
4th	81,547	93,485	4th	100,943	125,872	4th	81,651	87,776	171,735
5th	142,215	39,585	5th	145,980	52,495	5th	137,986	38,254	176,240
6th	104,046	90,033	6th	142,971	94,167	6th	115,622	....	160,688
LA:			LA:			LA:			
1st	(3)	....	1st	191,379	29,935	1st	174,614	....	180,570
2d	....	118,949	2d	....	(3)	2d	15,440	122,927	142,156
3d	(3)	....	3d	143,446	....	3d	130,323	....	150,342
4th	(3)	....	4th	122,678	43,600	4th	114,649	42,340	160,093
5th	(3)	....	5th	123,975	42,977	5th	85,744	86,718	172,462
6th	97,044	94,201	6th	165,637	72,192	6th	146,932	....	174,830
7th	....	(3)	7th	....	152,796	7th	....	138,659	159,710
ME:			ME:			ME:			
1st	79,160	134,335	1st	123,915	202,823	1st	97,931	172,646	270,577
2d	45,674	146,202	2d	79,522	219,783	2d	107,849	116,868	224,717
MD:			MD:			MD:			
1st	135,771	60,450	1st	165,293	91,022	1st	192,004	57,986	249,990
2d	125,162	74,275	2d	178,556	81,591	2d	88,954	105,718	194,672
3d	39,667	137,501	3d	53,827	169,347	3d	75,721	145,589	221,310
4th	21,518	129,139	4th	24,973	172,624	4th	34,890	131,644	166,729
5th	67,176	126,792	5th	89,019	166,231	5th	60,758	137,903	198,819
6th	127,802	73,728	6th	168,624	109,136	6th	147,825	75,575	223,400
7th	18,742	112,699	7th	19,773	134,066	7th	49,172	137,047	186,219
8th	133,145	87,497	8th	156,241	136,840	8th	103,587	112,788	217,974
MA:			MA:			MA:			
1st	48,055	121,863	1st	73,580	169,375	1st	66,061	137,841	212,216
2d	....	130,550	2d	....	196,670	2d	....	153,387	208,498
3d	79,174	108,613	3d	....	213,065	3d	....	155,697	212,304
4th	....	148,340	4th	56,553	200,638	4th	....	166,125	221,209

VOTES CAST FOR REPRESENTATIVES, RESIDENT COMMISSIONER, AND DELEGATES IN 1998, 2000, AND 2002—CONTINUED

[The figures, compiled from official statistics obtained by the Clerk of the House, show the votes for the Republican and Democratic nominees, except as otherwise indicated. Figures in the last column, for the 2002 election, may include totals for more candidates than the ones shown. The 2002 congressional districts reflect changes in apportionments resulting from the 2000 census.]

State and district	Vote cast in 1998		State and district	Vote cast in 2000		State and district	Vote cast in 2002		Total vote cast in 2002
	Republican	Democrat		Republican	Democrat		Republican	Democrat	
5th	52,725	127,418	5th	....	199,601	5th	69,337	122,562	214,022
6th	90,986	117,132	6th	83,501	205,324	6th	75,462	162,900	252,867
7th	56,977	137,178	7th	....	211,543	7th	....	170,968	236,013
8th	14,125	99,603	8th	....	144,031	8th	....	111,861	155,304
9th	....	150,667	9th	48,672	193,020	9th	....	168,055	235,866
10th	70,466	164,917	10th	81,192	234,675	10th	79,624	179,238	272,027
MI:			MI:			MI:			
1st	87,630	130,129	1st	117,300	169,649	1st	69,254	150,701	222,687
2d	146,854	63,573	2d	186,762	96,370	2d	156,937	61,749	222,907
3d	146,364	49,489	3d	179,539	91,309	3d	153,131	61,987	218,855
4th	155,343	....	4th	182,128	78,019	4th	149,090	65,950	218,573
5th	51,442	135,254	5th	59,274	184,048	5th	....	158,709	173,339
6th	113,292	45,358	6th	159,373	68,532	6th	126,936	53,793	183,517
7th	104,656	72,998	7th	147,369	86,080	7th	121,142	78,412	203,069
8th	84,254	125,169	8th	145,179	145,019	8th	156,525	70,920	230,597
9th	79,062	105,457	9th	92,926	158,184	9th	141,102	96,856	242,880
10th	94,027	108,770	10th	93,713	181,818	10th	137,339	77,053	216,928
11th	144,264	76,107	11th	170,790	124,053	11th	126,050	87,402	220,405
12th	79,619	105,824	12th	78,795	157,720	12th	61,502	140,970	206,528
13th	68,328	99,935	13th	79,445	160,084	13th	....	120,859	131,941
14th	16,140	126,321	14th	17,582	168,982	14th	26,544	145,285	174,608
15th	12,887	108,582	15th	14,336	140,609	15th	48,626	136,518	189,063
16th	54,121	116,145	16th	62,469	167,142				
MN:			MN:			MN:			
1st	131,233	108,420	1st	159,835	117,946	1st	163,570	92,165	265,982
2d	99,490	148,933	2d	138,957	138,802	2d	152,970	121,121	286,860
3d	203,731	66,505	3d	222,571	98,219	3d	213,334	82,575	296,218
4th	95,388	128,726	4th	83,852	130,403	4th	89,705	164,597	264,540
5th	60,035	145,535	5th	58,191	176,629	5th	66,271	171,572	255,982
6th	136,866	148,728	6th	170,900	176,340	6th	164,747	100,738	287,312
7th	66,562	169,907	7th	79,175	185,771	7th	90,342	170,234	260,813
8th	69,667	173,734	8th	79,890	210,094	8th	88,673	194,909	283,931
MS:			MS:			MS:			
1st	66,738	30,438	1st	145,967	59,763	1st	95,404	32,318	133,567
2d	....	80,284	2d	54,090	112,777	2d	69,711	89,913	163,050
3d	84,785	....	3d	153,899	54,151	3d	139,329	76,184	219,151
4th	61,551	73,252	4th	79,218	115,732	4th	34,373	121,742	161,868
5th	19,341	78,661	5th	35,309	153,264				
MO:			MO:			MO:			
1st	30,635	90,840	1st	42,730	149,173	1st	51,755	133,946	191,055
2d	142,313	57,565	2d	164,926	126,441	2d	167,057	77,223	248,828
3d	74,005	98,287	3d	100,967	147,222	3d	80,551	122,181	206,878
4th	51,005	133,173	4th	84,406	180,634	4th	64,451	142,204	210,238
5th	47,582	101,313	5th	66,439	159,826	5th	60,245	122,645	186,167
6th	51,679	136,774	6th	138,925	127,792	6th	131,151	73,202	208,088
7th	129,746	43,416	7th	202,305	65,510	7th	149,519	45,964	199,863
8th	104,271	59,426	8th	162,239	67,760	8th	135,144	50,686	188,321
9th	117,196	66,861	9th	172,787	111,662	9th	146,032	61,126	214,125
MT:			MT:			MT:			
At large	175,728	147,073	At large	211,418	189,971	At large	214,100	108,233	331,321
NE:			NE:			NE:			
1st	136,058	48,826	1st	155,485	72,859	1st	133,013	....	155,844
2d	106,782	55,722	2d	148,911	70,268	2d	89,917	46,843	142,014
3d	149,896	....	3d	182,117	34,944	3d	163,939	....	175,956
NV:			NV:			NV:			
1st	73,540	79,315	1st	101,276	118,469	1st	51,148	64,312	121,516
2d	201,623	....	2d	229,608	106,379	2d	149,574	40,189	201,343
						3d	100,378	66,659	178,994
NH:			NH:			NH:			
1st	104,430	51,783	1st	150,609	128,387	1st	128,993	85,426	221,987
2d	85,740	72,217	2d	152,581	110,367	2d	125,804	90,479	221,456
NJ:			NJ:			NJ:			
1st	27,855	90,279	1st	46,455	167,327	1st	....	121,846	131,389
2d	93,248	43,563	2d	155,187	74,632	2d	116,834	47,735	168,799
3d	97,508	55,248	3d	157,053	112,848	3d	123,375	64,364	189,739
4th	92,991	52,281	4th	158,515	87,956	4th	115,293	55,967	174,301
5th	106,304	55,487	5th	175,546	81,715	5th	118,881	76,504	199,851
6th	55,180	78,102	6th	62,454	141,698	6th	42,479	91,379	137,495
7th	77,751	65,776	7th	128,434	113,479	7th	106,055	74,879	183,002
8th	46,289	81,068	8th	60,606	134,074	8th	40,318	88,101	131,819
9th	47,817	91,330	9th	61,984	140,462	9th	42,088	97,108	139,196
10th	10,678	82,244	10th	18,436	133,073	10th	15,913	86,433	102,346
11th	100,910	44,160	11th	186,140	80,958	11th	132,938	48,477	183,678
12th	87,221	92,528	12th	145,511	146,162	12th	62,938	104,806	171,713
13th	14,615	70,308	13th	27,849	117,856	13th	16,852	72,605	92,731

VOTES CAST FOR REPRESENTATIVES, RESIDENT COMMISSIONER, AND DELEGATES IN 1998, 2000, AND 2002—CONTINUED

[The figures, compiled from official statistics obtained by the Clerk of the House, show the votes for the Republican and Democratic nominees, except as otherwise indicated. Figures in the last column, for the 2002 election, may include totals for more candidates than the ones shown. The 2002 congressional districts reflect changes in apportionments resulting from the 2000 census.]

State and district	Vote cast in 1998		State and district	Vote cast in 2000		State and district	Vote cast in 2002		Total vote cast in 2002
	Repub-lican	Demo-crat		Repub-lican	Demo-crat		Repub-lican	Demo-crat	
NM:			NM:			NM:			
1st	86,784	75,040	1st	107,296	92,187	1st	95,711	77,234	172,945
2d	85,077	61,796	2d	100,742	72,614	2d	79,631	61,916	141,629
3d	74,266	91,248	3d	65,979	135,040	3d	....	122,921	122,921
NY:			NY:			NY:			
1st	75,643	54,463	1st	111,003	97,299	1st	64,999	81,325	178,530
2d	71,760	37,949	2d	65,880	90,438	2d	48,239	75,845	160,213
3d	95,709	63,628	3d	122,820	91,948	3d	98,874	46,022	186,622
4th	64,509	86,692	4th	75,650	128,688	4th	61,473	85,496	180,253
5th	40,861	92,189	5th	56,046	127,233	5th	....	68,773	132,741
6th	....	73,235	6th	....	117,194	6th	....	68,718	111,818
7th	18,896	50,924	7th	24,592	78,207	7th	16,460	48,983	104,272
8th	18,383	108,408	8th	27,057	139,936	8th	18,623	71,996	141,576
9th	24,486	67,274	9th	40,866	96,348	9th	27,882	57,104	119,935
10th	5,577	81,368	10th	6,852	118,812	10th	....	72,313	117,571
11th	5,718	73,674	11th	7,088	105,321	11th	9,250	67,967	119,174
12th	7,405	53,269	12th	10,052	81,699	12th	....	43,809	84,765
13th	60,550	39,153	13th	95,696	55,763	13th	62,520	27,304	123,606
14th	32,458	104,351	14th	45,453	143,809	14th	30,053	85,029	151,606
15th	5,633	88,271	15th	6,906	124,415	15th	8,790	77,036	127,400
16th	2,457	65,957	16th	3,943	100,891	16th	3,916	48,411	78,454
17th	7,982	79,257	17th	11,513	112,748	17th	35,389	73,569	144,582
18th	....	91,623	18th	52,923	126,878	18th	....	95,396	190,018
19th	88,341	56,378	19th	133,963	82,082	19th	102,848	44,967	190,318
20th	98,546	61,753	20th	136,016	87,602	20th	125,335	45,878	222,534
21st	50,931	123,638	21st	60,333	157,773	21st	53,525	128,584	236,967
22d	87,786	81,296	22d	153,997	72,640	22d	52,499	92,336	192,271
23d	111,242	....	23d	110,634	38,049	23d	110,042	....	184,613
24th	101,689	31,011	24th	128,513	41,719	24th	108,017	....	202,632
25th	102,219	50,268	25th	132,120	64,533	25th	113,914	53,290	217,160
26th	47,084	99,249	26th	78,103	124,862	26th	105,807	41,140	213,994
27th	86,106	62,714	27th	144,011	69,870	27th	105,946	45,060	199,883
28th	50,926	118,856	28th	67,251	151,688	28th	45,125	94,209	179,708
29th	58,232	87,805	29th	68,958	115,685	29th	116,245	37,128	207,793
30th	91,350	55,199	30th	113,638	62,378				
31st	95,638	40,091	31st	143,584	45,193				
NC:			NC:			NC:			
1st	50,578	85,125	1st	62,198	124,171	1st	50,907	93,157	146,157
2d	72,997	100,550	2d	103,011	146,733	2d	50,965	100,121	153,184
3d	83,529	50,041	3d	121,940	74,058	3d	131,448	....	144,934
4th	93,469	129,157	4th	119,412	200,885	4th	78,095	132,185	216,046
5th	119,103	55,806	5th	172,489	....	5th	137,879	58,558	196,437
6th	112,740	....	6th	195,727	....	6th	151,430	....	167,497
7th	....	124,366	7th	66,463	160,185	7th	45,537	118,543	166,654
8th	67,505	64,127	8th	111,950	89,505	8th	80,298	66,819	149,736
9th	120,570	51,345	9th	181,161	79,382	9th	140,095	49,974	193,443
10th	118,541	....	10th	164,182	70,877	10th	102,768	65,587	173,292
11th	112,908	84,256	11th	146,677	112,234	11th	112,335	86,664	202,260
12th	62,070	82,305	12th	69,596	135,570	12th	49,588	98,821	151,239
						13th	77,688	100,287	183,270
ND:			ND:			ND:			
At large	87,511	119,668	At large	127,251	151,173	At large	109,957	121,073	231,030
OH:			OH:			OH:			
1st	92,421	82,003	1st	116,768	98,328	1st	110,760	60,168	170,928
2d	154,344	49,293	2d	204,184	64,091	2d	139,218	48,785	188,016
3d	50,544	114,198	3d	....	177,731	3d	111,630	78,307	189,951
4th	112,011	63,529	4th	156,510	67,330	4th	120,001	57,726	177,727
5th	123,979	61,926	5th	169,857	62,138	5th	126,286	51,872	188,254
6th	77,711	102,852	6th	96,966	138,849	6th	77,643	113,972	191,615
7th	120,765	49,780	7th	163,646	60,755	7th	113,252	45,568	167,632
8th	127,979	52,912	8th	179,756	66,293	8th	119,947	49,444	169,391
9th	30,312	130,793	9th	49,446	168,547	9th	46,481	132,236	178,717
10th	55,015	110,552	10th	48,930	167,063	10th	41,778	129,997	175,536
11th	18,592	115,226	11th	21,630	164,134	11th	36,146	116,590	152,736
12th	124,197	60,694	12th	139,242	115,432	12th	116,982	64,707	181,689
13th	72,666	116,309	13th	84,295	170,058	13th	55,357	123,025	178,382
14th	63,027	106,046	14th	71,432	149,184	14th	134,413	51,846	186,372
15th	113,846	49,334	15th	156,792	64,805	15th	108,193	54,286	162,479
16th	117,426	66,047	16th	162,294	62,709	16th	129,734	58,644	188,378
17th	57,703	123,718	17th	54,751	120,333	17th	62,188	94,441	184,674
18th	113,119	74,571	18th	152,325	79,232	18th	125,546	....	125,546
19th	126,786	64,090	19th	206,639	101,842				
OK:			OK:			OK:			
1st	91,031	56,309	1st	138,528	58,493	1st	119,566	90,649	214,955
2d	85,581	59,042	2d	81,672	107,273	2d	51,234	146,748	197,982

VOTES CAST FOR REPRESENTATIVES, RESIDENT COMMISSIONER, AND DELEGATES IN 1998, 2000, AND 2002—CONTINUED

[The figures, compiled from official statistics obtained by the Clerk of the House, show the votes for the Republican and Democratic nominees, except as otherwise indicated. Figures in the last column, for the 2002 election, may include totals for more candidates than the ones shown. The 2002 congressional districts reflect changes in apportionments resulting from the 2000 census.]

State and district	Vote cast in 1998		State and district	Vote cast in 2000		State and district	Vote cast in 2002		Total vote cast in 2002
	Republican	Democrat		Republican	Democrat		Republican	Democrat	
3d	89,832	55,163	3d	137,826	....	3d	148,206	....	196,090
4th	83,272	52,107	4th	114,000	54,808	4th	106,452	91,322	197,774
5th	103,217	48,182	5th	134,159	53,275	5th	121,374	63,208	195,051
6th	85,261	43,555	6th	95,635	63,106				
OR:			OR:			OR:			
1st	112,827	119,993	1st	115,303	176,902	1st	80,917	149,215	238,036
2d	132,316	74,924	2d	220,086	78,101	2d	181,295	64,991	252,284
3d	....	153,889	3d	64,128	181,049	3d	62,821	156,851	234,977
4th	64,143	157,524	4th	88,950	197,998	4th	90,523	168,150	263,481
5th	92,215	124,916	5th	118,631	156,315	5th	113,441	137,713	251,537
PA:			PA:			PA:			
1st	15,898	77,788	1st	19,920	149,621	1st	17,444	121,076	140,090
2d	16,001	102,763	2d	....	180,021	2d	20,988	150,623	171,611
3d	45,390	66,270	3d	59,343	130,528	3d	116,763	....	150,329
4th	58,485	103,183	4th	145,390	100,995	4th	130,534	71,674	202,218
5th	99,502	....	5th	147,570	....	5th	124,942	....	143,211
6th	54,579	85,374	6th	71,227	140,084	6th	103,648	98,128	201,791
7th	119,491	46,920	7th	172,569	93,687	7th	146,296	75,055	221,351
8th	93,697	48,320	8th	154,090	100,617	8th	127,475	76,178	203,687
9th	125,409	....	9th	184,401	....	9th	124,184	50,558	174,849
10th	84,275	83,760	10th	124,830	112,580	10th	152,017	....	164,159
11th	44,123	88,933	11th	66,699	131,948	11th	71,543	93,758	168,615
12th	46,239	100,529	12th	56,575	145,538	12th	44,818	124,201	169,028
13th	85,915	95,105	13th	126,501	146,026	13th	100,295	107,945	211,867
14th	52,745	83,355	14th	....	147,533	14th	....	123,323	123,412
15th	81,755	66,930	15th	118,307	103,864	15th	98,493	73,212	171,713
16th	95,979	40,092	16th	162,403	80,177	16th	119,046	....	134,597
17th	114,931	....	17th	166,236	66,190	17th	97,802	103,483	201,291
18th	46,945	98,363	18th	68,798	156,131	18th	119,885	79,451	199,349
19th	96,284	40,674	19th	168,722	61,538	19th	143,097	....	157,145
20th	....	97,885	20th	80,312	145,131				
21st	94,518	54,591	21st	135,164	87,018				
RI:			RI:			RI:			
1st	38,460	92,788	1st	61,522	123,442	1st	59,370	95,286	159,133
2d	38,170	110,917	2d	27,932	123,805	2d	37,767	129,390	169,610
SC:			SC:			SC:			
1st	118,414	....	1st	139,597	82,622	1st	127,562	....	142,425
2d	119,538	84,864	2d	154,338	110,672	2d	144,149	....	171,359
3d	129,047	....	3d	150,180	64,917	3d	119,644	55,743	178,195
4th	105,264	73,314	4th	150,436	....	4th	122,422	51,462	177,417
5th	66,367	95,696	5th	85,247	126,877	5th	....	121,912	141,972
6th	41,421	116,507	6th	50,005	138,053	6th	55,760	116,586	174,066
SD:			SD:			SD:			
At large	194,157	64,433	At large	231,083	78,321	At large	180,023	153,551	336,691
TN:			TN:			TN:			
1st	68,904	30,710	1st	157,828	....	1st	127,300	....	128,886
2d	90,860	....	2d	187,154	....	2d	146,887	37,035	185,981
3d	75,100	37,144	3d	139,840	75,785	3d	112,254	58,824	173,921
4th	62,829	42,627	4th	133,622	67,165	4th	85,680	95,989	184,300
5th	....	74,611	5th	50,386	149,277	5th	56,825	108,903	170,886
6th	62,277	75,055	6th	97,169	168,861	6th	57,397	117,119	177,628
7th	91,503	....	7th	171,056	71,587	7th	138,314	51,790	195,558
8th	....	76,803	8th	54,929	143,127	8th	45,853	117,811	167,970
9th	18,078	75,428	9th	....	143,298	9th	....	120,904	144,260
TX:			TX:			TX:			
1st	55,191	80,788	1st	91,912	118,157	1st	66,654	86,384	153,038
2d	56,891	81,556	2d	....	162,891	2d	53,656	85,492	140,501
3d	106,690	....	3d	187,486	67,233	3d	113,974	37,503	154,133
4th	58,954	82,989	4th	91,574	145,887	4th	67,939	97,304	168,285
5th	61,714	48,073	5th	100,487	82,629	5th	81,439	56,330	139,908
6th	112,957	40,112	6th	222,685	....	6th	115,396	45,404	164,037
7th	111,010	....	7th	183,712	60,694	7th	96,795	....	108,527
8th	123,372	....	8th	233,848	....	8th	140,575	....	150,926
9th	49,107	86,055	9th	87,165	130,143	9th	59,635	86,710	147,958
10th	....	116,127	10th	....	203,628	10th	....	114,428	135,624
11th	....	71,142	11th	85,546	105,782	11th	68,236	74,678	144,857
12th	66,740	39,084	12th	117,739	67,612	12th	121,208	....	131,931
13th	81,141	37,027	13th	117,995	54,343	13th	119,401	31,218	150,619
14th	84,459	68,014	14th	137,370	92,689	14th	102,905	48,224	151,129
15th	34,221	47,957	15th	106,570	....	15th	....	66,311	66,311
16th	....	67,486	16th	40,921	92,649	16th	....	72,383	72,383
17th	63,700	75,367	17th	72,535	120,670	17th	77,622	84,136	163,804
18th	....	82,091	18th	38,191	131,857	18th	27,980	99,161	128,926
19th	108,266	21,162	19th	170,319	....	19th	117,092	....	127,776
20th	28,347	50,356	20th	....	107,487	20th	....	68,685	68,685

VOTES CAST FOR REPRESENTATIVES, RESIDENT COMMISSIONER, AND DELEGATES IN 1998, 2000, AND 2002—CONTINUED

[The figures, compiled from official statistics obtained by the Clerk of the House, show the votes for the Republican and Democratic nominees, except as otherwise indicated. Figures in the last column, for the 2002 election, may include totals for more candidates than the ones shown. The 2002 congressional districts reflect changes in apportionments resulting from the 2000 census.]

State and district	Vote cast in 1998		State and district	Vote cast in 2000		State and district	Vote cast in 2002		Total vote cast in 2002
	Republican	Democrat		Republican	Democrat		Republican	Democrat	
21st	165,047	....	21st	251,049	73,326	21st	161,836	56,206	222,093
22d	87,840	45,386	22d	154,662	92,645	22d	100,499	55,716	159,084
23d	73,177	40,281	23d	119,679	78,274	23d	77,573	71,067	150,552
24th	40,105	56,321	24th	61,235	103,152	24th	38,332	73,002	112,894
25th	41,848	58,591	25th	68,010	106,112	25th	50,041	63,590	116,126
26th	120,332	....	26th	214,025	75,601	26th	123,195	37,485	164,678
27th	34,284	61,638	27th	54,660	102,088	27th	41,004	68,559	112,209
28th	....	71,849	28th	....	123,104	28th	26,973	71,393	100,420
29th	....	44,179	29th	29,606	84,665	29th	....	55,760	58,593
30th	21,338	57,603	30th	....	109,163	30th	28,981	88,980	119,817
						31st	111,556	44,183	161,484
						32d	100,226	44,886	147,902
UT:			UT:			UT:			
1st	109,708	49,307	1st	180,591	71,229	1st	109,265	66,104	179,412
2d	93,718	77,198	2d	107,114	145,021	2d	109,123	110,764	224,098
3d	100,830	....	3d	138,943	88,547	3d	103,598	44,533	153,643
VT:			VT:			VT:			
At large	[4]70,740	....	At large	[5]51,977	14,918	At large	[6]72,813	....	225,255
VA:			VA:			VA:			
1st	76,474	....	1st	151,344	97,399	1st	113,168	....	117,997
2d	....	67,975	2d	97,856	90,328	2d	104,081	....	124,622
3d	....	48,129	3d	....	137,527	3d	....	87,521	91,073
4th	....	64,563	4th	....	189,787	4th	108,733	....	111,041
5th	....	73,097	5th	....	[7]65,387	5th	95,360	54,805	150,233
6th	89,177	39,487	6th	153,338	....	6th	105,530	....	108,732
7th	77,044	....	7th	192,652	94,935	7th	113,658	49,854	163,665
8th	48,352	97,545	8th	88,262	164,178	8th	64,121	102,759	171,799
9th	55,918	87,163	9th	59,335	137,488	9th	....	100,075	152,183
10th	103,648	36,476	10th	238,817	....	10th	115,917	45,464	161,615
11th	91,603	....	11th	150,395	83,455	11th	135,379	....	163,298
WA:			WA:			WA:			
1st	99,910	112,726	1st	121,823	155,820	1st	84,696	114,087	205,034
2d	124,125	100,776	2d	134,660	146,617	2d	92,528	101,219	202,150
3d	99,855	120,364	3d	114,861	159,428	3d	74,065	119,264	193,329
4th	121,684	43,043	4th	143,259	87,585	4th	108,257	53,572	161,829
5th	110,040	73,545	5th	144,038	97,703	5th	126,757	65,146	202,282
6th	66,291	143,308	6th	79,215	164,853	6th	61,584	126,116	196,444
7th	....	183,076	7th	....	193,470	7th	46,256	156,300	211,003
8th	135,539	91,371	8th	183,255	104,944	8th	121,633	75,931	203,335
9th	61,108	111,948	9th	76,766	135,452	9th	63,146	95,805	163,710
WV:			WV:			WV:			
1st	....	105,191	1st	....	170,974	1st	....	110,941	111,261
2d	29,136	99,357	2d	108,769	103,003	2d	98,276	65,400	163,676
3d	....	78,814	3d	....	146,807	3d	37,229	87,783	125,012
WI:			WI:			WI:			
1st	108,475	81,164	1st	177,612	88,885	1st	140,176	63,895	208,613
2d	103,528	116,377	2d	154,632	163,534	2d	83,694	163,313	247,410
3d	51,001	128,256	3d	97,741	173,505	3d	69,955	131,038	208,581
4th	76,666	105,841	4th	101,811	163,622	4th	....	122,031	141,367
5th	33,506	121,129	5th	49,296	173,893	5th	191,224	....	222,012
6th	144,144	....	6th	179,205	96,125	6th	169,834	....	171,161
7th	75,049	115,613	7th	100,264	173,007	7th	81,518	146,364	227,955
8th	112,418	93,441	8th	211,388	71,575	8th	152,745	50,284	210,447
9th	175,533	....	9th	239,498	83,720				
WY:			WY:			WY:			
At large	100,687	67,399	At large	141,848	60,638	At large	110,229	65,961	182,152

[Table continues on next page]

VOTES CAST FOR REPRESENTATIVES, RESIDENT COMMISSIONER, AND DELEGATES IN 1998, 2000, AND 2002

[The figures, compiled from official statistics obtained by the Clerk of the House, show the votes for the Democratic and Republican nominees, except as otherwise indicated. Figures in the last column, for the 2002 election, may include totals for more candidates than the ones shown.]

Commonwealth of Puerto Rico	Vote						Total vote cast in 2002
	1998		2000		2002		
	New Progressive	Popular Democrat	New Progressive	Popular Democrat	New Progressive	Popular Democrat	
Resident Commissioner (4-year term)	....	....	905,690	983,488	....	....	....

District of Columbia	Vote						Total vote cast in 2002
	1998		2000		2002		
	Republican	Democrat	Republican	Democrat	Republican	Democrat	
Delegate	8,610	122,228	10,258	158,824	....	119,268	128,233

Guam	Vote						Total vote cast in 2002
	1998		2000		2002		
	Republican	Democrat	Republican	Democrat	Republican	Democrat	
Delegate	10,763	34,179	8,167	29,099	14,836	27,081	42,579

Virgin Islands	Vote						Total vote cast in 2002
	1998		2000		2002		
	Democrat	Independent	Democrat	Republican	Democrat	Independent	
Delegate	24,227	5,983	9,512	1,270	4,286	20,414	30,165

American Samoa	Vote						Total vote cast in 2002
	1998		2000		2002		
	Democrat	Republican	Democrat	Republican	Democrat	Republican	
Delegate	8,138	....	[8] 5,505	....	[9] 4,959	....	9,042

[1] Under Arkansas law, it is not required to tabulate votes for unopposed candidates.
[2] Under Florida law, the names of those with no opposition are not printed on the ballot.
[3] Under Louisiana law, the names of those with no opposition are not printed on the ballot.
[4] The Independent candidate was elected with 136,403 votes.
[5] The Independent candidate was elected with 196,118 votes.
[6] The Independent candidate was elected with 144,880 votes.
[7] The Independent candidate was elected with 143,312 votes.
[8] A runoff election was held on November 21, 2000.
[9] A runoff election was held on November 19, 2002.

SESSIONS OF CONGRESS

[Closing date for this table was July 8, 2003.]

MEETING DATES OF CONGRESS: Pursuant to a resolution of the Confederation Congress in 1788, the Constitution went into effect on March 4, 1789. From then until the 20th amendment took effect in January 1934, the term of each Congress began on March 4th of each odd-numbered year; however, Article I, section 4, of the Constitution provided that ''The Congress shall assemble at least once in every Year, and such Meeting shall be on the first Monday in December, unless they shall by law appoint a different day.'' The Congress therefore convened regularly on the first Monday in December until the 20th amendment became effective, which changed the beginning of Congress's term as well as its convening date to January 3rd. So prior to 1934, a new Congress typically would not convene for regular business until 13 months after being elected. One effect of this was that the last session of each Congress was a ''lame duck'' session. After the 20th amendment, the time from the election to the beginning of Congress's term as well as when it convened was reduced to two months. Recognizing that the need might exist for Congress to meet at times other than the regularly scheduled convening date, Article II, section 3 of the Constitution provides that the President ''may, on extraordinary occasions, convene both Houses, or either of them''; hence these sessions occur only if convened by Presidential proclamation. Except as noted, these are separately numbered sessions of a Congress, and are marked by an E in the session column of the table. Until the 20th amendment was adopted, there were also times when special sessions of the Senate were convened, principally for confirming Cabinet and other executive nominations, and occasionally for the ratification of treaties or other executive business. These Senate sessions were also called by Presidential proclamation (typically by the outgoing President, although on occasion by incumbents as well) and are marked by an S in the session column. MEETING PLACES OF CONGRESS: Congress met for the first and second sessions of the First Congress (1789 and 1790) in New York City. From the third session of the First Congress through the first session of the Sixth Congress (1790 to 1800), Philadelphia was the meeting place. Congress has convened in Washington since the second session of the Sixth Congress (1800).

Congress	Session	Convening Date	Adjournment Date	Length in days [1]	Recesses [2]		President pro tempore of the Senate [3]	Speaker of the House of Representatives
					Senate	House of Representatives		
1st	1	Mar. 4, 1789	Sept. 29, 1789	210			John Langdon, of New Hampshire	Frederick A.C. Muhlenberg, of Pennsylvania.
	2	Jan. 4, 1790	Aug. 12, 1790	221			......do.	
	3	Dec. 6, 1790	Mar. 3, 1791	88			......do.	
2d	S	Mar. 4, 1791	Mar. 4, 1791	1			......do.	
	1	Oct. 24, 1791	May 8, 1792	197			Richard Henry Lee, of Virginia	Jonathan Trumbull, of Connecticut.
	2	Nov. 5, 1792	Mar. 2, 1793	119			John Langdon, of New Hampshire.	
3d	S	Mar. 4, 1793	Mar. 4, 1793	1			......do.	
	1	Dec. 2, 1793	June 9, 1794	190			John Langdon, of New Hampshire; Ralph Izard, of South Carolina.	Frederick A.C. Muhlenberg, of Pennsylvania.
	2	Nov. 3, 1794	Mar. 3, 1795	121			Henry Tazewell, of Virginia.	
4th	S	June 8, 1795	June 26, 1795	19			......do.	
	1	Dec. 7, 1795	June 1, 1796	177			Henry Tazewell, of Virginia; Samuel Livermore, of New Hampshire.	Jonathan Dayton, of New Jersey.
	2	Dec. 5, 1796	Mar. 3, 1797	89			William Bingham, of Pennsylvania.	
5th	S	Mar. 4, 1797	Mar. 4, 1797	1				
	1–E	May 15, 1797	July 10, 1797	57			William Bradford, of Rhode Island	Do.
	S	July 17, 1798	July 19, 1798	3				
	2	Nov. 13, 1797	July 16, 1798	246			Jacob Read, of South Carolina; Theodore Sedgwick, of Massachusetts.	
	3	Dec. 3, 1798	Mar. 3, 1799	91			John Laurance, of New York; James Ross, of Pennsylvania.	
6th	1	Dec. 2, 1799	May 14, 1800	164			Samuel Livermore, of New Hampshire; Uriah Tracy, of Connecticut.	Theodore Sedgwick, of Massachusetts.
	2	Nov. 17, 1800	Mar. 3, 1801	107	Dec. 23–Dec. 30, 1800	Dec. 23–Dec. 30, 1800	John E. Howard, of Maryland; James Hillhouse, of Connecticut.	
7th	S	Mar. 4, 1801	Mar. 5, 1801	2				
	1	Dec. 7, 1801	May 3, 1802	148			Abraham Baldwin, of Georgia	Nathaniel Macon, of North Carolina.

	2	Dec. 6, 1802	Mar. 3, 1803	88			Stephen R. Bradley, of Vermont.	
8th	1–E	Oct. 17, 1803	Mar. 27, 1804	163			John Brown, of Kentucky; Jesse Franklin, of North Carolina.	Do.
	2	Nov. 5, 1804	Mar. 3, 1805	119			Joseph Anderson, of Tennessee.	
9th	1	Dec. 2, 1805	Apr. 21, 1806	141			Samuel Smith, of Maryland	Do.
	2	Dec. 1, 1806	Mar. 3, 1807	93			......do.	
10th	1–E	Oct. 26, 1807	Apr. 25, 1808	182			......do	Joseph B. Varnum, of Massachusetts.
	2	Nov. 7, 1808	Mar. 3, 1809	117			Stephen R. Bradley, of Vermont; John Milledge, of Georgia.	
11th	S	Mar. 4, 1809	Mar. 7, 1809	4				
	1	May 22, 1809	June 28, 1809	38			Andrew Gregg, of Pennsylvania	Do.
	2	Nov. 27, 1809	May 1, 1810	156			John Gaillard, of South Carolina.	
	3	Dec. 3, 1810	Mar. 3, 1811	91			John Pope, of Kentucky.	
12th	1–E	Nov. 4, 1811	July 6, 1812	245			William H. Crawford, of Georgia	Henry Clay, of Kentucky.
	2	Nov. 2, 1812	Mar. 3, 1813	122			......do.	
13th	1	May 24, 1813	Aug. 2, 1813	71			......do	Do.[4]
	2	Dec. 6, 1813	Apr. 18, 1814	134			Joseph B. Varnum, of Massachusetts; John Gaillard, of South Carolina.	Langdon Cheves, of South Carolina.[4]
	3–E	Sept. 19, 1814	Mar. 3, 1815	166			John Gaillard, of South Carolina.	
14th	1	Dec. 4, 1815	Apr. 30, 1816	148			......do	Henry Clay, of Kentucky.
	2	Dec. 2, 1816	Mar. 3, 1817	92			......do.	
15th	S	Mar. 4, 1817	Mar. 6, 1817	3			......do.	
	1	Dec. 1, 1817	Apr. 20, 1818	141	Dec. 24–Dec. 29, 1817	Dec. 24–Dec. 29, 1817	......do	Do.
	2	Nov. 16, 1818	Mar. 3, 1819	108			James Barbour, of Virginia.	
16th	1	Dec. 6, 1819	May 15, 1820	162			James Barbour, of Virginia; John Gaillard, of South Carolina.	Do.[5]
	2	Nov. 13, 1820	Mar. 3, 1821	111			John Gaillard, of South Carolina	John W. Taylor, of New York.[5]
17th	1	Dec. 3, 1821	May 8, 1822	157			......do	Philip P. Barbour, of Virginia.
	2	Dec. 2, 1822	Mar. 3, 1823	92			......do.	
18th	1	Dec. 1, 1823	May 27, 1824	178			......do	Henry Clay, of Kentucky.
	2	Dec. 6, 1824	Mar. 3, 1825	88			......do.	
19th	S	Mar. 4, 1825	Mar. 9, 1825	6			......do.	
	1	Dec. 5, 1825	May 22, 1826	169			Nathaniel Macon, of North Carolina	John W. Taylor, of New York.
	2	Dec. 4, 1826	Mar. 3, 1827	90			......do.	
20th	1	Dec. 3, 1827	May 26, 1828	175			Samuel Smith, of Maryland	Andrew Stevenson, of Virginia.
	2	Dec. 1, 1828	Mar. 3, 1829	93	Dec. 24–Dec. 29, 1828	Dec. 24–Dec. 29, 1828	......do.	
21st	S	Mar. 4, 1829	Mar. 17, 1829	14			......do.	
	1	Dec. 7, 1829	May 31, 1830	176			......do	Do.
	2	Dec. 6, 1830	Mar. 3, 1831	88			......do.	
22d	1	Dec. 5, 1831	July 16, 1832	225			Littleton Waller Tazewell, of Virginia	Do.
	2	Dec. 3, 1832	Mar. 2, 1833	91			Hugh Lawson White, of Tennessee.	
23d	1	Dec. 2, 1833	June 30, 1834	211			Hugh Lawson White, of Tennessee; George Poindexter, of Mississippi.	Do.[6]
	2	Dec. 1, 1834	Mar. 3, 1835	93			John Tyler, of Virginia	John Bell, of Tennessee.[6]
24th	1	Dec. 7, 1835	July 4, 1836	211			William R. King, of Alabama	James K. Polk, of Tennessee.
	2	Dec. 5, 1836	Mar. 3, 1837	89			......do.	
25th	S	Mar. 4, 1837	Mar. 10, 1837	7			......do.	
	1–E	Sept. 4, 1837	Oct. 16, 1837	43			......do	Do.
	2	Dec. 4, 1837	July 9, 1838	218			......do.	
	3	Dec. 3, 1838	Mar. 3, 1839	91			......do.	
26th	1	Dec. 2, 1839	July 21, 1840	233			......do	Robert M.T. Hunter, of Virginia.
	2	Dec. 7, 1840	Mar. 3, 1841	87			......do.	
27th	S	Mar. 4, 1841	Mar. 15, 1841	12			William R. King, of Alabama; Samuel L. Southard, of New Jersey.	

SESSIONS OF CONGRESS—CONTINUED

[Closing date for this table was July 8, 2003.]

MEETING DATES OF CONGRESS: Pursuant to a resolution of the Confederation Congress in 1788, the Constitution went into effect on March 4, 1789. From then until the 20th amendment took effect in January 1934, the term of each Congress began on March 4th of each odd-numbered year; however, Article I, section 4, of the Constitution provided that ''The Congress shall assemble at least once in every Year, and such Meeting shall be on the first Monday in December, unless they shall by law appoint a different day.'' The Congress therefore convened regularly on the first Monday in December until the 20th amendment became effective, which changed the beginning of Congress's term as well as its convening date to January 3rd. So prior to 1934, a new Congress typically would not convene for regular business until 13 months after being elected. One effect of this was that the last session of each Congress was a ''lame duck'' session. After the 20th amendment, the time from the election to the beginning of Congress's term as well as when it convened was reduced to two months. Recognizing that the need might exist for Congress to meet at times other than the regularly scheduled convening date, Article II, section 3 of the Constitution provides that the President ''may, on extraordinary occasions, convene both Houses, or either of them''; hence these sessions occur only if convened by Presidential proclamation. Except as noted, these are separately numbered sessions of a Congress, and are marked by an E in the session column of the table. Until the 20th amendment was adopted, there were also times when special sessions of the Senate were convened, principally for confirming Cabinet and other executive nominations, and occasionally for the ratification of treaties or other executive business. These Senate sessions were also called by Presidential proclamation (typically by the outgoing President, although on occasion by incumbents as well) and are marked by an S in the session column. MEETING PLACES OF CONGRESS: Congress met for the first and second sessions of the First Congress (1789 and 1790) in New York City. From the third session of the First Congress through the first session of the Sixth Congress (1790 to 1800), Philadelphia was the meeting place. Congress has convened in Washington since the second session of the Sixth Congress (1800).

Congress	Session	Convening Date	Adjournment Date	Length in days [1]	Recesses [2]		President pro tempore of the Senate [3]	Speaker of the House of Representatives
					Senate	House of Representatives		
	1–E	May 31, 1841	Sept. 13, 1841	106			Samuel L. Southard, of New Jersey	John White, of Kentucky.
	2	Dec. 6, 1841	Aug. 31, 1842	269			Willie P. Mangum, of North Carolina.	
	3	Dec. 5, 1842	Mar. 3, 1843	89			......do.	
28th	1	Dec. 4, 1843	June 17, 1844	196			......do	John W. Jones, of Virginia.
	2	Dec. 2, 1844	Mar. 3, 1845	92			......do.	
29th	S	Mar. 4, 1845	Mar. 20, 1845	17				
	1	Dec. 1, 1845	Aug. 10, 1846	253			Ambrose H. Sevier; David R. Atchison, of Missouri.	John W. Davis, of Indiana.
	2	Dec. 7, 1846	Mar. 3, 1847	87			David R. Atchison, of Missouri.	
30th	1	Dec. 6, 1847	Aug. 14, 1848	254			......do	Robert C. Winthrop, of Massachusetts.
	2	Dec. 4, 1848	Mar. 3, 1849	90			......do.	
31st	S	Mar. 5, 1849	Mar. 23, 1849	19			......do.	
	1	Dec. 3, 1849	Sept. 30, 1850	302			William R. King, of Alabama	Howell Cobb, of Georgia.
	2	Dec. 2, 1850	Mar. 3, 1851	92			......do.	
32d	S	Mar. 4, 1851	Mar. 13, 1851	10				
	1	Dec. 1, 1851	Aug. 31, 1852	275			......do	Linn Boyd, of Kentucky.
	2	Dec. 6, 1852	Mar. 3, 1853	88			David R. Atchison, of Missouri.	
33d	S	Mar. 4, 1853	Apr. 11, 1853	39			......do.	
	1	Dec. 5, 1853	Aug. 7, 1854	246			......do	Do.
	2	Dec. 4, 1854	Mar. 3, 1855	90			Lewis Cass, of Michigan; Jesse D. Bright, of Indiana.	
34th	1	Dec. 3, 1855	Aug. 18, 1856	260			Charles E. Stuart, of Michigan; Jesse D. Bright, of Indiana.	Nathaniel P. Banks, of Massachusetts.
	2–E	Aug. 21, 1856	Aug. 30, 1856	10			Jesse D. Bright, of Indiana.	
	3	Dec. 1, 1856	Mar. 3, 1857	93			James M. Mason, of Virginia.	
35th	S	Mar. 4, 1857	Mar. 14, 1857	11			James M. Mason, of Virginia; Thomas J. Rusk, of Texas.	
	1	Dec. 7, 1857	June 14, 1858	189	Dec. 23, 1857–Jan. 4, 1858	Dec. 23, 1857–Jan. 4, 1858	Benjamin Fitzpatrick, of Alabama	James L. Orr, of South Carolina.

	S	June 15, 1858	June 16, 1858	2				
	2	Dec. 6, 1858	Mar. 3, 1859	88	Dec. 23, 1858–Jan. 4, 1859	Dec. 23, 1858–Jan. 4, 1859	......do.	
36th	S	Mar. 4, 1859	Mar. 10, 1859	7			......do.	
	1	Dec. 5, 1859	June 25, 1860	202			Benjamin Fitzpatrick, of Alabama; Jesse D. Bright, of Indiana.	William Pennington, of New Jersey.
	S	June 26, 1860	June 28, 1860	3			Benjamin Fitzpatrick, of Alabama.	
	2	Dec. 3, 1860	Mar. 3, 1851	93			Solomon Foot, of Vermont.	
37th	S	Mar. 4, 1861	Mar. 28, 1861	25			......do.	
	1–E	July 4, 1861	Aug. 6, 1851	34			......do	Galusha A. Grow, of Pennsylvania.
	2	Dec. 2, 1861	July 17, 1862	228			......do.	
	3	Dec. 1, 1862	Mar. 3, 1863	93	Dec. 23, 1862–Jan. 5, 1863	Dec. 23, 1862–Jan. 5, 1863	......do.	
38th	S	Mar. 4, 1863	Mar. 14, 1863	11			......do.	
	1	Dec. 7, 1863	July 4, 1864	209	Dec. 23, 1863–Jan. 5, 1864	Dec. 23, 1863–Jan. 5, 1864	Solomon Foot, of Vermont; Daniel Clark, of New Hampshire.	Schuyler Colfax, of Indiana.
	2	Dec. 5, 1864	Mar. 3, 1865	89	Dec. 22, 1864–Jan. 5, 1865	Dec. 22, 1864–Jan. 5, 1865	Daniel Clark, of New Hampshire.	
39th	S	Mar. 4, 1865	Mar. 11, 1865	8			Lafayette S. Foster, of Connecticut.	
	1	Dec. 4, 1865	July 28, 1866	237	Dec. 6–Dec. 11, 1865 Dec. 21, 1865–Jan. 5, 1866	Dec. 6–Dec. 11, 1865 Dec. 21, 1865–Jan. 5, 1866	......do	Do.
	2	Dec. 3, 1866	Mar. 3, 1867	91	Dec. 20, 1866–Jan. 3, 1867	Dec. 20, 1866–Jan. 3, 1867	Benjamin F. Wade, of Ohio.	
40th	1	Mar. 4, 1867	Dec. 1, 1867	273	Mar. 30–July 3, 1867 July 20–Nov. 21, 1867	Mar. 30–July 3, 1867 July 20–Nov. 21, 1867	......do	Do.[7]
	S	Apr. 1, 1867	Apr. 20, 1867	20				
	2	Dec. 2, 1867	Nov. 10, 1858	345	Dec. 20, 1867–Jan. 6, 1868 July 27–Sept. 21, 1868 Sept. 21–Oct. 16, 1868 Oct. 16–Nov. 10, 1868	Dec. 20, 1867–Jan. 6, 1868 July 27–Sept. 21, 1868 Sept. 21–Oct. 16, 1868 Oct. 16–Nov. 10, 1868		
	3	Dec. 7, 1868	Mar. 3, 1869	87	Dec. 21, 1868–Jan. 5, 1869	Dec. 21, 1868–Jan. 5, 1869	......do	Theodore M. Pomeroy, of New York.[7]
41st	1	Mar. 4, 1869	Apr. 10, 1869	38			Henry B. Anthony, of Rhode Island	James G. Blaine, of Maine.
	S	Apr. 12, 1869	Apr. 22, 1869	11				
	2	Dec. 6, 1869	July 15, 1870	222	Dec. 22, 1869–Jan. 10, 1870	Dec. 22, 1869–Jan. 10, 1870	......do.	
	3	Dec. 5, 1870	Mar. 3, 1871	89	Dec. 23, 1870–Jan. 4, 1871	Dec. 22, 1870–Jan. 4, 1871	......do.	
42d	1	Mar. 4, 1871	Apr. 20, 1871	48			......do	Do.
	S	May 10, 1871	May 27, 1871	18			......do.	
	2	Dec. 4, 1871	June 10, 1872	190	Dec. 21, 1871–Jan. 8, 1872	Dec. 21, 1871–Jan. 8, 1872	......do.	
	3	Dec. 2, 1872	Mar. 3, 1873	92	Dec. 20, 1872–Jan. 6, 1873	Dec. 20, 1872–Jan. 6, 1873	......do.	
43d	S	Mar. 4, 1873	Mar. 26, 1873	23			Matthew H. Carpenter, of Wisconsin.	
	1	Dec. 1, 1873	June 23, 1874	204	Dec. 19, 1873–Jan. 5, 1874	Dec. 19, 1873–Jan. 5, 1874	......do	Do.
	2	Dec. 7, 1874	Mar. 3, 1875	87	Dec. 23, 1874–Jan. 5, 1875	Dec. 23, 1874–Jan. 5, 1875	Matthew H. Carpenter, of Wisconsin; Henry B. Anthony, of Rhode Island.	
44th	S	Mar. 5, 1875	Mar. 24, 1875	20			Thomas W. Ferry, of Michigan.	
	1	Dec. 6, 1875	Aug. 15, 1876	254	Dec. 20, 1875–Jan. 5, 1876	Dec. 21, 1875–Jan. 5, 1876	......do	Michael C. Kerr, of Indiana.[8]
	2	Dec. 4, 1876	Mar. 3, 1877	90			......do	Samuel J. Randall, of Pennsylvania.[8]
45th	S	Mar. 5, 1877	Mar. 17, 1877	13			......do.	
	1–E	Oct. 15, 1877	Dec. 3, 1877	50			......do	Do.
	2	Dec. 3, 1877	June 20, 1878	200	Dec. 15, 1877–Jan. 10, 1878	Dec. 15, 1877–Jan. 10, 1878	......do.	
	3	Dec. 2, 1878	Mar. 3, 1879	92	Dec. 20, 1878–Jan. 7, 1879	Dec. 20, 1878–Jan. 7, 1879	......do.	
46th	1–E	Mar. 18, 1879	July 1, 1879	106			Allen G. Thurman, of Ohio	Do.
	2	Dec. 1, 1879	June 16, 1880	199	Dec. 19, 1879–Jan. 6, 1880	Dec. 19, 1879–Jan. 6, 1880	......do.	
	3	Dec. 6, 1880	Mar. 3, 1881	88	Dec. 23, 1880–Jan. 5, 1881	Dec. 23, 1880–Jan. 5, 1881	......do.	
47th	S	Mar. 4, 1881	May. 20, 1881	78				
	S	Oct. 10, 1881	Oct. 29, 1881	20			Thomas F. Bayard, of Delaware; David Davis, of Illinois.	
	1	Dec. 5, 1881	Aug. 8, 1882	247	Dec. 22, 1881–Jan. 5, 1882	Dec. 22, 1881–Jan. 5, 1882	David Davis, of Illinois	J. Warren Keifer, of Ohio.

SESSIONS OF CONGRESS—CONTINUED

[Closing date for this table was July 8, 2003.]

MEETING DATES OF CONGRESS: Pursuant to a resolution of the Confederation Congress in 1788, the Constitution went into effect on March 4, 1789. From then until the 20th amendment took effect in January 1934, the term of each Congress began on March 4th of each odd-numbered year; however, Article I, section 4, of the Constitution provided that ''The Congress shall assemble at least once in every Year, and such Meeting shall be on the first Monday in December, unless they shall by law appoint a different day.'' The Congress therefore convened regularly on the first Monday in December until the 20th amendment became effective, which changed the beginning of Congress's term as well as its convening date to January 3rd. So prior to 1934, a new Congress typically would not convene for regular business until 13 months after being elected. One effect of this was that the last session of each Congress was a ''lame duck'' session. After the 20th amendment, the time from the election to the beginning of Congress's term as well as when it convened was reduced to two months. Recognizing that the need might exist for Congress to meet at times other than the regularly scheduled convening date, Article II, section 3 of the Constitution provides that the President ''may, on extraordinary occasions, convene both Houses, or either of them''; hence these sessions occur only if convened by Presidential proclamation. Except as noted, these are separately numbered sessions of a Congress, and are marked by an E in the session column of the table. Until the 20th amendment was adopted, there were also times when special sessions of the Senate were convened, principally for confirming Cabinet and other executive nominations, and occasionally for the ratification of treaties or other executive business. These Senate sessions were also called by Presidential proclamation (typically by the outgoing President, although on occasion by incumbents as well) and are marked by an S in the session column. MEETING PLACES OF CONGRESS: Congress met for the first and second sessions of the First Congress (1789 and 1790) in New York City. From the third session of the First Congress through the first session of the Sixth Congress (1790 to 1800), Philadelphia was the meeting place. Congress has convened in Washington since the second session of the Sixth Congress (1800).

Congress	Session	Convening Date	Adjournment Date	Length in days [1]	Recesses [2]		President pro tempore of the Senate [3]	Speaker of the House of Representatives
					Senate	House of Representatives		
	2	Dec. 4, 1882	Mar. 3, 1883	90			George F. Edmunds, of Vermont.	J. Warren Keifer, of Ohio.
48th	1	Dec. 3, 1883	July 7, 1884	218	Dec. 24, 1883–Jan. 7, 1884	Dec. 24, 1883–Jan. 7, 1884	......do	John G. Carlisle, of Kentucky.
	2	Dec. 1, 1884	Mar. 3, 1885	93	Dec. 24, 1884–Jan. 5, 1885	Dec. 24, 1884–Jan. 5, 1885	......do.	
49th	S	Mar. 4, 1885	Apr. 2, 1885	30				
	1	Dec. 7, 1885	Aug. 5, 1886	242	Dec. 21, 1885–Jan. 5, 1886	Dec. 21, 1885–Jan. 5, 1886	John Sherman, of Ohio	Do.
	2	Dec. 6, 1886	Mar. 3, 1887	88	Dec. 22, 1886–Jan. 4, 1887	Dec. 22, 1886–Jan. 4, 1887	John J. Ingalls, of Kansas.	
50th	1	Dec. 5, 1887	Oct. 20, 1888	321	Dec. 22, 1887–Jan. 4, 1888	Dec. 22, 1887–Jan. 4, 1888	......do	Do.
	2	Dec. 3, 1888	Mar. 3, 1889	91	Dec. 21, 1888–Jan. 2, 1889	Dec. 21, 1888–Jan. 2, 1889	......do.	
51st	S	Mar. 4, 1889	Apr. 2, 1889	30			......do.	
	1	Dec. 2, 1889	Oct. 1, 1890	304	Dec. 21, 1889–Jan. 6, 1890	Dec. 21, 1889–Jan. 6, 1890	......do	Thomas B. Reed, of Maine.
	2	Dec. 1, 1890	Mar. 3, 1891	93			Charles F. Manderson, of Nebraska.	
52d	1	Dec. 7, 1891	Aug. 5, 1892	251			......do	Charles F. Crisp, of Georgia.
	2	Dec. 5, 1892	Mar. 3, 1893	89	Dec. 22, 1892–Jan. 4, 1893	Dec. 22, 1892–Jan. 4, 1893	......do.	
53d	S	Mar. 4, 1893	Apr. 15, 1893	43			Charles F. Manderson, of Nebraska; Isham G. Harris, of Tennessee.	
	1–E	Aug. 7, 1893	Nov. 3, 1893	89			Isham G. Harris, of Tennessee	Do.
	2	Dec. 4, 1893	Aug. 28, 1894	268		Dec. 21, 1893–Jan. 3, 1894	......do.	
	3	Dec. 3, 1894	Mar. 3, 1895	97		Dec. 23, 1894–Jan. 3, 1895	Matt W. Ransom, of North Carolina; Isham G. Harris, of Tennessee.	
54th	1	Dec. 2, 1895	June 11, 1896	193			William P. Frye, of Maine	Thomas B. Reed, of Maine.
	2	Dec. 7, 1896	Mar. 3, 1897	87	Dec. 22, 1896–Jan. 5, 1897	Dec. 22, 1896–Jan. 5, 1897	......do.	
55th	S	Mar. 4, 1897	Mar. 10, 1897	11			......do.	
	1–E	Mar. 15, 1897	July 24, 1897	131			......do	Do.
	2	Dec. 6, 1897	July 8, 1898	215	Dec. 18, 1897–Jan. 5, 1898	Dec. 18, 1897–Jan. 5, 1898	......do.	
	3	Dec. 5, 1898	Mar. 3, 1899	89	Dec. 21, 1898–Jan. 4, 1899	Dec. 21, 1898–Jan. 4, 1899	......do.	
56th	1	Dec. 4, 1899	June 7, 1900	186	Dec. 20, 1899–Jan. 3, 1900	Dec. 20, 1899–Jan. 3, 1900	......do	David B. Henderson, of Iowa.
	2	Dec. 3, 1900	Mar. 3, 1901	91	Dec. 20, 1900–Jan. 3, 1901	Dec. 21, 1900–Jan. 3, 1901	......do.	
57th	S	Mar. 4, 1901	Mar. 9, 1901	6			......do.	

	1	Dec. 2, 1901	July 1, 1902	212	Dec. 19, 1901–Jan. 6, 1902	Dec. 19, 1901–Jan. 6, 1902	......do	Do.
	2	Dec. 1, 1902	Mar. 3, 1903	93	Dec. 20, 1902–Jan. 5, 1903	Dec. 20, 1902–Jan. 5, 1903	......do.	
58th ...	S	Mar. 5, 1903	Mar. 19, 1903	15			......do.	
	1–E	Nov. 9, 1903	Dec. 7, 1903	29			......do	Joseph G. Cannon, of Illinois.
	2	Dec. 7, 1903	Apr. 28, 1904	144	Dec. 19, 1903–Jan. 4, 1904	Dec. 19, 1903–Jan. 4, 1904	......do.	
	3	Dec. 5, 1904	Mar. 3, 1905	89	Dec. 21, 1904–Jan. 4, 1905	Dec. 21, 1904–Jan. 4, 1905	......do.	
59th ...	S	Mar. 4, 1905	Mar. 18, 1905	15			......do.	
	1	Dec. 4, 1905	June 30, 1906	209	Dec. 21, 1905–Jan. 4, 1906	Dec. 21, 1905–Jan. 4, 1906	......do	Do.
	2	Dec. 3, 1906	Mar. 3, 1907	91	Dec. 20, 1906–Jan. 3, 1907	Dec. 20, 1906–Jan. 3, 1907	......do.	
60th ...	1	Dec. 2, 1907	May 30, 1908	181	Dec. 21, 1907–Jan. 6, 1908	Dec. 21, 1907–Jan. 6, 1908	......do	Do.
	2	Dec. 7, 1908	Mar. 3, 1909	87	Dec. 19, 1908–Jan. 4, 1909	Dec. 19, 1908–Jan. 4, 1909	......do.	
61st	S	Mar. 4, 1909	Mar. 6, 1909	3			......do.	
	1–E	Mar. 15, 1909	Aug. 5, 1909	144			......do	Do.
	2	Dec. 6, 1909	June 25, 1910	202	Dec. 21, 1909–Jan. 4, 1910	Dec. 21, 1909–Jan. 4, 1910	......do.	
	3	Dec. 5, 1910	Mar. 3, 1911	89	Dec. 21, 1910–Jan. 5, 1911	Dec. 21, 1910–Jan. 5, 1911	......do.	
62d	1–E	Apr. 4, 1911	Aug. 22, 1911	141			......do.[9]	Champ Clark, of Missouri.
	2	Dec. 4, 1911	Aug. 26, 1912	267	Dec. 21, 1911–Jan. 3, 1912	Dec. 21, 1911–Jan. 3, 1912	Charles Curtis, of Kansas; Augustus O. Bacon, of Georgia; Jacob H. Gallinger, of New Hampshire; Henry Cabot Lodge, of Massachusetts; Frank B. Brandegee, of Connecticut.	
	3	Dec. 2, 1912	Mar. 3, 1913	92	Dec. 19, 1912–Jan. 2, 1913	Dec. 19, 1912–Jan. 2, 1913	Augustus O. Bacon, of Georgia; Jacob H. Gallinger, of New Hampshire.	
63d	S	Mar. 4, 1913	Mar. 17, 1913	14			James P. Clarke, of Arkansas.	
	1–E	Apr. 7, 1913	Dec. 1, 1913	239			......do	Do.
	2	Dec. 1, 1913	Oct. 24, 1914	328	Dec. 23, 1913–Jan. 12, 1914	Dec. 23, 1913–Jan. 12, 1914	......do.	
	3	Dec. 7, 1914	Mar. 3, 1915	87	Dec. 23–Dec. 28, 1914	Dec. 23–Dec. 28, 1914	......do.	
64th ...	1	Dec. 6, 1915	Sept. 8, 1916	278	Dec. 17, 1915–Jan. 4, 1916	Dec. 17, 1915–Jan. 4, 1916	......do[10]	Do.
	2	Dec. 4, 1916	Mar. 3, 1917	90	Dec. 22, 1916–Jan. 2, 1917	Dec. 22, 1916–Jan. 2, 1917	Willard Saulsbury, of Delaware[10]	
65th ...	S	Mar. 5, 1917	Mar. 16, 1917	12			......do.	
	1–E	Apr. 2, 1917	Oct. 6, 1917	188			......do	Do.
	2	Dec. 3, 1917	Nov. 21, 1918	354	Dec. 18, 1917–Jan. 3, 1918	Dec. 18, 1917–Jan. 3, 1918	......do.	
	3	Dec. 2, 1918	Mar. 3, 1919	92			......do.	
66th ...	1–E	May 19, 1919	Nov. 19, 1919	185	July 1–July 8, 1919	July 1–July 8, 1919	Albert B. Cummins, of Iowa	Frederick H. Gillett, of Massachusetts.
	2	Dec. 1, 1919	June 5, 1920	188	Dec. 20, 1919–Jan. 5, 1920	Dec. 20, 1919–Jan. 5, 1920	......do.	
	3	Dec. 6, 1920	Mar. 3, 1921	88			......do.	
67th ...	S	Mar. 4, 1921	Mar. 15, 1921	12			......do.	
	1–E	Apr. 11, 1921	Nov. 23, 1921	227	Aug. 24–Sept. 21, 1921	Aug. 24–Sept. 21, 1921	......do	Do.
	2	Dec. 5, 1921	Sept. 22, 1922	292	Dec. 22, 1921–Jan. 3, 1922	Dec. 22, 1921–Jan. 3, 1922	......do.	
	3–E	Nov. 20, 1922	Dec. 4, 1922	15			......do.	
	4	Dec. 4, 1922	Mar. 3, 1923	90			......do.	
68th ...	1	Dec. 3, 1923	June 7, 1924	188	Dec. 20, 1923–Jan. 3, 1924	Dec. 20, 1923–Jan. 3, 1924	......do	Do.
	2	Dec. 1, 1924	Mar. 3, 1925	93	Dec. 20–Dec. 29, 1924	Dec. 20–Dec. 29, 1924	......do.	
69th ...	S	Mar. 4, 1925	Mar. 18, 1925	15			Albert B. Cummins, of Iowa; George H. Moses, of New Hampshire.	
	1	Dec. 7, 1925	July 3, 1926	209	Dec. 22, 1925–Jan. 4, 1926	Dec. 22, 1925–Jan. 4, 1926	......do	Nicholas Longworth, of Ohio.
	2	Dec. 6, 1926	Mar. 4, 1927	88	Dec. 22, 1926–Jan. 3, 1927	Dec. 22, 1926–Jan. 3, 1927	......do.	
70th ...	1	Dec. 5, 1927	May 29, 1928	177	Dec. 21, 1927–Jan. 4, 1928	Dec. 21, 1927–Jan. 4, 1928	......do	Do.
	2	Dec. 3, 1928	Mar. 3, 1929	91	Dec. 22, 1928–Jan. 3, 1929	Dec. 22, 1928–Jan. 3, 1929	......do.	
71st	S	Mar. 4, 1929	Mar. 5, 1929	2			......do.	
	1–E	Apr. 15, 1929	Nov. 22, 1929	222	June 19–Aug. 19, 1929	June 19–Sept. 23, 1929	......do	Do.
	2	Dec. 2, 1929	July 3, 1930	214	Dec. 21, 1929–Jan. 6, 1930	Dec. 21, 1929–Jan. 6, 1930	......do.	
	S	July 7, 1930	July 21, 1930	15			......do.	

SESSIONS OF CONGRESS—CONTINUED

[Closing date for this table was July 8, 2003.]

MEETING DATES OF CONGRESS: Pursuant to a resolution of the Confederation Congress in 1788, the Constitution went into effect on March 4, 1789. From then until the 20th amendment took effect in January 1934, the term of each Congress began on March 4th of each odd-numbered year; however, Article I, section 4, of the Constitution provided that ''The Congress shall assemble at least once in every Year, and such Meeting shall be on the first Monday in December, unless they shall by law appoint a different day.'' The Congress therefore convened regularly on the first Monday in December until the 20th amendment became effective, which changed the beginning of Congress's term as well as its convening date to January 3rd. So prior to 1934, a new Congress typically would not convene for regular business until 13 months after being elected. One effect of this was that the last session of each Congress was a ''lame duck'' session. After the 20th amendment, the time from the election to the beginning of Congress's term as well as when it convened was reduced to two months. Recognizing that the need might exist for Congress to meet at times other than the regularly scheduled convening date, Article II, section 3 of the Constitution provides that the President ''may, on extraordinary occasions, convene both Houses, or either of them''; hence these sessions occur only if convened by Presidential proclamation. Except as noted, these are separately numbered sessions of a Congress, and are marked by an E in the session column of the table. Until the 20th amendment was adopted, there were also times when special sessions of the Senate were convened, principally for confirming Cabinet and other executive nominations, and occasionally for the ratification of treaties or other executive business. These Senate sessions were also called by Presidential proclamation (typically by the outgoing President, although on occasion by incumbents as well) and are marked by an S in the session column. MEETING PLACES OF CONGRESS: Congress met for the first and second sessions of the First Congress (1789 and 1790) in New York City. From the third session of the First Congress through the first session of the Sixth Congress (1790 to 1800), Philadelphia was the meeting place. Congress has convened in Washington since the second session of the Sixth Congress (1800).

Congress	Session	Convening Date	Adjournment Date	Length in days [1]	Recesses [2] Senate	Recesses [2] House of Representatives	President pro tempore of the Senate [3]	Speaker of the House of Representatives
	3	Dec. 1, 1930	Mar. 3, 1931	93	Dec. 20, 1930–Jan. 5, 1931	Dec. 20, 1930–Jan. 5, 1931	George H. Moses, of New Hampshire	Nicholas Longworth, of Ohio.
72d	1	Dec. 7, 1931	July 16, 1932	223	Dec. 22, 1931–Jan. 4, 1932	Dec. 22, 1931–Jan. 4, 1932	do	John N. Garner, of Texas.
	2	Dec. 5, 1932	Mar. 3, 1933	89			do.	
73d	S	Mar. 4, 1933	Mar. 6, 1933	3			do.	
	1–E	Mar. 9, 1933	June 15, 1933	99			Key Pittman, of Nevada	Henry T. Rainey, of Illinois.
	2	Jan. 3, 1934	June 18, 1934	167			do.	
74th	1	Jan. 3, 1935	Aug. 26, 1935	236			do	Joseph W. Byrns, of Tennessee.[11]
	2	Jan. 3, 1936	June 20, 1936	170	June 8–June 15, 1936	June 8–June 15, 1936	do	William B. Bankhead, of Alabama.[11]
75th	1	Jan. 5, 1937	Aug. 21, 1937	229			do	Do.
	2–E	Nov. 15, 1937	Dec. 21, 1937	37			do.	
	3	Jan. 3, 1938	June 16, 1938	165			do.	
76th	1	Jan. 3, 1939	Aug. 5, 1939	215			do	Do.[12]
	2–E	Sept. 21, 1939	Nov. 3, 1939	44			do.	
	3	Jan. 3, 1940	Jan. 3, 1941	366	July 11–July 22, 1940	July 11–July 22, 1940	Key Pittman, of Nevada; [13] William H. King, of Utah.[13]	Sam Rayburn, of Texas.[12]
77th	1	Jan. 3, 1941	Jan. 2, 1942	365			Pat Harrison, of Mississippi;[14] Carter Glass, of Virginia.[14]	Do.
	2	Jan. 5, 1942	Dec. 16, 1942	346			Carter Glass, of Virginia.	
78th	1	Jan. 6, 1943	Dec. 21, 1943	350	July 8–Sept. 14, 1943	July 8–Sept. 14, 1943	do	Do.
	2	Jan. 10, 1944	Dec. 19, 1944	345	Apr. 1–Apr. 12, 1944 June 23–Aug. 1, 1944 Sept. 21–Nov. 14, 1944	Apr. 1–Apr. 12, 1944 June 23–Aug. 1, 1944 Sept. 21–Nov. 14, 1944	do.	
79th	1	Jan. 3, 1945	Dec. 21, 1945	353	Aug. 1–Sept. 5, 1945	July 21–Sept. 5, 1945	Kenneth McKellar, of Tennessee	Do.
	2	Jan. 14, 1946	Aug. 2, 1946	201		Apr. 18–Apr. 30, 1946	do.	
80th	[15] 1	Jan. 3, 1947	Dec. 19, 1947	351	July 27–Nov. 17, 1947	July 27–Nov. 17, 1947	Arthur H. Vandenberg, of Michigan	Joseph W. Martin, Jr., of Massachusetts.
	[15] 2	Jan. 6, 1948	Dec. 31, 1948	361	June 20–July 26, 1948 Aug. 7–Dec. 31, 1948	June 20–July 26, 1948 Aug. 7–Dec. 31, 1948	do.	

81st	1	Jan. 3, 1949	Oct. 19, 1949	290			Kenneth McKellar, of Tennessee	Sam Rayburn, of Texas.
	2	Jan. 3, 1950	Jan. 2, 1951	365	Sept. 23–Nov. 27–1950	Apr. 6–Apr. 18, 1950 Sept. 23–Nov. 27, 1950	......do.	
82d	1	Jan. 3, 1951	Oct. 20, 1951	291		Mar. 22–Apr. 2, 1951 Aug. 23–Sept. 12, 1951	......do	Do.
	2	Jan. 8, 1952	July 7, 1952	182		Apr. 10–Apr. 22, 1952	......do.	
83d	1	Jan. 3, 1953	Aug. 3, 1953	213		Apr. 2–Apr. 13, 1953	Styles Bridges, of New Hampshire	Joseph W. Martin, Jr., of Massachusetts.
	2	Jan. 6, 1954	Dec. 2, 1954	331	Aug. 20–Nov. 8, 1954 Nov. 18–Nov. 29, 1954	Apr. 15–Apr. 22, 1954 Adjourned sine die Aug. 20, 1954	......do.	
84th	1	Jan. 5, 1955	Aug. 2, 1955	210	Apr. 4–Apr. 13, 1955	Apr. 4–Apr. 13, 1955	Walter F. George, of Georgia	Sam Rayburn, of Texas.
	2	Jan. 3, 1956	July 27, 1956	207	Mar. 29–Apr. 9, 1956	Mar. 29–Apr. 9, 1956	......do.	
85th	1	Jan. 3, 1957	Aug. 30, 1957	239	Apr. 18–Apr. 29, 1957	Apr. 18–Apr. 29, 1957	Carl Hayden, of Arizona	Do.
	2	Jan. 7, 1958	Aug. 24, 1958	230	Apr. 3–Apr. 14, 1958	Apr. 3–Apr. 14, 1958	......do.	
86th	1	Jan. 7, 1959	Sept. 15, 1959	252	Mar. 26–Apr. 7, 1959	Mar. 26–Apr. 7, 1959	......do	Do.
	2	Jan. 6, 1960	Sept. 1, 1960	240	Apr. 14–Apr. 18, 1960 May 27–May 31, 1960 July 3–Aug. 8, 1960	Apr. 14–Apr. 18, 1960 May 27–May 31, 1960 July 3–Aug. 15, 1960	......do.	
87th	1	Jan. 3, 1961	Sept. 27, 1961	268		Mar. 30–Apr. 10, 1961	......do	Do.[16]
	2	Jan. 10, 1962	Oct. 13, 1962	277		Apr. 19–Apr. 30, 1962	......do	John W. McCormack, of Massachusetts.[16]
88th	1	Jan. 9, 1963	Dec. 30, 1963	356		Apr. 11–Apr. 22, 1963	......do	Do.
	2	Jan. 7, 1964	Oct. 3, 1964	270	July 10–July 20, 1964 Aug. 21–Aug. 31, 1964	Mar. 26–Apr. 6, 1964 July 2–July 20, 1964 Aug. 21–Aug. 31, 1964	......do.	
89th	1	Jan. 4, 1965	Oct. 23, 1965	293			......do	Do.
	2	Jan. 10, 1966	Oct. 22, 1966	286	Apr. 7–Apr. 13, 1966 June 30–July 11, 1966	Apr. 7–Apr. 18, 1966 June 30–July 11, 1966	......do.	
90th	1	Jan. 10, 1967	Dec. 15, 1967	340	Mar. 23–Apr. 3, 1967 June 29–July 10, 1967 Aug. 31–Sept. 11, 1967 Nov. 22–Nov. 27, 1967	Mar. 23–Apr. 3, 1967 June 29–July 10, 1967 Aug. 31–Sept. 11, 1967 Nov. 22–Nov. 27, 1967	......do	Do.
	2	Jan. 15, 1968	Oct. 14, 1968	274	Apr. 11–Apr. 17, 1968 May 29–June 3, 1968 June 3–July 8, 1968 Aug. 2–Sept. 4, 1968	Apr. 11–Apr. 22, 1968 May 29–June 3, 1968 June 3–July 8, 1968 Aug. 2–Sept. 4, 1968	......do.	
91st	1	Jan. 3, 1969	Dec. 23, 1969	355	Feb. 7–Feb. 17, 1969 Apr. 3–Apr. 14, 1969 July 2–July 7, 1969 Aug. 13–Sept. 3, 1969 Nov. 26–Dec. 1, 1969	Feb. 7–Feb. 17, 1969 Apr. 3–Apr. 14, 1969 May 28–June 2, 1969 July 2–July 7, 1969 Aug. 13–Sept. 3, 1969 Nov. 6–Nov. 12, 1969 Nov. 26–Dec. 1, 1969	Richard B. Russell, of Georgia	Do.
	2	Jan. 19, 1970	Jan. 2, 1971	349	Feb. 10–Feb. 16, 1970 Mar. 26–Mar. 31, 1970 Sept. 2–Sept. 8, 1970 Oct. 14–Nov. 16, 1970 Nov. 25–Nov. 30, 1970 Dec. 22–Dec. 28, 1970	Feb. 10–Feb. 16, 1970 Mar. 26–Mar. 31, 1970 May 27–June 1, 1970 July 1–July 6, 1970 Aug. 14–Sept. 9, 1970 Oct. 14–Nov. 16, 1970 Nov. 25–Nov. 30, 1970 Dec. 22–Dec. 29, 1970	......do.	

SESSIONS OF CONGRESS—CONTINUED

[Closing date for this table was July 8, 2003.]

MEETING DATES OF CONGRESS: Pursuant to a resolution of the Confederation Congress in 1788, the Constitution went into effect on March 4, 1789. From then until the 20th amendment took effect in January 1934, the term of each Congress began on March 4th of each odd-numbered year; however, Article I, section 4, of the Constitution provided that ''The Congress shall assemble at least once in every Year, and such Meeting shall be on the first Monday in December, unless they shall by law appoint a different day.'' The Congress therefore convened regularly on the first Monday in December until the 20th amendment became effective, which changed the beginning of Congress's term as well as its convening date to January 3rd. So prior to 1934, a new Congress typically would not convene for regular business until 13 months after being elected. One effect of this was that the last session of each Congress was a ''lame duck'' session. After the 20th amendment, the time from the election to the beginning of Congress's term as well as when it convened was reduced to two months. Recognizing that the need might exist for Congress to meet at times other than the regularly scheduled convening date, Article II, section 3 of the Constitution provides that the President ''may, on extraordinary occasions, convene both Houses, or either of them''; hence these sessions occur only if convened by Presidential proclamation. Except as noted, these are separately numbered sessions of a Congress, and are marked by an E in the session column of the table. Until the 20th amendment was adopted, there were also times when special sessions of the Senate were convened, principally for confirming Cabinet and other executive nominations, and occasionally for the ratification of treaties or other executive business. These Senate sessions were also called by Presidential proclamation (typically by the outgoing President, although on occasion by incumbents as well) and are marked by an S in the session column. MEETING PLACES OF CONGRESS: Congress met for the first and second sessions of the First Congress (1789 and 1790) in New York City. From the third session of the First Congress through the first session of the Sixth Congress (1790 to 1800), Philadelphia was the meeting place. Congress has convened in Washington since the second session of the Sixth Congress (1800).

Congress	Session	Convening Date	Adjournment Date	Length in days[1]	Recesses[2]		President pro tempore of the Senate[3]	Speaker of the House of Representatives
					Senate	House of Representatives		
92d	1	Jan. 21, 1971	Dec. 17, 1971 ...	331	Feb. 11–Feb. 17, 1971 .... Apr. 7–Apr. 14, 1971 May 26–June 1, 1971 June 30–July 6, 1971 Aug. 6–Sept. 8, 1971 Oct. 21–Oct. 26, 1971 Nov. 24–Nov. 29, 1971	Feb. 10–Feb. 17, 1971 .... Apr. 7–Apr. 19, 1971 May 27–June 1, 1971 July 1–July 6, 1971 Aug. 6–Sept. 8, 1971 Oct. 7–Oct. 12, 1971 Oct. 21–Oct. 26, 1971 Nov. 19–Nov. 29, 1971	Richard B. Russell, of Georgia;[17] Allen J. Ellender, of Louisiana.[17]	Carl B. Albert, of Oklahoma.
	2	Jan. 18, 1972	Oct. 18, 1972 ...	275	Feb. 9–Feb. 14, 1972 .... Mar. 30–Apr. 4, 1972 May 25–May 30, 1972 June 30–July 17, 1972 Aug. 18–Sept. 5, 1972	Feb. 9–Feb. 16, 1972 .... Mar. 29–Apr. 10, 1972 May 24–May 30, 1972 June 30–July 17, 1972 Aug. 18–Sept. 5, 1972	Allen J. Ellender, of Louisiana;[18] James O. Eastland, of Mississippi.[18]	
93d	1	Jan. 3, 1973	Dec. 22, 1973 ...	354	Feb. 8–Feb. 15, 1973 .... Apr. 18–Apr. 30, 1973 May 23–May 29, 1973 June 30–July 9, 1973 Aug. 3–Sept. 5, 1973 Oct. 18–Oct. 23, 1973 Nov. 21–Nov. 26, 1973	Feb. 8–Feb. 19, 1973 .... Apr. 19–Apr. 30, 1973 May 24–May 29, 1973 June 30–July 10, 1973 Aug. 3–Sept. 5, 1973 Oct. 4–Oct. 9, 1973 Oct. 18–Oct. 23, 1973 Nov. 15–Nov. 26, 1973	James O. Eastland, of Mississippi	Do.
	2	Jan. 21, 1974	Dec. 20, 1974 ...	334	Feb. 8–Feb. 18, 1974 .... Mar. 13–Mar. 19, 1974 Apr. 11–Apr. 22, 1974 May 23–May 28, 1974 Aug. 22–Sept. 4, 1974 Oct. 17–Nov. 18, 1974 Nov. 26–Dec. 2, 1974	Feb. 7–Feb. 13, 1974 .... Apr. 11–Apr. 22, 1974 May 23–May 28, 1974 Aug. 22–Sept. 11, 1974 Oct. 17–Nov. 18, 1974 Nov. 26–Dec. 3, 1974	......do.	

94th ...	1	Jan. 14, 1975	Dec. 19, 1975 ...	340	Mar. 26–Apr. 7, 1975 May 22–June 2, 1975 June 27–July 7, 1975 Aug. 1–Sept. 3, 1975 Oct. 9–Oct. 20, 1975 Oct. 23–Oct. 28, 1975 Nov. 20–Dec. 1, 1975	Mar. 26–Apr. 7, 1975 May 22–June 2, 1975 June 26–July 8, 1975 Aug. 1–Sept. 3, 1975 Oct. 9–Oct. 20, 1975 Oct. 23–Oct. 28, 1975 Nov. 20–Dec. 1, 1975	......do	Do.
	2	Jan. 19, 1976	Oct. 1, 1976	257	Feb. 6–Feb. 16, 1976 Apr. 14–Apr. 26, 1976 May 28–June 2, 1976 July 2–July 19, 1976 Aug. 10–Aug. 23, 1976 Sept. 1–Sept. 7, 1976	Feb. 11–Feb. 16, 1976 Apr. 14–Apr. 26, 1976 May 27–June 1, 1976 July 2–July 19, 1976 Aug. 10–Aug. 23, 1976 Sept. 2–Sept. 8, 1976	......do.	
95th ...	1	Jan. 4, 1977	Dec. 15, 1977 ...	346	Feb. 11–Feb. 21, 1977 Apr. 7–Apr. 18, 1977 May 27–June 6, 1977 July 1–July 11, 1977 Aug. 6–Sept. 7, 1977	Feb. 9–Feb. 16, 1977 Apr. 6–Apr. 18, 1977 May 26–June 1, 1977 June 30–July 11, 1977 Aug. 5–Sept. 7, 1977 Oct. 6–Oct. 11, 1977	......do	Thomas P. O'Neill, Jr., of Massachusetts.
	2	Jan. 19, 1978	Oct. 15, 1978 ...	270	Feb. 10–Feb. 20, 1978 Mar. 23–Apr. 3, 1978 May 26–June 5, 1978 June 29–July 10, 1978 Aug. 25–Sept. 6, 1978	Feb. 9–Feb. 14, 1978 Mar. 22–Apr. 3, 1978 May 25–May 31, 1978 June 29–July 10, 1978 Aug. 17–Sept. 6, 1978	......do.	
96th ...	1	Jan. 15, 1979	Jan. 3, 1980	354	Feb. 9–Feb. 19, 1979 Apr. 10–Apr. 23, 1979 May 24–June 4, 1979 June 27–July 9, 1979 Aug. 3–Sept. 5, 1979 Nov. 20–Nov. 26, 1979 Adjourned sine die, Dec. 20, 1979	Feb. 8–Feb. 13, 1979 Apr. 10–Apr. 23, 1979 May 24–May 30, 1979 June 29–July 9, 1979 Aug. 2–Sept. 5, 1979 Nov. 20–Nov. 26, 1979	Warren G. Magnuson, of Washington ...	Do.
	2	Jan. 3, 1980	Dec. 16, 1980 ...	349	Apr. 3–Apr. 15, 1980 May 22–May 28, 1980 July 2–July 21, 1980 Aug. 6–Aug. 18, 1980 Aug. 27–Sept. 3, 1980 Oct. 1–Nov. 12, 1980 Nov. 25–Dec. 1, 1980	Feb. 13–Feb. 19, 1980 Apr. 2–Apr. 15, 1980 May 22–May 28, 1980 July 2–July 21, 1980 Aug. 1–Aug. 18, 1980 Aug. 28–Sept. 3, 1980 Oct. 2–Nov. 12, 1980 Nov. 21–Dec. 1, 1980	Warren G. Magnuson, of Washington; Milton Young, of North Dakota;[19] Warren G. Magnuson, of Washington.[19]	
97th ...	1	Jan. 5, 1981	Dec. 16, 1981 ...	347	Feb. 6–Feb. 16, 1981 Apr. 10–Apr. 27, 1981 June 25–July 8, 1981 Aug. 3–Sept. 9, 1981 Oct. 7–Oct. 14, 1981 Nov. 24–Nov. 30, 1981	Feb. 6–Feb. 17, 1981 Apr. 10–Apr. 27, 1981 June 26–July 8, 1981 Aug. 4–Sept. 9, 1981 Oct. 7–Oct. 13, 1981 Nov. 23–Nov. 30, 1981	Strom Thurmond, of South Carolina	Do.
	2	Jan. 25, 1982	Dec. 23, 1982 ...	333	Feb. 11–Feb. 22, 1982 Apr. 1–Apr. 13, 1982 May 27–June 8, 1982 July 1–July 12, 1982 Aug. 20–Sept. 8, 1982 Oct. 1–Nov. 29, 1982	Feb. 10–Feb. 22, 1982 Apr. 6–Apr. 20, 1982 May 27–June 2, 1982 July 1–July 12, 1982 Aug. 20–Sept. 8, 1982 Oct. 1–Nov. 29, 1982	......do	

SESSIONS OF CONGRESS—CONTINUED

[Closing date for this table was July 8, 2003.]

MEETING DATES OF CONGRESS: Pursuant to a resolution of the Confederation Congress in 1788, the Constitution went into effect on March 4, 1789. From then until the 20th amendment took effect in January 1934, the term of each Congress began on March 4th of each odd-numbered year; however, Article I, section 4, of the Constitution provided that ''The Congress shall assemble at least once in every Year, and such Meeting shall be on the first Monday in December, unless they shall by law appoint a different day.'' The Congress therefore convened regularly on the first Monday in December until the 20th amendment became effective, which changed the beginning of Congress's term as well as its convening date to January 3rd. So prior to 1934, a new Congress typically would not convene for regular business until 13 months after being elected. One effect of this was that the last session of each Congress was a ''lame duck'' session. After the 20th amendment, the time from the election to the beginning of Congress's term as well as when it convened was reduced to two months. Recognizing that the need might exist for Congress to meet at times other than the regularly scheduled convening date, Article II, section 3 of the Constitution provides that the President ''may, on extraordinary occasions, convene both Houses, or either of them''; hence these sessions occur only if convened by Presidential proclamation. Except as noted, these are separately numbered sessions of a Congress, and are marked by an E in the session column of the table. Until the 20th amendment was adopted, there were also times when special sessions of the Senate were convened, principally for confirming Cabinet and other executive nominations, and occasionally for the ratification of treaties or other executive business. These Senate sessions were also called by Presidential proclamation (typically by the outgoing President, although on occasion by incumbents as well) and are marked by an S in the session column. MEETING PLACES OF CONGRESS: Congress met for the first and second sessions of the First Congress (1789 and 1790) in New York City. From the third session of the First Congress through the first session of the Sixth Congress (1790 to 1800), Philadelphia was the meeting place. Congress has convened in Washington since the second session of the Sixth Congress (1800).

Congress	Session	Convening Date	Adjournment Date	Length in days [1]	Recesses [2]		President pro tempore of the Senate [3]	Speaker of the House of Representatives
					Senate	House of Representatives		
98th ...	1	Jan. 3, 1983	Nov. 18, 1983 ..	320	Jan. 3–Jan. 25, 1983 .... Feb. 3–Feb. 14, 1983 Mar. 24–Apr. 5, 1983 May 26–June 6, 1983 June 29–July 11, 1983 Aug. 4–Sept. 12, 1983 Oct. 7–Oct. 17, 1983	Jan. 6–Jan. 25, 1983 .... Feb. 17–Feb. 22, 1983 Mar. 24–Apr. 5, 1983 May 26–June 1, 1983 June 30–July 11, 1983 Aug. 4–Sept. 12, 1983 Oct. 6–Oct. 17, 1983	Strom Thurmond, of South Carolina	Thomas P. O'Neill, Jr., of Massachusetts.
	2	Jan. 23, 1984	Oct. 12, 1984 ...	264	Feb. 9–Feb. 20, 1984 .... Apr. 12–Apr. 24, 1984 May 24–May 31, 1984 June 29–July 23, 1984 Aug. 10–Sept. 5, 1984	Feb. 9–Feb. 21, 1984 .... Apr. 12–Apr. 24, 1984 May 24–May 30, 1984 June 29–July 23, 1984 Aug. 10–Sept. 5, 1984	......do.	
99th ...	1	Jan. 3, 1985	Dec. 20, 1985 ...	352	Jan. 7–Jan. 21, 1985 .... Feb. 7–Feb. 18, 1985 Apr. 4–Apr. 15, 1985 May 9–May 14, 1985 May 24–June 3, 1985 June 27–July 8, 1985 Aug. 1–Sept. 9, 1985 Nov. 23–Dec. 2, 1985	Jan. 3–Jan. 21, 1985 .... Feb. 7–Feb. 19, 1985 Mar. 7–Mar. 19, 1985 Apr. 4–Apr. 15, 1985 May 23–June 3, 1985 June 27–July 8, 1985 Aug. 1–Sept. 4, 1985 Nov. 21–Dec. 2, 1985	......do	Do.
	2	Jan. 21, 1986	Oct. 18, 1986 ...	278	Feb. 7–Feb. 17, 1986 .... Mar. 27–Apr. 8, 1986 May 21–June 2, 1986 June 26–July 7, 1986 Aug. 15–Sept. 8, 1986	Feb. 6–Feb. 18, 1986 .... Mar. 25–Apr. 8, 1986 May 22–June 3, 1986 June 26–July 14, 1986 Aug. 16–Sept. 8, 1986	......do.	

100th ..	1	Jan. 6, 1987	Dec. 22, 1987 ...	351	Jan. 6–Jan. 12, 1987 .... Feb. 5–Feb. 16, 1987 Apr. 10–Apr. 21, 1987 May 21–May 27, 1987 July 1–July 7, 1987 Aug. 7–Sept. 9, 1987 Nov. 20–Nov. 30, 1987	Jan. 8–Jan. 20, 1987 .... Feb. 11–Feb. 18, 1987 Apr. 9–Apr. 21, 1987 May 21–May 27, 1987 July 1–July 7, 1987 July 15–July 20, 1987 Aug. 7–Sept. 9, 1987 Nov. 10–Nov. 16, 1987 Nov. 20–Nov. 30, 1987	John C. Stennis, of Mississippi	James C. Wright, Jr., of Texas.
	2	Jan. 25, 1988	Oct. 22, 1988 ...	272	Feb. 4–Feb. 15, 1988 .... Mar. 4– Mar. 14, 1988 Mar. 31–Apr. 11, 1988 Apr. 29–May 9, 1988 May 27–June 6, 1988 June 29–July 6, 1988 July 14–July 25, 1988 Aug. 11–Sept. 7, 1988	Feb. 9–Feb. 16, 1988 .... Mar. 31–Apr. 11, 1988 May 26–June 1, 1988 June 30–July 7, 1988 July 14–July 26, 1988 Aug. 11–Sept. 7,1988	......do.	
101st ..	1	Jan. 3, 1989	Nov. 22, 1989 ..	324	Jan. 4–Jan. 20, 1989 .... Jan. 20–Jan. 25, 1989 Feb. 9–Feb. 21, 1989 Mar. 17–Apr. 4, 1989 Apr. 19–May 1, 1989 May 18–May 31, 1989 June 23–July 11, 1989 Aug. 4–Sept. 6, 1989	Jan. 4–Jan. 19, 1989 .... Feb. 9–Feb. 21, 1989 Mar. 23–Apr. 3, 1989 Apr. 18–Apr. 25, 1989 May 25–May 31, 1989 June 29–July 10, 1989 Aug. 5–Sept. 6, 1989	Robert C. Byrd, of West Virginia	James C. Wright, Jr., of Texas;[20] Thomas S. Foley, of Washington.[20]
	2	Jan. 23, 1990	Oct. 28, 1990 ...	260	Feb. 8–Feb. 20, 1990 .... Mar. 9–Mar. 20, 1990 Apr. 5–Apr. 18, 1990 May 24–June 5, 1990 June 28–July 10, 1990 Aug. 4–Sept. 10, 1990	Feb. 7–Feb. 20, 1990 .... Apr. 4–Apr. 18, 1990 May 25–June 5, 1990 June 28–July 10, 1990 Aug. 4–Sept. 5, 1990	......do.	
102d ...	1	Jan. 3, 1991	Jan. 3, 1992	366	Feb. 7–Feb. 19, 1991 .... Mar. 22–Apr. 9, 1991 Apr. 25–May 6, 1991 May 24–June 3, 1991 June 28–July 8, 1991 Aug. 2–Sept. 10, 1991 Nov. 27, 1991–Jan. 3, 1992	Feb. 6–Feb. 19, 1991 .... Mar. 22–Apr. 9, 1991 May 23–May 29, 1991 June 27–July 9, 1991 Aug. 2–Sept. 11, 1991 Nov. 27, 1991–Jan. 3, 1992	......do	Thomas S. Foley, of Washington.
	2	Jan. 3, 1992	Oct. 9, 1992	281	Jan. 3–Jan. 21, 1992 .... Feb. 7–Feb. 18, 1992 Apr. 10–Apr. 28, 1992 May 21–June 1, 1992 July 2–July 20, 1992 Aug. 12–Sept. 8, 1992	Jan. 3–Jan. 22, 1992 .... Apr. 10–Apr. 28, 1992 May 21–May 26, 1992 July 2–July 7, 1992 July 9–July 21, 1992 Aug. 12–Sept. 9, 1992	......do.	

SESSIONS OF CONGRESS—CONTINUED

[Closing date for this table was July 8, 2003.]

MEETING DATES OF CONGRESS: Pursuant to a resolution of the Confederation Congress in 1788, the Constitution went into effect on March 4, 1789. From then until the 20th amendment took effect in January 1934, the term of each Congress began on March 4th of each odd-numbered year; however, Article I, section 4, of the Constitution provided that ''The Congress shall assemble at least once in every Year, and such Meeting shall be on the first Monday in December, unless they shall by law appoint a different day.'' The Congress therefore convened regularly on the first Monday in December until the 20th amendment became effective, which changed the beginning of Congress's term as well as its convening date to January 3rd. So prior to 1934, a new Congress typically would not convene for regular business until 13 months after being elected. One effect of this was that the last session of each Congress was a ''lame duck'' session. After the 20th amendment, the time from the election to the beginning of Congress's term as well as when it convened was reduced to two months. Recognizing that the need might exist for Congress to meet at times other than the regularly scheduled convening date, Article II, section 3 of the Constitution provides that the President ''may, on extraordinary occasions, convene both Houses, or either of them''; hence these sessions occur only if convened by Presidential proclamation. Except as noted, these are separately numbered sessions of a Congress, and are marked by an E in the session column of the table. Until the 20th amendment was adopted, there were also times when special sessions of the Senate were convened, principally for confirming Cabinet and other executive nominations, and occasionally for the ratification of treaties or other executive business. These Senate sessions were also called by Presidential proclamation (typically by the outgoing President, although on occasion by incumbents as well) and are marked by an S in the session column. MEETING PLACES OF CONGRESS: Congress met for the first and second sessions of the First Congress (1789 and 1790) in New York City. From the third session of the First Congress through the first session of the Sixth Congress (1790 to 1800), Philadelphia was the meeting place. Congress has convened in Washington since the second session of the Sixth Congress (1800).

Congress	Session	Convening Date	Adjournment Date	Length in days[1]	Recesses[2]		President pro tempore of the Senate[3]	Speaker of the House of Representatives
					Senate	House of Representatives		
103d ...	1	Jan. 5, 1993	Nov. 26, 1993 ..	326	Jan. 7–Jan. 20, 1993 .... Feb. 4–Feb. 16, 1993 Apr. 7–Apr. 19, 1993 May 28–June 7, 1993 July 1–July 13, 1993 Aug. 7–Sept. 7, 1993 Oct. 7–Oct. 13, 1993 Nov. 11–Nov. 16, 1993	Jan. 6–Jan. 20, 1993 .... Jan. 27–Feb. 2, 1993 Feb. 4–Feb. 16, 1993 Apr. 7–Apr. 19, 1993 May 27–June 8, 1993 July 1–July 13, 1993 Aug. 6–Sept. 8, 1993 Sept. 15–Sept. 21, 1993 Oct. 7–Oct. 12, 1993 Nov. 10–Nov. 15, 1993	Robert C. Byrd, of West Virginia	Thomas S. Foley, of Washington.
	2	Jan. 25, 1994	Dec. 1, 1994	311	Feb. 11–Feb. 22, 1994 .... Mar. 26–Apr. 11, 1994 May 25–June 7, 1994 July 1–July 11, 1994 Aug. 25–Sept. 12, 1994 Oct. 8–Nov. 30, 1994	Jan. 26–Feb. 1, 1994 .... Feb. 11–Feb. 22, 1994 Mar. 24–Apr. 12, 1994 May 26–June 8, 1994 June 30–July 12, 1994 Aug. 26–Sept. 12, 1994 Oct. 8–Nov. 29, 1994	......do.	
104th..	1	Jan. 4, 1995	Jan. 3, 1996	365	Feb. 16–Feb. 22, 1995 .... Apr. 7–Apr. 24, 1995 May 26–June 5, 1995 June 30–July 10, 1995 Aug. 11–Sept. 5, 1995 Sept. 29–Oct. 10, 1995 Nov. 20–Nov. 27, 1995	Feb. 16–Feb. 21, 1995 .... Mar. 16–Mar. 21, 1995 Apr. 7–May 1, 1995 May 3–May 9, 1995 May 25–June 6, 1995 June 30–July 10, 1995 Aug. 4–Sept. 6, 1995 Sept. 29–Oct. 6, 1995 Nov. 20–Nov. 28, 1995	Strom Thurmond, of South Carolina	Newt Gingrich, of Georgia.

Congress	Session	Convening date	Adjournment date	Days	Recesses (Senate)	Recesses (House)	President pro tempore of the Senate	Speaker of the House
	2	Jan. 3, 1996	Oct. 4, 1996	276	Jan. 10–Jan. 22, 1996 Mar. 29–Apr. 15, 1996 May 24–June 3, 1996 June 28–July 8, 1996 Aug. 2–Sept. 3, 1996	Jan. 9–Jan. 22, 1996 Mar. 29–Apr. 15, 1996 May 23–May 29, 1996 June 28–July 8, 1996 Aug. 2–Sept. 4, 1996	......do.	
105th..	1	Jan. 7, 1997	Nov. 13, 1997	311	Jan. 9–Jan. 21, 1997 Feb. 13–Feb. 24, 1997 Mar. 21–Apr. 7, 1997 June 27–July 7, 1997 July 31–Sept. 2, 1997 Oct. 9–Oct. 20, 1997	Jan. 9–Jan. 20, 1997 Jan. 21–Feb. 4, 1997 Feb. 13–Feb. 25, 1997 Mar. 21–Apr. 8, 1997 June 26–July 8, 1997 Aug. 1–Sept. 3, 1997 Oct. 9–Oct. 21, 1997	......do	Do.
	2	Jan. 27, 1998	Dec. 19, 1998	327	Feb. 13–Feb. 23, 1998 Apr. 3–Apr. 20, 1998 May 22–June 1, 1998 June 26–July 6, 1998 July 31–Aug. 31, 1998 Adjourned sine die, Oct. 21, 1998.	Jan. 28–Feb. 3, 1998 Feb. 5–Feb. 11, 1998 Feb. 12–Feb. 24, 1998 Apr. 1–Apr. 21, 1998 May 22–June 3, 1998 June 25–July 14, 1998 Aug. 7–Sept. 9, 1998 Oct. 21–Dec. 17, 1998	......do.	
106th..	1	Jan. 6, 1999	Nov. 22, 1999	321	Feb. 12–Feb. 22, 1999 Mar. 25–Apr. 12, 1999 May 27–June 7, 1999 July 1–July 12, 1999 Aug. 5–Sept. 8, 1999	Jan. 6–Jan. 19, 1999 Jan. 19–Feb. 2, 1999 Feb. 12–Feb. 23, 1999 Mar. 25–Apr. 12, 1999 May 27–June 7, 1999 July 1–July 12, 1999 Aug. 6–Sept. 8, 1999	......do	J. Dennis Hastert, of Illinois.
	2	Jan. 24, 2000	Dec. 15, 2000	326	Feb. 10–Feb. 22, 2000 Mar. 9–Mar. 20, 2000 Apr. 13–Apr. 25, 2000 May 25–June 6, 2000 June 30–July 10, 2000 July 27–Sept. 5, 2000 Nov. 2–Nov. 14, 2000 Nov. 14–Dec. 5, 2000	Feb. 16–Feb. 29, 2000 Apr. 13–May 2, 2000 May 25–June 6, 2000 June 30–July 10, 2000 July 27–Sept. 6, 2000 Nov. 3–Nov. 13, 2000 Nov. 14–Dec. 4, 2000	......do.	
107th..	1	Jan. 3, 2001	Dec. 20, 2001	352	Jan. 8–Jan. 20, 2001 Feb. 15–Feb. 26, 2001 Apr. 6–Apr. 23, 2001 May 26–June 5, 2001 June 29–July 9, 2001 Aug. 3–Sept. 4, 2001 Oct. 18–Oct. 23, 2001 Nov. 16–Nov. 27, 2001	Jan. 6–Jan. 20, 2001 Jan. 20–Jan 30, 2001 Jan. 31–Feb. 6, 2001 Feb. 14–Feb. 26, 2001 Apr. 4–Apr. 24, 2001 May 26–June 5, 2001 June 28–July 10, 2001 Aug. 2–Sept. 5, 2001 Oct. 17–Oct. 23, 2001 Nov. 19–Nov. 27, 2001	Robert C. Byrd, of West Virginia;[21] Strom Thurmond, of South Carolina;[21] Robert C. Byrd, of West Virginia.[21]	Do.
	2	Jan. 23, 2002	Nov. 22, 2002	304	Jan. 29–Feb. 4, 2002 Feb. 15–Feb. 25, 2002 Mar. 22–Apr. 8, 2002 May 23–June 3, 2002 June 28–July 8, 202 Aug. 1–Sept. 3, 2002	Jan. 29–Feb. 4, 2002 Feb. 14–Feb. 26, 2002 Mar. 20–Apr. 9, 2002 May 24–June 4, 2002 June 28–July 8, 2002 July 27–Sept. 4, 2002	Robert C. Byrd, of West Virginia.	

SESSIONS OF CONGRESS—CONTINUED

[Closing date for this table was July 8, 2003.]

MEETING DATES OF CONGRESS: Pursuant to a resolution of the Confederation Congress in 1788, the Constitution went into effect on March 4, 1789. From then until the 20th amendment took effect in January 1934, the term of each Congress began on March 4th of each odd-numbered year; however, Article I, section 4, of the Constitution provided that ''The Congress shall assemble at least once in every Year, and such Meeting shall be on the first Monday in December, unless they shall by law appoint a different day.'' The Congress therefore convened regularly on the first Monday in December until the 20th amendment became effective, which changed the beginning of Congress's term as well as its convening date to January 3rd. So prior to 1934, a new Congress typically would not convene for regular business until 13 months after being elected. One effect of this was that the last session of each Congress was a ''lame duck'' session. After the 20th amendment, the time from the election to the beginning of Congress's term as well as when it convened was reduced to two months. Recognizing that the need might exist for Congress to meet at times other than the regularly scheduled convening date, Article II, section 3 of the Constitution provides that the President ''may, on extraordinary occasions, convene both Houses, or either of them''; hence these sessions occur only if convened by Presidential proclamation. Except as noted, these are separately numbered sessions of a Congress, and are marked by an E in the session column of the table. Until the 20th amendment was adopted, there were also times when special sessions of the Senate were convened, principally for confirming Cabinet and other executive nominations, and occasionally for the ratification of treaties or other executive business. These Senate sessions were also called by Presidential proclamation (typically by the outgoing President, although on occasion by incumbents as well) and are marked by an S in the session column. MEETING PLACES OF CONGRESS: Congress met for the first and second sessions of the First Congress (1789 and 1790) in New York City. From the third session of the First Congress through the first session of the Sixth Congress (1790 to 1800), Philadelphia was the meeting place. Congress has convened in Washington since the second session of the Sixth Congress (1800).

Congress	Session	Convening Date	Adjournment Date	Length in days [1]	Recesses [2]		President pro tempore of the Senate [3]	Speaker of the House of Representatives
					Senate	House of Representatives		
108th	1	Jan. 7, 2003			Feb. 14–Feb. 24, 2003 Apr. 11–Apr. 28, 2003 May 23–June 2, 2003 June 27–July 7, 2003	Jan. 8–Jan. 27, 2003 Feb. 13–Feb. 25, 2003 Apr. 12–Apr. 29, 2003 May 23–June 2, 2003 June 27–July 7, 2003	Ted Stevens, of Alaska.	J. Dennis Hastert, of Illinois.

[1] For the purposes of this table, a session's ''length in days'' is defined as the total number of calendar days from the convening date to the adjournment date, inclusive. It does not mean the actual number of days that Congress met during that session.

[2] For the purposes of this table, a ''recess'' is defined as any period of three or more complete days—excluding Sundays—when either the House of Representatives or the Senate is not in session. As listed, the recess periods also are inclusive of days only partially in the recess, i.e., the day (or days) when the House and Senate each adjourn to begin the recess, as well as the day (or days) when each body reconvenes at the end of the recess.

[3] The election and role of the President pro tempore has evolved considerably over the Senate's history. ''*Pro tempore* is Latin for 'for the time being'; thus, the post was conceived as a temporary presiding officer. In the eighteenth and nineteenth centuries, the Senate frequently elected several Presidents pro tempore during a single session. Since Vice Presidents presided routinely, the Senate thought it necessary to choose a President pro tempore only for the limited periods when the Vice President might be ill or otherwise absent.'' Since no provision was in place (until the 25th amendment was adopted in 1967) for replacing the Vice President if he died or resigned from office, or if he assumed the Presidency, the President pro tempore would continue under such circumstances to fill the duties of the chair until the next Vice President was elected. Since Mar. 12, 1890, however, Presidents pro tempore have served until ''the Senate otherwise ordered.'' Since 1949, while still elected, the position has gone to the most senior member of the majority party (see footnote 19 for a minority party exception). To gain a more complete understanding of this position, see Robert C. Byrd's *The Senate 1789–1989: Addresses on the History of the United States Senate*, vol. 2, ch. 6 ''The President Pro Tempore,'' pp. 167–183, from which the quotes in this footnote are taken. Also, a complete listing of the dates of election of the Presidents pro tempore is in vol. 4 of the Byrd series (*The Senate 1789–1989: Historical Statistics, 1789–1992*), table 6–2, pp. 647–653.

[4] Henry Clay resigned as Speaker on Jan. 19, 1814. He was succeeded by Langdon Cheves who was elected on that same day.

[5] Henry Clay resigned as Speaker on Oct. 28, 1820, after the sine die adjournment of the first session of the 16th Congress. He was succeeded by John W. Taylor who was elected at the beginning of the second session.

[6] Andrew Stevenson resigned as Speaker on June 2, 1834. He was succeeded by John Bell who was elected on that same day.

[7] Speaker Schuyler Colfax resigned as Speaker on the last day of the 40th Congress, Mar. 3, 1869, in preparation for becoming Vice President of the United States on the following day. Theodore M. Pomeroy was elected Speaker on Mar. 3, and served for only that one day.

[8] Speaker Michael C. Kerr died on Aug. 19, 1876, after the sine die adjournment of the first session of the 44th Congress. Samuel J. Randall was elected Speaker at the beginning of the second session.

[9] William P. Frye resigned as President pro tempore on Apr. 27, 1911.

[10] President pro tempore James P. Clarke died on Oct. 1, 1916, after the sine die adjournment of the first session of the 64th Congress. Willard Saulsbury was elected President pro tempore during the second session.

[11] Speaker Joseph W. Byrns died on June 4, 1936. He was succeeded by William B. Bankhead who was elected Speaker on that same day.

[12] Speaker William B. Bankhead died on Sept. 15, 1940. He was succeeded by Sam Rayburn who was elected Speaker on that same day.

[13] President pro tempore Key Pittman died on Nov. 10, 1940. He was succeeded by William H. King who was elected President pro tempore on Nov. 19, 1940.

[14] President pro tempore Pat Harrison died on June 22, 1941. He was succeeded by Carter Glass who was elected President pro tempore on July 10, 1941.

[15] President Harry S. Truman called the Congress into extraordinary session twice, both times during the 80th Congress. Each time Congress had essentially wrapped up its business for the year, but for technical reasons had not adjourned sine die, so in each case the extraordinary session is considered an extension of the regularly numbered session rather than a separately numbered one. The dates of these extraordinary sessions were Nov. 17 to Dec. 19, 1947, and July 26 to Aug. 7, 1948.

[16] Speaker Sam Rayburn died on Nov. 16, 1961, after the sine die adjournment of the first session of the 87th Congress. John W. McCormack was elected Speaker at the beginning of the second session.

[17] President pro tempore Richard B. Russell died on Jan. 21, 1971. He was succeeded by Allen J. Ellender who was elected to that position on Jan. 22, 1971.

[18] President pro tempore Allen J. Ellender died on July 27, 1972. He was succeeded by James O. Eastland who was elected President pro tempore on July 28, 1972.

[19] Milton Young was elected President pro tempore for one day, Dec. 5, 1980, which was at the end of his 36-year career in the Senate. He was Republican, which was the minority party at that time. Warren G. Magnuson resumed the position of President pro tempore on Dec. 6, 1980.

[20] James C. Wright, Jr., resigned as Speaker on June 6, 1989. He was succeeded by Thomas S. Foley who was elected on that same day.

[21] The 2000 election resulted in an even split in the Senate between Republicans and Democrats. From the date the 107th Congress convened on Jan. 3, 2001, until Inauguration Day on Jan. 20, 2001, Vice President Albert Gore tipped the scale to a Democratic majority, hence Robert C. Byrd served as President pro tempore during this brief period. When Vice President Richard B. Cheney took office on Jan. 20, the Republicans became the majority party, and Strom Thurmond was elected President pro tempore. On June 6, 2001, Republican Senator James Jeffords became an Independent, creating a Democratic majority, and Robert C. Byrd was elected President pro tempore on that day.

CEREMONIAL MEETINGS OF CONGRESS

The following ceremonial meetings of Congress occurred on the following dates, at the designated locations, and for the reasons indicated. Please note that Congress was not in session on these occasions.

July 16, 1987, 100th Congress, Philadelphia, Pennsylvania, Independence Hall and Congress Hall—In honor of the bicentennial of the Constitution and in commemoration of the Great Compromise of the Constitutional Convention.

September 6, 2002, 107th Congress, New York City, New York, Federal Hall—In remembrance of the victims and heroes of September 11, 2001, and in recognition of the courage and spirit of the City of New York.

JOINT SESSIONS AND MEETINGS, ADDRESSES TO THE SENATE OR THE HOUSE, AND INAUGURATIONS

1st–108th CONGRESSES, 1789–2003 [1]

The parliamentary difference between a joint session and a joint meeting has evolved over time. In recent years the distinctions have become clearer: a joint session is more formal, and occurs upon the adoption of a concurrent resolution; a joint meeting occurs when each body adopts a unanimous consent agreement to recess to meet with the other legislative body. Joint sessions typically are held to hear an address from the President of the United States or to count electoral votes. Joint meetings typically are held to hear an address from a foreign dignitary or visitors other than the President.

The Speaker of the House of Representatives usually presides over joint sessions and joint meetings; however, the President of the Senate does preside over joint sessions where the electoral votes are counted, as required by the Constitution.

In the earliest years of the Republic, 1789 and 1790, when the national legislature met in New York City, joint gatherings were held in the Senate Chamber in Federal Hall. In Philadelphia, when the legislature met in Congress Hall, such meetings were held in the Senate Chamber, 1790–1793, and in the Hall of the House of Representatives, 1794–1799. Once the Congress moved to the Capitol in Washington in 1800, the Senate Chamber again was used for joint gatherings through 1805. Since 1809, with few exceptions, joint sessions and joint meetings have occurred in the Hall of the House.

Presidential messages on the state of the Union were originally known as the ''Annual Message,'' but since the 80th Congress, in 1947, have been called the ''State of the Union Address.'' After President John Adams's Annual Message on November 22, 1800, these addresses were read by clerks to the individual bodies until President Woodrow Wilson resumed the practice of delivering them to joint sessions on December 2, 1913.

In some instances more than one joint gathering has occurred on the same day. For example, on January 6, 1941, Congress met in joint session to count electoral votes for President and Vice President, and then met again in joint session to receive President Franklin Delano Roosevelt's Annual Message.

Whereas in more recent decades, foreign dignitaries invited to speak before Congress have typically done so at joint meetings, in earlier times (and with several notable exceptions), such visitors were received by the Senate and the House separately, or by one or the other singly, a tradition begun with the visit of General Lafayette of France in 1824. At that time a joint committee decided that each body would honor Lafayette separately, establishing the precedent. (See fotnote 7 for more details.) Not all such occasions included formal addresses by such dignitaries (e.g., Lafayette's reception by the Senate in their chamber, at which he did not speak before they adjourned to greet him), hence the ''occasions'' listed in the third column of the table include not only addresses, but also remarks (defined as brief greetings or off-the-cuff comments often requested of the visitor at the last minute) and receptions. Relatively few foreign dignitaries were received by Congress before World War I.

Congress has hosted inaugurations since the first occasion in 1789. They always have been formal joint gatherings, and sometimes they also were joint sessions. Inaugurations were joint sessions when both houses of Congress were in session, and they processed to the ceremony as part of the business of the day. In many cases, however, one or both houses were not in session or were in recess at the time of the ceremony. In this table, inaugurations that were not joint sessions are listed in the second column. Those that were joint sessions are so identified and described in the third column.

JOINT SESSIONS AND MEETINGS, ADDRESSES TO THE SENATE OR THE HOUSE, AND INAUGURATIONS

[See notes at end of table]

Congress & Date	Type	Occasion, topic, or inaugural location	Name and position of dignitary (where applicable)
		NEW YORK CITY	
1st CONGRESS			
Apr. 6, 1789	Joint session	Counting electoral votes	N.A.
Apr. 30, 1789	......do	Inauguration and church service [2]	President George Washington; Right Reverend Samuel Provoost, Senate-appointed Chaplain.
Jan. 8, 1790	......do	Annual Message	President George Washington.
		PHILADELPHIA	
Dec. 8, 1790	......do	......do	Do.
2d CONGRESS			
Oct. 25, 1791	......do	......do	Do.
Nov. 6, 1792	......do	......do	Do.
Feb. 13, 1793	......do	Counting electoral votes	N.A.
3d CONGRESS			
Mar. 4, 1793	Inauguration	Senate Chamber	President George Washington.
Dec. 3, 1793	Joint session	Annual Message	Do.
Nov. 19, 1794	......do	......do	Do.
4th CONGRESS			
Dec. 8, 1795	......do	......do	Do.
Dec. 7, 1796	Joint session	Annual Message	Do.
Feb. 8, 1797	......do	Counting electoral votes	N.A.
5th CONGRESS			
Mar. 4, 1797	Inauguration	Hall of the House	President John Adams.
May 16, 1797	Joint session	Relations with France	Do.
Nov. 23, 1797	......do	Annual Message	Do.
Dec. 8, 1798	......do	......do	Do.
6th CONGRESS			
Dec. 3, 1799	......do	......do	Do.
Dec. 26, 1799	......do	Funeral procession and oration in memory of George Washington.[3]	Representative Henry Lee.
		WASHINGTON	
Nov. 22, 1800	......do	Annual Message	President John Adams.
Feb. 11, 1801	......do	Counting electoral votes [4]	N.A.
7th CONGRESS			
Mar. 4, 1801	Inauguration	Senate Chamber	President Thomas Jefferson.
8th CONGRESS			
Feb. 13, 1805	Joint session	Counting electoral votes	N.A.
9th CONGRESS			
Mar. 4, 1805	Inauguration	Senate Chamber	President Thomas Jefferson.
10th CONGRESS			
Feb. 8, 1809	Joint session	Counting electoral votes	N.A.
11th CONGRESS			
Mar. 4, 1809	Inauguration	Hall of the House	President James Madison.
12th CONGRESS			
Feb. 10, 1813	Joint session	Counting electoral votes	N.A.
13th CONGRESS			
Mar. 4, 1813	Inauguration	Hall of the House	President James Madison.
14th CONGRESS			
Feb. 12, 1817	Joint session	Counting electoral votes [5]	N.A.
15th CONGRESS			
Mar. 4, 1817	Inauguration	In front of Brick Capitol	President James Monroe.
16th CONGRESS			
Feb. 14, 1821	Joint session	Counting electoral votes [6]	N.A.
17th CONGRESS			
Mar. 5, 1821	Inauguration	Hall of the House	President James Monroe.
18th CONGRESS			
Dec. 9, 1824	Senate	Reception	General Gilbert du Motier, Marquis de Lafayette, of France.
Dec. 10, 1824	House [7]	Address	Speaker Henry Clay; General Gilbert du Motier, Marquis de Lafayette, of France.
Feb. 9, 1825	Joint session	Counting electoral votes [8]	N.A.

JOINT SESSIONS AND MEETINGS, ADDRESSES TO THE SENATE OR THE HOUSE, AND INAUGURATIONS—CONTINUED

[See notes at end of table]

Congress & Date	Type	Occasion, topic, or inaugural location	Name and position of dignitary (where applicable)
19th CONGRESS			
Mar. 4, 1825	Inauguration	Hall of the House	President John Quincy Adams.
20th CONGRESS			
Feb. 11, 1829	Joint session	Counting electoral votes	N.A.
21st CONGRESS			
Mar. 4, 1829	Inauguration	East Portico [9]	President Andrew Jackson.
22d CONGRESS			
Feb. 13, 1833	Joint session	Counting electoral votes	N.A.
23d CONGRESS			
Mar. 4, 1833	Inauguration	Hall of the House [10]	President Andrew Jackson.
Dec. 31, 1834	Joint session	Lafayette eulogy	Representative and former President John Quincy Adams; ceremony attended by President Andrew Jackson.
24th CONGRESS			
Feb. 8, 1837	......do	Counting electoral votes	N.A.
25th CONGRESS			
Mar. 4, 1837	Inauguration	East Portico	President Martin Van Buren.
26th CONGRESS			
Feb. 10, 1841	Joint session	Counting electoral votes	N.A.
27th CONGRESS			
Mar. 4, 1841	Inauguration	East Portico	President William Henry Harrison.
28th CONGRESS			
Feb. 12, 1845	Joint session	Counting electoral votes	N.A.
29th CONGRESS			
Mar. 4, 1845	Inauguration	East Portico	President James Knox Polk.
30th CONGRESS			
Feb. 14, 1849	Joint session	Counting electoral votes	N.A.
31st CONGRESS			
Mar. 5, 1849	Inauguration	East Portico	President Zachary Taylor.
July 10, 1850	Joint session	Oath of office to President Millard Fillmore. [11]	N.A.
32d CONGRESS			
Jan. 5, 1852	Senate	Reception	Louis Kossuth, exiled Governor of Hungary.
Jan. 7, 1852	House	Remarks and Reception	Do.
Feb. 9, 1853	Joint session	Counting electoral votes	N.A.
33d CONGRESS			
Mar. 4, 1853	Inauguration	East Portico	President Franklin Pierce.
34th CONGRESS			
Feb. 11, 1857	Joint session	Counting electoral votes	N.A.
35th CONGRESS			
Mar. 4, 1857	Inauguration	East Portico	President James Buchanan.
36th CONGRESS			
Feb. 13, 1861	Joint session	Counting electoral votes	N.A.
37th CONGRESS			
Mar. 4, 1861	Inauguration	East Portico	President Abraham Lincoln.
Feb. 22, 1862	Joint session	Reading of Washington's farewell address.	John W. Forney, Secretary of the Senate.
38th CONGRESS			
Feb. 8, 1865	......do	Counting electoral votes	N.A.
39th CONGRESS			
Mar. 4, 1865	Inauguration	East Portico	President Abraham Lincoln.
Feb. 12, 1866	Joint session	Memorial to Abraham Lincoln	George Bancroft, historian; ceremony attended by President Andrew Johnson.
40th CONGRESS			
June 9, 1868	House	Address	Anson Burlingame, Envoy to the U.S. from China, and former Representative.
Feb. 10, 1869	Joint session	Counting electoral votes	N.A.
41st CONGRESS			
Mar. 4, 1869	Inauguration	East Portico	President Ulysses S. Grant.
42d CONGRESS			
Mar. 6, 1872	House	Address	Tomomi Iwakura, Ambassador from Japan.

JOINT SESSIONS AND MEETINGS, ADDRESSES TO THE SENATE OR THE HOUSE, AND INAUGURATIONS—CONTINUED

[See notes at end of table]

Congress & Date	Type	Occasion, topic, or inaugural location	Name and position of dignitary (where applicable)
Feb. 12, 1873	Joint session	Counting electoral votes [12]	N.A.
43d CONGRESS			
Mar. 4, 1873	Inauguration	East Portico	President Ulysses S. Grant.
Dec. 18, 1874	Joint meeting	Reception and Remarks	Speaker James G. Blaine; David Kalakaua, King of the Hawaiian Islands.[13]
44th CONGRESS			
Feb. 1, 1877 Feb. 10, 1877 Feb. 12, 1877 Feb. 19, 1877 Feb. 20, 1877 Feb. 21, 1877 Feb. 24, 1877 Feb. 26, 1877 Feb. 28, 1877 Mar. 1, 1877 Mar. 2, 1877	Joint session	Counting electoral votes [14]	N.A.
45th CONGRESS			
Mar. 5, 1877	Inauguration	East Portico	President Rutherford B. Hayes.
46th CONGRESS			
Feb. 2, 1880	House	Address	Charles Stewart Parnell, member of Parliament from Ireland.
Feb. 9, 1881	Joint session	Counting electoral votes	N.A.
47th CONGRESS			
Mar. 4, 1881	Inauguration	East Portico	President James A. Garfield.
Feb. 27, 1882	Joint session	Memorial to James A. Garfield	James G. Blaine, former Speaker, Senator, and Secretary of State; ceremony attended by President Chester A. Arthur.
48th CONGRESS			
Feb. 11, 1885	Joint session	Counting electoral votes	N.A.
Feb. 21, 1885	......do	Completion of Washington Monument	Representative John D. Long; Representative-elect John W. Daniel,[15] ceremony attended by President Chester A. Arthur.
49th CONGRESS			
Mar. 4, 1885	Inauguration	East Portico	President Grover Cleveland.
50th CONGRESS			
Feb. 13, 1889	Joint session	Counting electoral votes	N.A.
51st CONGRESS			
Mar. 4, 1889	Inauguration	East Portico	President Benjamin Harrison.
Dec. 11, 1889	Joint session	Centennial of George Washington's first inauguration.	Melville W. Fuller, Chief Justice of the United States; ceremony attended by President Benjamin Harrison.
52d CONGRESS			
Feb. 8, 1893	......do	Counting electoral votes	N.A.
53d CONGRESS			
Mar. 4, 1893	Inauguration	East Portico	President Grover Cleveland.
54th CONGRESS			
Feb. 10, 1897	Joint session	Counting electoral votes	N.A.
55th CONGRESS			
Mar. 4, 1897	Inauguration	In front of original Senate Wing of Capitol.	President William McKinley.
56th CONGRESS			
Dec. 12, 1900	Joint meeting	Centennial of the Capital City	Representatives James D. Richardson and Sereno E. Payne, and Senator George F. Hoar; ceremony attended by President William McKinley.
Feb. 13, 1901	Joint session	Counting electoral votes	N.A.
57th CONGRESS			
Mar. 4, 1901	Inauguration	East Portico	President William McKinley.
Feb. 27, 1902	Joint session	Memorial to William McKinley	John Hay, Secretary of State; ceremony attended by President Theodore Roosevelt and Prince Henry of Prussia.
58th CONGRESS			
Feb. 8, 1905	......do	Counting electoral votes	N.A.

JOINT SESSIONS AND MEETINGS, ADDRESSES TO THE SENATE OR THE HOUSE, AND INAUGURATIONS—CONTINUED

[See notes at end of table]

Congress & Date	Type	Occasion, topic, or inaugural location	Name and position of dignitary (where applicable)
59th CONGRESS			
Mar. 4, 1905	Inauguration	East Portico	President Theodore Roosevelt.
60th CONGRESS			
Feb. 10, 1909	Joint session	Counting electoral votes	N.A.
61st CONGRESS			
Mar. 4, 1909	Inauguration	Senate Chamber [16]	President William Howard Taft.
Feb. 9, 1911	House	Address	Count Albert Apponyi, Minister of Education from Hungary.
62d CONGRESS			
Feb. 12, 1913	Joint session	Counting electoral votes	N.A.
Feb. 15, 1913	......do	Memorial for Vice President James S. Sherman.[17]	Senators Elihu Root, Thomas S. Martin, Jacob H. Gallinger, John R. Thornton, Henry Cabot Lodge, John W. Kern, Robert M. LaFollette, John Sharp Williams, Charles Curtis, Albert B. Cummins, George T. Oliver, James A. O'Gorman; Speaker Champ Clark; President William Howard Taft.
63d CONGRESS			
Mar. 4, 1913	Inauguration	East Portico	President Woodrow Wilson.
Apr. 8, 1913	Joint session	Tariff message	Do.
June 23, 1913	......do	Currency and bank reform message	Do.
Aug. 27, 1913	......do	Mexican affairs message	Do.
Dec. 2, 1913	......do	Annual Message	Do.
Jan. 20, 1914	......do	Trusts message	Do.
Mar. 5, 1914	......do	Panama Canal tolls	Do.
Apr. 20, 1914	......do	Mexico message	Do.
Sept. 4, 1914	......do	War tax message	Do.
Dec. 8, 1914	......do	Annual Message	Do.
64th CONGRESS			
Dec. 7, 1915	......do	......do	Do.
Aug. 29, 1916	Joint session	Railroad message (labor-management dispute).	Do.
Dec. 5, 1916	......do	Annual Message	Do.
Jan. 22, 1917	Senate	Planning ahead for peace	Do.
Feb. 3, 1917	Joint session	Severing diplomatic relations with Germany.	Do.
Feb. 14, 1917	......do	Counting electoral votes	N.A.
Feb. 26, 1917	......do	Arming of merchant ships	President Woodrow Wilson.
65th CONGRESS			
Mar. 5, 1917	Inauguration	East Portico	Do.
Apr. 2, 1917	Joint session	War with Germany	Do.
May 1, 1917	Senate	Address	René Raphaël Viviani, Minister of Justice from France; Jules Jusserand, Ambassador from France; address attended by Marshal Joseph Jacques Césaire Joffre, member of French Commission to U.S.
May 3, 1917	House	......do	Do.
May 5, 1917	......do	......do	Arthur James Balfour, British Secretary of State for Foreign Affairs.
May 8, 1917	Senate	......do	Do.
May 31, 1917	......do	......do	Ferdinando di'Savoia, Prince of Udine, Head of Italian Mission to U.S.
June 2, 1917	House	......do	Ferdinando di'Savoia, Prince of Udine, Head of Italian Mission to U.S.; Guglielmo Marconi, member of Italian Mission to U.S.
June 22, 1917	Senate	......do	Baron Moncheur, Chief of Political Bureau of Belgian Foreign Office at Havre.
June 23, 1917	House	......do	Boris Bakhmetieff, Ambassador from Russia.[18]
June 26, 1917	Senate	......do	Do.
June 27, 1917	House	......do	Baron Moncheur, Chief of Political Bureau of Belgian Foreign Office at Havre.
Aug. 30, 1917	Senate	......do	Kikujirō Ishii, Ambassador from Japan.
Sept. 5, 1917	House	......do	Do.
Dec. 4, 1917	Joint session	Annual Message/War with Austria-Hungary.	President Woodrow Wilson.
Jan. 4, 1918	......do	Federal operation of transportation systems.	Do.
Jan. 5, 1918	Senate	Address	Milenko Vesnic, Head of Serbian War Mission.

JOINT SESSIONS AND MEETINGS, ADDRESSES TO THE SENATE OR THE HOUSE, AND INAUGURATIONS—CONTINUED

[See notes at end of table]

Congress & Date	Type	Occasion, topic, or inaugural location	Name and position of dignitary (where applicable)
Jan. 8, 1918	House	Address	Milenko Vesnic, Head of Serbian War Mission.
Do	Joint session	Program for world's peace	President Woodrow Wilson.
Feb. 11, 1918	......do	Peace message	Do.
May 27, 1918	......do	War finance message	Do.
Sept. 24, 1918	Senate	Address and Reception [19]	Jules Jusserand, Ambassador from France; Vice President Thomas R. Marshall.
Sept. 30 1918	......do	Support of woman suffrage	President Woodrow Wilson.
Nov. 11, 1918	Joint session	Terms of armistice signed by Germany	Do.
Dec. 2, 1918	......do	Annual Message	Do.
Feb. 9, 1919	......do	Memorial to Theodore Roosevelt	Senator Henry Cabot Lodge, Sr.; ceremony attended by former President William Howard Taft.
66th CONGRESS			
June 23, 1919	Senate	Address	Epitácio da Silva Pessoa, President-elect of Brazil.
July 10, 1919	......do	Versailles Treaty	President Woodrow Wilson.
Aug. 8, 1919	Joint session	Cost of living message	Do.
Sept. 18, 1919	......do	Address	President pro tempore Albert B. Cummins; Speaker Frederick H. Gillett; Representative and former Speaker Champ Clark; General John J. Pershing.
Oct. 28, 1919	Senate	......do	Albert I, King of the Belgians.
Do	House	......do	Do.
Feb. 9, 1921	Joint session	Counting electoral votes	N.A.
67th CONGRESS			
Mar. 4, 1921	Inauguration	East Portico	President Warren G. Harding.
Apr. 12, 1921	Joint session	Federal problem message	Do.
July 12, 1921	Senate	Adjusted compensation for veterans of the World War [20].	Do.
Dec. 6, 1921	Joint session	Annual Message	Do.
Feb. 28, 1922	......do	Maintenance of the merchant marine	Do.
Aug. 18, 1922	......do	Coal and railroad message	Do.
Nov. 21, 1922	......do	Promotion of the American merchant marine.	Do.
Dec. 8, 1922	......do	Annual Message [21]	Do.
Feb. 7, 1923	......do	British debt due to the United States	Do.
68th CONGRESS			
Dec. 6, 1923	......do	Annual Message	President Calvin Coolidge.
Feb. 27, 1924	......do	Memorial to Warren G. Harding	Charles Evans Hughes, Secretary of State; ceremony attended by President Calvin Coolidge.
Dec. 15, 1924	......do	Memorial to Woodrow Wilson	Dr. Edwin Anderson Alderman, President of the University of Virginia; ceremony attended by President Calvin Coolidge.
Feb. 11, 1925	......do	Counting electoral votes	N.A.
69th CONGRESS			
Mar. 4, 1925	Inauguration	East Portico	President Calvin Coolidge.
Feb. 22, 1927	Joint session	George Washington birthday message	Do.
70th CONGRESS			
Jan. 25, 1928	House	Reception and Address	William Thomas Cosgrave, President of Executive Council of Ireland.
Feb. 13, 1929	Joint session	Counting electoral votes	N.A.
71st CONGRESS			
Mar. 4, 1929	Inauguration	East Portico	President Herbert Hoover.
Oct. 7, 1929	Senate	Address	James Ramsay MacDonald, Prime Minister of the United Kingdom.
Jan. 13, 1930	......do	Reception	Jan Christiaan Smuts, former Prime Minister of South Africa.
72d CONGRESS			
Feb. 22, 1932	Joint session	Bicentennial of George Washington's birth.	President Herbert Hoover.
May 31, 1932	Senate	Emergency character of economic situation in U.S.	Do.
Feb. 6, 1933	Joint meeting	Memorial to Calvin Coolidge	Arthur Prentice Rugg, Chief Justice of the Supreme Judicial Court of Massachusetts; ceremony attended by President Herbert Hoover.
Feb. 8, 1933	Joint session	Counting electoral votes	N.A.
73d CONGRESS			
Mar. 4, 1933	Inauguration	East Portico	President Franklin Delano Roosevelt.

JOINT SESSIONS AND MEETINGS, ADDRESSES TO THE SENATE OR THE HOUSE, AND INAUGURATIONS—CONTINUED

[See notes at end of table]

Congress & Date	Type	Occasion, topic, or inaugural location	Name and position of dignitary (where applicable)
Jan. 3, 1934	Joint session	Annual Message	President Franklin Delano Roosevelt.
May 20, 1934	......do	100th anniversary, death of Lafayette	André de Laboulaye, Ambassador of France; President Franklin Delano Roosevelt; ceremony attended by Count de Chambrun, great-grandson of Lafayette.
74th CONGRESS			
Jan. 4, 1935	......do	Annual Message	President Franklin Delano Roosevelt.
May 22, 1935	......do	Veto message	Do.
Jan. 3, 1936	......do	Annual Message	Do.
75th CONGRESS			
Jan. 6, 1937	......do	Counting electoral votes	N.A.
Do	......do	Annual Message	President Franklin Delano Roosevelt.
Jan. 20, 1937	Inauguration	East Portico	President Franklin Delano Roosevelt; Vice President John Nance Garner.[22]
Apr. 1, 1937	Senate	Address	John Buchan, Lord Tweedsmuir, Governor General of Canada.
Do	House	......do	Do.
Jan. 3, 1938	Joint session	Annual Message	President Franklin Delano Roosevelt.
76th CONGRESS			
Jan. 4, 1939	......do	......do	Do.
Mar. 4, 1939	......do	Sesquicentennial of the 1st Congress	Do.
May 8, 1939	Senate	Address	Anastasio Somoza Garcia, President of Nicaragua.
Do	House	......do	Do.
June 9, 1939	Joint meeting	Reception[23]	George VI and Elizabeth, King and Queen of the United Kingdom.
Sept. 21, 1939	Joint session	Neutrality address	President Franklin Delano Roosevelt.
Jan. 3, 1940	......do	Annual Message	Do.
May 16, 1940	......do	National defense message	Do.
77th CONGRESS			
Jan. 6, 1941	......do	Counting electoral votes	N.A.
Do	......do	Annual Message	President Franklin Delano Roosevelt.
Jan. 20, 1941	......do	Inauguration, East Portico	President Franklin Delano Roosevelt; Vice President Henry A. Wallace.
Dec. 8, 1941	......do	War with Japan	President Franklin Delano Roosevelt.
Dec. 26, 1941	Joint meeting[24]	Address	Winston Churchill, Prime Minister of the United Kingdom.
Jan. 6, 1942	Joint session	Annual Message	President Franklin Delano Roosevelt.
May 11, 1942	Senate	Address	Manuel Prado, President of Peru.
Do	House	......do	Do.
June 2, 1942	......do	......do	Manuel Luis Quezon, President of the Philippines.[25]
June 4, 1942	Senate	......do	Do.
June 15, 1942	......do	......do	George II, King of Greece.[26]
Do	House	......do	Do.
June 25, 1942	Senate	......do	Peter II, King of Yugoslavia.[26]
Do	House	......do	Do.
Aug. 6, 1942	Senate[27]	......do	Wilhelmina, Queen of the Netherlands.[26]
Nov. 24, 1942	House	......do	Carlos Arroyo del Río, President of Ecuador.
Nov. 25, 1942	Senate	......do	Do.
Dec. 10, 1942	House	......do	Fulgencio Batista, President of Cuba.
78th CONGRESS			
Jan. 7, 1943	Joint session	Annual Message	President Franklin Delano Roosevelt.
Feb. 18, 1943	Senate	Remarks	Madame Chiang Kai-shek, of China.
Do	House	Address	Do.
May 6, 1943	Senate	......do	Enrique Peñaranda, President of Bolivia.
Do	House	......do	Do.
May 13, 1943	Senate	......do	Edvard Beneš, President of Czechoslovakia.[26]
Do	House	......do	Do.
May 19, 1943	Joint meeting	Address	Winston Churchill, Prime Minister of the United Kingdom.
May 27, 1943	Senate	Remarks	Edwin Barclay, President of Liberia.
Do	House	Address	Do.
June 10, 1943	Senate	......do	President Hininio Moriñigo M., President of Paraguay.
Do	House	......do	Do.
Oct. 15, 1943	Senate	......do	Elie Lescot, President of Haiti.
Nov. 18, 1943	Joint meeting	Moscow Conference	Cordell Hull, Secretary of State.
Jan. 20, 1944	Senate	Address	Isaías Medina Angarita, President of Venezuela.
Do	House	......do	Do.
79th CONGRESS			
Jan. 6, 1945	Joint session	Counting electoral votes	N.A.

JOINT SESSIONS AND MEETINGS, ADDRESSES TO THE SENATE OR THE HOUSE, AND INAUGURATIONS—CONTINUED

[See notes at end of table]

Congress & Date	Type	Occasion, topic, or inaugural location	Name and position of dignitary (where applicable)
Jan. 6, 1945	Joint session	Annual Message	President Roosevelt was not present. His message was read before the Joint Session of Congress.
Jan. 20, 1945	Inauguration	South Portico, The White House[28]	President Franklin Delano Roosevelt; Vice President Harry S. Truman.
Mar. 1, 1945	Joint session	Yalta Conference	President Franklin Delano Roosevelt.
Apr. 16, 1945	......do	Prosecution of the War	President Harry S. Truman.
May 21, 1945	......do	Bestowal of Congressional Medal of Honor on Tech. Sgt. Jake William Lindsey.	General George C. Marshall, Chief of Staff, U.S. Army; President Harry S. Truman.
June 18, 1945	Joint meeting	Address	General Dwight D. Eisenhower, Supreme Commander, Allied Expeditionary Force.
July 2, 1945	Senate	United Nations Charter	President Harry S. Truman.
Oct. 5, 1945	Joint meeting	Address	Admiral Chester W. Nimitz, Commander-in-Chief, Pacific Fleet.
Oct. 23, 1945	Joint session	Universal military training message	President Harry S. Truman.
Nov. 13, 1945	Joint meeting	Address	Clement R. Attlee, Prime Minister of the United Kingdom.
May 25, 1946	Joint session	Railroad strike message	President Harry S. Truman.
July 1, 1946	......do	Memorial to Franklin Delano Roosevelt	John Winant, U.S. Representative on the Economic and Social Council of the United Nations; ceremony attended by President Harry S. Truman and Mrs. Franklin Delano Roosevelt.
80th CONGRESS			
Jan. 6, 1947	......do	State of the Union Address[29]	President Harry S. Truman.
Mar. 12, 1947	......do	Greek-Turkish aid policy	Do.
May 1, 1947	Joint meeting	Address	Miguel Alemán, President of Mexico.
Nov. 17, 1947	Joint session	Aid to Europe message	President Harry S. Truman.
Jan. 7, 1948	......do	State of the Union Address	Do.
Mar. 17, 1948	......do	National security and conditions in Europe.	Do.
Apr. 19, 1948	......do	50th anniversary, liberation of Cuba	President Harry S. Truman; Guillermo Belt, Ambassador of Cuba.
July 27, 1948	......do	Inflation, housing, and civil rights	President Harry S. Truman.
81st CONGRESS			
Jan. 5, 1949	......do	State of the Union Address	Do.
Jan. 6, 1949	......do	Counting electoral votes	N.A.
Jan. 20, 1949	......do	Inauguration, East Portico	President Harry S. Truman; Vice President Alben W. Barkley.
May 19, 1949	Joint meeting	Address	Eurico Gaspar Dutra, President of Brazil.
Aug. 9, 1949	House	......do	Elpidio Quirino, President of the Philippines.
Do	Senate	......do	Do.
Oct. 13, 1949	......do	......do	Jawaharlal Nehru, Prime Minister of India.
Do	House	......do	Do.
Jan. 4, 1950	Joint session	State of the Union Address	President Harry S. Truman.
Apr. 13, 1950	Senate	Address	Gabriel González-Videla, President of Chile.
May 4, 1950	......do	......do	Liaquat Ali Khan, Prime Minister of Pakistan.
Do	House	......do	Do.
May 31, 1950	Joint meeting	Address	Dean Acheson, Secretary of State.
July 28, 1950	Senate	......do	Chōjirō Kuriyama, member of Japanese Diet.
July 31, 1950	House	......do	Tokutarō Kitamura, member of Japanese Diet.
Aug. 1, 1950	......do	......do	Robert Gordon Menzies, Prime Minister of Australia.
Do	Senate	......do	Do.
82d CONGRESS			
Jan. 8, 1951	Joint session	State of the Union Address	President Harry S. Truman.
Feb. 1, 1951	Joint meeting[30]	North Atlantic Treaty Organization	General Dwight D. Eisenhower.
Apr. 2, 1951	Joint meeting	Address	Vincent Auriol, President of France.
Apr. 19, 1951	......do	Return from Pacific Command	General Douglas MacArthur.
June 21, 1951	......do	Address	Galo Plaza, President of Ecuador.
July 2, 1951	Senate	Addresses	Tadao Kuraishi, and Aisuke Okamoto, members of Japanese Diet.
Aug. 23, 1951	......do	Address	Zentarō Kosaka, member of Japanese Diet.
Sept. 24, 1951	Joint meeting	......do	Alcide de Gasperi, Prime Minister of Italy.
Jan. 9, 1952	Joint session	State of the Union Address	President Harry S. Truman.
Jan. 17, 1952	Joint meeting	Address	Winston Churchill, Prime Minister of the United Kingdom.

JOINT SESSIONS AND MEETINGS, ADDRESSES TO THE SENATE OR THE HOUSE, AND INAUGURATIONS—CONTINUED

[See notes at end of table]

Congress & Date	Type	Occasion, topic, or inaugural location	Name and position of dignitary (where applicable)
Apr. 3, 1952	Joint meeting	Address	Juliana, Queen of the Netherlands.
May 22, 1952	......do	Korea	General Matthew B. Ridgway.
June 10, 1952	Joint session	Steel industry dispute	President Harry S. Truman.
83d CONGRESS			
Jan. 6, 1953	......do	Counting electoral votes	N.A.
Jan. 20, 1953	......do	Inauguration, East Portico	President Dwight D. Eisenhower; Vice President Richard M. Nixon.
Feb. 2, 1953	......do	State of the Union Address	President Dwight D. Eisenhower.
Jan. 7, 1954	......do	......do	Do.
Jan. 29, 1954	Joint meeting	Address	Celal Bayar, President of Turkey.
May 4, 1954	......do	......do	Vincent Massey, Governor General of Canada.
May 28, 1954	......do	......do	Haile Selassie I, Emperor of Ethiopia.
July 28, 1954	......do	......do	Syngman Rhee, President of South Korea.
Nov. 12, 1954	Senate	Remarks	Shigeru Yoshida, Prime Minister of Japan.
Nov. 17, 1954	......do	Address [31]	Sarvepalli Radhakrishnan, Vice President of India.
Nov. 18, 1954	......do	Remarks	Pierre Mendès-France, Premier of France.
84th CONGRESS			
Jan. 6, 1955	Joint session	State of the Union Address	President Dwight D. Eisenhower.
Jan. 27, 1955	Joint meeting	Address	Paul E. Magliore, President of Haiti.
Mar. 16, 1955	Senate	......do	Robert Gordon Menzies, Prime Minister of Australia.
Do	House	......do	Do.
Mar. 30, 1955	Senate	......do	Mario Scelba, Prime Minister of Italy.
Do	House	......do	Do.
May 4, 1955	Senate	......do	P. Phibunsongkhram, Prime Minister of Thailand.
Do	House	......do	Do.
June 30, 1955	Senate	......do	U Nu, Prime Minister of Burma.
Do	House	......do	Do.
Jan. 5, 1956	Senate	......do	Juscelino Kubitschek de Oliverira, President-elect of Brazil.
Feb. 2, 1956	......do	......do	Anthony Eden, Prime Minister of the United Kingdom.
Do	House	......do	Do.
Feb. 29, 1956	Joint meeting	......do	Giovanni Gronchi, President of Italy.
Mar. 15, 1956	Senate	......do	John Aloysius Costello, Prime Minister of Ireland.
Do	House	......do	Do.
Apr. 30, 1956	Senate	......do	João Goulart, Vice President of Brazil.
May 17, 1956	Joint meeting	......do	Sukarno, President of Indonesia.
85th CONGRESS			
Jan. 5, 1957	Joint session	Middle East message	President Dwight D. Eisenhower.
Jan. 7, 1957	......do	Counting electoral votes	N.A.
Jan. 10, 1957	......do	State of the Union Address	President Dwight D. Eisenhower.
Jan. 21, 1957	......do	Inauguration, East Portico	President Dwight D. Eisenhower; Vice President Richard M. Nixon.
Feb. 27, 1957	House	Address	Guy Mollet, Premier of France.
Do	Senate	......do	Do.
May 9, 1957	Joint meeting	......do	Ngo Dinh Diem, President of Vietnam.
May 28, 1957	House	......do	Konrad Adenauer, Chancellor of West Germany.
Do	Senate	......do	Do.
June 20, 1957	......do	......do	Nobusuke Kishi, Prime Minister of Japan.
Do	House	......do	Do.
July 11, 1957	Senate	......do	Husseyn Shaheed Suhrawardy, Prime Minister of Pakistan.
Jan. 9, 1958	Joint session	State of the Union Address	President Dwight D. Eisenhower.
June 5, 1958	Joint meeting	Address	Theodor Heuss, President of West Germany.
June 10, 1958	Senate	......do	Harold Macmillan, Prime Minister of the United Kingdom.
June 18, 1958	Joint meeting	......do	Carlos F. Garcia, President of the Philippines.
June 25, 1958	House	......do	Muhammad Daoud Khan, Prime Minister of Afghanistan.
Do	Senate	......do	Do.
July 24, 1958	......do	......do	Kwame Nkrumah, Prime Minister of Ghana.
July 25, 1958	House	......do	Do.
July 29, 1958	Senate	......do	Amintore Fanfani, Prime Minister of Italy.
Do	House	......do	Do.
86th CONGRESS			
Jan. 9, 1959	Joint session	State of the Union Address	President Dwight D. Eisenhower.

JOINT SESSIONS AND MEETINGS, ADDRESSES TO THE SENATE OR THE HOUSE, AND INAUGURATIONS—CONTINUED

[See notes at end of table]

Congress & Date	Type	Occasion, topic, or inaugural location	Name and position of dignitary (where applicable)
Jan. 21, 1959	Joint meeting	Address	Arturo Frondizi, President of Argentina.
Feb. 12, 1959	Joint session	Sesquicentennial of Abraham Lincoln's birth.	Fredric March, actor; Carl Sandburg, poet.
Mar. 11, 1959	Joint meeting	Address	Jose Maria Lemus, President of El Salvador.
Mar. 18, 1959	......do	......do	Sean T. O'Kelly, President of Ireland.
May 12, 1959	......do	......do	Baudouin, King of the Belgians.
Jan. 7, 1960	Joint session	State of the Union Address	President Dwight D. Eisenhower.
Mar. 30, 1960	Senate	Address	Harold Macmillan, Prime Minister of the United Kingdom.
Apr. 6, 1960	Joint meeting	......do	Alberto Lleras-Camargo, President of Colombia.
Apr. 25, 1960	......do	......do	Charles de Gaulle, President of France.
Apr. 28, 1960	......do	......do	Mahendra, King of Nepal.
June 29, 1960	......do	......do	Bhumibol Adulyadej, King of Thailand.
87th CONGRESS			
Jan. 6, 1961	Joint session	Counting electoral votes	N.A.
Jan. 20, 1961	......do	Inauguration, East Portico	President John F. Kennedy; Vice President Lyndon B. Johnson.
Jan. 30, 1961	......do	State of the Union Address	President John F. Kennedy.
Apr. 13, 1961	Senate	Remarks	Konrad Adenauer, Chancellor of West Germany.
Apr. 18, 1961	House	Address	Constantine Karamanlis, Prime Minister of Greece.
May 4, 1961	Joint meeting	......do	Habib Bourguiba, President of Tunisia.
May 25, 1961	Joint session	Urgent national needs: foreign aid, defense, civil defense, and outer space.	President John F. Kennedy.
June 22, 1961	Senate	Remarks	Hayato Ikeda, Prime Minister of Japan.
Do	House	Address	Do.
July 12, 1961	Joint meeting	......do	Mohammad Ayub Khan, President of Pakistan.
July 26, 1961	House	......do	Abubakar Tafawa Balewa, Prime Minister of Nigeria.
Sept. 21, 1961	Joint meeting	......do	Manuel Prado, President of Peru.
Jan. 11, 1962	Joint session	State of the Union Address	President John F. Kennedy.
Feb. 26, 1962	Joint meeting	Friendship 7: 1st United States orbital space flight.	Lt. Col. John H. Glenn, Jr., USMC; Friendship 7 astronaut.
Apr. 4, 1962	......do	Address	João Goulart, President of Brazil.
Apr. 12, 1962	......do	......do	Mohammad Reza Shah Pahlavi, Shahanshah of Iran.
88th CONGRESS			
Jan. 14, 1963	Joint session	State of the Union Address	President John F. Kennedy.
May 21, 1963	Joint meeting	Flight of Faith 7 Spacecraft	Maj. Gordon L. Cooper, Jr., USAF, Faith 7 astronaut.
Oct. 2, 1963	Senate	Address	Haile Selassie I, Emperor of Ethiopia.
Nov. 27, 1963	Joint session	Assumption of office	President Lyndon B. Johnson.
Jan. 8, 1964	......do	State of the Union Address	Do.
Jan. 15, 1964	Joint meeting	Address	Antonio Segni, President of Italy.
May 28, 1964	......do	......do	Eamon de Valera, President of Ireland.
89th CONGRESS			
Jan. 4, 1965	Joint session	State of the Union Address	President Lyndon B. Johnson.
Jan. 6, 1965	......do	Counting electoral votes	N.A.
Jan. 20, 1965	......do [32]	Inauguration, East Portico	President Lyndon B. Johnson; Vice President Hubert H. Humphrey.
Mar. 15, 1965	Joint session	Voting rights	President Lyndon B. Johnson.
Sept. 14, 1965	Joint meeting	Flight of Gemini 5 Spacecraft	Lt. Col. Gordon L. Cooper, Jr., USAF; and Charles Conrad, Jr., USN; Gemini 5 astronauts.
Jan. 12, 1966	Joint session	State of the Union Address	President Lyndon B. Johnson.
Sept. 15, 1966	Joint meeting	Address	Ferdinand E. Marcos, President of the Philippines.
90th CONGRESS			
Jan. 10, 1967	Joint session	State of the Union Address	President Lyndon B. Johnson.
Apr. 28, 1967	Joint meeting	Vietnam policy	General William C. Westmoreland.
Aug. 16, 1967	Senate	Address	Kurt George Kiesinger, Chancellor of West Germany.
Oct. 27, 1967	Joint meeting	......do	Gustavo Diaz Ordaz, President of Mexico.
Jan. 17, 1968	Joint session	State of the Union Address	President Lyndon B. Johnson.
91st CONGRESS			
Jan. 6, 1969	......do	Counting electoral votes [33]	N.A.
Jan. 9, 1969	Joint meeting	Apollo 8: 1st flight around the moon	Col. Frank Borman, USAF; Capt. James A. Lowell, Jr., USN; Lt. Col. William A. Anders, USAF; Apollo 8 astronauts.
Jan. 14, 1969	Joint session	State of the Union Address	President Lyndon B. Johnson.

JOINT SESSIONS AND MEETINGS, ADDRESSES TO THE SENATE OR THE HOUSE, AND INAUGURATIONS—CONTINUED

[See notes at end of table]

Congress & Date	Type	Occasion, topic, or inaugural location	Name and position of dignitary (where applicable)
Jan. 20, 1969	Joint session [32]	Inauguration, East Portico	President Richard M. Nixon; Vice President Spiro T. Agnew.
Sept. 16, 1969	Joint meeting	Apollo 11: 1st lunar landing	Neil A. Armstrong; Col. Edwin E. Aldrin, Jr., USAF; and Lt. Col. Michael Collins, USAF; Apollo 11 astronauts.
Nov. 13, 1969	House	Executive-Legislative branch relations and Vietnam policy.	President Richard M. Nixon.
Do	Senate	......do	Do.
Jan. 22, 1970	Joint session	State of the Union Address	Do.
Feb. 25, 1970	Joint meeting	Address	Georges Pompidou, President of France.
June 3, 1970	......do	......do	Rafael Caldera, President of Venezuela.
Sept. 22, 1970	......do	Report on prisoners of war	Col. Frank Borman, Representative to the President on Prisoners of War.
92d CONGRESS			
Jan. 22, 1971	Joint session	State of the Union Address	President Richard M. Nixon.
Sept. 9, 1971	......do	Economic policy	Do.
Do	Joint meeting	Apollo 15: lunar mission	Col. David R. Scott, USAF; Col. James B. Irwin, USAF; and Lt. Col. Alfred M. Worden, USAF; Apollo 15 astronauts.
Jan. 20, 1972	Joint session	State of the Union Address	President Richard M. Nixon.
June 1, 1972	......do	European trip report	Do.
June 15, 1972	Joint meeting	Address	Luis Echeverria Alvarez, President of Mexico.
93d CONGRESS			
Jan. 6, 1973	Joint session	Counting electoral votes	N.A.
Jan. 20, 1973	Inauguration	East Portico	President Richard M. Nixon; Vice President Spiro T. Agnew.
Dec. 6, 1973	Joint meeting	Oath of office to, and Address by Vice President Gerald R. Ford.	Vice President Gerald R. Ford; ceremony attended by President Richard M. Nixon.
Do	Senate	Remarks and Reception	Vice President Gerald R. Ford.
Jan. 30 1974	Joint session	State of the Union Address	President Richard M. Nixon.
Aug. 12, 1974	......do	Assumption of office	President Gerald R. Ford.
Oct. 8, 1974	......do	Economy	Do.
Dec. 19, 1974	Senate	Address [34]	Vice President Nelson A. Rockefeller.
94th CONGRESS			
Jan. 15, 1975	Joint session	State of the Union Address	President Gerald R. Ford.
Apr. 10, 1975	......do	State of the World message	Do.
June 17, 1975	Joint meeting	Address	Walter Scheel, President of West Germany.
Nov. 5, 1975	......do	......do	Anwar El Sadat, President of Egypt.
Jan. 19, 1976	Joint session	State of the Union Address	President Gerald R. Ford.
Jan. 28, 1976	Joint meeting	Address	Yitzhak Rabin, Prime Minister of Israel.
Mar. 17, 1976	......do	......do	Liam Cosgrave, Prime Minister of Ireland.
May 18, 1976	......do	......do	Valery Giscard d'Estaing, President of France.
June 2, 1976	......do	......do	Juan Carlos I, King of Spain.
Sept. 23, 1976	......do	......do	William R. Tolbert, Jr., President of Liberia.
95th CONGRESS			
Jan. 6, 1977	Joint session	Counting electoral votes	N.A.
Jan. 12, 1977	......do	State of the Union Address	President Gerald R. Ford.
Jan. 20, 1977	Inauguration	East Portico	President Jimmy Carter; Vice President Walter F. Mondale.
Feb. 17, 1977	House	Address	José López Portillo, President of Mexico.
Feb. 22, 1977	Joint meeting	Address	Pierre Elliot Trudeau, Prime Minister of Canada.
Apr. 20, 1977	Joint session	Energy	President Jimmy Carter.
Jan. 19, 1978	......do	State of the Union Address	Do.
Sept. 18, 1978	......do	Middle East Peace agreements	President Jimmy Carter; joint session attended by Anwar El Sadat, President of Egypt, and by Menachem Begin, Prime Minister of Israel.
96th CONGRESS			
Jan. 23, 1979	......do	State of the Union Address	Do.
June 18, 1979	......do	Salt II agreements	Do.
Jan. 23, 1980	......do	State of the Union Address	Do.
97th CONGRESS			
Jan. 6, 1981	......do	Counting electoral votes	N.A.
Jan. 20, 1981	Joint session [32]	Inauguration, West Front	President Ronald Reagan; Vice President George Bush.

JOINT SESSIONS AND MEETINGS, ADDRESSES TO THE SENATE OR THE HOUSE, AND INAUGURATIONS—CONTINUED

[See notes at end of table]

Congress & Date	Type	Occasion, topic, or inaugural location	Name and position of dignitary (where applicable)
Feb. 18, 1981	Joint session	Economic recovery	President Ronald Reagan.
Apr. 28, 1981	......do	Economic recovery—inflation	Do.
Jan. 26, 1982	......do	State of the Union Address	Do.
Jan. 28, 1982	Joint meeting	Centennial of birth of Franklin Delano Roosevelt.	Dr. Arthur Schlesinger, historian; Senator Jennings Randolph; Representative Claude Pepper; Averell Harriman, former Governor of New York[35]; former Representative James Roosevelt, son of President Roosevelt.
Apr. 21, 1982	......do	Address	Beatrix, Queen of the Netherlands.
98th CONGRESS			
Jan. 25, 1983	Joint session	State of the Union Address	President Ronald Reagan.
Apr. 27, 1983	......do	Central America	Do.
Oct. 5, 1983	Joint meeting	Address	Karl Carstens, President of West Germany.
Jan. 25, 1984	Joint session	State of the Union Address	President Ronald Reagan.
Mar. 15, 1984	Joint meeting	Address	Dr. Garett FitzGerald, Prime Minister of Ireland.
Mar. 22, 1984	......do	......do	François Mitterand, President of France.
May 8, 1984	......do	Centennial of birth of Harry S. Truman	Representatives Ike Skelton and Alan Wheat; former Senator Stuart Symington; Margaret Truman Daniel, daughter of President Truman; and Senator Mark Hatfield.
May 16, 1984	......do	Address	Miguel de la Madrid, President of Mexico.
99th CONGRESS			
Jan. 7, 1985	Joint session	Counting electoral votes	N.A.
Jan. 21, 1985	Inauguration	Rotunda[36]	President Ronald Reagan; Vice President George Bush.
Feb. 6, 1985	Joint session	State of the Union Address	President Ronald Reagan.
Feb. 20, 1985	Joint meeting	Address	Margaret Thatcher, Prime Minister of the United Kingdom.
Mar. 6, 1985	......do	......do	Bettino Craxi, President of the Council of Ministers of Italy.
Mar. 20, 1985	......do	......do	Raul Alfonsin, President of Argentina.
June 13, 1985	......do	......do	Rajiv Gandhi, Prime Minister of India.
Oct. 9, 1985	......do	......do	Lee Kuan Yew, Prime Minister of Singapore.
Nov. 21, 1985	Joint session	Geneva Summit	President Ronald Reagan.
Feb. 4, 1986	......do	State of the Union Address	Do.
Sept. 11, 1986	Joint meeting	Address	Jose Sarney, President of Brazil.
Sept. 18, 1986	......do	......do	Corazon C. Aquino, President of the Philippines.
100th CONGRESS			
Jan. 27, 1987	Joint session	State of the Union Address	President Ronald Reagan.
Nov. 10, 1987	Joint meeting	Address	Chaim Herzog, President of Israel.
Jan. 25, 1988	Joint session	State of the Union Address	President Ronald Reagan.
Apr. 27, 1988	Joint meeting	Address	Brian Mulroney, Prime Minister of Canada.
June 23, 1988	......do	......do	Robert Hawke, Prime Minister of Australia.
101st CONGRESS			
Jan. 4, 1989	Joint session	Counting electoral votes	N.A.
Jan. 20, 1989	Inauguration	West Front	President George Bush; Vice President Dan Quayle.
Feb. 9, 1989	Joint session	Building a Better America	President George Bush.
Mar. 2, 1989	Joint meeting	Bicentennial of the 1st Congress	President Pro Tempore Robert C. Byrd; Speaker James C. Wright, Jr.; Representatives Lindy Boggs, Thomas S. Foley, and Robert H. Michel; Senators George Mitchell and Robert Dole; Howard Nemerov, Poet Laureate of the United States; David McCullough, historian; Anthony M. Frank, Postmaster General; former Senator Nicholas Brady, Secretary of the Treasury.
Apr. 6, 1989	Senate[37]	Addresses on the 200th anniversary commemoration of Senate's first legislative session.	Former Senators Thomas F. Eagleton and Howard H. Baker, Jr..
June 7, 1989	Joint meeting	Address	Benazir Bhutto, Prime Minister of Pakistan.
Oct. 4, 1989	......do	......do	Carlos Salinas de Gortari, President of Mexico.
Oct. 18, 1989	......do	......do	Roh Tae Woo, President of South Korea.

JOINT SESSIONS AND MEETINGS, ADDRESSES TO THE SENATE OR THE HOUSE, AND INAUGURATIONS—CONTINUED

[See notes at end of table]

Congress & Date	Type	Occasion, topic, or inaugural location	Name and position of dignitary (where applicable)
Nov. 15, 1989	Joint meeting	Address	Lech Walesa, chairman of Solidarnośc labor union, Poland.
Jan. 31, 1990	Joint session	State of the Union Address	President George Bush.
Feb. 21, 1990	Joint meeting	Address	Vaclav Hável, President of Czechoslovakia.
Mar. 7, 1990	......do	......do	Giulio Andreotti, President of the Council of Ministers of Italy.
Mar. 27, 1990	......do	Centennial of birth of Dwight D. Eisenhower.	Senator Robert Dole; Walter Cronkite, television journalist; Winston S. Churchill, member of British Parliament and grandson of Prime Minister Churchill; Clark M. Clifford, former Secretary of Defense; James D. Robinson III, chairman of Eisenhower Centennial Foundation; Arnold Palmer, professional golfer; John S.D. Eisenhower, former Ambassador to Belgium and son of President Eisenhower; Representatives Beverly Byron, William F. Goodling, and Pat Roberts.
June 26, 1990	......do	Address	Nelson Mandela, Deputy President of the African National Congress, South Africa.
Sept. 11, 1990	Joint session	Invasion of Kuwait by Iraq	President George Bush.
102d CONGRESS			
Jan. 29, 1991	......do	State of the Union Address	Do.
Mar. 6, 1991	......do	Conclusion of Persian Gulf War	Do.
Apr. 16, 1991	Joint meeting	Address	Violeta B. de Chamorro, President of Nicaragua.
May 8, 1991	House [38]	......do	General H. Norman Schwarzkopf.
May 16, 1991	Joint meeting	Address	Elizabeth II, Queen of the United Kingdom; joint meeting also attended by Prince Philip.
Nov. 14, 1991	......do	......do	Carlos Saul Menem, President of Argentina.
Jan. 28, 1992	Joint session	State of the Union Address	President George Bush.
Apr. 30, 1992	Joint meeting	Address	Richard von Weizsäcker, President of Germany.
June 17, 1992	......do	......do	Boris Yeltsin, President of Russia.
103d CONGRESS			
Jan. 6, 1993	Joint session	Counting electoral votes	N.A.
Jan. 20, 1993	Inauguration	West Front	President William J. Clinton; Vice President Albert Gore.
Feb. 17, 1993	Joint session	Economic Address [39]	President William J. Clinton.
Sept. 22, 1993	......do	Health care reform	Do.
Jan. 25, 1994	Joint session	State of the Union Address	Do.
May 18, 1994	Joint meeting	Address	Narasimha Rao, Prime Minister of India.
July 26, 1994	......do	Addresses	Hussein I, King of Jordan; Yitzhak Rabin, Prime Minister of Israel.
Oct. 6, 1994	......do	Address	Nelson Mandela, President of South Africa.
105th CONGRESS			
Jan. 24, 1995	Joint session	State of the Union Address	President William J. Clinton.
July 26, 1995	Joint meeting	Address	Kim Yong-sam, President of South Korea.[40]
Oct. 11, 1995	......do	Close of the Commemoration of the 50th Anniversary of World War II.	Speaker Newt Gingrich; Vice President Albert Gore; President Pro Tempore Strom Thurmond; Representatives Henry J. Hyde and G. V. "Sonny" Montgomery; Senators Daniel K. Inouye and Robert Dole; former Representative Robert H. Michel; General Louis H. Wilson (ret.), former Commandant of the Marine Corps.
Dec. 12, 1995	......do	Address	Shimon Peres, Prime Minister of Israel.
Jan. 30, 1996	Joint session	State of the Union Address	President William J. Clinton.
Feb. 1, 1996	Joint meeting	Address	Jacques Chirac, President of France.
July 10, 1996	......do	......do	Benyamin Netanyahu, Prime Minister of Israel.
Sept. 11, 1996	......do	......do	John Bruton, Prime Minister of Ireland.
105th CONGRESS			
Jan. 9, 1997	Joint session	Counting electoral votes	N.A.
Jan. 20, 1997	Inauguration	West Front	President William J. Clinton, Vice President Albert Gore.
Feb. 4, 1997	Joint session	State of the Union Address [41]	President William J. Clinton.
Feb. 27, 1997	Joint meeting	Address	Eduardo Frei, President of Chile.

JOINT SESSIONS AND MEETINGS, ADDRESSES TO THE SENATE OR THE HOUSE, AND INAUGURATIONS—CONTINUED

[See notes at end of table]

Congress & Date	Type	Occasion, topic, or inaugural location	Name and position of dignitary (where applicable)
Jan. 27, 1998	Joint session	State of the Union Address	President William J. Clinton.
June 10, 1998	Joint meeting	Address	Kim Dae-jung, President of South Korea.
July 15, 1998	......do	......do	Emil Constantinescu, President of Romania.
106th CONGRESS			
Jan. 19, 1999	Joint session	State of the Union Address	President William J. Clinton.
Jan. 27, 2000	......do	......do	Do.
Sept. 14, 2000	Joint meeting	Address	Atal Bihari Vajpayee, Prime Minister of India.
107th CONGRESS			
Jan. 6, 2001	Joint session	Counting electoral votes	N.A.
Jan. 20, 2001	Inauguration	West Front	President George W. Bush; Vice President Richard B. Cheney.
Feb. 27, 2001	Joint session	Budget message [39]	President George W. Bush.
Sept. 6, 2001	Joint meeting	Address	Vicente Fox, President of Mexico.
Sept. 20, 2001	Joint session	War on terrorism	President George W. Bush; joint session attended by Tony Blair, Prime Minister of the United Kingdom, by Tom Ridge, Governor of Pennsylvania, by George Pataki, Governor of New York, and by Rudolph Giuliani, Mayor of New York City.
Jan. 29, 2002	......do	State of the Union Address	President George W. Bush; joint session attended by Hamid Karzai, Chairman of the Interim Authority of Afghanistan.
108th CONGRESS			
Jan. 28, 2003	......do	......do	President George W. Bush.
July 17, 2003	Joint meeting	Address	Tony Blair, Prime Minister of the United Kingdom; joint meeting attended by Mrs. George W. Bush.

[1] Closing date for this table was July 17, 2003.

[2] The oath of office was administered to George Washington outside on the gallery in front of the Senate Chamber, after which the Congress and the President returned to the chamber to hear the inaugural address. They then proceeded to St. Paul's Chapel for the ''divine service'' performed by the Chaplain of the Congress. Adjournment of the ceremony did not occur until the Congress returned to Federal Hall.

[3] Funeral oration was delivered at the German Lutheran Church in Philadelphia.

[4] Because of a tie in the electoral vote between Thomas Jefferson and Aaron Burr, the House of Representatives had to decide the election. Thirty-six ballots were required to break the deadlock, with Jefferson's election as President and Burr's as Vice President on February 17. The Twelfth Amendment was added to the Constitution to prevent the 1800 problem from recurring.

[5] During most of the period while the Capitol was being reconstructed following the fire of 1814, the Congress met in the ''Brick Capitol,'' constructed on the site of the present Supreme Court building. This joint session took place in the Representatives' chamber on the 2d floor of the building.

[6] The joint session to count electoral votes was dissolved because the House and Senate disagreed on Missouri's status regarding statehood. The joint session was reconvened the same day and Missouri's votes were counted.

[7] While this occasion has historically been referred to as the first joint meeting of Congress, the Journals of the House and Senate indicate that Lafayette actually addressed the House of Representatives, with some of the Senators present as guests of the House (having been invited at the last minute to attend). Similar occasions, when members of the one body were invited as guests of the other, include the Senate address by Queen Wilhelmina of the Netherlands on Aug. 6, 1942, and the House address by General H. Norman Schwarzkopf on May 8, 1991.

[8] Although Andrew Jackson won the popular vote by a substantial amount and had the highest number of electoral votes from among the several candidates, he did not receive the required majority of the electoral votes. The responsibility for choosing the new President therefore devolved upon the House of Representatives. As soon as the Senators left the chamber, the balloting proceeded, and John Quincy Adams was elected on the first ballot.

[9] The ceremony was moved outside to accommodate the extraordinarily large crowd of people who had come to Washington to see the inauguration.

[10] The ceremony was moved inside because of cold weather.

[11] Following the death of President Zachary Taylor, Vice President Millard Fillmore took the Presidential oath of office in a special joint session in the Hall of the House.

[12] The joint session to count electoral votes was dissolved three times so that the House and Senate could resolve several electoral disputes.

[13] Because of a severe cold and hoarseness, the King could not deliver his speech, which was read by former Representative Elisha Hunt Allen, then serving as Chancellor and Chief Justice of the Hawaiian Islands.

[14] The contested election between Rutherford B. Hayes and Samuel J. Tilden created a constitutional crisis. Tilden won the popular vote by a close margin, but disputes concerning the electoral vote returns from four states deadlocked the proceedings of the joint session. Anticipating this development, the Congress had created a special commission of five Senators, five Representatives, and five Supreme Court Justices to resolve such disputes. The Commission met in the Supreme Court Chamber (the present Old Senate Chamber) as each problem arose. In each case, the Commission accepted the Hayes electors, securing his election by one electoral vote. The joint session was convened on 15 occasions, with the last on March 2, just three days before the inauguration.

[15] The speech was written by former Speaker and Senator Robert C. Winthrop, who could not attend the ceremony because of ill health.

[16] Because of a blizzard, the ceremony was moved inside, where it was held as part of the Senate's special session. President William Howard Taft took the oath of office and gave his inaugural address after Vice President James S. Sherman's inaugural address and the swearing-in of the new senators.

[17] Held in the Senate Chamber.

[18] Bakhmetieff represented the provisional government of Russia set up after the overthrow of the monarchy in March 1917 and recognized by the United States. The Bolsheviks took over in November 1917.

[19] The address and reception were in conjunction with the presentation to the Senate by France of two Sèvres vases in appreciation of the United States' involvement in World War I. The vases are today in the Senate lobby, just off the Senate floor. Two additional Sèvres vases were given without ceremony to the House of Representatives, which today are in the Rayburn Room, not far from the floor of the House.

[20] Senators later objected to President Harding's speech (given with no advance notice to most of the Senators) as an unconstitutional effort to interfere with the deliberations of the Senate, and Harding did not repeat visits of this kind.

[21] This was the first Annual Message broadcast live on radio.

[22] This was the first inauguration held pursuant to the Twentieth Amendment, which changed the date from March 4 to January 20. The Vice Presidential oath, which previously had been given earlier on the same day in the Senate Chamber, was added to the inaugural ceremony as well, but the Vice Presidential inaugural address was discontinued.

[23] A joint reception for the King and Queen of the United Kingdom was held in the Rotunda, authorized by Senate Concurrent Resolution 17, 76th Congress. Although the concurrent resolution was structured to establish a joint meeting, the Senate, in fact, adjourned rather than recessed as called for by the resolution.

[24] Held in the Senate Chamber.

[25] At this time, the Philippines was still a possession of the United States, although it had been made a self-governing commonwealth in 1935, in preparation for full independence in 1946. From 1909 to 1916, Quezon had served in the U.S. House of Representatives as the resident commissioner from the Philippines.

[26] In exile.

[27] For this Senate Address by Queen Wilhelmina, the members of the House of Representatives were invited as guests. This occasion has sometimes been mistakenly referred to as a joint meeting.

[28] The oaths of office were taken in simple ceremonies at the White House because the expense and festivity of a Capitol ceremony were thought inappropriate because of the war. The Joint Committee on Arrangements of the Congress was in charge, however, and both the Senate and the House of Representatives were present.

[29] This was the first time the term ''State of the Union Address'' was used for the President's Annual Message. Also, it was the first time the address was shown live on television.

[30] This was an informal meeting in the Coolidge Auditorium of the Library of Congress.

[31] Presentation of new ivory gavel to the Senate.

[32] According to the Congressional Record, the Senate adjourned prior to the inaugural ceremonies, even though the previously adopted resolution had stated the adjournment would come immediately following the inauguration. The Senate Journal records the adjournment as called for in the resolution, hence this listing as a joint session.

[33] The joint session to count electoral votes was dissolved so that the House and Senate could resolve the dispute regarding a ballot from North Carolina. The joint session was reconvened the same day and the North Carolina vote was counted.

[34] Rockefeller was sworn in as Vice President by Chief Justice Warren E. Burger, after which, by unanimous consent, he was allowed to address the Senate.

[35] Because the Governor had laryngitis, his speech was read by his wife, Pamela.

[36] The ceremony was moved inside because of extremely cold weather.

[37] These commemorative addresses were given in the Old Senate Chamber during a regular legislative session.

[38] For this House Address by General Schwarzkopf, the members of the Senate were invited as guests.

[39] This speech was mislabeled in many sources as a State of the Union Address.

[40] President Kim Yong-sam was in Washington for the dedication of the Korean Veterans' Memorial, held the day after this joint meeting.

[41] This was the first State of the Union Address carried live on the Internet.

REPRESENTATIVES UNDER EACH APPORTIONMENT

State	Constitutional apportionment	First Census, 1790	Second Census, 1800	Third Census, 1810	Fourth Census, 1820	Fifth Census, 1830	Sixth Census, 1840	Seventh Census, 1850	Eighth Census, 1860	Ninth Census, 1870	Tenth Census, 1880	Eleventh Census, 1890	Twelfth Census, 1900	Thirteenth Census, 1910 [1]	Fifteenth Census, 1930	Sixteenth Census, 1940	Seventeenth Census, 1950	Eighteenth Census, 1960	Nineteenth Census, 1970	Twentieth Census, 1980	Twenty-First Census, 1990	Twenty-Second Census, 2000
AL	......	......	......	[2]	3	5	7	7	6	8	8	9	9	10	9	9	9	8	7	7	7	7
AK	......	......	......	......	......	......	......	......	......	......	......	......	......	......	......	......	[2,3]	1	1	1	1	1
AZ	......	......	......	......	......	......	......	......	......	......	......	......	[2]	[4]1	1	2	2	3	4	5	6	8
AR	......	......	......	......	......	[2]	1	2	3	4	5	6	7	7	7	7	6	4	4	4	4	4
CA	......	......	......	......	......	......	[2]	[4]2	3	4	6	7	8	11	20	23	30	38	43	45	52	53
CO	......	......	......	......	......	......	......	......	......	[2]	1	2	3	4	4	4	4	4	5	6	6	7
CT	5	7	7	7	6	6	4	4	4	4	4	4	5	5	6	6	6	6	6	6	6	5
DE	1	1	1	2	1	1	1	1	1	1	1	1	1	1	1	1	1	1	1	1	1	1
FL	......	......	......	......	......	......	[2]	1	1	2	2	2	3	4	5	6	8	12	15	19	23	25
GA	3	2	4	6	7	9	8	8	7	9	10	11	11	12	10	10	10	10	10	10	11	13
HI	......	......	......	......	......	......	......	......	......	......	......	......	......	......	......	......	[2,3]	2	2	2	2	2
ID	......	......	......	......	......	......	......	......	......	......	[2]	1	1	2	2	2	2	2	2	2	2	2
IL	......	......	......	[2]	1	3	7	9	14	19	20	22	25	27	27	26	25	24	24	22	20	19
IN	......	......	......	[2]	3	7	10	11	11	13	13	13	13	13	12	11	11	11	11	10	10	9
IA	......	......	......	......	......	......	[2]	2	6	9	11	11	11	11	9	8	8	7	6	6	5	5
KS	......	......	......	......	......	......	......	[2]	[4]1	3	7	8	8	8	7	6	6	5	5	5	4	4
KY	[2]	[4]2	6	10	12	13	10	10	9	10	11	11	11	11	9	9	8	7	7	7	6	6
LA	......	......	......	[2]	3	3	4	4	5	6	6	6	7	8	8	8	8	8	8	8	7	7
ME	......	......	......	[5]	7	8	7	6	5	5	4	4	4	4	3	3	3	2	2	2	2	2
MD	6	8	9	9	9	8	6	6	5	6	6	6	6	6	6	6	7	8	8	8	8	8
MA	8	14	17	[5]20	13	12	10	11	10	11	12	13	14	16	15	14	14	12	12	11	10	10
MI	......	......	......	......	......	[2]	3	4	6	9	11	12	12	13	17	17	18	19	19	18	16	15
MN	......	......	......	......	......	......	......	[2]	2	3	5	7	9	10	9	9	9	8	8	8	8	8
MS	......	......	......	[2]	1	2	4	5	5	6	7	7	8	8	7	7	6	5	5	5	5	4
MO	......	......	......	[2]	[4]1	2	5	7	9	13	14	15	16	16	13	13	11	10	10	9	9	9
MT	......	......	......	......	......	......	......	......	......	......	[2]	1	1	2	2	2	2	2	2	2	1	1
NE	......	......	......	......	......	......	......	......	[2]	1	3	6	6	6	5	4	4	3	3	3	3	3
NV	......	......	......	......	......	......	......	......	[2]	1	1	1	1	1	1	1	1	1	1	2	2	3
NH	3	4	5	6	6	5	4	3	3	3	2	2	2	2	2	2	2	2	2	2	2	2
NJ	4	5	6	6	6	6	5	5	5	7	7	8	10	12	14	14	14	15	15	14	13	13
NM	......	......	......	......	......	......	......	......	......	......	......	......	[2]	[4]1	1	2	2	2	2	3	3	3
NY	6	10	17	27	34	40	34	33	31	33	34	34	37	43	45	45	43	41	39	34	31	29
NC	5	10	12	13	13	13	9	8	7	8	9	9	10	10	11	12	12	11	11	11	12	13
ND	......	......	......	......	......	......	......	......	......	......	[2]	1	2	3	2	2	2	2	1	1	1	1
OH	......	......	[2]	6	14	19	21	21	19	20	21	21	21	22	24	23	23	24	23	21	19	18
OK	......	......	......	......	......	......	......	......	......	......	......	......	[2]	8	9	8	6	6	6	6	6	5
OR	......	......	......	......	......	......	......	[2]	1	1	1	2	2	3	3	4	4	4	4	5	5	5
PA	8	13	18	23	26	28	24	25	24	27	28	30	32	36	34	33	30	27	25	23	21	19
RI	1	2	2	2	2	2	2	2	2	2	2	2	2	3	2	2	2	2	2	2	2	2
SC	5	6	8	9	9	9	7	6	4	5	7	7	7	7	6	6	6	6	6	6	6	6
SD	......	......	......	......	......	......	......	......	......	......	[2]	2	2	3	2	2	2	2	2	1	1	1
TN	......	[2]	3	6	9	13	11	10	8	10	10	10	10	10	9	10	9	9	8	9	9	9
TX	......	......	......	......	......	......	[2]	2	4	6	11	13	16	18	21	21	22	23	24	27	30	32
UT	......	......	......	......	......	......	......	......	......	......	......	[2]	1	2	2	2	2	2	2	3	3	3
VT	[2]	[4]2	4	6	5	5	4	3	3	3	2	2	2	2	1	1	1	1	1	1	1	1
VA	10	19	22	23	22	21	15	13	[6]11	9	10	10	10	10	9	9	10	10	10	10	11	11
WA	......	......	......	......	......	......	......	......	......	......	[2]	2	3	5	6	6	7	7	7	8	9	9
WV	......	......	......	......	......	......	......	......	[6]	3	4	4	5	6	6	6	6	5	4	4	3	3
WI	......	......	......	......	......	......	[2]	3	6	8	9	10	11	11	10	10	10	10	9	9	9	8
WY	......	......	......	......	......	......	......	......	......	......	[2]	1	1	1	1	1	1	1	1	1	1	1
Total	65	105	141	181	213	240	223	234	241	292	325	356	386	435	435	435	435	435	435	435	435	435

NOTE: The original apportionment of Representatives was assigned in 1787 in the Constitution and remained in effect for the 1st and 2d Congresses. Subsequent apportionments based on the censuses over the years have been figured using several different methods approved by Congress, all with the goal of dividing representation among the states as equally as possible. After each census up to and including the Thirteenth in 1910, Congress would enact a law designating the specific changes in the actual number of Representatives as well as the increase in the ratio of persons-per-Representative. After having made no apportionment after the Fourteenth census in 1920, Congress by statute in 1929 fixed the total number of Representatives at 435 (the number attained with the apportionment after the 1910 census), and since that time, only the ratio of persons-per-Representative has continued to increase, in fact, significantly so. Since the total is now fixed, the specific number of Representatives per state is adjusted after each census to reflect its percentage of the entire population. Since the Sixteenth Census in 1940, the ''equal proportions'' method of apportioning Representatives within the 435 total has been employed. A detailed explanation of the entire apportionment process can be found in *The Historical Atlas of United States Congressional Districts, 1789–1983.* Kenneth C. Martis, The Free Press, New York, 1982.

[1] No apportionment was made after the 1920 census.

[2] The following Representatives were added after the indicated apportionments when these states were admitted in the years listed. The number of these additonal Representatives for each state remained in effect until the next census's apportionment (with the exceptions of California and New Mexico, as explained in footnote 4). They are not included in the total for each column. In reading this table, please remember that the apportionments made after each census took effect with the election two years after the census date. As a result, in the table footnote 2 is placed for several states under the decade preceding the one in which it entered the Union, since the previous decade's apportionment was still in effect at the time of statehood. *Constitutional:* Vermont (1791), 2; Kentucky (1792), 2; *First:* Tennessee (1796), 1; *Second:* Ohio (1803), 1; *Third:* Louisiana (1812), 1; Indiana (1816), 1; Mississippi (1817), 1; Illinois (1818), 1; Alabama (1819), 1; Missouri (1821), 1; *Fifth:* Arkansas (1836), 1; Michigan (1837), 1; *Sixth:* Florida (1845), 1; Texas (1845), 2; Iowa (1846), 2; Wisconsin (1848), 2; California (1850), 2; *Seventh:* Minnesota (1858), 2; Oregon (1859), 1; Kansas (1861), 1; *Eighth:* Nevada (1864), 1; Nebraska (1867), 1; *Ninth:* Colorado (1876), 1; *Tenth:* North Dakota (1889), 1; South Dakota (1889), 2; Montana (1889), 1; Washington (1889), 1; Idaho (1890), 1; Wyoming (1890), 1; *Eleventh:* Utah (1896), 1; *Twelth:* Oklahoma (1907), 5; New Mexico (1912), 2; Arizona (1912), 1; *Seventeenth:* Alaska (1959), 1; Hawaii (1959), 1.

[3] When Alaska and then Hawaii joined the Union in 1959, the law was changed to allow the total membership of the House of Representatives to increase to 436 and then to 437, apportioning one new Representative for each of those states. The total

[4] Even though the respective censuses were taken before the following states joined the Union, Representatives for them were apportioned either because of anticipation of statehood or because they had become states in the period between the census and the apportionment, hence they are included in the totals of the respective columns. *First:* Vermont (1791); Kentucky (1792); *Fourth:* Missouri (1821); *Seventh:* California (1850); *Eighth:* Kansas (1861); *Thirteenth:* New Mexico (1912); Arizona (1912). (Please note: These seven states are also included in footnote 2 because they became states while the previous decade's apportionment was still in effect for the House of Representatives.) California's situation was unusual. It was scheduled for inclusion in the figures for the 1850 census apportionment; however, when the apportionment law was passed in 1852, California's census returns were still incomplete so Congress made special provision that the state would retain ''the number of Representatives [two] prescribed by the act of admission * * * into the Union until a new apportionment [i.e., after the 1860 census]'' would be made. The number of Representatives from California actually increased before the next apportionment to three when Congress gave the state an extra Representative during part of the 37th Congress, from 1862 to 1863. Regarding New Mexico, the 1911 apportionment law, passed by the 62d Congress in response to the 1910 census and effective with the 63d Congress in 1913, stated that ''if the Territor[y] of * * * New Mexico shall become [a State] in the Union before the apportionment of Representatives under the next decennial census [it] shall have one Representative * * *.'' When New Mexico became a state in 1912 during the 62d Congress, it was given two Representatives. The number was decreased to one beginning the next year in the 63d.

[5] The ''Maine District'' of Massachusetts became a separate state during the term of the 16th Congress, in 1820. For the remainder of that Congress, Maine was assigned one ''at large'' Representative while Massachusetts continued to have 20 Representatives, the number apportioned to it after the 1810 census. For the 17th Congress (the last before the 1820 census apportionment took effect), seven of Massachusetts's Representatives were reassigned to Maine, leaving Massachusetts with 13.

[6] Of the 11 Representatives apportioned to Virginia after the 1860 census, three were reassigned to West Virginia when that part of Virginia became a separate state in 1863. Since the Virginia seats in the House were vacant at that time because of the Civil War, all of the new Representatives from West Virginia were able to take their seats at once. When Representatives from Virginia reentered the House in 1870, only eight members represented it.

IMPEACHMENT PROCEEDINGS

The provisions of the United States Constitution which apply specifically to impeachments are as follows: Article I, section 2, clause 5; Article I, section 3, clauses 6 and 7; Article II, section 2, clause 1; Article II, section 4; and Article III, section 2, clause 3.

For the officials listed below, the date of impeachment by the House of Representatives is followed by the dates of the Senate trial, with the result of each listed at the end of the entry.

WILLIAM BLOUNT, a Senator of the United States from Tennessee; impeached July 7, 1797; tried Monday, December 17, 1798, to Monday, January 14, 1799; charges dismissed for want of jurisdiction.

JOHN PICKERING, judge of the United States district court for the district of New Hampshire; impeached March 2, 1803; tried Thursday, March 3, 1803, to Monday, March 12, 1804; removed from office.

SAMUEL CHASE, Associate Justice of the Supreme Court of the United States; impeached March 12, 1804; tried Friday, November 30, 1804, to Friday, March 1, 1805; acquitted.

JAMES H. PECK, judge of the United States district court for the district of Missouri; impeached April 24, 1830; tried Monday, April 26, 1830, to Monday, January 31, 1831; acquitted.

WEST H. HUMPHREYS, judge of the United States district court for the middle, eastern, and western districts of Tennessee; impeached May 6, 1862; tried Wednesday, May 7, 1862, to Thursday, June 26, 1862; removed from office and disqualified from future office.

ANDREW JOHNSON, President of the United States; impeached February 24, 1868; tried Tuesday, February 25, 1868, to Tuesday, May 26, 1868; acquitted.

WILLIAM W. BELKNAP, Secretary of War; impeached March 2, 1876; tried Friday, March 3, 1876, to Tuesday, August 1, 1876; acquitted.

CHARLES SWAYNE, judge of the United States district court for the northern district of Florida; impeached December 13, 1904; tried Wednesday, December 14, 1904, to Monday, February 27, 1905; acquitted.

ROBERT W. ARCHBALD, associate judge, United States Commerce Court; impeached July 11, 1912; tried Saturday, July 13, 1912, to Monday, January 13, 1913; removed from office and disqualified from future office.

GEORGE W. ENGLISH, judge of the United States district court for the eastern district of Illinois; impeached April 1, 1926; tried Friday, April 23, 1926, to Monday, December 13, 1926; resigned office Thursday, November 4, 1926; Court of Impeachment adjourned to December 13, 1926, when, on request of House managers, the proceedings were dismissed.

HAROLD LOUDERBACK, judge of the United States district court for the northern district of California; impeached February 24, 1933; tried Monday, May 15, 1933, to Wednesday, May 24, 1933; acquitted.

HALSTED L. RITTER, judge of the United States district court for the southern district of Florida; impeached March 2, 1936; tried Monday, April 6, 1936, to Friday, April 17, 1936; removed from office.

HARRY E. CLAIBORNE, judge of the United States district court of Nevada; impeached July 22, 1986; tried Tuesday, October 7, 1986, to Thursday, October 9, 1986; removed from office.

ALCEE L. HASTINGS, judge of the United States district court for the southern district of Florida; impeached August 3, 1988; tried Wednesday, October 18, 1989, to Friday, October 20, 1989; removed from office.

WALTER L. NIXON, judge of the United States district court for the southern district of Mississippi; impeached May 10, 1989; tried Wednesday, November 1, 1989, to Friday, November 3, 1989; removed from office.

WILLIAM JEFFERSON CLINTON, President of the United States; impeached December 19, 1998; tried Thursday, January 7, 1999, to Friday, February 12, 1999; acquitted.

DELEGATES, REPRESENTATIVES, AND SENATORS SERVING IN THE 1st–108th CONGRESSES [1]

As of June 12, 2003, 11,708 individuals have served: 9,833 only in the House of Representatives, 1,240 only in the Senate, and 635 in both Houses. Total serving in the House of Representatives (including individuals serving in both bodies) is 10,468. Total for the Senate (including individuals serving in both bodies) is 1,875.[2]

State	Date Became Territory	Date Entered Union	Delegates	Representatives Only	Senators Only	Both Houses	Total, Not Including Delegates
Alabama	Mar. 3, 1817	Dec. 14, 1819 (22d)	1	166	24	15	205
Alaska	Aug. 24, 1912	Jan. 3, 1959 (49th)	9	4	6	0	10
Arizona	Feb. 24, 1863	Feb. 14, 1912 (48th)	11	25	7	4	36
Arkansas	Mar. 2, 1819	June 15, 1836 (25th)	3	83	23	9	115
California		Sept. 9, 1850 (31st)		323	32	11	365
Colorado	Feb. 28, 1861	Aug. 1, 1876 (38th)	3	53	23	9	85
Connecticut		Jan. 9, 1788 (5th)		188	28	25	241
Delaware		Dec. 7, 1787 (1st)		47	35	14	96
Florida	Mar. 30, 1822	Mar. 3, 1845 (27th)	5	100	25	6	131
Georgia		Jan. 2, 1788 (4th)		246	37	21	304
Hawaii	June 14, 1900	Aug. 21, 1959 (50th)	10	6	2	3	11
Idaho	Mar. 3, 1863	July 3, 1890 (43d)	9	25	19	6	50
Illinois	Feb. 3, 1809	Dec. 3, 1818 (21st)	3	429	28	22	479
Indiana	May 7, 1800	Dec. 11, 1816 (19th)	3	294	27	17	338
Iowa	June 12, 1838	Dec. 28, 1846 (29th)	2	168	22	11	201
Kansas	May 30, 1854	Jan. 29, 1861 (34th)	2	104	22	9	135
Kentucky		June 1, 1792 (15th)		307	36	29	372
Louisiana	Mar. 24, 1804	Apr. 30, 1812 (18th)	2	142	34	13	189
Maine		Mar. 15, 1820 (23d)		141	18	18	177
Maryland		Apr. 28, 1788 (7th)		252	28	27	307
Massachusetts		Feb. 6, 1788 (6th)		383	20	28	431
Michigan	Jan. 11, 1805	Jan. 26, 1837 (26th)	7	245	24	14	284
Minnesota	Mar. 3, 1849	May 11, 1858 (32d)	3	119	25	11	155
Mississippi	Apr. 17, 1798	Dec. 10, 1817 (20th)	5	109	27	16	152
Missouri	June 4, 1812	Aug. 10, 1821 (24th)	3	289	34	9	332
Montana	May 26, 1864	Nov. 8, 1889 (41st)	5	26	13	6	45
Nebraska	May 30, 1854	Mar. 1, 1867 (37th)	6	85	28	7	120
Nevada	Mar. 2, 1861	Oct. 31, 1864 (36th)	2	25	19	6	50
New Hampshire		June 21, 1788 (9th)		117	35	26	178
New Jersey		Dec. 18, 1787 (3d)		297	48	14	359
New Mexico	Sept. 9, 1850	Jan. 6, 1912 (47th)	13	21	12	3	36
New York		July 26, 1788 (11th)		1,396	36	23	1,455
North Carolina		Nov. 21, 1789 (12th)		303	35	17	355
North Dakota [3]	Mar. 2, 1861	Nov. 2, 1889 (39th)	11	21	15	6	42
Ohio [4]		Mar. 1, 1803 (17th)	2	617	36	18	671
Oklahoma	May 2, 1890	Nov. 16, 1907 (46th)	4	71	11	5	87
Oregon	Aug. 14, 1848	Feb. 14, 1859 (33d)	2	56	31	5	92
Pennsylvania		Dec. 12, 1787 (2d)		992	32	21	1,044
Rhode Island		May 29, 1790 (13th)		61	36	10	107
South Carolina		May 23, 1788 (8th)		196	39	15	250
South Dakota [3]	Mar. 2, 1861	Nov. 2, 1889 (40th)	11	25	16	9	50
Tennessee		June 1, 1796 (16th)	2	242	39	18	299
Texas		Dec. 29, 1845 (28th)		229	21	10	260
Utah	Sept. 9, 1850	Jan. 4, 1896 (45th)	7	33	12	3	48
Vermont		Mar. 4, 1791 (14th)		80	24	15	119
Virginia		June 25, 1788 (10th)		379	25	26	430
Washington	Mar. 2, 1853	Nov. 11, 1889 (42d)	10	66	13	10	89
West Virginia		June 20, 1863 (35th)		91	22	8	121
Wisconsin	Apr. 20, 1836	May 29, 1848 (30th)	6	169	19	7	195
Wyoming	July 25, 1868	July 10, 1890 (44th)	4	14	17	3	34

[1] March 4, 1789 until June 12, 2003.

[2] Some of the larger states split into smaller states as the country grew westward (e.g., part of Virginia became West Virginia); hence, some individuals represented more than one state in the Congress.

[3] North and South Dakota were formed from a single territory on the same date, and they shared the same delegates before statehood.

[4] The Territory Northwest of the Ohio River was established as a district for purposes of temporary government by the Act of July 13, 1787. Virginia ceded the land beyond the Ohio River, and delegates representing the district first came to the 6th Congress on March 4, 1799.

NOTE: Information was supplied by the Congressional Research Service.

POLITICAL DIVISIONS OF THE SENATE AND HOUSE FROM 1855 TO 2003

[All Figures Reflect Immediate Result of Elections. Figures Supplied by the Clerk of the House]

Congress	Years	SENATE					HOUSE OF REPRESENTATIVES				
		No. of Senators	Democrats	Republicans	Other parties	Vacancies	No. of Representatives	Democrats	Republicans	Other parties	Vacancies
34th	1855–1857	62	42	15	5	....	234	83	108	43	....
35th	1857–1859	64	39	20	5	....	237	131	92	14	....
36th	1859–1861	66	38	26	2	....	237	101	113	23	....
37th	1861–1863	50	11	31	7	1	178	42	106	28	2
38th	1863–1865	51	12	39	....	....	183	80	103	....	....
39th	1865–1867	52	10	42	....	....	191	46	145	....	....
40th	1867–1869	53	11	42	....	....	193	49	143	....	1
41st	1869–1871	74	11	61	....	2	243	73	170	....	....
42d	1871–1873	74	17	57	....	....	243	104	139	....	....
43d	1873–1875	74	19	54	....	1	293	88	203	....	2
44th	1875–1877	76	29	46	....	1	293	181	107	3	2
45th	1877–1879	76	36	39	1	....	293	156	137	....	....
46th	1879–1881	76	43	33	....	....	293	150	128	14	1
47th	1881–1883	76	37	37	2	....	293	130	152	11	....
48th	1883–1885	76	36	40	....	....	325	200	119	6	....
49th	1885–1887	76	34	41	....	1	325	182	140	2	1
50th	1887–1889	76	37	39	....	....	325	170	151	4	....
51st	1889–1891	84	37	47	....	....	330	156	173	1	....
52d	1891–1893	88	39	47	2	....	333	231	88	14	....
53d	1893–1895	88	44	38	3	3	356	220	126	10	....
54th	1895–1897	88	39	44	5	....	357	104	246	7	....
55th	1897–1899	90	34	46	10	....	357	134	206	16	1
56th	1899–1901	90	26	53	11	....	357	163	185	9	....
57th	1901–1903	90	29	56	3	2	357	153	198	5	1
58th	1903–1905	90	32	58	....	....	386	178	207	....	1
59th	1905–1907	90	32	58	....	....	386	136	250	....	....
60th	1907–1909	92	29	61	....	2	386	164	222	....	....
61st	1909–1911	92	32	59	....	1	391	172	219	....	....
62d	1911–1913	92	42	49	....	1	391	228	162	1	....
63d	1913–1915	96	51	44	1	....	435	290	127	18	....
64th	1915–1917	96	56	39	1	....	435	231	193	8	3
65th	1917–1919	96	53	42	1	....	435	[1] 210	216	9	....
66th	1919–1921	96	47	48	1	....	435	191	237	7	....
67th	1921–1923	96	37	59	....	....	435	132	300	1	2
68th	1923–1925	96	43	51	2	....	435	207	225	3	....
69th	1925–1927	96	40	54	1	1	435	183	247	5	....
70th	1927–1929	96	47	48	1	....	435	195	237	3	....
71st	1929–1931	96	39	56	1	....	435	163	267	1	4
72d	1931–1933	96	47	48	1	....	435	[2] 216	218	1	....
73d	1933–1935	96	59	36	1	....	435	313	117	5	....
74th	1935–1937	96	69	25	2	....	435	322	103	10	....
75th	1937–1939	96	75	17	4	....	435	333	89	13	....
76th	1939–1941	96	69	23	4	....	435	262	169	4	....
77th	1941–1943	96	66	28	2	....	435	267	162	6	....
78th	1943–1945	96	57	38	1	....	435	222	209	4	....
79th	1945–1947	96	57	38	1	....	435	243	190	2	....
80th	1947–1949	96	45	51	....	....	435	188	246	1	....
81st	1949–1951	96	54	42	....	....	435	263	171	1	....
82d	1951–1953	96	48	47	1	....	435	234	199	2	....
83d	1953–1955	96	46	48	2	....	435	213	221	1	....
84th	1955–1957	96	48	47	1	....	435	232	203	....	....
85th	1957–1959	96	49	47	....	....	435	234	201	....	....
86th	1959–1961	98	64	34	....	....	[3] 436	283	153	....	....
87th	1961–1963	100	64	36	....	....	[4] 437	262	175	....	....
88th	1963–1965	100	67	33	....	....	435	258	176	....	1
89th	1965–1967	100	68	32	....	....	435	295	140	....	....
90th	1967–1969	100	64	36	....	....	435	248	187	....	....
91st	1969–1971	100	58	42	....	....	435	243	192	....	....
92d	1971–1973	100	54	44	2	....	435	255	180	....	....
93d	1973–1975	100	56	42	2	....	435	242	192	1	....
94th	1975–1977	100	60	37	2	....	435	291	144	1	....
95th	1977–1979	100	61	38	1	....	435	292	143	....	....
96th	1979–1981	100	58	41	1	....	435	277	158	....	....
97th	1981–1983	100	46	53	1	....	435	242	192	1	....
98th	1983–1985	100	46	54	....	....	435	269	166	....	....
99th	1985–1987	100	47	53	....	....	435	253	182	....	....
100th	1987–1989	100	55	45	....	....	435	258	177	....	....
101st	1989–1991	100	55	45	....	....	435	260	175	....	....
102d	1991–1993	100	56	44	....	....	435	267	167	1	....
103d	1993–1995	100	57	43	....	....	435	258	176	1	....
104th	1995–1997	100	48	52	....	....	435	204	230	1	....
105th	1997–1999	100	45	55	....	....	435	207	226	2	....
106th	1999–2001	100	45	55	....	....	435	211	223	1	....
107th	2001–2003	100	50	50	....	....	435	212	221	2	....
108th	2003–2005	100	48	51	1	....	435	204	229	1	1

[1] Democrats organized House with help of other parties.

[2] Democrats organized House because of Republican deaths.

[3] Proclamation declaring Alaska a State issued January 3, 1959.

[4] Proclamation declaring Hawaii a State issued August 21, 1959.

GOVERNORS OF THE STATES, COMMONWEALTH, AND TERRITORIES—2003

State, Commonwealth, or Territory	Capital	Governor	Party	Term of service	Expiration of term
STATE				*Years*	
Alabama	Montgomery	Bob Riley	Republican	[c] 4	Jan. 2007
Alaska	Juneau	Frank Murkowski	Republican	[c] 4	Dec. 2006
Arizona	Phoenix	Janet Napolitano	Democrat	[c] 4	Jan. 2007
Arkansas	Little Rock	Mike Huckabee	Republican	[e] 4	Jan. 2007
California	Sacramento	Gray Davis	Democrat	[c] 4	Jan. 2007
Colorado	Denver	Bill Owens	Republican	[c] 4	Jan. 2007
Connecticut	Hartford	John G. Rowland	Republican	[b] 4	Jan. 2007
Delaware	Dover	Ruth Ann Minner	Democrat	[c] 4	Jan. 2005
Florida	Tallahassee	Jeb Bush	Republican	[c] 4	Jan. 2007
Georgia	Atlanta	Sonny Perdue	Republican	[c] 4	Jan. 2007
Hawaii	Honolulu	Linda Lingle	Republican	[c] 4	Jan. 2007
Idaho	Boise	Dirk Kempthorne	Republican	[b] 4	Jan. 2007
Illinois	Springfield	Rod R. Blagojevich	Democrat	[b] 4	Jan. 2007
Indiana	Indianapolis	Frank O'Bannon	Democrat	[f] 4	Jan. 2005
Iowa	Des Moines	Tom Vilsack	Democrat	[b] 4	Jan. 2007
Kansas	Topeka	Kathleen Sebelius	Democrat	[c] 4	Jan. 2007
Kentucky	Frankfort	Paul E. Patton	Democrat	[c] 4	Dec. 2003
Louisiana	Baton Rouge	Mike Foster	Republican	[c] 4	Jan. 2004
Maine	Augusta	John Baldacci	Democrat	[c] 4	Jan. 2007
Maryland	Annapolis	Robert L. Ehrlich, Jr.	Republican	[c] 4	Jan. 2007
Massachusetts	Boston	Mitt Romney	Republican	[b] 4	Jan. 2007
Michigan	Lansing	Jennifer Granholm	Democrat	[b] 4	Jan. 2007
Minnesota	St. Paul	Tim Pawlenty	Republican	[b] 4	Jan. 2007
Mississippi	Jackson	Ronnie Musgrove	Democrat	[c] 4	Jan. 2004
Missouri	Jefferson City	Bob Holden	Democrat	[c] 4	Jan. 2005
Montana	Helena	Judy Martz	Republican	[c] 4	Jan. 2005
Nebraska	Lincoln	Mike Johanns	Republican	[c] 4	Jan. 2007
Nevada	Carson City	Kenny C. Guinn	Republican	[c] 4	Jan. 2007
New Hampshire	Concord	Craig Benson	Republican	[b] 2	Jan. 2005
New Jersey	Trenton	Jim McGreevey	Democrat	[c] 4	Jan. 2006
New Mexico	Santa Fe	Bill Richardson	Democrat	[c] 4	Jan. 2007
New York	Albany	George E. Pataki	Republican	[b] 4	Jan. 2007
North Carolina	Raleigh	Mike Easley	Democrat	[c] 4	Jan. 2005
North Dakota	Bismarck	John Hoeven	Republican	[b] 4	Jan. 2005
Ohio	Columbus	Bob Taft	Republican	[c] 4	Jan. 2007
Oklahoma	Oklahoma City	Brad Henry	Democrat	[c] 4	Jan. 2007
Oregon	Salem	Ted Kulongoski	Democrat	[f] 4	Jan. 2007
Pennsylvania	Harrisburg	Ed Rendell	Democrat	[c] 4	Jan. 2007
Rhode Island	Providence	Donald Carcieri	Republican	[c] 4	Jan. 2007
South Carolina	Columbia	Mark Sanford	Republican	[c] 4	Jan. 2007
South Dakota	Pierre	Mike Rounds	Republican	[c] 4	Jan. 2007
Tennessee	Nashville	Phil Bredeson	Democrat	[c] 4	Jan. 2007
Texas	Austin	Rick Perry	Republican	[b] 4	Jan. 2007
Utah	Salt Lake City	Michael O. Leavitt	Republican	[b] 4	Jan. 2005
Vermont	Montpelier	Jim Douglas	Republican	[b] 2	Jan. 2007
Virginia	Richmond	Mark R. Warner	Democrat	[a] 4	Jan. 2006
Washington	Olympia	Gary Locke	Democrat	[d] 4	Jan. 2005
West Virginia	Charleston	Bob Wise	Democrat	[c] 4	Jan. 2005
Wisconsin	Madison	Jim Doyle	Democrat	[b] 4	Jan. 2007
Wyoming	Cheyenne	Dave Freudenthal	Democrat	[c] 4	Jan. 2007
COMMONWEALTH OF					
Puerto Rico	San Juan	Sila Maria Calderon	[1] P.D.P.	[b] 4	Jan. 2005
TERRITORIES					
Guam	Agana	Felix Camacho	Republican	[c] 4	Jan. 2007
Virgin Islands	Charlotte Amalie	Charles W. Turnbull	Democrat	[c] 4	Jan. 2007
American Samoa	Pago Pago	Togiola T.A. Tulafono	Democrat	[c] 4	Jan. 2005
Northern Mariana Islands.	Saipan	Juan N. Babauta	Republican	[c] 4	Jan. 2006

[a] Cannot succeed himself. [b] No limit. [c] Can serve 2 consecutive terms. [d] Can serve 3 consecutive terms. [e] Can serve 4 consecutive terms. [f] Can serve no more than 8 years in a 12-year period.

[1] Popular Democratic Party.

PRESIDENTS AND VICE PRESIDENTS AND THE CONGRESSES COINCIDENT WITH THEIR TERMS [1]

President	Vice President	Service	Congresses
George Washington	John Adams	Apr. 30, 1789–Mar. 3, 1797	1, 2, 3, 4.
John Adams	Thomas Jefferson	Mar. 4, 1797–Mar. 3, 1801	5, 6.
Thomas Jefferson	Aaron Burr	Mar. 4, 1801–Mar. 3, 1805	7, 8.
Do	George Clinton	Mar. 4, 1805–Mar. 3, 1809	9, 10.
James Madison	......do. [2]	Mar. 4, 1809–Mar. 3, 1813	11, 12.
Do	Elbridge Gerry [3]	Mar. 4, 1813–Mar. 3, 1817	13, 14.
James Monroe	Daniel D. Tompkins	Mar. 4, 1817–Mar. 3, 1825	15, 16, 17, 18, 19
John Quincy Adams	John C. Calhoun	Mar. 4, 1825–Mar. 3, 1829	19, 20.
Andrew Jackson	......do. [4]	Mar. 4, 1829–Mar. 3, 1833	21, 22.
Do	Martin Van Buren	Mar. 4, 1833–Mar. 3, 1837	23, 24.
Martin Van Buren	Richard M. Johnson	Mar. 4, 1837–Mar. 3, 1841	25, 26.
William Henry Harrison [5]	John Tyler	Mar. 4, 1841–Apr. 4, 1841	27.
John Tyler		Apr. 6, 1841 –Mar. 3, 1845	27, 28.
James K. Polk	George M. Dallas	Mar. 4, 1845–Mar. 3, 1849	29, 30.
Zachary Taylor [5]	Millard Fillmore	Mar. 5, 1849–July 9, 1850	31.
Millard Fillmore		July 10, 1850–Mar. 3, 1853	31, 32.
Franklin Pierce	William R. King [6]	Mar. 4, 1853–Mar. 3, 1857	33, 34.
James Buchanan	John C. Breckinridge	Mar. 4, 1857–Mar. 3, 1861	35, 36.
Abraham Lincoln	Hannibal Hamlin	Mar. 4, 1861–Mar. 3, 1865	37, 38.
Do. [5]	Andrew Johnson	Mar. 4, 1865–Apr. 15, 1865	39.
Andrew Johnson		Apr. 15, 1865–Mar. 3, 1869	39, 40.
Ulysses S. Grant	Schuyler Colfax	Mar. 4, 1869–Mar. 3, 1873	41, 42.
Do	Henry Wilson [7]	Mar. 4, 1873–Mar. 3, 1877	43, 44.
Rutherford B. Hayes	William A. Wheeler	Mar. 4, 1877–Mar. 3, 1881	45, 46.
James A. Garfield [5]	Chester A. Arthur	Mar. 4, 1881–Sept. 19, 1881	47.
Chester A. Arthur		Sept. 20, 1881–Mar. 3, 1885	47, 48.
Grover Cleveland	Thomas A. Hendricks [8]	Mar. 4, 1885–Mar. 3, 1889	49, 50.
Benjamin Harrison	Levi P. Morton	Mar. 4, 1889–Mar. 3, 1893	51, 52.
Grover Cleveland	Adlai E. Stevenson	Mar. 4, 1893–Mar. 3, 1897	53, 54.
William McKinley	Garret A. Hobart [9]	Mar. 4, 1897–Mar. 3, 1901	55, 56.
Do. [5]	Theodore Roosevelt	Mar. 4, 1901–Sept. 14, 1901	57.
Theodore Roosevelt		Sept. 14, 1901–Mar. 3, 1905	57, 58.
Do	Charles W. Fairbanks	Mar. 4, 1905–Mar. 3, 1909	59, 60.
William H. Taft	James S. Sherman [10]	Mar. 4, 1909–Mar. 3, 1913	61, 62.
Woodrow Wilson	Thomas R. Marshall	Mar. 4, 1913–Mar. 3, 1921	63, 64, 65, 66, 67.
Warren G. Harding [5]	Calvin Coolidge	Mar. 4, 1921–Aug. 2, 1923	67.
Calvin Coolidge		Aug. 3, 1923–Mar. 3, 1925	68.
Do	Charles G. Dawes	Mar. 4, 1925–Mar. 3, 1929	69, 70.
Herbert C. Hoover	Charles Curtis	Mar. 4, 1929–Mar. 3, 1933	71, 72.
Franklin D. Roosevelt	John N. Garner	Mar. 4, 1933–Jan. 20, 1941	73, 74, 75, 76, 77.
Do	Henry A. Wallace	Jan. 20, 1941–Jan. 20, 1945	77, 78, 79.
Do. [5]	Harry S. Truman	Jan. 20, 1945–Apr. 12, 1945	79.
Harry S. Truman		Apr. 12, 1945–Jan. 20, 1949	79, 80, 81.
Do	Alben W. Barkley	Jan. 20, 1949–Jan. 20, 1953	81, 82, 83.
Dwight D. Eisenhower	Richard M. Nixon	Jan. 20, 1953–Jan. 20, 1961	83, 84, 85, 86, 87.
John F. Kennedy [5]	Lyndon B. Johnson	Jan. 20, 1961–Nov. 22, 1963	87, 88, 89.
Lyndon B. Johnson		Nov. 22, 1963–Jan. 20, 1965	88, 89.
Do	Hubert H. Humphrey	Jan. 20, 1965–Jan. 20, 1969	89, 90, 91.
Richard M. Nixon	Spiro T. Agnew [11]	Jan. 20, 1969–Dec. 6, 1973	91, 92, 93.
Do. [13]	Gerald R. Ford [12]	Dec. 6, 1973–Aug. 9, 1974	93.
Gerald R. Ford		Aug. 9, 1974–Dec. 19, 1974	93.
Do	Nelson A. Rockefeller [14]	Dec. 19, 1974–Jan. 20, 1977	93, 94, 95.
James Earl (Jimmy) Carter	Walter F. Mondale	Jan. 20, 1977–Jan. 20, 1981	95, 96, 97.
Ronald Reagan	George Bush	Jan. 20, 1981–Jan. 20, 1989	97, 98, 99, 100, 101.
George Bush	Dan Quayle	Jan. 20, 1989–Jan. 20, 1993	101, 102, 103.
William J. Clinton	Albert Gore	Jan. 20, 1993–Jan. 20, 2001	103, 104, 105, 106, 107.
George W. Bush	Richard B. Cheney	Jan. 20, 2001–	107, 108.

[1] From 1789 until 1933, the terms of the President and Vice President and the term of the Congress coincided, beginning on March 4 and ending on March 3. This changed when the 20th amendment to the Constitution was adopted in 1933. Beginning in 1934 the convening date for Congress became January 3, and beginning in 1937 the starting date for the Presidential term became January 20. Because of this change, the number of Congresses overlapping with a Presidential term increased from two to three, although the third only overlaps by a few weeks.

[2] Died Apr. 20, 1812.

[3] Died Nov. 23, 1814.

[4] Resigned Dec. 28, 1832, to become a United States Senator from South Carolina.

[5] Died in office.

[6] Died Apr. 18, 1853.

[7] Died Nov. 22, 1875.

[8] Died Nov. 25, 1885.

[9] Died Nov. 21, 1899.

[10] Died Oct. 30, 1912.

[11] Resigned Oct. 10, 1973.

[12] Nominated to be Vice President by President Richard M. Nixon on Oct. 12, 1973; confirmed by the Senate on Nov. 27, 1973; confirmed by the House of Representatives on Dec. 6, 1973; took the oath of office on Dec. 6, 1973 in the Hall of the House of Representatives. This was the first time a Vice President was nominated by the President and confirmed by the Congress pursuant to the 25th amendment to the Constitution.

[13] Resigned from office.

[14] Nominated to be Vice President by President Gerald R. Ford on Aug. 20, 1974; confirmed by the Senate on Dec. 10, 1974; confirmed by the House of Representatives on Dec. 19, 1974; took the oath of office on Dec. 19, 1974, in the Senate Chamber.

CAPITOL BUILDINGS AND GROUNDS

UNITED STATES CAPITOL

Overview of the Building and its Function

The United States Capitol is among the most architecturally impressive and symbolically important buildings in the world. It has housed the chambers of the Senate and the House of Representatives for more than two centuries. Begun in 1793, the Capitol has been built, burnt, rebuilt, extended, and restored; today, it stands as a monument not only to its builders but also to the American people and their government.

As the focal point of the government's legislative branch, the Capitol is the centerpiece of the Capitol Complex, which includes the six principal congressional office buildings and three Library of Congress buildings constructed on Capitol Hill in the 19th and 20th centuries.

In addition to its active use by Congress, the Capitol is a museum of American art and history. Each year, it is visited by millions of people from around the world.

A fine example of 19th-century neoclassical architecture, the Capitol combines function with aesthetics. Its design was derived from ancient Greece and Rome and evokes the ideals that guided the nation's founders as they framed their new republic. As the building was expanded from its original design, harmony with the existing portions was carefully maintained.

Today, the Capitol covers a ground area of 175,170 square feet, or about 4 acres, and has a floor area of approximately 16½ acres. Its length, from north to south, is 751 feet 4 inches; its greatest width, including approaches, is 350 feet. Its height above the base line on the east front to the top of the Statue of Freedom is 288 feet; from the basement floor to the top of the dome is an ascent of 365 steps. The building contains approximately 540 rooms and has 658 windows (108 in the dome alone) and approximately 850 doorways.

The building is divided into five levels. The first, or ground, floor is occupied chiefly by committee rooms and the spaces allocated to various congressional officers. The areas accessible to visitors on this level include the Hall of Columns, the Brumidi Corridor, the restored Old Supreme Court Chamber, and the Crypt beneath the Rotunda, where historical exhibits are presented.

The second floor holds the chambers of the House of Representatives (in the south wing) and the Senate (in the north wing) as well as the offices of the congressional leadership. This floor also contains three major public areas. In the center under the dome is the rotunda, a circular ceremonial space that also serves as a gallery of paintings and sculpture depicting significant people and events in the nation's history. The rotunda is 96 feet in diameter and rises 180 feet 3 inches to the canopy. The semicircular chamber south of the rotunda served as the Hall of the House until 1857; now designated National Statuary Hall, it houses part of the Capitol's collection of statues donated by the states in commemoration of notable citizens. The Old Senate Chamber northeast of the rotunda, which was used by the Senate until 1859, has been returned to its mid-19th-century appearance.

The third floor allows access to the galleries from which visitors to the Capitol may watch the proceedings of the House and the Senate when Congress is in session. The rest of this floor is occupied by offices, committee rooms, and press galleries.

The fourth floor and the basement/terrace level of the Capitol are occupied by offices, machinery rooms, workshops, and other support areas.

Location of the Capitol

The Capitol is located at the eastern end of the Mall on a plateau 88 feet above the level of the Potomac River, commanding a westward view across the Capitol Reflecting Pool to the Washington Monument 1.4 miles away and the Lincoln Memorial 2.2 miles away. The geographic location of the head of the Statue of Freedom that surmounts the Capitol dome is described by the National Geodetic Survey as latitude 38°53′23.31098″ north and longitude 77°00′32.62262″ west.

Before 1791, the Federal Government had no permanent site. The early Congresses met in eight different cities: Philadelphia, Baltimore, Lancaster, York, Princeton, Annapolis, Trenton, and New York City. The subject of a permanent capital for the government of the United States was first raised by Congress in 1783; it was ultimately addressed in Article I, Section 8 of the Constitution (1787), which gave the Congress legislative authority over ''such District (not exceeding ten Miles square) as may, by Cession of Particular States, and the Acceptance of Congress, become the Seat of the Government of the United States. . . .''

In 1788, the state of Maryland ceded to Congress ''any district in this State, not exceeding ten miles square,'' and in 1789 the State of Virginia ceded an equivalent amount of land. In accordance with the ''Residence Act'' passed by Congress in 1790, President Washington in 1791 selected the area that is now the District of Columbia from the land ceded by Maryland (private landowners whose property fell within this area were compensated by a payment of £25 per acre); that ceded by Virginia was not used for the capital and was returned to Virginia in 1846. Also under the provisions of that Act, he selected three commissioners to survey the site and oversee the design and construction of the capital city and its government buildings. The commissioners, in turn, selected the French-American engineer Peter Charles L'Enfant to plan the new city of Washington. L'Enfant's plan, which was influenced by the gardens at Versailles, arranged the city's streets and avenues in a grid overlaid with baroque diagonals; the result is a functional and aesthetic whole in which government buildings are balanced against public lawns, gardens, squares, and paths. The Capitol itself was located at the elevated east end of the Mall, on the brow of what was then called Jenkins' Hill. The site was, in L'Enfant's words, ''a pedestal waiting for a monument.''

SELECTION OF A PLAN

L'Enfant was expected to design the Capitol and to supervise its construction. However, he refused to produce any drawings for the building, claiming that he carried the design ''in his head''; this fact and his refusal to consider himself subject to the commissioners' authority led to his dismissal in 1792. In March of that year the commissioners announced a competition, suggested by Secretary of State Thomas Jefferson, that would award $500 and a city lot to whoever produced ''the most approved plan'' for the Capitol by mid-July. None of the 17 plans submitted, however, was wholly satisfactory. In October, a letter arrived from Dr. William Thornton, a Scottish-trained physician living in Tortola, British West Indies, requesting an opportunity to present a plan even though the competition had closed. The commissioners granted this request.

Thornton's plan depicted a building composed of three sections. The central section, which was topped by a low dome, was to be flanked on the north and south by two rectangular wings (one for the Senate and one for the House of Representatives). President Washington commended the plan for its ''grandeur, simplicity and convenience,'' and on April 5, 1793, it was accepted by the commissioners; Washington gave his formal approval on July 25.

BRIEF CONSTRUCTION HISTORY

1793–1829

The cornerstone was laid by President Washington in the building's southeast corner on September 18, 1793, with Masonic ceremonies. Work progressed under the direction of three architects in succession. Stephen H. Hallet (an entrant in the earlier competition) and George Hadfield were eventually dismissed by the commissioners because of inappropriate design changes that they tried to impose; James Hoban, the architect of the White House, saw the first phase of the project through to completion.

Construction was a laborious and time-consuming process: the sandstone used for the building had to be ferried on boats from the quarries at Aquia, Virginia; workers had to be induced to leave their homes to come to the relative wilderness of Capitol Hill; and funding was inadequate. By August 1796 the commissioners were forced to focus the entire work effort on the building's north wing so that it at least could be ready for government occupancy as scheduled. Even so, some third-floor rooms were still unfinished when the Congress, the Supreme Court, the Library of Congress, and the courts of the District of Columbia occupied the Capitol in late 1800.

In 1803, Congress allocated funds to resume construction. A year earlier, the office of the Commissioners had been abolished and replaced by a superintendent of the city of Washington. To oversee the renewed construction effort, B. Henry Latrobe was appointed surveyor of public buildings. The first professional architect and engineer to work in America, Latrobe modified Thornton's plan for the south wing to include space for offices and committee rooms; he also introduced alterations to simplify the construction work. Latrobe began work by removing a squat, oval, temporary building known as "the Oven," which had been erected in 1801 as a meeting place for the House of Representatives. By 1807 construction on the south wing was sufficiently advanced that the House was able to occupy its new legislative chamber, and the wing was completed in 1811.

In 1808, as work on the south wing progressed, Latrobe began the rebuilding of the north wing, which had fallen into disrepair. Rather than simply repair the wing, he redesigned the interior of the building to increase its usefulness and durability; among his changes was the addition of a chamber for the Supreme Court. By 1811, he had completed the eastern half of this wing, but funding was being increasingly diverted to preparations for a second war with Great Britain. By 1813, Latrobe had no further work in Washington and so he departed, leaving the north and south wings of the Capitol connected only by a temporary wooden passageway.

The War of 1812 left the Capitol, in Latrobe's later words, "a most magnificent ruin": on August 24, 1814, British troops set fire to the building, and only a sudden rainstorm prevented its complete destruction. Immediately after the fire, Congress met for one session in Blodget's Hotel, which was at Seventh and E Streets, NW. From 1815 to 1819, Congress occupied a building erected for it on First Street, NE, on part of the site now occupied by the Supreme Court Building. This building later came to be known as the Old Brick Capitol.

Latrobe returned to Washington in 1815, when he was rehired to restore the Capitol. In addition to making repairs, he took advantage of this opportunity to make further changes in the building's interior design (for example, an enlargement of the Senate Chamber) and introduce new materials (for example, marble discovered along the upper Potomac). However, he came under increasing pressure because of construction delays (most of which were beyond his control) and cost overruns; finally, he resigned his post in November 1817.

On January 8, 1818, Charles Bulfinch, a prominent Boston architect, was appointed Latrobe's successor. Continuing the restoration of the north and south wings, he was able to make the chambers for the Supreme Court, the House, and the Senate ready for use by 1819. Bulfinch also redesigned and supervised the construction of the Capitol's central section. The copper-covered wooden dome that topped this section was made higher than Bulfinch considered appropriate to the building's size (at the direction of President James Monroe and Secretary of State John Quincy Adams). After completing the last part of the building in 1826, Bulfinch spent the next few years on the Capitol's decoration and landscaping. In 1829, his work was done and his position with the government was terminated. In the 38 years following Bulfinch's tenure, the Capitol was entrusted to the care of the commissioner of public buildings.

1830–1868

The Capitol was by this point already an impressive structure. At ground level, its length was 351 feet 7½ inches and its width was 282 feet 10½ inches. Up to the year 1827—records from later years being incomplete—the project cost was $2,432,851.34. Improvements to the building continued in the years to come (running water in 1832, gas lighting in the 1840s), but by 1850 its size could no longer accommodate the increasing numbers of senators and representatives from newly admitted states. The Senate therefore voted to hold another competition, offering a prize of $500 for the best plan to extend the Capitol. Several suitable plans were submitted, some proposing an eastward extension of the building and others proposing the addition of large north and south wings. However, Congress was unable to decide between these two approaches, and the prize money was divided among five architects. Thus, the tasks of selecting a plan and appointing an architect fell to President Millard Fillmore.

Fillmore's choice was Thomas U. Walter, a Philadelphia architect who had entered the competition. On July 4, 1851, in a ceremony whose principal oration was delivered by Secretary of State Daniel Webster, the president laid the cornerstone in the northeast corner of the House wing. Over the next 14 years, Walter supervised the construction of the extension, ensuring their compatibility with the architectural style of the existing building. However, because the Aquia Creek sandstone used earlier had deteriorated noticeably, he chose to use marble for the exterior. For the veneer, Walter selected marble quarried at Lee, MA, and for the columns he used marble from Cockeysville, MD.

Walter faced several significant challenges during the course of construction. Chief among these was the steady imposition by the government of additional tasks without additional pay. Aside from his work on the Capitol extension, Walter designed the wings of the Patent Office building, extensions to the Treasury and Post Office buildings, and the Marine barracks in Pensacola and Brooklyn. When the Library of Congress in the Capitol's west central section was gutted by a fire in 1851, Walter was commissioned to restore it. He also encountered obstacles in his work on the Capitol extensions. His location of the legislative chambers was changed in 1853 at the direction of President Franklin Pierce, based on the suggestions of the newly appointed supervising engineer, Captain Montgomery C. Meigs. In general, however, the project progressed rapidly: the House of Representatives was able to meet in its new chamber on December 16, 1857, and the Senate first met in its present chamber on January 4, 1859. The old House chamber was later designated National Statuary Hall. In 1861 most construction was suspended because of the Civil War, and the Capitol was used briefly as a military barracks, hospital, and bakery. In 1862 work on the entire building was resumed.

As the new wings were constructed, more than doubling the length of the Capitol, it became apparent that the dome erected by Bulfinch no longer suited the building's proportions. In 1855 Congress voted for its replacement based on Walter's design for a new, fireproof cast-iron dome. The old dome was removed in 1856–56, and 5,000,000 pounds of new masonry was placed on the existing rotunda walls. Iron used in the dome construction had an aggregate weight of 8,909,200 pounds and was lifted into place by steam-powered derricks.

In 1859, Thomas Crawford's plaster model for the Statue of Freedom, designed for the top of the dome, arrived from the sculptor's studio in Rome. With a height of 19 feet 6 inches, the statue was almost 3 feet taller than specified, and Walter was compelled to make revisions to his design for the dome. When cast in bronze by Clark Mills at his foundry on the outskirts of Washington, it weighed 14,985 pounds. The statue was lifted into place atop the dome in 1863, its final section being installed on December 2 to the accompaniment of gun salutes from the forts around the city.

The work on the dome and the extension was completed under the direction of Edward Clark, who had served as Walter's assistant and was appointed Architect of the Capitol in 1865 after Walter's resignation. In 1866, the Italian-born artist Constantino Brumidi finished the canopy fresco, a monumental painting entitled *The Apotheosis of George Washington*. The Capitol extension was completed in 1868.

1869–1902

Clark continued to hold the post of Architect of the Capitol until his death in 1902. During his tenure, the Capitol underwent considerable modernization. Steam heat was gradually installed in the old Capitol. In 1874 the first elevator was installed, and in the 1880s electric lighting began to replace gas lights.

Between 1884 and 1891, the marble terraces on the north, west, and south sides of the Capitol were constructed. As part of the landscape plan devised by Frederick Law Olmsted, these terraces not only added over 100 rooms to the Capitol but also provided a broader, more substantial visual base for the building.

On November 6, 1898, a gas explosion and fire in the original north wing dramatically illustrated the need for fireproofing. The roofs over the Statuary Hall wing and the original north wing were reconstructed and fireproofed, the work being completed in 1902 by Clark's successor, Elliott Woods. In 1901 the space in the west central front vacated by the Library of Congress was converted to committee rooms.

1903–1970

During the remainder of Woods's service, which ended with his death in 1923, no major structural work was required on the Capitol. The activities performed in the building were limited chiefly to cleaning and refurbishing the interior. David Lynn, the Architect of the Capitol from 1923 until his retirement in 1954, continued these tasks. Between July 1949 and January 1951, the corroded roofs and skylights of both wings and the connecting corridors were replaced with new roofs of concrete and steel, covered with copper. The cast-iron and glass ceilings of the House and Senate chambers were replaced with ceilings of stainless steel and plaster, with a laylight of carved glass and bronze in the middle of each. The House and Senate chambers were completely redecorated, modern lighting was added, and acoustical problems were solved. During this renovation program, the House and Senate vacated their chambers on several occasions so that the work could progress.

The next significant modification made to the Capitol was the east front extension. This project was carried out under the supervision of Architect of the Capitol J. George Stewart, who served from 1954 until his death in 1970. Begun in 1958, it involved the construction of a new east front 32 feet 6 inches east of the old front, faithfully reproducing the sandstone structure in marble. The old sandstone walls were not destroyed; rather, they were left in place to become a part of the interior wall and are now buttressed by the addition. The marble columns of the connecting corridors were also moved and reused. Other elements of this project included repairing the dome, constructing a subway terminal under the Senate steps, reconstructing those steps, cleaning both wings, birdproofing the building, providing furniture and furnishings for 90 new rooms created by the extension, and improving the lighting throughout the building. The project was completed in 1962.

1971–PRESENT

During the nearly 25-year tenure (1971–1995) of Architect of the Capitol George M. White, FAIA, the building was both modernized and restored. Electronic voting equipment was installed in the House chamber in 1973; facilities were added to allow television coverage of the House and Senate debates in 1979 and 1986, respectively; and improved climate control, electronic surveillance systems, and new computer and communications facilities have been added to bring the Capitol up-to-date. The Old Senate Chamber, National Statuary Hall, and the Old Supreme Court Chamber, on the other hand, were restored to their mid-19th-century appearance in the 1970s.

In 1983, work began on the strengthening, renovation, and preservation of the west front of the Capitol. Structural problems had developed over the years because of defects in the original foundations, deterioration of the sandstone facing material, alterations to the basic building fabric (a fourth-floor addition and channeling of the walls to install interior utilities), and damage from the fires of 1814 and 1851 and the 1898 gas explosion

To strengthen the structure, over one thousand stainless steel tie rods were set into the building's masonry. More than 30 layers of paint were removed, and damaged stonework was repaired or replicated. Ultimately, 40 percent of the sandstone blocks were replaced with limestone. The walls were treated with a special consolidant and then painted to match the marble wings. The entire project was completed in 1987.

A related project, completed in January 1993, effected the repair of the Olmsted terraces, which had been subject to damage from settling, and converted the terrace courtyards into several thousand square feet of meeting space.

As the Capitol enters its third century, restoration and modernization work continues. Major projects completed in recent years include; repair and restoration of the House monumental stairs; conservation of the Statue of Freedom atop the Capitol dome; completion of the murals in the first-floor House corridors; preparation and publication of a new book on the artist Constantino Brumidi, whose paintings decorate much of the Capitol; preparation of a telecommunications plan for the Legislative Branch agencies; installation of an improved Senate subway system; construction of the Thurgood Marshall Federal Judiciary Building; construction of new House and Senate child care facilities and a new Senate Page school; and renovation, restoration, and modification of the interiors and exteriors of the Thomas Jefferson and John Adams Buildings of the Library of Congress.

The present Architect of the Capitol, Alan M. Hantman, FAIA, was appointed in January 1997. New and ongoing projects under his direction include rehabilitation of the Capitol dome; conservation of murals; improvement of speech-reinforcement, electrical, and fire-protection systems in the Capitol and the Congressional office buildings; work on security improvements within the Capitol Complex; restoration of the U.S. Botanic Garden Conservatory; the design and construction of the National Garden adjacent to the Botanic Garden Conservatory; renovation of the building systems in the Dirksen Senate Office Building; preparation and publication of the first comprehensive history of the Capitol to appear in a century; and construction of a new Capitol Visitor Center.

Work is now underway on the Capitol Visitor Center, which will make the U.S. Capitol more accessible, comfortable, secure, and informative for all visitors. Preparatory construction activities began in the fall of 2001, including relocation of utilities and visitor screening facilities, and implementation of a comprehensive tree preservation program. Major construction started in July 2002 and will be completed in 2005.

The CVC will be located underground on the East Front of the Capitol, so as to enhance rather than detract from the appearance of the Capitol and its historic Frederick Law Olmsted landscape. When completed, the CVC will contain 580,000 square feet on three levels, requiring a 196,000-square-foot excavation, or ''footprint,'' on the East Front of the Capitol. (For purposes of comparison, the Capitol itself encompasses 775,000 square feet.)

The project will include space for exhibits, visitor comfort, food service, two orientation theaters, an auditorium, gift shops, security, a service tunnel for truck loading and deliveries, mechanical facilities, storage, and much needed space for the House and Senate. When completed, the CVC will preserve and maximize public access to the Capitol while greatly enhancing the experience for the millions who walks its historic corridors and experience its monumental spaces every year.

All activities related to the Capitol Visitor Center take place under the direction of the Capitol Preservation Commission.

HOUSE OFFICE BUILDINGS

CANNON HOUSE OFFICE BUILDING

An increased membership of the Senate and House resulted in a demand for additional rooms for the accommodations of the Senators and Representatives. On March 3, 1903, the Congress authorized the erection of a fireproofed office building for the use of the House. It was designed by the firm of Carrere & Hastings of New York City in the Beaux Arts style. The first brick was laid July 5, 1905, in square No. 690, and formal exercises were held at the laying of the cornerstone on April 14, 1906, in which President Theodore Roosevelt participated. The building was completed and occupied January 10, 1908. A subsequent change in the basis of congressional representation made necessary the building of an additional story in 1913–14. The total cost of the building, including site, furnishings, equipment, and the subway connecting it with the U.S. Capitol, amounted to $4,860,155. This office building contains about 500 rooms, and was considered at the time of its completion fully equipped for all the needs of a modern building for office purposes. A garage was added in the building's courtyard in the 1960s.

Pursuant to authority in the Second Supplemental Appropriations Act, 1955, and subsequent action of the House Office Building Commission, remodeling of the Cannon Building began in 1966. The estimated cost of this work was $5,200,000. Pursuant to the provisions of Public Law 87–453, approved May 21, 1962, the building was named in honor of Joseph G. Cannon of Illinois, who was Speaker at the time the building was constructed.

LONGWORTH HOUSE OFFICE BUILDING

Under legislation contained in the authorization act of January 10, 1929, and in the urgent deficiency bill of March 4, 1929, provisions were made for an additional House office building, to be located on the west side of New Jersey Avenue (opposite the first House office building). The building was designed by the Allied Architects of Washington in the Neoclassical Revival style.

The cornerstone was laid June 24, 1932, and the building was completed on April 20, 1933. It contains 251 two-room suites and 16 committee rooms. Each suite and committee room is provided with a storeroom. Eight floors are occupied by members. The basement and subbasement contain shops and mechanical areas needed for the maintenance of the building. A cafeteria was added in the building's courtyard in the 1960s. The cost of this building, including site, furnishings, and equipment, was $7,805,705. Pursuant to the provisions of Public Law 87–453, approved May 21, 1962, the building was named in honor of Nicholas Longworth of Ohio, who was Speaker when the second House office building was constructed.

RAYBURN HOUSE OFFICE BUILDING AND OTHER RELATED CHANGES AND IMPROVEMENTS

Under legislation contained in the Second Supplemental Appropriations Act, 1955, provision was made for construction of a fireproof office building for the House of Representatives.

All work was carried forward by the Architect of the Capitol under the direction of the House Office Building Commission at a cost totaling $135,279,000.

The Rayburn Building is connected to the Capitol by a subway from the center of the Independence Avenue upper garage level to the southwest corner of the Capitol. Designs for the building were prepared by the firm of Harbeson, Hough, Livingston & Larson of Philadelphia, Associate Architects. The building contains 169 congressional suites; full-committee hearing rooms for 9 standing committees, 16 subcommittee hearing rooms, committee staff rooms and other committee facilities; a large cafeteria and other restaurant facilities; an underground garage accommodating 1,600 automobiles; and a variety of liaison offices, press and television facilities, maintenance and equipment shops or rooms, and storage areas. This building has nine stories and a penthouse for machinery.

The cornerstone was laid May 24, 1962, by John W. McCormack, Speaker of the House of Representatives. President John F. Kennedy participated in the cornerstone laying and delivered the address.

A portion of the basement floor was occupied beginning March 12, 1964, by House of Representatives personnel moved from the George Washington Inn property. Full occupancy of the Rayburn Building, under the room-filing regulations, was begun February 23, 1965, and completed April 2, 1965. Pursuant to the provisions of Public Law 87–453, approved May 21, 1962, the building was named in honor of Sam Rayburn of Texas, who was Speaker at the time the third House office building was constructed.

Two buildings have been purchased and adapted for office use by the House of Representatives. The eight-story Congressional Hotel across from the Cannon on C Street SE. was acquired in 1957 and subsequently altered for office use and a dormitory for the Pages. It has 124,000 square feet. It was known as House Office Building Annex No. 1, until it was named the ''Thomas P. O'Neill, Jr. House of Representatives Office Building'' in honor of the former Speaker of the House, pursuant to House Resolution 402, approved September 10, 1990. It was demolished in 2002 and the site made into a parking lot. House Office Building Annex No. 2, named the ''Gerald R. Ford House of Representatives Office Building'' by the same resolution, was acquired in 1975 from the General Services Administration. The structure, located at Second and D Streets SW., was built in 1939 for the Federal Bureau of Investigation as a fingerprint file archives. This building has approximately 432,000 square feet of space.

SENATE OFFICE BUILDINGS

RICHARD BREVARD RUSSELL SENATE OFFICE BUILDING

In 1891 the Senate provided itself with office space by the purchase of the Maltby Building, then located on the northwest corner of B Street (now Constitution Avenue) and New Jersey Avenue, NW. When it was condemned as an unsafe structure, senators needed safer and more commodious office space. Under authorization of the Act of April 28, 1904, square 686 on the northeast corner of Delaware Avenue and B Street NE. was purchased as a site for the Senate Office Building. The plans for the House Office Building were adapted for the Senate Office Building by the firm of Carrere & Hastings, with the exception that the side of the building fronting on First Street NE. was temporarily omitted. The cornerstone was laid without special exercises on July 31, 1906, and the building was occupied March 5, 1909. In 1931, the completion of the fourth side of the building was commenced. In 1933 it was completed, together with alterations to the C Street facade, and the construction of terraces, balustrades, and approaches. The cost of the completed building, including the site, furnishings, equipment and the subway connecting it with the United States Capitol, was $8,390,892.

The building was named the ''Richard Brevard Russell Senate Office Building'' by Senate Resolution 296, 92nd Congress, agreed to October 11, 1972, as amended by Senate Resolution 295, 96th Congress, agreed to December 3, 1979.

EVERETT MCKINLEY DIRKSEN SENATE OFFICE BUILDING

Under legislation contained in the Second Deficiency Appropriations Act, 1948, Public Law 80–785, provision was made for an additional office building for the United States Senate with limits of cost of $1,100,000 for acquisition of the site and $20,600,000 for constructing and equipping the building.

The construction cost limit was subsequently increased to $24,196. All work was carried forward by the Architect of the Capitol under the direction of the Senate Office Building Commission. The New York firm of Eggers & Higgins served as the consulting architect.

The site was acquired and cleared in 1948–49 at a total cost of $1,011,492.

A contract for excavation, concrete footings and mats for the new building was awarded in January 1955, in the amount of $747,200. Groundbreaking ceremonies were held January 26, 1955.

A contract for the superstructure of the new building was awarded September 9, 1955, in the amount of $17,200,000. The cornerstone was laid July 13, 1956.

As a part of this project, a new underground subway system was installed from the Capitol to both the Old and New Senate Office Buildings.

An appropriation of $1,000,000 for furniture and furnishings for the new building was provided in 1958. The building was accepted for beneficial occupancy October 15, 1958.

The building was named the ''Everett McKinley Dirksen Senate Office Building'' by Senate Resolution 296, 92nd Congress, agreed to October 11, 1972, and Senate Resolution 295, 96th Congress, agreed to December 3, 1979.

PHILIP A. HART SENATE OFFICE BUILDING

Construction as an extension to the Dirksen Senate Office Building was authorized on October 31, 1972; legislation enacted in subsequent years increased the scope of the project and established a total cost ceiling of $137,700,400. The firm of John Carl Warnecke & Associates served as Associate Architect for the project.

Senate Resolution 525, passed August 30, 1976, amended by Senate Resolution 295, 96th Congress, agreed to December 3, 1979, provided that upon completion of the extension it would be named the ''Philip A. Hart Senate Office Building'' to honor the senator from Michigan.

The contract for clearing of the site, piping for utilities, excavation, and construction of foundation was awarded in December 1975. Groundbreaking took place January 5, 1976. The contract for furnishing and delivery of the exterior stone was awarded in February 1977, and the contract for the superstructure, which included wall and roof systems and the erection of all exterior stonework, was awarded in October 1977. The contract for the first portion of the interior and related work was awarded in December 1978. A contract for interior finishing was awarded in July 1980. The first suite was occupied on November 22, 1982. Alexander Calder's mobile/stabile *Mountains and Clouds* was installed in the building's atrium in November 1986.

CAPITOL POWER PLANT

During the development of the plans for the Cannon and Russell Buildings, the question of heat, light, and power was considered. The Senate and House wings of the Capitol were heated by separate heating plants. The Library of Congress also had a heating plant for that building. It was determined that needs for heating and lighting and electrical power could be met by a central power plant.

A site was selected in Garfield Park. Since this park was a Government reservation, an appropriation was not required to secure title. The determining factors leading to the selection of this site were its proximity to the tracks of what is now the Penn Central Railroad and to the buildings to be served.

The dimensions of the Capitol Power Plant, which was authorized on April 28, 1904, and completed in 1910, were 244 feet 8 inches by 117 feet. There are two radial brick chimneys 174 feet in height (reduced from 212 feet to 174 feet in 1951–52) and 11 feet in diameter at the top.

The buildings originally served by the Capitol Power Plant were connected to it by a reinforced-concrete steam tunnel 7 feet high by 4½ feet wide, with walls approximately 12 inches thick. This tunnel originated at the Capitol Power Plant and terminated at the Senate Office Building, with connecting tunnels for the Cannon House Office Building, the Capitol, and the Library of Congress. Subsequently it was extended to the Government Printing Office and the Washington City Post Office, with steam lines extended to serve the Longworth House Office Building, the Supreme Court Building, the John Adams Building of the Library of Congress, and the Botanic Garden.

In September 1951, when the demand for electrical energy was reaching the maximum capacity of the Capitol Power Plant, arrangements were made to purchase electrical service from the local public utility company and to discontinue electrical generation. The heating and cooling functions of the Capitol Power Plant were expanded in 1935, 1939, 1958, 1973, and 1980. A new modernization and expansion project is now underway.

U.S. CAPITOL GROUNDS

A DESCRIPTION OF THE GROUNDS

Originally a wooded wilderness, the U.S. Capitol Grounds today provide a parklike setting for the Nation's Capitol, offering a picturesque counterpoint to the building's formal architecture. The grounds immediately surrounding the Capitol are bordered by a stone wall and cover an area of 58.8 acres. Their boundaries are Independence Avenue on the south, Constitution Avenue on the north, First Street NE./SE. on the east, and First Street NW./SW. on the west. Over 100 varieties of trees and bushes are planted around the Capitol, and thousands of flowers are used in seasonal displays. In contrast to the building's straight, neoclassical lines, most of the walkways in the grounds are curved. Benches along the paths offer pleasant spots for visitors to appreciate the building, its landscape, and the surrounding areas, most notably the Mall to the west.

The grounds were designed by Frederick Law Olmsted (1822–1903), who planned the landscaping of the area that was performed from 1874 to 1892. Olmsted, who also designed New York's Central Park, is considered the greatest American landscape architect of his day. He was a pioneer in the development of public parks in America, and many of his designs were influenced by his studies of European parks, gardens, and estates. In describing his plan for the Capitol grounds, Olmsted noted that ''The ground is in design part of the Capitol, but in all respects subsidiary to the central structure.'' Therefore, he was careful not to group trees or other landscape features in any way that would distract the viewer from the Capitol. The use of sculpture and other ornamentation has also been kept to a minimum.

Many of the trees on the Capitol grounds have historic or memorial associations. Among the oldest is the ''Cameron Elm'' near the House entrance. This tree was named in honor of the Pennsylvania Senator who ensured its preservation during Olmsted's landscaping project. Other trees commemorate members of Congress and other notable citizens, national organizations, and special events. In addition, over 30 states have made symbolic gifts of their state trees to the Capitol grounds. Many of the trees on the grounds bear plaques that identify their species and their historic significance. The eastern part of the grounds contains the greatest number of historic and commemorative trees.

At the East Capitol Street entrance to the Capitol plaza are two large rectangular stone fountains. The bottom levels now contain plantings, but at times in the past they have been used to catch the spillover from the fountains. At other times, both levels have held plantings. Six massive red granite lamp piers topped with light fixtures in wrought-iron cages, and 16 smaller bronze light fixtures, line the paved plaza. Seats are placed at intervals along the sidewalks. Three sets of benches are enclosed with wrought-iron railings and grilles; the roofed bench was originally a shelter for streetcar passengers.

The northern part of the grounds offers a shaded walk among trees, flowers, and shrubbery. A small, hexagonal brick structure named the Summer House may be found in the northwest corner of the grounds. This structure contains shaded benches, a central ornamental fountain, and three public drinking fountains. In a small grotto on the eastern side of the Summer House, a stream of water flows and splashes over rocks to create a pleasing sound and cool the summer breezes.

A Brief History of the Grounds Before Olmsted

The land on which the Capitol stands was first occupied by the Manahoacs and the Monacans, who were subtribes of the Algonquin Indians. Early settlers reported that these tribes occasionally held councils not far from the foot of the hill. This land eventually became a part of Cerne Abbey Manor, and at the time of its acquisition by the Federal Government it was owned by Daniel Carroll of Duddington.

The ''Residence Act'' of 1790 provided that the federal government should be established in a permanent location by the year 1800. In early March 1791 the commissioners of the city of Washington, who had been appointed by President George Washington, selected the French engineer Peter Charles L'Enfant to plan the new federal city. L'Enfant decided to locate the Capitol at the elevated east end of the Mall (on what was then called Jenkins' Hill); he described the site as ''a pedestal waiting for a monument.''

At this time the site of the Capitol was a relative wilderness partly overgrown with scrub oak. Oliver Wolcott, a signer of the Declaration of Independence, described the soil as an ''*exceedingly stiff* clay, becoming dust in dry and mortar in rainy weather.''

In 1825, a plan was devised for imposing order on the Capitol grounds, and it was carried out for almost 15 years. The plan divided the area into flat, rectangular grassy areas bordered by trees, flower beds, and gravel walks. The growth of the trees, however, soon deprived the other plantings of nourishment, and the design became increasingly difficult to maintain in light of sporadic and small appropriations. John Foy, who had charge of the grounds during most of this period, was ''superseded for political reasons,'' and the area was then maintained with little care or forethought. Many rapidly growing but short-lived trees were introduced and soon depleted the soil; a lack of proper pruning and thinning left the majority of the area's vegetation ill-grown, feeble, or dead. Virtually all was removed by the early 1870's, either to make way for building operations during Thomas U. Walter's enlargement of the Capitol or as required by changes in grading to accommodate the new work on the building or the alterations to surrounding streets.

The Olmsted Plan

The mid-19th-century extension of the Capitol, in which the House and Senate wings and the new dome were added, required also that the Capitol grounds be enlarged, and in 1874 Frederick Law Olmsted was commissioned to plan and oversee the project. As noted above, Olmsted was determined that the grounds should complement the building. In addition, he addressed an architectural problem that had persisted for some years: from the west (the growth of the city had nothing to do with the terraces)—the earthen terraces at the building's base made it seem inadequately supported at the top of the hill. The solution, Olmsted believed, was to construct marble terraces on the north, west, and south sides of the building, thereby causing it to ''gain greatly in the supreme qualities of stability, endurance, and repose.'' He submitted his design for these features in 1875, and after extensive study it was approved.

Work on the grounds began in 1874, concentrating first on the east side and then progressing to the west, north, and south sides. First, the ground was reduced in elevation. Almost 300,000 cubic yards of earth and other material were eventually removed, and over 200 trees were removed. New sewer, gas, and water lines were installed. The soil was then enriched with fertilizers to provide a suitable growth medium for new plantings. Paths and roadways were graded and laid.

By 1876, gas and water service was completed for the entire grounds, and electrical lamp-lighting apparatuses had been installed. Stables and workshops had been removed from the northwest and southwest corners. A streetcar system north and south of the west grounds had been relocated farther from the Capitol, and ornamental shelters were in place at the north and south car-track termini. The granite and bronze lamp piers and ornamental bronze lamps for the east plaza area were completed.

Work accelerated in 1877. By this time, according to Olmsted's report, ''altogether 7,837 plants and trees [had] been set out.'' However, not all had survived: hundreds were stolen or destroyed by vandals, and, as Olmsted explained, ''a large number of cattle [had] been caught trespassing.'' Other work met with less difficulty. Foot-walks were laid with artificial stone, a mixture of cement and sand, and approaches were paved with concrete. An ornamental iron trellis had been installed on the northern east-side walk, and another was under way on the southern walk.

The 1878 appointment of watchmen to patrol the grounds was quite effective in preventing further vandalism, allowing the lawns to be completed and much shrubbery to be added. Also in that year, the roads throughout the grounds were paved.

Most of the work required on the east side of the grounds was completed by 1879, and effort thus shifted largely to the west side. The Pennsylvania Avenue approach was virtually finished, and work on the Maryland Avenue approach had begun. The stone walls on the west side of the grounds were almost finished, and the red granite lamp piers were placed at the eastward entrance from Pennsylvania Avenue.

In the years 1880–82, many features of the grounds were completed. These included the walls and coping around the entire perimeter, the approaches and entrances, and the Summer House. Work on the terraces began in 1882, and most work from this point until 1892 was concentrated on these structures.

In 1885, Olmsted retired from superintendency of the terrace project; he continued to direct the work on the grounds until 1889. Landscaping work was performed to adapt the surrounding areas to the new construction, grading the ground and planting shrubs at the bases of the walls, as the progress of the masonry work allowed. Some trees and other types of vegetation were removed, either because they had decayed or as part of a careful thinning-out process.

In 1888, the wrought-iron lamp frames and railings were placed at the Maryland Avenue entrance, making it the last to be completed. In 1892, the streetcar track that had extended into grounds from Independence Avenue was removed.

The Grounds After Olmsted

In the last years of the 19th century, work on the grounds consisted chiefly of maintenance and repairs as needed. Trees, lawns, and plantings were tended, pruned, and thinned to allow their best growth. This work was quite successful: by 1894, the grounds were so deeply shaded by trees and shrubs that Architect of the Capitol Edward Clark recommended an all-night patrol by watchmen to ensure public safety. A hurricane in September 1896 damaged or destroyed a number of trees, requiring extensive removals in the following year. Also in 1897, electric lighting replaced gas lighting in the grounds.

Between 1910 and 1935, 61.4 acres north of Constitution Avenue were added to the grounds. Approximately 100 acres was added in subsequent years, bringing the total area to 274 acres. In 1981, the Architect of the Capitol developed the Master Plan for future development of the U.S. Capitol grounds and related areas.

Since 1983, increased security measures have been put into effect, including the installation of barriers at vehicular entrances. However, the area still functions in many ways as a public park, and visitors are welcome to use the walks to tour the grounds. Demonstrations and ceremonies are often held on the grounds. During the spring, many high-school bands perform in front of the Capitol, and a series of evening concerts by the bands of the Armed Forces is offered free of charge on the west front plaza. On various holidays, concerts by the National Symphony Orchestra are held on the west front lawn.

LEGISLATIVE BRANCH AGENCIES

CONGRESSIONAL BUDGET OFFICE

H2–405 Ford House Office Building, Second and D Streets SW., 20515
phone 226–2600, http://www.cbo.gov

[Created by Public Law 93–344]

Director.—Dan L. Crippen, 6–2700.
Deputy Director.—Barry B. Anderson, 6–2702.
Principal Associate Director.—William J. Gainer, 6–4945.
General Counsel.—Robert P. Murphy, 5–1971.
Assistant Director for—
Management, Business and Information Services.—Daniel F. Zimmerman, 6–2600.
Macroeconomic Analysis.—Robert A. Dennis, 6–2784.
Budget Analysis.—Robert A. Sunshine, 6–2800.
National Security.—J. Michael Gilmore, 6–2900.
Tax Analysis.—G. Thomas Woodward, 6–2687.
Health and Human Resources.—Steven M. Lieberman, 6–2668.
Microeconomic and Financial Studies.—Roger Hitchner, 6–2940.

GENERAL ACCOUNTING OFFICE

441 G Street NW., 20548, phone 512–3000
www.gao.gov

Comptroller General of the United States.—David M. Walker, 512–5500, fax 512–5507.
Chief Operating Officer.—Gene Dodaro, 512–5600.
Chief Mission Support Officer/Chief Financial Officer.—Sallyanne Harper, 512–5800.
General Counsel.—Tony Gamboa, 512–5400.
Deputy General Counsel.—Gary Kepplinger, 512–5207.
Office of Special Investigations.—Robert Cramer, 512–7455.

TEAMS

Applied Research and Methods.—Nancy Kingsbury, 512–2700.
Acquisition and Sourcing Management.—Jack Brock, 512–4841.
Defense Capabilities and Management.—Butch Hinton, 512–4300.
Education Workforce and Income Security.—Cindy Fagnoni, 512–7215.
Financial Management and Assurance.—Jeff Steinhoff, 512–2600.
Financial Markets and Community Investments.—Tom McCool, 512–8678.
Health Care.—Bill Scanlon, 512–7114.
Homeland Security and Justice.—Norm Rabkin, 512–9110.
Information Technology.—Joel Willemssen, 512–6408.
International Affairs and Trade.—Susan Westin, 512–3655.
National Preparedness (HSJ).—Randall Yim, 512–6787.
Natural Resources and Environment.—Bob Robinson, 512–3841.
Physical Infrastructure.—Mike Gryszkowiec, 512–2834.
Strategic Issues.—Vic Rezendes, 512–6806.

SUPPORT FUNCTIONS

Congressional Relations.—Gloria Jarmon, 512–4400.
External Liaison.—Jacquie Williams-Bridgers, 512–3101.
Field Offices.—John Anderson, 512–7200.
Inspector General (IG).—Frances Garcia, 512–5748.
Opportunity and Inclusiveness.—Ron Stroman, 512–6388.
Personnel Appeals Board.—Michael Wolf, 512–6137.
Public Affairs.—Jeff Nelligan, 512–4800.
Quality and Continuous Improvement.—Tim Bowling, 512–6100.

MISSION SUPPORT OFFICES

Deputy Chief Mission Support Officer/Chief Information Officer.—Tony Cicco, 512–6623.
Controller.—Stan Czerwinski, 512–6520.
Customer Relations.—Greg McDonald, 512–7228.
Human Capital Officer.—Jesse Hoskins, 512–5533.
Knowledge Services Officer.—Catherine Teti, 512–9255.
Professional Development Program.—Mark Gebicke, 512–4126.

GOVERNMENT PRINTING OFFICE

732 North Capitol Street NW., 20401

phone 512–0000, www.gpo.gov

gpoinfo@gpo.gov

OFFICE OF THE PUBLIC PRINTER

Public Printer.—Bruce R. James, 512–1000, fax 512–1347.
Deputy Public Printer.—William H. Turri, 512–2036, fax 512–1347.
Chief of Staff.—Frank A. Partlow, Jr., 512–1100, fax 512–1896.
Deputy Chief of Staff.—Robert C. Tapella, 512–1100, fax 512–1896.
Inspecter General.—Marc A. Nichols, 512–0039, fax 512–1352.
Director, Office of Equal Employment Opportunity.—Nadine L. Elzy, 512–2014, fax 512–0521.
Administrative Law Judge.—Kerry L. Miller, 512–0008, fax 512–1517.
General Counsel.—Anthony J. Zagami, 512–0033, fax 512–0076.
Deputy General Counsel.—Drew Spalding, 512–0033, fax 512–0076.
Director, Innovation and New Technology.—[Vacant].
Director, Congressional Relations.—Andrew M. Sherman, 512–1991, fax 512–1293.
Director, Public Affairs.—[Vacant].

CUSTOMER SERVICES

Managing Director.—Jim Bradley, 512–0111, fax 512–1347.
Superintendent of:
Congressional Publishing Services (formerly Congressional Printing Management Division).—Charles C. Cook, Sr., 512–0224, fax 512–1101.
Departmental Account Representative Division.—Spurgeon F. Johnson, Jr., 512–0238, fax 512–1260.
Typography and Design Division.—John W. Sapp, 512–0212, fax 512–1737.
Contract Management Division.—Levi D. Baisden, 512–0485, fax 512–1463.
Purchase Division.—James L. Leonard, 512–0528, fax 512–1671.
Regional Operations.—John D. Chapman, 512–0412, fax 512–0381.
Term Contracts Division.—Raymond T. Sullivan, 512–0320, fax 512–1368.
Director, Procurement Analysis and Review Staff.—John D. Chapman, 512–0376, fax 512–1848.
Director, Institute for Federal Printing and Electronic Publishing.—Carol F. Cini, 512–1116, fax 512–1255.

REGIONAL PRINTING PROCUREMENT OFFICES

Atlanta: 1888 Emery Street, Suite 110, Buckhead West, Atlanta, GA 30318–2542, (404) 605–9160, fax (404) 605–9185.

Manager.—Gary C. Bush.

Charleston Satellite Office: 2825 Avenue D., Charleston, SC 29405, (843) 743–2036, fax (843) 743–2068.

Manager.—[Vacant].

Assistant Manager.—Rebecca J. Coale.

Boston: 28 Court Square, Boston, MA 02108–2504, (617) 720–3680, fax (617) 720–0281.

Assistant Manager.—Fred W. Garlick.

Chicago: 200 North La Salle Street, Suite 810, Chicago, IL 60601–1055, (312) 353–3916, fax (312) 886–3163.

Manager.—Arnold R. Stenvog.

Columbus: 1335 Dublin Road, Suite 112–B, Columbus, OH 43215–7034, (614) 488–4616, fax (614) 488–4577.

Manager.—Aurelio E. Morales.

Dallas: U.S. Courthouse and Federal Office Building, 1100 Commerce Street, Room 7B7, Dallas, TX 75242–0395, (214) 767–0451, fax (214) 767–4101.

Manager.—[Vacant].

Assistant Manager.—Arthur Jacobson.

San Antonio Satellite Office: 1531 Connally Street, Suite 2, Lackland AFB, TX 78236–5514, (210) 675–1480, fax (210) 675–2429.

Assistant Manager.—[Vacant].

New Orleans Satellite Office: U.S. Customs Building, 423 Canal Street, Room 310, New Orleans, LA 70130–2352, (504) 589–2538, fax (504) 589–2542.

Assistant Manager.—Gerard J. Finnegan.

Oklahoma City Satellite Office: 3420 D Avenue, Suite 100, Tinker Air Force Base, OK 73145–9188, (405) 610–4146, fax (405) 610–4125.

Assistant Manager.—Timothy J. Ashcraft.

Denver: Denver Federal Center, Building 53, Room D–1010, Denver, CO 80225–0347, (303) 236–5292, fax (303) 236–5304.

Manager.—[Vacant].

Hampton, VA: 11836 Canon Boulevard, Suite 400, Newport News, VA 23606–2555, (757) 873–2800, fax (757) 873–2805.

Manager.—[Vacant].

Los Angeles: 12501 East Imperial Highway, Suite 110, Norwalk, CA 90650–3136, (562) 863–1708, fax (562) 863–8701.

Manager.—[Vacant].

Assistant Manager.—[Vacant].

San Diego Satellite Office: Valley Center Office Building, 2221 Camino Del Rio S., Suite 109, San Diego, CA 92108–3609, (619) 497–6050, fax (619) 497–6055.

Assistant Manager.—Eileen P. Hall-Splendorio.

New York: 201 Varick Street, Room 709, Seventh Floor, New York, NY 10014–4879, (212) 620–3321, fax (212) 620–3378.

Manager.—Ira Fishkin.

Assistant Manager.—[Vacant].

Philadelphia: Southampton Office Park, 928 Jaymore Road, Suite A190, Southampton, PA 18966–3820, (215) 364–6465, fax (215) 364–6479.

Manager.—Ira Fishkin.

Assistant Manager.—[Vacant].

Pittsburgh Satellite Office: Moorhead Federal Office Building, 1000 Liberty Avenue, Room 501, Pittsburgh, PA 15222–4000, (412) 395–6929, fax (412) 395–4894.

Assistant Manager.—[Vacant].

San Francisco: 536 Stone Road, Suite 1, Benicia, CA 94510–1170, (707) 748–1970, fax (707) 748–1980.

Manager.—John J. O'Connor.

Seattle: Federal Center South, 4735 East Marginal Way S., Seattle, WA 98134–2397, (206) 764–3726, fax (206) 764–3301.

Manager.—Michael J. Atkins.

St. Louis: 1222 Spruce Street, Room 1–205, St. Louis, MO 63103–2822, (314) 241–0349, fax (314) 241–4154.

Manager.—James A. Davidson.

Washington, DC: Rapid Response Center, Building 136, SE., Federal Center, 3rd and M Street, SE., Washington, DC 20403, (202) 755–2110, fax (202) 755–0287.

Manager.—[Vacant].

Assistant Manager.—Melvin R. Allen.

PUBLIC PRODUCTS AND SERVICES

Superintendent of Documents.—Judith C. Russell, 512–0571, fax 512–1434.
Deputy Superintendent of Documents.—Thomas C. Evans III, 512–1524.
Director of:
Documents Sales Service.—[Vacant].
Library Programs Service.—Ernest G. Baldwin, 512–1114, fax 512–1432.
Office of Electronic Information Dissemination.—Richard G. Davis, 512–1622, fax 512–1262.

GPO BOOKSTORES

Washington, DC, Metropolitan Area: GPO (Main) Bookstore, 710 North Capitol Street NW., Washington, DC 20401, (202) 512–0132, fax (202) 512–1355.
Laurel Sales Outlet, 8660 Cherry Lane, Laurel, MD 20707, (301) 953–7974, fax (301) 498–8995.

TO ORDER PUBLICATIONS:

Phone toll free (866) 512–1800 [DC area: (202) 512–1800], fax (202) 512–2250, mail orders to Superintendent of Documents, P.O. Box 371954, Pittsburgh PA 15250–7954, or order online from http://bookstore.gpo.gov. *GPO Access* technical support: gpoaccess@gpo.gov or toll free (888) 293–6498 [DC area (202) 512–1530].

PLANT OPERATIONS

Managing Director.—Robert E. Schwenk, 512–0707, fax 512–0740.
Deputy Managing Director of Plant Operations.—[Vacant].
Production Manager.—Jeffrey J. Bernazzoli, 512–0707.
Assistant Production Manager (night).—William C. Krakat, 512–0688, fax 512–0740.
Assistant to the Production Manager (night).—David Boddie, 512–0688.
Superintendent of:
Binding Division.—John W. Crawford, 512–0593, fax 512–1830.
Electronic Photocomposition Division.—Dannie E. Young, 512–0625, fax 512–1730.
Press Division.—George M. Domarasky, 512–0673, fax 512–1754.
Production Planning Division.—Philip J. Markett, Jr., 512–0233, fax 512–1569.
Manager, Quality Control and Technical Department.—Sylvia S.Y. Subt, 512–0766, fax 512–0015.
Engineering Service.—Dennis J. Carey (acting), 512–1031, fax 512–1418.
Materials Management Service.—[Vacant], 512–0935, fax 512–1518.

INFORMATION TECHNOLOGY AND SYSTEMS

Chief Information Officer.—[Vacant].
Manager of:
IRM Policy.—Reynold Schweickhart, 512–1913, fax 512–0740.
Electronic Systems Development Division.—Richard G. Leeds, Jr., 512–0029, fax 512–1756.
Graphic Systems Development Division.—Joel E. Reeves, 512–0731, fax 512–1840.

HUMAN RESOURCES

Chief Human Capital Officer.—Robert R. Carr, 512–1111, fax 512–2139.
Director of:
Office of Labor and Employee Relations.—Neal H. Fine, 512–0200, fax 512–1150.
Occupational Health and Environmental Services.—William T. Harris, 512–1210, fax 512–1505.
Office of Personnel.—[Vacant], 512–1111, fax 512–2139.

FINANCE AND ADMINISTRATION

Chief Financial Officer.—[Vacant].
Comptroller.—William L. Boesch, Jr., 512–2073, fax 512–1520.
Director of Budget.—William M. Guy, 512–0832, fax 512–1736.

LIBRARY OF CONGRESS

10 First Street SE., 20540, phone 707–5000, fax 707–5844

http://www.loc.gov

OFFICE OF THE LIBRARIAN, LM 608

Librarian of Congress.—James H. Billington, 707–5205.
Confidential Assistants to the Librarian: Timothy L. Robbins, Elizabeth A. Davis-Brown, 707–5205.
Deputy Librarian/Chief Operating Officer.—Donald L. Scott, 707–5215.
Chief of Staff.—Jo Ann C. Jenkins, 707–0351.
Director, Congressional Relations Office.—Geraldine Otremba, LM 611, 707–6577.
Director, Development Office.—Charles V. Stanhope (acting), LM 605, 707–2777.
Special Events Officer.—Kim H. Moden, LM 605, 707–1523.
Director, Communications Office.—Jill D. Brett, LM 105, 707–2905.
Editor, Calendar of Events.—Helen W. Dalrymple, 707–1940.
Editor, Library of Congress Information Bulletin.—Helen W. Dalrymple, 707–1940.
Editor, The Gazette.—Gail Fineberg, 707–9194.
General Counsel.—Elizabeth Pugh, LM 601, 707–6316.
Inspector General.—Karl W. Schornagel, LM 630, 707–6314.
Chief of Contracts and Grants Management.—William Barker (acting), LA 325, 707–6109.
The Librarian of Congress Emeritus.—Daniel J. Boorstin, LM 325, 707–1500.

OFFICE OF OPERATIONS MANAGEMENT AND TRAINING, LM 603

Chief.—Thomas Bryant (acting), 707–3867.

OFFICE OF SECURITY AND EMERGENCY PREPAREDNESS, LM G03

Director.—Kenneth Lopez, 707–8708.

OFFICE OF WORKFORCE DIVERSITY, LM 624

Director.—Gilbert Sandate, 707–4170.
Affirmative Action and Special Programs Office (LM 623), 707–5479.
Dispute Resolution Center, 707–4170.
Equal Employment Opportunity Complaints Office (LM 626), 707–6024.

OFFICE OF THE DIRECTOR FOR HUMAN RESOURCES SERVICES, LM 645

Director.—Teresa A. Smith, LM 645, 707–5659.
Special Assistants: Timothy W. Cannon, 707–6544; Michaline Dobrzeniecki, 707–7191.
Director, Office of:
Workforce Acquisitions.—William Ayers, Jr. (acting), 707–0289.
Workforce Management.—Charles Carron, LM 653, 707–6637.
Worklife Services Center.—Rafael E. Landrau, 707–8072.
Strategic Planning and Automation.—Dennis Hanratty, 707–0029.

OFFICE OF THE CHIEF FINANCIAL OFFICER, LM 613

Chief Financial Officer.—John D. Webster, 707–5189.
Accounting Operations Officer.—Nicole N. Sims, LM 617, 707–5547.
Budget Officer.—Kathryn B. Murphy, 707–5186.
Disbursing Officer.—Nicholas Roseto, 707–5202.
Financial Systems Officer.—Jamie L. McCullough, LM 617, 707–4160.
Strategic Planning Director.—Thomas Bryant, LM 603, 707–3867.

OFFICE OF THE DIRECTOR FOR INTEGRATED SUPPORT SERVICES, LM 327

Director.—Mary Berghaus Levering (acting), 707–1393.
Facility Services Officer.—Neal Graham (acting), 707–7512.
Health Services Officer.—Sandra Charles, LM G40, 707–8035.
Assistant Chief, Office Systems Services.—Jeffrey M. Guide, LM G23, 707–5590.
Safety Services Officer.—Robert Browne, LM B28, 707–6204.

OFFICE OF STRATEGIC INITIATIVES, LM 637

Associate Librarian for Strategic Initiatives/Chief Information Officer.—Laura E. Campbell, 707–3300.
Confidential Assistant to the Associate Librarian.—George Coulbourne, 707–7856.
Director, Digital Resource Managemant and Planning.—Molly H. Johnson, 707–0809.
Senior Advisor, Integration Management.—Elizabeth S. Dulabahn, 707–2369.
Director for Information Technology Services.—James M. Gallagher, LM G51, 707–5114.
Special Assistant to the Director.—Karen Caldwell, 707–3797.
Deputy Director.—[Vacant].
Data Administrator.—Mary Kay D. Ganning, 707–9709.
Resources Manager.—Mercedes Baird (acting), 707–9669.
Technology Assessment Manager.—James S. Graber, 707–9628.
Computer Operations Group, Group Leader.—Michael C. McClure (acting), 707–0912.
Group Leader for User Support.—Michael F. Handy, 707–8338.
Information Center Team, Team Leader.—James T. McGrory, 707–0141.
Telecommunications Administration Team, Team Leader.—Judith A. Conklin, 707–3165.
Telecommunications Team, Team Leader.—Michael C. McClure, 707–0912.
Group Leaders for Production Systems:
Group 1.—Richard W. Genter, 707–9577
Group 2.—Mercedes Baird, 707–9669
Group Leaders for Systems Development:
Group 1.—Alvert Q. Banks, 707–9562.
Group 2.—Maryle G. Ashley, 707–9641.
Group 3.—Richard W. Genter (acting), 707–9577.
Group 4.—Jane B. Mandelbaum, 707–4429.
Group Leader for Systems Engineering.—Michael F. Handy (acting), 707–8338.

LAW LIBRARY, OFFICE OF THE LAW LIBRARIAN, LM 240

Law Librarian.—Rubens Medina, 707–5065.
Director, Directorate of Law Library Services.—Margaret E. Whitlock, 707–5376.
Chief, Collection Services Office.—Rose Marie Clemandot, LM 233, 707–5067.
Chief, Public Services.—Robert N. Gee, LM 201, 707–0638.
Director, Directorate of Legal Research.—[Vacant].
Chief, Eastern Law Division.—Tao-tai Hsia, LM 235, 707–5085.
Chief, Western Law Division.—Kersi B. Shroff, LM 235, 707–7850.

LIBRARY SERVICES, OFFICE OF THE ASSOCIATE LIBRARIAN FOR LIBRARY SERVICES, LM 642

Associate Librarian.—Beacher J.E. Wiggins (acting), 707–6240.

Director for Acquisitions.—Nancy A. Davenport, 707–5137.

Fiscal Operations Officer.—Sylvia M. Csiffary, LM 633, 707–9444.

Chief of:

African/Asian Acquisitions and Overseas Operations.—Judy C. McDermott, LM 632, 707–5273.

Anglo American Acquisitions.—Michael W. Albin, LM B41, 707–5361.

European and Latin American Acquisitions.—Donald P. Panzera, LM G35, 707–5243.

Serial Record Division.—Maureen O. Landry, LM 515, 707–6428.

Director, Office for Area Studies Collections.—Carolyn T. Brown, LJ 100, 707–1902.

Chief of:

African and Middle Eastern Division.—Beverly Ann Gray, LJ 220, 707–2933.

Asian Division.—Hwa-Wei Lee, LJ 149, 707–5919.

European Division.—John Van Oudenaren, LJ 250, 707–4543.

Federal Research Division.—Robert L. Worden, LA 5282, 707–3909.

Hispanic Division.—Georgette M. Dorn, LJ 240, 707–2003.

Director, Office of Scholarly Programs.—Prosser Gifford, LJ 120, 707–1517.

Director of Cataloging.—Judith A. Mansfield (acting), 707–5333.

Chief of:

Arts and Sciences Cataloging Division.—Roman B. Worobec (acting), LM 501, 707–5342.

Cataloging in Publication Division.—John P. Celli, LM 542, 707–9797.

Cataloging Policy and Support Office.—Barbara B. Tillett, LA 311, 707–4714.

Decimal Classification Division.—Dennis M. McGovern (acting), LM 556, 707–6989.

History and Literature Cataloging Division.—Jeffrey Heynen, LM 541, 707–6015.

Regional and Cooperative Cataloging Division.—John D. Byrum, Jr., LM 535, 707–5196.

Social Sciences Cataloging Division.—Sime Letina (acting), LM 527, 707–0214.

Special Materials Cataloging Division.—Susan H. Vita, LM 547, 707–7211.

Director for National Services.—Beacher J.E. Wiggins (acting), 707–6240.

Chief, Cataloging Distribution Service.—Kathryn M. Mendenhall (acting), LA 206, 707–6121.

Director, Center for the Book.—John Y. Cole, Jr., LM 650, 707–5221.

Executive Director, Federal Library and Information Center Committee.—Susan M. Tarr, LA 217, 707–4801.

Interpretive Programs Officer.—Irene U. Chambers, LA G25, 707–5223.

Director, Office of National Library Service for the Blind and Physically Handicapped, TSA.—Frank K. Cylke, 707–5104.

Chief, Photoduplication Service.—Sandra M. Lawson (acting), LA 130, 707–5650.

Director, Publishing Office.—W. Ralph Eubanks, LM 602, 707–3892.

Retail Marketing Officer.—Anna S. Lee, LM 225Q, 707–7715.

Visitor Services Officer.—Teresa V. Sierra, 707–5277.

Director of Operations.—Clifford T. Cohen, 707–1858.

Chief of:

Automation Planning and Liaison Office.—Susan M. Hayduchok, LM 532, 707–0125.

Network Development and MARC Standards Office.—Sally H. McCallum, LM 639, 707–6237.

Technical Processing and Automation Instructions Office.—Judith P. Cannan, LM 530, 707–2031.

Director for Preservation.—Mark S. Roosa, 707–5213.

Chief of:

Binding and Collections Care Division.—[Vacant], LM G20, 707–9385.

Conservation Division.—Dianne van der Reyden, LM G38, 707–5634.

Preservation Reformatting Division.—John Mark Sweeney, LM G05, 707–5918.

Preservation Research and Testing Division.—Chandru J. Shahani, LM G38, 707–5607.

Director of:

American Folklife Center.—Peggy Bulger, LJ G59, 707–1745.

Public Service Collections.—Diane Nester Kresh, 707–5330.

Veterans History Project.—Ellen McCulloch-Lovell, LA 144, 707–0220.

Chief of:

Children's Literature Center.—Sybille A. Jagusch, LJ 100, 707–5535.

Collections Access, Loan and Management.—Steven J. Herman (acting), LJ G02, 707–7400.

Geography and Map Division.—John R. Hebert, LM B02, 707–8530.

Humanities and Social Sciences Divisions.—Stephen E. James, LJ 139A, 707–5530.

Manuscript Division.—James H. Hutson, LM 102, 707–5383.

Assistant Chief, Motion Picture, Broadcasting and Recorded Sound Division.—Gregory A. Lukow, LM 338, 707–5709.

Chief of:

Music Division.—Jon W. Newsom, LM 113, 707–5503.

Prints and Photographs Division.—Jeremy E. Adamson, LM 339, 707–5836.

Rare Book and Special Collections Division.—Mark G. Dimunation, LJ Dk A, 707–5434.

Science Technology and Business Division.—William J. Sittig, LA 5203, 707–5664.

Serial and Government Publications Division.—Karen Renninger, LM 133, 707–5096.

CONGRESSIONAL RESEARCH SERVICE, LM 203

Director.—Daniel P. Mulhollan, 707–5775.

Associate Directors for the offices of:

Finance and Administration.—Kathy A. Williams, LM 208, 707–6698.

Congressional Affairs and Counselor to the Director.—Kent M. Ronhovde, 707–7090.

Information Resources Management.—Stephanie V. Williams, LM 221, 707–5804.

Legislative Information.—Jeffrey C. Griffith, LM 208, 707–2475.

Workforce Development.—Bessie E.H. Alkisswani, LM 208, 707–8835.

Assistant Directors of:

American Law Division.—Richard C. Ehlke, LM 227, 707–6006.

Domestic Social Policy Division.—Royal Shipp, LM 323, 707–6228.

Foreign Affairs, Defense and Trade Division.—Charlotte P. Preece, LM 315, 707–7654.

Government and Finance Division.—Michael L. Koempel, LM 303, 707–0165.

Information Research Division.—Lynne K. McCay, LM 215, 707–1415.

Resources, Science and Industry Division.—John L. Moore, LM 423, 707–7232.

U.S. COPYRIGHT OFFICE, LM 403

Register of Copyrights and Associate Librarian for Copyright Services.—Marybeth Peters, 707–8350.

Staff Director.—Robert Dizard, Jr., 707–8350.

General Counsel.—David Carson, 707–8380.

Chief Operating Officer.—Robert Dizard, Jr., 707–8350.

Chief of:

Cataloging Division.—Joanna Roussis (acting), LM 513, 707–8040.

Examining Division.—Nanette Petruzzelli, LM 445, 707–8200.

Information and Reference Division.—James P. Cole, LM 453, 707–6800.

Licensing Division.—John E. Martin, Jr., LM 454, 707–8130.

Receiving and Processing Division.—Melissa Dadant, LM 435, 707–7700.

Associate Register for—

Policy and International Affairs.—Jule L. Sigall, LM 403, 707–8350.

National Copyright Programs.—Mary Berghaus Levering, LM 403, 707–8350.

Copyright Acquisitions Division.—Jewel Player, LM 438C, 707–7125.

UNITED STATES BOTANIC GARDEN

245 First Street, SW., Washington, DC 20024

(202) 225–8333 (information); (202) 226–8333 (receptionist)

http://www.usbg.gov

Director.—Alan M. Hantman, Architect of the Capitol, 228–1204.

Executive Director.—Holly H. Shimizu, 225–6670.

Administrative Officer.—Elizabeth A. Spar, 225–5002.

Public Programs Coordinator.—Christine A. Flanagan, 225–1269.

Horticulture Division Manager.—Robert Pennington, 225–6647.

Operations Division Manager.—John M. Gallagher, 225–6646.

THE CABINET

Vice President of the United States	RICHARD B. CHENEY.
Secretary of State	COLIN L. POWELL.
Secretary of the Treasury	JOHN W. SNOW.
Secretary of Defense	DONALD H. RUMSFELD.
Attorney General	JOHN ASHCROFT.
Secretary of the Interior	GALE NORTON.
Secretary of Agriculture	ANN VENEMAN.
Secretary of Commerce	DONALD L. EVANS.
Secretary of Labor	ELAINE CHAO.
Secretary of Health and Human Services	TOMMY THOMPSON.
Secretary of Housing and Urban Development	MEL MARTINEZ.
Secretary of Transportation	NORMAN Y. MINETA.
Secretary of Energy	SPENCER ABRAHAM.
Secretary of Education	RODERICK PAIGE.
Secretary of Veterans Affairs	ANTHONY PRINCIPI.
Secretary of Homeland Security	TOM RIDGE.
Director, Office of Management and Budget	JOSHUA B. BOLTEN.
U.S. Trade Representative	ROBERT ZOELLICK.
Director, Office of National Drug Control Policy	JOHN P. WALTERS.
Chief of Staff	ANDREW H. CARD, JR.

EXECUTIVE BRANCH

THE PRESIDENT

GEORGE W. BUSH, Republican, of Texas; born on July 6, 1946; raised in Midland and Houston, TX; education: Yale University (Bachelor's Degree); Harvard University (M.B.A.); military service: Texas Air National Guard; occupations: businessman (energy industry); Managing General Partner of the Texas Rangers (Major League Baseball team); public service: elected Governor of Texas on November 8, 1994; reelected as Governor on November 3, 1998; became the first Governor in Texas history to be elected to consecutive four-year terms; religion: Methodist; family: married to Laura; two children, Barbara and Jenna; elected President of the United States on November 7, 2000; took the oath of office on January 20, 2001.

EXECUTIVE OFFICE OF THE PRESIDENT

THE WHITE HOUSE OFFICE

1600 Pennsylvania Avenue, NW., 20500

Eisenhower Executive Office Building (EEOB), 17th Street and Pennsylvania Avenue, NW., 20500, phone 456–1414, http://www.whitehouse.gov

The President of the United States.—George W. Bush.
Deputy Assistant to the President and Director of Oval Office Operations.—Linda Gambatesa.
Personal Secretary to the President.—Ashley Estes.
Personal Aide to the President.—Blake Gottesman.

CABINET AFFAIRS

phone 456–2572

Deputy Assistant to the President and Cabinet Secretary.—Brian Montgomery.
Executive Assistant to the Director.—Taylor Hughes.
Deputy Assistant to the President and Deputy Cabinet Secretary.—Ed Ingle.
Special Assistant to the Cabinet Secretary.—Carrie Loy.
Associate Director of Cabinet Affairs: Matt Koch, Sarah Pfeifer, Ali Tubah.

CHIEF OF STAFF

phone 456–6798

Chief of Staff—Andrew H. Card, Jr.
Executive Assistant to the Chief of Staff and Scheduler.—Melissa Bennett.
Assistant to the President and Deputy Chief of Staff.—[Vacant].
Assistant to the President and Deputy Chief of Staff for Operations.—Joseph W. Hagin.

COMMUNICATIONS AND SPEECHWRITING

phone 456–7910, speechwriting phone 456–2763

Assistant to the President for Communications.—Dan Bartlett.
Deputy Assistant to the President for Communications.—Suzy DeFrancis.
Special Assistant to the President and Deputy Director of Communications for Production.—Scott Sforza.
Special Assistant to the President and Director of Communications for Planning.—Brian Besanceney.
Assistant to the President for Speechwriting and Policy Advisor.—Mike Gerson.
Deputy Assistant to the President and Deputy Director of Speechwriting.—John McConnell.

Special Assistant to the President and Director of Media Affairs.—Nicolle Devenish.
Special Assistant to the President and Senior Speechwriter to the President.—Matthew Scully.
Special Assistant to the President and Presidential Speechwriter.—Noam Neusner.
Deputy Assistant to the President and Director of Global Communications.—Tucker Eskew.
NSC Presidential Speechwriter.—Matthew Rees.
First Lady's Speechwriter.—Elizabeth Liptock.

OFFICE OF THE PRESS SECRETARY

Upper Press Office phone 456–2673, Lower Press Office phone 456–2580

Assistant to the President and White House Press Secretary.—Scott McClellan.
Assistant Press Secretaries: Adam Levine, Ashley Snee.
Deputy Assistant to the President and Principal Deputy Press Secretary.—[Vacant].

CORRESPONDENCE

phone 456–7610

Director of Presidential Correspondence.—Desiree Thompson Sayle.
Deputy Director of Presidential Correspondence.—Heidi Marquez Smith.
Editor/Quality Control.—Nancy Hansen.
Director of:
Agency Liaison.—Richard Henry, 456–5485.
Gift Unit.—Christa Bailey, 456–5457.
Mail Analysis.—Trudy Roddick, 456–5490.

WHITE HOUSE COUNSEL

phone 456–2632

Assistant to the President and White House Counsel.—Alberto R. Gonzales.
Executive Assistant to the Counsel.—Carrie Nelson.
Deputy Assistant to the President and Deputy Counsel to the President.—David Leitch.
Special Assistants to the President and Associate Counsels to the President: Chris Bartolomucci, Nanette Everson, Brett Kavanaugh, Jennifer Newstead, Benjamin Powell, Kyle Sampson, Ted Ullyott, Helgi Walker, Jennifer Brosnahan.

DOMESTIC POLICY COUNCIL

phone 456–5594

Assistant to the President for Domestic Policy.—Margaret Spellings.
Deputy Assistant to the President for Domestic Policy.—Jay Lefkowitz.
Special Assistant to the President for Domestic Policy on:
(Health).—Alan Gilbert.
(Justice).—Diana Schacht.
(HUD/Labor/Transportation).—Liz Dougherty.
(Child/Families).—Aquiles Suarez.
(Education).—David Dunn.

NATIONAL AIDS POLICY

phone 456–7320

Director.—Joseph O'Neill.

OFFICE OF FAITH-BASED AND COMMUNITY INITIATIVES

Deputy Assistant to the President and Director of Faith-Based and Community Initiative.—Jim Towey.

Associate Director for Law and Policy.—Stanley Carlson-Theis.

Director of Operations.—Michele Tennery (acting).

STRATEGIC INITIATIVES
phone 456–2369

Senior Advisor to the President.—Karl Rove.

Deputy Assistant to the President and Assistant to the Senior Advisor.—Israel Hernandez.

Executive Assistant to the Senior Advisor.—Susan Ralston.

FIRST LADY'S OFFICE
phone 456–7064

The First Lady.—Laura Bush.

Deputy Assistant to the President and Chief of Staff to the First Lady.—Andi Ball.

Special Assistant, Executive Assistant, and Personal Aide to the First Lady.—Lindsey Lineweaver.

Executive Assistant to the Chief of Staff.—Laurie McCord.

Director of Communications and Press Secretary to the First Lady.—Noelia Rodriguez

Deputy Press Secretary to the First Lady.—Barbara Knight.

Director of:

Correspondence for the First Lady.—Syndney Johnson.

Projects.—Anne Heiligenstein.

Scheduling.—January Zell.

Advance for the First Lady.—Terra Gray.

Deputy Director of Correspondence.—Sara Armstrong.

Special Assistant to the President and White House Social Secretary.—Cathy Fenton.

INTERGOVERNMENTAL AFFAIRS
phone 456–2896

Deputy Assistant to the President and Director for Intergovernmental Affairs.—Ruben Barrales.

Special Assistant to the President for Intergovernmental Affairs.—Deborah (Debbie) Spagnoli.

LEGISLATIVE AFFAIRS
phone 456–2230

Assistant to the President and Director of Legislative Affairs.— David Hobbs.

Deputy Assistant to the President and Deputy Director for Legislative Affairs.—Eric Pelletier.

Special Assistant to the Assistant to the President for Legislative Affairs.—Adam Ingols.

Deputy Assistant to the President for—

House Legislative Affairs.—Dan Keniry.

Senate Legislative Affairs.—Ziad Ojakli.

Director of Legislative Correspondence.—Brooke Manning.

MANAGEMENT AND ADMINISTRATION
phone 456–5400

Deputy Assistant to the President for Management Administration, and Oval Office Operations.—Linda Gambatesa.

NATIONAL ECONOMIC COUNCIL

phone 456–2800

Assistant to the President for Economic Policy and Director, National Economic Council.—Stephen Friedman.

Deputy Assistant to the President for Economic Policy and Deputy Director, National Economic Council.—Keith Hennessey.

Executive Assistant to the Director.—Jean Cooper.

Special Assistants to the President for Economic Policy: Doug Badger, Charles Blahous, Charles Conner, Robert (Bob) McNally, Brian Reardon, Kevin Warsh.

OFFICE OF THE VICE PRESIDENT

phone 456–1414

The Vice President.—Richard B. Cheney.

Chief of Staff.—Lewis Libby, EEOB, Room 276, 456–9000.

Deputy Chief of Staff.—Dean McGrath, EEOB, Room 276, 456–9000.

Counsel to the Vice President.—David Addington, EEOB, Room 268, 456–9089.

Counselor to the Vice President.—Catherine Martin, EEOB, Room 272, 456–9042.

Principal Deputy Assistant to the Vice President for National Security Affairs.—Eric Edelman, EEOB, Room 298, 456–9501.

Assistant to the Vice President for Legislative Affairs.—Candi Wolff, EEOB, Room 285, 456–6774.

Staff Assistant (Senate).—Sara Nokes, U.S. Capitol, Room S–212, 224–2424.

Assistant to the Vice President for Domestic Policy.—Cesar Conda, EEOB, Room 288, 456–2728.

Executive Assistant to the Vice President.—Debra Heiden, West Wing, 456–7549.

Deputy Assistant to the Vice President and Director of Operations.—Claire O'Donnell, EEOB, Room 269, 456–6770.

Assistant to the Vice President and Chief of Staff to Mrs. Cheney.—Lea Berman, EEOB, Room 200, 456–7458.

Deputy Assistant to the Vice President and Director of Scheduling.—Elizabeth Kleppe, EEOB, Room 279, 456–6773.

Director of Correspondence.—Cecelia Boyer, EEOB, Room 265, 456–9002.

POLITICAL AFFAIRS

phone 456–6257

Deputy Assistant to the President and Director of Political Affairs.—Ken Mehlman.

Executive Assistant.—Kate Walters.

Special Assistant to the President and Deputy Director of Political Affairs.—Matt Schlapp.

Associate Political Directors: Alicia Davis, Paul Dyck, Coddy Johnson, Sara Taylor, David Thomas.

PRESIDENTIAL PERSONNEL

phone 456–6676

Assistant to the President for Presidential Personnel.—Dina Powell.

Executive Assistant to the President for Presidential Personnel.—Raquel Cabral.

Special Assistants to the President and Associate Directors.—Jackie Arends, Katja Bullock, Rebecca Contreras, David Higbee, Elizabeth Hogan, Ed Moy, Liza Wright.

OFFICE OF PUBLIC LIAISON

phone 456–2380

Deputy Assistant to the President and Director of Public Liaison.—Lezlee Westine.

Special Assistants to the President and Deputy Directors of Public Liaison: Adam Goldman, Tim Goeglein.

Special Assistant to the Director.—Katy Hayes.

SCHEDULING

phone 456–5323

Deputy Assistant to the President and Director of Appointments and Scheduling.—Brad Blakeman.
Deputy Director of:
Appointments and Scheduling.—Kara Figg.
Scheduling (Surrogate Scheduling).—Adrian Gray.
Scheduling (Research).—Andrew Ciafardini.

ADVANCE

phone 456–5309

Deputy Assistant to the President and Director of Advance.—Gregory Jenkins.
Special Assistant to the President and Deputy Director of Advance—Event Coordination.—Craig Ray.
Special Assistant to the President and Deputy Director of Advance—Press.—Kelley Gannon.

STAFF SECRETARY

phone 456–2702

Assistant to the President and Staff Secretary.—Harriet Miers.
Special Assistants to the President and Staff Secretaries: Jonathan Burks, Karin Torgenson.
Executive Assistants to the Staff Secretary: Barbara Barclay, Debra Bird, Carol Cleveland.
Administrative Assistant to the Staff Secretary.—[Vacant].

WHITE HOUSE MILITARY OFFICE

phone 757–2151

Deputy Assistant to the President and Director.—RDML Michael H. Miller, USN.
Deputy Director.—[Vacant].
Director of Admission.—LT Robin A. MacLean, USN.
Logistics NCO.—SFC Kenneth Haskins, USA.
Air Force Aide to the President.—LTCOL John Newell.
Army Aide to the President.—MAJ James McAllister.
Coast Guard Aide to the President.—LCDR John Daly.
Marine Corps Aide to the President.—MAJ Paul Montanus.
Naval Aide to the President.—LCDR Greg Huffman.
Director of:
Policy, Plans and Requirements.—Paul J. Jackson.
Operations.—COL Rick Antaya, USAF.
Customer Support and Organization Development.—Gerald Suarez, Ph.D.
Security.—LTC Peter Coughlin, USA.
Financial Management.—LTC Jeffrey Field, USA.
Information Technology Management.—Karin Mills.
Presidential Food Service.—LT Francis X. Fuller, USN.
White House Transportation Agency.—Leroy Borden.
White House Medical Unit.—COL Richard J. Tubb, USAF.
Presidential Pilot's Office.—COL Mark Tillman, USAF.

COUNCIL OF ECONOMIC ADVISERS

Eisenhower Executive Office Building, phone (202) 395–5084
www.whitehouse.gov/cea

Chair.—N. Gregory Mankiw.
Chief of Staff.—Phillip Swagel.
Member.—Randall S. Kroszner.

COUNCIL ON ENVIRONMENTAL QUALITY

730 Jackson Place, NW., phone (202) 456–6224, www.whitehouse.gov/ceq

Chair.—James Connaughton.
Chief of Staff.—Phil Cooney.
Associate Director for—
Agriculture and Public Lands.—David Anderson.
Congressional Affairs.—Deb Fiddelke.
Energy and Transportation.—Brian Hannegan.
Environmental Policy.—Kameran Onley.
Global Environmental Affairs.—Kenneth Peel.
Natural Resources.—William Leary.
NEPA Oversight.—Horst Greczmiel.
Public Affairs.—Dana Perino.
Sustainable Development.—Allen Hecht.
Toxics and Environmental Protection.—Elizabeth Stolpe.
General Counsel.—Dinah Bear.
Deputy General Counsel.—Edward Boling.

CENTRAL INTELLIGENCE AGENCY

phone (703) 482–1100

Director.—George Tenet.
Executive Director.—A.B. Krongard.
Director of Congressional Affairs.—Stanley Moskowitz.
Congressional Inquiries.—[Vacant], (703) 482–6136.
General Counsel.—Scott Muller.

FOREIGN INTELLIGENCE ADVISORY BOARD

phone 456–2352

Executive Director.—Randy W. Deitering.

NATIONAL SECURITY COUNCIL

Eisenhower Executive Office Building, phone 456–9491

MEMBERS

The President.—George W. Bush.
The Vice President.—Richard Cheney.
The Secretary of State.—Colin L. Powell.
The Secretary of Defense.—Donald Rumsfeld.

STATUTORY ADVISERS

Director of Central Intelligence.—George Tenet.
Chairman, Joint Chiefs of Staff.—Gen. Richard B. Myers, USAF.
Assistant to the President for National Security Affairs.—Condoleezza Rice.
Assistant to the President and Deputy National Security Advisor.—Steve Hadley.

HOMELAND SECURITY COUNCIL

phone 456–1700

Assistant to the President and Homeland Security Advisor.—John Gordon.
Deputy Assistant to the President and Deputy Homeland Security Advisor.—Richard Falkenrath.

OFFICE OF ADMINISTRATION

Director and Special Assistant to the President.—Tim Campen.
Deputy Director.—[Vacant].
Chief, Office of:
Information.—Carlos Solari.
Operations.—Sandy Evans.
Finance.—James F. Daniel.
Director of:
EOP Security.—Jeffrey Thompson.
Equal Employment Opportunity.—Linda Sites.
Facilities Management.—Steven R. Beattie.
General Services Division.—Kenneth Hembree.
Human Resources.—Jon S. Laurich.

OFFICE OF MANAGEMENT AND BUDGET

Eisenhower Executive Office Building, phone 395–4840

Director.—Joshua B. Bolten.
Deputy Director.—Joel D. Kaplan.
Deputy Director for Management.—Clay Johnson III.
Executive Associate Director for Administration.—Austin Smythe.
Administrator, Office of:
Federal Procurement Policy.—Angela Styles.
Information and Regulatory Affairs.—John Graham.
Assistant Director for—
Budget.—Richard Emery.
Legislative Reference.—James J. Jukes.
Associate Director for—
Administration.—[Vacant].
Communications.—Trent Duffy.
Economic Policy.—J.D. Foster.
Human Resources Programs.—Jim Capretta.
General Government Programs.—Steve McMillin.
Legislative Affairs.—[Vacant].
National Security Programs.—Robin Cleveland.
Natural Resources, Energy and Science Programs.—Marcus Peacock.
General Counsel.—Phil Perry.

OFFICE OF NATIONAL DRUG CONTROL POLICY

750–17th Street, NW., phone 395–6738, fax 395–7251

Director.—John P. Walters, room 805, 395–6700.
Deputy Director.— Mary Ann Solberg, room 836, 395–6710.
Chief of Staff.—Christopher M. Marston, room 804, 395–7286.
Deputy Director, Office of Demand Reduction.—Andrea G. Barthwell, room 609, 395–6751.
Assistant Deputy Director.—[Vacant].
Deputy Director, Office of Supply Reduction.—Barry D. Crane, room 713, 396–6741.
Assistant Deputy Director.—[Vacant].
Deputy Director, Office of State and Local Affairs.—Scott M. Burns, room 661, 395–7252.
Assistant Deputy Director.—[Vacant].
General Counsel, Office of the General Counsel.—Edward H. Jurith, room 518, 395–6709.
Director, Counterdrug Technology Assessment Center.—Albert E. Brandenstein, room 731, 395–6758.
Associate Director, National Youth Anti-drug Media Campaign.—Alan M. Levitt, room 560, 395–6794.
Associate Director, Office of:
Intelligence.—Roger P. Mackin, room 755, 395–6764.
Legislative Affairs.—Christine E. Morden, room 825, 395–6655.
Management and Administration.—Michele C. Marx, room 326, 395–6883.
Planning and Budget.—Robert B. Eiss, room 333, 395–6725.
Public Affairs.—Thomas A. Riley, room 842, 395–6627.

OFFICE OF SCIENCE AND TECHNOLOGY POLICY

Eisenhower Executive Office Building, phone 456–7116, fax 456–6021
www.ostp.gov

Director.—John Marburger III.
Associate Director for—
Science.—Kathie Olsen.
Technology.—Richard Russell.
Chief of Staff and General Counsel.—Shana Dale.
Executive Secretary for—
National Science and Technology Council.—Ann Carlson.
Executive Director for President's Committee of Advisors on Science and Technology.—Stan Sokul.

OFFICE OF THE UNITED STATES TRADE REPRESENTATIVE

600 17th Street NW., phone 395–3230, www.ustr.gov

United States Trade Representative.—Robert Zoellick.
Deputy U.S. Trade Representative, Washington.—Peter F. Allgeier.
Deputy U.S. Trade Representative, Geneva.—Linnett F. Deily.
Associate U.S. Trade Representative.—Josette Shiner.
Chief of Staff.—Brian Gunderson.
Special Textile Negotiator.—David Spooner.
Chief Agricultural Negotiator.—Allen F. Johnson.
Counselor to the U.S. Trade Representative.—Harry Clark.
General Counsel.—John Veroneau.
Assistant U.S. Trade Representative for—
Administration.—John Hopkins.
Africa.—Florie Liser.
Agricultural Affairs.—James Murphy.
Asia and the Pacific.—Ralph Ives.
Congressional Affairs.—Matt Niemeyer.
Economic Affairs.—David Walters.
Environment and Natural Resources.—[Vacant].
Europe and the Mediterranean.—Cathy Novelli.
Industry.—Meredith Broadbent.
Intergovernmental Affairs and Public Liaison.—Christopher Padilla.
North Asian Affairs.—Wendy Cutler.
Monitoring and Enforcement.—Dan Brinza
North American Affairs.—[Vacant].
Office of the Americas.—Regina Vargo.
Policy Coordination.—Carmen Suro-Bredie.
Public/Media Affairs.—E. Richard Mills.
Services, Investment and Intellectual Property.—James Mendenhall.
Trade and Development.—Jon Rosenbaum.
Trade and Labor.—William Clatanoff.
World Trade Organization (WTO) and Multilateral Affairs.—Dorothy Dwoskin.

PRESIDENT'S COMMISSION ON WHITE HOUSE FELLOWSHIPS

phone 395–4522

Director.—Jocelyn White.
Associate Director.—Kelly Kenneally.
Administrative Officer.—Pandoria Nobles-Jones.
Education Director.—Marguerite Murer.
Associate Public Relations.—Karen Cruson.
Staff Assistant.—Elizabeth Jackson.

DEPARTMENT OF STATE

2201 C Street NW., 20520, phone 647–4000

COLIN L. POWELL, Secretary of State; born on April 5, 1937, in New York, NY; education: B.S., City College of New York; M.B.A., George Washington University; military and public service: Army ROTC; participated while attending City College of New York, and received a commission as a 2nd Lieutenant upon graduation; U.S. Army, served 1958–1993, rising to the rank of General (4 Stars); National Security Adviser for President Ronald Reagan, 1987–1989; Chairman of the Joint Chiefs of Staff, 1989–1993; Chairman, President's Summit for America's Future, 1997; Chairman, America's Promise—The Alliance for Youth, 1997–2000; awards: Presidential Medal of Freedom; Congressional Gold Medal; Presidential Citizens Medal; Secretary of State's Distinguished Service Medal; author: *My American Journey,* 1995; family: married to the former Alma Johnson; three children: Michael, Linda, and Anne; nominated by President George W. Bush to become the 65th Secretary of State, and was confirmed by the U.S. Senate on January 20, 2001.

OFFICE OF THE SECRETARY

Secretary of State.—Colin L. Powell, 647–5291.
Executive Assistant.—Craig Kelly, 647–9572.

OFFICE OF THE DEPUTY SECRETARY

Deputy Secretary of State.—Richard L. Armitage, room 7220, 647–9641.
Executive Assistant.—Robin Sakoda, 647–8931.

EXECUTIVE SECRETARIAT

Special Assistant and Executive Secretary.—Karl Hofmann, room 7224, 647–5301.
Deputy Executive Secretaries: Laurie J. Tracy, 647–6548; Marcia K. Wong, 647–5302; Elizabeth Whitaker, 647–8448.

POLICY PLANNING STAFF

Director.—Richard Haass, room 7531, 647–2972.
Principal Deputy Director.—Donald Steinberg, 647–2372.

AMBASSADOR-AT-LARGE FOR WAR CRIMES ISSUES

Ambassador-at-Large.—Pierre-Richard Prosper, room 7419A, 647–5074.
Deputy.—Michael Miklaucic, 647–6751.

UNDER SECRETARY FOR POLITICAL AFFAIRS

Under Secretary.—Marc Grossman, room 7240, 647–2471.
Executive Assistant.—Mark Wong, 647–1599.

UNDER SECRETARY FOR ECONOMIC, BUSINESS, AND AGRICULTURAL AFFAIRS

Under Secretary.—Alan Larson, room 7256, 647–7575.
Executive Assistant.—Peter Chase, 647–7674.

UNDER SECRETARY FOR ARMS CONTROL AND INTERNATIONAL SECURITY

Under Secretary.—John Bolton, room 7208, 647–1049.
Executive Assistant.—Fred Fleitz, 647–1749.

UNDER SECRETARY FOR MANAGEMENT

Under Secretary.—Grant S. Green Jr., room 7207, 647–1500.
Executive Assistant.—Richard Shinnick, 647–0501.

UNDER SECRETARY FOR GLOBAL AFFAIRS

Under Secretary.—Paula Dobriansky, room 7250, 647–6240.
Executive Assistant.—Jonathan Farrar, 647–7609.

UNDER SECRETARY FOR PUBLIC DIPLOMACY AND PUBLIC AFFAIRS

Under Secretary.—Patricia S. Harrison (acting), 647–9199.
Executive Assistant.—Doug Greene, 647–9105.

BUREAUS

AFRICAN AFFAIRS

Assistant Secretary.—Walter Kansteiner, room 6234, 647–4440.
Principal Deputy Assistant Secretary.—William Bellamy, 647–4493.
Deputy Assistant Secretaries: Pamela A. Bridgewater, 647–4485; Charles Snyder, 647–1818.

EAST ASIAN AND PACIFIC AFFAIRS

Assistant Secretary.—James Kelly, 647–9596.
Principal Deputy Assistant Secretary.—Donald Keyser, 647–4393.
Deputy Assistant Secretaries: Matthew Daley, 647–6904; Randall Schriver, 647–6910.

EUROPEAN AFFAIRS

Assistant Secretary.—Beth Jones, room 6226, 647–9626.
Principal Deputy Assistant Secretary.—Charles P. Ries, 647–6402.
Deputy Assistant Secretaries: Stephen Pifer, 647–5174; Janet L. Bogue, 647–6415; Robert Bradtke, 647–5142; Heather Conley, 647–6233; Lynn Pascoe, 647–5447.

NEAR-EASTERN AFFAIRS

Assistant Secretary.—William Burns, room 6242, 647–7209.
Principal Deputy Assistant Secretary.—James Larocco, 647–7207.
Deputy Assistant Secretary.—David Satterfield, 647–7170.

WESTERN HEMISPHERE AFFAIRS

Assistant Secretary.—Curt Struble (acting), room 6262, 647–8386.
Deputy Assistant Secretaries: Donald Camp, 736–4328; James Derham, 647–8562; Tom Shannon, 647–6754.

SOUTH ASIAN AFFAIRS

Assistant Secretary.—Christina Rocca, room 6254, 736–4325.
Deputy Assistant Secretary.—Michele J. Sison, 647–4331.

ADMINISTRATION

Assistant Secretary.—William A. Eaton, room 6330, 647–1492.
Procurement Executive.—Lloyd W. Pratsch, 647–1684.
Deputy Assistant Secretaries: Vince Chaverini, 647–1638; Lee R. Lohman, 647–2989; Frank Coulter, (703) 875–6956.

ARMS CONTROL

Assistant Secretary.—Stephen Rademaker, room 5930, 647–9610.
Principal Deputy Assistant Secretary.—R. Lucas Fischer, 647–8463.
Deputy Assistant Secretary.—Ambassador Donald Mahley (acting), 647–5999.

CONSULAR AFFAIRS

Assistant Secretary.—Mary A. Ryan, room 6811, 647–9576.
Principal Deputy Assistant Secretary.—Daniel B. Smith, 647–9577.

COORDINATOR FOR COUNTERTERRORISM

Ambassador-at-Large.—Cofer Black, room 2507, 647–9892.
Principal Deputy Assistant Secretary.—William Pope, 647–5278.
Deputy Coordinator.—Stephanie Kinney, 647–8536.

DEMOCRACY, HUMAN RIGHTS AND LABOR

Assistant Secretary.—Lorne W. Craner, room 7802, 647–2126.
Principal Deputy Assistant Secretary.—E. Michael Southwick, 647–2590.
Deputy Assistant Secretary.—John Scott Carpenter, 647–1783.

DIPLOMATIC SECURITY

Assistant Secretary.—Francis X. Taylor, room 6313, 647–6290.
Principal Deputy Assistant Secretary.—W. Ray Williams, 663–0538.
Deputy Assistant Secretary.—Lynn Dent, 647–3417.

DIRECTOR GENERAL OF THE FOREIGN SERVICE AND DIRECTOR OF PERSONNEL

Director General.—Ruth A. Davis, room 6218, 647–9898.
Principal Deputy Assistant Secretary.—Ruth A. Whiteside, 647–9438.
Deputy Assistant Secretaries: Linda Taglialatela, 647–5152; John Campbell, 647–5942.

ECONOMIC AND BUSINESS AFFAIRS

Assistant Secretary.—E. Anthony Wayne, room 6828, 647–7971.
Principal Deputy Assistant Secretary.—Shaun Donnelly, 647–5991.
Deputy Assistant Secretaries: Janice Bay, 647–9496; Anna Borg, 647–1498.

EDUCATIONAL AND CULTURAL AFFAIRS

Assistant Secretary.—Patricia de Stacy Harrison, 203–5111.
Deputy Assistant Secretaries: Brian Sexton, 619–5348; Marianne Craven (acting), 619–6409.

OFFICE OF CIVIL RIGHTS

Deputy Assistant Secretary.—Barbara Pope, room 4216, 647–9295.
Associate Director.—Patty Baldwin, 647–9295.

FINANCE AND MANAGEMENT POLICY

Chief Financial Officer.—Larry J. Eisenhart (acting), SA 1, H15800, 261–8620.
Executive Assistant.—[Vacant].

OFFICE OF FOREIGN MISSIONS

Deputy Assistant Secretary.—Theodore E. Strickler, 647–3416.

FOREIGN SERVICE INSTITUTE

Director.—Katherine Peterson, room F2103, (703) 302–6703.
Deputy Director.—Barry Wells, (703) 302–6707.

INTELLIGENCE AND RESEARCH

Assistant Secretary.—Carl W. Ford, Jr., room 6531, 647–9177.
Principal Deputy Assistant Secretary.—Thomas Fingar, 647–7826.
Deputy Assistant Secretaries: Joseph Le Baron, 647–1344; Carol A. Rodley, 647–7754; Bill Wood, 647–9633.

INTERNATIONAL INFORMATION PROGRAMS

Coordinator.—John P. Dwyer, 619–4545.
Deputy Coordinator.—Joe B. Johnson, 619–4545.

INTERNATIONAL NARCOTICS AND LAW ENFORCEMENT AFFAIRS

Assistant Secretary.—Paul Simons, room 7333, 647–8464.
Principal Deputy Assistant Secretary.—Deborah A. McCarthy, 647–6643.
Deputy Assistant Secretary.—Elizabeth Verville (acting), 647–6642.

INTERNATIONAL ORGANIZATION AFFAIRS

Assistant Secretary.—Kim R. Holmes, room 6323, 647–9600.
Principal Deputy Assistant Secretary.—James Swigert, 647–9602.
Deputy Assistant Secretary.—Richard Miller, 647–9604.

LEGAL ADVISER

The Legal Advisor.—William H. Taft IV, room 6423, 647–9598.

LEGISLATIVE AFFAIRS

Assistant Secretary.—Paul V. Kelly, room 7325, 647–4204.
Principal Deputy Assistant Secretary.—Michael C. Polt, 647–1050.
Deputy Assistant Secretary for Global Affairs.—James Terry, 647–2135.
Deputy Assistant Secretary (Senate).—[Vacant], 647–2135.
Deputy Assistant Secretary (House).—Carl N. Raether, 647–1048.

NONPROLIFERATION

Assistant Secretary.—John S. Wolf, room 3208, 647–1142.
Deputy Assistant Secretary.—Susan F. Burk, 647–6977.

OCEANS AND INTERNATIONAL ENVIRONMENTAL AND SCIENTIFIC AFFAIRS

Assistant Secretary.—John F. Turner, room 7831, 647–1554.
Principal Deputy Assistant Secretary.—Anthony Rock, 647–3004.
Deputy Assistant Secretaries: Jeffrey Burnham, 647–2232; Mary Beth West, 647–2396.

OFFICE OF THE INSPECTOR GENERAL

Inspector General.—[Vacant], room 6817, 647–9450.

POLITICAL–MILITARY AFFAIRS

Assistant Secretary.—Lincoln P. Bloomfield, Jr., room 6212, 647–9022.
Principal Deputy Assistant Secretary.—Gregory M. Suchan, 647–9023.
Deputy Assistant Secretaries: Kara Bue, 647–9023; Robert Maggi, 663–2861.

POPULATION, REFUGEES AND MIGRATION

Assistant Secretary.—Arthur E. Dewey, room 5824, 647–5767.
Principal Deputy Assistant Secretary.—Richard L. Greene, 647–5822.

PROTOCOL

Chief of Protocol.—Donald Ensenat, room 1232, 647–4543.
Deputy Chief.—David Pryor, 647–4120.

PUBLIC AFFAIRS

Assistant Secretary.—Richard Boucher, room 6800, 647–6607.
Principal Deputy Assistant Secretary.—Philip Reeker, 647–9606.
Deputy Assistant Secretary.—Robert A. Tappan, 647–6088.

UNITED STATES DIPLOMATIC OFFICES—FOREIGN SERVICE

(C= Consular Office, N= No Embassy or Consular Office)

LIST OF CHIEFS OF MISSION

AFGHANISTAN (Kabul).
Hon. Robert Patrick Finn.
ALBANIA (Tirana).
Hon. James Franklin Jeffery.
ALGERIA (Algiers).
Hon. Janet A. Sanderson.
ANDORRA (Vella) (N).
Hon. George L. Argyros, Sr.
ANGOLA (Luanda).
Hon. Christopher William Dell.
ANTIGUA AND BARBUDA
(St. John's) (N).
Hon. Earl Norfleet Phillips.
ARGENTINA (Buenos Aires).
Hon. James Donald Walsh.
ARMENIA (Yerevan).
Hon. John Malcolm Ordway.
AUSTRALIA (Canberra).
Hon. John Thomas Schieffer.
AUSTRIA (Vienna).
Hon. Lyons Brown, Jr.
AZERBAIJAN (Baku).
Hon. Ross L. Wilson.
BAHAMAS (Nassau).
Hon. J. Richard Blankenship.
BAHRAIN (Manama).
Hon. Ronald E. Neumann.
BANGLADESH (Dhaka).
Hon. Mary Ann Peters.
BARBADOS (Bridgetown) (N).
Hon. Earl Norfleet Phillips.
BELARUS (Minsk).
Hon. Michael G. Kozak.
BELGIUM (Brussels).
Hon. Stephen Brauer.
BELIZE (Belize City).
Hon. Russell F. Freeman.
BENIN (Contonou).
Hon. Wayne E. Neill.
BOLIVIA (La Paz).
Hon. David N. Greenlee.
BOSNIA-HERZEGOVINA (Sarajevo).
Hon. Clifford G. Bond.
BOTSWANA (Gaborone).
Hon. Joseph Huggins.
BRAZIL (Brasilia).
Hon. Donna Jean Hrinak.
BRUNEI DARUSSALAM
(Bandar Seri Begawan).
Hon. Gene B. Christy.
BULGARIA (Sofia).
Hon. James W. Pardew.
BURKINA FASO (Ouafadougou).
Hon. J. Anthony Holmes.
BURMA (Rangoon).
Hon. Carmen Martinez.
BURUNDI (Bujumbura).
Hon. James Howard Yellin.
CAMBODIA (Phnom Penh).
Hon. Charles Aaron Ray.
CAMEROON (Yaounde).
Hon. George McDade Staples.

CANADA (Ottawa).
Hon. Argeo Paul Celluci.
CAPE VERDE (Praia).
Hon. Donald C. Johnson.
CENTRAL AFRICAN REPUBLIC (Bangui).
Hon. Mattie R. Sharpless.
CHAD (N'Djamena).
Hon. Christopher Goldthwait.
CHILE (Santiago).
Hon. William R. Brownfield.
CHINA (Beijing).
Hon. Clark T. Randt, Jr.
COLOMBIA (Bogota).
Hon. Anne Woods Patterson.
COMOROS (Moroni) (N).
Hon. John Price.
CONGO, REPUBLIC OF (Brazzaville).
Hon. Robin Renee Sanders.
CONGO, DEMOCRATIC REPUBLIC OF (Kinshasa).
Hon. Aubrey Hooks.
COSTA RICA (San Jose).
Hon. John J. Danilovich.
COTE D'IVOIRE (Abidjan).
Hon. Arlene Render.
CROATIA (Zagreb).
Hon. Ralph Frank.
CUBA (Havana) (N).
Hon. James C. Cason.
CURACAO (Willemstad).
Hon. Deborah A. Bolten.
CYPRUS (Nicosia).
Hon. Michael Klosson.
CZECH REPUBLIC (Prague).
Hon. Craig Robert Stapleton.
DENMARK (Copenhagen).
Hon. Stuart A. Bernstein.
DJIBOUTI, REPUBLIC OF (Djibouti).
Hon. Donald Y. Yamamoto.
DOMINICAN REPUBLIC (Santo Domingo).
Hon. Hans H. Hertell.
EAST TIMOR (Dili).
Hon. Grover Joseph Rees III.
ECUADOR (Quito).
Hon. Kristie Anne Kenney.
EGYPT (Cairo).
Hon. C. David Welch.
EL SALVADOR (San Salvador).
Hon. Rose M. Likins.
EQUATORIAL GUINEA (Malabo) (N).
Hon. George McDade Staples.
ERITREA (Asmara).
Hon. Donald J. McConnell.
ESTONIA (Tallinn).
Hon. Joseph DeThomas.
ETHIOPIA (Addis Ababa).
Hon. Aurelia E. Brazeal.
FIJI (Suva) (N).
Hon. David L. Lyon.
FINLAND (Helsinki).
Hon. Bonnie McElveen-Hunter.
FRANCE (Paris).
Hon. Howard H. Leach.
GABONESE REPUBLIC (Libreville) (N).
Hon. Kenneth P. Moorefield.
GAMBIA (Banjul).
Hon. Jackson Chester McDonald.
GEORGIA (Tbilisi).
Hon. Richard Monroe Miles.
GERMANY (Berlin).
Hon. Daniel R. Coats.
GHANA (Accra).
Hon. Mary Carlin Yates.
GREECE (Athens).
Hon. Thomas J. Miller.
GRENADA (St. George) (N).
Hon. Earl Norfleet Phillips.
GUATEMALA (Guatemala).
Hon. John Randle Hamilton.
GUINEA (Conakry).
Hon. R. Barrie Walkley.
GUINEA-BISSAU (Bissau).
Hon. Richard Allan Roth.
GUYANA (Georgetown).
Hon. Ronald D. Godard.
HAITI (Port-au-Prince).
Hon. Brian Dean Curran.
HOLY SEE (Vatican City).
Hon. Jim Nicholson.
HONDURAS (Tegucigalpa).
Hon. Larry Leon Palmer.
HONG KONG (Hong Kong) (C).
Hon. James R. Keith.
HUNGARY (Budapest).
Hon. Nancy Goodman Brinker.
ICELAND (Reykjavik).
Hon. James Irvin Gadsden.
INDIA (New Delhi).
Hon. Robert D. Blackwill.
INDONESIA (Jakarta).
Hon. Ralph Leo Boyce, Jr.
IRELAND (Dublin).
[Vacant].
ISRAEL (Tel Aviv).
Hon. Daniel C. Kurtzer.
ITALY (Rome).
Hon. Melvin Sembler.
JAMAICA (Kingston).
Hon. Sue McCourt Cobb.
JAPAN (Tokyo).
Hon. Howard H. Baker, Jr.
JERUSALEM (C).
[Vacant].
JORDAN (Amman).
Hon. Edward W. Gnehm, Jr.
KAZAKHSTAN (Almaty).
Hon. Larry C. Napper.
KENYA (Nairobi).
Hon. Johnnie Carson.
KIRIBATI (Parawa) (N).
Hon. Michael J. Senko.
KOREA, REPUBLIC OF (Seoul).
Hon. Thomas C. Hubbard.
KOSOVO (Pristina) (N).
Hon. Reno Leon Harnish III.
KYRGYZ REPUBLIC (Bishkek).
Hon. John Martin O'Keefe.

KUWAIT (Kuwait City).
Hon. Richard Henry Jones.
LAOS PEOPLE'S DEMOCRATIC REPUBLIC (Vientiane).
Hon. Douglas Alan Hartwick.
LATVIA (Riga).
Hon. Brian E. Carlson.
LEBANON (Beirut).
Hon. Vincent Martin Battle.
LESOTHO (Maseru).
Hon. Robert Geers Loftis.
LIBERIA (Monrovia).
Hon. John W. Blaney.
LIECHTENSTEIN (Vaduz) (N).
[Vacant].
LITHUANIA (Vilnius).
Hon. John F. Tefft.
LUXEMBOURG (Luxembourg).
Hon. Peter Terpeluk, Jr.
MACEDONIA (Skopje).
Hon. Lawrence E. Butler.
MADAGASCAR (Antananarivo).
Hon. Wanda Nesbitt.
MALAWI (Lilongwe).
Hon. Roger A. Meece.
MALAYSIA (Kuala Lumpur).
Hon. Marie T. Huhtala.
MALDIVES (Male) (N).
Hon. E. Ashley Wills.
MALI (Bamako).
Hon. Vicki Huddleston.
MALTA (Valletta).
Hon. Anthony Horace Gioia.
MARSHALL ISLANDS (Majuro).
Hon. Michael J. Senko.
MAURITANIA (Nouakchott).
Hon. John W. Limbert.
MAURITIUS (Port Louis).
Hon. John Price.
MEXICO (Mexico City).
Hon. Antonio O. Garza, Jr.
MICRONESIA (Kolonia).
Hon. Larry Miles Dinger.
MOLDOVA (Chisinau).
Hon. Pamela Hyde Smith.
MONGOLIA (Ulaanbaatar).
Hon. John R. Dinger.
MOROCCO (Rabat).
Hon. Margaret DeBardeleben Tutwiler.
MOZAMBIQUE (Maputo).
Hon. Sharon P. Wilkinson.
NAMIBIA (Windhoek).
Hon. Kevin Joseph McGuire.
NAURU (Yaren) (N).
Hon. David L. Lyon.
NEPAL (Kathmandu).
Hon. Michael E. Malinowski.
NETHERLANDS (The Hague).
Hon. Clifford M. Sobel.
NEW ZEALAND (Wellington).
Hon. Charles J. Swindells.
NICARAGUA (Managua).
Hon. Barbara C. Moore.
NIGER (Niamey).
Hon. Gail Dennise Thomas Mathieu.
NIGERIA (Abuja).
Hon. Howard Franklin Jeter.
NORWAY (Oslo).
Hon. John D. Ong.
OMAN (Muscat).
Hon. Richard Lewis Baltimore III.
PAKISTAN (Islamabad).
Hon. Nancy J. Powell.
PALAU (Koror).
Hon. Francis Joseph Ricciardone, Jr.
PANAMA (Panama).
Hon. Linda Ellen Watt.
PAPUA NEW GUINEA (Port Moresby).
Hon. Suan S. Jacobs.
PARAGUAY (Asunción)
Hon. John F. Keane.
PERU (Lima).
Hon. John R. Dawson.
PHILIPPINES (Manila).
Hon. Francis J. Ricciardone, Jr.
POLAND (Warsaw).
Hon. Christopher Robert Hill.
PORTUGAL (Lisbon).
Hon. John N. Palmer.
QATAR (Doha).
Hon. Maureen Quinn.
ROMANIA (Bucharest).
Hon. Michael E. Guest.
RUSSIAN FEDERATION (Moscow).
Hon. Alexander R. Vershbow.
RWANDA (Kigali).
Margaret McMillion.
ST. KITTS AND NEVIS (Basseterrie) (N).
Hon. Earl Norfleet Phillips.
ST. LUCIA (Castries) (N).
Hon. Earl Norfleet Phillips.
ST. VINCENT AND THE GRENADINES (Kingstown) (N).
Hon. Earl Norfleet Phillips.
SAMOA (Apia) (N).
Hon. Charles Swindells.
SAO TOME AND PRINCIPE (Sao Tome) (N).
Hon. Kenneth P. Moorefield.
SAUDI ARABIA (Riyadh).
Hon. Robert W. Jordan.
SENEGAL (Dakar).
Hon. Richard Allan Roth.
SEYCHELLES (Victoria).
Hon. John Price.
SIERRA LEONE (Freetown).
Hon. Peter R. Chaveas.
SINGAPORE (Singapore).
Hon. Franklin L. Lavin.
SLOVAK REPUBLIC (Bratislava).
Hon. Ronald Weiser.
SLOVENIA (Ljubljana).
Hon. Johnny Young.
SOLOMON ISLANDS (Honiara) (N).
Hon. Susan S. Jacobs.
SOUTH AFRICA (Pretoria).
Hon. Cameron Hume.
SPAIN (Madrid).
Hon. George L. Argyros, Sr.

SRI LANKA (Colombo) (N).
Hon. E. Ashley Wills.
SUDAN (Khartoum).
[Vacant].
SURINAME (Paramaribo).
Hon. Daniel A. Johnson.
SWAZILAND (Mbabane).
Hon. James David McGee.
SWEDEN (Stockholm).
Hon. Charles A. Heimbold, Jr.
SWITZERLAND (Bern).
[Vacant].
SYRIAN ARAB REPUBLIC (Damascus).
Hon. Theodore H. Kattouf.
TAJIKISTAN (Dushanbe).
Hon. Franklin Pierce Huddle.
TANZANIA (Dar es Salaam).
Hon. Robert Royall.
THAILAND (Bangkok).
Hon. Darryl Norman Johnson.
TOGOLESE REPUBLIC (Lome).
Hon. Gregory Engle.
TONGA (Nuku'alofe) (N).
Hon. David L. Lyon.
TRINIDAD AND TOBAGO (Port-of-Spain).
Hon. Roy L. Austin.
TUNISIA (Tunis).
Hon. Rust Macpherson Deming.
TURKEY (Ankara).
Hon. W. Robert Pearson.
TURKMENISTAN (Ashgabat).
Hon. Laura E. Kennedy.
TUVALU (Funafuti) (N).
Hon. David L. Lyon.
UGANDA (Kampala).
Hon. Jimmy Kolker.
UKRAINE (Kiev).
Hon. Carlos Pascual.
UNITED ARAB EMIRATES (Abu Dhabi).
Hon. Marcelle M. Wahba.
UNITED KINGDOM (London).
Hon. William S. Farish.
URUGUAY (Montevideo).
Hon. Martin J. Silverstein.
UZBEKISTAN (Tashkent).
Hon. John Edward Herbst.
VANUATU (Port Moresby) (N).
Hon. Susan S. Jacobs.
VENEZUELA (Caracas).
Hon. Charles S. Shapiro.
VIETNAM (Hanoi).
Hon. Raymond Burghardt.
YEMEN (Sanaa).
Hon. Edmund James Hull.
YUGOSLAVIA (Belgrade) (C).
Hon. William Dale Montgomery.
ZAMBIA (Lusaka).
Hon. Martin George Brennan.
ZIMBABWE (Harare).
Hon. Joseph Gerard Sullivan.

UNITED STATES PERMANENT DIPLOMATIC MISSIONS TO INTERNATIONAL ORGANIZATIONS

UNITED NATIONS (New York).
Hon. John D. Negroponte.
ORGANIZATION OF AMERICAN STATES (Washington, DC).
Hon. Roger Francisco Noriega.
ORGANIZATION FOR SECURITY AND COOPERATION IN EUROPE (Vienna).
Hon. Stephan Michael Minikes.
UNITED NATIONS (Vienna).
Hon. Kenneth C. Brill.
NORTH ATLANTIC TREATY ORGANIZATION (Brussels).
Hon. R. Nicholas Burns.
ORGANIZATION FOR ECONOMIC COOPERATION AND DEVELOPMENT (Paris).
Hon. Jeanne L. Phillips.
UNITED NATIONS (Geneva).
Hon. Kevin E. Moley.
EUROPEAN UNION (Brussels).
Hon. Rockwell A. Schnabel.

DEPARTMENT OF THE TREASURY

15th and Pennsylvania Ave., NW., 20220, phone 622–2000, http://www.ustreas.gov

JOHN W. SNOW, Secretary of the Treasury; born on August 2, 1939, in Toledo, OH; education: Kenyon College, University of Toledo, B.A., 1962; University of Virginia, Ph.D. in Economics, 1965; George Washington University School of Law, LL.B., 1967; Kenyon College, Honorary Degree, LL.D., 1993; professional: Attorney; Assistant Professor of Economics, University of Maryland, 1965–67; Wheeler & Wheeler (law firm), 1967–72; Adjunct Professor of Law, George Washington University Law School, 1972–75; Assistant General Counsel, U.S. Department of Transportation (DOT), 1972–73; Deputy Assistant Secretary for Policy Plans, and International Affairs, DOT, 1973–74; Assistant Secretary for Governmental Affairs, DOT, 1974–75; Deputy Undersecretary, DOT, 1975–76; Administrator, National Highway Traffic Safety Administration, 1976–77; Visiting Professor of Economics, University of Virginia, 1977; Visiting Fellow, American Enterprise Institute, 1977; Vice President for Governmental Affairs, Chessie System, Inc., 1977–80; Senior Vice President for Corporate Services, CSX Corp., 1980–84; Executive Vice President, CSX Corp., 1984–85; President and Chief Executive Officer, Chessie System Railroads, 1985–86; President and Chief Executive Officer, CSX Rail Transport, 1986–87; President and Chief Executive Officer, CSX Transportation, 1987–88; President and Chief Operating Officer, CSX Corp., 1988–89; President and Chief Executive Officer, CSX Corp., 1989–91; Chairman, President, and Chief Executive Officer, CSX Corp., 1991–2002; religion: Episcopal; family: married to Carolyn Kalk Snow; children: Bradley, Ian, and Christopher; nominated by President George W. Bush to become the 73rd Secretary of the Treasury on December 9, 2002; and was confirmed by the U.S. Senate on January 30, 2003.

OFFICE OF THE SECRETARY

Secretary of the Treasury.—John W. Snow, room 3330, 622–1100.
Executive Assistant.—Deborah Grubbs, 622–0425.
Confidential Assistant.—Cheryl Matera, 622–0190.

OFFICE OF THE DEPUTY SECRETARY

Deputy Secretary.—[Vacant], room 3326, 622–1080.
Executive Assistants: Reavie Harvey, Marsha Valentic.
Senior Advisor.—Peter McPherson, room 3022, 622–1080.

OFFICE OF THE CHIEF OF STAFF

Chief of Staff.—Timothy Adams, room 3408, 622 1906.
Review Analyst.—Shirley Gathers.
Deputy Chief of Staff.—[Vacant].
Senior Advisor to the Secretary.—[Vacant].
Counselor to the Secretary.—Christopher Smith, room 3418, 622–4358.

OFFICE OF THE EXECUTIVE SECRETARY

Senior Advisor/Executive Secretary.—Jeffrey Kupfer, room 3408, 622–0064.
Deputy Executive Secretary.—Paul Curry, room 3414, 622–0298.
Review Analyst.—[Vacant].
Special Assistant to the Executive Secretary.—Benjamin Getto, room 3414, 622–2143.
Special Assistant to the Secretary (National Security).—Michael L. Romey, room 2049, 622–1841.
Senior National Intelligence Adviser.—Laurie Kurtzweg, room 2049, 622–1843.

OFFICE OF THE GENERAL COUNSEL

General Counsel.—David D. Aufhauser, room 3000, 622–0283.
Deputy General Counsel.—George Wolfe, 622–6362.
Associate Deputy General Counsel.—[Vacant].
Counselor to the General Counsel.—Thomas M. McGivern, room 3010, 622–2317.
Deputy Counselor to the General Counsel.—Traci J. Sanders, room 3014, 622–2744.
Administrative Officer.—Robert T. Foss, Jr., room 1421, 622–0302.
Assistant General Counsels:
Banking and Finance.—Roberta McInerney, room 2026, 622–1988.
Enforcement.—Michael T. Schmitz (acting), room 2000, 622–1931.
General Law and Ethics.—Kenneth R. Schmalzbach, room 1410, 622–0450.
International Affairs.—Russell L. Munk, room 2314, 622–1899.
Deputy Assistant General Counsels: Eleni Constantine, room 2014, 622–1934; Ellen McClain room 2000, 622–1931; Marilyn L. Muench, room 2013, 622–1986.
Chief Counsel, Foreign Assets Control.—Barbara C. Hammerle (acting), room 3123, 622–2410.
Counsel to the Inspector General for Tax Administration.—Mary Ann Curtin, room 3039, 622–4068.

OFFICE OF THE INSPECTOR GENERAL

Inspector General.—Jeffrey Rush, Jr., room 4436, 622–1090.
Deputy Inspector General.—Dennis S. Schindel, 622–1090.
Counsel to the Inspector General.—Richard Delmar, room 110, 927–0650.
Assistant Inspector General for Investigations.—Michael C. Tarr, room 500, 927–5260.
Deputy Assistant Inspector General for Investigations.—Elizabeth M. Redman.
Assistant Inspector General for Management Services.—Adam Silverman, room 510, 927–5200.
Assistant Inspector General for Audit.—Dennis S. Schindel, room 600, 927–5400.
Deputy Assistant Inspector General for Audit.—Marla Freedman, 927–5420.
Deputy Assistant Inspector General for Audit (CF0).—William Pugh, 927–5400.
Director of:
Human Resources.—Edith A. Greenip, room 510, 927–6552.
Asset Management.—Judy Mullen, room 510, 927–5023.

OFFICE OF THE ASSISTANT SECRETARY FOR LEGISLATIVE AFFAIRS

Assistant Secretary.—John Duncan, room 3025, 622–1900.
Deputy to the Assistant Secretary.—Tim Keeler, room 2124B, 622–0585.
Scheduling Coordinator.—Janet L. Jones, room 3025, 622–0581.
Legislative Assistant (Appropriations and Management).—Cherry Grayson, room 3025, 622–0555.
Senior Advisor.—David Merkel, room 3132, 622–0725.
Senior Legislative Specialist.—Andy Fishburn, room 3028, 622–6620.
Deputy Assistant Secretary for—
Appropriations and Management.—Art Cameron, room 3040, 622–1940.
Banking and Finance.—Laura Cox, room 2202, 622–6773.
Enforcement.—Katie Quinn, room 3021, 622–0725.
Tax and Budget.—James T. Young, room 3034, 622–1980.

OFFICE OF THE ASSISTANT SECRETARY FOR PUBLIC AFFAIRS

Assistant Secretary.—Robert Nichols (acting), room 3438, 622–2920.
Deputy Assistant Secretary.—Robert Nichols, room 2217, 622–2910.
Director (Public Education).—[Vacant], room 2222.
Director (Public Affairs).—Tony Fratto, room 2321, 622–2016.
Chief of Staff (Education).—[Vacant], room 1124.
Review Analyst and Scheduling Coordinator.—[Vacant], room 2217.

OFFICE OF THE UNDER SECRETARY FOR INTERNATIONAL AFFAIRS

Under Secretary.—John Taylor, room 3432, 622–0656.
Senior Advisors: Ramin Toloui, room 3425, 622–0395; Paul Ashin, room 4440, 622–2902.

OFFICE OF THE ASSISTANT SECRETARY FOR INTERNATIONAL AFFAIRS

Assistant Secretary.—Randal K. Quarles, room 3430, 622–1270.
Senior Advisor.—Meg Donovan, room 3425, 622–0659.
Staff Assistant.—Clara M. Robinson, room 3430, 622–1270.
Director of Program Services.—John McDowell, room 5457I, 622–1572.
Deputy Director.—Wilbur F. Monroe, room 3117, 622–1252.
Director, Office of:
International Banking and Securities Markets.—Wilbur F. Monroe (acting), room 3121, 622–1255.
International Monetary Policy.—Michele Shannon (acting), room 3101, 622–2352.
Foreign Exchange Operations.—Timothy DuLaney, room 2405, 622–2052.
Industrial Nations IMI and Global Analyses.—Robert Harlow (acting), room 3113, 622–0157.
East Asian Nations.—Albert Keidel (acting), room 4423, 622–0337.
Latin American and Caribbean Nations.—Steve Backes, room 5132H, 622–2876.
International Trade.—[Vacant], room 4109.
International Investment.—Gay S. Sills, room 4201, 622–9066.
Trade Finance.—Stephen F. Tvardek, room 2121, 622–1749.
International Financial Affairs.—T. Whittier Warthin, room 4401, 622–1733.
Central and Eastern European Nations.—Karen Mathiasen, room 5441J, 622–9190.
Middle Eastern and Central Asian Nations.—Anna Gelpern, room 54441C, 622–0603.
Technical Assistance.—Ged Smith, room 4000, 622–5787.
Middle East and South Asian Nations.—W. Larry McDonald, room 5400, 622–5504.
African Nations.—[Vacant], room 4407.
Development Banks.—Sara Paulson, room 3501, 622–1231.
International Debt Policy.—Michael Kaplan, room 3311, 622–6865.
Development Finance.—[Vacant], room 3317.
Deputy Assistant Secretary for—
International Development, Debt and Environmental Policy.—Williams E. Schuerch, room 3222, 622–0154.
International Monetary and Financial Policy.—Mark Sobel, room 3105, 622–0168.
Trade and Investment Policy.—[Vacant].
Eurasia and the Middle East.—Nancy Lee, room 5444D, 622–2916.
Technical Assistance Policy.—James H. Fall III, room 4422, 622–0667.
International Debt, Development and Quantitative Policy Analysis.—Clay Lowery, room 5132H, 622–0070.

OVERSEAS

U.S. Director of:
African Development Bank and Fund (Abidjan, Ivory Coast).—Cynthia Shepard Perry, 9–011–225–20–20–4015.
Asian Development Bank (Manila, Philippines).—Paul W. Speltz, 9–011–632–632–6050.
European Bank for Reconstruction and Development.—Mark Sullivan, 9–011–44–207–338–6502.
U.S. Executive Director of:
Inter-American Development Bank.—Jose Fourquet, 9–623–1033
International Bank for Reconstruction and Development.—Carole Brookins, 9–458–0110.
International Monetary Fund.—Nancy P. Jacklin, 9–623–7759.

OFFICE OF THE UNDER SECRETARY FOR DOMESTIC FINANCE

Under Secretary.—Peter R. Fisher, room 3312, 622–2044.
Senior Advisor.—[Vacant], room 2416.
Review Analyst.—Diana Ridgway, room 3312, 622–1703.

OFFICE OF THE FISCAL ASSISTANT SECRETARY

Fiscal Assistant Secretary.—Donald Hammond, room 2039, 622–0560.
Deputy Assistant.—Robert Reid, room 5323, 622–0550.
Director, Office of Cash and Debt Management.—David Monroe, room 5308, 622–1813.

FINANCIAL MANAGEMENT SERVICE

401 14th Street, SW., 20227, phone 874–6740, fax 874–6743

Commissioner.—Richard L. Gregg.
Deputy Commissioner.—Kenneth R. Papaj.
Assistant Commissioner for—
Agency Services.—Kerry Lanham.
Debt Management Services.—Martin Mills.
Federal Finance.—Bettsy H. Lane.
Financial Operations.—Judith R. Tillman.
Governmentwide Accounting.—D. James Sturgill.
Information Resources.—Nancy C. Fleetwood.
Management (Chief Financial Officer).—Scott Johnson.
Regional Operations.—Anthony Torrice.
Chief Counsel.—Debra Diener.
Director for Legislative and Public Affairs.—Alvina M. McHale.

BUREAU OF THE PUBLIC DEBT

E Street Building, Room 553, 20239, phone 219–3300, fax 219–3391

[Codified under U.S.C. 31, section 306]

Commissioner.—F. Van Zeck, 691–3500.
Deputy Commissioner.—Anne Meister.
Assistant Commissioner for—
Administration.—Glenn E. Ball, (304) 480–6514.
Office of Information Technology.—Cynthia Springer, (304) 480–6988.
Financing.—Carl Locken, 691–3550.
Public Debt Accounting.—Debra Hines, (304) 480–5101.
Office of Securities Operations.—John Swales, (304) 480–6515.
Office of Investor Services.—Frederick Pyatt, (304) 480–7730.
Chief Counsel.—Brian Ferrell, 691–3520.
Executive Director, Marketing Office.—Paul T. Vogelzang, 691–3535.

OFFICE OF THE ASSISTANT SECRETARY FOR ECONOMIC POLICY

Assistant Secretary.—Richard Clarida, room 3454, 622–2200.
Deputy Assistant Secretary for—
Macroeconomics Analysis.—[Vacant].
Policy Coordination.—James Carter, room 3445, 622–2220.
Microeconomic Analysis.—Mark Warshawsky, room 3445, 622–0563.
Director, Office of Microeconomic Analysis.—John Worth (acting), room 4423, 622–2683.
Director, Office of Macroeconomic Analysis.—Karen Hendershot (acting), room 2442, 622–1683.

OFFICE OF THE ASSISTANT SECRETARY FOR FINANCIAL INSTITUTIONS

Assistant Secretary.—Wayne A. Abernathy, room 2326, 622–2610.
Deputy Assistant Secretary, Office of:
Consumer Affairs and Community Policy.—Brian Tishuk (acting), room 3172, 622–0713.
Critical Infrastructure Protection and Compliance Policy.—Michael A. Dawson, room 3170, 622–0101
Financial Education.—Judy Chapa, room 2414, 622–5770.
Director, Office of:
Community Development Financial Institutions Fund.—Tony Brown, room 601, 622–8530.
Financial Institutions Policy.—Edward J. DeMarco, room 3160, 622–2792.
Financial Institutions and GSE Policy.—Gregory Zerzan, room 2416, 622–0430.
Sallie Mae Oversight.—Philip Quinn, room 5015, 622–0270.

OFFICE OF THE ASSISTANT SECRETARY FOR FINANCIAL MARKETS

Assistant Secretary.—Brian Carleton Roseboro, room 2334, 622–1715.
Deputy Assistant Secretary, Office of:
Accounting Operation.—Robert Reid, room 5323, 622–0550.
Fiscal Operations and Policy.—[Vacant].
Federal Finance.—Timothy Bitsberger, room 2334, 622–2245.
Government Financial Policy.—Roger Kodat, room 2412, 622–7073
Regulaotry, Tariff and Trade.—Timothy Skud (acting), room 4004, 622–0230.
Terrorism/Violent Crimes.—Juan Zarate, room 4328, 622–1466.
Director, Office of:
Advanced Counterfeit Deterrence.—Reese Fuller, room 5008, 622–1822.
Asset Forfeiture.—Raymond Dineen, room 700, 622–9600.
Cash and Debt Management.—David Monroe, room 5308, 622–1813.
Federal Finance Policy Analysis.—Norman K. Carleton, room 5011, 622–1855.
Foreign Assets Control.—R. Richard Newcomb, room 2233, 622–2500.
Government Financing.—Kerry Lanham, room SC–1, 622–2460.
Market Finance.—Paul F. Malvey, room 5020, 622–1881.
Money Laundering/Financial Crimes.—Danny Glaser, room 4406, 622–1943.
Trade and Tariff Affairs.—Timothy Skud, room 4004, 622–0230.

OFFICE OF THE ASSISTANT SECRETARY FOR TAX POLICY

Assistant Secretary.—Pamela Olson, room 3120, 622–0050.
Deputy Assistant Secretary for—
Regulatory Affairs.—Eric Solomon, room 3104, 622–0868.
Tax Analysis.—Drew Lyon, room 3064–A, 622–0120.
Tax Policy.—Gregory Jenner, room 3112, 622–0140.
Tax Legislative Counsel.—Helen Hubbard, room 3108, 622–1776.
Deputy Tax Legislative Counsel.—John Parcell (acting), room 1010, 622–2578.
Deputy Tax Legislative Counsels for—
Regulatory Affairs.—[Vacant].
Legislative Affairs.—[Vacant].
Deputy, International Tax Counsels: Carl Dubert, room 1018, 622–0222; Patricia Brown, room 5064, 622–1781.
Benefits Tax Counsel.—Bill Sweetnam, room 1000, 622–1357.
Director, Office of:
Tax Analysis.—Donald Kiefer, room 4116, 622–0269.
Economic Modeling and Computer Applications.—Paul Dobbins (acting), room 4138, 622–0848.
International Taxation.—William Randolph, room 5117, 622–0471.
Individual Taxation.—James R. Nunns, room 5406, 622–1328.
Business Taxation.—Geraldine A. Gerardi, room 4025, 622–1782.
Revenue Estimating.—Joel Platt, room 4112, 622–0259.

OFFICE OF THE ASSISTANT SECRETARY FOR MANAGEMENT / CHIEF FINANCIAL OFFICER

Assistant Secretary for Management.—Teresa Mullett Ressel (acting), room 2426, 622–0410.
Deputy Assistant for—
Information Systems/Chief Information Officer.—Mike Parker, room 2423, 622–1200.
Human Resources.—Earl Wright, room 6100, 622–1280.
Management Operations.—[Vacant], room 400–W, 622–0520.
Management and Budget.—Timothy Weatherford, room 2434, 622–2400.
Chiefs of:
Business Practices.—Mayi Canales, room 3E003, 927–7449.
Finance.—Seven Apps, room 3170, 622–2400.
Management and Administrative Programs.—Earl Wright (acting), room 6100, 622–1280.
Deputy Chief Financial Officer.—Barry K. Hudson, room 6253, 622–0750.
Director of:
Accounting and Internal Control.—James R. Lingebach, room 6263, 622–0818.
Asset Management.—Carolyn Austin-Diggs, room 400–W, 622–0022.
Budget.—Janice Lambert, room 6129, 622–8614.
Business Reengineering.—[Vacant].

Customer Service Consulting.—[Vacant].
Customer Service Infrastructure and Operations.—Patrick Hargett, room 12106, 622–7704.
Customer Solutions.—John Dyer (acting), room 2421, 622–0163.
Departmental Budget Execution.—Sandra M. Penny, room 6241, 622–1124.
Equal Opportunity.—Marcia Hall Coates, room 6069, 622–1170.
Facilities Management.—Wesley L. Hawley (acting), room 1400, 622–1350.
Financial Management.—[Vacant].
Financial Systems Integration.—David J. Epstein, room 6251, 622–0440.
IRS Management Board.—[Vacant].
IT Policy and Strategy.—Steve Bryant (acting), room 2111, 622–1549.
Information Services.—Veronica Marco, room 6901, 622–2477.
Information Systems Security.—Michelle Moldenhauer, room 3090, 622–1110.
Pensions.—Mary Beth Shaw, room 6267, 622–1068
Personnel Policy.—Ronald A. Glaser, room 6075, 622–1890.
Personnel Resources Division.—Barbara A. Borg, room 6109, 622–2209.
Printing and Graphics.—Melissa Hartman, room B–39, 622–1409.
Procurement.—[Vacant], room 400–W, 622–0520.
Procurement Services.—[Vacant].
Safety, Health and Environment.—Stuart Burns, room 6179, 622–0412.
Security.—Patrick J. Geary, room 3210, 622–3210.
Security/Infrastructure Protection.—[Vacant], room 2154, 622–1592.
Small and Disadvantaged Business Utilization.—Jody Falvey (acting), room 4W–704, 622–2826.
Strategic Planning and Evaluation.—Carl Froehlich, room 6133, 622–2228.
Travel and Special Events.—Lillian Wright (acting), room 6210, 622–0917.
Treasury Building.—David A. Lingrell, room 4170, 622–0877.
Treasury Executive Institute.—Marie Bauer, 622–9311.
Deputy Directors:
Outreach Programs.—Daniel F. Sturdivant, room 4W–703, 622–0375.
Pensions.—Peter Mackey, room 668, 622–0997.
FMD Accounting Officer.—John Roberts, room 200–E, 622–1067.

OFFICE OF THE TREASURER OF THE UNITED STATES

Treasurer.—[Vacant], 622–0100.
Special Assistants: Shirley L. Wheat; Karen Duncan.

UNITED STATES MINT

801 9th Street, NW., 20002, phone 354–7200, fax 756–6160

Director.—Henrietta Holsman Fore.
Executive Assistant to the Director.—Arnetta Cain.
Deputy Director.—David A. Lebryk.
Staff Assistant to the Deputy Director.—Pamela Carr.
Chief Counsel.—Dan Shaver.
Director of Legislative and Intergovernmental Affairs.—Madelyn Simmons.
Director of Public Affairs.—Becky Bailey.
Associate Director (Protection Strategic Business Unit).—William F. Daddio.
Deputy Director (Protection Strategic Business Unit).—Bill R. Bailey.
Associate Director/Chief Information Officer.—Jerry Horton.
Deputy Associate Director/Chief Information Officer.—Jay Mahanand.
Associate Director/Chief Financial Officer.—Jay Weinstein.
Deputy Associate Director/Deputy Chief Financial Officer.—Mike Green.
Associate Director (Numismatic Strategic Business Unit).—Gloria Eskridge.
Deputy Associate Director (Numismatic Strategic Business Unit).—Jim Riedford.
Associate Director (Circulating Strategic Business Unit).—Brad Cooper.
Deputy Associate Director (Circulating Strategic Business Unit).—Scott Myers.

BUREAU OF ENGRAVING AND PRINTING

14th and C Streets, NW., 20228, phone 874–2000

[Created by act of July 11, 1862; codified under U.S.C. 31, section 303]

Director.—Thomas A. Ferguson, 874–2000, fax 874–3879.
Chief Counsel.—Carrol H. Kinsey, 874–5363, fax 874–5710.
Associate Directors:
Chief Financial Officer.—Gregory D. Carper, 874–2020, fax 874–2025.
Chief Information Officer.—Ronald W. Falter, 874–3000, fax 927–1757.
Chief Operating Officer.—William W. Wills, 874–2030, fax 874–2034.
Associate Director for—
Management.—Joel C. Taub, 874–2040, fax 874–2043.
Technology.—Carla F. Kidwell, 874–2008, fax 874–2009.

OFFICE OF THE COMPTROLLER OF THE CURRENCY

250 E Street, SW., 20219, phone 874–5000

Comptroller.—John D. Hawke, Jr., 874–4900.
Chief of Staff/Sr. Deputy Comptroller (Public Affairs).—Mark A. Nishan (acting), 874–4880.
First Senior Deputy Comptroller/Chief Counsel.—Julie L. Williams, 874–5200.
Director for Congressional Liaison.—Carolyn Z. McFarlane, 874–4840.
Senior Deputy Comptroller of:
Midsize/Community Bank Supervision.—Timothy W. Long, 874–5020.
International and Economic Affairs.—Jonathan L. Fiechter, 874–5010.
Management.—Edward J. Hanley, 874–5080.
Large Bank Supervision.—Douglas W. Roeder, 874–4610.
Chief National Bank Examiner.—Emory W. Rushton, 874–2870.
Ombudsman.—Samuel P. Golden, (713) 336–4350.
Chief Information Officer.—Jackie Fletcher, 874–4480.

INTERNAL REVENUE SERVICE

Internal Revenue Building, 1111 Constitution Avenue, NW., 20224, phone 622–5000

[Created by act of July 1, 1862; codified under U.S.C. 26, section 7802]

Commissioner.—Mark W. Everson, 622–9511.
Deputy Commissioner, Services and Enforcement.—Bob Wenzel, 622–4255.
Commissioner of:
Large and Mid-Size Business.—Deborah Nolan, 283–8710.
Small Business/Self-Employed.—Dale Hart, 622–0600.
Tax Exempt and Government Entities.—Evelyn Petschek, 283–2500.
Wage and Investment.—Henry O. Lamar, Jr., 622–6860.
Chief, Criminal Investigation.—David B. Palmer, 622–3200.
Director, Office of Professional Responsibility.—Brien Downing, 694–1891.
Deputy Commissioner, Operations Support.—John M. Dalrymple, 622–6860.
Chief:
Information Officer.—W. Todd Grams, 622–6800.
Agency-Wide Shared Services.—Bill Boswell, 622–7500.
Financial Officer.—Eileen Powell (acting), 622–6400.
Human Capital Officer.—[Vacant].
Mission Assurance.—[Vacant].
Chief Counsel.—B. John Williams, Jr., 622–3300.
Chief, Appeals.—David Robison, 694–1800.
National Taxpayer Advocate.—Nina E. Olson, 622–6100.
Chief, EEO and Diversity.—John M. Robinson, 622–5400.
Director, Research, Analysis and Statistics.—Mark J. Mazur, 874–0100.
Chief, Communications and Liaison.—David R. Williams, 622–5440.
Inspector General TIGTA.—Pamela J. Gardiner (acting), 622–6500.

OFFICE OF THRIFT SUPERVISION

1700 G Street, NW., 20552, phone 906–6000, fax 906–7494, 906–7495

[Codified in U.S.C. 12, section 1462a]

Director.—James Gilleran, 906–6590.
Deputy Director.—Richard M. Riccobono, 906–6853.
Managing Director, Supervision.—Scott M. Albinson, 906–7984.
Chief Counsel.—Carolyn J. Buck, 906–6251.
Director of:
External Affairs.—Kevin Petrasic, 906–6288.
Information Systems, Administration and Finance (CEO and CIO).—Timothy T. Ward, 906–5666.

DEPARTMENT OF DEFENSE

The Pentagon 20301–1155, phone (703) 545–6700

fax (703) 695–3362/693–2161, www.defenselink.mil

DONALD H. RUMSFELD, Secretary of Defense; born on July 9, 1932, in Chicago, IL; education: A.B., Princeton University, 1954; military service: U.S. Navy, 1954–1957, served as a Naval aviator; professional: congressional assistant, 1958–1959; investment broker, 1960–1962; elected to the U.S. House of Representatives, 1963–1969; Assistant to the President, and Director of the Office of Economic Opportunity, 1969–1970; Counselor to the President, and Director of the Economic Stabilization Program, 1971–1972; U.S. Ambassador to NATO, 1973–1974; Chief of Staff for President Gerald R. Ford, 1974–1975; Secretary of Defense, 1975–1977; CEO, President, and then Chairman of G.D. Searle & Co., 1977–1985; private business, 1985–1990; Chairman and CEO of General Instrument Corp., 1990–1993; Chairman, Gilead Sciences, Inc., 1997–2000; nominated by President George W. Bush to become the 21st Secretary of Defense, and was confirmed by the U.S. Senate on January 20, 2001.

OFFICE OF THE SECRETARY

Pentagon, Room 3E880, 20301–1000, phone (703) 692–7100, fax (703) 697–9080

Secretary of Defense.—Donald H. Rumsfeld.

OFFICE OF THE DEPUTY SECRETARY

Pentagon, Room 3E944, 20301–1000, phone (703) 692–7150

Deputy Secretary of Defense.—Paul Wolfowitz.

EXECUTIVE SECRETARIAT

Pentagon, Room 3E880, 20301–1000, phone (703) 692–7125, fax (703) 697–9080

Executive Secretary.—COL James A. Whitmore, USAF.

UNDER SECRETARY OF DEFENSE FOR ACQUISITION AND TECHNOLOGY

Pentagon, Room 3E933, 20301, phone (703) 693–4265

Under Secretary.—Pete Aldridge.
Principal Deputy.—Michael Wynne.
Deputy Under Secretary for—
Industrial Policy.—Suzanne Patrick.
Installations and Environment.—Raymond F. DuBois.
Logistics.—Diane Morales.
Director, Small and Disadvantaged Business Utilization.—Frank M. Ramos.
Director, Defense Research and Engineering.—Ron Sega.
Deputy Under Secretary for—
Advanced Systems and Concepts.—Sue Payton.
Science and Technology.—Charles Holland.
Assistant to the Secretary of Defense for Nuclear and Chemical and Biological Defense Programs.—Dale Klein.

UNDER SECRETARY OF DEFENSE FOR POLICY

Pentagon, Room 4E808, 20301–2000, phone (703) 697–7200

Under Secretary.—Douglas Feith.
Principal Deputy Under Secretary.—Ryan Henry.
Assistant Secretary of Defense for—
International Security Affairs.—Peter Rodman.
International Security Policy.—Jack Dyer Crouch II.
Homeland Defense.—Paul McHale.
Special Operations and Low-Intensity Conflict.—[Vacant].
Defense Advisor, US Mission NATO.—Evan Galbraith.
Deputy Under Secretary (Technology Security Policy).—David Tarbell.

COMPTROLLER

Pentagon, Room 3E822, 20301–1100, phone (703) 695–3237

Under Secretary/Chief Financial Officer.—Dov Zakheim.
Principal Deputy Under Secretary.—Lawrence Lanzillotta.
Director, Program Analysis and Evaluation.—[Vacant].

PERSONNEL AND READINESS

Pentagon, Room 3E764, 20301–4000, phone (703) 695–5254

Under Secretary.—David S.C. Chu.
Principal Deputy Under Secretary.—Charles Abell.
Assistant Secretary for—
Health Affairs.—William Winkenwerder.
Reserve Affairs.—Thomas Hall.
Deputy Under Secretary for—
Readiness.—Paul Mayberry.
Program Integration.—Jeanne Fites.

GENERAL COUNSEL

Pentagon, Room 3E980, 20301–1600, phone (703) 695–3341, fax (703) 614–9789

General Counsel.—William J. Haynes.

OPERATIONAL TEST AND EVALUATION

Pentagon, Room 3A1073, 20301–1700, phone (703) 697–3654, fax (703) 693–5248

Director.—Thomas Christie.

INSPECTOR GENERAL

400 Army Navy Drive, Room 1000, Arlington VA 22202, phone (703) 604–8300
fax 604–8310, hotline 1–800–424–9098, hotline fax 604–8567

Inspector General.—Joseph Schmitz.

ASSISTANT SECRETARY FOR COMMAND, CONTROL, COMMUNICATIONS AND INTELLIGENCE (C^3I)

Pentagon, Room 3E172, 20301–3040, phone (703) 695–0348

Assistant Secretary.—John Stenbit.

ASSISTANT SECRETARY FOR LEGISLATIVE AFFAIRS

Pentagon, Room 3E966, 20301–1300, phone (703) 697–6210, fax (703) 697–8299

Assistant Secretary.—Powell Moore.

ASSISTANT TO THE SECRETARY OF DEFENSE FOR INTELLIGENCE OVERSIGHT

Crown Ridge Building, 4035 Ridge Top Road, Suite 210, Fairfax, VA 22030
phone (703) 275–6575

Assistant to the Secretary.—George B. Lotz II.

ASSISTANT SECRETARY FOR PUBLIC AFFAIRS

Pentagon, Room 2E800, 20301–1400, phone (703) 697–9312, fax (703) 695–1149
public inquiries (703) 697–5737

Assistant Secretary.—Larry DiRita (acting).

ADMINISTRATION AND MANAGEMENT

Pentagon, Room 3D972, 20301–1950, phone (703) 695–4436

Director.—Raymond F. DuBois.

DEPARTMENT OF DEFENSE FIELD ACTIVITIES

AMERICAN FORCES INFORMATION SERVICE

601 North Fairfax Street, Room 300, EFC Plaza, Alexandria, VA 22314
phone (703) 428–1200

Director.—Larry DiRita (acting).
Deputy Director.—[Vacant], room 300, (703) 428–1202.
General Counsel.—M. Filice, room 300, (703) 428–1204.
Director for Armed Forces Radio and Television Services.—Melvin W. Russell, room 360, (703) 428–0616.

DEPARTMENT OF DEFENSE EDUCATION ACTIVITY

4040 North Fairfax Drive, Arlington, VA 22203
school information (703) 696–4236

Director.—Dr. Joseph Tafoya.
Associate Director for Education.—Elizabeth Middlemiss.
Associate Director for Management.—Ms. Marilee Fitzgerald, (703) 696–3866.
General Counsel.—Maxanne Witkin, (703) 696–4387.

DEPARTMENT OF DEFENSE HUMAN RESOURCES ACTIVITY

4040 Fairfax Drive, Arlington, VA 22209, phone (703) 696–1036

Director.—David S.C. Chu.
Deputy Director.—Jeanne Fites.
Assistant Director.—Sharon Cooper, 696–0909.

TRICARE MANAGEMENT ACTIVITY

5111 Leesburg Pike, Falls Church, VA 22041, phone (703) 681–6909

Executive Director.—Thomas Carrato.
Deputy Director.—Diana Tabler.

DEFENSE PRISONER OF WAR / MISSING PERSONNEL OFFICE

1745 Jefferson Davis Highway, Suite 800, Arlington, VA 22201, phone (703) 602–2102

Director.—Jerry D. Jennings.
Deputy Director.—Alan Liotta.

OFFICE OF ECONOMIC ADJUSTMENT

400 Army Navy Drive, Suite 200, Arlington, VA 22202, phone (703) 604–6020

Director.—Paul J. Dempsey.
Deputy Director for Programs.—Patrick O'Brien, 604–5844.
Deputy Director for Management.—Dave Larson, 604–4828.
Sacramento Region Manager.—Anthony Gallegos, (916) 557–7365.

WASHINGTON HEADQUARTERS SERVICES

Pentagon, Room 3D972, 20301, phone (703) 695–4436

Director.—Raymond F. DuBois.
Director for—
Budget and Finance.—Joe Friedl, Jr., room 3B287, (703) 697–6760.
Correspondence and Directives.—Larry Curry, room 3B946, (703) 697–8261.
Federal Voting Assistance Office.—Polli Brunelli, room 14041, RPN, (703) 588–1584.
Information Operations and Reports.—Mary George (acting), room 1204, Crystal Gateway No. 3, 1215 Jefferson Davis Highway, Arlington VA 22202, (703) 604–4569.
Personnel and Security.—Janet E. Thompson, room 12063, RPN, (703) 588–0400.
Real Estate and Facilities.—Paul Haselbush, room 4A111, (703) 697–7241.
General Counsel.—Thomas R. Brooke, room 1E197, (703) 693–7374.
Freedom of Information and Security Review.—Henry McIntyre, room 2C757, (703) 697–4325.
Defense Privacy Office.—Vahn Moushegian, Jr., 920, CM4, 703 607–2943.

JOINT CHIEFS OF STAFF

OFFICE OF THE CHAIRMAN

Pentagon, Room 2E872, 20318–0001, phone (703) 697–9121

Chairman.—GEN Richard B. Myers, USAF.
Vice Chairman.—GEN Peter Pace, USMC, room 2E860, (703) 614–8948, (703) 614–2500.
Assistant to Chairman, Joint Chiefs of Staff.—VADM Walter F. Doran, USN, room 2E868, (703) 695–4605.

JOINT STAFF

Director.—LTG George W. Casey, USA, room 2E936, (703) 614–5221.
Vice Director.—MG James Hawkins, USA, room 2E936, (703) 614–5223.
Director for—
Manpower and Personnel, J–1.—BG Maria Cribbs, USAF, room 1E948, (703) 697–6098.
Intelligence, J–2.—MG Glen Shaffer, USN, room 1E880, (703) 697–9773.
Operations, J–3.—LTG Norton Schwartz, USMC, room 2D874, (703) 697–3702.
Logistics, J–4.—VADM G.S. Holder, USN, room 2E828, (703) 697–7000.
Strategic Plans and Policy, J–5.—LTG Walter Sharp, USA, room 2E996, (703) 695–5618.
Command, Control, Communications and Computer Systems, J–6.—LTG Joseph K. Kellogg, Jr., USA, room 2D860, (703) 695–6478.
Operational Plans and Interoperability, J–7.—BG Mark Hertling, USMC, room 2B865, (703) 697–9031.
Force Structure, Resource, and Assessment, J–8.—LTG James Cartwright, USAF, room 1E962, (703) 697–8853.

DEFENSE AGENCIES

MISSILE DEFENSE AGENCY

Pentagon, Room 1E1081, 20301–7100, phone (703) 695–8040

Director.—LTG Ronald T. Kadish, (703) 693–3025.
Deputy Director.—MG Peter C. Franklin, (703) 695–7060.

DEFENSE ADVANCED RESEARCH PROJECTS AGENCY

3701 North Fairfax Drive, Arlington, VA 22203, phone (703) 696–2444

Director.—Anthony Tether.
Deputy Director.—Jane Alexander, (703) 696–2402.

DEFENSE COMMISSARY AGENCY

Fort Lee, VA 23801, phone (804) 734–8721

Director.—MG Robert J. Courter, Jr., USA.
Executive Director for Operations and Product Support.—Scott E. Simpson.
Executive Director for Capital Investment.—Crosby H. Johnson.
Executive Director for Resources.—COL Ed Jones, USAF.

LIAISON OFFICE

Pentagon, Room 1B657, 20330–5130, phone (703) 614–9225

Director.—Daniel W. Schlater.

DEFENSE CONTRACT AUDIT AGENCY

**8725 John J. Kingman Road, Suite 2135, Fort Belvoir, VA 22060
phone (703) 767–3200**

Director.—William H. Reed.
Deputy Director.—Michael J. Thibault, (703) 767–3272.

DEFENSE FINANCE AND ACCOUNTING SERVICE

**Crystal Mall Building No. 3, 1931 Jefferson Davis Highway, Arlington, VA 22240
phone (703) 607–2616**

Director.—Thomas Bloom, room 425.
Principal Deputy Director.—RADM Mark A. Young, USN, room 425, (703) 607–1467.

DEFENSE INFORMATION SYSTEMS AGENCY

701 South Court House Road, Arlington, VA 22204, phone (703) 607–6020

Director.—LTG Harry D. Raduege, Sr., USAF, room 4222, (703) 607–6001.
Vice Director.—MG James D. Bryan, USA, room 4222, (703) 607–6010.

DEFENSE INTELLIGENCE AGENCY

Pentagon, Room 3E258, 20340–7400, phone (703) 695–0071

Director.—VADM Thomas R. Wilson, USN.
Deputy Director.—Mark W. Ewing, room 3E258, (703) 697–5128.

DEFENSE SECURITY SERVICE

1340 Braddock Place, Alexandria, VA 22314, phone (703) 325–5324

Director.—William A. Curtis (acting).
Deputy Director.—Michael G. Newman.

DEFENSE LEGAL SERVICES AGENCY

Pentagon, Room 3E980, 20301–1600, phone (703) 695–3341

Director/General Counsel.—William J. Haynes.
Principal Deputy Director.—Daniel Dell'Orto, (703) 697–7248.

DEFENSE LOGISTICS AGENCY

8725 John J. Kingman Road, Suite 2533, Ft. Belvoir, VA 22060 phone (703) 767–6666

Director.—VADM Keith W. Lippert, USN, (703) 767–5200.
Vice Director.—MG Mary L. Saunders, USAF, (703) 767–5222.

DEFENSE SECURITY COOPERATION AGENCY

1111 Jefferson Davis Highway, Suite 303, Arlington, VA 22202, phone (703) 604–6604

Director.—LTG Tome H. Walters, USAF.
Deputy Director.—Richard Millies (703) 604–6606.

NATIONAL IMAGERY AND MAPPING AGENCY

4600 Sangamore Road, Bethesda, MD 20816, phone (301) 227–7400

Director.—LTG James R. Clapper, Jr., USAF (Ret.).
Deputy Director.—Joanne Isham.

NATIONAL SECURITY AGENCY/CENTRAL SECURITY SERVICE

Ft. George G. Meade, MD 20755, phone (301) 688–6524

Director.—MG Michael V. Hayden, USAF.
Deputy Director.—William B. Black, Jr.

DEFENSE THREAT REDUCTION AGENCY

45045 Aviation Drive, Dulles, VA 20166, phone (703) 325–2102

Director.—MG Robert P. Bongiovi (acting), USAF.
Deputy Director.—MG Robert P. Bongiovi, USAF.

JOINT SERVICE SCHOOLS

DEFENSE ACQUISITION UNIVERSITY

President.—BG F. Anderson, Jr., (Ret.) (703) 845–6733.

JOINT MILITARY INTELLIGENCE COLLEGE

President.—A. Denis Clift, (202) 231–3344.

DEFENSE SYSTEMS MANAGEMENT COLLEGE

Commandant.—COL James R. Moran, USA, (703) 805–3360.

NATIONAL DEFENSE UNIVERSITY

Bldg. 62, 300 Fifth Avenue, Fort McNair, Washington, DC 20319 phone (202) 685–3912

President.—VADM Paul Gaffney, room 308, (202) 685–3922.
Vice President.— Daniel H. Simpson, (202) 685–3923.

INFORMATION RESOURCES MANAGEMENT COLLEGE

Dean of the College.—Robert D. Childs, (202) 685–3884.

ARMED FORCES STAFF COLLEGE

Commandant.—BG Franklin J. Blaisdell, USAF, room A201.

INDUSTRIAL COLLEGE OF THE ARMED FORCES

Commandant.—MG H. Mashburn, Jr., USMC, room 200, (202) 685–4337.

NATIONAL WAR COLLEGE

Commandant.—RADM Daniel R. Bowler, USN, room 113, (202) 685–4312.

UNIFORMED SERVICES UNIVERSITY OF THE HEALTH SCIENCES

4301 Jones Bridge Road, Bethesda, MD 20814, phone (301) 295–3030

President.—James A. Zimble, M.D., room A1018, (301) 295–3013.

DEPARTMENT OF THE AIR FORCE

Pentagon, 1670 Air Force, Washington, DC 20330–1670

phone (703) 697–7376, fax 693–7553

SECRETARY OF THE AIR FORCE

Secretary of the Air Force.—James G. Roche, room 4E871, 697–7376.
Confidential Assistant.—Debbie Henderson, room 4E871, 697–7376.
Senior Military Assistant.—COL Janet Therianos, room 4E864, 697–4181.
Deputy Military Assistant.—LTC Suzie Wells, room 4E864, 697–4181.
Military Aid.—MAJ Robert Armfield.
Protocol.—MAJ Karen Tibus, room 4E871, 697–7376.

SECAF/CSAF EXECUTIVE ACTION GROUP

Chief.—COL Paul Schafer, room 4E941, 697–5540.
Deputy Chief.—LTC Geo Frasier, 697–5540.

UNDER SECRETARY OF THE AIR FORCE

Pentagon, 1670 Air Force, Room 4E886, Washington, DC 20330, phone 697–1361

Under Secretary.—Peter B. Teets, 697–1361.
Confidential Assistant.—Elizabeth Owen.
Senior Military Assistant.—COL Warren Henderson.
Deputy Military Assistant.—LTC Ernesto Benavides.
Executive NCO.—MSgt Stuart Lemon.

DEPUTY UNDER SECRETARY FOR INTERNATIONAL AFFAIRS

Pentagon, 1080 Air Force, Room 4E236, Washington, DC 20330–1080

Rosslyn, 1500 Wilson Blvd., 8th Floor, Arlington, VA 22209

Deputy Under Secretary.—Willard H. Mitchell, 695–7262.
Assistant Deputy.—MG Ted M. McFarland, 588–8855.
Director of Policy.—Beth M. McCormick, 588–8860.
Director of Regional Affairs.—MG Jonathan S. Gration, 588–8820.
Executive Secretary.—Georgia Smothers, 695–7261.
Senior Executive Officer.—LTC Shannon Sullivan, 695–7262.
Executive Secretary.—Pamela Eichholz, 588–8800.
Executive Officers: MAJ Jim Federwisch, 588–8833; MAJ David Keller, 588–8828.

DIRECTOR FOR SMALL AND DISADVANTAGED BUSINESS UTILIZATION

Pentagon, 1060 Air Force, SAF/SB, Washington, DC 20330–1060

Director.—Joseph G. Diamond, 696–1103.

DEPUTY ASSISTANT SECRETARY FOR ENVIRONMENT, SAFETY AND OCCUPATIONAL HEALTH

Deputy Assistant Secretary.—Maureen T. Koetz, room 5C866, 697–9297.
Principal Deputy.—LTC Rebecca Brown, room 5C866, 695–5978.

Deputy for—

ESOH Integration.—COL Richard Ashworth, room 5C866, 697–1016.

Force Health Protection.—LTC Rebecca Brown, room 5C866, 695–5978.

Readiness for Guard and Reserve Affairs.—[Vacant].

Resource Management/Air Space and Ranges.—Robert McCann, room 5C866, 697–1019.

Safety.—Vance E. Lineberger, room 5C866, 693–7706.

Assistant Deputy for—

Environmental Planning.—LTC Jeff Cornell, room 5C866, 697–0997.

Pollution Prevention.—MAJ Sharon Spradling, room 5C866, 614–8458.

DEPUTY ASSISTANT SECRETARY FOR BASING AND INFRASTRUCTURE ANALYSIS

Deputy Assistant Secretary.—Michael Aimone, room 5C230, 697–2524.

Chief Base Transition.—COL Thomas Fleming, room 5C266, 692–9515.

Chief Joint Cross Service.—COL Kevin Erickson, room 5D260, 614–8666.

DIRECTOR OF LOGISTICS

Director.—Debbie Erickson, room 4D284, 692–9090.

Chief, Depot Operations and Strategy Planning.—MAJ Theresa Humphrey, room 4D284, 693–2185.

Chief, Weapons System Depot Integration.—Sandra Meckley, room 4D284, 695–6716.

DEPUTY ASSISTANT SECRETARY FOR INSTALLATIONS

Deputy Assistant Secretary.—Fred W. Kuhn, room 4C940, 695–3592.

Assistant for Installation Management.—John E.B. Smith, room 4C940, 593–9327.

Director for—

Facility Management Programs.—COL Edward J. Pokora, room 4C940, 697–7003.

Installation Policy.—COL William A. Formwalt, room 4C940, 695–6456.

MA.—COL Karen D. Kohlhaas, room 4C940, 693–9339.

Planning and Resources.—Jean A. Reynolds, room 4C940, 697–7244.

Real Estate Policy.—Barbara J. Jenkins, room 4C940, 697–7070.

Reserve Affairs.—COL Luis A. Vazquez, room 4C940, 693–9328.

Assistant for the Air National Guard Affairs.—COL Ron Sachse, room 4C940, 693–9339.

Secretary.—Pamela L. Coghill, room 4C940, 695–3592.

Administrative Assistant.—Everette Dewaine Longus, room 4C940, 697–4391.

AIR FORCE REAL PROPERTY AGENCY

Director.—Albert F. Lowas, Jr., (703) 696–5501.

Secretary.—Lisa Cannon, 696–5503.

Deputy Director.—Joyce Frank, 696–5502.

Deputy Secretary.—LaShelle Taylor, 696–5504.

Special Assistant for Public Affairs.—Shirley W. Curry, 696–5532.

Program Managers of:

Division A.—John Corradetti, 696–5250.

Division B.—Chips Johnson, 696–5546.

Division C.—Gene Aefsky (acting), 696–0326.

Division D.—Kenneth Reinertson, 696–5540.

Division EV.—Carol Ann Beda, 696–5534.

Chief of:

Real Estate Division.—Richard D. Jenkins, 696–5552.

Legal Counsel Division.—Douglas Heady, 696–5522.

Executive Services Division.—Joyce Truett, 696–5505.

Financial Management Division.—Kathy Peters, 696–5559.

AIR FORCE REVIEW BOARDS AGENCY

Director.—Joe G. Lineberger, AAFB, Building 1535, (240) 857–3137.

Deputy Director.—[Vacant], 857–3137.

Resource Assistant.—Brenda Thomas, 857–3137.

Chief, Review Boards Management.—CMSgt. Susan Ayala, 857–3119.

AIR FORCE BOARD FOR CORRECTION OF MILITARY RECORDS (AFBCMR)

Executive Director.—Mack M. Burton, AAFB, Building 1535, (240) 857–3502.
Deputy Executive Director.—Raymond H. Weller.
Chief Examiners; John J. D'Orazio; Rose Kirkpatrick; Donna Pittenger; Ralph Prete.
Superintendent, AFBCMR Information Management.—[Vacant], 857–3502.

AIR FORCE PERSONNEL COUNCIL

Director.—COL Wayne Newman, AAFB Building 1535, (240) 857–5325.
Senior Legal Advisor.—COL Felix Losco, 857–9043.
Senior Medical Advisor.—COL Horace Carson, 857–5353.
Chief, Air Force Discharge Review Board.—LTC Tom Hammen, 857–3504.
Air National Guard Advisor.—LTC Tom Hammen.
Decoration/Air Force Reserve Advisor.—COL Lee Tucker, 857–5342.
Executive Secretary/Attorney Advisor on Clemency/Parole Board.—James D. Johnston, 857–5329.
Executive Secretary, DOD Civilian/Military Service Review Board.—James D. Johnston.

AIR FORCE CIVILIAN APPELLATE REVIEW OFFICE

Director.—Rita Looney, AAFB Building 1535, (240) 857–7071.
Chief, Appellate Liaison Unit.—J. Hayward Kight, 857–3168.

ASSISTANT SECRETARY FOR MANPOWER AND RESERVE AFFAIRS

1660 Air Force Pentagon (4E1020), Washington, DC 20330

Assistant Secretary.—Hon. Michael L. Dominguez, (703) 697–2302.
MA.—BG Jose Portela, 693–9312.
Confidential Assistant.—Ruth N. Thornton, 695–6677.
Military Assistant.—COL Westanna H. Bobbitt, 697–2303.
Executive Officer.—MAJ Jerome Williams, 697–1258.
Executive Services.—[Vacant], room 4E985.
Superintendent.—[Vacant], 697–5828.

DEPUTY ASSISTANT SECRETARY FOR FORCE MANAGEMENT AND PERSONNEL

Deputy Assistant Secretary.—Kelly F. Craven, room 5E977, 614–4751.
IMA.—COL Jane Hess, 697–7783.
Executive Secretary.—Dottie A. Baltimore, 614–4751.
Assistant Deputy for—
Civilian Personnel.—Charlene M. Bradley, 614–4753.
Family Programs.—Linda Stephens-Jones, 693–9574.
Health Affairs.—Carol J. Thompson, 693–9764.
Manpower.—[Vacant], 614–4833.
Military Personnel.—COL Dave French, 693–9333.
Services and Force Support.—LTC Steve Jones, 693–9765.

DEPUTY ASSISTANT SECRETARY FOR RESERVE AFFAIRS

Deputy Assistant Secretary.—John C. Truesdell, room 5C938.
Secretary.—Rosa R. Ramirez, 697–6375.
IMA.—COL Christina Lafferty.
Assistant for—
Air Force Reserve Affairs Matters.—COL Klaus Hoehna, 693–9505.
ANG Matters.—COL Richard Stedding, Jr., 693–9504.
Enlisted Matters.—CMSgt. Gail Paich, 697–6429.
Military Executive for Air Reserve Forces Policy Division Committee.—MAJ Laura Hunter, 697–6430.

DEPUTY ASSISTANT SECRETARY FOR EQUAL OPPORTUNITY

Deputy Assistant Secretary.—Shirley A. Martinez, room 5D973, 697–6586.
Secretary.—Karen Sauls, 697–6586.
Program Manager.—Diane C. Wakeham, 614–1619.
Assistant Deputy for Military EO.—LTC Kevin Driscoll, 697–6583.

ASSISTANT SECRETARY FOR FINANCIAL MANAGEMENT AND COMPTROLLER OF THE AIR FORCE

Pentagon, 1130 Air Force, Washington, DC 20330

CGN, Air Force Cost Analysis Agency, Crystal Gateway North

1111 Jefferson Davis Highway, Suite 403, Arlington, VA 22202

Assistant Secretary.—Michael Montelongo, room 4E984, 693–6457.
Military Assistant.—LTC Mike Phelps, 695–0837.
Chief, Enlisted Matters.—CMSgt Larry P. Gonzales, 614–5437.

PRINCIPAL DEPUTY ASSISTANT SECRETARY FOR FINANCIAL MANAGEMENT

Principal Deputy Assistant Secretary.—Bruce S. Lemkin, 697–4464.
Military Assistant.—LTC (S) Angel (Manny) Maldonado, 695–0829.

EXECUTIVE SERVICES

Superintendent.—Patricia A. Tyler, room 4D181, 697–9992.
Chief, Information Management.—[Vacant].

DEPUTY ASSISTANT SECRETARY FOR BUDGET

Deputy Assistant Secretary.—MG Stephen Lorenz, 695–1875.
Executive Officer.—LTC Ricky T. Valentine, 695–1874.
Deputy.—Robert D. Stuart, 695–1877.
Executive Assistant.—SMSgt Angela Henderson, 695–1875.

DIRECTORATE OF BUDGET AND APPROPRIATIONS LIAISON

Director.—COL Brian E. Kistner, room 5D911, 614–8114.
Division Chief for—
Appropriations Liaison.—LTC Garry G. Sauner, 614–8112.
Budget Liaison.—[Vacant].

DIRECTORATE OF BUDGET MANAGEMENT AND EXECUTION

Director.—[Vacant].
Executive Officer.—MAJ James P. Gates.
Assistant for—
Future Budget System.—Dennis T. Bryson, SSC/SBFB, 201 E. Moore Drive, Gunter AFS, AL 36114–3005, (205) 596–2708.
Information Control.—Edward Parker, Pentagon, room 5D110, 614–7702.
Policy and Fiscal Control.—Marti A. Maust, room 5D110, 695–0305.
Special Programs.—Olga Crerar, room 5C132, 614–1319.
Revolving Funds.—[Vacant].

DIRECTORATE OF BUDGET INVESTMENT

Director.—Pat Zarodkiewicz, room 4D132, 614–4996.
Executive Officer.—MAJ James P. Gates.
Assistant for—
Aircraft Procurement and Technology Programs.—COL Richard Weathers, room 5C129, 614–5701.
Military Construction and Family Housing.—Michael J. Novel, room 5D110, 697–0166.
Integration Space and Technology.—Marilyn Thomas, room 5C116, 614–4996.
Security Assistance.—Patricia Vestal, room 4D223, 695–3980.

DIRECTORATE OF BUDGET OPERATIONS

Director.—BG Sandra A. Gregory, room 4D120, 697–0627.
Executive Officer.—LTC John Long.
Assistant for—
Integration Management.—COL Rory Cahoon, room 5D110, 614–4097.
Mission Operations.—COL Barbara S. Cain, 614–3801.
Personnel and Training.—COL Roger Bick, 695–4865.

DIRECTORATE OF BUDGET PROGRAMS

Director.—COL Dave Goossens, room 5D110, 614–7883.
Deputy Director.—LTC Carl Schweinfurth, room 5D110, 614–3113.

DEPUTY ASSISTANT SECRETARY FOR COST AND ECONOMICS

Deputy Assistant Secretary.—Richard K. Hartley, room 4D159, 697–5311.
Associate Deputy Assistant Secretary.—BJ White-Olson, 697–5313.
Executive Officer.—MAJ Kolin Rathmann, 697–5312.
Technical Director for Cost and Economics.—Jay Jordan, CGN, room 403, 604–0404.
Director, Economics and Business Management.—Stephen M. Connair, room 4D167, 693–0347.

DEPUTY ASSISTANT SECRETARY FOR FINANCIAL OPERATIONS

Deputy Assistant Secretary.—James E. Short, room 5E989, 697–2905.
Associate Deputy Assistant Secretary.—Richard (Gus) Gustafson, room 4E125, 693–7066.
Chief of Staff for Operations.—COL Patrick Coe, room 5E989, 697–3972.
Military Assistant.—CPT Dwayne LaHaye, room 5E989, 697–3831.
Director for—
FM Workforce Management.—Todd Schafer, room 4D160, 697–2657.
Financial Accounting and Reporting.—Anthony Colucci, room 4E139, 697–6465.
Audit Follow-up and Internal Management Controls.—Vaughn E. Schlunz, room 4D212, 697–3972.

ASSISTANT SECRETARY FOR ACQUISITION

Pentagon, 1060 Air Force, Washington, DC 20330

Rosslyn, 1500 Wilson Blvd., Arlington, VA 22209

Arlington, 1745 Jefferson Davis Highway, Suite 307, Arlington, VA 22202

Assistant Secretary.—Dr. Marvin R. Sambur, room 4E964, 697–6361.
Military Assistant.—COL Stephen Gray, 697–6990.
Executive Officer.—LTC Mark Murphy, 697–6362.

PRINCIPAL DEPUTY ASSISTANT SECRETARY FOR ACQUISITION

Principal Deputy Assistant Secretary.—LTG John D.W. Corley, room 4E964, 697–6363.
Executive Officer.—LTC Mark Beierle, 695–7311.
Senior Executive Enlisted Matters.—CMSgt. Gene Hopkins, room 4E959, 697–8331.

DEPUTY ASSISTANT SECRETARY FOR CONTRACTING

Deputy Assistant Secretary.—Charlie E. Williams, Jr., Rosslyn, 7th Floor, 588–7070.
Associate Deputy Assistant Secretary.—COL Maureen M. Clay, 7th Floor, 588–7010.
Chief, Contracting Action Group.—COL Kirk A. Stonerock, 7th Floor, 588–7009.
Chief, Contracting Operations Division.—Pamela Schwenke (acting), 7th Floor, 588–7050.
Chief, Resources and Analysis Division.—COL Wilma F. Slade, 7th Floor, 588–7011.
Chief, Policy and Implementation Division.—COL Robert D. Winiecki, 7th Floor, 588–7077.

DEPUTY ASSISTANT SECRETARY FOR ACQUISITION INTEGRATION

Deputy Assistant Secretary.—Blaise J. Durante, Rosslyn, 16th Floor, 588–7211.
Associate Deputy Assistant Secretary.—COL Richard W. Lombardi, 16th Floor, 696–0082.
Division of:
Management Policy.—Janet Hassan, 17th Floor, 588–7110.
Career Management and Resources.—Carolyn Willis, 17th Floor, 588–7120.
Program Integration.—Jeffrey Shelton, 16th Floor, 588–7232.
Operations Support.—COL Henry H. Dorton, Jr., 16th Floor, 588–7260.
Center for Excellence.—Marty Evans, 9th Floor, 253–1333.

CAPABILITY DIRECTORATE FOR INFORMATION DOMINANCE

Director.—BG Edward Mahan, Rosslyn, 12th Floor, 588–6346.
Deputy.—Bobby W. Smart, 12th Floor, 588–6350.
Division Chief for—
Congressional/Budget and Program Integration.—COL Mary A. Seibel (acting), 12th Floor, 588–6331.
C2 Future Capabilities.—LTC Tracy E. Tynan, 12th Floor, 588–6430.
C2 Platforms and Enablers.—LTC Daryl Hauk, 12th Floor, 588–6372.
Global Command and Control Systems.—COL Matthew R. Leavitt, 11th Floor, 588–7087.
IRS Platforms and Sensors.—COL Buck Arvin, 15th Floor, 588–2645.

CAPABILITY DIRECTORATE FOR GLOBAL REACH PROGRAMS

Director.—MG Wayne Hodges, Rosslyn, 14th Floor, 588–7752.
Deputy Director.—COL Paul M. Stipe, 14 Floor, 588–7756.
Division Chief for—
Mobility.—COL Jim Rivard, 14th Floor, 588–7757.
Program, Budget and Congressional.—COL(s) Ed Stanhouse, 15th Floor, 588–8330.
Tactical Airlift, SOF, and Trainer.—COL John W. Zahrt, 14th Floor, 588–7740.

CAPABILITY DIRECTORATE FOR SPECIAL PROGRAMS

Director.—COL David Bujold, Rosslyn, 15th Floor, 588–2117.
Deputy Director.—COL Ryan S. Dow, 15th Floor, 588–1631.
Division Chief for—
Advanced Sensors and Weapons.—COL Scott V. Sells, 15th Floor, 588–1463.
Operational and Export Policy.—LTC Kenneth S. Gurley, 15th Floor, 588–2083.
Special Program Operations.—LTC James R. Horeisi, 15th Floor, 588–2085.
Special Studies.—LTC William D. Oetting, 15th Floor, 588–2107.

CAPABILITY DIRECTORATE FOR GLOBAL POWER PROGRAMS

Director.—BG Mark Welsh III, Rosslyn, 11th Floor, 588–7171.
Deputy Director.—COL Robert K. Saxer, 11th Floor, 588–7177.
Division Chief for—
Air Superiority.—COL Robert M. Newton, 10th Floor, 588–6510.
Combat Support and Counter Air.—COL Doug Cooke, 11th Floor, 588–7178.
Fighter Bomber.—COL(s) Scotty Fairbairn, 10th Floor, 588–1201.
Program Integration Division.—Sue A. Lumpkins, 588–7181.

DEPUTY ASSISTANT SECRETARY FOR SCIENCE, TECHNOLOGY, AND ENGINEERING

Deputy Assistant Secretary.—Jim Engle, Rosslyn, 6th Floor, 588–7766.
Associate Deputy Assistant Secretary.—[Vacant].

AIR FORCE PROGRAM EXECUTIVE OFFICERS

Program Executive Officer for—
Airlift and Trainers.—BG Ted Bowlds, Rosslyn, 14th Floor, 588–7711.
Command and Control/Combat Support Systems.—BG Bob Dehnert, Rosslyn, 12th Floor, 588–6461.
Fighters and Bombers.—BG Rick Lewis, Rosslyn, 11th Floor, 588–7310.
Services.—Tim Beyland, 11th Floor, 588–7190.
Weapons.—Judy A. Stokley, 11th Floor, 588–1260.

JOINT STRIKE FIGHTER TECHNOLOGY PROGRAM

Program Executive Officer.—MG John L. Hudson, 1213 Jefferson Davis Highway, Crystal Gateway 4, Suite 600, Arlington, VA 22202, 602–7640.

JOINT LOGISTICS SYSTEMS CENTER

Commander.—Brian F. Drew, 1864 Fourth Street, Suite 1, Wright-Patterson AFB, OH 45433, (937) 255–0401.

ASSISTANT SECRETARY FOR SPACE

Pentagon, 1670 Air Force, Washington, DC 20330

Assistant Secretary.—Keith R. Hall, room 4E998, 693–5996.

PRINCIPAL DEPUTY ASSISTANT SECRETARY FOR SPACE

Principal Deputy Assistant Secretary.—Dennis Fitzgerald, (703) 808–1000.

GENERAL COUNSEL

Pentagon, 1740 Air Force, Washington, DC 20330

General Counsel.—Mary L. Walker.
Principal Deputy.—Daniel Ramos.
Military Assistant/Special Counsel.—LTC Kevin Baron, (703) 697–8418.
Deputy General Counsel for—
Installations and Environment.—Gina Guy, room 4C921, 695–4691.
Fiscal and Administrative Law.—Don W. Fox, room 4C916, 695–4975.
International Affairs.—Michael W. Zehner, room 4C941, 697–5196.
Contractor Responsibility.—Steven A. Shaw, Ballston, 588 0057.
Acquisition.—James Hughes, room 4D980, 697–3900.
Military Affairs.—W. Kipling Atlee, room 4C948, 695–5663.
Dispute Resolution.—Joseph McDade, room 4D1000, 693–7286.

INSPECTOR GENERAL

Pentagon, 1140 Air Force, Washington, DC 20330

Inspector General.—LTG Raymond P. Huot, room 4E1076, 697–6733.
Deputy Inspector General.—MG Jeff M. Musfeldt, 697–4351.
Executive Officer.—MAJ Kevin Adelsen, 697–4787.
Advisor for—
Reserve Matters.—COL Maureen Tritle, room 4E1082, 697–0066.
Air National Guard Matters.—COL Terry Davis, 588–1559.

OFFICE OF THE INSPECTOR GENERAL

Director of:

Inquiries Directorate.—COL James Worth, room 110, 588–1558.
Inspections.—COL Pat Ward, room 4E1081, 697–7050.
Special Investigations.—COL Michael McConnell, room 4E1081, 697–0411.
Senior Officials Inquiries.—COL Norman Schaule, room 4E119, 693–3579.

ADMINISTRATIVE ASSISTANT TO THE SECRETARY

Pentagon, 1720 Air Force, Washington, DC 20330

2221 South Clark Street, Arlington, VA 22202 (CP6)

220 Brookley Avenue, Bolling AFB, Washington, DC 20032 (BAFB1)

B–3 Brookley Avenue, Bolling AFB, Washington, DC 20032 (BAFB2)

Administrative Assistant.—William A. Davidson, Pentagon, room 4D881, 695–9492.
Deputy Administrative Assistant.—Robert E. Corsi, Jr., 695–9492.
Senior Executive Assistant.—LTC Sue Donnelly, 695–8806.
Executive Assistant.—MAJ John Owens, 695–8807.
Deputy Executive Assistant.—MSgt Susan Platz, 695–9492.

AIR FORCE ART PROGRAM OFFICE

Director.—Russell Kirk, room 5E271, 697–2858.

AIR FORCE CENTRAL ADJUDICATION FACILITY

Director.—COL Joseph Schott, BAFB1, (202) 767–9236.

AIR FORCE DECLASSIFICATION OFFICE

Director.—Linda Smith, CP6, Suite 600, 604–4665.

AIR FORCE DEPARTMENTAL PUBLISHING OFFICE

Director.—Carolyn Watkins-Taylor, BAFB2, room 302, (202) 404–2380.

AIR FORCE EXECUTIVE DINING FACILITY

General Manager.—Alfonso Sisneros, room 4C854, 697–1112.

FACILITIES SUPPORT DIVISION

Director.—Hector Dittamo, room 5E1083, 697–8222.

HUMAN RESOURCES AND MANPOWER DIVISION

Chief.—Patricia Robey, room 4C882, 697–1806.

PLANS, PROGRAMS AND BUDGET DIVISION

Director.—COL Gregory Bishop, room 5E117, 695–4007.

SECURITY AND SPECIAL PROGRAMS OVERSIGHT DIVISION

Director.—Barry Hennessey, room 5D972, 693–2013.

AUDITOR GENERAL

Pentagon, 1120 Air Force, Washington, DC 20330

4170 Hebble Creek Road, Building 280, Room 1, Wright-Patterson AFB, OH 45433 (WPAFB)

5023 Fourth Street, March ARB, CA 95218 (MARB)

2000 North 15th Street, Suite 506, Arlington, VA 22201 (ARLINGTON)

2509 Kennedy Circle, Brooks City-Base, TEXAS 78235

Auditor General.—James R. Speer, room 4E168, 614–5626.

AIR FORCE AUDIT AGENCY

Deputy Auditor General and Director of Operations.—Kenneth E. Gregory, room 4E168, (703) 614–5738.
Assistant Deputy Auditor General.—Michael V. Barbino, Arlington, (703) 696–8038.
Assistant Auditor General for—
Financial and Systems Audits.—Robert E. Dawes, MARB, (909) 655–7011.
Acquisition and Logistics Audits.—Theodore J. Williams, WPAFB, (937) 257–6355.
Support and Personnel Audits.—Maria S. Young, Brooks City-Base, (210) 536–1999.

DIRECTORATE OF LEGISLATIVE LIAISON

Pentagon, 1160 Air Force, Washington, DC 20330

Rayburn House Office Building, Washington, DC 20515 (RHOB)

Russell Senate Office Building, Washington, DC 20510 (RSOB)

Director.—BG Scott S. Custer, Pentagon, room 4D927, 697–8153.
Military Assistant to the Director.—BG Thomas L. Carter, 695–2650.
Executive Officer.—MAJ Robert Pavelko, 697–4142.
Deputy Executive Assistant.—SMSgt Andre L. Brown, 695–2650.
Chief of:
House Liaison Office.—COL David J. Scott, RHOB, room B322, (202) 685–4531.
Senate Liaison Office.—COL Bob Edmonds, RSOB, room SR182, (202) 685–2573.
Weapons Systems Liaison.—COL Derek S. Hess, room 4D961, 697–6711.
Programs and Legislation.—COL Bill Groves, room 5D927, 697–7950.
Congressional Action.—Skip Daly, room 5D928, 695–0137.
Air Operations.—Sandi J. Esty, room 5D912, 697–1500.
Congressional Inquiries.—COL Thomas W. Shubert, room 5D883.

DIRECTORATE OF PUBLIC AFFAIRS

Pentagon, 1690 Air Force, Washington, DC 20330

Arlington, 901 N. Stuart Street, Suite 803, Arlington, VA 22203

Director.—BG R.T. Rand, room 4D922, 697–6061.
Deputy Director.—COL Douglas D. McCoy, Jr.
Executive Officer.—MAJ Gary Scott.

MEDIA RELATIONS DIVISION

Chief of:
Media Relations.—LTC Susan E. Strednansky, room 5C879, 695–0640.
Operations.—MAJ Ed Worley, 697–4425.
Media Training.—T'Jae Gibson, room 5C885, 693–9089.

STRATEGIC COMMUNICATIONS

Assistant Director.—LTC Anne Morris, room 5C945, 697–6725.

RESOURCES DIVISION

Chief.—[Vacant].

SECURITY REVIEW

Chief.—[Vacant].

AIR FORCE NEWS AND INFORMATION

Chief, Internal Information.—COL Linda Leong, Arlington, room 803, 696–9159.
Assistant Director, Reserve Advisor.—COL Marly Houser, room 5C935, 697–6725.
Chief, Air Force Bands.—MAJ Mark Peterson, room 4A120, 695–2592.

PUBLIC COMMUNICATION

Chief.—LTC Robert Williams, room 4A120, 693–9094.
Public Affairs Advisors—
SECAF CAPT Chet Curtis, 695–8723.
CSAF LTC Woody Woodyard, 697–5630.
CMSAF MSgt. Beth Allen, 697–6205.

EXECUTIVE ISSUES GROUP

Chief.—COL Gary Halbert, room 5C945, 695–9425.

CHIEF OF STAFF

Pentagon, 1670 Air Force, Washington, DC 20330

Chief of Staff.—GEN John P. Jumper, room 4E925, 697–9225.
Executive Officer.—COL Judy Fedder.
Director, Operations Group.—COL Paul Schafer, room 4E941, 697–5540.
Vice Chief of Staff.—GEN Robert H. (Doc) Foglesong, room 4E936, 695–7911.
Assistant Vice Chief of Staff.—LTG Joseph H. Wehrle, room 4E944, 695–7913.
Chief Master Sergeant of the Air Force.—CMSAF Gerald R. Murray, room 4B948, 695–0498.

AIR FORCE STUDIES AND ANALYSIS AGENCY

Pentagon, 1570 Air Force, Washington, DC 20330

Rosslyn, 1777 North Kent Street, 6th, 7th, and 8th Floors, VA 22209

Director.—Dr. Jacqueline R. Henningsen, PhD, SES, 588–6966.
Vice Director.—COL Randal D. Fullhart, 588–6970.
Technical Director.—Daniel Barker, 588–6970.
Technical Advisor.—Dr. Francis McDonald, 588–8880.
Chief Analyst.—COL Jerry Diaz, 588–6910.

CHIEF OF SAFETY

9700 G. Avenue SE, Building 24499, Suite 240, Kirtland AFB, NM 87117

Chief of Safety/Commander, Air Force Safety Center.—MG Kenneth W. Hess, (505) 846–2372.

SAFETY ISSUES DIVISION (PENTAGON LIAISON)

Pentagon, 1400 Air Force, Washington, DC 20330

Director.—COL Gregory Alston, room 5E161, 693–7280.

SCIENTIFIC ADVISORY BOARD

Pentagon, 1180 Air Force, Washington, DC 20330

Chair.—Dr. Daniel E. Hastings, room 5D982, (703) 697–4811.
Vice Chair.—Heidi Shyu, room 5D982, 697–4811.
Military Director.—LTG John D.W. Corley, room 4E964, 697–6363.
Executive Director.—COL Charles D. Bowker, room 5D982, 697–8288.
Deputy Executive Director.—LTC Mark Nowack, room 5D982, 697–8652.
Military Assistants: MAJ Dwight Pavek, room 5D982, 697–4808; MAJ Christopher Berg, room 5D982, 697–4648.
Executive Assistants: TSgt Doug Payne, SSgt Ebony Rodriguez, room 5D982, 697–4811.

DIRECTORATE OF TEST AND EVALUATION

Pentagon, 1650 Air Force, Washington, DC 20330

Director.—John Manclark, room 4E995, 697–4774.

AIR FORCE HISTORIAN

500 Duncan Avenue, Box 94, Bolling Air Force Base, Washington, DC 20332 (BAFB)

Historian.—William (Bill) Heimdahl (acting), room 401, (202) 404–2167.
Executive Officer.—MAJ John Beaulieu, 404–2167.
Director, Air Force Historical Research Agency, Maxwell AFB, AL.—COL Carol Sikes, (334) 953–5342.

AIR FORCE SCIENTIST

Pentagon, 1075 Air Force, Washington, DC 20330

Chief Scientist.—Dr. Alexander Levis, room 4E288, 697–7842.
Military Assistant.—COL John Bedford, room 4E288, 697–7842.

AIR FORCE RESERVE

Pentagon, 1150 Air Force, Washington, DC 20330

Chief, Air Force Reserve/Commander, Air Force Reserve Command.—MG James E. Sherrard III, room 4E160, 695–9225.
Deputy.—BG William M. Rajczak, room 4E160, 614–7307.

NATIONAL GUARD BUREAU

1411 Jefferson Davis Highway, Arlington, VA 22202

Chief.—LTG H Steven Blum, JP–1, Crystal City, Suite 12000, (703) 607–2200.
Air National Guard:
Director.—LTG Daniel James III, JP–1, Crystal City, Suite 12200, 607–2408.
Deputy Director.—BG David Brubaker, JP–1, Crystal City, Suite 12200, 607–2408.

SURGEON GENERAL

Bolling AFB, 170 Luke Avenue, Building 5681, Suite 400, Washington, DC 20332

Surgeon General.—LTG George Peach Taylor, Jr., (202) 767–4765.
Deputy Surgeon General.—MG James Roudebush, 767–4766.
Executive Officers: COL Mark Hamilton, MAJ Brian Goviea, 767–4746.
Director for—
Congressional and Public Affairs.—Donna Tinsley, 767–4797.
Financial Management.—COL Robert Lenahan, 767–5706.
Expeditionary Operations.—MG Joseph Kelley, 767–0020.
Force Development.—MG Barbara Brannon, 767–4498.
Plans and Programs.—COL Gar Graham, 767–4864.
Modernization.—COL Pete Demitry, (703) 824–3155.

Corps Directors for—
Medical.—COL Mike Spaatz, 767–4455.
Biomedical Sciences.—COL James Young, 767–4498.
Nursing.—COL Linda Kisner, 767–4462.
Medical Services.—COL George Small, 767–4496.

CHIEF OF THE CHAPLAIN SERVICE

Bolling AFB, 112 Luke Avenue, Building 5683, Washington, DC 20032

Chief.—Chaplain (MG) Lorraine Potter, room 316, (202) 767–4577.
Deputy Chief.—Chaplain (BG) Charles Baldwin, room 313, (202) 767–4599.

JUDGE ADVOCATE GENERAL

Pentagon, 1420 Air Force, Washington, DC 20330

1501 Wilson Boulevard, Suite 810, Rosslyn, VA 22209 (ROSSLYN)

172 Luke Avenue, Suite 343, Bolling AFB, Washington, DC 20032 (BAFB)

Judge Advocate General.—MG Thomas J. Fiscus, Pentagon, room 4E112, 614–5732.
Deputy Judge Advocate General.—MG Jack L. Rives.
Director for—
Civil Law and Litigation.—COL Evan Haberman, Rosslyn, room 810, 696–9040.
USAF Judiciary.—COL Rebecca Weeks, BAFB, room 336, (202) 767–1535.
General Law.—Harlan G. Wilder, room 5E279, 614–4075.
International Law.—COL Jeanna Rueth, room 5C269, 695–9631.

LEGAL SERVICES

Commander, Air Force Legal Services Agency.—COL David Ehrhart, BAFB, room 336, (202) 404–8758.

DEPUTY CHIEF OF STAFF FOR AIR AND SPACE OPERATIONS

Pentagon, 1630 Air Force, Washington, DC 20330

GAL PL, 624 9th Street, NW., Suite 300, Washington, DC 20001

Deputy Chief of Staff.—LTG Ronald E. Keys, room 4E1032, 697–9991.
Assistant Deputy.—MG Randall M. Schmidt, 697–9881.
Mobilization Assistant.—BG Michael K. Lynch, room 4D1086, 697–3087.
Director, Security Forces.—BG James M. Shamess, room 1E270, 693–5494.
Deputy Director.—COL Kenneth M. Freeman.
Director, Homeland Security.—BG David E. Clary, room 4D237, 693–5726.
Deputy Director.—COL Steve Doss.
Director, Intelligence, Surveillance and Reconnaissance.—MG Ronald F. Sams, room 4A932, 695–5613.
Deputy Director.—BG John C. Koziol.
Director, Nuclear and Counter-Proliferation.—BG Robert L. Smolen, room 4C166, 695–5833.
Assistant Director.—SES Dr. Billy W. Mullins.
Deputy Director.—COL Rainer P. Stachowitz.
Director, Operations and Training.—MG Richard A. Mentemeyer, room 4E1046, 695–9067.
Deputy Director.—BG Norman R. Seip.
Director, Operational Capability Requirements.—MG Daniel P. Leaf, room 4E1021, 695–3018.
Deputy Director.—SES Harry C. Disbrow, Jr.
Director, Space Operations and Integration.—MG Franklin J. Blaisdell, room 4E1048, 693–9747.
Deputy Director.—COL R. Kent Traylor.
Director, Weather.—BG (Select) Thomas E. Stickford, room 4A1084, 614–7258.
Deputy Director.—COL H. Webster Tileston III.

Director, Operational Plans and Joint Matters.—MG(S) Michael C. Gould, room 4E1047, 614–2711.
Deputy Directors: COL Marc Felman.
Director, Executive Support.—LTC David R. Hinson.
Deputy Director.—MAJ Sean J. Neagle.

DEPUTY CHIEF OF STAFF FOR PERSONNEL

Pentagon, 1040 Air Force, Washington, DC 20330

Deputy Chief of Staff.—LTG Richard E. Brown III, room 4E194, 697–6088.
Assistant Deputy.—Roger M. Blanchard.
Chief, Personnel Issues Team.—COL (S) David Moore, room 4E185, 695–4212.
Director of:
Personnel Policy.—MG John Speigel, room 4E228, 697–1228.
Strategic Plans and Future Systems.—William Kelly, room 4E178, 697–5221.
Manpower and Organization.—BG William P. Ard, room 5A328, 692–1601.
Chief, Executive Services Group.—MAJ Darlene Cheatham, room 4E207, 697–2229.
Director, AF Senior Leader Management Office.—BG Richard S. Hassan, Crystal Gateway 3, Suite 102, 604–8126.
Director, Learning and Force Development.—MG Peter U. Sutton, room 4E144, 695–2144.

DEPUTY CHIEF OF STAFF FOR INSTALLATIONS AND LOGISTICS
Pentagon, 1030 Air Force, Washington, DC 20330
Crystal Gateway North, 1111 Jefferson Davis Highway, Arlington, VA 22202 (CGN)
Crystal Gateway 1, 1235 Jefferson Davis Highway, Arlington, VA 22202 (CG1)
Rosslyn, 1500 Wilson Boulevard, Arlington, VA 22209 (ROS)

Deputy Chief of Staff.—LTG Michael E. Zettler, Pentagon, room 4E260, 695–3153.
Assistant Deputy.—Susan A. O'Neal, Pentagon, room 4E260, 695–6236.
Director of:
Communication Operations.—BG (s) Ronnie D. Hawkins, ROS, Suite 220, 588–6100.
Innovation and Transformation.—Grover L. Dunn, Pentagon, room 5D967, 697–6559.
Logistics Readiness.—MG Craig P. Rasmussen, Pentagon, room 4B283, 697–1429.
Maintenance.—MG (s) Elizabeth A. Harrell, Pentagon, room 4E278, 695–4900.
Resources.—BG Arthur B. Morrill, Pentagon, room 4A272, 697–2822.
Services.—Arthur J. Myers, CGN, room 413, 604–0010.
The Civil Engineer.—MG L. Dean Fox, CG1, room 1000, 607–0200.

DEFENSE AGENCIES

DEFENSE COMMISSARY AGENCY

1300 E Avenue, Fort Lee, VA 23801, phone (804) 734–8330

Director.—MG Michael P. Wiedemer, USAF, 734–8717.
Deputy Director.—Patrick B. Nixon, 734–8720.
Executive Director for—
Capital Investment.—Crosby Johnson, 734–8721.
Operations and Product Support.—Bob Vitikacs, 734–8128.
Resource Management.—Ed Jones, 734–8706.

LIAISON OFFICE

Pentagon, Room 2E335, 20301, phone (703) 695–3265

Director.—Daniel W. Sclater.

ARMY AND AIR FORCE EXCHANGE SERVICE

3911 S. Walton Walker Boulevard, Dallas, TX 75236, phone 1–800–527–6790

Commander.—MG Kathryn G. Frost, USA.
Vice Commander.—BG Toreaser A. Steele, USAF.
Chief Operating Officer.—Marilyn Iverson.

WASHINGTON OFFICE/OFFICE OF THE BOARD OF DIRECTORS

National Center 1 (NC1), 2511 Jefferson Davis Highway, Suite 11600
Arlington, VA 22202, phone (703) 604–7523, DSN 664–7523

Director/Executive Secretary.—Robert A. Smith.
Deputy Director/Executive Assistant.—William J. Reid.

DEPUTY CHIEF OF STAFF FOR PLANS AND PROGRAMS

Pentagon, 1070 Air Force 20330

Deputy Chief of Staff.—LTG Duncan McNabb, room 4E124, 697–9472.
Director of Programs.—MG Kevin Chilton, room 5B279, 697–2405.
Deputy Director.—BG Raymond Johns, room 5B279, 697–2405.
Director for Strategic Planning.—MG Ronald Bath, room 5E171, 697–3117.

OFFICE OF THE CHIEF INFORMATION OFFICER

Pentagon, 1155 Air Force, Washington, DC 20330

Crystal Gateway 3 North, Arlington, Va 22202 (CG3)

Chief Information Officer.—John M. Gilligan, (703) 695–9698.
Executive Officer.—COL Jesse Citizen, 614–7891.
Director, Systems and Technology.—COL Norris Connelly, 601–4966.
Deputy Director.—COL Ross Miles, 601–4958.
Director, Plans and Policy.—COL Anne Leary, 601–3569.
Deputy Director.—LTC Bret Klassen, 601–3582.
Director, Resources and Analysis.—COL Michael Crane, 601–1169.
Deputy Director.—LTC Jeff Mercer, 601–3582.
Chief Architect.—Eric Skoog, (781) 377–6800.
Headquarters Air Force Chief Information Officer.—Jim Hundley, 601–3566.
Deputy.—LTC Rich Catington, 601–3567.

DEPUTY CHIEF OF STAFF FOR WARFIGHTING INTEGRATION

Pentagon, 1800 Air Force Pentagon, Washington, DC 20330

Deputy Chief of Staff.—LTG Leslie F. Kenne, room 4E212, (703) 695–6829.
Assistant.—Rob Thomas II, 697–1605.
Director of:
C4IER Infostructure.—MG Charles C. Croom, room 4B1060, 697–1326.
C4ISR Integration.—BG Dan R. Goodrich, room 4C1059, 695–1835.
C4ISR Architecture and Assessment.—David Tillotson, room 4C1059, 695–1839.
Resource Planning.—COL Daniel R. (Rick) Dinkins, room 4B1060, 697–3943.

DEPARTMENT OF THE ARMY

The Pentagon, 20310, phone (703) 695–2442

OFFICE OF THE SECRETARY

Pentagon, Room 3E700, 20310, phone (703) 695–3211, fax 697–8036

Secretary of the Army.—[Vacant].
Executive Officer.—COL Michael Oates, 695–1717.

OFFICE OF THE UNDER SECRETARY

Pentagon, Room 3E732, 20310–0102, phone (703) 695–4311, fax 695–1525

Under Secretary of the Army.—R. L. Brownlee.
Executive Officer.—COL Bruce Berwick, 697–6806.
Confidential Assistant.—Suzanne Ross.
Military Assistants: LTC Glen D. Lambkin, LTC Christopher Ross, LTC John K. Wood.

ASSISTANT SECRETARY FOR CIVIL WORKS

Pentagon, Room 3E446, 20310–0108, phone (703) 697–8986, fax 697–7401

Assistant Secretary.—[Vacant].
Principal Deputy Assistant Secretary.—[Vacant].
Executive Officer.—COL Richard J. Polo 697–9809.
Military Assistant.—LTC Richard Wagenaar 695–0482.
Administrative Officer.—Mark Lutz, 693–3656.
Deputy, Assistant Secretary for—
Policy and Legislation.—George Dunlop, 695–1370.
Management and Budget.—Claudia L. Tornblom, 695–1376.

ASSISTANT SECRETARY FOR FINANCIAL MANAGEMENT AND COMPTROLLER

Pentagon, Room 3A324, 20310–0109, phone (703) 614–4356

Assistant Secretary.—Sandra L. Pack.
Principal Deputy Assistant Secretary.—Ernest J. Gregory, 614–4337.
Executive Officer.—COL Aaron P. Gillison, 614–4337.
Deputy Assistant Secretary for—
Financial Operations.—COL William W. Landrum III, room 3A320A, 693–2741.
Resource Analysis and Business Practices.—Sharon Weinhold, room 3A712, 697–7399.
Army Budget.—MG Jerry Sinn, room 3A314, 614–4035.
Director for U.S. Cost and Economic Analysis Center.—COL Kenneth Ellis, 1421 Jefferson Davis Highway, Suite 9001, Arlington, VA 22202–3259, 601–4200.

ASSISTANT SECRETARY FOR INSTALLATIONS AND ENVIRONMENT

Pentagon, Room 3E464, 20310–0110, phone (703) 692–9801

Assistant Secretary.—Mario P. Fiori.
Principal Deputy Assistant Secretary.—Geoffrey G. Prosch, 692–9802.
Executive Officer.—COL Harold Chappell, 692–9804.

Deputy Assistant Secretary for—

Installations and Housing.—Joseph Whitaker, 697–8161, room 3E475.

Environment, Safety and Occupational Health.—Raymond J. Fatz, room 3D453, 697–1913.

Infrastructure and Analysis.—Craig College, room 3D453, 697–3388.

Privatizations and Partnerships.—William Armbruster, room 3D453, 692–9890.

ASSISTANT SECRETARY FOR MANPOWER AND RESERVE AFFAIRS

Pentagon, Room 2E468, 20310–0111, phone (703) 697–9253

Assistant Secretary.—Reginald J. Brown.

Principal Deputy Assistant Secretary.—Daniel B. Benning, room 2E460, 692–1292.

Executive Officer.—COL Tony Stamilio, 697–9253.

Deputy Assistant Secretary for—

Force Management, Manpower and Resources.—Sarah White, room 2E446, 695–9652.

Review Boards.—Karl Schneider, Crystal City #4, 607–1597.

Training, Readiness, and Mobility.—Daniel B. Denning, room 2E460, 692–1292.

Human Resources.—John P. McLaurin III, room 2E482, 697–2631.

ASSISTANT SECRETARY FOR ARMY ACQUISITION, LOGISTICS AND TECHNOLOGY

Pentagon, Room 2E672, 20310–0103, phone (703) 695–6153, fax 697–4003

Assistant Secretary.—Claude M. Bolton, Jr., 693–6153.

Chief of Staff.—COL Robert M. Brown, 695–5749.

Military Assistant.—LTC Bruce D. Lewis, 695–6742.

Military Deputy.—LTG John S. Caldwell, Jr., 697–0397.

Executive to Military Deputy.—LTC (P) Camille M. Nichols, 697–0356.

Deputy Assistant Secretary for—

Science and Technology.—Dr. A. Michael Andrews, room 3E620, 692–1830.

Policy and Procurement.—Earnestine Ballard (acting), room 2E661, 695–2488.

Plans, Programs and Resources.—Don Damstetter, room 2E673, 697–0387.

Deputy Assistant Secretary for Defense, Exports and Coopration.—Craig D. Hunter, 1777 N. Kent Street, North Plaza, 8th Floor, Rosslyn VA 22332, 588–8070.

GENERAL COUNSEL

Pentagon, Room 2E722, 20310–0104, phone (703) 697–9235, fax 697–6553

General Counsel.—Steven J. Morello.

Principal Deputy General Counsel.—Avon N. Williams, III.

Executive Officer/Special Counsel.—COL Frank B. Ecker, Jr.

Senior Deputy General Counsel.—Thomas W. Taylor, room 2E725, 695–0562.

Deputy General Counsel for—

Acquisition.—Levator Norsworthy, Jr., room 2E725, 697–5120.

Civil Works and Environment.—Earl H. Stockdale, Jr., room 2E725, 695–3024.

Ethics and Fiscal Law.—Matt Reres, room 2E725, 695–5105.

ADMINISTRATIVE ASSISTANT

Pentagon, Room 3E733, 20310–0105, phone (703) 695–2442, fax 697–6194

Administrative Assistant.—Joel B. Hudson.

Deputy Administrative Assistant.—Sandra R. Riley, 695–5879.

Director, Executive Support/Organizational Management.—Thomas Scullen, room 3D746, 697–7741.

Director of:

Internal Review.—George A. Sullivan, Taylor Building, 602–1774.

Network Infrastructure Services and Operations.—LTC Dennis Drakopoulos (acting), room BE882, 697–7848.

Resource Management.—Robert L. Jaworski, room 3D735, 695–8600.

Equal Employment Opportunity.—Debra A. Muse, Taylor Building, 604–2736.

Legal Services.—LTC Nathanael Causey, room 1C242, 697–5423.

Security and Safety.—COL William Long, room 1J663, 697–6432.

Logistics.—COL Catherine Schoonover, Taylor Building, 602–7856.

Administrative Services.—Fritz Kirklighter, 1525 Wilson Blvd., Rosslyn, VA 22209, (202) 374–6133.
Network Security (Pentagon).—Rick Anderson, room BF849D, 614–2719.
Data Center Services (Pentagon).—Dan Frye, room BF849D, 614–0312.
Telecommunications Center (Pentagon).—Marvin Owens, room 5A910, 697–8840.
Information Technology Integration (Pentagon).—Tom Krupp, room 4100, 588–8730.
U.S. Army Publishing Agency.—Emil Nazzaro, Hof I/room 1010, 325–6800.
Information Management Support Center.—Susan Fisher (acting), room 1E154, 695–4229.
Defense Contracting Command (Washington).—COL Joe E. Conley, room 1E230, 695–2005.
Defense Telecommunications Service (Washington).—Larry Miller, 1700 North Moore Street, Suite 1475, Arlington VA 22209–1903, 696–9596.
Human Resources.—Sherri V. Ward, room 1A881, 697–2691.
Space and Building Management Services (Washington).—Wes Blaine, room 1F202, 695–7555.
U.S. Army Visual Information Center.—Edward Jonas, room 5A928, 695–1798.
Support Services.—Lacy Saunders, room 3A145, 695–9024.

DIRECTOR OF INFORMATION SYSTEMS FOR COMMAND, CONTROL, COMMUNICATIONS AND COMPUTERS

Pentagon, Room 1A271, 20310–0107, phone (703) 695–4366, fax 695–3091

Chief Information Officer.—LTG Peter M. Cuviello.
Deputy Chief Information Officer.—David Borland, 695–6604.
Executive Officer.—COL Brian J. Donahue, 697–5503.
Director of:
Resource Integration.—Ms. Diane Armstrong, room 1A310, 614–0439.
Strategic Communications and Initiatives.—COL Edward M. Siomacco, room 1A266, 693–1327.
Information Operations, Networks and Space.—MG Steven W. Boutelle, room 2B855, 614–5666.
Enterprise Integration.—[Vacant].

INSPECTOR GENERAL

Pentagon, Room 1E736, 20310–1700, phone (703) 695–1500, fax 697–4705

Inspector General.—LTG Michael W. Ackerman.
Executive Officer.—COL Karl E. Tool, 695–1502.

AUDITOR GENERAL

3101 Park Center Drive, Alexandria, VA 22303, phone (703) 681–9809, fax 681–9860

Auditor General.—Francis E. Reardon.
Deputy Auditor General for—
Acquisition and Material Management.—Thomas Druzgal, 681–9839.
Installations Management.—Stephen E. Keefer, 681–9690.
Forces and Financial Management.—Joyce E. Morrow, 681–9574.
Policy and Operations Management.—Patrick J. Fitzgerald, 681–9820.

DEPUTY UNDER SECRETARY OF THE ARMY (INTERNATIONAL AFFAIRS)

Pentagon, Room 3E749, 20310–0102, phone (703) 697–5075

Deputy Under Secretary.—John W. McDonald.
Executive Officer.—COL Larry M Brom, 695–4392.
Administrative Assistant.—Clara E. Cavada.

DEPUTY UNDER SECRETARY OF THE ARMY (OPERATIONS RESEARCH)

Pentagon, Room 2E660, 20310–0102, phone (703) 695–0083, fax 693–3897

Deputy Under Secretary.—Walter W. Hollis.
Executive Officer.—COL Hoa Generazio, 697–0366.

LEGISLATIVE LIAISON

Pentagon, Room 1E416, 20310–1600, phone (703) 697–6767, fax 614–7599

Chief.—MG Guy C. Swan III, room 1E428.

Deputy Chief.—COL (P) Richard McCabe, room 1E428, 695–1235.

Special Assistant for Legislative Affairs for Intelligence.—Robert J. Winchester, room 1E428, 695–3918.

Executive Officer.—COL John L. Goetchius, Jr., room 1E428, 695–3524.

Chief of:

Congressional Inquiry.—Janet Fagan, room 1E423, 697–2583.

House Liaison.—COL Michael DeYoung, room B325, Rayburn House Office Building, Washington DC, (202) 225–3853.

Senate Liaison.—COL John Schorsch, room SR183, Senate Russell Office Building, Washington DC, (202) 224–2881.

Investigation and Legislative.—COL William Hudson, room 1E433, 697–2106.

Programs.—LTC Mike Delancy (acting), room 1E385, 693–8766.

PUBLIC AFFAIRS

Pentagon, Room 2B736, 20310–1500, phone (703) 695–5135, fax 693–8362

Chief.—MG Larry D. Gottardi.

Deputy Chief.—BG Robert Gaylord, 697–4482.

Executive Officer.—COL Lloyd W. Holloway, 697–4200.

Chief of Plans.—COL James M. Allen, room 2B733, 695–2743.

Chief of:

Media Relations Division.—COL Thomas J. Begines, room 2B739, 697–2564.

Information Strategy Division.—LTC (P) Stephen Campbell, room 2B720, 697–4640.

Community Relations and Outreach Division.—COL Fred Lydick, Taylor Building, room 11S18, 602–2591.

SMALL AND DISADVANTAGED BUSINESS UTILIZATION

Pentagon, Room 2A712, 20310–0106, phone (703) 695–9800, fax 693–3898

Director.—Tracey L. Pinson.

Deputy Director.—Paul L. Gardner (acting), 697–2868.

ARMED RESERVE FORCES POLICY COMMITTEE

Pentagon, Room 2D484, 20310–0112, phone (703) 695–5122, fax 695–6967

Chairman.—MG David R. Bockel.

Deputy Chairman.—MG Bennett Landreneau.

ARMY STAFF AND SELECTED AGENCIES

Pentagon, 20310–0200, phone (703) 695–2077

Chief of Staff.—GEN Eric K. Shinseki, room 3E668.

Vice Chief of Staff—GEN John M. Keane, room 3E666, 695–4371.

Director, CSA's Staff Group.—COL Michael D. Jones, 697–8363.

Director of Army Staff.—MG Antonio M. Taguba (acting), room 3E665, 695–3542.

Director, Office of:

Executive Commission and Control.—COL B. Kimo Gabriel, 695–7552.

Army Protocol.—Linda Jacobs, 697–0692.

Program Analysis and Evaluation.—BG David Melcher, room 3C718, 697–1475.

Test and Evaluation Management Agency.—Dr. John B. Foulkes, 695–8995.

Sergeant Major.—SMA Jack L. Tilley, 695–2150.

INTELLIGENCE

Pentagon, Room 2E408, 20310–1000, phone (703) 695–3033

Deputy Chief of Staff.—LTG Robert W. Noonan, Jr.

Executive Officer.—COL Michael W. Pick.

Assistant Deputy Chiefs: Terrance M. Ford, 697–4644; MG Alfonsa Gilley, 693–5889; MG Richard J. Quirk III, 695–3929; William H. Speer, 695–3929.

Director, Office of:
Foreign Intelligence.—COL William Slayton, room 2D428, 697–5484.
Information Management.—COL Lynn Schnurr, 693–7019.
Intelligence Policy.—COL James H. Harper, room 2D382, 695–1623.

LOGISTICS

Pentagon, Room 1A123, 20310–0500, phone (703) 695–4102, fax 614–6702

Deputy Chief of Staff.—LTG Charles S. Mahan, Jr.
Assistant Deputy Chiefs of Staff: LTG Claude V. Christianson, 697–5301; LTG Gary C. Wattnem, 695–4508.
Director, Office of:
Program Development.—Joe Billman, room 3B671, 695–4852.
Plans, Operations, and Readiness.—BG Jerome Johnson, room 3A670, 697–8007.
Projection and Distribution.—BG Jesus A. Mangual, room 3A720, 614–6186.
Sustainment.—BG Lloyd T. Waterman, room 3A662, 697–9081.

OPERATIONS AND PLANS

Pentagon, 20310–0400, phone (703) 695–2904

Deputy Chief of Staff.—LTG Richard A. Cody.
Assistant Deputy Chief of Staff.—MG James J. Lovelace, Jr.
Assistant Deputy Chief of Staff for—
Mobilization and Reserve Affairs.—BG Robert Chestnut, 695–3809.
Force Development.—MG James Grazioplene, room 1E148, 614–3809.
Director, Office of:
Strategy, Plans and Policy.—MG David Huntoon, 692–8805.
Training.—BG William Webster, 692–7332.
Requirements.—COL Michael Gaffney, 692–7902.
Force Management.—BG Dennis Hardy, 693–3154.
Operations Readiness and Mobilization.—BG Peter Chiarelli, 695–0526.

PERSONNEL

Pentagon, Room 2E460, 20310–0300, phone (703) 697–8060

Deputy Chief of Staff.—LTG John LeMoyne.
Assistant Deputy Chief of Staff.—MG Lawrence Adair, 692–1585.
Assistant Deputy Chief of Staff for Mobilization and Reserve Affairs.—MG Sue Dueitt, room 2D683, 614–3229.
Director, Office of:
Military Personnel Management.—BG Harry B. Axson, room 2C640–1, 614–7055.
Plans, Resources and Operations.—COL Mark R. Lewis, room 2B453, 697–5263.
Personnel Technologies.—Dr. Thomas Killion, room 2C674, 695–3048.
Human Resources.—BG Stephen Schook, room 2C678, 693–1850.
Civilian Personnel Management.—Elizabeth Throckmorton, Hoffman Bldg., 325–8724.

ASSISTANT CHIEF OF STAFF INSTALLATION MANAGEMENT

Pentagon, Room 1E668, 20310–0600, phone (703) 693–3233, fax 693–3507

Assistant Chief of Staff.—MG Larry J. Lust.
Deputy Assistant.—J.C. Menig.

CORPS OF ENGINEERS

GAO Building, 441 G Street, NW., Washington, DC 20314, phone (202) 761–0001

fax 761–0359

Chief.—LTG Robert B. Flowers.
Deputy Commander.—MG Milton Hunter, 761–0002.

SURGEON GENERAL

Skyline Place 6, Room 672, 5109 Leesburg Pike, Falls Church, VA 22041–3258

phone (703) 681–3000, fax 681–3167

Surgeon General.—LTG James B. Peake.
Deputy Surgeon General.—MG Kenneth L. Farmer, Jr., 681–3002.

NATIONAL GUARD BUREAU

1411 Jefferson Davis Highway, Arlington, VA 22202–3231, phone (703) 607–2200

Chief.—LTG Russell C. Davis.
Vice Chief.—MG Raymond F. Rees, 607–2204.
Director, Army National Guard.—MG Roger Schultz, 607–2352.

ARMY RESERVE

Pentagon, Room 1E729, 20310–2400, phone (703) 697–1784

Chief.—LTG Thomas J. Plewes.
Deputy Chief.—COL M. Bruce Westcott, 697–1260.
Deputy Chief (IMA).—COL David T. Zabecki, 695–1913.

JUDGE ADVOCATE

Pentagon, Room 1E739, 20310–2200, phone (703) 697–5151, fax 695–8370

Judge Advocate General.—MG Thomas J. Romig.
Assistant Judge Advocate General.—MG Michael J. Marchaud, 588–6720.
Assistant Deputy Chief for—
Civil Law and Litigation.—BG David P. Carey, room 704, 696–8114.
Military Law and Operations.—BG Scott C. Black, 693–5112.

CHIEF OF CHAPLAINS

Pentagon, Room 1E721, 20310–2700, phone (703) 695–1133, fax 695–9824

Chief.—MG Gaylord T. Gunhus.
Deputy Chief.—BG David H. Hicks, 695–1135.

LIAISON OFFICES

Pentagon, Room 2B476, 20310–2200, phone (703) 695–1327, fax 695–8370

USAREUR.—LTC Gene A. Maisano.
USA Forscoms/USA Tradoc.—LTC Steve Herold, 697–2591.

MAJOR ARMY COMMANDS

U.S. Army.—Joel B. Hudson, Headquarters, Department of the Army, Pentagon, Washington, DC 20310, (703) 395–2442.

U.S. Army Materiel Command.—Gen. Paul J. Kern, 5001 Eisenhower Avenue, room 1OE08, Alexandria, VA 22333–0001, (703) 617–9625.

U.S. Army Corps of Engineers.—LTG Robert B. Flowers, 441 G Street, NW, Washington, DC 20314–1000, (202) 761–0000.

U.S. Army Criminal Investigation Command.—MG Donald J. Ryder, 6010 6th Street, Fort Belvoir, VA 22060–5506, (703) 806–0400.

U.S. Army Forces Command.—GEN Larry R. Ellis, Fort McPherson, GA 30330–6000, (404) 464–5054.

U.S. Army Intelligence and Security Command.—MG Keith B. Alexander, 8825 Beulah Street, Fort Belvoir, VA 22060–5246, (703) 706–1603.

U.S. Army Medical Command/The Surgeon General.—LTG James B. Peake, 5109 Leesburg Pike, Falls Church, VA 22041, (703) 681–3000.

U.S. Army Military District of Washington.—MG James T. Jackson, Fort Lesley J. McNair, Washington, DC 20319–5000, (202) 685–2807.

U.S. Army Military Traffic Management Command.—MG Kenneth L. Privratsky, 200 Stovall Street, Hoffman Bldg. II, Alexandria, VA 22322–5000, (703) 428–3210.

U.S. Army Special Operations Command.—LTG Philip R. Kensinger, Fort Bragg, NC 28310–5200, (910) 432–3000.

U.S. Army Training and Doctrine Command.—GEN John N. Abrams, Fort Monroe, VA 23651–5000, (757) 788–3514.

U.S. Army South.—MG Alfred A. Valenzuela, Fort Buchanan, PR 00934–3400, (787) 707–5019.

Eighth U.S. Army.—LTG Daniel R. Zanini, APO AP 96205.

U.S. Army Pacific.—LTG Edwin P. Smith, Fort Shafter, Hawaii 96858–5100, (808) 438–2206.

U.S. Army Europe and 7th Army.—GEN Montgomery C. Meigs, APO AE 09014.

U.S. Army Space and Missile Defense Command.—LTG Joseph M. Cosumano, Jr., 1941 Jefferson Davis Highway, Suite 900, Arlington, VA 22215–0280, (703) 607–1873.

DEPARTMENT OF THE NAVY

Pentagon 20350–1000, phone (703) 695–3131

OFFICE OF THE SECRETARY OF THE NAVY

Pentagon, Room 4E686, phone (703) 695–3131

Secretary of the Navy.—Hon. H.T. Johnson.
Confidential Assistant.—J. Drennan, 695–4884.
Senior Military Assistant.—RADM J. Morgan, USN.
Executive Assistant and Marine Aide.—CAPT M. Jenkins, USN.
Deputy Executive Assistant and Naval Aide.—LCDR P. Tortora, USN.
Special Assistant for Business Initiatives.—D. Combs, room 4E775, 693–0258.
Administrative Aide.—CDR (S) L. Vasquez, USN, room 4E687, 695–5410.
Personal Aide.—CAPT L. Krsulich, USMC.
Special Assistant for—
Administrative Matters.—P. Matthews, room 4E687, 697–3334.
Legislation.—CDR J. Hannink, room 4D730, 697–6935.
Public Affairs.—CAPT K. Wensing, room 4D745, 697–7491.
Director, Division of:
Congressional Liaison Office.—YN1 R. Garris, USN, room 4C723, 695–3826.
Sensitive Correspondence.—YNC (SW) W. Ball, USN, room 4C729, 695–3800.

OFFICE OF THE UNDER SECRETARY OF THE NAVY

Pentagon, Room 4E732, phone (703) 695–3141

Under Secretary of the Navy.—[Vacant].
Executive Assistant and Naval Aide.—[Vacant].
Military Assistant and Marine Aide.—COL F. Ferguson, USMC.
Assistant for Administration.—J. La Raia, room 4E777, 697–0047.
Facilities and Support Services Division.—B. O'Donnell, room 5B731, 614–4290.
Director of:
Financial Management.—D. Nugent, AA/2507, 693–0321.
OPTI.—G. Wyckoff, room AA/4101, 695–6191.
SADBU.—N. Tarrant, WNY, 685–6485.
SHHRO.—W. Mann, room AA/2510, 693–0888.
Special Programs.—J. Moore, room AA/2517, 693–0933.
EEO Manager.—R. McGee, room AA/2052, 693–0202.
Assistant for Special Programs.—G. Osterman, room 5E689, 614–2613.

GENERAL COUNSEL

Pentagon, Room 4E724

Washington Navy Yard, Bldg. 36, 720 Kennon Street, SE., Washington, DC 20374
phone (703) 614–1994

General Counsel.—Hon. A.J. Mora.
Principal Deputy General Counsel.—T.F. Kranz, room 4D730, 614–5066.
Deputy General Counsel.—W. Molzahn.
Executive Assistant and Special Counsel.—CAPT D. O'Toole, JAGC, USN.
Associate General Counsel for—
Litigation.—F. Phelps, WNY/36, 685–6989.
Management.—A. Hildebrandt, room 4D730, 614–5066.
Assistant General Counsel for—
Ethics.—D. LaCroix, room NC–1, 604–8211.
Manpower and Reserve Affairs.—R. Cali, room 4D730, 614–5066.
Research, Development and Acquisition.—S. Krasik, room 4C748, 614–6985.
Military Assistant.—LTC R. Schieke, USMC, room 4D730, 614–5066.
Administrative Assistant.—LT P. Andreoli, USNR, room 5D830, 614–4472.

INSPECTOR GENERAL

1014 N Street, SE, Suite 100, Washington Navy Yard, DC 20374, phone (202) 433–2000

Inspector General.—VADM Tom Church.
Deputy Naval Inspector General.—Jill Vines Loftus.

LEGISLATIVE AFFAIRS

Room 5C760, phone (703) 697–7146, fax 697–1009

Chief.—RADM Gary Roughead.
Deputy Chief.—CAPT S.W. Gray.
Executive Assistant.—CDR Richard Clemmons.
Congressional Travel.—Paul B. Backe, room 5C765, 693–3764.
Public Affairs and Congressional Notifications.—CDR Conrad Chun, Sandra Latta, room 5C768, 695–0395; YNC (SW) Andre Dyson, room 5C832, 695–9359.
Director for Senate Liaison.—CAPT Mark Ferguson, room 182, (202) 685–6006.
Assistant Director for Senate Liaison.—CDR James C. Stein, (202) 685–6007.
Director for House Liaison.—CAPT Dale Lumme, room B324, (202) 225–7808.
Assistant Director for House Liaison.—CDR Lorin C. Selby, (202) 225–3075.
Director for Naval Programs.—CAPT Russel C. Keller, room 5C840, 693–2919.
Director for Legislation.—CAPT Mike McGregor, JAGC, room 5C800/5C771, 695–2776.

OFFICE OF INFORMATION

Pentagon, Room 4B463, phone (703) 697–7391

Chief.—RADM T. McCreary.
Deputy Chief.—CAPT Roxie Merritt.
Executive Assistant.—CDR Beci Brenton.
Assistant Chief for—
Administration and Resource Management.—William Mason, (703) 692–4747.
Media Operations.—CDR Conrad Chun, (703) 697–5342.
Naval Media Center.—CAPT Joseph Gradisher, (202) 433–5764.
Plans, Policy, and Community Programs.—CDR Corry Graham, (703) 697–0250.
Technology Integration.—Alan Goldstein, (703) 695–1887.

JUDGE ADVOCATE GENERAL

Pentagon, Room 5D834

Washington Navy Yard, 1322 Patterson Avenue, Suite 3000, Washington, DC 20374–5066
phone (703) 697–4610

Judge Advocate General.—RADM Michael Lohr.
Executive Assistant.—CAPT Russell L. Shaffer, (703) 614–7420.
Deputy Judge Advocate General.—RADM James E. McPherson.
Executive Assistant to the Deputy Judge Advocate General.—CDR James M. Ryan, (703) 614–7420, fax 697–4610.
Assistant Judge Advocate General for Civil Law.—CAPT Jane G. Dalton, WNY, Bldg. 33, (202) 685–5190 fax 685–5461.
Deputy Assistant Judge Advocate General for—
Administrative Law.—CAPT Eric E. Geisen, (703) 604–8200.
Admiralty.—CDR Scott Kenney, (202) 685–5075.
Claims, Investigations and Tort Litigation.—CAPT Paul M. Delaney, (202) 685–5920, fax 685–5484.
General Litigation.—CAPT Alex Whitaker, (202) 685–5075, fax 685–5472.
International and Operational Law.—CAPT David Grimord, (703) 697–9161.
Legal Assistance.—CDR Jennifer S. Herold, fax (202) 685–5486.
National Security Litigation and Intelligence Law.—CAPT James B. Norman, (202) 685–5464, fax 685–5467.
Assistant Judge Advocate General for Military Justice.—COL Kevin H. Winters, USMC, Building 111, 1st Floor, Washington Navy Yard, 20374–1111, (202) 685–7050, fax 685–7084.
Deputy Assistant Judge Advocate General for Criminal Law.—CAPT Kenneth R. Bryan, (USMC), (202) 685–7060, fax 685–7687.

Assistant Judge Advocate General for Operations and Management.—CAPT Robert W. Wedan, Jr., (202) 685–5190, fax 685–5461.

Deputy Assistant Judge Advocate General for—

Management and Plans.—CDR Jon E. Nelson, (202) 685–5218, fax 685–5479.

Military Personnel.—CDR Ann M. Delaney, (202) 685–5185, fax 685–5489.

Reserve and Retired Personnel Programs.—LCDR Frank Bustaman, (202) 685–5216, fax 685–5489.

Special Assistants to the Judge Advocate General—

Command Master Chief.—LNCM Renée S. Scheetz, (202) 685–5194, fax 685–5461.

Comptroller.—Dennis J. Oppman, (202) 685–5274, fax 685–5455.

Inspector General.—Joseph Scranton, (202) 685–5192, fax 685–5461.

Public Affairs Officer.—Carolyn Alison, (202) 685–5193, fax 685–5461.

OFFICE OF THE ASSISTANT SECRETARY OF THE NAVY FOR MANPOWER AND RESERVE AFFAIRS

Pentagon, Room 4E788, phone (703) 697–2180

Assistant Secretary.—Hon. W. Navas.

Executive Assistant and Naval Aide.—CAPT C. Noble, USN, 695–4537.

Military Assistant and Marine Aide.—LTC J. Andy, USMC, 697–0975.

Special Assistant for Military Law.—LCDR M. Moss, USN, room 5E827, 695–4367.

Administrative Assistant.—CWO3 W. Marin, 614–8288.

Director of Personnel Readiness Community Support.—B. Tate, room 5D800, 614–3553.

Deputy of:

Manpower Analysis and Assessment.—R. Beland, room 4E789, 695–4350.

Military Personnel.—A. Blair, room 4E789, 693–7700.

Reserve Affairs.—H. Barnum, room 5D833, 614–1327.

AGC.—R. Cali, room 4D730, 614–5066.

Staff Directors: CAPT S. Beaton, USN, room 5D833, 695–5302; C. Donovan, room 5D830, 614–3053; A. Khinoo, room 4E789, 695–2634; CDR C. Murphy, USN, room 5D800, 693–4489; CDR J. Slay, USN, room 4E789, 695–4356.

NAVAL COUNCIL OF PERSONNEL BOARDS

Washington Navy Yard, 720 Kennon Street SE., Room 309, Washington, DC 20374–5023
phone (202) 685–6407, fax 685–6610

Director.—CAPT William F. Eckert, Jr.

Counsel.—Roger R. Claussen.

Special Correspondence Officer.—Steven Neal.

Physical Evaluation Board.—COL Leif Larsen.

Naval Clemency and Parole Board.—LTC David Francis.

Naval Discharge Review Board.—LTC Wayne E. Briggs.

BOARD FOR CORRECTION OF NAVAL RECORDS

Arlington Annex Room 2432, Arlington, VA 20370–5100, phone (703) 614–9800
fax 614–9857

Executive Director.—W. Dean Pfieffer.

Deputy Executive Director.—Robert D. Zsalman.

Administrative Officer.—Ev Sellers.

BOARD FOR DECORATIONS AND MEDALS

Building 36 Washington Navy Yard, Washington, DC 20374–2001, phone (202) 685–6378

Senior Member.—VADM Albert Church.

Secretary to the Board.—LCDR Lisa Truesdale.

OFFICE OF THE ASSISTANT SECRETARY OF THE NAVY FOR RESEARCH, DEVELOPMENT AND ACQUISITION

Pentagon, Room 4E741, phone (703) 695–6315

Assistant Secretary.—Hon. J. Young, Jr.
Executive Assistant and Naval Aide.—CAPT W. Landay, USN, 697–4928.
Military Assistant and Marine Aide.—COL W. Taylor, USMC.
Deputy of:
Acquisition Management.—RADM R. Cowley, USN, room CP5/578, 602–2338.
Air Programs.—B. Balderson, room 5E715, 614–7794.
C4I/EW/Space Program.—Dr. D. Uhler, room PT1/1800, 602–6140.
Integrated Warfare Programs.—L. Wilson, room CM2/434, 602–1651.
International Programs.—[Vacant].
Littoral and Mine Warfare Programs.—COL J.K. Dodge, USMC (acting), room 5C738, 614–4794.
Logistics.—CAPT M. Ahern (acting), room 5E731, 697–2018.
Management and Budget.—CAPT J. Manna, USN (acting), room 5E785, 697–1091.
RDT&E.—Dr. M. McGrath, room 5E785, 697–1091.
Ship Programs.—CAPT R. Davis, USN (acting), room 5E813, 697–1710.
Acquisition and Career Management.—C. Stelloh-Garner, room CP5/362, 602–2835.
Manpower and Administration.—C. Horn, room 5D760, 614–5316.

ASSISTANT SECRETARY FOR FINANCIAL MANAGEMENT AND COMPTROLLER

Pentagon, Room 4E780, phone (703) 697–2325

Assistant Secretary.—Hon. D.M. Aviles.
Executive Assistant and Naval Aide.—CAPT W. Marriott, USN, room 4E768.
Director, Office of:
Budget.—RADM B. Engelhart, USN, room 4E348, 697–7105.
Financial Operations.—R. Haas, WNY, 685–6701.

ASSISTANT SECRETARY FOR INSTALLATIONS AND ENVIRONMENT

Pentagon, Room 4E729, phone (703) 693–4530

Assistant Secretary.—Hon. H.T. Johnson.
Executive Assistant and Naval Aide.—CAPT M. Jenkins, USN.
Deputy of:
Environment.—D. Schregardus, Rosslyn, 588–6676.
Infrastructure Analysis.—A. Davis, Rosslyn, 588–6611.
Installations and Facilities.—Wayne Arny, room 4E765, 693–4527.
Safety.—C. DeWitte, Rosslyn, 588–6680.
Assistant General Counsel for Installations and Environment.—T. Ledvina, room 5E677, 614–1090.
Confidential Assistant.—E. Davis.
Special Assistant/Scheduler.—GYSGT A. Sturgis, room 4E765, 693–4527.

DEPARTMENT OF THE NAVY CHIEF INFORMATION OFFICER

Chief Information Officer.—D. Wennergen, room PT1/2100, 602–1800.

CHIEF OF NAVAL OPERATIONS

Pentagon, Room 4E660, phone (703) 695–0532, fax 693–9408

Chief.—ADM V.E. Clark.
Vice Chief.—ADM W.J. Fallon.
Director, Naval Nuclear Propulsion Program.—ADM F.L. Bowman.
Special Assistant for—
Inspection Support.—VADM A.T. Church III.
Legal Services.—RADM Michael Lohr.
Legislative Support.—RADM Gary Roughead.
Material Inspections and Surveys.—RADM C.A. Kemp.

Naval Investigative Matters and Security.—D. Brant.
Public Affairs Support.—RADM S.R. Pietropaoli.
Safety Matters.—RADM D. Aronitzel.
Deputy Chief of Naval Operations for—
Logistics.—VADM Charles W. Moore, Jr.
Manpower.—VADM G.L. Hoewing.
Plans, Policy, and Operations.—VADM K.P. Green.
Resources, Warfare Requirements, and Assessments.—VADM M.G. Mullen.
Director, Office of:
Naval Intelligence.—RADM R.B. Porterfield.
Naval Medicine and Surgery.—VADM M.L. Cowan.
Naval Reserve.—VADM J.B. Totushek.
Naval Training.—VADM A.G. Harms, Jr.
Space and Electronic Warfare.—VADM R.W. Mayo.
Test and Evaluation and Technology Requirements.—RADM J.M. Cohen.
Chief of Chaplains.—[Vacant].
Oceanographer.—RADM T.J. Wilson III.

BUREAU OF MEDICINE AND SURGERY

Potomac Annex 23d and E Streets, Washington, DC 20372, phone (202) 762–3701
fax 653–0101

Chief.—VADM Michael L. Cowan, MC, USN.

NAVAL AIR SYSTEMS COMMAND

2531 Jefferson Plaza Building Nos. 1 and 2 Room 1200, Arlington, VA 20361
phone (703) 604–2822

Commander.—VADM Joseph W. Dyer, Jr.

NAVAL SEA SYSTEMS COMMAND

2531 Jefferson Davis Highway, Room 12E10 Building 3, Arlington, VA 22242
phone (703) 602–3381

Commander.—VADM Phillip M. Balisle.

NAVAL SUPPLY SYSTEMS COMMAND

Mechanicsburg, PA, phone (717) 790–6206

Commander.—VADM K.W. Lippert.

NAVAL HOSPITAL

Commanding Officer.—RADM Donald C. Arthur, Jr., (Medical Command), 8901 Wisconsin Avenue, Bethesda, MD 20614, (301) 295–2206.

NATIONAL NAVAL MEDICAL CENTER

Commander.—RADM Donald C. Arthur, Jr., (Medical Command), Bethesda, MD 20889 (301) 295–5800, fax 295–6521.

NAVAL NETWORK AND SPACE OPERATIONS COMMAND DETACHMENT

4401 Massachusetts Avenue, Washington, DC 20394, phone (202) 764–0356, fax 764–0357

Commander.—CAPT Gerda Edwards.

NAVAL FACILITIES ENGINEERING COMMAND

1322 Patterson Avenue, SE., Suite 1000, Washington Navy Yard, DC 20374
phone (202) 685–9002, fax 685–1463

Commander.—RADM Mike R. Johnson.

OFFICE OF NAVAL INTELLIGENCE

4251 Suitland Road, Washington, DC 20395, phone (301) 669–3001, fax 669–3099

Director.—RADM Richard B. Porterfield.

NAVAL CRIMINAL INVESTIGATIVE SERVICE COMMAND

716 Sicard Street SE, Suite 2000, Washington, DC 20388, phone (202) 433–8800, fax 433–9619

Director.—David L. Brant.

MILITARY SEALIFT COMMAND

Building No. 210, Washington Navy Yard, 9th and M Streets SE., Washington, DC 20398, phone (202) 685–5001, fax 685–5020

Commander.—VADM David L. Brewer.

JUDGE ADVOCATE GENERAL OF THE NAVY

Washington Navy Yard, 1322 Patterson Avenue, Washington, DC 20374
phone (202) 685–5190, fax 685–7151

Commander.—RADM Michael Lohr.

NAVAL SPACE COMMAND

Building 1700, 5280 Fourth Street, Dahlgren, VA 22448, phone (540) 653–6100

Commander.—RADM John P. Cryer III.

SPACE AND NAVAL WARFARE SYSTEMS COMMAND

14675 Lee Road, Chantilly, VA 20151, phone (703) 808–3000
fax 808–2779

Commander.—RADM Rand H. Fisher.

NAVAL DISTRICT OF WASHINGTON

901 M Street SE., Washington, DC 20374, phone 433–2777, fax 433–2207

Commandant.—RADM Christopher E. Weaver.
Chief of Staff.—CAPT Kathleen M. Cummings.

U.S. NAVAL ACADEMY

Annapolis, MD 21402, phone (410) 293–1000

Superintendent.—RADM Rodney P. Rempt, 293–1500.
Commandant of Midshipmen.—COL John R. Allen, 293–7005.

U.S. MARINE CORPS HEADQUARTERS

Pentagon, Room 4E714, Washington, DC, phone (703) 614–2500

Commandant.—GEN M.W. Hagee.
Assistant Commandant.—GEN W.L. Nyland.
Aide-de-Camp.—LTC F.W. Simonds.
Military Secretary.—COL J.C. Walker.
Sergeant Major of the Marine Corps.—SMAJ J. Estrada.
Legislative Assistant.—BG T.L. Corwin.
Counsel for the Commandant.—Peter M. Murphy.
Inspector General of the Marine Corps.—BG D. Thiessen.
Fiscal Director of the Marine Corps.—W.J. Wallhenhorst.
Chaplain.—CAPT L.V. Iasiello, USN.
Dental Officer.—COL A. Williams, US Army.
Judge Advocate.—BG J.L. Composto.
Medical Officer.—RADM (LH) R.D. Hufstader.
Deputy Chief of Staff for—
Aviation.—LTG M.A. Hough.
Installations and Logistics.—LTG R.L. Kelly.
Manpower and Reserve Affairs.—LTG G.L. Parks.
Plans, Policies, and Operations.—LTG E.R. Bedard.
Public Affairs.—BG M.A. Krusa-Dossin.
Programs and Resources.—LTG R. Mangus, (703) 614–3435.
Director of:
Intelligence.—BG M.E. Ennis.
Marine Corps History and Museums.—COL (Ret) J.W. Ripley.

MARINE BARRACKS

Eighth and I Streets SE., Washington DC 20390, phone (202) 433–4094

Commanding Officer.—COL D. O'Brien.

TRAINING AND EDUCATION COMMAND

Quantico, VA 22134, phone (703) 784–3730, fax 784–3724

Commanding General.—MG T.S. Jones.

DEPARTMENT OF JUSTICE

Main Justice Building

950 Pennsylvania Avenue, NW., Washington, DC 20530, phone (202) 514–2000
http://www.usdoj.gov

JOHN ASHCROFT, Attorney General, born on May 9, 1942, in Chicago, IL; education: Yale University, graduated with honors, 1964; University of Chicago School of Law, 1967; professional: taught business law at Southwest Missouri State University; and authored, or coauthored, several publications; public service: Missouri Auditor, 1973–1975; Missouri Attorney General, 1976–1985; Governor of Missouri, 1985–1993; Chairman, National Governors Association, 1991; U.S. Senate, 1995–2001; family: married to Janet Ashcroft, 1967; three children: Martha, John, and Andrew; nominated by George W. Bush to become the Attorney General of the United States on December 22, 2000, and was confirmed by the U.S. Senate on February 1, 2001.

OFFICE OF THE ATTORNEY GENERAL

Main Justice Building, Room 5111

Pennsylvania Avenue, NW., 20530, phone (202) 514–2001

Attorney General.—John Ashcroft.
Chief of Staff.—David T. Ayres, room 5216, 514–3892.
Deputy Chief of Staff and Counsel.—David M. Israelite, room 5222, 514–2291.
Counselor to the Attorney General.—Jeffrey Taylor, room 5110, 514–2107.
Counsel to the Attorney General: John Wood, 514–2001.
Director of Scheduling and Advance.—Andrew A. Beach, room 5133, 514–4195.
Advisor to the Attorney General and Deputy White House Liaison.—Susan M. Richmond, room 5214, 514–2927.
Confidential Assistant to the Attorney General.—Janet M. Potter, room 5111, 514–2001.

OFFICE OF THE DEPUTY ATTORNEY GENERAL

Main Justice Building, Room 4111, phone (202) 514–2101

Deputy Attorney General.—Larry D. Thompson.
Principal Associate Deputy Attorney General.—Stuart A. Levey, room 4115, 514–2269.
Chief of Staff.—Paul B. Murphy, room 4119, 305–3481.
Associate Deputy Attorneys General: Daniel P. Collins, room 4214, 514–6753; David Margolis, room 4113, 514–4945; Patrick Philbin, room 4222, 514–3744; Jonathan Tukel, room 4116, 514–8086; Christopher A. Wray, room 4208, 514–2105.
Senior Counsels to the Deputy Attorney General: Laura Baxter, room 4121, 514–9343; Stacey Duffy, room 4220, 305–1283; Bill Mateja, room 4131, 353–4435; James McAtamney, room 4311, 514–6907.
Counsel to the Deputy Attorney General.—Sigal Mandelker, room 4313, 616–1621.
Special Assistants to the Deputy Attorney General: Dawn Burton, room 4129, 305–0091; Wanda Martinson, room 4111, 514–2101.
Director, Faith Based and Community Initiatives Task Force.—Patrick Purtill, room 4409, 305–8283.
Chief Science Advisor.—Vahid Majida, room 4217, 305–7848.

OFFICE OF THE ASSOCIATE ATTORNEY GENERAL

Main Justice Building, Room 4633, phone (202) 514–9500

Associate Attorney General.—Robert D. McCallum, Jr., room 4633, 514–9500.
Principal Deputy Associate Attorney General.—Brian D. Boyle, room 4625, 305–1434.
Deputy Associate Attorneys General: David A. Higbee, room 4630, 616–0906; Jason Klitenic, room 4634, 305–1777.
Counsels to the Associate Attorney General: William Jordan, room 4621, 514–1968; Matthew L. Zabel, room 4632, 616–9475.
Confidential Assistant.—Currie Gunn, room 4633, 514–9500.

OFFICE OF DISPUTE RESOLUTION

Senior Counsel.—Linda Cinciotta, room 4619, 514–8910.

OFFICE OF THE SOLICITOR GENERAL

Main Justice Building, Room 5143, phone (202) 514–2201
www.usdjoj.gov.osg

Solicitor General.—Theodore B. Olson.
Principal Deputy Solicitor General.—Paul D. Clement, room 5143, 514–2206.
Deputy Solicitors General: Michael R. Dreeben, room 5623, 514–4285; Edwin S. Kneedler, room 5137, 514–3261.
Tax Assistant.—Kent L. Jones, room 5142, 514–3948.
Executive Officer.—Carolyn M. Brammer, room 3631, 514–5507.
Special Assistant.—Helen L. Voss, room 5143, 514–2201.
Legal Administrative Officer, Case Management Section.—Emily C. Spadoni, room 5614, 514–2218.
Chief, Research and Publications Section.—G. Shirley Anderson, room 6636, 514–3914.

OFFICE OF THE INSPECTOR GENERAL

RFK Main Justice Building, Room 4322, 950 Pennsylvania Avenue, NW., 20530
phone (202) 514–3435

Inspector General.—Glenn A. Fine.
Deputy Inspector General.—Robert L. Ashbaugh.
Counselor to the Inspector General.—Paul K. Martin.
Special Counsel.—Scott S. Dahl.
General Counsel.—Howard L. Sribnick, room 4316, 616–0646.
Assistant Inspectors General:
Audit.—Guy K. Zimmerman (NYAV), room 5000, 616–4633.
Evaluation and Inspections.—Paul A. Price (NYAV), room 6100, 616–4620.
Investigations.—Thomas J. Bondurant (NYAV), room 7100, 616–4760.
Management and Planning.—Gregory T. Peters (NYAV), room 7000, 616–4550.

OFFICE OF OVERSIGHT AND REVIEW

Director.—Carol F. Ochoa, room 4343, 616–0645.

REGIONAL AUDIT OFFICES

Washington: Domenic A. Zazzaro, 1425 New York Avenue, NW., room 6100, Washington, DC 20530, (202) 616–4688.
Computer Security and Information Technology Audit Office: Norman Hammonds, room 5000, (202) 616–3801.
Financial Statement Audit Office: Marilyn A. Kessinger, 1110 Vermont Avenue, NW., 8th Floor, Washington, DC 20530, (202) 616–4660.
Atlanta: Clark F. Cooper, Suite 1130, 75 Spring Street, Atlanta, GA 30303, (404) 331–5928.
Chicago: Carol S. Taraszka (acting), Suite 3510, Citicorp Center, 500 West Madison Street, Chicago, IL 60661, (312) 353–1203.
Dallas: George W. Stendell, Room 575, Box 4, 207 South Houston Street, Dallas, TX 75202–4724, (214) 655–5000.
Denver: David M. Sheeren, Suite 1603, Chencery Building, 1120 Lincoln Street, Denver, CO 80203, (303) 864–2000.
Philadelphia: Ferris B. Polk, Suite 201, 701 Market Street, Philadelphia, PA 19106, (215) 580–2111.
San Francisco: M. Thomas Clark, Suite 201, 1200 Bayhill Drive, San Bruno, CA 94066, (650) 876–9220.

REGIONAL INVESTIGATIONS OFFICES

Atlanta: Eddie D. Davis, 60 Forsyth Street, SW., Room 8M45, Atlanta, GA 30303, (404) 562–1980.

Boston: Thomas M. Hopkins, P.O. Box 2134, Boston, MA 02106, (617) 748–3218.

Chicago: Edward M. Dyner, P.O. Box 1802, Chicago, IL 60690, (312) 886–7050.

Colorado Springs: Craig Trautner, Suite 312, 111 S. Tejon Street, Colorado Springs, CO 80903, (719) 635–2366.

Dallas: James H. Mahon, Suite 551, Box 5, 207 S. Houston Street, Dallas, TX 75202, (214) 655–5076.

Detroit: Nicholas V. Candela, Suite 2001, 211 West Fort Street, Detroit, MI 48226, (313) 226–4005.

El Paso: Stephen P. Beauchamp, Suite 200, 4050 Rio Bravo, El Paso, TX 79902, (915) 577–0102.

Houston: Fred C. Ball, Jr., P.O. Box 610071, Houston, TX 77208, (713) 718–4888.

Los Angeles: Steve F. Turchek, Suite 655, 330 N. Brand Street, Glendale, CA 91203, (818) 543–1172.

McAllen: Wayne D. Beaman, Suite 510, Bentsen Tower, 1701 W. Business Highway 83, McAllen, TX 78501, (956) 618–8145.

Miami: Alan J. Hazen, Suite 312, 3800 Inverrary Boulevard, Ft. Lauderdale, FL 33319, (954) 535–2859.

New York: Ralph F. Paige, JFK Airport, P.O. Box 300999, Jamaica, NY 11430, (718) 553–7520.

Philadelphia: Kenneth R. Connaughton, Jr., P.O. Box 43508, Philadelphia, PA 19106, (215) 861–8755.

San Francisco: Norman K. Lau, Suite 220, 1200 Bayhill Drive, San Bruno, CA 94066, (650) 876–9058.

Seattle: Wayne Hawney, Suite 104, 620 Kirkland Way, Kirkland, WA 98033, (425) 828–3998.

Tucson: William L. King, Jr., P.O. Box 471, Tucson, AZ 85702, (520) 670–5243.

Washington: Charles T. Huggins, 1425 New York Avenue, NW., Suite 7100, Washington, DC 20530, (202) 616–4766.

Fraud Detection Office.—David R. Glendinning, room 7100, (202) 616–4766.

OFFICE OF LEGAL COUNSEL

Main Justice Building, Room 5229, phone (202) 514–2051

Assistant Attorney General.—M. Edward Whelan III (acting), room 5235, 514–2046.

Principal Deputy Assistant Attorney General.—M. Edward Whelan III, room 5235, 514–2046.

Deputy Assistant Attorneys General: Sheldon Bradshaw, room 5237, 514–3694; Noel J. Francisco, room 5236, 514–3744; Howard C. Nielson, Jr., room 5238, 514–2069.

Special Counsels: Paul P. Colborn, room 3230, 514–2048; Robert J. Delahunty, room 3229, 514–2054; Daniel L. Koffsky, room 3234, 514–2030.

Senior Counsel.—Rosemary A. Hart, room 3236, 514–2027.

Chief of Staff.—Frits H.H. Geurtsen, room 3316, 305–9250.

OFFICE OF LEGAL POLICY

Main Justice Building, Room 4234, phone (202) 514–4601

Assistant Attorney General.—Daniel J. Bryant (acting).

Principal Deputy Assistant Attorney General.—[Vacant], room 4238, 616–0038.

Deputy Assistant Attorneys General: Frank Campbell, room 7210, 514–2283; Michael Carrington, room 4224, 514–7473; Kevin R. Jones, room 7238, 514–4604.

Staff Director / Senior Counsel.—Brian A. Benczkowski, room 4228, 616–2004.

OFFICE OF PUBLIC AFFAIRS

Main Justice Building, Room 1220, phone (202) 514–2007

Director.—Barbara J. Comstock.

Deputy Directors: Mark C. Corallo, Monica M. Goodling, Gina M. Talamona.

OFFICE OF INFORMATION AND PRIVACY

Flag Building, Suite 570, phone (202) 514–3642

Co-Directors: Richard L. Huff and Daniel J. Metcalfe.
Deputy Director.—Melanie Ann Pustay.
Associate Director.—Kirsten J. Moncada.

OFFICE OF INTELLIGENCE POLICY AND REVIEW

Main Justice Building, Room 6150, phone (202) 514–3365

Counsel.—James A. Baker.
Deputy Counsel for—
Intelligence Operations.—Margaret A. Skelly-Nolen.
Intelligence Policy.—Mark A. Bradley (acting).

OFFICE OF PROFESSIONAL RESPONSIBILITY

20 Massachusetts Avenue, Suite 5100, phone (202) 514–3365

Counsel.—H. Marshall Jarrett.
Deputy Counsel.—Judith B. Wish.
Associate Counsels: William J. Birney, Paul L. Colby, Mary Anne Hoopes.
Assistant Counsels: James G. Duncan, Mark G. Fraase, Lyn A. Hardy, Neil C. Hurley, Tamara J. Kessler, Frederick C. Leiner, Mark S. Masling, Margaret S. McCarty, Simone E. Ross, Marlene M. Wahowiak, Barbara L. Ward, Karen A. Wehner, Alexander S. White, Candice M. Will.

PROFESSIONAL RESPONSIBILITY ADVISORY OFFICE

1325 Pennsylvania Avenue, National Theater Building, Suite 500, phone (202) 514–0458

Director.—Claudia J. Flynn.
Senior Advisor.—Barbara Kammerman.

OFFICE OF LEGISLATIVE AFFAIRS

Main Justice Building, Room 1145, phone (202) 514–2141

Assistant Attorney General.—William E. Moschella.
Special Counsel to the Assistant Attorney General.—M. Faith Burton, room 1141, 514–1653.
Principal Deputy Assistant Attorney General.—Jamie E. Brown, room 1143, 514–4054.

OFFICE OF INTERGOVERNMENTAL AND PUBLIC LIAISON

Main Justice Building, Room 1629, phone (202) 514–5530

Director.—Lori Sharpe Day.

OFFICE OF THE FEDERAL DETENTION TRUSTEE

1331 Pennsylvania Avenue, National Place Building, Suite 1210, phone (202) 353–4601

Director.—Claudia Hill.

JUSTICE MANAGEMENT DIVISION

RFK Main Justice Building, 950 Pennsylvania Avenue, NW., 20530

Rockville Building (ROC), 1151–D Seven Locks Road, Rockville, MD 20854

Bicentennial Building (BICN), 600 E Street NW., 20004

National Place Building (NPB), 1331 Pennsylvania Avenue, NW., 20530

Liberty Place Building (LPB), 325 7th Street NW., 20530

20 Massachusetts Avenue, NW., 20530

Patrick Henry Building (PHB), 601 D Street NW., 20530

Assistant Attorney General/Administration.—Paul R. Corts, room 1111, 514–3101.

Deputy Assistant Attorney General/Policy, Management and Planning.—[Vacant], room 1111, 514–3101.

Staff Directors for—

Department Ethics Office.—Stuart Frisch (acting), 1331 F Street, 514–8196.

Audit Liaison Office.—Vickie L. Sloan, 1331 F Street, 514–0469.

Office of General Counsel.—Stuart Frisch, General Counsel, (NPB), room 520, 514–3452.

Management and Planning.—David Orr (acting), (NPB), room 1400, 307–1800.

Security and Emergency Planning.—D. Jerry Rubino, room 6217, 514–2094.

Procurement Executive.—Leon J. Lofthaus (acting), room 1112, 514–1843.

Office of Small and Disadvantaged Business Utilization.—Joseph (Ken) Bryan, (NPB), room 1010, 616–0521.

Deputy Assistant Attorney General/Controller.—Leon J. Lofthaus (acting), room 1112, 514–1843.

Staff Directors for—

Budget.—Jolene Laurie Sullens, room 7601, 514–4082.

Finance.—Leon J. Lofthus (BICN), room 4070, 616–5800.

Procurement Services.—James Johnston (NPB), room 1000, 307–2000.

Asset Forfeiture Management Staff.—Michael Perez, room 6400, 20 Massachusetts Avenue, 616–8000.

Debt Collection Management.—Kathleen Haggerty (Liberty Place), 2nd Floor, 514–5343.

Deputy Assistant Attorney General, Human Resources/Administration.—Joanne W. Simms, room 1112, 514–5501.

Associate Assistant Attorney General for Federal Law Enforcement Training.—Thomas G. Milburn, Glynco, GA 31524, (912) 267–2914.

Staff Directors for—

Facilities and Administrative Services.—Stephen Myers (acting), (NPB), room 1050, 616–2995.

Library.—Blane Dessy, room 7535, 514–2133.

Personnel.—Debra Tomchek (NPB), room 1110, 514–6788.

Equal Employment Opportunity.—Ted McBurrows, 620 VT2, 616–4800.

Office of Attorney Recruitment and Management.—Louis DeFalaise, Suite 5200, 20 Massachusetts Avenue, 514–8900.

Consolidated Executive Office.—Willistine C. Brown, room 7113, 514–5537.

DOJ Executive Secretariat.—Kathie A. Harting, room 4412, 514–2063.

Deputy Assistant Attorney General/Information Resources Management and CIO.—Vance Hitch, room 1310–A, 514–0507.

Staff Directors for—

E-Government Services.—Mike Duffy, room 1314, 514–0507.

Policy and Planning.—Kevin Deeley (acting), room 1310, 514–4292.

Enterprise Solutions.—John Murray (PHB), room 4606, 514–0507.

IT Security.—Kevin Deeley (acting), (PHB), room 1600, 514–0507.

Operation Services.—Lisa Hooks (acting), room 1315, 514–3404.

ANTITRUST DIVISION

Main Justice Building, 950 Pennsylvania Avenue NW., 20530

City Center Building, 1401 H Street NW., 20530 (CCB)

Bicentennial Building, 600 E Street NW., 20530 (BICN)

Liberty Place Building, 325 Seventh Street NW., 20530 (LPB)

Patrick Henry Building, 601 D Street NW., 20530 (PHB)

Assistant Attorney General.—R. Hewitt Pate (acting), room 3109, 514–2401.
Deputy Assistant Attorneys General: James Griffin, room 3214, 514–3543; Deborah P. Majoras, room 3210, 514–0731; Edward T. Hand (acting), room 3119, 305–4517.
Director of:
Criminal Enforcement.—Scott D. Hammond, room 3217, 514–3543.
Economics Enforcement.—Kenneth Heyer, room 3112, 514–6995.
Operations.—Constance K. Robinson, room 3118, 514–3544.
Freedom of Information Act Officer.—Ann Lea Harding (LPB), room 200, 514–2692.
Executive Officer.—Thomas D. King (PHB), room 10150, 514–4005.
Section Chiefs:
Appellate.—Catherine G. O'Sullivan (PHB), room 10536, 514–2413.
Competition Policy.—[Vacant], (BICN), room 10900, 307–6665.
Economic Litigation.—Norman Familant (BICN), room 10800, 307–6323.
Economic Regulatory.—George A. Rozanski (BICN), room 10100, 307–6591.
Foreign Commerce.—Anne M. Purcell (acting), (PHB), room 10022, 514–5803.
Legal Policy.—Robert A. Potter (PHB), room 10124, 514–2512.
Litigation I.—Mark J. Botti (CCB), room 4000, 307–0827.
Litigation II.—J. Robert Kramer II (CCB), room 3000, 307–0924.
Litigation III.—James R. Wade (LPB), room 300, 616–5935.
National Criminal Enforcement.—Lisa M. Phelan (CCB), room 3700, 307–6694.
Networks and Technology.—Renata B. Hesse (BICN), room 9300, 514–5634.
Telecommunications and Media.—Nancy M. Goodman, (CCB), room 8000, 514–5621.
Transportation, Energy, and Agriculture.—Roger W. Fones (LPB), room 500, 307–6351.

FIELD OFFICES

California: Phillip H. Warren, 450 Golden Gate Avenue, Room 10–0101, Box 36046, San Francisco, CA 94102, (415) 436–6660.
Georgia: Nezida S. Davis, Richard B. Russell Building, 75 Spring Street SW., Suite 1176, Atlanta, GA 30303, (404) 331–7100.
Illinois: Marvin N. Price Jr., Rookery Building, 209 South LaSalle Street, Suite 600, Chicago, IL 60604, (312) 353–7530.
New York: Ralph T. Giordano, 26 Federal Plaza, Room 3630, New York, NY 10278, (212) 264–0391.
Ohio: Scott M. Watson, Plaza 9 Building, 55 Erieview Plaza, Suite 700, Cleveland, OH 44114, (216) 522–4070.
Pennsylvania: Robert E. Connolly, Curtis Center, One Independence Square West, 7th and Walnut Streets, Suite 650, Philadelphia, PA 19106, (215) 597–7405.
Texas: Duncan S. Currie, Thanksgiving Tower, 1601 Elm Street, Suite 4950, Dallas, TX 75201, (214) 880–9401.

CIVIL DIVISION

RFK Main Justice Building, 950 Pennsylvania Avenue, NW., 20530
(202) 514–3301 (MAIN)

20 Massachusetts Avenue, NW., 20530 (20MASS)

1100 L Street NW., 20530 (L ST)

National Place Building, 1331 Pennsylvania Avenue NW., 20530 (NATP)

1425 New York Avenue NW., 20530 (NYAV)

Patrick Henry Building, 601 D Street NW., 20530 (PHB)

Assistant Attorney General.—Robert D. McCallum, Jr. (MAIN), room 3141, 514–3301.
Senior Counsel.—William H. Jordan (MAIN), room 3605, 514–5421.

FEDERAL PROGRAMS BRANCH

Deputy Assistant Attorney General.—Shannen W. Coffin (MAIN), room 3137, 514–3310.

Directors: Felix Baxter (20MASS), room 7100, 514–4651; Joseph H. Hunt, room 7348, 514–1259; Jennifer D. Rivera (20MASS), room 6100, 514–3671.

Deputy Directors: Vincent M. Garvey (20MASS), room 7346, 514–3449; Sheila M. Lieber (20MASS), room 7102, 514–3786.

COMMERCIAL LITIGATION BRANCH

Deputy Assistant Attorney General.—Stuart E. Schiffer (MAIN), room 3607, 514–3306.

Directors: David M. Cohen, L Street, room 12124, 514–7300; Vito J. DiPietro, L Street, room 11116, 514–7223; Michael F. Hertz (PHB), room 9902, 514–7179; J. Christopher Kohn, L Street, room 10036, 514–7450.

Office of Foreign Litigation.—David Epstein, L Street, room 11006, 514–7455.

Deputy Directors: Joyce R. Branda (PHB), room 9904, 307–0231; Jeanne Davidson, L Street, room 12132, 307–0290; James M. Kinsella, L Street, room 12008, 307–1011; Sandra P. Spooner, L Street, room 10052, 514–7194.

Legal Officer.—James Gresser, Amerian Embassy, London, England, PSC 801, Box 42, FPO AE, New York, NY 09498-4042, 9+011–44–171–629–6794.

Attorney-in-Charge.—John J. Mahon (acting), Suite 339, 26 Federal Plaza, New York, NY 10278, FTS: (212) 264–9232.

TORTS BRANCH

Deputy Assistant Attorney General.—Jeffrey S. Bucholtz (MAIN), room 3127, 514–3045.

Directors: Gary W. Allen (NYAV), room 10122, 616–4000; Jeffery Axelrad (NATP), room 8098N, 616–4400; Sharon Y. Eubanks (NATP), room 115–02, 616–8280; J. Patrick Glynn (NATP), room 8028S, 616–4200; Helene M. Goldberg, (NYAV), room 8122, 616–4140.

Deputy Directors: JoAnn J. Bordeaux (NATP), room 8024S, 616–4204; John L. Euler (NYAV), room 3122, 616–4088; Paul F. Figley (NATP), room 8096N, 616–4248; Stephen D. Brody (NATP), room 1150–04, 616–1437.

Attorneys-in-Charge: Philip A. Berns, 450 Golden Gate Avenue, 10/6610, Box 36028, San Francisco, CA 94102–3463, FTS: (415) 436–6630; [Vacant], Suite 320, 26 Federal Plaza, New York, NY 10278–0140, FTS: (212) 264–0480.

APPELLATE STAFF

Deputy Assistant Attorney General.—Gregory G. Katsas (MAIN), room 3135, 514–4015.

Director.—Robert E. Kopp (PHB), room 9002, 514–3311.

Deputy Director.—William Kanter (PHB), room 9102, 514–4575.

CONSUMER LITIGATION

Deputy Assistant Attorney General.—Laura L. Flippin (MAIN), room 3131, 514–1258.

Director.—Eugene M. Thirolf (NATP), room 950N, 307–3009.

Deputy Director.—Lawrence G. McDade (NATP), room 950N, 307–0138.

IMMIGRATION LITIGATION

Deputy Assistant Attorney General.—Laura L. Flippin (MAIN), room 3131, 514–1258.

Director.—Thomas W. Hussey, (NATP), room 7026S, 616–4900.

Deputy Directors: Donald E. Keener, (NATP), room 7022S, 616–4878; David J. Kline (NATP), room 7006N, 616–4856; David M. McConnell (NATP), room 7260N, 616–4881.

MANAGEMENT PROGRAMS

Director.—Kenneth L. Zwick (MAIN), room 3140, 514–4552.

Directors, Office of:

Administration.—Shirley Lloyd, L Street, room 9008, 307–0016.

Planning, Budget, and Evaluation.—Linda S. Liner, L Street, room 9042, 307–0034.

Management Information.—Dorothy Bahr, L Street, room 8044, 307–0304.
Litigation Support.—Clarisse Abramidis, L Street, room 9126, 616–5014.
Policy and Management Operations.—Kevin Burket, L Street, room 8128, 616–8073.

CIVIL RIGHTS DIVISION

Main Justice Building, Room 3623, (202) 514–2151 (MAIN)

1425 New York Avenue, NW., 20035 (NYAV)

601 D Street, NW., 20004 (PHB)

100 Indiana Avenue, NW., 20004 (NALC)

1800 G Street, NW., 20004 (NWB)

www.usdoj.gov/crt

Assistant Attorney General.—Ralph F. Boyd, Jr., room 3623, 514–2151.
Deputy Assistant Attorneys General: Robert Neil Driscoll, room 3617, 353–0742; Loretta King, room 3343, 616–1278; Brad Schlozman, room 3337, 305–8060; J. Michael Wiggins, room 3623, 514–8696.
Counselor to the Assistant Attorney General.—Minh Vu, room 3615, 514–2938.
Counsels to the Assistant Attorney General for Civil Rights: James S. Angus, room 3342, 305–1119; Andrew Lelling, room 3618, 514–3845; Cynthia McKnight, room 3339, 305–0864; Hans von Spakovsky, room 3614, 305–9750.
Executive Officer.—DeDe Greene (NYAV), room 5058, 514–4224.
Section Chiefs:
Appellate.—David K. Flynn (PHB), room 5102, 514–2195.
Coordination and Review.—Merrily A. Friedlander (NYAV), room 6001, 307–2222.
Criminal.—Albert N. Moskowitz (PHB), room 5802, 514–3204.
Disability Rights.—John L. Wodatch (NYAV), room 4055, 307–2227.
Educational Opportunities.—Jeremiah Glassman (PHB), room 4002, 514–4092.
Employment Litigation.—David Palmer (PHB), room 4040, 514–3831.
Housing and Civil Enforcement.—Steven H. Rosenbaum (NWB), room 7002, 514–4713.
Special Counsel for Immigration Related Unfair Employment Practices.—[Vacant], (MAIN), room 9032, 616–5528.
Special Litigation.—Shanetta Brown Cutler (acting), (PHB), room 5114, 514–6255.
Voting.—Joseph D. Rich, (NWB), room 7254, 307–2767.

CRIMINAL DIVISION

Main Justice Building, Room 2107 (202) 514–2601 (MAIN)

Bond Building, 1400 New York Avenue NW., 20530 (BB)

1331 F Street NW., (F Street)

1301 New York Avenue, NW., 20530 (1301 NY)

Patrick Henry Building, 601 D Street, NW., (PHB)

Assistant Attorney General.—Michael Chertoff, room 2107, 514–7200.
Principal Deputy Assistant Attorney General.—John C. Keeney, room 2109, 514–2621.
Deputy Assistant Attorneys General: Alice Fisher, room 2212, 514–9725; John Malcolm, room 2113, 616–3930; Bruce Swartz, room 2119, 514–2333; Mary Lee Warren, room 2115, 514–3729.
Chief of Staff to the Assistant Attorney General.—Julie L. Myers, room 2100, 353–3600.
Deputy Chief of Staff and Senior Counsel to the Assistant Attorney General.—Richard M. Rogers, room 2208, 307–0030.
Counselor to the Assistant Attorney General.—Eric H. Jaso, room 2218, 514–9351.
Counsels to the Assistant Attorney General: David Nahmias, room 2214, 514–0169; Laura H. Parsky, room 2222, 616–1626.
Special Assistants to the Assistant Attorney General: Rajit Dosanjh, room 2121, 307–0084; Trent Luckenbill, room 2309, 514–1013; Sigal Mandelker, room 2309, 616–1621; James S. Reynolds, room 2315, 616–8664; John K. Wallace III, room 2116, 514–0940.
Executive Officer.—Sandra J. Bright (BB), room 5100, 514–2641.
Section Chiefs/Office Directors:
Appellate.—Patty M. Stemler (PHB), room 2606, 514–3521.
Asset Forfeiture and Money Laundering.—John Roth (BB), room 10100, 514–1263.

Capital Case Unit.—Margaret P. Griffey (PHB), room 6140, 353–9779.
Child Exploitation and Obscenity.—Andrew G. Oosterbaan (BB), room 6000, 514–5780.
Computer Crime and Intellectual Property.—Martha Stansell-Gramm (1301NY), suite 600, 514–1026.
Counterespionage.—John Dion (BB), room 9100, 514–1187.
Counterterrorism.—Barry Sabin (PHB), room 6500, 514–5000.
Domestic Security.—Teresa McHenry (acting), (1301NY), suite 6500, 514–0849.
Enforcement Operations.—Maureen Killion (1301NY), suite 1200, 514–6809.
Fraud.—Joshua R. Hochberg (BB), room 4100, 514–7023.
International Affairs.—Mary Ellen Warlow (1301NY), suite 900, 514–0000.
International Criminal Investigative Training Assistance Program.—Joseph Jones (acting), (1331 F), suite 500, 514–8881.
Narcotics and Dangerous Drugs.—Jodi Avergun (BB), room 11100, 514–0917.
Overseas Prosecutorial Development, Assistance and Training.—Carl Alexandre (1331 F), room 400, 514–1323.
Organized Crime and Racketeering.—Bruce Ohr (1301 NY), suite 700, 514–3594.
Organized Crime Drug Enforcement Task Forces.—[Vacant] (PHB), room 6426, 514–1860.
Policy and Legislation: Julie E. Samuels (1301 NY), suite 1000.
Public Integrity.—Noel Hillman (BB), room 12000, 514–1412.
Special Investigations.—Eli M. Rosenbaum (1301 NY), suite 200, 616–2492.

ENVIRONMENT AND NATURAL RESOURCES DIVISION

Main Justice Building, Room 2143 (202) 514–2701 (MAIN)

601 Pennsylvania Avenue, 20044 (PENN)

1425 New York Avenue NW., 20530 (NYAV)

501 D Street (PHB)

Assistant Attorney General.—Thomas L. Sansonetti, (MAIN), room 2143, 514–2701.
Principal Deputy Assistant Attorney General.—Kelly A. Johnson (MAIN), room 2141, 514–4760.
Deputy Assistant Attorneys General: Jeffrey Bossert Clark (MAIN), room 2607, 514–3370; John Cruden (MAIN), room 2611, 514–2718; Eileen Sobeck (MAIN), room 2135, 514–0943.
Counsels to the Assistant Attorney General: Andrew C. Emrich (MAIN), room 2607, 514–0624; Mary Neumayr (MAIN), room 2129, 514–0624.
Executive Officer.—Robert L. Bruffy (PHB), room 2038, 616–3147.
Section Chiefs:
Appellate.—James C. Kilbourne (PHB), room 8046, 514–2748.
Environmental Crimes.—David M. Uhlmann (PHB), room 2102, 305–0337.
Environmental Defense.—Letitia J. Grishaw (PHB), room 8002, 514–2219.
Environmental Enforcement.—Bruce Gelber (NYAV), room 13063, 514–4624.
General Litigation.—K. Jack Haugrud (PHB), room 3102, 305–0438.
Indian Resources.—Craig Alexander, (PHB), room 3016, 514–9080.
Land Acquisition.—Virginia P. Butler (PHB), room 3638, 305–0316.
Policy, Legislation, and Special Litigation.—Pauline M. Milius (PHB), room 8022, 514–2586.
Wildlife and Marine Resources.—Jean E. Williams (PHB), room 3902, 305–0210.

FIELD OFFICES

801 B Street, Suite 504, Anchorage, AK 99501–3657

Trial Attorneys: Regina Belt (907) 271–3456; Dean Dunsmore, (907) 271–5457; Bruce Landon (907) 271–5948.

999 18th Street, Suite 945, North Tower, Denver, CO 80202

Trial Attorneys: David Askman (303) 312–7247; Bruce Bernard (303) 312–7319; Bradley Bridgewater (303) 312–7318; Dave Carson (303) 312–7309; Jerry Ellington (303) 312–7321; Robert Foster (303) 312–7320; Jim Freeman (303) 312–7376; Dave Gehlert

(303) 312–7352; Mike Gheleta (303) 312–7303; Alan Greenberg (303) 312–7324; David Harder (303) 312–7328; Robert Homiak (303) 312–7353; Heidi Kukis (303) 312–7354; Lee Leininger, (303) 312–7322; John Moscato (303) 312–7346; Mark Nitcynski (303) 312–7388; Terry Petrie (303) 312–7327; Daniel Pinkston (303) 312–7397; Susan Schneider (303) 312–7308; Andrew Smith, (303) 312–7326; Andrew Walch (303) 312–7316.

Administrative Officer.—David Jones (303) 312–7387.

501 I Street, Suite 9–700, Sacramento, CA 95814–2322

Trial Attorneys: Maria Iizuka (916) 930–2202; Stephen Macfarlane (916) 930–2204; Charles Shockey (916) 930–2203.

301 Howard Street, Suite 1050, San Francisco, CA 94105–2001

Trial Attorneys: Matt Fogelson (415) 744–6470; David Glazer (415) 744–6477; Herb Johnson (415) 436–7159; Robert Mullaney (415) 744–6483; Bradley O'Brien (415) 744–6484; Angela O'Connell (415) 744–6485; Thomas Pacheco (415) 744–6480; Judith Rabinowitz (415) 744–6486; Mark Rigau (415) 744–6487; Noel Wise (415) 744–6471.

c/o NOAA/DARCNW, 7600 San Point Way NE, Seattle, WA 98115–0070

Trial Attorneys: Sean Carman (206) 526–6617; James Nicoli (206) 526–6616; David Spohr (206) 526–4603; Mike Zevenbergen (206) 526–6607.

One Gateway Center, Suite 6116, Newton Corner, MA 02158

Trial Attorneys: Catherine Fiske (617) 450–0444; Donald Frankel (617) 450–0442.

c/o U.S. Attorney's Office, 555 Pleasant Street, Suite 352, Concord, NH 03301

Trial Attorney.— Kristine Tardiff (603) 225–1562, ext. 283.

c/o U.S. Attorney's Office, 201 Third Street, NW., Suite 900, Albuquerque, NM 87102

Trial Attorney.—Andrew Smith, (505) 224–1468.

161 East Mallard Drive, Suite A, Boise, ID 83706

Trial Attorney.—David Negri, (208) 331–5943.

c/o U.S. Attorney's Office, 105 E. Pine Street, 2nd Floor, Missoula, MT 59802

Trial Attorney.—Robert Anderson, (406) 829–3322.

c/o U.S. Attorney's Office, Room 6–100, PJKK Federal Building, 300 Ala Moana Boulevard, Honolulu, HI 96850

Trial Attorney.—Sila DeRoma, (808) 541–2850.

483 Doe Run Road, Sequim, WA 98382

Appraiser.—James Eaton, (360) 582–0038.

1205 Via Escalante, Chula Vista, CA 91910

Trial Attorney.—Mike Reed, (619) 656–2273.

TAX DIVISION

Main Justice Building, 950 Pennsylvania Avenue NW., Room 4141, (202) 514–2901

Judiciary Center Building, 555 Fourth Street NW., 20001 (JCB)

Bicentennial Building, 600 E Street NW., 20004 (BICN)

Max Energy Tower, 7717 N. Harwood Street, Suite 400, Dallas, TX 75242 (MAX)

Patrick Henry Building, 601 D Street NW., 20004 (PHB)

Assistant Attorney General.—Eileen J. O'Connor, room 4601, 514–2901.

Deputy Assistant Attorneys General: Claire Fallon, room 4137, 514–5109 (Civil Matters); Mark V. Holmes, room 4609, 514–8665 (Chief of Staff); Richard T. Morrison, room 4613, 514–2901 (Appellate and Review); Rod J. Rosenstein, room 4603, 514–2915 (Criminal Matters).

Special Assistants: Christopher LaRosa (MAIN), room 4142, 307–6559; Cecilia Lutz (MAIN), room 4618, 514–5113; Ann Carroll Reid (MAIN), room 4138, 514–6636.

Senior Legislative Counsel.—Stephen J. Csontos (MAIN), room 4134, 307–6419.

Section Chiefs:

Central Region, Civil Trial.—Seth Heald (acting), (JCB), room 8921–B, 514–6502.

Eastern Region, Civil Trial.—David A. Hubbert (JCB) room 6126, 307–6426.

Northern Region, Civil Trial.—D. Patrick Mullarkey (JCB), room 7804–A, 307–6533.

Southern Region, Civil Trial.—Michael Kearns (JCB), room 6243–A, 514–5905.

Southwestern Region, Civil Trial.—Louise P. Hytken (MAX), room 4100, (214) 880–9725.

Western Region, Civil Trial.—Robert S. Watkins (JCB), room 7907–B, 307–6413.

Court of Federal Claims.—Mildred L. Seidman (JCB), room 8804–A, 307–6440.

Office of Review.—John DiCicco (JCB), room 6846, 307–6567.

Appellate.—Gary R. Allen (PHB), room 7038, 514–3361.

Criminal Enforcement, Northern Region.—Rosemary E. Paguni (BICN), room 5824, 514–2323.

Criminal Enforcement, Southern Region.—Thomas Zehnle (BICN), room 5135, 514–5112.

Criminal Enforcement, Western Region.—Ronald Cimino (BICN), room 5101, 514–5762.

Criminal Appeals and Tax Enforcement Policy.—Robert E. Lindsay (PHB), room 7002, 514–3011.

Executive Officer.—Joseph E. Young (PHB), room 7802, 616–0010.

Special Litigation Counsels: Jonathan S. Cohen (PHB), room 7028, 514–2970; Dennis M. Donohue (JCB), room 7104, 307–6492.

DRUG ENFORCEMENT ADMINISTRATION

Lincoln Place-1 (East), 600 Army-Navy Drive, Arlington, VA 22202 (LP–1)

Lincoln Place-2 (West), 700 Army-Navy Drive, Arlington, VA 22202 (LP–2)

Administrator.—Karen P. Tandy, room W–12060, 307–8000.

Executive Assistant.—Toni P. Purvis-Teresi, 307–8003.

Deputy Administrator.—John B. Brown III, room W–12058–F, 307–7345.

Executive Assistant.—Joel K. Fries, room W–12058–E, 307–8770.

Chief, Office of Congressional and Public Affairs.—Christopher L. Battle, room W–12228, 307–7363.

Chief, Executive Policy and Strategic Planning.—Russell F. Benson, room W11100, 307–7420.

Section Chiefs:

Congressional Affairs.—Emmett Highland (acting), room W–12100, 307–7423.

Demand Reduction.—Michael Dalich, room W–9164, 307–7936.

Public Affairs.—William R. Glaspy, room W–12100, 307–7977.

Information Services.—Donald E. Joseph, room W–12232, 307–7967.

Chief Counsel.—Cynthia R. Ryan, room W–12142–C, 307–7322.

Deputy Chief Counsel.—Robert C. Gleason, room E–12375, 307–8020.

Chief, Office of Administrative Law Judges.—Mary Ellen Bittner, room E–2129, 307–8188.

FINANCIAL MANAGEMENT DIVISION

Chief Financial Officer.—Frank M. Kalder, room W–12138, 307–7330.
Deputy Assistant Administrators for—
Finance.—Richard Kay, room E–7397, 307–7002.
Resource Management.—Charlotte A. Saunders, room E–7399, 307–4800.
Acquisition Management.—Christinia K. Sisk, room W–5100, 307–7777.
Section Chiefs:
Acquisition Management.—Jason Eickenhorst (acting), room W–5028, 307–7802.
Controls and Coordination.—David W. Kapaldo, room E–7395, 307–7080.
Evaluations and Planning.—Peter C. Linn, room E–7287, 307–7005.
Financial Integrity.—William S. Truitt, room E–7101, 307–7082.
Financial Operations.—Tammy Balas, room E–7165, 307–9933.
Financial Reports.—Kathleen Rodgers, room E–7165, 307–7062.
Financial Systems.—Daniel G. Gillette (acting), room E–7205, 307–7031.
Organization and Staffing Management.—Mark F. Bullard, room E–7331, 307–7059.
Policy and Transportation.—Barbara J. Joplin, room W–5010, 307–7808.
Program Liaison and Analysis.—Karin E. Franceschelli, room E–7259, 305–9149.
Statistical Services.—Patrick R. Gartin, room W–6300, 307–8276.

INSPECTIONS DIVISION

Chief Inspector.—George J. Cazenavette III, room W–12042A, 307–7358.
Deputy Chief Inspector, Office of:
Inspections.—Charles H. West, room W–4348, 307–8200.
Professional Responsibility.—John E. Driscoll, room W–4176, 307–8235.
Security Programs.—Mark S. Johnson, room W–2340, 307–3465.

OPERATIONS DIVISION

Chief of Operations.—Rogelio E. Guevara, room W–12050, 307–7340.
Special Agent-in-Charge, Aviation Division.—William C. Brown, Ft. Worth, TX (817) 837–2004.
Chiefs of:
Domestic Operations.—James L. Capra, room W–11070, 307–7927.
Operations Management.—William Simpson, Jr., room W–11148, 307–4200.
Section Chiefs of:
Caribbean and South America.—[Vacant], room W–8264, 307–7203.
Dangerous Drugs and Chemicals.—Dennis A. Wichern, room W–10128, 307–7490.
Domestic Asset Forfeiture.—James R. Fitzgerald, room E–11397, 307–7633.
Domestic Forfeiture Counsel.—John Hieronymus, room E–12105, 307–7636.
Europe/Africa/Asia and Canada.—Marshall Fisher, room W–10268, 307–4830.
Financial Operations.—Edward Guillen, room W–8300, 307–8396.
Investigative Support.—Roy Adams, room W–8316, 307–8923.
Local Impact.—Earl McKigney, room W–10034, 307–8918.
Mexico and Central America.—Douglas W. Hebert, room W–10106, 307–5582.
Operations Budget.—Anthony C. Marotta, room W–11254, 307–4218.
Policy and Planning.—Donald P. Augustine, room W–11250, 307–4211.
Tactical Enforcement.—Matthew G. Barnes, room W–6350, 307–8799.
Special Agent-in-Charge, Special Operations Division.—Joseph Keefe, Chantilly, VA (703) 488–4205.
Section Chiefs:
Latin America/Caribbean.—Jerome McArdle, Chantilly, VA (703) 488–4425.
Europe/Asia.—Patrick Cardiello, Chantilly, VA (703) 488–4338.
Special Projects.—Helen Bass, Chantilly, VA (703) 488–4311.
Southwest Border, Section A.—John S. Comer, Chantilly, VA (703) 488–4472.
Southwest Border, Section B.—Kevin Lane, Chantilly, VA (703) 488–4405.
Southwest Border, Section C.—Clay Price, Chantilly, VA (703) 488–4424.
Financial Investigations Unit.—Grant Murray, Chantilly, VA (703) 488–4264.
Deputy Assistant Administrator, Office of Diversion Control.—Laura M. Nagel, room E–6295, 307–7165.
Deputy Director.—Terrance W. Woodworth, room E–6293, 307–7163.
Section Chiefs:
Diversion/Planning/Resource.—Michael R. Mapes, room E–10285, 307–7197.
Chemical Control.—S. Scott Collier, room E–10165, 307–7204.

Drug and Chemical Evaluation.—Frank L. Sapienza, room E–6238, 307–7183.
Liaison and Policy.—Patricia Good, room E–6385, 307–7297.
Drug Operations.—Elizabeth Willis, room E–6171, 307–7194.
Registration and Progressive Support.—Richard A. Boyd, room E–6109, 307–4925.

Chief, Office of International Operations.—Martin W. Pracht, room W–11024, 307–4233.

Section Chiefs:

Central America and Mexico.—Michael McManus, room W–10202, 307–7472.
Europe/Mid-East.—Thomas Wade (acting), room W–10346, 307–4255.
Far East.—Michael Kula (acting), room W–10348, 307–7444.
South America.—John Emerson, room W–8344, 305–9108.
Caribbean Islands.—Frank Marrero, room W–8308, 307–1763.
Foreign Administrative Support.—Joseph P. Denehy, room W–11104, 353–0979.

INTELLIGENCE DIVISION

Assistant Administrator.—Steven W. Casteel, room W–12020A, 307–3607.

Director, El Paso Intelligence Center.—James S. Mavromatis, Building 11339, SSG Sims Street, El Paso, TX 79908–8098 (915) 760–2011.

Deputy Associate Administrator, Office of Intelligence Policy and Management.—Judith E. Bertini, room W–7176, 307–8748.

Section Chiefs:

Management and Program Support.—James A. Curtin, room W–7268, 307–7534.
Policy and Liaison.—Joan E. Zolak, room W–7030, 353–9620.

Deputy Assistant Administrator, Office of Strategic Intelligence.—Charles A. Gardner, room W–8072, 307–4294.

Section Chiefs:

Special Strategic Intelligence Section A.—Lourdes P. Border. room 8066, 307–8070.
Regional Strategic Intelligence.—[Vacant], room W–8258, 307–5442.

Deputy Assistant Administrator, Office of Investigative Intelligence.—Richard A. Tucker, room W–10190, 307–8050.

Section Chief of Worldwide Investigative Intelligence.—Craig Estancona, room W–10280, 307–8431.

Deputy Assistant Administrator, Office of Special Intelligence.—Dennis Morton, room E–5075A, 307–3650.

Section Chiefs:

Investigative Support.—Steve Casto, Chantilly, VA (703) 488–4246.
Operational Support.—Marilynn Nolan, room E–5015, 307–3645.
Technical Support.—Gisele Gatjanis, room E–5121A, 307–4872.
Data Management.—Sara Glazier, room E–5121B, 307–8796.

OPERATIONAL SUPPORT DIVISION

Assistant Administrator.—William B. Simpkins, room W–12142, 307–4730.

Deputy Assistant Administrator, Office of Administration.—James M. Whetstone, room W–9088, 307–7708.

Associate Deputy Assistant Administrator, Office of Administration.—G. Thomas Gitchel, room W–9174, 307–7708.

Section Chiefs:

Facilities and Finance.—William A. Kopitz, room W–5244, 307–7792.
Freedom of Information/Records Management.—Arthur W. Reed, room W–9174, 307–7711.
Administrative Operations.—Emmett T. Ridley, Jr., room W–5100–A, 307–7766.

Deputy Assistant Administrator, Office of Forensic Sciences.—Thomas J. Janovsky, room W–7342, 307–8866.

Associate Deputy Assistant Administrator, Office of Forsenic Sciences.—Alan B. Clark, room W–7344, 307–8868.

Section Chiefs:

Laboratory Operations.—Steven M. Sottolano, room W–7310, 307–8880.
Hazardous Waste Disposal.—Mary Greene, room W–7308, 307–8872.
Laboratory Support.—Rhesa G. Gilliland, room W–7348, 307–8785.

Deputy Assistant Administrator, Office of Investigative Technology.—Dale Zeisset, Gunston, VA (703) 495–6500.

Section Chiefs:

Communications and Polygraph Support.—Wayne A. Enders, Gunston, VA (703) 495–6520.

Telecommunications Intercept Support.—Donald Torres, Gunston, VA (703) 495–6550.

Surveillance Support.—Jon J. Sugrue, Gunston, VA (703) 495–6575.

Deputy Assistant Administrator, Office of Information Systems.—Dennis McCrary, room E–3105, 307–3653.

Section Chiefs:

Information Resources Management.—Ruth Torres, room E–3005, 307–9883.

Operations and Support.—Larry Castleberry, room E–3207, 307–9481.

Systems Applications.—John B. Taylor, room E–3105, 307–1797.

Special Projects.—Michelle M. Bower, room E–4111, 307–9896.

HUMAN RESOURCES DIVISION

Assistant Administrator.—Catherine J. Kasch, room W–3166, 307–4000.

Deputy Assistant Administrator, Office of Personnel.—[Vacant], room W–3166, 307–4000.

Section Chiefs:

Management & Employee Services.—Margaret A. Hager, room W–3058, 307–4015.

Recruitment and Placement.—Janis J. Johnson, room W–3242, 307–4055.

Equal Employment Opportunity Officer.—Barbara A. Lewis, room E–11275, 307–8888.

Career Board Executive Secretary.—Walter C. Morrison, room W–2268, 307–7349.

Chairman, Board of Professional Conduct.—Eli Madrid, room E–9333, 307–8980.

Special Agent-in-Charge, Office of Training.—John R. McCarty, DEA/FBI Academy, Building 1, Quantico, VA 22135 (703) 632–5010.

Assistant Special Agents-in-Charge:

Domestic Training Section 1.—Bill Faiella (703) 632–5110.

Domestic Training Section 2.—James Gregorious (703) 632–5310.

International Training Section.—Dominick D. Braccio, Jr., (703) 632–5330.

FIELD OFFICES

ATLANTA DIVISION:

Special Agent-in-Charge.—W. Michael Furgason, Sr., Room 740, 75 Spring Street SW, Atlanta, GA 30303 (404) 893–7000.

BOSTON DIVISION:

Special Agent-in-Charge.—Mark R. Trouville, JFK Federal Building, Room E–400, 15 Sudsbury Street, Boston, MA 02203 (617) 557–2100.

CARIBBEAN DIVISION:

Special Agent-in-Charge.—Jerome M. Harris, Metro Office Park, Building 17, Calle 2, Suite 500, Guaynabo, PR 00968–1706 (787) 775–1815.

CHICAGO DIVISION:

Special Agent-in-Charge.—Richard W. Sanders, Suite 1200, John C. Kluczynski Federal Building, 230 South Dearborn Street, Chicago, IL 60604 (312) 353–7875.

DALLAS DIVISION:

Special Agent-in-Charge.—Sherri F. Strange, 10160 Technology Boulevard East, Dallas, TX 75220 (214) 640–6900.

DENVER DIVISION:

Special Agent-in-Charge.—Robert Castillo, 115 Inverness Drive, East, Englewood, CO 80112 (303) 705–7300.

DETROIT DIVISION:

Special Agent-in-Charge.—Michael A. Braun, 431 Howard Street, Detroit, MI 48226 (313) 234–4000.

EL PASO DIVISION:

Special Agent-in-Charge.—Sandalio Gonzalez, 660 South Mesa Hills Drive, Suite 2000, El Paso, TX 79912 (915) 832–6000.

HOUSTON DIVISION:

Special Agent-in-Charge.—Kevin C. Whaley, 1433 West Loop South, Suite 600, Houston, TX 77027–9506 (713) 693–3000.

LOS ANGELES DIVISION:

Special Agent-in-Charge.—Michele Leonhart, 255 East Temple Street, 20th Floor, Los Angeles, CA 90012 (213) 621–6700.

MIAMI DIVISION:

Special Agent-in-Charge.—Thomas W. Raffanello, Phoenix Building, 8400 NW. 53rd Street, Miami, FL 33166 (305) 590–4870.

NEWARK DIVISION:

Special Agent-in-Charge.—Anthony D. Cammarato, 80 Mulberry Street, Second Floor, Newark, NJ 07102 (973) 273–5000.

NEW ORLEANS DIVISION:

Special Agent-in-Charge.—James D. Craig, Suite 1800, 3838 North Causeway Boulevard, Metaire, LA 70002 (504) 840–1100.

NEW YORK DIVISION:

Special Agent-in-Charge.—Anthony P. Placido, 99 10th Avenue, New York, NY 10011 (212) 337–3900.

PHILADELPHIA DIVISION:

Special Agent-in-Charge.—James M. Kason, 600 Arch Street, Philadelphia, PA 19106 (215) 861–3474.

PHOENIX DIVISION:

Special Agent-in-Charge.—Errol J. Chavez, Suite 301, 3010 North Second Street, Phoenix, AZ 85012 (602) 664–5600.

SAN DIEGO DIVISION:

Special Agent-in-Charge.—Michael S. Vigil, 4560 Viewridge Avenue, San Diego, CA 92123 (858) 616–4100.

SAN FRANCISCO DIVISION:

Special Agent-in-Charge.—Stephen C. Delgado, 450 Golden Gate Avenue, San Francisco, CA 94102 (415) 436–7900.

SEATTLE DIVISION:

Special Agent-in-Charge.—John M. Bott, 400 Second Avenue West, Seattle, WA 98119 (206) 553–5443.

ST. LOUIS DIVISION:

Special Agent-in-Charge.—William J. Renton, Jr., 317 South 16th Street, St. Louis, MO 63103 (314) 538–4770.

WASHINGTON, DC DIVISION:

Special Agent-in-Charge.—R.C. Gamble, 800 K Street, NW., Suite 500, Washington, DC 20001 (202) 305–4500.

OTHER DEA OFFICES

Special Agent-in-Charge.—James S. Mavromatis, El Paso Intelligence Center, Building 11339, SSG Sims Street, El Paso, TX 79908 (915) 760–2000.

Special Agent-in-Charge.—William C. Brown, Aviation Operations Division, 2300 Horizon Drive, Fort Worth, TX 76177 (817) 837–2000.

Special Agent-in-Charge.—Joseph D. Keefe, Special Operations Division, 14560 Avion Parkway, Chantilly, VA 20151 (703) 488–4200.

Special Agent-in-Charge.—John R. McCarty, Office of DEA Training Academy, P.O. Box 1475, Quantico, VA 22134 (703) 632–5000.

FOREIGN OFFICES

Ankara, Turkey: DEA / Justice, American Embassy Ankara, PSC 93, Box 5000, APO AE 09823, 9–011–90–312–468–6136.

Asuncion, Paraguay: DEA / Justice, American Embassy, Unit 4740, APO AA 34036, 9–011–595–21–210–738.

Athens, Greece: DEA / Justice, American Embassy Athens, PSC 108, Box 14, APO AE 09842, 9–011–30–1–643–4328.

Bangkok, Thailand: DEA / Justice, American Embassy Bangkok, APO AP 96546–0001, 9–011–662–205–4987.

Beijing, China: DEA/Justice, American Embassy Beijing, PSC 461, Box 50, FPO AP 96521–0002, 9–011–8610–8529–6880.

Belize, Country Office: DEA / Justice, American Embassy, Unit 7405, APO AA 34025, 9–011–501–233–3857.

Berlin, Germany: DEA / Justice, American Embassy, PSC 120, Box 3000, APO AE 09265, 9–011–49–30–8305–1460.

Bern, Switzerland: DEA / Justice, Bern Country Office, Department of State (Bern), Washington, DC 20521, 9–011–41–31–357–7367.

Bogota, Columbia: DEA / Justice, American Embassy, Unit 5116, APO AA 34038, 9–011–571–315–2121.

Brasilia, Brazil: DEA / Justice, American Embassy, Unit 3500, APO AA 34030, 9–011–55–61–323–6792.

Bridgetown, Barbados: DEA / Justice, American Embassy, FPO AA 34055, 9–1–246–437–6337.

Brussels, Belgium: DEA / Justice, Brussels Country Office, PSC 82, Box 002, APO AE 09710, 9–011–32–2–508–2420.

Buenos Aires, Argentina: DEA / Justice, American Embassy, Unit 4309, APO AA 34034, 9–011–5411–4811–4949.

Cairo, Egypt: DEA / Justice, Cairo Country Office, American Embassy, Unit 64900, Box 25, APO AE 09839–4900, 9–011–20–2–797–2461.

Canberra, Australia: DEA / Justice, American Embassy Canberra, APO AP 96549, 9–011–61–2–6214–5923.

Caracas, Venezuela: DEA / Justice, American Embassy, Unit 4962, APO AA 34037, 9–011–582–975–8910.

Cartagena, Resident Office: DEA / Justice, American Consulate, Unit 5141, APO AA 34038, 9–011–575–655–1423.

Chiang-Mai, Resident Office: DEA / Justice, American Consulate, Box C, APO AP 96546, 9–011–66–53–217–285.

Cochabamba, Resident Office: DEA / Justice, American Embassy, Unit 3913 (Cochabamba), APO AA 34032, 9–011–591–424–3320.

Copenhagen, Denmark: DEA / Justice, American Embassy Copenhagen, PSC 73, APO AE 09716, 9–011–45–35–42–26–80.

Curacao, Netherlands Antilles: DEA / Justice, Attn: Diplomatic Pouch, Washington, DC 20537, 9–011–582–975–8910.

Frankfurt, Resident Office: DEA / Justice, American Consulate General, PSC 115, Frankfurt / DEA, APO AE 09213, 9–011–49–69–7535–3770.

Freeport, Resident Office: DEA Freeport-Airport, P.O. Box 9009, Miami, FL 33159, 1–242–352–3392.

Guadalajara, Resident Office: DEA / Justice, Guadalajara Resident Office, P.O. Box 3088, Laredo, TX 78044–3088, 9–011–523–825–3064.

Guatemala City, Guatemala: DEA / Justice, American Embassy, Unit 3311, APO AA 34024, 9–011–502–331–4389.

Guayaquil, Resident Office: DEA / Justice, American Consulate General, Unit 5350, APO AA, 34039, 9–011–593–42–327–862.

The Hague, Netherlands: DEA / Justice, American Embassy, Unit 6707, Box 8, APO AE 09715, 9–011–31–70–310–9327.

Hanoi, Vietnam: DEA / Justice, American Embassy Hanoi, PSC 461, Box 400, FPO AP 96521, 9–011–772–1500, ext. 2357.

Hermosillo, Resident Office: DEA / Justice, Hermosillo Resident Office, P.O. Box 1689, Nogales, AZ 85628, 9–011–526–289–0220.

Hong Kong: DEA / Justice, American Consulate General, PSC 461, Box 16, FPO AP 96521, 9–852–2521–4536.

Istanbul: DEA / Justice, American Consulate General, PSC 97, Box 0002, APO AE 09327, 9–011–90–212–251–0160.

Juarez, Resident Office: P.O. Box 10545, El Paso, TX 79995, 9–011–521–611–1179.

Kingston, Jamaica: Kingston Country Office, Department of State, Washington, DC 20521, 9–1–876–929–4956.

Kuala Lumpur, Malaysia: DEA / Justice, American Embassy Kuala Lumpur, APO AP 96535, 9–011–603–2168–4957.

Lagos, Nigeria: DEA / Justice, American Embassy Lagos, Department of State, Attn: DEA / Justice, Washington, DC 20521, 9–011–234–1–261–9837.

La Paz, Bolivia: DEA / Justice, American Embassy, Unit 3913, APO AA 34032, 9–011–591–2–431481.

Lima, Peru: DEA / Justice, American Embassy, Unit 3810, APO AA 34031, 9–011–511–434–3058.

London, England: DEA / Justice, American Embassy, PSC 801, Box 08, FPO AE 09498, 9–011–44–20–7408–8026.

Lyon (INTERPOL): American Embassy Paris, DEA / Interpol, Lyon, PSC 116, APO AE 09777, 9–011–33–4–7244–7086.

Madrid, Spain: DEA / Justice, American Embassy Madrid, PSC 61, Box 0014, APO AE 09642, 9–011–34–91–587–2280.

Managua, Nicaragua: DEA / Justice, American Embassy Nicaragua, Unit 2701, Box 21, APO AA 34021, 9–011–505–266–2148.

Manila, Philippines: DEA / Justice, American Embassy, PSC 500, Box 11, FPO AP 96515, 9–011–632–523–1219.

Mazatlan, Resident Office: DEA / Justice, Mazatlan Resident Office, P.O. Box 2708, Laredo, TX 78044, 9–011–52–69–82–1715.

Merida: DEA / Justice, Merida Resident Office, P.O. Box 3087, Laredo, TX 78044, 9–011–529–925–8013.

Mexico City, Mexico: DEA / Justice, U.S. Embassy Mexico City, P.O. Box 9000–DEA, Brownsville, TX 78520, 9–011–525–080–2600.

Milan, Resident Office: DEA / Justice, American Consulate Milan, c/o American Embassy Rome, PSC 59, Box 60–M, APO AE 09624, 9–011–39–02–655–5766.

Monterrey, Resident Office: DEA / Justice, American Consulate General Monterrey, P.O. Box 3098, Laredo, TX 78044, 9–011–528–340–1299.

Moscow, Russia: DEA / Justice, American Embassy Moscow, PSC 77, APO AE 09721, 9–011–7–095–728–5218.

Nassau: Nassau Country Office, 3370 Nassau Place, Washington, DC 20521, 9–1–242–322–1700.

New Delhi, India: DEA / Justice, New Delhi Country Office, Department of State, Attn: DEA / Justice, Washington, DC 20521, 9–011–91–11–419–8495.

Nicosia, Cyprus: DEA / Justice, American Embassy, PSC 815, Box 1, FPO AE 09836, 9–011–357–2–777–086.

Ottawa, Canada: DEA / Justice, American Embassy Ottawa, P.O. Box 35, Ogdensburg, New York 13669, 9–1–613–238–5633.

Panama City, Panama: DEA / Justice, American Embassy, Unit 0945, APO AA 34002, 9–011–507–225–9685.

Paris, France: Justice, American Embassy Paris, PSC 116, Box D–401, APO AE 09777, 9–011–33–1–4312–7332.

Port-Au-Prince, Haiti: U.S. Department of State, Washington, DC 20521, 9–011–509–222–0200.

Port of Spain, Trinidad and Tobago: DEA / Justice, Port of Spain, Department of State, Washington, DC 20521, 9–1–868–628–8136.

Pretoria, South Africa: DEA / Justice, Pretoria Country Office, Department of State, Washington, DC 20521, 9–011–27–12–362–5009.

Quito, Ecuador: DEA / Justice, American Embassy, Unit 5338, APO AA 34039, 9–011–593–22–231–547.

Rangoon, Burma: DEA / Justice, American Embassy Rangoon, Box B, APO AP 96546, 9–011–95–1–285962.

Rome, Italy: DEA / Justice, American Embassy Rome, PSC 59, Box 22, APO AE 09624, 9–011–39–06–4674–2319.

San Jose, Costa Rica: DEA / Justice, American Embassy, Unit 2506, APO AA 34020, 9–011–506–220–2433.

San Salvador, El Salvador: American Embassy, Unit 3130, APO AA 34023, 9–011–503–278–6005.

Santa Cruz, Resident Office: DEA / Justice, American Embassy, Unit 3913 (Santa Cruz), APO AA 34032, 9–011–591–3–32–7153.

Santiago, Chile: DEA / Justice, American Embassy, Unit 4119, APO AA 34033, 9–011–56–2–330–3401.

Santo Domingo, Dominican Republic: DEA / Justice, American Embassy, Unit 5514, APO AA 34041, 9–1–301–985–9410.

Sao Paulo, Resident Office: DEA / Justice, American Embassy, Unit 3502, AP0 AA 34030, 9–011–55–11–852–6962.

Seoul, Korea: DEA / Justice, American Embassy Seoul, Unit 15550, APO AP 96205, 9–011–82–2–397–4260.

Singapore: DEA / Justice, American Embassy Singapore, PSC 470 DEA FPO 96507, 9–011–65–476–9021.

Songkhla, Resident Office: DEA / Justice, American Embassy, Box S, APO AP 96546, 9–011–66–74–324–236.

Tegucigalpa, Honduras: DEA / Justice, American Embassy, Unit 2912, APO AA 34022, 9–011–504–236–6780.

Tijuana, Resident Office: P.O. 439039, San Diego, CA 92143, 9–011–526–622–5110.

Tokyo, Japan: DEA / Justice, American Embassy Tokyo, Unit 45004, Box 224, APO AP 96337, 9–011–81–3–3224–5452.

Trinidad, Resident Office: DEA / Justice, American Embassy, Unit 3913 (Trinidad), APO AA 34032, 9–011–591–046–22561.

Udorn, Resident Office: DEA / Justice, American Embassy (Udorn), Box UD, APO AP 96546, 9–011–66–42–247–635.

Vienna, Austria: American Embassy Vienna, Department of State, Attn: DEA / Justice, Washington, DC 20521, 9–011–43–1–514–2251.

Vientiane, Laos: American Embassy Vientiane, Box V, APO AP 96546, 9–011–856–21–219–565.

FEDERAL BUREAU OF ALCOHOL, TOBACCO, FIREARMS, AND EXPLOSIVES (ATF)

650 Massachusetts Avenue, NW., 20226

OFFICE OF THE DIRECTOR

Director.—Bradley A. Buckles, (202) 927–8700.
Deputy Director.—Richard J. Hankinson, 927–8710.

OFFICE OF OMBUDSMAN

Ombudsman.—James H. McCall, 927–8151.
Associate Ombudsman.—Marianne Ketels, 927–3538.

STRATEGIC PLANNING OFFICE

Chief.—Wayne E. Miller, 927–4849.

OFFICE OF EQUAL OPPORTUNITY

Executive Assistant.—Anthony Torres, 927–8154.
Deputy Executive Assistant.—Oliver C. Allen, Jr., 927–8263.

OFFICE OF CHIEF COUNSEL

Chief Counsel.—Stephen R. Rubenstein (acting), 927–8224.
Deputy Chief Counsel.—Melanie S. Stinnett, 927–8211.

OFFICE OF FIREARMS, EXPLOSIVES AND ARSON

Assistant Director.—John Malone, 927–7940.
Deputy Assistant Director.—Wally Nelson.
Special Assistant.—Enrique Perez, 927–8489.
Chief of Staff.—Audrey Stucko, 927–7420.
Director of:
NIBIN Program.—Patricia Galupo, 927–8021.
Youth Crime Gun Interdiction Initiative.—William Kinsella, 927–8368.
Chief, Division of:
Arson and Explosives.—Carson Carroll, 927–7930.
FEA Services.—Mary Jo Hughes, 927–8045.
Firearms Program.—James Zammillo, 927–7953.
National Tracing Center.—Terry Austin, (304) 260–1505.
Deputy Chief, Division of:
Arson and Explosives.—Phillip Horbert, 927–7930.
Firearms Programs.—Terry Austin, 927–7770.

OFFICE OF SCIENCE AND TECHNOLOGY/CIO

Assistant Director/Chief Information Officer.—Marguerite R. Moccia, 927–8390.
Deputy Assistant Director.—Linda Y. Cureton.
Director, Laboratory Services.—Michael W. Ethridge, (240) 264–3700.
Chief of:
Audit Services Division.—Francis H. Frande, 927–8240.
E-Government Program Office.—Susan M. McCarron, 927–8572.
Fire Research Laboratory.—Rick Tontarski, (240) 264–3700.
Forensic Science Laboratory.—Donal McClamroch, (404) 417–2700.
Identification Section.—Nancy Davis, (404) 417–2704.
Information Services Division.—Robert J. Hughes, 927–7870.
Science and Technology Staff.—VaLerie Hill, 927–1610.
Technical Services Division.—Timothy A. McGinnis, (703) 948–2800.

OFFICE OF TRAINING AND PROFESSIONAL DEVELOPMENT

Assistant Director.—Mark Logan, 927–9380.
Deputy Assistant Director.—Richard Chase.
Deputy Chief, Career Development Division.—[Vacant], 927–7602.
Chief, ATF Academy.—Tony Robbins, (912) 267–2828.
Chief, Division of:
Leadership and Occupational Development.—Tom Klein, 927–8279.
Learning Systems Management.—Paul A. Leathem, 927–3156.
State, Local and International Training.—William D. Dwight, 927–3160.

OFFICE OF FIELD OPERATIONS

Assistant Director.—Paul M. Snabel, 927–7970.
Deputy Assistant Director for—
Central.—Guy K. Hummel, 927–7980.
East.—Edgar A. Domenech.
West.—James R. Switzer.
Chief of:
Field Management Staff.—Karl Anglin, 927–8090.
Operations Security.—Madison P. Townley, Sr., 927–1020.
Operations Support Branch.—Mary H. Warren, 927–8090.
Policy Development and Evaluation Section.—David H. Chipman, 927–8090.

OFFICE OF PUBLIC AND GOVERNMENTAL AFFAIRS

Assistant Director.—Kathleen Kiernan, 927–8500.
Executive Assistant.—Chuck Higman, 927–8490.
Deputy Executive Assistant.—Christine Smith.
Chief, Division of:
Disclosure.—Dorothy A. Chambers, 927–8344.
Public Affairs.—Andrew Lluberes, 927–8578.

OFFICE OF INSPECTION

Assistant Director.—Malcolm W. Brady, 927–7800.
Deputy Assistant Director.—Lewis P. Raden.
Special Agent in Charge, Division of:
Inspection.—Kenneth Massey, 927–4510.
Investigation.—Ron Comerford, (703) 756–6998.

OFFICE OF MANAGEMENT/CFO

Assistant Director/Chief Financial Officer.—William T. Earle, 927–8400.
Deputy Assistant Director.—Candace E. Moberly.
Director, New Building Projects Office.—Mignon Anthony, 927–3500.
Chief, Division of:
Acquisition and Property Management.—Efrain J. Fernandez, 927–8021.
Administrative Programs.—Harry Pass, 927–7706.
Financial Management/Deputy Chief Financial Officer.—Vivian Baran, 927–8420.
Management Analysis Staff.—Everett M. Tabourn, 927–8410.
Personnel.—John G. Duclos, 927–8556.
Director, New Building Projects Office.—Mignon Anthony, 927–3500.
Chair, Merit Promotion Board.—David Dottin, 927–7967.
Chair, Professional Review Board.—Steve L. Mathis, 927–8400.
Deputy Assistant Director Recruitment Center.—Donnie A. Carter, 927–5690.

FEDERAL BUREAU OF INVESTIGATION

J. Edgar Hoover Building (JEH), 935 Pennsylvania Avenue NW., Washington, DC 20535–0001, phone (202) 324–3000, http://www.fbi.gov

Director.—Robert S. Mueller III, room 7176, 324–3444.
Deputy Director.—Bruce J. Gebhardt, room 7142, 324–3315.
Executive Assistant Directors:
Administration.—W. Wilson Lowery, Jr., room 7142, 324–7101.
Counterintelligence.—Maureen A. Baginski.
Counterterrorism.—Pasquale J. D'Amuro, room 7116, 324–7045.
Law Enforcement Services.—Charles S. Prouty, room 7110, 324–4880.
Deputy Executive Assistant Director of Administration.—William L. Hooton, room 11703, 324–7129.
Assistant Directors:
Administrative Services Division.—Mark S. Bullock (acting), room 6012, 324–3514.
Counterintelligence Division.—David Szady, room 4012, 324–4614.
Counterterrorism Division.—Larry A. Mefford, room 5829, 324–2770.
Criminal Justice Information Services Division.—Michael D. Kirkpatrick, West Virginia Complex, Module C–3 (304) 625–2700.
Criminal Investigative Division.—Grant Ashley, room 5012, 324–4260.
Cyber Division.—Jana D. Monroe, room 3823, 324–1380.
Finance Division.—Tina W. Jonas, room 6032, 324–1345.
Information Resources Division.—Gregg D. (Skip) Bailey, room 9939, 324–4507.
Inspection Division.—Lynne A. Hunt, room 7825, 324–2901.
Investigative Technologies Division.—Thomas W. Richardson, A–217, ERF–Quantico, (703) 632–6100.
Laboratory Division.—Dwight E. Adams, 2501 Investigation Parkway, Quantico, VA 22135, (703) 632–7001.
Law Enforcement Services Division.—Louis F. Quijas, room 7110, 324–7126.
Office of the Chief Information Officer.—Darwin John, room 7128, 324–6165.
Office of Intelligence.—Steven C. McCraw, room 7869, 324–7606.
Office of Professional Responsibility.—Robert J. Jordan, room 7129, 324–8284.
Office of Public Affairs.—Cassandra M. Chandler (acting), room 7240, 324–5352.
Records Management Division.—Robert J. Garrity, Jr. (acting), room 11703, 324–7141.
Security Division.—Kenneth Senser, room 7128, 324–7112.
Training Division.—Patrick Patterson (acting), FBI Academy, Quantico, VA (703) 632–1100.
Offices:
Congressional Affairs.—Eleni P. Kalisch (acting), room 7240, 324–5051.
Equal Employment Opportunity Affairs.—EEO Officer Veronica Venture, room 7901, 324–4128.
International Operations.—Roderick L. Beverly, room 7443, 324–5904.
General Counsel.—Patrick Kelley (acting), room 7427, 324–6829.

FIELD DIVISIONS

Albany: 200 McCarty Avenue, Albany, NY 12209 (518) 465–7551.
Albuquerque: 415 Silver Avenue SW., Suite 300, Albuquerque, NM 87102 (505) 224–2000.
Anchorage: 101 East Sixth Avenue, Anchorage, AK 99501 (907) 258–5322.
Atlanta: 2635 Century Center Parkway, NE., Suite 400, Atlanta, GA 30345 (404) 679–9000.
Baltimore: 7142 Ambassador Road, Baltimore, MD 21244 (410) 265–8080.
Birmingham: 2121 Eighth Avenue North, Room 1400, Birmingham, AL 35203 (205) 326–6166.
Boston: One Center Plaza, Suite 600, Boston, MA 02108 (617) 742–5533.
Buffalo: One FBI Plaza, Buffalo, NY 14202 (716) 856–7800.
Charlotte: Wachovia Building, 400 South Tryon Street, Suite 900, Charlotte, NC 28285 (704) 377–9200.
Chicago: E.M. Dirksen Federal Office Building, 219 South Dearborn Street, Room 905, Chicago, IL 60604 (312) 431–1333.
Cincinnati: Federal Office Building, 550 Main Street, Room 9000, Cincinnati, OH 45202 (513) 421–4310.
Cleveland: 1501 Lakeside Avenue, Cleveland, OH 44114 (216) 522–1400.
Columbia: 151 Westpark Boulevard, Columbia, SC 29210 (803) 551–4200.
Dallas: J. Gordon Shanklin Building, One Justice Way, Dallas, TX 75220 (972) 559–5000.

Denver: Federal Office Building, 1961 Stout Street, Room 1823, Denver, CO 80294 (303) 629–7171.

Detroit: P.V. McNamara Federal Office Building, 477 Michigan Avenue, 26th Floor, Detroit, MI 48226 (313) 965–2323.

El Paso: 660 South Mesa Hills Drive, Suite 3000, El Paso, TX 79912 (915) 832–5000.

Honolulu: Kalanianaole Federal Office Building, 300 Ala Moana Boulevard, Room 4–230, Honolulu, HI 96850 (808) 566–4300.

Houston: 2500 East T.C. Jester, Suite 200, Houston, TX 77008 (713) 693–5000.

Indianapolis: Federal Office Building, 575 North Pennsylvania Street, Room 679, Indianapolis, IN 46204 (371) 639–3301.

Jackson: Federal Office Building, 100 West Capitol Street, Suite 1553, Jackson, MS 39269 (601) 948–5000.

Jacksonville: 7820 Arlington Expressway, Suite 200, Jacksonville, FL 32211 (904) 721–1211.

Kansas City: 1300 Summit, Kansas City, MO 64105 (816) 512–8200.

Knoxville: John J. Duncan Federal Office Building, 710 Locust Street, Room 600, Knoxville, TN 37902 (423) 544–0751.

Las Vegas: John Lawrence Bailey Building, 700 East Charleston Boulevard, Las Vegas, NV 89104 (702) 385–1281.

Little Rock: #24 Shackleford West Boulevard, Little Rock, AR 72211 (501) 221–9100.

Los Angeles: Federal Office Building, 11000 Wilshire Boulevard, Suite 1700, Los Angeles, CA 90024 (310) 477–6565.

Louisville: 600 Martin Luther King, Jr. Place, Room 500, Louisville, KY 40202 (502) 583–2941.

Memphis: Eagle Crest Building, 225 North Humphreys Boulevard, Suite 3000, Memphis, TN 38120 (901) 747–4300.

Miami: 16320 Northwest Second Avenue, Miami, FL 33169 (305) 944–9101.

Milwaukee: 330 East Kilbourn Avenue, Suite 600, Milwaukee, WI 53202 (414) 276–4684.

Minneapolis: 111 Washington Avenue South, Suite 100, Minneapolis, MN 55401 (612) 376–3200.

Mobile: 200 North Royal Street, Mobile, AL 36602 (334) 438–3674.

New Haven: 600 State Street, New Haven, CT 06511 (203) 777–6311.

New Orleans: 2901 Leon C. Simon Boulevard, New Orleans, LA 70126 (504) 816–3122.

New York: 26 Federal Plaza, 23rd Floor, New York, NY 10278 (212) 384–1000.

Newark: Claremont Tower Building, 11 Centre Place, Newark, NJ 07102 (973) 792–3000.

Norfolk: 150 Corporate Boulevard, Norfolk, VA 23502 (757) 455–0100.

Oklahoma City: 3301 West Memorial, Oklahoma City, OK 73134 (405) 290–7770.

Omaha: 10755 Burt Street, Omaha, NE 68114 (402) 493–8688.

Philadelphia: William J. Green, Jr., Federal Office Building, 600 Arch Street, Eighth Floor, Philadelphia, PA 19106 (215) 418–4000.

Phoenix: 201 East Indianola Avenue, Suite 400, Phoenix, AZ 85012 (602) 279–5511.

Pittsburgh: Martha Dixon Building, 3311 East Carson Street, Pittsburgh, PA 15203 (412) 432–4000.

Portland: Crown Plaza Building, 1500 Southwest First Avenue, Suite 401, Portland, OR 97201 (503) 224–4181.

Richmond: 1970 East Parham Road, Richmond, VA 23228 (804) 261–1044.

Sacramento: 4500 Orange Grove Avenue, Sacramento, CA 95841 (916) 481–9110.

Salt Lake City: 257 Towers Building, 257 East 200 South, Suite 1200, Salt Lake City, UT 84111 (801) 579–1400.

San Antonio: U.S. Post Office and Courthouse Building, 614 East Houston Street, Room 200, San Antonio, TX 78205 (210) 225–6741.

San Diego: Federal Office Building, 9797 Aero Drive, San Diego, CA 92123 (858) 565–1255.

San Francisco: 450 Golden Gate Avenue, 13th Floor, San Francisco, CA 64102 (415) 553–7400.

San Juan: U.S. Federal Office Building, 150 Chardon Avenue, Room 526, Hato Rey, PR 00918 (787) 754–6000.

Seattle: 1110 Third Avenue, Seattle, WA 98101 (206) 622–0460.

Springfield: 400 West Monroe Street, Suite 400, Springfield, IL 62704 (217) 522–9675.

St. Louis: 2222 Market Street, St. Louis, MO 63103 (314) 241–5357.

Tampa: Federal Office Building, 500 Zack Street, Room 610, Tampa, FL 33602 (813) 273–4566.

Washington Field Office: 601 Fourth Street NW., Washington, DC 20535 (202) 278–2000.

FEDERAL BUREAU OF PRISONS (BOP)

320 1st Street, NW., 20534, phone 1–888–317–8455 or

General Information Number (202) 305–2500

Director.—Harley G. Lappin, room 654, HOLC, 307–3250.
Director, National Institute of Corrections.—Morris L. Thigpen, Sr., 7th floor, 500 FRST, 307–3106 (0).
Assistant Director of:
Administration.—Bruce K. Sasser, 9th floor, 500 FRST, 307–3123.
Correctional Programs.—Michael B. Cooksey, room 554, HOLC, 307–3226.
General Counsel.—Christopher Erlewine, room 958C, HOLC, 307–3062.
Health Services.—MaryEllen Thomas, room 1054, HOLC, 307–3055.
Human Resources Management.—Keith Hall, room 454, HOLC, 307–3082.
Industries, Education, and Vocational Training.—Steve Schwalb, 8th floor, 400 FRST, 305–3500.
Information, Policy and Public Affairs.—Thomas R. Kane, room 641, HOLC, 514–6537.
Regional Director for—
Mid-Atlantic.—K.M. White, (301) 317–3100.
North Central.—G.L. Hershberger, (913) 621–3939.
Northeast.—Mickey Ray, (215) 521–7300.
South Central.—Ronald G. Thompson, (214) 224–3389.
Southeast.—R.E. Holt, (678) 686–1200.
Western.—Robert M. Haro, (925) 803–4700.
Telephone Directory Coordinator.—Jerry Vroegh, 307–3250.

OFFICE OF JUSTICE PROGRAMS (OJP)

810 7th Street, NW., 20531

Assistant Attorney General.—Deborah J. Daniels, room 6400, 307–5933.
Principal Deputy Assistant Attorney General.—Tracy Henke, room 6400, 307–5933.
Deputy Assistant Attorney General.—Cheri Nolan, room 6422, 307–5933.
Special Assistants to the Assistant Attorney General: Sean Costello, room 6400, 616–1700; Terrence Donahue, room 6352, 514–8353.
Manager, Equal Employment Opportunity.—Lori Bledsoe, 307–6013.
Director, American Indian and Alaska Native Affairs.—Norena A. Henry, 616–3205.

BUREAU OF JUSTICE ASSISTANCE

Director.—Richard Nedelkoff, room 4427, 514–6278.
Deputy Directors of:
Planning.—Harri J. Kramer, room 4345, 514–6094.
Policy.—Richard Ward III, room 4422, 616–6500.
Programs.—Camille Cain, room 4429, 514–6278.
Associate Deputy Director, Planning and Communications.—Eileen Garry, room 4206, 307–6226.
Senior Policy Manager.—Phillip Merkle, room 4121, 305–2550.

BUREAU OF JUSTICE STATISTICS

Director.—Lawrence A. Greenfeld, room 2409, 307–0765.
Senior Statistician, Research and Public Policy Issues.—Patrick A. Langan, room 2250, 616–3490.
Chiefs of:
Criminal History Improvement Program.—Carol G. Kaplan. room 2323, 307–0759.
Law Enforcement, Adjudication, and Federal Statistics.—Steven K. Smith, room 2338, 616–3485.
Planning, Management and Budget.—Maureen A. Henneberg, room 2402, 616–3282.

NATIONAL INSTITUTE OF JUSTICE

Director.—Sara V. Hart, room 7422, 307–2942.
Deputy Director.—Glenn Schmitt, room 7440, 307–2942.
Directors of:
Communications.—Gerold Soucy, room 7403, 616–3808.
Development.—Elizabeth Griffith, room 7123, 616–2008.
Development and Communications.—Cheryl Crawford Watson (acting), room 7118, 514–6210.
Drugs and Crime Research.—Henry Brownstein, room 6318, 305–8705.
International Center.—Jay Albansese, room 7110, 616–1960.
Investigative and Forensics Science.—Lisa Forman, room 7238, 307–6608.
Justice Systems Research.—Christopher Innes, room 7333, 307–2955.
Planning and Management.—Doug Horner, room 7423, 307–2942.
Research and Evaluation.—Thomas Feucht (acting), room 7337, 307–2949.
Research and Technology Development.—Trent DePersia, room 7252, 305–4686.
Science and Technology.—John Morgan (acting), room 7234, 305–0995.
Technology Assistance.—Marc Caplan, room 7224, 307–2956.
Technology Support.—Sharla Rausch, room 7227, 305–8628.
Program Executive, Critical Corrections Technology.—Larry Meachum, room 7241, 307–3593.

OFFICE OF JUVENILE JUSTICE AND DELINQUENCY PREVENTION

Administrator.—J. Robert Flores, room 3345, TWC, 307–5911.
Deputy Director.—William Woodruff, room 3241, TWC, 514–8053.
Directors of:
Child Protection.—Ronald C. Laney, room 3135, TWC, 616–7323.
Information Dissemination and Planning.—Catherine Doyle (acting), room 3312, TWC, 514–9208.
Special Emphasis.—Marilyn Roberts (acting), room 3141, TWC, 616–9055.
Research and Program Development.—Kathi Grasso, room 3347, TWC, 616–7567.
State and Tribal Assistance.—Roberta Dorn, room 3411, TWC, 616–3660.
Training and Technical Assistance.—Greg Thompson (acting), room 3407, TWC, 616–3663.

OFFICE FOR VICTIMS OF CRIME

Chief of Staff.—Jeannie Gregori, room 8331, 305–0093.
Director.—John W. Gillis, room 8332, 307–5983.
Deputy Director.—Carolyn A. Hightower, room 8328, 616–3586.
Directors of:
Special Projects.—Joyce Whatley (acting), room 8338, 305–1715.
State Compensation and Assistance.—Toni Thomas (acting), room 8242, 616–3579.
Technical Assistance, Publications and Information Resource.—Emily C. Martin (acting), room 8323, 616–3633.
Terrorism and International Victims.—Barbara Johnson, room 8340, 307–0012.

EXECUTIVE OFFICE FOR WEED AND SEED

Director.—Robert Samuels (acting), 616–1152.

OFFICE OF POLICE CORPS AND LAW ENFORCEMENT EDUCATION

Director.—Robbie Maxwell, room 3252, TWC, 305–8273.

OFFICE ON VIOLENCE AGAINST WOMEN

Chief of Staff.—Kris Rose, room 9325, TWC, 307–0466.
Director.—Diane Stuart (acting), room 9327, TWC, 307–0728.
Deputy Director.—Catherine Pierce, room 9426, TWC, 307–3913.
Assistant Directors: Lauren Nassikas, room 9212, TWC, 305–1792; Nadine Neufville, room 9213, TWC, 305–2590.
Special Assistant to the Director.—Omar Vargas, room 9303, TWC, 305–1821.

OFFICE OF CHIEF INFORMATION OFFICER

Chief Information Officer.—David Zeppieri, room 8411, 305–9071.
Deputy Chief Information Officer.—Chris Bruno, room 8425, 305–9071.

OFFICE OF ADMINISTRATION

Director.—Gary N. Silver, room 3424, 810 7th, 307–0087.
Director of:
Acquisition Management.—Patrick R. Fanning, room 3605, 307–0608.
Building and Support Services.—Bobby J. Railey, room 3418, 305–1549.
Personnel.—Leah Hollander, room 3330, 616–3272.

OFFICE FOR CIVIL RIGHTS

Director.—Michael Alston (acting), room 8122, 307–0692.

OFFICE OF THE COMPTROLLER

Comptroller.—Cynthia Schwimer, room 5248, 307–3186.
Deputy Comptroller.—James J. McKay, room 5252, 616–2687.
Directors of:
Accounting.—Marsha Barton, room 5322, 514–5579.
Financial Management.—Larry Hailes, room 5254, 514–7925.
Training and Policy.—Joanne Suttingon, room 5112, 305–2122.

OFFICE OF COMMUNICATIONS

Director.—Nancy Segerdahl, room 6338, 307–0703.
Deputy Director.—Glenda Kendrick, room 6118, 305–2467.

OFFICE OF GENERAL COUNSEL

General Counsel.—Rafael A. Maden, room 5418, 307–0790.
Principal Deputy General Counsel.—Gregory C. Brady, room 5328, 616–3254.
Deputy General Counsel.—John L. Pensinger, room 5420, 616–2370.

OFFICE OF BUDGET AND MANAGEMENT SERVICES

Director.—Kimberly Orben (acting), room 6240, 514–9337.

UNITED STATES MARSHALS SERVICE (USMS)

1735 Jefferson Davis Highway, Crystal Square III, Arlington, VA 22202

[Use (202) for 307 exchange and (703) for 557, 603, 416 and 285 exchanges]

fax (202) 307–5040

Director.—Benigno G. Reyna, Suite 1200, CS–3, 307–9001.
Deputy Director.—Donald A. Gambatesa, 307–9489.
Chief of Staff.—David F. Musel, 305–9546.
Counsel to the Director.—[Vacant], 307–5219.
Equal Employment Opportunity Officer.—Lisa Dickinson, Suite 103, 307–9048, fax 307–8765.

OFFICE OF DISTRICT AFFAIRS

Chief.—Arthur D. Roderick, Jr., Suite 1201, 307–9494.
Assistant Director.—Broadine M. Brown, 307–9032, fax 307–8340.
Chief Financial Officer, Management and Budget.—Edward Dolan, Suite 1100, 307–9193, fax 353–8340.

Chief Information Officer.—Diane Litman, (A), Suite 800, 307–9677, fax 307–5130.
Program Review.—Michael Urenko, Suite 870, 307–9749, fax 307–9773.
Security Programs.—James R. Ogan, Suite 1000, 307–9696, fax 307–9780.

OFFICE OF FINANCE

Chief.—Robert A. Whiteley, Suite 1110, 307–9320, fax (703) 603–0386.

INVESTIGATIVE SERVICES

24 Hour Communications Center, Penthouse, CS–3, 307–9000, fax 307–9177

Assistant Director.—Robert Finan II, Suite 1200, CS–4, 307–9707, fax 307–9299.
Witness Security.—Kearn Knowles, 307–9150, fax 307–9337.
Assistant Director of Judicial Security.—Sylvester E. Jones, Suite 600, 307–9860, fax 307–5206.

Court Security, Suite 600, CS–3, 307–9500, fax 307–5047

Assistant Director/Prisoner Services Division.—Lydia Blakey, (A), Suite 200, 307–5100, fax 305–9434.
Assistant Director, Justice Prisoner and Alien Transportation.—Kenneth Pakarek, Kansas City, MO (816) 374–6060, fax (816) 374–6040.

Air Operations, Alexandria, LA (318) 473–7536, fax (318) 473–7522.

Air Operations, OIC.—Jerry Hurd, Oklahoma City, OK (405) 680–3404, fax (405) 680–3466.

OFFICE OF THE GENERAL COUNSEL

Chief.—Gerald M. Auerbach, (A), Suite 1234, 307–9054, fax 307–9456.
Deputy General Counsel.—Luci Roberts, Suite 1229.
Assistant Director, Business Services.—Gary Mead, Suite 1100, 307–9395, fax 307–5026.
Director, Asset Forfeiture.—Katherine Deoudes, Suite 400, 307–9221, fax (703) 557–9751.
Central Courthouse Management Group.—Dave Barnes, Suite 300B, 353–8767, fax 353–7827.
National Procurement.—Pat Hanson, Suite 1124, 307–8640.
Assistant Director of:
Human Resources.—Suzanne Smith, Suite 890, LP–1, 307–9625, fax 307–9461.
Training.—Brian R. Beckwith, FLETC Building 70, Glynco, GA (912) 267–2731, fax (912) 267–2882.
Executive Services.—Michael Pearson (acting), Suite 1000, 307–9105, fax 307–9831.
Congressional Affairs.—John J. McNulty III, Suite 1001, 307–9220, fax 307–5228.
Public Affairs.—Don C. Hines, Suite 1001, 307–9065, fax 307–8729.
Internal Affairs.—Yvonne Bonner, Suite 900, 307–9155, fax 307–9779.
Telephone Directory Coordinator.—David M. Green, 307–5050.

OFFICE OF THE PARDON ATTORNEY

500 First Street, NW., Suite 400, 20530, phone (202) 616–6070

Pardon Attorney.—Roger C. Adams.
Deputy Pardon Attorney.—Susan M. Kuzma.
Administrative Officer.—William J. Dziwura.

U.S. PAROLE COMMISSION

5550 Friendship Boulevard, Room 420, Chevy Chase, MD 20815, phone (301) 492–5990 fax (301) 492–6694

Chairman.—Edward F. Reilly, Jr.
Chief of Staff.—Thomas W. Hutchinson.
Regional Commissioners: Cranston J. Mitchell, John R. Simpson.
Case Operations Administrator.—Stephen Husk.
Case Services Administrator.—Shelley Witenstein.

Executive Officer.—Judy I. Carter.
General Counsel.—Rockne Chickinell.
Research Administrator.—James Beck.
Staff Assistant to the Chairman.—Patricia W. Moore.

EXECUTIVE OFFICE FOR UNITED STATES TRUSTEES

20 Massachusetts Avenue NW., Washington, DC 20530, phone (202) 307–1391 (901E)

www.usdoj.gov/ust

Director.—Lawrence A. Friedman, room 8000.
Principal Deputy Director.—Martha L. Davis.
Deputy Director.—Clifford White III.
Associate Director.—Jeffrey M. Miller.
General Counsel.—Joseph Guzinski, 307–1399, room 8100.
Deputy General Counsel.—Esther I. Estryn, room 8102, 307–1320.
Assistant Directors Office of:
Administration.—Santal Manos, room 8200, 307–2926.
Research and Planning.—Sara L. Kistler (acting), room 8310, 307–3698.
Review and Oversight.—Sara L. Kistler (acting), room 8338, 307–3698.

U.S. TRUSTEES:

Region I:
Room 1184, 10 Causeway Street, Boston, MA 02222–1043 (617) 788–0400.
Suite 303, 537 Congress Street, Portland, ME 04101 (207) 780–3564.
Suite 200, 600 Main Street, Worchester, MA 01608 (508) 793–0555.
Suite 302, 66 Hanover Street, Manchester, NH 03101 (603) 666–7908.
Suite 910, 10 Dorrance Street, Providence, RI 02903 (401) 528–5551.

Region II:
21st floor, 33 Whitehall Street, New York, NY 10004 (212) 510–0500.
Suite 200, 74 Chapel Street, Albany, NY 12207 (518) 434–4553.
Suite 100, 42 Delaware Avenue, Buffalo, NY 14202 (716) 551–5541.
Long Island Federal Courthouse, 560 Federal Plaza, Central Islip, NY 11722–4456 (631) 715–7800.
Suite 1103, 265 Church Street, New Haven, CT 06510 (203) 773–2210.
Room 609, 100 State Street, Rochester, NY 14614 (716) 263–5812.
Room 105, 10 Broad Street, Utica, NY 13501 (315) 793–8191.

Region III:
Room 950 W, 601 Walnut Street, Philadelphia, PA 19106 (215) 597–4411.
Suite 2100, One Newark Center, Newark, NJ 07102 (973) 645–3014.
Suite 970, 1001 Liberty Avenue, Pittsburgh, PA 15222 (412) 644–4756.
Suite 1190, 228 Walnut Street, Harrisburg, PA 17101 or P.O. Box 969, Harrisburg, PA 17101 (717) 221–4515.
Suite 2313, 844 King Street, Wilmington, DE 19801 (302) 573–6491.

Region IV:
Suite 953, 1835 Assembly Street, Columbia, SC 29201 (803) 765–5250.
Room 210, 115 S. Union Street, Alexandria, VA 22314 (703) 557–7176.
Room 625, 200 Granby Street, Norfolk, VA 23510 (757) 441–6012.
Room 2025, 300 Virginia Street East, Charleston, WV 25301 (304) 347–3400.
First Campbell Square Building, 210 First Street SW., Suite 505, Roanoke, VA 24011 (540) 857–2806.
Suite 301, 600 East Main Street, Richmond, VA 23219 (804) 771–2310.
Suite 600, 6305 Ivy Lane, Greenbelt, MD 20770 (301) 344–6216.
Suite 350, 300 West Pratt Street, Baltimore, MD 21201 (410) 962–3910.

Region V:
Suite 2110, 400 Poydras Street, New Orleans, LA 70130 (504) 589–4018.
Suite 3196, 300 Fannin Street, Shreveport, LA 71101–3099 (318) 676–3456.
Suite 706, 100 West Capitol Street, Jackson, MS 39269 (601) 965–5241.

Region VI:
Room 9C60, 1100 Commerce Street, Dallas, TX 75242 (214) 767–8967.
Room 300, 110 North College Avenue, Tyler, TX 75702 (903) 590–1450.

Region VII:
Suite 3516, 515 Rusk Avenue, Houston, TX 77002 (713) 718–4650.
Room 230, 903 San Jacinto, Austin, TX 78701 (512) 916–5328.
Suite 533, 615 East Houston Street, San Antonio, TX 78205 (210) 472–4640.
Suite 1107, 606 N. Carancahua Street, Corpus Christi, TX 78476 (361) 888–3261.

Region VIII:
Suite 400, 200 Jefferson Avenue, Memphis, TN 38103 (901) 544–3251.
Suite 512, 601 W. Broadway, Louisville, KY 40202 (502) 582–6000.
Fourth floor, 31 East 11th Street, Chattanooga, TN 37402 (423) 752–5153.
Room 318, 701 Broadway, Nashville, TN 37203 (615) 736–2254.
Suite 803, 100 East Vine Street, Lexington, KY 40507 (859) 233–2822.

Region IX:
Suite 20–3300, BP Building, 200 Public Square, Cleveland, OH 44114 (216) 522–7800.
Suite 200, Schaff Building, 170 North High Street, Columbus, OH 43215–2403 (614) 469–7411.
Suite 2030, 36 East Seventh Street, Cincinnati, OH 45202 (513) 684–6988.
Suite 700, 211 W. Fort Street, Detroit, MI 48226 (313) 226–7999.
Suite 202, 330 Ionia NW. Grand Rapids, MI 49503 (616) 456–2002.

Region X:
Room 1000, 101 West Ohio Street, Indianapolis, IN 46204 (317) 226–6101.
Suite 1100, 401 Main Street, Peoria, IL 61602 (309) 671–7854.
Suite 555, 100 East Wayne Street, South Bend, IN 46601 (219) 236–8105.

Region XI:
Suite 3350, 227 West Monroe Street, Chicago, IL 60606 (312) 886–5785.
Room 430, 517 East Wisconsin Avenue, Milwaukee, WI 53202 (414) 297–4499.
Suite 304, 780 Regent Street, Madison, WI 53715 (608) 264–5522.

Region XII:
Suite 1015, U.S. Courthouse, 300 S. Fourth Street, Minneapolis, MN 55415 (612) 664–5500.
Suite 400, 225 Second Street SE., Cedar Rapids, IA 52401 (319) 364–2211.
Room 793, 210 Walnut Street, Des Moines, IA 50309–2108 (515) 284–4982.
Suite 502, 230 S. Philips Avenue, Sioux Falls, SD 57102–6321 (605) 330–4450.

Region XIII:
Suite 3440, 400 East 9th Street, Kansas City, MO 64106–1910 (816) 512–1940.
Suite 6353, 111 South 10th Street, St. Louis, MO 63102 (314) 539–2976.
Suite 201, 500 South Broadway, Little Rock, AR 72201–3344 (501) 324–7357.
Suite 1148, 111 South 18th Plaza, Omaha, NE 68102 (402) 221–4300.

Region XIV:
Suite 700, 2929 North Central Avenue, Phoenix, AZ 85012 or P.O. Box 36170, Phoenix, AZ 85067 (602) 640–2100.

Region XV:
Suite 600, 402 West Broadway Street, San Diego, CA 92101–8511 (619) 557–5013.
Suite 602, 1132 Bishop Street, Honolulu, HI 96813–2836 (808) 522–8150.

Region XVI:
725 South Figueroa, 26th floor, Los Angeles, CA 90017 (213) 894–6811.
Suite 9041, 411 W. Fourth Street, Santa Ana, CA 92701–8000 (714) 338–3401.
Suite 300, 3685 Main Street, Riverside, CA 92501 (909) 276–6990.
Suite 115, 21051 Warner Center Lane, Woodland Hills, CA 91367 (818) 716–8800.

Region XVII:
Suite 910, 250 Montgomery Street, San Francisco, CA 94104–3401 (415) 705–3300.
Suite 7–500, U.S. Courthouse, 501 I Street, Sacramento, CA 95814–2322 (916) 930–2100.
Suite 1110, 1130 O Street, Fresno, CA 93721 (559) 498–7400.
Suite 690N, 1301 Clay Street, Oakland, CA 94612–5217 (510) 637–3200.
Suite 430, 600 Las Vegas Boulevard South, Las Vegas, NV 89101 (702) 388–6600.
Suite 2129, 300 Booth Street, Reno, NV 89502 (775) 784–5335.
Room 268, 280 South First Street, San Jose, CA 95113 (408) 535–5525.

Region XVIII:
Room 600, 1200 Sixth Avenue, Seattle, WA 98101 (206) 553–2000.
Suite 213, 620 S.W. Main Street, Portland, OR 97205 (503) 326–4000.
Room 347, 304 North Eighth Street, Boise, ID 83702 (208) 334–1300.
Room 593, 920 West Riverside, Spokane, WA 99201 (509) 353–2999.
Suite 204, 301 Central Avenue, Great Falls, MT 59401 (406) 761–8777.
Suite 258, 605 West Fourth Avenue, Anchorage, AK 99501 (907) 271–2600.
Room 285, 211 East Seventh Avenue, Eugene, OR 97401 (541) 465–6330.

Region XIX:

Suite 1551, 999 Eighteenth Street, Denver, CO 80202 (303) 312–7230.
Suite 203, 308 West 21st Street, Cheyenne, WY 82001 (307) 772–2790.
Suite 100, 9 Exchange Place, Salt Lake City, UT 84111 (801) 524–5734.

Region XX:

Room 500, Epic Center, 301 North Main Street, Wichita, KS 67202 (316) 269–6637.
Suite 112, 421 Gold Street SW., Albuquerque, NM 87102 (505) 248–6544.
Suite 408, 215 Northwest Dean A. McGee Avenue, Oklahoma City, OK 73102 (405) 231–5950.
Suite 225, 224 S. Boulder Avenue, Tulsa, OK 74103 (918) 581–6670.

Region XXI:

Room 362, 75 Spring Street SW., Atlanta, GA 30303 (404) 331–4437.
Suite 301, 500 Tanca Street, San Juan, PR 00901 (787) 729–7444.
Room 1204, 51 Southwest First Avenue, Miami, FL 33130 (305) 536–7285.
Suite 302, 222 West Oglethorpe Avenue, Savannah, GA 31401 (912) 652–4112.
Suite 1200, 501 E. Polk Street, Tampa, FL 33602 (813) 228–2000.
Suite 510, 433 Cherry Street, Macon, GA 31201 (478) 752–3544.
Room 1038, 227 North Bronough Street, Tallahassee, FL 32301 (850) 942–8899.
Suite 620, 135 West Central Boulevard, Orlando, FL 32801 (407) 648–6301.

COMMUNITY RELATIONS SERVICE

600 E Street NW, Suite 6000, Washington, DC 20530, phone (202) 305–2935 fax 305–3009 (BICN)

Director.—Sharee M. Freeman.
Deputy Associate Director.—[Vacant].
Special Assistant to the Director.—Denice Gitsham, 305–3441.
Attorney Advisor.—George Henderson, 305–2964.
Media Affairs Officer.—Daryl Borgquist, 305–2966.

REGIONAL DIRECTORS

New England.—Martin A. Walsh, 408 Atlantic Avenue, Suite 222, Boston, MA 02110–1032 (617) 424–5715.

Northeast Region.—Reinaldo Rivera, Room 36–118, 26 Federal Plaza, New York, NY 10278 (212) 264–0700.

Mid-Atlantic Region.—Vermont McKinney, Customs House, Room 208, Second and Chestnut Streets, Philadelphia, PA 19106 (215) 597–2344.

Southeast Region.—Ozell Sutton, Citizens Trust Company Bank Building, Room 900, 75 Piedmont Avenue NE., Atlanta, GA 30303 (404) 331–6883.

Midwest Region.—Jesse Taylor, Xerox Center Building, 55 West Monroe Street, Suite 420, Chicago, IL 60603 (312) 353–4391.

Southwest Region.—Carmelita P. Freeman, 1420 West Mockingbird Lane, Suite 250, Dallas, TX 75247 (214) 655–8175.

Central Region.—Atkins Warren, 1100 Maine Street, Suite 320, Kansas City, MO 64106 (816) 426–7433.

Rocky Mountain Region.—Philip Arreola, 1244 Speer Boulevard, Room 650, Denver, CO 80204–3584 (303) 844–2973.

Northwest Region.—Rosa Melendez, Federal Office Building, 915 Second Avenue, Room 1898, Seattle, WA, 98174 (206) 220–6700.

Western Region.—Ron Wakabayashi, 888 South Figueroa Street, Suite 1880, Los Angeles, CA 90017 (213) 894–2941.

FOREIGN CLAIMS SETTLEMENT COMMISSION

Bicentennial Building, 600 E Street NW., Suite 6002, 20579, phone (202) 616–6975 (BICN)

Chair.—Mauricio J. Tamargo.
Chief Counsel.—David E. Bradley.
Special Assistant.—Patrick S. McArthur.
Commissioner.—Jeremy H.G. Ibrahim.
Administrative Officer.—Judith H. Lock, 616–6986.

OFFICE OF COMMUNITY ORIENTED POLICING SERVICES

1110 Vermont Avenue NW., 10th Floor, Washington, DC 20530, (202) 514–2058

Director.—Carl Peed, 616–2888.
Office Manager.—Laurel Matthews, 616–2888.
Administrative Assistant.—Sharon Baker, 616–2888.
Chief of Staff.—Timothy Quinn, 616–2888.
Deputy Director for—
Management.—Timothy Quinn (acting), 616–8122.
Grants/Monitoring.—[Vacant].
Community Policing Development.—Pam Cammarata (acting), 514–5793.

ADMINISTRATIVE DIVISION

Assistant Director.—Michael Vasquez (acting), 1100 VER, 4th floor, 616–5002.
Financial Officer.—Vivian Perry, 3rd floor, 514–3793.
Human Resources Program Coordinator.—[Vacant], 1100 VER, 4th floor, 514–8956.
Management Information Systems.—Michael Vasquez, 1100 VER, 2nd floor, 616–5002.
Supervisory Administrative Services Specialist.—Violet Graham, 1100 VER, 4th floor, 616–5002.

COMMUNICATIONS DIVISION

Assistant Director.—Maria Carolina Rozas, 1100 VER, 11th floor, 616–1728.

CONGRESSIONAL RELATIONS DIVISION

Assistant Director.—David Buchanan, 1100 VER, 11th floor, 514–9079.

INTERGOVERNMENTAL AND PUBLIC LIAISON DIVISION

Assistant Director.—David Buchanan (acting), 1100 VER, 11th floor, 514–9079.

GRANTS ADMINISTRATION DIVISION

Assistant Director.—Robert Phillips, 1100 VER, 10th floor, 616–3031.
Grant Regional Supervisors:

Michael Dame; Jamie French, 7th floor.
Keesha Thompson, 5th floor.
Cynthia Bowie, 9th floor.
Joseph Kuhns, 8th floor.

GRANT MONITORING DIVISION

Assistant Director.—[Vacant], 1100 VER, 10th floor, 514–9202.
Grant Monitoring Regional Supervisors: James Griffith; Juliette White.
General Counsel.—Lani Lee, 1100 VER, 12th floor, 514–3750.
Deputy General Counsel.—Charlotte C. Grzebien.
Associate General Counsels: Melissa Fieri-Fetrow; Jonya Wagner.

PROGRAM/POLICY SUPPORT AND EVALUATION

Assistant Director.—Pam Cammarata, 1100 VER, 10th floor, 514–2301.

TECHNICAL ASSISTANCE AND TRAINING DIVISION

Assistant Director.—Beverly Alford, 1100 VER, 10th floor, 514–5819.

EXECUTIVE OFFICE FOR IMMIGRATION REVIEW (EOIR)

Director.—Kevin D. Rooney, 2600 SKYT, (703) 305–0169.
Deputy Director.—Kevin A. Ohlson (acting).
Chief of Staff.—Paula Nasca, 305–1754.
Executive Secretariat.—Terry Samuels, 305–0169.
Assistant Director/General Counsel.—Charles Adkins Blanch, 305–0470.
Assistant Director of:
Administration.—Lawrence M. D'Elia, 2300 SKYT, 305–1171.
Management Programs.—Frances A. Mooney, 305–0289.
Planning and Analysis.—Amy Dale, 605–0445.
Chairman, Board of Immigration Appeals.—Lori L. Scialabba, 2400 SKYT, 305–1194.
Chief, Office of Administrative Hearing.—Jack E. Perkins, 2519 SKYT, 305–0864.
Deputy Chief, Office of Administrative Hearing.—Louis J. Ruffino, 2519 SKYT, 305–0864.
Chief, Office of Immigration Judge.—Michael J. Creppy, 2500 SKYT, 305–1247.
Deputy Chiefs, Immigration Judge.—Thomas L. Pullen, 2500 SKYT, 305–1247; Brian M. O'Leary.
Telephone Directory Coordinator.—Josetta M. Lamorella, (703) 305–1797.

EXECUTIVE OFFICE FOR UNITED STATES ATTORNEYS (EOUSA)

950 Pennsylvania Avenue, NW., Room 2621, 20530, phone 514–2121

Director.—Guy A. Lewis.
Deputy Directors: Robin C. Ashton; Theresa C. Bertucci, room 2621, 514–4506.
Chief of Staff.—Richard Byrne.
AGAC Liaison and United States Attorney's Manual.—Judith A. Beeman, room 2337, 514–4633.
Deputy Counsel to the Director.—Lynne M. Halbrooks, room 2617, 514–1023.
Senior Counsel to the Director.—Louis DeFalaise, room 2613, 616–2128.
Hearings Officer.—Naomi Miske, room 6800, BICN, 514–5719.
Office of Tribal Justice.—Tracy Toulou, room 2200C, 514–8812.
Assistant Director of:
Case Management.—Siobhan Sperin, room 7500, BICN, 616–6919.
Data Analysis.—Barbara Tone, room 2000, BICN, 616–6779.
Equal Employment.—Juan E. Milanes, room 524, NPB, 514–3982.
Evaluation and Review.—Chris Barnes, room 8500, BICN, 616–6776.
Execution.—Mary Ellen Wagner, room 8503, BICN, 616–6886.
Facilities Management and Support Service.—Trisha Bursey, room 2400, BICN, 616–6425.
FOIA and Privacy, FOIA Unit.—Marie O'Rourke, room 7300, BICN, 616–6757.
Formulation.—Alison Miner, room 8200, BICN, 717–6886.
Information Technology Security.—Ted Shelkey, room 9100, BICN, 616–6969.
LECC/Victim Witness Staff.—Camille Bennett (acting), room 2500, BICN, 616–6792.
Office Automation.—[Vacant], room 9100, BICN, 616–6969.
Personnel Management.—Linda Schwartz, room 8017, BICN, 616–6873.
Security Programs.—Tommie Barnes, room 2600, BICN, 616–6878.
Employee Assistance Program.—Eileen Grady, room 6800, BICN, 514–1036.
General Counsel.—Kenneth Blanco, room 2200, BICN, 514–4024.
Deputy General Counsels: Suzanne Bell, 514–4024; Leslie McClendon.
Director, Legal Education.—Michael W. Bailie, National Advocacy Center, 1620 Pendleton Street, Columbia, SC 29201, (803) 544–5100.
Deputy Director, Legal Programs.—Wendy Goggin, room 7600, BICN, 616–6444.
Chief Financial Officer.—Steve Parent, room 8300, BICN, 616–6886.
Chief Operating Officer.—David Downs, room 8100, BICN, 616–6600.
Associate Directors: Debora Cottrell, room 8100, BICN, 616–6600; Gail Williamson.
Chief Information Officer.—Zal Azmi, room 8009, BICN, 616–6973.
Telecommunications and Technology Development.—Harvey Press, room 6012, BICN, 616–6439.

INTERPOL—U.S. NATIONAL CENTRAL BUREAU

1301 New York Avenue, Room 4102, 20530, phone 616–9000

Director.—Edgar A. Adamson.
Deputy Director.—James M. Sullivan, room 4110.
Information Resources Manager.—Henry J. Coffman, room 4014.
General Counsel.—Kevin Smith, room 4419, 616–4103.
Assistant Director, Division of:
Administrative Services.—Aaron A. BoBo (acting), room 4114, 616–7983.
Alien/Fugitive Foreign Notice.—Martin Renkiewicz (acting), room 3026, 616–0310.
Drug Investigations.—Heidi L. Landgraf, room 4423, 616–3379.
Economic Crimes.—Albert Moy, room 3401, 616–3459.
Investigative Services.—Marconi O. Buchanan, room 3517, 616–5466.
State Liaison.—Michael D. Muth, room 4026, 616–8272.
Terrorism and Violent Crimes.—Stephen P. Markardt, room 3002, 616–0312.

NATIONAL DRUG INTELLIGENCE CENTER (NDIC)

319 Washington Street, Johnstown, PA 15901, phone (814) 532–4601

Email: NDIC.contacts@usdoj.gov

Liaison Office, 8201 Greensboro Drive, Suite 1001, McLean, VA 22102

phone (703) 556–8970

Director.—Michael T. Horn, (814) 532–4607.
Deputy Director.—Virgil D. Woolley, (814) 532–4978.
Chief of Staff.—MaryLou Rodgers, (814) 532–4974.
Legal Counsel.—Manuel A. Rodriguez, (814) 532–4616.
Chief of:
Congressional, Public, and Interagency Relations.—Charles F. Miller, (703) 556–8986.
Security and Classified Programs.—Steven R. Frank, (814) 532–4728.
Supervisor, Policies and Procedures.—Suzanne Craft (acting), (814) 532–4649.
Assistant Director, Intelligence.—Maurice E. Rinfret, (814) 532–4036.
Deputy Assistant Director, Intelligence.—Robert J. Rae, (814) 532–4069.
Deputy Assistant Director for Intelligence Policy.—Gregory T. Gatjanis, (703) 556–8997.
Chief of:
Eastern Region Branch.—Dean T. Scott (acting), (814) 532–4577.
Western Region Branch.—Matthew G. Maggio, (814) 532–4989.
Assistant Director, Document Exploitation.—John T. Counihan (acting), (814) 532–4684.
Deputy Chief Investigator, Document Exploitation.—Harry J. Keurner, Jr. (acting), (814) 532–4611.
Chief of:
Administrative Services Branch.—Karl F. Wenger, Jr., (814) 532–4628.
Document Exploitation Branch A.—Daniel G. Layton (acting), (814) 532–4759.
Document Exploitation Branch B.—Charles J. Rivetti, (814) 532–4654.
Intelligence Services Branch.—Bruce I. Merchant, (814) 532–4558.
Technical Services Branch.—David J. Bonski, (814) 532–4795.
Assistant Director, Intelligence Support Division.—David J. Mrozowski, (814) 532–4087.
Telephone Directory Coordinator.—Kelly Creighton, (703) 556–8982.

INTERPOL—U.S. NATIONAL CENTRAL BUREAU

NATIONAL DRUG INTELLIGENCE CENTER

DEPARTMENT OF THE INTERIOR

Interior Building, 1849 C Street 20240, phone (202) 208–3100, http://www.doi.gov

GALE NORTON, Secretary of the Interior; education: B.A., University of Denver, 1975; law degree, University of Denver, 1978; professional: Senior Attorney, Mountain States Legal Foundation, 1979–1983; Assistant to the Deputy Secretary of Agriculture, 1984–1985; Associate Solicitor at the Department of the Interior, 1985–1990; Colorado Attorney General, 1991–1999; Chair, Environment Committee for the Republican National Lawyers Association; General Counsel, Colorado Civil Justice League; awards: National Federalist Society Young Lawyer of the Year; and Colorado Women's Bar Association Mary Lathrop Trailblazer Award; family: married to John Hughes; nominated by President George W. Bush to become the 48th Secretary of the Interior, and was confirmed by the U.S. Senate on January 30, 2001.

OFFICE OF THE SECRETARY

Interior Building, Room 6156, phone 208–7351, fax 208–5048

Secretary of the Interior.—Gale Norton.
Special Assistant to the Secretary.—Patricia Connally.
Chief of Staff.—Brian Waidmann.
Deputy Chief of Staff.—Sue Ellen Wooldridge, 208–5504.
Counselors to the Secretary: Ann Klee, 208–6182; Michael Rossetti, 208–4123.
Director of External and Intergovernmental Affairs.—Kit Kimball, 208–1923.
Senior Adviser for Alaska Affairs.—Dru Pearce, 208–4177.

OFFICE OF THE DEPUTY SECRETARY

Interior Building, Room 6117, phone 208–6291

Deputy Secretary.—J. Steven Griles.
Associate Deputy Secretary.—James E. Cason.
Assistant Deputy Secretary.—Abraham E. Haspel.

OFFICE OF THE SPECIAL TRUSTEE FOR AMERICAN INDIANS

Interior Building, Room 5140, phone 208–4866, fax 208–7545

Special Trustee.—Ross O. Swimmer.

EXECUTIVE SECRETARIAT

Interior Building, Room 7212, phone 208–3181, fax 219–2100

Director.—Fay Iudicello.
Acting Deputy Director.—Dick Stephan, room 7217, 208–5257.

CONGRESSIONAL AND LEGISLATIVE AFFAIRS

Interior Building, Room 6256, phone 208–7693

Director of Congressional and Legislative Affairs and Counselor to the Secretary.—David L. Bernhardt.
Deputy Director of the Senate.—Chad Calvert, 208–7693.
Deputy Director, House of Representatives.—Teresa Davies, 208–7693.
Legislative Counsel.—Jane Lyder, Room 6245, 208–6706.

OFFICE OF COMMUNICATIONS

Interior Building, Room 6213, phone 208–6416

Director.—Eric Ruff.
Speech Writer.—Tina Kreisher.
Press Secretary.—Mark Pfeifle, room 6217.
Information Officers: Steve Brooks, Stephanie Hanna, Joan Moody, Frank Quimby, Hugh Vickery, John E. Wright, 208–6416.

OFFICE OF THE SOLICITOR

Interior Building, Room 6352, phone 208–4423

Solicitor.—William G. Myers III.
Deputy Solicitor.—Roderick E. Walston.
Associate Solicitor for—
Administration.—Edward Keable.
General Law.—Hugo Teufel.
Indian Affairs.—Edith Blackwell.
Land and Water.—Matthew J. McKeown.
Mineral Resources.—Fred Ferguson.
Parks and Wildlife.—Charles (Pete) Raynor.

OFFICE OF THE INSPECTOR GENERAL

Interior Building, Room 539, phone 208–5745, fax 219–3856

Inspector General.—Earl Devaney, room 5359.
Deputy Inspector General.—Mary Kendall Adler.
Association Inspector General for Whistle Blower Protection.—Richard Trinidad.
Assistant Inspector General for—
Administrative Service and Information Management.—Michael F. Wood.
Investigations.—David A. Montoya, 208–6752.
Audits.—Roger La Rouche, 208–4252.
Human Capitol Management.—Sharon D. Eller, 208–4618.

ASSISTANT SECRETARY FOR POLICY, MANAGEMENT AND BUDGET

Interior Building, Room 5110, phone 208–4203

Assistant Secretary.—Lynn Scarlett.
Counselor.—Daniel Jorjani.
Senior Advisor.—Robert Lamb.
Director, Office of Budget.—John D. Trezise, room 4100, 208–5308.
Deputy Assistant Secretary for—
Budget and Finance.—Nina Hatfield, 208–7966.
Human Resources and Workforce Diversity.—J. Michael Trujillo, room 5129, 208–4727.
Insular Affairs.—David Cohen, room 4328, 208–4736.
Law Enforcement and Security.—Larry Parkinson, room 7352, 208–5773.
Performance and Management.—Scott Cameron, room 5120, 208–1738.
Policy and International Affairs.—Chris Kearney, room 5124, 208–3219.

ASSISTANT SECRETARY FOR FISH AND WILDLIFE AND PARKS

Interior Building, Room 3156, phone 208–5347

Assistant Secretary.—Harold Craig Manson, room 3156, 208–5347.
Deputy Assistant Secretary.—Paul D. Hoffman, room 3156, 208–4416.
Deputy Assistant Secretary and Counselor.—P. David Smith, room 3154, 208–5378.
Senior Advisor to the Assistant Secretary.—Julie A. MacDonald, room 3144, 208–3928.

U.S. FISH AND WILDLIFE SERVICE

Interior Building, phone 208–4717, fax 208–6965

Director.—Steven A. Williams, 208–4717.
Deputy Directors: Matthew J. Hogan, 208–4545; Marshall P. Jones, Jr., 208–4545.
Chief, Office of Law Enforcement.—Kevin Adams, 208–3809.
Assistant Director for External Affairs.—Thomas O. Melius, 208–3809.
Chief, Division of:
Congressional and Legislative Affairs.—Alexandra Pitts, 208–5403.
Public Affairs.—Mitch Snow (acting), 208–4131.
Assistant Director for Migratory Birds and State Programs.—Paul Schmidt, 208–1050.
Chief, Office of Federal Aid.—Kris LaMontagne, (703) 358–2156.
Assistant Director for—
Endangered Species.—Gary Frazer, 208–4646.
Fisheries and Habitat Conservation.—Mamie Parker, 208–6394.
Business Management and Operations.—Paul Henne, (703) 358–1822.
National Wildlife Refuge System.—William Hartwig, 208–5333.
International Affairs.—Kenneth P. Stansell, 208–6393.
Budget, Planning, and Human Resources.—Denise Sheehan, 208–3736.
Chief, Division of Human Resources.—Kent Baum, (703) 358–1776.
Regional Directors:
Region 1.—David B. Allen, Eastside Federal Complex, 911 Northeast 11th Avenue, Portland, OR 97232, (503) 231–6118, fax (503) 872–2716.
California/Nevada Operations.—Steve Thompson, 2800 Cottage Way, Suite W2606, Sacramento, CA 95823, (916) 414–6486.
Region 2.—Dale Hall, PO Box 1306, Room 1306, 500 Gold Avenue SW., Albuquerque, NM 87103, (505) 248–6845.
Region 3.—Robyn Thorson, Federal Building, Fort Snelling, Twin Cities, MN 55111, (612) 725–3501.
Region 4.—Samuel D. Hamilton, 1875 Century Boulevard, Atlanta, GA 30345, (404) 679–4000, fax (404) 679–4006.
Region 5.—Rick Bennett (acting), 300 Westgate Center Drive, Hadley, MA 01035, (413) 253–8300, fax (413) 253–8308.
Region 6.—Ralph Morgenweck, PO Box 25486, Denver Federal Center, Denver, CO 80225, (303) 236–7920, fax (303) 236–8295.
Region 7.—Rowan Gould, 1011 East Tudor Road, Anchorage, AK 99503, (907) 786–3542, fax (907) 786–3306.

NATIONAL PARK SERVICE

Interior Building, Room 3104, phone 208–4621, fax 208–7625

Director.—Fran Mainella, room 3112, 208–4621.
Deputy Director.—Randy Jones, room 3113, 208–4621.
Associate Director for—
Cultural Resources, Stewardship and Partnership.—Kate Stevenson, room 3128, 208–7625.
Natural Resources Stewardship and Science.—Mike Soukup, room 3125, 208–3884.
Park Operations and Education.—Richard Ring, room 3130, 208–5651.
Professional Services.—Terrell Emmons, room 3127, 208–3264.
Assistant Director for—
External Affairs.—[Vacant].
Legislative and Congressional Affairs.—P. Daniel Smith, room 3210A, 208–5655.
Chief, Office of Public Affairs.—Dave Barna, room 3043, 208–6843.
Regional Directors:
Alaska Region.—Rob Arnberger, 2525 Gambell Street, Anchorage, AK 99503, (907) 257–2690, fax (907) 257–2510.
Northeast Region.—Marie Rust, 200 Chestnut Street, Philadelphia, PA 19106, (215) 597–7013, fax (215) 597–0815.
Midwest Region.—Ernest Quintana, 1709 Jackson Street, Omaha, NE, 68102, (402) 221–3448, fax (402) 341–2039.
National Capital Region.—Terry R. Carlstrom, (acting), 1100 Ohio Drive SW, Washington, DC 20242, (202) 619–7005, fax (202) 619–7220.

Intermountain Region.—Karen Wade, PO Box 25287, Denver, CO 80225, (303) 969–2500, fax (303) 969–2785.

Southeast Region.—William Schnek, 75 Spring Street SW, Atlanta, GA 30303, (404) 562–3100, fax (404) 331–3263.

Pacific Western Region.—Jon Jarvis, 600 Harrison Street, Suite 600, San Francisco, CA 94107, (415) 744–3876, fax (415) 744–4050.

ASSISTANT SECRETARY FOR INDIAN AFFAIRS

Interior Building, Room 4160, phone 208–7163

Assistant Secretary.—Aurene M. Martin (acting).

Deputy Assistant Secretary.—Aurene M. Martin.

Counselors to the Assistant Secretary: Mike Olsen, Theresa Rosier.

Special Assistant for Communications.—Daniel DuBray.

BUREAU OF INDIAN AFFAIRS

Interior Building, Room 4160, phone 208–5116

Director.—Terrance L. Virden.

Director, Office of:

Administration.—Debbie Clark.

Trust Responsibilities.—Jeff Lowman.

Tribal Services.—Michael Smith.

Director, Office of Indian Education Programs.—William Mehojah.

Deputy Director.—[Vacant].

Regional Directors:

Great Plains Region.—Paul Benjamin (acting), 115 Fourth Avenue SE, Aberdeen, SD 57401, (605) 226–7345, fax (602) 226–7446.

Southwest Region.—Robert Baracker, 615 First Street NW, Box 26567, Albuquerque, NM 87125, (505) 766–3171, fax (505) 766–1964.

Southern Plains Region.—Daniel J. Deerinwater, WCD Office Complex, Box 368, Anadarko, OK 73005, (405) 247–6673 Ext 314, fax (405) 247–2242.

Rocky Mountain Region.—Keith Beartusk, 316 North 26th Street, Billings, MT 58101, (406) 247–7943, fax (406) 247–7976.

Eastern Region.—Franklin Keel, 3701 North Fairfax Drive, Suite 260, Virginia Square, Arlington, VA 22203, (703) 235–2571, fax (703) 235–8610.

Alaska Region.—Niles Cesar, Federal Building, 3rd floor, PO Box 25520, Juneau, AK 99802, (907) 586–7177, fax (907) 586–7169.

Midwest Region.—Larry Morin, (acting), 331 Second Avenue South, Minneapolis, MN 55401, (612) 373–1000, fax (612) 373–1186.

Eastern Oklahoma Region.—Janet Hanna, Fifth and West Okmulgee, Muskogee, OK 74401, (918) 687–2296, fax (918) 687–2571.

Navajo Region.—Elouise Chicharello, PO Box 1060, Gallup, NM 87305, (505) 863–8314, fax (505) 863–8245.

Western Region.—Wayne C. Nordwall, One North First Street, PO Box 10, Phoenix, AZ 85001, (602) 379–6600, fax (602) 379–4413.

Northwest Region.—Stanley Speaks, 911 11th Avenue NE, Portland, OR 97232, (503) 231–6702, fax (503) 231–2201.

Pacific Region.—Clay Gregory (acting), 2800 Cottage Way, Sacramento, CA 95835, (916) 979–2600, fax (916) 979–2569.

ASSISTANT SECRETARY FOR LAND AND MINERALS MANAGEMENT

Interior Building, Room 7312, phone 208–6734, fax 208–3144

Assistant Secretary.—Rebecca W. Watson.

Deputy Assistant Secretary.—Patricia Morrison.

BUREAU OF LAND MANAGEMENT

Interior Building, Room 3314, phone 208–3801, fax 208–5242

Director.—Kathleen Clark, room 3314, 208–3801.
Deputy Director of:
Fire and Aviation.—Anne Jeffrey, room 5633, 208–4717.
Operations.—Francis R. Cherry, room 5660, 208–3801.
Programs and Policy.—James Hughes, 208–3801.
State Directors:
Alaska.—Henri Bisson, 222 West Seventh Avenue No. 13, Anchorage, AK 99513, (907) 271–5076, fax (907) 271–4596.
Arizona.—Elaine Y. Zielinski, 222 North Central Avenue, Phoenix, AZ 85004, (602) 417–9206, fax (602) 417–9398.
California.—Mike Pool, 2800 Cottage Way, Suite W1834, Sacramento, CA 95825, (916) 978–4600, fax (916) 978–4699.
Colorado.—Ron Wenker, 2850 Youngfield Street, Lakewood, CO 80215, (303) 239–3700, fax (303) 239–3934.
Eastern States.—Mike Nedd, 7450 Boston Boulevard, Springfield, VA 22153, (703) 440–1700, fax (703) 440–1701.
Idaho.—K. Lynn Bennett, 1387 South Vinnell Way, Boise, ID 83709, (208) 373–4000, fax (208) 373–3919.
Montana.—Thomas P. Lonnie, 5001 Southgate Drive, Billings, MT 59101, (406) 896–5298, fax (406) 896–5004.
Nevada.—Robert V. Abbey, P.O. Box 12000, Reno, NV 89520, (775) 861–6590, fax (775) 861–6601.
New Mexico.—Linda S.C. Rundell, P.O. Box 27115, Sante Fe, NM 87502, (505) 435–7501, fax (505) 435–7452.
Oregon.—Elaine Marquis-Brong, 333 SW 1st Avenue, Portland, OR 97204, (503) 808–6002, fax (503) 808–6308.
Utah.—Sally Wisely, 324 South State Street, 4th Floor, Salt Lake City, UT 84111, (801) 539–4010, fax (801) 539–4013.
Wyoming.—Bob Bennett, 5353 Yellowstone Road, PO Box 1828, Cheyenne, WY 82003, (307) 775–6256, fax (307) 775–6028.

MINERALS MANAGEMENT SERVICE

Interior Building, MS 4230 MIB, phone 208–3500, fax 208–7242

Director.—R.M. (Johnnie) Burton, 208–3500.
Deputy Director.—Walter D. Cruickshank, 208–3500.
Associate Director for—
Offshore Minerals Management.—Thomas Readinger, 208–3530.
Royalty Management.—Lucy Querques Denett, 208–3515.
Administration and Budget.—Robert E. Brown, 208–3220.
Policy and Management Improvement.—George Triebsch, 208–3398.
Chief, Office of Congressional Affairs.—[Vacant], 208–3985.
Other Continental Shelf Regions:
Alaska.—John T. Goll, 949 East 36th Avenue, Suite 300, Anchorage, AK 99508, (907) 271–6010.
Gulf of Mexico.—Chris C. Oynes, 1201 Elmwood Park Boulevard, New Orleans, LA 70123, (504) 736–2589, fax (504) 736–2589.
Pacific.—J. Lisle Reed, 770 Paseo Camarillo, Camarillo, CA 93010, (805) 389–7502.

SURFACE MINING RECLAMATION AND ENFORCEMENT

South Interior Building, Room 233, phone 208–4006, fax 219–3106

Director.—Jeffrey D. Jarrett.
Deputy Director.—Glenda Owens, room 233, SIB, 208–2807.
Assistant Director for Finance and Administration.—Carol Sampson, 208–2560.
Regional Director for—
Appalachian Coordinating Center.—Allen Klein, Three Parkway Center, Pittsburgh, PA 15220, (412) 937–2828, fax (412) 937–2903.
Mid-Continent Coordinating Center.—[Vacant].
Western Coordinating Center.—Brent T. Walquist, 1999 Broadway, Suite 3320, Denver, CO 80202, (303) 844–1401, fax (303) 844–1522.

Field Office Director for—

Alabama.—Arthur Abbs, 135 Gemini Circle, Suite 215, Homewood, AL 35209, (205) 290–7282, fax (205) 290–7280.

Indiana.—Andrew Gilmore, Minton-Capehart Federal Building, 575 North Pennsylvania Street, Room 301, Indianapolis, IN 46204, (317) 226–6700, fax (317) 226–6182.

Kentucky.—William Kovacic, 2675 Regency Road, Lexington, KY 40503, (606) 233–2894, fax (606) 233–2898.

New Mexico.—Willis Gainer, 505 Marquette Avenue NW, Suite 1200, Albuquerque, NM 87102, (505) 248–5070, fax (505) 248–5081.

Oklahoma.—Michael Wolfrom, 5100 East Skelley Drive, Suite 470, Tulsa, OK 74135, (918) 581–6430, fax (918) 581–6419.

Pennsylvania.—Beverly Brock (acting), Transportation Center, 415 Market Street, Suite 3C, Harrisburg, PA 17101, (717) 782–4036, fax (717) 782–3771.

Tennessee.—George Miller, 530 Gay Street, Suite 500, Knoxville, TN 37902, (423) 545–4103, fax (423) 545–4111.

Virginia.—Robert Penn, PO Drawer 1216, Big Stone Gap, VA 24219, (540) 523–0001, fax (540) 523–5053.

West Virginia.—Roger Calhoun, 1027 Virginia Street East, Charleston, WV 25301, (304) 347–7162, fax (304) 347–7170.

Wyoming.—Guy Padgett, 100 East B Street, Room 2128, Casper, WY 82601, (307) 261–6550, fax (307) 261–6552.

ASSISTANT SECRETARY FOR WATER AND SCIENCE

Interior Building, Room 7414, phone 208–3186, fax 208–6948

Assistant Secretary.—Bennett Raley, 208–3186.

Deputy Assistant Secretary.—R. Thomas Weimer, room 6654, 208–3136.

U.S. GEOLOGICAL SURVEY

The National Center, 12201 Sunrise Valley Drive, Reston, VA 20192

phone (703) 648–7411, fax (703) 648–4454

Director.—Charles G. Groat, 648–7411.

Deputy Director.—Robert E. Doyle, 648–7412.

Office of:

Administrative Policy and Services.—Carol Aten, (703) 648–7200.

Human Resources.—[Vacant]

Geographic Information Officer.—Karen Siderelis, (703) 648–5747.

Associate Directors for—

Geology.—P. Patrick Leahy, (703) 648–6600.

Geography.—Barbara J. Ryan, (703) 648–7413.

Water.—Robert M. Hirsch, (703) 648–5215.

Biology.—Susan D. Haseltine, (703) 648–4050.

Eastern Regional Director.—Bonnie A. McGregor, 1700 Leetown Road, Kearneysville, WV 25430, (304) 724–4521.

Central Regional Director.—Thomas J. Casadevall, P.O. Box 25046, Denver Federal Center, Building 810, Denver, CO 80225, (303) 202–4740.

Western Regional Director.—John (Doug) Buffington, 909 First Avenue, Suite 704, Seattle, WA 98104, (206) 220–4578.

BUREAU OF RECLAMATION

Interior Building, Room 7554, phone 513–0501, fax 513–0309

Commissioner.—John W. Keys III, room 7554, 513–0501.

Chief of Staff.—Robert J. Quint, room 7557, 513–0501.

Director of:

External and Intergovernmental Affairs.—Mark Limbaugh, 513–0615.

Congressional and Legislative Affairs.—Matt Eames, 513–0565.

Public Affairs.—Trudy Harlow, room 7542, 513–0575.

Director, Operations.—Jack Garner, room 7545, 513–0615.

Regional Directors:

Great Plains.—Maryanne Bach, P.O. Box 36900, Billings, MT 59107, (406) 247–7600, fax (406) 247–7793.

Lower Colorado.—Robert W. Johnson, P.O. Box 61470, Boulder City, NV 89006, (702) 293–8411, fax (702) 293–8416.

Mid-Pacific Region.—Kirk C. Rodgers, Federal Office Building, 2800 Cottage Way, Sacramento, CA 95825, (916) 978–5000, fax (916) 978–5599.

Pacific Northwest.—Bill McDonald, 1150 North Curtis Road, Suite 100, Boise, ID 83706, (208) 378–5012, fax (208) 378–5019.

Upper Colorado.—Rick Gold, 125 South State Street, room 6107, Salt Lake City, UT 84138, (801) 524–3600.

DEPARTMENT OF AGRICULTURE

Jamie L. Whitten Building, 1400 Independence Avenue, SW, Washington, DC 20250

phone (202) 720–3631, http://www.usda.gov

ANN VENEMAN, Secretary of Agriculture; education: B.A., University of California at Davis; M.A., University of California at Berkeley; J.D., Hastings College of Law; professional: attorney with Patton, Boggs & Blow, 1993–95; and with Nossanan, Guthner, Knox & Elliott, 1999–2001; public service: Secretary of the California Department of Food and Agriculture, 1995–99; U.S. Department of Agriculture, 1986–93; serving as Associate Administrator of the Foreign Agricultural Service, 1986–89; Deputy Under Secretary of Agriculture for International Affairs and Commodity Programs, 1989–91; and Deputy Secretary of Agriculture, 1991–93; community service: Close Up Foundation; serving as a board member for the nonpartisan civic education organization; nominated by President George W. Bush to become the 27th Secretary of Agriculture, and was fonfirmed by the U.S. Senate on January 20, 2001.

OFFICE OF THE SECRETARY

Secretary of Agriculture.—Ann Veneman, room 200–A, (202) 720–3631.
Chief of Staff.—Dale Moore.
Deputy Chief of Staff.—[Vacant].
Counsel for Trade.—David Hegwood.
Special Assistant to the President/Personnel.—Drew DeBerry.
Executive Secretariat.—Bruce Bundick, room 116–A, 720–7100.
Deputy Secretary.—James Moseley, room 202B–A, 720–6158.
Executive Assistant.—Deb Atwood, room 202B–A, 720–6158.
Chief Financial Officer.—Edward McPherson, room 143–W, 720–5539.
General Counsel.—Nancy Bryson, room 107–W, 720–3351.
Inspector General.—Phyllis Fong, room 117–W, 720–8001.
Chief Economist.—Keith Collins, room 227–E, 720–4164.
Chief Information Officer.—Scott Charbo, room 416–W, 720–3152.
Director of Communications.—[Vacant], room 402–A, 720–4623.
Under Secretary for Natural Resources and Environment.—Mark Rey.
Chief of Forest Service.—Dale Bosworth, Sidney R. Yates Building, 205–1661.
Chief of Natural Resources Conservation Service.—Bruce Knight, room 5105–S, BG, 720–4526.
Under Secretary for Farm and Foreign Agricultural Services.—J.B. Penn, room 205–E, 720–3111.
Administrator for—
Farm Services Agency.—James Little, room 3086–S, BG, 720–3467.
Foreign Agricultural Service.—A. Ellen Terpstra, room 5071–S, BG, 720–3935.
Under Secretary for Rural Development.—Thomas C. Dorr.
Administrator for—
Rural Business Service.—John Rosso, room 5045–S, 690–4730.
Rural Housing Service.—Arthur Garcia, 690–1533.
Rural Utilities Service.—Hilda Gay Legg, room 4051–S, 720–9540.
Under Secretary for Food, Nutrition and Consumer Services.—Eric Bost, room 240–E, 720–7711.
Administrator for Food and Nutrition Service.—Roberto Salazar, room 803, Park Center, 305–2062.
Under Secretary for Food Safety.—[Vacant].
Administrator for Food Safety and Inspection Service.—Garry McKee, room 331–E, 720–7025.
Under Secretary for Research, Education and Economics.—Joseph Jen, room 217–W, 720–8885.
Administrator for—
Agricultural Research Service.—Edward B. Knipling, room 302–A, 720–3656.
Cooperative State Research, Education, and Extension Service.—Colien Heffernan, room 304–A, 720–4423.

Economic Research Service.—Susan Offutt, room 4145, M. Street, 694–5000.
National Agricultural Statistics Service.—Ron Bosecker, room 417–S, BG, 720–2707.
Under Secretary for Marketing and Regulatory Service.—William Hawks, room 228–W, 720–4256.
Administrator for—
Agricultural Marketing Service.—Kenneth Clayton (acting), room 3071–S, 720–5115.
Animal and Plant Health Inspection Service.—Craig Reed, room 313–E, 720–3668.
Grain Inspection, Packers and Stockyards.—David Shipman (acting), room 1094–S, 720–0219.
Assistant Secretary for—
Administration.—Lou Gallegos, 720–3291.
Congressional and Intergovernmental Relations.—Mary Waters, room 213–A, 720–7095.
Director of:
Civil Rights.—David Winningham, room 326–W, 720–5212.
Congressional Relations.—Mary Waters, room 213–A, 720–7095.
Ethics.—Ray Sheehan, room 347–W, 720–2251.
Human Resources Management.—Ruthie Jackson, room 316–W, 720–3585.
Intergovernmental Affairs.—[Vacant].
Operations.—Priscilla Carey, room 1575–S, 720–3937.
Outreach.—[Vacant], 501 School Street, Suite 100, 720–6350.
Procurement and Property Management.—Warren R. Ashworth, Reporters Building, room 302, 720–9448.
Small and Disadvantaged Business Utilization.—Jim House, room 1566–S, 720–7117.
Office of Administrative Law Judges, Chief Judge.—James Hunt, room 1049–S, 720–6368.
Board of Contract Appeals.—Judge Edward Houry, Chairman, room 2916–S, 720–6110.
Office of the Judicial Officer.—William Jensen, 501 School Street, room 300–A, 720–7664.
Executive Operations—
Chief Economist.—Keith Collins, room 112–A, 720–4164.
Director, Office of:
Budget and Program Analysis.—Stephen B. Dewhurst, room 101–A, 720–7323.
Executive Secretariat.—Bruce Bundick, room 116–A, 720–7100.
National Appeals Division.—Roger J. Klurfeld, room 111–Park Center, (703) 305–2708.

GENERAL COUNSEL

Jamie L. Whitten Building, Room 107–W, phone 720–3351

General Counsel.—Nancy S. Bryson.
Deputy General Counsel.—James Michael Kelly.
Associate General Counsel for—
Civil Rights.—Arlean Leland, 720–1760.
International Affairs: Commodity Programs and Food Assistant Programs.—Thomas V. Conway, 720–6883.
Legislation, Litigation, General Law.—James Michael Kelly, 720–7219.
Natural Resources.—Jane Poling, 720–9311.
Regulatory and Marketing.—John Golden, 720–3155.
Rural Development.—David P. Grahn, 720–6187.
Deputy Associate General Counsel for Civil Rights Division.—Sadhna True, 720–3955.
Assistant General Counsel for—
Community Development.—Paul Loizeaux, 720–2508.
Electric and Telephone.—Terrance M. Brady, 720–2764.
Natural Resources.—[Vacant], 720–7121.
Assistant General Counsel, Division of:
Food and Nutrition.—Ronald Hill, 720–6181.
International Affairs and Commodity Programs.—Ralph Linden, 720–9246.
General Law.—Kenneth E. Cohen, 720–5565.
Legislation.—Michael Knipe, 720–5354.
Litigation.—Margaret Breinholt, 720–4733.
Marketing.—Kenneth Vail, 720–5293.
Regulatory.—Tom Walsh, 720–5550.
Resource Management Specialist.—Deborah L. Vita, 720–4861.
Trade Practices.—Mary Hobbie.

INSPECTOR GENERAL

Jamie L. Whitten Building, Room 117–W, phone 720–8001

Inspector General.—Phyllis K. Fong.
Deputy Inspector General.—Joyce Fleischmann, room 117–W, 720–7431.
Executive Assistant to the Inspector General.—[Vacant].
Assistant Inspector General for—
Audit.—Richard Long, room 403–E, 720–6945.
Investigations.—Jon Novak (acting), room 507–A, 720–3306.
Policy Development and Resources Management.—Paula F. Hayes, room 5–E, 720–6979.

ASSISTANT SECRETARY FOR ADMINISTRATION

Jamie L. Whitten Building, Room 240–W, phone 720–3291

Assistant Secretary for Administration.—Lou Gallegos.
Deputy Assistant Secretary for Administration.—John Surina.
Special Assistant.—Pat Porter.
Associate Assistant Secretary for Administration.—Clyde Thompson.

BOARD OF CONTRACT APPEALS

South Agriculture Building, Room 2916–S, phone 720–6110

Chairman and Administrative Judge.—Howard A. Pollack.
Vice Chair and Administrative Judge.—[Vacant], 720–2583.
Administrative Judges: Anne W. Westbrook, 720–7242; Joseph A. Vergilio, 720–2066.
Chief Counsel.—[Vacant], 720–6229.
Recorder.—Elaine M. Hillard, 720–7023.
Deputy Recorder.—Alice Vincent, 720–7023.
Legal Technician.—Natalie Krolczyk, room 2914–S, 720–7023.

OFFICE OF ADMINISTRATIVE LAW JUDGES

South Agriculture Building, Room 1049–S, phone 720–6383

Chief Administrative Law Judge.—James Hunt.
Secretary to the Chief Administrative Law Judge.—[Vacant].
Administrative Law Judge.—Jill S. Clifton, room, 1051–S, 720–8161.
Hearing Clerk.—Joyce A. Dawson, room 1081–S, 720–4443.

OFFICE OF THE JUDICIAL OFFICER

South Agriculture Building, Room 1449–S, phone 720–4764

Judicial Officer.—William G. Jensen.
Attorney Examiner.—Michael J. Stewart, 720–9268.

OFFICE OF SMALL AND DISADVANTAGED BUSINESS UTILIZATION

South Agriculture Building, Room 1566–S, phone 720–7117

Director.—James E. House.

OFFICE OF OPERATIONS

South Agriculture Building, Room 1575–S, phone 720–3937

Director.—Priscilla Carey.
Deputy Director.—Christopher A. Gomez, 720–1762.
Associate Director for Operations.—[Vacant], 720–3937.
Medical Officer.—Oleh Jacykewycw, room 1039, 720–3893.

OFFICE OF HUMAN RESOURCES MANAGEMENT

Jamie L. Whitten Building, Room 302–W, phone 720–3585

Director.—Ruthie Jackson.
Deputy Director.—Joseph Colantuoni, 720–3586.
Division Directors:
Executive Resources and Services.—Mary Jo Thompson, 720–2101.
Human Resources Services.—Clifton Taylor (acting), 720–5782.
Personnel Policy and Partnership.—Denise Leger-Lee, 720–3327.
Safety and Health Management.—James Stevens, 720–8248.
Workforce and Planning.—Clifton Taylor, 720–6104.

OFFICE OF CIVIL RIGHTS

Jamie L. Whitten Building Room 326–W, phone 720–5212

Director.—David Winningham.

OFFICE OF PROCUREMENT AND PROPERTY MANAGEMENT

Reporters Building, Room 302, phone 720–9448

Director.—Warren R. Ashworth.
Deputy Director.—Glenn Haggstrom.
Division Directors:
Procurement Policy.—David Shea, 720–6206.
Property Management.—Denise Hayes, 720–7283.

OFFICE OF THE CHIEF FINANCIAL OFFICER

Jamie L. Whitten Building, Room 143–W, phone 720–0727

Chief Financial Officer.—Ted McPherson.
Deputy Chief Financial Officer.—Pat Healy, room 143–W, 720–5539.
Associate Chief Financial Officer.—Wendy Snow, 501 School Street, 619–7636.
Division Chiefs:
Financial Systems Reporting and Analysis.—Pauline Myrick, room 3033–S, 720–1174.
Planning and Accountability.—Annie Walker Bradley (acting), room 5402–S, 720–1175.
Working Capital Fund Budget and Fiscal Services Division.—William King, room 4094–S, 720–1885.
Director, National Finance Center.—John Ortega, PO Box 60000, New Orleans LA 70160, (504) 255–5200, fax (504) 255–5548.
Foundation Financial Information Systems.—Wendy Snow, 501 School Street, 619–7636.

OFFICE OF THE CHIEF INFORMATION OFFICER

Jamie L. Whitten Building, Room 414–W, phone 720–8833

Chief Information Officer.—Scott Charbo.
Deputy Chief Information Officer.—Ira Hobbs, room 414–W, 720–8833.
Associate Chief Information Officers for—
Cyber Security.—Bill Hadesty, 690–0048.
E-Government.—Chris Niedermayer, 690–2118.
Information Resources Management.—Greg Parham, 720–5865.
National Information Technology Center.—Kathleen Rundle, P.O. Box 205, 8930 Ward Parkway, Kansas City, MO 64114, (816) 926–6501.
Telecommunications Services and Operations.—Jan Lilja, 720–8695.
Senior Policy Advisor for Field Service Center Oversight.—Richard Roberts (acting), 720–3482.
Supervisory Computer Specialist.—Ed Troup, 3825 East Mulberry Street, Fort Collins, CO 80524, (303) 498–1510.

OFFICE OF THE CHIEF ECONOMIST

Jamie L. Whitten Building, Room 112–A, phone 720–4164

Chief Economist.—Keith Collins.
Deputy Chief Economist.—Joseph Glauber, 720–6185.
Chairperson.—Gerald A. Bange, room 4414–S, 720–6030.
Chief Meteorologist.—Ray Motha, room 4414–S, 720–8651.
National Weather Service, Supervisory Meteorologist.—David Miskus, room 4414–S, 720–6030.
Global Change Program Office.—William Hohenstein, Reporters Building, room 4407–S, 720–6698.
Office of Energy Policy and New Uses.—Roger Conway, Reporters Building, room 361, 401–0461.
Office of Sustainable Development.—Adela Backiel, room 112–A, 720–2456.

OFFICE OF RISK ASSESSMENT AND COST BENEFIT ANALYSIS

South Agriculture Building, Room 5248–S, phone 720–8022

Director.—James Schaub.

OFFICE OF BUDGET AND PROGRAM ANALYSIS

Jamie L. Whitten Building, Room 101–A, phone 720–3323

Director.—Stephen B. Dewhurst.
Associate Director.—Lawrence Wachs, 720–5303.
Deputy Director, Budget, Legislative and Regulatory Systems.—Dennis Kaplan, room 102–E, 720–6667.
Deputy Director Program Analysis.—Scott Steele, room 126–W, 720–3396.

OFFICE OF THE EXECUTIVE SECRETARIAT

Jamie L. Whitten Building, Room 116–A, phone 720–7100

Director.—Bruce Bundick.
Deputy Director.—MaryAnn Swigart.

NATIONAL APPEALS DIVISION

3101 Park Center Drive, Room 1100, Alexandria VA 22302

Director.—Roger J. Klurfeld, (703) 305–2708.
Deputy Director.—M. Terry Johnson.

OFFICE OF COMMUNICATIONS

Jamie L. Whitten Building, Room 404–A, phone 720–4623

Director.—[Vacant].
Assistant Director.—Larry Quinn.
Deputy Director/Press Secretary.—Alisa Harrison.
Deputy Press Secretaries: Ed Loyd, Julie Quick.
Division Directors:
Administration and Information Services.—Johna Pierce.
Broadcast Media and Technology.—David Black.
Budget and Operations Services.—Ron DeMunbrun.
Constituent Affairs.—Patricia Klintberg.
Visual Communications.—Eva Cuevas.
Web Services and Distribution.—Kim Taylor.

UNDER SECRETARY FOR NATURAL RESOURCES AND ENVIRONMENT

Jamie L. Whitten Building, Room 21709–E, phone 720–7173

Under Secretary.—Mark Rey.
Deputy Under Secretary of:
Forestry.—Dave Tenny.
Conservation.—Mack Gray.

FOREST SERVICE

Sydney R. Yates Building, Fourth Floor, Auditors Building, 201 14th Street, SW., 20250
phone 205–1661

Chief.—Dale N. Bosworth.
Associate Chief.—Sally Collins.
Staff Directors:
Law Enforcement and Investigation.—William Wasley, 605–4690.
International Programs.—Valdis E. Mezainis, 205–1650.
Office of Communications.—George Lennon, 205–8333.

BUDGET AND FINANCE

Sydney R. Yates Building, First Floor, phone 205–1784

Deputy Chief/CFO.—Mary Sally Matiella, 205–1784.
Staff Directors:
Financial Management.—Dave Heerwagen, (703) 605–4763.
Program Development and Budget.—Hank Kashdan, 205–0987.

BUSINESS OPERATIONS

Sydney R. Yates Building, Second Floor, phone 205–1709

Deputy Chief.—Thomas Mills, 205–1655.
Associate Deputy Chief.—Gloria Manning, 205–1707.
Staff Assistant.—Ron Hooper.
Staff Directors:
Acquisition Management.—Robbie Chrishon, (703) 605–4744.
Civil Rights.—Kathy Gause, 205–1585.
Freedom of Information/Privacy Act.—Naomi Charboneau, (703) 605–4910.
Human Resources Management.—John Lopez, (703) 605–4532.
Information Resource Management.—Keith Jackson, (703) 605–4814.
Senior, Youth and Volunteer Programs.—Irving Thomas, (703) 605–4830.

NATIONAL FOREST SYSTEM

Sydney R. Yates Building, Third Floor, phone 205–1665

Deputy Chief.—Tom Thompson.
Associate Deputy Chiefs: Gloria Manning, Abigail Kimbell, 205–1465.
Staff Directors of:
Ecosystem Management Coordination.—Fred Norbury, 205–0895.
Engineering.—Vaughn Stokes, 205–1400.
Forest Management.—Jeanette Raiser.
Lands.—Jack Craven, 205–1248.
Minerals and Geology.—[Vacant], 205–1224.
Recreation.—Dave Holland, 205–1643.
Watershed and Air Management.—Jim Gladen, 205–1473.

PROGRAMS AND LEGISLATION

Sydney R. Yates Building, Fifth Floor, phone 205–1663

Chief.—Elizabeth Estill.
Associate Chief.—Susan Yonts-Shepherd, 205–1071.
Staff Assistant.—Scott Conroy, 205–1265.
Staff Chiefs of:
Legislative Affairs.—Tim DeCoster, 205–1637.
Policy Analysis.—Matiland Sharpe, 205–1775.
Strategic Planning and Resource Assessment.—[Vacant], 205–1235.

RESEARCH AND DEVELOPMENT

Sydney R. Yates Building, First Floor, phone 205–1665

Deputy Chief.—Robert Lewis, Jr., 205–1665.
Associate Deputy Chiefs: Bov Eav, Barbara C. Weber, 205–1702.
Staff Assistant.—Hao Tran, 205–1293.
Staff Directors of:
Resource Valuation and Use Research.—[Vacant], 205–1747.
Science Policy, Planning, Inventory and Information.—Richard W. Gulding, 205–1507.
Vegetation Management and Protection Research.—Jim Reaves, 205–1561.
Wildlife, Fish, Water and Air Research.—[Vacant], 205–1524.

STATE AND PRIVATE FORESTRY

Sydney R. Yates Building, Second Floor, phone 205–1567

Deputy Chief.—Joel Holtrop, 205–1657.
Associate Deputy Chief.—Robin Thompson, 205–1331.
Staff Assistant.—Stana Federighi, 205–1470.
Staff Directors of:
Conservation Education.—[Vacant], 205–5681.
Cooperative Forestry.—Larry Payne, 205–1389.
Fire and Aviation Management.—Jerry Williams, 205–1483.
Forest Health Protection.—Rob Nangold, 205–1600.

NATURAL RESOURCES CONSERVATION SERVICE

South Building, Room 5105–S, 720–4525

Chief.—Bruce I. Knight, 720–7246.
Associate Chief.—Thomas A. Weber, 720–4531.
Director of:
Civil Rights Staff.—Andrew Johnson, (301) 504–2180.
Conservation Communication Staff.—Terry Bish, 720–3210.
Legislative Affairs.—Douglas McKalip, 720–2771.
Strategic Natural Resource Issues Staff:
Special Assistants to the Chiefs: Dave Gagner, 720–2534; Gary A. Margheim, 690–2877/720–9480; Taylor Oldroyd, 720–1882; Christine Pytel, (301) 504–2201.
Deputy Chief of Management.—P. Dwight Holman, 720–6297.
Director & CIO, Information Technology Division.—Mary Thomas, (301) 504–2232.
Director of:
Correspondence Management.—Stephanie I. Edelen, 690–0023.
Financial Management Division.—Jack Crews, 720–5904.
Human Resources Management Division.—Karen Karlinchak, 720–2227.
Information Technology Center.—Jack Carlson, (970) 295–5576.
Management Services Division.—Edward M. Biggers, Jr., 720–4102.
National Employee Development Center.—Jerry Williamson, (817) 509–3241.
Deputy Chief, Programs.—Jose Acevedo, 720–4527.
Associate Deputy Chief.—Carol Jett, 720–6580.
Director of:
Animal Husbandry and Clean Water.—Tom Christensen, (301) 504–2196.
Conservation Operations Division.—Charles Whitmore (acting), 720–1845.

International Programs Division.—Jose Acevedo (acting), 720–2218.
Outreach Division.—Larry Holmes, (301) 504–2229.
Resource Conservation and Community Development Division.—Anne Dubey (acting), 720–2847.
Watersheds and Wetlands Division.—Harry Shawter (acting), 720–3534.

Science and Technology:
Deputy Chief.—Lawrence E. Clark, 720–4630.
Director of:
Conservation Engineering Division.—Ronald Marlow, 720–2520.
Ecological Sciences Division.—Diane F. Gelburd, 720–2587.
Resource Economics and Social Sciences Division.—Peter F. Smith, 720–5235.

Soil Survey and Resources Assessment:
Deputy Chief.—Maurice J. Mausbach, 690–4616.
Special Assistant to the Director.—Jeri I. Bere, 720–1881.
Director of:
Resource Assessment Division.—Carlos Heming, 720–8644.
Resource Inventory Division.—Wayne Maresch, (301) 504–2271.
Soil Survey Division.—Wayne Maresch (acting), 720–1820.

Strategic Planning and Accountability:
Deputy Chief.—Katherine C. Gugulis, 720–7847.
Director, Operations Management and Oversight Division.—Dana York, 720–8388.
Budget Planning and Analysis.—Brenda Thomas, 720–4533.
Strategic and Performance Planning Division.—Dan Lawson, 690–0467.

FARM SERVICE AGENCY

South Building, Room 3086–S, 720–3467.

Administrator.—Jim Little.
Associate Administrators:
Management.—[Vacant].
Programs.—[Vacant].
Executive Secretariat.—Sandra Smith, room 0071–S, 720–9564.
Civil Rights.—Sharon L. Holmes, 410–7197.
Legislative Liaison Staff.—Mary Helen Askins, room 3613–S, 720–3865.
Public Affairs Staff.—Eric Parsons, room 3624–S, 720–5237.
Economic and Policy Analysis Staff.—Larry A. Walker, room 3741–S, 720–3451.

Deputy Administrator for Farm Programs.—John Johnson, room 3612–S, 720–3175.
Assistant Deputy Administrator for Farm Programs.—Paul Gutierrez, 720–2070.
Production, Emergencies and Compliance Division.—Diane Sharp, room 4754, 720–7641.
Price Support Division.—Grady Bilberry, room 4095–S, 720–7901.
Conservation and Environmental Programs Division.—Robert Stephenson, room 4714–S, 720–6221.
Tobacco and Peanuts Division.—Daniel Stevens, room 5724, 720–8120.

Deputy Administrator for Loan Programs.—Carolyn Cooksie, room 3605–S, 720–4671.
Assistant Deputy Administrator.—Almeda Cole, (acting), room 3605–S, 720–7597.
Program Development and Economic Enhancement Division.—Bobby Reynolds, room 4919–S, 720–3647.
Loan Making Division.—James Radintz, room 5438–S, 720–1632.
Loan Servicing and Property Management Division.—Veldon Hall, room 5449–S, 720–4572.

Deputy Administrator for Field Operations.—Doug Frago, room 3092, 690–2807.
Assistant Deputy Administrator.—John W. Chott, Jr., room 8092, 690–2807.
Operations Review and Analysis Staff.—Thomas McCann, room 2720–S, 690–2532.
Area Offices:
Midwest Area.—[Vacant].
Northeast Area.—[Vacant].
Northwest Area.—[Vacant].
Southeast Area.—[Vacant].
Southwest Area.—[Vacant].

Deputy Administrator for Commodity Operations.—Bert Farrish, room 3080–S, 720–3217.
Assistant Deputy Administrator.—[Vacant].
Procurement and Donations Division.—Steve Mikkelson, room 5755, 720–5074.
Warehouse and Inventory Division.—Steve Gill (acting), room 5962–S, 720–2121.
Kansas City Commodity Office.—George Aldaya, (816) 926–6301.

Deputy Administrator for Management.—John Williams, room 3095–S, 720–3438.
Assistant Deputy Administrator.—[Vacant].
Management Services Division.—Chris Reagan, room 6603–S, 720–3138.
Human Resources Division.—Francis X. Riley, Jr., room 5200 (L-St), 418–8950.
Budget Division.—Dennis Taitano, room 4720–S, 720–3674.
Information Technology Services Division.—Francis Shehan, room 5768–S, 720–5320.
Financial Management Division.—Kristine Chadwick, room 1208 POC, 305–1386.
Kansas City Management Office.—[Vacant].

RISK MANAGEMENT AGENCY

South Building, Room 3053–S, 720–2803

Administrator.—Ross J. Davidson, Jr.
Associate Administrators: Byron E. Anderson, David C. Hatch.
Deputy Administrator for—
Compliance.—Michael Hand, room 6094–S, 720–0642.
Insurance Services.—Marian Jenkins (acting), room 6709–S, 720–5290.
Research and Development.—Timothy Witt, Kansas City, (816) 926–7394/7822.

FOREIGN AGRICULTURAL SERVICE

South Building, 14th and Independence Avenue, SW., room 5071, 20250
phone 720–3935, fax 690–2159

Administrator.—A. Ellen Terpstra, room 5071–S.
Associate Administrator.—Kenneth J. Roberts.
Confidential Assistant to the Administrator.—Lloyd Day.
Chief of Staff.—Gene Philhower.
General Sales Manager.—W. Kirk Miller.
Director of:
Budget Staff.—Hall G. Wynne, Jr., room 6083–S, 690–4052.
Civil Rights Staff.—Mae Johnson, room 6504–S, 720–7233.
Compliance Review Staff.—Robert Huttenlocker, room 4957–S, 720–6713.
Correspondence Unit.—Henry Noland (acting), room 6627–S, 720–7631.
External Affairs.—Roy Henwood, room 5071, 720–3935.
Information Division.—Maureen Quinn, room 5074–S, 720–3448.
Legislative Affairs Staff.—Sharon McClure (acting), room 5931–S, 720–6829.
Outreach and Exporter Assistance Staff.—Dale Miller (acting), room 3119–S, 720–5037.
Strategic Operations Staff.—David Pendlum, room 5080–S, 720–1293.

FOREIGN AGRICULTURAL AFFAIRS

Deputy Administrator.—Lyle Sebranek, room 5702–S, 720–6138.
Assistant Deputy Administrator for—
International Operations.—Weyland Beeghly, room 5702–S, 720–3253.
International Services.—Kathy Ting, room 6075–S, 720–7781.
Field Communications Officer.—Kathy Ting (acting), room 6072–S, 205–2930.
Representation and Foreign Visitors Protocol Staff Chief.—Allen Alexander, room 5088–S, 720–6725.
Area Officers:
Africa, Middle East, and Western Hemisphere.—Paul Hoffman, room 5094–S, 720–7053.
Eastern Europe and Eurasia.—James Denver, room 5099–S, 690–4053.
Europe.—John Wilson, room 5098–S, 690–3412.
North Asia.—Susan Schayes, room 5095–S, 720–3080.
South Asia and Oceania.—Steve Huete, room 5095–S,
Western Hemisphere.—Robert Hoff, room 5094–S, 720–3221.

INTERNATIONAL TRADE POLICY

Deputy Administrator.—Patricia Sheikh, room 5910–S, 720–6887.
Assistant Deputy Administrators: James Grueff, room 5908–S, 720–4055; Beverly Simmons, room 5914–S, 720–4433.

Director of:
Food Safety and Technical Services Division.—Bobby Richey, room 5545–S, 690–0929.
Multilateral Trade Negotiations Division.—Debra Henke, room 5530–S, 720–1324.
Deputy Directors: Charles Bertsch, room 5524–S, 720–6278; Sara Schwartz, room 5536–S, 720–6064.
Asia and Americas Division.—Brian Grunenfelder, room 5507–S, 720–2056.
Deputy Director.—Brenda Freeman, room 5511–S, 720–1291.
Europe, Africa, Middle East Division.—Robert Macke, room 5514–S, 720–1340.
Import Policies and Programs Division.—Richard Blabey, room 5533–S, 720–1061.
Deputy Director, Africa, Middle East, and South Asia.—Gary Meyer, room 5513–S, 720–2258.

EXPORT CREDITS

Deputy Administrator.—Mary T. Chambliss, room 4083–S, 720–6301.
Assistant Deputy Administrator.—Ira Branson, room 4083–S, 720–4274.
Director of:
Program Administration Division.—William Hawkins, room 4077–S, 720–3241.
Program Planning, Development and Evaluation Division.—Robin Tilsworth, room 4506–S, 720–4221.
Chief of:
Europe and Middle East Branch.—Mike Fay, room 4543–S, 720–0732.
Latin America, Caribbean, Africa and Asia Branch.—Lisa Twedt, room 4574–S, 720–2637.
Director of:
Operations Division.—Mark Rowse, room 4521–S, 720–6211.
Deputy Director.—[Vacant], room 4519–S, 720–0624.

COMMODITY AND MARKETING PROGRAMS

Deputy Administrator.—Franklin D. Lee, room 5089A–S, 720–4761.
Assistant Deputy Administrators: Kent Sisson, room 5089A–S, 720–7791; Randy Zeitner, room 5087–S, 720–1595.
Director of:
AgExport Services Division.—Dan Berman, room 4939–S, 720–6343.
Cotton, Oilseeds, Tobacco and Seeds Division.—J. Lawrence Blum, room 5646–S, 720–9516.
Dairy, Livestock and Poultry Division.—Howard Wetzel, room 5935–S, 720–8031.
Forest and Fishery Products Division.—Elizabeth Berry, room 4647–S, 720–0638.
Grain and Feed Division.—Robert Riemenschneider, room 5603–S, 720–6219.
Horticultural and Tropical Products Division.—Frank Tarrant, room 5649–S, 720–6590.
Marketing Operations Staff.—Denise Huttenlocker, room 4932–S, 720–4327.
Production Estimates and Assessment Division.—Allen Vandergriff, room 6053–S, 720–0888.

INTERNATIONAL COOPERATION AND DEVELOPMENT

Deputy Administrator.—Suzanne E. Heinen (acting), room 3008–S, 690–0776.
Assistant Deputy Administrators.—Jocelyn Brown, room 3010–S, 690–0775; Christian Foster, room 3002–S, 690–0776.
Directors for—
International Organization Affairs Division.—Lynne Reich, room 3005–S, 690–1823.
Food Industries Division.—Frank Fender, room 3241–S, 690–1339.
Research and Scientific Exchanges Division.—Carol Kramer-LeBlanc, room 3229–S, 720–8877.
Deputy Director.—Susan Owens, room 3229–S, 690–4872.
Development Resources Division.—Howard Anderson, room 3208–S, 690–1924.
Deputy Director.—Mark Holt, room 3208–S, 690–4872.
Leaders of:
Cochran Fellowship Program.—Margaret McDaniel (acting), room 3846–S, 690–1734.
Food Security Branch.—James Stevenson, room 3233–S, 720–0788.
Trade Investment Program.—Steve Beasley (acting), room 3247–S, 720–1347.
Trade Market Development and Policy Linkages Branch.—Gary Laidig, room 3236–S, 720–7481.

Professional Development Program.—Margaret Hively, room 3245–S, 690–1141.
Sustainable Agriculture and Resource Use Branch.—Richard Affleck, room 3235–S, 720–2589.

UNDER SECRETARY FOR RURAL DEVELOPMENT

Jamie L. Whitten Building, phone 720–4581

Under Secretary.—Thomas Dorr.
Deputy Under Secretary.—Gilbert Gonzalez.

OFFICE OF COMMUNITY DEVELOPMENT

Deputy Administrator for Community Development.—Louis Luna, 619–7980.
Associate Deputy Administrator.—J. Norman Reid, room 266, 260–6332.
Director of:
Community Resource Development.—Rick Wetherill (acting), room 266, 619–7983.
Empowerment Division.—Rick Wetherill, room 266, 619–7983.

OPERATIONS AND MANAGEMENT

NASA Building, Third Floor, phone 692–0200

Deputy Administrator.—Sherie Hinton-Henry, 692–0200.
Director of:
Budget Division.—Deborah Lawrence, 692–0122.
Civil Rights Staff.—Cheryl Prejean Greaux, 692–0204.
Financial Management Division.—John Purcell, 692–0080.
Legislative and Public Affairs.—Tim McNeilly (acting), 720–1019.
Policy and Analysis Division.—William French (acting), 690–9824.
Chief Financial Officer.—Christine Burgess (acting), (314) 457–4152.
Chief Information Officer.—Tom Hannah, 692–0212.
Assistant Administrator for—
Human Resources.—Diana Shermeyer (acting), 692–0222.
Procurement and Administration Services.—Sharon Randolph, 692–0207.
Program Manager for Alternate Dispute Resolution.—Bob Lovan, 690–2583.
Coordinator for Native American Affairs.—David Saffert, 720–0400.

RURAL HOUSING SERVICE

South Agriculture Building, Room 5014–S, phone 690–1533

Administrator.—Arthur A. Garcia.
Associate Administrator.—James Sellman.
Director, Program Support Staff.—Richard A. Davis, 720–9619.
Deputy Director.—Keith Suerdieck, 720–9619.
Deputy Administrator for Single Family.—David J. Vilano, 720–5177.
Director of:
Family Housing Direct Loan Division.—[Vacant], 720–1474.
Family Housing Guaranteed Loan Division.—Roger Glendenning, 720–1452.
Deputy Administrator for Multi-Family Housing.—[Vacant], 720–3773.
Director, Multi-Family Housing Processing Division.—Carl Wagner, 720–1604.
Deputy Director.—Sue Harris-Green, 720–1606.
Director of:
Guaranteed Loan Division.—Joyce Allen, 720–1505.
Direct Loan and Grant Processing Division.—Chadwick Parker, 720–1502.
Multi-Family Housing Portfolio Management Division, Direct Housing.—Stephanie White, 720–1600.
Deputy Director.—Janet Stouder, 720–9728.

RURAL BUSINESS-COOPERATIVE SERVICE

South Building, Room 5045–S, phone 690–4730

Administrator.—John Rosso, 690–4730.
Associate Administrator.—[Vacant].
Deputy Administrator for Business Programs.—William F. Hagy III, 720–7287.
Director of:
Business and Industry Division.—Carolyn Parker, 690–4103.
Cooperative Development Division.—John H. Wells, 720–3350.
Cooperative Marketing Division.—Thomas H. Stafford, 690–0368.
Cooperative Resources Management Division.—John R. Dunn, 690–1374.
Special Projects/Program Oversight Division.—Dwight A. Carmon, 690–4100.
Specialty Lenders Division.—[Vacant], 720–1400.
Deputy Administrator for Cooperative Services.—James Haskell (acting), 720–7558.
Statistics.—Eldon Erversull (acting), 720–3189.
Executive Director, National Sheep Industry Improvement Center.—Jay B. Wilson, 690–0632.

ALTERNATIVE AGRICULTURE RESEARCH AND COMMERCIALIZATION CORPORATION

South Building, Room 0156–S, phone 690–1633

Director.—Dr. Robert E. Armstrong.

RURAL UTILITIES SERVICE

South Building, Room 4051–S, phone 720–9540

Administrator.—Hilda Gay Legg, 720–9540.
Deputy Administrator.—Curtis M. Anderson, room 4048–S, 720–0962.
Program Advisor, Financial Services Staff.—Larry A. Belluzzo, room 4031–S, 720–1265.
Assistant Administrator for—
Electric Division.—Blaine D. Stockton, room 4037–S, 720–9545.
Program Accounting and Regulatory Analysis.—Kenneth M. Ackerman, room 4063–S, 720–9450.
Water and Environmental Programs.—Gary J. Morgan (acting), room 4048–S, 690–2670.
Director of:
Advanced Services Division.—Orren E. Cameron, room 2845–S, 690–4493.
Eastern Area, Telecommunications Program.—Kenneth Kuchno, room 2846–S, 690–4673.
Electric Staff Division.—George J. Bagnall, room 1246–S, 720–1900.
Northern Regional Electric Division.—Sally R. Price, room 0243–S, 720–1420.
Northwest Area, Telecommunications Program.—Jerry H. Brent, room 2835–S, 720–1025.
Power Supply Division.—Victor T Vu, room 270–S, 720–6436.
Southern Regional Electric Division.—Robert O. Ellinger, room 221–S, 720–0848.
Southwest Area, Telecommunications Program.—Ken B. Chandler, room 2808–S, 720–0800.
Telecommunications Standards Division.—Gerald Nugent, room 2868–S, 720–8663.
Assistant Administrator, Telecommunications Programs.—Roberta D. Purcell, room 4056–S, 720–9554.
Chief, Portfolio Management Branch.—Sewell Feddiman, Jr., room 2231–S, 720–9631.

UNDER SECRETARY FOR FOOD, NUTRITION AND CONSUMER SERVICES

Jamie L. Whitten Building, Room 240–E, phone 720–7711, fax 690–3100

Under Secretary.—Eric M. Bost.
Deputy Under Secretary.—Suzanne Bierman.
Executive Director, Center for Nutrition, Policy and Promotion.—Dr. Eric Hentges.

FOOD AND NUTRITION SERVICE

3101 Park Center Drive, Alexandria, VA 22302, phone (703) 305–2062

Administrator.—Roberto Salazar, room 906, 305–2062.
Associate Administrator.—George A. Braley, room 906, 305–2060.

COMMUNICATIONS AND GOVERNMENTAL AFFAIRS

Deputy Administrator.—Scott Mexic, room 920, 305–2281.
Director of:
Consumer and Community Affairs.—Pam Phillips, room 912, 305–2000.
Governmental Affairs.—Frank Ippolito, room 910, 305–2010.
Public Affairs.—Jean Daniel, room 920, 305–2286.

MANAGEMENT

Deputy Administrator.—David E. Arnette, room 314, (703) 305–2030.
Associate Deputy Administrator.—Floyd A. Wheeler, room 314, (703) 305–2032.
Director of:
Administrative Services Division.—Cherie Stallman, room 202, (703) 305–2231.
Human Resources Division.—Lehmer Sullivan, room 614, 305–2326.
Information Technology Division.—Christopher Beavers, room 304, 305–2754.

FINANCIAL MANAGEMENT

Deputy Administrator.—Gary Maupin, room 712, 305–2046.
Associate Deputy Administrator.—James Belcher, room 712, 605–0497.
Divisional Directors:
Accounting.—Rose McClyde, room 724, 305–2447.
Budget.—David Burr, room 708, 305–2189.

FOOD STAMP PROGRAM

Deputy Administrator.—Kate Coler, room 808, 305–2026.
Associate Deputy Administrator.—Bonny O'Neil, room 808, 305–2022.
Divisional Directors of:
Benefit Redemption.—Thomas O'Connor, room 400, 305–2756.
EBT Branch Coordination.—Lizabeth Silbermann, room 400, 305–2517.
Program Accountability.—[Vacant].
Program Development.—Arthur T. Foley, room 814, 305–2490.

SPECIAL NUTRITION PROGRAMS

Deputy Administrator.—Peter S. Murano, room 628, 305–2052.
Associate Administrator.—Ron Vogel, 305–2054.
Divisional Directors:
Child Nutrition.—Stan Garnets, room 620, 305–2590.
Food Distribution.—Phil Cohen (acting), room 500, 305–2680.
Supplemental Food Programs.—Patricia Daniels, room 520, 305–2746.

CENTER FOR NUTRITION POLICY AND PROMOTION

3101 Park Center Drive, Room 1032, Alexandria, VA 22302
phone (703) 305–7600, fax 305–3400

Executive Director.—Dr. Eric Hentges.
Deputy Executive Director.—Steve Christensen.
Director for—
Nutrition Policy and Analysis Staff.—Peter Basiotis.
Nutrition Promotion Staff.—Carole Davis.
Public Information and Governmental Affairs—John Webster.

FOOD SAFETY AND INSPECTION SERVICE

Jamie L. Whitten Building, Room 331–E, phone 720–7025, fax 690–0550

Administrator.—Garry McKee, 690–0550.
Associate Administrator.—Barbara Masters (acting), room 344–E, 720–5190.
U.S. Manager for Codex.—Ed Scarbrough, room 4861–S, 720–2057.

Director for—

Animal and Egg Production Food Safety.—Alice Thaler, room 2–S, 690–2683.

Biosciences.—Walter Hill, room 310, 690–6369.

Chemistry QA/QC Branch.—Jess Rajan, (706) 546–3447.

Congressional and Public Affairs.—Rob Larew, room 1175–S, 720–9113.

Data Analysis and Statistical Support.—Arshad Hussain, room 310–Annex, 205–0007.

EMS.—Barbara McNiff, room 1166–S, 690–3882.

Food Animal Science.—William James, room 318, 690–6566.

Food Safety Education.—Susan Conley, room 2932–S, 720–7943.

International Policy.—[Vacant].

Labeling and Consumer Protection.—Robert Post, room 602–A, 205–0279.

Laboratory Sample Data Management.—Patricia Abraham, room 308, 690–6382.

Meat and Poultry Advisory Committee.—Robert Tynan, room 617–Annex, 720–2982.

Program Evaluation and Improvement.—Jane Roth, room 3833–S, 720–6735.

Recall Management.—Armia Tawadrous, room 315–Aerospace, 690–6389.

Technology Program Development.—Charles Edwards, room 405–A, 205–0675.

Zoonotic Diseases and Residue Surveillance.—William James, room 318–Aerospace, 690–6566.

Deputy Administrator, Office of:

Field Operations.—William C. Smith, room 344–E, 720–8803.

Policy Program Development and Evaluation.—Philip S. Derfler, room 350–E, 720–2710.

Public Health and Science.—Karen Hulebak, room 341–E, 720–2644.

Associate Deputy Administrator.—Loren Lange (acting), room 341–E, 720–2644.

Senior Policy Manager, Federal, State and Local Government Relations.—William Leese, 1255 22nd Street NW., room 329, 418–8900.

UNDER SECRETARY FOR RESEARCH, EDUCATION AND ECONOMICS

Jamie L. Whitten Building, Room 214–W, phone 720–5923

Under Secretary.—Joseph J. Jen.

Deputy Under Secretary.—Rodney J. Brown, 720–8885.

AGRICULTURAL RESEARCH SERVICE

Administration Building, Room 303–A, phone 720–3656, fax 720–5427

Administrator.—Edward B. Knipling (acting), room 302–A, 720–3656.

Associate Administrator.—Caird E. Rexroad (acting), 720–3658.

Director of:

ARS Information Staff.—Sandy M. Hays, room 2251–G (301) 504–1638.

Budget and Program Management Staff.—Joseph S. Garbarino, room 358–A, 720–4421.

Civil Rights Staff.—Korona I. Prince, room 3552–S, 690–2244.

International Research Programs.—Arlyne Meyers (acting), room 1140–G (301) 504–4545.

Assistant Administrator, Office of Technology Transfer.—Michael Ruff, room 324–A (202) 720–3973.

ADMINISTRATIVE AND FINANCIAL MANAGEMENT

5601 Sunnyside Avenue, Beltsville, MD 20705–5108, Room 3–2154, phone (301) 504–1008

Deputy Administrator.—James H. Bradley, room 3–2157 (301) 504–1012.

Director of:

Acquisition, Property, and Telecommunications Division.—Larry Cullumber, room 2102–G (301) 504–1695.

Facilities Division.—Patrick Barry, room 1294 (301) 504–1151.

Financial Management Division.—Steven M. Helmrich, room 2190–G (301) 504–1257.

Human Resources Division.—Karen M. Brownell, room 1143–G (301) 504–1317.

NATIONAL AGRICULTURE LIBRARY

Route 1, Beltsville, MD 20705, phone (301) 504–5248, fax (301) 504–7042

Director.—Peter Young, room 200, (301) 504–5248.

Deputy Director.—Eleanor G. Frierson, room 200, 504–6780.

Director of:

Administration.—Linda Mooney, room 201, 504–5570.

Beltsville Agricultural Research Center.—Phyllis E. Johnson, room 223 B–003, 504–6078.

Information Systems Division.—Gary McCone, room 204 (301) 504–5018.

Public Affairs.—Len Carey, room 204, 504–6778.

Public Services Division.—Maria G. Pisa, room 203, 504–5834.

Technical Services Division.—Sally Sinn, room 203, 504–7294.

Associate Director of Beltsville Research Center.—Ronald F. Korcak, room 223 B–003, 504–5193.

NUTRITION RESEARCH CENTERS

Director, Beltsville Human Nutrition Research Center.—Ellen W. Harris, room 117 B–005, (301) 504–0610.

Director, U.S. National Arboretum.—Thomas S. Elias, room 100, (202) 245–4539.

Division Deputy Area Director of Facilities Management and Operations.—John Van de Vaarst, room 203 B–003, (301) 504–5664.

NATIONAL PROGRAM STAFF

5601 Sunnyside Avenue, Room 4–2152, Beltsville MD 20705–5134

phone (301) 504–5084

Deputy Administrator.—Dwayne R. Buxton, room 4–2150, 504–5084.

Program Planning Advisor.—David Rust, room 4–2144, 504–6233.

Associate Deputy Administrator for—

Animal Production, Product Value and Safety.—Caird E. Rexroad, Jr., room 4–2188, 504–7050.

Crop Production, Product Value and Safety.—Judith St. John, room 4–2204, 504–6252.

Natural Resources and Sustainable Agricultural Systems.—Allen R. Dedrick, room 4–2288, 504–7987.

AREA OFFICES

Director, Beltsville Area.—Phyllis E. Johnson, room 223, Building 003, BARC–West, Beltsville MD 20705, (301) 504–6078.

Associate Area Director.—Ron Korcak, room 223, Building 003, BARC–West, Beltsville MD 20705, (301) 504–5193.

Director, North Atlantic Area.—Wilda Martinez, 600 East Mermaid Line, Wyndmoor, PA 19038, (215) 233–6593.

Associate Area Director.—Hank Parker, (215) 233–6668.

Director, South Atlantic Area.—Karl Narang, PO Box 5677, College Station Road, Athens, GA 30604–5677, (706) 546–3311.

Associate Area Director.—Andrew Hammond, (706) 546–3328.

Director, Mid South Area.—Edgar King, Jr., PO Box 225, Stoneville, MS 38776, (601) 686–5265.

Associate Director.—Deborah Brennan, (662) 686–5266.

Director, Midwest Area.—Adrianna Hewings, room 2004, 1815 North University Street, Peoria, IL 61604–0000, (309) 681–6602.

Associate Director.—Darrell Cole, (309) 681–6600.

Director, Pacific West Area.—A.A. Betschart, room 2030, 800 Buchanan Street, Albany, CA 94710, (510) 559–6060.

Associate Director.—Michael Shannon, (510) 559–6071.

Director, Northern Plains Area.—Wilbert H. Blackburn, room S–150, 1201 Oakridge Road, Fort Collins, CO 80525–5562, (970) 229–5557.

Associate Area Director.—[Vacant], (970) 229–5595.

Director, Southern Plains Area.—Charles A. Onstad, Suite 230, 7607 Eastmark Drive, College Station, TX 77840, (409) 260–9346.

Associate Director.—James Coppedge, (409) 260–9346.

REGIONAL RESEARCH CENTERS

Director, Eastern Regional Research Center.—John P. Cherry, 600 East Mermaid Lane, Wyndmoor, PA 19038, (215) 233–6595.
Director, Western Regional Research Center.—James N. Seiber, 800 Buchanan Street, Albany, CA 94710–0000, (510) 559–5600.
Director, Southern Regional Research Center.—John Patrick Jordan, 1100 Robert E. Lee Boulevard, New Orleans, LA 70179–0000, (504) 286–4212.
Director, National Center for Agricultural Utilization Research.—Peter B. Johnsen, room 2038, 1815 North University Street, Peoria, IL 61604–0000, (309) 681–6541.

COOPERATIVE STATE RESEARCH, EDUCATION AND EXTENSION SERVICE

Jamie L. Whitten Building, Room 305–A, phone (202) 720–4423, fax 720–8987

Administrator.—Colien Heffernan.
Associate Administrator.—Gary Cunningham, 720–7441.
Deputy Administrator for—
Budget.—Tina Buch, room 332–A, 720–2675.
Communiucations.—Terry Meisenbach, room 4231, 720–2677.
Economic and Community Systems.—Alma Hobbs, room 4343, 720–5305.
Equal Opportunity Staff.—Curt DeVille, room 1230, 720–5843.
Extramural Programs.—Louise M. Ebaugh, room 2250, 401–6021.
Families, 4–H and Nutrition.—K. Jane Coulter, room 4329, 720–2326.
Information Systems and Technology Management.—Sarah J. Rockey, room 4122, 720–1766.
Natural Resources and Environment.—Dan Kugler, room 3231, 720–0740.
Planning and Accountability.—Cheryl Oros, room 1315, 690–1297.
Plant and Animal Systems.—Ralph Otto, room 3359, 401–5877.
Science and Education Resources Development.—George Cooper, room 3310, 401–2855.

ECONOMIC RESEARCH SERVICE

Administrator.—Susan E. Offutt, room N4145, (202) 694–5000.
Associate Administrator.—Philip Fulton, room N4150, 694–5000.
Division Directors:
Food and Rural Economics.—Betsey A. Kuhn, room N2168, 694–5400.
Information Services.—Paul H. Chan, room S2032, 694–5100.
Market and Trade Economics.—Neilson Conklin, room N5119, 694–5200.
Resource Economics.—Katherine R. Smith, room S4186, 694–5500.

NATIONAL AGRICULTURAL STATISTICS SERVICE

South Agriculture Building, Room 4117–S, phone 720–2707, fax 720–9013

Administrator.—R. Ronald Bosecker.
Associate Administrator.—Carol House, 720–2702.
Deputy Administrator for—
Field Operations.—Joseph T. Reilly, room 4133, 720–3638.
Programs and Products.—Richard D. Allen, room 5095, 690–8141.
Divisional Directors for—
Census and Survey.—Marshall Dantzler, room 6306, 720–4557.
Information Technology.—John P. Nealon, room 5847, 720–2984.
Research and Development.—George A. Hanuschak, room 305, Fairfax CBG, (703) 235–5211.
Statistics.—Steven D. Wiyatt, room 5810, 720–3896.

MARKETING AND REGULATORY PROGRAMS

Jamie A. Whitten Building, Room 228–W, phone (202) 720–4256, fax 720–5775

Under Secretary.—Bill Hawks.
Deputy Under Secretary.—Chuck Lambert, 720–4256.
Special Assistant to the Under Secretary.—Patrick Atagi, 720–5759.
Confidential Assistant to the Under Secretary.—Kimberly N. Smith, 720–4031.

AGRICULTURAL MARKETING SERVICE

South Agriculture Building, Room 3071–S, phone (202) 720–5115, fax 720–8477

Administrator.—A.J. Yates.
Associate Administrator.—Kenneth C. Clayton, room 3064–S, 720–4276.
Deputy Associate Administrator.—Charles R. Martin, rom 3064–S, 720–4024.

MARKETING PROGRAMS

Deputy Administrator for Compliance and Analysis Programs.—David N. Lewis, room 3529–S, 720–6766.
Deputy Administrator for—
Cotton Programs.—Norma McDill, room 2641–S, 720–3193.
Dairy Programs.—Richard M. McKee, room 2968–S, 720–4392.
Fruit and Vegetable Programs.—Robert C. Keeney, room 2077–S, 720–4722.
Livestock and Seed Programs.—Barry L. Carpenter, room 2092–S, 720–5705.
Poultry Programs.—Howard M. Magwire, room 3932–S, 720–4476.
Science and Technology.—Robert L. Epstein (acting), room 3507–S, 720–5231.
Tobacco Programs.—John P. Duncan III, room 502 Annex, 205–0567.
Transportation and Marketing.—Barbara C. Robinson, room 2510–S, 690–1300.

ANIMAL AND PLANT HEALTH INSPECTION SERVICE (APHIS)

Jamie L. Whitten Building, Room 312–E, phone (202) 720–3668, fax 720–3054

OFFICE OF THE ADMINISTRATOR

Administrator.—Bobby R. Acord.
Associate Administrator.—Peter Fernandez.
Chief of Staff.—Courtney R. Billet, room 308–E.
Director of Civil Rights Enforcement and Compliance.—Anna P. Grayson, room 1137–S, 720–6312.

LEGISLATIVE AND PUBLIC AFFAIRS

South Building, Room 1147–S, phone (202) 720–2511, fax 720–3982

Director.—Ralph R. Harding.
Deputy Director.—Lynn Quarles.
Assistant Director of:
Public Affairs.—Bethany Jones, (301) 734–7799.
Executive Correspondence.—Christina Myers, (301) 734–7776.
Freedom of Information.—Michael Marquis, (301) 734–7776.

POLICY AND PROGRAM DEVELOPMENT

4700 River Road, Riverdale, MD 20737

phone (301) 734–3771, fax (301) 734–5899

Director.—Kevin Shea, 734–5136.
Assistant Director.—William Wallace.
Unit Chiefs:
Planning, Evaluation and Monitoring.—Christine Zakarka, 734–8512.
Policy Analysis and Development.—Janet W. Berla, 734–8667.
Regulatory Analysis and Development.—Cynthia Howard (acting), 734–0682.
Risk Analysis.—[Vacant].

WILDLIFE SERVICES

South Building, Room 1624, phone (202) 720–2054, fax (202) 690–0053

Deputy Administrator.—William H. Clay.
Associate Deputy Administrator.—[Vacant].
Assistant Deputy Administrator.—Martin Mendoza.
Director for Operational Support.—Joanne Garrett, (301) 734–7921.

VETERINARY SERVICES

Jamie L. Whitten Building, Room 317–E, phone (202) 720–5193, fax 690–4171

Deputy Administrator.—W.R. DeHaven.
Administrative Officer.—Janet Alvestad (Ames), (515) 232–5785, CVB.
Associate Deputy Administrator for Regional Operations.—Dr. Andrea Morgan, 720–5193.
Assistant Deputy Administrator.—Dr. Valerie Ragan, (301) 734–3754.
Associate Deputy for Emergency Management.—[Vacant].
Director for—
Emergency Programs.—Joseph Annelli, (301) 794–8073.
Inspection and Compliance.—Steven A. Karli (Ames), (515) 232–5785.
Operational Support.—[Vacant].
Policy, Evaluation and Licensing.—Richard E. Hill, Jr, (515) 232–5785.
National Center of Import and Export.—Gary S. Colgrave, (301) 734–4356.
Chief Staff Veterinarian for National Animal Health Programs.—Michael Gilsdorf, (301) 734–6954.

INTERNATIONAL SERVICES

Jamie L. Whitten Building, Room 324–E, phone (202) 720–7593, fax 690–1484

Deputy Administrator.—Ralph Iwamoto.
Associate Deputy Administrator.—Nick Gutierrez, 720–7021.
Divisional Directors: Freida Skaggs (acting), (301) 734–5214; John Wyss, 734–3779.
Trade Support Team.—John Greifer, room 1128, 720–7677.

MARKETING AND REGULATORY PROGRAMS BUSINESS SERVICES

Jamie L. Whitten Building, Room 308–E, phone (202) 720–5213, fax 690–0686

Deputy Administrator.—William Hudnall.
Associate Deputy Administrator.—Joanne Munno.
Divisional Directors:
Budget and Accounting.—John Neesen, (301) 734–8014.
Investigative and Enforcement Services.—Alan Christian, (301) 734–6491.
Management Services.—Joanne L. Munno, (301) 734–6502.
MRP Human Resources.—Karen Benham, Ellen King, room 1709–S, 720–6377.
Resources Management Systems and Evaluation Staff.—Frank C. Vollmerhausen, (301) 734–8864.

PLANT PROTECTION AND QUARANTINE

Jamie L. Whitten Building, Room 302–E, phone (202) 720–5601, fax 690–0472

Deputy Administrator.—Richard I. Dunkle.
Associate Deputy Administrator.—Paul Eggert, 720–4441.
Assistant to the Deputy Administrator.—Jeffrey Grode, 720–5601.
Veterinary Medical Officer.—Le Ann Thomas, (301) 734–7633.
Director of:
Biocontrol.—Dale Meyerdirk, (301) 734–5667.
Center for Plant Health Science and Technology.—Gordon Gordh, (919) 513–2400.
Phytosanitary Issues Management.—Alan Green, (301) 734–8261.
Resource Management Support.—Terri Burrell, (301) 734–7764.
Technical Information Systems.—Allison Young, (301) 734–5518.

ANIMAL CARE

4700 River Road, Riverdale, MD 20737, phone (301) 734–4980, fax (301) 734–4328

Deputy Administrator.—Chester Gipson.
Associate Deputy Administrator.—Richard Watkins.

BIOTECHNOLOGY REGULATORY SERVICES

4700 River Road, Riverdale, MD 20737, phone (301) 734–7324, fax 734–8724

Deputy Administrator.—Cindy Smith.
Associate Deputy Administrator.—Rebecca Bech, 734–5716.
Assistant Deputy Administrator.—[Vacant].
Division Directors of:
Regulatory.—Rebecca Bech (acting), 734–5716.
Policy and International.—Ken Waters (acting), 734–8889.

GRAIN INSPECTION, PACKERS AND STOCKYARDS ADMINISTRATION

South Agriculture Building, Room 1094, phone (202) 720–0219, fax 205–9237

Administrator.—Donna Reifschneider.
Deputy Administrator for Grain Inspection.—David R. Shipman, room 1094, 720–9170.
Director of:
Civil Rights.—Eugene Bass, room 0623–S, 720–0216.
Compliance Division.—Neil Porter, room 1647–S, 720–8262.
Economic/Statistical Support.—Gerald Grinnell, room 1644–S, 720–7455.
Executive Resource Staff.—Robert Soderstrom, room 0634–S, 720–0231.
Field Management.—David Orr, room 2409–N, 720–0228.
Field Operations.—Daniel L. Van Ackeren, room 1642–S, 720–7063.
Information Staff.—Gregory J. Hawkins, room 1095–S, 720–3553.
International Affairs.—John Pitchford, room 1629–S, 720–0226.
Policy/Litigation Support.—Bruce Boor (acting), room 1638–S, 720–6951.
Technical Services Division.—Steven Tanner, Kansas City, MO (816) 891–0401.
Deputy Administrator for Packers and Stockyards Programs.—JoAnn Waterfield, room 1641–S, 720–7051.
Chief Information Officer.—Gerald Bromley, room 2446–S, 720–3204.

DEPARTMENT OF COMMERCE

Herbert C. Hoover Building

14th Street between Pennsylvania and Constitution Avenues 20230

phone 482–2000, http://www.doc.gov

DONALD L. EVANS, Secretary of Commerce; born in Houston, TX, in 1946; education: B.S. in mechanical engineering, University of Texas, 1969; M.B.A., University of Texas, 1973; fraternal organizations: Omicron Delta Kappa and Sigma Alpha Epsilon; professional: Tom Brown, Inc. (independent energy company), 1975–2000; served as Chairman of the Board of Directors, and Chief Executive Officer; public service: Board of Regents of the University of Texas, 1995–2000; elected as Chairman, 1997–2000; family: married to Susan Marinis Evans; three children; nominated by President George W. Bush to become the 34th Secretary of Commerce, and was confirmed by the U.S. Senate on January 20, 2001.

OFFICE OF THE SECRETARY

Secretary of Commerce.—Donald L. Evans, room 5858, 482–2112.
Deputy Secretary.—Samuel Bodman, room 5838, 482–4625.
Chief of Staff.—Alison Kaufman, room 5858, 482–4246.
Chief of Protocol.—Aimee Fleischer, room 5847, 482–3225.
Director, Office of:
Business Liaison.—Travis Thomas, room 5062, 482–1360.
Chief Information Officer.—Tom Pyke, room 5029B, 482–4797.
Executive Secretariat.—Fred Schwien, room 5516, 482–3934.
External Affairs.—Darren Grubb, room 5858, 482–2158.
Policy and Strategic Planning.—John Ackerly, room 5865, 482–3520.
Public Affairs.—Ron Bonjean, room 5415, 482–4883.
Scheduling.—Marilyn Abel, room 5883, 482–5880.
White House Liaison.—Aimee Fleishcher, room 5835, 482–1684.

GENERAL COUNSEL

General Counsel.—Ted Kassinger, room 5870, 482–4772.
Deputy General Counsel.—Jane Dana, room 5870, 482–4772.

ASSISTANT SECRETARY FOR LEGISLATIVE AND INTERGOVERNMENTAL AFFAIRS

Assistant Secretary.—Breanda L. Becker, room 5421, 482–3663.
Deputy Assistant Secretary for Trade Legislation.—Brett Palmer, room 5414, 482–1389.
Director for—
Legislative and Intergovernmental Affairs.—Karen A. Swanson-Woolf, room 5421, 482–3663.
Intergovernmental Affairs.—Elizabeth Dial, room 5414, 482–8017.

CHIEF FINANCIAL OFFICER (CFO) AND ASSISTANT SECRETARY FOR ADMINISTRATION

Herbert C. Hoover Building, Room 5830, 482–4951

Chief Financial Officer and Assistant Secretary.—Otto Wolff, room 5828.
Deputy Chief Financial Officer, Financial Management.—James Taylor, room 6827, 482–1207.
Deputy Assistant Secretary for Administration.—[Vacant].
Director for—
Acquisition Management.—Michael S. Sade, room 6422, 482–2773.
Administrative Services.—Denise Wells, room 6316, 482–1200.

Budget.—Barbara A. Retzlaff, room 5818, 482–4648.
Civil Rights.—Suzan J. Aramaki, room 6012, 482–0625.
Executive Budgeting and Assistance Management.—Robert F. Kugelman, room 6022, 482–4299.
Human Resources Management.—Deborah A. Jefferson, room 5001, 482–4807.
Management and Organization.—John J. Phelan III, room 5327, 482–3707.
Security.—Richard Yamamoto, room 1067, 482–4371.
Small and Disadvantaged Business Utilization.—Tlaloc J. Garcia, room 6411, 482–1472.

INSPECTOR GENERAL

Herbert C. Hoover Building, Room 7898–C, 482–4661

Inspector General.—Johnnie E. Frazier.
Deputy Inspector General.—Edward Blansitt, room 7898C, 482–3516.
Legislative and Intergovernmental Affairs Officer.—Jessica Rickenbach, room 7099–C, 482–3052.
Counsel to Inspector General.—Elizabeth T. Barlow, room 7892, room 482–5992.
Assistant Inspector General, Office of:
Auditing.—Larry B. Gross, room 7721, 482–1834.
Compliance and Administration.—Steven Garmon, room 7099C, 482–0231.
Inspections and Program Evaluations.—Jill A. Gross, room 7886–B, 482–2754.
Investigations.—Paul Buskirk, room 7614, 482–0934.
Systems Evaluation.—Judith J. Gordon, room 7876, 482–6186.

ECONOMICS AND STATISTICS ADMINISTRATION AFFAIRS

Herbert C. Hoover Building, Room 4848, phone 482–3727

Under Secretary for Economic Affairs.—Kathleen B. Cooper.
Deputy Under Secretary.—[Vacant].
Chief Counsel.—Roxie Jamison Jones, room 4868A, 482–5394.
Chief Economist.—Keith Hall, room 4842, 482–3523.
Associate Under Secretary for—
Communications.—Elizabeth R. Gregory, room 4836, 482–2760.
Congressional and Intergovernmental Affairs Specialist.—Clark L. Reid, room 4842, 482–3331.
Economic Information Officer.—Jane A. Callen, room 4855, 482–2235.
Director, Office of:
Economic Conditions.—Carl E. Cox, room 4861, 482–4871.
Policy Development.—Jeffrey L. Mayer, room 4858, 482–1727.
Management.—James K. White, room 4834, 482–2405.
Chief Information Officer and Director.—Kenneth S. Taylor, room 4880, 482–2853.
STAT–USA.—Forrest B. Williams, room 4886, 482–3429.
Chief Financial Officer, Finance and Administration.—Martin J. Rajk, room 4083, 482–4438.

BUREAU OF ECONOMIC ANALYSIS

1441 L Street NW., room 6006, phone (202) 606–9600

Director.—J. Steven Landefeld.
Deputy Director.—Rosemary Marcuss, room 6005, 606–9602.
Chief Economist.—Barbara Fraumeni, room 6063, 606–9603.
Chief Statistician.—Dennis J. Fixler, room 6065, 606–9607.
Chief Information Officer.—Alan C. Lorish, Jr., room 3050, 606–9910.
Associate Director for—
Industry Accounts.—Sumiye Okubo, room 6060, 606–9612.
International Economics.—Ralph H. Kozlow, room 6004, 606–9604.
Management and Chief Administrative Officer.—Suzette C. Kern, room 6027, 606–9616.
National Economic Accounts.—Brent R. Moulton, room 6062, 606–9606.
Regional Economics.—John W. Ruser, room 6064, 606–9605.
Division Chiefs:
Administrative Services.—C. Brian Grove, room 6026, 606–9624.
Balance of Payments.—Christopher L. Bach, room 8024, 606–9545.
Communications.—Karen Jeffries, room 3029, 606–9698.

Government.—Brooks B. Robinson, room 5068, 606–9778.
Industry Economics.—Ann M. Lawson, room 8066, 606–5584.
International Investment.—R. David Belli, room 7005, 606–9800.
National Income and Wealth.—Carol E. Moylan, room 5006, 606–9715.
Regional Economic Analysis.—John R. Kort, room 4048, 606–9221.
Regional Economic Measurement.—Robert L. Brown, room 4006, 606–9246.

THE CENSUS BUREAU

Federal Office Building 3, Silver Hill and Suitland Roads, Suitland, MD 20746, phone (301) 763–4778

Director.—Charles Louis Kincannon, room 2049, (301) 457–2135.
Deputy Director and Chief Operating Officer.—Hermann Habermann, room 2049, 763–2138.
Associate Director for—
Communications.—Lawrence A. Neal, room 2069, 763–2063.
Decennial Census.—Preston Jay Waite, room 2037, 763–3968.
Demographic Programs.—Nancy M. Gordon, room 2061, 763–2126.
Economic Programs.—Frederick T. Knickerbocker, room 2061, 763–2112.
Field Operations.—Marvin D. Raines, room 2027, 763–2072.
Finance and Administration.—Ted A. Johnson, room 2025, 763–3464.
Comptroller.—Andrew H. Moxam, room 3586, 763–9575.
Information Technology.—Richard W. Swartz, room 2065, 763–2117.
Methodology and Standards.—Cynthia Z.F. Clark, room 2031, 763–2160.
Assistant Director for—
Communications.—Laverne Vines Collins, room 2085, 763–8469.
Decennial Census.—Arnold A. Jackson, room 2018–2, 763–8626.
Economic Programs.—Thomas L. Mesenbourg, room 2069, 763–2932.
Information Technology.—Douglas Clift, room 1031, 763–5499.
Marketing and Customer Liaison.—Gloria Gutierrez, room 3051, 763–6560.
Division and Office Chiefs for—
Acquisition Division.—Michael L. Palensky, room G–314, 763–1818.
Administrative and Customer Services.—Walter C. Odom, Jr., room 2150, 763–2228.
Budget Division.—James E. Tyler, Jr., room 3430, 763–3903.
Client Support Office.—Ronald R. Swank, room 1373, 763–6846.
Company Statistics Division.—Ewen M. Wilson, room 1182, 763–3388.
Computer Assisted Survey Research Office.—Robert N. Tinari, 763–1420.
Computer Services Division.—Kenneth A. Riccini, Bowie Computer Center, 763–3922.
Congressional Affairs Office.—Jefferson Taylor, room 2073, 763–2171.
Customer Liaison Office.—Stanley J. Rolark, room 3634, 763–1305.
Decennial Management Division.—Teresa Angueira, room 2012–2, 763–1764.
Decennial Statistical Studies Division.—Rajendra Singh, room 2024, 763–9295.
Decennial Systems and Contract Management Office.—Michael J. Longini, room 2301, 763–2933.
Demographic Statistical Methods Division.—Alan Tupek, room 3705, 763–4287.
Demographic Surveys Division.—Chester E. Bowie, room 3324, 763–3773.
Economist Office.—Brad Jenson (acting), room 206, 763–6460.
Economic Planning and Coordination Division.—Shirin A. Ahmed, room 2584, 763–2558.
Economic Statistical Methods and Programming Division.—Howard Hogan, room 3015, 763–5870.
Equal Employment Opportunity Office.—Roy P. Castro, room 1229, 763–2853.
Field Division.—Brian Monaghan, room 1730, 763–7879.
Finance Division.—Joan P. Johnson, room 3582, 763–6803.
Financial and Administrative Systems Division.—James Aikman, room 3102, 763–3149.
Foreign Trade Division.—C. Harvey Monk, Jr., room 2104, 763–2255.
Geography Division.—Carol Van Horn (acting), room 651, 763–2131.
Governments Division.—[Vacant], room 407, 763–1489.
Housing and Household Economic Statistics.—Daniel H. Weinberg, room 1071, 763–3234.
Human Resources Division.—Tyra Dent Smith, room 3260, 763–5863.
Information Systems Support and Review Office.—J. Jerry Bell, room 1023, 763–1881.
Information Technology Security Office.—Timothy P. Ruland, room 1537, 763–2869.
Manufacturing and Construction.—William G. Bostic, Jr., room 2102–4, 763–4593.
Marketing Services Office.—John C. Kavaliunas, room 3021, 763–4090.

National Processing Center.—Judith N. Petty, (812) 218–3344.
Planning Research and Evaluation.—Ruth Ann Killion, room 1107–2, 763–2048.
Policy Office.—Gerald W. Gates, room 2430, 763–2515.
Population.—John F. Long, room 2011, 763–2071.
Public Information Office.—Kenneth C. Meyer, room 2705, 763–3100.
Security Office.—Harold L. Washington, Jr., room 1631, 763–1716.
Service Sector Statistics.—Mark E. Wallace, room 2633, 763–2683.
Statistical Research Division.—Tommy Wright, room 3203–4, 763–1702.
Systems Support.—Robert G. Munsey, room 1342, 763–2999.
Technologies Management Office.—Barbara M. LoPresti, room 1757, 763–7765.
Telecommunications Office.—Kenneth A. Riccini (acting), room 1101, 763–1793.

BUREAU OF INDUSTRY AND SECURITY

Herbert C. Hoover Building, Room 3898, phone (202) 482–1455

Under Secretary.—Kenneth I. Juster.
Deputy Under Secretary.—Karon Bhatia, room 3839, 482–5301.
Senior Advisor and Nonproliferation and Export Control International Cooperation Team Head.—Richard Capitt, room 3896, 482–1459.
Comptroller—Gay Shrum, room 6883, 482–1058.
Chief Information Officer.—Parick E. Heinig, room 6092, 482–4848.
Chief Counsel.—[Vacant].
Deputy Chief Counsel.—Jon Dyke, room 3839, 482–5301.
Assistant Secretary for Export Administration.—James J. Jochum, room 3886–C, 482–5491.
Deputy Assistant Secretary for Export Administration.—Matthew S. Borman, room 3886–C, 482–5711.
Assistant Secretary for Export Enforcement.—Lisa Prager (acting), room 3721, 482–5914.
Deputy Assistant Secretary.—Lisa A. Prager, room 3721, 482–5914.
Director, Office of:
Administration.—Miriam Cohen, room 3889, 482–1900.
Antiboycott Compliance.—Dexter M. Price, room 6098, 482–5914.
Congressional, Public and Intergovernmental Affairs.—Scott Kamins, room 3897, 482–0097.
Enforcement Analysis.—Thomas Andrukonis, room 4065, 482–4255.
Export Enforcement.—Mark D. Menefee, room 4616, 482–2252.
Exporter Services.—Eileen Albanese, room 1093, 482–0436.
Nonproliferation Controls and Treaty Compliance.—Steven C. Goldman, room 2093, 482–3825.
Planning, Evaluation and Management.—Jeannette Chiari, room 6883, 482–2117.
Strategic Industries and Economic Security.—Dan Hill, room 3878, 482–4506.
Strategic Trade and Foreign Policy Controls.—Joan Roberts (acting), room 2628, 482–4196.
Divisional Directors for—
Compliance Policy.—Robert Diamond, room 6098, 482–2060.
Export License Review and Compliance.—Carol Bryant, room 4065, 482–4255.
High Performance Computer Division.—Kimberly A. Smith, room 4065, 482–4255.
Preventive Enforcement Division.—Elizabeth Rosenkranz, room 4065, 482–4255.

ECONOMIC DEVELOPMENT ADMINISTRATION

Herbert C. Hoover Building, Room 7800, (202) 482–5081

Assistant Secretary.—David A. Sampson.
Deputy Assistant Secretary.—David Bearden, 482–4067.
Deputy Assistant Secretary, Office of:
Congressional Liaison and Program Research and Evaluation.—Nat Wienecke, room 7814–A, 482–2309.
Program Operations.—Sandy Baruah, room 7824, 482–3081.
Chief Counsel.—Claudia Nadig, room 7008, 482–4687.
Chief Financial Officer/Administrative Officer.—Mary Pleffner, room 7231, 482–5891.
Director, Office of:
Communications and Congressional Liaison.—Matt Crow, room 7814–A, 482–2309.
Congressional Director.—Paul Pisano, room 7814–A, 482–2309.
Research and National Technical Assistance.—[Vacant].

Director, Division of:

Accounting.—Joe Hurney, room 7215, 482–5271.
Budget.—Deborah Simmons, room 7108, 482–0540.
Economic Adjustment.—David Witochi, room 7527, 482–2659.
Information Systems.—Louise McGlathery, room 7112, 482–0526.
Liquidation.—Ken Kukovich, room 7830, 482–4965.
Operations Review and Analysis.—Pat Flynn, room 7015, 482–5353.
Planning and Development Assistance.—Tony Meyer, room 7317, 482–2127.
Public Works.—David McIlwain, room 7365, 482–5265.

INTERNATIONAL TRADE ADMINISTRATION

Under Secretary.—Grant D. Aldonas, room 3850, 482–2867.
Deputy Under Secretary.—Timothy J. Hauser, room 3842, 482–3917.
Deputy Under Secretary for Trade.—[Vacant].
Special Counselor.—Tracey McKibben, room 3427, 482–3500.
Counselor for Technology and Entrepreneurs.—Mario Cardullo, room 3427, 482–0978.
Legislative and Intergovernmental Affairs.—Brett Palmer, room 5421, 482–1389.
Public Affairs.—Julie Cram, room 3414, 482–3809.

ADMINISTRATION

Director and Chief Financial Officer.—Linda Moye Cheatham, room 3827, 482–5855.
Deputy Chief Financial Officer.—Jim Donahue, room 4112, 482–0210.
Director, Office of:
Human Resources Management.—Doris Brown, room 7060, 482–3505.
Organization and Management Support.—Mary Ann McFate, room 4001, 482–5436.

U.S. AND FOREIGN COMMERCIAL SERVICE

Assistant Secretary and Director General.—Maria Cino, room 3802, 482–5777.
Career Development and Assignment.—Rebecca Mann, room 1222, 482–5208.
Deputy Assistant Secretary for—
Domestic Operations.—Bruce Blakeman, room 3810, 482–4767.
Export Promotion Services.—John Klingelhut (acting), room 2810, 482–4767.
International Operations.—Karen Zens, room 3128, 482–6228.
Director for—
Africa, Near East and South Asia.—Babette Orr, room 1223, 482–0368.
East Asia and Pacific.—Ann Bacher, room 1223, 482–0423.
Europe.—Eric Sletten, room 3122, 482–5549.
Western Hemisphere.—Danny DeVito, room 1202, 482–2736.

ASSISTANT SECRETARY FOR IMPORT ADMINISTRATION

Assistant Secretary.—Joseph A. Spetrini (acting), room 3099, 482–1780.
Chief Counsel.—John D. McInerney, room 3622, 482–5589.
Foreign Trade Zones Executive Secretary.—Dennis Puccinelli, room 4008, 482–2862.
Director for—
Office of Accounting.—Neal Halper, room 3087–B, 482–2210.
Office of Policy.—Jeffrey May, room 3713, 482–4412.
Policy and Analysis.—Roland MacDonald, room 3713, 482–1768.
Statutory Import Programs Staff.—[Vacant].
Deputy Assistant Secretary for Antidumping Countervailing Duty Enforcement—
I.—Susan Kuhbach (acting), room 3099, 482–5497.
II.—Holly A. Kuga (acting), room 3099–B, 482–1780.
III.—Barbara Tillman (acting), room 3069–A, 482–2104.

ASSISTANT SECRETARY FOR MARKET ACCESS AND COMPLIANCE

Assistant Secretary.—William Henry Lash III, room 3868, 482–3022.
Deputy Assistant Secretary for—
Africa.—Gerald Feldman (acting), room 3819, 482–4925.
Asia and the Pacific.—Philip Agress (acting), room 2036, 482–5251.

Europe.—Charles Ludolph, room 3863, 482–5638.
Middle East and North Africa.—Molly Williamson, room 2329, 482–4651.
Western Hemisphere.—Regina Vargo, room 3826, 482–5324.
Agreements Compliance.—Stephen Jacobs, room 3043, 482–5767.

Director, Office of:
Africa.—Gerald Feldman, room 2037, 482–4227.
APEC (Asian and Asia-Pacific Economic Cooperation) Affairs.—[Vacant].
BISNIS (Business Information Service for the Newly Independent States).—Ann Grey (acting), room 800, 482–2299.
CEEBIC (Central and Eastern Europe Business Information Center).—Jay Burgess, room 800, 482–2645.
China Economic Area.—[Vacant].
Eastern Europe, Russia and the Newly Independent States.—Susanne Lotarski, room 3319, 482–1104.
European Union and Regional Affairs.—Eileen Hill, room 3513, 482–5276.
Japan.—Robert Francis, room 2328, 482–2425.
Latin America and the Caribbean.—Walter M. Bastian, room 3025, 482–2436.
Middle East and North Africa.—Thomas Parker, room 2029–B, 482–1860.
Multilateral Affairs.—Steward L. (Skip) Jones, Jr., room 3027, 482–2307.
NAFTA Secretariat.—Caratina Alston, room 2061, 482–5438.
North American Free Trade Agreement and Inter-American Affairs.—Juliet Bender, room 3024, 482–0305.

ASSISTANT SECRETARY FOR TRADE DEVELOPMENT

Assistant Secretary.—Linda Mysliwy Conlin, room 3832, 482–1461.
Executive Director.—Jonathan C. Menes, room 3832, 482–1112.
Deputy Assistant Secretary for—
Basic Industries.—Kevin Murphy, room 4043, 482–0614.
Environmental Technologies.—Carlos F. Montoulieu (acting), room 1001, 482–5225.
Information Technology Industries.—Michelle O'Neill, room 2003, 482–5908.
Service Industries and Finance.—Douglas C. Baker, room 1128, 482–5261.
Textiles, Apparel and Consumer Goods Industries.—James C. Leonard, room 3100, 482–3737.
Tourism Industries.—Helen Marano (acting), room 2073, 482–0140.
Chairman for Committee for the Implementation of Textile Agreements.—James C. Leonard, room 3100, 482–3737.
Director, Office of:
Advocacy Center.—Daniel J. Bloom, room 3814–A, 482–3896.
Aerospace.—Audrey Smerkanich, room 2128, 482–1229.
Automotive Affairs.—Henry P. Misisco, room 4036, 482–0554.
Consumer Goods.—Leslie Simon (acting), room 3013, 482–0337.
Electronic Commerce.—Patricia M. Sefcik, room 2003, 482–0216.
Energy, Infrastructure and Machinery.—Helen Burroughs, room 4411, 482–0169.
Environmental Technologies.—Carlos F. Montoulieu, room 1003, 482–5225.
Export Promotion Coordination.—Wendy Haimes Smith (acting), room 2003, 482–4501.
Export Trading Company Affairs.—Vanessa M. Bachman (acting), room 1800, 482–5131.
Finance.—David C. Bowie, room 1104, 482–3277.
Information Technologies.—Patricia Sefcik, room 2003, 482–0572.
Metals, Materials and Chemicals.—Robert C. Reiley, room 4039, 482–0575.
Microelectronics, Medical Equipment and Instrumentation.—Jeffrey Gren, room 1015, 482–2587.
Planning, Coordination and Resource Management.—Robert W. Pearson, room 3223, 482–4921.
Service Industries.—Keith Roth (acting), room 1124, 482–3575.
Telecommunications Technologies.—Terry Labat, room 4324, 482–4466.
Textiles and Apparel.—D. Michael Hutchinson, room 3100, 482–5078.
Trade and Economic Analysis.—Jeffrey Lins (acting), room 2815, 482–5145.
Trade Information Center.—Wendy Haimes Smith, room R–TIC, 482–0543.

PRESIDENT'S EXPORT COUNCIL

Room 2015, Department of Commerce 20230, phone (202) 482–1124.

[Authorized by Executive Orders 12131, 12534, 12551, 12610, 12692, 12774, 12869, and 12974 (May through September 1995)]

Staff:

Executive Director, Under Secretary of International Trade.—Grant D. Aldonas.
Executive Secretary/Staff Director.—Mark Chittum.

MINORITY BUSINESS DEVELOPMENT AGENCY

Director.—Ronald N. Langston, room 5055, (202) 482–5061.
Associate Director.—Edith McCloud, room 5088, 482–6224.
Chief Counsel.—Meena Elliot, room 5069, 482–5045.
Budget Division Chief.—Glen Clark, room 5089, 482–3341.

NATIONAL OCEANIC AND ATMOSPHERIC ADMINISTRATION

Under Secretary for Oceans and Atmosphere.—VADM Conrad C. Lautenbacher, Jr., room 5128, (202) 482–3436.
Deputy Under Secretary.—[Vacant], room 5810, 482–4569.
Assistant Secretary/Deputy Administrator.—James R. Mahoney, room 5804, 482–3567.
Chief Financial Officer/Chief Administrative Officer.—Sonya G. Stewart, room 6811, 482–2378.
Chief Scientist.—[Vacant].
General Counsel.—James Walpole, room 5814, 482–4080.
Director, Office of:
Education and Sustainable Development.—[Vacant].
International Affairs.—William Brennan, room 6228, 482–6196.
Legislative Affairs.—Brook Davis (acting), room 5225, 482–4981.
Marine and Aviation Operations/NOAA Commissioned Corps.—RADM Evelyn J. Fields, room 12837, (301) 713–1045.
Policy and Strategic Planning.—[Vacant].
Public and Constituent Affairs.—Jordan St. John, room 6217, 482–5647.

NATIONAL MARINE FISHERIES SERVICE

1315 East-West Highway, Silver Spring, MD 20910

Assistant Administrator.—William Hogarth, room 14555, (301) 713–2239.
Law Enforcement Chief.—Dale Jones, room 415, 427–2300.
Director, Office of:
Habitat Conservation.—Rolland A. Schmitten, room 15147, 713–2325.
Operations, Management and Information.—Alan Risenhoover (acting), room 14450, 713–2259.
Protected Resources.—Donald Knowles, room 13821, 713–2332.
Science and Technology.—William W. Fox, Jr., room 14350, 713–2367.
Sustainable Fisheries.—Bruce C. Morehead (acting), room 13350, 713–2334.

NATIONAL OCEAN SERVICE

Assistant Administrator.—Jamison Hawkins (acting), room 13632, (301) 713–3074.
Director, Office of Operational Oceanographic Products and Services.—Michael Szabados, room 6633, 713–2981.
Deputy Director.—Rick Edwing, room 662, 713–2981.
Chief Financial Officer/Chief Administrative Officer, Management and Budget.—Alan Neuschatz, room 13442, 713–3056.
Director, Office of:
Coast Survey.—CAPT David MacFarland, room 6147, 713–2770.
International Programs.—Charles Ehler, room 10414, 713–3078.
National Centers for Coastal Ocean Science.—Gary C. Matlock, room 8211, 713–3020.

National Geodetic Survey.—Charles W. Challstrom, room 8657, 713–3222.
NOAA Coastal Services.—Margaret A. Davidson, room 842, 740–1220.
Ocean and Coastal Resource Management.—Eldon Hout, room 10413, 713–3155.
Response and Restoration.—David Kennedy, room 10102, 713–2989.
Special Projects.—Daniel Farrow, room 9515, 713–3000.

NATIONAL ENVIRONMENTAL SATELLITE, DATA AND INFORMATION SERVICE

Assistant Administrator.—Gregory W. Withee, room 8338, (301) 713–3578.
International and Interagency Affairs Chief.—D. Brent Smith, room 7315, 713–2024.
Director, Office of:
Budget and Planning.—Thomas Williams, room 8342, 713–9230.
Chief Information.—Robert Mairs, room 8110, 713–9220.
Coastal Ocean Laboratory.—Wayne Wilmot, room 4651, 713–3272.
Environmental Information Services.—Ida Hakkarinen, room 7232, 713–0813.
Management Operations and Analysis.—Ralph P. Conlin, room 8132, 713–9210.
National Climatic Data.—Thomas R. Karl, room 557–C, (828) 271–4476.
National Geophysical Data Center.—Michael S. Loughridge, room 1B148, (303) 497–6215.
National Oceanographic Data Center.—H. Lee Dantzler, Jr., room 4820, 713–3270.
National Polar Orbiting Operational Environmental Satellite System Integrated Program.—John D. Cunningham, room 1450, 427–2070.
Research and Applications.—James F. Purdom, room 701, 763–8127.
Satellite Data Processing and Distribution.—Helen M. Wood, room 1069, 457–5120.
Satellite Operations.—Kathleen A. Kelly, room 0135, 457–5130.
Systems Development.—Gary K. Davis, room 3301, 457–5277.

NATIONAL WEATHER SERVICE

Assistant Administrator.—John J. Kelly, Jr., room 18150, (301) 713–0689.
Chief Financial Officer.—Irwin Ted David, room 18176, 713–0397.
Deputy Chief Financial Officer.—Steven Gallagher, room 18212, 713–0718.
Chief Information Officer.—Barry West, room 18122, 713–1360.
Director, Office of:
Climate, Water and Weather Services.—Gregory A. Mandt, room 14348, 713–0700.
Hydrologic Development.—Gary M. Carter, room 8212, 713–1658.
National Centers for Environmental Prediction.—Louis W. Uccellini, room 101, 763–8016.
Operational Systems.—John McNulty, room 16212, 713–0165.
Science and Technology.—John L. Hayes, room 15146, 713–1746.

OCEANIC AND ATMOSPHERIC RESEARCH

Assistant Administrator.—[Vacant].
Director of:
Aeronomy Laboratory.—Daniel L. Albritton, room 2A126, (303) 497–3134.
Air Resources Laboratory.—Bruce B. Hicks, room 3152, (301) 713–0684.
Atlantic Oceanographic and Meteorological Laboratory.—Kristina Katsaros, (305) 361–4300.
Climate Diagnostic Center.—Randall M. Dole, room ID–116, (303) 497–5812.
Geophysical Fluid Dynamics Laboratory.—Ants Leetmaa, (609) 452–6502.
Global Program Office.—Kenneth Mooney (acting), room 1210, (301) 427–6502.
Great Lakes Environmental Research Laboratory.—Stephen E. Brandt, (734) 741–2245.
National Sea Grant College Program.—Ronald Baird, room 11716, (301) 713–2448.
National Severe Storms Laboratory.—James Kimel, (405) 366–0429.
National Undersea Research Program.—Barbara S.P. Moore, room 11359, (301) 713–2427.
Pacific Marine Environmental Laboratory.—Eddie N. Bernard, (206) 526–6800.
Space Environmental Center.—Ernest Hildner, room 2C–108, (303) 497–3311.

PATENT AND TRADEMARK OFFICE
2021 Jefferson Davis Highway, Arlington, VA 22202
phone (703) 305–8600

Under Secretary for Intellectual Property/Director of U.S. Patent and Trade Office.—James Edward Rogan.
General Counsel.—James A. Toupin, 308–2000.
Management and Program Analyst.—Jewell Christian, 305–4240.
Deputy General Counsel for—
General Law.—Bernard J. Knight, Jr., 308–2000.
Intellectual Property Law and Solicitor.—John M. Whealan, 308–2000.

OFFICE OF THE DEPUTY UNDER SECRETARY AND DEPUTY DIRECTOR

Deputy Under Secretary.—Jon W. Dudas, (703) 305–8700.
Director of:
Enrollment and Discipline.—Harry I. Moatz, 306–4097.
Patent Quality Review.—Kay K. Kim, 305–3153.
Trademark Quality Review.—[Vacant].
Chief Administrative Judge for—
Patents.—Bruce H. Stoner, Jr., 308–9797.
Trademark.—J. David Sams, 308–9300.

CHIEF FINANCIAL OFFICER AND CHIEF ADMINISTRATIVE OFFICER

Chief Financial Officer/Administrative Officer.—JoAnne Bernard, (703) 305–9200.
Deputy Chief, for—
Administration.—John Hassett, 305–9200.
Finance/Comptroller.—[Vacant].
Director of:
Civil Rights.—Maria Campo, 305–8292.
Human Resources.—Sydney T. Rose, 305–8062.
Independent Inventor Programs.—Richard J. Apley, 306–5568.
Public Affairs.—Richard Maulsby, 305–8341.
Administrator for—
External Affairs.—Robert L. Stoll, 305–9300.
Quality Management and Training.—Mary Lee, 305–9100.
Space Acquisition.—Jo Anne Bernard, 308–5121.

COMMISSIONER FOR PATENTS

Commissioner.—Nicholas P. Godici, (703) 305–8800.
Deputy Commissioner.—Stephen G. Kunin, 305–8850.
Director, Office of:
International Liaison Staff.—Robert Saifer, 308–6853.
Patent and Cooperation Legal Administration Administrator.—Charles Pearson, 306–4154.
Patent Legal Administation.—Robert J. Spar, 308–5107.
Patent Policy Dissemination/Petitions.—Manuel A. Antonakas, 305–6199.
Deputy Commissioner for—
Patent Operations.—Esther M. Kepplinger, 305–8800.
Patent Resources and Planning.—Edward R. Kazenske, 305–8800.
Manager, Office of:
Initial Patent Examination.—Thomas I. Koontz, 308–0910.
Scientific and Technical Information Center.—Kristin Vajs, 308–0808.
Director, Office of:
Audit and Evaluation.—Karen M. Young, 305–9069.
Classification Operations.—Harold Smith, 305–5107.
Classification Support.—Duane Davis, 305–5762.
Patent and Cooperations Operations.—Robert Hafer, 308–2674.
Patent Financial Management.—John Mielcarek, 305–9214.
Patent Publications.—Richard A. Bawcombe, 305–8594.
Patent Resources Management.—Sally Middleton, 308–8594.
Planning and Capacity Analysis.—Bo Bounkong, 305–8800.
Search Systems.—Kay Melvin, 308–5188.

Administrator, Office of:
Patent Resources Administration Administrator.—Karen M. Young, 305–9069.
Search and Information Resources Administration.—Frederick Schmidt, 306–3105.

COMMISSIONER FOR TRADEMARKS

Commissioner.—Anne H. Chasser, (703) 306–3109.
Deputy Commissioner.—Robert M. Anderson, 308–8900.
Deputy Assistant Commissioner for Trademark Policy and Projects.—Lynne Beresford, 306–3109.
Chief Information Officer.—Douglas Bourgeois, 305–9400.
Deputy Chief Information Officer for—
Information Technology.—Ronald P. Hack, 305–9095.
System Modernization.—Wesley Gewehr, 305–9110.
Director, Office of:
Acquisition.—Ken Giese, 305–8642.
Architecture and Engineering.—Larry Cogut, 305–8685.
Customer Support.—Randy Bender, 305–8788.
Data Management.—Holly Higgins, 308–7393.
Development and Maintenance.—Robert Porter, 305–9172.
Information Dissemination Services.—[Vacant].
Public Records.—Patrick Rowe, 308–9743.
Product Assurance.—Jeffrey Wolfe, 305–9412.
System and Network Management.—Thomas Kenton, 305–9258.
Trademark Program Control.—Gary Cannon, 308–7200.
Trademark Services.—Ronald Williams, 305–1222.

TECHNOLOGY ADMINISTRATION

Under Secretary.—Phillip J. Bond, (202) 482–1575.
Deputy Under Secretary.—Benjamin H. Wu.
Director.—[Vacant].

OFFICE FOR TECHNOLOGY POLICY

Assistant Secretary.—Bruce P. Mehlman, (202) 482–5687.
Director, Office of:
International Policy.—Cathleen Campbell, 482–6351.
Technology Competitiveness.—Karen Laney-Cummings (acting), 482–6101.

NATIONAL INSTITUTE OF STANDARDS AND TECHNOLOGY

Director.—Dr. Arden L. Bement, Jr., (301) 975–2300.
Director for Congressional and Legislative Affairs.—Verna B. Hines, 975–3080.
Director of Administration/Chief Financial Officer.—Marilia A. Matos, 975–2390.
Deputy Director.—Karen H. Brown.
Human Resources Management Personnel Officer.—Ellen M. Dowd, 975–3000.
Chief, Office of Intelligent Processing of Materials.—Dale E. Hall (acting), 975–5658.
Comptroller, Financial Operations Division.—John C. McGuffin, 975–2291.
Budget Officer.—Thomas P. Kalusing, 975–2669.
Director, Office of:
Accounting.—Mary O. Houff (703) 605–6611.
Administration.—[Vacant].
Advanced Technology Program.—Marc G. Stanley (acting), 975–5187.
Budget and Financial Analysis.—Wayne J. Galliant, (703) 605–6471.
Building and Fire Research Laboratory.—Jack E. Snell, 975–6850.
Chemical Science and Technology Laboratory.—Hatch Semerjian, 975–8300.
Chemistry and Life Sciences.—Michael Walsh (acting), 975–5455.
Civil Rights.—Alvin C. Lewis, 975–2037.
Customer Relations.—Jon Birdsall, (703) 605–6102.
Database Services.—Jean Bowers, (703) 605–6227.
Economic Assessment.—Stephanie Shipp, 975–8978.
Electronics and Electrical Engineering Laboratory.—William E. Anderson, 975–2220.

Electronics and Photonics Technology.—Michael Schen, 975–6741.
International and Academic Affairs.—B. Stephen Carpenter, 975–4119.
Information Resources Management.—Keith Sinner, (703) 605–6310.
Information Services.—Mary-Deirdre Coraggio, 975–5158.
Information Technology and Applications.—Bettijoyce Lide (acting), 975–2218.
Information Technology Laboratory.—William O. Mehuron, 975–2900.
Manufacturing Engineering Laboratory.—Howard M. Bloom (acting), 975–3400.
Manufacturing Extension Partnership.—Kevin Carr, 975–5454.
Materials Science and Engineering Laboratory.—Leslie E. Smith, 975–5658.
Measurement Services.—Thomas E. Gills, 975–2016.
National Programs.—Stephen J. Thompson, 975–5042.
National Quality Program.—Harry S. Hertz, 975–2360.
National Technical Information.—Ronald E. Lawson, (703) 605–6400.
NIST/Boulder Laboratories.—Susan L. Sutherland, (303) 497–3237.
NIST Center for Neutron Research.—J. Michael Rowe, 975–6210.
Physics Laboratory.—Katherine B. Gebbie, 975–4201.
Product Development.—Edward J. Lehmann, (703) 605–6652.
Product Management.—Nancy Collins, (703) 605–6518.
Product Services.—[Vacant].
Program Office.—Michael P. Casassa (acting), 975–2667.
Programs Development.—J. Thomas Walker, 975–4176.
Regional Programs.—J. Michael Simpson (acting), 975–6454.
Standards Services.—Belinda L. Collins, 975–4000.
Technology Partnerships.—Bruce E. Mattson, 975–6501.
Technology Services.—Richard F. Kayser, 975–4500.

Chief, Division of:
Acquisition and Logistics.—Norman L. Osinski, 975–6348.
Advanced Network Technologies.—Kevin Mills, 975–3618.
Analytical Chemistry.—Willie E. May, 975–3108.
Atomic Physics.—Wolfgang L. Wiese, 975–3200.
Biotechnology.—Gary L. Gilliland, 975–2629.
Building Environment.—George Kelly, 975–5850.
Building Materials.—Geoffrey J. Frohnsdorff, 975–6706.
Ceramics.—Stephen W. Freiman, 975–6119.
Computer Security.—Edward Roback, 975–2934.
Convergent Information Systems.—Victor R. McCrary (acting), 975–4321.
Electricity.—James K. Olthoff (acting), 975–2400.
Electromagnetic Technology.—Richard E. Harris, (303) 497–3776.
Electron and Optical Physics.—Charles W. Clark, 975–3709.
Engineering, Maintenance, Safety and Support.—Stephen S. Salber, (303) 497–3886.
Fabrication Technology.—Mark E. Luce, 975–2159.
Facilities Services.—Susan J. Carscadden, 975–3301.
Financial Management Systems.—D. Michael Stogsdill, (301) 975–2179.
Financial Policy.—William A. Smoot, Jr., 975–2250.
Fire Safety Engineering.—David D. Evans, 975–6897.
Fire Sciences.—William L. Grosshandler, 975–2310.
Grants and Management.—George W. White, 975–8175.
Information Access.—Martin Herman, 975–4495.
Information Services and Computing.—Ray Hoffmann, 975–3240.
Ionizing Radiation.—Bert M. Coursey, 975–5584.
Intelligent Systems.—John M. Evans, 975–3418.
Management and Organization.—Sharon E. Bisco, 975–4074.
Manufacturing Metrology.—E. Clayton Teague, 975–6600.
Manufacturing Systems Integration.—Steven R. Ray, 975–3508.
Materials Reliability.—Fred R. Flickett, (303) 497–3268.
Mathematical and Computational Sciences.—Ronald F. Boisvert, 975–3800.
Metallurgy.—Carol A. Handwerker, 975–6158.
Occupational Health and Safety.—Rosamond A. Rutledge-Burns, 975–5818.
Optical Technology.—Albert C. Parr, 975–2316.
Optoelectronics.—Gordon W. Day, (303) 497–5204.
Physical and Chemical Properties.—Mickey Haynes, (303) 497–3247.
Plant Division.—Douglas F. Elznic, 975–6900.
Polymers.—Eric J. Amis, 975–6681.
Precision Engineering.—Dennis A. Swyt, 975–3463.
Public and Business Affairs.—Matthew Heyman, 975–2758.
Quantum Physics.—James E. Faller, (303) 492–6807.
Radio-Frequency Technology.—Dennis S. Friday, (303) 497–3131.

Semiconductor Electronics.—David G. Seiler, 975–2054.
Software Diagnostics and Conformance Testing.—Mark W. Skall, 975–3262.
Statistical Engineering.—Nell Sedransk, 975–2839.
Structures.—S. Shyam-Sunder, 975–6061.
Surface and Microanalysis Science.—Richard R. Cavanagh, 975–2368.
Time and Frequency.—Donald B. Sullivan, (303) 497–3772.
Associate Director for—
Business Development.—Walter L. Finch, (703) 605–6507.
Customer Services.—Sandra M. Rigby, 605–6100.
Financial and Administrative Management.—Paul Roberts, 605–6443.
Production Services.—Douglas Campion, 605–6214.

NATIONAL TELECOMMUNICATIONS AND INFORMATION ADMINISTRATION

Herbert C. Hoover Building, Room 4898, (202) 482–1840

Assistant Secretary for Communications and Information.—Nancy Victory.
Deputy Assistant Secretary.—[Vacant].
Director, Office of:
Chief Counsel.—Kathy Smith, 482–1816.
Communications and Information Infrastructure Assurance.—Daniel Hurley, 482–1116.
Congressional Affairs.—Jim Wasilewski, 482–1551.
Policy Coordination and Management.—[Vacant].
Spectrum Plans and Policies.—Frederick R. Wentland, 482–1850.
Associate Administrator of:
International Affairs.—Robin Layton (acting), 482–1866.
Policy Analysis and Development.—Kelly Levy, 482–1880.
Spectrum Management.—William T. Hatch, 482–1850.
Telecommunications and Information Applications.—Bernadette McGuire–Rivera, 482–5802.
Associate Administrator/Director, Institute for Telecommunications Sciences.—Val M. O'Day (acting), (303) 497–3500.

NATIONAL TECHNICAL INFORMATION SERVICE

Forbes Building, 5285 Port Royal Road, Room 200, Springfield, VA 22161
phone (703) 482–4093

Director.—Ronald E. Lawson, (703) 605–6400.
Deputy Director.—John Sopko, 605–6405.
Director, Office of:
Accounting.—Mary O. Houff, 605–6611.
Administration.—Rita Cunningham, 605–6449.
Budget and Financial Analysis.—Wayne J. Gallant, 605–6471.
Chief Information Officer.—Keith Sinner, 605–6310.
Customer Relations.—Jon Birdsall, 605–6102.
Database Services.—Jean Bowers, 605–6227.
Multi-Media and Online Services.—Patricia Gresham, 605–6123.
Policy Analyst.—Steven Needle, 605–6404.
Product Development.—Edward J. Lehmann, 605–6652.
Product Management.—Nancy Collins, 605–6518.
Product Services.—Douglas Campion, 605–6214.
Associate Director for—
Business Development.—Janice Long Coe, 605–6181.
Customer Services.—Sandra M. Rigby, 605–6100.
Financial and Administrative Management.—Paul Roberts, 605–6443.

DEPARTMENT OF LABOR

Frances Perkins Building, Third Street and Constitution Avenue, NW., 20210

phone (202) 693–5000, http://www.dol.gov

ELAINE L. CHAO, Secretary of Labor; education: B.A., Mount Holyoke College, 1975; M.B.A., Harvard University, 1979; she also studied at the Massachusetts Institute of Technology, Dartmouth College, and Columbia University; employment: Citicorp, 1979–1983; BankAmerica Capital Markets Group, 1984–1986; Distinguished Fellow, Heritage Foundation, 1996–2001; public service: White House Fellow, Office of Policy Development, 1983–1984; Deputy Maritime Administrator, Department of Transportation, 1986–1988; Chairwoman, Federal Maritime Commission, 1988–1989; Deputy Secretary of Transportation, 1989–1991; Peace Corps Director, 1991–1992; President and Chief Executive Officer of the United Way of America, 1992–1996; family: married to U.S. Senator Mitch McConnell (R–KY); recipient of many awards for her community service and professional accomplishments; and recipient of 11 honorary doctorate degrees from numerous colleges and universities; nominated by President George W. Bush to become the 24th Secretary of Labor, and was confirmed by the U.S. Senate on January 29, 2001.

OFFICE OF THE SECRETARY

phone 693–6000

Secretary of Labor.—Elaine L. Chao.
Executive Assistant.—Connie Johnston.
Chief of Staff.—Steven Law.
Counselor to the Secretary.—Andrew Siff.
Executive Secretariat.—Ruth D. Knouse, 693–6100.
Director of Scheduling and Advance.—Tina Henry, 693–6003.

OFFICE OF THE DEPUTY SECRETARY

Deputy Secretary.—D. Cameron Findlay, 693–6002.

OFFICE OF THE 21ST CENTURY WORKFORCE

Director.—[Vacant].
Deputy Director.—[Vacant].
Senior Counsel.—Alan Severson, 693–6490.

OFFICE OF FAITH BASED INITIATIVES

Director.—Brent Orrell, 693–6450.
Deputy Director.—Jacqueline Halbig.

ADMINISTRATIVE LAW JUDGES

Techworld, 800 K Street, NW., Suite 4148 20001–8002

Chief Administrative Law Judge.—John M. Vittone, 693–7542.

OFFICE OF MANAGING PARTNER

Associate Deputy Secretary for Adjudication.—[Vacant], room N–1519, 693–6234.

BENEFITS REVIEW BOARD

Chair.—Nancy S. Dolder, room N5101, 693–6300.

EMPLOYEES COMPENSATION APPEALS BOARD

Chairman.—Alec Koromilas, room N–2613, 693–6420.

ADMINISTRATIVE REVIEW BOARD

Chairman.—M. Cynthia Douglass, room S4309, 693–6200.

OFFICE OF SMALL BUSINESS PROGRAMS

Director.—Jose Lira, room C2318, 693–6460.

OFFICE OF DISABILITY EMPLOYMENT POLICY

Frances Perkins Building, Room S–1303, 693–7880, TTY 693–7881

Assistant Secretary.—W. Roy Grizzard, Ed.D.
Deputy Assistant Secretary.—Russell Harris (acting).
Chief of Staff.—J. Kim Cook, 693–7880.
Executive Assistant.—Nancy Skaggs.
Special Assistants: Robert Brostrom, Alice O'Steen.
Director of:
Office of Policy and Research.—Susan Parker.
Office of Operations.—John Davey.

ASSISTANT SECRETARY FOR CONGRESSIONAL AND INTERGOVERNMENTAL AFFAIRS

Frances Perkins Building, Room S2006, phone 693–4601

Assistant Secretary.—Kristine Iverson.
Staff Assistant.—Glenda Manning.
Deputy Assistant Secretary, Congressional.—Jennifer Jameson, room S–2220, 693–4600.
Deputy Assistant Secretary, Intergovernmental.—Karen Czarnecki, room S–2220, 693–4600.
Senior Legislative Officers:
Budget and Appropriations.—Adam Sullivan, room S–2220, 693–4600.
Employment Standards.—Elena Thompkins, room S–2220, 693–4600.
Employment and Training: Anthony Bedell, Mala Krishnamoorti, room S–2220, 693–4600.
Employment Benefits.—Bradford Campbell, room S–2220, 693–4600.
Workplace Safety and Health.—Bryan Little, room S–2220, 693–4600.
Congressional Research Assistants: Jana Hoisington, Elizabeth Keelan, Blair Palmer.
Senior Intergovernmental Officer.—Bettye Samuels, room S–2220, 693–4600.
Intergovernmental Officers: Christopher Bugbee, Maria Fuentes, room S–2220, 693–4600.
Administrative Officer.—Joycelyn Daniels, room S–1318, 693–4600.

REGIONAL OFFICES

Region I.—Connecticut, Maine, Massachusetts, New Hampshire, Rhode Island, Vermont.
Regional Representative.—[Vacant], One Congress Street, Boston, MA 02114–2023, (617) 565–2282.
Region II.—New York, New Jersey, Puerto Rico, Virgin Islands.
Regional Representative.—Angelica O. Tang, 201 Varick Street, Suite 605, New York, NY 10014–4811, (212) 337–2387.
Region III.—Pennsylvania, Delaware, District of Columbia, Maryland, Virginia, West Virginia.
Regional Representative.—[Vacant], 3535 Market Street, Philadelphia, PA 19104–3309, (215) 596–1116.
Region IV.—Alabama, Georgia, Florida, Kentucky, Mississippi, North Carolina, South Carolina, Tennessee.
Regional Representative.—[Vacant], Sam Nunn Atlanta Federal Center, 61 Forsyth Street, SW., Atlanta, GA 30303, (404) 562–2000.

Region V.—Illinois, Indiana, Michigan, Minnesota, Ohio, Wisconsin.
Regional Representative.—Robert Athey, 230 South Dearborn Street, Chicago, IL 60604, (312) 353–4703.

Region VI.—Texas, Arkansas, Louisiana, New Mexico, Oklahoma.
Regional Representative.—[Vacant], Federal Building, 525 Griffin Street, Dallas, TX 75202, (214) 767–6807.

Region VII.—Iowa, Kansas, Nebraska, Missouri.
Regional Representative.—[Vacant], City Center Square, 1100 Main Street, Kansas City, MO 64105–2112, (816) 426–6371.

Region VIII.—Colorado, Montana, North Dakota, South Dakota, Wyoming.
Regional Representative.—Rick Collins, 1999 Broadway, Suite 1600, Denver, CO 80202, (303) 844–1256.

Region IX.—California, Hawaii, Nevada, Arizona, Guam.
Regional Representative.—Judy Biviano Lloyd, 71 Stevenson Street, San Francisco, CA 94105, (415) 975–4042.

Region X.—Alaska, Idaho, Oregon, Washington.
Regional Representative.—Walter Liang, 1111 Third Avenue, Seattle, WA 98101–3212, (206) 553–0574.

ASSISTANT SECRETARY FOR PUBLIC AFFAIRS

Frances Perkins Building, Room S2514, phone 693–4650

Assistant Secretary.—Kathleen M. Harrington.
Deputy Assistant Secretary.—[Vacant].

REGIONAL OFFICES

Region I.—Connecticut, Maine, Massachusetts, New Hampshire, Rhode Island, Vermont.
Public Affairs Director.—John Chavez, JFK Federal Building, Government Center, Room E–120, Boston, MA 02203, (617) 565–2075.

Region IIA.—New York, Puerto Rico, Virgin Islands.
Regional Representative.—John Chavez, JFK Federal Building, Government Center, Room E–120, Boston, Massachusetts 02203, (617) 565–2075.

Region IIB.—New Jersey.
Regional Representative.—Kate Dugan, Room 14120, 3535 Market Street, Philadelphia, PA 19104, (215) 596–1147.

Region III.—Delaware, District of Columbia, Maryland, Pennsylvania, Virginia, West Virginia.
Public Affairs Director.—Kate Dugan, Room 14120, 3535 Market Street, Philadelphia, PA 19104, (215) 596–1147.

Region IV.—Alabama, Florida, Georgia, Kentucky, Mississippi, North Carolina, South Carolina, Tennessee.
Public Affairs Director.—Dan Fuqua, Atlanta Federal Center, 61 Forsyth SW, Suite 6B75, Atlanta, GA 30303, (404) 562–2078.

Region V.—Illinois, Indiana, Michigan, Minnesota, Ohio, Wisconsin.
Public Affairs Director.—Bradley Mitchell, Room 3192, 230 South Dearborn Street, Room 3192, Chicago, IL 60604, (312) 353–6976.

Region VI.—Arkansas, Louisiana, New Mexico, Oklahoma, Texas.
Public Affairs Director.—Diana Petterson, Room 734, 525 Griffin Street, Dallas, TX 75202, (214) 767–4777.

Region VII.—Iowa, Kansas, Missouri, Nebraska.
Public Affairs Specialist.—Norma Conrad, City Center Square, 11000 Main Street, Suite 1220, Kansas City, MO 64105, (816) 426–5490.

Region VIII.—Colorado, Montana, North Dakota, South Dakota, Utah, Wyoming.
Public Affairs Director.—Rich Kulczewski, 1999 Broadway, Suite 1640, Denver, CO 80202, (303) 844–1303.

Region IX.—Arizona, California, Guam, Hawaii, Nevada.
Public Affairs Director.—Tino Serrano, Suite 1035, 71 Stevenson Street, San Francisco, CA 94119–3766, (415) 975–4742.

Region X.—Alaska, Idaho, Oregon, Washington.
Public Affairs Director.—Mike Shimizu, Building B, Room 805, 1111 Third Avenue, Seattle WA, 98101, (206) 553–7620.

BUREAU OF INTERNATIONAL LABOR AFFAIRS

Frances Perkins Building, phone 693–4770

Deputy Under Secretary.—[Vacant].
Associate Deputies Under Secretary: Arnold Levine, Jorge Perez-Lopez.
Chief of Staff.—Martha Newton.
Director, Office of:
Foreign Relations.—James Perlmutter, 693–4785.
International Economic Affairs.—Jorge Perez-Lopez, 693–4888.
International Organizations.—Charles Spring, 693–4855.
National Administrative Office.—Lewis Karesh (acting), 693–4900.
International Child Labor Programs.—Marcia Eugenio (acting), 693–4843.

INSPECTOR GENERAL

Frances Perkins Building, Room S–5502, phone 693–5100

Inspector General.—Gordon S. Heddell.
Deputy Inspector General.—George J. Opfer.
Chief of Staff.—Nancy Ruiz de Gamboa.
Assistant Inspector General for—
Audit.—Elliot P. Lewis, room S–5518, 693–5168.
Investigations.—Stephen J. Cossu, room S–5014, 693–7034.
Legal Services.—Sylvia T. Horowitz, room S–1305, 693–5116.
Management and Policy.—[Vacant], room S–5020, 693–5191.

WOMEN'S BUREAU

Frances Perkins Building, Room S–3002, phone 693–6710

Director.—Shinae Chun.
Deputy Director.—Lisa Kruska.
Manager, National and Regional Operations.—Cornelia H. Moore, 693–6710.
Chief of:
Information and Support Services.—[Vacant], 693–6727.
Policy and Programs.—Collis Phillips, room S–3311, 693–6747.

EMPLOYEE BENEFITS SECURITY ADMINISTRATION

Frances Perkins Building, Room S–2524, phone 693–8300

Assistant Secretary.—Ann L. Combs.
Deputy Assistant Secretary for Policy.—Paul R. Zurawski.
Deputy Assistant Secretary.—Alan D. Lebowitz, room N–5677, 693–8315.
Chief of Staff.—Thomas Alexander, room S–2524, 693–8300.
Executive Assistant to the Deputy Assistant Secretary.—Sue Ugelow, 693–8315.
Confidential Assistant.—Rosita Hrobowski (acting).
Special Assistant.—[Vacant].
Senior Director for Policy and Legislative Analysis.—Morton Klevan, room N–5677, 693–8315.
Director of:
Program, Planning, Evaluation and Management.—Brian C. McDonnell, room N–5668, 693–8480.
Chief Accountant.—Ian Dingwall, room N–5459, 693–8360.
Enforcement.—Virginia Smith, room N–5702, 693–8440.
Exemption Determinations.—Ivan L. Strasfeld, room N–5649, 693–8540.
Information Management.—John Helms, room N–5459, 693–8600.
Program Services.—Sharon Watson, room N–5625, 693–8630.
Regulations and Interpretations.—Robert Doyle, room N–5669, 693–8500.
Policy and Research.—Joseph Piacentini (acting), room N–5718, 693–8410.

EMPLOYMENT STANDARDS ADMINISTRATION

Frances Perkins Building, Room S–2321, phone 693–0200

Assistant Secretary.—Victoria Lipnic.
Deputy Assistant Secretary.—D. Mark Wilson.
Chief of Staff.—Horace Cooper.
Special Assistants: Nicolee Ambrose, Corrie L. Fischel.
Administrator, Wage and Hour Division.—Tammy D. McCutchen, 693–0051.
Deputy Administrator for Policy.—Eric S. Dreiband.
Senior Policy Advisors: Dave Minsky, Alfred B. Robinson, Jr.
Director, Office of:
Planning and Analysis.—Nancy M. Flynn.
External Affairs.—Rae E. Glass.
Enforcement Policy.—Michael F. Ginley.
Wage Determinations.—William M. Gross.
Deputy Assistant Secretary, Office of Federal Contract Compliance Programs.—Charles E. James, Sr., 693–0101.
Deputy Director.—Bill Doyle.
Deputy Assistant Secretary, Office of Labor Management Programs.—Don Todd, 693–0202.
Director of Workers' Compensation Programs.—Shelby Hallmark, 693–0031.
Director, Division of:
Longshore and Harber Worker's Compensation.—Michael Niss.
Federal Employees Compensation.—Deborah Sanford.
Coal Mine Worker's Compensation.—James DeMarce.
Energy Employees Occupational Illness Compensation Program.—Peter Turcic.
Director, Office of Management, Administration and Planning.—Anne Baird-Bridges, 693–0608.
Deputy Director.—Patricia J. Vastano.
Coordinator, Equal Employment Opportunity Unit.—Kate Dorrell, 693–0024.

OFFICE OF THE ASSISTANT SECRETARY FOR ADMINISTRATION AND MANAGEMENT

Frances Perkins Building, Room S–2203, phone 693–4040

Assistant Secretary.—Patrick Pizzella.
Deputy Assistant Secretary for—
Operations.—Edward C. Hugler.
Budget and Strategic and Performance Planning.—James E. McMullen.
Special Assistants: Jeff Koch, John Pallasch.
Administrative Officer.—Noelia Fernandez.
Secretary.—Martie Boman.

DEPARTMENTAL BUDGET CENTER

Director.—Edward L. Jackson, room S–4020, 693–4090.
Staff Assistant.—Patricia Smith.
Deputy Director.—Richard V. French.
Office of:
Agency Budget Programs.—William C. Keisler, 693–4068.
Budget Policy and Systems.—Mark Wichlin, 693–4070.
Financial Management Operations.—Deborah Staton-Wright, S–5526, 693–4490.

CENTER FOR PROGRAM PLANNING AND RESULTS

Director.—Veronica C. Campbell, S–4020, 693–4069.
Office of:
Planning.—James D. Sullivan, 693–4076.
Performance Monitoring.—Donna Copson, 693–4087.

BUSINESS OPERATIONS CENTER

Director.—Al Stewart, room S–1524, 693–4028.
Deputy Director.—Kathy Alejandro, room S–1524, 693–4026.
Office of:
Emergency Operations.—Curtis Bartell, room 400, 800 K Street, NW., 693–7510.
Administrative Services.—[Vacant], room S–1522, 693–4036.
Procurement Services.—Daniel P. Murphy, room N–5416, 693–4570.
Acquisition and Management Support Services.—Karen Pedone, room S–1512, 693–7272.
Safety and Health Services.—Laurie Hileman, room C–3317, 693–6670.
Wirtz Labor Library.—Linda Parker, room N–2455, 693–6600.
Special Assistant.—Leonard A. Pettiford, room S–1522, 693–6665.

CIVIL RIGHTS CENTER

Director.—Annabelle T. Lockhart, room N–4123, 693–6500.
Staff Assistant.—Vicky Best-Morris.
Office of:
Compliance Assistance and Planning.—Gregory Shaw, 693–6501.
Enforcement/Internal and External.—Willie Alexander, 693–6501.
Mediation, Counseling and Evaluation.—[Vacant], 693–6504.
EEO Coordinator of Counselors.—Lillian Winstead, 693–6504.
Reasonable Accommodation Hotline.—Dawn Murray-Johnson, room N–4309, 693–6569.

HUMAN RESOURCES CENTER

Director.—Daliza Salas, room S–5526, 693–7600.
Deputy Director.—Jerry Lelchook, C–5526, 693–7600.
Office of:
Administration, Events Management and Assistive Services.—Sharon Woodward, C–5515, 693–7773.
Continuous Learning and Career Management.—Kim Green, room N–5460, 693–7630.
Employee Labor Management Relations.—Sandra Keppley, room N–5470, 693–7670.
Executive Resources and Personnel Security.—David LeDoux, room C–5508, 693–7800.
Human Resources Policy and Accountability.—Richard Kelley, room C–5470, 693–7720.
Human Resources Service Center.—Violet R. Parker, room C–5516, 693–7690.
Workforce Planning and Diversity.—Dennis Sullivan, room C–5522, 693–7740.
Worklife Programs.—[Vacant].

INFORMATION TECHNOLOGY CENTER

Director.—Keith Nelson (acting), room N–1301, 693–4567.
Administrative Officer.—Kathy Fox, 693–4215.
Human Resources Information Systems Unit.—Michael Miller, room N–2717, 693–4338.
Office of:
Technical Services.—Cornelius Johnson (acting Director), 693–4218.
Chief Information Officer Programs.—Hung Phan, 693–4209.
Systems Development and Integration.—Cornelius Johnson, 693–4170.
Customer Support and Field Operations.—[Vacant], 693–4567.
Government Benefits/Government Director.—Dennis Gusty, N–4309, 693–4205.
IT Help Desk.—7 a.m. to 7 p.m., room N–1505, 693–4444.

ASSISTANT SECRETARY FOR POLICY

Frances Perkins Building, Room S–2312, phone 693–5959

Assistant Secretary.—Chris Spear.
Chief of Staff.—Fay Ott, 693–5929.
Deputy Assistant Secretaries: Roland G. Droitsch, David Gray, 693–5900.
Associate Assistant Secretary.—Dana Barbieri.
Chief Economist.—Diana Furchgott-Roth, 693–5915.
Director, Office of:
Compliance Assistance Policy.—Barbara Bingham, 693–5080.
Regulatory Policy.—Kathleen Franks, 693–5072.
Programmatic Policy.—Ruth Samardick, 693–5075.
Research and Technical Policy.—David DeMers, 693–5906.

OFFICE OF THE SOLICITOR

Frances Perkins Building, phone 693–5260

Solicitor.—Howard M. Radzely, (acting).
Confidential Assistant.—Tina McCants.
Special Assistants: Craig W. Hukill, Timothy J. Keefer, Joseph B. Maher, Nancy M. Rooney, 693–5261.
Deputy Solicitor for—
National Operations.—Howard M. Radzely, 693–5261.
Regional Operations.—Ronald G. Whiting, 693–5262.
Planning and Coordination.—[Vacant].

OFFICE OF ADMINISTRATION, MANAGEMENT AND LITIGATION SUPPORT

Director.—Cecilia M. Holmes, room N–2414, 693–5405.
Financial Manager.—June M. Graft, room N–2427, 693–5433.
Personnel Officer.—Mary Pat Donelan, room N–2419, 693–5415.
EEO/Employee Relations.—Neilda Lee, room N–2419, 693–5424.
Litigation Support.—Alice L. Rapport, room N–2414, 693–5430.
Automation Information Services.—Georgette Price, room N–2414, 693–5428.
Internal Controls.—Brenda W. Murray, room N–2414, 693–5425.

DIVISION OF BLACK LUNG BENEFITS

Associate Solicitor.—Donald S. Shire, room N–2605, 693–5667.
Deputy Associate Solicitor.—Rae Ellen Frank James, 693–5656.
Counsel for—
Administrative Litigation and Legal Advice.—Michael J. Rutledge, 693–5666.
Appellate Litigation: Christian Barber; Patricia M. Nece, 693–5660.
Enforcement.—Edward Waldman, 693–5671.
Regional Litigation.—Brian E. Peters, 693–5663.

DIVISION OF CIVIL RIGHTS

Associate Solicitor.—Gary M. Buff, room N–2426, 693–5300.
Deputy Associate Solicitor.—Donald Shalhaub.
Counsel for—
Interpretations and Advice.—Suzan Chastain.
Litigation: Beverly Dankowitz, Richard Gilman.

DIVISION OF EMPLOYEE BENEFITS

Associate Solicitor.—Jeffrey L. Nesvet (acting), room S–4325, 693–5320.
Deputy Associate Solicitor.—Jeffrey L. Nesvet.
Counsel for—
Claims.—Catherine P. Carter.
Energy Employees Compensation.—Mark A. Reinhalter.
Longshore.—[Vacant].
Senior Trial Attorneys: John T. Gillelan II, Samuel J. Oshansky.

EMPLOYMENT AND TRAINING LEGAL SERVICES

Associate Solicitor.—Charles D. Raymond, room N–2101, 693–5710.
Deputy Associate Solicitor.—Jonathan H. Waxman, 693–5730.
Counsel for Litigation.—Harry L. Sheinfeld.
Counsel for—
Employment Compensation.—Michael N. Apfelbaum.
Employment and Immigration Programs.—Bruce W. Alter.
Senior Trial Attorney.—Vincent C. Costantino.

FAIR LABOR STANDARDS

Associate Solicitor.—Steve Mandel, room N–2716, 693–5555.
Deputy Associate Solicitor.—William Lesser.
Counsel for—
Appellate Litigation.—Paul L. Frieden, 693–5552.
Employment Standards.—Douglas J. Davidson.
Legal Advice.—Diane Heim.
Trial Litigation: Ellen Edmond, Anne P. Fugitt, Johnathan M. Kronheim.
Senior Trial Attorney.—William J. Stone.

DIVISION OF LABOR MANAGEMENT LAWS

Associate Solicitor.—Carol DeDeo, room N–2474, 693–5741.
Deputy Associate Solicitor.—Barron S. Widom, room N–2474, 693–5754.
Counsel for—
International Affairs/Opinions.—Donald D. Carter, 693–5739.
Litigation.—Dennis Paquette, 693–5758.

DIVISION OF LEGISLATION AND LEGAL COUNSEL

Associate Solicitor.—Robert A. Shapiro, room N–2428, 693–5500.
Deputy Associate Solicitor.—Bruce Cohen.
Counsel for—
Administrative Law: Peter D. Galvin, Miriam McD. Miller.
Ethics.—Robert Sadler.
Labor Relations.—Mark Maxin, 693–5520.
Legislative Reports.—Jill M. Otte.
Senior Attorney Advisers: Mark W. Morin; Seth D. Zinman.
Counsel for Opinions, Appropriations Law.—Myron Zeitz.

DIVISION OF MINE SAFETY AND HEALTH

1100 Wilson Boulevard, 22nd Floor, Arlington, VA 22209

Associate Solicitor.—Edward P. Clair, room 2222, (202) 693–9333.
Deputy Associate Solicitor.—Thomas A. Mascolino, room 2221.
Counsel for—
Appellate Litigation.—W. Christian Schumann, room 2220.
Coal Standards and Advice.—Heidi W. Strassler, room 2224.
Metal/Non-Metal Standards and Advice.—Deborah K. Green, room 2218.
Trial Litigation.—James B. Crawford, room 2219, 693–9335.
Senior Attorney Advisor.—Jerald S. Feingold.

DIVISION OF OCCUPATIONAL SAFETY AND HEALTH

Associate Solicitor.—Joseph M. Woodward, room S–4004, 693–5452.
Deputy Associate Solicitor.—Alexander Fernandez.
Counsel for—
Appellate Litigation: Bruce F. Justh, Ann Rosenthal, 693–5445.
General Legal Advice.—Robert W. Swain, 693–5445.
Health Standards.—Claudia Thurber, 693–5479.
Safety Standards.—George Henschel, 693–5445.
Trial and OSHRC Litigation.—Daniel Mick, 693–5445.
Senior Trial Attorneys: Kenneth Hellman, Charles F. James, 693–5445.
Senior Program Attorneys: Charles P. Gordon, 219–9468; Richard Pfeffer, 693–5449.

DIVISION OF PLAN BENEFITS SECURITY

Associate Solicitor.—Timothy D. Hauser, room N–4611, 693–5590.
Deputy Associate Solicitor.—Karen Handorf, 693–5600.
Counsel for—
Appellate and Special Litigation.—Elizabeth Hopkins.
Fiduciary Litigation.—Risa D. Sandler, 693–5592.

General Litigation.—Leslie Candied Perlman, 693–5593.
Regulation.—William White Taylor, 693–5583.
Senior Trial Attorneys: Michael A. Schloss, William Scott, William P. Tedesco, William E. Zuckerman, 693–5600.

DIVISION OF SPECIAL APPELLATE AND SUPREME COURT LITIGATION (SASCL)

Associate Solicitor.—Allen Feldman, room N–2700, 693–5760.
Deputy Associate Solicitor.—Nathaniel Spiller.
Senior Trial Attorneys: Ellen L. Beard, Michael Doyle, Mark S. Flynn, Elizabeth Hopkins, Edward D. Sieger, 693–5760.

OCCUPATIONAL SAFETY AND HEALTH ADMINISTRATION

Frances Perkins Building, Room S–2315, phone 693–2000

Assistant Secretary.—John Henshaw.
Deputy Assistant Secretaries: R. Davis Layne, Gary Visscher.
Director, Office of:
Equal Employment Opportunity.—Betty Gillis-Robinson, 693–2150.
Public Affairs.—Bonnie Friedman, 693–1999.
Director of:
Administrative Programs.—David Zeigler, 693–1600.
Construction and Engineering.—Russell B. Swanson, 693–2345.
Cooperative and State Programs.—Paula White.
Enforcement Programs.—Richard Fairfax, 693–2100.
Evaluation and Analysis.—Frank Froydma (acting), 693–2400.
Information Technology.—Cheryl Greeangh, 693–2400.
Science, Technology.—Ruth McCully, 693–2300.
Standards and Guidance.—Steven Witt, 693–1950.

EMPLOYMENT AND TRAINING ADMINISTRATION

Frances Perkins Building, Room S–2307, phone 693–2700

Assistant Secretary.—Emily Stover DeRocco.
Deputy Assistant Secretaries: Mason M. Bishop, David G. Dye, Thomas M. Dowd.
Administrator, Office of:
Apprenticeship Training, Employer and Labor Services.—Anthony Swoope, room N–4671, 693–2796.
Business Relations Group.—Gay Gilbert, N–4206, 693–3949.
EEO.—Jan T. Austin, N–4306, 693–3370.
Field Operations.—Jack Rapport, room C–4517, 693–3690.
Financial and Administrative Management.—Anna Goddard, room N–4470, 693–2800.
Job Corps.—Richard C. Trigg, room N–4463, 693–3000.
National Programs.—John R. Beverly III, room N–5306, 693–3540.
National Response.—Shirley M. Smith, room N–5422, 693–3500.
Outreach.—Jaime Fall, room N–4665, 693–2958.
Performance and Results.—Eric R. Johnson, room N–5306, 693–3031.
Policy Development, Evaluation and Research.—Maria Kniesler Flynn, room N–5637, 693–3700.
Technology.—Peter J. Brunner, room S–5206, 693–3420.
Workforce Investment.—Grace A. Kilbane, room S–4231, 693–3980.
Workforce Security.—Cheryl Atkinson, room S–4231, 693–3200.

MINE SAFETY AND HEALTH ADMINISTRATION

1100 Wilson Boulevard, Arlington, VA 22209–3939, phone (202) 693–9414, fax 693–9401, http://www.msha.gov

Assistant Secretary.—Dave D. Lauriski.
Deputy Assistant Secretaries: John R. Caylor, John R. Correll.
Chief of Staff.—Loretta M. Herrington.
Special Assistant.—Mark G. Ellis, 693–9406.

Director, Office of Information and Public Affairs.—Katherine Snyder, 693–9422.
Legislative and Policy Analyst.—Regina M. Flahie, 693–9435.
Administrator for—
Coal Mine Safety and Health.—Ray McKinney, 693–9502.
Metal and Nonmetal Mine Safety and Health.—Robert M. Friend, 693–9603.
Director for—
Administration and Management Office.—David L. Meyer, 693–9802.
Assessments Office.—Steve Webber, 693–9702.
Educational Policy and Development Office.—Jeffrey A. Duncan, 693–9572.
Program Evaluation and Information Resources.—George M. Fesak, 693–9752.
Standards, Regulations and Variances.—Marvin W. Nichols, Jr., 693–9442.
Technical Support.—Mark E. Skiles, 693–9472.

VETERANS' EMPLOYMENT AND TRAINING SERVICE

Frances Perkins Building, Room S–1313, phone 693–4700

Assistant Secretary.—Frederico Juarbe, Jr.
Deputy Assistant Secretary.—Charles S. Ciccolella.
Executive Assistant.—John Muckelbauer.
Special Assistant.—Vicki Sinnett.
Director, Management, Budget, and Agency Administrative Officer.—Harry Puente-Duany, 693–4750.
Operations and Programs.—Gordon Burke, 693–4707.
Chief of:
Compliance Assistance and Investigations Branch.—Norm Lance, 693–5731.
Employment and Training Program Division.—Robert Wilson, 693–4719.
Public Information Specialist.—[Vacant].
Director, Strategic Planning.—Ronald Drach, 693–4749.

REGIONAL OFFICES

Boston:
Administrator.—David Houle, (617) 565–2080.
Philadelphia:
Administrator.—John W. Hortiz, Jr., (215) 861–5390.
Atlanta:
Administrator.—William J. Bolls, Jr., (404) 562–2305.
Denver:
Administrator.—Ronald J. Bachman, (303) 844–1175.
Dallas:
Administrator.—Lester L. Williams, Jr., (214) 767–4987.
San Francisco:
Administrator.—Tom Pearson (acting), (360) 438–4600.

BUREAU OF LABOR STATISTICS

Postal Square Building, Suite 4040, 2 Massachusetts Avenue NE 20212, phone 691–7800

Commissioner.—Kathleen P. Utgoff, suite 4040, 691–7800.
Deputy Commissioner.—Lois L. Orr, 691–7802.
Associate Commissioners, Office of:
Administration.—Daniel J. Lacey, suite 4060, 691–7777.
Compensation and Working Conditions.—Katrina Reut, suite 4130, 691–6300.
Employment and Unemployment Statistics.—John M. Galvin, suite 4945, 691–6400.
Field Operations.—Robert A. Gaddie (acting), suite 2935, 691–5800.
Prices and Living Conditions.—Kenneth V. Dalton, suite 3120, 691–6960.
Productivity and Technology.—Marilyn E. Manser, suite 2150, 691–5600.
Publications and Special Studies.—Deborah P. Klein, suite 4110, 691–5900.
Survey Methods Research.—Stephen H. Cohen, suite 4080, 691–7372.
Technology and Survey Processing.—Thomas P. Zuromskis.

Assistant Commissioner, Office of:

Compensation Levels and Trends.—Mary McCarthy, suite 4130, 691–6302.
Consumer Prices and Price Indexes.—John D. Greenlees, suite 3130, 691–6950.
Current Employment Analysis.—Philip L. Rones, suite 4675, 691–6388.
Industrial Prices and Price Indexes.—Irwin B. Gerduk, suite 3840, 691–7700.
Industry Employment Statistics.—George S. Werking, suite 4840, 691–6528.
International Prices.—[Vacant].
Occupational Statistics and Employment Projections.—Michael W. Harrigan.
Safety, Health, and Working Conditions.—[Vacant].

Director of:

Survey Processing.—John D. Sinks, suite 5025, 691–7603.
Technology and Computing Services.—Rick Kryger (acting), suite 5025, 691–7606.

DEPARTMENT OF HEALTH AND HUMAN SERVICES

200 Independence Avenue SW 20201, http://www.hhs.gov

TOMMY G. THOMPSON, Secretary of Health and Human Services; born on November 19, 1941, in Elroy, WI; education: B.S., 1963, and J.D., 1966, University of Wisconsin-Madison; public service: Wisconsin State Assembly, 1966–1986; elected Assistant Assembly Minority Leader in 1973, and Assembly Minority Leader in 1981; Governor of Wisconsin, 1987–2001; has served as Chairman of the National Governors' Association, Midwestern Governors' Conference, and the Education Commission of the States; awards: Anti-Defamation League's Distinguished Public Service Award; Governing Magazine's Public Official of the Year Award; and the Horatio Alger Award; family: married to Sue Ann; three children; nominated by President George W. Bush to become the 19th Secretary of Health and Human Services, and was confirmed by the U.S. Senate on January 24, 2001.

OFFICE OF THE SECRETARY

Secretary of Health and Human Services.—Tommy G. Thompson, (202) 690–7000.
Staff Assistants to the Secretary: Linda Gyles, Mary Gerald.
Counselor to the Secretary.—Ladd Wiley, 690–7741.
Senior Advisor to the Secretary.—Mary Kay Mantho, 690–5400.

OFFICE OF THE DEPUTY SECRETARY

Deputy Secretary.—Claude A. Allen, (202) 690–6133.
Chief of Staff.—A. Scott Whitaker.
Deputy Chiefs of Staff: Andrew Knapp, Laura Lawlor, 690–5400.
Executive Secretary.—Ann Agnew, 690–5627.
Deputy Executive Secretary.—Dick Eisinger, 690–5627.
Director, Office of:
Global Health Affairs.—William Steiger, 690–6174.
Intergovernmental Affairs.—Regina Schofield, 690–6060.
Chair, Departmental Appeals Board.—Cecilia Sparks Ford, 690–5501.

ASSISTANT SECRETARY FOR LEGISLATION

Assistant Secretary-Designate.—Jennifer Young (acting).
Deputy Assistant Secretary for—
Congressional Liaison.—Paul Powell, 690–6786.
Health.—Jennifer Young, 690–7450.
Human Services.—Raissa Downs, 690–6311.
Planning and Budget.—Greg Hampton, 690–7627.

ASSISTANT SECRETARY FOR BUDGET, TECHNOLOGY AND FINANCE

Assistant Secretary.—Kerry Weems (acting), 690–6396.
Deputy Assistant Secretary for—
Budget.—William Beldon (acting), 690–7846.
Finance.—George H. Strader, 690–7084.
Information Resources Management.—Melissa Chapman, 690–6162.
Performance and Planning.—Kathleen Heuer, 690–6061.

ASSISTANT SECRETARY FOR PLANNING AND EVALUATION

Assistant Secretary.—William F. Raub (acting), 690–7858.
Principal Deputy Assistant Secretary.—William F. Raub, 690–7858.
Deputy Assistant Secretary for—
Disability, Aging, & Long Term Care Policy.—John Hoff, 690–6443.

Health Policy.—Ann-Marie Lynch, 690–6870.
Human Services Policy.—Don Winstead, 690–7409.
Science and Data Policy.—Jim Scanlon (acting), 690–5874.

ASSISTANT SECRETARY FOR ADMINISTRATION AND MANAGEMENT

Assistant Secretary.—Ed Sontag, 690–7431, fax 401–5207.
Principal Deputy Assistant Secretary.—Evelyn M. White, 690–7431.
Special Assistant.—Catherine Tyrell, 690–7431.
Deputy Assistant Secretary for Human Resources.—Rosemary Taylor, 690–6191.
Executive Officer, Office of the Secretary Executive Office.—Karen Norrell, 690–7591.
Director, Office of:
Acquisition Management and Policy.—Marc Weisman (acting), 690–8554.
Competitive Sourcing.—Robert Noonan (acting), 205–4650.
Grants Management Policy.—Charles Havekost (acting), 690–8443.
Secretary Equal Employment Office.—Barbara Barski-Carrow, 619–3677.

ASSISTANT SECRETARY FOR PUBLIC AFFAIRS

Assistant Secretary.—Kevin Keane, 690–7850.
Deputy Assistant Secretary for—
Policy and Communication.—Tracy Self, 690–7850.
Media.—Bill Pierce, 690–6343; fax 690–6247.
Director, Division of:
Freedom of Information/Privacy.—Ross Cirrincione, 690–7453.
News.—P. Campbell Gardett, 690–6343.

OFFICE FOR CIVIL RIGHTS

Director.—Richard Campanelli, 619–0403.
Principal Deputy Director.—Robinsue Frohboese, 619–0403.
Director for—
Resource Management Division.—Steven Melov, 619–0503.
Voluntary Compliance and Outreach Division.—Johnny Nelson, 619–2742.
Program, Policy and Training Division.—Claudia Schlosberg, 619–0553.
Senior Advisors, HIPPA Privacy Office: Kathleen Fyffe, Susan McAndrew, 205–8725.
Toll Free Voice Number (Nationwide)—1–800–368–1019.
Toll Free TDD Number (Nationwide)—1–800–527–7697.

OFFICE OF PUBLIC HEALTH AND SCIENCE

Assistant Secretary for Health.—Richard H. Carmona, M.D. (acting), (202) 690–7694.
The Surgeon General.—Richard H. Carmona, M.D., 443–4000.
Principal Deputy Assistant Secretary for Health.—Cristina Beato, M.D., 690–7694.
Deputy Assistant Secretary for Health.—Howard Zucker, M.D., (designee), 690–7694.
Deputy Assistant Secretary, Office of:
Minority Health.—Nathan Stinson, 443–5084.
Population Affairs.—Alma Golden, M.D., (301) 594–4001.
Women's Health.—Wanda Jones, 690–7650.
Disease Prevention and Health Promotion.—Carter Blakey (acting), (202) 401–6295.
HIV/AIDS Policy.—Christopher Bates (acting), (202) 690–5560.
Research Integrity.—Christopher Pascal, 443–3400.
President's Council on Physical Fitness and Sports.—Penelope Royall (acting), (202) 690–9000.

ASSISTANT SECRETARY FOR PUBLIC HEALTH EMERGENCY PREPAREDNESS

Assistant Secretary.—Jerome M. Hauer, 401–5840, fax 690–6512.
Senior Advisor.—James Reddig, 401–5833.
Director, Office of:
Planning and Emergency Response Coordination.—Robert Blitzer, 205–0872.
Research and Development Coordination.—Dr. Phillip Russell, 401–4861, fax 690–7412.
State and Local Preparedness.—Lily O. Engstrom, 205–2727.

OFFICE OF THE GENERAL COUNSEL

fax [Immediate Office] 690–7998, fax [Admin. Office] 690–5452

General Counsel.—Alex M. Azar, 690–7741.
Deputy General Counsel.—David S. Cade, 690–7721.
Legal Counsel.—E. Peter Urbanowicz, 690–7741.
Program Review.—Paula Stannard.
Regulations.—Stewart G. Simonson.
Associate General Counsel for—
Centers for Medicare and Medicaid Division.—Sheree Kanner, 619–0300.
Children, Family and Aging Division.—Robert Keith, 690–8005.
Civil Rights Division.—George Lyon, 619–0900.
Ethics Division/Special Counsel for Ethics.—Edgar Swindell, 690–7258.
Food and Drug Division.—Daniel Troy, (301) 827–1137.
General Law Division.—Katherine Drews, 619–0150.
Legislation Division.—Sondra Steigen Wallace, 690–7773.
Public Health Division.—[Vacant].

OFFICE OF THE INSPECTOR GENERAL

330 Independence Avenue, SW., 20201

Inspector General.—Dennis Durquette (acting), 619–3148.
Principal Deputy Inspector General.—Dennis Durquette (acting), 619–3148.
Chief Counsel to the Inspector General.—Lewis Morris, 619–0335.
Deputy Inspector General for—
Audit Services.—George Reeb (acting), 619–3155.
Evaluation and Inspections.—Joe Venegrin, 619–0480.
Investigations.—Vicki Shepard, 619–3208.
Management and Policy.—Brian Carman (acting), 619–3081.

ADMINISTRATION ON AGING

1 Massachusetts Avenue, SW., 20001

Assistant Secretary for Aging.—Josefina G. Carbonell, (202) 401–4541.
Deputy Assistant Secretary for—
Policy and Programs.—[Vacant], 401–4634.
Management.—Mike Magano, 357–3430.
Director for:
Office of Evaluation.—Frank Burns, 357–3516.
Executive Secretariat.—Harry Posman, 357–3540.
Center for Communications and Consumer Services.—Carol Crecy, 401–4541.
Center for Planning and Policy Development.—John Wren, 357–3460.
Center for Wellness and Community-Based Services.—[Vacant].

ADMINISTRATION FOR CHILDREN AND FAMILIES

370 L'Enfant Promenade SW., 20447

Assistant Secretary.—Wade F. Horn, (202) 401–9200.
Principal Deputy Assistant Secretary.—Christopher Gersten, 401–5180.
Deputy Assistant Secretary for—
Administration.—Curtis L. Coy, 401–9238.
Policy and External Affairs.—Martin Dannefelser, 401–6947.
Director, Regional Operations Staff.—Diann Dawson, 401–4802.
Commissioner for Administration on:
Children, Youth, and Families.—Joan E. Ohl, 205–8347.
Developmental Disabilities.—Patricia Morrissey, 690–6590.
Native Americans.—Quanah Stamps, 401–5590.
Associate Commissioner for—
Child Care Bureau.—Shannon Christian, 690–6782.
Children's Bureau.—Susan Orr, 205–8618.
Family and Youth Services Bureau.—Harry Wilson, 205–8102.
Head Start Bureau.—Wendy Hill, 205–8573.

Director, Office of:
Child Support Enforcement.—Sherri Heller, 401–9370.
Community Services.—Clarence Carter, 401–9333.
Family Assistance.—Andrew Bush, 401–9275.
Legislative Affairs and Budget.—Madeline Mocko, 401–9223.
Planning, Research and Evaluation.—Howard Rolston, 401–9220.
Public Affairs.—[Vacant].
Refugee Resettlement.—Nguyen Van Hanh.

AGENCY FOR TOXIC SUBSTANCES AND DISEASE REGISTRY

1600 Clifton Road NE, Atlanta, GA 30333

Administrator.—Julie L. Gerberding, (404) 639–7000.
Deputy Administrator.—David W. Fleming.
Assistant Administrator.—Henry Falk, 498–0004.
Deputy Assistant Administrator.—Peter J. McCumisky.

CENTERS FOR DISEASE CONTROL AND PREVENTION

1600 Clifton Road NE, Atlanta, GA 30333

Director.—Julie L. Gerberding, (404) 639–7000.
Deputy Directors for Public Health Science: David W. Fleming, F. Ed Thompson.
Chief Operating Officer.—William H. Gimson.
Chief of Staff.—Verla Neslund (acting).
Senior Advisor for Strategy and Innovation.—Kathy Cahill.
Associate Director for—
Communication.—Vicki Freimuth, 639–7290.
Global Health.—Steven Blount, 639–7420.
Minority Health.—Walter W. Williams, 639–7210.
Science.—Dixie E. Snider, 639–7240.
Washington.—Donald E. Shriber, (202) 690–8598.
Women's Health.—Yvonne Green, 639–7230.
Director, National Center for—
Birth Defects and Developmental Disabilities.—Jose Cordero, (770) 488–7150.
Chronic Disease Prevention and Health Promotion.—James S. Marks, (770) 488–5401.
Environmental Health.—Richard J. Jackson, (770) 488–7000.
Health Statistics.—Edward J. Sondik, (301) 458–4500.
HIV, STD, and TB Prevention.—Harold Jaffe, (404) 639–8000.
Infectious Disease.—James M. Hughes, (404) 639–3401.
Injury Prevention and Control.—Suzanne Binder, (770) 488–4696.
Director for—
National Immunization.—Walter A. Orenstein, (404) 639–8200.
National Institute for Occupational Safety and Health.—John Howard, (202) 401–6997.
Director, Program Office of:
Epidemiology.—Stephen B. Thacker, 639–3661.
Public Health Program.—Suzanne M. Smith, (770) 488–2402.
Director, Office of:
Equal Employment Opportunity.—[Vacant].
Health and Safety.—Robert H. Hill (acting), 639–2453.
Management and Operations.—Joseph R. Carter, 630–7010.
Program Planning and Evaluation.—Nancy Cheal (acting), 639–7060.

CENTERS FOR MEDICARE AND MEDICAID SERVICES

200 Independence Avenue, SW., 20201

Administrator.—Thomas Scully, (202) 690–6726.
Chief Operating Officer/Deputy Administrator.—Leslie Norwalk, (410) 786–3151.
Chief, Office of Actuary.—Rick Foster, (410) 786–6374.
Press Office.—Rob Sweezy, 690–6145.
Director, Office of:
Financial Standards and Quality.—Sean Tunis, (410) 786–6841.
Communications and Operations Support.—Jacquelyn White, 690–8390.
Equal Opportunity and Civil Rights.—Ramon Suris-Fernandez, (410) 786–5110.

Legislation.—Robert Foreman, 690–5960.
Strategic Planning.—Stu Guterman, 690–7063.
Director, Center for—
Beneficiary Choices.—Gail McGrath, (410) 786–4280.
Medicare Management.—Tom Grissom, 205–2505.
Medicaid and State Operations.—Dennis Smith, 690–7428.
Director, Office of:
Internal Customer Support.—Brenda Sykes, (410) 786–1051.
Financial Management.—Michelle Snyder, (410) 786–5448.
Information Services.—Gary Christoph, Ph.D., (410) 786–1800.
Administrator for—
Northeastern Consortium.—Judy Berek, (212) 264–4488.
Southern Consortium.—Rose Crum-Johnson, (404) 562–7150.
Midwestern Consortium.—Joe Tilghman, (816) 426–5233.
Western Consortium.—Linda Fuiz, (303) 844–2111.

FOOD AND DRUG ADMINISTRATION

5600 Fishers Lane, Rockville, MD 20857

Commissioner.—Mark B. McClellan, M.D., Ph.D., (301) 827–2410.
Deputy Commissioner.—Lester M. Crawford, DVM, Ph.D., 827–3310.
Principal Associate Commissioner.—Murray M. Lumpkin, M.D., 827–5709.
Chief Counsel.—Daniel E. Troy, (301) 827–1137.
Senior Advisor for Policy and Operations.—Serina N. Vandegrift, 827–9252.
Chief Mediator and Ombudsman.—[Vacant], 827–3390.
Associate Commissioner for—
Policy and Planning.—William K. Hubbard, 827–3370.
Management and Systems.—Jeffrey M. Weber, 255–6762.
Legislation.—Amit Sachdev, 827–0087.
Regulatory Affairs.—John Taylor, 827–3101.
Assistant Commissioner for—
Policy.—Jeffrey Shuren, 827–3360.
Planning.—Theresa Mullin, Ph.D., 827–5292.
Public Affairs.—Lawrence Bachorik, Ph.D., 827–6350.
Director, Center for—
Biologic Evaluation and Research.—Jesse Goodman, M.D., 827–0372.
Devices and Radiological Health.—David W. Feigal, M.D., 827–7975.
Drug Evaluation and Research.—Janet Woodcock, M.D., 594–5400.
Food Safety and Applied Nutrition.—Joseph A. Levitt, 436–1600.
Toxicological Research.—Daniel E. Casciano, Ph.D. (870) 543–7517.
Washington Operations, NCTR.—James J. MacGregor, 827–6696.
Veterinary Medicine.—Stephen Sundlof, D.V.M., Ph.D., 827–2950.
Director, Office of:
Executive Secretariat.—LaJuana Caldwell, 827–4450.
Executive Operations.—Linda Brna, 827–3440.
Equal Opportunity.—[Vacant], 827–4833.
Financial Management.—Helen Horn, 827–5001.
Human Resources and Management Services.—Mary L. Babcock, 827–4120.
Orphan Products Development.—Marlene Haffner, M.D., 827–3666.
Assistant Commissioner for—
International Programs.—Melinda Plaisier, 827–4480.
Special Health Issues.—Theresa A. Toigo, 827–4460.
Women's Health.—Susan Wood, Ph.D., 827–0305.

HEALTH RESOURCES AND SERVICES ADMINISTRATION

5600 Fishers Lane, Rockville, MD 20857

Administrator.—Elizabeth M. Duke, (301) 443–2216.
Deputy Administrator.—[Vacant].
Principal Advisor to the Administrator.—Steve Smith, 443–0506.
Chief Medical Officer.—William A. Robinson, 443–0458.
Associate Administrator for Management and Program Support.—John L. Nelson, 443–2053.

Associate Administrator, Bureau of:
Health Professions.—Kerry Nesseler, 443–5794.
HIV/AIDS.—Deborah Parham, 443–1993.
Maternal and Child Health.—Peter C. van Dyck, 443–2170.
Primary Health Care.—Sam S. Shekar, 443–4110.
Director, Office of:
Communications.—Kay Templeton Garvey, 443–3376.
Equal Opportunity and Civil Rights.—Patricia Mackey, 443–5636.
Information Resources Technology.—Catherine Flickinger, 443–9794.
Legislation.—Patricia Stroup, 443–1890.
Minority Health.—M. June Horner, 443–2964.
Planning and Evaluation.—Lyman van Nostrand, 443–2460.
Rural Health Policy.—Marcia Brand, 443–0835.
Special Programs.—Remy Aronoff (acting), 443–4134.

INDIAN HEALTH SERVICE

801 Thompson Avenue, Rockville, MD 20852

Director.—Charles W. Grim, DDS (acting), (301) 443–1083.
Senior Adviser to the Director.—W.L. Buck Martin.
Deputy Director.—Michel Lincoln.
Chief Medical Officer.—W. Craig Vanderwagen, M.D. (acting).
Director of:
Legislative Affairs.—Michael Mahsetky, 443–7261.
Equal Employment Opportunity.—Cecelia Heftel, 443–1108.
Field Operations.—Don J. Davis, 443–1083.
Headquarters Operations.—Duane Jeanotte, 443–1083.
Urban Indian Health Program.—James F. Cussen, 443–4680.
Director, Office of:
Public Affairs.—Tony Kendrick, 443–3593.
Tribal Programs.—Douglas P. Black, 443–1104.
Self-Governance.—Paula K. Williams, 443–7821.

NATIONAL INSTITUTES OF HEALTH

9000 Rockville Pike, Bethesda, MD 20892

Director.—Elias Zerhouni, (301) 496–2433.
Deputy Director.—Raynard S. Kingston, M.D., Ph.D., 496–7322.
Director/Executive Secretriat.—Dale Johnson (acting), 496–1461.
Executive Officer, Office of the Director.—John Jarman, 594–8231.
Legal Advisor, Office of the General Counsel.—Barbara McGarey, 496–6043.
Deputy Director, Office of:
Extramural Research.—Belinda Seto, Ph.D. (acting), 496–1096.
Intramural Research.—Michael M. Gottesman, M.D., 496–1921.
Management.—Charles Leasure, 496–3271.
Senior Advisor to the Director.—Ruth L. Kirschstein, M.D.
Associate Director for—
Administration.—Leamon Lee, Ph.D., (301) 496–4466.
AIDS Research.—Jack Whitescarver, Ph.D. (acting), 496–0357.
Behavioral and Social Science Research.—Virginia Cain, Ph.D. (acting), 402–1146.
Budget.—Donald Poppke (acting), 496–4477
Communications.—John Burklow, 496–4461.
Disease Prevention.—Barnett S. Kramer, M.D., M.P.H., 496–1508.
Legislative Policy and Analysis.—Marc Smolonsky, 496–3471.
Research on Women's Health.—Vivian W. Pinn, M.D., 402–1770.
Research Services.—Stephen A. Ficca, 496–2215.
Science Policy.—Lana Skirboll, Ph.D., 496–2122.
Director, Office of:
Community Liaison.—Thomas Gallagher, 496–3931.
Equal Opportunity.—Lawrence N. Self, 496–6301.
Human Resource Management.—Robert Hosenfeld, 496–3592.
Technology Transfer.—Mark Rohrbaugh, Ph.D., J.D., 594–7700.

Director of:
Fogarty International Center.—Gerald T. Keusch, 496–1415.
Warren Grant Magnuson Clinical Center.—John I. Gallin, M.D., 496–4114.
National Library of Medicine.—Donald A.B. Lindberg, M.D., 496–6221.
Director, National Center for—
Complementary and Alternative Medicine.—Stephen E. Straus, M.D., 435–5042.
Minority Health and Health Disparities.—John Ruffin, Ph.D., 402–2515.
Research Resources.—Judith L. Vaitukaitis, M.D., 496–5793.
Director, Center for—
Information Technology.—Alan S. Graeff, 496–5703.
Scientific Review.—Ellie Ehrenfeld, Ph.D., 435–1114.
Director, National Institute for—
Aging.—Richard J. Hodes, M.D., 496–9265.
Alcohol Abuse and Alcoholism.—T.K. Li, M.D., 443–3885.
Allergy and Infectious Diseases.—Anthony S. Fauci, M.D., 496–2263.
Arthritis, Musculoskeletal and Skin Diseases.—Stephen I. Katz, M.D., Ph.D., 496–4353.
Biomedical Imaging and Bioengineering.—Roderic Pettigrew, Ph.D., M.D., 435–6138.
Cancer.—Andrew von Eschenbach, M.D., 496–5615.
Child Health and Human Development.—Duane F. Alexander, M.D., 496–3454.
Deafness and Other Communication Disorders.—James F. Battey, Jr., 402–0900.
Dental and Craniofacial Research.—Lawrence Tabak, D.D.S., Ph.D., 496–3571.
Diabetes, Digestive and Kidney Diseases.—Allen M. Spiegel, M.D., 496–5877.
Drug Abuse.—Nora Volkow, M.D., 443–6480.
Environmental Health Sciences.—Kenneth Olden, Ph.D., (919) 541–3201.
Eye.—Paul A. Sieving, M.D., Ph.D., 496–2234.
General Medical Sciences.—Judith Greenberg, Ph.D. (acting), 594–2172.
Heart, Lung and Blood.—Claude Lenfant, M.D., 496–5166.
Human Genome Research.—Francis Collins, M.D., Ph.D., 496–0844.
Mental Health.—Thomas Insel, M.D., 443–3673.
Neurological Disorders and Stroke.—Audrey S. Penn, M.D., 496–9746.
Nursing Research.—Patricia A. Grady, Ph.D., R.N., 496–3885.

PROGRAM SUPPORT CENTER

5600 Fishers Lane, Rockville, MD 20857

Deputy Assistant Secretary.—Mike Blank, (301) 443–3921.
Senior Advisor.—John Sigmon.
Chief Financial Officer.—Tom Greene, 443–1478.
Director of:
Office of Operations.—Catherine Kualii, 443–0034.
Administrative Operations Service.—Heather Ransom (acting), 443–2516.
Budget and Management.—Jerrilyn Anderson, 443–1486.
Financial Management Service.—Tom Greene, 443–1478.
Human Resources Management.—Nancy Ward, 443–1200.
Office of Information Technology.—Jack Stoute (acting), 443–2365.
Federal Operational Health.—John Hisle, 594–0250.

SUBSTANCE ABUSE AND MENTAL HEALTH SERVICES ADMINISTRATION

5600 Fishers Lane Rockville, MD 20857

Administrator.—Charles Curie, 443–4795.
Deputy Administrator.—[Vacant].
Director, Equal Employment Opportunity.—Carmen Martinez, 443–4447.
Associate Administrator for—
Communications.—Mark Weber, 443–8956.
Minority Health.—DeLoris James-Hunter, 443–0365.
Policy and Program Coordination.—Daryl Kade, 443–4111.
Director, Center for—
Mental Health Services.—Gail Hutchings (acting), 443–0001.
Substance Abuse Prevention.—Beverly Watts Davis, 443–0365.
Substance Abuse Treatment.—H. Westley Clark, 443–5700.
Director, Office of:
Program Services.—Richard T. Kopanda, Executive Officer, 443–3875.
Applied Studies.—Donald Goldstone, 443–1038.

DEPARTMENT OF HOUSING AND URBAN DEVELOPMENT

Robert C. Weaver Federal Building, 451 Seventh Street, SW., 20410, phone (202) 708–1112, http://www.hud.gov

MEL MARTINEZ, Secretary of Housing and Urban Development; born on October 23, 1946, in Sagua La Grande, Cuba; in 1962, he came to the U.S. as part of the Catholic humanitarian effort Operation Pedro Pan; Catholic charitable groups then provided him temporary homes at two youth facilities; he was reunited with his family, in 1966, in Orlando, FL; education: B.A., Florida State University; law degree, Florida State University College of Law; professional: Attorney; law practice, 1973–1998; community service: Vice President, Board of Catholic Charities of the Orlando Diocese; active in numerous other community and charitable activities; public service: Chairman, Orange County, FL, 1998–2001; family: married to Kitty; three children: Lauren, John, and Andrew; nominated by President George W. Bush to become the 12th Secretary of Housing and Urban Development, and was confirmed by the U.S. Senate on January 23, 2001.

OFFICE OF THE SECRETARY

Secretary of Housing and Urban Development.—Mel Martinez, room 10000, 708–0417.
Chief of Staff.—Frank R. Jimenez, 708–2713.
Special Assistant to the Secretary.—Terry Couch.
Special Assistant to the Chief of Staff.—Pauline Lore, 708–2713.
Deputy Chief of Staff.—Phil Musser, 708–1781.
Deputy Chief of Staff for Policy and Programs.—Oscar Anderson, 708–1865.
Director, Center for Faith Based and Community Initiatives.—Ryan Streeter, 708–2404.
Executive Office for Administrative Operations and Management.—Marcella Belt, 708–3750.
Administrative Officer.—Marianne C. DeConti, 708–3750.

OFFICE OF THE DEPUTY SECRETARY

Deputy Secretary.—Alphonso Jackson, room 10100, 708–0123.
Staff Assistant.—Kimberly Snyder.
Special Assistant to the Deputy Secretary.—Margaret Lara.
Senior Advisor to the Deputy Secretary.—Camille Pierce.

ASSISTANT TO THE DEPUTY SECRETARY FOR FIELD POLICY AND MANAGEMENT

Assistant Deputy Secretary.—Pamela H. Patenaude, room 7106, 708–2426.

SMALL AND DISADVANTAGED BUSINESS UTILIZATION

Director.—Jo Baylor, room 3130, 708–1428.

OFFICE OF FAIR HOUSING AND EQUAL OPPORTUNITY

Assistant Secretary.—Carolyn Y. Peoples, room 5100, 708–4252.
General Deputy Assistant Secretary.—Floyd May.
Director, Office of Policy and Program Evaluation.—Bryan Greene, 708–1145.
Deputy Assistant Secretary for—
Enforcement Programs.—David Engel, 619–8046.
Operations and Management.—Karen A. Newton, 708–0768.
Economic Opportunity, Monitoring and Compliance.—[Vacant].

OFFICE OF ADMINISTRATION

Assistant Secretary/Chief Information Officer.—Vickers B. Meadows, room 10156, 708–0940.
General Deputy Assistant Secretary for Administration.—Fred Steckler.
Chief Technology Officer.—Gloria Parker, 708–1008.
Director, Office of the Executive Secretariat.—Cynthia A. O'Connor, 708–3054.
Chief Procurement Officer.—Dexter J. Sidney, 708–0600.
Deputy Assistant Secretary for—
Human Resource Management.—Barbara Edwards, 708–3946.
Operations.—Sherman R. Lancefield, 708–2268.

OFFICE OF GENERAL COUNSEL

General Counsel.—Richard A. Hauser, room 10214, 708–2244.
Deputy General Counsel for—
Equal Opportunity and Administrative Law.—Kathleen Koch, 708–3250.
Programs and Regulations.—[Vacant].
Litigation.—William C. White (acting), 708–0282.
Housing Finance Operations.—George L. Weidenfeller, 708–2864.
Associate General Counsel for—
Assisted Housing and Community Development.—Robert S. Kenison, 708–0212.
Finance and Regulatory Enforcement.—John P. Kennedy, 708–2203.
Human Resources.—Sam E. Hutchinson, 708–0888.
Insured Housing.—John J. Daly, 708–1274.
Legislation and Regulations.—Camille E. Acevedo, 708–1793.
Litigation.—Carole W. Wilson, 708–0300.
Fair Housing.—Harry L. Carey, 708–0570.
Director, Departmental Enforcement Center.—Jon L. Gant, 708–3354.

OFFICE OF COMMUNITY PLANNING AND DEVELOPMENT

Assistant Secretary.—Roy Bernardi, room 7100, 708–2690.
General Deputy Assistant Secretary.—Nelson Bregon (acting).
Deputy Assistant Secretary for—
Special Initiatives.—Anna Maria Farias, 708–2111.
Operations.—William Eargle, Jr., 708–2186.
Economic Development.—Donald Mains, 708–4091.
Special Needs.—Patricia Carlile, 708–1590.
Grant Programs.—Nelson Bregon, 708–1506.

OFFICE OF THE CHIEF FINANCIAL OFFICER

Chief Financial Officer.—Angela Antonelli, room 10234, 708–1946.
Deputy Chief Financial Officer.—De W. Ritchie.
Assistant Chief Financial Officer for—
Accounting.—Margaret E. White, 708–4474.
Financial Management.—James M. Martin, 708–0638.
Budget.—David M. Gibbons, 708–3296.
Systems.—Hartley M. Jones, 708–4474.

OFFICE OF THE INSPECTOR GENERAL

Inspector General.—Kenneth M. Donohue, Sr., room 8256, 708–0430.
Deputy Inspector General.—Michael P. Stephens.
Assistant Inspector General, Office of Audit.—James Heist, 708–0364.
Counsel to the Inspector General, Office of Legal Counsel.—Bryan Saddler, 708–1613.
Assistant Inspector General, Office of:
Management and Policy.—Dennis A. Raschka, 708–0006.
Investigation.—R. Joe Haban, 708–0390.

OFFICE OF HOUSING

Assistant Secretary/Federal Housing Commissioner.—John C. Weicher, 708–2601.
General Deputy Assistant Secretary.—Sean Cassidy.
Deputy Assistant Secretary for—
Multifamily Housing Programs.—Stillman Knight, 708–2495.
Single Family Housing.—John J. Connts (acting), 708–3175.
Regulatory Affairs and Manufactured Housing.—[Vacant], 708–6401.
Housing Operations.—Michael F. Hill, room 9138, 708–1104.
Finance and Budget.—Margaret A. Young, 708–2601.

ASSISTANT SECRETARY FOR CONGRESSIONAL AND INTERGOVERNMENTAL RELATIONS

Assistant Secretary.—Steven B. Nesmith, room 10120, 708–0005.
Deputy Assistant Secretary for—
Congressional Relations.—William M. Himpler, 708–0380.
Intergovernmental Relations.—Gregory Y. Hill.
Legislation.—L. Carter Cornick, 708–0005.

OFFICE OF LEAD HAZARD CONTROL

Director.—David E. Jacobs, room P3206, 755–4973.

OFFICE OF FEDERAL HOUSING ENTERPRISE OVERSIGHT

Director.—Armando Falcon, 414–6923.

OFFICE OF PUBLIC AND INDIAN HOUSING

Assistant Secretary.—Michael Liu, room 4100, 708–0950.
General Deputy Assistant Secretary.—Paula Blunt.
Deputy Assistant Secretary, for—
Policy, Programs and Legislative Initiatives.—Bessie Kong (acting), 708–0713.
Native American Programs.—Rodger J. Boyd, 708–7914.
Administration and Budget.—Robert Dalzell (acting), 708–0440.
Public Housing and Voucher Programs.—William Russell, 708–1380.
Troubled Agency Recovery.—David R. Ziaya (acting), 708–4016.
Public Housing Investments.—Milan Ozdinec, 708–8812.

OFFICE OF POLICY DEVELOPMENT AND RESEARCH

Assistant Secretary.—Alberto F. Trevino, room 8100, 708–1600.
General Deputy Assistant Secretary.—Darlene F. Williams.
Deputy Assistant Secretary for—
Economic Affairs.—Harold Bunce 708–3080.
International Affairs.—Shannon Sorzano, 708–0770.
Policy Development.—Christopher Lord, 708–3896.
Research, Evaluation and Monitoring.—[Vacant].

ASSISTANT SECRETARY FOR PUBLIC AFFAIRS

Assistant Secretary.—Diane Leneghan Tomb, room 10130, 708–0980.
General Deputy Assistant Secretary.—Douglas P. Duvall.
Director of Press Relations.—Kelley Keeler, 708–0685.

GOVERNMENT NATIONAL MORTGAGE ASSOCIATION

President.—Ronald A. Rosenfeld, room 6100, 708–0926.
Executive Vice President.—George S. Anderson.

Senior Vice President, Office of:
Management Operations.—Cheryl W. Owens, 708–2648.
Finance.—Michael J. Najjum, Jr., 401–2064.
Vice President, Office of:
Mortgage-Backed Securities.—Theodore B. Foster, 708–4141.
Program Operations.—Thomas R. Weakland, 708–2884.
Capital Markets.—Michael J. Frenz, 401–8970.

OFFICE OF MULTIFAMILY HOUSING ASSISTANCE RESTRUCTURING

Director.—Charles (Hank) Williams, 708–0001.

REAL ESTATE ASSESSMENT CENTER

Director.—Elizabeth A. Hanson, 708–4924.

OFFICE OF DEPARTMENTAL OPERATIONS AND COORDINATION

Director.—Frank L. Davis, room 2124, 708–2806.
Deputy Director.—Inez Banks-DuBose.
Coordinator, Southwest Border region, Colonias & Migrant/Farmworker Initiatives.—Maria S. Ortiz, 708–3086.

OFFICE OF DEPARTMENTAL EQUAL EMPLOYMENT OPPORTUNITY

Director.—William C. King, room 2106, 708–3362.

FIELD OFFICES

Boston, MA.—Kevin Keogh, Regional Director, Federal Building, Room 301, 10 Causeway Street, Boston, MA 02222–1092, (617) 994–8200.
Bangor, ME.—Loren W. Cole, Field Office Director, 202 Harlow Street, Chase Building, Suite 101, Bangor, ME 04402–1384, (207) 945–0467.
Burlington, VT.—Michael McNamara, Field Office Director, 159 Bank Street, Burlington, VT 05401, (802) 951–6290.
Hartford, CT.—Julie Fagan, Field Office Director, One Corporate Center, 19th Floor, Hartford, CT 06103–3220, (860) 240–4800, ext. 3100.
Manchester, NH.—James H. Barnes, Acting Field Office Director, Norris Cotton Federal Building, 275 Chestnut Street, Manchester, NH 03101–2487, (603) 666–7510, ext. 3903.
Providence, RI.—Nancy D. Smith, Field Office Director, Sixth Floor, 10 Weybosset Street, Providence, RI 02903–2818, (401) 528–5230.
New York, NY Regional.—Marisel Morales, Regional Director, 26 Federal Plaza, Suite 3541, New York, NY 10278–0068, (212) 264–8000.
Albany, NY.—Bob Scofield, Field Office Director, 52 Corporate Circle, Albany, NY 12203–5121, (518) 464–4200.
Buffalo, NY.—Stephen Banko, Field Office Director, Lafayette Court, Fifth Floor, 465 Main Street, Buffalo, NY 14203–1780, (716) 551–5755.
Camden, NJ.—Michael Worth, Field Office Director, Hudson Building, 800 Hudson Square, Second Floor, Camden, NJ 08102–1156, (856) 757–5081.
Newark, NJ.—Paul Aprigliano, Acting Field Office Director, One Newark Center, 13th Floor, Newark, NJ 07102–5260, (973) 622–7900.
Philadelphia, PA Regional.—Milton R. Pratt, Director, Wanamaker Building, 100 Penn Square East, Philadelphia, PA 19107–3380, (215) 656–0500.
Baltimore, MD.—Harold D. Young, Field Office Director, City Crescent Building, 10 South Howard Street, Fifth Floor, Baltimore, MD 21201–2505, (410) 962–2520.
Charleston, WV.—George H. Rodriguez, Field Office Director, Suite 708, 405 Capitol Street, Charleston, WV 25301–1795, (304) 347–7000.
Pittsburgh, PA.—Richard M. Nemoytin, Field Office Director, U.S. Post Office and Courthouse Building, 339 Sixth Avenue, Pittsburgh, PA 15222–2515, (412) 644–6436.
Richmond, VA.—Mary Ann Wilson, Field Office Director, 600 East Broad Street, Richmond, VA 23219–4920, (804) 771–2100.
Washington, DC.—James David Reeves, Field Office Director, 820 First Street, NE., Washington, DC 20002–4205, (202) 275–9200.

Wilmington, DE.—Diane Lello, Field Office Director, Suite 404, 920 King Street, Wilmington, DE 19801–3016, (302) 573–6300.

Atlanta, GA.—Brian Noyes, Regional Director, 40 Marietta St., Five Points Plaza, Atlanta, GA 30303–2806, (404) 331–4111.

Birmingham, AL.—Cindy Yarbrough, Field Office Director, 950 22nd St. N., Ste. 900, Birmingham, AL 35203–5302, (205) 731–2617.

Miami, FL.—Anthony Britto, Acting Director, 909 SE, First Avenue, Miami, FL 33131, (305) 536–4456.

Columbia, SC.—William D. Gregorie, Field Office Director, Strom Thurmond Federal Building, 1835 Assembly Street, Columbia, SC 29201–2480, (803) 765–5592.

Greensboro, NC.—Gary Dimmick, Acting Field Office Director, Koger Building, 2306 West Meadowview Road, Greensboro, NC 27401–3707, (336) 547–4001.

Jackson, MS.—Cassandra Terry, Acting Field Director, McCoy Federal Building, Room 910, 100 West Capitol Street, Jackson, MS 39269–1016, (601) 965–4757.

Jacksonville, FL.—Louis Ybarra, Acting Director, Southern Bell Tower, 301 West Bay Street, Suite 2200, Jacksonville, FL 32202–5121, (904) 232–2627.

Louisville, KY.—Ben Cook, Field Office Director, 601 West Broadway, Louisville, KY 40202, (502) 585–5251.

Knoxville, TN.—Mark J. Brezina Field Office Director, Suite 300, John J. Duncan Federal Building, 710 Locust Street, Knoxville, TN 37902–2526, (865) 545–4384.

Memphis, TN.—Yvonne F. Leander, Field Office Director, 200 Jefferson Ave, Suite 1200, Memphis, TN 38103–2335 (901) 544–3367.

Nashville, TN.—Edward Pringle, Field Office Director, Suite 200, 235 Cumberland Bend Drive, Nashville, TN 37228–1803, (615) 736–5213.

Orlando, FL.—Paul C. Ausley, Jr., Field Office Director, Langley Building, Suite 270, 3751 Maguire Boulevard, Orlando, FL 32803–3032, (407) 648–6441.

Caribbean.—Michael A. Colon, Field Office Director, New San Juan Building, 171 Carlos E. Chardon Avenue, San Juan, PR 00918–0903, (787) 766–5201.

Chicago, IL.—Joseph Galvan, Regional Director, Ralph H. Metcalfe Federal Building, 77 West Jackson Boulevard, Chicago, IL 60604–3507, (312) 353–5680.

Cincinnati, OH.—James Cunningham, Field Office Director, 15 E. Seventh St, Cincinnati, OH 45202–2401, (513) 684–3451.

Cleveland, OH.—Douglas W. Shelby, Field Office Director, Renaissance Building, 1350 Euclid Avenue, Suite 500, Cleveland, OH 44115–1815, (216) 522–4058.

Columbus, OH.—Thomas Leach, Field Office Director, 200 North High Street, Columbus, OH 43215–2463, (614) 469–2540.

Detroit, MI.—Dianne Johnson, Acting Field Office Director, Patrick V. McNamara Federal Building, 477 Michigan Avenue, Detroit, MI 48226–2592, (313) 266–7900.

Grand Rapids, MI.—Louis M. Berra, Field Office Director, Trade Center Building, Third Floor, 50 Louis Street, NW,, Grand Rapids, MI 49503–2633, (616) 456–2100.

Indianapolis, IN.—John Hall, Field Office Director, 151 North Delaware Street, Suite 1200, Indianapolis, IN 46204–2526, (317) 226–6303.

Milwaukee, WI.—Delbert F. Reynolds, Field Office Director, Henry S. Reuss Federal Plaza, Suite 1380, 310 West Wisconsin Avenue, Milwaukee, WI 53203–2289, (414) 297–3214.

Flint, MI.—Jason Gamlin, Field Office Director, The Federal Building, 1101 South Saginaw Street, Flint, MI 48502–1953, (810) 766–5112.

Minneapolis, MN.—Thomas T. Feeney, Field Office Director, 920 Second Street South, Minneapolis, MN 55402, (612) 370–3000.

Springfield, IL.—Anthony Randolph, Field Office Director, 320 West Washington, 7th Floor, Springfield, IL 62701, (217) 492–4120.

Albuquerque, NM.—Michael R. Griego, Field Office Director, 625 Silver Avenue, SW., Suite 100, Albuquerque, NM 87102, (505) 346–7320.

Dallas, TX.—[Vacant], Room 860, 525 Griffin Street, Dallas, TX 75202–5007, (214) 767–8300.

Houston, TX.—Richard Wilson, Field Office Director, Norfolk Tower, Suite 200, 2211 Norfolk, Houston, TX 77098–4096, (713) 313–2274.

Little Rock, AR.—Bessie Jackson, Field Office Director, 425 W. Capitol Avenue, Suite 900, Little Rock, AR 72201–3488, (501) 324–5931.

Lubbock, TX.—Miguel C. Rincon, Field Office Director, George H. Mahon Federal Building and United States Courthouse, Room 511, 1205 Texas Avenue, Lubbock, TX 79401–4093, (806) 472–7265.

New Orleans, LA.—Patricia Hoban-Moore, Field Office Director, Hale Boggs Federal Building, 501 Magazine Street, 9th Floor, New Orleans, LA 70130–3099, (504) 589–7201.

Oklahoma City, OK.—Kevin McNeely, Field Office Director, 500 W. Main Street, Suite 400, Oklahoma City, OK 73102–2233, (405) 553–7509.

San Antonio, TX.—Luz Day, Field Office Director, One Alamo Center, 106 South St. Mary's Street, San Antonio, TX 78205, (210) 475–6806.

Shreveport, LA.—Martha N. Sakre, Field Office Director, 401 Edwards Street, Suite 1510, Shreveport, LA 71101–5513, (318) 676–3440.

Tulsa, OK.—James S. Colgan, Field Office Director, 1516 S. Boston Ave., Ste. 100, Tulsa, OK 74119–4030, (918) 581–7434.

Kansas City, KS.—Macie Houston, Regional Director, Gateway Tower II, 400 State Avenue, Room 200, Kansas City, KS 66101–2406, (913) 551–5462.

Des Moines, IA.—William H. McNarney, Field Office Director, Room 239, 210 Walnut Street, Des Moines, IA 50309–2155, (515) 284–4512.

Omaha, NE.—Stan Quy, Field Office Director, 10909 Mill Valley Road, Suite 100, Omaha, NE 68154–3955, (402) 492–3101.

St. Louis, MO.—Roy E. Pierce, Field Office Director, 1222 Spruce Street, Suite 3207, St. Louis, MO 63103–2836, (314) 539–6583.

Denver, CO.—John K. Carson, Regional Director, First Interstate Tower North, 633 17th Street, 14th Floor, Denver, CO 80202–3607, (303) 672–5440.

Casper, WY.—Chris Stearns, Field Office Director, Federal Office Building, Room 1010, 100 East B Street, Casper, WY 82601–1969, (307) 261–6250.

Fargo, ND.—Joel Manske, Field Office Director, Federal Building, 657 Second Avenue North, Room 366, Fargo, ND 58108, (701) 239–5136.

Helena, MT.—Tom Friesen, Field Office Director, 7 W. 6th Ave, Helena, MT 59601, (406) 449–5050.

Salt Lake City, UT.—Dwight A. Peterson, Director, 125 South State Street, Suite 3001, Salt Lake City, UT 84138, (801) 524–6070.

Sioux Falls, SD.—Sheryl Miller, Field Office Director, 2400 W. 49th Street, Suite I–201, Sioux Falls, SD 57105–6558, (605) 330–4223.

San Francisco, CA.—Richard K. Rainey, Regional Director, Phillip Burton Federal Building and U.S. Courthouse, 450 Golden Gate Avenue, San Francisco, CA 94102–3448, (415) 436–6532.

Fresno, CA.—Ann Marie Sudduth, Field Office Director, 3125 Fresno St., Ste. 100, Fresno, CA, 93721–1718, (559) 487–5033.

Honolulu, HI.—Gordan Y. Furutani, Field Office Director, Seven Waterfront Plaza, Ala Moana Boulevard, Suite 3A, Honolulu, HI 96813–4918, (808) 522–8175.

Los Angeles, CA.—Jason Coughenour, Field Office Director, AT&T Center, 611 West Sixth Street, Suite 800, Los Angeles, CA 90017, (213) 894–8007.

Phoenix, AZ.—Rebecca Flanagan, Field Office Director, One N. Central Avenue, Suite 600, Phoenix, AZ 85004, (602) 379–7100.

Reno, NV.—Ken Lobene, Acting Field Office Director, 3702 S. Virginia St., Reno, NV 89502–6581, (775) 784–5383.

Sacramento, CA.—William Bolton, Field Office Director, 925 L Street, Sacramento, CA 95814, (916) 498–5220.

Fort Worth, TX.—Cynthia Leon, Regional Director, 801 Cherry St., P.O. Box 2905, Fort Worth, TX 76113–2905, (817) 978–5980.

San Diego, CA.—Charles J. Wilson, Field Office Director, Symphony Towers, 750 B St., Ste. 1600, San Diego, CA 92101–8131, (619) 557–5310.

Santa Ana, CA.—Theresa Camiling, Field Office Director, 1600 N. Broadway, Suite 101, Santa Ana, CA 92706–3927, (714) 796–5577.

Las Vegas, NV.—Ken Lobene, Field Office Director, Atrium Building, Suite 700, 333 North Rancho Drive, Las Vegas, NV 89106–3714, (702) 388–6500.

Tucson, AZ.—Sharon K. Atwell, Field Office Director, Security Pacific Bank Plaza, 160 North Stone Avenue, Suite 100, Tucson, AZ 85701–1467, (520) 670–6000.

Seattle, WA.—John W. Meyers, Regional Director, Seattle Federal Office Building, 909 First Avenue, Suite 200, Seattle, WA 98104–1000, (206) 220–5101.

Anchorage, AK.—Colleen Bickford, Field Office Director, University Plaza Building, 949 East 36th Avenue, Suite 401, Anchorage, AK 99508–4399, (907) 271–4663.

Boise, ID.—Constance Hogland, Field Office Director, Plaza IV, Suite 220, 800 Park Boulevard, Boise, ID 83712–7743, (208) 334–1990.

Portland, OR.—Thomas C. Cusack, Field Office Director, 400 Southwest Sixth Avenue, Suite 700, Portland, OR 97204–1632, (503) 326–2561.

Spokane, WA.—Arlene Patton, Field Office Director, U.S. Courthouse Bldg., 920 W. Riverside, Ste. 588, Spokane, WA 99201–1010, (509) 353–0674.

Tampa, FL.—Karen Jackson Sims, Field Office Director, 500 Zack Street, Suite 402, Tampa, FL 33602, (813) 228–2026.

Syracuse, NY.—Stephen Banko, Field Office Director, 128 Jefferson Street, Syracuse, NY 13202, (315) 477–0616.

DEPARTMENT OF TRANSPORTATION

400 Seventh Street SW., 20590

phone 366–4000, http://www.dot.gov

NORMAN Y. MINETA, Secretary of Transportation, born on November 12, 1931, in San Jose, CA; education: University of California, Berkeley, CA, 1953; military service: U.S. Army, 1953–56, served as an intelligence officer; professional: Mineta Insurance Agency; Lockheed Martin Corp.; public service: San Jose City Council, 1967–71; San Jose Mayor, 1971–1974; U.S. House of Representatives, 1975–1995; Chairman, National Civil Aviation Review Commission; Secretary of Commerce, 2000–2001; awards: Martin Luther King, Jr., Commemorative Medal, awarded by George Washington University, for contributions in the field of civil rights; family: married to Danealia (Deni) Mineta; he has two sons, David and Stuart Mineta, and two stepsons, Robert and Mark Brantner; nominated by President George W. Bush to become the 14th Secretary of Transportation, and was confirmed by the U.S. Senate on January 25, 2001.

OFFICE OF THE SECRETARY

Room 10200, phone 366–1111, fax 366–4508

[Created by the act of October 15, 1966; codified under U.S.C. 49]

Secretary of Transportation.—Norman Y. Mineta.
Chief of Staff.—John Flaherty, 366–1103.
Deputy Chief of Staff.—Martin Whitmer, 366–3377.
Deputy Secretary.—Michael Jackson, 366–2222.
Under Secretary of Transportation for Policy.—Jeffrey N. Shane, 366–1815.
Chairman, Board of Contract Appeals (Chief Administrative Judge).—Thaddeus V. Ware, room 5101, 366–4305.
Director, Office of:
Civil Rights.—Christopher Strobel (acting), 366–6524.
Executive Secretariat.—Michael Dannenhauer, room 10205, 366–4277.
Small and Disadvantaged Business Utilization.—Sean M. Moss, 366–1390.
Intelligence and Security.—Tom Falvey, room 10401, 366–6535.

GENERAL COUNSEL

General Counsel.—Kirk K, Van Tine, room 10428, 366–4702.
Deputy General Counsel.—Rosalind A. Knapp, 366–4713.
Special Counsel.—[Vacant].
Assistant General Counsel for—
Aviation Enforcement and Proceedings.—Samuel Podberesky, room 4116, 366–9342.
Environmental, Civil Rights and General Law.—Roberta D. Gabel, room 10102, 366–4710.
International Law.—Donald H. Horn, room 10105, 366–2972.
Legislation.—Thomas W. Herlihy, room 10100, 366–4687.
Litigation.—Paul M. Geier, room 4102, 366–4731.
Regulation and Enforcement.—Neil R. Eisner, room 10424, 366–4723.

INSPECTOR GENERAL

Inspector General.—Kenneth M. Mead, room 9210, 366–1959.
Deputy Inspector General.—Todd J. Zinser, room 9210, 366–6767.
Senior Counsel for Legal, Legislative and External Affairs.—Brian Dettelbach, room 9208, 366–8751.
Principal Assistant Inspector General for Auditing and Evaluation.—Alexis M. Stefani, room 9210, 366–1992.

Assistant Inspector General for—

Aviation Audits.—David A. Dobbs, room 9217, 366–0500.

Competition and Economic Analysis.—Mark Dayton, room 9134, 366–9970.

Financial and Information Technology Audits.—[Vacant].

Investigations.—Charles H. Lee, Jr., room 9210, 366–1967.

Surface and Maritime Programs.—Debra Ritt, room 9201, 366–5630.

Deputy Assistant Inspector General for—

Information Technology and Computer Security.—Rebecca Leng, room 9288, 366–1488.

Investigations.—Cecelia Rosser, room 9200, 366–8081.

Transportation Security and Hazardous Material.—Robin Hunt, 201 Mission Street, Suite 2130, San Francisco, CA, (415) 744–3090.

Director, Office of Human Resources.—Vivian Jarcho, room 7107, 366–1441.

Chief Technology Officer.—James Heminger, room 7117, 366–1968.

Chief Financial Officer and Chief Information Officer.—Jackie Weber, room 7117, 366–1495.

REGIONAL AUDIT OFFICES

Regional Program Directors:

Region II.—Michael E. Goldstein, Room 3134, 26 Federal Plaza, New York, NY 10278, (212) 264–8701.

Region III.—Earl Hedges, Suite 4500, City Cresent Building, 10 South Howard Street, Baltimore, MD 21201, (410) 962–3612.

Region IV.—Lou Dixon, Suite 17160, 61 Forsythe Street, SW, Atlanta, GA 30303 (404) 562–3770.

Region V.—Ronald H. Hoogenboom, 200 W. Adams Street, Suite 300, Chicago, IL 60606, (312) 353–0104.

Region VI.—Gary Lewis, Room 134A2, 819 Taylor Street, Fort Worth, TX 76102 (817) 978–3545.

Region IX.—Scott Macey (acting), 201 Mission Street, Suite 2310, San Francisco, CA 94105, (415) 744–3090.

Region X.—Darren Murphy, Room 644, 915 Second Avenue, Seattle WA, 98174, (206) 220–7754.

REGIONAL INVESTIGATIVE OFFICES

Special Agents-In-Charge:

Region I.—[Vacant].

Region II.—Ned E. Schwartz, Room 3134, 26 Federal Plaza, New York, NY 10278 (212) 264–8700.

Region IV.—William P. Tompkins, Suite 17160, 61 Forsythe Street, SW, Atlanta, GA 30303 (404) 562–3850.

Region V.—Dieter H. Harper, 200 W. Adams Street, Suite 300, Chicago, IL 60606, (312) 353–0106.

Region IX.—Hank W. Smedley, Suite 2310, 201 Mission Street, San Francisco, CA 94105, (415) 744–3090.

ASSISTANT SECRETARY FOR TRANSPORTATION POLICY

Assistant Secretary.—Emil Frankel, room 10305, 366–4540.

Deputy Assistant Secretary.—Joel Szabat.

ASSISTANT SECRETARY FOR AVIATION AND INTERNATIONAL AFFAIRS

Assistant Secretary.—Read Van de Water, room 10232, 366–8822.

Deputy Assistant Secretary.—Susan McDermott, room 10232, 366–4551.

Director, Office of:

International Transportation and Trade.—Bernestine Allen, room 10300, 366–4398.

International Aviation.—Paul Gretch, room 6402, 366–2423.

Aviation Analysis.—Randall Bennett, room 6401, 366–5903.

Planning and Special Projects.—James New, room 6426, 366–4868.

ASSISTANT SECRETARY FOR ADMINISTRATION

Assistant Secretary.—Vincent T. Taylor, room 10320, 366–2332.
Deputy Assistant Secretary.—Mari Barr Santangelo, room 7411, 366–4088.
Director, Office of:
Human Resource Management.—Mari Barr Santangelo (acting), room 7411, 366–4088.
Hearings, Chief Administrative Law Judge.—Judge Ronnie A. Yoder, room 5411C, 366–2142.
Senior Procurement Executive.—David J. Litman, room 7101D, 366–4263.
Security and Administrative Management.—Lee A. Privett, room 7404H, 366–4676.

ASSISTANT SECRETARY FOR BUDGET AND PROGRAMS

Assistant Secretary.—Donna McLean, room 10101, 366–9191.
Deputy Assistant Secretary.—Phyllis Scheinberg, room 10101, 366–9192.
Deputy Chief Financial Officer.—A. Thomas Park, room 10101, 366–9192.
Director, Office of:
Budget and Program Performance.—Lana Hurdle.
Financial Management.—A. Thomas Park, room 6101, 366–1306.

ASSISTANT SECRETARY FOR GOVERNMENTAL AFFAIRS

Assistant Secretary.—[Vacant], room 10408, 366–4573.
Deputy Assistant Secretary.—Shane Karr.

OFFICE OF PUBLIC AFFAIRS

Assistant to the Secretary and Director of Public Affairs.—Chet Lunner, room 10414, 366–4570.
Deputy Director.—Leonardo Alcivar, room 10414, 366–4531.
Assistant Director for—
Speech Writing and Research Division.—Harry Phillips, room 9419, 366–5822.
Media Relations Division.—William Adams, 366–5580.

BUREAU OF TRANSPORTATION STATISTICS

400 Seventh Street SW., Room 3103, 20590, phone 366–3282

Director.—Rick Kowaleski (acting), 366–6268.
Deputy Director.—Rick Kowaleski.

FEDERAL AVIATION ADMINISTRATION

800 Independence Avenue SW, 20591, phone 267–3484

Administrator.—Manon C. Blakey, 267–3111.
Chief of Staff.—David Mandell, 267–3111.
Senior Counsel to the Administrator.—Louise E. Maillett, 267–7417.
Executive Assistant to the Administrator.—Derra Brown, 267–3111.
Deputy Administrator.—Bobby Sturgell, 267–8111.
Senior Advisor to the Deputy Administrator.—Shirley S. Miller, 267–8111.
Director of:
Emergency Operations and Communication.—J. David Canoles, 493–4988.
Free Flight.—John F. Thornton, 220–3300.
Safety and Special Studies.—Darlene Freeman, 267–8111.
Security and Investigations.—Eugene Ross Hamory, 267–8537.
Operational Evolution Staff.—Charles E. Keegan, 267–7222.
Assistant Administrator for Financial Services.—John F. Hennigan (acting), 267–9105.
Deputy Assistant Administrator.—John F. Hennigan, 267–8928.
Director of:
Budget.—Alex Keenan, 267–8010
Cost and Performance Management.—Tim Lawler, 267–7140.
Financial Management.—David M. Zavada, 267–3018.

Assistant Administrator for Civil Rights.—Fanny Rivera, 267–3254.
Deputy Assistant Administrator.—Barbara A. Edwards, 267–3264.
Assistant Administrator for Aviation Policy, Planning and Environment.—Sharon L. Pinkerton, 267–3927.
Deputy Assistant Administrator.—[Vacant], 267–3927.
Director of:
Aviation Policy and Plans.—John M. Rodgers, 267–3274.
Environment and Energy.—Carl Burleson, 267–3576.
Chief Counsel.—Andrew B. Steinberg, 267–3222.
Deputy Chief Counsel.—James W. Whitlow, 267–3773.
Assistant Administrator for Government and Industry Affairs.—David Balloff, 267–3277.
Deputy Assistant Administrator.—David V. Broome, 267–8211.
Assistant Administrator for Human Resource Management.—Glenda M. Tate, 267–3458.
Deputy Assistant Administrator.—Mary Ellen Dix, 267–3850.
Deputy Assistant Administrator for Labor Relations.—Raymond B. Thoman, 267–3850.
Director of:
Accountability Board.—Maria Fernandez-Greczmiel, 267–3065.
Center for Management Devleopment.—Barbara J. Smith, (386) 446–7136.
Labor and Employee Relations.—Melvin Harns, 267–3979.
Organization, Learning and Development.—Barbara J. Smith (acting), 267–9041.
Personnel.—Roger M. Edwards, 267–3979.
Assistant Administrator for Information Services.—Daniel J. Mehan, 493–4570.
Deputy Assistant Administrator.—Arthur Pyster, 493–4570.
Director of Information Systems Security.—Michael F. Brown, 267–7104.
Assistant Administrator for Public Affairs.—Greg Martin, 267–3883.
Deputy Assistant Administrator.—Laura J. Brown, 267–3883.
Assistant Administrator for International Aviation.—Douglas E. Lavin, 267–3033.
Deputy Assistant Administrator.—[Vacant], 267–3927.
Director of:
Asia-Pacific.—Elizabeth E. Erickson, 65–6540–4114.
Europe, Africa, and Middle East.—Paul Feldman, (322) 508–2700.
International Aviation.—Ava L. Wilkerson, 267–3213.
Latin America-Caribbean.—Joaquin Archilla, (305) 716–3300.
Assistant Administrator for Regions and Center Operations.—Ruth Leverenz, 267–7369
Deputy Assistant Administrator.—[Vacant], 267–7369.
Regional Administrator for—
Alaskan.—Patrick N. Poe, (907) 271–5645.
Central.—Christopher Blum, (816) 329–3050.
Eastern.—Arlene B. Feldman, (718) 553–3000.
Great Lakes.—Cecelia Hunziker, (847) 294–7294.
New England.—Amy Lind Corbett, (781) 238–7020.
Northwest Mountain.—Tom Busker (acting), (425) 227–2001.
Southern.—Carolyn Blum, (404) 305–5000.
Southwest.—Ruth Leverenz, (817) 222–5001.
Western-Pacific.—William C. Withycombe, (310) 725–3550.
Director, Mike Monroney Aeronautical Center.—Lindy Ritz, (405) 954–4521.
Assistant Administrator for System Safety.—Christopher A. Hart, 267–3611.
Deputy Assistant Administrator.—Daniel C. Hedges, 267–3611.
Associate Administrator for Research and Acquisitions.—Charles E. Keegan, 267–7222.
Deputy Associate Administrator.—Dennis DeGaetano, 267–7222.
Director of:
Acquisitions.—Gilbert B. Devey, 267–8513.
Air Traffic Systems Development.—Gregory D. Burke, 493–0237.
Aviation Research.—Dr. Herman A. Rediess, 267–9251.
Business Management.—Lauraline Gregory, 267–3616.
Competitive Sourcing Acquisition.—Joann Kansier, 385–7749.
System Architecture and Investment Analysis.—John A. Scardina, 385–7100.
William J. Hughes Technical Center.—Dr. Anne Harlan, (609) 485–6641
Associate Administrator for Airports.—Woodie Woodward, 267–9471.
Deputy Associate Administrator.—Paul L. Galis, 267–8738.
Director of:
Airport Planning and Programming.—Catherline M. Lang, 267–8775.
Airport Safety and Standards.—David L. Bennett, 267–3053.
Associate Administrator for Commercial Space Transportation.—Patricia Grace Smith, 267–7793.
Deputy Associate Administrator.—Dr. George C. Nield, 267–7848.

Associate Administrator for Air Traffic Services.—Steven J. Brown, 267–7111.
Deputy Associate Administrator.—Peter H. Challan, 267–3133.
Director of:
Airway Facilities Service.—Steven B. Zaidman, 267–8181.
Air Traffic Service.—David B. Johnson, 267–3666.
Air Traffic Systems Requirements Service.—James H. Washington, 385–7500.
Independent Operational Test Evaluation.—A. Martin Phillips, 267–3341.
Runway Safety.—William S. Davis, 385–4778.
System Capacity.—Paula R. Lewis, 267–7370.
Terminal Business Service.—William Voss, 264–3000.
Associate Administrator for Regulation and Certification.—Nicholas A. Sabatini, 267–3131.
Deputy Associate Administrator.—Peggy Gilligan, 267–7804.
Director of:
Accident Investigation.—Steven B. Wallace, 267–9612.
Aircraft Certification Service.—John J. Hickey, 267–8235.
Flight Standards Service.—James Ballough, 267–8237.
Rulemaking.—Anthony F. Fazio, 267–9677.
Federal Air Surgeon.—Dr. Jon L. Jordan, 267–3535.

FEDERAL HIGHWAY ADMINISTRATION

Washington Headquarters, Nassif Building, 400 Seventh Street SW, 20590

Turner-Fairbank Highway Research Center (TFHRC)

6300 Georgetown Pike, McLean, VA 22201

Administrator.—Mary E. Peters, 366–0650.
Deputy Administrator.—J. Richard Capka, 366–2240.
Executive Director.—Frederick G. (Bud) Wright, 366–2242.
Chief Counsel.—James A. Rowland, room 4213, 366–0740.
Associate Administrator for—
Administration.—Michael J. Vecchietti, room 4316, 366–0604.
Civil Rights.—Edward W. Morris, Jr., room 4132, 366–0693.
Corporate Management.—Ronald C. Marshall, room 4208, 366–9393.
Federal Lands Highway.—Arthur E. Hamilton, room 6311, 366–9494.
Infrastructure.—King W. Gee, room 3212, 366–0371.
Operations.—Jeffrey F. Paniati, room 3401, 366–0408.
Planning, Environment, and Realty.—Cynthia J. Burbank, room 3212, 366–0116.
Policy.—Charles D. Nottingham, room 3317, 366–0585.
Professional Development.—Joseph S. Toole, room 800, 235–0500.
Public Affairs.—Bill Outlaw, room 4211, 366–0660.
Safety.—A. George Ostensen, room 3419, 366–2288.
Turner-Fairbank Highway Research Center.—Dennis C. Judycki, room T–306, 493–3999.

FIELD SERVICES

Organizationally report to Executive Director (HOA–3), Washington, DC

Eastern Field Office
Director.—Gene K. Fong, 10 S. Howard Street, Suite 4000, Baltimore, MD 21201, (410) 962–0093.
Southern Field Office
Director.—Eugene W. Cleckley, 61 Forsyth Street, SW., Suite 17T26, Atlanta, GA 30303, (404) 562–3570.
Western Field Office
Director.—Christine M. Johnson, 2520 West 4700 South, Suite 9C, Salt Lake City, UT 84114, (801) 967–5979.

RESOURCE CENTERS

Eastern Resource Center
Manager.—Joyce A. Curtis, 10 S. Howard Street, Suite 4000, Baltimore, MD 21201, (410) 962–0093
Midwestern Resource Center
Manager.—William R. Gary White, 19900 Governors Drive, Suite 301, Olympia Fields, IL 60461, (708) 283–3510.

Southern Resource Center

Manager.—Garrett (Gary) Corino, 61 Forsyth Street, SW., Suite 17T26, Atlanta, GA 30303, (404) 562–3570.

Western Resource Center

Manager.—C. Glenn Clinton, 201 Mission Street, Suite 2100, San Francisco, CA 94105, (415) 744–3102.

FEDERAL RAILROAD ADMINISTRATION

1120 Vermont Avenue, NW., 20590, (202) 493–6000, www.fra.dot.gov

Administrator.—Allan Rutter, room 7089, 493–6014.
Deputy Administrator.—Elizabeth Monro, room 7089, 493–6015.
Associate Administrator for—
Administration and Finance.—Margaret Reid, room 6077, 493–6024.
Policy and Program Development.—Jane H. Bachner (acting), room 7074, 493–6400.
Public Affairs.—Robert Gould, room 7086, 493–6024.
Railroad Development.—Mark E. Yachmetz, room 0729, 493–6381.
Safety.—George A. Gavila, room 6014, 493–6300.
Chief Counsel.—Mark Lindsey, room 7022, 493–6052.
Civil Rights Director.—Carl-Martin Ruiz, room 7096, 493–6010.
Budget Director.—DJ Stadler, room 6124, 493–6150.

REGIONAL OFFICES (RAILROAD SAFETY)

Region 1.—Northeastern. Connecticut, Maine, Massachusetts, New Hampshire, New Jersey, New York, Rhode Island, Vermont.
Regional Director.—Mark H. McKeon, Room 1077, 55 Broadway, Cambridge, MA 02142, (617) 494–2302.

Region 2.—Eastern. Delaware, District of Columbia, Maryland, Pennsylvania, Virginia, West Virginia, Ohio.
Regional Director.—David Myers, International Plaza, Suite 550, Philadelphia, PA 19113, (610) 521–8200.

Region 3.—Southern. Kentucky, Tennessee, Mississippi, North Carolina, South Carolina, Georgia, Alabama, Florida.
Regional Director.—Fred Denin, 61 Forsyth Street, NW., Suite 16T20, Atlanta, GA 30303, (404) 562–3800.

Region 4.—Central. Minnesota, Illinois, Indiana, Michigan, Wisconsin.
Regional Director.—Lawrence Hasvold, 200 W. Adams Street, Chicago, IL 60606, (312) 353–6203.

Region 5.—Southwestern. Arkansas, Louisiana, New Mexico, Oklahoma, Texas.
Regional Director.—John Megary, 4100 International Plaza, Suite 450, Ft. Worth, TX 96109, (817) 862–2200.

Region 6.—Midwestern. Iowa, Missouri, Kansas, Nebraska, Colorado.
Regional Director.—Darrell J. Tisor, DOT Building, 911 Locust Street, Suite 464, Kansas City, MO 64106, (816) 329–3840.

Region 7.—Western. Arizona, California, Nevada, Utah.
Regional Director.—Alvin L. Settle, 801 I Street, Suite 466, Sacramento, CA 95814 (916) 498–6540.

Region 8.—Northwestern. Idaho, Oregon, Wyoming, Montana, North Dakota, South Dakota, Washington, Alaska.
Regional Director.—Dick Clairmont, 703 Broadway, Murdock Executive Plaza, Suite 650, Vancouver, WA 98660, (360) 696–7536.

NATIONAL HIGHWAY TRAFFIC SAFETY ADMINISTRATION

400 Seventh Street SW, 20590

Administrator.—Dr. Jeffrey W. Runge, room 5220, 366–1836.
Deputy Administrator.—[Vacant].
Senior Associate Administrator for—
Injury Traffic and Control.—Brian McLaughlin, 366–1755.
Policy and Operation.—Bill Walsh, 366–2105.
Vehicle Safety.—Ronald Medford, 366–1810.

Associate Administrator for—
Administration.—Delmas Johnson, 366–1788.
Advance Research.—Raymond Owings, 366–1537.
Applied Research.—Joseph Kanathra, 366–4862.
Development and Delivery.—Marilena Amoni, 366–1755.
Enforcement.—Kenneth Weinstein, 366–9700.
External Affairs.—Scott Brenner, 366–2111.
Operation and Resource.—Marlene Markinson, 366–2121.
Planning, Evaluation and Budget.—Rose McMurray, 366–2550.
Rulemaking.—Stephen R. Kratzke, 366–1810.
Chief Information Officer.—Susan White, 366–0136.
Director, Office of:
Civil Rights.—George B. Quick, 366–0972.
Communication and Consumer Information.—Susan Gorcowski, 366–9550.
Legislative Affairs.—Wilfred Otero, 366–9263.
Chief Counsel.—Jacqueline Glassman, 366–9511.
Director, Executive Correspondence.—Linda Divelbiss, 366–1936.

REGIONAL OFFICES

Region I. Connecticut, Maine, Massachusetts, New Hampshire, Rhode Island, Vermont.
Regional Administrator.—[Vacant].
Region II. New York, New Jersey, Puerto Rico, Virgin Islands.
Regional Administrator.—Thomas M. Louizou, Suite 204, 222 Mamaroneck Avenue, White Plains, NY 10605, (914) 682–6162.
Region III. Delaware, District of Columbia, Maryland, Pennsylvania, Virginia, West Virginia.
Regional Administrator.—Elizabeth Baker, The Cresent Building, 10 South Howard Street, Suite 4000, Baltimore, MD 21201, (410) 961–7144.
Region IV. Alabama, Florida, Georgia, Kentucky, Mississippi, North Carolina, South Carolina, Tennessee.
Regional Administrator.—Troy Ayers, 100 Alabama Street SW, Suite 17T30, Atlanta, GA 30303–3106, (404) 562–3739.
Region V. Illinois, Indiana, Michigan, Minnesota, Ohio, Wisconsin.
Regional Administrator.—Donald J. McNamara, 19900 Governors Drive, Suite 201, Olympia Fields, IL 60461, (708) 503–8892.
Region VI. Arkansas, Louisiana, New Mexico, Oklahoma, Texas.
Regional Administrator.—George S. Chakiris, Room 8A38, 819 Taylor Street, Fort Worth, TX 76102–6177, (817) 978–3653.
Region VII. Iowa, Kansas, Missouri, Nebraska.
Regional Administrator.—Romell Cooks, PO Box 412515, Kansas City, MO 64141, (816) 926–7887.
Region VIII. Colorado, Montana, North Dakota, South Dakota. Utah, Wyoming.
Regional Administrator.—Louis R. DeCarolis, Fourth Floor, 555 Zang Street, Denver, CO 80228, (303) 969–6917.
Region IX. American Samoa, Arizona, California, Guam, Hawaii, Nevada.
Regional Administrator.—David Manning (acting), Suite 2230, 201 Mission Street, San Francisco, CA 94105, (415) 744–3089.
Region X. Alaska, Idaho, Oregon, Washington.
Regional Administrator.—Curtis Winston, Federal Building, Room 3140, 915 Second Avenue, Seattle, WA 98174, (206) 553–5934.

FEDERAL TRANSIT ADMINISTRATION

400 Seventh Street SW, 20590, phone 366–4040

Administrator.—Jennifer L. Dorn.
Deputy Administrator.—Robert Jamison.
Chief Counsel.—Will Sears, 366–4063.
Director, Office of:
Civil Rights.—Michael Winter.
Associate Administrator for—
Administration.—Tim Wolgast (acting).
Communications and Congressional Affairs.—Kristi Clemens.
Programs Management.—Hiram T. Walker.

Deputy Associate Administrator for—
Budget and Policy.—Bob Tuccillo, 366–4050.
Programs Management.—Lynn Sahaj.
Research, Demonstration and Innovation.—Barbara Sisson.

REGIONAL OFFICES

Region 1.—Connecticut, Maine, Massachusetts, New Hampshire, Rhode Island, Vermont.
Regional Administrator.—Richard H. Doyle, Transportation Systems Center, Kendall Square, Suite 920, 55 Broadway, Cambridge, MA 02142.
Region 2.—New Jersey, New York, Virgin Islands.
Regional Administrator.—Letitia Thompson, One Bowling Green, room 429, New York, NY 10004.
Region 3.—Delaware, District of Columbia, Maryland, North Carolina, Pennsylvania, Tennessee, Virginia, West Virginia.
Regional Administrator.—Herman Shipman (acting), Suite 500, 1760 Market Street, Philadelphia, PA 19103.
Region 4.—Alabama, Florida, Georgia, Kentucky, Mississippi, North Carolina, Puerto Rico, South Carolina, Tennessee.
Regional Administrator.—Jerry Franklin, 61 Forsyth Street, SW, Suite 17T50, Atlanta, GA 30303.
Region 5.—Illinois, Indiana, Michigan, Minnesota, Ohio, Wisconsin.
Regional Administrator.—Joel P. Ettinger, 200 West Adams Street, Suite 320, Chicago, IL 60606.
Region 6.—Arkansas, Louisiana, New Mexico, Oklahoma, Texas.
Regional Administrator.—Robert C. Patrick, Fritz Lanham Federal Building, 819 Taylor Street, room 8A36, Fort Worth, TX 76102.
Region 7.—Iowa, Kansas, Missouri, Nebraska.
Regional Administrator.—Mohktee Altmad, 901 Locust Street, Suite 404, Kansas City, MO 64131.
Region 8.—Colorado, Montana, North Dakota, South Dakota, Utah, Wyoming.
Regional Administrator.—Lee O. Waddleton, Columbine Place, 216 16th Street, Denver, CO 80202.
Region 9.—Arizona, California, Guam, Hawaii, Nevada, American Samoa.
Regional Administrator.—Leslie T. Rogers, Suite 2210, 201 Mission Street, San Francisco, CA 94105.
Region 10.—Alaska, Idaho, Oregon, Washington.
Regional Administrator.—Rick Krochalis, Suite 3142, 915 Second Avenue, Seattle, WA 98174.

SAINT LAWRENCE SEAWAY DEVELOPMENT CORPORATION

400 Seventh Street SW 20590, phone 366–0091, fax 366–7147

Administrator.—Albert Jacquez.
Director, Office of:
Budget and Logistics.—Kevin P. O'Malley.
Chief Counsel.—Marc C. Owen.
Trade Development and Public Affairs.—Rebecca McGill.

SEAWAY OPERATIONS

180 Andrews Street, PO Box 520, Massena, NY 13662–0520

phone (315) 764–3200, fax (315) 764–3235

Associate Administrator.—Salvatore L. Pisani.
Deputy Associate Administrator.—Carol A. Fenton.
Assistant.—Mary C. Fregoe.
Director, Office of:
Administration.—Mary Ann Hazel.
Engineering and Strategic Planning.—Stephen C. Hung.
Finance.—Edward Margosian.
Lock Operations.—Lori K. Curran.
Maintenance and Marine Services.—Peter Bashaw.

MARITIME ADMINISTRATION

400 Seventh Street SW, 20590, phone 366–5812

Maritime Administrator and Chairman, Maritime Subsidy Board.—William G. Schubert, room 7206, 366–5823.

Deputy Administrator.—Bruce J. Carlton (acting), room 7208, 366–1719.

Deputy Administrator for Inland Waterways and Great Lakes.—[Vacant].

Secretary, Maritime Administration and Maritime Subsidy Board.—Joel Richard, room 7210, 366–5746.

Chief Counsel and Member, Maritime Subsidy Board.—Robert B. Ostrom, room 7232, 366–5711.

Director, Office of:

Congressional and Public Affairs.—Robyn Boerstling, room 7206, 366–1707.

Associate Administrator for Administration.—Eileen S. Roberson, room 7216, 366–5802.

Deputy Associate Administrator for Administration.—Ralph W. Ferguson, room 7216, 366–5802.

Director, Office of:

Accounting.—John G. Hoban, room 7325, 366–5852.

Acquisition.—Tim Roark, room 7310, 366–5757.

Budget.—Lynn Ashe, room 7217, 366–5778.

Management and Information Services.—Richard A. Weaver, room 7301, 366–5816.

Personnel.—Raymond A. Pagliarini, room 2109, 366–4141.

Associate Administrator for Policy, International Trade.—Bruce J. Carlton, room 7218, 366–5772.

Director of:

International Activities.—Gregory Hall, room 7119, 366–5773.

Policy and Plans.—Janice G. Weaver, room 7123, 366–4468.

Statistical and Economic Analysis.—William B. Ebersold, room 8107, 366–2267.

Associate Administrator for Financial Approvals and Cargo Preference.—James J. Zok, room 8114, 366–0364.

Director, Office of:

Cargo Preference.—Thomas W. Harrelson, room 8118, 366–4610.

Financial and Rate Approvals.—Michael P. Ferris, room 8117, 366–2324.

Insurance and Shipping Analysis.—Edmond J. Fitzgerald, room 8117, 366–2400.

Associate Administrator for National Security.—James E. Caponiti, room 7300, 366–5400.

Director, Office of:

National Security Plans.—Thomas M. P. Christensen, room 7130, 366–5900.

Sealift Support.—Taylor E. Jones, II, room 7304, 366–2323.

Ship Operations.—William F. Trost, room 2122, 366–1875.

Associate Administrator for Shipbuilding.—Jean E. McKeever, room 8126, 366–5737.

Director of:

Insurance and Shipping Analysis.—Edmond J. Fitzgerald, room 8117, 366–2400.

Ship Financing.—Mitchell D. Lax, room 8122, 366–5744.

Shipbuilding and Marine Technology.—Joseph A. Byrne, room 8101, 366–1931.

Associate Administrator for Port, Intermodal and Environmental Activities.—Margaret D. Blum, room 7214, 366–4721.

Director, Office of:

Environmental Activities.—Michael C. Carter, room 7209, 366–8887.

Intermodal Development.—Richard L. Walker, room 7209, 366–8888.

Ports and Domestic Shipping.—Raymond R. Barberesi, room 7201, 366–4357.

FIELD ACTIVITIES

North Atlantic Region: *Director.*—Robert F. McKeon, 1 Bowling Green, room 418, New York, NY 10004, (212) 668–3330.

Central Region: *Director.*—John W. Carnes, 501 Magazine Street, room 1223, New Orleans, LA 70130, (504) 589–2000.

Great Lakes Region: *Director.*—Doris J. Bautch, Suite 185, 2860 S. River Road, Des Plaines, IL 60018, (847) 298–4535.

Western Region: *Director.*—Francis Johnston III, Suite 2200, 201 Mission Street, San Francisco, CA 94105, (415) 744–2580.

South Atlantic Region: *Director.*—M. Nuns Jain, Building 4D, Room 211, 7737 Hampton Boulevard, Norfolk, VA 23505, (757) 441–6393.

U.S. MERCHANT MARINE ACADEMY

Superintendent.—RADM Joseph D. Stewart, Kings Point, NY 11024, (516) 773–5000.
Assistant Superintendent for Academic Affairs (Academic Dean).—Dr. Warren F. Mazek, (516) 773–5000.

RESEARCH AND SPECIAL PROGRAMS ADMINISTRATION
400 Seventh Street SW, 20590, phone 366–4433

Administrator.—Samuel G. Bonasso (acting), room 8410, 366–4433.
Deputy Administrator.—Samuel G. Bonasso, room 8410, 366–4461.
Chief Counsel.—Elaine Joost, room 8407, 366–4400.
Director, Office of Civil Rights.—Helen E. Hagin, room 8419, 366–9638.
Associate Administrator for—
Hazardous Materials Safety.—Robert A. McGuire, room 8421, 366–0656.
Management and Administration.—Edward A. Brigham, room 7424, 366–4347.
Pipeline Safety.—Stacey Gerard, room 7128, 366–4595.
Program and Policy Support Staff.—[Vacant], room 8406, 366–4831.
Innovation, Research and Education.—Timothy Klein, room 7108, 366–4434.
Director, Office of Emergency Transportation.—[Vacant], room 8321, 366–5270.

TRANSPORTATION SAFETY INSTITUTE

Director.—Frank Tupper, 6500 South MacArthur Boulevard, Oklahoma City, OK 73125, (405) 954–3153.

VOLPE NATIONAL TRANSPORTATION SYSTEMS CENTER

Director.—Richard R. John, 55 Broadway, Kendall Square, Cambridge, MA 02142, (617) 494–2222.

HAZARDOUS MATERIALS SAFETY OFFICES

Eastern Region: *Chief.*—Colleen D. Abbenhaus, 820 Bear Tavern Road, Suite 306, West Trenton, NJ 08628, (609) 989–2256.

Central Region: *Chief.*—Kevin Boehne, Suite 478, 2350 East Devon Avenue, Des Plaines, IL 60018, (847) 294–8580.

Western Region: *Chief.*—Daniel Derwey, 3401 Centre Lake Drive, Suite 550–B, Ontario, CA 91764, (909) 937–3279.

Southern Region: *Chief.*—John Heneghan, 1701 Columbia Avenue, Suite 520, College Park, GA 30337, (404) 305–6120.

Southwest Region: *Chief.*—Billy Hines, 2320 LaBranch Street, room 2100, Houston, TX 77004, (713) 718–3950.

PIPELINE SAFETY OFFICES

Eastern Region: *Director.*—William H. Gute, 409 3rd Street, SW., Suite 300, Washington, DC 20024, (202) 260–8500.

Central Region: *Director.*—Ivan A. Huntoon, 901 Locust Street, Room 462, Kansas City, MO 64106, (816) 329–3800.

Western Region: *Director.*—Chris Hoidal, 12600 West Colfax Avenue, Suite A250, Lakewood, CO 80215, (303) 231–5701.

Southwest Region: *Director.*—Rodrick M. Seeley, 2320 LaBranch Street, Suite 2100, Houston, TX 77004, (713) 718–3748.

Southern Region: *Director.*—[Vacant], 61 Forsyth Street, Suite 6T15, Atlanta, GA 30303, (404) 562–3530.

SURFACE TRANSPORTATION BOARD

1925 K St. NW., 20423–0001, phone 565–1674

http://www.stb.dot.gov

Chairman.—Roger Nober, 565–1510.
Vice Chairman.—[Vacant].
Office of:
Compliance and Enforcement.—Melvin F. Clemens, 565–1573.
Congressionl and Public Services.—Dan G. King, 565–1594.
Economics, Environmental Analysis, and Administration.—Leland L. Gardner, 565–1526.
General Counsel.—Ellen D. Hanson, 565–1558.
Proceedings.—David M. Konschnik, 565–1600.
Secretary.—Vernon A. Williams, 565–1650.

DEPARTMENT OF ENERGY

James Forrestal Building, 1000 Independence Avenue SW 20585

phone (202) 586–5000, http://www.doe.gov

SPENCER ABRAHAM, Secretary of Energy; born on June 12, 1952, in East Lansing, MI; education: B.A., Michigan State University, 1974; J.D., Harvard University Law School, 1978; professional: Assistant Law Professor at Thomas M. Cooley Law School; Attorney at the law firm of Miller, Canfield, Paddock, and Stone; public service: Chairman, Michigan Republican Party, 1983–1990; Deputy Chief of Staff to the Vice President of the United States, Dan Quayle, 1990–1991; Co-Chairman of the National Republican Congressional Committee, 1991–1993; U.S. Senate, 1995–2001; organizations: Federalist Society; founder, *Harvard Journal of Law and Public Policy;* family: married to Jane Hershey Abraham; three children; nominated by President George W. Bush to become the 10th Secretary of Energy, and was confirmed by the U.S. Senate on January 20, 2001.

OFFICE OF THE SECRETARY

Secretary of Energy.—Spencer Abraham, 586–6210.
Deputy Secretary.—Kyle McSlarrow, 586–5500.
Under Secretary for Energy, Science, and Environment.—Robert Card, 586–7700.
Under Secretary for Nuclear Security.—Linton F. Brooks, 586–5555.
Inspector General.—Gregory H. Friedman, 586–4393.
General Counsel.—Lee Sarah Liberman Otis, 586–5281.
Secretary of Energy Advisory Board.—Craig R. Reed, 586–7092.
Assistant Secretary for—
Congressional and Intergovernmental Affairs.—Shannon D. Henderson (acting), 586–5450.
Energy Efficiency and Renewable Energy.—David K. Garman, 586–9220.
Environmental Management.—Jessie Hill Roberson, 586–7709.
Environment, Safety and Health.—Beverly Cook, 586–6151.
Fossil Energy.—Carl M. Smith, 586–6660.
Policy and International Affairs.—Vicky A. Bailey, 586–5800.
Administrator for Energy Information Administration.—Guy F. Caruso, 586–4361.
Director, Office of:
Management, Budget and Evaluation.—Bruce Carnes, 586–4171.
Civilian Radioactive Waste Management.—Margaret S. Y. Chu, 586–6842.
Economic Impact and Diversity.—Theresa Alvillar-Speake, 586–8383.
Fissile Materials Disposition.—Edward Siskin, 586–2695.
Hearings and Appeals.—George B. Breznay, 287–1566.
Nuclear Energy, Science and Technology.—William D. Magwood IV, 586–6630.
Science.—Dr. Raymond L. Orbach, 586–5430.
Worker and Community Transition.—Michael W. Owen, 586–7550.
Counterintelligence.—Stephen W. Dillard, 586–5901.
Intelligence.—John Russack, 586–2610.
Public Affairs.—Jeanne T. Lopatto, 586–4940.

MAJOR FIELD ORGANIZATIONS

OPERATIONS OFFICES

Managers:
Chicago.—Marvin Gunn, (708) 972–2110.
Idaho.—Elizabeth D. Sellers, (208) 526–5665.
Oak Ridge.—Gerald Boyd, (865) 576–4444.
Richland.—Keith Klein, (509) 376–7395.
Savannah River.—Jeffrey Allison, (803) 725–2405.

SITE OFFICES

Director, Oakland.—James Hirahara, (510) 637–1800.
Manager, Nevada.—Kathleen A. Carlson, (702) 295–3211.

NNSA SERVICE CENTER

Director, Albuquerque.—James Hirahara, (505) 845–6049.

FIELD OFFICES

Managers:
Golden.—John Kerston, (303) 275–3000.
Ohio.—Robert Warther, (937) 865–3977.
Rocky Flatts.—Gene Schmitt, (303) 966–2025.

ENERGY EFFICIENCY REGIONAL OFFICES

Directors:
Atlanta.—James R. Powell, (404) 562–0555.
Boston.—Hugh Saussy, (617) 565–9700.
Chicago.—Peter Dreyfuss, (312) 353–6749.
Denver.—Bill Becker, (303) 275–4826.
Philadelphia.—James M. Ferguson, (215) 656–6977.
Seattle.—Julie A. Riel, (206) 553–2875.

POWER MARKETING ADMINISTRATIONS

Administrator, Power Administration:
Bonneville.—Stephen J. Wright, (503) 230–5101.
Southeastern Area.—Charles A. Borchardt, (706) 213–3805.
Southwestern Area.—Michael A. Diehl, (918) 595–6601.
Western Area.—Michael S. Hacskaylo, (720) 962–7707.

OFFICE OF SCIENTIFIC AND TECHNICAL INFORMATION

Director.—Walter L. Warnick, (301) 903–7996.
Manager.—Robert Charles Morgan, (865) 576–1193.

NAVAL REACTORS OFFICES

Managers:
Pittsburgh.—Henry A. Cardinali, (412) 476–7200.
Schenectady.—Phil E. Salm, (518) 395–4690.

YUCCA MOUNTAIN SITE CHARACTERIZATION OFFICE

Project Manager.—W. John Arthur III, (702) 794–1300.

FOSSIL ENERGY FIELD OFFICES

Directors:
Albany Research Center (Oregon).—George J. Dooley III, (541) 967–5893.
National Energy Technology Lab.—Rita A. Bajura, (304) 285–4511.
Project Manager, Strategic Petroleum Reserve Project Office.—William C. Gibson Jr., (504) 734–4201.

NAVAL PETROLEUM RESERVES

Directors:
California.—James Curtis Killen, (661) 837–5000.
Colorado, Utah, Wyoming (Oil Shale Reserves).—Clarke D. Turner, (307) 261–5161.

FEDERAL ENERGY REGULATORY COMMISSION

Washington DC 20426

Chair.—Patrick Henry Wood III, (202) 502–8000.
Commissioners:
William L. Massey, (202) 502–8366.
Nora Mead Brownell, (202) 502–8383.
Executive Director and Chief Financial Officer.—Thomas R. Herlihy, (202) 502–8300.
Director, Office of External Affairs.—Kevin Cadden, (202) 502–8004.

DEPARTMENT OF EDUCATION

400 Maryland Avenue SW 20202

phone 401–3000, fax 401–0596, http://www.ed.gov

RODERICK R. PAIGE, Secretary of Education; born in Monticello, MS; education: B.A., Jackson State University; M.A. and Ph.D., Indiana University; professional: faculty member at the University of Cincinnati, Jackson State University, Utica Junior College, and the Dean of the College of Education at Texas Southern University; served as a trustee and an officer of the Board of Education of the Houston Independent School District, 1989–1994; Superintendent of the Houston Independent School District, 1994–2000; as Superintendent, Secretary Paige created the Peer Examination, Evaluation, and Redesign (PEER) Program, launched a system of charter schools, and introduced teacher incentive pay based on performance; organizations: Houston Job Partnership Council; Texas Business and Education Coalition; NAACP; American Leadership Forum; Education Commission of the States; and the Council of the Great City Schools; awards: Harold W. McGraw, Jr., Prize in Education; Richard R. Green Award; National Association of Black School Educators' Superintendent of the Year; and the American Association of School Administrators' National Superintendent of the Year; nominated by President George W. Bush to become the 7th Secretary of Education, and was confirmed by the U.S. Senate on January 20, 2001.

OFFICE OF THE SECRETARY

Room 7W301, phone 401–3000, fax 401–0596

Secretary of Education.—Roderick R. Paige.
Chief of Staff.—John Danielson, 401–7773.
Director, Office of Public Affairs.—John Gibbons, room 7C115, 401–0768, fax 401–3130 or 401–0954.

OFFICE OF THE DEPUTY SECRETARY

Room 7W310, phone 401–1000, fax 401–3095

Deputy Secretary.—William D. Hansen.
Chief of Staff.—James Manning, 7W314, 401–1000.
Office of Educational Technology.—John Bailey, 205–4280.
Office of Small and Disadvantaged Business Utilization.—Vi Jaramillo, 708–9820.

OFFICE FOR CIVIL RIGHTS

330 C Street SW, Room 5000, 20202, phone 205–5526, fax 205–9862 or 205–9889

Assistant Secretary.—Gerald Reynolds.
Deputy Assistant Secretary for Enforcement.—Ken Marcus (acting).
Special Assistant/Legal.—Kristen Schultz, room 51138, 205–3594.
Director of:
Enforcement, East.—Susan Bowers, room 5112A, 205–5596.
Enforcement, West.—Gary Jackson (acting), room SAV 3310, (260) 220–7900.
Resource Management Group.—Lester Slayton, room 5119, 205–8233.
Program Legal Group.—Louis Goldstein, room 5012–C, 205–9703.

OFFICE OF THE UNDER SECRETARY

Room 7E300, phone 401–1000, fax 260–7113 or 401–4353 or 205–7655

Under Secretary.—Eugene Hickok.
Chief of Staff.—Ronald Tomalis, 205–7762.
Director of:
Policy.—Christine Wolfe.
Policy and Program Studies Services.—Alan Ginsburg, 401–3132.

OFFICE OF INSPECTOR GENERAL

330 C Street, SW., Room 4006, 20202, phone 205–5439, fax 206–3821

Inspector General.—John Higgins, Jr., 205–5439.
Deputy Inspector General.—Tom Carter, 205–9327.
Counsel to the Inspector General.—Mary Mitchelson, 260–3556.
Assistant Inspector General for—
Audit Services.—Helen Lew, 205–9604.
Evaluation, Inspection and Management Services.—Cathy Lewis, 205–8639.

OFFICE OF THE GENERAL COUNSEL

Room 6E301, phone 401–6000, fax 205–2689

General Counsel.—Brian Jones.
Chief of Staff.—Charles R. Hokanson.
Senior Counsel.—Robert Wexler.
Deputy General Counsel of:
Program Service.—Steven Y. Winnick.
Postsecondary and Departmental Service.—Jonathan A. Vogel.
Departmental and Legislative Service.—Kent Talbert.
Executive Officer.—J. Carolyn Adams, 401–8340.

OFFICE OF SPECIAL EDUCATION AND REHABILITATIVE SERVICES

330 C Street, SW., Room 3006, 20202, phone 205–5465, fax 205–9252

Assistant Secretary.—Robert Pasternack.
Deputy Assistant Secretary.—Loretta Chittum, 205–5465.
Executive Administrator.—Andrew J. Pepin, room 3110, 205–9439.
Director of:
Office of Special Education Programs.—Stephanie Lee, 205–5507.
National Institute on Disability and Rehabilitation Research.—Steve Tingus, 205–8134.
Commissioner of Rehabilitation Services Administration.—Joanne Wilson, room 3026, 205–5482, fax 205–9874.

OFFICE OF THE CHIEF INFORMATION OFFICER

Room 2W301, phone 401–5848, fax 260–3761

Chief Information Officer.—William J. Leidinger, room 2W311, 260–0563 or 401–5848.
Deputy Chief Information Officer/Chief Technology Officer.—Craig B. Luigart, ROB–3, room 4082, 401–3200.
Director of:
Information Assurance and Enterprise Strategies.—Robert Davidson, ROB–3, room 4060, 205–5263.
Information Management.—Arthur Graham, ROB–3, room 4060, 260–0710.
Information Technology.—Stephen Fletcher (acting), room 2W307, 260–2645.

OFFICE OF LEGISLATION AND CONGRESSIONAL AFFAIRS

Room 6W301, phone 401–0020, fax 401–1438

Assistant Secretary.—Karen A. Johnson, 401–0020.
Deputy Assistant Secretary.—Clay Boothby, 205–8729.
Chief of Staff.—Camille Welborn, 401–0051.
Director of Communications for Legislation and Congressional Affairs.—Dallas Lawrence, 260–1974.
Congressional Affairs Liaisons:
Western Region.—Bill Knudsen, 401–3743.
Midwestern Region.—Ann Marie Pedersen, 205–1315.
Southeastern Region.—Amanda Hughes, 401–2035.
Northeastern Region.—Jon Keeling, 401–0023.

OFFICE OF INTERGOVERNMENTAL AND INTERAGENCY AFFAIRS

Room 5E313, phone 401–0404, fax 401–8607

Assistant Secretary.—Laurie Rich.
Chief of Staff.—Jennifer Gerber, room 5E327.
Deputy Assistant Secretary for—
Intergovernmental and Constituent Services.—Scott Jenkins, 205–5158.
Regional Services.—Terri Rayburn, 205–0678.
Corporate Liaison.—Kimberly Strycharz, 401–3728.
Senior Director for Community Services.—John McGrath, 401–1309.

OFFICE OF THE CHIEF FINANCIAL OFFICER

Room 4E313, phone 401–0085, fax 401–0006

Chief Financial Officer.—Jack Martin, 401–0477.
Deputy Chief Financial Officer.—Mark Carney, room 4E314, 401–0085.
Chief of Staff.—Mike McArdle, 358–2125.
Special Assistant / Operations.—[Vacant].
Director of:
Contracts and Purchasing Operations.—Glenn Perry, room 3929A, 7th and D Streets, SW., 20202, 708–8488, fax 205–0323.
Financial Improvement and Post Audit Operations.—Richard Mueller, room 4W103, 708–7770, fax 401–0082.
Grants Policy and Oversight Staff.—Blanca Rodriguez, 7th and D Streets, SW., room 3652, 20202, 260–8725, fax 205–0667.
Financial Management Operations.—Terry Bowie, room 4W202, 401–4144.
Financial Systems Operations.—Danny Harris, room 4E230, 401–0896.

OFFICE OF MANAGEMENT

Room 2W301, phone 401–5848, fax 260–3761

Assistant Secretary / Chief Information Officer.—William J. Leidinger, room 2W311, 260–0563 or 401–5848, fax 260–3761.
Deputy Assistant Secretaries: Stephen Fletcher, room 2W307, 260–2645, fax 260–3761; Michael Munoz, room 2W330, 401–5848, fax 260–3761.
Chief of Staff.—Nina Aten (acting), room 2W323, 205–4020, fax 260–3761.
Executive Officer.—Keith Berger, room 2W227, 401–0693, fax 401–3513.
Group Director of:
Human Resource Services.—Veronica D. Trietsch, room 2E314, 401–0553, fax 401–0520.
Process Performance Improvement Services.—Ann Manheimer, room 2W316, 205–8799.
Office of Hearings and Appeals.—Frank J. Furey, L'Enfant Plaza–2134, 619–9701, fax 619–9726.
Facility Services.—Steve Moore, room 2E315, 401–2349, fax 732–1534.
Security Services.—Michell Clark (acting), room 2W321, 260–7337, fax 260–3761.
Management Services.—George F. Green, room 2W226, 401–5931.

OFFICE OF FEDERAL STUDENT AID

830 First Street, NE., 20202, phone 377–3000, fax 275–5000

Chief Operating Officer.—Terri Shaw.
Chief of Staff.—Deborah Price.
Ombudsman.—Deb Wiley, room 41I1, 377–3801.
Chief Financial Officer.—Vicki Bateman, room 42G3, 377–3401.
Chief Information Officer.—Jerry Schubert, room 102E3, 377–3009.
Program Manager, Policy Liaison and Implementation Staff.—Jeff Baker, room 93G3, 377–4009.
General Manager of:
Administration and Workforce Support Services.—Calvin Thomas, room 22D1, 377–3011.
FSA Application and Delivery Services.—Kay Jacks, room 82E1, 377–4286.
Borrower Services.—Tom Pestka, room 41F1, 377–3015.
Communications Management Services.—Marianna O'Brien, room 11, 377–3095.
Financial Partners Services.—Kristie Hansen, room 112F1, 377–3301.
Enterprise Performance Management Services.—John Fare, room 92G2, 377–3707.

OFFICE OF POSTSECONDARY EDUCATION

1990 K Street, NW., 20006, phone 502–7750, fax 502–7677

Assistant Secretary.—Sally Stroup, 502–7715.
Chief of Staff.—Robert Lewis, 502–7713.
Deputy Assistant Secretary for—
Policy, Planning and Innovation.—Jeff Andrade, 502–7950.
Higher Education Programs.—Wilbert Bryant, 502–7555.

INSTITUTE OF EDUCATION SCIENCES

555 New Jersey Avenue, NW., Room 600, 20208, phone 219–1385, fax 219–1466

Director.—Russ Whitehurst.
Chief of Staff.—[Vacant].
Commissioner of:
National Center for Education Statistics.—[Vacant].
National Center for Education Evaluation and Regional Assistance.—[Vacant].
National Center for Education Research.—[Vacant].

OFFICE OF ELEMENTARY AND SECONDARY EDUCATION

400 Maryland Avenue, SW., Room 3W315, 20202, phone 401–0113, 205–0303

Assistant Secretary.—[Vacant].
Deputy Assistant Secretary.—Darla Marburger, 260–2032.
Chief of Staff.—Doug Mesecar, 401–0113.
Director of:
Impact Aid Programs.—Catherine Schagh, room 3E105, 260–3858, fax 205–0088.
Office of Migrant Education.—Francisco Garcia, room 3E317, 260–1164, fax 205–0089.
Office of Indian Education.—Victoria Vasques, 205–3687.
Student Achievement and School Accountability Programs.—Jackie Jackson (acting), 260–0826.
School Support and Technology Programs.—Sylvia Wright, 260–3778
Academic Improvement and Teacher Quality Programs.—Joseph Conaty, 260–8230.
Reading First.—Christopher Doherty, 401–2176.

OFFICE OF BILINGUAL EDUCATION AND MINORITY LANGUAGE AFFAIRS

330 C Street, SW., Room 5094, 20202, phone 205–5463, fax 205–8737 or 205–8680

Director.—Maria Hernandez Ferrier, 205–5463.
Deputy Director.—Marina Tse, 205–5463.
Senior Policy Advisor.—Kathleen Leos, 205–4037.

OFFICE OF VOCATIONAL AND ADULT EDUCATION

330 C Street, SW., Room 4090, 20202, phone 205–5451, fax 205–8748

Assistant Secretary.—[Vacant].
Deputy Assistant Secretary.—Hans Meeder, 205–9228.
Chief of Staff.—Amy Horton, 205–9289.
Special Assistant.—Joan Athen, 205–8224.
Confidential Assistant.—Ginger DeMint, 260–3570.

OFFICE OF SAFE AND DRUG-FREE SCHOOLS

400 Maryland Avenue, SW., phone 260–3954, fax 260–7767

Deputy Under Secretary.—Eric Andell, room 1E110, 205–4169.
Associate Deputy Under Secretary.—Bill Modzeleski, room 3E314, 260–1856.

OFFICE OF INNOVATION AND IMPROVEMENT

400 Maryland Avenue, SW., 20202, phone 205–4500

Deputy Under Secretary.—Nina Rees, 205–4484.
Associate Deputy Under Secretary for Policy: Michael Petrilli, 205–0653.
Special Assistant/School Choice Director.—Lori Yaklin, 401–1857.
Confidential Assistants: Megan Flock, 205–4499; Amber Hutchinson, 401–0850.

DEPARTMENT OF VETERANS AFFAIRS

Mail should be addressed to 810 Vermont Avenue, Washington DC 20420

http://www.va.gov

ANTHONY J. PRINCIPI, Secretary of Veterans Affairs; education: B.S., U.S. Navy Academy; J.D., Seton Hall University School of Law; military service: U.S. Navy, 1967–1990; Vietnam War veteran, receiving several decorations, including the Bronze Star with a ''V'' for Valor; public service: Veterans Administration, Deputy Administrator, 1983–1984; Staff Director for Senator Alan Simpson (R–WY), 1984–1986; Senate Committee on Veterans' Affairs, Republican Chief Counsel and Staff Director, 1984–1988; Deputy Secretary of Veterans Affairs, 1989–1992; Acting Secretary of Veterans Affairs, 1992–1993; professional: QTC Medical Services, Inc., serving as President; Luce, Forward, Hamilton & Scripps (law firm); Lockheed Martin IMS; family: married to Elizabeth Ann; three children; nominated by President George W. Bush to become the 4th Secretary of Veterans' Affairs, and was confirmed by the U.S. Senate on January 23, 2001.

OFFICE OF THE SECRETARY

Secretary of Veterans Affairs.—Anthony J. Principi, 273–4800.
Chief of Staff.—Nora E. Egan, 273–4808.
Deputy Chief of Staff.—Ronald Aument.
Special Assistant for Veterans Service Organizations Liaison.—Allen (Gunner) Kent, 273–4835.
General Counsel.—Tim S. McClain, 273–6660.
Inspector General.—Richard J. Griffin, 801 I Street, NW., 565–8620.
Chairman, Board of:
Contract Appeals.—Gary J. Krump, 1800 G Street, NW., 273–6743.
Veterans Appeals.—Eligah D. Clark, 811 Vermont Avenue, NW., 565–5001.

OFFICE OF THE DEPUTY SECRETARY

Deputy Secretary of Veterans Affairs.—Leo S. MacKay, Jr., 273–4817.
Director of:
Center for Minority Veterans.—Charles W. Nesby, 273–6708.
Center for Women Veterans.—Irene Trowell-Harris, 273–6193.
Employment Discrimination Complaint Adjudication.—Charles R. Delobe, 1722 I Street, NW., 254–0065.
Small and Disadvantaged Business Utilization.—Scott Denniston, 801 I Street, NW., 565–8124.
Regulation Policy and Management.—William A. Moorman, 273–9515.

ASSISTANT SECRETARY FOR CONGRESSIONAL AND LEGISLATIVE AFFAIRS

Assistant Secretary.—Gordon H. Mansfield, 273–5611.
Deputy Assistant Secretary for—
Legislative Affairs.—[Vacant].
Congressional Affairs.—[Vacant].

ASSISTANT SECRETARY FOR PUBLIC AND INTERGOVERNMENTAL AFFAIRS

Assistant Secretary.—Thomas G. Bowman (acting), 273–5750.
Deputy Assistant Secretary for—
Public Affairs.—Jeffrey E. Phillips, 273–5710.
Intergovernmental and International Affairs.—William McLemore, 273–5760.

ASSISTANT SECRETARY FOR POLICY, PLANNING, AND PREPAREDNESS

Assistant Secretary.—Claude M. Kicklighter, 273–5033.
Principal Deputy Assistant Secretary.—Dennis M. Duffy.
Deputy Assistant Secretary for—
Planning and Evaluation.—Gary A. Steinberg, 273–5068.
Policy.—David J. Balland, 273–5182.
Security and Law Enforcement.—John H. Baffa, 273–5500.
Director, Readiness and Emergency Preparedness.—Robert G. Claypool, M.D., 273–9276.

ASSISTANT SECRETARY FOR MANAGEMENT

Assistant Secretary.—William H. Campbell, 273–5589.
Principal Deputy Assistant Secretary.—D. Mark Catlett, 273–5583.
Deputy Assistant Secretary for—
Budget.—Rita Reed, 273–5289.
Finance.—Edward Murray (acting), 273–5504.
Acquisition and Materiel Management.—David S. Derr (acting), 273–6029.

ASSISTANT SECRETARY FOR INFORMATION AND TECHNOLOGY

Assistant Secretary.—John A. Gauss, Ph.D., RADM (ret) USN, 273–8842.
Deputy Assistant Secretary for Information and Technology Management.—Edward F. Meagher, 273–8855.

ASSISTANT SECRETARY FOR HUMAN RESOURCES AND ADMINISTRATION

Assistant Secretary.—William H. Campbell (acting), 273–4901.
Principal Deputy Assistant Secretary.—Robert W. Schultz, 273–5356.
Deputy Assistant Secretary for—
Human Resources Management.—Ventris Gibson, 273–4921.
Diversity Management and EEO.—Armando Rodriquez, 273–5888.
Resolution Management.—James S. Jones, 1575 I Street, NW., 501–2800.
Director, Office of Administration.—C.G. (Deno) Verenes, 273–5356.
Associate Deputy for Labor-Management Relations.—Ronald E. Cowles, 273–5369.

NATIONAL CEMETERY ADMINISTRATION

Under Secretary.—John W. Nicholson, 273–5146.
Deputy Under Secretary.—S. Eric Benson, 273–5153.
Senior Advisor.—Richard A. Wannemacher, Jr., 273–5235
Director of:
Field Programs.—Steve Muro, 273–5235.
Construction Management.—Robert B. Holbrook, 565–4830.
Finance and Planning.—Dan Tucker, 273–5157.
Memorial Programs Service.—David Schettler, 501–3100.
State Cemetery Grants Service.—G. William Jayne, 565–6152.
Communications Management Service.—Peggy McGee, 273–5175.
Information Systems Service.—Joseph Nosari, 273–5205.
Management Support Service.—Tom Balsanek, 273–5218.

VETERANS BENEFITS ADMINISTRATION

Under Secretary.—Daniel L. Cooper, 1800 G Street, NW., 273–6761.
Deputy Under Secretary.—William D. Stinger (acting).
Chief of Staff.—Lois Mittelstaedt.
Associate Deputy Under Secretary for—
Policy and Program Management.—Robert J. Epley, 273–6851.
Field Operations.—Michel Walcoff, 273–7259.
Chief Financial Officer.—James Bohmbach, 273–6728.
VA Deputy Chief Information Officer for Benefits.—K. Adair Martinez, 273–7004.

Director of:

Compensation and Pension.—Ronald Henke, 273–7203.

Education.—Judith A. Caden, 273–7132.

Employee Development and Training.—Dorothy Mackay, 273–5446.

Insurance.—Thomas Lastowka, 215–381–3100.

Loan Guaranty.—R. Keith Pedigo, 273–7331.

Vocational Rehabilitation and Employment.—Jeff Alger (acting), 273–7419.

VETERANS HEALTH ADMINISTRATION

Under Secretary.—Robert H. Roswell, M.D., 273–5781.

Deputy Under Secretary.—Jonathan B. Perlin, M.D., 273–5878.

Deputy Under Secretary for Health (DUSH) for Operations and Management.—Laura J. Miller, 273–5826.

Director, Network Support.—[Vacant].

Officer for—

Patient Care Services.—Thomas V. Holohan, M.D., 273–8474.

Public Health and Environmental Hazards.—Susan H. Mather, M.D., 273–8575.

Research and Development.—Nelda Wray, M.D., M.P.H., 254–0183.

DEPARTMENT OF HOMELAND SECURITY

U.S. Naval Security Station, 3801 Nebraska Avenue, NW., Washington, DC 20393

phone 282–8000

TOM RIDGE, Secretary of Homeland Security; born on August 26, 1945, in Pittsburgh's Steel Valley; education: earned a scholarship to Harvard University, graduated with honors, 1967; law degree, Dickinson School of Law; military service: U.S. Army; served as an infantry staff sergeant in Vietnam; awarded the Bronze Star for Valor; profession: Attorney; public service: Assistant District Attorney, Erie County, PA; U.S. House of Representatives, 1983–1995; Governor of Pennsylvania, 1995–2001; family: married to Michele; children: Lesley and Tommy; appointed by President George W. Bush as Office of Homeland Security Advisor, October 8, 2001; nominated by President Bush to become the 1st Secretary of Homeland Security on November 25, 2002, and was confirmed by the U.S. Senate on January 22, 2003.

OFFICE OF THE SECRETARY

Secretary of Homeland Security.—Tom Ridge.

OFFICE OF THE DEPUTY SECRETARY

Deputy Secretary of Homeland Security.—Gordon R. England.

OFFICE OF THE CHIEF OF STAFF

Chief of Staff.—Bruce Lawlor.

MANAGEMENT DIRECTORATE

Under Secretary.—Janet Hale.
- *Chief Financial Officer.*—Bruce Carnes.
- *Chief Information Officer.*—Steven Cooper.
- *Chief Human Capital Officer.*—Ronald James.

BORDER AND TRANSPORTATION SECURITY DIRECTORATE

Under Secretary.—Asa Hutchinson.
- *Assistant Secretary for Policy and Planning.*—Stewart Verdery.
- *Commissioner, Customs and Border Protection.*—Robert Bonner.
- *Administrator, Transportation Security Administration.*—James Loy.

SCIENCE AND TECHNOLOGY DIRECTORATE

Under Secretary.—Charles E. McQueary.

INFORMATION ANALYSIS AND INFRASTRUCTURE PROTECTION DIRECTORATE

Under Secretary.—Frank Libutti.
Assistant Secretary for Infrastructure Protection.—Robert Liscouski.

EMERGENCY PREPAREDNESS AND RESPONSE DIRECTORATE

Under Secretary.—Michael Brown.

UNITED STATES SECRET SERVICE

Director.—W. Ralph Basham.

UNITED STATES COAST GUARD

Commandant.—ADM Thomas H. Collins.

BUREAU OF CITIZENSHIP AND IMMIGRATION SERVICES

Director.—Eduardo Aguirre.

OFFICE OF COUNTERNARCOTICS

Counternarcotics Officer/U.S. Interdiction Coordinator.—Roger Mackin.

OFFICE OF STATE AND LOCAL GOVERNMENT COORDINATION

Director.—Josh Filler.

OFFICE OF NATIONAL CAPITAL REGION COORDINATION

Director.—Michael Byrne.

OFFICE OF THE INSPECTOR GENERAL

Inspector General.—Clark Ervin (acting).

OFFICE OF THE GENERAL COUNSEL

General Counsel.—Joe Whitley.

OFFICE OF THE PRIVACY OFFICER

Privacy Officer.—Nuala O'Connor Kelly.

OFFICE OF CIVIL RIGHTS AND CIVIL LIBERTIES

Civil Rights and Civil Liberties Officer.—Daniel Sutherland.

OFFICE OF THE PRIVATE SECTOR LIAISON

Special Assistant to the Secretary.—Al Martinez-Fonts.

OFFICE OF LEGISLATIVE AFFAIRS

Assistant Secretary.—Pam Turner.

OFFICE OF PUBLIC AFFAIRS

Assistant Secretary.—Susan Neely.

OFFICE OF INTERNATIONAL AFFAIRS

Director.—Cresencio Arcos.

INDEPENDENT AGENCIES, COMMISSIONS, BOARDS

ADVISORY COUNCIL ON HISTORIC PRESERVATION

1100 Pennsylvania Avenue NW, Suite 809, 20004

phone 606–8503, http://www.achp.gov

[Created by Public Law 89–665, as amended]

Chairman.—John L. Nau III, Houston, Texas.
Vice Chairman.—Bernadette Castro, Albany, New York.
Expert Members:
Bruce D. Judd, San Francisco, California.
Susan S. Schanlaber, Aurora, Illinois.
Ann Alexander Pritzlaff, Denver, Colorado.
Julia A. King, St. Leonard, Maryland.
Citizen Members:
Emily Summers, Dallas, Texas.
Carolyn J. Brackett, Nashville, Tennessee.
Native American Member:
Raynard C. Soon, Honolulu, Hawaii.
Governor.—Hon. Tim Pawlenty, St. Paul, Minnesota.
Mayor.—Hon. Bob Young, Augusta, Georgia.
Architect of the Capitol.—Hon. Alan M. Hantman, FAIA.
Secretary, Department of:
Agriculture.—Hon. Ann M. Veneman.
Interior.—Hon. Gale A. Norton.
Defense.—Hon. Donald H. Rumsfeld.
Transportation.—Hon. Norman Y. Mineta.
Administrator:
Environmental Protection Agency.—[Vacant].
General Services Administration.—Hon. Stephen A. Perry.
National Trust for Historic Preservation.—William B. Hart, Chairman, South Berwick, Maine.
National Conference of State Historic Preservation Officers.—Edward F. Sanderson, President, Providence, Rhode Island.

AFRICAN DEVELOPMENT FOUNDATION

1400 Eye Street NW, Suite 1000, 20005–2248, phone 673–3916, fax 673–3810

E-mail: info@adf.gov; Wb: www.adf.gov

[Created by Public Law 96–533]

BOARD OF DIRECTORS

Chairman.—Ernest G. Green.
Vice Chairman.—Willie Grace Campbell.
Private Members: [Vacant].
Public Members: [Vacant].

STAFF

President.—Nathaniel Fields.
Vice President.—[Vacant].
Advisory Committee Management.—[Vacant].
Congressional Liaison Officer.—Roger Ervin.

General Counsel.—Doris Mason Martin.
Budget and Finance Director.—Vicki L. Gentry.
Management and Information Systems.—Thomas F. Wilson.
Personnel Director.—[Vacant].
Program and Field Operations:
Region 1: Rama Bah.
Region 2: Christine Fowles.
Region 3: Kim Ward.
Region 4: Thomas R. Coogan.
Region 5: José Goncalves.

AMERICAN BATTLE MONUMENTS COMMISSION

Courthouse Plaza II, Suite 500, 2300 Clarendon Blvd., Arlington, VA 22201–3367

phone (703) 696–6902

[Created by Public Law 105–225]

Chairman.—GEN P.X. Kelly, U.S. Marine Corps (ret.).
Commissioners:
LTG Julius Becton, Jr., U.S. Army (ret.).
MG Patrick H. Brady, U.S. Army (ret.).
Honorable James B. Francis, Jr.
GEN Frederick M. Franks, U.S. Army (ret.).
Honorable Antonio Lopez.
Honorable Joseph E. Persico.
Honorable Sara A. Sellers.
Honorable Alan K. Simpson.
MG Will Hill Tankersley, U.S. Army (ret.).
BG Sue E. Turner, U.S. Air Force (ret.).
Secretary.—MG John P. Herrling, U.S. Army (ret.).
Executive Director.—Kenneth S. Pond.
Director for—
Engineering, Maintenance, and Operations.—Thomas R. Sole.
Finance.—Vincent Scatamacchia.
Personnel and Administration.—Theodore Gloukoff.
Procurement and Contracting.—William B. Owenby.

(Note: Public law changed to 105–225, August 1998; H.R. 1085).

AMERICAN NATIONAL RED CROSS

National Headquarters, 2025 E Street, NW., 20006, phone (202) 737–8300

HONORARY OFFICERS

Honorary Chairman.—George W. Bush, President of the United States.

CORPORATE OFFICERS

Chairman.—David T. McLaughlin.
President & CEO.—Marsha J. Evans.
General Counsel/Secretary.—Mary S. Elcano.

BOARD OF GOVERNORS

C=Elected by the Chartered Units

L=Elected by Board as Member-at-Large

P=Appointed by the President of the United States

Gina Adams (L).
Chris Allen (C).
Richard L. Armitage (P).
Sanford A. Belden (C).
Dr. Steven J. Bredehoeft (C).
Steven E. Carr (C).
Nita Clyde (L).
Douglas H. Dittrick (C).
Donald L. Evans (P).
Kathryn A. Forbes (C).
Bill J. Gagliano (C).
Dr. Lee A. Goldstein (C).

Karen K. Goodman (C)
William F. Grinnan, Jr. (C).
Carol Ann Haake (C).
Dr. Susan B. Hassmiller (C).
Michael W. Hawkins (C).
Edward A. Heidt, Jr. (C).
Joyce N. Hoffman (C).
Judith Richards Hope (L).
Jon M. Huntsman (L).
Gregory Kozmetsky (L).
Sherry Lansing (L).
Dr. William V. Lewis, Jr. (C).
Rex K. Linder (C).
Peter T. Loftin (L).
William Lucy (L).
Elaine M. Lyerly (C).
Dr. Allen W. Mathies, Jr. (C).
William F. McConnell, Jr. (C).
David T. McLaughlin (P).
E.R. Mitchell, Jr. (C).
Richard B. Myers (P).
Richard M. Niemiec (C).
Ross H. Ogden (C).
Roderick R. Paige (P).
Pat M. Powers (C).
Anthony J. Principi (P).
Thomas J. Ridge (P)
Glenn A. Sieber (C).
Nancylee A. Siebermann (C).
Brig. Gen. Robert L. Smolen (L).
E. Francine Stokes (C).
Tommy G. Thompson (P).
Christine K. Wilkinson (C).
Maurice W. Worth (C).

Chairman Emeritus.—Frank Stanton.

ADMINISTRATIVE OFFICERS

National Chair of Volunteers.—Mary H. DeKuyper.
Chief Diversity Officer.—Tony Polk.
Chief Financial Officer.—Robert P. McDonald.
Executive Vice President for—
Chapter Services Network.—James Krueger.
Disaster Services.—Terry Sicilia.
Executive Vice President & CEO, Biomedical Services.—Ramesh Thadani.
General Auditor.—Timothy Holmes.
Senior Vice President/Chief Information Officer.—Thomas Schwaninger.
Senior Vice President for—
Communications and Marketing.—Charles Connor.
Growth and Integrated Development.—Skip Seitz.
Human Resources.—Stanley H. Davis.
Quality and Regulatory.—[Vacant].
Vice President for—
Armed Forces Emergency Services.—Sue Richter.
Finance and Business Planning.—Brian Rhoa.
Government Relations.—Jan Lane.
Health, Safety and Community Services.—Scott Conner.
International Services.—Gerald Jones.

APPALACHIAN REGIONAL COMMISSION

1666 Connecticut Avenue NW 20235, phone (202) 884–7660, fax 884–7691

Federal Co-Chairman.—Anne B. Pope.
Alternate Federal Co-Chairman.—Richard J. Peltz.
States' Washington Representative.—G. William Walker.
Executive Director.—Thomas M. Hunter.
Congressional Affairs Officer.—Guy Land.

ARMED FORCES RETIREMENT HOME

3700 N. Capitol Street, NW., Box 1303, Washington, DC 20317

phone (202) 730–3077, fax 730–3166

Chief Operating Officer.—Timothy C. Cox.
Chief Financial Officer.—Steven G. McManus.

ARMED FORCES RETIREMENT HOME—WASHINGTON

3700 N. Capitol Street, NW., Washington, DC 20317

phone (202) 730–3229, fax 730–3127

Director.—COL Arnold Smith, USA.
Deputy Director.—CAPT(s) Paul Soares, USN.

ARMED FORCES RETIREMENT HOME—GULFPORT

1800 Beach Drive, Gulfport, MS 39507, phone (228) 897–4003, fax 897–4013

Director.—CAPT Jerald Ulmer, Sr., USN.
Deputy Director.—LCOL Wendy Van Dyke, USAF.

BOARD OF GOVERNORS OF THE FEDERAL RESERVE SYSTEM

Constitution Avenue and 20th Street 20551, phone (202) 452–3000

Chairman.—Alan Greenspan.
Vice Chair.—Roger W. Ferguson, Jr.
Members: Ben S. Bernanke; Susan Schmidt Bies; Edward M. Gramlich; Donald L. Kohn, Mark W. Olson.
Assistant to the Board and Director.—Donald J. Winn.
Assistants to the Board: Lynn Fox, Michelle A. Smith.
Deputy Congressional Liaison.—Winthrop P. Hambley.
Special Assistants to the Board: Rosanna Pianalto-Cameron, Dave Skidmore, John H. Lopez.

DIVISION OF INTERNATIONAL FINANCE

Director.—Karen H. Johnson.
Deputy Director.—David H. Howard.
Associate Director.—Thomas A. Conners.
Deputy Associate Directors: Richard T. Freeman, Steven B. Kamin.
Assistant Directors: Jon W. Faust, Joseph E. Gagnon, Michael P. Leahy, D. Nathan Sheets, Ralph W. Tryon.
Senior Advisers: Dale W. Henderson, William L. Helkie.
Adviser.—Willene A. Johnson.

DIVISION OF RESEARCH AND STATISTICS

Director.—David J. Stockton.
Deputy Directors: Edward C. Ettin, David Wilcox.
Associate Directors: Myron L. Kwast, Stephen D. Oliner, Patrick M. Parkinson, Lawrence Slifman, Charles S. Struckmeyer.
Deputy Associate Director.— Joyce K. Zickler.
Assistant Directors: J. Nellie Liang, S. Wayne Passmore, David L. Reifschneider, Janice Shack-Marquez, William L. Wascher III, Mary M. West, Alice Patricia White.
Senior Advisers: Glenn B. Canner, David S. Jones, Thomas D. Simpson.

DIVISION OF MONETARY AFFAIRS

Director.—Vincent Reinhart.
Deputy Directors: David E. Lindsey, Brian F. Madigan.
Deputy Associate Director.—William C. Whitesell.
Assistant Directors: James A. Clouse, William B. English.
Senior Adviser.—Richard D. Porter.
Special Assistant to the Board.—Normand R.V. Bernard.

DIVISION OF BANKING SUPERVISION AND REGULATION

Director.—Richard Spillenkothen.
Deputy Director.—Stephen C. Schemering.
Senior Associate Directors: Herbert A. Biern, Roger T. Cole, William A. Ryback.
Associate Directors: Gerald A. Edwards, Jr, Stephen M. Hoffman, Jr., James V. Houpt, Jack P. Jennings, Michael G. Martinson, Molly S. Wassom.
Deputy Associate Directors: Howard A. Amer, Norah M. Barger, Betsy Cross.
Assistant Directors: Deborah P. Bailey, Barbara J. Bouchard, Angela Desmond, James A. Embersit, Charles H. Holm, William G. Spaniel, David M. Wright.
Project Director, National Information Center.—William C. Schneider.

LEGAL DIVISION

General Counsel.—J. Virgil Mattingly, Jr.
Associate General Counsels: Scott G. Alvarez, Richard M. Ashton, Stephanie Martin, Kathleen M. O'Day.
Assistant General Counsels: Ann E. Misback, Stephen L. Siciliano, Katherine H. Wheatley, Cary K. Williams.

DIVISION OF CONSUMER AND COMMUNITY AFFAIRS

Director.—Dolores S. Smith.
Deputy Director.—Glenn E. Loney.
Senior Associate Director.—Sandra F. Braunstein.
Associate Directors: Adrienne D. Hurt, Irene Shawn McNulty.
Assistant Directors: James A. Michasels, Tonda E. Price.

OFFICE OF THE SECRETARY

Secretary.—Jennifer J. Johnson.
Deputy Secretary.—Robert deV. Frierson.
Assistant Secretary.—Margaret M. Shanks.

STAFF DIRECTOR FOR MANAGEMENT

Staff Director.—Stephen R. Malphrus.
EEO Programs Director.—Sheila Clark.

MANAGEMENT DIVISION

Director.—William R. Jones.
Deputy Director.—H. Fay Peters.
Associate Directors: Stephen J. Clark, Darrell R. Pauley, David L. Williams.
Assistant Directors: Christine M. Fields, Billy J. Sauls, Donald A. Spicer.

DIVISION OF INFORMATION TECHNOLOGY

Director.—Marianne M. Emerson.
Deputy Director.—Maureen T. Hannan.
Assistant Directors: Tillena G. Clark, Geary L. Cunningham, Wayne A. Edmondson, Po Kyung Kim, Susan F. Marycz, Sharon L. Mowry, Raymond Romero, Robert F. Taylor.

DIVISION OF SUPPORT SERVICES

Associate Director.—David L. Williams.

INSPECTOR GENERAL

Inspector General.—Barry R. Snyder.
Deputy Inspector General.—Donald L. Robinson.

DIVISION OF FEDERAL RESERVE BANK OPERATIONS AND PAYMENT SYSTEMS

Director.—Louise L. Roseman.
Associate Directors: Paul W. Bettge, Jeffrey C. Marquardt.
Assistant Directors: Kenneth D. Buckley, Joseph H. Hayes, Jr., Edgar A. Martindale III, Marsha W. Reidhill, Jeff J. Stehm, Jack K. Walton III.

COMMISSION OF FINE ARTS

401 F Street NW, National Building Museum, 20001

phone (202) 504–2200, fax 504–2195

Commissioners:
David M. Childs, New York, NY.
Donald A. Capoccia, New York, NY.
Barbaralee Diamonstein-Spielvogel, New York, NY.
Pamela Nelson, Dallas, TX.
Earl A. Powell III, Alexandria, VA.
Diana Balmori, New York, NY.
Elyn Zimmerman, New York, NY.
Secretary.—Charles H. Atherton, Washington, DC.

BOARD OF ARCHITECTURAL CONSULTANTS FOR THE OLD GEORGETOWN ACT

Mary Oehrlein, FAIA, chair.
John McCartney, FAIA.
Heather Willson CASS, FAIA.

COMMITTEE FOR PURCHASE FROM PEOPLE WHO ARE BLIND OR SEVERELY DISABLED

1421 Jefferson Davis Highway, Suite 10800, Jefferson Plaza 2

Arlington, VA 22202–3259, phone (703) 603–7740, fax 603–0655

Chairperson.—Steven B. Schwalb, Department of Justice.
Vice Chairperson.—LeRoy F. Saunders, private citizen (knowledgeable about obstacles to employment of persons who are blind).
Members:
[Vacant], Department of the Army.
Michael Sade, Department of Commerce.
[Vacant], General Services Administration.
Joanne M. Wilson, Department of Education.
William Mea, Department of Labor.
[Vacant], Department of Defense.
Timothy A. Beyland, Department of the Air Force.
Andrew D. Houghton, private citizen (representing nonprofit agency employees with other severe disabilities).
John Surina, Department of Agriculture.
Gary J. Krump, Department of Veterans Affairs.
RADM Justin D. McCarthy, Department of the Navy.
James H. Omvig, private citizen (representing nonprofit agency employees who are blind).

COMMODITY FUTURES TRADING COMMISSION

Three Lafayette Centre, 1155 21st Street NW 20581, phone 418–5000

fax 418–5521, http://www.cfta.gov

Chairman.—James E. Newsome, 418–5050.
Chief of Staff.—Scott Parsons, 418–5050.
Commissioners:
Barbara Pedersen Holum, 418–5070.
Walter L. Lukken, 418–5014.
Sharon Brown-Hruska, 418–5037.
Executive Director.—Madge A. Bolinger, 418–5160.
General Counsel.—Patrick McCarty, 418–5120.
Office of the Chief Economist.—James A. Overdahl, 418–5656.
Director, Division of:
Enforcement.—Gregory Mocek, 418–5320.
Clearing and Intermediary Oversight.—Jane Kang Thorps, 418–5108.
Market Oversight.—Michael Gorham, 418–5260.
Director, Office of:
External Affairs.—Alan C. Sobba, 418–5080.
Secretary.—Jean A. Webb, 418–5100.
Inspector General.—A. Roy Lavik, 418–5110.
International Affairs.—Andrea M. Corcoran, 418–5645.

REGIONAL OFFICES

Chicago: 525 West Monroe Street, Suite 1100, Chicago, IL 60601, (312) 596–0700, fax 596–0716.
Kansas City: 4900 Main Street, Suite 721, Kansas City, MO 64112, (816) 931–7600, fax 931–9643.
Minneapolis: 510 Grain Exchange Building, Minneapolis, MN 55415, (612) 370–3255, fax 370–3257.
New York: 140 Broadway, Suite 3747, New York, NY 10005, (646) 746–9700, fax 746–9938.

CONSUMER PRODUCT SAFETY COMMISSION

4330 East West Highway, Bethesda, MD 20814, phone (301) 504–6816
fax 504–0124, http://www.cpsc.gov

[Created by Public Law 92–573]

Chairperson.—Hal D. Stratton, 504–7900.
Commissioners: Mary Sheila Gall, 504–7901, Thomas H. Moore, 504–7902.
Executive Director.—Patricia M. Semple, 504–7907.
Deputy Executive Director.—Thomas W. Murr, Jr., 504–7907.
Secretary.—Todd A. Stevenson, 504–7923.
General Counsel.—William H. DuRoss, 504–7922.
Director, Congressional Relations.—John R. Horner, 504–7903.

CORPORATION FOR NATIONAL AND COMMUNITY SERVICE

1201 New York Avenue NW 20525, phone (202) 606–5000
http://www.cns.gov

[Executive Order 11603, June 30, 1971; codified in 42 U.S.C., section 4951]

Chief Executive Officer.—Dr. Leslie Lenkowsky.
Chief of Staff.—Amy Mack.
Chief Operating Officer.—[Vacant].
Chief Financial Officer.—Michelle Guillerman.
Inspector General.—Russell George, ext. 390.
Director of AmeriCorps.—Rosie Mauk, ext. 206.
General Counsel.—Frank Trinity (acting), ext. 256.
Director, National Senior Service Corps.—Tess Scannell (acting), ext 300.
Director, Learn and Serve America.—Dr. Amy Cohen (acting), ext. 484.
Director, Congressional and Intergovernmental Relations.—Katherine Hoehn, ext. 473.

DEFENSE NUCLEAR FACILITIES SAFETY BOARD

625 Indiana Avenue NW, Suite 700, 20004, phone 694–7000

fax 208–6518, http://www.dnfsb.gov

Chairman.—John T. Conway.
Vice Chairman.—A.J. Eggenberger.
Members: Joseph J. DiNunno, John E. Mansfield, R. Bruce Matthews.
General Counsel.—Richard A. Azzaro.
General Manager.—Kenneth M. Pusateri.
Technical Director.—Kent Fortenberry.

DELAWARE RIVER BASIN COMMISSION

Delaware River Basin Commission, PO Box 7360, West Trenton, NJ 08628

phone (609) 883–9500, fax (609) 883–9522

FEDERAL REPRESENTATIVES

Federal Commissioner.—BG Merdith (Bo) Temple, U.S. Army Corps of Engineers, North Atlantic Military Community, Brooklyn, NY 11252, (718) 491–8801.
First Alternate.—COL Gregory G. Bean, U.S. Army Corps of Engineers, North Atlantic Military Community, Brooklyn, NY 11252, (718) 491–8802.
Second Alternate and Advisor.—LTC Timothy Brown, District Engineer, U.S. Army Corps of Engineers, Wanamaker Building, 100 Pennsylvania Square, East Philadelphia, PA 19107 (215) 656–6501.

STAFF

Executive Director.—Carol R. Collier.
Commission Secretary.—Pamela M. Bush, Esq.
Chief Administrative Officer.—Richard C. Gore.
Public Information Officer.—Christopher M. Roberts.

ENVIRONMENTAL PROTECTION AGENCY

1200 Pennsylvania Avenue, NW., 20460, (202) 564–4700, http://www.epa.gov

Administrator.—Marianne Horinko (acting).
Deputy Administrator.—Stephen Johnson (acting).
Environmental Appeals Board: Scott Fulton, Ronald McCallham, Edward Reich, Kathie Stein.
Associate Administrator for—
Public Affairs.—Joe Martyak, 564–9828.
Congressional and Intergovernmental Relations.—Edward Krenik, 564–5200.
Policy, Economics and Innovation.—Jessica Furey, 564–4332.
Staff Offices, Director for—
Regional Operations.—Judy Kertcher, 564–3103.
Children's Health Protection.—[Vacant], 564–2188.
Civil Rights.—Karen Higginbotham (acting), 564–7272.
Science Advisory Board.—Vanessa Vu, 564–4533.
Director, Office of:
Small and Disadvantaged Business Utilization.—Jeanette Brown, 564–4100.
Cooperative Environmental Management.—Dalva Balkus, 564–9741.
Executive Secretariat.—William Meagher III, 564–7311.
Executive Support.—Diane Bazzle, 564–0444.
Administrative Law Judges.—Chief Judge Susan L. Biro, 564–6255.

ADMINISTRATION AND RESOURCES MANAGEMENT

Assistant Administrator.—Morris X. Winn, 564–4600.
Director, Office of:
Policy and Resources Management.—Sherry A. Kashak (acting), 564–1861.
Acquisition Management.—Judy S. Davis, 564–4310.
Administration and Resources Management.—William M. Henderson, Cincinnati, OH (513) 487–2026.

Contracts Management Division.—Tom O'Connell, Research Triangle Park, NC (919) 541–3044.
Administration.—Richard Lemley, 564–8400.
Grants and Debarment.—Howard F. Corcoran, 564–5310.
Human Resources and Organizational Services—Rafael Deleon, 564–4606.

OFFICE OF ENVIRONMENTAL INFORMATION

Assistant Administrator.—Kim T. Nelson, 564–6665.
Deputy Assistant Administrator.—Richard Otis, 564–6665.
Director, Office of:
Planning, Resources, and Outreach.—Wendy Cleland-Hamnett (acting), 564–4673.
Information Collection.—Mark Luttner, 566–1360.
Information, Analysis, and Access.—Elaine Stanley, 566–0600.
Technology Operations and Planning.—Mark Day, 566–0300.

AIR AND RADIATION

Assistant Administrator.—Jeffrey (Jeff) Holmstead, 564–7404.
Deputy Assistant Administrators: John Beale, 564–6229, Elizabeth Craig, 564–7403, Robert D. Brenner 564–1666.
Policy Analysis and Review.—Robert D. Brenner, 564–1677.
Program Management Operations.—Jerry A. Kurtzweg, 564–1234.
Director, Office of:
Air Quality Planning and Standards.—Steve Page, Research Triangle Park, NC (919) 541–5616.
Atmospheric Programs.—Brian J. McLean (acting), 564–9140.
Transportation and Air Quality.—Margo T. Oge, 564–1682.
Radiation and Indoor Air.—Elizabeth Cotsworth, 564–9320.

ENFORCEMENT AND COMPLIANCE ASSURANCE

Assistant Administrator.—John (JP) Peter Suarez (acting), 564–2440.
Principal Deputy Assistant Administrator.—Phyllis P. Harris (acting), 564–2440.
Director, Office of:
Administration and Resources Management Support.—David Swack, 564–2455.
Compliance.—Michael M. Stahl, 564–2280.
Criminal Enforcement, Forensics, and Training.—Leo D'Amico, 564–2480.
Federal Facilities Enforcement.—David Kling, 564–2510.
Federal Activities.—Anne Miller, 564–5400.
Regulatory Enforcement.—Walker B. Smith, 564–2220.
Environmental Justice.—Barry Hill, 564–2515.
Site Remediation Enforcement: Barry N. Breen, 564–5110.
Planning Policy Analysis and Communications.—Mary Kay Lynch, 564–2530.

CHIEF FINANCIAL OFFICER

Chief Financial Officer.—Linda M. Combs, 564–1151.
Director Office of:
Planning, Analysis, and Accountability.—David W. Ziegele, 564–9327.
Comptroller.—Joseph Dillon, 564–9673.

GENERAL COUNSEL

General Counsel.—Robert E. Fabricant, 564–8040.
Deputy General Counsel.—Lisa M. Jaeger, 564–8040.
Principal Deputy General Counsel.—Anna L. Wolgast, 564–8064.
Designated Agency Ethics Official.—Anna L. Wolgast.
Associate General Counsel for—
Air and Radiation Law Office.—Lisa K. Friedman, 564–7606.
Civil Rights Law Office.—Stephen Pressman (acting), 564–2738.
Cross-Cutting Issues Law Office.—James C. Nelson, 564–7622.
Finance and Operations Law Office.—Marla E. Diamond, 564–5323.

International Environmental Law Office.—[Vacant], 564–1810.
Pesticides and Toxic Substances Law Office.—Patricia Roberts, 564–5375.
Solid Waste and Emergency Response Law Office.—Earl Salo (acting), 564–7706.
Water Law Office.—Susan G. Lepow, 564–7700.

INSPECTOR GENERAL

Inspector General.—Nikki L. Tinsley, 566–0847.
Deputy Inspector General.—Gary L. Johnson, 566–0847.
Assistant Inspector General for—
Audit.—Melissa Heist, 566–0824.
Investigations.—Michael J. Speedling, 566–0819.
Program Evaluation.—Kwai Chan, 566–0832.
Congressional and Public Liaison.—Eileen McMahon, 566–2391.
Human Capital.—Bennie Salem, 566–0914.
Mission Systems.—Tommy Hwang, 566–2683.
Planning Analysis and Results.—Elissa Karpf, 566–2615.
Counsel to the Inspector General.—Mark Bialek, 566–0863.

INTERNATIONAL AFFAIRS

Assistant Administrator.—Judith E. Ayres, 564–6600.
Deputy Assistant Administrator.—Jerry Clifford, 564–6442.
Director, Office of:
International Environmental Policy.—Paul F. Cough, 564–6458.
Management Operations.—Kathy Petruccilli, 564–6605.
Technology Cooperation and Assistance.—Martin Dieu, 564–6439.
Western Hemisphere and Bilateral Affairs.—Joan Fidler, 564–6611.

PREVENTION, PESTICIDES AND TOXIC SUBSTANCES

Assistant Administrator.—Stephen Johnson, 564–2902.
Associate Assistant Administrator.—Adam J. Sharp, 564–2897.
Principal Deputy Assistant Administrator.—Susan B. Hazen, 260–2910.
Program Management Operations.—Marylouise M. Uhlig, 564–0545.
Director, Office of:
Pesticide Program.—Marcia E. Mulkey, (703) 305–7090.
Pollution Prevention and Toxics.—Charles Auer, 564–3810.
Science Coordination Policy.—Joseph J. Merenda, Jr., 564–8430.

RESEARCH AND DEVELOPMENT

Assistant Administrator for Research and Development.—Paul Gilman, Ph.D., 564–6620.
Director, Administrator for—
Resources Management and Administration.—Lek G. Kadeli, 564–6700.
Science.—William Farland, M.D., (acting), 564–6620.
Science Policy.—Kevin Teichman (acting), 564–6705.
Director, Office of:
National Center for Environmental Assessment.—George Alapas (acting), 564–3322.
National Center for Environmental Research.—Peter W. Preuss, 564–6825.
National Exposure Research Laboratory.—Gary J. Foley, Ph.D., 919–541–2106.
National Health and Environmental Effects Research Laboratory.—Lawrence W. Reiter, Ph.D., 919–541–2281.
Associate Director for—
Ecology.—[Vacant], 919–541–3554.
Health.—Harold Zenich, Ph.D., 919–541–2283.
National Risk Management Research Laboratory.—E. Timothy Oppelt, 513–569–7418.

SOLID WASTE AND EMERGENCY RESPONSE

Assistant Administrator.—Marianne Horinko, 566–0200.
Principal Deputy Assistant Administrator.—Barry Breen.
Associate Assistant Administrator.—Thomas P. Dunne.

Director, Office of:

Innovation Partnership and Communication Office.—Margorie Buckholtz, 566–0205.

Federal Facilities Restoration and Reuse Office.—James E. Woolford, (703) 603–9089.

Staff Director, Office of Program Management.—Devereaux Barnes, 566–1884.

Brownsfields Cleanup and Redevelopment.—Linda Garczynski, 566–2777.

Technology Innovation.—Walter W. Kovalick, Jr., 703–603–9910.

Chemical Emergency Preparedness and Prevention.—Debbie Y. Dietrich, 564–8600.

Emergency and Remedial Response (Superfund/Oil Programs).—Michael B. Cook, (703) 308–8790.

Solid Waste.—Robert Springer, (703) 308–8895.

Underground Storage Tanks.—Cliff Rothenstein, (703) 603–9900.

WATER

Assistant Administrator.—G. Tracy Mehan III, 564–5700.

Deputy Assistant Administrators: Benjamin Grumbles, Michael Shapiro, 560–5700.

Director, Office of:

American Indian Environmental.—Carol Jorgensen, 564–5887.

Ground Water and Drinking Water.—Cynthia C. Dougherty, 564–3750.

Science and Technology.—Geoffrey Grubbs, 566–0430.

Wastewater Management.—James Hanlon, 564–0748.

Wetlands, Oceans and Watersheds.—Diane Regas, 566–1146.

REGIONAL ADMINISTRATION

Region I (Boston): *Regional Administrator.*—Bob Varney, Federal Building, One Congress Street, Boston, MA 02114, (617) 918–1010.

Congressional Liaisons: Rudy Brown (617) 918–1031, Michael Ochs, (617) 918–1066.

Public Affairs.—[Vacant].

Region II (New York): *Regional Administrator.*—Jane M. Kenny, 290 Broadway, New York, NY 10007, (212) 637–5000.

Congressional Liaisons: Peter B. Brandt (212) 687–3654, Pat Carr (212) 637–3652, Barry Shore, (212) 637–3657.

Public Outreach.—[Vacant].

Region III (Philadelphia): *Regional Administrator.*—Donald S. Welsh, 1650 Arch Street, Philadelphia, PA 19103–2029, (215) 814–2900.

Congressional Liaison.—Michael F. Burke (215) 814–5100.

Public Out-Reach.—Patrick J. Boyle, (215) 814–5533.

Region IV (Atlanta): *Regional Administrator.*—James I. Palmer, Jr., 61 Forsyth Street SW, Atlanta, GA 30303–8960, (404) 562–8357.

Gulf of Mexico Program.—James D. Giattina, (404) 562–9470.

Congressional Liaison.—[Vacant].

Public Affairs.—[Vacant].

Region V (Chicago): *Regional Administrator.*—Thomas V. Skinner, 77 West Jackson Boulevard, Chicago, IL 60604–3507, (312) 886–3000.

Congressional Liaison.—Phillip Hoffman, (312) 886–4957.

Public Affairs.—Elissa Speizman, (312) 353–2077.

Region VI (Dallas): *Regional Administrator.*—Richard Greene, Fountain Place, 1445 Ross Avenue, 12th Floor, Suite 1200, Dallas, TX 75202–2733, (214) 665–2100.

Congressional Liaison.—Clovis Steib, (TX, NM, LA, AR, OK), (214) 665–2200.

External Affairs.—David W. Gray, (214) 665–2200.

Region VII (Kansas City): *Regional Administrator.*—James B. (Jim) Gulliford, 726 Minnesota Avenue, Kansas City, MO 66101, (913) 551–7306.

Congressional Liaison.—Karen Flournoy, (913) 551–7782.

Public Affairs.—[Vacant].

Region VIII (Denver): *Regional Administrator.*—Robert E. Roberts, 999 18th Street, Suite 500, Denver, CO 80202–2466, (303) 312–6308.

Congressional Liaison.—Sandra Johnston-Fells, (303) 312–6604.

External Affairs.—Sonya S. Pennock, (303) 312–6600.

Region IX (San Francisco): *Regional Administrator.*—Wayne Nastri, 75 Hawthorne Street, San Francisco, CA 94105, (415) 744–1001.

Congressional Liaisons: Brent Mayer, Sunny Nelson, (415) 744–1459.

External Affairs.—Mercedes Anaya, (415) 947–4288.

Region X (Seattle): *Regional Administrator.*—L. John Iani, 1200 Sixth Avenue, Seattle, WA 98101, (206) 553–1234.

Congressional Liaison.—Bill Dunbar, (206) 553–1203.

External Affairs.—Melanie Luh, (206) 553–1107.

EQUAL EMPLOYMENT OPPORTUNITY COMMISSION

1801 L Street 20507, phone (202) 663–4900

Chair.—Cari M. Dominguez, 663–4001, fax 663–4110.
Chief Operating Officer.—Leonora Guarraia.
Executive Assistant.—Karin W. Pedrick.
Senior Advisors: Lisa Fisher, Michael Richards.
Special Assistants: Terrie Dandy, Sandra Hobson, Christopher Kuczynski, Susan Murphy.
Vice Chair.—Naomi C. Earp, 663–4027, fax 663–7121.
Attorney Advisor.—Anthony Kaminski.
Special Assistants: Diane Fredericks, Awo Sarpong Ansu.

COMMISSIONERS

Commissioners: Paul Steven Miller, 663–4036, fax 663–7101; Leslie E. Silverman, 663–4099, fax 663–7086.
Senior Advisor.—R. Paul Richard.
Special Assistants: Antoinette M. Eates, Matthew Bradley.
Executive Officer.—Frances M. Hart, 663–4070, fax 663–4114.
General Counsel.—[Vacant], 663–4705, fax 663–4196.
Deputy General Counsel.—Nicholas M. Inzeo, (acting).
Legal Counsel.—David L. Frank, 663–4637, fax 663–4639.
Inspector General.—Aletha L. Brown, 663–4379, fax 663–7204.
Director, Office of:
Communications and Legislative Affairs.—H. Joan Ehrlich (acting), 663–4900, fax 663–4912.
Field Program.—Reuben Daniels, Jr., (acting), 663–4801, fax 663–4823.
Federal Operations.—Carlton M. Hadden, 663–4599, fax 663–7022.
Equal Employment Opportunity.—Jean M. Watson, 663–7081, fax 663–7003.

EXPORT-IMPORT BANK OF THE UNITED STATES

811 Vermont Avenue NW 20571, phone (800) 565–EXIM, fax 565–3380

President and Chairman.—Philip Merrill, room 1215, 565–3500.
Vice President and Vice Chairman.—[Vacant].
Executive Vice President.—James Lambright, room 1214, 565–3515.
Directors: J. Jospeh Grandmaison, room 1241, 565–3530; Vanessa Weaver, room 1229, 565–3520; April Foley, room 1257, 565–3540.
General Counsel.—Peter Saba, room 947, 565–3430.
Chief Financial Officer.—James K. Hess, room 1055, 565–3240.
Chief Information Officer.—Patrick O'Hare, room 1045, 565–3850.
Administrative Services.—George J. Sabo, room 1017, 565–3313.
Senior Vice President of:
Communications.—Lorrie Secrest, room 1267, 565–3200.
Congressional Affairs.—[Vacant], room 1261, 565–3230.
Credit Risk Management.—John McAdams, room 919, 565–3222.
Export Finance.—Jeffrey Miller, room 1115, 565–3225.
Trade Finance & Insurance.—John Emens, room 931, 565–3701.
Policy and Planning.—James Cruse, room 1243, 565–3761.
Resource Management.—Michael Cushing, room 1017, 565–3561.
Vice President of:
Business Credit.—Sam Z. Zytcer, room 903, 565–3782.
Country Risk and Economic Analysis.—[Vacant].
Engineering and Environment.—James Mahoney, room 1169, 565–3573.
Structured Finance.—Barbara O'Boyle, room 1005, 565–3699.
Transportation.—Robert Morin, room 1035, 565–3453.
Group Vice President of Small and New Business.—William W. Redway, room 919, 565–3633.
Directors of:
Equal Employment and Opportunity Diversity Program.—Kennie May, room 753, 565–3591.
Human Resources.—Elliot Davis, room 771, 565–3300.
Employee Development and Training.—Sherry Chaffin, room 751, 565–3592.

FARM CREDIT ADMINISTRATION

1501 Farm Credit Drive, McLean, VA 22102–5090

phone (703) 883–4000, fax 734–5784

[Reorganization pursuant to Public Law 99–205, December 23, 1985]

Chairperson.—Michael M. Reyna.
Members:
Douglas L. Flory.
Nancy C. Pellett.
Secretary.—Jeanette Brinkley.
Chief Operating Officer.—Cheryl Macias.
Director, Office of:
Chief Administrative Officer.—Philip Shebest, 883–4130.
Chief Information Officer.—Doug Valcour, 883–4166.
Chief Financial Officer.—W.B. Erwin, 883–4099.
Communication and Public Affairs.—Hal C. DeCell III (acting), 883–4056, fax 790–3260.
Congressional and Legislative Affairs.—Hal C. DeCell III, 883–4056, fax 790–3260.
Ombudsman.—Carl Clinefelter, 883–4241.
Policy and Analysis.—Michael Dunn, 883–4414.
Secondary Market Oversight.—Thomas McKenzie, 883–4277.
General Counsel.—Charles R. Rawls, 883–4020.
Inspector General.—Stephen Smith, 883–4030.
Chief Examiner and Director, Office of Examination.—Roland E. Smith, 883–4160.
Manager, Equal Employment Opportunity.—Eric Howard, 883–4144.

FEDERAL COMMUNICATIONS COMMISSION

445 12th Street SW, Washington, DC 20554, phone (202) 418–0200, http://www.fcc.gov

Chairman.—Michael K. Powell, room 8–B201, 418–1000.
Confidential Assistant.—Judith Mann.
Chief of Staff.—Marsha J. MacBride.
Senior Legal Advisor.—Bryan Tramont.
Legal Advisors: Christopher D. Libertelli, Susan M. Eid.
Commissioner.—Jonathan S. Adelstien, room 8–C302, 418–2300.
Confidential Assistant.—Katherine Lapin.
Senior Legal Advisor.—Lisa Zaina.
Legal Advisors: Barry Ohlson, Johanna Mikes.
Commissioner.—Kathleen Q. Abernathy, room 8–B115, 418–2400.
Confidential Assistant.—Elizabeth (Ann) Monahan.
Senior Legal Advisor.—Matthew Brill.
Legal Advisors: Jennifer Manner, Stacey Robinson.
Commissioner.—Michael Copps, room 8–A302, 418–2000.
Confidential Assistant.—Carolyn Conyers.
Senior Legal Advisor.—Jordan Goldstein.
Legal Advisors: Paul Margie, Jessica Rosenworcel.
Commissioner.—Kevin J. Martin, room 8–A204, 418–2100.
Confidential Assistant.—Ginger Clark.
Senior Legal Advisor.—Daniel Gonzalez.
Legal Advisors: Catherine Bohigian, Samuel Feder.
FCC NATIONAL CONSUMER CENTER, 1–888–225–5322; 1–888–835–5322 (TTY)

OFFICE OF STRATEGIC PLANNING AND POLICY ANALYSIS

Chief.—Jane Mago, room 7–C452, 418–2030.
Deputy Chief.—Kathleen O'Brien Ham.
Chief of Staff.—Maureen C. McLaughlin.

OFFICE OF MEDIA RELATIONS

Director.—David H. Fiske, room CY–C314, 418–0500.
Deputy Director.—Richard Diamond.

OFFICE OF LEGISLATIVE AFFAIRS

Director.—Martha Johnston, room 8–C432, 418–1900.
Deputy Director.—Paul Jackson.

OFFICE OF COMMUNICATIONS BUSINESS OPPORTUNITIES

Director.—Carolyn Fleming Williams, room 7–C204, 418–0990.

OFFICE OF ADMINISTRATIVE LAW JUDGES

Administrative Law Judges: Richard L. Sippel, room 1–C768, 418–2280; Arthur I. Steinberg, room 1–C861, 418–2255.

OFFICE OF GENERAL COUNSEL

General Counsel.—John A. Rogovin, room 8–C723, 418–1700.
Deputy General Counsel.—P. Michele Ellison.
Associate General Counsel.—Linda Kinney.

OFFICE OF INSPECTOR GENERAL

Inspector General.—H. Walker Feaster, room 2–C762, 418–0470.
Assistant Inspector General for—
Audits.—Thomas D. Bennett.

OFFICE OF MANAGING DIRECTOR

Managing Director.—Andrew S. Fishel, room 1–C144, 418–1919.
Deputy Managing Directors: Renee Licht, William Spencer.
Secretary.—Marlene Dortch, room TW–B204, 418–0300.
Deputy Secretary.—William F. Caton.
Associate Managing Director for Human Resources Management.—Michele C. Sutton, room 1–A100, 418–0137; 418–0126 (TTY); 418–0150 (Employment Verification).
Deputy Director.—Carol Nichols, room 1–A130, 418–0134.
Senior Policy Advisor.—Thomas Green, room 1–A161, 418–0116.

OFFICE OF ENGINEERING AND TECHNOLOGY

Chief.—Ed Thomas, room 7–C155, 418–2470.
Deputy Chiefs: Bruce A. Franca, Julius P. Knapp.

OFFICE OF WORKPLACE DIVERSITY

Director.—Barbara J. Douglas, room 5–C750, 418–1799.
Deputy Director.—Harvey Lee, room 5–C751.

MEDIA BUREAU

Chief.—W. Kenneth Ferree, room 3–C740, 418–7200.
Deputy Bureau Chiefs: William H. Johnson, room 3–C742; Robert H. Ratcliffe, room 3–C486.
Deputy Bureau Chief/Special Counsel on Broadband.—Kyle Dixon, room 2–C344, 418–7200.
Audio Services Division, 418–2700
Chief.—Peter H. Doyle, room 2–A360.
Deputy Chief.—Nina Shafran, room 2–A267.
Video Services Division, 418–1600.
Chief.—Barbara A. Kreisman, room 2–A666.
Deputy Chief.—James J. Brown, room 2–A663.

WIRELINE COMPETITION BUREAU

Chief.—William Maher, room 5–C450, 418–1500.
Senior Deputy Chief.—Jeffrey J. Carlisle, room 5–C356, 418–1500.
Deputy Chief.—Carol Mattey, room 5–C451, 418–1500.
Associate Bureau Chief.—Jane Jackson, room 5–C354, 418–1500.

ENFORCEMENT BUREAU

Chief.—David H. Solomon, room 7–C485, 418–7450.
Deputy Bureau Chief.—Linda Blair, Anne L. Weismann, room 7–C751, 418–7450.
Investigations and Hearing Division, 418–1420.
Chief.—Maureen F. Del Duca, room 3–B431.
Market Disputes Resolution Division, 418–7330.
Chief.—Alex Starr, room 5–848, 418–7248.
Deputy Chiefs: Lisa Griffin, room 5–C828, 418–7273; Radhika Karmarkar, room 5–A847, 418–1628.
Technical and Public Safety Division, 418–1160.
Chief.—Joseph P. Casey, room 7–A843, 418–1111.
Deputy Chiefs: Ricardo M. Durham, room 7–A744, 418–1160; James Dailey, room 7–C831, 418–1113.
Telecommunications Consumer Division, 418–7320.
Chief.—Colleen Heitkamp, room 3–C365, 418–0974.
Deputy Chief.—Kurt Schroeder, room 3–C366, 418–0966.
North East Region: Chicago, IL
Director.—Russell (Joe) D. Monie, (847) 376–2984.
Deputy Director.—Barry A. Bohoe.
South Central Region: Kansas City, MO
Director.—Dennis (Denny) P. Carlton, (816) 316–1243.
Western Region: San Diego, CA
Director.—Rebecca L. Dorch, (925) 416–9661.

INTERNATIONAL BUREAU

Chief.—Donald Abelson, room 6–C750, 418–0437.
Deputy Chiefs: Anna Gomez, room 6–C475, 418–0438; Roderick K. Porter, room 6–C752.
Satellite Division:
Chief.—Thomas S. Tycz, room 6–A665, 418–0719.
Deputy Chiefs: Fern Jarmulnek, room 6–A760; Cassandra Thomas, room 6–A666.

WIRELESS TELECOMMUNICATIONS BUREAU

Chief.—John B. Muleta, room 3–C252, 418–0600.
Deputy Bureau Chiefs: James D. Schlichting, room 3–C254; Gerald P. Vaughan, room 3–C250, 418–0600.
Commercial Wireless Division:
Chief.—William Kunze, room 4–C224, 418–7887.
Deputy Chiefs: Kathy Harris, room 4–C236, 418–0609; Roger Noel, room 4–B115, 418–0698; Jeffrey Steinberg, room 4–C222, 418–0896.
Public Safety & Private Wireless Division:
Chief.—D'Wana Terry, room 4–C321, 418–0680.
Deputy Chiefs: Ramona Melson (Legal), room 4–C322, 418–0680; Jeanne Kowalski (Public Safety), room 4–C324, 418–0680; Herbert W. Zeiler (Technical), room 4–C343, 418–0686.

CONSUMER AND GOVERNMENTAL AFFAIRS BUREAU

Chief.—Dane Snowden, room 5–C758, 418–1400.
Deputy Chiefs: Margaret M. Egler, room 5–C754; Kris Monteith, room 5–C755; Thomas D. Wyatt, room 5–A844.
Consumer Inquiries and Complaints Division:
Chief.—[Vacant].
Deputy Chief.—Sharon Bowers (Gettysburg), (717) 338–2531.

Reference Information Center Director.—Bill Cline, room CY–B533, 418–0267.
Consumer Affairs and Outreach Division:
Chief.—Martha Contee, room CY–B523, 418–2513.
Deputy Chief.—Irshad Abdal-Haqq, room 6–C466, 418–1444.

FIELD OFFICES

Atlanta: *Director.*—Fred L. Broce, Koger Center, 3575 Koger Boulevard, Ste. 320, Duluth, GA 30096, (707) 935–3370.

Boston: *Director.*—Vincent F. Kajunski, One Batterymarch Park, Quincy, MA 02169, (617) 786–7746.

Chicago: *Director.*—George M. Moffitt, Park Ridge Office Center, Room 306, 1550 Northwest Highway, Park Ridge, IL 60068, (847) 298–5412.

Columbia: *Director.*—Charles C. Magin, 9300 East Hampton Drive, Capitol Heights, MD 20743, (301) 725–1996.

Dallas: *Director.*—James D. Wells, 9330 LBJ Freeway, Room 1170, Dallas, TX 75243, (214) 575–6361.

Denver: *Director.*—Leo E. Cirbo, 215 S. Wadsworth Blvd., Suite 303, Lakewood, CO 80226, (303) 21–5212.

Detroit: *Director.*—James A. Bridgewater, 24897 Hathaway Street, Farmington Hills, MI 48335, (248) 471–5661.

Kansas City: *Director.*—Robert C. McKinney, 520 NE Colbern Road, Second Floor, Lee's Summit, MO 64086, (816) 316–1248.

Los Angeles: *Director.*—James R. Zoulek, Cerritos Corporate Towers, 18000 Studebaker Road, Room 660, Cerritos, CA 90701, (562) 860–7474.

New Orleans: *Director.*—James C. Hawkins, 2424 Edenborn Avenue, Room 460, Metarie, LA 70001, (504) 589–4966.

New York: *Director.*—Alexander J. Zimny, 201 Varick Street, Room 1151, New York, NY 10014, (212) 337–1865.

Philadelphia: *Director.*—John Rahtes, One Oxford Valley Office Building, Room 404, 2300 East Lincoln Highway, Langhorne, PA 19047, (215) 752–8549.

San Diego: *Director.*—Jim Zoulek (acting), Interstate Office Park, 4542 Ruffner Street, Room 370, San Diego, CA 92111, (858) 496–5111.

San Francisco: *Director.*—Thomas N. Van Stavern, 5653 Stoneridge Drive, Suite 105, Pleasanton, CA 94588, (925) 416–9717.

Seattle: *Director.*—Dennis Anderson, 11410 Northeast 122nd Way, Room 312, Kirkland, WA 98034, (425) 820–6271.

Tampa: *Director.*—Ralph M. Barlow, 2203 North Lois Avenue, Room 1215, Tampa, FL 33607, (813) 348–1741.

FEDERAL DEPOSIT INSURANCE CORPORATION

550 17th Street NW., 20429

phone (202) 736–0000, http://www.fdic.gov

Chairman.—Donald E. Powell.
Deputy to the Chairman and Chief Operating Officer.—John F. Bovenzi, 898–6949.
Vice Chairman.—John Reich, 898–3888.
Deputy.—Robert W. Russell, 898–8952.
Director.—[Vacant].
Deputy.—[Vacant].
Director.—John D. Hawke, Jr., 874–4900.
Deputy.—Tom Zemke, 898–6960.
Director.—James E. Gilleran, 906–6280.
Deputy.—Walter B. Mason, Jr., 898–6965.
Director, Office of Legislative Affairs.—Alice C. Goodman, 898–7055, fax 898–3745/7062.

FEDERAL ELECTION COMMISSION

999 E Street, NW., 20463

phone (202) 694–1000, Toll Free (800) 424–9530, fax 219–3880, http://www.fec.gov

Chairman.—Ellen L. Weintraub, 694–1035.
Vice Chairman.—Bradley A. Smith, 694–1011.
Commissioners:
Michael Toner, 694–1045.
Danny Lee McDonald, 694–1020.
Bradley Mason, 694–1050.
Scott E. Thomas, 694–1055, fax 219–8459.
Inspector General.—Lynne A. McFarland, 694–1015.
Staff Director.—James A. Pehrkon, 694–1007, fax 219–2338.
Deputy Staff Director.—Alison Doone, 694–1215.
Deputy Staff Director for Audit and Review.—Robert J. Costa, 494–1181.
Assistant Staff Director for—
Audit.—Joe Stoltz, 694–1209.
Disclosure.—Patricia K. Young, 694–1120.
Information Services.—Greg Scott, 694–1100.
Reports Analysis.—John D. Gibson, 694–1130.
Director for—
Office of Election Administration.—Penelope S. Bonsall, 694–1093.
Data Systems Development Division.—[Vacant].
Personnel and Labor Management Relations.—William J. Fleming, 694–1080.
Planning and Management.—John C. O'Brien, 694–1216.
General Counsel.—Lawrence H. Norton, 694–1650.
Associate General Counsel for—
Enforcement.—Rhonda Vosdingh, 694–1650.
Litigation.—Richard B. Bader, 694–1650.
Policy.—Rosemary Smith (acting), 694–1650.
Public Financing, Ethics and Special Projects.—Gregory R. Baker, 694–1650.
Administrative Officer.—Sylvia E. Butler, 694–1240.
Accounting Officer.—Brian Duffy, 694–1230.
Director of Congressional Affairs.—Christina H. VanBrakle, 694–1006, fax 219–2338.
EEO Director.—Patricia A. Brown, 694–1228.
Library Director (Law).—Leta L. Holley, 694–1600.
Press Officer.—Ronald M. Harris, 694–1220.

FEDERAL HOUSING FINANCE BOARD

1777 F Street NW 20006, phone 408–2500, fax 408–1435

[Created by the Financial Institutions Reform, Recovery, and Enforcement Act of August 9, 1989, 103 Stat. 354, 415]

Chairman.—John T. Korsmo, 408–2622.
Board of Directors:
John C. Weicher,* 708–3600.
Franz S. Leichter, 408–2986.
Allan I. Mendelowitz, 408–2587.
J. Timothy O'Neill, 408–2953.
Inspector General.—Edward Kelley, 408–2570.
General Counsel.—Arnie Intrater, 408–2536.
Director of Resource Management.—Judith L. Hofmann, 408–2586.
Director of Supervision.—Stephen M. Cross, 408–2980.

---

*The Secretary of Housing and Urban Development is one of the five Directors of the Federal Housing Finance Board. Secretary Martinez has designated John C. Weicher, the Assistant Secretary for Housing/Federal Housing Commissioner, to act for him on the Board of Directors of the Federal Housing Finance Board.

FEDERAL LABOR RELATIONS AUTHORITY

1400 K Street, NW., 20424–0001, phone (202) 218–7000, fax 482–6659

Chair.—Dale Cabaniss, 218–7900.
Chief of Staff.—Jill Crumpacker, 218–7945.
Chief Counsel.—Kirk Underwood.
Director, External Affairs.—[Vacant].
Director, Case Control.—Gail Reinhart, 218–7776.
Members:
Carol Waller Pope, 218–7920.
Chief Counsel.—Susan D. McCluskey.
Tony Armendariz, 218–7930.
Chief Counsel.—Steven H. Svartz.
General Counsel.—David L. Feder (acting), 218–7741.
Deputy General Counsel.—David L. Feder.
Assistant General Counsel for Appeals.—Richard Zorn.
Chief Administrative Law Judge.—Eli Nash, 218–7918.
Executive Director.—David M. Smith (acting), 218–7907.
Solicitor.—David M. Smith, 218–7907.
Inspector General.—Francine Eichler, 218–7744.
Collaboration and Alternative Dispute Resolution Program.—Andy Pizzi, 218–7933.
Federal Service Impasse Disputes Panel.—Becky Norton Dunlop, 218–7746.
Special Assistant to the Chairman.—Victoria Dutcher, 218–7746.
Executive Director.—H. Joseph Schimansky, 218–7991.
Foreign Service Impasse Disputes Panel.—Peter Tredick, 218–7746.
Foreign Service Labor Relations Board.—Dale Cabaniss, 218–7900.

REGIONAL OFFICES

Regional Directors:

Atlanta: Nancy A. Speight, Marquis Two Tower, Suite 701, 285 Peachtree Center Avenue, Atlanta, GA 30303, (404) 331–5212, fax (404) 331–5280.

Boston: Richard D. Zaiger, Suite 1500, 99 Summer Street, Boston, MA 02110, (617) 424–5731, fax 424–5743.

Chicago: William E. Washington, Suite 1150, 55 West Monroe, Chicago, IL 60603, (312) 886–3485, fax 886–5977.

Dallas: James E. Petrucci, Suite 926, LB 107, 525 Griffin Street, Dallas, TX 75202, (214) 767–4996, fax 767–0156.

Denver: Marjorie K. Thompson, Suite 100, 1244 Speer Boulevard, Denver, CO 80204, (303) 844–5226, fax 844–2774.

San Francisco: Gerald M. Cole, Suite 220, 901 Market Street, San Francisco, CA 94103, (415) 356–5002, fax 356–5017.

Washington, DC: William Persina (acting), Techworld Plaza, 800 K Street NW, Suite 910, Washington, DC 20001, (202) 482–6702, fax (202) 482–6724.

FEDERAL MARITIME COMMISSION

800 North Capitol Street NW., 20573, phone (202) 523–5725, fax 523–0014

OFFICE OF THE CHAIRMAN

Chairman.—Steven R. Blust, Jr., room 1000, 523–5911.
Counsel—Rachel Dickon-Matney.
Commissioner.—Delmond J.H. Won, room 1026, 523–5721.
Special Assistant.—Judy A. Crowe.
Commissioner.—Rebecca F. Dye, room 1038, 523–5715.
Counsel.—Edward L. Lee, Jr.
Commissioner.—Joseph E. Brennan, room 1032, 523–5723.
Counsel.—Steven D. Najarian.
Commissioner.—Harold J. Creel, Jr., room 1044, 523–5712.
Counsel.—Lucille L. Marvin.

OFFICE OF THE SECRETARY

Secretary.—Bryant L. VanBrakle, room 1046, 523–5725.
Assistant Secretary.—Theodore A. Zook.
Librarian.—David J. Vespa, room 1085, 523–5762.

GENERAL COUNSEL

General Counsel.—David R. Miles (acting), room 1018, 523–5740.
Deputy General Counsel.—[Vacant].

OFFICE OF EQUAL EMPLOYMENT OPPORTUNITY

Director.—Alice M. Blackmon, room 1052, 523–5806.

OFFICE OF ADMINISTRATIVE LAW JUDGES

Chief Judge.—Norman D. Kline, room 1089, 523–5750.

OFFICE OF THE INSPECTOR GENERAL

Inspector General.—Tony P. Kominoth, room 1054, 523–5863.

OFFICE OF THE EXECUTIVE DIRECTOR

Executive Director.—Bruce A. Dombrowski, room 1082, 523–5800.
Deputy Executive Director.—Austin L. Schmitt.
Director of:
Information Resources Management.—George D. Bowers, room 904, 523–5835.
Management Services.—Michael H. Kilby, room 924, 523–5900.
Budget and Financial Management.—Karon E. Douglass, room 916, 523–5770.
Human Resources.—Hatsie H. Charbonneau, room 924, 523–5773.

BUREAU OF TRADE ANALYSIS

Director.—Florence A. Carr, room 940, 523–5796.
Deputy Director.—Frank J. Schwarz.
Director of:
Agreements.—Jeremiah D. Hospital, room 940, 523–5793.
Economics and Competition Analysis.—Karen V. Gregory, room 940, 523–5845.
Service Contracts and Tariffs.—Mamie H. Black, room 940, 523–5856.

BUREAU OF CONSUMER COMPLAINTS AND LICENSING

Director.—Sandra L. Kusumoto, room 970, 523–5787.
Deputy Director.—Ronald D. Murphy.
Director of:
Consumer Complaints.—Joseph T. Farrell, 523–5807.
Passenger Vessels and Information Processing.—Anne E. Trotter, 523–5818.
Transportation Intermediaries.—Ralph W. Freibert, 523–5843.

BUREAU OF ENFORCEMENT

Director.—Vern W. Hill, room 900, 523–5783 or 523–5860.
Deputy Director.—Peter J. King.

AREA REPRESENTATIVES

Los Angeles.—Oliver E. Clark, (310) 514–4905.
Miami.—Andrew Margolis, (305) 536–4316, Eric O. Mintz, (305) 536–5529.
New Orleans.—Alvin N. Kellogg, (504) 589–6662.
New York.—Emanuel J. Mingione, (212) 637–2929.
Seattle.—Michael A. Moneck, (206) 553–0221.

FEDERAL MEDIATION AND CONCILIATION SERVICE

2100 K Street NW., Washington, DC 20427, phone (202) 606–8100, fax 606–4251

[Codified under 29 U.S.C. 172]

Director.—Peter J. Hurtgen.
Deputy Director.—C. Richard Barnes.
Chief of Staff.—John Toner.
General Counsel.—Arthur Pearlstein, 606–5444.
Director for—
International and ADR Services.—Richard Giacolone, 606–5445.
Director, FMCS Institute.—Gary R. Hattal, 606–9144.
Information Systems and Administrative Services.—Dan W. Funkhouser, 606–5477.
Arbitration Services.—Vella M. Traynham, 606–5111.
Budget and Finance.—Fran L. Leonard, 606–3661.
Human Resources.—William Carlisle, 606–5460.
Grants.—Jane A. Lorber, 606–8181.
Midwestern Region.—John F. Buettner (acting), (216) 522–4800.
Northeastern Region.—[Vacant].
Southern Region.—Fred W. Reebals, (404) 331–3995.
Upper Midwestern Region.—Scot L. Beckenbaugh, (612) 370–3300.
Western Region.—Barbara Wood, (510) 273–0100.

FEDERAL MINE SAFETY AND HEALTH REVIEW COMMISSION

601 New Jersey Avenue, NW., Suite 9500, Washington, DC 20001

phone (202) 434–9900, fax 343–9944

[Created by Public Law 95–164]

Chairperson.—Michael F. Duffy, room 9515, 434–9924.
Commissioners: Robert H. Beatty, Jr., room 9531, 434–9922; Stanley C. Suboleski, room 9523, 434–9921; [vacant].
Executive Director.—Richard L. Baker, room 9507, 434–9905.
Chief Administrative Law Judge.—David F. Barbour, room 8515, 434–958.
General Counsel.—Thomas Stock (acting), room 9547, 434–9935.

FEDERAL RETIREMENT THRIFT INVESTMENT BOARD

1250 H Street NW 20005, phone (202) 942–1600, fax 942–1676

[Authorized by 5 U.S.C. 8472]

Executive Director.—Gary A. Amelio, 942–1601.
General Counsel.—Elizabeth S. Woodruff, 942–1660.
Director, Office of:
Accounting.—David L. Black, 942–1610.
Administration.—Thomas L. Gray, (acting), 942–1670.
Automated Systems.—Lawrence Stiffler, 942–1440.
Investments and Benefits.—James B. Petrick, 942–1630.
Communications.—Veda R. Charrow, 942–1650.
External Affairs.—Thomas J. Trabucco, 942–1640.

Chairman.—Andrew M. Saul, 942–1660.
Board Members:
Scott B. Lukins.
Alejandro M. Sanchez.
Gordon J. Whiting.
Thomas A. Fink.

FEDERAL TRADE COMMISSION

600 Pennsylvania Avenue NW., 20580, phone 326–2195, http://www.ftc.gov

Chairman.—Timothy J. Muris, room 440, 326–2100.
Executive Assistant.—Martha Stringer, room 442, 326–3689.
Commissioners: Sheila F. Anthony, room 326, 326–2171; Thomas B. Leary, room 528, 326–2145; Orson Swindle, room 540, 326–2150; Mozelle W. Thompson, room 338, 326–3400.
Director, Office of:
Public Affairs.—Cathy MacFarlane, room 423, 326–2180.
Congressional Relations.—Anna H. Davis, room 406, 326–3680.
Executive Director.—Rosemarie Straight, room 426, 326–2207.
Deputy Executive Director.—Judith Bailey, room 422, 326–3609.
General Counsel.—William E. Kovacic, room 570, 326–3661.
Secretary.—Donald S. Clark, room 172, 326–2514.
Administrative Law Judges.—James P. Timony, room 112, 326–3635.
Inspector General.—Frederick J. Zirkel, room NJ1119, 326–2800.
Director, Bureau of Competition.—Joseph J. Simons, room 372, 326–3667.
Deputy Directors.—Susan A. Creighton, room 380, 326–2946; M. Sean Royall, room 378, 326–3663.
Consumer Protection.—J. Howard Beales III, room 470, 326–3665.
Deputy Directors: Lydia B. Parnes, room 474, 326–2676; Lee Peeler, room 476, 326–3090.
Economics.—David T. Scheffman, room 268, 326–3687.

REGIONAL DIRECTORS

East Central Region: John Mendenhall, Eaton Center, Suite 200, 1111 Superior Avenue, Cleveland, OH 44114, (216) 263–3455.
Midwest Region: C. Steve Baker, 55 East Monroe Street, Suite 1860, Chicago, IL 60603, (312) 960–5634.
Northeast Region: Barbara Anthony, One Bowling Green, Suite 318, New York, NY 10004, (212) 607–2829.
Northwest Region: Charles A. Harwood, 915 Second Avenue, Suite 2896, Seattle, WA 98174, (206) 220–6350.
Southeast Region: Andrea Foster, 60 Forsyth Street, Midrise Building, Suite 5M35, Atlanta, GA 30303, (404) 656–1390.
Southwest Region: Bradley Elbein, 1999 Bryan Street, Suite 2150, Dallas, TX 75201, (214) 979–9350.
Western Region—Los Angeles: Jeffrey Klurfeld, 18077 Wilshire Boulevard, Suite 700, Los Angeles, CA 90024–3679, (310) 824–4320.
Western Region—San Francisco: Jeffrey Klurfeld, 901 Market Street, Suite 570, San Francisco, CA 94103, (415) 848–5100.

FOREIGN–TRADE ZONES BOARD

1099 14th Street, NW., Franklin Court Building, Suite 4100W, Washington, DC 20005
phone (202) 482–2862, fax 482–0002

Chairman.—Donald L. Evans, Secretary of Commerce.
Members:
John W. Snow, Secretary of the Treasury.
Executive Secretary.—Dennis Puccinelli.

GENERAL SERVICES ADMINISTRATION

1800 F Street NW 20405, phone (202) 501–0800, http://www.gsa.gov

Administrator.—Stephen A. Perry, 501–0800.
Deputy Administrator.—Thurman M. Davis, Sr., 501–1226.
Chief of Staff.—David Safavian, 501–1216.
Associate Administrator, Office of Small Business Utilization.—Felipe Mendoza (acting), 501–1021.

Associate Administrator, Office of Civil Rights.—Madeline Caliendo, 501–0767.
Director of the Office of Civil Rights.—Regina Budd, 501–0767.
Associate Administrator, Office of Congressional and Intergovernmental Affairs.—Shawn McBurney, 501–0563.
Deputy Associate Administrator.—Gayland Barksdale (acting), 501–0563.
Associate Administrator, Office of Citizen Services and Communications.—M.J. Jameson, 501–0705.
Deputy Associate Administrator.—David Bethel (acting), 501–0705.
Inspector General.—Daniel R. Levinson, 501–0450.
Deputy Inspector General.—Joel S. Gallay, 501–1362.
Counsel to the Inspector General.—Kathleen S. Tighe, 501–1932.
Assistant Inspector General for Auditing.—Eugene L. Waszily, 501–0374.
Deputy Assistant Inspector General for Auditing.—[Vacant].
Assistant Inspector General for Investigations.—James E. Henderson, 501–1397.
Deputy Assistant Inspector General for Investigations.—Mark R. Woods, 501–1397.
Assistant Inspector General for Administration.—John C. Lebo, Jr. (acting), 501–2319.
Chairman, Board of Contract Appeals.—Stephen M. Daniels, 501–0585.
Vice Chairman.—Robert W. Parker, 501–0890.
Chief Counsel.—Margaret S. Pfunder, 501–0272.
Clerk.—Beatrice Jones, 501–0116.
Board Judges:
Anthony S. Borwick, 501–1852.
Stephen M. Daniels, 501–0585.
Martha H. DeGraff, 208–7922.
Allan H. Goodman, 501–0352.
Catherine B. Hyatt, 501–4594.
Edwin B. Neill, 501–0435.
Robert W. Parker, 501–0890.
Mary Ellen Coster Williams, 501–4668.
Chief People Officer.—Gail T. Lovelace, 501–0398.
Deputy Chief People Officer/Director of Management Services.—June V. Huber, 501–0796.
Chief Information Officer.—Frederick Alt, 501–2518.
Director of Human Resources Policy.—Ken Holecko, 501–0398.
General Counsel.—Raymond J. McKenna, 501–2200.
Associate General Counsel for—
General Law.—Eugenia D. Ellison, 501–1460.
Personal Property.—George N. Barclay, 501–1156.
Real Property.—Samuel J. Morris III, 501–0430.
Chief Financial Officer (B).—Kathleen M. Turco, 501–1721.
Director of:
Budget (BB).—Deborah Schilling, 501–0719.
Finance (BC).—Robert Shimshock, 501–0562.
Financial Management Systems (BD).—Jerry W. Cochran, 208–6968.
Controller (BE).—Ellen Warren (acting), 501–0562.
Chief Information Officer.—Michael Carleton, 501–1000.
Deputy Chief Information Officer.—[Vacant], 501–1000.
Director of Internetworking.—Eugene McNerney, 501–2812.
Chief Technology Officer.—Christopher Fornicker, 219–3393.
Associate Administrator, Office of Governmentwide Policy (M).—G. Martin Wagner, 501–8880.
Deputy Associate Administrator (M).—John G. Sindelar, 501–8880.
Executive Officer, Office of Governmentwide Policy (M).—Nancy Wong, 501–8880.
Deputy Associate Administrator for—
Acquisition Policy (MV).—David A. Drabkin, 501–1043.
Electronic Government and Technology (ME).—Mary J. Mitchell, 501–0202.
Real Property (MP).—David L. Bibb, 501–0856.
Transportation and Personal Property (MT).—Rebecca R. Rhodes, 501–1777.
Chief Information Officer for Governmentwide Policy (MJ).—Jack Finley, 501–1500.
Executive Director, Regulatory Information Service Center (MI).—Ronald C. Kelly, 482–7340.
Director, Committee Management Secretariat (MC).—James L. Dean, 273–3563.
Commissioner, Public Buildings Service.—F. Joseph Moravec, 501–1100.
Deputy Commissioner.—Paul Chistolini, 501–1100.
Chief of Staff.—Lea J. Uhre, 501–1100.
Chief Financial Officer.—Charles D'Agostino (acting), 501–0658.
Chief Information Officer.—Kay McNew, 501–9100.

Assistant Commissioner for—
Business Performance.—Paul M. Lynch, 501–0971.
Portfolio Management.—William H. Matthews, 501–0658.
Property Disposal.—Brian K. Polly, 501–0084.
Chief Architect.—Edward A. Feiner, 501–1888.
Director, Energy Center of Expertise.—Mark Ewing, 708–9296.
Commissioner, Federal Technology Service.—Sandra N. Bates, (703) 306–6020.
Deputy Commissioner.—Charles A. Self, (703) 306–6046.
Chief Financial Officer.—Anthony Tisone, (703) 306–6369.
Assistant Commissioner for—
Acquisition.—T. Keith Sandridge (acting), (703) 306–7800.
Chief Information Officer.—Jimmy Parker, (703) 306–6150.
Information Technology Solutions.—Robert E. Suda, (703) 306–6101.
Regional Services.—Margaret C. Binns, (703) 306–6508.
Sales.—Mary Whitley, (703) 306–6031.
Service Delivery.—John C. Johnson (acting), (703) 306–6200.
Service Development.—John C. Johnson, (703) 306–6007.
Commissioner, Federal Supply Service.—Donna D. Bennett, (703) 605–5400.
Deputy Commissioner.—Lester D. Gray, (703) 605–5400.
Chief of Staff.—Amanda G. Fredriksen, (703) 605–5400.
Assistant Commissioner, Office of:
Acquisition Management.—Patricia M. Mead, (703) 305–7933.
Business Management and Marketing.—Gary Feit, (703) 605–5640.
Commercial Acquisition.—Neal Fox, (703) 305–7901.
Controller.—Jon A. Jordan, (703) 605–5505.
Enterprise Planning.—John R. Roehmer, (703) 605–5480.
Global Supply.—Edward O'Hare, (703) 605–5515.
Information Chief Officer.—Donald P. Heffernan, (703) 305–5670.
Transportation and Property Management.—Joseph Jeu, (703) 605–5600.
Vehicle Acquisition and Leasing.—Barnaby Brasseux, (703) 605–5500.

REGIONAL OFFICES

National Capital Region: 7th and D Streets SW, Washington, DC 20407, (202) 708–9100.
Regional Administrator.—Donald C. Williams, 708–9100.
Deputy Administrator.—Ann Everett, 708–9100.
Assistant Regional Administrator for—
Federal Technology Service.—Craig F. Kennedy, 708–6100.
Public Buildings Service.—Anthony Costa, 708–5891.
Regional Counsel.—Sharon A. Roach, 708–5155.

New England Region: Thomas P. O'Neill Federal Building, 10 Causeway Street, Boston, MA 02222, (617) 565–5860.
Regional Administrator.—Dennis R. Smith, 565–5860.
Assistant Regional Administrator for—
Federal Technology Service.—William B. Horst, 565–5760.
Public Buildings Service.—Sandra DiBernardo, 565–5694.

Northeast and Caribbean Region: 26 Federal Plaza, New York, NY 10278, (212) 264–2600.
Regional Administrator.—Karl H. Reichelt, 264–2600.
Deputy Regional Administrator.—Steve Ruggiero, 264–2600.
Assistant Regional Administrator for—
Federal Supply Service.—Charles Weill, 264–3590.
Federal Technology Service.—Kerry Blette, 264–1257.
Public Buildings Service.—Alan Greenberg, 264–4282.

Mid-Atlantic Region: The Strawbridge's Building, 20 N. Eighth Street, Philadelphia, PA 19107, (215) 446–5100.
Regional Administrator.—Barbara L. Shelton, 446–4900.
Deputy Regional Administrator.—James A. Williams, 446–4900.
Assistant Regional Administrator for—
Federal Supply Service.—Jack R. Williams, 446–5000.
Federal Technology Service.—Paul J. McDermott, 446–5800.
Public Buildings Service.—Jan L. Ziegler, 446–4500.
Regional Counsel.—Robert J. McCall, 446–4946.

Southeast Sunbelt Region: 77 Forsyth Street, Suite 600, Atlanta, GA 30303, (404) 331–3200.

Regional Administrator.—Edwin E. Fielder, Jr., 331–3200.
Deputy Regional Administrator.—Jimmy H. Bridgeman, 331–3200.
Assistant Regional Administrator for—
Federal Supply Service.—William (Bill) Sisk, 331–5114.
Federal Technology Service.—Randall Witty, 331–5104.
Public Buildings Service.—Thomas Walker, 562–0262.

Great Lakes Region: 230 South Dearborn Street, Chicago, IL 60604, (312) 353–5395.

Regional Administrator.—James C. Handley, 353–5395.
Deputy Regional Administrator.—Joseph Demeo (acting), 353–5395.
Assistant Regional Administrator for—
Federal Supply Service.—Michael Gelber, 353–5504.
Federal Technology Service.—William A. Griessel, 886–3824.
Public Buildings Service.—J. David Hood, 353–5572.

Heartland Region: 1500 East Bannister Road, Kansas City, MO 64131, (816) 926–7201.

Regional Administrator.—Brad Scott, 926–7201.
Deputy Regional Administrator.—Clarence H. Rosser (acting), 926–7217.
Assistant Regional Administrator for—
Federal Supply Service.—Steve Triplett, 926–7245.
Federal Technology Service.—Ronald Q. Williams, 926–5192.
Public Buildings Service.—Buster Rosser, 926–7231.
Staff Support Service Directors:
Human Resources.—Nick Cave, (816) 926–7401.
Regional Counsel.—Samm Skare, (816) 926–7212.
Regional EEO Office.—Pinkie Mason, (816) 926–7349.
Finance Center.—Ed Nasalik, (816) 926–7625.
Office of Inspector General:
Audits.—Larry Elkin, (816) 926–7052.
Investigations.—John Kolze, (816) 926–7214.

Greater Southwest Region: 819 Taylor Street, Fort Worth, TX 76102, (817) 978–2321.

Regional Administrator.—Scott Armey, 978–2321.
Assistant Regional Administrator for—
Federal Supply Service.—Tyree Varnado, 978–2516.
Federal Technology Service.—Marcella F. Banks, 978–2871.
Public Buildings Service.—[Vacant], 978–2522.

Rocky Mountain Region: Building 41, Denver Federal Center, Denver, CO 80225, (303) 236–7329.

Regional Administrator.—Larry Trujillo, 236–7329.
Deputy Regional Administrator.—Benjamin F. Gonzales, 236–7329.
Assistant Regional Administrator for—
Federal Supply Service.—Kenneth M. Bowen, Jr., 236–7547.
Federal Technology Service.—Randall Touchton, 236–7319.
Public Buildings Service.—Paul F. Prouty, 236–7245.

Pacific Rim Region: 450 Golden Gate Avenue, room 5–2690, San Francisco, CA 94102, (415) 522–3001.

Regional Administrator.—Peter G. Stamison, 522–3001.
Deputy Regional Administrator.—Peter T. Glading, 522–3001.
Public Information Officer.—Bethany Rich, 522–3001.
Administrative Officer.—Kathryne McInturff, 522–3001.
Assistant Regional Administrator for—
Federal Supply Service.—John Boyan, 522–2777.
Federal Technology Service.—Ann Gladys, 522–4500.
Public Buildings Service.—Dan Voll, 522–3001.

Northwest/Arctic Region: GSA Center, 400 15th Street SW, Auburn, WA 98001, (253) 931–7000.

Regional Administrator.—Jon Kvistad, 931–7000.
Deputy Regional Administrator.—Bill DuBray, 931–7000.
Assistant Regional Administrator for—
Federal Supply Service.—Gary G. Casteel, 931–7115.
Federal Technology Service.—Gary G. Casteel (acting), 931–7115.
Public Buildings Service.—Robin G. Graf, 931–7200.

HARRY S. TRUMAN SCHOLARSHIP FOUNDATION

712 Jackson Place NW., 20006, phone (202) 395–4831, fax 395–6995

[Created by Public Law 93–642]

BOARD OF TRUSTEES

President.—Madeleine K. Albright.
Chairman Emeritus.—Elmer B. Staats.
Vice Chairman.—Ike Skelton, Representative from Missouri.
Secretary.—Mrs. Margaret Truman Daniel, New York, NY.
General Counsel.—C. Westbrook Murphy.
Members:
Rod Paige, Secretary of Education.
Christopher S. Bond, Senator from Missouri.
Jo Ann Emerson, Representative from Missouri.
Max Baucus, Senator from Montana.
Steven Zinter, Sixth Judicial Circuit from South Dakota.
Luis Rovira, Chief Justice (ret.) from Colorado.
Frederick G. Slabach, Dean, Florida Coastal School of Law.
Executive Secretary.—Louis H. Blair.
Deputy Executive Secretary.—Mary H. Tolar.
Program Officer.—Tonji W. Barrow.
2002–03 Resident Truman Scholar.—Angela Clements.

INTER-AMERICAN FOUNDATION

901 North Stuart Street, 10th Floor, Arlington, VA 22203, phone (703) 306–4301

Chairperson, Board of Directors.—Frank D. Yturria.
Vice Chair, Board of Directors.—Patricia Williams.
President.—David Valenzuela.
General Counsel.—Carolyn Karr.
Vice President for Programs.—Linda P. Borst.

INTERNATIONAL BROADCASTING BUREAU

[Created by Public Law 103–236]

The International Broadcasting Bureau (IBB) is composed of the Voice of America, WORLDNET Television and Film Service, and Radio and TV Marti. The Broadcasting Board of Governors oversees the operation of the IBB and provides yearly funding grants approved by Congress to two non-profit grantee corporations, Radio Free Europe / Radio Liberty and Radio Free Asia.

Director, International Broadcasting Bureau.—Seth Cropsey, 619–1088, fax 401–1327.
Director of:
Cuba Broadcasting.—Pedro Roig, (305) 437–7010, fax 437–7016.
Voice of America.—David Jackson, 619–3375, fax 260–2228.
WORLDNET Television and Film Service.—Marie Skiba (acting), 205–5600, fax 690–4952.
President, Radio Free Asia.—Richard Richter.
President, Radio Free Europe.—Thomas Dine.

BROADCASTING BOARD OF GOVERNORS

330 Independence Avenue SW, Suite 3360, 20547, phone 401–3736, fax 401–6605

Chairman.—Kenneth Y. Tomlinson.

GOVERNORS

Edward E. Kaufman
Robert M. Ledbetter, Jr.
Norm Pattiz
Joaquin F. Blaya
Blanquita Walsh Cullum
D. Jeffrey Hirschberg
Steven J. Simmons
Colin L. Powell
(ex officio)

STAFF

Executive Director.—Brian T. Conniff.
Deputy Executive Director.—Bruce Sherman.
Legal Counsel.—Carol Booker.
Program Review Officer.—Bruce Sherman.
Congressional Coordinator.—Susan Andross.
Communications Coordinator.—Joan Mower.
Chief Financial Officer.—Kelley Lehman Sullivan.
Executive Assistant.—Brenda Hardnett.
Research and Planning Coordinator.—Sherwood Demitz.
Program Review and Planning Officer.—Jim Morrow.
Special Projects Officer.—Oanh Tran.
Program Coordinator.—Bonnie Thompson.
Staff Assistants.—Mariam Azizkeya, Lori Dodson, Clark Pearson.

JOHN F. KENNEDY CENTER FOR THE PERFORMING ARTS

Washington, DC 20566, phone 416–8000, fax 416–8205

BOARD OF TRUSTEES

Honorary Chairs:
Mrs. Laura Bush
Senator Hillary Rodham Clinton
Mrs. George Bush
Mrs. Ronald Reagan
Mrs. Jimmy Carter
Mrs. Gerald R. Ford
Mrs. Lyndon B. Johnson

Officers:
Chairman.—James A. Johnson.
Vice Chairman.—Kenneth M. Duberstein.
Vice Chairman.—Alma Johnson Powell.
President.—Michael M. Kaiser.
Secretary.—Jean Kennedy Smith.
Assistant Secretary.—Ann Steck.
Treasurer.—Paul G. Stern.
Assistant Treasurer.—Henry Strong.

Members Appointed by the President of the United States:
Mrs. Anita Arnold
Mr. Smith Bagley
Mr. Robert B. Barnett
Mrs. Lois Phifer Betts
Mr. Ronald W. Burkle
Mrs. William N. Cafritz
Senator Jon S. Corzine
Mrs. Bo Derek
Dr. Ronald I. Dozoretz
Mr. Kenneth M. Duberstein
Mr. Melvyn Estrin
Mr. George Farias
Mr. Thomas C. Foley
Mr. David Girard-diCarlo
Mr. Albert B. Glickman
Mr. Roy Goodman
Mr. Vinod Gupta
Mrs. Anne Sewell Johnson
Mrs. Brenda LaGrange Johnson
Mr. James A. Johnson
Mr. James V. Kimsey
Mrs. Kathi Koll
Mrs. Marlene A. Malek
Mrs. Dorothy Swann McAuliffe
Mrs. Donna C. McLarty
The Hon. William F. McSweeney
Mr. Frank H. Pearl
Mrs. Alma Johnson Powell
Mrs. Catherine B. Reynolds
The Hon. Jean Kennedy Smith
Mr. Jay Stein
Mrs. Catherine Stevens
Mrs. Beatrice Walters
Mr. Mark W. Weiner
Mr. Thomas Wheeler

Ex Officio Members Designated by Act of Congress:
Colin L. Powell, Secretary of State.
Tommy Thompson, Secretary of Health and Human Services.
Rod Paige, Secretary of Education.
Edward M. Kennedy, Senator from Massachusetts.
William (Bill) Frist, Senate Republican Leader from Tennessee.
Tom Daschle, Senator from South Dakota.
Harry Reid, Senator from Nevada.
Ted Stevens, Senator from Alaska.
James L. Oberstar, Representative from Minnesota.
J. Dennis Hastert, Speaker of the U.S. House of Representatives from Illinois.
Nancy Pelosi, House Minority Leader from California.
Don Young, Representative from Alaska.
Jim Kolbe, Representative from Arizona.
Deborah Pryce, Representative from Ohio.

Patrick J. Kennedy, Representative from Rhode Island.
Anthony A. Williams, Mayor, District of Columbia.
Lawrence M. Small, Secretary, Smithsonian Institution.
James H. Billington, Librarian of Congress.
J. Carter Brown, Chairman, Commission of Fine Arts.
Fran Mainella, Director, National Park Service.
Founding Chairman.—Roger Stevens (deceased).
Chairman Emeritus.—James D. Wolfensohn.
Honorary Trustees:

James H. Evans
Alma Gildenhorn
Melvin R. Laird
Leonard L. Silverstein
Henry Strong

LEGAL SERVICES CORPORATION

750 First Street NE., 11th Floor 20002–4250, phone (202) 336–8800
fax (202) 336–8952

BOARD OF DIRECTORS

Douglas S. Eakeley, *Chair.*
LaVeeda M. Battle, *Vice Chair.*
Hulett H. Askew
John T. Broderick, Jr.
John N. Erlenborn
F. William McCalpin
Maria Luisa Mercado
Nancy H. Rogers
Thomas F. Smegal, Jr.
Ernestine P. Watlington
Edna Fairbanks-Williams

President.—John N. Erlenborn.
Vice President, Legal Affairs/General Counsel and Corporate Secretary.—Victor M. Fortuno.
Comptroller/Treasurer.—David Richardson.
Vice President of:
Programs.—Randi Youells.
Governmental Relations/Public Affairs.—Mauricio Vivero.
Compliance and Administration.—John Eidleman.
Inspector General.—Leonard J. Koczur.

NATIONAL AERONAUTICS AND SPACE ADMINISTRATION

300 E Street SW, Room 9F44, 20546, phone 358–0000
http://www.nasa.gov

OFFICE OF THE ADMINISTRATOR

Code A, Room 9F44, phone: 358–1010

Administrator.—Sean O'Keefe.
Executive Assistant.—Retha S. Whewell, 358–1801.
Secretary.—Denise Stewart, 358–1801.
Chief of Staff/White House Liaison.—Courtney Stadd, 358–1827.
Deputy Administrator.—Frederick D. Gregory, 358–1020.
Associate Deputy Administrator for Technical Programs.—Dr. Michael A. Greenfield, 358–1820.
Associate Deputy Administrator for Institutions.—James Jennings, 358–1809.
Chief Engineer.—Theron M. Bradley, room 9P80, 358–1823.
Chief Scientist.—Dr. Shannon W. Lucid, room 9S11, 358–4509.
Chief Health/Medical Officer.—Dr. Richard S. Williams, room 7P13, 358–2390.
Chief Information Officer (CIO).—Patricia Dunnington, room 6R82, 358–1824.

OFFICE OF THE CHIEF FINANCIAL OFFICER (CFO)

Code B, Room 8F72, phone: 358–2262

Chief Financial Officer (CFO).—[Vacant].
Deputy Chief Financial Officer for Financial Management.—Gwendolyn Brown.
Deputy Chief Financial Officer for Resources/Comptroller.—Steven Isakowitz.

OFFICE OF HEADQUARTERS OPERATIONS

Code C, Room 4V13, phone: 358–2100

Director for Headquarters Operations.—James Frelk.

OFFICE OF EQUAL OPPORTUNITY PROGRAMS

Code E, Room 4Y23, phone: 358–2167

Assistant Administrator for Equal Opportunity Programs.—Dr. Dorothy Hayden-Watkins.
Deputy Assistant Administrator.—[Vacant].

OFFICE OF HUMAN RESOURCES AND EDUCATION

Code F, Room 4V84, phone: 358–0520

Assistant Administrator.—Vicki A. Novak.

OFFICE OF THE GENERAL COUNSEL

Code G, Room 9W21, phone: 358–2450

General Counsel.—Paul G. Pastorek.
Deputy General Counsel.—Robert M. Stephens, room 9W23, 358–5055.

OFFICE OF PROCUREMENT

Code H, Room 3A70, phone: 358–2090

Assistant Administrator.—Thomas S. Luedtke.

OFFICE OF EXTERNAL RELATIONS

Code I, Room 7W19, phone: 358–0400

Assistant Administrator.—John D. Schumacher.
Deputy Assistant Administrator.—[Vacant].
Deputy Assistant Administrator (Space Flight).—Michael F. O'Brien, room 7U15, 358–0450.

OFFICE OF MANAGEMENT SYSTEMS

Code J, Room 6W17, phone: 358–2800

Assistant Administrator.—Jeffrey E. Sutton.

OFFICE OF SMALL AND DISADVANTAGED BUSINESS UTILIZATION

Code K, Room 9K70, phone: 358–2088

Assistant Administrator.—Ralph C. Thomas III.

OFFICE OF LEGISLATIVE AFFAIRS

Code L, Room 9L33, phone: 358–1948

Assistant Administrator.—Charles T. Horner III.
Deputy Assistant Administrator.—Mary D. Kerwin, room 9J11.

OFFICE OF SPACE FLIGHT

Code M, Room 7A11, phone: 358–2015

Associate Administrator.—William F. Readdy.
Deputy Associate Administrator.—Lynn F.H. Cline, room 7A70, 358–1200.
Deputy Associate Administrator for—
International Space Station and Space Shuttle.—Michael C. Kostelnik, room 7A70, 358–4424.

Assistant Associate Administrator for—
Advanced Systems.—John Mankins, room 7E80, 358–1448.
Institutional Assets Management.—Tom Cremins (acting), room 7L13, 358–1650.
Interagency Enterprise.—Albert DiMarcantonio, room 7E72, 358–1470.
Launch Services.—Karen Poniatowski, room 7C72, 358–2330.
Policy and Plans.—[Vacant].
Space Communications.—Robert E. Spearing, room 7B70, 358–2020.

OFFICE OF PUBLIC AFFAIRS

Code P, Room 9P37, phone: 358–1400

Assistant Administrator.—Glenn Mahone.
Deputy Assistant Administrator.—Dean Acosta.

OFFICE OF SAFETY AND MISSION ASSURANCE

Code Q, Room 5W21, phone: 358–2406

Associate Administrator.—Bryan D. O'Connor.
Deputy Associate Administrator.—James D. Lloyd, room 5U11, 358–1930.

OFFICE OF AEROSPACE TECHNOLOGY

Code R, Room 6A70, 358–4600

Associate Administrator.—Dr. Jeremiah F. Creedon.
Deputy Associate Administrator.—Dr. J. Victor Lebacqz, room 6A51, 358–4700.
Chief Technologist.—[Vacant].

OFFICE OF SPACE SCIENCE

Code S, Room 5A11, phone: 358–1409

Associate Administrator.—Dr. Edward J. Weiler.
Deputy Associate Administrator.—Chris Scolese, room 3A22, 358–1413.

OFFICE OF BIOLOGICAL AND PHYSICAL RESEARCH

Code U, Room 8G17, 358–0122

Associate Administrator.—Mary E. Kicza.
Deputy Associate Administrator (Science).—[Vacant], 358–0215.
Deputy Associate Administrator (Programs).—[Vacant], room 8E11, 358–0215.

OFFICE OF INSPECTOR GENERAL

Code W, Room 8S84, phone: 358–1220

Inspector General.—Robert W. Cobb.

OFFICE OF SECURITY MANAGEMENT AND SAFEGUARDS

Code X, Room 9U79, phone: 358–2010

Director.—David Saleeba.

OFFICE OF EARTH SCIENCE

Code Y, Room 5A70, phone: 358–2165

Associate Administrator.—Dr. Ghassem R. Asrar.
Deputy Associate Administrator.—Michael R. Luther, room 5A20, 358–0260.
Deputy Associate Administrator (Advanced Planning).—Dr. Mary Cleave, room 5B13, 358–2165.

NASA NATIONAL OFFICES

Air Force Space Command/XPX (NASA): Peterson Air Force Base, CO 80914.
NASA Senior Representative.—Stan Newberry, (719) 554–4900.

Ames Research Center: Moffett Field, CA 94035.
Director.—G. Scott Hubbard, (650) 604–5000.

Dryden Flight Research Center: P.O. Box 273, Edwards, CA 93523.
Director.—Kevin L. Petersen, (661) 276–3311.

Glenn Research Center at Lewisfield: 21000 Brookpark Road, Cleveland, OH 44135.
Director.—Donald J. Campbell, (216) 433–4000.

Goddard Institute for Space Studies: Goddard Space Flight Center, 2880 Broadway, New York, NY 10025.
Head.—Dr. James E. Hansen, (212) 678–5500.

Goddard Space Flight Center: 8800 Greenbelt Road, Greenbelt, MD 20771.
Director.—Alphonso V. Diaz, (301) 286–2000.

Jet Propulsion Laboratory: 4800 Oak Grove Drive, Pasadena, CA 91109.
Director.—Dr. Charles Elachi, (818) 354–4351.

Lyndon B. Johnson Space Center: Houston, TX 77058–3696.
Director.—Gen. Jefferson D. Howell, Jr., (281) 483–0123.

John F. Kennedy Space Center: Kennedy Space Center, FL 32899.
Director.—Gen. Roy D. Bridges, (321) 867–5000.

Langley Reseach Center: Hampton, VA 23681.
Director.—Delma C. Freeman, Jr. (acting), (757) 864–1000.

George C. Marshall Space Flight Center: Marshall Space Flight Center, AL 35812.
Director.—Arthur G. Stephenson, (256) 544–2121.

Michoud Assembly Facility: P.O. Box 29300, New Orleans, LA 70189.
Manager.—John K. White, (504) 257–3311.

NASA IV & V Facility: NASA Independent Verification and Validation Facility, 100 University Drive, Fairmont, WV 26554.
Director.—Nelson H. Keeler, (304) 367–8200.

NASA Management Office: Jet Propulsion Laboratory, 4800 Oak Grove Drive, Pasadena, CA 91109.
Director.—Dr. Robert A. Parker, (818) 354–5359.

John C. Stennis Space Center: Stennis Space Center, MS 39529.
Director.—William (Bill) W. Parsons, Jr., (228) 688–2211.

Vandenberg AFB: P.O. Box 425, Lompoc, CA 93438.
Manager.—Ted L. Oglesby, (805) 866–5859.

Wallops Flight Facility: Goddard Space Flight Center, Wallops Island, VA 23337.
Director.—Arnold Torres, (757) 824–1000.

White Sands Test Facility: Johnson Space Center, P.O. Drawer MM, Las Cruces, NM 88004.
Manager.—Joseph Fries, (505) 524–5771.

NASA OVERSEAS REPRESENTATIVES

Australia: APO AP 96549.
NASA Representative.—Neal Newman, phone: 011–61–2–6281–8501.

Europe: U.S. Embassy, Paris, PSC 116 APO AE 09777.
NASA Representative.—Karen C. Feldstein, phone: 011–33–1–4312–2100.

Japan: U.S. Embassy, Tokyo, Unit 45004, Box 235, APO AP, 96337–5004.
NASA Representative.—William Jordan, phone: 011–81–3–3224–5827.

Russia: U.S. Embassy, Moscow, PSC 77/NASA APO AE 09721.
NASA Representative.—Phillip Cleary, phone: (256) 961–6333.

Spain: PSC No. 61, Box 0037, APO AE 09642.
NASA Representative.—Ms. Ingrid Desilvestre, phone: 011–34–91–548–9250.

NATIONAL ARCHIVES AND RECORDS ADMINISTRATION

8601 Adelphi Road, College Park, MD 20740–6001

phone (301) 837–1600 http://www.nara.gov

[Created by Public Law 98–497]

Archivist of the United States.—John W. Carlin, fax (301) 837–3218.

Deputy Archivist of the United States and Chief of Staff.—Lewis J. Bellardo, fax (301) 837–3218.

Congressional and Public Affairs.—John A. Constance, (301) 837–1800, fax (301) 837–0311.

General Counsel.—Gary M. Stern, (301) 837–1750, fax (301) 837–0293.

Equal Employment Opportunity and Diversity Programs.—Robert Jew, (301) 837–1550, fax (301) 837–0869.

Policy and Communications Staff.—Lori A. Lisowski, (301) 837–1850, fax (301) 837–0319.

Information Security Oversight Office.—J. William Leonard, (301) 219–5250, fax (301) 219–5385.

National Historical Publications and Records Commission.—Max J. Evans, (202) 501–5600, fax (202) 501–5601.

Director, Office of:

Inspector General.—Paul Brachfeld, (301) 837–3000, fax (301) 837–3197.

Administrative Services.—Adrienne C. Thomas, (301) 837–3050, fax (301) 837–3217.

Federal Register.—Raymond A. Mosely, (202) 741–6000, fax (202) 741–6012.

Human Resources and Information Services.—L. Reynolds Cahoon, (301) 837–3670, fax (301) 837–3213.

Records Services, Washington, D.C.—Michael J. Kurtz, (301) 837–3110, fax (301) 837–3633.

Regional Records Services.—Thomas Mills, (301) 837–2950, fax (301) 837–1617.

REGIONAL OFFICES

Northeast Region, Headquarters: Waltham, MA. *Regional Director.*—Diane LeBlanc, (781) 663–0133.

Boston.—380 Trapelo Road, Waltham, MA 02452–6399, (781) 663–0130.

Pittsfield.—10 Conte Drive, Pittsfield, MA 01201–8230, (413) 236–3600.

New York City.—201 Varick St., New York, NY 10014–4811, (212) 401–1620.

Mid Atlantic Region, Headquarters: Philadelphia, PA. *Regional Director.*—V. Chapman Smith, (215) 305–2002.

Center City Philadelphia.—900 Market Street, Philadelphia, PA, 19107, (215) 597–3000.

Northeast Philadelphia.—14700 Townsend Road, Philadelphia, PA 19154, (215) 671–9027.

Southeast Region: *Regional Director.*—James McSweeney, (404) 763–7438.

Southeast Region.—1557 St. Joseph Avenue, East Point, GA 30344, (404) 763–7474.

Great Lakes Region, Headquarters: Chicago, IL, *Regional Director.*—David E. Kuehl, (773) 581–7816.

Chicago.—7358 South Pulaski Road, Chicago, IL 60629, (773) 581–9688.

Dayton.—3150 Springboro Road, Dayton, OH 45439, (513) 225–2852.

Central Plains Region: *Regional Director.*—R. Reed Whitaker, (816) 926–6920.

Central Plains Region.—2312 East Bannister Road, Kansas City, MO 64131, (816) 7271.

Southwest Region: *Regional Director.*—Kent C. Carter, (817) 334–5515.

Southwest Region.—501 W. Felix Street, Ft. Worth, TX 76115, (817) 334–5515.

Rocky Mountain Region: *Regional Director.*—Barbara Voss, (303) 236–0804.

Rocky Mountain Region.—Building 48, Denver Federal Center, Denver, CO 80225, (303) 236–0804.

Pacific Region, Headquarters: San Bruno, CA. *Director.*—Shirley J. Burton, (650) 876–9249.

Laguna Niguel.—24000 Avila Road, 1st Floor (East), Laguna Niguel, CA 92607, (949) 360–2641.

San Francisco.—1000 Commodore Drive, San Bruno, CA 94066, (415) 876–9001.

Pacific Alaska Region, Headquarters: Seattle, WA. *Regional Director.*—Steven M. Edwards, (206) 526–6501.

Seattle.—6125 Sand Point Way NE, Seattle, WA 98115, (206) 526–6501.

Anchorage.—654 West Third Avenue, Anchorage, AK 99501, (907) 721–2443.

National Personnel Records Center: *Director.*—Ronald L. Hindman, (314) 801–0574.

National Personnel Records Center.—9700 Page Avenue, St. Louis, MO 63132, (314) 538–4201.

Presidential Libraries.—Richard Claypoole, (301) 837–3250, fax (301) 837–3199.

Director for—

Herbert Hoover Library.—Timothy G. Walch, West Branch, IA 52358–0488, (319) 643–5301.

Franklin D. Roosevelt Library.—Cynthia M. Koch, Hyde Park, NY 12538–1999, (845) 486–7770.

Harry S. Truman Library.—Michael Devine, Independence, MO 64050–1798, (816) 833–1400.

Dwight D. Eisenhower Library.—Daniel D. Holt, Abilene, KS 67410–2900, (913) 263–4751.

John F. Kennedy Library.—Deborah Leff, Boston, MA 02125–3398, (617) 514–1600.

Lyndon Baines Johnson Library.—Betty Sue Flowers, Austin, TX 78705–5702, (512) 721–0200.

Gerald R. Ford Library.—Dennis A. Daellenbach, Ann Arbor, MI 48109–2114, (734) 741–2218.

Gerald R. Ford Museum.—Dennis A. Daellenbach, Grand Rapids, MI 49504–5353, (616) 451–9263.

Nixon Presidential Materials Staff.—Karl Weissenbach, College Park, MD 20740–6001, (301) 837–3290.

Jimmy Carter Library.—Jay E. Hakes, Atlanta, GA 30307–1498, (404) 331–3942.

Ronald Reagan Library.—R. Duke Blackwood, Simi Valley, CA 93065–0600, (800) 410–8354.

George Bush Library.—Edward Douglas Menarchik, College Station, TX 77845, (979) 691–4000.

Clinton Presidential Materials Project.—David E. Alsobrook, Little Rock, AR 72201, (501) 244–9756.

NATIONAL HISTORICAL PUBLICATIONS AND RECORDS COMMISSION

National Archives Building 20408, phone (202) 501–5610, fax (301) 501–5601

Members:

John W. Carlin, Archivist of the United States, Chairman, National Archives and Records Administration.

Justice David H. Souter, United States Supreme Court.

Christopher Dodd, Senator of Connecticut.

Tom Cole, Representative of Oklahoma.

Margaret P. Grafield, Director, Office of IRM Programs and Services, Department of State.

Alfred Goldberg, Historian, Office of the Secretary, Department of Defense.

James Hutson, Chief of Manuscripts Division, Library of Congress.

Nicholas C. Burckel, Dean of Libraries, Marquette University, Presidential Appointment.

David W. Brady, Hoover Institution, Stanford University, Presidential Appointment.

Barbara J. Fields, Professor of History, Columbia University, Organization of American Historians.

J. Kevin Graffagnino, Director, Vermont Historical Society, American Association for State and Local History.

Charles T. Cullen, President and Librarian, Newberry Library, Association for Documentary Editing.

Roy C. Turnbaugh, State Archivist of Oregon, National Association of Government Archives and Records Administrators.

Mary Maples Dunn, Co-Executive Officer, American Philosophical Society, American Historical Association.

Lee Stout, Head of Public Services and Outreach, Special Collections Department, Penn State University, Society of American Archivists.

Executive Director.—Max J. Evans, (202) 501–5610

NATIONAL ARCHIVES TRUST FUND BOARD

phone (301) 837–3550, fax (301) 837–3191

Members:

John W. Carlin, Archivist of the United States, *Chair.*

Bruce Cole, Chairman, National Endowment for the Humanities.

Donald V. Hammond, Fiscal Assistant Secretary, Department of the Treasury.

Secretary.—Evelyn A. Brown.

ADMINISTRATIVE COMMITTEE OF THE FEDERAL REGISTER

800 North Capitol Street, Washington, DC, phone (202) 741–6000

Members:
John W. Carlin, Archivist of the United States, *Chair*.
Rosemary Hart, Senior Counsel, Department of Justice.
Bruce James, The Public Printer of the United States.
Secretary.—Raymond A. Mosley, Director of the Federal Register, National Archives and Records Administration.

NATIONAL CAPITAL PLANNING COMMISSION

401 9th Street NW, North Lobby, Suite 500, 20576, phone (202) 482–7200
fax 482–7272

APPOINTIVE MEMBERS

Presidential Appointees:
John V. Cogbill, *Chairman.*
José L. Galvez.
Richard L. Friedman.
Mayoral Appointees:
Arrington Dixon.
Dr. Patricia Elwood, *Vice Chair.*
Ex Officio Members:
Anthony A. Williams, Mayor of the District of Columbia.
First Alternate.—Andrew Altman.
Second Alternate.—Ellen M. McCarthy.
Third Alternate.—Toni L. Griffin.
Linda W. Cropp, Chairman, Council of the District of Columbia.
First Alternate.—Robert E. Miller, Esq.
Second Alternate.—Christopher Murray.
Gale A. Norton, Secretary of the Interior.
First Alternate.—Fran P. Mainello.
Second Alternate.—Terry R. Carlstrom.
Third Alternate.—John G. Parsons.
Donald H. Rumsfeld, Secretary of Defense.
Alternate.—Jerry R. Shiplett.
Stephen A. Perry, Administrator, General Services Administration.
First Alternate.—F. Joseph Moravec.
Second Alternate.—Donald Williams.
Third Alternate.—Anthony E. Costa.
Fourth Alternate.—Craig King.
Fifth Alternate.—Michael S. McGill.
Susan Collins, Chairman, Senate Committee on Governmental Affairs.
First Alternate.—Cynthia Gooen Lesser.
Second Alternate.—Kevin Landy.
Third Alternate.—Kiersten Todt Coon.
Tom Davis, Chairman, House Committee on Government Reform.
Alternate.—Jennifer L. Hall.

EXECUTIVE STAFF

Executive Director.—Patricia E. Gallagher, 482–7211.
Deputy Executive Director.—Marcel C. Acosta, 482–7221.
Chief Operating Officer.—Connie M. Harshaw, 482–7220.
Community Planner.—Julia Koster, 482–7211.
Secretariat.—Deborah B. Young, 482–7228.
Executive Assistant.—Priscilla A. Brown, 482–7212.
Management Assistant.—LaWan L. Jenkins, 482–7225.
General Counsel.—Ash J. Jain, 482–7220.
Staff Attorney.—Wayne E. Costa, 482–7231.
Administrative Officer.—[Vacant].

Director, Office of:
Planning Research and Policy.—Joseph Kocy, 482–7275.
Urban Design & Plans Review.—Hillary Altman, 482–7244.
Plan and Project Implementation.—William G. Dowd, 482–7240.
Technology Development and Applications Support.—Michael Sherman, 482–7254.
Public Affairs Officer.—Lisa N. MacSpadden, 482–7263.

NATIONAL COMMISSION ON LIBRARIES AND INFORMATION SCIENCE

1110 Vermont Avenue NW., Suite 820, 20005

phone 606–9200, fax 606–9203, http://www.nclis.gov

[Created by Public Law 91–345]

Chairperson.—Martha B. Gould.
Vice Chairperson.—Joan R. Challinor, 3117 Hawthorne Street, NW, Washington, DC 20008.
Members:
James H. Billington, Librarian of Congress, Library of Congress, Washington, DC 20540.
Serves for the Librarian of Congress:
Nancy A. Davenport, Library of Congress, Madison Bldg., Room 642, Washington, DC 20540.
Jack E. Hightower, 5905 Doone Valley Court, Austin, TX 78731.
Robert S. Martin, Director, Institute of Museum and Library Services, 1100 Pennsylvania Avenue NW, Suite 510, Washington, DC 20506.
Bobby L. Roberts, Director, Central Arkansas Library System, 100 Rock Street, Little Rock, AR 72201.
Chairpersons Emeritus:
Charles Benton, 4411 N. Ravenswood Avenue, 3rd Floor, Chicago, IL 60640.
Frederick Burkhardt, Box 1067 Bennington, VT 05201.
Elinor M. Hashim, 5 King Arthur's Way #7, Newington, CT 06111.
Jerald C. Newman, 63 Captains Road, North Woodmere, NY 11581.
Charles E. Reid, 753 Charles Court, Ft. Lee, NJ 07024.

EXECUTIVE STAFF

Executive Director.—Robert S. Willard.
Director of Operations.—Madeleine C. McCain.
Secretary to the Staff.—[Vacant].
Administrative Officer.—Julie Yoon.

LIBRARY STATISTICS PROGRAM STAFF

Director, Statistics and Surveys.—Robert Molyneux.
Special Assistant, Technical.—Kim A. Miller.

NATIONAL COUNCIL ON DISABILITY

1331 F Street NW., Suite 850, 20004, phone 272–2004, fax 272–2022

Chairperson.—Lex Frieden, Houston, TX.
First Vice Chairperson.—Patricia Pound, Austin, TX.
Second Vice Chairperson.—Glenn Anderson, Little Rock, AR.
Executive Director.—Ethel D. Briggs.
Members:
Milton Aponte, Cooper City, FL.
Robert R. Davila, Ph.D., Pittsford, NY.
Barbara Gillcrist, Santa Fe, NM.
Graham Hill, Arlington, VA.
Joel I. Kahn, Wyoming, OH.
Young Woo Kang, Ph.D., Munster, IN.
Kathleen Martinez, Oakland, CA.
Carol Hughes Novak, Tampa, FL.
Marco Rodriguez, Elk Grove, CA.
David Wenzel, Scranton, PA.
Linda Wetters, Columbus, OH.
Kate Pew Wolters, Grand Rapids, MI.

NATIONAL CREDIT UNION ADMINISTRATION

1775 Duke Street, Alexandria, VA 22314–3428, phone (703) 518–6300, fax 518–6319

Chairman.—Dennis Dollar.
Chief of Staff and Counsel to acting Chairman.—Kirk Cuevas.
Confidential Assistant to the Chairman.—Marilynn Calderwood, 518–6307.
Special Assistant to the Chairman for Public Affairs.—Nicholas Owens, 518–6330.
Board Members.—JoAnn Johnson, Deborah Matz.
Executive Director.—J. Leonard Skiles, 518–6320.
Deputy Executive Director.—[Vacant].
General Counsel.—Robert M. Fenner, 518–6540.
Deputy General Counsel.—James J. Engel, 518–6540.
Inspector General.—Herb Yolles, 518–6350.
Deputy Inspector General.—William DeSarno, 518–6350.
Secretary to the Board.—Becky Baker.
Director, Office of:
Credit Union Development.—Anthony LaCreta, 518–6610.
Chief Financial Officer.—Dennis C. Winans, 518–6570.
Corporate Credit Unions.—Kent D. Buckham, 518–6640.
Examination and Insurance.—David M. Marquis, 518–6360.
Human Resources.—Sherry Turpenoff, 518–6510.
Chief Information Officer.—Doug Verner, 518–6440.
Public and Congressional Affairs.—Clifford R. Northup, 518–6330.
EEO.—Marilyn G. Gannon, 518–6325.
Strategic Program Support and Planning.—[Vacant].
Strategic Planning.—James L. Patrick, 518–6320.
Training and Development.—Leslie Armstrong, 518–6630.

REGIONAL OFFICES

Director, Office of:
Region I (Albany).—Mark A. Treichel, 9 Washington Square, Washington Avenue Extension, Albany, NY 12205, (518) 862–7400, fax 862–7420.
Region II (National Capital Region).—Edward Dupcak, Suite 4206, 1775 Duke Street, Alexandria, VA 22314, (703) 519–4600, fax 519–4620.
Region III (Atlanta).—Alonzo A. Swann III, Suite 1600, 7000 Central Parkway, Atlanta, GA 30328, (678) 443–3000, fax 443–3020.
Region IV (Chicago).—Melinda Love, Suite 125, 4225 Naperville Road, Lisle, IL 60532, (630) 955–4100, fax 955–4120.
Region V (Austin).—Jane Walters, Suite 5200, 4807 Spicewood Springs Road, Austin, TX 78759–8490, (512) 342–5600, fax 342–5620.
Region VI (Concord).—Robert Blatner, Suite 1350, 2300 Clayton Road, Concord, CA 94520, (925) 363–6200, fax 363–6220.
President, Asset Management and Assistance Center (Austin).—Mike Barton, Suite 5100, 4807 Spicewood Springs Road, Austin, TX 78759–8490, (512) 231–7900, fax 231–7920.

NATIONAL FOUNDATION ON THE ARTS AND THE HUMANITIES

Old Post Office Building, 1100 Pennsylvania Avenue, NW., 20506

NATIONAL ENDOWMENT FOR THE ARTS

Chairman.—Dana Gioia, 682–5414.
Senior Deputy Chairman.—Eileen B. Mason.
Deputy Chairman for—
Grants and Awards.—Patrice Walker Powell (acting), 682–5441.
Guidelines, Panel and Council Operations.—A.B. Spellman, 682–5421.
Management and Budget.—Laurence Baden, 682–5408.
Congressional and White House Liaison.—Ann Guthrie Hingston, 682–5434.
General Counsel.—Hope O'Keeffe (acting), 682–5418.
Policy Research and Analysis.—Keith Stephens (acting), 682–5424.
Inspector General.—Daniel Shaw, 682–5402.
Communications Director.—Felicia Knight, 682–5570.

THE NATIONAL COUNCIL ON THE ARTS

Chairman.—Dana Gioia.

Members:

Don V. Cogman
Mary D. Costa
Gordon Davidson
Katharine Cramer DeWitt
Makoto Fujimura
David H. Gelernter
Nathan Leventhal
Teresa Lozano Long
Maribeth Walton McGinley
Jerry Pinkney
Earl A. Powell III
Cleo Parker Robinson
Deedie Potter Rose
Karen Lias Wolff

Ex Officio Members:

Hon. Cass Ballenger
Hon. Buck McKeon

NATIONAL ENDOWMENT FOR THE HUMANITIES

http://www.neh.gov

Chairman.—Bruce Cole, 606–8310.
Deputy Chairman.—Lynne Munson, 606–8273.
Inspector General.—Sheldon L. Bernstein, 606–8350.
General Counsel.—Daniel Schneider, 606–8322.
Public Information Officer.—Joy Evans.
Public Affairs.—Noel Milan, 606–8446.
Strategic Planning.—Larry Myers, 606–8428.

NATIONAL COUNCIL ON THE HUMANITIES

Members:

Linda L. Aaker
Edward Ayers
Ira Berlin
Jewel Spears Brooker
Pedro Castillo
Celeste Colgan
Evelyn Edson
Elizabeth Fox-Genovese
Nathan Hatch
David Hertz
Amy Kass
Andrew Ladis
Wright Lassiter
Thomas Mallon
Wilfred McClay
Steven McKnight
Sidney McPhee
Naomi Shihab Nye
Lawrence Okamura
Michael Pack
James Stoner
Theodore Striggles
Marguerite Sullivan
Stephan Thernstrom
Jeffrey Wallin

FEDERAL COUNCIL ON THE ARTS AND THE HUMANITIES

Federal Council Members:

Dana Gioia, Chairman, National Endowment for the Arts.
Bruce Cole, Chairman, National Endowment for the Humanities.
Robert S. Martin, Director, Institute for Museum and Library Services.
Roderick R. Paige, Secretary, Department of Education.
Earl A. Powell III, Director, National Gallery of Art.
Harry S. Robinson III, Chairman, Commission of Fine Arts.
James H. Billington, Librarian of Congress, Library of Congress.
John W. Carlin, Archivist of the United States, National Archives and Records Administration.
F. Joseph Moravec, Commissioner, Public Buildings Service, General Services Administration.
Gale Norton, Secretary, Department of the Interior.
Rita Colwell, Director, National Science Foundation.
Jeri Thomson, Secretary of the Senate.
Lawrence M. Small, Secretary, Smithsonian Institution.
Fortney Pete Stark, Member, U.S. House of Representatives.
Donald L. Evans, Secretary, Department of Commerce.
Norman Y. Mineta, Secretary, Department of Transportation.
Judith Ann Rapanos, Chairman, National Museum Services Board.
Mel Martinez, Secretary, Department of Housing and Urban Development.
Elaine L. Chao, Secretary, Department of Labor.
Anthony J. Principi, Secretary, Department of Veterans Affairs.
Josefina G. Carbonell, Assistant Secretary for Aging, Department of Health and Human Services.

Staff Contact.—Alice M. Whelihan, Indemnity Administrator, National Endowment for the Arts, 682–5452.

INSTITUTE OF MUSEUM AND LIBRARY SERVICES

phone (202) 606–8536, fax 202–606–8591, http://www.imls.gov

[The Institute of Museum and Library Services was created by the Museum and Library Services Act of 1996, Public Law 104–208]

Director.—Robert S. Martin, 606–8536.
Deputy Directors: Schroeder Cherry, 606–0480, Mary Chute, 606–5419.
Director of:
Public and Legislative Affairs.—Mamie Bittner, 606–5227.
Budget and Administration.—Teresa LaHaie, 606–8536.
Research and Technology.—Rebecca Danvers, 606–2478.
State Programs.—Jane-Carol Heiser, 606–5252.
Museum Services.—Mary Estelle Kennelly, 606–8539.

NATIONAL MUSEUM SERVICES BOARD

Members:
Judith Ann Rapanos, Chair
David Donath
Nancy S. Dwight
A. Wilson Greene
Maria Mercedes Guillemard
Peter deCourey Hero
Thomas E. Lorentzen
Terry Maple
Elizabeth J. Pruet
Edwin Rigaud
Harry Robinson, Jr.
Beth LaRoche Walkup
Margaret Webster Scarlett
Ruth Tamura

NATIONAL COMMISSION ON LIBRARIES AND INFORMATION SCIENCE

Members:
Martha B. Gould, Chair
Joan R. Challinor, Vice Chair
Dr. James H. Billington, ex officio
Jack E. Hightower
Robert S. Martin, ex officio
Bobby L. Roberts
Nancy A. Davenport (for Dr. Billington)
Robert S. Willard, Executive Director

NATIONAL GALLERY OF ART

401 Constitution Avenue, NW., Washington, DC 20565, phone (202) 737–4215

fax (202) 289–5446

[Under the direction of the Board of Trustees of the National Gallery of Art]

Board of Trustees:
William H. Rehnquist, Chief Justice of the United States, ex officio.
Colin L. Powell, Secretary of State, ex officio.
John W. Snow, Secretary of the Treasury, ex officio.
Lawrence M. Small, Secretary of the Smithsonian Institution, ex officio.
Robert F. Erburu, Chairman.
Robert H. Smith, President.
Julian Ganz, Jr.
David O. Maxwell.
Victoria P. Sant.
Trustee Emerita.—Ruth Carter Stevenson.
Trustee Emeritus.—Alexander M. Laughlin.
Director.—Earl A. Powell III.
Deputy Director.—Alan Shestack.
Dean, Center for Advanced Study in the Visual Arts.—Elizabeth Cropper.
Administrator.—Darrell Willson.
Treasurer.—James E. Duff.
Secretary-General Counsel.—Elizabeth A. Croog.
External Affairs Officer.—Joseph J. Krakora.

NATIONAL LABOR RELATIONS BOARD

1099 14th Street, NW., 20570–0001

Personnel Locator (202) 273–4001, fax 273–4266

Chairman.—Robert J. Battista, 273–1770, fax 273–4270.
Chief Counsel.—Harold Datz, 273–1770.
Deputy Chief Counsel.—Kathleen Nixon, 273–1770.
Executive Assistant.—William B. Cowen, 273–1770.
Members:
Wilma B. Liebman, 273–1700.
Chief Counsel.—John F. Colwell, 273–1700.
Peter C. Schaumber, 273–1790.
Chief Counsel.—James R. Murphy, 273–1790.
Dennis P. Walsh, 273–1740.
Chief Counsel.—Gary W. Shinners, 273–1740.
R. Alexander Acosta, 273–1070.
Chief Counsel.—Peter Winkler (acting), 273–1070.
Executive Secretary.—[Vacant], 273–1940, fax 273–4270.
Deputy Executive Secretary.—Lester A. Heltzer, 273–1940.
Associate Executive Secretaries: Enid W. Weber, Hollace J. Enoch, Richard D. Hardick.
Solicitor.—Jeffrey D. Wedekind, 273–2910, fax 273–1962.
Inspector General.—Jane E. Altenhofen, 273–1960, fax 273–3244.
Director, Representation Appeals.—Lafe E. Solomon, 273–1980, fax 273–1962.
Deputy Director.—[Vacant].
Director, Division of Information.—David B. Parker, 273–1991, fax 273–1789.
Associate Director.—Patricia M. Gilbert.
Chief Administrative Law Judge.—Robert A. Giannasi, 501–8800, fax 501–8686.
Deputy Chief Administrative Law Judge.—Richard A. Scully, 501–8800.
Associate Chief Administrative Law Judges:
Joel P. Biblowitz, 120th West 45th Street—11th Floor, New York, NY 10036–5503, (212) 944–2941, fax 944–4904.
William N. Cates, 402 West Peachtree Street NW, Atlanta, GA 30308–3510, (404) 331–6652, fax 331–2061.
William L. Schmidt, Suite 300, 901 Market Street, San Francisco, CA 94103–1779, (415) 356–5255, fax 356–5254.

GENERAL COUNSEL

General Counsel.—Arthur F. Rosenfeld, 273–3700, fax 273–4483.
Deputy General Counsel.—John E. Higgins, Jr., 273–3700.
Assistant General Counsel.—Joseph F. Frankl, 273–3700.
Associate General Counsel, Division of Operations/Management.—Richard Siegel, 273–2900, fax 273–4274.
Deputy Associate General Counsel.—Anne Purcell, 273–2900.
Assistant General Counsels: James G. Paulsen, Jane C. Schnable, Shelley S. Korch, Nelson Levin.
Executive Assistant.—Carole K. Coleman.
Special Counsel: Joseph M. Davis, Peter A. Eveleth, Jennifer S. Kovachich, Barry F. Smith.
Associate General Counsel, Division of Advice.—Barry J. Kearney, 273–3800, fax 273–4275.
Deputy Associate General Counsel.—Ellen A. Farrell, 273–3800.
Assistant General Counsel for—
Regional Advice Branch.—David Colangelo, 273–3831.
Injunction Litigation Branch.—Judith I. Katz, 273–3810.
Legal Research and Policy Planning Branch.—Jacqueline A. Young, 273–3847.
Associate General Counsel, Division of Enforcement Litigation.—John H. Ferguson, 273–2950, fax 273–4244.
Appellate Court Branch:
Deputy Associate General Counsel.—Aileen Armstrong, 273–2960, fax 273–0191.
Deputy Branch Chief.—Linda Dreeben, 273–2966.
Supreme Court Branch:
Deputy Associate General Counsel.—[Vacant], 273–2954, fax 273–4283.
Assistant General Counsel.—John Arbab.
Special Litigation Branch:
Assistant General Counsel.—Margery E. Lieber, 273–2930, fax 273–1799.

Contempt Litigation Branch:
Assistant General Counsel.—Stanley R. Zirkin (acting), 273–3739, fax 273–4244.
Deputy Assistant General Counsel.—Daniel F. Collopy, 273–3745.
Director, Office of Appeals.—Yvonne T. Dixon, 273–3760, 273–4283.
Director, Division of Administration.—Gloria J. Joseph, 273–3890, fax 273–4266.
Deputy Director.—Frank V. Battle, 273–3890.

NATIONAL MEDIATION BOARD

1301 K Street NW., Suite 250 East, 20572, phone (202) 692–5000, fax 692–5080

Chairman.—Francis J. Duggan, 692–5019.
Board Members: Edward Fitzmaurice, 692–5016; Harry R. Hoglander, 692–5022.
Chief of Staff.—Benetta M. Mansfield, 692–5030.
Deputy Chief of Staff for—
Mediation.—Larry Gibbons, 692–5030.
Development and Technology.—Daniel Rainey, 692–5050.
Chief Financial/Information Officer.—June D.W. King, 692–5010.
General Counsel.—Mary L. Johnson, 692–5040.
Director, Arbitration Services.—Roland Watkins, 692–5055.

NATIONAL RESEARCH COUNCIL—NATIONAL ACADEMY OF SCIENCES NATIONAL ACADEMY OF ENGINEERING—INSTITUTE OF MEDICINE

2101 Constitution Avenue NW 20418, phone (202) 334–2000

The National Research Council, National Academy of Sciences, National Academy of Engineering, and Institute of Medicine, serves as an independent adviser to the Federal Government on scientific and technical questions of national importance. Although operating under a congressional charter granted the National Academy of Sciences in 1863, the National Research Council and its three parent organizations are private organizations, not agencies of the Federal Government, and receive no appropriations from Congress.

NATIONAL RESEARCH COUNCIL

Chairman.—Bruce M. Alberts, President, National Academy of Sciences, 334–2100.
Vice Chairman.—Wm. A. Wulf, President, National Academy of Engineering, 334–3200.
Executive Officer.—E. William Colglazier, 334–3000.
Director, Office of Congressional and Government Affairs.—James E. Jensen, 334–1601.

NATIONAL ACADEMY OF SCIENCES

President.—Bruce M. Alberts, 334–2100.
Vice President.—James S. Langer, University of California, Santa Barbara.
Home Secretary.—R. Stephen Berry, University of Chicago.
Foreign Secretary.—F. Sherwood Rowland, University of California, Irvine.
Treasurer.—Ronald L. Graham, University of California, San Diego.
Executive Officer.—E. William Colglazier, 334–3000.

NATIONAL ACADEMY OF ENGINEERING

President.—Wm. A. Wulf, 334–3200.
Chairman.—George M.C. Fisher (retired), Eastman Kodak Company.
Vice President.—Sheila E. Widnall, Massachusetts Institute of Technology.
Home Secretary.—W. Dale Compton, Purdue University.
Foreign Secretary.—Harold K. Forsen (retired), Bechtel Corporation.
Executive Officer.—Lance Davis, 334–3677.
Treasurer.—William L. Friend, National Labs.

INSTITUTE OF MEDICINE

President.—Harvey V. Fineberg, M.D., 334–3300.
Executive Officer.—Susanne Stoiber, 334–2177.

NATIONAL SCIENCE FOUNDATION

4201 Wilson Boulevard, Suite 1245, Arlington, VA 22230, http://www.nsf.gov

Director.—Rita R. Colwell, (703) 292–8000.
Deputy Director.—Joseph Bordogna, (703) 292–8000.
Inspector General.—Christine C. Boesz, (703) 292–7100.
Equal Opportunity Coordinator.—Ana A. Ortiz, (703) 292–8020.
Director, Office of:
Legislative and Public Affairs.—Curt Suplee, (703) 292–8070.
Polar Programs.—Karl Erb, (703) 292–8030.
Integrative Activities.—Nathaniel G. Pitts, (703) 292–8040.
General Counsel.—Lawrence Rudolph, (703) 292–8060.
Assistant Director for—
Biological Sciences.—Mary E. Clutter, (703) 292–8500.
Computer and Information Science and Engineering.—Peter Freeman, (703) 292–8900.
Education and Human Resources.—Judith A. Ramaley, (703) 292–8300.
Engineering.—John Brighton, (703) 292–8300.
Geosciences.—Margaret S. Leinen, (703) 292–8500.
Mathematical and Physical Sciences.—John Hunt (acting), (703) 292–8801.
Social, Behavorial, and Economic Sciences.—Norman M. Bradburn, (703) 292–8700.
Director, Office of:
Budget, Finance, and Award Management.—Thomas N. Cooley, (703) 292–8200.
Information and Resource Management.—Anthony Arnolie, (703) 292–8100.

NATIONAL SCIENCE BOARD

Chairman.—Warren M. Washington, (703) 292–7000.
Vice Chairman.—Diana Natalicio.
Executive Officer.—Gerry Glaser (acting).

MEMBERS

Barry C. Barish
Steven C. Beering
Ray M. Bowen
Delores M. Etter
Nina Fedoroff
Pamela A. Ferguson
Kenneth M. Ford
Daniel Hastings
Elizabeth Hoffman
Anita K. Jones
George M. Langford
Jane Lubchenco
Joseph A. Miller, Jr.
Douglas D. Randall
Robert C. Richardson
Michael G. Rossmann
Maxine Savitz
Luis Sequeira
Daniel Simberloff
JoAnne Vasquez
John A. White, Jr.
Mark S. Wrighton

NATIONAL TRANSPORTATION SAFETY BOARD

490 L'Enfant Plaza, SW., 20594, phone (202) 314–6000

Chairman.—Ellen G. Engleman, 314–6010, fax 314–6018.
Vice Chairman.—Mark V. Rosenker, 314–6004, fax 314–6027.
Members:
Richard Healing, 314–6058, fax 314–6035.
John J. Goglia, 314–6660, fax 314–6665.
Carol J. Carmody, 314–6020, fax 314–6027.
Executive Director.—[Vacant].
Managing Director.—Daniel Campbell, 314–6091, fax 314–6090.
General Counsel.—Ronald Battocchi, 314–6616, fax 314–6090.
Chief Financial Officer.—Steven Goldberg, 314–6212, fax 314–6261.
Director, Office of:
Aviation Safety.—John Clark, 314–6301, fax 314–6309.
Government Affairs/Family Affairs.—Brenda L. Yager, 314–6123, fax 314–6122.
Public Affairs.—Ted Lopatkiewicz, 314–6100, fax 314–6122.
Highway Safety.—Joseph Osterman, 314–6441, fax 314–6482.
Marine Safety.—Majorie Murtagh, 314–6450, fax 314–6454.
Railroad, Pipeline and Hazardous Materials Investigations.—Bob Chipkevich, 314–6461, fax 314–6482.
Research and Engineering.—Vernon Ellingstad, 314–6501, fax 314–6599.
Safety Recommendations/Accomplishments.—Elaine Weinstein, 314–6171, fax 314–6717.
Chief Administrative Law Judge.—William W. Fowler, Jr., 314–6150, fax 314–6158.

NEIGHBORHOOD REINVESTMENT CORPORATION

1325 G Street, NW., Room 800, 20005, phone (202) 220–2300, fax 376–2600

BOARD OF DIRECTORS

Chairman.—Edward M. Gramlich, Member, Board of Governors, Federal Reserve System.
Vice Chairman.—John Reich, Director, Federal Deposit Insurance Corporation.
Members:
John D. Hawke, Comptroller of the Currency, Department of the Treasury.
Julie Williams, First Senior Deputy Comptroller and Chief Counsel, U.S. Comptroller of the Currency Designate.
Mel Martinez, Secretary, Department of Housing and Urban Development.
James E. Gilleran, Director, Office of Thrift Supervision.
John C. Weicher, Assistant Secretary for Housing / Federal Housing Commissioner, Department of Housing and Urban Development.
Deborah Matz, Board Member, National Credit Union Administration.
Executive Director.—Ellen Lazar, 220–2410.
Chief Operating Officer.—Margo Kelly, (617) 450–0410/125.
Director for—
Public Policy and Legislative Affairs.—Steven Tuminaro, 220–2415.
Finance and Administration.—Allan Martin, 223–2390.
General Counsel / Secretary.—Jeffrey Bryson, 220–2372.
Internal Audit.—Frederick Udochi, 220–2409.
President / Chief Executive Officer, Neighborhood Housing Services of America.—Mary Widener, (510) 287–4201.
Manager, Congressional Affairs.—C.J. Hager, 220–2326.

NUCLEAR REGULATORY COMMISSION

Washington, DC 20555, phone (301) 415–7000, http//www.nrc.gov

[Authorized by 42 U.S.C. 5801 and U.S.C. 1201]

OFFICE OF THE CHAIRMAN

Chairman.—Nils J. Diaz, 415–1759.
Executive Assistant.—Maria Lopez-Otin, 415–1759.
Chief of Staff.—John W. Craig, 415–1750.
Administrative Assistant.—Vicki M. Bolling, 415–1759.
Administration and Communications Assistant.—Robert B. McOsker, 415–1750.
Legal Assistant.—Roger K. Davis, 415–1750.

COMMISSIONERS

Greta Joy Dicus.—415–1820.
Executive / Legal Assistant.—Bradley W. Jones.
Senior Technical Assistant for Materials.—Cynthia G. Jones, 415–1830.
Special Assistant.—Donna L. Smith.
Technical Assistants for—
Materials.—Joseph Olencz.
Reactors.—Thomas G. Hiltz.
Edward McGaffigan, Jr.—415–1800.
Executive / Technical Assistant for Materials.—Janet R. Schlueter, 415–1810.
Technical Assistants for Reactors: James E. Beall, Jeffry M. Sharkey.
Special Assistant.—Linda D. Lewis.
Jeffrey S. Merrifield—415–1850.
Special Assistant / Chief of Staff.—Lynne D. Stauss.
Legal Assistant.—Margaret M. Doane.
Technical Assistants for—
Materials.—John O. Thoma.
Reactors.—Brian C. McCabe.

STAFF OFFICES OF THE COMMISSION

Secretary.—Annette L. Vietti-Cook, 415–1969, fax 415–1672.
Commission Appellate Adjudication.—John F. Cordes, 415–1600, fax 415–1672.
Congressional Affairs.—Dennis K. Rathbun, 415–1776, fax 415–8571.
General Counsel.—Karen D. Cyr, 415–1743, fax 415–3725.
International Programs.—Janice Dunn Lee, 415–1780, fax 415–2400.
Public Affairs.—William M. Beecher, 415–8200, fax 415–3324.

ADVISORY COMMITTEE ON NUCLEAR WASTE

Chairman.—B. John Garrick, 415–7360.
(Contact: John T. Larkins, Executive Director, ACRS / ACNW, 415–7360, fax 415–5589/5422.)

ADVISORY COMMITTEE ON MEDICAL USES OF ISOTOPES

Committee Coordinator.—Mary Lou Roe, 415–7809.

ADVISORY COMMITTEE ON REACTOR SAFEGUARDS

Chairman.—Dana A. Powers, 415–7360,
(Contact: John T. Larkins, Executive Director, ACRS / ACNW, 415–7360, fax 415–5589/5422.)

ATOMIC SAFETY AND LICENSING BOARD PANEL

Chief Administrative Judge.—G. Paul Bollwerk III (acting), 415–7450, fax 415–5599.

INSPECTOR GENERAL

Inspector General.—Hubert Bell, 415–5930, fax 415–5091.
Deputy Inspector General.—David C. Lee, 415–5930.

CHIEF INFORMATION OFFICER

Chief Information Officer.—Jacqueline E. Silber (acting), 415–8700, fax 415–4246.

CHIEF FINANCIAL OFFICER

Chief Financial Officer.—Jesse L. Funches, 415–7322, fax 415–4236.

OFFICE OF THE EXECUTIVE DIRECTOR FOR OPERATIONS

Executive Director for Operations.—William D. Travers, 415–1700, fax 415–2162.
Deputy Executive Director for—
Regulatory Effectiveness.—Carl J. Paperiello, 415–1705, fax 415–2162.
Regulatory Programs.—William F. Kane, 415–1713, fax 415–2162.
Management Services.—Patricia G. Norry, 415–7443, fax 415–2162.

STAFF OFFICES OF THE EXECUTIVE DIRECTOR FOR OPERATIONS

Director, Office of:
Administration.—Michael L. Springer, 415–6222, fax 415–5400.
Enforcement.—Frank J. Congel, 415–2741, fax 415–3431.
Investigations.—Guy P. Caputo, 415–2373, fax 415–2370.
Human Resources.—Paul E. Bird, 415–7516, fax 415–5106.
Small Business and Civil Rights.—Irene P. Little, 415–7380, fax 415–5953.
State and Tribal Programs.—Paul H. Lohaus, 415–3340, fax 415–3502.

PROGRAM OFFICES

OFFICE OF NUCLEAR MATERIAL SAFETY AND SAFEGUARDS

Director.—Martin J. Virgilio, 415–7800, fax 415–5371.
Deputy Director.—Margaret V. Federline, 415–7358.
Divisional Directors:
Industrial and Medical Nuclear Safety.—Donald A. Cool, 415–7197.
Fuel Cycle Safety and Safeguards.—Michael F. Webber, 415–7212.
Waste Management.—John T. Greeves, 415–7437.
Spent Fuel Project Office.—E. William Brach, 415–8500.

OFFICE OF NUCLEAR REACTOR REGULATION

Director.—Samuel J. Collins, 415–1270, fax 415–1887.
Deputy Director.—Jon R. Johnson, 415–1272.
Associate Director for Project Licensing and Technical Analysis.—Brian Sheron, 415–1274.
Divisional Directors:
Engineering.—Jack R. Strosnider, 415–3298.
Licensing Project Management.—John A. Zwolinski, 415–1453.
Systems Safety and Analysis.—Suzanne Black (acting), 415–2884.
Associate Director for Inspection and Programs..—R. William Borchardt, 415–1284.
Divisional Directors:
Inspection Program Management.—Bruce A. Boger, 415–1004.
Regulory Improvement Programs.—David B. Matthews, 415–1199.

OFFICE OF NUCLEAR REGULATORY RESEARCH

Director.—Ashok C. Thadani, 415–6641, fax 415–5153.
Deputy Director.—Roy P. Zimmerman, 415–8003.
Divisional Directors:
Engineering Technology.—Michael E. Mayfield, 415–6207.
Risk Analysis and Applications.—Scott F. Newberry, 415–5790.
Systems Analysis and Regulatory Effectiveness.—Thomas L. King, 415–7499.

REGIONAL OFFICES

Regional Administrators:

Region I: Hubert J. Miller, 475 Allendale Road, King of Prussia, PA 19406, (610) 337–5299, fax 337–5324.
Deputy Regional Administrator.—James T. Wiggins, (610) 337–5359.
Divisional Directors:
Nuclear Materials Safety.—George C. Pangburn, (610) 337–5281.
Reactor Projects.—A. Rancy Blough, (610) 337–5229.
Reactor Safety.—Wayne D. Lanning, (610) 337–5126.

Region II: Luis A. Reyes, 61 Forsyth Street SE, Atlanta, GA 30303, (404) 562–4410, fax (404) 562–4766.
Deputy Regional Administrator.—Bruce S. Mallett, (404) 562–4411.
Divisional Directors:
Nuclear Materials Safety.—Douglas M. Collins, (404) 562–4700.
Reactor Projects.—Loren Plisco, (404) 562–4501.
Reactor Safety.—Charles Casto, (404) 562–4601.

Region III: James E. Dyer, 801 Warrensville Road, Lisle, IL 60532, (708) 829–9657, fax 515–1278.
Deputy Regional Administrator.—James L. Caldwell, 630–9658.
Divisional Directors:
Nuclear Materials Safety.—Cynthia D. Pederson, (630) 829–9800.
Reactor Projects.—Geoffrey E. Grant, (630) 829–9600.
Reactor Safety.—John A. Grobe, (630) 829–9700.

Region IV: Ellis W. Merschoff, Suite 400, 611 Ryan Plaza Drive, Arlington, TX 76011, (817) 860–8225, fax 860–8210.
Deputy Regional Administrator.—Thomas P. Gwynn, (817) 860–8226.
Divisional Directors:
Nuclear Materials Safety.—Dwight D. Chamberlain, (817) 860–8249.
Reactor Projects.—Kenneth E. Brockman, (817) 860–8140.
Reactor Safety.—Arthur T. Howell, (817) 860–8180.

OCCUPATIONAL SAFETY AND HEALTH REVIEW COMMISSION

1120 20th Street, NW., 20036, phone (202) 606–5398

[Created by Public Law 91–596]

Chairman.—W. Scott Railton, 606–2082.
Legal Advisor and Special Counsel.—Heather MacDougall.
Commissioner.—James M. Stephens, 606–5374.
Counsel to the Commissioner.—[Vacant].
Commissoner.—[Vacant].
Counsel to the Commissioner.—[Vacant].
Administrative Law Judges:
James Barkley, 425 Ivanhoe Street, Denver, CO 80220.
Sidney Goldstein, 1880 Arapahoe Street, Number 2608, Denver, CO 80202–1858.
Benjamin Loye, 3810 Marshall Street, Wheat Ridge, CO 80033.
Michael H. Schoenfeld, 1120 20th Street, NW, 9th Floor, Washington, DC 20036–3419.
Irving Sommer, 1951 Hopewood Drive, Falls Church, VA 22043.
Nancy L. Spies, 1365 Peachtree Street, NE, Room 240, Atlanta, GA 30309–3119.
Robert A. Yetman, McCormack Post Office and Courthouse, Room 420, Boston, MA 02109–4501.
Covette Rooney, 1120 20th Street, NW, 9th Floor, Washington, DC 20036–3419.
Marvin G. Bober, 1120 20th Street, NW, 9th Floor, Washington, DC 20036–3419.
Ken S. Welsch, 100 Alabama Street, SW, Building 1924, Room 2R90, Atlanta, GA 30303–3104.
Stephen J. Simko, 100 Alabama Street, SW, Building 1924, Room 2R90, Atlanta, GA 30303–3104.
General Counsel.—Earl R. Ohman, Jr.
Deputy General Counsel.—Patrick E. Moran, 606–5410.
Executive Director.—Patricia A. Randle, 606–5380.
Director for Management and Administrative Services.—Ledia E. Bernal, 606–5390.
Executive Secretary.—Ray H. Darling, Jr.
Public Information Officer.—Linda A. Gravely, 606–5398.

OFFICE OF GOVERNMENT ETHICS

1201 New York Avenue NW, Suite 500, 20005, phone (202) 208–8000, fax 208–8037

[Created by Act of October 1, 1989; codified in 5 U.S.C, section 401]

Director.—Amy L. Comstock.
Special Assistant.—James O'Sullivan.
Confidential Assistant.—Allison Balderston.
General Counsel.—Marilyn L. Glynn.
Deputy General Counsel.—Stuart Rick.
Deputy Director for—
Government Relations and Special Projects.—Jane S. Ley.
Agency Programs.—Jack Covaleski.
Administration and Information Management (CIO).—Daniel D. Dunning.
Deputy Chief of Information Resources Management.—James V. Parle.
Associate Director for—
Program Services Division.—Patricia C. Zemple.
Education Division.—Carolyn W. Chapman.
Program Review Division.—Edward W. Pratt.

OFFICE OF PERSONNEL MANAGEMENT

Theodore Roosevelt Building, 1900 E Street NW 20415–0001, phone (202) 606–2424
http://www.opm.gov

OFFICE OF THE DIRECTOR

Director.—Kay Coles James, (202) 606–1000.
Special Assistant to the Director.—Robert E. Beals.
Deputy Director.—Dan G. Blair.
Special Assistant to the Deputy Director.—Judy McCoy.

Chief of Staff.—Paul T. Conway.
Deputy Chief of Staff/Executive Secretariat.—Richard B. Lowe.
Deputy Chief of Staff.—Amber Roseboom.
White House Liaison.—Amanda Becker.
Senior Advisor for Homeland Security.—Steven R. Cohen.
Senior Policy Advisor to the Director and Chief Human Capital Officer.—Doris Hausser.
Special Assistant.—Gay Gardner (acting).
Senior Advisor for Investigative Operations and Agency Planning.—Eric M. Thorson.
Senior Advisor for Learning and Knowledge Management.—Thomas J. Towberman.
Director of CFC Operations.—Mara T. Patermaster, 606–2564.

OFFICE OF E-GOVERNMENT INITIATIVES

Program Director.—Norman Enger, 606–1000.
Special Assistant.—Jennifer L. Simmons.
Deputy Director.—Jeff T.H. Pon, 606–1472.

FEDERAL PREVAILING RATE ADVISORY COMMITTEE

Chair.—Mary R. Rose, 606–1500.
Staff Assistant.—Geraldine E. Coates.

OFFICE OF THE INSPECTOR GENERAL

Inspector General.—Patrick E. McFarland, 606–1200.
Executive Assistant.—A. Paulette Berry.
Deputy Inspector General.—Joseph R. Willever.
Assistant Inspector General for Legal Affairs.—E. Jeremy Hutton, 606–3807.
Counsel to the Inspector General.—Timothy C. Watkins, 606–2030.
Assistant Inspector General for Policy, Resources Management, and Oversight.—Daniel K. Marella, 606–2638.
Assistant Inspector General for Audits.—Harvey D. Thorp, 606–1200.
Deputy Assistant Inspector General for Audits.—Dennis K. Black, 606–4711.
Assistant Inspector General for Investigations.—Norbert E. Vint, 606–1200.
Deputy Assistant Inspector General for Investigations.—Charles W. Focarino, 606–3809.
Assistant Inspector General for Evaluation and Inspections.—[Vacant], 606–1200.

OFFICE OF THE GENERAL COUNSEL

General Counsel.—Mark A. Robbins, 606–1700.
Secretary.—Althea D. Elam.
Deputy General Counsel.—Kathie Ann Whipple.
Administrative Officer (OGC Administration).—Gloria V. Clark.
Associate General Counsel (Compensation, Benefits, Products, and Services).—James S. Green.
Assistant General Counsel (Merit Systems and Accountability Division).—James F. Hicks.

OFFICE OF CONGRESSIONAL RELATIONS

Director.—John C. Gartland, 606–1300.
Special Assistant to the Director.—Carlos E. Gomez.
Chief of:
House Affairs.—Jonathan J. Blyth.
Senate Affairs.—Dino L. Carluccio.
Congressional Liaison.—Charlene E. Luskey, B332 Rayburn House Office Building, (202) 632–6296, fax 632–0832.
Legislative Analysis.—Harry A. Wolf, 606–1424.
Administration and Confidential Assistant to the Director.—Kathi D. Ladner.

OFFICE OF COMMUNICATIONS AND PUBLIC LIAISON

Director.—Scott Hatch, 606–2402.
Deputy Director.—Susan Bryant.
Special Assistant.—Eldon Girdner.
Director of:
Web Design and Publications.—Vivian Mackey.
Public Liaison.—[Vacant].
Marketing.—[Vacant].
Press Relations.—[Vacant].
Administration/Budget.—Paul L. Holbert.
Speech Writers: Terri Hauser, Hans B. Petersen.

DIVISION FOR MANAGEMENT AND CHIEF FINANCIAL OFFICER

Associate Director.—Clarence C. Crawford, 606–1918.
Executive Officer/Senior Financial Advisor.—Gisele D. Jones.
Administrative Officer.—Patrice W. Mendonca, 606–2204.
Staff Assistant.—[Vacant], 606–1918.
Deputy Associate Director, Center for—
Contracting, Facilities, and Administrative Services Group.—Corey M. Rindner, 606–2200.
Financial Services and Deputy Chief Financial Officer.—William J. Washington, 606–1101.
Human Capital Management Services Group.—Mark D. Reinhold (acting), 606–2440.
Information Services and Chief Information Officer.—Janet L. Barnes, 606–2150.
Management Services.—Teresa M. Jenkins, 606–1918.
Chief, Center for—
Equal Employment Opportunity.—Michelle Payton-Kenner (acting), 606–2460.
Security and Emergency Actions.—[Vacant].

OFFICE OF HUMAN RESOURCES PRODUCTS AND SERVICES

Associate Director.—Stephen C. Benowitz, 606–0600.
Secretary.—Dee T. Harrell.
Resource Management Group.—Rich Liebl (acting), 606–2871.
Deputy Associate Director, Center for—
Eastern Management Development Group.—Barbara Smith, (304) 879–8000.
Federal Executive Institute.—Joseph R. Riddle (acting), (434) 980–6200.
Investigations Services.—Kathy Dillaman, (724) 794–5612.
Leadership Capacity Services.—[Vacant].
Retirement and Insurance Services Program.—Kathleen M. McGettigan, 606–0462.
Talent Services.—Nancy Randa, 606–0142.
Western Management Development Group.—Joe D. Wienand, (303) 671–1010.
Assistant Director for—
Examining and Consulting Services.—Linda M. Petersen (acting), 606–1527.
Operations.—Winona H. Varnon, 606–1042.
Retirement Services Programs.—Sidney M. Conley, 606–0300.
Insurance Services Programs.—Frank D. Titus, 606–0745.
RIS Support Services Program.—Maurice O. Duckett, 606–8089.

DIVISION FOR STRATEGIC HUMAN RESOURCES POLICY

Associate Director.—Ronald P. Sanders, 606–6500.
Staff Assistant.—Janice Johnson.
Deputy Associate Director, Center for—
Talent and Capacity Policy.—Ellen E. Tunstall, 606–6500.
Leadership and Executive Resources Policy.—Dee Everett (acting), 606–1050.
Pay and Performance Policy.—Donald J. Winstead, 606–2880.
Employee and Family Support Policy.—Abby L. Block (acting), 606–0770.
Workforce Planning and Policy Analysis.—Nancy H. Kichak, 606–9722.
Workforce Relations and Accountability Policy.—Jeffrey E. Sumberg, 606–2930.
HR Systems Requirements and Strategies.—Rhonda K. Diaz, 606–1126.

DIVISION FOR HUMAN CAPITAL LEADERSHIP AND MERIT SYSTEM ACCOUNTABILITY

Associate Director.—Marta Brito Perez, 606–1575.
Deputy Associate Director, Center for—
Merit System Compliance.—Conrad U. Johnson (acting), 606–2576.
Human Capital Implementation and Assessment.—Ann Ludwig, 606–2840.
Human Resources.—Michael J. Wilkin (acting), 606–1052.
Natural Resources Management.—[Vacant].
National Security.—[Vacant].
General Government.—Kevin E. Mahoney, 606–2820.
Small Agencies.—Dana K. Sitnick (acting), 606–2820.

OFFICE OF THE SPECIAL COUNSEL

1730 M Street, NW., Suite 300, 20036, phone (202) 653–7188

[Authorized by 5 U.S.C. 1101 and 5 U.S.C. 1211]

Special Counsel.—Elaine Kaplan, room 300, 653–7122.
Deputy Special Counsel.—Timothy Hannapel, 653–6006.
Outreach Director and Counsel.—Karen Dalheim, 653–8962.
Congressional and Public Affairs Division.—Jane McFarland, 653–5163.
Legal Counsel and Policy Division.—Erin McDonnell, 653–8971.
Investigation and Prosecution Divisions:
I.—William E. Reukauf, 653–6005.
II.—[Vacant].
III.—Cary Sklar, 653–6003.
Complaints and Disclosure Analysis Division.—Leonard Dribinsky, 653–7188.

PANAMA CANAL COMMISSION

Office of Transition Administration

1825 I Street NW., Suite 400, 20006, phone: (202) 775–4180; fax: 775–4184

[Created by Public Law 96–70]

Director.—William J. Connolly.
General Attorney.—R. David Ballenger.

IN PANAMA

Fiscal Officer.—Edward J. McAleer.

PEACE CORPS

1111 20th Street, NW., 20526, phone (202) 692–2000

Toll-Free Number (800) 424–8580, http://www.peacecorps.gov

[Created by Public Law 97–113]

OFFICE OF THE DIRECTOR

fax 692–2101

Director.—Gaddi H. Vasquez.
Deputy Director.—Josephine K. Olsen.
Chief of Staff.—Lloyd Pierson.
Deputy Chief of Staff/Congressional Relations Director.—Marie Wheat.
General Counsel.—Tyler Posey.
Communications Director.—Ellen Field.
Marketing Strategist.—Linda Isaac.
Press Secretary.—Barbara Daly.
Director of Planning, Policy and Analysis.—Kyo (Paul) Jhin.

American Diversity Program Director.—Shirley Everest.
Office of Private Sector Initiatives.—Nanci Brannan.
Overseas Executive Selection and Support Director.—[Vacant].
Printing Officer.—Susan Bloomer.
Inspector General.—Charles Smith.

OFFICE OF PLANNING, BUDGET, AND FINANCE

Chief Financial Officer.—Gopal Khanna (acting).
Budget Officer.—Janice Hagginbothom.
Office of Contracts Director.—George Schutter.
Office of Financial Services Director.—Stephanie Mitchell.

VOLUNTEER SUPPORT

Associate Director for Volunteer Support.—Steven Weinberg.
Director of:
Medical Services.—[Vacant].
Special Services.—[Vacant].

CRISIS CORPS

Director.—Dan Sullivan.

CENTER FOR FIELD ASSISTANCE AND APPLIED RESEARCH

Director.—Elizabeth Shays.

AFRICA OPERATIONS

Regional Director.—Henry McKoy.

EUROPE, MEDITERRANEAN, AND ASIA OPERATIONS

Regional Director.—Judy Van Rest.

INTER-AMERICA AND PACIFIC OPERATIONS

Regional Director.—Stephen Murphy.

ASSOCIATE DIRECTOR FOR MANAGEMENT

Associate Director/Management.—Chris Arnold.
Office of Administrative Services Director.—Michael Kole.
Office of Human Resource Management Director.—Daniel Janssen.
Office of Human Resource Management Deputy Director.—Bob Harrison.

CHIEF INFORMATION OFFICER

CIO.—Gopal Khanna.

VOLUNTEER RECRUITMENT AND SELECTION

Associate Director for Volunteer Recruitment and Selection.—Chuck Brooks.
Minority and National Recruitment Initiatives Director.—Wilfredo Sauri.
Office of Domestic Programs Director.—Allene Zanger.
Office of Domestic Programs Assistant Director for—
Fellows/USA Programs.—Michele Titi.
Returned Volunteer Services.—Shanta Swezy.
World Wise Schools.—Wayne Beslyn.

PEACE CORPS REGIONAL OFFICES

Atlanta: 100 Alabama Street, Building 1924, Suite 2R70, Atlanta, GA 30303, (404) 562–3456, fax (404) 562–3455 (FL, GA, TN, MS, AL, SC, PR).
Manager.—John Eaves.
Public Affairs Specialist.—Carla Murphy.

Boston: Ten Causeway Street, Room 450, Boston, MA 02222, (617) 565–5555, fax (617) 565–5539 (MA, VT, NH, RI, ME).
Manager.—James Arena-DeRosa.
Public Affairs Specialist.—Doreen Sabina.

Chicago: Xerox Center, 55 West Monroe Street, Suite 450, Chicago, IL 60603, (312) 353–4990, fax (312) 353–4192 (IL, IN, MO, MI, OH, KY).
Manager.—Virginia Koch.
Public Affairs Specialist.—Scot Roskelley.

Dallas: 207 South Houston Street, Room 527, Dallas, TX 75202, (214) 767–5435, fax (214) 767–5483 (TX, OK, LA, NM, AR).
Manager.—Abel Ruiz.
Public Affairs Specialist.—Jesus Garcia.

Denver: 1999 Broadway, Suite 2205, Denver, CO 80202–3050, (303) 844–7020, fax (303) 844–7010 (CO, KS, NE, UT, WY).
Manager.—Ann Conway.
Public Affairs Specialist.—Kristen Orr.

Los Angeles: 11000 Wilshire Boulevard, Suite 8104, Los Angeles, CA 90024, (310) 235–7444, fax (310) 235–7442 (Southern CA, AZ).
Manager.—Jill Andrews.
Public Affairs Specialist.—Michaela Brehm.

Minneapolis: 330 Second Avenue South, Suite 420, Minneapolis, MN 55401, (612) 348–1480, fax (612) 348–1474 (MN, WI, SD, ND, IA).
Manager.—David Belina.
Public Affairs Specialist.—Gary Lore.

New York: 201 Varick Street, Suite 1025, New York, NY 10014, (212) 352–5440, fax (212) 352–5442 (NY, NJ, CT, PA).
Manager.—Edwin Jorge.
Public Affairs Specialist.—Bartel Kendrick.

Rosslyn: 1525 Wilson Boulevard, Suite 250, Arlington, VA 22209, (703) 235–9191, fax (703) 235–9189 (DC, MD, NC, WV, DE, VA).
Manager.—Lynn Kneedler.
Public Affairs Specialist.—Sara Johnston.

San Francisco: 333 Market Street, Suite 600, San Francisco, CA 94105; (415) 977–8800, fax (415) 977–8803 (Northern CA, NV, HI).
Manager.—Harris Bostic II.
Public Affairs Specialist.—Dennis McMahon.

Seattle: 2001 Sixth Avenue, Suite 1776, Seattle, WA 98121, (206) 553–5490, fax (206) 553–2343 (WA, OR, ID, AK, MT).
Manager.—Wayne Blackwelder.
Public Affairs Specialist.—James Aquirre.

PENSION BENEFIT GUARANTY CORPORATION

1200 K Street 20005–4026, (202) 326–4000

BOARD OF DIRECTORS

Chairman.—Elaine L. Chao, Secretary of Labor.
Members:
John W. Snow, Secretary of the Treasury.
Donald L. Evans, Secretary of Commerce.

OFFICIALS

Executive Director.—Steven A. Kandarian, 326–4010.
Deputy Executive Director and—
Chief Operating Officer.—Joseph H. Grant, 326–4010.
Chief Financial Officer.—Hazel Broadnax, 326–4170.
Chief Management Officer.—John Seal, 326–4180.

Assistant Executive Director for Legislative Affairs.—Vincent Snowbarger, 326–4010.
Assistant Executive Director and Chief Technology Officer.—Richard W. Hartt, 326–4010.
Department Director for—
Budget.—Henry Thompson, 326–4120.
Communications and Public Affairs.—Randolph Clerihue, 326–4040.
Contracts and Controls Review.—Marty Boehem, 326–4161.
Corporate Finance and Negotiations and Chief Negotiator.—Andrea Schneider, 326–4070.
Corporate Policy and Research.—Stuart Sirkin, 326–4080.
Facilities and Services.—Janet A. Smith, 326–4150.
Financial Operations.—Theodore Winters, 326–4060.
Human Resources.—Sharon Barbee Fletcher, 326–4110.
Information Resources Management.—Cris Birch, 326–4130.
Insurance Operations.—Bennie Hagans, 326–4050.
Participant and Employer Appeals.—Harriet D. Verburg, 326–4090.
Procurement.—Robert W. Herting, 326–4160.
General Counsel.—James J. Keightley, 326–4020.
Inspector General.—Robert Emmons, 326–4030.

POSTAL RATE COMMISSION

1333 H Street NW., Suite 300, 20268–0001, phone (202) 789–6800, fax 789–6886

Chairman.—George A. Omas, 789–6801.
Vice Chairman.—Dana B. Covington, 789–6868.
Commissioners:
Dana B. Covington, 789–6868.
Ruth Y. Goldway, 789–6810.
Tony Hammond, 789–6805.
Chief Administrative Officer and Secretary.—Steven W. Williams, 789–6840.
General Counsel.—Stephen L. Sharfman, 789–6820.
Director, Office of:
Consumer Advocate.—Shelley S. Dreifuss, 789–6830.
Rates, Analysis and Planning.—Robert H. Cohen, 789–6850.

SECURITIES AND EXCHANGE COMMISSION

450 Fifth Street NW 20549, phone (202) 942–8088, TTY Relay Service 1–800–877–8339 fax 942–9628, http://www.sec.gov

THE COMMISSION

Chairman.—William Donaldson, 942–0100, fax 942–9646.
Managing Executive for—
External Affairs.—Laura Cox.
Operations.—Peter Derby.
Policy and Staff.—Patrick Von Bargen.
Counsel to the Chairman.—Consuelo Hitchcock, Stephen Jung, Fiona Philip.
Commissioners:
Paul Atkins, 952–0700, fax 942–9521.
Counsel to the Commissioner: Susan Ameel, Brent Fields, David Nason.
Roel Campos, 942–0500, fax 942–9647.
Counsel to the Commissioner: Scot Draeger, Heather Traeger, Kristina Wyatt.
Cynthia A. Glassman, 942–0600, fax 942–9666.
Counsel to the Commissioner: Mary Head, Rosemary Filou, Brian Stern.
Harvey Goldschmid, 942–0800, fax 942–9563.
Counsel to the Commissioner: Tracey Aronson, Daphne Chisolm, Luis DeLatorre.

OFFICE OF THE SECRETARY

Secretary.—Jonathan G. Katz, 942–7070.
Deputy Secretary.—Margaret H. McFarland, 942–7070.
Library Director.—Cindy Plisch, 942–7086.

OFFICE OF INVESTOR EDUCATION AND ASSISTANCE

Director.—Susan Ferris-Wyderko, 942–7040, fax 942–9634.

OFFICE OF EQUAL EMPLOYMENT OPPORTUNITY

Director.—Deborah K. Balducchi, 942–0044, fax 942–9547.

OFFICE OF FREEDOM OF INFORMATION AND PRIVACY ACT OPERATIONS

FOIA/Privacy Act Officer.—Barry D. Walters, 942–4320.

OFFICE OF THE CHIEF ACCOUNTANT

Chief Accountant.—Carol Stacey, 942–2960.
Deputy Chief Accountant.—Craig Olinger, 942–2960.
Chief Counsel.—Paula Dubberly, 942–2900.

OFFICE OF ECONOMIC ANALYSIS

Chief Economist.—Lawrence E. Harris, 942–8020, fax 942–9657.
Deputy Chief Economist.—Jonathan Sokobin, 942–8020.

OFFICE OF THE GENERAL COUNSEL

General Counsel.—Giovanni Prezioso, 942–0900, fax 942–9625.
Counselor to the General Counsel.—[Vacant].
Special Assistant for Management.—Virginia A. Mayberry, 942–0832.
Deputy General Counsel.—Meyer Eisenberg, 942–0966.
Ethics Counsel.—Barbara Hannigan, 942–0970.
Solicitor (Appellate Litigation and Bankruptcy).—Jacob H. Stillman, 942–0930.
Assistant General Counsels: (Principal Assistant), Eric Summergrad, 942–0911; (Bankruptcy and Appellate Litigation), Katharine Gresham, 942–0810; (Appellate Litigation), Randall Quinn, 942–0933.
Associate General Counsel for Litigation and Administrative Practice.—Richard M. Humes, 942–0875.
Assistant General Counsels: (Litigation and Administrative Practice), Melinda Hardy, 942–0877, Samuel Forstein, 942–0871; (Litigation and Contracting), George C. Brown, 942–0828.
Associate General Counsel for Legal Policy.—Meredith Mitchell, 942–0834.
Assistant General Counsels: (Investment Management, PUHCA and Administrative Law), Arthur Laby, 942–0958; (Market Regulation), Janice Mitnick, 942–0935; (Corporation Finance and Accounting), David Fredrickson, 942–0916; (Legislation and Financial Services), Stephen Jung, 942–0927.
Associate General Counsel for Counseling and Regulatory Policy.—Diane Sanger, 942–0960.
Associate General Counsel for Adjudication.—Anne E. Chafer, 942–0950.
Counselor for Adjudication.—William S. Stern, 942–0949.
Assistant General Counsels: (Principal Assistant), Joan Loizeaux, 942–0990, (Adjudication), Joan McCarthy, 942–0950.

DIVISION OF INVESTMENT MANAGEMENT

Director.—Paul F. Roye, 942–0720, fax 942–9659.
Deputy Director.—Cynthia M. Fornelli, 942–0720.
Senior Adviser to the Director.—Jennifer B. McHugh, 942–0720.
Associate Director, Chief Counsel.—Douglas J. Scheidt, 942–0666.
Assistant Chief Counsels: (International Issues), Alison M. Fuller, 942–0660; (Financial Institutions), Elizabeth G. Osterman, 942–0660.
Associate Director, Office of:
Disclosure & Insurance Product Regulation.—Susan Nash, 942–0630.
Legal and Disclosure.—Barry D. Miller, 942–0663.
Public Utility & Investment Company Regulation.—David B. Smith, 942–0525.
Regulatory Policy & Investment Adviser Regulation.—Robert E. Plaze, 942–0716.
Assistant Director, Office of:
Disclosure and Review No. 1.—Michael A. Lainoff, 942–0589.
Disclosure and Review No. 2.—Frank J. Donaty, 942–0585.
Disclosure Regulation.—Paul G. Cellupica, 942–0721.
Enforcement Liaison.—Barbara Chretien-Dar, 942–0535.

Financial Analysis.—Paul B. Goldman, 942–0510.
Insurance Products.—William J. Kotapish, 942–0670.
Investment Adviser Regulation.—Jennifer L. Sawin, 942–0719.
Investment Company Regulation.—Nadya B. Roytblat, 942–0564.
Public Utility Regulation.—Catherine A. Fisher, 942–0545.
Regulatory Policy.—C. Hunter Jones, 942–0690.
Chief Accountant (Office of Chief Accountant).—Brian D. Bullard, 942–0590.

DIVISION OF CORPORATION FINANCE

Director.—Alan Beller, 942–2929, fax 942–9525.
Deputy Director of:
Disclosure Operations.—Shelley E. Parratt, 942–2830.
Legal and Regulatory.—Martin Dunn, 942–2890.
Associate Directors:
Legal Office.—Paula Dubberly, 942–2900.
Regulatory.—Mauri L. Osheroff, 942–2840.
Chief Accountant.—Carol Stacey, 942–2960.
Disclosure Operations.—James Daly, 942–2881.
Chief, Office of:
Chief Counsel.—[Vacant], 942–2900.
EDGAR, Information and Analysis.—Herbert D. Scholl, 942–2930.
Enforcement Liaison.—[Vacant].
International Corporate Finance.—Paul Dudek, 942–2990.
Mergers and Acquisitions.—[Vacant], 942–2920.
Rulemaking.—Elizabeth Murphy, 942–2910.
Small Business Policy.—Gerald Laporte, 942–2950.
Assistant Directors: Karen Garnett, 942–1960; Peggy Fisher, 942–1880; Barbara Jacobs, 942–1800; Pamela Long, 942–1950; H. Christopher Owings, 942–1900; Jeffrey Reidler, 942–1840; John Reynolds, 942–2999; Todd Schiffman, 942–1760; H. Roger Schwall, 942–1870; Barry Summer, 942–1990; Max Webb, 942–1850.

DIVISION OF ENFORCEMENT

Director.—Stephen M. Cutler, 942–4500, fax 942–9636.
Senior Advisor.—Laurie Stegman, 942–4607.
Deputy Director.—Linda C. Thomsen, 942–4501.
Chief, Office of Internet Enforcement.—John R. Stark, 942–4803.
Associate Director.—Thomas C. Newkirk, 942–4550.
Assistant Directors: James T. Coffman, 942–4574; Cheryl J. Scarboro, 942–4583; Leonard W. Wang, 942–4828.
Associate Director.—Paul R. Berger, 942–4854.
Assistant Directors: Timothy N. England, 942–7109; Richard W. Grime, 942–4863; Russell G. Ryan, 942–4660; Richard C. Sauer, 942–4777.
Associate Director.—Lawrence A. West, 942–4631.
Assistant Directors: Charles Clark, 942–4731; Brian A. Ochs, 942–4740.
Chief, Market Surveillance.—Joseph J. Cella, 942–4559.
Associate Director.—Antonia Chion, 942–4567.
Assistant Directors: Christopher R. Conte, 942–4579; Scott W. Friestad, 942–4732; Yuri B. Zelinsky, 942–4890.
Chief Counsel.—Joan E. McKown, 942–4530.
Deputy Chief Counsel.—[Vacant].
Associate Chief Counsel.—Gretta J. Powers, 942–4756.
Assistant Chief Counsels: Nancy E. Allin, 942–4536; Charlotte L. Buford, 942–4758; Kenneth H. Hall, 942–4635; Kenneth R. Lench, 942–4755.
Chief Litigation Counsel.—David L. Kornblau, 942–4818.
Deputy Chief Litigation Counsel.—Peter H. Bresnan, 942–4788.
Chief Accountant.—[Vacant].
Associate Chief Accountants: Regina M. Barrett, 942–4524; Dwayne Brown, 942–4547; David M. Estabrook, 942–4814; Susan G. Markel, 942–4871; C. Gregory Scates, 942–4826.
Director, Regional Office Operations.—James A. Clarkson, 942–4580.

DIVISION OF MARKET REGULATION

Director.—Annette L. Nazareth, 942–0090, fax 942–9643.
Deputy Director.—Robert L.D. Colby, 942–0094.
Chief of Operations.—Herbert Brooks, 942–0150.
Counsel to the Director.—David S. Shillman, 942–0072.
Associate Director.—(Market Supervision), Elizabeth King, 942–0140.
Associate Director.—(Risk Management and Control), Larry Bergmann, 942–0770; Michael A. Macchiaroli, 942–0132.
Associate Director, Chief Counsel.—Catherine McGuire, 942–0061.
Deputy Chief Counsel.—Paula Jenson, 942–0073.
Assistant Directors: (Risk Management and Control), James Brigagliano, 942–0772; Jerry Carpenter, 942–4187; Thomas McGowan, 942–0177; JoAnne Swindler, 942–0750.
Assistant Directors: (Market Supervision), Katherine England, 942–0154; Terri Evans, 942–4162; Deborah L. Flynn, 942–0075; Nancy Sanow, 942–0796.

OFFICE OF INTERNATIONAL AFFAIRS

Director.—Ethiopis Tafara (acting), 942–2770, fax 942–9524.
Deputy Director.—[Vacant].
Assistant Directors: Elizabeth Jacobs, 942–2770; Robert D. Strahota, 942–2770; Ethiopis Tafara, 942–2770.

OFFICE OF LEGISLATIVE AFFAIRS

Director.—Jane Cobb, 942–0010, fax 942–9650.
Deputy Director.—Peter Kiernan.

OFFICE OF THE INSPECTOR GENERAL

Inspector General.—Walter J. Stachnik, 942–4660, fax 942–9653.
Deputy Inspector General.—Nelson N. Egbert, 942–4462.

OFFICE OF FILINGS AND INFORMATION SERVICES

Associate Executive Director.—Kenneth A. Fogash, 942–8938, fax (703) 914–1005.
Deputy Director.—Cecilia Wilkerson, 942–8928.
Associate Director.—Margaret Favor, 942–8920; Shirley Slocum, 942–8938.
Assistant Director.—Ronnette McDaniel, 942–8925.

OFFICE OF PUBLIC AFFAIRS

Director.—[Vacant], 942–0020, fax 942–9654.
Deputy Directors: John D. Heine, 942–0020; Herb Perone, 942–0020.

OFFICE OF FINANCIAL MANAGEMENT

Associate Executive Director.—Margaret J. Carpenter, 942–0340, fax (703) 914–0172.

OFFICE OF INFORMATION TECHNOLOGY

Associate Executive Director/Chief Information Officer.—Kenneth A. Fogash (acting), 942–8800; fax (703) 914–2621.

OFFICE OF ADMINISTRATIVE AND PERSONNEL MANAGEMENT

Associate Executive Director.—Jayne L. Seidman, 942–4000.

REGIONAL OFFICES

Northeast Regional Office: The Woolworth Building, 233 Broadway, New York, NY 10279, (646) 428–1500, fax (646) 428–1984.

Deputy Regional Director.—Edwin H. Nordlinger, 748–8038.

Assistant Regional Directors: Helene T. Glotzer, 428–1736; George N. Stepaniuk, 428–1910; David Rosenfeld, 428–1869; Alistaire Bambach, 428–1636; Caren Pennington, 428–1845; Leslie Kazon, 428–1778, Kay Lackey, 428–1790.

Associate Regional Directors: Robert B. Blackburn, 428–1610; Robert DeLeonardis, 428–1688; Barry Rashkover, 428–1856; Mark Schonfeld, 428–1650.

Associate Regional Director, Investment Management and Corporate Reorganization.—Douglas Scarff, 428–1660.

Assistant Regional Directors: Joseph Dimaria, 426–1692; Dorothy Eschwie, 428–1700; William Delmage, 428–1689.

Associate Regional Director, Broker/Dealer.—Robert A. Sollazzo, 428–1620.

Assistant Regional Directors: Broker/Dealer: Richard D. Lee, 428–1520; Linda Lettieri, 428–1797; Richard Heapy, 428–1753.

Boston District Office: 73 Tremont Street, Suite 600, Boston, MA 02108, (617) 424–5900, fax 424–5940.

District Administrator.—Juan Marcel Marcelino, 424–5934.

Assistant District Administrators: (Enforcement), David Bergers, 424–5927; Kate Poverman, 424–5936; (Regulation), Edward A. Ryan, Jr., 424–5935; Elizabeth Salini, 424–5931.

Philadelphia District Office: The Curtis Center, Suite 1005 East, 601 Walnut Street, Philadelphia, PA 19106, (215) 597–3100, fax 597–5885.

District Administrator.—Arthur Gabinet, 597–3106.

Associate District Administrator.—Joy G. Thompson, 597–6135.

Assistant District Administrators: (Enforcement), Merri Jo Gillette, 597–3191; C. David Horowitz, 597–3107.

Senior Assistant District Administrator (Regulation).—William R. Meck, 597–0789.

Assistant District Administrator (Regulation).—A. Laurence Ehrhart, 597–2983.

Southeast Regional Office: 801 Brickell Avenue, Suite 1800, Miami, FL 33131 (305) 982–6300, fax (305) 536–6300.

Regional Director.—David Nelson, 982–4120.

Assistant Regional Directors: (Enforcement), Ivan Harris, 982–6342; John C. Mattimore, 982–6357.

Assistant Regional Director.—John D. Mahoney, 982–6303.

Atlanta District Office: 3475 Lenox Road NE., Suite 1000, Atlanta, GA 30326, (404) 842–7600, fax 842–7666.

District Administrator.—Richard P. Wessel, 842–7610.

Associate District Administrator.—Ronald L. Crawford, 842–7630.

Assistant District Administrators: (Enforcement), Richard P. Murphy, 842–7665; (Regulation), Francis P. McGing, 842–7645.

Midwest Regional Office: 175 West Jackson Boulevard, Suite 900, Chicago, IL 60604, (312) 353–7390, fax 353–7398.

Regional Director.—Mary Keefe, 353–9338.

Associate Regional Directors: (Enforcement), Timothy Warren, 353–7394; (Regulation), John R. Brissman, 353–7436.

Assistant Regional Directors: (Enforcement), Daniel Gregus, 353–7423; Peter Chan, 353–7410; Jane Jarcho, 353–5479; David Medow, 353–5453; Scott J. Hlavacek, 353–1679; John R. Lee, 886–2247; (Regulation), Thomas Murphy, 886–8513; Lawrence Kendra, 886–8508; Thomas Kirk, 886–3956; Douglas Adams, 353–7402; Maureen Dempsey, 886–1496.

Central Regional Office: 1801 California Street, Suite 1500, Denver, CO 80202, (303) 844–1000, fax 844–1010.

Regional Director.—Randall J. Fons, 844–1000.

Associate Regional Director.—Donald M. Hoerl, 844–1060.

Assistant Regional Directors: (Enforcement), Edward A. Lewkowski, 844–1050; (Regulation), Katherine Addleman, 844–1070; Dale E. Coffin, 844–1040; Amy Norwood, 844–1029.

Fort Worth District Office: 801 Cherry Street, 19th Floor, Fort Worth, TX 76102, (817) 978–3821, fax 978–2700.

District Administrator.—T. Harold F. Degenhardt, 978–6469.

Assistant District Administrators: (Enforcement), Stephen Webster, 978–6459; (Regulation), Hugh M. Wright, 978–6474; Jeffrey Cohen, 978–6480.

Salt Lake District Office: 50 South Main Street, Suite 500, Salt Lake City, UT 84144, (801) 524–5796, fax 524–3558.

District Administrator.—Kenneth D. Israel, 524–6745.

Pacific Regional Office: 5670 Wilshire Boulevard, 11th Floor, Los Angeles, CA 90036, (213) 965–3998, fax 965–3816.

Regional Director.—Randall R. Lee, 965–3807.

Associate Regional Director (Enforcement).—Sandra J. Harris, 965–3962.

Assistant Regional Directors: (Enforcement), Lisa Gok, 965–3835; Kelly Bowers, 965–3924; Diana Tani, 965–3991.

Associate Regional Director (Regulation).—Rosalind R. Tyson, 965–3893.

Assistant Regional Directors: (Regulation), Michael P. Levitt, 525–2684; Paul Weiser, 525–3252; Cindy S. Wong, 965–3927.

San Francisco District Office: 44 Montgomery Street, Suite 1100, San Francisco, CA 94104, (415) 705–2500, fax 705–2501.

District Administrator.—Helane L. Morrison, 705–2450.

Assistant District Administrators: (Enforcement), Robert Mitchell, 705–2351; (Regulation), Daryl Hagel, 705–2340; Jennet Leong, 705–2452.

SELECTIVE SERVICE SYSTEM

1515 Wilson Boulevard, 4th Floor, Arlington, VA 22209–2425

phone (703) 605–4000, fax 605–4133, http://www.sss.gov

Director.—Lewis Brodsky (acting), 605–4010.

Deputy Director.—Lewis Brodsky.

Chief of Staff.—COL Richard A. Moore, 605–4010.

Office of General Counsel.—Rudy Sanchez, 605–4012.

Inspector General.—[Vacant].

Director for—

Operations.—Willie L. Blanding, Jr., 605–4066.

Information Management.—Norman W. Miller, 605–4110.

Resource Management.—Freida Brockington, 605–4032.

Public and Congressional Affairs.—Richard S. Flahavan, 605–4017, fax 605–4106.

Financial Management.—Carlo Verdino, 605–4020.

Registration Information Office, P.O. Box 94638, Palatine, IL 60094–4638, phone (847) 688–6888, fax (847) 688–2860.

SMALL BUSINESS ADMINISTRATION

409 Third Street, SW 20416

phone (202) 205–6600, fax (202) 205–7064, http://www.sbaonline.sba.gov

Administrator.—Hector V. Barreto, 205–6605.

Deputy Administrator.—Melanie Sabelhaus.

Counselor to the Administrator.—John Whitmore, 205–6605.

Chief of Staff.—Lisa Goeas, 205–6605.

Director of Executive Secretariat.—Sarah Rice Cutler (acting), 205–6608.

General Counsel.—David Javdan, 205–6642.

Chief Counsel for Advocacy.—Thomas M. Sullivan, 205–6533.

Inspector General.—Harry Damelin, 205–6580.

Chief Financial Officer.—Thomas Dumaresq, 205–6449.

Director, National Advisory Council.—Nancyellen Gentile, 205–6812.

Associate Administrator for—

Field Operations.—David Fredrickson, 205–6808.

Public Communications.—Sue Hensley, 205–6740.

Disaster Assistant.—Herb Mitchell, 205–6734.

Assistant Administrator for—

Congressional and Legislative Affairs.—[Vacant].

Hearings and Appeals.—Gloria Blazsik (acting), 401–8200.

Equal Employment Opportunity and Compliance.—Loyola Trujillo (acting), 205–6750.

Associate Deputy Administrator for Management and Administration.—Lloyd Blanchard, 205–6610.

Assistant Administrator for—

Administration.—Eugene Cornelius (acting), 205–6630.

Chief Information Officer.—[Vacant].

Human Capital Management.—Nancy Raum, 205–6780.

Associate Deputy Administrator for Capital Access.—Ronald Bew, 205–6557.
Associate Administrator for—
Business and Community Initiatives.—Ellen Thrasher (acting), 205–6665.
Small Business Development Centers.—Johnnie Albertson, 205–6766.
Financial Assistance.—James Riviera, 205–6490.
Investment.—Jeffrey Pierson, 205–6510.
Surety Guarantees.—Diane Neal (acting), 205–6540.
Assistant Administrator for—
International Trade.—Manuel Rosales, 205–6720.
Veterans' Affairs.—William Elmore, 205–6773.
Women's Business Ownership.—Wilma Goldstein, 205–6673.
Native American Affairs.—Thelma Stiffarm, 205–7364.
Associate Deputy Administrator for Government Contracting and Business Development.—Fred Armendariz, 205–6459.
Associate Administrator for—
Government Contracting.—Linda Williams, 205–6460.
Business Development.—Luz Hopewell, 205–6463.
Assistant Administrator for—
Size Standard.—Gary Jackson, 205–6618.
Technology.—Maurice Swinton, 205–6450.

SMITHSONIAN INSTITUTION

Smithsonian Institution Building—The Castle (SIB), 1000 Jefferson Drive, SW., 20560

phone 357–2700, http://www.smithsonian.org

The Smithsonian Institution is an independent trust instrumentality created in accordance with the terms of the will of James Smithson of England who in 1826 bequeathed his property to the United States of America "to found at Washington under the name of the Smithsonian Institution an establishment for the increase and diffusion of knowledge among men." Congress pledged the faith of the United States to carry out the trust in 1836 (Act of July 1, 1836, C. 252, 5 Stat. 64), and established the Institution in its present form in 1846 (August 10, 1846, C. 178, 9 Stat. 102), entrusting the management of the institution to its independent Board of Regents.

THE BOARD OF REGENTS

ex officio

Chief Justice of the United States.—William H. Rehnquist, Chancellor.
Vice President of the United States.—Richard B. Cheney.

Appointed by the President of the Senate
Hon. Thad Cochran
Hon. Bill Frist
Hon. Patrick Leahy

Appointed by the Speaker of the House
Hon. Sam Johnson
Hon. Ralph Regula
Hon. Robert T. Matsui

Appointed by Joint Resolution of Congress

Barber B. Conable, Jr.
Anne d'Harnoncourt
Dr. Hanna H. Gray
Dr. Manuel L. Ibáñez
Dr. Walter E. Massey
Dr. Patty Stonesifer
Alan G. Spoon
Roger Sant.
Wesley S. Williams, Jr.

OFFICE OF THE SECRETARY

Secretary.—Lawrence M. Small.
Executive Assistant to the Secretary.—James M. Hobbins, 357–1869.
Inspector General.—Thomas D. Blair, 275–2154.
Director of:
Policy and Analysis.—Carole M.P. Neves, 633–8065.
Director of Development.—[Vacant].
General Counsel.—John Huerta, 357–1997.

OFFICE OF THE UNDER SECRETARY FOR AMERICAN MUSEUMS AND NATIONAL PROGRAMS

Under Secretary.—Sheila P. Burke, 357–7033.
Director of:
Financial Affairs.—S. Anthony McCann, 357–4767.
Government Relations.—Nell Payne, 357–2962.
Communications and Public Affairs.—Evelyn Lieberman, 357–2627.
Special Events and Protocol.—Nicole L. Krakora, 357–2284.
National Programs.—Herma Hightower, 357–7037.
Operations.—[Vacant].
Arts and Industries Building.—Ellen Dorn, 786–9199.
Quadrangle Building.—Ronald W. Hawkins, 357–4586.
Accessibility Program.—Elizabeth Ziebarth, 786–2942.

AMERICAN MUSEUMS

Director of:
Anacostia Museum.—Steven Cameron Newsome, 610–3378.
Cooper-Hewitt, National Design Museum.—Paul Thompson, (212) 860–6868.
National Air and Space Museum.—Jack Dailey, 633–2350.
National Museum of American History.—Brent Glass, 357–2510.
National Museum of the American Indian.—W. Richard West, 287–2523.
National Portrait Gallery.—Marc Pachter, 275–1740.
National Postal Museum.—Allen Kane (acting), 633–9360.
Smithsonian American Art Museum.—Elizabeth Broun, 275–1515.
Curator-in-charge, Renwick Gallery.—Kenneth R. Trapp, 357–2533.

CULTURAL AND RESEARCH RESOURCES

Director of:
Archives of American Art.—Richard J. Wattenmaker, 275–2156.
Asian Pacific American Program.—Franklin Odo, 786–2963.
Center for Folklife Programs and Cultural Studies.—Richard Kurin, 275–1138.
Smithsonian Center for Latino Initiatives.—[Vacant].

NATIONAL PROGRAMS

Director of:
Smithsonian Affiliations Program.—Michael Carrigan, 633–9157.
Smithsonian Associates Program.—Mara Mayor, 357–2696.
Smithsonian Center for Education and Museum Studies.—Stephanie L. Norby (acting), 357–2624.
Smithsonian Institution Traveling Exhibition Service.—Anna Cohn, 357–3168, ext. 101.

OFFICE OF THE UNDER SECRETARY FOR FINANCE AND ADMINISTRATION

Under Secretary.—[Vacant].
Executive Assistant.—[Vacant].
Director of:
Exhibits Central.—Michael Headley, 357–1556, ext. 13.
Human Resources.—Carolyn E. Jones, 275–1100.
Smithsonian Institution Libraries.—Nancy Gwinn, 357–2240.

FINANCE

Chief Financial Officer.—Alice Maroni, 275–2020.
Comptroller.—Catheryne Hummel, 275–0300.
Treasurer.—Sudeep Anand, 275–0470.

Director, Office of:
Contracting.—John W. Cobert, 275–1600.
International Relations.—Francine Berkowitz, 357–4795.
Planning Management and Budget.—Bruce Dauer, 357–2917.

FACILITIES SERVICES

Facilities Engineering and Operations Director.—William W. Brubaker, 357–1873.
Director, Office of:
Safety and Environmental Management.—Roger Yankoupe, 275–1167.
Physical Plant.—Michael Sofield, 633–0101.
Protection Services.—James J. McLaughlin, 357–3375.

INFORMATION TECHNOLOGY

Chief Information Officer.—Dennis Shaw, 633–2800.
Director, Office of:
Systems Modernization.—Deron Burba, 633–7056.
Imaging, Printing, and Photographic Services.—[Vacant].
Smithsonian Archives.—Edie Hedlin, 357–3080.

OFFICE OF THE UNDER SECRETARY FOR SCIENCE

Under Secretary.—David Evans, 357–2903.
Director of:
Scientific Research Program.—Anthony Coates, 357–2903.
Scientific Diving Program.—Michael Lang, 786–2815.

SMITHSONIAN BUSINESS VENTURES DIVISION

Chief Executive Officer.—Gary M. Beer, 786–9141.
Chief Financial Officer.—Paul Wessel, 275–1612.
Publisher, Smithsonian Magazine.—Amy Wilkins, (212) 916–1313.
Editor, Smithsonian Magazine.—Carey Winfrey, 275–2202.
Chief Operating Officer, Mall Retail.—Gary Mercer.
Vice President, Consumer Marketing.—Scott Rockman, 916–1371.
Director of:
Catalogues.—Tom Holzfeind, 275–2192.
Corporate Development.—Jeanny Kim, 786–9141.
Merchandising.—Lisa Mazzio, 275–2191.
Product Development and Licensing.—Peter Reid, 275–1533.

INTERNATIONAL ART MUSEUMS DIVISION

Director.—Thomas W. Lentz, 357–7047.
Assistant Director for Administration.—[Vacant].
Administrative Coordinator/Scheduler.—Francie Woltz, 357–7047.
Senior Curator for Photography.—Merry Foresta, 275–1176.
Photography Assistant.—Jeana Foley, 633–9237.
Holocaust Research Historian.—[Vacant].

SOCIAL SECURITY ADMINISTRATION

International Trade Commission Building, 500 E Street SW, Washington, DC 20254, (ITCB)

Altmeyer Building, 6401 Security Boulevard, Baltimore, MD 21235, (ALTMB)

Annex Building, 6401 Security Boulevard, Baltimore, MD 21235, (ANXB)

National Computer Center, 6201 Security Boulevard, Baltimore, MD 21235, (NCC)

West High Rise Building, 6401 Security Boulevard, Baltimore, MD 21235, (WHRB)

East High Rise Building, 6401 Security Boulevard, Baltimore, MD 21235, (EHRB)

Gwynn Oak Building, 1710 Gwynn Oak Avenue, Baltimore, MD 21207, (GWOB)

Operations Building, 6401 Security Boulevard, Baltimore, MD 21235, (OPRB)

Metro West Tower Building, 300 North Greene Street, Baltimore, MD 21201, (MWTB)

Security West Tower, 1500 Woodlawn Drive, Baltimore, MD 21241, (SWTB)

One Skyline Tower, 5107 Leesburg Pike, Falls Church, VA 22041, (SKY)

http://www.ssa.gov

Commissioner.—Jo Anne Barnhart, ITCB, room 850, (202) 358–6000 or ALTMB, room 900, (410) 965–3120.
Deputy Commissioner.—James B. Lockhart III, ITCB, room 874, (202) 358–6041 or ALTMB, room 960, (410) 965–9000.
Chief of Staff.—Larry W. Dye, ITCB, room 858, (202) 358–6013 or ALTMB, room 900, (410) 966–8323.
Chief Information Officer.—Thomas P. Hughes, ALTMB, room 500, (410) 966–5738 or ITCB, room 870, (202) 358–6133.
Executive Secretary/Director Office of Executive Operations.—Veronica B. Henderson, ALTMB, room 942, (410) 966–8897.
Deputy Commissioner for Communications.—Terry Abbott, WHRB, room 4200, (410) 965–1720.
Assistant Deputy Commissioner.—Philip Gambino, WHRB, room 4200, (410) 965–1720.
Press Officer.—Jim Courtney, ALTMB, room 449, (410) 965–8904 or ITCB, room 866, (202) 358–6131.
Associate Commissioner, Office of:
Communication, Planning, Evaluation and Measurement.—C.J. McAuliffe (acting), WHRB, room 4300, (410) 965–2013.
Communications Policy and Technology.—Margy LaFond, WHRB, room 4100, (410) 965–4029.
External Affairs.—David Byrd, WHRB, room 4300, (410) 965–4023.
Public Inquiries.—Charles H. Mullen, WHRB, room 4200, (410) 965–2737.
Deputy Commissioner for Disability and Income Security Programs.—Martin H. Gerry, ALTMB, room 100, (410) 965–0100.
Assistant Deputy Commissioner.—Fritz G. Streckewald, ALTMB, room 100, (410) 965–6212.
Associate Commissioner, Office of:
International Programs.—Joseph Gribbin, ALTMB, room 142, (410) 965–7388.
Program Benefits.—Nancy Veillon, ALTMB, room 760, (410) 965–5961.
Disability.—Kenneth D. Nibali, ALTMB, room 560, (410) 965–3424.
Hearings and Appeals.—Rita Geier, SKY, room 1600, (703) 605–8200.
Program Support.—Ramona Frentz (acting), OPRB, room 2–Q–16, (410) 965–3658.
Employment Support Programs.—J. Kenneth McGill, ALTMB, room 107, (410) 965–3988.
Deputy Commissioner for Policy.—Paul Van de Water (acting), ITCB, room 826, (202) 358–6082.
Assistant Deputy Commissioner.—Paul Van de Water, ITCB, room 826, (202) 358–6082.
Associate Commissioner, Office of:
Research, Evaluation and Statistics.—Susan Grad (acting), OPRB, room 4–C–15, (410) 965–2841.
Disability and Income Assistance Policy.—Mark Nadel, ITCB, room 834, (202) 358–6114.
Retirement Policy.—[Vacant], ITCB, room 822, (202) 358–6100.

Deputy Commissioner for Operations.—Linda S. McMahon, WHRB, room 1204, (410) 965–3143.

Assistant Deputy Commissioner.—Mary Glenn-Croft, WHRB, room 1204, (410) 965–1880.

Associate Commissioner, Office of:

Public Service and Operations Support.—Roger McDonnell, WHRB, room 1224, (410) 965–4292.

Automation Support.—Mark Blatchford, WHRB, room 1126, (410) 966–8040.

Telephone Services.—Donnell Adams, ANX, room 4845, (410) 966–7758.

Electronic Services.—James Kissko, ANX, room 3845, (410) 965–2850.

Central Operations.—W. Burnell Hurt, SWTB, room 7000, (410) 966–7000.

Regional Commissioner for—

Boston: Manny Vaz (acting), JFK Federal Building, Government Center, Room 1900, Boston, MA 02203, (617) 565–2870.

New York: Beatrice Disman, 26 Federal Plaza, Room 40–102, New York, NY 10278, (212) 264–3915.

Philadelphia: Larry G. Massanari, P.O. Box 8788, 300 Spring Garden Street, Philadelphia, PA 19123, (215) 597–5157.

Atlanta: Paul Barnes, 61 Forsyth Street, Suite 23T30, Atlanta, GA 30303, (404) 562–5600.

Chicago: James F. Martin, Harold Washington Social Security Center, (P.O. Box 8280), 600 West Madison Street, Chicago, IL 60661, (312) 575–4000.

Dallas: Horace Dickerson, 1301 Young Street, Suite 500, Dallas, TX 75202, (214) 767–4210.

Kansas City: Michael Grochowski, Federal Office Building, 601 East 12th Street, Room 436, Kansas City, MO 64106, (816) 936–5700.

Denver: James Everett, Federal Office Building, 1961 Stout Street, Room 325, Denver, CO 80294, (303) 844–2388.

San Francisco: Pete Spencer, 75 Hawthorne Street, San Francisco, CA 94105, (415) 744–4676.

Seattle: Carmen M. Keller, 2201 Sixth Street, MS RX–50, Seattle, WA 98121, (206) 615–2103.

Deputy Commissioner for Finance, Assessment and Management.—Dale W. Sopper, ALTMB, room 800, (410) 965–2910.

Assistant Deputy Commissioner.—Tony Dinoto, ALTMB, room 800, (410) 965–2914.

Associate Commissioner, Office of:

Quality Assurance and Performance Assessment.—Thomas C. Evans, EHRB, room 600, (410) 965–3815.

Financial Policy and Operations.—Tony Dinoto (acting), EHRB, room 2150, (410) 965–3098.

Budget.—Robert M. Rothenberg, WHRB, room 2126, (410) 965–3501.

Acquisition and Grants.—James M. Fornataro, GWOB, room 1–A–7, (410) 965–9459.

Facilities Management.—Andria Childs, ALTMB, room 860, (410) 965–6789.

Publications and Logistics Management.—Gary Arnold, ANX, room 1540, (410) 965–4262.

Deputy Commissioner for Systems.—William Gray, ALTMB, room 400, (410) 965–7747.

Assistant Deputy Commissioner.—Kelly Croft, ALTMB, room 400, (410) 965–7481.

Associate Commissioner, Office of:

Retirement and Survivors Insurance Systems.—Carl Couchoud, WHRB, room 4–K–5, (410) 965–6290.

Systems Electronic Services.—Marsha R. Rydstrom, OPRB, room 4–S–3, (410) 965–3400.

Telecommunications and Systems Operations.—James E. Preissner, NCC, room 541, (410) 965–1500.

Enterprise Support, Architecture and Engineering.—Charles M. Wood, WHRB, room 3100, (410) 965–3780.

Disability and Supplemental Security Income Systems.—Peter V. Herrera, WHRB, room 3224, (410) 965–0413.

Earnings, Enumeration and Administrative Systems.—Judy Ziolkowski, WHRB, room 3124, (410) 965–5311.

Director, Office of:

Client/Server Configuration.—John Standridge (acting), NCC, room 553, (410) 965–6453.

Computer Operations Production Control.—Jacqueline Hill McCloud, NCC, room 471, (410) 965–1594.

Integrated Telecommunications Engineering.—Roland Washington, NCC, room 2240, (410) 965–6485.

Integration and Environmental Testing.—Gary Augustine, NCC, room 593, (410) 965–1205.

Monitoring and Online Systems.—[Vacant], NCC, room 591, (410) 965–2291.
National Network Services and Operations.—[Vacant], NCC, room 354, (410) 965–8182.
Network Engineering.—Gina Kotowski, NCC, room 560, (410) 965–2197.
Operational Capacity Performance Management.—Patrick Mooney, NCC, room 582, (410) 965–2116.
Operational Software Suport.—Nelson J. Brenneman, NCC, room 490, (410) 965–2241.
Resource Management and Acquisition.—Neil Whaley, NCC, room 570, (410) 965–6365.
Systems User Services and Facilities.—James Strickler, NCC, room 472, (410) 965–1536.
Telecommunications Security and Standards.—Ronald Burdinkski, NCC, room 592, (410) 965–1233.

Deputy Commissioner for Human Resources.—Dr. Reginald F. Wells, ALTMB, room 200, (410) 965–1900.
Assistant Deputy Commissioner.—Feli Sola-Carter, ALTMB, room 200, (410) 965–7642.
Associate Commissioner, Office of Personnel.—Sander K. Eckert, ANX, room 4170, (410) 965–3324.
Director, Office of:
Labor Management and Employee Relations.—Mark A. Anderson (acting), ANX, room 2170, (410) 965–3318.
Civil Rights and Equal Opportunity.—[Vacant].
Training.—Wayne Harmon, EHRB, room 100, (410) 966–8193.

Deputy Commissioner for Legislation and Congressional Affairs.—Diane B. Garro (acting), ITCB, room 826, (202) 358–6030, or ALTMB, room 152, (410) 965–2386.
Assistant Deputy Commissioner.—[Vacant].
Associate Commissioner for—
Legislative Relations.—[Vacant], ITCB, room 866, (202) 358–6030.
Legislative Development.—Webster Phillips, ITCB, room 813, (202) 358–6027 or ALTMB, room 146, (410) 965–3735.
Director for—
Disability Insurance Program.—Amy Snurr (acting), WHRB, room 3216, (410) 9 65–1835.
Legislative Research and Congressional Constituent Relations.—Marlow L. Mitchell, WHRB, room 3120, (410) 965–3533.
Supplemental Security Income Program.—Thomas M. Parrott, WHRB, room 3227, (410) 965–2617.
Old Age and Survivors Insurance Benefits.—Timothy J. Kelley, WHRB, room 3322, (410) 965–3293.
Program Administration and Financing.—Grayson G. Snurr, WHRB, room 3210, (410) 965–3288.

Chief Actuary.—Stephen C. Goss, ALTMB, room 700, (410) 965–3000.
Deputy Chief Actuary for—
Long Range.—Alice H. Wade, ALTMB, room 700, (410) 965–3002.
Short Range.—Eli N. Donkar, OPRB, room 4–N–29, (410) 965–3004.

General Counsel.—Lisa deSoto, ALTMB, room 600, (410) 965–0600.
Deputy General Counsel.—Thomas W. Crawley, ALTMB, room 600, (410) 965–3414.
Associate General Counsel for—
Program Litigation.—Charlotte Hardnett, ALTMB, room 624, (410) 965–3114.
General Law.—Michael G. Gallagher, ALTMB, room 560, (410) 965–3148.
Program Law.—John B. Watson, ALTMB, room 616, (410) 965–3137.
Regional Chief Counsel for—

Boston: Robert J. Triba, JFK Federal Building, Government Center, Room 625, Boston, MA 02203, (617) 565–4277.

New York: Barbara L. Spivak, 26 Federal Plaza, Suite 3904, New York, NY 12078, (212) 264–3650, ext. 222.

Philadelphia: James A. Winn, 300 Spring Garden Street, 6th Floor, Philadelphia, PA 19123, (215) 597–3300.

Atlanta: Mary Ann Sloan, Atlanta Federal Center, 61 Forsyth Street, SW, Suite 20T45, Atlanta, GA 30303, (404) 562–1010.

Chicago: Kim Leslie Bright, 200 West Adams Street, 30th Floor, Chicago, IL 60606, (312) 353–8201.

Dallas: Tina M. Waddell, 1301 Young Street, Suite 430, Dallas, TX 75202, (214) 767–3212.

Kansas City: Frank V. Smith, Federal Office Building, 601 East 12th Street, Room 535, Kansas City, MO 64106, (816) 936–5750.

Denver: Yvette G. Keesee (acting), Federal Office Building, 1961 Stout Street, Room 327, Denver, CO 80294, (303) 844–5459.

San Francisco: Janice L. Walli, 333 Market Street, Suite 1500, San Francisco, CA 94105, (415) 977–8943.

Seattle: Lucille Meis, 701 Fifth Avenue, Suite 2900, M/S 901, Seattle, WA 98104, (206) 615–2539.

Inspector General.—James G. Huse, Jr., ALTMB, room 300, (410) 966–8385.
Deputy Inspector General.—Jane E. Vezeris, ALTMB, room 300, (410) 966–8337.
Counsel to the Inspector General.—Kathy A. Buller, OPRB, room 4–M–1, (410) 965–6211.
Assistant Inspector General for—
Investigations.—Patrick O'Carroll, OPRB, room 4–S–1, (410) 965–7427.
Audit.—Steven L. Schaeffer, OPRB, room 4–L–1, (410) 965–9701.
Executive Operations.—Stephanie J. Palmer, ALTMB, room 300, (410) 965–9704.
Chief of Staff.—Richard A. Rohde, ALTMB, room 315, (410) 966–2436.

SUSQUEHANNA RIVER BASIN COMMISSION

COMMISSIONERS AND ALTERNATES

Federal Government.—BG Merdith (Bo) Temple (Chairman); COL Charles J. Fiala, Jr. (Alternate); COL John P. Carroll (Alternate).
New York.—John T. Hicks (Vice Chairman); Scott J. Foti (Alternate).
Pennsylvania.—Kathleen McGinty (Commissioner); Cathleen Myers (Alternate).
Maryland.—[Vacant] (Commissioner); Robert Summers (Alternate).

STAFF

1721 North Front Street, Harrisburg, PA 17102, phone (717) 238–0422

Executive Director.—Paul O. Swartz.
Chief Administrative Officer.—Duane A. Friends.
Chief, Watershed Assessment and Protection.—David W. Heicher.
Chief, Water Resources Management.—Glen DeWillie.
Director of Communications.—Susan S. Obleski.

STATE JUSTICE INSTITUTE

1650 King Street, Suite 600, Alexandria, VA 22314, phone (703) 684–6100

http://www.statejustice.org

BOARD OF DIRECTORS

Chairman.—Robert A. Miller.
Vice Chairmen.—Joseph F. Baca.
Secretary.—Sandra A. O'Connor.
Executive Committee Member.—Keith McNamara.
Members:

Terrence B. Adamson
Robert N. Baldwin
Carlos R. Garza
Sophia H. Hall
Tommy Jewell
Arthur A. McGiverin
Florence R. Murray

Officers:
Executive Director.—David I. Tevelin.
Deputy Director.—Kathy Schwartz.

TENNESSEE VALLEY AUTHORITY

One Massachusetts Avenue 20444, phone (202) 898–2999

Knoxville, TN 37902, phone (423) 632–2101

Chattanooga, TN 37401, phone (423) 751–0011

Muscle Shoals, AL 35660, phone (202) 386–2601

BOARD OF DIRECTORS

Chairman.—Glenn L. McCullough, Jr., (865) 632–2600 (Knoxville); (662) 690–3460 (Tupelo).
Directors: Skila Harris, (865) 632–3871 (Knoxville); William Baxter, (865) 632–2535 (Knoxville).
Chief Operating Officer.—Oswald J. (Ike) Zeringue, (423) 632–2366 (Knoxville).
Chief Nuclear Officer.—John A. Scalice, (423) 751–8682 (Chattanooga).
Chief Financial Officer.—David Smith, (423) 632–3987 (Knoxville).

CORPORATE VICE PRESIDENTS

Executive Vice Presidents:
Human Resources.—John E. Long, (865) 632–6307 (Knoxville).
Administration.—LeAnne Stribley, (865) 632–4352 (Knoxville).
Communications and Government Relations.—Ellen Robinson, (865) 632–3199 (Knoxville).
Customer Service and Marketing.—Mark O. Medord, (615) 882–2011 (Nashville).
General Counsel.—Maureen Dunn, (423) 632–2241 (Knoxville).
Inspector General.—Richard F. Chambers, (423) 632–4120 (Knoxville).

CHIEF OPERATING OFFICER ORGANIZATION

Bulk Power Trading.—Amy T. Burns, (423) 751–3907 (Chattanooga).
Performance Initiatives.—Ronald A. Loving, (865) 632–3435 (Knoxville).
Fossil Power Group.—Joseph R. Bynum, (423) 751–2601 (Chattanooga).
River System Operations and Environment.—Kathryn J. Jackson (423) 623–3141 (Knoxville).
TVA Nuclear.—John A. Scalice, (423) 751–8682 (Chattanooga).
Transmission/Power Supply.—W. Terry Boston, (423) 632–6000 (Chattanooga).
Power Resources & Operations Planning.—Gregory M. Vincent, (423) 751–4641 (Chattanooga).

WASHINGTON OFFICE

(202) 898–2999, fax (202) 898–2998

Vice President of Government Relations.—Linda Whitestone.
Washington Representatives: Justin Maierhofer, Scott Nielson, Nancy Townes.

U.S. TRADE AND DEVELOPMENT AGENCY

1621 North Kent Street, Suite 200, Arlington, VA 22209–2131, phone (703) 875–4357

Director.—Thelma J. Askey.
Deputy Director.—Barbara Bradford.
Chief of Staff.—Carl B. Kress.
General Counsel.—Leocadia I. Zak.
Assistant Director of Management.—Larry Bevan.
Assistant Director for Policy Planning.—Geoffrey Jackson.
Resource Advisor.—Micheal Hillier.
Congressional Relations Advisor.—Cherilyn Carruth.
Communications and Policy Advisor.—Donna Thiessen.
Regional Directors:
Africa and Middle East.—Henry D. Steingass.
Central/Eastern Europe.—Ned Cabot.
New Independent States.—Daniel D. Stein.
Asia and Pacific Islands.—Geoffrey Jackson.
Latin America and Caribbean.—Albert W. Angulo.

Economist/Evaluation Officer.—David Denny.
Grants Administrator.—Patricia Smith.
Financial Manager.—Noreen St. Louis.
Contracting Officer.—Della Glenn.
Administrative Officer.—Carolyn Hum.

U.S. ADVISORY COMMISSION ON PUBLIC DIPLOMACY

USIA Building, 301 Fourth Street SW., Room 600, 20547

phone (202) 619–4463, fax 619–5489

[Created by Executive Order 12048 and Public Law 96–60]

Chairman.—Harold C. Pachios.
Vice Chairman.—Charles H. Dolan.
Members: Penne Percy Korth, Lewis Manilow, Maria Elena Torano.
Senior Adviser.—Walter R. Roberts.
Executive Director.—Matt Lauer.
Administrative Officer.—Jamice Clayton.

U.S. COMMISSION ON CIVIL RIGHTS

624 Ninth Street NW., 20425, phone (202) 376–7700, fax (202) 376–7672

(Codified in 42 U.S.C., section 1975)

Chairperson.—Mary Frances Berry.
Vice Chairperson.—Cruz Reynoso.
Commissioners: Jennifer C. Braceras, Christopher Edly, Jr, Peter N. Kirsanow, Elsie M. Meeks, Russell G. Redenbaugh, Abigail Thernstrom.
Staff Director.—Les R. Jin.
Assistant Staff Director for Congressional Affairs.—[Vacant].
Deputy General Counsel.—Debra Carr, 376–8351.
Chief, Regional Programs Coordination Unit.—Ivy Davis, 376–7700.
Office of Civil Rights Evaluation.—Terri Dickerson, 376–8582.

U.S. HOLOCAUST MEMORIAL COUNCIL

The United States Holocaust Memorial Museum, 100 Raoul Wallenberg Place SW., 20024

phone 488–0400, fax (202) 488–2690

Officials:
Chair.—Fred S. Zeidman, Houston, TX.
Vice Chair.—Ruth B. Mandel, Princeton, NJ.
Director.—Sara J. Bloomfield, Washington, DC.

Members:
Sheldon G. Adelson, Las Vegas, NV.
Maya Angelou, Winston Salem, NC.
Susan Volchok Balaban, Bala Cynwyd, PA.
David Berger, Philadelphia, PA.
Tom A. Bernstein, New York, NY.
Rudy A. Boschwitz, Fridley, MN.
Lanny A. Breuer, Washington, DC.
Gila J. Bronner, Chicago, IL.
Norman Brownstein, Denver, CO.
Myron M. Cherry, Chicago, IL.
Stanley M. Chesley, Cincinnati, OH.
Debra Lerner Cohen, Washington, DC.
Sam Devinki, Kansas City, MO.
Kitty Dukakis, Brookline, MA.
Stuart E. Eizenstat, Chevy Chase, MD.
Susan Estrich, Los Angeles, CA.
Donald Etra, Los Angeles, CA.
David M. Flaum, Rochester, NY.
Pam Fleischaker, Oklahoma City, OK.
Joel M. Geiderman, Los Angeles, CA.
Michael C. Gelman, Bethesda, MD.
Harold Gershowitz, Chicago, IL.
William H. Gray III, Vienna, VA.
Barbara W. Grossman, Newton, MA.
Alice A. Kelikian, Cambridge, MA.
John F. Kordek, Arlington Heights, IL.
Frank R. Lautenberg, Rochelle Park, NJ.
William S. Lerach, San Diego, CA.
Mel Levine, Los Angeles, CA.
Deborah E. Lipstadt, Atlanta, GA.
Benjamin Meed, New York, NY.
Leo Melamed, Chicago, IL.
Harvey M. Meyerhoff, Baltimore, MD.
Set C. Momjian, Huntington Valley, PA.
Mervin G. Morris, Menlo Park, CA.

John T. Pawlikowski, Chicago, IL.
Burton P. Resnick, New York, NY.
Alvin H. Rosenfeld, Bloomington, IN.
Menachem Z. Rosensaft, New York, NY.
Eric F. Ross, South Orange, NJ.
Richard S. Sambol, Middletown, NJ.
Nathan Shapell, Beverly Hills, CA.
Mickey Shapiro, Farmington Hills, MI.
Jerome J. Shestack, Philadelphia, PA.
Ronald Steinhart, Dallas, TX.
Nechama Tec, Westport, CT.
Merryl H. Tisch, New York, NY.
Sonia Weitz, Peabody, MA.
Elie Wiesel, Boston, MA.
Karen B. Winnick, Beverly Hills, CA.
Aldona Z. Wos, Greensboro, NC.

Congressional Members:
Senate:
Barbara Boxer, Senator from California.
Norm Coleman, Senator from Minnesota.
Susan Collins, Senator from Maine.
Orrin G. Hatch, Senator from Utah.
Harry Reid, Senator from Nevada.
House of Representatives:
Christopher B. Cannon, Representative from Utah.
Eric I. Cantor, Representative from Virginia.
Martin Frost, Representative from Texas.
Tom Lantos, Representative from California.
Steven LaTourette, Representative from Ohio.
Ex Officio Members:
U.S. Department of:
Education.—Susan Sclafani.
Interior.—[Vacant].
State.—[Vacant].
Council Staff:
General Counsel.—Gerard Leval.
Secretary of the Council.—Jane M. Rizer.

U.S. INSTITUTE OF PEACE

1200 17th Street NW, Suite 200, 20036

phone (202) 457–1700, fax (202) 429–6063

BOARD OF DIRECTORS

Public Members:
Chairman.—Chester A. Crocker.
Vice Chairman.—Seymour Martin Lipset.
Members:
Betty Bumpers
Marc Leland
Barbara Snelling
Harriet Zimmerman
Holly Burkhalter
Maria Otero
Shibley Telhami
Ex Officio:
Assistant Secretary of Defense.—Douglas Feith (Secretary's Designate).
Assistant Secretary of State.—Lorne W. Craner (Secretary's Designate).
National Defense University.—VADM Paul G. Gaffney.
Officials:
President.—Richard H. Solomon.
Executive Vice President.—Harriet Hentges.
Vice President.—Charles Nelson.
Director of:
Education.—Pamela Aall.
Grants.—Judy Barsalou.
Jeannette Rankin Library Program.—Margarita Studemeister.
Jennings Randolph Fellowship Program.—Joseph L. Klaits.
Office of Administration.—Bernice Carney.
Office of Public Outreach.—John Brinkley.
Research and Studies.—Paul Stares.
Co-Director.—Bill Drennan.
Rule of Law.—Neil Kritz.
Training.—George Ward.
Acting Director.—Ray Caldwell.

Information and Communications Technology.—Sheryl Brown.
Publications.—Daniel Snodderly.
Religion and Peacemaking Initiative.—David Smock.
Balkans Initiative / Peace Operations.—Daniel Serwer.
Special Initiative on the Muslim World.—Rich Kauzlarich.
Virtual Diplomacy Initiative: Sheryl Brown, Margarita Studemeister.

U.S. AGENCY FOR INTERNATIONAL DEVELOPMENT

1300 Pennsylvania Avenue NW., Washington, DC 20523 phone (202) 712–0000

http://www.usaid.gov

Administrator.—Andrew S. Natsios, room 6.09, 712–4040, fax 216–3455.
Deputy Administrator.—Frederick Schieck, room 6.09, 712–4070.
Chief of Staff.—Douglas J. Aller, room 6.08, 712–0700.
Counselor.—William Pearson, room 6.08, 712–5010.
Executive Secretary.—Douglas J. Aller, room 6.08, 712–0700.
Assistant Administrator for—
Africa.—Constance Newman, room 4.08, 712–0500.
Asia and the Near East.—Wendy Chamberlin, room 4.09, 712–0200.
Europe and Eurasia.—Kent Hill, room 5.06, 712–0290.
Latin America and the Caribbean.—Adolfo Franco, room 5.09, 712–4800.
Program and Policy Coordination.—Patrick Cronin, room 6.08, 712–1430.
Democracy, Conflict and Humanitarian Assistance.—Roger Winter, room 8.06, 712–0100.
Global Health.—E. Anne Peterson, room 3.09, 712–1190.
Management.—John Marshall, room 6.09, 712–1200.
Legislative and Public Affairs.—J. Edward Fox, room 6.10, 712–4300.
Director of Equal Opportunity Programs.—Jessalyn L. Pendarvis, room 2.09, 712–1110.
Director of Small and Disadvantaged Business Utilization.—Marilyn Marton, room 7.08, 712–1500.
General Counsel.—John Gardner, room 6.06, 712–4476.
Inspector General.—Everett Mosley, room 6.06, 712–1150.

U.S. OVERSEAS PRIVATE INVESTMENT CORPORATION

1100 New York Avenue NW, Washington, DC 20527, (202) 336–8400

President and Chief Executive Officer.—Peter S. Watson.
Executive Vice President and Chief Operating Officer.—Ross J. Connelly.
Chief of Staff.—Joseph E. Flynn.
Vice President and General Counsel.—Mark Garfinkel.
Vice President and Chief Financial Officer.—Gary A. Keel.
Vice President for—
External Affairs.—Christopher Coughlin.
Finance.—Robert B. Drumheller.
Insurance.—Michael T. Lempres.
Investment Development and Economic Growth.—Daniel A. Nichols.
Investment Funds.—Cynthia L. Hostetler.
Investment Policy.—Virginia D. Green.
Director, Congressional Affairs.—Richard C. Horanburg, 336–8417.

BOARD OF DIRECTORS

Government Directors:
Andrew S. Natsios, Administrator, Agency for International Development.
Robert B. Zoellick, Deputy United States Trade Representative.
Peter S. Watson, President and Chief Executive Officer, Overseas Private Investment Corporation.
Alan P. Larson, Under Secretary of State for Economic, Business, and Agricultural Affairs, U.S. Department of State.
Grant D. Aldonas, Under Secretary of Commerce for International Trade, U.S. Department of Commerce.
John B. Taylor, Under Secretary for International Affairs, U.S. Department of Treasury.
D. Cameron Findlay, Deputy Secretary of Labor, U.S. Department of Labor.

Private Sector Directors:

Gary A. Barron, President, Strategic Alliance Partners, Aventura, Florida.

Samuel E. Ebbesen, President and CEO, Virgin Island Telephone Corporation, St. Thomas, Virgin Islands.

Collister Johnson, Jr., Senior Consultant, Mercer Management Consulting, Inc., Washington, DC.

George J. Kourpias, Retired President, International Association of Machinists and Aerospace Workers, Upper Marlboro, Maryland.

John L. Morrison, Chairman, Highland Capital, Minneapolis, Minnesota.

Diane M. Ruebling, Field Vice President, The Mony Group, Midvale, Utah.

Ned L. Siegel, President, The Siegel Group, Boca Raton, Florida.

C. William Swank, Retired Executive Vice President, Ohio Farm Bureau Federation, Westerville, Ohio.

Staff:

Board Counsel.—Mark Garfinkel, 336–8410.

Corporate Secretary.—Connie M. Downs, 336–8438.

U.S. INTERNATIONAL TRADE COMMISSION

500 E Street, SW., 20436

phone (202) 205–2000, fax 205–2798, http://www.usitc.gov

COMMISSIONERS

Chairman.—Deanna Tanner Okun, Republican, Idaho; term ending June 16, 2008; entered duty on January 3, 2000; designated Chairman for the term ending June 16, 2004.

Vice Chairman.—Jennifer A. Hillman, Democrat, Indiana; term ending December 16, 2006; entered duty on August 4, 1998; designated Vice Chairman for the term ending June 16, 2004.

Commissioners:

Marcia E. Miller, Democrat, Indiana; term ending December 16, 2003; entered duty on August 5, 1996.

Stephen Koplan, Democrat, Virginia; term ending June 16, 2005; entered duty on August 4, 1998.

Congressional Relations Officer.—Nancy M. Carman, 205–3151.

Secretary.—Marilyn R. Abbott, 205–2000.

Director, Office of External Relations.—Daniel F. Leahy, 205–3141.

Administrative Law Judges: Paul J. Luckern, 205–2694; Sidney Harris, 205–2692; Delbert Terrill, 708–4051, Charles E. Bullock, 205–2681.

General Counsel.—Lyn M. Schlitt, 205–3061.

Inspector General.—Kenneth Clarke, 205–2210.

Chief Information Officer.—Stephen A. McLaughlin, 205–3131.

Director, Office of:

Administration.—Stephen A. McLaughlin, 205–3131.

Economics.—Robert B. Koopman, 205–3216.

Equal Employment Opportunity.—Jacqueline A. Waters, 205–2240.

Finance.—Patricia Katsouros, 205–2682.

Industries.—Vern Simpson, 205–3296.

Investigations.—Robert Carpenter, 205–3160.

Operations.—Robert A. Rogowsky, 205–2230.

Human Resources.—Jeri L. Buchholz, 205–2651.

Tariff Affairs and Trade Agreements.—Eugene A. Rosengarden, 205–2595.

Unfair Import Investigations.—Lynn I. Levine, 205–2561.

Facilities Management.—Jonathan Brown, 205–2745.

Publishing.—Pamela Dyson, 205–2768.

U.S. MERIT SYSTEMS PROTECTION BOARD

1615 M Street, NW., 20419

phone (202) 653–6772, toll-free (800) 209–8960, fax 653–7130

[Created by Public Law 95–454]

Chairman.—Susanne T. Marshall.
Vice Chairman.—[Vacant].
Member.—[Vacant].
Chief of Staff.—Richard G. Banchoff.
General Counsel.—Martha Schneider.
Appeals Counsel.—Lynore Carnes.

REGIONAL OFFICES

Regional Directors:

Atlanta Regional Office: Covering Alabama, Florida, Georgia, Mississippi, South Carolina, Tennessee.—Thomas J. Lamphear, 10th Floor, 401 West Peachtree Street NW, Atlanta, GA 30308, (404) 730–2751, fax 730–2767.

Central Regional Office: Covering Illinois, Iowa, Kanas City, Kansas, Kentucky, Indiana, Michigan, Minnesota, Missouri, Ohio, Wisconsin.—Martin Baumgaertner, 31st Floor, 230 South Dearborn Street, Chicago, IL 60604, (312) 353–2923, fax 886–4231.

Dallas Field Office: Covering Arkansas, Louisiana, Oklahoma, Texas.—Sharon Jackson, Chief Administrative Judge, Room 620, 1100 Commerce Street, Dallas, TX 75242, (214) 767–0555, fax 767–0102.

Northeastern Regional Office: Covering Delaware, Maryland (except Montgomery and Prince Georges counties), Pennsylvania, New Jersey (except the counties of Bergen, Essex, Hudson, and Union), West Virginia.—Lonnie L. Crawford, U.S. Customhouse, Room 501, Second and Chestnut Streets, Philadelphia, PA 19106, (215) 597–9960, fax 597–3456.

Boston Field Office: Covering Connecticut, Maine, Massachusetts, New Hampshire, Rhode Island, Vermont.—William Carroll, Chief Administrative Judge, 99 Summer Street, Suite 1810, Boston, MA 02110, (617) 424–5700, fax (617) 424–5708.

New York Field Office: Covering New York, Puerto Rico, Virgin Islands, the following counties in New Jersey: Bergen, Essex, Hudson, Union.—Arthur Joseph, Chief Administrative Judge, Room 3137, 26 Federal Plaza, New York, NY 10278, (212) 264–9372, fax 264–1417.

Western Regional Office: Covering California and Nevada.—Amy Dunning, 250 Montgomery Street, Suite 400, 4th Floor, San Francisco, CA 94104, (415) 705–2935, fax (415) 705–2945.

Denver Field Office: Covering Arizona, Colorado, Kansas (except Kansas City), Montana, Nebraska, Nevada, New Mexico, North Dakota, South Dakota, Utah, Wyoming.—Joseph H. Harman, Chief Administrative Judge, 12567 West Cedar Drive, Suite 100, Lakewood, CO 80228, (303) 969–5101, fax (303) 969–5109.

Seattle Field Office: Covering Alaska, Hawaii, Idaho, Oregon, Washington, Pacific overseas.—Carl Berkenwald, Chief Administrative Judge, Room 1840, 915 Second Avenue, Seattle, WA 98174, (206) 220–7975, fax (206) 220–7982.

Washington Regional Office: Covering Washington, DC, Maryland (counties of Montgomery and Prince Georges, North Carolina, all overseas areas not otherwise covered), Virginia.—P.J. Winzer, Room 1109, 5203 Leesburg Pike, Falls Church, VA 22041, (703) 756–6250, fax (703) 756–7112.

U.S. POSTAL SERVICE

475 L'Enfant Plaza SW 20260–0010, phone (202) 268–2000

BOARD OF GOVERNORS

Albert Casey
LeGree S. Daniels
S. David Fineman
Alan Kessler
Ned R. McWherter
Robert F. Rider
John Walsh
John E. Potter, (Postmaster General)
John M. Nolan, (Deputy Postmaster General)

OFFICERS OF THE BOARD OF GOVERNORS

Secretary to the Board of Governors.—William T. Johnstone, 268–4800.
Deputy Secretary to the Board of Governors.—John Reynolds.

OFFICERS OF THE POSTAL SERVICE

Postmaster General, Chief Executive Officer.—John E. Potter, 268–2550.
Deputy Postmaster General.—John H. Nolan, 268–2525.
Chief Operating Officer and Executive Vice President.—Patrick R. Donahoe, 268–7500.
Chief Financial Officer and Senior Vice President.—Richard J. Strasser, Jr., 268–5272.
Chief Marketing Officer and Senior Vice President.—Anita J. Bizzotto, (703) 292–3676.
Chief Technology Officer and Senior Vice President.—Charles E. Bravo, 268–5470.
Chief Postal Inspector.—Lee Heath, 268–5616.
Inspector General.—David C. Williams, (703) 248–2300.
Senior Vice Presidents:
Capital Metro Operations.—Jerry D. Lane, (301) 548–1403.
Chief Technology Officer.—Robert L. Otto, 268–6900.
Consumer Advocate.—Francia G. Smith, 268–2281.
Controller.—Donna Peak, 268–4177.
Delivery and Retail.—Henry A. Pankey.
Diversity Development.—Murry Weatherall, 268–6566.
Employee Resource Management.—DeWitt Harris, 268–3783.
Engineering.—Thomas G. Day, (703) 280–7001.
Facilities.—Rudoloph K. Umscheid, (703) 526–2727.
General Counsel.—Mary Anne Gibbons, 268–2950.
Government Relations.—Ralph Moden, 268–2506.
Human Resources.—Suzanne Medvidovich, 268–4000.
International Business.—James P. Wade, (703) 292–3834.
Labor Relations.—Anthony Vegliante, 268–7852.
Network Operations Management.—Paul Vogel, 268–7666.
Operations.—John A. Rapp, 268–5381.
Pricing and Classification.—Stephen M. Kearney.
Product Development.—Nicholas F. Barranca, 268–5766.
Public Affairs and Communications.—Azeezaly S. Jaffer, 268–2143.
Sales.—Steve Hernandez (acting), (703) 292–3551.
Service and Market Development.—John R. Wargo, (703) 292–3800.
Strategic Planning.—Julie Moore (acting), 268–6257.
Supply Management.—Keith Strange, 268–4040.
Treasury.—Robert Pedersen, 268–2875.
Area Operations, Vice Presidents:
Eastern.—Alexander Lazaroff, (412) 494–2510.
Great Lakes.—Danny Jackson, (630) 539–5858.
New York Metro.—David L. Solomon, (718) 692–5611.
Northeast.—Jon M. Steele, (860) 285–7040.
Pacific.—Al Iniguez, (650) 635–3001.
Southeast.—William J. Brown, (901) 747–7333.
Southwest.—George L. Lopez, (214) 819–8650.
Western.—Craig G. Wade, (303) 313–5100.

U.S. RAILROAD RETIREMENT BOARD

844 North Rush Street, Chicago, IL 60611, phone (312) 751–4500, fax 751–4923, http://www.rrb.gov

Office of Legislative Affairs, 1310 G Street, Suite 500, 20005

phone (202) 272–7742, fax 272–7728, e-mail ola@rrb.gov

Chair.—Cherryl T. Thomas, (312) 751–4900, fax 751–7193.
Attorney Advisor to the Chair.—Rachel Simmons.
Labor Member.—V.M. Speakman, Jr., (312) 751–4905, fax 751–7194.
Assistants to the Labor Member: Robert E. Bergeron, James C. Boehner, Geraldine Clark, Michael Collins, Lawrence J. LaRocque.
Management Member.—Jerome F. Kever, (312) 751–4910, fax 751–7189.
Assistant to the Management Member.—Joseph Waechter.

Counsels to the Management Member: Robert M. Perbohner, Ann Chaney.
Inspector General.—Martin J. Dickman, (312) 751–4690, fax 751–4342.
SEO/General Counsel.—Steven A. Bartholow, (312) 751–4935, fax 751–7102.
Assistant to the SEO.—Charlene Kukla, (312) 751–4674, fax 751–7102.
Assistant General Counsel.—Marguerite Dadabo, (312) 751–4945, fax 751–7102.
Librarian.—Kay G. Collins, (312) 751–4927, fax 751–4924.
Director of:
Administration.—Henry Valiulis (acting), (312) 751–4990, fax 751–7197.
Assessment and Training.—Catherine A. Leyser, (312) 751–4757, fax 751–7190.
Equal Opportunity.—Lynn E. Cousins, (312) 751–4925, fax 751–7179.
Field Service.—Martha Barringer, (312) 751–4515, fax 751–3360.
Fiscal Operations.—Peter A. Larson, (312) 751–4590, fax 751–7171.
Hearings and Appeals.—Tom Sadler, (312) 751–4513, 751–7159.
Human Resources.—Keith Earley, (312) 751–4392, fax 751–7164.
Legislative Affairs.—Margaret S. Lindsley, (202) 272–7742, fax 272–7728.
Operations.—Robert J. Duda, (312) 751–4698, fax 751–7157.
Policy and Systems.—Ronald Russo, (312) 751–4984, fax 751–4650.
Programs.—Dorothy Isherwood, (312) 751–4980, fax 751–4333.
Public Affairs.—William O. Poulos, (312) 751–4777, fax 751–7154.
Resource Management Center.—Cecelia A. Freeman, (312) 751–4392, fax 751–7161.
Supply and Service.—Henry Valiulis, (312) 751–4565, fax 751–4923.
Chief Actuary.—Frank Buzzi, (312) 751–4915, fax 751–7129.
Chief, Benefit and Employment Analysis.—Marla Huddleston, (312) 751–4779, fax 751–7129.
Chief Financial Officer.—Kenneth P. Boehne, (312) 751–4930, fax 751–4931.
Supervisor, Quality Assurance.—Beatrice Sutter, (312) 751–4358, fax 751–3322.
Information Services—
Chief Information Officer.—Kenneth Zoll, (312) 751–7191; 751–7169.

REGIONAL OFFICES

Atlanta: Patricia R. Lawson, Suite 1703, 401 West Peachtree Street, Atlanta, GA 30308, (404) 331–2691, fax (404) 331–7234.
Denver: Louis E. Austin, Suite 3300, 1999 Broadway, Box 7, Denver, CO 80202, (303) 844–0800, fax (303) 844–0806.
Philadelphia: Richard D. Baird, 900 Market Street, Suite 304, Philadelphia, PA 19107, (215) 597–2647, fax (215) 597–2794.

U.S. SENTENCING COMMISSION

One Columbus Circle NE, Suite 2–500, South Lobby, 20002–8002

phone (202) 502–4500, fax (202) 502–4699

Chair.—Diana E. Murphy.
Vice Chairs:
Ruben Castillo, William K. Sessions III, John R. Steer.
Commissioner.—Michael E. O'Neill.
Commissioners, ex officio: Eric H. Jaso, Edward F. Reilly, Jr.
Staff Director.—Timothy B. McGrath, 502–4510.
Counsel/Executive Assistant to the Chair.—Frances Cook.
General Counsel.—Charles R. Tetzlaff, 502–4520.
Director of:
Administration.—Susan L. Winarsky, 502–4610.
Policy Analysis.—Louis W. Reedt (acting), 502–4530.
Monitoring.—J. Deon Haynes (acting), 502–4620.
Director and Chief Counsel of Office of Training.—Pamela G. Montgomery, 502–4540.
Special Counsel.—Judith M. Sheon, 502–4666.
Public Affairs Officer.—Michael Courlander, 502–4627.
Director of Legislative and Governmental Affairs.—Kenneth P. Cohen, 502–4627.
Public Information: 502–4590.
Publications Request Line: 502–4568.
Guideline Application Assistance HelpLine: 502–4545.

WASHINGTON METROPOLITAN AREA TRANSIT AUTHORITY

600 Fifth Street, NW., 20001, phone (202) 637–1234

CEO/General Manager.—Richard A. White.
Deputy General Manager for Operations.—James T. Gallagher.
General Counsel.—Cheryl C. Burke.
Chief of Staff/Secretary.—Harold M. Bartlett.
Chief Operation Officer for—
Bus Service.—Jack Requa.
Rail Service.—Lemuel M. Proctor.
Assistant General Manager for—
Capital Projects Management.—P. Takis Salpeas.
Communications.—Leona Agouridis.
System Safety and Risk Protection.—Frederick C. Goodine.
Workforce Development and Diversity Program.—William F. Scott.
Planning and Strategic Programs.—Edward L. Thomas.
Chief of:
Finances.—Peter Benjamin.
Transit Police Department.—Polly Hanson.
Director, Office of:
Intergovernmental Relations.—Deborah S. Lipman.
Media Relations.—Raymond Feldmann.

WASHINGTON NATIONAL MONUMENT SOCIETY

900 Ohio Drive, SW., Washington, DC 20024–2000, phone (202) 485–9683

[Organized 1833; chartered 1859; amended by Acts of August 2, 1876, October, 1888]

President Ex Officio.—George W. Bush, President of the United States.
Vice Presidents Ex Officio.—The Governors of the several States.
First Vice President.—James W. Symington, 1666 K Street, NW., Suite 500, Washington, DC 20006–2107, (202) 778–2107.
Second Vice President.—[Vacant].
Treasurer.—Henry Ravenel, Jr.
Secretary.—Fran Mainella, National Park Service, Department of the Interior.
Assistant Secretary.—Arnold Goldstein.
Members:
Christopher Addison
Vincent C. Burke, Jr.
Robert W. Duemling
Gilbert M. Grosvenor
Mrs. Potter Stewart
Richard P. Williams
C. Boyden Gray
George B. Hartzog, Jr.
John D.H. Kane
John A. Washington
Member Emeritus:
Harry F. Byrd, Jr.

WOODROW WILSON INTERNATIONAL CENTER FOR SCHOLARS

One Woodrow Wilson Plaza, phone 691–4000, fax 691–4001

1300 Pennsylvania Avenue NW., Washington, DC 20004–3027

(Under the direction of the Board of Trustees of Woodrow Wilson International Center for Scholars)

Director.—Lee H. Hamilton, 691–4202.
Deputy Director.—Michael Van Dusen, 691–4055.
Deputy Director for Planning and Management.—[Vacant].
Board of Trustees:
Chairman.—Joseph B. Gildenhorn.
Vice Chairman.—David A. Metzner.

Public Members:

Colin L. Powell, Secretary of State.
Roderick R. Paige, Secretary of Education.
Tommy G. Thompson, Secretary of Health and Human Services.
Bruce Cole, Chairman of the National Endowment for the Humanities.
Lawrence M. Small, Secretary of the Smithsonian Institution.
James H. Billington, Librarian of Congress.
John W. Carlin, Archivist of the United States.

Private Members:

Joseph A. Cari, Jr.
Carol Cartwright
Donald A. Garcia
Bruce S. Gelb
Daniel L. Lamaute
Tamala L. Longaberger
Thomas R. Reedy

JUDICIARY

SUPREME COURT OF THE UNITED STATES

One First Street NE 20543, phone 479–3000

WILLIAM HUBBS REHNQUIST, Chief Justice of the United States; born in Milwaukee, WI, October 1, 1924; son of William Benjamin and Margery Peck Rehnquist; married to Natalie Cornell of San Diego, CA; children: James, Janet, and Nancy, member of Faith Lutheran Church, Arlington, VA; served in the U.S. Army Air Corps in this country and overseas from 1943–46; discharged with the rank of sergeant; Stanford University, B.A., M.A., 1948; Harvard University, M.A., 1950; Stanford University, LL.B., 1952, ranking first in class; Order of the Coif; member of the Board of Editors of the Stanford Law Review; law clerk for Justice Robert H. Jackson, Supreme Court of the United States, 1952–53; private practice of law, Phoenix, AZ, 1953–69; engaged in a general practice of law with primary emphasis on civil litigation; appointed Assistant Attorney General, Office of Legal Counsel, by President Nixon in January 1969; nominated Associate Justice of the Supreme Court of the United States by President Nixon on October 21, 1971, confirmed December 10, 1971, sworn in on January 7, 1972; nominated by President Reagan as Chief Justice of the United States on June 17, 1986; sworn in on September 26, 1986.

JOHN PAUL STEVENS, Associate Justice of the Supreme Court of the United States; born in Chicago, IL, April 20, 1920; son of Ernest James and Elizabeth Street Stevens; A.B., University of Chicago, 1941, Phi Beta Kappa, Psi Upsilon; J.D. (*magna cum laude*), Northwestern University, 1947, Order of the Coif, Phi Delta Phi, co-editor, Illinois Law Review; married to Maryan Mulholland; children: John Joseph, Kathryn Jedlicka, Elizabeth Jane Sesemann, and Susan Roberta Mullen; entered active duty U.S. Navy in 1942, released as Lt. Commander in 1945 after WW II service, Bronz Star; law clerk to U.S. Supreme Court Justice Wiley Rutledge, 1947–48; admitted to Illinois bar, 1949; practiced law in Chicago, Poppenhusen, Johnston, Thompson and Raymond, 1949–52; associate counsel, Subcommittee on the Study of Monopoly Power, Judiciary Committee of the U.S. House of Representatives, 1951–52; partner, Rothschild, Stevens, Barry and Myers, Chicago, 1952–70; member of the Attorney General's National Committee to Study Antitrust Laws, 1953–55; lecturer in Antitrust Law, Northwestern University School of Law, 1950–54, and University of Chicago Law School, 1955–58; chief counsel, Illinois Supreme Court Special Commission to Investigate Integrity of the Judgment of *People* v. *Isaacs*, 1969; appointed U.S. Circuit Judge for the Seventh Circuit, October 14, 1970, entering on duty November 2, 1970, and serving until becoming an Associate Justice of the Supreme Court; nominated to the Supreme Court December 1, 1975, by President Ford; confirmed by the Senate December 17, 1975; sworn in on December 19, 1975.

SANDRA DAY O'CONNOR, Associate Justice of the Supreme Court of the United States; born in El Paso, TX, March 26, 1930; daughter of Harry A. and Ada Mae Wilkey Day; A.B. (with great distinction), Stanford University, 1950; LL.B., Stanford Law School, 1952; Order of the Coif, Board of Editors, Stanford Law Review; married to John Jay O'Connor III, 1952; children: Scott, Brian, and Jay; deputy county attorney, San Mateo County, CA, 1952–53; civilian attorney for Quartermaster Market Center, Frankfurt, Germany, 1954–57; private practice of law in Maryvale, AZ, 1958–60; assistant attorney general, Arizona, 1965–69; elected to the Arizona State senate, 1969–75; senate majority leader, 1974 and 1975; chairman of the State, County, and Municipal Affairs Committee in 1972 and 1973; also served on the Legislative Council, on the Probate Code Commission, and on the Arizona Advisory Council on Intergovernmental Relations; elected judge of the Maricopa County Superior Court, Phoenix, AZ, 1975–79; appointed to the Arizona Court of Appeals by Gov. Bruce Babbitt, 1979–81; nominated by President Reagan as Associate Justice of the U.S.

Supreme Court on July 7, 1981; confirmed by the U.S. Senate on September 22, 1981; and sworn in on September 25, 1981; member, National Board of Smithsonian Associates, 1981–present; president, board of trustees, The Heard Museum, 1968–74, 1976–81; member: Salvation Army Advisory Board, 1975–81, board of trustees, Stanford University, 1976–81, Board of Colonial Williamsburg Foundation, 1988 to present.

ANTONIN SCALIA, Associate Justice of the Supreme Court of the United States; born in Trenton, NJ, March 11, 1936; LL.B., Harvard Law School, 1960; note editor, Harvard Law Review; Sheldon fellow, Harvard University, 1960–61; married to Maureen McCarthy, September 10, 1960; children: Ann Forrest; Eugene, John Francis, Catherine Elisabeth, Mary Clare, Paul David, Matthew, Christopher James, and Margaret Jane; admitted to practice in Ohio (1962) and Virginia (1970); in private practice with Jones, Day, Cockley, and Reavis (Cleveland, OH), 1961–67; professor of law, University of Virginia Law School, 1967–74 (on leave 1971–74); general counsel, Office of Telecommunications Policy, Executive Office of the President, 1971–72; chairman, Administrative Conference of the United States, 1972–74; Assistant Attorney General, Office of Legal Counsel, U.S. Department of Justice, 1974–77; scholar in residence, American Enterprise Institute, 1977; professor of law, University of Chicago, 1977–82; appointed by President Reagan as Circuit Judge of the U.S. Court of Appeals for the District of Columbia Circuit; sworn in on August 17, 1982; appointed by President Reagan as Associate Justice of the U.S. Supreme Court; sworn in on September 26, 1986.

ANTHONY M. KENNEDY, Associate Justice of the Supreme Court of the United States; born in Sacramento, CA, July 23, 1936; son of Anthony James and Gladys McLeod Kennedy; married to Mary Davis, June 29, 1963; children: Justin Anthony, Gregory Davis, and Kristin Marie; Stanford University, 1954–57; London School of Economics, 1957–58; B.A., Stanford University, 1958; LL.B., Harvard Law School, 1961; associate, Thelen, Marrin, Johnson and Bridges, San Francisco, 1961–63; sole practitioner, Sacramento, 1963–67; partner, Evans, Jackson and Kennedy, Sacramento, 1967–75; professor of constitutional law, McGeorge School of Law, University of the Pacific, 1965–88; California Army National Guard, 1961; member: the Judicial Conference of the United States' Advisory Panel on Financial Disclosure Reports and Judicial Activities (subsequently renamed the Advisory Committee of Codes of Conduct), 1979–87; Committee on Pacific Territories, 1979–90 (chairman, 1982–90); board of the Federal Judicial Center, 1987–88; nominated by President Ford to U.S. Court of Appeals for the Ninth Circuit; sworn in on May 30, 1975; nominated by President Reagan as Associate Justice of the U.S. Supreme Court; sworn in on February 18, 1988.

DAVID HACKETT SOUTER, Associate Justice of the Supreme Court of the United States; born in Melrose, MA, September 17, 1939; son of Joseph Alexander and Helen Adams Hackett Souter; Harvard College, A.B., 1961, Phi Beta Kappa, selected Rhodes Scholar; Magdalen College, Oxford, 1963, A.B. in Jurisprudence, 1989, M.A., 1989; Harvard Law School, LL.B., 1966; associate, Orr and Reno, Concord, NH, 1966–68; assistant attorney general of New Hampshire, 1968–71; Deputy Attorney General of New Hampshire, 1971–76; Attorney General of New Hampshire, 1976–78; Associate Justice, New Hampshire Superior Court, 1978–83; Associate Justice, New Hampshire Supreme Court, 1983–90; member: Maine-New Hampshire Interstate Boundary Commission, 1971–75; New Hampshire Police Standards and Training Council, 1976–78; New Hampshire Governor's Commission on Crime and Delinquency, 1976–78; 1979–83; New Hampshire Judicial Council, 1976–78; Concord Hospital Board of Trustees, 1972–85 (president, 1978–84); New Hampshire Historical Society, 1968–present, (vice-president, 1980–85, trustee, 1976–85); Dartmouth Medical School, Board of Overseers, 1981–87; Merrimack County Bar Association, 1966–present; New Hampshire Bar Association, 1966–present; Honorary Fellow, American Bar Foundation; Honorary Fellow, American College of Trial Lawyers; Honorary Master of the Bench, Gray's Inn, London; Honorary Fellow, Magdalen College, Oxford; Associate, Lowell House, Harvard College; nominated by President Bush to U.S. Court of Appeals for the First Circuit; took oath May 25, 1990; nominated by President Bush as Associate Justice of the U.S. Supreme Court; took oath of office October 9, 1990.

CLARENCE THOMAS, Associate Justice of the Supreme Court of the United States; born in Pin Point, GA (near Savannah), June 23, 1948; son of M.C. and Leola Thomas; raised by his grandparents, Myers and Christine Anderson; married to Virginia Lamp, May 30, 1987; son Jamal Adeen by previous marriage; attended Conception Seminary, 1967–68; A.B. (*cum laude*), Holy Cross College, 1971; J.D., Yale Law School, 1974; admitted to practice in Missouri, 1974; assistant attorney general of Missouri, 1974–77; attorney in the law department of Monsanto Company, 1977–79; legislative assistant to Senator John Danforth, 1979–81; Assistant Secretary for Civil Rights, U.S. Department of Education, 1981–82; chairman, U.S. Equal Employment Opportunity Commission, 1982–90; nominated by President Bush to U.S. Court of Appeals for the District of Columbia Circuit; took oath March 12, 1990; nominated by President Bush as Associate Justice of the U.S. Supreme Court; took the constitutional oath on October 18, 1991 and the judicial oath on October 23, 1991.

RUTH BADER GINSBURG, Associate Justice of the Supreme Court of the United States; born March 15, 1933, Brooklyn, N.Y., the daughter of Nathan and Celia Amster Bader; married Martin Ginsburg, 1954; two children: Jane C. and James S.; B.A., Phi Beta Kappa, Cornell University, 1954; attended Harvard Law School, 1956–58; LL.B., Columbia Law School, 1959; law clerk to Edmund L. Palmieri, U.S. District Court, Southern District of New York, 1959–61; Columbia Law School Project on International Procedure, 1961–62, associate director, 1962–63; professor, Rutgers University School of Law, 1963–72; professor, Columbia Law School, 1972–80; Fellow, Center for Advanced Study in Behavioral Sciences, 1977–78; American Civil Liberties Union, general counsel, 1973–80; National Board of Directors, 1974–80; Women's Rights Project, founder and Counsel, 1972–80; American Bar Foundation Board of Directors, executive committee, secretary, 1979–89; American Bar Association Board of Editors, 1972–78; ABA Section on Individual Rights and Responsibilities, council member, 1975–81; American Law Institute, council member, 1978–93; American Academy of Arts and Sciences, Fellow, 1982–present; Council on Foreign Relations, 1975–present; nominated by President Carter as a Judge, U.S. Court of Appeals for the District of Columbia Circuit, sworn in on June 30, 1980; nominated Associate Justice by President Clinton, June 14, 1993, confirmed by the Senate, August 3, 1993, and sworn in August 10, 1993.

STEPHEN G. BREYER, Associate Justice of the Supreme Court of the United States; born in San Francisco, CA, August 15, 1938; son of Irving G. and Anne R. Breyer; married Joanna Hare, 1967, three children: Chloe, Nell, and Michael; A.B., Stanford University, 1959; B.A., Oxford University, Magdalen College, Marshall Scholar, 1961; LL.B., Harvard Law School, 1964; law clerk to Associate Justice Arthur J. Goldberg of the Supreme Court of the United States, 1964–65; special assistant to the Assistant Attorney General (Antitrust), Department of Justice, 1965–67; Assistant Special Prosecutor of the Watergate Special Prosecution Force, 1973; Special Counsel of the U.S. Senate Judiciary Committee, Subcommittee on Administrative Practices, 1974–75; Chief Counsel of the U.S. Senate Judiciary Committee, 1979–80; Professor of Law, Harvard Law School, 1970–80; (assistant professor, 1967–70; lecturer, 1980–94); professor, Kennedy School of Government, Harvard University, 1977–80; Nominated by President Carter as a Judge, U.S. Court of Appeals for the First Circuit, sworn in on December 10, 1980; Chief Judge, 1990–94; member, U.S. Sentencing Commission, 1985–89; member, Judicial Conference of the United States, 1990–94; nominated Associate Justice by President Clinton May 13, 1994, confirmed by the Senate July 29, 1994, and sworn in on August 3, 1994.

Officers of the Supreme Court

Clerk.—William K. Suter.
Librarian.—Judith Gaskell.
Marshal.—Pamela Talkin.
Reporter of Decisions.—Frank D. Wagner.
Counsel.—Scott Harris.
Curator.—Catherine Fitts.
Budget and Personnel Officer.—Cyril A. Donnelly.
Public Information Officer.—Kathleen L. Arberg.
Director of Data Systems.—Donna Clement.
Administrative Assistant to the Chief Justice.—Sally M. Rider.

UNITED STATES COURTS OF APPEALS

First Judicial Circuit (Districts of Maine, Massachusetts, New Hampshire, Puerto Rico, and Rhode Island).—*Chief Judge:* Michael Boudin. *Circuit Judges:* Juan R. Torruella; Bruce M. Selya; Sandra L. Lynch; Kermit V. Lipez; Jeffrey R. Howard. *Senior Circuit Judges:* Frank M. Coffin; Levin H. Campbell; Hugh H. Bownes; Conrad K. Cyr; Norman H. Stahl. *Circuit Executive:* Gary H. Wente, (617) 748–9613. *Clerk:* Richard C. Donovan, (617) 748–9057, John Joseph Moakley U.S. Courthouse, One Courthouse Way, Suite 2500, Boston, MA 02210.

Second Judicial Circuit (Districts of Connecticut, New York, and Vermont).—*Chief Judge:* John M. Walker, Jr. *Circuit Judges:* Dennis Jacobs; Guido Calabresi; José A. Cabranes; Fred I. Parker; Rosemary S. Pooler; Chester J. Straub; Robert D. Sack; Sonia Sotomayor; Robert Allen Katzmann; Barrington D. Parker, Jr.; Reena Raggi. *Senior Circuit Judges:* Wilfred Feinberg; James L. Oakes; Ellsworth A. Van Graafeiland; Thomas J. Meskill; Jon O. Newman; Richard J. Cardamone; Ralph K. Winter; Roger J. Miner; Joseph M. McLaughlin; Amalya L. Kearse; Pierre N. Leval. *Circuit Executive:* Karen Greve Milton, (212) 857–8700. *Clerk:* Roseann B. MacKechnie, (212) 857–8500, U.S. Courthouse, 40 Foley Square, New York, NY 10007–1581.

Third Judicial Circuit (Districts of Delaware, New Jersey, Pennsylvania, and Virgin Islands).—*Chief Judge:* Anthony J. Scirica. *Circuit Judges:* Dolores K. Sloviter; Richard L. Nygaard; Samuel H. Alito, Jr.; Jane R. Roth; Theodore A. McKee; Marjorie O. Rendell; Maryanne Trump Barry; Thomas L. Ambro; Julio M. Fuentes; D. Brooks Smith; Michael Chertoff. *Senior Circuit Judges:* Ruggero J. Aldisert; Max Rosenn; Joseph F. Weis, Jr.; Leonard I. Garth; Edward R. Becker; Walter K Stapleton; Morton I. Greenberg; Robert E. Cowen. *Circuit Executive:* Toby D. Slawsky, (215) 597–0718. *Clerk:* Marcia M. Waldron, (215) 597–2995, U.S. Courthouse, 601 Market Street, Philadelphia, PA 19106.

Fourth Judicial Circuit (Districts of Maryland, North Carolina, South Carolina, Virginia, and West Virginia).—*Chief Judge:* William W. Wilkin. *Circuit Judges:* H. Emory Widener, Jr.; Paul V. Niemeyer; J. Harvie Wilkinson III; J. Michael Luttig; Karen J. Williams; M. Blane Michael; Diana Gribbon Motz; William B. Traxler, Jr.; Robert B. King; Roger L. Gregory; Dennis W. Shedd. *Senior Circuit Judges:* Clyde H. Hamilton. *Circuit Executive:* Samuel W. Phillips, (804) 916–2184. *Clerk:* Patricia S. Connor, (804) 916–2700, Lewis F. Powell, Jr., U.S. Courthouse Annex, 1100 E. Main Street, Richmond, VA 23219.

Fifth Judicial Circuit (Districts of Louisiana, Mississippi, and Texas).—*Chief Judge:* Carolyn Dineen King. *Circuit Judges:* E. Grady Jolly; Patrick E. Higginbotham; W. Eugene Davis; Edith H. Jones; Jerry E. Smith; Jacques L. Wiener, Jr.; Rhesa H. Barksdale; Emilio M. Garza; Harold R. DeMoss, Jr.; Fortunato P. Benavides; Carl E. Stewart; James L. Dennis; Edith Brown Clement. *Senior Circuit Judges:* Reynaldo G. Garza; Thomas M. Reavley; Will Garwood; John M. Duhé, Jr. *Circuit Executive:* Gregory A. Nussel, (504) 310–7777. *Clerk:* Charles R. Fulbruge III, (504) 310–7700, John Minor Wisdom, U.S. Court of Appeals Building, 600 Camp Street, New Orleans, LA 70130–3425.

Sixth Judicial Circuit (Districts of Kentucky, Michigan, Ohio, and Tennessee).—*Chief Judge:* Boyce F. Martin, Jr. *Circuit Judges:* Danny J. Boggs; Alice M. Batchelder; Martha Craig Daughtrey; Karen Nelson Moore; R. Guy Cole, Jr.; Eric Lee Clay; Ronald Lee Gilman; Julie Smith Gibbons; John M. Rogers. *Senior Circuit Judges:* Albert J. Engel; Damon J. Keith; Cornelia G. Kennedy; Nathaniel R. Jones; Robert B. Krupansky; Harry W. Wellford; Ralph B. Guy, Jr.; David A. Nelson; James L. Ryan; Gilbert S. Merritt; Alan E. Norris; Richard F. Suhrheinrich; Eugene E. Siler, Jr. *Circuit Executive:* James A. Higgins, (513) 564–7200. *Clerk:* Leonard Green, (513) 564–7000, Potter Stewart U.S. Courthouse, 100 E. Fifth Street, Cincinnati, OH 45202.

Seventh Judicial Circuit (Districts of Illinois, Indiana, and Wisconsin).—*Chief Judge:* Joel M. Flaum. *Circuit Judges:* Richard A. Posner; John L. Coffey; Frank H. Easterbrook; Kenneth F. Ripple; Daniel A. Manion; Michael S. Kanne; Ilana Diamond Rovner; Diane P. Wood; Terence T. Evans; Ann Claire Williams. *Senior Circuit Judges:* Thomas E.

Fairchild; William J. Bauer; Richard D. Cudahy; Harlington Wood. *Circuit Executive:* Collins T. Fitzpatrick, (312) 435–5803. *Clerk:* Gino J. Agnello, (312) 435–5850, 2722 U.S. Courthouse, 219 S. Dearborn Street, Chicago, IL 60604.

Eighth Judicial Circuit (Districts of Arkansas, Iowa, Minnesota, Missouri, Nebraska, North Dakota, and South Dakota).—*Chief Judge:* James B. Loken. *Circuit Judges:* Theodore McMillian; Pasco M. Bowman II; Roger L. Wollman; Morris S. Arnold; Diana E. Murphy; Kermit E. Bye; William Jay Riley; Michael J. Melloy; Lavenski R. Smith. *Senior Circuit Judges:* Donald P. Lay; Gerald W. Heaney; Myron H. Bright; Richard S. Arnold; John R. Gibson; George G. Fagg; Frank J. Magill; C. Arlen Beam; David R. Hansen. *Circuit Executive:* Millie Adams, (314) 244–2600. *Clerk:* Michael E. Gans, (314) 244–2400, 111 S. Tenth Street, Suite 24.327, St. Louis, MO 63102.

Ninth Judicial Circuit (Districts of Alaska, Arizona, Central California, Eastern California, Northern California, Southern California, Guam, Hawaii, Idaho, Montana, Nevada, Northern Mariana Islands, Oregon, Eastern Washington and Western Washington).—*Chief Judge:* Mary M. Schroeder. *Circuit Judges:* Harry Pregerson; Stephen Reinhardt; Alex Kozinski; Diarmuid F. O'Scannlain; Stephen S. Trott; Pamela Ann Rymer; Thomas G. Nelson; Andrew J. Kleinfeld; Michael Daly Hawkins; A. Wallace Tashima; Sidney R. Thomas; Barry G. Silverman; Susan P. Graber; M. Margaret McKeown; Kim McLane Wardlaw; William A. Fletcher; Raymond C. Fisher; Ronald M. Gould; Richard A. Paez; Marsha S. Berzon; Richard C. Tallman; Johnnie B. Rawlinson; Richard R. Clifton; Jay S. Bybee. *Senior Circuit Judges:* James R. Browning; Herbert Y.C. Choy; Alfred T. Goodwin; J. Clifford Wallace; Joseph Tyree Sneed III; Procter Hug, Jr.; Otto R. Skopil, Jr.; Betty Binns Fletcher; Jerome Farris; Authur L. Alarcon; Warren J. Ferguson; Dorothy W. Nelson; William C. Canby, Jr.; Robert Boochever; Robert R. Beezer; Cynthia Holcomb Hall; Melvin Brunetti; John T. Noonan, Jr.; David R. Thompson; Edward Leavy; Ferdinand F. Fernandez. *Circuit Executive:* Gregory B. Walters, (415) 556–6162. *Clerk:* Cathy A. Catterson, (415) 556–9890, P.O. Box 193939, San Francisco, CA 94119–3939.

Tenth Judicial Circuit (Districts of Colorado, Kansas, New Mexico, Oklahoma, Utah, and Wyoming).—*Chief Judge:* Deanell R. Tacha. *Circuit Judges:* Stephanie K. Seymour; David M. Ebel; Paul J. Kelly, Jr.; Robert H. Henry; Mary Beck Briscoe; Carlos F. Lucero; Michael R. Murphy; Harris L. Hartz; Terrence L. O'Brien; Michael W. McConnell; Timothy Tymkovich. *Senior Circuit Judges:* William J. Holloway, Jr.; Robert H. McWilliams; James E. Barrett; Monroe G. McKay; John C. Porfilio; Stephen H. Anderson; Bobby R. Baldock; Wade Brorby. *Circuit Executive:* Elisabeth Shumaker, (303) 844–2067. *Clerk:* Patrick J. Fisher, (303) 844–3157, Byron White Courthouse, 1823 Stout Street, Denver, CO 80257.

Eleventh Judicial Circuit (Districts of Alabama, Florida, and Georgia).—*Chief Judge:* J.L. Edmondson. *Circuit Judges:* Gerald Bard Tjoflat; R. Lanier Anderson III; Stanley F. Birch, Jr.; Joel F. Dubina; Susan Harrell Black; Edward E. Carnes; Rosemary Barkett; Frank Mays Hull; Stanley Marcus; Charles Reginald Wilson. *Senior Circuit Judges:* John C. Godbold; Paul H. Roney; James C. Hill; Peter T. Fay; Phyllis A. Kravitch; Emmett Ripley Cox. *Circuit Executive:* Norman E. Zoller, (404) 335–6535. *Clerk:* Thomas K. Kahn, (404) 335–6100, 56 Forsyth Street NW., Atlanta, GA 30303.

UNITED STATES COURT OF APPEALS

FOR THE DISTRICT OF COLUMBIA CIRCUIT

333 Constitution Avenue 20001, phone 216–7300

DOUGLAS HOWARD GINSBURG, chief judge; born in Chicago, IL, May 25, 1946; son of Maurice and Katherine (Goodmont) Ginsburg; married to Claudia DeSecundy, May 31, 1968 (divorced); one child, Jessica J.E. Lubow; married to Hallee Perkins Morgan, May 9, 1981; children, Hallee Katherine Morgan and Hannah Maurice Morgan; education: diploma, Latin School of Chicago, 1963; B.S., Cornell University, 1970 (Phi Kappa Phi, Ives Award); J.D., University of Chicago, 1973 (Mecham Prize Scholarship 1970–73, Casper Platt Award, 1972, Order of Coif, Articles and Book Rev. Ed., 40 U. Chi. L. Rev.); bar admissions: Illinois (1973), Massachusetts (1982), U.S. Supreme Court (1984), U.S. Court of Appeals for the Ninth Circuit (1986). Member: Mont Pelerin Society, American Economic Association, Executive Council of Antitrust Section of the American Bar Association (ex officio, 1985–86 and 2000–03); law clerk to: Judge Carl McGowan, U.S. Court of Appeals for the District of Columbia Circuit, 1973–74; Associate Justice Thurgood Marshall, U.S. Supreme Court, 1974–75; previous positions: assistant professor, Harvard University Law School, 1975–81; Professor 1981–83; Deputy Assistant Attorney General for Regulatory Affairs, Antitrust Division, U.S. Department of Justice, 1983–84; Administrator for Information and Regulatory Affairs, Executive Office of the President, Office of Management and Budget, 1984–85; Assistant Attorney General, Antitrust Division, U.S. Department of Justice, 1985–86; visiting professor of law, Columbia University, New York City, 1987–88; lecturer in law, Harvard University, Cambridge, MA, 1987–90; foundation professor of law, George Mason University, Arlington, VA, 1988–; Charles J. Merriam visiting scholar, senior lecturer, University of Chicago Law School, 1990, 1992, 1994, 1996, 1998, and 2000. Appointed to U.S. Court of Appeals for the District of Columbia Circuit by President Ronald Reagan on October 14, 1986, taking the oath of office on November 10, 1986.

HARRY T. EDWARDS, circuit judge; born in New York, NY, November 3, 1940; son of George H. Edwards and Arline (Ross) Lyle; B.S., Cornell University, 1962; J.D. (with distinction), University of Michigan Law School, 1965; associate with Seyfarth, Shaw, Fairweather and Geraldson, 1965–70; professor of law, University of Michigan, 1970–75 and 1977–80; professor of law, Harvard University, 1975–77; visiting professor of law, Free University of Brussels, 1974; arbitrator of labor / management disputes, 1970–80; vice president, National Academy of Arbitrators, 1978–80; member (1977–79) and chairman (1979–80), National Railroad Passenger Corporation (Amtrak); Executive Committee of the Association of American Law Schools, 1979–80; public member of the Administrative Conference of the United States, 1976–80; International Women's Year Commission, 1976–77; American Bar Association Commission of Law and the Economy; coauthor of four books: *Labor Relations Law in the Public Sector, The Lawyer as a Negotiator, Higher Education and the Law*, and *Collective Bargaining and Labor Arbitration*; recipient of the Judge William B. Groat Alumni Award, 1978, given by Cornell University; the Society of American Law Teachers Award (for "distinguished contributions to teaching and public service"); the Whitney North Seymour Medal presented by the American Arbitration Association for outstanding contributions to the use of arbitration; and several Honorary Doctor of Laws degrees. Judge Edwards teaches law on a part-time basis; he has recently taught at Duke, Georgetown, Michigan, and Harvard Law Schools, and he is presently teaching a course in Federal Courts at N.Y.U.; A.B.A.; married to Pamela Carrington Edwards; children: Brent and Michelle; appointed to the U.S. Court of Appeals, February 20, 1980; served as chief judge September 15, 1994 to July 16, 2000; office: 5400 U.S. Courthouse, Washington, DC 20001.

DAVID BRYAN SENTELLE, circuit judge, U.S. Court of Appeals (District of Columbia Circuit); 273–0348; born in Canton, NC, February 12, 1943; son of Horace and Maude Sentelle; B.A., University of North Carolina at Chapel Hill, 1965; J.D. with honors, University of North Carolina School of Law, 1968; associate, Uzzell and Dumont, Charlotte, 1968–79; Assistant U.S. Attorney, Charlotte, 1970–74; North Carolina State District Judge,

1974–77; partner, Tucker, Hicks, Sentelle, Moon and Hodge, Charlotte, 1977–85; U.S. District Judge for the Western District of North Carolina, 1985–87; married to Jane LaRue Oldham; daughters: Sharon, Reagan, and Rebecca.

KAREN LECRAFT HENDERSON, circuit judge. [Biographical information not supplied, per Judge Henderson's request.]

A. RAYMOND RANDOLPH, circuit judge; born in Riverside, NJ, November 1, 1943; son of Arthur Raymond Randolph, Sr. and Marile (Kelly); two children: John Trevor and Cynthia Lee Randolph; married to Eileen Janette O'Connor, May 18, 1984. B.S., Drexel University, 1966; J.D., University of Pennsylvania Law School, 1969, *summa cum laude;* managing editor, University of Pennsylvania Law Review; Order of the Coif. Admitted to Supreme Court of the United States; Supreme Court of California; District of Columbia Court of Appeals; U.S. Courts of Appeals for the First, Second, Fourth, Fifth, Sixth, Seventh, Ninth, Eleventh, and District of Columbia Circuits. Memberships: American Law Institute. Law clerk to Judge Henry J. Friendly, U.S. Court of Appeals for the Second Circuit, 1969–70; Assistant to the Solicitor General, 1970–73; adjunct professor of law, Georgetown University Law Center, 1974–78; George Mason School of Law, 1992; Deputy Solicitor General, 1975–77; Special Counsel, Committee on Standards of Official Conduct, House of Representatives, 1979–80; special assistant attorney general, State of Montana (honorary), 1983–July 1990; special assistant attorney general, State of New Mexico, 1985–July 1990; special assistant attorney general, State of Utah, 1986–July 1990; advisory panel, Federal Courts Study Committee, 1989–July 1990; partner, Pepper, Hamilton and Scheetz, 1987–July 1990; appointed to the U.S. Court of Appeals for the District of Columbia Circuit by President George W. Bush on July 16, 1990, and took oath of office on July 20, 1990; chairman, Committee on Codes of Conduct, U.S. Judicial Conference, 1995–98; distinguished professor of law, George Mason Law School, 1999–present; recipient, Distinguished Alumnus Award, University of Pennsylvania Law School, 2002.

JUDITH W. ROGERS, circuit judge; born in New York, NY; A.B. (with honors), Radcliffe College, 1961; Phi Beta Kappa honors member; LL.B., Harvard Law School, 1964; LL.M., University of Virginia School of Law, 1988; law clerk, D.C. Juvenile Court, 1964–65; assistant U.S. Attorney for the District of Columbia, 1965–68; trial attorney, San Francisco Neighborhood Legal Assistance Foundation, 1968–69; Attorney, U.S. Department of Justice, Office of the Associate Deputy Attorney General and Criminal Division, 1969–71; general counsel, Congressional Commission on the Organization of the D.C. Government, 1971–72; legislative assistant to D.C. Mayor Walter E. Washington, 1972–79; corporation counsel for the District of Columbia, 1979–83; trustee, Radcliffe College, 1982–90; member of Visiting Committee to Harvard Law School, 1984–90. Appointed by President Ronald W. Reagan to the District of Columbia Court of Appeals as an Associate Judge on September 15, 1983; served as chief judge, November 1, 1988 to March 18, 1994; member of Executive Committee, Conference of Chief Justices, 1993–94. Appointed by President William Jefferson Clinton to the U.S. Court of Appeals for the District of Columbia Circuit on March 11, 1994, and entered on duty March 21, 1994.

DAVID S. TATEL, circuit judge; born in Washington, DC, March 16, 1942; son of Molly and Dr. Howard Tatel; B.A., University of Michigan, 1963; J.D., University of Chicago Law School, 1966; instructor, University of Michigan Law School, 1966–67; associate, Sidley and Austin, 1967–69, 1970–72; director, Chicago Lawyers' Committee for Civil Rights Under Law, 1969–70; director, National Lawyers' Committee for Civil Rights Under Law, 1972–74; director, Office for Civil Rights, U.S. Department of Health, Education and Welfare, 1977–79; associate and partner, Hogan and Hartson, 1974–77, 1979–94; lecturer, Stanford University Law School, 1991–92; board of directors, Spencer Foundation, 1987–97 (chair, 1990–97); board of directors, National Board for Professional Teaching Standards, 1997–2000; National Lawyers' Committee for Civil Rights Under Law, co-chair, 1989–91; Carnegie Foundation for the Advancement of Teachings, Board Member, current; admitted to practice law in Illinois in 1966 and the District Columbia in 1970; married to the former Edith Bassichis, 1965; children: Rebecca, Stephanie, Joshua, and Emily; appointed to the U.S. Court of Appeals for the District of Columbia Circuit by President William Jefferson Clinton on October 7, 1994, and entered on duty October 11, 1994.

MERRICK BRIAN GARLAND, circuit judge; born in Chicago, IL, November 13, 1952; A.B., Harvard University, 1974, *summa cum laude,* phi beta kappa; J.D., Harvard Law School, 1977, *magna cum laude,* articles editor, Harvard Law Review; law clerk to Judge Henry J. Friendly, U.S. Court of Appeals for the 2d Circuit, 1977–78; law clerk to Justice William J. Brennan, Jr., U.S. Supreme Court, 1978–79; Special Assistant to the Attorney General, 1979–81; associate then partner, Arnold and Porter, Washington, D.C., 1981–89; Assistant

U.S. Attorney, Washington, D.C., 1989–92; partner, Arnold and Porter, 1992–93; Deputy Assistant Attorney General, Criminal Division, U.S. Department of Justice, 1993–94; Principal Associate Deputy Attorney General, 1994–97; Lecturer on Law, Harvard Law School, 1985–86; Associate Independent Counsel, 1987–88. Admitted to the bars of the District of Columbia; U.S. District Court; Court of Appeals, District of Columbia Circuit; U.S. Courts of Appeals for the 4th, 9th, and 10th Circuits; and U.S. Supreme Court. Author: *Antitrust and State Action*, 96 Yale Law Journal 486 (1987); *Antitrust and Federalism,* 96 Yale Law Journal 1291 (1987); *Deregulation and Judicial Review,* 98 Harvard Law Review 505 (1985). Co-Chair, Administrative Law Section, District of Columbia Bar, 1991–94; member, American Law Institute. Appointed to the U.S. Court of Appeals for the District of Columbia Circuit on March 20, 1997.

SENIOR JUDGES

LAURENCE HIRSCH SILBERMAN, circuit judge; born in York, PA, on October 12, 1935; son of William Silberman and Anna (Hirsch); married to Rosalie G. Gaull on April 28, 1957; children: Robert Stephen Silberman, Katherine DeBoer Balaban, and Anne Gaull Otis; B.A., Dartmouth College, 1957; LL.B., Harvard Law School, 1961. Admitted to Hawaii bar, 1962; District of Columbia bar, 1973; associate, Moore, Torkildson and Rice, 1961–64; partner (Moore, Silberman and Schulze), Honolulu, 1964–67; attorney, National Labor Relations Board, Office of General Counsel, Appellate Division, 1967–69; Solicitor, Department of Labor, 1969–70; Under Secretary of Labor, 1970–73; partner, Steptoe and Johnson, 1973–74; Deputy Attorney General of the United States, 1974–75; Ambassador to Yugoslavia, 1975–77; President's Special Envoy on ILO Affairs, 1976; senior fellow, American Enterprise Institute, 1977–78; visiting fellow, 1978–85; managing partner, Morrison and Foerster, 1978–79 and 1983–85; executive vice president, Crocker National Bank, 1979–83; lecturer, University of Hawaii, 1962–63; board of directors, Commission on Present Danger, 1978–85, Institute for Educational Affairs, New York, NY, 1981–85, member: General Advisory Committee on Arms Control and Disarmament, 1981–85; Defense Policy Board, 1981–85; vice chairman, State Department's Commission on Security and Economic Assistance, 1983–84; American Bar Association (Labor Law Committee, 1965–72, Corporations and Banking Committee, 1973, Law and National Security Advisory Committee, 1981–85); Hawaii Bar Association Ethics Committee, 1965–67; Council on Foreign Relations, 1977–present; Judicial Conference Committee on Court Administration and Case Management, 1994; Adjunct Professor of Law (Administrative Law) Georgetown Law Center, 1987–94; 1997, 1999–present; Adjunct Professor of Law (Labor Law), Georgetown Law Center, 2002–present; Adjunct Professor of Law (Administrative Law) New York University Law School, 1995–96; appointed to the U.S. Court of Appeals for the District of Columbia Circuit by President Ronald Reagan on October 28, 1985.

STEPHEN F. WILLIAMS, circuit judge; born in New York, NY, September 23, 1936, son of Charles Dickerman Williams and Virginia (Fain); B.A., Yale, 1958, J.D., Harvard Law School, 1961. U.S. Army reserves, 1961–62; associate, Debevoise, Plimpton, Lyons and Gates, 1962–66; Assistant U.S. Attorney, Southern District of New York, 1966–69; associate professor and professor of law, University of Colorado School of Law, 1969–86; visiting professor of law, UCLA, 1975–76; visiting professor of law and fellow in law and economics, University Chicago Law School, 1979–80; visiting George W. Hutchison Professor of Energy Law, SMU, 1983–84; consultant to: Administrative Conference of the United States, 1974–76; Federal Trade Commission on energy-related issues, 1983–85; appointed to the U.S. Court of Appeals for the District of Columbia Circuit by President Ronald Reagan, June 16, 1986; member, American Law Institute; married to Faith Morrow, 1966; children: Susan, Geoffrey, Sarah, Timothy, and Nicholas.

OFFICERS OF THE UNITED STATES COURT OF APPEALS

FOR THE DISTRICT OF COLUMBIA CIRCUIT

Circuit Executive.—Jill C. Sayenga.
Clerk.—Mark J. Langer.
Chief Deputy Clerk.—Marilyn R. Sargent.
Chief, Legal Division.—Martha Tomich.

UNITED STATES COURT OF APPEALS

FEDERAL CIRCUIT

717 Madison Place 20439, phone 633–6550

HALDANE ROBERT MAYER, chief judge; born in Buffalo, NY, February 21, 1941; son of Haldane and Myrtle Mayer; educated in the public schools of Lockport, NY; B.S., U.S. Military Academy, West Point, NY, 1963; and J.D., Marshall-Wythe School of Law, The College of William and Mary in Virginia, 1971; editor-in-chief, *William and Mary Law Review,* Omicron Delta Kappa; admitted to practice in Virginia and the District of Columbia; board of directors, William and Mary Law School Association, 1979–85; served in the U.S. Army, 1963–75, in the Infantry and the Judge Advocate General's Corps; awarded the Bronze Star Medal, Meritorious Service Medal, Army Commendation Medal with Oak Leaf Cluster, Combat Infantryman Badge, Parachutist Badge, Ranger Tab, Ranger Combat Badge, Campaign and Service Ribbons; resigned from Regular Army and was commissioned in the U.S. Army Reserve, currently Lieutenant Colonel, retired; law clerk for Judge John D. Butzner, Jr., U.S. Court of Appeals for the Fourth Circuit, 1971–72; private practice with McGuire, Woods and Battle in Charlottesville, VA, 1975–77; adjunct professor, University of Virginia School of Law, 1975–77, 1992–94, George Washington University National Law Center, 1992–96; Special Assistant to the Chief Justice of the United States, Warren E. Burger, 1977–80; private practice with Baker and McKenzie in Washington, DC, 1980–81; Deputy and Acting Special Counsel (by designation of the President), U.S. Merit Systems Protection Board, 1981–82; appointed by President Reagan to the U.S. Claims Court, 1982; appointed by President Reagan to the U.S. Court of Appeals for the Federal Circuit, June 15, 1987; assumed duties of the office, June 19, 1987; assumed position of Chief Judge on December 25, 1997; Judicial Conference of the U.S. Committee on the International Appellate Judges Conference, 1988–91, Committee on Judicial Resources, 1990–97; member of the Judicial Conference of the United States, 1997–present; married Mary Anne McCurdy, August 13, 1966; two daughters, Anne Christian and Rebecca Paige.

PAULINE NEWMAN, circuit judge; born June 20, 1927, in New York, NY; daughter of Maxwell H. and Rosella G. Newman; B.A. degree from Vassar College in 1947; M.A. in pure science from Columbia University in 1948; Ph.D. degree in chemistry from Yale University in 1952; LL.B. degree from New York University School of Law in 1958; Doctor of Laws (honorary) from Franklin Pierce School of Law in 1991; admitted to the New York bar in 1958 and to the Pennsylvania bar in 1979; worked as research scientist for the American Cyanamid Co. from 1951–54; worked for the FMC Corp. from 1954–84 as patent attorney and house counsel and, since 1969, as director of the Patent, Trademark, and Licensing Department; on leave from FMC Corp. worked for the United Nations Educational, Scientific and Cultural Organization as a science policy specialist in the Department of Natural Sciences, 1961–62; offices in scientific and professional organizations include: member of Council of the Patent, Trademark and Copyright Section of the American Bar Association, 1982–84; board of directors of the American Patent Law Association, 1981–84; vice president of the United States Trademark Association, 1978–79, and member of the board of directors, 1975–76, 1977–79; board of governors of the New York Patent Law Association, 1970–74; president of the Pacific Industrial Property Association, 1978–80; executive committee of the International Patent and Trademark Association, 1982–84; board of directors: the American Chemical Society, 1973–75, 1976–78, 1979–81; American Institute of Chemists, 1960–66, 1970–76; member: board of trustees of Philadelphia College of Pharmacy and Science, 1983–84; patent policy board of State University of New York, 1983–84; national board of Medical College of Pennsylvania, 1975–84; board of directors of Research Corp., 1982–84; governmental committees include: State Department Advisory Committee on International Intellectual Property, 1974–84; advisory committee to the Domestic Policy Review of Industrial Innovation, 1978–79; special advisory committee on Patent Office Procedure and Practice, 1972–74; member of the U.S. Delegation to the Diplomatic Conference on the Revision of the Paris Convention for the Protection of Industrial Property, 1982–84; awarded Wilbur Cross Medal of Yale University Graduate School, 1989, the Jefferson Medal of the New Jersey Intellectual Property Law Association, 1988, the Award for Outstanding Contributions in the Intellectual Property Field of the Pacific Industrial Property Association, 1987; Vanderbilt Medal of New York University School of Law, 1995; Vasser College Distinguished Achievement Award, 2002; Distinguished Professor of Law, George Mason University School of Law (adjunct faculty); Council on Foreign Relations; appointed judge of the U.S. Court of Appeals for the Federal Circuit by President Reagan and entered upon duties of that office on May 7, 1984.

PAUL R. MICHEL, circuit judge; born February 3, 1941, in Philadelphia, PA; son of Lincoln M. and Dorothy Michel; educated in public schools in Wayne and Radnor, PA; B.A., Williams College, 1963; J.D., University of Virginia Law School, 1966; married Sally Ann Clark, 1965 (divorced, 1987); children, Sarah Elizabeth and Margaret Kelley; married Dr. Elizabeth Morgan, 1989; Second Lieutenant, U.S. Army Reserve (1966–72); admitted to practice: Pennsylvania (1967), U.S. district court (1968), U.S. circuit court (1969), and U.S. Supreme Court (1969); assistant district attorney, Philadelphia, PA (1967–71); Deputy District Attorney for Investigations (1972–74); Assistant Watergate Special Prosecutor (1974–75); assistant counsel, Senate Intelligence Committee (1975–76); deputy chief, Public Integrity Section, Criminal Division, U.S. Department of Justice (1976–78); ''Koreagate'' prosecutor (1976–78); Associate Deputy Attorney General (1978–81); Acting Deputy Attorney General (Dec. 1979-Feb. 1980); counsel and administrative assistant to Senator Arlen Specter (1981–88); nominated December 19, 1987 by President Ronald Reagan to be circuit judge, U.S. Court of Appeals for the Federal Circuit, confirmed by Senate on February 29, 1988, and assumed duties of the office on March 8, 1988.

ALAN D. LOURIE, circuit judge; born January 13, 1935, in Boston, MA; son of Joseph Lourie and Rose; educated in public schools in Brookline, MA; A.B., Harvard University, (1956); M.S., University of Wisconsin, (1958); Ph.D., University of Pennsylvania, (1965); and J.D., Temple University, (1970); married to the former L. Elizabeth D. Schwartz; children, Deborah L. Rapoport and Linda S. Lourie; employed at Monsanto Company (chemist, 1957–59); Wyeth Laboratories (chemist, literature scientist, patent liaison specialist, 1959–64); SmithKline Beecham Corporation, (Patent Agent, 1964–70; assistant director, Corporate Patents, 1970–76; director, Corporate Patents, 1976–77; vice president, Corporate Patents and Trademarks and Associate General Counsel, 1977–90); vice chairman of the Industry Functional Advisory Committee on Intellectual Property Rights for Trade Policy Matters (IFAC 3) for the Department of Commerce and the Office of the U.S. Trade Representative (1987–90); Treasurer of the Association of Corporate Patent Counsel (1987–89); President of the Philadelphia Patent Law Association (1984–85); member of the board of directors of the American Intellectual Property Law Association (formerly American Patent Law Association) (1982–85); member of the U.S. delegation to the Diplomatic Conference on the Revision of the Paris Convention for the Protection of Industrial Property, October–November 1982, March 1984; chairman of the Patent Committee of the Law Section of the Pharmaceutical Manufacturers Association (1980–85); member of Judicial Conference Committee on Financial Disclosure, 1990–98; member of the American Bar Association, the American Chemical Society, the Cosmos Club, and the Harvard Club of Washington; recipient of Jefferson Medal of the New Jersey Intellectual Property Law Association for outstanding contributions to intellectual property law, 1998; admitted to: Supreme Court of Pennsylvania, U.S. District Court for the Eastern District of Pennsylvania, U.S. Court of Appeals for the Third Circuit, U.S. Court of Appeals for the Federal Circuit, U.S. Supreme Court; nominated January 25, 1990, by President George Bush to be circuit judge, U.S. Court of Appeals for the Federal Circuit, confirmed by Senate on April 5, 1990, and assumed duties of the office on April 11, 1990.

RAYMOND C. CLEVENGER, III, circuit judge; born August 27, 1937, in Topeka, KS; son of R. Charles and Mary Margaret Clevenger; educated in the public schools in Topeka, Kansas, and at Phillips Academy, Andover, MA; B.A., Yale University, 1959; LL.B., Yale University, 1966; law clerk to Justice White, October term, 1966; practice of law at Wilmer, Cutler and Pickering, Washington, DC, 1967–90. Nominated by President George Bush on January 24, 1990, confirmed on April 27, 1990 and assumed duties on May 3, 1990.

RANDALL R. RADER, circuit judge; born April 21, 1949 in Hastings, NE, son of Raymond A. and Gloria R. Rader; higher education: B.A., Brigham Young University, 1971–74, (*magna cum laude*), Phi Beta Kappa; J.D., George Washington University Law Center, 1974–78; married the former Victoria Semenyuk: legislative assistant to Representative Virginia Smith; 1978–81: legislative director, counsel, House Committee on Ways and Means to Representative

Philip M. Crane; 1981–86: General Counsel, Chief Counsel, Subcommittee on the Constitution; 1987–88, Minority Chief Counsel, Staff Director, Subcommittee on Patents, Trademarks and Copyrights, Senate Committee on Judiciary; 1988–90: Judge, U.S. Claims Court; 1990–present, Circuit Judge, U.S. Court of Appeals for the Federal Circuit, nominated by President George Bush on June 12, 1990; confirmed by Senate August 3, 1990, sworn in August 14, 1990, recipient: Outstanding Young Federal Lawyer Award by Federal Bar Association, 1983; recipient: Jefferson Medal Award 2003; bar member: District of Columbia, 1978, Supreme Court of the United States, 1984, U.S. Claims Court, 1988, U.S. Court of Appeals for the Federal Circuit, 1990.

ALVIN A. SCHALL, circuit judge; born April 4, 1944, in New York City, NY; son of Gordon W. Schall and Helen D. Schall; preparatory education: St. Paul's School, Concord, NH, 1956–62, graduated *cum laude*; higher education: B.A., Princeton University, 1962–66; J.D., Tulane Law School, 1966–69; married to the former Sharon Frances LeBlanc, children: Amanda and Anthony. 1969–73: associate with the law firm of Shearman and Sterling in New York City; 1973–78: Assistant United States Attorney, Office of the United States Attorney for the Eastern District of New York; Chief of the Appeals Division, 1977–78; 1978–87: Trial Attorney, Senior Trial Counsel, Civil Division, United States Department of Justice, Washington, DC; 1987–88: member of the Washington, DC law firm of Perlman and Partners; 1988–92: Assistant to the Attorney General of the United States; 1992–Present: Circuit Judge, United States Court of Appeals for the Federal Circuit, appointed by President George Bush on August 17, 1992, sworn in on August 19, 1992. Author: ''Federal Contract Disputes and Forums,'' Chapter 9 in Construction Litigation: Strategies and Techniques, published by John Wiley and Sons (Wiley Law Publications), 1989. Bar memberships: State of New York (1970), District of Columbia (1980), Supreme Court of the United States (1989), U.S. Court of Appeals for the Second Circuit (1974), U.S. District Courts for the Eastern and Southern Districts of New York (1973), U.S. Court of Appeals for the District of Columbia Circuit (1991), United States District Court for the District of Columbia (1991), U.S. Court of Appeals for the Federal Circuit (1982), and U.S. Court of Federal Claims, formerly the U.S. Claims Court (1978).

WILLIAM CURTIS BRYSON, circuit judge; born August 19, 1945, in Houston, TX; A.B., Harvard University, 1969; J.D., University of Texas School of Law, 1973; married with two children; law clerk to Hon. Henry J. Friendly, circuit judge, U.S. Court of Appeals for the Second Circuit (1973–74), and Hon. Thurgood Marshall, associate justice, U.S. Supreme Court (1974–75); associate, Miller, Cassidy, Larroca and Lewin, Washington, DC (1975–78); Department of Justice, Criminal Division (1979–86), Office of Solicitor General (1978–79, 1986–94), and Office of the Associate Attorney General (1994); nominated in June 1994 by President Clinton to be circuit judge, U.S. Court of Appeals for the Federal Circuit, and assumed duties of the office on October 7, 1994.

ARTHUR J. GAJARSA, circuit judge; born March 1, 1941 in Norcia (Pro. Perugia), Italy; married to Melanie Gajarsa; five children; education: Rensselaer Polytechnic Institute, Troy, NY, 1958–62, B.S.E.E., Bausch and Lomb Medal, 1958, Benjamin Franklin Award, 1958; Catholic University of America, Washington, DC, 1968; M.A. in economics, graduate studies; J.D., Georgetown University Law Center, Washington, DC, 1967; career record: 1962–63, patent examiner, U.S. Patent Office, Department of Commerce; 1963–64, patent Adviser, U.S. Air Force, Department of Defense; 1964–67, patent adviser, Cushman, Darby and Cushman; 1967–68, law clerk to Judge Joseph McGarraghy, U.S. District Court for the District of Columbia, Washington, DC; 1968–69, attorney, Office of General Counsel, Aetna Life and Casualty Co.; 1969–71, special counsel and assistant to the Commissioner of Indian Affairs, Bureau of Indian Affairs, Department of Interior; 1971–72, associate, Duncan and Brown; 1972–78, partner, Gajarsa, Liss and Sterenbuch; 1978–80, partner, Garjarsa, Liss and Conroy; 1980–86, partner, Wender, Murase and White; 1987–97, partner and officer, Joseph Gajarsa, McDermott and Reiner, P.C.; registered patent agent, registered patent attorney, 1963; admitted to the D.C. Bar, U.S. District Court for the District of Columbia, and U.S. Court of Appeals for the District of Columbia, 1968; Connecticut State Bar, 1969; U.S. Supreme Court, 1971; Superior Court for D.C., Court of Appeals for D.C., 1972; U.S. Courts of Appeals for the Ninth and Federal Circuits, 1974; U.S. District Court for the Northern District of New York, 1980; awards: Sun and Balance Medal, Rensselaer Polytechnic Institute, 1990; Gigi Pieri Award, Camp Hale Association, Boston, MA, 1992; Rensselaer Key Alumni Award, 1992; 125th Anniversary Medal, Georgetown University Law Center, 1995; Order of Commendatore, Republic of Italy, 1995; Alumni Fellow Award, Rensselaer Alumni Association, 1996; Board of Directors: National Italian American Foundation, 1976–97, serving as general counsel, 1976–89, president, 1989–92, and vice chair, 1993–96; Rensselaer Neuman Foundation, trustee, 1973-present; Foundation for Improving Understanding of the Arts, trustee,

1982–96; Outward Bound, U.S.A., trustee, 1987–2002; John Carroll Society, Board of Governors, 1992–96; Rensselaer Polytechnic Institute, trustee, 1994-present; Georgetown University, regent, 1995–2001; Georgetown University Board of Directors, 2001–present; member: Federal, American, Federal Circuit, and D.C. Bar Associations; American Judicature Association; nominated for appointment on April 18, 1996 by President Clinton; confirmed by the Senate on July 31, 1997; entered service September 12, 1997.

RICHARD LINN, circuit judge; born in Brooklyn, NY, April 13, 1944; son of Marvin and Enid Linn; graduated in 1961 from Polytechnic Preparatory County Day School, Brooklyn, NY; received Bachelor of Electrical Engineering degree from Rensselaer Polytechnic Institute in 1965, and J.D. from Georgetown University Law Center in 1969; served as patent examiner at the U.S. Patent and Trademark Office, 1965–68; member of the founding Board of Governors of the Virginia State Bar Section on Patent, Trademark and Copyright Law, chairman, 1975; member of the American Bar Association Intellectual Property Law Section; the American Intellectual Property Law Association; the District of Columbia Bar Association Intellectual Property Section; the Virginia Bar Intellectual Property Law Section; and the Federal Circuit Bar Association; admitted to the Virginia Bar in 1969, the District of Columbia Bar in 1970, and the New York Bar in 1994; admitted to practice before the U.S. Supreme Court, the U.S. Courts of Appeals for the Fourth, Sixth, District of Columbia, and Federal Circuits, and the U.S. District Courts for the Eastern District of Virginia and the District of Columbia; partner, Marks and Murase, L.L.P., 1977–97, and member of the Executive Committee, 1987–97; partner, Foley and Lardner, 1997–99, Practice Group Leader, Electronics Practice Group, and Intellectual Property Department, 1997–99; recipient, Rensselaer Alumni Association Fellows Award for 2000; adjunct professor of law, George Washington University Law School, 2001-present; member, Advisory Board of the George Washington University Law School, 2001-present; Master, Giles S. Rich American Inn of Court, 2000-present; nominated to be Circuit Judge by President William J. Clinton on September 28, 1999, and confirmed by the Senate on November 19, 1999; assumed duties of the office on January 1, 2000.

TIMOTHY B. DYK, circuit judge; nominated for appointment on April 1, 1998 by President Clinton; confirmed by the Senate on May 24, 2000; entered on duty June 9, 2000; education: Harvard College, A.B. (*cum laude*), 1958; Harvard Law School, LL.B. (*magna cum laude*), 1961; prior employment: law clerk to Justices Reed and Burton (retired), 1961–62; law clerk to Chief Justice Warren, 1962–63; special assistant to Assistant Attorney General, Louis F. Oberdorfer, 1963–64; associate and partner, Wilmer, Cutler & Pickering, 1964–90; partner, and chair, of Issues & Appeals Practice area (until nomination) with Jones, Day, Reavis and Pogue, 1990–2000; and Adjunct Professor at Yale, University of Virginia and Georgetown Law Schools.

SHARON PROST, circuit judge; born Newburyport, MA; daughter of Zyskind and Ester Prost; educated in Hartford, CT; B.S., Cornell University, 1973; M.B.A., George Washington University, 1975; J.D., Washington College of Law, American University, 1979; admitted to practice in Washington, DC, 1979; LL.M., George Washington University School of Law, 1984; Labor Relations Specialist, U.S. Civil Service Commission, 1973–76; Labor Relations Specialist / Auditor, U.S. General Accounting Office, 1976–79; Trial Attorney, Federal Labor Relations Authority, 1979–82; Chief Counsel's Office, Department of Treasury, 1982–84; Assistant Solicitor, Associate Solicitor, and then Acting Solicitor, National Labor Relations Board, 1984–89; Adjunct Professor of Labor Law, George Mason University School of Law, 1986–87; Chief Labor Counsel, Senate Labor Committee—minority, 1989–93; Chief Counsel, Senate Judiciary Committee—minority, 1993–95; Deputy Chief Counsel, Senate Judiciary Committee—majority, 1995–2001; Chief Counsel, Senate Judiciary Committee—majority, 2001; appointed by President George W. Bush to the U.S. Court of Appeals for the Federal Circuit, September 21, 2001; assumed duties of the office, October 3, 2001; two sons, Matthew and Jeffrey.

DANIEL M. FRIEDMAN, senior judge; born New York, NY, February 8, 1916; son of Henry M. and Julia (Freedman) Friedman; attended the Ethical Culture Schools in New York City; A.B., Columbia College, 1937; LL.B., Columbia Law School, 1940; married to Leah L. Lipson (deceased), January 16, 1955; married to Elizabeth M. Ellis (deceased), October 18, 1975; admitted to New York bar, 1941; private practice, New York, NY, 1940–42; legal staff, Securities and Exchange Commission, 1942, 1946–51; served in the U.S. Army, 1942–46; Appellate Section, Antitrust Division, U.S. Department of Justice, 1951–59; assistant to the Solicitor General, 1959–62; second assistant to the Solicitor General, 1962–68; First Deputy Solicitor General, 1968–78; Acting Solicitor General, January–March 1977; nominated by President Carter as chief judge of the U.S. Court of Claims, March 22, 1978; confirmed by the Senate, May 17, 1978, and assumed duties of the office on May 24, 1978; as of October 1, 1982, continued in office as judge of the U.S. Court of Appeals for the Federal Circuit, pursuant to section 165, Federal Courts Improvement Act of 1982, Public Law 97–164, 96 Stat. 50.

GLENN LEROY ARCHER, JR., senior judge; born March 21, 1929, in Densmore, KS; son of Glenn L. and Ruth Agnes Archer; educated in Kansas public schools; B.A., Yale University, 1951; J.D., with honors, George Washington University Law School, 1954; married to Carole Joan Thomas; children: Susan, Sharon, Glenn III, and Thomas; First Lieutenant, Judge Advocate General's Office, U.S. Air Force, 1954–56; associate (1956–60) and partner (1960–81), Hamel, Park, McCabe and Saunders, Washington, DC; nominated in 1981 by President Ronald Reagan to be Assistant Attorney General for the Tax Division, U.S. Department of Justice, and served in that position from December 1981 to December 1985; nominated in October 1985 by President Ronald Reagan to be circuit judge, U.S. Court of Appeals for the Federal Circuit; took the oath of office as a Circuit Judge in December 1985; elevated to the position of Chief Judge on March 18, 1994, served in that capacity until December 24, 1997; took senior status beginning December 25, 1997.

S. JAY PLAGER, senior judge; born May 16, 1931, son of A.L. and Clara Plager; educated public schools, Long Branch, NJ; A.B., University of North Carolina, 1952; J.D., University of Florida, with high honors, 1958; LL.M., Columbia University, 1961; Phi Beta Kappa, Phi Kappa Phi, Order of the Coif, Holloway fellow, University of North Carolina; Editor-in-Chief, University of Florida Law Review; Charles Evans Hughes Fellow, Columbia University; three children; commissioned, Ensign U.S. Navy, 1952; active duty Korean conflict; honorable discharge as Commander, USNR, 1971; professor, Faculty of Law, University of Florida, 1958–64; University of Illinois, 1964–77; Indiana University School of Law, Bloomington, 1977–89; visiting research professor of law, University of Wisconsin, 1967–68; visiting fellow, Trinity College and visiting professor, Cambridge University, 1980; visiting scholar, Stanford University Law School, 1984–85; dean and professor, Indiana University School of Law, Bloomington, 1977–84; counselor to the Under Secretary, U.S. Department of Health and Human Services, 1986–87; Associate Director, Office of Management and Budget, Executive Office of the President of the United States, 1987–88; Administrator, Office of Information and Regulatory Affairs, Office of Management and Budget, Executive Office of the President of the United States, 1988–89; circuit judge, U.S. Court of Appeals for the Federal Circuit, appointed by President George Bush, November 1989.

OFFICERS OF THE UNITED STATES COURT OF APPEALS FOR THE FEDERAL CIRCUIT

Circuit Executive and Clerk of Court.—Jan Horbaly, (202) 312–5520.
Senior Technical Assistant.—Melvin L. Halpern, 312–3485.
Senior Staff Attorney.—Eleanor M. Thayer, 312–3490.
Administrative Services Officer.—Ruth A. Butler, 633–6588.
Circuit Librarian.—Patricia M. McDermott, 312–5500.
Automation and Technology Manager.—Larry Luallen, 312–3475.
Operations Officer.—Dale Bosley, 312–5517.
Chief Deputy Clerk for Administration.—Edward W. Hosken, Jr., 633–6550.
Chief Deputy Clerk for Operations.—Pamela Twiford, 633–6550.

UNITED STATES DISTRICT COURT FOR THE DISTRICT OF COLUMBIA

E. Barrett Prettyman U.S. Courthouse, 333 Constitution Avenue, Room 4106, 20001
phone (202) 354–3320, fax 354–3412

THOMAS F. HOGAN, chief judge; born in Washington, DC, May 31, 1938; son of Adm. Bartholomew W. (MC) (USN) Surgeon Gen., USN, 1956–62, and Grace (Gloninger) Hogan; married to Martha L. Wyrick (M.D.), July 16, 1966; one son, Thomas Garth; Georgetown Preparatory School, 1956; A.B., Georgetown University (classical), 1960; master's program, American and English literature, George Washington University, 1960–62; J.D., Georgetown University, 1965–66; Honorary Degree, Doctor of Laws, Georgetown University Law Center, May 1999; St. Thomas More Fellow, Georgetown University Law Center, 1965–66; American Jurisprudence Award: Corporation Law; member: bars of the District of Columbia and Maryland; law clerk to Hon. William B. Jones, U.S. District Court for the District of Columbia, 1966–67; counsel, Federal Commission on Reform of Federal Criminal Laws, 1967–68; private practice of law in the District of Columbia and Maryland, 1968–82; adjunct professor of law, Potomac School of Law, 1977–79; adjunct professor of law, Georgetown University Law Center, 1986–88; public member, officer evaluation board, U.S. Foreign Service, 1973; member: American Bar Association, State Chairman, Maryland Drug Abuse Education Program, Young Lawyers Section, 1970–73, District of Columbia Bar Association, Bar Association of the District of Columbia, Maryland State Bar Association, Montgomery County Bar Association, served on many committees, National Institute for Trial Advocacy, Defense Research Institute; chairman, board of directors, Christ Child Institute for Emotionally Ill Children, 1971–74; member, The Barristers, The Lawyers Club, USDC Executive Committee; Conference Committee on Administration of Federal Magistrates System 1988–91; Chairman Inter-Circuit Assignment Committee, 1990–; appointed judge of the U.S. District Court for the District of Columbia by President Ronald Reagan on October 4, 1982. Chief Judge June 19, 2001; member: Judicial Conference of the United States 2001–; Executive Committee of the Judicial Conference July 2001–.

ROYCE C. LAMBERTH, judge; born in San Antonio, TX, July 16, 1943; son of Nell Elizabeth Synder and Larimore S. Lamberth, Sr.; married Janis Kay Jost, June 17, 1979; South San Antonio High School, 1961; B.A., University of Texas at Austin, 1966; LL.B., University of Texas School of Law, 1967; permanent president, class of 1967, University of Texas School of Law; 1967–74, U.S. Army (Captain, Judge Advocate General's Corps, 1968–74; Vietnam Service Medal, Air Medal, Bronze Star with Oak Leaf Cluster, Meritorious Service Medal with Oak Leaf Cluster); 1974–87, assistant U.S. attorney, District of Columbia (chief, civil division, 1978–87); President's Reorganization Project, Federal Legal Representation Study, 1978–79; honorary faculty, Army Judge Advocate General's School, 1976; Attorney General's Special Commendation Award; Attorney General's John Marshall Award, 1982; vice chairman, Armed Services and Veterans Affairs Committee, Section on Administrative Law, American Bar Association, 1979–82, chairman, 1983–84; chairman, Professional Ethics Committee, 1989–91; co-chairman, Committee of Article III Judges, Judiciary Section 1989–present; chairman, Federal Litigation Section, 1986–87; chairman, Federal Rules Committee, 1985–86; deputy chairman, Council of the Federal Lawyer, 1980–83; chairman, Career Service Committee, Federal Bar Association, 1978–80; appointed judge, U.S. District Court for the District of Columbia by President Ronald Reagan, November 16, 1987; appointed by Chief Justice Rehnquist to be Presiding Judge of the United States Foreign Intelligence Surveillance Court, May 1995–2002.

GLADYS KESSLER, judge; born in New York, NY, January 22, 1938; Education: B.A., Cornell University, 1959; LL.B. Harvard Law School, 1962; member: American Judicature Society (board of directors, 1985–89); National Center for State Courts (board of directors, 1984–87); National Association of Women Judges (president, 1983–84); Women Judges' Fund for Justice, (president, 1980–82); Fellows of the American Bar Foundation; President's Council of Cornell Women; American Law Institute; American Bar Association—committees: Alternative Dispute Resolution, Bioethics and AIDS; Executive Committee, Conference of Federal Trial Judges; private law practice—partner, Roisman, Kessler and Cashdan, 1969–77; associate judge, Superior Court of the District of Columbia, 1977–94; court administrative activities: District of Columbia Courts Joint Committee on Judicial Administration, 1989–94; Domestic Violence Coordinating Council (chairperson, 1993–94); Multi-Door Dispute Resolution Program (supervising judge, 1985–90); family division, D.C. Superior Court (presiding judge, 1981–85); Einshac Institute Board of Directors; appointed judge, U.S. District Court for the District of Columbia by President Bill Clinton, June 16, 1994, and took oath of office, July 18, 1994; U.S. Judicial Conference Committee on Court Administration and Court Management; Frederick B. Abramson Memorial Foundation Board of Directors; Our Place Board of Directors; Vice Chair, District of Columbia Judicial Disabilities and Tenure Commissio.

PAUL L. FRIEDMAN, judge; born in Buffalo, NY, February 20, 1944; son of Cecil A. and Charlotte Wagner Friedman; married to Elizabeth Ann Zicherman, May 25, 1975; education: B.A. (political science), Cornell University, 1965; J.D., *cum laude,* School of Law, State University of New York at Buffalo, 1968; admitted to the bars of the District of Columbia, New York, U.S. Supreme Court, and U.S. Courts of Appeals for the D.C., Federal, Fourth, Fifth, Sixth, Seventh, Ninth and Eleventh Circuits; Law Clerk to Judge Aubrey E. Robinson, Jr., U.S. district court for the District of Columbia, 1968–69; Law Clerk to Judge Roger Robb, U.S. Court of Appeals for the District of Columbia Circuit, 1969–70; Assistant U.S. Attorney for the District of Columbia, 1970–74; assistant to the Solicitor General of the United States, 1974–76; associate independent counsel, Iran-Contra investigation, 1987–88, private law practice, White and Case (partner, 1979–94; associate, 1976–79); member: American Bar Association, Commission on Multidisciplinary Practice (1998–2000), District of Columbia bar (president, 1986–87), American Law Institute (1984) and ALI Council, 1998, American Academy of Appellate Lawyers, Bar Association of the District of Columbia, Women's Bar Association of the District of Columbia, Washington Bar Association, Hispanic Bar Association, Assistant United States Attorneys Association of the District of Columbia (president, 1976–77), Civil Justice Reform Act Advisory Group (chair, 1991–94), District of Columbia Judicial Nomination Commission (member, 1990–94; chair, 1992–94), Advisory Committee on Procedures, U.S. Court of Appeals for the D.C. Circuit (1982–88), Grievance Committee; U.S. District Court for the District of Columbia (member, 1981–87; chair, 1983–85); fellow, American College of Trial Lawyers; fellow, American Bar Foundation; board of directors: Frederick B. Abramson Memorial Foundation (president, 1991–94), Washington Area Lawyers for the Arts (1988–92), Washington Legal Clinic for the Homeless (member, 1987–92; vice-president 1988–91), Stuart Stiller Memorial Foundation (1980–94), American Judicature Society (1990–94), District of Columbia Public Defender Service (1989–92); member: Cosmos Club, Lawyers Club of Washington; appointed judge, U.S. District Court for the District of Columbia by President William Clinton, June 16, 1994, and took oath of office August 1, 1994; U.S. Judicial Conference Advisory Committee on Federal Criminal Rules.

RICARDO M. URBINA, judge; 55, sits on the United States District Court for the District of Columbia; born of an Honduran father and Puerto Rican mother in Manhattan, New York; attended Georgetown University and Georgetown Law Center before working as a staff attorney with the D.C. Public Defender Service; after a period of private practice with an emphasis on commercial litigation, joined the faculty of Howard University School of Law, directed the university's criminal justice clinic and taught criminal law, criminal procedure and torts; voted Professor of the Year by the Howard Law School student body, 1978; nominated to the D.C. Superior Court by President Carter, 1980; appointed to the bench as President Reagan's first presidential judicial appointment and the first Hispanic judge in the history of the District of Columbia, 1981; during his thirteen years on the Superior Court, Judge Urbina served as Chief Presiding Judge of the Family Division for three years and chaired the committee that drafted the Child Support Guidelines later adopted as the District of Columbia's child support law; managed a criminal calendar 1989–90 that consisted exclusively of first degree murder, rape and child molestation cases; designated by the Chief Judge to handle a special calendar consisting of complex civil litigation; twice recognized by the United States Department of Health and Human Services for his work with children and families; selected one of the Washingtonians of the Year by *Washington Magazine,* 1986; received Hugh Johnson Memorial Award for his many contributions to ". . . the creation of harmony among diverse elements of the community and the bar by D.C. Hispanic Bar Association;" received the Hispanic National Bar Association's 1993 award for demonstrated commitment to the "Preservation of Civil and Constitutional Rights of All Americans", and the 1995 NBC-Hispanic Magazine National VIDA Award in recognition of lifetime community service; adjunct professor at the George Washington University Law School since 1993; served as a visiting instructor of trial advocacy at the Harvard Law School, 1996–97; appointment by President Clinton to the U.S. District Court for the District of Columbia in 1994 made him the first Latino ever appointed to the federal bench in Washington, D.C. Bar Association, 1994; appointed by Chief Justice Rehnquist to serve on the Federal Judicial Conference Committee on Security, Space and Facilities, 1997; Latino Civil Rights Center presented him with the Justice Award in 1999; conferred Distinguished Adjunct Teacher Award by George Washington University Law School in 2001.

EMMET G. SULLIVAN, judge; born in Washington, DC, to Emmet A. Sullivan and the late Eileen G. Sullivan; graduated McKinley High School, 1964; B.A., Howard University, 1968; J.D., Howard University Law School, 1971; married to Nan Sullivan; two sons, Emmet and Erik; law clerk to Judge James A. Washington, Jr.; joined the law firm of Houston and Gardner, 1973–80, became a partner; thereafter was a partner with Houston, Sullivan and Gardner; board of directors of the D.C. Law Students in Court Program; D.C. Judicial Conference Voluntary Arbitration Committee; Nominating Committee of the Bar Association of the District of Columbia; U.S. District Court Committee on Grievances; adjunct professor at Howard University School of Law; member: National Bar Association, Washington Bar Association, Bar Association of the District of Columbia; appointed by President Reagan to the Superior Court of the District of Columbia as an associate judge, 1984; deputy presiding judge and presiding judge of the probate and tax division; chairperson of the rules committees for the probate and tax divisions; member: Court Rules Committee and the Jury Plan Committee; appointed by President George Bush to serve as an associate judge of the District of Columbia Court of Appeals, 1991; chairperson for the nineteenth annual judicial conference of the District of Columbia, 1994. The Conference theme was ''Rejuvenating Juvenile Justice—Responses to the Problems of Juvenile Violence in the District of Columbia''; appointed by chief judge Wagner, to chair the ''Task Force on Families and Violence for the District of Columbia Courts''; nominated to the U.S. District Court by President William Clinton on March 22, 1994; and confirmed by the U.S. Senate on June 15, 1994. Appointed by Chief Justice Rehnquist to serve on the Federal Judicial Conference Committee on Criminal Law, 1998; District of Columbia Judicial Disabilities and Tenure Commission, 1996–2001; presently serving on the District of Columbia Judicial Nomination Commission; presently serving on the Executive Committee of the Council for Court Excellence; first person in the District of Columbia to have been appointed to three judicial positions by three different U.S. Presidents.

JAMES ROBERTSON, judge; born Cleveland, OH, May 18, 1938; son of Frederick Irving and Doris (Byars) Robertson; married to Berit Selma Persson of Ange, Sweden, September 19, 1959; children: Stephen, Catherine, and Peter; educated at Western Reserve Academy, Hudson, OH; A.B., Princeton University, 1959 (Woodrow Wilson School); served as an officer in the U.S. Navy, on destroyers and in the Office of Naval Intelligence, 1959–64; LL.B., George Washington University, 1965 (editor-in-chief, George Washington Law Review); admitted to the bar of the District of Columbia, 1966; associate, Wilmer, Cutler and Pickering, 1965–69; chief counsel, litigation office, Lawyers' Committee for Civil Rights Under Law, Jackson, MS, 1969–70; executive director, Lawyers' Committee for Civil Rights Under Law, Washington, DC, 1971–72; partner, Wilmer, Cutler and Pickering, 1973–94; co-chair, Lawyers' Committee for Civil Rights Under Law, 1985–87; president, Southern Africa Legal Services and Legal Education Project, Inc., 1989–94; president, District of Columbia bar, 1991–92; fellow, American College of Trial Lawyers; fellow, American Bar Foundation; member, American Law Institute; Master, Edward Bennett Williams Inn of Court; appointed U.S. District Judge for the District of Columbia by President Clinton on October 11, 1994 and took oath of office on December 31, 1994; Member, Judicial Conference Committee on Information Technology, 1996–present.

COLLEEN KOLLAR–KOTELLY, judge; born in New York City; daughter of Konstantine and Irene Kollar; married to John Kotelly; attended bilingual schools in Mexico, Ecuador and Venezuela, and Georgetown Visitation Preparatory School in Washington, D.C.; received B.A. degree in English at Catholic University (Delta Epsilon Honor Society); received J.D. at Catholic University's Columbus School of Law (Moot Court Board of Governors); law clerk to Hon. Catherine B. Kelly, District of Columbia Court of Appeals, 1968–69; attorney, United States Department of Justice, Criminal Division, Appellate Section (1969–72); chief legal counsel, Saint Elizabeths Hospital, Department of Health and Human Services, 1972–84; received Saint Elizabeths Hospital Certificate of Appreciation, 1981; Meritorious Achievement Award from Alcohol, Drug Abuse and Mental Health Administration (ADAMHA), Department of Health and Human Services, 1981, appointed judge, Superior Court of the District of Columbia by President Ronald Reagan, October 3, 1984, took oath of office October 21, 1984; served as Deputy Presiding Judge, Criminal Division, January 1996–April 1997; received Achievement Recognition Award, Hispanic Heritage CORO Awards Celebration, 1996; appointed judge, U.S. District Court for the District of Columbia by President William Jefferson Clinton on March 26, 1997, took oath of office May 12, 1997;

appointed by Chief Justice Rehnquist to serve on the Financial Disclosure Committee, 2000–2002; Presiding Judge of the United States Foreign Intelligence Surveillance Court, 2002–present.

HENRY H. KENNEDY, Jr., judge; born in Columbia, South Carolina, February 22, 1948; son of Henry and Rachel Kennedy; married Altomease Rucker of Cleveland, Ohio, September 20, 1980; children: Morgan Rucker Kennedy and Alexandra Rucker Kennedy; A.B., Princeton University, 1970; J.D., Harvard University, 1973; admitted to the bar of the District of Columbia, 1973; Reavis, Pogue, Neal and Rose, 1972 and 1973; Assistant United States Attorney for the District of Columbia, 1973–76; United States Magistrate for the District of Columbia, April 1976–79; Judge, Superior Court of the District of Columbia, appointed by President Jimmy Carter, December 17, 1979; member: American Bar Foundation; District of Columbia Bar; Washington Bar Association; Bar Association of the District of Columbia; American Law Institute; member: The Barristers; Sigma Pi Phi; Epsilon Boule; Trustee, Princeton University; appointed judge, United States District Court for the District of Columbia, by President William Jefferson Clinton on September 18, 1997.

RICHARD W. ROBERTS, judge; born in New York, NY; son of Beverly N. Roberts and Angeline Tynes Roberts; married to Vonya B. McCann; children: Jordan and Jillian; graduate of the High School of Music and Art, 1970; A.B. Vassar College, 1974; M.I.A. School for International Training, 1978; J.D., Columbia Law School, 1978; Honors Program trial attorney, Criminal Section, Civil Rights Division, U.S. Department of Justice, Washington, D.C., 1978–1982; Associate, Covington and Burling, Washington, D.C., 1982–1986; Assistant U.S. Attorney, Southern District of NY, 1986–1988; Assistant U.S. Attorney, 1988–1993, then Principal Assistant U.S. Attorney, District of Columbia, 1993–1995; Chief, Criminal Section, Civil Rights Division, U.S. Department of Justice, Washington, DC, 1995–1998; adjunct professor of trial practice, Georgetown University Law Center, Washington, DC, 1983–1984; Guest faculty, Harvard Law School, Trial Advocacy Workshop, 1984 to present; admitted to bars of NY (1979) and DC (1983); U.S. District Court for District of Columbia, 1983; U.S. Court of Appeals for the D.C. Circuit, 1984; U.S. Supreme Court, 1985; U.S. District Court for the Southern District of NY and U.S. Court of Appeals for the Second Circuit, 1986; past or present member or officer of National Black Prosecutors Association; Washington Bar Association; National Conference of Black Lawyers; Department of Justice Association of Black Attorneys; Department of Justice Association of Hispanic Employees for Advancement and Development; DC Bar, Committee on Professionalism and Public Understanding About the Law; American Bar Association Criminal Justice Section Committees on Continuing Legal Education, and Race and Racism in the Criminal Justice System; ABA Task Force on the Judiciary; DC Circuit Judicial Conference Arrangements Committee; D.C. Judicial Conference Planning Committee; Edward Bennett Williams Inn of Court, Washington, DC, master; board of trustees, Vassar College; board of directors, Alumnae and Alumni of Vassar College; African American Alumni of Vassar College; Vassar Club of Washington, DC; Concerned Black Men, Inc., Washington DC Chapter; Sigma Pi Phi, Epsilon Boule; Council on Foreign Relations; DC Coalition Against Drugs and Violence; Murch Elementary School Restructuring Team; nominated as U.S. District Judge for the District of Columbia by President Clinton on January 27, 1998 and confirmed by the Senate on June 5, 1998. Took oath of office on July 31, 1998.

ELLEN SEGAL HUVELLE, judge; born in Boston, Massachusetts, June 3, 1948; daughter of Robert M. Segal, Esquire and Sharlee Segal; married to Jeffrey Huvelle, Esquire; children: Nicole and Justin; B.A., Wellesley College, 1970; Masters in City Planning, Yale University, 1972; J.D., *magna cum laude*, Boston College Law School, 1975 (Order of the Coif; Articles Editor of the law review); law clerk to Chief Justice Edward F. Hennessey, Massachusetts Supreme Judicial Court, 1975–1976; associate, Williams & Connolly, 1976–1984; partner, Williams & Connolly, 1984–1990; associate judge, Superior Court of the District of Columbia 1990–1999; member: American Bar Association, District of Columbia Bar; Women's Bar Association, Fellow of the American Bar Foundation, Master in the Edward Bennett Williams Inn of Court and member of the Inn's Executive Committee; instructor of Trial Advocacy at the University of Virginia Law School; member of Visiting Faculty at Harvard Law School's Trial Advocacy Workshop; Boston College Law School Board of Overseers; appointed judge, U.S. District Court for the District of Columbia by President Clinton in October 1999, and took oath of office on February 25, 2000.

REGGIE B. WALTON, judge; born in Donora, Pennsylvania, February 8, 1949; son of the late Theodore and Ruth (Garard) Walton; married to Debra A. Coats-Walton (M.D.); October 17, 1987; one daughter, Danon; B.A., West Virginia State College, 1971; J.D., American University, Washington College of Law, 1974; admitted to the bars of the Supreme

Court of Pennsylvania, 1974; United States District Court for the Eastern District of Pennsylvania, 1975; District of Columbia Court of Appeals, 1976; United States Court of Appeals for the District of Columbia Circuit, 1977; Supreme Court of the United States, 1980; United States District Court for the District of Columbia; Staff Attorney, Defender Association of Philadelphia, 1974–1976; Assistant United States Attorney for the District of Columbia, 1976–1980; Chief, Career Criminal Unit, Assistant United States Attorney for the District of Columbia, 1979–1980; Executive Assistant United States Attorney for the District of Columbia, 1980–1981; Associate Judge, Superior Court of the District of Columbia, 1981–1989; Deputy Presiding Judge of the Criminal Division, Superior Court of the District of Columbia, 1986–1989; Associate Director, Office of National Drug Control Policy, Executive Office of the President, 1989–1991; Senior White House Advisor for Crime, The White House, 1991; Associate Judge, Superior Court of the District of Columbia, 1991–2001; Presiding Judge of the Domestic Violence Unit, Superior Court of the District of Columbia, 2000; Presiding Judge of the Family Division, Superior Court of the District of Columbia, 2001; Instructor: National Judicial College, Reno, Nevada, 1999–present; Harvard University Law School, Trial Advocacy Workshop, 1994–present; National Institute of Trial Advocacy, Georgetown University Law School, 1983–present; Co-author, Pretrial Drug Testing—an Essential component of the National Drug Control Strategy, Brigham Young University Law Journal of Public Law (1991); Distinguished Alumnus Award, American University, Washington College of Law (1991); The William H. Hastie Award, The Judicial Council of the National Bar Association (1993); Commissioned as a Kentucky Colonel by the Governor (1990, 1991); Governor's Proclamation declaring April 9, 1991, Judge Reggie B. Walton Day in the State of Louisiana; The West Virginia State College National Alumni Association James R. Waddy Meritorious Service Award (1990); Secretary's Award, United States Department of Veterans Affairs (1990); Outstanding Alumnus Award, Ringgold High School (1987); Director's Award for Superior Performance as an Assistant United States Attorney (1980); Profiled in book entitled ''Black Judges on Justice: Prospectives From The Bench'' by Linn Washington (1995); appointed district judge, United States District Court for the District of Columbia by President George W. Bush, September 24, 2001, and took oath of office October 29, 2001.

JOHN D. BATES, judge; born in Elizabeth, NJ, October 11, 1946; son of Richard D. and Sarah (Deacon) Bates; married to Carol Ann Rhees, February 9, 1980; three children (Lauren, Brian and Kelly); B.A., Wesleyan University, 1968; J.D., University of Maryland School of Law, 1976; U.S. Army (1968–71, 1st Lt., Vietnam Service Medal, Bronze Star); law clerk to Hon. Roszel Thomsen, U.S. District Court for the District of Maryland, 1976–77; 1980–97, Assistant U.S. Attorney, District of Columbia (Chief, Civil Division, 1987–97); Director's Award for Superior Performance (1983); Attorney General's Special commendation Award (1986); Deputy Independent Counsel, Whitewater Investigation, 1995–1997; private practice of law, Miller & Chevalier (partner, 1998–2001), Chair of Government Contracts Litigation Department and member of Executive Committee), Steptoe & Johnson (associate, 1977–80); District of Columbia Circuit Advisory Committee for Procedures (1989–93); Civil Justice Reform Committee of the U.S. District Court for the District of Columbia (1996–2001); Treasurer, D.C. Bar (1992–93); Publications Committee, D.C. Bar (1991–97, Chair 1994–97); D.C. Bar Special Committee on Government Lawyers (1990–91); D.C. Bar Task Force on Civility in the Profession (1994–96); D.C. Bar Committee on Examination of Rule 49 (1995–96); Chairman, Litigation Section, Federal Bar Association (1986–89); Board of Directors, Washington Lawyers Committee for Civil Rights and Urban Affairs (1999–2001).

RICHARD J. LEON, judge; 53, born in South Natick, Massachusetts on December 3, 1949; son of Silvano B. Leon and Rita (O'Rorke) Leon; married to M-Christine Costa; one son, Nicholas Cavanagh; A.B., Holy Cross College, 1971, J.D., *cum laude,* Suffolk Law School, 1974; LL.M. Harvard Law School, 1981; Law Clerk to Chief Justice McLaughlin and the Associate Justices, Superior Court of Massachusetts, 1974–75; Law Clerk to Hon. Thomas F. Kelleher, Supreme Court of Rhode Island, 1975–76; admitted to bar, Rhode Island, 1975 and District of Columbia, 1991; Special Assistant U.S. Attorney, Southern District of New York, 1977–1978; Assistant Professor of Law, St. John's Law School, New York, 1979–1983; Senior Trial Attorney, Criminal Section, Tax Division, U.S. Department of Justice, 1983–1987; Deputy Chief Minority Counsel, U.S. House Select ''Iran-Contra'' Committee, 1987–1988; Deputy Assistant U.S. Attorney General, Environmental Division, 1988–1989; Partner, Baker & Hostetler, Washington, DC, 1989–1999; Commissioner, The White House Fellows Commission, 1990–1992; Chief Minority Counsel, U.S. House Foreign Affairs Committee ''October Suprise'' Task Force, 1992–1993; Special Counsel, U.S. House Banking Committee ''Whitewater'' Investigation, 1994; Special Counsel, U.S. House Ethics Reform Task Force, 1997; Adjunct Professor, Georgetown University Law Center, 1997–present; Partner, Vorys, Sater, Seymour and Pease, Washington, DC, 1999–2002; Commissioner, Judicial

Review Commission on Foreign Asset Control, 2000–2001; Master, Edward Bennett Williams Inn of Court; appointed U.S. District Judge for the District of Columbia by President George W. Bush on February 19, 2002; took oath of office on March 20, 2002.

ROSEMARY M. COLLYER, judge; born in White Plains, NY, November 19, 1945; daughter of Thomas C. and Alice Henry Mayers; married to Philip L. Collyer, June 22, 1968; one son; educated in parochial and public schools in Stamford, Connecticut; B.A., Trinity College, Washington, DC, 1968; J.D., University of Denver College of Law, 1977; practiced with Sherman & Howard, Denver, Colorado, 1977–1981; Chairman, Federal Mine Safety and Health Review Commission, 1981–1984 by appointment of President Ronald Reagan with Senate confirmation; General Counsel, National Labor Relations Board, 1984–1989 by appointment of President Ronald Reagan with Senate confirmation; private practice with Crowell & Moring LLP, Washington, DC 1989–2003; member and chairman of the firm's Management Committee; appointed U.S. District Judge for the District of Columbia by President George W. Bush and took oath of office on January 2, 2003.

SENIOR JUDGES

WILLIAM BENSON BRYANT, senior judge; born Wetumpka, AL, September 18, 1911; son of Benson and Alberta Bryant; married to Astaire A. Gonzalez (deceased), August 25, 1934; children: Astaire and William, Jr.; A.B., Howard University, 1932; LL.B., Howard University Law School, 1936; served in U.S. Army, World War II, 1943–47; member of the bar of the District of Columbia and of the Supreme Court of the United States; assistant U.S. attorney for the District of Columbia, 1951–54; private practice of law in District of Columbia as partner in firm of Houston, Bryant and Gardner, 1954–65; member: Committee on Admissions and Grievances of U.S. District Court for District of Columbia, 1959–65; District of Columbia Board of Appeals and Review, District of Columbia Special Police Trial Board, American Law Institute, National Lawyers' Club (honorary); appointed judge of the U.S. District Court for the District of Columbia Circuit by President Lyndon B. Johnson on July 11, 1965, and entered upon the duties of that office on August 16, 1965; served as chief judge, 1977–81; took senior judge status on January 31, 1982.

LOUIS FALK OBERDORFER, senior judge; born in Birmingham, AL, February 21, 1919; son of A. Leo and Stella Falk Oberdorfer; married to Elizabeth Weil of Montgomery, AL, July 31, 1941; children: John, Kathryn, Thomas, and William; A.B., Dartmouth College, 1939; LL.B., Yale Law School, 1946 (editor in chief, Yale Law Journal, 1941); admitted to the bar of Alabama, 1947, District of Columbia, 1949; U.S. Army, rising from private to captain, 1941–45; law clerk to Justice Hugo L. Black, 1946–47; attorney, Paul Weiss, Wharton, Garrison, 1947–51; partner, Wilmer, Cutler and Pickering, and predecessor firms, 1951–61 and 1965–77; Assistant Attorney General, Tax Division, U.S. Department of Justice, 1961–65; president, District of Columbia Bar, 1977; transition chief executive officer, Legal Services Corp., 1975; co-chairman, Lawyers' Committee for Civil Rights Under Law, 1967–69; member, Advisory Committee on Federal Rules of Civil Procedure, 1963–84; visiting lecturer, Yale Law School, 1966, 1971; adjunct professor, Georgetown Law Center, 1993–present; appointed judge of the U.S. District Court for the District of Columbia by President Jimmy Carter on October 11, 1977, and took oath of office on November 1, 1977; senior status July 31, 1992.

JOHN GARRETT PENN, senior judge; born in Pittsfield, MA, March 19, 1932; son of John and Eugenie Heyliger Penn; married to Ann Elizabeth Rollison of Lenox, MA, May 7, 1966; children: John, Karen, and David; A.B., University of Massachusetts (Amherst), 1954; LL.B., Boston University School of Law, 1957; admitted to the bars of Massachusetts, 1957 and District of Columbia, 1970; U.S. Army, first lieutenant, Judge Advocate General Corps, 1958–61; attorney, U.S. Department of Justice, Tax Division, 1961–70; trial attorney, 1961–65, reviewer, 1965–68, assistant chief, 1968–70; National Institute of Public Affairs Fellow, Woodrow Wilson School of Public and International Affairs, Princeton University, 1967–68; Awarded the Charles Hamilton Houston Medallion of Merit by the Washington Bar Association, May 1996; appointed judge, Superior Court of the District of Columbia by President Richard Nixon, October 1970; appointed judge, U.S. District Court for the District of Columbia by President Jimmy Carter, March 23, 1979, and took oath of office, May 15, 1979; Chief Judge March 1, 1992—July 21, 1997.

NORMA HOLLOWAY JOHNSON, senior judge; born in Lake Charles, LA; daughter of H. Lee and Beatrice Williams Holloway; married to Julius A. Johnson of St. Louis, MO, June 18, 1964; B.S., University of the District of Columbia, 1955; J.D., Georgetown

University Law Center, 1962; admitted to the bar of the District of Columbia, 1962; attorney, Civil Division, U.S. Department of Justice, 1963–67; Office of Corporation Counsel, District of Columbia, 1967–70; judge, Superior Court of the District of Columbia, 1970–80; appointed judge, U.S. District Court for the District of Columbia by President Jimmy Carter, May 12, 1980, and took oath of office, July 8, 1980; Chief Judge July 21, 1997 to June 18, 2001.

THOMAS PENFIELD JACKSON, judge; born Washington, DC, January 10, 1937; A.B., Dartmouth College, 1958; LL.B., Harvard Law School, 1964; line officer aboard U.S. Navy destroyer, 1958–61; admitted to bars of District of Columbia (1965), Maryland (1966), and U.S. Supreme Court (1970); private practice of law in the District of Columbia and Maryland, with firm of Jackson and Campbell, P.C., 1965–82; president, bar association of the District of Columbia, 1981–82; fellow, American College of Trial Lawyers; appointed judge of U.S. District Court for the District of Columbia by President Ronald Reagan, June 25, 1982; took senior status February, 2002.

OFFICERS OF THE UNITED STATES DISTRICT COURT FOR THE DISTRICT OF COLUMBIA

United States Magistrate Judges: Deborah A. Robinson; Alan Kay; John M. Facciola.
Clerk of Court.—Nancy Mayer-Whittington.
Administrative Assistant to the Chief Judge.—Sheldon L. Snook.
Bankruptcy Judge.—S. Martin Teel, Jr.
Bankruptcy Clerk of Court.—Denise Curtis.
Chief Probation Officer.—Richard A. Houck, Jr.

UNITED STATES COURT OF INTERNATIONAL TRADE

One Federal Plaza, New York NY 10278–0001, phone 212–264–2800

GREGORY W. CARMAN, chief judge, 1996–; born in Farmingdale, Long Island, NY, January 31, 1937; son of retired District Court Judge Willis B. and Marjorie Sosa Carman; B.A., St. Lawrence University, Canton, NY, 1958; national exchange student, 1956–57, studying at the University of Paris through Sweet Briar College Junior Year in France Program; J.D., St. John's University School of Law, (honors program), 1961; member, St. John's Law Review; University of Virginia Law School, JAG (with honors), 1962; Master in Taxation Program, New York University School of Law; Captain, U.S. Army, 1958–64, stationed with the 2d Infantry Division, Fort Benning, GA; awarded Army Commendation Medal for Meritorious Service, 1964; admitted to the New York bar, 1961; practiced law with the firm of Carman, Callahan & Sabino, Farmingdale, NY; admitted to practice in U.S. Court of Military Appeals, 1962; certified by Judge Advocate General to practice at general court martial trials, 1962; admitted to practice in the U.S. District Courts, Eastern District of New York and Southern District of New York, 1965; Second Circuit Court of Appeals, 1966; Supreme Court of the United States, 1967; U.S. Court of Appeals, District of Columbia, 1982; Councilman for the town of Oyster Bay, 1972–80; member, U.S. House of Representatives, 97th Congress; appointed to Banking, Finance and Urban Affairs Committee and Select Committee on Aging, 1981–82; member, International Trade, Investment and Monetary Policy Subcommittee of House Banking Committee, 1981–82; U.S. congressional delegate, International I.M.F. Conference, 1982; nominated by President Ronald Reagan, confirmed and appointed Judge of the U.S. Court of International Trade, March 2, 1983; served as Acting Chief Judge, 1991; became Chief Judge, 1996; Statutory Member, Judicial Conference of the United States; member, Executive Committee, Judicial Branch Committee, and Subcommittee on Long Range Planning of the Judicial Conference of the United States; member, Bicentennial Commission of Nassau County; Rotary International, 1964–present; named a Paul Harris Fellow of The Rotary Foundation of Rotary International; chairman, United Way, Town of Oyster Bay, 1973–76; member, Benevolent Protective Order of Elks; past president, Savings and Loan League Committee, New York Chapter of the American Bar Association; member: American Bar Association; Fellow, American Bar Foundation; member, New York State Bar Association; member and former chair, New York State Bar Association's Committee on Courts and the Community; recipient of 1996 Special Recognition Award from New York State Bar Association's Committee on Courts and the Community; director and member, Respect for Law Alliance, Inc.; member, Executive Committee and president-elect 2003–04 of the Theodore Roosevelt American Inn of Court; past president, Protestant Lawyers Association of Long Island; former member, Vestry, St. Thomas's Episcopal Church, Farmingdale, NY, 1992–94; Fellow, American College of Mortgage Attorneys; Phi Delta Phi legal fraternity; District Committee member, Nassau County Council of Boy Scouts of America, 1964 to present; past vice-chair, Paumanok Boy Scout District; former district chair, United Cerebral Palsy; member: Holland Society; recipient of 1999 Gold Medal for Distinguished Achievement in Jurisprudence from The Holland Society of New York; Doctor of Laws, *honoris causa*, Nova Southeastern University, 1999; Distinguished Jurist in Residence, Touro College Law Center, 2000; Doctor of Laws, *honoris causa*, St. John's University, 2002; Sigma Chi, social fraternity; married to Nancy Endruschat (deceased); children: Gregory Wright, Jr., John Frederick, James Matthew, and Mira Catherine; married to Judith L. Dennehy, 1995.

JANE A. RESTANI, judge; born February 27, 1948 in San Francisco, CA; parents, Emilia C. and Roy J. Restani; B.A., University of California at Berkeley, 1969; J.D., University of California at Davis, 1973; law review staff writer, 1971–72; articles editor, 1972–73; member, Order of the Coif; elected to Phi Kappa Phi Honor Society; admitted to the bar of the Supreme Court of the State of California, 1973; joined the civil division of the Department of Justice under the Attorney General's Honor Program, 1973 as a trial attorney; assistant chief commercial litigation section, civil division, 1976–80; director, commercial litigation branch, civil division, 1980–83; assumed the duties of a judge of the U.S. Court of International Trade on November 25, 1983; husband, Ira Bloom.

THOMAS J. AQUILINO, Jr., judge; born in Mount Kisco, NY, December 7, 1939; son of Thomas J. and Virginia B. (Doughty) Aquilino; attended Cornell University, 1957–59; B.A., Drew University, 1959–60, 1961–62; University of Munich, Germany, 1960–61; Free University of Berlin, Germany, 1965–66; J.D., Rutgers University School of Law, 1966–69; research assistant, Prof. L.F.E. Goldie (Resources for the Future—Ford Foundation) (1967–69); administrator, Northern Region, 1969; Jessup International Law Moot Court Competition; served in the U.S. Army, 1962–65; law clerk, Hon. John M. Cannella, U.S. district court for the Southern District of New York, 1969–71; attorney with Davis Polk and Wardwell, New York, 1971–85; admitted to practice New York, U.S. Supreme Court, U.S. Courts of Appeals for Second and Third Circuits, U.S. Court of International Trade, U.S. Court of Claims, U.S. district courts for Eastern, Southern and Northern Districts of New York, Interstate Commerce Commission; adjunct professor of law, Benjamin N. Cardozo School of Law, 1984–95; Mem., Drew University Board of Visitors, 1997–present; appointed by President Reagan on February 22, 1985; confirmed by U.S. Senate, April 3, 1985; married to Edith Berndt Aquilino; children: Christopher Thomas, Philip Andrew, Alexander Berndt.

DONALD C. POGUE, was appointed a Judge of the United States Court of International Trade (USCIT) by President Clinton in 1995; one of the nine members of the Court, he serves as chair of the Court's Long Range Planning Committee, and as a member of the Court's Technology Committee, and Education Committee; served as judge in Connecticut's Superior Court; appointed to the bench in 1994; served as chairman of Connecticut's Commission on Hospitals and Health Care; appointed as Commissioner by Governor O'Neill in 1989, and named chairman by Governor Weicker; practiced law in Hartford for 15 years with the firm of Kestell, Pogue, & Gould; lectured on labor law, at the University of Connecticut School of Law; assisted in teaching the Harvard Law School's program on negotiations and dispute resolution for lawyers; chaired the Connecticut Bar Association's Labor and Employment Law Section; graduated *magna cum laude,* Phi Beta Kappa from Dartmouth College; graduate work at the University of Essex, England; J.D., from Yale Law School; Masters of Philosophy, Yale University; listed in Martindale-Hubbell and in the Best Lawyers in America; resides in Connecticut with wife, Susan, since their marriage in 1971.

EVAN J. WALLACH, judge; born in Superior, AZ, November 11, 1949; son of Albert A. and Sara F. Wallach; married to Katherine Colleen Tobin, 1992; graduate of Acalanes High School, Lafayette, CA, 1967; attended Diablo Valley Junior College, Pleasant Hill, CA, 1967–68; news editor Viking Reporter; member Alfa Gamma Sigma, National Junior College Honor Society, member Junior Varsity Wrestling Team; enlisted United States Army, January, 1969, PVT–SGT, served as Recognizance Sergeant 8th Engineer Bn., 1st Calvary Division (Air Mobile), Republic of Vietnam, 1970–71, Bronze Star Medal, Air Medal, Valorous Unit Citation, Good Conduct Medal; attended University of Arizona, 1971–73, graduated B.A., Journalism (high honors), Phi Beta Kappa, Phi Kappa Phi, Kappa Tau Alfa, Rufenacht French language prize, Douglas Martin Journalism Scholarship; attended University of California, Berkeley, 1973–76, graduated J.D., 1976, research assistant to Prof. Melvin Eisenberg, member of University of California Honor Society; Associate (1976–82) and Partner (1983–95) Lionel Sawyer and Collins, Las Vegas, NV with emphasis on media representation; attended Cambridge University, Cambridge, England, LL.B. (international law) (honors), 1981, member Hughes Hall College Rowing Club, Cambridge University Tennis Club; General Counsel and Public Policy Advisor to U.S. Senator Harry Reid (D) of Nevada, 1987–88; served CAPT–MAJ Nevada Army National Guard, 1989–95; served as Attorney/Advisor, International Affairs Division; Office of the Judge Advocate General of the Army, February–June, 1991–92; Meritorious Service Medal (oak leaf cluster); Nevada Medal of Merit; General Counsel, Nevada Democratic Party, 1978–80, 1982–86; General Counsel, Reid for Congress campaign, 1982, 1984; Reid for Senate campaign, 1986, 1992; General Counsel, Bryan for Senate campaign, 1988; Nevada State Director, Mondale for President campaign, 1984; State Director, Nevada and Arizona Gore for President campaign, 1988; General Counsel Nevada Assembly Democratic Caucus, 1990–95; General Counsel, Society for Professional Journalists, 1988–95; General Counsel, Nevada Press Association, 1989–95; awarded American Bar Association Liberty Bell Award, 1993; Nevada State Press Association President's Award, 1994; Clark County School Librarians Intellectual Freedom Award, 1995; Law of War, Adjunct Professor, New York Law School, 1997–present; Brooklyn Law School 2000 to present; member Nevada Bar, 1977; District of Columbia, 1988; U.S. District Court, District of Nevada, 1977; Ninth Circuit Court of Appeals, 1989; author, Legal Handbook for Nevada Reporters (1994); Comparison of British and American Defense Based Prior Restraint, ICLQ (1984); Treatment of Crude Oil As A War Munition, ICLQ (1992); Three Ways Nevada Unconstitutionally Chills The Media; Nevada Lawyer (1994); Co-Editor, Nevada Civil Practice Handbook (1993). Extradition to the Rwandan War Crimes Tribunal: Is Another Treaty Required, USCLA Journal of International Law and Foreign Affairs, Spring/Summer, 1998. The Procedural and Evidentiary Rules of the Post World War II War Crimes Trials: Did They Provide An Outline For International Criminal Procedure? Columbia Journal of Translational Law, Spring, 1999; Webmaster, International Law of War Association, lawofwar.org; Afghanistan, Yamashita and Uchiyama: Does the Sauce Suit the Gander? The Army Lawyer, June 2003.

JUDITH M. BARZILAY, judge, U.S. Court of International Trade; born January 3, 1944, Russell, KS; husband, Sal (Doron) Barzilay; children, Ilan and Michael; parents, Arthur and Hilda Morgenstern; B.A., Wichita State University, 1965; M.L.S., Rutgers University School of Library and Information Science, 1971; J.D., Rutgers University School of Law, 1981, Moot Court Board, 1980–1981; trial attorney, U.S. Department of Justice (International Trade Field OFfice), 1983 to 1986; litigation associate, Siegel, Mandell and Davidson, New York, NY, 1986 to 1988; Sony Corporation of America, 1988 to 1998; customs and international trade counsel, 1988–1989; vice-president for import and export operations, 1989–1996; vice-president for government affairs, 1996–1998; executive board of the American Association of Exporters and Importers, 1993–1998; appointed by Treasury Secretary Robert Rubin to the Advisory Committee on Commercial Operations of the United States Customs Service, 1995–1998; nominated for appointment January 27, 1998 by President Clinton (D); sworn-in as judge June 3, 1998.

DELISSA A. RIDGWAY, judge; born June 28, 1955 in Kirksville, MO; B.A. (honors), University of Missouri-Columbia, 1975; graduate work, University of Missouri-Columbia, 1975–76; J.D., Northeastern University School of Law, 1979; Shaw Pittman Potts & Trowbridge (Washington, D.C.), 1979–94; Chair, Foreign Claims Settlement Commission of the U.S. (1994–98); U.S. Court of International Trade (1998-Present); Adjunct Professor of Law, Cornell Law School (1999–Present); Adjunct Professor of Law, Washington College of Law/The American University (1992–94); District of Columbia Bar, Secretary (1991–92), Board of Governors (1992–98); President, Women's Bar Association (1992–93); American Bar Association; Commission on Women in the Profession (2002–present); Federal Bar Association, National Council (1993–2002), Government Relations Committee (1996–present), Public Relations Committee Chair (1998–99); Founding Member of Board, D.C. Conference on Opportunities for Minorities in the Legal Profession (1992–93); Chair, D.C. Bar Summit on Women in the Legal Profession (1995–98); Fellow, American Bar Foundation; Member, American Law Institute; Fellow, Federal Bar Foundation; Earl W. Kintner Award of the Federal Bar Association (2000); Woman Lawyer of the Year, Washington, DC (2001).

RICHARD K. EATON, judge; District of Columbia; born in Walton, NY, August 22, 1948; married to Susan Henshaw Jones; two children: Alice and Elizabeth; attended Walton public schools; received B.A., Ithaca College, 1970; J.D., Union University Albany Law School, 1974; professional experience: Eaton and Eaton, partner (1975–76); Mudge Rose Guthrie Alexander & Ferdon, New York, NY, associate (1983–91) and Washington, DC, partner (1993–95); Stroock & Stroock & Lavan, Washington, DC, partner (1995–2000); served on the staff of Senator Daniel Patrick Moynihan (1977–79, 1980–83, 1991–93); confirmed by the United States Senate October 22, 1999.

TIMOTHY C. STANCEU, was appointed to the U.S. Court of International Trade by President George W. Bush and began serving on April 15, 2003. In assuming this responsibility, he returned to public service after a thirteen-year career in private practive in Washington, DC with the law firm Hogan & Hartson L.L.P, during which he represented clients in a variety of matters involving customs and international trade law. During the fifteen years prior to his law practice, Judge Stanceu's career in the Federal Government included a term as Deputy Director of the Office of Trade and Tariff Affairs at the U.S. Department of the Treasury, where his responsibilities involved the regulatory and enforcement matters of the U.S. Customs Service and other agencies. Prior to that position, he served as Special Assistant to the Treasury Department's Assistant Secretary for Enforcement and in several positions at the U.S. Environmental Protection Agency, where he concentrated on the development and review of regulations on various environmental subjects. Judge Stanceu is a native of Canton, Ohio. He is a 1973 graduate of Colgate University and received a law degree from the Georgetown University of Law Center in 1979.

NICHOLAS TSOUCALAS, senior judge; born August 24, 1926 in New York, NY; one of five children of George M. and Maria (Monogenis) Tsoucalas; received B.S. degree from Kent State University, 1949; received LL.B. from New York Law School, 1951; attended New York University Law School; entered U.S. Navy, 1944–46; reentered Navy, 1951–52 and served on the carrier, *U.S.S. Wasp;* admitted to New York bar, 1953; appointed Assistant U.S. Attorney for the Southern District of New York, 1955–59; appointed in 1959 as supervisor of 1960 census for the 17th and 18th Congressional Districts; appointed chairman, Board of Commissioners of Appraisal; appointed judge of Criminal Court of the City of New York, 1968; designated acting Supreme Court Justice, Kings and Queens Counties,

1975–82; resumed service as judge of the Criminal Court of the City of New York until June 1986; appointed judge of the U.S. Court of International Trade by President Ronald Reagan on September 9, 1985, and confirmed by U.S. Senate on June 6, 1986; assumed senior status on September 30, 1996; former chairman: Committee on Juvenile Delinquency, Federal Bar Association, and the Subcommittee on Public Order and Responsibility of the American Citizenship Committee of the New York County Lawyers' Association; founder of Eastern Orthodox Lawyers' Association; former president: Greek-American Lawyers' Association, and Board of Directors of Greek Orthodox Church of ''Evangelismos'', St. John's Theologos Society, and Parthenon Foundation; member, Order of Ahepa, Parthenon Lodge, F.A.M.; married to Catherine Aravantinos; two daughters: Stephanie (Mrs. Daniel Turriago) and Georgia (Mrs. Christopher Argyrople); five grandchildren.

R. KENTON MUSGRAVE, senior judge, U.S. Court of International Trade; born Clearwater, FL, September 7, 1927. Attended Augusta Academy (Virginia); B.A., University of Washington, 1948; editorial staff, Journal of International Law, Emory University; J.D., with distinction, Emory University, 1953; assistant general counsel, Lockheed Aircraft and Lockheed International, 1953–62; vice president and general counsel, Mattel, Inc., 1963–71; director, Ringling Bros. and Barnum and Bailey Combined Shows, Inc., 1968–72; commissioner, BSA (Atlanta), 1952–55; partner, Musgrave, Welbourn and Fertman, 1972–75; assistant general counsel, Pacific Enterprises, 1975–81; vice president, general counsel and secretary, Vivitar Corporation, 1981–85; vice president and director, Santa Barbara Applied Research Corp., 1982–87; trustee, Morris Animal Foundation, 1981–; director Emeritus, Pet Protection Society, 1981–; director, Dolphins of Shark Bay (Australia) Foundation, 1985–; trustee, The Dian Fossey Gorilla Fund, 1987–; trustee, The Ocean Conservancy, 2000–present; vice president and director, South Bay Social Services Group, 1963–70; director, Palos Verdes Community Arts Association, 1973–79; member, Governor of Florida's Council of 100, 1970–73; director, Orlando Bank and Trust, 1970–73; counsel, League of Women Voters, 1964–66; member, State Bar of Georgia, 1953–; State Bar of California, 1962–; Los Angeles County Bar Association, 1962–87 and chairman, Corporate Law Departments Section, 1965–66; admitted to practice before the U.S. Supreme Court, 1962; Supreme Court of Georgia, 1953; California Supreme Court, 1962; U.S. Customs Court, 1967; U.S. Court of International Trade, 1980. Married May 7, 1949 to former Ruth Shippen Hoppe, of Atlanta, GA. Three children: Laura Marie Musgrave (deceased), Ruth Shippen Musgrave, Esq., and Forest Kenton Musgrave. Nominated by President Ronald Reagan on July 1, 1987; confirmed by the Senate on November 9, and took oath of office on November 13, 1987.

RICHARD W. GOLDBERG, senior judge; born September 23, 1927 in Fargo, ND; J.D. from the University of Miami, 1952; served on active duty as an Air Force Judge Advocate, 1953–56; admitted to Washington, DC bar, Florida bar and North Dakota bar; from 1959 to 1983, owned and operated a regional grain processing firm in North Dakota; served as State Senator from North Dakota for eight years; taught military law for the Army and Air Force ROTC at North Dakota State University; was vice-chairman of the board of Minneapolis Grain Exchange; joined the Reagan administration in 1983 in Washington at the U.S. Department of Agriculture. Served as Deputy Under Secretary for International Affairs and Commodity Programs and later as Acting Under Secretary; in 1990 joined the Washington, DC law firm of Anderson, Hibey and Blair; appointed judge of the U.S. Court of International Trade in 1991; assumed senior status in 2001; married: two children, a daughter and a son.

OFFICERS OF THE UNITED STATES COURT OF INTERNATIONAL TRADE

Clerk.—Leo M. Gordon (212) 264–2814.

UNITED STATES COURT OF FEDERAL CLAIMS

Lafayette Square, 717 Madison Place NW 20005, phone (202) 219–9657

EDWARD J. DAMICH, chief judge; born in Pittsburgh, PA, June 19, 1948; son of John and Josephine (Lovrencic) Damich; A.B., St. Stephen's College, 1970; J.D., Catholic University, 1976; professor of law at Delaware School of Law of Widener University, 1976–84; served as a Law and Economics Fellow at Columbia University School of Law, where he earned his L.L.M. in 1983 and his J.S.D. in 1991; professor of law at George Mason University, 1984–98; appointed by President Bush to be a Commissioner of the Copyright Royalty Tribunal, 1992–93; Chief Intellectual Property Counsel for the Senate Judiciary Committee, 1995–98; appointed by President Clinton as judge, U.S. Court of Federal Claims, October 22, 1998; appointed by President Bush as chief judge, U.S. Court of Federal Claims, May 13, 2002; admitted to the Bars of the District of Columbia and Pennsylvania; member of the District of Columbia Bar Association, Pennsylvania Bar Association, American Bar Association, Supreme Court of the United States, the Federal Circuit and *Association litteraire et artistique internationale;* president of the National Federation of Croatian Americans, 1994–95. At present Judge Damich is an adjunct professor of law at the Georgetown University Law Center.

LAWRENCE M. BASKIR, judge; born in Brooklyn, NY, January 10, 1938; married to Marna Tucker, two children; graduated *magna cum laude*, Princeton University; A.B., Woodrow Wilson School of Public and International Affairs, 1959; LL.B., Harvard Law School, 1962; Principal Deputy General Counsel, Department of the Army, 1994–1998; private practice and Editor-In-Chief, Military Law Reporter, 1981–1994; Legislative Director to Senator Bill Bradley, 1979–1981; Deputy Assistant Secretary (Legislation), Office of the Secretary, Department of the Treasury, 1977–1979; Director, Vietnam Offender Study; Faculty Fellow, University of Notre Dame Law School, 1975–1977; Director, Presidential (Ford) Clemancy Board, White House, 1974–1975; Chief Counsel, Subcommittees on Constitutional Rights and Separation of Powers, Senate Judiciary Committee, Senator Sam J. Ervin, Chairman, 1967–1974; publications include *Chance and Circumstances: The Draft, the War and the Vietnam Generation*; consultant to Information Intelligence Committees, U.S. Congress; Adjunct Professor and Lecturer, Georgetown, Notre Dame, Catholic Law Schools, and American University; appointed judge of the U.S. Court of Federal Claims on October 22, 1998; chief judge, July 11, 2000 to May 10, 2002.

CHRISTINE ODELL COOK (O.C.) MILLER, judge; born in Oakland, CA, August 26, 1944; married to Dennis F. Miller; B.A., Stanford University, 1966; J.D., University of Utah College of Law, 1969; Comment Editor, Utah Law Review; Member, Utah Chapter Order of the Coif; Clerk to Chief Judge David T. Lewis, U.S. Court of Appeals for the 10th Circuit; trial attorney, Civil Division, U.S. Department of Justice; trial attorney, Federal Trade Commission, Bureau of Consumer Protection; Hogan and Hartson, litigation section; Pension Benefit Guaranty Corporation, Special Counsel; U.S. Railway Association, Assistant General Counsel; Shack and Kimball P.C., litigation; member of the Bars of the State of California and District of Columbia; Judge Miller was appointed by President Reagan on December 10, 1982, and confirmed as Christine Cook Nettsheim. She is a member of the University Club and the Cosmos Club. Judge Miller was reappointed by President Clinton on February 4, 1998.

MARIAN BLANK HORN, judge; born in New York, NY, 1943; daughter of Werner P. and Mady R. Blank; married to Robert Jack Horn; three daughters; attended Fieldston School, New York, NY, Barnard College, Columbia University and Fordham University School of Law; admitted to practice U.S. Supreme Court, 1973, Federal and State courts in New York, 1970, and Washington, DC, 1973; assistant district attorney, Deputy Chief Appeals Bureau, Bronx County, NY, 1969–72; attorney, Arent, Fox, Kintner, Plotkin and Kahn, 1972–73; adjunct professor of law, Washington College of Law, American University, 1973–76; litigation attorney, Federal Energy Administration, 1975–76; senior attorney, Office of General Counsel, Strategic Petroleum Reserve Branch, Department of Energy, 1976–79;

deputy assistant general counsel for procurement and financial incentives, Department of Energy, 1979–81; deputy associate solicitor, Division of Surface Mining, Department of the Interior, 1981–83; associate solicitor, Division of General Law, Department of the Interior, 1983–85; principal deputy solicitor and acting solicitor, Department of Interior, 1985–86; adjunct professor of law, George Washington University National Law Center, 1991–present; Woodrow Wilson Visiting Fellow, 1994; assumed duties of judge, U.S. Court of Federal Claims in 1986 and confirmed for a second term in 2003.

ROBERT HAYNE HODGES, JR., judge; born in Columbia, SC, September 11, 1944, son of Robert Hayne and Mary (Lawton) Hodges; educated in the public schools of Columbia, SC; attended Wofford College, Spartanburg, SC; B.S., University of South Carolina, 1966; J.D., University of South Carolina Law School, 1969; married to Ruth Nicholson (Lady) Hodges, August 23, 1963; three children; judge, U.S. Court of Federal Claims, March 12, 1990.

DIANE GILBERT SYPOLT, judge; born June 14, 1947, in Rochester, NY; daughter of Myron B. and Doris (Robie) Gilbert; married to Dwight D. Sypolt, October, 1995; children: Andrew and David; B.A., Smith College, 1969; visiting student at Stanford University Law School and Georgetown University Law Center, 1977–78; J.D., Boston University Law School, 1979; Boston University Alumnae Association Young Lawyers' Chair, 1989; law clerk, Judge Catherine B. Kelly, District of Columbia Court of Appeals, 1979–80; associate, Peabody, Lambert and Meyers, 1980–83; Assistant General Counsel, Office of Management and Budget, Executive Office of the President, 1983–86; Deputy General Counsel for Departmental Services, U.S. Department of Education, 1986–88; Acting General Counsel, U.S. Department of Education, 1988–89; Counselor to the Vice President of the United States, Counsel to the President's Competitiveness Council, 1989–90; nominated by President Bush as judge, U.S. Court of Federal Claims, on July 31, 1990, entered on duty October 22, 1990; admitted to the bars of the Commonwealth of Massachusetts and the District of Columbia; Master of the Federal American Inn of Court; Director, Federal Bar Association Affiliate Democracy Development Institute.

LYNN J. BUSH, judge; born in Little Rock, AR, December 30, 1948; daughter of John E. Bush III and Alice (Saville) Bush; one son, Brian Bush Ferguson; B.A., Antioch College, 1970, Thomas J. Watson Fellow; J.D., Georgetown University Law Center, 1976; admitted to the Arkansas Bar in 1976 and to the District of Columbia Bar in 1977; trial attorney, Commercial Litigation Branch, Civil Division, U.S. Department of Justice, 1976–1987; senior trial attorney, Naval Facilities Engineering Command, Department of the Navy, 1987–1989; counsel, Engineering Field Activity Chesapeake, Naval Facilities Engineering Command, Department of the Navy, 1989–1996; administrative judge, U.S. Department of Housing and Urban Development Board of Contract Appeals, 1996–1998; nominated by President William Jefferson Clinton as judge, U.S. Court of Federal Claims, June 22, 1998; and assumed duties of the office on October 26, 1998.

NANCY B. FIRESTONE, judge; born October 17, 1951, in Manchester, NH; B.A., Washington University, 1973; J.D., University of Missouri, Kansas City, 1977; one child: Amanda Leigh; attorney, Appellate Section and Environmental Enforcement Section, U.S. Department of Justice, Washington, D.C., 1977–1984; Assistant Chief, Policy Legislation and Special Litigation, Environment and Natural Resources Division, Department of Justice, Washington, D.C., 1984–1985; Deputy Chief, Environmental Enforcement Section, Department of Justice, Washington, D.C., 1985–1989; Associate Deputy Administrator, Environmental Protection Agency, Washington, D.C., 1989–1992; Judge, Environmental Appeals Board, Environmental Protection Agency, Washington, D.C., 1992–1995; Deputy Assistant Attorney General, Environment and Natural Resources Division, Department of Justice, Washington, D.C., 1995–1998; Adjunct Professor, Georgetown University Law Center, 1985–current; judge, U.S. Court of Federal Claims, December 4, 1998.

EMILY CLARK HEWITT, judge; born in Baltimore, MD, May 26, 1944; appointed Judge of the United States Court of Federal Claims on October 22, 1998; entered duty on November 10, 1998; educated at the Roland Park Country School, Baltimore, MD (1949–1962); Cornell University (A.B. 1966); Union Theological Seminary (M. Phil. 1975); Harvard Law School (J.D. c.l. 1978); ordained minister in the Episcopal Church (diaconate 1972; priesthood 1974); member, Bar of the Supreme Judicial Court of The Commonwealth of Massachusetts (1978); administrator, Cornell/Hofstra Upward Bound Program (1967–1969); lecturer, Union Theological Seminary (1972–1973; 1974–1975); assistant professor, Andover Newton Theological School (1973–1975); private practice of law, Hill & Barlow (1978–1993); council member, Real Property Section, Massachusetts Bar Association

(1983–1986); member, Executive Committee and chair, Practice Standards Committee, Massachusetts Conveyancers Association (1990–1992); General Counsel, U.S. General Services Administration (1993–1998); member, Administrative Conference of the United States (1993–1995); member, President's Interagency Council on Women (1995–1998).

FRANCIS M. ALLEGRA, judge; born October 14, 1957, in Cleveland, Ohio; married to Regina Allegra; one child (Domenic); B.A., Borromeo College of Ohio, 1978; J.D., Cleveland State University, 1981; judicial clerk to Chief Trial Judge Philip R. Miller, U.S. Court of Claims, 1981–82; associate, Squire, Sanders & Dempsey (Cleveland), 1982–84; line attorney, Appellate Section, then 1984–89, Counselor to the Assistant Attorney General, both with Tax Division, U.S. Department of Justice; 1994, Counselor to the Associate Attorney General then 1994–98, Deputy Associate Attorney General, both with the U.S. Department of Justice; judge, U.S. Court of Federal Claims, since October 22, 1998.

LAWRENCE J. BLOCK, judge, born in New York City, March 15, 1951; son of Jerome Block and Eve Silver; B.A., *magna cum laude,* New York University, 1973; J.D., The John Marshall Law School, 1981; law clerk for Hon. Roger J. Miner, United States District Court Judge for Northern District of New York, 1981–83; Associate, New York office of Skadden, Arps, Slate, Meagher and Flom, 1983–86; Attorney, Commercial Litigation Branch, U.S. Department of Justice, 1986; Senior Attorney-Advisor, Office of Legal Policy and Policy Development, U.S. Department of Justice, 1987–90; adjunct professor, George Mason University School of Law, 1990–91; acting general counsel for legal policy and deputy assistant general counsel for legal policy, U.S. Department of Energy, 1990–94; senior counsel, Senate Judiciary Committee, 1994–02; appointed by President George W. Bush on October 3, 2002, to a 15-years term as judge, U.S. Court of Federal Claims; admitted to the bar of Connecticut; admitted to practice in the U.S. Supreme Court, 1982, the U.S. Court of Appeals for the Eleventh Circuit, 1985, the United States District Court for the Eastern District of New York, 1985, the United States District Court for the northern district of New York, 1982.

SUSAN G. BRADEN, judge, born in Youngstown, OH, November 8, 1948, married to Thomas M. Susman, daughter (Daily); graduated Case Western Reserve University, B.A., 1970; Case Western Reserve University School of Law, J.D., 1973; Post graduate study Harvard Law School, Summer, 1979. Private practice, 1985–2003 (1997–2003 Baker & McKenzie); Federal Trade Commission: Special Counsel to Chairman, 1984–1985, Senior Attorney Advisor to Commissioner and Acting Chairman, 1980–1983; U.S. Department of Justice, Antitrust Division, Senior Trial Attorney, Energy Section, 1978–1980; Cleveland Field Office, 1973–1978. Special Assistant Attorney General for the State of Alabama, 1990; Consultant to the Administrative Conference of the United States, 1984–1985; 2000 Co-Chair, Lawyers for Bush-Cheney; General Counsel Presidential Debate for Dole-Kemp Campaign, 1996; Counsel to RNC Platform, 1996; Coordinator for Regulatory Reform and Antitrust Policy, Dole Presidential Campaign, 1995–1996; National Steering Committee, Lawyers for Bush-Quayle, 1992; Assistant General Counsel, Republican National Convention, 1988, 1992, 1996, 2000. Elected At-Large Member, D.C. Republican National Committee, 2000–2002; admitted to the Supreme Court of Ohio, 1973, U.S. District Court for the District of Columbia, 1980, U.S. Supreme Court, 1980; U.S. Court of Appeals for the District of Columbia, 1992; U.S. Court of Appeals for the Second Circuit, 1993, U.S. Court of Appeals for the Federal Circuit, 2001. Member of the American Bar Association (Council Member, Section on Administrative Law and Regulatory Practice, 1996–1999), Federal Circuit Bar Association, District of Columbia Bar Association, Computer Law Bar Association.

CHARLES F. LETTOW, judge, born in Iowa Falls, Iowa, February 10, 1941; son of Carl F. and Catherine Lettow; B.S.Ch.E. Iowa State University, 1962; LL.B. Stanford University, 1968, Order of the Coif; M.A. Brown University, 2001; Note Editor, Stanford Law Review; married to B. Sue Lettow; children: Renee Burnett, Carl Frederick II, John Stangland, and Paul Vorbeck; served U.S. Army, 1963–1965; law clerk to Judge Ben C. Duniway, U.S. Court of Appeals for the Ninth Circuit, 1968–1969, and Chief Justice Warren E. Burger, Supreme Court of the United States, 1969–1970; counsel, Council on Environmental Quality, Executive Office of the President, 1970–1973; associate (1973–1976) and partner (1976–2003), Cleary, Gottlieb, Steen & Hamilton, Washington, DC; admitted to practice before the U.S. Supreme Court, the U.S. Courts of Appeals for the D.C., Second, Third, Fourth, Fifth, Sixth, Eighth, Ninth, Tenth, and Federal Circuits, the U.S. District Courts for the District of Columbia, the Northern District of California, and the District of Maryland, and the U.S. Court of Federal Claims; member: American Law Institute, the American Bar Association, the D.C. Bar, the California State Bar, the Iowa State Bar Association, and the Maryland State Bar; nominated by President George W. Bush in 2001 and confirmed and took office in 2003.

MARY ELLEN COSTER WILLIAMS, judge; born in Flushing, NY, April 3, 1953; married to Mark Calhoun Williams; son: Justin; daughter: Jacquelyn; B.A. *summa cum laude* (Greek and Latin); MA (Latin), Catholic University, 1974; J.D. Duke University; Editorial Board, *Duke Law Journal,* 1976–1977; Admitted to the District of Columbia Bar. Associate, Fulbright and Jaworski, 1977–1979; Associate, Schnader, Harrison, Segal and Lewis, 1979–1983; Assistant U.S. Attorney, Civil Division, District of Columbia, 1983–1987; Partner—Janis, Schuelke, and Wechsler, 1987–1989; Administrative Judge, General Services Board of Contract Appeals March, 1989–July, 2003; Secretary, District of Columbia Bar, 1988–1989; Fellow, American Bar Foundation, Elected, 1985; Board of Directors, Bar Association of District of Columbia, 1985–1988; Chairman, Young Lawyers Section, Bar Association of District of Columbia, 1985–1986; Chair, Public Contract Law Section of American Bar Association 2002–03, Chair-Elect, Vice-Chair, Secretary, Council, 1995–2002; Delegate, Section of Public Contract Law, ABA House of Delegates 2003–04; Lecturer, Government Contract Law, 1989–Present.

VICTOR JOHN WOLSKI, judge; born in New Brunswick, NJ, November 14, 1962; son of Vito and Eugenia Wolski; B.A., B.S., University of Pennsylvania, 1984; J.D., University of Virginia School of Law, 1991; married to Lisa Wolski, June 3, 2000; admitted to Supreme Court of the United States, 1995; California Supreme Court, 1992; Washington Supreme Court, 1994; Oregon Supreme Court, 1996; District of Columbia Court of Appeals, 2001; U.S. Court of Appeals for the Ninth Circuit, 1993; U.S. Court of Appeals for the Federal Circuit, 2001; U.S. District Court for the Eastern District of California, 1993; U.S. District Court for the Northern District of California, 1995; U.S. Court of Federal Claims, 2001; U.S. District Court for the District of Columbia, 2002; research assistant, Center for Strategic and International Studies, 1984–85; research associate, Institute for Political Economy, 1985–88; Confidential Assistant and Speechwriter to the Secretary, U.S. Dept. of Agriculture, 1988; paralegal specialist, Office of the General Counsel, U.S. Dept. of Energy, 1989; law clerk to Judge Vaughn R. Walker, U.S. District Court for the Northern District of California, 1991–92; attorney, Pacific Legal Foundation, 1992–97; General Counsel, Sacramento County Republican Central Committee, 1995–97; Counsel to Senator Connie Mack, Vice-Chairman of the Joint Economic Committee, U.S. Congress, 1997–98; General Counsel and Chief Tax Adviser, Joint Economic Committee, U.S. Congress, 1999–2000; associate, Cooper, Carvin & Rosenthal, 2000–01; associate, Cooper & Kirk, 2001–03; nominated by President George W. Bush as judge, U.S. Court of Federal Claims, September 12, 2002, renominated January 7, 2003, confirmed by U.S. Senate July 9, 2003.

SENIOR JUDGES

KENNETH R. HARKINS, senior judge; born in Cadiz, OH, September 1, 1921; educated in public schools of Zandesville, OH; Ohio State University, B.A. (economics), 1943; LL.B., 1948; J.D., 1967; admitted to practice of law in Ohio, April, 1949; married to Helen Mae Dozer, 1942; children: M. Elaine and Richard A.; U.S. Army active duty, July, 1943 to June, 1946, 500 AFA Battalion, 14th Armored Division, private to 1st lieutenant; attorney, U.S. Housing and Home Finance Agency, 1949–51; trial attorney, Antitrust Division, Department of Justice, 1951–55; cocounsel, Antitrust Subcommittee, Judiciary Committee, House of Representatives, 1955–60; general counsel, Stromberg Carlson Division and Electronics Division, General Dynamics Corp., 1960–64; chief counsel, Antitrust Subcommittee, Judiciary Committee, House of Representatives, 1964–71; commissioner (trial judge), U.S. Court of Claims, 1971–82; judge, U.S. Court of Federal Claims, 1982–86, pursuant to Public Law 97–164, section 167(a), October 1, 1982 through November 30, 1986. Recalled to active service in senior status pursuant to 28 U.S.C., section 797, December 1, 1986; senior judge, 1986–present.

THOMAS J. LYDON, senior judge; born June 3, 1927 in Portland, ME; educated in the parochial and public schools in Portland; attended University of Maine, 1948–52, B.A.; Georgetown University Law Center, 1952–55, LL.B., 1956–57, LL.M.; trial attorney, Civil Division, Department of Justice, 1955–67; Chief, Court of Claims Section, Civil Division, 1967–72; trial commissioner (trial judge), U.S. Court of Claims, 1972 to September 30, 1982; judge, U.S. Claims Court, October 1, 1982–July 31, 1987; senior judge, August 1, 1987–present.

JAMES F. MEROW, senior judge; born in Salamanca, NY, March 16, 1932; educated in the public schools of Little Valley, NY and Alexandria, VA; A.B. (with distinction), The George Washington University, 1953; J.D. (with distinction), The George Washington University Law School, 1956; member: Phi Beta Kappa, Order of the Coif, Omicron Delta

Kappa; officer, U.S. Army Judge Advocate General's Corps, 1956–59; trial attorney-branch director, Civil Division, U.S. Department of Justice, 1959–78; trial judge, U.S. Court of Claims, 1978–82; judge, U.S. Court of Federal Claims since October 1, 1982 (reappointed by President Reagan to a 15-year term commencing August 5, 1983); member of Virginia State Bar, District of Columbia Bar, American Bar Association, and Federal Bar Association; married.

REGINALD W. GIBSON, senior judge; born in Lynchburg, VA, July 31, 1927; son of McCoy and Julia Gibson; son, Reginald S. Gibson, Jr.; educated in the public schools of Washington, DC; served in the U.S. Army, 1946–47; B.S., Virginia Union University, 1952; Wharton Graduate School of Business Administration, University of Pennsylvania, 1952–53; LL.B., Howard University School of Law, 1956; admitted to the District of Columbia Bar in 1957 and to the Illinois Bar in 1972; Internal Revenue agent, Internal Revenue Service, Washington, DC, 1957–61; trial attorney, tax division, criminal section, Department of Justice, Washington, DC, 1961–71; senior and later general tax attorney, International Harvester Co., Chicago, IL, 1971–82; judge, U.S. Court of Federal Claims, December 15, 1982–August 15, 1995; senior status, August 15, 1995–present.

JOHN PAUL WIESE, senior judge; born in Brooklyn, NY, April 19, 1934; son of Gustav and Margaret Wiese; B.A., *cum laude*, Hobart College, 1962, Phi Beta Kappa; LL.B., University of Virginia School of Law, 1965; married to Alice Mary Donoghue, June, 1961; one son, John Patrick; served U.S. Army, 1957–59; law clerk: U.S. Court of Claims, trial division, 1965–66, and Judge Linton M. Collins, U.S. Court of Claims, appellate division, 1966–67; private practice in District of Columbia, 1967–74 (specializing in government contract litigation); trial judge, U.S. Court of Claims, 1974–82; designated in Federal Courts Improvement Act of 1982 as judge, U.S. Court of Federal Claims, reappointed by President Reagan on October 14, 1986, to 15-year term as judge, U.S. Court of Federal Claims; admitted to bar of the District of Columbia, 1966; admitted to practice in the U.S. Supreme Court, the U.S. Court of Appeals for the Federal Circuit, the U.S. Court of Federal Claims; member: District of Columbia Bar Association and American Bar Association.

ROBERT J. YOCK, senior judge; born in St. James, MN, January 11, 1938; son of Dr. William J. and Erma Yock; B.A. St. Olaf College, 1959; J.D. University of Michigan Law School, 1962; married to Carla M. Moen, June 13, 1964; children: Signe Kara and Torunn Ingrid; admitted to the Minnesota Supreme Court in 1962; Court of Military Appeals, 1964; U.S. Supreme Court, 1965; U.S. District Court for the District of Minnesota, 1966; U.S. District Court for the District of Columbia, 1972; U.S. Court of Claims, 1979; and U.S. Court of Federal Claims, 1982; member: Minnesota State Bar Association, and District of Columbia Bar Association; served in the U.S. Navy, Judge Advocate General's Corps, 1962–66; private practice, St. Paul, MN, 1966–69; entered Government service as chief counsel to the National Archives and Record Services of the General Services Administration, 1969–70; executive assistant and legal advisor to the Administrator of General Services, 1970–72; assistant general counsel at GSA, 1972–77; trial judge, U.S. Court of Claims, 1977–82; designated by Public Law 97–164 as judge, U.S. Court of Federal Claims, 1982–83; renominated by President Reagan as judge, U.S. Court of Federal Claims, June 20, 1983, confirmed by U.S. Senate, August 4, 1983, reappointed to 15-year term, August 5, 1983.

LAWRENCE S. MARGOLIS, senior judge; born in Philadelphia, PA, March 13, 1935; son of Reuben and Mollie Margolis; B.A., Central High School, Philadelphia, PA; B.S. in mechanical engineering from the Drexel Institute of Technology (now Drexel University), 1957; J.D., George Washington University Law School, 1961; admitted to the District of Columbia Bar; patent examiner, U.S. Patent Office, 1957–62; patent counsel, Naval Ordnance Laboratory, White Oak, MD, 1962–63; assistant corporation counsel for the District of Columbia, 1963–66; attorney, criminal division, U.S. Department of Justice and special assistant U.S. attorney for District of Columbia, 1966–68; assistant U.S. attorney for the District of Columbia, 1968–71; appointed U.S. magistrate for District of Columbia in 1971; reappointed for a second 8-year term in 1979 and served until December, 1982 when appointed a judge, U.S. Court of Federal Claims; chairman, U.S. Court of Federal Claims: Security Committee, Building Committee, and Alternative Dispute Resolution Committee; chairman, American Bar Association, judicial administration division, 1980–81; chairman, National Conference of Special Court Judges, 1977–78; board of directors, Bar Association of the District of Columbia, 1970–72; editor: DC Bar Journal, 1966–73, Young Lawyers Newspaper editor, 1965–66; executive council, Young Lawyers Section, 1968–69; board of editors, The Judges' Journal and The District Lawyer; president, George Washington University National Law Association, 1983–84; president, George Washington Law Association, District of Columbia Chapter,

1975–76; board of governors, George Washington University General Alumni Association, 1978–85; fellow, Institute of Judicial Administration, 1993–; member, District of Columbia Judicial Conference; former member, board of directors, National Council of U.S. Magistrates; former president, Federal Bar Toastmasters; former technical editor, Federal Bar Journal; faculty, Federal Judicial Center; trustee, Drexel University, 1983–91; member, Rotary Club; Board of Managers, Central High (Philadelphia, PA); president, Washington, D.C. Rotary Club, 1988–89, District governor, 1991–92; American Bar Association Judicial Administration Division Award for distinguished service as chairman for 1980–81; Drexel University and George Washington University Distinguished Alumni Achievement Awards; Drexel University 100 (one of top 100 graduates); Center for Public Resources Alternative Dispute Resolution Achievement Award, 1987; George Washington University Community Service Award; married to Doris May Rosenberg, January 30, 1960; children: Mary Aleta and Paul Oliver; nominated by President Ronald Reagan as a judge on the U.S. Court of Federal Claims on September 27, 1982, confirmed by the Senate and received Commission on December 10, 1982, took oath of office on December 15, 1982.

MOODY R. TIDWELL III, senior judge; born in Miami, OK, February 15, 1939; son of Maj. Gen. M.R. Tidwell, Jr., and Dorothy (Thompson) Tidwell; married to Rena C. Tidwell; children: Gregory T. and Jeremy H.; B.A., Ohio Wesleyan University, 1961; J.D., Washington College of Law, American University; LL.M., National Law Center, George Washington University; admitted to the bar of the District of Columbia; admitted to practice in the U.S. Supreme Court, the U.S. Court of Appeals for the Federal Circuit and the U.S. Court of Federal Claims and various other circuit and U.S. district courts; attorney, General Accounting Office, 1965–69; associate solicitor, Divisions of General Law and Energy and Resources, Office of the Solicitor, U.S. Department of the Interior, 1969–77; staff director and vice chairman, Commission on Government Procurement, 1971–73; Associate Solicitor, Mine Safety and Health, Office of the Solicitor, U.S. Department of Labor, 1977–80; corporate secretary and board member, Keco Industries, Inc., 1979–82; deputy solicitor and counselor to the Secretary of the Interior, 1980–83; appointed and confirmed by the President as judge in the U.S. Court of Federal Claims, May 17, 1983.

LOREN ALLAN SMITH, senior judge; born December 22, 1944, in Chicago, IL; son of Alvin D. and Selma (Halpern) Smith; B.A., Northwestern University, 1966; J.D., Northwestern University School of Law, 1969; admitted to the Bars of the Illinois Supreme Court; the Court of Military Appeals; the U.S. Court of Appeals, District of Columbia Circuit; the U.S. Court of Appeals for the Federal Circuit; the U.S. Supreme Court; the U.S. Court of Federal Claims; honorary member: The University Club; consultant, Sidley and Austin Chicago, 1972–73; general attorney, Federal Communications Commission, 1973; assistant to the Special Counsel to the President, 1973–74; Special Assistant U.S. Attorney, District of Columbia, 1974–75; chief counsel, Reagan for President campaigns, 1976 and 1980; professor, Delaware Law School, 1976–84; distinguished lecturer at Columbus School of Law, The Catholic University of America and distinguished adjunct professor at George Mason University School of Law; deputy director, Executive Branch Management Office of Presidential Transition, 1980–81; Chairman, Administrative Conference of the Unites States, 1981–85; served as a member of the President's Cabinet Councils on Legal Policy and on Management and Administration; appointed judge of the U.S. Court of Federal Claims on July 11, 1985; entered on duty September 12, 1985; served as chief judge from January 14, 1986, until July 11, 2000; married.

ERIC G. BRUGGINK, senior judge; born in Kalidjati, Indonesia, September 11, 1949; naturalized U.S. citizen, 1961; married to Melinda Harris Bruggink; sons: John and David; B.A., *cum laude* (sociology), Auburn University, AL, 1971; M.A. (speech), 1972; J.D., University of Alabama, 1975; Hugo Black Scholar and Note and Comments Editor of Alabama Law Review; member, Alabama State Bar and District of Columbia Bar; served as law clerk to chief judge Frank H. McFadden, Northern District of Alabama, 1975–76; associate, Hardwick, Hause and Segrest, Dothan, AL, 1976–77; assistant director, Alabama Law Institute, 1977–79; director, Office of Energy and Environmental Law, 1977–79; associate, Steiner, Crum and Baker, Montgomery, AL, 1979–82; Director, Office of Appeals Counsel, Merit Systems Protection Board, 1982–86; judge, U.S. Court of Federal Claims, April 15, 1986.

WILKES COLEMAN ROBINSON, senior judge; born September 30, 1925 in Anniston, AL; B.A., University of Alabama, 1948; J.D., University of Virginia, 1951 member: Phi Beta Kappa, Phi Eta Sigma, Phi Alpha Theta, Kappa Alpha fraternity; associate attorney, Bibb and Hemphill, Anniston, AL, 1953–55; city recorder of Anniston, AL, 1953–55; judge, Juvenile and Domestic Relations Court, Calhoun County, AL, 1954–56; attorney: Gulf, Mobile and Ohio Railroad, 1956–58; asst. gen'l. attorney, Seaboard Airline Railroad Company,

1958–66; chief commerce counsel, Monsanto Company, 1966–70; vice president and general counsel, Marion Laboratories, Inc., 1970–80; president and member of board of directors, Gulf and Great Plains Legal Foundation, 1980–85; vice president and general counsel, S.R. Financial Group, Inc., 1986–87; judge, U.S. Court of Federal Claims, assumed duties July 10, 1987; member: Alabama State Bar, Virginia State Bar, Missouri State Bar, Kansas State Bar, U.S. Supreme Court Bar, Tenth Circuit Court of Appeals, Alabama and Missouri U.S. District Courts, U.S. Court of Federal Claims Bar; married to Julia Von P. Rowan; three children: Randolph C., Peyton H. and T. Wilkes C. Robinson.

BOHDAN A. FUTEY, senior judge; born in Ukraine, June 28, 1939; B.A., Western Reserve University, 1962; M.A., 1964; J.D., Cleveland Marshall Law School, 1968; partner, Futey and Rakowsky, 1968–72; chief assistant police prosecutor, city of Cleveland, 1972–74; executive assistant to the mayor of Cleveland, 1974–75; partner, Bazarko, Futey and Oryshkewych, 1975–84; chairman, U.S. Foreign Claims Settlement Commission, May, 1984–87; nominated judge of the U.S. Court of Federal Claims on January 30, 1987, and entered on duty, May 29, 1987; married to the former Myra Fur; three children: Andrew, Lidia, and Daria; member: District of Columbia Bar Association, the Ukrainian American Bar Association; Judge Futey is actively involved with Democratization and Rule of Law programs organized by the Judicial Conference of the United States, the Department of State, and the American Bar Association in Ukraine and Russia. He has participated in judicial exchange programs, seminars, and workshops and has been a consultant to the working group on Ukraine's Constitution and Ukrainian Parliament; Judge Futey is an advisor to the International Foundation for Election Systems (IFES); and the International Republican Institutes (IRI) democracy programs for Ukraine. He served as an official observer during the parliamentary and presidential elections in 1994 and 1998 and conducted briefings on Ukraine's election law for international observers; Judge Futey has lectured on Constitutional Law at the Ukrainian Free University in Munich and Passau University, Germany; also at Kyiv State University and Lviv University in Ukraine.

JAMES T. TURNER, senior judge; born March 12, 1938, in Clifton Forge, VA; B.A., Wake Forest University, 1960; LL.B., University of Virginia Law School, 1965; private practice of law, Williams, Worrell, Kelly and Greer, 1965–79; U.S. Magistrate for the eastern district of Virginia, 1979–87; president, National Council of U.S. Magistrates, 1984–85; judge, U.S. Court of Federal Claims since July 2, 1987; member of the American Bar Association, Virginia Bar Association, Virginia State Bar, Norfolk and Portsmouth Bar Association.

OFFICERS OF THE UNITED STATES COURT OF FEDERAL CLAIMS

Clerk.—Margaret M. Earnest, (202) 219–9657

UNITED STATES TAX COURT

400 Second Street 20217, phone (202) 606–8754

THOMAS B. WELLS, chief judge; born Akron, OH, July 2, 1945; married Mary Josephine Graham of Vidalia, GA in 1974; children: Kathryn and Graham; received B.S. degree from Miami University, Oxford, OH in 1967; J.D. degree from Emory University School of Law, Atlanta, GA in 1973; LL.M. degree (in Taxation) from New York University Graduate School of Law, New York, NY in 1978; attended Ohio Northern University School of Law, Ada, OH, served as managing editor of the law review until he transferred to Emory University School of Law in 1972; completed active duty in 1970 as a supply corps officer in the U.S. Naval Reserve after tours in Morocco and Vietnam; admitted to the practice of law in the State of Georgia and practiced law in Vidalia, GA with the law firm of Graham and Wells, P.C., served as county attorney for Toombs County, GA and city attorney for the city of Vidalia, GA until 1977, and in Atlanta with the law firm of Hurt, Richardson, Garner, Todd and Cadenhead until 1981 and with the law firm of Shearer and Wells, P.C. until his appointment to the U.S. Tax Court in 1986; member; American Bar Association (section of taxation); State Bar of Georgia, served as a member of its Board of Governors; Board of Editors of the Georgia State Bar Journal; active in the Atlanta Bar Association, served as editor of The Atlanta Lawyer; active in various tax organizations such as the Atlanta Tax Forum; the Atlanta Estate Planning Council, served as a director; and the North Atlanta Tax Council, served as a director; nominated by President Reagan and confirmed by the Senate as a judge of the U.S. Tax Court for a term of 15 years beginning October 12, 1986 to succeed Judge Richard C. Wilbur who retired.

MARY ANN COHEN, judge, California; born July 16, 1943, Albuquerque, NM; B.A., University of California at Los Angeles, 1964; J.D., University of Southern California, 1967; admitted to California Bar, 1967; private practice of law, Los Angeles, with firm of Abbott and Cohen, a professional corporation (and predecessors), 1967–82; member: American Bar Association (sections of taxation, litigation, and criminal justice), American Judicature Society, Attorney General's Advisory Committee on Tax Litigation, U.S. Department of Justice (1979–80); appointed to U.S. Tax Court, July 1982 to succeed Cynthia H. Hall; term expires September 24, 1997.

STEPHEN J. SWIFT, judge, California; born September 7, 1943, Salt Lake City, UT, son of Edward A. Swift and Maurine Jensen; married to Lorraine Burnell Facer, 1972; children: Carter, Stephanie, Spencer, Meredith, and Hunter; graduated, Menlo Atherton High School, Atherton, CA, 1961; B.A., Brigham Young University, political science, 1967; George Washington Law School, J.D. (with honors), 1970; trial attorney (honors program), tax division, U.S. Department of Justice, 1970–74; assistant U.S. attorney, tax division, U.S. attorney's office, San Francisco, CA 1974–77; vice president and senior tax counsel, tax department, BankAmerica N.T. and S.A., San Francisco, CA, 1977–83; adjunct professor, Graduate Tax Program, Golden Gate University, San Francisco, CA 1978–83; member: California Bar, District of Columbia Bar, and American Bar Association (section of taxation); appointed August 16, 1983 to the U.S. Tax Court for a 15-year term expiring August 16, 1998.

JOEL GERBER, judge, Virginia; born in Chicago, IL, July 16, 1940; married to Judith Smilgoff, 1963; three sons: Jay Lawrence, Jeffrey Mark, and Jon Victor; B.S., business administration, Roosevelt University, 1962; J.D., DePaul University, 1965; LL.M., taxation, Boston University Law School, 1968; admitted to the Illinois Bar, 1965; Georgia Bar, 1974; Tennessee Bar, 1978; member American Bar Association (section of taxation); served with U.S. Treasury Department, Internal Revenue Service as: trial attorney, Boston, MA, 1965–72; staff assistant, regional counsel/senior trial attorney, Atlanta, GA, 1972–76; district counsel, Nashville, TN, 1976–80; deputy chief counsel, Internal Revenue Service, Washington, DC, 1980–84; acting chief counsel, Internal Revenue Service, May 1983 to March 1984; recipient of a Presidential Meritorious Rank Award, 1983 and the Secretary of the Treasury's

Exceptional Service Award, 1984; lecturer, law, Vanderbilt University, 1976–80; appointed to the Tax Court for a 15-year term, beginning June 18, 1984, to succeed Senior Judge C. Moxley Featherston.

ROBERT PAUL RUWE, judge, Virginia; born July 3, 1941, Cincinnati, Ohio; married to Mary Kay Sayer, Cincinnati, Ohio, 1967; children: Paul, Michael, Christian, and Stephen; graduated Roger Bacon High School, St. Bernard, OH, 1959, Xavier University, Cincinnati, OH, 1963; J.D., Salmon P. Chase College of Law, 1970; admitted to Ohio bar, 1970; joined Office of Chief Counsel, Internal Revenue Service in 1970 and held the following positions, Trial Attorney (Indianapolis), Director, Criminal Tax Division, Deputy Associate Chief Counsel (Litigation), and Director, Tax Litigation Division; member, American Bar Association (Section of taxation); took oath of office as a judge of the U.S. Tax Court, November 20, 1987 for a 15-year term to succeed Judge Charles R. Simpson.

JOHN O. COLVIN, judge, Virginia; born November 17, 1946, Canton, OH; married Ava M. Belohlov in 1970; one son: Timothy; graduated from the University of Missouri (A.B., 1968), and Georgetown University Law Center (J.D., Masters of Law in Taxation, 1978). During college and law school, employed by Niedner, Niedner, Nack and Bodeux, St. Charles, MO; Missouri Attorney General John C. Danforth and Missouri State Representative Richard C. Marshall, Jefferson City, MO; and U.S. Senator Mark O. Hatfield and Congressman Thomas B. Curtis, Washington, DC; admitted to the practice of law in Missouri, 1971 and District of Columbia, 1974. Office of the Chief Counsel, U.S. Coast Guard, Washington, DC, 1971–75; served as tax counsel, Senator Bob Packwood, 1975–84; chief counsel, 1985–87, and chief minority counsel, 1987–88, U.S. Senate Finance Committee; officer of the Tax Section, Federal Bar Association since 1978, and adjunct professor of law, Georgetown University Law Center since 1987. Numerous civic and community activities; Judge Colvin was nominated by President Reagan and confirmed by the Senate as a Judge of the U.S. Tax Court for a term of 15 years beginning September 1, 1988 and expiring August 31, 2003. Judge Colvin filled a vacancy due to the resignation of Judge Samuel B. Sterrett.

JAMES S. HALPERN, judge, District of Columbia; born 1945, New York City; married to Nancy A. Nord; two children: W. Dyer and Hilary Ann; graduated from Hackley School, Terrytown, New York, 1963; Wharton School, University of Pennsylvania, B.S. 1967; Law School, University of Pennsylvania, J.D., 1972; Law School, New York University, LL.M. (in taxation) 1975; associate attorney, Mudge, Rose, Guthrie and Alexander, New York City, 1972–74; assistant professor of law, Law School, Washington and Lee University, 1975–76; assistant professor of law, St. John's University, New York City, 1976–78, visiting professor, Law School, New York University, 1978–79; associate attorney, Roberts and Holland, New York City, 1979–80; Principal Technical Advisor, Assistant Commissioner (Technical) and Associate Chief Counsel (Technical), Internal Revenue Service, Washington, DC, 1980–83; partner, Baker and Hostetler, Washington, DC, 1983–90; adjunct professor, Law School, George Washington University, Washington, DC, 1984–90; Colonel, U.S. Army Reserves; appointed to the U.S. Tax Court on July 3, 1990.

CAROLYN P. CHIECHI, judge, Maryland; born December 6, 1943, Newark, New Jersey; B.S., Georgetown, University, Washington, DC, *magna cum laude,* 1965 (Class Rank: 1); J.D., 1969 (Class Rank: 9); LL.M. (Taxation), 1971; admitted to the bar of the District of Columbia, 1969; served as attorney-advisor to Judge Leo H. Irwin, United States Tax Court, 1969–1971; practiced with the law firm of Sutherland, Asbill and Brennan, Washington, D.C. and Atlanta, Georgia (partner, 1976–1992; associate, 1971–1976); member, District of Columbia Bar (served as taxation section Tax Audits and Litigation Committee chairperson, 1987–1988); American Bar Association (Section of Taxation); Federal Bar Association (Section of Taxation); Women's Bar Association of the District of Columbia; elected fellow, American College of Tax Counsel; fellow, American Bar Foundation; member, Board of Regents, Georgetown University; member, National Law Alumni Board, Georgetown University; member, Stuart Stiller Memorial Foundation; appointed by the President to the U.S. Tax Court for a 15–year term beginning October 1, 1992.

DAVID LARO, judge, Michigan; born Flint, MI, March 3, 1942; married to the former Nancy Lynn Wolf on June 18, 1967; two children: Rachel Lynn and Marlene Ellen; graduated from the University of Michigan in 1964 with a B.A.; the University of Illinois Law School in 1967 with a J.D.; and New York University Law School in 1970 with an LL.M. in taxation; admitted to the bar of Michigan in 1968 and the United States District Court

(Eastern District) Michigan in 1968, United States Tax Court, 1971; former partner of Winegarden, Booth, Shedd, and Laro, Flint, MI, 1970–75; principal member, Laro and Borgeson, Flint, MI, 1975–86; principal member, David Laro, Attorney at Law, P.C., Flint, MI, 1986–92; of counsel to Dykema Gossett, Ann Arbor, MI, 1989–90; former president and chief executive officer of Durakon Industries, Inc., Lapeer, MI, 1989–91, and former chairman of the board of Durakon Industries, Inc., 1991–92; former chairman of the board of Republic Bank, Ann Arbor, MI, 1986–92, and vice chairman and co-founder of Republic Bancorp, Inc., Ann Arbor, MI, 1986–92. Regent, University of Michigan Board of Regents, Ann Arbor, MI, 1975–81; former member of the Michigan State Board of Education, 1982–83; former chairman of the Michigan State Tenure Commission, 1972–75; former commissioner, Civil Service Commission, Flint, MI, 1984–1985. Former Commissioner of Police, Flint Township, 1972–74; former member of the Political Leadership Program, the Institute for Public Policy and Social Research, Lansing, MI; frequent speaker and lecturer on tax matters for the Michigan Association of Certified Public Accountants, and the Michigan Institute of Continuing Legal Education and other professional and business groups and organizations; author of numerous articles on taxation; former member of the Ann Arbor Art Association Board of Directors, board member of the Holocaust Foundation (Ann Arbor); appointed to the Tax Court for a 15–year term beginning November 2, 1992, to fill vacancy created by Judge Jules G. Körner III, who assumed senior status.

MAURICE B. FOLEY, judge, Illinois; born March 28, 1960, Belleville, Illinois; married Cassandra LaNel Green; three children: Malcolm, Corinne, and Nathan; received a Bachelor of Arts degree from Swarthmore College, a Juris Doctor from Boalt Hall School of Law at the University of California at Berkeley, and a Master of Laws in Taxation from Georgetown University Law Center; prior to the appointment to the Court was an attorney for the Legislation and Regulations Division of the Internal Revenue Service, tax counsel for the United States Senate Committee on Finance and Deputy Tax Legislative Counsel in the Treasury's Office of Tax Policy; appointed to the Tax Court for a 15-year term beginning April 10, 1995 to succeed Judge Charles E. Clapp, II.

JUAN F. VASQUEZ, judge, Texas; born in San Antonio, TX on June 24, 1948; married to Mary Theresa (Terry) Schultz in 1970; two children: Juan, Jr. and Jaime; attended Fox Tech High School and San Antonio Junior College, A.D. (Data Processing); received B.B.A (Accounting) from the University of Texas in Austin in 1972; attended State University of New York in Buffalo, 1st year law school in 1975; graduate of University of Houston Law Center in 1977 with a J.D. and New York University Law School in 1978 with an LL.M. in Taxation. Certified in Tax Law by Texas Board of Legal Specialization in 1984; Certified Public Account Certificate from Texas in 1976 and California in 1974; admitted to the bar of Texas in 1977; United States Tax Court in 1978, United States District Court, Southern District of Texas in 1982 and Western District of Texas in 1985, Fifth Circuit Court of Appeals in 1982; private practice of Tax Law, 1987–April 1995; partner, Leighton, Hood and Vasquez, 1982–87, San Antonio, Texas; Trial Attorney, Office of Chief Counsel, Internal Revenue Service, Houston, TX, 1978–82; accountant, Coopers and Lybrand, Los Angeles, California, 1972–74; member American Bar Association (Tax Section); Texas State Bar (Tax and Probate Sections); Fellow of Texas and San Antonio Bar Foundations, Mexican American Bar Association (MABA) of San Antonio (Treasurer); Houston MABA; Texas MABA (Treasurer), National Association of Hispanic CPA's; San Antonio Chapter (founding member), College of State Bar of Texas, National Hispanic Bar Association, Member of Greater Austin Tax Litigation Association; served on Austin Internal Revenue Service District Director's Practitioner Liaison Committee, 1990–91, chairman, 1991; Judge Vasquez was nominated by President Clinton on September 14, 1994, and confirmed by the Senate on March 17, 1995, as a Judge of the United States Tax Court for a term of 15 years beginning on May 1, 1995 to succeed Judge Perry Shields who took senior status.

JOSEPH H. GALE, judge, Virginia; born August 26, 1953, in Smithfield, VA; received A.B., Philosophy, Princeton University, Princeton, New Jersey, 1976; J.D., University of Virginia School of Law, Charlottesville, VA, 1980, where he was a Dillard Fellow; practiced law as an associate attorney at Dewey Ballantine, Washington, DC, and New York, New York, 1980–83, and Dickstein, Shapiro and Morin, Washington, DC, 1983–85; served as Tax Legislative Counsel for Senator Daniel Patrick Moynihan (D–NY), 1985–88; administrative assistant and Tax Legislative Counsel, 1989; chief counsel, 1990–93; chief tax counsel, Committee on Finance, U.S. Senate, 1993–95; minority chief tax counsel, Senate Finance Committee, January 1995-July 1995; minority staff director and chief counsel, Senate Finance Committee, July 1995–January 1996; admitted to the District of Columbia Bar; member: American Bar Association, Section of Taxation; frequent speaker at professional conferences and seminars on various Federal income tax topics; appointed to Tax Court for a 15-year term beginning February 9, 1996, to succeed Judge Edna G. Parker, who assumed senior status.

MICHAEL B. THORNTON, judge; born February 9, 1954, in Hattiesburg, Mississippi. Married Alexandra Deane Thornton in 1992 and has two daughters, Michaela and Camille. Graduated from University of Southern Mississippi, B.S. in Accounting, *summa cum laude,* 1976, and M.S. in Accounting, 1997; University of Tennessee, M.A. in English Literature, 1979; Duke University School of Law, J.D. with distinction, 1982 (Order of the Coif, *Duke Law Journal* Editorial Board). Served as law clerk to the Honorable Charles Clark, Chief Judge, U.S. Court of Appeals for the Fifth Circuit (1983–1984). Practiced law as an Associate Attorney at Sutherland, Asbill and Brennan, Washington, D.C. (1982–1983 and summer 1981); and Miller and Chevalier, Chartered, Washington, D.C. (1985–1988). Served as Tax Counsel, U.S. House Committee on Ways and Means (1988–1993); Chief Minority Tax Counsel, U.S. House Committee on Ways and means (January 1995); Attorney-Adviser, U.S. Treasury Department (February-April 1995); and Deputy Tax Legislative Counsel (Tax Legislation) in the Office of Tax Policy, United States Treasury Department (April 1995-February 1998). Recipient of Treasury Secretary's Annual Award, U.S. Department of the Treasury, 1997; Meritorious Service Award, U.S. Department of the Treasury, 1998. Admitted to the District of Columbia Bar (1982). Appointed to the Tax Court for a 15-year term beginning March 8, 1998, to succeed Judge Lapsley W. Hamblen, Jr., who assumed senior status.

L. PAIGE MARVEL, judge, Baltimore, Maryland; born December 6, 1949, in Easton, Maryland. Education: College of Notre Dame, Baltimore, Maryland, B.A. *magna cum laude,* 1971; University of Maryland School of Law, Baltimore, Maryland, J.D. with honors, 1974. Member, Order of the Coif. Professional Experience: Garbis & Schwait, PA (Associate 1974–76; Shareholder 1976–1985); Garbis, Marvel & Junghans, PA (Shareholder 1985–1986); Melnicove, Kaufman, Weiner, Smouse & Garbis, PA (Shareholder 1986–1988); Venabel, Baetjer & Howard LLP (Partner 1988–1998). Practice concentrated in the areas of federal and state tax litigation (civil and criminal). Bar Associations: American Bar Association, Section of Taxation (Vice-Chair, Committee Operations 1993–95; Council Director 1989–92; Chair, Court Procedure Committee 1985–87); Maryland State Bar Association (Member, Board of Governors 1988–90, 1996–98; Chair, Taxation Section 1982–83); Federal Bar Association, Section of Taxation (Member, Section Council). Affiliations: Fellow, American Bar Foundation; Fellow, Maryland Bar Foundation; Fellow and Regent, American College of Tax Counsel; Member, American Law Institute; Advisor, ALI Restatement of Law Third-The Law Governing Lawyers 1988–1998; Member, University of Maryland Board of Visitors; Member, Loyola/Notre Dame Library, Inc. Board of Trustees; Co-editor, Procedure Department, *The Journal of Taxation* 1990–1998; member, Commissioner's Review Panel on IRS Integrity 1989–91; Member and Chair, Procedure Subcommittee, Commission to Revise the Annotated Code of Maryland; (Tax Provisions). Author of various articles and book chapters on tax and tax litigation topics. Frequent lecturer on tax and tax controversy topics. Married to Robert H. Dyer, Jr.; two children—Alex and Kelly Dyer. Appointed to the Tax Court for a 15-year term beginning April 6, 1998 to succeed Judge Lawrence A. Wright who assumed senior status.

HARRY A. HAINES, judge, Montana; married to the former Janet Meyers; three children: Eric, Rob, and Jeanne; B.A., St. Olaf College in Northfield, Minnesota; J.D., University of Montana Law School; LL.M., New York University School of Law, in taxation; practiced law with the firm of Worden, Thane & Haines, P.C., in Missoula, Montana; appointed April 22, 2003 as a judge of the United States Tax Court; appointed by President George W. Bush to the Tax Court for a 15-year term to succeed Judge Renato Beghe who assumed senior status.

JOSEPH ROBERT GOEKE, judge, Illinois; married to the former Linda Powers; three children: Robert, Benjamin, and Elizabeth; B.S., Xavier University in Cincinnati, OH; J.D., University of Kentucky College of Law; initially, with the Chief Counsel of the Internal Revenue Service and since 1998 with Mayer, Brown, Rowe and Maw in Chicago; appointed April 22, 2003 as a judge of the United States Tax Court; appointed by President George W. Bush to the Tax Court for a 15-year term to succeed Judge Herbert L. Chabot who assumed senior status.

ROBERT A. WHERRY, JR., judge, Colorado; married to the former Leslie Ross; two children: Richard and Marsha; B.S., J.D., University of Colorado at Boulder; LL.M., New

York University in taxation; practiced law for 30 years with Lentz, Evans, and King, P.C., in Denver, Colorado; appointed April 23, 2003, as a judge of the United States Tax Court; appointed by President George W. Bush to the Tax Court for a 15-year term to succeed Judge Laurence J. Whalen who assumed senior status.

SENIOR JUDGES

HOWARD A. DAWSON, JR., senior judge, Arkansas; born October 23, 1922, Okolona, AR, married to Marianne Atherholt; two daughters, Amy and Suzanne; graduated from University of North Carolina, B.S. in business administration, 1946; George Washington University Law School, J.D. with honors, 1949; president, Case Club; secretary-treasurer, Student Bar Association; private practice of law, Washington, DC, 1949–50; served with the U.S. Treasury Department, Internal Revenue Service, as follows: attorney, civil division, Office of Chief Counsel, 1950–53; civil advisory counsel, Atlanta District, 1953–57; regional counsel, Atlanta Region, 1958; personal assistant to Chief Counsel, December 1, 1958 to June 1, 1959; and assistant chief counsel (administration), June 1, 1959 to August 19, 1962; military service: U.S. Army Finance Corps, 1942–45; served 2 years in European theater; captain, Finance Corps, U.S. Army Reserve; member of District of Columbia Bar, Georgia Bar, American Bar Association (Section of Taxation), Federal Bar Association, National Lawyers Club, Delta Theta Phi Legal Fraternity, George Washington University Law Alumni Association; appointed on August 21, 1962, to the U.S. Tax Court for term expiring June 1, 1970; reappointed on May 21, 1970, to the U.S. Tax Court for a 15-year term expiring June 1, 1985; elected chief judge for a 2-year term beginning July 1, 1973; reelected chief judge for a 2-year term beginning July 1, 1975; again elected chief judge for a 2-year term beginning July 1, 1983. Assumed status as a senior judge on June 2, 1985. David L. Brennan Distinguished Visiting Professor of Law, University of Akron School of Law, spring term, 1986, professor of law and director, Graduate Tax Program, University of Baltimore School of Law, 1986–89; presently serving on senior status.

ARTHUR L. NIMS III, senior judge, New Jersey; elected chief judge for a 2-year term beginning June 1, 1988, re-elected chief judge beginning June 1, 1990; born January 3, 1923, Oklahoma City, OK; married to Nancy Chloe Keyes; two daughters; Deerfield Academy, Deerfield, MA; B.A., Williams College; LL.B., University of Georgia Law School; LL.M. (Tax), New York University Law School; served as an officer, lieutenant (jg.), U.S. Naval Reserve, on active duty in the Pacific theater during World War II; admitted to the bar of Georgia, 1949; and practiced in Macon, GA, 1949–51; served as special attorney, Office of the District Counsel, Internal Revenue Service, New York, NY, 1951–54; attorney, Legislation and Regulations Division, Chief Counsel's Office, Washington, DC, 1954–55; admitted to the bar of New Jersey, 1955; was with the law firm of McCarter and English, Newark, NJ, until 1979, having become a partner in 1961; served as secretary, Section of Taxation, American Bar Association, 1977–79; served as chairman, Section of Taxation, New Jersey State Bar Association, 1969–71; member, American Law Institute; appointed by the President to the U.S. Tax Court, June 21, 1979, to succeed Judge Arnold Raum, who assumed senior status; took office on June 29, 1979; assumed senior status June 1, 1992.

JULIAN I. JACOBS, senior judge, Maryland; born in Baltimore, MD, August 13, 1937; children: Richard and Jennifer; residence: Bethesda, MD; B.A., University of Maryland, 1958; LL.B., University of Maryland Law School, 1960; LL.M. (taxation), Georgetown Law Center, 1965; began legal career with the Internal Revenue Service, first in Washington, DC, drafting tax legislation and regulations from 1961–65, and then in Buffalo, NY, as a trial attorney in the regional counsel's office from 1965–67; entered private practice of law Baltimore City, 1967; partner, Baltimore law firm of Gordon, Feinblatt, Rothman, Hoffberger and Hollander, 1967, and remained until his appointment to the Tax Court on March 30, 1984, for a 15-year term to succeed Senior Judge Theodore Tannenwald, Jr.; chairman, study commission to improve the quality of the Maryland Tax Court, 1978, appointed by Maryland Gov. Blair Lee; member, several study groups to consider changes in the Maryland tax laws and as a commissioner on a commission to reorganize and recodify that article of Maryland law dealing with taxation, 1980, appointed by Maryland Gov. Harry Hughes; lecturer, tax seminars and professional programs; chairman, section of taxation, Maryland State Bar Association.

HERBERT L. CHABOT, senior judge, Maryland; born July 17, 1931, Bronx County, NY; married to Aleen Kerwin, 1951; four children: Elliot C., Donald J., Lewis A., and Nancy Jo; graduated, Stuyvesant High School, 1948; B.A. (*cum laude*), C.C.N.Y., 1952;

LL.B., Columbia University, 1957; LL.M. (taxation), Georgetown University, 1964; enlisted in U.S. Army for 2 years and Army Reserves (civil affairs units), 8 years; served on legal staff, American Jewish Congress, 1957–61; law clerk to tax court Judge Russell E. Train, 1961–65; served on staff of Congressional Joint Committee on Taxation, 1965–78; elected delegate, Maryland Constitutional Convention, 1967–68; adjunct professor, National Law Center, George Washington University, 1974–83; member, American Bar (tax section) and Federal Bar Associations; appointed to the U.S. Tax Court for a 15-year term, beginning April 3, 1978; reappointed for a second 15-year term in 1993.

LAURENCE J. WHALEN, judge, Oklahoma; born 1944, Philadelphia, PA; married Nan Shaver Whalen; son: E. Holmes Whalen; A.B., Georgetown University, 1967; J.D., Georgetown University Law Center, 1970; LL.M., 1971; special assistant to the Assistant Attorney General, 1971–72; trial attorney, tax division, 1971–75; private practice in Washington, DC, with Hamel and Park (now Hopkins, Sutter, Hamel and Park), 1977–84; also in Oklahoma City, OK, with Crowe and Dunlevy, 1984–87; member: Oklahoma Bar Association, District of Columbia Bar Association, American Bar Association, and Bar Association of the District of Columbia; appointed to the U.S. Tax Court, November 23, 1987.

RENATO BEGHE, judge, Illinois; born 1933, Chicago, Illinois; married to Bina House; four children and one grandchild; University of Chicago (A.B. 1951; J.D. 1954); Phi Beta Kappa; Order of the Coif and Law Review co-managing editor; Phi Gamma Delta; admitted New York bar 1955; practiced law with Carter, Ledyard and Milburn, New York City (associate 1954–65; partner 1965–83) and Morgan, Lewis and Bockius, New York City (1983–89); bar associations; Association of the Bar of the City of New York (Chairman, Art Law Committee, 1980–83); New York State Bar Association (tax section chairman 1977–78; Joint Practice Committee of Lawyers and Accountants, co-chairman, 1989–90); American Bar Association (Tax Section); International Bar Association; International Fiscal Association; member American Law Institute and American College of Tax Counsel; member America-Italy Society, Inc. and Honorable Order of Kentucky Counsel; appointed to the Tax Court for 15–year term beginning March 26, 1991, to fill vacancy created by resignation of Judge B. John Williams, Jr.

SPECIAL TRIAL JUDGES OF THE COURT

Robert N. Armen, Jr.; Lewis R. Carluzzo; D. Irvin Couvillion; John F. Dean; Daniel J. Dinan; Stanley J. Goldberg; John J. Pajak; Peter J. Panuthos (chief special trial judge); Carleton D. Powell, Norman H. Wolfe.

OFFICERS OF THE COURT

Clerk.—Charles S. Casazza, 606–2754.
Deputy Clerk.—Lynne L. Glasser.
Budget and Accounting Officer.—Washington B. Bowie.
Librarian.—Elsa Silverman.
Reporter.—John T. Fee.

UNITED STATES COURT OF APPEALS FOR THE ARMED FORCES[1]

450 E Street NW 20442–0001, phone 761–1448, fax 761–4672

SUSAN J. CRAWFORD, chief judge; born April 22, 1947, in Pittsburgh, PA; daughter of William E. and Joan B. Crawford; married to Roger W. Higgins of Geneva, NY, September 8, 1979; one child, Kelley S. Higgins; B.A., Bucknell University, Pennsylvania, 1969; J.D. (*cum laude*), Dean's Award, Arthur McClean Founder's Award, New England School of Law, Boston, MA, 1977; Career record: history teacher and coach of women's athletics, Radnor High School, Pennsylvania, 1969–74; associate, Burnett and Eiswert, Oakland, MD, 1977–79; Assistant State's Attorney, Garrett County, Maryland, 1978–1980; partner, Burnett, Eiswert and Crasford, 1979–81; instructor, Garrett County Community College, 1979–81; deputy general counsel, 1981–83, and general counsel, Department of the Army, 1983–89; special counsel to Secretary of Defense, 1989; inspector general, Department of Defense, 1989–91; member: bar of the Supreme Court of the United States; bar of the U.S. Court of Military Appeals, Maryland Bar Association, District of Columbia Bar Association, American Bar Association, Federal Bar Association, and the Edward Bennett Williams American Inn of Court; member: board of trustees, 1989–present, and Corporation, 1992–present, of New England School of Law; board of trustees, 1988–present, Bucknell University; nominated by President Bush as judge, U.S. Court of Military Appeals, February 19, 1991, for a term of 15 years; confirmed by the Senate on November 14, 1991, sworn in and officially assumed her duties on November 19, 1991. On October 1, 1999, she became the Chief Judge for a term of five years.

H.F. ''SPARKY'' GIERKE, associate judge; born March 13, 1943, in Williston, ND; son of Herman F. Gierke, Jr., and Mary Kelly Gierke; children: Todd, Scott, Craig, and Michelle; B.A., University of North Dakota, 1964; J.D., University of North Dakota, 1966; graduated basic course, the Judge Advocate General's School, Charlottesville, VA, 1967; graduated military judge course, the Judge Advocate General's School, Charlottesville, VA, 1969; active duty, U.S. Army judge advocate general's corps, 1967–71; private practice of law, 1971–83; served as a justice of the North Dakota supreme court from October 1, 1983 until appointment to U.S. Court of Military Appeals. Admitted to the North Dakota Bar, 1966; admitted to practice law before all North Dakota Courts, U.S. District Court for the District of North Dakota, U.S. District Court for the Southern District of Georgia, U.S. Court of Military Appeals, and U.S. Supreme Court; served as president of the State Bar Association of North Dakota in 1982–83; served as president of the North Dakota State's Attorneys Association in 1979–80; served on the board of governors of the North Dakota Trial Lawyers Association from 1977–83; served on the board of governors of the North Dakota State Bar Association from 1977–79 and from 1981–84; served as vice chairman and later chairman of the North Dakota Judicial Conference from June 1989 until November 1991. Fellow of the American Bar Foundation and the American College of Probate Counsel; member of the American Bar Association, American Judicature Society, Association of Trial Lawyers of America, Blue Key National Honor Fraternity, Kappa Sigma Social Fraternity, University of North Dakota President's Club; in 1984, received the Governor's Award from Governor Allen I. Olson for outstanding service to the State of North Dakota; in 1988 and again in 1991, awarded the North Dakota National Leadership Award of Excellence by Governor George A. Sinner; in 1989, selected as the Man of the Year by the Delta Mu Chapter of the Kappa Sigma Fraternity and as Outstanding Greek Alumnus of the University of North Dakota; also awarded the University of North Dakota Sioux Award (UND's alumni association's highest honor); in 1983–84, served as the first Vietnam era state commander of the North Dakota American Legion; in 1988–89, served as the first Vietnam era national commander of the American Legion; nominated by President Bush, October 1, 1991; confirmed by the Senate, November 14, 1991; sworn-in and assumed office on the U.S. Court of Military Appeals, November 20, 1991.

[1] Prior to October 5, 1994, United States Court of Military Appeals.

ANDREW S. EFFRON, associate judge; born in Stamford, CT, September 18, 1948; education: A.B., Harvard College, 1970; J.D., Harvard Law School, 1975; The Judge Advocate General's School, U.S. Army, 1976, 1983; legislative aide to the late Representative William A. Steiger, 1970–76 (two years full-time, the balance between school semesters); judge advocate, Office of the Staff Judge Advocate, Fort McClellan, Alabama, 1976–77; attorney-adviser, Office of the General Counsel, Department of Defense, 1977–87; Counsel, General Counsel, and Minority Counsel, Committee on Armed Services, U.S. Senate, 1987–96; nominated by President Clinton to serve on the U.S. Court of Appeals for the Armed Forces, June 21, 1996; confirmed by the Senate, July 12, 1996; took office on August 1, 1996.

JAMES E. BAKER, associate judge; born in New Haven, CT, on March 25, 1960; education: BA., Yale University, 1982; J.D., Yale Law School, 1990; Attorney, Department of State, 1990–1993; Counsel, President's Foreign Intelligence Advisory Board / Intelligence Oversight Board, 1993–1994; Deputy Legal Advisor, National Security Counsel, 1994–1997; Special Assistant to the President and Legal Advisor, National Security Counsel, 1997–2000; military service: U.S. Marine Corps and U.S. Marine Corp Reserve; nominated by President Clinton to serve on the U.S. Court of Appeals for the Armed Forces; began service on September 19, 2000.

CHARLES E. ERDMANN, associate judge; born in Great Falls, Montana on June 26, 1946; Education: BA, Montana State University, 1972; JD, University of Montana Law School, 1975; Air Force Judge Advocate Staff Officers Course, 1981; Air Command and Staff College, 1992; Air War College, 1994; Military Service: U.S. Marine Corps, 1967–1970; Air National Guard, 1981–2002 (retired as a Colonel); Employment: Assistant Montana Attorney General, 1975–76; Chief Counsel, Montana State Auditor's Office, 1976–78; Chief Staff Attorney, Montana Attorney General's Office, Antitrust Bureau; Bureau Chief, Montana Medicaid Fraud Bureau, 1980–82; General Counsel, Montana School Boards Association, 1982–86; Private Practice of Law, 1986–95; Associate Justice, Montana Supreme Court, 1995–97; Office of High Representative of Bosnia and Herzegovina, Judicial Reform Coordinator, 1998–99; Office of High Representative of Bosnia and Herzegovina, Head of Human Rights and Rule of Law Department, 1999; Chairman and Chief Judge, Bosnian Election Court, 2000–01; Judicial Reform and International Law Consultant, 2001–2002; appointed by President George W. Bush to serve on the U.S. Court of Appeals for the Armed Forces on October 9, 2002, commenced service on October 15, 2002.

WILLIAM HORACE DARDEN, senior judge; born in Union Point, GA, May 16, 1923; son of William W. and Sara (Newsom) Darden; B.B.A., University of Georgia, 1946; LL.B., University of Georgia, 1948; admitted to bar of Georgia and to practice before the Georgia Supreme Court, 1948; active duty in U.S. Navy from July 1, 1943 to July 3, 1946, when released to inactive duty as lieutenant (jg.); married to Mary Parrish Viccellio of Chatham, VA, December 31, 1949; children: Sara Newsom, Martha Hardy, William H., Jr., Daniel Hobson; secretary to U.S. Senator Richard B. Russell, 1948–51; chief clerk of U.S. Senate Committee on Armed Services, 1951–53; professional staff member and later chief of staff, U.S. Senate Committee on Armed Services, February 1953 to November 1968; received recess appointment as judge of the U.S. Court of Military Appeals from President Johnson on November 5, 1968, to succeed the late Judge Paul J. Kilday; took oath of office on November 13, 1968; nominated by President Johnson for the unexpired part of the term of the late Judge Paul J. Kilday ending May 1, 1976; confirmed by Senate on January 14, 1969; designated chief judge by President Nixon on June 23, 1971; resigned December 29, 1973; elected to become senior judge on February 11, 1974.

ROBINSON O. EVERETT, senior judge; born in Durham, NC, March 18, 1928; son of Reuben O. and Kathrine (Robinson) Everett; A.B. (*magna cum laude*), Harvard College, 1947; J.D. (*magna cum laude*), Harvard Law School, 1950; LL.M., Duke University, 1959; active duty in U.S. Air Force, 1951–53; thereafter served in U.S. Air Force Reserve and retired as colonel, 1978; married to Linda McGregor of Greensboro, NC, August 27, 1966; children: Robinson O., Jr., McGregor, and Lewis Moore; commissioner, U.S. Court of Military Appeals, 1953–55; private law practice, Durham, NC, 1955–80; assistant professor of law, 1950–51; adjunct professor of law, 1963–66; professor of law, Duke Law School, 1967–present; chairman Durham Urban Redevelopment Commission, 1958–75; counsel, 1961–64; consultant, 1964–66; Subcommittee on Constitutional Rights, Senate Committee on the Judiciary; chairman, Standing Committee on Military Law, American Bar Association, 1977–79; president, Durham County Bar Association, 1976–77; commissioner, National Conference of Commissioners on Uniform State Laws, 1961–73, 1977–present; member, American Law Institute, 1966–present; councillor, North Carolina State Bar, 1978–83; nominated by President Carter as judge of U.S. Court of Military Appeals, February 14, 1980, for the remainder of the term expiring May 1, 1981; unanimously confirmed by the Senate and designated chief judge by President Carter, March 28, 1980; took oath of office, April 16, 1980; term of office extended until April 15, 1990, by Act of December 23, 1980, Public Law 96–579, section 12, 94 Stat. 3369; term of office further extended until Sep. 30, 1990 by Act of November 29, 1989, Public Law 101–189, section 1301, 103 Stat 1575–76. Immediately upon his retirement at the end of his term on September 30, 1990, assumed status of senior judge and returned to full active service until January 1, 1992.

WALTER THOMPSON COX III, senior judge; born August 13, 1942, in Anderson, SC; son of Walter T. Cox and Mary Johnson Cox; married to Vicki Grubbs of Anderson, SC, February 8, 1963; children: Lisa and Walter; B.S., Clemson University, 1964; J.D. (*cum laude*), University of South Carolina School of Law, 1967; graduated Defense Language Institute (German), 1969; graduated basic course, the Judge Advocate General's School, Charlottesville, VA, 1967; studied procurement law at that same school, 1968. Active duty, U.S. Army judge advocate general's corps, 1964–72 (1964–67, excess leave to U.S.C. Law School). Private law practice, 1973–78. Elected resident judge, 10th Judicial Circuit, South Carolina, 1978–84; also served as acting associate justice of South Carolina supreme court, on the judicial council, on the circuit court advisory committee, and as a hearing officer of the judicial standards commission; member: bar of the Supreme Court of the United States; bar of the U.S. Court of Military Appeals; South Carolina Bar Association; Anderson County Bar Association; the American Bar Association; the South Carolina Trial Lawyers Association; the Federal Bar Association; and the Bar Association of the District of Columbia; has served as a member of the House of Delegates of the South Carolina Bar, and the Board of Commissioners on Grievances and Discipline. Nominated by President Reagan, as judge of U.S. Court of Military Appeals, June 28, 1984, for a term of 15 years; confirmed by the Senate, July 26, 1984; sworn-in and officially assumed his duties on September 6, 1984; retired on September 30, 1999 and immediately assumed status of senior judge on October 1, 1999 and returned to full active service until September 19, 2000.

EUGENE R. SULLIVAN, senior judge; born August 2, 1941, in St. Louis, MO; son of Raymond V. and Rosemary K. Sullivan; married to Lis U. Johansen of Ribe, Denmark, June 18, 1966; children: Kim A. and Eugene R. II; B.S., U.S. Military Academy, West Point, 1964; J.D., Georgetown Law Center, Washington, DC, 1971; active duty with the U.S. Army, 1964–69; service included duty with the 3rd Armored Division in Germany, and the 4th Infantry Division in Vietnam; R&D assignments with the Army Aviation Systems Command; one year as an instructor at the Army Ranger School, Ft. Benning, GA; decorations include: Bronze Star, Air Medal, Army Commendation Medal, Ranger and Parachutist Badges, Air Force Exceptional Civilian Service Medal. Following graduation from law school, clerked with U.S. Court of Appeals (8th Circuit), St. Louis, 1971–72; private law practice, Washington, DC, 1972–74; assistant special counsel, White House, 1974; trial attorney, U.S. Department of Justice, 1974–82; deputy general counsel, Department of the Air Force, 1982–84; general counsel of the Department of Air Force, 1984–86; Governor of Wake Island, 1984–86; presently serves on the Board of Governors for the West Point Society of the District of Columbia; the American Cancer Society (Montgomery County Chapter); nominated by President Reagan, as judge, U.S. Court of Military Appeals on February 25, 1986, and confirmed by the Senate on May 20, 1986, and assumed his office on May 27, 1986. President Bush named him the chief judge of the U.S. Court of Military Appeals, effective October 1, 1990, a position he held for five years. He retired on September 30, 2001 and immediately assumed status of senior judge and returned to full active service until Sept. 30, 2002.

OFFICERS OF THE U.S. COURT OF APPEALS FOR THE ARMED FORCES

Clerk of the Court.—William A. DeCicco.
Chief Deputy Clerk of the Court.—David A. Anderson.
Deputy Clerk for Opinions.—Kevin A. Doherty.
Administrative Officer.—Robert J. Bieber.
Librarian.—Agnes Kiang.

UNITED STATES COURT OF APPEALS FOR VETERANS CLAIMS

625 Indiana Avenue 20004, phone 501–5970

KENNETH B. KRAMER, chief judge; born February 19, 1942, in Chicago, IL; B.A., University of Illinois, 1963; J.D., Harvard Law School, 1966; admitted to the bars of the U.S. Supreme Court, the U.S. Court of Military Appeals, the State of Colorado, and the State of Illinois; commissioned in the U.S. Army, captain, Judge Advocate General's Corps, 1967–70; counsel, Army Physical Disability Evaluation Board, Fitzsimons Army Medical Center, Denver, CO; trial and defense counsel in general court-martial cases, chief of administrative law, and legal assistance officer, Fort Lewis, WA; practiced civil litigation law with Lord, Bissell and Brook, 1970; prosecutor, Office of the Deputy District Attorney, 4th Judicial District, Colorado, 1970–72; practiced law with Holme, Roberts and Owen, Colorado Springs, CO, 1972–74; practiced law with Floyd, Kramer and Lambrecht in Colorado, 1975–78; elected to the Colorado House of Representatives, 1973–78; serving as the chairman of the Rules Committee, and member of the Judiciary, Business Affairs and Labor, Education, Finance and Health Committees; elected to the U.S. House of Representatives, 1979–87; vice president, Aries Properties in Colorado Springs, CO, 1987; served as Assistant Secretary of the Army (Financial Management), 1988, until September 1989; confirmed by the U.S. Senate to the Court of Veterans Appeals on September 17, 1989; sworn in October 16, 1989;

JOHN J. FARLEY III, judge, of Bowie, MD; born July 30, 1942 in Hackensack, NJ to John J. Jr. and Patricia F. (Earle) Farley; married June 27, 1970 to Kathleen M. Wells; children: Maura, Brendan, Thomas, and Caitlin; A.B., economics, Holy Cross College, Worcester, MA, 1964; M.B.A., Columbia University Graduate School of Business, 1966 (Samuel Bronfman Fellow, Alpha Kappa Psi); J.D. (*cum laude*), Hofstra University School of Law, 1973 (first in class, editor-in-chief, Hofstra Law Review); served active duty as private, U.S. Army, 1966; released as Captain in 1970 after service in Vietnam, with Bronze Star with "V" device, three oak leaf clusters, Purple Heart with oak leaf cluster, Army Commendation Medal; career record 1973–78; attorney with the Department of Justice: trial attorney, torts section, 1978–80; assistant director for official immunity, torts branch, 1980–89; director, torts branch, with Civil Division, Department of Justice, 1989–present; admitted to: New York State Bar, 1974; District of Columbia Bar and U.S. Court of Appeals for D.C., 1975; U.S. Supreme Court Bar, 1977; author: "Robin Hood Jurisprudence: The Triumph of Equity in American Tort Law," 65 *St. John's Law Review* 997, 1991; "The New Kid on the Block: The United States Court of Veterans Appeals," *Federal Bar News and Journal*, volume 38, No. 9, Nov./Dec. 1991; "Personal Liability of Federal Investigators and Law Enforcement Officers," *Investigators Journal*, volume 2, Fall 1986; "Senior Executives' Personal Liability," 7, *Action* 4, May 1987; "The Fallout from Westfall," 8 Ibid. 3 March 1988; "From Liability to Immunity: The Roller Coaster Ride of 1988," *The Institute*, 1, February 1989; notable decisions: *Erspamer* v. *Derwinski,* 1990; *Rogozinski* v. *Derwinski,* 1990; *Gilbert* v. *Derwinski*, 1990; *Fegere* v. *Derwinski,* 1990; *Smith* v. *Derwinski,* 1991; *Ashley* v. *Derwinski,* 1992; *Darrow* v. *Derwinski*, 1992; *Zarycki* v. *Brown*, 1993; *Elcyzyn* v. *Brown*, 1994; recipient: Special Achievement Award, Department of Justice, 1979; First Civil Division Special Award for Superior Performance, Department of Justice, 1980; Senior Executive Service Special Achievement Awards, 1984 and 1988; Distinguished Alumni medal, Hofstra University School of Law, 1986; Dean's award for distinguised Hofstra Law School alumni, 1995; member: Federal Bar Association; Board of Directors, Amputee Coalition of America; John Carroll Society; Roman Catholic; nominated for appointment on August 29, 1989, by President Bush; confirmed by the Senate September 14, 1989; sworn in September 15, 1989.

DONALD L. IVERS, judge; born on May 6, 1941, in San Diego, CA; A.A., New Mexico Military Institute, 1961; B.A., University of New Mexico, 1963; J.D., American University, 1971; active duty in the U.S. Army, 1963–68, U.S., Europe, and Vietnam; retired from U.S. Army Reserve with the rank of lieutenant colonel; clerk, District of Columbia Superior

Court and the District of Columbia Court of Appeals; private practice of law with Brault, Graham, Scott and Brault, Washington, DC, 1972–78; chief counsel, Republican National Committee, 1978–81; chief counsel, Federal Highway Administration, 1981–85; director, Safety Review Task Force, U.S. Department of Transportation, 1984–85; general counsel, Veterans Administration, 1985–89; assistant to the Secretary, United States Department of Veterans Affairs, 1990; resides in Alexandria, VA; married, and the father of three children; nominated by President Bush, confirmed by the U.S. Senate in 1990; sworn in August 7, 1990.

JONATHAN ROBERT STEINBERG, judge; B.A., Cornell University, 1960; L.L.B., *cum laude,* University of Pennsylvania School of Law, 1963; research and note editor, University of Pennsylvania Law Review; Order of the Coif; research assistant, American Law Institute; law clerk for then Circuit Judge Warren E. Burger, U.S. Court of Appeals for the District of Columbia Circuit, 1963–64; attorney advisor, Peace Corps, 1964–68, and deputy general counsel, 1968–69; counsel, U.S. Senate Committee on Labor and Public Welfare (Subcommittee on Veterans' Affairs, Subcommittee on Railroad Retirement, and Special Subcommittee on Human Resources) 1969–77; chief counsel / staff director, U.S. Senate Committee on Veterans' Affairs, 1977–81 and 1987–90; minority chief counsel / staff director, Committee on Veterans' Affairs, 1981–87; admitted to bar of U.S. Court of Appeals for D.C. Circuit, May 1964; resides in Potomac, MD, with his wife Shellie; two adult children: Andrew and Amy; nominated by President Bush in May 1990, confirmed by the U.S. Senate in August 1990; sworn in on September 13, 1990.

WILLIAM P. GREENE, Jr., judge; born on July 27, 1943, in Bluefield, WV, to William and Dorothy Greene; married to Madeline Sinkford of Bluefield, WV; two children, William Robert, senior account executive for Dun and Bradstreet, Cincinnati, OH, and Jeffery P., officer and physician, United States Army Medical Corps, Tripler Army Medical Center, Hawaii, B.A., political science, West Virginia State College, 1965; J.D., Howard University, Washington, D.C., 1968; active duty in the United States Army Judge Advocate General's Corps following graduation from law school; as Judge Advocate, completed military education at the Basic, Advanced, and Military Judges' courses at The Judge Advocate General's School, the Army Command and General Staff College, Fort Leavenworth, KS, and the Army War College, Carlisle Barracks, PA; served as the Chief Prosecutor, Fort Knox, KY, 1969–97, and Chief Defense Counsel, Army Command, Hawaii, 1970–73; Army chief recruiter for lawyers 1974–77; Department Chair, Criminal Law Division, Judge Advocate General's School, Charlottesville, VA, 1981–84; Deputy Staff Judge Advocate, Third Infantry Division, Germany 1977–80; Staff Judge Advocate, Second Infantry Division, Korea 1984–85; following graduation from the United States Army War College, selected to serve as the Staff Judge Advocate of the United States Military Academy at West Point, NY, 1986–90, followed by another selection as Staff Judge Advocate at Fort Leavenworth, KS; retired from the United States Army as Colonel, 1993, receiving several awards during this service, including three Legions of Merit, three Meritorious Service Medals, and two Army Commendation Medals; appointed by the Attorney General of the United States as an Immigration Judge, Department of Justice, presiding over immigration cases in Maryland and Pennsylvania, June 1993—November 1997; nominated for appointment by President Clinton May 16, 1997; confirmed by the U.S. Senate November 7, 1997; sworn in November 24, 1997.

Officers of the U.S. Court of Veterans Appeals

Clerk of the Court.—Norman Y. Herring, 501–5980.
Operations Manager.—Anne P. Stygles.
Counsel and Court Reporter of Decisions.—Jack F. Lane.
Senior Staff Attorney (Central Legal Staff).—Jeffery N. Luthi.
Deputy Executive Officer.—Marlene Davis.
Librarian.—Bernard J. Sussman.

JUDICIAL PANEL ON MULTIDISTRICT LITIGATION

Thurgood Marshall Federal Judiciary Building, Room G–255, North Lobby, One Columbus Circle NE 20002, phone (202) 502–2800, fax 502–2888

(National jurisdiction to centralize related cases pending in multiple circuits and districts under 28 U.S.C. §§ 1407 & 2112)

Chairman.—Wm. Terrell Hodges, U.S. District Judge, Middle District of Florida.

Judges:

John F. Keenan, U.S. District Judge, Southern District of New York.
Bruce M. Selya, U.S. Court of Appeals Judge, First Circuit.
Julia Smith Gibbons, U.S. Court of Appeals Judge, Sixth Circuit.
D. Lowell Jensen, U.S. District Judge, Northern District of California.
J. Frederick Motz, U.S. District Judge, Chief Judge, District of Maryland.
Robert L. Miller, Jr., U.S. District Judge, Northern District of Indiana.

Executive Attorney.—Robert A. Cahn.

Clerk.—Michael J. Beck.

ADMINISTRATIVE OFFICE OF THE U.S. COURTS

Thurgood Marshall Federal Judiciary Building

One Columbus Circle, NE 20544, phone (202) 502–2600

Director.—Leonidas Ralph Mecham, 273–3000.
Associate Director, Management and Operations.—Clarence A. Lee, Jr., 273–3015.
Deputy Associate Director.—Cathy A. McCarthy, 502–1300.
Chief, Office of Audit.—Jeff Larioni, 502–1000.
Management Coordination and Planning Officer.—Cathy A. McCarthy, 502–1300.
Chief, Long-Range Planning Office.—William M. Lucianovic, 502–1300.
Associate Director and General Counsel.—William R. Burchill, Jr., 502–1100.
Deputy General Counsel.—Robert K. Loesche, 502–1100.
Assistant Director, Judicial Conference Executive Secretariat.—Karen K. Siegel, 502–2400.
Deputy Assistant Director, Judicial Conference Executive Secretariat.—Wendy Jennis, 02–2400.
Assistant Director, Legislative Affairs.—Michael W. Blommer, 502–1700.
Deputy Assistant Director for Legislative Affairs.—Daniel A. Cunningham, 502–1700.
Chief, Judicial Impact Office.—Richard A. Jaffe, 502–1700.
Assistant Director, Public Affairs.—David A. Sellers, 502–2600.
Assistant Director for Court Programs.—Noel J. Augustyn, 502–1500.
Deputy Assistant Director for Court Administration.—Glen K. Palman, 502–1500.
Chief of—
Electronic Access Program.—Mary Stickney, 502–1500.
Appellate Court and Circuit Administration Division.—JohnP. Hehman, 502–1520.
Bankruptcy Court Administration Division.—Glen K. Palman, 502–1540.
Court Administration Policy Staff.—Abel J. Mattos, 502–1560.
Defender Services Division.—Theodore J. Lidz, 502–3030.
District Court Administration Division.—Robert Lowney, 502–1570.
Federal Corrections and Supervision Division.—John M. Hughes, 502–1610.
Assistant Director for Facilities and Security.—Ross Eisenman, 502–1200.
Deputy Assistant Director for Facilities and Security.—William J. Lehman, 502–1200.
Chief of—
Court Security Office.—Dennis P. Chapas, 502–1280.
Policy and Resource Management Staff.—William J. Lehman (acting), 502–1200.
Space and Facilities Division.—Rodgers A. Stewart, 502–1340.
Assistant Director for Finance and Budget.—George H. Schafer, 502–2000.
Deputy Assistant Director for Finance and Budget.—Gregory D. Cummings, 502–2000.
Chief of—
Accounting and Financial Systems Division.—Philip L. McKinney, 502–2000.
Budget Division.—Bruce E. Johnson, 502–2100.
Financial Liaison Office.—Penny Jacobs Fleming, 502–2028.
Assistant Director for Human Resources and Statistics.—R. Townsend Robinson, 502–1170.
Chief of—
Employee Relations Office.—Trudi M. Morrison, 502–1380.
Human Resources Division.—Charlotte G. Peddicord, 502–3100.
Judiciary Benefits Program Office.—Lee Horvath, 502–1160.
Program and Workforce Development Division.—Maurice E. White, 502–1660.
Statistics Division.—Steven R. Schlesinger, 502–1440.
Assistant Director for Information Technology.—Melvin J. Bryson, 502–2300.
Deputy Assistant Director for Information Technology.—Barbara C. Macken, 502–2300.
Chief, Technology Officer.—Richard D. Fennell, 502–2300.
Chief of—
IT Applications Development Office.—Wendy R. Lageman, 502–2377.
IT Infrastructure Management Division.—Craig W. Jenkins, 502–2640.
IT Policy Staff.—Terry A. Cain, 502–3300.

IT Project Coordination Office.—Frank Dozier (acting), 502–2310.
IT Security Office.—Robert N. Sinsheimer, 502–2350.
IT Systems Deployment and Support Division.—Howard J. Grandier, 502–2700.
Assistant Director for Internal Services.—Laura C. Minor, 502–4200.
Deputy Assistant Director for Internal Services.—Nancy Lee Bradshaw, 502–4200.
Chief of—
AO Administrative Services Division.—Doreen G.B. Bydume, 502–1220.
AO Information Management Services Division.—John C. Chang, 502–2830.
AO Personnel Officer.—Cheri Thompson Reid, 502–3800.
AO Procurement Management Division.—Arnold Gildenhorn, 502–1330.
Assistant Director for Judges Programs.—Peter G. McCabe, 502–1800.
Deputy Assistant Director for Policy Development.—Jeffrey A. Hennemuth, 502–1800.
Chief of—
Analytical Services Office.—Ellyn L. Vail, 502–1180.
Article III Judges Division.—Margaret A. Irving (acting), 502–1860.
Bankruptcy Judges Division.—Francis F. Szczebak, 502–1900.
Magistrate Judges Division.—Thomas C. Hnatowski, 502–1830.
Rules Committee Support Office.—John K. Rabiej, 502–1820.

FEDERAL JUDICIAL CENTER

One Columbus Circle NE 20002–8003, phone (202) 502–4000

Director.—Judge Fern M. Smith, 502–4160, fax 502–4099.
Deputy Director.—Russell R. Wheeler, 502–4164, fax 502–4019.
Director of—
Communications Policy and Design.—Sylvan A. Sobel, 502–4250, fax 502–4077.
Judicial Education.—John S. Cooke, 502–4060, fax 502–4299.
Research.—James B. Eaglin, 502–4070, fax 502–4199.
Court Education.—Emily Z. Huebner, 502–4110, fax 502–4088.
Chief of—
Interjudicial Affairs Office.—Mira Gur-Arie, 502–4191, fax 502–4099.
Systems Innovations and Development Office.—Ted Coleman, 502–4223, fax 502–4288.
Federal Judicial History Office.—Bruce A. Ragsdale, 502–4181, fax 502–4077.

DISTRICT OF COLUMBIA COURTS

phone 879–1010

Executive Officer.—Anne B. Wicks, 879–1700.
Deputy Executive Officer.—Cheryl R. Bailey, 879–1700; fax 879–4829.
Director, Legislative, Intergovernmental and Public Affairs.—Leah Gurowitz, 879–1700.

DISTRICT OF COLUMBIA COURT OF APPEALS

500 Indiana Avenue 20001, phone 879-1010

Chief Judge.—Annice M. Wagner, 879–2770.
Associate Judges:
Michael W. Farrell, 879–2790.
Stephen H. Glickman, 879–2740.
Inez Smith Reid, 879–2726.
Vanessa Ruiz, 879–2761.
John A. Terry, 879–2780.
Frank E. Schwelb, 879–2730.
John M. Steadman, 879–2785.
Eric T. Washington, 879–2700.

Senior Judges: George R. Gallagher, 879–2768; John W. Kern III, 879–2754; William C. Pryor, 879–2745; Julia Cooper Mack, 879–2765; Theodore R. Newman, Jr., 879–2740; James A. Belson, 879–2760, Warren King, 626–8871; John M. Ferren, 879–2772; Frank Q. Nebeker, 879–2778.

Clerk.—Garland Pinkston, Jr., 879–2725.
Chief Deputy Clerk.—Joy A. Chapper, 879–2722.
Administration Director.—Steven J. Newman, 879–2738.
Admissions Director.—Clare M. Root, 879–2714.
Public Office Operations Director.—Jeanette E. Togans, 879–2702.
Senior Staff Attorney.—Rosanna M. Mason, 879–2718.

SUPERIOR COURT OF THE DISTRICT OF COLUMBIA

phone 879–1010

Chief Judge.—Rufus G. King III, 879–1600.

Associate Judges:
Geoffrey M. Alprin, 879–1577.
Judith Bartnoff, 879–1988.
John H. Bayly, Jr., 879–7874.
Ronna L. Beck, 879–1162.
James E. Boasberg, 879–4886.
Shellie F. Bowers, 879–1288.
Ana Blackburne-Rigsby, 879–0055.
Patricia A. Broderick, 879–8345.
A. Franklin Burgess, Jr., 879–1164.
Zoe Bush, 879–0023.
John M. Campbell, 879–1430.
Russell F. Canan, 879–1952.
Erik Christian, 879–1760.
Kaye K. Christian, 879–1668.
Natalia Combs Greene, 879–8350.
Harold L. Cushenberry, Jr., 879–4866.
Linda Kay Davis, 879–0050.
Rafael Diaz, 879–1125.
Herbert B. Dixon, Jr., 879–4808.
Stephanie Duncan-Peters, 879–1882.
Mildred M. Edwards, 879–7840.
Gerald I. Fisher, 879–8388.
Wendell P. Gardner, Jr., 879–1810.
Steffen W. Graae, 879–1244.
Brook Hedge, 879–1886.
William M. Jackson, 879–1909.
J. Ramsey Johnson, 879–8306.
Anita Josey-Herring, 879–1574.
Ann O'Regan Keary, 879–1863.
Noël A. Kramer, 879–1446.
Neal E. Kravitz, 879–8353.
Cheryl M. Long, 879–1200.
José M. López, 879–7877.
Lynn Lebowitz, 879–0441
George W. Mitchell, 879–1277.
Zinora Mitchell-Rankin, 879–7846.
Robert E. Morin, 879–1550.
Thomas J. Motley, 879–8377.
John M. Mott, 879–8393.
Hiram E. Puig-Lugo, 879–8370.
Michael L. Rankin, 879–1220.
Judith E. Retchin, 879–1866.
Robert I. Richter, 879–1422.
Robert Rigsby, 879–4344.
Maurice Ross, 879–1765.
Lee F. Satterfield, 879–1918.
Nan R. Shuker, 879–1207.
Mary A. Gooden Terrell, 879–1639.
Linda D. Turner, 879–1819.
Odessa F. Vincent, 879–0447.
Frederick H. Weisberg, 879–1066.
Susan R. Winfield, 879–1272.
Rhonda Reid Winston, 879–4750.
Melvin R. Wright, 879–8336.
Joan Zeldon, 879–1590.

Senior Judges:
Mary Ellen Abrecht, 879–7834.
Bruce D. Beaudin, 879–1575.
Leonard Braman, 879–1440.
Arthur L. Burnett, Sr., 879–4882.
Frederick D. Dorsey, 879–7837.
Stephen F. Eilperin, 879–1566.
George H. Goodrich, 879–1055.
Henry F. Greene, 879–1455.
Eugene N. Hamilton, 879–1727.
Margaret A. Haywood, 879–4633.
John R. Hess, 879–1420.
Bruce S. Mencher, 879–1358.
Stephen G. Milliken, 879–1823.
Gregory E. Mize, 879–1395.
Truman A. Morrison III, 879–1060.
Tim Murphy, 879–1099.
Robert S. Tignor, 879–1252.
Fred B. Ugast, 879–1890.
Paul R. Webber III, 879–1426.
Ronald P. Wertheim, 879–1170.
Peter H. Wolf, 879 –1088.
Patricia A. Wynn, 879–4630.

Clerk of the Court.—Duane B. Delaney, 879–1400.

GOVERNMENT OF THE DISTRICT OF COLUMBIA

COUNCIL OF THE DISTRICT OF COLUMBIA

John A. Wilson Building, 1350 Pennsylvania Avenue, NW, 20004, phone 724–8000

Council Chairman (at Large).—Linda W. Cropp, Suite 504, 724–8032.
Chairman Pro Tempore.—Jack Evans.
Council Members:
Jim Graham, Ward 1, Suite 406, 724–8181.
Jack Evans, Ward 2, Suite 106, 724–8058.
Kathleen Patterson, Ward 3, Suite 107, 724–8062.
Adrian Fenty, Ward 4, Suite 506, 724–8052.
Vincent B. Orange, Sr., Ward 5, Suite 108, 724–8028.
Sharon Ambrose, Ward 6, Suite 102, 724–8072.
Kevin P. Chavous, Ward 7, Suite 402, 724–8068.
Sandy (Sandra) Allen, Ward 8, Suite 408, 724–8045.
Council Members (at Large):
Harold Brazil, Suite 404, 724–8174.
Phil Mendelson, Suite 400, 724–8064.
Carol Schwartz, Suite 105, 724–8105.
David A. Catania, Suite 110, 724–7772.
Secretary to the Council.—Phyllis Jones, Suite 5, 724–8080.
General Counsel.—Charlotte Brookins-Hudson, Suite 4, 724–8026.
Budget Director.—Arte Blitzstein, Suite 508, 724–8139.

EXECUTIVE OFFICE OF THE MAYOR

Mayor of the District of Columbia.—Anthony A. Williams.
Chief of Staff.—Kelvin J. Robinson, Suite 509, 727–2643, fax 727–2975.
Executive Assistant to the Chief of Staff.—Lisa Johnson-Ingram, Suite 509, 727–2643, fax 727–2975.
Deputy Mayor for:
Children, Youth, Families and Elders.—Carolyn N. Graham, Suite 307, 727–8001, fax 727–0246.
Planning and Economic Development.—Eric W. Price, Suite 317, 727–6365, fax 727–6703.
Public Safety and Justice.—Margret Kellems, Suite 327, 727–4036, fax 727–8527.
Operations.—Herb Tillery, Suite 310, 727–6053, fax 727–9878.
Deputy Chief of Staff for:
Community Affairs.—Joy Arnold, Suite 527, 727–6770, fax 727–6895.
Policy and Legislative Affairs.—Gregory McCarthy, Suite 511, 727–6979, fax 727–3765.
Special Assistant to the Mayor.—Moddie Turray, 6th Floor, 727–2980, fax 727–6561.
Confidential Assistant to the Mayor.—Denise Grant, 6th Floor, 727–6263, fax 727–6561.
Executive Assistant to the Mayor.—Alicia Nunn, 6th Floor, 727–6263, fax 727–6561.
Director, Scheduling and Advance.—Joy Hilton, 5th Floor, 727–1681, fax 727–2357.
Deputy Director, Office of Communications.—Sharon Gang, Suite 533, 727–5011, fax 727–9561.
Director, Operations.—Marlene Jefferson, 5th Floor, 727–2643, fax 727–4683.
Secretary of the District of Columbia.—Beverly D. Rivers, Suite 419, 727–6306, fax 727–3582.
General Counsel to the Mayor.—Grace Lopes, Suite 327, 727–0872, fax 727–7743.
Inspector General.—Charles C. Maddox, 717 14th Street, NW., 5th Floor, 20005, 727–2540, fax 727–9903.
Senior Advisor:
Congressional Affairs.—Sabrina E. McNeal, Suite 511, 727–6979, fax 727–3765.
Education.—Michelle J. Walker, Suite 511, 727–6979, fax 727–3765.

Environmental Affairs.—Elizabeth Berry, Suite 512, 727–6979, fax 727–3765.
External and Regional Affairs.—Fonda Richardson, Suite 512, 727–2643, fax 727–7418.
Religious Affairs.—Carlton Pressley, Suite 211A, 727–1751, fax 727–5931.
Special Assistant, GLBT Affairs.—Wanda Alston, Suite 211A, 442–8150, fax 727–5931.

OFFICE OF THE CITY ADMINISTRATOR

City Administrator.—John A. Koskinen, 727–6053, fax 727–9878..
Executive Assistant to City Administrator.—Phyllis Kaiser-Dark.
Chief of Staff.—Alfreda Davis.
Director, Neighborhood Services.—Patrick J. Canavan.

COMMISSIONS

Arts and Humanities, 410 8th Street, NW., 5th Floor, 20004, 727–5613, fax 727–4135.
Executive Director.—Anthony Gittens.

National and Community Service, 441 4th Street, NW., Suite 1040S, 20001, 727–7943, fax 727–9198.
Executive Director.—Deborah Gist.

Social Services, 609 H Street, NE, 5th Floor, 20002, 727–5930, fax 727–1687.
Commissioner.—Adrianna Bucker (acting).

Taxicab Commission, 2041 Martin Luther King Jr. Avenue, SE., 2nd Floor, 20020, 645–6005, fax 889–3604.
Chairperson.—Lee Williams.

DEPARTMENTS

Asian and Pacific Islander Affairs, 441 4th Street, NW., Suite 805S, 20001, 727–3120, fax 727–9655.
Executive Director.—G. Greg Chen.

Child and Family Services Agency, 400 6th Street, SW., 5th Floor, 20024, 442–6100, fax 727–8885.
Director.—Olivia Golden.

Consumer and Regulatory Affairs, 941 North Capitol Street, NE., 9th Floor, 20002, 442–8947, fax 442–9444.
Director.—David Clark.

Contracting and Procurement, 441 4th Street, Suite 800, 20001, 724–4683, fax 727–3229.
Director.—Jacques Abadie.

Corrections Department, 1923 Vermont Avenue, NW., Room 207, 20001, 673–7361, fax 332–1470.
Director.—Odie Washington.

Employment Services, 609 H Street, NE., 20002, 671–1900, fax 673–6976.
Director.—Gregory P. Irish.

Fire and Emergency Medical Services, 1923 Vermont Avenue, NW., Suite 201, 20001, 673–3320, fax 462–0807.
Fire Chief.—Adrian Thompson.

Health Department, 825 North Capitol Street, NE., 20002, 442–5999, fax 442–4788.
Director.—James Buford, M.D.

Housing and Community Development, 801 North Capitol Street, NE., 8th floor, 20002, 442–7210, fax 442–9280.
Director.—Stanley Jackson (acting).

Human Rights, 441 4th Street, NW., Suite 570N, 20001, 727–4559, fax 724–5771.
Director.—Nadine Chandler Wilburn (acting).

Human Services, 2700 Martin Luther King Jr. Avenue, SE., 801 East Building, 20032, 279–6002, fax 279–6014.
Director.—[Vacant].

Insurance and Securities Regulation, 810 1st Street, NE., Suite 701, 20002, 727–8000, fax 535–1196.
Commissioner.—Lawrence H. Mirel.

Local Business Development, 441 4th Street, NW., Suite 970N, 20001, 727–3900, fax 727–6221.
Director.—Jacquelyn Flowers.

Mental Health, 77 P Street, NE., 4th Floor, 20002, phone 673–2200, fax 673–3433.
Director.—Martha Knisley (acting).

Metropolitan Police, 300 Indiana Avenue, NW., Room 5080, 20001, 727–4218, fax 727–9524.
Police Chief.—Charles H. Ramsey.

Motor Vehicles, 301 C Street, NW., Suite 1018, 20001, 724–2034, fax 727–5017.
Director.—Sherryl Hobbs-Newman.

Parks and Recreation, 3149 16th Street, NW., 20010, 673–7665, fax 673–2087.
Director.—Neil O. Albert.

Property Management, 441 4th Street, NW., Suite 1100S, 20001, 727–4400, fax 727–9877.
Director.—Timothy F. Dimond.

Public Works, 2000 14th Street, NW., 6th Floor, 20009, 673–6833, fax 671–0642.
Director.—Leslie Hotaling.

Transportation Department, 2000 14th Street, NW., 6th Floor, 20009, 673–6813, fax 671–0127.
Director.—Dan Tangherlini.

OFFICES

Aging, 441 Fourth Street, NW., Suite 900S, 20001, 724–5622,fax 724–4979.
Executive Director.—E. Veronica Pace.

Banking and Financial Institutions, 1400 L Street, NW., Suite 400, 20005, 727–1563, fax 727–1588.
Commissioner.—S. Kathryn Allen.

Boards and Commissions, 441 4th Street, NW., Suite 530S, 20001, 727–1372, fax 727–2359.
Director.—Ron Collins.

Cable Television, 2217 14th Street, NW., 20009, 671–0066, fax 332–7020.
Executive Director.—Darryl D. Anderson.

Chief Financial Officer, 1350 Pennsylvania Avenue, NW., Suite 209, 20004, 727–2476, fax 727–1643.
Chief Financial Officer.—Natwar M. Gandhi.

Chief Medical Examiner, 1910 Massachusetts Avenue, SE., Building 27, 20003, 698–9000, fax 698–9101.
Chief Medical Examiner.—Jonathan Arden.

Chief Technology Officer, 441 4th Street, NW., Suite 930S, 20001, 727–2277, fax 727–6857.
Chief Technology Officer.—Suzanne J. Peck.

Communications Office, 1350 Pennsylvania Avenue, NW., Suite 533, 20001, 727–5011, fax 727–9561.
Director.—Tony Bullock.

Community Outreach, 1350 Pennsylvania Avenue, NW., Suite 211A, 20001, 442–8150, fax 727–5931.
Director.—Linda Perkins (acting).

Corporation Counsel, 1350 Pennsylvania Avenue, NW., Suite 407 and 409, 20004, 724–3400, fax 724–6577.
Corporation Counsel.—Arabella Teal (acting).

Emergency Management Agency, 2000 14th Street, 8th Floor, 20009, 727–6161, fax 673–2290.
Director.—Peter LaPorte.

Labor Relations and Collective Bargaining, 441 4th Street, NW., Suite 200S, 20001, 724–4953, fax 727–6887.
Director.—Mary E. Leary.

Latino Affairs, 2000 14th Street, NW., 2nd Floor, 20009, 671–2825, fax 673–4557.
Director.—Christia Alou (acting).

Partnerships and Grants Development, 441 4th Street, NW., Suite 200S, 20001, 727–8900, fax 727–1652.
Director.—Lafayette Barnes.

Personnel Office, 441 4th Street, NW., Suite 300S, 20001, 442–9600, fax 727–6827.
Director.—Judy Banks (acting).

Planning Office, 801 North Capitol Street, NE., Suite 4000, 20002, 442–7600, fax 442–7638.
Director.—Andrew Altman.

Policy and Research Development, 1350 Pennsylvania Avenue, NW., Suite 511, 20004, 724–7696, fax 727–3765.
Director.—Sharon Anderson.

State Education, 441 4th Street, NW., Suite 350N, 20001, 727–6436, fax 727–2019.
State Education Officer.—C. Vannesa Spinner.

Veterans Affairs, 441 4th Street, NW., Suite 570S, 20001, 724–5454, fax 727–6329.
Director.—Kerwin Miller.

OTHER

Agency for HIV/AIDS, 717 14th Street, NW., Suite 600, 20005, 727–2500, fax 727–8471.
Administrator.—Ronald Lewis.

District of Columbia Housing Authority, 1133 North Capitol Street, NE., 20001, 535–1500, fax 535–1740.
Executive Director.—Michael P. Kelly.

District of Columbia Public Libraries, Martin Luther King Memorial Library (Main Library), 901 G Street, NW., Suite 400, 20001, 727–0321, fax 727–1129.
Director and State Librarian.—Molly Raphael.

District of Columbia Public Schools, 825 North Capitol Street, NW., Suite 9026, 20002, 442–5885, fax 442–5026.
Superintendent.—Paul L. Vance.

District of Columbia Sports Commission, 2400 East Capitol Street, SE., 20003, 547–9077, fax 547–7460.
Executive Director.—Robert D. Goldwater.

District Lottery and Charitable Games, 2101 Martin Luther King Jr. Avenue, SE., 20020, 645–8000, fax 645–7914.
Executive Director.—Anthony Cooper.

Parole Board, 633 Indiana Avenue, 8th Floor, 20001, 220–5450, fax 220–5466.
Chairperson.—Margaret Quick.

Superior Court of the District of Columbia, 500 Indiana Avenue, NW., Suite 3500, 20001, 879–1600, fax 879–7830.
Chief Judge.—Rufus G. King, III.

University of the District of Columbia, 4200 Connecticut Avenue, NW., 20008, 274–5100, fax 274–5304.
President.—William L. Pollard.

Washington Convention Center, 900 9th Street, NW., 20004, 371–3024, fax 789–8365.
General Manager.—Lewis Dawley.

DISTRICT OF COLUMBIA POST OFFICE LOCATIONS

900 Brentwood Road NE 20066–9998, General Information (202) 268–2000

Postmaster.—Delores D. Killett.

CLASSIFIED STATIONS

Station	Phone	Location / Zip Code
Anacostia	635–6307	2650 Naylor Rd. SE., 20020
Ben Franklin	523–2387	1200 Pennsylvania Ave. NW., 20044
B.F. Carriers	636–4484	900 Brentwood Rd. NE., 20004
Benning	523–2390	3937–½ Minnesota Ave. NE., 20019
Bolling AFB	767–4419	Bldg. 10 Brookley Avenue, 20332
Brightwood	523–2392	6323 Georgia Ave. NW., 20
Brookland	523–2133	3401 12th St. NE., 20017
Calvert	523–2907	2336 Wisconsin Ave. NW., 20007
Cleveland Park	523–2395	3430 Connecticut Ave. NW., 20008
Columbia Heights	635–5308	6510 Chillum Pl. NW., 20010
Congress Heights	523–2107	400 Southern Ave. SE., 20032
Customs House	635–5314	3178 Bladensburg Rd. NE., 20018
Dulles	(703) 471-1868	Dulles International Airport, 20041
Farragut	523–2506	1145 19th St. NW., 20033
Fort Davis	523–2152	3843 Pennsylvania Ave. SE., 20020
Fort McNair	523–2144	300 A. St. SW., 20319
Frederick Douglass	523–2980	Alabama Ave. SE., 20020
Friendship	523–2125	4005 Wisconsin Ave. NW., 20016
Georgetown	523–2405	1215 31st St. NW., 20007
Headsville	357–3029	Smithsonian Institute, 20560
Kalorama	523–2904	2300 18th St. NW., 20009
Lamond Riggs	523–2044	6200 North Capitol St. NW., 20
LeDroit Park	635–5311	416 Florida Ave. NW., 20001
L'Enfant Plaza	523–2013	458 L'Enfant Plaza SW., 20026
Martin L. King, Jr	523–2000	1400 L St. NW., 20043
McPherson	523–2393	1750 Pennsylvania Ave. NW, 20038
Mid City	523–2567	1408 14th St. NW., 20005
National Airport	523–2407	National Airport, 20001
National Capitol	523–2628	2 Massachusetts Ave. NE., 20002
Naval Research Lab	767–3426	4565 Overlook Ave., 20390
Navy Annex	694–2049	1668 D Street, 20335
Northeast	397–4813	1563 Maryland Ave. NE., 20002
Northwest	523–2569	5632 Connecticut Ave. NW., 20015
Palisades	523–2562	5136 MacArthur Blvd. NW., 20016
Pavilion Postique	523–2571	1100 Pennsylvania Ave. NW., 20004
Pentagon	(703) 695-6835	900 Brentwood Rd. NE., 20066
Petworth	523–2682	4211 9th St. NW., 20
Postal Square	523–2022	2 Massachusetts Ave. NW., 20002
Randle	584–3241	2341 Pennsylvania Ave. SE., 20023
River Terrace	523–2983	3621 Benning Rd. NE., 20019
Southeast	635–5300	327 7th St. SE., 20003
Southwest	635–5302	45 L St. SW., 20024
State Department	523–2573	2201 C St. NW., 20520
T Street	483–9580	1915 14th St. NW., 20009
Tech World	523–2400	800 K St. NW., 20001
Temple Heights	232–7613	1921 Florida Ave. NW., 20009
Twentieth Street	523–2410	2001 M St. NW., 20036
U.S. Naval	433–2216	940 M St. SE., 20374
V Street	523–2081	3300 V St. NE., 20018
Walter Reed	782–3768	6800 Georgia Ave. NW., 20012
Ward Place	523–2040	2121 Ward Pl. NW., 20037
Washington Main	636–1200	900 Brentwood Rd. NE., 20066
Washington Square	523–2631	1050 Connecticut Ave. NW., 20035
Watergate	965–2730	2512 Virginia Ave. NW., 20037
Woodridge	523–2414	2211 Rhode Island Ave. NE., 20018

INTERNATIONAL ORGANIZATIONS

EUROPEAN SPACE AGENCY (E.S.A.)

Headquarters: 8–10 Rue Mario Nikis, 75738 Paris Cedex 15, France

phone 011–33–1–5369–7654, fax 011–33–1–5369–7560

Chairman of the Council.—Per Tegnér.
Director General.—Antonio Rodota.
Member Countries:

Austria
Belgium
Denmark
Finland
France
Germany
Ireland
Italy
Netherlands
Norway
Portugal
Spain
Sweden
Switzerland
United Kingdom

Cooperative Agreement.—Canada.

European Space Operations Center (E.S.O.C.), Robert-Bosch-Str. 5, D–64293 Darmstadt, Germany, phone 011–49–6151–900, fax 011–49–6151–90495.

European Space Research and Technology Center (E.S.T.E.C.), Keplerlaan 1, NL–2201, AZ Noordwijk, ZH, The Netherlands, phone 011–31–71–565–6565; Telex: 844–39098, fax 011–31–71–565–6040.

European Space Research Institute (E.S.R.I.N.), Via Galileo Galilei, Casella Postale 64, 00044 Frascati, Italy. Phone, 011–39–6–94–18–01; fax 011–39–6–9418–0280.

Washington Office (E.S.A.), Suite 7800, 955 L'Enfant Plaza SW. 20024.
Head of Office.—Frederic Nordlund, 488–4158, fax: (202) 488–4930, *Frederic.Nordlund@esa.int.*

INTER-AMERICAN DEFENSE BOARD

2600 16th Street 20441, phone 939–6041, fax 387–2880

Chairman.—MG Carl H. Freeman, U.S. Army.
Vice Chairman.—MG Dardo Juan Antonio Parodi, Army, Argentina.
Secretary.—COL Ivan Corretjer, U.S. Air Force.
Vice Secretary.—1st LTC Martín Terrones, Army, Mexico.
Deputy Secretary for Administration.—MAJ Richard D. Phillips, U.S. Army.
Conference.—LT Armando Rodriguez, U.S. Air Force.
Finance.—Rick A. Diggs, U.S. Army.
Information Management.—MAJ William G. Beavers, U.S. Army.
Protocol.—LTC Eduardo Vargas, U.S. Air Force.
Staff Director.—GEN Rodolfo Interiano, Army, Honduras.
Staff Vice Director.—COL Jorge Izasa, Army, Colombia.

CHIEFS OF DELEGATION

Antigua and Barbuda.—Col. Trevor Thomas, Army.
Argentina.—Brigadier Horacio MIR González, Air Force.
Barbados.—LtCol. Alvin Quintyne, Defense Force.
Bolivia.—Division General Alfredo Abastos Baptista, Army.
Brazil.—Contraalmirante Carlos Araujo Eduardo Motta, Navy.
Chile.—Contraalmirante Alfredo Guiliano Ramírez, Navy.

Colombia.—Almirante Sergio E. García Torres, Navy.
Costa Rica.—Coronel Hernán Ramón Castro Hernández, Civilian Guard.
Dominican Republic.—Vicealmirante Rafael L. Monzón Brea, Navy.
Ecuador.—Coronel Luis Paredes, Army.
El Salvador.—Coronel Jorge Enrique Navas López, Air Force.
Guatemala.—BG Edgar Leonel Godoy Samaoya, Army.
Guyana.—Coronel Edward O. Collins, Defense Force.
Honduras.—Coronel Efraín A. Gutiérrez Ardón, Army.
Mexico.—BG Gilberto Hernández Andréu, Army.
Nicaragua.—BG Manuel Benito Salvatierra Rivera, Air Force.
Paraguay.—BG Luis Carlos Rene García Stautmeister, Army.
Peru.—MG Miguel Ángel Morón Buleje, Army.
Trinidad.—Brigadier John C.E. Sandy, Army.
United States.—MG Timothy A. Kinnan, Air Force.
Uruguay.—Brigadier José E. Mayo Hirigoyen, Air Force.
Venezuela.—Division General Héctor Centeno Cedeno, Air Force.

INTER-AMERICAN DEFENSE COLLEGE

Director.—MG Carl H. Freeman, U.S. Army.
Vice Director.—BG Marco Antonio Bonilla Reyes, Army, Honduras.
Chief of Studies.—Vicealmirante Mariano Gómez Barthelemy, Navy, Bolivia.

INTER-AMERICAN DEVELOPMENT BANK

1300 New York Avenue 20577, phone 623–1000

http://www.iadb.org

OFFICERS

President.—Enrique V. Iglesias (Uruguay).
Chief, Office of the President.—Euric A. Bobb.
Executive Vice President.—Dennis E. Flannery (United States).
Vice President for Planning and Administration.—Paulo Paiva.
Chief Advisor.—Joel A. Riley.
Director, Office of Evaluation and Oversight.—Stephen A. Quick.
Chief Economist.—Guillermo Calvo.
Auditor General.—William L. Taylor.
External Relations Advisor.—Mirna Liévando deMarques.
Associate Deputy Advisor.—Chris Sale.
Ombudsperson.—José Ignacio Estevez.
Manager, Office of:
Multilateral Investment Fund.—Donald F. Terry.
Information Technology and General Services.—Richard J. Herring.
Regional Operations Department 1.—Ricardo L. Santiago.
Deputy Manager.—Luisa C. Rains.
Regional Operations Support Office.—Rosa Olivia Villa Lawson.
Regional Operations Department 2—Miguel E. Martínez.
Deputy Manager.—Jairo Sanchez.
Regional Operations Department 3.—Ciro De Falco.
Deputy Manager.—Miguel A. Rivera.
Finance Department.—Charles O. Sethness.
Senior Deputy Manager-Treasurer.—Eloy B. Garcia.
Integration and Regional Programs Department.—Nohra Rey de Marulanda.
Deputy Manager.—Robert Devlin.
Private Sector Department.—Hiroshi Toyoda.
Deputy Manager.—Bernardo Frydman.
Sustainable Development Department.—Carlos M. Jarque.
Strategic Planning and Operational Policy Department.—Manuel Rapoport.
Human Resources.—Manuel Labrado.
General Counsel, Legal Department.—James Spinner.
Deputy General Counsel.—[Vacant].
Secretary.—Carlos Ferdinand.
Deputy Secretary.—Armando Chuecos.

BOARD OF EXECUTIVE DIRECTORS

Colombia and Peru.—Luis Guillermo Echeverri.
Alternate.—Jaime Piuto Tabini.
Bahamas, Barbados, Guyana, Jamaica, Trinidad and Tobago.—Luis A. Rodriguez.
Alternate.—Havelock Brewster.
Dominican Republic and Mexico.—Agustín García-López.
Alternate.—Héctor Santos.
Belize, Costa Rica, El Salvador, Guatemala, Haiti, Honduras, and Nicaragua.—José Carlos Quirce.
Alternate.—José Carlos Castañeda.
Panama and Venezuela.—José Alejandro Rojas.
Alternate.—Eduardo Linares.
Canada.—[Vacant].
Alternate.—Alan F. Gill.
Belgium, Germany, Israel, Italy, The Netherlands, and Switzerland.—Micheala Zintl.
Alternate.—Paolo Cappellacci.
Argentina and Haiti.—Richardo R. Carciofi.
Alternate.—Martín Bès.
United States.—José A. Fourquet.
Alternate.—Jorge L. Arrizurieta.
Brazil, and Suriname.—Martus Tavares.
Alternate.—Frederico Alvares.
Austria, Denmark, Finland, France, Norway, Spain, and Sweden.—Michel Planque.
Alternate.—Pekka Hukka.
Bolivia, Paraguay, and Uruguay.—Juan E. Notaro.
Alternate.—Jorge Crespo-Velasco.
Chile and Ecuador.—Germán Quintana.
Alternate.—Victor M. Acosta.
Croatia, Japan, Portugal, Slovenia, and United Kingdom.—Yoshihisa Ueda.
Alternate.—Toshitake Kurosawa.

INTER-AMERICAN TROPICAL TUNA COMMISSION

8604 La Jolla Shores Drive, La Jolla, CA 92037–1508, phone (858) 546–7100

fax (858) 546–7133, www.iattc.org

Director.—Robin L. Allen.

Costa Rican Commissioners:

Ligia Castro, Presidente Ejecutivo, Incopesca APDO, 333–5400, Puntarenas, Costa Rica, (506) 2907/807, fax (506) 296–2662; email: lcastro@gobnet.co.cr.

George Heigold, Compania Enlatadora Nacional, S.A. Apartado 82, Puntarenas, Costa Rica, (506) 661–0829/2625, fax (506) 661–1109; email: besilmon@racsa.co.cr.

Asdrubal Vasquez, Sardimar, S.A. Apartado Postal 549–7050, San Jose, Costa Rica, (506) 253–4321, fax (506) 225–9121; email: vasqueza@racsa.co.cr.

Ecuador Commissioners:

Lucia Fernández de De Genna, Subsecretaría de Recursos Pesqueros, Ministerio de Comercio Exterior, Industrialización y Pesca, AV. 9, De Octubre 200 y Pichincha, Edificio Banco Central, 70 Piso, Guayaquil, Ecuador, (593–4) 230–8222, fax (593–4) 256–1489; email: subsc01@subpesca.gov.ec.

Luis Torres, Director Probecuador, Subsecretaría de Recursos Pesqueros, Ministerio de Comercio Exterior, Industrialización y Pesca, AV. 9 De Octubre 200 y Pichincha, Edificio Banco Central, 70 Piso, Guayaquil, Ecuador, (593–4) 256–4300, ext. 103, 231–0814, fax (593–4) 256–1489/230–8413; email: Asesor01@subpcsca.gov.ec.

El Salvador Commissioners:

Roberto Interiano, Viceministro, Ministerio de Relaciones Exteriores, Calle Circunvalación No. 227, Colonia San Benito, Contiguo a Telemóvil, San Salvador, El Salvador, (503) 243–9667, fax (503) 243–9665; email: rintcriano@telesal.net.

Jorge Lopez Mendoza, Coordinador del Comité Consultivo Cientifico Nacional de Pesca y Acuicultura, tel/fax (503) 260–5524; email: cccnpesca@hotmail.com.

Mario Gonzalez Recinos, Director General, Cendepesca, Final 1 Av. Norte, Nueva, San Salvador, El Salvador, (503) 228–1066/0034, fax (503) 289–6125 / 228–0074; email: mgonzalez@sgsica.org.

Jose Emilio Suadi H., Viceministro, Ministerio de Agricultura y Ganaderia, Final 1 A. Avenida Norte y Ave. Manuel Gallardo, Nueva, San Salvador, El Salvador, (503) 288–9980, fax (503) 288–1938; email: jsuadi@mag.gov.sv.

French Commissioners:

Didier Ortolland, Ministry of Foreign Affairs, Direction des Affaires Juridiques, Sous-Direction du Droit de la Mer, Des Peches et De L'antarctique, 37, Quai D'orsay, 75007 Paris, France, 33 (01) 4317–5339, fax 33 (01) 4317–5505; email: didicr.ortolland@diplomatie. gouv.fr.

Daniel Silvestre, Secretariat General de la Mer, 16 Boulevard Raspail, 75007 Paris, France; email:daniel.silvestre@sgmer.pm.gouv.fr.

M. Sven-Erik Sjoden, Charge de Mission, Direction des Nations Unies et des Organisations Internationales, Ministere des Affairs Estrangeres, 37 Quai D'orsay, 75351 Paris, Cedex 07, France, (33–1) 43174659, fax (33–1) 43175558; email: svein-erik.sjoden@diplomatie.gouv.fr.

Xavier Vant, Direction des Peches Maritimes, Secretariat d'Etat a la Mer, 3 Place Fontenoy, 75700 Paris, France, (33–1) 4955–8236, fax (33–1) 4955–8200; email: xavier.vant@agriculture.gouv.fr.

Guatemala Commissioners:

Fraterno Diaz, Coordinator, Unipesca KM. 22, Carretera el Pacifico, Edificio la Ceiba, 3ER Nivel, Barcenas, Villa Nueva, Guatemala, (502) 630–5889/5883, fax (502) 630–5839; email: coorunipesca@c.net.gt.

Pablo Girón Muñoz, Viceministro, Ministerio de Agricultura, Ganaderia y Alimentación Recursos Hidrobiológicos y Alimentación, 7A Av. 12–90 Zona 13, Edificio Monja Blanca 1ER Nivel, Guatemala, (502) 362–4762, 331–0201, fax (502) 334–2784, 332–8302; email: vganaderia@intelnet.net.gt.

Japanese Commissioners:

Katsuma Hanafusa, Director for International Negotiation, Fisheries Policy Planning Department, Ministry of Agriculture, Forestry and Fisheries, 1–2–1 Kasumigaseki, Chiyoda-Ku, 100–8907 Tokyo, Japan, (81–3) 3591–1086, fax (81–3) 3502–0571; email: katsumahanafusa@nm.maff.go.jp.

Yoshiaki Ito, Director, Fishery Division, Ministry of Foreign Affairs, 2–11–1 Shibakouen Minato-Ku, 105–8519 Tokyo, Japan, (81–3) 6402–2234, fax (81–3) 6402–2233; email: yoshiaki.ito@mofa.go.jp.

Yamato Ueda, President, Federation of Japanese Tuna Fish Co-op Association, 2–3–22 Kudankita, Chiyoda-Ku, 102 Tokyo, Japan, (81–3) 3264–6167/6161, fax (81–3) 3234–7455; email: section1@intldiv.japantuna.or.ip.

Mexican Commissioners:

Maria Teresa Bandala, Directora de Medio Ambiente, Secretaría de Relaciones Exteriores, AV. Paseo de la Reforma 255, Piso 6, Colonia Cuauhtemoc, Mexico, D.F. 06500 Mexico, (52–5) 117–4354, fax (52–5) 117–4251; email: mbandala@sre.gob.mx.

Dr. Guillermo Compean Jiménez, Presidente, Instituto Nacional de la Pesca, Pitagoras #1320, Piso 8, Colonia Santa Cruz Atoyac, 06100 Mexico D.F., Mexico, (52–55) 5422–3002/5422–3009, fax (52–55) 5688–8418/5604–9169; email: compean@inp.semarnat.gob.mx.

Dr. Michel Dreyfus Leon, Director Del Pnaapd, Fidemar, Campus Cicese, Carretera Tijuana-Ensenada KM 107, 22860 Ensenada, B.C. México, (52–646) 174–5637, fax (52–646) 174–5639; email: dreyfus@cicese.mx.

Jerónimo Ramos Saenz Pardo, Conapesca, Av. Insurgentes Sur #489, Col. Condesa, 06100 México, D.F. México, (52–55) 5722–7392/8351, fax (52–55) 5574–0191; email: jramos.cnap@sagarpa.gob.mx.

Nicaraguan Commissioners:

Sergio Martinez Casco, Director, Cipa (Centro de Investigacion Pesqueras y Acuicolas, Apartado 2020, Managua, Nicaragua, (505) 270–0956, fax (505) 270–0977; email: semarca@tmx.com.ni.

Miguel Marenco Urcuyo, Director Ejecutivo, Adpesca, Apartado 2020, Managua, Nicaragua, (505) 270–0932/270–0946, fax (505) 270–0954; email: miguel.marenco@mific,gob.ni.

Panamanian Commissioner:

Arnulfo Luis Franco Rodriguez, Director Gral. de Recursos Marinos, Autoridad Maritima de Panama, Apartado 8062, Panama 7, Panama, (507) 232–8570/232–6117, fax (507) 232–6477; email: afranco@amp.gob.pa.

Peru Commissioners:

Dr. Leoncio Alvarez, Viceministro, Ministerio de la Producción, Calle Uno Oeste No. 60, Urb, Corpac, San Isidro, Lima 27 Perú, 51 (1) 224–3334, fax 51 (1) 224–2950; email:lalvarcz@minproduce.gob.pe.

Gládys Cárdenas, Instituto del Mar Perú, Apartado Postal 22, Lima, Peru, +51 (1) 429–7630, fax +51 (1) 420–0144; email: gcardenas@imarpe.gob.pe.

Patricia Durán, Ministerio de Relaciones Exteriores, Jr. Lampa 545, 7o. Piso, Lima, Lima 1 Perú, +51 (1) 311–2661, fax +51 (1) 311–2659; email: pduran@rroc.gob.pe.

Alberto Hart, Ministerio de Relaciones Exteriores, Jr. Lampa 545, 7o. Piso, Lima 1 Peru, +51 (1) 311–2653, fax +51 (1) 311–2659; email: ahart@rree.gob.pe.

Arnulfo Luis Franco Rodriguez, Director Gral. de Recursos Marinos, Autoridad Maritima de Panama, Apartado 8062, Panama 7, Panama, (507) 232–8570 / 232–6117, fax (507) 232–6477; email: afranco@amp.gob.pa.

United States Commissioners:

M. Austin Forman, 888 Southeast Third Avenue, Suite 501, Fort Lauderdale FL 33316, (954) 763–8111, fax (954) 522–1969; email: as01@bellsouth.net.

Dr. William Hogarth, Acting Assistant Administrator, National Marine Fisheries Service, 1315 East-West Highway, Silver Spring, MD 20910–3282, (301) 713–2239, fax (301) 713–2313; email: bill.hogarth@noaa.gov.

Dr. Rebecca Lent, Deputy Assistant Administration for Fisheries, National Marine Fisheries Service, 1315 East-West Highway, Silver Spring, MD 20910–3282, (301) 713–2239, fax (301) 713–1940; email: rebecca.lent@noaa.gov.

James T. McCarthy, 18708 Olmeda Place, San Diego CA 92128, (858) 485–9749, fax (858) 485–0172; email: tim@san.rr.com.

Vanuatuan Commissioners:

John Roosen, Commissioner of Maritime Affairs, Ministry of Maritime Affairs, P.O. Box 320, Marine Quay, Port Vila, Vanuatu, (678) 23128, fax (678) 22949; email: vma@vanuatu.com.vu.

A.N. Tillett, Marine & Cargo Surveyor, 663 Switzer Street, Tenth Avenue Terminal, San Diego, CA 92101, (619) 235–0766, fax (619) 235–6281; email: antillett@antillett.com.

Edward E. Weissman, Jorge Fishing, Inc., 2240 India St. San Diego, CA 92101, (619) 338–9984, fax (619) 338–9986; email: eweissman@aol.com.

Venezuelan Commissioner:

Francisco Ortisi, Jr., Vice-Presidente, Avencasa (Asociación Venezolana Camaronera, S.A.), Apartado Postal 47, Cerro Abajo, Carirubana, Venezuela, tel (58–269) 464–192 / 465–008, fax (58–269) 464–192 / 465–008; email: avecaisa@telcel.net.ve.

INTERNATIONAL BOUNDARY AND WATER COMMISSION, UNITED STATES AND MEXICO

UNITED STATES SECTION

The Commons, Building C, Suite 100, 4171 North Mesa, El Paso TX 79902–1441

phone (915) 832–4100, fax (915) 832–4190 www.ibwc.state.gov

Commissioner.—Carlos M. Ramirez (915) 832–4101.

Secretary.—Carlos Peña Jr. (915) 832–4105.

Principal Engineers:

Debra J. Little (915) 832–4147.

Carlos Marin (915) 832–4157.

Human Resources Director.—Robert Komp, (915) 832–4114.

Executive Engineer / Administrative Officer.—Robert Ortega, (915) 832–4118.

General Counsel / Legal Adviser.—Mario Lewis, (915) 832–4791.

MEXICAN SECTION

Avenida Universidad, No. 2180, Zona de El Chamizal, A.P. 1612–D, C.P. 32310, Ciudad Juarez, Chihuahua, Mexico

PO Box 10525, El Paso TX 79995.

phone 011–52–16–13–7311 or 011–52–16–13–7363 (Mexico)

Commissioner.—Arturo Herrera Solis.

Secretary.—Jose de Jesus Luevano Grano.

Principal Engineers: L. Antonio Rascon Mendoza, Gilberto Elizalde Hernandez.

INTERNATIONAL BOUNDARY COMMISSION, UNITED STATES AND CANADA

UNITED STATES SECTION

1250 23rd Street, Suite 100 20037, phone (202) 736–9100

Commissioner.—[Vacant].
Deputy Commissioner.—Kyle Hipsley.
Administrative Officer.—[Vacant].

CANADIAN SECTION

Room 555, 615 Booth Street, Ottawa ON, Canada K1A 0E9, phone (613) 995–4341

Commissioner.—Michael J. O'Sullivan.
Engineer to the Commission.—Al Arseneault.

INTERNATIONAL COTTON ADVISORY COMMITTEE

Headquarters: 1629 K Street Suite 702, 20006, secretariat@icac.org
phone 463–6660, fax 463–6950

(Permanent Secretariat of the Organization)

MEMBER COUNTRIES

Argentina
Australia
Belgium
Brazil
Burkina Faso
Cameroon
Chad
China (Taiwan)
Colombia
Côte d'Ivoire
Egypt
Finland
France
Germany
Greece
India
Iran
Israel
Italy
Japan
Korea, Republic of
Mali
Netherlands
Nigeria
Pakistan
Paraguay
Philippines
Poland
Russia
South Africa
Spain
Sudan
Switzerland
Syria
Tanzania
Togo
Turkey
Uganda
United Kingdom
United States
Uzbekistan
Zimbabwe

Executive Director.—Terry P. Townsend.
Statistician.—Gerald Estur.
Economists: Carlos Valderrama; Andrei Guitchounts.
Head of Technical Information Section.—M. Rafiq Chaudhry.
Manager Information Systems.—John Mulligan.
Administrative Officer.—Federico R. Arriola.

INTERNATIONAL JOINT COMMISSION, UNITED STATES AND CANADA

UNITED STATES SECTION

1250 23rd Street, Suite 100, 20440, phone (202) 736–9000, fax 467–0746, www.ijc.org

Chairman.—Dennis L. Schornacle.
Commissioners: Irene B. Brooks, Allen I. Olson.
Secretary.—Dr. Gerry Galloway.
Legal Adviser.—James G. Chandler.
Engineering Adviser.—Lisa Bourget.
Environmental Adviser.—Joel L. Fisher.
Public Information Officer.—Frank Bevacqua.
Ecologist.—Kay Austin.

CANADIAN SECTION

234 Laurier Avenue West, Ottawa, Ontario Canada K1P 6K6, phone (613) 995–2984, fax (613) 993–5583

Chairman.—Rt. Hon. Herb Gray.
Commissioners: Robert Gourd, Jack Blaney.
Secretary.—Murray Clamen.
Legal Adviser.—Michael Vechsler.
Engineering Adviser.—Edward A. Bailey.
Senior Environmental Adviser.—Tony Clarke.
Public Relations Adviser.—Fabien Lengellé.
Economics Adviser.—Ann MacKenzie.
Research Adviser.—Rudy Koop.

GREAT LAKES REGIONAL OFFICE

Eighth Floor, 100 Ouellette Avenue, Windsor, Ontario Canada N9A 6T3, phone (519) 257–6700 (Canada), (313) 226–2170 (U.S.)

Director.—Gail Krantzberg.
Public Affairs Officer.—Jennifer Day.

INTERNATIONAL LABOR ORGANIZATION

Headquarters: Geneva, Switzerland

Washington Branch Office, 1828 L Street, Suite 600, 20036, phone 653–7652, fax 653–7687, www.ilo.org

Liaison Office with the United Nations

220 East 42nd Street, Suite 3101, New York NY 10017–5806

International Labor Office (Permanent Secretariat of the Organization)
Headquarters Geneva:
Director General.—Juan Somavia.
Washington:
Director.—Anthony G. Freeman.
Assistant Director.—John R. Byrne.
Senior Advisor/Public Affairs.—Mary W. Covington.
Other Branch Offices: Bonn, London, Paris, Rome, Tokyo, Moscow.

INTERNATIONAL MONETARY FUND

700 19th Street 20431, phone (202) 623–7000

http://www.imf.org

MANAGEMENT AND SENIOR OFFICERS

Managing Director.—Horst Köhler.
First Deputy Managing Director.—Anne O. Krueger.
Deputy Managing Directors: Eduardo Aninat, Shigemitsu Sugisaki.
Economic Counsellor.—Kenneth S. Rogoff.
IMF Institute Director.—Mohsin S. Khan.
Legal Department General Counsel.—François P. Gianviti.
Departmental Directors:
Administration.—Brian C. Stuart.
African.—Abdoulaye Bio-Tchané.
Associate Director.—Ernesto Hernández-Catá.
Asia and Pacific.—David Burton.
European I.—Michael C. Deppler.
European II.—John Odling-Smee.
External Relations.—Thomas C. Dawson II.
Fiscal Affairs.—Theresa Ter-Minassian.

Middle Eastern.—George T. Abed.
Monetary and Exchange Affairs.—Stefan Ingves.
Policy Development and Review.—Timothy F. Geithner.
Research.—Kenneth S. Rogoff.
Secretary.—Shailendra Anjaria.
Statistics.—Carol S. Carson.
Treasurer.—Edward Brau.
Western Hemisphere.—Anoop Singh.

Bureau Directors:
Computing Services.—Warren N. Minami.
Language Services.—Patrick Delannoy.

Director Office of:
Budget and Planning.—Barry Potter.
Internal Audit and Inspection.—Alain Coune.

Regional Office for Asia and the Pacific Director.—Hiroyuki Hino.
Director Office in Europe (Paris).—Flemming Larsen.
Acting Director and Special Trade Representative (Geneva).—Grant B. Taplin.
Director and Special Representative to the United Nations.—Reinhard Munzberg.

EXECUTIVE DIRECTORS AND ALTERNATES

Executive Directors:

Sulaiman M. Al-Turki, represents Saudi Arabia.
Alternate.—Abudullah S. Al Azzuz.

Pierre Duquesne, represents France.
Alternate.—Sébastien Boitreaud.

Vilhjálmur Egilsson, represents Denmark, Estonia, Finland, Iceland, Latvia, Lithuania, Norway, Sweden.
Alternate.—Benny Andersen.

Hernán Oyarzábal, represents Costa Rica, El Salvador, Guatemala, Honduras, Mexico, Nicaragua, Spain, Venezuela, Republica Bolivariana de.
Alternate.—Mario Beauregard.

Ian E. Bennett, represents Antigua and Barbuda, the Bahamas, Barbados, Belize, Canada, Dominica, Grenada, Ireland, Jamaica, St. Kitts and Nevis, St. Lucia, St. Vincent and the Grenadines.
Alternate.—Nioclús A. O'Murchú.

Ismaila Usman, represents Angola, Botswana, Burundi, Eritrea, Ethiopia, Gambia, Kenya, Lesotho, Malawi, Mozambique, Namibia, Nigeria, Sierra Leone, South Africa, Sudan, Swaziland, Tanzania, Uganda, Zambia, Zimbabwe.
Alternate.—Peter J. Ngumbullu.

Yaga V. Reddy, represents Bangladesh, Bhutan, India, Sri Lanka.
Alternate.—R.A. Jayatissa.

Sri Mulyani Indrawati, represents Brunei Darussalam, Cambodia, Fiji, Indonesia, Lao People's Democratic Republic, Malaysia, Myanmar, Nepal, Singapore, Thailand, Tonga, Vietnam.
Alternate.—Ismail Alowi.

Fritz Zurbrügg, represents Azerbaijan, Kyrgyz Republic, Poland, Switzerland, Tajikistan, Turkmenistan, Uzbekistan, Serbia and Montenegro.
Alternate.—Wieslaw Szczuka.

Murilo Portugal, represents Brazil, Colombia, Dominican Republic, Ecuador, Guyana, Haiti, Panama, Suriname, Trinidad and Tobago.
Alternate.—Roberto Steiner.

Willy Kiekens, represents Austria, Belarus, Belgium, Czech Republic, Hungary, Kazakhstan, Luxembourg, Slovak Republic, Slovenia, Turkey.
Alternate.—Johann Prader.

Damian Ondo Mañe, represents Benin, Burkina Faso, Cameroon, Cape Verde, Central African Republic, Chad, Comoros, Congo, Democratic Republic of, Congo, Republic of, Côte d'Ivoire, Djibouti, Equatorial Guinea, Gabon, Guinea, Guinea-Bissau, Madagascar, Mali, Mauritania, Mauritius, Niger, Rwanda, Sǎo Tomé and Principe, Senegal, Togo.
Alternate.—Laurean W. Rutayisire.

Pier Carlo Padoan, represents Albania, Greece, Italy, Malta, Portugal, San Marino.
Alternate.—Harilaos Vittas.

Nancy P. Jacklin, represents United States.
Alternate.—Meg Lundsager.

Ken Yagi, represents Japan.
Alternate.—Haruyuki Toyama.

Abbas Mirakhor, represents Afghanistan Islamic State of, Algeria, Ghana, Iran, Islamic Republic of, Morocco, Pakistan, Tunisia.
Alternate.—Mohammed Daíri.
Guillermo Le Fort, represents Argentina, Bolivia, Chile, Paraguay, Peru, Uruguay.
Alternate.—A. Guillermo Zoccali.
Karlheinz Bischofberger, represents Germany.
Alternate.—Ruediger von Kleist.
A. Shakour Shaalan, represents Bahrain, Egypt, Iraq, Jordan, Kuwait, Lebanon, Libya Arab, Jamahiriya, Maldives, Oman, Qatar, Syrian Arab Republic, United Arab Emirates, Yemen, Republic of.
Alternate.—Oussama T. Kanaan.
Aleksei V. Mozhin, represents Russian Federation.
Alternate.—Andrei Lushin.
Michael J. Callaghan, represents Australia, Kiribati, Korea, Marshall Islands, Micronesia, Federated States of, Mongolia, New Zealand, Palau, Papua New Guinea, Philippines, Samoa, Seychelles, Solomon Islands, Vanuatu.
Alternate.—Michael H. Reddell.
Jeroen Kremers, represents Armenia, Bosnia and Herzegovina, Bulgaria, Croatia, Cyprus, Georgia, Israel, Macedonia, former Yugoslav Republic of, Moldova, Netherlands, Romania, Ukraine.
Alternate.—Yuriy G. Yakusha.
Wei Benhua, represents China.
Alternate.—Wang Xiaoyi.
Tom Schole, represents United Kingdom.
Alternate.—Martin A. Brooke.

INTERNATIONAL ORGANIZATION FOR MIGRATION

Headquarters: 17 Route Des Morillons (PO Box 71), CH1211, Geneva 19, Switzerland

Washington Mission: 1752 N Street, NW, Suite 700, 20036, phone (202) 862–1826

New York Mission: 122 East 42nd Street, Suite 1610, New York NY 10168–1610

phone (212) 681–7000

HEADQUARTERS

Director General.—Brunson McKinley (United States).
Deputy Director General.—Ndioro Ndiaye (Senegal).
Washington Regional Representative.—Frances E. Sullivan (United States).
New York Chief of Mission.—Andrew Bruce (New Zealand).

MEMBER STATES

Albania
Algeria
Angola
Argentina
Armenia
Australia
Austria
Azerbaijan
Bangladesh
Belgium
Belize
Benin
Bolivia
Bulgaria
Burkina Faso
Cambodia
Canada
Cape Verde
Chile
Colombia
Congo
Costa Rica
Cöte d'lvoire
Croatia
Cyprus
Czech Republic
Democratic Republic of the Congo
Denmark
Dominican Republic
Ecuador
Egypt
El Salvador
Finland
France
Gambia
Georgia
Germany
Greece
Guatemala
Guinea
Guinea-Bissau
Haiti
Honduras
Hungary
Ireland
Israel
Italy
Iran, Islamic Republic of
Japan
Jordan
Kazakhstan
Kenya

Kyrgyzstan
Latvia
Liberia
Lithuania
Luxembourg
Madagascar
Mali
Mexico
Morocco
Netherlands
Nicaragua
Nigeria
Norway
Pakistan
Panama
Paraguay
Peru
Philippines
Poland
Portugal
Republic of Korea
Romania
Rwanda
Senegal
Sierra Leone
Slovakia
Slovenia
South Africa
Sri Lanka
Sudan
Sweden
Switzerland
Tajikistan
Thailand
Tunisia
Uganda
Ukraine
United Kingdom of Great Britain and Northern Ireland
United Republic of Tanzania
United States of America
Uruguay
Venezuela
Yemen, Republic of
Yugoslavia
Zambia
Zimbabwe

STATES WITH OBSERVER STATUS

Afghanistan
Belarus
Bhutan
Bosnia and Herzegovina
Brazil
Burundi
China
Cuba
Estonia
Ethiopia
Ghana
Holy See
India
Indonesia
Jamaica
Libyan Arab Jamahiriya
Malta
Mozambique
Namibia
Nepal (Kingdom of)
New Zealand
Papua New Guinea
Republic of Moldova
Russian Federation
San Marino
Sao Tomé and Principe
Somalia
Spain
The former Yugoslav Republic of Macedonia
Turkey
Turkmenistan
Viet Nam
Sovereign Military Order of Malta

IOM OVERSEAS LIAISON AND OPERATIONAL OFFICES

Afghanistan, Herat
Albania, Tirana
Angola, Luanda
Argentina, Buenos Aires *
Armenia, Yerevan
Australia, Canberra City
Austria, Vienna *
Azerbaijan, Baku
Bangladesh, Dhaka
Belarus, Minsk
Belgium / Luxembourg, Brussels *
Bolivia, La Paz
Bosnia and Herzegovina, Sarajevo
Bulgaria, Sofia
Cambodia, Phnom Penh
Canada, Ottawa, Ontario
Cape Verde, Praia
Chile, Santiago de Chile
China, Hong Kong
Colombia, Bogotá
Congo, Brazzaville
Congo, (Democratic Republic of), Gombe, Kinshasa
Costa Rica, San José *
Côte D'Ivoire, Abidjan
Croatia, Zagreb
Cyprus, Nicosia
Czech Republic, Praha
Dominican Republic, Santo Domingo
East Timor, Dili
Ecuador, Quito
Egypt, Cairo *
El Salvador, San Salvador
Estonia, Tallinn
Ethiopia, Addis Ababa
Finland, Helsinki *
France, Paris
Gambia, Banjul
Georgia, Tbilisi
Germany, Berlin, Bonn
Ghana, Accra North
Greece, Athens
Guatemala, Ciudad de Guatemala
Guinea, Conakry
Guinea-Bissau, Guinea Bissau
Honduras, Tegucigalpa
Hungary, Budapest *
India, Ahmedabad
Indonesia, Jakarta, Kupang
Iran, Tehran
Ireland, Dublin
Italy, Roma *
Japan, Tokyo
Jordan, Amman
Kazakhstan, Almaty
Kenya, Nairobi *
Korea (Republic of), Seoul
Kyrgyz Republic, Bishkek City
Latvia, Riga
Lesotho, Maseru
Lithuania, Vilnius
Macedonia, Skopje
Mali, Bamako
Moldova, Chisinau
Nauru (Republic of)
Netherlands, Den Haag
Nicaragua, Managua
Norway, Oslo
Pakistan, Islamabad *
Papua New Guinea, Manus
Peru, Lima
Philippines, Manila *
Poland, Warszawa
Portugal, Lisbon
Romania, Bucharest
Russia, Moscow
Saudi Arabia, Riyadh
Senegal, Dakar *
Sierra Leone, Freetown
Slovak Republic, Bratislava
Slovenia, Ljubljana
South Africa, Pretoria
Spain, Madrid

Sri Lanka, Colombo
Sudan, Khartoum
Switzerland, Bern
Syrian Arab Republic, Damascus
Tajikistan, Dushanbe
Thailand, Bangkok *
Tunisia, Tunis
Turkey, Ankara
Turkmenistan, Ashgabad
Uganda, Kampala
Ukraine, Kiev
United Kingdom, London
United States of America, Washington, New York, Los Angeles, Miami, Rosemont
Uruguay, Montevideo
Venezuela, Caracas
Vietnam, Hanoi, Ho Chi Minh City
Yugoslavia (Federal Republic of), Belgrade, Prishtina
Zambia, Lusaka
Zimbabwe, Harare

INTERNATIONAL PACIFIC HALIBUT COMMISSION, UNITED STATES AND CANADA

Headquarters: University of Washington, Seattle, WA 98195

phone (206) 634–1838, fax (206) 632–2983

Mailing address: PO Box 95009, Seattle WA 98145–2009

American Commissioners:

Ralph G. Hoard, 4019 21st Avenue W., Seattle, WA 98199, (206) 282–0988, fax (206) 281–0329.

Mr. Drew Scalzi, 41685 Redoubt Circle, Homer, AK 99603, (907) 235–6359.

Dr. Jim Balsiger, National Marine Fisheries Service, PO Box 21668, Juneau, AK 99802, (907) 586–7221, fax (907) 586–7249.

Canadian Commissioners:

Dr. Richard J. Beamish, Pacific Biological Station, PO Box 100, Nanaimo, B.C., Canada V9R 5K6, (250) 756–7029, fax (250) 756–7333.

Cliff Atleo, PO Box 1218, Port Alberni, BC, Canada V9Y 7Ml, (250) 723–0188, fax (250) 723–1393.

John Secord, #301, 3680 W. 7th Avenue, Vancouver, BC, Canada V6R 1W4 (604) 734–1019, fax (604) 734–6962.

Director and Secretary (ex officio).—Dr. Bruce M. Leaman, PO Box 95009, Seattle, WA 98145–2009.

ORGANIZATION OF AMERICAN STATES

17th Street and Constitution Avenue, NW., 20006, phone (202) 458–3000, fax 458–3967

PERMANENT MISSIONS TO THE OAS

Antigua and Barbuda.—Ambassador Lionel Alexander Hurst, Permanent Representative, 3216 New Mexico Avenue NW., Washington DC 20016, phone (202) 362–5122, 5166 or 5211, fax 362–5225.

Argentina.—Ambassador Rodolfo Gil, Permanent Representative, 1816 Corcoran Street NW., Washington DC 20009, phone (202) 387–4142, 4146 or 4170, fax 328–1591.

The Bahamas.—Ambassador Joshua Sears, Permanent Representative, 2220 Massachusetts Avenue NW., Washington DC 20008, phone (202) 319–2660 to 2667, fax 319–2668.

Barbados.—Ambassador Michael I. King, Permanent Representative, 2144 Wyoming Avenue NW., Washington DC 20008, phone (202) 939–9200, 9201, 9202, fax 332–7467.

Belize.—Ambassador Lisa Shoman, Permanent Representative, 2535 Massachusetts Avenue NW., Washington DC 20008–3098, phone (202) 332–9636, ext. 3001, fax 332–6888.

Bolivia.—[Vacant]. Permanent Representative, 1819 H Street, NW., Suite 419, Washington, DC 20006, phone (202) 785–0218, fax 296–0563.

Brazil.—Ambassador Valter Pecly Moreira, Permanent Representative, 2600 Virginia Avenue NW., Suite 412, Washington DC 20037, phone (202) 333–4224, 4225 or 4226, fax 333–6610.

Canada.—Ambassador Paul Durand, Permanent Representative, 501 Pennsylvania Avenue NW., Washington DC 20001, phone (202) 682–1768, Ext. 7267, fax 682–7624.

Chile.—Ambassador Esteban Tomic Errázuriz, 2000 L Street NW., Suite 720, Washington DC 20036, phone (202) 887–5475, 5476, fax 775–0713.

* Mission with Regional Functions.

Colombia.—Ambassador Horacio Serpa, Permanent Representative, 1609 22nd Street NW., Washington DC 20008, phone 332–8003 or 8004, fax 234–9781.

Costa Rica.—Ambassador Walter Niehaus, Permanent Representative, 2112 S Street NW., Suite 300, Washington DC 20008, phone (202) 234–9280, fax 986–2274.

Dominica.—[Vacant], 3216 New Mexico Avenue NW., Washington, DC 20016, phone (202) 364–6781, fax 364–6791.

Dominican Republic.—Ambassador Ramón Quiñones, Permanent Representative, 1715 22nd Street NW., Washington DC 20008, phone (202) 332–9142, 6280, fax 232–5038.

Ecuador.—Ambassador Marcelo Hervas, Permanent Representative, 2535 15th Street NW., Washington DC 20009, phone (202) 234–1494 or 1692, fax 667–3482.

El Salvador.—Ambassador Margarita Escobar, Permanent Representative, 1211 Connecticut Avenue NW. Suite 401, Washington DC 20036, phone (202) 467–0054 or 4290, fax 467–4261.

Grenada.—Ambassador Denis G. Antoine, Permanent Representative, 1701 New Hampshire Avenue NW., Washington DC 20009, phone (202) 265–2561, fax 265–2468.

Guatemala.—Ambassador Victor Hugo Godoy, Permanent Representative, 1507 22nd Street NW., Washington DC 20037, phone (202) 833–4015, 4016, or 4017, fax 833–4011.

Guyana.—Ambassador Dr. M.A. Odeen Ishmael, Permanent Representative, 2490 Tracy Place NW., Washington DC 20008, phone (202) 265–6900 or 6901, fax 232–1297.

Haiti.—Ambassador Raymond Valcin, Interim Representative, 2311 Massachusetts Avenue NW., Washington DC 20008, phone (202) 332–4090 or 4092, fax 518–8742.

Honduras.—Ambassador Salvador Rodezno, Permanent Representative, 5100 Wisconsin Avenue NW., Suite 403, Washington DC 20016, phone (202) 362–9656 or 9657, fax 537–7170.

Jamaica.—Ambassador Seymour Mullings, Permanent Representative, 1520 New Hampshire Avenue NW., Washington DC 20036, phone (202) 986–0121, 0123, 452–0660, fax 452–9395.

Mexico.—Ambassador Miguel Ruíz-Cabañas, Permanent Representative, 2440 Massachusetts Avenue NW., Washington DC 20008, phone (202) 332–3663, 3664, 3984, fax 234–0602.

Nicaragua.—Ambassador Carmen Marina Gutierrez, Permanent Representative, 1627 New Hampshire Avenue NW., Washington DC 20009, phone (202) 332–1643 or 1644, fax 745–0710.

Panama.—Ambassador Juan Manuel Castulovich, Permanent Representative, 2201 Wisconsin Avenue NW., Suite 240, phone (202) 965–4826 or 4819, fax 965–4836.

Paraguay.—Ambassador Juan Enrique Chase Plate, Permanent Representative, 2022 Connecticut Avenue NW., Washington DC 20008, phone (202) 244–3003, fax 244–3005.

Peru.—Ambassador Eduardo Ferrero, Permanent Representative, 1901 Pennsylvania Avenue NW., Suite 402, Washington DC 20006, phone (202) 232–2281, fax 466–3068.

Saint Kitts and Nevis.—Ambassador Dr. Izben C. Williams, Permanent Representative, 3216 New Mexico Avenue NW., Washington DC 20016, phone (202) 686–2636, fax 686–5740.

Saint Lucia.—Ambassador Sonia M. Johnny, Permanent Representative, 3216 New Mexico Avenue NW., Washington, DC 20016, phone (202) 364–6792 thru 6795, fax 364–6723.

Saint Vincent and The Grenadines.— Ambassador Ellsworth I.A. John, Permanent Representative, 3216 New Mexico Avenue, NW., Washington DC 20016, phone (202) 364–6730, fax 364–6736.

Suriname.—Ambassador Henry Lothar Illes, Permanent Representative, 4301 Connecticut Avenue NW., Suite 462, Washington, DC 20008, phone (202) 244–7488, 7590, 7591 or 7592, fax 244–5878.

Trinidad and Tobago.—Ambassador Marina Valere, Interim Representative, 1708 Massachusetts Avenue NW., Washington DC 20036, phone (202) 467–6490, fax 785–3130.

United States of America.—Ambassador Thomas A. Shannon, Interim Representative, ARA/USOAS Bureau of Inter-American Affairs, Department of State, Room 6494, Washington DC 20520, phone (202) 647–9430, fax 647–0911.

Uruguay.—Ambassador Juan Enrique Fischer, Permanent Representative, 2801 New Mexico Avenue NW., Suite 1210, Washington DC 20007, phone (202) 333–0588 or 0687, fax 337–3758.

Venezuela.—Ambassador Jorge Valero Briceño, Permanent Representative, 1099 30th Street NW., Second Floor, Washington, DC 20007, phone (202) 342–5837 or 5838, fax 625–5657.

GENERAL SECRETARIAT

Secretary General.—Cesar Gaviria, 458–6836, fax 458–3624.
Chief of Staff to the Secretary General.—Fernando Jaramillo, 458–3841, fax 458–3624.
Assistant Secretary General.—Luigi Einaudi, 458–6046, fax 458–3011.
Chief of Staff to the Assistant Secretary General.—Sandra Honore, 458–3497.
Assistant Secretary for—
Legal Affairs.—Enrique Lagos, 458–3983.
Management.—James R. Harding, 458–3436.
Director General for Inter-American Agency for Cooperation and Development.—L. Ronald Scheman, 458–3510.
Directors:
Office of Protocol.—Ana C. O'Brien, 458–3718, fax 458–3722.
Department of Public Information.—Eduardo Del Buey (acting), 458–3760.
Inter-American Commission of Human Rights (ACHR)
Chairman.—Professor Helio Bicudo, 458–6002.
Executive Secretary.—Dr. Santiago Canton, 458–6002.
Inter-American Commission of Women (CIM)
Chairperson.—T.H. Indranie Chandarpal, 458–6084, fax 458–6094.
Executive Secretary.—Carmen Lomellin, 458–6084, fax 458–6094.
Inter-American Drug Abuse Control Commission (CICAD)
Chairman.—Dr. Alberto Soavarelli.
Executive Secretary.—David Beall, 458–3178.

ORGANIZATION FOR ECONOMIC COOPERATION AND DEVELOPMENT

Headquarters: 2 rue André-Pascal, 75775 Paris CEDEX 16, France

phone (331) 4524–8200, fax (331) 4524–8500

Secretary-General.—Donald J. Johnston.
Deputy Secretaries General: Richard Hecklinger, Seiichi Kondo, Herwig Schlogl.
Member Countries:

Australia
Austria
Belgium
Canada
Czech Republic
Denmark
Finland
France
Germany
Greece
Hungary
Iceland
Ireland
Italy
Japan
Korea
Luxembourg
Mexico
Netherlands
New Zealand
Norway
Poland
Portugal
Slovak Republic
Spain
Sweden
Switzerland
Turkey
United Kingdom
United States

OECD WASHINGTON CENTER

2001 L Street NW., #650, 20036, phone (202) 785–6323, fax (202) 785–0350

http://www.oecdwash.org

Heads of Center: Sandra Wilson and Matthew Brosius.

PAN AMERICAN SANITARY BUREAU

REGIONAL OFFICE OF THE WORLD HEALTH ORGANIZATION

525 23rd Street, NW., Washington DC 20037, phone (202) 974–3000, fax (202) 974–3663

PAN AMERICAN SANITARY BUREAU

Director.—Dr. Mirta Roses Periago, 974–3408.
Deputy Director.—Dr. David Brandling-Bennett, 974–3178.
Assistant Director.—[Vacant].
Director of:
Administration.—Mr. Eric Boswell, 974–3412.
Program Management.—Dr. Daniel López Acuña, 974–3221.

FIELD OFFICES

PAHO / WHO Caribbean Program Coordination, PO Box 508, Dayralls and Navy Garden Roads, Christ Church, Bridgetown, Barbados, phone (246) 426–3860 / 3865, fax 436–9779.

Caribbean Program Coordination (CPC).—Antigua and Barbuda, Barbados, Dominica, Grenada, St. Kitts and Nevis, Saint Lucia, St. Vincent and the Grenadines. Eastern Caribbean: Anguilla, British Virgin Islands, Montserrat. French Antilles: Guadaloupe, Martinique, St. Martin and St. Bartholomew, French Guiana.

PAHO / WHO Representatives:

Argentina, Dr. Juan Manuel Sotelo Figueiredo, Oficina Sanitaria Panamericana, Marcelo T. de Alvear 684, 4o. piso, 1058 Buenos Aires, Argentina, phone (54–11) 4312–5301 to 5304, fax 4311–9151.

Bahamas (*Turks and Caicos*), Dr. Richard Van West Charles, Union Court, Elizabeth Avenue, Nassau, Bahamas, phone (242) 326–7390, 7299, fax 326–7012.

Belize, Dr. Kathleen P. Israel, Belize City, Belize, phone (501–2) 448–85, 52, fax 309–17.

Bolivia, Dr. José Antonio Pagés, Representante de la OPS / OMS en Bolivia, Calle Victor Sanjines 2678, (Plaza España), 6to, Piso, La Paz, Bolivia, phone (591–2) 412–465, 303, 313, 397, fax 412–598.

Brazil, Dr. Jacobo Finkelman, Representante da OPAS / OMS no Brasil, Setor de Embaixadas Norte, Lote 19, 70800–400, Brasilia, D.F., Brasil, phone (55–61) 426–9595, 9550, 9500, fax 321–1922.

Chile, Dr. Henri Jouval Jr., Representante de la OPS / OMS en Chile, Avenida Providencia No. 1017, Piso 4 y 5, Santiago, Chile, phone (56–2) 264–9300, fax 264–9311.

Colombia, Dr. Eduardo Alvarez Peralta, Representante de la OPS / OMS en Colombia, Cra 7 74 21 piso 9, Edificio Aurora, Santafé de Bogotá, D.C., Colombia, phone (57–1) 347–8373, fax 254–7070.

Costa Rica, Dr. Philippe Lamy, Representante de la OPS / OMS en Costa Rica, Calle 16, Avenida 6 y 8, Distrito Hospital, San José, Costa Rica, phone (506) 258–5810, fax 258–5830.

Cuba, Dr. Eduardo Patricio Yépez, Representante de la OPS / OMS en Cuba, Oficina Sanitaria Panamericana, Calle 4 No. 407, entre 17 y 19 Vedado, La Habana, Cuba, phone (53–7), 552–526, 527, fax 662–075.

Dominican Republic, Dra. Socoro Gross, Representante de la OPS / OMS en República Dominicana, Calle Pepillo Salcedo, Plaza de la Salud, Edificio Cruz Roja / OPS / OMS, 2da, Planta, Santo Domingo, D.N., República Dominicana, phone (809) 562–1519, 1582, 1638, 1693, fax 544–0322.

Ecuador, Mr. Diego Victoria, Representante de la OPS / OMS en el Ecuador, Oficina Sanitaria Panamericana, Av. Amazonas 2889 y La Granja, Edificio Naciones Unidas Quito, Ecuador, phone (593–2) 246–0330, 0215, 0274, 0273, fax 246–0635.

El Salvador, Dr. Antonio Horacio Toro, Representante de la OPS / OMS en El Salvador, 73 Avenida Sur No. 135, Colonia Escalón, San Salvador, El Salvador, phone (503) 298–3491, 3306, fax 298–1168.

Guatemala, Dr. Pedro Luis Castellanos, Representante de la OPS / OMS en Guatemala, Oficina Sanitaria Panamericana, Avenida 15 de septiembre (7a avenida) 12–23, Zona 9, Edificio Etisa 3er. nivel, Plaza España, Guatemala, Guatemala, phone (011–502) 332–2032, fax 334–3804.

Guyana, Dr. Bernadette Theodore-Gandi, Lot 8 Brickdam Stabroek, Georgetown, Guyana, phone (592) 225–3000, fax 226–6654.

Haiti, Mrs. Lea Guido, Représentante de l'OPS / OMS en Haiti, ali., No. 295 Avenue John Brown, Port-au-Prince, Haiti, phone (53–7) 552–526, 527, fax 662–075.

Honduras, Dr. Carlos Samayoa Castillo, Representante de la OPS / OMS en Honduras, Oficina Sanitaria Panamericana, P.O. Box 728, Edificio Immobiliaria Caribe, Quinto Piso, Calle Principal, Colonia Lomas del Guijarro, Tegucigalpa, MDC, Honduras, phone (504) 221–3721, 3705, 7718, fax 221–3706.

Jamaica (Bermuda and Cayman), Dr. Manuel Peña, Old Oceana Building, 7th Floor, 2–4 King St., Kingston, Jamaica, phone (876) 967–4626, 4691, fax 967–5189.

Mexico, Dr. Joaquín Molina, Representante Interino de la OPS / OMS en México, Oficina Sanitaria Panamericana, Paseo de la Reforma #450, Pisos 2 y 3, Colonia Juárez, Delegación Cuauhtémoc, C.P. 06600, México, D.F. México, phone (525) 52–55–5207–3009, fax 52–55–5207–2964.

Nicaragua, Dr. Patricio Rojas, Representante de la OPS / OMS en Nicaragua, Oficina Sanitaria Panamericana, Complejo Nacional de Salud, Camino a la Sabana, Apartado Postal 1309, Managua, Nicaragua, phone (505–2) 89–4200, 4800, fax 89–4999.

Panama, Dr. Guadalupe Verdejo, Representante de la OPS / OMS en Panamá, Ministerio de Salud, Avenida Gorgas, Edif. 261, 2 piso, Ancón, Panamá, Panamá, phone (507) 262–0030, fax 262–4052.

Paraguay, Dr. Hernán Málaga, Representante de la OPS / OMS en Paraguay, Edificio ''Faro del Río'' Mcal. López 957 Esq. Estados Unidos, Asunción, Paraguay, phone (595–21) 450–495, 496, 497, fax 450–498.

Peru, Dr. Marie-Andrée Diouf, Representante de la OPS / OMS en Perú, Oficina Sanitaria Panamericana, Los Cedros 269, San Isidro, Lima 27, Perú, phone (51–1) 421–3030, fax 222–6405.

Suriname, Dr. Carol Vlassoff, Gravenstraat 60 (boven), Paramaribo, Suriname, phone (597) 471–676, fax 471–568.

Trinidad and Tobago, Dr. Lilian Reneau-Vernon, 49 Jerningham Avenue, Port-of-Spain, Trinidad, phone (868) 624–7524, 4376, 5642, 5928, fax 624–5643.

Uruguay, Dr. José Flusa Lima, Representante de la OPS / OMS en Uruguay, Avda. Brasil 2697, Apts. 5, 6 y 8, 2do. Piso, 11300, Montevideo, Uruguay, phone (598–2) 707–3581, 3589, 3590, fax 707–3530.

Venezuela (Netherlands Antilles), Dr. Isías Daniel Gutiérrez, Representante de la OPS / OMS en Venezuela, Oficina Sanitaria Panamericana, Avenida Sexta entre 5a y 6a, Transversal, Altamira, Caracas 1010, Venezuela, phone (212) 262–2085, fax 261–6069.

CENTERS

Caribbean Epidemiology Center (CAREC).—Dr. Carl James Hospedales, Director, 16–18 Jamaica Boulevard, Federation Park, Port-of Spain, Trinidad, phone (1–868) 622–4261, 4262, 3168, 3277, fax 622–2792.

Caribbean Food and Nutrition Institute (CFNI).—Dr. Fitzroy J. Henry, Director, University of the West Indies, Kingston 7, Jamaica, phone (1–876), 927–1540, 1541, 1927, fax 927–2657.

Field Office, United States-Mexico Border (FO / USMB).—Dr. Alfonso Ruiz, Chief, Pan American Sanitary Bureau, 5400 Suncrest Dr., Suite C–4, El Paso, Texas, 79912, phone (915) 845–5950, fax 845–4361.

Institute of Nutrition of Central America and Panama (INCAP).—Dr. Hernán Delgado, Director, Carretera Roosevelt, Zona 11, Guatemala, Guatemala, phone (011–502) 471–5655, fax 473–6529.

Latin American Center and Caribbean Center on Health Sciences Information (BIREME).—Mr. Abel Laerte Packer, Director, Rua Botucatú 862, Vila Clementino, CEP.04023–062, São Paulo, SP, Brasil, phone (011–55–11) 576–9800, fax 571–1919, 575–8868.

Latin American Center for Perinatology and Human Development (CLAP).—Dr. José Miguel Belizán, Director, Hospital de Clínicas, Piso 16, Montevideo, Uruguay, phone (011–598–2) 487–2929, 2930, 2931, 2933, fax 487–2593.

Pan American Institute for Food Protection and Zoonoses (INPPAZ).—Dr. Claudio Roberto Almeida, Director, Talcahuano 1660, B1640WAB–Martínez, Buenos Aires, Argentina, phone (011–54–11) 5789–4000, fax 4789–4013.

Pan American Center for Sanitary Engineering and Environmental Sciences (CEPIS).—Dr. Mauricio Pardón Ojeda, Director, Calle Los Pinos 259, Urbanización Camacho, Lima 12, Perú, phone 437–7019, fax 437–8289.

Pan American Foot-and-Mouth Disease Center (PANAFTOSA).—Dr. Eduardo Correa Melo, Director, Avenida Presidente Kennedy 7778, (Antiga Estrada Rio-Petrópolis), São Bento, Duque de Caxias, CEP 25040–000, Rio de Janeiro, Brasil, phone (011–55–21) 3661–9000, fax 3661–9001.

Regional Program on Bioethics.—Dr. Fernando Lolas Stepke, Director, Regional Program on Bioethics PAHO / WHO, Providencia 1017, Piso 7, Santiago de Chile, Chile, phone (011–56–2), 236–0330, fax 346–7219.

PERMANENT JOINT BOARD ON DEFENSE, CANADA-UNITED STATES

CANADIAN SECTION

MGen G.R. Pearkes Building, 101 Colonel By Drive

Ottawa, Ontario, Canada K1A OK2

phone (613) 995–6637

Chairman.—Jacques Saada, M.P., (613) 995–9287.

Members:

Foreign Affairs.—Jill Sinclair, 992–3402.

Policy.—MG Cameron Ross, 992–2769.

Navy.—Cmdre Jacques Gauvin, 945–0612.

Army.— BG Vince Kennedy, 945–0442.
Air Force.—BG Doug Langton, 992–7384.
MCC Chairman.—Cmdre Jean-Yves Forcier, 992–6191.
Foreign Affairs Secretary.—Lisa Helfand, 992–9263.
Military Secretary.—LtCol Ross Struthers, 995–6637.

UNITED STATES SECTION

2E977 Homeland Security Division, Pentagon, Washington, DC 20318

phone (703) 695–4477

Chairman.—Jack David, Room 2E977, (703) 695–4477.
Members:
Joint Staff.—MG Michael M. Dunn, Room 2E1008, 697–1887.
State Department.—Nancy Mason, Room 3917, State Department, (202) 647–2170.
Army.—MG David Huntoon, Room 2E387, 692–9388.
Navy.—RADM Joe Krol, Room N3N5B, 692–9291.
Air Force.—BG Mike Gould, Room 4E1047, 614–2711.
MCC Chairman.—BG Vincent Brooks, Room 2E980, 614–0243.
Political Secretary.—Tim Ryan, Room 3917, State Department, (202) 647–2475.
Military Secretary.—LtCol Dave Hafich, 695–4477.
Assistant Military Secretary.—TSgt Manuel Gonzales, Room 2E977, 695–4477.

SECRETARIAT OF THE PACIFIC COMMUNITY

B.P. D5, 98848 Noumea Cedex, New Caledonia, phone (687) 26.20.00, fax (687) 26.38.18, E-mail spc@spc.int, http://www.spc.int

Director-General.—Lourdes Pangelinan.
Senior Deputy Director General, Suva.—Dr. Jimmie Rodgers.
Deputy Director General, Noumea.—Yves Corbel.
Director of Corporate Services.—Louni Hanipale Mose.
Director of the Marine Resource Division.—Tim Adams.
Head of the Planning Unit.—Richard Mann.

U.S. Contact: Bureau of East Asian and Pacific Affairs, Office of Australia, New Zealand and Pacific Island Affairs, Department of State, Washington, DC 20520, phone (202) 647–9690, fax (202) 647–0118

Countries and Territories Covered by the SPC:

American Samoa
Australia
Cook Islands
Federated States of Micronesia
Fiji
France
French Polynesia
Guam
Kiribati
Marshall Islands
Nauru
New Caledonia
New Zealand
Niue
Northern Mariana Islands
Palau
Papua New Guinea
Pitcairn Islands
Samoa
Solomon Islands
Tokelau
Tonga
Tuvalu
United Kingdom
United States
Vanuatu
Wallis and Futuna

UNITED NATIONS

GENERAL ASSEMBLY

The General Assembly is composed of all 191 United Nations Member States.

SECURITY COUNCIL

The Security Council has 15 members. The United Nations Charter designates five States as permanent members, and the General Assembly elects 10 other members for two-year terms. The term of office for each non-permanent member of the Council ends on 31 December of the year indicated in parentheses next to its name.

The five permanent members of the Security Council are China, France, Russian Federation, United Kingdom and United States.

The 10 non-permanent members of the Council in 2003 are Angola (2004), Bulgaria (2003), Cameroon (2003), Chile (2004), Germany (2004), Guinea (2003), Mexico (2003), Pakistan (2004), Spain (2004), and Syria (2003).

ECONOMIC AND SOCIAL COUNCIL

The Economic and Social Council has 54 members, elected for three-year terms by the General Assembly. The term of office for each member expires on 31 December of the year indicated in parentheses next to its name. Voting in the Council is by simple majority; each member has one vote. In 2001, the Council is composed of the following 54 States:

Andorra (2003)
Argentina (2003)
Australia (2004)
Azerbaijan (2005)
Benin (2005)
Bhutan (2004)
Brazil (2003)
Burundi (2004)
Chile (2004)
China (2004)
Congo (2005)
Cuba (2005)
Ecuador (2005)
Egypt (2003)
El Salvador (2004)
Ethiopia (2003)
Finland (2004)
France (2005)
Georgia (2003)
Germany (2005)
Ghana (2004)
Greece (2005)
Guatemala (2004)
Hungary (2004)
India (2004)
Iran (2003)
Ireland (2005)
Italy (2003)
Jamaica (2005)
Japan (2005)
Kenya (2005)
Libya (2004)
Malaysia (2005)
Mozambique (2005)
Nepal (2003)
Netherlands (2003)
Nicaragua (2005)
Nigeria (2003)
Pakistan (2003)
Peru (2003)
Portugal (2005)
Qatar (2004)
Romania (2003)
Russian Federation (2004)
Republic of Korea (2003)
Saudi Arabia (2005)
Senegal (2005)
South Africa (2003)
Sweden (2004)
Uganda (2003)
Ukraine (2004)
United Kingdom (2004)
United States (2003)
Zimbabwe (2004)

TRUSTEESHIP COUNCIL

The Trusteeship Council has five members: China, France, Russian Federation, United Kingdom and the United States. With the independence of Palau, the last remaining United Nations trust territory, the Council formerly suspended operation on 1 November 1994. By a resolution adopted on that day, the Council amended its rules of procedure to drop the obligation to meet annually and agreed to meet as occasion required—by its decision or the decision of its President, or at the request of a majority of its members or the General Assembly or the Security Council.

INTERNATIONAL COURT OF JUSTICE

The International Court of Justice has 15 members, elected by both the General Assembly and the Security Council. Judges hold nine-year terms.

The current composition of the court is as follows: President Shi Jiuyong (China); Vice-President Raymond Ranjeva (Madagascar). Judges: Gilbert Guillaume (France), Abdul G. Koroma (Sierra Leone), Vladlen S. Vereshchetin (Russian Federation), Rosalyn Higgins (United Kingdom), Gonzalo Parra-Aranguren (Venezuela), Pieter H. Kooijmans (Netherlands), Francisco Rezek (Brazil), Awn Shawkat Al-Khasawneh (Jordan), Thomas Buergenthal (United States of America), Nabil Elaraby (Egypt), Hisashi Owada (Japan), Bruno Simma (Germany), and Peter Tomka (Slovakia).

The Registrar of the Court is Mr. Philippe Couvreur (Belgium).

UNITED NATIONS SECRETARIAT

One United Nations Plaza, New York NY 10017, (212) 963–1234, http://www.un.org

Secretary General.—Kofi A. Annan (Ghana).
Deputy Secretary.—Louise Fréchette (Canada).

EXECUTIVE OFFICE OF THE SECRETARY-GENERAL

Chief of Staff.—Iqbal Riza (Pakistan).
Assistant Secretary-General, Special Adviser.—Michael Doyle (USA).
Assistant Secretary-General, External Relations.—Gillian Sorensen (USA).
Special Assistant.—Elisabeth Lindenmayer (France).
Spokesman.—Fred Eckhard (USA).

OFFICE OF INTERNAL OVERSIGHT SERVICES

Under-Secretary-General.—Dileep Nair (Singapore).

OFFICE OF LEGAL AFFAIRS

Under-Secretary-General and Legal Counsel.—Hans Corell (Sweden).
Assistant Secretary General.—Ralph Zacklin (United Kingdom).

DEPARTMENT OF POLITICAL AFFAIRS

Under-Secretary-General.—Sir Kieran Prendergast (United Kingdom).
Assistant Secretary-General.—Tuliameni Kalomoh (Namibia).
Assistant Secretary-General.—Danilo Türk (Slovenia).

DEPARTMENT FOR DISARMAMENT AFFAIRS

Under-Secretary-General.—Jayantha Dhanapala (Sri Lanka).

DEPARTMENT OF PEACE-KEEPING OPERATIONS

Under-Secretary-General.—Jean-Marie Guehenno (France).
Assistant Secretary-General.—Hédi Annabi (Tunisia).
Assistant Secretary-General.—Michael Sheehan (USA).

OFFICE FOR THE COORDINATION OF HUMANITARIAN AFFAIRS

Under-Secretary-General, Emergency Relief Coordinator.—Kenzo Oshima (Japan).
Deputy Emergency Relief Coordinator.—Carolyn McAskie (Canada).

DEPARTMENT OF ECONOMIC AND SOCIAL AFFAIRS

Under-Secretary-General.—Nitin Desai (India).
Assistant Secretary-General.—Angela King (Jamaica).
Assistant Secretary-General.—Patrizio Civili (Italy).

DEPARTMENT OF GENERAL ASSEMBLY AND CONFERENCE MANAGEMENT

Under-Secretary-General.—Jian Chen (China).
Assistant Secretary-General.—Miles Stoby (Guyana).

DEPARTMENT OF PUBLIC INFORMATION

Under-Secretary-General.—Shashi Tharoor (India).

DEPARTMENT OF MANAGEMENT

Under-Secretary-General.—Catherine Bertini (USA).
Assistant Secretary-General, Controller.—Jean-Pierre Halbwachs (Mauritius).
Officer-in-Charge, Human Resources Management.—Dennis Beissel (USA).
Officer-in-Charge, Central Support Services.—Andrew Toh (Singapore).

OFFICE OF THE IRAQ PROGRAMME

Executive Director.—Benon Sevan (Cyprus).

OFFICE OF THE SPECIAL REPRESENTATIVE OF THE SECRETARY–GENERAL FOR CHILDREN AND ARMED CONFLICT

Under-Secretary-General.—Olara Otunnu (Cote d'Ivoire).

UNITED NATIONS FUND FOR INTERNATIONAL PARTNERSHIPS

Executive Director.—Amir A. Dossal (United Kingdom).

UNITED NATIONS AT GENEVA (UNOG)

Palais des Nations, 1211 Geneva 10, Switzerland, phone (41–22) 917–1234.
Director-General of UNOG.—Assistant Secretary-General Sergei A. Ordzhonikidze (Russian Federation).

UNITED NATIONS AT VIENNA (UNOV)

Vienna International Centre, PO Box 500, A–1400 Vienna, Austria, phone (43–1) 21345.
Director-General.—Antonio Maria Costa (Italy).

UNITED NATIONS INFORMATION CENTRE

1775 K Street, NW., Suite 400, Washington, DC 20006

phone: (202) 331–8670, fax: (202) 331–9191, email: unicwash@unicwash.org

http://www.unicwash.org

Director.—Catherine O'Neill (USA).
Deputy Director.—Dawn Calabia (USA).

REGIONAL ECONOMIC COMMISSIONS

Economic Commission for Africa (ECA), Africa Hall, P.O. Box 3001, Addis Ababa Ethiopia, phone (251–1) 51–72–00, fax (251–1) 51–44–16.
Executive Secretary.—K.Y. Amoako (Ghana).

Economic Commission for Europe (ECE) Palais des Nations, 1211 Geneva 10, Switzerland, phone (41–22) 917–2893.
Executive Secretary.—Brigita Schmognerova (Slovakia).

Economic Commission for Latin America and the Caribbean (ECLAC), Casilla 179–D, Santiago, Chile, phone (56–2) 210–2000, fax (56–2) 208–0252.
Executive Secretary.—José Antonio Ocampo (Colombia).

Economic and Social Commission for Asia and the Pacific (ESCAP), United Nations Building, Réjdamnern Avenue, Bangkok, Thailand, phone (66–2) 288–1234, fax (66–2) 288–1000.
Executive Secretary.—Hak-Su Kim (Republic of Korea).

Economic and Social Commission for Western Asia (ESCWA), P.O. Box 11–8575, Riad El-Solh Square, Beirut, Lebanon, phone 9611–981301, fax 9611– 981510.
Executive Secretary.—Mervat Tallawy (Egypt).

Regional Commissions, New York Office, (ECE, ESCAP, ECLAC, ECA, ESCWA), fax 963–1500.
Chief.—Sulafa Al-Bassam (Saudi Arabia).
Senior Economic Affairs Officer.—Kazi Rahman (Bangladesh).
Liaison Officer.—Margaret McCaffery (USA).
Documentation.—Maria Baquero (Ecuador).

FUNDS, PROGRAMMES, AND BODIES OF THE UNITED NATIONS

Advisory Committee on Administrative and Budgetary Questions (ACABQ), One United Nations Plaza, New York NY 10017, phone (212) 963–7456.
Chairman.—C.S.M. Mselle (UR of Tanzania).

Office of the High Commissioner for Human Rights, Palais des Nations, 8–14 Avenue de la Paix, 1211 Geneva 10, Switzerland, phone (41–22) 917–1234.
High Commissioner for Human Rights.—Sergio Vieira de Mello (Brazil).

International Civil Service Commission (ICSC), One United Nations Plaza, New York NY 10017, phone (212) 963–8464.
Chairman.—Mohsen Bel Hadj Amor (Tunisia).

Joint Inspection Unit (JIU), Palais des Nations, 1211 Geneva 10, Switzerland, phone (41–22) 917–1234.
Chairman.—Armando Duque González (Colombia).

Panel of External Auditors of the UN, Specialized Agencies and International Atomic Energy Agency, One United Nations Plaza, New York NY 10017, phone (212) 963–1234.
Chairman.—Shauket A. Fakie (South Africa).

United Nations Human Settlements Programme (UN–HABITAT), UN Office at Nairobi, PO Box 30030, Nairobi Kenya, phone (254–2) 621–1234.
Executive Director: Anna Kajumulo Tibaijuka (UR of Tanzania).

United Nations Children's Fund (UNICEF), UNICEF House, 3 UN Plaza, New York NY 10017, phone (212) 326–7000.
Executive Director.—Carol Bellamy (USA).

United Nations Conference on Trade and Development (UNCTAD), Palais des Nations, 8–14 Avenue de la Paix, 1211 Geneva 10, Switzerland, phone (41–22) 917–1234.
Secretary-General.—Rubens Ricupero (Brazil).

United Nations Development Fund for Women (UNIFEM), 304 East 45th Street, Sixth Floor, New York NY 10017, phone (212) 906–6400.
Director.—Noeleen Heyzer (Singapore).

United Nations Development Programme (UNDP), 1 United Nations Plaza, New York NY 10017, phone (212) 906–5000.
Administrator.—Mark Malloch Brown (United Kingdom).

United Nations Development Programme (UNDP), Liaison Office, 1775 K Street, NW., Suite 420, Washington DC 20006, phone (202) 331–9130.
Director.—Michael Marek.

United Nations Environment Programme (UNEP), PO Box 30552, Nairobi Kenya, phone (254–2) 621–1234.
Executive Director.—Klaus Topfer (Germany).

United Nations High Commissioner for Refugees (UNHCR), Case Postale 2500, CH–1211 Geneve 2 Depot, Switzerland, phone (41–22) 739–8111.
High Commissioner.—Ruud Lubbers (Netherlands).

United Nations High Commissioner for Refugees (UNHCR), Regional Office for the United States and the Caribbean, 1775 K Street, NW., Third Floor, Washington DC 20006, phone (202) 296–5191.
Representative.—Guenet Guevre-Christos.

United Nations Institute for Disarmament Research (UNIDIR), Palais des Nations, 1211 Geneva 10, Switzerland, phone (41–22) 917–4292.
Director.—Patricia Lewis (United Kingdom).

United Nations Institute for Training and Research (UNITAR), Palais des Nations, 1211 Geneva 10, Switzerland, phone (41–22) 798–5850.
Executive Director.—Marcel A. Boisard (Switzerland).

United Nations International Drug Control Programme (UNODC), PO Box 500, A–1400 Vienna, Austria, phone (43–1) 21345 ext. 4251.
Executive Director.—Antonio Maria Costa (Italy).

United Nations International Research and Training Institute for the Advancement of Women (INSTRAW), PO Box 21747, Santo Domingo, Dominican Republic, phone (1–809) 685–2111.
Officer-in-Charge.—Tatjana Sikoska.

United Nations Interregional Crime and Justice Research Institute (UNICRI), Via Giulia 52, 00186 Rome, Italy, phone (39–6) 687–7437.
Director.—Alberto Bradanini (Italy).

United Nations Office for Project Services (UNOPS), Room 1442, 220 East 42nd Street, New York NY 10017, phone (212) 906–6500.
Executive Director.—Gerald Walzer (Austria).

United Nations Population Fund (UNFPA), 220 East 42nd Street, New York NY 10017, phone (212) 297–5000.
Executive Director.—Thoraya Ahmed Obaid (Saudi Arabia).

United Nations Relief and Works Agency for Palestine Refugees in the Near East (UNRWA), Vienna International Centre, PO Box 700, A–1400 Vienna Austria, phone (43–1) 21345 ext. 4531.
Commissioner-General.—Peter Hansen (Denmark).

United Nations Research Institute for Social Development (UNRISD), Palais des Nations, 1211 Geneva 10, Switzerland, phone (41–22) 798–8400.
Director.—Thandika Mkandawire (Sweden).

United Nations Volunteers Programme (UNV), Postfach 260111, D–53153 Bonn Germany, phone (49–228) 815–2000.
Executive Coordinator.—Sharon Capeling-Alakija (Canada).

World Food Programme (WFP), 426 Via Cristoforo Colombo, 00145 Rome Italy, phone (39–6) 552–2821.
Executive Director.—James Morris (USA).

United Nations University (UNU), 53–70, Jingumae 5–Chome, Shibuya-Ku, Tokyo 150, Japan, phone (81–3) 3499–2811.
Rector.—Hans van Ginkel (Netherlands).

SPECIALIZED AGENCIES

Food and Agricuture Organization (FAO), Via delle Terme di Caracalla, 00100 Rome, Italy, phone (39–6) 52251.
Director-General.—Jacques Diouf (Senegal).

Food and Agriculture Organization, Liaison Office for North America, Suite 300, 2175 K Street, NW., Washington DC 20437, phone (202) 653–2400.
Director.—Charles Riemenschneider (USA).

International Civil Aviation Organization (ICAO), 1000 Sherbrooke Street West, Montreal, Quebec H3A 2R2 Canada, phone (1–514) 285–8221.
Secretary-General.—Renato Claudio Costa Pereira (Brazil).

International Fund for Agricultural Development (IFAD), Via del Serafico 107, 00142 Rome, Italy, phone (39–6) 54591.
President.—Lennart Bage (Sweden).
External Affairs Department, IFAD North American Liaison Office, Washington, DC, Suite 410, 1775 K Street, NW., Washington, DC 20006, phone (202) 331–9099.
Representative.—Vera Weill-Halle (USA).

International Labour Organization (ILO), 4, Routes des Morillons, Ch–1211 Geneva 22, Switzerland, phone (41–22) 799–6111.
Director-General.—Juan Somavia (Chile).
ILO Washington Branch Office, 1828 L Street, NW., Suite 801, Washington, DC 20036, phone (202) 653–7652.
Director.—Anthony Freeman (USA).

International Maritime Organization (IMO), 4 Albert Embankment, London SE1 7SR, England, phone (44–171) 735–7611.
Secretary-General.—William O'Neil (Canada).

International Monetary Fund (IMF), 700 19th Street NW, Washington, DC 20431, phone (202) 623–7000.
Managing Director.—Horst Köhler (Germany).

International Telecommunications Union (ITU), Palais des Nations, 1211 Geneva 20, Switzerland, phone (41–22) 730–5111.
Secretary-General.—Yoshio Utsumi (Japan).

United Nations Educational, Scientific and Cultural Organization (UNESCO), 7 Place de Fontenoy, 75732 Paris, 07 SP France, phone (33–1) 4568–1000.
Director-General.—Koichiro Matsuura (Japan).

United Nations Industrial Development Organization (UNIDO), PO Box 300, Vienna International Centre, A–1400 Vienna, Austria, phone (43–1) 21131–0.
Director-General.—Carlos Alfredo Magarinos (Argentina).

Universal Postal Union (UPU), Weltpoststrasse 4, Case Postale, 3000 Berne 15, Switzerland, phone (41–31) 350–3111.
Director-General.—Thomas E. Leavey (USA).

World Bank Group, 1818 H Street NW, Washington DC 20433, phone (202) 477–1234.
President.—James Wolfensohn (USA).

World Health Organization (WHO), 20 Avenue Appia, 1211 Geneva 27, Switzerland, phone (41–22) 791–2111.
Director-General.—Jong-Wook Lee (Republic of Korea).
World Health Organization Liaison Office, 1775 K Street NW, 4th Floor, Washington, DC 20006, phone (202) 331–9081.
Special Adviser to the Director-General.—Thomas Loftus (USA).

World Intellectual Property Organization (WIPO), 34 Chemin des Colombetts, 1211 Geneva 20, Switzerland, phone (41–22) 730–9111.
Director General.—Kamil Idris (Sudan).
World Intellectual Property Organization Coordination Office, 1775 K Street, NW., Washington, DC 20006, phone (202) 454–2460.
Coordinator.—Suzanne Stoll.

World Meteorological Organization (WMO), Case postale No.2300, CH–1211 Geneva 2, Switzerland, phone (41–22) 730–8111.
Secretary-General.—G.O.P. Obasi (Nigeria).

RELATED BODY

International Atomic Energy Agency (IAEA), PO Box 100, Vienna International Centre, A–1400 Vienna, Austria, phone (43–1) 2060–0.
Director General.—Mohamed Elbaradei (Egypt).
(The IAEA is an independent intergovernmental organization under the aegis of the UN).

SPECIAL REPRESENTATIVES OR ENVOYS OF THE SECRETARY–GENERAL

AFRICA

African Region:
Special Adviser for Special Assignments.—Ibrahim Gambari (Nigeria).
Special Representative for the Great Lakes Region.—Ibrahima Fall (Senegal).
Special Adviser.—Mohamed Sahnoun (Algeria).

Burundi:
Representative.—Berhanu Dinka (Ethiopia).

Central African Republic:
Representative.—General Lamine Cissé (Senegal).

Cote d'Ivoire:
Special Representative.—Albert Tevoedjre (Benin).

Democratic Republic of the Congo:
Special Representative.—Amos Namanga Ngongi (Cameroon).

Ethiopia / Eritrea:
Special Representative.—Legwaila Joseph Legwaila (Botswana).

Guinea-Bissau:
Representative.—David Stephen (United Kingdom).

Liberia:
Representative.—Abou Moussa (Chad).

Sierra Leone:
Special Representative.—Oluyemi Adeniji (Nigeria).

Somalia:
Representative.—Winston A. Tubman (Liberia).

Sudan:
Special Envoy.—Tom Eric Vraalsen (Norway).

West Africa:
Special Representative.—Ahmedou Ould-Abdallah (Mauritania).

Western Sahara:
Special Representative.—William Lacy Swing (United States).
Personal Envoy.—James A. Baker III (United States).

THE AMERICAS

Latin American Region:
Special Adviser.—Diego Cordovez (Ecuador).

Colombia:
Special Adviser.—James LeMoyne (United States).

Guatemala:
Representative.—Tom Koenigs (Germany).

Guyana-Venezuela:
Personal Representative.—Oliver Jackman (Barbados).

ASIA AND THE PACIFIC

Afghanistan:
Special Representative.—Lakhdar Brahimi (Algeria).

East Timor:
Special Representative.—Kamalesh Sharma (India).

Myanmar:
Special Envoy.—Razali Ismail (Malaysia).

Papua New Guinea:
Head of the United Nations Political Office in Bougainville.—Noel Sinclair (Guyana).

Tajikistan:
Representative.—Vladimir Sotirov (Bulgaria).

EUROPE

European Region:
Special Adviser.—Jean-Bernard Merimee (France).

Cyprus:
Special Adviser.—Alvaro de Soto (Peru).
Special Representative.—Zbigniew Wlosowicz (Poland).

Greece-Macedonia, Former Yugoslav Republic of:
Personal Envoy.—Matthew Nimetz (United States).

Georgia:
Special Representative.—Heidi Tagliavini (Switzerland).

Kosovo:
Special Representative.—Michael Steiner (Germany).

MIDDLE EAST

Territories Occupied by Israel:
Special Coordinator for the Middle East Peace Process and Personal Representative of the Secretary-General to the Palestine Liberation Organization.—Terje Roed-Larsen (Norway).

Iraq:
Special Adviser.—Rafeeuddin Ahmed (Pakistan).

Southern Lebanon:
Personal Representative.—Stafan de Mistura (Sweden).

OTHER HIGH LEVEL APPOINTMENTS

Children and Armed Conflict:
Special Representative.—Olara Otunnu (Uganda).

Commonwealth of Independent States (CIS):
Special Envoy.—Yuli Vorontsov (Russian Federation).

Gender Issues and Advancement of Women:
Special Adviser.—Angela King (Jamaica).

HIV / AIDS in Africa:
Special Envoy.—Stephen Lewis (Canada).

HIV / AIDS in Asia:
Special Envoy.—Nafis Sadik (Pakistan).

HIV / AIDS in the Caribbean Region:
Special Envoy.—George Alleyne (Barbados).

Human Rights:
Special Representative.—Hina Jilani (Pakistan).

Information and Communication Technologies (ICT):
Special Representative.—Jose Maria Figueres (Costa Rica).

Internally Displaced Persons:
Special Representative.—Francis Mading Deng (Sudan).

Least Developed Countries, Landlocked Developing Countries, and Small Island Developing States:
High Representative.—Anwarul K. Chowdhury (Bangladesh).

Sport for Development and Peace:
Special Adviser.—Adolf Ogi (Switzerland).

Millennium Development Goals:
Special Adviser.—Jeffrey D. Sachs (United States).

United Nations International School (UNIS):
Special Representative.—Silvia Fuhrman (United States).

United Nations University for Peace in Costa Rica:
Special Adviser and Rector of the University for Peace.—Maurice Strong (Canada).

WORLD BANK GROUP

The World Bank Group comprises five organizations: the International Bank for Reconstruction and Development (IBRD), the International Development Association (IDA), the International Finance Corporation (IFC), the Multilateral Investment Guarantee Agency (MIGA) and the International Centre for the Settlement of Investment Disputes (ICSID).

Headquarters: 1818 H Street NW., Room J1–060, 20433, (202) 458–5454, fax 522–1500; Public Information Center (Infoshop)

INTERNATIONAL BANK FOR RECONSTRUCTION AND DEVELOPMENT

President.—James D. Wolfensohn, 477–1234.
Managing Directors: Jeffrey Goldstein, 458–4001; Mamphela Ramphele, 473–2149; Shengman Zhang, 458–0242.
Managing Director and Executive Vice President.—Peter L. Woicke, 473–0381.
Vice President and General Counsel.—[Vacant].
Senior Vice President, Development Economics, and Chief Economist.—Nicholas H. Stern, 473–3774.
Senior Vice President and Chief Financial Officer.—Gary L. Perlin, 458–8111.
Vice President and Controller.—Fayezul Choudhury, 458–2100.
Vice President and Corporate Secretary.—Ngozi N. Okonjo-Iweala, 473–2888.
Vice President and Treasurer.—Graeme Wheeler, 458–5920.
Vice President of:
Middle East and North Africa.—Christiaan J. Poortman, 473–4946.
Latin America and the Caribbean.—David de Ferranti, 473–8729.
East Asia and Pacific.—Jemail-ud-din Kassum, 473–7723.
Europe and Central Asia.—Shigeo Katsu, 458–0602.
Africa.—Callisto Madavo, 458–2856.
South Asia.—Mieko Nishimizu, 458–0600.
Human Development Network.—Jean-Louis Sarbib, 473–2721.
Environmentally and Socially Sustainable Development Network.—Ian Johnson, 473–1053.
Poverty Reduction and Economic Management Network.—Gobind T. Nankani, 458–4641.
Infrastructure.—Nemat Talaat Shafik, 473–8632.
Human Resources.—Katherine Sierra, 473–6795.
Information Solutions Network.—Mohamed V. Muhsin, 473–5542.
External Affairs.—Ian A. Goldin, 458–0921.
Europe (External Affairs).—Jean-Francois Rischard, (33–1) 40 69 30 10.
Resource Mobilization and Cofinancing.—Geoffrey B. Lamb, 458–5522.
Network, Operational Policy and Country Services.—James W. Adams, 473–4084.
Strategy, Finance and Risk Management.—John Wilton, 458–0194.
World Bank Institute.—Frannie Leautier, 473–5307.
Director-General, Operations Evaluation.—Gregory K. Ingram, 473–1052.
Counselor to the President.—Matthew F. McHugh, 458–0309.
External Affairs Counselor.—John Donaldson, 473–1367.

OTHER WORLD BANK OFFICES

London: New Zealand House, 15th Floor, Haymarket, London SW1Y 4TE, England.
Geneva: 3, Chemin Louis Dunant, CP 66, CH 1211, Geneva 10, Switzerland.
Paris: 66, Avenue d'Iena, 75116 Paris, France.
Brussels: 10, rue Montoyer, B–1000 Brussels, Belgium.
Tokyo: Fukoku Seimei Building, 10th Floor, 2–2–2 Uchisawai-cho, Chiyoda-Ku, Tokyo 100, Japan.
Sydney: c/o South Pacific Project Facility, 89 York Street, Level 8, GPO Box 1612, Sydney, NSW 2000, Australia.
Frankfurt: Bockenheimer Landstrasse 109, 60325 Frankfurt am Main, Germany.

EXECUTIVE DIRECTORS AND ALTERNATES

Executive Director.—Carole Brookins (United States).
Alternate.—Robert B. Holland III (United States).
Executive Director.—Yuzo Harada (Japan).
Alternate.—Masanori Yoshida (Japan).
Executive Director.—Eckhard Deutscher (Germany).
Alternate.—Eckhardt Biskup (Germany).
Executive Director.—Pierre Duquesne (France).
Alternate.—Emmanuel Moulin (France).
Executive Director.—Tom Scholar (United Kingdom).
Alternate.—Rosemary B. Stevenson (United Kingdom).

Austria, Belarus, Belgium, Czech Republic, Hungary, Kazakhstan, Luxembourg, Slovak Republic, Slovenia, Turkey.
Executive Director.—Kurt Bayer (Austria).
Alternate.—Gino Alzetta (Belgium).

Costa Rica, El Salvador, Guatemala, Honduras, Mexico, Nicaragua, Spain, Venezuela (Republica Bolivariana de).
Executive Director.—Per Kurowski (Republica Bolivariana de Venezuela).
Alternate.—Maria Jesús Fernández (Spain).

Armenia, Bosnia and Herzegovina, Bulgaria, Croatia, Cyprus, Georgia, Israel, Macedonia (former Yugoslav Republic of), Moldova, Netherlands, Romania, Ukraine.
Executive Director.—Ad Melkert (Netherlands).
Alternate.—Tamara Solyanyk (Ukraine).

Antigua and Barbuda, Bahamas (The), Barbados, Belize, Canada, Dominica, Grenada, Guyana, Ireland, Jamaica, St. Kitts and Nevis, St. Lucia, St. Vincent and the Grenadines.
Executive Director.—Marcel Masse (Canada).
Alternate.—Sharon Weber (Jamaica).

Brazil, Colombia, Dominican Republic, Ecuador, Haiti, Panama, Philippines, Suriname, Trinidad and Tobago.
Executive Director.—Amaury Bier (Brazil).
Alternate.—Gill S. Beltran (Philippines).

Albania, Greece, Italy, Malta, Portugal, San Marino, Timor-Leste.
Executive Director.—Franco Passacantando (Italy).
Alternate.—Helena Cordeiro (Portugal).

Australia, Cambodia, Kiribati, Korea (Republic of), Marshall Islands, Micronesia (Federated States of), Mongolia, New Zealand, Palau, Papua New Guinea, Samoa, Solomon Islands, Vanuatu.
Executive Director.—Neil F. Hyden (Australia).
Alternate.—Dong-Soo Chin (Republic of Korea).

Angola, Botswana, Burundi, Eritrea, Ethiopia, Gambia (The), Kenya, Lesotho, Liberia, Malawi, Mozambique, Namibia, Nigeria, Seychelles, Sierra Leone, South Africa, Sudan, Swaziland, Tanzania, Uganda, Zambia, Zimbabwe.
Executive Director.—Louis K. Kasekende (Uganda).
Alternate.—J. Mills Jones (Liberia).

Bangladesh, Bhutan, India, Sri Lanka.
Executive Director.—Chander Mohan Vasudev (India).
Alternate.—Akbar Ali Khan (Bangladesh).

Afghanistan, Algeria, Ghana, Iran (Islamic Republic of), Iraq, Morocco, Pakistan, Tunisia.
Executive Director.—Tanwir Ali Agha (Pakistan).
Alternate.—Sid Ahmed Dib (Algeria).

Denmark, Estonia, Finland, Iceland, Latvia, Lithuania, Norway, Sweden.
Executive Director.—Finn Jonck (Denmark).
Alternate.—Inkeri Hirvensalo (Finland).

Azerbaijan, Kyrgyz Republic, Poland, Switzerland, Tajikistan, Turkmenistan, Uzbekistan, Yugoslavia (Fed. Rep. of).
Executive Director.—Pietro Veglio (Switzerland).
Alternate.—Jerzy Hylewski (Poland).

China.
Executive Director.—Zhu Guangyao (China).
Alternate.—Wu Jinkang (China).

Saudi Arabia.
Executive Director.—Yahya Abdullah M. Alyahya (Saudi Arabia).
Alternate.—Abdulrahman M. Almofadhi (Saudi Arabia).

Russian Federation.
Executive Director.—Alexey G. Kvasov (Russian Federation).
Alternate.—Eugene Miagkov (Russian Federation).

Bahrain, Egypt (Arab Republic of), Jordan, Kuwait, Lebanon, Libya, Maldives, Oman, Qatar, Syrian Arab Republic, United Arab Emirates, Yemen (Republic of).
Executive Director.—Mahdy Ismail Aljazzaf (Kuwait).
Alternate.—Mohamed Kamel Amr (Arab Republic of Egypt).
Brunei Darussalam, Fiji, Indonesia, Lao People's Democratic Republic, Malaysia, Myanmar, Nepal, Singapore, Thailand, Tonga, Vietnam.
Executive Director.—Rapee Asumpinpong (Thailand).
Alternate.—Hadiyanto (Indonesia).
Argentina, Bolivia, Chile, Paraguay, Peru, Uruguay.
Executive Director.—Alieto Guadagni (Argentina).
Alternate.—Alfonso C. Revollo (Bolivia).
Benin, Burkina Faso, Cameroon, Cape Verde, Central African Republic, Chad, Comoros, Congo (Democratic Republic of), Congo (Republic of), Cote d'lvoire, Djibouti, Equatorial Guinea, Gabon, Guinea, Guinea-Bissau, Madagascar, Mali, Mauritania, Mauritius, Niger, Rwanda, Sao Tome and Principe, Senegal, Togo.
Executive Director.—Paulo F. Gomes (Guinea-Bissau).
Alternate.—Louis Philippe Ong Seng (Mauritius).

INTERNATIONAL DEVELOPMENT ASSOCIATION

[The officers, executive directors, and alternates are the same as those of the International Bank for Reconstruction and Development.]

INTERNATIONAL FINANCE CORPORATION

President.—James D. Wolfensohn.
Executive Vice President.—Peter Lutz Woicke.
Vice President:
Human Resources and Administration.—Dorothy H. Berry.
Operations.—Assaad J. Jabre.
Portfolio and Risk Management.—Farida Khambata.
Legal.—Carol F. Lee.
Private Sector Development / Chief Economist.—Michael U. Klein.
Compliance Advisor / Ombudsman.—Meg Taylor.
Corporate Relations Unit Manager.—Joseph O'Keefe.
Financial Operations Unit.—Avi Hofman.
General Counsel and Director, Legal.—Jennifer A. Sullivan.
Operations Evaluation Group.—William E. Stevenson.
Controller's and Budgeting.—A.F. Shapiro.
Corporate Business Informatics / Chief Information Officer.—Guy-Pierre de Poerck.
Corporate Portfolio and Risk Management.—Marc A. Babin.
Credit Review.—Paul R. Hinchey.
Operations Strategy Group.—Bernard E. Sheahan.
Private Equity and Investment Funds.—T.C. Barger.
Syndications and International Securities.—S.L. Lazarus.
Agribusiness.—Jean-Paul Pinard.
Economics.—Guy Pierre Pfeffermann.
Environment and Social Development.—Gavin Murray.
Global Financial Markets Group.—Karl Voltaire.
Global Manufacturing and Services.—R.L. Ranken.
Global Information and Communications Technologies.—M.A. Khalil.
Oil, Gas, Mining and Chemicals.—Rashad-Rudolf Kaldany.
Infrastructure.—Francisco A. Tourreilles.
Small and Medium Enterprises.—Harold Rosen.
Health and Education.—G.M. Ellena.
Central and Eastern Europe.—Edward A. Nassim.
East Asia and Pacific.—Javed Hamid.
Latin America and Caribbean.—Bernard Pasquier.
Middle East and North Africa.—Sami Haddad.
South Asia.—Dimitris Tsitsiragos.
Southern Europe and Central Asia.—Khosrow K. Zamani.
Sub-Saharan Africa.—Haydee Celaya.

MULTILATERAL INVESTMENT GUARANTEE AGENCY

President.—James D. Wolfensohn.
Executive Vice President.—Motomichi Ikawa.
Director and Chief Financial Officer.—Amedee Prouvost.
Vice President and General Counsel.—Luis Dodero.
Vice President, Underwriting.—Roger Pruneau.
Director of:
Human Resources.—Tony Wan.
Investment Marketing Services.—Tessie San Martin.
Policy and Environment.—Gerald T. West.
Manager, Corporate Relations.—Moina Varkie.

OFFICE OF GUARANTEES

Vice President, Guarantees.—Roger Pruneau.
Manager, Operational Strategy, Syndication/Reinsurance.—Peter Jones.
Regional Managers:
Latin America and Caribbean, Europe and Central Asia:
Infrastructure, oil and gas, and mining.—Patricia Veevers-Carter.
Finance, manufacturing, agribusiness, and services.—Ileana Boza.
Africa, Asia and the Middle East:
Infrastructure, oil and gas, and mining.—Philippe Valahu.
Finance, agribusiness, manufacturing, services, and mining.—Mansour Kane.

OFFICE OF INVESTMENT MARKETING SERVICES

Director.—Tessie San Martin.
Managers:
Capacity Building and Investment Facilitation.—David Bridgman.
Information Products and Services.—John Wille.

OFFICE OF THE VICE PRESIDENT AND GENERAL COUNSEL, LEGAL AFFAIRS AND CLAIMS

Vice President and General Counsel.—Luis Dodero.
Chief Counsels: Srilal Perera, Lorin Weisenfeld.

FOREIGN DIPLOMATIC OFFICES IN THE UNITED STATES

AFGHANISTAN

Embassy of the Republic of Afghanistan
2341 Wyoming Avenue, NW., Washington, DC 20008
phone (202) 483–6410, fax (202) 483–6488
His Excellency Mohammad Ishaq Shahryar
Consular Office: New York, New York

ALBANIA

Embassy of the Republic of Albania
2100 S Street NW., Washington, DC 20008
phone (202) 223–4942, fax (202) 628–7342
His Excellency Dr. Fatos Tarifa
Ambassador E. and P.

ALGERIA

Embassy of the Democratic and Popular Republic of Algeria
2118 Kalorama Road NW., Washington, DC 20008
phone (202) 265–2800, fax (202) 667–2174
His Excellency Idriss Jazairy
Ambassador E. and P.

Iraqi Interests Section

1801 P Street NW., Washington, DC 20036
phone (202) 483–7500, fax (202) 462–5066

ANDORRA

Embassy of Andorra
Two United Nations Plaza, 25th Floor, New York, NY 10017
phone (212) 750–8064, fax (212) 750–6630
Ms. Jelena V. Pia-Comella
Minister Counselor

ANGOLA

Embassy of the Republic of Angola
2108 16th Street NW., Washington, DC 20009
phone (202) 785–1156, fax (202) 785–1258
Her Excellency Josefina Pitra Diakite
Ambassador E. and P.
Consular Offices:
New York, New York
Texas, Houston

ANTIGUA AND BARBUDA

Embassy of Antigua and Barbuda
3216 New Mexico Avenue, NW., Washington, DC 20016
phone (202) 362–5122/5166/5211, fax (202) 362–5225
His Excellency Lionel Alexander Hurst
Ambassador E. and P.
Consular Office: Florida, Miami

ARGENTINA

Embassy of the Argentine Republic
1600 New Hampshire Avenue, NW., Washington, DC 20009
phone (202) 238–6400, fax (202) 332–3171
His Excellency Eduardo Pablo Amadeo
Ambassador E. and P.
Consular Offices:
California, Los Angeles
Florida, Miami
Georgia, Atlanta
Illinois, Chicago
New York, New York
Texas, Houston

ARMENIA

Embassy of the Republic of Armenia
2225 R Street NW., Washington, DC 20008
phone (202) 319–1976, fax (202) 319–2982
His Excellency Arman John Kirakossian
Ambassador E. and P.
Consular Office: California, Los Angeles

AUSTRALIA

Embassy of Australia
1601 Massachusetts Avenue, NW., Washington, DC 20036–2273
phone (202) 797–3000, fax (202) 797–3168
His Excellency Michael Thawley
Ambassador E. and P.
Consular Offices:
California:
Los Angeles
San Francisco
Colorado, Denver
Georgia, Atlanta
Hawaii, Honolulu
Illinois, Chicago
Massachusetts, Boston
New York, New York

AUSTRIA

Embassy of Austria
3524 International Court NW., Washington, DC 20008–3027

phone (202) 895–6700, fax (202) 895–6750
His Excellency Peter Moser
Ambassador E. and P.
Consular Offices:
California:
Los Angeles
San Francisco
Colorado, Denver
Florida, Miami
Georgia, Atlanta
Hawaii, Honolulu
Illinois, Chicago
Louisiana, New Orleans
Michigan, Detroit
Minnesota, Minneapolis
Missouri, Kansas City
New York, New York
Pennsylvania, Philadelphia
Puerto Rico, San Juan
Texas, Houston

AZERBAIJAN

Embassy of the Republic of Azerbaijan
2741 34th Street NW., Washington, DC 20008
phone (202) 842–0001, fax (202) 842–0004
His Excellency Hafiz Mir Jalal Pashayev
Ambassador E. and P.

BAHAMAS

Embassy of the Commonwealth of The Bahamas
2220 Massachusetts Avenue, NW., Washington, DC 20008
phone (202) 319–2660, fax (202) 319–2668
His Excellency Joshua Sears
Ambassador E. and P.
Consular Offices:
Florida, Miami
New York, New York

BAHRAIN

Embassy of the State of Bahrain
3502 International Drive NW., Washington, DC 20008
phone (202) 342–0741, fax (202) 362–2192
Sheikh Khalifa Ali Al-Khalifa
Ambassador E. and P.
Consular Offices:
California, San Diego
New York, New York

BANGLADESH

Embassy of the People's Republic of Bangladesh
3510 International Drive NW., Washington, DC 20008
phone (202) 244–0183, fax (202) 244–5366
His Excellency Syed Hasan Ahmed
Ambassador E. and P.
Consular Offices:
California, Los Angeles
Hawaii, Honolulu
Louisiana, New Orleans
New York, New York

BARBADOS

Embassy of Barbados
2144 Wyoming Avenue, NW., Washington, DC 20008
phone (202) 939–9200, fax (202) 332–7467
His Excellency Michael Ian King
Ambassador E. and P.
Consular Offices:
California, Los Angeles
Florida, Miami
New York, New York

BELARUS

Embassy of the Republic of Belarus
1619 New Hampshire Avenue, NW., Washington, DC 20009
phone (202) 986–1604, fax (202) 986–1805
His Excellency Mikhail Khvostov
Ambassador E. and P.
Consular Office: New York, New York

BELGIUM

Embassy of Belgium
3330 Garfield Street NW., Washington, DC 20008
phone (202) 333–6900, fax (202) 333–3079
His Excellency Franciskus Van Daele
Ambassador E. and P.
Consular Offices:
California, Los Angeles
Georgia, Atlanta
Illinois, Chicago
New York, New York
Texas, Houston

BELIZE

Embassy of Belize
2535 Massachusetts Avenue, NW., Washington, DC 20008
phone (202) 332–9636, fax (202) 332–6888
Her Excellency Lisa Shoman
Ambassador E. and P.
Consular Offices:
California, Los Angeles
Puerto Rico, San Juan
Texas, Houston

BENIN

Embassy of the Republic of Benin
2124 Kalorama Road NW., Washington, DC 20008
phone (202) 232–6656, fax (202) 265–1996
His Excellency Segbe Cyrille Oguin
Ambassador E. and P.

BHUTAN

Consular Office:
New York, New York

BOLIVIA

Embassy of the Republic of Bolivia
3014 Massachusetts Avenue, NW., Washington, DC 20008
phone (202) 483–4410, fax (202) 328–3712
Her Excellency Jaime Aparicio
Ambassador E. and P.
Consular Offices:
California, San Francisco
Florida, Miami
Georgia, Atlanta
Massachusetts, Boston
New York, New York
Texas, Houston

BOSNIA AND HERZEGOVINA

Embassy of Bosnia and Herzegovina
2109 E Street NW., Washington, DC 20037
phone (202) 337–1500, fax (202) 337–1502
His Excellency Igor Davidovic
Ambassador E. and P.
Consular Office: New York, New York

BOTSWANA

Embassy of the Republic of Botswana
1531–1533 New Hampshire Avenue, NW., Washington, DC 20036
phone (202) 244–4990, fax (202) 244–4164
His Excellency Lapologang Caesar Lekoa
Ambassador E. and P.

BRAZIL

Brazilian Embassy
3006 Massachusetts Avenue, NW., Washington, DC 20008
phone (202) 238–2700, fax (202) 238–2827
His Excellency Rubens Antonio Barbosa
Ambassador E. and P.
Consular Offices:
California:
Los Angeles
San Francisco
Florida, Miami
Illinois, Chicago
Massachusetts, Boston
New York, New York
Puerto Rico, San Juan
Texas, Houston

BRUNEI

Embassy of the State of Brunei Darussalam
3520 International Court NW., Washington, DC 20008
phone (202) 237–1838, fax (202) 885–0560
His Excellency Pengiran Anak Dato Puteh
Ambassador E. and P.

BULGARIA

Embassy of the Republic of Bulgaria
1621 22nd Street NW., Washington, DC 20008
phone (202) 387–0174, fax (202) 234–7973
Her Excellency Elena Poptodorova
Ambassador E. and P.
Consular Office: New York, New York

BURKINA FASO

Embassy of the Burkina Faso
2340 Massachusetts Avenue, NW., Washington, DC 20008
phone (202) 332–5577, fax (202) 667–1882
His Excellency Tertius Zongo
Ambassador E. and P.

BURMA

Embassy of the Union of Burma
2300 S Street NW., Washington, DC 20008–4089
phone (202) 332–9044, fax (202) 332–9046
His Excellency U Linn Myaing
Ambassador E. and P.
Consular Office: New York, New York

BURUNDI

Embassy of the Republic of Burundi
2233 Wisconsin Avenue, NW., Suite 212, Washington, DC 20007
phone (202) 342–2574, fax (202) 342–2578
His Excellency Antoine Ntamobwa
Ambassador E. and P.

CAMBODIA

Royal Embassy of Cambodia
4530 16th Street NW., Washington, DC 20011
phone (202) 726–7742, fax (202) 726–8381
His Excellency Roland Eng
Ambassador E. and P.

CAMEROON

Embassy of the Republic of Cameroon
2349 Massachusetts Avenue, NW., Washington, DC 20008
phone (202) 265–8790, fax (202) 387–3826
His Excellency Jerome Mendouga
Ambassador E. and P.

CANADA

Embassy of Canada
501 Pennsylvania Avenue, NW., Washington, DC 20001
phone (202) 682–1740, fax (202) 682–7726
His Excellency Michael Kergin
Ambassador E. and P.

Consular Offices:
California:
Los Angeles
San Francisco
San Jose
Florida, Miami
Georgia, Atlanta
Illinois, Chicago
Massachusetts, Boston
Michigan, Detroit
Minnesota, Minneapolis
New Jersey, Princeton
New York:
Buffalo
New York
Texas, Dallas
Washington, Seattle

CAPE VERDE

Embassy of the Republic of Cape Verde
3415 Massachusetts Avenue, NW., Washington, DC 20007
phone (202) 965–6820, fax (202) 965–1207
His Excellency Jose Brito
Ambassador E. and P.
Consular Office:
Massachusetts, Boston

CENTRAL AFRICAN REPUBLIC

Embassy of Central African Republic
1618 22nd Street NW., Washington, DC 20008
phone (202) 483–7800, fax (202) 332–9893
His Excellency Emmanuel Touaboy
Ambassador E. and P.
Consular Office:
California, Los Angeles

CHAD

Embassy of the Republic of Chad
2002 R Street NW., Washington, DC 20009
phone (202) 462–4009, fax (202) 265–1937
His Excellency Hassaballah Ahmat Soubiane
Ambassador E. and P.

CHILE

Embassy of the Republic of Chile
1732 Massachusetts Avenue, NW., Washington, DC 20036
phone (202) 785–1746, fax (202) 887–5579
His Excellency Andrés Bianchi
Ambassador E. and P.
Consular Offices:
California:
Los Angeles
San Francisco
Florida, Miami
Illinois, Chicago
New York, New York
Pennsylvania, Philadelphia
Puerto Rico, San Juan
Texas, Houston

CHINA

Embassy of the People's Republic of China
2300 Connecticut Avenue, NW., Washington, DC 20008
phone (202) 328–2500, fax (202) 588–0032
His Excellency Jiechi Jang
Ambassador E. and P.
Consular Offices:
California:
Los Angeles
San Francisco
Illinois, Chicago
New York, New York
Texas, Houston

COLOMBIA

Embassy of Colombia
2118 Leroy Place NW., Washington, DC 20008
phone (202) 387–8338, fax (202) 232–8643
His Excellency Luis Alberto Moreno
Ambassador E. and P.
Consular Offices:
California:
Los Angeles
San Francisco
Florida, Miami
Georgia, Atlanta
Illinois, Chicago
Louisiana, New Orleans
Massachusetts, Boston
New York, New York
Puerto Rico, San Juan
Texas, Houston

COMOROS

Embassy of the Federal and Islamic Republic of the Comoros
420 East 50th Street, New York, NY 10022
phone (212) 972–8010, fax (202) 983–4712
[Ambassador departed January 31, 1999]
Consular Office: New York, New York

CONGO, DEMOCRATIC REPUBLIC OF

Embassy of the Democratic Republic of the Congo
1800 New Hampshire Avenue, NW., Washington, DC 20009
phone (202) 234–7690, fax (202) 234–2609
Her Excellency Faida Mitifu
Ambassador E. and P.

CONGO, REPUBLIC OF

Embassy of the Republic of the Congo
4891 Colorado Avenue, NW., Washington, DC 20011

phone (202) 726–5500, fax (202) 726–1860
His Excellency Serge Mombouli
Ambassador E. and P.

COOK ISLANDS

Consular Offices:
California, Los Angeles
Hawaii, Honolulu

COSTA RICA

Embassy of Costa Rica
2114 S Street NW., Washington, DC 20008
phone (202) 234–2945, fax (202) 265–4795
His Excellency Jamie Daremblum
Ambassador E. and P.
Consular Offices:
California:
Los Angeles
San Francisco
Florida:
Miami
Tampa
Georgia, Atlanta
Illinois, Chicago
Louisiana, New Orleans
Massachusetts, Boston
New Mexico, Albuquerque
New York, New York
North Carolina, Durham
Pennsylvania, Philadelphia
Puerto Rico, San Juan
Texas:
Austin
Houston
San Antonio

CÔTE D'IVOIRE

Embassy of the Republic of Côte d'Ivoire
3421 Massachusetts Avenue, NW., Washington, DC 20007
phone (202) 797–0300, fax (202) 462–9444
His Excellency Dago Pascal Kokora
Ambassador E. and P.
Consular Offices:
California, San Francisco

CROATIA

Embassy of the Republic of Croatia
2343 Massachusetts Avenue, NW., Washington, DC 20008
phone (202) 588–5899, fax (202) 588–8937
His Excellency Dr. Ivan Grdesic
Ambassador E. and P.
Consular Offices:
California, Los Angeles
Illinois, Chicago
Minnesota, St. Paul
New York, New York

CYPRUS

Embassy of the Republic of Cyprus
2211 R Street NW., Washington, DC 20008
phone (202) 462–5772, fax (202) 483–6710
Her Excellency Erato Kozakou-Marcoullis
Ambassador E. and P.
Consular Offices:
California, Los Angeles
New York, New York
Texas, Houston

CZECH REPUBLIC

Embassy of the Czech Republic
3900 Spring of Freedom Street NW., Washington, DC 20008
phone (202) 274–9100, fax (202) 966–8540
His Excellency Martin Palous
Ambassador E. and P.
Consular Offices:
California:
Los Angeles
San Francisco
New York, New York
Pennsylvania, Philadelphia

DENMARK

Royal Danish Embassy
3200 Whitehaven Street NW., Washington, DC 20008–3683
phone (202) 234–4300, fax (202) 328–1470
His Excellency Ulrik A. Federspiel
Ambassador E. and P.
Consular Offices:
California, Los Angeles
Illinois, Chicago
New York, New York

DJIBOUTI

Embassy of the Republic of Djibouti
1156 15th Street NW., Suite 515, Washington, DC 20005
phone (202) 331–0270, fax (202) 331–0302
His Excellency Roble Olhaye
Ambassador E. and P.

DOMINICA

Embassy of the Commonwealth of Dominica
3216 New Mexico Avenue, NW., Washington, DC 20016
phone (202) 364–6781, fax (202) 364–6791
[Ambassador departed October 12, 2001]
Consular Office: New York, New York

DOMINICAN REPUBLIC

Embassy of the Dominican Republic
1715 22nd Street NW., Washington, DC 20008
phone (202) 332–6280, fax (202) 265–8057
His Excellency Hugo M. Guilliani Cury

Ambassador E. and P.
Consular Offices:
- Alabama, Mobile
- California, San Francisco
- Florida:
  - Jacksonville
  - Miami
- Illinois, Chicago
- Louisiana, New Orleans
- Massachusetts, Boston
- Minnesota, Minneapolis
- New York, New York
- Pennsylvania, Philadelphia
- Puerto Rico:
  - Mayaguez
  - Ponce
  - San Juan

ECUADOR

Embassy of Ecuador
2535 15th Street NW., Washington, DC 20009
phone (202) 234–7200, fax (202) 265–6385
Carlos A. Jativa
Minister
Consular Offices:
- California:
  - Los Angeles
  - San Francisco
- Florida, Miami
- Illinois, Chicago
- Louisiana, New Orleans
- Nevada, Las Vegas
- New Jersey, Newark
- New York, New York
- Pennsylvania, Philadelphia
- Texas, Houston

EGYPT

Embassy of the Arab Republic of Egypt
3521 International Court NW., Washington, DC 20008
phone (202) 895–5400, fax (202) 244–4319/5131
His Excellency M. Nabil Fahmy
Ambassador E. and P.
Consular Offices:
- California, San Francisco
- Illinois, Chicago
- New York, New York
- Texas, Houston

EL SALVADOR

Embassy of El Salvador
2308 California Street NW., Washington, DC 20008
phone (202) 265–9671, fax (202) 332–2225
His Excellency René Antonio Leon
Ambassador E. and P.
Consular Offices:
- California:
  - Los Angeles
  - San Francisco
- Florida, Miami
- Illinois, Chicago
- Louisiana, New Orleans
- Massachusetts, Boston
- New York, New York
- Puerto Rico, Bayamon
- Texas:
  - Dallas
  - Houston

EQUATORIAL GUINEA

Embassy of the Republic of Equatorial Guinea
2020 16th Street NW., Washington, DC 20009
phone (202) 518–5700, fax (202) 518–5252
His Excellency Teodoro Biyogo Nsue
Ambassador E. and P.

ERITREA

Embassy of the State of Eritrea
1708 New Hampshire Avenue, NW., Washington, DC 20009
phone (202) 319–1991, fax (202) 319–1304
His Excellency Girma Asmerom
Ambassador E. and P.
Consular Office: California, Oakland

ESTONIA

Embassy of Estonia
1730 M Street, NW., Suite 503, Washington, DC 20036
phone (202) 588–0101, fax (202) 588–0108
His Excellency Sven Jürgenson
Ambassador E. and P.
Consular Office: New York, New York

ETHIOPIA

Embassy of Ethiopia
3506 International Drive NW., Washington, DC 20008
phone (202) 364–1200, fax (202) 686–9551
His Excellency Kassahun Ayele
Ambassador E. and P.

FIJI

Embassy of the Republic of the Fiji Islands
2233 Wisconsin Avenue, NW., Suite 240, Washington, DC 20007
phone (202) 337–8320, fax (202) 337–1996
Anare Jale
Ambassador E. and P.

FINLAND

Embassy of Finland
3301 Massachusetts Avenue, NW., Washington, DC 20008

phone (202) 298–5800, fax (202) 298–6030
His Excellency Jukka Valtasaari
Ambassador E. and P.
Consular Offices:
California:
Los Angeles
San Francisco
Massachusetts, Boston
New York, New York

FRANCE

Embassy of France
4101 Reservoir Road NW., Washington, DC 20007
phone (202) 944–6000, fax (202) 944–6166
His Excellency Jean David Levitte
Ambassador E. and P.
Consular Offices:
California:
Los Angeles
San Francisco
Florida, Miami
Georgia, Atlanta
Illinois, Chicago
Louisiana, New Orleans
Massachusetts, Boston
New York, New York
Texas, Houston

GABON

Embassy of the Gabonese Republic
2034 20th Street NW., Washington, DC 20009
phone (202) 797–1000, fax (202) 332–0668
His Excellency Jules Marius Ogouebandja
Ambassador E. and P.
Consular Office: New York, New York

GAMBIA, THE

Embassy of The Gambia
1156 15th Street NW., Suite 1000, Washington, DC 20005
phone (202) 785–1399, fax (202) 785–1430
Leana Manga Sagnia Seck
Minister-Counselor
Consular Office: California, Los Angeles

GEORGIA, REPUBLIC OF

Embassy of the Republic of Georgia
1615 New Hampshire Avenue, NW., Suite 300, Washington, DC 20009
phone (202) 387–2390, fax (202) 393–4537
His Excellency Levan Mikeladze
Ambassador E. and P.

GERMANY, FEDERAL REPUBLIC OF

Embassy of the Federal Republic of Germany
4645 Reservoir Road NW., Washington, DC 20007–1998
phone (202) 298–8140, fax (202) 298–4249
His Excellency Wolfgang Friedrich Ischinger
Ambassador E. and P.
Consular Offices:
California:
Los Angeles
San Francisco
Florida, Miami
Georgia, Atlanta
Illinois, Chicago
Massachusetts, Boston
Michigan, Detroit
New York, New York
Texas, Houston

GHANA

Embassy of Ghana
3512 International Drive NW., Washington, DC 20008
phone (202) 686–4520, fax (202) 686–4527
His Excellency Alan J. Kyerematen
Ambassador E. and P.
Consular Offices:
Georgia, Altanta
New York, New York

GREAT BRITAIN

See United Kingdom of Great Britain and Northern Ireland

GREECE

Embassy of Greece
2221 Massachusetts Avenue, NW., Washington, DC 20008
phone (202) 939–5800, fax (202) 939–5824
His Excellency Alexandre Philon
Ambassador E. and P.
Consular Offices:
California:
Los Angeles
San Francisco
Georgia, Atlanta
Illinois, Chicago
Louisiana, New Orleans
Massachusetts, Boston
New York, New York
Texas, Houston

GRENADA

Embassy of Grenada
1701 New Hampshire Avenue, NW., Washington, DC 20009
phone (202) 265–2561, fax (202) 265–2468
His Excellency Denis G. Antoine
Ambassador E. and P.
Consular Offices:
Florida, Ft. Lauderdale
New York, New York

GUATEMALA

Embassy of Guatemala
2220 R Street NW., Washington, DC 20008
phone (202) 745–4952, fax (202) 745–1908
His Excellency Antonio Arenales Forno
Ambassador E. and P.
Consular Offices:
California:
Los Angeles
San Francisco
Colorado, Denver
Florida, Miami
Illinois, Chicago
New York, New York
Texas, Houston

GUINEA

Embassy of the Republic of Guinea
2112 Leroy Place NW., Washington, DC 20008
phone (202) 483–9420, fax (202) 483–8688
His Excellency Alpha Oumar Rafiou Barry
Ambassador E. and P.

GUINEA-BISSAU

Embassy of the Republic of Guinea-Bissau
P.O. Box 33813, Washington, DC 20033
phone (301) 947–3958
Henrique Adriano Da Silva
Minister-Counselor

GUYANA

Embassy of Guyana
2490 Tracy Place NW., Washington, DC 20008
phone (202) 265–6900, fax (202) 232–1297
His Excellency Dr. Mohammed Ali Odeen Ishmael
Ambassador E. and P.
Consular Office: New York, New York

HAITI

Embassy of the Republic of Haiti
2311 Massachusetts Avenue, NW., Washington, DC 20008
phone (202) 332–4090, fax (202) 745–7215
Harry Frantz Leo
Minister-Counselor
Consular Offices:
Florida, Miami
Illinois, Chicago
Massachusetts, Boston
New York, New York
Puerto Rico, San Juan

THE HOLY SEE (VATICAN CITY)

Apostolic Nunciature
3339 Massachusetts Avenue, NW., Washington, DC 20008
phone (202) 333–7121, fax (202) 337–4036
His Excellency The Most Reverend Gabriele Montalvo
Apostolic Nuncio

HONDURAS

Embassy of Honduras
3007 Tilden Street NW., Suite 4–M, Washington, DC 20008
phone (202) 966–7702, fax (202) 966–9751
His Excellency Mario Miguel Canahuati
Ambassador E. and P.
Consular Offices:
Arizona, Phoenix
California:
Los Angeles
San Francisco
Florida:
Jacksonville
Miami
Georgia, Atlanta
Illinois, Chicago
Louisiana, New Orleans
Maryland, Baltimore
Massachusetts, Boston
Michigan, Detroit
New York, New York
Puerto Rico, San Juan
Texas, Houston

HUNGARY

Embassy of the Republic of Hungary
3910 Shoemaker Street NW., Washington, DC 20008
phone (202) 362–6730, fax (202) 966–8135
His Excellency Andras Simonyi
Ambassador E. and P.
Consular Offices:
California, Los Angeles
Colorado, Denver
Florida, Miami
New York, New York
Ohio, Cleveland

ICELAND

Embassy of the Republic of Iceland
1156 15th Street NW., Suite 1200, Washington, DC 20005
phone (202) 265–6653, fax (202) 265–6656
His Excellency Helgi Agustsson
Ambassador E. and P.
Consular Offices:
California, Los Angeles
Florida:
Hollywood
Tallahassee
Georgia, Atlanta
Illinois, Chicago

Minnesota, Minneapolis
New York, New York
Washington, Seattle

INDIA

Embassy of India
2107 Massachusetts Avenue, NW., Washington, DC 20008
phone (202) 939–7000, fax (202) 265–4351
His Excellency Lalit Mansingh
Ambassador E. and P.
Consular Offices:
California, San Francisco
Hawaii, Honolulu
Illinois, Chicago
New York, New York
Texas, Houston

INDONESIA

Embassy of the Republic of Indonesia
2020 Massachusetts Avenue, NW., Washington, DC 20036
phone (202) 775–5200, fax (202) 775–5365
Soemadi Djoko M. Brotodiningrat
Ambassador E. and P.
Consular Offices:
California:
Los Angeles
San Francisco
Illinois, Chicago
New York, New York
Texas, Houston

IRAN

See Pakistan

IRAQ

See Algeria

IRELAND

Embassy of Ireland
2234 Massachusetts Avenue, NW., Washington, DC 20008
phone (202) 462–3939, ext. 232, fax (202) 232–5993
His Excellency Noel Fahey
Ambassador E. and P.
Consular Offices:
California, San Francisco
Illinois, Chicago
Massachusetts, Boston
New York, New York

ISRAEL

Embassy of Israel
3514 International Drive NW., Washington, DC 20008
phone (202) 364–5500, fax (202) 364–5610
His Excellency Daniel Ayalon
Ambassador E. and P.
Consular Offices:
California:
Los Angeles
San Francisco
Florida, Miami
Georgia, Atlanta
Illinois, Chicago
Massachusetts, Boston
New York, New York
Pennsylvania, Philadelphia
Texas, Houston

ITALY

Embassy of Italy
3000 Whitehaven Street NW., Washington, DC 20008
phone (202) 612–4400, fax (202) 518–2154
His Excellency Sergio Vento
Ambassador E. and P.
Consular Offices:
California:
Los Angeles
San Francisco
Florida, Miami
Illinois, Chicago
Massachusetts, Boston
Michigan, Detroit
New York, New York
Pennsylvania, Philadelphia
Texas, Houston

IVORY COAST

See Côte d'Ivoire

JAMAICA

Embassy of Jamaica
1520 New Hampshire Avenue, NW., Washington, DC 20036
phone (202) 452–0660, fax (202) 452–0081
His Excellency Seymour Edward Mullings
Ambassador E. and P.
Consular Offices:
Florida, Miami
New York, New York

JAPAN

Embassy of Japan
2520 Massachusetts Avenue, NW., Washington, DC 20008
phone (202) 238–6700, fax (202) 328–2187
His Excellency Royozo Kato
Ambassador E. and P.
Consular Offices:
Alabama, Mobile
Alaska, Anchorage
Arizona, Phoenix

California:
Los Angeles
San Diego
San Francisco
Colorado, Denver
Connecticut, Avon
Florida, Miami
Georgia, Atlanta
Guam, Agana
Hawaii, Honolulu
Illinois, Chicago
Indiana, Indianapolis
Louisiana, New Orleans
Massachusetts, Boston
Michigan, Detroit
Minnesota, Minneapolis
Missouri:
Kansas City
St. Louis
New York:
Buffalo
New York
North Carolina, High Point
Ohio, Columbus
Oklahoma, Oklahoma City
Oregon, Portland
Pennsylvania, Philadelphia
Puerto Rico, San Juan
Tennessee, Nashville
Texas, Houston
Houston
Mariana Islands
Washington, Seattle
Wyoming, Casper

JORDAN

Embassy of the Hashemite Kingdom of Jordan
3504 International Drive NW., Washington, DC 20008
phone (202) 966–2664, fax (202) 966–3110
His Excellency Karim Kawar
Ambassador E. and P.
Consular Offices:
Illinois, Chicago
Texas, Houston

KAZAKHSTAN

Embassy of the Republic of Kazakhstan
1401 16th Street NW., Washington, DC 20036
phone (202) 232–5488, fax (202) 232–5845
His Excellency Kanat B. Saudabayev
Ambassador E. and P.
Consular Office: New York, New York

KENYA

Embassy of the Republic of Kenya
2249 R Street NW., Washington, DC 20008
phone (202) 387–6101, fax (202) 462–3829
Telex: 197376
His Excellency Yusuf Abdulrahman Nzibo
Ambassador E. and P.
Consular Offices:
California, Los Angeles
New York, New York

KIRIBATI

Consular Office: Hawaii, Honolulu

KOREA, REPUBLIC OF

Embassy of the Republic of Korea
2450 Massachusetts Avenue, NW., Washington, DC 20008
phone (202) 939–5600, fax (202) 232–0117
His Excellency Sung-Joo Han
Ambassador E. and P.
Consular Offices:
Alaska, Anchorage
California:
Los Angeles
San Francisco
Florida, Miami
Georgia, Atlanta
Guam, Agana
Hawaii, Honolulu
Illinois, Chicago
Louisiana, New Orleans
Massachusetts, Boston
Minnesota, Minneapolis
New York, New York
Oregon, Portland
Puerto Rico, San Juan
Texas, Houston
Washington, Seattle

KUWAIT

Embassy of the State of Kuwait
2940 Tilden Street, NW., Washington, DC 20008
phone (202) 966–0702, fax (202) 966–0517
His Excellency Sheikh Salem Abdullah Al Jaber Al-Sabah
Ambassador E. and P.

KYRGYZSTAN

Embassy of the Kyrgyz Republic
1732 Wisconsin Avenue, NW., Washington, DC 20007
phone (202) 338–5141, fax (202) 338–5139
His Excellency Baktybek Abdrissaev
Ambassador E. and P.
Consular Offices:
New York, New York
Texas, Houston

LAOS

Embassy of the Lao People's Democratic Republic
2222 S Street NW., Washington, DC 20008

phone (202) 332–6416, fax (202) 332–4923
His Excellency Phanthong Phommahaxay
Ambassador E. and P.

LATVIA

Embassy of Latvia
4325 17th Street NW., Washington, DC 20011
phone (202) 726–8123, fax (202) 726–6785
His Excellency Aivis Ronis
Ambassador E. and P.

LEBANON

Embassy of Lebanon
2560 28th Street NW., Washington, DC 20008
phone (202) 939–6300, fax (202) 939–6324
His Excellency Farid Abboud
Ambassador E. and P.
Consular Offices:
California, Los Angeles
Michigan, Detroit
New York, New York

LESOTHO

Embassy of the Kingdom of Lesotho
2511 Massachusetts Avenue, NW., Washington, DC 20008
phone (202) 797–5533, fax (202) 234–6815
His Excellency Molelekeng E. Rapolaki
Ambassador E. and P.
Consular Office:
Louisiana, New Orleans

LIBERIA

Embassy of the Republic of Liberia
5201 16th Street NW., Washington, DC 20011
phone (202) 723–0437, fax (202) 723–0436
Aaron B. Kollie
Minister
Consular Offices:
California:
Los Angeles
San Francisco
Georgia, Atlanta
Illinois, Chicago
Michigan, Detroit
New York, New York

LIECHTENSTEIN

Embassy of the Principality of Liechtenstein
1300 Eye Street, NW., Suite 550 W, Washington, DC 20005
phone (202) 216–0460, fax (202) 216–0459
Her Excellency Claudia Fritsche
Ambassador E. and P.

LITHUANIA

Embassy of the Republic of Lithuania
2622 16th Street NW., Washington, DC 20009
phone (202) 234–5860, fax (202) 328–0466
His Excellency Vygaudas Usackas
Ambassador E. and P.
Consular Offices:
California, Los Angeles
Illinois, Chicago
New York, New York

LUXEMBOURG

Embassy of Grand Duchy of Luxembourg
2200 Massachusetts Avenue, NW., Washington, DC 20008
phone (202) 265–4171, fax (202) 328–8270
Her Excellency Arlette Conzemius
Ambassador E. and P.
Consular Offices:
California, San Francisco
Illinois, Chicago
Missouri, Kansas City
New York, New York

MACEDONIA

Embassy of the Former Yugoslav Republic of Macedonia
1101 30th Street, NW., Suite 302, Washington, DC 20007
phone (202) 337–3063, fax (202) 337–3093
His Excellency Nikola Dmitrov
Ambassador E. and P.
Consular Office: New York, New York

MADAGASCAR

Embassy of the Republic of Madagascar
2374 Massachusetts Avenue, NW., Washington, DC 20008
phone (202) 265–5525, fax (202) 265–3034
His Excellency Narisoa Rajaonarivony
Ambassador E. and P.
Consular Office: New York, New York

MALAWI

Embassy of the Republic of Malawi
2408 Massachusetts Avenue, NW., Washington, DC 20008
phone (202) 797–1007, fax (202) 265–0976
His Excellency Tony Kandiero
Ambassador E. and P.

MALAYSIA

Embassy of Malaysia
3516 International Court, NW., Washington, DC 20008
phone (202) 572–9700, fax (202) 572–9882
His Excellency Sheikh Abdul Khalid Ghazzali
Ambassador E. and P.
Consular Offices:
California, Los Angeles
New York, New York

MALDIVES

Embassy of the Republic of Maldives
800 2nd Avenue, Suite 400E, New York, NY 10017
phone (212) 599–6195
His Excellency Dr. Mohamed Latheef
Ambassador E. and P.

MALI

Embassy of the Republic of Mali
2130 R Street NW., Washington, DC 20008
phone (202) 332–2249, fax (202) 332–6603
His Excellency Abdoulaye Diop
Ambassador E. and P.

MALTA

Embassy of Malta
2017 Connecticut Avenue, NW., Washington, DC 20008
phone (202) 462–3611/12, fax (202) 387–5470
His Excellency John Lowell
Ambassador E. and P.
Consular Offices:
- California, San Francisco
- Michigan, Detroit
- Minnesota, St. Paul
- New York, New York
- Texas, Houston

MARSHALL ISLANDS

Embassy of the Republic of the Marshall Islands
2433 Massachusetts Avenue, NW., Washington, DC 20008
phone (202) 234–5414, fax (202) 232–3236
His Excellency Banny De Brum
Ambassador E. and P.
Consular Office: Hawaii, Honolulu

MAURITANIA

Embassy of the Islamic Republic of Mauritania
2129 Leroy Place NW., Washington, DC 20008
phone (202) 232–5700, fax (202) 319–2623
His Excellency Mohamedou Ould Michel
Ambassador E. and P.

MAURITIUS

Embassy of the Republic of Mauritius
4301 Connecticut Avenue, NW., Suite 441, Washington, DC 20008
phone (202) 244–1491/92, fax (202) 966–0983
His Excellency Usha Jeetah
Ambassador E. and P.

MEXICO

Embassy of Mexico
1911 Pennsylvania Avenue, NW., Washington, DC 20006
phone (202) 728–1600, fax (202) 728–1698
His Excellency Juan José Bremer Martino
Ambassador E. and P.
Consular Offices:
- Arizona:
  - Douglas
  - Nogales
  - Phoenix
  - Tucson
  - Yuma
- California:
  - Calexico
  - Fresno
  - Los Angeles
  - Oxnard
  - Sacramento
  - San Bernardino
  - San Diego
  - San Francisco
  - San Jose
  - Santa Ana
- Colorado, Denver
- Florida:
  - Miami
  - Orlando
- Georgia, Atlanta
- Illinois, Chicago
- Indiana, Indianapolis
- Louisiana, New Orleans
- Massachusetts, Boston
- Michigan, Detroit
- Missouri, Kansas City
- Nebraska, Omaha
- Nevada, Las Vegas
- New Mexico, Albuquerque
- New York, New York
- Oregon, Portland
- Pennsylvania, Philadelphia
- Puerto Rico, San Juan
- Texas:
  - Austin
  - Brownsville
  - Corpus Christi
  - Dallas
  - Del Rio
  - Eagle Pass
  - El Paso
  - Houston
  - Laredo
  - McAllen
  - Midland
  - San Antonio
- Utah, Salt Lake City
- Washington:
  - Seattle

MICRONESIA

Embassy of the Federated States of Micronesia
1725 N Street NW., Washington, DC 20036
phone (202) 223–4383, fax (202) 223–4391

His Excellency Jesse Bibiano Marehalau
Ambassador E. and P.
Consular Offices:
Guam, Tamuning
Hawaii, Honolulu

MOLDOVA

Embassy of the Republic of Moldova
2101 S Street NW., Washington, DC 20008
phone (202) 667–1130, fax (202) 667–1240
His Excellency Mihail Manoli
Ambassador E. and P.

MONACO

Consular Offices:
California:
Los Angeles
San Francisco
Florida, Miami
Illinois, Chicago
Massachusetts, Boston
New York, New York
Texas, Dallas

MONGOLIA

Embassy of Mongolia
2833 M Street NW., Washington, DC 20007
phone (202) 333–7117, fax (202) 298–9227
His Excellency Bold Ravdan
Ambassador E. and P.
Consular Offices:
California, San Francisco
New York, New York

MOROCCO

Embassy of the Kingdom of Morocco
1601 21st Street NW., Washington, DC 20009
phone (202) 462–7979, fax (202) 265–0161, 462–7643
His Excellency Aziz Mekouar
Ambassador E. and P.
Consular Office:
New York, New York

MOZAMBIQUE

Embassy of the Republic of Mozambique
1990 M Street NW., Suite 570, Washington, DC 20036
phone (202) 293–7146, fax (202) 835–0245
His Excellency Armando Alexandre Panguene
Ambassador E. and P.

NAURU

Consular Office: Guam, Agana

NAMIBIA

Embassy of the Republic of Namibia
1605 New Hampshire Avenue, NW., Washington, DC 20009
phone (202) 986–0540, fax (202) 986–0443
His Excellency Leonard Nangolo Iipumbu
Ambassador E. and P.
Consular Office: Michigan, Detroit

NEPAL

Royal Nepalese Embassy
2131 Leroy Place NW., Washington, DC 20008
phone (202) 667–4550, fax (202) 667–5534
His Excellency Jai Pratap Rana
Ambassador E. and P.
Consular Offices:
California:
Los Angeles
San Francisco
New York, New York
Ohio, Cleveland

NETHERLANDS

Royal Netherlands Embassy
4200 Linnean Avenue, NW., Washington, DC 20008
phone (202) 244–5300, fax (202) 364–6511
His Excellency Boudewijn van Eenennaam
Ambassador E. and P.
Consular Offices:
California:
Los Angeles
Florida, Miami
Illinois, Chicago
Massachusetts, Boston
New York, New York
Texas, Houston

NEW ZEALAND

Embassy of New Zealand
37 Observatory Circle NW., Washington, DC 20008
phone (202) 328–4800, fax (202) 667–5227
His Excellency John Wood
Ambassador E. and P.
Consular Offices:
California, Los Angeles
New York, New York

NICARAGUA

Embassy of the Republic of Nicaragua
1627 New Hampshire Avenue, NW., Washington, DC 20009
phone (202) 939–6570, fax (202) 939–6542
His Excellency Carlos Jose Ulvert Sanchez
Ambassador E. and P.
Consular Offices:
California, Los Angeles
Florida, Miami
Louisiana, New Orleans
New York, New York
Puerto Rico, San Juan
Texas, Houston

NIGER

Embassy of the Republic of Niger
2204 R Street NW., Washington, DC 20008
phone (202) 483–4224, fax (202) 683–3169
His Excellency Joseph Diatta
Ambassador E. and P.

NIGERIA

Embassy of the Federal Republic of Nigeria
3519 International Court, NW., Washington, DC 20008
phone (202) 986–8400, fax (202) 775–1385
His Excellency Jibril Muhammad Aminu
Ambassador E. and P.
Consular Offices:
Georgia, Atlanta
New York, New York

NORWAY

Royal Norwegian Embassy
2720 34th Street NW., Washington, DC 20008–2714
phone (202) 333–6000, fax (202) 333–0543
His Excellency Knut Vollebaek
Ambassador E. and P.
Consular Offices:
California:
Los Angeles
San Francisco
Florida, Miami
Illinois, Chicago
Minnesota, Minneapolis
New York, New York
Texas, Houston

OMAN

Embassy of the Sultanate of Oman
2535 Belmont Road NW., Washington, DC 20008
phone (202) 387–1980, fax (202) 745–4933
His Excellency Mohamed Ali Al Khusaiby
Ambassador E. and P.

PAKISTAN

Embassy of Pakistan
3517 International Court, NW., Washington, DC 20008
phone (202) 243–6500, fax (202) 686–1534
Her Excellency Ashraf Jehangir Qazi
Ambassador E. and P.
Consular Offices:
California:
Los Angeles
Sunnyvale
Massachusetts, Boston
New York, New York

Iranian Interests Section

2209 Wisconsin Avenue, NW., Washington, DC 20007
phone (202) 965–4990

PALAU

Embassy of the Republic of Palau
1800 K Street, NW., Suite 714, Washington, DC 20006
phone (202) 452–6814, fax (202) 452–6281
His Excellency Hersey Kyota
Ambassador E. and P.
Consular Office: Guam, Tamuning

PANAMA

Embassy of the Republic of Panama
2862 McGill Terrace NW., Washington, DC 20008
phone (202) 483–1407, fax (202) 483–8413
His Excellency Roberto Alfaro Estripeaut
Ambassador E. and P.
Consular Offices:
California, San Francisco
Florida:
Miami
Tampa
Georgia, Atlanta
Hawaii, Honolulu
Illinois, Chicago
Louisiana, New Orleans
Massachusetts, Boston
New York, New York
Pennsylvania, Philadelphia
Puerto Rico, San Juan
Texas, Houston

PAPUA NEW GUINEA

Embassy of Papua New Guinea
1779 Massachusetts Avenue, NW., Suite 805, Washington, DC 20036
phone (202) 745–3680, fax (202) 745–3679
Graham Michael
Counselor
Consular Offices:
California, Los Angeles
Texas, Houston

PARAGUAY

Embassy of Paraguay
2400 Massachusetts Avenue, NW., Washington, DC 20008
phone (202) 483–6960, fax (202) 234–4508
Her Excellency Leila Teresa Rachid Cowles
Ambassador E. and P.
Consular Offices:
California, Los Angeles
Florida, Miami
Kansas, Kansas City
Louisiana, New Orleans
New York, New York

PERU

Embassy of Peru
1700 Massachusetts Avenue, NW., Washington, DC 20036
phone (202) 833–9860, fax (202) 659–8124
His Excellency Roberto Danino
Ambassador E. and P.
Consular Offices:
California:
Los Angeles
San Francisco
Colorado, Denver
Connecticut, Hartford
Florida, Miami
Illinois, Chicago
Massachusetts, Boston
New Jersey, Paterson
New York, New York
Puerto Rico, San Juan
Texas, Houston

PHILIPPINES

Embassy of the Philippines
1600 Massachusetts Avenue, NW., Washington, DC 20036
phone (202) 467–9300/63, fax (202) 328–7614, 467–9417
His Excellency Albert Ferreros Del Rosario
Ambassador E. and P.
Consular Offices:
California:
Los Angeles
San Diego
San Francisco
Georgia, Atlanta
Guam, Agana
Hawaii, Honolulu
Illinois, Chicago
Louisiana, New Orleans
New York, New York
Texas, Houston

POLAND

Embassy of the Republic of Poland
2640 16th Street NW., Washington, DC 20009
phone (202) 234–3800, fax (202) 328–6271
His Excellency Przemyslaw Grudzinski
Ambassador E. and P.
Consular Offices:
California, Los Angeles
Illinois, Chicago
New York, New York

PORTUGAL

Embassy of Portugal
2125 Kalorama Road NW., Washington, DC 20008
phone (202) 328–8610, fax (202) 462–3726
His Excellency Pedro Catarino
Ambassador E. and P.
Consular Offices:
California:
Los Angeles
San Francisco
Massachusetts:
Boston
New Bedford
New Jersey, Newark
New York, New York
Rhode Island, Providence

QATAR

Embassy of the State of Qatar
4200 Wisconsin Avenue, NW., Suite 200, Washington, DC 20016
phone (202) 274–1603, fax (202) 237–0061
His Excellency Bader Omar Al Dafa
Ambassador E. and P.
Consular Office: Texas, Houston

ROMANIA

Embassy of Romania
1607 23rd Street NW., Washington, DC 20008
phone (202) 332–4846, fax (202) 232–4748
His Excellency Dumitru Sorin Ducaru
Ambassador E. and P.
Consular Offices:
California, Los Angeles
Illinois, Chicago
Massachusetts, Boston
Michigan, Detroit
New York, New York

RUSSIA

Embassy of the Russian Federation
2650 Wisconsin Avenue, NW., Washington, DC 20007
phone (202) 298–5700, fax (202) 298–5735
His Excellency Yury Viktorovich Ushakov
Ambassador E. and P.
Consular Offices:
Alaska, Anchorage
California, San Francisco
Hawaii, Honolulu
New York, New York
Utah, Salt Lake City
Washington, Seattle

RWANDA

Embassy of the Republic of Rwanda
1714 New Hampshire Avenue, NW., Washington, DC 20009
phone (202) 232–2882, fax (202) 232–4544
His Excellency Zac Nsenga
Ambassador E. and P.
Consular Office: Illinois, Chicago

SAINT KITTS AND NEVIS

Embassy of Saint Kitts and Nevis
3216 New Mexico Avenue, NW., Washington, DC 20016
phone (202) 686–2636, fax (202) 686–5740
His Excellency Izben Cordinal Williams
Ambassador E. and P.
Consular Offices:
Georgia, Atlanta
Texas, Dallas

SAINT LUCIA

Embassy of Saint Lucia
3216 New Mexico Avenue, NW., Washington, DC 20016
phone (202) 364–6792, fax (202) 364–6723
Her Excellency Sonia Merlyn Johnny
Ambassador E. and P.
Consular Offices:
Florida, Miami
New York, New York

SAINT VINCENT AND THE GRENADINES

Embassy of Saint Vincent and the Grenadines
3216 New Mexico Avenue, NW., Washington, DC 20016
phone (202) 364–6730, fax (202) 364–6736
His Excellency Ellsworth I.A. John
Ambassador E. and P.
Consular Offices:
California, Los Angeles
Louisiana, New Orleans
New York, New York

SAMOA

Embassy of the Independent State of Samoa
800 2nd Avenue, Suite 400J, New York, NY 10017
phone (212) 599–6196, fax (212) 599–0797
His Excellency Tuiloma Neroni Slade
Ambassador E. and P.
Consular Office: Hawaii, Honolulu

SAN MARINO

Consular Office: New York, New York

SAO TOME AND PRINCIPE

Consular Office: Illinois, Chicago

SAUDI ARABIA

Embassy of Saudi Arabia
601 New Hampshire Avenue, NW., Washington, DC 20037
phone (202) 342–3800, fax (202) 944–5983
His Royal Highness Prince Bandar Bin Sultan
Ambassador E. and P.
Consular Offices:
California, Los Angeles
New York, New York
Texas, Houston

SENEGAL

Embassy of the Republic of Senegal
2112 Wyoming Avenue, NW., Washington, DC 20008
phone (202) 234–0540, fax (202) 332–6315
His Excellency Dr. Amadou Lamine Ba
Ambassador E. and P.
Consular Offices:
Louisiana, New Orleans
Massachusetts, Boston
New York, New York

SERBIA & MONTENEGRO

Embassy of Serbia & Montenegro
2134 Kaloram road, NW., Washington, DC 20008
phone (202) 332–0333, fax (202) 332–3933
His Excellency Ivan Vujacic
Ambassador E. and P.
Consular Offices:
Colorado, Denver
Illinois, Chicago
Wyoming, Cheyenne

SEYCHELLES

Embassy of the Republic of Seychelles
800 2nd Avenue, Suite 400C, New York, NY 10017
phone (212) 972–1785, fax (212) 972–1786
His Excellency Claude Sylvestre Morel
Ambassador E. and P.
Consular Office: Washington, Seattle

SIERRA LEONE

Embassy of Sierra Leone
1701 19th Street NW., Washington, DC 20009
phone (202) 939–9261, fax (202) 483–1793
His Excellency Ibrahim M. Kamara
Ambassador E. and P.

SINGAPORE

Embassy of the Republic of Singapore
3501 International Place NW., Washington, DC 20008
phone (202) 537–3100, fax (202) 537–0876
Her Excellency Heng Chee Chan
Ambassador E. and P.
Consular Offices:
California:
Las Angeles
San Francisco
Illinois, Chicago
New York, New York

SLOVAK REPUBLIC

Embassy of the Slovak Republic
3523 International Court NW., Washington, DC 20008
phone (202) 237–1054, fax (202) 237–6438
Peter Kmec
Counselor

SLOVENIA

Embassy of the Republic of Slovenia
1525 New Hampshire Avenue, NW., Washington, DC 20036
phone (202) 667–5363, fax (202) 667–4563
His Excellency Davorin Kracun
Ambassador E. and P.
Consular Offices:
New York, New York
Ohio, Cleveland

SOLOMON ISLANDS

Embassy of the Solomon Islands
800 2nd Avenue, Suite 400L, New York, NY 10017
phone (212) 599–6192, fax (212) 661–8925
Jeremiah Manele
Counselor

SOMALIA

Embassy of the Somali Democratic Republic
(Embassy ceased operations May 8, 1991)

SOUTH AFRICA

Embassy of the Republic of South Africa
3051 Massachusetts Avenue, NW., Washington, DC 20008
phone (202) 232–4400, fax (202) 265–1607
Ronald Thandabantu G. Nhlapo
Minister
Consular Offices:
Alabama, Mobile
California, Los Angeles
Illinois, Chicago
New York, New York

SPAIN

Embassy of Spain
2375 Pennsylvania Avenue, NW., Washington, DC 20037
phone (202) 452–0100, fax (202) 833–5670
His Excellency Francisco Javier Ruperez
Ambassador E. and P.
Consular Offices:
Alabama, Mobile
California:
Los Angeles
San Francisco
Florida, Miami
Illinois, Chicago
Louisiana, New Orleans
Massachusetts, Boston
New York, New York
Puerto Rico, San Juan
Texas, Houston

SRI LANKA

Embassy of the Democratic Socialist Republic of Sri Lanka
2148 Wyoming Avenue, NW., Washington, DC 20008
phone (202) 483–4025, fax (202) 232–7181
His Excellency Devinda Rohan Subasinghe
Ambassador E. and P.
Consular Offices:
California, Los Angeles
Georgia, Atlanta
New York, New York

SUDAN

Embassy of the Republic of the Sudan
2210 Massachusetts Avenue, NW., Washington, DC 20008
phone (202) 338–8565, fax (202) 667–2406
Khidir Haroun Ahmed
Minister

SURINAME

Embassy of the Republic of Suriname
4301 Connecticut Avenue, NW., Suite 460, Washington, DC 20008
phone (202) 244–7488, fax (202) 244–5878
His Excellency Henry L. Illes
Ambassador E. and P.
Consular Office: Florida, Miami

SWAZILAND

Embassy of the Kingdom of Swaziland
1712 New Hampshire Avenue, NW., Washington, DC 20009
phone (202) 234–5002, fax (202) 234–8254
Her Excellency Mary M. Kanya
Ambassador E. and P.

SWEDEN

Embassy of Sweden
1501 M Street, NW., Suite 900, Washington, DC 20005
phone (202) 467–2600, fax (202) 467–2699
His Excellency Jan K. Eliasson
Ambassador E. and P.
Consular Offices:
California:
Los Angeles
San Francisco
Illinois, Chicago
Minnesota, Minneapolis
New York, New York

SWITZERLAND

Embassy of Switzerland
2900 Cathedral Avenue, NW., Washington, DC 20008
phone (202) 745–7900, fax (202) 387–2564
His Excellency Christian Blickenstorfer
Ambassador E. and P.

Consular Offices:
  California:
    Los Angeles
    San Francisco
  Georgia, Atlanta
  Illinois, Chicago
  Massachusetts, Boston
  New York, New York
  Texas, Houston

Cuban Interests Section

Embassy of Switzerland
2630 16th Street, NW 20009
phone (202) 797–8518
Dagoberto Rodriguez Barrera
Counselor

SYRIA

Embassy of the Syrian Arab Republic
2215 Wyoming Avenue, NW., Washington, DC 20008
phone (202) 232–6313, fax (202) 234–9548
His Excellency Dr. Rostom Al Zoubi
Ambassador E. and P.
Consular Offices:
  California, Los Angeles
  Michigan, Detroit
  Texas, Houston

TAJIKISTAN

Embassy of the Republic of Tajikistan
1725 K Street, NW., Suite 409, Washington, DC 20006
phone (202) 223–6090, fax (202) 223–6091
His Excellency Khamrokhon Zaripov
Ambassador E. and P.

TANZANIA

Embassy of the United Republic of Tanzania
2139 R Street NW., Washington, DC 20008
phone (202) 939–6125, 884–1080, fax (202) 797–7408
His Excellency Andrew Mhando Daraja
Ambassador E. and P.

THAILAND

Royal Thai Embassy
1024 Wisconsin Avenue, NW., Suite 401, Washington, DC 20007
phone (202) 944–3600, fax (202) 944–3611
His Excellency Sakthip Krairiksh
Ambassador E. and P.
Consular Offices:
  Alabama, Montgomery
  California, Los Angeles
  Colorado, Denver
  Florida, Coral Gables
  Georgia, Atlanta
  Hawaii, Honolulu
  Illinois, Chicago
  Massachusetts, Boston
  New York, New York
  Oklahoma, Tulsa
  Puerto Rico, Hato Rey
  Texas:
    Dallas
    El Paso
    Houston

TOGO

Embassy of the Republic of Togo
2208 Massachusetts Avenue, NW., Washington, DC 20008
phone (202) 234–4212, fax (202) 232–3190
His Excellency Akoussoulelou Bodjona
Ambassador E. and P.

TONGA

Embassy of the Kingdom of Tonga
250 East 51st Street, New York, NY 10022
phone (917) 369–1025, fax (917) 369–1024
Her Excellency Sonatane Tua Taumoepeau Tupou
Ambassador E. and P.
Consular Office: California, San Francisco

TRINIDAD AND TOBAGO

Embassy of the Republic of Trinidad and Tobago
1708 Massachusetts Avenue, NW., Washington, DC 20036–1975
phone (202) 467–6490, fax (202) 785–3130
Her Excellency Marina Annette Valere
Ambassador E. and P.
Consular Offices:
  Florida, Miami
  New York, New York

TUNISIA

Embassy of Tunisia
1515 Massachusetts Avenue, NW., Washington, DC 20005
phone (202) 862–1850, fax (202) 862–1858
His Excellency Hatem Atallah
Ambassador E. and P.
Consular Office: California, San Francisco

TURKEY

Embassy of the Republic of Turkey
2525 Massachusetts Avenue, NW., Washington, DC 20008
phone (202) 612–6700, fax (202) 612–6744
His Excellency Dr. Osman Faruk Logoglu
Ambassador E. and P.
Consular Offices:
  California:
    Los Angeles
    Oakland
  Georgia, Atlanta
  Illinois, Chicago

Kansas, Mission Hills
Maryland, Baltimore
New York, New York
Texas, Houston
Washington, Seattle

TURKMENISTAN

Embassy of Turkmenistan
2207 Massachusetts Avenue, NW., Washington, DC 20008
phone (202) 588–1500, fax (202) 588–0697
His Excellency Meret Bairamovich Orazov
Ambassador E. and P.

UGANDA

Embassy of the Republic of Uganda
5911 16th Street, NW., Washington, DC 20011
phone (202) 726–7100, fax (202) 726–1727
Her Excellency Edith Grace Ssempala
Ambassador E. and P.

UKRAINE

Embassy of Ukraine
3350 M Street, NW., Washington, DC 20007
phone (202) 333–0606, fax (202) 333–0817
His Excellency Kostyantyn Gryshchenko
Ambassador E. and P.
Consular Offices:
Illinois, Chicago
New York, New York

UNITED ARAB EMIRATES

Embassy of the United Arab Emirates
3522 International Court NW., Washington, DC 20008
phone (202) 243–2400, fax (202) 243–2432
His Excellency Alasri Saeed Aldhahri
Ambassador E. and P.

UNITED KINGDOM OF GREAT BRITAIN AND NORTHERN IRELAND

British Embassy
3100 Massachusetts Avenue, NW., Washington, DC 20008
phone (202) 588–6500, fax (202) 588–7870
Anthony Brenton
Minister
Consular Offices:
California:
Los Angeles
San Francisco
Colorado, Denver
Florida:
Miami
Orlando
Georgia, Atlanta
Illinois, Chicago
Massachusetts, Boston
New York, New York
Texas:
Dallas
Houston
Washington, Seattle

URUGUAY

Embassy of Uruguay
1913 I Street, NW., Washington, DC 20006
phone (202) 331–1313, fax (202) 331–8142
His Excellency Hugo Fernandez Faingold
Ambassador E. and P.
Consular Offices:
California, Los Angeles
Florida, Miami
Illinois, Chicago
New York, New York

UZBEKISTAN

Embassy of the Republic of Uzbekistan
1746 Massachusetts Avenue, NW., Washington, DC 20036
phone (202) 887–5300, fax (202) 293–6804
His Excellency Shavkat Shodiyevich Khamrakulov
Ambassador E. and P.
Consular Offices:
Colorado, Denver
New York, New York
Washington, Seattle

VENEZUELA

Embassy of the Republic of Venezuela
1099 30th Street, NW., Washington, DC 20007
phone (202) 342–2214, fax (202) 342–6820
His Excellency Bernardo Alvarez Herrera
Ambassador E. and P.
Consular Offices:
California, San Francisco
Florida, Miami
Illinois, Chicago
Louisiana, New Orleans
Massachusetts, Boston
New York, New York
Puerto Rico, San Juan
Texas, Houston

VIETNAM

Embassy of Vietnam
1233 20th Street, NW., Suite 400, Washington, DC 20036
phone (202) 861–0737, fax (202) 861–0917
His Excellency Chien Tam Nguyen
Ambassador E. and P.
Consular Office: California, San Francisco

YEMEN

Embassy of the Republic of Yemen
2600 Virginia Avenue, NW., Suite 705, Washington, DC 20037

phone (202) 965–4760, fax (202) 337–2017
His Excellency Abdulwahab A. Al-Hajjri
Ambassador E. and P.
Consular Office: Michigan, Detroit

YUGOSLAVIA

Permanent Mission of the Federal Republic of Yugoslavia to the U.N.
854 5th Avenue, New York, NY 10021
phone (212) 879–8700, fax (212) 879–8705
Vladislav Jovanovic
Ambassador E. and P.

ZAMBIA

Embassy of the Republic of Zambia
2419 Massachusetts Avenue, NW., Washington, DC 20008
phone (202) 265–9717, fax (202) 332–0826
Her Excellency Inonge Mbikusita Lewanika
Ambassador E. and P.

ZIMBABWE

Embassy of the Republic of Zimbabwe
1608 New Hampshire Avenue, NW., Washington, DC 20009
phone (202) 332–7100, fax (202) 483–9326
His Excellency Simbi Veke Mubako
Ambassador E. and P.

EUROPEAN UNION

Delegation of the European Commission
2300 M Street, NW., Washington, DC 20037
phone (202) 862–9500, fax (202) 429–1766
His Excellency Guenter Burghardt
Ambassador E. and P. (Head of Delegation)

The following is a list of countries with which diplomatic relations have been severed:

After each country, in parenthesis, is the name of the country's protecting power in the United States.

CUBA (Switzerland)
IRAN (Pakistan)
IRAQ (Algeria)

PRESS GALLERIES*

SENATE PRESS GALLERY

The Capitol, Room S–316, phone 224–0241

Director.—S. Joseph Keenan
Deputy Director.—Joan McKinney
Senior Media Coordinator.—Merri I. Baker
Media Coordinators:
James D. Saris
Wendy A. Oscarson
Amy M. Harkins

HOUSE PRESS GALLERY

The Capitol, Room H–315, phone 225–3945, 225–6722

Superintendent.—Jerry L. Gallegos
Deputy Superintendent.—Justin J. Supon
Assistant Superintendents:
Emily T. Dupree
Drew Cannon
Ric Andersen
Laura Reed

STANDING COMMITTEE OF CORRESPONDENTS

Scott Shepard, Cox News Service, *Chairman*
Jack Torry, Columbus Dispatch, *Secretary*
Jim Drinkard, USA Today
Mary Agnes Carey, Congressional Quarterly
Jesse Holland, The Associated Press

RULES GOVERNING PRESS GALLERIES

1. Administration of the press galleries shall be vested in a Standing Committee of Correspondents elected by accredited members of the galleries. The Committee shall consist of five persons elected to serve for terms of two years. Provided, however, that at the election in January 1951, the three candidates receiving the highest number of votes shall serve for two years and the remaining two for one year. Thereafter, three members shall be elected in odd-numbered years and two in even-numbered years. Elections shall be held in January. The Committee shall elect its own chairman and secretary. Vacancies on the Committee shall be filled by special election to be called by the Standing Committee.

2. Persons desiring admission to the press galleries of Congress shall make application in accordance with Rule 34 of the House of Representatives, subject to the direction and control of the Speaker and Rule 33 of the Senate, which rules shall be interpreted and administered by the Standing Committee of Correspondents, subject to the review and an approval by the Senate Committee on Rules and Administration.

3. The Standing Committee of Correspondents shall limit membership in the press galleries to bona fide correspondents of repute in their profession, under such rules as the Standing Committee of Correspondents shall prescribe.

*Information is based on data furnished and edited by each respective gallery.

4. Provided, however, that the Standing Committee of Correspondents shall admit to the galleries no person who does not establish to the satisfaction of the Standing Committee all of the following:

(a) That his or her principal income is obtained from news correspondence intended for publication in newspapers entitled to second-class mailing privileges.

(b) That he or she is not engaged in paid publicity or promotion work or in prosecuting any claim before Congress or before any department of the government, and will not become so engaged while a member of the galleries.

(c) That he or she is not engaged in any lobbying activity and will not become so engaged while a member of the galleries.

5. Members of the families of correspondents are not entitled to the privileges of the galleries.

6. The Standing Committee of Correspondents shall propose no change or changes in these rules except upon petition in writing signed by not less than 100 accredited members of the galleries.

The above rules have been approved by the Committee on Rules and Administration.

J. DENNIS HASTERT,
Speaker of the House of Representatives.

TRENT LOTT,
Chairman, Senate Committee on Rules and Administration.

MEMBERS ENTITLED TO ADMISSION

PRESS GALLERIES

Abbott, Charles: Reuters
Abboud, Leila: Wall Street Journal
Abell, John: Reuters
Abrahms, Douglas: Gannett News Service
Abrams, James: Associated Press
Abramson, Jill: New York Times
Ackerman, Liza: Congressional Quarterly
Adair, William: St. Petersburg Times
Adams, Rebecca: Congressional Quarterly
Adcock, Beryl: Knight Ridder
Agres, Theodore: Washington Times
Ahmann, Timothy: Reuters
Aida, Hirotsugu: Kyodo News
Akashi, Kazuyasu: Jiji Press
Akita, Hiroyuki: Nikkei
Albanesius, Chloe: National Journal's Technology Daily
Alday, Ricardo: Notimex Mexican News Agency
Alden, Edward: Financial Times
Aldinger, Charles: Reuters
Alexander, Andrew: Cox Newspapers
Alexander, Charles: Reuters
Aljadi, Adnan: Kuwait News Agency
Allen, JoAnne: Reuters
Allen, Jonathan: Congressional Quarterly
Allen, Karen: Scripps Howard News Service
Allen, Michael: Washington Post
Allen, Victoria: Reuters
Allen, III, Charles: Bloomberg News
Alonso-Zaldivar, Ricardo: Los Angeles Times
Alpert, Bruce: New Orleans Times-Picayune
Al-Sowayel, Naila: Saudi Press Agency
Amano, Masashi: Yomiuri Shimbun
Ambrose, Jay: Scripps Howard News Service
Amosu, Akwe: AllAfrica.com
Anason, Dean: American Banker
Anderson, Curt: Associated Press
Anderson, Nick: Los Angeles Times
Anderson, Mark: Dow Jones Newswires
Andrejczak, Matt: CBS MarketWatch
Andrews, Caesar: Gannett News Service
Andrews, Edmund: New York Times
Angle, Martha: Congressional Quarterly
Anidjar, Patrick: Agence France-Presse
Anklam, Jr., Fred: USA Today
Anselmo, Joseph: Congressional Quarterly
Aoki, Masaaki: Kyodo News
Appleby, Julie: USA Today
Archibald, George: Washington Times
Armas, Genaro: Associated Press
Arnold, Laurence: Associated Press
Arnone, Michael: Chronicle of Higher Education
Arthur, William: Bloomberg News
Asher, James: Knight Ridder
Asher, Julie: Catholic News Service
Asher, Robert: Washington Post
Ashizuka, Tomoko: Nikkei
Aslam, Abid: AFX News
Asseo, Laurie: Bloomberg News
Atallah, Ayda: Financial Times
Aukofer, Frank: Artists & Writers Syndicate
Aulston, Von: New York Times
Auster, Elizabeth: Cleveland Plain Dealer
Austin, Janet: Congressional Quarterly
Aversa, Jeannine: Associated Press
Aziakou, Gerard: Agence France-Presse
Azpiazu, Maria: EFE News Services
Babington, Charles: Washington Post
Bachelet, Pablo: Reuters
Backover, Andrew: USA Today
Bacon, John: USA Today
Baer, Susan: Baltimore Sun
Bailey, Ruby: Detroit Free Press
Baker, Chris: Washington Times
Baker, Frank: Associated Press
Baker, Gerard: Financial Times
Baldor, Lolita: Associated Press
Ball, Micheal: Energy Argus
Balluck, Kyle: WashingtonPost.com
Baltimore, Chris: Reuters
Balz, Daniel: Washington Post
Banales, Jorge: Congressional Quarterly
Banales, Jorge: EFE News Services
Banks, Adelle: Religion News Service
Barazia, Virginia: Congressional Quarterly
Barbara, Philip: Reuters
Barbaro, Michael: Washington Post
Barfield Berry, Deborah: Newsday
Barker, Jeffrey: Baltimore Sun
Barnett, James: Oregonian
Barnett, Pamela: CongressDaily
Barollier, Pascal: Agence France-Presse
Barr, Gary: Washington Post
Barrera, Ruben: Notimex Mexican News Agency
Barrett, Devlin: Associated Press
Barrett, Greg: Gannett News Service
Barrett, Terrence: Bloomberg News
Barry, Theresa: Bloomberg News
Barshay, Jill: Congressional Quarterly
Bartash, Jeffrey: CBS MarketWatch

MEMBERS ENTITLED TO ADMISSION—Continued

Barton, Paul: Arkansas Democrat-Gazette
Bashir, Mustafa: Saudi Press Agency
Basken, Paul: Bloomberg News
Bater, Jeffrey: Dow Jones Newswires
Batt, Tony: Stephens Media Group
Battaile, Janet: New York Times
Baumgardner, Neil: Defense Daily
Baygents, Ronald: Kuwait News Agency
Baylin, Joshua: Bloomberg News
Bazinet, Kenneth: New York Daily News
Beattie, Alan: Financial Times
Beattie, Jeff: Energy Daily
Beck, Ellen: United Press International
Beck, Tobin: United Press International
Becker, Elizabeth: New York Times
Beckner, Erica: Market News International
Beckner, Steven: Market News International
Beddall, Katherine: Agence France-Presse
Beech, Eric: Reuters
Begos, Jr., Kevin: Winston-Salem Journal
Behn, Sharon: Washington Times
Behr, Peter: Washington Post
Bendavid, Naftali: Chicago Tribune
Benedetto, Richard: USA Today
Benenson, Robert: Congressional Quarterly
Benincasa, Robert: Gannett News Service
Benjamin, Mark: United Press International
Benkelman, Susan: Congressional Quarterly
Benson, Miles: Newhouse News Service
Benton, Nell: Congressional Quarterly
Berardelli, Phil: United Press International
Berke, Richard: New York Times
Berry, John: Washington Post
Bethel, Alison: Detroit News
Bettelheim, Adriel: Congressional Quarterly
Bicknell, Arwen: Congressional Quarterly
Bicknell, John: Congressional Quarterly
Bilski, Christina: Nikkei
Binder, David: New York Times
Bishop, Ian: Lowell Sun Media News Group
Bishop, Sam: Fairbanks Daily News Miner
Biskupic, Joan: USA Today
Bivins, Larry: Gannett News Service
Bjerga, Alan: Wichita Eagle
Blackwell, Rob: American Banker
Bland, Melissa: Reuters
Blankley, Tony: Washington Times
Bliss, Jeffrey: Bloomberg News
Bliss, Lynn: Dow Jones Newswires
Block, Sandra: USA Today
Blomquist, Brian: New York Post
Blum, Justin: Washington Post
Blumenthal, Les: McClatchy Newspapers
Bohan, Caren: Reuters
Bold, Michael: McClatchy Newspapers
Boliek, Brooks: Hollywood Reporter
Bonilla, Laura: Agence France-Presse
Bono, Agostino: Catholic News Service
Boodhoo, Niaia: Reuters
Borenstein, Seth: Knight Ridder
Borger, Julian: London Guardian
Borkowski, Monica: New York Times
Borrego, Anne Marie: Chronicle of Higher Education
Bosman, Julie: New York Times
Bosworth, Geoffrey: Congressional Quarterly
Boudreau, Wendy: Congressional Quarterly
Bourge, Christian: United Press International
Bovee, Timothy: Associated Press
Bowers, Faye: Christian Science Monitor
Bowman, Curtis Lee: Scripps Howard News Service
Bowman, Tom: Baltimore Sun
Boyd, Robert: Knight Ridder
Brady, Erik: USA Today
Brainard, Jeffrey: Chronicle of Higher Education
Branch-Brioso, Karen: St. Louis Post Dispatch
Brasher, Philip: Des Moines Register
Braun, Stephen: Los Angeles Times
Bravin, Jess: Wall Street Journal
Bremner, Faith: Gannett News Service
Briand, Xavier: Reuters
Bridis, Ted: Associated Press
Brinkley, Joel: New York Times
Bristol, Nellie: Health News Daily
Brock, Gregory: New York Times
Broder, David: Washington Post
Broder, Jonathan: Congressional Quarterly
Brodmann, Ronald: Congressional Quarterly
Brodsky, Arthur: Congressional Quarterly
Brogan, Pamela: Gannett News Service
Brooks, David: La Jornada
Brosnan, James: Scripps Howard News Service
Brown, Andrew: Knight Ridder
Brown, David: Washington Post
Brown, Rene: Hartford Courant
Brownstein, Ronald: Los Angeles Times
Brune, Thomas: Newsday
Bumiller, Elisabeth: New York Times
Bunis, Dena: Orange County Register
Burd, Stephen: Chronicle of Higher Education
Burke, Alecia: Congressional Quarterly
Burns, Judith: Dow Jones Newswires
Burns, Robert: Associated Press
Burns, Susan: Cox Newspapers
Bustos, Sergio: Gannett News Service
Butler, Amy: Bloomberg News
Butler, David: Congressional Quarterly
Butler, Steven: Knight Ridder
Butters, Patrick: Scripps Howard News Service
Cahir, William: Newhouse News Service
Calamur, Krishnadev: United Press International
Calmes, Jackie: Wall Street Journal
Camia, Catalina: Gannett News Service
Camire, Dennis: Gannett News Service
Campbell, Chris: Scripps Howard News Service

MEMBERS ENTITLED TO ADMISSION—Continued

Canan, Micheal: Scripps Howard News Service
Canas, Rafael: EFE News Services
Canellos, Peter: Boston Globe
Canizares, Alex: Bloomberg News
Cantlupe, Joe: Copley News Service
Capaccio, Anthony: Bloomberg News
Caplan, Abby: Energy Argus
Cardman, Michael: Education Daily
Caretto, Ennio: Il Corriere Della Sera
Carey, Mary Agnes: Congressional Quarterly
Carnevale, Dan: Chronicle of Higher Education
Carnevale, Mary: Wall Street Journal
Carney, David: Tech Law Journal
Carr, Rebecca: Cox Newspapers
Carreno, Jose: El Universal
Carroll, James: Congressional Quarterly
Carroll, James: Louisville Courier Journal
Carroll, Rebecca: Associated Press
Carter, Thomas: Washington Times
Cason, James: La Jornada
Casper, Lucian: Basler Zeitung
Cass, Connie: Associated Press
Casteel, Chris: Daily Oklahoman
Cazalas, Robert: Congressional Information Bureau
Chaddock, Gail: Christian Science Monitor
Chaffin, Joshua: Financial Times
Chambliss, Eva Lauren: London Evening Standard
Chang, Tsung-Chih: United Daily News
Charles, Deborah: Reuters
Chase, Katharine: Education Daily
Chatterjee, Sumana: Knight Ridder
Chebium, Raju: Gannett News Service
Chen, Edwin: Los Angeles Times
Chen, Jay: Central News Agency
Chen, Shawn: National Journal's Technology Daily
Chiantaretto, Mariuccia: Il Giornale
Chikazawa, Moriyasu: Kyodo News
Choi, Donald: US–Asian News Service
Christensen, Mike: Congressional Quarterly
Christie, Rebecca: Dow Jones Newswires
Chu, Patrick: Bloomberg News
Chwallek, Gabriele: German Press Agency/DPA
Ci, Guihang: China Wen Hui Bao Daily
Cienski, Jan: National Post
Cindemir, Mehmet: Hurriyet
Clark, Andrew: Reuters
Clark, Colin: Congressional Quarterly
Clark, Drew: National Journal's Technology Daily
Clarke, David: Congressional Quarterly
Clavel, Guy: Agence France-Presse
Clemetson, Lynette: New York Times
Cloud, David: Wall Street Journal
Clymer, Adam: New York Times
Coache, Wendy: Associated Press
Cobb, Jr., Charles: AllAfrica.com
Cocco, Marie: Newsday
Cochran, John: Congressional Quarterly
Cockel, Christopher: China Post
Codrea, George: Congressional Quarterly
Coghill, Kim: BioWorld Today
Cohen, Robert: Newark Star-Ledger
Cohen, Ronald: Gannett News Service
Cohn, D'Vera: Washington Post
Cohn, Peter: Congressional Quarterly
Coile, Zachary: San Francisco Chronicle
Cole, Justin: AFX News
Coleman, Michael: Albuquerque Journal
Collie, Kristen: Hearst Newspapers
Collins, Chris: USA Today
Collins, Michael: Scripps Howard News Service
Collinson, Stephen: Agence France-Presse
Coman, Julian: London Sunday Telegraph
Condon, Jr., George: Copley News Service
Conkey, Christopher: Wall Street Journal
Conlon, Chuck: Congressional Quarterly
Connolly, Ceci: Washington Post
Connor, John: Dow Jones Newswires
Conrad, Dennis: Associated Press
Constantine, Gus: Washington Times
Cook, David: Christian Science Monitor
Coombs, Jr., Francis: Washington Times
Cooper, Helene: Wall Street Journal
Cooper, Kent: Political Money Line
Cooper, Richard: Los Angeles Times
Cooper, Sonya: Bloomberg News
Copeland, Peter: Scripps Howard News Service
Copp, Tara: Scripps Howard News Service
Corbett Dooren, Jennifer: Dow Jones Newswires
Cornwell, Rupert: London Independent
Cornwell, Susan Jean: Reuters
Cortes, Lorenzo: Defense Daily
Covington, Robert: Reuters
Cowan, Richard: Reuters
Cox, Jim: USA Today
Coyne, Martin: Air Daily
Crabtree, Susan: Daily Variety
Cranford, John: Congressional Quarterly
Crawford, Craig: Congressional Quarterly
Crawley, John: Reuters
Crenshaw, Albert: Washington Post
Crites, Alice: Washington Post
Crutsinger, Martin: Associated Press
Cubbison, Christopher: USA Today
Cummings, Jeanne: Wall Street Journal
Curl, Joseph: Washington Times
Curtius, Mary: Los Angeles Times
Cushman, Jr., John: New York Times
Czarniak, Chet: USAToday.com
D'Arcy, Janice: Hartford Courant
Da Costa, Mario Navarro: ABIM News Agency
Dalglish, Arthur: Cox Newspapers
Dalrymple, Mary: Associated Press
Daly, Corbett: AFX News
Daly, Matthew: Associated Press

MEMBERS ENTITLED TO ADMISSION—Continued

Daly, Richard: Congressional Quarterly
Dangond, Silvia: El Columbiano
Dao, James: New York Times
Dart, Robert: Cox Newspapers
Davenport, Todd: American Banker
Davidson, Lee: Deseret News
Davidson, Paul: USA Today
Davies, Frank: Miami Herald
Davila, Juan: Associated Press
Davis, David: Congressional Quarterly
Davis, Joyce: Knight Ridder
Davis, Julie: Baltimore Sun
Davis, Robert: USA Today
Davis, Robert: Wall Street Journal
Davis, Tina: Energy Daily
Day, Kathleen: Washington Post
De Carlo, Cesare: La Nazione
De Roquefeuil, Christophe: Agence France-Presse
de Toledano, Ralph: National News Research Syndicate
Deans, Jr., Robert: Cox Newspapers
Deantonio, Farid: La Nacion USA
DeBarros, Anthony: USA Today
Debeusscher, Phillippe: Agence France-Presse
DeBose, Brian: Washington Times
Decker, Susan: Bloomberg News
DeFrank, Thomas: New York Daily News
Deibel, Mary: Scripps Howard News Service
Del Giudice, Vincent: Bloomberg News
Del Riccio, Cristiano: ANSA Italian News Agency
Delaney, Thomas: Associated Press
Delgado, Jose: El Nuevo Dia
Delollis, Barbara: USA Today
DeMarco, Edward: Bloomberg News
Denniston, Lyle: Boston Globe
DePledge, Derrick: Gannett News Service
Dermody, William: USA Today
Dermota, Kenneth: Agence France-Presse
Despeignes, Peronet: Financial Times
Dessouky, Dean: Saudi Press Agency
Detzel, Thomas: Oregonian
Deutsch, Jack: Congressional Quarterly
Dewar, Helen: Washington Post
Diamond, John: USA Today
Diaz, Kevin: Minneapolis Star Tribune
Diemer, Thomas: Cleveland Plain Dealer
Dinan, Stephen: Washington Times
Dine, Philip: St. Louis Post-Dispatch
Dinesh, Manimoli: Oil Daily
Dinmore, Guy: Financial Times
Divis, Dee Ann: United Press International
Dlouhy, Jennifer: Congressional Quarterly
Dobbin, Muriel: McClatchy Newspapers
Dobbs, Micheal: Washington Post
Dobbyn, Timothy: Reuters
Dodd, Michael: USA Today
Dodge, Catherine: Bloomberg News
Dodge, Robert: Dallas Morning News
Doering, Christopher: Reuters
Doggett, Tom: Reuters
Doherty, Robert: Reuters
Donmoyer, Ryan: Bloomberg News
Donnelly, John: Boston Globe
Dono, Linda: Gannett News Service
Dooley, Kerry: Bloomberg News
Dorning, Mike: Chicago Tribune
Doty, Cate: New York Times
Doublet, Jean-Louis: Agence France-Presse
Doughty, Stuart: Reuters
Douglas, William: Newsday
Dowd, Maureen: New York Times
Downey, Kirstin: Washington Post
Doyle, Michael: McClatchy Newspapers
Drajem, Mark: Bloomberg News
Drawbaugh, Kevin: Reuters
Dreazen, Yochi: Wall Street Journal
Drinkard, Jim: USA Today
Drogin, Robert: Los Angeles Times
Drummond, Bob: Bloomberg News
Duff, Susanna: Bond Buyer
Duggan, Loren: Congressional Quarterly
Duin, Julia: Washington Times
Dunham, Will: Reuters
Dunne, Nancy: Financial Times
Dunphy, Harry: Associated Press
Durbin, Dee-Ann: Associated Press
Dusseau, Brigitte: Agence France-Presse
Eaton, Sabrina: Cleveland Plain Dealer
Eccleston, Roy: Australian
Eckert, Toby: Copley News Service
Eckstrom, Kevin: Religion News Service
Edmonds Crang, Sarah: Reuters
Edmonds, Jr., Ronald: Associated Press
Edmonson, George: Atlanta Journal-Constitution
Edsall, Thomas: Washington Post
Efron, Sonni: Los Angeles Times
Efstathiou, James: Bloomberg News
Egan, Mark: Reuters
Eggen, Daniel: Washington Post
Eguigure, Maria: La Nacion USA
Eilperin, Juliet: Washington Post
Eisler, Peter: USA Today
Eisman, Dale: Virginian-Pilot
El Nasser, Haya: USA Today
Eldridge, Earle: USA Today
Elgood, Giles: Reuters
Ellicott, Val: Gannett News Service
Ellis, Julie: LRP Publications
Ellis, Kristi: Fairchild News Service
Elsner, Alan: Reuters
Emerson, Jason: LRP Publications
Endo, Seiji: Akahata
Enoch, Daniel: Bloomberg News
Enrich, David: States News Service

MEMBERS ENTITLED TO ADMISSION—Continued

Epstein, Edward: San Francisco Chronicle
Epstein, Keith: Tampa Tribune
Eskovitz, Joel: Scripps Howard News Service
Espo, David: Associated Press
Esterhazy, Yvonne: Financial Times-Deutschland
Estevez, Dolia: El Financiero
Estill, Jerry: Associated Press
Eversley, Melanie: Atlanta Journal-Constitution
Fabi, Randolph: Reuters
Faen, Wang: Xinhua News Agency
Fagan, Amy: Washington Times
Faler, Brian: Washington Post
Faltin, Cornel: Springer Foreign News Service
Faltin, Frauke: Springer Foreign News Service
Farah, Douglas: Washington Post
Farah, Joseph: WorldNetDaily.com
Farrell, Greg: USA Today
Farrell, John: Denver Post
Fatsis, Stefan: Wall Street Journal
Fazzino, Elysa: Il Secolo XIX
Fears, Darryl: Washington Post
Featherstone, Charles: Saudi Press Agency
Feazel, R. Michael: Communications Daily
Feer, Jason: Energy Argus
Feld, Karen: Capital Connections
Feldman, Carole: Associated Press
Feldmann, Linda: Christian Science Monitor
Felker, Edward: SNG Newspapers
Feller, Ben: Associated Press
Felsenthal, Mark: Reuters
Feng, Shaojie: China Legal Daily
Ferguson, Alexander: Reuters
Ferguson, Andrew: Bloomberg News
Ferguson, Ellyn: Gannett News Service
Ferrari, Francisco: Agence France-Presse
Ferraro, Thomas: Reuters
Ferrechio, Susan: Congressional Quarterly
Ferreira, Anton: Reuters
Ferris, Craig: Bond Buyer
Fessenden, Helen: Congressional Quarterly
Fetterman, Mindy: USA Today
Fialka, John: Wall Street Journal
Fibich, Linda: Newhouse News Service
Field, Kelly: Congressional Quarterly
Fields, Gary: Wall Street Journal
Files III, John: New York Times
Filipczyk, Kathleen: LRP Publications
Filteau, Jerome: Catholic News Service
Fineman, Mark: Los Angeles Times
Finkel, David: Washington Post
Fiore, Faye: Los Angeles Times
Fireman, Kenneth: Newsday
Firestone, David: New York Times
Fischer, Karin: Charleston (WVA) Daily Mail
Flaherty, Mary Pat: Washington Post
Flamini, Roland: United Press International
Flanders, Gwen: USA Today
Flattau, Edward: Global Horizons Syndicate
Fleming, Alexandria: Washington Times
Fletcher, Michael: Washington Post
Flippen, Carli: Energy Argus
Fogarty, Thomas: USA Today
Foster-Simeon, Ed: USA Today
Fox, Maggie: Reuters
Fram, Alan: Associated Press
Frandsen, Jon: Gannett News Service
Frank, Thomas: Newsday
Fraze, Barbara: Catholic News Service
Frederick, Don: Los Angeles Times
Freedman, Andrew: Congressional Quarterly
Freedman, Dan: Hearst Newspapers
Freedman, Daniel: Associated Press
Freking, Kevin: Arkansas Democrat-Gazette
Frenk, Clara: USAToday.com
Friedman, Lisa: Los Angeles Daily News
Friend, Tim: USA Today
Friesner, Margery: ANSA Italian News Agency
Fritz, Sara: St. Petersburg Times
Frommer, Frederick: Associated Press
Fruitrich, Chris: Congressional Quarterly
Fryer, Alex: Seattle Times
Fu, Norman: China Times
Fuhrig, Frank: German Press Agency/DPA
Fukase, Atsuko: Nikkei
Fulton, April: CongressDaily
Funk, Timothy: Charlotte Observer
Furlow, Robert: Associated Press
Galianese, Joseph: Associated Press
Gallen, Claire: Agence France-Presse
Galloway, Joseph: Knight Ridder
Gamboa, Suzanne: Associated Press
Gambrell, Kathy: United Press International
Gamerman, Ellen: Baltimore Sun
Gardett, Peter: Energy Argus
Gardiner, Andrew: USA Today
Gardner, Patrick: Tokyo-Chunichi Shimbun
Garver, Rob: American Banker
Gay, Lance: Scripps Howard News Service
Gearan, Anne: Associated Press
Gedda, George: Associated Press
Geewax, Marilyn: Cox Newspapers
Gehrke, Robert: Associated Press
Geimann, Stephen: Bloomberg News
Geracimos, Ann: Washington Times
Gersema, Emily: Associated Press
Gerstenzang, James: Los Angeles Times
Gerth, Jeff: New York Times
Gertz, William: Washington Times
Getter, Lisa: Los Angeles Times
Gettinger, Steve: Bloomberg News
Ghazarian, Stephane: Agence France-Presse
Ghent, Bill: CongressDaily
Giacomo, Carol: Reuters
Gibson, Andreas: Associated Press

MEMBERS ENTITLED TO ADMISSION—Continued

Gibson, Gail: Baltimore Sun
Gibson, William: South Florida Sun-Sentinel
Gilbert, Craig: Milwaukee Journal Sentinel
Gildea, Kerry: Defense Daily
Gillman, Todd: Dallas Morning News
Ginsburg, Steven: Reuters
Giroux, Gregory: Congressional Quarterly
Glain, Steven: Boston Globe
Glanz, William: Washington Times
Glass, Pamela: Le Mauricien
Glass, Robert: Associated Press
Glendinning, David: Health News Daily
Glover, K. Daniel: National Journal's Technology Daily
Go, Gwangchul: Korea Economic Daily
Godfrey, John: Dow Jones Newswires
Goffe, Shelia: Congressional Quarterly
Goldbacher, Raymond: USA Today
Golden, Jim: Gannett News Service
Goldenberg, Suzanne: London Guardian
Goldreich, Samuel: Congressional Quarterly
Goldstein, Amy: Washington Post
Goldstein, Daniel: Bloomberg News
Goldstein, David: Kansas City Star
Goldstein, Jacobo: La Tribuna
Goldstein, Steven: Philadelphia Inquirer
Golle, Vince: Bloomberg News
Gomez, Sergio: El Tiempo
Gonzalez, David: Associated Press
Gonzalez, Enrique: El Pais
Gonzalez, Maria: El Norte & Reforma
Goo, Sara: Washington Post
Goodman, Adrianne: Los Angeles Times
Gordon, D. Craig: Newsday
Gordon, Greg: McClatchy Newspapers
Gordon, Gregory: Minneapolis Star Tribune
Gordon, Marcy: Associated Press
Gordon, Michael: New York Times
Gosselin, Peter: Los Angeles Times
Goto, Shihoko: United Press International
Graham, Bradley: Washington Post
Graham-Silverman, Adam: Congressional Quarterly
Gramaglia, Giampiero: ANSA Italian News Agency
Greczyn, Mary: Communications Daily
Green, Mark: Daily Oklahoman
Greenberg, Brigitte: Communications Daily
Greenberger, Robert: Wall Street Journal
Greenburg, Jan: Chicago Tribune
Greene, David: Baltimore Sun
Greene, Robert: Bloomberg News
Greenhouse, Linda: New York Times
Grenz-Marcuse, Gabrielle: Agence France-Presse
Greve, Frank: Knight Ridder
Grier, Peter: Christian Science Monitor
Griffith, Stephanie: Agence France-Presse
Grimaldi, James: Washington Post
Groppe, Maureen: Gannett News Service
Grove, Benjamin: Las Vegas Sun
Gruenwald, Juliana: CongressDaily
Gruley, Bryan: Wall Street Journal
Grunwald, Michael: Washington Post
Guggenheim, Ken: Associated Press
Gugliotta, Guy: Washington Post
Guinto, Joseph: Investor's Business Daily
Gulino, Denny: Market News International
Gundersen, Heather: Associated Press
Gunther, Markus: Westdeutsche Allgemeine
Hackett, Laurel: Scripps Howard News Service
Hagenbaugh, Barbara: USA Today
Hager, George: USA Today
Haggerty, Maryann: Washington Post
Hall, Glenn: Bloomberg News
Hall, John: Media General News Service
Hall, Mimi: USA Today
Hallam, Kristen: Bloomberg News
Hallock, Kimberly: Congressional Quarterly
Halloran, Liz: Hartford Courant
Hallow, Ralph: Washington Times
Hamalainen, Aloysia: St. Louis Post-Dispatch
Hamann, Carlos: Agence France-Presse
Hamatani, Koji: Akahata
Hamburger, Thomas: Wall Street Journal
Hamill, Kevin: Reuters
Hamilton, Martha: Washington Post
Hananel, Sam: Associated Press
Hanner, Kenneth: Washington Times
Harden, Patrick: LRP Publications
Hardin, Peter: Richmond Times-Dispatch
Harding, James: Financial Times
Hargrove, Thomas: Scripps Howard News Service
Harland, Janis: New York Times
Harnden, Toby: London Daily Telegraph
Harper, Jennifer: Washington Times
Harper, Tim: Toronto Star
Harrell, Peter: Congressional Quarterly
Harrington, Caitlin: Congressional Quarterly
Harris, Hamil: Washington Post
Hartcher, Peter: Australian Financial Review
Hartman, Carl: Associated Press
Hartnagel, Nancy: Catholic News Service
Hartson, Merrill: Associated Press
Harwood, John: Wall Street Journal
Hasan, Khalid: Lahore Daily Times
Hastings, Maribel: La Opinion
Havemann, Joel: Los Angeles Times
Hawkings, David: Congressional Quarterly
Hawkins, Chuck: Congressional Quarterly
Hazar, Hasan: Turkiye Daily
Healy, Robert: Congressional Quarterly
Heavey, Susan: Reuters
Hebel, Sara: Chronicle of Higher Education
Hebert, H. Josef: Associated Press
Hedges, Michael: Houston Chronicle
Hedges, Stephen: Chicago Tribune

MEMBERS ENTITLED TO ADMISSION—Continued

Hedgpeth, Dana: Washington Post
Heil, Emily: CongressDaily
Heilbrunn, Jacob: Los Angeles Times
Heilprin, John: Associated Press
Heller, Marc: Watertown Daily Times
Heller, Michele: American Banker
Helm, Mark: Hearst Newspapers
Hendel, Caitlin: Congressional Quarterly
Hendel, John: United Press International
Henderson, Joan: Restructuring Today
Henderson, Stephen: Knight Ridder
Hendren, John: Los Angeles Times
Hendrie, Paul: Bloomberg News
Henriksson, Karin: Svenska Dagbladet
Henry, John: Houston Chronicle
Hepinstall, Sonya: Reuters
Herman, Edith: Communications Daily
Herms-Drath, Viola: Handelsblatt
Hernandez, Raymond: New York Times
Hess, David: CongressDaily
Hess, Pamela: United Press International
Hicks, Travis: Education Daily
Hiestand, Michael: USA Today
Higa, Liriel: Congressional Quarterly
Higgins, Marguerite: Washington Times
Higgins, Sean: Investor's Business Daily
Hill, Patrice: Washington Times
Hillburg, William: Los Angeles Newspaper Group
Hillman, G. Robert: Dallas Morning News
Hilzenrath, David: Washington Post
Hines, Cragg: Houston Chronicle
Hines, Elizabeth: New York Times
Hinton, Earl: Associated Press
Hirsch, Claudia: Market News International
Hisae, Masahiko: Kyodo News
Hishinuma, Takao: Yomiuri Shimbun
Hitt, Greg: Wall Street Journal
Ho, David: Associated Press
Hoffecker, Leslie: Los Angeles Times
Hoffman, Lisa: Scripps Howard News Service
Holland, Gina: Associated Press
Holland, Jesse: Associated Press
Holland, Judy: Hearst Newspapers
Holly, Christopher: Energy Daily
Holmes, Charles: Cox Newspapers
Holmes, Steven: New York Times
Holzer, Linda: USA Today
Honawar, Vaishali: Washington Times
Hook, Janet: Los Angeles Times
Hoopes, Cora: Roll Call Report Syndicate
Hopgood, Mei-Ling: Dayton Daily News
Hopkins, Andrea: Reuters
Hopkins, Cheyenne: Reuters
Horrock, Nicholas: United Press International
Horwich, Lee: USA Today
Hoskinson, Jr., Charles: Agence France-Presse
Hosler, Karen: Baltimore Sun
Hotakainen, Rob: Minneapolis Star Tribune
House, Billy: Arizona Republic
Howell, Deborah: Newhouse News Service
Hoy, Anne: Newsday
Hoyt, Clark: Knight Ridder
Hsu, Spencer: Washington Post
Hu, Xiaoming: Xinhua News Agency
Huber, Christopher: Associated Press
Hudson, Audrey: Washington Times
Hughes, John: Bloomberg News
Hughes, Michael: Associated Press
Hughes, Siobhan: Congressional Quarterly
Hughey, Ann: Bloomberg News
Hujer, Marc: Sueddeutsche Zeitung
Hulse, Carl: New York Times
Hultman, Tamela: AllAfrica.com
Hume, Lynn: Bond Buyer
Hunley, Johnathan: Fredericksburg Freelance-Star
Hunt, Katherine: Reuters
Hunt, Terence: Associated Press
Hurlburt, Sid: USA Today
Hurt, Charles: Washington Times
Hutcheson, Ron: Knight Ridder
Hutchinson, Martin: United Press International
Ibarguen, Diego: Knight Ridder
Ida, Tetsuji: Kyodo News
Ikeda, Nestor: Associated Press
Ilustre, Josefina: Philippine Daily Inquirer
Ip, Gregory: Wall Street Journal
Iqbal, Anwar: United Press International
Ishiaia, Tsutomu: Asahi Shimbun
Ito, Toshiyuki: Yomiuri Shimbun
Ivanovich, David: Houston Chronicle
Jackler, Rosalind: USA Today
Jackson, David: Dallas Morning News
Jacoby, Mary: St. Petersburg Times
Jaffe, Greg: Wall Street Journal
Jahn, Daniel: Agence France-Presse
Jalonick, Mary Clare: Congressional Quarterly
James III, Frank: Chicago Tribune
Jansen, Bart: Portland Press Herald
Jarreau, Patrick: Le Monde
Jaspin, Elliot: Cox Newspapers
Jehl, Douglas: New York Times
Jelinek, Pauline: Associated Press
Jensen, Kristin: Bloomberg News
Jing, Hui: Epoch Times
Johnson, Angela: Newsday
Johnson, Carrie: Washington Post
Johnson, David: Scripps Howard News Service
Johnson, Glen: Boston Globe
Johnson, Kevin: USA Today
Johnson, Sandy: Associated Press
Johnson, Timothy: Miami Herald
Johnston, David: New York Times
Jones, Brent: USA Today
Jones, David: Washington Times

MEMBERS ENTITLED TO ADMISSION—Continued

Jones, Del: USA Today
Jones, Kerry: Congressional Quarterly
Jones, Robert: Scripps Howard News Service
Jordan, Charles: CongressDaily
Jordan, Lara: Associated Press
Joseph, Lori: USA Today
Joy, Patricia: Congressional Quarterly
Joyce, Stacy: Reuters
Jung, Daniel: WashingtonPost.com
Justice, Glen: Bloomberg News
Kady II, Martin: Congressional Quarterly
Kagan, Daniel: United Press International
Kammer, Jerry: Copley News Service
Kampeas, Ron: Associated Press
Kanno, Michiyo: Tokyo-Chunichi Shimbun
Kaplan, Peter: Reuters
Kapochunas, Rachel: San Francisco Chronicle
Karey, Gerald: Platts News Service
Kashiyama, Yukio: Sankei Shimbun
Kassou, Abderrahmane: Maghreb Arabe Presse
Kastner, Kevin: Market News International
Kawano, Toshifumi: Mainichi Shimbun
Keefe, Stephen: Nikkei
Keen, Judith: USA Today
Keeter, Hunter: Defense Daily
Kelley, Jack: USA Today
Kelley, Matt: Omaha World Herald
Kelley, Matthew: Associated Press
Kellogg, Sarah: Newhouse News Service
Kelly, Dennis: USA Today
Kelly, Erin: Gannett News Service
Kelly, Nancy: American Metal Market
Kelotra, Ritu: Congressional Quarterly
Kemper, Robert: Chicago Tribune
Kemper, Vicki: Los Angeles Times
Kendall, Jr., Charles: National News Research Syndicate
Kenen, Joanne: Reuters
Kennedy, Helen: New York Daily News
Kennedy, Simon: Bloomberg News
Kerr, Jennifer: Associated Press
Kertes, Noella: Congressional Quarterly
Kesen, Hideo: Sankei Shimbun
Kessler, Glenn: Washington Post
Kessner, Brennan: Defense Daily
Kesten, Lou: Associated Press
Keto, Laurin: Dow Jones Newswires
Keynes, Alana: Education Daily
Kiely, Kathy: USA Today
Kilian, Michael: Chicago Tribune
Kim, Eun Kyung: Associated Press
King, Ledyard S.R.: Gannett News Service
King, Llewellyn: Energy Daily
King, Jr., Neil: Wall Street Journal
King, Peter: Congressional Quarterly
Kingdom, Arthur: Restructuring Today
Kinoshita, Hideomi: Kyodo News
Kipling, Bogdan: Kipling News Service
Kirchhoff, Sue: USA Today
Kirkland, Michael: United Press International
Kirsanov, Dmitry: Itar-Tass News Agency
Kishida, Yoshida: Jiji Press
Kivlan, Terence: Newhouse News Service
Klein Jr., Gilbert: Media General News Service
Kline, Alan: American Banker
Kniazkov, Maxim: Agence France-Presse
Knowlton, Brian: International Herald Tribune
Knox, Olivier: Agence France-Presse
Koar, Juergen: Stuttgarter Zeitung
Koff, Stephen: Cleveland Plain Dealer
Koffler, Keith: CongressDaily
Kogure, Satoko: Jiji Press
Kohn, Francis: Agence France-Presse
Komori, Yoshihisa: Sankei Shimbun
Koning, Rachel: CBS MarketWatch
Kopecki, Dawn: Dow Jones Newswires
Koring, Paul: Toronto Globe and Mail
Kornblut, Anne: Boston Globe
Kosukegawa, Yoichi: Kyodo News
Koydl, Wolfgang: Sueddeutsche Zeitung
Kralev, Nicholas: Washington Times
Kramer, Reed: AllAfrica.com
Kranish, Michael: Boston Globe
Krawzak, Paul: Copley News Service
Krebs, Brian: WashingtonPost.com
Kreisher, Otto: Copley News Service
Krim, Jonathan: Washington Post
Krishnaswami, Sridhara: Hindu
Kronholz, June: Wall Street Journal
Kuckro, Rod: Oil Daily
Kuhnhenn, James: Knight Ridder
Kuk, Kiyon: Segye Times
Kulish, Nicholas: Wall Street Journal
Kumar, Aparna: Associate Press
Kumar, Dinesh: Communications Daily
Kumode, Mitsura: Tokyo-Chunichi Shimbun
Kuntz, Philip: Wall Street Journal
Kuo, Wu-hueng: Central News Agency
Kwon, Soon-Taek: Korea Dong-A Ilbo
Kyan, Seiko: Kyodo News
La Franchi, Howard: Christian Science Monitor
Labaton, Stephen: New York Times
Labriny, Azeddine: Saudi Press Agency
Lagomarsino, Deborah: Dow Jones Newswires
Lakely, James: Washington Times
Lamb, David: Los Angeles Times
Lambrecht, William: St. Louis Post-Dispatch
Lambro, Donald: Washington Times
Landay, Jonathan: Knight Ridder
Landers, James: Dallas Morning News
Landry, Catherine: Platts News Service
Lane, Earl: Newsday
Lane, Terry: Communications Daily
Lang, Michael: Asahi Shimbun

MEMBERS ENTITLED TO ADMISSION—Continued

Lanman, Scott: Bloomberg News
Lardner, George: Washington Post
LaRoue, Jr., James: Congressional Information Bureau
Lavin, Carl: New York Times
Lawrence, Jill: USA Today
Le Roux, Gildas: Agence France-Presse
Leary, Warren: New York Times
Leavitt, Paul: USA Today
Lebedev, Ivan: Itar-Tass News Agency
Lebling, Madonna: Washington Post
Lee, Christopher: Washington Post
Lee, Hyo-joon: Joong Ang Ilbo
Lee, Jennifer: New York Times
Lee, Matthew: Agence France-Presse
Lee, Mi Sook: Munwha Ilbo
Lee, Richard: Media General News Service
Lee, Seung Chull: Kyung Hyang Shinmun
Leen, Jeff: Washington Post
Lehming, Malte: Der Tagesspiegel
Leinwand, Donna: USA Today
Leland, Jennifer: Tokyo-Chunichi Shimbun
Lemke, Tim: Washington Times
Leonard, Mary: Boston Globe
Lerman, David: Newport News Daily Press
Lesparre, Michael: Roll Call Report Syndicate
Lester, William: Associated Press
Leubsdorf, Carl: Dallas Morning News
Lever, Robert: Agence France-Presse
Levin, Alan: USA Today
Lewis, Charles: Hearst Newspapers
Lewis, Finlay: Copley News Service
Lewis, Katherine: Dallas Morning News
Lewis, Katherine: Newhouse News Service
Lewis, Neil: New York Times
Li, Zhengxin: China Economic Daily
Libbon, Mark: Syracuse Post-Standard
Lichtblau, Eric: New York Times
Lieberman, Brett: Harrisburg Patriot-News
Lightman, David: Hartford Courant
Lin, Betty: World Journal
Lindell, Chuck: Austin American Statesman
Linder, Craig: States News Service
Lindsey, David: USA Today
Ling, Christina: Reuters
Lipman, Laurence: Palm Beach Post
Little, Robert: Baltimore Sun
Litvan, Laura: Bloomberg News
Liu, Ping: China Times
Liu, Kuen-yuan: Central News Agency
Lizama, Orlando: EFE News Services
Lobe, James: Inter Press Service
Lobsenz, George: Energy Daily
Lochhead, Carolyn: San Francisco Chronicle
Locy, Toni: USA Today
Logan, Christopher: Congressional Quarterly
Logan, Rebecca: EFE News Services
Lohmeyer, Suzette: WashingtonPost.com
Long, Drew: LRP Publications
Lopez, Jose: Notimex Mexican Newsm Agency
Loren, Jennifer: Associated Press
Lorente, Rafael: South Florida Sun-Sentinel
Louven, Alexandra: Boersen-Zeitung
Lowrey, Dan: Dow Jones Newswires
Lowy, Joan: Scripps Howard News Service
Lueck, Sarah: Wall Street Journal
Lumpkin, John: Associated Press
Lyons, Johnathan: Reuters
Lytle, Tamara: Orlando Sentinel
MacDonald, David: McClendon News Service
MacDonald, John: Hartford Courant
MacFarland, Margo: CongressDaily
MacInnis, Laura: Reuters
MacMillan, Robert: WashingtonPost.com
MacPhersen, Karen: Pittsburgh Post-Gazette
Machacek, John: Gannett News Service
Mackenzie, Hillary: Southam News of Canada
Madden, Mike: Gannett News Service
Majano, Rosendo: EFE News Services
Malone, Julia: Cox Newspapers
Maloy, Timothy: United Press International
Malseed, Mark: Washington Post
Mann, William: Associated Press
Mannion, James: Agence France-Presse
Mao, Lei: Xinhua News Agency
Marano, Louis: United Press International
Marchand, Ann: WashingtonPost.com
Marchi, Stefano: Il Tempo
Marcus, Jeffrey: WashingtonPost.com
Marcus, Ruth: Washington Post
Marcy, Steven: Energy Argus
Margasak, Lawrence: Associated Press
Marino, Marie: Gannett News Service
Marklein, Mary Beth: USA Today
Markoe, Lauren: Columbia State
Marlantes, Elizabeth: Christian Science Monitor
Marley, Jefferson: WashingtonPost.com
Marolo, Bruno: L'Unita
Marquis, Christopher: New York Times
Marshall, Stephen: USAToday.com
Martin, Gary: San Antonio Express-News
Martin, Harold: United Press International
Martinez, Gebe: Congressional Quarterly
Martinez, Pablo Sandino: La Nacion USA
Mason, Julie: Houston Chronicle
Massie, Alex: Edinburgh Scotsman
Masterson, Karen: Houston Chronicle
Matsui, Masanori: Nikkei
Matthews, Mark: Baltimore Sun
Matthews, Robert Guy: Wall Street Journal
Matusic, Karen: Oil Daily
Mayer, Caroline: Washington Post
Maymi, Javier: El Vocero de Puerto Rico
Maynard, Michael: CBS MarketWatch
McCaffrey, Shannon: Knight Ridder

MEMBERS ENTITLED TO ADMISSION—Continued

McCarthy, Mike: German Press Agency/DPA
McCarthy, Thomas: Los Angeles Times
McCarty, Philip: Dow Jones Newswires
McCaslin, John: Washington Times
McCord, Nancy: Financial Times
McCrehan, Jeff: Christian Science Monitor
McCutcheon, Chuck: Newhouse News Service
McDonough, Siobhan: Associated Press
McDowell, Julie: Energy Argus
McFeatters, Ann: Pittsburgh Post-Gazette
McFeatters, Dale: Scripps Howard News Service
McGee, Frank: Congressional Quarterly
McGinley, Laurie: Wall Street Journal
McGregor, Deborah: Financial Times
McGrory, Mary: Washington Post
McGuire, David: WashingtonPost.com
McIntyre, Allison: Los Angeles Times
McKeaney, Kristy: Bloomberg News
McKee, Michael: Bloomberg News
McKenna, Barrie: Toronto Globe and Mail
McKinnon, John: Wall Street Journal
McLean, Renwick: New York Times
McLoone, Sharon: National Journal's Technology Daily
McManus, Doyle: Los Angeles Times
McMurray, Jeffrey: Associated Press
McNeil, Margaret: CBS MarketWatch
McQuaid, John: New Orleans Times-Picayune
McQuillan, Laurence: USA Today
McQuillan, Mark: Bloomberg News
Meadows, Clifton: New York Times
Means, Marianne: Hearst Newspapers
Mears, Frances: Gannett News Service
Meckler, Laura: Associated Press
Meddis, Saverio: USAToday.com
Meek, James: New York Daily News
Meinert, Dori: Copley News Service
Mekay, Emad: Inter Press Service
Melendez, Michele: Newhouse News Service
Memmott, Mark: USA Today
Mentzer, Thomas: Scripps Howard News Service
Mercer, Marsha: Media General News Service
Merida, Kevin: Washington Post
Merline, John: USA Today
Meszoly, Robin: Bloomberg News
Meyer, Joshua: Los Angeles Times
Michaels, Jim: USA Today
Michalski, Patty: USAToday.com
Middleton, Chris: Market News International
Middleton, Otesa: Dow Jones Newswires
Miga, Andrew: Boston Herald
Mikkelsen, Randall: Reuters
Milbank, Dana: Washington Post
Miller, Alan: Los Angeles Times
Miller, David: Congressional Quarterly
Miller, Greg: Los Angeles Times
Miller, Jeff: Allentown Morning Call
Miller, Judith: New York Times
Miller, Kevin: Bloomberg News
Miller, Leslie: Associated Press
Miller, Marilee: Congressional Quarterly
Miller, Steven: Washington Times
Miller, Todd: Kyodo News
Millership, Peter: Reuters
Milligan, Susan: Boston Globe
Millikan, Jay: Congressional Quarterly
Mills, Betty: Griffin-Larrabee News Service
Mills, Michael: Congressional Quarterly
Mitchell, Brian: Investor's Business Daily
Mitchell, Charles: CongressDaily
Mitchell, Kirsten: Media General News Service
Mitchell, Steve: United Press International
Mitkevicius, Adom: Asahi Shimbun
Mittelstadt, Michelle: Dallas Morning News
Mitton, Roger: Singapore Straits Times
Miura, Toshiaki: Asahi Shimbun
Miyasaka, Yoshio: Kyodo News
Mizushima, Toshio: Yomiuri Shimbun
Mohammed, Arshad: Reuters
Molenkamp, Sarah: Congressional Quarterly
Mollison, Andrew: Cox Newspapers
Monahan, Elaine: London Times
Mondics, Christopher: Philadelphia Inquirer
Moniz, Dave: USA Today
Monoson, Theodore: Casper Star-Tribune
Montgomery, Christine: USAToday.com
Montgomery, David: Fort Worth Star-Telegram
Montgomery, David: Washington Post
Montgomery, Scott: Congressional Quarterly
Moon, Julie: US-Asian News Service
Morgan, Dan: Washington Post
Moriarty, JoAnn: Newhouse News Service
Moritsugu, Ken: Knight Ridder
Moriyasu, Ken: Nikkei
Morris, James: Dallas Morning News
Morris, Vincent: New York Post
Morrison, Blake: USA Today
Morrison, James: Washington Times
Morrison, Joanne: Reuters
Moscoso, Eunice: Cox Newspapers
Moss, Desda: CongressDaily
Mueller, Mark: Energy Argus
Mueller, Sarah: Newsday
Mueller, Thomas: German Press Agency/DPA
Mulkern, Anne: Denver Post
Mulligan, John: Providence Journal
Munoz, Acebes Cesar: EFE News Services
Murata, Junichi: Jiji Press
Murayama, Tomohiro: Asahi Shimbun
Murdock, Deroy: Scripps Howard News Service
Murray, Brendan: Bloomberg News
Murray, Frank: Washington Times
Murray, Shailagh: Wall Street Journal
Murray, Shanon: Daily Deal

MEMBERS ENTITLED TO ADMISSION—Continued

Murray, William: Bloomberg News
Music, Kimberley: Oil Daily
Mussenden, Sean: Orlando Sentinel
Myers, Jim: Tulsa World
Myers, Michael: Myers News Service
N'Diaye, Yali: Market News International
Nacheman, Allen: Agence France-Presse
Nagata, Kazuo: Yomiuri Shimbun
Nagourney, Adam: New York Times
Nail, Dawson: Communications Daily
Nakajima, Tetsuo: Mainichi Shimbun
Nakamura, Hiroko: Yomiuri Shimbun
Nakano, Tetsuya: Jiji Press
Narayanan, Vinuraj: USA Today
Nasso, Laura: Il Corriere Della Sera
Nather, David: Congressional Quarterly
Neal, Terry: WashingtonPost.com
Neergaard, Lauran: Associated Press
Neikirk, William: Chicago Tribune
Nelson, Deborah: Los Angeles Times
Nelson Fitzhugh, Soni: United Press International
Nesmith, Jeff: Cox Newspapers
Neubauer, Chuck: Los Angeles Times
Neuman, Johanna: Los Angeles Times
New, Kevin: Medical Device Daily
New, William: National Journal's Technology Daily
Newman, Emily: Bond Buyer
Nicholas, Peter: Philadelphia Inquirer
Nichols, Bill: USA Today
Nichols, John: WashingtonPost.com
Nicholson, Jonathan: Reuters
Niehaus, Wanita: Scripps Howard News Service
Nielsen, David: Scripps Howard News Service
Nishimura, Yoichi: Asahi Shimbun
Niven, Michael: Energy Argus
Nomiyama, Chizu: Reuters
Nordness, Anne: Congressional Quarterly
Norman, Jane: Des Moines Register
Norton, C. JoAnne: Bloomberg News
Norton, Monica: Newsday
Norton, Stephen: Congressional Quarterly
Norville, Lancelot: Associated Press
Novak, Robert: Chicago Sun-Times
Nutting, Brian: Congressional Quarterly
Nutting, Rex: CBS MarketWatch
Nyitray, Joseph: Congressional Quarterly
O'Brien, Nancy: Catholic News Service
O'Connell, James: Bloomberg News
O'Donnell, Jayne: USA Today
O'Donnell Jr., John: Baltimore Sun
O'Keefe, Mark: Newhouse News Service
O'Reilly II, Joseph: Bloomberg News
O'Rourke, Lawrence: McClatchy Newspapers
O'Sullivan, John: United Press International
O'Toole, Thomas: USA Today
Oelrich, Christiane: German Press Agency/DPA
Oestreicher-Gross, Jill: Reuters
Ogata, Kakuya: Kyodo News
Oh, Diane: Asahi Shimbun
Olchowy, Mark: Associated Press
Oliphant, Cortright: Oliphant News Service
Oliphant, Robert: Oliphant News Service
Oliphant, Thomas: Boston Globe
Olmsted, Daniel: United Press International
Olson, Elizabeth: New York Times
Oppel, Richard: New York Times
Orin, Deborah: New York Post
Orndorff, Mary: Birmingham News
Orol, Ron: Daily Deal
Orr, J. Scott: Newark Star-Ledger
Oshima, Uichiro: Tokyo-Chunichi Shimbun
Ostermann, Dietmar: Frankfurter Rundschau
Ota, Alan: Congressional Quarterly
Ota, Masakatsu: Kyodo News
Ottaway, David: Washington Post
Ourlian, Robert: CongressDaily
Overberg, Paul: USA Today
Pace, Anthony: Associated Press
Pace, David: Associated Press
Page, Clarence: Chicago Tribune
Page, Susan: USA Today
Pallotto, Adam: Congressional Quarterly
Palmer, Doug: Reuters
Palo, Vanessa: Associated Press
Parasuram, T.V.: Press Trust of India
Pardue, Douglas: USA Today
Parker, Laura: USA Today
Parks, Daniel: Congressional Quarterly
Parry, Robert: Bloomberg News
Pasternak, Judy: Los Angeles Times
Patrick, Robert: Los Angeles Times
Patrick, Steven: Congressional Quarterly
Pattison, Mark: Catholic News Service
Patton, Scott: Oil Daily
Peacock, Steve: Communications Daily
Pear, Robert: New York Times
Pearlstein, Steven: Washington Post
Peck, Louis: CongressDaily
Pelofsky, Jeremy: Reuters
Pena, Maria: EFE News Services
Pennybacker, Mary: Associated Press
Perine, Keith: Congressional Quarterly
Pesce, Carolyn: USA Today
Petersen, Rosemary: Copley News Service
Peterson, Jonathan: Los Angeles Times
Peterson, Karen: USA Today
Peterson, Margaret: National Journal's Technology Daily
Pfleger, Katherine: Seattle Times
Phelps, Timothy: Newsday
Phillips, Don: Washington Post
Phillips, Heather: San Jose Mercury News
Phillips, Michael: Wall Street Journal
Philpott, Thomas: Military Update

MEMBERS ENTITLED TO ADMISSION—Continued

Pianin, Eric: Washington Post
Pickler, Nedra: Associated Press
Pike, David: Los Angeles Daily Journal
Pincus, Walter: Washington Post
Pine, Art: Bloomberg News
Pino-Marina, Christina: WashingtonPost.com
Platero, Mario Calvo: Il Sole 24 Ore
Pleming, Susan: Reuters
Plocek, Joseph: Market News International
Plungis, Jeff: Detroit News
Poirier, John: Reuters
Polyakova, Susan: Communications Daily
Pontarelli, Erika: Agence France-Presse
Poole, Janet: Agence France-Presse
Pope, Charles: Seattle Post-Intelligencer
Posner, Michael: CongressDaily
Povich, Elaine: Newsday
Powell, Stewart: Hearst Newspapers
Powelson, Richard: Scripps Howard News Service
Power, Stephen: Wall Street Journal
Powers, Ronald: Associated Press
Price, Deborah: Detroit News
Price, Elizabeth: Dow Jones Newswires
Price, Marc: Associated Press
Priest, Dana: Washington Post
Prothero, P. Mitchell: United Press International
Pruden, Wesley: Washington Times
Pruitt, Phil: USAToday.com
Przybyla, Heidi: Bloomberg News
Puchol, Fernando: EFE News Services
Puente, Maria: USA Today
Puertas, Jose: Agence France-Presse
Pugh, Anthony: Knight Ridder
Purce, Melinda: Associated Press
Purdum, Todd: New York Times
Purger, Tibor: Magyar Szo
Pusey, Allen: Dallas Morning News
Putman, Eileen: Associated Press
Putrich, Gayle: Congressional Quarterly
Puzzanghera, James: San Jose Mercury News
Pylas, Panagiotis: AFX News
Quaid, Libby: Associated Press
Raab, Charlotte: Agence France-Presse
Raasch, Charles: Gannett News Service
Radelat, Ana: Gannett News Service
Raffaelli, Jean: Agence France-Presse
Raimon, Marcelo: ANSA Italian News Agency
Raivio, Jyri: Helsingin Sanomat
Ramadan, Wafik: L'Orient—Le Jour
Rambourg, Gersende: Agence France-Presse
Ramey, Joanna: Fairchild News Service
Ramjug, Peter: Reuters
Ramstack, Thomas: Washington Times
Rankin, Robert: Knight Ridder
Rapp, David: Congressional Quarterly
Rater, Philippe: Agence France-Presse
Raum, Thomas: Associated Press
Rauscher, Jr., Carl: Cox Newspapers
Ray, Eric: Congressional Quarterly
Raymond, Anthony: Political Money Line
Rebello, Joseph: Dow Jones Newswires
Reber, Paticia: German Press Agency/DPA
Recer, Paul: Associated Press
Recio, Maria: Fort Worth Star-Telegram
Reddy, Anitha: Washington Post
Reeves, Pamela: Scripps Howard News Service
Rega, John: Bloomberg News
Rehm, Barbara: American Banker
Rehring, Emily: Oil Daily
Rehrmann, Laura: Gannett News Service
Reid, Tim: London Times
Reilly, Sean: Mobile Register
Reinert-Mason, Patty: Houston Chronicle
Reiss, Cory: New York Times Regional News
Remez, Michael: Hartford Courant
Rennie, David: London Daily Telegraph
Retter, Daphne: Congressional Quarterly
Reynard, Pascal: Agence France-Presse
Reynolds, Maura: Los Angeles Times
Riccardi, Emenuele: ANSA Italian News Agency
Rich, Spencer: CongressDaily
Richardson, Betty: Congressional Quarterly
Riche, Pascal: Liberation
Richey, Warren: Christian Science Monitor
Richter, Joseph: Bloomberg News
Richter, Paul: Los Angeles Times
Richwine, Lisa: Reuters
Rickett, Keith: Associated Press
Ricks, Tom: Washington Post
Riddell, Jr., John: Associated Press
Riechmann-Kepler, Deb: Associated Press
Riehl, Jonathan: Congressional Quarterly
Riley, John: USAToday.com
Rios, Delia: Newhouse News Service
Risen, James: New York Times
Riskind, Jonathan: Columbus Dispatch
Risser, William: USA Today
Rivero, Maria Isabel: German Press Agency/DPA
Rizzo, Katherine: Congressional Quarterly
Robb, Greg: AFX News
Robbins, Carla: Wall Street Journal
Roberts III, William: Bloomberg News
Robinson, James: Los Angeles Times
Robinson, John: Defense Daily
Robinson, Melissa: Associated Press
Robinson, Stuart: Congressional Quarterly
Roff, Peter: United Press International
Rogers, David: Wall Street Journal
Roland, Neil: Bloomberg News
Rosales, Jorge: La Nacion
Rose, Alexander: National Post
Rosen, James: McClatchy Newspapers
Rosenbaum, David: New York Times
Rosenberg, Eric: Hearst Newspapers

MEMBERS ENTITLED TO ADMISSION—Continued

Rosenkrantz, Holly: Bloomberg News
Rosenstein, Bruce: USA Today
Rosenthal, Harry: Associated Press
Ross, Patrick: Communications Daily
Ross, Sonya: Associated Press
Roth, Bennett: Houston Chronicle
Roth, Susan: Gannett News Service
Rousseaux, Charles: Washington Times
Rovner, Julie: CongressDaily
Rowley, James: Bloomberg News
Roybal, Peter: Congressional Quarterly
Rubin, Hannah: Education Daily
Rubin, James: Bloomberg News
Rucker, Teri: National Journal's Technology Daily
Rudell, Brent: Congressional Quarterly
Ruiz, Phillip: Los Angeles Times
Rulon, Malia: Associated Press
Runningen, Roger: Bloomberg News
Ruskin, Liz: Anchorage Daily News
Ryan, Richard: Detroit News
Ryan, Timothy: Reuters
Safire, William: New York Times
Saiyid, Amena: Energy Argus
Sakai, Katushiko: Jiji Press
Sakajiri, Nobuyoshi: Asahi Shimbun
Salant, Jonathan: Associated Press
Salhani, Claude: United Press International
Sammon, William: Washington Times
Sanchez, Humberto: Bond Buyer
Sandalow, Marc: San Francisco Chronicle
Sanders, Edmund: Los Angeles Times
Sands, David: Washington Times
Sanger, David: New York Times
Santana, Tamra: Bloomberg News
Santini, Jean-Louis: Agence France-Presse
Sarasohn, Judy: Washington Post
Sasazawa, Kyoichi: Yomiuri Shimbun
Satariano, Adam: Congressional Quarterly
Sato, Chiyako: Mainichi Shimbun
Saunders, John: Toronto Globe and Mail
Savage, David: Los Angeles Times
Sawaki, Nori: Tokyo-Chunichi Shimbun
Sawyer, Jon: St. Louis Post-Dispatch
Scally, William: William Scally Reports
Scarborough, Rowan: Washington Times
Schatz, Joseph: Congressional Quarterly
Scheibel, Kenneth: Washington Bureau News
Schemo, Diana: New York Times
Schlesinger, Jacob: Wall Street Journal
Schlesinger, Robert: Boston Globe
Schmick, Bill: Bloomberg News
Schmid, Randolph: Associated Press
Schmid, Sharon: Wall Street Journal
Schmidt, Peter: Chronicle of Higher Education
Schmidt, Robert: Bloomberg News
Schmitt, Eric: New York Times
Schmitt, Richard: Los Angeles Times
Schnakenberg, Lea Ann: German Press Agency/DPA
Schneider, Andrew: St. Louis Post-Dispatch
Schneider, Greg: Washington Post
Schoof, Renee: Knight Ridder
Schouten, Fredreka: Gannett News Service
Schrader, Esther: Los Angeles Times
Schram, Martin: Scripps Howard News Service
Schroeder, Michael: Wall Street Journal
Schuler, Kate: Congressional Quarterly
Schwartz, Leland: States News Service
Schwed, Craig: Gannett News Service
Schweid, Barry: Associated Press
Scott, Heather: Market News International
Scott, Katherine: Gannett News Service
Scrivo, Karen: CongressDaily
Seelye, Katharine: New York Times
Seeman, Bruce: Newhouse News Service
Sefton, Dru: Newhouse News Service
Seib, Gerald: Wall Street Journal
Seiberg, Jaret: Daily Deal
Selingo, Jeffrey: Chronicle of Higher Education
Seper, Jerry: Washington Times
Sergent, Jennifer: Scripps Howard News Service
Serrano, Richard: Los Angeles Times
Settles, Mary: McClatchy Newspapers
Sevastopulo, Demetri: Financial Times
Shaffrey, Mary: Washington Times
Shalal-Esa, Andrea: Reuters
Shanker, Thomas: New York Times
Shapiro, Walter: USA Today
Sharn, Lori: CongressDaily
Shaw, Gwyneth: Orlando Sentinel
Shaw, John: Market News International
Shea, Griffin: Agence France-Presse
Shearer, Cody: Shearer and Glen News
Sheehan, Theresa: Market News International
Sheikh, Nezar: Saudi Press Agency
Shek, Katherine: LRP Publications
Shelly, Nedra: Cleveland Plain Dealer
Shenon, Philip: New York Times
Shepard, Scott: Cox Newspapers
Sher, Andrew: Chattanooga Times/Free Press
Sherman, Mark: Associated Press
Sherry, Mike: Congressional Quarterly
Sherzai, Magan: Agence France-Presse
Shesgreen, Deirdre: St. Louis Post-Dispatch
Shibata, Gaku: Yomiuri Shimbun
Shields, Mark: Creators Syndicate
Shimada, Testsuya: Kyodo News
Shiver, Jr., Jube: Los Angeles Times
Shogren, Elizabeth: Los Angeles Times
Shoup, Megan: Asahi Shimbun
Sia, Richard: CongressDaily
Sichelman, Lew: United Media
Siciliano, John: Saudi Press Agency
Sigurdson, Todd: Associated Press

MEMBERS ENTITLED TO ADMISSION—Continued

Silva, Rodrigo: Associated Press
Silvassy, Kathleen: Congressional Quarterly
Silverstein, Kenneth: Los Angeles Times
Simison, Robert: Bloomberg News
Simmons Robinson, Deborah: Washington Times
Simon, Richard: Los Angeles Times
Simpson, Cam: Chicago Tribune
Singer, Paul: Chicago Tribune
Sipher, Anthony: Yomiuri Shimbun
Sirhal, Maureen: National Journal's Technology Daily
Sisk, Richard: New York Daily News
Sitov, Andrei: Itar-Tass News Agency
Skarzenski, Ronald: New York Times
Skiba, Katherine: Milwaukee Journal Sentinel
Skorneck, Carolyn: Congressional Quarterly
Skrzycki, Cindy: Washington Post
Slater, Jim: Agence France-Presse
Slavin, Barbara: USA Today
Smith, Christopher: Salt Lake Tribune
Smith, Donna: Reuters
Smith, Elliot: USA Today
Smith, Jeffrey: Washington Post
Smith, Sylvia: Ft. Wayne Journal Gazette
Smith, Tiffany: USA Today
Smitherman, Laura: Bloomberg News
Snider, Keith: Bloomberg News
Snider, Mike: USA Today
Sniffen, Michael: Associated Press
Snyder, Charles: Taipei Times
Sobczyk, Joseph: Bloomberg News
Solis Jr., Carlos: Jiji Press
Solomon, Deborah: Wall Street Journal
Solomon, John: Associated Press
Somerville, Glenn: Reuters
Soraghan, Michael: Denver Post
Sorokin, Ellen: Washington Times
Sorrells, Niels: Congressional Quarterly
Sotero, Paulo: O Estado De S. Paulo
Southwell, Charles: Congressional Quarterly
Spang, Thomas: Rheinische Post
Sparshott, Jeffrey: Washington Times
Spence, Timothy: Hearst Newspapers
Spencer, George: Restructuring Today
Sperry, Paul: WorldNetDaily.com
Spiegel, Peter: Financial Times
Spinner, Jackie: Washington Post
Spors, Kelly: Wall Street Journal
Sprengelmeyer, Michael: Scripps Howard News Service
Squitieri, Tom: USA Today
St. Onge, Jeffery: Bloomberg News
Stainer, M. Maria: Washington Times
Standeford, Dugie: Communications Daily
Stanglin, Douglas: USA Today
Stanton, John: CongressDaily
Starks, Tim: New York Sun
Staub, Ignaz: Tages Anzeiger
Stearns, Matthew: Kansas City Star
Steele, Stephen: Catholic News Service
Steiger, Jana: Congressional Quarterly
Stein, Jeff: Congressional Quarterly
Stempleman, Neil: Reuters
Stephens, Joe: Washington Post
Stern, Christopher: Washington Post
Stern, Marcus: Copley News Service
Sternberg, Steve: USA Today
Sternberg, William: USA Today
Stevens, Allison: Congressional Quarterly
Stevenson, Johnny: Wall Street Journal
Stevenson, Richard: New York Times
Stewart, B. Scott: Sankei Shimbun
Stinson, Jeffrey: USA Today
Stohr, Greg: Bloomberg News
Stolberg, Sheryl: New York Times
Stolley, Anne Marie: Bloomberg News
Stone, Andrea: USA Today
Storey, David: Reuters
Stoullig, Jean-Michel: Agence France-Presse
Stout, David: New York Times
Straub, Bill: Scripps Howard News Service
Straub, Noelle: Boston Herald
Straw, Joseph: New Haven Register
Streck, Michael: Die Tageszeitung
Strobel, Warren: Knight Ridder
Strong, Thomas: Associated Press
Strope, Leigh: Associated Press
Struck, Myron: States News Service
Sudyatmiko, Karina: Suara Pembaruan
Suissa Zeimet, Corinne: Agence France-Presse
Sujono, Djono: Suara Merdeka
Sullivan, Andy: Reuters
Sullivan, Jack: Associated Press
Sullivan, Laura: Baltimore Sun
Sumikawa, Yuriko: Kyodo News
Sunohara, Tsuyoshi: Nikkei
Supervielle, Ana Baron: Clarin
Superville, Darlene: Associated Press
Surzhanskiy, Andrey: Itar-Tass News Agency
Sutherland, Rita: Scripps Howard News Service
Swarns, Rachel: New York Times
Sweet, Lynn: Chicago Sun-Times
Swindell, Bill: Congressional Quarterly
Swisher, Lawrence: Northwest Newspapers
Szekely, Peter: Reuters
Tackett, R. Michael: Chicago Tribune
Takahashi, Akira: Kyodo News
Takegawa, Masanori: Mainichi Shimbun
Takeuchi, Takeshi: Dow Jones Newswires
Tan, Weibing: Xinhua News Agency
Tan, Xinmu: Xinhua News Agency
Tanzi, Alexandre: Bloomberg News
Taylor, Andrew: Congressional Quarterly
Taylor, Cynthia: Boston Globe

MEMBERS ENTITLED TO ADMISSION—Continued

Tedards, Frank: Cox Newspapers
Temman, Francis: Agence France-Presse
Terzian, Philip: Providence Journal
Tetreault, Stephan: Stephens Media Group
Theimer, Sharon: Associated Press
Thomas, Helen: Hearst Newspapers
Thomas, Karen: USA Today
Thomas, Richard: Roll Call Report Syndicate
Thomasson, Dan: Scripps Howard News Service
Thomma, Steven: Knight Ridder
Thompson, Alan: Scripps Howard News Service
Thompson, Jake: Omaha World-Herald
Thompson, Jason: WashingtonPost.com
Thompson, Laura: American Banker
Thorn, Willy: Catholic News Service
Thornburg, Ryan: WashingtonPost.com
Thyfault, Mary: CongressDaily
Tierney, John: New York Times
Tilove, Jonathan: Newhouse News Service
Timberg, Robert: Baltimore Sun
Timberlake, Jeanene: Communications Daily
Timmons, Karen: Scripps Howard News Service
Tinsley, Elisa: USA Today
Toedtman, James: Newsday
Togasawa, Hidetoshi: Mainichi Shimbun
Tokito, Mineko: Yomiuri Shimbun
Toles, Tom: Washington Post
Tomkin, Robert: Congressional Quarterly
Tomkins, Richard: United Press International
Tomson, Bill: Oster Dow Jones
Toner, Robin: New York Times
Toppo, Gregory: USA Today
Torobin, Jeremy: Congressional Quarterly
Torres, Carlos: Bloomberg News
Torres, Craig: Bloomberg News
Torry, Jack: Columbus Dispatch
Torry, Saundra: USA Today
Toshi, Eiji: Jiji Press
Totten, Russell: Yomiuri Shimbun
Toyoda, Yochi: Tokyo-Chunichi Shimbun
Toyokazu, Kondo: Sankei Shimbun
Trott, Nancy: Associated Press
Trott, William: Reuters
Truslow, Hugh: New York Times
Tsao, Yu Fen: Liberty Times
Tumulty, Brian: Gannett News Service
Tunks, Larry: Congressional Quarterly
Turner, Douglas: Buffalo News
Tyler, Patrick: New York Times
Tyson, Ann Scott: Christian Science Monitor
Tyson, James: Bloomberg News
Ullmann, Owen: USA Today
Urban, Peter: Connecticut Post
Urbanski, Kara: LRP Publications
Vadum, Matthew: Bond Buyer
Vaida, Bara: National Journal's Technology Daily
Val Mitjavila: Eusebio, La VanGuardia
Valbrun, Marjorie: Wall Street Journal
van der Linden, Frank: United States Press
Vande Hei, Jim: Washington Post
Vanden Brook, Tom: USA Today
Vander Haar, William: Associated Press
Vanichkin, Pavel: Itar-Tass News Agency
Vasquez, Patricia: Oil Daily
Vaughan, Martin: CongressDaily
Veazey, Walter: Scripps Howard News Service
Vekshin, Alison: Stephens Media Group
Vergano, Dan: USA Today
Viccora, Andrew: LRP Publications
Vicini, James: Reuters
Vidal Liy, Macarena: EFE News Services
Vieth, Warren: Los Angeles Times
Vineys, Kevin: Associated Press
Vise, Dan: Washington Post
Vitucci, Claire: Riverside Press-Enterprise
Vogel, Stephen: Washington Post
Von Drehle, David: Washington Post
Vorman, Julie: Reuters
Waggoner, John: USA Today
Wagman, Robert: Newspaper Enterprise
Wagner, Jr., John: McClatchy Newspapers
Waitz, Nancy: Reuters
Walcott, John: Knight Ridder
Wald, Matthew: New York Times
Walker, Martin: United Press International
Walsh, Bill: New Orleans Times-Picayune
Walsh, Campion: Dow Jones Newswires
Walsh, Edward: Washington Post
Walte, Juan: USA Today
Walton-James, Vickie: Chicago Tribune
Wang, Hong: Epoch Times
Ward, Jon: Washington Times
Warminsky, Joseph: Congressional Quarterly
Warrick, Joby: Washington Post
Washington, Wayne: Boston Globe
Watanabe, Tsutomu: Asahi Shimbun
Watanabe, Yosuke: Kyodo News
Waterman, Shaun: United Press International
Waters, Donald: Associated Press
Watson II, Ripley: Bloomberg News
Watson, Roland: London Times
Watson, Traci: USA Today
Watters, Susan: Fairchild News Service
Watts, William: CBS MarketWatch
Wayne, Leslie: New York Times
Webb, Fletcher: Associated Press
Webb, Thomas: Saint Paul Pioneer Press
Weber, Joseph: Washington Times
Weber, Maya: CongressDaily
Weglarczyk, Bartosz: Gazeta Wyborcza
Wegner, Mark: CongressDaily
Wehrman, Jessica: Scripps Howard News Service
Weintraub, Lisa: Congressional Quarterly
Weiser, Carl: Gannett News Service

MEMBERS ENTITLED TO ADMISSION—Continued

Weisman, Jonathan: Washington Post
Weisman, Steven: New York Times
Weiss, Rick: Washington Post
Welch, James: USA Today
Welch, William: USA Today
Wells, Billie Jean: Gannett News Service
Wells, Robert: Dow Jones Newswires
Wessel, David: Wall Street Journal
West, Paul: Baltimore Sun
Westphal, David: McClatchy Newspapers
Wetzel, Hubert: Financial Times
Wetzstein, Cheryl: Washington Times
Wheeler, Lawrence: Gannett News Service
White, Dina: Chicago Tribune
White, Gordon: Washington Telecommunications
White, Jr., Joseph: Associated Press
White, Keith: CongressDaily
Whitesides, John: Reuters
Whitney, David: McClatchy Newspapers
Whittle, Richard: Dallas Morning News
Wibisono, Christianto: Suara Pembaruan
Wibisono, Jasmine: Suara Pembaruan
Wiessler, David: Reuters
Wigfield, Mark: Dow Jones Newswires
Wiggins, Clayton: Wall Street Journal
Wilke, John: Wall Street Journal
Wilkie, Dana: Copley News Service
Wilkinson, Marian: Sydney Morning Herald
Wilkinson, Mark: Reuters
Willard, Anna: Reuters
Williams, David: Agence France-Presse
Williams, Joelle: Mainichi Shimbun
Williams, Leticia: CBS MarketWatch
Willing, Richard: USA Today
Willman, David: Los Angeles Times
Wilson, Christopher: Reuters
Wilson, Kinsey: USAToday.com
Wilson, Martha: Scripps Howard News Service
Wingfield, Brian: New York Times
Wingfield, Frederick: Associated Press
Winicour, Daniel: Congressional Quarterly
Winkler, Herbert: German Press Agency/DPA
Winski, Joe: Bloomberg News
Witcher, Tim: Agence France-Presse
Witcover, Jules: Baltimore Sun
Witham, Larry: Washington Times
Witt, Howard: Chicago Tribune
Witter, Willis: Washington Times
Wodele, Greta: CongressDaily
Wolf, Jim: Reuters
Wolf, Richard: USA Today
Wolfe, Elizabeth: Associated Press
Wolfe, Kathryn: Congressional Quarterly
Woo, Yee Ling: Congressional Quarterly
Wood, David: Newhouse News Service
Wood, Winston: Wall Street Journal
Woods, Michael: Pittsburgh Post-Gazette
Woodward, Bob: Washington Post
Woutat, Donald: Los Angeles Times
Wright, Gregory: Gannett News Service
Wright, Ivan: Associated Press
Wright, Jonathan: Reuters
Wright, Robin: Los Angeles Times
Wu, Jianyou: Guangming Daily
Wynn, Randall: Congressional Quarterly
Wysocki, Jr., Bernard: Wall Street Journal
Xiao-Jing, Du: China Press
Xinghui, Zhang: China Youth Daily
Yamawaki, Takeshi: Asahi Shimbun
Yan, Feng: Xinhua News Agency
Yancey, Matthew: Associated Press
Yaukey, John: Gannett News Service
Ying, He: Xinhua News Agency
Yoder, Eric: Washington Post
Yoon, Gook-Han: Han-Kyoreh Shinmun
Yoshida, Toru: Nikkei
Yoshitsugu, Hiroshi: Nikkei
Yost, Benjamin: Associated Press
Yost, Pete: Associated Press
Young, Alison: Knight Ridder
Young, Jeffrey: Health News Daily
Young, Samantha: Stephens Media Group
Yu, Xiaokui: Guangming Daily
Yule, Robert: Asahi Shimbun
Yun, Linda: Yomiuri Shimbun
Zabarenko, Deborah: Reuters
Zagaroli, Lisa: Detroit News
Zakaria, Tabassum: Reuters
Zalewski, Witold: Polish Press Agency
Zaneski, Cyril: CongressDaily
Zapor, Patricia: Catholic News Service
Zaro, Erin: Saudi Press Agency
Zeleny, Jeff: Chicago Tribune
Zeller, Frank: German Press Agency/DPA
Zengerle, Patricia: Reuters
Zeranski, Todd: Bloomberg News
Zeuthen, Kasper: Yomiuri Shimbun
Zhang, Mengjun: Science and Technology Daily
Zhao, Guangjun: China Legal Daily
Zhenhua, Wang: Xinhua News Agency
Zhu, Xingfu: Shanghai Wenhui Daily
Ziegler, Julie: Bloomberg News
Zimmerman, Carol: Catholic News Service
Zitner, Aaron: Los Angeles Times
Zoroya, Gregg: USA Today
Zremski, Jerry: Buffalo News
Zuckerbrod, Nancy: Associated Press
Zuckman, Jill: Chicago Tribune

NEWSPAPERS REPRESENTED IN PRESS GALLERIES

House Gallery 225–3945, 225–6722 Senate Gallery 224–0241

ABIM News Agency—(703) 243–2104; 1344 Merrie Ridge Road, McLean VA 22101: Mario Navarro Da Costa.

AFX News—(202) 414–0711; 1015 15th Street, Suite 500, Washington, DC 20005: Abid Aslam, Justin Cole, Corbett Daly, Panagiotis Pylas, Greg Robb.

ANSA Italian News Agency—(202) 628–3317; 1285 National Press Building, Washington, DC 20045: Giampiero Gramaglia, Cristiano Del Riccio, Margery Friesner, Marcelo Raimon, Emenuele Riccardi.

Agence France-Presse—(202) 414–0602; 1015 15th Street, Suite 500, Washington, DC 20005: Patrick Anidjar, Gerard Aziakou, Pascal Barollier, Katherine Beddall, Laura Bonilla, Guy Clavel, Stephen Collinson, Christophe De Roquefeuil, Phillippe Debeusscher, Kenneth Dermota, Jean-Louis Doublet, Brigitte Dusseau, Francisco Ferrari, Claire Gallen, Stephane Ghazarian, Gabrielle Grenz-Marcuse, Stephanie Griffith, Carlos Hamann, Charles Hoskinson, Jr., Daniel Jahn, Maxim Kniazkov, Olivier Knox, Francis Kohn, Gildas Le Roux, Matthew Lee, Robert Lever, James Mannion, Allen Nacheman, Erika Pontarelli, Janet Poole, Jose Puertas, Charlotte Raab, Jean Raffaelli, Gersende Rambourg, Philippe Rater, Pascal Reynard, Jean-Louis Santini, Griffin Shea, Magan Sherzai, Jim Slater, Jean-Michel Stoullig, Francis Temman, David Williams, Tim Witcher, Corinne Suissa Zeimet.

Air Daily—(202) 349–2861; 1700 K Street, Suite 1202, Washington, DC 20006: Martin Coyne.

Akahata—(202) 393–5238; 978 National Press Building, Washington, DC 20045: Seiji Endo, Koji Hamatani.

Albuquerque Journal—(202) 662–7488; 1111 National Press Building, Washington, DC 20045: Michael Coleman.

AllAfrica.com—(202) 546–0777; 920 M Street, SE., Washington, DC 20003: Akwe Amosu, Charles Cobb, Jr., Tamela Hultman, Reed Kramer.

Allentown Morning Call—(202) 824–8216; 1325 G Street, Suite 200, Washington, DC 20005: Jeff Miller.

American Banker—(202) 347–5529; 1325 G Street, Suite 900, Washington, DC 20005: Dean Anason, Rob Blackwell, Todd Davenport, Rob Garver, Michele Heller, Alan Kline, Barbara Rehm, Laura Thompson.

American Metal Market—(202) 393–7750; 943 National Press Building, Washington, DC 20045: Nancy Kelly.

Anchorage Daily News—(202) 383–0007; 420 National Press Building, Washington, DC 20045: Liz Ruskin.

Arizona Republic—(202) 906–8136; 1100 New York Avenue, 2nd Floor, Washington, DC 20005: Billy House.

Arkansas Democrat-Gazette—(202) 662–7690; 1190 National Press Building, Washington, DC 20045: Paul Barton, Kevin Freking.

Artists & Writers Syndicate—(703) 820–4232; 6325 Beachway Drive, Falls Church, VA 22044: Frank Aukofer.

Asahi Shimbun—(202) 783–1000; 1022 National Press Building, Washington, DC 20045: Tsutomu Ishiaia, Michael Lang, Adom Mitkevicius, Toshiaki Miura, Tomohiro Murayama, Yoichi Nishimura, Diane Oh, Nobuyoshi Sakajiri, Megan Shoup, Takeshi Yamawaki, Robert Yule, Tsutomu Watanabe.

Associate Press—(202) 776–9400; 2021 K Street, 6th Floor, Washington, DC 20006: James Abrams, Curt Anderson, Genaro Armas, Laurence Arnold, Jeannine Aversa, Frank Baker, Lolita Baldor, Devlin Barrett, Timothy Bovee, Ted Bridis, Robert Burns, Rebecca Carroll, Connie Cass, Wendy Coache, Dennis Conrad, Martin Crutsinger, Mary Dalrymple, Matthew Daly, Juan Davila, Thomas Delaney, Harry Dunphy, Dee-Ann Durbin, Ronald Edmonds, Jr., David Espo, Jerry Estill, Carole Feldman, Ben Feller, Alan Fram, Daniel Freedman, Frederick Frommer, Robert Furlow, Joseph Galianese, Suzanne Gamboa, Anne Gearan, George Gedda, Robert Gehrke, Emily Gersema, Andreas Gibson, Robert Glass, David Gonzalez, Marcy Gordon, Ken Guggenheim, Heather Gundersen, Sam Hananel, Carl Hartman, Merrill Hartson, H. Josef Hebert, John Heilprin, Earl Hinton, Gina Holland, Christopher Huber, Michael Hughes, David Ho, Jesse Holland, Terence Hunt, Nestor Ikeda, Pauline Jelinek, Sandy Johnson, Lara Jordan, Ron Kampeas, Matthew Kelley, Jennifer Kerr, Lou Kesten, Eun Kyung Kim, Aparna Kumar, William Lester, Jennifer Loren, John Lumpkin, William Mann, Lawrence Margasak, Siobhan McDonough, Jeffrey McMurray, Leslie Miller, Laura Meckler, Lauran Neergaard, Lancelot Norville, Mark Olchowy, Anthony Pace, David Pace, Vanessa Palo, Mary Pennybacker, Nedra Pickler, Ronald Powers, Marc Price, Melinda Purce, Eileen Putman, Libby Quaid, Thomas Raum, Paul Recer, Keith Rickett, John Riddell, Jr., Deb Riechmann-Kepler, Melissa Robinson, Harry Rosenthal, Sonya Ross, Malia Rulon, Jonathan Salant, Randolph Schmid, Barry Schweid, Mark Sherman, Todd Sigurdson, Rodrigo Silva, Michael Sniffen, John Solomon, Thomas Strong, Leigh Strope, Jack Sullivan, Darlene Superville, Sharon Theimer, Nancy Trott, William Vander Haar, Kevin Vineys, Donald Waters, Fletcher Webb,

NEWSPAPERS REPRESENTED—Continued

Joseph White, Jr., Frederick Wingfield, Elizabeth Wolfe, Ivan Wright, Matthew Yancey, Benjamin Yost, Pete Yost, Nancy Zuckerbrod.

Atlanta Journal-Constitution—(202) 887–8380; 400 N. Capitol Street, Suite 750, Washington, DC 20001: George Edmonson, Melanie Eversley.

Austin American Statesman—(202) 887–8329; 400 N. Capitol Street, Suite 750, Washington, DC 20001: Chuck Lindell.

Australian—(202) 628–7079; 446 National Press Building, Washington, DC 20045: Roy Eccleston.

Australian Financial Review—(202) 639–8084; 1331 Pennsylvania Avenue, #904, Washington, DC 20004: Peter Hartcher.

Baltimore Sun—(202) 416–0268; 1627 K Street, Suite 1100, Washington, DC 20006: Susan Baer, Jeffrey Barker, Tom Bowman, Julie Davis, Ellen Gamerman, Gail Gibson, David Greene, Karen Hosler, Robert Little, Mark Matthews, John O'Donnell Jr., Laura Sullivan, Robert Timberg, Paul West, Jules Witcover.

Basler Zeitung—(202) 986–7542; 1526 Corcoran Street, NW., Washington, DC 20009: Lucian Casper.

BioWorld Today—(202) 719–7816; 4301 Connecticut Avenue, Suite 330, Washington, DC 22302: Kim Coghill.

Birmingham News—(202) 383–7837; 1101 Connecticut Avenue, Suite 300, Washington, DC 20036: Mary Orndorff.

Bloomberg News—(202) 624–1847; 1399 New York Avenue, 11th Floor, Washington, DC 20005: Charles Allen III, Alex Canizares, William Arthur, Laurie Asseo, Terrence Barrett, Theresa Barry, Paul Basken, Joshua Baylin, Jeffrey Bliss, Amy Butler, Anthony Capaccio, Sonya Cooper, Patrick Chu, Susan Decker, Vincent Del Giudice, Edward DeMarco, Catherine Dodge, Ryan Donmoyer, Kerry Dooley, Mark Drajem, Bob Drummond, James Efstathiou, Daniel Enoch, Andrew Ferguson, Stephen Geimann, Steve Gettinger, Daniel Goldstein, Vince Golle, Robert Greene, Glenn Hall, Kristen Hallam, Paul Hendrie, John Hughes, Ann Hughey, Kristin Jensen, Glen Justice, Simon Kennedy, Scott Lanman, Laura Litvan, Kristy McKeaney, Michael McKee, Mark McQuillan, Robin Meszoly, Kevin Miller, Brendan Murray, William Murray, C. JoAnne Norton, James O'Connell, Joseph O'Reilly II, Robert Parry, Art Pine, Heidi Przybyla, John Rega, Joseph Richter, William Roberts III, Neil Roland, Holly Rosenkrantz, James Rowley, James Rubin, Roger Runningen, Tamra Santana, Bill Schmick, Robert Schmidt, Robert Simison, Laura Smitherman, Keith Snider, Joseph Sobczyk, Jeffery St. Onge, Greg Stohr, Anne Marie Stolley, Alexandre Tanzi, Carlos Torres, Craig Torres, James Tyson, Ripley Watson II, Joe Winski, Todd Zeranski, Julie Ziegler.

Boersen-Zeitung—(202) 229–0200; 1779 Church Street, Washington, DC 20036: Alexandra Louven.

Bond Buyer—(202) 434–0307; 1325 G Street, Suite 900, Washington, DC 20005: Susanna Duff, Craig Ferris, Lynn Hume, Emily Newman, Humberto Sanchez, Matthew Vadum.

Boston Globe—(202) 857–5050; 1130 Connecticut Avenue, Suite 520, Washington, DC 20036: Peter Canellos, Lyle Denniston, John Donnelly, Steven Glain, Glen Johnson, Anne Kornblut, Michael Kranish, Mary Leonard, Susan Milligan, Thomas Oliphant, Robert Schlesinger, Cynthia Taylor, Wayne Washington.

Boston Herald—(202) 6381796; 988 National Press Building, Washington, DC 20045: Andrew Miga, Noelle Straub.

Buffalo News—(202) 737–3188; 1141 National Press Building, Washington, DC 20045: Douglas Turner, Jerry Zremski.

Capital Connections—(202) 337–2044; 1698 32nd Street, NW., Washington, DC 20007: Karen Feld.

Casper Star-Tribune—(202) 669–6392; 1090 Vermont Avenue, 10th Floor, Washington, DC 20005: Theodore Monoson.

Catholic News Service—(202) 541–3268; 3211 Fourth Street, NE., Washington, DC 20017: Julie Asher, Agostino Bono, Barbara Fraze, Jerome Filteau, Nancy Hartnagel, Nancy O'Brien, Mark Pattison, Stephen Steele, Willy Thorn, Patricia Zapor, Carol Zimmerman.

CBS MarketWatch—(202) 824–0548; 620 National Press Building, Washington, DC 20045: Matt Andrejczak, Jeffrey Bartash, Rachel Koning, Michael Maynard, Margaret McNeil, Rex Nutting, William Watts, Leticia Williams.

Central News Agency—(202) 628–2738; 1173 National Press Building, Washington, DC 20045: Jay Chen, Wu-hueng Kuo, Kuen-yuan Liu.

Charleston (WVA) Daily Mail—(202) 662–8732; 1255 National Press Building, Washington, DC 20045: Karin Fischer.

Charlotte Observer—(202) 383–6057; 700 National Press Building, Washington, DC 20045: Timothy Funk.

Chattanooga Times/Free Press—(202) 662–7651; 1190 National Press Building, Washington, DC 20045: Andrew Sher.

Chicago Sun-Times—(202) 662–8808; 1206 National Press Building, Washington, DC 20045: Robert Novak, Lynn Sweet.

Chicago Tribune—(202) 824–8227; 1325 G Street, Suite 200, Washington, DC 20005: Naftali Bendavid, Mike Dorning, Jan Greenburg, Stephen Hedges, Frank James III, Robert Kemper, Michael Kilian, William Neikirk, Clarence Page, Cam Simpson, Paul Singer, R. Michael Tackett, Vickie Walton-James, Dina White, Howard Witt, Jeff Zeleny, Jill Zuckman.

NEWSPAPERS REPRESENTED—Continued

China Economic Daily—(703) 698–8579; 3305 Crest Haven Court, Falls Church, VA 22042: Zhengxin Li.

China Legal Daily—(703) 413–9251; 2111 Jefferson Davis Hwy #1109-Sth, Arlington, VA 22202: Shaojie Feng, Guangjun Zhao.

China Post—(301) 335–1359; 11750–B Apt. #2231 Old Georgetown, Bethesda, MD 20852: Christopher Cockel.

China Press—(703) 289–6651; 3207 Allen Street, #301, Falls Church, VA 22042: Du Xiao-Jing.

China Times—(202) 347–5670; 952 National Press Building, Washington, DC 20045: Norman Fu, Ping Liu.

China Wen Hui Bao Daily—(703) 521–2371; 1600 S. Eads Street, #1134–N, Arlington, VA 22202: Guihang Ci.

China Youth Daily—(703) 979–6080; 1900 S. Eads St., #1003, Arlington, VA 22202: Zhang Xinghui.

Christian Science Monitor—(202) 785–4400; 910 16th Street, Suite 200, Washington, DC 20006: Faye Bowers, Gail Chaddock, David Cook, Linda Feldmann, Peter Grier, Howard La Franchi, Elizabeth Marlantes, Jeff McCrehan, Warren Richey, Ann Scott Tyson.

Chronicle of Higher Education—(202) 466–1075; 1255 23rd Street, Washington, DC 20037: Michael Arnone, Anne Marie Borrego, Jeffrey Brainard, Stephen Burd, Dan Carnevale, Sara Hebel, Peter Schmidt, Jeffrey Selingo.

Clarin—(202) 737–4850; 539 14th Street Suite 1271, Washington, DC 20045: Ana Baron Supervielle.

Cleveland Plain Dealer—(202) 638–1366; 930 National Press Building, Washington, DC 20045: Elizabeth Auster, Thomas Diemer, Sabrina Eaton, Stephen Koff, Nedra Shelly.

Columbia State—(202) 383–6032; 700 National Press Building, Washington, DC 20045: Lauren Markoe.

Columbus Dispatch—(202) 824–6765; 400 North Capitol Street, Suite 850, Washington, DC 20001: Jonathan Riskind, Jack Torry.

Communications Daily—(202) 872–9200; 2115 Ward Court, Washington, DC 20037: R. Michael Feazel, Mary Greczyn, Brigitte Greenberg, Edith Herman, Dinesh Kumar, Terry Lane, Dawson Nail, Steve Peacock, Susan Polyakova, Patrick Ross, Dugie Standeford, Jeanene Timberlake.

CongressDaily—(202) 261–0385; 1501 M Street, Suite 300, Washington, DC 20005: Pamela Barnett, April Fulton, Bill Ghent, Juliana Gruenwald, Emily Heil, David Hess, Charles Jordan, Keith Koffler, Margo MacFarland, Charles Mitchell, Desda Moss, Robert Ourlian, Louis Peck, Michael Posner, Spencer Rich, Julie Rovner, Karen Scrivo, Lori Sharn, Richard Sia, John Stanton, Mary Thyfault, Martin Vaughan, Maya Weber, Mark Wegner, Keith White, Greta Wodele, Cyril Zaneski.

Congressional Information Bureau—(703) 516–4801; 5001 Lee Hwy, Suite 102, Arlington, VA 20007: Robert Cazalas, James LaRoue, Jr.

Congressional Quarterly—(202) 887–8500; 1414 22nd Street, Washington, DC 20007: Rebecca Adams, Liza Ackerman, Jonathan Allen, Martha Angle, Joseph Anselmo, Janet Austin, Jorge Banales, Virginia Barazia, Jill Barshay, Robert Benenson, Susan Benkelman, Nell Benton, Adriel Bettelheim, Arwen Bicknell, John Bicknell, Geoffrey Bosworth, Wendy Boudreau, Jonathan Broder, Ronald Brodmann, Arthur Brodsky, Alecia Burke, David Butler, Mary Agnes Carey, James Carroll, Mike Christensen, Colin Clark, David Clarke, John Cochran, George Codrea, Peter Cohn, Chuck Conlon, John Cranford, Craig Crawford, Richard Daly, David Davis, Jack Deutsch, Jennifer Dlouhy, Loren Duggan, Susan Ferrechio, Helen Fessenden, Kelly Field, Andrew Freedman, Chris Fruitrich, Gregory Giroux, Shelia Goffe, Samuel Goldreich, Adam Graham-Silverman, Kimberly Hallock, Peter Harrell, Caitlin Harrington, David Hawkings, Chuck Hawkins, Robert Healy, Caitlin Hendel, Liriel Higa, Siobhan Hughes, Mary Clare Jalonick, Kerry Jones, Patricia Joy, Martin Kady II, Ritu Kelotra, Noella Kertes, Peter King, Christopher Logan, Gebe Martinez, Frank McGee, David Miller, Marilee Miller, Jay Millikan, Michael Mills, Sarah Molenkamp, Scott Montgomery, David Nather, Anne Nordness, Stephen Norton, Brian Nutting, Joseph Nyitray, Alan Ota, Adam Pallotto, Daniel Parks, Steven Patrick, Keith Perine, Gayle Putrich, David Rapp, Eric Ray, Daphne Retter, Betty Richardson, Jonathan Riehl, Katherine Rizzo, Stuart Robinson, Peter Roybal, Brent Rudell, Adam Satariano, Joseph Schatz, Kate Schuler, Mike Sherry, Kathleen Silvassy, Carolyn Skorneck, Niels Sorrells, Charles Southwell, Jana Steiger, Jeff Stein, Allison Stevens, Bill Swindell, Andrew Taylor, Robert Tomkin, Jeremy Torobin, Larry Tunks, Joseph Warminsky, Lisa Weintraub, Daniel Winicour, Kathryn Wolfe, Yee Ling Woo, Randall Wynn.

Connecticut Post—(202) 662–8927; 1255 National Press Building, Washington, DC 20045: Peter Urban.

Copley News Service—(202) 737–7686; 1100 National Press Building, Washington, DC 20045: Joe Cantlupe, George Condon, Jr., Toby Eckert, Jerry Kammer, Paul Krawzak, Otto Kreisher, Finlay Lewis, Dori Meinert, Rosemary Petersen, Marcus Stern, Dana Wilkie.

Cox Newspapers—(202) 887–8361; 400 N. Capitol Street, Suite 750, Washington, DC 20001: Andrew Alexander, Susan Burns, Rebecca Carr, Arthur Dalglish, Robert Dart, Robert Deans, Jr., Marilyn Geewax, Charles Holmes, Elliot Jaspin, Julia Malone, Andrew Mollison, Eunice Moscoso, Jeff Nesmith, Carl Rauscher, Jr., Scott Shepard, Frank Tedards.

Creators Syndicate—(202) 662–1255; 1009 National Press Building, Washington, DC 20045: Mark Shields.

Daily Deal—(202) 429–2995; 1775 K Street, Suite 590, Washington, DC 20006: Shanon Murray, Ron Orol, Jaret Seiberg.

NEWSPAPERS REPRESENTED—Continued

Daily Oklahoman—(202) 662–7547; 914 National Press Building, Washington, DC 20045: Chris Casteel, Mark Green.

Daily Variety—(202) 463–3705; 1627 K Street, Washington, DC 20006: Susan Crabtree.

Dallas Morning News—(202) 661–8417; 1325 G Street, Suite 250, Washington, DC 20005: Robert Dodge, Todd Gillman, G. Robert Hillman, David Jackson, James Landers, Carl Leubsdorf, Katherine Lewis, Michelle Mittelstadt, James Morris, Allen Pusey, Richard Whittle.

Dayton Daily News—(202) 887–8329; 400 North Capitol Street, Suite 750, Washington, DC 20001: Mei-Ling Hopgood.

Defense Daily—(703) 522–5655; 1111 N. 19th Street, Suite 503, Arlington, VA 22209: Neil Baumgardner, Lorenzo Cortes, Kerry Gildea, Hunter Keeter, Brennan Kessner, John Robinson.

Denver Post—(202) 662–8730; 1255 National Press Building, Washington, DC 20045: John Farrell, Anne Mulkern, Michael Soraghan.

Der Tagesspiegel—(202) 234–2168; 766 A Chireh Street, NW., Washington, DC 20036: Malte Lehming.

Des Moines Register—(202) 906–8137; 1100 New York Avenue, Washington, DC 20005: Philip Brasher, Jane Norman.

Deseret News—(202) 737–5311; 1061 National Press Building, Washington, DC 20045: Lee Davidson.

Detroit Free Press—(202) 383–6036; 700 National Press Building, Washington, DC 20045: Ruby Bailey.

Detroit News—(202) 662–7382; 1148 National Press Building, Washington, DC 20045: Alison Bethel, Jeff Plungis, Deborah Price, Richard Ryan, Lisa Zagaroli.

Die Tageszeitung—(202) 462–6824; 1721 Newton Street, NW., Washington, DC 20020: Michael Streck.

Dow Jones Newswires—(202) 862–9256; 1025 Connecticut Avenue, Suite 1100, Washington, DC 20036: Mark Anderson, Jeffrey Bater, Lynn Bliss, Judith Burns, Rebecca Christie, John Connor, Jennifer Corbett Dooren, John Godfrey, Laurin Keto, Dawn Kopecki, Deborah Lagomarsino, Dan Lowrey, Otesa Middleton, Elizabeth Price, Philip McCarty, Joseph Rebello, Takeshi Takeuchi, Campion Walsh, Robert Wells, Mark Wigfield.

Edinburgh Scotsman—(202) 277–9368; 2515 13th Street, Apt. #408, Washington, DC 20009: Alex Massie.

Education Daily—(202) 312–6083; 1333 M Street, Suite 100 East, Washington, DC 20005: Michael Cardman, Katharine Chase, Travis Hicks, Alana Keynes, Hannah Rubin.

EFE News Services—(202) 745–7692; 1252 National Press Building, Washington, DC 20045: Cesar Munoz Acebes, Maria Azpiazu, Jorge Banales, Rafael Canas, Macarena Vidal Liy, Orlando Lizama, Rebecca Logan, Rosendo Majano, Maria Pena, Fernando Puchol.

El Columbiano—(703) 683–6786; 2402 Comeron Mills Road, Alexandria, VA 22302: Silvia Dangond.

El Financiero—(703) 707–0236; 2300 Darius Lane, Reston, VA 20191: Dolia Estevez.

El Norte–Reforma—(202) 628–0031; 1126 National Press Building, Washington, DC 20045: Maria Gonzalez.

El Nuevo Dia—(202) 662–7360; 1053 National Press Building, Washington, DC 20045: José Delgado.

El Pais—(202) 638–7604; 1134 National Press Building, Washington, DC 20045: Enrique Gonzalez.

El Tiempo—(202) 607–5929; 2402 Cameron Mills Road, Alexandria, VA 22302: Sergio Gomez.

El Universal—(202) 662–7190; 1193 National Press Building, Washington, DC 20045: Jose Carreno.

El Vocero de Puerto Rico—(703) 914–1557; 4524 Airlie Way, Annadale, VA 22003: Javier Maymi.

Energy Argus—(202) 349–2860; 1012 14th Street, Suite 1500, Washington, DC 20005: Abby Caplan, Micheal Ball, Jason Feer, Carli Flippen, Peter Gardett, Steven Marcy, Julie McDowell, Mark Mueller, Michael Niven, Amena Saiyid.

Energy Daily—(202) 662–9739; 1325 G Street, Suite 1003, Washington, DC 20005: Jeff Beattie, Tina Davis, Christopher Holly, Llewellyn King, George Lobsenz.

Epoch Times—(301) 963–3134; 7602 Quincewood Court, Rockville, MD 20855: Hui Jing, Hong Wang.

Fairbanks Daily News Miner—(202) 662–8721; 1255 National Press Building, Washington, DC 20045: Sam Bishop.

Fairchild News Service—(202) 662–8828; 954 National Press Building, Washington, DC 20045: Kristi Ellis, Joanna Ramey, Susan Watters.

Financial Times—(202) 434–0987; 700 13th Street, Suite 555, Washington, DC 20005: Edward Alden, Ayda Atallah, Gerard Baker, Alan Beattie, Joshua Chaffin, Peronet Despeignes, Guy Dinmore, Nancy Dunne, James Harding, Nancy McCord, Deborah McGregor, Demetri Sevastopulo, Peter Spiegel, Hubert Wetzel.

Financial Times-Deutschland—(202) 737–5377; 700 13th Street, Suite 555, Washington, DC 20005: Yvonne Esterhazy.

Fort Worth Star-Telegram—(202) 383–6016; 700 National Press Building, Washington, DC 20045: David Montgomery, Maria Recio.

Frankfurter Rundschau—(301) 762–9661; 5011 Keokuk Street, Bethesda, MD 20816: Dietmar Ostermann.

Fredericksburg Freelance-Star—(540) 368–5004; 616 Amelia Street, Fredericksburg, VA 22401: Johnathan Hunley.

Ft. Wayne Journal Gazette—(202) 879–6710; 551 National Press Building, Washington, DC 20045: Sylvia Smith.

Gannett News Service—(703) 854–5898; 7950 Jones Branch Drive, McClean VA, 22107: Caesar Andrews, Marie Marino, Craig Schwed.

NEWSPAPERS REPRESENTED—Continued

Gannett News Service—(202) 906–8133; 1100 New York Avenue, Washington, DC 20005: Douglas Abrahms, Greg Barrett, Robert Benincasa, Larry Bivins, Faith Bremner, Pamela Brogan, Sergio Bustos, Catalina Camia, Dennis Camire, Raju Chebium, Ronald Cohen, Derrick DePledge, Linda Dono, Val Ellicott, Ellyn Ferguson, Jon Frandsen, Jim Golden, Maureen Groppe, Erin Kelly, Ledyard S.R. King, John Machacek, Mike Madden, Frances Mears, Charles Raasch, Ana Radelat, Laura Rehrmann, Susan Roth, Fredreka Schouten, Katherine Scott, Brian Tumulty, Carl Weiser, Billie Jean Wells, Lawrence Wheeler, Gregory Wright, John Yaukey.

Gazeta Wyborcza—(202) 887–8336; 400 North Capitol Street, #750, Washington, DC 20001: Bartosz Weglarczyk.

German Press Agency–DPA—(202) 662–1220; 969 National Press Building, Washington, DC 20045: Gabriele Chwallek, Frank Fuhrig, Mike McCarthy, Thomas Mueller, Christiane Oelrich, Paticia Reber, Maria Isabel Rivero, Lea Ann Schnakenberg, Herbert Winkler, Frank Zeller.

Global Horizons Syndicate—(202) 966–8636; 1330 New Hampshire Avenue, Washington, DC 20036: Edward Flattau.

Griffin-Larrabee News Service—(202) 554–3579; 2404 Davis Avenue, Alexandria, VA 22302: Betty Mills.

Guangming Daily—(202) 363–0628; 4816 Butterworth Place, NW., Washington, DC 20016: Jianyou Wu, Xiaokui Yu.

Handelsblatt—(202) 965–0563; 3206 Q Street, Washington, DC 20007: Viola Herms-Drath.

Han-Kyoreh Shinmun—(202) 347–7411; 3305 Cannongate Road, Washington, DC 22031: Gook-Han Yoon.

Harrisburg Patriot-News—(202) 383–7833; 1101 Connecticut Avenue, Suite 300, Washington, DC 20036: Brett Lieberman.

Hartford Courant—(202) 824–8452; 1325 G Street, Suite 200, Washington, DC 20005: Rene Brown, Janice D'Arcy, Liz Halloran, David Lightman, John MacDonald, Michael Remez.

Health News Daily—(301) 657–9830; 5550 Friendship Boulevard, Suite 1, Chevy Chase, MD 20815: Nellie Bristol, David Glendinning, Jeffrey Young.

Hearst Newspapers—(202) 263–6400; 1850 K Street, NW., Suite 1000, Washington, DC 20006: Kristen Collie, Dan Freedman, Mark Helm, Judy Holland, Charles Lewis, Marianne Means, Stewart Powell, Eric Rosenberg, Timothy Spence, Helen Thomas.

Helsingin Sanomat—(202) 955–7956; 1726 M Street, NW., Suite #700, Washington, DC 20036: Jyri Raivio.

Hindu—(301) 654–9038; 4701 Willard Avenue, #1531, Chevy Chase, MD 20815: Sridhara Krishnaswami.

Hollywood Reporter—(202) 833–8845; 910 17th Street, NW., Washington, DC 20006: Brooks Boliek.

Houston Chronicle—(202) 393–6880; 1341 G Street, Suite 201, Washington, DC 20005: Michael Hedges, David Ivanovich, Julie Mason, Karen Masterson, Cragg Hines, John Henry, Patty Reinert-Mason, Bennett Roth.

Hurriyet—(301) 564–6691; 16 Grove Ridge Court, Rockville, MD 20852: Mehmet Cindemir.

Il Corriere Della Sera—(202) 879–6733; 450 National Press Building, Washington, DC 20045: Ennio Caretto, Laura Nasso.

Il Giornale—(202) 237–1019; 2841 Arizona Terrace, Washington, DC 20016: Mariuccia Chiantaretto.

Il Secolo XIX—(202) 957–8522; 3030 44th Street, NW., Washington, DC 20026: Elysa Fazzino.

Il Sole 24 Ore—(202) 879–6733; 450 National Press Building, Washington, DC 20045: Mario Calvo Platero.

Il Tempo—(202) 306–4737; 3140 Wisconsin Avenue, Washington, DC 20016: Stefano Marchi.

Inter Press Service—(202) 662–7160; 1293 National Press Building, Washington, DC 20045: James Lobe, Emad Mekay.

International Herald Tribune—(202) 862–0357; 1150 15th Street, Washington, DC 20071: Brian Knowlton.

Investor's Business Daily—(202) 728–2150; 1701 K Street, Suite 550, Washington, DC 20006: Joseph Guinto, Sean Higgins, Brian Mitchell.

Itar-Tass News Agency—(202) 662–7080; 1004 National Press Building, Washington, DC 20045: Dmitry Kirsanov, Ivan Lebedev, Andrei Sitov, Andrey Surzhanskiy, Pavel Vanichkin.

Jiji Press—(202) 783–4330; 550 National Press Building, Washington, DC 20045: Kazuyasu Akashi, Yoshida Kishida, Satoko Kogure, Junichi Murata, Tetsuya Nakano, Katushiko Sakai, Carlos Solis Jr., Eiji Toshi.

Joong Ang Ilbo—(202) 347–0122; 839 National Press Building, Washington, DC 20045: Hyo-joon Lee.

Kansas City Star—(202) 383–6105; 700 National Press Building, Washington, DC 20045: David Goldstein, Matthew Stearns.

Kipling News Service—(301) 929–0760; 12611 Farnell Drive, Silver Spring, MD 20906: Bogdan Kipling.

Knight Ridder—(202) 383–6004; 700 National Press Building, Washington, DC 20045: Beryl Adcock, James Asher, Seth Borenstein, Robert Boyd, Andrew Brown, Steven Butler, Sumana Chatterjee, Joyce Davis, Joseph Galloway, Frank Greve, Stephen Henderson, Clark Hoyt, Ron Hutcheson, Diego Ibarguen, James Kuhnhenn, Jonathan Landay, Shannon McCaffrey, Ken Moritsugu, Anthony Pugh, Robert Rankin, Renee Schoof, Warren Strobel, Steven Thomma, John Walcott, Alison Young.

Korea Dong-A Ilbo—(202) 347–4097; 974 National Press Building, Washington, DC 20045: Soon-Taek Kwon.

NEWSPAPERS REPRESENTED—Continued

Korea Economic Daily—(202) 347–2014; 909 National Press Building, Washington, DC 20045: Gwangchul Go.

Kuwait News Agency—(202) 347–5554; 906 National Press Building, Washington, DC 20045: Adnan Aljadi, Ronald Baygents.

Kyodo News—(202) 347–5767; 400 National Press Building, Washington, DC 20045: Hirotsugu Aida, Masaaki Aoki, Moriyasu Chikazawa, Masahiko Hisae, Tetsuji Ida, Hideomi Kinoshita, Yoichi Kosukegawa, Seiko Kyan, Todd Miller, Yoshio Miyasaka, Kakuya Ogata, Masakatsu Ota, Testsuya Shimada, Yuriko Sumikawa, Akira Takahashi, Yosuke Watanabe.

Kyung Hyang Shinmun—(703) 241–5511; 1914 Autumn Chase Court, Falls Church, VA 22043: Seung Chull Lee.

La Jornada—(202) 547–5852; 132 North Carolina Avenue, SE., Washington, DC 20003: David Brooks, James Cason.

La Nacion—(202) 628–7907; 1193 National Press Building, Washington, DC 20045: Jorge Rosales.

La Nacion USA—(703) 998–9493; 2615–A Shirlington Road, Arlington VA, 22206: Farid Deantonio, Maria Eguigure, Pablo Sandino Martinez.

La Nazione—(202) 347–0245; 450 National Press Building, Washington, DC 20045: Cesare De Carlo.

La Opinion—(202) 662–1240; 962 National Press Building, Washington, DC 20045: Maribel Hastings.

La Tribuna—(202) 737–5349; 1193 National Press Building, Washington, DC 20045: Jacobo Goldstein.

La VanGuardia—(301) 229–1695; 6812 Algonquin Avenue, Bethesda, MD 20817: Eusebio Val Mitjavila.

Lahore Daily Times—(703) 280–5832; 9019 Bowler Drive, Fairfax, VA, 22031: Khalid Hasan.

Las Vegas Sun—(202) 662–7245; 529 National Press Building, Washington, DC 20045: Benjamin Grove.

Le Mauricien—(301) 424–3884; 1084 Pipestem Place, Potomac, MD 20854: Pamela Glass.

Le Monde—(202) 347–2520; 1826 Biltmore Street, Washington, DC 20009: Patrick Jarreau.

Liberation—(202) 249–9343; 4127 Harrison Street, Washington, DC 20015: Pascal Riche.

Liberty Times—(202) 879–6765; 1294 National Press Building, Washington, DC 20045: Yu Fen Tsao.

London Daily Telegraph—(202) 393–5195; 1331 Pennsylvania Avenue, #904, Washington, DC 20004: Toby Harnden, David Rennie.

London Evening Standard—(607) 589–7306; 8 Jefferson Avenue, Takoma Park, MD 20912: Eva Lauren Chambliss.

London Guardian—(202) 223–2486; 1730 Rhode Island Avenue, #502, Washington, DC 20036: Julian Borger, Suzanne Goldenberg.

London Independent—(202) 467–4460; 1726 M Street, Suite 700, Washington, DC 20008: Rupert Cornwell.

London Sunday Telegraph—(202) 393–5195; 1331 Pennsylvania Avenue, Suite 904, Washington, DC 20004: Julian Coman.

London Times—(202) 349–7659; 446 National Press Building, Washington, DC 20045: Elaine Monahan, Tim Reid, Roland Watson.

L'Orient–Le Jour—(202) 842–3681; 1045 31st Street, #404, Washington, DC 20007: Wafik Ramadan.

Los Angeles Daily Journal—(202) 484–8255; 1 First Street, NE., Pressroom, Washington, DC 20543: David Pike.

Los Angeles Daily News—(202) 662–8731; 1255 National Press Building, Washington, DC 20045: Lisa Friedman.

Los Angeles Newspaper Group—(202) 662–8925; 1255 National Press Building, Washington, DC 20045: William Hillburg.

Los Angeles Times—(202) 293–4650; 1875 I Street, Suite 1100, Washington, DC 20006: Ricardo Alonso-Zaldivar, Nick Anderson, Stephen Braun, Ronald Brownstein, Edwin Chen, Richard Cooper, Mary Curtius, Robert Drogin, Sonni Efron, Mark Fineman, Faye Fiore, Don Frederick, James Gerstenzang, Lisa Getter, Adrianne Goodman, Peter Gosselin, Joel Havemann, Jacob Heilbrunn, John Hendren, Leslie Hoffecker Janet Hook, Vicki Kemper, David Lamb, Thomas McCarthy, Allison McIntyre, Doyle McManus, Joshua Meyer, Alan Miller, Greg Miller, Deborah Nelson, Chuck Neubauer, Johanna Neuman, Judy Pasternak, Robert Patrick, Jonathan Peterson, Maura Reynolds, Paul Richter, James Robinson, Phillip Ruiz, Edmund Sanders, David Savage, Richard Schmitt, Esther Schrader, Jube Shiver, Jr., Elizabeth Shogren, Richard Serrano, Kenneth Silverstein, Richard Simon, Warren Vieth, David Willman, Donald Woutat, Robin Wright, Aaron Zitner.

Louisville Courier Journal—(202) 906–8141; 1100 New York Avenue, NW., Washington, DC 20005: James Carroll.

Lowell Sun Media News Group—(202) 662–8926; 1255 National Press Building, Washington, DC 20045: Ian Bishop.

LRP Publications—(703) 684–5244; 1555 King Street, Suite 200, Alexandria, VA 22314: Julie Ellis, Jason Emerson, Kathleen Filipczyk, Patrick Harden, Drew Long, Katherine Shek, Kara Urbanski, Andrew Viccora.

L'Unita—(202) 237–1050; 2841 Arizona Terrace, Washington, DC 20045: Bruno Marolo.

Maghreb Arabe Presse—(703) 538–7780; 6018 Woodley Road, McLean, VA 22101: Abderrahmane Kassou.

Magyar Szo—(202) 904–4433; 1775 Massachusetts Avenue, Suite 207, Washington, DC 20036: Tibor Purger.

NEWSPAPERS REPRESENTED—Continued

Mainichi Shimbun—(202) 737–2817; 340 National Press Building, Washington, DC 20045: Toshifumi Kawano, Tetsuo Nakajima, Chiyako Sato, Masanori Takegawa, Hidetoshi Togasawa, Joelle Williams.

Market News International—(202) 371–2121; 552 National Press Building, Washington, DC 20045: Erica Beckner, Steven Beckner, Denny Gulino, Claudia Hirsch, Kevin Kastner, Chris Middleton, Yali N'Diaye, Joseph Plocek, Heather Scott, John Shaw, Theresa Sheehan.

McClatchy Newspapers—(202) 383–0017; 420 National Press Building, Washington, DC 20045: Les Blumenthal, Michael Bold, Muriel Dobbin, Michael Doyle, Greg Gordon, Lawrence O'Rourke, James Rosen, Mary Settles, John Wagner, Jr., David Westphal, David Whitney.

McClendon News Service—(202) 797–8467; 2933 28th Street, NW., Washington, DC 20008: David MacDonald.

Media General News Service—(202) 662–7670; 1214 National Press Building, Washington, DC 20045: John Hall, Gilbert Klein Jr., Richard Lee, Marsha Mercer, Kirsten Mitchell.

Medical Device Daily—(202) 719–7814; 4301 Conneticut Avenue, Suite 330, Washington, DC 20008: Kevin New.

Miami Herald—(202) 383–6054; 700 National Press Building, Washington, DC 20045: Frank Davies, Timothy Johnson.

Military Update—(703) 830–6863; P.O. Box 23111, Centreville, VA 20120: Thomas Philpott.

Milwaukee Journal Sentinel—(202) 662–7290; 940 National Press Building, Washington, DC 20045: Craig Gilbert, Katherine Skiba.

Minneapolis Star Tribune—(202) 383–0003; 420 National Press Building, Washington, DC 20045: Kevin Diaz, Gregory Gordon, Rob Hotakainen.

Mobile Register—(202) 383–7815; 1101 Connecticut Avenue, Suite 300, Washington, DC 20036: Sean Reilly.

Munwha Ilbo—(202) 662–7342; 1148 National Press Building, Washington, DC 20045: Mi Sook Lee.

Myers News Service—(202) 4791130; 8213 Taunton Place, Springfield, VA 22152: Michael Myers.

National Journal's Technology Daily—(202) 261–0364; 1501 M Street, Suite 300, Washington, DC 20005: Chloe Albanesius, Shawn Chen, Drew Clark, K. Daniel Glover, Sharon McLoone, William New, Margaret Peterson, Teri Rucker, Maureen Sirhal, Bara Vaida.

National News Research Syndicate—(202) 223–1196; 500 23rd Street, NW., Washington, DC 20037: Charles Kendall, Jr., Ralph de Toledano.

National Post—(202) 638–7055; 529 14th Street, NW., Suite 529, Washington, DC 20045: Jan Cienski, Alexander Rose.

New Haven Register—(202) 737–5654; 1331 Pennsylvania Avenue, NW., Washington, DC 20004: Joseph Straw.

New Orleans Times-Picayune—(202) 383–7817; 1101 Connecticut Avenue, Suite 300, Washington, DC 20036: Bruce Alpert, John McQuaid, Bill Walsh.

New York Daily News—(202) 467–6770; 1615 M Street, Suite 720, Washington, DC 20036: Kenneth Bazinet, Thomas DeFrank, Helen Kennedy, James Meek, Richard Sisk.

New York Post—(202) 393–1787; 1114 National Press Building, Washington, DC 20045: Brian Blomquist, Vincent Morris, Deborah Orin.

New York Sun—(202) 628–1040; 1331 Pennsylvania Avenue, NW., #904N, Washington, DC 20004: Tim Starks.

New York Times—(202) 862–0300; 1627 I Street, Suite 700, Washington, DC 20006: Jill Abramson, Edmund Andrews, Von Aulston, Janet Battaile, Elizabeth Becker, Richard Berke, David Binder, Monica Borkowski, Julie Bosman, Joel Brinkley, Gregory Brock, Elisabeth Bumiller, Lynette Clemetson, Adam Clymer, John Cushman, Jr., James Dao, Cate Doty, Maureen Dowd, John Files III, David Firestone, Jeff Gerth, Michael Gordon, Linda Greenhouse, Janis Harland, Raymond Hernandez, Elizabeth Hines, Steven Holmes, Carl Hulse, Douglas Jehl, David Johnston, Stephen Labaton, Carl Lavin, Warren Leary, Jennifer Lee, Neil Lewis, Eric Lichtblau, Christopher Marquis, Renwick McLean, Clifton Meadows, Judith Miller, Adam Nagourney, Elizabeth Olson, Richard Oppel, Robert Pear, Todd Purdum, James Risen, David Rosenbaum, William Safire, David Sanger, Diana Schemo, Eric Schmitt, Katharine Seelye, Thomas Shanker, Philip Shenon, Ronald Skarzenski, Richard Stevenson, Sheryl Stolberg, David Stout, Rachel Swarns, John Tierney, Robin Toner, Hugh Truslow, Patrick Tyler, Matthew Wald, Leslie Wayne, Steven Weisman, Brian Wingfield.

New York Times Regional News—(202) 862–0382; Cory Reiss.

Newark Star-Ledger—(202) 383–7823; 1101 Connecticut Avenue, Suite 300, Washington, DC 20036: Robert Cohen, J. Scott Orr.

Newhouse News Service—(202) 383–7835; 1101 Connecticut Avenue, Suite 300, Washington, DC 20036: Miles Benson, William Cahir, Deborah Howell, Linda Fibich, Sarah Kellogg, Terence Kivlan, Katherine Lewis, Chuck McCutcheon, Michele Melendez, JoAnn Moriarty, Mark O'Keefe, Delia Rios, Bruce Seeman, Dru Sefton, Jonathan Tilove, David Wood.

Newport News Daily Press—(202) 824–8224; 1325 G Street, NW., Suite 200, Washington, DC 20005: David Lerman.

Newsday—(202) 628–8481; 1730 Pennsylvania Avenue, #850, Washington, DC 20006: Deborah Barfield Berry, Thomas Brune, Marie Cocco, William Douglas, Anne Hoy, Kenneth Fireman, Thomas Frank,

NEWSPAPERS REPRESENTED—Continued

D. Craig Gordon, Angela Johnson, Earl Lane, Sarah Mueller, Monica Norton, Timothy Phelps, Elaine Povich, James Toedtman.

Newspaper Enterprise—(301) 320–5559; 6008 Osceola Road, Bethesda, MD 20816: Robert Wagman.

Nikkei—(202) 393–1388; 815 Conneticut Avenue, Suite 310, Washington, DC 20006: Hiroyuki Akita, Tomoko Ashizuka, Christina Bilski, Atsuko Fukase, Stephen Keefe, Masanori Matsui, Ken Moriyasu, Toru Yoshida, Hiroshi Yoshitsugu.

Northwest Newspapers—(202) 546–2547; 316 3rd Street, NE., Washington, DC 20002: Lawrence Swisher.

Notimex Mexican News Agency—(202) 347–5227; 425 National Press Building, Washington, DC 20045: Ricardo Alday, Ruben Barrera, Jose Lopez.

O Estado De S. Paulo—(202) 628–3752; 700 13th Street, Suite 555, Washington, DC 20005: Paulo Sotero.

Oil Daily—(202) 662–0739; 1401 New York Avenue, Suite 500, Washington, DC 20005: Manimoli Dinesh, Rod Kuckro, Karen Matusic, Kimberley Music, Scott Patton, Emily Rehring, Patricia Vasquez.

Oliphant News Service—(202) 298–7226; P.O. Box 9808, Washington, DC 20016: Cortright Oliphant, Robert Oliphant.

Omaha World Herald—(202) 662–7270; 836 National Press Building, Washington, DC 20045: Matt Kelley, Jake Thompson.

Orange County Register—(202) 628–6381; 1295 National Press Building, Washington, DC 20045: Dena Bunis.

Oregonian—(202) 383–7819; 1101 Connecticut Avenue, Suite 300, Washington, DC 20036: James Barnett, Thomas Detzel.

Orlando Sentinel—(202) 824–8233; 1325 G Street, Suite 200, Washington, DC 20005: Tamara Lytle, Sean Mussenden, Gwyneth Shaw.

Oster Dow Jones—(202) 646–0088; 1025 Connecticut Avenue, Washington, DC 20006: Bill Tomson.

Palm Beach Post—(202) 887–8340; 400 N. Capitol Street, Suite 750, 20001: Laurence Lipman.

Philadelphia Inquirer—(202) 383–6046; 700 National Press Building, Washington, DC 20045: Steven Goldstein, Christopher Mondics, Peter Nicholas.

Philippine Daily Inquirer—(703) 685–2665; 841 South Glebe Road, Arlington, VA 22204: Josefina Ilustre.

Pittsburgh Post-Gazette—(202) 662–7075; 955 National Press Building, Washington, DC 20045: Karen MacPhersen, Ann McFeatters, Michael Woods.

Platts News Service—(202) 383–2251; 1200 G Street, Suite 1100, Washington, DC 20005: Gerald Karey, Catherine Landry

Polish Press Agency—(301) 365–1099; 7505 Democracy Blvd. #A413, Bethesda, MD 20817: Witold Zalewski.

Political Money Line—(202) 628–0618; 50 F Street, Suite 1198, Washington, DC 20001: Kent Cooper, Anthony Raymond.

Portland Press Herald—(202) 488–1119; 10056 Maple Leaf Drive, Gaithersburg, MD 20886: Bart Jansen.

Press Trust of India—(301) 951–8657; 4450 South Park Avenue, Suite 1719, Chevy Chase, MD 20815: T.V. Parasuram.

Providence Journal—(202) 661–8423; 1325 G Street, Suite 250, Washington, DC 20005: John Mulligan, Philip Terzian.

Religion News Service—(202) 383–7863; 1101 Connecticut Avenue, Suite 350, Washington, DC 20036: Adelle Banks, Kevin Eckstrom.

Restructuring Today—(202) 298–8201; 4418 MacArthur Blvd., Washington, DC 20007: Joan Henderson, Arthur Kingdom, George Spencer.

Reuters—(202) 898–8391; 1333 H Street, Suite 410, Washington, DC 20005: Charles Abbott, John Abell, Timothy Ahmann, Charles Aldinger, Charles Alexander, JoAnne Allen, Victoria Allen, Pablo Bachelet, Chris Baltimore, Philip Barbara, Eric Beech, Melissa Bland, Caren Bohan, Niaia Boodhoo, Xavier Briand, Deborah Charles, Andrew Clark, Susan Jean Cornwell, Robert Covington, Richard Cowan, Sarah Edmonds Crang, John Crawley, Timothy Dobbyn, Christopher Doering, Tom Doggett, Robert Doherty, Stuart Doughty, Kevin Drawbaugh, Will Dunham, Mark Egan, Giles Elgood, Alan Elsner, Randolph Fabi, Mark Felsenthal, Alexander Ferguson, Thomas Ferraro, Anton Ferreira, Maggie Fox, Carol Giacomo, Steven Ginsburg, Kevin Hamill, Susan Heavey, Sonya Hepinstall, Andrea Hopkins, Cheyenne Hopkins, Katherine Hunt, Stacy Joyce, Peter Kaplan, Joanne Kenen, Christina Ling, Johnathan Lyons, Laura MacInnis, Randall Mikkelsen, Peter Millership, Arshad Mohammed, Joanne Morrison, Jonathan Nicholson, Chizu Nomiyama, Jill Oestreicher-Gross, Doug Palmer, Jeremy Pelofsky, Susan Pleming, John Poirier, Peter Ramjug, Lisa Richwine, Timothy Ryan, Andrea Shalal-Esa, Donna Smith, Glenn Somerville, Neil Stempleman, David Storey, Andy Sullivan, Peter Szekely, William Trott, James Vicini, Julie Vorman, Nancy Waitz, John Whitesides, David Wiessler, Mark Wilkinson, Anna Willard, Christopher Wilson, Jim Wolf, Jonathan Wright, Deborah Zabarenko, Tabassum Zakaria, Patricia Zengerle.

Rheinische Post—(301) 299–5777; 10201 Windsor View Drive, Potomac, MD 20854: Thomas Spang.

Richmond Times-Dispatch—(202) 662–7669; 1214 National Press Building, Washington, DC 20045: Peter Hardin.

Riverside Press-Enterprise—(202) 661–8422; 1325 G Street, Suite 250, Washington, DC 20045: Claire Vitucci.

NEWSPAPERS REPRESENTED—Continued

Roll Call Report Syndicate—(202) 737–1888; 1297 National Press Building, Washington, DC 20045: Cora Hoopes, Michael Lesparre, Richard Thomas.

Saint Paul Pioneer Press—(202) 383–6032; 700 National Press Building, Washington, DC 20045: Thomas Webb.

Salt Lake Tribune—(202) 662–8897; 1255 National Press Building, Washington, DC 20045: Christopher Smith.

San Antonio Express-News—(202) 298–6920; 1701 Pennsylvania Avenue, #610, Washington, DC 20006: Gary Martin.

San Francisco Chronicle—(202) 737–7134; 1085 National Press Building, Washington, DC 20045: Zachary Coile, Edward Epstein, Rachel Kapochunas, Carolyn Lochhead, Marc Sandalow,

San Jose Mercury News—(202) 383–6043; 700 National Press Building, Washington, DC 20045: Heather Phillips, James Puzzanghera.

Sankei Shimbun—(202) 347–2842; 330 National Press Building, Washington, DC 20045: Yukio Kashiyama, Hideo Kesen, Yoshihisa Komori, B. Scott Stewart, Kondo Toyokazu.

Saudi Press Agency—(202) 861–0324; 1155 15th Street, Suite 1111, Washington, DC 20005: Naila Al-Sowayel, Mustafa Bashir, Dean Dessouky, Charles Featherstone, Azeddine Labriny, Nezar Sheikh, John Siciliano, Erin Zaro.

Science and Technology Daily—(703) 734–9288; 1827 Barbee Street, McLean, VA 22101: Mengjun Zhang.

Scripps Howard News Service—(202) 4082715; 1090 Vermont Avenue, Suite 1000, Washington, DC 20005: Karen Allen, Jay Ambrose, Curtis Lee Bowman, James Brosnan, Patrick Butters, Chris Campbell, Micheal Canan, Michael Collins, Peter Copeland, Tara Copp, Mary Deibel, Joel Eskovitz, Lance Gay, Laurel Hackett, Thomas Hargrove, Lisa Hoffman, David Johnson, Robert Jones, Joan Lowy, Dale McFeatters, Thomas Mentzer, Deroy Murdock, Wanita Niehaus, David Nielsen, Richard Powelson, Pamela Reeves, Martin Schram, Jennifer Sergent, Michael Sprengelmeyer, Bill Straub, Rita Sutherland, Dan Thomasson, Alan Thompson, Karen Timmons, Walter Veazey, Jessica Wehrman, Martha Wilson.

Seattle Post-Intelligencer—(202) 298–6920; 1701 Pennsylvania Avenue, #610, Washington, DC 20006: Charles Pope.

Seattle Times—(202) 662–7456; 920 National Press Building, Washington, DC 20045: Alex Fryer, Katherine Pfleger.

Segye Times—(202) 637–0587; 909 National Press Building, Washington, DC 20045: Kiyon Kuk.

Shanghai Wenhui Daily—(703) 521–2371; 1600 S Eads Street, Suite 1134N, Arlington, VA 22202: Xingfu Zhu.

Shearer and Glen News—(202) 462–6070; 2708 Cathedral Avenue, NW., Washington, DC 20008: Cody Shearer.

Singapore Straits Times—(202) 662–8727; 916 National Press Building, Washington, DC 20045: Roger Mitton.

SNG Newspapers—(202) 662–7240; 1183 National Press Building, Washington, DC 20045: Edward Felker.

South Florida Sun-Sentinel—(202) 824–8225; 1325 G Street, Suite 200, Washington, DC 20005: William Gibson, Rafael Lorente.

Southam News of Canada—(202) 662–7225; 1206 National Press Building, Washington, DC 20045: Hillary Mackenzie.

Springer Foreign News Service—(202) 342–3103; 4830 Brandywine Street, Washington, DC 20016: Cornel Faltin, Frauke Faltin.

St. Louis Post Dispatch—(202) 298–6880; 1701 Pennsylvania Avenue, #550, Washington, DC 20006: Karen Branch-Brioso, Philip Dine, Aloysia Hamalainen, William Lambrecht, Jon Sawyer, Andrew Schneider, Deirdre Shesgreen.

St. Petersburg Times—(202) 463–0574; 1100 Connecticut Avenue, #1300, Washington, DC 20036: William Adair, Sara Fritz, Mary Jacoby.

States News Service—(202) 628 3100; 1331 Pennsylvania Avenue, NW., #232, Washington, DC 20004: David Enrich, Craig Linder, Leland Schwartz, Myron Struck.

Stephens Media Group—(202) 783–1760; 666 11th Street, Suite 535, Washington, DC 20001: Tony Batt, Stephan Tetreault, Alison Vekshin, Samantha Young.

Stuttgarter Zeitung—(301) 983–0735; 11204 Powder Horn Drive, Potomac, MD 20854: Juergen Koar.

Suara Merdeka—(301) 946–9553; 2700 Hardy Avenue, Silver Spring, MD 20902: Djono Sujono.

Suara Pembaruan—(703) 534–6014; 1908 Armand Court, Falls Church, VA 22043: Karina Sudyatmiko, Christianto Wibisono, Jasmine Wibisono.

Sueddeutsche Zeitung—(202) 965–5253; 3636 S Street, NW., Washington, DC 20007: Marc Hujer.

Sueddeutsche Zeitung—(301) 610–9460; 1741 Crestview Drive, Bethesda, MD 20854: Wolfgang Koydl.

Svenska Dagbladet—(202) 362–8253; 3601 Connecticut Avenue, #622, Washington, DC 20008: Karin Henriksson.

Sydney Morning Herald—(202) 737–6359; 1331 Pennsylvania Avenue, Suite 904, Washington, DC 20005: Marian Wilkinson.

Syracuse Post-Standard—(202) 383–7818; 1101 Connecticut Avenue, Suite 300, Washington, DC 20036: Mark Libbon.

NEWSPAPERS REPRESENTED—Continued

Tages Anzeiger—(202) 467–4780; 2000 M Street, Suite 370, Washington, DC 20036: Ignaz Staub.

Taipei Times—(301) 942–2442; P.O. Box 571, Garrett Park, MD 20898: Charles Snyder.

Tampa Tribune—(202) 662–7673; 1214 National Press Building, Washington, DC 20045: Keith Epstein.

Tech Law Journal—(202) 364–8882; P.O. Box 15186, Washington, DC 20003: David Carney.

Tokyo-Chunichi Shimbun—(202) 783–9479; 1012 National Press Building, Washington, DC 20045: Patrick Gardner, Michiyo Kanno, Mitsura Kumode, Jennifer Leland, Uichiro Oshima, Nori Sawaki, Yochi Toyoda.

Toronto Globe and Mail—(202) 662–7167; 2000 M Street, Suite 330, Washington, DC 20036: Paul Koring, Barrie McKenna, John Saunders.

Toronto Star—(202) 662–7390; 982 National Press Building, Washington, DC 20045: Tim Harper.

Tulsa World—(202) 484–1424; 1417 North Inglewood Street, Arlington, VA 22205: Jim Myers.

Turkiye Daily—(202) 253–3289; 12704 Hallman Court, North, Potomac, MD 20878: Hasan Hazar.

United Daily News—(202) 737–6426; 1099 National Press Building, Washington, DC 20045: Tsung-Chih Chang.

United Media—(301) 494–0430; 3330 Blue Heron Drive, N. Chesapeake, MD 20732: Lew Sichelman.

United Press International—(202) 898–8238; 1510 H Street, Washington, DC 20005: Ellen Beck, Tobin Beck, Mark Benjamin, Phil Berardelli, Christian Bourge, Krishnadev Calamur, Dee Ann Divis, Soni Nelson Fitzhugh, Roland Flamini, Kathy Gambrell, Shihoko Goto, John Hendel, Pamela Hess, Nicholas Horrock, Martin Hutchinson, Anwar Iqbal, Daniel Kagan, Michael Kirkland, Timothy Maloy, Louis Marano, Harold Martin, Steve Mitchell, John O'Sullivan, Daniel Olmsted, P. Mitchell Prothero, Peter Roff, Claude Salhani, Richard Tomkins, Martin Walker, Shaun Waterman.

United States Press—(301) 654–1872; 5301 Westbard Circle, #247, Bethesda, MD 20816: Frank van der Linden.

USA Today—(202) 906–8179; 1100 New York Avenue, NW., Washington, DC 20005: Richard Benedetto, Joan Biskupic, Jim Drinkard, Peter Eisler, Greg Farrell, Gwen Flanders, Barbara Hagenbaugh, George Hager, Mimi Hall, Linda Holzer, Kevin Johnson, Judith Keen, Kathy Kiely, Sue Kirchhoff, Jill Lawrence, Donna Leinwand, Alan Levin, Toni Locy, Laurence McQuillan, Dave Moniz, Bill Nichols, Susan Page, Barbara Slavin, Tiffany Smith, Tom Squitieri, Andrea Stone, William Welch, Richard Wolf.

USA Today—(703) 854–4521; 7950 Jones Branch Drive, McLean, VA 22108: Fred Anklam, Jr., Julie Appleby, Andrew Backover, John Bacon, Sandra Block, Erik Brady, Tom Vanden Brook, Chris Collins, Jim Cox, Christopher Cubbison, Paul Davidson, Robert Davis, Anthony DeBarros, Barbara Delollis, William Dermody, John Diamond, Michael Dodd, Earle Eldridge, Mindy Fetterman, Thomas Fogarty, Ed Foster-Simeon, Tim Friend, Andrew Gardiner, Raymond Goldbacher, Michael Hiestand, Lee Horwich, Sid Hurlburt, Rosalind Jackler, Brent Jones, Del Jones, Lori Joseph, Dennis Kelly, Jack Kelley, Paul Leavitt, David Lindsey, Mary Beth Marklein, Mark Memmott, John Merline, Jim Michaels, Blake Morrison, Vinuraj Narayanan, Haya El Nasser, Jayne O'Donnell, Thomas O'Toole, Paul Overberg, Douglas Pardue, Laura Parker, Carolyn Pesce, Karen Peterson, Maria Puente, William Risser, Bruce Rosenstein, Walter Shapiro, Elliot Smith, Mike Snider, Douglas Stanglin, Steve Sternberg, William Sternberg, Jeffrey Stinson, Karen Thomas, Elisa Tinsley, Gregory Toppo, Saundra Torry, Owen Ullmann, Dan Vergano, John Waggoner, Juan Walte, Traci Watson, James Welch, Richard Willing, Gregg Zoroya.

US–Asian News Service—(703) 525–5164; 3443 North Randolph Street, Arlington, VA 22207: Donald Choi, Julie Moon.

USAToday.com—(703) 854–8054; 7950 Jones Branch Drive, McLean VA, 22108: Chet Czarniak, Clara Frenk, Stephen Marshall, Saverio Meddis, Patty Michalski, Christine Montgomery, Phil Pruitt, John Riley, Winsey Wilson.

Virginian-Pilot—(703) 913–9872; 7802 Glenister Drive, Springfield, VA 22152: Dale Eisman.

Wall Street Journal—(202) 862–6663; 1025 Connecticut Avenue, Suite 800, Washington, DC 20036: Leila Abboud, Jess Bravin, Jackie Calmes, Mary Carnevale, David Cloud, Christopher Conkey, Helene Cooper, Jeanne Cummings, Robert Davis, Yochi Dreazen, Stefan Fatsis, John Fialka, Gary Fields, Robert Greenberger, Bryan Gruley, Thomas Hamburger, John Harwood, Greg Hitt, Gregory Ip, Greg Jaffe, Neil King, Jr., June Kronholz, Nicholas Kulish, Philip Kuntz, Sarah Lueck, Robert Guy Matthews, Laurie McGinley, John McKinnon, Shailagh Murray, Michael Phillips, Stephen Power, Carla Robbins, David Rogers, Jacob Schlesinger, Sharon Schmid, Michael Schroeder, Gerald Seib, Deborah Solomon, Kelly Spors, Johnny Stevenson, Marjorie Valbrun, David Wessel, Clayton Wiggins, John Wilke, Winston Wood, Bernard Wysocki, Jr.

Washington Bureau News—(202) 293–3003; 1325 18th Street, Suite 302, Washington, DC 20036: Kenneth Scheibel.

Washington Post—(202) 334–7410; 1150 15th Street, Washington, DC 20071: Michael Allen, Robert Asher, Charles Babington, Daniel Balz, Michael Barbaro, Gary Barr, Peter Behr, John Berry, David Broder, David Brown, Justin Blum, D'Vera Cohn, Ceci Connolly, Albert Crenshaw, Alice Crites, Kathleen Day, Helen Dewar, Micheal Dobbs, Kirstin Downey, David Von Drehle, Thomas Edsall, Daniel Eggen, Juliet Eilperin, Brian Faler, Douglas Farah, Darryl Fears, David Finkel, Mary Pat Flaherty, Michael Fletcher, Amy Goldstein, Sara Goo, Bradley Graham, James Grimaldi, Michael Grunwald,

NEWSPAPERS REPRESENTED—Continued

Guy Gugliotta, Maryann Haggerty, Martha Hamilton, Hamil Harris, Dana Hedgpeth, Jim Vande Hei, David Hilzenrath, Spencer Hsu, Carrie Johnson, Glenn Kessler, Jonathan Krim, George Lardner, Madonna Lebling, Christopher Lee, Jeff Leen, Mark Malseed, Ruth Marcus, Caroline Mayer, Mary McGrory, Kevin Merida, Dana Milbank, David Montgomery, Dan Morgan, David Ottaway, Steven Pearlstein, Don Phillips, Eric Pianin, Walter Pincus, Dana Priest, Anitha Reddy, Tom Ricks, Judy Sarasohn, Greg Schneider, Cindy Skrzycki, Jeffrey Smith, Jackie Spinner, Joe Stephens, Christopher Stern, Tom Toles, Dan Vise, Stephen Vogel, Edward Walsh, Joby Warrick, Jonathan Weisman, Rick Weiss, Bob Woodward, Eric Yoder.

Washington Telecommunications—(703) 461–7183; 1006 Harrison Circle, Alexandria, VA 22304: Gordon White.

Washington Times—(202) 636–3289; 3600 New York Avenue NE., Washington, DC 20002: Theodore Agres, George Archibald, Chris Baker, Sharon Behn, Tony Blankley, Thomas Carter, Gus Constantine, Francis Coombs, Jr., Joseph Curl, Brian DeBose, Stephen Dinan, Julia Duin, Amy Fagan, Alexandria Fleming, Ann Geracimos, William Gertz, William Glanz, Ralph Hallow, Kenneth Hanner, Jennifer Harper, Marguerite Higgins, Patrice Hill, Vaishali Honawar, Audrey Hudson, Charles Hurt, David Jones, Nicholas Kralev, James Lakely, Donald Lambro, Tim Lemke, John McCaslin, Steven Miller, James Morrison, Frank Murray, Wesley Pruden, Thomas Ramstack, Deborah Simmons Robinson, Charles Rousseaux, William Sammon, David Sands, Rowan Scarborough, Jerry Seper, Mary Shaffrey, Ellen Sorokin, Jeffrey Sparshott, M. Maria Stainer, Jon Ward, Joseph Weber, Cheryl Wetzstein, Larry Witham, Willis Witter.

WashingtonPost.com—(703) 469–2618; 1515 N. Courthouse Road, Arlington, VA 22201: Kyle Balluck, Daniel Jung, Brian Krebs, Suzette Lohmeyer, Ann Marchand, Jeffrey Marcus, Jefferson Marley, Robert MacMillan, David McGuire, Terry Neal, John Nichols, Christina Pino-Marina, Jason Thompson, Ryan Thornburg.

Watertown Daily Times—(202) 662–7085; 1001 National Press Building, Washington, DC 20045: Marc Heller.

Westdeutsche Allgemeine—(202) 363–7791; 4611 47th Street, Washington, DC 20016: Markus Gunther.

Wichita Eagle—(202) 383–6055; 700 National Press Building, Washington, DC 20045: Alan Bjerga.

William Scally Reports—(202) 362–2382; 2918 Legation Street, Washington, DC 20015: William Scally.

Winston-Salem Journal—(202) 662–7672; 1214 National Press Building, Washington, DC 20045: Kevin Begos, Jr.

World Journal—(202) 215–1710; 1099 National Press Building, Washington, DC 20045: Betty Lin.

WorldNetDaily.com—(703) 8150685; 8665 Sudley Road, Suite 605, Manasses, VA 20110: Joseph Farah, Paul Sperry.

Xinhua News Agency—(202) 661–8181; 1145 National Press Building, Washington, DC 20045: Wang Faen, Xiaoming Hu, Lei Mao, Weibing Tan, Xinmu Tan, Feng Yan, He Ying, Wang Zhenhua.

Yomiuri Shimbun—(202) 783–0363; 802 National Press Building, Washington, DC 20045: Masashi Amano, Takao Hishinuma, Toshiyuki Ito, Toshio Mizushima, Kazuo Nagata, Hiroko Nakamura, Kyoichi Sasazawa, Gaku Shibata, Anthony Sipher, Mineko Tokito, Russell Totten, Linda Yun, Kasper Zeuthen.

PRESS PHOTOGRAPHERS' GALLERY*

PRESS PHOTOGRAPHERS' GALLERY

The Capitol, Room S–317, 224–6548

www.senate.gov/galleries/photo

Director.—Jeffrey S. Kent.
Deputy Director.—Mark A. Abraham.
Assistant Director.—Sonya Hebert.

STANDING COMMITTEE OF PRESS PHOTOGRAPHERS

Tim Dillon, *Chairman*
Dennis Brack, *Secretary-Treasurer*
Scott Applewhite
James Colburn
Stephen Crowley
Win McNamee

RULES GOVERNING PRESS PHOTOGRAPHERS' GALLERY

1. (a) Administration of the Press Photographers' Gallery is vested in a Standing Committee of Press Photographers consisting of six persons elected by accredited members of the Gallery. The Committee shall be composed of one member each from Associated Press Photos; Reuters News Pictures or AFP Photos; magazine media; local newspapers; agency or freelance member; and one at-large member. The at-large member may be, but need not be, selected from media otherwise represented on the Committee; however no organization may have more than one representative on the Committee.

(b) Elections shall be held as early as practicable in each year, and in no case later than March 31. A vacancy in the membership of the Committee occurring prior to the expiration of a term shall be filled by a special election called for that purpose by the Committee.

(c) The Standing Committee of the Press Photographers' Gallery shall propose no change or changes in these rules except upon petition in writing signed by not less than 25 accredited members of the gallery.

2. Persons desiring admission to the Press Photographers' Gallery of the Senate shall make application in accordance with Rule 33 of the Senate, which rule shall be interpreted and administered by the Standing Committee of Press Photographers subject to the review and approval of the Senate Committee on Rules and Administration.

3. The Standing Committee of Press photographers shall limit membership in the photographers' gallery to bona fide news photographers of repute in their profession and Heads of Photographic Bureaus under such rules as the Standing Committee of Press Photographers shall prescribe.

4. Provided, however, that the Standing Committee of Press Photographers shall admit to the gallery no person who does not establish to the satisfaction of the Committee all of the following:

(a) That any member is not engaged in paid publicity or promotion work or in prosecuting any claim before Congress or before any department of the Government, and will not become so engaged while a member of the gallery.

---

*Information is based on data furnished and edited by each respective gallery.

(b) That he or she is not engaged in any lobbying activity and will not become so engaged while a member of the gallery.

The above rules have been approved by the Committee on Rules and Administration.

J. DENNIS HASTERT,
Speaker, House of Representatives.

TRENT LOTT,
Chairman, Senate Committee on Rules and Administration.

MEMBERS ENTITLED FOR ADMISSION

PRESS PHOTOGRAPHERS' GALLERY

Allen, John T.: Washington Post
Alleruzzo, Maya: Washington Times
Alpert, Brian F.: Keystone Press Agency
Alswang, Ralph: Freelance
Anderson, Christopher: Freelance
Applewhite, J. Scott: Associated Press Photos
Archambault, Charles: U.S. News & World Report
Arias, Juana L.: Washington Post
Ashe, James F.: Freelance
Ashley, Douglas G.: Suburban Communications Corp.
Attlee, Tracey A.: Freelance
Aubry, Timothy R.: Reuters News Pictures
Augustino, Jocelyn: Freelance
Ballard, Karen: Freelance
Barouh, Stan: Freelance
Barrett, Steve E.: Freelance
Baughman, J. Ross: Washington Times
Baylen, Elizabeth: Washington Times
Beals, Herman: Reuters News Pictures
Beiser, H. Darr: USA/Today
Benavides, Mauricio: Freelance
Bengiveno, Nicole: New York Times
Benic, Patrick T.: Freelance
Bentley, PF: Newsweek
Berg, Lisa: Freelance
Bernasconi, Francisco: New York Times
Biber, Mehmet: Hurriyet
Susan, Biddle: Washington Post
Jeremy, Bigwood: Freelance
Bingham, Mary (Molly): Freelance
Binks, Porter L.: Sports Illustrated
Blass, Eileen, M.: USA/Today
Bloom, Richard: National Journal
Bochatey, Terry F.: Reuters News Pictures
Boitano, Stephen J.: Freelance
Borea, Roberto: Associated Press Photos
Boston, Bernard N.: Bryce Mountain Courier
Bouchard, Renee M.: Freelance
Bowe, Christy: ImageCatcher News
Bowmer, Frederick S.: Associated Press Photos
Brack, William D: Black Star
Brantley, James: Washington Times
Bridges, George S.: Knight Ridder Tribune News Service
Brooks, Dudley: Washington Post
Brown, Robert A.: Richmond Times Dispatch
Brown, Stephen R.: Freelance
Bui, Khue: Newsweek
Burke, Lauren V.: Freelance
Burnett, David: Contact Press Images
Burns, David S.: Photo Trends, Inc.
Butler, Thomas: The Hill
Calvert, Mary F.: Washington Times
Cameron, Gary A.: Reuters News Pictures
Carioti, Richard A.: Washington Post
Cavanaugh, Matthew T.: Freelance
Cedeno, Ken: Freelance
Ceneta, Manuel B.: Freelance
Chang, Cyrena: The Journal Newspapers
Chikwendu, Jahi: Washington Post
Clark, Bill: Scripps Howard News Service
Clark, Kevin: Washington Post
Clement, Richard: Reuters News Pictures
Cobb, Jodi: National Geographic
Cohen, Marshall H.: Bigmarsh News Photos
Colburn, James E.: Time Magazine
Connor, Michael: Washington Times
Cook, Dennis: Associated Press Photos
Cooke, John: Credit Union Times
Coppage, Gary R.: Photo Press International
Corder, Chris: United Press International
Cramp, Stacey: Legal Times
Crandall, Bill: Freelance
Crandall, Rob: Freelance
Crowley, Stephen: New York Times
Curtis, Rob: Army Times Publishing
Cutts, Peter J.: Freelance
D'Angelo, Rebecca: Freelance
DeArmas, Adrienne: Apix
DeGyor, Henrik: Post-Newsweek Media
Devadas, Rajan: Front Line
Dharapak, Charles: Associated Press Photos
DiBari, Jr., Michael: Freelance
Dillon, Timothy P.: USA/Today
DiPasquale, Jill: Army Times Publishing
Douliery, Olivier: Post-Newsweek Media
Downing, Lawrencc: Reuters News Pictures
Doyle, Kevin W.: Freelance
Du Cille, Michael: Washington Post
Eddins, Jr., Joseph M.: Washington Times
Edmonds, Ronald: Associated Press Photos
Elfers, Steve: Army Times Publishing
Ellis, Richard: Getty Images
Ellsworth, Katie: Newsweek
Emanuel, Hector: Freelance
Evstafiev, Mikhail: Reuters News Pictures
Falk, Steven M.: The Philadelphia Daily News
Falls, Jr., John W.: Freelance
Fenster, J. Adam: Post-Newsweek Media
Ferrell, Scott: CQ Weekly

MEMBERS ENTITLED FOR ADMISSION—Continued

Ficara, John F.: Freelance
Fitz-Patrick, Bill: Freelance
Fiume, Gregory C.: Freelance
Foster, Jacqueline Mia: Freelance
Fox, Travis: Wash. Post Newsweek Interactive
Franklin, Ross D.: Washington Times
Franko, Jeff: Gannett News Service
Frazza, Luke:Agence France-Presse
Fremson, Ruth: New York Times
Gainer, Denny: USAToday.com
Gamarra, Ruben F.: Notimex
Garcia, Mannie: Freelance
Geissinger, Michael A.: Freelance
Gifford, Porter: Freelance
Gilbert, Patrice J.: Freelance
Gillis, John A.: United Press International
Godfrey, Mark: Freelance
Goulait, Bert V.: Washington Times
Graham, Douglas: Roll Call
Graves, Thomas A: Freelance
Gripas, Yuri: Sipa Press
Guzy, Carol: Washington Post
Hall, John: Associated Press Photos
Halstead, Dirck: The Digital Journalist
Hamburg, Harry: New York Daily News
Harrington, John H.: Black Star
Harris, Steven J.: Polaris Images
Hartmann, Paul: Freelance
Helber, Stephen: Associated Press Photos
Herbert, Gerald: Associated Press Photos
Hershorn, Gary: Reuters News Pictures
Hittle, David E.: Freelance
Holden, Peter: World & I
Holloway, David S.: Apix
Hosefros, Paul: New York Times
Jackson, Lawrence: Associated Press Photos
Jacobs, Vance: Freelance
Jaffe, Stephen: Agence France-Presse
Jennings, Stan: Jennings Publications
Johnson, Richard D.: Freelance
Johnson, Cynthia: Freelance
Johnston, Frank B.: Washington Post
Joseph, Marvin: Washington Post
Juarez, Miguel: Reforma
Kahn, Nikki: Freelance
Kang, Hyungwon: Reuters News Pictures
Katz, Martin I.: Chesapeake News Service
Kennedy, Chuck: Knight Ridder Tribune News Service
Kennerly, David H.: Newsweek
Kent, Jeff: Director
Kim, Yunghi: Freelance
Kittner, Sam: Freelance
Kleinfeld, Michael: United Press International
Kleponis, Chris: Freelance
Kon, Toshiyuki: The Yomiuri Shimbun
Kossoff, Leslie: Freelance
Kozak, Richard: Insight Magazine
Kraft, Brooks: Time Magazine
Lamarque, Kevin: Reuters News Pictures
Lamkey, Jr., Rod A.: Washington Times
Latimer, Bronwen: U.S. News & World Report
LaVor, Martin L.: Freelance
Lee, Chang W.: New York Times
Lessig, Alan: Federal Times
Lewter, Lani R.: Global News Photo
Lipski, Richard A.: Washington Post
Liss, Steve: Time Magazine
Lopez, Jose: New York Times
LoScalzo, Jim: U.S. News & World Report
Lowy, Benjamin: Freelance
Lu, Mingxiang: Xinhua News Agency
Lueders, Martin: Freelance
Lustig, Raymond J.: Washington Post
Lutzky, Micheal: Washington Post
Lynaugh, Michael: Freelance
Lynch, Liz: National Journal
Lynch, M. Patricia: Frontiers News Magazine
MacMillan, Jeffrey G.: U.S. News & World Report
Maddaloni, Chris: Roll Call
Madrid, Michael: USA/Today
Mallin, Jay: Impact Visuals
Mallory, Tyler: Freelance
Mara, Melina: Seattle Post Intelligencer
Markel, Brad: Capri
Marks, Donovan: Freelance
Marquette, Joseph C.: European Press Association
Martineau, Gerald: Washington Post
Monsivais, Pablo Martinez: Associated Press Photos
Mathieson, Greg E.: MAI Photo Agency
McCrehin, Jud: Army Times Publishing
McDonnell, John: Washington Post
McKay, Richard D.: Cox Newspapers
McNamee, Win: Reuters News Pictures
Menashe, Isaac: Freelance
Meyers, Keith: New York Times
Mills, Douglas: New York Times
Molloy, Michelle: Newsweek
Morris, Christopher: Time Magazine
Morris, Larry E.: Washington Post
Morrissey, Heather: Gannett News Service
Mosley, Leigh H: Freelance
Murphy, Timothy A.: Freelance
Musi, Vincent J.: Time Magazine
Naltchayan, Joyce: Agence France-Presse
Nelson, Andrew P.: Christian Science Monitor
Newton, Gregg: Reuters News Pictures
Nipp, Lisa: Freelance
Nozzoli, Akram: Saudi Press Agency
O'Leary, William P: Washington Post
Ommanney, Charles: Newsweek
Otfinowski, Danuta: Freelance
Owen, Clifford: Washington Times
Pajic, Kamenko: Freelance
Panagos, Dimitrios: Greek American News Agency

MEMBERS ENTITLED FOR ADMISSION—Continued

Parcels, James A.: Washington Post
Parker, Howard (Hank) H.: Freelance
Parsons, Nate: Washington Post
Pastor, Nancy: Washington Times
Patterson, Kathryn B.: USA Today
Pearson, Robert L.: Agence France-Presse
Perkins, Lucien: Washington Post
Perry, William: Freelance
Persson, Jessica: Reuters News Pictures
Petros, Bill: Freelance
Philpott, William: Freelance
Poleski, David: Freelance
Powers, Carol T.: Freelance
Price, Brian: Times Community Newspapers
Prichard, James W.: Education Week
Purcell, Steven: Freelance
Raab, Susana A.: Freelance
Raimondo, Lois: Washington Post
Rasmussen, Randy L.: Oregonian
Reed, Jason: Reuters News Pictures
Reeder, Robert A: Washington Post
Reinhard, Rick: Freelance
Remsberg, Edwin H.: Getty Images
Ricardel, Vincent J.: Freelance
Richards, Paul J.: Agence France-Presse
Richardson, Joel M.: Washington Post
Riecken, Astrid: Washington Times
Riley, Molly: Reuters News Pictures
Roberts, Nicholas: Freelance
Robinson, Scott: Freelance
Robinson-Chavez, Michael: Washington Post
Roggenbrodt, Jacqueline: Freelance
Ronay, Vivian: Freelance
Rosenbaum, Daniel: Washington Times
Rossetti, Amy: Media General
Ryan, Patrick: The Hill
Sachs, Arnold: Consolidated News Pictures
Sachs, Ronald M.: Consolidated News Pictures
Salisbury, Barbara L.: The Gazette
Schaeffer, Sandra L.: MAI Photo Agency
Schroeder, Bjorn O.: German Newspaper Group
Schumacher, Karl H.: Freelance
Schwartz, David S.: Freelance
Schwarz, Ira J.: Freelance
Scull, David: Freelance
Sell, Blake P.: Sipa Press
Shell, Mary: Time Magazine
Shelley, Allison: Education Week
Silverman, Joseph A.: Washington Times
Simon, Martin: Corbis Saba
Sloan, Timothy: Agence France-Presse
Smith, Dayna: Washington Post
Sommer, Emilie: Freelance
Souza, Peter J.: Chicago Tribune
Spillers, Linda J.: Freelance
Springer, Mike: Zuma Press
Starr, Adele: Freelance
Stenzel, Maria: National Geographic
Stephenson, Al: Freelance
Sudyatmiko, Karina: Suara Pembaruan
Sykes, Jack W.: Professional Pilot Magazine
Sypher, Mark F.: Fauquier Times-Democrat
Takeda, Yasushi: Shukan Shincho, Shinchosha Co.
Tefft-Soraghan, Jessica: Washington Times
Temchine, Michael: Freelance
Theiler, Michael: Reuters News Pictures
Thew, Shawn: European Press Association
Thiessen, Mark: National Geographic
Thomas, Margaret: Washington Post
Thomas, Ronald W.: Freelance
Thresher, James M.: Washington Post
Trippett, Robert: Sipa Press
Turner, Tyrone: Freelance
Usher, Chris: Apix
Van Riper, Frank A.: Washingtonpost.com
Varias, Stelios A.: Reuters News Pictures
Visser, Robert: Photopress Washington
Vosin, Sarah L.: Washington Post
Votaw, Jr., Charles W.: Freelance
Vucci, Evan: European Press Association
Wagreich, Ian: Freelance
Walker, Diana: Time Magazine
Walker, Harry E.: Knight Ridder Tribune News Service
Walsh, Susan: Associated Press Photos
Ward, Fred: Black Star
Watkins, Jr., Frederick L.: Johnson Publishing Co.
Whitesell, Gregory: Insight Magazine
Williams, Tom: Roll Call
Williamson, Michael: Washington Post
Wilson, Jim: New York Times
Wilson, Mark L.: Getty Images
Wines, Heather: Gannett News Service
Wolf, Lloyd: Freelance
Wollenberg, Roger L.: United Press International
Wong, Alex: Getty Images
Woodall, Andrea B.: Washington Post
Woodward, Tracy L.: Washington Post
Wright, Donald A.: Freelance
Yim, Heesoon: HANA
Zaklin, Stefan: Freelance
Ziffer, Steve: Freelance
Zinn, Warren: Army Times Publishing

SERVICES REPRESENTED

(Service and telephone number, office address, and name of representative)

AGENCE FRANCE-PRESSE—(202) 414–0551; 1015 15th Street, NW., Suite 500, Washington, DC 20005: Frazza, Luke; Jaffe, Stephen; Naltchayan, Joyce; Pearson, Robert; Richards, Paul; Sloan, Timothy.

APIX—(202) 262–7112; 638 6th Street, NE., Washington, DC 20002: DeArmas, Adrienne; Holloway, David; Usher, Chris.

ARMY TIMES—(703) 750–8170; 6883 Commercial Drive, Springfield, VA 22159: Curtis, Rob; DiPasquale, Jill; Elfers, Steve; McCrehin, Jud; Zinn, Warren.

ASSOCIATED PRESS—(202) 776–9510; 2021 K Street, NW., Washington, DC 20006: Applewhite, J. Scott; Borea, Roberto; Bowmer, Frederick; Cook, Dennis; Dharapak, Charles; Edmonds, Ronald; Hall, John; Helber, Stephen; Herbert, Gerald; Jackson, Lawrence; Martinez Monsivais, Pablo; Walsh, Susan.

BLACK STAR—(703) 547–1176; 7704 Tauxemont Rd, Alexandria, VA 22308: Brack, William; Harrington, John; Ward, Fred.

CAPRI PRESS—(717) 757–2962; 485 Sundale Drive, York, PA 17402: Markel, Brad.

CHESAPEAKE NEWS SERVICE—(410) 484–3500; 2534 Old Court Road, Baltimore, MD 21022: Katz, Martin.

CHICAGO TRIBUNE—(202) 824–8200; 1325 G Street, NW., Suite 200, Washington, DC 20005: Souza, Peter.

CHRISTIAN SCIENCE MONITOR—(617) 450–2000; 1 Norway Street, Boston, MA 02115: Nelson, Andrew.

CONGRESSIONAL QUARTERLY—(202) 822–1431; 1414 22nd Street, NW., Washington, DC 20037: Ferrell, Scott.

CONSOLIDATED NEWS PICTURES—(202) 543–3203; 209 Pennsylvania Avenue, SE., Washington, DC 20003: Sachs, Ronald; Sachs, Arnold.

CONTACT PRESS IMAGES—(212) 481–6910; 116 E Street, New York, NY 10016: Burnett, David.

COX NEWSPAPERS—(202) 331–0900; 2000 Pennsylvania, Avenue, NW., Washington, DC 20006: McKay, Richard.

CREDIT UNION TIMES—(301) 845–7820; 8507 Inspiration Avenue, Walkersville, MD 21793: Cooke, John.

EDUCATION WEEK—(301) 280–3100; 6935 Arlington Road, Suite 100, Bethesda, MD 20814: Prichard, James; Shelley, Allison.

EUROPEAN PRESSPHOTO AGENCY—(202) 288–1029; 1252 National Press Building, 529 14th Street, NW., Washington, DC 20045: Marquette, Joseph; Thew, Shawn; Vucci, Evan.

FROINTIERS NEWS MAGAZINE—(301) 229–0635; P.O. Box 634, Glen Echo, MD 20812: Lynch, Patricia.

GANNETT NEWS SERVICE—(703) 854–3675; 7950 Jones Branch Drive, McLean, VA 22107: Franko, Jeff; Morrissey, Heather; Wines, Heather.

GERMAN NEWSPAPER GROUP—(202) 244–5013; 4100 Massachusetts Avenue, Washington, DC 20016: Schroeder, Bjorn.

GETTY IMAGES—(202) 861–8551; One Hudson Place, 75 Varick Street, New York, NY 10013: Ellis, Richard; Wilson, Mark, Wong, Alex.

GREEK AMERICAN NEWS AGENCY—(202) 332–2727; 107 Frederick Avenue, Babylon, NY 11702: Panagos, Dimitrios.

HANA—(202) 393–1166; 1111 National Press Building, Washington, DC 20045: Yim, Heesoon.

HURRIYET—(703) 978–8073; 8919 Moreland Lane, Annandale, VA 22003: Biber, Mehmet.

IMAGECATCHER NEWS—(202) 483–3791; 3133 Connecticut Avenue, NW., Washington, DC 20008: Bowe, Christy.

INSIGHT—(202) 636–3000; 3600 New York Avenue, NE., Washington, DC 20002: Kozak, Richard; Whitesell, Gregory.

JENNINGS PUBLICATIONS—(301) 946–5538; 2600 Plyers Mill Road, Silver Spring, MD 20902: Jennings, Stan.

JOHNSON PUBLISHING CO.—(202) 393–5860; 1750 Pennsylvania Avenue, NW., Washington, DC 20006: Watkins, Jr. Frederick.

KEYSTONE PRESS AGENCY—(212) 924–8123; 202 East 42nd Street, New York, NY 10017: Alpert, Brian.

KNIGHT RIDDER TRIBUNE—(202) 383–6169; 790 National Press Building, Washington, DC 20045: Bridges, George; Kennedy, Charles; Harry Walker.

LAVOR GROUP—(703) 765–7187; 7710 Lookout Court, Alexandria, VA 22306: LaVor, Martin.

LEGAL TIMES—(202) 457–0686; 1730 M Street, NW., Suite 802, Washington, DC 20036: Cramp, Stacey.

SERVICES REPRESENTED—Continued

MAI PHOTO AGENCY—(703) 968–0030; 6601 B Ashmere Lane, Centreville, VA 22020: Mathieson, Greg; Schaeffer, Sandra.

MEDIA GENERAL—(202) 662–7660; 14010 Smoketown Road, Woodbridge, VA 22192: Rossetti, Amy.

NATIONAL GEOGRAPHIC—(202) 857–7000; 1145 17th Street, NW., Washington, DC 20036: Cobb, Jodi; Stenzel, Maria; Thiessen, Mark.

NATIONAL JOURNAL—(202) 739–8400; 1501 M Street, NW., Suite 300, Washington, DC 20005: Bloom, Richard; Lynch, Liz.

NEW YORK TIMES—(202) 862–0300; 1627 Eye Street, NW., Washington, DC 20006: Bengiveno, Nicole; Bernasconi, Francisco; Crowley, Stephen; Fremson, Ruth; Hosefros, Paul; Lee, Chang; Lopez, Jose; Meyers, Keith; Mills, Douglas; Wilson, Jim.

NEWSWEEK—(202) 626–2085; 1750 Pennsylvania Avenue, NW., Washington, DC 20006: Bentley, PF; Bui, Khue; Ellsworth, Katie; Kennerly, David; Molloy, Michelle; Ommanney, Charles.

NOTIMEX—(202) 347–5227; 529 14th Street, NW., Washington, DC 20009: Gamarra, Ruben.

OREGONIAN—(503) 221–8370; 1320 SW Broadway, Portland, OR 97201: Rasmussen, Randy.

PHOTO PRESS INTERNATIONAL—(703) 548–7172; 2 East Glebe Road, Alexandria, VA 22305: Coppage, Gary.

PHOTOPRESS WASHINGTON—(202) 234–8787; National Press Building, Suite 2105, Washington, DC 20045: Visser, Robert.

POST-NEWSWEEK—(301) 670–2011; 1200 Quince Orchard Lane, Gaithersburg, MD 20878: DeGyor, Henrik; Douliery, Olivier; Fenster, J. Adam.

PROFESSIONAL PILOT MAGAZINE—(703) 370–0606; 3014 Colvin Street, Alexandria, VA 22314: Sykes, Jack.

REFORMA—(202) 628–0031; 1126 National Press Building, Washington, DC 20045: Juarez, Miguel.

REUTERS NEWS PICTURES—(202) 898–8333; 1333 H Street, NW., Suite 410, Washington, DC 20005: Aubry, Timothy; Beals, Herman; Bochatey, Terry; Cameron, Gary; Clement, Richard; Downing, Lawrence; Evstafiev, Mikhail; Hershorn, Gary; Kang, Hyungwon; Lamarque, Kevin; McNamee, Win; Newton, Gregg; Reed, Jason; Riley, Molly; Theiler, Michael; Varias, Stelios.

RICHMOND TIMES DISPATCH—(804) 649–6486; 333 East Grace Street, Richmond, VA 23219: Brown, Robert.

ROLL CALL—(202) 824–6800; 50 F Street, NW., 7th Floor, Washington, DC 20001: Graham, Douglas; Maddaloni, Chris; Williams, Tom.

SCRIPPS HOWARD—(202) 408–2723; 1090 Vermont Avenue, NW., 10th Floor, Washington, DC 20005: Clark, Bill.

SIPA PRESS—(212) 463–0150; 30 West 21st Street, New York, NY 10010: Trippett, Robert; Gripas, Yuri; Sell, Blake.

SHUKAN SHINCHO, SHINCHOSHA CO.—(703) 243–1569; 2001 North Adams Street, #715, Arlington, VA 22201: Takeda, Yasushi.

SPORTS ILLUSTRATED—(212) 522–3325; 1271 Avenue of the Americas, Room 1970, New York, NY 10020: Binks, Porter.

SUBURBAN COMMUNICATIONS CORP.—(810) 645–5164; 872 Dursley Road, Bloomfield Hills, ME 48304: Ashley, Douglas.

THE HILL—(202) 628–8525; 733 15th Street, Washington, DC 20005: Butler, Thomas; Ryan, Patrick.

TIME—(202) 861–4062; 555 12th Street, NW., Suite 600, Washington, DC 20004: Colburn, James; Kraft, Brooks; Liss, Steve; Morris, Christopher; Musi, Vincent; Shell, Mary; Walker, Diana.

US NEWS AND WORLD REPORT—(202) 955–2210; 1050 Thomas Jefferson Street, NW., Washington, DC 20007: Archambault, Charles; Latimer, Bronwen; LoScalzo, Jim; MacMillan, Jeffrey.

USA TODAY—(703) 854–5216; 7950 Jones Branch Road, McLean, VA 22107: Patterson, Kathryn; Beiser, H. Darr; Blass, Eileen; Dillon, Timothy; Madrid, Michael; Gainer, Denny.

UNITED PRESS INTERNATIONAL—(202) 387–7965; 1510 H Street, NW., Washington, DC 20005: Gillis, John; Kleinfeld, Michael; Wollenberg, Roger.

WASHINGTON POST—(202) 334–7380; 1150 15th Street, NW., Washington, DC 20079: Allen, John; Arias, Juana; Biddle, Susan; Brooks, Dudley; Carioti, Richard; Chikwendu, Jahi; Clark, Kevin; Du Cille, Michael; Guzy, Carol; Johnston, Frank; Joseph, Marvin; Lipski, Richard; Lustig, Raymond; Lutzky, Micheal; Martineau, Gerald; McDonnell, John; Morris, Larry; O'Leary, William; Parcels, James; Parsons, Nate; Perkins, Lucien; Raimondo, Lois; Reeder, Robert; Richardson, Joel; Robinson-Chavez, Michael; Smith, Dayna; Thomas, Margaret; Thresher, James; Vosin, Sarah; Williamson, Michael; Woodall, Andrea; Woodward, Tracy.

WASHINGTON TIMES—(202) 636–3000; 3600 New York Avenue, NE., Washington, DC 20002: Alleruzzo, Maya; Baughman, J. Ross; Baylen, Elizabeth; Brantley, James; Calvert, Mary; Connor, Michael; Eddins, Jr., Joseph; Franklin, Ross; Goulait, Bert; Lamkey, Jr., Rod; Owen, Clifford; Pastor, Nancy; Riecken, Astrid; Rosenbaum, Daniel; Silverman, Joseph; Tefft-Soraghan, Jessica.

SERVICES REPRESENTED—Continued

WORLD & I—(202) 636–4004; 3600 New York Avenue, NE., Washington, DC 20002: Holden, Peter.

XINHUA NEWS AGENCY—(703) 875–0086; 1740N 14th Street, Arlington, VA 22209: Lu, Mingxiang.

FREELANCE

Freelance—Alswang, Ralph; Anderson, Christopher; Ashe, James; Attlee, Tracey; Augustino, Jocelyn; Ballard, Karen; Barouh, Stan; Barrett, Steve; Benavides, Mauricio; Benic, Patrick; Berg, Lisa; Bigwood, Jeremy; Bingham, Mary; Boitano, Stephen; Bouchard, Renee; Brown, Stephen; Burke, Lauren; Cavanaugh, Matthew; Cedeno, Ken; Ceneta, Manuel; Crandall, Bill; Crandall, Rob; Cutts, Peter; D'Angelo, Rebecca; DiBari, Jr., Michael; Doyle, Kevin; Emanuel, Hector; Falls, Jr., John; Ficara, John; Fitz-Patrick, Bill; Fiume, Gregory; Foster, Jacqueline Mia; Garcia, Mannie; Geissinger, Michael; Gifford, Porter; Gilbert, Patrice; Godfrey, Mark; Graves, Thomas; Hartmann, Paul; Hittle, David; Jacobs, Vance; Johnson, Richard; Johnson, Cynthia; Kahn, Nikki; Kim, Yunghi; Kittner, Sam; Kleponis, Chris; Kossoff, Leslie; LaVor, Martin; Lowy, Benjamin; Lueders, Martin; Lynaugh, Michael; Mallory, Tyler; Marks, Donovan; Menashe, Isaac; Mosley, Leigh; Murphy, Timothy; Nipp, Lisa; Otfinowski, Danuta; Pajic, Kamenko; Parker, Howard (Hank); Perry, William; Petros, Bill; Philpott, William; Poleski, David; Powers, Carol; Purcell, Steven; Raab, Susana; Reinhard, Rick; Ricardel, Vincent; Roberts, Nicholas; Robinson, Scott; Roggenbrodt, Jacqueline; Ronay, Vivian; Schumacher, Karl; Schwartz, David; Schwarz, Ira; Scull, David; Sommer, Emilie; Spillers, Linda; Springer, Mike; Starr, Adele; Stephenson, Al; Temchine, Michael; Thomas, Ronald; Turner, Tyrone; Votaw, Jr., Charles; Wagreich, Ian; Wolf, Lloyd; Wright, Donald; Zaklin, Stefan; Ziffer, Steve.

WHITE HOUSE NEWS PHOTOGRAPHERS' ASSOCIATION

PO 7119, Washington, DC 20044–7119, phone 785–5230

webmaster@whnpa.org www.whnpa.org

OFFICERS

Susan A. Walsh, Associated Press, *President*
Doug Wilkes, WTTG–TV, *Vice President*
Bob Pearson, Agence France Press, *Secretary*
Jeffrey D. Lawrence, Knight-Ridder Tribune, *Treasurer*

EXECUTIVE BOARD

Susan Biddle (Washington Post)
Dennis Brack (Black Star)
Ed Eaves (NBC News)
Travis Fox (Washingtonpost.com)
Mike Horan (WTTG-TV)
Cliff Owen (Washington Times)

MEMBERS REPRESENTED

Abraham, Mark: Freelance
Aceto, Lorie H.: Smithsonian Institution
Ake, J. David: Associated Press
Alberter Jr., William: CNN / Team Video Services
Allen, Tom: Washington Post
Alleruzzo, Maya: Washington Times
Allmond, Douglas: ABC
Almanza, Armando: Ventana Productions
Amos, James: Freelance
Andrews, Nancy: Detroit Free Press
Applewhite, J. Scott: Associated Press
Apt Johnson, Roslyn: WJLA–TV / Freelance
Archambault, Charles: U.S. News & World Report
Arias, Juana: Washington Post
Arrington, Percy: NBC
Ashley, Douglas: Freelance
Atherton, James K.W.: (life member)
Attlee, Tracey: Freelance
Aubry, Tim: Reuters
Aufdem-Brinke, Ronald: Freelance
Austin, Suzanne M.: Freelance
Auth, William: U.S. News & World Report
Babington-Heina, Martin Benjamin: Freelance
Bacheler, Peter: Freelance
Baughman, J. Ross: Washington Times
Beene, Richard: AFP Photo
Beiser, H.Darr: USA Today
Bennett, Ronald T.: HUD
Biddle, Susan: Washington Post
Binks, Porter: Sports Illustrated
Black, Brad: ABC News
Blair, James P.: Freelance
Blaylock, Kenneth L.: (life member)
Bochatey, Terry: Reuters
Bodnar, John: CNN
Boi, Hoan Pham: CBS News
Boitano, Stephen J.: Freelance
Boston, Bernie: Boston Photography & Marketing
Boswell Jr., Victor: Freelance
Bowe, Christy: ImageCatcher News
Bozick, Peter: Freelance
Brack, Dennis: Black Star
Brandon, Alex: Freelance
Brantley, James R.: Washington Times
Bridges, George Stubbs: Knight Ridder Tribune
Brooks, Dudley: Washington Post
Brown, Stephen: Freelance
Brown Sr., Henry M.: ABC
Bruce, Woodall Andrea: Washington Post
Bryan, Beverly: WJLA–TV
Burgess, Robert Harrison: Freelance
Burke, Lauren Victoria: Freelance
Burnett, David: Contact Press Images
Butler, Francis: Freelance

MEMBERS REPRESENTED—Continued

Cain, Stephen: ABC–TV
Calvert, Mary F.: Washington Times
Cameron, Gary: Reuters
Cannarozzi, Melissa: Washington Post
Carlisle, Stephen Daniel: Fuji Photo Film U.S.A., Inc.
Casey, Sean: NBC–4
Cassetta, Guido: Freelance
Castner, Edward: Freelance
Castoro, Susan Mary: Associated Press
Cedeno, Ken:
Chandler, Rod R.: Duffy Wall & Associaties
Chase, David: Cox Broadcasting
Chikwendiu, Jahi: Washington Post
Cirace, Robert: CNN
Cissell, James R.: The Freedom Forum
Clark, Bill: Scripps Howard
Clarkson, Rich: Clarkson & Associaties
Cobb, Jodi: National Geographic
Cohen, Marshall: Big Marsh News
Cohen, Stuart A.: Freelance
Cola, Craig: Washington Post Newsweek Interactive
Colburn, Jim: Time
Conger, Dean: Freelance
Cook, Dennis: Associated Press
Coppage, Gary R.: Photo Press International
Costello II, Thomas T.: Asbury Park Press
Crane, Arnold: Freelance
Craven Jr., Thomas:
Crawford, Walter: WJLA–TV
Crowley, Stephen: The New York Times
Cuong, Pham: CBS
Curley, Tom: Fuji Photo Film U.S.A. Inc.
Curran, Patrick J.: WTTG–TV
Curtis, Rob: Army Times Publishing
Dale, Bruce: Freelance
Darcey, Richard: (life member)
Daugherty, Bob: Associated Press
de la Cruz, Benedict: Washingtonpost.com
Dennehey, Paul: (life member)
Desantis, Dominic: Freelance
Desfor, Max: (life member)
Deslich, Steve: Knight Ridder Tribune Photo Service
DiMarco Jr., Salvatore: Time Magazine
Doane, Martin Call: WJLA–TV
Dodson, Richard: NBC
Downing, Larry: Reuters
Doyle, Anne: Fairfax Hospital Media Center
Drapkin, Arnold H.: TIME Magazine
duCille, Michel: Washington Post
Dukehart Jr., Thomas: WUSA–TV
Dunmire, John: WTTG–TV
Eaves, Ed: NBC News
Eddins, Joseph M.: Washington Times
Edmonds, Ron: Associated Press
Edrington, Michael Gordon: U.S. Army Visual Information Center
Ehrenberg Jr., Richard: ABC News
Elbert II, Joseph: Washington Post
Elfers, Stephen: Army Times Publishing Co.
Elvington, Glenn: Liveshots DC
Epstein, Linda D.: Knight Ridder Tribune
Estrada, Peter J.: WJLA–TV
Ewing, David: Freelance
Fagan, Bill: Noritsu America Corporation
Falk, Steven: Philadelphia Daily News
Feldman, Randy: Viewpoint Communications Inc.
Ferrell, Scott Joseph: Congressional Quarterly
Fiedler Jr., James: American Online
Fielman, Sheldon: NBC News
Fine, Holly: ABC
Fine, Paul: ABC
Finnigan, Vincent: Finnigan & Associates
Fitz-Patrick, Bill: Freelance
Fletcher, John E. (Jack): (life member)
Folwell, Frank: USA Today
Fookes, Gary: Freelance
Forcucci, Michael: WJLA–TV
Forner, Jim: WTTG–TV
Foss, Philip: ProTech
Fox, Travis Gerard: Washingtonpost.com
Foy, Mary Lou: Washington Post
Frame, John: WTTG–TV
Franklin, Ross: Washington Times
Frazza, Luke: AFP
Freeman, Roland: Freelance
Fridrich, George: NBC
Garcia, Mannie: Freelance
Garfinkel, Xeriqua: Freelance
Geissinger, Michael: Freelance
Gertler Lindsey, Debra: Washington Post
Gibson, Craig: Freelance
Gilbert, Kevin T.: The Arkhaven Group
Gilgannon, Pege: WJLA
Gilka, Robert: (life member)
Gmiter, Bernard: ABC News
Goodman, Jeffrey: NBC/Freelance
Goulait, Bert: Washington Times
Goulding, David: Emotion Pictures
Grace, Arthur: Freelance
Grieser Jr., Robert: ATL Picture Text Agency
Guzy, Carol: Washington Post
Halstead, Dirck: Time
Hamburg, Harry: NY Daily News
Harrington, John: Freelance
Harrity, Charles: U.S. News & World Report
Harvey, Alan: NBC
Hastings III, Sidney James: Sun Publications
Heikes, Darryl: Freelance
Heilemann, Tami: Department of Interior
Herbert, Gerald: Washington Times
Hernandez, Carlos Eleuterio: WTTG–TV
Herndon, Craig: Washington Post
Hershorn, Gary: Reuters

MEMBERS REPRESENTED—Continued

Herstatt, Steve: Fuji Photo Film U.S.A. Inc.
Hillian, Vanessa Barnes: Washington Post
Hinds, Hugh: WJLA–TV
Hoiland, Harald: WUSA–TV
Horan, Michael: WTTG–TV
Hoyt, Michael: Catholic Standard
Imai, Kesaharu: World Photo Press
Insana, Dominick: Fuji Photo Film U.S.A. Inc.
Irby, Kenneth F.: Poynter Institute
Johnson, Kenneth: ABC–TV
Johnson, Maurice: (life member)
Johnston, Frank: Washington Post
Jones, Nelson P.: WTTG–TV
Joy, Richard C.: Ventana Productions
Kahn, Nikki: Freelance
Kang, Hyungwon: Freelance
Katz, Marty: Chesapeake News Service
Kennedy, Thomas: Washington Post Newseek Interactive
Kennedy, Charles: Freelance
Kennerly, David Hume: Newsweek
Kent, Jeffrey S.: Press Photographers' Gallery
Kim, Yunghi: Freelance/Contact
Kinlaw, Worth: TVS @ CNN
Kinney, Barbara: Reuters
Kittner, Sam: Freelance
Kobersteen, Kent: National Geographic
Koppelman, Mitch: Reuters
Kossoff, Leslie E.: LK Photos
Krebs, Lawrence: WMAL
Krieger, Barbara: NBC/WRC–TV
Lamarque, Kevin: Reuters
Lambert, Ken: Associated Press
Lambert, H.M. Skip: (life member)
Larsen, Gregory: Freelance
Latimer, Bronwen: U.S. News & World Report
Lavies, Bianca: Freelance
LaVor, Marty: Freelance
Lawrence, Jeffrey Dean: Knight-Ridder Tribune
Lehnhardt, Brian Douglas: U.S. Army
Levin, Larry: Freelance
Levy, John:
Levy, Glenn Ann: Freelance
Lewin, Jim: Image Delivery Systems, Inc
Lion, Harold: Lion Recording Services, Inc.
Lipski, Richard: Washington Post
Lloyd Jr., Raymond L.: NYANG USAF
Lockhart, June:
Lodovichetti, Arthur:
Loehrke, Timothy Don: Army Times
Lopez, Jose: New York Times
Lorek, Stanley: ABC
LoScalzo, James: US News & World Report
Love, Diane: International Center of Photography
Luce, Robert John: Fuji Photo Film USA
Lustig, Ray: Washington Post
Lutzky, Michael: Washington Post
Lynch Jr., Robert J.: WTTG–TV
Lyons, Paul: NET
MacDonald, Charles Wayne: National Geographic Channel
MacDonald, Jim: Canadian TV Network
MacMillan, Jeffrey: US News & World Report
Madrid, Michael A.: USA Today
Maggiolo, Vito: CNN
Manley, Jerold: Freelance
Mark, Leighton: Associated Press
Markel, Harry W.: Fuji Photo Film USA
Marks, Donovan: Washington National Cathedral
Maroon, Fred:
Marquette, Joseph: Associated Press
Martin Jr., James T.: ABC News
Martineau, Gerald: Washington Post
Martinez Monsivais, Pablo: Associated Press
Mason, Thomas: WTTG–TV
Massey, Toby: Associated Press
Mathieson, Greg E.: MAI Photo News Agency, Inc.
Maze, Stephanie: Maze Productions Inc.
Mazer-Field, Joni: Freelance
Mazzatenta, O. Louis: Freelance
McCarthy III, Edward F.X.: Hudson Valley Black Press
McCrehin, Jud: Army Times Publishing Co.
McDonnell, Suzanne: Shortenz DC
McDonnell, John: Washington Post
McDougall, Ian: Reuters Television
McKay, Richard: Cox Newspapers
McNamee, Wallace: Freelance
McNamee, Win: Reuters
McNay, James E.: San Jose State University
Mendelsohn, Matthew: USA Today
Milenic, Alexander: Freelance
Mills, Doug: Associated Press
Mishoe Jr., Philip: ABC
Mitchell, Bruce: Fuji Photo Film U.S.A., Inc.
Mole, Robert: NBC
Morris, Larry: Washington Post
Murphy, Timothy: Freelance
Murphy, John: Freelance
Murray, Timothy: KalenVentana Productions
Musolf, Patricia: The Tiffen Company
Nakashima, Giuliana: Washington Post
Naltchayan, Joyce: Agence France Presse
Natoli, Sharon: Freelance
Nelson, Andrew Paul: Christian Science Monitor
Newton, Jonathan A.: Washington Post
Nighswander, Larry: Ohio University
Nighswander, Marcia: Ohio University
Nisselson, Evan: Eye Tide Media Inc.
Nolan, David S.: Nolan & Company
Norling, Richard A.: Freelance
Oates, Walter: (life member)
Ohlson, Kevin David: U.S. Air Force
O'Keefe, Dennis: Freelance
O'Leary, William: Washington Post

MEMBERS REPRESENTED—Continued

Ours, Karen Leslie: WJLA–TV Channel 7
Owen, Cliff: Washington Times
Pajic, Kamenko: Freelance
Panzer, Chester: NBC–WRC
Parcell, James: Washington Post
Partlow, Wayne: Associated Press
Patterson, Kathryn: USA Today
Patterson, Jay: ABC
Pearson, Robert: AFP
Pelletier, Richard: Kodak Professional
Pensinger, Douglas Alan: Allsport Photography
Perkins, Lucian: Washington Post
Peterson, Jr., Robert: Freelance
Petras, William: NBC
Petros, Bill: Freelance
Pinczuk, Murray: Freelance
Poleski, David: Photo Press International
Poole, John: Washington Post Newsweek Interactive
Popper, Andrew: Business Week
Potasznik, David: Point of View Productions
Powell Jr., William: NBC
Powers, Carol: (active)
Proser, Michael: ABC–News
Raab, Susana Alicia: Freelance
Raimondo, Lois: Washington Post
Reeder, Robert: Washington Post
Reinstein, Mark: Freelance
Rensberger, Scott Alan: Freelance
Richards, Paul J.: AFP
Richards, Roger Maris: Washington Times
Richardson, Joel: Washington Post
Riecken, Astrid: Washington Times
Riffle, Luke John: Ventana Productions
Riley, Molly: Reuters
Robinson Sr., Clyde: NBC
Robinson-Chavez, Michael: Washington Post
Ronay, Vivian: Freelance
Rosenbaum, Daniel: Washington Times
Rossetti, Amy: Potomac News
Roth, Rebecca Susan: USA Today Weekend
Roth Jr., Johnie: NBC
Ruland, Brian G: U.S. Army White House Communications Agency
Russell, James R.: Defense Information School
Rysak, F. David: WTTG–TV
Sachs, Arnie: Consolidated News Photos
Sachs, Ronald M.: Consolidated News Photos
Saltzman, Ron: Fuji Photo Film U.S.A., Inc.
Saunders, Ray Keller: Washington Post
Schaeffer, Sandra Lynne: MAI Photo News Agency
Schmick, Paul: Freelance
Schule, James: Fox News Network
Schumacher, Karl: Freelance
Schwarz, Ira: Freelance
Scicchitano, Carmine D.: NBC
Semiatin, Morris: Morris Semiatin-Photographer
Shannon, Dennis: CBS News
Shelley, Allison L.: Education Week
Shlemon, Christopher: Independent TV News
Shutt, Charles: Communications Consultant
Sikes, Laura Ann: Freelance
Silverman, Joe: Washington Times
Singelis, Phaedra: Washington Post.com
Sisson, Robert: Macro/Nature Photography
Smith, Dayna: Washington Post
Souza, Peter: Chicago Tribune
Spillers, Linda Jean: Freelance
Stearns, Stan: Freelance
Stein, Norman: Sinclair Broadcast Group
Stein III, Arthur: Freelance
Stephenson, Al: Freelance
Stoddard, Mark: Freelance
Strong, Bob: Reuters
Suddeth, Richard: Freelance
Swanson, Richard: Freelance
Sweets, Fred: Associated Press
Swenson, Gordon: ABC
Swiatkowski, Edward:
Sykes, Jack: Professional Pilot Magazine
Tama, Mario: Freelance
Tasnadi, Charles: (life member)
Taylor, Medford: Freelance
Tefft-Soraghan, Jessica: Washington Times
Thalman, Mark: Ventana Productions
Thew, Shawn A.: Freelance
Thomas, Margaret: Washington Post
Thomas, Ronald: World Bank Group
Thresher, James: Washington Post
Thumma, Barry: Retired
Tinsley, Jeff: Smithsonian Institution
Torelli, Joseph: Avid Technology
Traver, Joseph R.: Freelance
Trippett, Robert: Sipa Press
Tsuboi, Kazua: World Photo Press
Tuckson D.D.S., Coleman: Consolidated News Pictures
Tuel, Ted Richard: Ventana Productions
Usher, Chris R.: Freelance
Valeri, Charlene: National Geographic
Van Riper, Frank: Freelance
Varias, Stelios: Reuters
Verna, Tressa: NBC–News Dateline
Voisin, Sarah L.: Washington Post
Walker, Diana: Time Magazine
Walker, Harry E.: Knight Ridder Tribune Photo
Wallace, Jim: Smithsonian Institution
Walsh, Susan: Associated Press
Walter, Charles A.: National Geographic
Ward, Fred: Black Star
Watrud, Donald: WTTG–TV
Waugh, William: Associated Press
Weik, David: ABC
Weller, George: Freelance
Wells, Jim: Freelance
Whyte, Paul: USA Today
Wilkes, Douglas: WTTG–TV

MEMBERS REPRESENTED—Continued

Williams, Robert: NBC News
Williams, Thomas L: Roll Call Newspaper
Williams, Milton: Freelance
Williams, Christopher James: U.S. Navy
Williamson, Michael: Washington Post
Wilson, Jamal: Freelance
Wilson, James: New York Times
Wilson, Woodrow R.: (life member)
Woodward, Tracy: Washington Post
Woszczyna, Jaroslaw T.: Expess Magazine
Wright, David R.: Knight Ridder Tribune
Yates II, H. William: CBS News Freelance
Yazdanfar, Mohammad: RezaSheyda Photography
Yokota, Victoria: Freelance
Young, Bruce: The Evans-McCan Group
Young, Jennifer Law: The Evans-McCan Group
Zacharias, Dan: Fuji Photo Film U.S.A., Inc.
Zervos, Stratis: Qwest Digital Media
Zinn, Warren Todd: Army Times
Zlotky, Alan: Washington Times

RADIO AND TELEVISION CORRESPONDENTS' GALLERIES*

SENATE RADIO AND TELEVISION GALLERY

The Capitol, Room S–325, 224–6421

Director—Lawrence J. Janezich
Deputy Director—Jane Ruyle
Senior Media Coordinator—Michael Lawrence
Media Coordinators: Michael Mastrian, Sara Robertson

HOUSE RADIO AND TELEVISION GALLERY

The Capitol, Room H–321, 225–5214

Director—Tina Tate
Deputy Director—Beverly Braun
Assistant for Administrative Operations—Gail Davis
Assistant for Technical Operations—Olga Ramirez Kornacki
Assistants: Andrew Elias, Gerald Rupert

EXECUTIVE COMMITTEE OF THE RADIO AND TELEVISION CORRESPONDENTS' GALLERIES

Joe Johns, NBC News, *Chair*
Jerry Bodlander, Associated Press Radio
Bob Fuss, CBS News
Edward O'Keefe, ABC News
Dave McConnell, WTOP Radio
Richard Tillery, The Washington Bureau
David Wellna, NPR News

RULES GOVERNING RADIO AND TELEVISION CORRESPONDENTS' GALLERIES

1. Persons desiring admission to the Radio and Television Galleries of Congress shall make application to the Speaker, as required by Rule 34 of the House of Representatives, as amended, and to the Committee on Rules and Administration of the Senate, as required by Rule 33, as amended, for the regulation of Senate wing of the Capitol. Applicants shall state in writing the names of all radio stations, television stations, systems, or news-gathering organizations by which they are employed and what other occupation or employment they may have, if any. Applicants shall further declare that they are not engaged in the prosecution of claims or the promotion of legislation pending before Congress, the Departments, or the independent agencies, and that they will not become so employed without resigning from the galleries. They shall further declare that they are not employed in any legislative or executive department or independent agency of the Government, or by any foreign government or representative thereof; that they are not engaged in any lobbying activities; that they

*Information is based on data furnished and edited by each respective gallery.

do not and will not, directly or indirectly, furnish special information to any organization, individual, or group of individuals for the influencing of prices on any commodity or stock exchange; that they will not do so during the time they retain membership in the galleries. Holders of visitors' cards who may be allowed temporary admission to the galleries must conform to all the restrictions of this paragraph.

2. It shall be prerequisite to membership that the radio station, television station, system, or news-gathering agency which the applicant represents shall certify in writing to the Radio and Television Correspondents' Galleries that the applicant conforms to the foregoing regulations.

3. The applications required by the above rule shall be authenticated in a manner that shall be satisfactory to the Executive Committee of the Radio and Television Correspondents' Galleries who shall see that the occupation of the galleries is confined to bona fide news gatherers and/or reporters of reputable standing in their business who represent radio stations, television stations, systems, or news-gathering agencies engaged primarily in serving radio stations, television stations, or systems. It shall be the duty of the Executive Committee of the Radio and Television Correspondents' Galleries to report, at its discretion, violation of the privileges of the galleries to the Speaker or to the Senate Committee on Rules and Administration, and pending action thereon, the offending individual may be suspended.

4. Persons engaged in other occupations, whose chief attention is not given to—or more than one-half of their earned income is not derived from—the gathering or reporting of news for radio stations, television stations, systems, or news-gathering agencies primarily serving radio stations or systems, shall not be entitled to admission to the Radio and Television Galleries. The Radio and Television Correspondents' List in the Congressional Directory shall be a list only of persons whose chief attention is given to or more than one-half of their earned income is derived from the gathering and reporting of news for radio stations, television stations, and systems engaged in the daily dissemination of news, and of representatives of news-gathering agencies engaged in the daily service of news to such radio stations, television stations, or systems.

5. Members of the families of correspondents are not entitled to the privileges of the galleries.

6. The Radio and Television Galleries shall be under the control of the Executive Committee of the Radio and Television Correspondents' Galleries, subject to the approval and supervision of the Speaker of the House of Representatives and the Senate Committee on Rules and Administration.

Approved.

J. DENNIS HASTERT,
Speaker, House of Representatives.

TRENT LOTT,
Chairman, Senate Committee on Rules and Administration.

MEMBERS ENTITLED TO ADMISSION

RADIO AND TELEVISION CORRESPONDENTS' GALLERIES

Abbott, Kimberly: CNN
Abdallah, Khalil: CNN
Abdul-Jawad, Walid: Freelancer
Abe, Takaaki: Nippon TV Network
Abed, Nader: Al-Jazeera TV/Peninsula
Aberman, Samara: Newshour with Jim Lehrer
Abramson, Larry: National Public Radio
Abuelhawa, Daoud: MBC–TV (Middle East Broadcast Center)
Aburahma, Eyad: Al-Jazeera TV/Peninsula
Ackerman, Thomas: Belo Capital Bureau
Ackland, Matt: WTTG–Fox Television
Adams, Douglas A.: NBC News
Adams, James M.: WRC–TV/NBC–4
Adhicary, Dave: Freelancer
Adlerblum, Robin Carol: CBS News
Adrine, Lynne: ABC NEWS
Afsharian, Maria: NBC News
Aguirre, Bertrand: French Television TF1
Ahlers, Michael M.: CNN
Ahmed, Lukman: MBC–TV (Middle East Broadcast Center)
Ahn, Jaehoon: Radio Free Asia
Aiello, Bud: National Public Radio
Akassy, Hugues-Denver: HDA Pictures, Inc./Orbite
Al-Aqidi, Dalia: MBC–TV (Middle East Broadcast Center)
Albano, Thomas: CBS News
Alberter, William: CNN/TVS
Aleemi, Akmal: Voice of America
Alexander, Kenneth: C–SPAN
Aliaga, Julio E.: CNN
Allard, John: ABC News
Alldredge, Thomas: C–SPAN
Allen, Darrell: Worldnet Television
Allen, Jennifer: Capitol Pulse
Allen, Joy: WJLA–TV/Newschannel 8
Allen, Michael: WRC–TV/NBC–4
Allison, Lynn: WETA–TV
Allmond, Douglas: ABC News
Alnwick, Melanie: WTTG–Fox Television
Alonzo, Frances: Freelancer
Alrawi, Khaldoun: APTN
Alvey, Jay: WRC–TV/NBC–4
Ambinder, Marc: ABC News
Ammerman, Stuart: Freelancer
Amperiadis, Dimitrios: Hellenic Broadcast Corporation (ERT)
Anastasi, Patrick G.: NBC News
Anderson, Charles: CNN/TVS
Anderson, Kevin: BBC
Andrews, Wyatt: CBS News
Angle, James L.: Fox Newschannel
Anglim, John: WTTG–Fox Television
Annaheim, Brett: C–SPAN
Anstey, Alexander: Independent Television News (ITN)
Anyse, Alana M.: Cox Broadcasting
Apokis, Dimitrios: Hellenic Broadcast Corporation (ERT)
Appleman, Emily: Capitol Pulse
Aragon, Carlos: WPWC–AM (Radio Fiesta)
Arcega, Milandro: WRC–TV/NBC–4
Arena, Bruno: Freelancer
Arena, Kelli: CNN
Arenstein, Howard: CBS News
Armfield, Robert: Fox Newschannel
Armstrong, Phyllis: WUSA–TV
Armstrong, Richard: WUSA–TV
Arndts, Ulrich: German Television/ARD
Arrington, Percy: NBC News
Arsenault, Adrienne: CBC
Artesona, Eva: Cataluna TV/TV3
Aryankalayil, Babu: Al-Jazeera TV/Peninsula
Asberg, Stefan: Swedish Television
Ashburn, Lauren: USA Today Live
Asher, Julie: Fox Newschannel
Aslan, Berkin: Capitol Pulse
Aspery, Gregory: Tribune Broadcasting
Aspiazu, Maria: Telemundo Network
Assuras, Thalia: CBS News
Atkinson, Rodney: CNN/TVS
Attkinson, Barry: CBS News
Audas, Tamzen: BBC
Audick, George: Freelancer
Aufdem-Brinke, Ronald: Freelancer
Augenstein, Neal: WTOP Radio
Autrey, Steven: CBC
Avary, Max: Radio Free Asia
Azais, Jean-Pasca: French Television TF1
Babington-Heina, Martin: WRC–TV/NBC–4
Baccam, Dara: Voice of America
Bachenheimer, Stephan: German Television N24/SAT 1
Bachmann, Thorsten: German Television/ARD
Bacon, Jason: WJLA–TV/Newschannel 8
Badrian, Jonathan: The Washington Bureau
Bagnato, Sharyl: CBS News
Bagwall, Thomas: Freelancer
Baham, Tooo: C–SPAN
Bailor, Michelle: C–SPAN

MEMBERS ENTITLED TO ADMISSION—Continued

Bairer, Bret: Fox Newschannel
Baker, Cissy: Tribune Broadcasting
Baker, Craig: CNN
Baker, Les: Fox Newschannel
Bakova, Olga: Slovak Radio
Baktar, Reza: CNN/TVS
Ballou, Jeffrey: WTTG–Fox Television
Balsamo, James: Grace Digital Media
Baltimore, Dennis: Fox Newschannel
Banaszak, Brendan: National Public Radio
Banes, Hildegard: Austrian Radio ORF
Bangura, Benneh: CBS News
Banigan, Mike: CNN/TVS
Banionis, Asta: Radio Free Europe/Radio Liberty
Banks, Katherine: WRC–TV/NBC–4
Banville, Lee M.: Newshour with Jim Lehrer
Barber, Gregory J.: Newshour with Jim Lehrer
Barbour, Lantz: Freelancer
Barker, Edward: C–SPAN
Barnard, Bob: WTTG–Fox Television
Barnes, Audrey: WRC–TV/NBC–4
Barnes, Peter: Hearst-Argyle Television
Barnett, Christina-Marie: Hearst-Argyle Television
Barnett, James: CNN
Barnett, Pamela: Free Speech Radio News
Barnhart, Marsha J.: Radio Free Asia
Barr, Amy: C–SPAN
Barr, Bruce: CBS News
Barreda, Eric: Freelancer
Barrett, Ted: CNN
Bartlett, Cameron: Freelancer
Bartlett, Stephen: Freelancer
Bascom, Jon: ABC News
Basinger, Stuart: Fox Newschannel
Baskerville, Kia: CBS News
Baskin, Robert: Public Affairs Television (Bill Moyers)
Basu, Arin: Radio Free Asia
Bates, Deborah: C–SPAN
Batten, Rodney S.: NBC News
Bauer, John H.: Freelancer
Bauer, Udo: Deutsche Welle TV
Baumann, Robert: Grace Digital Media
Baumel, Susan: Voyage Productions
Bavaud, Pierre: Swiss Broadcasting
Bawa, Malini: Freelancer
Beall, Gary Glenn: NBC News
Beamon, Ta'Adhmeeka: Freelancer
Beasley, David: Radio Free Asia
Beaucar, Kelley O.: Fox Newschannel
Beaudin, Emery Robert: Worldnet Television
Beausoleil, Garry: SRN News (SALEM)
Becker, Bruce: Fox Newschannel
Becker, Frank K.: WJLA–TV/Newschannel 8
Beckman, Jennifer: APTN
Bedard, Marie-Eve: CBC
Beery, Nic: Mobile Video Services
Beesley, Kevin J.: Voyage Productions
Behrens, Paul: CBC
Bell, Bradley: WJLA–TV/Newschannel 8
Bell, Ross: Capitol Pulse
Bella, Rick D.: Fox Newschannel
Bellone, Dominic: NBC News
Belmar, Adam: ABC News
Bender, Bob: ABC News
Bender, Sharon: Belo Capital Bureau
Bennett, Kevin: Discovery Times Channel
Bennett, Shephard B.: C–SPAN
Bensen, Jackie: WRC–TV/NBC–4
Benson, Adam: CNN
Benson, Pamela S.: CNN
Bentley, David: Freelancer
Benton, Molly: C–SPAN
Benz, Kathy: CNN
Berger, Catherine: CNN
Berger, Deborah: CNN
Berk, Jay: CNN/TVS
Berman, David: CNN/TVS
Bernardini, Laura: CNN
Berrou, Loick: French Television TF1
Betsch, Michael L.: CNSNews.com
Betsill, Brett: C–SPAN
Beyer, Kevin: Freelancer
Bicudo, Pedro A.: RTP Portuguese Public Television
Biddle, Michael: C–SPAN
Bintrim, Tim Raymond: CNN/TVS
Bisney, John: CNN Radio
Blackman, Jay: NBC News
Blackman, Keith: NBC News
Blake, Stephanie: AP–Broadcast
Blakeslee, Carol: Newshour with Jim Lehrer
Blakey, Rea: CNN
Blanchet, Sharon: BBC
Blandburg, Victor: WJLA–TV/Newschannel 8
Blatter, Christiane: German Television/ZDF
Blitzer, Wolf: CNN
Block, Melissa: National Public Radio
Blooston, Victoria: NBC News
Blount, Jeffery: NBC News
Bluey, Robert B.: CNSNews.com
Blumberg, Sarah: Freelancer
Blumstein, Eve: Fox Newschannel
Bly, Denny: WUSA–TV
Bodlander, Gerald: AP–Broadcast
Bodnar, John: CNN/TVS
Bogle, Christopher: Worldnet Television
Bogley, John: Court TV (Metro Teleproductions)
Bohannon, Camille: AP–Broadcast
Bohannon, Joseph: NBC News
Bohn, Kevin: CNN
Bolter, Brian: WTTG–Fox Television
Bonzagni, George: SRN News (SALEM)
Bookhultz, Bruce: WUSA–TV
Borniger, Charles: Freelancer

MEMBERS ENTITLED TO ADMISSION—Continued

Borniger, Herta: German Television/ARD
Borrasso, Jennifer: SRN News (Salem)
Borzage, Frank E.: Freelancer
Bost, Mark: WUSA–TV
Boswell, Elizabeth: Fox Newschannel
Boughton, Bryan: Fox Newschannel
Bounnak, Thao-Mo: Radio Free Asia
Bowen, Timothy: WETA–TV
Boyd, Janet E.: Fox Newschannel
Boyd, John D.: NBC News
Boyd, Wayne: Freelancer
Boysha, Judy A.: AP–Broadcast
Braddel, Andrew: AP–Broadcast
Bradley, Michelle: Fox Newschannel
Bragale, Charles: WRC–TV/NBC–4
Bramson, Robert E.: ABC News
Brandkamp, Jonathan D.: Voice of America
Brannock, Michael: C–SPAN
Bransford, Fletcher: Fox Newschannel
Bratton, Michael G.: WUSA–TV
Brawner, Donald: WETA–TV
Breed, Richard: Freelancer
Breiterman, Charles: ABC News
Brennan, Christine: CNN
Brickhill, Robert Lee: CNN
Bridgforth, Turner: Freelancer
Brieger, Annette: Freelancer
Brinberg, Clarie: CNN
Brisson, Stephanie: CTV–Canadian Television
Britell, Penny: CBS News
Brittain, Becky: CNN
Brock, Alan Matth: WJLA–TV/Newschannel 8
Broffman, Craig A.: CNN
Broleman, Mike: Freelancer
Brooks, Michael: CNN
Brooks, Sam: ABC News
Broullire, Bridget: Hearst-Argyle Television
Brower, Brooke: ABC News
Brown, Almadale: NBC News
Brown, Cecile P.: CBS News
Brown, Christopher: Freelancer
Brown, Christopher: NBC News
Brown, Dwight: Freelancer
Brown, Edgar: Fox Newschannel
Brown, H. Metric: ABC News
Brown, Jeffrey: Newshour with Jim Lehrer
Brown, Jennifer: CBC
Brown, Karen E.: WJLA–TV/Newschannel 8
Brown, Malcolm: Feature Story News
Brown, Melissa: WJLA–TV/Newschannel 8
Brown, Paul: C–SPAN
Brown, Steve: CNSNews.com
Brown, Tracy Ann: APTN
Browne, Allison: Metro Networks
Bruce, Andrea: CBS News
Brumbaugh, Kathleen: Grace Digital Media
Bruner, Caroline Hall: Fox Newschannel
Bruns, Aaron: Fox Newschannel
Bruns, Jayne Hilary: ABC News
Bryant, Nick: BBC
Buchanan, Douglas: WUSA–TV
Buchanan, Michael: WUSA–TV
Buchanan, Michael: BBC
Buchdahl, Hannah: CNN
Buckhorn, Burke: CNN/TVS
Buckingham, Joesph: WETA–TV
Buckland, Carol E.: CNN
Buckley, Freda: C–SPAN
Budeiri, Dana: Al-Jazeera TV/Peninsula
Buel, Meredith S.: Voice of America
Buhrow, Tom: German Television/ARD
Bullard, Larry: WRC–TV/NBC–4
Bullock, Peter: Reuters Television
Bullock, Thomas: National Public Radio
Bundock, Susan J.: C–SPAN
Bunyan, Maureen: WJLA–TV/Newschannel 8
Burch, Kevin: C–SPAN
Burdick, Leslie: C–SPAN
Burke, James: C–SPAN
Burns, Alison: Cox Broadcasting
Burns, James E.: CNSNews.com
Bussey, Eliza: Reuters Television
Butler, Norman: Freelancer
Buttar, Jasmin: BBC
Butterworth, David: Newshour with Jim Lehrer
Byrne, Barbara: WETA–TV
Byrne, Joseph J.: Talk Radio News Service
Byrne, Matthew: CNN
Cabarcos, Tomas: Telemundo Network
Cabot, Heather: Freelancer
Cacas, Max: Capitol Hill Bureau from PRI
Cadoret, Remi: French Television TF1
Cagas, Elaine: CNN
Caggiano, Gabriel: MBC–TV (Middle East Broadcast Center)
Caldwell, Traci L.: CBS News
Calfat, Marcel: CBC
Callan, Elizabeth: Newshour with Jim Lehrer
Cameron, Carl: Fox Newschannel
Cameron, Ian: ABC News
Campbell, Arch: WRC–TV/NBC–4
Campbell, Christopher: Freelancer
Campbell, Shawn Corey: National Public Radio
Candia, Kirsten: German Television/ZDF
Canipe, LuAnn: WJLA–TV/Newschannel 8
Cao, Huidong: Radio Free Asia
Caplan, Craig: C–SPAN
Capra, Anthony: NBC News
Capuchinho, Marcelo: RTP Portuguese Public Television
Caravello, David: CBS News
Carey, Julie: WRC–TV/NBC–4
Carlson, Brett: Freelancer
Carlson, Chris: ABC News
Carlson, Melissa: Voice of America

MEMBERS ENTITLED TO ADMISSION—Continued

Carlsson, Leif: Swedish Television
Carlsson, Lisa: Swedish Television
Carney, Keith: FedNet
Carothers, Josh: Potomac Radio News
Carpel, Michael: Fox Newschannel
Carpio, Erick: Telemundo Network
Carr, Martin: WETA–TV
Carrier, Therese: CBC
Carrillo, Silvio: CNN
Carroll, Patricia: C–SPAN
Carver, Darryl: WJLA–TV/Newschannel 8
Carver, Tom: BBC
Casey, Sean: WRC–TV/NBC–4
Cassano, Joseph: Telemundo Network
Cassidy, David Mart: Belo Capital Bureau
Castiel, Carol: Voice of America
Castillo-Trentin, Jorge: Freelancer
Castner, Edward: Freelancer
Castro, Carlos: WTTG–Fox Television
Catrett, David Keith: CNN/TVS
Causey, Mike: WTOP Radio
Cavaiola, Michael: C–SPAN
Cavin, Anthony: CBS News
Cecil, Brenda: Grace Digital Media
Centanni, Steve: Fox Newschannel
Cesa, Jessica A.: NBC News
Cesar, Ronald: Voice of America
Chadwick, Alex: National Public Radio
Chaffin, Joshua: Free Speech Radio News
Chaggaris, Steven: CBS News
Chamberlain, Richard: Tribune Broadcasting
Chamberland, Bethany A.: CNN
Champ, Henry: CBC
Chang, Nike: Broadcasting Corporation of China
Chapman, Irwin: Bloomberg Television
Charbonneau, Melissa A.: CBC
Charpa, Silvia: German Broadcasting Systems/ARD
Chase, David: Cox Broadcasting
Chattman, Tanya: C–SPAN
Chavez, Miguel: Telemundo Network
Chavez, Roby: WTTG–Fox Television
Chaytor, David: WJLA–TV/Newschannel 8
Chen, Joie: CBS News
Chen, Joseph: Voice of America
Chen, Yi Qiu: CTI–TV (China)
Chenevey, Steve: Freelancer
Chernenkoff, Kelly: Fox Newschannel
Cherquis, Gustavo: Telemundo Network
Cheshire, Joshua: FedNet
Cheval, Stephanie: France 2 Television
Chicca, Trish: CNN
Chick, Jane: Freelancer
Chikata, Kenti: Nippon TV Network
Childs, Nick: BBC
Choi, Chang Young: MBC–TV Korea (Munhwa)
Choi, Myung-Ghil: MBC–TV Korea (Munhwa)
Chophel, Lobsang: Radio Free Asia
Christian, George: CBS News
Christianson, Nancy: C–SPAN
Chu, Jennifer: Living on Earth
Chun, Sooil: Radio Free Asia
Chung, Patrice: Fox Newschannel
Chung, Royd: To the Contrary (Persephone Productions)
Cilberti, David: Tribune Broadcasting
Ciralsky, Adam: CBS News
Clap, Nathan: Freelancer
Clapman, Leah: Newshour with Jim Lehrer
Clark, James: C–SPAN
Clark, Nary: Video News Service
Clark, Theodore: National Public Radio
Clarke, Jim: WJLA–TV/Newschannel 8
Clarke, John: Reuters Television
Clarkson, Russell: Newshour with Jim Lehrer
Clavijo, Ernesto E.: Univision News
Clayton, Delia V.: Capitol Pulse
Clemann, William: WUSA–TV
Clogston, Juanita: Freelancer
Clugston, Gregory: SRN News (Salem)
Cockerham, Rick: Fox Newschannel
Cocklin, Anne: Freelancer
Cocklin, Steve: Freelancer
Coffman, Mary: Medill News Service
Cofske, Harvey: Grace Digital Media
Cohan, Stacey: WUSA–TV
Cohen, Josh: C–SPAN
Cohen, Stuart: Freelancer
Cohencious, Robert: Native American Television
Coil, Holley: WTTG–Fox Television
Colby, Alfred: CBS News
Cole, Bryan: Fox Newschannel
Cole, Robert: Voice of America
Coleman, Carole: Irish Radio and Television (RTE)
Coles, David: Newshour with Jim Lehrer
Colgan, Jill: Australian Broadcasting Corporation
Collingwood, Eloise: C–SPAN
Collins, Bruce: C–SPAN
Collins, Maxine: Independent Television News (ITN)
Collins, Michael J.: Voice of America
Collins, Nicole: Fox Newschannel
Collins, Pat: WRC–TV/NBC–4
Collinson, Luke Alexander: Independent Television News (ITN)
Comport, Caroline J.: Tribune Broadcasting
Conan, Neal: National Public Radio
Conlin, Sheila: NBC Newschannel
Conner, Carrie: CNN
Conner, Eric: Fox Newschannel
Conner, Leslie: C–SPAN
Connolly, Carrie: WJLA–TV/Newschannel 8
Connor, Gail: APTN
Conover, Katie: Fox Newschannel
Conover, William: C–SPAN
Conrad, Monique: BET Nightly News

MEMBERS ENTITLED TO ADMISSION—Continued

Contreras, Jorge: Univision News
Contreras, Lalnie: AP–Broadcast
Conway, Zoe: Independent Television News (ITN)
Cook, James: CNN/TVS
Cook, Peter: Freelancer
Cooke, David: Grace Digital Media
Coolidge, Richard: ABC News
Cooper, Caroline: ABC News
Cooper, Fred C.: Voice of America
Cooper, George: CNN
Cooper, John: Freelancer
Cooper, Rebecca J.: WJLA–TV/Newschannel 8
Corbey, Robert: Freelancer
Corcoran, Patricia: WTTG–Fox Television
Corera, Gordon: BBC
Correa, Pedro: Telemundo Network
Corum, Paul H.: CBS News
Costantini, Bob: WJLA–TV/Newschannel 8
Cottom, Everett: Freelancer
Coudoux, Sylvain: NHK–Japan Broadcasting
Coulter, Pam: ABC News
Coupet, Sorine: CBC
Courson, Paul S.: CNN
Courtoglous, Melanie: Freelancer
Couvillion, Ronald: Freelancer
Covert, Cal: Freelancer
Cowen, Joshua: CNN
Cox, Kristina: Capitol Pulse
Cox, Merrilee: ABC News
Cox, Wayne M.: ABC News
Craca, Thomas: Freelancer
Cratty, Carol A.: CNN
Crawford, Robert: ABC News
Crawford, Sonya: ABC News
Crawford, Walter: WJLA–TV/Newschannel 8
Crawley, Plummer: Freelancer
Crenshaw, Elizabeth: WRC–TV/NBC–4
Cridland, Jeffrey: WUSA–TV
Croley, Adam: Capitol Pulse
Cronen, Elizabeth: WETA–TV
Crosariol, Paul M.: Potomac Television
Crosby, Josef: The Washington Bureau
Crosswhite, Karla: CNN
Crowley, Candy Alt: CNN
Crowley, Dennis: United News and Information
Crutchfield, Curtis: Prince George's Community Television
Cruz, Damon: CNN
Crystal, Lester M.: Newshour with Jim Lehrer
Csongos, Frank T.: Radio Free Europe/ Radio Liberty
Cuddy, Matthew: CNBC
Cullum, James W.: Talk Radio News Service
Culpepper, Kathy: Metro Networks
Cunha, John: CNN/TVS
Cuong, Pham Gia: CBS News
Curran, Patrick J.: Freelancer
Currier, Liam: C–SPAN
Curry, Thomas J.: MSNBC/ NBC News
Curry, Traci: CNN
Curtis, Alexander: C–SPAN
Cyr, Emily Michelle: WUSA–TV
D'Alberto, Emily A.: CNN
D'Annibale, Thomas J.: ABC News
Daell, Michelle: WTTG–Fox Television
Dager, Elizabeth: SRN News (Salem)
Dajani, Rula: Al-Jazeera TV/Peninsula
Daly, Jennifer: NBC Newschannel
Daly, John: CBS News
Daniels, Brady G.: NBC News
Daschle, Kelly: APTN
Dashevsky, Arik: Washington News Network
Date, Jack: CNN
Dauchess, Matthew: C–SPAN
Daugherty, Jeffery: Worldnet Television
Davalos, Anna: Freelancer
Davenport, Alice H.: Newshour with Jim Lehrer
Davenport, Anne: Newshour with Jim Lehrer
Davieaud, Helene: French Television TF1
Davis, Haary L.: WRC–TV/NBC–4
Davis, John: CNN/TVS
Davis, Kristin: CNN
Davis, Patrick A.: CNN
Davis, Tiffani M.: ABC News
Davis-Hopper, Regan: WJLA–TV/Newschannel 8
Dawson, Wendy: Fox Newschannel
de Guise, Louis: CBC
De Keyser, Greta: Belgian Radio and TV/VRT
de Sola, David: Freelancer
DeMark, Michael: Freelancer
DeMoss, Gary: Freelancer
DePuyt, Bruce: WJLA–TV/Newschannel 8
DeSantis, Dominic: Freelancer
DeSimone, Bridget: Newshour with Jim Lehrer
DeVito, Andrea: Fox Newschannel
DeWitt, Terry T.: ABC News
Debreczeni, Sonia Y.: WJLA–TV/Newschannel 8
Deckel, Yaron: Israel Television and Radio
Decker, Jonathan P.: USA Radio Network
Deger, Anne H.: Hamilton Productions
DelaForet, Andre D.: NBC News
Delboni, Chris: CBC
Dentzer, Susan: Newshour with Jim Lehrer
Dew, Kyneesha: C–SPAN
DiCarlo, Patricia: WTTG–Fox Television
DiMassimo, Richard: Native American Television
Diakides, Anastasia N.: CNN
Diamond, Aaron: France 2 Television
Diamond, Darryl: CNN/TVS
Diarra, Sofia: BBC
Dickerson, Anne: German Television N24/SAT 1
Dickie, Mary Theresa: AP–Broadcast
Diel, Heike: German Television/ZDF
Dietrich, Geoff: CNN
Diller, Jeremy: Hearst-Argyle Television

MEMBERS ENTITLED TO ADMISSION—Continued

Dillon, H. Estel: NBC Newschannel
Dimmler, Erika: CNN
Dimsdale, John: Marketplace Radio
Dinardo, Anne Marie: C–SPAN
Dine, Laura: Newshour with Jim Lehrer
Disselkamp, Henry: ABC News
Dixon-Gumm, Penny: Voice of America
Dixson, Charles H.: CBS News
Doane, Martin C.: WJLA–TV/Newschannel 8
Dockins, Pamela: AP–Broadcast
Doebele, Connie: C–SPAN
Doherty, Peter M.: ABC News
Dolcimascolo, Carolyn: WTTG–Fox Television
Dolma, Dana: Radio Free Asia
Donahue, Ed: AP–Broadcast
Donald, William: Freelancer
Donovan, Christopher: NBC News
Donovan, Jeffrey: Radio Free Europe/Radio Liberty
Donovan, Mary Ellen: WRC–TV/NBC–4
Dore, Margaret: Freelancer
Dorjee, Karma: Radio Free Asia
Dorn, Jason M.: Tribune Broadcasting
Dorsey, Tony: WRC–TV/NBC–4
Dougherty, Mark: Tech TV
Dougherty, Martin: CNN/TVS
Dougherty, Paul: Freelancer
Douglass, Linda D.: ABC News
Dow, Angela: Capitol Pulse
Doyle, Geoffrey C.: NBC News
Drew, Catherine: Feature Story News
Drew, Sarah: Freelancer
Drew, William: BBC
Drum, Jonathan E.: Belo Capital Bureau
DuBreuil, James: ABC News
Dubroff, Rich: CNN
Dudley, Phil: CTV–Canadian Television
Duke, Megan: CNN
Dukehart, Thomas: WUSA–TV
Dumont, Jonathan: CNN
Dunaway, John: CNN
Duncan, Benjamin: Capitol Pulse
Duncan, Emily: Potomac Radio News
Duncan, Michael J.: Potomac Radio News
Duncan, Robert: National Public Radio
Duncan, Victoria: NBC News
Duncanson, Annie: BBC
Dunlavey, Dennis: ABC News
Dunlop, William: European Broadcasting Union
Dunmire, John P.: WTTG–Fox Television
Dunn, Lauren: WJLA–TV/Newschannel 8
Dunston, Andre: WJLA–TV/Newschannel 8
Dupree, Jamie: Cox Broadcasting
Durham, Deborah: Univision News
Durham, Lisa: CNN
Dyer, Lois: CBS News
Ebersohl, Kevin: WUSA–TV
Ebinger, Jonathan: ABC News
Ebitty-Doro, Estelle: AP–Broadcast
Echevarria, Pedro L.: C–SPAN
Echols, Jerry: Fox Newschannel
Eck, Christina: Deutsche Press Agency
Eckert, Barton: Washington News Network
Edmond, Danaj: NBC News
Edwards, Dana: WUSA–TV
Egusquiza, Mariella: Televisa News Network (ECO)
Eisenbarth, Ron: C–SPAN
Eisenhuth, Alfred S.: Freelancer
el-Bardicy, Thabet: Al-Jazeera TV/Peninsula
el-Hamalawy, Mahmoud: Al-Jazeera TV/Peninsula
Elbadry, Hanan H.: Egyptian TV
Eldridge, James W.: Fox Newschannel
Eldridge, Mercedes: Washington Bureau News Service
Eldridge, Michael: Washington Bureau News Service
Eldridge, Steve: WTOP Radio
Ellard, Nancy: NBC Newschannel
Ellenwood, Gary: C–SPAN
Eller, Robert E.: AP–Broadcast
Elving, Ronald: National Public Radio
Elvington, Glenn: BET Nightly News
Emanuel, Mike: Fox Newschannel
Engel, Seth: C–SPAN
Epstein, Steve: Freelancer
Erbe, Bonnie: To the Contrary (Persephone Productions)
Eriksen, Wenke: Norwegian Broadcasting
Erlenborn, Daniel: NBC News
Ermolovich, Kate: Freelancer
Ernst, Charolotte: TV2 Denmark
Escalona, Alejandro: Voice of America
Espinoza, Cholene: Talk Radio News Service
Estepp, Jeff: Prince George's Community Television
Evans, Kendall: CNBC
Evans, Laura: WTTG–Fox Television
Evans, Sarah: NBC News
Everly, Thomas: Freelancer
Ewing, Samara Martin: WUSA–TV
Fabian, Kathleen: CNN
Fabic, Greg: C–SPAN
Faerber, Fritz: AP–Broadcast
Falcone, David: APTN
Falson, Al: Freelancer
Fancher, William: American Family Radio
Fang, Sabrina: Tribune Broadcasting
Fant, Barbara: NBC News
Farag, Aziz Fahmy: MBC–TV (Middle East Broadcast Center)
Farid, Mahtab: Voice of America
Farkas, Daniel: CNN/TVS
Farkas, Mark: C–SPAN
Farley, Jim: WTOP Radio
Farrar, Amy: CNN
Farrell, Kathryn: CNN
Farzam, Parichehr: Voice of America

MEMBERS ENTITLED TO ADMISSION—Continued

Faulkner, Michael: CBS News
Fausto, Ramon: Reuters Television
Faw, Robert: NBC News
Feather, Richard: Ventana Productions
Feeney, Susan: National Public Radio
Feig, Christy: CNN
Feldman, Clifford: FedNet
Feldman, Elizabeth: WRC–TV/NBC–4
Feldman, Randy: Viewpoint Communications
Fendrick, Anne-Marie: NHK–Japan Broadcasting
Feng, Xiao Ming: Radio Free Asia
Fensterer, Julia: German Television/ARD
Ferder, Bruce: Freelancer
Ferringno, Tony: WJLA–TV/Newschannel 8
Ferris, Shaye: CNN
Ferry, Scott: AP–Broadcast
Fessler, Pamela: National Public Radio
Fetzer, Robert: Grace Digital Media
Fiedler, Hartmut: Austrian Radio ORF
Fiegel, Eric James: CNN
Field, Andrew: Freelancer
Fielder, John Paul: Tribune Broadcasting
Fields, Matthew: NBC News
Fielman, Sheldon: NBC News
Fierro, Juan Martinez: Cadena Cope (Spain)
Finamore, Charles: ABC News
Finney, Richard: Radio Free Asia
Finnigan, Michael: Freelancer
Fischer, Elizabeth: NBC News
Fischoff, Michael: WJLA–TV/Newschannel 8
Fishel, Justin: Fox Newschannel
Fitzmaurice, Frank: WETA–TV
Fitzpatrick, Craig: Voice of America
Fitzwilliams, Malcolm: APTN
Flannery, Amy: Freelancer
Fleeson, Richard: C–SPAN
Fleischman, Philip: SRN News (Salem)
Fleming, Eileen: AP–Broadcast
Flood, Randolph: Native American Television
Flores, Cesar: Freelancer
Flores, Juan: C–SPAN
Flower, Kevin: CNN
Flynn, Michael: WUSA–TV
Foelmer-Suchorski, Kristin: Freelancer
Fogarty, Erin: NBC News
Fogarty, Kevin: Reuters Television
Forcucci, Michael: WJLA–TV/Newschannel 8
Ford, Michael: Freelancer
Ford, Sam: WJLA–TV/Newschannel 8
Forman, David: NBC News
Forrest, James M: WRC–TV/NBC–4
Forrest, Kerri: NBC News
Forte, B.J.: WJLA–TV/Newschannel 8
Foster, Carl: C–SPAN
Foster, Lesli: WUSA–TV
Foster, Scott: NBC News
Foster, Tom: Freelancer
Foty, Tom: Freelancer
Foundas, John: WTTG–Fox Television
Fox, Jan: WUSA–TV
Fox, Michael C.: WUSA–TV
Fox, Peggy: WUSA–TV
Fox, Peter: Reuters Television
Frame, John: WTTG–Fox Television
Francis, Elliott: WJLA–TV/Newschannel 8
Francis, Fredrick N.: NBC News
Frankel, Bruce: French Television TF1
Franken, Robert: CNN
Fraser, Jr., Wilfred R.: NBC News
Frayer, Lauren: AP–Broadcast
Frazier, William: C–SPAN
Freedman, Allan: Newshour with Jim Lehrer
Freeland, Eric: WJLA–TV/Newschannel 8
Frei, Matt: BBC
French, Francis P.: Freelancer
Friar, David J.: AP–Broadcast
Fridrich, George: Freelancer
Frieden, Terry: CNN
Friedman, David: Freelancer
Fritz, Hans Peter: Austrian Radio ORF
Frost, Lovisa: Talk Radio News Service
Fry, Jim: Belo Capital Bureau
Fryer, Alan: CTV–Canadian Television
Fulk, Elizabeth: CNN
Furlow, Tony: CBS News
Furst, David: Voyage Productions
Fuss, Bob: CBS News
Futrowsky, David: Fox Newschannel
G. Visley, Andrew: AP–Broadcast
Gabala, Rick: C–SPAN
Gabriel, Oscar Wells: AP–Broadcast
Gadsden, Ginger: USA Today Live
Gaffney, Dennis: Freelancer
Gafner, Randall: Freelancer
Gaither, Karen: C–SPAN
Galdabini, Christian: Freelancer
Galfetti, Michele: Swiss Broadcasting
Galindo, Michael Travis: Freelancer
Gallagher, Bill: C–SPAN
Gallagher, Jr., Joseph: Voice of America
Gallasch, Hillery: Deutsche Welle TV
Gallo, Dan: Fox Newschannel
Gandara, Francisca: Freelancer
Gangel, Jamie: NBC News
Garber, Harriet: CBS News
Garcia, Aurora: Ventana Productions
Garcia, Edith: Telemundo Network
Garcia, Gerardo: USA Today Live
Garcia, Guillermo: Reuters Television
Garcia, Jon Dominic: ABC News
Garcia, Patricia Villon: Prince George's Community Television
Gardella, Richard: NBC News
Gardner, Cy: Freelancer
Gargagliano, Richard: Native American Television

MEMBERS ENTITLED TO ADMISSION—Continued

Gargiulo, Michael: WTTG–Fox Television
Garraty, Timothy C.: CNN/TVS
Garrett, Major: Fox Newschannel
Gary, Garney: C–SPAN
Gato, Pablo: Telemundo Network
Gavnit, Holly Carol: WTTG–Fox Television
Gawad, Atef: Freelancer
Gebhardt, William A: NBC News
Geldon, Ben: CNN
Gembara, Deborah: Reuters Television
Genter, Joyce: C–SPAN
Gentilo, Richard: APTN
Gentry, Pamela: BET Nightly News
Gentry, Robert H.: TV Asahi
George, Maurice: CNN/TVS
George-Kanentiio, Douglas M.: Native American Television
Gergely, Valer: Voice of America
Gerhard, Cara: National Public Radio
Gersh, Darren: Nightly Business Report
Getter, John: The Washington Bureau
Geyelin, Philip: Freelancer
Ghadishah, Arash: ABC News
Giammetta, Max: WTTG–Fox Television
Gibbons, Gavin: Freelancer
Gibson, Jake: Freelancer
Gibson, Jennifer: CNN
Gibson, Jr., Frank L.: NBC News
Gibson, Sheri: NBC Newschannel
Giebel, Edward: Freelancer
Gilbert, Ben: National Public Radio
Giles, Frank: CBS News
Gilgannon, Pege: WJLA–TV/Newschannel 8
Gillespie, Maria: Fox Newschannel
Gillette, David: WETA–TV
Gilman, Jeff: WTTG–Fox Television
Gilmore, John: CNN
Gilmour, Karen: CBS News
Ginsburg, Benson: CBS News
Giroux, Dorothee: CBC
Giusto, Thomas: ABC News
Gjelten, Tom: National Public Radio
Gladstone, Jennifer: Sinclair Broadcast Group
Glass, Evan: CNN
Glassman, Matt: WRC–TV/NBC–4
Gleason, Norma: C–SPAN
Glennon, John: Freelancer
Glusing III, Edward: Sinclair Broadcast Group
Gmiter, Bernard: ABC News
Gold, Peter: Fuji Television
Gold, Walter: Washington News Network
Goldfein, Michael: Belo Capital Bureau
Goldman, David: Prince George's Community Television
Goldman, Jeff Scott: CBS News
Goldsmith, Timothy: Fox Newschannel
Goler, Wendell: Fox Newschannel
Gollust, David A.: Voice of America
Gomez, Augusto G.: Freelancer
Gong, Xiao: Radio Free Asia
Gonyea, Don: National Public Radio
Gonzalez, Carlos Alberto: WTTG–Fox Television
Gonzalez, John: WJLA–TV/Newschannel 8
Goodknight, Charles A.: WJLA-TV/Newschannel 8
Goodman, Jeffrey: Freelancer
Goodman, Susan: Voyage Productions
Gordemer, Barry: National Public Radio
Gordon, Chris Herbert: WRC–TV/NBC–4
Gordon, Stuart: ABC News
Gorman, James: APTN
Gottlieb, Brian: Newshour with Jim Lehrer
Gottlieb, Carl: Sinclair Broadcast Group
Gottschalk, Irene: Discovery Times Channel
Gould, Robert: C–SPAN
Goulding, David: Freelancer
Grabow, Barton: National Public Radio
Gracey, David: CNN
Gradison, Robin: ABC News
Granda, Marco: Univision News
Granena, Marc: Freelancer
Grant, Miles: WJLA–TV/Newschannel 8
Grasso, Neil: CBS News
Graves, Lindsay: Freelancer
Gray, Sean: C–SPAN
Grayson, Gisele: National Public Radio
Graziano, Julieann: WTTG–Fox Television
Greco, John J.: NBC News
Green, Erin: NBC News
Green, Molette: WJLA–TV/Newschannel 8
Greenbaum, Adam: NBC Newschannel
Greenblatt, Larry: Viewpoint Communications
Greene, James M.: NBC News
Greene, Laura: ABC News
Greene, Thomas: CNN/TVS
Greenfield, Heather: AP–Broadcast
Greenwood, John K.: WRC–TV/NBC–4
Greenwood, William: ABC News
Gregory, David: NBC News
Greiner, Nicholas: Freelancer
Griffin, Eileen: WETA–TV
Griffin, Kevin: Freelancer
Griffitts, William: Mobile Video Services
Groenhuijsen, Charles: NOS Dutch Public Broadcasting
Gross, Andrew F.: NBC News
Gross, Eddie S.: CNN/TVS
Gross, Joshua D.: CBS News
Grove, Mark C.: Freelancer
Gruber, Martin: Freelancer
Guastadisegni, Richard: WJLA–TV/Newschannel 8
Guise, Gregory: WUSA–TV
Gundy-Rice, Dorry: Freelancer
Gunning, Meredith: Hearst-Argyle Television
Gurney, Ben: BBC
Gursky, Gregg L.: Fox Newschannel

MEMBERS ENTITLED TO ADMISSION—Continued

Guthrie, Erin: Sinclair Broadcast Group
Gutmann, Hanna: Washington Radio & Press Service
Gutnikoff, Robert: APTN
Guzman, Armando: TV Azteca
Gwadz, Joel: Freelancer
Haberstick, Fred: Fox Newschannel
Hackett, Steve: WJLA–TV/Newschannel 8
Hackley, Dana: Sinclair Broadcast Group
Hager, Mary: CBS News
Hager, Robert M.: NBC News
Hagerty, Michael E.: Freelancer
Haggerty, Patrick B.: WGN Radio/U.S. Farm Report
Hakel, Peter: WJLA–TV/Newschannel 8
Hale, Brian P.: ABC News
Halfpenny, Sara: BBC
Halkett, Kimberly: Freelancer
Hall, Christine.: CNSNews.com
Hall, Richard: C–SPAN
Haller, Klaus: German Television/ARD
Haller, Sylvie: NBC News
Halton, David: CBC
Hamberg, Steve: Viewpoint Communications
Hamilton, Christopher: CNN/TVS
Hamilton, Jay: Hamilton Productions
Hamilton, John: Hamilton Productions
Hamilton, Jonathan: National Public Radio
Hammer, Michael J.: AP–Broadcast
Hampton, Cheryl: National Public Radio
Handelsman, Steve: NBC Newschannel
Handly, James: WRC–TV/NBC–4
Hanka, Roland: German Television/ARD
Hanlon, Carl P.: Global TV Canada
Hann, Stephen: Marketplace Radio
Hanna, Kate Albright: CNN
Hanner, Mark D.: CBS News
Hanoura, Hamada: C–SPAN
Hansen, Eric: C–SPAN
Hanson, Chris: C–SPAN
Hara, Kyoji Nippon TV Network
Harding, Alejandro: Video News Service
Harding, William: Freelancer
Hardy, Arthur: CNN
Harkness, Stephen: C–SPAN
Harleston, Robb: C–SPAN
Harmeyer, Nancy: Fox Newschannel
Harmon, Susan Bullard: CBS News
Harper, Elizabeth: Newshour with Jim Lehrer
Harper, Steven: Freelancer
Harrington, Craig J.: WTTG–Fox Television
Harris, Glenn: WJLA–TV/Newschannel 8
Harris, Richard: National Public Radio
Harris, Roy J.: Freelancer
Harrison, Elizabeth: C–SPAN
Harter, John R.: WJLA–TV/Newschannel 8
Hartge, John: Freelancer
Hartman, Brian: ABC News
Harvey, Alan: NBC News
Haselton, Brennan: WTOP Radio
Hash, James: WUSA–TV
Hass, Thomas: Freelancer
Hatch, Jocelyn: Freelancer
Hawke, Anne: National Public Radio
Hayes, Mary: WTTG–Fox Television
Hayley, Harold Paul: NBC News
Haynes, Maurice: C–SPAN
Hays, Guerin: CNN
Hayward, Jacqueline: WUSA–TV
Haywood, Barry: Freelancer
Hazelton, Jacqueline: AP–Broadcast
Headen, Greg: Fox Newschannel
Headline, William: European Broadcasting Union
Healey, Sean: Freelancer
Hearn, Josephine: Hedrick Smith Productions/ Frontline
Heffley, William: C–SPAN
Heik, Jens: Freelancer
Hendin, Robert: CBS News
Hendren, Karen: Freelancer
Hendricks, Mark B.: CBC
Henneburg, Mary Janne: Fox Newschannel
Henrehan, John: WTTG–Fox Television
Henriquez, Andrea: Television Naciaonal De Chile (TVN)
Henry, Chas: WTOP Radio
Henry, Jonelle P.: C–SPAN
Henry, Robert: Grace Digital Media
Henschel, Kara Woods: WJLA–TV/Newschannel 8
Herald, Vernon: CNN/TVS
Herbas, Francis: C–SPAN
Hering, Ruth Kristen: European Broadcasting Union
Herman, Lawrence: WJLA–TV/Newschannel 8
Hernandez, Carlos E.: WTTG–Fox Television
Hernandez, Eugneio: APTN
Hertrick, Jeff: Freelancer
Hesse-Kastein, Sebastian: German Public Radio/ARD
Hester, Deirdre: CBS News
Heyman, Leslye: C–SPAN
Heywood, Harry B.: ABC News
Hickman, Stacy: Fox Newschannel
Hill, Dallas: C–SPAN
Hillard, Timothy: KOMO–TV
Hindes, Wally: AP–Broadcast
Hinds, Hugh: Freelancer
Hirsh, Stephen: Fox Newschannel
Hirzel, Conrad: CNN/TVS
Hitchcock, Jennifer: Hearst-Argyle Television
Hix, Leta: C–SPAN
Ho, Rowena: Radio Free Asia
Ho, Stephanie J.: Voice of America
Hoai, Than: Video News Service
Hobson, Lee J.: Court TV (Metro Teleproductions)
Hoch, Maureen: Newshour with Jim Lehrer
Hodge, Darnley: WJLA–TV/Newschannel 8
Hodges, Debbie: Capitol Pulse

MEMBERS ENTITLED TO ADMISSION—Continued

Hoffman, Babette: Newshour with Jim Lehrer
Hoffmaster, Robert: C–SPAN
Hofler, Julie: CNN
Hogensen, Scott Alan.: CNSNews.com
Holland, John F.: NBC News
Holland, Sarah B.: CNN
Hollenbeck, Paul: Freelancer
Holley, Julie S.: WJLA–TV/Newschannel 8
Holly, Derrill: AP–Broadcast
Holman, Kwami: Newshour with Jim Lehrer
Holmes, Horace: WJLA–TV/Newschannel 8
Holtschneider, Joseph: Mobile Video Services
Hood, Mary: Freelancer
Hooper, Molly: Fox Newschannel
Hoover, Toni: Freelancer
Hopkins, Adrienne M.: Fox Newschannel
Hopkins, Brian: WJLA–TV/Newschannel 8
Hopkins, Joseph L.R.: Voice of America
Hopper, David: Freelancer
Hormuth, Thomas: WJLA–TV/Newschannel 8
Horne, LaTanya E.: WJLA–TV/Newschannel 8
Horne, Roger: German Television Agency
Hosford, Matthew A.: NBC News
Houston, Chris: WUSA–TV
Houston, Karen Gray: WTTG–Fox Television
Howard, Hillary: WUSA–TV
Howell, George: C–SPAN
Howell, Shelly: AP–Broadcast
Hoye, Matthew: CNN
Hoyt, Anne: Telemundo Network
Huang, Laura: Radio Free Asia
Huda, Jasmine: Fox Newschannel
Hudson, Christian: CNN
Hudson, Don: WJLA–TV/Newschannel 8
Hudson, Ira John: WRC–TV/NBC–4
Huff, Dan: APTN
Huff, Priscilla: Feature Story News
Huffman, Ashley: CNN
Hugel, Dave: CNN/TVS
Hughes, James: Freelancer
Hughes, Sarah: Voyage Productions
Hume, Brit: Fox Newschannel
Hume, Kim: Fox Newschannel
Hung, Shirley: CNN
Hunter, Roger: C–SPAN
Hunter, Ryan: WUSA–TV
Hurley, Charles: CNN
Hurt, James: NBC Newschannel
Husain, Mishal: BBC
Hutcherson, Trudy Marie: Freelancer
Hutchins, Stacy: Belo Capital Bureau
Hyater, John: WETA–TV
Ide, Charles: WETA–TV
Ifill, Gwen: Newshour with Jim Lehrer
Iiyama, Laura: Freelancer
Ilustre, Josefina: ABS–CBN (Philippines)
Ing, Lance: USA Today Live
Ingram, Shermaze: Newshour with Jim Lehrer
Irving, John: Metro Networks
Ishaq, Salim I.: NBC News
Iverson, Matthew: Grace Digital Media
Jackson, Brooks: CNN
Jackson, Roberta: C–SPAN
Jackson, Ryan: Cox Broadcasting
Jacobs, Philip H.: WRC–TV/NBC–4
Jacobson, Murrey: Newshour with Jim Lehrer
Jaconi, Michelle: NBC News
Jacques, Virg: Freelancer
Jaffe, Gary M.: Voice of America
Jaje, Joanne: NBC News
James, Karen L.: CNBC
Jamison, Christina: NBC News
Jamison, Dennis: CBS News
Japaridze, NuNu: CNN
Jarvis, Debbi: WRC–TV/NBC–4
Jarvis, Julie: NBC Newschannel
Jaskot, Sheila: WTTG–Fox Television
Javadi, Afshin: Freelancer
Javers, Eamon: CNBC
Jeffries, Katherine: C–SPAN
Jenkins, David: CNN/TVS
Jennings, Alicia: NBC News
Jennings, Edward B.: Freelancer
Jensen, Heidi: ABC News
Jermin, Ede R.: WRC–TV/NBC–4
Jessen, Peeter: Freelancer
Jia, Wei-ye: The Washington Bureau
Jiadai, Yang: Radio Free Asia
Jimenez, Martin: CNN/TVS
Johnke, Tracy: AP–Broadcast
Johns, Joseph: NBC News
Johnsen, Kyle: CNN
Johnson, Bruce: WUSA–TV
Johnson, Darryl B.: Freelancer
Johnson, Irene: WJLA–TV/Newschannel 8
Johnson, Jeffrey S.: CNSNews.com
Johnson, Kenneth: ABC News
Johnson, Kevin: Cox Broadcasting
Johnson, Kia: Reuters Television
Johnson, Lanny: Freelancer
Johnson, Lanora Booker: Cox Broadcasting
Johnson, Leroy: NBC News
Johnson, Obin: CBS News
Johnson, Sasha: CNN
Johnson, Sherrie: Freelancer
Johnston, Derek: Freelancer
Johnston, Jeffrey: CBS News
Jones, Alvin: FedNet
Jones, Alvin: Freelancer
Jones, Gwyneth: NBC News
Jones, Hannelore: German Public Radio/ARD
Jones, James: Voyage Productions
Jones, Kim: C–SPAN
Jones, Lyrone Steven: WTTG–Fox Television

MEMBERS ENTITLED TO ADMISSION—Continued

Jones, Morris: Sinclair Broadcast Group
Jones, Nelson: WTTG–Fox Television
Jones, Victoria: Talk Radio News Service
Joost, Nathalie: WTTG–Fox Television
Jordan, Rosiland: NBC News
Jouffriault, Pascal: Freelancer
Joy, Michael: Freelancer
Joy, Richard: Ventana Productions
Joya, Steve E.: ABC News
Joyce, Christopher: National Public Radio
Jubar, Muriel: Grace Digital Media
Judd, Jackie: ABC News
Juenger, Georg: German Television/ZDF
Kabbaj, Abdel Hakim: Freelancer
Kahn, Michael W.: AP–Broadcast
Kalbfeld, Brad: AP–Broadcast
Kaldan, Jon: Danish Broadcasting Corporation
Kalfopulos, Joy: ABC News
Kamberi, Dolkun: Radio Free Asia
Kane, James F.: ABC News
Kanehira, Shigenori: Tokyo Broadcasting System
Kaplan, William: Court TV (Metro Teleproductions)
Karimi, Nazira: Radio Free Europe/Radio Liberty
Karl, Jonathan: CNN
Karson, Danielle: Voyage Productions
Katkov, Mark: CBS News
Katz, Barry: C–SPAN
Katz, Hubert B.: Voice of America
Katz, Ivan: Freelancer
Katz, Jeffrey: National Public Radio
Kay, Katty: BBC
Kaye, Mathew D.: Berns Bureau
Kaye, Stephanie: Voyage Productions
Keating, Timothy: Freelancer
Keator, John C.: National Public Radio
Kehnemui, Sharon: Fox Newschannel
Kehoe, Steven: C–SPAN
Kelemen, Michele: National Public Radio
Kelleher, Kristine: APTN
Kellerman, Mike: SBS Radio (Australia)
Kelley, Alice: German Television/ZDF
Kelley, Daniela: Fox Newschannel
Kelley, Jonathan: C–SPAN
Kellog-Wheeler, Ashley: WJLA–TV/Newschannel 8
Kelly, Ariana: To the Contrary (Persephone Productions)
Kelly, Sean: CNN
Kelly, Terry: Freelancer
Kempf, Deborah: ABC News
Kendall, Brent: Capitol Pulse
Kenin, Justine: National Public Radio
Kennedy, Robert: C–SPAN
Kennedy, Suzanne: WJLA–TV/Newschannel 8
Kenny, Justin: Reuters Television
Kent, Peter: Freelancer
Kenyon, Linda: SRN News (Salem)
Kerchner, Eric: ABC News
Kerr, Roxane: C–SPAN
Kersey, Philip: Fox Newschannel
Kerslake, Louise: BBC
Kessler, Jonathan: Freelancer
Ketcham, Lewis: C–SPAN
Kethewell, Christian: APTN
Keyes, Charley: CNN
Khananányev, Grigory: Fox Newschannel
Kharel, Ram C.: Sagarmatha Television
Kiker, Douglas: CBS News
Kim, Eugene: AP–Broadcast
Kim, Yonho: Radio Free Asia
King, Colleen: CBS News
King, Donna: Freelancer
King, Gregory: WETA–TV
King, John C.: CNN
King, Kevin: C–SPAN
King, Kevin: WUSA–TV
King, Kristi: WTOP Radio
King, Kyle: Voice of America
Kingsley, Kimberly: WTOP Radio
Kinlaw, Worth: CNN/TVS
Kinney, Laura: Hearst-Argyle Television
Kinney, Michael: Freelancer
Kinney, Michael: WTTG–Fox Television
Kirk, Beverly: NBC Newschannel
Kirtz, Julie: Freelancer
Kiyasu, Adilson: CNN/TVS
Kizer, James S.: WRC–TV/NBC–4
Klayman, Elliot: Freelancer
Klein, Konstantin: Freelancer
Klein, Robert: Freelancer
Klein, Susan: National Public Radio
Kline, Heidi Curley: Capitol Pulse
Kline, Jeffrey: Hispanic Radio Network
Kloehn, Pat: CNN
Knight, Terrence: National Public Radio
Knoller, Mark: CBS News
Knott, James Jeffery: CNN
Knott, John: ABC News
Koch, Kathleen: CNN
Koch, Kay: German Television/ZDF
Kojovic, Predrag: Reuters Television
Koller, Frank: CBC
Kolodziejczak, Thomas: Tribune Broadcasting
Konrad, Monika: ABC News
Koolhof, Vanessa M.: WUSA–TV
Kopecky, Dave: Freelancer
Kopel, Genevieve: Talk Radio News Service
Kornely, Michael: Belo Capital Bureau
Kornely, Sharon: Medill News Service
Kos, Martin A.: Freelancer
Koslow, Marc: NBC News
Kotke, Wolfgan: Freelancer
Kovach, Robert S.: CNN
Kozel, Sandy: AP–Broadcast
Kramer, Amy: ABC News
Krebs, Joe: WRC–TV/NBC–4

MEMBERS ENTITLED TO ADMISSION—Continued

Krenindler, Virginia Coyne: NBC Newschannel
Kretman, Lester A.: NBC News
Kreuz, Greta: WJLA–TV/Newschannel 8
Kross, Kathryn: CNN
Krupin, David: Freelancer
Kube, Courtney: NBC News
Kulsziski, Peter: Freelancer
Kupper, Carmen: Freelancer
Kupperman, Tamara: NBC News
Kurcias, Martin R.: National Public Radio
Kure, Fumihiko Nippon TV Network
Kutler, Rebecca: CNN
Kwan, Vivian: Radio Free Asia
Kwasniak, Sarah: Sinclair Broadcast Group
LaComa, Lawrence: Deutsche Welle TV
LaFollette, Marianna: Freelancer
LaSalla, Susan: NBC News
LaTorre, Frank: CBS News
Labott, Elise: CNN
Laboy, Tony: C–SPAN
Lai, Yuk-Chong: Radio Free Asia
Lamb, Brian P.: C–SPAN
Lambidakis, Stephanie: CBS News
Lan, Tanya: Radio Free Asia
Landay, Woodrow: Australian Broadcasting Corporation
Landers, John: Freelancer
Landwehr, Arthur: German Public Radio/ARD
Landy, Hope: C–SPAN
Lane, Christopher: WETA–TV
Lane, Lisa: NHK–Japan Broadcasting
Langley, Larry: CNN/TVS
Langmade, Brigette: Cox Broadcasting
Larade, Darren: C–SPAN
Larsen, Greogory: Freelancer
Lassen, Kim: Danish Broadcasting Corporation
Laughlin, Ara: Prince George's Community Television
Lavallee, Michael: Tokyo Broadcasting System
Lawton, Kim: Religion & Ethics Newsweekly
Lazar, Robert: C–SPAN
Lazernik, Ira: WTTG–Fox Television
LeBrecht, Thelma: AP–Broadcast
LeCroy, Lillian: Fox Newschannel
LeCroy, Philip: Fox Newschannel
LeMay, Gabriel: Freelancer
Leahigh, Pamela: CNN/TVS
Leake, Myron A.: CNN/TVS
Leamy, Elisabeth: WTTG–Fox Television
Lee, Donald A.: CBS News
Lee, Dong Hyuk: Radio Free Asia
Lee, Edward: WETA–TV
Lee, Hun-min: Taiwan Television
Lee, Kyu: Radio Free Asia
Lee, Sarah: Freelancer
Lee, Soo Kyung: Radio Free Asia
Lee, Yeon Cheol: Voice of America
Lee, Yvonne: CNN
Leeds, Larry: Native American Television
Lehrer, Jim: Newshour with Jim Lehrer
Lehrman, Margaret: NBC News
Leidelmeyer, Ronald: WRC–TV/NBC–4
Leiken, Katherine: Freelancer
Leimbach, Elizabeth: Capitol Pulse
Leissner, Janet: CBS News
Leist, Elizabeth: NBC News
Lelle, Werner: Freelancer
Lendzian, Gundula: German Television/ZDF
Lent, David: Freelancer
Lentz, Rudiger: Deutsche Welle TV
Leong, Dexter: Freelancer
Leong, H. Ming: WJLA–TV/Newschannel 8
Lescalier, Francois: French Television TF1
Leshan, Bruce: WUSA–TV
Leshner, Matt: Freelancer
Lester, Paul: Prince George's Community Television
Levine, Michael: Fox Newschannel
Lewandowski, Mary E.: CNN
Lewine, Frances L.: CNN
Lewis, Edward: Fox Newschannel
Lewis, Jerry: WETA–TV
Lewis, John Elliott: WJLA–TV/Newschannel 8
Lewis, Penelope: Freelancer
Lewis, Stephen: NBC News
Lewis, Steve: CNBC
Leyne, Jon: BBC
Li, Denise: CBS News
Li, Yue: Radio Free Asia
Liao, Xiao Qiang: Radio Free Asia
Liasson, Mara: National Public Radio
Lien, Johnathan: CBS News
Liffiton, Bruce: Freelancer
Lilling, Dave: Court TV (Metro Teleproductions)
Lilly, Judlyne: WTOP Radio
Limbach, Francis J.: AP–Broadcast
Lin, Yu-Chu: NHK–Japan Broadcasting
Linda, Winslow: Newshour with Jim Lehrer
Lindberg, Lyle H.: Worldnet Television
Lindblom, Mark: FedNeT
Linden, Kim: CNN
Lindo, Viviana Avila: Caracol TV
Lisle, John D.: WJLA–TV/Newschannel 8
Little, Craig: WTTG–Fox Television
Litzenblatt, Seth: KTUU–TV
Liu, Ted: Radio Free Asia
Lively, Lydia: NBC News
Lloyd, Stacy: Fox Newschannel
Lodoe, Kalden: Radio Free Asia
Loescher, Skip: CNN
Loeschke, Paul: C–SPAN
Loftus, Kevin: Freelancer
Logan, Russell: C–SPAN
Long, Chris: C–SPAN
Long, Culver J.: Freelancer
Long, James V.: NBC News

MEMBERS ENTITLED TO ADMISSION—Continued

Long, Robert: WRC–TV/NBC–4
Loomans, Kathryn: AP–Broadcast
Lopez, Liliana: NBC News
Lopez, Rene: KTUU–TV
Lora, Willie A.: CNN
Lorek, Stanley: ABC News
Lormand, John: SRN News (Salem)
Loucks, William: CBC
Loughlin, Sean: CNN
Loughran, Heather: CBC
Lowe, Matt: CBS News
Lowe, Rachael Myers: Cadena Cope (Spain)
Lowman, Wayne: Fox Newschannel
Lu, Lucy: Radio Free Asia
Lucas, Dave: WJLA–TV/Newschannel 8
Lucas, Sean: Sinclair Broadcast Group
Lucchini, Maria Rosa: Univision News
Luck, David: C–SPAN
Ludden, Jennifer: National Public Radio
Ludwig, Robert: WETA–TV
Ludwin, James: AP–Broadcast
Luhn, Laurie: Fox Newschannel
Lukas, Jayne: Freelancer
Lumpkin, Beverley C.: ABC News
Lupo, Michael: Capitol Pulse
Lutt, Howard: CNN/TVS
Lutterbeck, Deborah: Reuters Television
Lutz, Ellsworth: ABC News
Luzquinos, Julio: Freelancer
Ly, Sherri: WTTG–Fox Television
Lyles, Brigitte: Fox Newschannel
Lynch, Donald H.: WETA–TV
Lynch, Laura: CBC
Lynn, John: CNN
Lyon, Michael: Fox Newschannel
MacDonald, Jim: CTV–Canadian Television
MacDonald, Neil: CBC
MacSpadden, Ian: Reuters Television
Macholz, Wolfgang: German Television/ZDF
Madden, Thomas: FedNet
Madigan, Bob: WTOP Radio
Madigan, Erin M.: Stateline.org
Maeder, Rudolf: Swiss Broadcasting
Maer, Peter: CBS News
Maguire, Stephen: Freelancer
Magwenya, Vincent: Australian Broadcasting Corporation
Mahdawi, Nezam: Al-Jazeera TV/Peninsula
Majchrowitz, Michael: Cox Broadcasting
Majerus, Marlis: WTOP2 (Federal News Radio)
Malin, Susan: Newshour with Jim Lehrer
Mallory, Brenda N.: WRC–TV/NBC–4
Malone, James: Voice of America
Malveaux, Suzanne: CNN
Manes, Lisa: CNN/TVS
Mangus, Richard: WMAL Radio
Mann, Jonathon: WJLA–TV/Newschannel 8
Manning, Jason: Newshour with Jim Lehrer
Manresa, Elizabeth: WJLA–TV/Newschannel 8
Marantz, Michael: WTTG–Fox Television
Marchione, Mark Antho: CNN/TVS
Marcus, Michael: CNN/TVS
Marcus, Ralph: CNN/TVS
Marks, Simon: Feature Story News
Marlovits, Johnannes: Austrian Radio ORF
Marno, Michael: Fox Newschannel
Marques, Antonio: Freelancer
Marriott, Mai: Freelancer
Marriott, Marc: Freelancer
Marriott, Michael: Freelancer
Marshall, Mark: Freelancer
Marshall, Melanie: BBC
Marshall, Nancy: Voyage Productions
Martin, David: Australian Broadcasting Corporation
Martin, David: CBS News
Martin, James: ABC News
Martin, Neville: Grace Digital Media
Martin, Wisdom: WTTG–Fox Television
Martinez, Luis: ABC News
Martinez-Bustos, Lillian
Martino, Jeff: Freelancer
Masayuki, Nakazato: Tokyo Broadcasting System
Mason, Cecelia: West Virginia Public Broadcasting
Mathers, Alexandra: CBS News
Matheu, Joe: CBC
Mathews, George D.: CNN
Mathis, Jimmy: WTTG–Fox Television
Matkosky, Timothy: WBAL–TV
Matsuyama, Toshiyuki: Fuji Television
Mattesky, Thomas A.: CBS News
Matthews, Claude L.: Freelancer
Matthews, Kathleen: WJLA–TV/Newschannel 8
Matthews, Lisa N.: AP–Broadcast
Matthews, Valerie: C–SPAN
Maxwell, Darraine: ABC News
Mayes, Michael: WETA–TV
Mayhew, Dwight: NBC Newschannel
Mayhew, Linda: Grace Digital Media
Mazariegos, Mark: BET Nightly News
McAlary, David E.: Voice of America
McBride, Heather: Prince George's Community Television
McCabe, Lauren Kathleen: Freelancer
McCaffrey, Chris: USA Today Live
McCaleb, Ian: Fox Newschannel
McCally, John: Fox Newschannel
McCann, Michael: C–SPAN
McCann, Sean P.: C–SPAN
McCarren, Andrea: WJLA–TV/Newschannel 8
McCarthy, Kate: C–SPAN
McCarthy, Lark: WTTG–Fox Television
McCarty, D. Jay: Freelancer
McCarty, Dennis: CNN/TVS
McCash, Doug: Freelancer
McCathran, Scott: WTTG–Fox Television
McCaughan, Kristen: CNN

MEMBERS ENTITLED TO ADMISSION—Continued

McCaughan, Timothy: CNN
McClam, Kevin: Freelancer
McCleery, Kathleen: Newshour with Jim Lehrer
McClellan, Maxwell: CBS News
McClure, Tipp: Reuters Television
McConnaughy, Brian: ABC News
McConnell, Dave: WTOP Radio
McCorkell, Meghan: WJLA–TV/Newschannel 8
McCrary, Ron: C–SPAN
McDermott, Frank: WUSA–TV
McDermott, Richard: NBC Newschannel
McDonald, Natashka: Radio Bilingue
McDougall, Ian: Reuters Television
McFadden, Kerith: CNN
McGath, Sarah L.: Sinclair Broadcast Group
McGill, Sharon: Channel One News
McGinn, Anne: Fox Newschannel
McGlinchy, James: CBS News
McGrath, Mark: ABC News
McGrath, Megan: WRC–TV/NBC–4
McGrath, Patrick: WTTG–Fox Television
McGreevy, Allen: BBC
McGuire, Bradley: C–SPAN
McGuire, Lorna: Freelancer
McGuire, Michael: CBS News
McHenry, Bob: WUSA–TV
McHenry, Brian: Freelancer
McKelway, Doug: WJLA–TV/Newschannel 8
McKenna, Kate: AP–Broadcast
McKenna, Patrick T.: WRC–TV/NBC–4
McKenna, William: Freelancer
McKinney, Haven L.: Freelancer
McKnight, William Charles: WUSA–TV
McLean, George: Capitol Pulse
McLeod, Malkia: Capitol Pulse
McManamon, Erin T.: Hearst-Argyle Television
McManus, Kevin A.: NBC Newschannel
McManus, Michael: CNN
McMartin, Philip: AGDAY
McMearty, Mike: WTOP Radio
McMenamin, Eileen: CNN
McMichael, Samuel J.: Freelancer
McMinn, Nan Hee: Grace Digital Media
McMorris, Ebony Nicole: NBC News
McNulty, Edward: National Public Radio
McQuay, William: National Public Radio
McQueen Martin, Michel: ABC News
McQuone, Kerry: WJLA–TV/Newschannel 8
McWethy, John: ABC News
Means, Jeffrey Wendell: Voice of America
Mears, Carroll Ann: NBC News
Mears, William: CNN
Mebane, William: National Public Radio
Meeks, Brock Nola: NBC News
Meghani, Sagar: AP–Broadcast
Meier, Christiane: German Television/ARD
Meier, Markus: German Television Agency
Mejia, Douglas: Telemundo Network
Melendy, David R: AP–Broadcast
Melinescu, Cecilia: Romanian Television
Melinescu, Nicolae: Romanian Television
Mellman, Ira: Clear Channel Communications
Mellom, Soheila: Freelancer
Meltzer, Ari: Tribune Broadcasting
Meluza, Lourdes: Univision News
Meraz, Gregorio: Televisa News Network (ECO)
Mercurio, John: CNN
Merobshoev, Seeno: C–SPAN
Meserve, Jeanne: CNN
Meyer, Jill Rosenbaum: CBS News
Meyer, Kerry: Grace Digital Media
Meyer, Lisa: AP–Broadcast
Meyer, Richard: CBS News
Michael, Horan: WTTG–Fox Television
Michael, Michelle: WRC–TV/NBC–4
Michaud, Bryant: AP–Broadcast
Michaud, Robert: Belo Capital Bureau
Michel, Theresa: C–SPAN
Michele, Kelemen: National Public Radio
Mickelson, Matthew: Freelancer
Migas, Portia R.: ABC News
Mihalisko, Michael: Radio Free Europe/ Radio Liberty
Miklaszewski, James: NBC News
Mikoda, Akihiro: NHK–Japan Broadcasting
Mikus, Andrea: SRN News (Salem)
Milenic, Alexander: Freelancer
Milford, Robert H.: Mobile Video Services
Millar, Lisa: Australian Broadcasting Corporation
Miller, Andrew: C–SPAN
Miller, Annette L.: Newshour with Jim Lehrer
Miller, Avery: ABC News
Miller, Beth: BBC
Miller, Doreen Gentzler: WRC–TV/NBC–4
Miller, Paul: CNN/TVS
Milller, Mitchell: WTOP Radio
Mills, Jim: Fox Newschannel
Mills, Katherine: C–SPAN
Mills, Susan L.: Newshour with Jim Lehrer
Milstein, Jeff: CNN
Minner, Richard: NBC News
Minott, Gloria: WPFW–FM
Mir, Abner S.: Radio Free Asia
Mitchell, Andrea: NBC News
Mitchell, Patricia Davis: CNN
Mitchell, Traci: Freelancer
Mitnick, Steven E.: Freelancer
Mitric, Julia: National Public Radio
Miura, Kenichi Nippon TV Network
Miyake, Yuko: Tokyo Broadcasting System
Mizumoto, Rika: TV ASAHI
Mo, Nai Chian: Phoenix Satellite Television
Mogg, Stephanie.: TV Asahi
Mohen, Peter: CNN/TVS

MEMBERS ENTITLED TO ADMISSION—Continued

Molineaux, Diana: Cataluna Radio
Molino, Heather: WJLA–TV/Newschannel 8
Monack, David: C–SPAN
Monange, Arielle: France 2 Television
Mong, Bryan: NHK–Japan Broadcasting
Montague, William: Danish Broadcasting Corporation
Montaut, Hector: Televisa News Network (ECO)
Monte, John: Freelancer
Montenegro, Lori: Telemundo Network
Montenegro, Norma: Univision News
Montero, Luisa: Telemundo Network
Mooar, Brian: Freelancer
Moore, Abe: Medill News Service
Moore, Garrette: C–SPAN
Moore, Jessica: Newshour with Jim Lehrer
Moore, Linwood: C–SPAN
Moore, Peter: CNN/TVS
Moore, Robert: Independent Television News (ITN)
Moore, Terrence: Metro Networks
Morahan, Lawrence.: CNSNews.com
Moran, James M.: Freelancer
Moran, Molly: Freelancer
Morano, Marc: CNSNews.com
Moreno, Rosa M.: European Broadcasting Union
Morgan, Howard: SRN News (Salem)
Mori, Yugo: Tokyo Broadcasting System
Morrell, Geoff: ABC News
Morris, Amy: WTOP Radio
Morris, Diane: C–SPAN
Morris, Holly: WTTG–Fox Television
Morris, W. Harrison: CNN/TVS
Morrisette, Roland: Bloomberg Television
Morrison, Bridget: C–SPAN
Morse, Richard: CNN/TVS
Mort, Stephen: Feature Story News
Morton, Bruce: CNN
Morton, Dan: C–SPAN
Mortreux, Vincent: French Television TF1
Moseley, Terry: Reuters Television
Moses, Lester: NBC News
Mosettig, Michael D.: Newshour with Jim Lehrer
Mosley, Joseph: CNN/TVS
Mosley, Matt: Ventana Productions
Mottola, Lorraine: Freelancer
Mountcastle, Katharine: CBS News
Mueller, John: Freelancer
Muhammad, Alverda Ann: National Scene News
Muhammad, Askia: National Scene News
Muir, Robert: Reuters Television
Mukaiyama, Akio: Tokyo Broadcasting System
Mulveny, Jason: French Television TF1
Munoz, Luis: CNN/TVS
Murai, Masamobu:: TV TOKYO
Muratani, Tateki: Fuji Television
Murotani, Makiko: Tokyo Broadcasting System
Murphy, Fran: WJLA–TV/Newschannel 8
Murphy, John: CBS News
Murphy, Kathy: C–SPAN
Murphy, Terence: C–SPAN
Murphy, Thomas: CNN/TVS
Murray, Alan S.: CNBC
Murray, Andrew: C–SPAN
Murray, Matt: WJLA–TV/Newschannel 8
Murray, Matthew: Tribune Broadcasting
Murray, Timothy K.: Ventana Productions
Murrow, Keith W.: Tech TV
Murtaugh, Peter: Grace Digital Media
Musa, Imad: Al-Jazeera TV/Peninsula
Muse, Lowell: National Public Radio
Muse, Pat Lawson: WRC–TV/NBC–4
Musha, Jilil: Radio Free Asia
Musha, Masami: NHK–Japan Broadcasting
Myers, Adolyn A.: NBC News
Myers, Dayna K.: Newshour with Jim Lehrer
Myers, Lisa M.: NBC News
Nagle, Erin C: Fox Newschannel
Nakano, Hirofumi Nippon TV Network
Namgyal, Tseten: Radio Free Asia
Narahari, Priya: European Broadcasting Union
Nash, John C.: WETA–TV
Nason, Andrew: C–SPAN
Naus, Angela: CBC
Naylor, Brian: National Public Radio
Neale, Tracey: WTTG–Fox Television
Nealer, Stephanie Mann: Voice of America
Neapolitan, Michael: Grace Digital Media
Neel, Joe R.: National Public Radio
Nelson, Donna: NBC News
Nelson, James: Fox Newschannel
Nelson, Marie: ABC News
Nelson, Nicole: Prince George's Community Television
Nelson, Suzanne: CNN
Ness, Eric: Potomac Radio News
Neto, Joaquim: Mobile Video Services
Neustadt, James J.: WRC–TV/NBC–4
Nevins, Elizabeth: NBC News
Newberry, Tom: NBC Newschannel
Nguyen, An: Radio Free Asia
Nguyen, Anh: Freelancer
Nguyen, Phuong G.: ABC News
Nguyen, Viet Tien: Radio Free Asia
Nicolaidis, Virginia: CNN
Nielsen, John: National Public Radio
Niland, Marty: AP–Broadcast
Ninoseki, Yoshio: Fuji Television
Nishiumi, Setsu: Fuji Television
Nix, Jack: Washington News Network
Nixon, Adam: Freelancer
Nixon, Charles: WETA–TV
Noble, Jeff: CNN/TVS
Nocciolo, Ernest G.: CNN/TVS
Nocciolo, Valerie T.: CNN/TVS
Noce, Julie: European Broadcasting Union
Nolen, John: CBS News

MEMBERS ENTITLED TO ADMISSION—Continued

Nori, Joel: Capitol Pulse
Norins, Jamie: Potomac Television
Norland, Dean E.: ABC News
Norling, Richard: Freelancer
Norman, Dennis: CNN/TVS
Norris, Christopher: Freelancer
Norris, James F.: CNN/TVS
Norris, Michele: National Public Radio
Novy, Michele: Fox Newschannel
Nugroho, Irawan: Voice of America
Nurenberg, Gary: Freelancer
Nurnberger, Lisa: Voyage Productions
Nyane, Khin: Radio Free Asia
Nyberg, Pertti Mikael: MTV3 (Finland)
O'Berry, D. Kerry: Freelancer
O'Brien, David: Freelancer
O'Brien, John: Court TV (Metro Teleproductions)
O'Connell, Benjamin: C–SPAN
O'Connor, Thomas: Freelancer
O'Day, Andrew: CBS Marketwatch
O'Donell, Norah: NBC News
O'Donnell, Barry: Grace Digital Media
O'Donnell, Patrick: Freelancer
O'Hara, Victoria: National Public Radio
O'Keefe, Edward F.: ABC News
O'Leary, John F.: ABC News
O'Leary, John: CBC
O'Leary, Karen: CBC
O'Shea, Daniel J.: Freelancer
O'Toole, Quinn: National Public Radio
Oajacos, Anna: WRC–TV/NBC–4
Oates, Kim: WTOP2 (Federal News Radio)
Oberti, Ralf: Television Naciaonal De Chile (TVN)
Och, Philip: Fox Newschannel
Offerman, Claudia: German Television/ZDF
Ogata, Kerry: CNN
Oinonen, Tarja: Finnish Broadcasting Company (YLE)
Okita, Teri: CBS News
Olick, Diana: CNBC
Oliver, LaFontaine: Radio One
Ong, Ling: Freelancer
Oo, Thein H.: Radio Free Asia
Orchard, Mark: BBC
Orgel, Paul: C–SPAN
Orr, K. Robert: CBS News
Osborne, Kyle: WJLA–TV/Newschannel 8
Osgood, Gabi: German Television/ZDF
Osman, Hafez: Al-Jazeera TV/Peninsula
Ota, Kazuhiko.: TV Asahi
Otsuka, Mika: TV Tokyo
Ottersbach, Cornelia: Deutsche Welle TV
Ouezada, Cristian: Video News Service
Overby, Peter: National Public Radio
Overdiek, Timotheus: NOS Dutch Public Broadcasting
Owen, Andrea: ABC News
Owens, Cheryl: C–SPAN
Oziel, David: Washington News Network
Ozsancak, Hakan: APTN
Pacheco, Sarah: CNN/TVS
Page, David: CBC
Palca, Joe: National Public Radio
Pancoe, Virginia: WJLA–TV/Newschannel 8
Pannell, Ian: BBC
Pantaze, Adrien: Freelancer
Panzer, Chester: WRC–TV/NBC–4
Pappas, Icarus N. (Ike): Washington News Network
Parenti, Alisa: WJLA–TV/Newschannel 8
Parker, Beth: WTTG–Fox Television
Parker, Julie: WJLA–TV/Newschannel 8
Parker, Shaun: Freelancer
Parker, Tanya: C–SPAN
Parks, Chadwick Ryan: NBC News
Parnell, Sara: The Washington Bureau
Parshall, Janet: SRN News (Salem)
Pastre, Dominique: Fox Newschannel
Patrick, Daniel: WUSA–TV
Patterson, George: Freelancer
Patterson, Pamela: Freelancer
Pauls, Hartmut: Freelancer
Paulsen, Beverley: Freelancer
Payne, Scott: Freelancer
Peacock, Grant: Freelancer
Peaks, Gershon: Reuters Television
Pearson, Hampton: CNBC
Pearson, Mark: Freelancer
Pegues, Susan Nippon TV Network
Peltier, Yves: CBC
Pena, Celinda: WUSA–TV
Penaloza, Marisa: National Public Radio
Penebre, Peter: Freelancer
Penniman, Judy: ABC News
Pennybacker, Gail: WJLA–TV/Newschannel 8
Pennybacker, Jen: Ventana Productions
Perez, Ines I.: Freelancer
Pergram, Chad: Capitol Hill Bureau from PRI
Perkins, Veron K.: C–SPAN
Perl, Drora: Israel Army Radio/Galei-Tzahal
Perry, Andrea: C–SPAN
Peslis, Chris: Fox Newschannel
Pessin, Donald: Reuters Television
Peters, Michael: CNN/TVS
Peterson III, Robert J.: Freelancer
Peterson, Gordon: WUSA–TV
Peterson, James P.: Freelancer
Peterson, Kavan: Stateline.org
Peterson, Laura: NHK–Japan Broadcasting
Peterson, Rebecca: CBS News
Peterson, Robert J.: Freelancer
Petras, William: NBC News
Pettit, Debra: NBC News
Pexton, Ken: Freelancer
Peyton, Michael: Freelancer
Pham, Jacqueline: Fox Newschannel

MEMBERS ENTITLED TO ADMISSION—Continued

Pham, Tran: ABC News
Phillips, Gurvir: WUSA–TV
Phillips, Nicole: Freelancer
Phillips, Steven: Reuters Television
Pickett, Paul: C–SPAN
Pickup, Michael: ABC News
Piedrahita, Ronald: Freelancer
Pierce, Maura: C–SPAN
Piette, Didier: European Broadcasting Union
Piltz, Eberhard: German Television/ZDF
Pinczuk, Murray: Freelancer
Pinkas, Boris: Freelancer
Pinto, Lauren: Austrian Radio ORF
Pinzon, Wingel: Telemundo Network
Piskounov, Eugene: Russian State TV and Radio (RTR)
Pitocco, Nickolas: C–SPAN
Pitra, Katharine: Public Affairs Television (Bill Moyers)
Pitsinger, Geraldine: Fox Newschannel
Pizarro, Fernando: Univision News
Plante, William: CBS News
Plater, Christopher: WJLA–TV/Newschannel 8
Pletnikov, Stanislav: Russian State TV and Radio (RTR)
Plotkin, Mark: WTOP Radio
Poley, Michael: CNN
Popkin, James K.: NBC News
Popovic, Boris: Capitol Pulse
Porter, Almon L.: C–SPAN
Posey, Luther: CBS News
Potisk, Steven F.: AP–Broadcast
Potts, Nina-Maria: Feature Story News
Powell, Dennis: ABC News
Powell, Shannon: Fox Newschannel
Pozniak, Stephen: WJLA–TV/Newschannel 8
Prah, Pamela: Stateline.org
Pratt, Jim: WUSA–TV
Preloh, Anne: C–SPAN
Presutti, Carolyn: Belo Capital Bureau
Price, Steve: Freelancer
Primmer, Ryan: Freelancer
Prior, James R.: Native American Television
Privitera, Alexander: German Television N24/SAT 1
Puckett, Richard: Dispatch Broadcast Group
Pugliese, Pat: Freelancer
Quinn, Diana: CBS News
Quinn, Jason: Freelancer
Quinn, John D.: Worldnet Television
Quinn, Mary: ABC News
Quinnette, John Jay: CNN/TVS
Quinonez, Omar: Freelancer
Rabbage, Mark: BBC
Rabin, Mark: Freelancer
Racki, Jason D.: Australian Broadcasting Corporation
Rad, Ali: Freelancer
Rager, Bryan: Reuters Television
Rahal, Hugo: Al-Jazeera TV/Peninsula
Rahman, Nadia: Al-Jazeera TV/Peninsula
Rainey, R. Brian: Fox Newschannel
Ramos, Raul: Univision News
Rampy, Grant: Tribune Broadcasting
Ramshaw, Gregg: Newshour with Jim Lehrer
Rarey, Richard Howell: National Public Radio
Rathner, Jeffrey: WETA–TV
Ratliff, Walter: APTN
Ratner, Ellen: Talk Radio News Service
Ratner, Victor: ABC News
Raval, Aditya: ABC News
Raval, Nikhil: C–SPAN
Ravin, Dan: CBS News
Ray, Branden: CNN
Ray, John: Feature Story News
Raymer, Katelynn Reckord: Nightly Business Report
Reagan, Cheryl: Grace Digital Media
Reals, Gary: WUSA–TV
Reals, Tucker: APTN
Reap, Patrick T.: CNN
Reaume, Greogory: CBC
Redding, William: ABC News
Reddoor, Charles: Native American Television
Redpath-Buckley, Julia: National Public Radio
Reese, Courtenay: NBC News
Reese, Orla: AP–Broadcast
Reeve, Richard: WJLA–TV/Newschannel 8
Regan, James: C–SPAN
Reich, Sharon: Freelancer
Reilly, Robert: C–SPAN
Reimann, Fritz: Swiss Broadcasting
Reinsel, Ed: Freelancer
Reis, Sean: NBC News
Remillard, Michele: Fox Newschannel
Rensberger, Scott: TV2 Denmark
Repke, Amy: WUSA–TV
Reuter, Cynthia: C–SPAN
Reyes, Victor: Telemundo Network
Reynolds, Judy: Religion & Ethics Newsweekly
Reynolds, Robert: CNBC
Reynolds, Talesha: ABC News
Rhodes, Elizabeth: Fox Newschannel
Rice, Alan Gregory: NBC News
Rich, Lauren: Hearst-Argyle Television
Richard, Sylvain: CBC
Rickard, Michael: WTTG–Fox Television
Riese, Hans-Peter: German Broadcasting Systems/ARD
Riess, Steffanie: German Television/ZDF
Riggs, James W.: CNN/TVS
Riggs, Tyrone W.: CNN/TVS
Riha, Anne Marie: Fox Newschannel
Riley, Heather: CNN
Riner, Corbett: Fox Newschannel
Ritchie, Thomas: APTN

MEMBERS ENTITLED TO ADMISSION—Continued

Rivero, Raul Jorge: WUSA–TV
Rizzolo, Lisa: Fox Newschannel
Roach, Amy: C–SPAN
Robach, Amy: WTTG–Fox Television
Robbins, Francisco: CBS News
Roberson, David: European Broadcasting Union
Roberson, Hilary: Irish Radio and Television (RTE)
Roberts, Corinne B.: ABC News
Roberts, John: CBS News
Roberts, Nathan: WJLA–TV/Newschannel 8
Roberts, Susan: WJLA–TV/Newschannel 8
Robertson, Greg: CNN/TVS
Robinson, Daniel: Voice of America
Robinson, Douglas: Austrian Radio ORF
Robinson, Earle: Freelancer
Robinson, Laura: CNN
Robinson, Margaret: Newshour with Jim Lehrer
Robinson, Querry: Fox Newschannel
Rocha, Juan: Ventana Productions
Rocha, Sam: RCN–TV (Colombia)
Roche, J. Michael: Freelancer
Rochelle, Carl: NBC News
Rockler, Julia: The Washington Bureau
Rockwood, Ryan: Religion & Ethics Newsweekly
Rodgers, William F.: Voice of America
Rodriguez, Janet: CNN
Rodriguez, Martine: C–SPAN
Rogers, Lauren: ABC News
Rogers, Nicole: Fox Newschannel
Rohrbeck, Douglas: Fox Newschannel
Rokus, Brian: CNN
Rollins, Bonnie: NBC Newschannel
Romilly, George: ABC News
Rommelmeyer, Pamela: SRN News (Salem)
Roof, Peter: Freelancer
Roome, Adrianna: Washington News Network
Rose, Francis: C–SPAN
Rose, Jeff: WJLA–TV/Newschannel 8
Rose, Joseph: WJLA–TV/Newschannel 8
Roselli, H. Michael: CNN
Rosen, James: Fox Newschannel
Rosen, Rachel: CNN
Rosenbaum, Peter: Grace Digital Media
Rosenbaum, Thea: German Television/ARD
Rosenberg, Gary: ABC News
Rosenberg, Howard L.: ABC News
Rosenberg, James: Voyage Productions
Rosenberg, Jeffrey: National Public Radio
Rosgaard, Jessica: CNN
Rossetti-Meyer, Misa: Grace Digital Media
Rossignol, Florence: CTV–Canadian Television
Roston, Aram: Freelancer
Rotan, Eric: WJLA–TV/Newschannel 8
Rotatori, Beth Ann: CNN
Rotchford, Karin: Newshour with Jim Lehrer
Roth, Johnie F.: NBC News
Roth, Linda: CNN
Roth, Theodore: Freelancer
Rowe, Hildrun: German Television/ZDF
Rowe, Jo Ann: Rowe News Service
Rowe, Tom: Reuters Television
Royce, Lindy: CNN
Roycratt, David: WUSA–TV
Rozentals, Karina: BBC
Ruby, Tracy: C–SPAN
Rucci, Susan Ruth: CBS News
Rudd, Michael: WJLA–TV/Newschannel 8
Ruddle, Richard: Native American Television
Rudin, Ken: National Public Radio
Ruggiero, Diane: CNN
Russell, Dedrick: WJLA–TV/Newschannel 8
Russell, Eugene: WTTG–Fox Television
Russell, Roxanne: CBS News
Russert, Timothy: NBC News
Rutherford, John H.: NBC News
Ruttenberg, Margie: WRC–TV/NBC–4
Ryan, Emily: Hearst-Argyle Television
Ryan, Jason: ABC News
Ryan, Jennifer: WUSA–TV
Ryan, Marty: Fox Newschannel
Ryan, Mike: Potomac Television
Rysak, Francis David: WTTG–Fox Television
Saal, Matthew: NBC News
Sable, Julia: Radio Free Asia
Sabo, Lara: Belo Capital Bureau
Saffelle, Jeffrey Lynn: Global TV Canada
Sagalyn, Daniel: Newshour with Jim Lehrer
Saiciuc, Doina: Romanian Radio
Sala, Salvador: Cataluna TV/TV3
Sales, Leigh: Australian Broadcasting Corporation
Salinas, Mary Alice: WRC–TV/NBC–4
Salkoff, Brooke-Hart: NBC Newschannel
Salvador, Steve: CNN
Sampy, David: Independent Television News (ITN)
Sanchez, Pablo: Univision News
Sanders-Smith, Sherry: C–SPAN
Sandiford, Michele: C–SPAN
Sandy, David: Freelancer
Sanfuentes, Jose A.: NBC News
Santana, Elvira: APTN
Santer, Sarah: Fox Newschannel
Santos, Augusto: CNN
Santos, Jeff: Regional News Network
Santos, Jose: Belo Capital Bureau
Sargeant, Nancy Lyons: AP–Broadcast
Sargent, Mark: WTTG–Fox Television
Sarkisian, Vatche: MBC–TV (Middle East Broadcast Center).
Sarmiento, Domingo: CNN
Sarvamaa, Petri: Finnish Broadcasting Company (YLE)
Sasson, Aaron: Freelancer
Satchell, David: WUSA–TV
Sathianarayanan, Ranjini: WJLA-TV/Newschannel 8
Saunders, Kevin: Capitol Pulse

MEMBERS ENTITLED TO ADMISSION—Continued

Savage, Craig: Fox Newschannel
Savoy, Greg: Global TV Canada
Sawka, Andrew Nippon TV Network
Scanlan, Bill: C–SPAN
Scanlon, Jason: Fox Newschannel
Scanlon, Mary: C–SPAN
Schaefer, Eugenia: NBC News
Schaefer, James: WJLA–TV/Newschannel 8
Schaff, Michael: CBC
Schalch, Kathleen: National Public Radio
Schall, Fred: Freelancer
Schantz, Kristine K.: CNN
Scharf, Jason: APTN
Schaverien, Natalie: BBC
Schenardoah, Michelle: Native American Television
Scherer, David: CNN/TVS
Scheschkewitz, Daniel: Deutsche Welle TV
Scheuer, John: C–SPAN
Scheuer, Stefan: German Television/ARD
Schiavone, Louise: CNN
Schiefer, Bob: CBS News
Schiff, Brian R.: Voice of America
Schifferis, Stephen: BBC
Schiller, Vivian: Discovery Times Channel
Schindler, Max: NBC News
Schlachter, Therese: Freelancer
Schlegel, Barry C.: CNN/TVS
Schleicher, Anne M.: Newshour with Jim Lehrer
Schlesinger, Patricia: German Television/ARD
Schloemer, Hans-Peter: Freelancer
Schlosberg, Andrew: TV Tokyo
Schneider, Inka: German Television/ARD
Schoene, Philip: WETA–TV
Schoenholtz, Howard: ABC News
Schoenmann, Donald: Viewpoint Communications
Schroeder, Anne: CNN
Schuiten, Jeroen: European Broadcasting Union
Schule, James R.: Fox Newschannel
Schulken, Sonja Deaner: Tribune Broadcasting
Schulte-Ebbert, Martin: German Television/ARD
Schultz, James J.: Fox Newschannel
Schultz, Ronald: Hearst-Argyle Television
Schultz, Teri: Fox Newschannel
Schultz-Burkel, Gunnar: German Broadcasting Systems/ARD
Schultze, F. Kevin: WJLA–TV/Newschannel 8
Schumaker, Carrie: AP–Broadcast
Schwarte, Georg: German Television/ARD
Schwartz, Harry Andrew: Fox Newschannel
Schweiger, Ellen: C–SPAN
Schweitzer, Gareth: Talk Radio News Service
Schweitzer, Murray H.: WRC–TV/NBC–4
Scicchitano, Carmine: NBC News
Scott, Amy E.: Marketplace Radio
Scott, Graham: Austrian Radio ORF
Scott, Harry Lee: Radio Free Asia
Scott, Ivan: Freelancer
Scott, Linda J.: Newshour with Jim Lehrer
Scott, Michael: ABC News
Scott, Raquel: CNN
Scott, Sarah: Freelancer
Scruggs, Wesley: NBC News
Scuderi, Donna: SRN News (Salem)
Scullin, Robin: C–SPAN
Scully, Steven: C–SPAN
Seabrook, Andrea: National Public Radio
Seabrook, Willliam: WETA–TV
Sears, Carl V.: NBC News
Seem, Thomas H.: CBS News
Segraves, Mark: WJLA–TV/Newschannel 8
Seidman, Joel: NBC News
Seium, Michael: Washington News Network
Selma, Reginald G: CNN/TVS
Serafin, Barry: ABC News
Serensits, Joseph: ABC News
Sergay, Richard G.: ABC News
Serna, Adriana Ahmad: CMI Television (Colombia)
Serper, Noelle: Religion & Ethics Newsweekly
Serrell, Gene Paul: CBC
Settle, Jeremy: WUSA–TV
Sewell, Leslie: Freelancer
Seymour, Allison: WTTG–Fox Television
Shaffir, Kimberlee: CBS News
Shalhoup, Joseph: NBC News
Shand, Christina: Fox Newschannel
Shand, Susan: Freelancer
Shannon, Dennis: CBS News
Shapiro, Joseph: National Public Radio
Shastri, Namgyal: Voice of America
Shattuck, Megan: CNN
Shaughnessy, Lawrence: Freelancer
Shaul, Lisa: CNN
Shaw, Heather: CNN
Shaw, Larry: ABC News
Shedrick, Daniel: APTN
Shelton, Steve: Fox Newschannel
Shenandoah, Joanne: Native American Television
Shepherd, Sarah: CNN
Sherman, Keisha L.: Freelancer
Sherwood, Tom: WRC–TV/NBC–4
Shih, Che-Wei: TVBS
Shine, Thomas Andrew: ABC News
Shire, Robert: Freelancer
Shively, Caroline: Freelancer
Shlemon, Chris: Independent Television News (ITN)
Shockley, Milton T.: WRC–TV/NBC–4
Shoffner, Harry: Freelancer
Shon, Robert: WTTG–Fox Television
Shott, David: Fox Newschannel
Shovelan, John: Australian Broadcasting Corporation
Showell, Andre: Freelancer
Shuster, David: NBC News
Shwe, Nyein: Radio Free Asia
Shweiki, Stephanie: Swiss Broadcasting

MEMBERS ENTITLED TO ADMISSION—Continued

Sicoli, Dean: CNN
Sides, James E.: C–SPAN
Sieg, Betareh: Voice of America
Siegel, Robert: National Public Radio
Siegfriedt, Anita: C–SPAN
Sierra, Joann: CNN
Silberbrandt, Allan: TV2 Denmark
Silberner, Joanne: National Public Radio
Silman, Jimmie: WUSA–TV
Silver, Darwin: WETA–TV
Silver, David: Freelancer
Silver, Janet E.: Australian Broadcasting Corporation
Silver, Torri: Prince George's Community Television
Silverberg, Hank: WTOP Radio
Silverman, Kip: Freelancer
Silverthorne, Robert: Freelancer
Simeone, Nick: Voice of America
Simmons, Jane Adams: CNBC
Simmons, Y. Sean: Freelancer
Simon, Laura D.: Radio France
Simons, John: CNN/TVS
Simpson, Carole: ABC News
Simpson, Gary: C–SPAN
Simpson, Ross: AP–Broadcast
Singer, Lauren: NBC News
Singleton, Erica L.: Prince George's Community Television
Sinn, Patricia: Cataluna TV/TV3
Sirgany, Aleen: CBS News
Sisco, Paul: Freelancer
Sit, David C.: Newshour with Jim Lehrer
Skeans, Ronald: Grace Digital Media
Skehan, Andrea Roane: WUSA–TV
Skomal, Paul: Freelancer
Slade, Jim: ABC News
Slattery, Julie: Bloomberg Television
Slen, Peter: C–SPAN
Slewka, Stephanie: Freelancer
Slie, Charles: Freelancer
Sloane, Ward C.: CBS News
Slobogin, Kathy: CNN
Slone, Sean: C–SPAN
Small, Matt: AP–Broadcast
Small, William: Bloomberg Television
Smee, Bill: Discovery Times Channel
Smelser, Judith: Feature Story News
Smith, Bob: CNN
Smith, Candace: AP–Broadcast
Smith, Carroll: CNN/TVS
Smith, David: Independent Television News (ITN)
Smith, Hedrick: Hedrick Smith Productions/ Frontline
Smith, Jason H.: WTTG–Fox Television
Smith, Mark S.: AP–Broadcast
Smith, Philip: Belo Capital Bureau
Smith, Raeshawn: Freelancer
Smith, Shirley: AP–Broadcast
Smith, Stephanie: Capitol Pulse
Smith, Terence: Newshour with Jim Lehrer
Smith, William: Hearst-Argyle Television
Sneed, Kimberly: NBC News
Snow, Kate: CNN
Snow, Tony: Fox Newschannel
Sobola, Michael: Ventana Productions
Soh, June: Voice of America
Sokolova, Elena: Russian State TV and Radio (RTR)
Solorzano, Gilbert: Freelancer
Soltysiak, Tansy: CNN
Soneira, Robert: Freelancer
Sorenson, Randall: Freelancer
Soucy, Peggy: European Broadcasting Union
Southern, Joel L: Alaska Public Radio Network
Southworth, Cal R.: National Public Radio
Sozio, George: Freelancer
Spain, Thomas: CNN/TVS
Speck, Alan: C–SPAN
Spector, Teresa: Fox Newschannel
Speer, John C.: National Public Radio
Speights, Eric V.: ABC News
Speiser, Matthew: CNN
Spektor, Eleanor: CNN
Spellman, Jim: CNN
Spelman, Paul: Hearst-Argyle Television
Spence, Robert: C–SPAN
Spencer, Christina M.: WJLA–TV/Newschannel 8
Spencer, Darcy: Freelancer
Sperrozza, Diana: Discovery Times Channel
Spevak, Joe: WTTG–Fox Television
Spire, Richard H.: CBS News
Spoerry, Philip: CNN
Sponder, Myron: Talk Radio News Service
Sproul, Robin: ABC News
St. James, Greg: C–SPAN
St. John, Jonathan: CNN
St. Onge, Derek: CNN/TVS
St. Pierre, Christine: CBC
Stage, Tina: Bloomberg Television
Stanford, David E.: CBS News
Stang, Tim: Bloomberg Television
Starddard, Gregory: WUSA–TV
Stark, Lisa: ABC News
Starks, Bill: WRC–TV/NBC–4
Starling, Walter: Freelancer
Staton, Thomas: Freelancer
Statter, Louis: WUSA–TV
Staude, Linda: German Television/ARD
Staude, Vaar: TV2 NORWAY
Stavitsky, Irina: APTN
Stearns, Scott: Voice of America
Stein, Cari: To the Contrary (Persephone Productions)
Stellabotta, Nancy: CBC
Stephanopoulos, George: ABC News

MEMBERS ENTITLED TO ADMISSION—Continued

Stephens, Mark: WRC–TV/NBC–4
Stepney, Eric: C–SPAN
Stetson, Chris: Fox Newschannel
Steuart, Elizabeth: NBC News
Stevenson, Carrie: CNN
Stevenson, Louis: WTTG–Fox Television
Steverson, Simone: National Public Radio
Stewart, Andrew: SRN News (Salem)
Stewart, James D.: CBS News
Stewart, Robin A.: Ventana Productions
Stirland, Sarah: Capitol Pulse
Stix, Gabriel: CBS News
Stoddard, Rick: C–SPAN
Stolley, Anna: Fox Newschannel
Stone, Carolyn: CNN/TVS
Storper, David: C–SPAN
Strand, Paul L.: CBC
Strass, Nina: AP–Broadcast
Strickland, Kenneth: NBC News
Stringer, Ashley: Grace Digital Media
Strong, David: Freelancer
Stubblefield, Abraham: WJLA–TV/Newschannel 8
Stubbs, James: CNN/TVS
Stultz, Amanda: Reuters Television
Stumpo, Donald: WRC–TV/NBC–4
Sturgis, Lisa C.: Fox Newschannel
Styles, Julian: CNN
Suarez, Fernando J.: CBS News
Suarez, Rafael A.: Newshour with Jim Lehrer
Suddeth, Rick: Freelancer
Suh, Young-Ho: MBC–TV Korea (Munhwa)
Suissa, Jimmy: CNN/TVS
Sullivan, Virginia L.: National Public Radio
Summers, Elizabeth: Newshour with Jim Lehrer
Summers, Patrick: Fox Newschannel
Surbey, Jason: C–SPAN
Surc, Matej: RTV Slovenija
Sutherland, Leigh: NBC News
Suto, Ena.: TV Asahi
Swain, Jayme: Freelancer
Swain, Susan M.: C–SPAN
Swain, Todd M.: Mobile Video Services
Swanier, Sherrell: CNN
Swann, Michael: WRC–TV/NBC–4
Sweeney, David: National Public Radio
Sweet, Mark: CNN
Sweetapple, Dan: Australian Broadcasting Corporation
Sylvester, Lisa B.: ABC News
Syrjanen, Janne: Freelancer
Szaroleta, Marjorie: AP–Broadcast
Szechenyi, Nicholas: Fuji Television
Tabata, Tadashi.: TV ASAHI
Tabbs, Kelvin: Freelancer
Taglienti, Ernie: Freelancer
Tait, Ted: BBC
Taiton, Abbi: CNN
Takahashi, Yusuke: NHK–Japan Broadcasting
Takashima, Hajime.: TV Asahi
Talley, Stephen: Capitol Pulse
Tamboli, Jay: Talk Radio News Service
Tamerlani, George: Reuters Television
Tan, Janet: Radio Free Asia
Tarrant, Philippa: BBC
Tate, Deborah: Voice of America
Taylor, Allyson Ross: CBS News
Taylor, Daniel: CNN/TVS
Taylor, Tanisha N.: WUSA–TV
Teboe, Mark: Freelancer
Teeples, Joseph: C–SPAN
Tendencia, Editha: European Broadcasting Union
Terrell-Heath, Angela: Nightly Business Report
Terry, Janet: WUSA–TV
Teshima, Ryuichi: NHK–Japan Broadcasting
Thakral, Shelley: BBC
Thalman, Mark: Ventana Productions
Than, Hla Hla: Voice of America
Thanos, Georgeanne: ABC News
Thinn, Soe: Radio Free Asia
Thoman, Eric: C–SPAN
Thomas, Amy Jo: ABC News
Thomas, Andrew: Freelancer
Thomas, Bert: Fox Newschannel
Thomas, Evelyn: CBS News
Thomas, Gary P.: Voice of America
Thomas, Jeanette: BBC
Thomas, Kenneth: Freelancer
Thomas, Marguerie: Talk Radio News Service
Thomas, Pierre G.: ABC News
Thomas, Sharahn: National Public Radio
Thomas, Shari: Freelancer
Thomas, Valerie: CBC
Thomas, Will: WTTG–Fox Television
Thompson, Jerry: CNN/TVS
Thompson, Jr., Joseph: Freelancer
Thompson, Margita: CNN
Thompson, Ron: Radio One
Thornton, Theodore: Freelancer
Till, Morgan: Newshour with Jim Lehrer
Tiller, Arthur: C–SPAN
Tillery, Richard: The Washington Bureau
Tillman, Thomas E.: CBS News
Tilman, Ai Nippon TV Network
Tilman, Brandon: C–SPAN
Tin, Annie: C–SPAN
Tinnefeld, Norbert: German Television/ARD
Tobias, Ed: AP–Broadcast
Todd, Brian: CNN
Tofani, Jeffrey T.: Voice of America
Tolliver, Terri: WTTG–Fox Television
Tollkuhn, Eckhard: Freelancer
Tollkuhn, Felicity: Austrian Radio ORF
Tomko, Joe: Video News Service
Tomko, Stephen: Video News Service
Tomlinson, Kathy: CTV–Canadian Television

MEMBERS ENTITLED TO ADMISSION—Continued

Tong, Scott: Newshour with Jim Lehrer
Topgyal, Benpa: Radio Free Asia
Torgenson, Ande: Fox Newschannel
Torvalds, Nils: Finnish Broadcasting Company (YLE)
Totenberg, Nina: National Public Radio
Touhey, Emmanuel: C–SPAN
Toulouse, Anne: Reuters Television
Trammell, Michael: WUSA–TV
Travis, Scott: Freelancer
Traynham, Peter C.: CBS News
Trengrove, James: Newshour with Jim Lehrer
Triay, Andres P.: CBS News
Trivic, Branka: Radio Free Europe/Radio Liberty
Truitt, Susan: WUSA–TV
Trujillo, Alicia: BBC
Tschida, Stephen: WJLA–TV/Newschannel 8
Tucker, Elke: German Television/ZDF
Tuel, Ted: Nightly Business Report
Tully, Andrew: Radio Free Europe/Radio Liberty
Tuohey, Kenneth: CNN/TVS
Tureck, Matthew: NBC Newschannel
Turner, Al Douglas: ABC News
Turner, Martin: BBC
Turner, Renee: Freelancer
Turner, Terry: Freelancer
Turnham, Steve: CNN
Tursun, Nabijan: Radio Free Asia
Tutman, Dan D.: CBS News
Tyler, Laurence: CNN/TVS
Tyler, Raven: Newshour with Jim Lehrer
Tyler, Thomas J.: CNN/TVS
Tzemach, Gayle: ABC News
Uchimiya, Ellen: Fox Newschannel
Udenans, Vija: ABC News
Uhl, Kim: CNN/TVS
Ulery, Brad: APTN
Uliano, Richard J.: CNN Radio
Ulloa, Victor: CBS News
Umeh, Maureen: WTTG–Fox Television
Umrani, Anthony R.: CNN/TVS
Urbina, Adrienne: Newshour with Jim Lehrer
Urbina, Luis: WRC–TV/NBC–4
Ure, Laurie: CNN
Usaeva, Nadia: Radio Free Asia
Valcarrel, Gus: APTN
Valderrama, Anna: Reuters Television
Vallese, Julie: CNN
Vample, Ron: AP–Broadcast
van den Nieuwendijk, Hans: NOS Dutch Public Broadcasting
Van Susteren, Greta: Fox Newschannel
Van der Bellen, Erin: WRC–TV/NBC–4
VanArsdale, Vicki: Bloomberg Television
Vance, Denise: APTN
Vance, Jim: WRC–TV/NBC–4
VanderVeen, Lawrence: Mobile Video Services
VanderVeen, Paul: Freelancer
Vaughan, Scott: Freelancer
Vecchione, Allan: Sinclair Broadcast Group
Vennell, Vicki: ABC News
Vergara, Sandra: RCN–TV (Colombia)
Veronelli, Alessio: Swiss Broadcasting
Vicario, Virginia A.: ABC News
Vicary, Lauren H.: AP–Broadcast
Vines, Andrew: The Washington Bureau
Vinson, Bryce: Fox Newschannel
Viqueira, Michael J.: NBC News
Visioli, Todd: Fox Newschannel
Vizcarra, Mario: Univision News
von Brocke-Doman, Evelin: Freelancer
Vorachak, Phaysarn: Radio Free Asia
Voth, Charles: WETA–TV
Voughn, Michael: WJLA–TV/Newschannel 8
Vukmer, David: NBC News
Wagner, Martin: German Public Radio/ARD
Wagner, Paul: WTTG–Fox Television
Wailand, Kate: CNN
Walde, Thomas: German Television/ZDF
Walker, Brian: APTN
Walker, James William: WJLA–TV/Newschannel 8
Walker, Joey Daniel: CNN/TVS
Walker, Tom.: Dispatch Broadcast Group
Wallace, John L.: Fox Newschannel
Wallace, Zelda: Cox Broadcasting
Walsh, Deirdre: CNN
Walsh, Mary E.: CBS News
Walter, Mike: USA Today Live
Walters, Del: WJLA–TV/Newschannel 8
Walton, J. N'oeyz: Freelancer
Walz, Mark: CNN/TVS
Wang, April: Radio Free Asia
Waqfi, Wajd: Al-Jazeera TV/Peninsula
Ward, Derrick: WTOP Radio
Warehime, Keith: C–SPAN
Warner, Craig: CBS News
Warner, Margaret: Newshour with Jim Lehrer
Warner, Tarik: WJLA–TV/Newschannel 8
Washburn, Kevin: C–SPAN
Washington, Erik: CBS News
Washington, Ervin: Nightly Business Report
Wasserman, Michele: Hamilton Productions
Waters, Hunter: CNN
Watkins, Duane: WTTG–Fox Television
Watrel, Jane: Freelancer
Watrud, Don: WTTG–Fox Television
Watson, Robert: BBC
Watts, Michael: CNN
Wauzer, John S.: Freelancer
Waxler, Gary: Freelancer
Webb, David: WJLA–TV/Newschannel 8
Webb, Justin Oliver: BBC
Webster, Aaron S.: Freelancer
Weglarczyk, Izabela BBC Polish Section
Wehinger, Amy: Fox Newschannel

MEMBERS ENTITLED TO ADMISSION—Continued

Wei, J. Naghshineh: Talk Radio News Service
Wei, Jing: Phoenix Satellite Television
Weidenbosch, Glenn E.: ABC News
Weilhammer, Francoise: Swiss Broadcasting
Weiner, Eric: Tokyo Broadcasting System
Weiner, Nancy: ABC News
Weinfeld, Michael: AP–Broadcast
Weininger, Alexandria: WJLA–TV/Newschannel 8
Weinstein, Richard: C–SPAN
Weisman, Josh: Fox Newschannel
Weiss, Jason: Medill News Service
Weisskopf, Arlene: Freelancer
Weldonm, Jody: Sinclair Broadcast Group
Wells, Courtney: Fox Newschannel
Welna, David: National Public Radio
Wendy, Carla: Fox Newschannel
Werner, Dan: Newshour with Jim Lehrer
Wertheimer, Linda C.: National Public Radio
Wheeler, Danette: NBC News
Wheelock, Robert: ABC News
Whelton, Danielle: CNN
White, Lauren Harris: Hearst-Argyle Television
Whiteman, Doug: AP–Broadcast
Whitley, Walter: Fox Newschannel
Whitney, Ian: Washington Bureau News Service
Whitney, Michael: Washington Bureau News Service
Whittington, Christopher: NBC News
Widmer, Christopher: CBS News
Wiesen, Stefan: Freelancer
Wik, Snorre: NBC Newschannel
Wildman, James: National Public Radio
Wilk, Wendy: WTTG–Fox Television
Wilkes, Douglas H.: WTTG–Fox Television
Wilkinson, Wendla: NBC News
Will, George: ABC News
Williams, Candace A.: Voice of America
Williams, Daniel: SKY NEWS
Williams, David E.: CNN
Williams, Derek: WTOP Radio
Williams, Jeffrey L: Cox Broadcasting.
Williams, John: Freelancer
Williams, Juan: National Public Radio
Williams, Keith: WUSA–TV
Williams, LaTanya: C–SPAN
Williams, Louis A.: NBC News
Williams, Michael: NBC Newschannel
Williams, Robert T: NBC News
Williams, Steven: Freelancer
Williams, Wendell: Metro Networks
Willingham, Valerie A.: WRC–TV/NBC–4
Willis, Anne Marie: Fox Newschannel
Willis, Judy: Newshour with Jim Lehrer
Wilmeth, Mary: NBC News
Wilner, Elizabeth: ABC News
Wilson, Brian: Fox Newschannel
Wilson, Edwin: WJLA–TV/Newschannel 8
Wilson, George: Radio One
Wilson, John: AP–Broadcast
Wilson, Justin: C–SPAN
Wilson, Kristin: Freelancer
Wilson, Leigh: CBS News
Wilson, Marcus: ABC News
Wilson, Mark: CBS News
Wilson, Stephanie: WUSA–TV
Wilson, Toni: CNN
Windham, Ronald: Tribune Broadcasting
Winslow, David: AP–Broadcast
Winterhalter, Ruthann: C–SPAN
Winters, Paul: C–SPAN
Winthrop, Tony: Freelancer
Witte, Joel: Ventana Productions
Witten, Robert: NBC News
Wittstock, Melinda: Capitol Hill Bureau from PRI
Wixted, Kathleen: C–SPAN
Woerner, Holly: ABC News
Wolfe, Lisa: WTOP Radio
Wolfe, Randy: NBC Newschannel
Wolff, Sarah: CBS News
Wolfson, Charles: CBS News
Wolfson, Paula: Voice of America
Wood, Alden: CBS News
Wood, Barry: Voice of America
Wood, Christopher: C–SPAN
Wood, Wayne C.: WRC–TV/NBC–4
Woodard, Alicia C.: WTTG–Fox Television
Woodruff, Judy: CNN
Woods, Stephanie: Nightly Business Report
Woolman, Shiloh: Bloomberg Television
Wordock, Colleen: Bloomberg Television
Wordock, John: CBS Marketwatch
Worth, Barbara: AP–Broadcast
Worthy, Cardozar: WJLA–TV/Newschannel 8
Wotring, Melanie: WJLA–TV/Newschannel 8
Wright, Brad: CNN
Wright, Christopher: Fox Newschannel
Wright, Cindy: WJLA–TV/Newschannel 8
Wright, Dale: WJLA–TV/Newschannel 8
Wright, Kelly: Fox Newschannel
Wu, Hsiang-San: Taiwan Television
Xiao, Yan: Phoenix Satellite Television
Xu, Susie: CNN
Yaklyvich, Brian: CNN/TVS
Yam, Raymond: Voice of America
Yamakawa, Madoka: Fuji Television
Yamamura, Mitsuru: NHK–Japan Broadcasting
Yamashita, Takeshi: NHK–Japan Broadcasting
Yancy, Shawn: WTTG–Fox Television
Yang, Carter: CBS News
Yang, Eun: WRC–TV/NBC–4
Yang, Sungwon: Radio Free Asia
Yao, Charlene: Formosa TV
Ydstie, John: National Public Radio.
Ye, Mary: Radio Free Asia

MEMBERS ENTITLED TO ADMISSION—Continued

Yektafar, Babak: C–SPAN
Yeshi, Lobsang: Radio Free Asia
Yianopoulos, Karen: NBC News
Yingling, Rob: Freelancer
Yoon, Robert: CNN
Young, Bob: Freelancer
Young, Jerome: CBC
Young, Melissa: ABC News
Young, Paul: Freelancer
Young, Rick: Hedrick Smith Productions/Frontline
Young, Saundra: CNN
Yu, Minjung Nippon TV Network
Yui, Hideki: NHK–Japan Broadcasting
Yuille, Jennifer: CNN
Zang, Guohua: CTI–TV (China)
Zayed, Nahedah: Fox Newschannel
Zeffler, Markus: German Television N24/SAT 1
Zervos, Stratis: Freelancer
Zhang, Huchen: Voice of America
Zhang, Jing: Voice of America
Zheng, Yeeli Hua: Phoenix Satellite Television
Zhou, Zhou: Phoenix Satellite Television
Zhuo, Qun: WETA–TV
Zilberstein, Shirley: CNN
Zmidzinski, Andrew: WJLA–TV/Newschannel 8
Zodun, Albert N.: WRC–TV/NBC–4
Zosso, Elizabeth: CNN/TVS
Zumwalt, Maya: Fox Newschannel
Zurkhang, Karma: Radio Free Asia
Zvaners, Martins: Radio Free Europe/Radio Liberty

NETWORKS, STATIONS, AND SERVICES REPRESENTED

Senate Gallery 224–6421 House Gallery 225–5214

ABC NEWS—(202) 222–7700; 1717 DeSales Street, NW 20036: Lynne Adrine, John Allard, Douglas Allmond, Marc Ambinder, Jon Bascom, Adam Belmar, Bob Bender, Robert E. Bramson, Charles Breiterman, Sam Brooks, Brooke Brower, H. Metric Brown, Jayne Hilary Bruns, Ian Cameron, Chris Carlson, Richard Coolidge, Caroline Cooper, Pam Coulter, Merrilee Cox, Wayne M. Cox, Robert Crawford, Sonya Crawford, Thomas J. D'Annibale, Tiffani M. Davis, Terry T. DeWitt, Henry Disselkamp, Peter M. Doherty, Linda D. Douglass, James DuBreuil, Dennis Dunlavey, Jonathan Ebinger, Charles Finamore, Jon Dominic Garcia, Arash Ghadishah, Thomas Giusto, Bernard Gmiter, Stuart Gordon, Robin Gradison, Laura Greene, William Greenwood, Brian P. Hale, Brian Hartman, Harry B. Heywood, Heidi Jensen, Kenneth Johnson, Steve E. Joya, Jackie Judd, Joy Kalfopulos, James F. Kane, Deborah Kempf, Eric Kerchner, John Knott, Monika Konrad, Amy Kramer, Stanley Lorek, Beverley C Lumpkin, Ellsworth Lutz, James Martin, Michel McQueen Martin, Luis Martinez, Darraine Maxwell, Brian McConnaughy, Mark McGrath, John McWethy, Portia R. Migas, Avery Miller, Geoff Morrell, Marie Nelson, Phuong G. Nguyen, Dean E. Norland, Edward F. O'Keefe, John F. O'Leary, Andrea Owen, Judy Penniman, Tran Pham, Michael Pickup, Dennis Powell, Mary Quinn, Victor Ratner, Aditya Raval, William Redding, Talesha Reynolds, Corinne B. Roberts, Lauren Rogers, George Romilly, Gary Rosenberg, Howard L. Rosenberg, Jason Ryan, Howard Schoenholtz, Michael Scott, Barry Serafin, Joseph Serensits, Richard G. Sergay, Larry Shaw, Thomas Andrew Shine, Carole Simpson, Jim Slade, Eric V. Speights, Robin Sproul, Lisa Stark, George Stephanopoulos, Lisa B. Sylvester, Georgeanne Thanos, Amy Jo Thomas, Pierre G. Thomas, Al Douglas Turner, Gayle Tzemach, Vija Udenans, Vicki Vennell, Virginia A. Vicario, Glenn E. Weidenbosch, Nancy Weiner, Robert Wheelock, George Will, Elizabeth Wilner, Marcus Wilson, Holly Woerner, Melissa Young.

ABS–CBN (PHILIPPINES)—(703) 685–2665; 841 South Glebe Road, Arlington, VA 22204: Josefina Ilustre.

AGDAY—(574) 631–1313; 54516 Business U.S. 31 North, South Bend, IN 46637: Philip McMartin.

ALASKA PUBLIC RADIO NETWORK—(202) 944–2394; 4023 Beecher Street, NW., #3, Washington, DC 20007: Joel L. Southern.

AL–JAZEERA TV/PENINSULA—(202) 467–5601; 1825 K Street, NW., 9th Floor 20006: Nader Abed, Eyad Aburahma, Babu Aryankalayil, Dana Budeiri, Rula Dajani, Thabet el-Bardicy, Mahmoud el-Hamalawy, Nezam Mahdawi, Imad Musa, Hafez Osman, Hugo Rahal, Nadia Rahman, Wajd Waqfi.

AMERICAN FAMILY RADIO—(703) 378–0942; 15250 Louis Mill Drive, Chantilly, VA 20151: William Fancher.

AP–BROADCAST—(202) 736–9500; 1825 K Street, NW 20006: Stephanie Blake, Gerald Bodlander, Camille Bohannon, Judy A. Boysha, Andrew Braddel, Lalnie Contreras, Mary Theresa Dickie, Pamela Dockins, Ed Donahue, Estelle Ebitty-Doro, Robert E. Eller, Fritz Faerber, Scott Ferry, Eileen Fleming, Lauren Frayer, David J. Friar, Oscar Wells Gabriel, Heather Greenfield, Michael J. Hammer, Jacqueline Hazelton, Wally Hindes, Derrill Holly, Shelly Howell, Tracy Johnke, Michael W. Kahn, Brad Kalbfeld, Eugene Kim, Sandy Kozel, Thelma LeBrecht, Francis J. Limbach, Kathryn Loomans, James Ludwin, Lisa N. Matthews, Kate McKenna, Sagar Meghani, David R. Melendy, Lisa Meyer, Bryant Michaud, Marty Niland, Steven F. Potisk, Orla Reese, Nancy Lyons Sargeant, Carrie Schumaker, Ross Simpson, Matt Small, Candace Smith, Mark S. Smith, Shirley Smith, Nina Strass, Marjorie Szaroleta, Ed Tobias, Ron Vample, Lauren H. Vicary, Andrew G. Visley, Michael Weinfeld, Doug Whiteman, John Wilson, David Winslow, Barbara Worth.

APTN—(202) 736–9595; 1825 K Street, NW 20006: Khaldoun Alrawi, Jennifer Beckman, Tracy Ann Brown, Gail Connor, Kelly Daschle Waiel El Nour, David Falcone, Malcolm Fitzwilliams, Richard Gentilo, James Gorman, Robert Gutnikoff, Eugneio Hernandez, Dan Huff, Kristine Kelleher, Christian Kethewell, Hakan Ozsancak, Walter Ratliff, Tucker Reals, Thomas Ritchie, Elvira Santana, Jason Scharf, Daniel Shedrick, Irina Stavitsky, Brad Ulery, Gus Valcarrel, Denise Vance, Brian Walker.

AUSTRALIAN BROADCASTING CORPORATION—(202) 466–8575; 529 14th Street, NW., #510 20045: Jill Colgan, Woodrow Landay, David Martin, Vincent Magwenya, Lisa Millar, Jason D. Racki, Leigh Sales, John Shovelan, Janet E. Silver, Dan Sweetapple.

AUSTRIAN RADIO ORF—(202) 822–9570; 1206 Eton Court, NW 20007: Hildegard Banes, Hartmut Fiedler, Hans Peter Fritz, Johnannes Marlovits, Lauren Pinto, Douglas Robinson, Graham Scott, Felicity Tollkuhn.

BBC—(202) 223–2050; 2030 M Street, NW., #350 20036: Kevin Anderson, Tamzen Audas, Sharon Blanchet, Nick Bryant, Michael Buchanan, Jasmin Buttar, Tom Carver, Nick Childs, Gordon Corera, Sofia Diarra, William Drew, Annie Duncanson, Matt Frei, Ben Gurney, Sara Halfpenny, Mishal Husain, Katty Kay, Louise Kerslake, Jon Leyne, Melanie Marshall, Allen McGreevy, Beth Miller, Mark Orchard,

NETWORKS, STATIONS, AND SERVICES REPRESENTED—Continued

Ian Pannell, Mark Rabbage, Karina Rozentals, Natalie Schaverien, Stephen Schifferis, Ted Tait, Philippa Tarrant, Shelley Thakral, Jeanette Thomas, Alicia Trujillo, Martin Turner, Robert Watson, Justin Oliver Webb.

BBC POLISH SECTION—(202) 841–3291; 400 North Capitol Street, NW 20001: Izabela Weglarczyk.

BELGIAN RADIO AND TV/VRT—(202) 466–8793; 2000 M Street, NW., #365 20036: Greta De Keyser.

BELO CAPITAL BUREAU—(202) 661–8400; 1325 G Street, NW 20045: Thomas Ackerman, Sharon Bender, David Mart Cassidy, Jonathan E Drum, Jim Fry, Michael Goldfein, Stacy Hutchins, Michael Kornely, Robert Michaud, Carolyn Presutti, Lara Sabo, Jose Santos, Philip Smith.

BERNS BUREAU—(202) 314–5165; P.O. Box 2939 20013: Mathew D. Kaye.

BET NIGHTLY NEWS—(202) 783–0537; 400 North Capitol Street, NW., #361 20001: Monique Conrad, Glenn Elvington, Pamela Gentry, Mark Mazariegos.

BLOOMBERG TELEVISION—(202) 624–1866; 1399 New York Avenue, NW 20005: Irwin Chapman, Roland Morrisette, Julie Slattery, William Small, Tim Stang, Tina Stage, Vicki VanArsdale, Shiloh Woolman, Colleen Wordock.

BROADCASTING CORPORATION OF CHINA—(703) 691–0091; 9328 Branchside Lane, Fairfax, VA 22031: Nike Chang.

CADENA COPE (SPAIN)—(202) 686–1982; 4904 Belt Road, NW 20016; Juan Martinez Fierro.

CANCERPAGE.COM—(703) 287–9421; 1430 Spring Hill Road, McLean, VA 22102: Rachael Myers Lowe.

CAPITOL HILL BUREAU FROM PRI—(202) 251–5730; P.O. Box 77796 20013: Max Cacas, Chad Pergram, Melinda Wittstock.

CAPITOL PULSE—(202) 454–5289; 209 Pennsylvania Avenue, SE., #207/600 20003: Jennifer Allen, Emily Appleman, Berkin Aslan, Ross Bell, Delia V. Clayton, Kristina Cox, Adam Croley, Angela Dow, Benjamin Duncan, Debbie Hodges, Brent Kendall, Heidi Curley Kline, Elizabeth Leimbach, Michael Lupo, George McLean, Malkia McLeod, Joel Nori, Boris Popovic, Kevin Saunders, Stephanie Smith, Sarah Stirland, Stephen Talley.

CARACOL TV—(202) 236–7995; 529 14th Street, NW 20045: Viviana Avila Lindo.

CATALUNA RADIO—(202) 686–6558; 3001 Veazey Terrace, NW., #116 20008: Diana Molineaux.

CATALUNA TV/TV3—(202) 785–0580; 1620 I Street, NW., #150 20006: Eva Artesona, Salvador Sala, Patricia Sinn.

CBC—(202) 383–2900; 529 14 Street, NW., #500 20045: Adrienne Arsenault, Marie-Eve Bedard, Jennifer Brown, Marcel Calfat, Henry Champ, Sorine Coupet, Louis de Guise, Dorothee Giroux, David Halton, Frank Koller, William Loucks, Heather Loughran, Laura Lynch, Neil MacDonald, Angela Naus, Karen O'Leary, Yves Peltier, Greogory Reaume, Sylvain Richard, Christine St. Pierre.

CBN NEWS—(202) 833–2707; 1111 19th Street, NW., #950 20036: Steven Autrey, Paul Behrens, Therese Carrier, Melissa A. Charbonneau, Mark B. Hendricks, John O'Leary, David Page, Michael Schaff, Gene Paul Serrell, Nancy Stellabotta, Paul L. Strand, Valerie Thomas, Jerome Young.

CBN RADIO NETWORK (BRAZIL)—(202) 363–5640; 5246 Loughboro Road, NW 20016: Chris Delboni, Joe Matheu.

CBS MARKETWATCH—(202) 824–0573; 529 14th Street, NW 20045: Andrew O'Day, John Wordock.

CBS NEWS—(202) 457–4444; 2020 M Street, NW 20036: Robin Carol Adlerblum, Thomas Albano, Wyatt Andrews, Howard Arenstein, Thalia Assuras, Sharyl Attkinson Barry Bagnato, Benneh Bangura, Bruce Barr, Kia Baskerville, Penny Britell, Cecile P. Brown, Andrea Bruce, Traci L. Caldwell, David Caravello, Anthony Cavin, Steven Chaggaris, Joie Chen, George Christian, Adam Ciralsky, Alfred Colby, Paul H. Corum, Pham Gia Cuong, John Daly, Charles H. Dixson, Lois Dyer, Michael Faulkner, Tony Furlow, Bob Fuss, Harriet Garber, Frank Giles, Karen Gilmour, Benson Ginsburg, Jeff Scott Goldman, Neil Grasso, Joshua D. Gross, Mary Hager, Mark D. Hanner, Susan Bullard Harmon, Robert Hendin, Deirdre Hester, Dennis Jamison, Obin Johnson, Jeffrey Johnston, Mark Katkov, Douglas Kiker, Colleen King, Mark Knoller, Stephanie Lambidakis, Frank LaTorre, Donald A. Lee, Janet Leissner, Denise Li, Johnathan Lien, Matt Lowe, Peter Maer, David Martin, Alexandra Mathers, Thomas A. Mattesky, Maxwell McClellan, James McGlinchy, Michael McGuire, Jill Rosenbaum Meyer, Richard Meyer, Katharine Mountcastle, John Murphy, John Nolen, Teri Okita, K. Robert Orr, Rebecca Peterson, William Plante, Luther Posey, Diana Quinn, Mark Rabin, Dan Ravin, Francisco Robbins, John Roberts, Susan Ruth Rucci, Roxanne Russell, Bob Schiefer, Thomas H. Seem, Kimberlee Shaffir, Dennis Shannon, Aleen Sirgany, Ward C. Sloane, Richard H. Spire, David E. Stanford, James D. Stewart, Gabriel Stix, Fernando J. Suarez, Allyson Ross Taylor, Evelyn Thomas, Thomas E. Tillman, Peter C. Traynham, Andres P. Triay, Dan D. Tutman, Victor Ulloa, Mary E. Walsh, Craig Warner, Erik Washington, Christopher Widmer, Kristin Wilson, Leigh Wilson, Mark Wilson, Sarah Wolff, Charles Wolfson, Alden Wood, Carter Yang.

CHANNEL ONE NEWS—(202) 296–5937; 1825 K Street, NW., #501 20006: Sharon McGill.

CLEAR CHANNEL COMMUNICATIONS—(301) 255–4399; 1801 Rockville Pike, 6th Floor, Rockville, MD 20852: Ira Mellman.

CMI TELEVISION (COLOMBIA)—(571) 337–7500; Diagonal 22A N 43–65 Bogota, Colombia: Adriana Ahmad Serna.

NETWORKS, STATIONS, AND SERVICES REPRESENTED—Continued

CNBC—(202) 467–5400; 1025 Conecticut Avenue, NW 20036: Matthew Cuddy, Kendall Evans, Karen L. James, Eamon Javers, Steve Lewis, Alan S. Murray, Diana Olick, Hampton Pearson, Robert Reynolds, Jane Adams Simmons.

CNN—(202) 898–7900 First Street, NE 20002: Kimberly Abbott, Khalil Abdallah, Michael M. Ahlers, Julio E. Aliaga, Kelli Arena, Craig Baker, James Barnett, Ted Barrett, Adam Benson, Pamela S. Benson, Kathy Benz, Catherine Berger, Deborah Berger, Laura Bernardini, Rea Blakey, Wolf Blitzer, Kevin Bohn, Christine Brennan, Robert Lee Brickhill, Clarie Brinberg, Becky Brittain, Craig A. Broffman, Michael Brooks, Hannah Buchdahl, Carol E. Buckland, Matthew Byrne, Elaine Cagas, Silvio Carrillo, Bethany A. Chamberland, Trish Chicca, Carrie Conner, George Cooper, Paul S. Courson, Joshua Cowen, Carol A. Cratty, Karla Crosswhite, Candy Alt Crowley, Damon Cruz, Traci Curry, Emily A.D'Alberto, Jack Date, Kristin Davis, Patrick A. Davis, Anastasia N. Diakides, Geoff Dietrich, Erika Dimmler, Rich Dubroff, Megan Duke, Jonathan Dumont, John Dunaway, Lisa Durham, Kathleen Fabian, Amy Farrar, Kathryn Farrell, Christy Feig, Shaye Ferris, Eric James Fiegel, Kevin Flower, Robert Franken, Terry Frieden, Elizabeth Fulk, Ben Geldon, Jennifer Gibson, John Gilmore, Evan Glass, David Gracey, Kate Albright Hanna, Arthur Hardy, Guerin Hays, Julie Hofler, Sarah B. Holland, Matthew Hoye, Christian Hudson, Ashley Huffman, Shirley Hung, Charles Hurley, Brooks Jackson, NuNu Japaridze, Kyle Johnsen, Sasha Johnson, Jonathan Karl, Sean Kelly, Charley Keyes, John C. King, Pat Kloehn, James Jeffery Knott, Kathleen Koch, Robert S. Kovach, Amy Kramer, Kathryn Kross, Rebecca Kutler, Elise Labott, Yvonne Lee, Mary E. Lewandowski, Frances L. Lewine, Kim Linden, Skip Loescher, Willie A. Lora, Sean Loughlin, John Lynn, Suzanne Malveaux, George D. Mathews, Kristen McCaughan, Timothy McCaughan, Kerith McFadden, Michael McManus, Eileen McMenamin, William Mears, John Mercurio, Jeanne Meserve, Jeff Milstein, Patricia Davis Mitchell, Bruce Morton, Suzanne Nelson, Virginia Nicolaidis, Kerry Ogata, Michael Poley, Branden Ray, Patrick T. Reap, Heather Riley, Laura Robinson, Janet Rodriguez, Brian Rokus, H. Michael Roselli, Rachel Rosen, Jessica Rosgaard, Beth Ann Rotatori, Linda Roth, Lindy Royce, Diane Ruggiero, Steve Salvador, Augusto Santos, Domingo Sarmiento, Kristine K Schantz, Louise Schiavone, Anne Schroeder, Raquel Scott, Megan Shattuck, Lisa Shaul, Heather Shaw, Sarah Shepherd, Dean Sicoli, Joann Sierra, Kathy Slobogin, Bob Smith, Kate Snow, Tansy Soltysiak, Matthew Speiser, Eleanor Spektor, Jim Spellman, Philip Spoerry, Jonathan St. John, Carrie Stevenson, Julian Styles, Sherrell Swanier, Mark Sweet, Abbi Taiton, Margita Thompson, Brian Todd, Steve Turnham, Laurie Ure, Julie Vallese, Kate Wailand, Deirdre Walsh, Hunter Waters, Michael Watts, Danielle Whelton, David E. Williams, Toni Wilson, Judy Woodruff, Brad Wright, Susie Xu, Robert Yoon, Saundra Young, Jennifer Yuille, Shirley Zilberstein.

CNN RADIO—(202) 515–2229; 820 First Street, NE 20002: John Bisney, Richard J. Uliano.

CNN/TVS—(202) 898–7670; 820 First Street, NE 20002: William Alberter, Charles Anderson, Rodney Atkinson, Reza Baktar, Mike Banigan, Jay Berk, David Berman, Tim Raymond Bintrim, John Bodnar, Burke Buckhorn, David Keith Catrett, James Cook, John Cunha, John Davis, Darryl Diamond, Martin Dougherty, Daniel Farkas, Timothy C. Garraty, Maurice George, Thomas Greene, Eddie S. Gross, Christopher Hamilton, Vernon Herald, Conrad Hirzel, Dave Hugel, David Jenkins, Martin Jimenez, Worth Kinlaw, Adilson Kiyasu, Larry Langley, Pamela Leahigh, Myron A. Leake, Howard Lutt, Lisa Manes, Mark Antho Marchione, Michael Marcus, Ralph Marcus, Dennis McCarty, Paul Miller, Peter Mohen, W. Harrison Moore Peter Morris, Richard Morse, Joseph Mosley, Luis Munoz, Thomas Murphy, Jeff Noble, Ernest G. Nocciolo, Valerie T. Nocciolo, Dennis Norman, James F. Norris, Sarah Pacheco, Michael Peters, John Jay Quinnette, James W. Riggs, Tyrone W. Riggs, Greg Robertson, David Scherer, Barry C. Schlegel, Reginald G Selma, John Simons, Carroll Smith, Thomas Spain, Derek St. Onge, Carolyn Stone, James Stubbs, Jimmy Suissa, Daniel Taylor, Jerry Thompson, Kenneth Tuohey, Laurence Tyler, Thomas J. Tyler, Kim Uhl, Anthony R. Umrani, Joey Daniel Walker, Mark Walz, Brian Yaklyvich, Elizabeth Zosso.

CNSNEWS.COM—(703) 683–9733; 325 South Patrick Street, Alexandria, VA 22314: Michael L. Betsch, Robert B Bluey, Steve Brown, James E. Burns, Christine Hall, Scott Alan Hogensen, Jeffrey S. Johnson, Lawrence Morahan, Marc Morano.

COURT TV (METRO TELEPRODUCTIONS)—(202) 828–0366; 1400 East West Highway, Suite 628, Silver Spring, MD 20910: John Bogley, Lee J. Hobson, William Kaplan, Dave Lilling, John O'Brien.

COX BROADCASTING—(202) 777–7000; 400 North Capitol Street, NW., #750 20001: Alana M. Anyse, Alison Burns, David Chase, Jamie Dupree, Ryan Jackson, Lanora Booker Johnson, Kevin Johnson, Brigette Langmade, Michael Majchrowitz, Zelda Wallace, Jeffrey L. Williams.

C–SPAN—(202) 737–3220; 400 North Capitol Street, NW., #650 20001: Kenneth Alexander, Thomas Alldredge, Brett Annaheim, Tooo Baham, Michelle Bailor, Edward Barker, Amy Barr, Deborah Bates, Afrika Bell Kathuria, Shephard B Bennett, Molly Benton, Brett Betsill, Michael Biddle, Michael Brannock, Paul Brown, Freda Buckley, Susan J. Bundock, Kevin Burch, Leslie Burdick, James Burke, Craig Caplan, Patricia Carroll, Michael Cavaiola, Tanya Chattman, Nancy Christianson, James Clark, Josh Cohen, Eloise Collingwood, Bruce Collins, Leslie Conner, William Conover, Liam Currier, Alexander Curtis, Matthew Dauchess, Kyneesha Dew, Anne Marie Dinardo, Connie Doebele, Pedro L. Echevarria, Ron Eisenbarth, Gary Ellenwood, Seth Engel, Greg Fabic, Mark Farkas, Richard Fleeson, Juan Flores, Carl Foster, William Frazier, Rick Gabala, Karen Gaither, Bill Gallagher, Garney Gary,

NETWORKS, STATIONS, AND SERVICES REPRESENTED—Continued

Joyce Genter, Norma Gleason, Robert Gould, Sean Gray, Richard Hall, Hamada Hanoura, Eric Hansen, Chris Hanson, Stephen Harkness, Robb Harleston, Elizabeth Harrison, Maurice Haynes, William Heffley, Jonelle P. Henry, Francis Herbas, Leslye Heyman, Dallas Hill, Leta Hix, Robert Hoffmaster, George Howell, Roger Hunter, Roberta Jackson, Katherine Jeffries, Kim Jones, Barry Katz, Steven Kehoe, Jonathan Kelley, Robert Kennedy, Roxane Kerr, Lewis Ketcham, Kevin King, Tony Laboy, Brian P. Lamb, Hope Landy, Darren Larade, Robert Lazar, Paul Loeschke, Russell Logan, Chris Long, David Luck, Valerie Matthews, Michael McCann, Sean P. McCann, Kate McCarthy, Ron McCrary, Bradley McGuire, Seeno Merobshoev, Theresa Michel, Andrew Miller, Katherine Mills, David Monack, Garrette Moore, Linwood Moore, Diane Morris, Bridget Morrison, Dan Morton, Kathy Murphy, Terence Murphy, Andrew Murray, Andrew Nason, Benjamin O'Connell, Paul Orgel, Cheryl Owens, Tanya Parker, Veron K. Perkins, Andrea Perry, Paul Pickett, Maura Pierce, Nickolas Pitocco, Almon L. Porter, Anne Preloh, Nikhil Raval, James Regan, Robert Reilly, Cynthia Reuter, Amy Roach, Martine Rodriguez, Francis Rose, Tracy Ruby, Sherry Sanders-Smith, Michele Sandiford, Bill Scanlan, Mary Scanlon, John Scheuer, Ellen Schweiger, Robin Scullin, Steven Scully, James E. Sides, Anita Siegfriedt, Gary Simpson, Peter Slen, Sean Slone, Alan Speck, Robert Spence, Greg St. James, Eric Stepney, Rick Stoddard, David Storper, Jason Surbey, Susan M. Swain, Joseph Teeples, Eric Thoman, Arthur Tiller, Brandon Tilman, Annie Tin, Emmanuel Touhey, Keith Warehime, Kevin Washburn, Richard Weinstein, LaTanya Williams, Justin Wilson, Ruthann Winterhalter, Paul Winters, Kathleen Wixted, Christopher Wood, Babak Yektafar.

CTI–TV (CHINA)—(202) 331–9110; 1825 K Street, NW., #716 20006: Yi Qiu Chen, Guohua Zang.

CTV–CANADIAN TELEVISION—(202) 466–3595; 2000 M Street, NW., #330 20036: Stephanie Brisson, Phil Dudley, Alan Fryer, Jim MacDonald, Florence Rossignol, Kathy Tomlinson.

DANISH BROADCASTING CORPORATION—(202) 785–1957; 2030 M Street, NW., #700 20036: Jon Kaldan, Kim Lassen, William Montague.

DEUTSCHE PRESS AGENCY—(202) 662–1220; 969 14th Street, NW 20045: Christina Eck.

DEUTSCHE WELLE TV—(202) 785–5730; 2000 M Street, #335 20036: Udo Bauer, Hillery Gallasch, Lawrence LaComa, Rudiger Lentz, Cornelia Ottersbach, Daniel Scheschkewitz.

DISCOVERY TIMES CHANNEL—(240) 662–2189; 1 Discovery Place, Silver Spring, MD 20910: Kevin Bennett, Irene Gottschalk, Vivian Schiller, Bill Smee, Diana Sperrozza.

DISPATCH BROADCAST GROUP—400 North Capitol Street, #850 20001: Richard Puckett, Tom Walker.

EGYPTIAN TV—(202) 293–9371; 2000 M Street, NW., #300 20036: Hanan H. Elbadry.

EUROPEAN BROADCASTING UNION—(202) 775–1295; 2000 M Street, NW., #300, 20036: William Dunlop, William Headline, Ruth Kristen Hering, Rosa M. Moreno, Priya Narahari, Julie Noce, Didier Piette, Jeroen Schuiten, Editha Tendencia, David Roberson, Peggy Soucy.

FEATURE STORY NEWS—(202) 296–9012; 1730 Rhode Island Avenue, NW 20036: Malcolm Brown, Catherine Drew, Priscilla Huff, Simon Marks, Stephen Mort, Nina-Maria Potts, John Ray, Judith Smelser.

FEDNET—(202) 393–7300; 50 F Street, NW., Suite #1C 20001: Keith Carney, Joshua Cheshire, Clifford Feldman, Alvin Jones, Mark Lindblom, Thomas Madden.

FINNISH BROADCASTING COMPANY (YLE)—(202) 785–2087; 2030 M Street, NW., #700 20036: Tarja Oinonen, Petri Sarvamaa, Nils Torvalds.

FORMOSA TV—(202) 775–8112; 1825 K Street, NW., #17, 20006: Charlene Yao.

FOX NEWSCHANNEL—(202) 824–6300; 400 North Capitol Street, NW 20001: James L. Angle, Robert Armfield, Julie Asher, Bret Bairer, Les Baker, Dennis Baltimore, Stuart Basinger, Kelley O. Beaucar, Bruce Becker, Eve Blumstein, Elizabeth Boswell, Bryan Boughton, Janet E. Boyd, Michelle Bradley, Fletcher Bransford, Edgar Brown, Caroline Hall Bruner, Aaron Bruns, Carl Cameron, Michael Carpel, Steve Centanni, Kelly Chernenkoff, Patrice Chung, Rick Cockerham, Bryan Cole, Nicole Collins, Eric Conner, Katie Conover, Wendy Dawson, Rick D. Bella, Andrea DeVito, Jerry Echols, James W. Eldridge, Mike Emanuel, Justin Fishel, David Futrowsky, Dan Gallo, Major Garrett, Maria Gillespie, Timothy Goldsmith, Wendell Goler, Gregg L. Gursky, Fred Haberstick, Nancy Harmeyer, Greg Headen, Mary Janne Henneburg, Stacy Hickman, Stephen Hirsh, Molly Hooper, Adrienne M. Hopkins, Jasmine Huda, Brit Hume, Kim Hume, Sharon Kehnemui, Daniela Kelley, Philip Kersey, Grigory Khananyev, Lillian LeCroy, Philip LeCroy, Michael Levine, Edward Lewis, Stacy Lloyd, Wayne Lowman, Laurie Luhn, Brigitte Lyles, Michael Lyon, Michael Marno, Ian McCaleb, John McCally, Anne McGinn, Jim Mills, Erin C. Nagle, James Nelson, Michele Novy, Philip Och, Dominique Pastre, Chris Peslis, Jacqueline Pham, Geraldine Pitsinger, Shannon Powell, R. Brian Rainey, Michele Remillard, Elizabeth Rhodes, Anne Marie Riha, Corbett Riner, Lisa Rizzolo, Querry Robinson, Nicole Rogers, Douglas Rohrbeck, James Rosen, Marty Ryan, Sarah Santer, Craig Savage, Jason Scanlon, James R. Schule, James J. Schultz, Teri Schultz, Harry Andrew Schwartz, Christina Shand, Steve Shelton, David Shott, Tony Snow, Teresa Spector, Chris Stetson, Anna Stolley, Lisa C. Sturgis, Patrick Summers, Bert Thomas, Ande Torgenson, Ellen Uchimiya, Greta Van Susteren, Bryce Vinson, Todd Visioli, John L. Wallace, Amy Wehinger, Josh Weisman, Courtney Wells, Carla Wendy, Walter Whitley, Anne Marie Willis, Brian Wilson, Christopher Wright, Kelly Wright, Nahedah Zayed, Maya Zumwalt.

NETWORKS, STATIONS, AND SERVICES REPRESENTED—Continued

FRANCE 2 TELEVISION—(202) 833–1818; 2000 M Street, NW 20036: Stephanie Cheval, Aaron Diamond, Arielle Monange.

FREE SPEECH RADIO NEWS—(212) 209–2811; 1929 Martin Luther King Jr. Way, #73, Berkeley, CA 94704: Pamela Barnett, Joshua Chaffin.

FRENCH TELEVISION TF1—(202) 223–3642; 2100 M Street, NW., #302, 20037: Bertrand Aguirre, Jean-Pascal Azais, Loick Berrou, Remi Cadoret, Helene Davieaud, Bruce Frankel, Francois Lescalier, Vincent Mortreux, Jason Mulveny.

FUJI TELEVISION—(202) 347–1600; 529 14th Street, NW., #330, 20045: Peter Gold, Toshiyuki Matsuyama, Tateki Muratani, Yoshio Ninoseki, Setsu Nishiumi, Nicholas Szechenyi, Madoka Yamakawa.

GERMAN BROADCASTING SYSTEMS/ARD—(202) 944–5290; 1200 Eton Court, NW., #100 20007: Silvia Charpa, Hans-Peter Riese, Gunnar Schultz-Burkel.

GERMAN PUBLIC RADIO/ARD—(202) 625–6203; 1200 Eton Court, NW., #200 20007: Hannelore Jones, Sebastian Hesse-Kastein, Arthur Landwehr, Martin Wagner.

GERMAN TELEVISION AGENCY—(202) 393–7571; 529 14th Street, NW., #1199 20045: Roger Horne, Markus Meier.

GERMAN TELEVISION N24/SAT 1—(202) 331–7883; 1620 I Street, NW 20006: Stephan Bachenheimer, Anne Dickerson, Alexander Privitera, Markus Zeffler.

GERMAN TELEVISION/ARD—(202) 298–6535; 3132 M Street, NW 20007: Ulrich Arndts, Thorsten Bachmann, Herta Borniger, Tom Buhrow, Martin Schulte-Ebbert, Julia Fensterer, Klaus Haller, Roland Hanka, Christiane Meier, Thea Rosenbaum, Stefan Scheuer, Patricia Schlesinger, Inka Schneider, Georg Schwarte, Linda Staude, Norbert Tinnefeld.

GERMAN TELEVISION/ZDF—(202) 333–3909; 1077 31st Street, NW 20007: Christiane Blatter, Kirsten Candia, Heike Diel, Georg Juenger, Alice Kelley, Gundula Koch Kay Lendzian, Wolfgang Macholz, Claudia Offerman, Gabi Osgood, Eberhard Piltz, Steffanie Riess, Hildrun Rowe, Elke Tucker, Thomas Walde.

GLOBAL TV CANADA—(202) 824–6770; 400 North Capitol Street, NW 20001: Carl P. Hanlon, Jeffrey Lynn Saffelle, Greg Savoy.

GRACE DIGITAL MEDIA—(202) 775–0894; 1919 M Street, NW., #200 20036: James Balsamo, Robert Baumann, Kathleen Brumbaugh, Brenda Cecil, Harvey Cofske, David Cooke, Robert Fetzer, Robert Henry, Matthew Iverson, Muriel Jubar, Neville Martin, Linda Mayhew, Nan Hee McMinn, Kerry Meyer, Peter Murtaugh, Michael Neapolitan, Barry O'Donnell, Cheryl Reagan, Peter Rosenbaum, Misa Rossetti-Meyer, Ronald Skeans, Ashley Stringer.

HAMILTON PRODUCTIONS—(703) 734–5444; 7732 Georgetown Pike, McLean, VA 22102: Anne H. Deger, Jay Hamilton, John Hamilton, Michele Wasserman.

HDA PICTURES, INC./ORBITE—(202) 332–9019; 2231 California Street, NW., #301 20008: Hugues-Denver Akassy.

HEARST-ARGYLE TELEVISION—(202) 457–0220; 1825 K Street, NW., #720 20006: Peter Barnes, Christina-Marie Barnett, Bridget Broullire, Jeremy Diller, Michael Finnigan, Meredith Gunning, Jennifer Hitchcock, Laura Kinney, Erin T. McManamon, Lauren Rich, Emily Ryan, Ronald Schultz, William Smith, Paul Spelman, Lauren Harris White.

HEDRICK SMITH PRODUCTIONS/FRONTLINE—(301) 654–9848; 6935 Wisconsin Avenue, #208 Chevy Chase, MD 20815: Josephine Hearn, Hedrick Smith, Rick Young.

HELLENIC BROADCAST CORPORATION (ERT)—(202) 223–5423; 4201 Massachusetts Avenue, NW., #A249C 20016: Dimitrios Amperiadis, Dimitrios Apokis.

HISPANIC RADIO NETWORK—(202) 637–8800; 740 National Press Building 20045: Jeffrey Kline.

INDEPENDENT TELEVISION NEWS (ITN)—(202) 429–9080; 400 North Capitol Street, NW., Suite 899, 20001: Alexander Anstey, Maxine Collins, Luke Alexander Collinson, Zoe Conway, Robert Moore, David Sampy, Chris Shlemon, David Smith.

IRISH RADIO AND TELEVISION (RTE)—(202) 223–7989; 2000 M Street, NW., #315, 20036: Carole Coleman, Hilary Roberson.

ISRAEL ARMY RADIO/GALEI–TZAHAL—(301) 622–1591; 112 Shaw Avenue, Silver Spring, MD 20904: Drora Perl.

ISRAEL TELEVSION AND RADIO—(202) 331–2859; 1620 I Street, NW 20006: Yaron Deckel.

KOMO–TV—(202) 265–3229; 1317 Rhode Island Avenue, NW., #201, 20005: Timothy Hillard.

KTUU–TV—(202) 661–0065; 400 North Capitol Street, #850, NW 20001: Seth Litzenblatt, Rene Lopez.

LIVING ON EARTH—(617) 868–8810; 8 Story Street, Cambridge, MA 02138–4956: Jennifer Chu.

MARKETPLACE RADIO—(202) 223–6699; 1333 H Street, NW., Suite 600 West, 20005: John Dimsdale, Stephen Hann, Amy E. Scott.

MBC–TV (MIDDLE EAST BROADCAST CENTER)—(202) 898–8047; 1510 H Street, NW., #B2, 20005: Daoud Abuelhawa, Lukman Ahmed, Dalia Al-Aqidi Gabriel Caggiano, Aziz Fahmy Farag, Vatche Sarkisian.

MBC–TV KOREA (MUNHWA)—(202) 347–4147; 529 14th Street, NW., #1131, 20045: Chang Young Choi, Myung-Ghil Choi, Young-Ho Suh.

MEDILL NEWS SERVICE—(202) 347–8700; 1325 G Street, Suite 730, NW 20005: Mary Coffman, Sharon Kornely, Abe Moore, Jason Weiss.

NETWORKS, STATIONS, AND SERVICES REPRESENTED—Continued

METRO NETWORKS—(301) 628–2700; 400 North Capitol Street, NW., #G–50, 20001: Allison Browne, Kathy Culpepper, John Irving, Terrence Moore, Wendell Williams.

MOBILE VIDEO SERVICES—(202) 331–8882; 1620 I Street, #1000, NW 20006: Nic Beery, William Griffitts, Joseph Holtschneider, Robert H. Milford, Joaquim Neto, Todd M. Swain, VanderVeen.

MSNBC/NBC NEWS—(202) 824–6704; 400 North Capitol Street, #850, NW 20001: Thomas J. Curry.

MTV3 (FINLAND)—(202) 364–2880; 6144 Utah Avenue, NW 20015: Pertti Mikael Nyberg.

NATIONAL PUBLIC RADIO—(202) 513–2000; 635 Massachusetts Avenue, NW 20001: Larry Abramson, Bud Aiello, Brendan Banaszak, Melissa Block, Thomas Bullock, Shawn Corey Campbell, Alex Chadwick, Theodore Clark, Neal Conan, Robert Duncan, Ronald Elving, Susan Feeney, Pamela Fessler, Cara Gerhard, Ben Gilbert, Tom Gjelten, Don Gonyea, Barry Gordemer, Barton Grabow, Gisele Grayson, Jonathan Hamilton, Cheryl Hampton, Richard Harris, Anne Hawke, Christopher Joyce, Jeffrey Katz, John C. Keator, Michele Kelemen, Justine Kenin, Susan Klein, Terrence Knight, Martin R. Kurcias, Mara Liasson, Jennifer Ludden, Edward McNulty, William McQuay, William Mebane, Kelemen Michele, Julia Mitric, Lowell Muse, Brian Naylor, Joe R. Neel, John Nielsen, Michele Norris, Victoria O'Hara, Quinn O'Toole, Peter Overby, Joe Palca, Marisa Penaloza, Richard Howell Rarey, Julia Redpath-Buckley, Jeffrey Rosenberg, Ken Rudin, Kathleen Schalch, Andrea Seabrook, Joseph Shapiro, Robert Siegel, Joanne Silberner, Cal R. Southworth, John C. Speer, Simone Steverson, Virginia L. Sullivan, David Sweeney, Sharahn Thomas, Nina Totenberg, David Welna, Linda C. Wertheimer, James Wildman, Juan Williams, John Ydstie.

NATIONAL SCENE NEWS—(202) 898–7670; 1718 M Street, NW., #333, 20036: Alverda Ann Muhammad, Askia Muhammad.

NATIVE AMERICAN TELEVISION—(703) 771–7469; 444 North Capitol Street, NW., #601C, 20001: Robert Cohencious, Richard DiMassimo, Randolph Flood, Richard Gargagliano, Douglas M. George-Kanentiio, Larry Leeds, James R. Prior, Charles Reddoor, Richard Ruddle, Michelle Schenardoah, Joanne Shenandoah.

NBC NEWS—(202) 885–4210; 4001 Nebraska Avenue, NW 20016: Douglas A. Adams, Maria Afsharian, Patrick G. Anastasi, Percy Arrington, Rodney Sim Batten, Gary Glenn Beall, Dominic Bellone, Jay Blackman, Keith Blackman, Victoria Blooston, Jeffery Blount, Joseph Bohannon, John D. Boyd, Almadale Brown, Christopher Brown, Anthony Capra, Jessica A. Cesa, Brady G. Daniels, Andre D. DelaForet, Christopher Donovan, Geoffrey C. Doyle, Victoria Duncan, Danaj Edmond, Daniel Erlenborn, Sarah Evans, Barbara Fant, Robert Faw, Matthew Fields, Sheldon Fielman, Elizabeth Fischer, Erin Fogarty, David Forman, Kerri Forrest, Scott Foster, Fredrick N Francis, Wilfred R. Fraser, Jr., Jamie Gangel, Richard Gardella, William A. Gebhardt, Frank L. Gibson, Jr., John J. Greco, Erin Green, James M. Greene, David Gregory, Andrew F. Gross, Robert M. Hager, Sylvie Haller, Alan Harvey, Harold Paul Hayley, John F. Holland, Matthew A. Hosford, Salim I. Ishaq, Philip Jacobs, Michelle Jaconi, Joanne Jaje, Christina Jamison, Alicia Jennings, Joseph Johns, Leroy Johnson, Gwyneth Jones, Rosiland Jordan, Marc Koslow, Lester A. Kretman, Courtney Kube, Tamara Kupperman, Susan Alic LaSalla, Margaret Lehrman, Elizabeth Leist, Stephen Lewis, Lydia Lively, James V. Long, Liliana Lopez, Ebony Nicole McMorris, Carroll Ann Mears, Brock Nola Meeks, James Miklaszewski, Richard Minner, Andrea Mitchell, Lester Moses, Adolyn A. Myers, Lisa M. Myers, Donna Nelson, Elizabeth Nevins, Norah O'Donell, Chadwick Ryan Parks, William Petras, Debra Pettit, James K. Popkin, Courtenay Reese, Sean Reis, Alan Gregory Rice, Carl Rochelle, Johnie F. Roth, Timothy Russert, John H. Rutherford, Matthew Saal, Jose A. Sanfuentes, Eugenia Schaefer, Max Schindler, Carmine Scicchitano, Wesley Scruggs, Carl V. Sears, Joel Seidman, Joseph Shalhoup, David Shuster, Lauren Singer, Kimberly Sneed, Elizabeth Steuart, Kenneth Strickland, Leigh Sutherland, Michael J. Viqueira, David Vukmer, Danette Wheeler, Christopher Whittington, Wendla Wilkinson, Louis A. Williams, Robert T Williams, Mary Wilmeth, Robert Witten, Karen Yianopoulos.

NBC NEWSCHANNEL—(202) 783–2615; 400 North Capitol Street, NW., #850, 20001: Turner Bridgforth, Sheila Conlin, Jennifer Daly, H. Estel Dillon, Nancy Ellard, Sheri Gibson, Adam Greenbaum, Steve Handelsman, James Hurt, Julie Jarvis, Beverly Kirk, Virginia Coyne Krenindler, Dwight Mayhew, Richard McDermott, Kevin A. McManus, Tom Newberry, Bonnie Rollins, Brooke-Hart Salkoff, Matthew Tureck, Snorre Wik, Michael Williams, Randy Wolfe.

NEWSHOUR WITH JIM LEHRER—(703) 998–2870; 2700 S. Quincy Street, #250, Arlington, VA 22206: Samara Aberman, Lee M. Banville, Gregory J. Barber, Carol Blakeslee, Jeffrey Brown, David Butterworth, Elizabeth Callan, Leah Clapman, Russell Clarkson, David Coles, Lester M. Crystal, Alice H. Davenport, Anne Davenport, Susan Dentzer, Bridget DeSimone, Laura Dine, Allan Freedman, Brian Gottlieb, Elizabeth Harper, Maureen Hoch, Babette Hoffman, Kwami Holman, Gwen Ifill, Shermaze Ingram, Murrey Jacobson, Jim Lehrer, Susan Malin, Jason Manning, Kathleen McCleery, Annette L. Miller, Susan L. Mills, Jessica Moore, Michael D. Mosettig, Dayna K. Myers, Gregg Ramshaw, Margaret Robinson, Karin Rotchford, Daniel Sagalyn, Anne M. Schleicher, Linda J. Scott, David C. Sit, Terence Smith, Rafael A. Suarez, Elizabeth Summers, Morgan Till, Scott Tong, James Trengrove, Raven Tyler, Adrienne Urbina, Margaret Warner, Dan Werner, Judy Willis, Linda Winslow.

NETWORKS, STATIONS, AND SERVICES REPRESENTED—Continued

NHK–JAPAN BROADCASTING—(202) 828–5180; 2030 M Street, NW., #706, 20036: Sylvain Coudoux, Anne-Marie Fendrick, Lisa Lane, Yu-Chu Lin, Akihiro Mikoda, Bryan Mong, Masami Musha, Laura Peterson, Yusuke Takahashi, Ryuichi Teshima, Mitsuru Yamamura, Takeshi Yamashita, Hideki Yui.

NIGHTLY BUSINESS REPORT—(202) 682–9029; 1325 G Street, #1005, NW 20005: Darren Gersh, Katelynn Reckord Raymer, Angela Terrell-Heath, Ted Tuel, Ervin Washington, Stephanie Woods.

NIPPON TV NETWORK—(202) 638–0890; 529 14th Street, #1036, NW 20045: Takaaki Abe, Kenti Chikata, Kyoji Hara, Fumihiko Kure, Kenichi Miura, Hirofumi Nakano, Susan Pegues, Andrew Sawka, Ai Tilman, Minjung Yu.

NORWEGIAN BROADCASTING—(202) 785–1481; 2030 M Street, NW., #700, 20036: Wenke Eriksen.

NOS DUTCH PUBLIC BROADCASTING—(202) 466–8793; 2000 M Street, NW., #365, 20036: Charles Groenhuijsen, Hans van den Nieuwendijk, Timotheus Overdiek.

PHOENIX SATELLITE TELEVISION—(202) 824–6585; 400 North Capitol Street, NW., #550, 20001: Nai Chian Mo, Jing Wei, Yan Xiao, Yeeli Hua Zheng, Zhou Zhou.

POTOMAC RADIO NEWS—(202) 244–2781; 3130 Wisconsin Avenue, NW., #519, 20016: Josh Carothers, Emily Duncan, Michael J Duncan, Eric Ness, Mike Ryan.

POTOMAC TELEVISION—(202) 783–6464; 529 14th Street, NW., #480, 20045: Paul M. Crosariol, Jamie Norins, Mike Ryan.

PRINCE GEORGE'S COMMUNITY TELEVISION—(301) 386–4085; 9475 Lottsford Road, Largo, MD 20774: Curtis Crutchfield, Jeff Estepp, Patricia Villon Garcia, David Goldman, Ara Laughlin, Paul Lester, Heather McBride, Nicole Nelson, Torri Silver, Erica L. Singleton.

PUBLIC AFFAIRS TELEVISION (BILL MOYERS)—(212) 560–8600; 450 West 33rd Street, 7th Floor, NY, NY 10001: Robert Baskin, Katharine Pitra.

RADIO BILINGUE—(202) 234–0280; 1420 N Street, NW., #101, 20005: Natashka McDonald.

RADIO FRANCE—(202) 965–1327; 4512 Q Lane, NW 20007: Laura D. Simon.

RADIO FREE ASIA—(202) 530–4900; 2025 M Street, NW., #300, 20036: Jaehoon Ahn, Max Avary, Marsha J. Barnhart, Arin Basu, David Beasley, Thao-Mo Bounnak, Huidong Cao, Lobsang Chophel, Sooil Chun, Dana Dolma, Karma Dorjee, Xiao Ming Feng, Richard Finney, Xiao Gong, Rowena Ho, Laura Huang, Yang Jiadai, Dolkun Kamberi, Yonho Kim, Vivian Kwan, Yuk-Chong Lai, Tanya Lan, Dong Hyuk Lee, Dong Hywk Lee, Kyu Lee, Soo Kyung Lee, Yue Li, Xiao Qiang Liao, Ted Liu, Kalden Lodoe, Lucy Lu, Abner S. Mir, Jilil Musha, Tseten Namgyal, An Nguyen, Viet Tien Nguyen, Khin Nyane, Thein H. Oo, Julia Sable, Harry Lee Scott, Nyein Shwe, Janet Tan, Soe Thinn, Benpa Topgyal, Nabijan Tursun, Nadia Usaeva, Phaysarn Vorachak, April Wang, Sungwon Yang, Mary Ye, Lobsang Yeshi, Karma Zurkhang.

RADIO FREE EUROPE/RADIO LIBERTY—(202) 457–6900; 1201 Connecticut Avenue, NW., 11th Floor, 20036: Asta Banionis, Frank T. Csongos, Jeffrey Donovan, Nazira Karimi, Michael Mihalisko, Branka Trivic, Andrew Tully, Martins Zvaners.

RADIO ONE—(301) 306–1111; 5900 Princess Garden Parkway, Lanham, MD 20706: LaFontaine Oliver, Ron Thompson, George Wilson.

RCN–TV (COLOMBIA)—(202) 572–0389; 1825 K Street, NW., #501, 20006: Sam Rocha, Sandra Vergara.

REGIONAL NEWS NETWORK—(202) 347–7631; 400 North Capitol Street, NW., #775, 20001: Jeff Santos.

RELIGION & ETHICS NEWSWEEKLY—(202) 216–2384; 1333 H Street, NW., 6th Floor, 20005: Kim Lawton, Judy Reynolds, Ryan Rockwood, Noelle Serper.

REUTERS TELEVISION—(202) 898–0056; 1333 H Street, NW., 6th Floor, 20005: Peter Bullock, Eliza Bussey, John Clarke, Kevin Fogarty, Peter Fox, Guillermo Garcia, Deborah Gembara, Kia Johnson, Justin Kenny, Predrag Kojovic, Deborah Lutterbeck, Ian MacSpadden, Tipp McClure, Ian McDougall, Terry Moseley, Robert Muir, Gershon Peaks, Donald Pessin, Steven Phillips, Bryan Rager, Fausto Ramon, Jr., Tom Rowe, Amanda Stultz, George Tamerlani, Anne Toulouse, Anna Valderrama.

ROMANIAN RADIO—(202) 625–6284; 2519 39th Street, NW., #102, 20007: Doina Saiciuc.

ROMANIAN TELEVISION—(202) 248–7140; 2511 Q Street, NW., #201, 20007: Cecilia Melinescu, Nicolae Melinescu.

ROWE NEWS SERVICE—(301) 977–6252; 922 Beacon Square Ct., #324, Gaithersburg, MD 20878: Jo Ann Rowe.

RTP PORTUGUESE PUBLIC TELEVISION—(202) 783–0095; 1120 G Street, NW., #270, 20005: Pedro A. Bicudo, Marcelo Capuchinho.

RTV SLOVENIJA—(703) 845–8171; 1462 South Greenmount Drive, #107, Alexandria, VA 22311: Matej Surc.

RUSSIAN STATE TV AND RADIO (RTR)—(202) 298–5748; 2650 Wisconsin Avenue, NW 20007: Eugene Piskounov, Elena Sokolova, Stanislav Pletnikov.

SAGARMATHA TELEVISION—(703) 926–9530; P.O. Box 12272, Burke, VA 22009: Ram C. Kharel.

SBS RADIO (AUSTRALIA)—(202) 452–5552; 4808 Arburis Avenue, Rockville, MD 20853: Mike Kellerman.

SINCLAIR BROADCAST GROUP—(410) 568–2123; 10706 Beaver Dam Road, Hunt Valley, MD 21030: Jennifer Gladstone, Edward Glusing III, Carl Gottlieb, Erin Guthrie, Dana Hackley, Morris Jones, Sarah Kwasniak, Sean Lucas, Sarah L. McGath, Allan Vecchione, Jody Weldonm, Cindy Wright.

NETWORKS, STATIONS, AND SERVICES REPRESENTED—Continued

SKY NEWS—(202) 864–6583; #550, North Capitol Street, 20001: Daniel Williams.

SLOVAK RADIO—(202) 244–4971; 4418 35th Street, NW 20008: Olga Bakova.

SRN NEWS (SALEM)—(703) 528–6213; 1901 North Moore Street, #201, Arlington, VA 22209: Garry Beausoleil, George Bonzagni, Jennifer Borrasso, Gregory Clugston, Elizabeth Dager, Philip Fleischman, Linda Kenyon, John Lormand, Andrea Mikus, Howard Morgan, Janet Parshall, Pamela Rommelmeyer, Donna Scuderi, Andrew Stewart.

STATELINE.ORG—(202) 339–6146; 1101 30th Street, NW., #301, 20007: Erin M. Madigan, Kavan Peterson, Pamela Prah.

SWEDISH TELEVISION—(202) 785–1727; 2030 M Street, NW 20036: Stefan Asberg, Leif Carlsson, Lisa Carlsson.

SWISS BROADCASTING—(202) 429–9668; 2000 M Street, NW 20036: Pierre Bavaud, Michele Galfetti, Rudolf Maeder, Fritz Reimann, Stephanie Shweiki, Alessio Veronelli, Francoise Weilhammer.

TAIWAN TELEVISION—(202) 223–6642; 1825 K Street, NW., #717, 20036: Hun-min Lee, Hsiang-San Wu.

TALK RADIO NEWS SERVICE—(202) 337–5322; 2514 Mill Road, NW 20007: Joseph J. Byrne, James W. Cullum, Cholene Espinoza, Lovisa Frost, Victoria Jones, Genevieve Kopel, Ellen Ratner, Gareth Schweitzer, Myron Sponder, Jay Tamboli, Marguerie Thomas, J. Naghshineh Wei.

TECH TV—(202) 775–9754; 1620 I Street, NW., #1000, 20006: Peter Barnes, Mark Dougherty, Keith W. Murrow.

TELEMUNDO NETWORK—(703) 820–8333; 2775 South Quincy Street, #100, Arlington, VA 22206: Maria Aspiazu, Tomas Cabarcos, Erick Carpio, Joseph Cassano, Miguel Chavez, Gustavo Cherquis, Pedro Correa, Edith Garcia, Pablo Gato, Anne Hoyt, Lillian Martinez-Bustos, Douglas Mejia, Lori Montenegro, Luisa Montero, Wingel Pinzon, Victor Reyes.

TELEVISA NEWS NETWORK (ECO)—(202) 714–8446; 1825 K Street, NW., #718, 20006: Mariella Egusquiza, Gregorio Meraz, Hector Montaut.

TELEVISION NACIAONAL DE CHILE (TVN)—(202) 483–2392; 2407 15th Street, NW., #410, 20009: Andrea Henriquez, Ralf Oberti.

THE WASHINGTON BUREAU—(202) 347–6396; 400 North Capitol Street, NW., #775, 20001: Jonathan Badrian, Josef Crosby, John Getter, Wei-ye Jia, Sara Parnell, Julia Rockler, Richard Tillery, Andrew Vines.

TOKYO BROADCASTING SYSTEM—(202) 393–3800; 1088 National Press Building, 20045: Shigenori Kanehira, Michael Lavallee, Nakazato Masayuki, Yuko Miyake, Yugo Mori, Akio Mukaiyama, Makiko Murotani, Eric Weiner.

TO THE CONTRARY (PERSEPHONE PRODUCTIONS)—(202) 973–0079; 1825 K Street, NW., #501, 20006: Royd Chung, Bonnie Erbe, Ariana Kelly, Cari Stein.

TRIBUNE BROADCASTING—(202) 824–8444; 1325 G Street, NW., #200, 20005: Gregory Aspery, Cissy Baker, Richard Chamberlain, David Cilberti, Caroline J. Comport, Jason M. Dorn, Sabrina Fang, John Paul Fielder, Michael Kinney, Thomas Kolodziejczak, Ari Meltzer, Matthew Murray, Grant Rampy, Sonja Deaner Schulken, Ronald Windham.

TV ASAHI—(202) 347–2933; 670 National Press Building, 20045: Robert H. Gentry, Rika Mizumoto, Stephanie Mogg, Kazuhiko Ota, Ena Suto, Tadashi Tabata, Hajime Takashima.

TVBS—(202) 310–5449; 1333 H Street, NW., 5th Floor, 20007: Che-Wei Shih.

TV AZTECA—(703) 927–4664; 3800 Dade Drive, Annandale, VA 22003: Armando Guzman.

TV TOKYO—(202) 638–0441; 529 14th Street, NW., #803, 20045: Masamobu Murai, Mika Otsuka, Andrew Schlosberg.

TV2 DENMARK—(202) 828–4555; 2030 M Street, NW., #375, 20036: Charolotte Ernst, Scott Rensberger, Allan Silberbrandt.

TV2 NORWAY—(202) 466–7505; 2000 M Street, NW., #380, 20036: Vaar Staude.

UNITED NEWS AND INFORMATION—(202) 783–2002; 1057–D National Press Building, 20045: Dennis Crowley.

UNIVISION NEWS—(202) 783–7155; 444 North Capitol Street, NW., #601G, 20001: Ernesto E. Clavijo, Jorge Contreras, Deborah Durham, Marco Granda, Maria Rosa Lucchini, Lourdes Meluza, Norma Montenegro, Fernando Pizarro, Raul Ramos, Pablo Sanchez, Mario Vizcarra.

USA RADIO NETWORK—(202) 237–0870; 3101 New Mexico Avenue, NW., #55G, 20016: Jonathan P. Decker.

USA TODAY LIVE—(703) 854–7610; 7950 Jones Branch Drive, McLean, VA 22108: Lauren Ashburn, Ginger Gadsden, Gerardo Garcia, Lance Ing, Chris McCaffrey, Mike Walter.

VENTANA PRODUCTIONS—(202) 785–5112; 1825 K Street, NW., #501, 20006: Richard Feather, Aurora Garcia, Richard Joy, Matt Mosley, Timothy K. Murray, Jen Pennybacker, Juan Rocha, Michael Sobola, Robin A. Stewart, Mark Thalman, Joel Witte.

VIDEO NEWS SERVICE—(202) 365–3693; 1825 K Street, NW., #501, 20006: Nary Clark, Alejandro Harding, Than Hoai, Cristian Ouezada, Joe Tomko, Stephen Tomko.

VIEWPOINT COMMUNICATIONS—(301) 565–1650; 8607 Second Avenue, #402, Silver Spring, MD, 20910: Randy Feldman, Larry Greenblatt, Steve Hamberg, Donald Schoenmann.

NETWORKS, STATIONS, AND SERVICES REPRESENTED—Continued

VOICE OF AMERICA—(202) 619–2702; 330 Independence Avenue, SW., 20237: Akmal Aleemi, Dara Baccam, Jonathan D. Brandkamp, Meredith S. Buel, Melissa Carlson, Carol Castiel, Ronald Cesar, Joseph Chen, Robert Cole, Michael J. Collins, Fred C. Cooper, Penny Dixon-Gumm, Alejandro Escalona, Mahtab Farid, Parichehr Farzam, Craig Fitzpatrick, Joseph Gallagher, Jr., Valer Gergely, David A. Gollust, Stephanie J. Ho, Joseph L.R. Hopkins, Gary M. Jaffe, Hubert B. Katz, Kyle King, Yeon Cheol Lee, James Malone, David E. McAlary, Jeffrey Wendell Means, Stephanie Mann Nealer, Irawan Nugroho, Daniel Robinson, William F. Rodgers, Brian R. Schiff, Namgyal Shastri, Betareh Sieg, Nick Simeone, June Soh, Scott Stearns, Deborah Tate, Hla Hla Than, Gary P. Thomas, Jeffrey T. Tofani, Candace A. Williams, Paula Wolfson, Barry Wood, Raymond Yam, Huchen Zhang, Jing Zhang.

VOYAGE PRODUCTIONS—(202) 276–2848; 1825 K Street, NW., #501, 20006: Susan Baumel.

WAMU–FM—(202) 885–1233; 4000 Brandywine Street, NW 20016: Kevin J. Beesley, David Furst, Susan Goodman, Sarah Hughes, James Jones, Danielle Karson, Stephanie Kaye, Nancy Marshall, Lisa Nurnberger, James Rosenberg.

WASHINGTON BUREAU NEWS SERVICE—(202) 255–8695; 7475 Swan Point Way, Columbia, MD, 21045: Mercedes Eldridge, Michael Eldridge, Ian Whitney, Michael Whitney.

WASHINGTON NEWS NETWORK—(202) 628–4000; 400 North Capitol Street, NW., #650, 20001: Arik Dashevsky, Barton Eckert, Walter Gold, Jack Nix, David Oziel, Icarus N. (Ike) Pappas, Adrianna Roome, Michael Seium.

WASHINGTON RADIO & PRESS SERVICE—(301) 229–2576; 6702 Pawtucket Road, Bethesda, MD 20817: Hanna Gutmann.

WBAL–TV—(410) 467–3000; 3800 Hooper Avenue, Baltimore, MD 21211: Timothy Matkosky.

WEST VIRGINIA PUBLIC BROADCASTING—(304) 876–9313; P.O. Box 3210, Shepherdstown, WV 25443: Cecelia Mason.

WETA–TV—(703) 998–1800; 2775 South Quincy Street, Arlington, VA 22206: Lynn Allison, Timothy Bowen, Donald Brawner, Joesph Buckingham, Barbara Byrne, Martin Carr, Elizabeth Cronen, Frank Fitzmaurice, David Gillette, Eileen Griffin, John Hyater, Charles Ide, Gregory King, Christopher Lane, Edward Lee, Jerry Lewis, Robert Ludwig, Donald H. Lynch, Michael Mayes, John C. Nash, Charles Nixon, Jeffrey Rathner, Philip Schoene, Willliam Seabrook, Darwin Silver, Charles Voth, Qun Zhuo.

WGN RADIO/U.S. FARM REPORT—(301) 942–1996; 9915 Hillridge Drive, Kensington, MD 20895: Patrick B. Haggerty.

WJLA–TV/NEWSCHANNEL 8—(202) 364–7715; 1100 Wilson Boulevard, Arlington, VA 22209: Joy Allen, Jason Bacon, Frank K. Becker, Bradley Bell, Victor Blandburg, Alan Matth Brock, Karen E. Brown, Melissa Brown, Maureen Bunyan, LuAnn Canipe, Darryl Carver, David Chaytor, Jim Clarke, Carrie Connolly, Rebecca J. Cooper, Bob Costantini, Walter Crawford, Regan Davis-Hopper, Sonia Y. Debreczeni, Bruce DePuyt, Martin C. Doane, Lauren Dunn, Andre Dunston, Tony Ferringno, Michael Fischoff, Michael Forcucci, Sam Ford, B.J. Forte, Elliott Francis, Eric Freeland, Pege Gilgannon, John Gonzalez, Charles A Goodknight, Miles Grant, Molette Green, Richard Guastadisegni, Steve Hackett, Peter Hakel, Glenn Harris, John R. Harter, Kara Woods Henschel, Lawrence Herman, Darnley Hodge, Julie S. Holley, Horace Holmes, Brian Hopkins, Thomas Hormuth, LaTanya E. Horne, Don Hudson, Irene Johnson, Ashley Kellog-Wheeler, Suzanne Kennedy, Greta Kreuz, H. Ming Leong, John Elliott Lewis, John D Lisle, Dave Lucas, Jonathon Mann, Elizabeth Manresa, Kathleen Matthews, Andrea McCarren, Meghan McCorkell, Doug McKelway, Kerry McQuone, Heather Molino, Fran Murphy, Matt Murray, Kyle Osborne, Virginia Pancoe, Alisa Parenti, Julie Parker, Gail Pennybacker, Christopher Plater, Stephen Pozniak, Richard Reeve, Nathan Roberts, Susan Roberts, Jeff Rose, Joseph Rose, Eric Rotan, Michael Rudd, Dedrick Russell, Ranjini Sathianarayanan, James Schaefer, F. Kevin Schultze, Mark Segraves, Christina M. Spencer, Abraham Stubblefield, Stephen Tschida, Michael Voughn, James William Walker, Del Walters, Tarik Warner, David Webb, Nancy Weiner, Alexandria Weininger, Edwin Wilson, Cardozar Worthy, Melanie Wotring, Cindy Wright, Dale Wright, Andrew Zmidzinski.

WMAL RADIO—(202) 686–3100; 4400 Jenifer Street, NW 20015: Richard Mangus.

WORLDNET TELEVISION—(202) 401–8272; 330 Independence Avenue, SW 20547: Darrell Allen, Emery Robert Beaudin, Christopher Bogle, Jeffery Daugherty, Lyle H. Lindberg, John D. Quinn.

WPFW–FM—(202) 588–0999; 2390 Champlain Street, NW 20009: Gloria Minott.

WPWC–AM (RADIO FIESTA)—(703) 494–0100; 14416 Jefferson Davis Hwy #20 Woodbridge, VA 22191: Carlos Aragon.

WRC–TV/NBC–4—(202) 885–4111; 400 Nebraska Avenue, NW 20016: James M. Adams, Michael Allen, Jay Alvey, Milandro Arcega, Martin Babington-Heina, Katherine Banks, Audrey Barnes, Jackie Bensen, Charles Bragale, Larry Bullard, Arch Campbell, Julie Carey, Sean Casey, Pat Collins, Elizabeth Crenshaw, Anna Davalos, Harry L. Davis, Mary Ellen Donovan, Tony Dorsey, Elizabeth Feldman, James M. Forrest, Matt Glassman, Chris Herbert Gordon, John K. Greenwood, James Handly, Ira John Hudson, Philip H. Jacobs, Debbi Jarvis, Ede R. Jermin, James S. Kizer, Joe Krebs, Ronald Leidelmeyer, Robert Long, Brenda N. Mallory, Megan McGrath, Patrick T. McKenna, Michelle Michael, Doreen Gentzler Miller, Pat Lawson Muse, James J. Neustadt, Anna Oajacos, Chester Panzer, Margie Ruttenberg, Mary Alice Salinas, Murray H. Schweitzer, Tom Sherwood, Milton T. Shockley, Bill Starks, Mark

NETWORKS, STATIONS, AND SERVICES REPRESENTED—Continued

Stephens, Donald Stumpo, Michael Swann, Luis Urbina, Erin Van der Bellen, Jim Vance, Valerie A. Willingham, Wayne C. Wood, Eun Yang, Albert N. Zodun.

WTOP RADIO—(202) 895–5060; 3400 Idaho Avenue, NW 20016: Neal Augenstein, Mike Causey, Steve Eldridge, Jim Farley, Brennan Haselton, Chas Henry, Kristi King, Kimberly Kingsley, Judlyne Lilly, Bob Madigan, Dave McConnell, Mike McMearty, Mitchell Milller, Amy Morris, Mark Plotkin, Hank Silverberg, Derrick Ward, Derek Williams, Lisa Wolfe.

WTOP2 (FEDERAL NEWS RADIO)—(202) 895–5086; 3400 Idaho Avenue, NW 20016: Marlis Majerus, Kim Oates.

WTTG–FOX TELEVISION—(202) 895–3000; 5151 Wisconsin Avenue, NW 20016: Matt Ackland, Melanie Alnwick, John Anglim, Jeffrey Ballou, Bob Barnard, Brian Bolter, Carlos Castro, Roby Chavez, Holley Coil, Patricia Corcoran, Michelle Daell, Craig Little, Patricia DiCarlo, Carolyn Dolcimascolo, John P. Dunmire, Laura Evans, John Foundas, John Frame, Michael Gargiulo, Holly Carol Gavnit, Max Giammetta, Jeff Gilman, Carlos Alberto Gonzalez, Julieann Graziano, Craig J. Harrington, Mary Hayes, John Henrehan, Carlos E. Hernandez, Michael Horan, Karen Gray Houston, Sheila Jaskot, Lyrone Steven Jones, Nelson Jones, Nathalie Joost, Michael Kinney, Ira Lazernik, Elisabeth Leamy, Sherri Ly, Michael Marantz, Wisdom Martin, Jimmy Mathis, Lark McCarthy, Scott McCathran, Patrick McGrath, Holly Morris, Tracey Neale, Beth Parker, Michael Rickard, Amy Robach, Eugene Russell, Francis David Rysak, Mark Sargent, Allison Seymour, Robert Shon, Jason H. Smith, Joe Spevak, Louis Stevenson, Will Thomas, Terri Tolliver, Maureen Umeh, Paul Wagner, Duane Watkins, Don Watrud, Wendy Wilk, Douglas H. Wilkes, Alicia C. Woodard, Shawn Yancy.

WUSA–TV—(202) 895–5999; 4100 Wisconsin Avenue, NW 20016: Phyllis Armstrong, Richard Armstrong, Mark Bernard Bost, Denny Bly, Bruce Bookhultz, Mark Bost, Michael G. Bratton, Douglas Buchanan, Michael Buchanan, William Clemann, Stacey Cohan, Jeffrey Cridland, Emily Michelle Cyr, Thomas Dukehart, Kevin Ebersohl, Dana Edwards, Michael Flynn, Lesli Foster, Jan Fox, Michael C. Fox, Peggy Fox, Gregory Guise, James Hash, Jacqueline Hayward, Chris Houston, Hillary Howard, Ryan Hunter, Bruce Johnson, Kevin King, Vanessa M. Koolhof, Bruce Leshan, Samara Martin Ewing, Frank McDermott, Bob McHenry, William Charles McKnight, Daniel Patrick, Celinda Pena, Gordon Peterson, Gurvir Phillips, Jim Pratt, Gary Reals, Amy Repke, Raul Jorge Rivero, David Roycratt, Jennifer Ryan, David Satchell, Jeremy Settle, Jimmie Silman, Andrea Roane Skehan, Gregory Starddard, Louis Statter, Tanisha N. Taylor, Janet Terry, Michael Trammell, Susan Truitt, Keith Williams, Stephanie Wilson.

FREELANCERS: Walid Abdul-Jawad, Dave Adhicary, Frances Alonzo, Stuart Ammerman, Bruno Arena, George Audick, Ronald Aufdem-Brinke, Thomas Bagwall, Lantz Barbour, Eric Barreda, Malini Bawa, Cameron Bartlett, Stephen Bartlett, John H. Bauer, Ta'Adhmeeka Beamon, David Bentley, Kevin Beyer, Sarah Blumberg, Charles Borniger, Frank E. Borzage, Wayne Boyd, Richard Breed, Annette Brieger, Mike Broleman, Christopher Brown, Dwight Brown, Norman Butler, Heather Cabot, Christopher Campbell, Brett Carlson, Edward Castner, Steve Chenevey, Jane Chick, Nathan Clap, Juanita Clogston, Anne Cocklin, Steve Cocklin, Stuart Cohen, Peter Cook, John Cooper, Robert Corbey, Everett Cottom, Melanie Courtoglous, Ronald Couvillion, Cal Covert, Thomas Craca, Plummer Crawley, Patrick J. Curran, Anna Davalos, Michael DeMark, Gary DeMoss, William Donald, Margaret Dore, Dominic DeSantis, Paul Dougherty, Sarah Drew, Alfred S. Eisenhuth, Steve Epstein, Kate Ermolovich, Thomas Everly, Al Falson, Bruce Ferder, Andrew Field, Michael Finnigan, Amy Flannery, Cesar Flores, Kristin Foelmer-Suchorski, Michael Ford, Tom Foster, Tom Foty, Francis P. French, David Friedman, George Fridrich, Randall Gafner, Dennis Gaffney, Christian Galdabini, Michael Travis Galindo, Cy Gardner, Francisca Gandara, Atef Gawad, Philip Geyelin, Gavin Gibbons, Jake Gibson, Edward Giebel, Jeffrey Goodman, Marc Granena, Lindsay Graves, Martin Gruber, John Glennon, Augusto G. Gomez, Mark C. Grove, Nicholas Greiner, Kevin Griffin, Joel Gwadz, Dorry Gundy-Rice, David Goulding, Michael E. Hagerty, Kimberly Halkett, William Harding, Steven Harper, Roy J. Harris, John Hartge, Thomas Hass, Jocelyn Hatch, Barry Haywood, Jens Heik, Sean Healey, Karen Hendren, Jeff Hertrick, Hugh Hinds, Paul Hollenbeck, Mary Hood, Toni Hoover, David Hopper, James Hughes, Trudy Marie Hutcherson, Laura Iiyama, Virg Jacques, Afshin Javadi, Edward B. Jennings, Peeter Jessen, Darryl B. Johnson, Lanny Johnson, Sherrie Johnson, Derek Johnston, Alvin Jones, Pascal Jouffriault, Michael Joy, Abdel Hakim Kabbaj, Ivan Katz, Terry Kelly, Peter Kent, Jonathan Kessler, Timothy Keating, Donna King, Michael Kinney, Julie Kirtz, Elliot Klayman, Konstantin Klein, Robert Klein, Dave Kopecky, Martin A. Kos, Wolfgan Kotke, David Krupin, Peter Kulsziski, Carmen Kupper, Marianna LaFollette, John Landers, Gregoory Larsen, Sarah Lee, Katherine Leiken, Werner Lelle, David Lent, Gabriel LeMay, Dexter Leong, Matt Leshner, Penelope Lewis, Bruce Liffiton, Kevin Loftus, Culver J. Long, Jayne Lukas, Julio Luzquinos, Stephen Maguire, Antonio Marques, Mai Marriott, Marc Marriott, Michael Marriott, Mark Marshall, Jeff Martino, Claude L. Matthews, D. Jay McCarty, Doug McCash, Kevin McClam, William McKenna, Lauren Kathleen McCabe, Samuel J. McMichael, Lorna McGuire, Brian McHenry, Haven L. McKinney, Soheila Mellom, Matthew Mickelson, Alexander Milenic, Traci Mitchell, Steven E. Mitnick, John Monte, Brian Mooar, James M. Moran, Molly Moran, Lorraine Mottola, John Mueller, Anh Nguyen, Adam Nixon, Richard Norling, Christopher Norris, Gary Nurenberg, D. Kerry O'Berry, David O'Brien, Thomas O'Connor, Partick O'Donnell, Daniel J. O'Shea, Ling

NETWORKS, STATIONS, AND SERVICES REPRESENTED—Continued

Ong, Shaun Parker, Adrien Pantaze, George Patterson, Pamela Patterson, Hartmut Pauls, Beverley Paulsen, Scott Payne, Grant Peacock, Mark Pearson, Peter Penebre, Ines I. Perez, James P. Peterson, Robert J. Peterson III, Robert J. Peterson, Ken Pexton, Michael Peyton, Nicole Phillips, Ronald Piedrahita, Boris Pinkas, Murray Pinczuk, Steve Price, Ryan Primmer, Pat Pugliese, Jason Quinn, Omar Quinonez, Mark Rabin, Ali Rad, Sharon Reich, Ed Reinsel, Earle Robinson, J. Michael Roche, Peter Roof, Aram Roston, Theodore Roth, Jo Anne Rowe, David Sandy, Aaron Sasson, Fred Schall, Therese Schlachter, Hans-Peter Schloemer, Ivan Scott, Sarah Scott, Leslie Sewell, Susan Shand, Lawrence Shaughnessy, Keisha L Sherman, Robert Shire, Caroline Shively, Harry Shoffner, Andre Showell, David Silver, Kip Silverman, Robert Silverthorne, Y. Sean Simmons, Paul Sisco, Paul Skomal, Stephanie Slewka, Charles Slie, Raeshawn Smith, David de Sola, Gilbert Solorzano, Robert Soneira, Thomas Staton, Randall Sorenson, George Sozio, Darcy Spencer, Walter Starling, David Strong, Rick Suddeth, Jayme Swain, Janne Syrjanen, Kelvin Tabbs, Ernie Taglienti, Mark Teboe, Joseph Thompson, Jr., Andrew Thomas, Kenneth Thomas, Shari Thomas, Theodore Thornton, Eckhard Tollkuhn, Scott Travis, Jorge Castillo-Trentin, Renee Turner, Terry Turner, Scott Vaughan, Paul VanderVeen, Evelin von Brocke-Doman, J. N'oeye Walton, Jane Watrel, John S. Wauzer, Gary Waxler, Aaron S. Webster, Stefan Wiesen, Arlene Weisskopf, John Williams, Steven Williams, Kristin Wilson, Tony Winthrop, Rob Yingling, Bob Young, Paul Young, Stratis Zervos.

PERIODICAL PRESS GALLERIES*

HOUSE PERIODICAL PRESS GALLERY

The Capitol, H–304, 225–2941

Director.—Robert M. Zatkowski.
Assistant Directors: Laura Eckart, Robert L. Stallings.

SENATE PERIODICAL PRESS GALLERY

The Capitol, S–320, 224–0265

Director.—Edward V. Pesce.
Assistant Directors: Kristyn N. Kline, Justin Wilson.

EXECUTIVE COMMITTEE OF CORRESPONDENTS

Lorraine Woellert, Business Week, Chairman
Heidi Glenn, Tax Notes, Secretary-Treasurer
Richard E. Cohen, National Journal
Tim Curran, Roll Call
Douglas Waller, Time Magazine
Terence Samuel, U.S. News & World Report
Katherine M. Stimmel, BNA News

RULES GOVERNING PERIODICAL PRESS GALLERIES

1. Persons eligible for admission to the Periodical Press Galleries must be bona fide resident correspondents of reputable standing, giving their chief attention to the gathering and reporting of news. They shall state in writing the names of their employers and their additional sources of earned income; and they shall declare that, while a member of the Galleries, they will not act as an agent in the prosecution of claims, and will not become engaged or assist, directly or indirectly, in any lobbying, promotion, advertising, or publicity activity intended to influence legislation or any other action of the Congress, nor any matter before any independent agency, or any department or other instrumentality of the Executive branch; and that they will not act as an agent for, or be employed by the Federal, or any State, local or foreign government or representatives thereof; and that they will not, directly or indirectly, furnish special or ''insider'' information intended to influence prices or for the purpose of trading on any commodity or stock exchange; and that they will not become employed, directly or indirectly, by any stock exchange, board of trade or other organization or member thereof, or brokerage house or broker engaged in the buying and selling of any security or commodity. Applications shall be submitted to the Executive Committee of the Periodical Correspondents' Association and shall be authenticated in a manner satisfactory to the Executive Committee.

2. Applicants must be employed by periodicals that regularly publish a substantial volume of news material of either general, economic, industrial, technical, cultural, or trade character. The periodical must require such Washington coverage on a continuing basis and must be owned and operated independently of any government, industry, institution, association, or lobbying organization. Applicants must also be employed by a periodical that is published for profit and is supported chiefly by advertising or by subscription, or by a periodical meeting the conditions in this paragraph but published by a nonprofit organization that, first, operates independently of any government, industry, or institution and, second, does not engage, directly or indirectly, in any lobbying or other activity intended to influence any matter before Congress or before any independent agency or any department or other instrumentality of the Executive branch. House organs are not eligible.

*Information is based on data furnished and edited by each respective gallery.

3. Members of the families of correspondents are not entitled to the privileges of the galleries.

4. The Executive Committee may issue temporary credentials permitting the privileges of the galleries to individuals who meet the rules of eligibility but who may be on short-term assignment or temporarily residing in Washington.

5. Under the authority of rule 6 of the House of Representatives and of rule 33 of the Senate, the Periodical Galleries shall be under the control of the Executive Committee, subject to the approval and supervision of the Speaker of the House of Representatives and the Senate Committee on Rules and Administration. It shall be the duty of the Executive Committee, at its discretion, to report violations of the privileges of the galleries to the Speaker or the Senate Committee on Rules and Administration, and pending action thereon, the offending correspondent may be suspended. The committee shall be elected at the start of each Congress by members of the Periodical Correspondents' Association and shall consist of seven members with no more than one member from any one publishing organization. The committee shall elect its own officers and a majority of the committee may fill vacancies on the committee. The list in the Congressional Directory shall be a list only of members of the Periodical Correspondents' Association.

J. DENNIS HASTERT,
Speaker, House of Representatives.

TRENT LOTT,
Chairman, Senate Committee on Rules and Administration.

MEMBERS ENTITLED TO ADMISSION

PERIODICAL PRESS GALLERIES

Abramson, Julie: Insight Magazine
Ackerman, Spencer: New Republic
Ackley, Kate: American Lawyer Media
Acord, David: Food Chemical News
Adams, Christopher J.: BNA News
Adde, Nicholas L.: Army Times Publishing Co.
Adelsberger, Bernard: Army Times Publishing Co.
Ahearn, David M.: King Publishing Group
Aiken, Deborah: Tax Notes
Aker, Janet A.: FDC Reports
Albiniak, Paige: Broadcasting & Cable
Albright, Stephen: CD Publications
Alexander, Lisa Michele: Tax Notes
Alexis, Alexei: BNA News
Alford, Carrie Ann: CD Publications
Allen, Jodie T.: U. S. News & World Report
Allen, LaQuesha: Tax Notes
Allizon, Marie B.: Internewsletter
Almeras, Jon S.: Tax Notes
Aluise, Beth: National News Syndicate
Aluise, Susan J.: National News Syndicate
Alvey, Jennifer: Public Utilities Fortnightly
Amber, Michelle: BNA News
Ament, Lucy: Food Chemical News
Amolsch, Arthur L.: FTC Watch
Analore, Andrew: Inside Mortgage Finance
Anand, Vineeta: Crain Communications
Anft, Michael: Chronicle of Higher Education
Anselmo, Joseph: Washington Techway
Anthes, Gary H.: IDG Communications
Antonides, David S.: Tax Notes
Aplin, Donald G.: BNA News
Archer, Jeffrey Robert: Education Week
Armbrister, Trevor: Reader's Digest
Armes, Leroy: BNA News
Arnold, Andrew: Business Publishers
Arnone, Michael: Chronicle of Higher Education
Arnoult, Sandra: Penton Media Inc.
Arora, Vasantha: News India Times
Ashton, Jerome C.: BNA News
Ashworth, Jerry: Thompson Publishing Group
Asker, James R.: Aviation Week
Assam, Cecelia M.: BNA News
Atkins, Pamela: BNA News
Atkinson, Peter: Army Times Publishing Co.
Atwood, John F.: Washington Service Bureau
August, Lissa: Time Inc.
Aukofer, Matthew: Business Publishers
Ayayo, Herman P.: Tax Notes
Aycock, Elizabeth Wheatly: American Lawyer Media
Ayers, Carl Albert: UCG
Ayoub, Nina Cary: Chronicle of Higher Education
Bacheldor, Beth: CMP Media Inc.
Bacon, Lance M.: Army Times Publishing Co.
Bacon, Jr., Perry: Time Inc.
Baghdadi, Ramsey: FDC Reports
Bailey, Laura: Army Times Publishing Co.
Ballard, Tanya N.: Government Executive
Bancroft, John: Inside Mortgage Finance
Barak, Sarah: Thompson Publishing Group
Barber, Jeffrey: McGraw-Hill
Barbieri, Richard: American Lawyer Media
Barnes, Fred: Weekly Standard
Barnes, James A.: National Journal
Barnes, Julian: U. S. News & World Report
Barnett, Megan L.: U. S. News & World Report
Barone, Michael: U. S. News & World Report
Barrett, Brendan: Washington Techway
Barry, John A.: Newsweek
Bartlett, Thomas: Chronicle of Higher Education
Bartscht, Jill F.: National Journal
Basinger, Julianne: Chronicle of Higher Education
Batzler, Lloyd: Government Computer News
Baumann, David: National Journal
Beaman, William P.: Reader's Digest
Beatty-Brown, Marantha: Federal Publications
Beaven, Lara W.: Inside Washington Publishers
Beck, Robert E.: Federal Employees News Digest
Becker, Loren: BNA News
Beckley, Elizabeth: Crain Communications
Bedard, Paul: U. S. News & World Report
Beers, Allison: Food Chemical News
Beinart, Peter: New Republic
Bell, John C.: Tax Notes
Bell, Kevin A.: Tax Notes
Belton, Beth: Business Week
Bender, Lisa: Tax Notes
Bennett, Alison: BNA News
Bennett, Heather: Tax Notes
Bennett, John T.: Inside Washington Publishers
Bennett, Lorraine: Inside Washington Publishers
Bennett, Ralph: Reader's Digest
Benton, Nicholas F.: Falls Church News Press
Berger, James R.: Washington Trade Daily
Berger, Mary: Washington Trade Daily
Berger, Mitchell: Thompson Publishing Group
Bergin, Christopher: Tax Notes
Berkowitz, Debra: Research Institute of America Group
Berkowitz, Lois: Title I Report
Berlau, John: Insight Magazine

MEMBERS ENTITLED TO ADMISSION, PERIODICAL PRESS GALLERIES—Continued

Berman, Dan: Environment & Energy Publishing
Bernstein, Aaron: Business Week
Bernstein, Amy L.: CD Publications
Bernstein, Daniel: Institutional Investor
Bernstein, Jeremy: Inside Washington Publishers
Besser, James David: New York Jewish Week
Best, Frank M.: U. S. Medicine
Beswick, Ellen: Natural Gas Intelligence
Betts, Mitch: IDG Communications
Bhambhani, Dipka: Government Computer News
Bier-Myers, Jennifer: American Lawyer Media
Bigman-Galimore, Cabral: FDC Reports
Billings, Deborah: BNA News
Billings, Erin: Roll Call
Billitteri, Thomas J.: Chronicle of Higher Education
Bilodeau, Otis: American Lawyer Media
Binney, Erin: Washington Service Bureau
Birnbaum, Jeffrey H.: Time Inc.
Bivens, Matt: Nation
Black, Chris: Roll Call
Blair, Bridgette: Army Times Publishing Co.
Blair, Julie R.: Education Week
Blalock, Cecelia: Periodicals News Service
Blanchard, Tericke: FDC Reports
Blank, Peter L.: Kiplinger Washington Editors
Block, Jonathan M.: Inside Washington Publishers
Blum, Debra: Chronicle of Higher Education
Blum, Vanessa: American Lawyer Media
Blumenstyk, Goldie: Chronicle of Higher Education
Boahene, Adwoa K.: FDC Reports
Bobbitt, Alla Rutstein: FDC Reports
Bockhorn, Lee: Weekly Standard
Bodnar, Janet: Kiplinger Washington Editors
Bolen, Cheryl: BNA News
Boles, Margaret: Telecommunications Reports
Bolton, Alexander: The Hill
Bond, David: Aviation Week
Bond, Jeremy: Business Publishers
Booker, Simeon S.: Jet/Ebony
Borcherson-Keto, Sarah A.: CCH Inc.
Borger, Gloria: U. S. News & World Report
Boris, Joseph P.: Inside Washington Publishers
Borja, Rhea: Education Week
Borrego, Anne Marie: Chronicle of Higher Education
Borrus, Amy: Business Week
Bottorff, David: BNA News
Bowen, Michael: Radio & Records
Bowman, Darcia Harris: Education Week
Boyce, Clayton W.: Traffic World
Boye, Will: Institutional Investor
Boyles, William Robert: Health Market Survey
Bracken, Leonard: BNA News
Brady, Matthew T.: American Banker Newsletters
Brager, Mark E.: FDC Reports
Bramnick, Andrew: Federal Publications
Brand, Peter: The Hill
Brandolph, David Barry: BNA News
Brandon, George E.: Kiplinger Washington Editors
Brandon, Priscilla T.: Kiplinger Washington Editors
Brant, Martha: Newsweek
Braun, Kevin D.: Environment & Energy Publishing
Bray, Sarah: Chronicle of Higher Education
Breen, Tim: Environment & Energy Publishing
Bresnahan, John: Roll Call
Brevetti, Rossella: BNA News
Brinkley, Curtis Mark: Army Times Publishing Co.
Brion, Theresa Markley: Research Institute of America Group
Bristow, Melissa Star: Kiplinger Washington Editors
Britt, Angela L.: BNA News
Broderick, Brian J.: BNA News
Bronson, Richard James: BNA News
Brooks, David: Weekly Standard
Brooks, George A.: Inside Mortgage Finance
Brostoff, Steven: National Underwriter
Brown, Carrie: CD Publications
Brown, David: Army Times Publishing Co.
Brown, Janet M.: Press Associates
Brown, Jill: Atlantic Information Services
Brown, Malina: Inside Washington Publishers
Brown, Patricia: McGraw-Hill/Aero
Brown, Steven G.: CD Publications
Browning, Graeme: Federal Computer Week
Bruce, R. Christian: BNA News
Brugger, Abigail Benezra: Thompson Publishing Group
Brumfiel, Geoff: Nature
Bruninga, Susan: BNA News
Brunori, David E.: Tax Notes
Bryant, Sue: BNA News
Buntin, John: Governing
Burden, Lisa D.: Thompson Publishing Group
Burger, Timothy J.: Time Inc.
Burkhart, Lori: Public Utilities Fortnightly
Burlage, John D.: Army Times Publishing Co.
Burton, Douglas: Insight Magazine
Busche, Linda: UCG
Bushell, Brian Andrew: Rolling Stone
Bushweller, Kevin C.: Education Week
Buskirk, Howard: Telecommunications Reports
Butcher, Lauren: Thompson Publishing Group
Butchock, Steve: Medical Devices Report
Butler, Amy: Inside Washington Publishers
Butts, Thomas: IMAS Publishing
Byerrum, Ellen: BNA News
Byrne, James: CD Publications
Byus, Jonathan D.: Insight Magazine
Cabrera, Raul: BNA News
Cahlink, George: Government Executive
Cain, Derrick: BNA News
Calabresi, Massimo: Time Inc.
Caldwell, Christopher: Weekly Standard
Callahan, Joanne: McGraw-Hill
Cannon, Carl M.: National Journal
Cannon, Mary Angela: U. S. News & World Report

MEMBERS ENTITLED TO ADMISSION, PERIODICAL PRESS GALLERIES—Continued

Cano, Craig S.: McGraw-Hill
Canonica, Rocco: Natural Gas Intelligence
Carey, John A.: Business Week
Carlile, Amy: Roll Call
Carlson, Caron: EWeek
Carlson, Jeffrey E.: CCH Inc.
Carlson, Scott: Chronicle of Higher Education
Carlson, Tucker: Weekly Standard
Carnahan, Ira: Forbes
Carnevale, Dan: Chronicle of Higher Education
Carney, Eliza Newlin: National Journal
Carney, James: Time Inc.
Carney, Timothy: Evans-Novak Political Report
Carpenter, Alison: Washington Service Bureau
Carpenter, Lee: National Journal
Carr, Jennifer: Tax Notes
Carroll, Catherine Anne: Education Week
Carter, Cynthia: Washington Business Information
Cartwright, Linda A.: Green Sheets
Casey, Kendra: BNA News
Cash, Catherine: McGraw-Hill
Cassidy, Jonathan: The Hill
Cassidy, William B.: Traffic World
Cassin, Ann: Title I Report
Castelli, Christopher J.: Inside Washington Publishers
Castellon, David: Army Times Publishing Co.
Caterinicchia, Dan: Federal Computer Week
Caterinicchia, Matthew: Federal Computer Week
Catts, Timothy Philip: Tax Notes
Cauthen, Carey: Thompson Publishing Group
Cavallaro, Gina: Army Times Publishing Co.
Cavanagh, Sean: Education Week
Cavas, Christopher: Army Times Publishing Co.
Cecala, Guy David: Inside Mortgage Finance
Chait, Jonathan: New Republic
Chapman, Stephen: Food Chemical News
Chappell, Kevin: Jet/Ebony
Chappie, Damon: Roll Call
Check, Erika: Nature
Cherkasky, Mara: Thompson Publishing Group
Cherry, Sheila R.: Insight Magazine
Chibbaro, Jr., Louis M.: Washington Blade
Childress, Rasheeda Crayton: Business Publishers
Chineson, Joel: American Lawyer Media
Chourey, Sarita: The Hill
Chronister, Gregory M.: Education Week
Ciampoli, Paul: Natural Gas Intelligence
Cillizza, Chris: Roll Call
Clapp, Stephen: Food Chemical News
Clark, Colin: Army Times Publishing Co.
Clark, Kim: U. S. News & World Report
Clark, Ryan A.: Thompson Publishing Group
Clark, Sharon Lynn: CD Publications
Clark, Timothy B.: Government Executive
Clarke-Gomez, Irene: BNA News
Clement, Julie: Inside Mortgage Finance
Clemetson, Lynette: Newsweek
Clemmitt, Marcia: Healthcare Information
Clift, Eleanor: Newsweek
Cline, Regina P.: BNA News
Coffin, James B.: Public Lands News
Cohen, Richard E.: National Journal
Cohn, Elizabeth Schwinn: Chronicle of Higher Education
Cohn, Laura: Business Week
Colarusso, Laura: Army Times Publishing Co.
Colarusso, Laura M: Inside Washington Publishers
Coleman, Cari: Thompson Publishing Group
Coleman, Janet: FDC Reports
Colenso, Robert: Army Times Publishing Co.
Collins, Brian: National Mortgage News
Collins, Jr., Donald: Time Inc.
Collogan, David L.: McGraw-Hill/Aero
Combemale, Martine: Milan Presse
Combs, Jennifer: BNA News
Compart, Andrew: Travel Weekly
Conconi, Charles N.: Washingtonian
Condon, Erin: Government Information Services
Connole, Patrick: McGraw-Hill
Conradi, Melissa: Governing
Conroy, Declan: BNA News
Cook, Barbara C.: Business Travel News
Cook, Steven: BNA News
Cook, Jr., Charles E.: Cook Political Report
Cooper, Catherine: Green Sheets
Cooper, Mary H.: CQ Researcher
Cooper, Matthew: Time Inc.
Corbett, Warren: Set-Aside Alert
Corley, Matilda Monroe: BNA News
Corn, David: Nation
Cosgrove, Anita Kelly: Capitol City Publishers
Costa, Keith J.: Inside Washington Publishers
Cottle, Michelle: New Republic
Coughlin, Brett: UCG
Couillard, Lauren: BNA News
Cowden, Richard H.: BNA News
Cox, Matthew: Army Times Publishing Co.
Coyle, Marcia: National Law Journal
Crader, Benjamin Boyce: Weekly Standard
Craig, David Brian: Army Times Publishing Co.
Crain, Chris: Washington Blade
Craver, Martha L.: Kiplinger Washington Editors
Crawley, Vince: Army Times Publishing Co.
Crea, Joseph Ross: Washington Blade
Crider, Richie: Washington Business Information
Crock, Stan: Business Week
Croft, John W.: Aviation Week
Crowley, Mary E.: CD Publications
Crowley, Michael: New Republic
Crowne, James D.: BNA News
Cruickshank, Paula L.: CCH Inc.
Curran, John: Telecommunications Reports
Curran, Timothy: Roll Call
Curry, Leonard: Washington Crime News Services
Curthoys, Kathleen: Army Times Publishing Co.

MEMBERS ENTITLED TO ADMISSION, PERIODICAL PRESS GALLERIES—Continued

Curtis, Victoria: Telecommunications Reports
Cusack, Robert: The Hill
Cusick, Daniel: Environment & Energy Publishing
Cutler, Mark: BNA News
D'Agostino, Joseph A.: Human Events
Dalecki, Kenneth B.: Kiplinger Washington Editors
Dalton, Matthew: Inside Washington Publishers
Daniels, Alex: Washington Techway
Dannheisser, Ralph: Green Sheets
Darcey, Sue: Pesticide Report
Datta, Veena: Federal Publications
Daukantas, Patricia: Government Computer News
Davidson, Daniel: Army Times Publishing Co.
Davidson, Deirdre: American Lawyer Media
Davidson, Mark: McGraw-Hill
Davies, Lira Behrens: McGraw-Hill
Davies, Stephen: Endangered Species & Wetlands Report
Davis, Brett: McGraw-Hill/Aero
Davis, Michelle R.: Education Week
Davis, Paris D.: Metro Herald Newspaper
Davis, Shannon: Inside Washington Publishers
Davis, Steve: Food Chemical News
Day, Jeff: BNA News
DeMott, Kathryn: International Medical News Group
Dealey, Sam: The Hill
Dealey, Sam J.: Weekly Standard
Dean, Joshua: Government Executive
Degen, Colin: Business Publishers
Deigh, Gloria: BNA News
Dembeck, Chet: Army Times Publishing Co.
Dembicki, Matthew: Kiplinger Washington Editors
Denton, Judith: Insight Magazine
Dervarics, Charles: Business Publishers
DiMascio, Jennifer: Inside Washington Publishers
Diamond, Phyllis: BNA News
Dickerson, John F.: Time Inc.
Dickinson, Amy: Time Inc.
Diegmueller, Karen: Education Week
Dineen, John: Green Sheets
Dinges, Tomas: Hispanic Link News Service
Dizard, Wilson: Government Computer News
Doan, Michael F.: Kiplinger Washington Editors
Dobias, Matthew: UCG
Dobson, Jon: FDC Reports
Doi, Ayako: Japan Digest
Doman, Kimberlee Smith: BNA News
Domone, Dana: BNA News
Donlan, Thomas G.: Barron's
Donnelly, John M.: King Publishing Group
Donnelly, Sally: Time Inc.
Donoghue, James A.: Penton Media Inc.
Doolan, Kelley: McGraw-Hill
Dorobek, Christopher J.: Federal Computer Week
Doster, Dennis A.: Government Information Services
Dove, Andrew: FDC Reports
Downes, Bob: Travel Trade
Doyle, John M.: McGraw-Hill/Aero
Doyle, Kenneth P.: BNA News
Dressel, Althea: Tax Notes
DuMond, Marge: National Journal
Duff, Susanna: Crain Communications
Duffy, Jennifer: Cook Political Report
Duffy, Michael: Time Inc.
Duffy, Thomas: Inside Washington Publishers
Dufour, Jeff: The Hill
Duncan, Leslie A.: Green Sheets
Dunham, Nancy: UCG
Dunham, Richard S.: Business Week
Dunlap, Karin R.: CCH Inc.
Dunn, William: Research Institute of America Group
Dupont, Daniel G.: Inside Washington Publishers
Duran, Nicole: Roll Call
Durkin, Tish: National Journal
Dwyer, Paula: Business Week
Earle, Geoff: The Hill
Easterbrook, Gregg: New Republic
Eastland, Terry: Weekly Standard
Eckstein, Adam: FDC Reports
Edmondson, Thomas: BNA News
Edmonson, Robert G.: Traffic World
Edney, Hazel Trice: Afro American Newspapers
Edwards, Charles J.: Government Information Services
Edwards, Randall: Federal Computer Week
Edwards, Thomas J.: CD Publications
Ege, Konrad: Blatter
Eggerton, John S.: Broadcasting & Cable
Egna, Martin: CCH Inc.
Ehrenhalt, Alan: Governing
Eisele, Albert: The Hill
Eiserer, Elaine R.: Business Publishers
Eiserer, Leonard A. C.: Business Publishers
Eisler, Kim: Washingtonian
Elfin, Dana: BNA News
Ellis, Isobel L.: National Journal
Emery, Gail: Washington Technology
Engdahl, Elizabeth: American Lawyer Media
Epatko, Larisa: Environment & Energy Publishing
Ericksen, Charles: Hispanic Link News Service
Esquivel, J. Jesus: Proceso
Evangelauf, Jean: Chronicle of Higher Education
Evans, Jeffrey: International Medical News Group
Evans, Julie C.: FDC Reports
Evelyn, Jamilah: Chronicle of Higher Education
Ewing, Laurence Lee: McGraw-Hill/Aero
Eyman, Nicole: Kiplinger Washington Editors
Fabian, Thecla: Business Publishers
Fajardo, Jacqueline: CCH Inc.
Fallows, James: Atlantic Monthly
Falvella-Garraty, Susan: Irish Echo
Farrar, Loren S.: Penton Media Inc.
Farrell, Elizabeth: Chronicle of Higher Education

MEMBERS ENTITLED TO ADMISSION, PERIODICAL PRESS GALLERIES—Continued

Fedak, Laura Lee: Thompson Publishing Group
Feiler, Jeremy: Inside Washington Publishers
Felsher, Murray: Washington Remote Sensing Letter
Feltman, Peter E.: CCH Inc.
Ferguson, Brett: BNA News
Ferullo, Michael: BNA News
Fetterolf, Amanda: Exchange Monitor Publications
Fickling, Amy L.: Telecommunications Reports
Field, David: Airline Business
Fineman, Howard: Newsweek
Fiorino, Frances: Aviation Week
Fischer, Craig: Pace Publications
Fishbein, Lawrence I.: Kiplinger Washington Editors
Fitzpatrick, Erika: Capitol City Publishers
Fitzpatrick, James F.: BNA News
Fleet, Leslie G.: BNA News
Fleming, Christopher T.: Healthcare Information
Fletcher, Jay: Business Publishers
Flint, Perry: Penton Media Inc.
Foer, Franklin: New Republic
Fogg, E. Piper: Chronicle of Higher Education
Fonder, Melanie: The Hill
Fong, Tony: Crain Communications
Foradori, Angela: The Hill
Foster, Andrea: Chronicle of Higher Education
Foster, Brooke: Washingtonian
Foster, Lawrence D.: McGraw-Hill
Fotos, Christopher: McGraw-Hill/Aero
Foullon, Danielle: FDC Reports
Fourney, Susan: Government Executive
Fox, Kara: Washington Blade
Francis, Eileen: FDC Reports
Frank, Diane: Federal Computer Week
Franklin, Mary Beth: Kiplinger Washington Editors
Franz, Damon: Environment & Energy Publishing
Fraser, Katharine: McGraw-Hill
Frater, Elisabeth: National Journal
Freddoso, David A.: Human Events
Freedberg, Jr., Sydney J.: National Journal
Freeman, Allison: Environment & Energy Publishing
Freeman, William: Penton Media Inc.
French, Matthew: Federal Computer Week
Frick, Robert L.: Kiplinger Washington Editors
Frieden, Joyce: International Medical News Group
Friel, Brian: Government Executive
Frost, Brendan DuBois: CCH Inc.
Fruehling, Douglas: Roll Call
Fulghum, David: Aviation Week
Fullerton, Jane: Farm Journal
Funk, Deborah: Army Times Publishing Co.
Gable, Eryn: Environment & Energy Publishing
Gallagher, Dylan: Penton Media Inc.
Gallagher, John: Traffic World
Galley, Michelle W.: Education Week
Garcia, Rodney D.: Thompson Publishing Group
Garfield, Bob: Crain Communications
Garner, W. Lynn: Green Sheets
Garretson, Cara: IDG Communications
Gasparello, Linda Ann: King Publishing Group
Gatty, Mary Ann: Periodicals News Service
Gegax, Thomas Trent: Newsweek
Gehring, John: Education Week
Geisel, Jerome M.: Crain Communications
Geman, Benjamin: Inside Washington Publishers
Genauer, Abraham: The Hill
George, Nicole: Japan Digest
Gerber, Michael: The Hill
Gerecht, Michael: CD Publications
Gersemann, Olaf: Wirtschaftswoche
Gettlin, Robert H.: National Journal
Gewertz, Catherine: Education Week
Gewin, Virginia: Nature
Ghosh, Chandrani: Forbes
Gibb, Steven K.: Inside Washington Publishers
Gilbert, Lorraine S.: BNA News
Gilcrest, Laura: Food Chemical News
Gillies, Andrew: Forbes
Gillis, Christopher: American Shipper
Gilston, Samuel M.: Gilston Communications Group
Ginsbach, Pam D.: BNA News
Gizzi, John: Human Events
Glass, Andrew J.: The Hill
Gleckman, Howard: Business Week
Glenn, David G.: Chronicle of Higher Education
Glenn, Heidi: Tax Notes
Glenzer, Michael: Exchange Monitor Publications
Gnaedinger, Chuck: Tax Notes
Go, Annabelle: Government Information Services
Goebes, Robert L.: BNA News
Goindi, Geeta: Express India
Goldberg, Kirsten: Cancer Letter
Goldberg, Paul: Cancer Letter
Goldfarb, Bruce: Washington Business Information
Goldman, Ted: American Lawyer Media
Goldstein, Andrew Daniel: Time Inc.
Goldstein, Lisa Fine: Education Week
Goldstein, Peter: Kiplinger Washington Editors
Goldstein, Sid: Pace Publications
Goldwasser, Joan: Kiplinger Washington Editors
Goldwyn, Brant: BNA News
Golub, Barbra: Research Institute of America Group
Goode, Darren: Inside Washington Publishers
Goode, Stephen Ray: Insight Magazine
Goodhue, David: Inside Washington Publishers
Goodwin, Anne B.: BNA News
Goodwine, Velma: Research Institute of America Group
Gordon, Kelly J.: Thompson Publishing Group
Gordon, Meryl: Elle
Gorman, S. Siobhan: National Journal
Gose, Ben: Chronicle of Higher Education
Goulder, Robert: Tax Notes
Goyal, Raghubir: Asia Today
Grabow, Colin: Defense Focus
Grass, Michael: Roll Call

MEMBERS ENTITLED TO ADMISSION, PERIODICAL PRESS GALLERIES—Continued

Green, Charles A.: National Journal
Greenberg, Kevin M.: FDC Reports
Greenblatt, Alan: Governing
Greene, Elizabeth: Chronicle of Higher Education
Greene, Jenna: American Lawyer Media
Gregg, Diana I.: BNA News
Gregorits, Angela: BNA News
Grodsky, Dawn: Inside Washington Publishers
Groner, Jonathan: American Lawyer Media
Gross, Grant: IDG News Service
Grossman, Elaine M.: Inside Washington Publishers
Gruber, Amelia: Government Executive
Gruber, Peter: Focus
Gruenberg, Mark J.: Press Associates
Grupe', Bob: Business Publishers
Gruss, Jean: Kiplinger Washington Editors
Guay, Thomas: Progressive Business Publications
Guerra, John: Billing World Magazine
Gunter, Chris: Nature
Gurdon, Hugo: The Hill
Guterman, Lila: Chronicle of Higher Education
Gutman, Roy: Newsweek
Guttman, George: Tax Notes
Hadley, Richard D.: UCG
Hafner, Lauren: FDC Reports
Hagen, Scott: Insight Magazine
Hagstrom, Jerry: National Journal
Halonen, Douglas J.: Crain Communications
Hamilton, Amy: Tax Notes
Hammond, Brian: Telecommunications Reports
Hammond, Sarah Spencer: Business Publishers
Hand, Mark: Public Utilities Fortnightly
Haney, Joe: National Journal
Haniffa, Abdul Aziz: India Abroad
Hansard, Sara: Crain Communications
Hansen, Brian: CQ Researcher
Hansen, David: CCH Inc.
Hanson, Christine M.: Federal Publications
Hanson, Melinda: BNA News
Harbert, Tam: Electronic Business
Harbrecht, Douglas A.: Business Week
Hardy, Michael: Federal Computer Week
Hargreaves, Jonathan: FDC Reports
Harkins, Donna: Insight Magazine
Harkness, Peter A.: Governing
Harman, Thomas: Inside Washington Publishers
Harmon, Sonya V.: Tax Notes
Harras, Steven: BNA News
Harrington, Timothy P.: FDC Reports
Harris, Donna L.: Crain Communications
Harris, Joann Christine: Tax Notes
Harris, Lona C.: Time Inc.
Harris, Shane: Government Executive
Harrison, Catherine: FDC Reports
Harrison, Tom: McGraw-Hill
Haseley, Donna: Inside Washington Publishers
Hasson, Judith B.: Federal Computer Week
Hatch, David M.: Crain Communications
Hawana, Joanne: FDC Reports
Hawkins, Andrew: FDC Reports
Hawkins, Dana: U. S. News & World Report
Hayes, Lisa L.: Thompson Publishing Group
Hayes, Peter S.: BNA News
Hayes, Stephen F.: Weekly Standard
Hazard, Charles: Insight Magazine
Hearn, Edward T.: Multichannel News
Heath, Erin J.: National Journal
Hebert, Adam: Inside Washington Publishers
Heckathorn, Mark E.: Natural Gas Week
Hedges, Joyce: BNA News
Heflin, Jay: UCG
Hegland, Corine: National Journal
Henderson, Kristina: Inside Washington Publishers
Hendrie, Caroline: Education Week
Hennig, Jutta: Inside Washington Publishers
Henning, Jonathan: Defense Focus
Henning, Lily: American Lawyer Media
Henry, Corey Neal: Inside Washington Publishers
Henry, Edward M.: Roll Call
Henry, Natalie: Environment & Energy Publishing
Herard, Vladimire: CD Publications
Hernandez, Luis: Thompson Publishing Group
Heron, Liz: Inside Washington Publishers
Hertzfeld, Laura: McGraw-Hill
Hess, Glenn H.: Chemical Market Reporter
Hess, Ryan E.: MII Publications
Heyd, Cindy Ann: Tax Notes
Hickey, Jennifer: Insight Magazine
Hickey, Kathleen: Traffic World
Hicks, Travis: CD Publications
Hiebert, Murray: Far Eastern Economic Review
Higgins, John: Business Publishers
Hilburn, Matthew: Army Times Publishing Co.
Hill, Keith M.: BNA News
Hill, Richard: BNA News
Hillgren, Sonja: Farm Journal
Hiruo, Elaine: McGraw-Hill
Hobbs, M. Nielsen: FDC Reports
Hobbs, Susan: BNA News
Hocking, Bryanna: Roll Call
Hodge, Nathan: King Publishing Group
Hodierne, Robert: Army Times Publishing Co.
Hoff, David: Education Week
Hoffman, Donald: Government Information Services
Hoffman, Rebecca: BNA News
Hofmann, Mark A.: Crain Communications
Hofmeister, Elizabeth W.: BNA News
Holland, Bill: Billboard Magazine
Hollingsworth, Catherine: BNA News
Holly, Tricia: Travel Agent Magazine
Holmes, Allan T.: Federal Computer Week
Holmes, Natalie C.: Capitol City Publishers
Hoover, Eric: Chronicle of Higher Education
Hoover, Kent: Washington Business Journal

MEMBERS ENTITLED TO ADMISSION, PERIODICAL PRESS GALLERIES—Continued

Horner, Dan: McGraw-Hill
Horwood, Rachel Jane: Economist
Hosenball, Mark: Newsweek
Hotta, Yoshio: Yomiuri America
Hoversten, Paul: McGraw-Hill/Aero
Howard, Joe: Radio & Records
Hsu, Emily: Inside Washington Publishers
Hsu, Susan: Business Publishers
Hubbard, Catherine A.: CCH Inc.
Hughes, Jr., John D.: Aviation Week
Hunter, Gabrielle: FTC Watch
Hurst, Marianne Delinda: Education Week
Hutchens, George: CD Publications
Hutnyan, Joseph: McGraw-Hill
Ichniowski, Thomas F.: McGraw-Hill
Idaszak, Jerome: Kiplinger Washington Editors
Iekel, John F.: Thompson Publishing Group
Imperio, Winnie Anne: International Medical News Group
Ingersoll, Stephanie: BNA News
Ingram, Michael: UCG
Irvin, Helen D.: BNA News
Isikoff, Michael: Newsweek
Iyengar, Sunil: FDC Reports
Jackman, Frank: McGraw-Hill
Jackson, Anthony: Time Inc.
Jackson, Irvin L.: Inside Washington Publishers
Jackson, Joab: Washington Technology
Jackson, Rochelle D.: BNA News
Jackson, Valarie: McGraw-Hill
Jackson, Whitney L.: UCG
Jackson, William K.: Government Computer News
Jacobson, Louis: National Journal
Jaffe, Harry S.: Washingtonian
Jagadeesan, Gomati: Inside Washington Publishers
James, Betty: Federal Publications
Jeffrey, Terence P.: Human Events
Jenkins, Scott: FDC Reports
Johnson, Alisa: BNA News
Johnson, Fawn: BNA News
Johnson, Greg: Inside Mortgage Finance
Johnson, Kimberly E.: McGraw-Hill/Aero
Johnson, Michael R.: Telecommunications Reports
Johnson, Regina: McGraw-Hill
Johnston, Gretel: IDG Communications
Johnston, Robert C.: Education Week
Jones, David: McGraw-Hill
Jones, George: CCH Inc.
Jones, Helen: BNA News
Jones, Joyce: Black Enterprise
Jones, Mary Lynn: The Hill
Jonson, Nicholas G.: McGraw-Hill/Aero
Jordan, Anne: Governing
Jordan, Brian D.: McGraw-Hill
Jordan, Bryant: Army Times Publishing Co.
Joseph, Ludwina: Outlook
Joslyn, Heather: Chronicle of Higher Education
Jost, Kenneth W.: CQ Researcher
Jowers, Karen Grigg: Army Times Publishing Co.
Judis, John: New Republic
June, Audrey Williams: Chronicle of Higher Education
Kachman, Michael: Insight Magazine
Kalb, Deborah: The Hill
Kallioinen, Anna: Washington Service Bureau
Kane, Paul: Roll Call
Kansagor, Gayle: Telecommunications Reports
Kaplan, Hugh B.: BNA News
Kaplan, Jonathan: The Hill
Karpavich, Todd: CD Publications
Karpf, Ben: U. S. Medicine
Kasper, Kara: FDC Reports
Kasperowicz, Peter: Inside Washington Publishers
Kass, Marcia B.: BNA News
Kassabian, Gloria B.: Business Week
Kauffman, Tim: Army Times Publishing Co.
Kaufman, Bruce S.: BNA News
Kaufman, Gail: Army Times Publishing Co.
Kavanagh, Susan: Washington Service Bureau
Kavruck, Deborah A.: Washington Counseletter
Kavruck, Samuel: Washington Counseletter
Keane, Angela Greiling: Traffic World
Keen, Lisa Melinda: Washington Blade
Keller, Amy M.: Roll Call
Keller, Bess: Education Week
Keller, Gail: BNA News
Kelley, Jaimie: FDC Reports
Kellogg, Alex P.: Chronicle of Higher Education
Kelly, Cathy: FDC Reports
Kelly, Patrice Wingert: Newsweek
Kelly, Spencer: UCG
Kendrick, Adrienne: Tax Notes
Kent, Christina: Physician's Weekly
Keplinger, Carolyn: McGraw-Hill
Kessler, Elaine: BNA News
Khan, Altaf U.: BNA News
Khor, Lena: FDC Reports
Kidney, Steve: CD Publications
Kiernan, Vincent: Chronicle of Higher Education
Kilian, Martin: Die Weltwoche
Kim, Angela: McGraw-Hill/Aero
Kim, Helen: Government Information Services
Kime, Patricia: Army Times Publishing Co.
King, Llewellyn W.: King Publishing Group
Kinnard, Meg: National Journal
Kintisch, Eli: Jewish Forward
Kiplinger, Austin H.: Kiplinger Washington Editors
Kirby, Paul: Telecommunications Reports
Kirkell, Sarah M. W.: Tax Notes
Kirkland, John Robert: BNA News
Kisliuk, Bill: American Lawyer Media
Kitfield, James: National Journal
Kittross, David: CD Publications
Klaidman, Daniel: Newsweek
Klein, Eric: UCG
Klein, Judith: National Journal

MEMBERS ENTITLED TO ADMISSION, PERIODICAL PRESS GALLERIES—Continued

Kleine-Brockhoff, Thomas: Die Zeit
Kleiner, Henry E.: Business Publishers
Klimko, Frank: CD Publications
Kline, Jerry Lee: Thompson Publishing Group
Knapik, Michael: McGraw-Hill
Knestout, Brian: Kiplinger Washington Editors
Knutson, Ted: CD Publications
Koch, Andrew: Jane's Information Group
Koch, Kathy: CQ Researcher
Kohut, John J.: Cook Political Report
Kolidakis, Vonronica: BNA News
Kondracke, Morton M.: Roll Call
Koons, Jennifer: Environment & Energy Publishing
Kosnett, Jeffrey: Kiplinger Washington Editors
Kosova, Weston: Newsweek
Koss, Geoffrey: Inside Washington Publishers
Kosterlitz, Julie A.: National Journal
Kovski, Alan: Utility Spotlight
Kraft, Scott: UCG
Kramer, David: Science & Government Report
Kramer, Linda: Time Inc.
Kramer, Steven R.: King Publishing Group
Kriz, Margaret E.: National Journal
Kubetin, W. Randy: BNA News
Kucher, Liane: McGraw-Hill
Kuhn, Mark: CD Publications
Kulman, Linda: U. S. News & World Report
Kurtz, Josh: Roll Call
LaBrecque, Louis C.: BNA News
LaFon, Carolyn Wright: Tax Notes
Labash, Matthew: Weekly Standard
Laffler, Mary Jo: FDC Reports
Lally, Rosemarie: Thompson Publishing Group
Lamb, Kevin: Human Events
Lamb, Robyn: UCG
Lamoreaux, Denise: Thompson Publishing Group
Lane, Patrick: Inside Washington Publishers
Langel, Stephen: Inside Washington Publishers
Lankford, Kimberly: Kiplinger Washington Editors
Lardner, Richard: Inside Washington Publishers
Larose, Marni D.: Chronicle of Higher Education
Larsen, Kathy Carolin: McGraw-Hill
Larson, Adrianne: McGraw-Hill/Aero
Lash, Steve: Business Publishers
Last, Jonathan: Weekly Standard
Lauerman, Kerry: Salon Magazine
Laurent, Anne: Government Executive
Laurenzo, Ron: King Publishing Group
Lavelle, Marianne: U. S. News & World Report
Lawrence, Richard: Traffic World
Lazenby, Edith: Food Chemical News
LeSueur, Steve: Washington Technology
Leavitt, David I.: Environment & Energy Publishing
Lechy, Emily: Government Information Services
Lederman, Douglas: Chronicle of Higher Education
Lee, Georgiana: National Mortgage News
Lee, Ken: Radio Business Report
Leithauser, Tom: Telecommunications Reports
Lekus, Eric: BNA News
Lemov, Penelope: Governing
Leopold, George: CMP Media Inc.
Lerer, Lisa: National Journal
Lesher, Sarah: The Hill
Leske, Gisela: Der Spiegel
Levine, Daniel R.: Reader's Digest
Levine, Samantha: U. S. News & World Report
Levy, Sara E.: Telecommunications Reports
Lewis, Nicole: Chronicle of Higher Education
Liang, John: Inside Washington Publishers
Lindeman, Ralph: BNA News
Lindsay, Drew: Washingtonian
Lipman, Harvy: Chronicle of Higher Education
Lipowicz, Alice: CD Publications
Lipper, Tamara: Newsweek
Lisagor, Megan: Federal Computer Week
Lithwick, Dahlia Hannah: Slate
Lizza, Ryan: New Republic
LoRusso, Dina: Thompson Publishing Group
Lockett, Brian A.: BNA News
Logan, Christopher P.: Exchange Monitor Publications
Logue, Wayne: Research Institute of America Group
Lopes, Gregory: Inside Washington Publishers
Lorch, Donatella: Newsweek
Lord, Mary C.: U. S. News & World Report
Lorenzetti, Maureen Shields: Oil & Gas Journal
Losey, Stephen: Army Times Publishing Co.
Lott, Steven: McGraw-Hill/Aero
Loveless, William E.: McGraw-Hill
Lovern, Edward: Crain Communications
Lowe, Christian: Army Times Publishing Co.
Lowe, Paul: Aviation International News
Lowther, William A.: Mail on Sunday
Lubold, Gordon: Army Times Publishing Co.
Luccioli, Colleen: Environment & Energy Publishing
Lucier, James P.: Insight Magazine
Lum, Benjamin: FDC Reports
Lumb, Jacquelyn: Washington Service Bureau
Lunney, Kellie: Government Executive
Lustig, Joe: Thompson Publishing Group
Lutterbeck, Claus: Stern
Lynch, Kerry: McGraw-Hill/Aero
Ma, Jason: Inside Washington Publishers
MacDonald, Neil: Technology Commercialization
MacDonald, Sam: Insight Magazine
MacKeil, Brian: Army Times Publishing Co.
MacRae, Catherine: Inside Washington Publishers
Macarelli, Nicholas: FDC Reports
Macilwain, Colin: Nature
Madrigal, Jacqueline: Radio & Records
Maggs, John J.: National Journal
Magill, Barbara: Thompson Publishing Group
Magnusson, Paul: Business Week
Mahoney, Fabia H.: BNA News

MEMBERS ENTITLED TO ADMISSION, PERIODICAL PRESS GALLERIES—Continued

Maier, Timothy: Insight Magazine
Maixner, Edward: Farm Progress News
Maloney, Christopher: MII Publications
Mandell, Dara: Jewish Press
Mangu-Ward, Katherine: Weekly Standard
Mani, Meredith Billman: Inside Washington Publishers
Mann, Paul S.: Aviation Week
Manning, Robert F.: Tax Notes
Mannix, Margaret: U. S. News & World Report
Manzo, Kathleen K.: Education Week
Marcisz, Christopher: Inside Washington Publishers
Marcoux, Michel: FDC Reports
Marcucci, Carl: Radio Business Report
Mariani, Michele: Governing
Mariani, Patricia: Federal Publications
Markley, Mary Ann Grena: BNA News
Marois, Denise: McGraw-Hill/Aero
Marre, Klaus: Inside Washington Publishers
Marsan, Carolyn Duffy: IDG Communications
Marshall, Joshua: Salon Magazine
Martinez, Arlene Vanessa: Hispanic Link News Service
Marvin, Robert: McGraw-Hill
Masci, David: CQ Researcher
Mathis, Lisa: BNA News
Mathur, Vandana: Kiplinger Washington Editors
Matloff, Rebecca A.: FDC Reports
Matthews, Jim: McGraw-Hill/Aero
Matthews, Martha: BNA News
Matthews, S. William: Federal Computer Week
Matthews, Sidney William: Army Times Publishing Co.
Matus, Victorino: Weekly Standard
Matusow-Nelson, Barbara: Washingtonian
Maurer, Henry Kevin: Inside Washington Publishers
Mauro, Tony: American Lawyer Media
Mayer, Jane: New Yorker
Maze, Richard: Army Times Publishing Co.
Mazumdar, Anandashankar: BNA News
Mazzetti, Mark: U. S. News & World Report
McBeth, Karen: McGraw-Hill
McCaffery, Gregory: BNA News
McCaney, Kevin: Government Computer News
McCaughan, Michael: FDC Reports
McClenahen, John: Penton Media Inc.
McConnell, William: Broadcasting & Cable
McCormack, Richard: Manufacturing News
McCormally, Kevin: Kiplinger Washington Editors
McCracken, Rebecca P.: BNA News
McDermott, Kevin: Research Institute of America Group
McFadden, Edward: Reader's Digest
McGeehon, Dale: Business Publishers
McGoffin, Michael J.: Research Institute of America Group
McGolrick, Susan J.: BNA News
McGovern, Susan: Washington Business Information
McGrath, Courtney B.: Kiplinger Washington Editors
McHugh, Jane Claire: Army Times Publishing Co.
McHugh, Mark Sean: American Shipper
McInerney, Susan: BNA News
McIntosh, Toby: BNA News
McLane, Paul J.: IMAS Publishing
McLaughlin, Matthew J.: Government Computer News
McLemee, Scott: Chronicle of Higher Education
McManus, Brooke E.: FDC Reports
McMurtrie, Beth: Chronicle of Higher Education
McNamee, Michael D.: Business Week
McPartlin, Martha: CD Publications
McTague, James: Barron's
McTague, Rachel S.: BNA News
McVearry, Rachel D.: Thompson Publishing Group
McVicker, William: Recall
Mechcatie, Elizabeth: International Medical News Group
Meldrum, Sarah: Pace Publications
Melillo, Wendy: Adweek Magazine
Menke, Susan: Government Computer News
Menon, Veena: Inside Washington Publishers
Mercurio, John: Roll Call
Meredith, Jeff: Exchange Monitor Publications
Merrill, Jessica E.: FDC Reports
Merrion, Paul Robert: Crain Communications
Methvin, Eugene: Reader's Digest
Meyers, David B.: Roll Call
Michael, Sara: Federal Computer Week
Michels, Jennifer: Travel Agent Magazine
Mientka, Matthew: U. S. Medicine
Miller, Jason: Government Computer News
Miller, John J.: National Review
Miller, Julie A.: Title I Report
Miller, Karla L.: Tax Notes
Miller, Margaret: BNA News
Miller, Reed J.: FDC Reports
Miller, Richard: Business Week
Miller, W. Kent: Army Times Publishing Co.
Miller, William H.: Penton Media Inc.
Milligan, Michael: Travel Weekly
Minikon, Patricia: Federal Publications
Minton-Beddoes, Zanny: Economist
Mitchell, John: Reader's Digest
Mitchell, Robert W.: Thompson Publishing Group
Miura, Lauren: Environment & Energy Publishing
Mohr, Patti: Tax Notes
Mokhiber, Russell: Corporate Crime Reporter
Mola, Roger Andrew: Aviation International News
Monastersky, Richard: Chronicle of Higher Education
Monroe, John: Federal Computer Week
Montwieler, Nancy: BNA News
Moore, James Gerry: Kiplinger Washington Editors

MEMBERS ENTITLED TO ADMISSION, PERIODICAL PRESS GALLERIES—Continued

Moore, Jennifer L.: Chronicle of Higher Education
Moore, Miles David: Crain Communications
Moore, Nancy J.: BNA News
Moore, Pamela Susan: Capitol Publications
Moore, Tom: Federal Employees News Digest
Moragne, Lenora: Black Congressional Monitor
Morales, Cecilio: MII Publications
Morehead, Nicholas: UCG
Morehouse, Macon: Time Inc.
Moreno-Hines, Mia: Tax Notes
Morgan, Jill: Billing World Magazine
Morin, Christopher Scott: Thompson Publishing Group
Morring, Jr., Frank: Aviation Week
Morris, Jefferson F.: McGraw-Hill/Aero
Morris, Jodie: National Journal
Morris, Walter: FDC Reports
Morrison, David Carlisle: Credit Union Times
Morrissey, James A.: Textile World
Morton, Peter: Financial Post
Mosquera, Mary: UCG
Mowbray, Joel: National Review
Moylan, Brian: Washington Blade
Mullen, Richard: King Publishing Group
Mullen, Thomas: Healthcare Information
Muller, Stephanie L.: Thompson Publishing Group
Mullins, Brody: Roll Call
Mulrine, Anna: U. S. News & World Report
Mundy, Alicia: CableWorld
Munoz, German: News Bites
Munro, Neil P.: National Journal
Munsey, Christopher: Army Times Publishing Co.
Muolo, Paul: National Mortgage News
Muradian, Vago: Army Times Publishing Co.
Murdoch, Joyce M.: National Journal
Murray, Mark: National Journal
Mutcherson-Ridley, Joyce: CCH Inc.
Muth, Katherine P.: Sedgwick Publishing
Najor, Pamela: BNA News
Nalbone, Heather M.: CD Publications
Namian, Tina Fritz: Research Institute of America Group
Nance, Scott: King Publishing Group
Nash, James L.: Penton Media Inc.
Nations, Deborah L. Acomb: National Journal
Naylor, Sean D.: Army Times Publishing Co.
Neill, Alex: Army Times Publishing Co.
Nelson, Suzanne: Roll Call
Neuder, Lisa R.: CCH Inc.
Neusner, Noam: U. S. News & World Report
Newkumet, Christopher J.: McGraw-Hill
Newman, Bernard: BNA News
Newman, Richard J.: U. S. News & World Report
Nichols, Hans: The Hill
Nicklin, Julie L.: Chronicle of Higher Education
Nir, Ori: The Forward
Noah, Timothy Robert: Slate
Nordwall, Bruce D.: Aviation Week
Norris, Gail Lawyer: Capitol City Publishers
North, David M.: Aviation Week
Novack, Janet: Forbes
Novak, Viveca: Time Inc.
O'Beirne, Kate Walsh: National Review
O'Brien, Sarah: Crain Communications
O'Connor, Erin: Research Institute of America Group
O'Connor, Patrick: The Hill
O'Hara, Colleen M.: Federal Computer Week
O'Meara, Kelly: Insight Magazine
O'Toole, Thomas: BNA News
Oberdorfer, Carol: BNA News
Obey, Douglas: Inside Washington Publishers
Ochs, Natalie A.: FDC Reports
Ognanovich, Nancy: BNA News
Oliphant, James: American Lawyer Media
Olsen, Florence: Chronicle of Higher Education
Olson, Lynn: Education Week
Onley, Dawn S.: Government Computer News
Onley, Gloria R.: BNA News
Oram, Mark Alexander: McGraw-Hill
Orleans, Anne: Washington New Observer
Orosco, Cynthia: Hispanic Link News Service
Orr, Christopher: New Republic
Orrick, Sarah: Congressional Digest
Orth, Maureen: Vanity Fair
Ostroff, Jim: Kiplinger Washington Editors
Osvath, Rebecca: FDC Reports
Otto, Mitchell Alexander: BNA News
Padmanabhan, Anant R.: FDC Reports
Page, Paul: Traffic World
Pak, Janne Kum Cha: USA Journal
Palmer, Avery: Inside Washington Publishers
Pannell, Susan J.: BNA News
Pappalardo, Denise: IDG Communications
Parish, David O.: MII Publications
Parisi, Gretchen: Thompson Publishing Group
Parker, John: Economist
Parker, Susan T.: Natural Gas Intelligence
Parrish, Molly R.: Pace Publications
Parten, Constance: BNA News
Parthasarathy, Hemai: Nature
Paschal, Mack Arthur: BNA News
Patton, Oliver B.: Heavy Duty Trucking
Paulson, Kathryn: FDC Reports
Paulson, William Clifford: FDC Reports
Paynter, Jennifer D.: MII Publications
Pazanowski, Bernard J.: BNA News
Peckenpaugh, Jason: Government Executive
Pekow, Charles: LP/Gas
Peniston, Brad: Army Times Publishing Co.
Perlman, Ellen: Governing
Pershing, Benjamin: Roll Call
Peters, Katherine M.: Government Executive
Peters, Sally: International Medical News Group
Petersen, Tina: McGraw-Hill
Peterson, Donna M.: Army Times Publishing Co.

MEMBERS ENTITLED TO ADMISSION, PERIODICAL PRESS GALLERIES—Continued

Pettigrew, Sharon Rae: IMAS Publishing
Pexton, Patrick: National Journal
Phibbs, Pat: BNA News
Phillips, Cathleen: Tax Notes
Phillips, Vanessa: UCG
Phinney, David: Army Times Publishing Co.
Piemonte, Philip M.: Washington Business Information
Pierce, Emily: Roll Call
Pietras, Seth: FDC Reports
Pilson, Karen: BNA News
Pimley, D. Ward: BNA News
Pines, Jeffrey: CD Publications
Piotrowski, Matt: McGraw-Hill
Plotz, David: Slate
Plummer, Anne: Inside Washington Publishers
Podesta, Jane: Time Inc.
Polachek, Jay S.: Public Utilities Fortnightly
Polen, Benjamin: Satellite Business News
Pollan, Sarah: FDC Reports
Pollard, Rebecca: American Lawyer Media
Polley, Mary Elizabeth: Food Chemical News
Polster, Nathaniel: HLB Newsletter
Ponnuru, Ramesh: National Review
Porado, Philip: UCG
Postal, Arthur D.: American Banker Newsletters
Postel, Danny: Chronicle of Higher Education
Powell, Kendall: Nature
Powers, Martha C.: Mid-Atlantic Research
Powers, William: National Journal
Precht, Paul: Inside Washington Publishers
Preston, Mark: Roll Call
Preston, Meredith: BNA News
Prevatt, Elizabeth: IMAS Publishing
Prochoroff, Alan: UCG
Pryde, Joan: Kiplinger Washington Editors
Pueschel, Matt: U. S. Medicine
Pulley, John L.: Chronicle of Higher Education
Quenqua, Douglas: PR Week
Rabil, Daniel: McGraw-Hill
Radford, Bruce W.: Public Utilities Fortnightly
Radow, Jonathan: FDC Reports
Radziejewska, Natalia: Tax Notes
Ragavan, Chitra: U. S. News & World Report
Raju, Manu: Inside Washington Publishers
Ramirez, Rosa Maria: Hispanic Link News Service
Rankin, Ken: Lebhar-Friedman Publications
Ranson, Lori: McGraw-Hill/Aero
Ratnam, Gopal: Army Times Publishing Co.
Rawson, Kathleen E.: FDC Reports
Razzi, Elizabeth A.: Kiplinger Washington Editors
Reddy, Tarun: Institutional Investor
Rees, Elizabeth: Inside Washington Publishers
Rees, John: Mid-Atlantic Research
Reese, April G.: Environment & Energy Publishing
Reichard, John: Washington Healthbeat
Reid, Karla S.: Education Week
Reid, Kenneth: Washington Information Source
Reisman, Adam: UCG
Rheault, Magali: Kiplinger Washington Editors
Rhein, Jr., Reginald W.: Scrip World Pharmaceutical News
Ribas, Jorge Luis: Government Information Services
Richard, Alan: Education Week
Richardson, Jenn: Army Times Publishing Co.
Rickman, Johnathan: Tax Notes
Ridgeway, James: Village Voice
Riley, Karen Jane: Clinica
Rinke, Daniel: CCH Inc.
Ritter, Nancy M.: Thompson Publishing Group
Ritterpusch, Kurt: BNA News
Rizer, Steven: KLA Group
Rizzo, Katherine: BNA News
Robb, Karen: Army Times Publishing Co.
Robelen, Erik: Education Week
Roberts, Edward S.: Credit Union Journal
Roberts, Sharon: Time Inc.
Roberts, Vanessa Jo: Government Computer News
Roberts, Victoria: BNA News
Robertson, Jack W.: CMP Media Inc.
Robinson, Linda: U. S. News & World Report
Robinson, Paulette J.: Metro Herald Newspaper
Robinson, Thomas Steven: Mass Transit Lawyer
Rockwell, L. Mark: Wireless Week
Rodeffer, Mark H.: National Journal
Rodriguez, Eva: American Lawyer Media
Rodriguez, Fresia: Hispanic Link News Service
Rodriguez, Paul M.: Insight Magazine
Roeder, Linda: BNA News
Rogers, Adam: Newsweek
Rogers, Amy: CMP Media Inc.
Rogers, Warren: Associated Features
Roha, Ronaleen: Kiplinger Washington Editors
Rohde, Peter: Inside Washington Publishers
Rohrer, S. Scott: National Journal
Rojas, Warren A.: Tax Notes
Rolfsen, Bruce: Army Times Publishing Co.
Rollins, Jonathan: Insight Magazine
Rollow, Jake: Hispanic Link News Service
Romanello, Michael: Telecommunications Reports
Roosevelt, Ann: King Publishing Group
Rose, Lois C.: BNA News
Rose, Phil: Professional Pilot Magazine
Rosen, Jeffrey: New Republic
Rosenberg, Debra: Newsweek
Roston, Eric: Time Inc.
Roth, Siobhan: American Lawyer Media
Rothenberg, Stuart: Rothenberg Political Report
Rothman, Heather M.: BNA News
Rothstein, Betsy: The Hill
Rovetto, Edward: Telecommunications Reports
Roy, Daniel J.: BNA News
Ruark, Jennifer K.: Chronicle of Higher Education
Rubin, Courtney: Washingtonian
Rugaber, Chris: BNA News
Rushford, Greg: Rushford Report

MEMBERS ENTITLED TO ADMISSION, PERIODICAL PRESS GALLERIES—Continued

Ryan, Denise: Tax Notes
Ryan, Margaret L.: McGraw-Hill
Saba, Monica: Radio & Records
Saccomano, Ann: Traffic World
Sack, Joetta L.: Education Week
Safford, David T.: BNA News
Sala, Susan J.: BNA News
Saldarini, Katy: Government Executive
Saletan, William: Slate
Saloom, Elizabeth: Federal Employees News Digest
Salt, Matthew: Washington Business Information
Salzano, Carlo J.: Waterways Journal
Sami, Tamra: Washington Information Source
Sammon, Richard: Kiplinger Washington Editors
Samuel, Terence: U. S. News & World Report
Samuelsohn, Darren: Environment & Energy Publishing
Samuelson, Robert: Newsweek
Sangillo, Gregg Thomas: National Journal
Santiago, Annette R.: McGraw-Hill/Aero
Sarkar, Dibya: Federal Computer Week
Sarkis, Paul A.: BNA News
Sartipzadeh, S. Ali: BNA News
Satchell, Michael John: U. S. News & World Report
Sattler, Cheryl: Government Information Services
Savodnik, Peter: The Hill
Savoor, Namrata: Washington Service Bureau
Sawchuk, Stephen: Government Information Services
Schaffer, Michael: U. S. News & World Report
Schatz-Guthrie, Kathy: Tax Notes
Scherman, Bob: Satellite Business News
Schmidt, Mike: McGraw-Hill
Schmitt, Christopher: U. S. News & World Report
Schmollinger, Christian D.: Natural Gas Week
Schneider, Andrew C.: Kiplinger Washington Editors
Schneider, Martin A.: Exchange Monitor Publications
Schneider, Mary Ellen: Inernational Medical News Group
Schoenberg, Tom: American Lawyer Media
Schofield, Adrian: McGraw-Hill/Aero
Schomisch, Jeffrey: Thompson Publishing Group
Schorr, Burt: UCG
Schoultz, Cathleen O'Connor: BNA News
Schuff, Sally: Farm Progress News
Schultz, Evan P.: American Lawyer Media
Schulz, John D.: Traffic World
Schulz, William: Reader's Digest
Schuster, Elizabeth: Thompson Publishing Group
Schwartz, Cindy: FDC Reports
Schwartz, Lauren: FDC Reports
Scorza, John Forrest: CCH Inc.
Scott, Cordia: Tax Notes
Scott, Dean: Kiplinger Washington Editors
Scott, Douglas: CD Publications
Scribner, Amy: Thompson Publishing Group
Scully, Megan: Inside Washington Publishers
Seckora, Melissa: The Hill
Sedlak, Teresa: Time Inc.
Segarra, Shane: Hispanic Link News Service
Seidenberg, John: Federal Employees News Digest
Selinger, Marc: McGraw-Hill/Aero
Serafini, Marilyn Werber: National Journal
Sergeon, Janet L.: BNA News
Setze, Karen Jeanne: Tax Notes
Seyler, David P.: Radio Business Report
Sfiligoj, Mark L.: Kiplinger Washington Editors
Shafer, Jack: Slate
Shah, Neil: Inside Washington Publishers
Shannon, Darren: Travel Agent Magazine
Shannon, Elaine: Time Inc.
Shapiro, Elizabeth: UCG
Shea, Richard L.: Federal Publications
Shehzad, Noor: FDC Reports
Sheppard, Doug: Tax Notes
Sherfy, Elizabeth Jean: Thompson Publishing Group
Sherman, Jason: Army Times Publishing Co.
Sherman, Mark W.: Business Publishers
Sherrod, Lawrence: Satellite Business News
Shields, Todd: Adweek Magazine
Shipman, William Matthew: Inside Washington Publishers
Shomper, Corie: Business Publishers
Shoop, Thomas J.: Government Executive
Shute, Nancy: U. S. News & World Report
Sian, Maria: Insight Magazine
Sidey, Hugh S.: Time Inc.
Sidor, Tara: Inside Washington Publishers
Silva, Jeffrey S.: Crain Communications
Silverberg, David: The Hill
Silverman, Bridget L.: FDC Reports
Silverman, Jennifer: International Medical News Group
Simendinger, Alexis A.: National Journal
Simmons, Nancy F.: BNA News
Simon, Harvey: McGraw-Hill/Aero
Simon, Roger: U. S. News & World Report
Simon, Seena: Army Times Publishing Co.
Singleton, Joe: Inside Washington Publishers
Sinha, Vandana: Government Computer News
Sirak, Michael: Jane's Information Group
Skilling, Kenneth: BNA News
Skinner, David: Weekly Standard
Skolnik, Sarah: Time Inc.
Skovron, James W.: BNA News
Slaughter, David A.: Thompson Publishing Group
Slavin, Erik: UCG
Smaglik, Paul: Nature
Small, John R.: BNA News
Smallen, Jill: National Journal
Smallwood, Scott: Chronicle of Higher Education
Smith, Anne: Kiplinger Washington Editors
Smith, Douglas: Tax Notes
Smith, Eileen B.: Thompson Publishing Group

MEMBERS ENTITLED TO ADMISSION, PERIODICAL PRESS GALLERIES—Continued

Smith, Guy D.: The Hill
Smith, John Allen: Thompson Publishing Group
Smith, Joseph: CD Publications
Smith, Marcus J.: UCG
Smith, Rhonda: Washington Blade
Snyder, Jim: Inside Washington Publishers
Sobieraj, Sandra: Time Inc.
Socha, Evamarie: Washington Technology
Solomon, Burt: National Journal
Solomon, Francis: Inside Mortgage Finance
Solomon, Goody L.: News Bites
Soloway, Colin: Newsweek
Sommerfield, Margaret N.: Chronicle of Higher Education
Sostek, Anya: Governing
Spangler, Matthew: McGraw-Hill
Speaker, Scott C.: Natural Gas Week
Speights, Michael David: Business Publishers
Spence, Charles F.: General Aviation News
Spencer, Duncan: The Hill
Spencer, Patricia S.: BNA News
Spieler, Rebecca: FDC Reports
Splete, Heidi: International Medical News Group
Spoerl, Gerhard: Der Spiegel
Spotswood, Stephen: U. S. Medicine
Sprague, Dean: Budget & Program
Sprague, John: Budget & Program
Spun, Brandon Evan: Insight Magazine
Stam, John: BNA News
Stanley, Scott: Insight Magazine
Stanton, John Roberts: Inside Washington Publishers
Stanton, Lynn E.: Telecommunications Reports
Starr, Alexandra: Business Week
Starr, Beth: BNA News
Stavros, Richard: Public Utilities Fortnightly
Steele, Zaira: Steele Communications
Stein, Keith: King Publishing Group
Stein, Lisa: U. S. News & World Report
Steinberg, Julie: BNA News
Steinke, Scott A.: FDC Reports
Steis, Alexander Beswick: Natural Gas Intelligence
Stempeck, Brian: Environment & Energy Publishing
Stephens, Hampton: Inside Washington Publishers
Stevens, Allison: The Hill
Stewart, William H.: Thompson Publishing Group
Stichter, Charlotte: Federal Publications
Stimmel, Katherine M.: BNA News
Stimson, Leslie: IMAS Publishing
Stockdale, Grant: King Publishing Group
Stoffer, Harry: Crain Communications
Stokeld, Frederick W.: Tax Notes
Stoler, Judith: Time Inc.
Stone, Gregory M.: Mobile Radio Technology
Stone, Peter H.: National Journal
Stover, Kathy A.: Thompson Publishing Group
Stowell, Alan M.: BNA News
Stratton, Sheryl: Tax Notes
Straub, Noelle: The Hill
Strong, Eric: McGraw-Hill
Struglinski, Suzanne: Environment & Energy Publishing
Stulin, Jamie L.: FDC Reports
Sturges, Peyton M.: BNA News
Suellentrop, Chris: Slate
Sugarman, Carole: Food Chemical News
Suggs, Welch: Chronicle of Higher Education
Sullivan, Colin: Environment & Energy Publishing
Sullivan, Drew: National Journal
Sullivan, John H.: BNA News
Sullivan, Monica C.: National Journal
Sullivan, Patrick: Tax Notes
Sultan, Michael: Natural Gas Week
Summer, Prairie: Inside Washington Publishers
Sutter, Susan M.: FDC Reports
Svitak, Amy: Army Times Publishing Co.
Swanson, Ian: Inside Washington Publishers
Sweeney, Frederick: CD Publications
Sweeney, Jeanne: Title I Report
Sweeting, Paul: Reed Business Information
Swibel, Matthew: Forbes
Swinson, Angela: BNA News
Sybor, Adrian: BNA News
Tacconelli, Gail: Newsweek
Talley, Kenneth: BNA News
Talwani, Sanjay: IMAS Publishing
Tapper, Jake: Salon Magazine
Tatum, Melanie: McGraw-Hill
Taube, Herman: Jewish Forward
Taylor, Richard: Business Publishers
Taylor, Ronald: BNA News
Taylor, Stuart S.: National Journal
Taylor, Vincent: UCG
Teinowitz, Ira: Crain Communications
Temin, Thomas R.: Government Computer News
Terry, Rob: Washington Techway
Terry, Shawn: McGraw-Hill
Teske, Steven: BNA News
Thibodeau, Patrick: IDG Communications
Thomas, Griff: Congressional Digest
Thomas, Richard: Newsweek
Thomas, Steele: FDC Reports
Thompson, Mark J.: Time Inc.
Thormeyer, Robert J.: McGraw-Hill
Thorn, Judith: BNA News
Thorndike, Joseph: Tax Notes
Thurneysen-Lukow, Rachel: Newsweek
Tiboni, Francis: Army Times Publishing Co.
Tice, James S.: Army Times Publishing Co.
Tieman, Jeff: Crain Communications
Tiernan, Tom: McGraw-Hill
Tilley-Hinckle, Elizabeth: Washington Business Information
Timmerman, Kenneth R.: Insight Magazine
Tinkelman, Joseph: BNA News
Tobias, Susan Meader: Thompson Publishing Group
Todaro, Jane: Business Week

MEMBERS ENTITLED TO ADMISSION, PERIODICAL PRESS GALLERIES—Continued

Toloken, Steve: Crain Communications
Tomson, Bill: Exchange Monitor Publications
Torregrossa, Steven J.: Tax Notes
Torrieri, Marisa: UCG
Tosh, Dennis A.: Thompson Publishing Group
Towns, Otis: Set-Aside Alert
Tracy, Tennille: Inside Washington Publishers
Treadway, Todd L.: Kiplinger Washington Editors
Trigoboff, Dan: Broadcasting & Cable
Trimble, Stephan: McGraw-Hill/Aero
Triplett, Michael R.: BNA News
Trotter, Andrew: Education Week
Trowbridge, Gordon: Army Times Publishing Co.
Tsimekles, Diane: Army Times Publishing Co.
Tsui, Amy: BNA News
Tucker, Miriam E.: International Medical News Group
Tumulty, Karen: Time Inc.
Twachtman, Gregory: McGraw-Hill
Udoff, David: Natural Gas Week
Uhlendorf, Karl: FDC Reports
Urdan, Rachel: Inside Washington Publishers
Vample, Gwendolyn C.: Thompson Publishing Group
Van Atta, Dale: Reader's Digest
Van Der Werf, Martin: Chronicle of Higher Education
Van Dongen, Rachel: Roll Call
Vasishtha, Preeti: Government Computer News
Vasse, Aimee: FDC Reports
Vaughan, Martin: Inside Washington Publishers
Verhoff, Thaddeus: BNA News
Verton, Daniel: IDG Communications
Viadero, Debra: Education Week
Victor, Kirk: National Journal
Vidas, Chris: BNA News
Villamana, Molly: Environment & Energy Publishing
Vinch, Charles: Army Times Publishing Co.
Voelz, Martha: Chronicle of Higher Education
Von Zeppelin, Cristina L.: Forbes
Wachter, Kerri: International Medical News Group
Wagner, Anne: National Journal
Wait, Patience: Washington Technology
Wakeman, Nick: Washington Technology
Walczak, Lee: Business Week
Walker, Christopher: FDC Reports
Walker, Richard: Government Computer News
Wall, Robert: Aviation Week
Wallace, Nicole: Chronicle of Higher Education
Waller, Douglas C.: Time Inc.
Wallison, Ethan: Roll Call
Walsh, Gertrude: Government Computer News
Walsh, Kenneth T.: U. S. News & World Report
Walsh, Mark: Education Week
Walsh, Sharon: Chronicle of Higher Education
Walter, Amy: Cook Political Report
Walton, Robert: McGraw-Hill
Ware, Andrew: Natural Gas Week
Ware, Patricia: BNA News
Warner, Veronica Lynn: Tax Notes
Wasch, Adam: BNA News
Washington, Debbie: Inside Washington Publishers
Waterfield, Larry: Vance Publishing
Watkins, Steve: Army Times Publishing Co.
Wear, Benjamin Frank: Education Week
Weaver, Heather Forsgren: Crain Communications
Weber, Rick: Inside Washington Publishers
Webster, James C.: Webster Communications
Wechsler, Jill: Pharmaceutical Executive
Weil, Jenny: McGraw-Hill
Weinstein, Gary A.: BNA News
Weinstock, Matthew: Government Executive
Weisberg, Jacob: Slate
Weisskopf, Michael: Time Inc.
Welch, Jake: National Journal
Welch, Wayne M.: CD Publications
Wells, Robert J.: Tax Notes
Welsh, William E.: Washington Technology
Werble, Cole Palmer: FDC Reports
Werner, Karen Leigh: BNA News
West, Donald V.: Broadcasting & Cable
Whalen, John M.: BNA News
Wheeler, David L.: Chronicle of Higher Education
Wheeler, Scott L.: Insight Magazine
Whelan, David: Chronicle of Higher Education
White, Elizabeth A.: BNA News
White, Frank: McGraw-Hill
White, Rodney: McGraw-Hill
Whitelaw, Kevin: U. S. News & World Report
Whitman, David deF.: U. S. News & World Report
Whittington, Lauren: Roll Call
Wiener, Leonard: U. S. News & World Report
Wieser, Eric M.: Business Publishers
Wilcox, Melynda D.: Kiplinger Washington Editors
Wilczek, Michael J.: McGraw-Hill
Wildavsky, Ben: U. S. News & World Report
Wildstrom, Stephen H.: Business Week
Wilhelm, Ian: Chronicle of Higher Education
Wilkerson, John: Inside Washington Publishers
Willen, Mark: Kiplinger Washington Editors
Willenson, Kim: Japan Digest
Williams, Audrey Y.: Chronicle of Higher Education
Williams, Eileen J.: BNA News
Williams, Grant: Chronicle of Higher Education
Williams, Jeanne: Capitol City Publishers
Williams, Jeffrey: Satellite Business News
Williams, Risa: Tax Notes
Wilson, George C.: National Journal
Wilson, Stanley E.: Institutional Investor
Windish, David F.: Tax Notes
Winebrenner, Jane A.: BNA News
Winograd, Erin Q.: Inside Washington Publishers
Winograd, Jeffrey L.: BNA News
Winston, Sherie: McGraw-Hill

MEMBERS ENTITLED TO ADMISSION, PERIODICAL PRESS GALLERIES—Continued

Winter, Thomas S.: Human Events
Wisniowski, Charles: CD Publications
Witkin, Gordon: U. S. News & World Report
Witt, Elder: Governing
Wittman, Amy: Army Times Publishing Co.
Wittman, John: Army Times Publishing Co.
Woellert, Lorraine: Business Week
Wolffe, Richard: Newsweek
Wolszon, Jamie: Inside Washington Publishers
Wolverton, Bradley: Chronicle of Higher Education
Woods, Randy: Inside Washington Publishers
Woodward, Emily: Army Times Publishing Co.
Woodworth, Esther M.: Tax Notes
Wooldridge, Adrian: Economist
Wright, Charlotte: Business Publishers
Wright, Joseph Michael: National Journal
Wright, Michelle A.: Washington Business Information
Wyand, Michael W.: BNA News
Yachnin, Jennifer: Roll Call
Yaksick, George L.: CCH Inc.
Yamazaki, Kazutami: Washington Watch
Yancey, Kimberly: Tax Notes
Yang, Catherine T.: Business Week
Yarborough, Mary Helen: Thompson Publishing Group
Yasin, Rutrell: Federal Computer Week
Yates, Marshall: KLA Group
Yerkey, Gary G.: BNA News
Yochelson, Mindy: BNA News
Yohannan, Suzanne: Inside Washington Publishers
York, Anthony: Salon Magazine
York, Byron: National Review
Yorke, Jeffrey: Radio & Records
Young, Jeffrey R.: Chronicle of Higher Education
Young, Kathryn M.: Penton Media Inc.
Yuill, Barbara: BNA News
Zagorin, Adam: Time Inc.
Zehr, Mary Ann: Education Week
Zeller, Shawn: National Journal
Zengerle, Jason: New Republic
Ziegler, Mollie: Army Times Publishing Co.
Zung, Robert Te-Kang: BNA News
Zurcher, Anthony W.: Congressional Digest
Zurlo, Jeanne: Washington Service Bureau

PERIODICALS REPRESENTED IN PRESS GALLERIES

House Gallery 225–2941, Senate Gallery 224–0265

ADWEEK MAGAZINE—(202) 833–8184; 910 17th Street, Suite 215, Washington, DC 20005: Wendy Melillo, Todd Shields.

AFRO AMERICAN NEWSPAPERS—(202) 291–9310; 1612 14th Street, NW., Washington, DC 20009: Hazel Trice Edney.

AIRLINE BUSINESS—(703) 836–7442; 333 N. Fairfax Street, Suite 301, Alexandria, VA 22314: David Field.

AMERICAN BANKER NEWSLETTERS—(202) 434–0335; 1325 G Street, NW., Suite 900, Washington, DC 20005: Matthew T. Brady, Arthur D. Postal.

AMERICAN LAWYER MEDIA—(202) 828–0348; 1730 M Street, NW., Suite 802, Washington, DC 20036: Kate Ackley, Elizabeth Wheatly Aycock , Richard Barbieri, Jennifer Bier-Myers, Otis Bilodeau, Vanessa Blum, Joel Chineson, Deirdre Davidson, Elizabeth Engdahl, Ted Goldman, Jenna Greene, Jonathan Groner, Lily Henning, Bill Kisliuk, Tony Mauro, James Oliphant, Rebecca Pollard, Eva Rodriguez, Siobhan Roth, Tom Schoenberg, Evan P. Schultz.

AMERICAN SHIPPER—(202) 347–1678; National Press Building, Room 1269, Washington, DC 20045: Christopher Gillis, Mark Sean McHugh.

ARMY TIMES PUBLISHING CO.—(703) 750–8670; 6883 Commercial Drive, Springfield, VA 22159: Nicholas L. Adde, Bernard Adelsberger, Peter Atkinson, Lance M. Bacon, Laura Bailey, Bridgette Blair, Curtis Mark Brinkley, David Brown, John D. Burlage, David Castellon, Gina Cavallaro, Christopher Cavas, Colin Clark, Laura Colarusso, Robert Colenso, Matthew Cox, David Brian Craig, Vince Crawley, Kathleen A. Curthoys, Daniel Davidson, Chet Dembeck, Deborah M. Funk, Matthew Hilburn, Robert Hodierne, Bryant Jordan, Karen Grigg Jowers, Tim Kauffman, Gail Kaufman, Patricia Kime, Stephen Losey, Christian Lowe, Gordon Lubold, Brian MacKeil, Sidney William Matthews, Richard Maze, Jane Claire McHugh, W. Kent Miller, Christopher Munsey, Vago Muradian, Sean D. Naylor, Alex Neill, Brad Peniston, Donna M. Peterson, David Phinney, Gopal Ratnam, Jenn Richardson, Karen Robb, Bruce Rolfsen, Jason Sherman, Seena Simon, Amy Svitak, Francis Tiboni, James S. Tice, Gordon Trowbridge, Diane Tsimekles, Charles Vinch, Steve Watkins, Amy Wittman, John Wittman, Emily Woodward, Mollie Ziegler.

ASIA TODAY—(202) 271–1100; 27025 McPhearson Square, Washington, DC 20038: Raghubir Goyal.

ASSOCIATED FEATURES—(202) 965–0802; 1622 30th Street, NW., Washington, DC 20007: Warren Rogers.

ATLANTIC INFORMATION SERVICES—(202) 775–9008; 1100 17th Street, NW., Suite 300, Washington, DC 20036: Jill Brown.

ATLANTIC MONTHLY—(202) 333–9211; 4780 Dexter Street, Washington, DC 20007–1015: James Fallows.

AVIATION INTERNATIONAL NEWS—(301) 963–9253; 8020 Needwood Road, #101, Derwood, MD 20855: Paul Lowe, Roger Mola.

AVIATION WEEK—(202) 833–2305; 1200 G Street, NW., Suite 200, Washington, DC 20005: James R. Asker, David Bond, John W. Croft, Frances Fiorino, David Fulghum, John D. Hughes, Jr., Paul S. Mann, Frank Morring, Jr., Bruce D. Nordwall, David M. North, Robert Wall.

BNA NEWS—(202) 452–4200; 1231 25th Street, NW., Washington, DC 20037: Christopher J. Adams, Alexei Alexis, Michelle Amber, Donald G. Aplin, Leroy Armes, Jerome C. Ashton, Cecelia M. Assam, Pamela S. Atkins, Loren Becker, Alison Bennett, Deborah Billings, Cheryl Bolen, David Bottorff, Leonard Bracken, David Barry Brandolph, Rossella Brevetti, Angela L. Britt, Brian J. Broderick, Richard James Bronson, R. Christian Bruce, Susan Bruninga, Sue Bryant, Ellen Byerrum, Raul Cabrera, Derrick Cain, Kendra Casey, Irene Clarke-Gomez, Regina P. Cline, Jennifer Combs, Declan Conroy, Steven Cook, Matilda Monroe Corley, Lauren Couillard, Richard H. Cowden, James D. Crowne, Mark Cutler, Jeff Day, Gloria Deigh, Phyllis Diamond, Kimberlee Smith Doman, Dana J. Domone, Kenneth P. Doyle, Thomas Edmondson, Dana Elfin, Brett Ferguson, Michael Ferullo, James F. Fitzpatrick, Leslie G. Fleet, Lorraine S. Gilbert, Pam D. Ginsbach, Robert L. Goebes, Brant Goldwyn, Anne B. Goodwin, Diana I. Gregg, Angela Gregorits, Melinda Hanson, Steven Harras, Peter S. Hayes, Joyce Hedges, Keith M. Hill, Richard Hill, Susan Hobbs, Rebecca Hoffman, Elizabeth W. Hofmeister, Catherine Hollingsworth, Stephanie Ingersoll, Helen D. Irvin, Rochelle D. Jackson, Alisa Johnson, Fawn Johnson, Helen Jones, Hugh B. Kaplan, Marcia B. Kass, Bruce S. Kaufman, Gail S. Keller, Elaine Kessler, Altaf U. Khan, John Robert Kirkland, Vonronica Kolidakis, W. Randy Kubetin, Louis C. LaBrecque, Eric Lekus, Ralph Lindeman, Brian Alexander Lockett, Fabia H. Mahoney, Mary Ann Grena Manley, Lisa Mathis, Martha Matthews, Anandashankar Mazumdar, Gregory C. McCaffery, Rebecca Pearl McCracken, Susan J. McGolrick, Susan McInerney, Toby McIntosh, Rachel McTague,

PERIODICALS REPRESENTED IN PRESS GALLERIES—Continued

Margaret Miller, Nancy H. Montwieler, Nancy Moore, Pamela Najor, Bud Newman, Thomas O'Toole, Carol Oberdorfer, Nancy Ognanovich, Gloria R. Onley, Mitchell Alexander Otto, Susan J. Pannell, Constance Parten, Mack Paschal, Bernard Pazandowski, Pat Phibbs, Karen Pilson, D. Ward Pimley, Meredith Preston, Kurt Ritterpusch, Katherine Rizzo, Victoria Roberts, Linda Roeder, Lois C. Rose, Heather M. Rothman, Daniel J. Roy, Chris Rugaber, David T. Safford, Susan J. Sala, Paul A. Sarkis, S. Ali Sartipzadeh, Cathleen O'Connor Schoultz, Janet L. Sergeon, Nancy F. Simmons, Kenneth H. Skilling, James W. Skovron, John R. Small, Patricia S. Spencer, John Stam, Beth L. Starr, Julie A. Steinberg, Katherine M. Stimmel, Alan M. Stowell, Peyton Mackay Sturges, John H. Sullivan, Angela Swinson, Adrian Sybor, Kenneth Talley, Ronald Taylor, Steven Teske, Judith Thorn, Joseph Tinkelman, Michael R. Triplett, Amy Tsui, Thaddeus Verhoff, Chris Vidas, Patricia Ware, Adam Wasch, Gary A. Weinstein, Karen Leigh Werner, John M. Whalen, Elizabeth A. White, Eileen J. Williams, Jane A. Winebrenner, Jeffrey L. Winograd, Michael W. Wyand, Gary G. Yerkey, Mindy Yochelson, Barbara Yuill, Robert Te-Kang Zung.

BARRON'S—(202) 862–6606; 1025 Connecticut Avenue, NW., Suite 800, Washington, DC 20036: Thomas G. Donlan, James McTague.

BILLBOARD MAGAZINE—(202) 833–8692; 910 17th Street, NW., Suite 215, Washington, DC 20006: Bill Holland.

BILLING WORLD MAGAZINE—(703) 734–7050,2618; 7918 Jones Branch Drive, 3rd Floor, McLean, VA 22102: John Guerra, Jill Morgan.

BLACK CONGRESSIONAL MONITOR—(202) 488–8879; P.O. Box 75035, Washington, DC 20013: Lenora Moragne.

BLACK ENTERPRISE—(202) 544–3143; 1507 Massachusetts Avenue, SE., Washington, DC 20003: Joyce Jones.

BLATTER—(301) 699–3908; 4506 32nd Street, Mt. Rainier, MD 20712: Konrad Ege.

BROADCASTING & CABLE—(202) 463–3708; 1627 K Street, NW., Washington, DC 20006: Paige Albiniak, John S. Eggerton, William McConnell, Dan Trigoboff, Donald V. West.

BUDGET & PROGRAM—(202) 628–3860; P. O. Box 6269, Washington, DC 20015: Dean Sprague, John Sprague.

BUSINESS PUBLISHERS—(301) 587–6300; 8737 Colesville Road, Suite 1100, Silver Spring, MD 20910: Andrew Arnold, Matthew Aukofer, Jeremy Bond, Rasheeda Crayton Childress, Colin Degen, Charles Dervarics, Elaine R. Eiserer, Leonard A. C. Eiserer, Thecla Fabian, Jay Fletcher, Bob Grupe, Sarah Spencer Hammond, John Higgins, Susan Hsu, Henry E. Kleiner, Steve Lash, Dale McGeehon, Mark W. Sherman, Corie Shomper, Michael David Speights, Richard Taylor, Eric M. Wieser, Charlotte Wright.

BUSINESS TRAVEL NEWS—(703) 642–6422; P. O. Box 11269, Alexandria, VA 22312: Barbara C. Cook.

BUSINESS WEEK—(202) 383–2120; 1200 G Street, NW., Suite 1100, Washington, DC 20005: Beth Belton, Aaron Bernstein, Amy Borrus, John A. Carey, Laura Cohn, Stan Crock, Richard S. Dunham, Paula Dwyer, Howard Gleckman, Douglas A. Harbrecht, Gloria B. Kassabian, Paul Magnusson, Michael D. McNamee, Richard Miller, Alexandra Starr, Jane Todaro, Lee Walczak, Stephen H. Wildstrom, Lorraine Woellert, Catherine T. Yang.

CCH INC.—(202) 259–0012; 1015 15th Street, NW., Suite 1000, Washington, DC 20005: Sarah A. Borchersen-Keto, Jeffrey E. Carlson, Paula L. Cruickshank, Karin R. Dunlap, Martin Egna, Jacqueline E. Fajardo, Peter E. Feltman, Brendan DuBois Frost, David Hansen, Catherine A. Hubbard, George G. Jones, Joyce Mutcherson-Ridley, Lisa R. Neuder, Daniel Rinke, John Forrest Scorza, George L. Yaksick.

CD PUBLICATIONS—(301) 588–6380; 8204 Fenton Street, Silver Spring MD 20910: Stephen Albright, Carrie Ann Alford, Amy L. Bernstein, Carrie Brown, Steven Brown, James S. Byrne, Sharon Lynn Clark, Mary E. Crowley, Thomas J. Edwards, Michael Gerecht, Vladimire Herard, Travis Hicks, George Hutchens, Todd Karpovich, Steve Kidney, David Kittross, Frank Klimko, Ted Knutson, Mark A. Kuhn, Alice Lipowicz, Martha McPartlin, Heather M. Nalbone, Jeffrey Pines, Douglas Scott, Joseph Smith, Frederick Sweeney, Wayne M. Welch, Charles Wisniowski.

CMP MEDIA INC.—(202) 383–4783; 601 13th Street, NW., Suite 560 South, Washington, DC 20005: Beth Bacheldor, George Leopold, Jack W. Robertson, Amy Rogers.

CQ RESEARCHER—(202) 887–8637; 1414 22nd Street, NW., Washington, DC 20037: Mary H. Cooper, Brian Hansen, Kenneth W. Jost, Kathy Koch, David Masci.

CABLEWORLD—(703) 683–2933; 209A S. Union Street, Alexandria, VA 22314: Alicia Mundy.

CANCER LETTER—(202) 362–1809; 3821 Woodley Road NW., Washington, DC 20016: Kirsten Goldberg, Paul Goldberg.

CAPITOL CITY PUBLISHERS—(703) 525–3080; 605 10th Street NE, Washington, DC 20002: Anita Kelly Cosgrove, Erika Fitzpatrick, Natalie C. Holmes, Gail Lawyer Norris, Jeanne M. Williams.

CAPITOL PUBLICATIONS—(202) 312–6088; 1333 H Street, NW., Washington, DC 20005: Pamela Susan Moore.

CHEMICAL MARKET REPORTER—(202) 393–1444; 1057 C National Press Building, Washington, DC 20045: Glenn H. Hess.

PERIODICALS REPRESENTED IN PRESS GALLERIES—Continued

CHRONICLE OF HIGHER EDUCATION—(202) 466–1031; 1255 23rd Street, NW., Washington, DC 20037: Michael Anft, Michael Arnone, Nina Cary Ayoub, Thomas Bartlett, Julianne Basinger, Thomas J. Billitteri, Debra E. Blum, Goldie Blumenstyk, Anne Marie Borrego, Sarah Bray, Scott Carlson, Dan Carnevale, Elizabeth Schwinn Cohn, Jean Evangelauf, Jamilah Evelyn, Elizabeth Farrell, E. Piper Fogg, Andrea Foster, David G. Glenn, Benjamin P. Gose, Elizabeth Greene, Lila Guterman, Eric Hoover, Heather Joslyn, Audrey Williams June, Alex P. Kellogg, Vincent Kiernan, Marni D. Larose, Doug Lederman, Nicole Lewis, Harvy Lipman, Scott McLemee, Beth McMurtrie, Richard Monastersky, Jennifer Lynn Moore, Julie L. Nicklin, Florence Olsen, Danny Postel, John L. Pulley, Jennifer K. Ruark, Scott Smallwood, Margaret N. Sommerfeld, Welch Suggs, Martin Van Der Werf, Martha Voelz, Nicole Wallace, Sharon Walsh, David L. Wheeler, David Whelan, Ian Wilhelm, Audrey Y. Williams, Grant Williams, Bradley Wolverton, Jeffrey R. Young.

CLINICA—(301) 927–1485; 4004 Jefferson Street, Hyattsville MD 20781: Karen Jane Riley.

CONGRESSIONAL DIGEST—(202) 333–7332; 1525B 29th Street, NW., Washington, DC 20007: Sarah Orrick, Griff Thomas, Anthony W. Zurcher.

COOK POLITICAL REPORT—(202) 739–8525; 1501 M Street, NW., Suite 300, Washington, DC 20005: Charles E. Cook, Jr., Jennifer Duffy, John J. Kohut, Amy Walter.

CORPORATE CRIME REPORTER—(202) 737–1680; 1209 National Press Building, Washington, DC 20045: Russell Mokhiber.

CRAIN COMMUNICATIONS—(202) 662–7219; 814 National Press Building, Washington, DC 20045: Vineeta Anand, Elizabeth Beckley, Susanna Duff, Tony Fong, Bob Garfield, Jerome M. Geisel, Douglas J. Halonen, Sara Hansard, Donna L. Harris, David M. Hatch, Mark A. Hofmann, Edward Lovern, Paul Robert Merrion, Miles David Moore, Sarah O'Brien, Jeffrey S. Silva, Harry Stoffer, Ira Teinowitz, Jeff Tieman, Steve Toloken, Heather Forsgren Weaver.

CREDIT UNION JOURNAL—(202) 393–1285; 1325 G Street, NW., Suite 910, Washington, DC 20005: Edward S. Roberts.

CREDIT UNION TIMES—(703) 379–2626; 4600 South Four Mile Run, Suite 930, Arlington, VA 22204: David Carlisle Morrison.

DEFENSE FOCUS—(703) 528–3770; 1300 North 17th Street, 11th Floor, Arlington, VA 22209: Colin Grabow, Jonathan Henning.

DER SPIEGEL—(202) 347–5222; 1202 National Press Building, Washington, DC 20045: Gisela Leske, Dr. Gerhard Spoerl.

DIE WELTWOCHE—(202) 210–1950; 2026 16th Street, NW., #5, Washington, DC 20009: Martin Kilian.

DIE ZEIT—(202) 223–0165; 1730 Rhode Island Avenue, NW., Suite 502, Washington, DC 20036: Thomas Kleine-Brockhoff.

EWEEK—(703) 875–9443; 900 N. Randolph Street #1811, Arlington, VA 22203: Caron Carlson.

ECONOMIST—(202) 783–5753; 1331 Pennsylvania Avenue, NW., Suite 510, Washington, DC 20004: Rachel Jane Horwood, Zanny Minton-Beddoes, John Parker, Adrian Wooldridge.

EDUCATION WEEK—(202) 364–4114; 6935 Arlington Road, Suite 100, Bethesda, MD 20814: Jeffrey Robert Archer, Julie R. Blair, Rhea R. Borja, Darcia Harris Bowman, Kevin C. Bushweller, Catherine Anne Carroll, Sean Cavanagh, Gregory M. Chronister, Michelle R. Davis, Karen Diegmueller, Michelle W. Galley, John Gehring, Catherine Gewertz, Lisa Fine Goldstein, Caroline Hendrie, David Hoff, Marianne Delinda Hurst, Robert Charles Johnston, Bess Keller, Kathleen K. Manzo, Lynn Olson, Karla S. Reid, Alan Richard, Erik Robelen, Joetta L. Sack, Andrew Trotter, Debra Viadero, Mark Walsh, Benjamin Frank Wear, Mary Ann Zehr.

ELECTRONIC BUSINESS—(301) 738–0071; P.O. Box 4190, Rockville, MD 20849–4190: Tam Harbert.

ELLE—(202) 462–2951; 3133 Connecticut Avenue, NW., Suite 315, Washington, DC 20008: Meryl Gordon.

ENDANGERED SPECIES & WETLANDS REPORT—(301) 891–3791; 6717 Poplar Avenue, Takoma Park MD 20912: Stephen Davies.

ENVIRONMENT & ENERGY PUBLISHING—(202) 737–4340; 122 C Street, NW., Suite 722, Washington, DC 20001: Dan Berman, Kevin D. Braun, Tim Breen, Daniel Cusick, Larisa Epatko, Damon Franz, Allison Freeman, Eryn Gable, Natalie Henry, Jennifer Koons, David I. Leavitt, Colleen Luccioli, Lauren Miura, April G. Reese, Darren Samuelsohn, Brian Stempeck, Suzanne Struglinski, Colin Sullivan, Molly Villamana.

EVANS-NOVAK POLITICAL REPORT—(202) 393–4340; 1750 Pennsylvania Avenue, NW., Washington, DC 20006: Timothy Carney.

EXCHANGE MONITOR PUBLICATIONS—(202) 296–2814; 1725 K Street NW Suite 1203, Washington, DC 20006: Amanda Fetterolf, Michael Glenzer, Christopher P. Logan, Jeff Meredith, Martin A. Schneider, Bill Tomson.

EXPRESS INDIA—(703) 893–5565; 1541 Wellingham Court, Vienna, VA 22182: Geeta Goindi.

FDC REPORTS—(301) 657–9830; 5550 Friendship Boulevard, Suite One, Chevy Chase MD 20815: Janet A. Aker,Barbara Ewing, Ramsey Baghdadi, Cabral Bigman-Galimore, Tericke Blanchard, Adwoa K. Boahene, Alla Rutstein Bobbitt, Mark E. Brager, Janet Coleman, Jon Dobson, Andrew Dove, Adam Eckstein, Julie Evans, Danielle Foullon, Eileen Francis, Kevin M. Greenberg, Lauren Hafner, Jonathan Hargreaves, Timothy P. Harrington, Catherine Harrison, Joanne Hawana, Andrew Hawkins, M. Nielsen

PERIODICALS REPRESENTED IN PRESS GALLERIES—Continued

Hobbs, Sunil Iyengar, Scott Jenkins, Kara Kasper, Jaimie Kelley, Cathy Heinze Kelly, Lena Khor, Mary Jo Laffler, Benjamin Lum, Nicholas Macarelli, Michel Marcoux, Rebecca A. Matloff, Michael McCaughan, Brooke E. McManus, Jessica E. Merrill, Reed J. Miller, Walter Morris, Natalie A. Ochs, Rebecca Osvath, Anant R. Padmanabhan, Kathryn Paulson, William Clifford Paulson, Seth Pietras, Sarah Pollan, Jonathan Radow, Kathleen Rawson, Cindy Schwartz, Lauren Schwartz, Noor Shehzad, Bridget L. Silverman, Rebecca S. Spieler, Scott A. Steinke, Jamie L. Stulin, Susan M. Sutter, Steele Thomas, Karl Uhlendorf, Aimee Vasse, Christopher Walker, Cole Palmer Werble.

FTC WATCH—(202) 639–0581; 601 Indiana Avenue, Washington, DC 20004: Arthur L. Amolsch, Gabrielle Hunter.

FALLS CHURCH NEWS PRESS—(703) 532–3267; 929 West Broad Street, Suite 200, Falls Church, VA 22046: Nicholas F. Benton.

FAR EASTERN ECONOMIC REVIEW—(202) 862–9286; 1025 Connecticut Avenue, NW., Suite 800, Washington, DC 20036: Murray Hiebert.

FARM JOURNAL—(703) 331–3073; 12161 Cheshire Court, Bristow, VA 20136: Jane Fullerton, Sonja Hillgren.

FARM PROGRESS NEWS—(202) 554–2092; 496 Fillmore Street, Herndon, VA 20170: Edward Maixner.

FARM PROGRESS NEWS—(202) 484–0744; 520 N Street, SW., Suite S–514, Washington, DC 20024: Sally Schuff.

FEDERAL COMPUTER WEEK—(703) 876–5139; 3141 Fairview Park Drive, Suite 777, Falls Church, VA 22042: Graeme Browning, Dan Caterinicchia, Matthew Caterinicchia, Christopher Dorobek, Randall Edwards, Diane Frank, Matthew French, Michael Hardy, Judith B. Hasson, Allan T. Holmes,Molly Ferrara, Megan Lisagor, S. William Matthews, Sara Michael, John Monroe, Colleen M. O'Hara, Dibya Sarkar, Rutrell Yasin.

FEDERAL EMPLOYEES NEWS DIGEST—(703) 648–9551; 1850 Centennial Park Drive, Suite 520, Reston, VA 20191: Robert Beck, Tom Moore, Elizabeth Saloom, John Seidenberg.

FEDERAL PUBLICATIONS—(202) 828–0299; 901 15th Street, NW., Suite 1010, Washington, DC 20005: Marantha Beatty-Brown, Andrew Bramnick, Veena Datta, Christine M. Hanson, Betty James, Patricia Mariani, Patricia Minikon, Richard L. Shea, Charlotte Stichter.

FINANCIAL POST—(202) 842–1190; National Press Club Suite 206, Washington, DC 20045: Peter Morton.

FOCUS—(301) 581–0999; 8515 Rosewood Drive, Bethesda MD 20814: Peter Gruber.

FOOD CHEMICAL NEWS—(202) 887–6320,116; 1725 K Street, NW., Suite 506, Washington, DC 20006: David Acord, Lucy Ament, Allison Beers, Stephen Chapman, Stephen Clapp, Steve Davis, Laura Gilcrest, Edith Lazenby, Mary Elizabeth Polley, Carole Sugarman.

FORBES—(202) 785–1480; 1101 17th Street, NW., Suite 409, Washington, DC 20036: Ira Carnahan, Chandrani Ghosh, Andrew Gillies, Janet Novack, Matthew Swibel, Cristina L. von Zeppelin.

GENERAL AVIATION NEWS—(301) 330–2715; 1915 Windjammer Way, Gaithersburg, MD 20879: Charles F. Spence.

GILSTON COMMUNICATIONS GROUP—(301) 570–4544; 4816 Sweetbirch Drive, Rockville, MD 20853: Samuel M. Gilston.

GOVERNING—(202) 862–1436; 1100 Connecticut Avenue, NW., Suite 1300, Washington, DC 20036: John Buntin, Melissa Conradi, Alan Ehrenhalt, Alan Greenblatt, Peter A. Harkness, Anne Jordan, Penelope Lemov, Michele Mariani, Ellen Perlman, Anya Sostek, Elder Witt.

GOVERNMENT COMPUTER NEWS—(202) 772–2581; 10 G Street NE, Suite 500, Washington, DC 20002: Lloyd Batzler, Dipka Bhambhani, Patricia Daukantas, Wilson Dizard, William K. Jackson, Kevin McCaney, Matthew J. McLaughlin, Susan Menke, Jason Miller, Dawn S. Onley, Vanessa Jo Roberts, Vandana Sinha, Thomas R. Temin, Preeti Vasishtha, Richard Walker, Gertrude Walsh.

GOVERNMENT EXECUTIVE—(202) 739–8500; 1501 M Street, NW., Suite 300, Washington, DC 20005: Tanya N. Ballard, George Cahlink, Timothy B. Clark, Joshua C. Dean, Susan Fourney, Brian Friel, Amelia Gruber, Shane Harris, Anne Laurent, Kellie Lunney, Jason Peckenpaugh, Katherine M. Peters, Katy Saldarini, Thomas J. Shoop, Matthew Weinstock.

GOVERNMENT INFORMATION SERVICES—(202) 739–9733; 1725 K Street, NW., Suite 700, Washington, DC 20006: Erin Condon, Dennis A. Doster, Charles J. Edwards, Annabelle Go, Donald Hoffman, Helen Kim, Emily Lechy, Jorge Luis Ribas, Cheryl Sattler, Stephen Sawchuk.

GREEN SHEETS—(202) 546–2220; 406 E Street SE., Washington, DC 20003: Linda A. Cartwright, Catherine Cooper, Ralph Dannheisser, John Dineen, Leslie Ann Duncan, W. Lynn Garner.

HLB NEWSLETTER—(301) 770–1884; 5901 Montrose Road, Suite N408, Rockville, MD 20852: Nathaniel Polster.

HEALTH MARKET SURVEY—(202) 362–5408; 5437 Connecticut Avenue, Suite 708, Washington, DC 20015: William Robert Boyles.

HEALTHCARE INFORMATION—(202) 233–0010; 740 National Press Building, Washington, DC 20045: Marcia Clemmitt, Christopher T. Fleming, Thomas Mullen.

HEAVY DUTY TRUCKING—(703) 683–9935; 802 S. Overlook Drive, Alexandria, VA 22305: Oliver B. Patton.

PERIODICALS REPRESENTED IN PRESS GALLERIES—Continued

HISPANIC LINK NEWS SERVICE—(202) 234–0280; 1420 N Street, NW., Washington, DC 20016: Tomas Dinges, Charles Ericksen, Arlene Vanessa Martinez, Cynthia Orosco, Rosa Maria Ramirez, Fresia Rodriguez, Jake Rollow, Shane Segarra.

HUMAN EVENTS—(202) 216–0601,444; One Massachusetts Avenue, NW., Washington, DC 20001: Joseph A. D'Agostino, David Freddoso, John Gizzi, Terence P. Jeffrey, Kevin Lamb, Thomas S. Winter.

IDG COMMUNICATIONS—(202) 879–6724; 1201 F Street, NW., Suite 850, Washington, DC 20004: Gary H. Anthes, Mitch Betts, Cara Garretson, Gretel Johnston, Carolyn Duffy Marsan, Denise Pappalardo, Patrick Thibodeau, Daniel Verton.

IDG NEWS SERVICE—(301) 604–6250; 906 Phillip Powers Drive, Baltimore, MD 21231: Grant Gross.

IMAS PUBLISHING—(703) 998–7600; 5827 Columbia Pike, Falls Church, VA 22041: Thomas Butts, Paul J. McLane, Sharon Rae Pettigrew, Elizabeth Prevatt, Leslie Stimson, Sanjay Talwani.

INDIA ABROAD—(703) 218–0790; 5026 Huntwood Manor Drive, Fairfax, VA 22030: Abdul Aziz Haniffa.

INERNATIONAL MEDICAL NEWS GROUP—(301) 816–8735; 12230 Wilkens Avenue, Rockville MD 20852: Mary Ellen Schneider.

INSIDE MORTGAGE FINANCE—(301) 951–1240; 7910 Woodmont Avenue, Suite 1010, Bethesda, MD 20814: Andrew Analore, John Bancroft, George A. Brooks, Guy David Cecala, Julie Clement, Greg Johnson, Francis Solomon.

INSIDE WASHINGTON PUBLISHERS—(703) 414–5003; 1225 Jefferson Davis Highway, Suite 1400, Arlington, VA 22202: Lara W. Beaven, John T. Bennett, Lorraine Bennett, Jeremy Bernstein, Jonathan M. Block, Joseph P. Boris, Malina Brown, Amy Butler, Christopher J. Castelli, Laura M. Colarusso, Keith J. Costa, Matthew Dalton, Shannon Davis, Jennifer DiMascio, Thomas Patrick Duffy, Daniel G. Dupont, Jeremy Feiler, Benjamin Geman, Steven K. Gibb, Darren Goode, David Goodhue, Dawn Grodsky, Elaine M. Grossman, Thomas Harman, Donna Haseley, Adam Hebert, Kristina Henderson, Jutta Hennig, Corey Neal Henry, Liz Heron, Emily Hsu, Irvin L. Jackson, Gomati Jagadeesan, Peter Kasperowicz, Geoffrey Koss, Patrick Lane, Stephen Langel, Richard Lardner, John Liang, Gregory Lopes, Jason Ma, Catherine MacRae, Meredith Billman Mani, Christopher Marcisz, Klaus Marre, Henry Kevin Maurer, Veena Menon, Douglas Obey, Avery Palmer, Anne Plummer, Paul Precht, Manu Raju, Elizabeth Rees, Peter Rohde, Megan Scully, Neil Shah, William Matthew Shipman, Tara Sidor, Joe Singleton, Jim Snyder, John Roberts Stanton, Hampton Stephens, Prairie Summer, Ian Swanson, Tennille Tracy, Rachel Urdan, Martin Vaughan, Debbie Washington, Rick Weber, John Wilkerson, Erin Q. Winograd, Jamie Wolszon, Randy Woods, Suzanne Yohannan.

INSIGHT MAGAZINE—(202) 636–8846; 3600 New York Avenue, NE, Washington, DC 20002: Julie Abramson, John Berlau, Douglas Burton, Jonathan D. Byus, Sheila R. Cherry, Judith Denton, Stephen Ray Goode, Scott Hagen, Donna Harkins, Charles Hazard, Jennifer Hickey, Michael Kachman, James P. Lucier, Sam MacDonald, Timothy Maier, Kelly O'Meara, Paul M. Rodriguez, Jonathan Rollins, Maria C.Sian, Brandon Evan Spun, Scott Stanley, Kenneth R. Timmerman, Scott L. Wheeler.

INSTITUTIONAL INVESTOR—(202) 393–5555; 1319 F Street, NW., Suite 805, Washington, DC 20004: Daniel Bernstein, Will Boye, Tarun Reddy, Stanley Eugene Wilson.

INTERNATIONAL MEDICAL NEWS GROUP—(301) 816–8790; 12230 Wilkins Avenue, Rockville, MD 20852: Kathryn DeMott, Jeffrey Evans, Joyce Frieden, Winnie Anne Imperio, Elizabeth Mechcatie, Sally Peters, Jennifer Silverman, Heidi Splete, Miriam E. Tucker, Kerri Wachter.

INTERNEWSLETTER—(202) 347–4575; 1063 National Press Building, Washington, DC 20045: Marie B. Allizon.

IRISH ECHO—(301) 404–9773; 9534 Fernwood Road, Bethesda, MD 20817: Susan Falvella-Garraty.

JANE'S INFORMATION GROUP—(703) 236–2435; 1340 Braddock Place, Suite 300, Alexandria, VA 22314: Andrew R. Koch, Michael C. Sirak.

JAPAN DIGEST—(703) 931–2500; 3424 Barger Drive, Falls Church, VA 22044: Ayako Doi, Nicole George, Kim Willenson.

JET/EBONY—(202) 393–5860; 1750 Pennsylvania Avenue, NW., Suite 1201, Washington, DC 20006: Simeon S. Booker, Kevin Chappell.

JEWISH FORWARD—(202) 879–6720; National Press Building, Suite 1049, Washington, DC 20045: Eli Kintisch.

JEWISH FORWARD—(301) 530–8109; 10500 Rockville Pike, Suite 604, Rockville, MD 20852: Herman Taube.

JEWISH PRESS—(202) 861–2317; 2130 P Street NW #405, Washington, DC 20036: Dara Mandell.

KLA GROUP—(703) 866–2844; 7324 Bath Street, Springfield, VA 22150: Steven M. Rizer, Marshall Yates.

KING PUBLISHING GROUP—(202) 662–9729; 1325 G Street, NW., Suite 1003, Washington, DC 20005: David Ahearn, Rita Robinson,John M. Donnelly, Linda Ann Gasparello, Nathan Hodge, Llewellyn W. King, Steven R. Kramer, Ron Laurenzo, Richard Mullen, Scott Nance, Ann Roosevelt, Keith Stein, Grant Stockdale.

KIPLINGER WASHINGTON EDITORS—(202) 887–6452; 1729 H Street, NW., Washington, DC 20006: Peter L. Blank, Janet Bodnar, George E. Brandon, Priscilla T. Brandon, Melissa Star Bristow, Martha L. Craver, Kenneth B. Dalecki, Matthew Dembicki, Michael F. Doan, Nicole Eyman, Lawrence I.

PERIODICALS REPRESENTED IN PRESS GALLERIES—Continued

Fishbein, Mary Beth Franklin, Robert L. Frick, Peter Goldstein, Joan Goldwasser, Jean Gruss, Jerome Idaszak, Austin H. Kiplinger, Brian P. Knestout, Jeffrey Kosnett, Kimberly Lankford, Vandana Mathur, Kevin McCormally, Courtney B. McGrath, James Gerry Moore, Jim Ostroff, Joan Pryde, Elizabeth A. Razzi, Magali Rheault, Ronaleen Roha, Richard Sammon, Andrew C. Schneider, Dean Scott, Mark Sfiligoj, Anne Smith, Todd L. Treadway, Melynda D. Wilcox, Mark Willen.

LP/GAS—(301) 493–6926; 5225 Pooks Hill Road #118N, Bethesda, MD 20814: Charles Pekow.

LEBHAR–FRIEDMAN PUBLICATIONS—(301) 924–3033; 17735 Striley Drive, Ashton, MD 20861: Ken Rankin.

MII PUBLICATIONS—(202) 347–4822; 733 15th Street, NW., Suite 900, Washington, DC 20005: Ryan E. Hess, Christopher Maloney, Cecilio Morales, David O. Parish II, Jennifer Paynter.

MAIL ON SUNDAY—(202) 547–7980; 510 Constitution Avenue, NE, Washington, DC 20002–5926: William A. Lowther.

MANUFACTURING NEWS—(703) 750–2664; P.O.Box 36, Annandale, VA 22003: Richard McCormack.

MASS TRANSIT LAWYER—(703) 548–5177; 1216 Michigan Court, Alexandria, VA 22314: Thomas Steven Robinson.

MCGRAW–HILL—(202) 383–2183; 1200 G Street, NW., Suite 1000, Washington, DC 20005: Jeffrey Barber, Joanne Callahan, Craig S. Cano, Catherine Cash, Patrick Connole, Mark Davidson, Lira Behrens Davies, Kelley Doolan, Lawrence D. Foster, Katharine Fraser, Tom Harrison, Laura Hertzfeld, Elaine Hiruo, Dan Horner, Joseph D. Hutnyan, Thomas F. Ichniowski, Frank Jackman, Valarie Jackson, Regina Johnson, David Jones, Brian D. Jordan, Carolyn Keplinger, Michael Knapik, Liane Kucher, Kathy Carolin Larsen, William E. Loveless, Robert Marvin, Karen McBeth, Christopher J. Newkumet, Mark Alexander Oram, Tina Petersen, Matt Piotrowski, Daniel Rabil, Margaret L. Ryan, Mike Schmidt, Matthew Spangler, Eric Strong, Melanie Tatum, Shawn Terry, Robert J. Thormeyer, Tom Tiernan, Gregory Twachtman, Robert Walton, Gloria Kassabian,Jenny Weil, Frank White, Rodney A. White, Michael J. Wilczek, Sherie Winston.

MCGRAW–HILL/AERO—(202) 383–2401; 1200 G Street, NW., Suite 200, Washington, DC 20005: Patricia Brown, David L. Collogan, Brett Davis, John Doyle, Laurence Lee Ewing, Christopher Fotos, Paul Hoversten, Kimberly E. Johnson, Nicholas G. Jonson, Angela Kim, Adrianne Larson, Steven Lott, Kerry Lynch, Denise Marois, Jim Matthews, Jefferson F. Morris, Lori Ranson, Annette R. Santiago, Adrian Schofield, Marc Selinger, Harvey Simon, Stephen Trimble.

MEDICAL DEVICES REPORT—(703) 361–6472; 7643 Bland Drive, Manassas, VA 20109: Steve Butchock.

METRO HERALD NEWSPAPER—(703) 548–8891; 901 North Washington Street, Suite 603, Alexandria, VA 22314: Paris D. Davis, Paulette J. Robinson.

MID–ATLANTIC RESEARCH—800,227–7140; 2805 St. Paul Street, Baltimore, MD 21218: Martha C. Powers, John Rees.

MILAN PRESSE—(301) 907,7580; 7711 Tilbury Street, Bethesda MD 20814: Martine Combemale.

MOBILE RADIO TECHNOLOGY—(703) 684–8548; P. O. Box 25693, Alexandria, VA 22313: Gregory M. Stone.

MULTICHANNEL NEWS—(202) 463–3737; 1627 K Street, NW., 10th Floor, Washington, DC 20006: Edward T. Hearn.

NATION—(240) 899–1510; 110 Maryland Avenue, NE., Suite 308, Washington, DC 20002: Matt Bivens, David Corn.

NATIONAL JOURNAL—(202) 739–8425; 1501 M Street, NW., Suite 300, Washington, DC 20005: James A. Barnes, Jill F. Bartscht, David Baumann, Carl M. Cannon, Eliza Newlin Carney, Lee Carpenter, Richard E. Cohen, Marge DuMond, Tish Durkin, Isobel Ellis, Elisabeth Frater, Sydney J. Freedberg, Jr., Robert H. Gettlin, S. Siobhan Gorman, Charles A. Green, Jerry Hagstrom, Joe Haney, Erin J. Heath, Corine Hegland, Louis Jacobson, Meg Kinnard, James Kitfield, Judith Klein, Julie A. Kosterlitz, Margaret E. Kriz, Lisa Lerer, John J. Maggs, Jodie Morris, Neil P. Munro, Joyce M. Murdoch, Mark Murray, Deborah L. Acomb Nations, Patrick Pexton, William Powers, Mark H. Rodeffer, S. Scott Rohrer, Gregg Thomas Sangillo, Marilyn Werber Serafini, Alexis Simendinger, Jill Smallen, Burt Solomon, Peter Stone, Drew Sullivan, Monica C. Sullivan, Stuart S. Taylor, Jr., Kirk Victor, Anne Wagner, Jake Welch, George C. Wilson, Joseph Michael Wright, Shawn Zeller.

NATIONAL LAW JOURNAL—(202) 828–0360; 1730 M Street, NW., Washington, DC 20036: Marcia Coyle.

NATIONAL MORTGAGE NEWS—(202) 434–0323; 1325 G Street, NW., Suite 910, Washington, DC 20005: Brian Collins, Georgiana Lee, Paul Muolo.

NATIONAL NEWS SYNDICATE—(703) 356–6599; 1350 Beverly Road, Suite 115–229, McLean, VA 22101: Beth Aluise, Susan J. Aluise.

NATIONAL REVIEW—(202) 543–9226; 219 Pennsylvania Avenue, SE., Washington, DC 20003: John J. Miller, Joel Mowbray, Kate Walsh O'Beirne, Ramesh Ponnuru, Byron York.

NATIONAL UNDERWRITER—(202) 783–8443; 1249 National Press Building, Washington, DC 20045: Steven Brostoff.

NATURAL GAS INTELLIGENCE—(703) 318–8848; 22648 Glenn Drive, Suite 305, Sterling, VA 20164: Ellen Beswick, Rocco Canonica, Paul Ciampoli, Susan T. Parker, Alexander Beswick Steis.

PERIODICALS REPRESENTED IN PRESS GALLERIES—Continued

NATURAL GAS WEEK—(202) 662–0718; 1401 New York Avenue, NW., Suite 500, Washington, DC 20005: Mark E. Heckathorn, Christian D. Schmollinger, Scott C. Speaker, Michael Sultan, David Udoff, Andrew Ware.

NATURE—(202) 737–4628; 968 National Press Building, Washington, DC 20045: Geoff Brumfiel, Erika Check, Ramani Gnanasambat, Virginia Gewin, Chris Gunter, Colin Macilwain, Hemai Parthasarathy, Kendall Powell, Paul Smaglik.

NEW REPUBLIC—(202) 508–4444; 1331 H Street, NW., Suite 700, Washington, DC 20005: Spencer Ackerman, Peter Beinart, Jonathan Chait, Michelle Cottle, Michael Crowley, Gregg Easterbrook, Franklin Foer, John B. Judis, Ryan Lizza,Laura Obolinski, Christopher Orr, Jeffrey Rosen, Jason Zengerle.

NEW YORK JEWISH WEEK—(703) 978–4724; 8713 Braeburn Drive, Annandale, VA 22203: James David Besser.

NEW YORKER—(202) 296–5840; 1156 15th Street, NW., Washington, DC 20005: Jane Mayer.

NEWS BITES—(202) 723–2477; 1712 Taylor Street, NW., Washington, DC 20011: German Munoz, Goody L. Solomon.

NEWS INDIA TIMES—(703) 455–6394; 7911 Edinburgh Drive, Springfield, VA 22153: Vasantha Arora.

NEWSWEEK—(202) 626–2050; 1750 Pennsylvania Avenue, NW., Suite 1220, Washington, DC 20006: John A. Barry, Martha Brant, Lynette Clemetson, Eleanor Clift, Howard Fineman, Thomas Trent Gegax, Roy Gutman, Mark Hosenball, Michael Isikoff, Patrice Wingert Kelly, Daniel Klaidman, Weston Kosova, Tamara Lipper, Donatella Lorch, Adam Rogers, Debra Rosenberg, Robert Samuelson, Colin Soloway, Gail G. Tacconelli, Richard K. Thomas, Rachel Thurneysen-Lukow, Richard Wolffe.

OIL & GAS JOURNAL—(301) 365–5510; 9704 Corkran Lane, Bethesda, MD 20817: Maureen Shields Lorenzetti.

OUTLOOK—(202) 452–1462; 1255 New Hampshire Avenue, NW., Suite 630, Washington, DC 20036: Ludwina Joseph.

PR WEEK—(202) 543–5040; 731 6th Street SE., Washington, DC 20003: Douglas Quenqua.

PACE PUBLICATIONS—(202) 835–1771; 1900 L Street, NW., Suite 312, Washington, DC 20036: Craig Fischer, Sid Goldstein, Sarah Meldrum, Molly R. Parrish.

PENTON MEDIA INC.—(202) 659–8500; 1350 Connecticut Avenue, NW., Suite 902, Washington, DC 20036: Sandra Arnoult, James A. Donoghue, Loren S. Farrar, Perry Flint, William A. Freeman III, Dylan Gallagher, John McClenahen, William H. Miller, James L. Nash, Kathryn Young.

PERIODICALS NEWS SERVICE—(301) 725–2756; 9206 Vollmerhausen Road, Jessup MD 20794: Cecelia Blalock, Mary Ann Gatty.

PESTICIDE REPORT—(301) 864–3088; 3918 Oglethorpe Street, Hyattsville MD 20782: Sue Darcey.

PHARMACEUTICAL EXECUTIVE—(301) 656–4634; 7715 Rocton Avenue, Chevy Chase, MD 20815: Jill Wechsler.

PHYSICIAN'S WEEKLY—(202) 783–6521; 499 National Press Building, Washington, DC 20045: Christina Kent.

PRESS ASSOCIATES—(202) 898–4825; 1000 Vermont Avenue, NW., Suite 101, Washington, DC 20005: Janet M. Brown, Mark J. Gruenberg.

PROCESO—(202) 737–1538; 529 14th Street, NW., Suite 480, Washington, DC 20045: J. Jesus Esquivel.

PROFESSIONAL PILOT MAGAZINE—(703) 370–0606; 3014 Colvin Street, Alexandria, VA 22314: Phil Rose.

PROGRESSIVE BUSINESS PUBLICATIONS—(410) 349–8200; 1528 Circle Drive, Annapolis, MD 21401: Thomas Guay.

PUBLIC LANDS NEWS—(202) 638–7529; 1010 Vermont Avenue, NW., Suite 708, Washington, DC 20005: James B. Coffin.

PUBLIC UTILITIES FORTNIGHTLY—(703) 847–7761; 8229 Boone Boulevard, Suite 401, Vienna, VA 22182: Jennifer Alvey, Lori Burkhart, Mark Hand, Jay S. Polachek, Bruce W. Radford, Richard Stavros.

RADIO & RECORDS—(202) 463–3930; 888 17th Street NW Suite 310, Washington, DC 20006: Michael Bowen, Joe Howard, Jacqueline Madrigal, Monica Saba, Jeffrey Yorke.

RADIO BUSINESS REPORT—(703) 719–9500; 6208–B Old Franconia Road, Alexandria, VA 22310: Ken Lee, Carl A. Marcucci, David P. Seyler.

READER'S DIGEST—(202) 223–9520; 1730 Rhode Island Avenue, NW., Suite 406, Washington, DC 20036: Trevor Armbrister, William P. Beaman, Ralph Kinney Bennett, Daniel R. Levine, Edward McFadden, Eugene H. Methvin, John Mitchell, William Schulz, Dale Van Atta.

RECALL—(301) 460–8821; 14208 Oakvale Street, Rockville, MD 20853: William McVicker.

REED BUSINESS INFORMATION—(202) 463–3736; 1627 K Street, NW., Washington, DC 20002: Paul Sweeting.

RESEARCH INSTITUTE OF AMERICA GROUP—(703) 706–0214; 1325 G Street, NW., Suite 910, Washington, DC 20005: Debra Berkowitz, Theresa Markley Brion, William Dunn, Barbra Golub, Velma D. Goodwine, Wayne Logue, Kevin McDermott, Michael J. McGoffin, Tina Fritz Namian, Erin O'Connor.

ROLL CALL—(202) 824–6800; 50 F Street, NW., Suite 700, Washington, DC 20001: Erin Billings, Chris Black, John Bresnahan, Amy Carlile, Damon Chappie, Chris Cillizza, Timothy Curran, Nicole

PERIODICALS REPRESENTED IN PRESS GALLERIES—Continued

Duran, Douglas Fruehling, Michael Grass, Ed Henry, Bryanna Hocking, Paul Kane, Amy M. Keller, Morton M. Kondracke, Josh Kurtz, John Mercurio, David B. Meyers, Brody Mullins, Suzanne Nelson, Benjamin Pershing, Emily Pierce, Mark Preston, Rachel Van Dongen, Ethan Wallison, Lauren Whittington, Jennifer Yachnin.

ROLLING STONE—(781) 639–9650; 8567 Yoder Street, Manassas, VA 20110: Brian Andrew Bushell.

ROTHENBERG POLITICAL REPORT—(202) 546–2822; 50 F Street, NW., 7th Floor, Washington, DC 20001: Stuart Rothenberg.

RUSHFORD REPORT—(703) 938–9420; 261 Commons Drive, Vienna, VA 22810: Greg Rushford.

SALON MAGAZINE—(202) 265–2007; 1642 R Street, NW., Washington, DC 20009: Kerry Lauerman, Joshua Marshall, Jake Tapper, Anthony York.

SATELLITE BUSINESS NEWS—(202) 785–0505; 1990 M Street, NW., Suite 510, Washington, DC 20036: Benjamin Polen, Bob Scherman, Lawrence Sherrod, Jeffrey Williams.

SCIENCE & GOVERNMENT REPORT—(301) 889–0562; P.O. Box 190, Churchton, MD 20733: David Kramer.

SCRIP WORLD PHARMACEUTICAL NEWS—(301) 229–7910; 6102 Princeton Avenue, Glen Echo, MD 20812: Reginald W. Rhein, Jr..

SEDGWICK PUBLISHING—(703) 237–7962; 5209 N. 30th Street, Arlington, VA 22207: Katherine P. Muth.

SET–ASIDE ALERT—(202) 364–6473; 4201 Connecticut Avenue, #610, Washington, DC 20008: Warren Corbett, Otis Towns.

SLATE—(202) 387–2298; 1800 M Street, NW., Suite 330, Washington, DC 20036: Dahlia Hannah Lithwick, Timothy Robert Noah, David Plotz, William Saletan, Jack Shafer, Chris Suellentrop, Jacob Weisberg.

STEELE COMMUNICATIONS—(301) 916–7132; 11109 Yellow Leaf Way, Germantown, MD 20876: Zaira Steele.

STERN—(301) 365–6629; 9133 Vendome Drive, Bethesda, MD 20817: Claus Lutterbeck.

TAX NOTES—(703) 533–4417; 6830 North Fairfax Drive, Arlington, VA 22213: Deborah Aiken, Lisa Michele Alexander, LaQuesha Allen, Jon S. Almeras, David S. Antonides, Herman P. Ayayo, John C. Bell, Kevin A. Bell, Lisa J. Bender, Heather Bennett, Christopher E. Bergin, David E. Brunori, Jennifer Carr, Timothy Philip Catts, Althea Dressel, Heidi Glenn,Pat Price, Chuck Gnaedinger, Robert Goulder, George Guttman, Amy Hamilton, Sonya V. Harmon, Joann Christine Harris, Cindy Ann Heyd, Adrienne Kendrick, Sarah M. W. Kirkell, Carolyn Wright LaFon, Robert F. Manning, Karla L. Miller, Patti Mohr, Mia Moreno-Hines, Cathleen M. Phillips, Natalia Radziejewska, Johnathan Alexander Rickman, Warren A. Rojas, Denise Ryan, Kathy Schatz-Guthrie, Cordia Scott, Karen Jeanne Setze, Doug Sheppard, Douglas Smith, Frederick Stokeld, Sheryl Stratton, Patrick Sullivan, Joseph Thorndike, Steven J. Torregrossa, Veronica Lynn Warner, Robert J. Wells, Risa Williams, David F. Windish, Esther M. Woodworth, Kimberly Yancey.

TECHNOLOGY COMMERCIALIZATION—(703) 522–6648; P.O. Box 10060, Arlington, VA 22210: Neil MacDonald.

TELECOMMUNICATIONS REPORTS—(202) 312–6084; 1333 H Street, NW., Suite 100 East, Washington, DC 20005: Margaret Boles, Howard Buskirk, John Curran, Victoria Curtis, Amy L. Fickling, Brian Hammond, Michael R. Johnson, Gayle Kansagor, Paul Kirby, Tom Leithauser, Sara E. Levy, Michael Romanello, Edward Rovetto, Lynn E. Stanton.

TEXTILE WORLD—(703) 437–4079; 1702 Red Oak Circle, Reston, VA 22090: James A. Morrissey.

THE FORWARD—(202) 879–6740; 5412 N. 26th Street, Arlington, VA 22207: Ori Nir.

THE HILL—(202) 628–8529; 733 15th Street, NW., Suite 1140, Washington, DC 20005: Alexander Bolton, Peter Brand, Jonathan Cassidy, Sarita Chourey, Robert Cusack, Sam Dealey, Jeff Dufour, Geoff Earle, Albert Eisele, Melanie Fonder, Angela Foradori, Abraham Genauer, Michael Gerber, Andrew J. Glass, Hugo Gurdon, Mary Lynn Jones, Deborah Kalb, Jonathan Kaplan, Sarah Lesher, Hans Nichols, Patrick O'Connor, Betsy Rothstein, Peter Savodnik, Melissa Seckora, David Silverberg, Guy D. Smith, Duncan Spencer, Allison Stevens, Noelle Straub.

THOMPSON PUBLISHING GROUP—(202) 739–9719; 1725 K Street, NW., Suite 700, Washington, DC 20006: Jerry Ashworth, Sarah Barak, Mitchell Berger, Abigail Benezra Brugger, Lisa D. Burden, Lauren Butcher, Carey Cauthen, Mara Cherkasky, Ryan A. Clark, Cari Coleman, Laura Lee Fedak, Rodney D. Garcia, Kelly J. Gordon, Lisa L. Hayes, Luis Hernandez, John F. Iekel, Jerry Lee Kline, Rosemarie Lally, Denise Lamoreaux, Dina LoRusso, Joe Lustig, Barbara Magill, Rachel D. McVearry, Robert W. Mitchell, Christopher Scott Morin, Stephanie L. Muller, Gretchen Parisi, Nancy M. Ritter, Jeffrey Schomisch, Elizabeth Schuster, Amy Scribner, Elizabeth Jean Sherfy, David A. Slaughter, Eileen B. Smith, John Allen Smith, William H. Stewart, Kathy A. Stover, Susan Meader Tobias, Dennis A. Tosh, Gwendolyn C. Vample, Mary Helen Yarborough.

TIME INC.—(202) 861–4065; 555 12th Street, NW., Washington, DC 20004: Lissa August, Perry Bacon, Jr., Jeffrey H. Birnbaum, Timothy Burger, Massimo Calabresi, James Carney, Donald Collins, Jr., Matthew Cooper, John F. Dickerson, Amy Dickinson, Sally Donnelly, Michael Duffy, Andrew Daniel Goldstein, Lona C. Harris, Anthony Jackson, Linda Kramer, Macon Morehouse, Viveca Novak, Jane Podesta, Sharon Roberts, Eric Roston, Teresa Sedlak, Elaine Shannon, Hugh S. Sidey, Sarah Skolnik,

PERIODICALS REPRESENTED IN PRESS GALLERIES—Continued

Sandra Sobieraj, Judith Stoler, Mark J. Thompson, Karen Tumulty, Douglas C. Waller, Michael Weisskopf, Adam Zagorin.

TITLE I REPORT—(202) 363–5534; 215 E. Del Ray Avenue, Alexandria, VA 22301: Lois Berkowitz, Ann Cassin, Julie A. Miller, Jeanne Sweeney.

TRAFFIC WORLD—(202) 661–3372; 1270 National Press Building, Washington, DC 20045: Clayton W. Boyce, William B. Cassidy, Robert G. Edmonson, John Gallagher, Kathleen Hickey, Angela Greiling Keane, Richard Lawrence, Paul Page, Ann Saccomano, John D. Schulz.

TRAVEL AGENT MAGAZINE—(202) 393–6281; 529 14th Street, NW., Suite 1291, Washington, DC 20045: Tricia Holly, Jennifer Michels, Darren Shannon.

TRAVEL TRADE—(703) 451–5130; P. O. Box 2430, Springfield, VA 22152: Bob Downes.

TRAVEL WEEKLY—(202) 463–3732; 1627 K Street, NW., 10th Floor, Washington, DC 20006: Andrew Compart, Michael Milligan.

U. S. MEDICINE—(202) 463–6000; 2021 L Street, NW., Suite 400, Washington, DC 20036: Frank M. Best, Ben Karpf, Matthew Mientka, Matt Pueschel, Stephen Spotswood.

U.S. NEWS & WORLD REPORT—(202) 955–2401; 1050 Thomas Jefferson Street, NW., Washington, DC 20007: Jodie T. Allen, Julian E. Barnes, Megan L. Barnett, Michael Barone, Paul Bedard, Gloria Borger, Mary Angela Cannon, Kim Clark, Dana Hawkins, Linda Kulman, Marianne Lavelle, Samantha Levine, Mary C. Lord, Margaret Mannix, Mark Mazetti, Anna Mulrine, Noam Neusner, Richard J. Newman, Chitra Ragavan, Linda Robinson, Terence Samuel,Lynne Edwards, Michael John Satchell, Michael Schaffer, Christopher Schmitt, Nancy Shute, Roger Simon, Lisa Stein, Kenneth T. Walsh, Kevin Whitelaw.

UNITED COMMUNICATIONS GROUP—(301) 816–8950,2363; 11300 Rockville Pike, Suite 1100, Rockville, MD 20852: Carl Albert Ayers, Linda Busche, Brett Coughlin, Matthew Dobias, Nancy Dunham, Richard D. Hadley, Jay Heflin, Michael Ingram, Whitney L. Jackson, Spencer Kelly, Eric Klein, Scott Kraft, Robyn Lamb, Nicholas Morehead, Mary Mosquera, Vanessa Phillips, Philip Porado, Alan Prochoroff, Adam Reisman, Burt Schorr, Elizabeth Shapiro, Erik Slavin, Marcus J. Smith, Vincent Taylor, Marisa Torrieri.

USA JOURNAL—(703) 379–2520; 250 S. Reynolds Street, #1309, Alexandria, VA 22304: Janne Kum Cha Pak.

UTILITY SPOTLIGHT—(703) 525–1524; 4300 Old Dominion Drive, #903, Arlington, VA 22207: Alan Kovski.

VANCE PUBLISHING—(703) 451–7941; 7124 Hanks Place, Springfield, VA 22153: Larry Waterfield.

VANITY FAIR—(202) 342–2126; 3124 Woodley Road, Washington, DC 20008: Maureen Orth.

VILLAGE VOICE—(202) 332–1818; 1312 18th Street, NW., Washington, DC 20036: James Ridgeway.

WASHINGTON BLADE—(202) 797–7000; 1408 U Street, NW., Second Floor, Washington, DC 20009: Louis M. Chibbaro, Jr., Chris Crain, Joseph Ross Crea, Kara Fox, Lisa Melinda Keen, Brian Moylan, Rhonda M. Smith.

WASHINGTON BUSINESS INFORMATION—(703) 538–7666; 300 N. Washington Street, Suite 200, Falls Church, VA 22046: Cynthia Carter, Richie Crider, Bruce Goldfarb, Susan McGovern, Philip M. Piemonte, Matthew Salt, Elizabeth Tilley-Hinkle, Michelle A. Wright.

WASHINGTON BUSINESS JOURNAL—(703) 816–0330; 1555 Wilson Boulevard, Suite 400, Arlington, VA 22209: Kent Hoover.

WASHINGTON COUNSELETTER—(202) 244–6709; 5712 26th Street, NW., Washington, DC 20015: Deborah Kavruck, Samuel Kavruck.

WASHINGTON CRIME NEWS SERVICES—(202) 662–7035; National Press Building, Suite 960D, Washington, DC 20045: Leonard Curry.

WASHINGTON HEALTHBEAT—(301) 495–3063; 9595 Caroline Avenue, Silver Spring, MD 20901: John Reichard.

WASHINGTON INFORMATION SOURCE—(703) 779–8777; 4 Loudon Street, SE., Leesburg, VA 20175: Kenneth Reid, Tamra Sami.

WASHINGTON NEW OBSERVER—(301) 657–1966; 5101 River Road, Suite 1204, Bethesda, MD 20816: Anne Orleans.

WASHINGTON REMOTE SENSING LETTER—(202) 393–3640; 1057–B National Press Building, Washington, DC 20045: Murray Felsher.

WASHINGTON SERVICE BUREAU—(202) 312–6604; 1015 15th Street, NW., Suite 1000, Washington, DC 20005: John F. Atwood, Erin Binney, Alison Carpenter, Anna Kallioinen, Susan Kavanagh, Jacquelyn Lumb, Namrata Savoor, Jeanne Zurlo.

WASHINGTON TECHNOLOGY—(202) 772–2575; 10 G Street, NE., Suite 500, Washington, DC 20002: Gail Emery, Joab Jackson, Steve LaSueur, Evamarie Socha, Patience Wait, Nick Wakeman, William Welsh.

WASHINGTON TECHWAY—(703) 469–2992; 1515 N. Courthouse Road, Arlington, VA 22201: Joseph Anselmo, Brendan Barrett, Alex Daniels, Rob Terry.

WASHINGTON TRADE DAILY—(301) 946–0817; 2104 National Press Building, Washington, DC 20045: James R. Berger, Mary Berger.

PERIODICALS REPRESENTED IN PRESS GALLERIES—Continued

WASHINGTON WATCH—(301) 897–4145; 5014 Cloister Drive, Rockville, MD 20852: Kazutami Yamazaki.

WASHINGTONIAN—(202) 296–3600; 1828 L Street, NW., Suite 200, Washington, DC 20036: Charles N. Conconi, Kim Eisler, Brooke Foster, Harry S. Jaffe, Drew Lindsay, Barbara Matusow-Nelson, Courtney Rubin.

WATERWAYS JOURNAL—(703) 524–2490; 5220 North Carlin Springs Road, Arlington, VA 22203–1307: Carlo J. Salzano.

WEBSTER COMMUNICATIONS—(703) 525–4512; 3835 N. 9th Street, Suite 401W, Arlington, VA 22203: James C. Webster.

WEEKLY STANDARD—(202) 293–4900; 1150 17th Street, NW., Suite 505, Washington, DC 20036: Fred Barnes, Lee Bockhorn, David Brooks, Christopher Caldwell, Tucker Carlson, Benjamin Boyce Crader, Sam J. Dealey, Terry Eastland, Stephen F. Hayes, Matthew Labash, Jonathan Last, Katherine Mangu-Ward, Victorino Matus, David Skinner.

WIRELESS WEEK—(202) 463–3702; 1627 K Street, NW., 10th Floor, Washington, DC 20006: L. Mark Rockwell.

WIRTSCHAFTSWOCHE—(202) 238–0130; 1779 Church Street, NW., Washington, DC 20036: Olaf Gersemann.

YOMIURI AMERICA—(703) 525–0576; 2100 Lee Highway, Suite 524, Arlington, VA 22201: Yoshio Hotta.

CONGRESSIONAL DISTRICT MAPS

ALABAMA—Congressional Districts—(7 Districts)

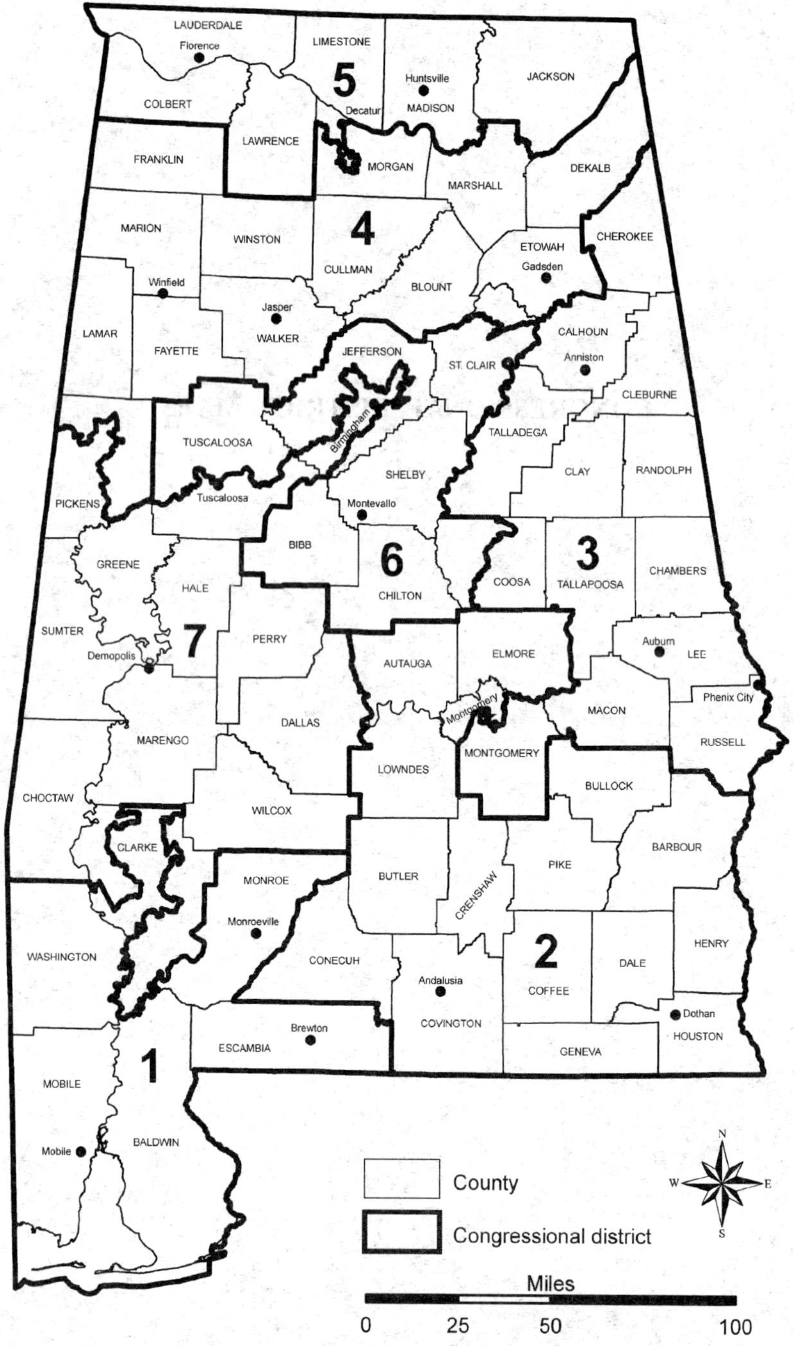

ALASKA—Congressional District—(1 District At Large)

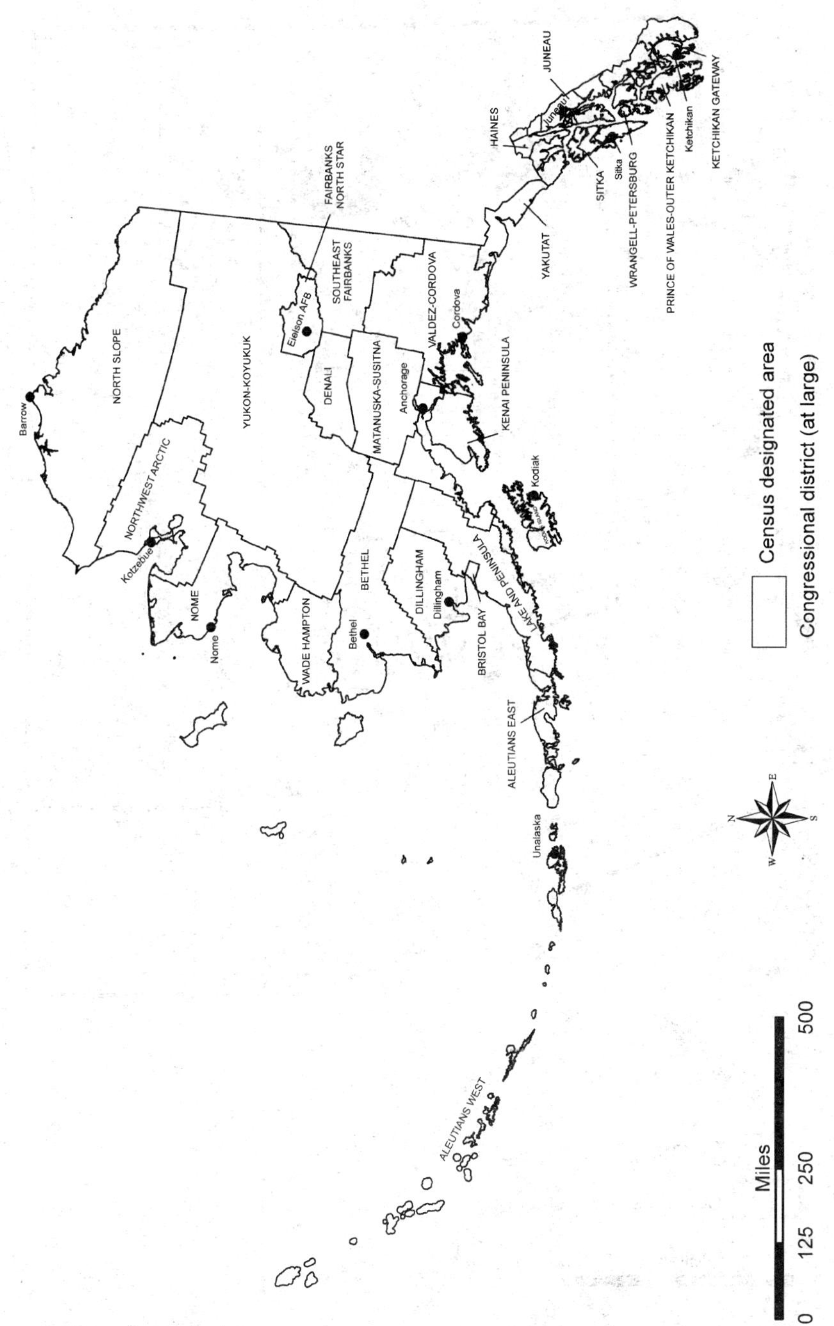

ARIZONA—Congressional Districts—(8 Districts)

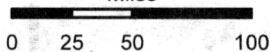

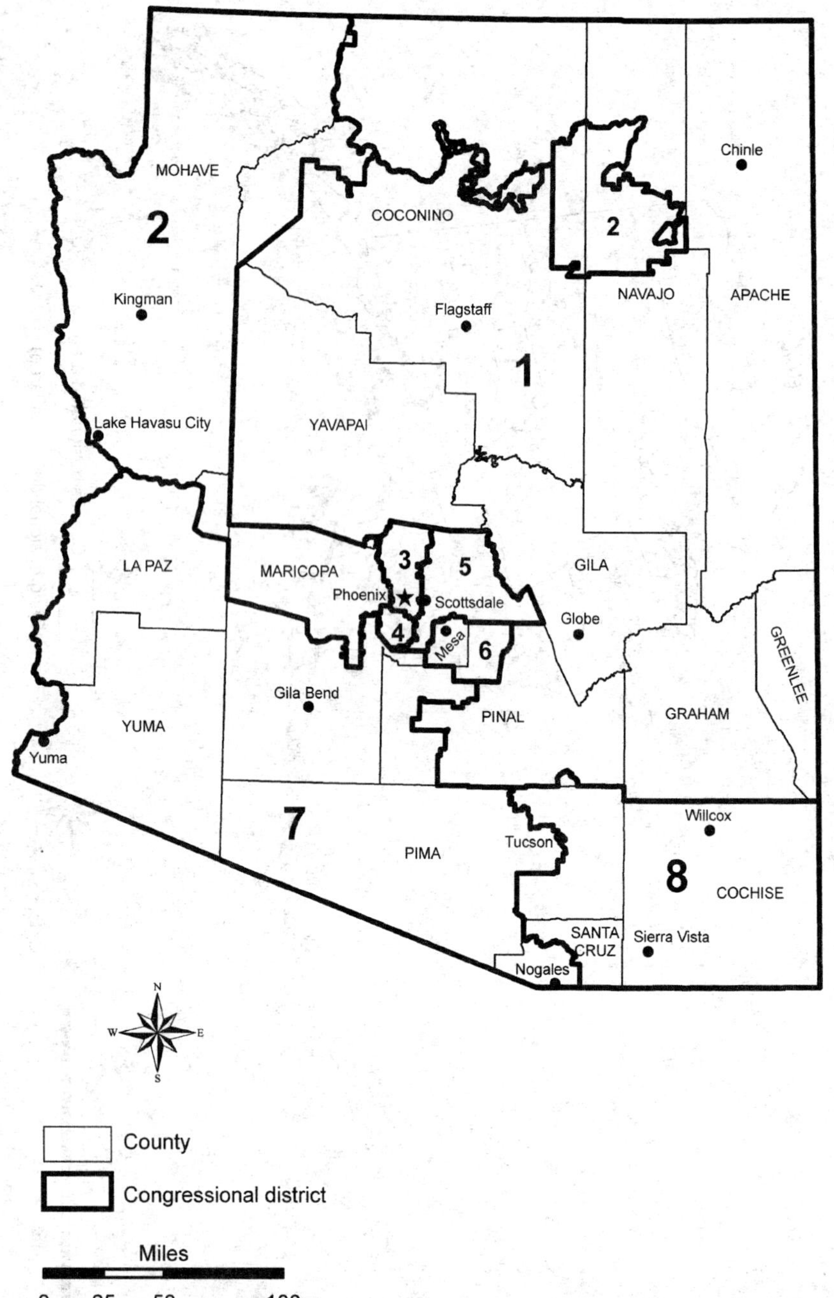

ARKANSAS—Congressional Districts—(4 Districts)

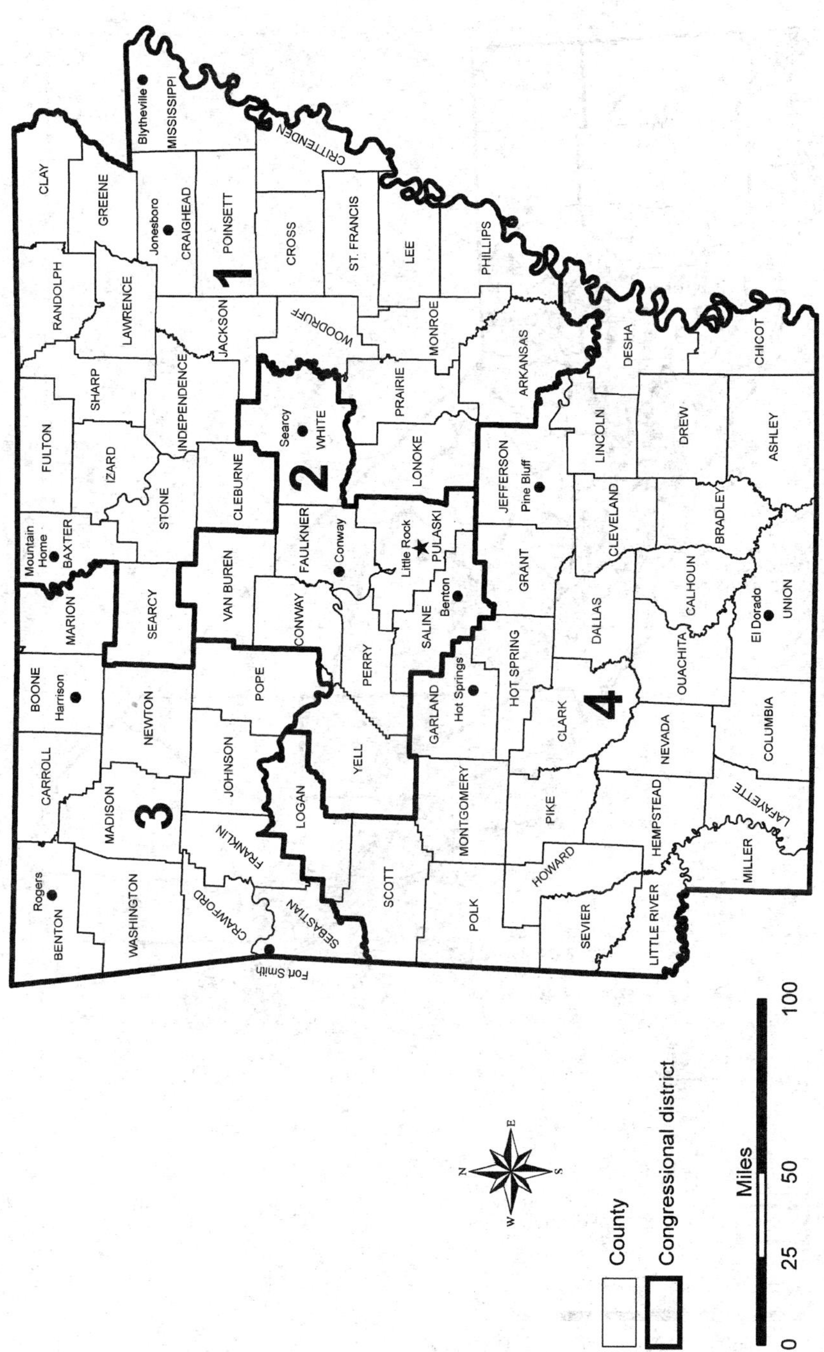

CALIFORNIA—Congressional Districts—(53 Districts)

COLORADO —Congressional Districts—(7 Districts)

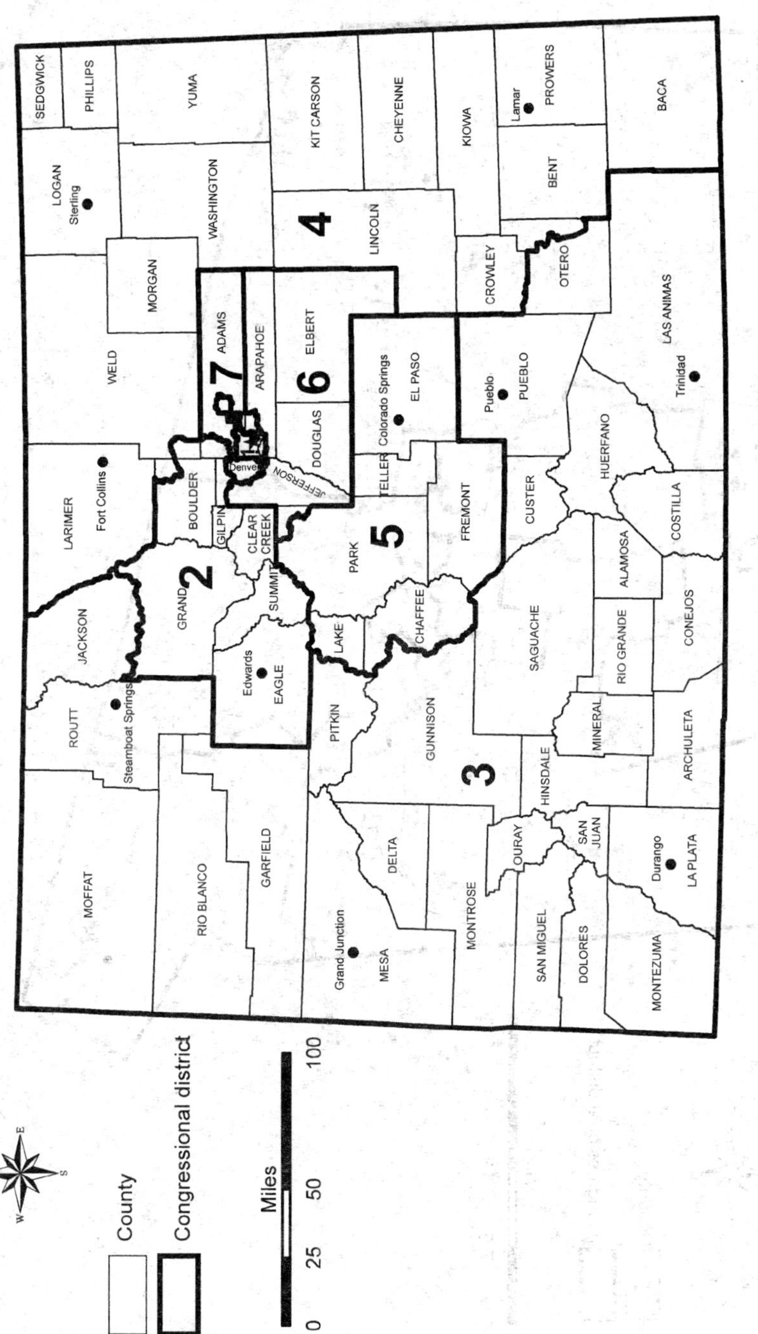

CONNECTICUT—Congressional Districts—(5 Districts)

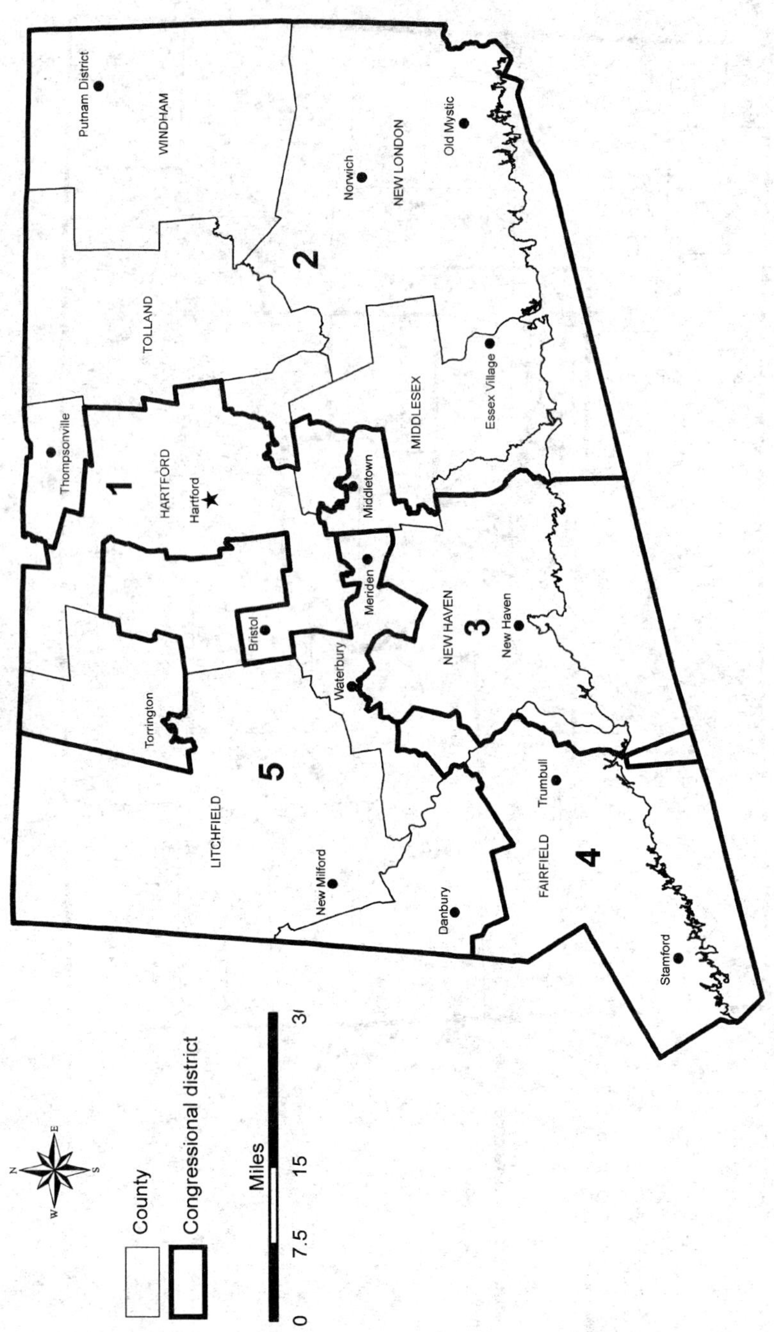

DELAWARE—Congressional District—(1 District At Large)

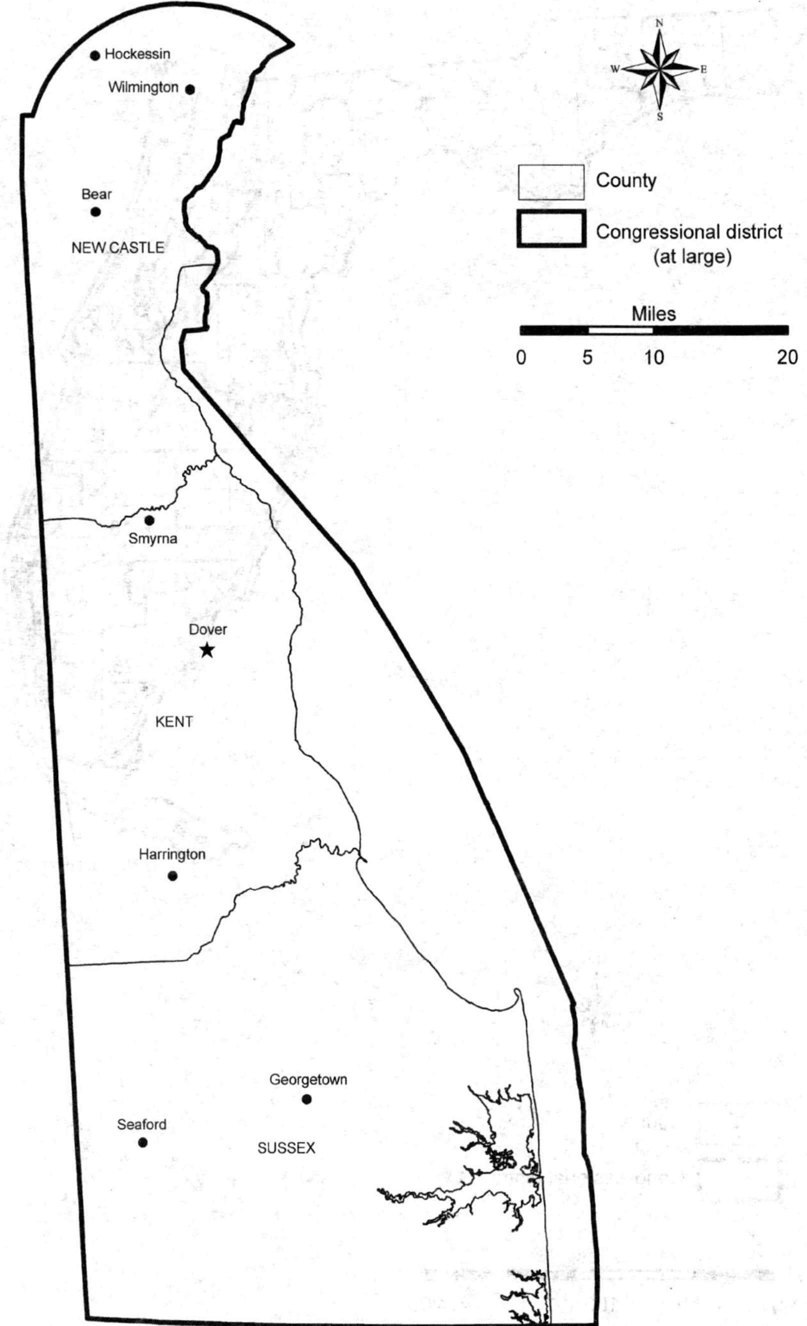

FLORIDA—Congressional Districts—(25 Districts)

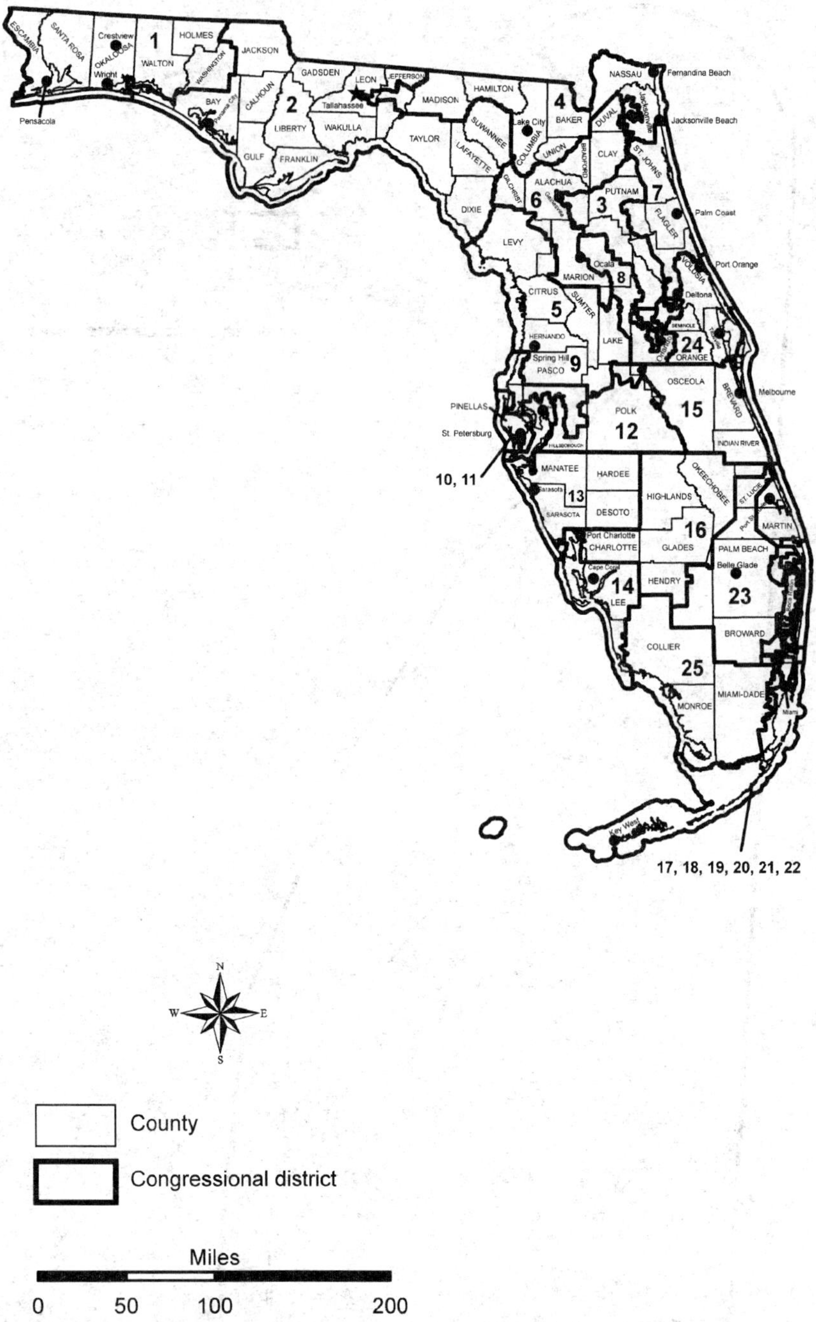

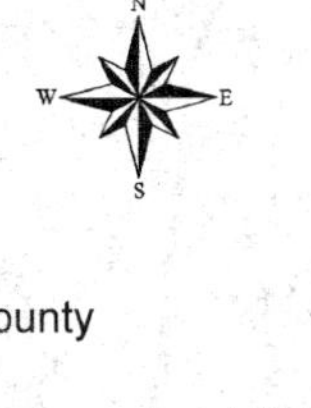

County

Congressional district

Miles

0 50 100 200

GEORGIA—Congressional Districts—(13 Districts)

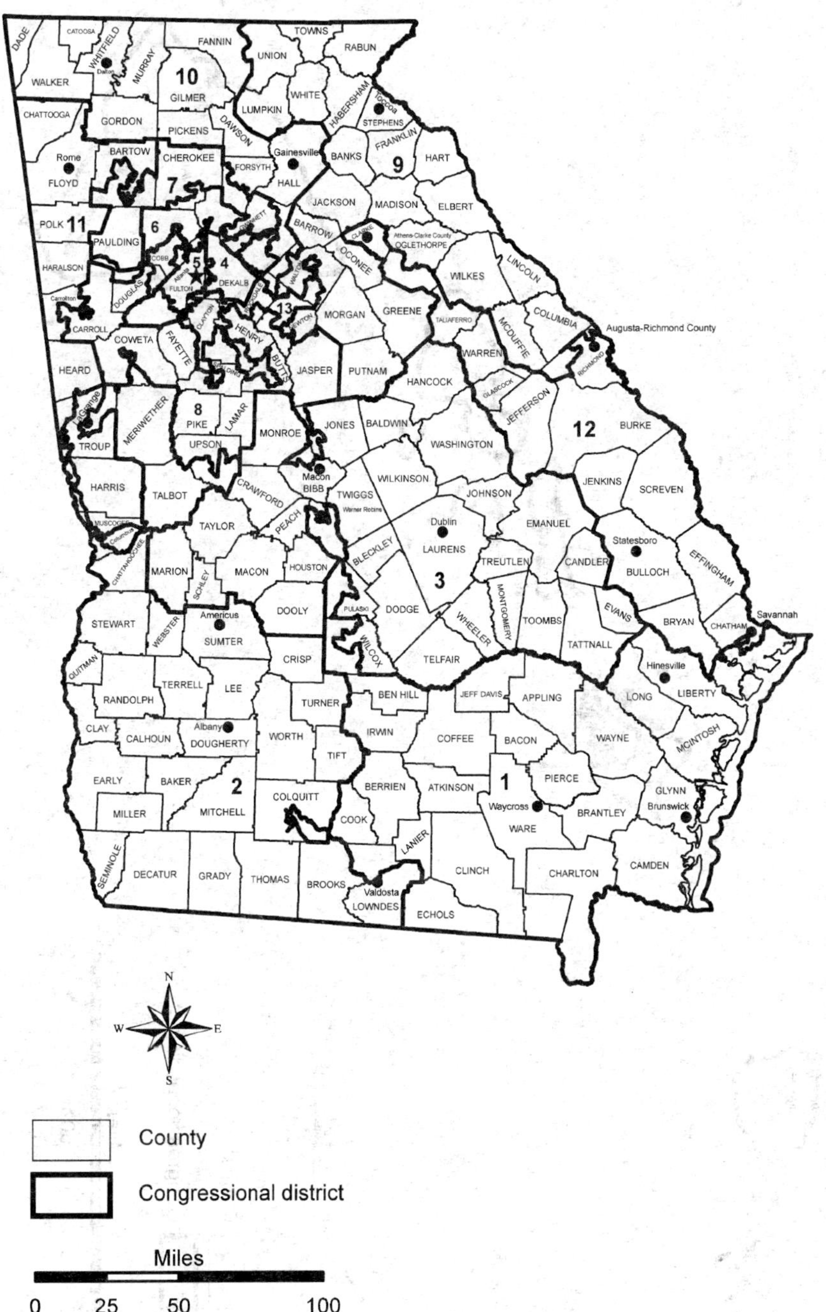

HAWAII—Congressional Districts—(2 Districts)

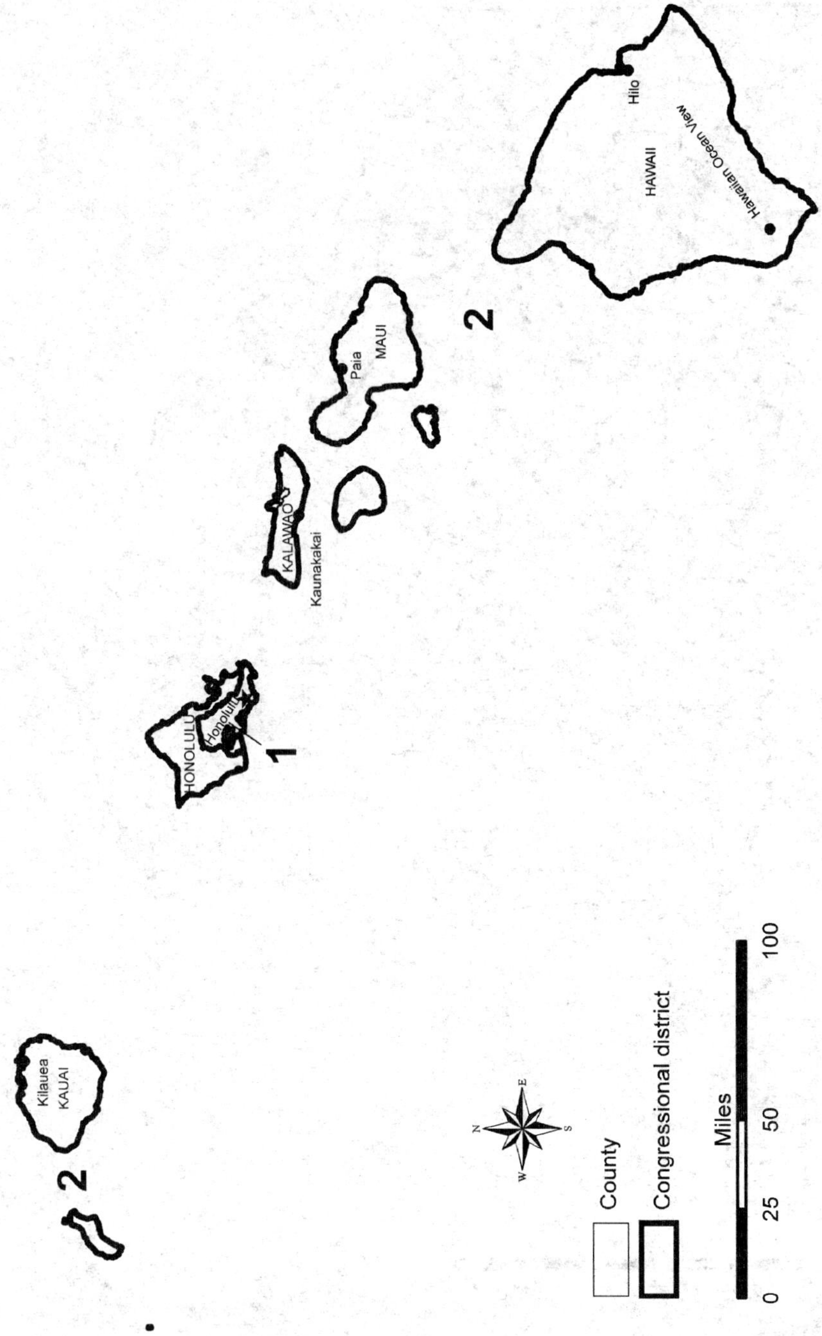

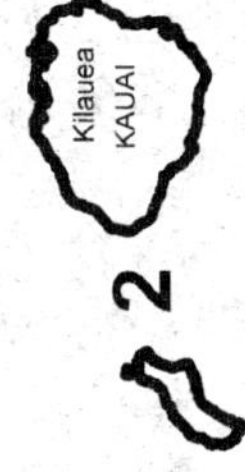

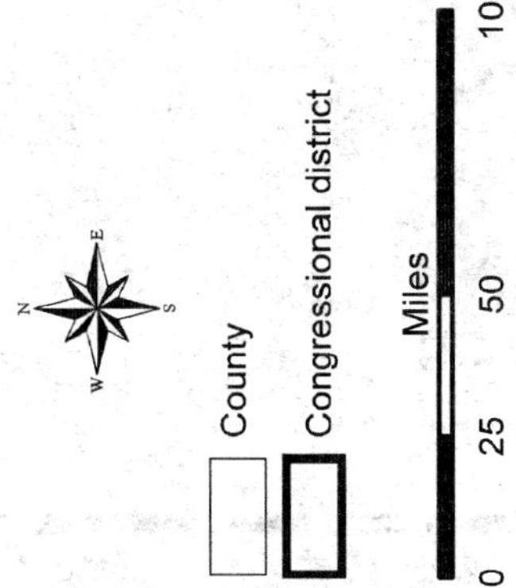

IDAHO—Congressional Districts—(2 Districts)

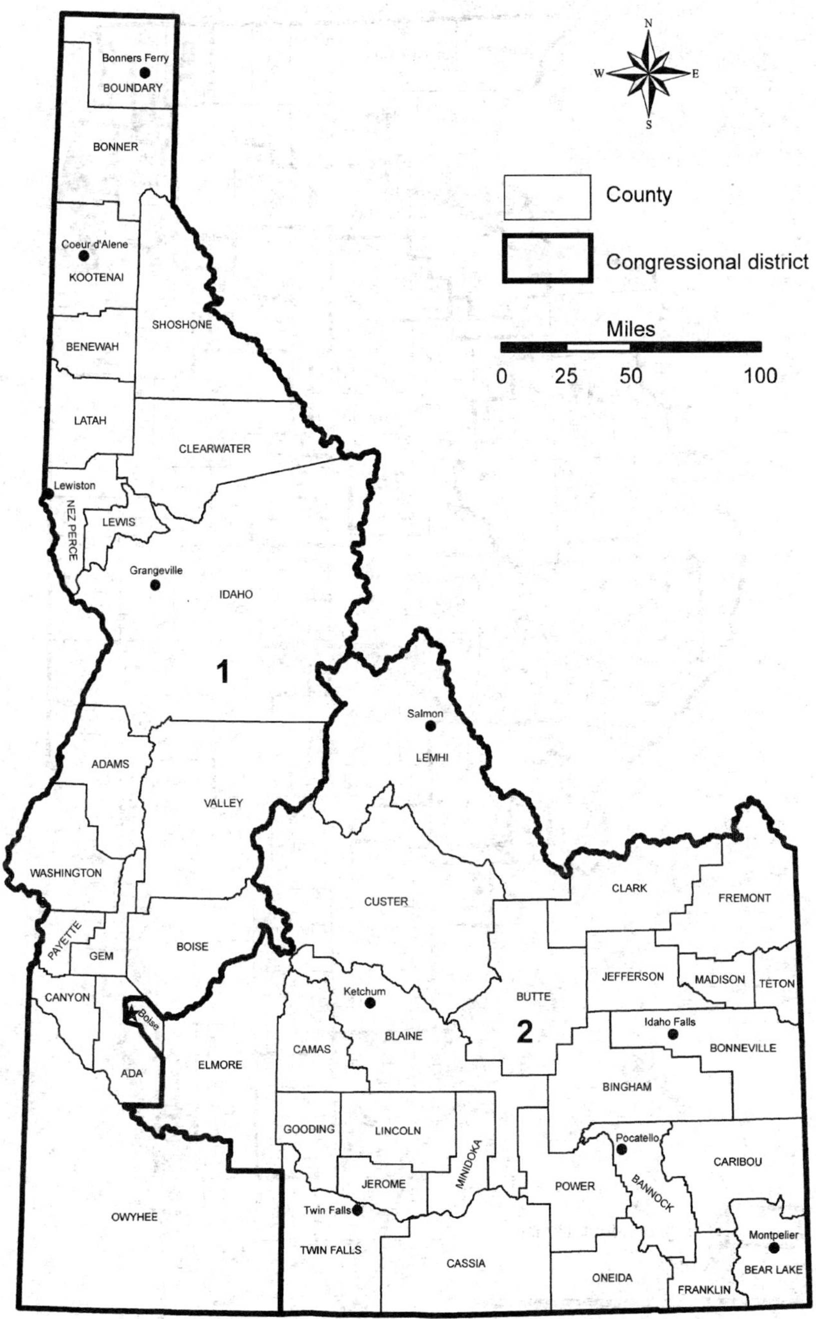

ILLINOIS—Congressional Districts—(19 Districts)

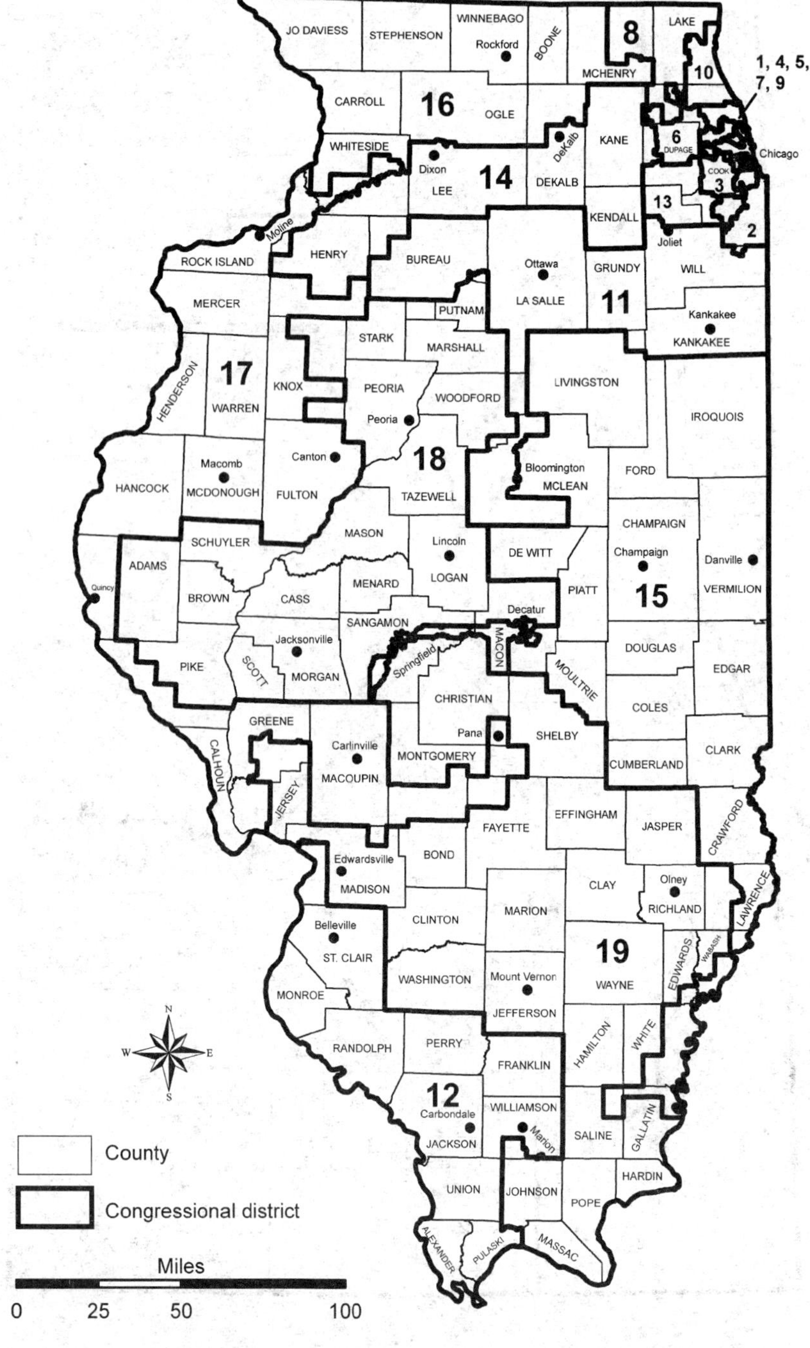

INDIANA—Congressional Districts—(9 Districts)

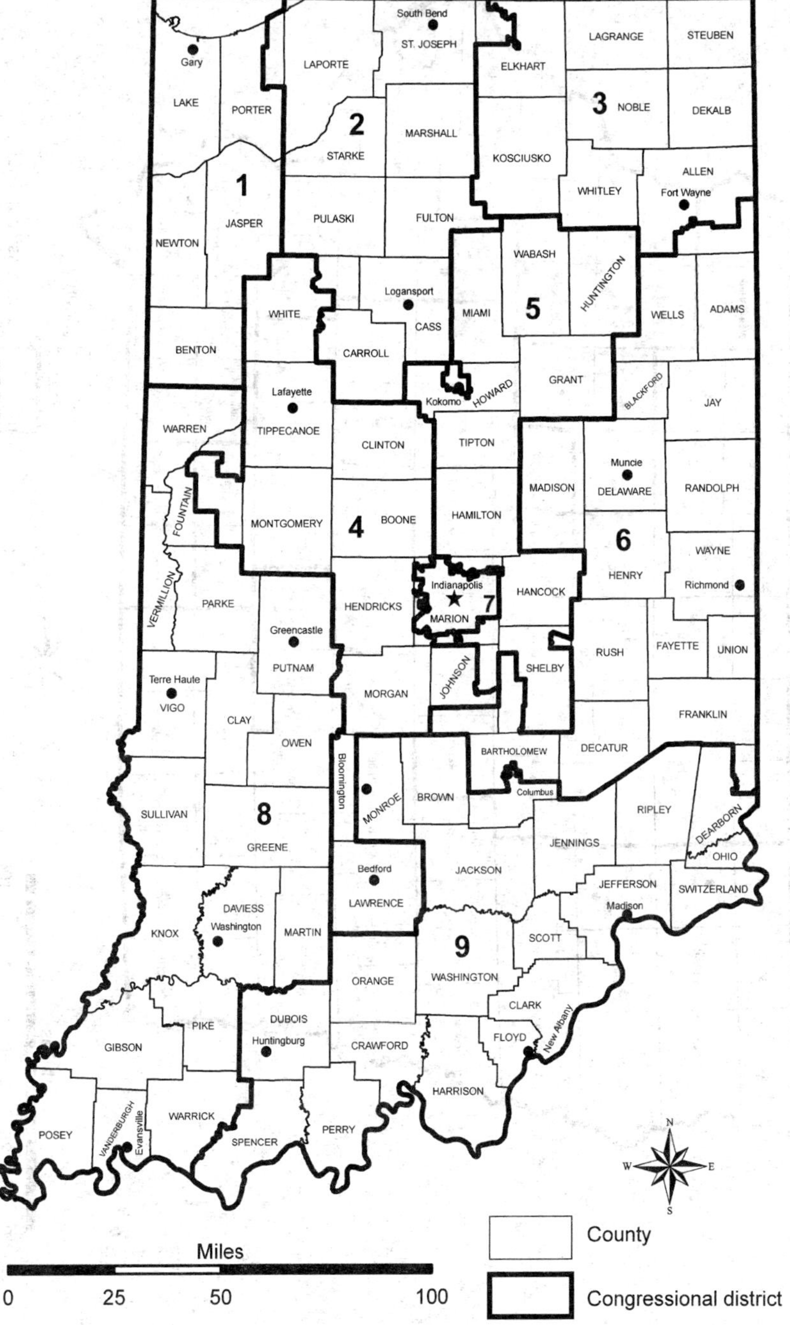

IOWA—Congressional Districts—(5 Districts)

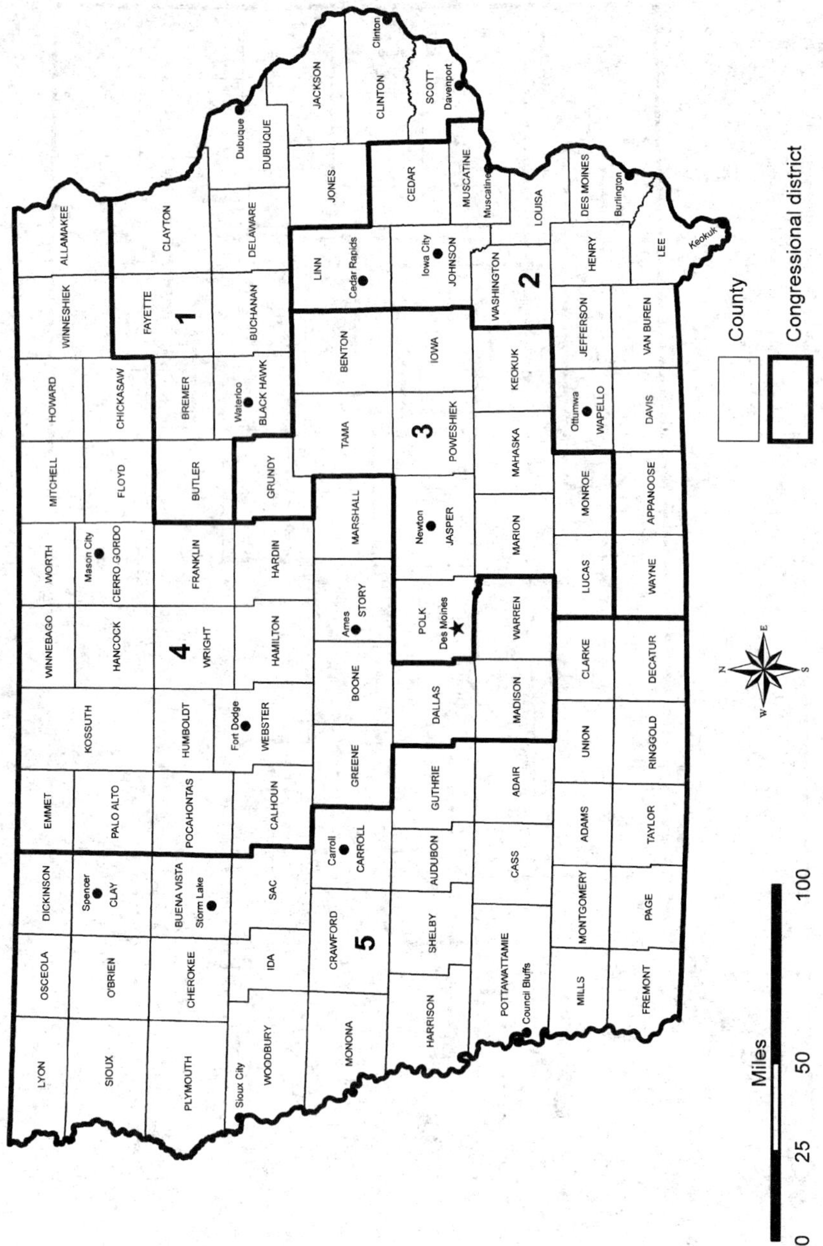

KANSAS—Congressional Districts—(4 Districts)

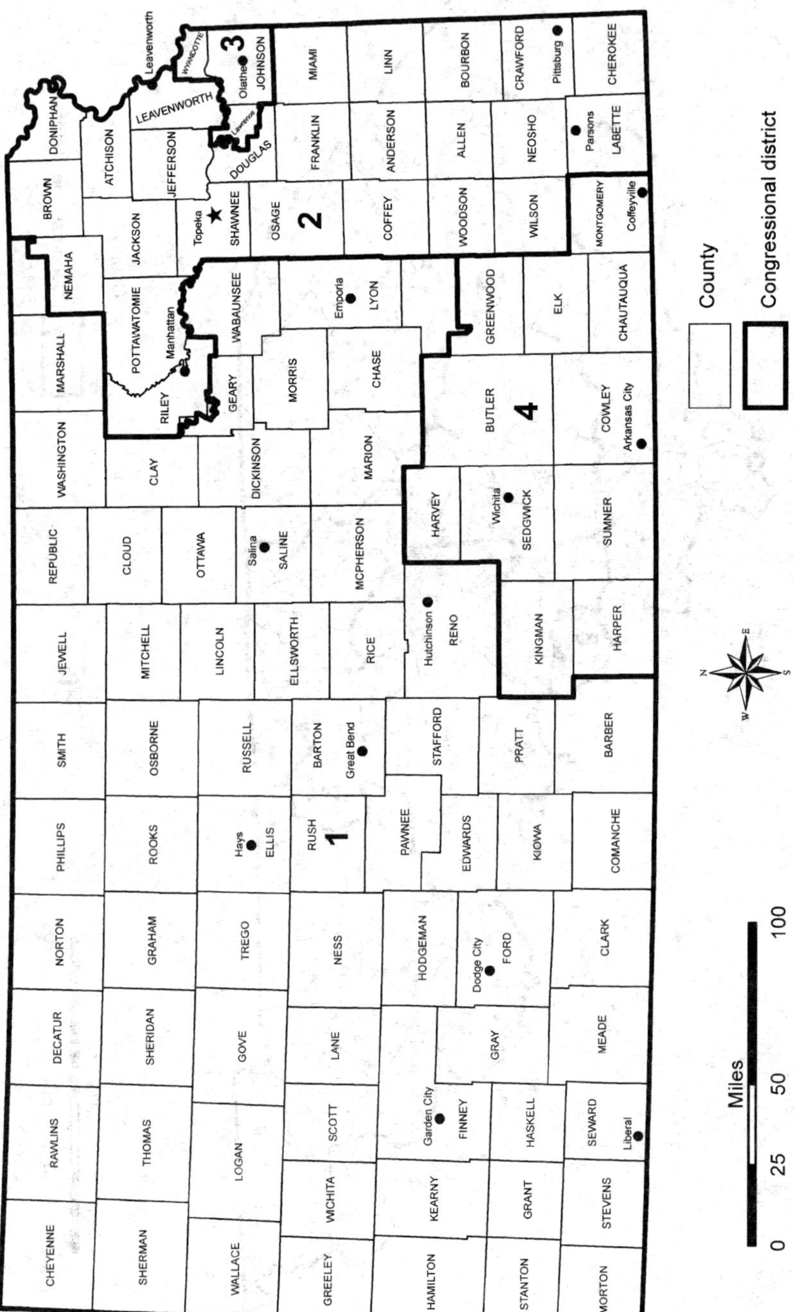

KENTUCKY—Congressional Districts—(6 Districts)

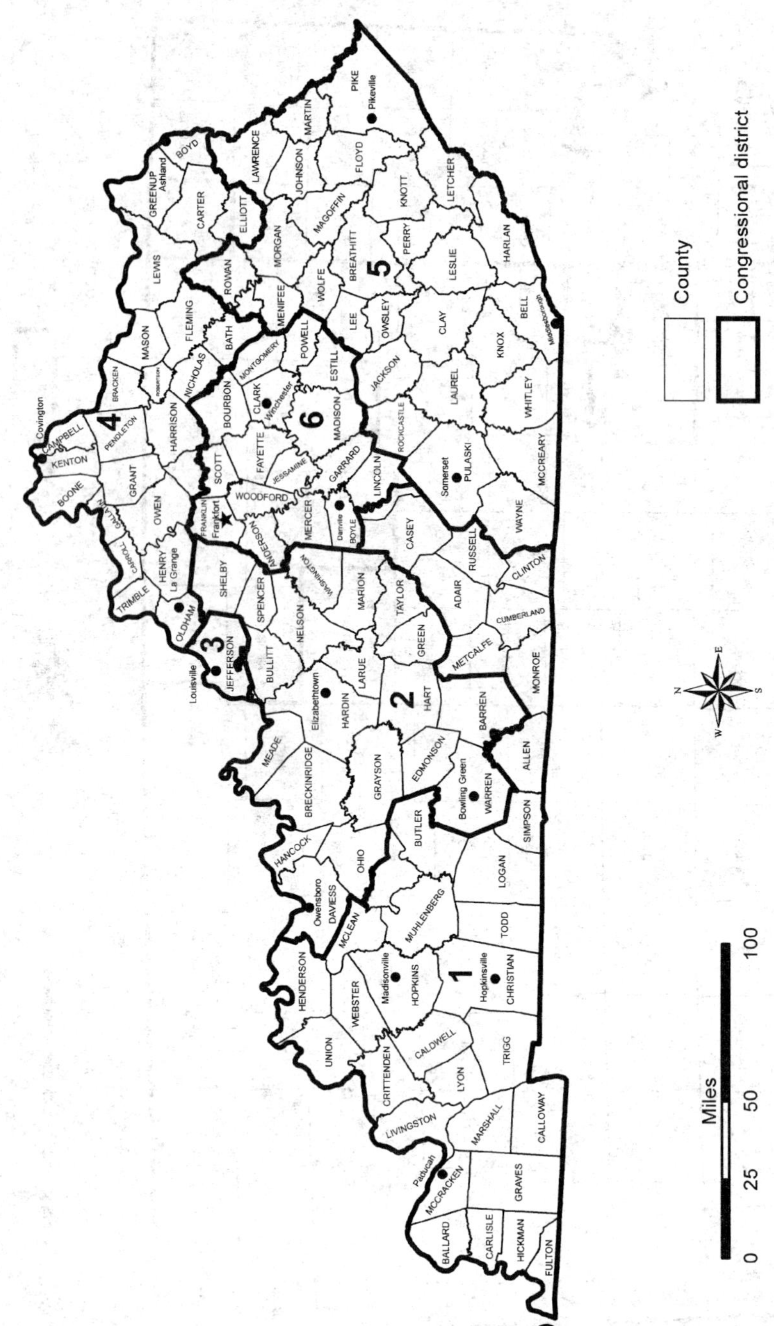

LOUISIANA—Congressional Districts—(7 Districts)

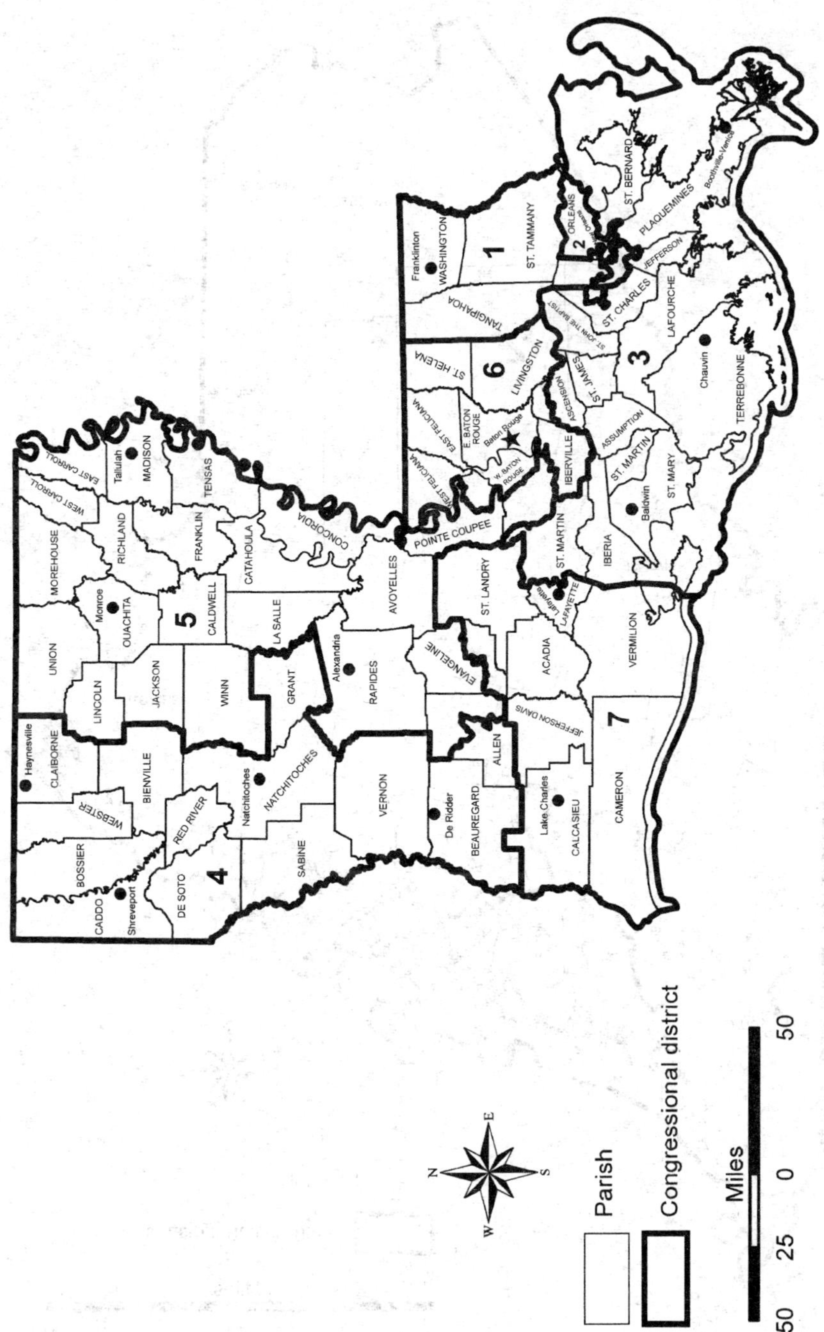

MAINE—Congressional Districts—(2 Districts)

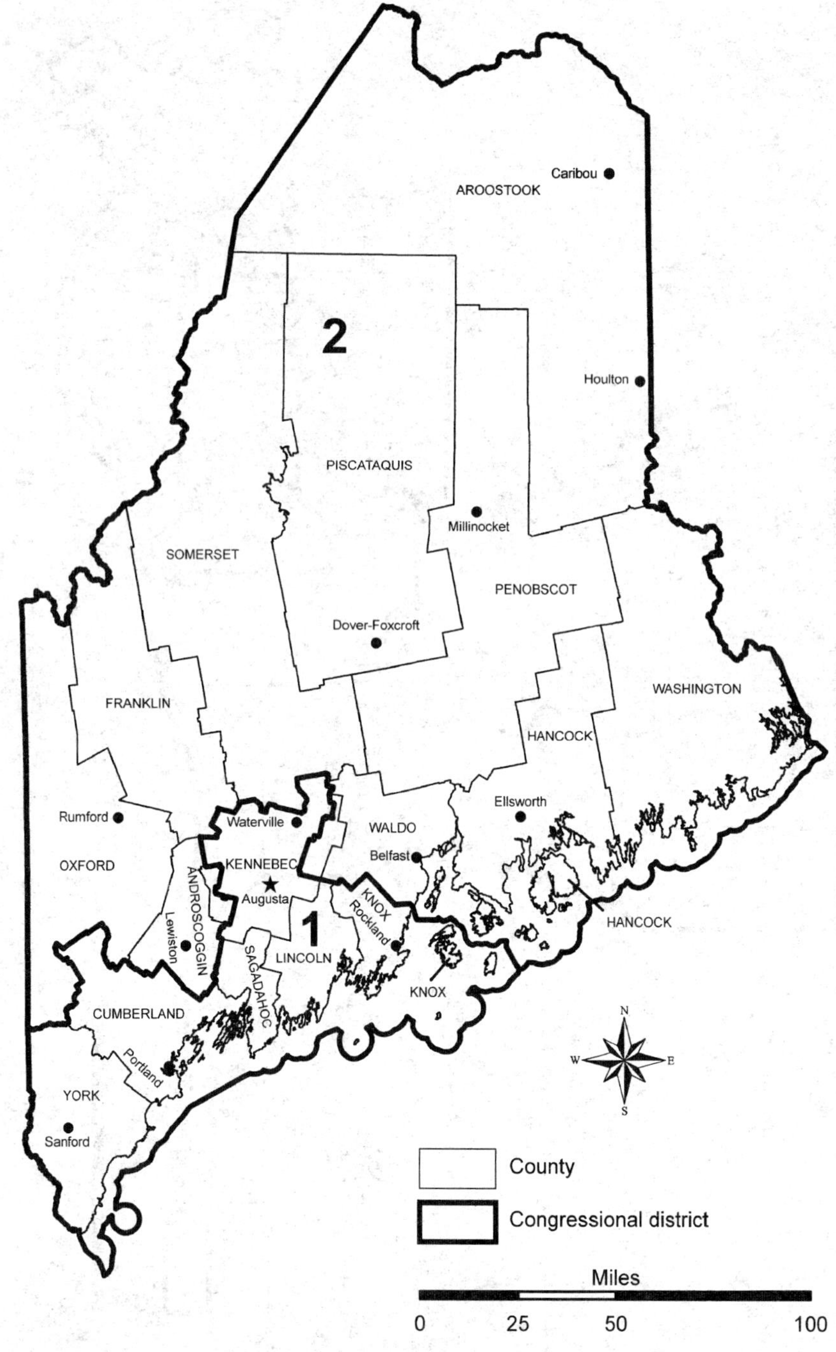

MARYLAND—Congressional Districts—(8 Districts)

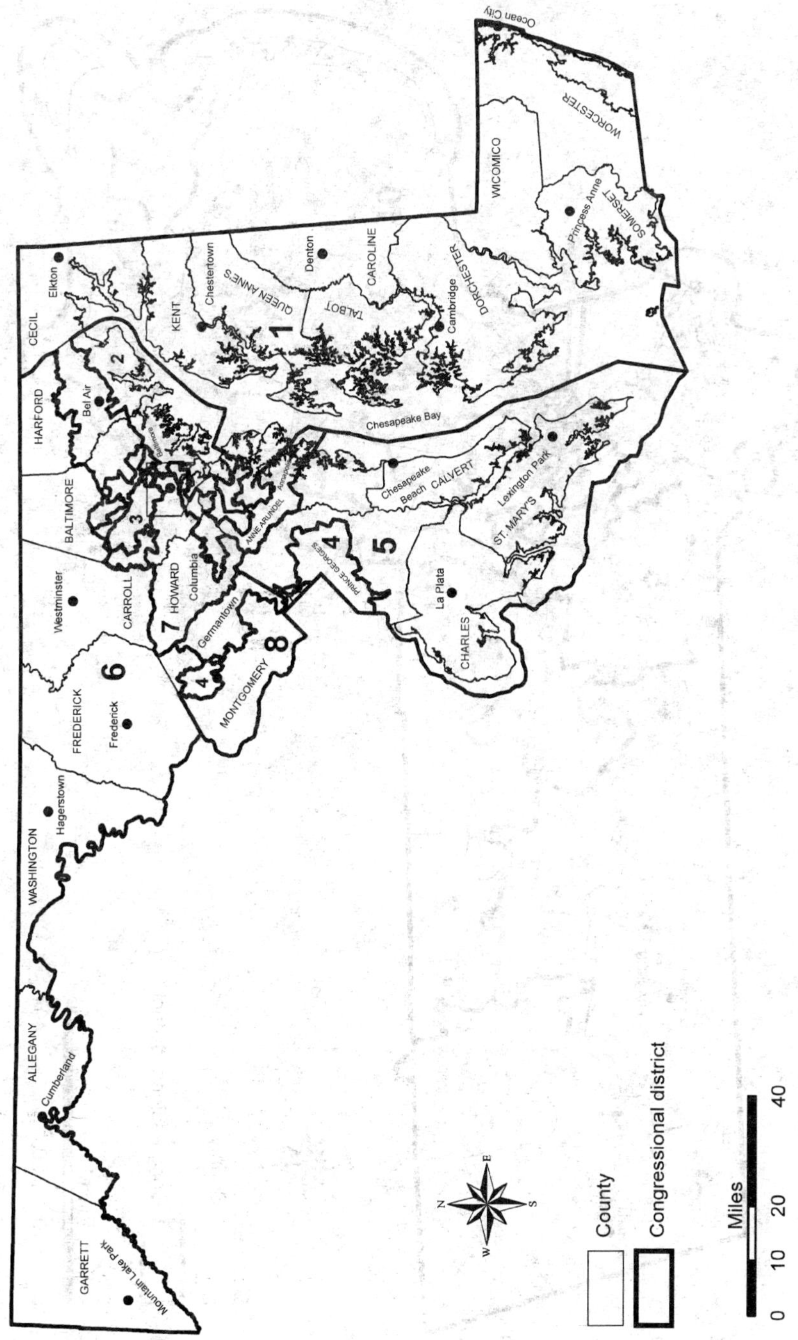

MASSACHUSETTS—Congressional Districts—(10 Districts)

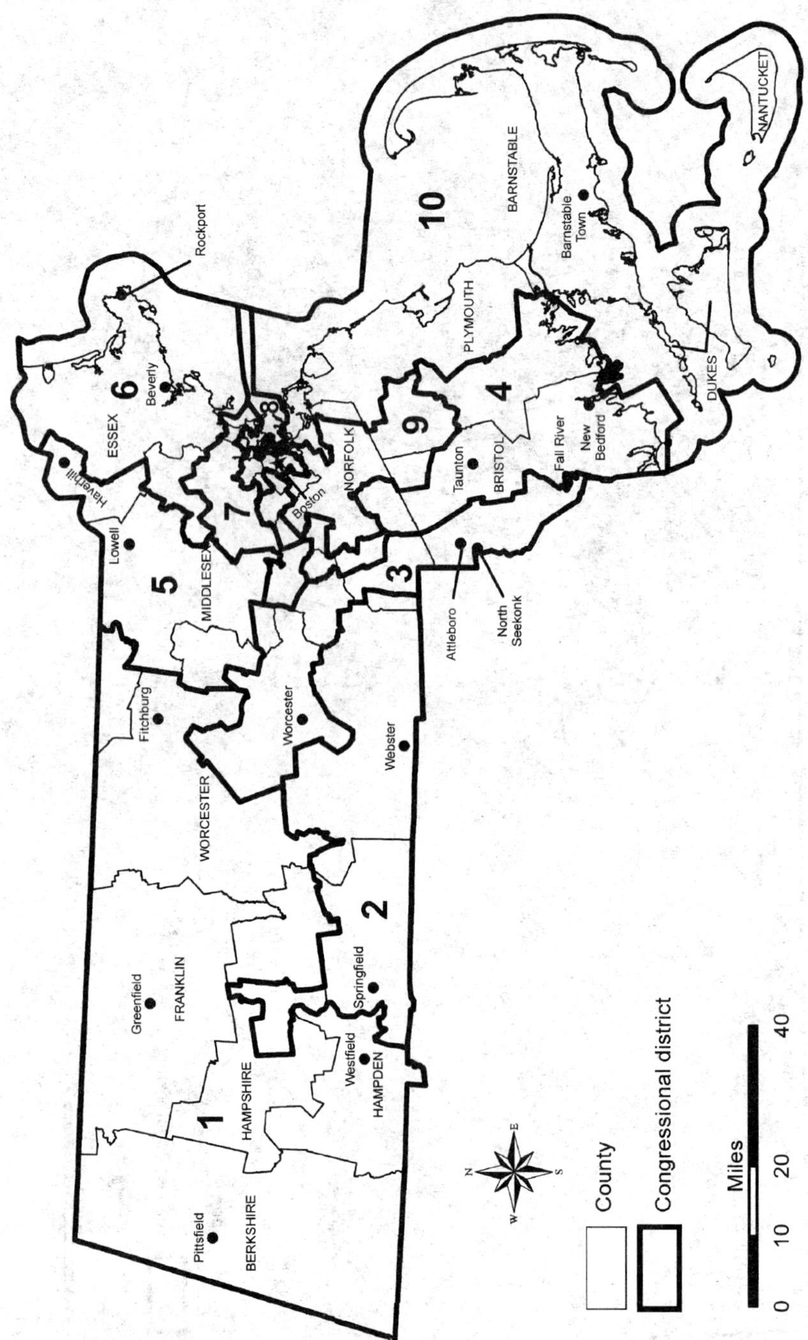

MICHIGAN—Congressional Districts—(15 Districts)

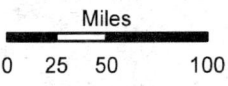

MINNESOTA—Congressional Districts—(8 Districts)

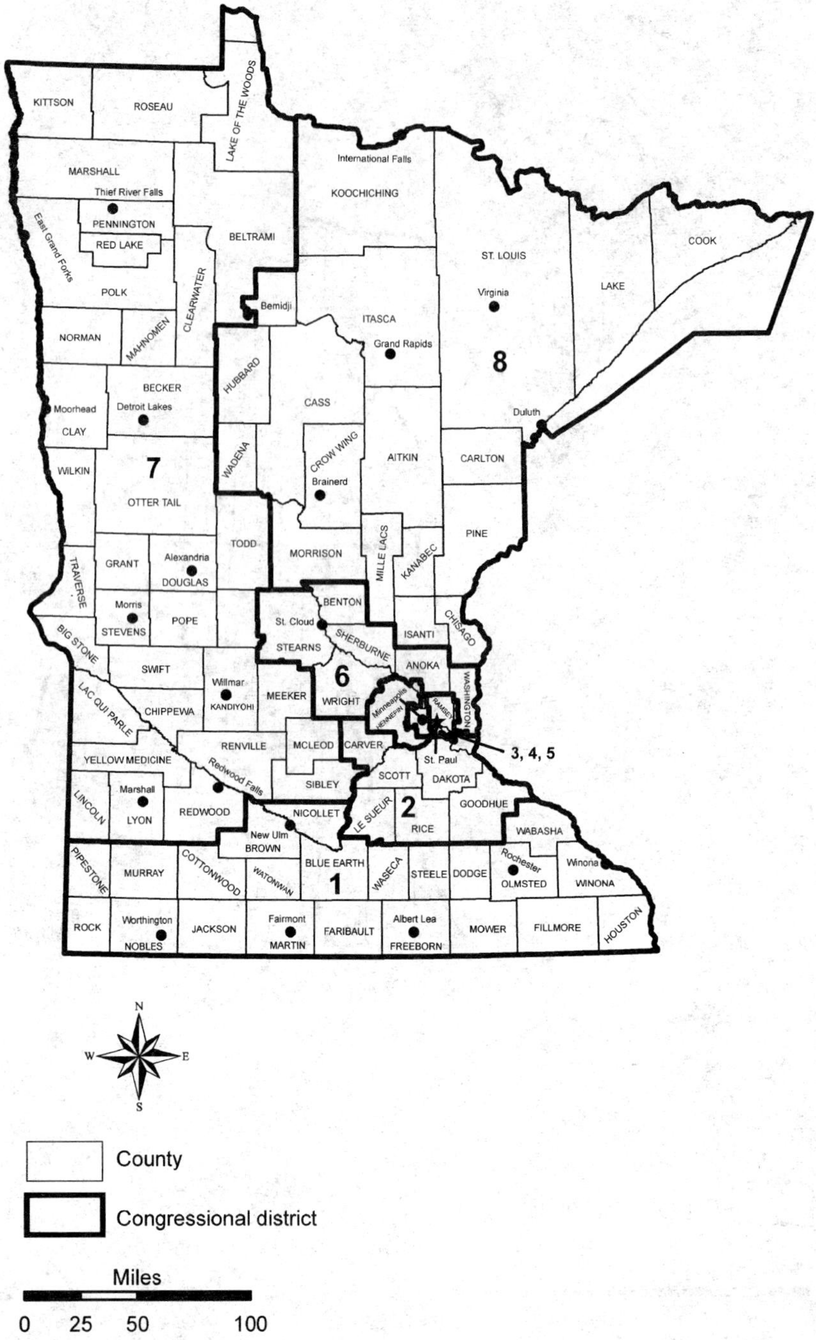

KITTSON
ROSEAU
LAKE OF THE WOODS
MARSHALL
Thief River Falls
PENNINGTON
RED LAKE
East Grand Forks
POLK
BELTRAMI
Bemidji
CLEARWATER
NORMAN
MAHNOMEN
International Falls
KOOCHICHING
ITASCA
Grand Rapids
ST. LOUIS
Virginia
LAKE
COOK
8
Duluth
CARLTON
PINE
AITKIN
CASS
HUBBARD
WADENA
CROW WING
Brainerd
BECKER
Detroit Lakes
Moorhead
CLAY
WILKIN
7
OTTER TAIL
TODD
MORRISON
MILLE LACS
KANABEC
TRAVERSE
GRANT
Alexandria
DOUGLAS
Morris
STEVENS
POPE
BENTON
St. Cloud
STEARNS
SHERBURNE
ISANTI
CHISAGO
ANOKA
WASHINGTON
BIG STONE
SWIFT
Willmar
KANDIYOHI
MEEKER
6
WRIGHT
Minneapolis
HENNEPIN
RAMSEY
St. Paul
3, 4, 5
LAC QUI PARLE
CHIPPEWA
RENVILLE
MCLEOD
CARVER
YELLOW MEDICINE
Redwood Falls
SIBLEY
SCOTT
DAKOTA
LINCOLN
Marshall
LYON
REDWOOD
NICOLLET
LE SUEUR
2
RICE
GOODHUE
WABASHA
New Ulm
BROWN
PIPESTONE
MURRAY
COTTONWOOD
WATONWAN
BLUE EARTH
1
WASECA
STEELE
DODGE
Rochester
OLMSTED
Winona
WINONA
ROCK
Worthington
NOBLES
JACKSON
Fairmont
MARTIN
FARIBAULT
Albert Lea
FREEBORN
MOWER
FILLMORE
HOUSTON

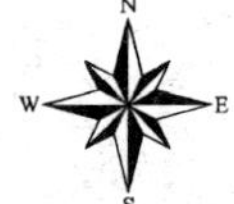

County

Congressional district

Miles

0 25 50 100

MISSISSIPPI—Congressional Districts—(4 Districts)

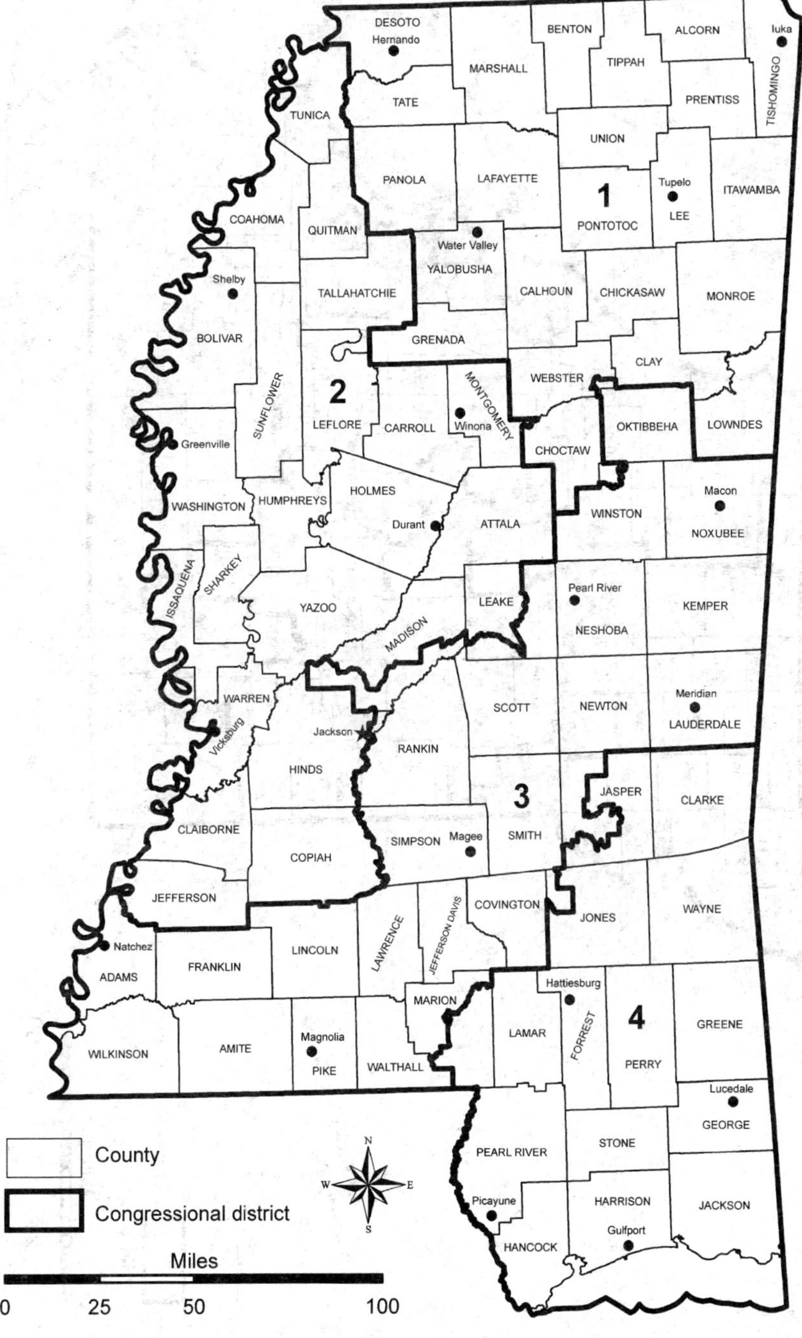

MISSOURI—Congressional Districts—(9 Districts)

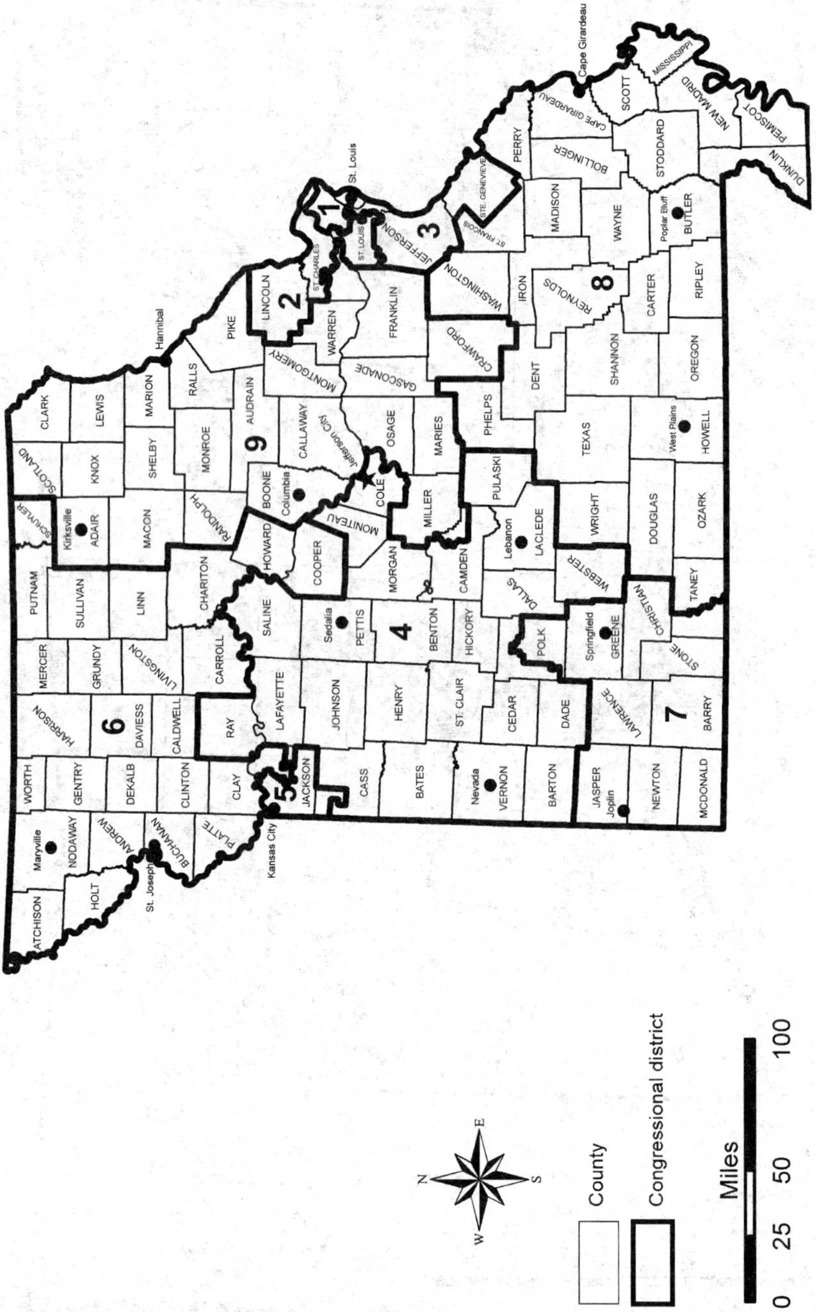

CLARK LEWIS MARION Hannibal RALLS PIKE LINCOLN St. Louis ST. CHARLES ST. LOUIS 1 2 3 JEFFERSON STE. GENEVIEVE PERRY Cape Girardeau CAPE GIRARDEAU SCOTT MISSISSIPPI NEW MADRID PEMISCOT DUNKLIN STODDARD BOLLINGER MADISON ST. FRANCOIS WAYNE BUTLER Poplar Bluff 8 REYNOLDS IRON WASHINGTON FRANKLIN WARREN MONTGOMERY GASCONADE CRAWFORD DENT SHANNON CARTER RIPLEY OREGON HOWELL West Plains TEXAS PHELPS MARIES OSAGE CALLAWAY AUDRAIN 9 MONROE SHELBY KNOX SCOTLAND SCHUYLER ADAIR Kirksville MACON RANDOLPH BOONE Columbia Jefferson City COLE MONITEAU MILLER PULASKI LACLEDE Lebanon WRIGHT DOUGLAS OZARK TANEY WEBSTER CHRISTIAN STONE GREENE Springfield POLK DALLAS CAMDEN MORGAN COOPER HOWARD CHARITON LINN SULLIVAN PUTNAM MERCER GRUNDY LIVINGSTON CARROLL SALINE PETTIS Sedalia 4 BENTON HICKORY CEDAR DADE LAWRENCE 7 BARRY ST. CLAIR HENRY JOHNSON LAFAYETTE RAY CALDWELL DAVIESS 6 HARRISON WORTH GENTRY DEKALB CLINTON CLAY 5 JACKSON CASS BATES VERNON Nevada BARTON JASPER Joplin NEWTON MCDONALD Kansas City PLATTE BUCHANAN St. Joseph ANDREW NODAWAY Maryville HOLT ATCHISON

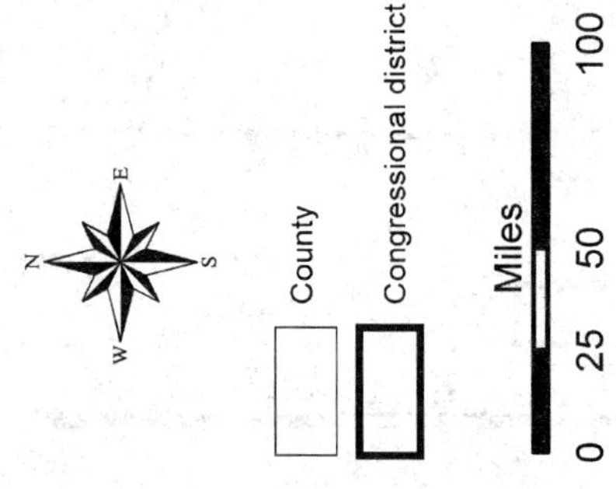

MONTANA—Congressional District—(1 District At Large)

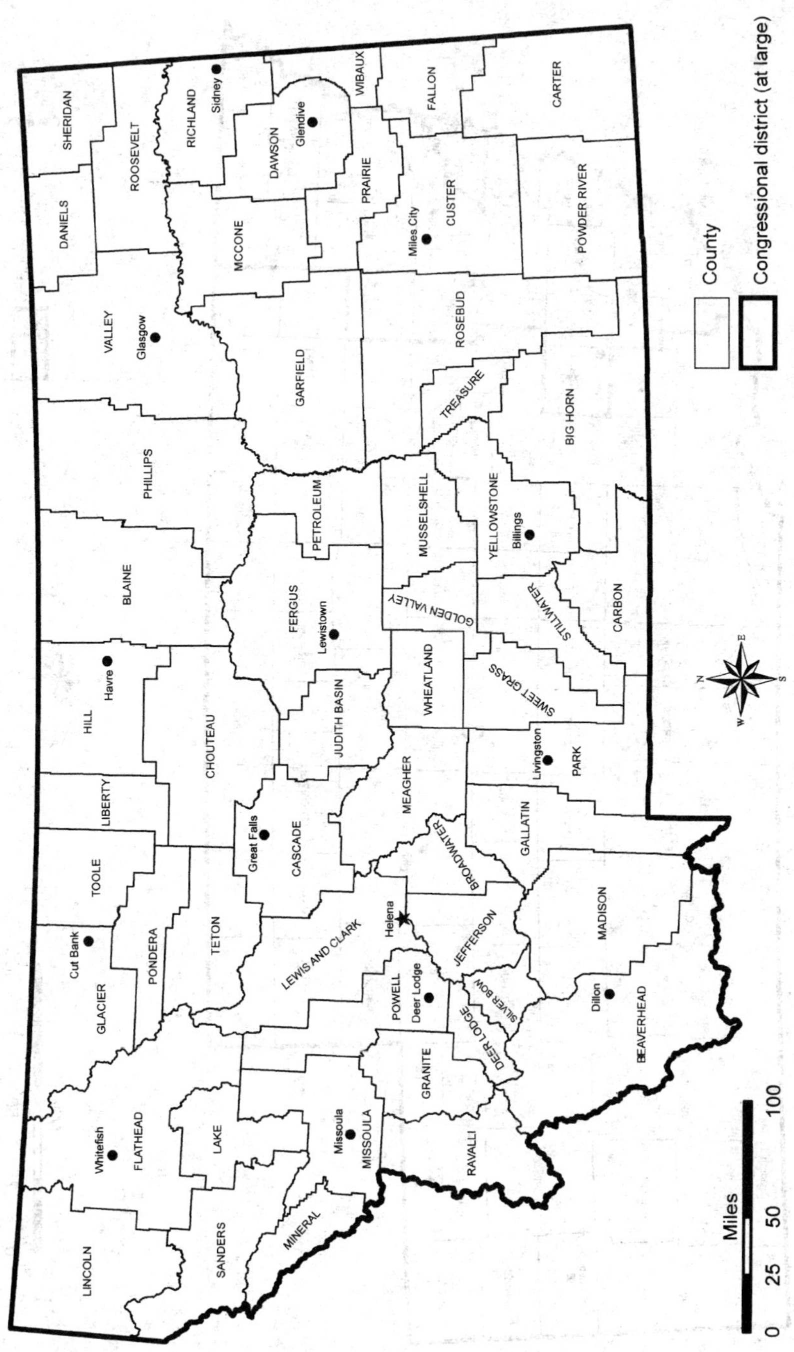

NEBRASKA—Congressional Districts—(3 Districts)

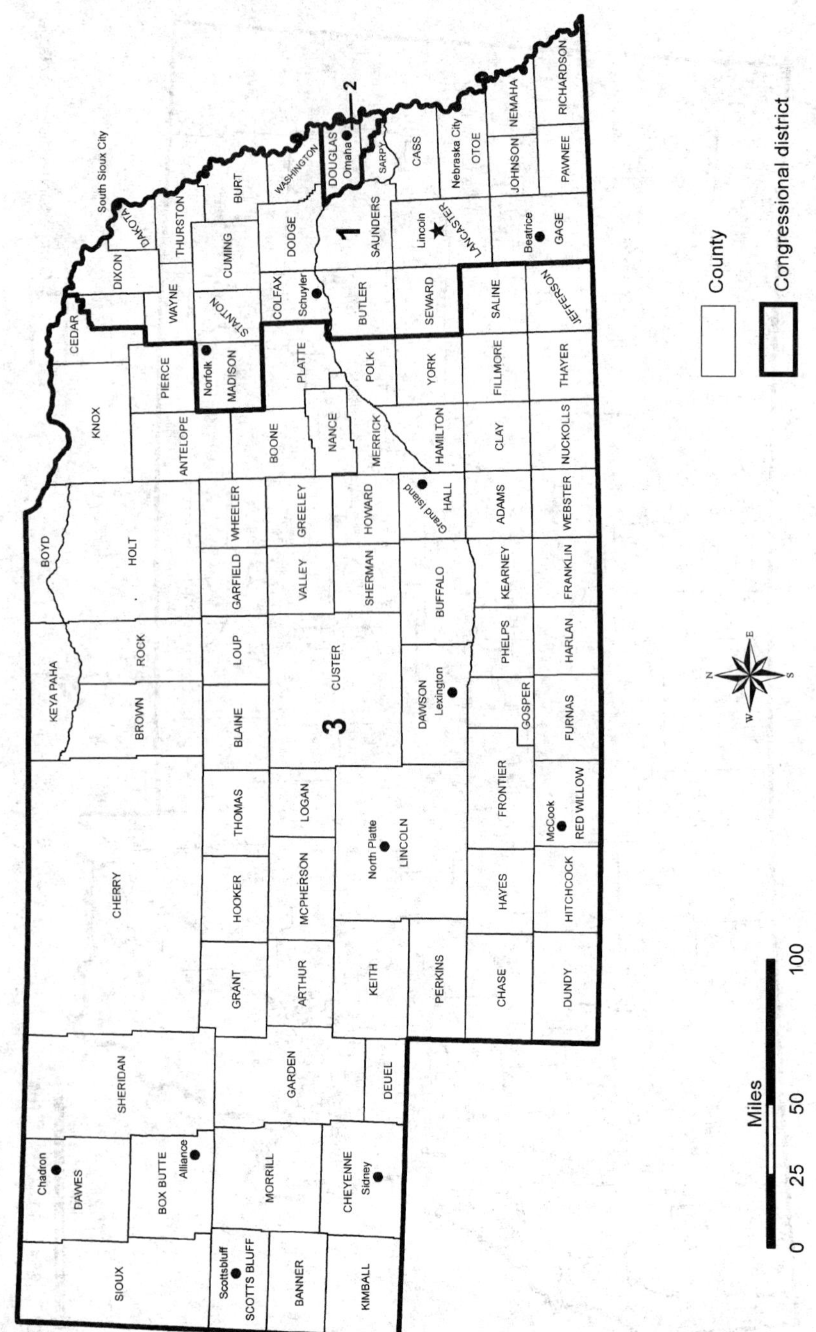

NEVADA—Congressional Districts—(3 Districts)

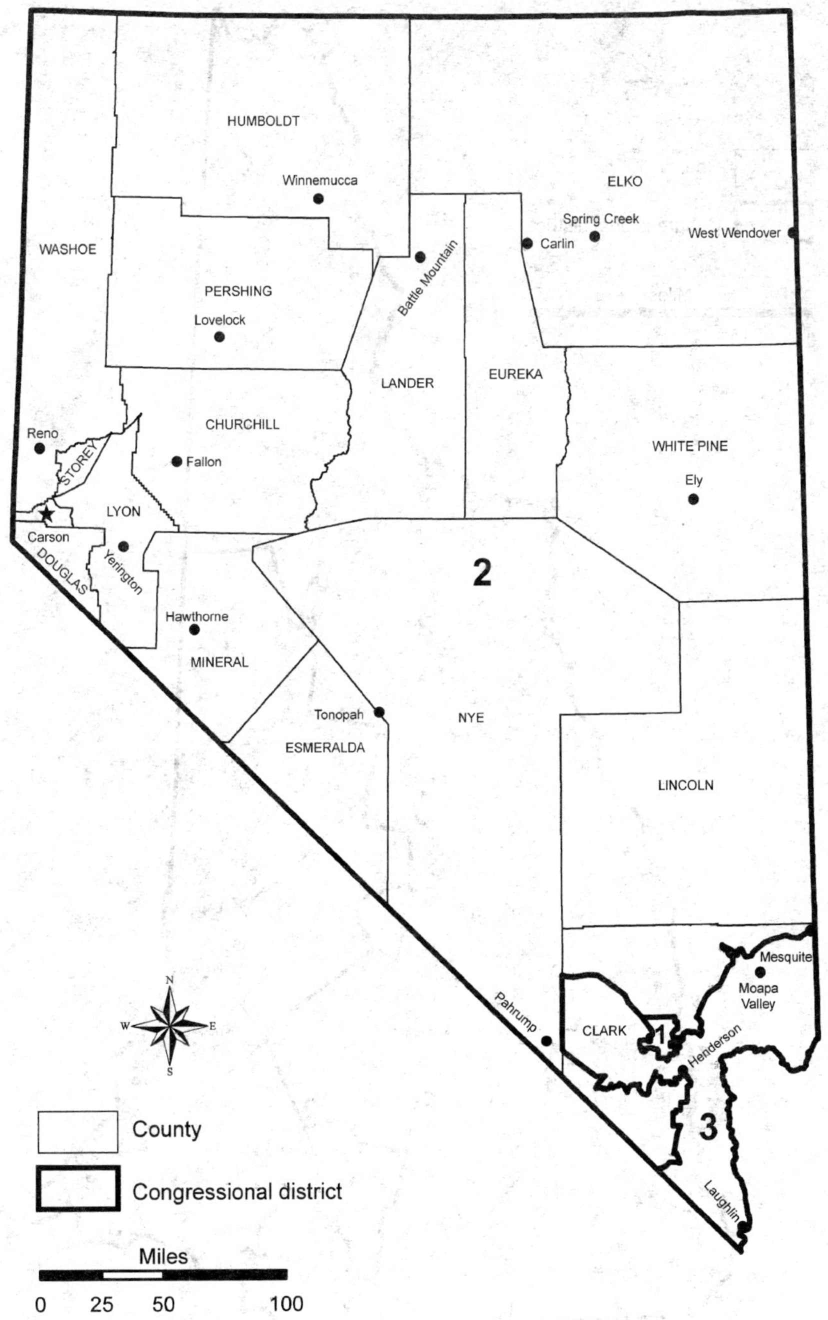

NEW HAMPSHIRE—Congressional Districts—(2 Districts)

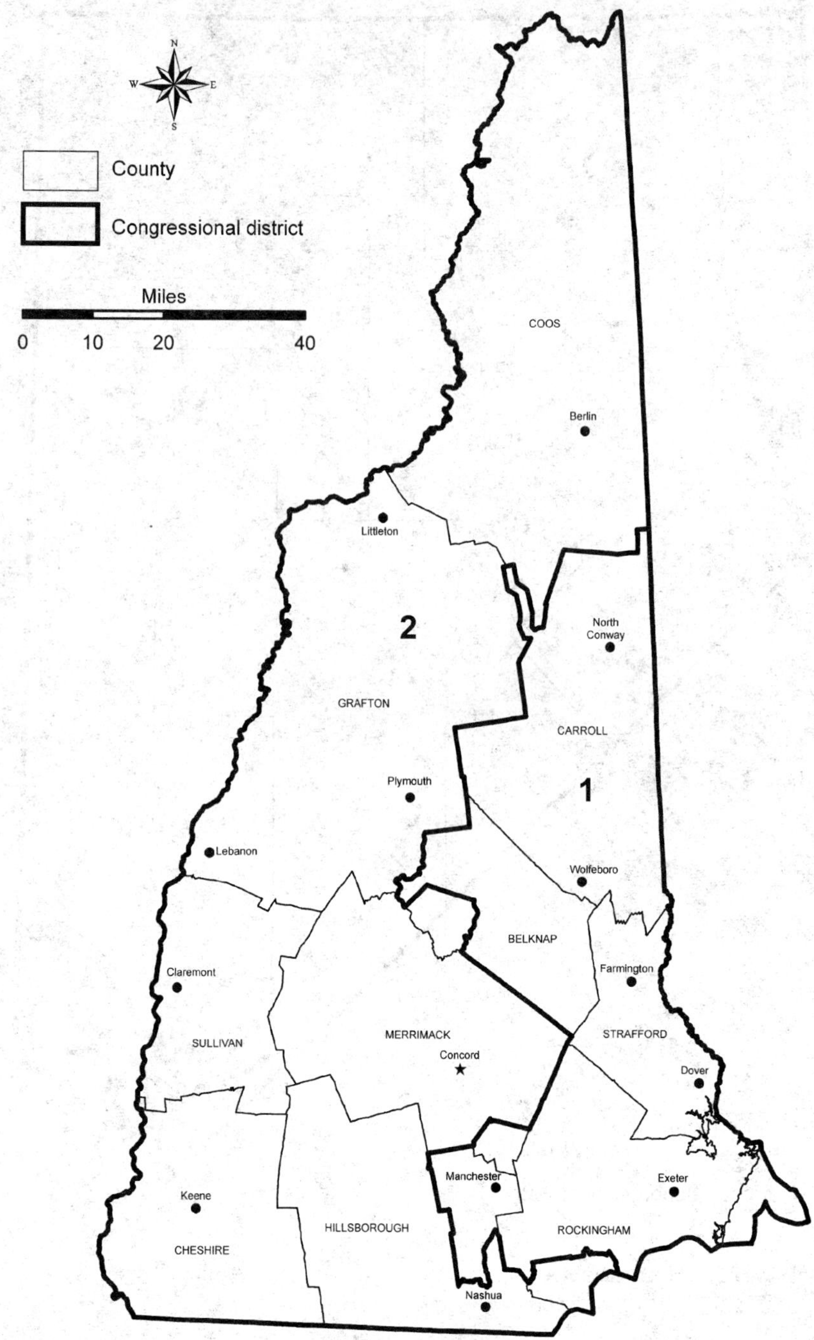

NEW JERSEY—Congressional Districts—(13 Districts)

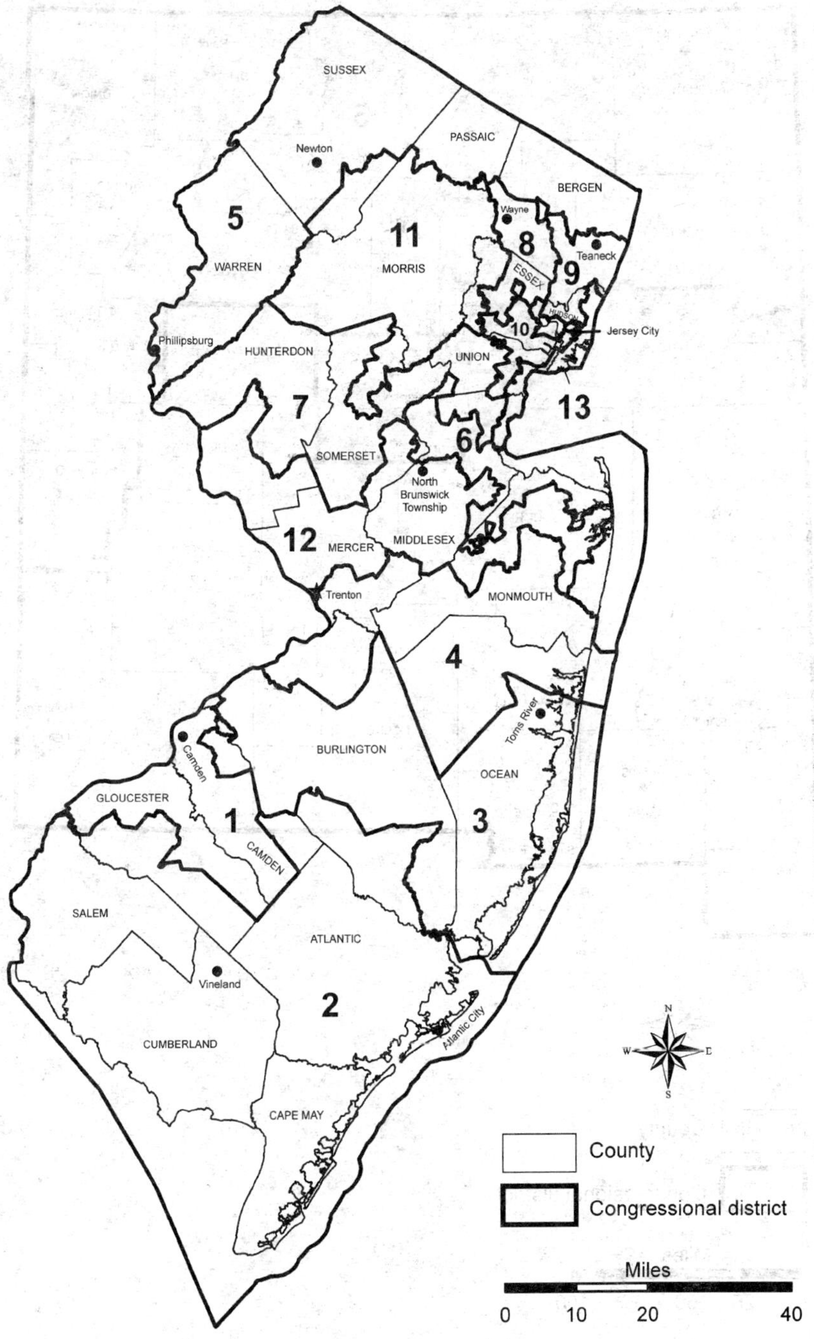

NEW MEXICO—Congressional Districts—(3 Districts)

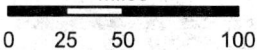

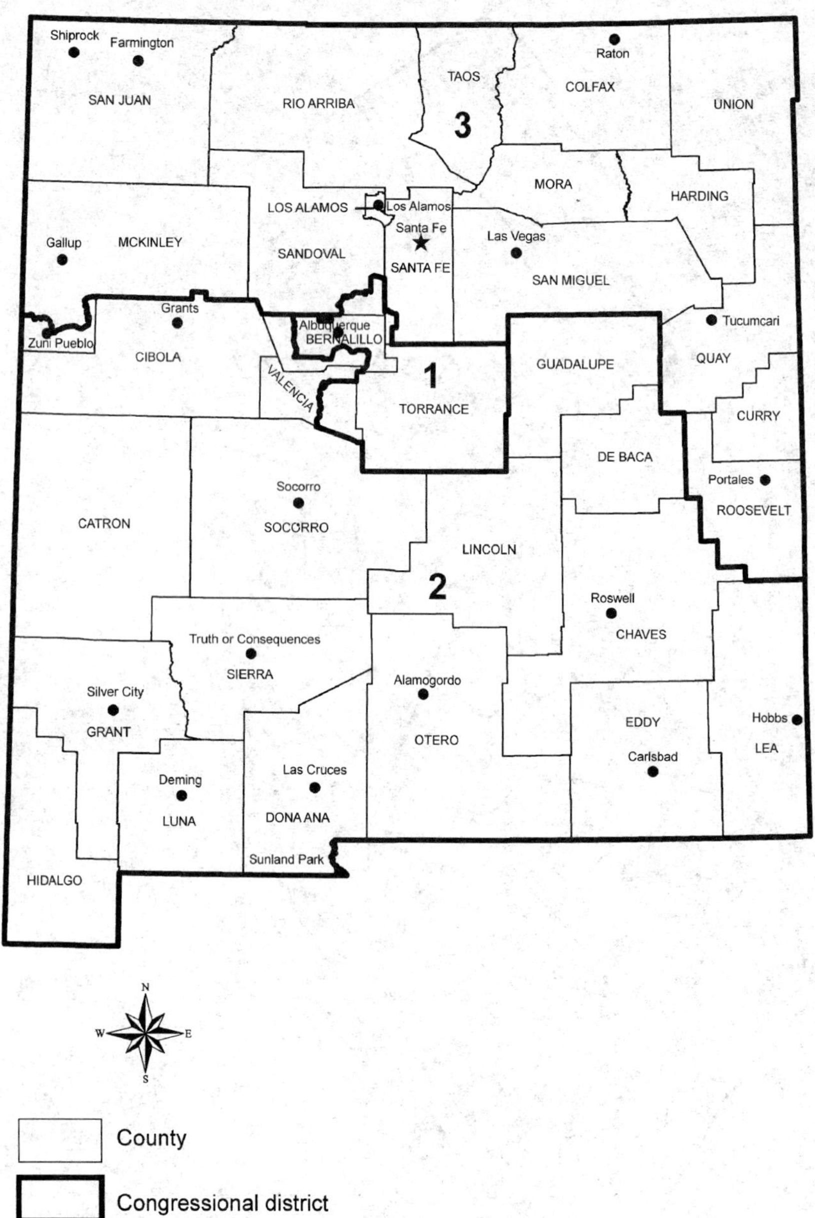

NEW YORK—Congressional Districts—(29 Districts)

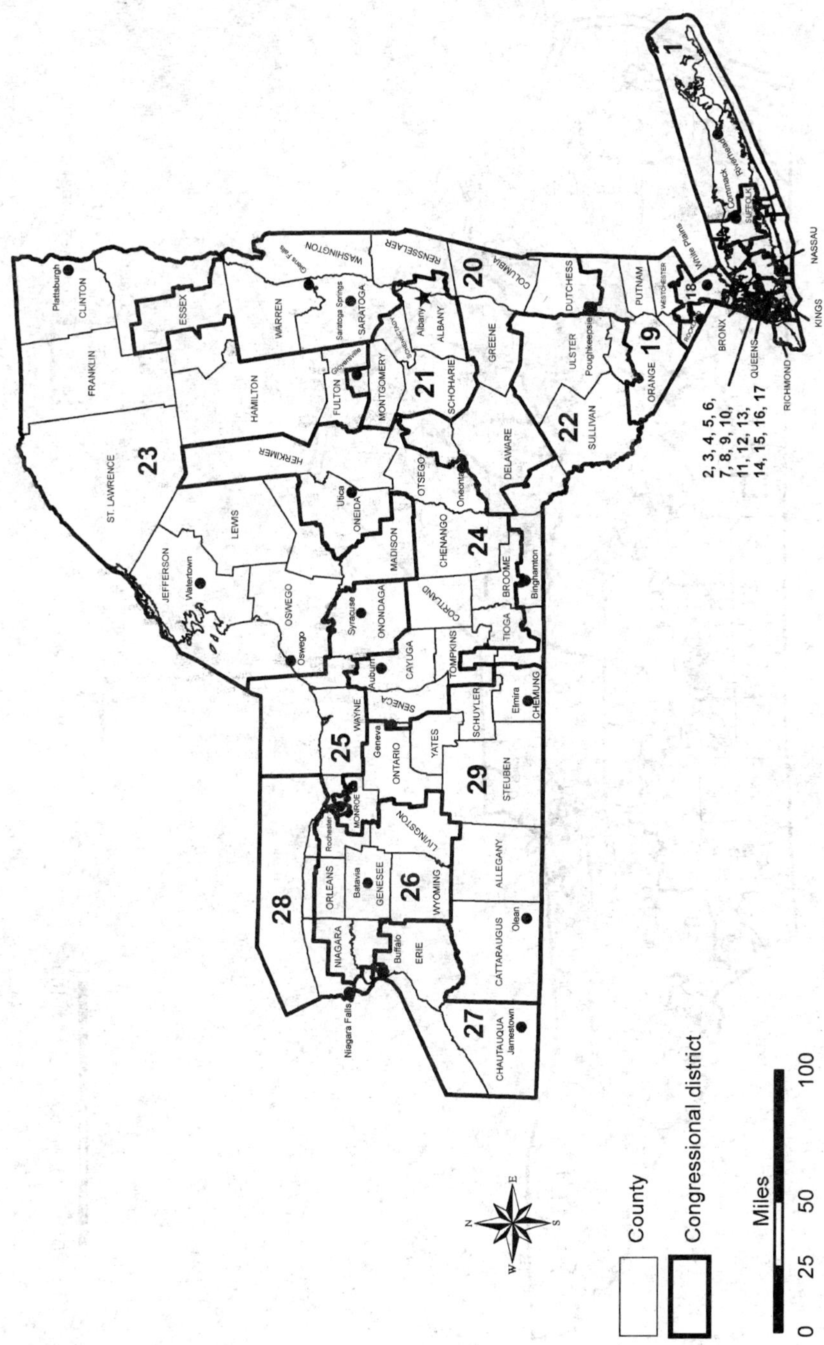

NORTH CAROLINA—Congressional Districts—(13 Districts)

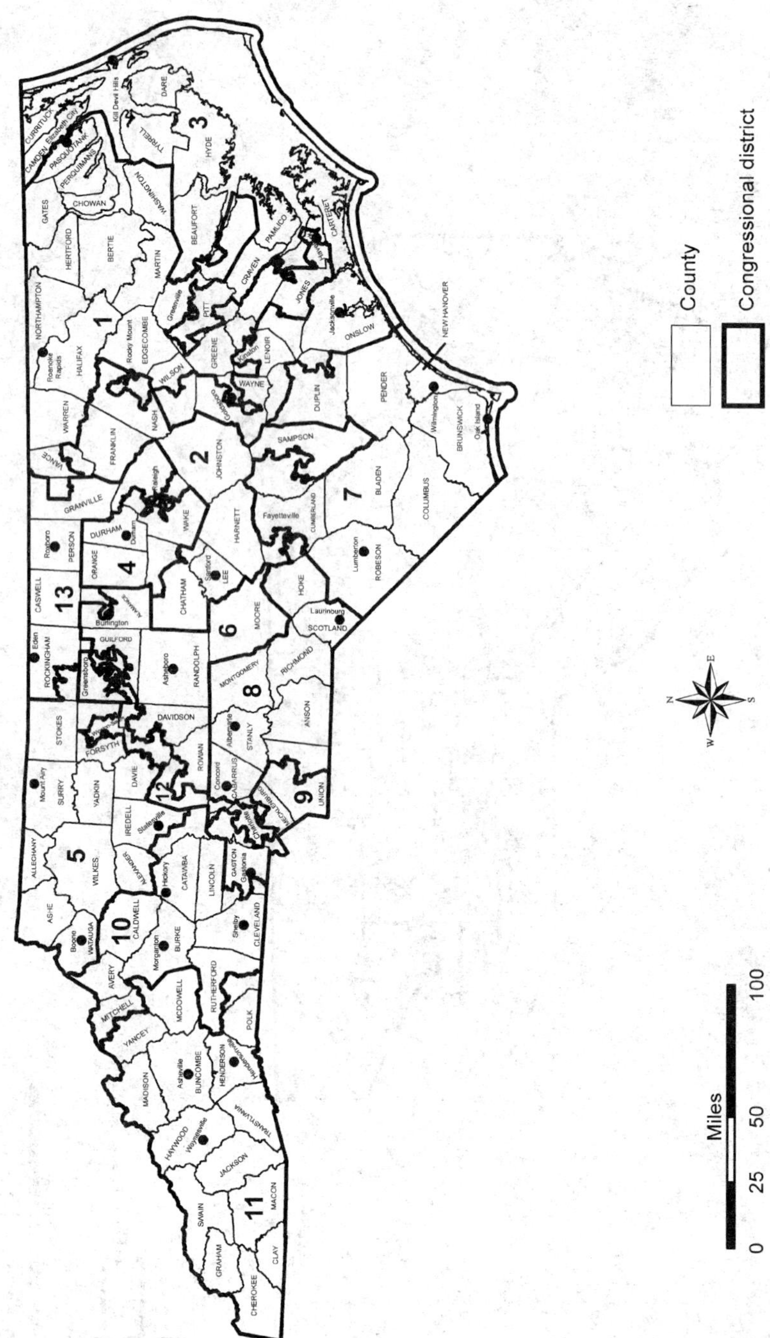

NORTH DAKOTA—Congressional District—(1 District At Large)

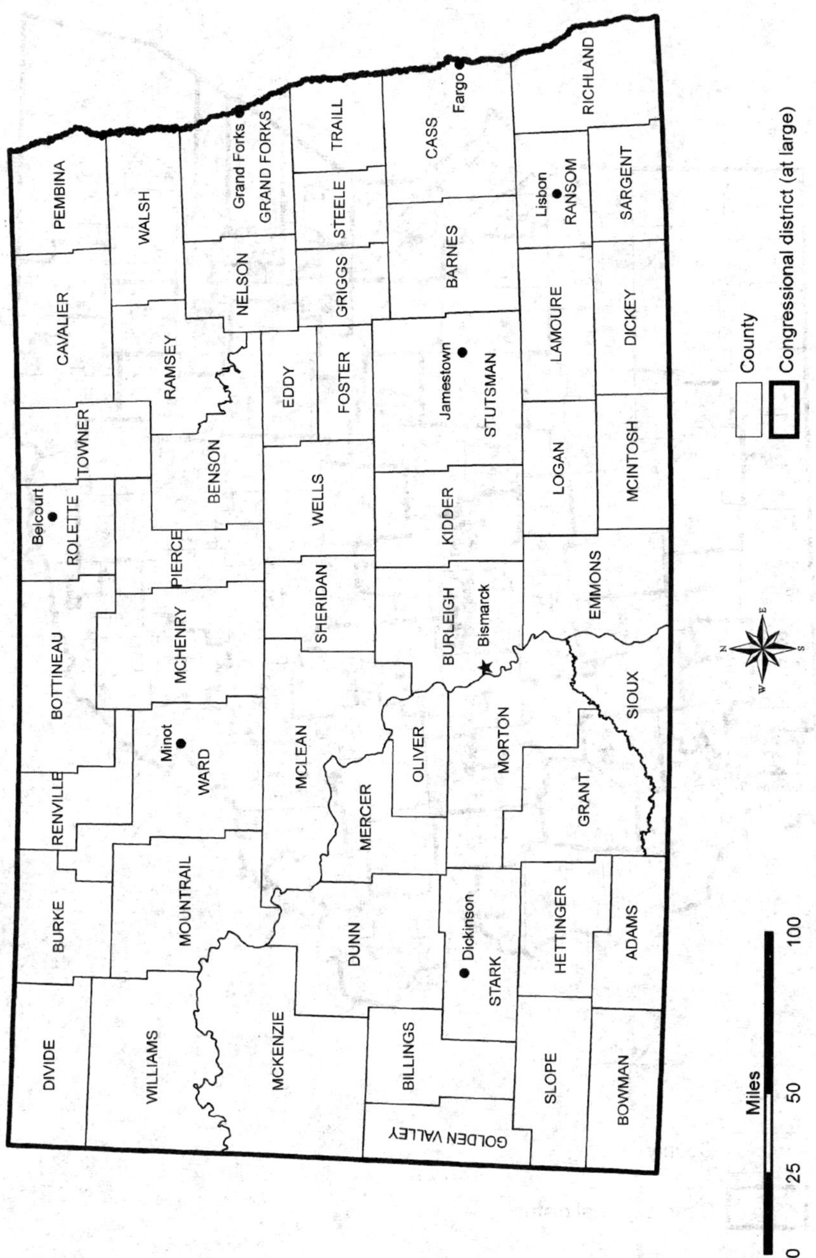

OHIO—Congressional Districts—(18 Districts)

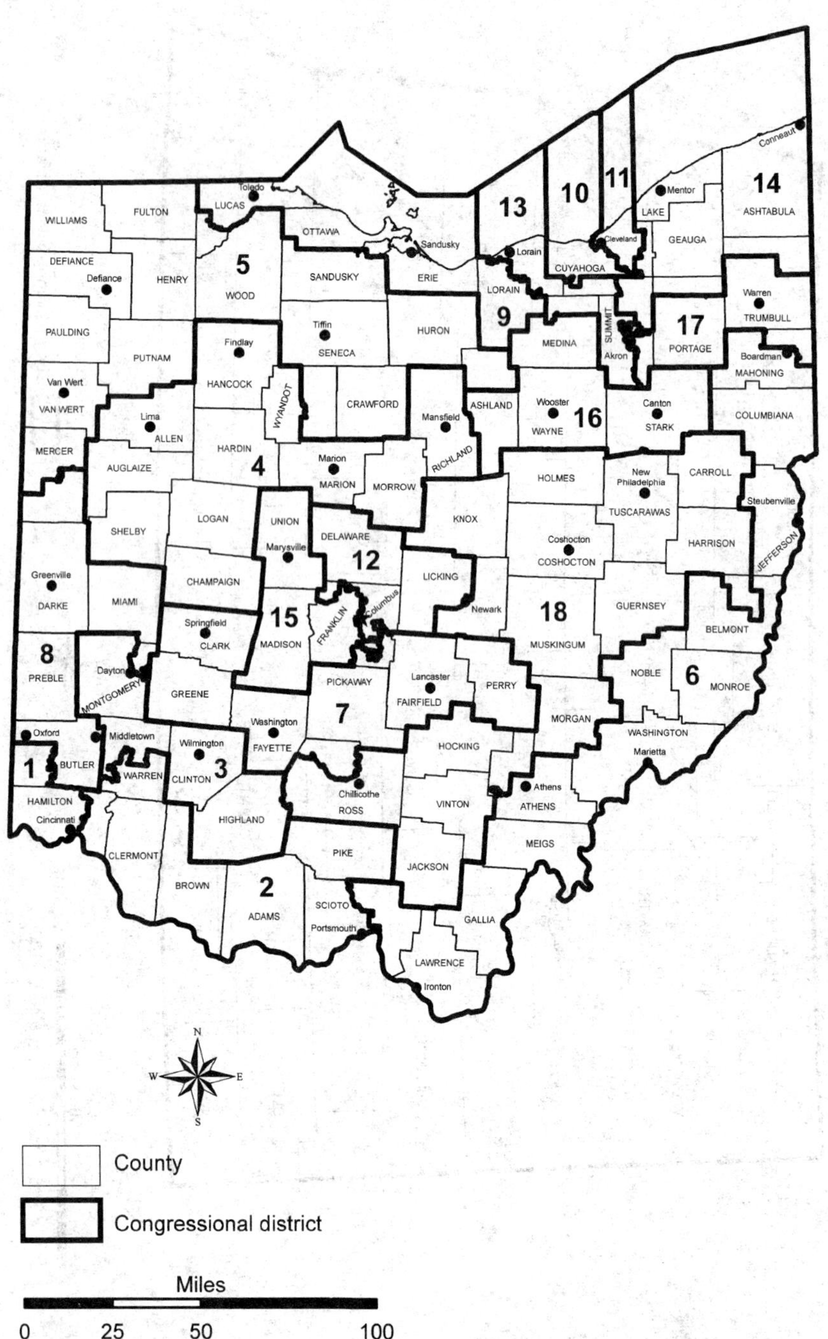

OKLAHOMA—Congressional Districts—(5 Districts)

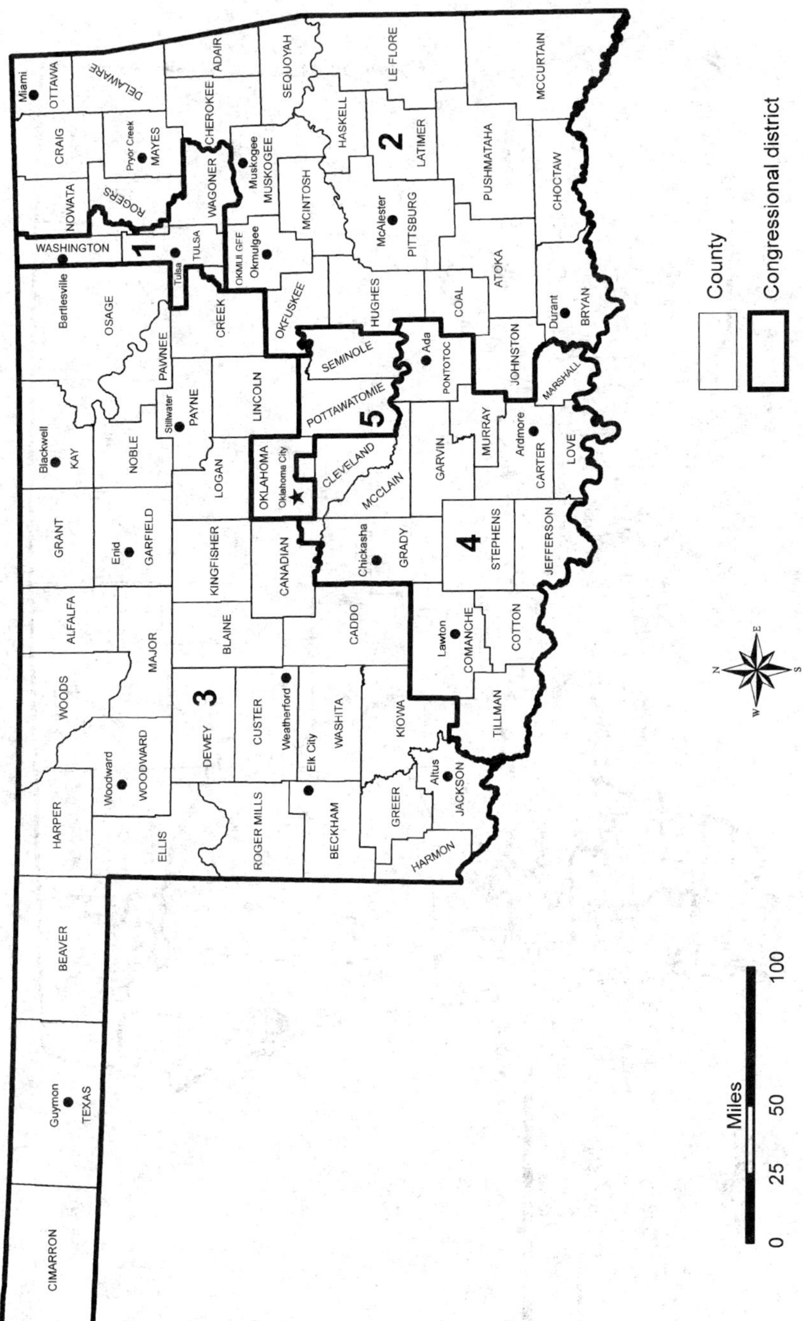

OREGON—Congressional Districts—(5 Districts)

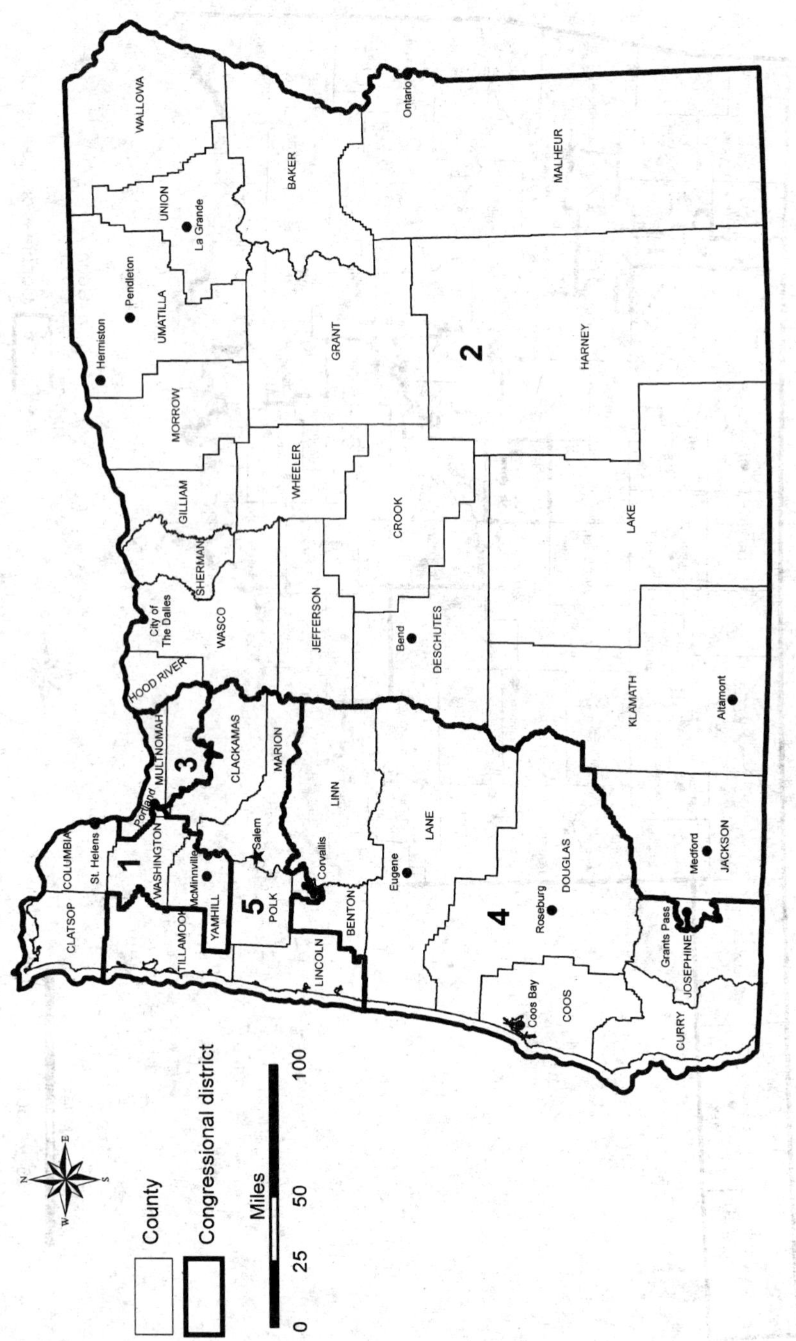

PENNSYLVANIA—Congressional Districts—(19 Districts)

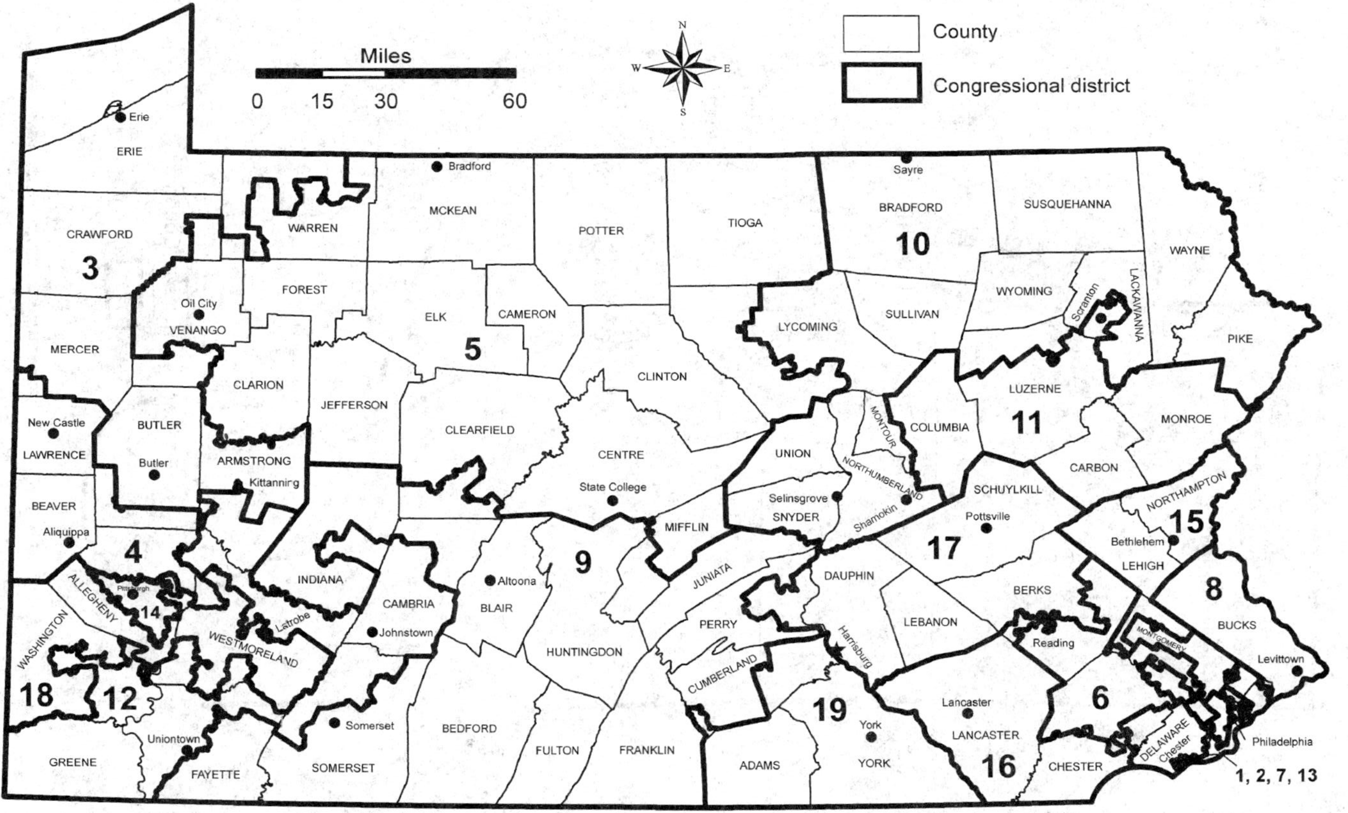

RHODE ISLAND—Congressional Districts—(2 Districts)

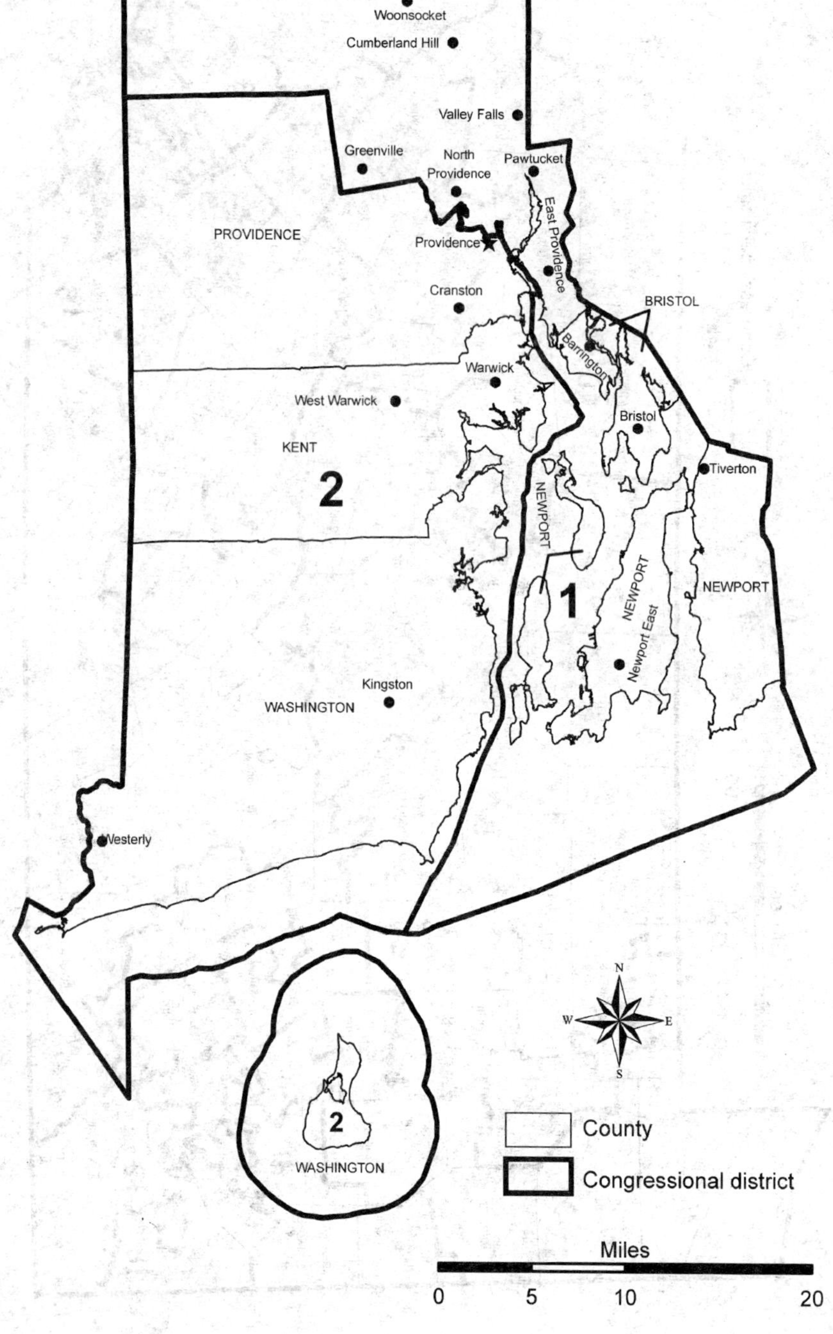

SOUTH CAROLINA—Congressional Districts—(6 Districts)

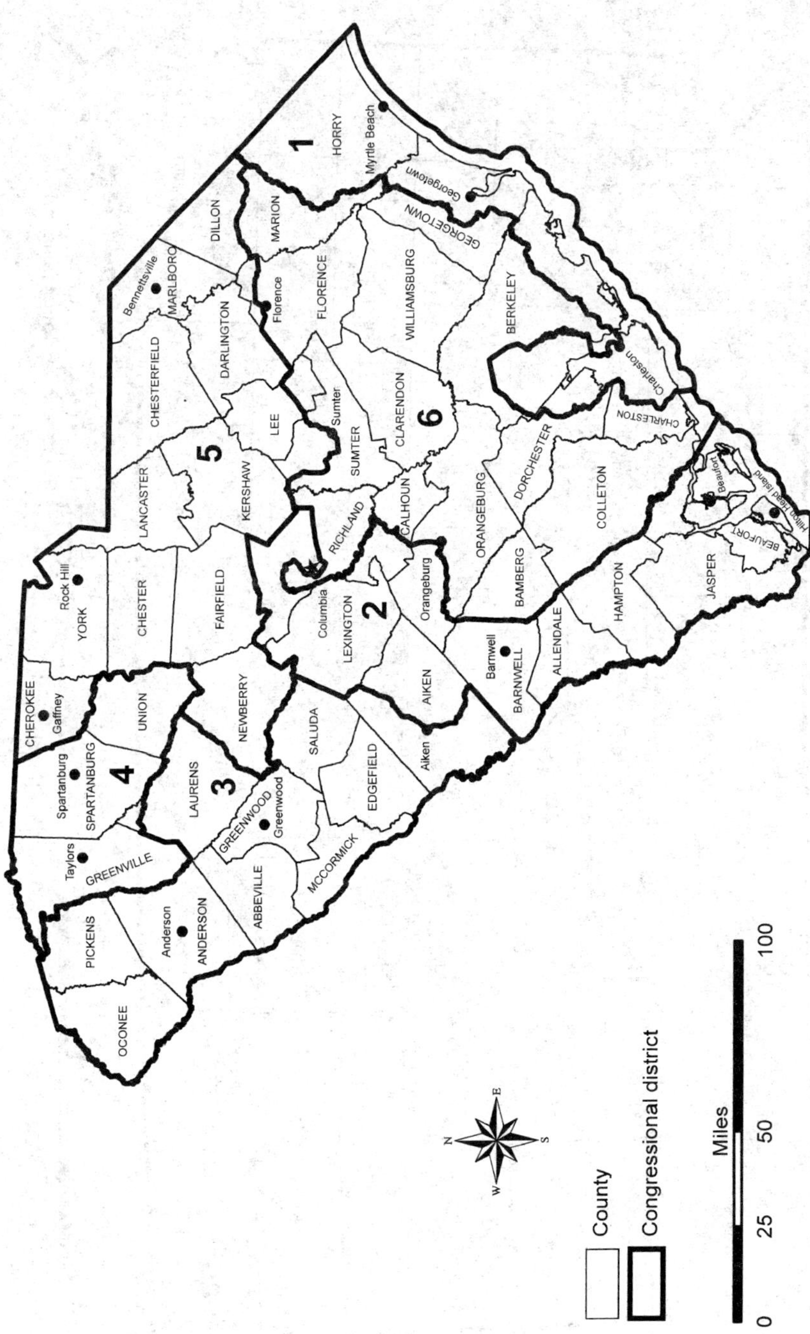

SOUTH DAKOTA—Congressional District—(1 District At Large)

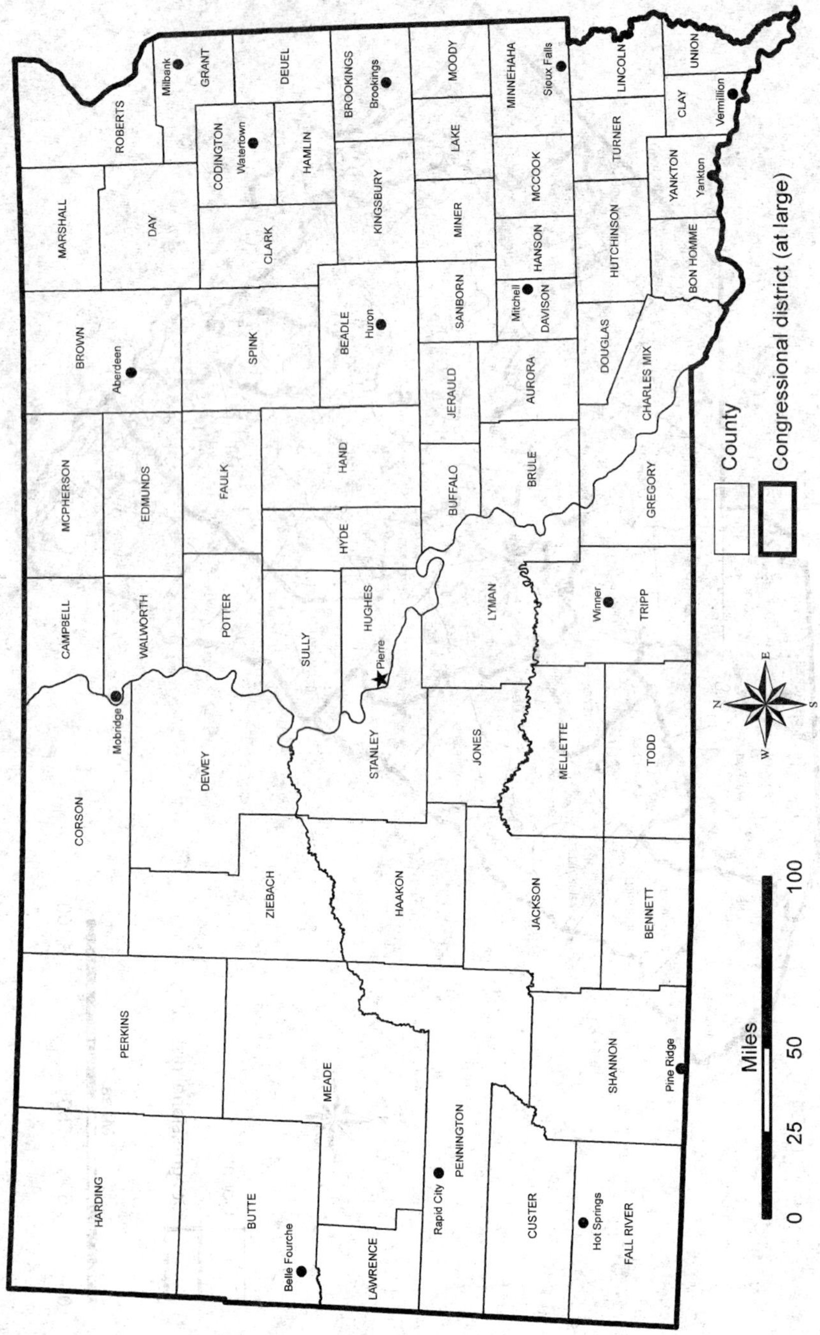

TENNESSEE—Congressional Districts—(9 Districts)

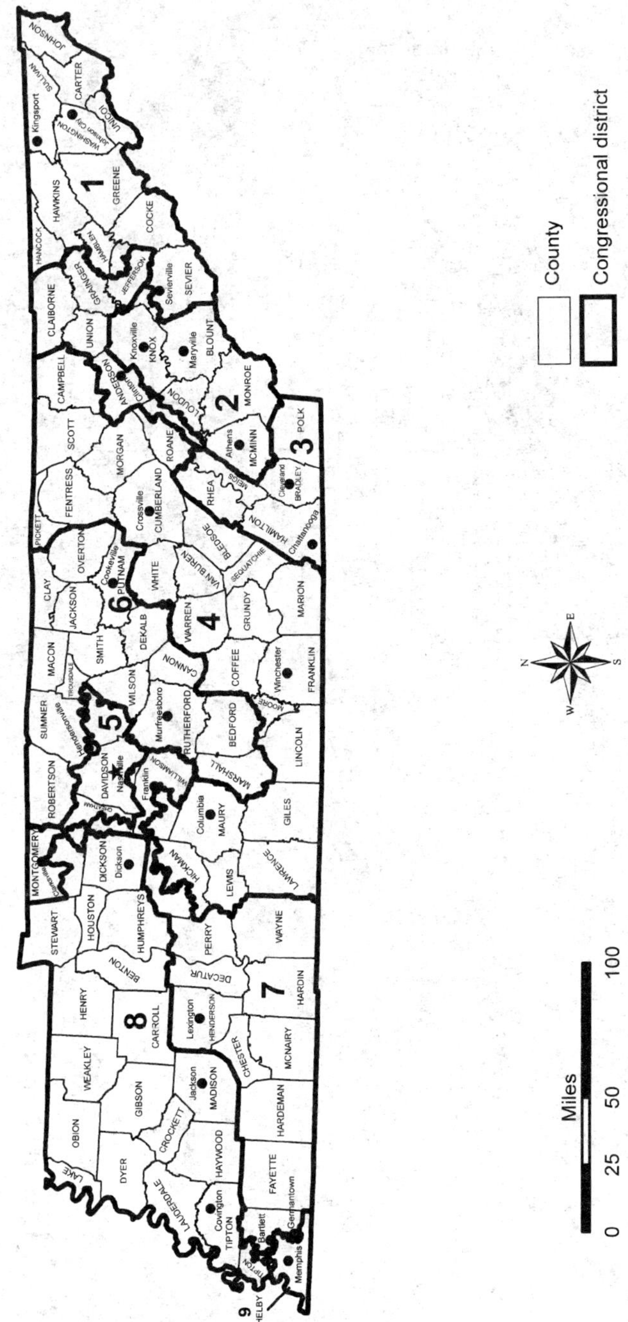

TEXAS—Congressional Districts—(32 Districts)

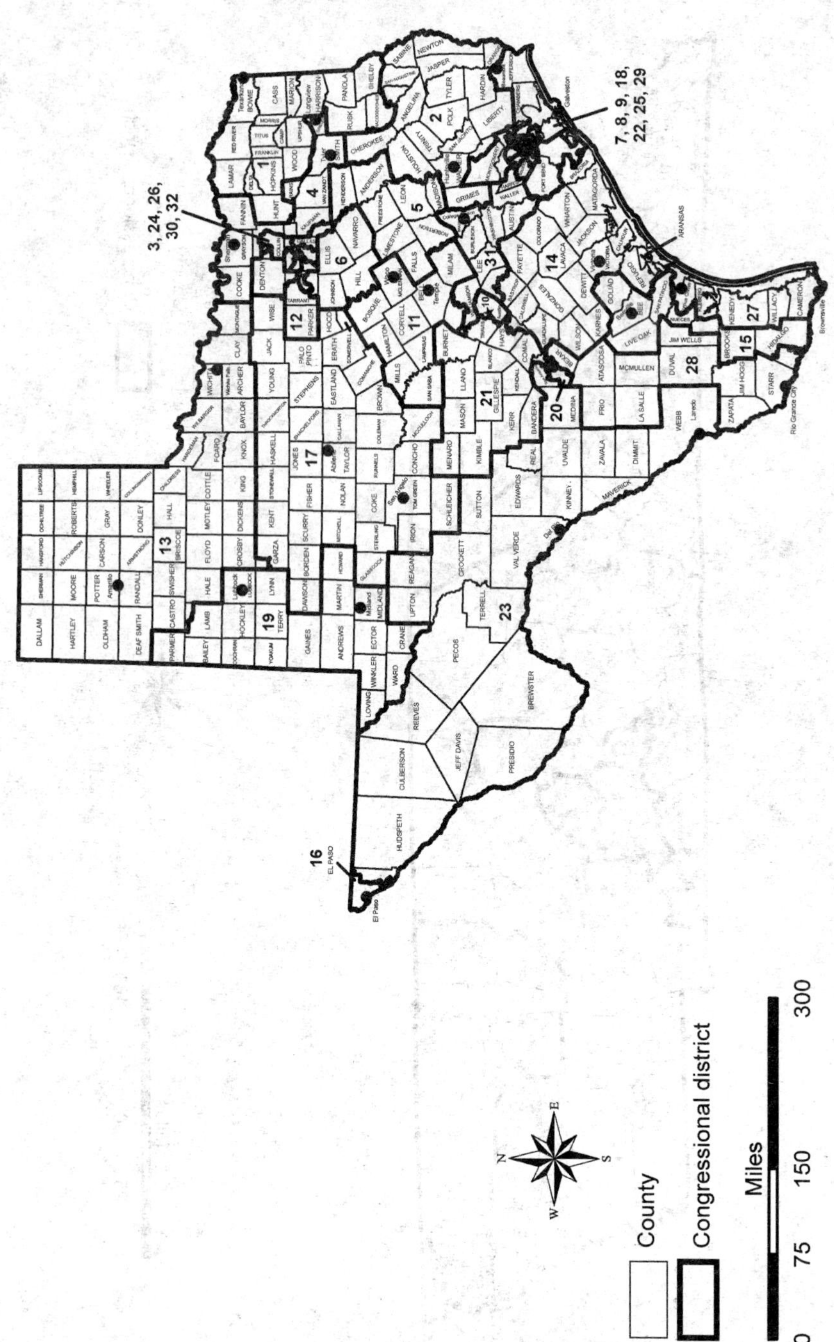

UTAH—Congressional Districts—(3 Districts)

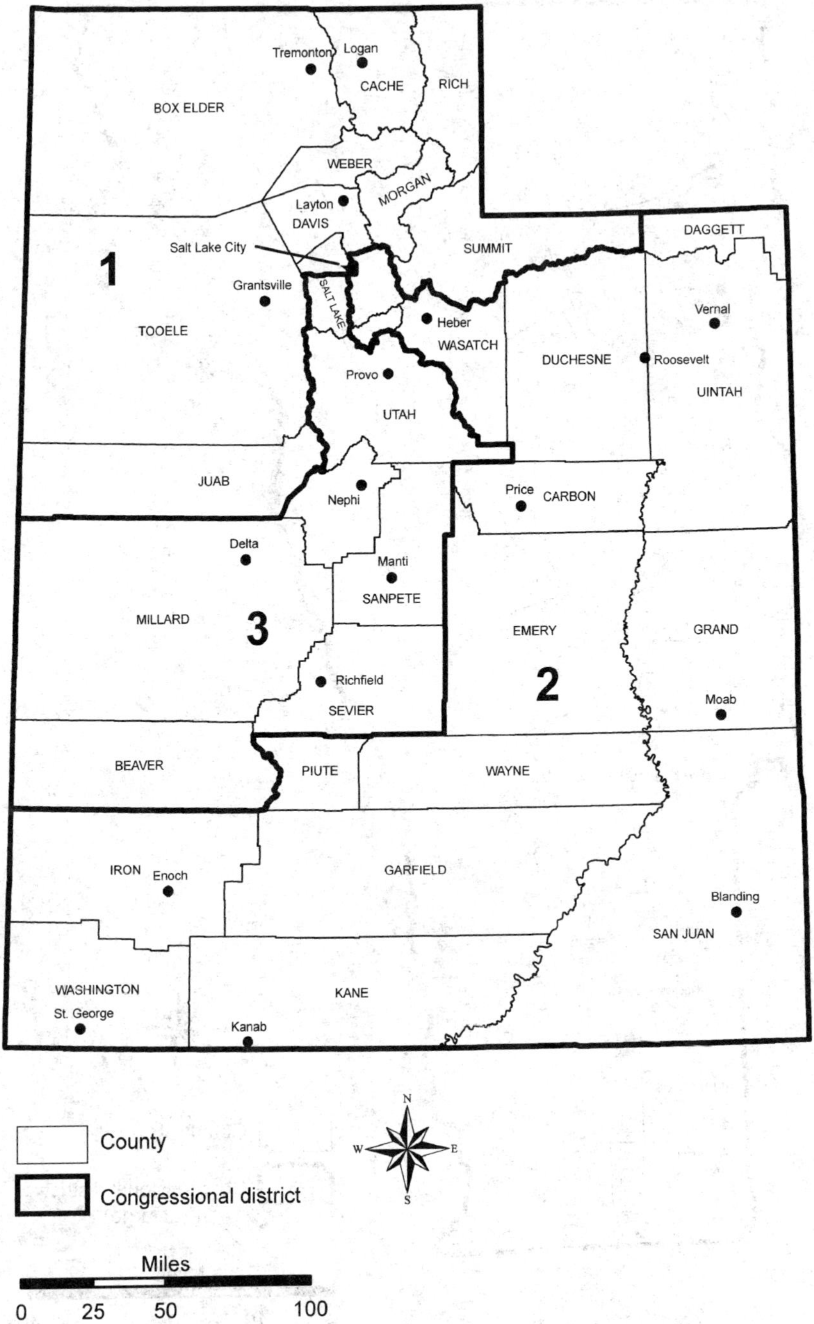

Tremonton
Logan
CACHE
RICH
BOX ELDER
WEBER
MORGAN
Layton
DAVIS
Salt Lake City
SUMMIT
DAGGETT
1
Grantsville
SALT LAKE
Heber
WASATCH
Vernal
TOOELE
DUCHESNE
Roosevelt
UINTAH
Provo
UTAH
JUAB
Nephi
Price
CARBON
Delta
Manti
SANPETE
MILLARD
3
EMERY
GRAND
Richfield
SEVIER
2
Moab
BEAVER
PIUTE
WAYNE
IRON
Enoch
GARFIELD
Blanding
SAN JUAN
WASHINGTON
St. George
KANE
Kanab
N
W
E
S
County
Congressional district
Miles
0
25
50
100

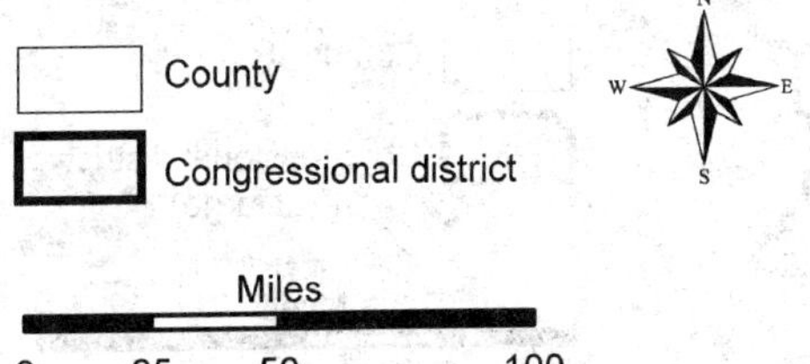

VERMONT—Congressional District—(1 District At Large)

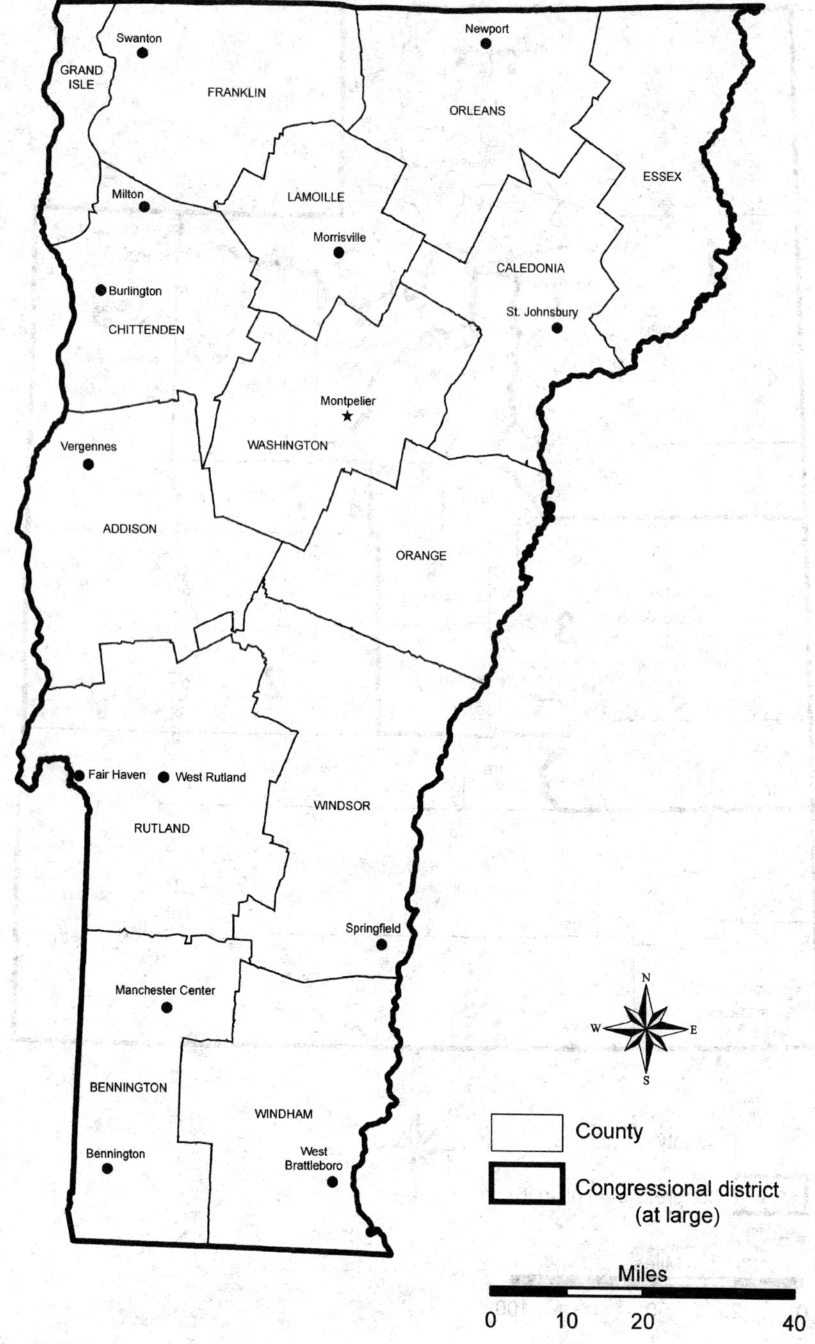

VIRGINIA—Congressional Districts—(11 Districts)

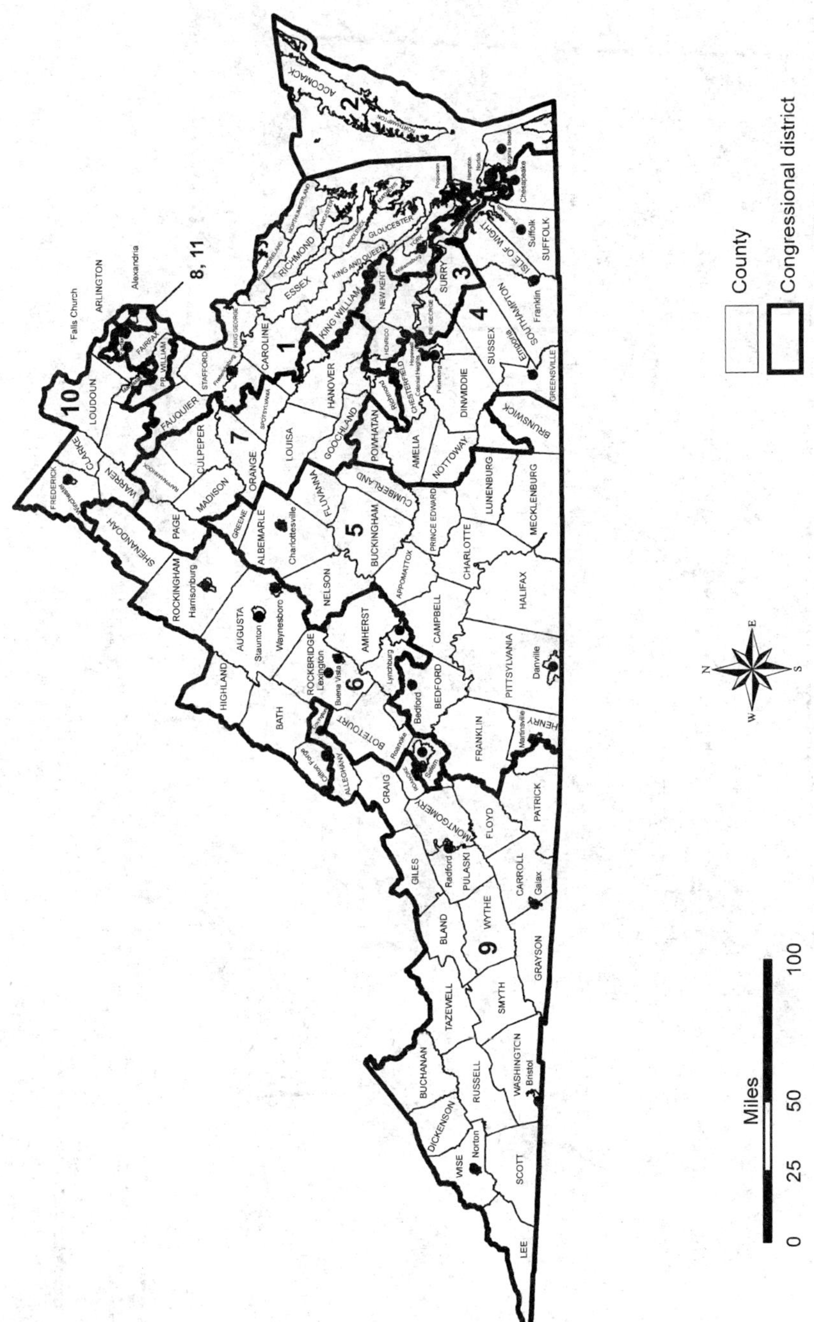

WASHINGTON—Congressional Districts—(9 Districts)

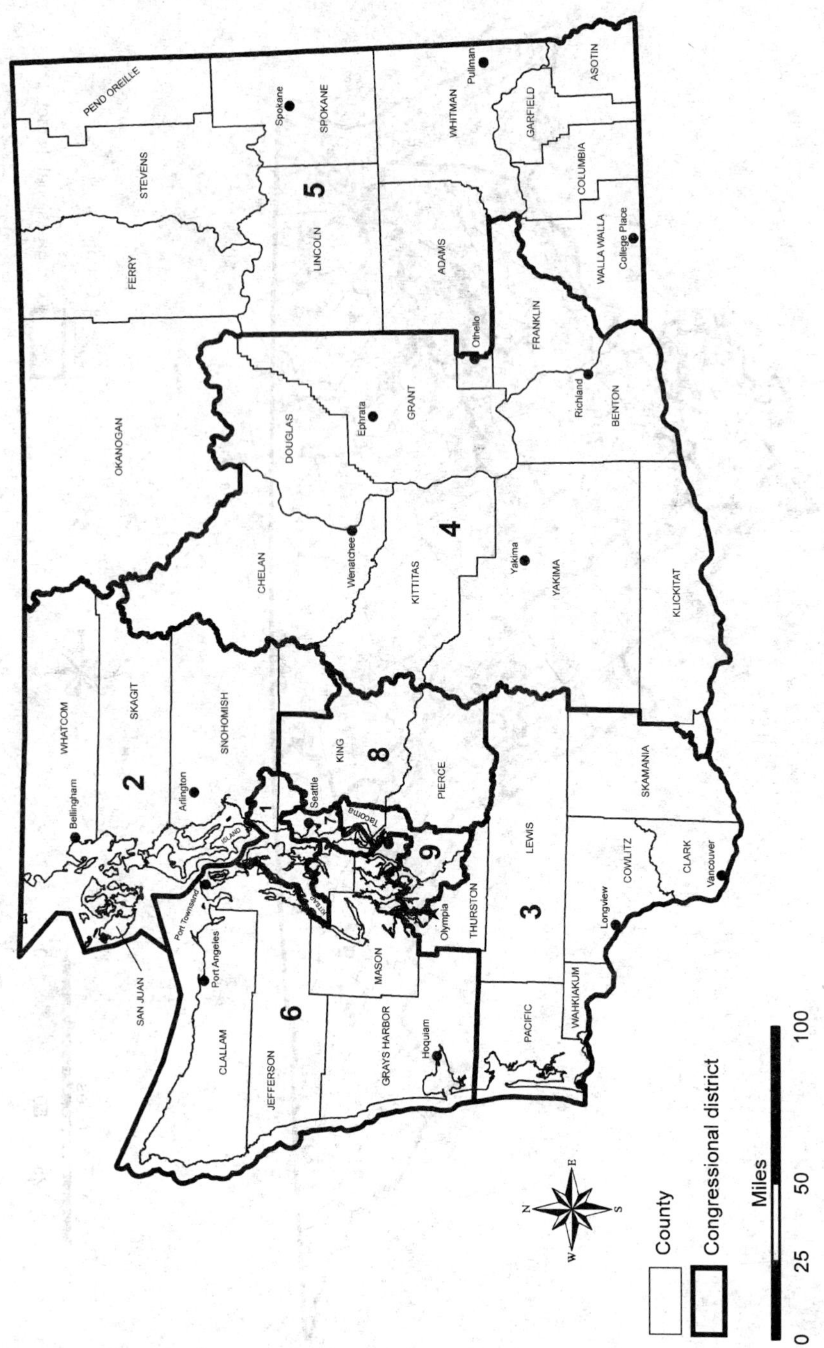

WEST VIRGINIA—Congressional Districts—(3 Districts)

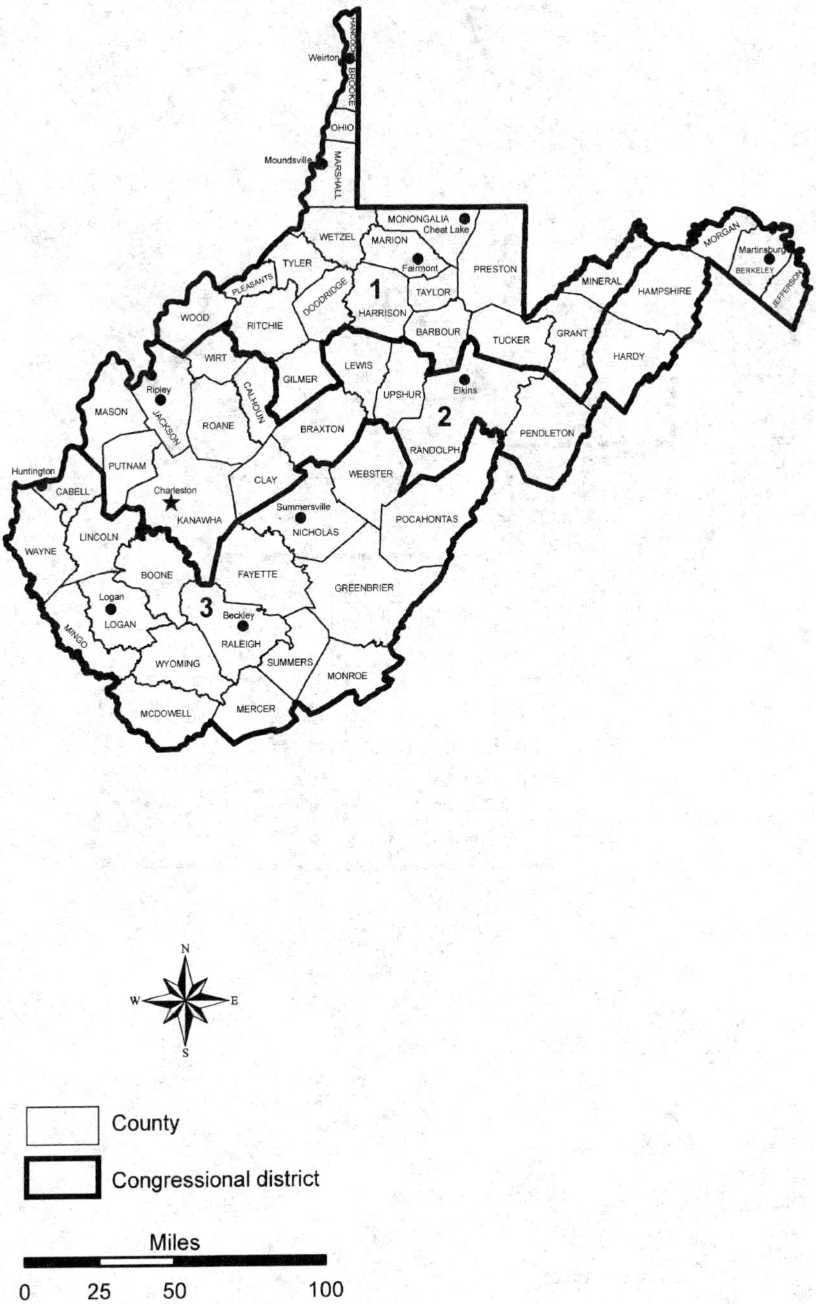

County

Congressional district

Miles

0 25 50 100

WISCONSIN—Congressional Districts—(8 Districts)

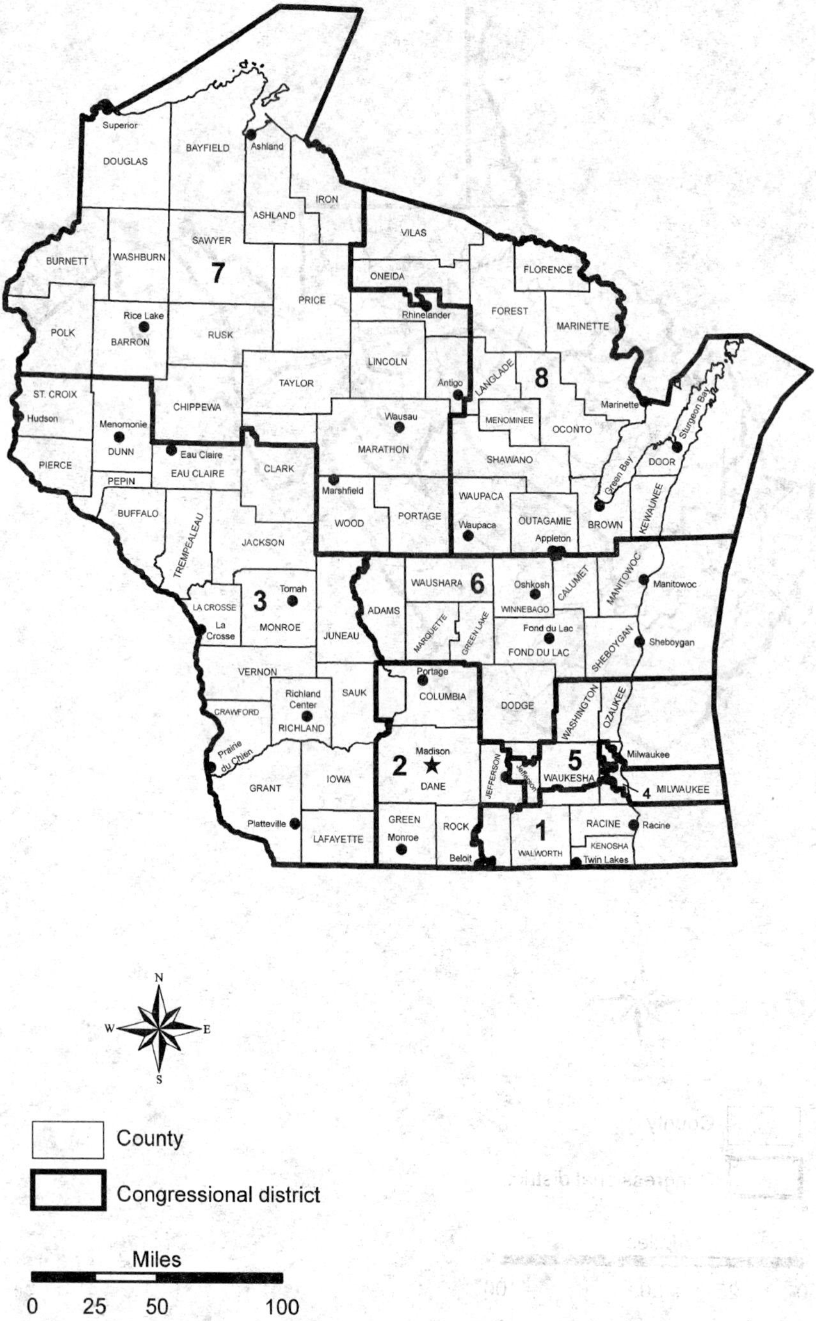

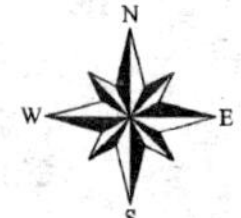

County

Congressional district

Miles

0 25 50 100

WYOMING—Congressional District—(1 District At Large)

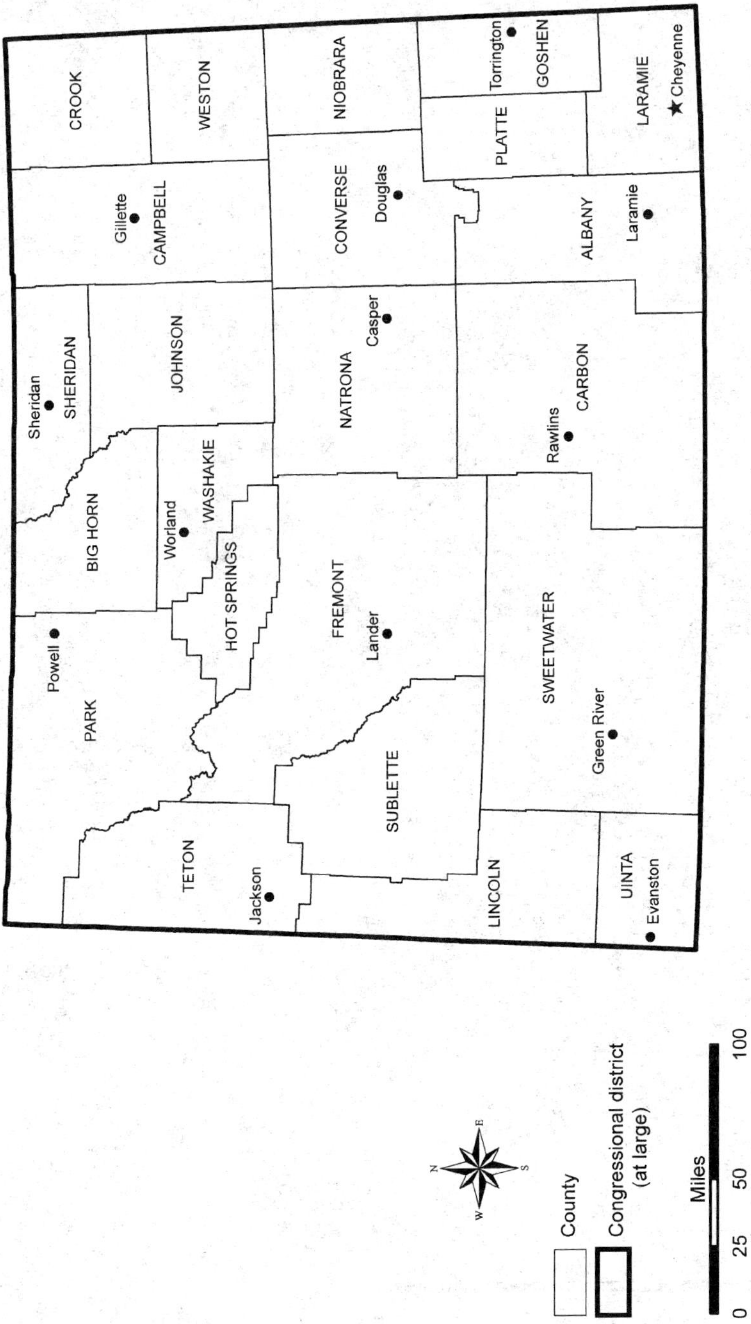

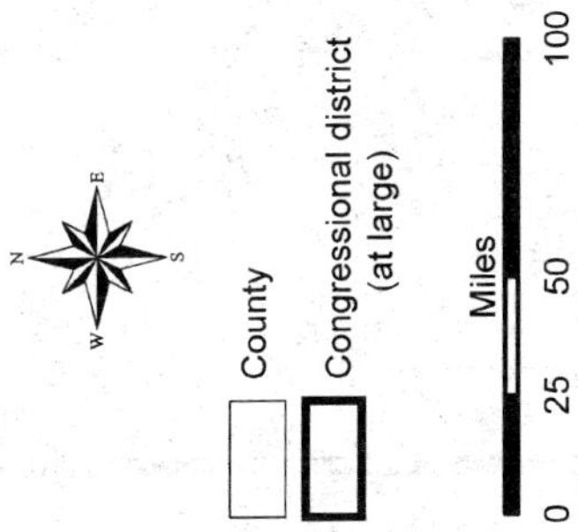

AMERICAN SAMOA—(1 Delegate At Large)

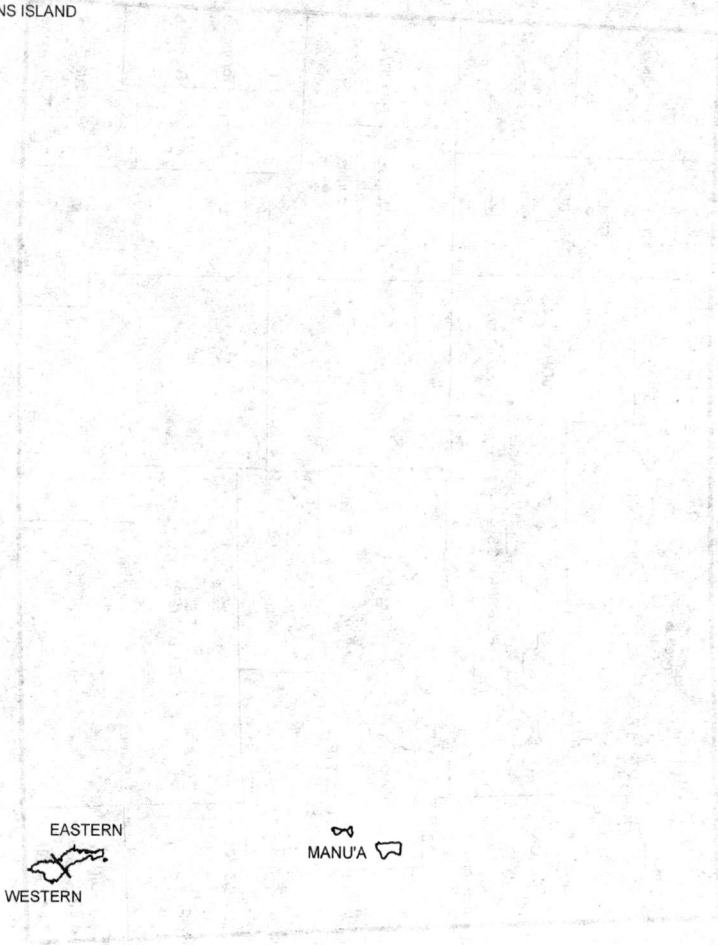

SWAINS ISLAND

EASTERN

MANU'A

WESTERN

ROSE ISLAND

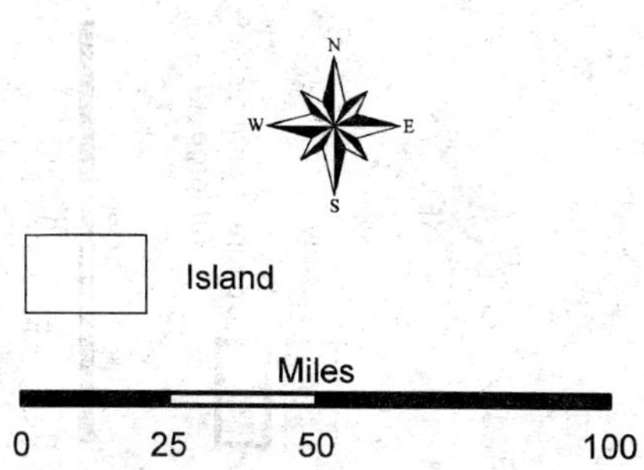

DISTRICT OF COLUMBIA—(1 Delegate At Large)

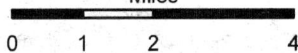

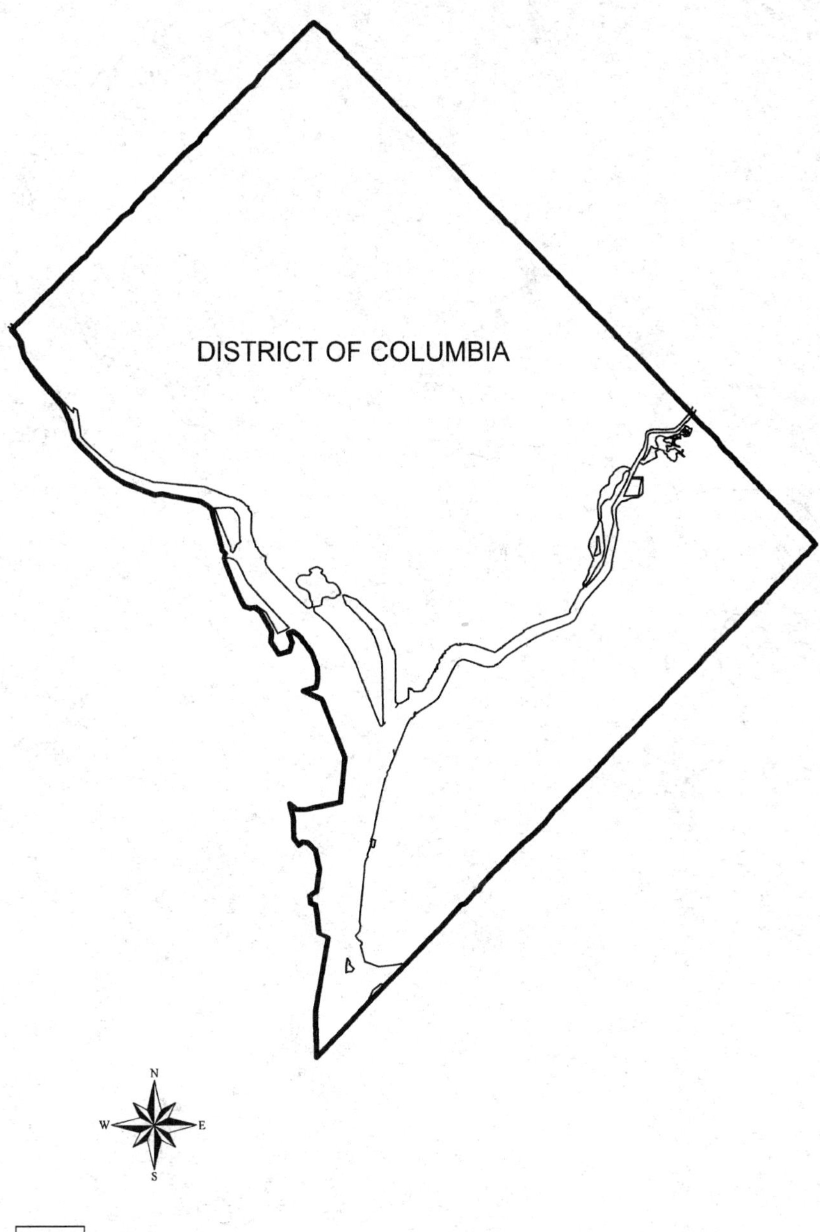

GUAM—(1 Delegate At Large)

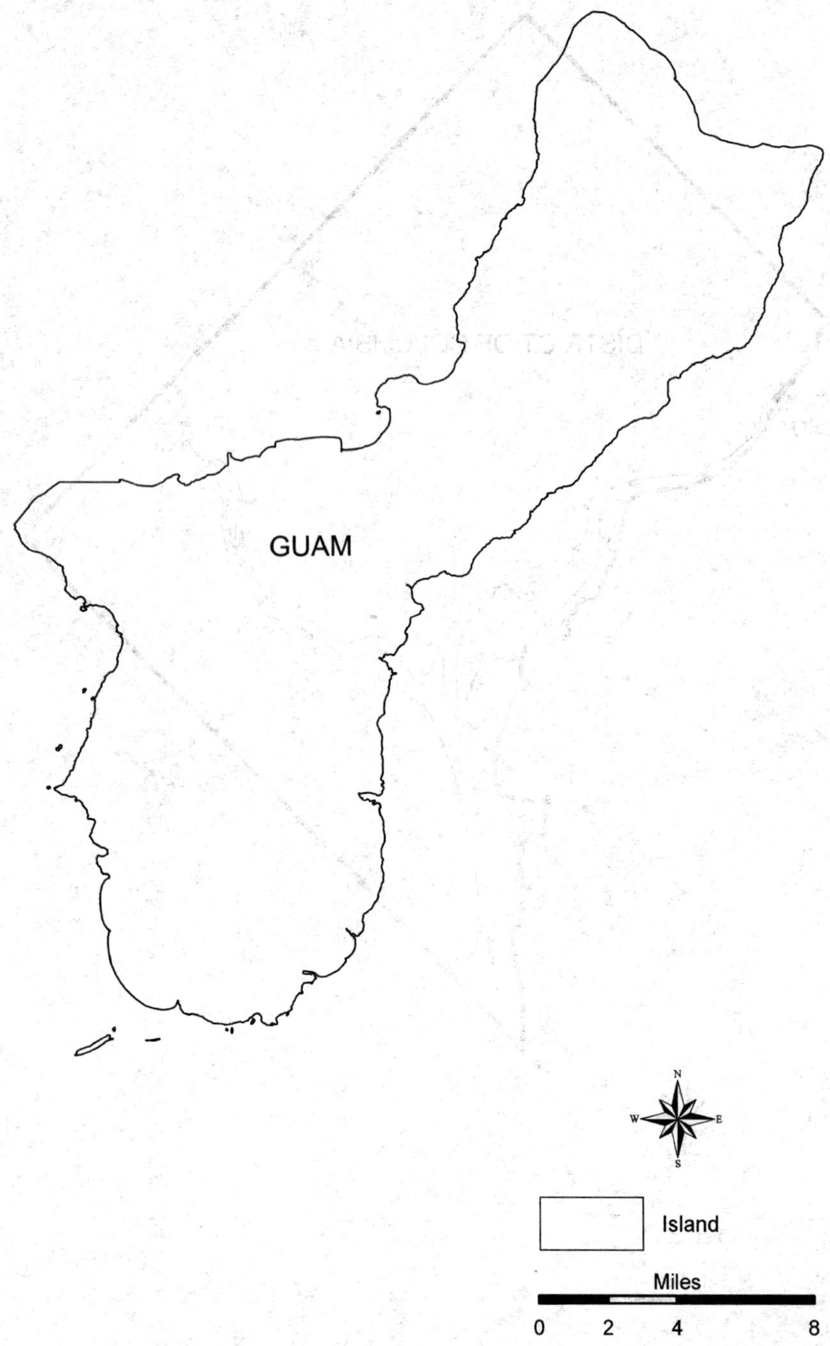

PUERTO RICO—(1 Resident Commissioner At Large)

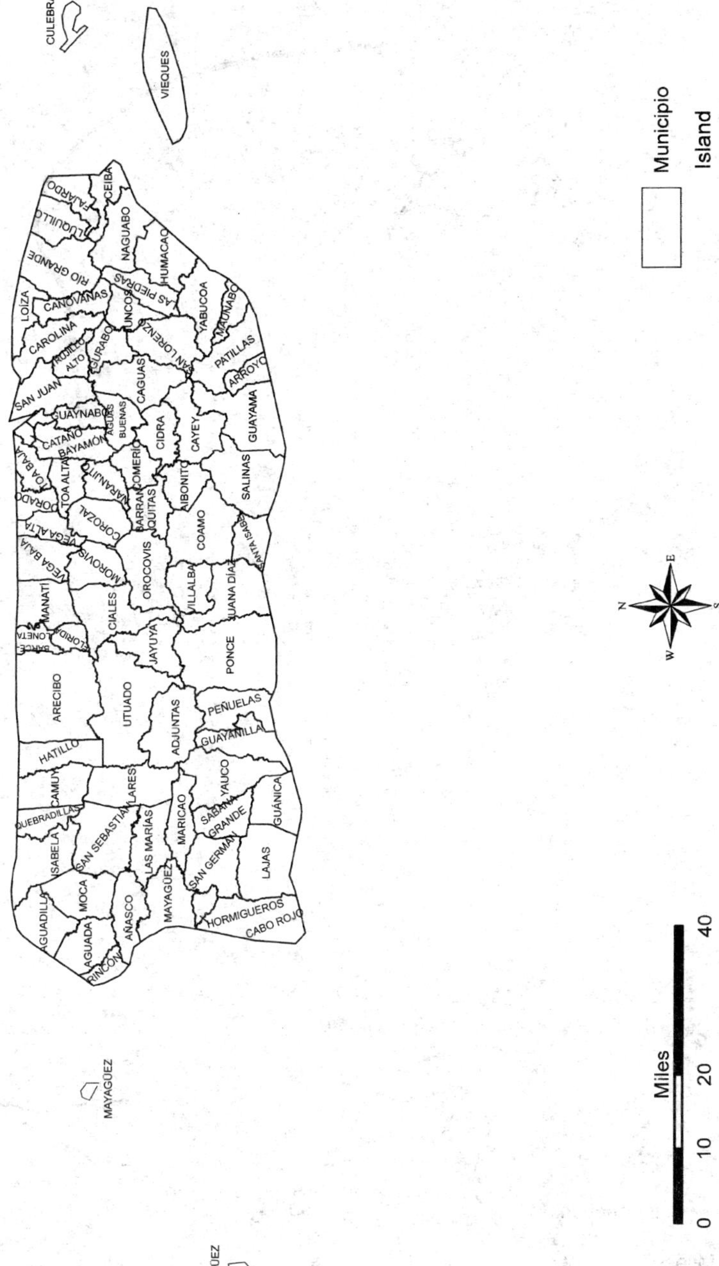

THE VIRGIN ISLANDS OF THE UNITED STATES—(1 Delegate At Large)

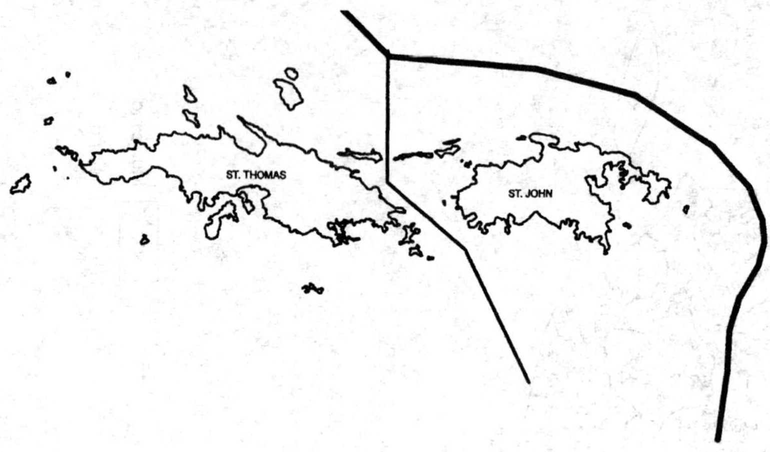

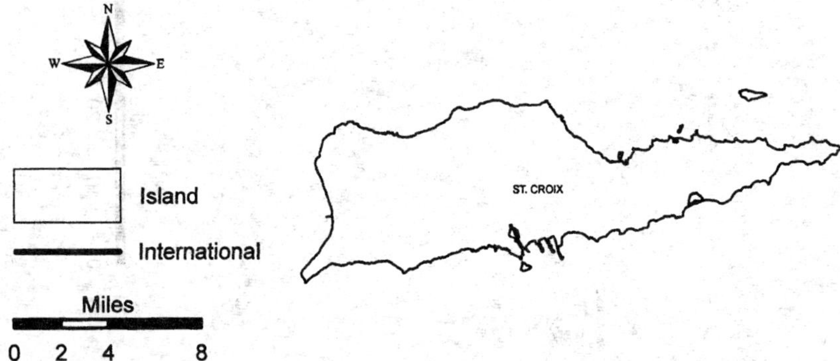

NAME INDEX

E

L

W

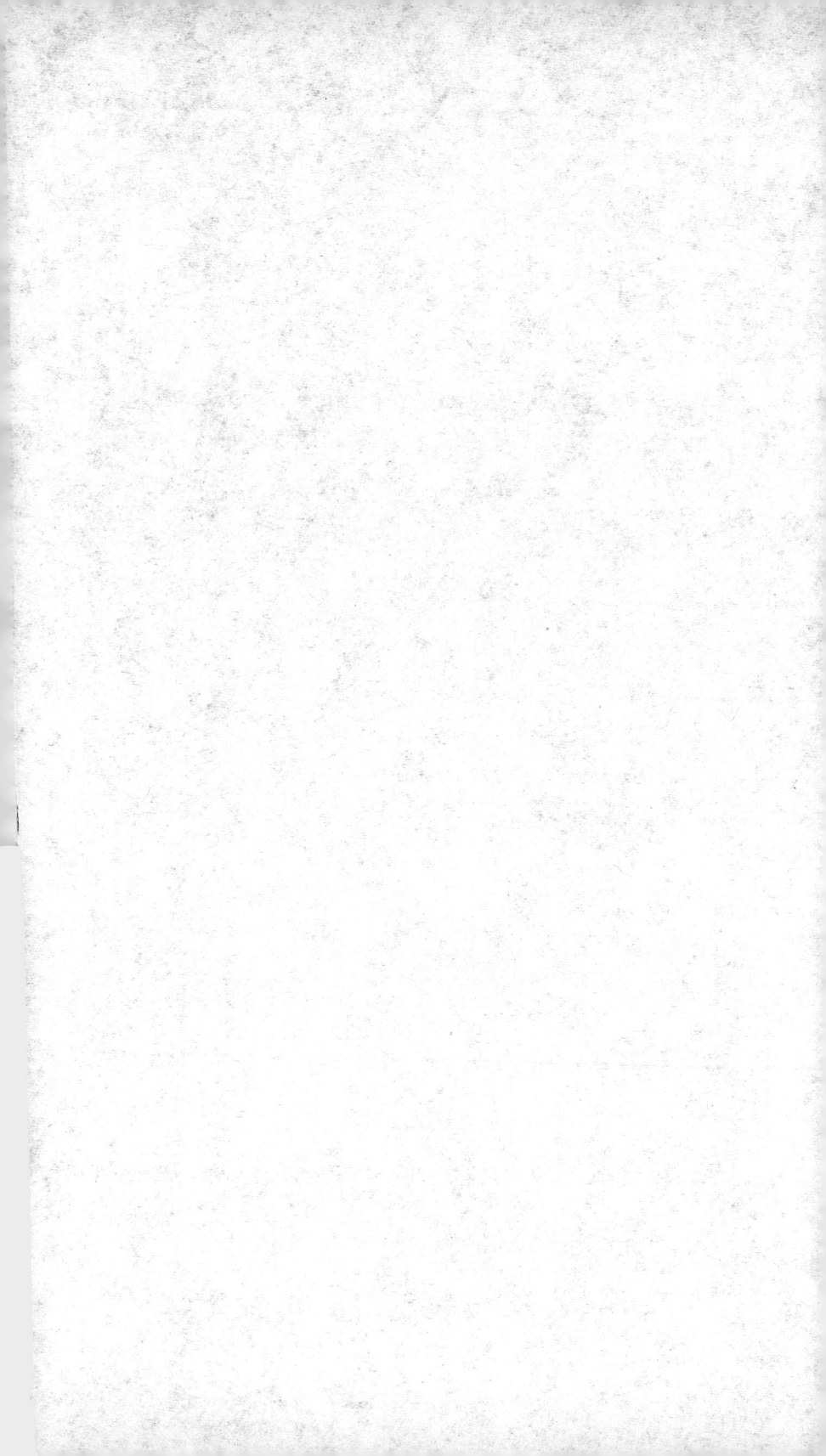

Margin Index:

To use, bend book and align index marker with black-edged page mark in text.